Why Do You Need This New Edition?

*Here are six great reasons
why you should buy
this new edition of*
**The Necessary
Shakespeare**

1. **"Reading Shakespeare in the Twenty-First Century"** has been updated. This section offers practical strategies for readers new to Shakespeare.

2. **The General Introduction** has been significantly revised to provide easier navigation.

3. **"Films and Videos as a Guide to the Study of Shakespeare,"** has been thoroughly updated and revised for the seventh edition. This helpful appendix offers an annotated filmography and advice on how to use films and videos on how to study a play.

4. **Throughout the text, you'll find woodcuts and other illustrations,** many of them new, depicting famous persons, animals, social customs, pastimes, hobbies, costuming conventions, themes, myths, and the like from the world that Shakespeare knew.

5. **"Shakespeare's World: A Visual Portfolio"** includes more than 10 new illustrations with many representing pivotal stage productions.

6. **Thoroughly revised and updated notes and glosses** give you help by translating unusual or unfamiliar language into clear and accessible modern explanations.

The
Necessary
Shakespeare

The Necessary Shakespeare

Fourth Edition

Edited by

David Bevington

The University of Chicago

PEARSON

Boston   Columbus   Indianapolis   New York   San Francisco
Upper Saddle River   Amsterdam   Cape Town   Dubai   London   Madrid
Milan   Munich   Paris   Montréal   Toronto   Delhi   Mexico City   São Paulo
Sydney   Hong Kong   Seoul   Singapore   Taipei   Tokyo

Senior Sponsoring Editor: Katharine Glynn
Assistant Editor: Rebecca Gilpin
Senior Marketing Manager: Sandra McGuire
Executive Digital Producer: Stefanie Snajder
Digital Project Manager: Janell Lantana
Production Manager: S.S. Kulig
Project Coordination, Text Design, and Electronic Page Makeup: Integra
Cover Designer/Manager: Wendy Ann Fredericks
Cover Art: Scene still from *Shakespeare in Love*, 1998. © Miramax Films/Universal Pictures/
    The Kobal Collection/Sparham, Laurie; *background art:* © Fotalia
Senior Manufacturing Buyer: Dennis Para
Printer/Binder: Courier Corporation
Cover Printer: Lehigh-Phoenix Color

Credits and acknowledgments borrowed from other sources and reproduced, with permission, in this textbook appear on the appropriate page within text.

Library of Congress Cataloging-in-Publication Data

Shakespeare, William, 1564–1616.
  [Selections. 2013]
  The necessary Shakespeare/edited by David Bevington, The University of Chicago.—Fourth edition.
    pages cm
  Includes bibliographical references and index.
  ISBN-13: 978-0-321-88094-9
  ISBN-10: 0-321-88094-3
  1. Shakespeare, William, 1564–1616—Criticism and interpretation. I. Bevington, David M. II. Title.
  PR2759.B64 2013
  822.3'3—dc23

                                                                          2012043850

10 9 8 7 6 5 4 3 2 1—CRK—16 15 14 13

www.pearsonhighered.com

ISBN 10:   0-321-88094-3
ISBN 13: 978-0-321-88094-9

CONTENTS

Preface viii

Shakespeare's World: A Visual Portfolio   following page xxxii

PREFACE

The Necessary Shakespeare distills the best, the oftenest read, the most often produced of Shakespeare's great plays. By publishing this selection in a compact paperback edition, my hope is to expose a new broader student audience to the work of perhaps the greatest author in the history of the English language.

Of the thirty-eight or so plays and various poems written by or attributed to Shakespeare, this collection offers twenty plays and the sonnets. I have made these selections based on the response of Shakespeare instructors across the country who indicated which works are truly "necessary" in the undergraduate classroom. I have also tried to select plays that are frequently performed or widely available on film or video.

I include seven romantic comedies, four English history plays, seven of the great tragedies, and two romances. Cutting is always a thankless task, and I have omitted some works that some readers will miss: *Troilus and Cressida, The Second Part of King Henry the Fourth, Coriolanus*, and *Cymbeline* might well be on such a list. Even so, I hope that this collection does represent the best and best known of his work. It covers Shakespeare's favorite genres; it shows his development from the early *The Taming of the Shrew* and *Richard the Third* to the late *The Tempest*; it shows him as an amazing poet as well as dramatist. My hope is that such a volume will find a real use in personal libraries and classrooms.

The arrangement of the plays in this volume under the categories of comedies, histories, tragedies, and romances is close to that of the First Folio of 1623, in which Shakespeare's plays were grouped under three categories of comedies, histories, and tragedies (the romances were included under "comedies"). They were published posthumously by two of his erstwhile colleagues in the acting company known as the King's Men. The poems and sonnets were published separately.

My edition of *The Complete Works of Shakespeare* (seventh edition, Pearson, 2014) is available for more complete coverage. Over the course of its publishing history, I have profited greatly from the consultation of various friends and colleagues at colleges and universities all over the world. In each case I showed the consultant all the materials I had prepared—the Shakespeare text, the commentary notes, the textual notes, the introduction—and sought that person's aid in revision. These friends have aided me through progressive reconsiderations of the work. Other colleagues helped me with the plays and poems omitted from this present volume. I want to extend my warmest thanks to all.

In this present edition, I have also selected from the front matter and appendices of the 2014 edition of *The Complete Works of Shakespeare*. The choices here are an attempt to respond to the desires of representative readers and users of the volume. They helped me decide that we should keep the introductory material on life in Shakespeare's England, the drama before Shakespeare, London theatres and dramatic companies, Shakespeare's life and work, how to read Shakespeare, Shakespeare's language, and Shakespeare criticism. All of these sections have been brought up to date, especially the materials on Shakespeare criticism. I have added substantially to the bibliography, to make it as up-to-date as possible.

In the appendices, I have kept the material on Canon, Dates, and Early Texts, and on sources. An essay on "Shakespeare in Performance," by Professor Lois Potter of the University of Delaware, brings performance history up to date with an emphasis on film and television. An updated Appendix on Films and Videos as a Guide to the Study of Shakespeare provides an extensive filmography or film biography, listing the best and most available of films or videos for each play in this edition. I have revised the bibliographies to focus on the works contained in this edition. I have recast the index. Readers and teachers seem to appreciate having an index, although many editions do not include one. I have kept this as part of the volume.

KEY FEATURES OF THE FOURTH EDITION

- **"Reading Shakespeare in the Twenty-First Century,"** an updated essay that opens the general introduction, poses questions about the relevance and difficulty of Shakespeare for contemporary students and offers practical strategies for readers new to Shakespeare.
- **"Shakespeare's Language,"** in the general introduction, has been completely rewritten in order to better introduce Shakespeare's idioms and vocabulary to novice readers.
- **"Films and Videos as a Guide to the Study of Shakespeare,"** is an updated appendix for the fourth edition, offering an annotated filmography and advice on how to use films and videos to study a play.
- **Thoroughly revised and updated notes and glosses** provide contemporary readers the support they need to understand Elizabethan language and idioms in accessible and clear modern language, line by line.
- **A richly illustrated general introduction** provides readers with the historical and cultural background required to understand Shakespeare's works in context.
- **"Shakespeare's World: A Visual Portfolio"** provides 16 pages of full-color illustrations to help readers visualize Renaissance life and culture and to trace the history of significant performances on stage and screen. Nearly one-third of these color images are new to this edition and are drawn from Shakespeare productions from around the globe.
- Woodcuts and other illustrations throughout the volume from the sixteenth and seventeenth centuries, depicting famous persons, animals, social customs, pastimes, hobbies, costuming conventions, themes, myths, and the like from the world that Shakespeare knew.
- For those who prefer the convenience of studying online, *The Complete Works of Shakespeare* is now available as a Pearson eText. The eText offers complete note-taking capabilities so you can mark the text as you would a printed page. Housed within MyLiteratureLab, this dynamic online tool provides engaging multimedia resources that personalize, stimulate, and measure learning for each student.

SUPPLEMENTS

The following supplements are available free when ordered with this text. Please consult your local Pearson representative if you would like to set up a value pack.

Evaluating a Performance, **by Mike Greenwald,** informs students about stage and theatrical performance and helps them to become more critical viewers of dramatic productions (ISBN 0-321-09541-3).

Screening Shakespeare: Using Film to Understand the Plays, **by Michael Greer,** is a brief, practical guide to select feature films of the most commonly taught plays (ISBN 0-321-19479-9).

David Bevington
2012

GENERAL INTRODUCTION

READING SHAKESPEARE IN THE TWENTY-FIRST CENTURY

Why read Shakespeare today? He lived some four centuries ago. He wrote in an earlier form of English that needs getting used to. His vocabulary is daunting. He and his audiences lived in a world that was remarkably different from ours: a world of religious wars between Catholic and Protestant, of competing monarchies, and of extreme contrasts between the wealth of a tiny wealthy ruling elite and the poverty of a huge underclass composed largely of agricultural laborers. Travel was unsafe and sanitation conditions were rudimentary. Shakespeare dramatizes the lives of ancient kings and personages that are not an immediate part of our own history. He is familiar with old myths and legends that are no longer current today. Given these circumstances, how can Shakespeare hope to be relevant?

Until recently, Shakespeare was more a required subject in schools and colleges than is the case today. As a mandatory subject, he was resisted like any inflexible requirement. Why study something simply because it is a traditional part of the curriculum? Isn't that boring? In an age when we are inclined to be wary of dead European white male authors, isn't Shakespeare a prime candidate for dismissal? He is all of those things: dead, European, white, and male.

Yet Shakespeare lives, despite these hazards, in the theater, in film and video, and in the classroom. The evidence is all around us. Enrollments are up in colleges and universities, largely on a voluntary basis. And Shakespeare has enjoyed a remarkable revival in film and video. See Appendix 4 at the back of this volume for an extensive account of plays available in films and video, along with a selective play-by-play filmography giving dates, directors, and leading actors.

Here we might name some of the greatest Shakespeare films of the twentieth and twenty-first centuries, to make the point of Shakespeare's great popularity on screen. Mary Pickford and Douglas Fairbanks Sr. starred as Kate and Petruchio in the first full-length talking film of a Shakespeare play, *The Taming of the Shrew*, 1929. Max Reinhardt's *A Midsummer Night's Dream*, 1935, starred Mickey Rooney as Puck and James Cagney as Bottom the Weaver, along with some other Hollywood celebrities. Franco Zeffirelli cast Richard Burton and Elizabeth Taylor as Petruchio and Kate in his *The Taming of the Shrew* (1967), Leonard Whiting and Olivia Hussey as the title characters in his *Romeo and Juliet* (1968), and Mel Gibson as the protagonist in his *Hamlet* (1990), along with Glenn Close as Gertrude, Helena Bonham Carter as Ophelia, Ian Holm as Polonius, Alan Bates as Claudius, and Paul Scofield as the Ghost.

Laurence Olivier achieved great success in 1944 with his full-length color film of *Henry V*, produced during World War II to encourage patriotic support for the war effort against Germany. Olivier's *Hamlet*, 1948, *Richard III*, 1955, and *Othello*, 1965, were no less popular.

Orson Welles's *Macbeth*, 1948, and *Othello*, 1952, were conscious attempts to show that the United States could match the British film industry in Shakespearean high art. Welles's *Chimes at Midnight* (1965), with himself in the role of Falstaff, combined elements of *1* and *2 Henry IV* and bits of *The Merry Wives of Windsor* to produce a moving account of Prince Hal's friendship with, and ultimate rejection of, Falstaff.

Another wave of Shakespeare films began in 1989 with Kenneth Branagh's highly successful *Henry V*, challenging the patriotism of Olivier's 1944 version with a more matter-of-fact appraisal of warmaking. *Much Ado About Nothing* followed in 1993 with Branagh as Benedick and his then wife Emma Thompson as Beatrice, along with Denzel Washington as Don Pedro, Keanu Reeves as Don John, and Michael Keaton as Dogberry. Branagh repeated the surefire stratagem of employing star actors in his four-hour *Hamlet*, 1996, with himself as Hamlet, Julie Christie as Gertrude, Kate Winslet as Ophelia, Derek Jacobi as Claudius, and a host of cameo appearances by Jack Lemmon (Marcellus), Gérard Depardieu (Reynaldo), Robin Williams (Osric), Billy Crystal (the Gravedigger), and Charlton Heston (the Player King). More recent have been Branagh's *Love's Labour's Lost* (2000) and *As You Like It* (2006).

Other famous directors on the Shakespeare scene have included Akira Kurosawa, with his *Throne of Blood*, 1957, based on *Macbeth*, and his *Ran*, 1985, based on *King Lear*; Grigori Kozintsev, with two notable Russian films, *Hamlet*, 1964, and *King Lear*, 1970; Peter Brook, directing *King Lear* in 1971 with Paul Scofield in the lead role; Trevor Nunn, directing *Antony and Cleopatra* (1974), *The Comedy of Errors* (1978), *Macbeth* (1979), *Othello* (1990), and *Twelfth Night* (1996); Peter Hall, directing *A Midsummer Night's Dream* (1969); Roman Polanski, directing *Macbeth* (1971); Julie Taymor, directing *Titus Andronicus* (1999) and *The Tempest* (2010), with Helen Mirren as a female protagonist named Prospera; Baz Luhrmann, directing *Romeo + Juliet* (1996); Michael Almereyda, directing *Hamlet* (2000); Michael Radford, directing Al Pacino, Jeremy Irons, and others in *The Merchant of Venice* (2004), based on a Broadway production; Gregory Doran, directing *Macbeth* (2004), with Antony Sher in the title role; Gregory Doran, directing David Tennant, Patrick Stewart, and others in a TV film version of *Hamlet* based on a stage production for the Royal Shakespeare Company (2009); Trevor Nunn, directing *King Lear* (2009), with Ian McKellen as King Lear; Nicholas Hytner, directing *Hamlet* (2010), with Rory Kinnear in the title role; Ralph Fiennes, directing *Coriolanus* (2011), with Fiennes himself in the title role; and still others.

Film adaptations are a sure sign of Shakespeare's popularity today. Along with the films of Akira Kurosawa listed above, one thinks immediately of *West Side Story*, 1961, based on *Romeo and Juliet*; *Kiss Me, Kate*, 1953, based on *The Taming of the Shrew*; Gil Junger's *10 Things I Hate About You*, 1999, based on the same play; Tim Blake Nelson's *O*, 2001, based on *Othello*; and *Shakespeare in Love*, 1998, containing some fine scenes from *Romeo and Juliet*. Again, there are many others.

Recent stage productions of Shakespeare's plays have also enjoyed as great a success, albeit necessarily for less-global audiences. Ian McKellen in *King Lear* (2007) has toured intercontinentally to positive reviews. Greg Doran had great success at the Swan Theatre in Stratford-upon-Avon with his *Othello* (2004), starring Antony Sher as Iago. Sher was no less astonishing as Richard III at Stratford-upon-Avon in 1984. Equally wonderful in the same role were Ian McKellen at London's National Theatre in 1990 and Simon Russell Beale at Stratford in 1992. Patrick Stewart has been very well received in *Macbeth* (London, 2007). Some of the best film versions we have began as stage productions, including Olivier's *Richard III*, Branagh's *Henry V*, McKellen and Dench in *Macbeth*, McKellen and Willard White in *Othello*, *West Side Story*, *Kiss Me, Kate*, and still others. *Much Ado About Nothing* was produced by Joseph Papp and directed by A. J. Antoon at the New York Shakespeare Festival in Delacorte Theatre in 1972 before it was telecast the following year. The enduring popularity of outdoor summer performances in New York's Central Park is confirmed by the fact that fans will wait in line for hours to see the productions. Other festivals and repertory Shakespeare companies at Stratford in Canada, Stratford-upon-Avon in England; Ashland, Oregon; Washington, D.C.; Chicago; and many others are no less a mark of tribute to Shakespeare as a preeminently successful writer for the stage. Shakespeare has become big business.

Seeing one or more productions of a Shakespeare play is often a very good way to start. Films are easily rented or otherwise obtained in video, and watching a film is something we all generally enjoy. Seeing a play in the theater can certainly be no less engrossing, but the opportunities come far less often, so the thing to do is to take advantage of film or video. A common experience today is for viewers, in the theater or watching a screen, to be surprised with how clear the story can be and how good acting can really help with interpretation. Watching a play, even for the first time, one scarcely notices how some forms of expression might seem a little archaic or unfamiliar. Fine actors deliver the lines with their own well-trained comprehension, so that what they say to each other or in soliloquy sounds intelligible and persuasive.

When one reads a play for the first time, probably the best thing to do is to ignore the notes for the moment and try to hear voices saying the lines as they would in a performance. We can take advantage of the notes in a subsequent reading, as we retrace our steps and stop to reflect on the meanings of unfamiliar terms. Reading a play, by Shakespeare or anyone else, is a challenging and exciting assignment, because as readers our task is in effect to produce and direct the play in our heads. We need to imagine the setting, whether indoors or outdoors, with scenic effects and furniture as needed. We need to clothe the actors in appropriate garb and give them the hand props called for in the script. We need to decide what age the actors are and what they look like. As Shakespeare says to his spectators in the opening chorus of Henry V:

> Piece out our imperfections with your thoughts.
> Into a thousand parts divide one man,
> And make imaginary puissance.
> Think, when we talk of horses, that you see them
> Printing their proud hoofs i'th' receiving earth.

Shakespeare asks us to adorn the actors with our thoughts and "Carry them here and there, jumping o'er times." We are in charge of the show. Classroom discussion can be invaluable, of course. But one needs to take individual initiative and be an active, imaginative reader. One needs to ask questions all the time: why is a character saying what he or she is saying to another character? Where are the changes in tempo or "beat" in a scene? What happens when someone else enters or exits? What are the characters trying to do in a particular scene? What are they after? How do they change under the pressure of observation and conversation?

Why read Shakespeare, when some more modern dramatist or novelist or poet or short story writer might seem more available and relevant? Each reader or viewer must answer this for him- or herself, of course, but the general view down through the centuries is that Shakespeare is an extraordinary poet and that he excels in the breadth and incisiveness of his depictions of human experience. As a poet he commands an extraordinary range of vocabulary and image-making. His vocabulary is roughly twice that of his nearest competitor in English and American literature. He has a formidable talent in his use of verse forms, from blank verse to rhymed couplets to the fourteen-line sonnet to various lyric stanzas. His prose is admirably flexible, especially for comedy. He thinks in images, as all great poets do. He says things so well that countless utterances of his have become proverbial: "Neither a borrower nor a lender be," "The apparel oft proclaims the man," "Frailty, thy name is woman," "The time is out of joint," "Brevity is the soul of wit," "To be or not to be, that is the question," "Thus conscience doth make cowards of us all," "Get thee to a nunnery," "There's a divinity that shapes our ends, rough-hew them how we will," and on and on. All these are chosen from *Hamlet*; the list could be substantially extended just in this one play. Shakespeare is an important architect of the English language as we have come to know it.

Then, too, we have in Shakespeare's writings a remarkable breadth of human experience, analyzed and depicted with acumen and compassionate understanding. His characters fall in love, experience jealousy and rivalry, cope with parental obtuseness, learn what it is like to challenge the authority of a parent, experience frustra- tion in personal ambitions, suffer neglect and misunderstanding. As they grow older, they often encounter religious doubt, go through the dark night of skeptical uncertainty and loss of faith, know what it is to become middle-aged and fearful of a decline in sexual potency and physical strength, and discover to their horror their own capacity for evil, even to the point of killing another human being. They sometimes experience the total disillusionment of misanthropy and misogyny, feel shame and the need to be forgiven, and worry about retirement from the world. One beautiful thing about this richly complex portrait of human striving is that it paints a chronological portrait of the life of the human being from childhood to middle years and then to a decline toward death, all of this brilliantly laid out by Shakespeare as his plays and poems move from early to late. The plays and poems are the biography of what it is to be human.

The fact that Shakespeare's world is very different from ours ought to be an added incentive for wanting to read him, not a detraction. We all need to know more about other cultures and other value systems, in our world today and in the past. Strangeness can give us a perspective on ourselves. It can give us the chance to question our values by comparing them with what other peoples in other eras have believed in.

This is only a sketch of the author from whom we can hope to learn so much about ourselves. The place to begin, perhaps, is to locate Shakespeare in the England and the London in which he lived and worked. What was England like in the late sixteenth and early seventeenth centuries, while he was alive, from 1564 to 1616? In what ways did it differ from our modern world? What insights into his work can we derive by seeing him in the context of his personal environment?

LIFE IN SHAKESPEARE'S ENGLAND

England during Shakespeare's lifetime (1564–1616) was a proud nation with a strong sense of national identity, but it was also a small nation by modern standards. Probably not more than five million people lived in the whole of England, considerably fewer than now live in London. England's territories in France were no longer extensive, as they had been during the fourteenth century and earlier; in fact, by the end of Queen Elizabeth's reign (1558–1603), England had virtually retired from the territories she had previously controlled on the Continent, especially in France. Wales was a conquered principality. England's overseas empire in America had scarcely begun, with the Virginia settlement established in the 1580s. Scotland was not yet a part of Great Britain; union with Scotland would not take place until 1707,

The plowman

"Enclosure" was a problem throughout the sixteenth century in England. Croplands were converted into pasturage. The livelihood of the plowman was threatened by the pasturing of sheep and the growing production of wool.

despite the fact that King James VI of Scotland assumed the English throne in 1603 as James I of England. Ireland, although declared a kingdom under English rule in 1541, was more a source of trouble than of economic strength. The last years of Elizabeth's reign, especially from 1597 to 1601, were plagued by the rebellion of the Irish under Hugh O'Neill, Earl of Tyrone. Thus, England of the sixteenth and early seventeenth centuries was both small and isolated.

THE SOCIAL AND ECONOMIC BACKGROUND

By and large, England was a rural land. Much of the kingdom was still wooded, though timber was being used increasingly in manufacturing and shipbuilding. The area of the Midlands, today heavily industrialized, was at that time still a region of great trees, green fields, and clear streams. England's chief means of livelihood was agriculture. This part of the economy was generally in a bad way, however, and people who lived off the land did not share in the prosperity of many Londoners. A problem throughout the sixteenth century was that of "enclosure": the conversion by rich landowners of croplands into pasturage. Farmers and peasants complained bitterly that they were being dispossessed and starved for the benefit of livestock. Rural uprisings and food riots were common, to the dismay of the authorities. Some Oxfordshire peasants arose in 1596, threatening to massacre the gentry and march on London; other riots had occurred in 1586 and 1591. There were thirteen riots in Kent alone during Elizabeth's reign. Unrest continued into the reign of James I, notably the Midlands' rising of 1607. Although the

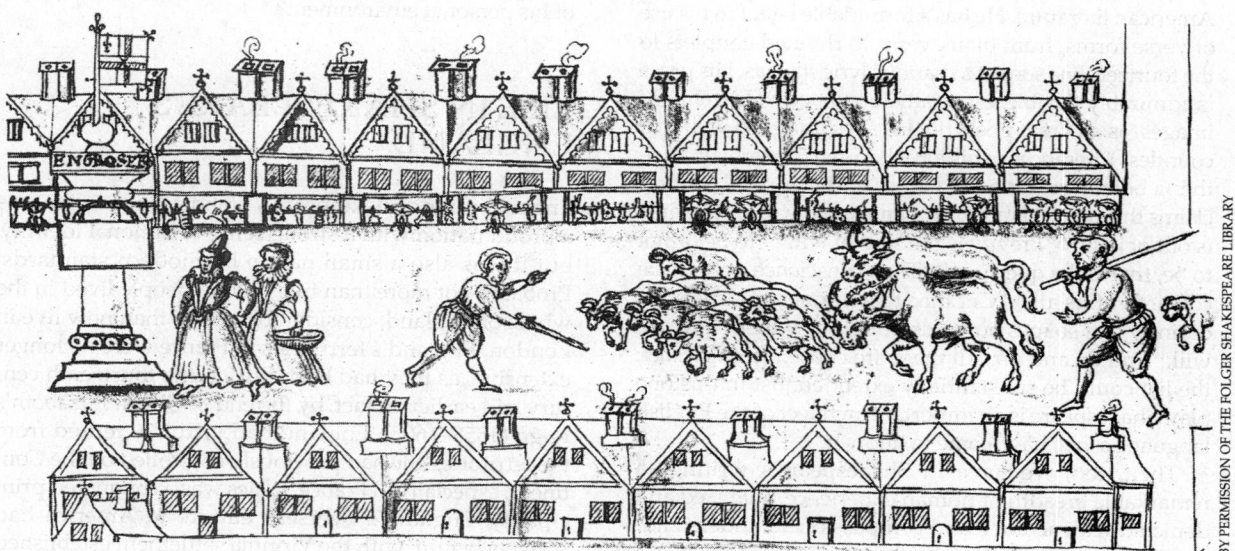

Sixteenth-century London was a city teeming with activity. Pedestrians were often forced to make way for the livestock being driven through the streets.

government did what it could to inhibit enclosure, the economic forces at work were too massive and too inadequately understood to be curbed by governmental fiat. The absence of effective bureaucracies or agencies of coercion compounded the difficulty of governmental control. Pasture used large areas with greater efficiency than crop farming and required far less labor. The wool produced by the pasturing of sheep was needed in ever increasing amounts for the manufacture of cloth.

The wool industry also experienced occasional economic difficulties, to be sure; overexpansion in the early years of the sixteenth century created a glutted market that collapsed disastrously in 1551, producing widespread unemployment. Despite such fluctuations and reversals, however, the wool industry at least provided handsome profits for some landowners and middlemen. Mining and manufacture in coal, iron, tin, copper, and lead, although insignificant by modern standards, also were expanding at a significant rate. Trading companies exploited the rich new resources of the Americas, as well as of eastern Europe and the Orient. Queen Elizabeth aided economic development by keeping England out of war with her continental enemies as long as possible, despite provocations from those powers and despite the eagerness of some of her advisers to retaliate.

Certainly England's economic condition was better than the economic condition of the rest of the Continent; an Italian called England "the land of comforts." Yet although some prosperity did exist, it was not evenly distributed. Especially during Shakespeare's first years in London, in the late 1580s and the 1590s, the gap between rich and poor grew more and more extreme. Elizabeth's efforts at peacemaking were no longer able to prevent years of war with the Catholic powers of the Continent. Taxation grew heavier, and inflation proceeded at an unusually rapid rate during this period. A succession of bad harvests compounded the miseries of those who dwelled on the land. When the hostilities on the Continent ceased for a time in about 1597, a wave of returning veterans added to unemployment and crime. The rising prosperity experienced by Shakespeare and other fortunate Londoners was undeniably real, but it was not universal. Nowhere was the contrast between rich and poor more visible than in London.

COURTESY, GUILDHALL LIBRARY, CORPORATION OF LONDON

This detail from a 1572 map of London shows closely packed buildings intersected with throroughfares, with gardens and open spaces on the outskirts.

BY PERMISSION OF THE FOLGER SHAKESPEARE LIBRARY

London Bridge, lined with shops, houses, and severed heads on poles, provided a colorful route for those traveling between the north and south banks of the Thames. A number of Elizabethan theaters, including the Globe, were located on the south bank.

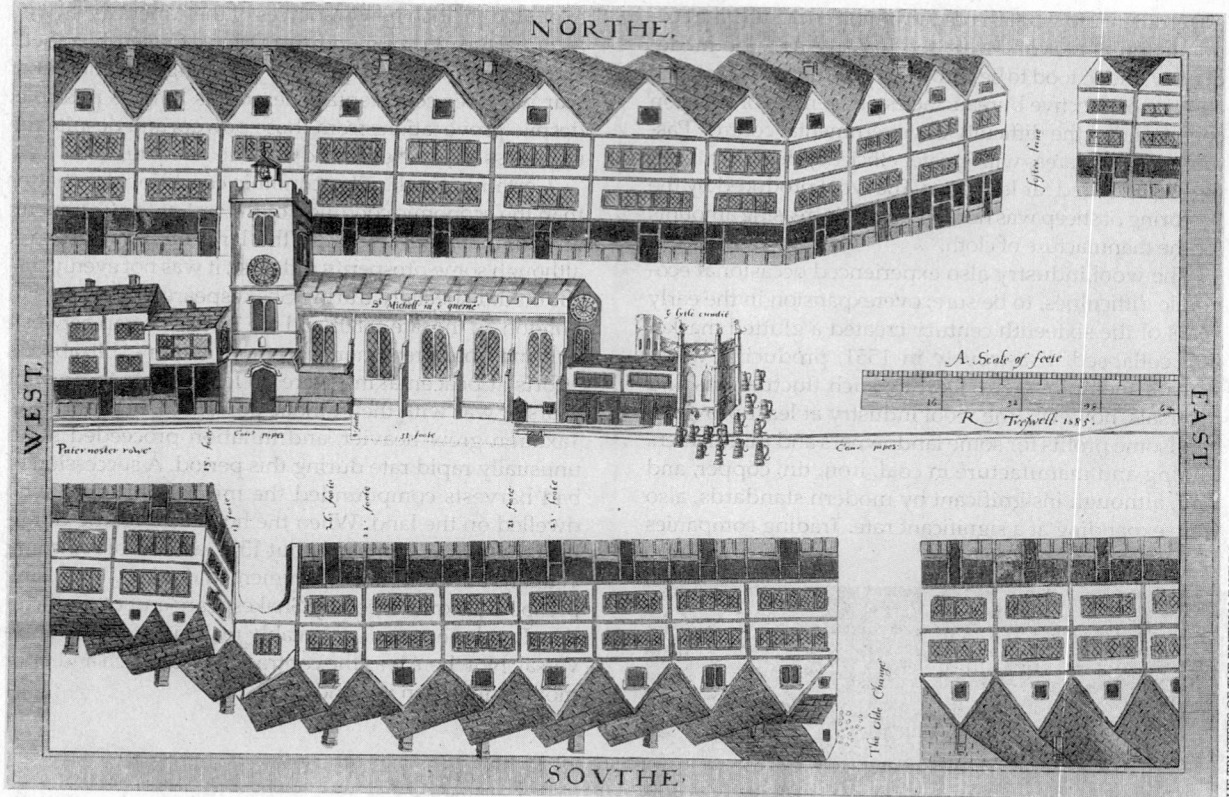

The taverns of Cheapside in London were popular and occasionally rowdy.

London

Sixteenth-century London was at once more attractive and less attractive than twenty-first-century London. It was full of trees and gardens; meadows and cultivated lands reached in some places to its very walls. Today we can perhaps imagine the way in which it bordered clear streams and green fields when we approach from a distance some noncommercial provincial city such as Lincoln, York, or Hereford. Partly surrounded by its ancient wall, London was by no means a large metropolis. With 190,000 to 200,000 inhabitants in the city proper and its suburbs, it was nonetheless the largest city of Europe, and its dominance among English cities was even more striking; in 1543–1544, London paid thirty times the subsidy of Norwich, then the second-largest city in the kingdom (15,000 inhabitants). Although London's population had expanded into the surrounding area in all directions, the city proper stretched along the north bank of the Thames River from the old Tower of London on the east to St. Paul's Cathedral and the Fleet Ditch on the west—a distance of little more than a mile. Visitors approaching London from the south bank of the Thames (the Bankside) and crossing London Bridge could see virtually all of this exciting city lying before them. London Bridge itself was one of the major

attractions of the city, lined with shops and richly decorated on occasion for the triumphal entry of a king or queen.

Yet London had its grim and ugly side as well. On London Bridge could sometimes be seen the heads of executed traitors. The city's houses were generally small and crowded; its streets were often narrow and filthy. In the absence of sewers, open ditches in the streets served to collect and carry off refuse. Frequent epidemics of the bubonic plague were the inevitable result of unsanitary conditions and medical ignorance. Lighting of the streets at night was generally nonexistent, and the constabulary was notoriously unreliable. Shakespeare gives us unforgettable satires of night watchmen and bumbling police officials in *Much Ado About Nothing* (Dogberry and the night watch) and *Measure for Measure* (Constable Elbow). Prostitution thrived in the suburbs, conveniently located, although beyond the reach of the London authorities. Again, we are indebted to Shakespeare for a memorable portrayal in *Measure for Measure* of just such a demimonde (Mistress Overdone the bawd, Pompey her pimp, and various customers). Houses of prostitution were often found in the vicinity of the public theaters, since the theaters also took advantage of suburban locations to escape the stringent regulations imposed by London's

Lord Mayor and Council of Aldermen. The famous Globe Theatre, for example, was on the south bank of the Thames, a short distance west of London Bridge. Another theatrical building (called simply "The Theatre"), used earlier by Shakespeare and the Lord Chamberlain's players, was located in Finsbury Fields, a short distance across Moorfields from London's northeast corner. The suburbs also housed various con games and illegal operations, some of them brilliantly illustrated (and no doubt exaggerated) in Ben Jonson's *The Alchemist* (1610).

Roughly half of London's total population, perhaps 100,000 people, lived within its walls, and as many more in the suburbs. The royal palace of Whitehall, Westminster Abbey (then known as the Abbey Church of St. Peter), the Parliament House, and Westminster Hall were well outside London, two miles or so to the west on the Thames River. They remain today in the same location, in Westminster, although the metropolis of London has long since surrounded these official buildings.

Travel

Travel was still extremely painful and slow because of the poor condition of the roads. Highway robbers were a constant threat. (The celebrated highway robbery in Shakespeare's *1 Henry IV* takes place at Gads Hill, on the main road between London and Canterbury.) English inns seem to have been good, however, and certainly much better than the inns of the Continent. Travel on horseback was the most common method of transportation, and probably the most comfortable, since coach building was a new and imperfect art. Coaches of state, some of which we see in prints and pictures of the era, were lumbering affairs, no doubt handsome enough in processions, but springless, unwieldly, and hard to pull. Carts and wagons were used for carrying merchandise, but packsaddles were safer and quicker. Under such difficulties, no metropolitan area such as London could possibly have thrived in the interior. London depended for its commercial greatness upon the Thames River and its access to the North Sea.

Commerce

When Elizabeth came to the English throne in 1558, England's chief foreign trade was with Antwerp, Bruges, and other Belgian cities. Antwerp was an especially important market for England's export of wool cloth. This market was seriously threatened, however, since the Low Countries were under the domination of the Catholic King of Spain, Philip II. When Philip undertook to punish his Protestant subjects in the Low Countries for their religious heresy, many of Elizabeth's counselors and subjects urged her to come to the defense of England's Protestant neighbors and trading allies. Elizabeth held back. Philip's armies attacked Antwerp in 1576 and again in 1585,

putting an end to the commercial ascendancy of that great northern European metropolis. Perhaps as many as one-third of Antwerp's merchants and artisans settled in London, bringing with them their expert knowledge of commerce and manufacture. The influx of so many skilled workers and merchants into London produced problems of unemployment and overcrowding but contributed nevertheless to London's emergence as a leading port of trade.

English ships assumed a dominant position in Mediterranean trade, formerly carried on mainly by the Venetians. In the Baltic Sea, England competed successfully in trade that had previously been controlled by the Hanseatic League. Bristol thrived on commerce with Ireland and subsequently on trade with the Western Hemisphere. Boston and Hull increased their business with Scandinavian ports. The Russia Company was founded in 1555; the Levant Company became the famous East India Company in 1600; and the Virginia Company opened up trade with the New World in the Western Hemisphere. Fisheries were developed in the North Sea, in the waters north of Ireland, and off the banks of Newfoundland. Elizabeth and her ministers encouraged this commercial expansion.

The Poor Laws and Apprenticeship

Despite the new prosperity experienced by many Elizabethans, especially in London, unemployment remained a serious problem. The suppresssion of the monasteries in 1536–1539, as part of Henry VIII's reformation of the Catholic Church, had dispossessed a large class of persons who were not easily reemployed. Other causes of unemployment, such as the periodic collapse of the wool trade, dispossession of farm workers by enclosure of land, the sudden influx of skilled artisans from Antwerp, and the

Although some Elizabethans rose to great wealth, poverty and unemployment were widespread.

THE BRITISH LIBRARY

return of army veterans, have already been mentioned. Elizabethan parliaments attempted to cope with the problem of unemployment but did so in ways that seem unduly harsh today. Several laws were passed between 1531, when the distinction between those poor needing charity and those unwilling to work first became law, and 1597–1598. The harshest of the laws was that of 1547, providing that vagabonds be branded and enslaved for two years; escape was punishable by death or life enslavement. This act was repealed in 1549, but subsequent acts of 1572 and 1576 designated ten classes of vagrants and required municipal authorities to provide work for the healthy unemployed of each town or parish. This localization of responsibility laid the basis for what has been known historically as the "poor rate" (a local tax levied for the support of the poor) and for that sinister institution, the workhouse. The provisions of this act remained in force for centuries. The most comprehensive laws were those of the Parliament of 1597–1598, which repeated many provisions of earlier acts and added harsh, punitive penalties intended to send vagabonds back to the parishes in which they had been born or had last worked. After 1597, no begging was permitted; the poor were supposed to be provided for by the "poor rate" already established.

Regulations for apprentices were no less strict. An act of Parliament of 1563, known as the Statute of Artificers, gave the craft trades of England—still organized as medieval guilds—virtually complete authority over the young persons apprenticed to a trade. The law severely limited access to apprenticeship to sons of families with estates worth at least forty shillings of income. Apprenticeship usually began between the ages of fourteen and seventeen and lasted for a period of not less than seven years. During this time, the young worker lived with the family of the employer. Without such an extensive apprenticeship, entry into the skilled crafts was virtually impossible. Apprenticeships were not open, however, in all guilds, and the law courts subsequently ruled that apprenticeship rules did not apply to crafts developed after 1563, so that exceptions did exist. All able-bodied workers not bound to crafts were supposed to work in agriculture. Acting companies, such as the company Shakespeare joined, were not technically organized as guilds, though the boys who played women's parts were in some cases at least bound by the terms of apprenticeship; a number of the adult actors belonged to one London guild or another and could use that status to apprentice boys. We do not know whether Shakespeare actually served such an indenture before becoming a full member of his acting company.

Social Change

The opportunities for rapid economic advance in Elizabethan England, though limited almost entirely to those who were already prosperous, did produce social change and a quality of restlessness in English society. "New men" at court were an increasing phenomenon under the Tudor monarchs, especially Henry VII and Henry VIII, who tended to rely on loyal counselors of humble origin rather than on the once-too-powerful nobility. Cardinal Wolsey, for example, rose from obscurity to become the most mighty subject of Henry VIII's realm, with a newly built residence (Hampton Court) rivaling the splendor of the King's own palaces. He was detested as an upstart by old aristocrats, such as the Duke of Norfolk, and his sudden fall was as spectacular as had been his rise to power. The Earl of Leicester, Queen Elizabeth's first favorite, was a descendant of the Edmund Dudley who had risen from unpretentious beginnings to great eminence under Henry VII, Queen Elizabeth's grandfather. Although Queen Elizabeth did not contribute substantially to the new aristocracy—she created only three peers from 1573 onward—new and influential families were numerous throughout the century. Conversely, the ancient families discovered that they were no longer entrusted with positions of highest authority. To be sure, the aristocracy remained at the apex of England's social structure. New aspirants to power emulated the aristocracy by purchasing land and building splendid residences, rather than defining themselves as a rich new "middle class." Bourgeois status was something the new men put behind them as quickly as they could. Moreover, social mobility could work in both directions: upward and downward. Many men were quickly ruined by the costly and competitive business of seeking favor at the Tudor court. The poor, in a vast majority, enjoyed virtually no rights at all. Nonetheless, the Elizabethan era was one of greater opportunity for rapid social and economic advancement among persons of wealth than England had heretofore known.

Increased economic contacts with the outside world inevitably led to the importation of new styles of living. Such new fashions, together with the rapid changes now possible in social position, produced a reaction of dismay from those who feared the destruction of traditional English values. Attitudes toward Italy veered erratically between condemnation and admiration: on the one hand, Italy was the home of the Catholic Church and originator of many supposedly decadent fashions, whereas, on the other hand, Italy was the cradle of humanism and the country famed for Venice's experiment in republican government. To many conservative Englishmen, the word *Italianate* connoted a whole range of villainous practices, including diabolical methods of torture and revenge: poisoned books of devotion that would kill the unsuspecting victims who kissed them, ingeniously contrived chairs that would close upon the person who sat in them, and the like. The revenge plays of Shakespeare's contemporaries, such as *Antonio's Revenge* by John Marston, *The Revenger's Tragedy* probably by Thomas Middleton, and *The White Devil* by John Webster, offer spectacular caricatures of the

This brothel scene, featuring gambling or dicing, illustrates some of the vices that were attributed to the corrupting influence from abroad.

so-called Italianate style in murder. The name of Italy was also associated with licentiousness, immorality, and outlandish fashions in clothes. France, too, was accused of encouraging such extravagances in dress as ornamented headdresses, stiffly pleated ruffs, padded doublets, puffed or double sleeves, and richly decorated hose. Rapid changes in fashion added to the costliness of being up to date and thereby increased the outcry against vanity in dress. Fencing, dicing, the use of cosmetics, the smoking of tobacco, the drinking of imported wines, and almost every vice known to humanity were attributed by angry moralists to the corrupting influence from abroad.

Not all Englishmen deplored continental fashion, of course. Persons of advanced taste saw the importation of European styles as a culturally liberating process. Fashion thus became a subject of debate between moral traditionalists and those who welcomed the new styles. The controversy was a bitter one, with religious overtones, in which the reformers' angry accusations became increasingly extreme. This attack on changing fashion was, in fact, an integral part of the Puritan movement. It therefore stressed the sinfulness, not only of extravagance in clothing, but also of the costliness in building great houses and other such worldly pursuits. Those whose sympathies were Puritan became more and more disaffected with the cultural values represented by the court, and thus English society drifted further and further toward irreconcilable conflict.

Shakespeare's personal views on this controversy are hard to determine and do not bear importantly on his achievement as an artist. Generally, however, we can observe that his many references to changes in fashion cater neither to the avant-garde nor to reactionary traditionalists. Shakespeare's audience was, after all, a broadly national one. It included many well-informed Londoners who viewed "Italianate" fashion neither with enthusiasm nor with alarm, but with satiric laughter. Such spectators would certainly have seen the point, for example, in Mercutio's witty diatribe at the expense of the new French style

in fencing. The object of his scorn is Tybalt, who, according to Mercutio, "fights as you sing prick song" and fancies himself to be "the very butcher of a silk button." "Is not this a lamentable thing," asks Mercutio rhetorically, "that we should be thus afflicted with these strange flies, these fashionmongers, these pardon-me's, who stand so much on the new form that they cannot sit at ease on the old bench?" (*Romeo and Juliet*, 2.4.20–35). In a similar vein, Shakespeare's audience would have appreciated the joking in *The Merchant of Venice* about England's servile imitation of continental styles in clothes. "What say you, then, to Falconbridge, the young baron of England?" asks Nerissa of her mistress Portia concerning one of Portia's many suitors. Portia replies, "How oddly he is suited! I think he bought his doublet in Italy, his round hose in France, his bonnet in Germany, and his behavior everywhere" (1.2.64–74). Court butterflies in Shakespeare's plays who bow and scrape and fondle their plumed headgear, like Le Beau in *As You Like It* and Osric in *Hamlet*, are the objects of ridicule. Hotspur in *1 Henry IV*, proud northern aristocrat that he is, has nothing but contempt for an effeminate courtier, "perfumèd like a milliner," who has come from King Henry to discuss the question of prisoners (1.3.36). Throughout Shakespeare's plays, the use of cosmetics generally has the negative connotation of artificial beauty used to conceal inward corruption, as in Claudius's reference to "the harlot's cheek, beautied with plast'ring art" (*Hamlet*, 3.1.52). Yet Shakespeare's treatment of newness in fashion is never shrill in tone. Nor does he fail in his dramas to give an honorable place to the ceremonial use of wealth and splendid costuming. His plays thus avoid both extremes in the controversy over changing fashions, though they give plentiful evidence as to the liveliness and currency of the topic.

Shakespeare also reflects a contemporary interest in the problem of usury, especially in *The Merchant of Venice*. Although usury was becoming more and more of a necessity, emotional attitudes toward it changed only slowly. The traditional moral view condemned usury as forbidden by Christian teaching; on the other hand, European governments of the sixteenth century found themselves increasingly obliged to borrow large sums of money. The laws against usury were alternatively relaxed and enforced, according to the economic exigencies of the moment. Shakespeare's plays capture the Elizabethan ambivalence of attitude toward this feared but necessary practice (see Introduction to *The Merchant of Venice*). Similarly, most Englishmen had contradictory attitudes toward what we today would call the law of supply and demand in the marketplace. Conservative moralists complained bitterly when merchants exploited the scarcity of some commodity by forcing up prices; the practice was denounced as excessive profit taking and declared to be sinful, like usury. In economic policy, then, as in matters of changing fashion or increased social mobility, many Englishmen were ambivalent about the perennial conflict between the old order and the new.

Elizabethan Houses

Those fortunate Englishmen who grew wealthy in the reign of Elizabeth took special pleasure in building themselves fine new houses with furnishings to match. Chimneys were increasingly common, so that smoke no longer had to escape through a hole in the roof. Pewter, or even silver, dishes took the place of the wooden spoon and trencher. Beds, and even pillows, became common. Carpets were replacing rushes as covering for the floors; wainscoting, tapestries or hangings, and pictures appeared on the walls; and glass began to be used extensively for windows.

Despite the warnings of those moralists who preached against the vanity of worldly acquisition, domestic comfort made considerable progress in Elizabethan England. Many splendid Tudor mansions stand today, testifying to the important social changes that had taken place between the strife-torn fifteenth century and the era of relative peace under Elizabeth. The battlement, the moat, the fortified gate, and the narrow window used for archery or firearms generally disappeared in favor of handsome gardens and terraces. At the lower end of the social scale, the agricultural laborers who constituted the great mass of the English population were generally poor, malnourished, and uneducated, but they seem to have enjoyed greater physical security than did their ancestors

Tudor mansions were often splendid, with impressive gardens and terraces. Shown here is Little Moreton Hall, in Cheshire, built in 1559.

in the fifteenth century and no longer needed to bring their cows, pigs, and poultry into their dwellings at night in order to protect them from thieves. City houses, of which many exist today, were often large and imposing structures, three or four stories in height, and framed usually of strong oak, with the walls filled in with brick and plaster. Although the frontage on the streets of London was usually narrow, many houses had trees and handsome gardens at the rear. Of course London also had its plentiful share of tenements for the urban poor.

With the finer houses owned by the fortunate elite came features of privacy that had been virtually unknown to previous generations. Life in the household of a medieval lord had generally focused on the great hall, which could serve variously as the kitchen, dining hall, and sitting room for the entire family and its retainers. The men drank in the hall in the evenings and slept there at night. The new dwellings of prosperous Elizabethans, on the other hand, featured private chambers into which the family and the chief guests could retire.

The Elizabethans built well. Not only do we still admire their houses, but also we can see from their oriel windows and stained glass, their broad staircases, their jewels, and their costumes that they treasured the new beauty of their lives made possible by the culture of the Renaissance. Although the graphic and plastic arts did not thrive in England to the same extent as in Italy, France, and the Low Countries, England made lasting achievements in architecture, as well as in music, drama, and all forms of literature.

THE POLITICAL AND RELIGIOUS BACKGROUND

England under the Tudors suffered from almost unceasing religious conflict. The battle over religion affected every aspect of life and none more so than politics. At the very beginning of the Tudor reign, to be sure, England's problem was not religious but dynastic. Henry VII, the first of the Tudor kings, brought an end to the devastating civil wars of the fifteenth century with his overthrow

On Sundays crowds gathered to listen to the sermon at St. Paul's Cathedral, the subject of this anonymous painting dated 1616.

The Knights of the Garter belonged to the highest order of knighthood; many were influential courtiers and favorites of Queen Elizabeth. A masterful politician, Elizabeth remained unmarried throughout her life. A marriage would have upset the political balance and would have committed her to one foreign nation or to one constituency at home.

of Richard III at the battle of Bosworth Field in 1485. The civil wars thus ended were the so-called Wars of the Roses, between the Lancastrian House of Henry VI (symbolized by the red rose) and the Yorkist House of Edward IV (symbolized by the white rose). Shakespeare chose these eventful struggles as the subject for his first series of English history plays, from *Henry VI* in three parts to *Richard III.* The House of Lancaster drew its title from John of Gaunt, Duke of Lancaster, father of Henry IV and great-grandfather of Henry VI; the House of York drew its title from Edmund Langley, Duke of York, great-grandfather of Edward IV and Richard III. Because John of Gaunt and Edmund Langley had been brothers, virtually all the noble contestants in this War of the Roses were cousins, caught in a remorseless dynastic struggle for control of the English crown. Many of them lost their lives in the fighting. By 1485, England was exhausted from civil conflict. Although Henry VII's own dynastic claim to the throne was weak, he managed to suppress factional opposition and to give England the respite from war so desperately needed. His son, Henry VIII, inherited a throne in 1509 that was more secure than it had been in nearly a century.

Henry VIII's notorious marital difficulties, however, soon brought an end to dynastic security and civil accord. Moreover, religious conflict within the Catholic Church was growing to the extent that a break with Rome appeared inevitable. Henry's marriage troubles precipitated that momentous event. Because he divorced his first wife, Katharine of Aragon, in 1530 without the consent of Rome, he was excommunicated by the pope. His response in 1534 was to have himself proclaimed "Protector and only Supreme Head of the Church and Clergy of England." This decisive act signaled the beginning of the Reformation in England, not many years after Martin Luther's momentous break with the papacy in 1517 and the consequent beginning of Lutheran Protestantism on the Continent. In England, Henry's act of defiance split the Church and the nation. Many persons chose Sir Thomas More's path of martyrdom rather than submit to Henry's new title as supreme head of the English church. Henry's later years did witness a period of retrenchment in religion, after the downfall of Thomas Cromwell in 1540, and indeed Henry's break with Rome had had its origin in political and marital strife as well as in matters of dogma and liturgy. Nevertheless, the establishment of an English church was now an accomplished fact. The accession of Henry's ten-year-old son Edward VI in 1547 gave reformers an opportunity to bring about rapid changes in English Protestantism. Archbishop Cranmer's forty-two articles of religion (1551) and his prayer book laid the basis for the Anglican Church of the sixteenth century.

The death of the sickly Edward VI in 1553 brought with it an intense crisis in religious politics and a

temporary reversal of England's religious orientation. The Duke of Northumberland, Protector and virtual ruler of England in Edward's last years, attempted to secure a Protestant succession and his own power by marrying his son to Lady Jane Grey, a granddaughter of Henry VII, whom Edward had named heir to the throne, but the proclamation of Lady Jane as Queen ended in failure. She was executed, as were her husband and father-in-law. For five years, England returned to Catholicism under the rule of Edward's elder sister Mary, daughter of the Catholic Queen Katharine of Aragon. The crisis accompanying such changes of government during this mid-century period was greatly exacerbated by the fact that all three of Henry VIII's living children were considered illegitimate by one faction or another of the English people. In Protestant eyes, Mary was the daughter of the divorced Queen Katharine, whose marriage to Henry had never been valid because she had previously been the spouse of Henry VIII's older brother Arthur. This Arthur had died at a young age, in 1502, shortly after his state marriage to the Spanish princess. If, as the Protestants insisted, Arthur had consummated the marriage, then Katharine's subsequent union with her deceased husband's brother was invalid, and Henry was free, instead, to marry Anne Boleyn—the mother-to-be of Elizabeth. In Catholic eyes, however, both Elizabeth and her brother Edward VI (son of Jane Seymour, Henry VIII's third wife) were the bastard issue of Henry's bigamous marriages; Henry's one and only true marriage in the Catholic faith was that to Katharine of Aragon. Edward and Elizabeth were regarded by many Catholics, at home and abroad, not only as illegitimate children, but also as illegitimate rulers, to be disobeyed and even overthrown by force. Thus, dynastic and marital conflicts became matters of grave political consequence.

Because of these struggles, Elizabeth's accession to the throne in 1558 remained an uncertainty until the last moment. Once she actually became ruler, England returned once more to the Protestant faith. Even then, tact and moderation were required to prevent open religious war. Elizabeth's genius at compromise prompted her to seek a middle position for her church, one that combined an episcopal form of church government (owing no allegiance to the pope) with an essentially traditional form of liturgy and dogma. As much as was practicable, she left matters up to individual conscience; she drew the line, however, where matters of conscience tended to "exceed their bounds and grow to be matter of faction." In practice, this meant that she did not tolerate avowed Catholics on the religious right or Protestant sects who denied the doctrine of the Trinity on the religious left. The foundation for this so-called Elizabethan compromise was the thirty-nine articles, adopted in 1563 and based in many respects upon Cranmer's forty-two articles of 1551. The compromise did not please everyone, of course, but it did achieve a remarkable degree of consensus during Elizabeth's long reign.

Queen Elizabeth and Tudor Absolutism

Elizabeth had to cope with a religiously divided nation and with extremists of both the right and the left who wished her downfall. She was a woman, in an age openly skeptical of women's ability or right to rule. Her success in dealing with such formidable odds was in large measure the result of her personal style as a monarch. Her combination of imperious will and femininity and her brilliant handling of her many contending male admirers have become legendary. She remained unmarried throughout her life, in part, at least, because marriage would have upset the delicate balance she maintained among rival groups, both foreign and domestic. Marriage would have committed her irretrievably to either one foreign nation or one constituency at home. She chose instead to bestow her favor on certain courtiers, notably Robert Dudley (whom she elevated to be the Earl of Leicester) and, after Leicester's death in 1588, Robert Devereux, second Earl of Essex. Her relationship with these men, despite her partiality to them, was marked by her outbursts of tempestuous jealousy. In addition, she relied on the staid counsel of her hard-working ministers: Lord Burghley, Sir Francis Walsingham, Burghley's son Robert Cecil, and a few others.

In her personal style as monarch, Elizabeth availed herself of the theory of absolute supremacy. Under all the Tudors, England was, nominally at least, an absolute monarchy in an age when many of England's greatest rivals—France, Spain, the Holy Roman Empire—were also under absolutist rule. "Absolutism" meant that the monarch served for life, could not legally be removed from office, and was normally succeeded by his eldest son—all of this bolstered by claims of divine sanction, though the claims were frequently contested. The rise of absolutism throughout Renaissance Europe was the result of an increase of centralized national power and a corresponding decrease in autonomous baronial influence. Henry VII's strong assertion of his royal authority at the expense of the feudal lords corresponded roughly in time with the ascendancy of Francis I of France (1515) and Charles V of the Holy Roman Empire (1519). Yet England had long enjoyed a tradition of rule by consensus. When Elizabeth came to the throne, England was already in some ways a "limited" monarchy. Parliament, and especially the members of the House of Commons, claimed prerogatives of their own and were steadily gaining in both experience and power. In the mid-1560s, for example, the Commons made repeated attempts to use parliamentary tax-levying authority as a means of obliging Elizabeth to name a Protestant successor to the throne. The attempt, despite its failure to achieve its immediate goal, was significant; the Commons had shown that they

were a force to be reckoned with. Even though Elizabeth made skillful rhetorical use of the theory of absolutism, portraying herself as God's appointed deputy on earth, her idea of absolutism should not be confused with despotism. To be sure, Elizabeth learned to avoid parliamentary interference in her affairs whenever possible; there were only thirteen sessions of Parliament in her forty-five years of rule. Still, Parliament claimed the right to establish law and to levy taxes on which the monarchy had to depend. Elizabeth needed all her considerable diplomatic skills in dealing with her parliaments and with the English people, who were self-reliant and proud of their reputation for independence. Elizabeth had more direct authority over her Privy Council, since she could appoint its members herself, yet even here she consulted faithfully with them on virtually everything she did. Nor were her closest advisers reluctant to offer her advice. Many vocal leaders in her government, including Walsingham and Leicester, urged the Queen during the 1570s and 1580s to undertake a more active military role on the Continent against the Catholic powers. So did her later favorite, the Earl of Essex. With remarkable tact, she managed to retain the loyalty of her militant and sometimes exasperated counselors and yet keep England out of war with Spain until that country actually launched an invasion attempt in 1588 (the Great Armada).

Catholic Opposition

During her early years, Elizabeth sought through her religious compromise to ease the divisions of her kingdom and attempted to placate her enemies abroad (notably Philip of Spain) rather than involve England in a costly war. For about twelve years, while England's economy gained much-needed strength, this policy of temporizing succeeded. Yet Elizabeth's more extreme Catholic opponents at home and abroad could never be reconciled to the daughter of that Protestant "whore," Anne Boleyn. England's period of relative accommodation came to an end in 1569 and 1570, with Catholic uprisings in the north and with papal excommunication of the English Queen. As a declared heretic, Elizabeth's very life was in danger; her Catholic subjects were encouraged by Rome to disobey her and to seek means for her violent overthrow.

Conspirators did, in fact, make attempts on the Queen's life, notably in the so-called Babington conspiracy of 1586, named for one of the chief participants. This plot, brought to light by Secretary of State Walsingham, sought to place Mary, Queen of Scots, on the English throne in Elizabeth's stead. Mary was Elizabeth's kinswoman; Mary's grandmother, sister to Henry VIII, had been married to James IV of Scotland. So long as Elizabeth remained childless, Mary was a prominent heir to the English throne. Catholics pinned their hopes on her succession, by force if necessary; Protestant leaders urged was translated in 1595; *The Prince* was not translated until 1640.) Nevertheless, his writings were available in Italian, French, and Latin editions and in manuscript English translations. His ideas certainly had a profound impact on the England of the 1590s. Marlowe caricatures the Italian writer in his *The Jew of Malta,* but he clearly was fascinated by what Machiavelli had to say. Shakespeare, too, reveals a complex awareness. However much he may lampoon the Machiavellian type of conscienceless villain in *Richard III,* he shows us more-plausible pragmatists in *Richard II* and *1 Henry IV.* Conservative theories of the divine right of kings are set in debate with the more heterodox ambitions of Henry Bolingbroke (who then adopts the most orthodox of political vocabularies once he is king). Bolingbroke is not a very attractive figure, but he does succeed politically where Richard has failed.

Shakespeare thus reveals himself as less a defender of the established order than as a great dramatist able to give sympathetic expression to the aspirations of all sides in a tense political struggle. His history plays have been variously interpreted either as defenses of monarchy or as subtle pleas for rebellion, but the consensus today is that the plays use political conflict as a way of probing the motivations of social behavior. To be sure, the plays do stress the painful consequences of disorder and present, on the whole, an admiring view of monarchy (especially in *Henry V*), despite the manifest limitations of that institution. Certainly, we can sense that Shakespeare's history plays were written for a generation of Englishmen who had experienced political crisis and who could perceive issues of statecraft in Shakespeare's plays that were relevant to England's struggles in the 1580s and the 1590s. The play of *King John,* for example, deals with a king whose uncertain claim to the throne is challenged by France and the papacy in the name of John's nephew, Arthur; Elizabeth faced a similar situation in her dilemma over her kinswoman, Mary, Queen of Scots. Elizabeth also bitterly acknowledged the cogency of a popular analogy comparing her reign with that of King Richard II. And when Shakespeare's play about Bolingbroke's overthrow of Richard was apparently revived for political purposes shortly before the Earl of Essex's abortive rebellion against Elizabeth in 1601, Shakespeare's acting company had some explaining to do to the authorities (see Introduction to *Richard II*). Nevertheless, Shakespeare's attitudes toward the issues of his own day are ultimately unknowable and unimportant, since his main concern seems to have been with the dramatization of political conflict rather than with the urging of a polemical position.

Shakespeare on Religion

Our impressions of Shakespeare's personal sympathies in religion are similarly obscured by his refusal to use his art for polemical purposes. To be sure, members of his moth-er's family in Warwickshire seem to have remained loyal to Catholicism, and his father, John Shakespeare, may conceivably have undergone financial and other difficulties in Stratford for reasons of faith. (See "Shakespeare's Family" below, in the section on Shakespeare's Life and Work.) Certainly Shakespeare himself displays a familiarity with some Catholic practices and theology, as when the Ghost of Hamlet's father speaks of being "Unhousled, disappointed, unaneled" (i.e., not having received last rites) at the time of his murder (*Hamlet,* 1.5.78). Nonetheless, we see in his plays a spectrum of religious attitudes portrayed with an extraordinary range of insight. In matters of doctrine, his characters are at various times acquainted with Catholic theology or with the controversy concerning salvation by faith or good works (see *Measure for Measure,* 1.2.24–5), and yet a consistent polemical bias is absent. Some Catholic prelates are schemers, like Pandulph in *King John.* Ordinarily, however, Shakespeare's satirical digs at ecclesiastical pomposity and hypocrisy have little to do with the Catholic question. Cardinal Beaufort in *1 Henry VI* is a political maneuverer, but so are many of his secular rivals. Cardinal Wolsey in *Henry VIII* is motivated by personal ambition rather than by any sinister conspiracy of the international church. Many of Shakespeare's nominally Catholic clerics, such as Friar Laurence in *Romeo and Juliet* or Friar Francis in *Much Ado About Nothing,* are gentle and well-intentioned people, even if occasionally bumbling. We can certainly say that Shakespeare consistently avoids the chauvinistic anti-Catholic baiting so often found in the plays of his contemporaries.

The same avoidance of extremes can be seen in his portrayal of Protestant reformers, though the instances in this case are few. Malvolio in *Twelfth Night* is fleetingly compared with a "Puritan" (2.3.139–46), although Shakespeare insists that no extensive analogy can be made. Angelo in *Measure for Measure* is sometimes thought to be a critical portrait of the Puritan temperament. Even if this were so, Shakespeare's satire is extremely indirect compared with the lampoons written by his contemporaries Ben Jonson and Thomas Dekker.

Stuart Absolutism

Queen Elizabeth's successor, James I of the Scottish House of Stuarts, reigned from 1603 to 1625. Even more than Elizabeth, he was a strong believer in the divinely appointed authority of kings; whereas she had insisted on divine sanction, James and his successor, Charles, called it a divine right. Although James succeeded easily to the throne in 1603, since he was Protestant, with a legitimate claim of descent from Henry VIII, the English people did not take to this foreigner from the north. James was eccentric in his personal habits, and the English were always inclined to be suspicious of the Scots in any case. As a result, James was less successful in dealing with the heterogeneous and antagonistic forces that Elizabeth had kept in precarious balance. At the Hampton Court Conference of 1604, relations quickly broke down between James and the Puritan wing of the church, so that even its more moderate adherents joined forces with the separatists. James had similar difficulties with an increasingly radical group in the House of Commons. In the widening rift between the absolutists and those who defended the supremacy of Parliament, James's court moved toward the right. Catholic sympathies at court became common. Civil war was still a long way off and by no means inevitable; the beheading of King Charles I (James's son) would not occur until 1649. Still, throughout James's reign, the estrangement between the right and the left was becoming more and more uncomfortable. The infamous Gunpowder Plot of 1605, in which Guy Fawkes and other Catholic conspirators were accused of having plotted to blow up the houses of Parliament, raised hysteria to a new intensity. Penal laws against papists were harshly enforced. The Parliament of 1614 included in its membership John Pym, Thomas Wentworth, and John Eliot—men who were to become turbulent spokesmen against taxes imposed without parliamentary grant, imprisonment without the stating of specific criminal charges, and other purported abuses of royal power. The polarization of English society naturally affected the London theaters. Popular London audiences (generally sympathetic with religious reform) eventually grew disaffected with the stage, while even the popular acting companies came under the increasing domination of the court. Shakespeare's late plays reflect the increasing influence of a courtly audience.

THE INTELLECTUAL BACKGROUND

Renaissance Cosmology

In learning, as in politics and religion, Shakespeare's England was a time of conflict and excitement. Medieval ideas of a hierarchical and ordered creation were under attack but were still widely prevalent and were used to justify a hierarchical order in society itself. According to the so-called Ptolemaic system of the universe, formulated by Ptolemy of Alexandria in the second century A.D., the earth stood at the center of creation. Around it moved, in nine concentric spheres, the heavenly bodies of the visible universe, in order as follows (from the earth outward): the moon, Mercury, Venus, the sun, Mars, Jupiter, Saturn, the fixed stars on a single plane, and lastly the *primum mobile,* imparting motion to the whole system. (See the accompanying illustration.) Some commentators proposed alternate arrangements or speculated as to the existence of one or two additional spheres, in particular a "crystalline sphere" between the fixed stars and the *primum mobile*. These additional spheres were needed to

cope with matters not adequately explained in Ptolemaic astronomy, such as the precession of the equinoxes. More troublesomely, the seemingly erratic retrograde motion of the planets—that is, the refusal of Mars and other planets to move around the earth in steady orbit—called forth increasingly ingenious theories, such as Tycho Brahe's scheme of epicycles. Still, the conservative appeal of the earth-centered cosmos remained very strong. How could one suppose that the earth was not at the center of the universe?

The *primum mobile* was thought to turn the entire universe around the earth once every twenty-four hours. Simultaneously, the individual heavenly bodies moved more slowly around the earth on their individual spheres, constantly changing position with respect to the fixed stars. The moon, being the only heavenly body that seemed subject to change in its monthly waxing and waning, was thought to represent the boundary between the unchanging universe and the incessantly changing world. Beneath the moon, in the "sublunary" sphere, all creation was subject to death as a result of Adam's fall from grace; beyond the moon lay perfection. Hell was imagined to exist deep within the earth, as in Dante's *Inferno,* or else outside the *primum mobile* and far below the created universe in the realm of chaos, as in Milton's *Paradise Lost.*

Heaven, or the Empyrean, stood, according to most Ptolemaic systems, at the top of the universe. Between heaven and earth dwelled the nine angelic orders, each associated with one of the nine concentric spheres. According to a work attributed to Dionysius the Areopagite, *On the Heavenly Hierarchy* (fifth century A.D.), the nine angelic orders consisted of three hierarchies. Closest to God were the contemplative orders of Seraphim, Cherubim, and Thrones; next, the intermediate orders of Dominions, Powers, and Virtues; and finally the active orders of Principalities, Archangels, and Angels. These last served as God's messengers and intervened from time to time in the affairs of mortals. Ordered life among humans, although manifestly imperfect when compared with the eternal bliss of the angelic orders, still modeled itself on that platonic idea of perfect harmony. Thus the state, the church, and the family all resembled one another because they resembled (however distantly) the kingdom of God. Richard Hooker, in his *Of the Laws of Ecclesiastical Polity* (1594–1597), defends the established Church of England in terms that emanate from a comparable idea of a divine, creative, and ordering law of nature "Whose seat is the bosom of God, whose voice the harmony of the world."

The devils of hell were fallen angels, with Satan as their leader. Such evil spirits might assume any number of shapes, such as demons, goblins, wizards, or witches. Believers in evil spirits generally made no distinction between orthodox Christian explanations of evil and the more primitive folklore of witchcraft. Belief in witchcraft was widespread indeed; King James I took the matter

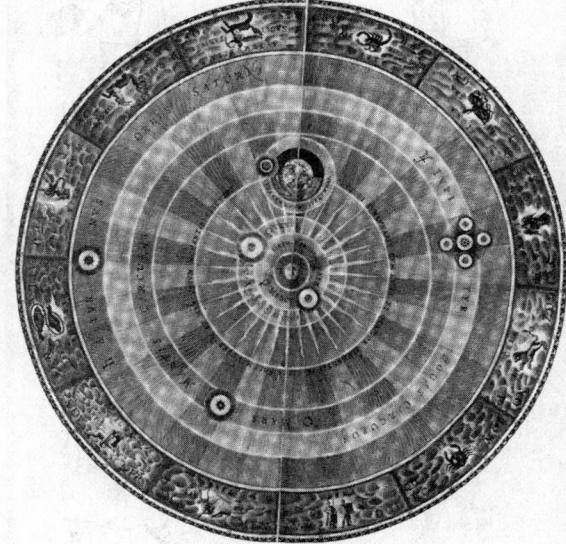

*Hic canet errantê Lunam,Solisq; labores
Arcturuq;,pluuiasq; hyad.geinosq; triões*

*Ptolemy's earth-centered system of the universe (top) was
challenged by the sun-centered system of Copernicus (bottom)
with the publishing of* De revolutionibus orbium coelestium
*in 1543. Shakespeare, like other major poets of the English Renais-
sance, poetically represents the universe in cosmic terms as
described by Ptolemy, but also reflects uncertainties generated
by the new cosmology.*

very seriously. So did Reginald Scot's *The Discovery of
Witchcraft* (1584), though its author also attempted to confute what he regarded as ignorant superstition and char-
latanism. Throughout Shakespeare's lifetime, belief and
skepticism about such matters existed side by side.

A similar ambiguity pertained to belief in the Ptolemaic universe itself. All major poets of the Renaissance,
including Shakespeare, Spenser, and Milton (who completed *Paradise Lost* after 1660), represented the universe
in cosmic terms essentially as described by Ptolemy. Yet
Nicolaus Copernicus's revolutionary theory of a sun-centered solar system (*De revolutionibus orbium coelestium*,
published on the Continent in 1543) and the discovery of
a new star in Cassiopeia in 1572 stimulated much new
thought. Galileo Galilei, born in the same year as Shakespeare (1564), published in 1610 the results of his tele-
scopic examinations of Jupiter's moons, thereby further
confirming Copernicus's hypothesis. Although the news
of Galileo's astounding discovery came too late to affect
any but the latest of Shakespeare's plays, a sense of excitement and dislocation was apparent throughout most of
the years of his writing career. Thomas Nashe, in 1595,
referred familiarly to Copernicus as the author "who held
that the sun remains immobile in the center of the world,
and that the earth is moved about the sun" (Nashe, *Works*,
ed. R. B. McKerrow, 1904–1910, 3.94). John Donne lamented in 1611–1612 that the "new philosophy" (i.e., the new
science) "calls all in doubt." Skeptical uncertainty about
the cosmos was on the rise. The poetic affirmations in
Renaissance art of traditional ideas of the cosmos can best
be understood as a response to uncertainty—a statement
of faith in an age of increasing skepticism.

Alchemy and Medicine

In all areas of Renaissance learning, the new and the old
science were juxtaposed. Alchemy, for example, made
important contributions to learning, despite its superstitious character. Its chief goal was the transformation of
base metals into gold, on the assumption that all metals
were ranked on a hierarchical scale and could be raised
from lower to higher positions on that scale by means of
certain alchemical techniques. Other aims of alchemy
included the discovery of a universal cure for diseases and
of a means for preserving life indefinitely. Such aims
encouraged quackery and prompted various exposés,
such as Chaucer's "The Canon's Yeoman's Tale" (late
fourteenth century) and Jonson's *The Alchemist* (1610). Yet
many of the procedures used in alchemy were essentially
chemical procedures, and the science of chemistry
received a valuable impetus from constant experimentation. Queen Elizabeth was seriously interested in alchemy
throughout her life.

In physics, medicine, and psychology, as well, older
concepts vied with new. Traditional learning apportioned

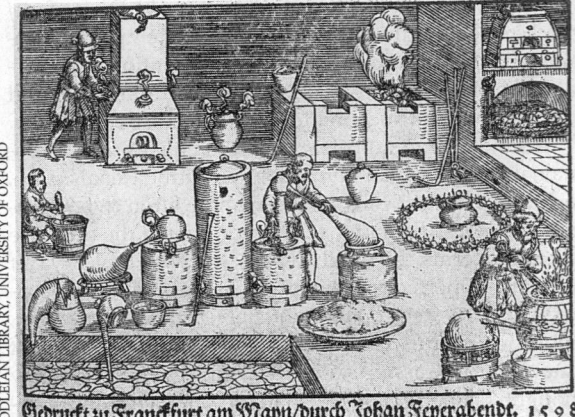

Gedruckt zu Franckfurt am Mayn/durch Johan Feyerabendt. 1598.

Alchemists employed relatively sophisticated equipment in their futile search for the "philosopher's stone," a reputed substance supposed to possess the property of changing other metals into gold and silver.

all physical matter into four elements: earth, air, fire, and water. Each of these was thought to be a different combination of the four "qualities" of the universe: hot, cold, moist, and dry. Earth combined cold and dry; air, hot and moist; fire, hot and dry; and water, cold and moist. Earth and water were the baser or lower elements, confined to the physical world; fire and air were aspiring elements, tending upward. Humans, as a microcosm of the larger universe, contained in themselves the four elements. The individual's temperament, or "humor" or "complexion," depended on which "humor" predominated in that person. The four humors in humans corresponded to the four elements of physical matter. The blood was hot and moist, like air; yellow bile, or choler, was hot and dry, like fire; phlegm was cold and moist, like water; and black bile was cold and dry, like earth. A predominance of blood in an individual created a sanguine or cheerful temperament (or humor), yellow bile produced a choleric or irascible temperament, phlegm produced a phlegmatic or stolid temperament, and black bile produced a melancholic temperament. Diet could affect the balance among these humors, since an excess of a particular food would stimulate overproduction of one humor. The stomach and the liver, which converted food into humors, were regarded as the seat of human passions. The spleen was thought to be the seat of laughter, sudden impulse, or caprice, and also melancholy. (Hotspur, in *1 Henry IV*, is said to be "governed by a spleen," 5.2.19.) Strong emotional reactions could be explained in terms of the physiology of the humors: in anger, the blood rushed to the head and thereby produced a flush of red color and staring eyes; in fear, the blood migrated to the heart and thus left the face and liver pale, and so on. Sighs supposedly cost the heart a drop of blood, while wine could refortify it (as Falstaff

insists in *2 Henry IV*, 4.3.90–123). The signs of youth were warmth and moisture, as in Desdemona's "hot and moist" hand (*Othello*, 3.4.39); those of age were "a moist eye, a dry hand, a yellow cheek, a white beard, a decreasing leg, an increasing belly" (*2 Henry IV*, 1.2.179–81). A common remedy for illness was to let blood and thereby purge the body of unwanted humors.

The name traditionally associated with such theories was that of Galen, the most celebrated of ancient writers on medicine (c. 130 A.D.). A more revolutionary name was that of Paracelsus, a famous German physician (c. 1493–1541) who attacked the traditional medical learning of his time and urged a more unfettered, pragmatic research into pharmacy and medicine. Such experimentalism bore fruit in the anatomical research of Vesalius (1514–1564) and in William Harvey's investigations of the circulation of the blood (c. 1616). Nevertheless, the practice of medicine in Renaissance times remained under the influence of the "humors" theory until quite late, and its ideas are found throughout Shakespeare's writings.

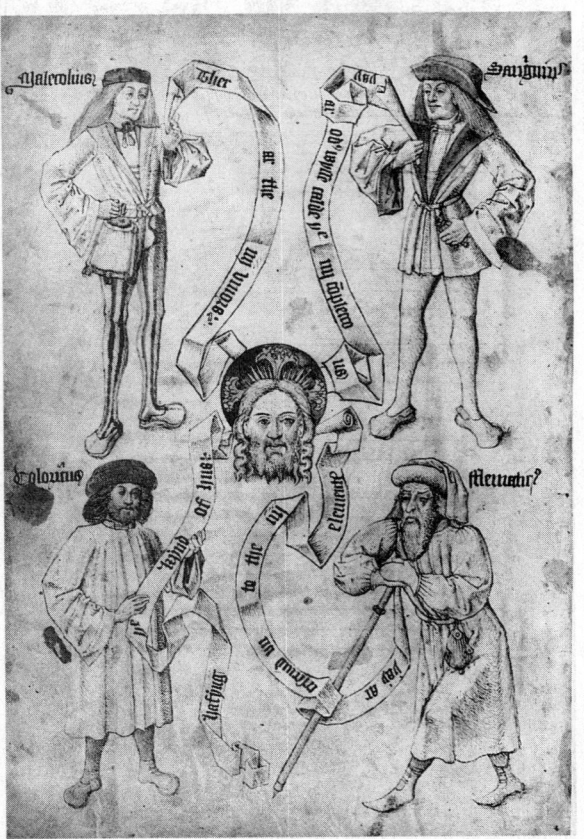

The four humors of black bile, blood, yellow bile (or choler), and phlegm, as shown in this illustration from an illuminated manuscript, were believed to govern the human personality by producing a disposition toward melancholic, sanguine, choleric, or phlegmatic temperaments.

Learning

In learning generally, and in theories of education, new ideas conflicted with old. The curriculum of schools and colleges in the Renaissance was inherited largely from the Middle Ages and displayed many traditional characteristics. The curriculum consisted of the seven Liberal Arts: a lower division, called the trivium, composed of grammar, rhetoric, and logic; and an upper division, called the quadrivium, composed of arithmetic, geometry, astronomy, and music. In addition, there were the philosophical studies associated chiefly with Aristotle: natural philosophy, ethics, and metaphysics.

Aristotle's name had a towering influence in medieval times and remained important to the Renaissance as well. Even among his Renaissance admirers, however, Aristotle proved more compelling in practical matters than in the abstract scholastic reasoning associated with his name in the Middle Ages. The Italian Aristotelians whose work made its way into England were interested primarily in the science of human behavior. Aristotelian ethics was for them a practical subject, telling people how to live usefully and well and how to govern themselves politically. Rhetoric was the science of persuasion, enabling people to use eloquence for socially useful goals. Poetry was a kind of rhetoric, a language of persuasion that dramatists, too, might use for morally pragmatic ends.

At the same time, new thinkers were daring to attack Aristotle by name as a symbol of traditional medieval thought. The attack was not always fair to Aristotle himself, whose work had been bent to the *a priori* purposes of much medieval scholasticism. Nevertheless, his name had assumed such symbolic importance that he had to be confronted directly. The Huguenot logician Petrus Ramus (1515–1572), defiantly proclaiming that "everything that Aristotle taught is false," argued for rules of logic as derived from observation. He urged, for example, that his students learn about rhetoric from observing in detail Cicero's effect on his listeners, rather than by the rote practice of syllogism. Actually, Ramus's thought was less revolutionary in its concepts of logic than in the tremendous ferment of opinion caused by his iconoclastic teaching.

A basic issue at stake in the anti-Aristotelian movement was that of traditional authority versus independent observation. How do people best acquire true knowledge—through the teachings of their predecessors or through their own discovery? The issue had profound implications for religious truth as well: should individuals heed the collective wisdom of the earthly church or read the Bible with their individual perceptions as their guide? Is "reason" an accretive wisdom handed down by authority or a quality of the individual soul? Obviously, a middle ground exists between the two extremes, and no new thinker of the Renaissance professed to abandon entirely the use of ancient authority. For men like Henricus Agrippa (1486–1535) and Sir Francis Bacon (1561–1626), however, scholastic tradition had exerted its oppressive influence far too long. Authority needed to be examined critically and scientifically. Bacon, in his *The Advancement of Learning* (1605), fought against the blind acceptance of ancient wisdom and argued that "knowledge derived from Aristotle, and exempted from liberty of examination, will not rise again higher than the knowledge of Aristotle." Sir Walter Ralegh and others joined in the excited new search for what human "reason" could discover when set free from scholastic restraint. Such belief in the perfectibility of human reason owed some of its inspiration to Italian Neoplatonic humanists like Giovanni Pico della Mirandola (1463–1494), who, in his *Oration on the Dignity of Man*, celebrated a human race "constrained by no limits," in accordance with the potential of its own free will. The new learning did not seem to trouble these men in their religious faith, although a tension between scientific observation and faith in miracles was to become plentifully evident in the seventeenth century.

The Nature of Humankind

Medieval thought generally assigned to humankind a uniquely superior place in the order of creation on earth. That assumption of superiority rested on biblical and patristic teachings about the hierarchy of creation, in which humanity stood at the apex of physical creation nearest God and the angels. Humankind was thus supreme on earth in the so-called chain of being. Human reason, though subject to error because of sinfulness, enabled humans to aspire toward divinity. Humans were, in the view of medieval philosophers, the great amphibians, as well as the microcosm of the universe, part bestial and part immortal, doomed by Adam's fall to misery and death in this life but promised eternal salvation through Christ's atonement. Right reason, properly employed, could lead to the truths of revealed Christianity and thus give humankind a glimpse of the heavenly perfection one day to be ours. Renaissance Neoplatonism, as expounded, for example, in the writings of Marsilio Ficino, Pico della Mirandola, and Baldassare Castiglione (in *The Courtier*, translated by Sir Thomas Hoby in 1561), offered humanity a vision of a platonic ladder, extending from the perception of physical beauty to contemplation of the platonic idea of beauty and finally to the experiencing of God's transcendent love.

Protestant thought of the Renaissance did not wholly disagree with this formulation, but it did place a major new emphasis on human reprobation. The idea was not new, for Saint Augustine (354–430) had insisted on human depravity and our total dependence on God's inscrutable grace, but, in the years of the Reformation, this theology took on a new urgency. Martin Luther

(1483–1540), by rejecting veneration of the Virgin Mary and the saints and by taking away the sacraments of confession and penance, by which individual Christians could seek the institutional comforts of the Catholic Church, exposed the individual sinner to agonies of conscience that could result in a sense of alienation and loss. The rewards were great for those who found new faith in God's infinite goodness, but the hazards of predestinate damnation were fearsome to those who were less sure of their spiritual welfare. Luther's God was inscrutable, majestic, and infallible. Luther's God decreed salvation for the elect and damnation for all others, and His will could not be challenged or questioned. The individual was to blame for sin, even though God hardened the hearts of the reprobate. John Calvin (1509–1564) placed even greater stress on predestinate good and evil and insisted that the grace of salvation was founded on God's freely given mercy that humans could not possibly deserve. Salvation was God's to give or withhold as He wished; humans might not repine that in His incomprehensible wisdom God has "barred the door of life to those whom He has given over to damnation." Faced with such

a view of human spiritual destiny, the individual Christian's lot was one of potential tragedy. The human soul was a battleground of good and evil.

Michel de Montaigne (1533–1592), Shakespeare's great French contemporary, provided a very different and heterodox way of thinking about human imperfection. In his "Apology for Raymond Sebond" and other of his essays, Montaigne questioned the assumption of humanity's superiority to the animal kingdom, and in doing so gave Shakespeare a fundamentally different way to consider the nature of humankind—a way that reflects itself, for example, in Hamlet's observations on humans as "quintessence of dust." Montaigne stressed humans' arrogance, vanity, and frailty. He was unconvinced of humanity's purported moral superiority to the animals and argued that animals are no less endowed with a soul. Montaigne undermined, in other words, the hierarchy in which the human race was the unquestioned master of the physical world, just as Copernican science overturned the earth-centered cosmos and Machiavelli's political system dismissed as an improbable fiction the divinely constituted hierarchy of the state. Montaigne's very choice of

This guide, graphically setting forth the ideals to which every English gentlewoman and gentleman should aspire, illustrates the Renaissance concept that outward deportment and accomplishments should correctly and invariably mirror a person's inner nature.

Shakespeare's World
A Visual Portfolio

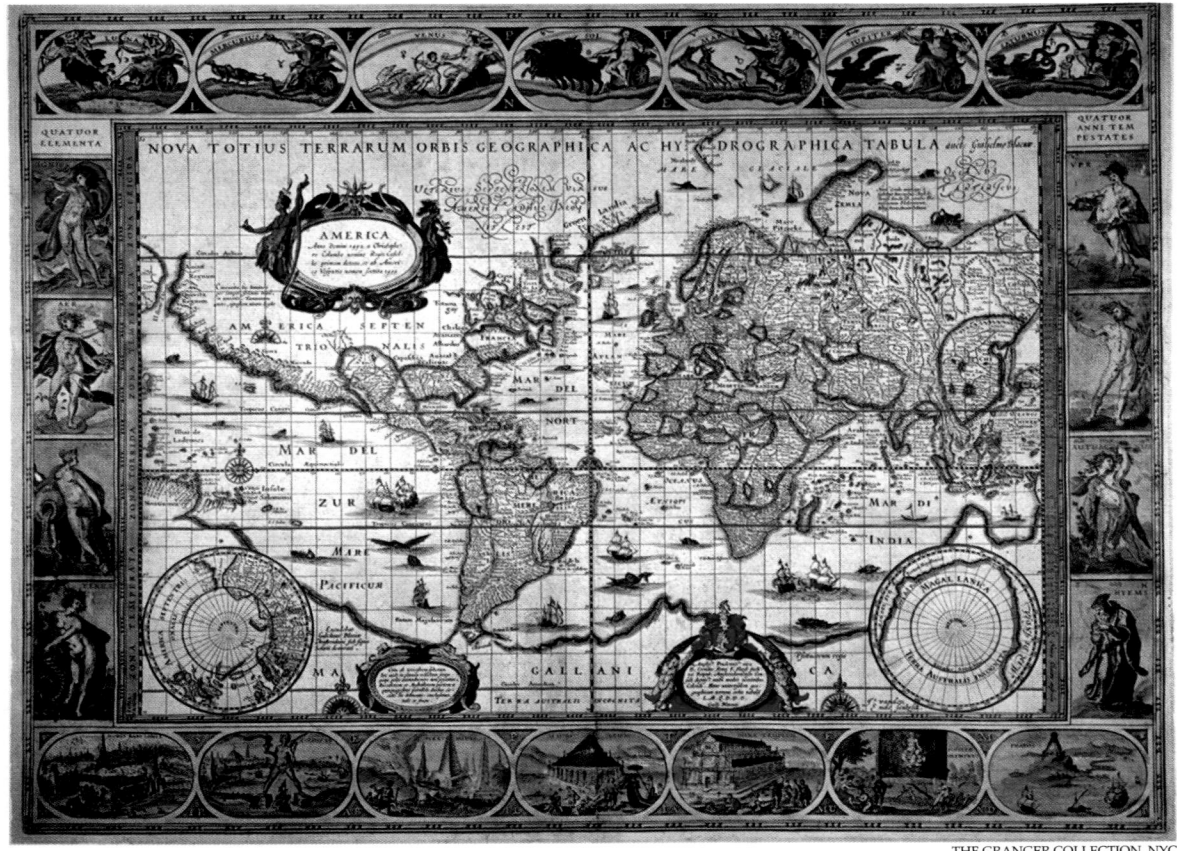

PLATE 1. The Seventeenth-Century World. *Dutch cartographer Willem Janszoon Blaeu (1571–1638) produced this map in 1635. Around the border are panels depicting the four elements, the seven known planets, the four seasons, and the seven wonders of the world. While the establishment of English settlements in North America expanded the scope of the early seventeenth-century world, England in Shakespeare's day still remained both small and isolated.*

PLATE 2. London in Shakespeare's Time. *In this anonymous seventeenth-century painting, the theaters of Southwark are clearly visible in the left foreground, flags flying. London Bridge crosses the River Thames into the city, where St Paul's Cathedral dominates the central skyline. The Tower of London is visible on the right. The many boats on the Thames are evidence of the vital role the river played in the city's emerging importance in national and international trade.*

Plate 3. The Painting of a Lifetime. *This painting of the life of Sir Henry Unton (1557?–1596), probably commissioned by his widow, shows the important events of his life. In the lower right, we see him at birth, in his mother's arms. Above that, we see him as a student at Oxford. The top center depicts his travels to Europe and his expedition to the Netherlands ("Low Countries") under the command of the Earl of Leicester. Below that, we see various scenes in Wadley House, his residence, including a feast with masquers in festive dress, led in procession by Diana and Mercury. His death and burial are pictured in the lower left corner.*

PLATE 4. Queen Elizabeth I. *Few monarchs have ever influenced an age so pervasively and left their stamp on it so permanently as did Elizabeth I during her reign from 1558-1603. Elizabeth is celebrated in this portrait that commemorates the English defeat of the Spanish Armada in 1588. A mythology developed around the Queen, linked to her virginity and devotion to her people. With her right hand on the globe, she is shown here in all her glory as the empress of the world.*

PLATE 5. King James I. *James I, King of England from 1603–1625, was the first of the Stuart dynasty. His name is linked to one of the most creative periods in the history of the theater: that of the Jacobean drama. "Jacobean" is derived from* Jacobus, *the Latin word for James.*

PLATE 6. Social Class in Shakespeare's Time. *Social classes and fashions in Shakespeare's day were clearly defined. People were required by English law to dress according to their social status. Shown here are a workman (top), carrying his tools; "a presumptuous woman" (center), gaudily attired beyond her appointed station; and a "gentleman" (bottom), privileged to wear his apparel.*

PLATE 7. Ben Jonson. *Chief dramatic rival for public acclaim during Shakespeare's later years was Ben Jonson (1572–1637). Jonson, a poet, playwright, and literary critic, was a noted scholar of classical literature and a good friend of Shakespeare. The First Folio of 1623 contains a poetic eulogy of Shakespeare written by Jonson.*

PLATE 8. Edward Alleyn. *Edward Alleyn (1566–1626) won great acclaim in the roles of Tamburlaine and Doctor Faustus, among many others. As leading player of Lord Strange's Men and then the Lord Admiral's Men, he became a prominent rival of Richard Burbage of the Lord Chamberlain's Men. This was the company in which Shakespeare served as actor-sharer and playwright, starting in 1594. Alleyn was also the founder of Dulwich College.*

PLATE 9. Falstaff and Crew. *William Hogarth's painting, "Falstaff Examining His Recruits from Henry IV," dates from 1730. Sir John Falstaff was one of Shakespeare's most popular characters, appearing in parts 1 and 2 of* Henry IV *as well as* The Merry Wives of Windsor. *Falstaff, in the red jacket and feathered hat, here reviews his ragged recruits in a scene from* 2 Henry IV *(3.2).*

PLATE 10. *A Midsummer Night's Dream. Peter Brook's brilliantly revisionary stage production for the Royal Shakespeare Company in 1970 set* A Midsummer Night's Dream *in a brightly lit white box peopled with jugglers and athletic trapeze artists who tumbled and dashed about after one another with abandon. Here, Titania, under the spell of a love potion, embraces the weaver, Bottom, whom Puck has mischievously given an ass's ears and a clown nose. (The clown nose is Brook's invention; Shakespeare's script calls for an ass's head.)*

PLATE 11. *The Taming of the Shrew. Franco Zeffirelli directed the 1967 film version that features real-life husband and wife Elizabeth Taylor and Richard Burton as Kate and Petruchio.*

Plate 12. ***A Midsummer's Summer Night Dream.*** *Bottom and Titania from the production directed by Jean Louise Martinoty with music by Benjamin Britten staged at the National Opera of Nancy.*

POL EMILE/SIPA/NEWSCOM

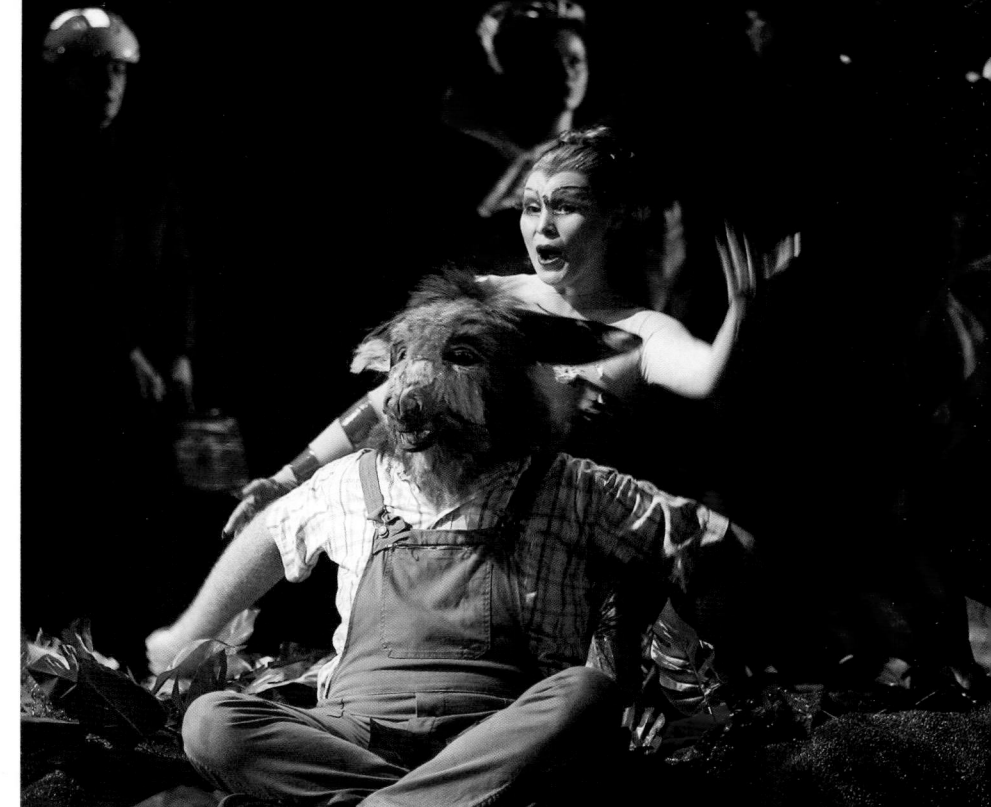

Plate 13. ***Much Ado About Nothing.*** *This 2010 Parisian adaption titled* Beaucoup de Bruit Pour Rien *featured Vincent Caire and Gael Collins along with Theatre du Ranalagh company actors.*

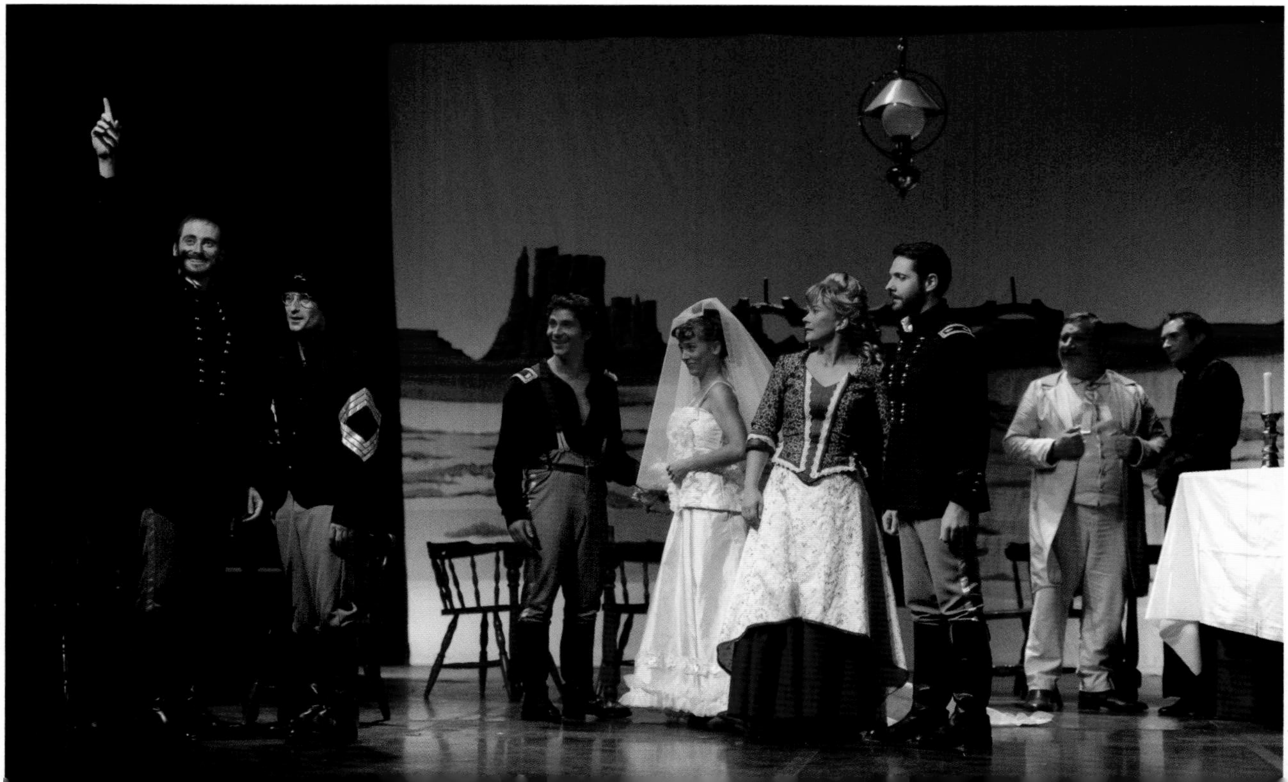

RAYMOND DELALANDE/SIPA/NEWSCOM

Plate 14. *Romeo and Juliet.* Leonardo DiCaprio and Claire Danes along with Miriam Margolyes, Pete Postlethwaite, and John Leguizamo star in this 1996 film adaption directed by Baz Luhrmann. The film retains much of the original dialogue, set in a modern city closely resembling Los Angeles or Miami (though filmed in part in Mexico City), with gas stations that are set afire, gang warfare, nouveau riche mansions, New Age priests, MTV sound track, and much more.

Plate 15. *Hamlet.* Peter Brook's production of Hamlet *featured English actors Adrian Lester and Bruce Meyers. The production was staged in the Theatre of Bouffes du Nord in Paris as part of the 29th Paris Autumn Festival in 2000.*

Plate 16. *King Lear. Kazunori Akitaya as Gloucester shown after being brutally blinded in this 1991 Tokyo Globe Company production.*

PLATE 17. *King Lear.*
Written and directed by Akira Kurosawa, the 1985 film Ran *is a retelling of* King Lear *transposing the plot into 16th century Japanese life, culture, and images. Stars include Tatsuya Nakadi and Akira Terao.*

PLATE 18. *The Tempest.* Jasper Britton played Caliban in this 2000 production staged at Shakespeare's Globe Theatre. Britton's legendary performance included such actions as spitting fish-heads into the audience.

PLATE 19. *The Tempest.* Forbidden Planet, *the 1956 film produced by Nicholas Nayfack, is an adaptation of* The Tempest *as a journey into space. Directed by Fred McLeod Wilcox, it features Walter Pidgeon as the Prospero-like Doctor Morbius, Anne Francis as the Miranda-like Altaira, Leslie Nielsen as the Ferdinand-like Commander J.J. Adams, and Robby the Robot as the Ariel-like servant to Doctor Morbius.*

PLATE 20. *Macbeth. Umabatha Theatre Company as they rehearse* The Zulu Macbeth, *a reimagining of Shakespeare's play. It was performed at the London Globe Theatre in 2001.*

PLATE 21. *Measure for Measure. The 2012 production was performed by the Umabatha Theatre Company in Taiwan.*

PLATE 22. *Richard III. Ian McKellan stars in the 1995 film directed by Richard Loncraine. Others actors who appeared in the film include Annette Bening, Jim Broadbent, Robert Downey Jr., Nigel Hawthorne, Kristin Scott Thomas, Maggie Smith, John Wood and Dominic West. The film changes the play's setting to 1930s Britain under a fascist regime.*

PLATE 23. *Twelfth Night. Ben Kingsley as Feste in director Trevor Nunn's 1996 film. The film cast includes Helena Bonham Carter, Richard E. Grant, and Imogen Stubbs.*

PLATE 24. *The Winter's Tale. Phyllida Hancock appeared as Perdita in a Royal Shakespeare Company 1992 production held at the Barbican Theatre in London. Regarded as a landmark production, it was hailed by critics and played to packed houses both in Stratford and London.*

the essay as his favorite literary form bespeaks his commitment to attempts and explorations, rather than to definite solutions; etymologically, the very word "essay" signifies an exploration or inquiry. Montaigne was not alone in his skepticism about human nature; his ideas had much in common with Bernardino Telesio's *De Rerum Natura* and with the writings of the Italian Giordano Bruno. Montaigne was followed in the seventeenth century by that overpowering iconoclast, Thomas Hobbes, who extended the concept of mechanical laws governing human society and human psychology. Hobbes postdates Shakespeare, to be sure, but one has only to consider Iago's philosophy of the assertive individual will (in *Othello*) or Edmund's contempt for his father Gloucester's astrological pieties (in *King Lear*) to see the enormous impact on Shakespeare of the new heterodoxies of his age. Shakespeare makes us aware that skeptical thought can be used by dangerous men like Iago, Edmund, and Richard III to promote their own villainies in a world no longer held together by the certitudes of traditional faith, but he also shows us the gullibility of some traditionalists and the abuses of power that can be perpetrated in the name of ancient and divine privilege by a king like Richard II. Above all, Shakespeare delights in the play of mind among competing ideas, inviting us to wonder, for example, if Caliban in *The Tempest* is not invested with natural qualities that Prospero, his Christian colonizer, does not sufficiently understand and whether some of the other supposedly civilized Europeans who come to Caliban's island do not have a great deal to learn from its uncivilized beauty.

THE DRAMA BEFORE SHAKESPEARE

When William Shakespeare made his first acquaintance with the professions of acting and playwriting in the late 1580s, the English theater was already a flourishing institution with a long and complex history. In order to understand what opportunities it offered Shakespeare, we need to look briefly at that history.

The Liturgical Drama

The sixth-century Catholic Church had been largely responsible for closing down the late Roman theater, with its bloody gladiatorial contests and its pervasive moral decadence. Thereafter, for about four centuries, the theater officially did not exist in western Europe. Paradoxically, it was the Church in the tenth century that sponsored the beginnings of a new dramatic form within the liturgy (the prescribed form of worship) of the Church itself. This dramatic activity perhaps began as an insertion into the regular service of a "trope" or musical composition designed to be sung antiphonally by members of a monastic community. The earliest of these may have been composed for Easter morning, at the supremely important moment of Christ's Resurrection. The Mass itself had long displayed semidramatic characteristics, and the first Easter expansions must not have seemed particularly revolutionary to anyone involved. The simplest of the early tropes (though perhaps not the first), composed at St. Gall in Switzerland some time early in the tenth century, consists merely of a chanted interrogation, "*Quem quaeritis in sepulchro, Christicolae?*" ("Whom do you seek in the sepulcher, O followers of Christ?"), and a chanted response, "*Jesum Nazarenum crucifixum, o caelicolae*" ("Jesus of Nazareth who was crucified, O heaven-dwellers"), followed by an announcement that Christ is risen as He had predicted. From other early texts of this sort, we can guess that this simple antiphon was accompanied by some stylized semidramatic assignment of roles to members of the religious community as the three Marys visiting Christ's tomb and as the angels guarding the tomb. At any rate, tenth-century tropes of Easter soon included use of simple costumes, physical movement toward the tomb, and appropriate gestures.

Other actions were appropriate to such a dramatic representation of the Resurrection: the visit of the disciples to the sepulchre, the appearance of Christ as a gardener to Mary Magdalene, and his appearance to the disciples on the road to Emmaus. Moreover, other seasons of the year afforded similar opportunities, especially Christmas; the crèche was already a venerable custom, and Christmas tropes may have originated as early as Easter tropes or possibly even earlier.

In any event, Christmas liturgical dramatic activity grew apace, perhaps more rapidly than at Easter because of the sacred inhibitions associated with the Resurrection. By the twelfth century, Christmas liturgical drama had become lengthy and complex, including not only the visit of the shepherds and the Magi, but also the slaughter of the innocents and the flight into Egypt. Simultaneously, liturgical plays were developed for other festivals in the liturgical calendar. Some were in the vernacular: by the end of the twelfth century, an Anglo-Norman poet had written a play of Adam featuring the creation of humankind, the expulsion from the garden of Eden, the slaughter of Abel by Cain, and a lengthy procession of prophets announcing the advent of Christ. Such early vernacular plays may well have influenced the development of Latin liturgical drama. The twelfth century also saw a play about Daniel in the lions' den, various Saint Nicholas plays in which that popular saint performed miracles, a play at Tegernsee about the Antichrist, a play about the conversion of Saint Paul, and many others. In other words, by 1200 or thereabouts, the liturgical drama had produced plays of considerable length and complexity for numerous religious festivals throughout the individual saints and martyrs rather than, as in the cycles, telling the entire divine history of the human race as incorporated chiefly in the Old and New Testaments. Some particular cases, to be sure, incorporated features of both saints' lives and Corpus Christi drama. The story of Mary Magdalene, for example, was derived in part from the biblical accounts of her meetings with Christ, but the narrative had been enormously expanded to include legendary reports of her travels and miraculous deeds as a saint. St. Paul was another biblical figure whose sudden conversion and subsequent travels gave to his story the characteristics of a typical saint's life. As a group, however, saints' plays offered more emphasis on miraculous conversion from sin to grace and on the wondrous intervention of saints in the lives of ordinary people than did the Corpus Christi cycles.

Allegorical characters in the morality play Hickescorner were Contemplation, Pity, Free Will, Imagination, Hickescorner, and Perseverance.

Shakespeare's debt to saints' plays is indirect and hard to demonstrate. Some of his history plays reveal a pattern of conversion followed by glorious acts, as in the saga of Henry V, but this story was inherent in the myth of Henry V that Shakespeare inherited. Comedies of repentance, such as *Measure for Measure* and *The Winter's Tale,* show us a pattern of redemptive sorrow and renewal in which the protagonist is given an almost miraculous second chance. Shakespeare's late romances are especially illuminated by this tradition of conversion narratives. We cannot be sure, however, that he encountered such stories through saints' plays (which were suppressed by the English Reformation), since nondramatic sources, such as the Legenda Aurea (or Golden Legend) of the lives of the saints, were more immediately available to him.

Shakespeare's awareness of the morality play is easier to prove. Indeed, this genre had survived well enough into the late sixteenth century to make a significant impact on the plays of Shakespeare, Ben Jonson, and others. The morality play chose as its distinctive mode the allegorical rendition of humanity's spiritual journey through life to an eventual preparation for death and judgment before God. Allegory was not unknown in the cycles or in the saints' plays, but it became the staple of the morality play. The earliest texts, from the sixteenth century, include *The Castle of Perseverance, Mankind,* and *Everyman.* Although the last of these focuses atypically on the moment of death, more-typical early morality plays tell a story of spiritual struggle and eventual triumph over sin. This simple plot had an advantage over the cycles and saints' plays in that it could be adapted to the religious and social controversies of the era. The Corpus Christi cycles and saints' plays were, after all, tied to biblical or legendary events; when Reformation authorities sought to suppress the "idolatrous" representation of God on stage or banned worship of the Virgin Mary and the saints, the cycles and saints' plays were doomed. Even though they were occasionally staged late enough in the sixteenth century for Shakespeare to have seen performances, they belonged chiefly to an earlier, pre-Reformation era. The morality play, on the other hand, thrived on controversy. Its plot of soul struggle between the forces of good and evil for the allegiance of Mankind or Everyman, and his wavering progress toward eventual salvation, could and did frequently serve as a vehicle for portraying many social phenomena of the sixteenth century.

In John Skelton's political morality play called *Magnificence* (1515–1518), for example, the protagonist is a representative king figure who must choose between evil counselors urging fiscal extravagance on the one hand and wise counselors urging fiscal prudence on the other hand. The plot, telling of the King's temptation and his choosing of the wrong path before he is finally awakened to his folly, is essentially that of nonpolitical morality plays—such as *Hickescorner*, or *Youth* (c. 1513–1520), in which the human protagonist inevitably succumbs to temptation but is eventually rescued through divine guidance. The issues in Skelton's play have embraced secular as well as spiritual concerns, while the simple story line and the dramatic structure have remained virtually unchanged. The study of a "historical" type, in this case a king, enables such a play to comment on contemporary history and yet appeal simultaneously to a universal moral pattern. Skelton's play may allude indirectly to the fiscal recklessness of Henry VIII under Cardinal Wolsey's persuasive tutelage, but it discusses fiscal responsibility in general terms that also apply to any king—or to any human. Shakespeare's English history plays, especially the early plays about Henry VI and Richard III, owe an important debt to the tradition of the political morality, as exemplified by *Magnificence*.

Shakespeare's history play *King John* studies a king who had actually been the protagonist of the first play to represent an English monarch, *King Johan*, by John Bale (1538, later revised). Although Shakespeare may not have consulted Bale's play directly, Bale still had made an impressive contribution to the English history play by demonstrating how the morality structure could be used in the analysis of political crises. His play is an avowedly Protestant tract in the guise of a morality play, depicting its historical protagonist as a victim of Catholic duplicity and hence an example of what sixteenth-century England had to fear from its Catholic enemies. Later popular plays, combining a morality structure with a passionate interest in history and contemporary political theory, include Thomas Preston's *Cambises* (1560–1561) and John Pickering's *Horestes* (1567).

During the Reformation, the morality play was used polemically by both the Protestants and the Catholics. Dramatists were often commissioned by governmental authorities to write plays for public performance by touring actors, as weapons of ideological persuasion. In Protestant plays, such as *Lusty Juventus* (c. 1547–1553) or *New Custom* (c. 1570), the villainous Vices were depicted as Catholic tempters; in Catholic plays, such as *Republica* (1553, during the reign of Queen Mary), the Vices were Protestant. The protean flexibility of the morality formula enabled it to adapt itself to many different situations in this way. Polemical drama put ideology ahead of artistic concern, to be sure, but constant experimentation with new forms provided the popular drama of midcentury England with much-needed practical experience. One permutation of the Reformation morality play, for example, proved of considerable importance to the development of English tragedy. In some Protestant morality plays that Calvinistically stress humankind's innate depravity—such as William Wager's *Enough Is as Good as a Feast* (c. 1559–1570) and Nathaniel Woodes's *The Conflict of Conscience* (1570–1581)—spiritual struggle ends in failure rather than in triumph for the human protagonist. Among the great English tragedies of the late sixteenth century, Christopher Marlowe's *Doctor Faustus* (c. 1588) is most obviously indebted to such dramatic renditions of spiritual despair, but Shakespeare's *Macbeth* and other plays may also have learned something from a native homiletic tradition in tragedy.

In staging and acting, as well, the morality play served as an important transition from late medieval religious drama to the drama of the late sixteenth century. In its origins, as seen, for example, in *The Castle of Perseverance* (early fifteenth century), the morality play had been staged like many of the cycles or saints' plays, such as *Mary Magdalene*, that is, in the round, with an open acting area surrounded by acting scaffolds on the periphery. The morality play developed great flexibility in its staging, however, just as it had developed flexibility in its approach to contemporary political or social issues. *Mankind* (c. 1471) required only an acting platform, raised probably on trestles to a height of four or five feet, and a curtain backdrop through which the actors could enter and exit. A stage of this simplicity could be carried anywhere in England and set up at a moment's notice—on a village green, in a town hall, or in the banqueting hall of a lord's manor. The troupe acting *Mankind* was vastly more efficient and transportable than the company of twenty-two or more actors required for *The Castle of Perseverance; Mankind* required only six actors.

Troupes of four or five men and one boy apprentice (for women's roles) were quite standard in early Tudor England. Similar or even smaller troupes enacted folk plays and miracle plays, the texts of which are regrettably not as extensively preserved as those of morality plays. Such troupes traveled the length and breadth of the country and dominated the field of popular entertainment from the late fifteenth century until Shakespeare's day. They were, in fact, the professional ancestors of the Shakespearean acting company. Under the direction of their leading player, who often acted the part of Vice since it was usually the choice role of the morality play, the actors were organized as repertory companies able to perform a number of plays on short notice and to present a remarkably large number of roles by the doubling of parts. They grew slowly in size as they prospered, but they retained their traditional organization. The best of the troupes gravitated to London, where, in 1576, a troupe of perhaps six or eight men and two boys founded England's first permanent theater. Shakespeare's company, the Lord Chamberlain's Men (later the King's Men), was only slightly larger than this, with perhaps ten actors who were partners or "sharers" in the company, two or more boys, and a few hired hands. Shakespeare's early plays, moreover, were sometimes structured for presentation by just such a company, much as earlier popular plays had been structured, with considerable doubling of

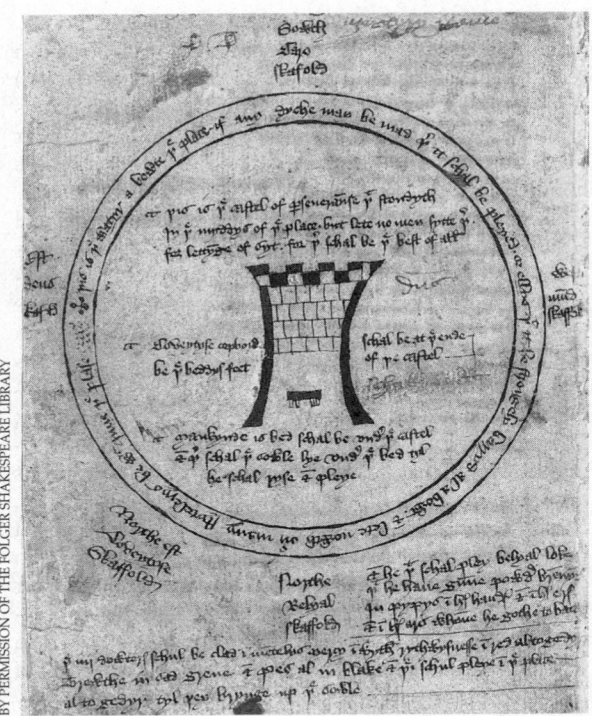

A fifteenth-century diagram for the presentation of The Castle of Perseverance *shows the scaffolds surrounding the open acting area with the castle in the center.*

parts and with a multiplicity of episodes allowing for the sequential presentation of numerous minor roles. The early history plays about Henry VI and Richard III are especially illustrative of this structural tradition.

Shakespeare's references to morality drama suggest a real familiarity. Prince Hal jestingly caricatures Falstaff as "that roasted Manningtree ox with the pudding in his belly, that reverend Vice, that grey iniquity, that father ruffian, that vanity in years . . . that old white-bearded Satan" (*1 Henry IV,* 2.4.447–58). Manningtree, in Essex, appears to have been renowned for its annual fair at which plays were acted and great-sized oxen were roasted; the Vice, as we have seen, was the chief comic tempter of most morality plays. Falstaff himself refers to the Vice's traditional dagger of lath in his contemptuous remarks about Justice Shallow: "And now is this Vice's dagger become a squire" (*2 Henry IV,* 3.2.317–18). Feste, in *Twelfth Night,* exits at one point with a promise to the audience that he will return soon "Like to the old Vice," with his "dagger of lath" and "his rage and his wrath" (4.2.121–32). Kent, in *King Lear,* speaks of Goneril as having taken "Vanity the puppet's part against the royalty of her father" (2.2.36–7), as though she were a personified representation of Pride in a morality play. The evocation of that

genre strengthens our perception that good and evil are indeed battling over Lear's destiny on a cosmic scale. Richard III explicitly compares himself to "the formal Vice, Iniquity" in his use of sinister double entendres and his boasting to the audience of his cleverness (3.1.82–3).

Shakespeare's specific references to late medieval drama are less important, however, than his larger indebtedness to it. His use of a structural tradition of episodic multiplicity and of alternation between seriousness and comedy is especially evident in the early history plays. Of equal significance is his indebtedness to the Vice, the comic tempter of the morality play whose sinister but fascinating techniques of evil persuasion had become an enduring part of Tudor popular drama. The Vice's boastful and chortling brand of villainy is still clearly recognizable, though transmuted into superb poetry, in the insinuations of Richard III, Aaron the Moor (in *Titus Andronicus*), Iago (in *Othello*), and Edmund (in *King Lear*). As Bernard Spivack has argued, in his *Shakespeare and the Allegory of Evil,* Shakespeare's secular vision of the contest between good and evil for human souls owes much to the morality tradition and to other forms of medieval drama.

Early Tudor Humanist Drama

The development of the morality play and of other medieval drama, briefly sketched in the preceding sections, tells only one part of the story of sixteenth-century drama. The trend we have observed in morality drama, toward the depiction of contemporary English life, manifested itself also in other kinds of plays that were not so plainly derived from the religious drama of the Middle Ages. A relatively new influence was that of classical and neoclassical drama, from the ancient classical world and from Renaissance Europe. Important, too, were the secular kinds of dramatic entertainment that had flourished in the English court even before the advent of neoclassicism. Early Tudor drama for courtly and well-educated audiences was heterogeneous because it reflected so many diverse impulses: the intensified renewal of classical learning that had come about through the activities of the new humanists, the ferment of ideologies introduced by the Reformation, the increase in social mobility in the Tudor court, and the like. In varying proportions, the courtly and intellectual drama of the period borrowed from the English morality play, from courtly pastimes such as the "disguising" (a kind of masque) and the dialogue or *débat,* from secular farce and romance, from classical and neoclassical literature, and even from the Corpus Christi cycles and saints' plays. The mixture, experimental and often uneven, was nonetheless stimulating because it attempted to fuse English culture with the thought of neoclassical Europe. This drama was usually staged in courtly surroundings, such as the banqueting halls of the aristocracy. (See "The

Tudor Hall" below, in the section on London Theaters and Dramatic Companies.)

Especially important in the development of this early Tudor drama were the humanists who associated themselves with Sir Thomas More and his patron Cardinal Morton. These men were, like their counterparts in Italy and elsewhere on the Continent, intensely devoted to the revival of classical learning in all its aspects—art, architecture, literary texts, historical knowledge, and politics—and thus to the enhancement of the human spirit. Their shared ideals can be seen in the plays that they wrote or sponsored. Henry Medwall, chaplain to Cardinal Morton, wrote a morality play called *Nature* (c. 1490–1501) that reveals an interest in Aristotelian ethics, as well as in traditional Christian ideas of salvation. Medwall also wrote *Fulgens and Lucrece* (c. 1490–1500), the earliest extant play in England to use an ancient Roman setting and a secular romantic love plot. The heroine, Lucrece, chooses the love of a virtuous but untitled "new" man at court in preference to a haughty and degenerate aristocrat. This *débat* was derived from *De Vera Nobilitate* by Buonaccorso of Pistoia, an ardent Italian humanist. Despite its ancient setting and romantic plot, it is also unmistakably relevant to the struggle between "new" men and old aristocrats in the court of Henry VII. Both of Medwall's plays were printed by John Rastell, another humanist in the service of Cardinal Morton. Rastell, who married More's sister, wrote a humanist interlude called *The Nature of the Four Elements* (c. 1517–1518), in which he excitedly discussed the latest scientific theories concerning the roundness of the world and other such new ideas. He is probably the author of *Of Gentleness and Nobility* (c. 1527–1530) as well, a play that iconoclastically asks whether monarchy and the inheritance of property are not social evils that ideally ought to be abolished. The influence of Thomas More's *Utopia* on this play is unmistakable.

John Heywood, son-in-law of John Rastell, was the most important and versatile dramatist of the humanist group. All his plays, except *Witty and Witless*, which has been preserved only in manuscript, were printed by John Rastell or his son, William Rastell. Heywood's plays fall into two groups: the courtly disputations, such as *The Play of Love, The Play of the Weather,* and *Witty and Witless* (c. 1525–1533), and the more popular farces that may have been intended for popular audiences as well, such as *The Pardoner and the Friar, The Four PP,* and *John John the Husband* (c. 1513–1533). In the first group, *Weather* reveals a characteristic attention to humanist and courtly themes. In an obvious analogy to the Tudor concept of an absolutist yet benevolent monarchy, the various petitioners of the play complain to Jupiter about the weather but are finally persuaded to be grateful for the mixed weather that is provided them. Heywood is suggesting, in other words, that the English monarchy must bestow its favors impartially on all classes of persons and that all subjects

ought to recognize the essential soundness of the social order as it presently exists. Heywood's second group of plays, on the other hand, eschews such courtly and political themes for a broader slapstick comedy, in the vein of Chaucerian fabliau and French farce.

In addition to these humanist plays written by members of the Sir Thomas More circle, the learned drama of early Tudor England included many plays written for schoolboys or for the choristers attached to royal and noble households. The plays written under such auspices tended to reveal a much stronger interest in classical and neoclassical drama than did the plays written for popular audiences. Schoolmasters wrote dramatic texts derived from the classics for educational purposes; at court, sophisticated audiences were interested in the latest dramatic fashions from Italy or France. Ancient Greek drama did not receive nearly so much attention, however, as the Latin drama of Terence (c. 186–159 B.C.), Plautus (c. 254–184 B.C.), and Seneca (c. 4 B.C. –65 A.D.). These Latin authors had long been used as schoolboys' texts, though they were frequently expurgated or allegorized into the terms of Christian morality in order to render them suitable for schoolboys' sensibilities. This academic tradition, on the Continent and in England, produced a number of imitative plays that could be acted by boys as part of their training in classical languages. Some plays, such as John Palsgrave's *Acolastus* (1540), were intended to be read rather than acted. Many others were Latin biblical plays in classical guise, such as Thomas Watson's *Absalom* (c. 1535–1544) and George Buchanan's *Jephthes* (1540–1545).

At court and in noble households, choristers were becoming noted for their acting ability. They performed chiefly during seasons of revels, such as in the Christmas season. They did not appear commercially before public audiences during the early Tudor period, as did the players of moralities and popular interludes. The Children of the Royal Chapel are known to have presented plays as early as 1506. The boys of St. Paul's School acted before King Henry VIII in 1528. Later, in the 1570s and 1580s, these children's groups were organized into professional acting companies. Children's plays were generally written by schoolmasters or choirmasters. The plays were heavily influenced by continental traditions and often depicted themes, such as that of the Prodigal Son, that were congenial to boys of school age. *Nice Wanton* (1547–1553) offers an instance of this sort. Biblical themes were common and were sometimes used to urge a political lesson in the presence of a courtly audience. *Godly Queen Hester* (1525–1529), for example, seems to defend the cause of Katharine of Aragon and to denounce the machinations of Cardinal Wolsey. *Jacob and Esau* (1547–1553) draws an unflattering comparison between the unregenerate Esau and those who refuse to abandon the Catholic faith. Classical subjects were, of course, much in

Early Tudor drama employed the talents of boy actors on stage such as this company, the Children of the Royal Chapel.

demand as a way of educating youth, as in *Appius and Virginia* (1559–1567) and in Richard Edwards's *Damon and Pythias* (c. 1565).

Early Comedy

Schoolboys' drama was also vitally important in the development of classical or "regular" comedy on the English stage. Native morality drama was often highly comic, to be sure, especially in its depiction of the resourceful and scheming Vice; but English drama still had much to learn from classical examples about play construction and about the presentation of various types of characters. Perhaps the two best-known early English "regular" comedies were *Ralph Roister Doister* and *Gammer Gurton's Needle*.

Ralph Roister Doister, by Nicholas Udall, at one time headmaster of Eton, was acted probably between 1552 and 1554 by boy actors. Its staging is essentially that of neoclassical comedy, with two houses facing onto a street. The play employs a classical five-act structure and preserves the unities of time and place. (According to classical and neoclassical theory, a play's action should be limited to one location—a city, for example—and to a single day.) Stock comic types include the *miles gloriosus,* or braggart soldier, and the parasite. At the same time, Udall has transformed his heroine, usually a courtesan in Plautus's racy comedies, into a winsomely pious Englishwoman named Christian Custance. Ralph Roister Doister, the braggardly type for whom the play is named, is foiled in his mean-spirited determination to win Christian Custance away from her true love, Gawin Goodluck. Almost all the characters virtuously conspire to expose Ralph for his effrontery and pretended bravery; even Matthew Merrygreek, the fun-loving parasite, proves ultimately to be on the side of decency and fair play. Throughout, Udall has adapted Roman comedy to English customs and mores.

Gammer Gurton's Needle, written by William Stevenson, fellow of Christ's College, Cambridge, at about the same time as *Ralph Roister Doister,* is similarly designed for student acting. Stock Roman characters are transformed into hearty English types. Diccon the Bedlam, who engineers the farcical action of the lost needle, resembles not only the Roman parasite but also the English natural fool or zany. To some extent, he also reminds us of the mischievous and inventive Vice of the morality play. Other characters are even less purely Roman in their origin: Hodge, the clownish servant; Dame Chat, the shrewish neighbor; and Dr. Rat, the impoverished and ill-trained clergyman who spends most of his time drinking and complaining about his wretched lot. The play is an educated college man's indulgent laugh at his country neighbors. Yet the play is, like *Ralph Roister Doister,* classically structured into five acts, with a single stage setting that preserves the unities of time and place.

In 1566, the members of Gray's Inn saw a production of George Gascoigne's *Supposes,* translated from the Italian of Ariosto (1509). Because it was a translation and not an English adaptation, this play preserves essentially in their original form the stock character types of neoclassical comedy: the parasite, the pantaloon or miserly aged rival in love, the overly watchful father, the clever servant, the bawdy nurse, and so on. The heroine, though no longer a Roman courtesan as in the comedies of the much-imitated Latin dramatist Plautus, is nonetheless a self-possessed and sophisticated young woman who conducts a secret affair for some time without being detected by her father. The mores of this continental play must have seemed challengingly cosmopolitan to its fashionable courtly and intellectual audience. Just as importantly, the play offered graceful prose language as its medium, rather than the homely English verse of *Ralph Roister Doister* and *Gammer Gurton's Needle. Supposes* provided a new model for neoclassical comedy and was to become (with some of its continental morality anglicized) a source for Shakespeare's *The Taming of the Shrew.* Indeed, Shakespeare learned much about play construction, dialogue, and characterization from neoclassical comedies of this sort; perhaps his earliest comedy, *The Comedy of Errors,* owes a great deal to Plautus and to neoclassical imitators of that Latin comic writer. Another early Italian comedy in English, *The Bugbears,* was adapted from Grazzini's *La Spiritata* and acted in about 1563–1565 by boy actors.

Early Tragedy

In early English tragedy, as in early comedy, native and neoclassical traditions coalesced and sometimes clashed. Native conceptions of tragedy had partly originated in two great medieval commonplaces: the "wheel of fortune" and the "fall of princes." Both were incorporated in Chaucer's "The Monk's Tale" and its source, Boccaccio's *De Casibus Virorum Illustrium,* which presented moral examples from the lives of famous men. Chaucer had defined "tragedy" as the story of a great person "that stood in greet prosperitee, / And is yfallen out of heigh degree / Into myserie, and endeth wrecchedly." His examples, taken from Boccaccio, included Lucifer, Adam, Samson, Hercules, Julius Caesar, and others. These were men or evil beings who had either fallen through sinful pride or had been brought low through the inevitable turn of fortune's wheel. Both types of tragedy illustrated to the medieval mind the folly of trusting to worldly expectations. The "fall of princes" tradition was extended into Elizabethan times through John Lydgate's Chaucerian imitation, *The Fall of Princes*, and its Tudor sequel, *The Mirror for Magistrates* (1559, with many subsequent revisions and enlargements). The morality play contributed a pattern similar to that of Satan's tragic fall through pride; and, although the mankind figure of early morality plays invariably was recovered to God's grace by the end of the play, some early Elizabethan Calvinistic moralities (such as *Enough Is as Good as a Feast* or *The Longer Thou Livest the More Fool Thou Art*) featured human protagonists who were eternally damned. As we have already seen, Elizabethan moralities of this sort anticipated the tragic pattern of Marlowe's *Doctor Faustus*.

Native traditions of tragedy evolved quite independent of classical tragic drama and were, in some ways, strikingly different from it. Christian morality often served as a major explanation of the cause of tragic fall in medieval tragedy. Moreover, the focus was broad and cosmic, as in *Doctor Faustus*. Scenes of comic depravity often alternated with scenes of tragic seriousness, especially in the morality plays. Classical tragedy, on the other hand, usually focused on a moment of crisis in the protagonist's life and presented this crisis in its full, tragic intensity, without the undercutting of comic effect. In classical tragedy generally, narrative interest was subordinated to dramatic or lyrical interest. Unity of action, as understood by Renaissance theorists of drama, necessarily included unity of time and place. Thus, the gap between native and classical tragedy was potentially vast.

Perhaps the earliest tragedy based on classical models in England was Thomas Norton and Thomas Sackville's *Gorboduc*, presented before Queen Elizabeth at Whitehall on January 18, 1562. The play attempted to offer Queen Elizabeth political advice on the need for naming a Protestant successor, by way of a cautionary example in the fratricidal strife between Gorboduc's two sons. Although Sir Philip Sidney later complained about the play's violation of the unities in the fifth act, he praised it otherwise as "an exact model of all tragedies." To be sure, native concepts of tragedy are observable in *Gorboduc*, especially in its use of an ancient British setting and in its moral and Christian explanations of the causes of tragedy. Nevertheless, the classical element predominates.

This classical element is basically Senecan. Ancient Greek tragedy was relatively unknown to Elizabethan England except through Seneca's Roman adaptations. Seneca's ten plays were all translated into English by 1581 and had long been read in the schools as models of rhetoric (just as Terence and Plautus were also read). Seneca's plays were, in fact, closet dramas, intended to be recited rather than acted. Seneca provided *Gorboduc* with a model for its long declamatory speeches, its occasional passages of stichomythia (rapid one-line exchange of dialogue), its five-act structure punctuated by dumb shows, and its supernatural agents prognosticating doom. Moreover, *Gorboduc*'s blank verse, created to approximate the Latin meters of Seneca, set a style for blank verse tragedy that dominated the English stage throughout Shakespeare's career. (Blank verse had been used shortly before *Gorboduc* by the Earl of Surrey in his translations from Virgil's *Aeneid*, but never before in drama.) *Gorboduc* also made an important contribution to the English history play by its use of chronicle materials in a tragic setting.

Other Senecan plays followed, written at first for gentlemanly audiences of the universities and the Inns of Court, rather than for the popular stage. One such was George Gascoigne's *Jocasta* (1566). In 1588, eight gentlemen of Gray's Inn, including Thomas Hughes and Francis Bacon, presented before the Queen a drama similar in form to *Gorboduc*, called *The Misfortunes of Arthur*. This tragedy borrows from Seneca not only chorus, messengers, and machinery, but also ideas, sentiments, and heightened language. Like *Gorboduc*, *The Misfortunes of Arthur* is somewhat free with the classical unities. Also, it is based upon the chronicle history of Britain, which was to become one of the chief sources of subject matter for English tragedy.

Another principal source for tragic writers was the Italian short story, which, because it was also impassioned and serious, offered many themes to writers of tragedy. *Gismond of Salerne* dramatizes a well-known Italian tale and, like *Gorboduc* and *The Misfortunes of Arthur*, is Senecan in form and nature. It was acted before the Queen in 1566 or 1568. In the same storehouse of narrative,

Shakespeare was later to find his source for *Othello*, as well as for such comedies as *The Merchant of Venice* and *Measure for Measure*. *Romeo and Juliet* was based on a English poem which in turn drew from an Italian source.

Sir Philip Sidney as Dramatic Critic

The kind of tragedy that Shakespeare and other popular dramatists wrote in the late sixteenth and early seventeenth centuries is not rigorously classical. It preserves many of the elements of English tragedy already enumerated: a broad narrative focus, frequent violations or total ignoring of the classical unities of time and place, the inclusion of comedy, and the like. Tragedy of this sort might never have developed in England to so high a point or might never have been accepted as the prevailing form of tragedy but for two things: in the first place, few Elizabethan dramatists learned their craft by studying the classical rules; in the second place, the Elizabethan audience, with a taste for native English drama, demanded new, varied, and sensational plots, accompanied by vaudeville clownery and songs. Such popular drama was often condemned by those critics who were familiar with classical literature, but to have made English tragedy conform with classical rules would have meant changing its nature. In France, where in Shakespeare's time the drama came under the control of the court and the learned classes, tragedy developed according to classical rules into the drama of Corneille and Racine; in England, on the other hand, Shakespeare and his contemporaries created a kind of tragedy particularly their own.

The most famous neoclassical critic of the age, Sir Philip Sidney, took vigorous exception to the kind of tragedy in vogue during the 1580s. His views are set forth in *The Defence of Poesy*, written in 1581 or slightly later:

Our tragedies and comedies not without cause cried out against, observing rules neither of honest civility nor skillful poetry, excepting *Gorboduc*—again I say of those that I have seen. Which notwithstanding as it is full of stately speeches and well-sounding phrases, climbing to the height of Seneca his style, and as full of notable morality, which it doth most delightfully teach, and so obtain the very end of poesy, yet in truth it is very defective in the circumstances, which grieves me, because it might not remain as an exact model of all tragedies. For it is faulty both in place and time, the two necessary companions of all corporal actions. For where the stage should alway represent but one place, and the uttermost time presupposed in it should be, both by Aristotle's precept and common reason, but one day, there is both many days and many places inartificially imagined.

But if it be so in *Gorboduc*, how much more in all the rest? where you shall have Asia of the one side and Afric of the other, and so many other under-kingdoms, that the player, when he comes in, must ever begin with telling where he is, or else the tale will not be conceived. Now you shall have three ladies walk to gather flowers, and then we must believe the stage to be a garden. By and by we hear news of shipwreck in the same place; then we are to blame if we accept it not for a rock. Upon the back of that comes out a hideous monster with fire and smoke, and then the miserable beholders are bound to take it for a cave. While in the meantime two armies fly in, represented with four swords and bucklers, and then what hard heart will not receive it for a pitched field?

Now of time they are much more liberal. For ordinary it is that two young princes fall in love; after many traverses she is got with child, delivered of a fair boy; he is lost, groweth a man, falleth in love, and is ready to get another child,—and all this in two hours space; which how absurd it is in sense even sense may imagine, and art hath taught, and all ancient examples justified, and at this day the ordinary players in Italy will not err in....

Later he tells us that English plays are "neither right tragedies nor right comedies"; instead, they mingle clowns and kings with "neither decency nor discretion."

To be sure, Sidney's criticism is never narrowly classical; in the essay as a whole, he affirms the power of the artist to range freely in the world of wit and imagination and to create artifacts that are more universally "true" than either philosophy or history. At the same time, his strictures against the contemporary English stage do invoke classical ideals of unity that many dramatists and audiences ignored. Popular audiences of the time seem to have had no more difficulty imagining the lapse of twenty years than the lapse of two hours. Nor were they troubled by scenic shifts from one continent to another, or by shifts in tone from the comic to the pathetic, the grotesque, or the tragic. Because native English drama had never paid much attention to classical precept, it worked out its own sense of cohesion according to different criteria of multiplicity, alternating effects, sudden juxtapositions, typological recurrence, and the like.

John Lyly, George Peele, and Robert Greene

In facing the problem of understanding just what Elizabethan drama was and how it became what it was, we must recognize that the classification of drama into comedy and tragedy by the ancients does not tell the whole story. Even when we add the history or chronicle play to these two divisions of drama, we have, at best, a rough classification that leaves out a great deal and implies that these three forms were sharply discriminated. In fact, Elizabethan drama is, generally speaking, a blend of many elements. Nearly all Elizabethan tragedies have in them comic scenes and by-plots; most comedies have in them serious issues that might conceivably result in disaster; and history plays are often capable of being classified as comedies or as tragedies. To appreciate further this protean quality of genre in early Elizabethan drama, we might consider the varied works of a number of dramatists whose practice was successful on the stage and who influenced Shakespeare and his immediate contemporaries. Of these, John Lyly is one of the most important.

John Lyly (1554?–1606), grandson of the grammarian William Lyly or Lilly, educated at Oxford and Cambridge, first acquired fame not as a dramatist, but as a writer of prose. His *Euphues, The Anatomy of Wit*, published in 1578, and its sequel, *Euphues and His England* (1580), stand as the most sensational and brilliant effort in the struggle of English Renaissance prose to acquire a conscious artistic manner. The style is, to a remarkable extent, composed of rhetorical devices: antithesis, personification, rhetorical question, metaphor, simile, and, above all, balance reinforced by alliteration. Recondite tidbits and fanciful legends about natural history are garnered from Plutarch, Pliny, and many other writers. The overall result is a kind of handbook for the courtier, the lover, the traveler, and the statesman. Lyly's deliberately outrageous style was imitated by dozens of other writers, including Robert Greene and Thomas Lodge, and seems to have set a new fashion of smart speech in the court of Queen Elizabeth. "Euphuism" itself had a vast influence on the style of the drama and other literature, both in poetry and in prose. Shakespeare is one of those who imitated and also ridiculed euphuistic speech. (For amusing examples of Shakespeare's parodying of the euphuistic style, see Falstaff's speech in *1 Henry IV*, 2.4.396 ff., beginning "for though the camomile, the more it is trodden on the faster it grows, yet youth, the more it is wasted the sooner it wears," or Don Armado's love letter in *Love's Labor's Lost*, 4.1.61 ff.: "Shall I command thy love? I may. Shall I enforce thy love? I could. Shall I entreat thy love? I will," and so on.)

Lyly was also the author of at least eight comedies, written to suit the taste of the court and possibly all acted before the Queen by the children of the Chapel Royal or of St. Paul's School. The plays are often courtly debates in the tradition of Medwall's *Fulgens and Lucrece*, with much combat of wits and philosophical argument. These comedies are also sufficiently modeled on Plautus or Terence to indicate that the characteristic features of Latin comedy by this time (1580–1590) had become naturalized on the English stage. *Mother Bombie*, for example, is an adaptation of Latin comedy, containing such stock figures as the pedant, the rascally servant, the duped parent, the parasite, and the aged lover, although, as usual, in Lyly the clownery has an English flavor as well.

Indeed, however much Lyly may recall classical Latin comedy, he is most important as the inventor of a fanciful type of love comedy to which Shakespeare was significantly indebted in several of his plays. Lyly's *Sappho and Phao, Endymion*, and *Midas* have romantic plots derived from Ovidian mythology. *Galatea* uses a pastoral setting for its love story and male disguises for the heroines, as in *As You Like It. Love's Metamorphosis* and *The Woman in the Moon* are also pastoral comedies. *Campaspe*, like *The Merchant of Venice*, portrays conflicts of love and friendship. Lyly's flattery of Queen Elizabeth through topical allegory and his appeal to a courtly clientele are, to be sure, modes that Shakespeare does not generally adopt. On the other hand, Shakespeare learned a good deal from Lyly's sensitive portrayal of the psychology of love. The depiction is often wryly comic: Lyly's men abase themselves before women, vacillate between idealization and misogyny, and not infrequently fail as wooers—much as the young lords do in Shakespeare's most Lylyan play, *Love's Labor's Lost*. Shakespeare's lovers generally work toward a more successful and realistic completion of romantic expectations, but Shakespeare's interest in love comedy began, in part, with what Lyly had achieved.

George Peele (1558?–1597) was also active as a dramatist around the time that Shakespeare first came to London. Peele's *The Arraignment of Paris* (1581) offers a quality of blank verse not previously seen in comedy and shows how classical legend could be adapted to a thoroughly English celebration of the nation and its Queen. *The Old Wives' Tale* (c. 1588–1594) is a seemingly naive but actually skillful medley of folk legends in the spirit of popular romance. *David and Bethsabe* (c. 1581–1594) dramatizes a familar biblical narrative in terms of erotic love and kingly power. Peele also contributed importantly to the new and burgeoning genre of the English history play with his *Edward I* (1590–1593); it is, like other history plays of the Armada era, jingoistically anti-Spanish and features a popular folk-hero king who understands and respects the proud local customs of his people. *The Battle of Alcazar* (1588–1589), another play of the Armada era, revels in the exotic world of Africa and the Middle East, in the vaunting heroic vein of Christopher Marlowe's *Tamburlaine*. Peele also devised two London civic pageants.

Robert Greene (1558–1592), more than any other dramatist, opened up for Shakespeare the world of Greek romance—the kind of fiction ultimately derived from Heliodorus, Achilles Tatius, and other protonovelists of the Mediterranean world in the second through fourth centuries. The Greeks of that era were the merchants, traders, sailors, and schoolmasters of the Roman Empire, and the early form of prose romance they created was a reflection of the adventurous life they lived. This romantic fiction reveled in strange and improbable encounters, piracies, the exposure of infant children to the elements and their eventual restoration as grown-ups to their aging parents, the separation and reunion of indistinguishable twins, and many other plot devices rendered familiar to us in the writings of Renaissance authors for whom this kind of sensationalism was every bit as interesting and worthy of imitation as the classics of Virgil and Ovid. Stories of the Greek kind, translated into various languages and ultimately into English, were to serve as models for a number of Shakespeare's late romances, especially *Pericles, The Winter's Tale*, and *Cymbeline*. Indeed, the plot of *The Winter's Tale* came to Shakespeare by way of Greene's prose romance, *Pandosto.*

From Greek romantic fiction, Greene devised a type of plucky romantic heroine for his plays and novels that Shakespeare was to develop further in his comedies. The society depicted by Greek romance gave women great liberty, and, like them, Greene's heroines are independent, witty, and resourceful, though at the same time feminine. Greene's dramas are almost the first modern productions in which women are in any degree represented as assuming a relatively dignified station in a mutually supportive love relationship with a man.

Greene also borrowed from Greek romantic fiction, and from other sources, especially for pastoral fiction. His plays, particularly *James IV* and *Friar Bacon and Friar Bungay* (c. 1589–1592), give us that blend of the pastoral and the romantic which the world has enjoyed in *As You Like It* and *Love's Labor's Lost. Friar Bacon* is particularly noteworthy for its multiple plot, its resourceful heroine, and its embracing of serious issues in a comic world. Greene must be regarded as the first great master of plot in English comedy.

Greene may also have written *George a Greene, the Pinner of Wakefield* (1587–1593), a play that exalts the virtues of England's yeoman class in defiance of the aristocracy and all foreign foes. The hero, George, is a patriot, a scorner of hereditary titles, and a representative of the common people against vested interests. As a new breed of English folk hero, he is so invincible that even Robin Hood must yield to his authority. The appeal of this dream of power to the artisans and yeomen in Greene's popular audiences must have been heady indeed.

Shortly before he fell victim to the notorious debaucheries of his bohemian existence (he was reported to have died from a surfeit of pickled herring and Rhenish wine), Greene wrote many pamphlets, some about London roguery, some about his own hard usage at the hands of the world. In one of the latter, *Greene's Groatsworth of Wit Bought with a Million of Repentance* (1592), he gave us our first personal reference to Shakespeare. (See "The Only Shake-scene in a Country" in the biographical account of Shakespeare's life and work, below.) Shakespeare was, of course, not the only dramatist to be influenced by Greene; Anthony Munday, Thomas Dekker, and most of the popular dramatists of the next decade were similarly indebted to Greene's example.

Thomas Kyd and Christopher Marlowe

While romantic comedy was being shaped and developed in the hands of Lyly, Peele, and Greene, Senecan tragedy was also finding its proponents on the English stage. Lucius Annaeus Seneca (c. 4 B.C.–65 A.D.), a Roman statesman and stoic philosopher during the reign of the emperor Nero, wrote tragedies of a severely formal cast based on the tragedies of Aeschylus, Sophocles, and Euripides. Although never performed in Seneca's lifetime and indeed written as "closet" dramas, they became immensely influential on dramatists of later generations, especially during the Renaissance on the Continent and in England. The greatest genius in adapting Senecan action to the English theater was Thomas Kyd (1558–1594). His influence on his contemporaries and on later dramatists was immense; *The Spanish Tragedy* (c. 1583–1587) was probably acted more times during the sixteenth century than any other English play and became a pattern for subsequent revenge drama. Although Senecan tradition by no means accounts for all of the play's successful qualities, it remains a central part. Kyd catches the unabashed brutality and horror of the Senecan story and reveals it openly. Instead of having the action reported as taking place off the stage, as in Seneca and in most classical tragedy, he presents it directly. For tales of Greek mythology, he substitutes a modern story

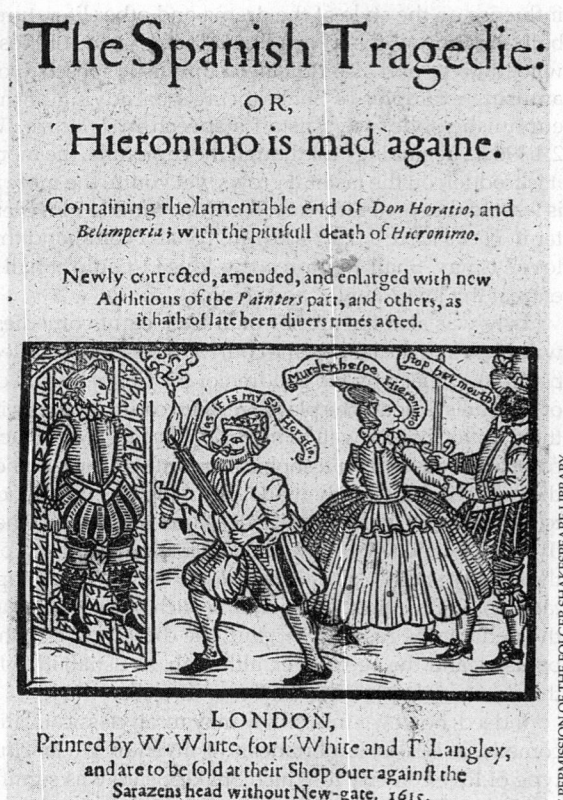

Thomas Kyd's The Spanish Tragedy *was perhaps the most popular play of the sixteenth century; it was performed more than any other English drama of the time. The Spanish Tragedy served as a pattern and influenced subsequent revenge drama—including Shakespeare's* Hamlet.

of love, conspiracy, murder, and political intrigue. He retains the Senecan ghost, the revenge motive, the spirit of stoicism, and a modified form of the chorus. The play deals both seriously and sensationally with the conflicting codes of revenge and Christian faith in God's providence. The protagonist Hieronimo, confronted with his son's murder and seemingly unable to obtain justice through the state, finds his pleas to the heavens unanswered and turns instead to a revenge that hardens his spirit and requires his own violent death as payment. The action is presided over by the spirit of Revenge, a chorus-like figure whose aims share nothing in common with Christian views of justice and mercy. *The Spanish Tragedy* is also noteworthy for a style that is a tour de force of rhetorical figures, such as anaphora and oxymoron—an achievement both imitated and mocked by later dramatists. Probably Kyd is also the author of the first dramatic version of the story of Hamlet.

Kyd's work gave rise to a series of revenge plays, not only in his own time, but also later, in 1600 and the years following, when the revenge tragedy again became fashionable. Moreover, Kyd seems to have had a shaping influence on Greene and on Marlowe. For example, Marlowe's *The Jew of Malta* (c. 1589), in its verbal extravagance and sensational intrigue, seems particularly indebted to *The Spanish Tragedy.*

Nevertheless, however much Kyd may have contributed in matters of style and form, Marlowe remains the leader in the great English type of Elizabethan tragedy. He shaped the genre that subsequently was perfected by Shakespeare. His achievement is all the more remarkable when we consider that he was born in the same year as Shakespeare (1564) and died in 1593, when Shakespeare had written no more than six or seven of his earliest plays. Marlowe's great contribution to English drama was a type of protagonist expressing something of the aspiration of the very Renaissance itself. Tamburlaine thirsts for world conquest; Dr. Faustus would go to the utmost bounds of knowledge and the power which knowledge gives; and Barabas in *The Jew of Malta* sets no limit to his longing for wealth.

Structurally, *Tamburlaine* (1587–1588) is a good deal closer to the English popular morality play than to classical drama. Each of the play's two parts consists of a linear sequence of conquests by the humbly born but seemingly invincible Tamburlaine, until at last death ends his glory. Because many characters appear in one episode only, the cast is large and yet within the capacities of an Elizabethan acting company. Doubling of parts, as in Shakespeare's early history plays, is both common and necessary. Structural unity is achieved through thematic repetition rather than through a narrowing of the narrative focus. At the same time, the language of *Tamburlaine* is rich and new in its vibrant appeal to limitless human aspiration. The Elizabethan playgoer is invited to forget moral considerations

in evaluating the play's ruthless hero and to revel instead in the intoxicating spectacle of a baseborn shepherd "threat'ning the world with high astounding terms."

A profound ambivalence permeates all of Marlowe's plays and gives them a restless, brilliant energy that is characteristic of the times for which they were written. Tamburlaine is both a remorseless butcher of his enemies and a superhuman quester. He is fierce, mysterious, oriental, exotic, unknowable; as the projection of a universal human dream of aspiration, he is to be both admired and feared. Barabas in *The Jew of Malta* is at once colossally rich and colossally evil. Similarly, the protagonist of *Doctor Faustus* (c. 1588–1589) is both a sinner who falls from grace and a noble but doomed Overreacher (as Harry Levin describes him), daring like Icarus to fly toward the sun. In medieval and Christian orthodox terms, Faustus is guilty of pride, the deadliest of the Deadly Sins; but in Renaissance terms he at least fleetingly resembles Prometheus, challenging the hierarchy of an oppressive and outmoded universe. In its free mixture of comedy and tragedy and its wholesale disregard of the classical unities, *Doctor Faustus* brilliantly demonstrates

The title page of the 1616 edition of Christopher Marlowe's Doctor Faustus *shows Faustus's conjuration of the devil. The play illustrates native rather than classical traditions of tragedy in its disregard of the unities and its free use of comedy.*

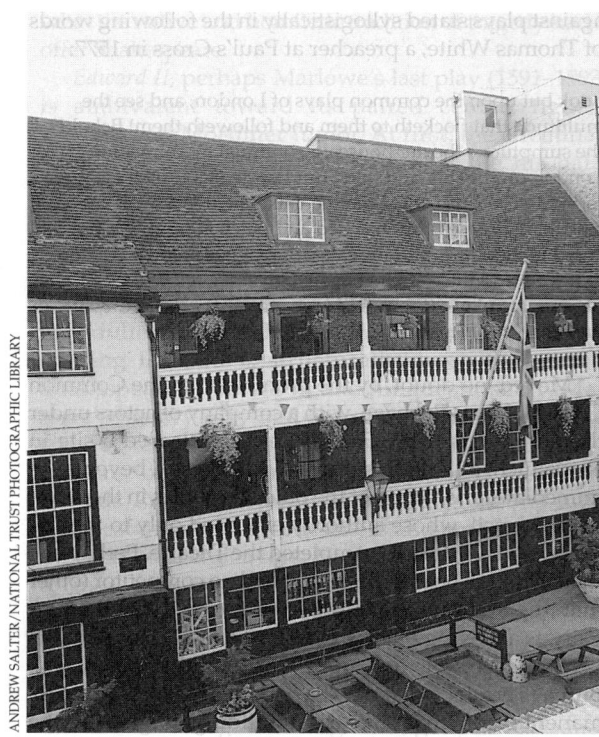

The George Inn of Southwark, England, London's only surviving galleried inn, was destroyed by fire in 1676 but rebuilt the following year with two galleries instead of the original three. Despite these changes, the George Inn gives us the best picture we have of the kind of space in which traveling companies could mount their plays on bare platform stages.

playwrights, were numerous and often heard: namely, that classical antiquity gave precedent for dramatic spectacles; that by drawing a true picture of both the bad and the good in life, plays enabled people to choose the good; that people should have wholesome amusement; and that plays provided livelihood for loyal subjects of the Queen.

Of these arguments, to be sure, the Privy Council made little use, resting the case for plays instead on what was, no doubt, an unanswerable argument: that since the players were to appear before Her Majesty, especially during the Christmas/Shrovetide period, the players needed practice in order to prepare themselves to please the royal taste. A good deal of politic fencing ensued, and, so far as orders, complaints, and denunciations were concerned, the reforming opposition had much the better of it. The preachers thundered against plays. Pamphleteers denounced all matters pertaining to the stage: Stephen Gosson in *The School of Abuse, Containing a Pleasant Invective Against Poets, Pipers, Players, Jesters and Suchlike Caterpillars of a Commonwealth* (1579) and other works; Philip Stubbes in *The Anatomy of Abuses* (1583); and finally and most furiously of all, William Prynne in *Histrio-Mastix:*

The Players' Scourge or Actor's Tragedy (1633). Gosson spoke of plays as "the inventions of the devil, the offerings of idolatry, the pomp of worldlings, the blossoms of vanity, the root of apostacy, food of iniquity, riot and adultery." "Detest them," he warned. "Players are masters of vice, teachers of wantonness, spurs to impurity, the sons of idleness."

At first, such diatribes represented an extreme reforming opinion obviously not shared by a majority of London viewers. They kept coming to plays, and the flourishing public theaters attracted the talents of the age's leading dramatists. An ominous note of polarization was sounded, however, early in the reign of James I (1603–1625), when the rift between the Puritans and the court broke into open antagonism. After about 1604, when James alienated the Puritans at the Hampton Court Conference, the split between popular audiences and the best drama of the age became increasingly evident. Shakespeare's company, now the King's Men, gravitated, whether through choice or necessity, toward the precinct of the court. Although the public theater, with its capacity for large audiences, continued to serve as a lively center of theatrical activity, Puritan opposition to the stage gathered momentum. Many dramatists, in turn, grew more satirical of London customs and more attuned to courtly tastes. Eventually, Puritan hostility to the theater was at least part of the motive behind Parliament's order to close the theaters in 1642.

The Public Theaters

A year or more after Burbage built the Theatre in 1576, the Curtain was put up near it by Philip Henslowe, or possibly by Henry Laneman, or Lanman. About ten years later, Philip Henslowe built the Rose, the first playhouse on the Bankside (the southern bank of the Thames River). In 1599, James Burbage's sons Richard and Cuthbert dismantled the Theatre because of trouble about the lease of the land and rebuilt it as the Globe on the Bankside. This Globe playhouse burned on June 29, 1613, from the discharge of cannon backstage during a performance of *All Is True*, a play thought to be identical with Shakespeare's *Henry VIII*. The Globe was rebuilt, probably in its original polygonal form—that is, essentially round, with a large number of sides. In 1600, Henslowe built the Fortune as a theater for the Lord Admiral's Men, who were chief rivals to the Lord Chamberlain's Men. The companies were differently organized, in that the Lord Chamberlain's Men were joint sharers in their own enterprise and owners of their own theatrical building, whereas Henslowe owned the Fortune (and the Rose before it) and served as landlord to the Admiral's Men—no doubt profiting handsomely from their activities.

Various records of these theatrical buildings have survived. One such record is the Fortune contract, preserved at Dulwich College among other invaluable papers of

Philip Henslowe, theatrical entrepreneur and father-in-law of the famous Edward Alleyn of the Lord Admiral's Men. The contract for building the Fortune was let to the same contractor who had built the new Globe, and, since the specifications required that the Fortune should be like the Globe in all its main features, except that it was to be square instead of polygonal, we may gain from these specifications an idea of the Globe. A second documentary record is a drawing of the Swan, a Bankside theater, accompanying a description of the playhouse by Johannes De Witt, who visited London in 1596. The drawing, which was discovered in the University Library at Utrecht, is the work of one Van Buchell and may be based on drawings by De Witt himself. Besides the Fortune contract and the Swan drawing, we have two or three little pictures of the Elizabethan public stage on the title pages of published plays, the most important being that on the title page of William Alabaster's *Roxana* (1632). Just recently, in 1989, the discovery and excavation of the foundations of the Rose playhouse and partial excavation of the Globe playhouse foundations in Southwark, together with the construction of a modern replica of the Globe playhouse near the site of these two theaters, have

This drawing of an Elizabethan public stage appeared on the title page of the published version of William Alabaster's play Roxana *(1632).*

added invaluable archeological information about the dimensions of that acting arena.

The London Public Stage

From these documents and pictures and from scattered references to the theaters, as well as from extended studies of stage directions and scenic conditions in plays themselves, we have a fairly clear idea of the public stage in London. Its features are these: a pit about seventy feet in diameter, usually circular and open to the sky; surrounding this, galleries in three tiers, containing the most expensive seats; and a rectangular stage, about forty-three by twenty-seven feet, wider than it was deep, raised about five and one-half feet above the surface of the yard, sometimes built on trestles so that it could be removed if the house was also customarily used for bear-baiting and bullbaiting. The flat, open stage usually contained one trapdoor. Part of the stage was afforded some protection from the weather by a brightly decorated wooden roof supported by posts, constituting the "heavens." Above this roof was a "hut," perhaps containing suspension gear for ascents and descents. (The Rose appears originally to have been generally smaller than what is described here, with a stage that tapered toward the front to a width of only twenty-five feet or so. The building was somewhat expanded in 1592 but was still small compared with other theaters. The original building shows no certain evidence of a roof over the stage supported by pillars, but the later building appears to have had roof pillars at the front of the stage.)

At the back of the stage was a partition wall, the "tiring-house facade," with at least two doors in it connecting the stage with the actors' dressing rooms or "tiring house." In the Rose, the tiring-house facade seems to have curved with the polygonal shape of the theater building, but in the DeWitt drawing the Swan facade looks perfectly straight across. Some theaters appear to have had no more than two doors, left and right, as shown in the Swan drawing; other theaters may have had a third door in the center. The arrangement of the Globe playhouse in this important matter cannot be finally determined, although some particular scenes from Shakespeare's plays seem to demand a third door. In any case, the so-called inner stage, long supposed to have stood at the rear of the Elizabeth stage, almost certainly did not exist. A more modest "discovery space" could be provided at one of the curtained doors when needed, as for example in *The Tempest* when Ferdinand and Miranda are suddenly "discovered" at their game of chess by Prospero. Such scenes never called for extensive action within the discovery space, however, and, indeed, the number of such discoveries in Elizabethan plays is very few. Well-to-do spectators who may have been seated in the gallery above the rear of the stage could not see into the discovery

This diagram of the Swan Theatre (left) by Van Buchell (c. 1596), based on the observations of Johannes De Witt, shows features of the public playhouse shared by James Burbage's Theatre and the Globe. To the right, a modern rendition of a typical Elizabethan playhouse shows the acting platform with spectators standing around three sides of it in the "yard," and a roofed hut above the acting area. Like the Globe and other open theaters, the design of the Swan seems to resemble the Elizabethan innyard with an added stage.

space. Accordingly, it was used sparingly and only for brief visual effects. Otherwise, the actors performed virtually all their scenes on the open stage. Sometimes curtains were hung over the tiring-house facade between the doors to facilitate scenes of concealment, as when Polonius and Claudius eavesdrop on Hamlet and Ophelia.

An upper station was sometimes used as an acting space, but not nearly so often as was once supposed. The gallery seats above the stage, sometimes known as the "Lord's room," were normally sold to well-to-do spectators. (We can see such spectators in the Swan drawing and in Alabaster's *Roxana*.) Occasionally, these box seats could be used by the actors, as when Juliet appears at her window (it is never called a balcony). In military sequences, as in the *Henry VI* plays, the tiring-house facade could represent the walls of a besieged city, with the city's defenders appearing "on the walls" (i.e., in the gallery above the stage) in order to parley with the besieging enemy standing below on the main stage. Such scenes were relatively infrequent, however, and usually required only a small number of persons to be aloft. A music room, when needed, could be located in one of the gallery boxes over the stage, but public theaters did not emulate the private stages with music rooms and music between the acts until some time around 1609.

The use of scenery was almost wholly unknown on the Elizabethan public stage, although we do find occasional hints of the use of labels to designate a certain door or area as a fixed location (as, perhaps, in *The Comedy of Errors*). For the most part, the scene was unlimited and the concept of space was fluid. No proscenium arch or curtain stood between the actors and the audience, and so the action could not be easily interrupted. Only belatedly did the public companies adopt the private-theater practice of entr'acte music, as we have seen. Most popular Elizabethan plays were written to be performed nonstop. Five-act structure had little currency, especially at first, and the occasional act divisions in the published versions of Shakespeare's plays may be nonauthorial. Acting tempo was brisk. The Prologue of *Romeo and Juliet* speaks of "the two hours' traffic of our stage." Plays were performed in the afternoons and had to be completed by dark in order to allow the audience to return safely to London. During the winter season, playing time was severely restricted. Outbreaks of plague often occasioned the closing of the theaters, especially in warm weather.

A capacity audience for the popular theaters came to about 2,000 to 3,000 persons. (The recently excavated Rose playhouse foundations suggest an audience there of around 2,000.) For the most part, the audience was

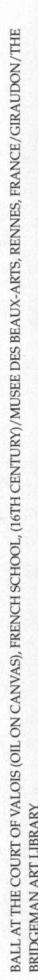

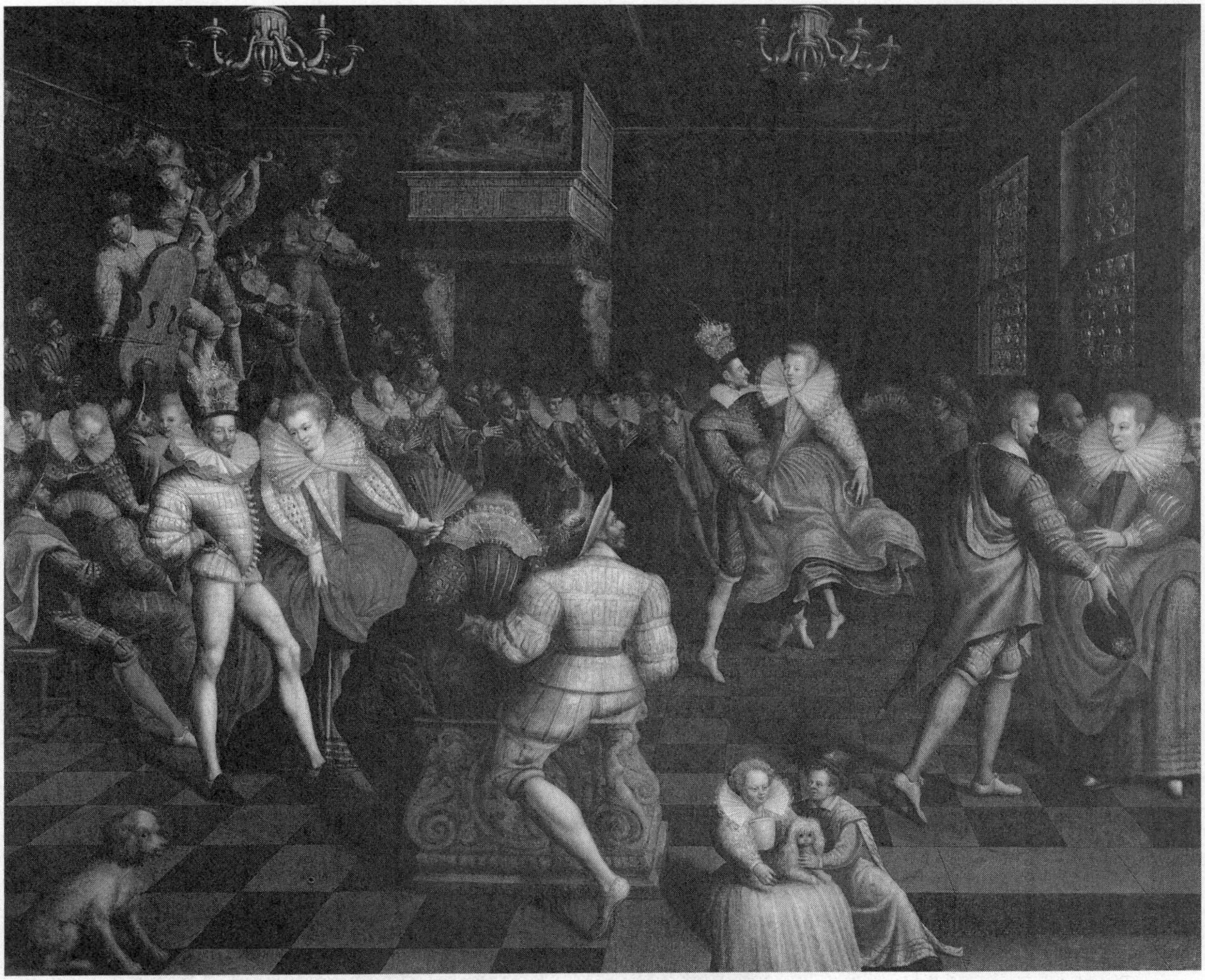

BALL AT THE COURT OF VALOIS (OIL ON CANVAS), FRENCH SCHOOL, (16TH CENTURY)/MUSEE DES BEAUX-ARTS, RENNES, FRANCE/GIRAUDON/THE BRIDGEMAN ART LIBRARY

Elizabethan dancers, shown above, perform on a stage below a gallery of musicians. Imported stage designs from Italy made more use of perspective scenery than did the commercial theaters.

affluent, consisting chiefly of the gentry and of London's substantial mercantile citizenry who paid two to three pence or more for gallery seats or the "Lord's room," but the ample pit or yard also provided room for small shopkeepers and artisans who stood for a penny. The spectators were lively, demanding, and intelligent. Although Shakespeare does allow Hamlet to refer disparagingly on one occasion to the "groundlings" who "for the most part are capable of nothing but inexplicable dumbshows and noise" (*Hamlet*, 3.2.11–12), Shakespeare appealed to the keenest understanding of his whole audience, thereby achieving a breadth of vision seldom found in continental courtly drama of the same period. The vitality and financial success of the Elizabethan public theater is without parallel in English history. The city of London itself, in 1600 or so, had only about 100,000 inhabitants, yet throughout Shakespeare's career several companies were competing simultaneously for this audience and constantly producing new plays. Most new plays ran for only a few performances, so that the acting companies were always in rehearsal with new shows. The actors needed phenomenal memories and a gift of improvisation as well. Their acting seems to have been of a high caliber, despite the speed with which they worked. Among other things, many of them were expert fencers and singers.

The London public stage inherited many of its practices from native and medieval traditions. The fluid, open stage, with spectators on four sides, recalled the arena staging of many early Corpus Christi cycles, saints' plays, and morality plays. The adult professional companies were, as we have seen, descended from the itinerant troupes that had acted their plays throughout England in guildhalls, private residences, monastic houses and schools, and perhaps occasionally outdoors on booth stages (though the evidence for this last possible venue is scarce). The Elizabethan tiring-house facade and platform stage may have owed much to the kinds of theatrical space that touring actors had known, and perhaps to the arrangement of a booth stage and a trestle platform set up against one wall of an innyard, where the guests of the inn could enjoy a performance, along with standing spectators in the yard. When the itinerant actors had set up their plays in noblemen's banqueting halls or at court, at any rate, they encountered another space that had an important influence on their concept of a theater: the Tudor hall. We must next examine the significance of this indoor theatrical setting.

The Tudor Hall

The Tudor banqueting hall played a major part in the staging of much early Tudor drama. Medwall's *Fulgens and Lucrece,* one of the earliest such plays, was written to be performed during the intervals of a state banquet. The patrician guests were seated at tables, while servingmen bustled to and fro or stood crowded together at the doors in the hall "screen." This screen or partition traversed the lower end of the rectangular hall, providing a passageway to the kitchens and to the outside. Its doors—often two, sometimes three—were normally curtained to prevent drafts. This arrangement of the doors bears an interesting resemblance to that of many playhouses in late Elizabethan England, both public and private. Moreover, hall screens and passageways were normally surmounted by a gallery, where musicians could play—an archi-

tectural feature markedly resembling the upper galleries of late Elizabethan theaters. Could the Tudor hall screen provide a natural facade for dramatic action? Perhaps it did, although records from Shakespeare's era only rarely document an actual performance in front of the screen, whereas performances were common at the upper end of the hall in front of the dais or in the midst of the hall, where the persons of highest social rank sitting on the dais would have had the best view. The actors of *Fulgens and Lucrece* clearly made use of the doorways in the hall screen, sometimes joking with the servingmen as the actors pushed their way into the hall, but they probably acted in the center, among the spectators' tables. John Heywood's *Play of the Weather* calls for a similar *mise en scène.* Although this ready-made "stage" sufficed for most Tudor plays, the actors sometimes provided additional stage structures; *Weather,* for example, calls for a throne room into which Jupiter can retire without leaving the hall. Similar structures could represent a shop, an orchard, a mountain, or what have you.

Guild and town halls, where players on tour performed before the mayor and council (and sometimes a wider public), provided a similar physical environment, except that we cannot be sure that such spaces had galleries in the sixteenth century. Since the gallery is not necessary for many Tudor plays, the players may well have gained experience in halls of this kind that influenced their techniques of staging once they had gravitated to London.

Although both medieval and continental drama offered traditions of multiple staging, in which a series of simultaneously visible and adjacent structures would

The Tudor banqueting hall provided a place to "stage" much early Tudor drama. The actors performed on the floor, among the tables of the guests. The Middle Temple Hall, shown here, later served as the location for a performance of Shakespeare's Twelfth Night *on February 2, 1602. The Middle Temple is one of the Inns of Court, where young men studied law and occasionally relaxed by staging dramatic entertainments.*

represent as fixed locations all the playing areas needed for the performance of a play, Tudor indoor staging seems to have made less use of this method than was once supposed. Nor did the various indoor theaters of Tudor England make extensive use of neoclassical staging from Italy, with its street scene in perspective created by means of lath-and-canvas stage "houses." Italian scenery of this sort came into use sooner in the court masque than in regular drama. Nevertheless, we do find in the Tudor indoor theater a neoclassical tendency toward a fixed locale, in preference to the unlimited open stage. *Gammer Gurton's Needle*, for example, acted probably in a university hall, seems to have used one stage structure, or possibly one door, to represent Gammer's house throughout the action, and another to represent Dame Chat's house. Shakespeare may have been influenced by this kind of fixed-locale staging in *The Comedy of Errors*. (Alan Nelson's *Early Cambridge Theaters*, 1994, is an important resource for school staging.)

The Private Stage

Despite such influences on the public stage, the most significant contribution of the Tudor hall and its hall screen was to the so-called private stage of the late Elizabethan period—"private" in the sense of being intended for a more select and courtly audience than that which frequented the "public" theaters. In the 1570s, choir boys began performing professionally to courtly and intellectual audiences in London. The choir boys had long performed plays for the royal and noble households to which they were attached, but in the 1570s they were, in effect, organized into professional acting companies. Sebastian

A reconstruction of the Second Blackfriars, featuring a rectangular stage, a tiring house with three doors, and a gallery.

PHOTO BY LAUREN D. ROGERS/AMERICAN SHAKESPEARE CENTER

Westcote and the Children of Paul's may have originated this enterprise. Their theater was apparently some indoor hall in the vicinity of St. Paul's in London, outfitted much like the typical domestic Tudor hall to which the boys had grown accustomed. Comparable indoor "private" theaters soon followed at Blackfriars and Whitefriars.

At some point, a low stage was constructed in front of the hall screen, and seats were provided for all the spectators. Many of these seats were in the "pit," or what we would call the "orchestra," facing toward the stage at one end of the rectangular room. Other seats were in galleries along both sides of the room; these were quite elaborate in the so-called Second Blackfriars of 1596 and provided two or three tiers of seats. Elegant box seats stood at either side of the stage itself. The Second Blackfriars had a permanently built tiring house to the rear of the stage, with probably three doors. Above it was a gallery used variously as a lord's room, a music room, and an upper station for occasional acting.

The private theater flourished during the 1580s and again after 1598–1599, having been closed down during most of the 1590s because of its satirical activities. Although it was a commercial theater, it was "private" in its clientele, because its high price of admission (sixpence) excluded those who could stand in the yards of the "public" theaters for a penny (roughly the equivalent of an hour's wage for a skilled worker). Plays written for the more select audiences of the "private" theaters tended to be more satirical and oriented to courtly values than those written for the "public" theaters, although the distinction is by no means absolute.

London Private Theaters

The important private theaters of Shakespeare's London were two in the precinct, or "liberty," of Blackfriars, an early one in Whitefriars about which little is known, a later one there, and a theater at Paul's, the exact location and nature of which is not known. In the thirteenth century, the mother house of the Dominican friars, or Blackfriars, was established on the sloping ground between St. Paul's Cathedral and the river. It was a sizable institution, ultimately covering about five acres of ground. It stood on the very border of the city and, after the custom of the time, was made a liberty; that is to say, it had its own local government and was removed from the immediate jurisdiction of the city of London. After the suppression of the friary and the confiscation of its lands, the jealousy existing between the Privy Council, representing the crown, and the mayor and aldermen, representing the city and probably also the rights of property holders, prevented the district of the Blackfriars from losing its political independence of the municipality. It was still a liberty and therefore attractive to players and other persons wishing to avoid the London authorities. At the same time, aristocrats residing in the area required protection, and the Crown had certain rights still in its control.

From 1576 to 1584, the Children of the Queen's Chapel, one of the two most important companies of boy actors, had used a hall in the precinct of Blackfriars in which to act their plays. Here were acted at least some of John Lyly's plays. In 1596, James Burbage purchased property in this precinct and seems to have spent a good deal of money in its adaptation for use as an indoor theater (the so-called Second Blackfriars). He probably appreciated its advantages over Cripplegate or the Bankside of greater proximity to London and of protection against the elements, particularly for use in winter. But the aristocratic residents of the Blackfriars, by petition to the Privy Council, prevented him from making use of his theater. Plays within the city proper had only recently been finally and successfully prohibited, and the petitioners no doubt objected to their intrusion into Blackfriars, on the grounds that the plays and their crowds were a nuisance.

Burbage's new indoor theater may have lain idle from the time of its preparation until 1600; but, in any case, in that year it became the scene of many plays. It was let by lease for the use of the Children of the Chapel, who in 1604 became the Children of the Queen's Revels. Their theater managers brought into their service a number of new dramatists—Ben Jonson, John Marston, George Chapman, and later John Webster. The vogue of the plays acted by the Children of the Chapel was so great as to damage the patronage of the established companies and to compel them to go on the road. Out of this rivalry between the children and the adult actors arose that open competition alluded to in *Hamlet* (2.2.328–362) and sometimes referred to today as the "War of the Theaters." The skirmishes were relatively brief, arising in part from a clash of personalities among Jonson, Marston, and Thomas Dekker, but the debate between public and private acting companies was significant as an indication of whether London drama would continue to play to large popular audiences or would increasingly turn to a more courtly clientele. In 1608, the Burbage interests secured the evacuation of the lease, so that the theater in Blackfriars became the winter playhouse of Shakespeare's company from that time forward.

System of Patronage

In 1572, common players of interludes, along with minstrels, bearwards, and fencers, were included within the hard terms of the act for the punishment of vagabonds, provided that such common players were not enrolled as the servants of a baron of the realm or of some honorable person of greater degree. The result was a system of patronage of theatrical companies in Elizabethan and Jacobean times, according to which players became the "servants" of some nobleman or of some member of the royal family.

By the time Shakespeare came to London in the late 1580s, many of these companies were already in existence, some of which long antedated the passage of the act of 1572. Provincial records of the visits of players, to be sure, sometimes failed to distinguish actors from acrobats or other public performers who were similarly organized. Nonetheless, we have evidence that various companies of players performed in London and elsewhere in the late 1580s, under the patronage of the Queen, the Earl of Worcester, the Earl of Leicester, the Earl of Oxford, the Earl of Sussex, the Lord Admiral, and Charles, Lord Howard of Effingham. These companies were eventually much reduced in number; usually only three adult companies acted at any given time in London during Shakespeare's prime. In addition, the children's companies, privately controlled, acted intermittently but at times very successfully. The most important of these were the Children of the Chapel and Queen's Revels and the Children of Paul's, but there were also boy players of Windsor, Eton College, the Merchant Taylors, Westminster, and other schools.

Shakespeare and the London Theatrical Companies

We know that by 1592 Shakespeare had arrived in London and had achieved sufficient notice as a young playwright to arouse the resentment of a rival dramatist, Robert Greene. In that year, shortly before he died, Greene—or possibly his editor after Greene's death—lashed out at an "upstart crow, beautified with our feathers," who had had the audacity to fancy himself "the only Shake-scene in a country" (*Groats-worth of Wit*). This petulant outburst was plainly directed at Shakespeare, since Greene included in his remarks a parody of some lines from *3 Henry VI*. As a university man and an established dramatist, Greene seems to have resented the intrusion into his profession of a mere player who was not university trained. This "upstart crow" was achieving a very real success on the London stage. Shakespeare had probably already written *The Comedy of Errors, Love's Labor's Lost, The Two Gentlemen of Verona*, the *Henry VI* plays, and *Titus Andronicus*, and perhaps also *Richard III* and *The Taming of the Shrew*.

For which acting company or companies had he written these plays, however? By 1594, we know that Shakespeare was an established member of the Lord Chamberlain's company, important enough, in fact, to have been named, along with Will Kempe and Richard Burbage, as payee for court performances on December 26 and 28 of 1594. But when had he joined the Chamberlain's Men, and for whom had he written and acted previously? These are the problems of the so-called dark years, during which Shakespeare came to London (perhaps around 1587) and got started on his career.

One prestigious acting company he could have joined was the Earl of Leicester's company, led by James Burbage, father of Shakespeare's later colleague, Richard Burbage.

Leicester was a favorite minister of Queen Elizabeth until his death in 1588, and his company of actors received from the Queen in 1574 an extraordinary patent to perform plays anywhere in England, despite all local prohibitions, provided that the plays were approved beforehand by the master of the Queen's Revels. Since an act of 1572 had outlawed all unlicensed troupes, Leicester's Men and similar companies attached to important noblemen were given a virtual monopoly over public acting. In 1576, Burbage built the Theatre for his company in the northeast suburbs of London. This group also toured the provinces: Leicester's company visited Stratford-upon-Avon in 1587. Conceivably, Shakespeare served an apprenticeship in this company, though no evidence exists to prove a connection. Leicester's company had lost some of its prominence in 1583, when several of its best men joined the newly formed Queen's Men, with Richard Tarlton as its most famous actor. The remaining members of Leicester's company disbanded in 1588 upon the death of the Earl, and many of its principal actors ultimately became part of Lord Strange's company. These probably included George Bryan, Will Kempe, and Thomas Pope, all of whom subsequently went on to become Lord Chamberlain's Men.

Lord Strange's (The Earl of Derby's) Men

The Queen's Men gained an extraordinary prominence in the 1580s, as Scott McMillin and Sally-Beth MacLean have shown in the *Queen's Men and Their Plays* (1998). This acting group was assembled under royal sponsorship, as an instrument of furthering the Protestant Reformation through its performances of plays, and did so with notable success, although it then declined rapidly in the early 1590s, chiefly because as a touring company it was unprepared to compete with the new companies that learned how to succeed in the metropolis by staging a wide variety of plays in a fixed London theater. Prominent among the acting companies to which Shakespeare could have belonged when he came to London, probably in the late 1580s, were Lord Strange's Men, the Lord Admiral's Men, the Earl of Pembroke's Men, and the Earl of Sussex's Men. Scholars have long speculated that Shakespeare may have joined the company of Ferdinando Stanley, Lord Strange (who in 1593 became the Earl of Derby). The names of George Bryan, Will Kempe, and Thomas Pope appear on a roster of Strange's company in 1593, along with those of John Heminges and Augustine Phillips. All of these men later became part of the Lord Chamberlain's company, most of them when it was first formed in 1594. Shakespeare's name does not appear on the 1593 Lord Strange's list (which was a license for touring in the provinces), but he may possibly have stayed in London to attend to his writing while the company toured. Certainly, an important number of his later associates belonged to this group.

Clowns were enormously popular on the Elizabethan stage. Of the many Elizabethan clowns whose names are known to us, Richard Tarlton is one of the most famous. (Will Kempe, in Shakespeare's company, the Lord Chamberlain's Men, is another; see pp. lxx–lxxi.) Tarlton is shown here inside an elaborate letter T, dancing a jig with his pipe and tabor. Such jigs were often used at the conclusion of a play.

During the years from 1590 to 1594, some of Lord Strange's Men appear to have joined forces on occasion with Edward Alleyn and others of the Admiral's Men. This impressive combination of talents enjoyed a successful season in 1591–1592, with six performances at court. Alleyn's father-in-law, Philip Henslowe, recorded in his *Diary* the performances of the combined players in early 1592, probably at the Rose Theatre. Their repertory included a *Harey the vj* and a *Titus & Vespacia*. The latter play is, however, no longer thought to have any connection with Shakespeare's *Titus Andronicus*; and the *Harey the vj* may or may not have been Shakespeare's, since *3 Henry VI* was (according to its 1595 title page) acted by Pembroke's Men rather than Lord Strange's Men. If Shakespeare was a member of the Strange-Admiral's combination in 1591–1592, we are at a loss to explain why Henslowe's 1592 list records so many performances of plays by Marlowe, Greene, Kyd, and others, but none that are certainly by Shakespeare. On the other hand, the *Harey the vj* may be his, and the title page of the 1594 quarto of *Titus Andronicus* does list the Earl of Derby's Men as performers of the play, in addition to the Earl of Pembroke's and the Earl of Sussex's Men. (Lord Strange's Men became officially known as the Earl of Derby's Men when Lord Strange was made an earl in September 1593.) At any rate, the company disbanded when the Earl died in April 1594, leaving them without a patron. The connection with the Admiral's Men was discontinued, with Alleyn returning to the Admiral's Men and the rest of the group forming a new company under the patronage of Henry Carey, first Lord Hunsdon, the Lord Chamberlain.

The Earl of Pembroke's Men

The other company to which Shakespeare is most likely to have belonged prior to 1594 is the Earl of Pembroke's company. This group came to grief in 1593–1594, evidently as a result of virulent outbursts of the plague, which had kept the theaters closed during most of 1592 and 1593. Pembroke's Men were forced to tour the provinces and then to sell a number of their best plays to the booksellers. Henslowe wrote to Alleyn in September 1593 of the extreme financial plight of Pembroke's company: "As for my lord of Pembroke's [Men], which you desire to know where they be, they are all at home and has been this five or six weeks, for they cannot save their charges [expenses] with travel, as I hear, and were fain to pawn their parell [apparel] for their charge." Soon thereafter this company disbanded.

Pembroke's Men were associated with a significant number of Shakespeare's early plays. Among the playbooks they evidently sold in 1593–1594 were *The Taming of a Shrew* and *The True Tragedy of Richard Duke of York*. The first of these was published in 1594 with the assertion that it had been "sundry times acted by the Right Honorable the Earle of Pembroke his Servants." Although the text of this quarto is not Shakespeare's play as we know it but, instead, an anonymous version, most scholars now feel certain that it was an imitation of Shakespeare's play and that the work performed by Pembroke's Men was, in fact, Shakespeare's. The same conclusion pertains to a performance in 1594 of "*the Tamynge of a Shrowe*" at Newington Butts, a playhouse south of London Bridge. Henslowe's *Diary* informs us that the actors on this occasion were either the Lord Chamberlain's or the Lord Admiral's Men. The probability, then, is that Shakespeare's *The Taming of the Shrew* passed from Pembroke's Men to the Chamberlain's Men when Pembroke's company collapsed in 1593–1594.

The True Tragedy of Richard Duke of York, published in 1595, was a seemingly unauthorized quarto of Shakespeare's *3 Henry VI*. Its title page declared that it had been "sundry times acted by the Right Honorable the Earl of Pembroke his Servants." Probably they acted *2 Henry VI* as well, to which part three was a sequel. In addition, the 1594 quarto of *Titus Andronicus* mentions on its title page the Earl of Pembroke's Servants, although the Earl of Derby's and the Earl of Sussex's Men are named there as well. Thus, Pembroke's Men performed as many as four of Shakespeare's early plays—more than we can assign to any other known company. Nevertheless, their claim to Shakespeare remains uncertain. We simply do not know who acted several of Shakespeare's earliest plays, such as *The Comedy of Errors*, *Love's Labor's Lost*, and *The Two Gentlemen of Verona*. Lord Strange's (Derby's) men, as we have seen, did act something called *Harey the vj* and are named on the 1594 title page of *Titus Andronicus*. Sussex's Men may conceivably have owned for a time some early Shakespearean plays that later went to the Lord Chamberlain's Men, such as *Titus Andronicus*. The Queen's Men, although associated with no known Shakespeare play, other than the old *King Lear* (acted jointly with Sussex's Men in 1593), were a leading company during the years in question. All we can say for sure is that the difficulties of 1592–1593 with the plague and the death of the Earl of Derby in 1594 led to a major reshuffling of the London acting companies. From this reshuffling emerged in 1594 the Lord Chamberlain's company, with Shakespeare and Richard Burbage (whose earlier history is also difficult to trace) as two of its earliest and most prominent members.

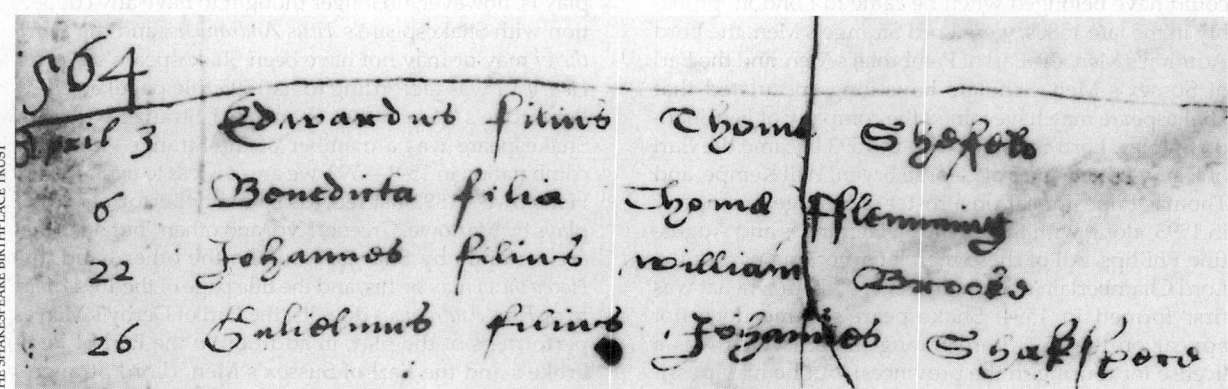

The earliest written reference to William Shakespeare is this record of his christening in the register of Holy Trinity Church at Stratford, April 26, 1564. The entry reads, "Gulielmus filius Johannes Shakspere."

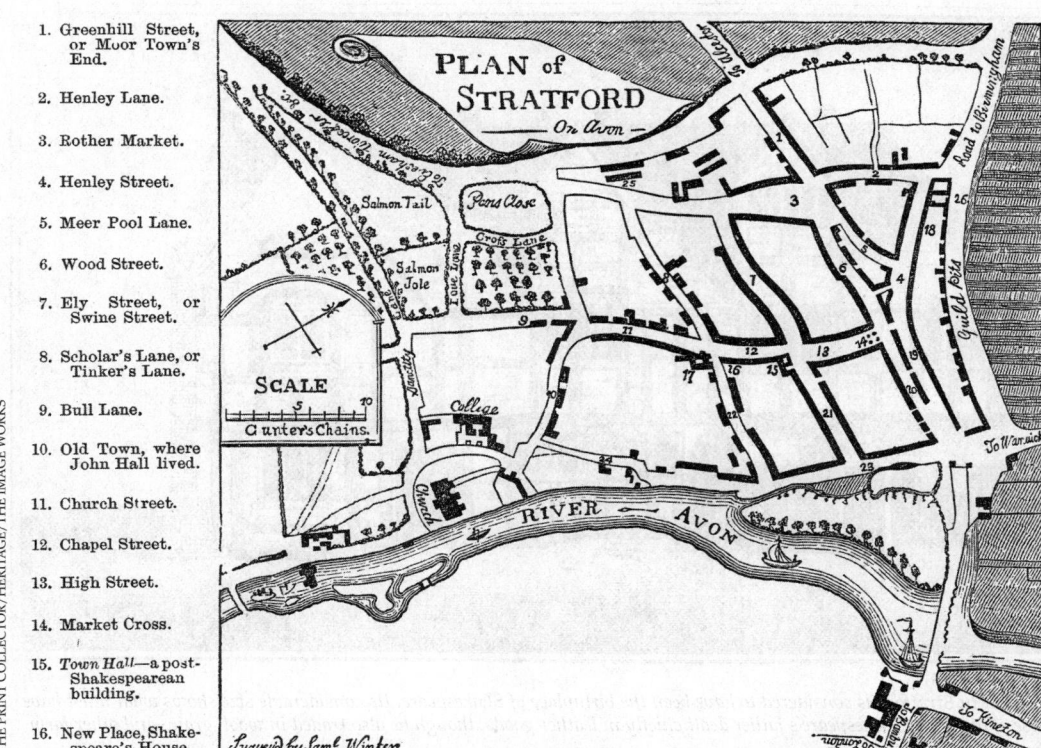

1. Greenhill Street, or Moor Town's End.

2. Henley Lane.

3. Rother Market.

4. Henley Street.

5. Meer Pool Lane.

6. Wood Street.

7. Ely Street, or Swine Street.

8. Scholar's Lane, or Tinker's Lane.

9. Bull Lane.

10. Old Town, where John Hall lived.

11. Church Street.

12. Chapel Street.

13. High Street.

14. Market Cross.

15. *Town Hall*—a post-Shakespearean building.

16. New Place, Shakespeare's House.

17. Guild Chapel, Grammar School and Guild Hall.

18. Shakespeare's birth-place.

19. Back Bridge Street.

20. Bridge, or Fore Bridge Street.

21. Sheep Street.

22. Chapel Lane.

23. Buildings known as Waterside.

24. Southam's Lane.

25. *Dissenters' Meeting House* (post-Shakespearean.)

26. *White Lion* (post-Shakespearean).

[The Mill and Mill Bridge are indicated on the river at the left-hand corner of the map. Bridge Town lies in the right-hand corner. The Great Western Railway's modern station at Stratford is built on ground to the right of the road "to Alcester."]

The town of Stratford-upon-Avon as Shakespeare knew it. The house in which he is considered to have been born is on Henley Street (number 2); the larger house he purchased in 1597, New Place, is on Chapel Street (number 16).

SHAKESPEARE'S LIFE AND WORK

THE EARLY YEARS, 1564–C. 1594

Stratford-upon-Avon

About Shakespeare's place of birth, Stratford-upon-Avon, there is no doubt. He spent his childhood there and returned periodically throughout his life. During most or all of his long professional career in London, his wife and children lived in Stratford. He acquired property and took some interest in local affairs. He retired to Stratford and chose to be buried there. Its Warwickshire surroundings lived in his poetic imagination.

The Stratford of Shakespeare's day was a "handsome small market town" (as described by William Camden) of perhaps 1,500 inhabitants, with fairly broad streets and half-timbered houses roofed with thatch. It could boast of a long history and an attractive setting on the river Avon. A bridge of fourteen arches, built in 1496 by Sir Hugh Clopton, Lord Mayor of London, spanned the river. Beside the Avon stood Trinity Church, built on the site of a Saxon monastery. The chapel of the Guild of the Holy

Trinity, dating from the thirteenth century, and an old King Edward VI grammar school were buildings of note. Stratford had maintained a grammar school at least since 1424 and probably long before that. It was a town without the domination of clergy, aristocracy, or great wealth. It lay in a rich agricultural region, in the county of Warwickshire. To the north of Stratford lay the Forest of Arden.

Shakespeare's Family

The family that bore the name of Shakespeare was well distributed throughout England, but was especially numerous in Warwickshire. A name "Saquespee," in various spellings, is found in Normandy at an early date. It means, according to J. Q. Adams, "to draw out the sword quickly." That name, in the form "Sakspee," with many variants, is found in England; also the name "Saksper," varying gradually to the form "Shakespeare." It may have been wrought into that form by the obvious military meaning of "one who shakes the spear."

Our first substantial records of the family begin with Richard Shakespeare, who was, in all probability, Shakespeare's grandfather, a farmer living in the village of

This house on Henley Street in Stratford is considered to have been the birthplace of Shakespeare. Its considerable size shows what must have been an important house of business. Shakespeare's father dealt chiefly in leather goods, though he also traded in wool, grain, and other farm produce.

Snitterfield four miles from Stratford. He was a tenant on the property of Robert Arden of Wilmcote, a wealthy man with the social status of gentleman. Richard Shakespeare died about 1561, possessed of an estate valued at the very respectable sum of thirty-eight pounds and seventeen shillings.

His son John made a great step forward in the world by his marriage with Mary Arden, daughter of his father's landlord. John Shakespeare had some property of his own and through his wife acquired a good deal more. He moved from Snitterfield to Stratford at some date before 1552. He rose to great local importance in Stratford and bought several houses, among which was the one on Henley Street traditionally identified as Shakespeare's birthplace. William Shakespeare was born in 1564 and was baptized on April 26. The exact date of his birth is not known, but traditionally we celebrate it on April 23, the feast day of St. George, England's patron saint. (The date is at least plausible in view of the practice of baptizing infants shortly after birth.) The house in which Shakespeare was probably born, though almost entirely rebuilt and changed in various and unknown ways during the years that have intervened since Shakespeare's birth, still stands. It is of considerable size, having four rooms on the ground floor, and must, therefore, have been an important business house in the Stratford of those days. John Shakespeare's occupation seems to

have been that of a tanner and glover; that is, he cured skins, made gloves and some other leather goods, and sold them in his shop. He was also a dealer in wool, grain, malt, and other farm produce.

The long story, beginning in 1552, of John Shakespeare's success and misfortunes in Stratford is attested to by many borough records. He held various city offices. He was ale taster (inspector of bread and malt), burgess (petty constable), affeeror (assessor of fines), city chamberlain (treasurer), alderman, and high bailiff of the town—the highest municipal office in Stratford. At some time around 1576, he applied to the Herald's office for the right to bear arms and style himself a gentleman. This petition was later to be renewed and successfully carried through to completion by his famous son. In 1577 or 1578, however, when William was as yet only thirteen or fourteen years old, John Shakespeare's fortunes began a sudden and mysterious decline. He absented himself from council meetings. He had to mortgage his wife's property and showed other signs of being in financial difficulty. He became involved in serious litigation and was assessed heavy fines. Although he kept his position on the corporation council until 1586 or 1587, he was finally replaced as alderman because of his failure to attend. Conceivably, John Shakespeare's sudden difficulties were the result of persecution for his Catholic faith, since John's wife's family had remained loyal to Catholicism, and the old faith

The interior of the Stratford grammar school: a late and not very reliable tradition claims that Shakespeare's desk was third from the front on the left-hand side.

was being attacked with new vigor in the Warwickshire region in 1577 and afterward. This hypothesis is unsubstantial, however, especially in view of the fact that some Catholics and Puritans seem to have held posts of trust and to have remained prosperous in Stratford during this period. In the last analysis, we have little evidence as to John Shakespeare's religious faith or as to the reasons for his sudden reversal of fortune.

The family of Shakespeare's mother could trace its ancestry back to the time of William the Conqueror, and Shakespeare's father, in spite of his troubles, was a citizen of importance. John Shakespeare made his mark, instead of writing his name, but so did other men of the time who we know could read and write. His offices, particularly that of chamberlain, and the various public functions he discharged indicate that he must have had some education.

Shakespeare in School

Nicholas Rowe, who published in 1709 the first extensive biographical account of Shakespeare, reports the tradition that Shakespeare studied "for some time at a Free-School." Although the list of students who actually attended the King's New School at Stratford-upon-Avon in the late sixteenth century has not survived, we cannot doubt that Rowe is reporting accurately. Shakespeare's father, as a leading citizen of Stratford, would scarcely have spurned the benefits of one of Stratford's most prized institutions. The town had had a free school since the thirteenth century, at first under the auspices of the Church. During the reign of King Edward VI (1547–1553), the Church lands were expropriated by the Crown, and the town of Stratford was granted a corporate charter. At this time, the school was reorganized as the King's New School, named in honor of the reigning monarch. It prospered. Its teachers, or "masters," regularly held degrees from Oxford during Shakespeare's childhood and received salaries that were superior to those of most comparable schools.

Much has been learned about the curriculum of such a school. A child would first learn the rudiments of reading and writing English by spending two or three years in a "petty" or elementary school. The child learned to

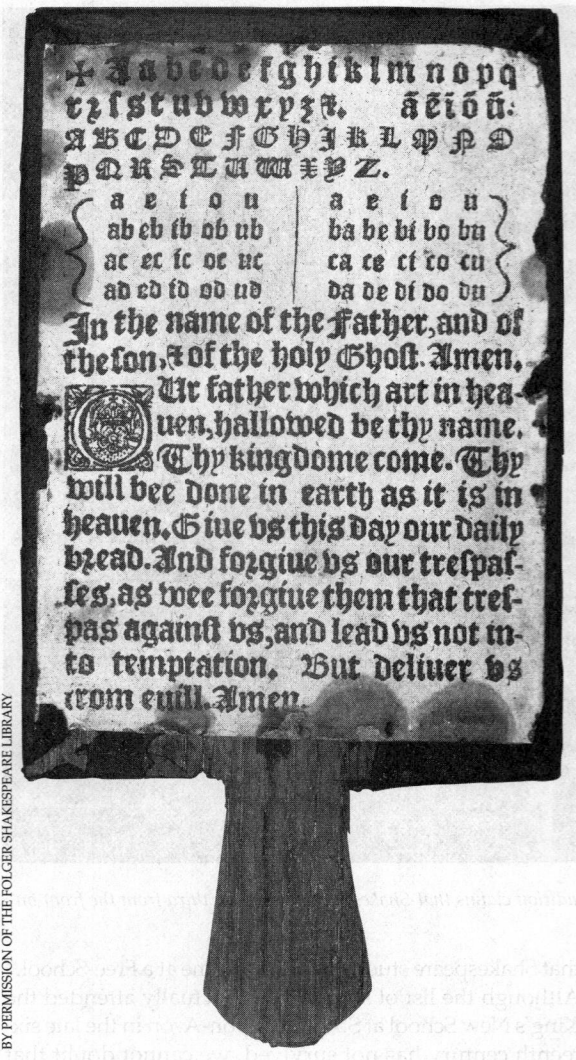

The hornbook pictured here—showing the alphabet and the Lord's Prayer—was part of a child's education in Shakespeare's time.

read from a "hornbook," a single sheet of paper mounted on a board and protected by a thin transparent layer of horn, on which was usually printed the alphabet in small and capital letters and the Lord's Prayer. The child would also practice an ABC book with catechism. When the child had demonstrated the ability to read satisfactorily, the child was admitted, at about the age of seven, to the grammar school proper. Here the day was a rigorous one, usually extending from 6 A.M. in the summer or 7 A.M. in the winter until 5 P.M. Intervals for food or brief recreation came at midmorning, noon, and midafternoon. Holidays occurred at Christmas, Easter, and Whitsuntide (usually late May and June), comprising perhaps forty days in all through the year. Discipline was strict, and physical punishment was common.

Latin formed the basis of the grammar school curriculum. The scholars studied grammar, read ancient writers, recited, and learned to write in Latin. A standard text was the *Grammatica Latina* by William Lilly or Lyly, grandfather of the later Elizabethan dramatist John Lyly. The scholars also became familiar with the *Disticha de Moribus* (moral proverbs) attributed to Cato, *Aesop's Fables,* the *Eclogues* of Baptista Spagnuoli Mantuanus or Mantuan (alluded to in *Love's Labor's Lost*), the *Eclogues* and *Aeneid* of Virgil, the comedies of Plautus or Terence (sometimes performed in Latin by the children), Ovid's *Metamorphoses* and other of his works, and possibly some Horace and Seneca.

Shakespeare plentifully reveals in his dramatic writings an awareness of many of these authors, especially Plautus (in *The Comedy of Errors*), Ovid (in *A Midsummer Night's Dream* and elsewhere), and Seneca (in *Titus Andronicus*). Although he often consulted translations of these authors, he seems to have known the originals as well. He had, in Ben Jonson's learned estimation, "small Latin and less Greek"; the tone is condescending, but the statement does concede that Shakespeare had some of both. He would have acquired some Greek in the last years of his grammar schooling. By twentieth-century standards, Shakespeare had a fairly comprehensive amount of training in the ancient classics, certainly enough to account for the general, if unscholarly, references we find in the plays.

Shakespeare's Marriage

When Shakespeare was eighteen years old, he married Anne Hathaway, a woman eight years his senior. (The inscription on her grave states that she was sixty-seven when she died in August 1623.) The bishop's register of Worcester, the central city of the diocese, shows for November 27, 1582, the issue of a bishop's license for the marriage of William Shakespeare and Anne "Whately"; the bond of sureties issued next day refers to her as "Hathaway." She has been identified with all reasonable probability as Agnes (or Anne) Hathaway, daughter of the then recently deceased Richard Hathaway of the hamlet of Shottery, a short distance from Stratford.

The obtaining of a license was not normally required for a marriage. William Shakespeare and Anne Hathaway seem to have applied for a license on this occasion because they wished to be married after only one reading of the banns rather than the usual three. (The reading of the banns, or announcement in church of a forthcoming marriage, usually on three successive Sundays, enabled any party to object to the marriage if he or she knew of any legal impediment.) Since the reading of all banns was suspended for long periods during Advent (before Christmas) and Lent (before Easter), a couple intending to marry shortly before Christmas might have had to wait until April before the banns could be read thrice. Accordingly, the bishop not uncommonly granted a license permitting

A schoolroom in Tudor England.

couples to marry during the winter season with only one reading of the banns. To obtain such a license, two friends of the bride's family had to sign a bond obligating themselves to pay the bishop up to forty pounds, should any impediment to the marriage result in a legal action against the bishop for having issued the license.

The actual record of the marriage in a parish register has not survived, but presumably the couple were married shortly after obtaining the license. They may have been married in Temple Grafton, where Anne had relatives. The couple took up residence in Stratford. Anne was already pregnant at the time of the marriage, for she

The substantial farmhouse owned by the Hathaways of Shottery, originally known as "Hewland" but now almost universally famous as Anne Hathaway's Cottage.

gave birth to a daughter, Susanna, on May 26, 1583. The birth of a child six months after the wedding may explain the need for haste the previous November. These circumstances, and Anne's considerable seniority in age to William, have given rise to much speculation about matters that can never be satisfactorily resolved. We do know that a formal betrothal in the presence of witnesses could legally validate a binding relationship, enabling a couple to consummate their love without social stigma. We know also that Shakespeare dramatized the issue of premarital contract and pregnancy in *Measure for Measure*. Whether Shakespeare entered into such a formal relationship with Anne is, however, undiscoverable.

On February 2, 1585, Shakespeare's only other children, the twins Hamnet and Judith, were baptized in Stratford Church. The twins seem to have been named after Shakespeare's friends and neighbors, Hamnet Sadler, a baker, and his wife, Judith.

The Seven "Dark" Years

From 1585, the year in which his twins were baptized, until 1592, when he was first referred to as an actor and dramatist of growing importance in London, Shakespeare's activities are wholly unknown. Presumably, at some time during this period he made his way to London and entered its theatrical world, but otherwise we can only record traditions and guesses as to what he did between the ages of 21 and 28.

One of the oldest and most intriguing suggestions comes from John Aubrey, who, in collecting information in the late seventeenth century about actors and dramatists for his "Minutes of Lives," sought the help of one William Beeston. John Dryden believed Beeston to be "the chronicle of the stage," and Aubrey seems also to have had a high opinion of Beeston's theatrical knowledge. In his manuscript, Aubrey made a note to himself: "W. Shakespeare—quaere [i.e., inquire of] Mr. Beeston, who knows most of him." Aubrey then cites Beeston as his authority for this tradition about Shakespeare:

Though, as Ben Jonson says of him, that he had but little Latin and less Greek, he understood Latin pretty well, for he had been in his younger years a schoolmaster in the country.

Beeston had been a theatrical manager all his life. He was the son of the actor Christopher Beeston, who had been a member of Shakespeare's company, probably from 1596 until 1602, and who therefore had occasion to know Shakespeare well.

Shakespeare's own grammar school education would not have qualified him to be the master of a school, but he could have served as "usher" or assistant to the master. The idea that Shakespeare may have taught in this way is not unattractive. Although, as we have seen, he had some acquaintance with Plautus, Ovid, and other classical writers through his own grammar school reading, a stint as schoolmaster would have made these authors more familiar and readily accessible to him when he began writing his plays and nondramatic poems. His earliest works—*The Comedy of Errors, Love's Labor's Lost, Titus Andronicus, Venus and Adonis, The Rape of Lucrece*—show most steadily and directly the effect of his classical reading. Schoolteaching experience might have encouraged his ambitions to be a writer, like Marlowe or Greene, who went to London not to be actors but to try their hands at poetry and playwriting. All in all, however, it seems more probable that Shakespeare became a young actor rather than a schoolteacher.

Another tradition about the years from 1585 to 1592 asserts that Shakespeare served part of an apprenticeship in Stratford. This suggestion comes to us from one John Dowdall, who, traveling through Warwickshire in 1693, heard the story from an old parish clerk who was showing him around the town of Stratford. According to this parish clerk, Shakespeare had been bound as apprentice to a butcher but ran away from his master to London, where he was received into a playhouse as "servitor." John Aubrey records a similar tradition: "When he [Shakespeare] was a boy he exercised his father's trade." Aubrey believed this trade to have been that of a butcher. Moreover, says Aubrey, "When he killed a calf, he would do it in a high style, and make a speech." No other evidence confirms, however, that Shakespeare was a runaway apprentice. The allusion to "killing a calf" may, instead, refer to an ancient rural amusement in which the slaughter of a calf was staged behind a curtain for the entertainment of visitors at county fairs. Conceivably, Shakespeare's participation in such a game during his youth may have given rise to the tradition that he had been a butcher's apprentice.

Another legend, that of Shakespeare's deer stealing, has enjoyed wide currency. We are indebted for this story to the Reverend Richard Davies, who, some time between 1688 and 1709, jotted down some gossipy interpolations in the manuscripts of the Reverend William Fulman. (Fulman himself was an antiquarian who had collected a number of notes about Shakespeare and Stratford.) According to Davies, Shakespeare was "much given to all unluckiness in stealing venison and rabbits, particularly from Sir ——— Lucy, who had him oft whipped and sometimes imprisoned and at last made him fly his native country, to his great advancement." This tradition has led to speculation by Nicholas Rowe that Justice Shallow of *2 Henry IV* and *The Merry Wives of Windsor* is a satirical portrait of Sir Thomas Lucy of Charlecote Hall and that Shakespeare even composed an irreverent ballad about Lucy that added to the urgency of Shakespeare's departure for London. In fact, however, there is no compelling reason to believe that Shallow is based on Lucy, on Justice William Gardiner of Surrey (as Leslie Hotson insists), or on any live Elizabethan. We don't know that Shakespeare ever drew contemporary portraits in his plays, as is sometimes alleged; is Polonius in *Hamlet* Lord Burghley, for example, or is he Shakespeare's original portrait of a minister of state who is also a busybody? Nor do we know if the deer-slaying incident took place at all. It makes interesting fiction but unreliable biography.

Shakespeare's Arrival in London

Because of the total absence of reliable information concerning the seven years from 1585 to 1592, we do not know how Shakespeare got his start in the theatrical world. He may have joined one of the touring companies that came to Stratford and then accompanied the players to London. Edmund Malone offered the unsupported statement (in 1780) that Shakespeare's "first office in the theater was that of prompter's attendant." Presumably, a young man from the country would have had to begin at the bottom. Shakespeare's later work certainly reveals an intimate and practical acquaintance with technical matters of stagecraft. In any case, his rise to eminence as an actor and a writer seems to have been rapid. He was fortunate also in having at least one prosperous acquaintance in London, Richard Field, formerly of Stratford and the son of an associate of Shakespeare's father. Field was a printer, and in 1593 and 1594 he published two handsome editions of Shakespeare's first serious poems, *Venus and Adonis* and *The Rape of Lucrece.*

"The Only Shake-scene in a Country"

The first allusion to Shakespeare after his Stratford days is a vitriolic attack on him. It occurs in *Greene's Groatsworth of Wit Bought with a Million of Repentance,* written by Robert Greene during the last months of his wretched existence (he died in poverty in September 1592). A famous passage in this work lashes out at the actors of the public theaters for having deserted Greene and for bestowing their favor instead on a certain upstart dramatist. The passage warns three fellow dramatists and University Wits, Christopher Marlowe, Thomas Nashe, and George Peele, to abandon the writing of plays before they fall prey to a similar ingratitude. The diatribe runs as follows:

> . . . Base minded men all three of you, if by my misery you be not warned. For unto none of you (like me) sought those burs to cleave—those puppets, I mean, that spake from our mouths, those antics garnished in our colors. Is it not strange that I, to whom they all have been beholding, is it not like that you, to whom they all have been beholding, shall (were ye in that case as I am now) be both at once of them forsaken? Yes, trust them not. For there is an upstart crow, beautified with our feathers, that with his "Tiger's heart wrapped in a player's hide" supposes he is as well able to bombast out a blank verse as the best of you, and, being an absolute *Johannes Factotum,* is in his own conceit the only Shake-scene in a country.

The "burs" here referred to are those who have forsaken Greene in his poverty for the rival playwright "Shakescene"—an obvious hit at Shakespeare. The sneer at a *"Johannes Factotum"* suggests another dig at Shakespeare for being a jack-of-all-trades—actor, playwright, poet, and theatrical handyman in the directing and producing of plays. The most unmistakable reference to Shakespeare, however, is to be found in the burlesque line, "Tiger's heart wrapped in a player's hide," modeled after "Oh, tiger's heart wrapped in a woman's hide!" from 3 *Henry VI* (1.4.137). Shakespeare's success as a dramatist had led to an envious outburst from an older, disappointed rival. (Did Shakespeare possibly have this attack in mind some years later when he has Polonius object, in *Hamlet,* 2.2.111–12, "'beautified' is a vile phrase"?)

Soon after Greene's death, Henry Chettle, who had seen the manuscript through the press (and who today some believe to have written the attack himself), issued an apology in his *Kind-Heart's Dream* that may refer to Shakespeare. The apology begins with a disclaimer of all personal responsibility for the incident and with Chettle's insistence that he has neither known nor wishes to know Marlowe (whom Greene's pamphlet had accused of atheism). Toward another unidentified playwright, on the other hand, Chettle expresses genuine concern and regret that Chettle had not done more to soften the acerbity of Greene's vitriol:

> The other, whom at that time I did not so much spare as since I wish I had, for that, as I have moderated the heat of living writers and might have used my own discretion (especially in such a case, the author being dead), that I did not I am as sorry as if the original fault had been my fault; because myself have seen his demeanor no less civil than he excellent in the quality he professes. Besides, divers of worship have reported his uprightness of dealing, which argues his honesty and his facetious grace in writing that approves his art.

If the unnamed person here is to be understood as Shakespeare, it represents him in a most attractive light. Chettle freely admits to having been impressed by this person's civility. He praises the dramatist as "excellent in the quality he professes," that is, excellent as an actor. Chettle notes with approval that the man he is describing enjoys the favor of certain persons of importance, some of whom have borne witness to his uprightness in dealing. *Greene's Groatsworth of Wit,* then, with its rancorous attack on Shakespeare, has paradoxically led to the plausible inference (though not certain in its identification) that in 1592 Shakespeare was regarded as a man of pleasant demeanor, honest reputation, and acknowledged skill as an actor and writer.

Dramatic Apprenticeship

By the end of the year 1594, when after the long plague the theatrical companies were again permitted to act before London audiences, we find Shakespeare as a member of the Lord Chamberlain's company. Probably he had already written *The Comedy of Errors, Love's Labor's Lost, The Two Gentlemen of Verona,* the *Henry VI* plays, and *Titus Andronicus.* (*A Love's Labor's Won,* mentioned by Francis Meres in 1598, is possibly either a lost play or an alternate title for one of the extant comedies.) He may also have completed *The Taming of the Shrew, A Midsummer Night's Dream, Richard III, King John,* and *Romeo and Juliet.* Although some scholars still question his authorship in part or all of *Titus* and the *Henry VI* plays, no one questions that they are from the period around 1590.

Shakespeare's early development is hard to follow because of difficulties in exact dating of the early plays and because some of the texts (such as *Love's Labor's Lost*) may have been later revised. As a learner making rapid progress in the skill of his art, Shakespeare was also subjected to outside influences that can only partly be determined. Among these influences, we may be sure, were the plays of his contemporary dramatists. If we could define these influences and form an idea of the kinds of plays acceptable on the stage during Shakespeare's early period, we could better understand the milieu in which he began his work.

Fortunately, we know a fair amount concerning the dramatic repertory in London during Shakespeare's early years. Henslowe's *Diary,* for example, records the daily performances of plays by the Lord Strange's Men, in conjunction with the Admiral's Men, from February 19, 1592, to June 22, 1592. Many of their plays unfortunately are lost, but enough of them are preserved to indicate the sorts of drama then in vogue. The Strange-Admiral's repertory included Christopher Marlowe's *The Jew of Malta,* Robert Greene's *Orlando Furioso* and *Friar Bacon and Friar Bungay,* Robert Greene and Thomas Lodge's *A Looking Glass for London and England,* Thomas Kyd's *The Spanish Tragedy,* the anonymous *A Knack to Know a Knave,* and possibly George Peele's *The Battle of Alcazar* and Shakespeare's *1 Henry VI.* We find, in other words, a tragedy with a villain as hero, a romantic comedy masquerading as a heroic play, a love comedy featuring a lot of magic, a biblical moral, England's first great revenge tragedy, a popular satiric comedy aimed at dissolute courtiers and usurers, a history play about Portugal's African empire, and an English history play. The titles of other works now lost suggest a similar amalgam of widely differing genres.

Comparatively few plays may have been written during the period when plays were forbidden because of the long plague of 1592–1594. When the Lord Chamberlain's Men and the Lord Admiral's Men acted under Henslowe's management at the suburban theater of Newington Butts from June 3–13, 1594, their repertories seem to have consisted largely of old plays. In this brief period, they are thought to have acted *Titus Andronicus,*

Hamlet (the pre-Shakespearean version), *The Taming of a Shrew* (quite possibly Shakespeare's version), *The Jew of Malta,* a lost play called *Hester and Ahasuerus,* and others.

The Lord Admiral's Men probably moved soon afterwards in 1594 to the Rose on the Bankside, across the River Thames from the city of London, where they continued to play under Henslowe's management until 1603. During the years 1594–1597, Henslowe kept in his *Diary* a careful record of their plays and of the sums of money taken in. This circumstance enables us to know a great deal more about the repertory of Shakespeare's rival company than we can ever know about his own. When the Lord Admiral's Men began again in 1594, they had five of Marlowe's plays. They seem also to have had Peele's *Edward I,* Kyd's *The Spanish Tragedy,* and a Henry V play. They may also have had plays by both Greene and Peele (Henslowe's chaotic spelling makes it hard to determine), although some of the principal dramas of these two authors had probably ceased to be acted.

We do not know as much about the repertory of the Lord Chamberlain's company as we do about that of the Lord Admiral's Men. We know enough, however, to be sure that in 1594 both companies were acting the same sorts of plays that had been on the boards in 1592. We have, therefore, grounds for assuming that, in spite of the loss of many plays (some of which may have been important), the chief contemporary influences upon Shakespeare during his early period were those of Marlowe, Greene, Peele, and Kyd. As an actor possibly in Lord Strange's company or the Earl of Pembroke's company, he would have been familiar with their plays.

Shakespeare learned also from Lyly, though perhaps more from reading Lyly's plays than from actually seeing or performing in them. The boy actors for whom Lyly wrote were forced by the authorities to suspend acting in about 1591 because of their tendency toward controversial satire, and a number of Lyly's plays were printed at that time. As a theatrical figure, therefore, Lyly belonged really to the previous decade.

The Early Plays

Although Shakespeare's genius manifests itself in his early work, his indebtedness to contemporary dramatists and to classical writers is also more plainly evident than in his later writings. His first tragedy, *Titus Andronicus* (c. 1589–1592), is more laden with quotations and classical references than any other tragedy he wrote. Its genre owes much to the revenge play that had been made so popular by Thomas Kyd. Like Kyd, Shakespeare turns to Seneca but also reveals on stage a considerable amount of sensational violence in a manner that is distinctly not classical. For his first villain, Aaron the Moor, Shakespeare borrows some motifs from the morality play and its gleefully sinister tempter, the Vice. Shakespeare may also

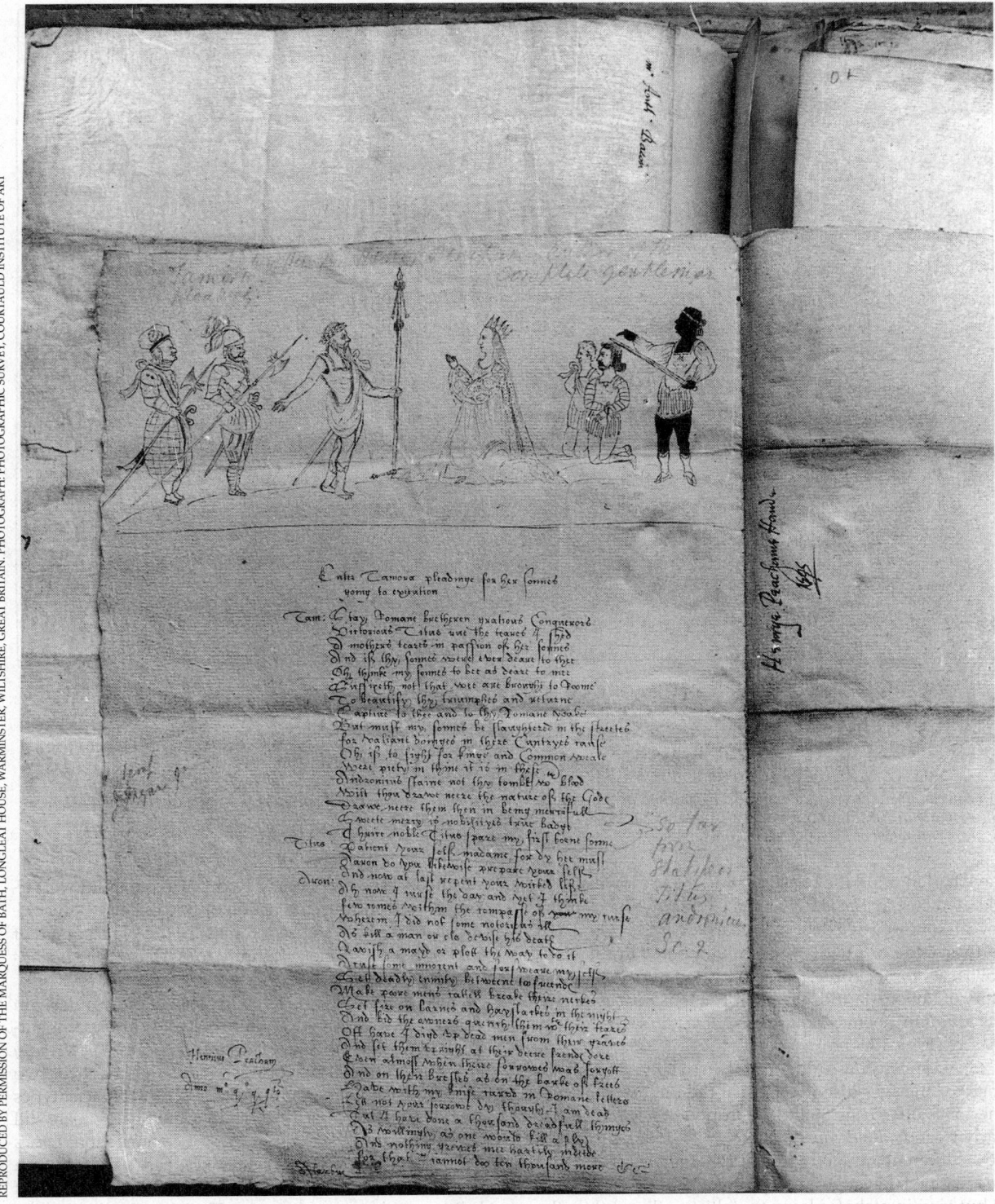

A contemporary illustration of Titus Andronicus, *the earliest of Shakespeare's tragedies. Shakespeare's early plays demonstrated that he was more than a slavish imitator of predecessors such as Kyd and Marlowe.*

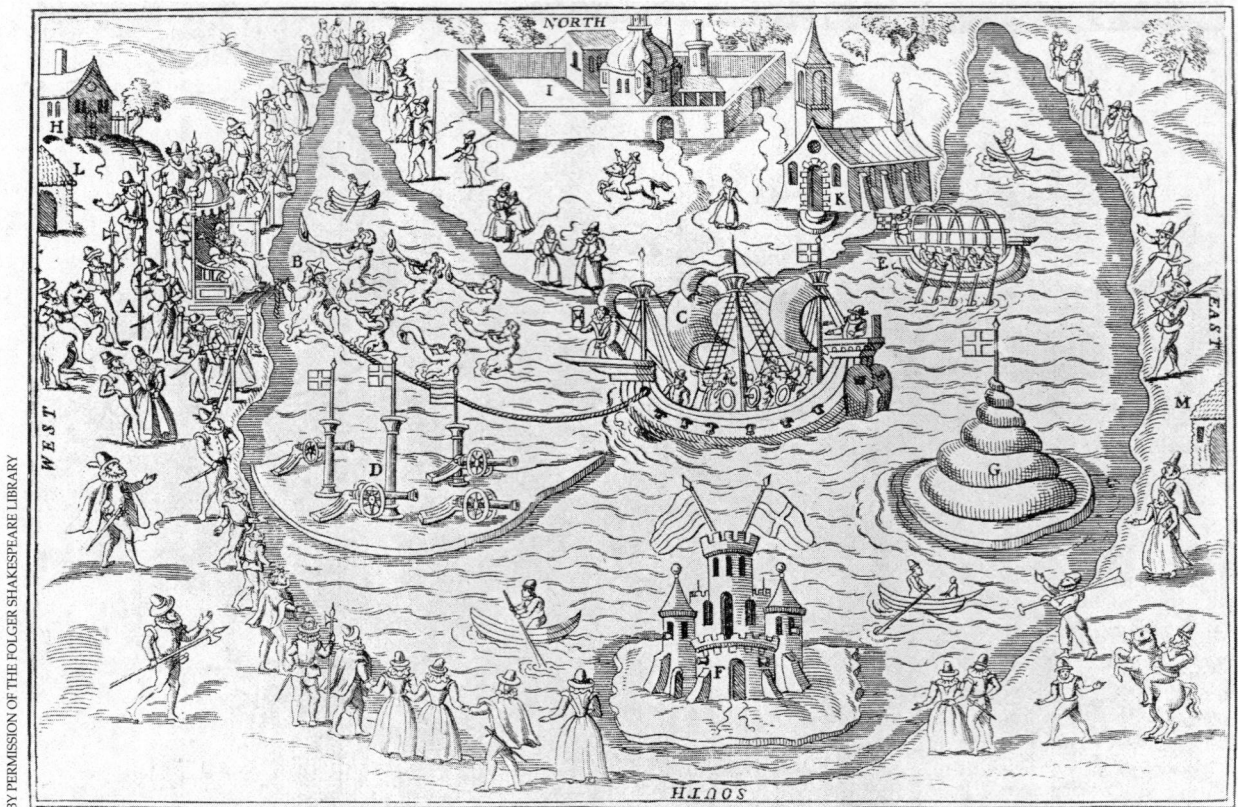

THE GREAT POND AT ELVETHAM
arranged for the Second Day's Entertainment.

A. Her Majestie's presence seate and traine. B. Nereus and his followers. C. The pinnace of Neæra and her musicke. D. The Ship-ile.
E. A boate with musicke, attending on the pinnace of Neæra. F. The Fort-mount. G. The Snaile-mount. H. The Roome of Estate.
I. Her Majestie's Court. K. Her Majestie's Wardrop. L. The place whence Silvanus and his companie issued.

An entertainment presented by the Earl of Hertford to Queen Elizabeth during her visit to Elvetham in 1591 is seemingly referred to by Shakespeare in A Midsummer Night's Dream, *2.1.157–64. The scene shows an elaborate water pageant in honor of the Queen, who appears enthroned at the left of the picture.*

have had in mind the boastful antics of Marlowe's Vice-like Barabas, in *The Jew of Malta*. Certainly, Shakespeare reveals an extensive debt in his early works to Ovid and to the vogue of Ovidian narrative poetry in the early 1590s, as, for example, in his repeated allusions to the story of Philomela and Tereus (in *Titus Andronicus*) and in his Ovidian poems, *Venus and Adonis* and *The Rape of Lucrece* (1593, 1594).

Shakespeare was still questing for a suitable mode in tragedy and was discovering that the English drama of the 1590s offered no single, clear model. His only other early tragedy, *Romeo and Juliet* (c. 1594–1596), proved to be as different a tragedy from *Titus Andronicus* as could be imagined. Revenge is still prominent in *Romeo and Juliet* but is ultimately far less compelling a theme than the brevity of love and the sacrifice the lovers make of themselves to one another. Shakespeare's source is not the

revenge drama of Seneca or Kyd, but a romantic love narrative derived from the fiction of Renaissance Italy. Elements of comedy so predominate in the play's first half that one senses a closer affinity to *A Midsummer Night's Dream* than to *The Spanish Tragedy*.

Shakespeare discovered his true bent more quickly in comedy than in tragedy. Again, however, he experimented with a wide range of models and genres. *The Comedy of Errors* (c. 1589–1594) brings together elements of two plots from the Latin drama of Plautus. The character types and situations are partly derivative, but Shakespeare still reveals an impressive skill in plot construction. *Love's Labor's Lost* (c. 1588–1597) is Shakespeare's most Lylyan early comedy, with its witty debates and its amicable, if brittle, war between the sexes. The play also features an array of humorous characters, including a clownish bumpkin, a country slut, a fantastic courtier, a pedant, a country curate, and the like, whose mannerisms and wordplay add to the rich feast of language in a play that centers its attention on proper and improper styles. *The Two Gentlemen of Verona* (c. 1590–1594) and *The Taming of the Shrew* (c. 1590–1593) are derived from Italianate romantic fiction and comedy. In both, Shakespeare skillfully combines simultaneous plots that offer contrasting views on love and friendship. (*The Taming of the Shrew* makes effective use of a "frame" plot involving a group of characters who serve as audience for the rest of the play.) *A Midsummer Night's Dream* (c. 1595), with its four brilliantly interwoven actions involving court figures, lovers, fairies, and Athenian tradesmen, shows us Shakespeare already at the height of his powers in play construction, even though the comic emphasis on love's irrationality in this play is still in keeping with Shakespeare's early style. The early comedies do not ignore conflict and danger, as we see in the threatened execution of Egeon in *The Comedy of Errors* and the failure of courtships in *Love's Labor's Lost*, but these plays do not as yet fully explore the social dilemmas of *The Merchant of Venice*, the narrowly averted catastrophe of *Much Ado About Nothing*, or the melancholy vein of *As You Like It* and *Twelfth Night*. On stage, early comedies such as *The Comedy of Errors* and *The Taming of the Shrew* are as hilariously funny as anything Shakespeare ever wrote.

Shakespeare's early history plays show a marked affinity with those of Marlowe, Peele, and Greene. Yet today Shakespeare is given more credit for pioneering in the genre of the English history play than he once was. If all the *Henry VI* plays (c. 1589–1592) are basically his, as scholars now often allow, he had more imitators in this genre than predecessors. He scored a huge early success with the heroic character of Lord Talbot in *1 Henry VI*, and by the time Richard Duke of Gloucester had emerged from the *Henry VI* plays to become King Richard III, Shakespeare's fame as a dramatist was assured. He had, of course, learned much from Marlowe's "mighty line" in *Tamburlaine* (1587–1588) and perhaps from Peele's *The Battle of Alcazar* (1588–1589). The anonymous *Famous Victories of Henry V* (1583–1588) must have preceded and influenced his work. Even so, Shakespeare had done much more than simply "beautify" himself with the "feathers" of earlier dramatists, as Greene (or Chettle) enviously charged. Even in his earliest work, Shakespeare already displayed an extraordinary ability to transcend the models from which he learned.

SHAKESPEARE IN THE THEATER, C. 1594–1601

By the year 1594, Shakespeare had already achieved a considerable reputation as a poet and dramatist. We should not be surprised that many of his contemporaries thought of his nondramatic writing as his most significant literary achievement. Throughout his lifetime, in fact, his con-

temporary fame rested, to a remarkable degree, on his nondramatic poems, *Venus and Adonis, The Rape of Lucrece*, and the *Sonnets* (which were circulated in manuscript prior to their unauthorized publication in 1609). One of the earliest tributes suggesting the importance of the poems is found in an anonymous commendatory verse prefixed to Henry Willobie's *Willobie His Avisa* (1594). It summarizes the plot and theme of *The Rape of Lucrece*:

> Though *Collatine* have dearly bought,
> To high renown, a lasting life,
> And found—that most in vain have sought—
> To have a fair and constant wife,
>   Yet Tarquin plucked his glistering grape,
>   And Shakespeare paints poor Lucrece' rape.

Richard Barnfield, in his *Poems in Divers Humors* (1598), praised the "honey-flowing vein" of Shakespeare's *Venus and Adonis* and *The Rape of Lucrece*.

Yet Shakespeare's plays were also highly regarded by his contemporaries, even if those plays were accorded a literary status below that given to the narrative and lyrical poems. Francis Meres insisted, in 1598, that Shakespeare deserved to be compared not only with Ovid for his verse, but also with Plautus and Seneca for his comedies and tragedies:

> As the soul of Euphorbus was thought to live in Pythagoras, so the sweet, witty soul of Ovid lives in mellifluous and honey-tongued Shakespeare: witness his *Venus and Adonis*, his *Lucrece*, his sugared sonnets among his private friends, etc.
>
> As Plautus and Seneca are accounted the best for comedy and tragedy among the Latins, so Shakespeare among the English is the most excellent in both kinds for the stage: for comedy, witness his *Gentlemen of Verona*, his *Errors*, his *Love's Labor's Lost*, his *Love's Labor's Won*, his *Midsummer Night's Dream*, and his *Merchant of Venice*; for tragedy, his *Richard the II*, *Richard the III*, *Henry the IV*, *King John*, *Titus Andronicus*, and his *Romeo and Juliet*.

Comedy and tragedy were, after all, literary forms sanctioned by classical precept. By calling some of Shakespeare's English history plays "tragedies," Meres endowed them with the respectability of an ancient literary tradition, recognizing, too, that many of Shakespeare's historical plays culminate in the death of an English king.

John Weever, too, in his epigram *Ad Gulielmum Shakespeare* in *Epigrams in the Oldest Cut and Newest Fashion* (1599), mentioned not only the ever-popular narrative poems, but also *Romeo and Juliet* and a history play about one of the Richards:

> Honey-tongued Shakespeare! When I saw thine issue,
> I swore Apollo got them and none other:
> Their rosy-tainted features clothed in tissue,
> Some heaven-born goddess said to be their mother;
> Rose-cheeked Adonis, with his amber tresses,
> Fair fire-hot Venus, charming him to love her;

Falstaff and Mistress Quickly are shown here in a composite theatrical illustration of about 1662. The engraving, used as the frontispiece to Francis Kirkman's The Wits, or Sport upon Sport, *also shows other theatrical types. Visible are candelabras and footlights for stage lighting and a curtained area used perhaps for "discoveries." Spectators are visible in the gallery above, as they are also in the De Witt drawing of the Swan Theatre on p. xlviii and in Alabaster's* Roxana *on p. xlvii.*

Chaste Lucretia virgin-like her dresses,
Proud lust-stung Tarquin seeking still to prove her;
Romeo, Richard—more whose names I know not.
Their sugared tongues and power-attractive beauty
Say they are saints, although that saints they show not,
For thousands vows to them subjective duty;
They burn in love thy children. Shakespeare het them.
Go, woo thy muse more nymphish brood beget them.

Even Gabriel Harvey, an esteemed classical scholar and friend of Edmund Spenser, considered Shakespeare's play *Hamlet* to be worthy of no less praise than the best of the Ovidian poems. Harvey's comments are to be found in a marginal note to a copy of Speght's *Chaucer*, written down some time between 1598 and 1601:

The younger sort takes much delight in Shakespeare's *Venus and Adonis*, but his *Lucrece* and his tragedy of *Hamlet, Prince of Denmark* have it in them to please the wiser sort.

Shakespeare's growing fame was even such that his dramatic characters began to enter into the intellectual life of the time. The name of Falstaff became a byword almost as soon as he made his appearance on the stage. The references were not always friendly. A play written to be performed by the rival Admiral's company in answer to *1 Henry IV*, called *Sir John Oldcastle* (1599), took Falstaff to task for being a "pampered glutton" and an "aged counsellor to youthful sin." Evidently, the authors of this attack were offended by the fact that Falstaff had been named "Oldcastle" in an early version of *1 Henry IV*,

thereby dishonoring the name of one whom many Puritans regarded as a martyr to their cause (see the Introduction to *1 Henry IV*). Generally, however, the references during this period to Falstaff and his cronies were fond. In a letter to a friend in London, for example, Sir Charles Percy fretted jocosely that his prolonged stay in the country among his rustic neighbors might cause him to "be taken for Justice Silence or Justice Shallow" (1600). In another letter, from the Countess of Southampton to her husband (written seemingly in 1599), Falstaff's name had become so familiar that it was used apparently as a privately understood substitute for the name of some real person in an item of court gossip:

All the news I can send you, that I think will make you merry, is that I read in a letter from London that Sir John Falstaff is by his Mistress Dame Pintpot made father of a godly miller's thumb, a boy that's all head and very little body; but this is a secret.

Shakespeare's immense popularity as a dramatist was bound to invite some resentment. One irreverent reaction is found in the so-called *Parnassus* trilogy (1598–1603). The three plays in this series consist of *The Pilgrimage to Parnassus* and *The Return from Parnassus*, in two parts, all of which were acted by the students of St. John's College, Cambridge.

These *Parnassus* plays take a mordantly satirical view of English life around 1600, from the point of view of university graduates attempting to find gainful employment. The graduates discover, to their vocal dismay, that they must seek the patronage of fashion-mongering courtiers,

Henry Fuseli's nineteenth-century interpretation of Falstaff shows him in the tavern in Eastcheap with Doll Tearsheet on his lap while Prince Hal and Poins, disguised as tapsters, enter from behind. Falstaff is perhaps saying, "Peace, good Doll, do not speak like a death's-head" (2 Henry IV, 2.4.233–4).

complacent justices of the peace, professional acting companies who offer them pitifully small wages, and the like. One especially foolish patron, to whom the witty Ingenioso applies for a position, is a poetaster named Gullio. This courtly fop aspires to be a fashionable poet himself, and agrees to hire Ingenioso if the latter will help him with his verse writing. In fact, however, as Ingenioso scornfully observes in a series of asides, Gullio's verses are "nothing but pure Shakespeare and shreds of poetry that he hath gathered at the theaters." Most of all, Gullio loves to plagiarize from *Venus and Adonis* and *Romeo and Juliet.* With unparalleled presumption, he actually requests Ingenioso to compose poems "in two or three divers veins, in Chaucer's, Gower's and Spenser's and Mr. Shakespeare's," which Gullio will then pass off as his own inspiration. When Ingenioso does so extempore, producing, among other things, a fine parody of *Venus and Adonis,* Gullio is as delighted as a child. Although he admires Spenser, Chaucer, and Gower, Gullio confesses that Shakespeare is his favorite; he longs to hang Shakespeare's portrait "in my study at the court" and vows he will sleep with *Venus and Adonis* under his pillow (*The Return from Parnassus*, Part I, 1009–1217). Later on (lines 1875–1880), some university graduates trying out as actors in Shakespeare's company are requested to recite a few famous

lines from the beginning of *Richard III*—lines that, in the satirical context of this play, sound both stereotyped and bombastic. Shakespeare's fame made him an easy target for university "wits" who regarded the theater of London as lowbrow. Still, the portrait throughout is more satirical of those who plagiarize and idolize Shakespeare than of the dramatist's own work. In their backhanded tribute, the *Parnassus* authors make plain that Shakespeare was a household name even at the universities.

Shakespeare's Career and Private Life

During the years from 1594 to 1601, Shakespeare seems to have prospered as an actor and writer for the Lord Chamberlain's Men. Whether he had previously belonged to Lord Strange's company or to the Earl of Pembroke's company, or possibly to some other group, is uncertain, but we know that he took part in 1594 in the general reorganization of the companies, out of which emerged the Lord Chamberlain's company. In 1595, his name appeared, for the first time, in the accounts of the Treasurer of the Royal Chamber as a member of the Chamberlain's company of players, which had presented two comedies before Queen Elizabeth at Greenwich in the Christmas season of 1594. This company usually performed at the Theatre, northeast of London, from 1594 until 1599, when they moved to the Globe playhouse south of the Thames. They seem to have been the victors in the intense economic rivalry between themselves and the Lord Admiral's company at the Rose playhouse, under Philip Henslowe's management. Fortunately for all the adult companies, the boys' private theatrical companies were shut down during most of the 1590s. Shakespeare's company enjoyed a phenomenal success, and in a short time it became the most successful theatrical organization in England.

The nucleus of the Chamberlain's company in 1594 was the family of Burbage. James Burbage, the father, was owner of the Theatre, Cuthbert Burbage was a manager, and Richard Burbage became the principal actor of the troupe. Together the Burbages owned five "shares" in the

First among the actors in Shakespeare's company was Richard Burbage (1567–1619). He played Hamlet, Othello, King Lear, and presumably other major roles including Macbeth, Antony, Coriolanus, and Prospero.

company, entitling them to half the profits. Shakespeare and four other principal actors—John Heminges, Thomas Pope, Augustine Phillips, and Will Kempe—owned one share each. Not only was Shakespeare a full sharing actor, but also he was the principal playwright of the company. He was named as a chief actor in the 1616 edition of Ben Jonson's *Every Man in His Humor,* performed by the Chamberlain's company in 1598. Later tradition reports, with questionable reliability, that Shakespeare specialized in "kingly parts" or in the roles of older men, such as Adam in *As You Like It* and the Ghost in *Hamlet.* Shakespeare was more celebrated as a playwright than as an actor, and his acting responsibilities may well have diminished as his writing reputation grew. The last occasion on which he is known to have acted was in Jonson's *Sejanus* in 1603.

His prosperity appears in the first record of his residence in London. The tax returns, or Subsidy Rolls, of a parliamentary subsidy granted to Queen Elizabeth for the year 1596 show that Shakespeare was a resident in the parish of St. Helen's, Bishopsgate, near the Theatre, and was assessed at the respectable sum of five pounds. By the next year, Shakespeare had evidently moved to Southwark, near the Bear Garden, for the returns from Bishopsgate show his taxes delinquent. He was later located and the taxes paid.

In 1596, Shakespeare suffered a serious personal loss: the death of his only son Hamnet, at the age of eleven. Hamnet was buried at Stratford in August.

Shakespeare acquired property in Stratford during these years, as well as in London. In 1597 he purchased New Place, a house of importance and one of the two largest in Stratford. Shakespeare's family entered the house as residents shortly after the purchase and contin-ued to live there until long after Shakespeare's death. The last of his family, his granddaughter, Lady Bernard, died in 1670, and New Place was sold.

Shakespeare was also interested in the purchase of land at Shottery in 1598. He was listed among the chief holders of corn and malt in Stratford that same year and sold a load of stone to the Stratford corporation in 1599.

No less suggestive of Shakespeare's rapid rise in the world is his acquisition of the right to bear arms, or, in other words, his establishment in the rank and title of gentleman. The Herald's College in London preserves two drafts of a grant of arms to Shakespeare's father, devised by one William Dethick and dated October 20, 1596. Although we may certainly believe that the application was put forward by William Shakespeare, John Shakespeare was still living, and the grant was drawn up in the father's name. The device for Shakespeare's coat of arms makes a somewhat easy use of the meaning of his name:

Gold on a bend sables, a spear of the first steeled argent. And for his crest of cognizance a falcon, his wings displayed argent, standing on a wreath of his colors, supporting a spear, gold steeled as aforesaid, set upon a helmet with mantles and tassels, as hath been accustomed and doth more plainly appear depicted on this margent.

According to one of the documents in the grant, John Shakespeare, at the height of his prosperity as a Stratford burgher, had applied twenty years before to the Herald's College for authority to bear arms. The family may not have been able to meet the expense of seeing the application through, however, until William Shakespeare had made his fortune. The grant of heraldic honors to John Shakespeare was confirmed in 1599.

This recreation of what New Place purportedly looked like during Shakespeare's ownership suggests that it must have indeed been an imposing structure. It was warmed by ten fireplaces and had surrounding grounds that included two gardens and two barns.

A lawsuit during this period gives us a rather baffling glimpse into Shakespeare's life in the theater. From a writ discovered by Leslie Hotson (*Shakespeare Versus Shallow*, 1931) in the records of the Court of the Queen's Bench, Michaelmas term 1596, we learn that a person named William Wayte sought "for fear of death" to have William Shakespeare, Francis Langley, and two unknown women bound over to keep the peace. Earlier in the same term, moreover, Francis Langley had sworn out a similar writ against this same William Wayte and his stepfather William Gardiner, a justice of the peace in Surrey. Langley was owner of the Swan playhouse on the bankside, near the later-built Globe. His quarrel with Gardiner and Wayte appears to have jeopardized all the acting companies that performed plays south of the Thames, for William Gardiner's jurisdiction included the Bankside theater district. Gardiner and Wayte vengefully tried to drive the theaters out of the area. Possibly Shakespeare's company acted occasionally at the Swan in 1596. Hotson speculates that Shakespeare retaliated by immortalizing Gardiner and Wayte as Shallow and Slender in *The Merry Wives of Windsor*. The date of 1596 is too early for that play, and we do not know that Shakespeare drew contemporary portraits in his drama, but we can wonder if lawsuits of this sort gave him no very high opinion of the law's delay and the insolence of office.

During this period Shakespeare's plays began to appear occasionally in print. His name was becoming such a drawing card that it appeared on the title pages of the second and third quartos of *Richard II* (1598), the second quarto of *Richard III* (1598), *Love's Labor's Lost* (1598), and the second quarto of *1 Henry IV* (1599).

In 1599, the printer William Jaggard sought to capitalize unscrupulously on Shakespeare's growing reputation by bringing out a slender volume of twenty or twenty-one poems called *The Passionate Pilgrim*, attributed to Shakespeare. In fact, only five of the poems were assuredly his, and none of them was newly composed for the occasion. Three came from *Love's Labor's Lost* (published in 1598) and two from Shakespeare's as yet unpublished sonnet sequence.

Contemporary Drama

Shakespeare was without doubt the leading dramatist of the period from 1594 to 1601, not only in our view, but also in that of his contemporaries. The earlier group of dramatists from whom he had learned so much—Lyly, Greene, Marlowe, Peele, Kyd, Nashe—were either dead or no longer writing plays. The group of dramatists who were to rival him in the 1600s and eventually surpass him in contemporary popularity had not yet become well known.

Ben Jonson's early career is obscure. He may have written an early version of his *A Tale of a Tub* in 1596 and *The Case Is Altered* in 1597, though both were later revised. Unquestionably, his first major play was *Every Man in His Humor* (1598), in which Shakespeare acted. This comedy did much to establish the new vogue of comedy of humors, a realistic and satirical kind of drama featuring "humors" characters whose personalities are dominated by some exaggerated trait. We are invited to laugh at the country simpleton, the jealous husband, the overly careful father, the cowardly braggart soldier, the poetaster, and the like. Shakespeare responded to the vogue of humors comedy in his *Henry IV* plays and *The Merry Wives*. Jonson followed his great success with *Every Man Out of His Humor* (1599), an even more biting vision of human folly. George Chapman also deserves important credit for the establishment of humors comedy, with his *The Blind Beggar of Alexandria* (1596) and *An Humorous Day's Mirth* (1597).

Despite the emergence of humors comedy, however, with its important anticipations of Jacobean and even Restoration comedy of manners, the prevailing comedy to be seen on the London stage between 1595 and 1601 was romantic comedy. William Haughton wrote *Englishmen for My Money* in 1598. Thomas Dekker's *Old Fortunatus*, the dramatization of a German folktale, appeared in 1599. Dekker's *The Shoemaker's Holiday* (1599), despite its seemingly realistic touches of life among the apprentices of London, is a thoroughly romanticized saga of rags to riches. A young aristocrat disguises himself as a shoemaker to woo a mayor's daughter; love conquers social rank, and the King himself sentimentally blesses the union. Thomas Heywood wrote heroical romances and comedies, perhaps including *Godfrey of Boulogne* (1594), although most of his early works have disappeared. The boys' private theaters were closed during most of the 1590s, until 1598–1599, and thus the child actors could not perform the satirical comedies at which they were so adept.

Patriotic history drama also continued to flourish on the public stage during those years when Shakespeare wrote his best history plays. Heywood wrote the two parts of *Edward IV* between 1592 and 1599. The anonymous *Edward III* appeared in 1595 or earlier, enough in the vein of Shakespeare's histories that it is sometimes attributed (albeit on uncertain and impressionistic grounds) to him. *Sir Thomas More*, by Munday, Dekker, Chettle, and perhaps Heywood, was written sometime in the later 1590s and very probably revised by Shakespeare himself. Chettle and Munday wrote a trilogy of plays about *Robert, Earl of Huntingdon*, or Robin Hood (1598–1599), on themes that remind us of Shakespeare's *As You Like It*. These plays were performed by the Admiral's Men, who also produced the two parts of *Sir John Oldcastle* (1599–1600) by Drayton, Hathway, Munday, and others, in rivalry with Shakespeare's *Henry IV* plays.

Shakespeare's Work

Shakespeare thus wrote his greatest history plays for an audience that knew the genre well. The history play had first become popular just at the start of Shakespeare's career, during the patriotic aftermath of the defeat of the Spanish Armada (1588). Shakespeare himself did much to establish the genre. He wrote first his four-play series dealing with the Lancastrian wars of the fifteenth century, and then went backwards in historical time to King John's reign and to the famous reigns of Henry IV and Henry V.

His romantic comedies were also written for audiences that knew what to expect from the genre. From the comedies of Greene, Peele, Munday, and the rest, as well as Shakespeare himself, Elizabethan audiences were thoroughly familiar with such conventions as fairy charms, improbable adventures in forests, heroines disguised as young men, shipwrecks, love overcoming differences in social rank, and the like. Yet the conventions also demanded more than mere horseplay or foolish antics. Plays of this sort customarily affirmed "wholesome" moral values and appealed to generosity and decency. They were written, like the history plays, for a socially diversified, though generally intelligent and well-to-do, audience.

Several critical terms have been used to suggest the special quality of Shakespeare's comedies during this period of the later 1590s. "Romantic comedy" implies first of all a story in which the main action is about love, but it can also imply elements of the improbable and the miraculous. (The difference between the "romantic comedies" of the later 1590s and the "romances" of Shakespeare's last years, 1606–1613, is that, in part at least, romantic comedy seeks to "make wonder familiar," whereas the romances seek to make the familiar wonderful.) "Philosophical comedy" emphasizes the moral, and sometimes Christian idealism, underlying many of these comedies of the 1590s: the quest for deep and honest understanding between men and women in *Much Ado About Nothing*, the awareness of an eternal and spiritual dimension to love in *The Merchant of Venice*, and the theme of love as a mysterious force able to regenerate a

corrupted social world from which it has been banished in *As You Like It*. "Love-game comedy" pays particular attention to the witty battle of the sexes that we find in several of these plays. "Festive comedy" urges the celebratory nature of comedy, especially in *Twelfth Night* and the *Henry IV* plays, in which Saturnalian revelry must contend against grim and disapproving forces of sobriety. "Comedy of forgiveness," although applicable to only a limited number of plays of this period (especially *Much Ado*), stresses the unexpected second chance that the world of comedy extends to even the most undeserving of heroes; Claudio is forgiven his ill treatment of Hero, although the play's villain, Don John, is not.

Shakespeare in the Theater, c. 1601–1608

When the Globe, the most famous of the London public playhouses, was built in 1599, one-half interest in the property was assigned to the Burbage family, especially to the brothers Cuthbert and Richard Burbage. The other half was divided among five actor-sharers: Shakespeare, Will Kempe, Thomas Pope, Augustine Phillips, and John Heminges. Kempe left the company, however, in 1599 and subsequently became a member of the Earl of Worcester's Men. His place as leading comic actor was taken by Robert Armin, an experienced man of the theater and occasional author, whose comic specialty was the role of the wise fool. We can observe in Shakespeare's plays the effects of Kempe's departure and of Armin's arrival. Kempe had apparently specialized in clownish and rustic parts, such as those of Dogberry in *Much Ado*, Lancelot Gobbo in *The Merchant of Venice*, and Bottom in *A Midsummer Night's Dream*. (We know that he played Dogberry because his name appears in the early quarto, derived from the play manuscript; similar evidence links his name to the role of Peter in *Romeo and Juliet*.) For Armin, on the other hand,

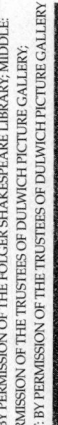

Among the members of Shakespeare's acting company were John Lowin, William Sly, and Nathaniel Field.

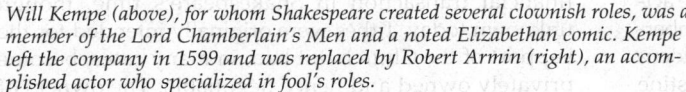

Will Kempe (above), for whom Shakespeare created several clownish roles, was a member of the Lord Chamberlain's Men and a noted Elizabethan comic. Kempe left the company in 1599 and was replaced by Robert Armin (right), an accomplished actor who specialized in fool's roles.

Shakespeare evidently created such roles as Touchstone in *As You Like It*, Feste in *Twelfth Night*, Lavatch in *All's Well That Ends Well*, and the Fool in *King Lear*.

Other shifts in personnel can sometimes be traced in Shakespeare's plays, especially changes in the number and ability of the boy actors (whose voices would suddenly start to crack at puberty). Shakespeare makes an amusing point about the relative size of two boy actors, for example, in *A Midsummer Night's Dream* and in *As You Like It*; this option may have been available to him only at certain times. On the other hand, not all changes in the company roster can be related meaningfully to Shakespeare's dramatic development. Augustine Phillips, who died in 1605, was a full actor-sharer of long standing in the company, but his "type" of role was probably not sharply differentiated from that of several of his associates. Shakespeare's plays, after all, involve many important supporting roles, and versatility in the undertaking of such parts must have been more common than specialization. (Phillips is remembered also for his last will and testament: he left a bequest of "a thirty shillings piece in gold" to "my fellow, William Shakespeare," and similar bequests to other members of the troupe.)

With the reopening of the boys' acting companies in 1598–1599, a serious economic rivalry sprang up between them and the adult companies. The Children of the Chapel Royal occupied the theater in Blackfriars, and the Children of Paul's probably acted in their own singing school in St. Paul's churchyard. Their plays exploited a new vogue for satire. The satiric laughter was often directed at the city of London and its bourgeois inhabitants:

socially ambitious tradesmen's wives, Puritan zealots, and the like. Other favorite targets included parvenu knights at court, would-be poets, and hysterical governmental officials. The price of admission at the private theaters was considerably higher than at the Globe or Rose, so the clientele tended to be more fashionable. Sophisticated authors like Ben Jonson, George Chapman, and John Marston tended to find writing for the boy actors more rewarding literarily than writing for the adult players.

One manifestation of the rivalry between public and private theaters was the so-called War of the Theaters, or Poetomachia. In part, this was a personal quarrel between Jonson on one side and Marston and Thomas Dekker on the other. Underlying this quarrel, however, was a serious hostility between a public theater and one that catered more to the elite. Dekker, with Marston's encouragement, attacked Jonson as a literary dictator and snob—one who subverted public decency. Jonson replied with a fervent defense of the artist's right to criticize everything that the artist sees wrong. The major plays in the exchange (1600–1601) were Jonson's *Cynthia's Revels*, Dekker and Marston's *Satiromastix*, and Jonson's *The Poetaster*.

Shakespeare allows Hamlet to comment on the theatrical rivalry (2.2.330–62), with seeming regret for the fact that the boys have been overly successful and that many adult troupes have been obliged to tour the provinces. Most of all, though, Hamlet's remarks deplore the needless bitterness on both sides. The tone of kindly remonstrance makes it seem unlikely that Shakespeare took an active part in the fracas. To be sure, in the Cambridge play *2 Return from Parnassus* (1601–1603), the character called

Will Kempe does assert that his fellow actor, Shakespeare, had put down the famous Ben Jonson:

Why, here's our fellow Shakespeare puts them all down, ay, and Ben Jonson, too. Oh, that Ben Jonson is a pestilent fellow! He brought up Horace giving the poets a pill, but our fellow Shakespeare hath given him a purge that made him bewray his credit (lines 1809–1813).

Nevertheless, no play exists in which Shakespeare did put down Jonson, and the reference may be instead to *Satiromastix*, which was performed by Shakespeare's company. Or perhaps "put down" means simply "surpassed." In fact, Shakespeare and Jonson remained on cordial terms, despite their differences in artistic outlook.

Upon the death of Queen Elizabeth in 1603 and the accession to the throne of King James I, Shakespeare's company added an important new success to their already great prosperity. According to a document of instruction from King James to his Keeper of the Privy Seal, dated May 19, 1603, and endorsed as "The Players' Privilege," the acting company that had formerly been the Lord Chamberlain's Men now became the King's company. The document names Shakespeare, Richard Burbage, Augustine Phillips, John Heminges, Henry Condell, Will Sly, Robert Armin, Richard Cowley, and Lawrence Fletcher—the last, an actor who had played before the King and the Scottish court in 1599 and 1601. These players are accorded the usual privileges of exercising their art anywhere within the kingdom and are henceforth to be known as the King's company. The principal members of the troupe also were appointed to the honorary rank of Grooms of the Royal Chamber. We therefore find them duly recorded in the Accounts of the Master of the Wardrobe on March 15, 1604, as recipients of the customary grants of red cloth, so that they, dressed in the royal livery, might take part in the approaching coronation procession of King James. The same men are mentioned in these grants as in the Players' Privilege. Shakespeare's name stands second in the former document and first in the latter. In a somewhat similar manner, the King's players, as Grooms of the Royal Chamber, were called in attendance on the Spanish ambassador at Somerset House in August 1604.

The Revels Accounts of performances at court during the winter season of 1604–1605 contain an unusually full entry, listing several of Shakespeare's plays. The list includes *Othello, The Merry Wives of Windsor, Measure for Measure,* "The play of Errors," *Love's Labor's Lost, Henry V,* and *The Merchant of Venice.* The last play was "again commanded by the King's majesty," and so was performed a second time. This list also sporadically notes the names of "the poets which made the plays," ascribing three of these works to "Shaxberd." (Probably the final *d* is an error for *e,* since the two characters are easily confused in Elizabethan handwriting; the word represents "Shaxbere" or "Shaxpere.") The entire entry was once called into question as a possible forgery but is now generally regarded as authentic.

A number of records during this period show us glimpses of Shakespeare as a man of property. On May 1, 1602, John and William Combe conveyed to Shakespeare one hundred and seven acres of arable land, plus twenty acres of pasture in the parish of Old Stratford, for the sizable payment of three hundred and twenty pounds. The deed was delivered to Shakespeare's brother Gilbert and not to the poet, who was probably at that time occupied in London. On September 28 of the same year, Shakespeare acquired the title to "one cottage and one garden by estimation a quarter of an acre," located opposite his home (New Place) in Stratford.

Shakespeare made still other real-estate investments in his hometown. In 1605 he purchased an interest in the tithes of Stratford and adjacent villages from one Ralph Hubaud for the considerable sum of four hundred and forty pounds. The purchasing of tithes was a common financial transaction in Shakespeare's time, though unknown today. Tithes were originally intended for the support of the Church but had, in many cases, become privately owned and hence negotiable. The owners of tithes paid a fixed rental sum for the right to collect as many of these taxes as they could, up to the total amount due under the law. Shakespeare seems, on this occasion in 1605, to have bought from Ralph Hubaud a one-half interest, or "moiety," in certain tithes of Stratford and vicinity. Later, probably in 1609, Shakespeare was one of those who brought a bill of complaint before the Lord Chancellor, requesting that certain other titheholders be required to come into the High Court of Chancery and make answer to the complaints alleged, namely, that they had not paid their proportional part of an annual rental of twenty-seven pounds, thirteen shillings, and four pence on the whole property in the tithes to one Henry Barker. This Barker had the theoretical right to foreclose on the entire property if any one of the forty-two titheholders failed to contribute his share of the annual fee. The suit was, in effect, a friendly one, designed to ensure that all those who were supposed to contribute did so on an equitable and businesslike basis.

We learn from the Stratford Registers of baptism, marriage, and burial of the changes in Shakespeare's family during this period. His father died in 1601, his brother Edmund in 1607, and his mother in 1608. On June 5, 1607, his daughter Susanna was married to Dr. John Hall in Holy Trinity Church, Stratford. Their first child, and Shakespeare's first grandchild, Elizabeth, was christened in the same church on February 21, 1608.

Shakespeare's Reputation, 1601–1608

Allusions to Shakespeare are frequent during this period of his life. One amusing reference is not literary but professes to tell about Shakespeare's prowess as a lover and rival of his good friend and theatrical colleague, Richard Burbage. Perhaps the joke was just a good bawdy story and should not be taken too seriously, but it is nonetheless one of the few anecdotes that date from Shakespeare's lifetime. Our informant is John Manningham, a young law student, who notes in his commonplace book in 1602 the following:

13 March 1601 [1602] . . . Upon a time, when Burbage played Richard III there was a citizen grew so far in liking with him that, before she went to the play, she appointed him to come that night unto her by the name of Richard the Third. Shakespeare, overhearing their conclusion, went before, was entertained and at his game ere Burbage came. Then message being brought that Richard the Third was at the door, Shakespeare caused return to be made that William the Conqueror was before Richard the Third. Shakespeare's name William.

Other allusions of the time are more literary. Shakespeare's greatness is, by this time, taken for granted. Anthony Scoloker, for example, in his epistle prefatory to *Diaphantus, or the Passions of Love* (1604), attempts to describe an excellent literary work in this way:

It should be like the never-too-well read Arcadia . . . or to come home to the vulgar's element, like friendly Shakespeare's tragedies, where the comedian rides, when the tragedian stands on tip-toe. Faith, it should please all, like Prince Hamlet.

The antiquarian William Camden includes Shakespeare's name among his list of England's greatest writers in his *Remains of a Greater Work Concerning Britain* (1605):

These may suffice for some poetical descriptions of our ancient poets. If I would come to our time, what a world could I present to you out of Sir Philip Sidney, Edmund Spenser, Samuel Daniel, Hugh Holland, Ben Jonson, Thomas Campion, Michael Drayton, George Chapman, John Marston, William Shakespeare, and other most pregnant wits of these our times, whom succeeding ages may justly admire.

An attempt to use one of Shakespeare's plays for political purposes had some potentially serious repercussions. Two days before the abortive rebellion of the Earl of Essex on February 7, 1601, Shakespeare's company was commissioned to perform a well-known play in its repertory about King Richard II. This play must almost surely have been Shakespeare's. Evidently, the purpose of this extraordinary performance was to awaken public sympathy for Essex by suggesting that Queen Elizabeth was another Richard II, surrounded by corrupt favorites and deaf to the pleas of her subjects. Essex's avowed intention was to remove from positions of influence those men whom he considered his political enemies. Fortunately, Shakespeare's company was later exonerated of any blame in the affair (see the Introduction to *Richard II*).

Perhaps no other allusion to Shakespeare during this period can suggest so well as the following quotation the extent to which Shakespeare's plays had become familiar to English citizens everywhere. The quotation is taken from the notes of a certain Captain Keeling, commander of the East India Company's ship *Dragon,* off Sierra Leone, in the years 1607 and 1608:

1607, Sept. 5. I sent the interpreter, according to his desire, aboard the *Hector,* where he broke fast, and after came aboard me, where we gave the tragedy of *Hamlet.*

30. Captain Hawkins dined with me, where my companions acted *King Richard the Second.*

[March 31.] I invited Captain Hawkins to a fish dinner and had *Hamlet* acted aboard me, which I permit to keep my people from idleness and unlawful games or sleep.

Other Drama of the Period

Even without Shakespeare, the early Jacobean drama in England would rank as one of the most creative periods in the history of all theater. (The word *Jacobean* is derived from *Jacobus,* the Latin form of the name of King James I.) Shakespeare's earlier contemporaries—Lyly, Greene, Marlowe, Peele, Kyd—were dead or silent, but another generation of playwrights was at hand. George Chapman, John Marston, and Ben Jonson all began writing plays shortly before 1600. So did Thomas Dekker and Thomas Heywood, whose dramatic output, often in collaboration, would prove to be considerable. Francis Beaumont, John Fletcher, Cyril Tourneur, and Thomas Middleton emerged into prominence in about 1606 or 1607. John Webster collaborated with Dekker and others in such plays as *Westward Ho* and *Sir Thomas Wyatt* around 1604, although he did not write his great tragedies until 1609–1614. Lesser talents, such as Henry Chettle, Anthony Munday, Henry Porter, John Day, and William Haughton, continued to pour forth an abundant supply of workmanlike plays. As Shakespeare's career developed, therefore, he enjoyed the fellowship and, no doubt, the rivalry of a remarkably gifted and diverse group of practicing dramatists.

Early Jacobean drama is, on the whole, characteristically different from the late Elizabethan drama that had preceded it. Other dramatists besides Shakespeare mirror his shift of focus from romantic comedies and patriotic histories to "problem" plays and tragedies. The boys' companies, reopening in 1598–1599 after virtually a decade of silence, did much to set the new tone. They avoided almost entirely the English history play, with its muscularly heroic style, so unsuited for the acting capabilities of boys. Besides, sophisticated audiences were sated with jingoistic fare, and even in the public theaters the genre had pretty well run its course. The fashion of the moment turned instead to revenge tragedy and satiric comedy.

The Jacobean revenge play owed much of its original inspiration to Thomas Kyd's *The Spanish Tragedy* (c. 1587), with its influential conventions: the intervention of supernatural forces, the feigned madness of the avenger, his difficulty in ascertaining the true facts of the murder, his morbid awareness of the conflict between human injustice and divine justice, his devising of a play within the play, and his invention of ingenious methods of slaughter in the play's gory ending. Kyd may also have written an early version of *Hamlet* featuring similar motifs. Shakespeare confronted cosmic issues of justice and human depravity in his revenge tragedy, *Hamlet* (c. 1599–1601), as indeed Kyd had done, but most followers of Kyd preferred to revel in the sensationalism of the genre. Some private-theater dramatists, such as Marston, subjected the conventions of the genre to caricature. Marston's revenge plays, written chiefly for Paul's boys and (after 1604) for the Children of the Queen's Revels, include *Antonio's Revenge* (1599–1601) and *The Malcontent* (1600–1604). These dramas are marked by flamboyantly overstated cynicism and are, in many ways, as close to satire as they are to tragedy. Marston had, in fact, made his first reputation as a nondramatic satirist, with *The Metamorphosis of Pygmalion's Image* and *The Scourge of Villainy* in 1598. His plays represent a continuation in dramatic form of the techniques of the Roman satirist. The typical Marstonian avenger, such as Malevole in *The Malcontent*, is an exaggeratedly unattractive authorial spokesman, pouring forth venomous hatred upon the loathsome and degenerate court in which he finds himself.

Similar in their exaggerated pursuit of the grotesque and the morbid are Cyril Tourneur's *The Atheist's Tragedy* (1607–1611) and a play formerly attributed to Tourneur but probably by Thomas Middleton, *The Revenger's Tragedy* (1606–1607). These plays are brilliant in the plotting of impossible situations and in the invention of cunning Italianate forms of torture and murder. Any sympathetic identification with the characters of these plays is sacrificed in the interests of technical virtuosity. As a result, the plays are more ironic than cathartic in their effect; we are overwhelmed by life's dark absurdities rather than ennobled by a vision of humanity's tragic grandeur. *The Tragedy of Hoffman, or A Revenge for a Father* by Henry Chettle (Admiral's Men, 1602) is similarly grotesque and lacking in sympathy for its revenger hero. To be sure, George Chapman's *Bussy D'Ambois* (1600–1604) and its sequel, *The Revenge of Bussy D'Ambois* (1607–1612), are thoughtful plays about human aspiration, in the vein of Marlowe's *Tamburlaine*, but even these plays employ a good deal of Senecan bloody melodrama.

The revenge play enjoyed a great popularity on the public stage and (in a caricatured form) on the private stage. The public theater did, however, cater also to its Puritan-leaning audiences, with more pious and moral tragedy. *Arden of Feversham* (c. 1591) is a good early example of what has come to be called domestic or homiletic tragedy. In the studiously plain style of a broadside ballad, it sets forth the facts of an actual murder that had occurred in 1551 and had been reported in Holinshed's *Chronicles*. The play interprets those events earnestly and providen-

tially. The most famous play in the genre of domestic tragedy is Thomas Heywood's *A Woman Killed with Kindness* (1603). It tells, not of a murder, but of an adultery, for which the goodhearted but offending wife must be perpetually banished by her grieving husband. The play succeeds in elevating the private sorrows of its ordinary characters to tragic stature. The moral stances appear to be unambiguous: adultery is a heinous offense but can be transcended by Christian forgiveness; dueling is evil. Still, a mix of sympathies is perhaps reflective of shifting public attitudes toward the role of women in marriage. Other plays in the vein of domestic tragedy include *A Yorkshire Tragedy* (1605–1608), *The Miseries of Enforced Marriage* (1605–1606), and *Two Lamentable Tragedies* (c. 1594–1598).

In comedy, the greatest writer of the period besides Shakespeare was Ben Jonson. His predilection was toward the private theater, though he continued to write occasionally for the public stage as well. To an ever-increasing extent, he fixed his satirical gaze on those values and institutions which Thomas Heywood cherished: the city of London, its bourgeois citizens, its traditional approach to morality, and its religious zeal. *Every Man Out of His Humor* (1599), written for the Chamberlain's Men, features a foolish, uxorious citizen, his socially aspiring wife, and her fashionmongering lover—humors types that were to appear again and again in the genre of satirical comedy known as "city comedy." (See Brian Gibbons, *Jacobean City Comedy*, 1968.) *Volpone* (1605–1606), though technically not a London city comedy, since it purportedly takes place in Venice, castigates greed among lawyers, businessmen, and other professional types. *The Alchemist* (1610) ridicules the affectations of petty shopkeepers, lawyers' clerks, Puritan divines, and others. *Bartholomew Fair* (1614) and *The Alchemist* give us Jonson's most memorable indictment of the Puritans.

Numerous other writers contributed to humors comedy and city comedy. George Chapman probably deserves more credit than he usually receives for having helped determine the shape of humors comedy in his *The Blind Beggar of Alexandria* (1596), *An Humorous Day's Mirth* (1597), *All Fools* (1599–1604), *May-Day* (1601–1609), *The Gentleman Usher* (1602–1604), and others. Francis Beaumont, assisted perhaps by John Fletcher, ridicules London grocers and apprentices for their naive tastes in romantic chivalry in *The Knight of the Burning Pestle* (1607–1610). Some satire in this vein, to be sure, is reasonably good-humored. *Eastward Ho!* (1605), by Chapman, Jonson, and Marston, is genially sympathetic toward the lifestyle of the small shopkeeper, even though the play contains a good deal of satire directed at social climbing and sharp business practices. Thomas Dekker's collaboration with Thomas Middleton on *The Honest Whore* (Part I, 1604) gives us an amused and yet warm portrayal of a linen draper who succeeds in business by insisting that the customer is always right. Dekker often shows a wry but generous appreciation of bourgeois ethics, as in *The Shoemaker's Holiday* (1599). Yet even he turns against the Puritans in *If This Be Not a Good Play, the Devil Is in It* (1611–1612).

Marston shows his talent for city comedy in *The Dutch Courtesan* (1603–1605). Perhaps the most ingratiating and truly funny of the writers of city comedy, however, is Middleton. His *A Trick to Catch the Old One* (1604–1607) illustrates the tendency of Jacobean comedy to move away both from Shakespeare's romantic vein and Jonson's morally satirical vein toward a more lighthearted comedy of manners, anticipating the style of Restoration comedy. One of Middleton's most hilarious and philosophically unpretentious plays, though plotted with great ingenuity of situation, is *A Mad World, My Masters* (1604–1607). *Michaelmas Term*, written about the same time, exposes the sharp practices of usurers and lawyers. All these Middleton plays were written for Paul's boys.

Romantic comedy, though overshadowed by humors and city comedy during the 1600s, still held forth at the public theaters. A leading exponent was Thomas Heywood, in such plays as *The Fair Maid of the West*, or *A Girl Worth Gold* (1597–1610). Heywood also wrote English history plays designed to prove the sturdiness and historical importance of the London citizenry he so loved, as in *Edward IV* (1597–1599), *The Four Prentices of London* (c. 1600), and *If You Know Not Me You Know Nobody* (1605). Classical tragedy also continued to be written, despite the vogue of revenge tragedy. Ben Jonson rather dogmatically illustrated his classical theories of tragedy in *Sejanus* (1603) and *Catiline* (1611). Samuel Daniel wrote *Philotas* in 1604 and a revision of his *Cleopatra* in 1607. Heywood's *The Rape of Lucrece* appeared in 1606–1608. These are not, however, the immortal tragedies for which the Jacobean period is remembered.

Shakespeare's Work, 1601–1608

Shakespeare's plays of this period are characteristically Jacobean in their fascination with the dark complexities of sexual jealousy, betrayal, revenge, and social conflict. The comedies are few in number and lack the joyous affirmation we associate with *Twelfth Night* and earlier plays. *Measure for Measure*, for example, is not about young men and women happily in love, but about premarital sex and the insoluble problems that arise when vice-prone men attempt to legislate morality for their fellow mortals. Angelo, self-hating and out of emotional control, is a tragic hero providentially rescued from his own worst self. The Duke and Isabella must use ethically dubious means—the bed trick—to effect their virtuous aims. Comedy in the play deals darkly in terms of prostitution, slander, and police inefficiency.

All's Well That Ends Well, though less grim than *Measure for Measure* in its confrontation of human degeneracy, does apply a similar bed trick as its central plot device. Just as important, the obstacles to love are internal and psychological, rather than external; that is, the happy union of Bertram and Helena is delayed, not by parental objections or by accident (as in *Romeo and Juliet* and *A Midsummer Night's Dream*), but by Bertram's unreadiness for the demands of a mature marital relationship. *Troilus and Cressida* is a play in which love is paralyzed by a combination of external and internal forces. Troilus must hand Cressida over to the Greeks because his code of honor bids him put his country's cause before his own, and yet that code of "honor" is based on Paris's rape of Helen. Cressida simply gives herself up to Diomedes, knowing she is not strong enough to stand alone in a moral wilderness. The combatants in

Raphael Holinshed's Chronicles of England, Scotland, and Ireland, *which was published (1577, 2nd edition in 1587) before Shakespeare's career began, served as principal historic source for many plays, including* Macbeth, King Lear, *and* Cymbeline, *as well as the history plays. Here, in a woodcut from the* Chronicles, Macbeth *and* Banquo *are shown encountering the three weird sisters.*

the greatest war in all history turn out to be petty bickerers who play nasty games on one another and sulk when their reputations are impugned. The cause for which both sides fight is squalid and senseless.

In *Hamlet*, Shakespeare explores similar dilemmas posed by human carnality. Women, in Hamlet's misogynistic angst, are too often frail; men are too often importunate and brutal. How is a thoughtful person to justify his or her own existence? Should one struggle actively against injustice and personal wrong? How can one know what is really true or foresee the complex results of action? How, in *Othello*, can the protagonist resist temptation and inner weakness, prompting him to destroy the very thing on which his happiness depends? Is Macbeth tempted to sin by the weird sisters and his wife, or is the choice to murder Duncan ultimately his? To what extent is humanity responsible for its tragic fate? Most of all, in *King Lear*, are the heavens themselves indifferent to human bestiality? Must Cordelia die? Yet, despite these overwhelmingly pessimistic questions, and the tragic consequences they imply for all human life, Shakespeare's "great" tragedies affirm at least the nobility of humanity's striving to know itself, and the redeeming fact that human goodness does exist (in Desdemona, Duncan, Cordelia), even if those who practice goodness are often slaughtered.

The Roman or classical tragedies are something apart from the "great" tragedies. They are more ironic in tone, more dispiriting, though they, too, affirm an essential nobility in humanity. Brutus misguidedly leads a revolution against Caesar but dies loyal to his great principles. Timon of Athens proves the appalling ingratitude of his fellow creature and resolutely cuts himself off from all human contact. Coriolanus proclaims himself an enemy of the Roman people and seeks to destroy them for their ingratitude, though he is compromised and destroyed at last by his promptings of human feeling. Antony, too, is pulled apart by an irreconcilable conflict. Yet, in this play at least, Shakespeare achieves, partly through the greatness of Cleopatra, a triumph over defeat that seems to offer a new resolution of humanity's tragic dilemma.

THE LATE YEARS: 1608–1616

In the summer of 1608, Shakespeare's acting company signed a twenty-one-year lease for the use of the Blackfriars playhouse, an indoor and rather intimate, artificially lighted theater inside the city of London, close to the site of St. Paul's Cathedral. A private theater had existed on this spot since 1576, when the Children of the Chapel and then Paul's boys began acting their courtly plays for paying spectators in a building that had once belonged to the Dominicans, or Black Friars. James Burbage had begun construction in 1596 of the so-called Second Blackfriars theater in the same building. Although James encountered opposition from the residents of the area and died before

he could complete the work, James's son Richard did succeed in opening the new theater in 1600. At first, he leased it (for twenty-one years) to a children's company, but when that company was suppressed in 1608 for offending the French ambassador in a play by George Chapman, Burbage seized the opportunity to take back the unexpired lease and to set up Blackfriars as the winter playhouse for his adult company, the King's Men. By this time, the adult troupes could plainly see that they needed to cater more directly to courtly audiences than they once had done. Their popular audiences were becoming increasingly disenchanted with the drama. Puritan fulminations against the stage gained in effect, especially when many playwrights refused to disguise their satirical hostility toward Puritans and the London bourgeoisie.

Several of Shakespeare's late plays may have been acted both at the Globe and at Blackfriars. The plays he wrote after 1608–1609—*Cymbeline, The Winter's Tale*, and *The Tempest*—all show the distinct influence of the dramaturgy of the private theaters. Also, we know that an increasing number of Shakespeare's plays were acted at the court of King James. *Othello, King Lear*, and *The Tempest* are named in court revels accounts, and *Macbeth* dramatizes Scottish history with a seemingly explicit reference to King James as the descendant of Banquo, who bears the "twofold balls and treble scepters" (4.1.121); James had received a double coronation as King of England and Scotland, and took seriously his assumed title as King of Great Britain, France, and Ireland. On the other hand, Shakespeare's plays certainly continued to be acted at the Globe to the very end of his career. The 1609 quarto of *Pericles* advertises that it was acted "by his Majesty's Servants, at the Globe on the Bankside." The 1608 quarto of *King Lear* mentions a performance at court and assigns the play to "His Majesty's servants playing usually at the Globe on the Bankside." Simon Forman saw *Macbeth, Cymbeline*, and *The Winter's Tale* at the Globe. Finally, a performance of *Henry VIII* on June 29, 1613, resulted in the burning of the Globe to the ground, though afterwards it soon was rebuilt.

Shakespeare's last plays, written with a view to Blackfriars and the court, as well as to the Globe, are now usually called "romances" or "tragicomedies," or sometimes both. Although they were not known by these terms in Shakespeare's day—they were grouped with the comedies in the First Folio of 1623, except for *Cymbeline*, which was placed among the tragedies—the very ambiguity about the genre in this arrangement is suggestive of an uncertainty as to whether they were seen as predominantly comic or tragic. The term "romance" suggests a return to the kind of story Robert Greene had derived from Greek romance: tales of adventure, long separation, and tearful reunion, involving shipwreck, capture by pirates, riddling prophecies, children set adrift in boats or abandoned on foreign shores, the illusion of death and subsequent restoration to life, the revelation of the identity of long-lost children by

COURTESY, GUILDHALL LIBRARY, CORPORATION OF LONDON

This section of Wenceslaus Hollar's "Long View" of London dates from 1647, some years after Shakespeare's death, but gives nonetheless a fine view of two theater buildings on the south bank of the Thames River, across from the city. The two labels of "The Globe" and "Beere bayting" should in fact be reversed; the Globe (rebuilt in 1613) appears to the left and below the bearbaiting arena.

birthmarks, and the like. The term "tragicomedy" suggests a play in which the protagonist commits a seemingly fatal error or crime, or (as in *Pericles*) suffers an extraordinarily adverse fortune to test his patience; in either event, he must experience agonies of contrition and bereavement until he is providentially delivered from his tribulations. The tone is deeply melancholic and resigned, although suffused also with a sense of gratitude for the harmonies that are mysteriously restored.

The appropriateness of such plays to the elegant atmosphere of Blackfriars and the court is subtle but real. Although one might suppose at first that old-fashioned naiveté would seem out of place in a sophisticated milieu, the naiveté is only superficial. Tragicomedy and pastoral romance were, in the period from 1606 to 1610, beginning to enjoy a fashionable courtly revival. The leading practitioners of the new genre were Beaumont and Fletcher, though Shakespeare made a highly significant contribution. Perhaps sophisticated audiences responded to pastoral and romantic drama as the nostalgic evocation of an idealized past, a chivalric "golden world" fleetingly recovered through an artistic journey back to naiveté and inno-

cence. The evocation of such a world demands the kind of studied but informal artifice we find in many tragicomic plays of the period: the elaborate masques and allegorical shows, the descents of enthroned gods from the heavens (as in *Cymbeline*), the use of quaint Chorus figures like Old Gower or Time (in *Pericles* and *The Winter's Tale*), and the quasi-operatic blend of music and spectacle. At their best, such plays powerfully compel belief in the artistic world thus artificially created. The very improbability of the story becomes, paradoxically, part of the means by which an audience must "awake its faith" in a mysterious truth.

Shakespeare did not merely ape the new fashion in tragicomedy and romance. In fact, he may have done much to establish it. His *Pericles*, written seemingly in about 1606–1608 for the public stage before Shakespeare's company acquired Blackfriars, anticipated many important features, not only of Shakespeare's own later romances, but also of Beaumont and Fletcher's *The Maid's Tragedy* and *Philaster* (c. 1608–1611). Still, Shakespeare was on the verge of retirement, and the future belonged to Beaumont and Fletcher. Gradually, Shakespeare disengaged himself, spending more and more time in Stratford. His last-known stint as an actor was in Jonson's *Sejanus* in 1603. Some time in 1611 or 1612, he probably gave up his lodgings in London, though he still may have returned for such occasions as the opening performance of *Henry VIII* in 1613. He continued to be one of the proprietors of the newly rebuilt Globe, but his involvement in its day-to-day operations dwindled.

Shakespeare's Reputation, 1608–1616

Shakespeare's reputation among his contemporaries was undiminished in his late years, even though Beaumont and Fletcher were the new rage at the Globe and Blackfriars. Among those who apostrophized Shakespeare was John Davies of Hereford in *The Scourge of Folly* (entered in the Stationers' Register in 1610):

> To our English Terence, Mr. Will Shakespeare.
>
> Some say, good Will, which I, in sport, do sing:
> Hadst thou not played some kingly parts in sport,
> Thou hadst been a companion for a king,
> And been a king among the meaner sort.
> Some others rail. But, rail as they think fit,
> Thou hast no railing, but a reigning, wit.
> And honesty thou sow'st, which they do reap,
> So to increase their stock which they do keep.

The following sonnet is from *Run and a Great Cast* (1614) by Thomas Freeman:

> To Master W. Shakespeare.
>
> Shakespeare, that nimble Mercury thy brain
> Lulls many hundred Argus-eyes asleep,
> So fit, for all thou fashionest thy vein,

At th' horse-foot fountain thou hast drunk full deep.
Virtue's or vice's theme to thee all one is.
Who loves chaste life, there's *Lucrece* for a teacher;
Who list read lust, there's *Venus and Adonis,*
True model of a most lascivious lecher.
Besides, in plays thy wit winds like Meander,
Whence needy new composers borrow more
Than Terence doth from Plautus or Menander.
But to praise thee aright, I want thy store.
    Then let thine own works thine own worth upraise,
    And help t' adorn thee with deservèd bays.

Ben Jonson took a more critical view, though he also admired Shakespeare greatly. In the Induction to his *Bartholomew Fair* (1631 edition), Jonson compared the imaginary world he presented in his play with the more improbable fantasies of romantic drama:

If there be never a servant-monster i' the fair, who can help it?
He [the author, Jonson] says; nor a nest of antics? He is loath to
make Nature afraid in his plays, like those that beget tales,
Tempests, and suchlike drolleries to mix his head with other
men's heels.

From this, one judges that Jonson had in mind not only *The Tempest*, but also Shakespeare's other late romances. He similarly protested in the Prologue to his 1616 edition of *Every Man in His Humor* that his own playwriting was free of the usual romantic claptrap:

Where neither Chorus wafts you o'er the seas,
Nor creaking throne comes down the boys to please,
Nor nimble squib is seen to make afeard
The gentlewomen, nor rolled bullet heard
To say it thunders, nor tempestuous drum
Rumbles to tell you when the storm doth come.

Still, Shakespeare's reputation was assured. John Webster paid due homage, in his note To the Reader accompanying *The White Devil* (1612): to "the right happy and copious industry of M. *Shakespeare*, M. *Dekker*, & M. *Heywood*," along with Chapman, Jonson, Beaumont, and Fletcher.

Records of the Late Years

Shakespeare's last recorded investment in real estate was the purchase of a house in Blackfriars, London, in 1613. There is no indication he lived there, for he had retired to Stratford. He did not pay the full purchase price of one hundred and forty pounds, and the mortgage deed executed for the unpaid balance furnishes one of the six unquestioned examples of his signature.

John Combe, a wealthy bachelor of Stratford and Shakespeare's friend, left him a legacy of five pounds in his will at the time of Combe's death in 1613. At about the same time, John's kinsman William Combe began a controversial attempt to enclose Welcombe Common, that is, to convert narrow strips of arable land to pasture. Pre-

sumably, Combe was interested in a more efficient means of using the land. Enclosure was, however, an explosive issue, since many people feared they would lose the right to farm the land and would be evicted to make room for cattle and sheep. Combe attempted to guarantee Shakespeare and other titheholders that they would lose no money. He offered similar assurances to the Stratford Council, but the townspeople were adamantly opposed. Shakespeare was consulted by letter as a leading titheholder. The letter is lost, but, presumably, it set forth the Council's reasons for objecting to enclosure. Shakespeare's views on the controversy remain unknown. Eventually, the case went to the Privy Council, where Combe was ordered to restore the land to its original use.

One of the most interesting documents from these years consists of the records of a lawsuit entered into in 1612 by Stephen Belott against his father-in-law, Christopher Mountjoy, a Huguenot maker of women's ornamental headdresses who resided on Silver Street, St. Olave's parish, London. Belott sought to secure the payment of a dower promised him at the time of his marriage to Mountjoy's daughter. In this suit, Shakespeare was summoned as a witness and made deposition on five interrogatories. From this document we learn that Shakespeare was a lodger in Mountjoy's house at the time of the marriage in 1604 and probably for some time before that, since he states in his testimony that he had known Mountjoy for more than ten years. Shakespeare admitted that, at the solicitation of Mountjoy's wife, he had acted as an intermediary in the arrangement of the marriage between Belott and Mountjoy's daughter. Shakespeare declared himself unable, however, to recall the exact amount of the portion or the date on which it was to have been paid. Shakespeare's signature to his deposition is authentic and one of the best samples of his handwriting that we have.

In January 1616, Shakespeare drew up his last will and testament with the assistance of his lawyer Francis Collins, who had aided him earlier in some of his transactions in real estate. On March 25, 1616, Shakespeare revised his will in order to provide for the marriage of his daughter Judith and Thomas Quiney in that same year. Shakespeare's three quavering signatures, one on each page of this document, suggest that he was in failing health. The cause of his death on April 23 is not known. An intriguing bit of Stratford gossip is reported by John Ward, vicar of Holy Trinity in Stratford from 1662 to 1689, in his diary: "Shakespeare, Drayton, and Ben Jonson had a merry meeting, and it seems drank too hard, for Shakespeare died of a fever there contracted." The report comes fifty years after Shakespeare's death, however, and is hardly an expert medical opinion.

The will disposes of all the property of which Shakespeare is known to have died possessing, the greater share of it going to his daughter Susanna. His recently married daughter, Judith, received a dowry, a provision for any children that might be born of her marriage, and other gifts. Ten pounds went to the poor of Stratford; Shakespeare's sword went to Mr. Thomas Combe; twenty-six shillings and eight pence apiece went to Shakespeare's fellow actors Heminges, Burbage, and Condell to buy them mourning rings; and other small bequests went to various other friends and relatives.

An interlineation contains the bequest of Shakespeare's "second best bed with the furniture" that is, the hangings, to his wife. Anne's name appears nowhere else in the will. Some scholars, beginning with Edmund Malone, have taken this reference as proof of an unhappy marriage, confirming earlier indications, such as the hasty wedding to a woman who was William's senior by eight years and his prolonged residence in London for twenty years or more, seemingly without his family. The evidence is inconclusive, however. Shakespeare certainly supported his family handsomely, acquired much property in Stratford, and retired there when he might have remained still in London. Although he showed no great solicitude for Anne's well-being in the will, her rights were protected by law; a third of her husband's estate went to her without having to be mentioned in the will. New Place was to be the home of Shakespeare's favorite daughter, Susanna, wife of the distinguished Dr. John Hall. Anne Shakespeare would make her home with her daughter

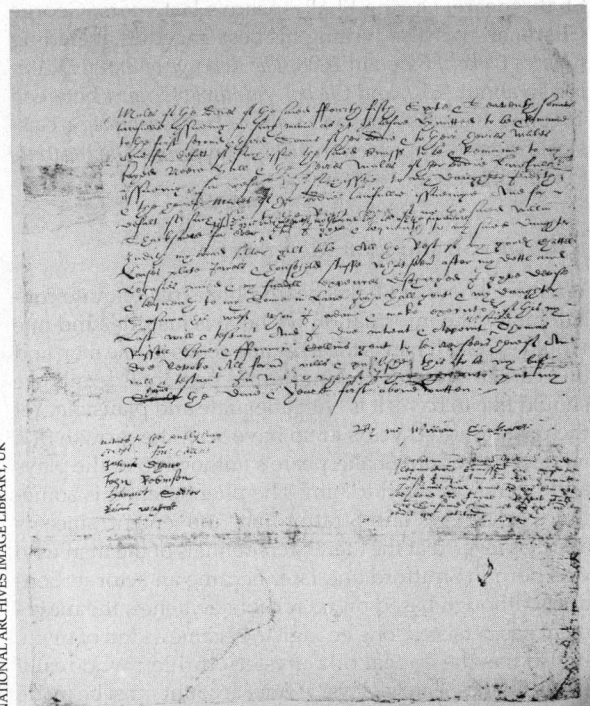

As with so many other things in his life, the curious terms of Shakespeare's will have led to endless and provocative conjecture.

and, with her dower rights secured by law, would be quite as wealthy as she would need to be.

The date of Shakespeare's death (April 23, 1616) and his age (his fifty-third year) are inscribed on his monument. This elaborate structure, still standing in the chancel of Trinity Church, Stratford, was erected some time before 1623 by the London stonecutting firm of Gheerart Janssen and his sons. Janssen's shop was in Southwark, near the Globe, and may have been familiar to the actors. The bust of Shakespeare is a conventional sort of statuary for its time. Still, it is one of the only two contemporary likenesses we have. The other is the Droeshout engraving of Shakespeare in the Folio of 1623.

The epitaph on the monument reads as follows:

Iudicio Pylium, genio Socratem, arte Maronem;
Terra tegit, populus maeret, Olympus habet.
Stay, passenger. Why goest thou by so fast?
Read, if thou canst, whom envious Death hath placed
Within this monument: Shakespeare, with whom
Quick Nature died, whose name doth deck this tomb
Far more than cost, sith all that he hath writ
Leaves living art but page to serve his wit.

Obiit anno domini 1616,
Aetatis 53, die 23 April.

These lines, of which the beginning Latin couplet compares Shakespeare with Nestor (King of Pylos) for wise judgment, Socrates for genius, and Virgil (Maro) for poetic art, and avers that the earth covers him, people grieve for him, and Mount Olympus (that is, heaven) has him, indicate the high reputation he enjoyed at the time of his death. More widely known, perhaps, are the four lines inscribed over Shakespeare's grave near the north wall of the chancel. A local tradition assigns them to Shakespeare himself and implies that he wrote them "to suit the capacity of clerks and sextons," whom he wished apparently to frighten out of the idea of opening the grave to make room for a new occupant:

Good friend, for Jesus' sake forbear
To dig the dust enclosèd here.
Blest be the man that spares these stones,
And curst be he that moves my bones.

Whether Shakespeare actually wrote these lines cannot, however, be determined.

Other Dramatists

The most significant new development in the drama of the period from about 1608 to 1616, apart from Shakespeare's new interest in romance and tragicomedy, was the emergence of the famous literary partners Francis Beaumont and John Fletcher. Beaumont, the son of a distinguished lawyer, studied for a while at Oxford and then at the Inner Temple before drifting into a literary career. In 1613, he married an heiress and retired almost completely from the theater. John Fletcher was the son of Richard Fletcher, Queen Elizabeth's chaplain and later Bishop of London. The young man probably studied at Cambridge. The father died in 1596 heavily in debt, leaving the young Fletcher to support a family of eight children. Fletcher became a professional writer, earning his living as chief dramatist for the King's Men. He was Shakespeare's successor. Fletcher's cousins, Giles and Phineas Fletcher, gained some reputation as poets. Beaumont and Fletcher, who were close friends, regarded themselves also as poets and as members of the "tribe of Ben"—the disciples of the great Ben Jonson who often gathered together at the Mermaid Tavern for an evening of witty literary conversation.

> What things have we seen
> Done at the Mermaid! heard words that have been
> So nimble, and so full of subtle flame,
> As if that every one from whence they came
> Had meant to put his whole wit in a jest,
> And had resolved to live a fool the rest
> Of his dull life!

> *(Master Francis Beaumont's Letter to Ben Jonson)*

Beaumont and Fletcher actually collaborated on only about seven plays: *The Woman Hater,* a comedy (1606); *The Maid's Tragedy*, a tragedy (1608–1611); *Philaster,* a tragicomedy (1608–1610); *Cupid's Revenge*, a tragedy (c. 1607–1612); *The Coxcomb,* a comedy (1608–1610); *A King and No King,* a tragicomedy (1611); *The Scornful Lady,* a tragicomedy (1613–1616); and perhaps one or two others. They may have collaborated on *The Knight of the Burning Pestle* (c. 1607–1610), though it was chiefly Beaumont's. Beaumont also wrote *Mask of the Inner Temple and Gray's Inn* (1613). Fletcher unassisted wrote *The Faithful Shepherdess* (1608–1609), *The Night Walker* (c. 1611), *Bonduca* (1611–1614), *Valentinian* (1610–1614), and others. He also collaborated with several other writers, including Massinger, Middleton, Field, and Rowley. Importantly, he seems to have collaborated with Shakespeare on *The Two Noble Kinsmen* (1613–1616) and, probably, on *Henry VIII.* Eventually, most of these various dramatic enterprises were gathered together in 1647 as the works of Beaumont and Fletcher. They have remained known as such ever since, partly because the original collaboration of these two men did so much to set a new style in coterie drama.

The plays they wrote together, such as *The Maid's Tragedy* and *Philaster,* offer an interesting comparison with Shakespeare's contemporary writing in a similar genre. Beaumont and Fletcher often employ exotic settings, like Rhodes or Sicily. In such an environment, refined aristocratic characters are caught in dynastic struggles or in a rarified conflict between love and honor. They must cope with stereotyped villains, such as tyrants or shamelessly lustful courtiers. The sentiments are lofty, the rhetoric is mannered; elaborately contrived situations are offered with no pretense of verisimilitude. The characters live according to lofty chivalric codes and despise ill breeding above all else. In the plotting of the tragicomic reversal, the audience is sometimes deliberately deceived into believing something that is not true, so that the sudden happy outcome arrives as a theatrically contrived surprise. Disguising and masking are common motifs. The audience is deliberately made aware throughout of the play's theatrical artifice, statuesque scene building, and titillating sensationalism.

Although Shakespeare wrote no tragedies after *Coriolanus,* great tragedy did continue to appear on the Jacobean stage. John Webster wrote his two most splendid plays, *The White Devil* and *The Duchess of Malfi,* between 1609 and 1614. Both contain elements of the still-popular revenge tradition. They also manage to achieve a vision of triumphant human dignity in defeat that merits comparison with Shakespeare's greatest tragic achievement. Still to come were *The Changeling* (1622) by Thomas Middleton and William Rowley, *Women Beware Women* (c. 1620–1627) by Middleton, *'Tis Pity She's a Whore* (1629?–1633) by John Ford, and others. Although these tragedies are more concerned with the grotesque than are Shakespeare's great tragedies, and more obsessed with abnormal human psychology (incest, werewolfism, and the like), they are nonetheless sublime achievements in art. The genius of the age for tragedy did not die with Shakespeare. During Shakespeare's last years, George Chapman was also writing his best tragedies, including *Charles Duke of Byron* in 1608, *The Revenge of Bussy D'Ambois* in about 1610, and *Chabot, Admiral of France* between 1611 and 1622. Ben Jonson's *Catiline His Conspiracy,* a classical tragedy, appeared in 1611; Marston's *The Insatiate Countess,* in about 1610.

The Anti-Stratfordian Movement

What we know of Shakespeare's life is really quite considerable. The information we have is just the kind one would expect. It hangs together and refers to one man and one career. Though lacking in the personal details we should like to have, it is both adequate and plausible. Yet the past hundred years or so have seen the growth of a tendency to doubt Shakespeare's authorship of the plays and poems ascribed to him. The phenomenon is sometimes called the "anti-Stratfordian" movement, since its attack is leveled at the literary credentials of the man who was born in Stratford and later became an actor in London. Although based on no reliable evidence, the movement has persisted long enough to become a kind of myth. It also has the appeal of a mystery thriller: who really wrote Shakespeare's plays? A brief account must be made here of the origins of the anti-Stratfordian movement.

Beginning in the late eighteenth century, and especially in the mid-nineteenth century, a few admirers of

Shakespeare began to be troubled by the scantiness of information about England's greatest author. As we have already seen, good reasons exist for the scarcity: the great London fire of 1666 that destroyed many records, the relatively low social esteem accorded to popular dramatists during the Elizabethan period, and the like. Also, we do actually know more about Shakespeare than about most of his contemporaries in the theater, despite the difficulties imposed by the passage of time. Still, some nineteenth-century readers saw only that they knew far less about Shakespeare than about many authors of more recent date.

Moreover, the impressions of the man did not seem to square with his unparalleled literary greatness. William Shakespeare had been brought up in a small country town; were his parents cultured folk or even literate? No record of his schooling has been preserved; was Shakespeare himself able to read and write, much less write immortal plays and poems? The anti-Stratfordians did not deny the existence of a man called Shakespeare from Stratford-upon-Avon, but they found it incredible that such a person should be connected with the works ascribed to him. Mark Twain, himself an anti-Stratfordian, was fond of joking that the plays were not by Shakespeare but by another person of the same name. Beneath the humor in this remark lies a deep-seated mistrust: how could a country boy have written so knowledgeably and eloquently about the lives of kings and queens? Where could such a person have learned so much about the law, about medicine, about the art of war, about heraldry? The puzzle seemed a genuine one, even though no one until the late eighteenth century had thought to question Shakespeare's authorship of the plays—least of all his colleagues and friends, such as Ben Jonson, who admitted that Shakespeare's classical learning was "small" but insisted that Shakespeare was an incomparable genius.

The first candidate put forward in the anti-Stratfordian cause as the "real" author of the plays was Sir Francis Bacon, a reputable Elizabethan writer with connections at court and considerable cultural attainments. Yet the ascription of the plays to Bacon was based on no documentary evidence. It relied, instead, on the essentially snobbish argument that Bacon was better born and purportedly better educated than Shakespeare—an argument that appealed strongly to the nineteenth century in which a university education was becoming more and more a distinctive mark of the cultivated person. The assertion of Bacon's authorship was also based on a conspiratorial theory of history; that is, its believers had to assume the existence of a mammoth conspiracy in Elizabethan times, in which Shakespeare would allow his name to be used by Bacon as a *nom de plume* and in which Shakespeare's friends, such as Ben Jonson, would take part. (Jonson knew Shakespeare too well, after all, to have been duped for a period of almost twenty years.) The motive for such an arrangement, presumably, was that Bacon did not deign to lend his dignified name to the writing of popular plays (since they were considered subliterary) and so chose a common actor named Shakespeare to serve as his alter ego. This theory of an elaborate hoax involving England's greatest literary giant has proved powerfully attractive to modern writers like Mark Twain, who have sometimes referred to themselves as rebels against the cultural "Establishment" of their own times.

The claim that Bacon wrote Shakespeare's works was soon challenged in the name of other prominent Elizabethans: the Earl of Oxford, the Earl of Southampton, Anthony Bacon, the Earl of Rutland, the Earl of Devonshire, Christopher Marlowe, and others. Since documentary claims as to Bacon's authorship of the Shakespearean canon were nonexistent, other Elizabethans could be proposed to fill his role just as satisfactorily as Bacon himself. The anti-Stratfordian movement gained momentum and came to include several prominent persons, including Delia Bacon and Sigmund Freud, as well as Mark Twain. One of the appeals of the anti-Stratfordian movement in recent years has proved to be a kind of amateur sleuthing or scholarship, carried on by professional lawyers, doctors, and the like, who have explored Shakespeare's interest in law and medicine as a hobby and have convinced themselves that Shakespeare's wisdom in these subjects entitles him to claim a better birth than that of a glover's son from Stratford. Ingenious efforts at "deciphering" hidden meanings in the works have been adduced to prove one authorship claim or another. The academic "Establishments" of modern universities have been accused of perpetuating Shakespeare's name out of mere vested self-interest: Shakespeare scholarship is an industry, and its busy workers need to preserve their source of income.

We must ask in all seriousness, however, whether such assertions are not offering answers to nonexistent questions. Responsible scholarship has admirably dispelled the seeming mystery of Shakespeare's humble beginnings. T. W. Baldwin, for example, in *William Shakspere's Petty School* (1943) and *William Shakspere's Small Latine and Lesse Greeke* (1944), has shown just what sort of classical training Shakespeare almost surely received in the free grammar school of Stratford. It is precisely the sort of training that would have enabled him to use classical authors as he does, with the familiarity of one who likes to read. His Latin and Greek were passable but not strong; he often consulted modern translations, as well as classical originals. Just as importantly, Shakespeare's social background was, in fact, typical of many of the greatest writers of the English Renaissance. He earned his living by his writing, and thus had one of the strongest of motives for success. So did his contemporaries Marlowe (who came from a shoemaker's family) and Jonson (whose stepfather was a brickmason). Greene, Peele, Nashe, and many others sold plays and other writings for a livelihood. Although a few wellborn persons, such as

Bacon and Sir Philip Sidney, also made exceptional contributions to literature, and although a number of courtiers emulated Henry VIII and Elizabeth as gifted amateurs in the arts, the court was not the direct or major source of England's literary greatness. Most courtiers were not, like Shakespeare, professional writers. A man like Bacon lacked Shakespeare's connection with a commercial acting company. Surely the theater was a more relevant "university" for Shakespeare than Oxford or Cambridge, where most of his studies would have been in ancient languages and in divinity.

HOW TO READ SHAKESPEARE

In the short essay on "Reading Shakespeare in the Twenty-First Century" at the head of the General Introduction to this book, I have suggested that anyone newly coming on Shakespeare, and finding the language difficult, might do well to adopt several strategies. One is to see the play that interests you, or is assigned for class study, in performance. Many excellent film interpretations are available on film or in video, and are discussed in Appendix 4 at the end of this volume. Good actors can make a Shakespeare play seem entirely intelligible and moving.

Another approach is to read the play to oneself, or aloud with friends, without at first consulting the notes, taking the play it as it comes, as a script for performance. Hear Shakespeare's words in your head. Ask, as you read, why the characters are saying what they say, to one another or to themselves. What is motivating their arguments, their pleadings with one another, their boasts, their anxieties? Shakespeare is wonderful at creating character. Listen for verbal traits that distinguish them one from another. How do Romeo's vocabulary and images differ from those of Juliet? In what ways does Juliet's father, old Capulet, create such a distinctive impression of who he is by the way he goes about determining that his only daughter will marry a young man of his choice? In what ways does Hermia's father, old Egeus, define himself for us in *A Midsummer Night's Dream* by his equally stubborn insistence that Hermia marry his choice, Demetrius, rather than the young man she loves, Lysander? How is King Claudius, in *Hamlet*, revealed to us by his suave explanations as to why he has so quickly married his widowed sister-in-law after the unexpected and sudden death of her husband, Claudius's older brother?

Because Shakespeare's characters live so vividly in the ways they speak, our job as readers of his plays is to stage a given play in our minds as we read. Imagine yourself as director, coaching the actors as to whether they should at various times speak tenderly, or ironically, or angrily, or in a sullen whisper or defiant outburst. In your imagination as you read, try to hear what characters are arguing about. What is at issue? Why do things matter to them? What is

Juliet thinking about when she gives such evasive answers to her father about his plans for her to marry Count Paris? What is Romeo thinking about when he has slain Juliet's cousin Tybalt in a street quarrel and must now face the certainty of his being punished for that homicide? How does Shakespeare go about portraying through the spoken word the anguish of a young man who knows that he has betrayed his vows of undying loyalty to Juliet?

Such questions prompt others that we must think about as we read. What is it that has prompted Romeo to refuse to fight the angry Tybalt at first but then to challenge Tybalt to a duel in revenge for Tybalt's having slain Romeo's dear friend Mercutio? The emotional necessity of avenging that deed, Romeo's wish to show himself manly in a quarrel—how are these considerations balanced off against his promises to Juliet?

Shakespeare loves hard questions. Is misfortune partly to blame for the tragic outcome of *Romeo and Juliet*, particularly when the letter written by Friar Lawrence to Romeo in banishment fails to reach him in time, or is the tragedy centered around Romeo's ill-considered killing of Tybalt, or is the tragic cause to be found more in the long-standing quarrel setting Capulets against Montagues? Shakespeare not only loves hard questions, he refuses to give simple answers. Does Hamlet hesitate to avenge his father's murder because he is emotionally confused or because the very nature of action requires careful deliberation? Why is Claudius, in *Hamlet*, unable to pray that he be forgiven for having murdered his own brother? Did Queen Gertrude have any foreknowledge of this crime before it was committed?

Hard questions like these require careful reading, but they also should add real excitement to the adventure of reading Shakespeare. He challenges us at every turn. The rewards are that we are invited by Shakespeare into consideration of issues that matter deeply to us as human beings: love, friendship, physical attraction, marriage, jealousy, self-betrayal, inconstancy, forgiveness, fear of death, renunciation, affirmation, and so much else.

When Shakespeare wrote his plays and poems, some four centuries ago, the English language was in transition from the Middle English of Geoffrey Chaucer to the modern English we speak and read today. Chaucer's English is notably different from ours, though still recognizably the same language. The opening of *The Canterbury Tales* reads as follows:

Whan that April with his shoures soote
The droghte of March hath perced to the roote,

that is to say,

When April with its sweet showers
Has pierced to the root the drought of March.

Shakespeare's English, sometimes called Early Modern English, is more familiar than that, and is assisted too by the fact that Shakespeare editions today generally modernize spellings and pronunciation. This present edition does so. We can modernize Shakespeare in a way that isn't quite possible with Chaucer, because Shakespeare is closer to modern English.

Still, differences are marked. Shakespeare regularly uses "he hath" and "she hath" for "he has" and "she has." He uses a personal form in the second-person singular that we have lost: "thou art" for "you are," "I would thou wert" for "I wish you would," "How camest thou" for "How did you come." Many European languages, including French, Italian, Spanish, and German, retain the personal form here, as an intimate form of address among family and friends, and Quakers do so still in English, but the rest of us have lost that personal form of address. In so doing, we have lost a nuance of language that can be eloquently meaningful; expressions of tender feeling are marked as such by the personal pronoun.

What's more, Elizabethan language can express power relationships this way: parents address their children as "thee" and "thou," while children show their respect for parents by using the more formal "you." Addressing someone who is not a family member or intimate friend as "thou" can be terribly insulting. When Tybalt says to Mercutio, in Act 3, scene 1 of *Romeo and Juliet*, "Mercutio, thou consortest with Romeo" (line 44), Mercutio correctly interprets this as offensive and so a fight begins. And when Romeo, now married to Tybalt's cousin Juliet, though without Tybalt's knowledge, uses the personal pronoun to Tybalt as a kinsman by marriage ("Tybalt, the reason that I have to love thee," etc., lines 61 ff.), Tybalt misinterprets this as an insult. "Boy," he shouts back, "this shall not excuse the injuries / That thou hast done me," etc., lines 65 ff.). "Boy" is deeply insulting, too. As readers of Shakespeare, we need to learn to read these linguistic signals.

Colloquial expressions change rapidly in any language, and for that reason the colloquialisms in Shakespeare are apt to sound unfamiliar. "Marry, come up, I trow," says the Nurse in *Romeo and Juliet* (2.5.62), meaning something like "Goodness gracious, what's all this fuss about?" It is an exclamation of impatient reproof, occasioned by what Juliet has just said to the Nurse. "Marry" is a common mild oath, originally meaning "By the Virgin Mary." "Go to" is a familiar expostulation, as when Capulet is rebuking his nephew Tybalt for creating dissension over Romeo's having crashed the dance at the Capulets' house. "Go to, go to," says Capulet, "You are a saucy boy" (1.5.83–4). The Nurse's speech is full of colloquialisms: "by the rood" ("by Christ's cross"), "by my halidom" ("by all things holy," but confused popularly with "by my Holy Dame"), "now by my maidenhead at twelve year old" ("now by the virginity I still had when I was twelve"), "Nay, I do bear a brain" ("My memory is as keen as can be"), and much more (1.3.1–44). These col-

orful speech patterns help characterize the Nurse as of lower social station than the Capulets whom she serves. The commentary notes and glossary can help with unfamiliar speech patterns of this sort.

Shakespeare's impressively large vocabulary contains many words no longer current in English, and, to complicate matters still further, sometimes look familiar but with a different meaning in Shakespeare's day. *An* and *An if* can both mean "if." *Wherefore* means "why." *Withal* usually simply means "with." Sometimes words convey their modern meaning along with others that are lost. *Brave* can mean "gallant, full of courage," but it more commonly means "elegantly dressed, decked out in finery," or simply "splendid." *Fond* can be tricky for us today: "fond of" can mean having a fond feeling for someone or something, but "fond" is more likely to mean "foolish, doting." *Travel* often suggests both "journey" and "hard labor, travail"; the common early spelling, "trauaile," captures the fruitful ambiguity. *Large* can mean "large" in our sense; it also suggests "liberal, bounteous, lavish." *Liberal* has a similar multiplicity of meanings: "genteel, wellborn, refined, free of speech, unrestrained, licentious." *Front* can mean "forehead." A *humor* is a mood, fancy, temperament, cast of mind; it can also be one of the four "humors" of the body that determine temperament. *Like* can mean "likely," as in Juliet's "If he be marrièd, / My grave is like to be my wedding bed" (1.5.135-6). The notes and glossary are helpful here, buttressed by an awareness on the part of the reader that terms can mean something quite apart from their normal meaning today.

Shakespeare often writes in verse, though he is also a master of prose. Verse takes getting used to. Shakespeare's favorite verse form by far is the so-called blank-verse line, in iambic pentameter. That means that each line has essentially five "feet," or metrical units. "Penta" means five, from the Latin. The "feet" in this verse form have two syllables each, normally with no stress on the first syllable and a stress on the second. Words like "todáy," "remárk," "imménse," and "suppóse" are all naturally iambic; we stress the second syllables of these words when we talk. Iambic pentameter is a verse form that more closely approximates the rhythms of English speech than other verse forms; that is presumably why it is so often used by English poets and dramatists.

Shakespeare's blank verse, then, normally has ten syllables per line, with five stresses interspersed with unaccented syllables. Here is an example from Romeo's first speech as he enters the garden below Juliet's window in Act 2, scene 2 of *Romeo and Juliet*. He is alone on stage:

> But sóft, what líght through yónder wíndow bréaks?
> It ís the éast, and Júliet ís the sún.
> Aríse, fair sún, and kíll the énvious móon,
> Who ís alréady síck and pále with gríef
> That thóu her máid art fár more fáir than shé.

We can observe here that words of more than one syllable are placed so that the stress falls on the right syllable: yónder wíndow, Júliet, Aríse, énvious, alréady. Actually, two of these words have three syllables of which the third is an added unaccented syllable: Júliet, énvious, both spoken almost as in two syllables. A certain delicate variation in the pattern of unstressed/stressed can help prevent a sing-song effect. Then we note that the important words are stressed: sóft, líght, bréaks, ís, éast, sún, kíll, móon, síck, pále, gríef, thóu, máid, fár, fáir, shé. These words are nouns, pronouns, verbs, and adjectives. Left generally unstressed are functional words such as prepositions and conjunctions: through, and, with.

SHAKESPEARE'S LANGUAGE

How are we as readers to proceed, in view of these unfamiliar qualities of Shakespeare's English? As we've already suggested, watching a film or video can be a good place to start, along with a reading to oneself or with friends that continually asks the questions, who are these characters that speak, and why are they speaking as they do? What are they arguing about? Other questions need to be considered as well. Again, it can be helpful to imagine oneself as a director of a production. We as readers have to stage the play in our imaginations.

Where is the action taking place in any given scene, and why are the characters here? Shakespeare is wonderfully helpful at giving us the information we need, if we read carefully; everything is to be found in what the characters say. Why does Shakespeare begin *Hamlet* with two guardsmen nervously talking to each other about their relieving of the watch? We learn shortly that it is midnight, and that the weather is very cold; the actors tell us this. Why are they so apprehensive? What is about to happen? A ghost suddenly appears. Whose spirit is this, and why is it walking in Denmark in the dead of night? What does the Ghost look like? What is it wearing? We learn shortly that it appears "in the same figure like the King that's dead." What King? How did he die? The men on watch, now joined by Hamlet's friend Horatio, agree that the resemblance of this Ghost to the dead king is striking. But why will the Ghost not answer Horatio's asking the Ghost why it has thus appeared in such a frightening shape? Why is it important that Horatio is a "scholar" if he is to speak to this Ghost?

The play thus begins with many unanswered questions, creating a sense of mystery and dread. But as we read, the conversation of the men on watch provides some answers. The dead Danish king, Hamlet's father, had fought and won a duel with the King of Norway, thereby obliging Norway to become a client state of Denmark; now that the Danish king has suddenly died,

the Norwegian King's nephew, Fortinbras, is bent on invading Denmark to recover Norway's lost rights. Denmark is busy arming itself to resist that invasion. If as readers we concentrate on what we are learning that is necessary to the plot, the difficulties of language should fall into place.

What props are needed for this scene? We are not actually putting together a production as we read, so that we need not worry about practicalities that would be considered in the shop creating costumes and props, but we need to bring the scene alive in our imaginations as we read. What weapons are the guards carrying as they challenge one another and then the Ghost? The weapon is called a "partisan" in line 144; a note in the edition will explain that this is a long-handled spear, much like the halberd or battle-axe with a sharp pike that is mentioned elsewhere in Shakespeare. The particular weapon matters less than how it is deployed. Why is it that the guards' attempts to strike at it with their partisans are ineffectual? Presumably the Ghost is a disembodied spirit. The actors can easily mime an action of swinging at the Ghost, missing him but in such a way that the visual impression for the audience is one of invulnerability.

What does it mean when we learn, in scene 2, that the Ghost "wore his beaver up" and that he bore a countenance "more in sorrow than in anger"? Why are we told that "His beard was grizzled," that is, "A sable silvered," just as when old King Hamlet was still alive? These are telling details to which we want to pay attention as we read. They suggest here that the Ghost's face was indeed visible to the audience and to the Guard in scene 1, because the visor of his helmet was in its upright position, allowing the wearer to be seen. The details help confirm that this was indeed the ghost of the dead king. The very fact of the Ghost's having appeared in armor was presumably a signal of the warlike state of Denmark as well as pointing to Hamlet senior's warlike valor and armed might. All these details are revealing as we read.

Horatio presumably is not dressed like the ordinary guardsmen on duty, even if he is probably cloaked against the cold. Horatio is a gentleman. Class differences were visibly marked by costume in Shakespeare's day, and, as we read, we would do well to be sensitive to such differences. In the play's second scene, we should note that Hamlet is dressed in mourning black, whereas evidently the courtiers and their new king and queen have set aside black for something more colorful. As the new king has said to them, it has befitted the court to mourn a royal death for a time, but the time has come to move toward something more normal and even festive, mixing "mirth in funeral" and "dirge in marriage." These signals are eloquent testimonials to the haste with which Claudius has married his brother's widow. To Hamlet, such haste is unseemly, even outrageous; to the King and his court, the time has come to move on. As readers, we must be attuned to these visible distinctions. Costuming can at once enable an audience to distinguish a king from a Franciscan friar or a soothsayer or an apothecary or a fairy. We as readers must supply these staging requirements with our thoughts if we are to savor properly the gradations of rank that were so integral a part of courtly life in the Elizabethan era.

Reading a play differs in these matters from reading a short story or a novel. In such prose genres, the author has ample opportunity to spell out for the readers exactly how persons are dressed, where they live, what personal habits they practice, and the rest. Drama, and especially the highly poetic drama of an author like Shakespeare, must convey the story through dialogue. Stage directions can be provided, of course, although they tend to be sparse in the drama of Shakespeare because he was an actor in the company for which he wrote, and was thus at hand to help with blocking, gesture, inflections of speech, and the like. Reading today these scripts that were written for an acting company some 400 years ago invites us to write our own stage directions, in effect.

When the Chorus of *Henry V* opens the play with an appeal to his audience, his words are wonderfully pertinent to us as attentive readers. This is part of what he says:

> On your imaginary forces work.
> Suppose within the girdles of these walls
> Are now contained two mighty monarchies,
> Whose high upreareéd and abutting fronts
> The perilous narrow ocean parts asunder.
> Piece out our imperfections with your thoughts:
> Into a thousand parts divide one man,
> And make imaginary puissance.
> Think, when we talk of horses, that you see them
> Printing their proud hoofs i'th' receiving earth.
> For 'tis your thoughts that now must deck our kings,
> Carry them here and there, jumping o'er times,
> Turning the accomplishments of many years
> Into an hourglass.

This is precisely what we must do as readers. Theatrical performance, in Shakespeare's view, is a kind of shorthand, a set of clues that we as readers (or viewers in the theater) much augment with our imaginative reconstruction of how the whole thing is to look and sound and take on meaning. We must visualize horses when they are talked about. We must suppose a world of human action that can encompass a battle between two kingdoms, or between two families, or indeed between the elemental forces of good and evil. We must "piece out" the imperfections of a stage presentation or the dramatist's script with our thoughts, making "imaginary puissance." We must understand that actions of several years can be compressed "into an hourglass"—a shorthand expression for the time needed for performance. Our sense of place must be equally flexible, as we move

from Venice to Cyprus in *Othello* or from the royal court to Scotland and thence to England's southwest counties and finally to Dover cliffs in the course of *King Lear*.

Once you have read through the play in this way of bringing it to life as a theatrical experience, and have (if possible) supplemented that journey by savoring the play in a good performance in film or video (or, best of all, on stage if a production is available), you will then be in a good position to go back through the play with the assistance of the notes and commentary, including the Introduction. The information here can be invaluable, and will, we hope, enrich and test the perceptions you have already begun to form in your first reading. The reason I am suggesting that you postpone the notes to this second stage is that you should first try to enjoy the play as performance, just as you would if you were seeing it on stage or in film, even if seeing it for the first time. Let it roll over you as you react to its power, its humor, its brilliant insights. Shakespeare's plays work splendidly for those who encounter them for the first time in performance. Do what you can to give yourself that pleasure. For now, when the language seems difficult, go right on and listen to what is being said.

For a more detailed essay on the topic we have been discussing here, with illustrations from *A Midsummer Night's Dream, Romeo and Juliet, 1 Henry IV, Hamlet, King Lear*, and *The Tempest*, you might want to take a look at my *How to Read a Shakespeare Play* (Oxford: Blackwell Publishing, 2006). If you are interested in a further discussion of Shakespeare's style as it develops from his early to his late work, the pronunciation of Shakespeare's language in its own day, his conventions of grammar and rhetoric, and his vocabulary, I can refer you to earlier editions of *The Complete Works of Shakespeare* (sixth edition, 2008) or *The Necessary Shakespeare*; this present, shorter account of Shakespeare's English takes the place of those more specialized analyses. Similarly, the section in previous editions on "Editions and Editors of Shakespeare" is omitted here as of specialized interest; it too is available in those earlier editions.

SHAKESPEARE CRITICISM

In his own time, Shakespeare achieved a reputation for immortal greatness that is astonishing when we consider the low regard in which playwrights were then generally held. Francis Meres compared him to Ovid, Plautus, and Seneca, and proclaimed Shakespeare to be England's most excellent writer in both comedy and tragedy. John Weever spoke of "honey-tongued Shakespeare." The number of such praising allusions is high. Even Ben Jonson, a learned writer strongly influenced by the classical tradition, lauded Shakespeare as "a monument without a tomb," England's best poet, exceeding

Chaucer, Spenser, Beaumont, Kyd, and Marlowe. In tragedy, Jonson compared Shakespeare with Aeschylus, Euripides, and Sophocles; in comedy, he insisted Shakespeare had no rival even in "insolent Greece or haughty Rome." This tribute appeared in Jonson's commendatory poem written for the Shakespeare First Folio of 1623.

To be sure, Jonson had more critical things to say about Shakespeare. Even in the Folio commendatory poem, Jonson could not resist a dig at Shakespeare's "small Latin, and less Greek." To William Drummond of Hawthornden, he objected that Shakespeare "wanted art" because in a play (*The Winter's Tale*) he "brought in a number of men saying they had suffered shipwreck in Bohemia, where there is no sea near by some hundred miles." In *Timber, or Discoveries*, Jonson chided Shakespeare for his unrestrained facility in writing. "The players have often mentioned it as an honor to Shakespeare, that in his writing, whatsoever he penned he never blotted out [a] line. My answer hath been, would he had blotted a thousand." In a prologue to his own play, *Every Man in His Humor* (1616 edition), Jonson satirized English history plays (such as Shakespeare's) that "with three rusty swords, / And help of some few foot-and-half-foot words, / Fight over York and Lancaster's long jars, / And in the tiring-house bring wounds to scars." He also jeered at plays lacking unity of time in which children grow to the age of sixty or older and at nonsensical romantic plays featuring fireworks, thunder, and a chorus that "wafts you o'er the seas."

These criticisms are all of a piece. As a classicist himself, Jonson held in high regard the classical unities. He deplored much English popular drama, including some of Shakespeare's plays, for their undisciplined mixture of comedy and tragedy. Measured against his cherished ideals of classical decorum and refinement of language, Shakespeare's histories and the late romances—*Pericles, Cymbeline, The Winter's Tale,* and *The Tempest*—seemed irritatingly naive and loose-jointed. Yet Jonson knew that Shakespeare had an incomparable genius, superior even to his own. Jonson's affection and respect for Shakespeare seem to have been quite unforced. In the midst of his critical remarks in *Timber,* he freely conceded that "I loved the man, and do honor his memory (on this side idolatry) as much as any. He was indeed honest, and of an open and free nature, had an excellent fantasy, brave notions, and gentle expressions."

The Age of Dryden and Pope

Jonson's attitude toward Shakespeare lived on into the Restoration period of the late seventeenth century. A commonplace of that age held it proper to "admire" Ben Jonson but to "love" Shakespeare. Jonson was the more correct poet, the better model for imitation. Shakespeare often had to be rewritten according to the sophisticated tastes of the Restoration (see Appendix 3 for an account of Restoration stage adaptations of Shakespeare), but he

was also regarded as a natural genius. Dryden reflected this view in his *Essay of Dramatic Poesy* (1668) and his *Essay on the Dramatic Poetry of the Last Age* (1672). Dryden condemned *The Winter's Tale, Pericles,* and several other late romances for "the lameness of their plots" and for their "ridiculous incoherent story" which is usually "grounded on impossibilities." Not only Shakespeare, he charged, but several of his contemporaries "neither understood correct plotting nor that which they call *the decorum of the stage.*" Had Shakespeare lived in the Restoration, Dryden believed, he would doubtless have written "more correctly" under the influence of a language that had become more "courtly" and a wit that had grown more "refined." Shakespeare, he thought, had limitless "fancy" but sometimes lacked "judgment." Dryden regretted that Shakespeare had been forced to write in "ignorant" times and for audiences who "knew no better." Like Jonson, nevertheless, Dryden had the magnanimity to perceive that Shakespeare transcended his limitations. Shakespeare, said Dryden, was "the man who of all modern and perhaps ancient poets had the largest and most comprehensive soul." From a classical writer, this was high praise indeed.

Alexander Pope's edition of Shakespeare (1725) was based upon a similar estimate of Shakespeare as an untutored genius. Pope freely "improved" Shakespeare's language, rewriting lines and excising those parts he considered vulgar, in order to rescue Shakespeare from the barbaric circumstances of his Elizabethan milieu. Other critics of the Restoration and early eighteenth century who stressed Shakespeare's "natural" genius and imaginative powers were John Dennis, Joseph Addison, and the editors Nicholas Rowe and Lewis Theobald.

The Age of Johnson

Shakespeare was not without his detractors during the late seventeenth and early eighteenth centuries; after all, classical criticism tended to distrust imagination and fancy. Notable among the harsher critics of the Restoration period was Thomas Rymer, whose *Short View of Tragedy* (1692) included a famous attack on *Othello* for making too much out of Desdemona's handkerchief. In the eighteenth century, Voltaire spoke out sharply against Shakespeare's violation of the classical unities, though Voltaire also had some admiring things to say.

The most considered answer to such criticism in the later eighteenth century was that of Dr. Samuel Johnson, in his edition of Shakespeare's plays and its great preface (1765). Shakespeare, said Johnson, is the poet of nature who "holds up to his readers a faithful mirror of manners and of life. His characters are not modified by the customs of particular places, unpracticed by the rest of the world. . . . In the writings of other poets a character is too often an individual; in those of Shakespeare it is commonly a species." Johnson's attitudes were essentially classical in that he praised Shakespeare for being universal, for having provided a "just representation of general nature," and for having stood the test of time. Yet Johnson also magnanimously praised Shakespeare for having transcended the classical rules. Johnson triumphantly vindicated the mixture of comedy and tragedy in Shakespeare's plays and the supposed indecorum of his characters.

Of course, Johnson did not praise everything he saw. He objected to Shakespeare's loose construction of plot, careless huddling together of the ends of his plays, licentious humor, and, above all, the punning wordplay. He deplored Shakespeare's failure to satisfy the demands of poetic justice, especially in *King Lear,* and he regretted that Shakespeare seemed more anxious to please than to instruct. Still, Johnson did much to free Shakespeare from the constraint of an overly restrictive classical approach to criticism.

The Age of Coleridge

With the beginning of the Romantic period, in England and on the Continent, Shakespeare criticism increasingly turned away from classical precept in favor of a more spontaneous and enthusiastic approach to Shakespeare's creative genius. The new Shakespeare became indeed a rallying cry for those who now deplored such "regular" dramatic poets as Racine and Corneille. Shakespeare became a seer, a bard with mystic powers of insight into the human condition. Goethe, in *Wilhelm Meister* (1796), conceived of Hamlet as the archetypal "Romantic" poet: melancholic, delicate, and unable to act.

Critical trends in England moved toward similar conclusions. Maurice Morgann, in his *Essay on the Dramatic Character of Sir John Falstaff* (1777), glorified Falstaff into a rare individual of courage, dignity, and—yes—honor. To do so, Morgann had to suppress much evidence as to Falstaff's overall function in the *Henry IV* plays. Dramatic structure, in fact, did not interest him; his passion was "character," and his study of Falstaff reflected a new Romantic preoccupation with character analysis. Like other character critics who followed him, Morgann tended to move away from the play itself and into a world where the dramatic personage being considered might lead an independent existence. What would it have been like to know Falstaff as a real person? How would he have behaved on occasions other than those reported by Shakespeare? Such questions fascinated Morgann and others because they led into grand speculations about human psychology and philosophy. Shakespeare's incomparably penetrating insights into character prompted further investigations of the human psyche.

Other late eighteenth-century works devoted to the study of character included Lord Kames's *Elements of Criticism* (1762), Thomas Whately's *Remarks on Some of the Characters of Shakespeare* (1785), William Richardson's *Philosophical Analysis and Illustration of Some of Shakespeare's Remarkable Characters* (1774), and William Jackson's *Thirty Letters on Various Subjects* (1782). Morgann spoke for this school of critics when he insisted, "It may be fit to consider them [Shakespeare's characters] rather as historic than dramatic beings; and, when occasion requires, to account for their conduct from the whole of character, from general principles, from latent motives, and from policies not avowed."

Samuel Taylor Coleridge, the greatest of the English Romantic critics, was profoundly influenced by character criticism, both English and continental. He himself made important contributions to the study of character. His conception of Hamlet, derived in part from Goethe and Hegel, as one who "vacillates from sensibility, and procrastinates from thought, and loses the power of action in the energy of resolve," was to dominate nineteenth-century interpretations of Hamlet. His insight into Iago's evil nature—"the motive-hunting of a motiveless malignity"—was also influential.

Nevertheless, Coleridge did not succumb to the temptation, as did so many character critics, of ignoring the unity of an entire play. Quite to the contrary, he affirmed in Shakespeare an "organic form" or "innate" sense of shape, developed from within, that gave new meaning to Shakespeare's fusion of comedy and tragedy, his seeming anachronisms, his improbable fictions, and his supposedly rambling plots. Coleridge heaped scorn on the eighteenth-century idea of Shakespeare as a "natural" but untaught genius. He praised Shakespeare not for having mirrored life, as Dr. Johnson had said, but for having created an imaginative world attuned to its own internal harmonies. He saw Shakespeare as an inspired but deliberate artist who fitted together the parts of his imaginative world with consummate skill. "The judgment of Shakespeare is commensurate with his genius."

In all this, Coleridge was remarkably close to his German contemporary and rival, August Wilhelm Schlegel, who insisted that Shakespeare was "a profound artist, and not a blind and wildly luxuriant genius." In Shakespeare's plays, said Schlegel, "The fancy lays claim to be considered as an independent mental power governed according to its own laws." Between them, Coleridge and Schlegel utterly inverted the critical values of the previous age, substituting "sublimity" and "imagination" for universality and trueness to nature.

Other Romantic critics included William Hazlitt (*Characters of Shakespear's Plays,* 1817), Charles Lamb (*On the Tragedies of Shakespeare,* 1811), and Thomas De Quincey (*On the Knocking at the Gate in Macbeth,* 1823). Hazlitt reveals a political liberalism characteristic of a number of Romantic writers in his skeptical view of Henry V's absolutism and his imperialist war against the French. John Keats has some penetrating things to say in his letters about Shakespeare's "negative capability," or his ability to see into characters' lives with an extraordinary self-effacing sympathy. As a whole, the Romantics were enthusiasts of Shakespeare, and sometimes even idolaters. Yet they consistently refused to recognize him as a man of the theater. Lamb wrote, "It may seem a paradox, but I cannot help being of the opinion that the plays of Shakespeare are less calculated for performance on a stage than those of almost any other dramatist whatever." Hazlitt similarly observed: "We do not like to see our author's plays acted, and least of all, *Hamlet*. There is no play that suffers so much in being transferred to the stage." These hostile attitudes toward the theater reflected, in part, the condition of the stage in nineteenth-century England. In part, however, these attitudes were the inevitable result of character criticism, or what Lamb called the desire "to know the internal workings and movements of a great mind, of an Othello or a Hamlet for instance, the *when* and the *why* and the *how far* they should be moved." This fascination with character swept everything before it during the Romantic period.

A. C. Bradley and the Turn of the Century

The tendency of nineteenth-century criticism, then, was to exalt Shakespeare as a poet and a philosopher rather than as a playwright, and as a creator of immortal characters whose "lives" might be studied as though existing independent of a dramatic text. Not infrequently, this critical approach led to a biographical interpretation of Shakespeare through his plays, on the assumption that what he wrote was his own spiritual autobiography and a key to his own fascinating character. Perhaps the most famous critical study in this line was Edward Dowden's *Shakspere: A Critical Study of His Mind and Art* (1875), in which he traced a progression from Shakespeare's early exuberance and passionate involvement through brooding pessimism to a final philosophical calm.

At the same time, the nineteenth century also saw the rise of a more factual and methodological scholarship, especially in the German universities. Dowden, in fact, reflected this trend as well, for one of the achievements of philological study was to establish with some accuracy the dating of Shakespeare's plays and thus make possible an analysis of his artistic development. Hermann Ulrici's *Über Shakespeares dramatische Kunst* (1839) and Gott-fried Gervinus's edition of 1849 were among the earliest studies to interest themselves in Shakespeare's chronological development.

The critic who best summed up the achievement of nineteenth-century Shakespeare criticism was A. C. Bradley, in his *Shakespearean Tragedy* (1904) and other studies. *Shakespearean Tragedy* dealt with the four "great"

tragedies: *Hamlet, Othello, King Lear,* and *Macbeth.* Bradley revealed his Romantic tendencies in his focus on psychological analysis of character, but he also brought to his work a scholarly awareness of the text that had been missing in some earlier character critics. His work continues to have considerable influence today, despite modern tendencies to rebel against nineteenth-century idealism. To Bradley, Shakespeare's tragic world was ultimately explicable and profoundly moral. Despite the overwhelming impression of tragic waste in *King Lear,* he argued, we as audience experience a sense of compensation and completion that implies an ultimate pattern in human life. "Good, in the widest sense, seems thus to be the principle of life and health in the world; evil, at least in these worst forms, to be a poison. The world reacts against it violently, and, in the struggle to expel it, is driven to devastate itself." Humanity must suffer because of its fatal tendency to pursue some extreme passion, but humanity learns through suffering about itself and the nature of its world. We as audience are reconciled to our existence through purgative release; we smile through our tears. Cordelia is wantonly destroyed, but the fact of her transcendent goodness is eternal. Although in one sense she fails, said Bradley, she is "in another sense superior to the world in which [she] appears; is, in some way which we do not seek to define, untouched by the doom that overtakes [her]; and is rather set free from life than deprived of it."

Historical Criticism

The first major twentieth-century reaction against character criticism was that of the so-called historical critics. (On the later critical movement known as the New Historicism, see below, following "Jan Kott and the Theater of the Absurd.") These critics insisted on a more hardheaded and skeptical appraisal of Shakespeare through better understanding of his historical milieu: his theater, his audience, and his political and social environment. In good part, this movement was the result of a new professionalism of Shakespearean studies in the twentieth century. Whereas earlier critics—Dryden, Pope, Johnson, and Coleridge—had generally been literary amateurs in the best sense, early twentieth-century criticism became increasingly the province of those who taught in universities. Historical research became a professional activity. Bradley himself was Professor of English Literature at Liverpool and Oxford, and did much to legitimize the incorporation of Shakespeare into the humanities curriculum. German scholarship produced the first regular periodical devoted to Shakespeare studies, *Shakespeare-Jahrbuch,* to be followed in due course in England and America by *Shakespeare Survey* (beginning in 1948), *Shakespeare Quarterly* (1950), and *Shakespeare Studies* (1965).

From the start, historical criticism took a new look at Shakespeare as a man of the theater. Sir Walter Raleigh

(Professor of English Literature at Oxford, not to be confused with his Elizabethan namesake) rejected the Romantic absorption in psychology and turned his attention instead to the artistic methods by which plays affect theater-going spectators. The poet Robert Bridges insisted that Shakespeare had often sacrificed consistency and logic for primitive theatrical effects designed to please his vulgar audience. Bridges's objections were often based on a serious lack of information about Shakespeare's stage, but they had a healthy iconoclastic effect nonetheless on the scholarship of his time. In Germany, Levin Schücking pursued a similar line of reasoning in his *Character Problems in Shakespeare's Plays* (1917, translated into English in 1922). Schücking argued that Shakespeare had disregarded coherent structure and had striven instead for vivid dramatic effect ("episodic intensification") in his particular scenes. Schücking's *The Meaning of Hamlet* (1937) explained the strange contradictions of that play as resulting from primitive and brutal Germanic source materials which Shakespeare had not fully assimilated.

A keynote for historical critics of the early twentieth century was the concept of artifice or convention in the construction of a play. Perhaps the leading spokesman for this approach was E. E. Stoll, a student of G. L. Kittredge of Harvard University, himself a leading force in historical scholarship in America. Stoll vigorously insisted, in such works as *Othello: An Historical and Comparative Study* (1915), *Hamlet: An Historical and Comparative Study* (1919), and *Art and Artifice in Shakespeare* (1933), that a critic must never be sidetracked by moral, psychological, or biographical interpretations. A play, he argued, is an artifice arising out of its historical milieu. Its conventions are implicit agreements between playwright and spectator. They alter with time, and a modern reader who is ignorant of Elizabethan conventions is all too apt to be misled by his own post-Romantic preconceptions. For example, a calumniator like Iago in *Othello* is conventionally supposed to be believed by the other characters on stage. We do not need to speculate about the "realities" of Othello's being duped, and, in fact, we are likely to be led astray by such Romantic speculations. Stoll went so far as to affirm, in fact, that Shakespearean drama intentionally distorts reality through its theatrical conventions, in order to fulfill its own existence as artifice. *Hamlet* is not a play about delay, but a revenge story of a certain length, containing many conventional revenge motifs, such as the ghost and the "mousetrap" scheme used to test the villain, and deriving many of its circumstances from Shakespeare's sources; delay is a conventional device needed to continue the story to its conclusion.

Stoll's zeal led to excessive claims for historical criticism, as one might expect in the early years of a pioneering movement. At its extreme, historical criticism came close to implying that Shakespeare was a mere product of his environment. Indeed, the movement owed many of its evolutionist assumptions to the supposedly scientific "social Darwinism" of Thomas Huxley and other late nineteenth-century social philosophers. In more recent years, however, the crusading spirit has given way to a more moderate historical criticism that continues to be an important part of Shakespearean scholarship.

Alfred Harbage, for example, in *As They Liked It* (1947) and *Shakespeare and the Rival Traditions* (1952), has analyzed the audience for which Shakespeare wrote and the rivalry between popular and elite theaters in the London of his day. Harbage sees Shakespeare as a popular dramatist writing for a highly intelligent, enthusiastic, and socially diversified audience. More recently, in *The Privileged Playgoers of Shakespeare's London, 1576–1642* (1981), Ann Jennalie Cook has qualified Harbage's view, arguing that Shakespeare's audience was, for the most part, affluent and well connected. G. E. Bentley has amassed an invaluable storehouse of information about *The Jacobean and Caroline Stage* (1941–1968), just as E. K. Chambers earlier had collected documents and data on *The Elizabethan Stage* (1923). Other studies by these historical scholars include Chambers's *William Shakespeare: A Study of Facts and Problems* (1930), and Bentley's *Shakespeare and His Theatre* (1964) and *The Profession of Dramatist in Shakespeare's Time* (1971). T. W. Baldwin exemplifies the historical scholar who, like Stoll, claims too much for the method; nevertheless, much information on Shakespeare's schooling, reading, and professional theatrical life is available in such works as *William Shakspere's Small Latine and Lesse Greeke* (1944) and *The Organization and Personnel of the Shakespearean Company* (1927). Hardin Craig uses historical method in *An Interpretation of Shakespeare* (1948).

Historical criticism has contributed greatly to our knowledge of the staging of Shakespeare's plays. George Pierce Baker, in *The Development of Shakespeare as a Dramatist* (1907), continued the line of investigation begun by Walter Raleigh. Harley Granville-Barker brought to his *Prefaces to Shakespeare* (1930, 1946) a wealth of professional theatrical experience of his own. Ever since his time, the new theatrical method of interpreting Shakespeare has been based to an ever increasing extent on a genuine revival of interest in Shakespearean production. John Dover Wilson shows an awareness of the stage in *What Happens in Hamlet* (1935) and *The Fortunes of Falstaff* (1943). At its best, as in John Russell Brown's *Shakespeare's Plays in Performance* (1966), in John Styan's *Shakespeare's Stagecraft* (1967), in Michael Goldman's *Shakespeare and the Energies of Drama* (1972), and in Alan Dessen's *Elizabethan Drama and the Viewer's Eye* (1977) and his *Recovering Shakespeare's Theatrical Vocabulary* (1995), this critical method reveals many insights into the text that are hard to obtain without an awareness of theatrical technique.

Supporting this theatrical criticism, historical research has learned a great deal about the physical nature of Shakespeare's stage. J. C. Adams's well-known model of the Globe Playhouse, as presented in Irwin Smith's *Shakespeare's Globe Playhouse: A Modern Reconstruction* (1956), is now generally discredited in favor of a simpler building, as reconstructed by C. Walter Hodges (*The Globe Restored*, 1953, 2nd edition, 1968), Bernard Beckerman (*Shakespeare at the Globe*, 1962, 2nd edition, 1967), Richard Hosley ("The Playhouses and the Stage" in *A New Companion to Shakespeare Studies*, edited by K. Muir and S. Schoenbaum, 1971, and several other good essays), T. J. King (*Shakespearean Staging, 1599–1642*, 1971), and others. Information on the private theaters, such as the Blackfriars, where Shakespeare's plays were also performed, appears in William Armstrong, *The Elizabethan Private Theatres* (1958); Richard Hosley, "A Reconstruction of the Second Blackfriars" (*The Elizabethan Theatre*, 1969); Glynne Wickham, *Early English Stages* (1959–1972); and others. For further information on innyard theaters and on courtly or private theaters, see the contributions of Herbert Berry, D. F. Rowan, W. Reavley Gair, and others cited in the bibliography at the end of this volume.

A related pursuit of historical criticism has been the better understanding of Shakespeare through his dramatic predecessors and contemporaries. Willard Farnham, in *The Medieval Heritage of Elizabethan Tragedy* (1936), traces the evolution of native English tragedy through the morality plays of the early Tudor period. J. M. R. Margeson's *The Origins of English Tragedy* (1967) broadens the pattern to include still other sources for Elizabethan ideas on dramatic tragedy. Bernard Spivack, in *Shakespeare and the Allegory of Evil* (1958), sees Iago, Edmund, Richard III, and other boasting villains in Shakespeare as descendants of the morality Vice. In *Shakespeare and the Idea of the Play* (1962), Anne Righter (Barton) traces the device of the play-within-the-play and the metaphor of the world as a stage back to medieval and classical ideas of dramatic illusion. Irving Ribner's *The English History Play in the Age of Shakespeare* (1959, revised 1965) examines Shakespeare's plays on English history in the context of the popular Elizabethan genre to which they belonged. Robert Weimann's *Shakespeare and the Popular Tradition in the Theatre* (translated from the German in 1978) is a Marxist study in the social dimension of dramatic form and function. Many other studies of this sort could be cited, including Glynne Wickham's *Shakespeare's Dramatic Heritage* (1969), Oscar J. Campbell's *Shakespeare's Satire* (1943), M. C. Bradbrook's *Themes and Conventions of Elizabethan Tragedy* (1935), and S. L. Bethell's *Shakespeare and the Popular Dramatic Tradition* (1944).

Another important concern of historical criticism has been the relationship between Shakespeare and the ideas of his age—cosmological, philosophical, and political.

Among the first scholars to study Elizabethan cosmology were Hardin Craig in *The Enchanted Glass* (1936) and A. O. Lovejoy in *The Great Chain of Being* (1936). As their successor, E. M. W. Tillyard provided in *The Elizabethan World Picture* (1943) a definitive view of the conservative and hierarchical values that Elizabethans were supposed to have espoused. In *Shakespeare's History Plays* (1944), Tillyard extended his essentially conservative view of Shakespeare's philosophical outlook to the histories, arguing that they embody a "Tudor myth" and thereby lend support to the Tudor state. Increasingly, however, critics have disputed the extent to which Shakespeare in fact endorsed the "establishment" values of the Elizabethan world picture. Theodore Spencer, in *Shakespeare and the Nature of Man* (1942), discusses the impact on Shakespeare of radical new thinkers like Machiavelli, Montaigne, and Copernicus. In political matters, Henry A. Kelly's *Divine Providence in the England of Shakespeare's Histories* (1970) has challenged the existence of a single "Tudor myth" and has argued that Shakespeare's history plays reflect contrasting political philosophies set dramatically in conflict with one another. M. M. Reese's *The Cease of Majesty* (1961) also offers a graceful corrective to Tillyard's lucid but occasionally one-sided interpretations. Revisions in this direction continue in the work of the so-called new historicists and cultural materialists, to be discussed below.

Historical criticism has also yielded many profitable specialized studies, in which Shakespeare is illuminated by a better understanding of various sciences of his day. Lily Bess Campbell approaches Shakespearean tragedy through Renaissance psychology in *Shakespeare's Tragic Heroes: Slaves of Passion* (1930). Paul Jorgensen uses Elizabethan documents on the arts of war and generalship in his study *Shakespeare's Military World* (1956). Many similar studies examine Shakespeare in relation to law, medicine, and other professions.

"New" Criticism

As we have seen, historical criticism is still an important part of Shakespeare criticism; for better or worse, it is the stuff of some research-oriented universities and their Ph.D. programs. Since its beginning, however, historical criticism has had to face a critical reaction, generated, in part, by its own utilitarian and fact-gathering tendencies. The suggestions urged by Stoll and others that Shakespeare was the product of his cultural and theatrical environment tended to obscure his achievement as a poet. Amassing of information about Shakespeare's reading or his theatrical company often seemed to inhibit the scholar from responding to the power of words and images.

Such at any rate was the rallying cry of the *Scrutiny* group in England, centered on F. R. Leavis, L. C. Knights, and Derek Traversi, and the "new" critics in America, such as Cleanth Brooks. The new critics demanded close attention to the poetry without the encumbrance of historical research. Especially at first, the new critics were openly hostile to any criticism distracting readers from the text. The satirical force of the movement can perhaps best be savored in L. C. Knights's "How Many Children Had Lady Macbeth?" (1933), prompted by the learned appendices in Bradley's *Shakespearean Tragedy*: "When was the murder of Duncan first plotted? Did Lady Macbeth really faint? Duration of the action in *Macbeth*. Macbeth's age. 'He has no children.'"

In part, the new critical movement was (and still is) a pedagogical movement, a protest against the potential dryness of historical footnoting and an insistence that classroom study of Shakespeare ought to focus on a response to his language. Cleanth Brooks's "The Naked Babe and the Cloak of Manliness" (in *The Well Wrought Urn*, 1947) offers to the teacher a model of close reading that focuses on imagery and yet attempts to see a whole vision of the play through its language. G. Wilson Knight concentrates on imagery and verbal texture, sometimes to the exclusion of the play as a whole, in his *The Wheel of Fire* (1930), *The Imperial Theme* (1931), *The Shakespearian Tempest* (1932), *The Crown of Life* (1947), and others. William Empson is best known for his *Seven Types of Ambiguity* (1930) and *Some Versions of Pastoral* (1935). Derek Traversi's works include *An Approach to Shakespeare* (1938), *Shakespeare: The Last Phase* (1954), *Shakespeare: From Richard II to Henry V* (1957), and *Shakespeare: The Roman Plays* (1963). Perhaps the greatest critic of this school has been L. C. Knights, whose books include *Explorations* (1946), *Some Shakespearean Themes* (1959), *An Approach to Hamlet* (1960), and *Further Explorations* (1965). T. S. Eliot's perceptive and controversial observations have also had an important influence on critics of this school. Other studies making good use of the new critical method include Robert Heilman's *This Great Stage* (1948) and *Magic in the Web* (1956). Many of these critics are concerned not only with language, but also with the larger moral and structural implications of Shakespeare's plays as discovered through a sensitive reading of the text.

More specialized studies of Shakespearean imagery and language include Caroline Spurgeon's *Shakespeare's Imagery and What It Tells Us* (1935). Its classifications are now recognized to be overly statistical and restricted in definition, but the work has nonetheless prompted valuable further study. Among later works are Sister Miriam Joseph's *Shakespeare's Use of the Arts of Language* (1947, partly reprinted in *Rhetoric in Shakespeare's Time*, 1962), Wolfgang Clemen's *The Development of Shakespeare's Imagery* (1951), and M. M. Mahood's *Shakespeare's Wordplay* (1957). The study of prose has not received as much attention as that of poetry, although Brian Vickers's *The Artistry of Shakespeare's Prose* (1968) and Milton Crane's *Shakespeare's Prose* (1951) make significant contributions.

See also Edward Armstrong's *Shakespeare's Imagination* (1963) and Kirby Farrell's *Shakespeare's Creation: The Language of Magic and Play* (1975).

A more recent development in studies of Shakespeare's imagery has led to the examination of visual images in the theater as part of Shakespeare's art. Reginald Foakes ("Suggestions for a New Approach to Shakespeare's Imagery," *Shakespeare Survey*, 5, 1952, 81–92) and Maurice Charney (*Shakespeare's Roman Plays: The Function of Imagery in the Drama*, 1961) were among the first to notice that Caroline Spurgeon and other "new" critics usually excluded stage picture in their focus on verbal image patterns. Yet Shakespeare's extensive involvement with the practicalities of theatrical production might well lead one to suspect that he arranges his stage with care and that the plays are full of hints as to how he communicates through visual means. Costume, properties, the theater building, the blocking of actors in visual patterns onstage, expression, movement—all of these contribute to the play's artistic whole. Francis Fergusson analyzes the way in which the Elizabethan theatrical building provides *Hamlet* with an eloquently expressive idea of order and hierarchy, against which are ironically juxtaposed Claudius's acts of killing a king and marrying his widow (*The Idea of a Theater*, 1949). Other studies of stage imagery include Ann Pasternak Slater's *Shakespeare the Director* (1982) and David Bevington's *Action Is Eloquence: Shakespeare's Language of Gesture* (1984).

Another call for expansion of the occasionally narrow limits of "new" criticism comes from the so-called Chicago school of criticism, centered on R. S. Crane, Richard McKeon, Elder Olson, Bernard Weinberg, and others, who, in the 1950s and 1960s, espoused a formal or structural approach to criticism, using Aristotle as its point of departure. Crane was reacting to the new critics who, in his view, restricted the kinds of answers they could obtain by limiting themselves to one methodology. Critics hostile to the Chicago school have responded, to be sure, that Crane's own approach tends to produce its own dogmatism. Formalist analyses of Shakespeare plays are to be found, for example, in the work of W. R. Keast, Wayne Booth, and Norman Maclean; see *Critics and Criticism*, edited by R. S. Crane (1952) and the bibliography at the back of this book.

Psychological Criticism

In a sense, Freudian and other psychological criticism continues the "character" criticism of the nineteenth century. Freudian critics sometimes follow a character into a world outside the text, analyzing Hamlet (for instance) as though he were a real person whose childhood traumas can be inferred from the symptoms he displays. The most famous work in this vein is *Hamlet and Oedipus* (1910, revised 1949), by Freud's disciple, Ernest Jones. According to Jones, Hamlet's delay is caused by an oedipal trauma. Hamlet's uncle, Claudius, has done exactly what Hamlet himself incestuously and subconsciously wished to do: kill his father and marry his mother. Because he cannot articulate these forbidden impulses to himself, Hamlet is paralyzed into inactivity. Jones's critical analysis thus assumes, as did such Romantic critics as Coleridge, that the central problem of *Hamlet* is one of character and motivation: why does Hamlet delay? Many modern critics would deny that this is a problem or would insist, at least, that by setting such a problem, Jones has limited the number of possible answers. Avi Erlich proposes an entirely different psychological reading of the play in *Hamlet's Absent Father*, 1977. Psychological criticism sometimes also reveals its affinities with nineteenth-century character criticism in its attempt to analyze Shakespeare's personality through his plays, as though the works constituted a spiritual autobiography. The terminology of psychological criticism is suspect to some readers because it is at least superficially anachronistic when dealing with a Renaissance writer. The terminology is also sometimes overburdened with technical jargon.

Nonetheless, psychological criticism has afforded many insights into Shakespeare not readily available through other modes of perception. Jones's book makes clear the intensity of Hamlet's revulsion toward women as a result of his mother's inconstancy. At a mythic level, Hamlet's story certainly resembles that of Oedipus, and Freudian criticism is often at its best when it shows us this universal aspect of the human psyche. Freudian terminology need not be anachronistic when it deals with timeless truths. Psychological criticism can reveal to us Shakespeare's preoccupation with certain types of women in his plays, such as the domineering and threatening masculine type (Joan of Arc, Margaret of Anjou) or, conversely, the long-suffering and patient heroine (Helena in *All's Well*, Hermione in *The Winter's Tale*). Psychological criticism is perhaps most useful in studying family relationships in Shakespeare. It also has much to say about the psychic or sexual connotations of symbols. Influential books include Norman O. Brown's *Life Against Death: The Psychoanalytical Meaning of History* (1959) and Norman Holland's *Psychoanalysis and Shakespeare* (1966) and *The Shakespearean Imagination* (1964).

Richard Wheeler's *Turn and Counter-Turn: Shakespeare's Development and the Problem Comedies* (1981) applies psychoanalytic method to a study of Shakespeare's development, in which, as Wheeler sees it, the sonnets and the problem plays are pivotal as Shakespeare turns from the safely contained worlds of romantic comedy (with nonthreatening heroines) and the English history play (in which women are generally denied anything more than a marginal role in state affairs) to the tragedies, in which sexual conflict is shown in all its potentially terrifying destructiveness. Wheeler's completion of C. L. Barber's *The Whole*

Journey: Shakespeare's Power of Development (1986) continues the study of Shakespeare's development in the late plays. The dichotomies of gender and genre urged in these studies and continued by Linda Bamber (*Comic Women, Tragic Men: A Study of Gender and Genre in Shakespeare*, 1982), among others, have been challenged by Jonathan Goldberg in his essay, "Shakespearean Inscriptions: The Voicing of Power," in *Shakespeare and the Question of Theory* (edited by Patricia Parker and Geoffrey Hartman, 1985). A collection of essays under the editorship of Murray Schwartz and Coppélia Kahn, *Representing Shakespeare* (1980), affords a sample of work by Janet Adelman, David Wilbern, Meredith Skura, David Sundelson, Madelon Gohlke Sprengnether, Joel Fineman, and others.

Much psychoanalytic criticism of the 1980s has sought to displace Freud's emphasis upon the relation of son and father in the oedipal triangle in favor of attention to the mother and child preoedipal relation; a model here is the work of Karen Horney (e.g., *Neurosis and Human Growth: The Struggle Toward Self-Realization*, 1950). Jacques Lacan (*Écrits*, translated by Alan Sheridan, 1977) and Erik Erikson (*Childhood and Selfhood*, 1978) are also prominent theorists in the post-Freudian era. Despite such changes, the psychoanalytic critic still attempts to discover in the language of the play the means by which he or she can reconstruct an early stage in the development of one or more of the dramatic characters.

Mythological Criticism

Related to psychological criticism is the search for archetypal myth in literature, as an expression of the "collective unconscious" of the human race. Behind such an approach lie the anthropological and psychological assumptions of Jung and his followers. One of the earliest studies of this sort was Gilbert Murray's *Hamlet and Orestes* (1914), analyzing the archetype of revenge for a murdered father. Clearly this custom goes far back into tribal prehistory and emerges in varying but interrelated forms in many different societies. This anthropological universality enables us to look at Hamlet as the heightened manifestation of an incredibly basic story. *Hamlet* gives shape to urgings that are a part of our innermost social being. The struggle between the civilized and the primitive goes on in us as in the play *Hamlet*.

The vast interdisciplinary character of mythological criticism leaves it vulnerable to charges of speculativeness and glib theorizing. At its best, however, mythological criticism can illuminate the nature of our responses as audience to a work of art. Northrop Frye argues, in *A Natural Perspective* (1965), that we respond to mythic patterns by imagining ourselves participating in them communally. The Greek drama emerged, after all, from Dionysiac ritual. All drama celebrates in one form or another the primal myths of vegetation, from the death of the year to the renewal or resurrection of life. In his most influential book, *Anatomy of Criticism* (1957), Frye argues that mythic criticism presents a universal scheme for the investigation of all literature, or all art, since art is itself the ordering of our most primal stirrings. Frye sees in drama (as in other literature) a fourfold correspondence to the cyclical pattern of the year: comedy is associated with spring, romance with summer, tragedy with autumn, and satire with winter. Historically, civilization moves through a recurrent cycle from newness to decadence and decay; this cycle expresses itself culturally in a progression from epic and romance to tragedy, to social realism, and, finally, to irony and satire before the cycle renews itself. Thus, according to Frye, the genres of dramatic literature (and of other literary forms as well) have an absolute and timeless relationship to myth and cultural history. That is why we as audience respond so deeply to form and meaning as contained in genre. C. L. Barber, in *Shakespeare's Festive Comedy* (1959), makes a similar argument: our enjoyment of comedy arises from our intuitive appreciation of such "primitive" social customs as Saturnalian revels, May games, and fertility rites. John Holloway offers an anthropological study of Shakespeare's tragedies in *The Story of the Night* (1961).

Frye's critical system has not been without its detractors. For example, Frederick Crews (*Psychoanalysis and Literary Process*, 1970) argues that Frye's system is too self-contained in its ivory tower and too much an abstract artifact of the critical mind to be "relevant" to the social purposes of art. Nevertheless, Frye continues to be one of the most influential critics of the late twentieth century.

Typological Criticism

Another controversy of the later twentieth century has to do with the Christian interpretation of Shakespeare. Do the images and allusions of Shakespeare's plays show him to be deeply immersed in a Christian culture inherited from the Middle Ages? Does he reveal a typological cast of mind, so common in medieval literature, whereby a story can suggest through analogy a universal religious archetype? For example, does the mysterious Duke in *Measure for Measure* suggest to us a God figure, hovering unseen throughout the play to test human will and then to present humanity with an omniscient but merciful judgment? Is the wanton slaughter of the good Cordelia in *King Lear* reminiscent of the Passion of Christ? Can Portia in *The Merchant of Venice* be seen as an angelic figure descending from Belmont into the fallen human world of Venice? Often the operative question we must ask is: "How far should such analogy be pursued?" Richard II unquestionably likens himself to Christ betrayed by the disciples, and at times the play evokes images of Adam banished from Paradise, but do these allusions coalesce into a sustained analogy?

Among the most enthusiastic searchers after Christian meaning are J. A. Bryant, in *Hippolyta's View* (1961); Roy Battenhouse, in *Shakespearean Tragedy: Its Art and Christian Premises* (1969); and R. Chris Hassel, in *Renaissance Drama and the English Church* (1979) and *Faith and Folly in Shakespeare: Romantic Comedies* (1980). Their efforts have encountered stern opposition, however. One notable dissenter is Roland M. Frye, whose *Shakespeare and Christian Doctrine* (1963) argues that Shakespeare cannot be shown to have known much Renaissance theology and that, in any case, his plays are concerned with human drama rather than with otherworldly questions of damnation or salvation. Frye's argument stresses the incompatibility of Christianity and tragedy, as does also D. G. James's *The Dream of Learning* (1951) and Clifford Leech's *Shakespeare's Tragedies and Other Studies in Seventeenth-Century Drama* (1950). Virgil Whitaker's *The Mirror Up to Nature* (1965) sees religion as an essential element in Shakespeare's plays but argues that Shakespeare uses the religious knowledge of his audience as a shortcut to characterization and meaning, rather than as an ideological weapon. The controversy will doubtless long continue, even though the typological critics have had to assume a defensive posture.

Jan Kott and the Theater of the Absurd

At an opposite extreme from the Christian idealism of most typological critics is the iconoclasm of those who have been disillusioned by recent events in history. One who brilliantly epitomizes political disillusionment in the aftermath of World War II, especially in Eastern Europe, is Jan Kott. The evocative debunking of romantic idealism set forth in his *Shakespeare Our Contemporary* (1964, translated from the Polish) has enjoyed enormous influence since the 1960s, especially in the theater. Kott sees Shakespeare as a dramatist of the absurd and the grotesque. In this view, Shakespearean plays are often close to "black" comedy or comedy of the absurd, as defined by Antonin Artaud (*The Theatre and Its Double*, 1958) and Jerzy Grotowski (*Towards a Poor Theatre*, 1968). Indeed, Kott has inspired productions that expose traditional values to skepticism and ridicule. Portia and Bassanio in *The Merchant of Venice* become scheming adventurers; Henry V becomes a priggish warmonger. History is for Kott a nightmare associated with his country's experience in World War II, and Shakespeare's modernity can be seen in his sardonic portrayal of political opportunism and violence. Even *A Midsummer Night's Dream* is a play of disturbingly erotic brutality, Kott argues. Here is an interpretation of Shakespeare that was bound to have an enormous appeal in a world confronted by the assassinations of the Kennedys and Martin Luther King Jr.; by incessant war in the Middle East, Southeast Asia, and much of the third world; by the threat of nuclear annihilation and ecological disaster; and by political leadership generally perceived as interested only in the public-relations techniques of self-preservation. An essentially ironic view of politics and, more broadly, of human nature has informed a good deal of criticism since Kott's day and has led to the dethronement of E. M. W. Tillyard and his essentially positive view of English patriotism and heroism in the history plays.

New Historicism and Cultural Materialism

A more recent way of investigating Shakespeare through the demystifying perspective of modern experience—the so-called new historicism— has focused on the themes of political self-fashioning and role playing in terms of power and subversion. This critical school has paid close attention to historians and cultural anthropologists like Lawrence Stone (*The Crisis of the Aristocracy, 1558–1641*, 1965) and Clifford Geertz (*Negara: The Theatre State in Nineteenth-Century Bali,* 1980), who explore new ways of looking at the relationship between historical change and the myths generated to bring it about or to retain power. Geertz analyzes the way in which the ceremonies and myths of political rule can, in effect, become a self-fulfilling reality; kings and other leaders, acting out their roles in ceremonials designed to encapsulate the myth of their greatness and divine origin, essentially become what they have created in their impersonations of power. Such a view of political authority is an inherently skeptical one, seeing government as a process of manipulating illusions. When Shakespeare's English history plays—or indeed any plays dealing with conflicts of authority—are analyzed in these terms, subversion and containment become important issues. Do the plays of Shakespeare and other Renaissance dramatists celebrate the power of the Tudor monarchs, or do they question and undermine assumptions of hierarchy? Did Elizabethan drama serve to increase skepticism and pressure for change, or was it, conversely, a way of easing that pressure so that the power structure could remain in force?

The "new historicism" is a name applied to a kind of literary criticism practiced in America, prominently by Stephen Greenblatt. Especially influential have been his *Renaissance Self-Fashioning* (1980), *Shakespearean Negotiations* (1988), and his editing of the journal *Representations*. Those who pursue similar concerns, including Louis Montrose, Stephen Orgel, Richard Helgerson, Don E. Wayne, Frank Whigham, Richard Strier, Jonathan Goldberg, David Scott Kastan, and Steven Mullaney, share Greenblatt's goals to a greater or lesser extent and think of themselves only with important reservations as "new historicists"; the term is misleadingly categorical, and Greenblatt, among others, is eager to enlarge the parameters of the method rather than to allow it to harden into an orthodoxy. (Greenblatt, in fact, prefers the term "poetics of culture" to "new historicism," even though the latter phrase remains better known.) Still,

these critics do generally share a number of common concerns. Among the ways in which new historicists seek to separate themselves from earlier historical critics is by denying that the work of art is a unified and self-contained product of an independent creator in masterful control of the meaning of the work. Instead, the new historicists represent the work as shot through with the multiple and contradictory discourses of its time. New historicists also deny the notion that art merely "reflects" its historical milieu; instead, they argue that art is caught up in, and contributes to, the social practices of its time. Although the boundary between new and old historical criticism is often hard to draw, in general the new historicists are apt to be skeptical of the accepted canon of literary texts and are drawn to a markedly politicized reading of Renaissance plays. One finds everywhere in the new historicism a deep ambivalence toward political authority.

Mikhail Bakhtin's provocative ideas on carnival (*L'Oeuvre de François Rabelais et la Culture Populaire du Moyen Age,* 1970) have had an important influence in new historical circles, as reflected, for example, in the work of Michael Bristol (*Carnival and Theatre: Plebeian Culture and the Structure of Authority in Renaissance England,* 1985), Peter Stallybrass, Gail Paster, and others. Like new historicism, this critical approach looks at so-called high cultural entertainment, including Shakespeare, in relation to the practices of popular culture, thereby breaking down the distinction between "high" and "popular." Literary and nonliterary texts are subjected to the same kind of serious scrutiny. Popular origins of the theater receive new attention, as in Robert Weimann's *Shakespeare and the Popular Tradition in the Theater: Studies in the Social Dimension of Dramatic Form and Function* (published in German in 1967 and in English translation in 1978).

Cultural materialism, in Britain, takes an analogous approach to the dethroning of canonical texts and the emphasis on art as deeply implicated in the social practices of its time but differs from American new historicism on the issue of change. New historicism is sometimes criticized for its lack of a model for change and for its reluctant belief, instead (in Greenblatt's formulation especially), that all attempts at subversion through art are destined to be contained by power structures in society; art permits the expression of heterodox points of view, but only as a way of letting off steam, as it were, and thereby easing the pressures for actual radical change. British cultural materialism, in contrast, is more avowedly committed not only to radical political interpretation, but also to rapid political change, partly in response to what are perceived to be more deeply rooted class differences than are found in America. Jonathan Dollimore's *Radical Tragedy* (1984) and *Political Shakespeare* (1985), edited by Dollimore and Alan Sinfield, enlist the dramatist on the side of class struggle. So do *Alternative Shakespeares*, edited by John Drakakis (1985), and Terry Eagleton's *Shakespeare and Society* (1967) and *William Shakespeare*

(1986). Raymond Williams, not himself a Shakespearean critic, is an acknowledged godfather of the movement.

Feminist Criticism

Feminist criticism is such an important and diverse field that it has necessarily and productively reached into a number of related disciplines, such as cultural anthropology and its wealth of information about family structures. In his *The Elementary Structures of Kinship* (1949, translated 1969) and other books, Claude Lévi-Strauss analyzes the way in which men, as fathers and as husbands, control the transfer of women from one family to another in an "exogamous" marital system designed to strengthen commercial and other ties among men. Recent feminist criticism has had a lot to say about patriarchal structures in the plays and poems of Shakespeare, some of it building upon Lévi-Strauss's analysis of patriarchy; see, for example, Karen Newman, "Portia's Ring: Unruly Women and Structures of Exchange in *The Merchant of Venice*," *Shakespeare Quarterly*, 38 (1987), 10–33, and Lynda Boose, "The Father and the Bride in Shakespeare," *PMLA*, 97 (1982), 325–47. Coppélia Kahn has examined the ideology of rape in *The Rape of Lucrece*, showing how the raped woman is devalued by the shame that attaches to her husband even though she is innocent (*Shakespeare Studies*, 9, 1976, 45–72).

Another important source of insight for feminist criticism is the anthropological work on rites of passage by Arnold Van Gennep (*The Rites of Passage*, translated by M. B. Vizedom and G. L. Caffee, 1960) and Victor Turner (*The Ritual Process*, 1969), among others. The focus here is on the dangers of transition at times of birth, puberty, marriage, death, and other turning points of human life. Feminist criticism, in dealing with such crises of transition, concerns itself not only with women's roles, but also more broadly with gender relations, with family structures, and with the problems that males encounter in their quest for mature sexual identity. Coppélia Kahn's *Man's Estate; Masculine Identity in Shakespeare* (1981) looks particularly at the difficulty of the male in confronting the hazards of maturity. Robert Watson's *Shakespeare and the Hazards of Ambition* (1984) also looks at the male in the political context of career and self-fashioning. Marjorie Garber's *Coming of Age in Shakespeare* (1981) takes a broad look at maturation.

As these titles suggest, the models are often psychological, as well as anthropological. One focus of feminist criticism is the role of women in love and marriage. Feminist critics disagree among themselves as to whether the portrait painted by Shakespeare and other Elizabethan dramatists is a hopeful one, as argued, for example, by Juliet Dusinberre in *Shakespeare and the Nature of Women* (1975, 1996), or repressive, as argued by Lisa Jardine in *Still Harping on Daughters: Women and Drama in the Age of Shakespeare* (1983). Recent historians add an important perspective, especially Lawrence Stone in his *The Family, Sex, and Marriage in England, 1500–1800* (1977). Did the Protestant emphasis on marriage as a morally elevated and reciprocal relationship have the paradoxical effect of arousing in men an increased hostility and wariness toward women and a resulting increase in repression and violence? Or, as David Underdown suggests, should we look to economic explanations of hostility and wariness toward women in the Renaissance? His studies indicate that repression of women is greatest in regions of the country where their place in the economy offers the possibility of their having some control over family finances. (See *Revel, Riot, and Rebellion: Popular Culture in England, 1603–1660*, 1985, pp. 73–105, especially p. 99.)

Certainly, recent criticism has paid a lot of attention to male anxieties about women in Shakespeare's plays, as various male protagonists resolve to teach women a lesson (*The Taming of the Shrew*), succumb to dark fantasies of female unfaithfulness (*Much Ado About Nothing, Othello*), or are overwhelmed by misogynistic revulsion (*Hamlet, King Lear*). It is as though Shakespeare, in his plays and poems, works through the problems that men experience throughout their lives in their relationships with women, from the insecurities of courtship to the desire for possession and control in marriage, and from jealous fears of betrayal to the longing for escape into middle-age sexual adventure (as in *Antony and Cleopatra*). The late plays show us the preoccupation of the aging male with the marriages of his daughters (another form of betrayal) and with the approach of death.

Recently, feminist criticism has begun to increase its historical consciousness. Critics such as Gail Paster, Jean Howard, Phyllis Rackin, Dympna Callaghan, Lorraine Helms, Jyotsna Singh, Alison Findlay, Lisa Jardine, and Karen Newman focus on the construction of gender in early modern England in terms of social and material conditions, abandoning the nonhistorical psychological model of earlier feminist criticism. See the bibliography at the end of this book for feminist studies by these and other feminist critics, including Catherine Belsey, Carol Neely, Peter Erickson, Meredith Skura, Marianne Novy, Margo Hendricks, Kim Hall, Philippa Berry, Frances Dolan, Mary Beth Rose, Valerie Traub, Susan Zimmerman, Lynda Boose, and Ania Loomba. Gender studies concerned with issues of same-sex relationships have made important contributions in recent years, in the work of Bruce Smith, Laurie Shannon, Jonathan Goldberg, Stephen Orgel, Leonard Barkan, Mario DiGangi, and others.

Poststructuralism and Deconstruction

A major influence today in Shakespeare criticism, as in virtually all literary criticism of recent date, is the school of analysis known as poststructuralism or deconstruction; the terms, though not identical, significantly overlap. This school derives its inspiration originally from the work of certain French philosophers and critics, chief among whom are Ferdinand de Saussure, a specialist in linguistics, Michel Foucault, a historian of systems of discourse, and Jacques Derrida, perhaps the most highly visible exponent and practitioner of deconstruction. The ideas of these men were first introduced into American literary criticism by scholars at Yale such as Geoffrey Hartman, J. Hillis Miller, and Paul De Man. The ideas are controversial and difficult.

Poststructuralism and deconstruction begin with an insistence that language is a system of difference—one in which the signifiers (such as words and gestures) are essentially arbitrary to the extent that "meaning" and "authorial intention" are virtually impossible to fix precisely; that is, language enjoys a potentially infinite subjectivity. To an extent, this approach to the subjectivity of meaning in a work of art resembles "new" criticism in its mistrust of "message" in literature, but the new method goes further. It resists all attempts at paraphrase, for example, insisting that the words of a text cannot be translated into other words without altering something vital; indeed, there is no way of knowing if an author's words will strike any two readers or listeners in the same way. The very concept of an author has been challenged by Michel Foucault ("What Is an Author?" in *Language, Counter-Memory, Practice*, edited by Donald F. Bouchard, 1977). Deconstruction proclaims that there is no single identifiable author in the traditional sense; instead of a single text, we have a potentially infinite number of texts.

Both the theory and practice of deconstruction remain highly controversial. Although poststructuralism and deconstruction owe a debt to the general philosophical theory of signs and symbols known as semiotics, in which the function of linguistic signs is perceived to be artificially constructed, the new method also calls into question the very distinctions on which the discipline of semiotics is based. Derrida builds upon the work of Saussure and yet goes well beyond him in an insistence that words (signifiers) be left in play rather than attached to their alleged meaning (signifieds). Frank Lentricchia (*After the New Criticism*, 1980) takes the Yale school critics to task for interpreting Derrida in too formalist and apolitical a sense. Despite disagreements among theorists, nevertheless, the approach has deeply influenced Shakespeare criticism as a whole by urging critics to consider the suppleness with which signifiers (words) in the Shakespearean text are converted by listeners and readers into some approximation of meaning.

The ramifications of poststructuralism and deconstruction are increasingly felt in other forms of criticism, even those at least nominally at odds with poststructuralist assumptions. Some radical textual critics, for example, are fascinated by the unsettling prospects of the deconstructed text. What does one edit and how does one go about editing when words are to be left in play, to the infinite regress of meaning? The problems are acutely examined in a collection of essays called *The Division of the Kingdom*, edited by Gary Taylor and Michael Warren, on the two early and divergent texts of *King Lear* (1983). The method of linguistic analysis known as "speech-act theory," developed by the philosopher J. L. Austin as a way of exploring how we perform certain linguistic acts when we swear oaths or make asseverations and the like, is sharply at variance with deconstruction in its premises about a correlation between speech and intended meaning, and yet it, too, can help us understand the instability of spoken or written language in Shakespeare. Joseph Porter's *The Drama of Speech Acts* (1979), for example, looks at ways in which Shakespeare's characters in the plays about Henry IV and Henry V reveal, through their language of oath making and oath breaking, asseveration, and the like, their linguistic adaptability or lack of adaptability to historical change. Richard II resists historical change in the very way he speaks; Prince Hal embraces it. A third related field of analysis that is interested in the instability of meaning in Shakespeare's texts is metadramatic criticism, where the focus is on ways in which dramatic texts essentially talk about the drama itself, about artistic expression, and about the artist's quest for immortality in art. James Calderwood's *Shakespearean Metadrama* (1971) is an influential example.

At its extreme, then, deconstructive criticism comes close to undermining all kinds of "meaningfulness" in artistic utterance and to being thus at war with other methods of interpretation. Still, deconstruction continues to remain influential, because it also usefully challenges complacent formulations of meaning and because it promotes such a subtle view of linguistic complexity.

At its best, late twentieth-century criticism transcends the splintering effect of a heterogeneous critical tradition to achieve a synthesis that is at once unified and multiform in its vision. The pluralistic approach aims at overall balance and a reinforcement of one critical approach through the methodology of another. Many of the works already cited in this introduction refuse to be constricted by methodological boundaries. The best historical criticism makes use of close explication of the text where appropriate; image patterns can certainly reinforce mythological patterns; typological interpretation, when sensibly applied, serves the cause of image study. Some fine books are so eclectic in their method that one hesitates to apply the label of any one critical school. Among such works are Maynard Mack's *King Lear in Our Time* (1965), David Young's *Something of Great Constancy: The Art of A Midsummer Night's Dream* (1966), R. G. Hunter's *Shakespeare and the Comedy of Forgiveness* (1965), Janet Adelman's *The Common Liar: An Essay on "Antony and Cleopatra"* (1973), Stanley Cavell's "The Avoidance of Love: A Reading of King Lear," in *Must We Mean What We Say?* (1969, reprinted in *Disowning Knowledge in Seven Plays of Shakespeare*, 2003), and Paul Jorgensen's *Our Naked Frailties: Sensational Art and Meaning in Macbeth* (1971).

Into the Twenty-First Century

The sense of where we are in the twenty-first century in Shakespeare criticism reflects the uncertainties and guardedly hopeful expectations of the academic profession as a whole. The period of the 1970s and 1980s, described previously, was one of extraordinary ferment, brought on by a host of developments: the Vietnam War and its aftermath, the assassinations of the Kennedys and Martin Luther King Jr., the impact of French linguistic and philosophical thought on American intellectual writing, the frustrations of many academics with Reaganomics and their consequent fascination with British Marxism, emerging demands on behalf of minorities and women, a revolution in social and sexual mores accompanied by a backlash in the name of "family values," conflict over American foreign policy in the Middle East (Israel, Iraq), and much more. The result was what must be regarded as a genuine revolution in methods of critical analysis and reading. The literary text became multivalent, ambiguous, deconstructed, dethroned as a unique artifact, and was seen, instead, as a product of and contributing to its social and intellectual environment. The author became a construction of criticism and of a new kind of literary history.

Shakespeare studies have taken a lead in all of this new exploration. Although one of the postmodern demands has been for a recanonizing of literature in favor of newer literature, works by women and minorities, and works from countries other than Britain and the United States instead of the traditional canon of dead white European males, Shakespeare not only has survived this recanonization but also has become more prominent than ever. Other Renaissance writers such as Ben Jonson, John Webster, Thomas Dekker, Thomas Nashe, John Lyly, Edmund Spenser, and even Christopher Marlowe, John Milton, and John Donne have been the victims of declining enrollments in classes generally, but Shakespeare triumphs. Why?

One compelling answer is that Shakespeare is simply indispensable to postmodern critical inquiry. His texts are so extraordinarily responsive that new questions put to them—about the changing role of women, about cynicism in the political process, about the protean near-indeterminacy of meaning in language—evoke insights that are hard to duplicate in other literary texts. Shakespeare does not seem out of date. The very impulse of so much recent criticism to claim Shakespeare as "our contemporary," attuned to our own skepticisms and disillusionment and even despair (as in the writings of Jan Kott, for example), attests to his unparalleled engagement with the issues about which we care so deeply. Even those who argue that Shakespeare exhibits the male hang-ups of a patriarchal society and that he is a social snob who glorifies aristocracy and warfare do not see Shakespeare as a writer who is out of touch with the values of our contemporary society but, rather, as one who gives eloquent testimonial to structures that were alive in our cultural past and with which we sense a continuum today even if outward circumstances have changed. The best scholarship does not condemn Shakespeare for believing in kingship or for sometimes showing men as victorious in the battle of the sexes; instead, that criticism is interested in the whole process of the literary text's participation in the creation of culture. Even when recent scholarship is concerned with examining class and gender issues to clarify some of the systematic oppressiveness of early modern culture, it does so generally in an attempt to negotiate the relationship of the present to the past, rather than assuming a superiority in our modern world's approaches to issues of class, gender, and ethnicity.

To be sure, a number of Shakespeare's plays are in trouble today because they make us uncomfortable about these issues. *The Merchant of Venice* is, in the eyes of many, almost unproduceable, because the anti-Semitic emotions it explores are so distasteful. It is less often assigned now in classrooms than it once was, even though, when it is taught or produced onstage, it can lead to extraordinarily searching discussions of painful but real issues. The same is true of *The Taming of the Shrew*, which is being taken from the shelves of more than a few libraries because of its apparent flaunting of sexist behavior toward women. *Othello* offends some readers and viewers because of its racist language and, in the view of some, racial stereotypes. Yet, the power of Shakespeare's language continues to exert its spell despite, and in part because of, these troubling conflicts over the role of dramatic art in modern society.

The world of Shakespeare criticism today, after two decades or so of revolution, is seemingly one of consolidation. At a March 1995 meeting of the Shakespeare Association of America in Chicago, many conferees wondered: Where is the profession going? What are the hot new issues? Who are the new critics that no one wants to miss? And, in fact, there seemed to be little dramatic excitement of this sort, little agreement as to any discernible new trend. To some, this is frustrating. Where does one turn for real creativity after a thoroughgoing revolution such as we have experienced?

To others, a time of stocktaking is potentially healthy. There seems to be relatively little interest in turning the clock back; postmodernism and indeterminacy have changed the critical landscape for better and for worse. Now that this new landscape begins to seem familiar, however, new members of the profession seem less anxious to resolve their own identity crises in terms of affiliating with some critical school or other. The critical challenges are there, not so stridently new as they were ten years ago, and adaptable to various uses.

The result is increasing variety in the kinds of critical work being done. Some of it is recognizably traditional, dealing with stage history and conditions of performance during Shakespeare's lifetime, as, for example, in T. J. King, *Casting Shakespeare's Plays: London Actors and Their Roles* (1992); William Ingram, *The Business of Playing: The Beginnings of the Adult Professional Theater in Elizabethan London* (1992); David Bradley, *From Text to Performance in the Elizabethan Theatre: Preparing the Play for the Stage* (1992); David Mann, *The Elizabethan Player: Contemporary Stage Representation* (1991); John H. Astington, ed., *The Development of Shakespeare's Theater* (1992); Andrew Gurr, *Playgoing in Shakespeare's London* (1987, 2nd edition, 1996) and *The Shakespearian Playing Companies* (1996); and Roslyn Lander Knutson, *The Repertory of Shakespeare's Company, 1594–1613* (1991). Background and historical studies of the conditions that helped produce Shakespeare's theater can sometimes be informatively revisionist in the sense of toppling cherished older notions without at the same time being postmodern in approach. Examples here might include Richard Dutton, *Mastering the Revels: The Regulation and Censorship of English Renaissance Drama* (1991); Scott McMillin and Sally-Beth MacLean, *The Queen's Men and Their Plays* (1998); and Leeds Barroll, *Politics, Plague, and Shakespeare's Theater: The Stuart Years* (1991).

Other studies are more openly revisionist in a postmodern vein, sometimes in dealing with hypotheses about bibliography and textual studies, as in Margreta de Grazia, *Shakespeare Verbatim: The Reproduction of Authenticity and the 1790 Apparatus* (1991), and Grace Ioppolo, *Revising Shakespeare* (1991). The New Folger Library Shakespeare, edited by Barbara Mowat and Paul Werstine (1992—), gives a more measured approach. The Arden Shakespeare is currently bringing out new critical editions of all the plays in individual volumes (Arden 3), as are the New Cambridge Shakespeare and the Oxford Shakespeare. Occasionally a conservative counterblast is heard, as in Brian Vickers's entertaining, learned, and feisty polemic, *Appropriating Shakespeare: Contemporary Critical Quarrels* (1993). A forum of essays edited by Ivo Kamps, called *Shakespeare Left and Right*, gives us a chance to weigh arguments from various sides.

What the contemporary critical scene does best is to free critics to be who they are and to write without paying dues to any particular affiliation. The results are refreshingly diverse. Among the books of the 1990s that show this spread of critical approaches are Karen Newman, *Fashioning Femininity and the English Renaissance Drama* (1991); Bruce R. Smith, *Homosexual Desire in Shakespeare's England* (1991); Janet Adelman, *Suffocating Mothers: Fantasies of Maternal Origin in Shakespeare's Plays, "Hamlet" to "The Tempest"* (1992); Alan Sinfield, *Faultlines: Cultural Materialism and the Politics of Dissident Reading* (1992); Valerie Traub, *Desire and Anxiety: Circulations of Sexuality in Shakespearean Drama* (1992); Richard Burt, *Licensed by Authority: Ben Jonson and the Discourses of Censorship* (1993);

Linda Charnes, *Notorious Identity: Materializing the Subject in Shakespeare* (1993); Lars Engle, *Shakespearean Pragmatism: Market of His Time* (1993); Gail Kern Paster, *The Body Embarrassed: Drama and the Disciplines of Shame in Early Modern England* (1993); Meredith Anne Skura, *Shakespeare the Actor and the Purposes of Playing* (1993); Frances E. Dolan, *Dangerous Familiars: Representations of Domestic Crime in England, 1550–1700* (1994); Kim F. Hall, *Things of Darkness: Economies of Race and Gender in Early Modern England* (1994); Jean Howard, *The Stage and Social Struggle in Early Modern England* (1994); Robert Watson, *The Rest Is Silence: Death as Annihilation in the English Renaissance* (1994); Katharine Eisaman Maus, *Inwardness and Theatre in the English Renaissance Drama* (1995); Louis Montrose, *The Purpose of Playing: Shakespeare and the Cultural Politics of the Elizabethan Theatre* (1996); Patricia Parker, *Shakespeare from the Margins: Language, Culture, Context* (1996); Jean E. Howard and Phyllis Rackin, *Engendering a Nation: A Feminist Account of Shakespeare's English Histories* (1997); and David Scott Kastan, ed., *A Companion to Shakespeare* (1999).

These same qualities of excellence in diverse critical approaches can be sampled in many studies of Shakespeare in the first decade of the twenty-first century, as for example in Stephen Greenblatt, *Hamlet in Purgatory* (2001); Anthony B. Dawson and Paul Yachnin, *The Culture of Playgoing in Shakespeare's England* (2001); David Scott Kastan, *Shakespeare and the Book* (2001); Mary Beth Rose, *Gender and Heroism in Early Modern Literature* (2002); Stephen Orgel, *The Authentic Shakespeare* (2002); Ania Loomba, *Shakespeare, Race, and Colonialism* (2002); Laurie Shannon, *Sovereign Amity: Figures of Friendship in Shakespeare's Contexts* (2002); Richard Dutton and Jean E. Howard, eds., *A Companion to Shakespeare's Works*, in 4 vols. (2003); B. J. and Mary Sokol, *Shakespeare, Law, and Marriage* (2003); Stephen Orgel, *Imagining Shakespeare* (2003); Stanley Wells, *Shakespeare: For All Time* (2003); Stephen Greenblatt, *Will in the World: How Shakespeare Became Shakespeare* (2004); Marjorie Garber, *Shakespeare After All* (2004); Andrew Gurr, *The Shakespeare Company, 1594–1642* (2004); Gale Paster, *Humoring the Body: Emotions and the Renaissance Stage* (2004); James S. Shapiro, *A Year in the Life of William Shakespeare, 1599* (2005); Phyllis Rackin, *Shakespeare and Women* (2005); Robin Headlam Wells, *Shakespeare's Humanism* (2005); Russ McDonald, *Shakespeare's Late Style* (2006); Peter Holland, *Shakespeare, Memory, and Performance* (2006); John D. Cox, *Seeming Knowledge: Shakespeare and Skeptical Faith* (2007); Margreta de Grazia, *"Hamlet" without Hamlet* (2007); Jonathan Bate, *Soul of the Age: A Biography of the Mind of William Shakespeare* (2009); James Shapiro, *Contested Will: Who Wrote Shakespeare?* (2010); Stanley Wells, *Shakespeare, Sex, and Love* (2010); Richard Strier, *The Unrepentant Renaissance: From Petrarch to Shakespeare* (2011); Catherine Richardson, *Shakespeare and Material Culture* (2011); and Lois Potter, *The Life of William Shakespeare* (2012). For other suggestions, see recent entries in the bibliography at the back of this volume.

Ex dono Wilh. Iaggard Typographi aᵒ 1623

Mr. WILLIAM
SHAKESPEARES

COMEDIES,
HISTORIES, &
TRAGEDIES.

Publiſhed according to the True Originall Copies.

Martin Droeſhout ſculpſit London.

LONDON ―
Printed by Iſaac Iaggard, and Ed. Blount. 1623.

Martin Droeshout's engraving on the title page of the First Folio is one of only two authentic likenesses of Shakespeare in existence.

A CATALOGVE

of the ſeuerall Comedies, Hiſtories, and Tragedies contained in this Volume.

COMEDIES.

He Tempeſt.	Folio 1.
The two Gentlemen of Verona.	20
The Merry Wiues of Windſor.	38
Meaſure for Meaſure.	61
The Comedy of Errours.	85
Much adoo about Nothing.	101
Loues Labour loſt.	122
Midſommer Nights Dreame.	145
The Merchant of Venice.	163
As you Like it.	185
The Taming of the Shrew.	208
All is well, that Ends well.	230
Twelfe-Night, or what you will.	255
The Winters Tale.	304

HISTORIES.

The Life and Death of King John.	Fol. 1.
The Life & death of Richard the ſecond.	23

The Firſt part of King Henry the fourth.	46
The Second part of K. Henry the fourth.	74
The Life of King Henry the Fift.	69
The Firſt part of King Henry the Sixt.	96
The Second part of King Hen. the Sixt.	120
The Third part of King Henry the Sixt.	147
The Life & Death of Richard the Third.	173
The Life of King Henry the Eight.	205

TRAGEDIES.

The Tragedy of Coriolanus.	Fol. 1.
Titus Andronicus.	31
Romeo and Juliet.	53
Timon of Athens.	80
The Life and death of Julius Cæsar.	109
The Tragedy of Macbeth.	131
The Tragedy of Hamlet.	152
King Lear.	283
Othello, the Moore of Venice.	310
Anthony and Cleopater.	346
Cymbeline King of Britaine.	369

John Heminges and Henry Condell, Shakespeare's fellow actors, gathered contents for the First Folio, published in 1623. They collected thirty-six plays in the volume, omitting Pericles and The Two Noble Kinsmen. Troilus and Cressida is included in most copies of the First Folio but is not listed here in the contents.

The Comedies

The Taming of the Shrew

*T*he *Taming of the Shrew* (c. 1592–1594) shows Shakespeare's comic genius at its best. At the same time, it shares with his other early plays an anticipation of the directions that his genius is to take in *Much Ado About Nothing* and other comedies of the later 1590s. By skillfully juxtaposing two plots and an induction, or framing plot, it offers contrasting views on the battle of the sexes. This debate on the nature of the love relationship will continue through many later comedies. The play also adroitly manipulates the device of mistaken identity, as in *The Comedy of Errors,* inverting appearance and reality, dreaming and waking, and the master-servant relationship in order to create a transformed Saturnalian world anticipating that of *A Midsummer Night's Dream* and *Twelfth Night.*

The induction sets up the theme of illusion, using an old motif known as "The Sleeper Awakened" (as found, for example, in *The Arabian Nights*). This device frames the main action of the play, giving to it an added perspective. *The Taming of the Shrew* purports, in fact, to be a play within a play, an entertainment devised by a witty nobleman as a practical joke on a drunken tinker, Christopher Sly. The jest is to convince Sly that he is not Sly at all, but an aristocrat suffering delusions. Outlandishly dressed in new finery, Sly is invited to witness a play from the gallery over the stage. In a rendition called *The Taming of a Shrew* (printed in 1594 and now generally thought to be taken from an earlier version of Shakespeare's play, employing a good deal of conscious originality along with some literary borrowing and even plagiarism), the framing plot concludes by actually putting Sly back out on the street in front of the alehouse where he was found. He awakes, recalls the play as a dream, and proposes to put the vision to good use by taming his own wife. Whether this ending reflects an epilogue now lost from the text of Shakespeare's play cannot be said, but it does reinforce the idea of the play as Sly's fantasy. Like Puck at the end of *A Midsummer Night's Dream*, urging us to dismiss what we have seen as the product of our own slumbering, Sly continually reminds us that the play is only an illusion or shadow.

With repeated daring, Shakespeare calls attention to the contrived nature of his artifact, the play. When, for example, Sly is finally convinced that he is, in fact, a noble lord recovering from madness and lustily proposes to hasten off to bed with his long-neglected wife, we are comically aware that the "wife" is an impostor, a young page in disguise. Yet this counterfeiting of roles is no more unreal than the employment of Elizabethan boy-actors for the parts of Katharina and Bianca in the "real" play. As we watch Sly watching a play, levels of meaning intersect in this evocative fashion. Again, the paintings offered to Sly by his new attendants call attention to art's ability to confound illusion and reality. In one painting, Cytherea is hidden by reeds "Which seem to move and wanton with her breath, / Even as the waving sedges play wi'th'wind," and, in another painting, Io appears "As lively painted as the deed was done" (Induction, 2.50–6). Sly's function, then, is that of the naive observer who inverts illusion and reality in his mind, concluding that his whole previous life of tinkers and alehouses and Cicely Hackets has been unreal. As his attendants explain to him, "These fifteen years you have been in a dream, / Or when you waked, so waked as if you slept." We as audience laugh at Sly's naiveté, and yet we, too, are moved and even transformed by an artistic vision that we know to be illusory.

Like Sly, many characters in the main action of the play are persuaded, or contrive, to be what they are not. Lucentio and Tranio exchange roles of master and servant. Bianca's supposed tutors are, in fact, her wooers, using their lessons to disguise messages of love. Katharina is prevailed upon by her husband, Petruchio, to declare that the sun is the moon and that an old gentleman (Vincentio) is a fair young maiden. Vincentio is publicly informed that he is an impostor and that the "real" Vincentio (the Pedant) is at that very moment looking at him out of the window of his son Lucentio's house. This last ruse does not fool the real Vincentio, but it nearly succeeds in fooling everyone else. Baptista Minola is about to commit Vincentio to jail for the infamous slander of asserting that the supposed Lucentio is only a servant in disguise. Vincentio, as the newly arrived stranger, is able to see matters as they really are, but the dwellers of Padua have grown so accustomed to the mad and improbable fictions of their life that they are not easily awakened to reality.

Such illusions have the effect of challenging the norms of social order. If a servant can playact at being the master so successfully that no one can tell the difference, are we to understand that social distinctions are mere arbitrary constructions? If Sly can become a lord by wearing the right clothes and speaking blank verse (as in the Induction, 2.68 and following), might audience members similarly raise their status? The theater promotes such skeptical questions, since it is in the business of dressing actors up as persons of whatever rank the playwright chooses. Surely one of the pleasures of theatrical performance for Elizabethan audiences was that of dreaming of social advancement or social control. At the same time, this theater treats such a liberating experience as holiday or farcical nightmare, and as Saturnalian escape; we realize as audience that we will return to the norms of our daily lives after having visited an imagined space where anything is possible.

Shakespeare multiplies his devices of illusion by combining two entirely distinct plots, each concerned, at least in part, with the comic inversion of appearance and reality: the shrew-taming plot involving Petruchio and Kate, and the more conventional romantic plot involving Lucentio and Bianca. The latter plot is derived from the *Supposes* of George Gascoigne, a play first presented at Gray's Inn (one of the Inns of Court) in 1566, as translated from Ariosto's neoclassical comedy, *I Suppositi*, 1509. (Ariosto's work, in turn, was based upon Terence's *Eunuchus* and Plautus's *Captivi*.) The "Supposes" are mistaken identities or misunderstandings, the kind of hilarious farcical mix-ups with which Shakespeare had already experimented in *The Comedy of Errors*. Shakespeare has, as usual, both romanticized his source and moralized it in a characteristically English way. The heroine, who in the Roman comedy of Plautus and Terence would have been a courtesan, and who in *Supposes* is made pregnant by her clandestine lover, remains thoroughly chaste in Shakespeare's comedy. Consequently, she has no need for a pander, or go-between, such as the bawdy Duenna or Nurse of *Supposes*. The satire directed at the heroine's unwelcome old wooer Gremio is far less savage than in *Supposes*, where the "pantaloon," Dr. Cleander, is a villainously corrupt lawyer epitomizing the depravity of "respectable" society. Despite Shakespeare's modifications, however, the basic plot remains an effort to foil parental authority. The young lovers, choosing

each other for romantic reasons, must fend off the materialistic calculations of their parents.

In a stock situation of this sort, the character types are also conventional. Gremio, the aged wealthy wooer, is actually labeled a "pantaloon" in the text (3.1.36–7) to stress his neoclassical ancestry. (Lean and foolish old wooers of this sort were customarily dressed in pantaloons, slippers, and spectacles on the Italian stage.) Gremio is typically "the graybeard," and Baptista Minola is "the narrow-prying father" (3.2.145–6). Even though Shakespeare renders these characters far less unattractive than in *Supposes*, their worldly behavior still invites reprisal from the young. Since Baptista Minola insists on selling his daughter Bianca to the highest bidder, it is fitting that her wealthiest suitor (the supposed Lucentio) should turn out in the end to be a penniless servant (Tranio) disguised as a man of affluence and position. In his traditional role as the clever servant of neoclassical comedy, Tranio skillfully apes the mannerisms of respectable society. He can deal in the mere surfaces— clothes or reputation—out of which a man's social importance is created, and can even furnish himself with a rich father. Gremio and Baptista deserve to be foiled, because they accept the illusion of respectability as real.

Even the romantic lovers of this borrowed plot are largely conventional. To be sure, Shakespeare emphasizes their virtuous qualities and their sincerity. He adds Hortensio (not in *Supposes*) to provide Lucentio with a genuine, if foolish, rival and Bianca with two wooers closer to her age than old Gremio. Lucentio and Bianca deserve their romantic triumph; they are self-possessed, witty, and steadfast to each other. Yet we know very little about them, nor have they seen deeply into each other. Lucentio's love talk is laden with conventional images in praise of Bianca's dark eyes and scarlet lips. At the play's end, he discovers, to his surprise, that she can be willful, even disobedient. Has her appearance of virtue concealed something from him and from us? Because the relationship between these lovers is superficial, they are appropriately destined to a superficial marriage as well. The passive Bianca becomes the proud and defiant wife.

By contrast, Petruchio and Kate are the more interesting lovers, whose courtship involves mutual self-discovery. Admittedly, we must not overstate the case. Especially at first, these lovers are also stock types: the shrew tamer and his proverbially shrewish wife. (The word *shrew*, originally signifying a wicked or malignant man, often applied to the devil or to a malignant planet, had come to mean a scolding or turbulent wife.) Although Shakespeare seems not to have used any single source for this plot, he was well acquainted with crude, misogynistic stories demonstrating the need for putting women in their place. In a ballad called *A Merry Jest of a Shrewd and Curst Wife, Lapped in Morel's Skin* (printed c. 1550), for example, the husband tames his shrewish wife by flaying her bloody with birch rods and then wrapping her in the freshly salted skin of a plow horse named Morel. (This shrewish wife, like Kate, has an obedient and gentle younger sister who is their father's favorite.) Other features of Shakespeare's plot can be found in similar tales: the tailor scolded for devising a gown of outlandish fashion (Gerard Legh's *Accidence of Armory*, 1562), the wife obliged to agree with her husband's assertion of some patent falsehood (Don Juan Manuel's *El Conde Lucanor*, c. 1335), and the three husbands' wager on their wives' obedience (*The Book of the Knight of La Tour-Landry*, printed 1484). In the raw spirit of this sexist tradition, so unlike the refined Italianate sentiment of his other plot, Shakespeare introduces Petruchio as a man of reckless bravado who is ready to marry the ugliest or sharpest-tongued woman alive so long as she is rich. However much he may be later attracted by Kate's fiery spirit, his first attraction to her is crassly financial. Kate is, moreover, a troublesomely defiant young woman at first, described by the men who know her as "intolerable curst / And shrewd and froward," and aggressive in her bullying of Bianca. She and Petruchio meet as grotesque comic counterparts.

At the play's end, the traditional pattern of male dominance and female acquiescence is still prominent. Kate is allowed food, sleep, and sex only when she yields to a socially ordained patriarchal framework in which a husband is the princely ruler of his wife. Kate is not like the young heroines of many other Shakespearean comedies (Portia in *The Merchant of Venice* and Rosalind in *As You Like It*, for example) who wittily guide their immature and overly romantic young men toward a pragmatic view of love and marriage; in this play, Kate is the one who must be mastered by the self-assured male. Her shrewishness is an open threat to male control in the marital bond, and, accordingly, the play's comic finale celebrates containment of this threat in her, along with a sharp reminder of the resistance to be endured by other husbands who have failed to tame their shrews.

Within this male-oriented frame of reference, however, Petruchio and Kate are surprisingly like Benedick and Beatrice of *Much Ado About Nothing*. Petruchio, for all his rant, is increasingly drawn to Kate by her spirit. As wit-combatants, they are worthy of one another's enmity—or love. No one else in the play is a fit match for either of them. Kate, too, is attracted to Petruchio, despite her war of words. Her anger is part defensive protection, part testing of his sincerity. If she is contemptuous of the wooers she has seen till now, she has good reason to be. We share her condescension toward the aged Gremio or the laughably inept Hortensio. She rightly fears that her father wishes to dispose of her so that he may auction off Bianca to the wealthiest competitor. Kate's jaded view of such marriage brokering is entirely defensible. Not surprisingly, she first views Petruchio, whose professed intentions are far from reassuring, as another mere adventurer in love. She is impressed by his "line" in wooing her but needs to test his constancy and sincerity. Marriage for her

would be a serious step, since social convention allows a dominant role for the husband; can she hope that she and Petruchio will arrive at some sort of understanding in which her role as wife and partner will be an honorable one? She puts down most men with a shrewish manner that challenges their very masculinity; Petruchio is the first man to counter her wit and energy with his own. Can she learn to live with this man?

Kate's rejection of men has not left her very happy, however genuine her disdain is for most of those who have come to woo. Petruchio's "schooling" can be seen as addressing that unhappiness, even if his purpose is unremittingly masculine in its assumption that a rebellious wife has to be "tamed" as one would tame a hawk. Having wooed and partly won her, Petruchio tests her with his late arrival at the marriage, his unconventional dress, and his crossing all her desires. Like the hawk-tamer, Petruchio uses harsh physical means, including deprivation of food and drink. He treats Kate as his chattel, and never wavers in his certainty that he is right to do so. Other males applaud his success and wish only to follow his example. The resolution is in these terms manifestly more sexist than in *Much Ado About Nothing*; it is as though Shakespeare works his way through the problems of sexual conflict from this early, very masculine play to a more complex and mutual accommodation in his later comedies.

At the same time, it is possible to see *The Taming of the Shrew* as a play in which a genuine accommodation is reached, even if it is on the man's terms with the woman being given no choice. The play may encourage the view that Petruchio's treatment of Kate, no matter how temporarily harsh, is ultimately benign in its intent. Petruchio, by his outlandish behavior of overturning tables and scolding servants, shows Kate an ugly picture of what her refractoriness is like. He succeeds by insisting on what, arguably, she may desire too: a well-defined relationship tempered by mutual respect and love. In this interpretation, Kate may gain something by the play's end. Her closing speech, with its fine blend of irony and self-conscious hyperbole, together with its seriousness of concern, can be read as expressing the way in which her independence of spirit and her newfound acceptance of a domestic rule are successfully fused, enabling her to gain widespread applause instead of opprobrium.

This is by no means the only way of reading the final scene, as modern productions often make clear: Kate emerges in various stage productions as more or less contented, or as simply resigned, or as cruelly brainwashed, or as only playing the role of obedient wife to get what she wants. The uncertainty of interpretation is one of the great pleasures and challenges today, in a world for which ideas about marriage have manifestly shifted since Shakespeare wrote. Even so, the play offers common ground in its appreciation for the seriousness of the issue and in its wonderful transparency as a text that offers itself up for rival interpretations.

The Taming of the Shrew

[*Dramatis Personae*

CHRISTOPHER SLY, *a tinker and beggar,*
HOSTESS *of an alehouse,*
A LORD,
A PAGE, SERVANTS, HUNTSMEN,
PLAYERS,

} *Persons in the Induction*

BAPTISTA, *a rich gentleman of Padua*
KATHARINA, *the shrew, also called Katharine and Kate, Baptista's elder daughter*
BIANCA, *Baptista's younger daughter*

PETRUCHIO, *a gentleman of Verona, suitor to Katharina*
GRUMIO, *Petruchio's servant*
CURTIS, NATHANIEL, PHILIP, JOSEPH, NICHOLAS, PETER, *and other servants of Petruchio*

GREMIO, *elderly suitor to Bianca*
HORTENSIO, *suitor to Bianca*
LUCENTIO, *son of Vincentio, in love with Bianca*
TRANIO, *Lucentio's servant*
BIONDELLO, *Lucentio's servant*
VINCENTIO, *a gentleman of Pisa*
A PEDANT (*or Merchant*) *of Mantua*
A WIDOW, *courted by Hortensio*

A TAILOR
A HABERDASHER
AN OFFICER
Other Servants of Baptista and Lucentio

SCENE: *Padua, and Petruchio's country house in Italy; the Induction is located in the countryside and at a Lord's house in England*]

[Induction.1]

Enter Beggar (Christopher Sly) and Hostess.

SLY I'll feeze you, in faith.   1
HOSTESS A pair of stocks, you rogue!   2
SLY You're a baggage. The Slys are no rogues. Look in   3
the chronicles; we came in with Richard Conqueror.   4
Therefore *paucas pallabris*, let the world slide. Sessa!   5
HOSTESS You will not pay for the glasses you have
burst?
SLY No, not a denier. Go by, Saint Jeronimy, go to thy   8
cold bed and warm thee.   9

HOSTESS I know my remedy; I must go fetch the third-   10
borough.   [*Exit.*]   11
SLY Third, or fourth, or fifth borough, I'll answer him   12
by law. I'll not budge an inch, boy. Let him come, and   13
kindly.   *Falls asleep.*   14

Wind horns [*within*]. *Enter a Lord from hunting, with his train.*

LORD
Huntsman, I charge thee, tender well my hounds.   15
Breathe Merriman—the poor cur is embossed—   16
And couple Clowder with the deep-mouthed brach.   17
Saw'st thou not, boy, how Silver made it good   18
At the hedge corner, in the coldest fault?   19

Induction.1. Location: Before an alehouse and, subsequently, before the Lord's house nearby. (See lines 75, 135.)
1 feeze you i.e., fix you, get even with you   **2 A . . . stocks** i.e., I'll have you put in the stocks   **3 baggage** contemptible woman or prostitute.   **4 Richard** (Sly's mistake for "William.")   **5 paucas pallabris** i.e., *pocas palabras,* "few words." (Spanish.)   **Sessa** (Of doubtful meaning; perhaps "be quiet," "cease," or "let it go.")   **8 denier** French copper coin of little value.   **Go . . . Jeronimy** (Sly's variation of an often quoted line from Kyd's *The Spanish Tragedy,* urging caution.)   **8–9 go . . . thee** (Perhaps a proverb; see *King Lear,* 3.4.46–7.)

10–11 thirdborough constable.   **12 Third** (Sly shows his ignorance; the *third* in "thirdborough" derives from the Old English word *frith,* "peace.")   **13 by law** in the law courts.   **14 kindly** welcome. (Said ironically.)   **14.1 Wind** Blow   **14.2 train** retinue.   **15 tender** care for   **16 Breathe Merriman** Give the dog Merriman time to recover its breath.   **embossed** foaming at the mouth from exhaustion   **17 couple** leash together.   **deep-mouthed brach** bitch hound with the deep baying voice.   **18 made it good** i.e., picked up the lost scent   **19 in the coldest fault** when the scent was lost by a *fault* or break in the scent.

5

I would not lose the dog for twenty pound.

FIRST HUNTSMAN
Why, Bellman is as good as he, my lord.
He cried upon it at the merest loss,   22
And twice today picked out the dullest scent.
Trust me, I take him for the better dog.

LORD
Thou art a fool. If Echo were as fleet,
I would esteem him worth a dozen such.
But sup them well and look unto them all.   27
Tomorrow I intend to hunt again.

FIRST HUNTSMAN   I will, my lord.

LORD [seeing Sly]
What's here? One dead, or drunk? See, doth he
    breathe?

SECOND HUNTSMAN [examining Sly]
He breathes, my lord. Were he not warmed with ale,
This were a bed but cold to sleep so soundly.

LORD
Oh, monstrous beast, how like a swine he lies!
Grim death, how foul and loathsome is thine image!   34
Sirs, I will practice on this drunken man.   35
What think you, if he were conveyed to bed,
Wrapped in sweet clothes, rings put upon his fingers,   37
A most delicious banquet by his bed,   38
And brave attendants near him when he wakes,   39
Would not the beggar then forget himself?

FIRST HUNTSMAN
Believe me, lord, I think he cannot choose.   41

SECOND HUNTSMAN
It would seem strange unto him when he waked.

LORD
Even as a flatt'ring dream or worthless fancy.   43
Then take him up, and manage well the jest.
Carry him gently to my fairest chamber,
And hang it round with all my wanton pictures.
Balm his foul head in warm distillèd waters,   47
And burn sweet wood to make the lodging sweet.
Procure me music ready when he wakes,
To make a dulcet and a heavenly sound.   50
And if he chance to speak, be ready straight,   51
And with a low submissive reverence   52
Say, "What is it Your Honor will command?"
Let one attend him with a silver basin
Full of rosewater and bestrewed with flowers;
Another bear the ewer, the third a diaper,   56
And say, "Will 't please Your Lordship cool your
    hands?"
Someone be ready with a costly suit,
And ask him what apparel he will wear;
Another tell him of his hounds and horse,   60
And that his lady mourns at his disease.   61

Persuade him that he hath been lunatic,
And when he says he is, say that he dreams,   63
For he is nothing but a mighty lord.
This do, and do it kindly, gentle sirs.   65
It will be pastime passing excellent,   66
If it be husbanded with modesty.   67

FIRST HUNTSMAN
My lord, I warrant you we will play our part
As he shall think by our true diligence   69
He is no less than what we say he is.

LORD
Take him up gently, and to bed with him,
And each one to his office when he wakes.   72
          [Some bear out Sly.] Sound trumpets [within].
Sirrah, go see what trumpet 'tis that sounds.   73
                              [Exit a Servingman.]
Belike some noble gentleman that means,   74
Traveling some journey, to repose him here.

          Enter [a] Servingman.

How now? Who is it?

SERVINGMAN   An't please Your Honor, players   76
That offer service to Your Lordship.

          Enter Players.

LORD
Bid them come near.—Now, fellows, you are welcome.

PLAYERS   We thank Your Honor.

LORD
Do you intend to stay with me tonight?

FIRST PLAYER
So please Your Lordship to accept our duty.   81

LORD
With all my heart. This fellow I remember
Since once he played a farmer's eldest son.—
'Twas where you wooed the gentlewoman so well.
I have forgot your name, but sure that part
Was aptly fitted and naturally performed.

SECOND PLAYER
I think 'twas Soto that Your Honor means.

LORD
'Tis very true. Thou didst it excellent.
Well, you are come to me in happy time,   89
The rather for I have some sport in hand   90
Wherein your cunning can assist me much.   91
There is a lord will hear you play tonight.
But I am doubtful of your modesties,   93
Lest, overeyeing of his odd behavior—   94
For yet His Honor never heard a play—
You break into some merry passion   96

---

22 cried . . . loss bayed to signal his recovery of the scent after it had been
completely lost   27 sup them well feed them a good supper
34 image likeness (since sleep was regarded as a likeness of death).
35 practice on play a joke on   37 sweet perfumed   38 banquet light
repast   39 brave finely arrayed   41 cannot choose is bound to.
43 fancy flight of imagination.   47 Balm Bathe, anoint   50 dulcet melodious   51 straight at once   52 reverence bow   56 ewer jug, pitcher.
diaper towel   60 horse horses   61 disease i.e., mental derangement.

63 when . . . is i.e., when he says he must be mad indeed. (The is is
stressed.)   65 kindly naturally (and thus persuasively).   gentle kind
66 passing surpassingly   67 husbanded with modesty managed
with decorum.   69 As so that.   by as a result of   72 office duty
73 Sirrah (Usual form of address to inferiors.)   74 Belike Perhaps
76 An't If it   81 So please If it please.   duty expression of respect
and dutiful service.   89 happy opportune   90 The rather for the
more so since   91 cunning professional skill   93 doubtful apprehensive.   modesties discretion, self-control   94 overeyeing of witnessing   96 merry passion outburst of laughter

And so offend him; for I tell you, sirs,
If you should smile, he grows impatient.
FIRST PLAYER
  Fear not, my lord, we can contain ourselves,
  Were he the veriest antic in the world.   100
LORD [*to a Servingman*]
  Go, sirrah, take them to the buttery,   101
  And give them friendly welcome every one.
  Let them want nothing that my house affords.   103
                 Exit one with the Players.
  Sirrah, go you to Barthol'mew my page,
  And see him dressed in all suits like a lady.   105
  That done, conduct him to the drunkard's chamber,
  And call him "madam," do him obeisance.   107
  Tell him from me, as he will win my love,   108
  He bear himself with honorable action
  Such as he hath observed in noble ladies
  Unto their lords by them accomplishèd.   111
  Such duty to the drunkard let him do
  With soft low tongue and lowly courtesy,
  And say, "What is't Your Honor will command,
  Wherein your lady and your humble wife
  May show her duty and make known her love?"
  And then with kind embracements, tempting kisses,
  And with declining head into his bosom,
  Bid him shed tears, as being overjoyed
  To see her noble lord restored to health,
  Who for this seven years hath esteemèd him   121
  No better than a poor and loathsome beggar.
  And if the boy have not a woman's gift
  To rain a shower of commanded tears,
  An onion will do well for such a shift,   125
  Which in a napkin being close conveyed   126
  Shall in despite enforce a watery eye.   127
  See this dispatched with all the haste thou canst.
  Anon I'll give thee more instructions.   129
                 Exit a Servingman.
  I know the boy will well usurp the grace,   130
  Voice, gait, and action of a gentlewoman.
  I long to hear him call the drunkard husband,
  And how my men will stay themselves from laughter   133
  When they do homage to this simple peasant.
  I'll in to counsel them. Haply my presence   135
  May well abate the overmerry spleen   136
  Which otherwise would grow into extremes.
                     [Exeunt.]

                 ♣

---

100 **veriest antic** oddest buffoon or eccentric   101 **buttery** pantry, or a room for storing liquor (in butts) and other provisions   103 **want** lack   105 **in all suits** in every detail. (With a pun on *suits* of clothes.) 107 **do him obeisance** show him dutiful respect.   108 **him** i.e., the page Bartholomew.   **as he will** if he wishes to   111 **by them accomplishèd** performed by the ladies.   121 **him** himself   125 **shift** purpose   126 **napkin** handkerchief.   **close** secretly   127 **in despite** i.e., notwithstanding a natural inclination to laugh rather than cry 129 **Anon** Soon   130 **usurp** assume   133 **And how** i.e., and to see how   135 **I'll in** I'll go in   136 **spleen** mood. (The spleen was the supposed seat of laughter and anger.)

[Induction.2]

Enter aloft the drunkard [Sly], with attendants;
some with apparel, basin, and ewer and other
appurtenances; and Lord.

SLY   For God's sake, a pot of small ale.   1
FIRST SERVINGMAN
  Will't please Your Lordship drink a cup of sack?   2
SECOND SERVINGMAN
  Will't please Your Honor taste of these conserves?   3
THIRD SERVINGMAN
  What raiment will Your Honor wear today?
SLY   I am Christophero Sly. Call not me "Honor" nor
"Lordship." I ne'er drank sack in my life; and if you
give me any conserves, give me conserves of beef.   7
Ne'er ask me what raiment I'll wear, for I have no
more doublets than backs, no more stockings than   9
legs, nor no more shoes than feet—nay, sometimes
more feet than shoes, or such shoes as my toes look   11
through the overleather.   12
LORD
  Heaven cease this idle humor in Your Honor!   13
  Oh, that a mighty man of such descent,
  Of such possessions and so high esteem,
  Should be infusèd with so foul a spirit!
SLY   What, would you make me mad? Am not I Christopher Sly, old Sly's son of Burton-heath, by birth a   18
peddler, by education a cardmaker, by transmutation   19
a bearherd, and now by present profession a tinker?   20
Ask Marian Hacket, the fat alewife of Wincot, if she   21
know me not. If she say I am not fourteen pence on   22
the score for sheer ale, score me up for the lyingest   23
knave in Christendom. What, I am not bestraught: 24
here's—
THIRD SERVINGMAN
  Oh, this it is that makes your lady mourn!
SECOND SERVINGMAN
  Oh, this is it that makes your servants droop!
LORD
  Hence comes it that your kindred shuns your house,
  As beaten hence by your strange lunacy.   29
  Oh, noble lord, bethink thee of thy birth.
  Call home thy ancient thoughts from banishment,   31
  And banish hence these abject lowly dreams.
  Look how thy servants do attend on thee,
  Each in his office ready at thy beck.   34

Induction.2. Location: A bedchamber in the Lord's house.
0.1 *aloft* i.e., in the gallery over the rear facade of the stage   **1 small** weak (and therefore cheap)   **2 sack** sweet Spanish wine (suited for a gentleman to drink).   **3 conserves** candied fruit.   **7 conserves of beef** preserved (salted) beef.   **9 doublets** men's jackets   **11 as that** **12 overleather** upper leather of the shoe.   **13 idle humor** foolish whim   **18 Burton-heath** (Perhaps Barton on the Heath, about sixteen miles from Stratford, the home of Shakespeare's aunt.)   **19 cardmaker** maker of cards or combs used to prepare wool for spinning **20 bearherd** keeper of a performing bear.   **tinker** pot mender. **21 alewife** woman who keeps an alehouse.   **Wincot** small village about four miles from Stratford. (The parish register shows that there were Hackets living there in 1591.)   **22–3 on the score** in debt (since such reckonings were originally notched or scored on a stick)   **23 sheer** nothing but.   **score me up for** reckon me to be   **24 bestraught** distracted   **29 As** as if   **31 ancient** former   **34 beck** nod.

Wilt thou have music? Hark, Apollo plays,   *Music.* 35
And twenty cagèd nightingales do sing.
Or wilt thou sleep? We'll have thee to a couch,
Softer and sweeter than the lustful bed
On purpose trimmed up for Semiramis.   39
Say thou wilt walk; we will bestrew the ground.   40
Or wilt thou ride? Thy horses shall be trapped,   41
Their harness studded all with gold and pearl.
Dost thou love hawking? Thou hast hawks will soar
Above the morning lark. Or wilt thou hunt?
Thy hounds shall make the welkin answer them   45
And fetch shrill echoes from the hollow earth.

FIRST SERVINGMAN
Say thou wilt course, thy greyhounds are as swift   47
As breathèd stags, ay, fleeter than the roe.   48

SECOND SERVINGMAN
Dost thou love pictures? We will fetch thee straight
Adonis painted by a running brook,   50
And Cytherea all in sedges hid,   51
Which seem to move and wanton with her breath,   52
Even as the waving sedges play wi'th'wind.

LORD
We'll show thee Io as she was a maid,   54
And how she was beguilèd and surprised,
As lively painted as the deed was done.   56

THIRD SERVINGMAN
Or Daphne roaming through a thorny wood,   57
Scratching her legs that one shall swear she bleeds,
And at that sight shall sad Apollo weep,
So workmanly the blood and tears are drawn.   60

LORD
Thou art a lord, and nothing but a lord.
Thou hast a lady far more beautiful
Than any woman in this waning age.   63

FIRST SERVINGMAN
And till the tears that she hath shed for thee
Like envious floods o'errun her lovely face,   65
She was the fairest creature in the world;
And yet she is inferior to none.   67

SLY
Am I a lord? And have I such a lady?
Or do I dream? Or have I dreamed till now?
I do not sleep: I see, I hear, I speak,
I smell sweet savors, and I feel soft things.
Upon my life, I am a lord indeed,
And not a tinker nor Christopher Sly.
Well, bring our lady hither to our sight,

And once again a pot o'th' smallest ale.

SECOND SERVINGMAN
Will 't please Your Mightiness to wash your hands?
Oh, how we joy to see your wit restored!   77
Oh, that once more you knew but what you are!   78
These fifteen years you have been in a dream,
Or when you waked, so waked as if you slept.

SLY
These fifteen years! By my fay, a goodly nap.   81
But did I never speak of all that time?   82

FIRST SERVINGMAN
Oh, yes, my lord, but very idle words;
For though you lay here in this goodly chamber,
Yet would you say ye were beaten out of door,
And rail upon the hostess of the house,   86
And say you would present her at the leet   87
Because she brought stone jugs and no sealed quarts.   88
Sometimes you would call out for Cicely Hacket.

SLY
Ay, the woman's maid of the house.

THIRD SERVINGMAN
Why, sir, you know no house, nor no such maid,
Nor no such men as you have reckoned up,
As Stephen Sly, and old John Naps of Greet,   93
And Peter Turf, and Henry Pimpernel,
And twenty more such names and men as these,
Which never were, nor no man ever saw.

SLY
Now Lord be thankèd for my good amends!   97

ALL
Amen.

Enter [the Page as a] lady, with Attendants.

SLY   I thank thee. Thou shalt not lose by it.   98

PAGE
How fares my noble lord?

SLY   Marry, I fare well,   99
For here is cheer enough. Where is my wife?

PAGE
Here, noble lord. What is thy will with her?

SLY
Are you my wife, and will not call me husband?
My men should call me "lord"; I am your goodman.   103

PAGE
My husband and my lord, my lord and husband;
I am your wife in all obedience.

SLY
I know it well.—What must I call her?

LORD   Madam.

35 **Apollo** i.e., as god of music   39 **Semiramis** legendary queen of
Assyria, famous for her voluptuousness.   40 **bestrew** i.e., scatter
rushes on   41 **trapped** adorned   45 **welkin** sky, heavens   47 **course**
hunt the hare   48 **breathèd** in good physical condition, with good
wind. **roe** small, swift deer.   50 **Adonis** a young huntsman with
whom Venus is vainly in love. (See Ovid's *Metamorphoses*, Book 10,
and Shakespeare's poem, *Venus and Adonis*.)   51 **Cytherea** one of the
names for Venus (because of her association with the island of
Cytherea). **sedges** grassy marsh plants   52 **wanton** play seductively
54 **Io** a woman who, according to Ovid, was seduced by Jove concealed in a mist and afterwards transformed into a heifer   56 **as** as if
57 **Daphne** a wood nymph beloved by Apollo, changed by Diana into
a laurel tree to preserve her from Apollo's assault (*Metamorphoses*,
Book 1)   60 **workmanly** skillfully   63 **waning** degenerate   65 **envious** spiteful   67 **yet** even today

77 **wit** mental faculties   78 **knew but** only knew   81 **fay** faith   82 **of**
during   86 **house** tavern   87 **present** bring accusation against. **leet**
manorial court   88 **sealed quarts** quart containers officially stamped
as a guarantee of that capacity. (The irregular stoneware quarts might
be used to cheat customers.)   93 **Stephen . . . Greet** (A Stephen Sly
lived in Stratford during Shakespeare's day. *Greet* is a Gloucestershire
hamlet not far from Stratford. The Folio reading, "Greece," is an easy
misreading if Shakespeare wrote "Greete.")   97 **amends** recovery.
98 **Thou . . . it** i.e., I will reward your solicitude toward me.
99 **Marry** (A mild oath, derived from "by Mary.")   **fare well** (1) am
fine (2) have plenty of good *cheer* (line 100), refreshment   103 **goodman** (A homely term for "husband.")

SLY   Al'ce madam, or Joan madam?

LORD

    Madam, and nothing else. So lords call ladies.

SLY

    Madam wife, they say that I have dreamed

    And slept above some fifteen year or more.

PAGE

    Ay, and the time seems thirty unto me,

    Being all this time abandoned from your bed.   112

SLY

    'Tis much.—Servants, leave me and her alone.—

    Madam, undress you and come now to bed.

PAGE

    Thrice-noble lord, let me entreat of you

    To pardon me yet for a night or two,

    Or, if not so, until the sun be set.

    For your physicians have expressly charged,

    In peril to incur your former malady,

    That I should yet absent me from your bed.

    I hope this reason stands for my excuse.

SLY   Ay, it stands so that I may hardly tarry so long. But   122

    I would be loath to fall into my dreams again. I will

    therefore tarry in despite of the flesh and the blood.

Enter a [Servingman as] messenger.

SERVINGMAN

    Your Honor's players, hearing your amendment,

    Are come to play a pleasant comedy,

    For so your doctors hold it very meet,   127

    Seeing too much sadness hath congealed your blood,

    And melancholy is the nurse of frenzy.

    Therefore they thought it good you hear a play

    And frame your mind to mirth and merriment,

    Which bars a thousand harms and lengthens life.

SLY   Marry, I will let them play it. Is not a comonty a   133

    Christmas gambold or a tumbling-trick?   134

PAGE

    No, my good lord, it is more pleasing stuff.

SLY   What, household stuff?   136

PAGE   It is a kind of history.   137

SLY   Well, we'll see 't. Come, madam wife, sit by my side

    and let the world slip; we shall ne'er be younger.   139

              [They sit over the stage.] Flourish.

❧

1.1

Enter Lucentio and his man, Tranio.

LUCENTIO

    Tranio, since for the great desire I had

    To see fair Padua, nursery of arts,   2

    I am arrived fore fruitful Lombardy,   3

    The pleasant garden of great Italy,

    And by my father's love and leave am armed

    With his good will and thy good company,

    My trusty servant, well approved in all,   7

    Here let us breathe and haply institute   8

    A course of learning and ingenious studies.   9

    Pisa, renownèd for grave citizens,

    Gave me my being, and my father first—   11

    A merchant of great traffic through the world,   12

    Vincentio, come of the Bentivolii.   13

    Vincentio's son, brought up in Florence,   14

    It shall become to serve all hopes conceived   15

    To deck his fortune with his virtuous deeds.   16

    And therefore, Tranio, for the time I study,   17

    Virtue and that part of philosophy

    Will I apply that treats of happiness   19

    By virtue specially to be achieved.

    Tell me thy mind, for I have Pisa left

    And am to Padua come as he that leaves

    A shallow plash to plunge him in the deep,   23

    And with satiety seeks to quench his thirst.

TRANIO

    Mi perdonate, gentle master mine.   25

    I am in all affected as yourself,   26

    Glad that you thus continue your resolve

    To suck the sweets of sweet philosophy.

    Only, good master, while we do admire

    This virtue and this moral discipline,

    Let's be no stoics nor no stocks, I pray,   31

    Or so devote to Aristotle's checks   32

    As Ovid be an outcast quite abjured.   33

    Balk logic with acquaintance that you have,   34

    And practice rhetoric in your common talk.   35

    Music and poesy use to quicken you;   36

1.1 Location: Padua. A street before Baptista's house.
2 Padua . . . arts (Padua's was one of the most renowned of universities during Shakespeare's time.)   **3 am arrived fore** have arrived at, or at the gates of, before. (Padua is not in Lombardy, but imprecise maps may have allowed Shakespeare to think of Lombardy as comprising all of northern Italy.)   **7 approved** tested and proved trustworthy   **8 breathe** pause, settle down.   **haply institute** begin, as circumstances permit   **9 ingenious** i.e., "ingenuous," liberal, befitting a wellborn person   **11 first** i.e., before me   **12 of great traffic** involved in extensive trade   **13 come of** descended from   **14–16 Vincentio's . . . deeds** It will befit Vincentio's son, brought up in Florence, to fulfill all the hopes of his family by adding virtuous deeds to what fortune has bestowed on him.   **17 for . . . study** for my term of study   **19 apply** study.   treats of discusses, concerns   **23 plash** pool   **25 *Mi perdonate*** Pardon me   **26 affected** disposed   **31 stocks** persons devoid of feeling, like wooden posts. (With a play on *stoics*.)   **32 devote** devoted.   **checks** restraints   **33 As** so that.   **Ovid** Latin love poet. (Used here to typify amorous light entertainment, as contrasted with the constraining philosophic study of Aristotle.)   **34 Balk logic** Argue, bandy words.   **acquaintance** acquaintances   **35 common talk** ordinary conversation.   **36 Music . . . you** Use music and poetry to refresh yourself

112 abandoned banished   **122 stands** (1) is the case (2) punningly, "is giving me an erection." The joke picks up on *stands*, meaning "serves," in line 121.   **127 meet** suitable   **133 Marry . . . play it** (Perhaps the Folio punctuation should be emended to "Marry, I will. Let them play it.")   **comonty** (Sly's approximation of "comedy.")   **134 gambold** (Sly's version of "gambol," frolicsome merrymaking and leaping about.)   **136 household stuff** i.e., domestic doings.   **137 history** story.   **139.1 *They sit over the stage*** (Possibly the Lord and some servingmen exeunt here or at line 113. At 1.1.249 ff., a servingman, the Page, and Sly speak, while the Lord is no longer heard from.)

The mathematics and the metaphysics,
Fall to them as you find your stomach serves you.   38
No profit grows where is no pleasure ta'en.
In brief, sir, study what you most affect.   40

LUCENTIO
Gramercies, Tranio, well dost thou advise.   41
If, Biondello, thou wert come ashore,   42
We could at once put us in readiness
And take a lodging fit to entertain
Such friends as time in Padua shall beget.
But stay awhile, what company is this?

TRANIO
Master, some show to welcome us to town.   47

Enter Baptista with his two daughters, Katharina and Bianca; Gremio, a pantaloon; [and] Hortensio, suitor to Bianca. Lucentio [and] Tranio stand by.

BAPTISTA
Gentlemen, importune me no farther,
For how I firmly am resolved you know:
That is, not to bestow my youngest daughter
Before I have a husband for the elder.
If either of you both love Katharina,
Because I know you well and love you well,
Leave shall you have to court her at your pleasure.

GREMIO
To cart her rather. She's too rough for me.   55
There, there, Hortensio, will you any wife?

KATHARINA [*to Baptista*]
I pray you, sir, is it your will
To make a stale of me amongst these mates?   58

HORTENSIO
"Mates," maid? How mean you that? No mates for you,
Unless you were of gentler, milder mold.

KATHARINA
I'faith, sir, you shall never need to fear;
Iwis it is not halfway to her heart.   62
But if it were, doubt not her care should be
To comb your noddle with a three-legged stool,   64
And paint your face, and use you like a fool.   65

HORTENSIO
From all such devils, good Lord deliver us!

GREMIO   And me too, good Lord!

TRANIO [*aside to Lucentio*]
Husht, master, here's some good pastime toward.   68

That wench is stark mad or wonderful froward.   69

LUCENTIO [*aside to Tranio*]
But in the other's silence do I see
Maid's mild behavior and sobriety.
Peace, Tranio!

TRANIO [*aside to Lucentio*]
Well said, master. Mum, and gaze your fill.

BAPTISTA
Gentlemen, that I may soon make good
What I have said—Bianca, get you in.
And let it not displease thee, good Bianca,
For I will love thee ne'er the less, my girl.

KATHARINA   A pretty peat! It is best   78
Put finger in the eye, an she knew why.   79

BIANCA
Sister, content you in my discontent.—
Sir, to your pleasure humbly I subscribe.   81
My books and instruments shall be my company,
On them to look and practice by myself.

LUCENTIO [*aside to Tranio*]
Hark, Tranio, thou mayst hear Minerva speak.   84

HORTENSIO
Signor Baptista, will you be so strange?   85
Sorry am I that our good will effects   86
Bianca's grief.

GREMIO   Why will you mew her up,   87
Signor Baptista, for this fiend of hell,
And make her bear the penance of her tongue?   89

BAPTISTA
Gentlemen, content ye. I am resolved.
Go in, Bianca.   [*Exit Bianca.*]
And for I know she taketh most delight   92
In music, instruments, and poetry,
Schoolmasters will I keep within my house
Fit to instruct her youth. If you, Hortensio,
Or, Signor Gremio, you know any such,
Prefer them hither; for to cunning men   97
I will be very kind, and liberal
To mine own children in good bringing up.
And so farewell.—Katharina, you may stay,
For I have more to commune with Bianca.   *Exit.*   101

KATHARINA
Why, and I trust I may go too, may I not?
What, shall I be appointed hours,   103
As though, belike, I knew not what to take,   104
And what to leave? Ha!   *Exit.*   105

GREMIO   You may go to the devil's dam. Your gifts are   106
so good, here's none will hold you.—Their love is not   107

---

38 stomach inclination, appetite   **40 affect** find pleasant.   **41 Gramercies** Many thanks   **42 Biondello** (Lucentio apostrophizes his absent servant.)   **come ashore** (Padua, though inland, is given a harbor by Shakespeare, unless he is thinking of the canals that crossed northern Italy in the sixteenth century.)   **47.2 pantaloon** foolish old man, a stock character in Italian comedy   **55 cart** carry in a cart through the streets by way of punishment or public exposure. (With a play on *court*.)   **58 stale** laughingstock. (With a play on the meaning "harlot," since a harlot might well be carted.)   **mates** rude fellows. (But Hortensio takes the word in the sense of "husband.")   **62 Iwis . . . heart** indeed, marriage is not even halfway suited to my inclination. (Katharina speaks of herself in the third person here and in line 63.)   **64 comb your noddle** rake your head   **65 paint** i.e., make red with scratches   **68 toward** in prospect.

69 wonderful froward incredibly perverse.   **78–9 A . . . why** i.e., A fine spoiled darling she is! She does well to put on a show of weeping, knowing what's good for her. (Said sardonically.)   **81 pleasure** will.   **subscribe** submit.   **84 Minerva** goddess of wisdom   **85 strange** distant, unfeeling.   **86 effects** causes   **87 mew** coop (as one would a falcon)   **89 her . . . her** i.e., Bianca . . . Katharina's   **92 for** because   **97 Prefer** recommend.   **cunning** skillful, learned   **101 commune** discuss   **103 appointed hours** given a timetable   **104–5 As . . . leave?** as though, forsooth, I didn't know how to choose for myself?   **106 dam** mother.   **gifts** endowments. (Said ironically.)   **107 hold** detain.   **Their love** i.e., The love of women

so great, Hortensio, but we may blow our nails to- 108
gether and fast it fairly out. Our cake's dough on both 109
sides. Farewell. Yet, for the love I bear my sweet 110
Bianca, if I can by any means light on a fit man to teach
her that wherein she delights, I will wish him to 112
her father.

HORTENSIO   So will I, Signor Gremio. But a word, I pray.
Though the nature of our quarrel yet never brooked 115
parle, know now, upon advice, it toucheth us both, 116
that we may yet again have access to our fair mistress
and be happy rivals in Bianca's love, to labor and effect
one thing specially.

GREMIO   What's that, I pray?

HORTENSIO   Marry, sir, to get a husband for her sister.

GREMIO   A husband? A devil.

HORTENSIO   I say a husband.

GREMIO   I say a devil. Think'st thou, Hortensio, though
her father be very rich, any man is so very a fool to be 125
married to hell?

HORTENSIO   Tush, Gremio, though it pass your patience 127
and mine to endure her loud alarums, why, man, there 128
be good fellows in the world, an a man could light on 129
them, would take her with all faults, and money 130
enough.

GREMIO   I cannot tell. But I had as lief take her dowry 132
with this condition: to be whipped at the high cross 133
every morning.

HORTENSIO   Faith, as you say, there's small choice in
rotten apples. But come, since this bar in law makes us 136
friends, it shall be so far forth friendly maintained till
by helping Baptista's eldest daughter to a husband we
set his youngest free for a husband, and then have to't 139
afresh. Sweet Bianca! Happy man be his dole! He that 140
runs fastest gets the ring. How say you, Signor 141
Gremio?

GREMIO   I am agreed, and would I had given him the
best horse in Padua to begin his wooing that would
thor-oughly woo her, wed her, and bed her and rid the
house of her! Come on.   *Exeunt ambo. Manent* 146
                                 Tranio and Lucentio.

TRANIO
I pray, sir, tell me, is it possible
That love should of a sudden take such hold?

LUCENTIO
Oh, Tranio, till I found it to be true,
I never thought it possible or likely.
But see, while idly I stood looking on,

I found the effect of love in idleness, 152
And now in plainness do confess to thee,
That art to me as secret and as dear 154
As Anna to the Queen of Carthage was, 155
Tranio, I burn, I pine, I perish, Tranio,
If I achieve not this young modest girl.
Counsel me, Tranio, for I know thou canst;
Assist me, Tranio, for I know thou wilt.

TRANIO
Master, it is no time to chide you now.
Affection is not rated from the heart. 161
If love have touched you, naught remains but so,
"Redime te captum quam queas minimo." 163

LUCENTIO
Gramercies, lad. Go forward. This contents; 164
The rest will comfort, for thy counsel's sound. 165

TRANIO
Master, you looked so longly on the maid, 166
Perhaps you marked not what's the pith of all. 167

LUCENTIO
Oh, yes, I saw sweet beauty in her face,
Such as the daughter of Agenor had, 169
That made great Jove to humble him to her hand, 170
When with his knees he kissed the Cretan strand. 171

TRANIO
Saw you no more? Marked you not how her sister
Began to scold and raise up such a storm
That mortal ears might hardly endure the din?

LUCENTIO
Tranio, I saw her coral lips to move,
And with her breath she did perfume the air.
Sacred and sweet was all I saw in her.

TRANIO [*aside*]
Nay, then, 'tis time to stir him from his trance.—
I pray, awake, sir. If you love the maid,
Bend thoughts and wits to achieve her. Thus it stands:
Her elder sister is so curst and shrewd 181
That till the father rid his hands of her,
Master, your love must live a maid at home, 183
And therefore has he closely mewed her up,
Because she will not be annoyed with suitors. 185

LUCENTIO
Ah, Tranio, what a cruel father's he!
But art thou not advised he took some care 187
To get her cunning schoolmasters to instruct her? 188

TRANIO
Ay, marry, am I, sir; and now 'tis plotted.

108–9 blow . . . together i.e., twiddle our thumbs, wait patiently
109 fast . . . out abstain as best we can.   **109–10 Our cake's . . . sides**
i.e., We're both out of luck, getting nowhere.   **112 wish** commend
115-16 brooked parle tolerated conference   **116 advice** reflection.
toucheth concerns   **125 very a** utterly a   **127 pass** exceed
128 alarums i.e., loud, startling noises. (In military terms, a call to
arms.)   **129 an** if   **130 would** who would   **132 I cannot tell** i.e., I
don't know about that, don't know what to say.   **had as lief** would
as willingly   **133 high cross** cross set on a pedestal in a marketplace
or center of a town   **136 bar in law** legal impediment, i.e., Baptista's
refusal to receive suitors for Bianca   **139 have to't** renew combat
140 Happy . . . dole! i.e., May happiness be the reward of him who
wins! (Proverbial.)   **141 the ring** (An allusion to the sport of riding at
the ring, with quibble on "wedding ring" and also sexual sense, "vul-
var ring.")   **146 s.d.** *ambo* both.   *Manent* They remain onstage

152 love in idleness i.e., (1) desire bred by idleness (2) a popular name
for the pansy, thought to induce love   **154 secret** trusted, intimate
155 Anna confidante of her sister Dido, Queen of Carthage, beloved of
Aeneas   **161 rated** driven away by chiding   **163 Redime . . . minimo**
Buy yourself out of bondage for as little as you can. (From Terence's
Eunuchus as quoted in William Lilly's *Latin Grammar*.)   **164 Gramercies** Thanks   **165 The rest** the rest of what you have to say   **166 so
longly** (1) for such a long time (2) so longingly   **167 marked** noted.
pith core, essence   **169 daughter of Agenor** Europa, beloved of Jove;
Jove took the form of a bull in order to abduct her   **170 him** himself
171 kissed i.e., knelt on   **181 curst and shrewd** shrewish and ill-
natured   **183 must . . . home** must remain unattached, unmated
185 Because so that   **187 advised** aware (that)   **188 cunning** expert

LUCENTIO
I have it, Tranio.

TRANIO   Master, for my hand,   190
Both our inventions meet and jump in one.   191

LUCENTIO
Tell me thine first.

TRANIO   You will be schoolmaster
And undertake the teaching of the maid:
That's your device.

LUCENTIO   It is. May it be done?

TRANIO
Not possible; for who shall bear your part
And be in Padua here Vincentio's son,
Keep house and ply his book, welcome his friends,   197
Visit his countrymen, and banquet them?

LUCENTIO
Basta, content thee, for I have it full.   199
We have not yet been seen in any house,
Nor can we be distinguished by our faces
For man or master. Then it follows thus:
Thou shalt be master, Tranio, in my stead,
Keep house, and port, and servants, as I should.   204
I will some other be, some Florentine,
Some Neapolitan, or meaner man of Pisa.   206
'Tis hatched and shall be so. Tranio, at once
Uncase thee. Take my colored hat and cloak.   208
When Biondello comes, he waits on thee,
But I will charm him first to keep his tongue.   210

TRANIO   So had you need.
In brief, sir, sith it your pleasure is,   212
And I am tied to be obedient—
For so your father charged me at our parting,
"Be serviceable to my son," quoth he,
Although I think 'twas in another sense—
I am content to be Lucentio,
Because so well I love Lucentio.
                    [*They exchange clothes.*]

LUCENTIO
Tranio, be so, because Lucentio loves.
And let me be a slave t'achieve that maid
Whose sudden sight hath thralled my wounded eye.   221

                    Enter Biondello.

Here comes the rogue.—Sirrah, where have you been?

BIONDELLO
Where have I been? Nay, how now, where are you?
Master, has my fellow Tranio stol'n your clothes?
Or you stol'n his? Or both? Pray, what's the news?

LUCENTIO
Sirrah, come hither. 'Tis no time to jest,
And therefore frame your manners to the time.   227
Your fellow Tranio here, to save my life,
Puts my apparel and my countenance on,   229

And I for my escape have put on his;
For in a quarrel since I came ashore,
I killed a man, and fear I was descried.   232
Wait you on him, I charge you, as becomes,   233
While I make way from hence to save my life.
You understand me?

BIONDELLO   I, sir?—Ne'er a whit.   235

LUCENTIO
And not a jot of Tranio in your mouth.
Tranio is changed into Lucentio.

BIONDELLO
The better for him. Would I were so, too!

TRANIO
So could I, faith, boy, to have the next wish after,
That Lucentio indeed had Baptista's youngest
    daughter.
But, sirrah, not for my sake, but your master's, I
    advise
You use your manners discreetly in all kind of com-
    panies.
When I am alone, why, then I am Tranio,
But in all places else your master Lucentio.

LUCENTIO   Tranio, let's go.
One thing more rests, that thyself execute: 246
To make one among these wooers. If thou ask me
    why,
Sufficeth my reasons are both good and weighty.   248
                    Exeunt.

                    The presenters above speak.

FIRST SERVINGMAN
My lord, you nod. You do not mind the play.   249

SLY   Yes, by Saint Anne, do I. A good matter, surely.
Comes there any more of it?

PAGE [*as lady*]   My lord, 'tis but begun.

SLY   'Tis a very excellent piece of work, madam lady.
Would 'twere done!   *They sit and mark.*   254

                    ❦

[1.2]

                    Enter Petruchio and his man, Grumio.

PETRUCHIO
Verona, for a while I take my leave
To see my friends in Padua, but of all   2
My best belovèd and approvèd friend,
Hortensio; and I trow this is his house.   4
Here, sirrah Grumio, knock, I say.

GRUMIO   Knock, sir? Whom should I knock? Is there any
man has rebused Your Worship?   7

PETRUCHIO   Villain, I say, knock me here soundly.   8

---

190 **for my hand** (A mild oath.)   191 **inventions** plans.   **jump** tally,
agree   197 **Keep . . . book** entertain guests and pursue his studies
199 *Basta* Enough.   **full** i.e., fully thought out.   204 **port** state, style
of living   206 **meaner** of a lower social class   208 **Uncase thee**
remove your outer garments.   210 **charm** i.e., command, persuade
212 **sith** since   221 **Whose . . . thralled** the sudden sight of whom has
captured   227 **frame** adapt, suit   229 **countenance** bearing, manner

232 **descried** observed.   233 **as becomes** as is suitable   235 **I, sir**
(Lucentio may hear this as "Ay, sir.")   **Ne'er a whit** Not in the least.
246 **rests** remains to be done   248 **Sufficeth** it suffices that
248.2 *presenters* characters of the Induction, whose role it is to "present" the play proper   249 **mind** attend to   254 **s.d. mark** observe.
1.2. **Location: Padua. Before Hortensio's house.**
2 **of all** above all   4 **trow** believe   7 **rebused** (A blunder for
"abused.")   8 **Villain** i.e., Wretch. (A term of abuse.)   **me** i.e., for me.
(But Grumio, perhaps intentionally, misunderstands.)

GRUMIO Knock you here, sir? Why, sir, what am I, sir,
that I should knock you here, sir?

PETRUCHIO
Villain, I say, knock me at this gate,   11
And rap me well, or I'll knock your knave's pate.

GRUMIO
My master is grown quarrelsome. I should knock
you first,   13
And then I know after who comes by the worst.   14

PETRUCHIO Will it not be?   15
Faith, sirrah, an you'll not knock, I'll ring it.   16
I'll try how you can *sol fa* and sing it.   17
He wrings him by the ears.

GRUMIO
Help, masters, help! My master is mad.   18

PETRUCHIO
Now knock when I bid you, sirrah villain.

Enter Hortensio.

HORTENSIO How now, what's the matter? My old
friend Grumio and my good friend Petruchio? How
do you all at Verona?

PETRUCHIO
Signor Hortensio, come you to part the fray?
Con tutto il cuore ben trovato, may I say.   24

HORTENSIO
Alla nostra casa ben venuto,   25
Molto onorato signor mio Petruchio.—   26
Rise, Grumio, rise. We will compound this quarrel.   27

GRUMIO Nay, 'tis no matter, sir, what he 'leges in Latin.   28
If this be not a lawful cause for me to leave his service!
Look you, sir: he bid me knock him and rap him
soundly, sir. Well, was it fit for a servant to use his
master so, being perhaps, for aught I see, two-and-   32
thirty, a pip out?   33
Whom would to God I had well knocked at first!
Then had not Grumio come by the worst.

PETRUCHIO
A senseless villain! Good Hortensio,
I bade the rascal knock upon your gate,
And could not get him for my heart to do it.   38

GRUMIO Knock at the gate? Oh, heavens! Spake you
not these words plain, "Sirrah, knock me here, rap me
here, knock me well, and knock me soundly"? And
come you now with "knocking at the gate"?   42

PETRUCHIO
Sirrah, begone, or talk not, I advise you.

HORTENSIO
Petruchio, patience. I am Grumio's pledge.   44
Why, this's a heavy chance twixt him and you,   45
Your ancient, trusty, pleasant servant Grumio.   46
And tell me now, sweet friend, what happy gale
Blows you to Padua here from old Verona?

PETRUCHIO
Such wind as scatters young men through the world
To seek their fortunes farther than at home,
Where small experience grows. But in a few,   51
Signor Hortensio, thus it stands with me:
Antonio, my father, is deceased,
And I have thrust myself into this maze,
Happily to wive and thrive as best I may.   55
Crowns in my purse I have, and goods at home,   56
And so am come abroad to see the world.

HORTENSIO
Petruchio, shall I then come roundly to thee   58
And wish thee to a shrewd, ill-favored wife?   59
Thou'dst thank me but a little for my counsel.
And yet I'll promise thee she shall be rich,
And very rich. But thou'rt too much my friend,
And I'll not wish thee to her.

PETRUCHIO
Signor Hortensio, twixt such friends as we
Few words suffice. And therefore, if thou know
One rich enough to be Petruchio's wife—
As wealth is burden of my wooing dance—   67
Be she as foul as was Florentius' love,   68
As old as Sibyl, and as curst and shrewd   69
As Socrates' Xanthippe, or a worse,   70
She moves me not, or not removes, at least,   71
Affection's edge in me, were she as rough   72
As are the swelling Adriatic seas.
I come to wive it wealthily in Padua;
If wealthily, then happily in Padua.

GRUMIO Nay, look you, sir, he tells you flatly what his
mind is. Why, give him gold enough and marry him
to a puppet or an aglet-baby, or an old trot with ne'er   78
a tooth in her head, though she have as many diseases
as two-and-fifty horses. Why, nothing comes amiss, so   80
money comes withal.   81

---

11 **gate** door   13–14 **I should . . . worst** i.e., You're asking me to hit
you—and I know who then will get the worst of it.   15 **Will it not
be?** i.e., Aren't you going to do what I said?   16 **an** if.   **ring it** sound
loudly, using a circular knocker or a bell. (With a pun on *wring*.)
17 **I'll . . . sing it** i.e., I'll make you cry out. (To *sol fa* is to sing a scale.)
18 **masters** i.e., sirs. (Addressed to the audience.)   24 **Con . . . trovato**
With all my heart, well met   25–6 **Alla . . . Petruchio** Welcome to our
house, my much-honored Signor Petruchio. (Italian.)   27 **compound**
settle   28 **'leges** alleges   32–3 **two . . . out** i.e., drunk, or not quite
right in the head. (Derived from the card game called *one-and-thirty*.)

33 **a pip** a spot on a playing card. (Hence, *a pip out* means "off by
one," or "one in excess of thirty one.")   38 **for my heart** i.e., for my
life   42 **come you now with** do you now change your tune to

44 **pledge** surety.   45 **this's . . . chance** this is a sad occurrence
46 **ancient** long-standing.   **pleasant** merry   51 **in a few** in short
55 **Happily** with good luck. (*Happily* and *haply* were not always distinguished.)   56 **Crowns** Gold coins   58 **come roundly** speak
plainly   59 **shrewd** shrewish.   **ill-favored** ill-natured (? Kate is not
"ugly," the usual meaning of this term; see line 85.)   67 **burden**
undersong, i.e., basis   68 **foul** ugly.   **Florentius' love** (An allusion
to John Gower's version in *Confessio Amantis* of the fairy tale of the
knight who promises to marry an ugly old woman if she solves the
riddle he must answer. After the fulfillment of all promises, she
becomes young and beautiful. Another version of this story is
Chaucer's "Tale of the Wife of Bath," from *The Canterbury Tales*.)
69 **Sibyl** prophetess of Cumae, to whom Apollo gave as many
years of life as she held grains of sand in her hand   70 **Xanthippe**
the philosopher's notoriously shrewish wife   71 **moves** affects,
disturbs. (Setting up wordplay on *removes*.)   72 **Affection's edge**
the keen edge of desire   78 **aglet-baby** small figure carved on the
metal tip of a lace, i.e., a tiny baby.   **trot** hag   80 **so** provided
81 **withal** with it.

HORTENSIO
Petruchio, since we are stepped thus far in,
I will continue that I broached in jest.   83
I can, Petruchio, help thee to a wife
With wealth enough, and young and beauteous,
Brought up as best becomes a gentlewoman.
Her only fault, and that is faults enough,
Is that she is intolerable curst   88
And shrewd, and froward, so beyond all measure   89
That, were my state far worser than it is,   90
I would not wed her for a mine of gold.
PETRUCHIO
Hortensio, peace! Thou know'st not gold's effect.
Tell me her father's name and 'tis enough;
For I will board her, though she chide as loud   94
As thunder when the clouds in autumn crack.   95
HORTENSIO
Her father is Baptista Minola,
An affable and courteous gentleman.
Her name is Katharina Minola,
Renowned in Padua for her scolding tongue.
PETRUCHIO
I know her father, though I know not her,
And he knew my deceasèd father well.
I will not sleep, Hortensio, till I see her;
And therefore let me be thus bold with you
To give you over at this first encounter,   104
Unless you will accompany me thither.
GRUMIO [to Hortensio]   I pray you, sir, let him go while
the humor lasts. O' my word, an she knew him as well   107
as I do, she would think scolding would do little good
upon him. She may perhaps call him half a score
knaves or so. Why, that's nothing; an he begin once,
he'll rail in his rope tricks. I'll tell you what, sir: an she 111
stand him but a little, he will throw a figure in her face   112
and so disfigure her with it that she shall have no more   113
eyes to see withal than a cat. You know him not, sir.   114
HORTENSIO
Tarry, Petruchio, I must go with thee,
For in Baptista's keep my treasure is.   116
He hath the jewel of my life in hold,   117
His youngest daughter, beautiful Bianca,
And her withholds from me and other more,   119
Suitors to her and rivals in my love,
Supposing it a thing impossible,
For those defects I have before rehearsed,   122
That ever Katharina will be wooed.
Therefore this order hath Baptista ta'en,   124
That none shall have access unto Bianca

Till Katharine the curst have got a husband.
GRUMIO   Katharine the curst!
A title for a maid of all titles the worst.
HORTENSIO
Now shall my friend Petruchio do me grace,   129
And offer me disguised in sober robes
To old Baptista as a schoolmaster
Well seen in music, to instruct Bianca,   132
That so I may by this device at least
Have leave and leisure to make love to her,   134
And unsuspected court her by herself.

Enter Gremio [with a paper], and Lucentio dis-
guised [as a schoolmaster].

GRUMIO   Here's no knavery! See, to beguile the old   136
folks, how the young folks lay their heads together!
Master, master, look about you. Who goes there, ha?
HORTENSIO
Peace, Grumio, it is the rival of my love.
Petruchio, stand by awhile.   [*They stand aside.*]
GRUMIO [*aside*]
A proper stripling and an amorous!   141
GREMIO [*to Lucentio*]
Oh, very well, I have perused the note.   142
Hark you, sir, I'll have them very fairly bound—
All books of love, see that at any hand—   144
And see you read no other lectures to her.   145
You understand me. Over and beside
Signor Baptista's liberality,
I'll mend it with a largess. Take your paper too,   148
[*giving Lucentio the note*]
And let me have them very well perfumed,   149
For she is sweeter than perfume itself
To whom they go to. What will you read to her?
LUCENTIO
Whate'er I read to her, I'll plead for you
As for my patron, stand you so assured,
As firmly as yourself were still in place—   154
Yea, and perhaps with more successful words
Than you, unless you were a scholar, sir.
GREMIO
Oh, this learning, what a thing it is!
GRUMIO [*aside*]
Oh, this woodcock, what an ass it is!   158
PETRUCHIO   Peace, sirrah!
HORTENSIO [*coming forward*]
Grumio, mum!—God save you, Signor Gremio.
GREMIO
And you are well met, Signor Hortensio.   161
Trow you whither I am going? To Baptista Minola.   162

83 that I broached what I began   88–9 intolerable . . . froward intol-
erably ill-natured and willful   90 state estate   94 board woo aggressively, accost, have intercourse with, rape   95 crack make an
explosive noise.   104 give you over leave you   107 humor whim.
O' my word, an On my word, if   111 he'll . . . tricks i.e., he has tricks
up his sleeve to answer her scolding.   112–14 he will . . . cat i.e., he
will utterly dazzle and disable her with his rhetorical tricks. (A *figure*
is a figure of speech.)   116 keep (1) place to store treasure (2) keeping
117 in hold (1) in his custody (2) in his stronghold   119 And . . . more
and witholds her from me and others besides   122 rehearsed related,
described   124 this order these measures

129 grace a favor   132 seen skilled   134 make love to woo
136 Here's no knavery! (Said sarcastically.)   141 proper stripling
handsome young fellow. (Said ironically, in reference to Gremio.)
142 note (Evidently, a list of books for Bianca's tutoring.)
144 see see to.   at any hand in any case   145 read . . . lectures teach
no other lessons   148 mend improve, increase.   largess gift of
money.   149 them i.e., the books   154 as as if.   still in place present
all the time   158 woodcock (A bird easily caught; proverbially stupid.)   161 you are well met i.e., how opportune to meet you just
now   162 Trow Know

I promised to inquire carefully
About a schoolmaster for the fair Bianca,
And by good fortune I have lighted well   165
On this young man, for learning and behavior
Fit for her turn, well read in poetry   167
And other books—good ones, I warrant ye.
HORTENSIO
'Tis well. And I have met a gentleman
Hath promised me to help me to another,   170
A fine musician to instruct our mistress.
So shall I no whit be behind in duty
To fair Bianca, so beloved of me.
GREMIO
Beloved of me, and that my deeds shall prove.
GRUMIO [aside]   And that his bags shall prove.   175
HORTENSIO
Gremio, 'tis now no time to vent our love.   176
Listen to me, and if you speak me fair,   177
I'll tell you news indifferent good for either. 178
Here is a gentleman whom by chance I met,
Upon agreement from us to his liking,   180
Will undertake to woo curst Katharine,
Yea, and to marry her, if her dowry please.
GREMIO   So said, so done, is well.   183
Hortensio, have you told him all her faults?
PETRUCHIO
I know she is an irksome brawling scold.
If that be all, masters, I hear no harm.   186
GREMIO
No? Say'st me so, friend? What countryman?
PETRUCHIO
Born in Verona, old Antonio's son.
My father dead, his fortune lives for me,
And I do hope good days and long to see.   190
GREMIO
Oh, sir, such a life with such a wife were strange. 191
But if you have a stomach, to't, i' God's name.   192
You shall have me assisting you in all.
But will you woo this wildcat?
PETRUCHIO   Will I live?
GRUMIO
Will he woo her? Ay, or I'll hang her.
PETRUCHIO
Why came I hither but to that intent?
Think you a little din can daunt mine ears?
Have I not in my time heard lions roar?
Have I not heard the sea, puffed up with winds,
Rage like an angry boar chafèd with sweat?
Have I not heard great ordnance in the field,   201
And heaven's artillery thunder in the skies?

Have I not in a pitchèd battle heard   203
Loud 'larums, neighing steeds, and trumpets' clang? 204
And do you tell me of a woman's tongue,
That gives not half so great a blow to hear
As will a chestnut in a farmer's fire?   207
Tush, tush! Fear boys with bugs.
GRUMIO   For he fears none.   208
GREMIO   Hortensio, hark.
This gentleman is happily arrived,   210
My mind presumes, for his own good and ours.
HORTENSIO
I promised we would be contributors
And bear his charge of wooing, whatsoe'er.   213
GREMIO
And so we will, provided that he win her.
GRUMIO
I would I were as sure of a good dinner.   215

   Enter Tranio, brave [as Lucentio], and
   Biondello.

TRANIO
Gentlemen, God save you. If I may be bold,
Tell me, I beseech you, which is the readiest way
To the house of Signor Baptista Minola?
BIONDELLO   He that has the two fair daughters, is't he
you mean?
TRANIO   Even he, Biondello.   221
GREMIO
Hark you, sir, you mean not her to—
TRANIO
Perhaps him and her, sir. What have you to do?   223
PETRUCHIO
Not her that chides, sir, at any hand, I pray.   224
TRANIO
I love no chiders, sir.—Biondello, let's away.
LUCENTIO [aside]
Well begun, Tranio.
HORTENSIO   Sir, a word ere you go.
Are you a suitor to the maid you talk of, yea or no?
TRANIO
An if I be, sir, is it any offense?
GREMIO
No, if without more words you will get you hence.
TRANIO
Why, sir, I pray, are not the streets as free
For me as for you?
GREMIO   But so is not she.
TRANIO
For what reason, I beseech you?
GREMIO   For this reason, if you'll know,
That she's the choice love of Signor Gremio.

165 lighted alighted   167 Fit for her turn suited to her needs. (Something that is true in more ways than Gremio realizes.)   170 Hath . . . another who has promised to help me to obtain another   175 bags moneybags   176 vent express   177 speak me fair deal with me courteously   178 indifferent equally   180 Upon . . . liking who, if we agree to terms satisfactory to him   183 So . . . is well i.e., That's all very well, when his deeds match his words (which may not be soon).   186 masters good sirs   190 And . . . see and I hope to see many happy days.   191 were would be   192 a stomach an appetite, inclination   201 ordnance artillery.   field battlefield

203 a pitchèd battle a planned battle set in orderly array (unlike a skirmish)   204 'larums calls to arms   207 chestnut (Chestnuts roasted will pop open or explode with a loud report.)   208 Fear . . . bugs. Frighten children with bugbears, bogeymen.   210 happily fortunately, just when needed   213 charge expense   215.1 brave elegantly dressed   221 Even he Yes, precisely, he   223 Perhaps . . . do? i.e., Perhaps I mean to woo both Baptista Minola and Katharina, sir. What's that to you?   224 at any hand on any account

HORTENSIO
> That she's the chosen of Signor Hortensio.

TRANIO
> Softly, my masters! If you be gentlemen,
> Do me this right: hear me with patience.
> Baptista is a noble gentleman,
> To whom my father is not all unknown;   238
> And were his daughter fairer than she is,
> She may more suitors have, and me for one.
> Fair Leda's daughter had a thousand wooers;   241
> Then well one more may fair Bianca have,
> And so she shall. Lucentio shall make one,
> Though Paris came in hope to speed alone.   244

GREMIO
> What, this gentleman will out-talk us all!

LUCENTIO
> Sir, give him head. I know he'll prove a jade.   246

PETRUCHIO
> Hortensio, to what end are all these words?

HORTENSIO [to Tranio]
> Sir, let me be so bold as ask you,   248
> Did you yet ever see Baptista's daughter?

TRANIO
> No, sir, but hear I do that he hath two,
> The one as famous for a scolding tongue
> As is the other for beauteous modesty.

PETRUCHIO
> Sir, sir, the first's for me. Let her go by.   253

GREMIO
> Yea, leave that labor to great Hercules,
> And let it be more than Alcides' twelve.   255

PETRUCHIO
> Sir, understand you this of me, in sooth: 256
> The youngest daughter, whom you hearken for,   257
> Her father keeps from all access of suitors,
> And will not promise her to any man
> Until the elder sister first be wed.
> The younger then is free, and not before.

TRANIO
> If it be so, sir, that you are the man
> Must stead us all, and me amongst the rest;   263
> And if you break the ice and do this feat,
> Achieve the elder, set the younger free
> For our access, whose hap shall be to have her   266
> Will not so graceless be to be ingrate.   267

HORTENSIO
> Sir, you say well, and well you do conceive.   268
> And since you do profess to be a suitor,
> You must, as we do, gratify this gentleman,   270

---

238 **all** entirely   241 **Leda's daughter** Helen of Troy   244 **Though . . . alone** even if Paris (who abducted Helen from her husband, Menelaus) were to come in hopes of succeeding above all others. 246 **Sir . . . jade** Sir, give him a loose bridle; i.e., let him talk freely. I know he'll prove to be a worthless horse, soon tired.   248 **as ask** as to ask   253 **Let her go by** Pass over her.   255 **And . . . twelve** (Hercules, called *Alcides* because he was the reputed grandson of Alcaeus, had to perform twelve huge labors.)   256 **of me** from me. **sooth** truth   257 **hearken for** seek to win   263 **Must stead** who must help 266 **whose hap** he whose good fortune   267 **to be ingrate** as to be ungrateful.   268 **conceive** understand.   270 **gratify this gentleman** reward Petruchio

---

> To whom we all rest generally beholding.   271

TRANIO
> Sir, I shall not be slack. In sign whereof,
> Please ye we may contrive this afternoon,   273
> And quaff carouses to our mistress' health,   274
> And do as adversaries do in law—   275
> Strive mightily, but eat and drink as friends.

GRUMIO, BIONDELLO
> Oh, excellent motion! Fellows, let's be gone.   277

HORTENSIO
> The motion's good indeed, and be it so.
> Petruchio, I shall be your *ben venuto*.   *Exeunt.* 279

❖

[2.1]

Enter Katharina and Bianca [with her hands tied].

BIANCA
> Good sister, wrong me not, nor wrong yourself,
> To make a bondmaid and a slave of me.
> That I disdain. But for these other goods,   3
> Unbind my hands, I'll pull them off myself,   4
> Yea, all my raiment, to my petticoat,
> Or what you will command me will I do,
> So well I know my duty to my elders.

KATHARINA
> Of all thy suitors here I charge thee tell
> Whom thou lov'st best. See thou dissemble not.

BIANCA
> Believe me, sister, of all the men alive
> I never yet beheld that special face
> Which I could fancy more than any other.

KATHARINA
> Minion, thou liest. Is't not Hortensio?   13

BIANCA
> If you affect him, sister, here I swear   14
> I'll plead for you myself but you shall have him.   15

KATHARINA
> Oh, then belike you fancy riches more.   16
> You will have Gremio to keep you fair.   17

BIANCA
> Is it for him you do envy me so?
> Nay, then, you jest, and now I well perceive
> You have but jested with me all this while.
> I prithee, sister Kate, untie my hands.

KATHARINA *(strikes her)*
> If that be jest, then all the rest was so.

Enter Baptista.

---

271 **beholding** beholden, indebted.   273 **contrive** manage our affairs, pass the time   274 **quaff carouses** drink toasts   275 **adversaries** opposing lawyers   277 **motion** suggestion.   279 *ben venuto* welcome, i.e., host.
2.1. Location: Padua. Baptista's house.
3 **for** as for.   **goods** i.e., clothes, jewels, love tokens   4 **Unbind** if you will unbind   13 **Minion** Hussy   14 **affect** love   15 **but . . . him** if necessary for you to win him.   16 **belike** perhaps   17 **fair** resplendent with finery.

BAPTISTA
    Why, how now, dame, whence grows this
        insolence?—
    Bianca, stand aside. Poor girl, she weeps.
    Go ply thy needle, meddle not with her.—   25
    For shame, thou hilding of a devilish spirit,   26
    Why dost thou wrong her that did ne'er wrong thee?
    When did she cross thee with a bitter word?   28

KATHARINA
    Her silence flouts me, and I'll be revenged.   29
                                [*She*] *flies after Bianca.*

BAPTISTA
    What, in my sight? Bianca, get thee in.   *Exit* [*Bianca*].

KATHARINA
    What, will you not suffer me? Nay, now I see   31
    She is your treasure, she must have a husband;
    I must dance barefoot on her wedding day,   33
    And for your love to her lead apes in hell.   34
    Talk not to me. I will go sit and weep
    Till I can find occasion of revenge.   [*Exit.*]

BAPTISTA
    Was ever gentleman thus grieved as I?
    But who comes here?   38

    Enter Gremio, Lucentio [*as a schoolmaster*] *in the
    habit of a mean man, Petruchio, with* [*Hortensio as
    a musician, and*] *Tranio* [*as Lucentio*] *with his boy*
    [*Biondello*] *bearing a lute and books.*

GREMIO   Good morrow, neighbor Baptista.

BAPTISTA   Good morrow, neighbor Gremio. God save
    you, gentlemen.

PETRUCHIO
    And you, good sir. Pray, have you not a daughter
    Called Katharina, fair and virtuous?

BAPTISTA
    I have a daughter, sir, called Katharina.

GREMIO
    You are too blunt. Go to it orderly.   45

PETRUCHIO
    You wrong me, Signor Gremio; give me leave.—   46
    I am a gentleman of Verona, sir,
    That, hearing of her beauty and her wit,
    Her affability and bashful modesty,
    Her wondrous qualities and mild behavior,
    Am bold to show myself a forward guest
    Within your house, to make mine eye the witness
    Of that report which I so oft have heard.
    And, for an entrance to my entertainment,   54
    I do present you with a man of mine,
                            [*presenting Hortensio*]
    Cunning in music and the mathematics,   56

    To instruct her fully in those sciences,   57
    Whereof I know she is not ignorant.
    Accept of him, or else you do me wrong.   59
    His name is Litio, born in Mantua.

BAPTISTA
    You're welcome, sir, and he, for your good sake.
    But for my daughter Katharine, this I know,   62
    She is not for your turn, the more my grief.

PETRUCHIO
    I see you do not mean to part with her,
    Or else you like not of my company.   65

BAPTISTA
    Mistake me not, I speak but as I find.
    Whence are you, sir? What may I call your name?

PETRUCHIO
    Petruchio is my name, Antonio's son,
    A man well known throughout all Italy.

BAPTISTA
    I know him well. You are welcome for his sake.   70

GREMIO
    Saving your tale, Petruchio, I pray,   71
    Let us that are poor petitioners speak too.
    Bacare! You are marvelous forward.   73

PETRUCHIO
    Oh, pardon me, Signor Gremio, I would fain be doing. 74

GREMIO
    I doubt it not, sir, but you will curse your wooing.—
    Neighbors, this is a gift very grateful, I am sure of   76
    it. [*To Baptista*] To express the like kindness, my-
    self, that have been more kindly beholding to you
    than any, freely give unto you this young scholar
    [*presenting Lucentio*], that hath been long studying at
    Rheims, as cunning in Greek, Latin, and other
    languages as the other in music and mathematics. His   82
    name is Cambio. Pray, accept his service.   83

BAPTISTA   A thousand thanks, Signor Gremio.—Wel-
    come, good Cambio. [*To Tranio*] But, gentle sir,
    methinks you walk like a stranger. May I be so bold to
    know the cause of your coming?

TRANIO
    Pardon me, sir, the boldness is mine own,
    That, being a stranger in this city here,
    Do make myself a suitor to your daughter,
    Unto Bianca, fair and virtuous.
    Nor is your firm resolve unknown to me
    In the preferment of the eldest sister.
    This liberty is all that I request,   93
    That, upon knowledge of my parentage,
    I may have welcome 'mongst the rest that woo,   95
    And free access and favor as the rest.   97

---

25 **meddle not with** have nothing to do with   26 **hilding** vicious
(hence worthless) beast   28 **cross** contradict, thwart   29 **flouts**
mocks, insults   31 **suffer me** let me have my own way.   33, 34 **dance
. . . day, lead . . . hell** (Popularly supposed to be the fate of old maids.)
38.2 *habit* dress.   *mean* of low social station. (Said here of a schoolmaster.)   45 **orderly** in a properly orderly manner.   46 **give me leave**
excuse me, let me do this my way.   54 **entrance** entrance fee.
entertainment reception   56 **Cunning** skillful

57 **sciences** subjects, branches of knowledge   59 **Accept of** Accept
62 **for** as for   65 **like not of** do not like   70 **know** know of. (See also
lines 104–5.)   71 **Saving** With all due respect for   73 *Bacare!* Stand
back!   74 **fain** gladly.   **doing** getting on with the business. (With
sexual suggestion.)   76 **grateful** pleasing   82 **the other** i.e., Hortensio   83 **Cambio** (In Italian, appropriately, the word means "change"
or "exchange.")   93 **In the preferment of** in the precedence you give
to   95 **upon knowledge of** when you know about   97 **favor** leave,
permission

And toward the education of your daughters
I here bestow a simple instrument,
And this small packet of Greek and Latin books.
If you accept them, then their worth is great.
                    [*Biondello brings forward the lute and books.*]

BAPTISTA
Lucentio is your name? Of whence, I pray?   102

TRANIO
Of Pisa, sir, son to Vincentio.

BAPTISTA
A mighty man of Pisa. By report
I know him well. You are very welcome, sir.
[*To Hortensio*] Take you the lute, [*to Lucentio*] and
    you the set of books;
You shall go see your pupils presently.—
Holla, within!

                    Enter a Servant.

                              Sirrah, lead these gentlemen
To my daughters, and tell them both
These are their tutors. Bid them use them well.
                    [*Exit Servant, with Lucentio and Hortensio.*]
We will go walk a little in the orchard,
And then to dinner. You are passing welcome,   112
And so I pray you all to think yourselves.

PETRUCHIO
Signor Baptista, my business asketh haste,
And every day I cannot come to woo.
You knew my father well, and in him me,
Left solely heir to all his lands and goods,
Which I have bettered rather than decreased.
Then tell me, if I get your daughter's love,
What dowry shall I have with her to wife?

BAPTISTA
After my death the one half of my lands,
And in possession twenty thousand crowns.   122

PETRUCHIO
And for that dowry I'll assure her of   123
Her widowhood, be it that she survive me,   124
In all my lands and leases whatsoever.
Let specialties be therefore drawn between us,   126
That covenants may be kept on either hand.

BAPTISTA
Ay, when the special thing is well obtained,
That is, her love; for that is all in all.

PETRUCHIO
Why, that is nothing, for I tell you, father,   130
I am as peremptory as she proud-minded;
And where two raging fires meet together,
They do consume the thing that feeds their fury.
Though little fire grows great with little wind,
Yet extreme gusts will blow out fire and all.
So I to her, and so she yields to me,   136

For I am rough and woo not like a babe.

BAPTISTA
Well mayst thou woo, and happy be thy speed!   138
But be thou armed for some unhappy words.

PETRUCHIO
Ay, to the proof, as mountains are for winds,   140
That shakes not, though they blow perpetually.   141

            Enter Hortensio [as Litio], with his head broke.

BAPTISTA
How now, my friend, why dost thou look so pale?

HORTENSIO
For fear, I promise you, if I look pale.   143

BAPTISTA
What, will my daughter prove a good musician?

HORTENSIO
I think she'll sooner prove a soldier.   145
Iron may hold with her, but never lutes.   146

BAPTISTA
Why then, thou canst not break her to the lute?   147

HORTENSIO
Why, no, for she hath broke the lute to me.
I did but tell her she mistook her frets,   149
And bowed her hand to teach her fingering,
When, with a most impatient devilish spirit,
"Frets, call you these?" quoth she, "I'll fume with
    them."
And with that word she struck me on the head,
And through the instrument my pate made way;
And there I stood amazèd for a while,   155
As on a pillory, looking through the lute,   156
While she did call me rascal fiddler
And twangling Jack, with twenty such vile terms,   158
As had she studied to misuse me so.   159

PETRUCHIO
Now, by the world, it is a lusty wench!   160
I love her ten times more than e'er I did.
Oh, how I long to have some chat with her!

BAPTISTA [*to Hortensio*]
Well, go with me, and be not so discomfited.
Proceed in practice with my younger daughter;   164
She's apt to learn and thankful for good turns.—
Signor Petruchio, will you go with us,
Or shall I send my daughter Kate to you?

PETRUCHIO
I pray you, do.   *Exeunt. Manet Petruchio.*
            I'll attend her here,   168
And woo her with some spirit when she comes.

---

102 **Lucentio . . . name?** (Baptista may have learned this information from a note accompanying the books and lute.)   112 **passing** exceedingly   122 **in possession** in immediate possession   123 **for** in exchange for   124 **widowhood** i.e., widow's share of the estate. **be it that she** if she should   126 **specialties** terms of contract   130 **father** father-in-law   136 **So I** i.e., So I behave, like an extreme gust of wind

138 **happy . . . speed!** may fortune give you success!   140 **to the proof** i.e., in armor, proof against her shrewishness   141 **shakes** shake   141.1 *broke* with a bleeding cut. (Hortensio usually appears on stage with his head emerging through a broken lute.)   143 **promise** assure   145 **I think . . . soldier** i.e., She's better suited for the manly career of soldiering.   146 **hold with** hold out against   147 **break** train. (With pun in the next line.)   149 **frets** ridges or bars on the fingerboard of the lute. (But Kate puns on the sense of "fume," "be indignant.")   155 **amazèd** bewildered   156 **As on a pillory** as if with my head in a wooden collar used as punishment   158 **Jack** knave   159 **As . . . so** as if she had planned how to abuse me so.   160 **lusty** lively   164 **practice** instruction   168 s.d. *Manet* He remains onstage

Say that she rail, why then I'll tell her plain
She sings as sweetly as a nightingale.
Say that she frown, I'll say she looks as clear   172
As morning roses newly washed with dew.
Say she be mute and will not speak a word,
Then I'll commend her volubility
And say she uttereth piercing eloquence.   176
If she do bid me pack, I'll give her thanks,   177
As though she bid me stay by her a week.
If she deny to wed, I'll crave the day   179
When I shall ask the banns and when be married.   180
But here she comes; and now, Petruchio, speak.

    Enter Katharina.

Good morrow, Kate, for that's your name, I hear.
KATHARINA
Well have you heard, but something hard of hearing.   183
They call me Katharine that do talk of me.
PETRUCHIO
You lie, in faith, for you are called plain Kate,
And bonny Kate, and sometimes Kate the curst;
But Kate, the prettiest Kate in Christendom,
Kate of Kate Hall, my superdainty Kate,
For dainties are all Kates, and therefore, Kate,   189
Take this of me, Kate of my consolation: 190
Hearing thy mildness praised in every town,
Thy virtues spoke of, and thy beauty sounded,   192
Yet not so deeply as to thee belongs,
Myself am moved to woo thee for my wife.   194
KATHARINA
Moved? In good time! Let him that moved you hither   195
Remove you hence. I knew you at the first
You were a movable.
PETRUCHIO   Why, what's a movable?   197
KATHARINA
A joint stool.
PETRUCHIO   Thou hast hit it. Come, sit on me.   198
KATHARINA
Asses are made to bear, and so are you.   199
PETRUCHIO
Women are made to bear, and so are you.
KATHARINA
No such jade as you, if me you mean.   201
PETRUCHIO
Alas, good Kate, I will not burden thee,   202

For knowing thee to be but young and light.   203
KATHARINA
Too light for such a swain as you to catch,   204
And yet as heavy as my weight should be.
PETRUCHIO
Should be? Should—buzz!
KATHARINA   Well ta'en, and like a buzzard.   206
PETRUCHIO
Oh, slow-winged turtle, shall a buzzard take thee?
KATHARINA
Ay, for a turtle, as he takes a buzzard.
PETRUCHIO
Come, come, you wasp, i'faith you are too angry.   209
KATHARINA
If I be waspish, best beware my sting.
PETRUCHIO
My remedy is then to pluck it out.
KATHARINA
Ay, if the fool could find it where it lies.
PETRUCHIO
Who knows not where a wasp does wear his sting?
In his tail.
KATHARINA   In his tongue.
PETRUCHIO   Whose tongue?
KATHARINA
Yours, if you talk of tales, and so farewell.   217
PETRUCHIO
What, with my tongue in your tail? Nay, come again.
Good Kate, I am a gentleman—
KATHARINA   That I'll try.
                              She strikes him.
PETRUCHIO
I swear I'll cuff you if you strike again.
KATHARINA   So may you lose your arms.
If you strike me, you are no gentleman,
And if no gentleman, why then no arms.   223
PETRUCHIO
A herald, Kate? Oh, put me in thy books!   224
KATHARINA   What is your crest, a coxcomb?   225
PETRUCHIO
A combless cock, so Kate will be my hen.   226
KATHARINA
No cock of mine. You crow too like a craven.   227

---

172 clear serene   **176 piercing** moving   **177 pack** begone   **179 deny** refuse.   **crave the day** ask her to name the day   **180 ask the banns** have a reading of the required announcement in church of a forth-coming marriage   **183 heard, hard** (Pronounced nearly alike.) **189 all Kates** (With a quibble on "cates," confections, delicacies.) **190 of me** from me.   **consolation** comfort   **192 sounded** proclaimed. (With a quibble on "plumbed," as indicated by *deeply* in the next line.) **194 moved** impelled. (Followed by wordplay on the more literal meaning of *move* and *remove*.)   **195 In good time!** Forsooth! Indeed! **197 movable** (1) one easily changed or dissuaded (2) an article of furniture.   **198 A joint stool** a well-fitted stool made by an expert crafts-man.   **199 bear** carry. (With puns in the following lines suggesting "bear children" and "support a man during sexual intercourse.") **201 jade** an ill-conditioned horse   **202 burden** (1) oppress with a heavy load—a term appropriate to *asses* and *bear* in line 199, since asses are beasts of *burden* (2) lie on during sexual intercourse, impregnate. (See notes on lines 199 and 203.)

203 For knowing because I know.   **light** (1) of delicate stature (2) las-civious (3) lacking a *burden* (see previous line) in the musical sense of lacking a bass undersong or accompaniment (4) elusive (in the fol-lowing line).   **204 swain** young rustic in love   **206 Should . . . buzz!** (Petruchio puns on *be* and "bee," and uses *buzz* in perhaps three senses: [1] an interjection of impatience or contempt [2] a bee's sound [3] a rumor being buzzed about, to which, he implies, Kate had better listen.)   **buzzard** (1) figuratively, a fool (2) in the next line, an inferior kind of hawk, fit only to overtake a slow-winged *turtle* or turtledove, as Petruchio might overtake Kate (3) a buzzing insect, caught by a turtledove.   **209 wasp** i.e., waspish, scolding woman. (But suggested by *buzzard*, buzzing insect.)   **217 talk of tales** i.e., idly tell stories. (With pun on "tail.")   **223 no arms** no coat of arms. (With pun on *arms* as limbs of the body.)   **224 books** (1) books of heraldry, heraldic registers (2) grace, favor.   **225 crest** (1) armorial device (2) a rooster's comb, setting up the joke on *coxcomb*, the cap of the court fool **226 A combless cock** i.e., A gentle rooster. (With suggestion of the male sexual organ.)   **so** provided that   **227 a craven** a cock that is not "game" or willing to fight.

PETRUCHIO
Nay, come, Kate, come. You must not look so sour.

KATHARINA
It is my fashion when I see a crab.   229

PETRUCHIO
Why, here's no crab, and therefore look not sour.

KATHARINA   There is, there is.

PETRUCHIO
Then show it me.

KATHARINA   Had I a glass, I would.

PETRUCHIO   What, you mean my face?

KATHARINA   Well aimed of such a young one.   234

PETRUCHIO
Now, by Saint George, I am too young for you.

KATHARINA
Yet you are withered.

PETRUCHIO   'Tis with cares.

KATHARINA   I care not.

PETRUCHIO
Nay, hear you, Kate. In sooth, you scape not so.   237

KATHARINA
I chafe you if I tarry. Let me go.   238

PETRUCHIO
No, not a whit. I find you passing gentle.   239
'Twas told me you were rough, and coy, and sullen,   240
And now I find report a very liar,   241
For thou art pleasant, gamesome, passing courteous, 242
But slow in speech, yet sweet as springtime flowers. 243
Thou canst not frown, thou canst not look askance,   244
Nor bite the lip, as angry wenches will,
Nor hast thou pleasure to be cross in talk;   246
But thou with mildness entertain'st thy wooers,   247
With gentle conference, soft and affable.   248
Why does the world report that Kate doth limp?
Oh, sland'rous world! Kate like the hazel twig
Is straight and slender, and as brown in hue
As hazelnuts, and sweeter than the kernels.
Oh, let me see thee walk. Thou dost not halt.   253

KATHARINA
Go, fool, and whom thou keep'st command.   254

PETRUCHIO
Did ever Dian so become a grove   255
As Kate this chamber with her princely gait?
Oh, be thou Dian, and let her be Kate,
And then let Kate be chaste and Dian sportful!   258

KATHARINA
Where did you study all this goodly speech?   259

PETRUCHIO
It is extempore, from my mother wit.   260

KATHARINA
A witty mother! Witless else her son.   261

PETRUCHIO   Am I not wise?   262

KATHARINA   Yes, keep you warm.   263

PETRUCHIO
Marry, so I mean, sweet Katharine, in thy bed.
And therefore, setting all this chat aside,
Thus in plain terms: your father hath consented
That you shall be my wife; your dowry 'greed on;
And will you, nill you, I will marry you.   268
Now, Kate, I am a husband for your turn,   269
For by this light, whereby I see thy beauty—
Thy beauty that doth make me like thee well—
Thou must be married to no man but me.

*Enter Baptista, Gremio, [and] Tranio [as
Lucentio].*

For I am he am born to tame you, Kate,
And bring you from a wild Kate to a Kate   274
Conformable as other household Kates.   275
Here comes your father. Never make denial;
I must and will have Katharine to my wife.

BAPTISTA
Now, Signor Petruchio, how speed you with my
daughter?   278

PETRUCHIO
How but well, sir, how but well?
It were impossible I should speed amiss.

BAPTISTA
Why, how now, daughter Katharine, in your dumps? 281

KATHARINA
Call you me daughter? Now, I promise you,   282
You have showed a tender fatherly regard,
To wish me wed to one half-lunatic,
A madcap ruffian and a swearing Jack,   285
That thinks with oaths to face the matter out.   286

PETRUCHIO
Father, 'tis thus: yourself and all the world
That talked of her have talked amiss of her.
If she be curst, it is for policy,   289
For she's not froward, but modest as the dove.   290
She is not hot, but temperate as the morn.
For patience she will prove a second Grissel,   292
And Roman Lucrece for her chastity.   293
And to conclude, we have 'greed so well together
That upon Sunday is the wedding day.

---

229 **crab** crab apple.   234 **aimed of** guessed for.   **young** i.e., inexperienced. (But Petruchio picks up the word in the sense of "strong," "virile.")   237 **scape** escape   238 **chafe** irritate, arouse   239 **passing** very. (Also in line 242.)   240 **coy** disdainful   241 **a very** an utter   242 **pleasant, gamesome** merry, spirited   243 **But slow** never anything but slow   244 **askance** scornfully   246 **cross in talk** always contradicting   247 **entertain'st** receive   248 **conference** conversation   253 **halt** limp.   254 **whom thou keep'st command** i.e., order about those whom you employ, your servants, not me.   255 **Dian** Diana, goddess of the hunt and of chastity.   **become** adorn   258 **sportful** amorous.   259 **study** memorize   260 **mother wit** native intelligence.

261 **Witless . . . son** i.e., Without the intelligence inherited from her, he would have none at all.   262–3 **wise . . . warm** (An allusion to the proverbial phrase "enough wit to keep oneself warm.")   268 **will you, nill you** whether you're willing or not   269 **for your turn** to suit you   274 **wild Kate** (With a quibble on "wildcat.")   275 **Conformable** compliant   278 **speed** fare, get on   281 **in your dumps** in low spirits.   282 **promise** assure   285 **Jack** ill-mannered fellow   286 **face** brazen   289 **policy** cunning, ulterior motive   290 **froward** willful, perverse   292 **Grissel** patient Griselda, the epitome of wifely patience and devotion (whose story was told by Chaucer in "The Clerk's Tale" of *The Canterbury Tales* and earlier by Boccaccio and Petrarch)   293 **Roman Lucrece** Lucretia, a Roman lady who took her own life after her chastity had been violated by the Tarquin prince, Sextus. (Shakespeare tells the story in *The Rape of Lucrece.*)

KATHARINA
I'll see thee hanged on Sunday first.
GREMIO Hark, Petruchio, she says she'll see thee
hanged first.
TRANIO
Is this your speeding? Nay then, good night our part! 299
PETRUCHIO
Be patient, gentlemen. I choose her for myself.
If she and I be pleased, what's that to you?
'Tis bargained twixt us twain, being alone,
That she shall still be curst in company.
I tell you, 'tis incredible to believe
How much she loves me. Oh, the kindest Kate!
She hung about my neck, and kiss on kiss
She vied so fast, protesting oath on oath,   307
That in a twink she won me to her love.
Oh, you are novices! 'Tis a world to see   309
How tame, when men and women are alone,
A meacock wretch can make the curstest shrew.—   311
Give me thy hand, Kate. I will unto Venice
To buy apparel gainst the wedding day.—   313
Provide the feast, father, and bid the guests.
I will be sure my Katharine shall be fine.   315
BAPTISTA
I know not what to say. But give me your hands.
God send you joy, Petruchio! 'Tis a match.
GREMIO, TRANIO
Amen, say we. We will be witnesses.
PETRUCHIO
Father, and wife, and gentlemen, adieu.
I will to Venice. Sunday comes apace.
We will have rings, and things, and fine array;
And kiss me, Kate. We will be married o'Sunday. 322
Exeunt Petruchio and Katharine [separately].
GREMIO
Was ever match clapped up so suddenly?   323
BAPTISTA
Faith, gentlemen, now I play a merchant's part, 324
And venture madly on a desperate mart.   325
TRANIO
'Twas a commodity lay fretting by you;   326
'Twill bring you gain, or perish on the seas.
BAPTISTA
The gain I seek is quiet in the match.
GREMIO
No doubt but he hath got a quiet catch.   329
But now, Baptista, to your younger daughter.
Now is the day we long have looked for.
I am your neighbor, and was suitor first.

TRANIO
And I am one that love Bianca more
Than words can witness, or your thoughts can guess.
GREMIO
Youngling, thou canst not love so dear as I.
TRANIO
Graybeard, thy love doth freeze.
GREMIO   But thine doth fry.
Skipper, stand back. 'Tis age that nourisheth.   337
TRANIO
But youth in ladies' eyes that flourisheth.
BAPTISTA
Content you, gentlemen, I will compound this strife. 339
'Tis deeds must win the prize, and he of both   340
That can assure my daughter greatest dower   341
Shall have my Bianca's love.
Say, Signor Gremio, what can you assure her?
GREMIO
First, as you know, my house within the city
Is richly furnishèd with plate and gold,   345
Basins and ewers to lave her dainty hands;   346
My hangings all of Tyrian tapestry;   347
In ivory coffers I have stuffed my crowns;   348
In cypress chests my arras counterpoints,   349
Costly apparel, tents, and canopies,   350
Fine linen, Turkey cushions bossed with pearl,   351
Valance of Venice gold in needlework,   352
Pewter and brass, and all things that belongs
To house or housekeeping. Then at my farm
I have a hundred milch kine to the pail,   355
Sixscore fat oxen standing in my stalls,
And all things answerable to this portion.   357
Myself am struck in years, I must confess,   358
And if I die tomorrow, this is hers,
If whilst I live she will be only mine.
TRANIO
That "only" came well in.—Sir, list to me:
I am my father's heir and only son.
If I may have your daughter to my wife,
I'll leave her houses three or four as good,
Within rich Pisa walls, as any one
Old Signor Gremio has in Padua,
Besides two thousand ducats by the year   367
Of fruitful land, all which shall be her jointure.— 368
What, have I pinched you, Signor Gremio?
GREMIO
Two thousand ducats by the year of land!
[*Aside*] My land amounts not to so much in all.—
That she shall have, besides an argosy   372

299 speeding success.   **good night our part** good-bye to what we
hoped to get.   **307 vied** went me one better, kiss for kiss   **309 a
world** worth a whole world   **311 meacock** cowardly   **313 gainst** in
anticipation of   **315 fine** elegantly dressed.   **322 kiss me** (Petruchio
probably kisses her.)   **323 clapped up** settled (by a shaking of hands)
324 Faith In faith   **325 desperate mart** risky venture.   **326 lay fretting** i.e., which lay in storage being destroyed by moths, weevils, or
spoilage. (With a pun on "chafing.")   **329 quiet catch** (Said ironically;
Gremio is sure that Kate will be anything but quiet.)

337 Skipper Flighty fellow   **339 compound** settle   **340 deeds**
(1) actions (2) legal deeds.   **he of both** the one of you two   **341
dower** portion of a husband's estate settled on his wife in his will.
(Also at line 387 and 4.4.45.)   **345 plate** silver utensils   **346 ewers to
lave** pitchers to wash   **347 hangings** draperies hung on beds and
walls.   **Tyrian** dark red or purple   **348 crowns** five-shilling coins
349 arras counterpoints counterpanes of tapestry   **350 tents** bed curtains   **351 Turkey** Turkish.   **bossed** embossed   **352 Valance** fringes
of drapery around the canopy or bed frame   **355 milch kine to the
pail** dairy cattle   **357 answerable to** on the same scale as   **358 struck**
advanced   **367 ducats** gold coins   **368 Of** from.   **jointure** marriage
settlement.   **372 argosy** merchant vessel of the largest size

That now is lying in Marseilles road.   373
[*To Tranio*] What, have I choked you with an argosy?

TRANIO
Gremio, 'tis known my father hath no less
Than three great argosies, besides two galliases   376
And twelve tight galleys. These I will assure her,   377
And twice as much, whate'er thou off'rest next.

GREMIO
Nay, I have offered all. I have no more,
And she can have no more than all I have.
[*To Baptista*] If you like me, she shall have me and
    mine.

TRANIO
Why then, the maid is mine from all the world,
By your firm promise. Gremio is outvied.   383

BAPTISTA
I must confess your offer is the best;
And, let your father make her the assurance,   385
She is your own; else, you must pardon me.
If you should die before him, where's her dower?

TRANIO
That's but a cavil. He is old, I young.   388

GREMIO
And may not young men die, as well as old?

BAPTISTA
Well, gentlemen, I am thus resolved:
On Sunday next, you know
My daughter Katharine is to be married.
Now, on the Sunday following shall Bianca
Be bride [*to Tranio*] to you, if you make this assurance;
If not, to Signor Gremio.
And so I take my leave, and thank you both.   *Exit.*

GREMIO
Adieu, good neighbor.—Now I fear thee not.
Sirrah, young gamester, your father were a fool
To give thee all, and in his waning age
Set foot under thy table. Tut, a toy!   400
An old Italian fox is not so kind, my boy.   *Exit.*

TRANIO
A vengeance on your crafty withered hide!
Yet I have faced it with a card of ten.   403
'Tis in my head to do my master good.
I see no reason but supposed Lucentio
Must get a father, called supposed Vincentio—
And that's a wonder. Fathers commonly
Do get their children; but in this case of wooing,   408
A child shall get a sire, if I fail not of my cunning.
                                                    Exit.

❧

373 road roadstead, harbor.   **376 galliases** heavy, low-built vessels
377 tight watertight   **383 outvied** outbidden.   **385 let** provided
388 but a cavil merely a frivolous objection.   **400 Set . . . toy!** i.e.,
become a dependent in your household. Tut, nonsense!   **403 faced . . .
ten** brazened it out with only a ten-spot of cards.   **408 get** beget.
(With a play on *get*, "obtain," in line 406.)

3.1

Enter Lucentio [*as Cambio*], *Hortensio* [*as
Litio*], *and Bianca.*

LUCENTIO
Fiddler, forbear. You grow too forward, sir.
Have you so soon forgot the entertainment
Her sister Katharine welcomed you withal?

HORTENSIO
But, wrangling pedant, this is   4
The patroness of heavenly harmony.
Then give me leave to have prerogative,   6
And when in music we have spent an hour,
Your lecture shall have leisure for as much.   8

LUCENTIO
Preposterous ass, that never read so far
To know the cause why music was ordained!   10
Was it not to refresh the mind of man
After his studies or his usual pain?   12
Then give me leave to read philosophy,   13
And, while I pause, serve in your harmony.   14

HORTENSIO
Sirrah, I will not bear these braves of thine.   15

BIANCA
Why, gentlemen, you do me double wrong
To strive for that which resteth in my choice.
I am no breeching scholar in the schools;   18
I'll not be tied to hours nor 'pointed times,
But learn my lessons as I please myself.
And, to cut off all strife, here sit we down.
[*To Hortensio*] Take you your instrument, play you the
    whiles;   22
His lecture will be done ere you have tuned.

HORTENSIO
You'll leave his lecture when I am in tune?

LUCENTIO
That will be never. Tune your instrument.
                    [*Hortensio moves aside and tunes.*]

BIANCA   Where left we last?
LUCENTIO   Here, madam. [*He reads.*]
    "*Hic ibat Simois; hic est Sigeia tellus;*   28
    Hic steterat Priami regia celsa senis."   29
BIANCA   Conster them.   30
LUCENTIO   "*Hic ibat,*" as I told you before, "*Simois,*" I
    am Lucentio, "*hic est,*" son unto Vincentio of Pisa, "*Sigeia
    tellus,*" disguised thus to get your love; "*Hic
    steterat,*" and that Lucentio that comes a-wooing,
    "*Priami,*" is my man Tranio, "*regia,*" bearing my port,   35
    "*celsa senis,*" that we might beguile the old panta-   36
    loon.   37

3.1. Location: The same.
4 this i.e., Bianca   **6 prerogative** precedence   **8 lecture** lesson
10 To know as to know   **12 usual pain** regular labors.   **13 read** teach
14 serve in present, serve up   **15 braves** insults   **18 breeching
scholar** i.e., schoolboy liable to be whipped   **22 the whiles** meantime
28–9 Hic . . . senis Here flowed the river Simois; here is the Sigeian
land; here stood the lofty palace of old Priam. (Ovid, *Heroides,* 1.33–4.)
30 Conster Construe   **35 bearing my port** i.e., pretending to be me
36–7 pantaloon foolish old man, i.e., Gremio.

HORTENSIO   Madam, my instrument's in tune.

BIANCA   Let's hear. [He plays.] Oh, fie! The treble jars.

LUCENTIO   Spit in the hole, man, and tune again.   40
                                    [Hortensio moves aside.]

BIANCA   Now let me see if I can conster it: *"Hic ibat*
   Simois," I know you not, *"hic est Sigeia tellus,"* I trust
   you not; *"Hic steterat Priami,"* take heed he hear us not,
   "regia," presume not, *"celsa senis,"* despair not.

HORTENSIO
   Madam, 'tis now in tune.   [He plays again.]

LUCENTIO   All but the bass.

HORTENSIO
   The bass is right, 'tis the base knave that jars.
   [Aside] How fiery and forward our pedant is!
   Now, for my life, the knave doth court my love.
   Pedascule, I'll watch you better yet.   49

BIANCA [to Lucentio]
   In time I may believe, yet I mistrust.

LUCENTIO
   Mistrust it not, for, sure, Aeacides   51
   Was Ajax, called so from his grandfather.

BIANCA
   I must believe my master; else, I promise you,
   I should be arguing still upon that doubt.
   But let it rest.—Now, Litio, to you:
   Good master, take it not unkindly, pray,
   That I have been thus pleasant with you both.   57

HORTENSIO [to Lucentio]
   You may go walk, and give me leave awhile.
   My lessons make no music in three parts.

LUCENTIO
   Are you so formal, sir? Well, I must wait.   60
   [Aside] And watch withal; for, but I be deceived,   61
   Our fine musician groweth amorous.
                            [He moves aside.]

HORTENSIO
   Madam, before you touch the instrument,
   To learn the order of my fingering,   64
   I must begin with rudiments of art,
   To teach you gamut in a briefer sort,   66
   More pleasant, pithy, and effectual
   Than hath been taught by any of my trade.
   And there it is in writing, fairly drawn.   69
                         [He gives her a paper.]

BIANCA
   Why, I am past my gamut long ago.

HORTENSIO
   Yet read the gamut of Hortensio.

BIANCA [reads]
   "Gamut I am, the ground of all accord,   72
   A re, to plead Hortensio's passion;
   B mi, Bianca, take him for thy lord,   74
   C fa ut, that loves with all affection.   75
   D sol re, one clef, two notes have I;   76
   E la mi, show pity, or I die."   77
   Call you this gamut? Tut, I like it not.
   Old fashions please me best; I am not so nice   79
   To change true rules for odd inventions.

           Enter a [Servant as] messenger.

SERVANT
   Mistress, your father prays you leave your books
   And help to dress your sister's chamber up.
   You know tomorrow is the wedding day.

BIANCA
   Farewell, sweet masters both. I must be gone.

LUCENTIO
   Faith, mistress, then I have no cause to stay.
        [Exeunt Bianca, Servant, and Lucentio.]

HORTENSIO
   But I have cause to pry into this pedant.
   Methinks he looks as though he were in love.
   Yet if thy thoughts, Bianca, be so humble
   To cast thy wandering eyes on every stale,   89
   Seize thee that list. If once I find thee ranging,   90
   Hortensio will be quit with thee by changing.   *Exit.*   91

                      ❖

[3.2]

   Enter Baptista, Gremio, Tranio [as Lucentio],
   Katharine, Bianca, [Lucentio as Cambio], and
   others, attendants.

BAPTISTA [to Tranio]
   Signor Lucentio, this is the 'pointed day
   That Katharine and Petruchio should be married,
   And yet we hear not of our son-in-law.
   What will be said? What mockery will it be,   4
   To want the bridegroom when the priest attends   5
   To speak the ceremonial rites of marriage?
   What says Lucentio to this shame of ours?

---

40 Spit in the hole i.e., to make the peg stick   **49 *Pedascule*** (A word contemptuously coined by Hortensio, presumably the vocative of an invented Latinism, *pedasculus,* "little pedant.")   **51 Mistrust** (Lucentio plays upon Bianca's *mistrust* in line 50, in which she expresses skepticism about his secret wooing; his answer seeks to reassure her, while at the same time in "Litio's" hearing he seems to emphasize the truth of his instruction as he goes on with his lesson from the *Heroides.* Her reply is ambiguous in the same way.)   **Aeacides** descendant of Aeacus, King of Aegina, father of Telamon and grandfather of Ajax   **57 pleasant** merry   **60 formal** precise   **61 but** unless   **64 order** method   **66 gamut** the scale, from the alphabet name (*gamma*) of the first note plus *ut,* its syllable name, now commonly called *do.* (The *gamut* of Hortensio begins on G instead of on C.)   **69 drawn** set out, copied.

72 ground bass note, foundation.   **accord** harmony   **74 *B mi*** (With a suggestion of "be my.")   **75 *fa ut*** (The note C is the fourth note, or *fa,* of a scale based on G but is the first note, *ut,* or *do,* of the more universal major scale based on C. Similarly, D is the fifth note, or *sol,* in the G scale but is the second, or *re,* in the C scale; similarly, with E as sixth and third.)   **76 two notes** (Hinting at Hortensio's disguise.)   **77 *E la mi*** (Suggesting "Ill am I.")   **79 nice** capricious   **89 stale** ridiculous rival   **90 Seize . . . list** let him who wants you have her.   **ranging** inconstant. (The metaphor is that of a straying hawk.)   **91 be quit** get even.   **changing** loving another.   **3.2. Location: Padua. Before Baptista's house.**   **4 What . . . said?** What will people say?   **5 want** lack

KATHARINA
No shame but mine. I must, forsooth, be forced
To give my hand opposed against my heart
Unto a mad-brain rudesby full of spleen,   10
Who wooed in haste and means to wed at leisure.
I told you, I, he was a frantic fool,
Hiding his bitter jests in blunt behavior.
And, to be noted for a merry man,   14
He'll woo a thousand, 'point the day of marriage,
Make friends, invite, and proclaim the banns,   16
Yet never means to wed where he hath wooed.
Now must the world point at poor Katharine
And say, "Lo, there is mad Petruchio's wife,
If it would please him come and marry her!"

TRANIO
Patience, good Katharine, and Baptista, too.
Upon my life, Petruchio means but well,
Whatever fortune stays him from his word.   23
Though he be blunt, I know him passing wise;   24
Though he be merry, yet withal he's honest.   25

KATHARINA
Would Katharine had never seen him, though!
                                        Exit weeping.

BAPTISTA
Go, girl, I cannot blame thee now to weep,
For such an injury would vex a very saint,
Much more a shrew of thy impatient humor.

                Enter Biondello.

BIONDELLO   Master, master! News, and such old news   30
as you never heard of!
BAPTISTA   Is it new and old too? How may that be?
BIONDELLO   Why, is it not news to hear of Petruchio's
coming?
BAPTISTA   Is he come?
BIONDELLO   Why, no, sir.
BAPTISTA   What, then?
BIONDELLO   He is coming.
BAPTISTA   When will he be here?
BIONDELLO   When he stands where I am and sees you
there.
TRANIO   But say, what to thine old news?   42
BIONDELLO   Why, Petruchio is coming in a new hat and
an old jerkin; a pair of old breeches thrice turned; a   44
pair of boots that have been candle-cases, one buckled,   45
another laced; an old rusty sword ta'en out of the town
armory, with a broken hilt, and chapeless; with two   47
broken points; his horse hipped, with an old mothy   48

saddle and stirrups of no kindred; besides, possessed   49
with the glanders and like to mose in the chine, trou-   50
bled with the lampass, infected with the fashions, full   51
of windgalls, sped with spavins, rayed with the yel-   52
lows, past cure of the fives, stark spoiled with the stag-   53
gers, begnawn with the bots, swayed in the back and   54
shoulder-shotten; near-legged before, and with a half-   55
cheeked bit and a headstall of sheep's leather which,   56
being restrained to keep him from stumbling, hath   57
been often burst and now repaired with knots; one
girth six times pieced, and a woman's crupper of   59
velour, which hath two letters for her name fairly   60
set down in studs, and here and there pieced
with packthread.   62
BAPTISTA   Who comes with him?
BIONDELLO   Oh, sir, his lackey, for all the world capari-   64
soned like the horse; with a linen stock on one leg and   65
a kersey boot-hose on the other, gartered with a red   66
and blue list; an old hat, and the humor of forty fan-   67
cies pricked in 't for a feather—a monster, a very mon-   68
ster in apparel, and not like a Christian footboy or a
gentleman's lackey.
TRANIO
'Tis some odd humor pricks him to this fashion;   71
Yet oftentimes he goes but mean-appareled.   72
BAPTISTA   I am glad he's come, howsoe'er he comes.
BIONDELLO   Why, sir, he comes not.
BAPTISTA   Didst thou not say he comes?
BIONDELLO   Who? That Petruchio came?
BAPTISTA   Ay, that Petruchio came.
BIONDELLO   No, sir, I say his horse comes, with him on
his back.
BAPTISTA   Why, that's all one.   80
BIONDELLO
Nay, by Saint Jamy,

---

10 **rudesby** unmannerly fellow.   **spleen** i.e., changeable temper
14 **to be noted for** in order to get a reputation as   16 **banns** wedding
announcement   23 **Whatever . . . word** whatever accident keeps him
from fulfilling his promise.   24 **passing** exceedingly   25 **merry**
given to joking   30 **old** rare; and referring to Petruchio's old clothes
42 **to** about   44 **jerkin** man's jacket.   **turned** i.e., with the material
reversed to get more wear   45 **candle-cases** i.e., discarded boots,
used only as a receptacle for candle ends   47 **chapeless** without the
chape, the metal plate or mounting of a scabbard, especially that
which covers the point   48 **points** tagged laces for attaching hose to
doublet.   **hipped** lamed in the hip. (Almost all the diseases here
named are described in Gervase Markham's *How to Choose, Ride,
Train, and Diet both Hunting Horses and Running Horses . . . Also a Discourse of Horsemanship*, probably first published in 1593.)

49 **of no kindred** that don't match   50 **glanders** contagious disease in
horses causing swelling beneath the jaw and mucous discharge from
the nostrils.   **mose in the chine** suffer from glanders   51 **lampass** a
thick, spongy flesh growing over a horse's upper teeth and hindering
his eating.   **fashions** i.e., farcins, or farcy, a disease like glanders
52 **windgalls** soft tumors or swellings generally found on the fetlock
joint, so called from having been supposed to contain air.   **sped** far
gone.   **spavins** a disease of the hock, marked by a small bony enlargement inside the leg.   **rayed** bespattered, defiled   52–3 **yellows** jaundice   53 **fives** avives, a glandular disease causing swelling behind the
ear   53–4 **stark . . . staggers** completely destroyed by a disease causing
palsylike staggering   54 **bots** parasitic worms   55 **shoulder-shotten**
with sprained or dislocated shoulder.   **near-legged before** with knock-
kneed forelegs   55–6 **half-cheeked** bit one to which the bridle is
attached halfway up the cheek or sidepiece and thus not giving sufficient control over the horse   56 **headstall** part of the bridle over the
head.   **sheep's leather** (i.e., of inferior quality; pigskin was used for
strongest harness)   57 **restrained** drawn back   59 **girth** saddle-strap
passing under the horse's belly.   **pieced** mended.   **crupper** leather
loop passing under the horse's tail and fastened to the saddle
60 **velour** velvet.   **two . . . name** her initials   62 **packthread** twine for
securing parcels.   64–5 **for . . . caparisoned** in all respects outfitted
65 **stock** stocking   66 **kersey boot-hose** overstocking of coarse material
for wearing under boots   67 **list** strip of cloth   67–8 **the humor . . .**
feather a trite motto incised in it instead of a feather   68 **pricked**
pinned.   **for** in place of   71 **humor pricks** whim that spurs   72 **mean-**
appareled poorly dressed.   80 **all one** the same thing.

I hold you a penny,   82
A horse and a man
Is more than one,
And yet not many.

Enter Petruchio and Grumio.

PETRUCHIO
Come, where be these gallants? Who's at home?

BAPTISTA   You are welcome, sir.

PETRUCHIO   And yet I come not well.   88

BAPTISTA   And yet you halt not.   89

TRANIO
Not so well appareled as I wish you were.

PETRUCHIO
Were it better, I should rush in thus.   91
But where is Kate? Where is my lovely bride?
How does my father? Gentles, methinks you frown.
And wherefore gaze this goodly company,
As if they saw some wondrous monument,   95
Some comet, or unusual prodigy?   96

BAPTISTA
Why, sir, you know this is your wedding day.
First were we sad, fearing you would not come,
Now sadder that you come so unprovided.   99
Fie, doff this habit, shame to your estate,   100
An eyesore to our solemn festival!

TRANIO
And tell us, what occasion of import
Hath all so long detained you from your wife
And sent you hither so unlike yourself?

PETRUCHIO
Tedious it were to tell, and harsh to hear.
Sufficeth I am come to keep my word,   106
Though in some part enforcèd to digress,   107
Which at more leisure I will so excuse
As you shall well be satisfied withal.
But where is Kate? I stay too long from her.
The morning wears; 'tis time we were at church.

TRANIO
See not your bride in these unreverent robes.
Go to my chamber. Put on clothes of mine.

PETRUCHIO
Not I, believe me. Thus I'll visit her.

BAPTISTA
But thus, I trust, you will not marry her.

PETRUCHIO
Good sooth, even thus. Therefore ha' done with
    words.   116
To me she's married, not unto my clothes.
Could I repair what she will wear in me   118
As I can change these poor accoutrements,
'Twere well for Kate and better for myself.

But what a fool am I to chat with you,
When I should bid good morrow to my bride
And seal the title with a lovely kiss!   *Exit.* 123

TRANIO
He hath some meaning in his mad attire.
We will persuade him, be it possible,
To put on better ere he go to church.

BAPTISTA
I'll after him, and see the event of this.   127
            Exit [with all but Tranio and Lucentio].

TRANIO
But, sir, to love concerneth us to add   128
Her father's liking, which to bring to pass,
As I before imparted to Your Worship,   130
I am to get a man—whate'er he be
It skills not much, we'll fit him to our turn—   132
And he shall be Vincentio of Pisa
And make assurance here in Padua
Of greater sums than I have promisèd.
So shall you quietly enjoy your hope
And marry sweet Bianca with consent.

LUCENTIO
Were it not that my fellow schoolmaster
Doth watch Bianca's steps so narrowly,
'Twere good, methinks, to steal our marriage,   140
Which once performed, let all the world say no,
I'll keep mine own, despite of all the world.

TRANIO
That by degrees we mean to look into,
And watch our vantage in this business.   144
We'll overreach the graybeard, Gremio,
The narrow-prying father, Minola,   146
The quaint musician, amorous Litio,   147
All for my master's sake, Lucentio.

Enter Gremio.

Signor Gremio, came you from the church?

GREMIO
As willingly as e'er I came from school.

TRANIO
And is the bride and bridegroom coming home?

GREMIO
A bridegroom, say you? 'Tis a groom indeed,   152
A grumbling groom, and that the girl shall find.

TRANIO
Curster than she? Why, 'tis impossible.

GREMIO
Why, he 's a devil, a devil, a very fiend.

TRANIO
Why, she's a devil, a devil, the devil's dam.   156

---

82 **hold** wager   88 **I come not well** i.e., I am not made to feel welcome; or, I come admittedly not well appareled.   89 **halt** limp, move slowly   91 **Were it** Even if it (my apparel) were. **rush** come quickly. (Referring to *halt not* in line 89.)   95 **monument** portent   96 **prodigy** omen.   99 **unprovided** ill equipped.   100 **habit** outfit. **estate** position, station   106 **Sufficeth** It is enough that   107 **digress** i.e., deviate   116 **Good sooth** i.e., Yes, indeed   118 **Could . . . me** If I could amend in my character what she'll have to put up with

123 **lovely** loving   127 **event** outcome   128 **to love . . . add** besides obtaining the love of the lady, it behooves us to add   130 **to Your Worship** (Tranio privately drops the fiction that he is Lucentio's master.)   132 **skills** matters   140 **steal our marriage** elope   144 **watch our vantage** look out for our best opportunity, advantage   146 **narrow-prying** suspicious, watchful   147 **quaint** skillful   152 **'Tis a groom indeed** A fine bridegroom he is. (Said ironically, with pun on the sense of "servant," "rough fellow.")   156 **dam** mother.

GREMIO
Tut, she's a lamb, a dove, a fool to him.   157
I'll tell you, Sir Lucentio. When the priest
Should ask if Katharine should be his wife,   159
"Ay, by Gog's wouns," quoth he, and swore so loud   160
That all amazed the priest let fall the book,
And as he stooped again to take it up,
This mad-brained bridegroom took him such a cuff   163
That down fell priest and book, and book and priest.
"Now take them up," quoth he, "if any list."   165

TRANIO
What said the wench when he rose again?

GREMIO
Trembled and shook, forwhy he stamped and swore   167
As if the vicar meant to cozen him.   168
But after many ceremonies done
He calls for wine. "A health!" quoth he, as if
He had been aboard, carousing to his mates   171
After a storm; quaffed off the muscatel
And threw the sops all in the sexton's face,   173
Having no other reason
But that his beard grew thin and hungerly   175
And seemed to ask him sops as he was drinking.   176
This done, he took the bride about the neck
And kissed her lips with such a clamorous smack
That at the parting all the church did echo.
And I seeing this came thence for very shame,
And after me, I know, the rout is coming.   181
Such a mad marriage never was before.   *Music plays.*
Hark, hark! I hear the minstrels play.

Enter Petruchio, Kate, Bianca, Hortensio [as Litio],
Baptista, [with Grumio, and train].

PETRUCHIO
Gentlemen and friends, I thank you for your pains.
I know you think to dine with me today,
And have prepared great store of wedding cheer;
But so it is my haste doth call me hence,
And therefore here I mean to take my leave.

BAPTISTA
Is't possible you will away tonight?

PETRUCHIO
I must away today, before night come.
Make it no wonder. If you knew my business,   191
You would entreat me rather go than stay.
And, honest company, I thank you all   193
That have beheld me give away myself
To this most patient, sweet, and virtuous wife.
Dine with my father, drink a health to me,
For I must hence; and farewell to you all.

TRANIO
Let us entreat you stay till after dinner.

PETRUCHIO
It may not be.

GREMIO   Let me entreat you.

PETRUCHIO
It cannot be.

KATHARINA   Let me entreat you.

PETRUCHIO
I am content.

KATHARINA   Are you content to stay?

PETRUCHIO
I am content you shall entreat me stay;
But yet not stay, entreat me how you can.

KATHARINA
Now, if you love me, stay.

PETRUCHIO   Grumio, my horse.   204

GRUMIO   Ay, sir, they be ready. The oats have eaten the   205
horses.   206

KATHARINA   Nay, then,
Do what thou canst, I will not go today,
No, nor tomorrow—not till I please myself.
The door is open, sir; there lies your way.
You may be jogging whiles your boots are green.   211
For me, I'll not be gone till I please myself.   212
'Tis like you'll prove a jolly, surly groom,   213
That take it on you at the first so roundly.   214

PETRUCHIO
Oh, Kate, content thee. Prithee, be not angry.

KATHARINA
I will be angry. What hast thou to do?—   216
Father, be quiet. He shall stay my leisure.   217

GREMIO
Ay, marry, sir, now it begins to work.   218

KATHARINA
Gentlemen, forward to the bridal dinner.
I see a woman may be made a fool
If she had not a spirit to resist.

PETRUCHIO
They shall go forward, Kate, at thy command.—
Obey the bride, you that attend on her.
Go to the feast, revel and domineer,   224
Carouse full measure to her maidenhead,   225
Be mad and merry, or go hang yourselves.
But for my bonny Kate, she must with me.   227
Nay, look not big, nor stamp, nor stare, nor fret;   228
I will be master of what is mine own.
She is my goods, my chattels; she is my house,
My household stuff, my field, my barn,
My horse, my ox, my ass, my anything;   232
And here she stands, touch her whoever dare.

---

157 **a fool to** i.e., a pitiable weak creature compared with
159 **Should ask** came to the point (in the service) where he is directed
to ask   160 **Gog's wouns** God's (Christ's) wounds   163 **took** gave,
struck   165 **list** choose.   167 **forwhy** for   168 **cozen** cheat
171 **aboard** aboard ship   173 **sops** cakes or bread soaked in the wine
175 **hungerly** hungry looking, having a starved or famished look
176 **And . . . drinking** and seemed to invite the throwing in his face of
what Petruchio was drinking.   181 **rout** crowd, wedding party
191 **Make it no wonder** Don't be surprised.   193 **honest** worthy, kind

204 **horse** horses.   205–6 **oats . . . horses** (A comic inversion.)
211 **be . . . green** (Proverbial for "getting an early start," with a sarcastic allusion to his unseemly attire.)   **green** fresh, new.   212 **For** As
for   213 **like** likely.   **jolly** (Said sarcastically.)   214 **take it on you**
i.e., throw your weight around.   **roundly** unceremoniously.
216 **What . . . do?** What business is it of yours?   217 **stay my leisure**
wait until I am ready.   218 **now . . . work** now it starts.   224 **domineer** feast riotously   225 **to her maidenhead** to her loss of virginity
227 **for** as for   228 **big** threatening   232 **ox . . . anything** (This catalogue of a man's possessions is from the Tenth Commandment.)

I'll bring mine action on the proudest he   234
That stops my way in Padua.—Grumio,
Draw forth thy weapon. We are beset with thieves.   236
Rescue thy mistress, if thou be a man.—
Fear not, sweet wench, they shall not touch thee, Kate!
I'll buckler thee against a million.   239
        Exeunt Petruchio, Katharina, [and Grumio].

BAPTISTA
Nay, let them go—a couple of quiet ones!
GREMIO
Went they not quickly, I should die with laughing.
TRANIO
Of all mad matches never was the like.
LUCENTIO
Mistress, what's your opinion of your sister?
BIANCA
That, being mad herself, she's madly mated.
GREMIO
I warrant him, Petruchio is Kated.   245
BAPTISTA
Neighbors and friends, though bride and bridegroom
   wants   246
For to supply the places at the table,   247
You know there wants no junkets at the feast.   248
Lucentio, you shall supply the bridegroom's place,
And let Bianca take her sister's room.
TRANIO
Shall sweet Bianca practice how to bride it?   251
BAPTISTA
She shall, Lucentio.—Come, gentlemen, let's go.
        Exeunt.

❖

[4.1]

Enter Grumio.

GRUMIO   Fie, fie on all tired jades, on all mad masters,   1
and all foul ways! Was ever man so beaten? Was ever   2
man so rayed? Was ever man so weary? I am sent be-   3
fore to make a fire, and they are coming after to warm
them. Now, were not I a little pot and soon hot, my   5
very lips might freeze to my teeth, my tongue to the
roof of my mouth, my heart in my belly, ere I should
come by a fire to thaw me. But I with blowing the fire   8
shall warm myself; for, considering the weather, a
taller man than I will take cold.—Holla, ho! Curtis!   10

Enter Curtis.

CURTIS   Who is that calls so coldly?

GRUMIO   A piece of ice. If thou doubt it, thou mayst
slide from my shoulder to my heel with no greater a
run but my head and my neck. A fire, good Curtis!   14
CURTIS   Is my master and his wife coming, Grumio?
GRUMIO   Oh, ay, Curtis, ay, and therefore fire, fire! Cast   16
on no water.   17
CURTIS   Is she so hot a shrew as she's reported?
GRUMIO   She was, good Curtis, before this frost. But,
thou know'st, winter tames man, woman, and beast;
for it hath tamed my old master and my new mistress
and myself, fellow Curtis.
CURTIS   Away, you three-inch fool! I am no beast.   23
GRUMIO   Am I but three inches? Why, thy horn is a foot,   24
and so long am I, at the least. But wilt thou make a fire,   25
or shall I complain on thee to our mistress, whose
hand—she being now at hand—thou shalt soon feel,
to thy cold comfort, for being slow in thy hot office?   28
CURTIS   I prithee, good Grumio, tell me, how goes the
world?
GRUMIO   A cold world, Curtis, in every office but thine,
and therefore fire. Do thy duty, and have thy duty, for   32
my master and mistress are almost frozen to death.
CURTIS   There's fire ready, and therefore, good Grumio,
the news.
GRUMIO   Why, "Jack boy, ho, boy!" and as much news   36
as wilt thou.
CURTIS   Come, you are so full of coney-catching.   38
GRUMIO   Why, therefore fire, for I have caught extreme
cold. Where's the cook? Is supper ready, the house
trimmed, rushes strewed, cobwebs swept, the serv-   41
ingmen in their new fustian, the white stockings, and   42
every officer his wedding garment on? Be the Jacks   43
fair within, the Jills fair without, the carpets laid, and   44
everything in order?
CURTIS   All ready; and therefore, I pray thee, news.
GRUMIO   First, know my horse is tired, my master and
mistress fallen out.   48
CURTIS   How?
GRUMIO   Out of their saddles into the dirt—and thereby   50
hangs a tale.   51

---

234 action (1) lawsuit (2) attack   **236 Draw** (Perhaps Petruchio and Grumio actually draw their swords.)   **239 buckler** shield, defend **245 Kated** (Gremio's invention for "mated and matched with Kate.") **246–7 wants For to supply** are not present to fill   **248 there wants no junkets** there is no lack of sweetmeats   **251 bride it** play the bride. **4.1. Location: Petruchio's country house. A table is set out, with seats. 1 jades** ill-conditioned horses   **2 ways** roads.   **3 rayed** bespattered. **5 a little . . . hot** (Proverbial expression for a person of small stature soon angered.)   **8 come by** find   **10 taller** (With play on the meaning "better," "finer.")

14 run running start   **16–17 Cast . . . water** (Alludes to the round "Scotland's burning," in which the phrase "Fire, fire!" is followed by "Pour on water, pour on water.")   **23 three-inch fool** (Another reference to Grumio's size.)   **I am no beast** (Curtis protests being called *fellow* by Grumio, since Grumio in line 20 has paralleled himself with *beast*.)   **24–5 Why . . . least** (Grumio hints that Curtis is a beast with a prominent *horn*, and hence a cuckold; suggesting too that Grumio's *horn*, i.e., *penis*, is as long as Curtis's or longer.)   **28 hot office** i.e., duty of providing a fire.   **32 have thy duty** have what's coming to you, your due   **36 Jack . . . boy** (The first line of another round or catch.)   **38 coney-catching** cheating, trickery. (With wordplay on *catch*, or round, like "Jack boy, ho, boy" in line 36.) **41 rushes** (Used to cover the floor.)   **42 fustian** coarse cloth of cotton and flax   **43 officer** household servant.   **Jacks** (1) servingmen (2) drinking vessels, usually of leather and hence needing to be clean *within*   **44 Jills** (1) maidservants (2) "gills," drinking vessels holding a quarter pint, often of metal and hence in need of polishing *without*. (Grumio may joke that the maidservants cannot be expected to be clean *within*.)   **48 fallen out** quarreling. (But with a pun on the literal sense in line 50.)   **50–1 thereby hangs a tale** there's quite a story to tell about that. (But with a risible suggestion of hanging by one's *tail*.)

CURTIS Let's ha 't, good Grumio.   52
GRUMIO Lend thine ear.
CURTIS Here.
GRUMIO There.   [*He cuffs Curtis.*]
CURTIS This 'tis to feel a tale, not to hear a tale.
GRUMIO And therefore 'tis called a sensible tale, and   57
this cuff was but to knock at your ear and beseech
listening. Now I begin: Imprimis, we came down a   59
foul hill, my master riding behind my mistress—   60
CURTIS Both of one horse?   61
GRUMIO What's that to thee?
CURTIS Why, a horse.
GRUMIO Tell thou the tale. But hadst thou not crossed   64
me, thou shouldst have heard how her horse fell and
she under her horse; thou shouldst have heard in how
miry a place, how she was bemoiled, how he left her   67
with the horse upon her, how he beat me because her
horse stumbled, how she waded through the dirt to
pluck him off me, how he swore, how she prayed that
never prayed before, how I cried, how the horses ran
away, how her bridle was burst, how I lost my
crupper, with many things of worthy memory, which   73
now shall die in oblivion and thou return unexperi-
enced to thy grave.
CURTIS By this reckoning he is more shrew than she.
GRUMIO Ay, and that thou and the proudest of you all
shall find when he comes home. But what talk I of   78
this? Call forth Nathaniel, Joseph, Nicholas, Philip,
Walter, Sugarsop, and the rest. Let their heads be
sleekly combed, their blue coats brushed, and their   81
garters of an indifferent knit; let them curtsy with their   82
left legs, and not presume to touch a hair of my
master's horsetail till they kiss their hands. Are they
all ready?
CURTIS They are.
GRUMIO Call them forth.
CURTIS [*calling*] Do you hear, ho? You must meet my
master to countenance my mistress.   89
GRUMIO Why, she hath a face of her own.
CURTIS Who knows not that?
GRUMIO Thou, it seems, that calls for company to
countenance her.
CURTIS I call them forth to credit her.   94

Enter four or five Servingmen.

GRUMIO Why, she comes to borrow nothing of them.
NATHANIEL Welcome home, Grumio!
PHILIP How now, Grumio?
JOSEPH What, Grumio!
NICHOLAS Fellow Grumio!
NATHANIEL How now, old lad?

GRUMIO Welcome, you; how now, you; what, you; fellow, you—and thus much for greeting. Now, my
spruce companions, is all ready, and all things neat?   103
NATHANIEL All things is ready. How near is our
master?
GRUMIO E'en at hand, alighted by this; and therefore
be not—Cock's passion, silence! I hear my master.   107

Enter Petruchio and Kate.

PETRUCHIO
Where be these knaves? What, no man at door
To hold my stirrup nor to take my horse?   109
Where is Nathaniel, Gregory, Philip?
ALL SERVANTS Here, here, sir, here, sir.
PETRUCHIO
Here, sir! Here, sir! Here, sir! Here, sir!
You loggerheaded and unpolished grooms!
What, no attendance? No regard? No duty?
Where is the foolish knave I sent before?   115
GRUMIO
Here, sir, as foolish as I was before.
PETRUCHIO
You peasant swain, you whoreson, malt-horse
drudge!   117
Did I not bid thee meet me in the park
And bring along these rascal knaves with thee?
GRUMIO
Nathaniel's coat, sir, was not fully made,
And Gabriel's pumps were all unpinked i'the heel.   121
There was no link to color Peter's hat,   122
And Walter's dagger was not come from sheathing.   123
There were none fine but Adam, Ralph, and Gregory;   124
The rest were ragged, old, and beggarly.
Yet, as they are, here are they come to meet you.
PETRUCHIO
Go, rascals, go and fetch my supper in.
                                    Exeunt Servants.
[*He sings.*] "Where is the life that late I led?   128
Where are those—" Sit down, Kate, and welcome.—   129
                                    [*They sit at table.*]
Soud, soud, soud, soud!   130

Enter Servants with supper.

Why, when, I say?—Nay, good sweet Kate, be
merry.—   131
Off with my boots, you rogues! You villains, when?
                    [*A Servant takes off Petruchio's boots.*]
[*He sings.*] "It was the friar of orders gray,   133
                    As he forth walkèd on his way—"   134

52 **ha 't** have it   57 **sensible** (1) capable of being felt (2) showing good sense   59 **Imprimis** In the first place   60 **foul** muddy   61 **of** on   64 **crossed** thwarted, interrupted   67 **bemoiled** befouled with mire   73 **crupper** (See 3.2.59.)   **of worthy** worthy of   78 **what** why   81 **blue coats** (Usual dress for servingmen.)   82 **indifferent** well-matched, identical   89 **countenance** pay respects to. (With a following pun on the meaning "face.")   94 **credit** pay respects to. (With another pun following, on "extend financial credit.")

103 **spruce** lively, trim in appearance   107 **Cock's passion** By God's (Christ's) suffering   109 **hold my stirrup** i.e., help me dismount   115 **before** ahead. (With pun in next line on "previously.")   117 **swain** rustic.   **whoreson ... drudge** worthless plodding work animal, such as would be used on a treadmill to grind malt.   121 **pumps** low-cut shoes.   **unpinked** lacking in eyelets or in orna-mental tracing in the leather   122 **link** blacking made from burnt "links" or torches   123 **sheathing** being fitted with a sheath.   124 **fine** well clothed   128–9 **Where ... those** (A fragment of a lost ballad, probably lamenting the man's loss of freedom in marriage.)   130 **Soud** (A nonsense song, or expression of impatience, or perhaps "food!")   131 **when** (An exclamation of impatience.)   133–4 **"It ... way"** (A fragment of a lost ballad, probably bawdy.)

Out, you rogue! You pluck my foot awry.   135
                    [*He kicks the Servant.*]
Take that, and mend the plucking of the other.—   136
Be merry, Kate.—Some water, here. What, ho!

    Enter one with water.

Where's my spaniel Troilus? Sirrah, get you hence,
And bid my cousin Ferdinand come hither—
                    [*Exit Servant.*]
One, Kate, that you must kiss and be acquainted with.
Where are my slippers? Shall I have some water?
Come, Kate, and wash, and welcome heartily.
          [*A Servant offers water, but spills some.*]
You whoreson villain, will you let it fall?
                    [*He strikes the Servant.*]

KATHARINA
Patience, I pray you, 'twas a fault unwilling.   144
PETRUCHIO
A whoreson, beetleheaded, flap-eared knave!—   145
Come, Kate, sit down. I know you have a stomach.   146
Will you give thanks, sweet Kate, or else shall I?—   147
What's this? Mutton?
FIRST SERVANT   Ay.
PETRUCHIO   Who brought it?
PETER   I.
PETRUCHIO
'Tis burnt, and so is all the meat.
What dogs are these? Where is the rascal cook?
How durst you, villains, bring it from the dresser   151
And serve it thus to me that love it not?
There, take it to you, trenchers, cups, and all.   153
          [*He throws the meat, etc., at them.*]
You heedless jolt-heads and unmannered slaves!   154
What, do you grumble? I'll be with you straight.   155
                    [*They run out.*]
KATHARINA
I pray you, husband, be not so disquiet.
The meat was well, if you were so contented.   157
PETRUCHIO
I tell thee, Kate, 'twas burnt and dried away,
And I expressly am forbid to touch it;
For it engenders choler, planteth anger,   160
And better 'twere that both of us did fast,
Since, of ourselves, ourselves are choleric,   162
Than feed it with such overroasted flesh.
Be patient. Tomorrow 't shall be mended,
And for this night we'll fast for company.   165
Come, I will bring thee to thy bridal chamber.   166
                              Exeunt.

    Enter Servants severally.

NATHANIEL   Peter, didst ever see the like?
PETER   He kills her in her own humor.   168

    Enter Curtis.

GRUMIO   Where is he?
CURTIS   In her chamber,
Making a sermon of continency to her,   171
And rails, and swears, and rates, that she, poor soul,   172
Knows not which way to stand, to look, to speak,
And sits as one new risen from a dream.
Away, away! For he is coming hither.   [*Exeunt.*]

    Enter Petruchio.

PETRUCHIO
Thus have I politicly begun my reign,   176
And 'tis my hope to end successfully.
My falcon now is sharp and passing empty,   178
And till she stoop she must not be full-gorged,   179
For then she never looks upon her lure.
Another way I have to man my haggard,   181
To make her come and know her keeper's call:
That is, to watch her, as we watch these kites   183
That bate and beat and will not be obedient.   184
She ate no meat today, nor none shall eat.
Last night she slept not, nor tonight she shall not.
As with the meat, some undeservèd fault
I'll find about the making of the bed,
And here I'll fling the pillow, there the bolster,
This way the coverlet, another way the sheets.
Ay, and amid this hurly I intend   191
That all is done in reverent care of her.
And in conclusion she shall watch all night,   193
And if she chance to nod I'll rail and brawl,
And with the clamor keep her still awake.
This is a way to kill a wife with kindness;
And thus I'll curb her mad and headstrong humor.   197
He that knows better how to tame a shrew,
Now let him speak. 'Tis charity to show.   *Exit.* 199

    ❖

[4.2]

    *Enter Tranio [as Lucentio] and Hortensio
    [as Litio].*

TRANIO
Is't possible, friend Litio, that Mistress Bianca
Doth fancy any other but Lucentio?
I tell you, sir, she bears me fair in hand.   3

---

135 Out (Exclamation of anger or reproach.)   **136 mend the plucking of** do a better job of pulling off   **144 unwilling** not intentional.
145 beetleheaded i.e., blockheaded (since a *beetle* is a pounding tool)
146 stomach appetite. (With a suggestion also of "temper.")
147 give thanks say grace   **151 dresser** one who "dresses" or prepares the food; or, sideboard   **153 trenchers** wooden dishes or plates
154 jolt-heads blockheads   **155 with you straight** after you at once (to get even for this).   **157 if . . . contented** if you had chosen to be pleased with it.   **160 choler** the humor or bodily fluid, hot and dry in character, that supposedly produced ill temper and was thought to be aggravated by the eating of roast meat   **162 of ourselves** by our natures   **165 for company** together.   **166.2 severally** separately.

168 He . . . humor He subdues her shrewishness with his own greater shrewishness.   **171 sermon of continency** lecture on self-restraint
172 rates scolds.   **that** so that   **176 politicly** with skillful calculation
178 sharp hungry.   **passing** very   **179 stoop** fly down to the lure
181 man tame, assert masculine authority over.   **haggard** wild female hawk; hence, an intractable woman   **183 watch her** keep her watching, i.e., awake.   **kites** a kind of hawk. (With a pun on *Kate*.)
184 bate and beat beat the wings impatiently and flutter away from the hand or perch   **191 hurly** commotion.   **intend** pretend
193 watch stay awake   **197 humor** disposition.   **199 'Tis charity to show** This is to perform an act of Christian benevolence. (On the rhyme with *shrew*, see also the play's final lines.)
4.2. Location: Padua. Before Baptista's house.
3 bears . . . hand gives me encouragement, leads me on.

HORTENSIO
Sir, to satisfy you in what I have said,   4
Stand by and mark the manner of his teaching.
                                    [*They stand aside.*]

        Enter Bianca [and Lucentio as Cambio].

LUCENTIO
Now, mistress, profit you in what you read?   6
BIANCA
What, master, read you? First resolve me that.   7
LUCENTIO
I read that I profess, *The Art to Love*.   8
BIANCA
And may you prove, sir, master of your art!
LUCENTIO
While you, sweet dear, prove mistress of my heart!
              [*They move aside and court each other.*]
HORTENSIO [*to Tranio, coming forward*]
Quick proceeders, marry! Now, tell me, I pray,   11
You that durst swear that your mistress Bianca
Loved none in the world so well as Lucentio.
TRANIO
Oh, despiteful love! Unconstant womankind!   14
I tell thee, Litio, this is wonderful.   15
HORTENSIO
Mistake no more. I am not Litio,
Nor a musician, as I seem to be,
But one that scorn to live in this disguise   18
For such a one as leaves a gentleman   19
And makes a god of such a cullion.   20
Know, sir, that I am called Hortensio.
TRANIO
Signor Hortensio, I have often heard
Of your entire affection to Bianca;   23
And since mine eyes are witness of her lightness,   24
I will with you, if you be so contented,
Forswear Bianca and her love forever.
HORTENSIO
See how they kiss and court! Signor Lucentio,
Here is my hand, and here I firmly vow
                                    [*giving his hand*]
Never to woo her more, but do forswear her,
As one unworthy all the former favors
That I have fondly flattered her withal.   31
TRANIO
And here I take the like unfeignèd oath,
Never to marry with her though she would entreat.
Fie on her, see how beastly she doth court him!
HORTENSIO
Would all the world but he had quite forsworn!   35

For me, that I may surely keep mine oath,   36
I will be married to a wealthy widow,
Ere three days pass, which hath as long loved me
As I have loved this proud disdainful haggard.   39
And so farewell, Signor Lucentio.
Kindness in women, not their beauteous looks,
Shall win my love. And so I take my leave,
In resolution as I swore before.   [*Exit.*]   43
TRANIO [*as Lucentio and Bianca come forward again*]
Mistress Bianca, bless you with such grace
As 'longeth to a lover's blessèd case!   45
Nay, I have ta'en you napping, gentle love,   46
And have forsworn you with Hortensio.
BIANCA
Tranio, you jest. But have you both forsworn me?
TRANIO
Mistress, we have.
LUCENTIO   Then we are rid of Litio.
TRANIO
I' faith, he'll have a lusty widow now,   50
That shall be wooed and wedded in a day.
BIANCA   God give him joy!
TRANIO   Ay, and he'll tame her.
BIANCA   He says so, Tranio?
TRANIO
Faith, he is gone unto the taming-school.
BIANCA
The taming-school! What, is there such a place?
TRANIO
Ay, mistress, and Petruchio is the master,
That teacheth tricks eleven-and-twenty long   58
To tame a shrew and charm her chattering tongue.

                        Enter Biondello.

BIONDELLO
Oh, master, master, I have watched so long
That I am dog-weary, but at last I spied
An ancient angel coming down the hill   62
Will serve the turn.
TRANIO   What is he, Biondello?   63
BIONDELLO
Master, a marcantant, or a pedant,   64
I know not what, but formal in apparel,
In gait and countenance surely like a father.
LUCENTIO   And what of him, Tranio?
TRANIO
If he be credulous and trust my tale,
I'll make him glad to seem Vincentio,
And give assurance to Baptista Minola

---

4 satisfy convince   **6 read** (Evidently, both Bianca and "Cambio" carry books.)   **7 resolve** answer   **8 I read . . . *Love*** I read what I practice, Ovid's *Ars Amatoria*.   **11 proceeders** (1) workers, doers (2) candidates for academic degrees (as suggested by the phrase *master of your art* in line 9)   **14 despiteful** cruel   **15 wonderful** cause for wonder.   **18 scorn** scorns   **19 such a one** i.e., Bianca   **20 cullion** base fellow. (Referring to "Cambio"; literally, *cullion* means "testicle.")   **23 entire** sincere   **24 lightness** wantonness   **31 fondly** foolishly   **35 Would . . . forsworn!** i.e., May everyone in the world forsake her except the penniless "Cambio," and may she thus get what she deserves!

36 For As for   **39 haggard** wild hawk.   **43 In resolution** determined   **45 'longeth** belongs   **46 ta'en you napping** taken you by surprise   **50 lusty** merry, lively   **58 eleven . . . long** i.e., right on the money. (Alluding to the card game called "one-and-thirty" referred to at 1.2.32–3.)   **62 ancient angel** i.e., fellow of the good old stamp. (Literally, an "angel" or gold coin bearing the stamp of the archangel Michael and thus distinguishable from more recent debased coinage.)   **63 Will . . . turn** who will serve our purposes.   **64 marcantant** merchant.   **pedant** schoolmaster. (Though at lines 90–1 he speaks more like a merchant.)

As if he were the right Vincentio.
Take in your love, and then let me alone.　72

　　　　　　　[*Exeunt Lucentio and Bianca.*]

Enter a Pedant.

PEDANT
God save you, sir!
TRANIO　　　　　　　And you sir! You are welcome.
Travel you farre on, or are you at the farthest?　74
PEDANT
Sir, at the farthest for a week or two,
But then up farther, and as far as Rome,
And so to Tripoli, if God lend me life.
TRANIO
What countryman, I pray?
PEDANT　　　　　　　Of Mantua.
TRANIO
Of Mantua, sir? Marry, God forbid!
And come to Padua, careless of your life?
PEDANT
My life, sir? How, I pray? For that goes hard.　81
TRANIO
'Tis death for anyone in Mantua
To come to Padua. Know you not the cause?
Your ships are stayed at Venice, and the Duke,　84
For private quarrel twixt your Duke and him,
Hath published and proclaimed it openly.
'Tis marvel, but that you are but newly come,
You might have heard it else proclaimed about.
PEDANT
Alas, sir, it is worse for me than so,　89
For I have bills for money by exchange　90
From Florence, and must here deliver them.
TRANIO
Well, sir, to do you courtesy,
This will I do, and this I will advise you—
First, tell me, have you ever been at Pisa?
PEDANT
Ay, sir, in Pisa have I often been,
Pisa renownèd for grave citizens.
TRANIO
Among them know you one Vincentio?
PEDANT
I know him not, but I have heard of him;
A merchant of incomparable wealth.
TRANIO
He is my father, sir, and, sooth to say,
In count'nance somewhat doth resemble you.
BIONDELLO [*aside*]　As much as an apple doth an oy-
ster, and all one.　103
TRANIO
To save your life in this extremity,
This favor will I do you for his sake;
And think it not the worst of all your fortunes
That you are like to Sir Vincentio.

His name and credit shall you undertake,　108
And in my house you shall be friendly lodged.
Look that you take upon you as you should.　110
You understand me, sir. So shall you stay
Till you have done your business in the city.
If this be courtesy, sir, accept of it.
PEDANT
Oh, sir, I do, and will repute you ever　114
The patron of my life and liberty.
TRANIO
Then go with me to make the matter good.　116
This, by the way, I let you understand:
My father is here looked for every day
To pass assurance of a dower in marriage　119
Twixt me and one Baptista's daughter here.
In all these circumstances I'll instruct you.
Go with me to clothe you as becomes you.

　　　　　　　　　　　　　　Exeunt.

❖

4.[3]

Enter Katharina and Grumio.

GRUMIO
No, no, forsooth, I dare not for my life.
KATHARINA
The more my wrong, the more his spite appears.　2
What, did he marry me to famish me?
Beggars that come unto my father's door
Upon entreaty have a present alms;　5
If not, elsewhere they meet with charity.
But I, who never knew how to entreat,
Nor never needed that I should entreat,
Am starved for meat, giddy for lack of sleep,
With oaths kept waking, and with brawling fed.
And that which spites me more than all these wants,
He does it under name of perfect love,
As who should say, if I should sleep or eat　13
'Twere deadly sickness or else present death.
I prithee, go and get me some repast,
I care not what, so it be wholesome food.　16
GRUMIO　　What say you to a neat's foot?　17
KATHARINA
'Tis passing good. I prithee, let me have it.　18
GRUMIO
I fear it is too choleric a meat.
How say you to a fat tripe finely broiled?
KATHARINA
I like it well. Good Grumio, fetch it me.
GRUMIO
I cannot tell. I fear 'tis choleric.　22
What say you to a piece of beef and mustard?

---

108 credit reputation　**110 take upon you** play your part　**114 repute you** regard you as　**116 make . . . good** carry out the plan　**119 pass assurance** convey a legal guarantee
4.3. Location: Petruchio's house. A table is set out, with seats.
2 my wrong the wrong done to me　**5 present** immediate. (As in line 14.)　**13 As who** as if one　**16 so** so long as　**17 neat's** ox's　**18 passing** extremely　**22 I cannot tell** I don't know what to say.

---

72 let me alone leave things to me.　**74 farre** farther　**81 goes hard** is serious indeed.　**84 stayed** detained　**89 than so** than that　**90 bills . . . exchange** promissory notes　**103 all one** no matter.

KATHARINA
A dish that I do love to feed upon.

GRUMIO
Ay, but the mustard is too hot a little.

KATHARINA
Why then, the beef, and let the mustard rest. 26

GRUMIO
Nay then, I will not. You shall have the mustard,
Or else you get no beef of Grumio.

KATHARINA
Then both, or one, or anything thou wilt.

GRUMIO
Why then, the mustard without the beef.

KATHARINA
Go, get thee gone, thou false, deluding slave,
                              [She] beats him.
That feed'st me with the very name of meat! 32
Sorrow on thee and all the pack of you,
That triumph thus upon my misery!
Go, get thee gone, I say.

        Enter Petruchio and Hortensio with meat.

PETRUCHIO
How fares my Kate? What, sweeting, all amort? 36

HORTENSIO
Mistress, what cheer?

KATHARINA   Faith, as cold as can be.

PETRUCHIO
Pluck up thy spirits; look cheerfully upon me.
Here, love, thou see'st how diligent I am
To dress thy meat myself and bring it thee. 40
I am sure, sweet Kate, this kindness merits thanks.
What, not a word? Nay, then thou lov'st it not,
And all my pains is sorted to no proof.— 43
Here, take away this dish.

KATHARINA   I pray you, let it stand.

PETRUCHIO
The poorest service is repaid with thanks,
And so shall mine before you touch the meat.

KATHARINA   I thank you, sir.

HORTENSIO
Signor Petruchio, fie, you are to blame.
Come, Mistress Kate, I'll bear you company.

PETRUCHIO [aside to Hortensio]
Eat it up all, Hortensio, if thou lovest me.—
Much good do it unto thy gentle heart!
Kate, eat apace. And now, my honey love,
Will we return unto thy father's house
And revel it as bravely as the best, 54
With silken coats and caps and golden rings,
With ruffs, and cuffs, and farthingales, and things, 56
With scarves, and fans, and double change of brav'ry, 57
With amber bracelets, beads, and all this knav'ry.

What, hast thou dined? The tailor stays thy leisure, 59
To deck thy body with his ruffling treasure. 60

        Enter Tailor [with a gown].

Come, tailor, let us see these ornaments.
Lay forth the gown.

        Enter Haberdasher [with a cap].

                  What news with you, sir?

HABERDASHER
Here is the cap Your Worship did bespeak. 63

PETRUCHIO
Why, this was molded on a porringer— 64
A velvet dish. Fie, fie, 'tis lewd and filthy. 65
Why, 'tis a cockle or a walnut shell, 66
A knack, a toy, a trick, a baby's cap. 67
Away with it! Come, let me have a bigger.

KATHARINA
I'll have no bigger. This doth fit the time, 69
And gentlewomen wear such caps as these.

PETRUCHIO
When you are gentle, you shall have one too, 71
And not till then.

HORTENSIO [aside] That will not be in haste.

KATHARINA
Why, sir, I trust I may have leave to speak,
And speak I will. I am no child, no babe.
Your betters have endured me say my mind, 75
And if you cannot, best you stop your ears.
My tongue will tell the anger of my heart,
Or else my heart, concealing it, will break.
And rather than it shall, I will be free
Even to the uttermost, as I please, in words.

PETRUCHIO
Why, thou say'st true. It is a paltry cap,
A custard-coffin, a bauble, a silken pie. 82
I love thee well in that thou lik'st it not.

KATHARINA
Love me or love me not, I like the cap,
And it I will have, or I will have none.

                  [Exit Haberdasher.]

PETRUCHIO
Thy gown? Why, ay. Come, tailor, let us see't.
Oh, mercy, God, what masquing stuff is here? 87
What's this, a sleeve? 'Tis like a demicannon. 88
What, up and down carved like an apple tart? 89
Here's snip, and nip, and cut, and slish and slash,
Like to a censer in a barber's shop. 91
Why, what i' devil's name, tailor, call'st thou this?

---

26 let . . . rest i.e., forget about the mustard. 32 very mere 36 all amort dejected, dispirited. 40 dress prepare 43 is . . . proof have proved to be to no purpose. 54 bravely splendidly 56 farthingales hooped petticoats 57 brav'ry finery

59 stays awaits 60 ruffling treasure finery trimmed with ruffles. 63 bespeak order. 64 porringer porridge bowl 65 lewd vile 66 cockle cockleshell 67 trick trifle 69 fit the time suit the current fashion 71 gentle mild. (Petruchio plays on Kate's *gentlewomen,* line 70, i.e., women of high social station.) 75 endured me say suffered me to say 82 custard-coffin pastry crust for a custard 87 masquing i.e., suited only for a masque 88 demicannon large cannon. 89 What . . . tart? What, carved from one end to the other with slits like those in the crust of an apple tart? (Such slits in gowns were designed to reveal the fabric underneath.) 91 censer perfuming pan having an ornamental lid

HORTENSIO [aside]
  I see she's like to have neither cap nor gown.   93
TAILOR
  You bid me make it orderly and well,
  According to the fashion and the time.
PETRUCHIO
  Marry, and did. But if you be remembered,   96
  I did not bid you mar it to the time.
  Go hop me over every kennel home,   98
  For you shall hop without my custom, sir.
  I'll none of it. Hence, make your best of it.
KATHARINA
  I never saw a better fashioned gown,
  More quaint, more pleasing, nor more
    commendable.   102
  Belike you mean to make a puppet of me.   103
PETRUCHIO
  Why, true, he means to make a puppet of thee.
TAILOR
  She says Your Worship means to make a puppet of her.
PETRUCHIO
  Oh, monstrous arrogance! Thou liest, thou thread,
    thou thimble,   106
  Thou yard, three-quarters, half-yard, quarter, nail!   107
  Thou flea, thou nit, thou winter cricket, thou!   108
  Braved in mine own house with a skein of thread?   109
  Away, thou rag, thou quantity, thou remnant,   110
  Or I shall so be-mete thee with thy yard   111
  As thou shalt think on prating whilst thou liv'st!   112
  I tell thee, I, that thou hast marred her gown.
TAILOR
  Your Worship is deceived. The gown is made
  Just as my master had direction.
  Grumio gave order how it should be done.
GRUMIO   I gave him no order. I gave him the stuff.   117
TAILOR
  But how did you desire it should be made?
GRUMIO   Marry, sir, with needle and thread.
TAILOR
  But did you not request to have it cut?
GRUMIO   Thou hast faced many things.   121
TAILOR   I have.
GRUMIO   Face not me. Thou hast braved many men;   123
  brave not me. I will neither be faced nor braved. I say   124
  unto thee, I bid thy master cut out the gown, but I did
  not bid him cut it to pieces. Ergo, thou liest.   126
TAILOR   Why, here is the note of the fashion to testify.
            [He displays his bill.]
PETRUCHIO   Read it.

GRUMIO   The note lies in 's throat if he say I said so.   129
TAILOR [reads]   "Imprimis, a loose-bodied gown—"   130
GRUMIO   Master, if ever I said loose-bodied gown,   131
  sew me in the skirts of it and beat me to death with a
  bottom of brown thread. I said a gown.   133
PETRUCHIO   Proceed.
TAILOR [reads]   "With a small compassed cape—"   135
GRUMIO   I confess the cape.
TAILOR [reads]   "With a trunk sleeve—"   137
GRUMIO   I confess two sleeves.
TAILOR [reads]   "The sleeves curiously cut."   139
PETRUCHIO   Ay, there's the villainy.
GRUMIO   Error i'the bill, sir, error i'the bill. I commanded
  the sleeves should be cut out and sewed up again, and
  that I'll prove upon thee, though thy little finger be   143
  armed in a thimble.
TAILOR   This is true that I say. An I had thee in place   145
  where, thou shouldst know it.   146
GRUMIO   I am for thee straight. Take thou the bill, give   147
  me thy mete-yard, and spare not me.   148
HORTENSIO   God-a-mercy, Grumio, then he shall have   149
  no odds.   150
PETRUCHIO   Well, sir, in brief, the gown is not for me.
GRUMIO   You are i'the right, sir, 'tis for my mistress.
PETRUCHIO   Go, take it up unto thy master's use.   153
GRUMIO [to the Tailor]   Villain, not for thy life! Take up
  my mistress' gown for thy master's use!
PETRUCHIO   Why sir, what's your conceit in that?   156
GRUMIO
  Oh, sir, the conceit is deeper than you think for: 157
  Take up my mistress' gown to his master's use!
  Oh, fie, fie, fie!
PETRUCHIO [aside to Hortensio]
  Hortensio, say thou wilt see the tailor paid.
  [To Tailor] Go, take it hence. Begone, and say no more.
HORTENSIO [aside to the Tailor]
  Tailor, I'll pay thee for thy gown tomorrow.
  Take no unkindness of his hasty words.
  Away, I say. Commend me to thy master.
                      Exit Tailor.
PETRUCHIO
  Well, come, my Kate. We will unto your father's
  Even in these honest, mean habiliments.   166
  Our purses shall be proud, our garments poor,
  For 'tis the mind that makes the body rich;
  And as the sun breaks through the darkest clouds,

---

93 like likely   96 Marry . . remembered I did indeed. But if you rec-
ollect   98 hop . . . home hop on home over every street gutter
102 quaint elegant   103 Belike Perhaps   106–10 thou thread . . .
remnant Petruchio attacks the tailor's proverbial thinness and effeminacy using metaphors from tailoring.   107 nail a measure of length
for cloth: 2 ¼ inches.   108 nit louse egg   109 Braved Defied.   with
by   110 quantity fragment   111 be-mete measure, i.e., thrash.   yard
yardstick   112 think on prating i.e., remember this thrashing and
think twice before talking so again   117 stuff material.
121 faced trimmed, decked   123 Face Bully.   braved dressed finely
124 brave defy   126 Ergo Therefore

129 lies in 's throat i.e., lies utterly   130 Imprimis First   131 loose-
bodied gown (Grumio plays on loose, "wanton"; a gown fit for a
prostitute.)   133 bottom i.e., ball or skein. (A weaver's term for the
bobbin.)   135 compassed flared, cut on the bias so as to fall in a circle
137 trunk full, wide   139 curiously elaborately   143 prove upon
thee prove by fighting you   145–6 in place where in a suitable place
147 bill (1) the note ordering the gown (2) a weapon, a halberd
148 mete-yard measuring stick   149 God-a-mercy Thanks   150 no
odds no advantage. (The contest between Grumio and the Tailor will
be evenly matched.)   153 take it up take it away.   use i.e., whatever
use he can make of it. (But Grumio deliberately misinterprets both
expressions in a bawdy sense.)   156 conceit idea   157 deeper more
serious. (But continuing the sexual idea of lifting up the dress and
entering for sexual "use," as in lines 155 and 158.)   166 honest, mean
habiliments respectable, plain clothes.

So honor peereth in the meanest habit.   170
What, is the jay more precious than the lark
Because his feathers are more beautiful?
Or is the adder better than the eel
Because his painted skin contents the eye?   174
Oh, no, good Kate; neither art thou the worse
For this poor furniture and mean array.   176
If thou account'st it shame, lay it on me.
And therefore frolic; we will hence forthwith,
To feast and sport us at thy father's house.
[*To Grumio*] Go call my men, and let us straight
     to him;
And bring our horses unto Long Lane end.
There will we mount, and thither walk on foot.
Let's see, I think 'tis now some seven o'clock,
And well we may come there by dinnertime.   184

KATHARINA
I dare assure you, sir, 'tis almost two,
And 'twill be suppertime ere you come there.

PETRUCHIO
It shall be seven ere I go to horse.
Look what I speak, or do, or think to do,   188
You are still crossing it.—Sirs, let 't alone.   189
I will not go today, and ere I do,
It shall be what o'clock I say it is.

HORTENSIO [*aside*]
Why, so this gallant will command the sun.   192

                                   [*Exeunt.*]

❖

[4.4]

*Enter Tranio [as Lucentio], and the Pedant
dressed like Vincentio [booted].*

TRANIO
Sir, this is the house. Please it you that I call?

PEDANT
Ay, what else? And but I be deceived,   2
Signor Baptista may remember me,   3
Near twenty years ago, in Genoa—   4

TRANIO
Where we were lodgers at the Pegasus.—   5
'Tis well; and hold your own in any case   6
With such austerity as 'longeth to a father.

Enter Biondello.

PEDANT
I warrant you. But, sir, here comes your boy.
'Twere good he were schooled.   9

TRANIO
Fear you not him.—Sirrah Biondello,
Now do your duty throughly, I advise you.   11
Imagine 'twere the right Vincentio.   12

BIONDELLO   Tut, fear not me.   13

TRANIO
But hast thou done thy errand to Baptista?

BIONDELLO
I told him that your father was at Venice
And that you looked for him this day in Padua.

TRANIO [*giving money*]
Thou'rt a tall fellow. Hold thee that to drink.   17
Here comes Baptista. Set your countenance, sir.   18

*Enter Baptista, and Lucentio [as Cambio].
[The] Pedant [stands] bareheaded.*

Signor Baptista, you are happily met.   19
[*To the Pedant*] Sir, this is the gentleman I told you of.
I pray you, stand good father to me now;
Give me Bianca for my patrimony.

PEDANT   Soft, son!—   23
Sir, by your leave, having come to Padua
To gather in some debts, my son Lucentio
Made me acquainted with a weighty cause
Of love between your daughter and himself;
And, for the good report I hear of you   28
And for the love he beareth to your daughter
And she to him, to stay him not too long,   30
I am content, in a good father's care,
To have him matched. And if you please to like   32
No worse than I, upon some agreement
Me shall you find ready and willing
With one consent to have her so bestowed;   35
For curious I cannot be with you,   36
Signor Baptista, of whom I hear so well.

BAPTISTA
Sir, pardon me in what I have to say.
Your plainness and your shortness please me well.
Right true it is your son Lucentio here
Doth love my daughter, and she loveth him,
Or both dissemble deeply their affections.
And therefore, if you say no more than this,
That like a father you will deal with him
And pass my daughter a sufficient dower,   45
The match is made, and all is done.
Your son shall have my daughter with consent.

TRANIO
I thank you, sir. Where then do you know best   48
We be affied and such assurance ta'en   49
As shall with either part's agreement stand?   50

---

170 **peereth . . . habit** peeps through the humblest attire.
174 **painted** colorfully patterned   176 **furniture** furnishings of attire
184 **dinnertime** i.e., about noon.   188 **Look what** Whatever
189 **still crossing** always contradicting or defying   192 **so** at this rate
4.4. Location: Padua. Before Baptista's house.
0.2 **booted** (signifying travel)   2 **but** unless   3–4 **Signor . . . Genoa**
(The Pedant rehearses what he is to say.)   5 **Where . . . Pegasus**
(Tranio is coaching the Pedant in further details of his story.)   **the
Pegasus** i.e., an inn, so named after the famous winged horse of classical myth.   6 **hold your own** play your part   9 **schooled** i.e.,
rehearsed in his part.

11 **throughly** thoroughly   12 **right** real   13 **fear not me** don't worry
about my doing my part.   17 **tall** fine.   **Hold . . . drink** Take that
and buy a drink.   18 **Set your countenance** i.e., Put on the expression of an austere father (line 7).   19 **happily** fortunately   23 **Soft**
i.e., Steady, take it easy   28 **for** because of   30 **to stay him not** not to
keep him waiting   32 **like** i.e., approve of the match   35 **one** i.e.,
firm   36 **curious** overly particular   45 **pass** settle on, give
48–50 **Where . . . stand?** Where in your view is the best place for
us to be betrothed and for legal assurances to be made that will
confirm an agreement satisfactory to both parties?

BAPTISTA

Not in my house, Lucentio, for you know
Pitchers have ears, and I have many servants.
Besides, old Gremio is heark'ning still,   53
And happily we might be interrupted.   54

TRANIO

Then at my lodging, an it like you.   55
There doth my father lie, and there this night   56
We'll pass the business privately and well.   57
Send for your daughter by your servant here.
    [*He indicates Lucentio, and winks at him.*]
My boy shall fetch the scrivener presently.   59
The worst is this, that at so slender warning
You are like to have a thin and slender pittance. 61

BAPTISTA

It likes me well. Cambio, hie you home,
And bid Bianca make her ready straight.
And if you will, tell what hath happened:
Lucentio's father is arrived in Padua,
And how she's like to be Lucentio's wife.
                              [*Exit Lucentio.*]

BIONDELLO

I pray the gods she may with all my heart!

TRANIO

Dally not with the gods, but get thee gone.
                              Exit [*Biondello*].
Signor Baptista, shall I lead the way?
Welcome! One mess is like to be your cheer.   70
Come, sir, we will better it in Pisa.

BAPTISTA   I follow you.   72
                Exeunt [*Tranio, Pedant, and Baptista*].

    Enter Lucentio [*as Cambio*] *and Biondello.*

BIONDELLO   Cambio!
LUCENTIO   What say'st thou, Biondello?
BIONDELLO   You saw my master wink and laugh upon
you?
LUCENTIO   Biondello, what of that?
BIONDELLO   Faith, nothing; but he's left me here behind
to expound the meaning or moral of his signs and to-   79
kens.
LUCENTIO   I pray thee, moralize them.   81
BIONDELLO   Then thus. Baptista is safe, talking with   82
the deceiving father of a deceitful son.
LUCENTIO   And what of him?
BIONDELLO   His daughter is to be brought by you to
the supper.
LUCENTIO   And then?
BIONDELLO   The old priest at Saint Luke's church is at
your command at all hours.
LUCENTIO   And what of all this?

BIONDELLO   I cannot tell, except they are busied about a   91
counterfeit assurance. Take you assurance of her   92
cum privilegio ad imprimendum solum. To th'   93
church take the priest, clerk, and some sufficient hon-   94
est witnesses.
If this be not that you look for, I have no more to say,   96
But bid Bianca farewell forever and a day.
                              [*Biondello starts to leave.*]
LUCENTIO   Hear'st thou, Biondello?
BIONDELLO   I cannot tarry. I knew a wench married in
an afternoon as she went to the garden for parsley to
stuff a rabbit, and so may you, sir. And so, adieu, sir.
My master hath appointed me to go to Saint Luke's, to
bid the priest be ready to come against you come with   103
your appendix.   *Exit.*   104
LUCENTIO

I may, and will, if she be so contented.
She will be pleased; then wherefore should I doubt?
Hap what hap may, I'll roundly go about her.   107
It shall go hard if Cambio go without her.   *Exit.*   108

                              ❧

[4.5]

    Enter Petruchio, Kate, [*and*] *Hortensio.*

PETRUCHIO

Come on, i'God's name, once more toward our father's.   1
Good Lord, how bright and goodly shines the moon!

KATHARINA

The moon? The sun. It is not moonlight now.

PETRUCHIO

I say it is the moon that shines so bright.

KATHARINA

I know it is the sun that shines so bright.

PETRUCHIO

Now, by my mother's son, and that's myself,
It shall be moon, or star, or what I list   7
Or ere I journey to your father's house.—   8
Go on, and fetch our horses back again—
Evermore crossed and crossed, nothing but crossed!

HORTENSIO [*to Katharina*]

Say as he says, or we shall never go.

KATHARINA

Forward, I pray, since we have come so far,
And be it moon, or sun, or what you please;
An if you please to call it a rush candle,   14

---

91 except unless   **92 counterfeit assurance** pretended betrothal
agreement.   **Take . . . of her** Legalize your claim to her (by marriage)
93 cum . . . solum with exclusive printing rights. (A copyright formula
often appearing on the title pages of books, here jokingly applied to
the marriage and to procreation as an act of imprinting.)   **94 suffi-**
cient meeting the legal requirement in number and social standing
96 that you look for what you are looking for   **103 against you come**
in anticipation of your arrival   **104 appendix** something appended,
i.e., the bride. (Continuing the metaphor of printing.)   **107 roundly . . .**
her set about marrying her in no uncertain terms.   **108 It . . . her** i.e.,
I'm determined to have her. (With pun about erection.)
4.5. Location: A road on the way to Padua.
1 our father's our father's house.   **7 list** please   **8 Or ere** before
14 a rush candle a rush dipped into tallow; hence a very feeble light

---

53 heark'ning still continually listening   **54 happily** haply   **55 an it**
like if it please   **56 lie** lodge   **57 pass** transact   **59 scrivener** notary,
one to draw up contracts.   **presently** at once.   **61 like** likely.
slender pittance i.e., scanty banquet.   **70 mess** dish.   **cheer** entertainment.   **72.1 Exeunt** (Technically, the cleared stage may mark a
new scene, but the conversation of Lucentio and Biondello suggests
that they come creeping back on stage as the others leave rather than
doing the errands Baptista and Tranio bid them.)   **79 moral** hidden
meaning   **81 moralize** elucidate   **82 safe** i.e., safely out of the way

Henceforth I vow it shall be so for me.

PETRUCHIO
I say it is the moon.

KATHARINA   I know it is the moon.

PETRUCHIO
Nay, then you lie. It is the blessèd sun.

KATHARINA
Then, God be blessed, it is the blessèd sun.
But sun it is not, when you say it is not,
And the moon changes even as your mind.
What you will have it named, even that it is,
And so it shall be so for Katharine.

HORTENSIO
Petruchio, go thy ways. The field is won.   23

PETRUCHIO
Well, forward, forward. Thus the bowl should run,
And not unluckily against the bias.   25
But soft! Company is coming here.

          Enter Vincentio.

[*To Vincentio*] Good morrow, gentle mistress. Where
     away?—   27
Tell me, sweet Kate, and tell me truly too,
Hast thou beheld a fresher gentlewoman?
Such war of white and red within her cheeks!
What stars do spangle heaven with such beauty
As those two eyes become that heavenly face?—
Fair lovely maid, once more good day to thee.—
Sweet Kate, embrace her for her beauty's sake.

HORTENSIO [*aside*]
'A will make the man mad, to make a woman of him. 35

KATHARINA [*embracing Vincentio*]
Young budding virgin, fair, and fresh, and sweet,
Whither away, or where is thy abode?
Happy the parents of so fair a child!
Happier the man whom favorable stars
Allots thee for his lovely bedfellow!   40

PETRUCHIO
Why, how now, Kate? I hope thou art not mad.
This is a man, old, wrinkled, faded, withered,
And not a maiden, as thou say'st he is.

KATHARINA
Pardon, old father, my mistaking eyes,
That have been so bedazzled with the sun
That everything I look on seemeth green.   46
Now I perceive thou art a reverend father.
Pardon, I pray thee, for my mad mistaking.

PETRUCHIO
Do, good old grandsire, and withal make known
Which way thou travelest—if along with us,
We shall be joyful of thy company.

VINCENTIO
Fair sir, and you, my merry mistress,
That with your strange encounter much amazed me,

My name is called Vincentio, my dwelling Pisa,
And bound I am to Padua, there to visit
A son of mine, which long I have not seen.

PETRUCHIO
What is his name?

VINCENTIO   Lucentio, gentle sir.

PETRUCHIO
Happily met, the happier for thy son.
And now by law as well as reverend age
I may entitle thee my loving father.
The sister to my wife, this gentlewoman,
Thy son by this hath married. Wonder not,   62
Nor be not grieved. She is of good esteem,   63
Her dowry wealthy, and of worthy birth;
Besides, so qualified as may beseem   65
The spouse of any noble gentleman.
Let me embrace with old Vincentio,
And wander we to see thy honest son,   68
Who will of thy arrival be full joyous.
                              [*He embraces Vincentio.*]

VINCENTIO
But is this true? Or is it else your pleasure,
Like pleasant travelers, to break a jest   71
Upon the company you overtake?

HORTENSIO
I do assure thee, father, so it is.

PETRUCHIO
Come, go along, and see the truth hereof,
For our first merriment hath made thee jealous.   75
                         Exeunt [all but Hortensio].

HORTENSIO
Well, Petruchio, this has put me in heart.   76
Have to my widow! And if she be froward,   77
Then hast thou taught Hortensio to be untoward.   78
                                           Exit.

                    ❧

[5.1]

*Enter Biondello, Lucentio [no longer disguised],
and Bianca. Gremio is out before [and stands
aside].*

BIONDELLO   Softly and swiftly, sir, for the priest is
ready.

LUCENTIO   I fly, Biondello. But they may chance to need
thee at home; therefore leave us.

BIONDELLO   Nay, faith, I'll see the church a' your back,   5
and then come back to my master's as soon as I can.
                [Exeunt Lucentio, Bianca, and Biondello.]

---

62 by this by this time   **63 esteem** reputation   **65 so qualified** having
such qualities.   **beseem** befit   **68 wander** go (having changed plans)
71 pleasant humorous, jocular.   **break a jest** play a practical joke
75 jealous suspicious.   **76 put me in heart** encouraged me.   **77 Have
to** i.e., Now for.   **froward** perverse   **78 untoward** unmannerly.
5.1. Location: Padua. Before Lucentio's house.
0.2 out before i.e., onstage first. (Gremio does not see Biondello,
Lucentio, and Bianca as they steal to church, or else he does not
recognize Lucentio in his own person.)   **5 a' your back** at your
back, behind you. (Biondello first wants to see them in church
and safely married.)

---

23 go thy ways i.e., well done, carry on.   **25 against the bias** off its
proper course. (The *bias* is an off-center weight in a bowling ball
enabling the bowler to roll the ball in an oblique or curving path.)
27 Where away? Where are you going?   **35 'A** He   **40 Allots** allot
46 green young and fresh.

GREMIO
I marvel Cambio comes not all this while.

Enter Petruchio, Kate, Vincentio, Grumio, with attendants.

PETRUCHIO
Sir, here's the door. This is Lucentio's house.
My father's bears more toward the marketplace;   9
Thither must I, and here I leave you, sir.

VINCENTIO
You shall not choose but drink before you go.   11
I think I shall command your welcome here,
And by all likelihood some cheer is toward.   *Knock.* 13

GREMIO [*advancing*] They're busy within. You were
best knock louder.   15

Pedant looks out of the window.

PEDANT What's he that knocks as he would beat down
the gate?

VINCENTIO Is Signor Lucentio within, sir?

PEDANT He's within, sir, but not to be spoken withal.   19

VINCENTIO What if a man bring him a hundred pound
or two to make merry withal?

PEDANT Keep your hundred pounds to yourself. He
shall need none, so long as I live.

PETRUCHIO [*to Vincentio*] Nay, I told you your son was
well beloved in Padua.—Do you hear, sir? To leave
frivolous circumstances, I pray you, tell Signor Lucentio that his father is come from Pisa and is here at the   26
door to speak with him.

PEDANT Thou liest. His father is come from Padua and   29
here looking out at the window.

VINCENTIO Art thou his father?

PEDANT Ay, sir, so his mother says, if I may believe
her.

PETRUCHIO [*to Vincentio*] Why, how now, gentleman!
Why, this is flat knavery, to take upon you another   35
man's name.

PEDANT Lay hands on the villain. I believe 'a means to
cozen somebody in this city under my countenance.   38

Enter Biondello.

BIONDELLO [*aside*] I have seen them in the church
together, God send 'em good shipping! But who is   40
here? Mine old master Vincentio! Now we are undone
and brought to nothing.

VINCENTIO [*seeing Biondello*] Come hither, crackhemp.   43

BIONDELLO I hope I may choose, sir.   44

---

9 **father's** i.e., father-in-law's, Baptista's. **bears** lies. (A nautical
term.) **11 You . . . but** i.e., I insist that **13 cheer is toward** entertainment is in prospect. **15.1** *window* i.e., probably the gallery to the
rear, over the stage. **19 withal** with. **26 circumstances** matters
29 from Padua i.e., from Padua, where we are right now. (Often
emended to "from Mantua," "from Pisa," "to Padua," etc.)
35 flat downright **38 cozen** cheat. **under my countenance** by pretending to be me. **40 good shipping** bon voyage, good fortune.
43 crackhemp i.e., rogue likely to end up being hanged. **44 choose**
do as I choose

VINCENTIO Come hither, you rogue. What, have you
forgot me?

BIONDELLO Forgot you? No, sir. I could not forget you,
for I never saw you before in all my life.

VINCENTIO What, you notorious villain, didst thou
never see thy master's father, Vincentio?

BIONDELLO What, my old worshipful old master? Yes,
marry, sir, see where he looks out of the window.

VINCENTIO Is't so, indeed?   *He beats Biondello.*

BIONDELLO Help, help, help! Here's a madman will
murder me.   [*Exit.*]

PEDANT Help, son! Help, Signor Baptista!
                       [*Exit from the window.*]

PETRUCHIO Prithee, Kate, let's stand aside and see the
end of this controversy.   [*They stand aside.*]

*Enter [below] Pedant with servants, Baptista,
[and] Tranio [as Lucentio].*

TRANIO Sir, what are you that offer to beat my servant?   59

VINCENTIO What am I, sir? Nay, what are you, sir? O
immortal gods! Oh, fine villain! A silken doublet, a velvet hose, a scarlet cloak, and a copintank hat! Oh, I am   62
undone, I am undone! While I play the good husband   63
at home, my son and my servant spend all at the university.

TRANIO How now, what's the matter?

BAPTISTA What, is the man lunatic?

TRANIO Sir, you seem a sober ancient gentleman by
your habit, but your words show you a madman.   69
Why, sir, what 'cerns it you if I wear pearl and gold?   70
I thank my good father, I am able to maintain it.   71

VINCENTIO Thy father! Oh, villain, he is a sailmaker in
Bergamo.

BAPTISTA You mistake, sir, you mistake, sir. Pray, what
do you think is his name?

VINCENTIO His name! As if I knew not his name! I have
brought him up ever since he was three years old, and
his name is Tranio.

PEDANT Away, away, mad ass! His name is Lucentio,
and he is mine only son, and heir to the lands of me,
Signor Vincentio.

VINCENTIO Lucentio! Oh, he hath murdered his master!
Lay hold on him, I charge you, in the Duke's name.
Oh, my son, my son! Tell me, thou villain, where is my
son Lucentio?

TRANIO Call forth an officer.

[Enter an Officer.]

Carry this mad knave to the jail. Father Baptista, I
charge you see that he be forthcoming.   88

VINCENTIO Carry me to the jail?

GREMIO Stay, officer, he shall not go to prison.

BAPTISTA Talk not, Signor Gremio. I say he shall go to
prison.

---

59 **offer** dare, presume **62 copintank** high-crowned, sugar-loaf
shape **63 good husband** careful provider, manager **69 habit** clothing **70 'cerns** concerns **71 maintain** afford **88 forthcoming** ready
to stand trial when required.

GREMIO   Take heed, Signor Baptista, lest you be coney- 93
catched in this business. I dare swear this is the right 94
Vincentio.

PEDANT   Swear, if thou dar'st.

GREMIO   Nay, I dare not swear it.

TRANIO   Then thou wert best say that I am not Lucentio. 98

GREMIO   Yes, I know thee to be Signor Lucentio.

BAPTISTA   Away with the dotard! To the jail with him!

Enter Biondello, Lucentio, and Bianca.

VINCENTIO   Thus strangers may be haled and abused. 101
—Oh, monstrous villain!

BIONDELLO   Oh! We are spoiled and—yonder he is. 103
Deny him, forswear him, or else we are all undone.
*Exeunt Biondello, Tranio, and Pedant as fast as
may be. [Lucentio and Bianca] kneel.*

LUCENTIO
Pardon, sweet father.

VINCENTIO   Lives my sweet son?

BIANCA
Pardon, dear father.

BAPTISTA   How hast thou offended?
Where is Lucentio?

LUCENTIO   Here's Lucentio,
Right son to the right Vincentio,
That have by marriage made thy daughter mine,
While counterfeit supposes bleared thine eyne. 110

GREMIO
Here's packing, with a witness, to deceive us all! 111

VINCENTIO
Where is that damnèd villain Tranio,
That faced and braved me in this matter so? 113

BAPTISTA
Why, tell me, is not this my Cambio?

BIANCA
Cambio is changed into Lucentio. 115

LUCENTIO
Love wrought these miracles. Bianca's love
Made me exchange my state with Tranio, 117
While he did bear my countenance in the town, 118
And happily I have arrivèd at the last
Unto the wishèd haven of my bliss.
What Tranio did, myself enforced him to;
Then pardon him, sweet father, for my sake.

VINCENTIO   I'll slit the villain's nose, that would have
sent me to the jail.

BAPTISTA *[to Lucentio]*   But do you hear, sir? Have you
married my daughter without asking my good will?

VINCENTIO   Fear not, Baptista, we will content you. Go 127
to. But I will in, to be revenged for this villainy. 128
Exit.

BAPTISTA   And I, to sound the depth of this knavery.
Exit.

LUCENTIO   Look not pale, Bianca. Thy father will not
frown.   *Exeunt [Lucentio and Bianca].*

GREMIO
My cake is dough, but I'll in among the rest, 132
Out of hope of all but my share of the feast.   *[Exit.]* 133

KATHARINA   Husband, let's follow, to see the end of
this ado.

PETRUCHIO   First kiss me, Kate, and we will.

KATHARINA   What, in the midst of the street?

PETRUCHIO   What, art thou ashamed of me?

KATHARINA   No, sir, God forbid, but ashamed to kiss.

PETRUCHIO
Why, then let's home again. *[To Grumio]* Come, sirrah,
let's away.

KATHARINA
Nay, I will give thee a kiss. *[She kisses him.]* Now pray
thee, love, stay.

PETRUCHIO
Is not this well? Come, my sweet Kate.
Better once than never, for never too late.   *Exeunt.* 143

❧

5.[2]

*Enter Baptista, Vincentio, Gremio, the Pedant,
Lucentio, and Bianca; [Petruchio, Kate, Hortensio,] Tranio, Biondello, Grumio, and [the]
Widow; the servingmen with Tranio bringing
in a banquet.*

LUCENTIO
At last, though long, our jarring notes agree, 1
And time it is, when raging war is done,
To smile at scapes and perils overblown. 3
My fair Bianca, bid my father welcome,
While I with selfsame kindness welcome thine.
Brother Petruchio, sister Katharina,
And thou, Hortensio, with thy loving widow,
Feast with the best, and welcome to my house.
My banquet is to close our stomachs up 9
After our great good cheer. Pray you, sit down, 10
For now we sit to chat as well as eat.   *[They sit.]*

PETRUCHIO
Nothing but sit and sit, and eat and eat!

BAPTISTA
Padua affords this kindness, son Petruchio.

PETRUCHIO
Padua affords nothing but what is kind.

93–4 **coney-catched** tricked   98 **wert best** might as well
101 **haled** hauled about, maltreated   103 **spoiled** ruined   110 **supposes** suppositions, false appearances. (With an allusion to Gascoigne's *Supposes*, an adaptation of *I Suppositi* by Ariosto, from
which Shakespeare took the Lucentio-Bianca plot of intrigue.)
eyne eyes.   111 **Here's . . . all!** Here's evidence of a conspiracy, no
mistake about it!   113 **faced and braved** stood up to and defied
115 **Cambio is changed** (A pun. *Cambio* in Italian means "change"
or "exchange.")   117 **state** social station   118 **countenance** appearance, identity

127–8 **Go to** i.e., Don't worry. (An expression of impatience or annoyance.)   132 **My . . . dough** i.e., I'm out of luck, I failed
133 **Out . . . but** having hope for nothing other than   143 **once** at
some time. (Compare with "better late than never.")
5.2. Location: Padua. Lucentio's house.
1 **long** after long time   3 **scapes** close calls   9 **stomachs** (1) appetites
(2) quarrels   10 **cheer** i.e., wedding feast

HORTENSIO
    For both our sakes, I would that word were true.
PETRUCHIO
    Now, for my life, Hortensio fears his widow.   16
WIDOW
    Then never trust me if I be afeard.   17
PETRUCHIO
    You are very sensible, and yet you miss my sense:
    I mean Hortensio is afeard of you.
WIDOW
    He that is giddy thinks the world turns round.
PETRUCHIO
    Roundly replied.
KATHARINA   Mistress, how mean you that?   21
WIDOW   Thus I conceive by him.   22
PETRUCHIO
    Conceives by me! How likes Hortensio that?
HORTENSIO
    My widow says, thus she conceives her tale.   24
PETRUCHIO
    Very well mended. Kiss him for that, good widow.
KATHARINA
    "He that is giddy thinks the world turns round":
    I pray you, tell me what you meant by that.
WIDOW
    Your husband, being troubled with a shrew,
    Measures my husband's sorrow by his woe.   29
    And now you know my meaning.
KATHARINA
    A very mean meaning.
WIDOW   Right, I mean you.   31
KATHARINA
    And I am mean indeed, respecting you.   32
PETRUCHIO   To her, Kate!   33
HORTENSIO   To her, widow!
PETRUCHIO
    A hundred marks, my Kate does put her down.   35
HORTENSIO   That's my office.
PETRUCHIO
    Spoke like an officer. Ha' to thee, lad!   37
                            [He] drinks to Hortensio.
BAPTISTA
    How likes Gremio these quick-witted folks?
GREMIO
    Believe me, sir, they butt together well.   39
BIANCA
    Head, and butt! An hasty-witted body   40
    Would say your head and butt were head and horn.   41

VINCENTIO
    Ay, mistress bride, hath that awakened you?
BIANCA
    Ay, but not frighted me. Therefore I'll sleep again.
PETRUCHIO
    Nay, that you shall not. Since you have begun,
    Have at you for a bitter jest or two!   45
BIANCA
    Am I your bird? I mean to shift my bush;   46
    And then pursue me as you draw your bow.
    You are welcome all.
                    Exit Bianca [with Katharina and the Widow].
PETRUCHIO
    She hath prevented me. Here, Signor Tranio,   49
    This bird you aimed at, though you hit her not.   50
    Therefore a health to all that shot and missed.   51
                                    [He offers a toast.]
TRANIO
    Oh, sir, Lucentio slipped me like his greyhound,   52
    Which runs himself and catches for his master.
PETRUCHIO
    A good swift simile, but something currish.   54
TRANIO
    'Tis well, sir, that you hunted for yourself.
    'Tis thought your deer does hold you at a bay.   56
BAPTISTA
    Oho, Petruchio! Tranio hits you now.
LUCENTIO
    I thank thee for that gird, good Tranio.   58
HORTENSIO
    Confess, confess, hath he not hit you here?
PETRUCHIO
    'A has a little galled me, I confess;   60
    And as the jest did glance away from me,
    'Tis ten to one it maimed you two outright.
BAPTISTA
    Now, in good sadness, son Petruchio,   63
    I think thou hast the veriest shrew of all.
PETRUCHIO
    Well, I say no. And therefore for assurance   65
    Let's each one send unto his wife;
    And he whose wife is most obedient
    To come at first when he doth send for her
    Shall win the wager which we will propose.
HORTENSIO
    Content. What's the wager?
LUCENTIO   Twenty crowns.
PETRUCHIO   Twenty crowns!
    I'll venture so much of my hawk or hound,   72
    But twenty times so much upon my wife.

16 for my life upon my life.   **fears** is afraid of   **17 afeard** frightened
(by Hortensio).   **21 Roundly** Boldly, bluntly   **22 Thus . . . him** i.e.,
That's what I think of him, Petruchio. (But Petruchio takes up
conceives in the sense of "is made pregnant.")   **24 conceives** intends,
interprets. (With a possible pun on *tale* and "tail.")   **29 his** his own
31 very mean contemptible. (But the Widow takes up *mean* in the
sense of "have in mind," and Kate replies in the sense of "moderate
in shrewishness.")   **32 respecting** compared to   **33 To her** (A cry used
to egg on fighting roosters.)   **35 marks** coins worth thirteen shillings
four pence.   **put her down** overcome her. (But Hortensio takes up the
phrase in a bawdy sense.)   **37 officer** (playing on Hortensio's speaking of his *office* or function).   **Ha'** Have, i.e., Here's   **39 butt** butt heads
40 An hasty-witted body A quick-witted person   **41 head and horn**
(Alluding to the familiar joke about cuckolds' horns.)

45 Have at you for Here comes   **46 Am . . . bush** i.e., If you mean to
shoot your barbs at me, I intend to move out of the way, as a bird
would fly to another bush. (With a possible bawdy double meaning;
bush can suggest pubic hair.)   **49 prevented** forestalled   **50 This bird**
i.e., Bianca, whom Tranio courted (*aimed at*) in his disguise as Lucentio   **51 a health** a toast   **52 slipped** unleashed   **54 swift** (1) quick-
witted (2) concerning swiftness.   **currish** (1) ignoble (2) concerning
dogs.   **56 deer** (Punning on "dear.")   **does . . . bay** turns on you like
a cornered animal and holds you at a distance.   **58 gird** sharp, biting
jest   **60 galled** scratched, chafed   **63 sadness** seriousness   **65 assurance** proof   **72 of** on

LUCENTIO A hundred then.

HORTENSIO Content.

PETRUCHIO A match. 'Tis done.

HORTENSIO Who shall begin?

LUCENTIO That will I.
Go, Biondello, bid your mistress come to me.

BIONDELLO I go.   *Exit.*

BAPTISTA
Son, I'll be your half Bianca comes.   81

LUCENTIO
I'll have no halves; I'll bear it all myself.

       Enter Biondello.

How now, what news?

BIONDELLO
Sir, my mistress sends you word
That she is busy and she cannot come.

PETRUCHIO
How? She's busy and she cannot come?
Is that an answer?

GREMIO   Ay, and a kind one too.
Pray God, sir, your wife send you not a worse.

PETRUCHIO I hope better.

HORTENSIO
Sirrah Biondello, go and entreat my wife
To come to me forthwith.   *Exit Biondello.*

PETRUCHIO   Oho, entreat her!
Nay, then she must needs come.

HORTENSIO   I am afraid, sir,
Do what you can, yours will not be entreated.

       Enter Biondello.

Now, where's my wife?

BIONDELLO
She says you have some goodly jest in hand.
She will not come. She bids you come to her.

PETRUCHIO
Worse and worse. She will not come!
Oh, vile, intolerable, not to be endured!—
Sirrah Grumio, go to your mistress.
Say I command her come to me.   *Exit [Grumio].*

HORTENSIO
I know her answer.

PETRUCHIO   What?

HORTENSIO   She will not.

PETRUCHIO
The fouler fortune mine, and there an end.   102

       Enter Katharina.

BAPTISTA
Now, by my halidom, here comes Katharina!   103

KATHARINA
What is your will, sir, that you send for me?

PETRUCHIO
Where is your sister, and Hortensio's wife?

KATHARINA
They sit conferring by the parlor fire.

PETRUCHIO
Go fetch them hither. If they deny to come,
Swinge me them soundly forth unto their husbands.   108
Away, I say, and bring them hither straight.

                [Exit Katharina.]

LUCENTIO
Here is a wonder, if you talk of a wonder.

HORTENSIO
And so it is. I wonder what it bodes.

PETRUCHIO
Marry, peace it bodes, and love, and quiet life,
An aweful rule, and right supremacy,   113
And, to be short, what not that's sweet and happy.

BAPTISTA
Now, fair befall thee, good Petruchio!   115
The wager thou hast won, and I will add
Unto their losses twenty thousand crowns,
Another dowry to another daughter,
For she is changed, as she had never been.   119

PETRUCHIO
Nay, I will win my wager better yet,
And show more sign of her obedience,
Her new-built virtue and obedience.

       Enter Kate, Bianca, and [the] Widow.

See where she comes and brings your froward wives
As prisoners to her womanly persuasion.—
Katharine, that cap of yours becomes you not.
Off with that bauble. Throw it underfoot.

                [She obeys.]

WIDOW
Lord, let me never have a cause to sigh
Till I be brought to such a silly pass!   128

BIANCA
Fie, what a foolish duty call you this?

LUCENTIO
I would your duty were as foolish, too.
The wisdom of your duty, fair Bianca,
Hath cost me a hundred crowns since suppertime.

BIANCA
The more fool you, for laying on my duty.   133

PETRUCHIO
Katharine, I charge thee tell these headstrong women
What duty they do owe their lords and husbands.

WIDOW
Come, come, you're mocking. We will have no telling.

PETRUCHIO
Come on, I say, and first begin with her.

WIDOW She shall not.

PETRUCHIO
I say she shall—and first begin with her.

---

81 **be your half** take half your bet   **102 there an end** that's that.
103 **by my halidom** (Originally an oath by the holy relics, but confused with an oath to the Virgin Mary.)

108 **Swinge** thrash. **me** i.e., at my behest. (*Me* is used colloquially.)
113 **aweful rule** authority commanding awe or respect **115 fair**
befall thee good luck to you, and congratulations **119 as . . . been** as
if she had never existed, i.e., she is totally changed. **128 pass** state of
affairs. **133 laying** wagering

KATHARINA

Fie, fie! Unknit that threatening, unkind brow,
And dart not scornful glances from those eyes
To wound thy lord, thy king, thy governor.
It blots thy beauty as frosts do bite the meads,   143
Confounds thy fame as whirlwinds shake fair buds,   144
And in no sense is meet or amiable.
A woman moved is like a fountain troubled,   146
Muddy, ill-seeming, thick, bereft of beauty;
And while it is so, none so dry or thirsty   148
Will deign to sip or touch one drop of it.
Thy husband is thy lord, thy life, thy keeper,
Thy head, thy sovereign; one that cares for thee,
And for thy maintenance commits his body
To painful labor both by sea and land,   153
To watch the night in storms, the day in cold,   154
Whilst thou liest warm at home, secure and safe;
And craves no other tribute at thy hands
But love, fair looks, and true obedience—
Too little payment for so great a debt.
Such duty as the subject owes the prince,
Even such a woman oweth to her husband;
And when she is froward, peevish, sullen, sour,   161
And not obedient to his honest will,   162
What is she but a foul contending rebel
And graceless traitor to her loving lord?
I am ashamed that women are so simple   165
To offer war where they should kneel for peace,
Or seek for rule, supremacy, and sway,
When they are bound to serve, love, and obey.
Why are our bodies soft, and weak, and smooth,
Unapt to toil and trouble in the world,   170
But that our soft conditions and our hearts   171
Should well agree with our external parts?

---

143 **meads** meadows   144 **Confounds thy fame** ruins your reputation   146 **moved** angry   148 **none . . . thirsty** there is no one so
thirsty that he   153 **painful** onerous   154 **watch** stay awake
throughout   161 **peevish** obstinate   162 **to his honest will** (Kate
may suggest that she will be obedient when his will is decent and virtuous, not that his will is always so.)   165 **simple** foolish   170 **Unapt
to** unfit for   171 **conditions** qualities

Come, come, you froward and unable worms!   173
My mind hath been as big as one of yours,   174
My heart as great, my reason haply more,
To bandy word for word and frown for frown;
But now I see our lances are but straws,
Our strength as weak, our weakness past compare,   178
That seeming to be most which we indeed least are.   179
Then vail your stomachs, for it is no boot,   180
And place your hands below your husband's foot,
In token of which duty, if he please,
My hand is ready; may it do him ease.   183

PETRUCHIO

Why, there's a wench! Come on, and kiss me, Kate.

[*They kiss.*]

LUCENTIO

Well, go thy ways, old lad, for thou shalt ha 't.   185

VINCENTIO

'Tis a good hearing when children are toward.   186

LUCENTIO

But a harsh hearing when women are froward.

PETRUCHIO   Come, Kate, we'll to bed.

We three are married, but you two are sped.   189
[*To Lucentio*] 'Twas I won the wager, though you hit
  the white,   190
And, being a winner, God give you good night!   191

Exit Petruchio [*with Katharina*].

HORTENSIO

Now go thy ways. Thou hast tamed a curst shrew.   192

LUCENTIO

'Tis a wonder, by your leave, she will be tamed so.

[*Exeunt.*]

---

173 **unable worms** i.e., poor feeble creatures.   174 **big** haughty
178 **as weak** i.e., as weak as straws   179 **That seeming to be** seeming
to be that   180 **Then . . . boot** Then lower your pride, for it is no use
striving   183 **do him ease** give him pleasure.   185 **go thy ways** well
done.   **ha 't** have it, the prize.   186 **'Tis . . . toward** i.e., One likes to
hear when children are obedient.   189 **We . . . sped** i.e., All we three
men have taken wives, but you two are done for (*sped*) through disobedient wives.   190 **the white** the center of the target. (With quibble
on the name of Bianca, which in Italian means "white.")   191 **being**
since I am   192 **shrew** pronounced "shrow" (and thus spelled in the
Folio). See also 4.1.198 and 5.2.28.

A Midsummer Night's Dream

One of the many astonishing achievements in *A Midsummer Night's Dream* (c. 1594–1595) is its development of the motif of love as an imaginative journey from a world of social conflict into a fantasy world created by the artist, ending in a return to a reality that has itself been partly transformed by the experience of the journey. As the lovers in this play flee from the Athenian law to lose themselves in the forest, they reveal and discover in themselves the simultaneously hilarious and horrifying effects of sexual desire. Moreover, their journey suggests the extent to which love or desire is itself an act of imagination, not unlike the imagination that underlies the creation of art. The fifth act especially invites us to see theatrical experience as like a dream, at times nightmarish but at its best an emancipating foray into an imagined space wholly beyond the realm of ordinary human happenings. Shakespeare gives us an earlier hint of an imaginary sylvan landscape in *The Two Gentlemen of Verona*, but not until *A Midsummer Night's Dream* is the idea fully realized. The motif of contrasting worlds, one of social convention and the other of visionary fantasy, will remain an enduring preoccupation of Shakespeare to the very last. This visionary world haunts the imagination with some of the most poetic passages of the entire Shakespeare canon, from Titania's evocation of her bond of affection with her votaress "in the spicèd Indian air by night" (2.1.123–37) to Oberon's memory of a mermaid singing on a dolphin's back (2.1.150–4). Containing the highest percentage of rhymed verse in all of Shakespeare's plays, *A Midsummer Night's Dream* calls attention to the seemingly magical capacity of words to weave spells not only on the characters but on the audience as well.

In construction, *A Midsummer Night's Dream* is a skillful interweaving of four plots involving four groups of characters: the court party of Theseus, the four young lovers, the fairies, and the "rude mechanicals" or would-be actors. Felix Mendelssohn's incidental music for the play evokes the contrasting textures of the various groups: Theseus's hunting horns and ceremonial wedding marches, the lovers' soaring and throbbing melodies, the fairies' pianissimo staccato, the tradesmen's clownish bassoon. Moreover, each plot is derived from its own set of source materials. The action involving Theseus and Hippolyta, for example, owes several details to Thomas North's translation (1579) of Plutarch's *Lives of the Noble Grecians and Romans*, to Chaucer's *Knight's Tale* and perhaps to his *Legend of Good Women*, and to Ovid's *Metamorphoses* (in the Latin text or in Arthur Golding's popular Elizabethan translation). The lovers' story, meanwhile, is Italianate and Ovidian in tone and also, in the broadest sense, follows the conventions of plot in Plautus's and Terence's Roman comedies, although no particular source is known. Shakespeare's rich fairy lore, by contrast, is part folk tradition and part learned. For some of his material he seems to have turned to written sources, such as the French romance *Huon of Bordeaux* (translated into English by 1540), Robert Greene's play *James IV* (c. 1591), and Edmund Spenser's *The Faerie Queene*, II.i.8 (1590). Similarly, he may have taken Titania's name from the *Metamorphoses*, where it is used as an epithet for both Diana and Circe. At the same time, in his creation of Mustardseed, Cobweb, Mote, and Peaseblossom, Shakespeare also pays homage to a rich body of unwritten sources that are, for the most part, no longer accessible. Changeling children, mortals kidnapped by fairy queens, men transformed to beasts by evil spells: these were the stuff of oral tales circulated by firesides on winter nights. Finally, for Bottom the weaver and company, Shakespeare's primary inspiration was doubtless his own theatrical experience, although even here he is indebted to Ovid for the story of Pyramus and Thisbe, and probably to Apuleius's *Golden Ass* (translated by William Adlington, 1566) for Bottom's transformation.

Each of the four main plots in *A Midsummer Night's Dream* contains one or more pairs of lovers whose happiness has been frustrated by misunderstanding or parental opposition. Theseus and Hippolyta, once enemies in battle, become husband and wife; their court marriage, constituting the overplot of the play, provides a framework for other dramatic actions that similarly oscillate between conflict and harmony. In fact, Theseus's actions are instrumental in setting in motion and finally resolving the tribulations of the other characters. In the beginning of the play, for example, the lovers flee from Theseus's Athenian law; at the end, they are awakened by him from their dream. As the king and queen of fairies come to Athens to celebrate Theseus's wedding, they exchange jealous accusations: Oberon accuses his queen of being overly partial to Theseus, while she is critical of Oberon's attentions to Hippolyta. These plots of the Athenian and the fairy monarchs are drawn even more closely together by the common practice in today's theater of doubling the parts of Theseus and Oberon, Hippolyta and Titania (also, frequently, Philostrate and Puck). The broadly comic action of Bottom the Weaver and his companions is drawn into the overall design by means of their deciding to use the forest of Athens as the place where they will rehearse their performance of "Pyramus and Thisbe" in anticipation of the wedding festivities.

The tragic love story of Pyramus and Thisbe, although it seems absurdly ill suited to a wedding, reminds us of the discord and potentially fatal misunderstandings that threaten even the best of relationships between men and women. For all his graceful bearing and princely authority, Theseus is a conquering male who freely admits that he has won the love of Hippolyta with his sword, doing her "injuries" (1.1.17). He never questions that the accord between them should now be stated in terms of male ascendancy over the female. The Amazonian Hippolyta may accept with good grace the marriage she previously resisted with all her might, like Kate in *The Taming of the Shrew*, and yet, in many recent stage productions, the actress playing Hippolyta has found it easy to cast doubt on the presumed tranquility of this forthcoming marriage by a display of feminist impatience at Theseus's urbanely patriarchal ways. The reconciliation of Oberon and Titania, meanwhile, reinforces the hierarchy of male over female in no uncertain terms. Having taught Titania a lesson for trying to keep a changeling boy from him, Oberon relents and eventually frees Titania from her debasing enchantment. She does not reproach him with so much as a word when she is awakened from her "vision." Even so, the very existence of the abundantly female space of Titania's bower where, surrounded by her attendants, she has acted out desires that she thought were her own, poses an alternative to patriarchy. The four young lovers end up happily paired, but only after they have experienced rejection, rivalry, hatred, and the desire to kill; the final resolution of this plot would not be possible if Demetrius were not left under the spell of the fairy love-juice. Thus, Theseus's wedding provides a ceremonial occasion of harmony and reconciliation but in such a way as to highlight the difficulties that have beset the drama's various couples.

Despite Theseus's cheerful preoccupation with marriage, his court embodies at first a stern attitude toward young love. As administrator of the law, Theseus must accede to the remorseless demands of Hermia's father, Egeus. The inflexible Athenian law sides with parentage, age, male dominance, wealth, and position against youth and romantic choice in love. The penalties are harsh: death or perpetual virginity—and virginity is presented in this comedy (despite the nobly chaste examples of Christ, St. Paul, and Queen Elizabeth) as a fate worse than death. Egeus is a familiar type, the interfering parent found in the Roman comedy of Plautus and Terence (and in Shakespeare's *Romeo and Juliet*). Indeed, the lovers' story is distantly derived from Roman comedy, which conventionally celebrated the triumph of young love over the machinations of age and wealth. Lysander reminds us that "the course of true love never did run smooth," and he sees its enemies as being chiefly external: the conflicting interests of parents or friends; mismating with respect to years and blood, war, death, or sickness (1.1.134–42). This description clearly applies to "Pyramus and Thisbe," and it is tested by the action of *A Midsummer Night's Dream* as a whole (as well as by other early Shakespearean plays, such as *Romeo and Juliet*). The archetypal story, whether ending happily or sadly, is an evocation of love's difficulties in the face of social hostility and indifference.

While Shakespeare uses several elements of Roman comedy in setting up the basic conflicts of his drama, he also introduces important modifications from the beginning. For example, he discards one conventional confrontation of classical and neoclassical comedy, in which the heroine must choose between an old, wealthy suitor supported by her family and the young but impecunious darling of her heart. Lysander is equal to his rival in social position, income, and attractiveness. Egeus's demand, therefore—that Hermia marry Demetrius rather than Lysander—seems simply arbitrary and unjust. Shakespeare emphasizes in this way the irrationality of Egeus's harsh insistence on being obeyed and of Theseus's rather complacent acceptance of the law's inequity. Spurned by an unfeeling social order, Lysander and Hermia are compelled to elope. To be sure, in the end Egeus proves to be no formidable threat; even he must admit the logic of permitting the lovers to couple as they ultimately desire. Thus, the obstacles to love are seen from the start as fundamentally superficial and indeed almost whimsical. Egeus is as heavy a villain as we are likely to find in this *jeu d'esprit*. Moreover, the very irrationality of his position prepares the way for an ultimate resolution of the conflict. Nevertheless, by the end of the first act, the supposedly rational world of conformity and duty, by its customary insensitivity to youthful happiness, has set in motion a temporary escape to a fantasy world where the law cannot reach.

In the forest, all the lovers—including Titania and Bottom—undergo a transforming experience engineered by the mischievous Puck. This experience demonstrates the universal power of love, which can overcome the queen of fairies as readily as the lowliest of humans. It also suggests the irrational nature of love and its affinity to enchantment, witchcraft, and even madness. Love is seen as an affliction taken in through the frail senses, particularly the eyes. When it strikes, the victim cannot choose but to embrace the object of his or her infatuation. By his amusing miscalculations, Puck shuffles the four lovers through various permutations with mathematical predictability. First, two gentlemen compete for one lady, leaving the second lady sadly unrequited in love; then everything is at cross-purposes, with each gentleman pursuing the lady who is in love with the other man; then the two gentlemen compete for the lady they both previously ignored. Finally, of course, Jack shall have his Jill—whom else should he have? The couples are properly united, as they evidently were at some time prior to the commencement of the play, when Demetrius had been romantically attached to Helena and Lysander to Hermia.

Their experience in the forest is an unsettling one for the four young lovers. Although some of them seek out the forest as a refuge from the Athenian law, the place rapidly takes on the darker aspect of a nightmare. Hermia awakens from sleep to find Lysander gone and soon discovers that her dream of a serpent eating her heart away while Lysander watches smiling (2.2.155–6) is all too prophetically true. The forest is a place of testing of the lovers, and the test appears at first to show how they are all their own worst enemies. Helena, having been rejected by Demetrius, can only suppose that she is being mocked, with Lysander and Demetrius both paying court to her. Next, it occurs to her that Hermia must be part of their conspiracy, too. Even though Hermia and Helena recall to each other the selfless devotion they have known as young friends, they become hated rivals in their present mood of self-pity and injured self-regard. The threshold of sexual awakening, it would seem, confronts them with a hazardous rite of passage—one that is especially threatening to the nonsexual friendship of their adolescent years. The two young men respond to similar conflicts by turning on one another in characteristically aggressive male ways. Puck allows them to playact their intended mayhem in a way that cannot harm them and then brings all four lovers together where they can awaken from their nightmare of imagined persecution. How much do they remember? Have they been changed by their journey in the forest? The lovers convey a sense of confusion, of an unreconciled dissonance of perspective in which "everything seems double" (4.1.189). As the lovers return to the daylight world of Athens and the court, their experiences assume the unreality of a remembered dream, like "far-off mountains turnèd into clouds" (4.1.187). When they thus awaken and return to the daylight world of Athens and the court, their renewed love and friendship are presumably deepened by their perception of how narrowly they have escaped from their own self-destructive imaginings. Their new happiness, they see, is better than they have deserved.

We sense that Puck is by no means unhappy about his knavish errors and manipulations: "Lord, what fools these mortals be!" (3.2.115). Along with the other fairies in this play, Puck takes his being and his complex motivation from many denizens of the invisible world. As the agent of all-powerful love, Puck compares himself to Cupid. The love juice he administers comes from Cupid's flower, "love-in-idleness." Like Cupid, Puck acts at the behest of the gods, and yet he wields a power that the chiefest of the gods themselves cannot resist. Essentially, however, Puck is less a classical love deity than a prankish folk spirit, such as we find in every folklore: gremlin, leprechaun, hobgoblin, and the like. Titania's fairies recognize Puck as the folk figure Robin Goodfellow, able to deprive a beer barrel of its yeast so that it spoils rather than ferments. Puck characterizes himself as a practical joker, pulling stools out from under old ladies.

Folk wisdom imagines the inexplicable and unaccountable events in life to be caused by invisible spirits who laugh at mortals' discomfiture and mock them for mere sport. Puck is related to these mysterious spirits dwelling in nature, who must be placated with gifts and ceremonies. Although Shakespeare restricts Puck to a benign sportive role in dealing with the lovers or with Titania, the actual folk legends about Puck mentioned in this play are frequently disquieting. Puck is known to "mislead night wanderers, laughing at their harm" (2.1.39); indeed, he demonstrates as much with Demetrius and Lysander, leading them on through the forest to the point of exhaustion, even though we perceive the sportful intent. At the play's end, Puck links himself and his fellows with the ghoulish apparitions of death and night: wolves howling at the moon, screech owls, shrouds, gaping graves. Associations of this sort go beyond mere sportiveness to the witchcraft and demonology involving spirits rising from the dead. Even Oberon's assurance that the fairies will bless all the marriages of this play, shielding their progeny against mole, harelip, or other birth defects, carries the implication that such misfortunes can be caused by offended spirits. The magic of this play is thus explicitly related to deep irrational powers and forces capable of doing great harm, although, to be sure, the spirit of comedy keeps such veiled threats safely at a distance in *A Midsummer Night's Dream*.

Oberon and Titania, in their view of the relationship between gods and humans, reflect yet another aspect of the fairies' spiritual ancestry. The king and queen of fairies assert that, because they are immortal, their regal quarrels in love must inevitably have dire consequences on earth, either in the love relationship of Theseus and Hippolyta or in the management of the weather. Floods, storms, diseases, and sterility abound, "And this same progeny of evils comes / From our debate, from our dissension. / We are their parents and original" (2.1.115–17). This motif of the gods' quarreling over human affairs reminds us of Homer and Virgil. At the same time, in this lighthearted play the motif is more nearly mock-epic than truly epic. The consequences of the gods' anger are simply mirth-provoking, most of all in Titania's love affair with Bottom the weaver.

The story of Bottom and Titania is simultaneously classical and folk in nature. In a playfully classical mode, this love affair between a god and an earthy creature underscores humanity's double nature. Bottom himself becomes half man and half beast, even if he is more ludicrously comic than the centaurs, satyrs, griffins, sphinxes, and other amphibious beings of classical mythology. Some ballads of the early modern period tell of humans transformed into beasts, or of mortals kidnapped by a fairy queen; see, for example, "Tam Lin" and "Thomas Rhymer." Bottom is an especially comic example of metamorphosis because he reverses the usual pattern of a human head and an animal body: instead, his head is animal, his body human. His very name suggests the solid nature of his fleshly being (*bottom* is appropriately also a weaving term). He and Titania represent the opposites of flesh and spirit, miraculously yoked for a time in a twofold vision of humankind's absurd and ethereal nature.

A play bringing together fairies and mortals inevitably raises questions of illusion and reality. These questions reach their greatest intensity in the presentation of "Pyramus and Thisbe." This play within a play focuses our attention on the familiarly Shakespearean metaphor of art as illusion and of the world itself as a stage on which men and women are merely players. As Theseus observes, apologizing for the ineptness of the tradesmen's performance, "the best in this kind are but shadows" (5.1.210); that is, Shakespeare's own play is of the same order of reality as Bottom's play. Puck too, in his epilogue, invites any spectator offended by Shakespeare's play to dismiss it as a mere dream—as, indeed, the play's very title suggests. Theseus goes even further, linking dream to the essence of imaginative art, although he does so in a clearly critical and rather patronizing way. The artist, he says, is like the maniac or the lover in his or her frenzy of inspiration, giving "to airy nothing / A local habitation and a name" (5.1.16–17). Artistic achievements are too unsubstantial for Theseus; from his point of view they are the products of mere fantasy and irrationality, mere myths or fairy stories or old wives' tales. Behind this critical persona defending the "real" world of his court, however, we can hear Shakespeare's characteristically self-effacing defense of "dreaming."

"Pyramus and Thisbe," like the larger play surrounding it, attempts to body forth "the forms of things unknown." The play within the play gives us personified moonshine, a speaking wall, and an apologetic lion. Of course, it is an absurdly bad play, full of lame epithets, bombastic alliteration, and bathos. In part, Shakespeare here is satirizing the abuses of a theater he had helped reform. The players' chosen method of portraying imaginative matters is ridiculous and calls forth deliciously wry comments from the courtly spectators on stage: "Would you desire lime and hair to speak better?" (5.1.164–5). At the same time, those spectators on stage are actors in our play. Their sarcasms render them less sympathetic in our eyes; we see that their kind of sophistication is as restrictive as it is illuminating. Bottom and his friends have conceived moonshine and lion as they did because these simple men are so responsive to the terrifying power of art. A lion might frighten the ladies and get the men hanged. Theirs is a primitive faith, naive but strong, and in this sense it contrasts favorably with the jaded rationality of the court party. Theseus's valuable reminder that all art is only "illusion" is thus juxtaposed with Bottom's insistence that imaginative art has a reality of its own.

Theseus above all embodies the sophistication of the court in his description of art as a frenzy of seething brains. Ironically, Theseus's genial scoffing at "These antique fables" and "these fairy toys" (5.1.3) would seem to efface his own identity as the figure of legend. Limited by his own skepticism, Theseus seems to have forgotten his own forest wanderings, led by Titania through the "glimmering night" (2.1.77). Bottom, contrastingly, has experienced "a most rare vision," such a dream as is "past the wit of man to say what dream it was" (4.1.203–5). He alone can claim to have been the lover of the queen of fairies; and, although his language cannot adequately describe the experience, Bottom will see it made into a ballad called "Bottom's Dream." Shakespeare leaves the status of his fantasy world deliberately complex; Theseus's lofty denial of dreaming is too abrupt. Even if the Athenian forest world can be made only momentarily substantial in the artifact of Shakespeare's play, we as audience respond to its tantalizing vision. We emerge back into our lives wondering if the fairies were "real"; that is, we are puzzled by the relationship of these artistic symbols to the tangible concreteness of our daily existence. Unless our perceptions have been thus enlarged by sharing in the author's dream, we have not surrendered to the imaginative experience.

Recent performances of this enduringly popular play suggest how open it is to varying interpretation and especially to postmodern views of love and politics as thoroughly unsettling in their irrationality. Nineteenth-century staging generally preferred to see the play as a gossamer delight of diminutive gilded-winged fairies and prankish hobgoblins, all underscored by the romantic strains of Mendelssohn's incidental music. More recently, and especially after World War II, theater and film versions have responded to a darker view. Inspired by Jan Kott's *Shakespeare Our Contemporary* (1964), a book written from the perspective of Soviet-dominated eastern Europe of the Cold War, Peter Brook's brilliantly revisionary stage version for the Royal Shakespeare Theater in 1970 set the play in a brightly lit white box peopled with jugglers and athletic trapeze artists who tumbled and dashed about after one another with abandon. A fisted arm thrust between the legs of Bottom the Weaver as he was carried off stage from his rendezvous with Queen Titania suggested a triumphant phallus.

Brook's avowed aim of freeing the play from what he saw as an oppressive tradition has proved to be immensely influential. Ever since, the young lovers have learned to express their sexual energies through vigorous pursuit and physical contact. Feminist insights have enriched the role of Queen Hippolyta: formerly a captive queen resigned to her marriage to Theseus, she has become in many productions a champion of Hermia's right to resist her father's patriarchal insistence on his will. Puck, in many a recent production, is the denizen of a drug culture, with the love potion as the weed he gleefully distributes. The experience of the forest becomes a drug-induced "high," for audiences as for the actors. The fairies, sometimes played by adult and hairy males, can exhibit a steak of cruelty. The doubling of some central roles, notably Theseus/Oberon, Hippolyta/Titania, and Philostrate/Puck, has given ironic emphasis to parallels between human society and fairyland. Throughout, modern productions have tended to exploit disenchantment with traditional social structures and the surging energy of sexual self-discovery. These modern interpretations are arguably neither more nor less "true" to Shakespeare's text than earlier or more "traditional" versions. What they do demonstrate is the play's remarkable permeability and openness to differing views.

A Midsummer Night's Dream

[*Dramatis Personae*

THESEUS, *Duke of Athens*

HIPPOLYTA, *Queen of the Amazons, betrothed to Theseus*
PHILOSTRATE, *Master of the Revels*
EGEUS, *father of Hermia*

HERMIA, *daughter of Egeus, in love with Lysander*
LYSANDER, *in love with Hermia*
DEMETRIUS, *in love with Hermia and favored by Egeus*
HELENA, *in love with Demetrius*

OBERON, *King of the Fairies*
TITANIA, *Queen of the Fairies*
PUCK, *or* ROBIN GOODFELLOW

SCENE: *Athens, and a wood near it*]

PEASEBLOSSOM,
COBWEB,
MOTE, } *fairies attending Titania*
MUSTARDSEED,
Other FAIRIES *attending*

PETER QUINCE, *a carpenter,*
NICK BOTTOM, *a weaver,*
FRANCIS FLUTE, *a bellows mender,*
TOM SNOUT, *a tinker,*
SNUG, *a joiner,*
ROBIN STARVELING, *a tailor,*

} *representing* {
PROLOGUE
PYRAMUS
THISBE
WALL
LION
MOONSHINE

Lords and Attendants on Theseus and Hippolyta

[1.1]

Enter Theseus, Hippolyta, [and Philostrate,]
with others.

THESEUS
Now, fair Hippolyta, our nuptial hour
Draws on apace. Four happy days bring in
Another moon; but, oh, methinks, how slow
This old moon wanes! She lingers my desires,   4
Like to a stepdame or a dowager   5
Long withering out a young man's revenue.   6

HIPPOLYTA
Four days will quickly steep themselves in night;   7
Four nights will quickly dream away the time;
And then the moon, like to a silver bow
New bent in heaven, shall behold the night
Of our solemnities.

THESEUS   Go, Philostrate,   11
Stir up the Athenian youth to merriments.
Awake the pert and nimble spirit of mirth.
Turn melancholy forth to funerals;
The pale companion is not for our pomp.   15
                                       [*Exit Philostrate.*]
Hippolyta, I wooed thee with my sword   16
And won thy love doing thee injuries;
But I will wed thee in another key,
With pomp, with triumph, and with reveling.   19

Enter Egeus and his daughter Hermia, and
Lysander, and Demetrius.

EGEUS
Happy be Theseus, our renownèd duke!

THESEUS
Thanks, good Egeus. What's the news with thee?

EGEUS
Full of vexation come I, with complaint
Against my child, my daughter Hermia.—
Stand forth, Demetrius.—My noble lord,
This man hath my consent to marry her.—
Stand forth, Lysander.—And, my gracious Duke,
This man hath bewitched the bosom of my child.—
Thou, thou Lysander, thou hast given her rhymes
And interchanged love tokens with my child.
Thou hast by moonlight at her window sung
With feigning voice verses of feigning love,   31
And stol'n the impression of her fantasy   32
With bracelets of thy hair, rings, gauds, conceits,   33

Knacks, trifles, nosegays, sweetmeats—messengers   34
Of strong prevailment in unhardened youth.   35
With cunning hast thou filched my daughter's heart,
Turned her obedience, which is due to me,
To stubborn harshness. And, my gracious Duke,
Be it so she will not here before Your Grace   39
Consent to marry with Demetrius,
I beg the ancient privilege of Athens:
As she is mine, I may dispose of her,
Which shall be either to this gentleman
Or to her death, according to our law
Immediately provided in that case.   45

THESEUS
What say you, Hermia? Be advised, fair maid.
To you your father should be as a god—
One that composed your beauties, yea, and one
To whom you are but as a form in wax
By him imprinted, and within his power
To leave the figure or disfigure it.   51
Demetrius is a worthy gentleman.

HERMIA
So is Lysander.

THESEUS   In himself he is;
But in this kind, wanting your father's voice,   54
The other must be held the worthier.

HERMIA
I would my father looked but with my eyes.

THESEUS
Rather your eyes must with his judgment look.

HERMIA
I do entreat Your Grace to pardon me.
I know not by what power I am made bold,
Nor how it may concern my modesty
In such a presence here to plead my thoughts;
But I beseech Your Grace that I may know
The worst that may befall me in this case
If I refuse to wed Demetrius.

THESEUS
Either to die the death or to abjure   65
Forever the society of men.
Therefore, fair Hermia, question your desires,
Know of your youth, examine well your blood,   68
Whether, if you yield not to your father's choice,
You can endure the livery of a nun,   70
For aye to be in shady cloister mewed,   71
To live a barren sister all your life,
Chanting faint hymns to the cold fruitless moon.
Thrice blessèd they that master so their blood
To undergo such maiden pilgrimage;
But earthlier happy is the rose distilled   76
Than that which, withering on the virgin thorn,
Grows, lives, and dies in single blessedness.

1.1. Location: Athens. Theseus's court.
4 lingers frustrates   **5 stepdame** stepmother.   **a dowager** i.e., a
widow (whose right of inheritance from her dead husband is eating
into her son's estate)   **6 withering out** causing to dwindle
7 Four . . . night (The image is of the day sinking into the ocean as
night comes on.)   **11 solemnities** festive ceremonies of marriage.
15 companion fellow. (A pale complexion is linked to melancholy.)
pomp ceremonial magnificence.   **16 with my sword** i.e., in a military
engagement against the Amazons, when Hippolyta was taken captive
19 triumph public festivity   **31 feigning** (1) counterfeiting
(2) faining, desirous   **32 And . . . fantasy** and made her fall in love
with you (imprinting your image on her imagination) by stealthy and
dishonest means   **33 gauds, conceits** playthings, fanciful trifles

34 Knacks . . . sweetmeats knicknacks, trinkets, bouquets, candies
35 prevailment in influence on   **39 Be it so** if   **45 Immediately**
directly, with nothing intervening   **51 leave** i.e., leave unaltered
54 kind respect.   **wanting** lacking.   **voice** approval   **65 die the**
death be executed by legal process   **68 blood** passions   **70 livery**
habit, costume   **71 aye** ever.   **mewed** shut in. (Said of a hawk, poultry, etc.)   **76 earthlier happy** happier as respects this world.
distilled i.e., to make perfume

HERMIA
    So will I grow, so live, so die, my lord,
    Ere I will yield my virgin patent up   80
    Unto His Lordship, whose unwishèd yoke
    My soul consents not to give sovereignty.

THESEUS
    Take time to pause, and by the next new moon—
    The sealing day betwixt my love and me
    For everlasting bond of fellowship—
    Upon that day either prepare to die
    For disobedience to your father's will,
    Or else to wed Demetrius, as he would,
    Or on Diana's altar to protest   89
    For aye austerity and single life.

DEMETRIUS
    Relent, sweet Hermia, and, Lysander, yield
    Thy crazèd title to my certain right.   92

LYSANDER
    You have her father's love, Demetrius;
    Let me have Hermia's. Do you marry him.

EGEUS
    Scornful Lysander! True, he hath my love,
    And what is mine my love shall render him.
    And she is mine, and all my right of her
    I do estate unto Demetrius.   98

LYSANDER
    I am, my lord, as well derived as he,   99
    As well possessed; my love is more than his;   100
    My fortunes every way as fairly ranked,   101
    If not with vantage, as Demetrius';   102
    And, which is more than all these boasts can be,
    I am beloved of beauteous Hermia.
    Why should not I then prosecute my right?
    Demetrius, I'll avouch it to his head,   106
    Made love to Nedar's daughter, Helena,
    And won her soul; and she, sweet lady, dotes,
    Devoutly dotes, dotes in idolatry
    Upon this spotted and inconstant man.   110

THESEUS
    I must confess that I have heard so much,
    And with Demetrius thought to have spoke thereof;
    But, being overfull of self-affairs,   113
    My mind did lose it. But, Demetrius, come,
    And come, Egeus, you shall go with me;
    I have some private schooling for you both.   116
    For you, fair Hermia, look you arm yourself   117
    To fit your fancies to your father's will,   118
    Or else the law of Athens yields you up—
    Which by no means we may extenuate—   120
    To death or to a vow of single life.
    Come, my Hippolyta. What cheer, my love?
    Demetrius and Egeus, go along.   123

    I must employ you in some business
    Against our nuptial, and confer with you   125
    Of something nearly that concerns yourselves.   126

EGEUS
    With duty and desire we follow you.
            Exeunt [all but Lysander and Hermia].

LYSANDER
    How now, my love, why is your cheek so pale?
    How chance the roses there do fade so fast?

HERMIA
    Belike for want of rain, which I could well   130
    Beteem them from the tempest of my eyes.   131

LYSANDER
    Ay me! For aught that I could ever read,
    Could ever hear by tale or history,
    The course of true love never did run smooth;
    But either it was different in blood—   135

HERMIA
    Oh, cross! Too high to be enthralled to low.   136

LYSANDER
    Or else misgrafted in respect of years—   137

HERMIA
    Oh, spite! Too old to be engaged to young.

LYSANDER
    Or else it stood upon the choice of friends—   139

HERMIA
    Oh, hell, to choose love by another's eyes!

LYSANDER
    Or if there were a sympathy in choice,   141
    War, death, or sickness did lay siege to it,
    Making it momentany as a sound,   143
    Swift as a shadow, short as any dream,
    Brief as the lightning in the collied night   145
    That in a spleen unfolds both heaven and earth,   146
    And ere a man hath power to say "Behold!"
    The jaws of darkness do devour it up.
    So quick bright things come to confusion.   149

HERMIA
    If then true lovers have been ever crossed,   150
    It stands as an edict in destiny.
    Then let us teach our trial patience,   152
    Because it is a customary cross,
    As due to love as thoughts, and dreams, and sighs,
    Wishes, and tears, poor fancy's followers.   155

LYSANDER
    A good persuasion. Therefore, hear me, Hermia: 156
    I have a widow aunt, a dowager
    Of great revenue, and she hath no child.
    From Athens is her house remote seven leagues;   159
    And she respects me as her only son.   160

---

80 **patent** privilege   89 **protest** vow   92 **crazèd** cracked, unsound
98 **estate unto** settle or bestow upon   99 **as well derived** as well born
and descended   100 **possessed** endowed with wealth   101 **fairly**
handsomely   102 **vantage** superiority   106 **head** i.e., face   110 **spotted** i.e., morally stained   113 **self-affairs** my own concerns
116 **schooling** admonition   117 **look you arm** take care you prepare
118 **fancies** likings, thoughts of love   120 **extenuate** mitigate, relax
123 **go** i.e., come

125 **Against** in preparation for   126 **nearly that** that closely
130 **Belike** Very likely   131 **Beteem** grant, afford   135 **blood** hereditary rank   136 **cross** vexation.   137 **misgrafted** ill grafted, badly
matched   139 **friends** relatives   141 **sympathy** agreement
143 **momentany** lasting but a moment   145 **collied** blackened (as
with coal dust), darkened   146 **in a spleen** in a swift impulse, in a
violent flash.   **unfolds** reveals   149 **confusion** ruin.   150 **ever
crossed** always thwarted   152 **teach . . . patience** i.e., teach ourselves
patience in this trial   155 **fancy's** amorous passion's   156 **persuasion** doctrine.   159 **seven leagues** about 21 miles   160 **respects**
regards

There, gentle Hermia, may I marry thee,
And to that place the sharp Athenian law
Cannot pursue us. If thou lovest me, then,
Steal forth thy father's house tomorrow night;
And in the wood, a league without the town,   165
Where I did meet thee once with Helena
To do observance to a morn of May,   167
There will I stay for thee.

HERMIA   My good Lysander!
I swear to thee, by Cupid's strongest bow,
By his best arrow with the golden head,   170
By the simplicity of Venus' doves,   171
By that which knitteth souls and prospers loves,
And by that fire which burned the Carthage queen   173
When the false Trojan under sail was seen,   174
By all the vows that ever men have broke,
In number more than ever women spoke,
In that same place thou hast appointed me
Tomorrow truly will I meet with thee.

LYSANDER
Keep promise, love. Look, here comes Helena.

        Enter Helena.

HERMIA
God speed, fair Helena! Whither away?   180

HELENA
Call you me fair? That "fair" again unsay.
Demetrius loves your fair. Oh, happy fair!   182
Your eyes are lodestars, and your tongue's sweet air 183
More tunable than lark to shepherd's ear   184
When wheat is green, when hawthorn buds appear.
Sickness is catching. Oh, were favor so,   186
Yours would I catch, fair Hermia, ere I go;
My ear should catch your voice, my eye your eye,
My tongue should catch your tongue's sweet melody.
Were the world mine, Demetrius being bated,   190
The rest I'd give to be to you translated.   191
Oh, teach me how you look and with what art
You sway the motion of Demetrius' heart.   193

HERMIA
I frown upon him, yet he loves me still.

HELENA
Oh, that your frowns would teach my smiles such
    skill!

HERMIA
I give him curses, yet he gives me love.

HELENA
Oh, that my prayers could such affection move!   197

HERMIA
The more I hate, the more he follows me.

HELENA
The more I love, the more he hateth me.

HERMIA
His folly, Helena, is no fault of mine.

HELENA
None, but your beauty. Would that fault were mine!

HERMIA
Take comfort. He no more shall see my face.
Lysander and myself will fly this place.
Before the time I did Lysander see   204
Seemed Athens as a paradise to me.   205
Oh, then, what graces in my love do dwell,
That he hath turned a heaven unto a hell?

LYSANDER
Helen, to you our minds we will unfold.
Tomorrow night, when Phoebe doth behold   209
Her silver visage in the watery glass,   210
Decking with liquid pearl the bladed grass,   211
A time that lovers' flights doth still conceal,   212
Through Athens' gates have we devised to steal.

HERMIA
And in the wood, where often you and I
Upon faint primrose beds were wont to lie,   215
Emptying our bosoms of their counsel sweet,   216
There my Lysander and myself shall meet,
And thence from Athens turn away our eyes
To seek new friends and stranger companies.   219
Farewell, sweet playfellow. Pray thou for us,
And good luck grant thee thy Demetrius!
Keep word, Lysander. We must starve our sight
From lovers' food till morrow deep midnight.

LYSANDER
I will, my Hermia.   *Exit Hermia.*
                Helena, adieu!
As you on him, Demetrius dote on you!
                        Exit Lysander.

HELENA
How happy some o'er other some can be!   226
Through Athens I am thought as fair as she.
But what of that? Demetrius thinks not so;
He will not know what all but he do know.
And as he errs, doting on Hermia's eyes,
So I, admiring of his qualities.
Things base and vile, holding no quantity,   232
Love can transpose to form and dignity.
Love looks not with the eyes, but with the mind,
And therefore is winged Cupid painted blind.

Nor hath Love's mind of any judgment taste;   236
Wings and no eyes figure unheedy haste.   237
And therefore is Love said to be a child,
Because in choice he is so oft beguiled.   239
As waggish boys in game themselves forswear,   240
So the boy Love is perjured everywhere.
For ere Demetrius looked on Hermia's eyne,   242
He hailed down oaths that he was only mine;
And when this hail some heat from Hermia felt,
So he dissolved, and showers of oaths did melt.
I will go tell him of fair Hermia's flight.
Then to the wood will he tomorrow night
Pursue her; and for this intelligence   248
If I have thanks, it is a dear expense.   249
But herein mean I to enrich my pain,
To have his sight thither and back again.   *Exit.*

❖

[1.2]

*Enter Quince the carpenter, and Snug the
joiner, and Bottom the weaver, and Flute the
bellows mender, and Snout the tinker, and
Starveling the tailor.*

QUINCE   Is all our company here?
BOTTOM   You were best to call them generally, man by   2
man, according to the scrip.   3
QUINCE   Here is the scroll of every man's name which
is thought fit, through all Athens, to play in our inter- 5
lude before the Duke and the Duchess on his wedding   6
day at night.
BOTTOM   First, good Peter Quince, say what the play
treats on, then read the names of the actors, and so
grow to a point.   10
QUINCE   Marry, our play is "The most lamentable com-   11
edy and most cruel death of Pyramus and Thisbe."
BOTTOM   A very good piece of work, I assure you, and
a merry. Now, good Peter Quince, call forth your
actors by the scroll. Masters, spread yourselves.
QUINCE   Answer as I call you. Nick Bottom, the weaver.   16
BOTTOM   Ready. Name what part I am for, and proceed.
QUINCE   You, Nick Bottom, are set down for Pyramus.
BOTTOM   What is Pyramus? A lover or a tyrant?
QUINCE   A lover, that kills himself most gallant for love.
BOTTOM   That will ask some tears in the true performing
of it. If I do it, let the audience look to their eyes. I will
move storms; I will condole in some measure. To the   23
rest—yet my chief humor is for a tyrant. I could play   24

Ercles rarely, or a part to tear a cat in, to make all split.   25
    "The raging rocks
    And shivering shocks
    Shall break the locks
       Of prison gates;
    And Phibbus' car   30
    Shall shine from far
    And make and mar
       The foolish Fates."
This was lofty! Now name the rest of the players. This is
Ercles' vein, a tyrant's vein. A lover is more condoling.
QUINCE   Francis Flute, the bellows mender.
FLUTE   Here, Peter Quince.
QUINCE   Flute, you must take Thisbe on you.
FLUTE   What is Thisbe? A wandering knight?
QUINCE   It is the lady that Pyramus must love.
FLUTE   Nay, faith, let not me play a woman. I have a
beard coming.
QUINCE   That's all one. You shall play it in a mask, and   43
you may speak as small as you will.   44
BOTTOM   An I may hide my face, let me play Thisbe too.   45
I'll speak in a monstrous little voice: "Thisne, Thisne!"
"Ah, Pyramus, my lover dear! Thy Thisbe dear, and
lady dear!"
QUINCE   No, no, you must play Pyramus, and Flute, you
Thisbe.
BOTTOM   Well, proceed.
QUINCE   Robin Starveling, the tailor.
STARVELING   Here, Peter Quince.
QUINCE   Robin Starveling, you must play Thisbe's
mother. Tom Snout, the tinker.
SNOUT   Here, Peter Quince.
QUINCE   You, Pyramus' father; myself, Thisbe's father;
Snug, the joiner, you, the lion's part; and I hope here is
a play fitted.
SNUG   Have you the lion's part written? Pray you, if it
be, give it me, for I am slow of study.
QUINCE   You may do it extempore, for it is nothing but
roaring.
BOTTOM   Let me play the lion too. I will roar that I will
do any man's heart good to hear me. I will roar that I
will make the Duke say, "Let him roar again, let him
roar again."
QUINCE   An you should do it too terribly, you would
fright the Duchess and the ladies, that they would
shriek; and that were enough to hang us all.
ALL   That would hang us, every mother's son.
BOTTOM   I grant you, friends, if you should fright the
ladies out of their wits, they would have no more discretion but to hang us; but I will aggravate my voice   74
so that I will roar you as gently as any sucking dove; I   75
will roar you an 'twere any nightingale.   76

---

236 Nor . . . taste i.e., Nor has Love, which dwells in the fancy or
imagination, any least bit of judgment or reason   **237 figure** signify
239 in choice in choosing.   **beguiled** self-deluded, making unaccountable choices.   **240 waggish** playful, mischievous.   **game** sport,
jest   **242 eyne** eyes. (Old form of plural.)   **248 intelligence** information   **249 a dear expense** i.e., a trouble worth taking on my part.
1.2. Location: Athens.
2 generally (Bottom's blunder for "individually.")   **3 scrip** script.
5–6 interlude play   **10 grow to** come to   **11 Marry** (A mild oath;
originally the name of the Virgin Mary.)   **16 Bottom** (As a weaver's
term, a *bottom* was an object around which thread was wound.)
23 condole lament, arouse pity   **24 humor** inclination

25 Ercles Hercules. (The tradition of ranting came from Seneca's
Hercules Furens.)   **tear a cat** i.e., rant.   **make all split** i.e., cause a stir,
bring the house down.   **30 Phibbus' car** Phoebus's, the sun god's,
chariot   **43 That's all one** It makes no difference.   **44 small** high-
pitched   **45 An** If. (Also at line 68.)   **74 aggravate** (Bottom's blunder
for "moderate.")   **75 roar you** i.e., roar for you.   **sucking dove** (Bottom conflates *sitting dove* and *sucking lamb*, two proverbial images of
innocence.)   **76 an 'twere** as if it were

QUINCE   You can play no part but Pyramus; for Pyramus is a sweet-faced man, a proper man as one shall   78
see in a summer's day, a most lovely gentlemanlike
man. Therefore you must needs play Pyramus.

BOTTOM   Well, I will undertake it. What beard were I
best to play it in?

QUINCE   Why, what you will.

BOTTOM   I will discharge it in either your straw-color   84
beard, your orange-tawny beard, your purple-in-grain   85
beard, or your French-crown-color beard, your perfect   86
yellow.

QUINCE   Some of your French crowns have no hair at all,   88
and then you will play barefaced. But, masters, here
are your parts. [*He distributes parts.*] And I am to
entreat you, request you, and desire you to con them   91
by tomorrow night, and meet me in the palace wood,
a mile without the town, by moonlight. There will we
rehearse; for if we meet in the city, we shall be dogged
with company, and our devices known. In the mean-   95
time I will draw a bill of properties, such as our play   96
wants. I pray you, fail me not.

BOTTOM   We will meet, and there we may rehearse most
obscenely and courageously. Take pains, be perfect.   99
Adieu.

QUINCE   At the Duke's oak we meet.

BOTTOM   Enough. Hold, or cut bowstrings.   *Exeunt.*   102

❖

[2.1]

Enter a Fairy at one door, and Robin Goodfellow
[Puck] at another.

PUCK
How now, spirit, whither wander you?

FAIRY
Over hill, over dale,
　　Thorough bush, thorough brier,   3
Over park, over pale,   4
　　Thorough flood, thorough fire,
I do wander everywhere,
Swifter than the moon's sphere;   7
And I serve the Fairy Queen,
To dew her orbs upon the green.   9
The cowslips tall her pensioners be.   10
In their gold coats spots you see;

Those be rubies, fairy favors;   12
　　In those freckles live their savors.   13
I must go seek some dewdrops here
And hang a pearl in every cowslip's ear.
Farewell, thou lob of spirits; I'll be gone.   16
Our Queen and all her elves come here anon.   17

PUCK
The King doth keep his revels here tonight.
Take heed the Queen come not within his sight.
For Oberon is passing fell and wrath,   20
Because that she as her attendant hath
A lovely boy, stolen from an Indian king;
She never had so sweet a changeling.   23
And jealous Oberon would have the child
Knight of his train, to trace the forests wild.   25
But she perforce withholds the lovèd boy,   26
Crowns him with flowers, and makes him all her joy.
And now they never meet in grove or green,
By fountain clear, or spangled starlight sheen,   29
But they do square, that all their elves for fear   30
Creep into acorn cups and hide them there.

FAIRY
Either I mistake your shape and making quite,
Or else you are that shrewd and knavish sprite   33
Called Robin Goodfellow. Are not you he
That frights the maidens of the villagery,   35
Skim milk, and sometimes labor in the quern,   36
And bootless make the breathless huswife churn,   37
And sometimes make the drink to bear no barm,   38
Mislead night wanderers, laughing at their harm?   39
Those that "Hobgoblin" call you, and "Sweet Puck,"   40
You do their work, and they shall have good luck.
Are you not he?

PUCK　　　　　　　Thou speakest aright;
I am that merry wanderer of the night.
I jest to Oberon and make him smile
When I a fat and bean-fed horse beguile,   45
Neighing in likeness of a filly foal;   46
And sometimes lurk I in a gossip's bowl   47
In very likeness of a roasted crab,   48
And when she drinks, against her lips I bob
And on her withered dewlap pour the ale.   50
The wisest aunt, telling the saddest tale,   51

---

78 proper handsome   **84 discharge** perform.   **your** i.e., you know
the kind I mean   **85 purple-in-grain** dyed a very deep red. (From
grain, the name applied to the dried insect used to make the dye.)
86 French-crown-color i.e., color of a French crown, a gold coin
88 crowns heads bald from syphilis, the "French disease"   **91 con**
memorize   **95 devices** plans   **96 draw a bill** draw up a list
99 obscenely (An unintentionally funny blunder, whatever Bottom
meant to say.)   **perfect** i.e., letter-perfect in memorizing your parts.
102 Hold . . . bowstrings (An archers' expression, not definitely
explained, but probably meaning here "keep your promises, or give
up the play.")
2.1. Location: A wood near Athens.
3 Thorough through   **4 pale** enclosure   **7 sphere** orbit   **9 dew**
sprinkle with dew.   **orbs** circles, i.e., fairy rings (circular bands of
grass, darker than the surrounding area, caused by fungi enriching
the soil)   **10 pensioners** retainers, members of the royal bodyguard

12 favors love tokens   **13 savors** sweet smells.   **16 lob** country
bumpkin   **17 anon** at once.   **20 passing fell** exceedingly angry.
wrath wrathful   **23 changeling** child exchanged for another by the
fairies.   **25 trace** range through   **26 perforce** forcibly   **29 fountain**
spring.   **starlight sheen** shining starlight   **30 square** quarrel
33 shrewd mischievous.   **sprite** spirit   **35 villagery** village population   **36 Skim milk** i.e., steal the cream.   **quern** hand mill (where
Puck presumably hampers the grinding of grain)   **37 bootless** in
vain. (Puck prevents the cream from turning to butter.)   **huswife**
housewife   **38 barm** head on the ale. (Puck prevents the barm or
yeast from producing fermentation.)   **39 Mislead night wanderers**
i.e., mislead with false fire those who walk abroad at night (hence
earning Puck his other names of Jack o' Lantern and Will o' the Wisp)
40 Those . . . Puck i.e., Those who call you by the names you favor
rather than those denoting the mischief you do   **45 bean-fed** full of
beans   **46 a filly foal** a mare (in heat)   **47 gossip's** old woman's
48 crab crab apple   **50 dewlap** loose skin on neck   **51 aunt** old
woman.   **saddest** most serious

DEMETRIUS
    Tempt not too much the hatred of my spirit,
    For I am sick when I do look on thee.

HELENA
    And I am sick when I look not on you.

DEMETRIUS
    You do impeach your modesty too much   214
    To leave the city and commit yourself   215
    Into the hands of one that loves you not,
    To trust the opportunity of night
    And the ill counsel of a desert place   218
    With the rich worth of your virginity.

HELENA
    Your virtue is my privilege. For that   220
    It is not night when I do see your face,
    Therefore I think I am not in the night;
    Nor doth this wood lack worlds of company,
    For you, in my respect, are all the world.   224
    Then how can it be said I am alone
    When all the world is here to look on me?

DEMETRIUS
    I'll run from thee and hide me in the brakes, 227
    And leave thee to the mercy of wild beasts.

HELENA
    The wildest hath not such a heart as you.
    Run when you will. The story shall be changed:
    Apollo flies and Daphne holds the chase,   231
    The dove pursues the griffin, the mild hind   232
    Makes speed to catch the tiger—bootless speed, 233
    When cowardice pursues and valor flies!

DEMETRIUS
    I will not stay thy questions. Let me go!   235
    Or if thou follow me, do not believe
    But I shall do thee mischief in the wood.

HELENA
    Ay, in the temple, in the town, the field,
    You do me mischief. Fie, Demetrius!
    Your wrongs do set a scandal on my sex.   240
    We cannot fight for love, as men may do;
    We should be wooed and were not made to woo.
                     [Exit Demetrius.]
    I'll follow thee and make a heaven of hell,
    To die upon the hand I love so well.
                         [Exit.] 244

OBERON
    Fare thee well, nymph. Ere he do leave this grove
    Thou shalt fly him, and he shall seek thy love.

               Enter Puck.

    Hast thou the flower there? Welcome, wanderer.

PUCK
    Ay, there it is.   [He offers the flower.]

OBERON   I pray thee, give it me.
    I know a bank where the wild thyme blows,   249
    Where oxlips and the nodding violet grows,   250
    Quite overcanopied with luscious woodbine,   251
    With sweet muskroses and with eglantine.   252
    There sleeps Titania sometime of the night,   253
    Lulled in these flowers with dances and delight;
    And there the snake throws her enameled skin, 255
    Weed wide enough to wrap a fairy in.   256
    And with the juice of this I'll streak her eyes 257
    And make her full of hateful fantasies.
    Take thou some of it, and seek through this grove.
                 [He gives some love juice.]
    A sweet Athenian lady is in love
    With a disdainful youth. Anoint his eyes,
    But do it when the next thing he espies
    May be the lady. Thou shalt know the man
    By the Athenian garments he hath on.
    Effect it with some care, that he may prove
    More fond on her than she upon her love;   266
    And look thou meet me ere the first cock crow.

PUCK
    Fear not, my lord, your servant shall do so.
                     Exeunt [separately].

❖

[2.2]

    Enter Titania, Queen of Fairies, with her train.

TITANIA
    Come, now a roundel and a fairy song;   1
    Then, for the third part of a minute, hence—
    Some to kill cankers in the muskrose buds,   3
    Some war with reremice for their leathern wings 4
    To make my small elves coats, and some keep back
    The clamorous owl, that nightly hoots and wonders
    At our quaint spirits. Sing me now asleep.   7
    Then to your offices, and let me rest.

           Fairies sing.

FIRST FAIRY
    You spotted snakes with double tongue,   9
      Thorny hedgehogs, be not seen;
    Newts and blindworms, do no wrong;   11
      Come not near our Fairy Queen.

---

214 impeach call into question **215 To leave** by leaving **218 desert**
deserted **220 privilege** safeguard, warrant. **For that** Because
224 in my respect as far as I am concerned, in my esteem
227 brakes thickets **231 Apollo . . . chase** (In the ancient myth,
Daphne fled from Apollo and was saved from rape by being transformed into a laurel tree; here it is the female who *holds the chase*, or
pursues, instead of the male.) **232 griffin** a fabulous monster with
the head and wings of an eagle and the body of a lion. **hind** female
deer **233 bootless** fruitless **235 stay** wait for, put up with.
questions talk or argument. **240 Your . . . sex** i.e., The wrongs that
you do me cause me to act in a manner that disgraces my sex.
244 upon by

249 blows blooms **250 oxlips** flowers resembling cowslip and primrose **251 woodbine** honeysuckle **252 muskroses** a kind of large,
sweet-scented rose. **eglantine** sweetbrier, another kind of rose.
253 sometime of for part of **255 throws** sloughs off, sheds
256 Weed garment **257 streak** anoint, touch gently **266 fond on**
doting on
2.2. Location: The wood.
1 roundel dance in a ring **3 cankers** cankerworms (i.e., caterpillars
or grubs) **4 reremice** bats **7 quaint** dainty **9 double** forked
11 Newts water lizards. (Considered poisonous, as were *blindworms*—
small snakes with tiny eyes—and spiders.)

CHORUS [*dancing*]
  Philomel, with melody   13
  Sing in our sweet lullaby;
  Lulla, lulla, lullaby, lulla, lulla, lullaby.
    Never harm
    Nor spell nor charm
  Come our lovely lady nigh.
  So good night, with lullaby.

FIRST FAIRY
  Weaving spiders, come not here;
  Hence, you long-legged spinners, hence!
  Beetles black, approach not near;
  Worm nor snail, do no offense.   23

CHORUS [*dancing*]
  Philomel, with melody
  Sing in our sweet lullaby;
  Lulla, lulla, lullaby, lulla, lulla, lullaby.
    Never harm
    Nor spell nor charm
  Come our lovely lady nigh.
  So good night, with lullaby.   [*Titania sleeps.*]

SECOND FAIRY
  Hence, away! Now all is well.
  One aloof stand sentinel.   32
    [*Exeunt Fairies, leaving one sentinel.*]

  *Enter Oberon [and squeezes the flower on
  Titania's eyelids].*

OBERON
  What thou see'st when thou dost wake,
  Do it for thy true love take;
  Love and languish for his sake.
  Be it ounce, or cat, or bear,   36
  Pard, or boar with bristled hair,   37
  In thy eye that shall appear
  When thou wak'st, it is thy dear.
  Wake when some vile thing is near.   [*Exit.*]

  Enter Lysander and Hermia.

LYSANDER
  Fair love, you faint with wand'ring in the wood;
  And to speak truth, I have forgot our way.
  We'll rest us, Hermia, if you think it good,
  And tarry for the comfort of the day.

HERMIA
  Be it so, Lysander. Find you out a bed,
  For I upon this bank will rest my head.

LYSANDER
  One turf shall serve as pillow for us both;
  One heart, one bed, two bosoms, and one troth.   48

HERMIA
  Nay, good Lysander, for my sake, my dear,
  Lie further off yet. Do not lie so near.

LYSANDER
  Oh, take the sense, sweet, of my innocence!   51
  Love takes the meaning in love's conference.   52
  I mean that my heart unto yours is knit,
  So that but one heart we can make of it;
  Two bosoms interchainèd with an oath—
  So then two bosoms and a single troth.
  Then by your side no bed-room me deny,
  For lying so, Hermia, I do not lie.   58

HERMIA
  Lysander riddles very prettily.
  Now much beshrew my manners and my pride   60
  If Hermia meant to say Lysander lied.
  But, gentle friend, for love and courtesy
  Lie further off, in human modesty.
  Such separation as may well be said
  Becomes a virtuous bachelor and a maid,
  So far be distant; and, good night, sweet friend.
  Thy love ne'er alter till thy sweet life end!

LYSANDER
  Amen, amen, to that fair prayer, say I,
  And then end life when I end loyalty!
  Here is my bed. Sleep give thee all his rest!

HERMIA
  With half that wish the wisher's eyes be pressed!   71
    [*They sleep, separated by a short distance.*]

  Enter Puck.

PUCK
  Through the forest have I gone,
  But Athenian found I none
  On whose eyes I might approve   74
  This flower's force in stirring love.
  Night and silence.—Who is here?
  Weeds of Athens he doth wear.
  This is he, my master said,
  Despisèd the Athenian maid;
  And here the maiden, sleeping sound,
  On the dank and dirty ground.
  Pretty soul, she durst not lie
  Near this lack-love, this kill-courtesy.
  Churl, upon thy eyes I throw
  All the power this charm doth owe.   85
    [*He applies the love juice.*]
  When thou wak'st, let love forbid   86
  Sleep his seat on thy eyelid.   87
  So awake when I am gone,
  For I must now to Oberon.   *Exit.*

  Enter Demetrius and Helena, running.

HELENA
  Stay, though thou kill me, sweet Demetrius!

---

13 Philomel the nightingale. (Philomela, daughter of King Pandion, was transformed into a nightingale, according to Ovid's *Metamorphoses* 6, after she had been raped by her sister Procne's husband, Tereus.) **23 offense** harm. **32 sentinel** (Presumably Oberon is able to outwit or intimidate this guard.) **36 ounce** lynx **37 Pard** leopard **48 troth** faith, trothplight.

51–2 take . . . conference take my meaning in an innocent sense, with generosity and sympathy! True lovers do so when they converse. **58 lie** tell a falsehood. (With a riddling pun on *lie*, "recline.") **60 beshrew** (A mild oath.) **71 With . . . pressed!** i.e., I return half that wish, so that you, the wisher, may sleep well too (instead of Sleep giving all his rest to me)! **74 approve** test **85 owe** own. **86–7 let . . . eyelid** may love, heretofore denied, be enthroned in your eyes.

DEMETRIUS
    I charge thee, hence, and do not haunt me thus.
HELENA
    Oh, wilt thou darkling leave me? Do not so.   92
DEMETRIUS
    Stay, on thy peril! I alone will go.   [*Exit.*]   93
HELENA
    Oh, I am out of breath in this fond chase!   94
    The more my prayer, the lesser is my grace.   95
    Happy is Hermia, wheresoe'er she lies,   96
    For she hath blessèd and attractive eyes.
    How came her eyes so bright? Not with salt tears;
    If so, my eyes are oft'ner washed than hers.
    No, no, I am as ugly as a bear,
    For beasts that meet me run away for fear.
    Therefore no marvel though Demetrius   102
    Do, as a monster, fly my presence thus.   103
    What wicked and dissembling glass of mine   104
    Made me compare with Hermia's sphery eyne?   105
    But who is here? Lysander, on the ground?
    Dead, or asleep? I see no blood, no wound.
    Lysander, if you live, good sir, awake.
LYSANDER [*awaking*]
    And run through fire I will for thy sweet sake.
    Transparent Helena! Nature shows art,   110
    That through thy bosom makes me see thy heart.
    Where is Demetrius? Oh, how fit a word
    Is that vile name to perish on my sword!
HELENA
    Do not say so, Lysander; say not so.
    What though he love your Hermia? Lord, what
        though?
    Yet Hermia still loves you. Then be content.
LYSANDER
    Content with Hermia? No! I do repent
    The tedious minutes I with her have spent.
    Not Hermia but Helena I love.
    Who will not change a raven for a dove?
    The will of man is by his reason swayed,   121
    And reason says you are the worthier maid.
    Things growing are not ripe until their season;
    So I, being young, till now ripe not to reason.   124
    And, touching now the point of human skill,   125
    Reason becomes the marshal to my will
    And leads me to your eyes, where I o'erlook   127
    Love's stories written in love's richest book.
HELENA
    Wherefore was I to this keen mockery born?   129
    When at your hands did I deserve this scorn?
    Is't not enough, is't not enough, young man,
    That I did never—no, nor never can—
    Deserve a sweet look from Demetrius' eye,

But you must flout my insufficiency?
Good troth, you do me wrong, good sooth, you do,   135
In such disdainful manner me to woo.
But fare you well. Perforce I must confess
I thought you lord of more true gentleness.   138
Oh, that a lady, of one man refused,   139
Should of another therefore be abused!   *Exit.* 140
LYSANDER
    She sees not Hermia. Hermia, sleep thou there,
    And never mayst thou come Lysander near!
    For as a surfeit of the sweetest things
    The deepest loathing to the stomach brings,
    Or as the heresies that men do leave   145
    Are hated most of those they did deceive,   146
    So thou, my surfeit and my heresy,
    Of all be hated, but the most of me!   148
    And, all my powers, address your love and might 149
    To honor Helen and to be her knight!   *Exit.*
HERMIA [*awaking*]
    Help me, Lysander, help me! Do thy best
    To pluck this crawling serpent from my breast!
    Ay me, for pity! What a dream was here!
    Lysander, look how I do quake with fear.
    Methought a serpent ate my heart away,
    And you sat smiling at his cruel prey.   156
    Lysander! What, removed? Lysander! Lord!
    What, out of hearing? Gone? No sound, no word?
    Alack, where are you? Speak, an if you hear;   159
    Speak, of all loves! I swoon almost with fear.   160
    No? Then I well perceive you are not nigh.
    Either death, or you, I'll find immediately.
                    Exit. [*The sleeping Titania remains.*]

                            ❧

[3.1]

Enter the clowns [*Quince, Snug, Bottom, Flute,
Snout, and Starveling*].

BOTTOM   Are we all met?
QUINCE   Pat, pat; and here's a marvelous convenient   2
    place for our rehearsal. This green plot shall be our
    stage, this hawthorn brake our tiring-house, and we   4
    will do it in action as we will do it before the Duke.
BOTTOM   Peter Quince?
QUINCE   What sayest thou, bully Bottom?   7
BOTTOM   There are things in this comedy of Pyramus
    and Thisbe that will never please. First, Pyramus must
    draw a sword to kill himself, which the ladies cannot
    abide. How answer you that?
SNOUT   By'r lakin, a parlous fear.   12

92 **darkling** in the dark   93 **on thy peril** i.e., on pain of reprisal if you don't obey me and stay.   94 **fond** doting   95 **my grace** the favor I obtain.   96 **lies** dwells   102–3 **no marvel . . . thus** i.e., no wonder that Demetrius flies from me as from a monster.   104 **glass** mirror 105 **compare** compare myself.   **sphery eyne** eyes as bright as stars in their spheres.   110 **Transparent** Radiant, pure.   **art** skill, magic power   121 **will** desire   124 **ripe not** have not ripened   125 **touching . . . skill** reaching now the age of mature judgment   127 **o'erlook** read over   129 **Wherefore** Why

135 **Good troth, good sooth** i.e., Indeed, truly   138 **lord of** i.e., possessor of.   **gentleness** courtesy.   139 **of** by   140 **abused** ill treated. 145–6 **as . . . deceive** as renounced heresies are hated most by those persons who formerly were deceived by them   148 **Of . . . of** by . . . by   149 **address** direct, apply   156 **prey** act of preying   159 **an if** if 160 **of all loves** for love's sake.
3.1. **Location: The action is continuous.**
0.1 *clowns* rustics   2 **Pat** On the dot, punctually   4 **brake** thicket. **tiring-house** attiring area, hence backstage   7 **bully** i.e., worthy, jolly, fine fellow   12 **By'r lakin** By our ladykin, i.e., the Virgin Mary. **parlous** perilous, alarming

STARVELING   I believe we must leave the killing out, when all is done.   14

BOTTOM   Not a whit. I have a device to make all well. Write me a prologue, and let the prologue seem to say,   16 we will do no harm with our swords, and that Pyramus is not killed indeed; and for the more better assurance, tell them that I, Pyramus, am not Pyramus but Bottom the weaver. This will put them out of fear.

QUINCE   Well, we will have such a prologue, and it shall be written in eight and six.   22

BOTTOM   No, make it two more: let it be written in eight and eight.

SNOUT   Will not the ladies be afeard of the lion?

STARVELING   I fear it, I promise you.

BOTTOM   Masters, you ought to consider with yourself, to bring in—God shield us!—a lion among ladies is a   28 most dreadful thing. For there is not a more fearful   29 wildfowl than your lion living, and we ought to look to 't.

SNOUT   Therefore another prologue must tell he is not a lion.

BOTTOM   Nay, you must name his name, and half his face must be seen through the lion's neck, and he himself must speak through, saying thus or to the same defect: "Ladies," or "Fair ladies, I would wish you," or   37 "I would request you," or "I would entreat you, not to fear, not to tremble; my life for yours. If you think I   39 come hither as a lion, it were pity of my life. No, I am   40 no such thing; I am a man as other men are." And there indeed let him name his name, and tell them plainly he is Snug the joiner.

QUINCE   Well, it shall be so. But there is two hard things: that is, to bring the moonlight into a chamber; for, you know, Pyramus and Thisbe meet by moonlight.

SNOUT   Doth the moon shine that night we play our play?

BOTTOM   A calendar, a calendar! Look in the almanac. Find out moonshine, find out moonshine.

[They consult an almanac.]

QUINCE   Yes, it doth shine that night.

BOTTOM   Why then may you leave a casement of the great chamber window where we play open, and the moon may shine in at the casement.

QUINCE   Ay; or else one must come in with a bush of   55 thorns and a lantern and say he comes to disfigure, or   56 to present, the person of Moonshine. Then there is another thing: we must have a wall in the great cham-ber; for Pyramus and Thisbe, says the story, did talk through the chink of a wall.

SNOUT   You can never bring in a wall. What say you, Bottom?

BOTTOM   Some man or other must present Wall. And let him have some plaster, or some loam, or some rough-   64 cast about him, to signify wall; or let him hold his   65 fingers thus, and through that cranny shall Pyramus and Thisbe whisper.

QUINCE   If that may be, then all is well. Come, sit down, every mother's son, and rehearse your parts. Pyramus, you begin. When you have spoken your speech, enter into that brake, and so everyone according to his cue.

Enter Robin [Puck].

PUCK [*aside*]
What hempen homespuns have we swagg'ring here   72
So near the cradle of the Fairy Queen?   73
What, a play toward? I'll be an auditor;   74
An actor, too, perhaps, if I see cause.

QUINCE   Speak, Pyramus. Thisbe, stand forth.

BOTTOM [*as Pyramus*]
"Thisbe, the flowers of odious savors sweet—"

QUINCE   Odors, odors.

BOTTOM   "—Odors savors sweet;
So hath thy breath, my dearest Thisbe dear.
But hark, a voice! Stay thou but here awhile,
And by and by I will to thee appear."   *Exit.*

PUCK   A stranger Pyramus than e'er played here. [*Exit.*]   83

FLUTE   Must I speak now?

QUINCE   Ay, marry, must you; for you must understand he goes but to see a noise that he heard, and is to come again.

FLUTE [*as Thisbe*]
"Most radiant Pyramus, most lily-white of hue,
Of color like the red rose on triumphant brier,   89
Most brisky juvenal and eke most lovely Jew,   90
As true as truest horse that yet would never tire.
I'll meet thee, Pyramus, at Ninny's tomb."

QUINCE   "Ninus' tomb," man. Why, you must not speak   93 that yet. That you answer to Pyramus. You speak all your part at once, cues and all. Pyramus, enter. Your   95 cue is past; it is "never tire."

FLUTE   Oh—"As true as truest horse that yet would never tire."   97

[*Enter Puck, and Bottom as Pyramus with the ass head.*]

---

14 when all is done i.e., when all is said and done.   **16 Write me** i.e., Write at my suggestion. (*Me* is used colloquially.)   **22 eight and six** alternate lines of eight and six syllables, a common ballad measure. **28 lion among ladies** (A contemporary pamphlet tells how, at the christening in 1594 of Prince Henry, eldest son of King James VI of Scotland, later James I of England, a "blackamoor" instead of a lion drew the triumphal chariot, since the lion's presence might have "brought some fear to the nearest.")   **29 fearful** fear-inspiring **37 defect** (Bottom's blunder for "effect.")   **39 my life for yours** i.e., I pledge my life to make your lives safe.   **40 it were . . . life** i.e., I should be sorry, by my life; or, my life would be endangered. **55–6 bush of thorns** bundle of thornbush fagots. (Part of the accou-trements of the man in the moon, according to the popular notions of the time, along with his lantern and his dog.)   **56 disfigure** (Quince's blunder for "figure," "represent.")

64–5 roughcast a mixture of lime and gravel used to plaster the out-side of buildings   **72 hempen homespuns** i.e., rustics dressed in homespun fabric made from hemp   **73 cradle** i.e., Titania's bower **74 toward** about to take place.   **83 A stranger . . . here** The strangest Pyramus you ever saw.   **89 triumphant** magnificent   **90 brisky juvenal** lively youth.   **eke** also.   **Jew** (A desperate attempt to rhyme with *hue*, inspired perhaps by the first syllable of *juvenal*.)   **93 Ninus'** Ninus was the mythical founder of Nineveh (whose wife, Semiramis, was supposed to have built the walls of Babylon where the story of Pyramus and Thisbe takes place)   **95 part** (An actor's *part* was a script consisting only of his speeches and their cues.)   **97.1–2 with the ass head** (This stage direction, taken from the Folio, presumably refers to a standard stage property.)

BOTTOM
"If I were fair, Thisbe, I were only thine." 98

QUINCE   Oh, monstrous! Oh, strange! We are haunted.
Pray, masters! Fly, masters! Help!

[*Exeunt Quince, Snug, Flute,
Snout, and Starveling.*]

PUCK
I'll follow you: I'll lead you about a round, 101
    Through bog, through bush, through brake,
        through brier.
Sometimes a horse I'll be, sometimes a hound,
    A hog, a headless bear, sometimes a fire; 104
And neigh, and bark, and grunt, and roar, and burn,
Like horse, hound, hog, bear, fire, at every turn. *Exit.*

BOTTOM   Why do they run away? This is a knavery of
them to make me afeard.

Enter Snout.

SNOUT   Oh, Bottom, thou art changed! What do I see on
thee?

BOTTOM   What do you see? You see an ass head of your
own, do you?   [*Exit Snout.*]

Enter Quince.

QUINCE   Bless thee, Bottom, bless thee! Thou art trans- 113
lated.   *Exit.* 114

BOTTOM   I see their knavery. This is to make an ass of
me, to fright me, if they could. But I will not stir from
this place, do what they can. I will walk up and down
here, and I will sing, that they shall hear I am not
afraid.   [*He sings.*]
    The ouzel cock so black of hue, 120
        With orange-tawny bill,
    The throstle with his note so true, 122
        The wren with little quill— 123

TITANIA [*awaking*]
What angel wakes me from my flow'ry bed?

BOTTOM [*sings*]
    The finch, the sparrow, and the lark,
        The plainsong cuckoo gray, 126
    Whose note full many a man doth mark,
        And dares not answer nay— 128
    For indeed, who would set his wit to so foolish a bird? 129
    Who would give a bird the lie, though he cry "cuckoo" 130
    never so? 131

TITANIA
I pray thee, gentle mortal, sing again.
Mine ear is much enamored of thy note;
So is mine eye enthrallèd to thy shape;
And thy fair virtue's force perforce doth move me 135
On the first view to say, to swear, I love thee.

BOTTOM   Methinks, mistress, you should have little reason for that. And yet, to say the truth, reason and love
keep little company together nowadays—the more the
pity that some honest neighbors will not make them
friends. Nay, I can gleek upon occasion. 141

TITANIA
Thou art as wise as thou art beautiful.

BOTTOM   Not so, neither. But if I had wit enough to get
out of this wood, I have enough to serve mine own 144
turn. 145

TITANIA
Out of this wood do not desire to go.
Thou shalt remain here, whether thou wilt or no.
I am a spirit of no common rate. 148
The summer still doth tend upon my state, 149
And I do love thee. Therefore, go with me.
I'll give thee fairies to attend on thee,
And they shall fetch thee jewels from the deep,
And sing while thou on pressèd flowers dost sleep.
And I will purge thy mortal grossness so
That thou shalt like an airy spirit go.—
Peaseblossom, Cobweb, Mote, and Mustardseed! 156

*Enter four Fairies [Peaseblossom, Cobweb,
Mote, and Mustardseed].*

PEASEBLOSSOM   Ready.
COBWEB   And I.
MOTE   And I.
MUSTARDSEED   And I.
ALL   Where shall we go?

TITANIA
Be kind and courteous to this gentleman.
Hop in his walks and gambol in his eyes; 160
Feed him with apricots and dewberries, 161
With purple grapes, green figs, and mulberries;
The honey bags steal from the humble-bees,
And for night tapers crop their waxen thighs, 164
And light them at the fiery glowworms' eyes, 165
To have my love to bed and to arise;
And pluck the wings from painted butterflies
To fan the moonbeams from his sleeping eyes.
Nod to him, elves, and do him courtesies.

PEASEBLOSSOM   Hail, mortal!
COBWEB   Hail!
MOTE   Hail!
MUSTARDSEED   Hail!

BOTTOM   I cry Your Worships mercy, heartily. I beseech 174
Your Worship's name.

COBWEB   Cobweb.

---

98 If Even if. **fair** handsome. **were** would be **101 about a round**
roundabout **104 fire** will-o'-the-wisp **113–14 translated** transformed. **120 ouzel cock** male blackbird **122 throstle** song thrush
123 with little quill with small pipe, i.e., high-pitched note; or else
with small feathers **126 plainsong** singing a melody without variations **128 dares . . . nay** i.e., cannot deny that he is a cuckold
129 set his wit to employ his intelligence to answer **130 give . . . lie**
call the bird a liar **131 never so** ever so much. **135 thy . . . force**
the power of your unblemished excellence

141 gleek jest **144–5 serve . . . turn** answer my purpose. **148 rate**
rank, value. **149 still . . . state** always waits upon me as a part of my
royal retinue **156 Mote** i.e., speck. (The two words *moth* and *mote*
were pronounced alike, and both meanings may be present.) **160 in
his eyes** in his sight (i.e., before him) **161 dewberries** blackberries
164 night . . . thighs (The waxen thighs of the bumble-bee are to be
fashioned into wax candles to light Bottom's way in the dark.) **165
eyes** (In fact, the light is emitted by the abdomen. *Eyes* may be
metaphorical.) **174 I cry . . . mercy** I beg pardon of Your Worships
(for presuming to ask a question)

BOTTOM   I shall desire you of more acquaintance, good 177
Master Cobweb. If I cut my finger, I shall make bold 178
with you.—Your name, honest gentleman?   179

PEASEBLOSSOM   Peaseblossom.

BOTTOM   I pray you, commend me to Mistress Squash, 181
your mother, and to Master Peascod, your father. 182
Good Master Peaseblossom, I shall desire you of more
acquaintance too.—Your name, I beseech you, sir?

MUSTARDSEED   Mustardseed.

BOTTOM   Good Master Mustardseed, I know your 186
patience well. That same cowardly, giantlike ox-beef 187
hath devoured many a gentleman of your house. I
promise you, your kindred hath made my eyes water 189
ere now. I desire you of more acquaintance, good
Master Mustardseed.

TITANIA
Come wait upon him; lead him to my bower.
The moon methinks looks with a wat'ry eye;
And when she weeps, weeps every little flower,   194
Lamenting some enforcèd chastity.   195
Tie up my lover's tongue; bring him silently.   196

Exeunt.

❦

[3.2]

Enter [Oberon,] King of Fairies.

OBERON
I wonder if Titania be awaked;
Then, what it was that next came in her eye,
Which she must dote on in extremity.

[Enter] Robin Goodfellow [Puck].

Here comes my messenger. How now, mad spirit?
What night-rule now about this haunted grove?   5

PUCK
My mistress with a monster is in love.
Near to her close and consecrated bower,   7
While she was in her dull and sleeping hour,   8
A crew of patches, rude mechanicals,   9
That work for bread upon Athenian stalls,   10
Were met together to rehearse a play
Intended for great Theseus' nuptial day.
The shallowest thickskin of that barren sort,   13
Who Pyramus presented, in their sport   14
Forsook his scene and entered in a brake.   15
When I did him at this advantage take,

An ass's noll I fixèd on his head.   17
Anon his Thisbe must be answerèd,
And forth my mimic comes. When they him spy,   19
As wild geese that the creeping fowler eye,   20
Or russet-pated choughs, many in sort,   21
Rising and cawing at the gun's report,
Sever themselves and madly sweep the sky,   23
So, at his sight, away his fellows fly;
And, at our stamp, here o'er and o'er one falls;
He "Murder!" cries and help from Athens calls.
Their sense thus weak, lost with their fears thus
    strong,   27
Made senseless things begin to do them wrong,   28
For briers and thorns at their apparel snatch;
Some, sleeves—some, hats; from yielders all things
    catch.   30
I led them on in this distracted fear
And left sweet Pyramus translated there,
When in that moment, so it came to pass,
Titania waked and straightway loved an ass.

OBERON
This falls out better than I could devise.
But hast thou yet latched the Athenian's eyes   36
With the love juice, as I did bid thee do?

PUCK
I took him sleeping—that is finished too—
And the Athenian woman by his side,
That, when he waked, of force she must be eyed.   40

Enter Demetrius and Hermia.

OBERON
Stand close. This is the same Athenian.

PUCK
This is the woman, but not this the man.

[They stand aside.]

DEMETRIUS
Oh, why rebuke you him that loves you so?
Lay breath so bitter on your bitter foe.

HERMIA
Now I but chide; but I should use thee worse,
For thou, I fear, hast given me cause to curse.
If thou hast slain Lysander in his sleep,
Being o'er shoes in blood, plunge in the deep,   48
And kill me too.
The sun was not so true unto the day
As he to me. Would he have stolen away
From sleeping Hermia? I'll believe as soon
This whole earth may be bored, and that the moon   53
May through the center creep, and so displease
Her brother's noontide with th'Antipodes.   55

---

177 I . . . acquaintance I crave to be better acquainted with you
178–9 If . . . you (Cobwebs were used to stanch bleeding.)
181 Squash unripe pea pod   **182 Peascod** ripe pea pod   **186–7 your
patience** what you have endured. (Mustard is eaten with beef.)
189 water (1) weep for sympathy (2) smart, sting   **194 And . . .
flower** (Dew was thought to fall from the heavens in greater proportion as the moon shown fully.)   **195 enforcèd** violated. (The moon is
associated throughout the play with the goddess Diana and chastity.)
196 Tie . . . tongue (Presumably Bottom is braying like an ass.)
3.2. Location: The wood.
5 night-rule diversion or misrule for the night   **7 close** secret   **8 dull**
drowsy   **9 patches** clowns, fools.   **rude mechanicals** ignorant artisans   **10 stalls** market booths   **13 barren sort** stupid company or
crew   **14 presented** acted   **15 scene** playing area

---

17 noll noddle, head   **19 mimic** actor   **20 fowler** hunter of game
birds   **21 russet-pated choughs** reddish brown or gray-headed jackdaws.   **in sort** in a flock   **23 Sever themselves** i.e., scatter
27–8 Their . . . wrong Their weakened physical senses, disabled by
their strong fears, made it seem to them as though inanimate things
in the forest were attacking them   **30 from . . . catch** the forest
snatches away everything from those who yield to it.   **36 latched**
snared, taken prisoner   **40 of force** perforce   **48 Being o'er shoes**
having waded in so far   **53 whole** solid   **55 Her . . . Antipodes** i.e.,
the sun's noontime on the opposite side of the earth, among the people who live there, the Antipodes.

It cannot be but thou hast murdered him;
So should a murderer look, so dead, so grim.   57

DEMETRIUS
So should the murdered look, and so should I,
Pierced through the heart with your stern cruelty.
Yet you, the murderer, look as bright, as clear
As yonder Venus in her glimmering sphere.

HERMIA
What's this to my Lysander? Where is he?   62
Ah, good Demetrius, wilt thou give him me?

DEMETRIUS
I had rather give his carcass to my hounds.

HERMIA
Out, dog! Out, cur! Thou driv'st me past the bounds
Of maiden's patience. Hast thou slain him, then?
Henceforth be never numbered among men.
Oh, once tell true, tell true, even for my sake: 68
Durst thou have looked upon him being awake?   69
And hast thou killed him sleeping? Oh, brave touch!   70
Could not a worm, an adder, do so much?   71
An adder did it; for with doubler tongue   72
Than thine, thou serpent, never adder stung.

DEMETRIUS
You spend your passion on a misprised mood.   74
I am not guilty of Lysander's blood,
Nor is he dead, for aught that I can tell.

HERMIA
I pray thee, tell me then that he is well.

DEMETRIUS
And if I could, what should I get therefor?   78

HERMIA
A privilege never to see me more.
And from thy hated presence part I so.
See me no more, whether he be dead or no.   Exit.

DEMETRIUS
There is no following her in this fierce vein.
Here therefore for a while I will remain.
So sorrow's heaviness doth heavier grow   84
For debt that bankrupt sleep doth sorrow owe,   85
Which now in some slight measure it will pay,   86
If for his tender here I make some stay.   87
          [He] lie[s] down [and sleeps].

OBERON
What hast thou done? Thou hast mistaken quite
And laid the love juice on some true love's sight.
Of thy misprision must perforce ensue   90
Some true love turned, and not a false turned true.

PUCK
Then fate o'errules, that, one man holding troth,   92
A million fail, confounding oath on oath.   93

OBERON
About the wood go swifter than the wind,
And Helena of Athens look thou find.
All fancy-sick she is and pale of cheer   96
With sighs of love, that cost the fresh blood dear.   97
By some illusion see thou bring her here.
I'll charm his eyes against she do appear.   99

PUCK
I go, I go, look how I go,
Swifter than arrow from the Tartar's bow.   [Exit.] 101

OBERON [applying love juice to Demetrius's eyes]
Flower of this purple dye,
Hit with Cupid's archery,
Sink in apple of his eye.   104
When his love he doth espy,
Let her shine as gloriously
As the Venus of the sky.
When thou wak'st, if she be by,
Beg of her for remedy.

          Enter Puck.

PUCK
Captain of our fairy band,
Helena is here at hand,
And the youth, mistook by me,
Pleading for a lover's fee.   113
Shall we their fond pageant see?   114
Lord, what fools these mortals be!

OBERON
Stand aside. The noise they make
Will cause Demetrius to awake.

PUCK
Then will two at once woo one;
That must needs be sport alone.   119
And those things do best please me
That befall preposterously.   121
          [They stand aside.]

          Enter Lysander and Helena.

LYSANDER
Why should you think that I should woo in scorn?
     Scorn and derision never come in tears.
Look when I vow, I weep; and vows so born,   124
     In their nativity all truth appears.   125
How can these things in me seem scorn to you,
Bearing the badge of faith to prove them true?

HELENA
You do advance your cunning more and more.   128
     When truth kills truth, oh, devilish-holy fray!   129
These vows are Hermia's. Will you give her o'er?
     Weigh oath with oath, and you will nothing weigh;

---

57 dead deadly, or deathly pale   **62 to** to do with   **68 once** once and for all   **69 being awake** when he was awake.   **70 brave touch!** fine stroke! (Said ironically.)   **71 worm** serpent   **72 doubler** (1) more forked (2) more deceitful   **74 You . . . mood** Your anger is misdirected.   **78 therefor** in return for that.   **84–7 So . . . stay** The heaviness of sorrow grows still heavier when sleepiness adds to the weariness caused by sorrow, which debt to sleepiness I will now repay in part if I can stop here and accept what sleep has to offer.
90 misprision mistake   **92–3 Then . . . oath** If so, then fate prevails; for each male who is able to keep true faith in love, a million will fail, breaking oath on oath.

96 fancy-sick lovesick.   **cheer** face   **97 sighs . . . dear** (Each sigh was supposed to cost the heart a drop of blood.)   **99 against . . . appear** in anticipation of her coming.   **101 Tartar's bow** (Tartars were famed for their skill with the bow.)   **104 apple** pupil   **113 fee** privilege, reward.   **114 fond pageant** foolish spectacle   **119 alone** unequaled.   **121 preposterously** out of the natural order.   **124 Look when** Whenever   **124–5 vows . . . appears** i.e., vows made by one who is weeping give evidence thereby of their sincerity.
128 advance carry forward, display   **129 When . . . truth** i.e., When one of your vows cancels the other

Your vows to her and me, put in two scales,
Will even weigh, and both as light as tales.   133

LYSANDER
I had no judgment when to her I swore.

HELENA
Nor none, in my mind, now you give her o'er.

LYSANDER
Demetrius loves her, and he loves not you.

DEMETRIUS [*awaking*]
O Helen, goddess, nymph, perfect, divine!
To what, my love, shall I compare thine eyne?
Crystal is muddy. Oh, how ripe in show   139
Thy lips, those kissing cherries, tempting grow!
That pure congealèd white, high Taurus' snow,   141
Fanned with the eastern wind, turns to a crow   142
When thou hold'st up thy hand. Oh, let me kiss
This princess of pure white, this seal of bliss! 144

HELENA
Oh, spite! Oh, hell! I see you all are bent
To set against me for your merriment.   146
If you were civil and knew courtesy,
You would not do me thus much injury.
Can you not hate me, as I know you do,
But you must join in souls to mock me too?   150
If you were men, as men you are in show,
You would not use a gentle lady so—
To vow, and swear, and superpraise my parts,   153
When I am sure you hate me with your hearts.
You both are rivals, and love Hermia,
And now both rivals to mock Helena.
A trim exploit, a manly enterprise,   157
To conjure tears up in a poor maid's eyes
With your derision! None of noble sort   159
Would so offend a virgin and extort   160
A poor soul's patience, all to make you sport.

LYSANDER
You are unkind, Demetrius. Be not so.
For you love Hermia; this you know I know.
And here, with all good will, with all my heart,
In Hermia's love I yield you up my part;
And yours of Helena to me bequeath,
Whom I do love, and will do till my death.

HELENA
Never did mockers waste more idle breath.

DEMETRIUS
Lysander, keep thy Hermia; I will none.   169
If e'er I loved her, all that love is gone.
My heart to her but as guestwise sojourned,   171
And now to Helen is it home returned,
There to remain.

LYSANDER   Helen, it is not so.

DEMETRIUS
Disparage not the faith thou dost not know,
Lest, to thy peril, thou aby it dear.   175
Look where thy love comes; yonder is thy dear.

    Enter Hermia.

HERMIA
Dark night, that from the eye his function takes, 177
The ear more quick of apprehension makes;
Wherein it doth impair the seeing sense,
It pays the hearing double recompense.
Thou art not by mine eye, Lysander, found;
Mine ear, I thank it, brought me to thy sound.
But why unkindly didst thou leave me so?

LYSANDER
Why should he stay, whom love doth press to go?

HERMIA
What love could press Lysander from my side?

LYSANDER
Lysander's love, that would not let him bide—
Fair Helena, who more engilds the night
Than all yon fiery oes and eyes of light.   188
Why seek'st thou me? Could not this make thee
   know
The hate I bear thee made me leave thee so?

HERMIA
You speak not as you think. It cannot be.

HELENA
Lo, she is one of this confederacy!
Now I perceive they have conjoined all three
To fashion this false sport, in spite of me.   194
Injurious Hermia, most ungrateful maid!
Have you conspired, have you with these contrived
To bait me with this foul derision?   197
Is all the counsel that we two have shared—   198
The sisters' vows, the hours that we have spent
When we have chid the hasty-footed time
For parting us—oh, is all forgot?
All schooldays' friendship, childhood innocence?
We, Hermia, like two artificial gods   203
Have with our needles created both one flower,
Both on one sampler, sitting on one cushion,
Both warbling of one song, both in one key,
As if our hands, our sides, voices, and minds
Had been incorporate. So we grew together,   208
Like to a double cherry, seeming parted,
But yet an union in partition,
Two lovely berries molded on one stem;
So, with two seeming bodies but one heart,
Two of the first, like coats in heraldry,   213
Due but to one and crownèd with one crest.   214
And will you rend our ancient love asunder,
To join with men in scorning your poor friend?
It is not friendly, 'tis not maidenly.

---

133 tales lies. **139 show** appearance **141 Taurus'** Taurus was a lofty
mountain range in Asia Minor **142 turns to a crow** i.e., seems black
by contrast **144 seal** pledge **146 set against** attack **150 in souls**
i.e., heart and soul **153 superpraise** overpraise. **parts** qualities
157 trim pretty, fine. (Said ironically.) **159 sort** character, quality
160 extort twist, torture **169 will none** i.e., want no part of her.
171 to . . . sojourned only visited with her

175 aby pay for **177 his** its **188 oes** spangles (here, stars) **194 in
spite of me** to vex me. **197 bait** torment, as one sets on dogs to bait
a bear **198 counsel** confidential talk **203 artificial** skilled in art or
creation **208 incorporate** of one body. **213–14 Two . . . crest** i.e., we
have two separate bodies, just as a coat of arms in heraldry can be
represented twice on a shield but surmounted by a single crest.

Our sex, as well as I, may chide you for it,
Though I alone do feel the injury.

HERMIA
I am amazèd at your passionate words.
I scorn you not. It seems that you scorn me.

HELENA
Have you not set Lysander, as in scorn,
To follow me and praise my eyes and face?
And made your other love, Demetrius,
Who even but now did spurn me with his foot,
To call me goddess, nymph, divine, and rare,
Precious, celestial? Wherefore speaks he this
To her he hates? And wherefore doth Lysander
Deny your love, so rich within his soul,
And tender me, forsooth, affection,   230
But by your setting on, by your consent?
What though I be not so in grace as you,   232
So hung upon with love, so fortunate,
But miserable most, to love unloved?
This you should pity rather than despise.

HERMIA
I understand not what you mean by this.

HELENA
Ay, do! Persever, counterfeit sad looks,   237
Make mouths upon me when I turn my back,   238
Wink each at other, hold the sweet jest up.   239
This sport, well carried, shall be chronicled.   240
If you have any pity, grace, or manners,
You would not make me such an argument.   242
But fare ye well. 'Tis partly my own fault,
Which death, or absence, soon shall remedy.

LYSANDER
Stay, gentle Helena; hear my excuse,
My love, my life, my soul, fair Helena!

HELENA
Oh, excellent!

HERMIA [to Lysander]   Sweet, do not scorn her so.

DEMETRIUS [to Lysander]
If she cannot entreat, I can compel.   248

LYSANDER
Thou canst compel no more than she entreat.
Thy threats have no more strength than her weak
      prayers.—
Helen, I love thee, by my life, I do!
I swear by that which I will lose for thee,
To prove him false that says I love thee not.

DEMETRIUS [to Helena]
I say I love thee more than he can do.

LYSANDER
If thou say so, withdraw, and prove it too.   255

DEMETRIUS
Quick, come!

HERMIA   Lysander, whereto tends all this?

LYSANDER
Away, you Ethiope!
                        [He tries to break away from Hermia.]

DEMETRIUS   No, no; he'll   257
Seem to break loose; take on as you would follow,   258
But yet come not. You are a tame man. Go!

LYSANDER [to Hermia]
Hang off, thou cat, thou burr! Vile thing, let loose,   260
Or I will shake thee from me like a serpent!

HERMIA
Why are you grown so rude? What change is this,
Sweet love?

LYSANDER   Thy love? Out, tawny Tartar, out!
Out, loathèd med'cine! O hated potion, hence!   264

HERMIA
Do you not jest?

HELENA   Yes, sooth, and so do you.   265

LYSANDER
Demetrius, I will keep my word with thee.

DEMETRIUS
I would I had your bond, for I perceive
A weak bond holds you. I'll not trust your word.   268

LYSANDER
What, should I hurt her, strike her, kill her dead?
Although I hate her, I'll not harm her so.

HERMIA
What, can you do me greater harm than hate?
Hate me? Wherefore? Oh, me, what news, my love?   272
Am not I Hermia? Are not you Lysander?
I am as fair now as I was erewhile.   274
Since night you loved me; yet since night you left me.
Why, then you left me—oh, the gods forbid!—
In earnest, shall I say?

LYSANDER   Ay, by my life!
And never did desire to see thee more.
Therefore be out of hope, of question, of doubt;
Be certain, nothing truer. 'Tis no jest
That I do hate thee and love Helena.

HERMIA [to Helena]
Oh, me! You juggler! You cankerblossom!   282
You thief of love! What, have you come by night
And stol'n my love's heart from him?

HELENA   Fine, i'faith!
Have you no modesty, no maiden shame,
No touch of bashfulness? What, will you tear
Impatient answers from my gentle tongue?
Fie, fie! You counterfeit, you puppet, you!   288

HERMIA
"Puppet"? Why, so! Ay, that way goes the game.
Now I perceive that she hath made compare
Between our statures; she hath urged her height,
And with her personage, her tall personage,

---

230 **tender** offer   232 **grace** favor   237 **sad** grave, serious
238 **mouths** i.e., mows, faces, grimaces. **upon** at   239 **hold . . . up**
keep up the joke.   240 **carried** carried out, brought off   242 **argument** subject for a jest.   248 **entreat** i.e., succeed by entreaty
255 **withdraw . . . too** i.e., withdraw with me and prove your claim
in a duel. (The two gentlemen are armed.)

257 **Ethiope** (Referring to Hermia's relatively dark hair and complexion; see also *tawny Tartar* six lines later.)   258 **take on as** act as if,
make a fuss as if   260 **Hang off** Let go   264 **med'cine** i.e., poison
265 **sooth** truly   268 **weak bond** i.e., Hermia's arm. (With a pun on
bond, "oath," in the previous line.)   272 **what news** what is the matter   274 **erewhile** just now.   282 **cankerblossom** worm that destroys
the flower bud, or wild rose.   288 **puppet** (1) counterfeit (2) dwarfish
woman (in reference to Hermia's smaller stature)

Her height, forsooth, she hath prevailed with him.
And are you grown so high in his esteem
Because I am so dwarfish and so low?
How low am I, thou painted maypole? Speak!
How low am I? I am not yet so low
But that my nails can reach unto thine eyes.

[She flails at Helena but is restrained.]

HELENA
I pray you, though you mock me, gentlemen,
Let her not hurt me. I was never curst;   300
I have no gift at all in shrewishness;
I am a right maid for my cowardice.   302
Let her not strike me. You perhaps may think,
Because she is something lower than myself,   304
That I can match her.

HERMIA   Lower? Hark, again!

HELENA
Good Hermia, do not be so bitter with me.
I evermore did love you, Hermia,
Did ever keep your counsels, never wronged you,
Save that, in love unto Demetrius,
I told him of your stealth unto this wood.   310
He followed you; for love I followed him.
But he hath chid me hence and threatened me   312
To strike me, spurn me, nay, to kill me too.   313
And now, so you will let me quiet go,   314
To Athens will I bear my folly back
And follow you no further. Let me go.
You see how simple and how fond I am.   317

HERMIA
Why, get you gone. Who is't that hinders you?

HELENA
A foolish heart, that I leave here behind.

HERMIA
What, with Lysander?

HELENA   With Demetrius.

LYSANDER
Be not afraid; she shall not harm thee, Helena.

DEMETRIUS
No, sir, she shall not, though you take her part.

HELENA
Oh, when she is angry, she is keen and shrewd.   323
She was a vixen when she went to school;
And though she be but little, she is fierce.

HERMIA
"Little" again? Nothing but "low" and "little"?—
Why will you suffer her to flout me thus?
Let me come to her.

LYSANDER   Get you gone, you dwarf!
You minimus, of hind'ring knotgrass made!   329
You bead, you acorn!

DEMETRIUS   You are too officious
In her behalf that scorns your services.
Let her alone. Speak not of Helena;

Take not her part. For, if thou dost intend   333
Never so little show of love to her,
Thou shalt aby it.

LYSANDER   Now she holds me not.   335
Now follow, if thou dar'st, to try whose right,
Of thine or mine, is most in Helena.   *[Exit.]*

DEMETRIUS
Follow? Nay, I'll go with thee, cheek by jowl.   338

[Exit, following Lysander.]

HERMIA
You, mistress, all this coil is 'long of you.   339
Nay, go not back.

HELENA   I will not trust you, I,   340
Nor longer stay in your curst company.
Your hands than mine are quicker for a fray;
My legs are longer, though, to run away.   *[Exit.]*

HERMIA
I am amazed and know not what to say.   *Exit.*

[Oberon and Puck come forward.]

OBERON
This is thy negligence. Still thou mistak'st,
Or else commit'st thy knaveries willfully.

PUCK
Believe me, king of shadows, I mistook.
Did not you tell me I should know the man
By the Athenian garments he had on?
And so far blameless proves my enterprise
That I have 'nointed an Athenian's eyes;
And so far am I glad it so did sort,   352
As this their jangling I esteem a sport.   353

OBERON
Thou see'st these lovers seek a place to fight.
Hie therefore, Robin, overcast the night;   355
The starry welkin cover thou anon   356
With drooping fog as black as Acheron,   357
And lead these testy rivals so astray
As one come not within another's way.   359
Like to Lysander sometimes frame thy tongue,   360
Then stir Demetrius up with bitter wrong;   361
And sometimes rail thou like Demetrius.
And from each other look thou lead them thus,
Till o'er their brows death-counterfeiting sleep
With leaden legs and batty wings doth creep.   365
Then crush this herb into Lysander's eye,   366

[giving herb]

Whose liquor hath this virtuous property,   367
To take from thence all error with his might   368
And make his eyeballs roll with wonted sight.   369
When they next wake, all this derision   370
Shall seem a dream and fruitless vision,

---

300 **curst** shrewish   302 **right** true.   **for** for all   304 **something**
somewhat   310 **stealth** stealing away   312 **chid me hence** driven me
away with his scolding   313 **spurn** kick   314 **so** if only   317 **fond**
foolish   323 **keen and shrewd** fierce and shrewish.   329 **minimus**
diminutive creature.   **knotgrass** a weed, an infusion of which was
thought to stunt the growth

333 **intend** give sign of   335 **aby** pay for   338 **cheek by jowl** i.e.,
side by side.   339 **coil** turmoil, dissension.   **'long of** on account of
340 **go not back** i.e., don't retreat. (Hermia is again proposing a fight.)
352 **so far** at least to this extent.   **sort** turn out   353 **As** in that
355 **Hie** Hasten   356 **welkin** sky   357 **Acheron** river of Hades (here
representing Hades itself)   359 **As** that   360 **frame thy tongue** fashion your speech   361 **wrong** insults   365 **batty** batlike   366 **this
herb** i.e., the antidote (mentioned in 2.1.184) to love-in-idleness
367 **virtuous** efficacious   368 **his** its   369 **wonted** accustomed
370 **derision** laughable business

And she in mild terms begged my patience,
I then did ask of her her changeling child,
Which straight she gave me, and her fairy sent
To bear him to my bower in Fairyland.
And, now I have the boy, I will undo
This hateful imperfection of her eyes.
And, gentle Puck, take this transformèd scalp
From off the head of this Athenian swain,
That he, awaking when the other do,   65
May all to Athens back again repair,   66
And think no more of this night's accidents
But as the fierce vexation of a dream.
But first I will release the Fairy Queen.
                              [*He squeezes an herb on her eyes.*]
        Be as thou wast wont to be;
        See as thou wast wont to see.
        Dian's bud o'er Cupid's flower   72
        Hath such force and blessèd power.
Now, my Titania, wake you, my sweet queen.

TITANIA [*awaking*]
My Oberon! What visions have I seen!
Methought I was enamored of an ass.

OBERON
There lies your love.

TITANIA   How came these things to pass?
Oh, how mine eyes do loathe his visage now!

OBERON
Silence awhile. Robin, take off this head.
Titania, music call, and strike more dead
Than common sleep of all these five the sense.   81

TITANIA
Music, ho! Music, such as charmeth sleep!   [*Music.*]   82

PUCK [*removing the ass head*]
Now, when thou wak'st, with thine own fool's eyes
        peep.

OBERON
Sound, music! Come, my queen, take hands with me,
And rock the ground whereon these sleepers be.
                                      [*They dance.*]
Now thou and I are new in amity,
And will tomorrow midnight solemnly   87
Dance in Duke Theseus' house triumphantly,
And bless it to all fair prosperity.
There shall the pairs of faithful lovers be
Wedded, with Theseus, all in jollity.

PUCK
        Fairy King, attend, and mark:
        I do hear the morning lark.

OBERON
        Then, my queen, in silence sad,   94
        Trip we after night's shade.
        We the globe can compass soon,
        Swifter than the wand'ring moon.

TITANIA
        Come, my lord, and in our flight
        Tell me how it came this night
        That I sleeping here was found
        With these mortals on the ground.
                  Exeunt [*Oberon, Titania, and Puck*].
                              Wind horn [*within*].

        Enter Theseus and all his train; [*Hippolyta,
        Egeus*].

THESEUS
Go, one of you, find out the forester,
For now our observation is performed;   103
And since we have the vaward of the day,   104
My love shall hear the music of my hounds.
Uncouple in the western valley; let them go.   106
Dispatch, I say, and find the forester.
                              [*Exit an Attendant.*]
We will, fair queen, up to the mountain's top
And mark the musical confusion
Of hounds and echo in conjunction.

HIPPOLYTA
I was with Hercules and Cadmus once   111
When in a wood of Crete they bayed the bear   112
With hounds of Sparta. Never did I hear   113
Such gallant chiding; for, besides the groves,   114
The skies, the fountains, every region near
Seemed all one mutual cry. I never heard
So musical a discord, such sweet thunder.

THESEUS
My hounds are bred out of the Spartan kind,   118
So flewed, so sanded; and their heads are hung   119
With ears that sweep away the morning dew;
Crook-kneed, and dewlapped like Thessalian bulls;   121
Slow in pursuit, but matched in mouth like bells,   122
Each under each. A cry more tunable   123
Was never holloed to nor cheered with horn   124
In Crete, in Sparta, nor in Thessaly.
Judge when you hear. [*He sees the sleepers.*] But soft!
        What nymphs are these?   126

EGEUS
My lord, this is my daughter here asleep,
And this Lysander; this Demetrius is;
This Helena, old Nedar's Helena.
I wonder of their being here together.   130

THESEUS
No doubt they rose up early to observe
The rite of May, and hearing our intent,

---

65 other others   **66 repair** return   **72 Dian's bud** (Perhaps the flower of the *agnus castus* or chaste-tree, supposed to preserve chastity; or perhaps referring simply to Oberon's herb by which he can undo the effects of "Cupid's flower," the love-in-idleness of 2.1.166–8.)
81 these five i.e., the four lovers and Bottom   **82 charmeth** brings about, as though by a charm   **87 solemnly** ceremoniously
94 sad solemn

103 observation i.e., observance to a morn of May (1.1.167)
104 vaward vanguard, i.e., earliest part   **106 Uncouple** Set free for the hunt   **111 Cadmus** mythical founder of Thebes. (This story about him is unknown.)   **112 bayed** brought to bay   **113 hounds of Sparta** (A breed famous in antiquity for their hunting skill.)   **114 chiding** i.e., yelping   **118 kind** strain, breed   **119 So flewed** similarly having large hanging chaps or fleshy covering of the jaw.   **sanded** of sandy color   **121 dewlapped** having pendulous folds of skin under the neck.   **Thessalian** from Thessaly, in Greece   **122–3 matched . . . each** i.e., harmoniously matched in their various cries like a set of bells, from treble down to bass.   **123 cry** pack of hounds.   **tunable** well tuned, melodious   **124 cheered** encouraged   **126 soft** i.e., gently, wait a minute.   **130 of** at

Came here in grace of our solemnity.　　　　133
But speak, Egeus. Is not this the day
That Hermia should give answer of her choice?

EGEUS　　It is, my lord.

THESEUS
Go bid the huntsmen wake them with their horns.
　　　　　　　　　　　　　　[Exit an Attendant.]

Shout within. Wind horns. They all start up.

Good morrow, friends. Saint Valentine is past.　　138
Begin these woodbirds but to couple now?

LYSANDER
Pardon, my lord.　　　　　　　　　　[They kneel.]

THESEUS　　　　I pray you all, stand up.
　　　　　　　　　　　　　　　　[They stand.]
I know you two are rival enemies;
How comes this gentle concord in the world,
That hatred is so far from jealousy
To sleep by hate and fear no enmity?

LYSANDER
My lord, I shall reply amazedly,
Half sleep, half waking; but as yet, I swear,
I cannot truly say how I came here.
But, as I think—for truly would I speak,
And now I do bethink me, so it is—
I came with Hermia hither. Our intent
Was to be gone from Athens, where we might,
Without the peril of the Athenian law—

EGEUS
Enough, enough, my lord; you have enough.
I beg the law, the law, upon his head.
They would have stol'n away; they would, Demetrius,
Thereby to have defeated you and me,
You of your wife and me of my consent,
Of my consent that she should be your wife.

DEMETRIUS
My lord, fair Helen told me of their stealth,
Of this their purpose hither to this wood,
And I in fury hither followed them,
Fair Helena in fancy following me.　　　　162
But, my good lord, I wot not by what power—
But by some power it is—my love to Hermia,
Melted as the snow, seems to me now
As the remembrance of an idle gaud　　　166
Which in my childhood I did dote upon;
And all the faith, the virtue of my heart,
The object and the pleasure of mine eye,
Is only Helena. To her, my lord,
Was I betrothed ere I saw Hermia,
But like a sickness did I loathe this food;
But, as in health, come to my natural taste,
Now I do wish it, love it, long for it,
And will forevermore be true to it.

THESEUS
Fair lovers, you are fortunately met.
Of this discourse we more will hear anon.

Egeus, I will overbear your will;
For in the temple, by and by, with us
These couples shall eternally be knit.
And, for the morning now is something worn,　　181
Our purposed hunting shall be set aside.
Away with us to Athens. Three and three,
We'll hold a feast in great solemnity.　　184
Come, Hippolyta.
　　　[Exeunt Theseus, Hippolyta, Egeus, and train.]

DEMETRIUS
These things seem small and undistinguishable,
Like far-off mountains turnèd into clouds.

HERMIA
Methinks I see these things with parted eye,　　188
When everything seems double.

HELENA　　　　　　　　　　So methinks;
And I have found Demetrius like a jewel,　　190
Mine own, and not mine own.

DEMETRIUS　　　　　　　　Are you sure　　191
That we are awake? It seems to me
That yet we sleep, we dream. Do not you think
The Duke was here, and bid us follow him?

HERMIA
Yea, and my father.

HELENA　　　　　　And Hippolyta.

LYSANDER
And he did bid us follow to the temple.

DEMETRIUS
Why, then, we are awake. Let's follow him,
And by the way let us recount our dreams.
　　　　　　　　　　　　　　[Exeunt the lovers.]

BOTTOM [awaking]　When my cue comes, call me, and I
will answer. My next is "Most fair Pyramus." Heigh-
ho! Peter Quince! Flute, the bellows mender! Snout,
the tinker! Starveling! God's my life, stolen hence and　202
left me asleep! I have had a most rare vision. I have
had a dream, past the wit of man to say what dream
it was. Man is but an ass if he go about to expound this　205
dream. Methought I was—there is no man can tell
what. Methought I was—and methought I had—but
man is but a patched fool if he will offer to say what　208
methought I had. The eye of man hath not heard, the　209
ear of man hath not seen, man's hand is not able to　210
taste, his tongue to conceive, nor his heart to report,　211
what my dream was. I will get Peter Quince to write
a ballad of this dream. It shall be called "Bottom's　213
Dream," because it hath no bottom; and I will sing it　214
in the latter end of a play, before the Duke. Peradventure, to make it the more gracious, I shall sing it at her　216
death.　　　　　　　　　　　　　　　　[Exit.]

---

181 **for** since.　**something** somewhat　184 **in great solemnity** with great ceremony.　188 **parted** i.e., improperly focused　190–1 **like . . . own** i.e., something precious that seems mine and yet so mysteriously found that I can hardly believe it is mine.　202 **God's** May God save　205 **go about** attempt　208 **patched** wearing motley, i.e., a dress of various colors.　**offer** venture　209–11 **The eye . . . report** (Bottom garbles 1 Corinthians 2:9.)　213 **ballad** (The proper medium for relating sensational stories and preposterous events.)　214 **hath no bottom** is unfathomable　216 **her** Thisbe's (?)

---

133 **in . . . solemnity** in honor of our wedding ceremony.　138 **Saint Valentine** (Birds were supposed to choose their mates on Saint Valentine's Day.)　162 **in fancy** driven by love　166 **idle gaud** worthless trinket

Consider, then, we come but in despite.
  We do not come, as minding to content you, 113
Our true intent is. All for your delight
  We are not here. That you should here repent you,
The actors are at hand; and, by their show,
You shall know all that you are like to know.

THESEUS   This fellow doth not stand upon points. 118

LYSANDER   He hath rid his prologue like a rough colt; he 119
knows not the stop. A good moral, my lord: it is not 120
enough to speak, but to speak true.

HIPPOLYTA   Indeed, he hath played on his prologue like
a child on a recorder: a sound, but not in government. 123

THESEUS   His speech was like a tangled chain: nothing 124
impaired, but all disordered. Who is next?

Enter Pyramus [Bottom], and Thisbe [Flute],
and Wall [Snout], and Moonshine [Starveling],
and Lion [Snug].

PROLOGUE
Gentles, perchance you wonder at this show;
  But wonder on, till truth make all things plain.
This man is Pyramus, if you would know;
  This beauteous lady Thisbe is, certain.
This man with lime and roughcast doth present
  Wall, that vile wall which did these lovers sunder;
And through Wall's chink, poor souls, they are content
  To whisper. At the which let no man wonder.
This man with lantern, dog, and bush of thorn
  Presenteth Moonshine; for, if you will know,
By moonshine did these lovers think no scorn 136
  To meet at Ninus' tomb, there, there to woo.
This grisly beast, which Lion hight by name, 138
  The trusty Thisbe coming first by night
Did scare away, or rather did affright;
  And as she fled, her mantle she did fall, 141
  Which Lion vile with bloody mouth did stain.
Anon comes Pyramus, sweet youth and tall, 143
  And finds his trusty Thisbe's mantle slain;
Whereat, with blade, with bloody, blameful blade,
  He bravely broached his boiling bloody breast. 146
And Thisbe, tarrying in mulberry shade,
  His dagger drew, and died. For all the rest,
Let Lion, Moonshine, Wall, and lovers twain
At large discourse, while here they do remain. 150
    Exeunt Lion, Thisbe, and Moonshine.

THESEUS   I wonder if the lion be to speak.

DEMETRIUS   No wonder, my lord. One lion may, when
many asses do.

WALL
In this same interlude it doth befall 154
That I, one Snout by name, present a wall;
And such a wall as I would have you think

---

113 **minding** intending 118 **stand upon points** (1) heed niceties or
small points (2) pay attention to punctuation in his reading. (The
humor of Quince's speech is in the blunders of its punctuation.)
119 **rid** ridden. **rough** unbroken 120 **stop** (1) stopping of a colt by
reining it in (2) punctuation mark. 123 **recorder** wind instrument
like a flute. **government** control. 124 **nothing** not at all 136 **think
no scorn** think it no disgraceful matter 138 **hight** is called 141 **fall**
let fall 143 **tall** courageous 146 **broached** stabbed 150 **At large** in
full, at length 154 **interlude** play

That had in it a crannied hole or chink,
Through which the lovers, Pyramus and Thisbe,
Did whisper often, very secretly.
This loam, this roughcast, and this stone doth show
That I am that same wall; the truth is so.
And this the cranny is, right and sinister, 162
Through which the fearful lovers are to whisper.

THESEUS   Would you desire lime and hair to speak
better?

DEMETRIUS   It is the wittiest partition that ever I heard 166
discourse, my lord.

[Pyramus comes forward.]

THESEUS   Pyramus draws near the wall. Silence!

PYRAMUS
O grim-looked night! O night with hue so black! 169
  O night, which ever art when day is not!
O night, O night! Alack, alack, alack,
  I fear my Thisbe's promise is forgot.
And thou, O wall, O sweet, O lovely wall,
  That stand'st between her father's ground and
    mine,
Thou wall, O wall, O sweet and lovely wall,
  Show me thy chink, to blink through with mine
    eyne.   *[Wall makes a chink with his fingers.]*
Thanks, courteous wall. Jove shield thee well for
  this.
  But what see I? No Thisbe do I see.
O wicked wall, through whom I see no bliss!
  Cursed be thy stones for thus deceiving me!

THESEUS   The wall, methinks, being sensible, should 181
curse again. 182

PYRAMUS   No, in truth, sir, he should not. "Deceiving
me" is Thisbe's cue: she is to enter now, and I am to
spy her through the wall. You shall see, it will fall pat 185
as I told you. Yonder she comes.

Enter Thisbe.

THISBE
O wall, full often hast thou heard my moans
  For parting my fair Pyramus and me.
My cherry lips have often kissed thy stones,
  Thy stones with lime and hair knit up in thee.

PYRAMUS
I see a voice. Now will I to the chink,
  To spy an I can hear my Thisbe's face. 192
Thisbe!

THISBE   My love! Thou art my love, I think.

PYRAMUS
  Think what thou wilt, I am thy lover's grace, 194
And like Limander am I trusty still. 195

THISBE
And I like Helen, till the Fates me kill. 196

---

162 **right and sinister** from right to left 166 **partition** (1) wall (2) section of a learned treatise or oration 169 **grim-looked** grim-looking
181 **sensible** capable of feeling 182 **again** in return. 185 **pat** exactly
192 **an** if 194 **lover's grace** i.e., gracious lover 195, 196 **Limander,
Helen** (Blunders for "Leander" and "Hero.")

PYRAMUS

Not Shafalus to Procrus was so true.   197

THISBE

As Shafalus to Procrus, I to you.

PYRAMUS

Oh, kiss me through the hole of this vile wall!

THISBE

I kiss the wall's hole, not your lips at all.

PYRAMUS

Wilt thou at Ninny's tomb meet me straightway?

THISBE

'Tide life, 'tide death, I come without delay.   202

[*Exeunt Pyramus and Thisbe.*]

WALL

Thus have I, Wall, my part dischargèd so;
And, being done, thus Wall away doth go.   [*Exit.*]

THESEUS   Now is the mural down between the two
neighbors.

DEMETRIUS   No remedy, my lord, when walls are so
willful to hear without warning.   208

HIPPOLYTA   This is the silliest stuff that ever I heard.

THESEUS   The best in this kind are but shadows; and the   210
worst are no worse, if imagination amend them.

HIPPOLYTA   It must be your imagination then, and not
theirs.

THESEUS   If we imagine no worse of them than they of
themselves, they may pass for excellent men. Here
come two noble beasts in, a man and a lion.

Enter Lion and Moonshine.

LION

You, ladies, you, whose gentle hearts do fear
    The smallest monstrous mouse that creeps on
        floor,
May now perchance both quake and tremble here,
    When lion rough in wildest rage doth roar.
Then know that I, as Snug the joiner, am   221
A lion fell, nor else no lion's dam;   222
For, if I should as lion come in strife
Into this place, 'twere pity on my life.

THESEUS   A very gentle beast, and of a good conscience.

DEMETRIUS   The very best at a beast, my lord, that e'er I
saw.

LYSANDER   This lion is a very fox for his valor.   228

THESEUS   True; and a goose for his discretion.   229

DEMETRIUS   Not so, my lord, for his valor cannot carry
his discretion, and the fox carries the goose.

THESEUS   His discretion, I am sure, cannot carry his
valor; for the goose carries not the fox. It is well. Leave
it to his discretion, and let us listen to the moon.

MOON

This lanthorn doth the hornèd moon present—   235

DEMETRIUS   He should have worn the horns on his   236
head.   237

THESEUS   He is no crescent, and his horns are invisible 238
within the circumference.

MOON

This lanthorn doth the hornèd moon present;
Myself the man i'th' moon do seem to be.

THESEUS   This is the greatest error of all the rest. The
man should be put into the lanthorn. How is it else the
man i'th' moon?

DEMETRIUS   He dares not come there for the candle, for   245
you see it is already in snuff.   246

HIPPOLYTA   I am aweary of this moon. Would he would
change!

THESEUS   It appears, by his small light of discretion, that
he is in the wane; but yet, in courtesy, in all reason, we
must stay the time.

LYSANDER   Proceed, Moon.

MOON   All that I have to say is to tell you that the lanthorn is the moon, I, the man i'th' moon, this thornbush my thornbush, and this dog my dog.

DEMETRIUS   Why, all these should be in the lanthorn,
for all these are in the moon. But silence! Here comes
Thisbe.

Enter Thisbe.

THISBE

This is old Ninny's tomb. Where is my love?

LION [*roaring*]   Oh!

DEMETRIUS   Well roared, Lion.

[*Thisbe runs off, dropping her mantle.*]

THESEUS   Well run, Thisbe.

HIPPOLYTA   Well shone, Moon. Truly, the moon shines
with a good grace.

[*The Lion worries Thisbe's mantle.*]

THESEUS   Well moused, Lion.   265

Enter Pyramus.   [*Exit Lion.*]

DEMETRIUS   And then came Pyramus.

LYSANDER   And so the lion vanished.

PYRAMUS

Sweet Moon, I thank thee for thy sunny beams;
    I thank thee, Moon, for shining now so bright;
For, by thy gracious, golden, glittering gleams,
    I trust to take of truest Thisbe sight.
        But stay, oh, spite!
        But mark, poor knight,
    What dreadful dole is here?   274
        Eyes, do you see?
        How can it be?

---

197 Shafalus, Procrus (Blunders for "Cephalus" and "Procris," also famous lovers.)   **202 'Tide** Betide, come   **208 willful** willing.   **without warning** i.e., without warning the parents. (Demetrius makes a joke on the proverb "Walls have ears.")   **210 in this kind** of this sort.   **shadows** likenesses, representations   **221–2 am . . . dam** enact the part of a fierce lion, but otherwise am not really a lion. (*Dam* means "mother"; in Shakespeare's source the beast is a lioness.)   **228 is . . . valor** i.e., his valor consists of craftiness and discretion.   **229 a goose . . . discretion** i.e., as discreet as a goose, that is, more foolish than discreet.

235 lanthorn (This original spelling, "lanthorne," may suggest a play on the *horn* of which lanterns were made and also on a cuckold's horns; however, the spelling "lanthorne" is not used consistently for comic effect in this play or elsewhere. At 5.1.134, for example, the word is "lanterne" in the original.)   **236–7 on his head** (As a sign of cuck-oldry.)   **238 crescent** a waxing moon   **245 for the** because of the, for fear of the   **246 in snuff** (1) offended (2) in need of snuffing or trim-ming.   **265 moused** shaken, torn, bitten   **274 dole** grievous event

Oh, dainty duck! Oh, dear!
    Thy mantle good,
    What, stained with blood?
Approach, ye Furies fell!   280
    O Fates, come, come,   281
    Cut thread and thrum;   282
    Quail, crush, conclude, and quell!   283

THESEUS   This passion, and the death of a dear friend,   284
would go near to make a man look sad.   285

HIPPOLYTA   Beshrew my heart, but I pity the man.   286

PYRAMUS
Oh, wherefore, Nature, didst thou lions frame?   287
Since lion vile hath here deflowered my dear,
Which is—no, no, which was—the fairest dame
That lived, that loved, that liked, that looked with
    cheer.   290
    Come, tears, confound,
    Out, sword, and wound
The pap of Pyramus;   293
    Ay, that left pap,
    Where heart doth hop.   [He stabs himself.]
Thus die I, thus, thus, thus.
    Now am I dead,
    Now am I fled;
My soul is in the sky.
    Tongue, lose thy light;
    Moon, take thy flight.   [Exit Moonshine.]
Now die, die, die, die, die.   [Pyramus dies.]

DEMETRIUS   No die, but an ace, for him; for he is   303
but one.   304

LYSANDER   Less than an ace, man; for he is dead, he is
nothing.

THESEUS   With the help of a surgeon he might yet
recover, and yet prove an ass.   308

HIPPOLYTA   How chance Moonshine is gone before
Thisbe comes back and finds her lover?

THESEUS   She will find him by starlight.

[Enter Thisbe.]

Here she comes; and her passion ends the play.

HIPPOLYTA   Methinks she should not use a long one for
such a Pyramus. I hope she will be brief.

DEMETRIUS   A mote will turn the balance, which Pyra-   315
mus which Thisbe, is the better: he for a man, God   316
warrant us; she for a woman, God bless us.

LYSANDER   She hath spied him already with those sweet
eyes.

DEMETRIUS   And thus she means, videlicet: 320

THISBE
    Asleep, my love?
    What, dead, my dove?
O Pyramus, arise!
    Speak, speak. Quite dumb?
    Dead, dead? A tomb
Must cover thy sweet eyes.
    These lily lips,
    This cherry nose,
These yellow cowslip cheeks,
    Are gone, are gone!
    Lovers, make moan.
His eyes were green as leeks.
    O Sisters Three,   333
    Come, come to me,
With hands as pale as milk;
    Lay them in gore,
    Since you have shore   337
With shears his thread of silk.
    Tongue, not a word.
    Come, trusty sword,
Come, blade, my breast imbrue!   341
            [She stabs herself.]
    And farewell, friends.
    Thus Thisbe ends.
    Adieu, adieu, adieu.   [She dies.]

THESEUS   Moonshine and Lion are left to bury the dead.

DEMETRIUS   Ay, and Wall too.

BOTTOM [starting up, as Flute does also]   No, I assure you,
the wall is down that parted their fathers. Will it please
you to see the epilogue, or to hear a Bergomask dance   349
between two of our company?

[The other players enter.]

THESEUS   No epilogue, I pray you; for your play needs
no excuse. Never excuse; for when the players are all
dead, there need none to be blamed. Marry, if he that
writ it had played Pyramus and hanged himself in
Thisbe's garter, it would have been a fine tragedy; and
so it is, truly, and very notably discharged. But, come,
your Bergomask. Let your epilogue alone. [A dance.]
The iron tongue of midnight hath told twelve.   358
Lovers, to bed, 'tis almost fairy time.
I fear we shall outsleep the coming morn
As much as we this night have overwatched.   361
This palpable-gross play hath well beguiled   362
The heavy gait of night. Sweet friends, to bed.   363
A fortnight hold we this solemnity,
In nightly revels and new jollity.   [Exeunt.]

    Enter Puck [carrying a broom].

---

280 **Furies fell** fierce avenging goddesses of Greek myth.   281 **Fates**
the three goddesses (Clotho, Lachesis, Atropos) of Greek myth who
spun, drew, and cut the thread of human life   282 **thread and thrum**
i.e., everything—the good and bad alike; literally, the warp in weaving and the loose end of the warp   283 **Quail** overpower. **quell** kill,
destroy.   284–5 **This . . . sad** i.e., If one had other reason to grieve,
one might be sad, but not from this absurd portrayal of passion.
286 **Beshrew** Curse. (A mild curse.)   287 **frame** create.   290 **cheer**
countenance.   293 **pap** breast   303 **ace** the side of the die featuring
the single pip, or spot. (The pun is on *die* as a singular of *dice*; Bottom's performance is not worth a whole *die* but rather one single face
of it, one small portion.)   304 **one** (1) an individual person
(2) unique.   308 **ass** (With a pun on *ace*.)   315 **mote** small particle
315–16 **which . . . which** whether . . . or

320 **means** moans, laments. (With a pun on the meaning, "lodge a formal complaint.") **videlicet** to wit   333 **Sisters Three** the Fates
337 **shore** shorn   341 **imbrue** stain with blood.   349 **Bergomask
dance** a rustic named from Bergamo, a province in the state of
Venice   358 **iron tongue** i.e., of a bell. **told** counted, struck
("tolled")   361 **overwatched** stayed up too late.   362 **palpable-gross**
palpably gross, obviously crude   363 **heavy** drowsy, dull

PUCK

Now the hungry lion roars,
  And the wolf behowls the moon,
Whilst the heavy plowman snores,   368
  All with weary task fordone.   369
Now the wasted brands do glow,   370
  Whilst the screech owl, screeching loud,
Puts the wretch that lies in woe
  In remembrance of a shroud.
Now it is the time of night
  That the graves, all gaping wide,
Every one lets forth his sprite,   376
  In the churchway paths to glide.
And we fairies, that do run
  By the triple Hecate's team.   379
From the presence of the sun,
  Following darkness like a dream,
Now are frolic. Not a mouse   382
  Shall disturb this hallowed house.
I am sent with broom before,
To sweep the dust behind the door.   385

  Enter [Oberon and Titania,] King and Queen of
  Fairies, with all their train.

OBERON

Through the house give glimmering light,
  By the dead and drowsy fire;
Every elf and fairy sprite
  Hop as light as bird from brier;
And this ditty, after me,
Sing, and dance it trippingly.

TITANIA

First, rehearse your song by rote,   392
To each word a warbling note.
Hand in hand, with fairy grace,
Will we sing, and bless this place.
                            [Song and dance.]

OBERON

Now, until the break of day,
Through this house each fairy stray.
To the best bride-bed will we,
Which by us shall blessèd be;
And the issue there create   400
Ever shall be fortunate.
So shall all the couples three
Ever true in loving be;
And the blots of Nature's hand
Shall not in their issue stand;
Never mole, harelip, nor scar,
Nor mark prodigious, such as are   407
Despisèd in nativity,
Shall upon their children be.
With this field dew consecrate,   410
Every fairy take his gait,   411
And each several chamber bless,   412
Through this palace, with sweet peace;
And the owner of it blest
Ever shall in safety rest.
Trip away; make no stay;
Meet me all by break of day.
              Exeunt [Oberon, Titania, and train].

PUCK [to the audience]

If we shadows have offended,
Think but this, and all is mended,
That you have but slumbered here   420
While these visions did appear.
And this weak and idle theme,
No more yielding but a dream,   423
Gentles, do not reprehend.
If you pardon, we will mend.   425
And, as I am an honest Puck,
If we have unearnèd luck
Now to scape the serpent's tongue,   428
We will make amends ere long;
Else the Puck a liar call.
So, good night unto you all.
Give me your hands, if we be friends,   432
And Robin shall restore amends.   [Exit.] 433

368 heavy tired   369 fordone exhausted.   370 wasted brands
burned-out logs   376 Every . . . sprite every grave lets forth its ghost
379 triple Hecate's (Hecate ruled in three capacities: as Luna or Cynthia in heaven, as Diana on earth, and as Proserpina in hell.)
382 frolic merry.   385 behind from behind, or else like sweeping the
dirt under the carpet. (Robin Goodfellow was a household spirit who
helped good housemaids and punished lazy ones, but he could, of
course, be mischievous.)   392 rehearse recite

400 issue offspring.   create created   407 prodigious monstrous,
unnatural   410 consecrate consecrated   411 take his gait go his way
412 several separate   420 That . . . here i.e., that it is a "midsummer
night's dream"   423 No . . . but yielding no more than   425 mend
improve.   428 serpent's tongue i.e., hissing   432 Give . . . hands
Applaud   433 restore amends give satisfaction in return.

The Merchant of Venice

Although Shylock is the most prominent character in *The Merchant of Venice*, he takes part in neither the beginning nor the ending of the play. And, although the play's title might seem to suggest that he is the "merchant" of Venice, Shylock is, strictly speaking, a moneylender whose usury is portrayed as the very opposite of true commerce. His vengeful struggle to obtain a pound of flesh from Antonio contrasts with the various romantic episodes woven together in this play: Bassanio's choosing of Portia by means of the caskets, Gratiano's wooing of Nerissa, Jessica's elopement with Lorenzo, Lancelot Gobbo's changing of masters, and the episode of the rings. In all these stories, a Christian ethic of generosity, love, and risk-taking friendship is set in pointed contrast with a non-Christian ethic that is seen, from a Christian point of view, as grudging, resentful, and self-calculating. Yet this contrasting vision is made problematic by the deplorable behavior of some Christians. In stage productions today, Belmont and its inhabitants are apt to seem frivolous, pleasure-loving, hedonistic, and above all racist in their insular preference for their own economically and culturally privileged position. The play invites us to question the motives of Shylock's enemies. It makes us (today, at least, after the terrors of the German Holocaust) uncomfortable at the insularity of a Venetian ethic that has no genuine place for non-Christians or cultural outsiders. The most painful question of all, for us, is to wonder whether the play assumes for its own dramatic purposes a Christian point of view, however much it sees a genuine and understandable motive in Shylock's desire for revenge. The problem of divided sympathies is exacerbated because Shylock's structural function in the play is essentially that of the villain in a love comedy. His remorseless pursuit of Antonio darkens the mood of the play, and his overthrow signals the providential triumph of love and friendship, even though that triumph is not without its undercurrent of wry melancholy. Before we examine the painful issue of anti-Semitism more closely,

we need to establish the structural context of this love comedy as a whole.

Like many of Shakespeare's philosophical and festive comedies, *The Merchant of Venice* presents two contrasting worlds—one fantasy-like and the other marked by conflict and anxiety. To an extent, these contrasting worlds can be identified with the locations of Belmont and Venice. Belmont, to which the various happy lovers and their friends eventually retire, is a place of magic and romance. As its name implies, it is on a mountain, and it is reached by a journey across water. As often happens in fairy stories, on this mountain dwells a princess who must be won by means of a riddling contest. We usually see Belmont at night. Music surrounds it, and women preside over it. Even its caskets, houses, and rings are essentially feminine symbols. Venice, on the other hand, is a place of bustle and economic competition, seen most characteristically in the heat of the day. It lies low and flat, at a point where rivers reach the sea. Men preside over its contentious marketplace and its haggling law courts. Actually, the opposition of Venice and Belmont is not quite so clear-cut: Venice contains much compassionate friendship, whereas Belmont is subject to the arbitrary command of Portia's dead father. (Portia somewhat resembles Jessica in being imprisoned by her father's will.) Even though Portia descends to Venice in the angelic role of mercy giver, she also remains very human: sharp-tongued and even venomous in caricaturing her unwelcome wooers, crafty in her legal maneuvering, saucily prankish in her torturing of Bassanio about the rings. For all its warmth and generosity, Belmont is also the embodiment of an insular Christian culture that makes room for outsiders only when they convert to Christian mores. The traits that Shylock carries to an unpleasant extreme are needed in moderation by the Venetians, notably thrift, promise-keeping, and prudent self-interest; only when the Christians temper their penchant for reckless extravagance, legal sophistry or even theft, and risk-taking is a happy resolution possible. Nevertheless, the polarity of two contrasting localities and two groups of characters is vividly real in this play.

The play's opening scene, from which Shylock is excluded, sets forth the interrelated themes of friendship, romantic love, and risk or "hazard." The merchant who seemingly fulfills the title role, Antonio, is the victim of a mysterious melancholy. He is wealthy enough and surrounded by friends, but something is missing from his life. He assures his solicitous companions that he has no financial worries, for he has been too careful to trust all his cargoes to one sea vessel. Antonio, in fact, has no idea why he is so sad. The question is haunting. What is the matter? Perhaps the answer is to be found in a paradox: those who strive to prosper in the world's terms are doomed to frustration, not because prosperity will necessarily elude them, but because it will not satisfy the spirit. "You have too much respect upon the world," argues the carefree Gratiano. "They lose it that do buy it with much care" (1.1.74–5). Portia and Jessica, too, are at first afflicted by a melancholy that stems from the incompleteness of living isolated lives, with insufficient opportunities for love and sacrifice. They must learn, as Antonio learns with the help of his dear friend Bassanio, to seek happiness by daring to risk everything for friendship. Antonio's risk is most extreme: only when he has thrown away concern for his life can he discover what there is to live for.

At first, Bassanio's request for assistance seems just as materialistic as the worldliness from which Antonio suffers. Bassanio proposes to marry a rich young lady, Portia, in order to recoup his fortune lost through prodigality, and he needs money from Antonio so that he may woo Portia in proper fashion. She is "richly left," the heiress of a dead father, a golden fleece for whom this new Jason will make a quest. Bassanio's adventure is partly commercial. Yet his pilgrimage for Portia is magnanimous as well. The occasional modern practice of playing Bassanio and Portia as cynical antiheroes of a "black" comedy points up the problematic character of their materialism and calculation, but it gives only one aspect of the portrayal. Bassanio has lost his previous fortune through the amiable faults of reckless generosity and a lack of concern for financial prudence. The money he must now borrow, and the fortune he hopes to acquire, are to him no more than a means to carefree happiness. Although Portia's rich dowry is a strong consideration, he describes her also as "fair and, fairer than that word,/Of wondrous virtues" (1.1.162–3). Moreover, he enjoys the element of risk in wooing her. It is like shooting a second arrow in order to recover one that has been lost—double or nothing. This gamble, or "hazard," involves risk for Antonio as well as for Bassanio, and it ultimately brings a double reward to them both—spiritual as well as financial. Unless one recognizes these aspects of Bassanio's quest, as well as the

clear fairy-tale quality with which Shakespeare deliberately invests this part of the plot, one cannot properly assess Bassanio's role in this romantic comedy.

Bassanio's quest for Portia can, in fact, never succeed until he disavows the very financial considerations that brought him to Belmont in the first place. This is the paradox of the riddle of the three caskets, an ancient parable stressing the need for choosing by true substance rather than by outward show. To choose "what many men desire," as the Prince of Morocco does, is to pin one's hopes on worldly wealth; to believe that one "deserves" good fortune, as the Prince of Aragon does, is to reveal a fatal pride in one's own merit. Bassanio perceives that, in order to win true love, he must "give and hazard all he hath" (2.7.9). He is not "deceived with ornament" (3.2.74). Just as Antonio must risk all for friendship, and just as Bassanio himself must later be willing to risk losing Portia for the sake of true friendship (in the episode of the rings), Bassanio must renounce worldly ambition and beauty before he can be rewarded with success. Paradoxically, only those who learn to subdue such worldly desires may then legitimately enjoy the world's pleasures. Only they have acknowledged the hierarchical subservience of the flesh to the spirit. These are the philosophical truisms of Renaissance Neoplatonism, depicting love as a chain or ladder from the basest carnality to the supreme love of God for humanity. On this ladder, perfect friendship and spiritual union are more sublimely Godlike than sexual fulfillment. This idealism may seem a strange doctrine for Bassanio the fortune hunter, but, actually, its conventional wisdom simply confirms his role as romantic hero. He and Portia are not denied worldly happiness or erotic pleasure; they are merely asked to give first thought to their Christian duty in marriage.

For Portia, marriage represents both a gain and a loss. She can choose only by her dead father's will; the patriarchal system, according to which a woman is given in marriage by her father to a younger man, is seemingly able to extend its control even beyond the grave. The prospect of marrying the Prince of Morocco or the Prince of Aragon dismays her, and yet she persists in her vow of obedience and is eventually rewarded by the man of her choice. It is as though the benign father knew how to set the terms of choice in such a way that the "lottery" of the caskets would turn out right for her. When she accepts Bassanio, too, she must make a difficult choice, for in legal terms she makes Bassanio master over everything she owns. Portia is at once spirited and submissive, able to straighten out Venice's legal tangles when all the men have failed and yet ready to call Bassanio her lord. Her teasing him about the ring is a sign that she will make demands of him in marriage, but it is a testing that cannot produce lasting disharmony so long as Bassanio is truly loyal. Portia is, from Bassanio's male point of view, the perfect woman: humanly attainable and yet never seriously threatening. Guided by her, Bassanio makes the potentially hazardous transition from the male-oriented friendships of Venice (especially with Antonio) to heterosexual union. Portia is more fortunate than Jessica, who must break with her faith and her father in order to find marital happiness. The two women are alike, however, in that they experience the play's central paradox of losing the world in order to gain the world. Through them, we see that this paradox illuminates the casket episode, the struggle for the pound of flesh, the elopement of Jessica, the ring episode, and even the comic foolery of Lancelot Gobbo.

Shylock, in his quest for the pound of flesh, represents, as seen from a Christian point of view, a denial of all the paradoxical truths just described. As a usurer, he refuses to lend money interest-free in the name of friendship. Instead of taking risks, he insists on his bond. He spurns mercy and demands strict justice. By calculating all his chances too craftily, he appears to win at first but must eventually lose all. He has "too much respect upon the world" (1.1.74). His God is the Old Testament God of Moses, the God of wrath, the God of the Ten Commandments, with their forbidding emphasis on "Thou shalt not." (This oversimplified contrast between Judaism and Christianity was commonplace in Shakespeare's time.) Shylock abhors stealing but admires equivocation as a means of out-maneuvering a competitor; he approvingly cites Jacob's ruse to deprive Laban of his sheep (1.3.69–88). Any tactic is permissible so long as it falls within the realm of legality and contract.

Shylock's ethical outlook, then, justifies both usury and the old dispensation of the Jewish law. The two are philosophically combined, just as usury and Judaism had become equated in the popular imagination of Renaissance Europe. Even though lending at interest was becoming increasingly necessary and common, old prejudices against it still persisted. Angry moralists pointed out that the New Testament had condemned usury and that Aristotle had described money as barren. To breed money was therefore regarded as unnatural. Usury was considered sinful because it did not involve the usual risks of commerce; the lender was assured against loss of his principal by the posting of collateral and, at the same time, was sure to earn a handsome interest. The usurer seemed to be getting something for nothing. For these reasons, usury was sometimes declared illegal. Its practitioners were viewed as corrupt and grasping, hated as misers. In some European countries, Jews were permitted to practice this un-Christian living (and permitted to do very little else) and then, hypocritically, were detested for performing un-Christian deeds. Ironically, the moneylenders of England were Christians, and few Jews were to be found in any professions. Nominally excluded since Edward I's reign, the Jews had returned in small numbers to London but did not practice their Judaism openly.

They attended Anglican services as required by law and then worshiped in private, relatively undisturbed by the authorities. Shylock may not be based on observation from London life. He is derived from continental tradition and reflects a widespread conviction that Jews and usurers were alike in being un-Christian and sinister.

Shylock is unquestionably sinister, even if he also invites sympathy. He bears an "ancient grudge" against Antonio simply because Antonio is "a Christian." We recognize in Shylock the archetype of the supposed Jew who wishes to kill a Christian and obtain his flesh. In early medieval anti-Semitic legends of this sort, the flesh thus obtained was imagined to be eaten ritually during Passover. Because some Jews had once persecuted Christ, all were unfairly presumed to be implacable enemies of all Christians. These anti-Semitic superstitions were likely to erupt into hysteria at any time, as in 1594 when Dr. Roderigo Lopez, a Portuguese Jewish physician, was accused of having plotted against the life of Queen Elizabeth and of Don Antonio, pretender to the Portuguese throne. Christopher Marlowe's *The Jew of Malta* was revived for this occasion, enjoying an unusually successful run of fifteen performances, and scholars have often wondered if Shakespeare's play was not written under the same impetus. On this score, the evidence is inconclusive, and the play might have been written any time between 1594 and 1598 (when it is mentioned by Francis Meres), but, in any case, Shakespeare has made no attempt to avoid the anti-Semitic nature of his story.

To offset the portrayal of Jewish villainy, however, the play also dramatizes the possibility of conversion to Christianity, suggesting that Judaism is more a matter of benighted faith than of ethnic origin. Converted Jews were not new on the stage: they had appeared in medieval cycle drama, in the Croxton *Play of the Sacrament* (late fifteenth century), and more recently in *The Jew of Malta*, in which Barabas' daughter Abigail falls in love with a Christian and eventually becomes a nun. Shylock's daughter Jessica similarly embraces Christianity as Lorenzo's wife and is received into the happy comradeship of Belmont. Shylock is forced to accept Christianity, presumably for the benefit of his eternal soul (though today we find this deeply offensive, and it is sometimes cut from stage productions). Earlier in the play, Antonio repeatedly indicates his willingness to befriend Shylock if the latter will only give up usury, and he is even cautiously hopeful when Shylock offers him an interest-free loan: "The Hebrew will turn Christian; he grows kind" (1.3.177). To be sure, Antonio's denunciation of Shylock's usurious Judaism has been vehement and personal; we learn that he has spat on Shylock's gaberdine and kicked him as one would kick a dog. This violent disapproval offers no opportunity for the toleration of cultural and religious differences that we expect today from people of good will, but at least Antonio is prepared to accept Shylock if Shylock will embrace the Christian faith and its ethical responsibilities. Whether the play itself endorses Antonio's Christian point of view as normative or insists on a darker reading by making us uneasy with intolerance is a matter of unceasing critical debate. Quite possibly, the play's power to disturb emanates—at least in part—from the dramatic conflict of irreconcilable sets of values.

To Antonio, then, as well as to other Venetians, true Christianity is both an absolute good from which no deviation is possible without evil and a state of faith to which aliens may turn by abjuring the benighted creeds of their ancestors. By this token, the Prince of Morocco is condemned to failure in his quest for Portia, not so much because he is black as because he is an infidel, one who worships "blind fortune" and therefore chooses a worldly rather than a spiritual reward. Although Portia pertly dismisses him with "Let all of his complexion choose me so" (2.7.79), she professes earlier to find him handsome and agrees that he should not be judged by his complexion (2.1.13–22). Unless she is merely being hypocritical, she means by her later remark that black-skinned people are generally infidels, just as Jews are as a group un-Christian. Such pejorative thinking about persons as types is no doubt distressing and suggests—at least to a modern audience—the cultural limitation of Portia's view, but, in any case, it shows her to be no less well disposed toward black suitors than toward others who are also alien. She is glad not to be won by the Prince of Aragon because he, too, though nominally a Christian, is too self-satisfied and proud. All persons, therefore, may aspire to truly virtuous conduct, and those who choose virtue are equally blessed; however, the terms of defining that ideal in this play are essentially Christian. Jews and Blacks may rise spiritually only by abandoning their pagan creeds for the new dispensation of charity and forgiveness.

The superiority of Christian teaching to the older Jewish dispensation was, of course, a widely accepted notion of Shakespeare's time. After all, these were the years when people fought and died to maintain their religious beliefs. Today, the notion of a single true church is less widely held, and we have difficulty understanding why anyone would wish to force conversion on Shylock. Modern productions find it tempting to portray Shylock as a victim of bigotry and to put great stress on his heartrending assertions of his humanity: "Hath not a Jew eyes? . . . If you prick us, do we not bleed?" (3.1.56–62). Shylock does indeed suffer from his enemies, and his sufferings add a tortured complexity to this play—even, one suspects, for an Elizabethan audience. Those who profess Christianity must surely examine their own motives and conduct. Is it right to steal treasure from Shylock's house along with his eloped daughter? Is it considerate of Jessica and Lorenzo to squander Shylock's turquoise ring, the gift of his wife Leah, on a monkey? Does Shylock's vengeful insistence on law justify the quibbling counter-

measures devised by Portia even as she piously declaims about mercy? Do Shylock's misfortunes deserve the mirthful parodies of Solanio ("My daughter! Oh, my ducats!") or the hostile jeering of Gratiano at the conclusion of the trial? Because he stands outside Christian faith, Shylock can provide a perspective whereby we see the hypocrisies of those who profess a higher ethical code. Nevertheless, Shylock's compulsive desire for vengeance according to an Old Testament code of an eye for an eye cannot be justified by the wrongdoings of any particular Christian. In the play's control of an ethical point of view, such deeds condemn the doer rather than undermine the Christian standards of true virtue as ideally expressed. Shakespeare humanizes Shylock by portraying him as a believable and sensitive man, and he shows much that is to be regretted in Shylock's Christian antagonists, but he also allows Shylock to place himself in the wrong by his refusal to forgive his enemies.

Shylock thus loses everything through his effort to win everything on his own terms. His daughter, Jessica, by her elopement, follows an opposite course. She characterizes her father's home as "hell," and she resents being locked up behind closed windows. Shylock detests music and the sounds of merriment; Jessica's new life in Belmont is immersed in music. He is old, suspicious, miserly; she is young, loving, adventurous. Most important, she seems to be at least part Christian when we first see her. As Lancelot jests half in earnest, "If a Christian did not play the knave and get thee, I am much deceived" (2.3.11–12). Her removal from Shylock's house involves theft, and her running from Venice is, she confesses, an "unthrift love." Paradoxically, however, she sees this recklessness as of more blessed effect than her father's legalistic caution. As she says, "I shall be saved by my husband. He hath made me a Christian" (3.5.17–18).

Lancelot Gobbo's clowning offers a similarly paradoxical comment on the tragedy of Shylock. Lancelot debates whether or not to leave Shylock's service in terms of a soul struggle between his conscience and the devil (2.2.1–29). Conscience bids him stay, for service is a debt, a bond, an obligation, whereas abandonment of one's indenture is a kind of rebellion or stealing away. Yet Shylock's house is "hell" to Lancelot as it is to Jessica. Comparing his new master with his old, Lancelot observes to Bassanio, "You have the grace of God, sir, and he hath enough." Service with Bassanio involves imprudent risks, since Bassanio is a spendthrift. The miserly Shylock rejoices to see the ever hungry Lancelot, this "huge feeder," wasting the substance of a hated Christian. Once again, however, Shylock will lose everything in his grasping quest for security. Another spiritual renewal occurs when Lancelot encounters his old and nearly blind father (2.2). In a scene echoing the biblical stories of the Prodigal Son and of Jacob and Esau, Lancelot teases the old man with false rumors of Lancelot's own death in order to make their reunion seem all the more unexpected and precious. The illusion of loss gives way to joy: Lancelot is, in language adapted from the liturgy, "your boy that was, your son that is, your child that shall be."

In the episode of the rings, we encounter a final playful variation on the paradox of winning through losing. Portia and Nerissa cleverly present their new husbands with a cruel choice: disguised as a doctor of law and his clerk, who have just saved the life of Antonio from Shylock's wrath, the two wives ask nothing more for their services than the rings they see on the fingers of Bassanio and Gratiano. The two husbands, who have vowed never to part with these wedding rings, must therefore choose between love and friendship. Portia knows well enough that Bassanio's obedience to the Neoplatonic ideal of disinterested friendship is an essential part of his virtue. Just as he previously renounced beauty and riches before he could deserve Portia, he must now risk losing her for friendship's sake. The testing of the husbands' constancy does border at times on gratuitous harshness and exercise of power, for it deals with the oldest of masculine nightmares: cuckoldry. Wives are not without weapons in the struggle for control in marriage, and Portia and Nerissa enjoy trapping their new husbands in a no-win situation. Still, the threat is easily resolved by the dispelling of farcically mistaken identities. The young men have been tricked into bestowing their rings on their wives for a second time in the name of perfect friendship, thereby confirming a relationship that is both platonic and fleshly. As Gratiano bawdily points out in the play's last line, the ring is both a spiritual and a sexual symbol of marriage. The resolution of this illusory quarrel also brings to an end the merry battle of the sexes between wives and husbands. Having hinted at the sorts of misunderstandings that afflict even the best of human relationships and having proved themselves wittily able to torture and deceive their husbands, Portia and Nerissa submit at last to the patriarchal norms of their age and to the authority of Bassanio and Gratiano.

Bassanio's marriage to Portia represents a heterosexual fulfillment of their courtship that leaves Antonio without a partner at the play's end. He is, to be sure, included in the camaraderie of Belmont, but a part of the sacrifice he has made for Bassanio is to give that young man the freedom and means to marry as he chooses. Antonio's attachment for Bassanio is a deeply loving one, and is sometimes portrayed as homosexual in modern productions. The force of Antonio's attachment to Bassanio should not be underestimated. At the same time, he does appear to be truly willing for the young man to marry. In this sense, the marriage represents a completion in which friendship and love are fully complementary. Heterosexual union is, in this play and in Shakespearean comedy generally, a dominant and theatrically conventional resolution; but it is so without denying that there

are other forms of human happiness. Whether or not Antonio is entirely content with his final role as a kind of benign older friend we cannot be sure, but his pronouncements in the final act are all aimed at encouraging the harmony between husband and wife that he has risked his life to enable.

As defined by the accepted notions of gender relations in Shakespeare's time, then, all appears to be in harmony in Belmont. The disorders of Venice have been left far behind, however imperfectly they may have been resolved. Jessica and Lorenzo contrast their present happiness with the sufferings of less fortunate lovers of long ago: Troilus and Cressida, Pyramus and Thisbe, Aeneas and Dido, Jason and Medea. The tranquil joy found in Belmont is attuned to the music of the spheres, the singing of the "young-eyed cherubins" (5.1.62), although with a proper Christian humility the lovers also realize that the harmony of immortal souls is infinitely beyond their comprehension. Bound in by the grossness of the flesh, "this muddy vesture of decay" (5.1.64), they can only reach toward the bliss of eternity through music and the perfect friendship of true love. Even in their final joy, accordingly, the lovers find an incompleteness that lends a wistful and slightly melancholy reflective tone to the play's ending. That sense of imperfection is accentuated for us by our awareness that the play's serious problems of gender relations, friendship, and anti-Semitism have by no means been fully resolved; the final concord is one that arises out of discord. Even so, this concluding sense of the unavoidable incompleteness of all human life is of a very different order from that earlier melancholy of isolation and lack of commitment experienced by Portia, Jessica, Antonio, and others.

In performance, the play has prompted both hostile and genuinely sympathetic responses for Shylock. The traditional anti-Semitic interpretation in early stage history manifested itself, for instance, in the performance of George Frederick Cooke in 1803–1804, "bent with age and ugly with mental deformity, grinning with deadly malice, with the venom of his heart congealed in the expression of his countenance, sullen, morose, gloomy, inflexible" (these are William Hazlitt's words). Still other renditions made use of the red wig and hooked nose of the stereotypical stage Jew that associated Shylock with Judas Iscariot. Conversely, Edmund Kean, in 1814, evoked such sympathy as to make the Christians in the play seem hypocrites by comparison. Henry Irving in 1879, and Beerbohm Tree in 1908, combined a kind of ancient dignity with pathos. George C. Scott, at the New York Shakespeare Festival in 1962, acted Shylock as a persecuted and desperate man surrounded by powerful enemies. Laurence Olivier's anguished Shylock (1970, subsequently televised) showed up the Christians as complacent members of a bigoted Venetian social world of privilege and exclusivity. A production in Weimar, Germany, in 1995, commemorating the fiftieth anniversary of the liberation of the concentration camp at nearby Buchenwald, captured what is so horrendously problematic in the play by imagining what it would be like if enacted by German officers and guards amusing themselves with amateur theatricals during wartime and assigning three Jewish inmates to the roles of Shylock, Tubal, and Jessica. Perhaps no Shakespeare play raises more painful issues today for us to think hard about than *The Merchant of Venice.*

The Merchant of Venice

[*Dramatis Personae*

THE DUKE OF VENICE
ANTONIO, *a merchant of Venice*
BASSANIO, *his friend, suitor to Portia*
GRATIANO, *a follower of Bassanio, in love with Nerissa*
SOLANIO, ⎫ *friends to Antonio*
SALERIO, ⎭ *and Bassanio*
LORENZO, *in love with Jessica*
LEONARDO, *servant to Bassanio*

PORTIA, *a rich heiress of Belmont*
NERISSA, *her waiting-gentlewoman*
BALTHASAR, *servant to Portia*
STEPHANO, *servant to Portia*

THE PRINCE OF MOROCCO, *suitor to Portia*
THE PRINCE OF ARAGON, *suitor to Portia*
A MESSENGER *to Portia*

SHYLOCK, *a rich Jew*
JESSICA, *his daughter*
TUBAL, *a Jew, Shylock's friend*
LANCELOT GOBBO, *a clown, servant to Shylock and then to Bassanio*
OLD GOBBO, *Lancelot's father*

Magnificoes of Venice, Officers of the Court of Justice, Jailor, Servants to Portia, and other Attendants

SCENE: *Partly at Venice and partly at Belmont, the seat of Portia*]

[1.1]

Enter Antonio, Salerio, and Solanio.

ANTONIO
  In sooth, I know not why I am so sad.   1
  It wearies me, you say it wearies you;
  But how I caught it, found it, or came by it,
  What stuff 'tis made of, whereof it is born,
  I am to learn;   5
  And such a want-wit sadness makes of me   6
  That I have much ado to know myself.

SALERIO
  Your mind is tossing on the ocean,
  There where your argosies with portly sail,   9
  Like signors and rich burghers on the flood,   10
  Or as it were the pageants of the sea,   11
  Do overpeer the petty traffickers   12
  That curtsy to them, do them reverence,   13
  As they fly by them with their woven wings.   14

SOLANIO
  Believe me, sir, had I such venture forth,   15
  The better part of my affections would

1.1. Location: A street in Venice.
1 In sooth Truly.   **sad** morose, dismal-looking.   **5 am to learn** have yet to learn   **6 such … of me** such sadness makes me so distracted, lacking in good sense

9 argosies large merchant ships. (So named from *Ragusa*, the modern city of Dubrovnik.)   **portly** majestic   **10 signors** gentlemen.   **flood** sea   **11 pageants** mobile stages used in plays or processions **12 overpeer** look down upon   **13 curtsy** i.e., bob up and down, or lower topsails in token of respect (*reverence*)   **14 woven wings** canvas sails.   **15 venture forth** investment at risk

I have a mind presages me such thrift   175
That I should questionless be fortunate.

ANTONIO

Thou know'st that all my fortunes are at sea;
Neither have I money nor commodity   178
To raise a present sum. Therefore go forth.   179
Try what my credit can in Venice do;
That shall be racked even to the uttermost   181
To furnish thee to Belmont, to fair Portia.
Go presently inquire, and so will I,   183
Where money is, and I no question make   184
To have it of my trust or for my sake.   *Exeunt.*   185

❖

[1.2]

Enter Portia with her waiting woman, Nerissa.

PORTIA   By my troth, Nerissa, my little body is aweary   1
of this great world.

NERISSA   You would be, sweet madam, if your miseries   3
were in the same abundance as your good fortunes
are; and yet, for aught I see, they are as sick that surfeit   5
with too much as they that starve with nothing. It is
no mean happiness, therefore, to be seated in the   7
mean. Superfluity comes sooner by white hairs, but   8
competency lives longer.   9

PORTIA   Good sentences, and well pronounced.   10

NERISSA   They would be better if well followed.

PORTIA   If to do were as easy as to know what were
good to do, chapels had been churches and poor
men's cottages princes' palaces. It is a good divine that   14
follows his own instructions. I can easier teach twenty
what were good to be done than to be one of the
twenty to follow mine own teaching. The brain may
devise laws for the blood, but a hot temper leaps o'er   18
a cold decree; such a hare is madness, the youth, to
skip o'er the meshes of good counsel, the cripple. But   20
this reasoning is not in the fashion to choose me a   21
husband. Oh, me, the word "choose"! I may neither   22
choose who I would nor refuse who I dislike; so is the
will of a living daughter curbed by the will of a dead   24
father. Is it not hard, Nerissa, that I cannot choose one
nor refuse none?

NERISSA   Your father was ever virtuous, and holy men
at their death have good inspirations; therefore the

lottery that he hath devised in these three chests of
gold, silver, and lead, whereof who chooses his mean-   30
ing chooses you, will no doubt never be chosen by
any rightly but one who you shall rightly love. But   32
what warmth is there in your affection towards any of
these princely suitors that are already come?

PORTIA   I pray thee, overname them, and as thou nam-   35
est them I will describe them; and according to my
description level at my affection.   37

NERISSA   First, there is the Neapolitan prince.

PORTIA   Ay, that's a colt indeed, for he doth nothing but   39
talk of his horse, and he makes it a great appropriation   40
to his own good parts that he can shoe him him-   41
self. I am much afeard my lady his mother played false
with a smith.

NERISSA   Then is there the County Palatine.   44

PORTIA   He doth nothing but frown, as who should say,   45
"An you will not have me, choose." He hears merry   46
tales and smiles not. I fear he will prove the weeping   47
philosopher when he grows old, being so full of un-   48
mannerly sadness in his youth. I had rather be mar-   49
ried to a death's-head with a bone in his mouth than
to either of these. God defend me from these two!

NERISSA   How say you by the French lord, Monsieur   52
Le Bon?

PORTIA   God made him, and therefore let him pass for a
man. In truth, I know it is a sin to be a mocker, but
he! Why, he hath a horse better than the Neapolitan's,
a better bad habit of frowning than the Count Palatine;
he is every man in no man. If a throstle sing, he   58
falls straight a-capering. He will fence with his own   59
shadow. If I should marry him, I should marry twenty
husbands. If he would despise me, I would forgive
him, for if he love me to madness, I shall never re-   62
quite him.

NERISSA   What say you, then, to Falconbridge, the   64
young baron of England?

PORTIA   You know I say nothing to him, for he understands not me, nor I him. He hath neither Latin,
French, nor Italian, and you will come into the court   68
and swear that I have a poor pennyworth in the Eng-   69
lish. He is a proper man's picture, but alas, who can   70
converse with a dumb show? How oddly he is suited!   71
I think he bought his doublet in Italy, his round hose   72

---

175 **presages** i.e., that presages.   **thrift** profit and good fortune
178 **commodity** merchandise   179 **a present sum** ready money.
181 **racked** stretched   183 **presently** immediately   184 **no question
make** have no doubt   185 **of my trust** on the basis of my credit as a
merchant.   **sake** i.e., personal sake.
1.2. Location: Belmont. Portia's house.
1 **troth** faith   3 **would be** would have reason to be (weary)
5 **surfeit** overindulge   7 **mean** small. (With a pun; see next note.)
7–8 **in the mean** having neither too much nor too little.   8 **comes
sooner by** acquires sooner   9 **competency** modest means   10 **sentences** maxims.   **pronounced** delivered.   14 **divine** clergyman
18 **blood** (Thought of as a chief agent of the passions, which in turn
were regarded as the enemies of reason.)   20 **meshes** nets. (Used
here for hunting hares.)   **good counsel, the cripple** (Wisdom is portrayed as old and no longer agile.)   20–2 **But . . . husband** But this
talk is not the way to help me choose a husband.   24 **will . . . will**
volition . . . testament

30 **who** whoever.   **his** i.e., the father's   32 **rightly** correctly . . . **rightly** truly   35 **overname them** name them over   37 **level** aim,
guess   39 **colt** i.e., wanton and foolish young man. (With a punning
appropriateness to his interest in horses.)   40 **appropriation** addition
41 **good parts** accomplishments   44 **County Palatine** a count entitled
to supreme jurisdiction in his province.   45 **as who should say** as
one might say   46 **An** If.   **choose** i.e., do as you please.   47–8 **the
weeping philosopher** i.e., Heraclitus of Ephesus, a melancholic and
retiring philosopher of about 500 B.C., often contrasted with Democri-
tus, the "laughing philosopher"   49 **sadness** melancholy   52 **How
. . . by** What do you have to say about   58 **he is . . . no man** i.e., he
borrows aspects from everyone but has no character of his own.
throstle thrush   59 **straight** at once   62 **if** even if   64 **say you . . . to**
do you say about. (But Portia wittily puns, in her reply, on the literal
sense of "speak to.")   68–70 **come . . . English** i.e., bear witness that I
can speak very little English.   70 **He . . . picture** i.e., He looks handsome   71 **dumb show** pantomime.   **suited** dressed.   72 **doublet**
upper garment corresponding to a jacket.   **round hose** short, puffed-
out breeches

in France, his bonnet in Germany, and his behavior 73
everywhere.

NERISSA   What think you of the Scottish lord, his
neighbor?

PORTIA   That he hath a neighborly charity in him, for he
borrowed a box of the ear of the Englishman and swore 78
he would pay him again when he was able. I think the
Frenchman became his surety and sealed under for an- 80
other. 81

NERISSA   How like you the young German, the Duke of
Saxony's nephew?

PORTIA   Very vilely in the morning, when he is sober,
and most vilely in the afternoon, when he is drunk.
When he is best he is a little worse than a man, and
when he is worst he is little better than a beast. An 87
the worst fall that ever fell, I hope I shall make shift to 88
go without him.

NERISSA   If he should offer to choose, and choose the 90
right casket, you should refuse to perform your father's
will if you should refuse to accept him.

PORTIA   Therefore, for fear of the worst, I pray thee, set
a deep glass of Rhenish wine on the contrary casket, 94
for if the devil be within and that temptation without, 95
I know he will choose it. I will do anything, Nerissa, 96
ere I will be married to a sponge.

NERISSA   You need not fear, lady, the having any of
these lords. They have acquainted me with their de-
terminations, which is indeed to return to their home
and to trouble you with no more suit, unless you may
be won by some other sort than your father's imposi- 102
tion depending on the caskets. 103

PORTIA   If I live to be as old as Sibylla, I will die as chaste 104
as Diana, unless I be obtained by the manner of my 105
father's will. I am glad this parcel of wooers are so rea- 106
sonable, for there is not one among them but I dote on
his very absence, and I pray God grant them a fair
departure.

NERISSA   Do you not remember, lady, in your father's
time, a Venetian, a scholar and a soldier, that came
hither in company of the Marquess of Montferrat?

PORTIA   Yes, yes, it was Bassanio—as I think, so was
he called.

NERISSA   True, madam. He, of all the men that ever my
foolish eyes looked upon was the best deserving a fair
lady.

PORTIA   I remember him well, and I remember him
worthy of thy praise.

Enter a Servingman.

How now, what news?

SERVINGMAN   The four strangers seek for you, madam, 121
to take their leave; and there is a forerunner come from 122
a fifth, the Prince of Morocco, who brings word the
Prince his master will be here tonight.

PORTIA   If I could bid the fifth welcome with so good
heart as I can bid the other four farewell, I should be
glad of his approach. If he have the condition of a saint 127
and the complexion of a devil, I had rather he should 128
shrive me than wive me. 129
Come, Nerissa. [*To Servingman*] Sirrah, go before. 130
Whiles we shut the gate upon one wooer, another
knocks at the door.   *Exeunt.*

[1.3]

Enter Bassanio with Shylock the Jew.

SHYLOCK   Three thousand ducats, well.   1

BASSANIO   Ay, sir, for three months.

SHYLOCK   For three months, well.

BASSANIO   For the which, as I told you, Antonio shall
be bound.

SHYLOCK   Antonio shall become bound, well.

BASSANIO   May you stead me? Will you pleasure me? 7
Shall I know your answer?

SHYLOCK   Three thousand ducats for three months and
Antonio bound.

BASSANIO   Your answer to that.

SHYLOCK   Antonio is a good man.   12

BASSANIO   Have you heard any imputation to the
contrary?

SHYLOCK   Ho, no, no, no, no! My meaning in saying he
is a good man is to have you understand me that he is
sufficient. Yet his means are in supposition. He hath an 17
argosy bound to Tripolis, another to the Indies. I understand, moreover, upon the Rialto, he hath a third 19
at Mexico, a fourth for England, and other ventures he
hath squandered abroad. But ships are but boards, 21
sailors but men. There be land rats and water rats,
water thieves and land thieves—I mean pirates—and
then there is the peril of waters, winds, and rocks. The
man is, notwithstanding, sufficient. Three thousand
ducats. I think I may take his bond.

BASSANIO   Be assured you may.   27

SHYLOCK   I will be assured I may; and that I may be 28
assured, I will bethink me. May I speak with Antonio?

---

121 **four** (Nerissa actually names six suitors; possibly a sign of revision or the author's early draft.)   122 **forerunner** herald   127 **condition** disposition, character   128 **complexion of a devil** (Devils were thought to be black; but *complexion* can also mean "temperament," "disposition.")   129 **shrive me** pardon me, excuse me from having to be wooed. (Literally, act as my confessor and give absolution.)
130 **Sirrah** (Form of address to social inferior.)
1.3. Location: Venice. A public place.
1 **ducats** gold coins   7 **stead** supply, assist.   **pleasure** oblige
12 **good** (Shylock means "solvent," a good credit risk; Bassanio interprets it in the moral sense.)   17 **sufficient** i.e., a good security.   **in supposition** doubtful, uncertain.   19 **the Rialto** the merchants' exchange in Venice and the center of commercial activity   21 **squandered** scattered   27, 28 **assured** (Bassanio means that Shylock may trust Antonio, whereas Shylock means that he will obtain legal assurances.)

---

73 **bonnet** hat   78 **borrowed** received. (But with a play on the idea of something that must be repaid.)   80–1 **became . . . another** offered to back up the Scottish lord and promised (with as solemn a vow as if he were signing and sealing a document) to add a blow of his own. (An allusion to the age-old alliance of the French and the Scots against the English.)   87 **An** If   88 **fall** befall.   **make shift** manage   90 **offer** undertake   94 **Rhenish wine** a German white wine from the Rhine Valley.   **contrary** i.e., wrong   95 **if** even if   96 **it** i.e., the tempting red wine.   102 **sort** means. (With perhaps a suggestion too of "casting or drawing of lots.")   102–3 **imposition** command, charge   104 **Sibylla** the Cumaean Sibyl, to whom Apollo gave as many years as there were grains in her handful of sand   105 **Diana** goddess of chastity and of the hunt   106 **parcel** assembly, group

BASSANIO   If it please you to dine with us.

SHYLOCK   Yes, to smell pork, to eat of the habitation
which your prophet the Nazarite conjured the devil   32
into. I will buy with you, sell with you, talk with you,
walk with you, and so following, but I will not eat   34
with you, drink with you, nor pray with you. What
news on the Rialto? Who is he comes here?

Enter Antonio.

BASSANIO   This is Signor Antonio.

SHYLOCK [*aside*]
How like a fawning publican he looks!   38
I hate him for he is a Christian,   39
But more for that in low simplicity   40
He lends out money gratis and brings down   41
The rate of usance here with us in Venice.   42
If I can catch him once upon the hip,   43
I will feed fat the ancient grudge I bear him.   44
He hates our sacred nation, and he rails,   45
Even there where merchants most do congregate,
On me, my bargains, and my well-won thrift,
Which he calls interest. Cursèd be my tribe
If I forgive him!

BASSANIO   Shylock, do you hear?

SHYLOCK   I am debating of my present store,   50
And, by the near guess of my memory,
I cannot instantly raise up the gross   52
Of full three thousand ducats. What of that?
Tubal, a wealthy Hebrew of my tribe,
Will furnish me. But soft, how many months   55
Do you desire? [*To Antonio*] Rest you fair, good
signor!
Your Worship was the last man in our mouths.   57

ANTONIO
Shylock, albeit I neither lend nor borrow
By taking nor by giving of excess,   59
Yet, to supply the ripe wants of my friend,   60
I'll break a custom. [*To Bassanio*] Is he yet possessed   61
How much ye would?   62

SHYLOCK   Ay, ay, three thousand ducats.

ANTONIO   And for three months.

SHYLOCK
I had forgot—three months, you told me so.
Well then, your bond. And let me see—but hear
you,
Methought you said you neither lend nor borrow
Upon advantage.

ANTONIO   I do never use it.   68

SHYLOCK
When Jacob grazed his uncle Laban's sheep—   69
This Jacob from our holy Abram was,   70
As his wise mother wrought in his behalf,
The third possessor; ay, he was the third—   72

ANTONIO
And what of him? Did he take interest?

SHYLOCK
No, not take interest, not as you would say
Directly interest. Mark what Jacob did.
When Laban and himself were compromised   76
That all the eanlings which were streaked and pied   77
Should fall as Jacob's hire, the ewes, being rank,   78
In end of autumn turnèd to the rams,
And when the work of generation was   80
Between these woolly breeders in the act,
The skillful shepherd peeled me certain wands,   82
And in the doing of the deed of kind   83
He stuck them up before the fulsome ewes,   84
Who then conceiving did in eaning time   85
Fall parti-colored lambs, and those were Jacob's.   86
This was a way to thrive, and he was blest;
And thrift is blessing, if men steal it not.   88

ANTONIO
This was a venture, sir, that Jacob served for,   89
A thing not in his power to bring to pass,
But swayed and fashioned by the hand of heaven.
Was this inserted to make interest good?   92
Or is your gold and silver ewes and rams?

SHYLOCK
I cannot tell. I make it breed as fast.   94
But note me, signor—

ANTONIO   Mark you this, Bassanio,
The devil can cite Scripture for his purpose.   96
An evil soul producing holy witness
Is like a villain with a smiling cheek,
A goodly apple rotten at the heart.
Oh, what a goodly outside falsehood hath!

SHYLOCK
Three thousand ducats. 'Tis a good round sum.
Three months from twelve, then let me see, the rate—

ANTONIO
Well, Shylock, shall we be beholding to you?   103

SHYLOCK
Signor Antonio, many a time and oft
In the Rialto you have rated me   105
About my moneys and my usances.
Still have I borne it with a patient shrug,

---

32 Nazarite Nazarene. (For the reference to Christ's casting evil spirits into a herd of swine, see Matthew 8:30–2, Mark 5:1–13, and Luke 8:32–3.)   **34 so following** so forth   **38 publican** Roman tax gatherer (a term of opprobrium; see Luke 18:9–14); or, innkeeper   **39 for** because   **40 low simplicity** humble foolishness   **41 gratis** without charging interest   **42 usance** usury, interest   **43 upon the hip** i.e., at my mercy. (A figure of speech from wrestling; see Genesis 32:24–9.)   **44 fat** until fatted for the kill   **45 our sacred nation** i.e., the Hebrew people   **50 I am . . . store** I am considering my current supply of money   **52 gross** total   **55 soft** i.e., wait a minute   **57 Your . . . mouths** i.e., We were just speaking of you. (But with ominous connotation of devouring; compare line 44.)   **59 excess** interest   **60 ripe wants** pressing needs   **61 possessed** informed   **62 ye would** you want.   **68 advantage** interest.

69 Jacob (See Genesis 27, 30:25–43.)   **70 Abram** Abraham   **72 third** i.e., after Abraham and Isaac.   **possessor** i.e., of the birthright of which, with the help of Rebecca, he was able to cheat Esau, his elder brother   **76 compromised** agreed   **77 eanlings** young lambs or kids.   **pied** spotted   **78 hire** wages, share.   **rank** in heat   **80 work of generation** mating   **82 peeled . . . wands** i.e., partly stripped the bark of some sticks. (*Me* is used colloquially.)   **83 deed of kind** i.e., copulation   **84 fulsome** lustful, well-fed   **85 eaning** lambing   **86 Fall** give birth to   **88 thrift** thriving, profit   **89 venture . . . for** uncertain commercial venture on which Jacob risked his wages   **92 inserted . . . good** brought in to justify the practice of usury.   **94 I cannot tell** i.e., I don't know about that.   **96 devil . . . Scripture** (See Matthew 4:6.)   **103 beholding** beholden, indebted   **105 rated** berated, rebuked

For sufferance is the badge of all our tribe.   108
You call me misbeliever, cutthroat dog,
And spit upon my Jewish gaberdine,   110
And all for use of that which is mine own.
Well then, it now appears you need my help.
Go to, then. You come to me and you say,   113
"Shylock, we would have moneys"—you say so,
You, that did void your rheum upon my beard   115
And foot me as you spurn a stranger cur   116
Over your threshold. Moneys is your suit.   117
What should I say to you? Should I not say,
"Hath a dog money? Is it possible
A cur can lend three thousand ducats?" Or
Shall I bend low, and in a bondman's key,   121
With bated breath and whispering humbleness,   122
Say this:
"Fair sir, you spit on me on Wednesday last,
You spurned me such a day, another time
You called me dog, and for these courtesies
I'll lend you thus much moneys"?

ANTONIO
I am as like to call thee so again,   128
To spit on thee again, to spurn thee too.
If thou wilt lend this money, lend it not
As to thy friends, for when did friendship take
A breed for barren metal of his friend?   132
But lend it rather to thine enemy,   133
Who, if he break, thou mayst with better face   134
Exact the penalty.

SHYLOCK   Why, look you how you storm!
I would be friends with you and have your love,
Forget the shames that you have stained me with,
Supply your present wants, and take no doit   138
Of usance for my moneys, and you'll not hear me.
This is kind I offer.   140

BASSANIO   This were kindness.   141

SHYLOCK   This kindness will I show.
Go with me to a notary, seal me there
Your single bond; and, in a merry sport,   144
If you repay me not on such a day,
In such a place, such sum or sums as are
Expressed in the condition, let the forfeit
Be nominated for an equal pound   148
Of your fair flesh, to be cut off and taken
In what part of your body pleaseth me.

ANTONIO
Content, in faith. I'll seal to such a bond
And say there is much kindness in the Jew.

BASSANIO
You shall not seal to such a bond for me!
I'll rather dwell in my necessity.   154

ANTONIO
Why, fear not, man, I will not forfeit it.
Within these two months—that's a month before
This bond expires—I do expect return
Of thrice three times the value of this bond.

SHYLOCK
O father Abram, what these Christians are,
Whose own hard dealings teaches them suspect
The thoughts of others! Pray you, tell me this:
If he should break his day, what should I gain
By the exaction of the forfeiture?
A pound of man's flesh taken from a man
Is not so estimable, profitable neither,   165
As flesh of muttons, beefs, or goats. I say
To buy his favor I extend this friendship.
If he will take it, so; if not, adieu.   168
And for my love, I pray you, wrong me not.   169

ANTONIO
Yes, Shylock, I will seal unto this bond.

SHYLOCK
Then meet me forthwith at the notary's.
Give him direction for this merry bond,
And I will go and purse the ducats straight,
See to my house, left in the fearful guard   174
Of an unthrifty knave, and presently
I'll be with you.   Exit.

ANTONIO   Hie thee, gentle Jew.—   176
The Hebrew will turn Christian; he grows kind.

BASSANIO
I like not fair terms and a villain's mind.

ANTONIO
Come on. In this there can be no dismay;
My ships come home a month before the day.
                                                   [Exeunt.]

❖

[2.1]

[Flourish of cornets.] Enter [the Prince of]
Morocco, a tawny Moor all in white, and three
or four followers accordingly, with Portia, Nerissa, and their train.

MOROCCO
Mislike me not for my complexion,
The shadowed livery of the burnished sun,   2
To whom I am a neighbor and near bred.   3
Bring me the fairest creature northward born,
Where Phoebus' fire scarce thaws the icicles,   5
And let us make incision for your love

---

108 **sufferance** endurance   110 **gaberdine** loose outer garment like a
cape or mantle   113 **Go to** (An exclamation of impatience or annoyance.)   115 **rheum** spittle   116 **spurn** kick   117 **suit** request.
121 **bondman's key** serf's tone of voice   122 **bated** subdued
128 **like** likely   132 **A breed . . . metal** offspring from money, which
cannot naturally breed. (One of the oldest arguments against usury
was that it was thereby "unnatural.")   **of** from   133 **to** as if to
134 **Who** from whom.   **break** fail to pay on time   138 **doit** a Dutch
coin of very small value   140 **kind** kindly   141 **were** would be (if
seriously offered)   144 **single bond** bond signed alone without other
security; unconditional. (Shylock pretends the *condition*, line 147, is
only a joke.)   148 **nominated for** named, specified as.   **equal** exact

154 **dwell** remain   165 **estimable** valuable   168 **so** well and good
169 **wrong me not** do not think evil of me.   174 **fearful** to be mistrusted   176 **gentle** gracious, courteous. (With a play on "gentile.")
2.1. Location: Belmont. Portia's house.
0.3 *accordingly* similarly (i.e., dressed in white and dark-skinned like
Morocco)   **2 shadowed livery** i.e., dark complexion, worn as though
it were a costume of the sun's servants   **3 near bred** closely related.
5 Phoebus' i.e., the sun's

To prove whose blood is reddest, his or mine.   7
I tell thee, lady, this aspect of mine   8
Hath feared the valiant. By my love I swear,   9
The best-regarded virgins of our clime
Have loved it too. I would not change this hue,
Except to steal your thoughts, my gentle queen.

PORTIA
In terms of choice I am not solely led
By nice direction of a maiden's eyes;   14
Besides, the lott'ry of my destiny
Bars me the right of voluntary choosing.
But if my father had not scanted me,   17
And hedged me by his wit to yield myself   18
His wife who wins me by that means I told you,   19
Yourself, renownèd prince, then stood as fair   20
As any comer I have looked on yet
For my affection.

MOROCCO   Even for that I thank you.   22
Therefore, I pray you, lead me to the caskets
To try my fortune. By this scimitar
That slew the Sophy and a Persian prince,   25
That won three fields of Sultan Solyman,   26
I would o'erstare the sternest eyes that look,   27
Outbrave the heart most daring on the earth,
Pluck the young sucking cubs from the she-bear,
Yea, mock the lion when 'a roars for prey,   30
To win thee, lady. But alas the while!
If Hercules and Lichas play at dice   32
Which is the better man, the greater throw
May turn by fortune from the weaker hand.
So is Alcides beaten by his page,
And so may I, blind Fortune leading me,
Miss that which one unworthier may attain,
And die with grieving.

PORTIA   You must take your chance,
And either not attempt to choose at all
Or swear before you choose, if you choose wrong
Never to speak to lady afterward
In way of marriage. Therefore be advised.   42

MOROCCO
Nor will not. Come, bring me unto my chance.   43

PORTIA
First, forward to the temple. After dinner   44
Your hazard shall be made.

MOROCCO   Good fortune then!
To make me blest or cursed'st among men.

                          [Cornets, and] exeunt.

                              ❖

7 **reddest** (Red blood was regarded as a sign of courage.)   8 **aspect**
visage   9 **feared** frightened   14 **nice direction** careful guidance
17 **scanted** limited   18 **wit** wisdom   18–19 **yield . . . who** give
myself to be the wife of him who   20 **then . . . fair** would then have
looked as attractive and stood as fair a chance. (With a play on "fair-
skinned.")   22 **For my** of gaining my   25 **Sophy** Shah of Persia
26 **fields** battles.   **Solyman** a Turkish sultan ruling from 1520 to 1566
27 **o'erstare** outstare   30 **'a** he   32 **Lichas** a page of Hercules
(Alcides). See the note for 3.2.55.   42 **be advised** take warning, consider.   43 **Nor will not** i.e., Nor indeed will I violate the oath.   44 **to
the temple** i.e., in order to take the oaths.

[2.2]

Enter [Lancelot] the clown, alone.

LANCELOT   Certainly my conscience will serve me to   1
run from this Jew my master. The fiend is at mine
elbow and tempts me, saying to me, "Gobbo, Lancelot
Gobbo, good Lancelot," or "Good Gobbo," or "Good
Lancelot Gobbo, use your legs, take the start, run
away." My conscience says, "No, take heed, honest
Lancelot, take heed, honest Gobbo," or, as aforesaid,
"Honest Lancelot Gobbo, do not run; scorn running
with thy heels." Well, the most courageous fiend bids   9
me pack. " Fia!" says the fiend. "Away!" says the fiend. 10
"For the heavens, rouse up a brave mind," says the   11
fiend, "and run." Well, my conscience, hanging about   12
the neck of my heart, says very wisely to me, "My hon-   13
est friend Lancelot, being an honest man's son," or
rather an honest woman's son—for indeed my father
did something smack, something grow to, he had a   16
kind of taste—well, my conscience says, "Lancelot,   17
budge not." "Budge," says the fiend "Budge not," says
my conscience. "Conscience," say I, "you counsel
well." "Fiend," say I, "you counsel well." To be ruled by
my conscience, I should stay with the Jew my master,
who, God bless the mark, is a kind of devil; and to run 22
away from the Jew, I should be ruled by the fiend, who,
saving your reverence, is the devil himself. Certainly
the Jew is the very devil incarnation; and, in my con-   25
science, my conscience is but a kind of hard conscience
to offer to counsel me to stay with the Jew. The fiend
gives the more friendly counsel. I will run, fiend. My
heels are at your commandment. I will run.

Enter Old Gobbo, with a basket.

GOBBO   Master young man, you, I pray you, which is   30
the way to master Jew's?
LANCELOT   [*aside*]   Oh, heavens, this is my true-
begotten father, who, being more than sand-blind,   33
high-gravel-blind, knows me not. I will try confusions   34
with him.
GOBBO   Master young gentleman, I pray you, which is
the way to master Jew's?
LANCELOT   Turn up on your right hand at the next
turning, but at the next turning of all on your left;
marry, at the very next turning, turn of no hand, but   40
turn down indirectly to the Jew's house.

2.2. **Location: Venice. A street.**
0.1 *clown* (1) country bumpkin (2) comic type in an Elizabethan acting company   1 **serve** permit   9 **with thy heels** i.e., emphatically.
(With a pun on the literal sense.)   10 **pack** begone.   **Fia!** i.e., Via,
away!   11 **For the heavens** i.e., In heaven's name   12–13 **hanging . . .
heart** i.e., timidly   16–17 **did something . . . taste** i.e., had a tendency to lechery   22 **God . . . mark** (An expression by way of apology for
introducing something potentially offensive, as also in *saving your
reverence* in line 24.)   25 **incarnation** (Lancelot means "incarnate.")
30 **you** (Gobbo uses the formal *you* but switches to the familiar *thou*,
line 88, when he accepts Lancelot as his son.)   33 **sand-blind** dim-
sighted   34 **high-gravel-blind** blinder than sand-blind. (A term
seemingly invented by Lancelot.)   **try confusions** (Lancelot's blunder for "try conclusions," i.e., experiment, though his error is comically apt.)   40 **marry** i.e., by the Virgin Mary, indeed. (A mild
interjection.)   **of no hand** neither right nor left

GOBBO   By God's sonties, 'twill be a hard way to hit.   42
Can you tell me whether one Lancelot, that dwells
with him, dwell with him or no?

LANCELOT   Talk you of young Master Lancelot? [*Aside*]
Mark me now; now will I raise the waters.—Talk you   46
of young Master Lancelot?

GOBBO   No master, sir, but a poor man's son. His father,   48
though I say't, is an honest exceeding poor man and,
God be thanked, well to live.   50

LANCELOT   Well, let his father be what 'a will, we talk   51
of young Master Lancelot.

GOBBO   Your Worship's friend, and Lancelot, sir.   53

LANCELOT   But I pray you, ergo, old man, ergo, I be-   54
seech you, talk you of young Master Lancelot?

GOBBO   Of Lancelot, an't please Your Mastership.

LANCELOT   Ergo, Master Lancelot. Talk not of Master
Lancelot, father, for the young gentleman, according   58
to Fates and Destinies and such odd sayings, the Sis-   59
ters Three and such branches of learning, is indeed   60
deceased, or, as you would say in plain terms, gone to
heaven.

GOBBO   Marry, God forbid! The boy was the very staff
of my age, my very prop.

LANCELOT   Do I look like a cudgel or a hovel post, a   65
staff, or a prop? Do you know me, father?

GOBBO   Alack the day, I know you not, young gentleman. But I pray you, tell me, is my boy, God rest his
soul, alive or dead?

LANCELOT   Do you not know me, father?

GOBBO   Alack, sir, I am sand-blind. I know you not.

LANCELOT   Nay, indeed, if you had your eyes you
might fail of the knowing me; it is a wise father that   73
knows his own child. Well, old man, I will tell you   74
news of your son. [*He kneels.*] Give me your blessing.
Truth will come to light; murder cannot be hid long; a
man's son may, but in the end truth will out.

GOBBO   Pray you, sir, stand up. I am sure you are not
Lancelot, my boy.

LANCELOT   Pray you, let's have no more fooling about
it, but give me your blessing. I am Lancelot, your   81
boy that was, your son that is, your child that shall be.   82

GOBBO   I cannot think you are my son.

LANCELOT   I know not what I shall think of that; but I
am Lancelot, the Jew's man, and I am sure Margery
your wife is my mother.

GOBBO   Her name is Margery indeed. I'll be sworn, if
thou be Lancelot, thou art mine own flesh and blood.
Lord worshiped might he be, what a beard hast thou   89
got! Thou hast got more hair on thy chin than Dobbin
my fill horse has on his tail.   91

LANCELOT [*rising*]   It should seem then that Dobbin's
tail grows backward. I am sure he had more hair of   93
his tail than I have of my face when I last saw him.   94

GOBBO   Lord, how art thou changed! How dost thou and
thy master agree? I have brought him a present. How
'gree you now?

LANCELOT   Well, well; but for mine own part, as I have
set up my rest to run away, so I will not rest till   99
I have run some ground. My master's a very Jew. Give   100
him a present? Give him a halter! I am famished in his   101
service; you may tell every finger I have with my ribs.   102
Father, I am glad you are come. Give me your present   103
to one Master Bassanio, who indeed gives rare new   104
liveries. If I serve not him, I will run as far as God has   105
any ground. Oh, rare fortune! Here comes the man. To
him, father, for I am a Jew if I serve the Jew any longer.   107

Enter Bassanio, with [Leonardo and] a follower
or two.

BASSANIO   You may do so, but let it be so hasted that   108
supper be ready at the farthest by five of the clock. See   109
these letters delivered, put the liveries to making, and
desire Gratiano to come anon to my lodging.

[*Exit a Servant.*]

LANCELOT   To him, father.

GOBBO [*advancing*]   God bless Your Worship!

BASSANIO   Gramercy. Wouldst thou aught with me?   114

GOBBO   Here's my son, sir, a poor boy—   115

LANCELOT   Not a poor boy, sir, but the rich Jew's man,
that would, sir, as my father shall specify—

GOBBO   He hath a great infection, sir, as one would say,   118
to serve—

LANCELOT   Indeed, the short and the long is, I serve the
Jew, and have a desire, as my father shall specify—

GOBBO   His master and he, saving Your Worship's
reverence, are scarce cater-cousins—   123

LANCELOT   To be brief, the very truth is that the Jew,
having done me wrong, doth cause me, as my father,
being, I hope, an old man, shall frutify unto you—   126

GOBBO   I have here a dish of doves that I would bestow
upon Your Worship, and my suit is—

LANCELOT   In very brief, the suit is impertinent to   129
myself, as Your Worship shall know by this honest old
man, and, though I say it, though old man, yet poor
man, my father.

---

42 sonties little saints   **46 raise the waters** i.e., start tears.   **48 master**
(The title was applied to gentlefolk only.)   **50 well to live** prospering,
in good health.   **51 'a** he   **53 Your . . . Lancelot** (Again, Old Gobbo
denies that Lancelot is entitled to be called "Master.")   **54 ergo** therefore. (But Lancelot may use this Latin word with no particular meaning in mind.)   **58 father** (1) old man (2) father   **59–60 the Sisters**
Three the three Fates   **65 hovel post** post holding up a hovel or open
shed   **73–4 it is . . . child** (Reverses the proverb "It is a wise child
that knows his own father.")   **81–2 your . . . shall be** (Echoes the
Gloria from the Book of Common Prayer: "As it was in the beginning,
is now, and ever shall be.")   **89 beard** (Stage tradition has Old Gobbo
mistaking Lancelot's long hair for a beard.)   **91 fill horse** cart horse

93 grows backward grows at the wrong end.   **94 of** on   **99 set up**
my rest determined, risked all. (A metaphor from the card game
primero, in which a final wager is made, with a pun also on *rest* as
"place of residence.")   **not rest** i.e., not stop running. (More punning
on *rest*.)   **100 very** veritable.   **Jew** (1) Hebrew (2) grasping old
usurer.   **101 halter** hangman's noose.   **102 tell** count.   **tell . . . ribs**
(Comically reverses the usual saying of counting one's ribs with one's
fingers.)   **103 Give me** Give. (*Me* suggests "on my behalf.")
104 rare splendid   **105 liveries** uniforms or costumes for servants.
107 a Jew i.e., a villain. (Punning on the literal sense in *the Jew*. Compare with line 100.)   **108 hasted** hastened, hurried   **109 farthest** latest   **114 Gramercy** Many thanks.   **aught** anything   **115 poor**
(1) unfortunate (2) penniless (contrasted with *rich* in the next line)
118 infection (Blunder for "affection" or "inclination.")   **123 cater-**
cousins good friends   **126 frutify** (Lancelot may be trying to say
"fructify," but he means "certify" or "notify.")   **129 impertinent**
(Blunder for "pertinent.")

SHYLOCK   So do I his.

LANCELOT   And they have conspired together. I will
not say you shall see a masque, but if you do, then it
was not for nothing that my nose fell a-bleeding on
Black Monday last at six o'clock i'th' morning, falling   26
out that year on Ash Wednesday was four year in
th'afternoon.

SHYLOCK
What, are there masques? Hear you me, Jessica:
Lock up my doors, and when you hear the drum
And the vile squealing of the wry-necked fife,   31
Clamber not you up to the casements then,
Nor thrust your head into the public street
To gaze on Christian fools with varnished faces,   34
But stop my house's ears—I mean my casements.
Let not the sound of shallow fopp'ry enter
My sober house. By Jacob's staff I swear   37
I have no mind of feasting forth tonight.
But I will go.—Go you before me, sirrah.
Say I will come.

LANCELOT   I will go before, sir. [Aside to Jessica] Mistress, look out at window, for all this;
     There will come a Christian by,
     Will be worth a Jewess' eye.   [Exit.]

SHYLOCK
What says that fool of Hagar's offspring, ha?   45

JESSICA
His words were "Farewell, mistress," nothing else.

SHYLOCK
The patch is kind enough, but a huge feeder,   47
Snail-slow in profit, and he sleeps by day   48
More than the wildcat. Drones hive not with me;
Therefore I part with him, and part with him
To one that I would have him help to waste
His borrowed purse. Well, Jessica, go in.
Perhaps I will return immediately.
Do as I bid you. Shut doors after you.
Fast bind, fast find—   55
A proverb never stale in thrifty mind.   Exit.

JESSICA
Farewell, and if my fortune be not crossed,
I have a father, you a daughter, lost.   Exit.

❖

[2.6]

Enter the masquers, Gratiano and Salerio.

GRATIANO
This is the penthouse under which Lorenzo   1

Desired us to make stand.

SALERIO   His hour is almost past.

GRATIANO
And it is marvel he outdwells his hour,   4
For lovers ever run before the clock.

SALERIO
Oh, ten times faster Venus' pigeons fly   6
To seal love's bonds new-made than they are wont   7
To keep obligèd faith unforfeited.   8

GRATIANO
That ever holds. Who riseth from a feast   9
With that keen appetite that he sits down?
Where is the horse that doth untread again   11
His tedious measures with the unbated fire   12
That he did pace them first? All things that are
Are with more spirit chasèd than enjoyed.
How like a younger or a prodigal   15
The scarfèd bark puts from her native bay,   16
Hugged and embracèd by the strumpet wind!   17
How like the prodigal doth she return,
With overweathered ribs and ragged sails,   19
Lean, rent, and beggared by the strumpet wind!   20

Enter Lorenzo.

SALERIO
Here comes Lorenzo. More of this hereafter.

LORENZO
Sweet friends, your patience for my long abode,   22
Not I, but my affairs, have made you wait.
When you shall please to play the thieves for wives,
I'll watch as long for you then. Approach;   25
Here dwells my father Jew.—Ho! Who's within?   26

[Enter] Jessica, above [in boy's clothes].

JESSICA
Who are you? Tell me for more certainty,
Albeit I'll swear that I do know your tongue.

LORENZO   Lorenzo, and thy love.

JESSICA
Lorenzo, certain, and my love indeed,
For who love I so much? And now who knows
But you, Lorenzo, whether I am yours?   32

LORENZO
Heaven and thy thoughts are witness that thou art.

JESSICA [throwing down a casket]
Here, catch this casket. It is worth the pains.
I am glad 'tis night, you do not look on me,

---

26 Black Monday Easter Monday. (Lancelot's talk of omens is perhaps intentional gibberish, a parody of Shylock's fears.)   31 wry-
necked i.e., played with the musician's head awry; or possibly
comparing the fife's *vile squealing* to the call of the wryneck, a bird
with a high-pitched call and a writhing movement of head and neck
34 varnished faces i.e., painted masks   37 Jacob's staff (See Genesis
32:10 and Hebrews 11:21.)   45 Hagar's offspring (Hagar, a gentile
and Abraham's servant, gave birth to Ishmael; both mother and son
were cast out after the birth of Isaac.)   47 patch fool   48 profit profitable labor   55 Fast . . . find i.e., Keep your property secure and you
will always know where it is. (Proverbial.)
2.6. Location: Before Shylock's house, as in 2.5.
1 penthouse projecting roof or upper story of a house

4 it . . . hour i.e., it is surprising that he is late   6–8 Oh, ten . . . unforfeited i.e., Oh, lovers are ten times more alacritous in their first
pledge of love than in keeping faith in a long-term commitment.
(*Venus' pigeons* are the doves that draw her chariot.)   9 ever holds
always holds true.   11 untread retrace   12 measures paces
15 younger i.e., younger son, as in the parable of the Prodigal Son
(Luke 15). (Often emended to *younker*, youth.)   16 scarfèd bark sailing vessel festooned with flags or streamers   17 strumpet i.e., inconsistent, variable. (Likened metaphorically to the harlots with whom
the Prodigal Son wasted his fortune.)   19 overweathered ribs i.e.,
weather-beaten and leaking timbers   20 rent torn   22 your patience
i.e., I beg your patience.   abode delay   25 watch keep watch
26 father i.e., father-in-law   32 But you better than you

For I am much ashamed of my exchange.   36
But love is blind, and lovers cannot see
The pretty follies that themselves commit,   38
For if they could, Cupid himself would blush
To see me thus transformèd to a boy.

LORENZO
Descend, for you must be my torchbearer.

JESSICA
What, must I hold a candle to my shames?   42
They in themselves, good sooth, are too too light.   43
Why, 'tis an office of discovery, love,   44
And I should be obscured.

LORENZO   So are you, sweet,
Even in the lovely garnish of a boy.   46
But come at once,
For the close night doth play the runaway,   48
And we are stayed for at Bassanio's feast.   49

JESSICA
I will make fast the doors, and gild myself   50
With some more ducats, and be with you straight.
                         [Exit above.]

GRATIANO
Now, by my hood, a gentle and no Jew.   52

LORENZO
Beshrew me but I love her heartily,   53
For she is wise, if I can judge of her,
And fair she is, if that mine eyes be true,
And true she is, as she hath proved herself;
And therefore, like herself, wise, fair, and true,
Shall she be placèd in my constant soul.

         Enter Jessica [below].

What, art thou come? On, gentlemen, away!
Our masquing mates by this time for us stay.   60
             Exit [with Jessica and Salerio;
             Gratiano is about to follow them].

         Enter Antonio.

ANTONIO   Who's there?

GRATIANO   Signor Antonio?

ANTONIO
Fie, fie, Gratiano! Where are all the rest?
'Tis nine o'clock; our friends all stay for you.
No masque tonight. The wind is come about;
Bassanio presently will go aboard.
I have sent twenty out to seek for you.

GRATIANO
I am glad on 't. I desire no more delight
Than to be under sail and gone tonight.   *Exeunt.*

❖

[2.7]

[Flourish of cornets.] Enter Portia, with [the
Prince of] Morocco, and both their trains.

PORTIA
Go, draw aside the curtains and discover   1
The several caskets to this noble prince.   2
Now make your choice.   *[The curtains are drawn.]*

MOROCCO
The first, of gold, who this inscription bears,   4
"Who chooseth me shall gain what many men desire";
The second, silver, which this promise carries,
"Who chooseth me shall get as much as he deserves";
This third, dull lead, with warning all as blunt,   8
"Who chooseth me must give and hazard all he hath."
How shall I know if I do choose the right?

PORTIA
The one of them contains my picture, Prince.
If you choose that, then I am yours withal.   12

MOROCCO
Some god direct my judgment! Let me see,
I will survey th'inscriptions back again.
What says this leaden casket?
"Who chooseth me must give and hazard all he hath."
Must give—for what? For lead? Hazard for lead?
This casket threatens. Men that hazard all
Do it in hope of fair advantages.
A golden mind stoops not to shows of dross.   20
I'll then nor give nor hazard aught for lead.   21
What says the silver with her virgin hue?
"Who chooseth me shall get as much as he deserves."
As much as he deserves! Pause there, Morocco,
And weigh thy value with an even hand.   25
If thou be'st rated by thy estimation,   26
Thou dost deserve enough; and yet enough
May not extend so far as to the lady;
And yet to be afeard of my deserving
Were but a weak disabling of myself.   30
As much as I deserve? Why, that's the lady.
I do in birth deserve her, and in fortunes,
In graces, and in qualities of breeding;
But more than these, in love I do deserve.
What if I strayed no farther, but chose here?
Let's see once more this saying graved in gold: 36
"Who chooseth me shall gain what many men desire."
Why, that's the lady; all the world desires her.
From the four corners of the earth they come
To kiss this shrine, this mortal breathing saint.   40
The Hyrcanian deserts and the vasty wilds   41
Of wide Arabia are as throughfares now
For princes to come view fair Portia.

---

36 **exchange** change of clothes.   38 **pretty** ingenious, artful   42 **hold a candle** i.e., stand by and witness. (With a play on the idea of acting as torchbearer.)   43 **light** (1) immodest (2) illuminated.   44 **'tis . . . discovery** i.e., torchbearing is intended to shed light on matters   46 **garnish** outfit, trimmings   48 **close** dark, secretive.   **doth . . . runaway** i.e., is quickly passing   49 **stayed** waited   50 **gild** adorn. (Literally, cover with gold.)   52 **by my hood** (An asseveration.)   **gentle** gracious person. (With pun on "gentile," as at 2.4.34.)   53 **Beshrew** i.e., A mischief on. (A mild oath.)   60 **stay** wait. (Also in line 64.)

2.7. Location: Belmont. Portia's house.
0.2 *trains* followers   1 **discover** reveal   2 **several** different, various   4 **who** which   8 **dull** (1) dull-colored (2) blunt.   **all as blunt** as blunt as lead   12 **withal** with it.   20 **dross** worthless matter. (Literally, the impurities cast off in the melting down of metals.)   21 **nor give** neither give   25 **even** impartial   26 **estimation** worth   30 **disabling** underrating   36 **graved** engraved   40 **mortal breathing** living   41 **Hyrcanian** (Hyrcania was the country south of the Caspian Sea celebrated for its wildness.)   **vasty** vast

The watery kingdom, whose ambitious head
Spits in the face of heaven, is no bar   45
To stop the foreign spirits, but they come,   46
As o'er a brook, to see fair Portia.
One of these three contains her heavenly picture.
Is't like that lead contains her? 'Twere damnation   49
To think so base a thought; it were too gross   50
To rib her cerecloth in the obscure grave.   51
Or shall I think in silver she's immured,   52
Being ten times undervalued to tried gold?   53
Oh, sinful thought! Never so rich a gem
Was set in worse than gold. They have in England   55
A coin that bears the figure of an angel   56
Stamped in gold, but that's insculped upon;   57
But here an angel in a golden bed
Lies all within. Deliver me the key.
Here do I choose, and thrive I as I may!

PORTIA
There, take it, Prince; and if my form lie there,   61
Then I am yours.
                            [*He unlocks the golden casket.*]
MOROCCO   Oh, hell! What have we here?
A carrion Death, within whose empty eye   63
There is a written scroll! I'll read the writing.
[*He reads.*]
        "All that glisters is not gold;
        Often have you heard that told.
        Many a man his life hath sold
        But my outside to behold.   68
        Gilded tombs do worms infold.
        Had you been as wise as bold,
        Young in limbs, in judgment old,
        Your answer had not been inscrolled.   72
        Fare you well; your suit is cold."
    Cold, indeed, and labor lost.
    Then, farewell, heat, and welcome, frost!
Portia, adieu. I have too grieved a heart
To take a tedious leave. Thus losers part.   77
                    Exit [*with his train. Flourish of cornets.*]
PORTIA
A gentle riddance. Draw the curtains, go.
Let all of his complexion choose me so.   79
                    [*The curtains are closed, and*] *exeunt.*

❧

---

45 Spits (The image is of huge waves breaking at sea.)   **46 spirits** i.e.,
men of courage   **49 like** likely   **50 base** (1) ignoble (2) low in the
natural scale, as with lead, a *base* metal   **50–1 it were . . . grave** i.e., it
would be too gross an insult to inter her, as it were, wrapped in a
waxed cloth, in a lead casket.   **52 immured** enclosed, confined
53 Being . . . gold which has only one-tenth the value of assayed and
purified gold.   **55 set** fixed, as a precious stone, in a border of metal
56 coin i.e., the gold coin known as the *angel*, which bore the device
of the archangel Michael treading on the dragon   **57 insculped upon**
merely engraved upon the surface   **61 form** image   **63 carrion
Death** death's-head   **68 But** only   **72 inscrolled** i.e., written on this
scroll.   **77 part** depart.   **79 complexion** temperament (not merely
skin color)

[2.8]

Enter Salerio and Solanio.

SALERIO
Why, man, I saw Bassanio under sail.
With him is Gratiano gone along,
And in their ship I am sure Lorenzo is not.
SOLANIO
The villain Jew with outcries raised the Duke,   4
Who went with him to search Bassanio's ship.
SALERIO
He came too late. The ship was under sail.
But there the Duke was given to understand
That in a gondola were seen together
Lorenzo and his amorous Jessica.
Besides, Antonio certified the Duke
They were not with Bassanio in his ship.
SOLANIO
I never heard a passion so confused,   12
So strange, outrageous, and so variable
As the dog Jew did utter in the streets:
"My daughter! Oh, my ducats! Oh, my daughter!
Fled with a Christian! Oh, my Christian ducats!
Justice! The law! My ducats, and my daughter!
A sealèd bag, two sealèd bags of ducats,
Of double ducats, stol'n from me by my daughter!
And jewels, two stones, two rich and precious
    stones,
Stol'n by my daughter! Justice! Find the girl!
She hath the stones upon her, and the ducats."
SALERIO
Why, all the boys in Venice follow him,
Crying his stones, his daughter, and his ducats.   24
SOLANIO
Let good Antonio look he keep his day,   25
Or he shall pay for this.
SALERIO   Marry, well remembered.
I reasoned with a Frenchman yesterday,   27
Who told me, in the narrow seas that part   28
The French and English, there miscarrièd
A vessel of our country richly fraught.   30
I thought upon Antonio when he told me,
And wished in silence that it were not his.
SOLANIO
You were best to tell Antonio what you hear.
Yet do not suddenly, for it may grieve him.
SALERIO
A kinder gentleman treads not the earth.
I saw Bassanio and Antonio part.
Bassanio told him he would make some speed
Of his return; he answered, "Do not so.
Slubber not business for my sake, Bassanio,   39
But stay the very riping of the time;   40

2.8. Location: Venice. A street.
4 raised roused   **12 passion** passionate outburst   **24 stones** (In the
boys' jeering cry, the *two stones* suggest testicles; see line 20.)   **25 look . . .
day** see to it that he repays his loan on time   **27 reasoned** talked
28 narrow seas English Channel   **30 fraught** freighted.   **39 Slubber
not business** Don't do the business hastily and badly   **40 But . . . time**
i.e., pursue your business at Belmont until it is brought to completion

And for the Jew's bond which he hath of me,   41
Let it not enter in your mind of love.   42
Be merry, and employ your chiefest thoughts
To courtship and such fair ostents of love   44
As shall conveniently become you there."
And even there, his eye being big with tears,   46
Turning his face, he put his hand behind him,   47
And with affection wondrous sensible   48
He wrung Bassanio's hand; and so they parted.

SOLANIO
I think he only loves the world for him.   50
I pray thee, let us go and find him out
And quicken his embracèd heaviness   52
With some delight or other.

SALERIO   Do we so.   *Exeunt.*

❋

[2.9]

Enter Nerissa and a Servitor.

NERISSA
Quick, quick, I pray thee, draw the curtain straight.   1
The Prince of Aragon hath ta'en his oath,
And comes to his election presently.   3
                   [*The curtains are drawn back.*]

[*Flourish of cornets.*] *Enter [the Prince of]*
Aragon, his train, and Portia.

PORTIA
Behold, there stand the caskets, noble Prince.
If you choose that wherein I am contained,
Straight shall our nuptial rites be solemnized;
But if you fail, without more speech, my lord,
You must be gone from hence immediately.

ARAGON
I am enjoined by oath to observe three things:
First, never to unfold to anyone   10
Which casket 'twas I chose; next, if I fail
Of the right casket, never in my life
To woo a maid in way of marriage;
Lastly,
If I do fail in fortune of my choice,
Immediately to leave you and be gone.

PORTIA
To these injunctions everyone doth swear
That comes to hazard for my worthless self.

ARAGON
And so have I addressed me. Fortune now   19
To my heart's hope! Gold, silver, and base lead.
"Who chooseth me must give and hazard all he hath."

You shall look fairer ere I give or hazard.
What says the golden chest? Ha, let me see:
"Who chooseth me shall gain what many men desire."
What many men desire! That "many" may be meant
By the fool multitude, that choose by show,   26
Not learning more than the fond eye doth teach,   27
Which pries not to th'interior, but like the martlet   28
Builds in the weather on the outward wall,   29
Even in the force and road of casualty.   30
I will not choose what many men desire,
Because I will not jump with common spirits   32
And rank me with the barbarous multitudes.
Why then, to thee, thou silver treasure-house!
Tell me once more what title thou dost bear:
"Who chooseth me shall get as much as he deserves."
And well said too; for who shall go about
To cozen fortune, and be honorable   38
Without the stamp of merit? Let none presume   39
To wear an undeservèd dignity.
Oh, that estates, degrees, and offices   41
Were not derived corruptly, and that clear honor
Were purchased by the merit of the wearer!
How many then should cover that stand bare?   44
How many be commanded that command?   45
How much low peasantry would then be gleaned   46
From the true seed of honor, and how much honor   47
Picked from the chaff and ruin of the times
To be new-varnished? Well, but to my choice: 49
"Who chooseth me shall get as much as he deserves."
I will assume desert. Give me a key for this,
And instantly unlock my fortunes here.
                        [*He opens the silver casket.*]

PORTIA
Too long a pause for that which you find there.

ARAGON
What's here? The portrait of a blinking idiot,
Presenting me a schedule! I will read it.   55
How much unlike art thou to Portia!
How much unlike my hopes and my deservings!
"Who chooseth me shall have as much as he
     deserves."
Did I deserve no more than a fool's head?
Is that my prize? Are my deserts no better?

PORTIA
To offend and judge are distinct offices   61
And of opposèd natures.

ARAGON   What is here?   62

41 **for** as for   42 **of** preoccupied with   44 **ostents** expressions, shows
46 **there** thereupon, then   47 **behind him** (Antonio turns away in
tears while extending his hand back to Bassanio.)   48 **affection wondrous sensible** wondrously sensitive and keen emotion   50 **he . . .
him** i.e., Bassanio is all he lives for.   52 **quicken . . . heaviness**
lighten the sorrow he has embraced
2.9. Location: Belmont. Portia's house.
0.1 *Servitor* servant   1 **straight** at once.   3 **election presently** choice
immediately.   10 **unfold** disclose   19 **addressed me** prepared myself
(by this swearing).

26 **By** for, to signify   27 **fond** foolish   28 **martlet** swift   29 **in**
exposed to   30 **force . . . casualty** power and path of mischance.
32 **jump** agree   38 **cozen** cheat   39 **stamp** seal of approval
41 **estates, degrees** status, social rank   44 **cover . . . bare** i.e., wear
hats (of authority) who now stand bareheaded.   45 **How . . . command?** How many then should be servants that are now masters?
46 **gleaned** culled out and discarded   47 **the true seed of honor** i.e.,
persons of noble descent   49 **new-varnished** i.e., having the luster of
their true nobility restored to them.   55 **schedule** written paper.
61–2 **To offend . . . natures** i.e., You have no right, having submitted
your case to judgment, to attempt to judge your own case; or, it is not
for me to say, since I've been the indirect cause of your discomfiture.

[*He reads.*]"The fire seven times tried this;   63
    Seven times tried that judgment is
    That did never choose amiss.
    Some there be that shadows kiss;   66
    Such have but a shadow's bliss.
    There be fools alive, iwis,   68
    Silvered o'er, and so was this.   69
    Take what wife you will to bed;
    I will ever be your head.   71
    So begone; you are sped."   72

Still more fool I shall appear   73
By the time I linger here.   74
With one fool's head I came to woo,
But I go away with two.
Sweet, adieu. I'll keep my oath,
Patiently to bear my wroth.   78
                [*Exeunt Aragon and train.*]

PORTIA
Thus hath the candle singed the moth.
Oh, these deliberate fools! When they do choose,   80
They have the wisdom by their wit to lose.

NERISSA
The ancient saying is no heresy:
Hanging and wiving goes by destiny.

PORTIA   Come, draw the curtain, Nerissa.
                [*The curtains are closed.*]

Enter Messenger.

MESSENGER
Where is my lady?

PORTIA   Here. What would my lord?   85

MESSENGER
Madam, there is alighted at your gate
A young Venetian, one that comes before
To signify th'approaching of his lord,
From whom he bringeth sensible regreets,   89
To wit, besides commends and courteous breath,   90
Gifts of rich value. Yet I have not seen   91
So likely an ambassador of love.
A day in April never came so sweet,
To show how costly summer was at hand,   94
As this fore-spurrer comes before his lord.   95

PORTIA
No more, I pray thee. I am half afeard
Thou wilt say anon he is some kin to thee,
Thou spend'st such high-day wit in praising him.   98
Come, come, Nerissa, for I long to see
Quick Cupid's post that comes so mannerly.   100

NERISSA
Bassanio, Lord Love, if thy will it be!   *Exeunt.*

❦

[3.1]

[Enter] Solanio and Salerio.

SOLANIO   Now, what news on the Rialto?

SALERIO   Why, yet it lives there unchecked that Anto-nio   2
hath a ship of rich lading wrecked on the narrow   3
seas—the Goodwins, I think they call the place, a   4
very dangerous flat, and fatal, where the carcasses of   5
many a tall ship lie buried, as they say, if my gossip   6
Report be an honest woman of her word.   7

SOLANIO   I would she were as lying a gossip in that as
ever knapped ginger or made her neighbors believe   9
she wept for the death of a third husband. But it is
true, without any slips of prolixity or crossing the   11
plain highway of talk, that the good Antonio, the   12
honest Antonio—oh, that I had a title good enough to
keep his name company!—

SALERIO   Come, the full stop.   15

SOLANIO   Ha, what sayest thou? Why, the end is, he
hath lost a ship.

SALERIO   I would it might prove the end of his losses.

SOLANIO   Let me say "amen" betimes, lest the devil   19
cross my prayer, for here he comes in the likeness of   20
a Jew.

Enter Shylock.

How now, Shylock, what news among the merchants?

SHYLOCK   You knew, none so well, none so well as
you, of my daughter's flight.

SALERIO   That's certain. I for my part knew the tailor
that made the wings she flew withal.   26

SOLANIO   And Shylock for his own part knew the bird
was fledge, and then it is the complexion of them all   28
to leave the dam.   29

SHYLOCK   She is damned for it.

SALERIO   That's certain, if the devil may be her judge.

SHYLOCK   My own flesh and blood to rebel!

SOLANIO   Out upon it, old carrion! Rebels it at these   33
years?   34

SHYLOCK   I say my daughter is my flesh and my blood.

---

63 The fire . . . this This silver has been seven times tested and purified   **66 shadows** illusions   **68 iwis** certainly   **69 Silvered o'er** i.e.,
with silver hair and so apparently wise   **71 I . . . head** i.e., you will
always have a fool's head, be a fool.   **72 sped** done for.   **73–4 Still . . .
here** i.e., I shall seem all the greater fool for wasting any more time
here.   **78 wroth** sorrow, unhappy lot (a variant of *ruth*); or, anger.
80 deliberate reasoning, calculating   **85 my lord** (A jesting response
to "my lady.")   **89 sensible regreets** tangible gifts, greetings
90 commends greetings.   **breath** speech   **91 Yet** Heretofore
94 costly lavish, rich   **95 fore-spurrer** herald, harbinger
98 high-day holiday (i.e., extravagant)   **100 post** messenger

3.1. Location: Venice. A street.
2 yet . . . unchecked i.e., a rumor is spreading undenied   **3–4 the narrow seas** the English Channel, as at 2.8.28   **4 Goodwins** Goodwin
Sands, off the Kentish coast near the Thames estuary   **5 flat** shoal,
sandbank   **6 tall** gallant   **6-7 gossip Report** i.e., Dame Rumor
9 knapped nibbled   **11 slips of prolixity** lapses into long-winded-
ness; or, long-winded lies. *Slips* may be the cuttings or offshoots of
tediousness.   **11–12 crossing . . . talk** deviating from honest, plain
speech   **15 Come . . . stop** Finish your sentence; rein in your tongue
as a horse is checked in its manage.   **19 betimes** while there is yet
time   **20 cross** thwart; make the sign of the cross following
26 the wings . . . withal i.e., the disguise she escaped in. (With a play
on *wings* or ornamented shoulder flaps sewn on garments.)
28 fledge ready to fly.   **complexion** natural disposition, as at 2.7.79
29 dam mother.   **33–4 Rebels . . . years?** (Solanio pretends to interpret Shylock's cry about the rebellion of his own flesh and blood as
referring to his own carnal desires, his own erection.)

SALERIO   There is more difference between thy flesh and
hers than between jet and ivory, more between your   37
bloods than there is between red wine and Rhenish.   38
But tell us, do you hear whether Antonio have had any
loss at sea or no?

SHYLOCK   There I have another bad match! A bankrupt,   41
a prodigal, who dare scarce show his head on the
Rialto; a beggar, that was used to come so smug upon
the mart! Let him look to his bond. He was wont to   44
call me usurer. Let him look to his bond. He was wont
to lend money for a Christian courtesy. Let him look to
his bond.

SALERIO   Why, I am sure, if he forfeit, thou wilt not take
his flesh. What's that good for?

SHYLOCK   To bait fish withal. If it will feed nothing else,
it will feed my revenge. He hath disgraced me, and
hindered me half a million, laughed at my losses,
mocked at my gains, scorned my nation, thwarted my
bargains, cooled my friends, heated mine enemies;
and what's his reason? I am a Jew. Hath not a Jew
eyes? Hath not a Jew hands, organs, dimensions, senses, affections, passions? Fed with the same food, hurt
with the same weapons, subject to the same diseases,
healed by the same means, warmed and cooled by the
same winter and summer, as a Christian is? If you
prick us, do we not bleed? If you tickle us, do we not
laugh? If you poison us, do we not die? And if you
wrong us, shall we not revenge? If we are like you in
the rest, we will resemble you in that. If a Jew wrong
a Christian, what is his humility? Revenge. If a   65
Christian wrong a Jew, what should his sufferance be   66
by Christian example? Why, revenge. The villainy you
teach me I will execute, and it shall go hard but I will   68
better the instruction.

Enter a Man from Antonio.

MAN   Gentlemen, my master Antonio is at his house
and desires to speak with you both.

SALERIO   We have been up and down to seek him.   72

Enter Tubal.

SOLANIO   Here comes another of the tribe. A third
cannot be matched, unless the devil himself turn Jew.   74
Exeunt gentlemen [Solanio, Salerio, with Man].

SHYLOCK   How now, Tubal, what news from Genoa?
Hast thou found my daughter?

TUBAL   I often came where I did hear of her, but cannot
find her.

SHYLOCK   Why, there, there, there, there! A diamond
gone, cost me two thousand ducats in Frankfort! The   80
curse never fell upon our nation till now; I never felt it   81

till now. Two thousand ducats in that, and other
precious, precious jewels. I would my daughter were
dead at my foot, and the jewels in her ear! Would she
were hearsed at my foot, and the ducats in her coffin!   85
No news of them? Why, so—and I know not what's
spent in the search. Why, thou loss upon loss! The
thief gone with so much, and so much to find the
thief, and no satisfaction, no revenge! Nor no ill luck
stirring but what lights o' my shoulders, no sighs but
o' my breathing, no tears but o' my shedding.

TUBAL   Yes, other men have ill luck too. Antonio, as I
heard in Genoa—

SHYLOCK   What, what, what? Ill luck, ill luck?

TUBAL   Hath an argosy cast away, coming from Tripolis.   95

SHYLCOK   I thank God, I thank God. Is it true, is it true?

TUBAL   I spoke with some of the sailors that escaped the
wreck.

SHYLOCK   I thank thee, good Tubal. Good news, good
news! Ha, ha! Heard in Genoa?

TUBAL   Your daughter spent in Genoa, as I heard, one
night fourscore ducats.

SHYLOCK   Thou stick'st a dagger in me. I shall never see
my gold again. Fourscore ducats at a sitting? Fourscore ducats?

TUBAL   There came divers of Antonio's creditors in my
company to Venice that swear he cannot choose but
break.   108

SHYLOCK   I am very glad of it. I'll plague him, I'll torture
him. I am glad of it.

TUBAL   One of them showed me a ring that he had of
your daughter for a monkey.

SHYLOCK   Out upon her! Thou torturest me, Tubal. It
was my turquoise; I had it of Leah when I was a   114
bachelor. I would not have given it for a wilderness of
monkeys.

TUBAL   But Antonio is certainly undone.

SHYLOCK   Nay, that's true, that's very true. Go, Tubal,
fee me an officer; bespeak him a fortnight before. I will   119
have the heart of him if he forfeit, for were he out of
Venice I can make what merchandise I will. Go, Tubal,   121
and meet me at our synagogue. Go, good Tubal; at our
synagogue, Tubal.   *Exeunt [separately].*

❖

[3.2]

*Enter Bassanio, Portia, Gratiano, [Nerissa,]
and all their trains.*

PORTIA

I pray you, tarry. Pause a day or two
Before you hazard, for in choosing wrong   2
I lose your company. Therefore forbear awhile.
There's something tells me—but it is not love—
I would not lose you; and you know yourself
Hate counsels not in such a quality.   6

---

37 jet a black, hard mineral, here contrasted with the whiteness of
ivory and Jessica's fair complexion   **38 Rhenish** i.e., a German white
wine from the Rhine valley. (Salerio seems to prefer the white wine as
more refined than the red.)   **41 match** bargain.   **44 mart** marketplace, Rialto.   **65 what . . . Revenge** i.e., in what spirit does the Christian receive the injury, that of Christian humility? No, he seeks
revenge.   **66 his sufferance** the Jew's patient endurance   **68 it shall
. . . but** i.e., assuredly; unless difficulties intervene   **72 up and down**
i.e., everywhere   **74 matched** i.e., found to match them   **80–1 The
curse** God's curse (such as the plagues visited upon Egypt in Exodus
7–12)

85 hearsed coffined   **95 cast away** shipwrecked   **108 break** go bankrupt.   **114 Leah** Shylock's wife   **119 fee** hire.   **officer** bailiff.
bespeak engage   **121 make . . . I** I will drive whatever bargains I
please.
3.2. Location: Belmont. Portia's house.
2 in choosing if you choose   **6 quality** way, manner.

And there is such confusion in my powers
As, after some oration fairly spoke
By a belovèd prince, there doth appear
Among the buzzing pleasèd multitude,
Where every something being blent together
Turns to a wild of nothing save of joy
Expressed and not expressed. But when this ring
Parts from this finger, then parts life from hence.
Oh, then be bold to say Bassanio's dead!

NERISSA
My lord and lady, it is now our time,
That have stood by and seen our wishes prosper,
To cry, "good joy." Good joy, my lord and lady!

GRATIANO
My lord Bassanio and my gentle lady,
I wish you all the joy that you can wish—
For I am sure you can wish none from me.
And when Your Honors mean to solemnize
The bargain of your faith, I do beseech you
Even at that time I may be married too.

BASSANIO
With all my heart, so thou canst get a wife.

GRATIANO
I thank Your Lordship, you have got me one.
My eyes, my lord, can look as swift as yours.
You saw the mistress, I beheld the maid;
You loved, I loved; for intermission
No more pertains to me, my lord, than you.
Your fortune stood upon the caskets there,
And so did mine too, as the matter falls;
For wooing here until I sweat again,
And swearing till my very roof was dry
With oaths of love, at last, if promise last,
I got a promise of this fair one here
To have her love, provided that your fortune
Achieved her mistress.

PORTIA   Is this true, Nerissa?

NERISSA
Madam, it is, so you stand pleased withal.

BASSANIO
And do you, Gratiano, mean good faith?

GRATIANO   Yes, faith, my lord.

BASSANIO
Our feast shall be much honored in your marriage.

GRATIANO   We'll play with them the first boy for a thousand ducats.

NERISSA   What, and stake down?

GRATIANO   No, we shall ne'er win at that sport, and
stake down.

*Enter Lorenzo, Jessica, and Salerio, a messenger
from Venice.*

But who comes here? Lorenzo and his infidel?
What, and my old Venetian friend Salerio?

BASSANIO
Lorenzo and Salerio, welcome hither,
If that the youth of my new interest here
Have power to bid you welcome.—By your leave,
I bid my very friends and countrymen,
Sweet Portia, welcome.

PORTIA   So do I, my lord.
They are entirely welcome.

LORENZO
I thank Your Honor. For my part, my lord,
My purpose was not to have seen you here,
But, meeting with Salerio by the way,
He did entreat me, past all saying nay,
To come with him along.

SALERIO   I did, my lord,
And I have reason for it. Signor Antonio
Commends him to you.   [*He gives Bassanio a letter.*]

BASSANIO   Ere I ope his letter,
I pray you tell me how my good friend doth.

SALERIO
Not sick, my lord, unless it be in mind,
Nor well, unless in mind. His letter there
Will show you his estate.   [*Bassanio*] open[s] *the letter.*

GRATIANO [*indicating Jessica*]
Nerissa, cheer yond stranger, bid her welcome.
Your hand, Salerio. What's the news from Venice?
How doth that royal merchant, good Antonio?
I know he will be glad of our success.
We are the Jasons; we have won the fleece.

SALERIO
I would you had won the fleece that he hath lost.

PORTIA
There are some shrewd contents in yond same paper
That steals the color from Bassanio's cheek—
Some dear friend dead, else nothing in the world
Could turn so much the constitution
Of any constant man. What, worse and worse?
With leave, Bassanio; I am half yourself,
And I must freely have the half of anything
That this same paper brings you.

BASSANIO   O sweet Portia,
Here are a few of the unpleasant'st words
That ever blotted paper! Gentle lady,
When I did first impart my love to you,
I freely told you all the wealth I had
Ran in my veins, I was a gentleman;
And then I told you true. And yet, dear lady,

---

177 **powers** faculties   181–3 **Where . . . expressed** i.e., in which every individual utterance, being blended and confused, turns into a hubbub of joy.   187 **That** we who   191 **For . . . me** i.e., I'm sure I can't wish you any more joy than you could wish for yourselves, or, I'm sure your wishes for happiness cannot take away from my happiness.   195 **so** provided   198 **maid** (Nerissa is a lady-in-waiting, not a house servant.)   199 **intermission** delay (in loving)   202 **falls** falls out, happens   203 **sweat again** sweated repeatedly   204 **roof** roof of my mouth   205 **if promise last** i.e., if Nerissa's promise should last, hold out. (With a play on *last* and *at last*, "finally.")   209 **so** provided   213 **We'll . . . boy** We'll wager with them to see who has the first male heir   215 **stake down** cash placed in advance. (But Gratiano, in his reply, turns the phrase into a bawdy joke; *stake down* to him suggests a non-erect phallus.)

221 **youth . . . interest** i.e., newness of my household authority   223 **very true**   232 **Commends him** desires to be remembered   236 **estate** situation.   237 **stranger** alien   239 **royal merchant** i.e., chief among merchants   241 **Jasons . . . fleece** (Compare with 1.1.170–2.)   243 **shrewd** cursed, grievous   247 **constant** settled, not swayed by passion   248 **With leave** With your permission

Rating myself at nothing, you shall see
How much I was a braggart. When I told you
My state was nothing, I should then have told you   259
That I was worse than nothing; for indeed
I have engaged myself to a dear friend,
Engaged my friend to his mere enemy,   262
To feed my means. Here is a letter, lady,
The paper as the body of my friend,
And every word in it a gaping wound
Issuing lifeblood. But is it true, Salerio?
Hath all his ventures failed? What, not one hit?   267
From Tripolis, from Mexico, and England,
From Lisbon, Barbary, and India,
And not one vessel scape the dreadful touch
Of merchant-marring rocks?

SALERIO   Not one, my lord.   271
Besides, it should appear that if he had
The present money to discharge the Jew   273
He would not take it. Never did I know   274
A creature that did bear the shape of man
So keen and greedy to confound a man.   276
He plies the Duke at morning and at night,
And doth impeach the freedom of the state   278
If they deny him justice. Twenty merchants,
The Duke himself, and the magnificoes   280
Of greatest port have all persuaded with him,   281
But none can drive him from the envious plea   282
Of forfeiture, of justice, and his bond.

JESSICA
When I was with him I have heard him swear
To Tubal and to Chus, his countrymen,   285
That he would rather have Antonio's flesh
Than twenty times the value of the sum
That he did owe him; and I know, my lord,
If law, authority, and power deny not,
It will go hard with poor Antonio.

PORTIA [to Bassanio]
Is it your dear friend that is thus in trouble?

BASSANIO
The dearest friend to me, the kindest man,
The best-conditioned and unwearied spirit   293
In doing courtesies, and one in whom
The ancient Roman honor more appears
Than any that draws breath in Italy.

PORTIA   What sum owes he the Jew?

BASSANIO
For me, three thousand ducats.

PORTIA   What, no more?
Pay him six thousand, and deface the bond;   299
Double six thousand, and then treble that,
Before a friend of this description

Shall lose a hair through Bassanio's fault.
First go with me to church and call me wife,
And then away to Venice to your friend;
For never shall you lie by Portia's side
With an unquiet soul. You shall have gold
To pay the petty debt twenty times over.
When it is paid, bring your true friend along.
My maid Nerissa and myself meantime
Will live as maids and widows. Come, away!
For you shall hence upon your wedding day.
Bid your friends welcome, show a merry cheer;   312
Since you are dear bought, I will love you dear.   313
But let me hear the letter of your friend.

BASSANIO [reads] "Sweet Bassanio, my ships have all
miscarried, my creditors grow cruel, my estate is
very low, my bond to the Jew is forfeit; and since in
paying it, it is impossible I should live, all debts are
cleared between you and I if I might but see you at
my death. Notwithstanding, use your pleasure. If
your love do not persuade you to come, let not my
letter."

PORTIA
O love, dispatch all business, and begone!

BASSANIO
Since I have your good leave to go away,
I will make haste; but till I come again
No bed shall e'er be guilty of my stay,
Nor rest be interposer twixt us twain.   Exeunt.

❖

[3.3]

*Enter [Shylock] the Jew and Solanio and Antonio
and the Jailer.*

SHYLOCK
Jailer, look to him. Tell not me of mercy.
This is the fool that lent out money gratis.   2
Jailer, look to him.

ANTONIO   Hear me yet, good Shylock.

SHYLOCK
I'll have my bond. Speak not against my bond.
I have sworn an oath that I will have my bond.
Thou called'st me dog before thou hadst a cause,
But since I am a dog, beware my fangs.
The Duke shall grant me justice. I do wonder,
Thou naughty jailer, that thou art so fond   9
To come abroad with him at his request.   10

ANTONIO   I pray thee, hear me speak.

SHYLOCK
I'll have my bond. I will not hear thee speak.
I'll have my bond, and therefore speak no more.
I'll not be made a soft and dull-eyed fool,   14
To shake the head, relent, and sigh, and yield
To Christian intercessors. Follow not.
I'll have no speaking. I will have my bond.   *Exit Jew.*

---

259 **state** estate   262 **mere** absolute   267 **hit** success.   271 **merchant-marring** capable of damaging a merchant ship   273 **present** available. **discharge** pay off   274 **He** i.e., Shylock   276 **confound** destroy   278 **doth . . . state** i.e., calls in question the ability of Venice to defend legally the freedom of commerce of its citizens   280 **magnificoes** chief men of Venice   281 **port** dignity.   **persuaded** argued   282 **envious** malicious   285 **Chus** the Bishops' Bible spelling of *Cush*, son of Ham and grandson of Noah. *Tubal* was son of Japheth and grandson of Noah (Genesis 10:2, 6).   293 **best-conditioned** best-natured   299 **deface** erase

312 **cheer** countenance   313 **dear . . . dear** at great cost . . . dearly.   **3.3. Location: Venice. A street.**   2 **gratis** free (of interest).   9 **naughty** worthless, wicked.   **fond** foolish   10 **abroad** outside   14 **dull-eyed** easily duped

SOLANIO
  It is the most impenetrable cur
  That ever kept with men.

ANTONIO   Let him alone.   19
  I'll follow him no more with bootless prayers.   20
  He seeks my life. His reason well I know:
  I oft delivered from his forfeitures
  Many that have at times made moan to me;
  Therefore he hates me.

SOLANIO   I am sure the Duke
  Will never grant this forfeiture to hold.

ANTONIO
  The Duke cannot deny the course of law;
  For the commodity that strangers have   27
  With us in Venice, if it be denied,
  Will much impeach the justice of the state,
  Since that the trade and profit of the city   30
  Consisteth of all nations. Therefore go.
  These griefs and losses have so bated me   32
  That I shall hardly spare a pound of flesh
  Tomorrow to my bloody creditor.—
  Well, jailer, on. Pray God Bassanio come
  To see me pay his debt, and then I care not.   *Exeunt.*

❖

[3.4]

*Enter Portia, Nerissa, Lorenzo, Jessica, and
[Balthasar,] a man of Portia's.*

LORENZO
  Madam, although I speak it in your presence,
  You have a noble and a true conceit   2
  Of godlike amity, which appears most strongly   3
  In bearing thus the absence of your lord.
  But if you knew to whom you show this honor,   5
  How true a gentleman you send relief,
  How dear a lover of my lord your husband,   7
  I know you would be prouder of the work
  Than customary bounty can enforce you.   9

PORTIA
  I never did repent for doing good,
  Nor shall not now; for in companions
  That do converse and waste the time together,   12
  Whose souls do bear an equal yoke of love,
  There must be needs a like proportion   14
  Of lineaments, of manners, and of spirit;   15
  Which makes me think that this Antonio,
  Being the bosom lover of my lord,   17
  Must needs be like my lord. If it be so,
  How little is the cost I have bestowed
  In purchasing the semblance of my soul   20

          From out the state of hellish cruelty!   21
  This comes too near the praising of myself;
  Therefore no more of it. Hear other things:
  Lorenzo, I commit into your hands
  The husbandry and manage of my house   25
  Until my lord's return. For mine own part,
  I have toward heaven breathed a secret vow
  To live in prayer and contemplation,
  Only attended by Nerissa here,
  Until her husband and my lord's return.
  There is a monastery two miles off,
  And there we will abide. I do desire you
  Not to deny this imposition,   33
  The which my love and some necessity
  Now lays upon you.

LORENZO   Madam, with all my heart,
  I shall obey you in all fair commands.

PORTIA
  My people do already know my mind,   37
  And will acknowledge you and Jessica
  In place of Lord Bassanio and myself.
  So fare you well till we shall meet again.

LORENZO
  Fair thoughts and happy hours attend on you!

JESSICA
  I wish Your Ladyship all heart's content.

PORTIA
  I thank you for your wish and am well pleased
  To wish it back on you. Fare you well, Jessica.
                 Exeunt [Jessica and Lorenzo].
  Now, Balthasar,
  As I have ever found thee honest-true,
  So let me find thee still. Take this same letter,
                     [giving a letter]
  And use thou all th'endeavor of a man
  In speed to Padua. See thou render this
  Into my cousin's hands, Doctor Bellario;
  And look what notes and garments he doth give thee,   51
  Bring them, I pray thee, with imagined speed   52
  Unto the traject, to the common ferry   53
  Which trades to Venice. Waste no time in words,   54
  But get thee gone. I shall be there before thee.

BALTHASAR
  Madam, I go with all convenient speed.   *[Exit.]*

PORTIA
  Come on, Nerissa, I have work in hand
  That you yet know not of. We'll see our husbands
  Before they think of us.

NERISSA   Shall they see us?

PORTIA
  They shall, Nerissa, but in such a habit   60
  That they shall think we are accomplishèd   61
  With that we lack. I'll hold thee any wager,   62

---

19 kept associated, dwelt   **20 bootless** unavailing   **27 commodity**
facilities or privileges for trading.   **strangers** noncitizens, including
Jews   **30 Since that** since   **32 bated** reduced
3.4. Location: Belmont. Portia's house.
2 conceit understanding   **3 amity** friendship and love   **5 to whom . . .
honor** i.e., Antonio, who you honor by sending money to relieve him
7 lover friend   **9 Than . . . you** than ordinary benevolence can make
you.   **12 waste** spend   **14 must be needs** must be   **15 lineaments**
physical features   **17 bosom lover** dear friend   **20 the semblance of
my soul** i.e., Antonio, so like my Bassanio

21 From . . . cruelty from the cruel state in which he presently stands.
25 husbandry and manage care and management   **33 deny this
imposition** refuse this charge imposed   **37 people** servants   **51 look
what** whatever   **52 imagined** all imaginable   **53 traject** ferry. (Italian
traghetto.)   **common** public   **54 trades** plies back and forth
60 habit apparel, garb   **61 accomplishèd** supplied   **62 that** that
which. (With a bawdy suggestion.)

When we are both accoutered like young men
I'll prove the prettier fellow of the two,
And wear my dagger with the braver grace,
And speak between the change of man and boy
With a reed voice, and turn two mincing steps
Into a manly stride, and speak of frays
Like a fine bragging youth, and tell quaint lies,   69
How honorable ladies sought my love,
Which I denying, they fell sick and died—
I could not do withal! Then I'll repent,   72
And wish, for all that, that I had not killed them;
And twenty of these puny lies I'll tell,   74
That men shall swear I have discontinued school   75
Above a twelvemonth. I have within my mind   76
A thousand raw tricks of these bragging Jacks,   77
Which I will practice.

NERISSA   Why, shall we turn to men?   78

PORTIA   Fie, what a question's that,
If thou wert near a lewd interpreter!
But come, I'll tell thee all my whole device   81
When I am in my coach, which stays for us
At the park gate; and therefore haste away,
For we must measure twenty miles today.   *Exeunt.* 84

❖

[3.5]

Enter [Lancelot the] clown and Jessica.

LANCELOT   Yes, truly, for look you, the sins of the father are to be laid upon the children; therefore, I prom-   2
ise you, I fear you. I was always plain with you, and   3
so now I speak my agitation of the matter. Therefore   4
be o' good cheer, for truly I think you are damned.
There is but one hope in it that can do you any good,
and that is but a kind of bastard hope, neither.   7

JESSICA   And what hope is that, I pray thee?

LANCELOT   Marry, you may partly hope that your father got you not, that you are not the Jew's daughter.   10

JESSICA   That were a kind of bastard hope, indeed! So
the sins of my mother should be visited upon me.

LANCELOT   Truly, then, I fear you are damned both by
father and mother. Thus when I shun Scylla, your   14
father, I fall into Charybdis, your mother. Well, you   15
are gone both ways.   16

JESSICA   I shall be saved by my husband. He hath made   17
me a Christian.

LANCELOT   Truly, the more to blame he! We were   19
Christians enough before, e'en as many as could well   20
live one by another. This making of Christians will   21
raise the price of hogs. If we grow all to be pork eaters,
we shall not shortly have a rasher on the coals for   23
money.   24

Enter Lorenzo.

JESSICA   I'll tell my husband, Lancelot, what you say.
Here he comes.

LORENZO   I shall grow jealous of you shortly, Lancelot,
if you thus get my wife into corners.

JESSICA   Nay, you need not fear us, Lorenzo. Lancelot
and I are out. He tells me flatly there's no mercy for me   30
in heaven because I am a Jew's daughter; and he says
you are no good member of the commonwealth, for in
converting Jews to Christians you raise the price of
pork.

LORENZO   [*to Lancelot*]   I shall answer that better to the
commonwealth than you can the getting up of the
Negro's belly. The Moor is with child by you, Lancelot.   37

LANCELOT   It is much that the Moor should be more   38
than reason; but if she be less than an honest woman,   39
she is indeed more than I took her for.   40

LORENZO   How every fool can play upon the word! I
think the best grace of wit will shortly turn into   42
silence, and discourse grow commendable in none
only but parrots. Go in, sirrah, bid them prepare for
dinner.

LANCELOT   That is done, sir. They have all stomachs.   46

LORENZO   Goodly Lord, what a wit-snapper are you!
Then bid them prepare dinner.

LANCELOT   That is done too, sir, only "cover" is the   49
word.

LORENZO   Will you cover then, sir?   51

LANCELOT   Not so, sir, neither. I know my duty.   52

LORENZO   Yet more quarreling with occasion! Wilt thou   53
show the whole wealth of thy wit in an instant? I pray
thee, understand a plain man in his plain meaning: go
to thy fellows, bid them cover the table, serve in the
meat, and we will come in to dinner.   57

LANCELOT   For the table, sir, it shall be served in; for the   58
meat, sir, it shall be covered; for your coming in to   59

---

69 **quaint** elaborate, clever   72 **do withal** help it.   74 **puny** childish
75–6 **I . . . twelvemonth** i.e., that I am no mere schoolboy.   76 **Above**
more than   77 **Jacks** fellows   78 **turn to** turn into. (But Portia sees
the occasion for a bawdy quibble on the idea of "turning toward,
lying next to.")   81 **device** plan   84 **measure** traverse
3.5. Location: Belmont. Outside Portia's house.
2–3 **promise** assure   3 **fear you** fear for you.   4 **my agitation of** my
sense of agitation about   7 **bastard** i.e., unfounded. (But also anticipating the usual meaning in lines 9–10.)   **neither** i.e., to be sure.
10 **got** begot   14, 15 **Scylla, Charybdis** twin dangers of the *Odyssey*,
12.255, a monster and a whirlpool guarding the straits presumably
between Italy and Sicily. (*Fall into* plays on the idea of entering the
female sexual anatomy.)   16 **gone** done for   17 **I . . . husband**
(Compare 1 Corinthians 7:14: "the unbelieving wife is sanctified by
the husband.")

19–20 **We . . . enough** There were enough of us Christians   21 **one by
another** (1) as neighbors (2) off one another.   23 **rasher** i.e., of bacon
23–4 **for money** even for ready money, at any price.   30 **are out** have
fallen out.   37 **The Moor** (Lancelot has evidently impregnated some
woman of the household, who, being of African heritage, is referred
to as both "Negro" and "Moor.")   38–40 **It is . . . for** i.e., It is a matter
of concern that the Moor is larger (being pregnant) than usual, larger
than she should be; but if it turns out that she is less than perfectly
chaste, she is something more than I originally supposed. (Lancelot
professes to be surprised by what has happened. With wordplay on
less/more and *more/Moor*.)   42 **the best . . . wit** true wittiness   46 **They
. . . stomachs** The guests all have appetites, and are prepared in that
sense. (Lancelot quibbles with Lorenzo's meaning that the cooks and
servants should be told to get dinner ready.)   49, 51 **cover** spread the
table for the meal. (But in line 52 Lancelot uses the word to mean
"put on one's hat.")   52 **my duty** i.e., my duty to remain bareheaded.
53 **Yet . . . occasion!** i.e., Still quibbling at every opportunity!
57 **meat** food   58 **For** As for.   **table** (Here Lancelot quibblingly takes
the word to mean the food itself.)   59 **covered** (Here used in the
sense of providing a cover for each separate dish.)

dinner, sir, why, let it be as humors and conceits shall   60
govern.   *Exit [Lancelot the] clown.*

LORENZO
Oh, dear discretion, how his words are suited!   62
The fool hath planted in his memory
An army of good words; and I do know
A many fools, that stand in better place,   65
Garnished like him, that for a tricksy word   66
Defy the matter. How cheer'st thou, Jessica?   67
And now, good sweet, say thy opinion:
How dost thou like the Lord Bassanio's wife?

JESSICA
Past all expressing. It is very meet   70
The Lord Bassanio live an upright life,
For, having such a blessing in his lady,
He finds the joys of heaven here on earth;
And if on earth he do not merit it,
In reason he should never come to heaven.   75
Why, if two gods should play some heavenly match
And on the wager lay two earthly women,   77
And Portia one, there must be something else   78
Pawned with the other, for the poor rude world   79
Hath not her fellow.

LORENZO   Even such a husband   80
Hast thou of me as she is for a wife.

JESSICA
Nay, but ask my opinion too of that!

LORENZO
I will anon. First let us go to dinner.

JESSICA
Nay, let me praise you while I have a stomach.   84

LORENZO
No, pray thee, let it serve for table talk;
Then, howsome'er thou speak'st, 'mong other things
I shall digest it.

JESSICA   Well, I'll set you forth.   *Exeunt.* 87

❋

[4.1]

*Enter the Duke, the Magnificoes, Antonio, Bas-
sanio, [Salerio,] and Gratiano [with others. The
judges take their places.]*

DUKE   What, is Antonio here?
ANTONIO   Ready, so please Your Grace.

DUKE
I am sorry for thee. Thou art come to answer   3
A stony adversary, an inhuman wretch
Uncapable of pity, void and empty
From any dram of mercy.

ANTONIO   I have heard   6
Your Grace hath ta'en great pains to qualify   7
His rigorous course; but since he stands obdurate
And that no lawful means can carry me
Out of his envy's reach, I do oppose   10
My patience to his fury and am armed
To suffer with a quietness of spirit
The very tyranny and rage of his.   13

DUKE
Go one, and call the Jew into the court.

SALERIO
He is ready at the door. He comes, my lord.

Enter Shylock.

DUKE
Make room, and let him stand before our face.—   16
Shylock, the world thinks, and I think so too,
That thou but leadest this fashion of thy malice   18
To the last hour of act, and then 'tis thought   19
Thou'lt show thy mercy and remorse more strange   20
Than is thy strange apparent cruelty;   21
And where thou now exacts the penalty,
Which is a pound of this poor merchant's flesh,
Thou wilt not only loose the forfeiture,   24
But, touched with human gentleness and love,
Forgive a moiety of the principal,   26
Glancing an eye of pity on his losses
That have of late so huddled on his back—
Enough to press a royal merchant down
And pluck commiseration of his state   30
From brassy bosoms and rough hearts of flint,   31
From stubborn Turks and Tartars never trained
To offices of tender courtesy.
We all expect a gentle answer, Jew.

SHYLOCK
I have possessed Your Grace of what I purpose,   35
And by our holy Sabaoth have I sworn   36
To have the due and forfeit of my bond.
If you deny it, let the danger light   38
Upon your charter and your city's freedom!   39
You'll ask me why I rather choose to have
A weight of carrion flesh than to receive
Three thousand ducats. I'll not answer that,
But say it is my humor. Is it answered?   43
What if my house be troubled with a rat
And I be pleased to give ten thousand ducats

60 humors and conceits whims and fancies   62 Oh, dear discretion
Oh, what precious discrimination.   suited suited to the occasion
65 A many many.   better place higher social station   66 Garnished
i.e., furnished with words, or with garments   66–7 that . . . matter
who for the sake of ingenious wordplay torture the plain meaning.
67 How cheer'st thou i.e., What cheer, how are you doing   70 meet
fitting   75 In reason it stands to reason. (Jessica jokes that for Bassanio to receive unmerited bliss on earth—unmerited because no person can earn bliss through his or her own deserving—is to run the
risk of eternal damnation.)   77 lay stake   78 else more   79 Pawned
staked, wagered   80 fellow equal.   84 stomach (1) appetite (2) inclination.   87 digest (1) ponder, analyze (2) "swallow," put up with.
(With a play also on the gastronomic sense.)   set you forth (1) serve
you up, as at a feast (2) set forth your praises.
4.1. Location: Venice. A court of justice. Benches, etc., are provided
for the justices.

3 answer defend yourself against. (A legal term.)   6 dram sixty
grains apothecaries' weight, a tiny quantity   7 qualify moderate
10 envy's malice's   13 tyranny cruelty   16 our (The royal plural.)
18 That . . . fashion that you only maintain this pretense or form
19 the last . . . act the brink of action   20 remorse pity.   strange
remarkable   21 strange unnatural, foreign.   apparent (1) manifest,
overt (2) seeming   24 loose release, waive   26 moiety part, portion
30 of for   31 brassy unfeeling, hard like brass   35 possessed
informed   36 Sabaoth Lord of Hosts   38 danger injury
39 Upon . . . freedom (See 3.2.278.)   43 humor whim.

To have it baned? What, are you answered yet?   46
Some men there are love not a gaping pig,   47
Some that are mad if they behold a cat,
And others, when the bagpipe sings i'th' nose,
Cannot contain their urine; for affection,   50
Mistress of passion, sways it to the mood
Of what it likes or loathes. Now, for your answer:
As there is no firm reason to be rendered
Why he cannot abide a gaping pig,   54
Why he a harmless necessary cat,   55
Why he a woolen bagpipe, but of force   56
Must yield to such inevitable shame
As to offend, himself being offended,
So can I give no reason, nor I will not,
More than a lodged hate and a certain loathing   60
I bear Antonio, that I follow thus
A losing suit against him. Are you answered?   62

BASSANIO
This is no answer, thou unfeeling man,
To excuse the current of thy cruelty.   64

SHYLOCK
I am not bound to please thee with my answers.

BASSANIO
Do all men kill the things they do not love?

SHYLOCK
Hates any man the thing he would not kill?

BASSANIO
Every offense is not a hate at first.

SHYLOCK
What, wouldst thou have a serpent sting thee twice?

ANTONIO
I pray you, think you question with the Jew.   70
You may as well go stand upon the beach
And bid the main flood bate his usual height;   72
You may as well use question with the wolf   73
Why he hath made the ewe bleat for the lamb;
You may as well forbid the mountain pines
To wag their high tops and to make no noise
When they are fretten with the gusts of heaven;   77
You may as well do anything most hard
As seek to soften that—than which what's harder?—
His Jewish heart. Therefore, I do beseech you,
Make no more offers, use no farther means,
But with all brief and plain conveniency
Let me have judgment, and the Jew his will.

BASSANIO [to Shylock]
For thy three thousand ducats here is six.

SHYLOCK
If every ducat in six thousand ducats
Were in six parts, and every part a ducat,
I would not draw them. I would have my bond.   87

DUKE
How shalt thou hope for mercy, rendering none?

SHYLOCK
What judgment shall I dread, doing no wrong?   89
You have among you many a purchased slave,
Which, like your asses and your dogs and mules,
You use in abject and in slavish parts,   92
Because you bought them. Shall I say to you,
"Let them be free, marry them to your heirs!
Why sweat they under burdens? Let their beds
Be made as soft as yours, and let their palates
Be seasoned with such viands"? You will answer   97
"The slaves are ours." So do I answer you:
The pound of flesh which I demand of him
Is dearly bought, is mine, and I will have it.
If you deny me, fie upon your law!
There is no force in the decrees of Venice.
I stand for judgment. Answer: shall I have it?

DUKE
Upon my power I may dismiss this court,   104
Unless Bellario, a learnèd doctor,   105
Whom I have sent for to determine this,   106
Come here today.

SALERIO   My lord, here stays without   107
A messenger with letters from the doctor,
New come from Padua.

DUKE
Bring us the letters. Call the messenger.   [Exit one.]

BASSANIO
Good cheer, Antonio. What, man, courage yet!
The Jew shall have my flesh, blood, bones, and all,
Ere thou shalt lose for me one drop of blood.

ANTONIO
I am a tainted wether of the flock,   114
Meetest for death. The weakest kind of fruit   115
Drops earliest to the ground, and so let me.
You cannot better be employed, Bassanio,
Than to live still and write mine epitaph.

Enter Nerissa [dressed like a lawyer's clerk].

DUKE
Came you from Padua, from Bellario?

NERISSA
From both, my lord. Bellario greets Your Grace.
[She presents a letter. Shylock whets his knife on his shoe.]

BASSANIO
Why dost thou whet thy knife so earnestly?

SHYLOCK
To cut the forfeiture from that bankrupt there.

GRATIANO
Not on thy sole, but on thy soul, harsh Jew,
Thou mak'st thy knife keen; but no metal can,
No, not the hangman's ax, bear half the keenness   125
Of thy sharp envy. Can no prayers pierce thee?   126

---

46 **baned** poisoned.   47 **love** who love.   **gaping pig** pig roasted whole with its mouth open   50 **affection** feeling, desire   54, 55, 56 **he, he, he** one person, another, yet another   55 **necessary** i.e., useful for catching rats and mice   56 **woolen** i.e., with flannel-covered bag   60 **lodged** settled, steadfast.   **certain** unwavering, fixed   62 **losing** unprofitable   64 **current** flow, tendency   70 **think** bear in mind.   **question** argue   72 **And . . . height** and bid the ocean put an end to its usual high tide   73 **use question with** interrogate   77 **fretten** fretted, i.e., disturbed, ruffled   87 **draw** receive

89 **wrong** legal wrong.   92 **parts** duties, capacities   97 **such viands** food such as you eat.   104 **Upon** In accordance with   105 **doctor** person of learning. (Here, of law.)   106 **determine this** resolve this legal dispute   107 **stays without** waits outside   114 **wether** ram, especially a castrated ram   115 **Meetest** fittest   125 **hangman's** executioner's.   **keenness** (1) sharpness (2) savagery   126 **envy** malice.

SHYLOCK
 No, none that thou hast wit enough to make.
GRATIANO
 Oh, be thou damned, inexecrable dog,   128
 And for thy life let Justice be accused!   129
 Thou almost mak'st me waver in my faith
 To hold opinion with Pythagoras   131
 That souls of animals infuse themselves
 Into the trunks of men. Thy currish spirit
 Governed a wolf who, hanged for human slaughter,   134
 Even from the gallows did his fell soul fleet,   135
 And, whilst thou layest in thy unhallowed dam,   136
 Infused itself in thee; for thy desires
 Are wolvish, bloody, starved, and ravenous.
SHYLOCK
 Till thou canst rail the seal from off my bond,   139
 Thou but offend'st thy lungs to speak so loud.   140
 Repair thy wit, good youth, or it will fall
 To cureless ruin. I stand here for law.   142
DUKE
 This letter from Bellario doth commend
 A young and learnèd doctor to our court.
 Where is he?
NERISSA   He attendeth here hard by
 To know your answer, whether you'll admit him.
DUKE
 With all my heart. Some three or four of you
 Go give him courteous conduct to this place.
                                      [Exeunt some.]
 Meantime the court shall hear Bellario's letter.
 [He reads.] "Your Grace shall understand that at the   150
 receipt of your letter I am very sick; but in the instant
 that your messenger came, in loving visitation was
 with me a young doctor of Rome. His name is Balthasar. I acquainted him with the cause in controversy
 between the Jew and Antonio the merchant. We
 turned o'er many books together. He is furnished with
 my opinion, which, bettered with his own learning,
 the greatness whereof I cannot enough commend,
 comes with him, at my importunity, to fill up Your   159
 Grace's request in my stead. I beseech you, let his lack
 of years be no impediment to let him lack a reverend   161
 estimation, for I never knew so young a body with so
 old a head. I leave him to your gracious acceptance,
 whose trial shall better publish his commendation."   164

      Enter Portia for Balthasar [*dressed like a doctor
      of laws, escorted*].

128 **inexecrable** thoroughly execrable 129 **And . . . accused!** and may
Justice herself be accused for allowing you to live! 131 **Pythagoras**
ancient Greek philosopher who argued for the transmigration of souls
134 **hanged for human slaughter** (A possible allusion to the Elizabethan practice of trying and punishing animals for various crimes.)
135 **fell** fierce, cruel. **fleet** flit, i.e., pass from the body 136 **dam**
mother. (Usually used of animals.) 139 **rail** remove by your abusive
language 140 **Thou but offend'st** you merely injure 142 **cureless**
incurable 150 **[He reads.]** (In many modern editions, the reading of
the letter is assigned to a clerk, but the original text gives no such indication.) 159 **comes with him** accompanies him in the form of my
learned opinion. **importunity** insistence 161 **to let him lack** such as
would deprive him of 164 **whose . . . commendation** the demonstration of whose excellence will proclaim what is commendable in him
better than my letter can. 164.1 *for* i.e., disguised as

You hear the learn'd Bellario, what he writes;
And here, I take it, is the doctor come.—
Give me your hand. Come you from old Bellario?
PORTIA
 I did, my lord.
DUKE   You are welcome. Take your place.
                          [*Portia takes her place.*]
 Are you acquainted with the difference   169
 That holds this present question in the court?
PORTIA
 I am informèd throughly of the cause.   171
 Which is the merchant here, and which the Jew?
DUKE
 Antonio and old Shylock, both stand forth.
                 [*Antonio and Shylock stand forth.*]
PORTIA
 Is your name Shylock?
SHYLOCK   Shylock is my name.
PORTIA
 Of a strange nature is the suit you follow,
 Yet in such rule that the Venetian law   176
 Cannot impugn you as you do proceed.—   177
 You stand within his danger, do you not?
ANTONIO
 Ay, so he says.
PORTIA   Do you confess the bond?
ANTONIO
 I do.
PORTIA   Then must the Jew be merciful.
SHYLOCK
 On what compulsion must I? Tell me that.
PORTIA
 The quality of mercy is not strained.   182
 It droppeth as the gentle rain from heaven
 Upon the place beneath. It is twice blest: 184
 It blesseth him that gives and him that takes.
 'Tis mightiest in the mightiest; it becomes
 The thronèd monarch better than his crown.
 His scepter shows the force of temporal power,   188
 The attribute to awe and majesty,   189
 Wherein doth sit the dread and fear of kings.
 But mercy is above this sceptered sway;
 It is enthronèd in the hearts of kings;
 It is an attribute to God himself;
 And earthly power doth then show likest God's
 When mercy seasons justice. Therefore, Jew,
 Though justice be thy plea, consider this,
 That in the course of justice none of us   197
 Should see salvation. We do pray for mercy,
 And that same prayer doth teach us all to render
 The deeds of mercy. I have spoke thus much
 To mitigate the justice of thy plea,   201
 Which if thou follow, this strict court of Venice
 Must needs give sentence 'gainst the merchant there.

169 **difference** argument 171 **throughly** thoroughly. **cause** case.
176 **rule** order 177 **impugn** find fault with 182 **strained** forced,
constrained. 184 **is twice blest** grants a double blessing 188 **His**
i.e., The monarch's 189 **attribute to** symbol of 197 **justice** divine
justice 201 **To . . . plea** i.e., to show the way in which your call for
justice needs to be mitigated or reduced in severity

SHYLOCK
My deeds upon my head! I crave the law,   204
The penalty and forfeit of my bond.

PORTIA
Is he not able to discharge the money?

BASSANIO
Yes, here I tender it for him in the court,
Yea, twice the sum. If that will not suffice,
I will be bound to pay it ten times o'er,
On forfeit of my hands, my head, my heart.
If this will not suffice, it must appear
That malice bears down truth. And I beseech you,   212
Wrest once the law to your authority.   213
To do a great right, do a little wrong,
And curb this cruel devil of his will.

PORTIA
It must not be. There is no power in Venice
Can alter a decree establishèd.
'Twill be recorded for a precedent,
And many an error by the same example
Will rush into the state. It cannot be.

SHYLOCK
A Daniel come to judgment! Yea, a Daniel!   221
O wise young judge, how I do honor thee!

PORTIA
I pray you, let me look upon the bond.

SHYLOCK [giving the bond]
Here 'tis, most reverend doctor, here it is.

PORTIA
Shylock, there's thrice thy money offered thee.

SHYLOCK
An oath, an oath! I have an oath in heaven.
Shall I lay perjury upon my soul?
No, not for Venice.

PORTIA   Why, this bond is forfeit,
And lawfully by this the Jew may claim
A pound of flesh, to be by him cut off
Nearest the merchant's heart.—Be merciful.
Take thrice thy money; bid me tear the bond.

SHYLOCK
When it is paid according to the tenor.   233
It doth appear you are a worthy judge.
You know the law. Your exposition
Hath been most sound. I charge you by the law,
Whereof you are a well-deserving pillar,
Proceed to judgment. By my soul I swear
There is no power in the tongue of man
To alter me. I stay here on my bond.   240

ANTONIO
Most heartily I do beseech the court
To give the judgment.

PORTIA   Why then, thus it is:
You must prepare your bosom for his knife.

SHYLOCK
O noble judge! O excellent young man!

PORTIA
For the intent and purpose of the law
Hath full relation to the penalty   246
Which here appeareth due upon the bond.

SHYLOCK
'Tis very true. O wise and upright judge!
How much more elder art thou than thy looks!

PORTIA
Therefore lay bare your bosom.

SHYLOCK   Ay, his breast.
So says the bond, doth it not, noble judge?
"Nearest his heart," those are the very words.

PORTIA
It is so. Are there balance here   253
To weigh the flesh?

SHYLOCK   I have them ready.

PORTIA
Have by some surgeon, Shylock, on your charge,   255
To stop his wounds, lest he do bleed to death.

SHYLOCK
Is it so nominated in the bond?

PORTIA
It is not so expressed, but what of that?
'Twere good you do so much for charity.

SHYLOCK
I cannot find it. 'Tis not in the bond.

PORTIA
You, merchant, have you anything to say?

ANTONIO
But little. I am armed and well prepared.—   262
Give me your hand, Bassanio; fare you well!
Grieve not that I am fall'n to this for you,
For herein Fortune shows herself more kind
Than is her custom. It is still her use   266
To let the wretched man outlive his wealth
To view with hollow eye and wrinkled brow
An age of poverty; from which ling'ring penance
Of such misery doth she cut me off.
Commend me to your honorable wife.
Tell her the process of Antonio's end,   272
Say how I loved you, speak me fair in death;   273
And, when the tale is told, bid her be judge
Whether Bassanio had not once a love.   275
Repent but you that you shall lose your friend,   276
And he repents not that he pays your debt.
For if the Jew do cut but deep enough,
I'll pay it instantly with all my heart.   279

BASSANIO
Antonio, I am married to a wife,
Which is as dear to me as life itself;
But life itself, my wife, and all the world

---

204 My . . . head! (Compare the cry of the crowd at Jesus' crucifixion: "His blood be on us, and on our children," Matthew 27:25.) 212 bears down truth overwhelms righteousness. 213 Wrest once for once, forcibly subject 221 Daniel (In the Apocrypha's story of Susannah and the Elders, Daniel is the young man who rescues Susannah from her false accusers.) 233 tenor conditions. 240 stay stand, insist

246 Hath . . . to is fully in accord with 253 balance scales 255 Have by Have ready at hand. on your charge at your personal expense 262 armed i.e., fortified in spirit 266 still her use i.e., commonly Fortune's practice 272 process story, manner 273 speak me fair speak well of me 275 a love a friend's love. 276 Repent but you Grieve only 279 with . . . heart (1) wholeheartedly (2) literally, with my heart's blood.

Are not with me esteemed above thy life.
I would lose all, ay, sacrifice them all
Here to this devil, to deliver you.

PORTIA
Your wife would give you little thanks for that,
If she were by to hear you make the offer.   287

GRATIANO
I have a wife who, I protest, I love;
I would she were in heaven, so she could
Entreat some power to change this currish Jew.

NERISSA
'Tis well you offer it behind her back;
The wish would make else an unquiet house.

SHYLOCK
These be the Christian husbands. I have a daughter;
Would any of the stock of Barabbas   294
Had been her husband rather than a Christian!—
We trifle time. I pray thee, pursue sentence.   296

PORTIA
A pound of that same merchant's flesh is thine.
The court awards it, and the law doth give it.

SHYLOCK   Most rightful judge!

PORTIA
And you must cut this flesh from off his breast.
The law allows it, and the court awards it.

SHYLOCK
Most learnèd judge! A sentence!—Come, prepare.

PORTIA
Tarry a little; there is something else.
This bond doth give thee here no jot of blood;
The words expressly are "a pound of flesh."
Take then thy bond, take thou thy pound of flesh,
But in the cutting it if thou dost shed
One drop of Christian blood, thy lands and goods
Are by the laws of Venice confiscate
Unto the state of Venice.

GRATIANO
O upright judge! Mark, Jew. O learnèd judge!

SHYLOCK
Is that the law?

PORTIA   Thyself shalt see the act;
For, as thou urgest justice, be assured
Thou shalt have justice, more than thou desir'st.

GRATIANO
O learnèd judge! Mark, Jew, a learnèd judge!

SHYLOCK
I take this offer, then. Pay the bond thrice
And let the Christian go.

BASSANIO   Here is the money.

PORTIA   Soft!   318
The Jew shall have all justice. Soft, no haste.   319
He shall have nothing but the penalty.

GRATIANO
O Jew! An upright judge, a learnèd judge!

PORTIA
Therefore prepare thee to cut off the flesh.
Shed thou no blood, nor cut thou less nor more
But just a pound of flesh. If thou tak'st more
Or less than a just pound, be it but so much
As makes it light or heavy in the substance   326
Or the division of the twentieth part   327
Of one poor scruple, nay, if the scale do turn   328
But in the estimation of a hair,
Thou diest, and all thy goods are confiscate.

GRATIANO
A second Daniel, a Daniel, Jew!   331
Now, infidel, I have you on the hip.   332

PORTIA
Why doth the Jew pause? Take thy forfeiture.

SHYLOCK
Give me my principal, and let me go.

BASSANIO
I have it ready for thee. Here it is.

PORTIA
He hath refused it in the open court.
He shall have merely justice and his bond.

GRATIANO
A Daniel, still say I, a second Daniel!
I thank thee, Jew, for teaching me that word.

SHYLOCK
Shall I not have barely my principal?

PORTIA
Thou shalt have nothing but the forfeiture,
To be so taken at thy peril, Jew.

SHYLOCK
Why, then the devil give him good of it!
I'll stay no longer question.   [*He starts to go.*]

PORTIA   Tarry, Jew!   344
The law hath yet another hold on you.
It is enacted in the laws of Venice,
If it be proved against an alien
That by direct or indirect attempts
He seek the life of any citizen,
The party 'gainst the which he doth contrive
Shall seize one half his goods; the other half
Comes to the privy coffer of the state,   352
And the offender's life lies in the mercy   353
Of the Duke only, 'gainst all other voice.   354
In which predicament, I say, thou stand'st;
For it appears, by manifest proceeding,
That indirectly and directly too
Thou hast contrived against the very life
Of the defendant; and thou hast incurred
The danger formerly by me rehearsed.   360
Down therefore, and beg mercy of the Duke.   361

---

287 **by** nearby   294 **Barabbas** a thief whom Pontius Pilate set free instead of Christ in response to the people's demand (see Mark 15); also, the villainous protagonist of Marlowe's *The Jew of Malta*
296 **trifle** waste.   **pursue** proceed with   318 **Soft!** i.e., Not so fast!
319 **all justice** precisely what the law provides.

326 **substance** mass or gross weight   327 **division** fraction
328 **scruple** twenty grains apothecaries' weight, a small quantity
331 **Daniel** (See line 221 above and note.)   332 **on the hip** i.e., at a disadvantage. (A phrase from wrestling.)   344 **I'll . . . question** I'll stay no further pursuing of the case.   352 **privy coffer** private treasury   353 **lies in** lies at   354 **'gainst . . . voice** without appeal
360 **The danger . . . rehearsed** the penalty already cited by me.
361 **Down** Down on your knees

GRATIANO

Beg that thou mayst have leave to hang thyself!
And yet, thy wealth being forfeit to the state,
Thou hast not left the value of a cord;
Therefore thou must be hanged at the state's charge.   365

DUKE

That thou shalt see the difference of our spirit,
I pardon thee thy life before thou ask it.
For half thy wealth, it is Antonio's;   368
The other half comes to the general state,
Which humbleness may drive unto a fine.   370

PORTIA

Ay, for the state, not for Antonio.   371

SHYLOCK

Nay, take my life and all! Pardon not that!
You take my house when you do take the prop
That doth sustain my house. You take my life
When you do take the means whereby I live.

PORTIA

What mercy can you render him, Antonio?

GRATIANO

A halter gratis! Nothing else, for God's sake.   377

ANTONIO

So please my lord the Duke and all the court
To quit the fine for one half of his goods,   379
I am content, so he will let me have   380
The other half in use, to render it,   381
Upon his death, unto the gentleman
That lately stole his daughter.
Two things provided more: that for this favor
He presently become a Christian;   385
The other, that he do record a gift
Here in the court of all he dies possessed   387
Unto his son Lorenzo and his daughter.

DUKE

He shall do this, or else I do recant
The pardon that I late pronouncèd here.   389

PORTIA

Art thou contented, Jew? What dost thou say?

SHYLOCK

I am content.

PORTIA   Clerk, draw a deed of gift.

SHYLOCK

I pray you, give me leave to go from hence;
I am not well. Send the deed after me,
And I will sign it.

DUKE   Get thee gone, but do it.

GRATIANO

In christening shalt thou have two godfathers.
Had I been judge, thou shouldst have had ten more,   397

To bring thee to the gallows, not the font.
                                        Exit [Shylock].

DUKE *[to Portia]*

Sir, I entreat you home with me to dinner.

PORTIA

I humbly do desire Your Grace of pardon.
I must away this night toward Padua,
And it is meet I presently set forth.   402

DUKE

I am sorry that your leisure serves you not.
Antonio, gratify this gentleman,   404
For in my mind you are much bound to him.
                        Exeunt Duke and his train.

BASSANIO *[to Portia]*

Most worthy gentleman, I and my friend
Have by your wisdom been this day acquitted
Of grievous penalties, in lieu whereof,   408
Three thousand ducats due unto the Jew
We freely cope your courteous pains withal.   410
                                [He offers money.]

ANTONIO

And stand indebted over and above
In love and service to you evermore.

PORTIA

He is well paid that is well satisfied,
And I, delivering you, am satisfied,
And therein do account myself well paid.
My mind was never yet more mercenary.
I pray you, know me when we meet again.   417
I wish you well, and so I take my leave.
                                [She starts to leave.]

BASSANIO

Dear sir, of force I must attempt you further.   419
Take some remembrance of us as a tribute,
Not as fee. Grant me two things, I pray you:
Not to deny me, and to pardon me.   422

PORTIA

You press me far, and therefore I will yield.
Give me your gloves, I'll wear them for your sake.   424
And, for your love, I'll take this ring from you.   425
Do not draw back your hand; I'll take no more,
And you in love shall not deny me this.

BASSANIO

This ring, good sir? Alas, it is a trifle!
I will not shame myself to give you this.

PORTIA

I will have nothing else but only this;
And now, methinks, I have a mind to it.

BASSANIO

There's more depends on this than on the value.

---

365 charge expense.   **368 For** As for   **370 Which . . . fine** i.e., which
penitence on your part may persuade me to reduce to a fine.
371 Ay . . . Antonio i.e., Yes, the state's half may be reduced to a fine,
but not Antonio's half.   **377 halter** hangman's noose   **379 To . . .
goods** i.e., to cancel the fine of one-half of Shylock's estate owed to
the state of Venice (line 352)   **380 so** provided that   **381 in use** in
trust (until Shylock's death)   **385 presently** at once   **387 of . . . possessed** i.e., what remains of the portion not placed under Antonio's
trust (which will also go to Lorenzo and Jessica)   **389 late** lately
397 ten more i.e., to make up a jury of twelve. (Jurors were colloquially termed *godfathers.*)

402 meet necessary, suitable   **404 gratify** reward   **408 in lieu
whereof** in return for which   **410 cope** requite   **417 know . . . again**
i.e., consider our acquaintance well established. (But punning on
know in the sense of "recognize" and "have sexual relations with"—
meanings that are hidden from Bassanio by Portia's disguise.)
419 of force of necessity.   **attempt** urge   **422 pardon me** i.e., pardon
my presumption in pressing the matter.   **424 gloves** (Perhaps Bassanio
removes his gloves, thereby revealing the ring that "Balthasar" asks of
him.)   **425 for your love** i.e., for friendship's sake—a polite phrase, but
with ironic double meaning as applied to husband and wife

The dearest ring in Venice will I give you,   433
And find it out by proclamation.
Only for this, I pray you, pardon me.

PORTIA
I see, sir, you are liberal in offers.   436
You taught me first to beg, and now, methinks,
You teach me how a beggar should be answered.

BASSANIO
Good sir, this ring was given me by my wife,
And when she put it on she made me vow
That I should neither sell nor give nor lose it.

PORTIA
That 'scuse serves many men to save their gifts.
An if your wife be not a madwoman,   443
And know how well I have deserved this ring,
She would not hold out enemy forever
For giving it to me. Well, peace be with you!
                    Exeunt [*Portia and Nerissa*].

ANTONIO
My lord Bassanio, let him have the ring.
Let his deservings and my love withal
Be valued 'gainst your wife's commandement.   449

BASSANIO
Go, Gratiano, run and overtake him;
Give him the ring, and bring him, if thou canst,
Unto Antonio's house. Away, make haste!
                    Exit Gratiano [*with the ring*].
Come, you and I will thither presently,
And in the morning early will we both
Fly toward Belmont. Come, Antonio.   *Exeunt.*

❧

[4.2]

Enter [*Portia and*] *Nerissa* [*still disguised*].

PORTIA [*giving a deed to Nerissa*]
Inquire the Jew's house out; give him this deed   1
And let him sign it. We'll away tonight
And be a day before our husbands home.
This deed will be well welcome to Lorenzo.

Enter Gratiano.

GRATIANO   Fair sir, you are well o'erta'en.   5
My lord Bassanio upon more advice   6
Hath sent you here this ring and doth entreat
Your company at dinner.   [*He gives a ring.*]

PORTIA   That cannot be.
His ring I do accept most thankfully,
And so, I pray you, tell him. Furthermore,
I pray you, show my youth old Shylock's house.

GRATIANO
That will I do.

NERISSA   Sir, I would speak with you.
[*Aside to Portia*] I'll see if I can get my husband's
    ring,
Which I did make him swear to keep forever.

PORTIA [*aside to Nerissa*]
Thou mayst, I warrant. We shall have old swearing   15
That they did give the rings away to men;
But we'll outface them, and outswear them too.—   17
Away, make haste! Thou know'st where I will tarry.

NERISSA [*to Gratiano*]
Come, good sir, will you show me to this house?
                    [*Exeunt, Portia separately from the others.*]

❧

[5.1]

Enter Lorenzo and Jessica.

LORENZO
The moon shines bright. In such a night as this,
When the sweet wind did gently kiss the trees
And they did make no noise, in such a night
Troilus methinks mounted the Trojan walls   4
And sighed his soul toward the Grecian tents
Where Cressid lay that night.

JESSICA   In such a night
Did Thisbe fearfully o'ertrip the dew,   7
And saw the lion's shadow ere himself,
And ran dismayed away.

LORENZO   In such a night
Stood Dido with a willow in her hand   10
Upon the wild sea banks, and waft her love   11
To come again to Carthage.

JESSICA   In such a night
Medea gathered the enchanted herbs   13
That did renew old Aeson.

LORENZO   In such a night
Did Jessica steal from the wealthy Jew   15
And with an unthrift love did run from Venice   16
As far as Belmont.

JESSICA   In such a night
Did young Lorenzo swear he loved her well,
Stealing her soul with many vows of faith,
And ne'er a true one.

LORENZO   In such a night
Did pretty Jessica, like a little shrew,
Slander her love, and he forgave it her.

JESSICA
I would out-night you, did nobody come.   23
But hark, I hear the footing of a man.   24

Enter [*Stephano,*] *a messenger.*

LORENZO
Who comes so fast in silence of the night?

---

433 **dearest** most expensive   436 **liberal** generous   443 **An if** If
449 **commandement** (Pronounced in four syllables.)
4.2. Location: Venice. A street.
1 **this deed** i.e., the deed of gift   5 **you . . . o'erta'en** I'm happy to
have caught up with you.   6 **advice** consideration

15 **old** plenty of   17 **outface** boldly contradict
5.1. Location: Belmont. Outside Portia's house.
4 **Troilus** Trojan prince deserted by his beloved, Cressida, after she had
been transferred to the Greek camp   7 **Thisbe** beloved of Pyramus
who, arranging to meet him by night, was frightened by a lion and fled;
the tragic misunderstanding of her absence led to the suicides of both
lovers. (See *A Midsummer Night's Dream*, Act 5.)   10 **Dido** Queen of
Carthage, deserted by Aeneas.   **willow** (A symbol of forsaken love.)
11 **waft** wafted, beckoned   13 **Medea** famous sorceress of Colchis who,
after falling in love with Jason and helping him to gain the Golden
Fleece, used her magic to restore youth to Aeson, Jason's father
15 **steal** (1) escape (2) rob   16 **unthrift** prodigal   23 **out-night** i.e.,
outdo in the verbal games we've been playing   24 **footing** footsteps

STEPHANO   A friend.

LORENZO

A friend? What friend? Your name, I pray you,
   friend?

STEPHANO

Stephano is my name, and I bring word
My mistress will before the break of day
Be here at Belmont. She doth stray about
By holy crosses, where she kneels and prays   31
For happy wedlock hours.   Who comes with her?

STEPHANO

None but a holy hermit and her maid.
I pray you, is my master yet returned?

LORENZO

He is not, nor we have not heard from him.
But go we in, I pray thee, Jessica,
And ceremoniously let us prepare
Some welcome for the mistress of the house.

Enter [Lancelot, the] clown.

LANCELOT   Sola, sola! Wo ha, ho! Sola, sola!   39

LORENZO   Who calls?

LANCELOT   Sola! Did you see Master Lorenzo? Master
   Lorenzo, sola, sola!

LORENZO   Leave holloing, man! Here.

LANCELOT   Sola! Where, where?

LORENZO   Here.

LANCELOT   Tell him there's a post come from my mas-   46
ter, with his horn full of good news: my master will be   47
here ere morning.   [*Exit.*]

LORENZO

Sweet soul, let's in, and there expect their coming.   49
And yet no matter. Why should we go in?
My friend Stephano, signify, I pray you,   51
Within the house, your mistress is at hand,
And bring your music forth into the air.

[*Exit Stephano.*]

How sweet the moonlight sleeps upon this bank!
Here will we sit and let the sounds of music
Creep in our ears. Soft stillness and the night
Become the touches of sweet harmony.   57
Sit, Jessica. [*They sit.*] Look how the floor of heaven
Is thick inlaid with patens of bright gold.   59
There's not the smallest orb which thou behold'st
But in his motion like an angel sings,
Still choiring to the young-eyed cherubins.   62
Such harmony is in immortal souls,
But whilst this muddy vesture of decay   64
Doth grossly close it in, we cannot hear it.   65

[*Enter musicians.*]

Come, ho, and wake Diana with a hymn!   66
With sweetest touches pierce your mistress' ear
And draw her home with music.   *Play music.*

JESSICA

I am never merry when I hear sweet music.

LORENZO

The reason is, your spirits are attentive.   70
For do but note a wild and wanton herd,
Or race of youthful and unhandled colts,   72
Fetching mad bounds, bellowing and neighing loud,
Which is the hot condition of their blood;
If they but hear perchance a trumpet sound,
Or any air of music touch their ears,
You shall perceive them make a mutual stand,   77
Their savage eyes turned to a modest gaze
By the sweet power of music. Therefore the poet   79
Did feign that Orpheus drew trees, stones, and
   floods,   80
Since naught so stockish, hard, and full of rage   81
But music for the time doth change his nature.   82
The man that hath no music in himself,
Nor is not moved with concord of sweet sounds,
Is fit for treasons, stratagems, and spoils;   85
The motions of his spirit are dull as night
And his affections dark as Erebus.   87
Let no such man be trusted. Mark the music.

Enter Portia and Nerissa.

PORTIA

That light we see is burning in my hall.
How far that little candle throws his beams!
So shines a good deed in a naughty world.   91

NERISSA

When the moon shone, we did not see the candle.

PORTIA

So doth the greater glory dim the less.
A substitute shines brightly as a king
Until a king be by, and then his state   95
Empties itself, as doth an inland brook
Into the main of waters. Music! Hark!   97

NERISSA

It is your music, madam, of the house.

PORTIA

Nothing is good, I see, without respect.   99
Methinks it sounds much sweeter than by day.

NERISSA

Silence bestows that virtue on it, madam.

PORTIA

The crow doth sing as sweetly as the lark
When neither is attended; and I think   103
The nightingale, if she should sing by day,

---

31 holy crosses wayside shrines   **39 Sola** (Imitation of a post horn.)
46 post courier   **47 horn** (Lancelot jestingly compares the courier's
post horn to a cornucopia; perhaps too with a glance at the frayed jest
about cuckolds' horns.)   **49 expect** await   **51 signify** make known
57 Become suit.   **touches** strains, notes (produced by the fingering of
an instrument)   **59 patens** thin, circular plates of metal   **62 Still
choiring** continually singing.   **young-eyed** eternally clear-sighted.
(In Ezekiel 10:12, the bodies and wings of cherubim are "full of eyes
round about.")   **64 muddy . . . decay** i.e., mortal flesh   **65 close it in**
i.e., enclose the soul.   **hear it** i.e., hear the music of the spheres.

66 Diana (Here, goddess of the moon; compare with 1.2.105.)
70 spirits are attentive (The spirits would be in motion within the
body in merriment, whereas in sadness they would be drawn to the
heart and, as it were, busy listening.)   **72 race** herd   **77 mutual** common or simultaneous   **79 poet** perhaps Ovid, with whom the story of
Orpheus was a favorite theme   **80 Orpheus** legendary musician.
drew attracted, charmed.   **floods** rivers   **81 stockish** unfeeling
82 his its (a tree, a stone, etc.)   **85 spoils** acts of pillage   **87 Erebus** a
place of primeval darkness on the way to Hades.   **91 naughty**
wicked   **95 his** i.e., the substitute's   **97 main of waters** sea.
99 respect comparison, context.   **103 attended** listened to

When every goose is cackling, would be thought
No better a musician than the wren.
How many things by season seasoned are   107
To their right praise and true perfection!
Peace, ho! The moon sleeps with Endymion   109
And would not be awaked.   [*The music ceases.*]

LORENZO   That is the voice,
Or I am much deceived, of Portia.

PORTIA
He knows me as the blind man knows the cuckoo,
By the bad voice.

LORENZO   Dear lady, welcome home.

PORTIA
We have been praying for our husbands' welfare,
Which speed, we hope, the better for our words.   115
Are they returned?

LORENZO   Madam, they are not yet;
But there is come a messenger before,
To signify their coming.

PORTIA   Go in, Nerissa.
Give order to my servants that they take
No note at all of our being absent hence;
Nor you, Lorenzo; Jessica, nor you. [*A tucket sounds.*] 121

LORENZO
Your husband is at hand. I hear his trumpet.
We are no telltales, madam, fear you not.

PORTIA
This night, methinks, is but the daylight sick;   124
It looks a little paler. 'Tis a day
Such as the day is when the sun is hid.

*Enter Bassanio, Antonio, Gratiano, and their
followers.*

BASSANIO
We should hold day with the Antipodes,   127
If you would walk in absence of the sun.   128

PORTIA
Let me give light, but let me not be light;   129
For a light wife doth make a heavy husband,   130
And never be Bassanio so for me.
But God sort all! You are welcome home, my lord.   132

BASSANIO
I thank you, madam. Give welcome to my friend.
This is the man, this is Antonio,
To whom I am so infinitely bound.

PORTIA
You should in all sense be much bound to him,   136
For, as I hear, he was much bound for you.   137

ANTONIO
No more than I am well acquitted of.   138

PORTIA
Sir, you are very welcome to our house.
It must appear in other ways than words;
Therefore I scant this breathing courtesy.   141

GRATIANO [*to Nerissa*]
By yonder moon I swear you do me wrong!
In faith, I gave it to the judge's clerk.
Would he were gelt that had it, for my part,   144
Since you do take it, love, so much at heart.

PORTIA
A quarrel, ho, already? What's the matter?

GRATIANO
About a hoop of gold, a paltry ring
That she did give me, whose posy was   148
For all the world like cutler's poetry
Upon a knife, "Love me, and leave me not."

NERISSA
What talk you of the posy or the value?
You swore to me, when I did give it you,
That you would wear it till your hour of death
And that it should lie with you in your grave.
Though not for me, yet for your vehement oaths
You should have been respective and have kept it.   156
Gave it a judge's clerk! No, God's my judge,
The clerk will ne'er wear hair on 's face that had it.

GRATIANO
He will, an if he live to be a man.   159

NERISSA
Ay, if a woman live to be a man.

GRATIANO
Now, by this hand, I gave it to a youth,
A kind of boy, a little scrubbèd boy   162
No higher than thyself, the judge's clerk,
A prating boy, that begged it as a fee.   164
I could not for my heart deny it him.

PORTIA
You were to blame—I must be plain with you—
To part so slightly with your wife's first gift,
A thing stuck on with oaths upon your finger,
And so riveted with faith unto your flesh.
I gave my love a ring and made him swear
Never to part with it; and here he stands.
I dare be sworn for him he would not leave it,
Nor pluck it from his finger, for the wealth
That the world masters. Now, in faith, Gratiano,   174
You give your wife too unkind a cause of grief.
An 'twere to me, I should be mad at it.   176

BASSANIO [*aside*]
Why, I were best to cut my left hand off
And swear I lost the ring defending it.

GRATIANO
My lord Bassanio gave his ring away

107 **season** fit occasion. (But playing on the idea of seasoning, spices.)
109 **Endymion** a shepherd loved by the moon goddess, who caused
him to sleep a perennial sleep in a cave on Mount Latmos where she
could visit him   115 **Which . . . words** who prosper and return
speedily, we hope, because we prayed for them.   121 **s.d. *tucket***
flourish on a trumpet   124 **sick** i.e., made pale by the approach of
dawn   127–8 **We . . . sun** i.e., If you, Portia, like a second sun, would
always walk about during the sun's absence, we should never have
night but would enjoy daylight even when the Antipodes, those who
dwell on the opposite side of the globe, enjoy daylight.   129 **be light**
be wanton, unchaste   130 **heavy** sad. (With wordplay on the antithesis of *light* and *heavy*.)   132 **sort** decide, dispose   136 **in all sense** in
every way, with every reason   136–7 **bound . . . bound** Portia plays
on (1) obligated (2) indebted and imprisoned

138 **acquitted of** freed from and amply repaid (by thanks and love).
141 **scant . . . courtesy** make brief these empty (i.e., merely verbal)
compliments.   144 **gelt** gelded, castrated.   **for my part** as far as I'm
concerned   148 **posy** a motto on a ring   156 **respective** mindful,
careful   159 **an if** if   162 **scrubbèd** diminutive   164 **prating** chattering   174 **masters** owns.   176 **An** If.   **mad** beside myself

Unto the judge that begged it and indeed
Deserved it too; and then the boy, his clerk,
That took some pains in writing, he begged mine;
And neither man nor master would take aught   183
But the two rings.

PORTIA [*to Bassanio*]   What ring gave you, my lord?
Not that, I hope, which you received of me.

BASSANIO
If I could add a lie unto a fault,
I would deny it; but you see my finger
Hath not the ring upon it. It is gone.

PORTIA
Even so void is your false heart of truth.
By heaven, I will ne'er come in your bed
Until I see the ring!

NERISSA [*to Gratiano*]   Nor I in yours
Till I again see mine.

BASSANIO   Sweet Portia,
If you did know to whom I gave the ring,
If you did know for whom I gave the ring,
And would conceive for what I gave the ring,
And how unwillingly I left the ring,
When naught would be accepted but the ring,
You would abate the strength of your displeasure.

PORTIA
If you had known the virtue of the ring,   199
Or half her worthiness that gave the ring,
Or your own honor to contain the ring,   201
You would not then have parted with the ring.
What man is there so much unreasonable,
If you had pleased to have defended it
With any terms of zeal, wanted the modesty   205
To urge the thing held as a ceremony?   206
Nerissa teaches me what to believe:
I'll die for't but some woman had the ring.

BASSANIO
No, by my honor, madam! By my soul,
No woman had it, but a civil doctor,   210
Which did refuse three thousand ducats of me
And begged the ring, the which I did deny him
And suffered him to go displeased away—   213
Even he that had held up the very life
Of my dear friend. What should I say, sweet lady?
I was enforced to send it after him.
I was beset with shame and courtesy.
My honor would not let ingratitude
So much besmear it. Pardon me, good lady!   219
For by these blessèd candles of the night,   220
Had you been there, I think you would have begged
The ring of me to give the worthy doctor.

PORTIA
Let not that doctor e'er come near my house.
Since he hath got the jewel that I loved,
And that which you did swear to keep for me,
I will become as liberal as you: 226

I'll not deny him anything I have,
No, not my body nor my husband's bed.
Know him I shall, I am well sure of it.   229
Lie not a night from home. Watch me like Argus;   230
If you do not, if I be left alone,
Now, by mine honor, which is yet mine own,   232
I'll have that doctor for my bedfellow.

NERISSA
And I his clerk; therefore be well advised   234
How you do leave me to mine own protection.

GRATIANO
Well, do you so. Let not me take him, then!   236
For if I do, I'll mar the young clerk's pen.   237

ANTONIO
I am th'unhappy subject of these quarrels.

PORTIA
Sir, grieve not you; you are welcome notwithstanding.

BASSANIO
Portia, forgive me this enforcèd wrong,
And in the hearing of these many friends
I swear to thee, even by thine own fair eyes
Wherein I see myself—

PORTIA   Mark you but that!
In both my eyes he doubly sees himself;
In each eye, one. Swear by your double self,   245
And there's an oath of credit.

BASSANIO   Nay, but hear me.   246
Pardon this fault, and by my soul I swear
I never more will break an oath with thee.

ANTONIO
I once did lend my body for his wealth,   249
Which, but for him that had your husband's ring,
Had quite miscarried. I dare be bound again,
My soul upon the forfeit, that your lord   252
Will nevermore break faith advisedly.   253

PORTIA
Then you shall be his surety. Give him this,   254
And bid him keep it better than the other.
     [*She gives the ring to Antonio, who gives it to Bassanio.*]

ANTONIO
Here, Lord Bassanio. Swear to keep this ring.

BASSANIO
By heaven, it is the same I gave the doctor!

PORTIA
I had it of him. Pardon me, Bassanio,
For by this ring the doctor lay with me.

NERISSA
And pardon me, my gentle Gratiano,
For that same scrubbèd boy, the doctor's clerk,
In lieu of this last night did lie with me.   262
       [*Presenting her ring.*]

---

183 **aught** anything   199 **virtue** moral efficacy   201 **contain** keep
safe   205 **wanted the modesty** who would have been so lacking in
consideration as   206 **urge** insist upon receiving. **ceremony** something
sacred   210 **civil doctor** i.e., doctor of civil law   213 **suffered**
allowed   219 **it** i.e., my honor.   220 **blessèd . . . night** i.e., stars
226 **liberal** generous (sexually as well as otherwise)

229 **Know** (With the suggestion of carnal knowledge.)   230 **from**
away from.   **Argus** mythological monster with a hundred eyes
232 **honor** (1) honorable name (2) chastity   234 **be well advised** take
care   236 **take** apprehend   237 **pen** (With sexual double meaning.)
245 **double** i.e., deceitful   246 **of credit** worthy to be believed. (Said
ironically.)   249 **wealth** welfare   252 **My . . . forfeit** at the risk of
eternal damnation   253 **advisedly** intentionally.   254 **surety** guarantor.   262 **In lieu of** in return for

GRATIANO
　Why, this is like the mending of highways
　In summer, where the ways are fair enough.　264
　What, are we cuckolds ere we have deserved it?　265
PORTIA
　Speak not so grossly. You are all amazed.
　Here is a letter; read it at your leisure.

　　　　　　　　　　[*She gives a letter.*]

　It comes from Padua, from Bellario.
　There you shall find that Portia was the doctor,
　Nerissa there her clerk. Lorenzo here
　Shall witness I set forth as soon as you,
　And even but now returned; I have not yet
　Entered my house. Antonio, you are welcome,
　And I have better news in store for you
　Than you expect. Unseal this letter soon.

　　　　　　　　　　[*She gives him a letter.*]

　There you shall find three of your argosies
　Are richly come to harbor suddenly.
　You shall not know by what strange accident
　I chancèd on this letter.
ANTONIO　　　　　　　　　I am dumb.　279
BASSANIO [*to Portia*]
　Were you the doctor and I knew you not?
GRATIANO [*to Nerissa*]
　Were you the clerk that is to make me cuckold?
NERISSA
　Ay, but the clerk that never means to do it,
　Unless he live until he be a man.
BASSANIO
　Sweet doctor, you shall be my bedfellow.

When I am absent, then lie with my wife.
ANTONIO
　Sweet lady, you have given me life and living;
　For here I read for certain that my ships
　Are safely come to road.
PORTIA　　　　　　　　How now, Lorenzo?　288
　My clerk hath some good comforts too for you.
NERISSA
　Ay, and I'll give them him without a fee.

　　　　　　　　　　[*She gives a deed.*]

　There do I give to you and Jessica,
　From the rich Jew, a special deed of gift,
　After his death, of all he dies possessed of.
LORENZO
　Fair ladies, you drop manna in the way　294
　Of starved people.
PORTIA　　　　　　　It is almost morning,
　And yet I am sure you are not satisfied
　Of these events at full. Let us go in;
　And charge us there upon inter'gatories,　298
　And we will answer all things faithfully.
GRATIANO
　Let it be so. The first inter'gatory
　That my Nerissa shall be sworn on is
　Whether till the next night she had rather stay　302
　Or go to bed now, being two hours to day.
　But were the day come, I should wish it dark
　Till I were couching with the doctor's clerk.　305
　Well, while I live I'll fear no other thing
　So sore as keeping safe Nerissa's ring.　　*Exeunt.* 307

288 road anchorage.　**294 manna** the food from heaven that was miraculously supplied to the Israelites in the wilderness (Exodus 16) **298 And . . . inter'gatories** and put questions to us (as in a court of law)　**302 stay** wait　**305 couching** going to bed　**307 ring** (With sexual suggestion.)

264 are fair enough i.e., are not in need of repair.　**265 cuckolds** husbands whose wives are unfaithful　**279 dumb** at a loss for words.

BELMONT, AVENUE TO PORTIA'S HOUSE, ACT IIV, SCENE I, FROM 'THE MERCHANT OF VENICE', FROM THE BOYDELL SHAKESPEARE GALLERY, PUBLISHED LATE 19TH CENTURY (LITHO), HODGES, WILLIAM (1744–97) (AFTER)/PRIVATE COLLECTION/KEN WELSH/THE BRIDGEMAN ART LIBRARY

Much Ado About Nothing

Much Ado About Nothing belongs to a group of Shakespeare's most mature romantic comedies, linked by similar titles, that also includes *As You Like It* and *Twelfth Night* (subtitled *What You Will*). All date from the period 1598 to 1600. These plays are the culmination of Shakespeare's exuberant, philosophical, and festive vein in comedy, with only an occasional anticipation of the darker problem comedies of the early 1600s. They also parallel the culmination of Shakespeare's writing of history plays, in *Henry IV* and *V*.

Much Ado excels in combative wit and in swift, colloquial prose. It differs, too, from several other comedies (including *A Midsummer Night's Dream* and *The Merchant of Venice*) in that it features no journey of the lovers, no heroine disguised as a man, no envious court or city contrasted with an idealized landscape of the artist's imagination. Instead, the prevailing motif is that of the mask. Prominent scenes include a masked ball (2.1), a charade offstage in which the villainous Borachio misrepresents himself as the lover of Hero (actually Margaret in disguise), and a marriage ceremony with the supposedly dead bride masking as her own cousin (5.3). The word *Nothing* in the play's title, pronounced rather like *noting* in the English of Elizabethan London and vicinity, suggests a pun on the idea of overhearing as well as of musical notation; it also has a bawdy connotation, as when Hamlet wryly suggests to Ophelia that "Nothing" is "a fair thought to lie between maids' legs" (*Hamlet*, 3.2.116–18; see also *Othello*, 3.3.317, where Iago responds to his wife's "I have a thing for you" with a degrading sexual insult). Overhearings are constant and are essential to the process of both misunderstanding (as in the false rumor of Don Pedro's wooing Hero for himself) and clarification (as in the discovery by the night watch of the slander done to Hero's reputation, or in the revelation to Beatrice and Benedick of each other's true state of mind). The masks, or roles, that the characters incessantly assume are, for the most part, defensive and inimical to mutual understanding. How can they be dispelled? It is the search for candor and self-awareness in relationships with others, the quest for honesty and respect beneath conventional outward appearances, that provides the journey in this play.

Structurally, the play contrasts two pairs of lovers. The ladies, Beatrice and Hero, are cousins and close friends. The gentlemen, Benedick and Claudio, Italian gentlemen and fellow officers under the command of Don Pedro, have returned from the war, in which they have fought bravely. These similarities chiefly serve, however, to accentuate the differences between the two couples. Hero is modest, retiring, usually silent, and obedient to her father's will. Claudio appears ideally suited to her, since he is also respectful and decorous. They are conventional lovers in the roles of romantic hero and naive heroine. Beatrice and Benedick, on the other hand, are renowned for "a kind of merry war" between them. Although obviously destined to come together, they are seemingly too independent and skeptical of convention to be tolerant and accepting in love. They scoff so at romantic sentimentality that they cannot permit themselves to drop their satirical masks. Yet, paradoxically, their relationship is ultimately more surefooted because of their refusal to settle for the illusory cliches of many young wooers.

As in some of his other comic double plots (*The Taming of the Shrew*, for example), Shakespeare has linked together two stories of diverse origins and contrasting tones in order to set off one against the other. The Hero-Claudio plot is Italianate in flavor and origin, sensational, melodramatic, and potentially tragic. In fact, the often told story of the maiden falsely slandered did frequently end in disaster—as, for example, in Edmund Spenser's *Faerie Queene*, 2.4 (1590). Spenser was apparently indebted to Ariosto's *Orlando Furioso* (translated into English by Sir John Harington, 1591), as were Peter Beverly in *The Historie of Ariodanto and Ieneura* (1566) and Richard Mulcaster in his play *Ariodante and Genevora* (1583).

Shakespeare seems to have relied more on the Italian version by Matteo Bandello (Lucca, 1554) and its French translation by Belleforest, *Histoires Tragiques* (1569). Still other versions have been discovered, both nondramatic and dramatic, although it cannot be established that Shakespeare was reworking an old play. Various factual inconsistencies in Shakespeare's text (such as Leonato's wife Innogen and a "kinsman" who are named briefly in both quarto and Folio but have no roles in the play) can perhaps be explained by Shakespeare's having worked quickly from more than one source.

Shakespeare's other plot, of Benedick and Beatrice, is much more English and his own. The battle of the sexes is a staple of English medieval humor (Chaucer's Wife of Bath, the Wakefield play of *Noah*) and of Shakespeare's own early comedy: Berowne and Rosaline in *Love's Labor's Lost*, Petruchio and Katharina in *The Taming of the Shrew*. The merry war of Benedick and Beatrice is Shakespeare's finest achievement in this vein and was to become a rich legacy in the later English comedy of William Congreve, Oscar Wilde, and George Bernard Shaw. The tone is lighthearted, bantering, and reassuring, in contrast with the Italianate mood of vengeance and duplicity in the Claudio-Hero plot. No less English are the clownish antics of Dogberry and his crew, representing still another group of characters although not a separate plot. Like Constable Dull in *Love's Labor's Lost* or the tradesmen of *A Midsummer Night's Dream*, the buffoons of *Much Ado* function in a nominally Mediterranean setting but are nonetheless recognizable London types. Their preposterous antics not only puncture the ominous mood threatening our enjoyment of the main plot but also, absurdly enough, even help to abort a potential crime. When Dogberry comes, laughter cannot be far behind.

The two plots provide contrasting perspectives on the nature of love. Because it is sensational and melodramatic, the Claudio-Hero plot stresses situation at the expense of character. The conspiracy that nearly overwhelms the lovers is an engrossing story, but they themselves remain one-dimensional. They interest us more as conventional types, and hence as foils to Benedick and Beatrice, than as lovers in their own right. Benedick and Beatrice, on the other hand, are psychologically complex. Clearly, they are fascinated with each other. Beatrice's questions in the first scene, although abusive in tone, betray her concern for Benedick's welfare. Has he safely returned from the wars? How did he bear himself in battle? Who are his companions? She tests his moral character by high standards, suspecting that he will fail because she demands so much. We are not surprised when she lectures her docile cousin, Hero, on the folly of submitting to parental choice in marriage: "It is my cousin's duty to make curtsy and say, 'Father, as it please you.' But yet for all that, cousin, let him be a handsome fellow, or else

make another curtsy and say, 'Father, as it please me' " (2.1.49–52). Beatrice remains single not from love of spinsterhood but from insistence on a nearly perfect mate. Paradoxically, she who is the inveterate scoffer is the true idealist. And we know from her unceasing fascination with Benedick that he, of all the men in her acquaintance, comes closest to her mark. The only fear preventing the revelation of her love—a not unnatural fear, in view of the insults she and Benedick exchange—is that he will prove faithless and jest at her weakness.

Benedick is similarly hemmed in by his posturing as "a professed tyrant to their sex." Despite his reputation as a perennial bachelor and his wry amusement at Claudio's newfound passion, Benedick confesses in soliloquy (2.3.8–34) that he could be won to affection by the ideal woman. Again, his criteria are chiefly those of temperament and moral character, although he by no means spurns wealth, beauty, and social position; the happiest couples are those well matched in fortune's gifts. "Rich she shall be, that's certain; wise, or I'll none; virtuous, or I'll never cheapen her; fair, or I'll never look on her; mild, or come not near me; noble, or not I for an angel; of good discourse, an excellent musician, and her hair shall be of what color it please God." This last self-mocking concession indicates that Benedick is aware of how impossibly much he is asking. Still, there is one woman, Beatrice, who may well possess all of these qualities except mildness. Even her sharp wit is part of her admirable intelligence. She is a match for Benedick, and he is a man who would never tolerate the submissive conventionality of someone like Hero. All that appears to be lacking, in fact, is any sign of fondness on Beatrice's part. For him to make overtures would be to invite her withering scorn—not to mention the I-told-you-so mockery of his friends.

Benedick and Beatrice have been playing the game of verbal abuse for so long that they scarcely remember how it started—perhaps as a squaring-off between the only two intelligences worthy of contending with each other, perhaps as a more profoundly defensive reaction of two sensitive persons not willing to part lightly with their independence. They seem to have had a prior relationsip with each other that ended unhappily. They know that intimate involvement with another person is a complex matter—one that can cause heartache. Yet the masks they wear with each other are scarcely satisfactory. At the masked ball (2.1), we see how hurtful the "merry war" has become. Benedick, attempting to pass himself off as a stranger in a mask, abuses Beatrice by telling her of her reputation for disdain; but she, perceiving who he is, retaliates by telling him as a purported stranger what she "really" thinks of Benedick. These devices cut deeply and confirm the worst fears of each. Ironically, these fears can be dispelled only by the virtuous deceptions practiced on them by their friends. Once Benedick is assured that Beatrice secretly loves him, masking her affection with scorn, he acquires the confidence he needs to make a commitment, and vice versa in her case. The beauty of the virtuous deceptions, moreover, is that they are so plausible—because, indeed, they are essentially true. Benedick overhears himself described as a person so satirical that Beatrice dare not reveal her affection, for fear of being repulsed (2.3). Beatrice learns that she is indeed called disdainful by her friends (3.1). Both lovers respond generously to these revelations, accepting the accusations as richly deserved and placing no blame on the other. As Beatrice proclaims to herself, "Contempt, farewell, and maiden pride, adieu!" The relief afforded by this honesty is genuine and lasting.

Because Claudio knows so little about Hero and is content with superficial expectations, he is vulnerable to a far uglier sort of deception. Claudio's first questions about Hero betray his romantically stereotyped attitudes and his willingness to let Don Pedro and Hero's father, Leonato, arrange a financially advantageous match. Claudio treasures Hero's outward reputation for modesty, an appearance easily besmirched. When a false rumor suggests that Don Pedro is wooing the lady for himself, Claudio's response is predictably cliché-ridden: all's fair in love and war, you can't trust friends in an affair of the heart, and so farewell Hero. The rumor has a superficial plausibility about it, especially when the villainous Don John steps into the situation. Motivated in part by pure malice and the sport of ruining others' happiness, Don John speaks to the masked Claudio at the ball (2.1) as though he were speaking to Benedick and, in this guise, pretends to reveal the secret "fact" of Don Pedro's duplicity in love. (The device is precisely that used by Beatrice to put down Benedick in the same scene.) With this specious confirmation, Claudio leaps to a wrong conclusion, thereby judging both his friend and mistress to be false. He gives them no chance to speak in their own defense. To be sure, Hero's father and uncle have also believed in the false report and have welcomed the prospect of Don Pedro as Hero's husband. She herself raises no objection to the prospect of marriage with the older man. Don Pedro is, after all, a prince of presumably enormous wealth, power, and social status, well above that of Leonato and his well-to-do but bourgeois family; when he asks (perhaps as a pleasantry) if Beatrice will have him as her husband, her polite refusal seems tinged with a note of regret (2.1.303–21). These attractive features in Don Pedro tend to excuse the general willingness to accept the idea of him as a splendidly suitable husband for Hero. Even so, Claudio has revealed a lack of faith resulting from his slender knowledge of Hero and of himself.

The nearly tragic "demonstration" of Hero's infidelity follows the same course, because Claudio has not learned from his first experience. Once again, the villainous Don John first implants the insidious suggestion in Claudio's mind, then creates an illusion entirely plausible to the senses, and finally confirms it with Borachio's testimony. What Claudio and Don Pedro have actually seen is Margaret wooed at Hero's window, shrouded in the dark of night and seen from "afar off in the orchard." The power of suggestion is enough to do the rest. Don John's method, and his pleasure in evil, are much like those of his later counterparts, Iago in *Othello* and Edmund in *King Lear*. Indeed, John is compared with the devil, who has power over mortals' frail senses but must rely on their complicity and acquiescence in evil. Claudio is once again led to denounce faithlessly the virtuous woman whose loyalty he no longer deserves. Yet his fault is typically human and is shared by Don Pedro. Providence gives him a second chance, through the ludicrous and bumbling intervention of Dogberry's night watch. These men overhear the plot of Don John as soon as it is announced to us, so that we know justice will eventually prevail, even though it will also be farcically delayed. Once again, misunderstanding has become "much ado about nothing," an escalating of recriminations based on a purely chimerical assumption that must eventually be deflated. The painful experience is not without value, for it tests the characters' spiritual worth in a crisis. Beatrice, like Friar Francis, shows herself to be a person of unshakable faith in goodness. Benedick, though puzzled and torn in his loyalties, also passes the test and proves himself worthy of Beatrice. Claudio is found wanting, and indeed is judged by many modern readers and audiences to be wholly inadequate, but Hero forgives and accepts him anyway. In her role as the granter of a merciful second chance, she foreshadows the beatifically symbolic nature of many of Shakespeare's later heroines.

Much Ado comes perhaps closer to potentially tragic action than Shakespeare's other festive comedies, though *The Merchant of Venice* is another, and so are late romances like *Cymbeline* and *The Winter's Tale* that *Much Ado* can be said to anticipate in the serious matter of slander against a virtuous heroine. Most strikingly, Claudio's failure is unnervingly like that of Othello. The fact that both men are too easily persuaded to reject and humiliate the innocent women they love suggests a deep inadequacy in each. The tempters (Don John, Iago) cannot alone be blamed; the male lovers themselves are too prone to believe the worst of women. In Claudio we can see a vulnerability in the very way he looks at courtship and marriage. As Benedick jests, Claudio talks almost as though he wants to buy Hero (1.1.172). Certainly his attitude is acquisitive and superficial; as the conquering hero returned from the wars, he is ready to settle down into married respectability, and he needs a socially eligible wife. He desires Hero for her beauty, for her wealth and family connections, and above all for her modesty and her reputation for virginal purity. These

HERO   My cousin means Signor Benedick of Padua.

MESSENGER   Oh, he's returned, and as pleasant as ever 35
he was.

BEATRICE   He set up his bills here in Messina and chal- 37
lenged Cupid at the flight; and my uncle's fool, reading 38
the challenge, subscribed for Cupid and challenged 39
him at the bird-bolt. I pray you, how many hath he 40
killed and eaten in these wars? But how many hath he
killed? For indeed I promised to eat all of his killing.

LEONATO   Faith, niece, you tax Signor Benedick too 43
much, but he'll be meet with you, I doubt it not. 44

MESSENGER   He hath done good service, lady, in these
wars.

BEATRICE   You had musty victual, and he hath holp to 47
eat it. He is a very valiant trencherman; he hath an 48
excellent stomach. 49

MESSENGER   And a good soldier too, lady.

BEATRICE   And a good soldier to a lady, but what is he 51
to a lord? 52

MESSENGER   A lord to a lord, a man to a man, stuffed 53
with all honorable virtues.

BEATRICE   It is so, indeed, he is no less than a stuffed 55
man. But for the stuffing—well, we are all mortal. 56

LEONATO   You must not, sir, mistake my niece. There is
a kind of merry war betwixt Signor Benedick and her.
They never meet but there's a skirmish of wit between
them.

BEATRICE   Alas! He gets nothing by that. In our last
conflict, four of his five wits went halting off, and now 62
is the whole man governed with one; so that if he have
wit enough to keep himself warm, let him bear it for a
difference between himself and his horse, for it is all 65
the wealth that he hath left to be known a reasonable 66
creature. Who is his companion now? He hath every 67
month a new sworn brother. 68

MESSENGER   Is't possible?

BEATRICE   Very easily possible. He wears his faith but as 70
the fashion of his hat; it ever changes with the next
block. 72

MESSENGER   I see, lady, the gentleman is not in your 73
books. 74

BEATRICE   No. An he were, I would burn my study. But 75
I pray you, who is his companion? Is there no young
squarer now that will make a voyage with him to the 77
devil?

MESSENGER   He is most in the company of the right
noble Claudio.

BEATRICE   Oh, Lord, he will hang upon him like a 81
disease! He is sooner caught than the pestilence, and
the taker runs presently mad. God help the noble 83
Claudio! If he have caught the Benedick, it will cost 84
him a thousand pound ere 'a be cured. 85

MESSENGER   I will hold friends with you, lady. 86

BEATRICE   Do, good friend.

LEONATO   You will never run mad, niece. 88

BEATRICE   No, not till a hot January. 89

MESSENGER   Don Pedro is approached.

*Enter Don Pedro, Claudio, Benedick, Balthasar,
and [Don] John the Bastard.*

DON PEDRO   Good Signor Leonato, are you come to
meet your trouble? The fashion of the world is to 92
avoid cost, and you encounter it. 93

LEONATO   Never came trouble to my house in the
likeness of Your Grace. For trouble being gone,
comfort should remain; but when you depart from
me, sorrow abides and happiness takes his leave.

DON PEDRO   You embrace your charge too willingly.—I 98
think this is your daughter.

[Presenting himself to Hero.]

LEONATO   Her mother hath many times told me so.

BENEDICK   Were you in doubt, sir, that you asked her?

LEONATO   Signor Benedick, no; for then were you a
child.

DON PEDRO   You have it full, Benedick. We may guess 104
by this what you are, being a man. Truly, the lady
fathers herself. Be happy, lady, for you are like an 106
honorable father.

BENEDICK   If Signor Leonato be her father, she would
not have his head on her shoulders for all Messina, as 109
like him as she is.   *[Don Pedro and Leonato talk aside.]*

BEATRICE   I wonder that you will still be talking, Signor
Benedick. Nobody marks you.

BENEDICK   What, my dear Lady Disdain! Are you yet
living?

BEATRICE   Is it possible disdain should die while she
hath such meet food to feed it as Signor Benedick? 116

---

35 pleasant jocular   **37 bills** placards, advertisements   **38 at the
flight** to a long-distance archery contest. (Beatrice mocks Benedick's
pretentions as a lady killer.)   **my uncle's fool** (Perhaps a professional fool in her uncle's service.)   **39 subscribed for** accepted on
behalf of   **40 bird-bolt** a blunt-headed arrow used for fowling.
(Sometimes used by children because of its relative harmlessness
and thus conventionally appropriate to Cupid.)   **43 tax** disparage
44 meet even, quits   **47 musty victual** stale food.   **holp** helped
48 valiant trencherman great eater   **49 stomach** appetite. (With a
mocking suggestion also of "courage.")   **51 soldier to a lady** lady
killer. (With a play on *to/too.*)   **52 to** compared to   **53 stuffed**
amply supplied   **55–6 a stuffed man** i.e., a figure stuffed to resemble a man.   **56 the stuffing** i.e., what he's truly made of.   **well . . .
mortal** i.e., well, we all have our faults.   **62 five wits** i.e., not the
five senses, but the five faculties: memory, imagination, judgment,
fantasy, common sense.   **halting** limping   **65 difference** heraldic
feature distinguishing a junior member or branch of a family. (With
a play on the usual sense.)   **65–7 it is . . . creature** i.e., his feeble wit
is all he has left to identify him as rationally human.   **68 sworn
brother** brother in arms (*frater juratus*, an allusion to the ancient
practice of swearing brotherhood).   **70 faith** allegiance, or fidelity
72 block mold for shaping hats.

73–4 in your books in favor with you, in your good books. (But Beatrice, in her reply, takes *books* in the literal sense of something to be
found in a library.)   **75 An** If. (Also in line 131.)   **77 squarer** quarreler   **81 he** i.e., Benedick   **83 presently** immediately   **84 the
Benedick** i.e., as if this were a disease   **85 'a** he   **86 hold friends**
keep on friendly terms (so as not to earn your enmity)   **88 run mad**
i.e., "catch the Benedick"   **89 not . . . January** i.e., not any time soon.
92 your trouble i.e., the expense of entertaining me and my retinue.
93 encounter go to meet   **98 charge** social responsibility and
expense   **104 have it full** are well answered   **106 fathers herself**
shows by appearance who her father is.   **109 his head** i.e., with
Leonato's white beard and signs of age   **116 meet** suitable. (With a
pun on "meat.")

Courtesy itself must convert to disdain, if you come in 117
her presence.

BENEDICK   Then is courtesy a turncoat. But it is certain
I am loved of all ladies, only you excepted; and I
would I could find in my heart that I had not a hard
heart, for truly I love none.

BEATRICE   A dear happiness to women! They would 123
else have been troubled with a pernicious suitor. I
thank God and my cold blood I am of your humor for 125
that. I had rather hear my dog bark at a crow than a 126
man swear he loves me.

BENEDICK   God keep Your Ladyship still in that mind!
So some gentleman or other shall scape a predestinate 129
scratched face.

BEATRICE   Scratching could not make it worse, an 'twere
such a face as yours were. 132

BENEDICK   Well, you are a rare parrot-teacher. 133

BEATRICE   A bird of my tongue is better than a beast of 134
yours. 135

BENEDICK   I would my horse had the speed of your
tongue and so good a continuer. But keep your way, 137
i'God's name; I have done.

BEATRICE   You always end with a jade's trick. I know 139
you of old.

DON PEDRO   That is the sum of all, Leonato. Signor 141
Claudio and Signor Benedick, my dear friend Leonato
hath invited you all. I tell him we shall stay here at the
least a month, and he heartily prays some occasion
may detain us longer. I dare swear he is no hypocrite,
but prays from his heart.

LEONATO   If you swear, my lord, you shall not be forsworn. [To Don John] Let me bid you welcome, my
lord, being reconciled to the Prince your brother. I owe 149
you all duty.

DON JOHN   I thank you. I am not of many words, but I
thank you.

LEONATO   Please it Your Grace lead on? 153

DON PEDRO   Your hand, Leonato. We will go together. 154
                        Exeunt. Manent Benedick and Claudio.

CLAUDIO   Benedick, didst thou note the daughter of
Signor Leonato?

BENEDICK   I noted her not, but I looked on her. 157

CLAUDIO   Is she not a modest young lady?

BENEDICK   Do you question me as an honest man
should do, for my simple true judgment? Or would

you have me speak after my custom, as being a
professed tyrant to their sex? 162

CLAUDIO   No, I pray thee, speak in sober judgment.

BENEDICK   Why, i'faith, methinks she's too low for a 164
high praise, too brown for a fair praise, and too little
for a great praise. Only this commendation I can afford
her, that were she other than she is, she were unhandsome, and being no other but as she is, I do not like
her.

CLAUDIO   Thou thinkest I am in sport. I pray thee, tell
me truly how thou lik'st her.

BENEDICK   Would you buy her, that you inquire after
her?

CLAUDIO   Can the world buy such a jewel?

BENEDICK   Yea, and a case to put it into. But speak you 175
this with a sad brow? Or do you play the flouting Jack, 176
to tell us Cupid is a good hare-finder and Vulcan a rare 177
carpenter? Come, in what key shall a man take you, to 178
go in the song? 179

CLAUDIO   In mine eye she is the sweetest lady that ever
I looked on.

BENEDICK   I can see yet without spectacles, and I see no
such matter. There's her cousin, an she were not possessed with a fury, exceeds her as much in beauty as the 184
first of May doth the last of December. But I hope you
have no intent to turn husband, have you?

CLAUDIO   I would scarce trust myself, though I had
sworn the contrary, if Hero would be my wife.

BENEDICK   Is't come to this? In faith, hath not the world 189
one man but he will wear his cap with suspicion? Shall 190
I never see a bachelor of threescore again? Go to, 191
i'faith; an thou wilt needs thrust thy neck into a yoke,
wear the print of it and sigh away Sundays. Look, Don 193
Pedro is returned to seek you.

                        Enter Don Pedro.

DON PEDRO   What secret hath held you here, that you
followed not to Leonato's?

BENEDICK   I would Your Grace would constrain me to 197
tell.

DON PEDRO   I charge thee on thy allegiance.

BENEDICK   You hear, Count Claudio. I can be secret as a
dumb man—I would have you think so—but on my
allegiance, mark you this, on my allegiance! He is in
love. With who? Now that is Your Grace's part. Mark 203
how short his answer is: with Hero, Leonato's short
daughter.

117 convert change   123 dear happiness precious piece of luck
125–6 I am . . . that I am of the same disposition in that matter, i.e., of
loving no one.   129 scape escape.   predestinate inevitable (for any
man who should woo Beatrice)   132 were i.e., is.   133 rare outstanding.   parrot-teacher i.e., one who would teach a parrot well, because
you merely "parrot" my lines.   134 of my tongue taught to speak
like me, i.e., incessantly   134–5 of yours taught to speak like you.
137 and . . . continuer i.e., and as much staying power in running as
you have in talking.   139 a jade's trick i.e., an ill-tempered horse's
habit of slipping its head out of the collar or stopping suddenly (just
as Benedick proposes to abandon this exchange of witticisms when
he thinks he has had the last word).   141 sum of all (Don Pedro and
Leonato have been conversing apart on other matters.)   149 being
since you are   153 Please it May it please   154 go together i.e., go
arm in arm (thus avoiding the question of precedence in order of
leaving).   154.1 Manent They remain onstage   157 noted her not
gave her no special attention

162 tyrant one cruel or pitiless in attitude   164 low short   175 case
(1) jewel case (2) clothing, outer garments. (There is also a bawdy
play on the meaning "female pudenda.")   176 sad serious.   flouting
Jack i.e., mocking rascal   177–8 to tell . . . carpenter? i.e., are you
mocking us with nonsense? (Cupid was blind, not sharp-eyed like a
hunter, and Vulcan was a blacksmith, not a carpenter.)   178–9 to . . .
song as the song expresses it. (Alluding perhaps to some popular
song.)   184 with a fury by an avenging, infernal spirit   189–90 hath
. . . suspicion? i.e., isn't there a man left alive who will regard marriage with a jaundiced eye? (A cap might be used, unsuccessfully perhaps, in an attempt to hide a cuckold's horns.)   191 Go to (An
expression of impatience.)   193 wear . . . Sundays i.e., display the
marks of your domestic enslavement resignedly.   197 constrain
order   203 part speaking part. (I.e., to say, "With who?")

CLAUDIO   If this were so, so were it uttered.   206

BENEDICK   Like the old tale, my lord: "It is not so, nor   207
'twas not so, but indeed, God forbid it should be so."

CLAUDIO   If my passion change not shortly, God forbid
it should be otherwise.

DON PEDRO   Amen, if you love her, for the lady is very
well worthy.

CLAUDIO   You speak this to fetch me in, my lord.   213

DON PEDRO   By my troth, I speak my thought.   214

CLAUDIO   And in faith, my lord, I spoke mine.

BENEDICK   And by my two faiths and troths, my lord, I   216
spoke mine.

CLAUDIO   That I love her, I feel.

DON PEDRO   That she is worthy, I know.

BENEDICK   That I neither feel how she should be loved
nor know how she should be worthy is the opinion
that fire cannot melt out of me. I will die in it at the
stake.

DON PEDRO   Thou wast ever an obstinate heretic in the
despite of beauty.   225

CLAUDIO   And never could maintain his part but in the   226
force of his will.   227

BENEDICK   That a woman conceived me, I thank her;
that she brought me up, I likewise give her most humble thanks. But that I will have a recheat winded in my   230
forehead or hang my bugle in an invisible baldrick, all   231
women shall pardon me. Because I will not do them   232
the wrong to mistrust any, I will do myself the right to
trust none; and the fine is, for the which I may go the   234
finer, I will live a bachelor.   235

DON PEDRO   I shall see thee, ere I die, look pale with
love.

BENEDICK   With anger, with sickness, or with hunger,
my lord, not with love. Prove that ever I lose more   239
blood with love than I will get again with drinking,   240
pick out mine eyes with a ballad-maker's pen and   241
hang me up at the door of a brothel house for the sign   242
of blind Cupid.

DON PEDRO   Well, if ever thou dost fall from this faith,
thou wilt prove a notable argument.   245

BENEDICK   If I do, hang me in a bottle like a cat and   246
shoot at me, and he that hits me, let him be clapped on
the shoulder and called Adam.   248

DON PEDRO   Well, as time shall try:
"In time the savage bull doth bear the yoke."   250

BENEDICK   The savage bull may; but if ever the sensible
Benedick bear it, pluck off the bull's horns and set
them in my forehead, and let me be vilely painted, and
in such great letters as they write, "Here is good horse
to hire," let them signify under my sign, "Here you
may see Benedick the married man."

CLAUDIO   If this should ever happen, thou wouldst be
horn-mad.   258

DON PEDRO   Nay, if Cupid have not spent all his quiver
in Venice, thou wilt quake for this shortly.   260

BENEDICK   I look for an earthquake too, then.   261

DON PEDRO   Well, you will temporize with the hours. In   262
the meantime, good Signor Benedick, repair to
Leonato's. Commend me to him, and tell him I will
not fail him at supper, for indeed he hath made great
preparation.

BENEDICK   I have almost matter enough in me for such   267
an embassage; and so I commit you—   268

CLAUDIO   To the tuition of God. From my house, if I had   269
it—

DON PEDRO   The sixth of July. Your loving friend,
Benedick.

BENEDICK   Nay, mock not, mock not. The body of your
discourse is sometime guarded with fragments, and   274
the guards are but slightly basted on neither. Ere you   275
flout old ends any further, examine your conscience.   276
And so I leave you.   *Exit.*

CLAUDIO
My liege, Your Highness now may do me good.   278

DON PEDRO
My love is thine to teach. Teach it but how,
And thou shalt see how apt it is to learn
Any hard lesson that may do thee good.

CLAUDIO
Hath Leonato any son, my lord?

DON PEDRO
No child but Hero; she's his only heir.
Dost thou affect her, Claudio?

CLAUDIO   O my lord,   284

---

206 If . . . uttered If this were true, it might be told in words to this
effect.   **207 old tale** (In the English fairy tale known as "Mr. Fox," a
murderous wooer, discovered in his crimes by the lady he seeks to
marry and victimize, repeatedly disclaims her recital of what she has
seen by the refrain here set in quotations. The story is a variant of the
theme known as "the Robber Bridegroom." Benedick uses it mockingly here to characterize Claudio's reluctance to admit his "crime" of
falling in love.)   **213 fetch me in** get me to confess   **214 By my troth**
By my faith, upon my word. (A mild oath.)   **216 by . . . troths** as it
were, by my loyalty to you both   **225 despite** contempt   **226–7 in . . .
will** by mere obstinacy (which, as defined by the Schoolmen, was the
state of the heretic).   **230–2 But that . . . me** i.e., Women must pardon
me for refusing to have a horn placed on my head as if I were a cuckold. (A *recheat* is a hunting call sounded [*winded*] on a horn to assemble the hounds; a *baldrick* is a strap that supports the horn, here
invisible because the horn is the metaphorical one of cuckoldry.)
234 fine conclusion   **234–5 go the finer** be more finely dressed (since
without a wife I will have more money to spend on clothing).
239 Prove If you can prove   **239–40 lose . . . drinking** (According to
Elizabethan theory, each sigh cost the heart a drop of blood, whereas
blood was replenished by wine.)   **241 ballad-maker's pen** i.e., such
as would be used to write love ballads or satires   **242 sign** painted
sign, such as hung over inns and shops   **245 notable argument** notorious subject for conversation, example.

246 bottle wicker or leather basket (to hold the cat sometimes used as
an archery target)   **248 Adam** (Probably refers to Adam Bell, archer
outlaw of the ballads.)   **250 In . . . yoke** (Proverbial.)   **258 horn-mad**
stark mad. (From the fury of horned beasts; with allusion to cuckoldry.)   **260 Venice** (A city noted for licentiousness.)   **quake** (With a
pun on *quiver* in the previous line.)   **261 I . . . then** i.e., My falling in
love will be at least as rare as an earthquake.   **262 temporize . . .
hours** come to terms, or become milder, in time. (With perhaps a
bawdy pun on *hours,* "whores," pronounced something like "hoors.")
267 matter wit, intelligence   **268 embassage** mission.   **and so . . . you**
(A conventional close, which Claudio and Don Pedro mockingly play
with as though it were the complimentary close of a letter.)
269 tuition protection   **274 guarded** ornamented, trimmed
275 guards . . . neither trimmings are tenuously stitched on at best,
have only the flimsiest connection.   **276 flout old ends** quote or recite
mockingly proverbial tags of wisdom (as well as fragments of cloth, or
the *ends* of letters that Claudio and Don Pedro have been parodying).
examine your conscience look to your own behavior or speech.
278 do me good do me some good, help me.   **284 affect** love

When you went onward on this ended action,   285
I looked upon her with a soldier's eye,
That liked, but had a rougher task in hand
Than to drive liking to the name of love.
But now I am returned and that war thoughts   289
Have left their places vacant, in their rooms
Come thronging soft and delicate desires,
All prompting me how fair young Hero is,
Saying, I liked her ere I went to wars.

DON PEDRO
Thou wilt be like a lover presently
And tire the hearer with a book of words.
If thou dost love fair Hero, cherish it,
And I will break with her and with her father,   297
And thou shalt have her. Was't not to this end
That thou began'st to twist so fine a story?   299

CLAUDIO
How sweetly you do minister to love,
That know love's grief by his complexion!   301
But lest my liking might too sudden seem,
I would have salved it with a longer treatise.   303

DON PEDRO
What need the bridge much broader than the flood?   304
The fairest grant is the necessity.   305
Look what will serve is fit. 'Tis once: thou lovest, 306
And I will fit thee with the remedy.
I know we shall have reveling tonight;
I will assume thy part in some disguise
And tell fair Hero I am Claudio,
And in her bosom I'll unclasp my heart
And take her hearing prisoner with the force
And strong encounter of my amorous tale.
Then after to her father will I break,
And the conclusion is, she shall be thine.
In practice let us put it presently.   *Exeunt.*

❧

[1.2]

Enter Leonato and an old man [Antonio],
brother to Leonato, [meeting].

LEONATO   How now, brother, where is my cousin,   1
your son? Hath he provided this music?

ANTONIO   He is very busy about it. But brother, I can
tell you strange news that you yet dreamt not of.

LEONATO   Are they good?   5

ANTONIO   As the event stamps them, but they have a 6
good cover; they show well outward. The Prince and   7

Count Claudio, walking in a thick-pleached alley in   8
mine orchard, were thus much overheard by a man of   9
mine: the Prince discovered to Claudio that he loved 10
my niece your daughter and meant to acknowledge it
this night in a dance, and if he found her accordant, he 12
meant to take the present time by the top and instantly 13
break with you of it.

LEONATO   Hath the fellow any wit that told you this?   15

ANTONIO   A good sharp fellow. I will send for him, and
question him yourself.

LEONATO   No, no; we will hold it as a dream till it
appear itself. But I will acquaint my daughter withal,
that she may be the better prepared for an answer, if
peradventure this be true. Go you and tell her of it.

[*Enter Antonio's Son, with a musician and*
others.]

Cousins, you know what you have to do.—Oh, I cry   22
you mercy, friend; go you with me, and I will use your   23
skill.—Good cousin, have a care this busy time.
Exeunt.

❧

[1.3]

Enter Sir [Don] John the Bastard and Conrade,
his companion.

CONRADE   What the goodyear, my lord! Why are you   1
thus out of measure sad?   2

DON JOHN   There is no measure in the occasion that
breeds; therefore the sadness is without limit.

CONRADE   You should hear reason.   5

DON JOHN   And when I have heard it, what blessing
brings it?

CONRADE   If not a present remedy, at least a patient
sufferance.   9

DON JOHN   I wonder that thou, being, as thou say'st
thou art, born under Saturn, goest about to apply a   11
moral medicine to a mortifying mischief. I cannot hide 12
what I am: I must be sad when I have cause and smile
at no man's jests, eat when I have stomach and wait   14
for no man's leisure, sleep when I am drowsy and
tend on no man's business, laugh when I am merry   16
and claw no man in his humor.   17

CONRADE   Yea, but you must not make the full show of
this till you may do it without controlment. You have   19
of late stood out against your brother, and he hath   20
ta'en you newly into his grace, where it is impossible 21
you should take true root but by the fair weather that

285 ended action military action now ended   289 now now that
297 break open the subject. (As also in line 314.)   299 twist draw out
the thread of   301 his complexion its outward appearance.
303 salved soothed, eased the way for   304 What need Why need be.
flood river.   305 The fairest . . . necessity The best thing to do is simply what is necessary.   306 Look what Whatever.   'Tis once In
short, once and for all. (This speech of Don Pedro's is overheard by a
servant of Antonio's, as we learn in the next scene.)
1.2. Location: Leonato's house.
1 cousin kinsman   5 they i.e., the news. (Often treated as a plural
noun, as at 2.1.167.)   6 event outcome   6–7 they . . . cover (The
image is of a printed book, promising well by its cover.)

8 thick-pleached alley walk lined with dense hedges of intertwined
shrubs   9 orchard garden.   man servant   10 discovered disclosed
12 accordant agreeing, consenting   13 take . . . top i.e., seize the
opportunity. (Proverbially, Occasion was imagined bald in the back of
the head but with a forelock hair in the front that opportunistically
could be grabbed.)   15 wit sense, intelligence   22–3 cry you mercy
beg your pardon   23 friend (Addressed perhaps to the musician.)
1.3. Location: Leonato's house.
1 What the goodyear i.e., What the deuce   2 out of measure immoderately   5 hear listen to   9 sufferance endurance.   11 under Saturn
(Hence, of a morose disposition.)   11–12 goest . . . mischief endeavor
to cure with moral commonplaces a deadly disease.   14 stomach
appetite   16 tend on attend to   17 claw flatter.   humor whim.
19 controlment restraint.   20 stood out rebelled   21 grace favor

you make yourself. It is needful that you frame the 23
season for your own harvest.

DON JOHN   I had rather be a canker in a hedge than a 25
rose in his grace, and it better fits my blood to be dis- 26
dained of all than to fashion a carriage to rob love from 27
any. In this, though I cannot be said to be a flattering
honest man, it must not be denied but I am a plain-
dealing villain. I am trusted with a muzzle and 30
enfranchised with a clog; therefore I have decreed not 31
to sing in my cage. If I had my mouth, I would bite; if
I had my liberty, I would do my liking. In the
meantime let me be that I am, and seek not to alter me.

CONRADE   Can you make no use of your discontent?

DON JOHN   I make all use of it, for I use it only. Who 36
comes here?

Enter Borachio.

What news, Borachio?

BORACHIO   I came yonder from a great supper. The
Prince your brother is royally entertained by Leonato,
and I can give you intelligence of an intended mar- 41
riage.

DON JOHN   Will it serve for any model to build mischief
on? What is he for a fool that betroths himself to 44
unquietness?

BORACHIO   Marry, it is your brother's right hand. 46

DON JOHN   Who, the most exquisite Claudio?

BORACHIO   Even he.

DON JOHN   A proper squire! And who, and who? Which 49
way looks he?

BORACHIO   Marry, one Hero, the daughter and heir of
Leonato.

DON JOHN   A very forward March chick! How came 53
you to this?

BORACHIO   Being entertained for a perfumer, as I was 55
smoking a musty room, comes me the Prince and 56
Claudio, hand in hand, in sad conference. I whipped 57
me behind the arras, and there heard it agreed upon 58
that the Prince should woo Hero for himself and,
having obtained her, give her to Count Claudio.

DON JOHN   Come, come, let us thither. This may prove
food to my displeasure. That young start-up hath all 62
the glory of my overthrow. If I can cross him any way, 63
I bless myself every way. You are both sure, and will 64
assist me?

CONRADE   To the death, my lord.

DON JOHN   Let us to the great supper. Their cheer is the
greater that I am subdued. Would the cook were o' my 68
mind! Shall we go prove what's to be done? 69

BORACHIO   We'll wait upon Your Lordship.   *Exeunt.*

[2.1]

Enter Leonato, his brother [Antonio], Hero his
daughter, and Beatrice his niece [with Margaret
and Ursula].

LEONATO   Was not Count John here at supper?

ANTONIO   I saw him not.

BEATRICE   How tartly that gentleman looks! I never can 3
see him but I am heartburned an hour after. 4

HERO   He is of a very melancholy disposition.

BEATRICE   He were an excellent man that were made 6
just in the midway between him and Benedick. The
one is too like an image and says nothing, and the 8
other too like my lady's eldest son, evermore tattling. 9

LEONATO   Then half Signor Benedick's tongue in Count
John's mouth, and half Count John's melancholy in
Signor Benedick's face—

BEATRICE   With a good leg and a good foot, uncle, and
money enough in his purse, such a man would win
any woman in the world, if 'a could get her good will. 15

LEONATO   By my troth, niece, thou wilt never get thee a
husband if thou be so shrewd of thy tongue. 17

ANTONIO   In faith, she's too curst. 18

BEATRICE   Too curst is more than curst. I shall lessen
God's sending that way; for it is said, "God sends a 20
curst cow short horns," but to a cow too curst he sends 21
none.

LEONATO   So, by being too curst, God will send you no
horns.

BEATRICE   Just, if he send me no husband, for the which 25
blessing I am at him upon my knees every morning
and evening. Lord, I could not endure a husband with
a beard on his face! I had rather lie in the woolen. 28

LEONATO   You may light on a husband that hath no
beard.

BEATRICE   What should I do with him? Dress him in my
apparel and make him my waiting-gentlewoman? He
that hath a beard is more than a youth, and he that
hath no beard is less than a man; and he that is more
than a youth is not for me, and he that is less than a
man, I am not for him. Therefore I will even take

23 **frame** fashion   25 **canker** dog rose, one that grows wild rather
than being cultivated in formal gardens   26 **blood** mood, disposition
27 **fashion . . . love** counterfeit a behavior to gain undeserved attention   30–1 **I . . . clog** I am trusted only with my muzzle on and am
allowed freedom only to the extent of being hampered by a heavy
wooden block   31 **decreed** determined   36 **I . . . only** Discontent is
my only resource, and I cultivate it alone.   41 **intelligence** news
44 **What . . . fool** What kind of fool is he   46 **Marry** By the Virgin
Mary, i.e., indeed   49 **proper squire** fine young man. (Said contemptuously.)   53 **forward March chick** precocious young thing (like a
chick hatched early).   55 **entertained for** hired as   56 **smoking**
sweetening the air of (with aromatic smoke).   **comes me** comes. (*Me*
is used colloquially, as also in line 58.)   57 **sad** serious   58 **arras**
tapestry, wall hanging   62 **start-up** upstart   63 **cross** thwart
64 **sure** trustworthy

68–9 **o' my mind** i.e., of a mind to poison the food.   69 **prove** try out
2.1. Location: Leonato's house.
3 **tartly** sour of disposition   4 **heartburned** afflicted with heartburn or
indigestion   6 **He were** A man would be   8 **image** statue   9 **my . . .
son** i.e., a spoiled child.   **tattling** chattering.   15 **'a** he   17 **shrewd**
sharp   18 **curst** shrewish.   20 **that way** in that respect   21 **curst** i.e.,
savage, vicious. (God proverbially takes care that vicious creatures are
limited in their ability to do harm.)   25 **Just** Right, exactly so.   **no
husband** If Beatrice has no husband, there can be no prospect of cuckold's horns. (She may also be jesting about a short penis here and in
lines 20–2.)   28 **in the woolen** between blankets, without sheets.

and whatsoever comes athwart his affection ranges   6
evenly with mine. How canst thou cross this mar-   7
riage?

BORACHIO   Not honestly, my lord, but so covertly that
no dishonesty shall appear in me.

DON JOHN   Show me briefly how.

BORACHIO   I think I told Your Lordship, a year since,   12
how much I am in the favor of Margaret, the waiting
gentlewoman to Hero.

DON JOHN   I remember.

BORACHIO   I can, at any unseasonable instant of the   16
night, appoint her to look out at her lady's chamber
window.

DON JOHN   What life is in that, to be the death of this
marriage?

BORACHIO   The poison of that lies in you to temper. Go   21
you to the Prince your brother; spare not to tell him
that he hath wronged his honor in marrying the renowned Claudio—whose estimation do you mightily   24
hold up—to a contaminated stale, such a one as Hero.   25

DON JOHN   What proof shall I make of that?

BORACHIO   Proof enough to misuse the Prince, to vex   27
Claudio, to undo Hero, and kill Leonato. Look you for
any other issue?   29

DON JOHN   Only to despite them I will endeavor any-   30
thing.

BORACHIO   Go, then, find me a meet hour to draw Don   32
Pedro and the Count Claudio alone. Tell them that you
know that Hero loves me. Intend a kind of zeal both to   34
the Prince and Claudio, as—in love of your brother's   35
honor, who hath made this match, and his friend's
reputation, who is thus like to be cozened with the   37
semblance of a maid—that you have discovered thus.   38
They will scarcely believe this without trial. Offer
them instances, which shall bear no less likelihood   40
than to see me at her chamber window, hear me call
Margaret Hero, hear Margaret term me Claudio; and   42
bring them to see this the very night before the
intended wedding—for in the meantime I will so
fashion the matter that Hero shall be absent—and
there shall appear such seeming truth of Hero's
disloyalty that jealousy shall be called assurance and   47
all the preparation overthrown.   48

DON JOHN   Grow this to what adverse issue it can, I will   49
put it in practice. Be cunning in the working this, and
thy fee is a thousand ducats.   51

BORACHIO   Be you constant in the accusation, and my
cunning shall not shame me.

DON JOHN   I will presently go learn their day of mar-   54
riage.   *Exit [with Borachio].*

✦

[2.3]

Enter Benedick alone.

BENEDICK   Boy!

[Enter Boy.]

BOY   Signor?

BENEDICK   In my chamber window lies a book. Bring it
hither to me in the orchard.   4

BOY   I am here already, sir.   5

BENEDICK   I know that, but I would have thee hence and
here again.   *Exit [Boy].*
I do much wonder that one man, seeing how much
another man is a fool when he dedicates his behaviors
to love, will, after he hath laughed at such shallow follies in others, become the argument of his own scorn   11
by falling in love; and such a man is Claudio. I have
known when there was no music with him but the   13
drum and the fife, and now had he rather hear the   14
tabor and the pipe. I have known when he would have   15
walked ten mile afoot to see a good armor, and now   16
will he lie ten nights awake carving the fashion of a   17
new doublet. He was wont to speak plain and to the   18
purpose, like an honest man and a soldier, and now is
he turned orthography—his words are a very fantas-   20
tical banquet, just so many strange dishes. May I be so
converted and see with these eyes? I cannot tell; I think
not. I will not be sworn but Love may transform me to
an oyster, but I'll take my oath on it, till he have made
an oyster of me, he shall never make me such a fool.
One woman is fair, yet I am well; another is wise, yet
I am well; another virtuous, yet I am well; but till all
graces be in one woman, one woman shall not come
in my grace. Rich she shall be, that's certain; wise, or
I'll none; virtuous, or I'll never cheapen her; fair, or I'll   30
never look on her; mild, or come not near me; noble,   31
or not I for an angel; of good discourse, an excellent   32
musician, and her hair shall be of what color it please
God. Ha! The Prince and Monsieur Love. I will hide
me in the arbor.   *[He hides.]*

Enter Prince [Don Pedro], Leonato, Claudio.

DON PEDRO   Come, shall we hear this music?

6–7 whatsoever . . . mine whatever crosses his inclination runs parallel
with mine.   **12 since** ago   **16 unseasonable** unsuitable, unseemly
21 lies in rests with.   **temper** mix, compound.   **24–5 whose . . . up** and
emphasize how much you admire his reputation   **25 stale** prostitute
27 misuse abuse, deceive   **29 issue** outcome. (With a pun on children
as the product of marriage; cf. 4.1.132.)   **30 despite** torture, injure
32 meet suitable   **34 Intend** Pretend   **35 as** i.e., saying as follows. (The
words between the dashes are to be understood as instructions to Don
John as to what he is to say.)   **37 like** likely.   **cozened** deceived,
cheated   **38 semblance** semblance only, outward appearance.
discovered revealed   **40 instances** proofs   **42 hear . . . Claudio** (Many
editors read *Borachio* for *Claudio*. The present reading may be defended
if one imagines that, by arrangement with Margaret, Borachio is playing
the part of Claudio, but the reading may also be an inconsistency.)
47 jealousy suspicion.   **assurance** certainty   **48 preparation** i.e., for
marriage   **49 Grow this** Let this ripen   **51 ducats** gold coins.

54 presently immediately
2.3. Location: Leonato's garden.
4 orchard garden.   **5 I . . . already** i.e., I will be so quick as to use no
time at all. (But Benedick quibbles on the literal sense.)   **11 argument**
subject   **13-14 there was . . . fife** i.e., his only commitment was to soldiering   **15 tabor . . . pipe** (Symbols of peaceful merriment and wooing.)   **16 armor** suit of armor   **17 carving** planning   **18 doublet** jacket.
20 turned orthography become fastidious and fashionable in his choice
of language   **30 I'll none** I'll have none of her.   **cheapen** make a bid
for. (The idea of lessening her value by using her may also be suggested,
though historically it is a later meaning.)   **31, 32 noble, angel** (Each of
these words involves a pun on the meaning "a coin," a noble being
worth six shillings eightpence and an angel, ten shillings.)

CLAUDIO
Yea, my good lord. How still the evening is,
As hushed on purpose to grace harmony!   38
DON PEDRO [*apart to them*]
See you where Benedick hath hid himself?
CLAUDIO [*apart in reply*]
Oh, very well, my lord. The music ended,   40
We'll fit the kid-fox with a pennyworth.   41

Enter Balthasar with music.

DON PEDRO
Come, Balthasar, we'll hear that song again.
BALTHASAR
Oh, good my lord, tax not so bad a voice   43
To slander music any more than once.
DON PEDRO
It is the witness still of excellency   45
To put a strange face on his own perfection.   46
I pray thee, sing, and let me woo no more.   47
BALTHASAR
Because you talk of wooing, I will sing,   48
Since many a wooer doth commence his suit   49
To her he thinks not worthy, yet he woos,   50
Yet will he swear he loves.
DON PEDRO   Nay, pray thee, come,   51
Or if thou wilt hold longer argument,
Do it in notes.
BALTHASAR   Note this before my notes: 53
There's not a note of mine that's worth the noting.
DON PEDRO
Why, these are very crotchets that he speaks!   55
Note, notes, forsooth, and nothing.   [*Music.*]   56
BENEDICK [*aside*]   Now, divine air! Now is his soul rav-   57
ished! Is it not strange that sheeps' guts should hale   58
souls out of men's bodies? Well, a horn for my money,   59
when all's done.

The Song.

BALTHASAR
Sigh no more, ladies, sigh no more.
Men were deceivers ever,
One foot in sea and one on shore,
To one thing constant never.

---

38 As as if.   **grace harmony** do honor to music.   **40 The music ended** When the music is over   **41 We'll ... pennyworth** i.e., we'll give our sly victim more than he bargained for. (A *kid-fox* is presumably a young fox, as in beast fable; *kid*, i.e., young goat, also suggests one whom they are stalking as their quarry. Claudio may be referring to some children's game.)   **43 tax** task   **45–6 It ... perfection** It is always characteristic of excellence to pretend not to know its own skill.   **47 woo** entreat   **48–51 Because ... he loves** (Balthasar modestly claims to be unworthy of being *wooed*, i.e., entreated, but will comply, since he knows Don Pedro speaks with the hyperbole all wooers use in addressing women they actually consider unworthy.)   **53 notes** music.   **55 crotchets** (1) whims, fancies (2) musical notes of brief duration   **56 nothing** (With a pun on *noting;* the two words were pronounced alike. Compare the same pun in the title of the play, where *Nothing* suggests "noting," or eavesdropping.)   **57 air** melody.   **58 sheeps' guts** strings on musical instruments.   **hale** draw   **59 a horn** a hunting horn, a more masculine instrument than a lute. (But with a perhaps unconscious allusion to a cuckold's horns.)

Then sigh not so, but let them go,
  And be you blithe and bonny,   66
Converting all your sounds of woe
  Into Hey nonny, nonny.   68

Sing no more ditties, sing no moe,   69
  Of dumps so dull and heavy;   70
The fraud of men was ever so,
  Since summer first was leavy.   72
Then sigh not so, but let them go,
  And be you blithe and bonny,
Converting all your sounds of woe
  Into Hey nonny, nonny.

DON PEDRO   By my troth, a good song.
BALTHASAR   And an ill singer, my lord.
DON PEDRO   Ha, no, no, faith, thou sing'st well enough
for a shift.   80
BENEDICK [*aside*]   An he had been a dog that should   81
have howled thus, they would have hanged him, and
I pray God his bad voice bode no mischief. I has as
lief have heard the night raven, come what plague   84
could have come after it.
DON PEDRO   Yea, marry, dost thou hear, Balthasar? I   86
pray thee, get us some excellent music, for tomorrow
night we would have it at the Lady Hero's chamber
window.
BALTHASAR   The best I can, my lord.
DON PEDRO   Do so. Farewell.   *Exit Balthasar.*
Come hither, Leonato. What was it you told me of
today, that your niece Beatrice was in love with Signor
Benedick?
CLAUDIO   Oh, ay! [*Aside to Pedro*] Stalk on, stalk on; the   95
fowl sits.—I did never think that lady would have   96
loved any man.
LEONATO   No, nor I neither, but most wonderful that she
should so dote on Signor Benedick, whom she hath in
all outward behaviors seemed ever to abhor.
BENEDICK [*aside*]   Is't possible? Sits the wind in that   101
corner?   102
LEONATO   By my troth, my lord, I cannot tell what to
think of it but that she loves him with an enraged   104
affection; it is past the infinite of thought.   105
DON PEDRO   Maybe she doth but counterfeit.
CLAUDIO   Faith, like enough.   107
LEONATO   Oh, God, counterfeit? There was never counterfeit of passion came so near the life of passion as she
discovers it.   110
DON PEDRO   Why, what effects of passion shows she?
CLAUDIO [*aside to them*]   Bait the hook well; this fish will
bite.

---

66 blithe and bonny cheerful and carefree   **68 Hey nonny, nonny** (A nonsense refrain.)   **69 moe** more   **70 dumps** mournful songs; also, dances   **72 leavy** leafy.   **80 for a shift** in a pinch.   **81 An** If. (Also in line 161.)   **84 lief** willingly.   **night raven** a bird of night, portending disaster   **86 Yea, marry** (A continuation of Don Pedro's speech preceding Benedick's aside.)   **95–6 Stalk . . . sits** i.e., Proceed stealthily; the hunted bird is hiding in the bush.   **101–2 Sits . . . corner?** Is that the way the wind is blowing?   **104 enraged** maddened with passion   **105 infinite** farthest reach. (It's unbelievable but true.)   **107 like** likely   **110 discovers** betrays

LEONATO   What effects, my lord? She will sit you—you 114
heard my daughter tell you how.

CLAUDIO   She did indeed.

DON PEDRO   How, how, I pray you? You amaze me. I
would have thought her spirit had been invincible
against all assaults of affection.

LEONATO   I would have sworn it had, my lord—especially against Benedick.

BENEDICK [aside]   I should think this a gull but that the 122
white-bearded fellow speaks it. Knavery cannot, sure,
hide himself in such reverence.

CLAUDIO [apart to them]   He hath ta'en th'infection.
Hold it up.   126

DON PEDRO   Hath she made her affection known to
Benedick?

LEONATO   No, and swears she never will. That's her
torment.

CLAUDIO   'Tis true, indeed. So your daughter says.
"Shall I," says she, "that have so oft encountered him 132
with scorn, write to him that I love him?"

LEONATO   This says she now when she is beginning to
write to him, for she'll be up twenty times a night, and
there will she sit in her smock till she have writ a sheet 136
of paper. My daughter tells us all.

CLAUDIO   Now you talk of a sheet of paper, I remember
a pretty jest your daughter told us of.

LEONATO   Oh, when she had writ it and was reading it
over, she found "Benedick" and "Beatrice" between
the sheet?

CLAUDIO   That.   143

LEONATO   Oh, she tore the letter into a thousand half- 144
pence; railed at herself, that she should be so immod- 145
est to write to one that she knew would flout her. "I 146
measure him," says she, "by my own spirit, for I
should flout him if he writ to me. Yea, though I love
him, I should."

CLAUDIO   Then down upon her knees she falls, weeps,
sobs, beats her heart, tears her hair, prays, curses: "O
sweet Benedick! God give me patience!"

LEONATO   She doth indeed; my daughter says so. And
the ecstasy hath so much overborne her that my 154
daughter is sometime afeard she will do a desperate
outrage to herself. It is very true.

DON PEDRO   It were good that Benedick knew of it by
some other, if she will not discover it.   158

CLAUDIO   To what end? He would make but a sport of
it and torment the poor lady worse.

DON PEDRO   An he should, it were an alms to hang him. 161
She's an excellent sweet lady, and, out of all suspicion, 162
she is virtuous.

CLAUDIO   And she is exceeding wise.

DON PEDRO   In everything but in loving Benedick.

LEONATO   O my lord, wisdom and blood combating in 166

so tender a body, we have ten proofs to one that blood
hath the victory. I am sorry for her, as I have just
cause, being her uncle and her guardian.

DON PEDRO   I would she had bestowed this dotage on 170
me. I would have doffed all other respects and made 171
her half myself. I pray you, tell Benedick of it, and hear 172
what 'a will say.

LEONATO   Were it good, think you?

CLAUDIO   Hero thinks surely she will die; for she says
she will die if he love her not, and she will die ere she
make her love known, and she will die if he woo her,
rather than she will bate one breath of her accustomed 178
crossness.   179

DON PEDRO   She doth well. If she should make tender 180
of her love, 'tis very possible he'll scorn it; for the man,
as you know all, hath a contemptible spirit.   182

CLAUDIO   He is a very proper man.   183

DON PEDRO   He hath indeed a good outward happiness. 184

CLAUDIO   Before God, and in my mind, very wise.   185

DON PEDRO   He doth indeed show some sparks that are
like wit.

CLAUDIO   And I take him to be valiant.

DON PEDRO   As Hector, I assure you; and in the manag- 189
ing of quarrels you may say he is wise, for either he
avoids them with great discretion or undertakes them
with a most Christian-like fear.

LEONATO   If he do fear God, 'a must necessarily keep
peace. If he break the peace, he ought to enter into a
quarrel with fear and trembling.

DON PEDRO   And so will he do, for the man doth fear
God, howsoever it seems not in him by some large 197
jests he will make. Well, I am sorry for your niece. Shall
we go seek Benedick and tell him of her love?

CLAUDIO   Never tell him, my lord. Let her wear it out 200
with good counsel.   201

LEONATO   Nay, that's impossible. She may wear her
heart out first.

DON PEDRO   Well, we will hear further of it by your
daughter. Let it cool the while. I love Benedick well,
and I could wish he would modestly examine himself,
to see how much he is unworthy so good a lady.

LEONATO   My lord, will you walk? Dinner is ready.

                                              [They walk aside.]

CLAUDIO   If he do not dote on her upon this, I will never 209
trust my expectation.

DON PEDRO   Let there be the same net spread for her;
and that must your daughter and her gentlewomen
carry. The sport will be when they hold one an opinion 213
of another's dotage, and no such matter; that's the 214

---

114 sit you i.e., sit. (You is used idiomatically.)   122 gull trick, deception.   but except for the fact   126 Hold it up Keep up the jest.
132 she i.e., Beatrice   136 smock chemise   143 That i.e., That's it.
144–5 halfpence i.e., small pieces   146 flout mock   154 overborne
overwhelmed   158 discover reveal   161 alms good deed. (Hanging
would be too good for him.)   162 out of beyond   166 blood natural
feeling

170 dotage doting affection   171 doffed put or turned aside.
respects considerations   172 half myself i.e., my wife.   178 bate
abate   179 crossness perversity, contrariety.   180 tender offer
182 contemptible contemptuous   183 proper handsome   184 outward happiness fortune in his good looks.   185 Before God i.e., By
God, you're absolutely right   189 Hector the mightiest of the Trojans   197 by to judge by.   large broad, indelicate   200 wear it out
eradicate it   201 counsel reflection, deliberation.   209 upon as a
result of, after   213 carry carry out.   213–14 they . . . dotage each
believes the other to be in love   214 no such matter the reality is
quite otherwise

scene that I would see, which will be merely a dumb   215
show. Let us send her to call him in to dinner.   216

[*Exeunt Don Pedro, Claudio, and Leonato.*]

BENEDICK [*coming forward*]   This can be no trick. The
conference was sadly borne. They have the truth of   218
this from Hero. They seem to pity the lady. It seems
her affections have their full bent. Love me? Why, it   220
must be requited. I hear how I am censured. They say
I will bear myself proudly if I perceive the love come
from her; they say too that she will rather die than give
any sign of affection. I did never think to marry. I must
not seem proud; happy are they that hear their detrac-   225
tions and can put them to mending. They say the lady   226
is fair; 'tis a truth, I can bear them witness; and virtuous; 'tis so, I cannot reprove it; and wise but for loving   228
me; by my troth, it is no addition to her wit, nor no
great argument of her folly, for I will be horribly in
love with her. I may chance have some odd quirks and   231
remnants of wit broken on me, because I have railed
so long against marriage. But doth not the appetite
alter? A man loves the meat in his youth that he cannot endure in his age. Shall quips and sentences and   235
these paper bullets of the brain awe a man from the   236
career of his humor? No, the world must be peopled.   237
When I said I would die a bachelor, I did not think I
should live till I were married. Here comes Beatrice.
By this day, she's a fair lady! I do spy some marks of
love in her.

Enter Beatrice.

BEATRICE   Against my will I am sent to bid you come in
to dinner.
BENEDICK   Fair Beatrice, I thank you for your pains.
BEATRICE   I took no more pains for those thanks than
you take pains to thank me. If it had been painful I
would not have come.
BENEDICK   You take pleasure then in the message?
BEATRICE   Yea, just so much as you may take upon a   249
knife's point and choke a daw withal. You have no   250
stomach, signor. Fare you well.   *Exit.*   251
BENEDICK   Ha! "Against my will I am sent to bid you
come in to dinner." There's a double meaning in that.
"I took no more pains for those thanks than you took
pains to thank me." That's as much as to say, "Any
pains that I take for you is as easy as thanks." If I do
not take pity of her, I am a villain; if I do not love her,
I am a Jew. I will go get her picture.   *Exit.*

❧

[3.1]

*Enter Hero and two gentlewomen, Margaret
and Ursula.*

HERO
Good Margaret, run thee to the parlor.
There shalt thou find my cousin Beatrice
Proposing with the Prince and Claudio.   3
Whisper her ear and tell her I and Ursley   4
Walk in the orchard, and our whole discourse
Is all of her. Say that thou overheard'st us,
And bid her steal into the pleachèd bower,   7
Where honeysuckles, ripened by the sun,
Forbid the sun to enter, like favorites,
Made proud by princes, that advance their pride   10
Against that power that bred it. There will she hide
her,   11
To listen our propose. This is thy office.   12
Bear thee well in it and leave us alone.   13
MARGARET
I'll make her come, I warrant you, presently.   [*Exit.*]   14
HERO
Now, Ursula, when Beatrice doth come,
As we do trace this alley up and down,   16
Our talk must only be of Benedick.
When I do name him, let it be thy part
To praise him more than ever man did merit.
My talk to thee must be how Benedick
Is sick in love with Beatrice. Of this matter
Is little Cupid's crafty arrow made,
That only wounds by hearsay.

Enter Beatrice [behind].

Now begin,   23
For look where Beatrice, like a lapwing, runs   24
Close by the ground, to hear our conference.
URSULA [*to Hero*]
The pleasant'st angling is to see the fish
Cut with her golden oars the silver stream   27
And greedily devour the treacherous bait.
So angle we for Beatrice, who even now
Is couchèd in the woodbine coverture.   30
Fear you not my part of the dialogue.   31
HERO [*to Ursula*]
Then go we near her, that her ear lose nothing
Of the false sweet bait that we lay for it.
[*They approach the bower.*]
No, truly, Ursula, she is too disdainful;
I know her spirits are as coy and wild   35
As haggards of the rock.
URSULA   But are you sure   36

215–16 **dumb show** pantomime (lacking their usual banter)
218 **sadly borne** soberly conducted.   220 **have . . . bent** i.e., are fully
engaged. (The image is of a bow pulled taut.)   225–6 **that . . . mending** that can hear themselves criticized and undertake to remedy the
defect.   228 **reprove** refute   231 **quirks** witty conceits or jokes
235 **sentences** saws, maxims   236 **paper bullets** i.e., words
237 **career of his humor** pursuit of his inclination. (In horsemanship,
a *career* is a short gallop.)   249–50 **just . . . withal** i.e., very little. (A
daw or jackdaw is a common blackbird, smaller than a crow.)
251 **stomach** appetite

3.1. Location: Leonato's garden.
3 **Proposing** conversing   4 **Ursley** (A nickname for *Ursula*.)
7 **pleachèd** formed by densely interwoven branches   10–11 **that . . . it**
i.e., who dare set themselves up against the very princes who advanced
them.   12 **listen our propose** listen to our conversation.   **office** responsibility.   13 **leave us alone** leave the rest to us.   14 **presently** immediately.   16 **trace** walk   23 **only . . . hearsay** wounds by mere report.
24 **lapwing** bird of the plover family   27 **oars** i.e., fins   30 **Is . . . coverture** is hid in the honeysuckle bower.   31 **Fear . . . dialogue** Don't worry
about my not holding up my part in the conversation.   35 **coy** disdainful   36 **As . . . rock** as untamed female hawks in mountainous terrain.

That Benedick loves Beatrice so entirely?

HERO
So says the Prince and my new-trothèd lord.

URSULA
And did they bid you tell her of it, madam?

HERO
They did entreat me to acquaint her of it;
But I persuaded them, if they loved Benedick,
To wish him wrestle with affection
And never to let Beatrice know of it.

URSULA
Why did you so? Doth not the gentleman
Deserve as full as fortunate a bed   45
As ever Beatrice shall couch upon?   46

HERO
O god of love! I know he doth deserve
As much as may be yielded to a man;
But Nature never framed a woman's heart
Of prouder stuff than that of Beatrice.
Disdain and scorn ride sparkling in her eyes,
Misprizing what they look on, and her wit   52
Values itself so highly that to her
All matter else seems weak. She cannot love, 54
Nor take no shape nor project of affection,   55
She is so self-endearèd.

URSULA   Sure I think so,   56
And therefore certainly it were not good
She knew his love, lest she'll make sport at it.

HERO
Why, you speak truth. I never yet saw man,
How wise, how noble, young, how rarely featured, 60
But she would spell him backward. If fair-faced, 61
She would swear the gentleman should be her
    sister;
If black, why, Nature, drawing of an antic,   63
Made a foul blot; if tall, a lance ill-headed;
If low, an agate very vilely cut;   65
If speaking, why, a vane blown with all winds;
If silent, why, a block movèd with none.
So turns she every man the wrong side out
And never gives to truth and virtue that
Which simpleness and merit purchaseth.   70

URSULA
Sure, sure, such carping is not commendable.

HERO
No, not to be so odd and from all fashions   72
As Beatrice is cannot be commendable.
But who dare tell her so? If I should speak,
She would mock me into air; oh, she would laugh me 75
Out of myself, press me to death with wit.   76

Therefore let Benedick, like covered fire,
Consume away in sighs, waste inwardly.   78
It were a better death than die with mocks,
Which is as bad as die with tickling.

URSULA
Yet tell her of it. Hear what she will say.

HERO
No, rather I will go to Benedick
And counsel him to fight against his passion.
And truly, I'll devise some honest slanders   84
To stain my cousin with. One doth not know
How much an ill word may empoison liking.

URSULA
Oh, do not do your cousin such a wrong!
She cannot be so much without true judgment—
Having so swift and excellent a wit
As she is prized to have—as to refuse   90
So rare a gentleman as Signor Benedick.

HERO
He is the only man of Italy,
Always excepted my dear Claudio.

URSULA
I pray you, be not angry with me, madam,
Speaking my fancy: Signor Benedick,
For shape, for bearing, argument, and valor, 96
Goes foremost in report through Italy.

HERO
Indeed, he hath an excellent good name.

URSULA
His excellence did earn it ere he had it.
When are you married, madam?

HERO
Why, every day, tomorrow. Come, go in.   101
I'll show thee some attires and have thy counsel
Which is the best to furnish me tomorrow.
                              [They walk away.]

URSULA [to Hero]
She's limed, I warrant you. We have caught her,
    madam.   104

HERO [to Ursula]
If it prove so, then loving goes by haps;   105
Some Cupid kills with arrows, some with traps. 106
                      [Exeunt Hero and Ursula.]

BEATRICE [coming forward]
What fire is in mine ears? Can this be true?   107
    Stand I condemned for pride and scorn so much?
Contempt, farewell, and maiden pride, adieu!
    No glory lives behind the back of such.   110
And Benedick, love on; I will requite thee,
    Taming my wild heart to thy loving hand.   112

45–6 as full . . . upon i.e., as good a wife as Beatrice.   52 Misprizing
undervaluing, despising   54 weak unimportant.   55 project conception, idea   56 self-endearèd full of self-love.   60 How however.
rarely excellently   61 spell him backward i.e., speak contrarily of
him by characterizing his virtues as vices.   63 black dark.   antic
buffoon, grotesque figure   65 agate i.e., diminutive person. (Alluding to the small figures cut in agate for rings.)   70 simpleness
integrity, plainness.   purchaseth earn, deserve.   72 from contrary to
75–6 she . . . myself she would mockingly put me down   76 press
me to death (Pressing to death with weights was the usual punishment for those accused of crimes who refused to plead either guilty
or not guilty.)

78 Consume . . . sighs (An allusion to the belief that each sigh cost the
heart a drop of blood.)   84 honest slanders i.e., slanders that do not
involve her virtue   90 prized esteemed   96 argument skill in discourse   101 every day, tomorrow tomorrow and every day thereafter.   104 limed caught, like a bird in birdlime, a sticky substance
spread on branches to trap the birds that perch on them   105 by haps
by chance   106 Some Cupid kills Cupid kills some   107 What . . .
ears? (An allusion to the old saying that a person's ears burn when
one is being discussed in one's absence.)   110 No . . . such Nothing is
gained by hiding behind such defenses.   112 Taming . . . hand
(A figure derived from the taming of the hawk by the hand of
the falconer.)

If thou dost love, my kindness shall incite thee
　　To bind our loves up in a holy band;　　　　　　　　114
For others say thou dost deserve, and I
Believe it better than reportingly.　　　　　　　　　*Exit.* 116

❖

[3.2]

Enter Prince [Don Pedro], Claudio, Benedick,
and Leonato.

DON PEDRO   I do but stay till your marriage be con-   1
summate, and then go I toward Aragon.   2
CLAUDIO   I'll bring you thither, my lord, if you'll   3
vouchsafe me.   4
DON PEDRO   Nay, that would be as great a soil in the   5
new gloss of your marriage as to show a child his new
coat and forbid him to wear it. I will only be bold with   7
Benedick for his company, for from the crown of his
head to the sole of his foot he is all mirth. He hath
twice or thrice cut Cupid's bowstring, and the little
hangman dare not shoot at him. He hath a heart as   11
sound as a bell, and his tongue is the clapper, for what
his heart thinks his tongue speaks.
BENEDICK   Gallants, I am not as I have been.
LEONATO   So say I. Methinks you are sadder.   15
CLAUDIO   I hope he be in love.
DON PEDRO   Hang him, truant! There's no true drop of   17
blood in him, to be truly touched with love. If he be
sad, he wants money.   19
BENEDICK   I have the toothache.   20
DON PEDRO   Draw it.   21
BENEDICK   Hang it!   22
CLAUDIO   You must hang it first and draw it after-
wards.
DON PEDRO   What, sigh for the toothache?
LEONATO   Where is but a humor or a worm.   26
BENEDICK   Well, everyone can master a grief but he that   27
has it.
CLAUDIO   Yet say I, he is in love.
DON PEDRO   There is no appearance of fancy in him,   30
unless it be a fancy that he hath to strange disguises;   31
as, to be a Dutchman today, a Frenchman tomorrow,
or in the shape of two countries at once, as, a German
from the waist downward, all slops, and a Spaniard   34
from the hip upward, no doublet. Unless he have a   35

fancy to this foolery, as it appears he hath, he is no fool   36
for fancy, as you would have it appear he is.   37
CLAUDIO   If he be not in love with some woman, there
is no believing old signs. 'A brushes his hat o'
mornings. What should that bode?
DON PEDRO   Hath any man seen him at the barber's?
CLAUDIO   No, but the barber's man hath been seen with
him, and the old ornament of his cheek hath already   43
stuffed tennis balls.   44
LEONATO   Indeed he looks younger than he did by the
loss of a beard.
DON PEDRO   Nay, 'a rubs himself with civet. Can you   47
smell him out by that?   48
CLAUDIO   That's as much as to say the sweet youth's in
love.
DON PEDRO   The greatest note of it is his melancholy.   51
CLAUDIO   And when was he wont to wash his face?   52
DON PEDRO   Yea, or to paint himself? For the which I   53
hear what they say of him.   54
CLAUDIO   Nay, but his jesting spirit, which is now crept
into a lute string and now governed by stops.   56
DON PEDRO   Indeed, that tells a heavy tale for him.
Conclude, conclude he is in love.
CLAUDIO   Nay, but I know who loves him.
DON PEDRO   That would I know too. I warrant, one that
knows him not.
CLAUDIO   Yes, and his ill conditions; and, in despite of   62
all, dies for him.
DON PEDRO   She shall be buried with her face upwards.   64
BENEDICK   Yet is this no charm for the toothache. Old
signor, walk aside with me. I have studied eight or
nine wise words to speak to you, which these hobby-   67
horses must not hear.   *[Exeunt Benedick and Leonato.]*   68
DON PEDRO   For my life, to break with him about   69
Beatrice.
CLAUDIO   'Tis even so. Hero and Margaret have by this   71
played their parts with Beatrice, and then the two
bears will not bite one another when they meet.

Enter [Don] John the Bastard.

DON JOHN   My lord and brother, God save you!
DON PEDRO   Good e'en, brother.   75
DON JOHN   If your leisure served, I would speak with
you.
DON PEDRO   In private?

---

114 **band** bond   116 **better than reportingly** on better evidence than
mere report.
3.2. Location: Leonato's house.
1–2 **consummate** consummated   3 **bring** escort   4 **vouchsafe** allow
5 **soil** stain   7 **be bold with** ask   11 **hangman** executioner; rogue.
(Playfully applied to Cupid.)   15 **sadder** more serious.   17 **truant**
i.e., from love.   19 **wants** lacks   20 **toothache** (Thought to be a common ailment of lovers.)   21 **Draw** Extract. (But Claudio jokes on the
method of executing traitors, who were hanged first and then cut
down alive and drawn, i.e., disemboweled, and finally quartered.)
22 **Hang it!** Confound it!   26 **Where** Where there.   **humor or a**
worm (A toothache was ascribed to "humors," or unhealthy secre-
tions, and to actual worms in the teeth.)   27 **grief** pain.   **but** except
30 **fancy** love   31 **fancy** whim, liking   34 **slops** loose breeches
35 **no doublet** i.e., with a hip-length cloak in place of, or covering, the
close-fitting doublet.

36–7 **fool for fancy** i.e., lover   43–4 **the old . . . tennis balls** i.e.,
Benedick's beard has gone to stuff tennis balls. (He appears onstage
beardless in this scene for the first time.)   47 **civet** perfume derived
from the civet cat.   48 **smell him out** (1) discern his secret (2) smell
him coming   51 **note** mark   52 **wont** accustomed.   **wash** i.e., with
cosmetics; similarly with *paint* in the next line   53–4 **For . . . him**
That's what I hear people saying about him.   56 **stops** (1) frets on the
fingerboard (2) restraints.   62 **ill conditions** bad qualities   64 **buried**
. . . upwards i.e., as the faithful, not as a suicide, who were sometimes
buried face downwards (?). (There is also a sexual suggestion of her
being smothered under Benedick, continuing the joke on *dies for him*,
meaning to have an orgasm.)   67–8 **hobbyhorses** i.e., buffoons.
(Originally, figures in a morris dance made to resemble a horse and
rider.)   69 **For** Upon.   **break** speak   71 **Margaret** (Ursula joined
Hero in playing the trick on Beatrice, but Margaret has been in on it.)
75 **e'en** evening, i.e., afternoon

DON JOHN   If it please you. Yet Count Claudio may hear,
for what I would speak of concerns him.
DON PEDRO   What's the matter?
DON JOHN   [*to Claudio*] Means Your Lordship to be married tomorrow?
DON PEDRO   You know he does.
DON JOHN   I know not that, when he knows what I
know.
CLAUDIO   If there be any impediment, I pray you
discover it.   88
DON JOHN   You may think I love you not. Let that
appear hereafter, and aim better at me by that I now   90
will manifest. For my brother, I think he holds you   91
well and in dearness of heart hath holp to effect your   92
ensuing marriage—surely suit ill spent and labor ill
bestowed.
DON PEDRO   Why, what's the matter?
DON JOHN   I came hither to tell you, and, circumstances   96
shortened—for she has been too long a-talking of—   97
the lady is disloyal.   98
CLAUDIO   Who, Hero?
DON JOHN   Even she—Leonato's Hero, your Hero,
every man's Hero.
CLAUDIO   Disloyal?
DON JOHN   The word is too good to paint out her   103
wickedness. I could say she were worse; think you of
a worse title, and I will fit her to it. Wonder not till fur-   105
ther warrant. Go but with me tonight, you shall see her   106
chamber window entered, even the night before her
wedding day. If you love her then, tomorrow wed her;
but it would better fit your honor to change your
mind.
CLAUDIO   May this be so?
DON PEDRO   I will not think it.
DON JOHN   If you dare not trust that you see, confess not   113
that you know. If you will follow me, I will show you   114
enough; and when you have seen more and heard
more, proceed accordingly.
CLAUDIO   If I see anything tonight why I should not
marry her, tomorrow in the congregation, where I
should wed, there will I shame her.
DON PEDRO   And, as I wooed for thee to obtain her, I
will join with thee to disgrace her.
DON JOHN   I will disparage her no farther till you are my
witnesses. Bear it coldly but till midnight, and let the   123
issue show itself.   124
DON PEDRO   O day untowardly turned!   125
CLAUDIO   O mischief strangely thwarting!
DON JOHN   O plague right well prevented! So will you
say when you have seen the sequel.   [*Exeunt.*]

❧

88 **discover** reveal   90 **aim better at** judge better of.   **that** that which
91–2 **holds you well** thinks well of you   92 **holp** helped   96–7 **circumstances shortened** without unnecessary details   97 **a-talking of**
under discussion (by us)   98 **disloyal** unfaithful.   103 **paint out** portray in full   105–6 **till further warrant** till further proof appears.
113–14 **If . . . know** i.e., If you are unwilling to believe what you see,
then don't claim to know the truth.   123 **coldly** calmly   124 **issue**
outcome   125 **untowardly turned** wretchedly altered.

[3.3]

*Enter Dogberry and his compartner [Verges]
with the Watch.*

DOGBERRY   Are you good men and true?
VERGES   Yea, or else it were pity but they should suffer
salvation, body and soul.   3
DOGBERRY   Nay, that were a punishment too good for
them, if they should have any allegiance in them,   5
being chosen for the Prince's watch.
VERGES   Well, give them their charge, neighbor Dog-   7
berry.
DOGBERRY   First, who think you the most desartless   9
man to be constable?
FIRST WATCH   Hugh Oatcake, sir, or George Seacoal, for
they can write and read.
DOGBERRY   Come hither, neighbor Seacoal. [*Seacoal, or
Second Watch, steps forward.*] God hath blessed you
with a good name. To be a well-favored man is the gift   15
of fortune, but to write and read comes by nature.
SEACOAL   Both which, Master Constable—
DOGBERRY   You have. I knew it would be your answer.
Well, for your favor, sir, why, give God thanks, and
make no boast of it; and for your writing and reading,
let that appear when there is no need of such vanity.
You are thought here to be the most senseless and fit   22
man for the constable of the watch; therefore bear you
the lantern. This is your charge: you shall comprehend   24
all vagrom men; you are to bid any man stand, in the   25
Prince's name.
SEACOAL   How if 'a will not stand?
DOGBERRY   Why, then, take no note of him, but let him
go, and presently call the rest of the watch together
and thank God you are rid of a knave.
VERGES   If he will not stand when he is bidden, he is
none of the Prince's subjects.
DOGBERRY   True, and they are to meddle with none but
the Prince's subjects. You shall also make no noise in
the streets; for, for the watch to babble and to talk is
most tolerable and not to be endured.   36
WATCH   We will rather sleep than talk. We know what
belongs to a watch.   38
DOGBERRY   Why, you speak like an ancient and most   39
quiet watchman, for I cannot see how sleeping should
offend. Only have a care that your bills be not stolen.   41
Well, you are to call at all the alehouses and bid those
that are drunk get them to bed.
WATCH   How if they will not?

3.3. Location: A street.
3 **salvation** (A blunder for "damnation.")   5 **allegiance** (For "treachery.")   7 **charge** instructions   9 **desartless** (For "deserving.")
15 **a good name** (Sea coal was high-grade coal shipped from Newcas-
tle, not the charcoal usually sold by London colliers.)   **well-favored**
good-looking   22 **senseless** (For "sensible.")   24 **comprehend** (For
"apprehend.")   25 **vagrom** vagrant.   **stand** stand still, stop   36 **tolerable** (For "intolerable.")   37 WATCH (Here and at lines 44, 48, 53,
and 66 Shakespeare's text does not specify which watchman speaks.
These lines are sometimes assigned to the Second Watch, Seacoal, but
could be spoken by others of the watch.)   38 **belongs to** are the
duties of   39 **ancient** venerable, experienced   41 **bills** pikes, with
axes fixed to long poles

DOGBERRY   Why, then, let them alone till they are sober. If they make you not then the better answer, you may say they are not the men you took them for.

WATCH   Well, sir.

DOGBERRY   If you meet a thief, you may suspect him, by virtue of your office, to be no true man; and for such 50 kind of men, the less you meddle or make with them, 51 why, the more is for your honesty. 52

WATCH   If we know him to be a thief, shall we not lay hands on him?

DOGBERRY   Truly, by your office you may, but I think they that touch pitch will be defiled. The most 56 peaceable way for you, if you do take a thief, is to let him show himself what he is and steal out of your company.

VERGES   You have been always called a merciful man, partner.

DOGBERRY   Truly, I would not hang a dog by my will, much more a man who hath any honesty in him.

VERGES   If you hear a child cry in the night, you must call to the nurse and bid her still it.

WATCH   How if the nurse be asleep and will not hear us?

DOGBERRY   Why, then, depart in peace and let the child wake her with crying, for the ewe that will not hear her lamb when it baas will never answer a calf when he bleats.

VERGES   'Tis very true.

DOGBERRY   This is the end of the charge: you, Constable, are to present the Prince's own person. If you meet 74 the Prince in the night, you may stay him.

VERGES   Nay, by'r Lady, that I think 'a cannot. 76

DOGBERRY   Five shillings to one on't, with any man that knows the statutes, he may stay him; marry, not without the Prince be willing, for indeed the watch ought to offend no man, and it is an offense to stay a man against his will.

VERGES   By'r Lady, I think it be so.

DOGBERRY   Ha, ah ha! Well, masters, good night. An there be any matter of weight chances, call up me. Keep your fellows' counsels and your own, and good night. Come, neighbor. [He starts to leave with Verges.]

SEACOAL   Well, masters, we hear our charge. Let us go sit here upon the church bench till two, and then all to bed.

DOGBERRY   One word more, honest neighbors. I pray you, watch about Signor Leonato's door, for the wedding being there tomorrow, there is a great coil 92 tonight. Adieu. Be vigitant, I beseech you. 93

Exeunt [Dogberry and Verges].

Enter Borachio and Conrade.

BORACHIO   What, Conrade!

SEACOAL   [aside] Peace! Stir not.

BORACHIO   Conrade, I say!

CONRADE   Here, man. I am at thy elbow.

BORACHIO   Mass, and my elbow itched; I thought there 98 would a scab follow. 99

CONRADE   I will owe thee an answer for that. And now, 100 forward with thy tale.

BORACHIO   Stand thee close, then, under this penthouse, 102 for it drizzles rain, and I will, like a true drunkard, 103 utter all to thee.

SEACOAL   [aside] Some treason, masters. Yet stand 105 close. 106

BORACHIO   Therefore know I have earned of Don John a thousand ducats.

CONRADE   Is it possible that any villainy should be so dear? 110

BORACHIO   Thou shouldst rather ask if it were possible any villainy should be so rich; for when rich villains 112 have need of poor ones, poor ones may make what price they will.

CONRADE   I wonder at it.

BORACHIO   That shows thou art unconfirmed. Thou 116 knowest that the fashion of a doublet, or a hat, or a cloak, is nothing to a man. 118

CONRADE   Yes, it is apparel.

BORACHIO   I mean, the fashion. 120

CONRADE   Yes, the fashion is the fashion.

BORACHIO   Tush, I may as well say the fool's the fool. But see'st thou not what a deformed thief this fashion 123 is?

SEACOAL   [aside] I know that Deformed. 'A has been a vile thief this seven year; 'a goes up and down like a 126 gentleman. I remember his name.

BORACHIO   Didst thou not hear somebody?

CONRADE   No, 'twas the vane on the house.

BORACHIO   See'st thou not, I say, what a deformed thief this fashion is, how giddily 'a turns about all the hot bloods between fourteen and five-and-thirty, sometimes fashioning them like Pharaoh's soldiers in the reechy painting, sometime like god Bel's priests in the 134 old church-window, sometime like the shaven 135 Hercules in the smirched worm-eaten tapestry, where 136 his codpiece seems as massy as his club? 137

50 true honest   51 meddle or make have to do   52 is it is   56 they . . . defiled (A commonplace, derived from Ecclesiasticus 13:1.)
74 present represent   76 by'r Lady i.e., by Our Lady. (A mild oath.)
92 coil to-do   93 vigitant (For "vigilant.")

98 Mass i.e., By the Mass.   my elbow itched (Proverbially, a warning against questionable companions.)   99 scab i.e., scoundrel. (With play on literal meaning.)   100 owe thee an answer answer later
102 penthouse overhanging structure   103 true drunkard (Alludes to the commonplace that the drunkard tells all; Borachio's name in Spanish means "drunkard.")   105–6 stand close stay hidden.
110 dear expensive.   112 rich well-paid   116 unconfirmed inexperienced.   118 is . . . man does not make the man. (But Conrade plays on the phrase in the sense of "means nothing to a man.")   120 I . . . fashion i.e., My emphasis was on the mere fashion, not on the apparel itself. (But Conrade wittily refuses to allow the difference.)
123 deformed thief i.e., so called because fashion takes such varied and extreme shapes and because it impoverishes those who follow fashion   126 up and down about, here and there   134 reechy dirty, grimy. (Perhaps this painting is of the Israelites passing through the Red Sea.)   god Bel's priests (Probably alludes to the story of Bel and the Dragon, from the apocryphal Book of Daniel, depicted in a stained-glass window.)   135–6 shaven Hercules (A reference either to young Hercules at the crossroads, choosing between virtue and vice, or in the service of Omphale—see 2.1.242, note—or, confusedly, to the story of Samson.)   137 codpiece decorative pouch at the front of a man's breeches (indelicately conspicuous in this tapestry)

CONRADE All this I see, and I see that the fashion wears 138
out more apparel than the man. But art not thou 139
thyself giddy with the fashion, too, that thou hast
shifted out of thy tale into telling me of the fashion?

BORACHIO Not so, neither. But know that I have tonight
wooed Margaret, the Lady Hero's gentlewoman, by
the name of Hero. She leans me out at her mistress' 144
chamber window, bids me a thousand times good
night—I tell this tale vilely; I should first tell thee how
the Prince, Claudio, and my master, planted and
placed and possessed by my master Don John, saw 148
afar off in the orchard this amiable encounter. 149

CONRADE And thought they Margaret was Hero?

BORACHIO Two of them did, the Prince and Claudio,
but the devil my master knew she was Margaret; and
partly by his oaths, which first possessed them, partly
by the dark night, which did deceive them, but chiefly
by my villainy, which did confirm any slander that
Don John had made, away went Claudio enraged;
swore he would meet her, as he was appointed, next
morning at the temple, and there, before the whole
congregation, shame her with what he saw o'ernight
and send her home again without a husband.

SEACOAL We charge you, in the Prince's name, stand!

FIRST WATCH Call up the Right Master Constable. We 162
have here recovered the most dangerous piece of 163
lechery that ever was known in the commonwealth. 164

SEACOAL And one Deformed is one of them. I know
him; 'a wears a lock. 166

CONRADE Masters, masters—

FIRST WATCH You'll be made bring Deformed forth, I
warrant you.

CONRADE Masters—

SEACOAL Never speak, we charge you. Let us obey you 171
to go with us.

BORACHIO We are like to prove a goodly commodity, 173
being taken up of these men's bills. 174

CONRADE A commodity in question, I warrant you. 175
Come, we'll obey you.   *Exeunt.*

❖

[3.4]

Enter Hero, and Margaret and Ursula.

HERO Good Ursula, wake my cousin Beatrice, and
desire her to rise.

URSULA I will, lady.

HERO And bid her come hither.

URSULA Well.   [*Exit.*] 5

MARGARET Troth, I think your other rabato were better. 6

HERO No, pray thee, good Meg, I'll wear this.

MARGARET By my troth, 's not so good, and I warrant 8
your cousin will say so.

HERO My cousin's a fool, and thou art another. I'll wear
none but this.

MARGARET I like the new tire within excellently, if the 12
hair were a thought browner; and your gown's a most 13
rare fashion, i'faith. I saw the Duchess of Milan's gown
that they praise so.

HERO Oh, that exceeds, they say. 16

MARGARET By my troth, 's but a nightgown in respect 17
of yours: cloth o' gold, and cuts, and laced with silver, 18
set with pearls, down sleeves, side sleeves, and skirts, 19
round underborne with a bluish tinsel. But for a fine, 20
quaint, graceful, and excellent fashion, yours is worth 21
ten on't. 22

HERO God give me joy to wear it! For my heart is
exceeding heavy.

MARGARET 'Twill be heavier soon by the weight of a
man.

HERO Fie upon thee! Art not ashamed?

MARGARET Of what, lady? Of speaking honorably? Is
not marriage honorable in a beggar? Is not your lord 29
honorable without marriage? I think you would have
me say, "saving your reverence, a husband." An bad 31
thinking do not wrest true speaking, I'll offend 32
nobody. Is there any harm in "the heavier for a husband"? None, I think, an it be the right husband and
the right wife; otherwise 'tis light, and not heavy. Ask 35
my Lady Beatrice else. Here she comes.

Enter Beatrice.

HERO Good morrow, coz.

BEATRICE Good morrow, sweet Hero.

HERO Why, how now? Do you speak in the sick tune? 39

BEATRICE I am out of all other tune, methinks.

MARGARET Clap 's into "Light o 'love." That goes 41
without a burden; do you sing it, and I'll dance it. 42

BEATRICE Ye light o' love with your heels! Then, if your 43
husband have stables enough, you'll see he shall lack
no barns. 45

MARGARET Oh, illegitimate construction! I scorn that 46
with my heels. 47

6 **rabato** tall collar supporting a ruff, stiffened with wire or starch
8 **troth, 's** faith, it is 12 **tire within** headdress in the inner room
13 **hair** hairpiece attached to the *tire* (line 12) 16 **exceeds** i.e., exceeds
comparison 17 **nightgown** dressing gown 17–18 **in respect of** compared to 18 **cuts . . . silver** slashes in a garment revealing the underlying fabic, and laced with silver thread 19 **down sleeves** tight-fitting
sleeves to the wrist. **side sleeves** secondary ornamental sleeves hanging from the shoulder 20 **round underborne** with a lining around the
edge of the skirt. **tinsel** cloth, usually silk, interwoven with threads of
silver or gold. 21 **quaint** elegant 22 **on't** of it. 29 **in** even in
31 **saving . . . husband** (By this apologetic formula, Margaret suggests
that Hero is too prudish even to hear the word *husband* mentioned.)
An bad If bawdy 32 **wrest** misinterpret 35 **light** harmless. (With a
play on the meaning "wanton.") 39 **tune** i.e., mood. 41 **Clap 's** Let's
shift. **Light o' love** (A popular song.) 42 **burden** bass accompaniment. (With play on the idea of "the weight of a man.") 43 **Ye . . .
heels!** i.e., You're light-heeled, wanton! 45 **barns** (With pun on
"bairns," children.) 46 **illegitimate construction** false inference. (But
with a play on the idea of bastard "bairns.") 47 **with my heels** (A
proverbial expression of scorn.)

138–9 **fashion . . . man** i.e., fashion prompts the discarding of clothes
faster than honest use. 144 **leans me** leans. (*Me* is an emphatic
marker.) 148 **possessed** (misleadingly) informed; also, perhaps, possessed, as by the devil 149 **amiable** amorous 162 **Right Master
Constable** (A comic title on the pattern of "Right Worshipful," etc.)
163 **recovered** (For "discovered.") 164 **lechery** (For "treachery.")
166 **lock** lock of hair hanging down on the left shoulder; the lovelock.
171 **obey** (For "oblige," "command.") 173 **commodity** goods
acquired 174 **taken up** (1) arrested (2) obtained on credit. **bills**
(1) pikes (2) bonds given as security. 175 **in question** (1) subject to
judicial examination (2) of doubtful value
3.4. Location: Leonato's house.
5 **Well** Very well, as you wish.

BEATRICE   'Tis almost five o'clock, cousin; 'tis time you
were ready. By my troth, I am exceeding ill. Heigh-ho!

MARGARET   For a hawk, a horse, or a husband? 50

BEATRICE   For the letter that begins them all, H. 51

MARGARET   Well, an you be not turned Turk, there's no 52
more sailing by the star. 53

BEATRICE   What means the fool, trow? 54

MARGARET   Nothing, I; but God send everyone their
heart's desire!

HERO   These gloves the Count sent me, they are an
excellent perfume. 58

BEATRICE   I am stuffed, cousin. I cannot smell. 59

MARGARET   A maid, and stuffed! There's goodly catching of cold.

BEATRICE   Oh, God help me, God help me! How long
have you professed apprehension? 63

MARGARET   Ever since you left it. Doth not my wit 64
become me rarely?

BEATRICE   It is not seen enough; you should wear it in 66
your cap. By my troth, I am sick. 67

MARGARET   Get you some of this distilled *carduus bene-* 68
dictus, and lay it to your heart. It is the only thing for a 69
qualm. 70

HERO   There thou prick'st her with a thistle.

BEATRICE   *Benedictus!* Why *benedictus?* You have some
moral in this *benedictus.* 73

MARGARET   Moral? No, by my troth, I have no moral
meaning, I meant plain holy thistle. You may think 75
perchance that I think you are in love. Nay, by'r Lady,
I am not such a fool to think what I list, nor I list not to 77
think what I can, nor indeed I cannot think, if I would
think my heart out of thinking, that you are in love or 79
that you will be in love or that you can be in love. Yet
Benedick was such another, and now is he become a 81
man. He swore he would never marry, and yet now, 82
in despite of his heart, he eats his meat without grudg- 83
ing; and how you may be converted I know not, but 84
methinks you look with your eyes as other women do.

BEATRICE   What pace is this that thy tongue keeps?

MARGARET   Not a false gallop. 87

Enter Ursula.

50 For ... husband? (*Heigh-ho* might be a cry of encouragement in the
hunt or else "Heigh-ho for a husband!" as at 2.1.305.)   **51 H** (With a
pun on "ache," pronounced "aitch." Beatrice complains of aching with a
cold.)   **52 turned Turk** i.e., turned apostate to the true faith (by violat-
ing your oath not to become a lover)   **52–3 no ... star** no more navigat-
ing by the North Star, i.e., no certain truth in which to trust.   **54 trow** I
wonder.   **58 perfume** (Gloves were often perfumed.)   **59 stuffed** i.e.,
stuffed up with a cold. (But Margaret takes it in a bawdy sense.)   **63
professed** apprehension made claim to be witty.   **64 left it** gave it up.
(Margaret gibes at Beatrice's pretending not to know what the joking is
all about.)   **66–7 wear ... cap** i.e., wear it prominently visible, as a fool
wears his coxcomb. (Beatrice jokes that Margaret's supposed wit is
imperceptible.)   **68–9 carduus benedictus** the blessed thistle, noted for
medicinal properties. (With a pun on "Benedick.")   **70 a qualm** an
attack of nausea (or misgiving).   **73 moral** hidden meaning   **75 holy
thistle** the blessed thistle or *carduus benedictus* of 68–9.   **77 list** please
79 think ... thinking i.e., rack my brains   **81 such another** i.e., seemingly proof against love   **81–2 a man** i.e., like other men.   **83–4 eats ...
grudging** i.e., is content to be like other men, to be in love   **87 Not ...
gallop.** i.e., I'm not speaking at a false pace, at a canter; I speak the
truth.

URSULA   Madam, withdraw. The Prince, the Count,
Signor Benedick, Don John, and all the gallants of the
town are come to fetch you to church.

HERO   Help to dress me, good coz, good Meg, good
Ursula.   *[Exeunt.]*

✣

[3.5]

*Enter Leonato and the Constable [Dogberry]
and the Headborough [Verges].*

LEONATO   What would you with me, honest neighbor?

DOGBERRY   Marry, sir, I would have some confidence 2
with you that decerns you nearly. 3

LEONATO   Brief, I pray you, for you see it is a busy time
with me.

DOGBERRY   Marry, this it is, sir.

VERGES   Yes, in truth it is, sir.

LEONATO   What is it, my good friends?

DOGBERRY   Goodman Verges, sir, speaks a little off the 9
matter—an old man, sir, and his wits are not so blunt 10
as, God help, I would desire they were, but, in faith,
honest as the skin between his brows. 12

VERGES   Yes, I thank God I am as honest as any man
living that is an old man and no honester than I.

DOGBERRY   Comparisons are odorous. *Palabras*, neigh- 15
bor Verges.

LEONATO   Neighbors, you are tedious.

DOGBERRY   It pleases Your Worship to say so, but we are
the poor Duke's officers. But truly, for mine own part, 19
if I were as tedious as a king, I could find in my heart 20
to bestow it all of Your Worship. 21

LEONATO   All thy tediousness on me, ah?

DOGBERRY   Yea, an 'twere a thousand pound more than
'tis; for I hear as good exclamation on Your Worship as 24
of any man in the city, and though I be but a poor man,
I am glad to hear it.

VERGES   And so am I.

LEONATO   I would fain know what you have to say.

VERGES   Marry, sir, our watch tonight, excepting Your 29
Worship's presence, ha' ta'en a couple of as arrant 30
knaves as any in Messina.

DOGBERRY   A good old man, sir; he will be talking. As
they say, when the age is in, the wit is out. God help 33
us, it is a world to see! Well said, i'faith, neighbor 34

3.5. Location: Leonato's house.
0.2 *Headborough* local constable   **2 confidence** (A blunder for
"conference.")   **3 decerns** (For "concerns.")   **9 Goodman** (Title of a
person under the social rank of gentleman.)   **10 blunt** (He means
"sharp.")   **12 honest ... brows** (Proverbial expression of honesty.)
15 odorous (For "odious.")   *Palabras* (For *pocas palabras*, "few
words" in Spanish.)   **19 poor Duke's officers** (For "Duke's poor officers.")   **20 tedious** (Dogberry evidently thinks *tedious* means "rich.")
21 of on   **24 exclamation** (Possibly for "acclamation.")   **29 tonight**
last night   **29–30 excepting ... presence** (The normal meaning,
"with the exception of your honored self," comically implies that
Leonato is an even more arrant knave than the men arrested. Verges
probably means, "begging Your Worship's pardon.")   **30 ha' ta'en**
have taken   **33 when ... out** (An adaptation of the proverb, "When
ale is in, wit is out.")   **34 a world** i.e., wonderful. (Proverbial.)

VERGES. Well, God's a good man. An two men ride ₃₅
of a horse, one must ride behind. An honest soul, ₃₆
i'faith, sir, by my troth he is, as ever broke bread. But, God
is to be worshiped, all men are not alike, alas, good
neighbor!

LEONATO   Indeed, neighbor, he comes too short of you.

DOGBERRY   Gifts that God gives.

LEONATO   I must leave you.

DOGBERRY   One word, sir. Our watch, sir, have indeed
comprehended two aspicious persons, and we would ₄₄
have them this morning examined before Your Worship.

LEONATO   Take their examination yourself and bring
it me. I am now in great haste, as it may appear
unto you.

DOGBERRY   It shall be suffigance.   ₅₀

LEONATO   Drink some wine ere you go. Fare you well.

[Enter a Messenger.]

MESSENGER   My lord, they stay for you to give your
daughter to her husband.

LEONATO   I'll wait upon them. I am ready.   ₅₄

[Exeunt Leonato and Messenger.]

DOGBERRY   Go, good partner, go, get you to Francis Sea- ₅₅
coal. Bid him bring his pen and inkhorn to the jail. We ₅₆
are now to examination these men.   ₅₇

VERGES   And we must do it wisely.

DOGBERRY   We will spare for no wit, I warrant you.
Here's that shall drive some of them to a noncome. ₆₀
Only get the learned writer to set down our excom- ₆₁
munication, and meet me at the jail.   [Exeunt.] ₆₂

❖

[4.1]

*Enter Prince [Don Pedro], [Don John the]
Bastard, Leonato, Friar [Francis], Claudio,
Benedick, Hero, and Beatrice [with attendants].*

LEONATO   Come, Friar Francis, be brief—only to the
plain form of marriage, and you shall recount their
particular duties afterwards.

FRIAR   You come hither, my lord, to marry this lady?

CLAUDIO   No.

LEONATO   To be married to her. Friar, you come to
marry her.

FRIAR   Lady, you come hither to be married to this
Count?

HERO   I do.

FRIAR   If either of you know any inward impediment ₁₁

why you should not be conjoined, I charge you on
your souls to utter it.

CLAUDIO   Know you any, Hero?

HERO   None, my lord.

FRIAR   Know you any, Count?

LEONATO   I dare make his answer: none.

CLAUDIO   Oh, what men dare do! What men may do!
What men daily do, not knowing what they do!

BENEDICK   How now? Interjections? Why, then, some be ₂₀
of laughing, as, ah, ha, he!   ₂₁

CLAUDIO
Stand thee by, Friar.—Father, by your leave,   ₂₂
Will you with free and unconstrainèd soul
Give me this maid, your daughter?

LEONATO
As freely, son, as God did give her me.

CLAUDIO
And what have I to give you back, whose worth
May counterpoise this rich and precious gift?   ₂₇

DON PEDRO
Nothing, unless you render her again.

CLAUDIO
Sweet Prince, you learn me noble thankfulness.   ₂₉

[He hands Hero to Leonato.]

There, Leonato, take her back again.
Give not this rotten orange to your friend;
She's but the sign and semblance of her honor.   ₃₂
Behold how like a maid she blushes here!
Oh, what authority and show of truth
Can cunning sin cover itself withal!
Comes not that blood as modest evidence   ₃₆
To witness simple virtue? Would you not swear,   ₃₇
All you that see her, that she were a maid,
By these exterior shows? But she is none:
She knows the heat of a luxurious bed.   ₄₀
Her blush is guiltiness, not modesty.

LEONATO
What do you mean, my lord?

CLAUDIO   Not to be married,   ₄₂
Not to knit my soul to an approvèd wanton.   ₄₃

LEONATO
Dear my lord, if you, in your own proof,   ₄₄
Have vanquished the resistance of her youth,
And made defeat of her virginity—

CLAUDIO
I know what you would say: if I have known her,   ₄₇
You will say, she did embrace me as a husband,
And so extenuate the forehand sin.   ₄₉
No, Leonato,
I never tempted her with word too large,   ₅₁

But, as a brother to his sister, showed
Bashful sincerity and comely love.

HERO
And seemed I ever otherwise to you?

CLAUDIO
Out on thee, seeming! I will write against it.   55
You seem to me as Dian in her orb,   56
As chaste as is the bud ere it be blown;   57
But you are more intemperate in your blood
Than Venus, or those pampered animals
That rage in savage sensuality.

HERO
Is my lord well, that he doth speak so wide?   61

LEONATO
Sweet Prince, why speak not you?

DON PEDRO   What should I speak?
I stand dishonored, that have gone about   63
To link my dear friend to a common stale.   64

LEONATO
Are these things spoken, or do I but dream?

DON JOHN
Sir, they are spoken, and these things are true.

BENEDICK   This looks not like a nuptial.

HERO   "True"! Oh, God!   68

CLAUDIO   Leonato, stand I here?
Is this the Prince? Is this the Prince's brother?
Is this face Hero's? Are our eyes our own?

LEONATO
All this is so. But what of this, my lord?

CLAUDIO
Let me but move one question to your daughter,   73
And by that fatherly and kindly power   74
That you have in her, bid her answer truly.

LEONATO [to Hero]
I charge thee do so, as thou art my child.

HERO
Oh, God defend me, how am I beset!
What kind of catechizing call you this?   78

CLAUDIO
To make you answer truly to your name.

HERO
Is it not Hero? Who can blot that name
With any just reproach?

CLAUDIO   Marry, that can Hero!
Hero itself can blot out Hero's virtue.   82
What man was he talked with you yesternight
Out at your window betwixt twelve and one?
Now, if you are a maid, answer to this.

HERO
I talked with no man at that hour, my lord.

DON PEDRO
Why, then are you no maiden. Leonato,
I am sorry you must hear. Upon mine honor,
Myself, my brother, and this grievèd Count   89
Did see her, hear her, at that hour last night
Talk with a ruffian at her chamber window,
Who hath indeed, most like a liberal villain,   92
Confessed the vile encounters they have had
A thousand times in secret.

DON JOHN
Fie, fie, they are not to be named, my lord,
Not to be spoke of!
There is not chastity enough in language
Without offense to utter them. Thus, pretty lady,
I am sorry for thy much misgovernment.   99

CLAUDIO
O Hero, what a Hero hadst thou been
If half thy outward graces had been placed
About thy thoughts and counsels of thy heart!
But fare thee well, most foul, most fair! Farewell,
Thou pure impiety and impious purity!
For thee I'll lock up all the gates of love,   105
And on my eyelids shall conjecture hang,   106
To turn all beauty into thoughts of harm,
And never shall it more be gracious.   108

LEONATO
Hath no man's dagger here a point for me?
                              [Hero swoons.]

BEATRICE
Why, how now, cousin, wherefore sink you down?   110

DON JOHN
Come, let us go. These things, come thus to light,
Smother her spirits up.
              [Exeunt Don Pedro, Don John, and Claudio.]

BENEDICK
How doth the lady?

BEATRICE   Dead, I think. Help, uncle!
Hero, why, Hero! Uncle! Signor Benedick! Friar!

LEONATO
O Fate, take not away thy heavy hand!
Death is the fairest cover for her shame
That may be wished for.

BEATRICE   How now, cousin Hero?

FRIAR   Have comfort, lady.

LEONATO
Dost thou look up?

FRIAR   Yea, wherefore should she not?   119

LEONATO
Wherefore? Why, doth not every earthly thing
Cry shame upon her? Could she here deny
The story that is printed in her blood?   122
Do not live, Hero, do not ope thine eyes;
For, did I think thou wouldst not quickly die,
Thought I thy spirits were stronger than thy shames,   125

---

55 Out . . . seeming! i.e., Shame on you, a mere semblance of good!
56 Dian . . . orb i.e., Diana, goddess of chastity, enthroned in the
moon   57 be blown open, flowering   61 wide wide of the mark.
63 gone about undertaken   64 stale whore.   68 True (A response
to Don John's use of the term.)   73 move put   74 kindly natural
78 catechizing formal questioning used by the Church to teach the
principles of faith. The first question in the Church of England's catechism is, "What is your name?"   82 Hero itself The very name of
Hero (who, in the story of Hero and Leander, is the faithful tragic
heroine)

89 grievèd (1) aggrieved, wronged (2) struck with grief   92 liberal
licentious   99 much misgovernment gross misconduct.   105 For
thee Because of you   106 conjecture evil suspicion   108 be gracious
seem attractive, graceful.   110, 119 wherefore why   122 blood i.e.,
blushes.   125 spirits life-giving energies, vital powers

Myself would, on the rearward of reproaches,   126
Strike at thy life. Grieved I I had but one?
Chid I for that at frugal nature's frame?   128
Oh, one too much by thee! Why had I one?
Why ever wast thou lovely in my eyes?
Why had I not with charitable hand
Took up a beggar's issue at my gates,   132
Who, smirchèd thus and mired with infamy,
I might have said, "No part of it is mine;
This shame derives itself from unknown loins"?
But mine, and mine I loved, and mine I praised,   136
And mine that I was proud on, mine so much
That I myself was to myself not mine,   138
Valuing of her—why, she, oh, she, is fallen   139
Into a pit of ink, that the wide sea   140
Hath drops too few to wash her clean again
And salt too little which may season give   142
To her foul-tainted flesh!

BENEDICK   Sir, sir, be patient.
For my part, I am so attired in wonder,
I know not what to say.

BEATRICE
Oh, on my soul, my cousin is belied!

BENEDICK
Lady, were you her bedfellow last night?

BEATRICE
No, truly, not; although, until last night,
I have this twelvemonth been her bedfellow.

LEONATO
Confirmed, confirmed! Oh, that is stronger made
Which was before barred up with ribs of iron!   151
Would the two princes lie and Claudio lie,
Who loved her so that, speaking of her foulness,
Washed it with tears? Hence from her! Let her die.

FRIAR   Hear me a little;
For I have only been silent so long
And given way unto this course of fortune   157
By noting of the lady. I have marked
A thousand blushing apparitions
To start into her face, a thousand innocent shames
In angel whiteness beat away those blushes,
And in her eye there hath appeared a fire
To burn the errors that these princes hold
Against her maiden truth. Call me a fool;
Trust not my reading nor my observations,
Which with experimental seal doth warrant   166
The tenor of my book; trust not my age,   167
My reverence, calling, nor divinity,
If this sweet lady lie not guiltless here
Under some biting error.

LEONATO   Friar, it cannot be.
Thou see'st that all the grace that she hath left
Is that she will not add to her damnation

A sin of perjury; she not denies it.
Why seek'st thou then to cover with excuse
That which appears in proper nakedness?   175

FRIAR
Lady, what man is he you are accused of?

HERO
They know that do accuse me; I know none.
If I know more of any man alive
Than that which maiden modesty doth warrant,   179
Let all my sins lack mercy! O my father,
Prove you that any man with me conversed   181
At hours unmeet or that I yesternight   182
Maintained the change of words with any creature,   183
Refuse me, hate me, torture me to death!   184

FRIAR
There is some strange misprision in the princes.   185

BENEDICK
Two of them have the very bent of honor;   186
And if their wisdoms be misled in this,
The practice of it lives in John the Bastard,   188
Whose spirits toil in frame of villainies.   189

LEONATO
I know not. If they speak but truth of her,
These hands shall tear her; if they wrong her honor,
The proudest of them shall well hear of it.
Time hath not yet so dried this blood of mine,
Nor age so eat up my invention,   194
Nor fortune made such havoc of my means,
Nor my bad life reft me so much of friends,   196
But they shall find, awaked in such a kind,   197
Both strength of limb and policy of mind,   198
Ability in means, and choice of friends,
To quit me of them throughly.

FRIAR   Pause awhile,   200
And let my counsel sway you in this case.
Your daughter here the princes left for dead,   202
Let her awhile be secretly kept in,   203
And publish it that she is dead indeed.
Maintain a mourning ostentation,   205
And on your family's old monument   206
Hang mournful epitaphs, and do all rites
That appertain unto a burial.

LEONATO
What shall become of this? What will this do?   209

FRIAR
Marry, this, well carried, shall on her behalf   210
Change slander to remorse. That is some good.
But not for that dream I on this strange course,   212

126 on . . . reproaches following this public disgrace   128 Chid
Chided.   frame plan, order.   132 Took . . . issue taken up a beggar's
child   136 mine i.e., my own daughter   138–9 That . . . her i.e., that I
set no value on myself in caring so much for her   140 that such that
142 season preservative   151 before already   157 given . . . fortune
yielded to this turn of events   166–7 Which . . . book i.e., by means
of which observations and experience I have confirmed what I
learned from books

175 proper true   179 warrant sanction, permit   181 Prove you if you
prove   182 unmeet improper   183 Maintained the change held
exchange   184 Refuse disown   185 misprision mistake, misunderstanding   186 Two . . . honor i.e., Don Pedro and Claudio are wholly
honorable   188 practice scheming   189 frame contriving   194 eat
eaten. (Pronounced "et.")   invention power to plan (vengeance)
196 reft robbed   197 kind manner   198 policy shrewdness
200 quit . . . throughly settle accounts with them thoroughly.
202 the princes i.e., (whom) Don Pedro and Claudio   203 in in hiding, at home   205 Maintain . . . ostentation Perform all the outward
signs of mourning   206 monument burial vault   209 become of
result from   210 carried managed   212 not for that not for that
reason alone

But on this travail look for greater birth.   213
She—dying, as it must be so maintained,
Upon the instant that she was accused—
Shall be lamented, pitied, and excused
Of every hearer; for it so falls out
That what we have we prize not to the worth   218
Whiles we enjoy it, but, being lacked and lost,
Why then we rack the value, then we find   220
The virtue that possession would not show us
Whiles it was ours. So will it fare with Claudio.
When he shall hear she died upon his words,   223
Th'idea of her life shall sweetly creep
Into his study of imagination,   225
And every lovely organ of her life   226
Shall come appareled in more precious habit,   227
More moving-delicate, and full of life,
Into the eye and prospect of his soul,   229
Than when she lived indeed. Then shall he mourn,
If ever love had interest in his liver,   231
And wish he had not so accusèd her,
No, though he thought his accusation true.
Let this be so, and doubt not but success   234
Will fashion the event in better shape   235
Than I can lay it down in likelihood.   236
But if all aim but this be leveled false,   237
The supposition of the lady's death
Will quench the wonder of her infamy.
And if it sort not well, you may conceal her,   240
As best befits her wounded reputation,
In some reclusive and religious life,   242
Out of all eyes, tongues, minds, and injuries.   243

BENEDICK
Signor Leonato, let the Friar advise you.
And though you know my inwardness and love   245
Is very much unto the Prince and Claudio,
Yet, by mine honor, I will deal in this
As secretly and justly as your soul
Should with your body.

LEONATO   Being that I flow in grief,   249
The smallest twine may lead me.

FRIAR
'Tis well consented. Presently away;   251
    For to strange sores strangely they strain the cure.   252
Come, lady, die to live. This wedding day
    Perhaps is but prolonged. Have patience, and
    endure.   254
                    Exit [with all but Benedick and Beatrice].
BENEDICK   Lady Beatrice, have you wept all this while?

BEATRICE   Yea, and I will weep a while longer.
BENEDICK   I will not desire that.
BEATRICE   You have no reason. I do it freely.   258
BENEDICK   Surely I do believe your fair cousin is
    wronged.
BEATRICE   Ah, how much might the man deserve of me
    that would right her!
BENEDICK   Is there any way to show such friendship?
BEATRICE   A very even way, but no such friend.   264
BENEDICK   May a man do it?
BEATRICE   It is a man's office, but not yours.   266
BENEDICK   I do love nothing in the world so well as you.
    Is not that strange?
BEATRICE   As strange as the thing I know not. It were as
    possible for me to say I loved nothing so well as you.
    But believe me not; and yet I lie not. I confess nothing,
    nor I deny nothing. I am sorry for my cousin.
BENEDICK   By my sword, Beatrice, thou lovest me.
BEATRICE   Do not swear and eat it.   274
BENEDICK   I will swear by it that you love me, and I will
    make him eat it that says I love not you.   276
BEATRICE   Will you not eat your word?
BENEDICK   With no sauce that can be devised to it. I
    protest I love thee.   279
BEATRICE   Why, then, God forgive me!
BENEDICK   What offense, sweet Beatrice?
BEATRICE   You have stayed me in a happy hour. I was   282
    about to protest I loved you.
BENEDICK   And do it with all thy heart.
BEATRICE   I love you with so much of my heart that
    none is left to protest.   286
BENEDICK   Come, bid me do anything for thee.
BEATRICE   Kill Claudio.
BENEDICK   Ha! Not for the wide world.
BEATRICE   You kill me to deny it. Farewell.   [Going.]
BENEDICK   Tarry, sweet Beatrice.
BEATRICE   I am gone, though I am here. There is no love   292
    in you. Nay, I pray you, let me go.
BENEDICK   Beatrice—
BEATRICE   In faith, I will go.
BENEDICK   We'll be friends first.
BEATRICE   You dare easier be friends with me than fight
    with mine enemy.
BENEDICK   Is Claudio thine enemy?
BEATRICE   Is 'a not approved in the height a villain, that   300
    hath slandered, scorned, dishonored my kinswoman?
    Oh, that I were a man! What, bear her in hand until   302
    they come to take hands, and then, with public accus-
    ation, uncovered slander, unmitigated rancor—Oh,   304
    God, that I were a man! I would eat his heart in the
    marketplace.

213 on this travail from this effort (which is metaphorically like the *travail*, or labor, of childbirth)   **218 to the worth** as fully as it deserves   **220 rack** stretch, extend   **223 upon** in consequence of   **225 Into . . . imagination** into his thoughts   **226 organ . . . life** aspect of her when she was alive   **227 habit** apparel   **229 prospect** range of vision   **231 interest in** claim upon.   **liver** (The supposed seat of the passion of love.)   **234 success** i.e., what succeeds or happens in time as my plan unfolds   **235 event** outcome   **236 lay . . . likelihood** anticipate its probable course.   **237 if . . . false** i.e., if every other aim miscarry   **240 sort** turn out   **242 reclusive** cloistered   **243 injuries** insults.   **245 inwardness and love** close friendship   **249 Being . . . grief** Since I overflow in grief   **251 Presently** Immediately   **252 For . . . cure** for strange diseases require strange and desperate cures.   **254 prolonged** deferred.

258 You . . . reason (Beatrice twists Benedick's "I wish you weren't so unhappy," line 257, into "There's no need for you to bid me stop weeping.")   **264 even** direct, straightforward   **266 office** duty   **274 eat it** i.e., eat your words.   **276 eat it** i.e., eat my sword, be stabbed by it   **279 protest** affirm. (Also in line 283.)   **282 stayed** stopped.   **in . . . hour** at an appropriate moment.   **286 protest** object. (With a play on the sense of "affirm" in 279 and 283.)   **292 gone** i.e., in spirit   **300 approved in the height** proved in the highest degree   **302 bear her in hand** delude Hero with false hopes   **304 uncovered** open, unconcealed

BENEDICK   Hear me, Beatrice—

BEATRICE   Talk with a man out at a window! A proper   308
saying!   309

BENEDICK   Nay, but Beatrice—

BEATRICE   Sweet Hero! She is wronged, she is slandered,
she is undone.

BENEDICK   Beat—

BEATRICE   Princes and counties! Surely, a princely testi-   314
mony, a goodly count, Count Comfect; a sweet gallant,   315
surely! Oh, that I were a man for his sake! Or that I had
any friend would be a man for my sake! But manhood
is melted into curtsies, valor into compliment, and
men are only turned into tongue, and trim ones too.   319
He is now as valiant as Hercules that only tells a lie   320
and swears it. I cannot be a man with wishing, there-   321
fore I will die a woman with grieving.

BENEDICK   Tarry, good Beatrice. By this hand, I love
thee.

BEATRICE   Use it for my love some other way than
swearing by it.

BENEDICK   Think you in your soul the Count Claudio
hath wronged Hero?

BEATRICE   Yea, as sure as I have a thought or a soul.

BENEDICK   Enough, I am engaged. I will challenge him.   330
I will kiss your hand, and so I leave you. By this hand,
Claudio shall render me a dear account. As you hear   332
of me, so think of me. Go comfort your cousin. I must
say she is dead. And so, farewell. [*Exeunt separately.*]

[4.2]

*Enter the Constables [Dogberry and Verges]
and the Town Clerk [Sexton] in gowns, Borachio, [Conrade, and Watch].*

DOGBERRY   Is our whole dissembly appeared?   1

VERGES   Oh, a stool and a cushion for the sexton.
[*Stool and cushion are brought. The Sexton sits.*]

SEXTON   Which be the malefactors?

DOGBERRY   Marry, that am I and my partner.   4

VERGES   Nay, that's certain; we have the exhibition to   5
examine.

SEXTON   But which are the offenders that are to be
examined? Let them come before Master Constable.

DOGBERRY   Yea, marry, let them come before me. [*The
prisoners are brought forward.*] What is your name,
friend?

BORACHIO   Borachio.

DOGBERRY   Pray, write down Borachio.—Yours, sirrah?   13

CONRADE   I am a gentleman, sir, and my name is
Conrade.

DOGBERRY   Write down Master Gentleman Conrade.
Masters, do you serve God?

CONRADE, BORACHIO   Yea, sir, we hope.

DOGBERRY   Write down that they hope they serve God;
and write God first, for God defend but God should   20
go before such villains! Masters, it is proved already
that you are little better than false knaves, and it will
go near to be thought so shortly. How answer you for
yourselves?

CONRADE   Marry, sir, we say we are none.

DOGBERRY   A marvelous witty fellow, I assure you, but   26
I will go about with him. [*To Borachio*] Come you   27
hither, sirrah. A word in your ear. Sir, I say to you, it is
thought you are false knaves.

BORACHIO   Sir, I say to you we are none.

DOGBERRY   Well, stand aside. 'Fore God, they are both
in a tale. Have you writ down that they are none?   32

SEXTON   Master Constable, you go not the way to
examine. You must call forth the watch that are their
accusers.

DOGBERRY   Yea, marry, that's the eftest way. Let the   36
watch come forth.—Masters, I charge you in the
Prince's name accuse these men.

SEACOAL   This man said, sir, that Don John, the Prince's
brother, was a villain.

DOGBERRY   Write down Prince John a villain. Why, this
is flat perjury, to call a prince's brother villain.   42

BORACHIO   Master Constable—

DOGBERRY   Pray thee, fellow, peace. I do not like thy
look, I promise thee.

SEXTON   What heard you him say else?

FIRST WATCH   Marry, that he had received a thousand
ducats of Don John for accusing the Lady Hero
wrongfully.

DOGBERRY   Flat burglary as ever was committed.

VERGES   Yea, by Mass, that it is.   51

SEXTON   What else, fellow?

SEACOAL   And that Count Claudio did mean, upon his   53
words, to disgrace Hero before the whole assembly,   54
and not marry her.

DOGBERRY   Oh, villain! Thou wilt be condemned into
everlasting redemption for this.   57

SEXTON   What else?

WATCH   This is all.   59

SEXTON   And this is more, masters, than you can deny:
Prince John is this morning secretly stolen away. Hero
was in this manner accused, in this very manner
refused, and upon the grief of this suddenly died.—
Master Constable, let these men be bound and
brought to Leonato's. I will go before and show him
their examination.   [*Exit.*]

308–9 proper saying likely story.   **314 counties** counts.   **315 count**
(1) the title (2) declaration of complaint in an indictment (3) account.
Comfect candy or sweetmeat   **319 are . . . tongue** have become mere
(flattering) voices.   **trim** nice, elegant, fine. (Used ironically.)
320–1 He . . . swears it A man need only tell lies and swear they are
true to gain a reputation for bravery nowadays.   **330 I am engaged** I
pledge myself.   **332 dear** costly
4.2. Location: The jail.
1 dissembly (A blunder for "assembly.")   **4 that am I** (Dogberry evidently understands *malefactors* to mean "factors," agents.)   **5 exhibition** (Possibly for "commission.")   **13 sirrah** (Used to address
inferiors; Conrade objects.)

20 defend forbid   **26 witty** clever, cunning   **27 go about with** get
the better of, deal with   **32 in a tale** in agreement.   **36 eftest** (Some
sort of invention for "easiest" or "deftest.")   **42 perjury** (Dogberry
means "slander.")   **51 by Mass** by the Mass   **53–4 upon his words**
on the basis of Borachio's testimony   **57 redemption** (Dogberry
means "damnation.")   **59 WATCH** (Perhaps both Seacoal and his partner speak.)

DOGBERRY   Come, let them be opinioned.   67

VERGES   Let them be in the hands—

CONRADE   Off, coxcomb!

DOGBERRY   God's my life, where's the sexton? Let him   70
write down the Prince's officer coxcomb. Come, bind
them. Thou naughty varlet!   72

CONRADE   Away! You are an ass, you are an ass.

DOGBERRY   Dost thou not suspect my place? Dost thou   74
not suspect my years? Oh, that he were here to write   75
me down an ass! But masters, remember that I am an
ass; though it be not written down, yet forget not that
I am an ass. No, thou villain, thou art full of piety, as   78
shall be proved upon thee by good witness. I am a
wise fellow, and, which is more, an officer, and, which
is more, a householder, and, which is more, as pretty
a piece of flesh as any is in Messina, and one that
knows the law, go to, and a rich fellow enough, go to,
and a fellow that hath had losses, and one that hath
two gowns and everything handsome about him.—
Bring him away. Oh, that I had been writ down an ass!
Exeunt.

✦

[5.1]

Enter Leonato and his brother [Antonio].

ANTONIO
If you go on thus, you will kill yourself;
And 'tis not wisdom thus to second grief   2
Against yourself.

LEONATO   I pray thee, cease thy counsel,
Which falls into mine ears as profitless
As water in a sieve. Give not me counsel,
Nor let no comforter delight mine ear
But such a one whose wrongs do suit with mine.   7
Bring me a father that so loved his child,
Whose joy of her is overwhelmed like mine,
And bid him speak of patience;
Measure his woe the length and breadth of mine,   11
And let it answer every strain for strain,   12
As thus for thus, and such a grief for such,
In every lineament, branch, shape, and form;
If such a one will smile and stroke his beard,
Bid sorrow wag, cry "hem!" when he should groan,   16
Patch grief with proverbs, make misfortune drunk   17
With candle wasters, bring him yet to me,   18
And I of him will gather patience.
But there is no such man. For, brother, men
Can counsel and speak comfort to that grief
Which they themselves not feel; but tasting it,

Their counsel turns to passion, which before
Would give preceptial medicine to rage,   24
Fetter strong madness in a silken thread,
Charm ache with air and agony with words.   26
No, no, 'tis all men's office to speak patience   27
To those that wring under the load of sorrow,   28
But no man's virtue nor sufficiency   29
To be so moral when he shall endure   30
The like himself. Therefore give me no counsel.
My griefs cry louder than advertisement.   32

ANTONIO
Therein do men from children nothing differ.   33

LEONATO
I pray thee, peace. I will be flesh and blood;
For there was never yet philosopher
That could endure the toothache patiently,
However they have writ the style of gods   37
And made a push at chance and sufferance.   38

ANTONIO
Yet bend not all the harm upon yourself.
Make those that do offend you suffer, too.

LEONATO
There thou speak'st reason. Nay, I will do so.
My soul doth tell me Hero is belied,
And that shall Claudio know; so shall the Prince
And all of them that thus dishonor her.

Enter Prince [Don Pedro] and Claudio.

ANTONIO
Here comes the Prince and Claudio hastily.

DON PEDRO
Good e'en, good e'en.

CLAUDIO   Good day to both of you.

LEONATO
Hear you, my lords—

DON PEDRO   We have some haste, Leonato.

LEONATO
Some haste, my lord! Well, fare you well, my lord.
Are you so hasty now? Well, all is one.   49

DON PEDRO
Nay, do not quarrel with us, good old man.

ANTONIO
If he could right himself with quarreling,   51
Some of us would lie low.

CLAUDIO   Who wrongs him?   52

LEONATO
Marry, thou dost wrong me, thou dissembler, thou!   53
Nay, never lay thy hand upon thy sword;
I fear thee not.

CLAUDIO   Marry, beshrew my hand   55
If it should give your age such cause of fear.

---

67 opinioned (For "pinioned.")   **70 God's** May God save
72 naughty wicked   **74 suspect** (For "respect.")   **75 my years** (With
an unconscious suggestion of "my ears," i.e., ass's ears.)   **78 piety**
(For "impiety.")
5.1. Location: Near Leonato's house.
2 second assist, encourage   **7 suit with** match   **11 Measure his woe**
let his woe equal in scope   **12 answer . . . for strain** correspond, pang
for pang. (With a musical sense also of echoing a refrain.)   **16 wag** be
off.   **cry "hem"** i.e., clear the throat as before some wordy speech
17 drunk i.e., insensible to pain   **18 candle wasters** those who waste
candles by late study, bookworms, moral philosophers

24 preceptial consisting of precepts   **26 air** mere breath, words
27 office duty   **28 wring** writhe   **29 sufficiency** ability, power
30 moral prone to moralizing   **32 advertisement** advice, counsel.
33 Therein . . . differ i.e., It is childish to be so inconsolable.   **37 writ . . .
gods** uttered godlike wisdom   **38 made . . . sufferance** scoffed at misfortune and suffering.   **49 all is one** it makes no difference.   **51 he** i.e.,
Leonato   **52 Some of us** i.e., Don Pedro and Claudio   **53 thou** (Used
contemptuously instead of the more polite *you.*)   **55 beshrew** curse

In faith, my hand meant nothing to my sword.   57

LEONATO

Tush, tush, man, never fleer and jest at me.   58
I speak not like a dotard nor a fool,
As under privilege of age to brag
What I have done being young or what would do
Were I not old. Know, Claudio, to thy head,   62
Thou hast so wronged mine innocent child and me
That I am forced to lay my reverence by,   64
And with gray hairs and bruise of many days
Do challenge thee to trial of a man.   66
I say thou hast belied mine innocent child.
Thy slander hath gone through and through her
    heart,
And she lies buried with her ancestors—
Oh, in a tomb where never scandal slept,
Save this of hers, framed by thy villainy!   71

CLAUDIO

My villainy?

LEONATO   Thine, Claudio, thine, I say.

DON PEDRO

You say not right, old man.

LEONATO   My lord, my lord,
I'll prove it on his body if he dare,
Despite his nice fence and his active practice,   75
His May of youth and bloom of lustihood.   76

CLAUDIO

Away! I will not have to do with you.

LEONATO

Canst thou so daff me? Thou hast killed my child.   78
If thou kill'st me, boy, thou shalt kill a man.

ANTONIO

He shall kill two of us, and men indeed.
But that's no matter; let him kill one first.
Win me and wear me! Let him answer me.   82
Come follow me, boy. Come, sir boy, come follow me,
Sir boy, I'll whip you from your foining fence!   84
Nay, as I am a gentleman, I will.

LEONATO   Brother—

ANTONIO

Content yourself. God knows I loved my niece,   87
And she is dead, slandered to death by villains
That dare as well answer a man indeed
As I dare take a serpent by the tongue.
Boys, apes, braggarts, jacks, milksops!

LEONATO   Brother Antony—

ANTONIO

Hold you content. What, man! I know them, yea,
And what they weigh, even to the utmost scruple—   94
Scambling, outfacing, fashionmonging boys,   95

That lie and cog and flout, deprave and slander,   96
Go anticly, show outward hideousness,   97
And speak off half a dozen dangerous words   98
How they might hurt their enemies, if they durst,
And this is all.

LEONATO

But brother Antony—

ANTONIO   Come, 'tis no matter.

Do not you meddle; let me deal in this.

DON PEDRO

Gentlemen both, we will not wake your patience.   103
My heart is sorry for your daughter's death;
But, on my honor, she was charged with nothing
But what was true and very full of proof.

LEONATO   My lord, my lord—

DON PEDRO   I will not hear you.

LEONATO

No? Come, brother, away! I will be heard.

ANTONIO

And shall, or some of us will smart for it.   110

Exeunt ambo [Leonato and Antonio].

Enter Benedick.

DON PEDRO

See, see, here comes the man we went to seek.

CLAUDIO   Now, signor, what news?

BENEDICK   Good day, my lord.

DON PEDRO   Welcome, signor. You are almost come to
part almost a fray.

CLAUDIO   We would like to have had our two noses   116
snapped off with two old men without teeth.   117

DON PEDRO   Leonato and his brother. What think'st
thou? Had we fought, I doubt we should have been   119
too young for them.

BENEDICK   In a false quarrel there is no true valor. I came
to seek you both.

CLAUDIO   We have been up and down to seek thee, for
we are high-proof melancholy and would fain have it   124
beaten away. Wilt thou use thy wit?

BENEDICK   It is in my scabbard. Shall I draw it?

DON PEDRO   Dost thou wear thy wit by thy side?

CLAUDIO   Never any did so, though very many have
been beside their wit. I will bid thee draw as we do the   129
minstrels, draw to pleasure us.   130

DON PEDRO   As I am an honest man, he looks pale. Art
thou sick, or angry?

CLAUDIO   What, courage, man! What though care killed
a cat, thou hast mettle enough in thee to kill care.

BENEDICK   Sir, I shall meet your wit in the career, an you   135
charge it against me. I pray you, choose another subject.   136

---

57 my . . . sword I had no intention of using my sword.   **58 fleer** sneer,
jeer   **62 head** i.e., face   **64 my reverence** i.e., the reverence due old
age   **66 trial of a man** manly contest, i.e., duel.   **71 framed** devised
75 nice fence dexterous swordsmanship. (Said contemptuously.)   **76
lustihood** bodily vigor.   **78 daff** doff, brush aside   **82 Win . . . me!**
(A proverbial expression, used as a challenge, meaning he'll have to
overcome me before he can claim me as a prize.)   **answer me** i.e., in
a duel.   **84 foining** thrusting   **87 Content yourself** i.e., Don't try to
stop me.   **94 scruple** small measure of weight   **95 Scambling . . .
boys** contentious, swaggering, dandified boys

96 cog cheat.   **deprave** defame, traduce   **97 anticly** fantastically
dressed.   **hideousness** frightening appearance   **98 dangerous**
threatening, haughty   **103 wake your patience** put your patience to
any further test.   **110.1 ambo** both   **116 We had . . . had** We almost
had   **117 with** by   **119 doubt** fear, suspect. (Said ironically.)   **124
high-proof** to the highest degree.   **fain** gladly
129 beside their wit out of their wits. (Playing on *by thy side* in line
127.)   **130 draw** (1) draw your weapon (2) draw a bow across a musical instrument   **135 career** short gallop at full speed (as in a tourney).
an if   **136 charge** level (as a weapon)

CLAUDIO   Nay, then, give him another staff. This last 138
was broke cross. 139

DON PEDRO   By this light, he changes more and more. I
think he be angry indeed.

CLAUDIO   If he be, he knows how to turn his girdle. 142

BENEDICK   Shall I speak a word in your ear?

CLAUDIO   God bless me from a challenge!

BENEDICK [aside to Claudio]   You are a villain. I jest not. I
will make it good how you dare, with what you dare,
and when you dare. Do me right, or I will protest your 147
cowardice. You have killed a sweet lady, and her death
shall fall heavy on you. Let me hear from you.

CLAUDIO   Well, I will meet you, so I may have good
cheer. 151

DON PEDRO   What, a feast, a feast?

CLAUDIO   I'faith, I thank him, he hath bid me to a calf's 153
head and a capon, the which if I do not carve most 154
curiously, say my knife's naught. Shall I not find a 155
woodcock too? 156

BENEDICK   Sir, your wit ambles well; it goes easily. 157

DON PEDRO   I'll tell thee how Beatrice praised thy wit
the other day. I said thou hadst a fine wit. "True," said
she, "a fine little one." "No," said I, "a great wit."
"Right," says she, "a great gross one." "Nay," said I, "a
good wit." "Just," said she, "it hurts nobody." "Nay," 162
said I, "the gentleman is wise." "Certain," said she,
"a wise gentleman." "Nay," said I, "he hath the 164
tongues." "That I believe," said she, "for he swore a 165
thing to me on Monday night which he forswore on
Tuesday morning. There's a double tongue; there's
two tongues." Thus did she, an hour together, trans- 168
shape thy particular virtues. Yet at last she concluded 169
with a sigh, thou wast the proper'st man in Italy. 170

CLAUDIO   For the which she wept heartily and said she
cared not.

DON PEDRO   Yea, that she did. But yet for all that, an if
she did not hate him deadly, she would love him
dearly. The old man's daughter told us all. 175

CLAUDIO   All, all. And, moreover, God saw him when 176
he was hid in the garden. 177

DON PEDRO   But when shall we set the savage bull's
horns on the sensible Benedick's head?

CLAUDIO   Yea, and text underneath, "Here dwells 180
Benedick, the married man"?

BENEDICK   Fare you well, boy. You know my mind. I
will leave you now to your gossiplike humor. You
break jests as braggarts do their blades, which, God be 184
thanked, hurt not.—My lord, for your many courtesies I thank you. I must discontinue your company.
Your brother the bastard is fled from Messina. You
have among you killed a sweet and innocent lady. For
my Lord Lackbeard there, he and I shall meet, and till
then peace be with him.   [Exit.]

DON PEDRO   He is in earnest.

CLAUDIO   In most profound earnest, and, I'll warrant
you, for the love of Beatrice.

DON PEDRO   And hath challenged thee?

CLAUDIO   Most sincerely.

DON PEDRO   What a pretty thing man is when he goes 196
in his doublet and hose and leaves off his wit! 197

CLAUDIO   He is then a giant to an ape; but then is an ape 198
a doctor to such a man. 199

DON PEDRO   But, soft you, let me be. Pluck up, my heart, 200
and be sad. Did he not say my brother was fled? 201

*Enter Constables, [Dogberry and Verges, and
the Watch, with] Conrade and Borachio.*

DOGBERRY   Come you, sir. If Justice cannot tame you,
she shall ne'er weigh more reasons in her balance. 203
Nay, an you be a cursing hypocrite once, you must be 204
looked to.

DON PEDRO   How now, two of my brother's men
bound? Borachio one!

CLAUDIO   Hearken after their offense, my lord. 208

DON PEDRO   Officers, what offense have these men
done?

DOGBERRY   Marry, sir, they have committed false report;
moreover, they have spoken untruths; secondarily,
they are slanders; sixth and lastly, they have belied a 213
lady; thirdly, they have verified unjust things; and to
conclude, they are lying knaves.

DON PEDRO   First, I ask thee what they have done;
thirdly, I ask thee what's their offense; sixth and lastly,
why they are committed; and to conclude, what you
lay to their charge.

CLAUDIO   Rightly reasoned, and in his own division; 220
and, by my troth, there's one meaning well suited. 221

DON PEDRO   Who have you offended, masters, that you
are thus bound to your answer? This learned consta- 223
ble is too cunning to be understood. What's your
offense?

---

138 staff spear shaft.   **139 broke cross** i.e., broken by clumsily allowing the spear to break crosswise against the opponent's shield. (In
other words, Claudio accuses Benedick of having failed in his sally of
wit.)   **142 turn his girdle** i.e., turn his sword belt around so that he's
ready to fight. (A proverbial expression of uncertain meaning.)
147 Do me right Give me satisfaction.   **protest** proclaim before witnesses   **151 cheer** entertainment. (Claudio is ready to fight, he says,
for the pleasant diversion it should offer.)   **153–6 calf's head, capon,
woodcock** (In the proposed feast of dueling, Claudio plans to carve
various dishes connoting foolishness, effeminate cowardice, and stupidity.)   **155 curiously** daintily.   **naught** good for nothing.
157 ambles i.e., minces along   **162 good** (1) keen (2) harmless.   **Just**
Exactly   **164 a wise gentleman** i.e., an old fool.   **164–5 hath the
tongues** masters several languages.   **168–9 trans-shape** distort, turn
the wrong side out   **170 proper'st** handsomest   **175 old man's
daughter** i.e., Hero   **176–7 God . . . garden** (Alluding to the trick
played on Benedick to love Beatrice, and also to Genesis 3:8.)
180 text (In 1.1.251–6, Benedick vowed that, if he were ever to fall in
love, his friends might set a bull's horns on his head and label him
"Benedick the married man.")

184 as . . . blades i.e., as braggarts furtively damage their blades to
make it appear they have been fighting fiercely   **196–7 goes . . . wit**
goes about fully dressed like a rational creature but forgets to equip
himself with good sense.   **198–9 He . . . man** i.e., Such a man looks
like a hero in a fool's eyes, but actually the fool is a wise man compared to him.   **200–1 soft . . . be sad** wait a minute, not so fast; let me
think. Rouse yourself, my heart, and be serious.   **201.1–2** (The quarto
placement of this stage direction after line 197 suggests that Dogberry
is visible, strutting and fussing with his prisoners, before he speaks.)
203 ne'er . . . balance never again weigh arguments of reason in her
scales. (But the pronunciation of *reason* as "raisin" invokes the comic
image of a shopkeeper weighing produce.)   **204 cursing** accursed.
once in a word   **208 Hearken after** Inquire into   **213 slanders** (For
"slanderers.")   **220 his own division** its own partition in a logical
arrangement. (Said ironically.)   **221 well suited** nicely dressed up in
the trappings of language.   **223 bound** (Playing on the meanings
"pinioned" and "headed for a destination.")   **answer** trial, account.

BORACHIO   Sweet Prince, let me go no farther to mine answer. Do you hear me, and let this count kill me. I have deceived even your very eyes. What your wisdoms could not discover, these shallow fools have brought to light, who in the night overheard me confessing to this man how Don John your brother incensed me to slander the Lady Hero, how you were 232 brought into the orchard and saw me court Margaret in Hero's garments, how you disgraced her when you should marry her. My villainy they have upon record, which I had rather seal with my death than repeat over to my shame. The lady is dead upon mine and 237 my master's false accusation; and, briefly, I desire nothing but the reward of a villain.

DON PEDRO   [to Claudio]
Runs not this speech like iron through your blood?

CLAUDIO
I have drunk poison whiles he uttered it.

DON PEDRO   [to Borachio]
But did my brother set thee on to this?

BORACHIO   Yea, and paid me richly for the practice of it. 243

DON PEDRO
He is composed and framed of treachery,
And fled he is upon this villainy.   245

CLAUDIO
Sweet Hero! Now thy image doth appear
In the rare semblance that I loved it first.   247

DOGBERRY   Come, bring away the plaintiffs. By this time 248
our sexton hath reformed Signor Leonato of the 249
matter. And masters, do not forget to specify, when 250
time and place shall serve, that I am an ass.

VERGES   Here, here comes Master Signor Leonato, and
the sexton, too.

*Enter Leonato, his brother [Antonio], and the
Sexton.*

LEONATO
Which is the villain? Let me see his eyes,
That when I note another man like him,
I may avoid him. Which of these is he?

BORACHIO
If you would know your wronger, look on me.

LEONATO
Art thou the slave that with thy breath hast killed
Mine innocent child?

BORACHIO   Yea, even I alone.

LEONATO
No, not so, villain, thou beliest thyself.
Here stand a pair of honorable men—   261
A third is fled—that had a hand in it.
I thank you, princes, for my daughter's death.
Record it with your high and worthy deeds.
'Twas bravely done, if you bethink you of it.

CLAUDIO
I know not how to pray your patience,
Yet I must speak. Choose your revenge yourself;

Impose me to what penance your invention   268
Can lay upon my sin. Yet sinned I not
But in mistaking.

DON PEDRO   By my soul, nor I.
And yet, to satisfy this good old man,
I would bend under any heavy weight
That he'll enjoin me to.

LEONATO
I cannot bid you bid my daughter live—
That were impossible—but, I pray you both,
Possess the people in Messina here   276
How innocent she died; and if your love
Can labor aught in sad invention,   278
Hang her an epitaph upon her tomb,
And sing it to her bones; sing it tonight.
Tomorrow morning come you to my house,
And since you could not be my son-in-law,
Be yet my nephew. My brother hath a daughter,
Almost the copy of my child that's dead,
And she alone is heir to both of us.   285
Give her the right you should have giv'n her cousin, 286
And so dies my revenge.

CLAUDIO   O noble sir,
Your overkindness doth wring tears from me!
I do embrace your offer; and dispose   289
For henceforth of poor Claudio.   290

LEONATO
Tomorrow then I will expect your coming;
Tonight I take my leave. This naughty man   292
Shall face to face be brought to Margaret,
Who I believe was packed in all this wrong,   294
Hired to it by your brother.

BORACHIO   No, by my soul, she was not,
Nor knew not what she did when she spoke to me,
But always hath been just and virtuous
In anything that I do know by her.   299

DOGBERRY   Moreover, sir, which indeed is not under 300
white and black, this plaintiff here, the offender, did 301
call me ass. I beseech you, let it be remembered in his
punishment. And also the watch heard them talk of
one Deformed. They say he wears a key in his ear and 304
a lock hanging by it and borrows money in God's 305
name, the which he hath used so long and never paid 306
that now men grow hardhearted and will lend nothing for God's sake. Pray you, examine him upon that point.

LEONATO   I thank thee for thy care and honest pains.

DOGBERRY   Your Worship speaks like a most thankful
and reverend youth, and I praise God for you.

LEONATO   There's for thy pains.   [He gives money.]

DOGBERRY   God save the foundation!   314

---

268 **Impose me to** Impose on me   276 **Possess** inform   278 **aught** to
any extent   285 **heir to both** (Leonato overlooks Antonio's son mentioned in 1.2.2.)   286 **right** equitable treatment. (Quibbling on "rite,"
"ceremony.")   289 **dispose** you may dispose   290 **For henceforth** for
the future   292 **naughty** wicked   294 **packed** involved as an accomplice   299 **by** concerning   300–1 **under . . . black** written down in
black and white   304–5 **key . . . by it** (This is what Dogberry has
made out of the lovelock mentioned in 3.3.166.)   305–6 **in God's
name** (A phrase of the professional beggar.)   314 **God . . . foundation!** (A formula of those who received alms at religious houses or
charitable foundations.)

232 **incensed** incited   237 **upon** in consequence of   243 **practice** cunning execution   245 **upon** i.e., having committed   247 **rare semblance** splendid likeness   248 **plaintiffs** (For "defendants.")
249 **reformed** (For "informed.")   250 **specify** (For "testify"?)
261 **honorable men** i.e., Don Pedro and Claudio, men of rank

LEONATO   Go, I discharge thee of thy prisoner, and I
thank thee.
DOGBERRY   I leave an arrant knave with Your Worship,
which I beseech Your Worship to correct yourself, for
the example of others. God keep Your Worship! I wish
Your Worship well. God restore you to health! I
humbly give you leave to depart; and if a merry meet-   321
ing may be wished, God prohibit it! Come, neighbor.   322
[Exeunt Dogberry and Verges.]
LEONATO
Until tomorrow morning, lords, farewell.
ANTONIO
Farewell, my lords. We look for you tomorrow.
DON PEDRO
We will not fail.
CLAUDIO   Tonight I'll mourn with Hero.
LEONATO *[to the Watch]*
Bring you these fellows on.—We'll talk with Margaret,
How her acquaintance grew with this lewd fellow.   327
Exeunt [separately].

❧

[5.2]

Enter Benedick and Margaret, [meeting].

BENEDICK   Pray thee, sweet Mistress Margaret, deserve
well at my hands by helping me to the speech of   2
Beatrice.
MARGARET   Will you then write me a sonnet in praise of
my beauty?
BENEDICK   In so high a style, Margaret, that no man   6
living shall come over it, for in most comely truth thou   7
deservest it.
MARGARET   To have no man come over me! Why, shall
I always keep below stairs?   10
BENEDICK   Thy wit is as quick as the greyhound's
mouth; it catches.
MARGARET   And yours as blunt as the fencer's foils,
which hit but hurt not.
BENEDICK   A most manly wit, Margaret; it will not hurt
a woman. And so, I pray thee, call Beatrice. I give thee   16
the bucklers.   17
MARGARET   Give us the swords. We have bucklers of
our own.
BENEDICK   If you use them, Margaret, you must put in
the pikes with a vice, and they are dangerous weapons   21
for maids.

MARGARET   Well, I will call Beatrice to you, who I think
hath legs.   *Exit Margaret.*
BENEDICK   And therefore will come.
[He sings.] "The god of love,   26
    That sits above,
    And knows me, and knows me,
    How pitiful I deserve—"   29
I mean in singing; but in loving, Leander the good   30
swimmer, Troilus the first employer of panders, and a   31
whole bookful of these quondam carpetmongers,   32
whose names yet run smoothly in the even road of a
blank verse, why, they were never so truly turned over   34
and over as my poor self in love. Marry, I cannot show   35
it in rhyme. I have tried. I can find out no rhyme to
"lady" but "baby," an innocent rhyme; for "scorn,"   37
"horn," a hard rhyme; for "school," "fool," a babbling   38
rhyme; very ominous endings. No, I was not born
under a rhyming planet, nor I cannot woo in festival
terms.

Enter Beatrice.

Sweet Beatrice, wouldst thou come when I called thee?
BEATRICE   Yea, signor, and depart when you bid me.
BENEDICK   Oh, stay but till then!   *[She starts to leave.]*
BEATRICE   "Then" is spoken; fare you well now. And
yet, ere I go, let me go with that I came, which is, with   46
knowing what hath passed between you and Claudio.
BENEDICK   Only foul words; and thereupon I will kiss
thee.
BEATRICE   Foul words is but foul wind, and foul wind
is but foul breath, and foul breath is noisome; there-   51
fore I will depart unkissed.
BENEDICK   Thou hast frighted the word out of his right   53
sense, so forcible is thy wit. But I must tell thee plainly,
Claudio undergoes my challenge; and either I must
shortly hear from him, or I will subscribe him a   56
coward. And I pray thee now tell me, for which of my
bad parts didst thou first fall in love with me?
BEATRICE   For them all together, which maintained so
politic a state of evil that they will not admit any good   60
part to intermingle with them. But for which of my
good parts did you first suffer love for me?   62
BENEDICK   Suffer love! A good epithet. I do suffer love   63
indeed, for I love thee against my will.
BEATRICE   In spite of your heart, I think. Alas, poor
heart, if you spite it for my sake I will spite it for yours,
for I will never love that which my friend hates.
BENEDICK   Thou and I are too wise to woo peaceably.

---

321 give you leave (For "ask your leave.")   **322 prohibit** (For "permit.")   **327 lewd** wicked, worthless
**5.2. Location: Leonato's garden (? At the scene's end, Leonato's
house is some distance away.)**
2 to the speech of to speak with   **6 style** (1) poetic style (2) stile,
stairs over a fence   **7 come over** (1) excel beyond (2) traverse, as one
would cross a stile (3) in Margaret's next speech, the phrase is taken
to mean "mount sexually."   **comely** good. (With an allusion to Margaret's beauty.)   **10 keep below stairs** dwell in the servants' quarters.
16–17 I . . . bucklers i.e., I acknowledge myself beaten (in repartee).
(Bucklers are shields with spikes [pikes] in their centers. Margaret
uses the word in a bawdy sense in her reply.)   **21 pikes** spikes in the
center of a shield.   **vice** screw. (Benedick's bawdy sense continues
Margaret's jest.)

26–9 The god . . . deserve (The beginning of an old song by William
Elderton.)   **29 How . . . deserve** how I deserve pity. (But Benedick
uses the phrase to mean "how little I deserve.")   **30 Leander** lover of
Hero of Sestos; he swam the Hellespont nightly to see her until he
drowned   **31 Troilus** lover of Cressida, whose affair was assisted by
her uncle Pandarus   **32 quondam carpetmongers** ladies' men of old,
such as one might find in the carpeted boudoirs of the women they
woo   **34–5 over and over** i.e., head over heels   **37 innocent** childish
38 hard (1) exact (2) unpleasant, because of the association with cuckold's horns   **46 that I came** what I came for   **51 noisome** noxious
53 his its   **56 subscribe** formally proclaim in writing   **60 politic** prudently governed   **62 suffer** (1) experience (2) feel the pain of
63 epithet expression.

BEATRICE   It appears not in this confession. There's not ⁶⁹
one wise man among twenty that will praise himself.

BENEDICK   An old, an old instance, Beatrice, that lived ⁷¹
in the time of good neighbors. If a man do not erect in ⁷²
this age his own tomb ere he dies, he shall live no ⁷³
longer in monument than the bell rings and the ⁷⁴
widow weeps. ⁷⁵

BEATRICE   And how long is that, think you?

BENEDICK   Question: why, an hour in clamor and a ⁷⁷
quarter in rheum. Therefore is it most expedient for ⁷⁸
the wise, if Don Worm, his conscience, find no imped- ⁷⁹
iment to the contrary, to be the trumpet of his own
virtues, as I am to myself. So much for praising myself,
who, I myself will bear witness, is praiseworthy. And
now tell me, how doth your cousin?

BEATRICE   Very ill.

BENEDICK   And how do you?

BEATRICE   Very ill too.

BENEDICK   Serve God, love me, and mend. There will I
leave you too, for here comes one in haste.

Enter Ursula.

URSULA   Madam, you must come to your uncle. Yonder's old coil at home. It is proved my lady Hero hath ⁹⁰
been falsely accused, the Prince and Claudio mightily
abused, and Don John is the author of all, who is fled ⁹²
and gone. Will you come presently? ⁹³

BEATRICE   Will you go hear this news, signor?

BENEDICK   I will live in thy heart, die in thy lap, and be ⁹⁵
buried in thy eyes; and moreover I will go with thee to
thy uncle's.   *Exeunt.*

❖

[5.3]

*Enter Claudio, Prince [Don Pedro, Balthasar],
and three or four with tapers.*

CLAUDIO   Is this the monument of Leonato?

A LORD   It is, my lord.

CLAUDIO   [*reading from a scroll*]

Epitaph.

"Done to death by slanderous tongues
    Was the Hero that here lies.
Death, in guerdon of her wrongs, ⁵
    Gives her fame which never dies.
So the life that died with shame
Lives in death with glorious fame."

Hang thou there upon the tomb,
Praising her when I am dumb.

[*He hangs up the scroll.*]
Now, music, sound, and sing your solemn hymn.

Song.

BALTHASAR
Pardon, goddess of the night, ¹²
Those that slew thy virgin knight; ¹³
For the which, with songs of woe,
Round about her tomb they go.
Midnight, assist our moan;
Help us to sigh and groan,
    Heavily, heavily.
Graves, yawn and yield your dead,
Till death be utterèd, ²⁰
    Heavily, heavily.

CLAUDIO
Now, unto thy bones good night!
Yearly will I do this rite.

DON PEDRO
Good morrow, masters. Put your torches out.
The wolves have preyed; and look, the gentle day, ²⁵
Before the wheels of Phoebus, round about ²⁶
Dapples the drowsy east with spots of gray.
Thanks to you all, and leave us. Fare you well.

CLAUDIO
Good morrow, masters. Each his several way. ²⁹

DON PEDRO
Come, let us hence, and put on other weeds, ³⁰
And then to Leonato's we will go.

CLAUDIO
And Hymen now with luckier issue speed's ³²
Than this for whom we rendered up this woe.

Exeunt.

❖

[5.4]

*Enter Leonato, Benedick, [Beatrice], Margaret,
Ursula, old man [Antonio], Friar [Francis, and]
Hero.*

FRIAR
Did I not tell you she was innocent?

LEONATO
So are the Prince and Claudio, who accused her
Upon the error that you heard debated.
But Margaret was in some fault for this, ³
Although against her will, as it appears ⁵
In the true course of all the question. ⁶

---

69 It . . . confession i.e., You don't show your wisdom in praising
yourself for being wise.   71 instance proverb (i.e., "He has ill neighbors that is fain to praise himself")   72 time . . . neighbors good old
times (when one's neighbors spoke well of one).   73–5 he shall . . .
weeps i.e., he will be memorialized only during the (brief) time of the
funeral service and the official mourning.   77 Question i.e., An easy
question, which I will answer as follows.   clamor noise (of the bell)
78 rheum tears (of the widow).   79 Don . . . conscience (The action
of the conscience was traditionally described as the gnawing of a
worm; compare with Mark 9:44–8.)   90 old coil great confusion
92 abused deceived   93 presently immediately.   95 die (With the
common connotation of "experience sexual climax.")
5.3. Location: A churchyard.
5 guerdon recompense

12 goddess of the night i.e., Diana, moon goddess, patroness of
chastity   13 knight i.e., follower   20 utterèd fully expressed
25 have preyed i.e., have done their preying   26 wheels of Phoebus
i.e., chariot of the sun god   29 several separate   30 weeds garments
32 And . . . speed's And may the god of marriage favor us with better
fortune
5.4. Location: Leonato's house.
3 Upon on the basis of   5 against her will unintentionally   6 question investigation.

ANTONIO
Well, I am glad that all things sorts so well.   7
BENEDICK
And so am I, being else by faith enforced   8
To call young Claudio to a reckoning for it.
LEONATO
Well, daughter, and you gentlewomen all,
Withdraw into a chamber by yourselves,
And when I send for you, come hither masked.
The Prince and Claudio promised by this hour
To visit me. You know your office, brother:
You must be father to your brother's daughter,
And give her to young Claudio.   *Exeunt ladies.*
ANTONIO
Which I will do with confirmed countenance.   17
BENEDICK
Friar, I must entreat your pains, I think.   18
FRIAR   To do what, signor?
BENEDICK
To bind me or undo me—one of them.   20
Signor Leonato, truth it is, good signor,
Your niece regards me with an eye of favor.
LEONATO
That eye my daughter lent her. 'Tis most true.   23
BENEDICK
And I do with an eye of love requite her.
LEONATO
The sight whereof I think you had from me,   25
From Claudio, and the Prince. But what's your will?   26
BENEDICK
Your answer, sir, is enigmatical.
But, for my will, my will is your good will   28
May stand with ours, this day to be conjoined
In the state of honorable marriage,
In which, good Friar, I shall desire your help.
LEONATO
My heart is with your liking.
FRIAR   And my help.
Here comes the Prince and Claudio.

        Enter Prince [Don Pedro] and Claudio, and
        two or three other.

DON PEDRO
Good morrow to this fair assembly.
LEONATO
Good morrow, Prince. Good morrow, Claudio.
We here attend you. Are you yet determined   36
Today to marry with my brother's daughter?
CLAUDIO
I'll hold my mind, were she an Ethiope.
LEONATO
Call her forth, brother. Here's the Friar ready.
                            [Exit Antonio.]

DON PEDRO
Good morrow, Benedick. Why, what's the matter,
That you have such a February face,
So full of frost, of storm, and cloudiness?
CLAUDIO
I think he thinks upon the savage bull.   43
Tush, fear not, man! We'll tip thy horns with gold,
And all Europa shall rejoice at thee,   45
As once Europa did at lusty Jove   46
When he would play the noble beast in love.
BENEDICK
Bull Jove, sir, had an amiable low,
And some such strange bull leapt your father's cow
And got a calf in that same noble feat
Much like to you, for you have just his bleat.

        Enter [Leonato's] brother [Antonio], Hero,
        Beatrice, Margaret, [and] Ursula, [the ladies
        masked].

CLAUDIO
For this I owe you. Here comes other reckonings.   52
Which is the lady I must seize upon?
ANTONIO
This same is she, and I do give you her.
CLAUDIO
Why then, she's mine. Sweet, let me see your face.
LEONATO
No, that you shall not, till you take her hand
Before this friar and swear to marry her.
CLAUDIO
Give me your hand before this holy friar.
I am your husband, if you like of me.   59
HERO *[unmasking]*
And when I lived, I was your other wife;
And when you loved, you were my other husband.
CLAUDIO
Another Hero!
HERO   Nothing certainer.
One Hero died defiled, but I do live,
And surely as I live, I am a maid.
DON PEDRO
The former Hero! Hero that is dead!
LEONATO
She died, my lord, but whiles her slander lived.   66
FRIAR
All this amazement can I qualify,   67
When, after that the holy rites are ended,
I'll tell you largely of fair Hero's death.   69
Meantime let wonder seem familiar,   70
And to the chapel let us presently.   71
BENEDICK
Soft and fair, Friar. Which is Beatrice?   72

---

7 sorts turn out   **8 being . . . enforced** since otherwise I would be
enforced by my promise to Beatrice   **17 confirmed countenance**
straight face.   **18 entreat your pains** beg your help   **20 undo** (1) ruin
(2) untie, unbind   **23 That . . . her** (Alludes to Hero's role in tricking
Beatrice into confessing her love for Benedick.)   **25–6 The sight . . .**
Prince (Alludes to their role in tricking Benedick into confessing his
love for Beatrice.)   **28 for** as for.   **is** is that   **36 yet** still

43 I . . . bull (A jocular reminiscence of the conversation in 1.1.250 ff.)
45 Europa Europe   **46 Europa** a princess whom Jove approached in
the form of a white bull and bore on his back through the sea to Crete
52 I owe you i.e., I'll pay you back later (for calling me a calf and a
bastard).   **other reckonings** i.e., other matters to be settled first.
59 like of care for   **66 but whiles** only while   **67 qualify** moderate
69 largely at large, in full   **70 let . . . familiar** treat these marvels as
ordinary matters   **71 let us presently** let us go at once.   **72 Soft and**
fair i.e., Wait a minute

BEATRICE [*unmasking*]
I answer to that name. What is your will?

BENEDICK
Do not you love me?

BEATRICE　　　　　　　Why, no, no more than reason.

BENEDICK
Why, then your uncle and the Prince and Claudio
Have been deceived. They swore you did.

BEATRICE
Do not you love me?

BENEDICK　　　　　　　Troth, no, no more than reason.

BEATRICE
Why, then my cousin, Margaret, and Ursula　　78
Are much deceived, for they did swear you did.

BENEDICK
They swore that you were almost sick for me.

BEATRICE
They swore that you were well-nigh dead for me.

BENEDICK
'Tis no such matter. Then you do not love me?

BEATRICE
No, truly, but in friendly recompense.

LEONATO
Come, cousin, I am sure you love the gentleman.　84

CLAUDIO
And I'll be sworn upon't that he loves her;
For here's a paper written in his hand,
A halting sonnet of his own pure brain,　　87
Fashioned to Beatrice.　　　　　　[*He shows a paper.*]

HERO　　　　　　　　And here's another
Writ in my cousin's hand, stol'n from her pocket,
Containing her affection unto Benedick.
　　　　　　　　　　　　[*She shows another paper.*]

BENEDICK　A miracle! Here's our own hands against our　91
hearts. Come, I will have thee, but by this light I take　92
thee for pity.

BEATRICE　I would not deny you, but by this good day,
I yield upon great persuasion, and partly to save your
life, for I was told you were in a consumption.　96

---

78 my cousin i.e., Hero　**84 cousin** i.e., niece　**87 halting** limping.
his own pure purely his own　**91–2 against our hearts** i.e., to prove
our hearts guilty as charged.　**96 in a consumption** i.e., wasting
away in sighs.

BENEDICK　Peace! I will stop your mouth. [*Kissing her.*]

DON PEDRO　How dost thou, Benedick, the married
man?

BENEDICK　I'll tell thee what, Prince: a college of wit-　100
crackers cannot flout me out of my humor. Dost thou
think I care for a satire or an epigram? No. If a man　102
will be beaten with brains, 'a shall wear nothing hand-　103
some about him. In brief, since I do purpose to marry,　104
I will think nothing to any purpose that the world can
say against it; and therefore never flout at me for what　106
I have said against it; for man is a giddy thing, and this
is my conclusion. For thy part, Claudio, I did think to
have beaten thee, but in that thou art like to be my　109
kinsman, live unbruised, and love my cousin.

CLAUDIO　I had well hoped thou wouldst have denied
Beatrice, that I might have cudgeled thee out of thy
single life, to make thee a double-dealer, which out of　113
question thou wilt be, if my cousin do not look　114
exceeding narrowly to thee.　　　　　　　　　　115

BENEDICK　Come, come, we are friends. Let's have a
dance ere we are married, that we may lighten our
own hearts and our wives' heels.

LEONATO　We'll have dancing afterward.

BENEDICK　First, of my word! Therefore play, music.　120
Prince, thou art sad. Get thee a wife, get thee a wife.
There is no staff more reverend than one tipped with　122
horn.　　　　　　　　　　　　　　　　　　　123

Enter Messenger.

MESSENGER
My lord, your brother John is ta'en in flight
And brought with armèd men back to Messina.

BENEDICK　Think not on him till tomorrow. I'll devise
thee brave punishments for him. Strike up, pipers!　127
　　　　　　　　　　　　　　　Dance. [*Exeunt.*]

---

100 college assembly　**102–4 If . . . him** i.e., If a man allows himself
to be cowed by ridicule, he'll never dare dress handsomely or do anything conspicuous that will draw attention.　**106 flout** mock　**109 in
that** in view of the fact that.　**like** likely　**113 a double-dealer** (1) a
married man (2) a deceiver, adulterer　**114–15 look . . . narrowly** to
keep close watch over　**120 of** on　**122–3 tipped with horn** (Alludes
to the usual joke about cuckolds, as at line 44.)　**127 brave** fine

As You Like It

As You Like It represents, together with *Much Ado About Nothing* and *Twelfth Night*, the summation of Shakespeare's achievement in festive, happy comedy during the years 1598–1601. *As You Like It* contains several motifs found in other Shakespearean comedies: the journey from a jaded court into a transforming sylvan environment and back to a revitalized court (as in *A Midsummer Night's Dream*); hence, a contrasting of two worlds in the play—one presided over by a virtuous but exiled older brother and the other, by a usurping younger brother (as in *The Tempest*); the heroine disguised as a man (as in *The Merchant of Venice*, *The Two Gentlemen of Verona*, *Cymbeline*, and *Twelfth Night*); and a structure of multiple plotting in which numerous groups of characters are thematically played off against one another (as in several of Shakespeare's comedies). What chiefly distinguishes this play from the others, however, is the nature and function of its pastoral setting—the Forest of Arden.

The Forest of Arden is seen in many perspectives. As a natural wilderness, it is probably most like the real forest Shakespeare knew near Stratford-upon-Avon in Warwickshire—a place capable of producing the vulgarity of an Audrey or the bumptious clowning of a William. The forest bears the name of Shakespeare's mother, Mary Arden, the daughter of a prosperous Warwickshire farmer. Its name also owes something to the forest in Shakespeare's source, *Rosalynde*, based in turn on the forest of Ardennes in France. No less vividly, the place recalls for us Nottinghamshire and the Sherwood Forest of Robin Hood, where persons in retreat from a society seemingly beyond repair find refuge in a mythic folk world purged of social injustice. As the "golden world" (1.1.114), the forest evokes an even deeper longing for a mythological past age of innocence and plenty, when humans shared some attributes of the giants and the gods. This myth has its parallel in the biblical Garden of Eden, before the human race experienced "the penalty of Adam" (2.1.5). Finally, in another of its aspects, the forest is Arcadia, a pastoral landscape embodied in an ancient and sophisticated literary tradition and peopled by the likes of Corin, Silvius, and Phoebe.

All but the first of these Ardens, compared and contrasted with one another, involve some idealization, not only of nature and the natural landscape, but also of the human condition. These various Ardens place our real life in a complex perspective and force us to a fresh appraisal of our own ordinary existence. Duke Senior, for example, describes the forest environment as a corrective for the evils of society. He addresses his followers in the forest as "my co-mates and brothers in exile" (2.1.1), suggesting a kind of social equality that he could never know in the cramped formality of his previous official existence. The banished Duke Senior and his followers have had to leave behind their lands and revenues in the grip of the usurping Duke Frederick. No longer rich, though adequately provided with life's necessities, the Duke and his "merry men" live "like the old Robin Hood of England" and "fleet the time carelessly as they did in the golden world" (1.1.111–14). In this friendly society, a strong communal sense replaces the necessity for individual proprietorship. All comers are welcome, with food for all.

There are no luxuries in the forest, to be sure, but even this spare existence affords relief from the decadence of courtly life. "Sweet are the uses of adversity" (2.1.12), insists Duke Senior. He welcomes the cold of winter because it teaches him the true condition of humanity and of himself. The forest is serenely impartial: neither malicious nor compassionate. Death, and even killing for food, are an inevitable part of forest existence. The Duke concedes that his presence in the forest means the slaughter of deer, who were the original inhabitants; Orlando and Adam find that death through starvation in the forest is all too real a possibility. The forest is never guilty of the degrading perversity of humans at their worst, but it is also incapable of charity and forgiveness.

Shakespeare's sources reflect the complexity of his vision of Arden. The original of the Orlando story, which Shakespeare may not have used directly, is *The Cook's Tale of Gamelyn*, found in a number of manuscripts of *The Canterbury Tales* and wrongly attributed to Chaucer. This hearty English romance glorifies the rebellious and even violent spirit of its Robin Hood hero, the neglected youngest son Gamelyn, who, aided by faithful old Adam the Spencer, evades his wicked eldest brother in a cunning and bloody escape. As king of the outlaws in Sherwood Forest, Gamelyn eventually triumphs over his eldest brother (now the sheriff) and sees him hanged. Here, then, originates the motif of refuge from social injustice in Arden, even though most of the actual violence has been omitted from Shakespeare's version. (A trio of Robin Hood plays on a similar theme, beginning in 1598 with Anthony Munday's *The Downfall of Robert Earl of Huntingdon After Called Robin Hood*, was being performed with great success by the Admiral's company, chief rivals of the Lord Chamberlain's company to which Shakespeare belonged.)

As You Like It is clearly indebted to Thomas Lodge's *Rosalynde: Euphues' Golden Legacy* (published in 1590), a prose narrative version of the Gamelyn story in the ornate Euphuistic style of the 1580s. (Lodge's Epistle to the Gentleman Readers, casually inviting them to be pleased with this story if they are so inclined—"*If you like it, so*"—probably gave Shakespeare a hint for the name of his play.) Lodge accentuated the love story with its courtship in masquerade, provided some charming songs, and introduced the pastoral love motif involving Corin, Silvius, Phoebe, and Ganymede. Shakespeare's ordering of episode is generally close to that of Lodge. Pastoral literature, which had become a literary rage in the 1580s and early 1590s, owing particularly to Edmund Spenser's *Shepheardes Calendar* (1579) and Philip Sidney's *Arcadia* (1590), traced its ancestry through such Renaissance continental writers as Jorge de Montemayor, Jacopo Sannazaro, and Giovanni Battista Guarini to the so-called Greek romances, and finally back to the eclogues of Virgil, Theocritus, and Bion. A literary mode that had begun originally as a realistic evocation of difficult country life had become, in the Renaissance, an elegant vehicle for the loftiest and most patrician sentiments in love, for philosophic debate, and even for extensive political analysis and satire of the clergy.

Shakespeare's alterations and additions give us insight into his method of construction and his thematic focus. Whereas Lodge cheerfully accepts the pastoral conventions of his day, Shakespeare exposes those conventions to some criticism and considerable irony. Alongside the mannered and literary Silvius and Phoebe, he places William and Audrey, as peasantlike a couple as ever drew milk from a cow's teat. The juxtaposition holds up to crit-

ical perspective the rival claims of the literary and natural worlds by examining the defects of each in relation to the strengths of the other. William and Audrey are Shakespeare's own creation, based presumably on observation and also on the dramatic convention of the rustic clown and wench, as exemplified earlier in his Costard and Jaquenetta (*Love's Labor's Lost*).

Equally original, and essential to the many-sided debate concerning the virtues of the court versus those of the country, are Touchstone and Jaques. Touchstone is a professional court fool, dressed in motley, a new comic type in Shakespeare, created apparently in response to the recent addition to the Lord Chamberlain's company of the brilliant actor Robert Armin. Jaques is also a new type, the malcontent satirist, reflecting the very latest literary vogue in the nondramatic poetry and in drama of George Chapman, John Marston, and Ben Jonson. (The so-called private theaters, featuring boy actors, reopened in 1598–1599 after nearly a decade of enforced silence and proceeded at once to specialize in satirical drama; the public theaters like the Globe, the Rose, and the Swan sometimes joined in.) Touchstone and Jaques complement one another as critics and observers—one laughing at human folly with quizzical comic detachment and the other satirizing it with self-righteous scorn. Once we have been exposed to this assortment of newly created characters, we can no longer view either pastoral life or pastoral love as simply as Lodge and some other writers of the period portray them.

When *As You Like It* is compared with its chief source, Shakespeare can also be seen to have altered and considerably softened the characters of the wicked brothers Oliver and Frederick. Whereas Lodge's Saladyne is motivated by a greedy desire to seize his younger brother Rosader's property, Shakespeare's Oliver is envious of Orlando's natural goodness and popularity. As he confesses in soliloquy, Orlando is "so much in the heart of the world and especially of my own people . . . that I am altogether misprized" (1.1.159–61). In his warped way, Oliver desires to be more like Orlando, and in the enchanted forest of Arden he eventually becomes so. Duke Frederick, too, is plainly envious of goodness. Trying to persuade his daughter Celia of the need for banishing Rosalind, he argues, "thou wilt show more bright and seem more virtuous / When she is gone" (1.3.79–80). In spite of his obsession with the mere "seeming" of virtue, Duke Frederick acknowledges the power of a goodness that will eventually convert him along with the rest. Penitence and conciliation replace the vengeful conclusion of Lodge's novel, in which the nobles of France finally overthrow and execute the usurping king. Although Shakespeare's resolutions are sudden, like all miracles they attest to the inexplicable power of goodness.

The court of Duke Frederick is "the envious court," identified by this fixed epithet. In it, brothers turn unnaturally against brothers: the younger Frederick usurps his older brother's throne, whereas the older Oliver denies the younger Orlando his birthright of education. In still another parallel, both Rosalind and Orlando find themselves mistrusted as the children of Frederick's political enemies, Duke Senior and Sir Rowland de Boys. A daughter and a son are held to be guilty by association. "Thou art thy father's daughter. There's enough" (1.3.56), Frederick curtly retorts in explaining Rosalind's exile. And to Orlando, triumphant in wrestling with Charles, Frederick asserts, "I would thou hadst been son to some man else" (1.2.214). Here again, Frederick plaintively reveals his envy of goodness, even if at present any potential for goodness in him is thwarted by tyrannous whim. Many of Frederick's entourage might also be better persons if they only knew how to escape the insincerities of their courtly life. Charles the wrestler, for example, places himself at Oliver's service, and yet he would happily avoid breaking Orlando's neck if to do so were consistent with self-interest. Even Le Beau, the giddy fop so delighted at first with the cruel sport of wrestling, takes Orlando aside at some personal risk to warn him of Duke Frederick's foul humor. Ideally, Le Beau would prefer to be a companion of Orlando's "in a better world than this" (1.2.275). The vision of a regenerative Utopia secretly abides in the heart of this courtly creature.

It is easier to anatomize the defects of a social order than to propound solutions. As have other creators of visionary landscapes (including Thomas More in his *Utopia*), Shakespeare uses playful debate to elicit complicated responses on the part of his audience. Which is preferable, the court or the country? Jaques and Touchstone are adept gadflies, incessantly pointing out contradictions and ironies. Jaques, the malcontent railer derived from literary satire, takes delight in being out of step with everyone. Seemingly, his chief reason for having joined the others in the forest is to jibe at their motives for being there. To their song about the rejection of courtly ambition he mockingly supplies another verse, charging them with having left their wealth and ease out of mere willfulness (2.5.46–54). With ironic appropriateness, Jaques eventually decides to remain in the forest in the company of Frederick; Jaques cannot thrive on resolution and harmony. His humor is "melancholy," from which, as he observes, he draws consolation as a weasel sucks eggs (2.5.11–12). The others treat him as a sort of profane jester whose soured conceits add relish to their enjoyment of the forest life.

Despite his affectation, however, Jaques is serious and even excited in his defense of satire as a curative form of laughter (2.7.47–87). The appearance of Touchstone in the forest has reaffirmed in Jaques his profound commitment to a view of life as an absurd process of decay governed by inexorable time. His function in such a life is to be mor-

dant, unsparing. As literary satirist, he must be free to awaken people's minds to their own folly. To Duke Senior's protestation that the satirist is merely self-indulgent and licentious, Jaques counters with a thoughtful and classically Horatian defense of satire as an art form devoted not to libelous attacks on individuals but to exposing types of folly. Any observer who feels individually portrayed merely condemns himself or herself by confessing his or her resemblance to the type. This particular debate between Duke Senior and Jaques ends, appropriately, in a draw. The Duke's point is well taken, for Jaques's famous "Seven Ages of Man" speech, so often read out of context, occurs in a scene that also witnesses the sacrifices and brave deeds that Orlando and Adam are prepared to undertake for each other. The feeling bond between the generations that they share refutes Jaques's wry narrative of isolated self-interest. As though in answer to Jaques's acid depiction of covetous old age, we see old Adam's self-sacrifice and trust in Providence. Instead of "mere oblivion," we see charitable compassion prompting Duke Senior to aid Orlando and Orlando to aid Adam. Perhaps this vision seems of a higher spiritual order than that of Jaques. Nonetheless, without him the forest would lack a satirical perspective that continually requires us to reexamine our romantic assumptions about human happiness.

Touchstone's name suggests that he similarly offers a multiplicity of viewpoints. (A touchstone is a kind of stone used to test for gold and silver.) He shares with Jaques a skeptical view of life, but for Touchstone the inconsistency and absurdity of life are occasions for wit and humor rather than melancholy and cynicism. As a professional fool, he observes that many supposedly sane men are more foolish than he—as, for example, in their elaborate dueling code of the Retort Courteous and the Reply Churlish, leading finally to the Lie Circumstantial and the Lie Direct. He is fascinated by the games people make of their lives and is amused by their inability to be content with what they already have. Of the shepherd's life, he comments, "In respect that it is solitary, I like it very well; but in respect that it is private, it is a very vile life" (3.2.15–16). This paradox, though nonsensical, captures the restlessness of human striving for a life that can somehow combine the peaceful solitude of nature with the convenience and excitement of city life. Although Touchstone marries, even his marriage is a spoof of the institution rather than a serious attempt at commitment. Like all fools, who in Renaissance times were regarded as a breed apart, Touchstone exists outside the realm of ordinary human responses. There he can comment disinterestedly on human folly. He is prevented, however, from sharing fully in the human love and conciliation with which the play ends. He and Jaques are not touched by the play's regenerative magic;

Jaques will remain in the forest, and Touchstone will remain forever a childlike entertainer.

The regenerative power of Arden, as we have seen, is not the forest's alone. What saves Orlando is the human charity practiced by him and by Duke Senior, who, for all his love of the forest, longs to rejoin that human society where he has "with holy bell been knolled to church" (2.7.120). Civilization at its best is no less necessary to the human spirit than is the natural order of the forest. In love, also, perception and wisdom must be combined with nature's gifts. Orlando, when we first see him, is a young man of the finest natural qualities but admittedly lacking experience in the nuances of complex human relationships. Nowhere does his lack of sophistication betray him more unhappily than in his first encounter with Rosalind, following the wrestling match. In response to her unmistakable hints of favor, he stands ox-like, tongue-tied. Later, in the forest, his first attempts at self-education in love lead him into an opposite danger: an excess of platitudinous manners parading in the guise of Petrarchism. (The Italian sonneteer Francis Petrarch has given to the language a name for the stereotypical literary mannerisms we associate with courtly love: the sighing and self-abasement of the young man, the chaste denial of love by the woman whom he worships, and the like.) Orlando's newfound self-abasement and idealization of his absent mistress are as unsatisfactory as his former naiveté. The sonnets he hangs on trees are deserving of the delicious parody they get from Touchstone. Orlando must learn from Rosalind that a quest for true understanding in love avoids the extreme of pretentious mannerism as well as that of mere artlessness. Orlando as Petrarchan lover too much resembles Silvius, the lovesick young man, cowering before the imperious will of his coy mistress Phoebe. This stereotyped relationship, taken from the pages of fashionable pastoral romance, represents a posturing that Rosalind hopes to cure in Silvius and Phoebe even as she will also cure Orlando.

Rosalind is, above all, the realistic one, the plucky Shakespearean heroine showing her mettle in the world of men, emotionally more mature than her lover. Her concern is with a working and clear-sighted relationship in love, and to that end she daringly insists that Orlando learn something of woman's changeable mood. Above all, she must disabuse him of the dangerously misleading clichés of the Petrarchan love myth. When he protests he would die for love of Rosalind, she lectures him mockingly in her guise of Ganymede: "No, faith, die by attorney. The poor world is almost six thousand years old, and in all this time there was not any man died in his own person, videlicet, in a love cause." She debunks the legends of Troilus and Leander, youths supposed to have died for love who, if they had ever really existed, would no doubt have met with more prosaic ends. "But these are all lies. Men have died from time to time, and worms have eaten them, but not for love" (4.1.89–102). Rosalind wants Orlando to know that women are not goddesses but frail human beings who can be giddy, jealous, infatuated with novelty, irritatingly talkative, peremptory, and hysterical (4.1.142–9), though she is circumspect as to whether women can also be unfaithful. Orlando must be taught that love is a madness (3.2.390), and he must be cured, not of loving Rosalind, but of worshiping her with unrealistic expectations that can lead only to disillusionment. Rosalind teaches him, as Portia does Bassanio in *The Merchant of Venice,* but she does not seriously threaten him with wantonness. Her disguise as Ganymede provides for her the perfect role in Orlando's approach to sexual manhood: he can learn to love "Ganymede" as a friend and then make the transition to heterosexual union in his blessed discovery that the friend is also the lover. Rosalind's own rite of passage is easier; for all her reliance on her loving friendship with Celia, or "Aliena," she is ready to exclaim, "But what talk we of fathers, when there is such a man as Orlando?" (3.4.36–7). She is spiritedly independent, even more so than Portia; whereas Portia's choice of husband is controlled by her father from his grave, Rosalind picks for herself. To be sure, Duke Senior is certainly happy that she marries Orlando, and she is glad to be reunited with her father, but her choice in marriage is very much her own. The forest is indeed a place where she can encounter her father "man to man," as it were, and be liberated from him while coming to terms with a patriarchal world. She is ready to give herself to Orlando, but she must educate him first. When Orlando has been sufficiently tested as to patience, loyalty, and understanding, she unmasks herself to him and simultaneously unravels the plot of ridiculous love we have come to associate with Silvius and Phoebe.

Rosalind's disguise name, Ganymede, has connotations that suggest ways in which human sexuality can be partly understood as socially constructed. If Rosalind in disguise as Ganymede wins the affection and eventually the love of Orlando, while her father and the other forest dwellers are equally taken in by the disguise, are maleness and femaleness chiefly matters of sartorial convention and superficial appearance? When Phoebe falls in love with Ganymede, is not her infatuation a way of showing that the roles of the sexes can be put on and off? Theatrically, the device of having a young male actor play Rosalind who then disguises him/herself as a young man adds to the witty confusion of sexual identities by introducing homoerotic possibilities. Not only can the roles of the sexes be put on and off, sexual desire itself is unstable, attaching itself to effeminate or sexually indeterminate young men like Ganymede, who is described as being "Of female favor" and "Like a ripe sister"

(4.3.87–8; compare *Twelfth Night*, 1.4.31–4, where Orsino says of "Cesario" that "all is semblative a woman's part"). Both Phoebe and Orlando are in some ways attracted to Ganymede; when Rosalind says of Orlando that "his kissing is as full of sanctity as the touch of holy bread" (3.4.13–14), she seems to suggest that Orlando has kissed her in her male disguise. Mythologically Ganymede is Zeus's or Jupiter's young male lover as well as cupbearer. The very role of boy actors in an all-male acting company must have struck some viewers as homoerotically suggestive.

At the same time, the motif of disguise enables the play to pursue a serious point about love and friendship. Orlando can speak frankly and personally to "Ganymede" as a perfect friend, one who can enable him as a young man still faced with the uncertainties and hazards of courtship to traverse the potentially difficult transition from male-to-male friendship into adult heterosexuality. The relationship closely anticipates that of "Cesario" and Orsino in *Twelfth Night*, where once again a powerful and loving attraction to a sexually ambiguous young man/woman ripens into mature love when the older man has been educated by the experience of loving friendship. Both plays depict heterosexual courtship as full of dangers for the male. In *As You Like It*, Rosalind is at pains to coach Orlando in what to expect from unruly women; and indeed, Rosalind's very readiness to wear male apparel bespeaks her daring intrusion into a man's world, even if Shakespeare carefully hedges this threat by insisting on Rosalind's hesitancy in being so bold. Rosalind is thus, like Portia in *The Merchant of Venice*, both spirited and eventually ready to comply with the mores of a male-dominated world.

By becoming Orlando's teacher, Rosalind is able to claim a strong position in their friendship and in our estimate of her remarkable worthiness. Posing as Ganymede, Rosalind can observe and test Orlando and thereby learn the truth about his capability for lifelong fidelity as only another man would have the opportunity to do. Once a loving friendship has grown strong between them, the unmasking of Rosalind's sexual identity makes possible a physical union between them to confirm and express the spiritual. In these terms, the play's happy ending affirms marriage as an institution, not simply as the expected denouement. The procession to the altar is synchronous with the return to civilization's other institutions, made whole again not solely by the forest but by the power of goodness embodied in Rosalind, Orlando, Duke Senior, and the others who persevere.

As You Like It

[*Dramatis Personae*

DUKE SENIOR, *a banished duke*
DUKE FREDERICK, *his usurping brother*
ROSALIND, *daughter of Duke Senior, later disguised as*
   GANYMEDE
CELIA, *daughter of Duke Frederick, later disguised as* ALIENA

OLIVER,
JAQUES,   } *sons of Sir Rowland de Boys*
ORLANDO,

AMIENS, }
JAQUES, } *lords attending Duke Senior*

LE BEAU, *a courtier attending Duke Frederick*
CHARLES, *a wrestler in the court of Duke Frederick*

ADAM, *an aged servant of Oliver and then Orlando*
DENNIS, *a servant of Oliver*

TOUCHSTONE, *the* CLOWN *or* FOOL

CORIN, *an old shepherd*
SILVIUS, *a young shepherd, in love with Phoebe*
PHOEBE, *a shepherdess*
WILLIAM, *a country youth, in love with Audrey*
AUDREY, *a country wench*
SIR OLIVER MAR-TEXT, *a country vicar*

HYMEN, *god of marriage*

Lords and Attendants waiting on Duke Frederick and Duke
   Senior

SCENE: *Oliver's house; Duke Frederick's court; and the Forest of Arden*]

1.1

Enter Orlando and Adam.

ORLANDO   As I remember, Adam, it was upon this fash- 1
ion bequeathed me by will but poor a thousand 2
crowns and, as thou say'st, charged my brother on his 3
blessing to breed me well; and there begins my 4
sadness. My brother Jaques he keeps at school, and 5
report speaks goldenly of his profit. For my part, he 6
keeps me rustically at home—or, to speak more
properly, stays me here at home unkept; for call you 8
that "keeping" for a gentleman of my birth, that
differs not from the stalling of an ox? His horses are
bred better, for besides that they are fair with their 11
feeding, they are taught their manage, and to that end 12

riders dearly hired. But I, his brother, gain nothing 13
under him but growth, for the which his animals on
his dunghills are as much bound to him as I. Besides
this nothing that he so plentifully gives me, the
something that nature gave me his countenance 17
seems to take from me. He lets me feed with his
hinds, bars me the place of a brother, and as much as 19
in him lies, mines my gentility with my education. 20
This is it, Adam, that grieves me; and the spirit of my
father, which I think is within me, begins to mutiny
against this servitude. I will no longer endure it,
though yet I know no wise remedy how to avoid it.

Enter Oliver.

ADAM   Yonder comes my master, your brother.
ORLANDO   Go apart, Adam, and thou shalt hear how 26
he will shake me up.   [*Adam stands aside.*] 27
OLIVER   Now, sir, what make you here? 28

1.1. Location: The garden of Oliver's house.
1–3 it was . . . crowns it was in this way that I was left, by the terms of my father's will, a mere thousand crowns or £250 **3 crowns** coins worth five shillings. **3–4 charged . . . well** my brother was instructed as a condition of my father's blessing to educate me well
5 My . . . school My oldest brother Oliver maintains my other brother, Jaques, at university **6 profit** progress. **8 stays** detains. **unkept** poorly supported **11–12 fair . . . feeding** kept well groomed with good diet **12 manage** manège, paces and maneuvers in the art of horsemanship

13 riders trainers. **dearly** expensively **17 countenance** behavior; (neglectful) patronage **19 hinds** farm hands. **bars me** excludes me from **19–20 as much . . . education** with all the power at his disposal, undermines my right to be educated as a gentleman. **26 Go apart** Stand aside **27 shake me up** abuse me. **28 make** do. (But Orlando takes it in the more usual sense.)

ORLANDO   Nothing. I am not taught to make anything.

OLIVER   What mar you then, sir?   30

ORLANDO   Marry, sir, I am helping you to mar that   31
which God made, a poor unworthy brother of yours,
with idleness.

OLIVER   Marry, sir, be better employed, and be naught   34
awhile.   35

ORLANDO   Shall I keep your hogs and eat husks with   36
them? What prodigal portion have I spent, that I   37
should come to such penury?   38

OLIVER   Know you where you are, sir?   39

ORLANDO   Oh, sir, very well: here in your orchard.   40

OLIVER   Know you before whom, sir?

ORLANDO   Ay, better than him I am before knows me.
I know you are my eldest brother, and in the gentle   43
condition of blood you should so know me. The cour-   44
tesy of nations allows you my better, in that you are   45
the firstborn, but the same tradition takes not away
my blood, were there twenty brothers betwixt us. I   47
have as much of my father in me as you, albeit I confess your coming before me is nearer to his reverence.   49

OLIVER   What, boy!   [He strikes Orlando.]

ORLANDO   Come, come, elder brother, you are too
young in this.   [He seizes Oliver by the throat.]   52

OLIVER   Wilt thou lay hands on me, villain?   53

ORLANDO   I am no villain. I am the youngest son of Sir
Rowland de Boys. He was my father, and he is thrice   55
a villain that says such a father begot villains. Wert
thou not my brother, I would not take this hand from
thy throat till this other had pulled out thy tongue for
saying so. Thou hast railed on thyself.   59

ADAM   Sweet masters, be patient! For your father's   60
remembrance, be at accord.   61

OLIVER   Let me go, I say.

ORLANDO   I will not till I please. You shall hear me. My
father charged you in his will to give me good education. You have trained me like a peasant, obscuring
and hiding from me all gentlemanlike qualities. The   66
spirit of my father grows strong in me, and I will no
longer endure it; therefore allow me such exercises as   68
may become a gentleman, or give me the poor allotery   69
my father left me by testament. With that I will go buy
my fortunes.   [He releases Oliver.]

OLIVER   And what wilt thou do? Beg when that is
spent? Well, sir, get you in. I will not long be troubled
with you; you shall have some part of your will. I pray   74
you, leave me.

ORLANDO   I will no further offend you than becomes me
for my good.

OLIVER   [to Adam]   Get you with him, you old dog.

ADAM   Is "old dog" my reward? Most true, I have lost
my teeth in your service. God be with my old master!
He would not have spoke such a word.

                    Exeunt Orlando [and] Adam.

OLIVER   Is it even so? Begin you to grow upon me? I will   82
physic your rankness and yet give no thousand   83
crowns neither.—Holla, Dennis!   84

            Enter Dennis.

DENNIS   Calls Your Worship?

OLIVER   Was not Charles, the Duke's wrestler, here to
speak with me?

DENNIS   So please you, he is here at the door and   88
importunes access to you.

OLIVER   Call him in.   [Exit Dennis.]
'Twill be a good way; and tomorrow the wrestling is.

            Enter Charles.

CHARLES   Good morrow to Your Worship.   92

OLIVER   Good Monsieur Charles, what's the new news
at the new court?

CHARLES   There's no news at the court, sir, but the old
news: that is, the old Duke is banished by his younger
brother the new Duke, and three or four loving lords
have put themselves into voluntary exile with him,
whose lands and revenues enrich the new Duke;   99
therefore he gives them good leave to wander.   100

OLIVER   Can you tell if Rosalind, the Duke's daughter,
be banished with her father?

CHARLES   Oh, no; for the Duke's daughter, her cousin, so
loves her, being ever from their cradles bred together,   104
that she would have followed her exile or have died to   105
stay behind her. She is at the court and no less beloved   106
of her uncle than his own daughter, and never
two ladies loved as they do.

OLIVER   Where will the old Duke live?

CHARLES   They say he is already in the Forest of Arden,
and a many merry men with him; and there they live
like the old Robin Hood of England. They say many
young gentlemen flock to him every day and fleet the   113
time carelessly as they did in the golden world.   114

OLIVER   What, you wrestle tomorrow before the new
Duke?

---

30 mar ("To make or mar" is a commonplace antithesis.)   **31 Marry**
i.e., Indeed. (Originally an oath by the Virgin Mary.)   **34–5 be**
naught awhile i.e., stay in your place, don't grumble.   **36–8 Shall . . .**
penury? (Alluding to the story of the Prodigal Son, in Luke 15:11–32,
who, having wasted his "portion" or inheritance, had to tend swine
and eat with them.)   **39 where** in whose presence. (But Orlando sarcastically takes the more literal meaning.)   **40 orchard** garden.
43–4 in . . . blood acknowledging the bond of our being of gentle
birth   **44–5 courtesy of nations** recognized custom (of primogeni-
ture, whereby the eldest son inherits all the land)   **47 blood** (1) gentlemanly lineage (2) spirit   **49 is nearer . . . reverence** is closer to his
position of authority (as head of family).   **52 young** inexperienced
(at fighting)   **53 villain** i.e., wicked fellow. (But Orlando plays on the
literal meaning of "bondman" or "serf," as well as Oliver's meaning.)
55 he anyone   **59 railed on thyself** insulted your own blood.
60–1 your father's remembrance the sake of your father's memory
66 qualities (1) characteristics (2) accomplishments.   **68 exercises**
employments   **69 allottery** portion

74 will (1) desire (2) portion from your father's will (3) willfulness
(i.e., you'll get what is coming to you).   **82 grow upon me** take liberties with me; grow too big for your breeches.   **83 physic your rank-**
ness apply medicine to your overweening   **84 neither** either.
88 So please you If you please   **92 Good morrow** Good morning
99 whose all of whose   **100 good leave** full permission   **104 being**
they being   **105–6 died to stay** died from being forced to stay
113 fleet pass   **114 carelessly** free from care.   **golden world** the primal age of innocence and ease from which humankind was thought
to have degenerated. (See Ovid, *Metamorphoses* 1.)

CHARLES　Marry, do I, sir; and I came to acquaint you with a matter. I am given, sir, secretly to understand that your younger brother Orlando hath a disposition to come in disguised against me to try a fall. Tomor- 120 row, sir, I wrestle for my credit, and he that escapes 121 me without some broken limb shall acquit him well. 122 Your brother is but young and tender, and for your love I would be loath to foil him, as I must for my 124 own honor if he come in. Therefore, out of my love to you, I came hither to acquaint you withal, that either 126 you might stay him from his intendment or brook 127 such disgrace well as he shall run into, in that it is a thing of his own search and altogether against my will. 129

OLIVER　Charles, I thank thee for thy love to me, which thou shalt find I will most kindly requite. I had myself notice of my brother's purpose herein and have by underhand means labored to dissuade him from it, but 133 he is resolute. I'll tell thee, Charles, it is the stubbornest young fellow of France, full of ambition, an envious 135 emulator of every man's good parts, a secret and 136 villainous contriver against me his natural brother. 137 Therefore use thy discretion. I had as lief thou didst 138 break his neck as his finger. And thou wert best look 139 to't; for if thou dost him any slight disgrace, or if he 140 do not mightily grace himself on thee, he will practice 141 against thee by poison, entrap thee by some treacher- ous device, and never leave thee till he hath ta'en thy life by some indirect means or other; for I assure thee, and almost with tears I speak it, there is not one so young and so villainous this day living. I speak but brotherly of him, but should I anatomize him to thee as 147 he is, I must blush and weep, and thou must look pale and wonder.

CHARLES　I am heartily glad I came hither to you. If he come tomorrow, I'll give him his payment. If ever he go alone again, I'll never wrestle for prize more. And 152 so God keep Your Worship!

OLIVER　Farewell, good Charles.　　　　*Exit* [*Charles*]. Now will I stir this gamester. I hope I shall see an end of 155 him; for my soul, yet I know not why, hates nothing more than he. Yet he's gentle, never schooled and yet 157 learned, full of noble device, of all sorts enchantingly 158 beloved, and indeed so much in the heart of the world and especially of my own people, who best know him, 160 that I am altogether misprized. But it shall not be so 161

long; this wrestler shall clear all. Nothing remains but 162 that I kindle the boy thither, which now I'll go about. 163
　　　　　　　　　　　　　　　　　　　　　　　　Exit.

❖

1.2

Enter Rosalind and Celia.

CELIA　I pray thee, Rosalind, sweet my coz, be merry. 1
ROSALIND　Dear Celia, I show more mirth than I am mistress of, and would you yet I were merrier? Unless you could teach me to forget a banished father, you must not learn me how to remember any extraordi- 5 nary pleasure.
CELIA　Herein I see thou lov'st me not with the full weight that I love thee. If my uncle, thy banished 8 father, had banished thy uncle, the Duke my father, so thou hadst been still with me, I could have taught 10 my love to take thy father for mine. So wouldst thou, if the truth of thy love to me were so righteously 12 tempered as mine is to thee. 13
ROSALIND　Well, I will forget the condition of my estate 14 to rejoice in yours.
CELIA　You know my father hath no child but I, nor none is like to have. And truly, when he dies thou 17 shalt be his heir, for what he hath taken away from thy father perforce I will render thee again in affection. By 19 mine honor, I will, and when I break that oath, let me turn monster. Therefore, my sweet Rose, my dear Rose, be merry.
ROSALIND　From henceforth I will, coz, and devise sports. Let me see, what think you of falling in love?
CELIA　Marry, I prithee, do, to make sport withal. But 25 love no man in good earnest, nor no further in sport neither than with safety of a pure blush thou mayst in 27 honor come off again. 28
ROSALIND　What shall be our sport, then?
CELIA　Let us sit and mock the good huswife Fortune 30 from her wheel, that her gifts may henceforth be be- stowed equally.
ROSALIND　I would we could do so, for her benefits are mightily misplaced, and the bountiful blind woman 34 doth most mistake in her gifts to women.
CELIA　'Tis true, for those that she makes fair she scarce 36 makes honest, and those that she makes honest she 37 makes very ill-favoredly. 38

---

120 **a fall** a bout of wrestling.　121 **credit** reputation　122 **shall . . . well** (1) must exert himself very skillfully (2) will be lucky indeed. 124 **foil** defeat　126 **withal** with this　127 **stay . . . intendment** restrain him from his intent.　**brook** endure　129 **search** seeking 133 **underhand** unobtrusive　135–6 **envious emulator** malicious dis- parager　136 **parts** qualities　137 **contriver** plotter.　**natural** blood 138 **lief** willingly　139–40 **thou . . . to't** you'd better beware　140–1 **if he . . . on thee** if he fails to distinguish himself at your expense 141 **practice** plot　147 **brotherly** as a brother should.　**anatomize** analyze　152 **go alone** walk unassisted　155 **gamester** sportsman. (Said sardonically.)　157 **gentle** gentlemanly　158 **noble device** lofty aspiration.　**sorts** classes of people.　**enchantingly** as if they were under his spell　160 **people** servants　161 **misprized** undervalued, scorned.

162 **clear all** solve everything.　163 **kindle . . . thither** inflame Orlando with desire to go to the wrestling match
1.2. Location: Duke Frederick's court. A place suitable for wrestling.
1 **sweet my coz** my sweet cousin　5 **learn** teach　8 **that** with which 10 **so** provided that　12–13 **righteously tempered** harmoniously composed　14 **condition of my estate** state of my fortunes　17 **like** likely　19 **perforce** by force　25 **sport** pastimes　27 **pure** (1) mere (2) innocent　28 **come off** retire, leave　30 **huswife** one who man- ages household affairs and operates the spinning wheel. (Shake- speare conflates this wheel with the commonplace wheel of Fortune.) *Huswife* is used derogatorily here, with a suggestion of "hussy." 34 **bountiful blind woman** i.e., Fortune　36 **scarce** rarely　37 **honest** chaste　38 **ill-favoredly** ugly.

ROSALIND   Nay, now thou goest from Fortune's office to
Nature's. Fortune reigns in gifts of the world, not in   40
the lineaments of Nature.   41

Enter [Touchstone the] Clown.

CELIA   No; when Nature hath made a fair creature, may
she not by Fortune fall into the fire? Though Nature   43
hath given us wit to flout at Fortune, hath not Fortune   44
sent in this fool to cut off the argument?
ROSALIND   Indeed, there is Fortune too hard for Nature,   46
when Fortune makes Nature's natural the cutter-off of   47
Nature's wit.   48
CELIA   Peradventure this is not Fortune's work neither   49
but Nature's, who perceiveth our natural wits too dull
to reason of such goddesses and hath sent this natural   51
for our whetstone; for always the dullness of the fool   52
is the whetstone of the wits.—How now, wit, whither   53
wander you?   54
TOUCHSTONE   Mistress, you must come away to your
father.
CELIA   Were you made the messenger?
TOUCHSTONE   No, by mine honor, but I was bid to
come for you.
ROSALIND   Where learned you that oath, Fool?
TOUCHSTONE   Of a certain knight that swore by his
honor they were good pancakes and swore by his   62
honor the mustard was naught. Now I'll stand to it the   63
pancakes were naught and the mustard was good,
and yet was not the knight forsworn.   65
CELIA   How prove you that in the great heap of your
knowledge?
ROSALIND   Ay, marry, now unmuzzle your wisdom.
TOUCHSTONE   Stand you both forth now. Stroke your
chins, and swear by your beards that I am a knave.
CELIA   By our beards, if we had them, thou art.
TOUCHSTONE   By my knavery, if I had it, then I were;
but if you swear by that that is not, you are not
forsworn. No more was this knight, swearing by his
honor, for he never had any; or if he had, he had
sworn it away before ever he saw those pancakes or
that mustard.
CELIA   Prithee, who is't that thou mean'st?
TOUCHSTONE   One that old Frederick, your father, loves.
CELIA   My father's love is enough to honor him enough.
Speak no more of him; you'll be whipped for taxation   81
one of these days.

TOUCHSTONE   The more pity that fools may not speak
wisely what wise men do foolishly.
CELIA   By my troth, thou sayest true; for since the little   85
wit that fools have was silenced, the little foolery that   86
wise men have makes a great show. Here comes
Monsieur Le Beau.

Enter Le Beau.

ROSALIND   With his mouth full of news.
CELIA   Which he will put on us as pigeons feed their   90
young.
ROSALIND   Then shall we be news-crammed.
CELIA   All the better; we shall be the more mar-   93
ketable.—*Bonjour,* Monsieur Le Beau. What's the   94
news?
LE BEAU   Fair princess, you have lost much good sport.
CELIA   Sport? Of what color?   97
LE BEAU   What color, madam? How shall I answer you?
ROSALIND   As wit and fortune will.
TOUCHSTONE   Or as the Destinies decrees.
CELIA   Well said. That was laid on with a trowel.   101
TOUCHSTONE   Nay, if I keep not my rank—   102
ROSALIND   Thou loosest thy old smell.
LE BEAU   You amaze me, ladies. I would have told you   104
of good wrestling, which you have lost the sight of.
ROSALIND   Yet tell us the manner of the wrestling.
LE BEAU   I will tell you the beginning, and if it please
Your Ladyships you may see the end, for the best is yet   108
to do, and here, where you are, they are coming to   109
perform it.
CELIA   Well, the beginning, that is dead and buried.   111
LE BEAU   There comes an old man and his three sons—
CELIA   I could match this beginning with an old tale.
LE BEAU   Three proper young men, of excellent growth   114
and presence—
ROSALIND   With bills on their necks, "Be it known unto   116
all men by these presents."   117
LE BEAU   The eldest of the three wrestled with Charles,
the Duke's wrestler, which Charles in a moment threw
him and broke three of his ribs, that there is little hope
of life in him. So he served the second, and so the   121
third. Yonder they lie, the poor old man their father
making such pitiful dole over them that all the behold-   123
ers take his part with weeping.
ROSALIND   Alas!
TOUCHSTONE   But what is the sport, monsieur, that the
ladies have lost?
LE BEAU   Why, this that I speak of.

---

40 gifts of the world e.g., riches and power   **41 the lineaments of
Nature** the features that Nature provides (like beauty or ugliness).
41.1 *Touchstone* a stone used to test for gold and silver   **43 she** the
woman whom Nature has made beautiful   **44 flout** scoff   **46 there**
in that instance   **47–8 when . . . wit** i.e., when Fortune makes this
natural half-wit (Touchstone) the cutter-off of witty dialogue that our
natural gifts enable us to engage in. (A *natural* here means a born
idiot; also in line 51.)   **49 Peradventure** Perhaps   **51 to reason . . .
goddesses** to engage in debate about Reason and Nature   **52 whetstone** grinding stone against which to sharpen things (in this case,
wit)   **52–3 the dullness . . . wits** i.e., the mindless things said by an
idiot serve as material on which to sharpen our wits.   **53–4 whither
wander you** (An allusion to the expression "wandering wits.")
62 pancakes fritters (which might be made of meat and so require
mustard)   **63 naught** worthless.   **stand to it** maintain, argue
65 forsworn perjured.   **81 taxation** censure, slander

85–6 since . . . silenced (Perhaps refers specifically to the Bishops'
order of June 1599 banning satirical books.)   **90 put on** force upon
93–4 marketable i.e., like animals that have been crammed with food
before being sent to market.   **97 color** kind.   **101 with a trowel**
thick.   **102 rank** i.e., status as a wit. (But Rosalind plays on the sense
of "stench.")   **104 amaze** bewilder   **108–9 yet to do** still to come
111 the beginning tell us what has already occurred   **114 proper**
handsome   **116 bills** proclamations   **117 these presents** the present
document. (Rosalind uses this legal phrase to pun on *presence* in line
115.)   **121 So** Similarly   **123 dole** lamentation

TOUCHSTONE   Thus men may grow wiser every day. It is the first time that ever I heard breaking of ribs was sport for ladies.

CELIA   Or I, I promise thee.   132

ROSALIND   But is there any else longs to see this broken 133 music in his sides? Is there yet another dotes upon rib 134 breaking?—Shall we see this wrestling, cousin?

LE BEAU   You must if you stay here, for here is the place appointed for the wrestling, and they are ready to perform it.

CELIA   Yonder, sure, they are coming. Let us now stay and see it.

Flourish. Enter Duke [Frederick], Lords, Orlando, Charles, and attendants.

DUKE FREDERICK   Come on. Since the youth will not be entreated, his own peril on his forwardness.   142

ROSALIND   [to Le Beau]   Is yonder the man?

LE BEAU   Even he, madam.

CELIA   Alas, he is too young! Yet he looks successfully.   145

DUKE FREDERICK   How now, daughter and cousin? Are 146 you crept hither to see the wrestling?

ROSALIND   Ay, my liege, so please you give us leave.   148

DUKE FREDERICK   You will take little delight in it, I can tell you, there is such odds in the man. In pity of the 150 challenger's youth I would fain dissuade him, but he 151 will not be entreated. Speak to him, ladies; see if you can move him.

CELIA   Call him hither, good Monsieur Le Beau.

DUKE FREDERICK   Do so. I'll not be by.   [He steps aside.]

LE BEAU   [to Orlando]   Monsieur the challenger, the princess calls for you.

ORLANDO   [approaching the ladies]   I attend them with all respect and duty.

ROSALIND   Young man, have you challenged Charles the wrestler?

ORLANDO   No, fair princess. He is the general chal- 162 lenger. I come but in, as others do, to try with him the 163 strength of my youth.

CELIA   Young gentleman, your spirits are too bold for your years. You have seen cruel proof of this man's strength. If you saw yourself with your eyes or knew 167 yourself with your judgment, the fear of your adven- 168 ture would counsel you to a more equal enterprise. We 169 pray you, for your own sake, to embrace your own safety and give over this attempt.

ROSALIND   Do, young sir. Your reputation shall not therefore be misprized. We will make it our suit to the 173 Duke that the wrestling might not go forward.

ORLANDO   I beseech you, punish me not with your hard thoughts, wherein I confess me much guilty to deny 176 so fair and excellent ladies anything. But let your fair eyes and gentle wishes go with me to my trial, wherein if I be foiled, there is but one shamed that was never gracious, if killed, but one dead that is willing to 180 be so. I shall do my friends no wrong, for I have none to lament me; the world no injury, for in it I have nothing. Only in the world I fill up a place which may 183 be better supplied when I have made it empty.

ROSALIND   The little strength that I have, I would it were with you.

CELIA   And mine, to eke out hers.

ROSALIND   Fare you well. Pray heaven I be deceived 188 in you!   189

CELIA   Your heart's desires be with you!

CHARLES   Come, where is this young gallant that is so desirous to lie with his mother earth?

ORLANDO   Ready, sir, but his will hath in it a more modest working.   194

DUKE FREDERICK   You shall try but one fall.

CHARLES   No, I warrant Your Grace, you shall not entreat him to a second, that have so mightily persuaded him from a first.

ORLANDO   You mean to mock me after; you should not have mocked me before. But come your ways.   200

ROSALIND   Now Hercules be thy speed, young man!   201

CELIA   I would I were invisible, to catch the strong fellow by the leg.   [Orlando and Charles] wrestle.

ROSALIND   Oh, excellent young man!

CELIA   If I had a thunderbolt in mine eye, I can tell who 205 should down.   Shout. [Charles is thrown.]   206

DUKE FREDERICK   No more, no more.

ORLANDO   Yes, I beseech Your Grace. I am not yet well 208 breathed.   209

DUKE FREDERICK   How dost thou, Charles?

LE BEAU   He cannot speak, my lord.

DUKE FREDERICK   Bear him away.—What is thy name, young man?   [Charles is borne out.]

ORLANDO   Orlando, my liege, the youngest son of Sir Rowland de Boys.

DUKE FREDERICK   I would thou hadst been son to some man else. The world esteemed thy father honorable, But I did find him still mine enemy. Thou shouldst have better pleased me with this deed Hadst thou descended from another house. But fare thee well; thou art a gallant youth. I would thou hadst told me of another father.

Exit Duke [with train, and others. Rosalind and Celia remain; Orlando stands apart from them.]

---

132 **promise** assure   133 **any else** anyone else who   133–4 **broken music** literally, music arranged in parts for different instruments; here applied to the breaking of ribs   134 **another** another who 142 **entreated . . . forwardness** i.e., entreated to desist, let the risk be blamed upon his own rashness.   145 **successfully** i.e., as if he would be successful.   146 **cousin** i.e., niece.   148 **so . . . leave** if you will permit us.   150 **there . . . man** Charles is such an odds-on favorite to win.   151 **fain** willingly   162–3 **the general challenger** the one who is ready to take on all comers. (Orlando is the challenger in a more limited sense.)   167–8 **If . . . judgment** If you saw yourself objectively   169 **equal** i.e., where the odds are more equal   173 **misprized** despised, undervalued.

176 **wherein** though.   **to deny** in denying   180 **gracious** looked upon with favor   183 **Only . . . I** In the world I merely 188–9 **deceived in you** i.e., mistaken in fearing you will lose. 194 **modest working** decorous endeavor (than to lie with one's mother earth. For a man to lie with his mother is to commit incest.) 200 **come your ways** come on.   201 **Hercules be thy speed** may Hercules help you   205 **If . . . eye** i.e., If I were Zeus or Jupiter 206 **down** fall.   208–9 **well breathed** warmed up.

CELIA [*to Rosalind*]
   Were I my father, coz, would I do this?
ORLANDO [*to no one in particular*]
   I am more proud to be Sir Rowland's son,
   His youngest son, and would not change that calling 223
   To be adopted heir to Frederick.
ROSALIND [*to Celia*]
   My father loved Sir Rowland as his soul,
   And all the world was of my father's mind.
   Had I before known this young man his son,
   I should have given him tears unto entreaties   228
   Ere he should thus have ventured.
CELIA [*to Rosalind*]   Gentle cousin,
   Let us go thank him and encourage him.
   My father's rough and envious disposition
   Sticks me at heart.—Sir, you have well deserved. 232
   If you do keep your promises in love
   But justly as you have exceeded all promise,   234
   Your mistress shall be happy.
ROSALIND [*giving him a chain from her neck*] Gentleman, 235
   Wear this for me, one out of suits with fortune, 236
   That could give more, but that her hand lacks means. 237
   [*To Celia*] Shall we go, coz?
CELIA   Ay.—Fare you well, fair gentleman.
                    [*Rosalind and Celia start to leave.*]
ORLANDO [*aside*]
   Can I not say, "I thank you"? My better parts
   Are all thrown down, and that which here stands up
   Is but a quintain, a mere lifeless block.   241
ROSALIND [*to Celia*]
   He calls us back. My pride fell with my fortunes;
   I'll ask him what he would.—Did you call, sir? 243
   Sir, you have wrestled well and overthrown
   More than your enemies.
CELIA   Will you go, coz?
ROSALIND   Have with you.—Fare you well.   247
                    Exit [*with Celia*].
ORLANDO
   What passion hangs these weights upon my tongue?
   I cannot speak to her, yet she urged conference. 249
   O poor Orlando, thou art overthrown!
   Or Charles or something weaker masters thee.   251

   Enter Le Beau.

LE BEAU
   Good sir, I do in friendship counsel you
   To leave this place. Albeit you have deserved
   High commendation, true applause, and love,
   Yet such is now the Duke's condition   255
   That he misconsters all that you have done.   256
   The Duke is humorous. What he is indeed   257
   More suits you to conceive than I to speak of.   258

ORLANDO
   I thank you, sir. And, pray you, tell me this:
   Which of the two was daughter of the Duke
   That here was at the wrestling?
LE BEAU
   Neither his daughter, if we judge by manners,
   But yet indeed the taller is his daughter.   263
   The other is daughter to the banished Duke,
   And here detained by her usurping uncle
   To keep his daughter company, whose loves
   Are dearer than the natural bond of sisters.
   But I can tell you that of late this Duke
   Hath ta'en displeasure gainst his gentle niece,
   Grounded upon no other argument   270
   But that the people praise her for her virtues
   And pity her for her good father's sake;
   And, on my life, his malice gainst the lady
   Will suddenly break forth. Sir, fare you well.   274
   Hereafter, in a better world than this,   275
   I shall desire more love and knowledge of you.
ORLANDO
   I rest much bounden to you. Fare you well.   277
                    [*Exit Le Beau.*]
   Thus must I from the smoke into the smother,   278
   From tyrant Duke unto a tyrant brother.
   But heavenly Rosalind!   *Exit.*

❖

1.3

   Enter Celia and Rosalind.

CELIA   Why, cousin, why, Rosalind! Cupid have mercy!
   Not a word?
ROSALIND   Not one to throw at a dog.
CELIA   No, thy words are too precious to be cast away
   upon curs. Throw some of them at me. Come, lame   5
   me with reasons.   6
ROSALIND   Then there were two cousins laid up, when
   the one should be lamed with reasons and the other
   mad without any.
CELIA   But is all this for your father?
ROSALIND   No, some of it is for my child's father. Oh,   11
   how full of briers is this working-day world!
CELIA   They are but burrs, cousin, thrown upon thee in   13
   holiday foolery. If we walk not in the trodden paths,   14
   our very petticoats will catch them.   15
ROSALIND   I could shake them off my coat. These burrs
   are in my heart.

---

223 **change that calling** exchange that name and vocation   228 **unto**
in addition to   232 **Sticks** stabs   234 **But justly** exactly   235 **s.d.**
chain (See 3.2.178, where Celia speaks of a chain given to Orlando by
Rosalind.)   236 **out . . . fortune** (1) whose petitions to Fortune are
rejected (2) not wearing the livery of Fortune, not in her service
237 **could** would   241 **quintain** wooden figure used as a target in
tilting   243 **would** wants.   247 **Have with you** I'll go with you.
249 **urged conference** invited conversation.   251 **Or** Either   255 **con-**
dition disposition   256 **misconsters** misconstrues   257 **humorous**
capricious.   258 **conceive** imagine, understand

263 **taller** (Perhaps a textual error for *smaller* or *lesser*, or else an inconsistency on Shakespeare's part; at 1.3.113, Rosalind is shown to be the
taller.)   270 **argument** reason   274 **suddenly** very soon   275 **in . . .**
world in better times   277 **bounden** indebted   278 **from . . . smother**
i.e., out of the frying pan into the fire. (*Smother* means "a dense suffocating smoke.")
1.3. Location: Duke Frederick's court.
5–6 **lame . . . reasons** throw some explanations (for your silence) at
me.   11 **my child's father** one who might father my children, i.e.,
Orlando.   13–15 **They . . . them** i.e., You are making too much of
minor difficulties; one catches such burrs on one's clothes constantly
if one strays from the path of propriety (by falling into the folly of
love). (*Holiday* and *working-day*, lines 12 and 14, form a crucial comic
binary in this play.)

CELIA   Hem them away.   18

ROSALIND   I would try, if I could cry "hem" and have   19
him.

CELIA   Come, come, wrestle with thy affections.

ROSALIND   Oh, they take the part of a better wrestler than
myself.

CELIA   Oh, a good wish upon you! You will try in time,   24
in despite of a fall. But, turning these jests out of   25
service, let us talk in good earnest. Is it possible, on   26
such a sudden, you should fall into so strong a liking
with old Sir Rowland's youngest son?

ROSALIND   The Duke my father loved his father dearly.

CELIA   Doth it therefore ensue that you should love his
son dearly? By this kind of chase, I should hate him,   31
for my father hated his father dearly; yet I hate not   32
Orlando.

ROSALIND   No, faith, hate him not, for my sake.   34

CELIA   Why should I not? Doth he not deserve well?   35

Enter Duke [Frederick], with Lords.

ROSALIND   Let me love him for that, and do you love
him because I do.—Look, here comes the Duke.

CELIA   With his eyes full of anger.

DUKE FREDERICK   *[to Rosalind]*
Mistress, dispatch you with your safest haste
And get you from our court.

ROSALIND   Me, uncle?

DUKE FREDERICK   You, cousin.   40
Within these ten days if that thou be'st found
So near our public court as twenty miles,
Thou diest for it.

ROSALIND   I do beseech Your Grace
Let me the knowledge of my fault bear with me.
If with myself I hold intelligence   45
Or have acquaintance with mine own desires,
If that I do not dream or be not frantic—   47
As I do trust I am not—then, dear uncle,
Never so much as in a thought unborn
Did I offend Your Highness.

DUKE FREDERICK   Thus do all traitors.
If their purgation did consist in words,   51
They are as innocent as grace itself.
Let it suffice thee that I trust thee not.

ROSALIND
Yet your mistrust cannot make me a traitor.
Tell me whereon the likelihood depends.

DUKE FREDERICK
Thou art thy father's daughter. There's enough.   56

ROSALIND
So was I when Your Highness took his dukedom;
So was I when Your Highness banished him.
Treason is not inherited, my lord;
Or, if we did derive it from our friends,   60
What's that to me? My father was no traitor.
Then, good my liege, mistake me not so much
To think my poverty is treacherous.   63

CELIA   Dear sovereign, hear me speak.

DUKE FREDERICK
Ay, Celia, we stayed her for your sake,   65
Else had she with her father ranged along.   66

CELIA
I did not then entreat to have her stay;
It was your pleasure and your own remorse.   68
I was too young that time to value her,   69
But now I know her. If she be a traitor,
Why, so am I. We still have slept together,   71
Rose at an instant, learned, played, eat together,   72
And wheresoe'er we went, like Juno's swans   73
Still we went coupled and inseparable.

DUKE FREDERICK
She is too subtle for thee; and her smoothness,
Her very silence, and her patience
Speak to the people, and they pity her.
Thou art a fool. She robs thee of thy name,   78
And thou wilt show more bright and seem more
virtuous
When she is gone. Then open not thy lips.
Firm and irrevocable is my doom   81
Which I have passed upon her; she is banished.

CELIA
Pronounce that sentence then on me, my liege!
I cannot live out of her company.

DUKE FREDERICK
You are a fool.—You, niece, provide yourself.   85
If you outstay the time, upon mine honor,
And in the greatness of my word, you die.   87
                                Exit Duke [with Lords].

CELIA
O my poor Rosalind, whither wilt thou go?
Wilt thou change fathers? I will give thee mine.   89
I charge thee, be not thou more grieved than I am.

ROSALIND
I have more cause.

CELIA   Thou hast not, cousin.
Prithee, be cheerful. Know'st thou not the Duke
Hath banished me, his daughter?

ROSALIND   That he hath not.

---

18 **Hem** (1) Tuck (2) Cough (since you say they are in the chest.) A *bur*
can be something that sticks in the throat.   19 **cry "hem"** attract
Orlando's attention by coughing. (But with the suggestion too of a
bawd's warning cry to the lovers whose secrecy is being guarded.
With a pun on *"hem"* and *him*.)   24–5 **Oh . . . fall** i.e., Good luck to
you; you'll undertake to wrestle with Orlando sooner or later, despite
the danger of your being thrown down. (With sexual suggestion.)
25–6 **turning . . . service** i.e., dismissing this banter   31 **By . . . chase**
To pursue this line of reasoning   32 **dearly** intensely   34 **faith** in
truth   35 **Why . . . not?** Why shouldn't I hate him, i.e., love him?
(Celia has just argued by chop-logic, in lines 30-2, that to love is to
hate and vice versa.)   40 **cousin** i.e., niece.   45 **if . . . intelligence** If I
understand my own feelings   47 **If that** if.   **frantic** insane   51 **purgation** clearing of guilt. (A medical, legal, and theological metaphor.)

56 **There's enough** That's reason enough.   60 **friends** relatives
63 **To think** as to think   65 **stayed** kept   66 **ranged** roamed
68 **remorse** compassion.   69 **that time** at that time   71 **still** continually   72 **at an instant** at the same time.   **eat** ate   73 **Juno's swans**
i.e., yoked together. (Though according to Ovid it was Venus, not
Juno, who used swans to draw her chariot.)   78 **name** reputation
81 **doom** sentence   85 **provide yourself** get ready.   87 **in . . . word**
upon my authority as Duke   89 **change** exchange

CELIA

No, hath not? Rosalind lacks then the love
Which teacheth thee that thou and I am one.
Shall we be sundered? Shall we part, sweet girl?
No, let my father seek another heir.
Therefore devise with me how we may fly,
Whither to go, and what to bear with us.
And do not seek to take your change upon you,   100
To bear your griefs yourself and leave me out;
For, by this heaven, now at our sorrows pale,   102
Say what thou canst, I'll go along with thee.

ROSALIND   Why, whither shall we go?

CELIA

To seek my uncle in the Forest of Arden.

ROSALIND

Alas, what danger will it be to us,
Maids as we are, to travel forth so far!
Beauty provoketh thieves sooner than gold.

CELIA

I'll put myself in poor and mean attire   109
And with a kind of umber smirch my face;   110
The like do you. So shall we pass along
And never stir assailants.

ROSALIND   Were it not better,
Because that I am more than common tall,
That I did suit me all points like a man?   114
A gallant curtal ax upon my thigh,   115
A boar spear in my hand, and—in my heart
Lie there what hidden woman's fear there will—
We'll have a swashing and a martial outside,   118
As many other mannish cowards have
That do outface it with their semblances.   120

CELIA

What shall I call thee when thou art a man?

ROSALIND

I'll have no worse a name than Jove's own page,
And therefore look you call me Ganymede.   123
But what will you be called?

CELIA

Something that hath a reference to my state:
No longer Celia, but Aliena.   126

ROSALIND

But, cousin, what if we assayed to steal   127
The clownish fool out of your father's court?
Would he not be a comfort to our travel?   129

CELIA

He'll go along o'er the wide world with me.
Leave me alone to woo him. Let's away,   131
And get our jewels and our wealth together,
Devise the fittest time and safest way
To hide us from pursuit that will be made

After my flight. Now go we in content   135
To liberty, and not to banishment.   *Exeunt.*

❖

2.1

Enter Duke Senior, Amiens, and two or three
Lords, [dressed] like foresters.

DUKE SENIOR

Now, my co-mates and brothers in exile,
Hath not old custom made this life more sweet   2
Than that of painted pomp? Are not these woods
More free from peril than the envious court?
Here feel we not the penalty of Adam,   5
The seasons' difference, as the icy fang   6
And churlish chiding of the winter's wind,
Which when it bites and blows upon my body
Even till I shrink with cold, I smile and say
"This is no flattery; these are counselors
That feelingly persuade me what I am."
Sweet are the uses of adversity,
Which, like the toad, ugly and venomous,   13
Wears yet a precious jewel in his head;   14
And this our life, exempt from public haunt,   15
Finds tongues in trees, books in the running brooks,
Sermons in stones, and good in everything.

AMIENS

I would not change it. Happy is Your Grace
That can translate the stubbornness of fortune
Into so quiet and so sweet a style.

DUKE SENIOR

Come, shall we go and kill us venison?
And yet it irks me the poor dappled fools,   22
Being native burghers of this desert city,   23
Should in their own confines with forkèd heads   24
Have their round haunches gored.

FIRST LORD   Indeed, my lord,
The melancholy Jaques grieves at that,
And in that kind swears you do more usurp   27
Than doth your brother that hath banished you.
Today my lord of Amiens and myself
Did steal behind him as he lay along   30
Under an oak whose antique root peeps out   31
Upon the brook that brawls along this wood,   32
To the which place a poor sequestered stag   33
That from the hunter's aim had ta'en a hurt
Did come to languish. And indeed, my lord,
The wretched animal heaved forth such groans

---

100 change change of fortune   **102 pale** (Heaven is pale in sympathy with their plight.)   **109 mean** lowly   **110 umber** yellow-brown pigment (to give a tanned appearance appropriate to countrywomen)   **114 suit me all points** outfit myself in all ways   **115 curtal ax** broad cutting sword   **118 swashing** swaggering   **120 outface . . . semblances** bluff their way through with mere appearances.   **123 Ganymede** Jupiter's cupbearer. (The name used for disguise also in Lodge's *Rosalynde*.)   **126 Aliena** the estranged one.   **127 assayed** undertook   **129 travel** (1) movement from place to place (2) labor, hardship (*travail*)   **131 Leave . . . him** Leave it to me to persuade him.

135 content contentment
2.1. Location: The Forest of Arden.
2 old custom long experience   **5–6 feel . . . difference** we don't mind the consequences of Adam's original sin—the hardship of the seasons. (*Not* is often emended to *but*.)   **6 as** such as   **13–14 like . . . head** (Alludes to the widespread belief that the toad was a poisonous creature but with a jewel embedded in its head that worked as an antidote.)   **15 exempt** cut off.   **haunt** society   **22 fools** innocents   **23 burghers** citizens.   **desert city** uninhabited place   **24 forkèd heads** barbed hunting arrows, but also suggesting antlers   **27 kind** regard   **30 along** stretched out   **31 antique** (1) ancient or (2) *antic*, "gnarled"   **32 brawls** noisily flows   **33 sequestered** separated (from the herd)

That their discharge did stretch his leathern coat
Almost to bursting, and the big round tears
Coursed one another down his innocent nose   39
In piteous chase. And thus the hairy fool,
Much markèd of the melancholy Jaques,   41
Stood on th'extremest verge of the swift brook,   42
Augmenting it with tears.

DUKE SENIOR   But what said Jaques?
Did he not moralize this spectacle?   44

FIRST LORD
Oh, yes, into a thousand similes.
First, for his weeping into the needless stream: 46
"Poor deer," quoth he, "thou mak'st a testament   47
As worldings do, giving thy sum of more   48
To that which had too much." Then, being there alone,   49
Left and abandoned of his velvet friends: 50
"'Tis right," quoth he, "thus misery doth part   51
The flux of company." Anon a careless herd,   52
Full of the pasture, jumps along by him   53
And never stays to greet him. "Ay," quoth Jaques,
"Sweep on, you fat and greasy citizens;   55
'Tis just the fashion. Wherefore do you look   56
Upon that poor and broken bankrupt there?"   57
Thus most invectively he pierceth through   58
The body of the country, city, court,
Yea, and of this our life, swearing that we
Are mere usurpers, tyrants, and what's worse,   61
To fright the animals and to kill them up   62
In their assigned and native dwelling place.

DUKE SENIOR
And did you leave him in this contemplation?

SECOND LORD
We did, my lord, weeping and commenting
Upon the sobbing deer.

DUKE SENIOR   Show me the place.
I love to cope him in these sullen fits,   67
For then he's full of matter.   68

FIRST LORD   I'll bring you to him straight.   *Exeunt.*   69

❖

2.2

Enter Duke [Frederick], with Lords.

DUKE FREDERICK
Can it be possible that no man saw them?
It cannot be. Some villains of my court
Are of consent and sufferance in this.   3

FIRST LORD
I cannot hear of any that did see her.   4
The ladies, her attendants of her chamber,
Saw her abed, and in the morning early
They found the bed untreasured of their mistress.

SECOND LORD
My lord, the roynish clown, at whom so oft   8
Your Grace was wont to laugh, is also missing.
Hisperia, the princess' gentlewoman,
Confesses that she secretly o'erheard
Your daughter and her cousin much commend
The parts and graces of the wrestler   13
That did but lately foil the sinewy Charles,
And she believes wherever they are gone
That youth is surely in their company.

DUKE FREDERICK
Send to his brother. Fetch that gallant hither.   17
If he be absent, bring his brother to me;   18
I'll make him find him. Do this suddenly,   19
And let not search and inquisition quail   20
To bring again these foolish runaways.   *Exeunt.*   21

❖

2.3

Enter Orlando and Adam, [meeting].

ORLANDO   Who's there?
ADAM
What, my young master? Oh, my gentle master,
Oh, my sweet master, oh, you memory   3
Of old Sir Rowland! Why, what make you here?   4
Why are you virtuous? Why do people love you?
And wherefore are you gentle, strong, and valiant?
Why would you be so fond to overcome   7
The bonny prizer of the humorous Duke?   8
Your praise is come too swiftly home before you.
Know you not, master, to some kind of men
Their graces serve them but as enemies?
No more do yours. Your virtues, gentle master,   12
Are sanctified and holy traitors to you.

---

39 Coursed chased   **41 markèd of** observed by   **42 th'extremest
verge** the very edge   **44 moralize** draw out the hidden meaning of
46 needless having no need of more water. (Weeping deer are common in literature.)   **47 testament** will   **48 worldings** worldly men
48–9 giving . . . much bequeathing your superabundance of wealth
to heirs who are already too wealthy.   **49 being** the deer being
50 of by.   **velvet** i.e., prosperous. (Velvet was an appropriately rich
dress for a courtier; the term also alludes here to the deers' velvety
coat or to the covering of their antlers during rapid growth.)
51 'Tis right i.e., That's how it goes   **51–2 thus . . . company** thus
the miserable are separated from and forgotten by the herd.
52 careless (1) carefree (2) uncaring   **53 the pasture** i.e., good food
55 greasy fat and unctuously prosperous, like rich burghers or *citizens*   **56–7 Wherefore . . . there?** Why do you even bother to glance
at that poor physically shattered deer there? (*Broken* also hints at a
financial ruin appropriate to *citizens* in line 55.)   **58 invectively** in
the most bitter terms   **61 what's worse** whatever is worse than
these   **62 up** off, utterly   **67 cope** encounter   **68 matter** substance.
69 straight at once.

2.2. Location: Duke Frederick's court.
3 Are . . . this have conspired in and permitted this.   **4 her** Celia.
8 roynish scurvy, rascally. (Literally, covered with scale or scurf.)
13 parts good qualities   **17 Send . . . hither** i.e., Send word to Oliver
to bring Orlando here.   **18 he** i.e., Orlando.   **his brother** i.e., Oliver.
(Or possibly referring to Jaques de Boys, the other brother.)   **19 suddenly** speedily   **20 inquisition quail** investigation fail   **21 again**
back
2.3. Location: Before Oliver's house.
3 memory likeness, reminder   **4 what make you** what are you doing
7 fond to foolish as to   **8 bonny prizer** sturdy prizefighter.
humorous temperamental   **12 No . . . yours** Your fine qualities serve
you no better than that.

Oh, what a world is this, when what is comely
Envenoms him that bears it!

ORLANDO
Why, what's the matter?

ADAM   O unhappy youth,
Come not within these doors! Within this roof
The enemy of all your graces lives.
Your brother—no, no brother; yet the son—
Yet not the son, I will not call him son
Of him I was about to call his father—
Hath heard your praises, and this night he means   22
To burn the lodging where you use to lie   23
And you within it. If he fail of that,
He will have other means to cut you off.
I overheard him and his practices.   26
This is no place, this house is but a butchery.   27
Abhor it, fear it, do not enter it.

ORLANDO
Why, whither, Adam, wouldst thou have me go?

ADAM
No matter whither, so you come not here.   30

ORLANDO
What, wouldst thou have me go and beg my food?
Or with a base and boist'rous sword enforce   32
A thievish living on the common road?
This I must do or know not what to do;
Yet this I will not do, do how I can.
I rather will subject me to the malice
Of a diverted blood and bloody brother.   37

ADAM
But do not so. I have five hundred crowns,
The thrifty hire I saved under your father,   39
Which I did store to be my foster nurse
When service should in my old limbs lie lame   41
And unregarded age in corners thrown.   42
Take that, and He that doth the ravens feed,   43
Yea, providently caters for the sparrow,   44
Be comfort to my age! Here is the gold; [offering gold]
All this I give you. Let me be your servant.
Though I look old, yet I am strong and lusty,   47
For in my youth I never did apply
Hot and rebellious liquors in my blood,
Nor did not with unbashful forehead woo   50
The means of weakness and debility;   51
Therefore my age is as a lusty winter,
Frosty but kindly. Let me go with you.   53
I'll do the service of a younger man
In all your business and necessities.

ORLANDO
Oh, good old man, how well in thee appears
The constant service of the antique world,   57
When service sweat for duty, not for meed!   58
Thou art not for the fashion of these times,
Where none will sweat but for promotion,
And having that do choke their service up   61
Even with the having. It is not so with thee.   62
But, poor old man, thou prun'st a rotten tree,
That cannot so much as a blossom yield
In lieu of all thy pains and husbandry.   65
But come thy ways. We'll go along together,
And ere we have thy youthful wages spent,
We'll light upon some settled low content.   68

ADAM
Master, go on, and I will follow thee
To the last gasp, with truth and loyalty.
From seventeen years till now almost fourscore
Here livèd I, but now live here no more.
At seventeen years many their fortunes seek,
But at fourscore it is too late a week;   74
Yet fortune cannot recompense me better
Than to die well and not my master's debtor.

                                              Exeunt.

❖

2.4

Enter Rosalind for Ganymede, Celia for Aliena,
and Clown, alias Touchstone.

ROSALIND   Oh, Jupiter, how weary are my spirits!

TOUCHSTONE   I care not for my spirits, if my legs were
    not weary.

ROSALIND   I could find in my heart to disgrace my man's
    apparel and to cry like a woman; but I must comfort   5
    the weaker vessel, as doublet and hose ought to show   6
    itself courageous to petticoat. Therefore courage, good
    Aliena!

CELIA   I pray you, bear with me. I cannot go no further.

TOUCHSTONE   For my part, I had rather bear with you
    than bear you; yet I should bear no cross if I did bear 11
    you, for I think you have no money in your purse.

ROSALIND   Well, this is the Forest of Arden.

TOUCHSTONE   Ay, now am I in Arden; the more fool I.
    When I was at home I was in a better place, but
    travelers must be content.

    Enter Corin and Silvius.

---

22 **your praises** people's praise of you   23 **use** are accustomed
26 **practices** plots.   27 **place** place for you   30 **so** provided that
32 **boist'rous** rough   37 **diverted blood** kinship diverted from the
natural source   39 **thrifty . . . saved** wages I thriftily saved   41 **lie
lame** i.e., be performed only lamely   42 **And . . . thrown** and when I
will be neglected and thrown aside because of my old age.   43–4 **and
He . . . sparrow** i.e., and may God, who guards over all His creatures
(see Luke 12:6, 22-4, Psalms 147:9, etc.)   47 **lusty** vigorous   50–1 **Nor
. . . debility** nor did I with shameless countenance chase after pleasures that would have weakened and disabled me   53 **Frosty** i.e.,
white-haired

57 **constant** faithful.   **antique** ancient (as in the Golden Age)
58 **sweat** sweated.   **meed** reward.   61–2 **do choke . . . having** i.e.,
cease serving once they have gained promotion.   65 **lieu of** return
for   68 **low content** lowly contented state.   74 **too . . . week** i.e., too
late in life
2.4 Location: The Forest of Arden.
0.1. for i.e., disguised as   **5–6 comfort the weaker vessel** (The First
Epistle of Peter 3:7, bids husbands give honor to their wives "as unto
the weaker vessel.")   **6 doublet and hose** close-fitting jacket and
breeches; typical male attire   **11 cross** (1) burden (2) coin having on it
a figure of a cross

ROSALIND   Ay, be so, good Touchstone.—Look you
who comes here, a young man and an old in solemn
talk.   [*They stand aside and listen.*]

CORIN
That is the way to make her scorn you still.

SILVIUS
Oh, Corin, that thou knew'st how I do love her!

CORIN
I partly guess, for I have loved ere now.

SILVIUS
No, Corin, being old, thou canst not guess,
Though in thy youth thou wast as true a lover
As ever sighed upon a midnight pillow.
But if thy love were ever like to mine—
As sure I think did never man love so—
How many actions most ridiculous
Hast thou been drawn to by thy fantasy?   29

CORIN
Into a thousand that I have forgotten.

SILVIUS
Oh, thou didst then never love so heartily!
If thou remember'st not the slightest folly
That ever love did make thee run into,
Thou hast not loved.
Or if thou hast not sat as I do now,
Wearing thy hearer in thy mistress' praise,   36
Thou hast not loved.
Or if thou hast not broke from company
Abruptly, as my passion now makes me,
Thou has not loved.
O Phoebe, Phoebe, Phoebe!   *Exit.*

ROSALIND
Alas, poor shepherd! Searching of thy wound,   42
I have by hard adventure found mine own.   43

TOUCHSTONE   And I mine. I remember, when I was in
love I broke my sword upon a stone and bid him take   45
that for coming a-night to Jane Smile; and I remember   46
the kissing of her batler and the cow's dugs that her   47
pretty chapped hands had milked; and I remember   48
the wooing of a peascod instead of her, from whom I   49
took two cods and, giving her them again, said with   50
weeping tears, "Wear these for my sake." We that are   51
true lovers run into strange capers; but as all is mortal   52
in nature, so is all nature in love mortal in folly.   53

ROSALIND   Thou speak'st wiser than thou art ware of.   54

TOUCHSTONE   Nay, I shall ne'er be ware of mine own   55
wit till I break my shins against it.   56

ROSALIND
Jove, Jove! This shepherd's passion
Is much upon my fashion.   58

TOUCHSTONE
And mine, but it grows something stale with me.   59

CELIA
I pray you, one of you question yond man
If he for gold will give us any food.
I faint almost to death.

TOUCHSTONE   [*to Corin*]   Holla: you, clown!   62

ROSALIND
Peace, Fool! He's not thy kinsman.

CORIN   Who calls?

TOUCHSTONE
Your betters, sir.

CORIN   Else are they very wretched.

ROSALIND
Peace, I say.—Good even to you, friend.   65

CORIN
And to you, gentle sir, and to you all.

ROSALIND
I prithee, shepherd, if that love or gold   67
Can in this desert place buy entertainment,   68
Bring us where we may rest ourselves and feed.
Here's a young maid with travel much oppressed,
And faints for succor.

CORIN   Fair sir, I pity her   71
And wish, for her sake more than for mine own,
My fortunes were more able to relieve her;
But I am shepherd to another man
And do not shear the fleeces that I graze.   75
My master is of churlish disposition,   76
And little recks to find the way to heaven   77
By doing deeds of hospitality.
Besides, his cote, his flocks, and bounds of feed   79
Are now on sale, and at our sheepcote now,
By reason of his absence, there is nothing
That you will feed on. But what is, come see,   82
And in my voice most welcome shall you be.   83

ROSALIND
What is he that shall buy his flock and pasture?   84

CORIN
That young swain that you saw here but erewhile,   85
That little cares for buying anything.

ROSALIND
I pray thee, if it stand with honesty,   87
Buy thou the cottage, pasture, and the flock,
And thou shalt have to pay for it of us.   89

---

29 **fantasy** love imaginings. 36 **Wearing** wearing out 42 **Searching of** Probing 43 **hard adventure** painful experience 45–6 **I broke ... Smile** (In his parody of a distraught lover, Touchstone imagines himself attacking a stone as if it were his rival for a country maiden named Jane Smile. *A-night* means "by night.") 47 **batler** club for beating clothes in process of washing. **dugs** udder 48–51 **I ... sake** (Touchstone absurdly imagines himself courting a pea plant as though it were Jane Smile and exchanging pea pods with her by way of love tokens.) 52 **mortal** subject to death 53 **mortal** typically human, frail 54 **ware** aware 55–6 **Nay ... against it** (Touchstone, as a professional fool, laughs at the idea of stumbling on or discovering his own capacity for saying something wise. His use of *ware* plays on [1] aware [2] wary.)

58 **upon** after, according to 59 **something** somewhat 62 **clown** yokel. (But Rosalind then alludes to the word as it applies to Touchstone as a court fool or clown.) 65 **even** evening, i.e., afternoon 67 **if that** if 68 **desert** uninhabited. **entertainment** provision 71 **for succor** for lack of food. 75 **do ... fleeces** i.e., do not obtain the profits from the flock 76 **churlish** miserly 77 **recks** reckons 79 **cote** cottage. **bounds of feed** range of pasture 82 **That ... feed on** suitable for your refined tastes. 83 **in my voice** insofar as I have authority to speak 84 **What** Who 85 **but erewhile** just now 87 **stand** be consistent 89 **have to pay** have the money

CELIA
And we will mend thy wages. I like this place   90
And willingly could waste my time in it.   91

CORIN
Assuredly the thing is to be sold.
Go with me. If you like upon report
The soil, the profit, and this kind of life,
I will your very faithful feeder be   95
And buy it with your gold right suddenly.   *Exeunt.* 96

❋

2.5

Enter Amiens, Jaques, and others. [A table is set out.]

Song.

AMIENS [*sings*]
Under the greenwood tree
Who loves to lie with me,   2
And turn his merry note   3
Unto the sweet bird's throat,   4
Come hither, come hither, come hither.
Here shall he see
No enemy
But winter and rough weather.

JAQUES   More, more, I prithee, more.
AMIENS   It will make you melancholy, Monsieur Jaques.
JAQUES   I thank it. More, I prithee, more. I can suck melancholy out of a song as a weasel sucks eggs. More, I prithee, more.
AMIENS   My voice is ragged. I know I cannot please you.   14
JAQUES   I do not desire you to please me, I do desire you to sing. Come, more, another stanzo. Call you   16 'em "stanzos"?
AMIENS   What you will, Monsieur Jaques.
JAQUES   Nay, I care not for their names; they owe me   19 nothing. Will you sing?   20
AMIENS   More at your request than to please myself.
JAQUES   Well then, if ever I thank any man, I'll thank you; but that they call "compliment" is like th'en-   23 counter of two dog-apes, and when a man thanks   24 me heartily, methinks I have given him a penny and he renders me the beggarly thanks. Come, sing; and   26 you that will not, hold your tongues.
AMIENS   Well, I'll end the song.—Sirs, cover the while;   28 the Duke will drink under this tree.—He hath been all this day to look you.   [*Food and drink are set out.*] 30

JAQUES   And I have been all this day to avoid him. He is too disputable for my company. I think of as many   32 matters as he, but I give heaven thanks and make no boast of them. Come, warble, come.

Song.

AMIENS [*sings*]
Who doth ambition shun
And loves to live i'th' sun,   36
Seeking the food he eats   37
And pleased with what he gets,
All together here.
Come hither, come hither, come hither.
Here shall he see
No enemy
But winter and rough weather.

JAQUES   I'll give you a verse to this note that I made   43 yesterday in despite of my invention.   44
AMIENS   And I'll sing it.
JAQUES   Thus it goes:

If it do come to pass
That any man turn ass,
Leaving his wealth and ease,
A stubborn will to please,
Ducdame, ducdame, ducdame,   51
Here shall he see
Gross fools as he,
An if he will come to me.

AMIENS   What's that "ducdame"?
JAQUES   'Tis a Greek invocation, to call fools into a circle. I'll go sleep, if I can; if I cannot, I'll rail against all the firstborn of Egypt.   58
AMIENS   And I'll go seek the Duke. His banquet is pre-   59 pared.   *Exeunt [separately].*

❋

2.6

Enter Orlando and Adam.

ADAM   Dear master, I can go no further. Oh, I die for food! Here lie I down and measure out my grave. Farewell, kind master.   [*He lies down.*]

---

32 **disputable** inclined to dispute   36 **live i'th' sun** dwell in the open air, without the cares of the court   37 **Seeking** hunting for   43 **note** tune   44 **in . . . invention** i.e., without needing to make use of my powerful rhetorical skills. (The nonsense that follows will make a mockery of true invention.)   51 **Ducdame** (Probably a nonsense term devised to puzzle Jaques's hearers, although with intriguing resemblances to phrases in Romany, *dukrà me*, "I foretell," or Welsh *Dewch da mi*, "Come with (or to) me," or dog-Latin *Duc ad me*, "Lead him to me," or simply "Duke damn me.")   58 **firstborn of Egypt** (In Exodus 12:28–33, the firstborn of Egypt are slain by the Lord as the enemies of Moses and the Israelites, who, like the Duke and his followers, are in exile.)   59 **banquet** wine and dessert after dinner. (This repast, now prepared on stage, seemingly is to remain there during the short following scene.)
2.6. Location: The forest. The scene is continuous. By convention we understand that Adam and Orlando are in a different part of the forest and do not "see" the table remaining onstage.

---

90 **mend** improve   91 **waste** spend   95 **feeder** dependent, servant
96 **right suddenly** without delay.
2.5. Location: The forest.
2 **Who** anyone who.   **lie** dwell   3–4 **And . . . throat** and tune his song to the bird's voice   14 **ragged** hoarse.   16 **stanzo** (The word *stanza*, variously spelled, was newfangled and therefore of ironic interest to Jaques.)   19–20 **they owe me nothing** (Jaques speaks of names as of something valuable only when written as signatures to a bond of indebtedness.)   23 **that** what.   **"compliment"** courtesy   24 **dog-apes** dog-faced baboons   26 **beggarly** effusive, like the thanks of a beggar   28 **cover the while** set the table for a meal meanwhile   30 **to look** looking for

ORLANDO   Why, how now, Adam? No greater heart in
thee? Live a little, comfort a little, cheer thyself a little.   5
If this uncouth forest yield anything savage, I will   6
either be food for it or bring it for food to thee. Thy   7
conceit is nearer death than thy powers. For my sake   8
be comfortable; hold death awhile at the arm's end. I   9
will here be with thee presently, and if I bring thee not
something to eat, I will give thee leave to die; but if
thou diest before I come, thou art a mocker of my
labor. Well said! Thou look'st cheerly, and I'll be with   13
thee quickly. Yet thou liest in the bleak air. Come, I
will bear thee to some shelter; and thou shalt not die
for lack of a dinner, if there live anything in this desert.
[*He picks up Adam.*] Cheerly, good Adam!   *Exeunt.*

❧

2.7

Enter Duke Senior and Lords, like outlaws.

DUKE SENIOR
I think he be transformed into a beast,
For I can nowhere find him like a man.

FIRST LORD
My lord, he is but even now gone hence.
Here was he merry, hearing of a song.

DUKE SENIOR
If he, compact of jars, grow musical,   5
We shall have shortly discord in the spheres.   6
Go seek him. Tell him I would speak with him.

Enter Jaques.

FIRST LORD
He saves my labor by his own approach.

DUKE SENIOR
Why, how now, monsieur, what a life is this,
That your poor friends must woo your company!
What, you look merrily.

JAQUES
A fool, a fool! I met a fool i'th' forest,
A motley fool. A miserable world!   13
As I do live by food, I met a fool,
Who laid him down and basked him in the sun,
And railed on Lady Fortune in good terms,
In good set terms, and yet a motley fool.   17
"Good morrow, Fool," quoth I. "No, sir," quoth he,
"Call me not fool till heaven hath sent me fortune."   19
And then he drew a dial from his poke   20
And, looking on it with lackluster eye,
Says very wisely, "It is ten o'clock.

Thus we may see," quoth he, "how the world wags.   23
'Tis but an hour ago since it was nine,
And after one hour more 'twill be eleven;
And so from hour to hour we ripe and ripe,
And then from hour to hour we rot and rot,
And thereby hangs a tale." When I did hear
The motley fool thus moral on the time,   29
My lungs began to crow like Chanticleer,   30
That fools should be so deep-contemplative,
And I did laugh sans intermission   32
An hour by his dial. Oh, noble fool!
A worthy fool! Motley's the only wear.   34

DUKE SENIOR   What fool is this?

JAQUES
Oh, worthy fool! One that hath been a courtier,
And says, if ladies be but young and fair,
They have the gift to know it. And in his brain,   38
Which is as dry as the remainder biscuit   39
After a voyage, he hath strange places crammed   40
With observation, the which he vents   41
In mangled forms. Oh, that I were a fool!
I am ambitious for a motley coat.

DUKE SENIOR
Thou shalt have one.

JAQUES   It is my only suit,   44
Provided that you weed your better judgments
Of all opinion that grows rank in them   46
That I am wise. I must have liberty
Withal, as large a charter as the wind,   48
To blow on whom I please, for so fools have.
And they that are most gallèd with my folly,   50
They most must laugh. And why, sir, must they so?
The "why" is plain as way to parish church:
He that a fool doth very wisely hit   53
Doth very foolishly, although he smart,   54
Not to seem senseless of the bob. If not,   55
The wise man's folly is anatomized   56
Even by the squand'ring glances of the fool.   57
Invest me in my motley; give me leave   58
To speak my mind, and I will through and through
Cleanse the foul body of th'infected world,   60
If they will patiently receive my medicine.

DUKE SENIOR
Fie on thee! I can tell what thou wouldst do.

JAQUES
What, for a counter, would I do but good?   63

---

5 comfort comfort yourself   **6 uncouth** strange, wild   **7–8 Thy conceit . . . powers** You imagine you are nearer death than you really are.
9 comfortable comforted   **13 Well said!** Well done!
2.7. Location: The forest; the scene is continuous. (A repast, set out for the Duke in 2.5, has remained onstage during 2.6.)
5 compact of jars composed of discords   **6 the spheres** the concentric spheres of the old Ptolemaic solar system (which, by their movement, were thought to produce harmonious music).   **13 motley** wearing motley, the parti-colored dress of the professional jester
17 set carefully composed   **19 Call . . . fortune** (An allusion to the proverb "Fortune favors fools.")   **20 dial** pocket sundial or watch.
poke pouch or pocket

23 wags goes.   **29 moral** moralize   **30 crow** i.e., laugh merrily.
Chanticleer a rooster   **32 sans** without   **34 only wear** only thing worth wearing.   **38 know it** i.e., put their beauty to advantage.
39 dry (According to Elizabethan physiology, a dry brain was marked by a strong memory but a slowness of apprehension.)   **remainder** left over   **40 places** (1) nooks and corners (2) rhetorical topics
41 vents utters   **44 suit** (1) request (2) suit of clothes   **46 rank** wildly, coarsely   **48 Withal** in addition.   **charter** license, privilege   **50 gallèd** rubbed sore   **53–5 He . . . bob** He whom a fool wittily attacks behaves very foolishly, no matter how much he feels the sting, unless he pretends to be unaware of the taunt.   **55–7 If not . . . fool** Otherwise, the folly of even a wise person is dissected and laid open even by the variously directed shots of wit made by the fool.   **58 Invest** Array   **60 Cleanse** purge. (A medical metaphor.)   **63 counter** (1) thing of no intrinsic value, a metal disk used in counting (2) parry

DUKE SENIOR
Most mischievous foul sin, in chiding sin.
For thou thyself hast been a libertine,
As sensual as the brutish sting itself;
And all th'embossèd sores and headed evils
That thou with license of free foot hast caught
Wouldst thou disgorge into the general world.

JAQUES   Why, who cries out on pride
That can therein tax any private party?
Doth it not flow as hugely as the sea,
Till that the weary very means do ebb?
What woman in the city do I name,
When that I say the city woman bears
The cost of princes on unworthy shoulders?
Who can come in and say that I mean her,
When such a one as she, such is her neighbor?
Or what is he of basest function
That says his bravery is not on my cost,
Thinking that I mean him, but therein suits
His folly to the mettle of my speech?
There then, how then? What then? Let me see
    wherein
My tongue hath wronged him. If it do him right,
Then he hath wronged himself. If he be free,
Why then my taxing like a wild goose flies,
Unclaimed of any man.—But who comes here?

Enter Orlando [with his sword drawn].

ORLANDO
Forbear, and eat no more!

JAQUES   Why, I have eat none yet.

ORLANDO
Nor shalt not, till necessity be served.

JAQUES
Of what kind should this cock come of?

DUKE SENIOR
Art thou thus boldened, man, by thy distress,
Or else a rude despiser of good manners,
That in civility thou seem'st so empty?

ORLANDO
You touched my vein at first. The thorny point
Of bare distress hath ta'en from me the show
Of smooth civility; yet am I inland bred

66 **brutish sting** carnal impulse   67 **th'embossèd** the swollen.
headed evils sores that have come to a head   68 **license . . . foot** the
licentious freedom of a libertine   69 **disgorge** vomit   70–1 **who . . .
party?** what true satirist inveighs against extravagance in dress with
only some private individual in mind?   72–3 **Doth . . . ebb?** Is not
pride as universal as the sea, overflowing everywhere until it finally
ebbs like the tide, having exhausted what it fed upon?   75–6 **When . .
. shoulders?** when I characterize the typical citizen's wife as dressing
herself in finery that is costly enough to adorn a prince?   77 **come in**
i.e., come into court as a complainant   79–82 **Or . . . speech?** Or who
is he of even the lowest social standing that does not object to my
saying that sartorial finery is a fit subject for my satirical spleen,
thinking I am satirizing him when his own folly shows how well he
fits the contents of my speech?   84–7 **If . . . man** If my satirical sketch
fits him, then he condemns himself by resembling my portrait of
folly. If he does not resemble my sketch, my criticism does him no
harm.   88 **have eat** have eaten. (Pronounced "et.")   90 **Of . . . of?**
What sort of fighting cock is this?   94 **You . . . first** Your first supposition is correct.   96 **inland bred** i.e., raised in the center of civilization rather than on the outskirts

And know some nurture. But forbear, I say.
He dies that touches any of this fruit
Till I and my affairs are answerèd.

JAQUES
An you will not be answered with reason, I must die.

DUKE SENIOR
What would you have? Your gentleness shall force
More than your force move us to gentleness.

ORLANDO
I almost die for food, and let me have it!

DUKE SENIOR
Sit down and feed, and welcome to our table.

ORLANDO
Speak you so gently? Pardon me, I pray you.
I thought that all things had been savage here,
And therefore put I on the countenance
Of stern commandment. But whate'er you are
That in this desert inaccessible,
Under the shade of melancholy boughs,
Lose and neglect the creeping hours of time;
If ever you have looked on better days,
If ever been where bells have knolled to church,
If ever sat at any good man's feast,
If ever from your eyelids wiped a tear
And know what 'tis to pity and be pitied,
Let gentleness my strong enforcement be,
In the which hope I blush and hide my sword.
    [He sheathes his sword.]

DUKE SENIOR
True is it that we have seen better days,
And have with holy bell been knolled to church,
And sat at good men's feasts, and wiped our eyes
Of drops that sacred pity hath engendered.
And therefore sit you down in gentleness,
And take upon command what help we have
That to your wanting may be ministered.

ORLANDO
Then but forbear your food a little while,
Whiles, like a doe, I go to find my fawn
And give it food. There is an old poor man
Who after me hath many a weary step
Limped in pure love. Till he be first sufficed,
Oppressed with two weak evils, age and hunger,
I will not touch a bit.

DUKE SENIOR   Go find him out,
And we will nothing waste till you return.

ORLANDO
I thank ye; and be blest for your good comfort!
    [Exit.]

DUKE SENIOR
Thou see'st we are not all alone unhappy.
This wide and universal theater
Presents more woeful pageants than the scene
Wherein we play in.

JAQUES   All the world's a stage,

97 **nurture** education, training.   99 **answerèd** satisfied.   100 **An** If.
reason (A pun on "raisin" plays upon *fruit* in line 98.)   110 **melancholy** dark, shadowy   113 **knolled** knelled, rung   124 **upon command** for the asking   125 **wanting** need   131 **weak evils** disabilities
causing weakness   133 **waste** consume

And all the men and women merely players.
They have their exits and their entrances,
And one man in his time plays many parts,
His acts being seven ages. At first the infant,
Mewling and puking in the nurse's arms.   143
Then the whining schoolboy, with his satchel
And shining morning face, creeping like snail
Unwillingly to school. And then the lover,
Sighing like furnace, with a woeful ballad
Made to his mistress' eyebrow. Then a soldier,
Full of strange oaths and bearded like the pard,   149
Jealous in honor, sudden, and quick in quarrel,   150
Seeking the bubble reputation
Even in the cannon's mouth. And then the justice,
In fair round belly with good capon lined,   153
With eyes severe and beard of formal cut,
Full of wise saws and modern instances;   155
And so he plays his part. The sixth age shifts
Into the lean and slippered pantaloon,   157
With spectacles on nose and pouch on side,
His youthful hose, well saved, a world too wide
For his shrunk shank; and his big manly voice,   160
Turning again toward childish treble, pipes
And whistles in his sound. Last scene of all,   162
That ends this strange, eventful history,
Is second childishness and mere oblivion,   164
Sans teeth, sans eyes, sans taste, sans everything.   165

Enter Orlando, with Adam.

DUKE SENIOR
Welcome. Set down your venerable burden
And let him feed.
ORLANDO   I thank you most for him.
                              [*He sets down Adam.*]
ADAM   So had you need.
I scarce can speak to thank you for myself.
DUKE SENIOR
Welcome. Fall to. I will not trouble you
As yet to question you about your fortunes.—
Give us some music, and, good cousin, sing.   173
                    [*They eat, while Orlando and Duke Senior*
                                          converse apart.]

Song.

AMIENS [*sings*]
        Blow, blow, thou winter wind.
        Thou art not so unkind
                As man's ingratitude.
        Thy tooth is not so keen,
        Because thou art not seen,
                Although thy breath be rude.   179

Heigh-ho, sing heigh-ho, unto the green holly.   180
Most friendship is feigning, most loving mere
    folly.
        Then heigh-ho, the holly!
            This life is most jolly.
    Freeze, freeze, thou bitter sky,
    That dost not bite so nigh   185
        As benefits forgot.
    Though thou the waters warp,   187
    Thy sting is not so sharp
        As friend remembered not.
Heigh-ho, sing heigh-ho, unto the green holly.
Most friendship is feigning, most loving mere
    folly.
        Then heigh-ho, the holly!
            This life is most jolly.

DUKE SENIOR [*to Orlando*]
If that you were the good Sir Rowland's son,   194
As you have whispered faithfully you were   195
And as mine eye doth his effigies witness   196
Most truly limned and living in your face,   197
Be truly welcome hither. I am the Duke
That loved your father. The residue of your fortune,   199
Go to my cave and tell me.—Good old man,
Thou art right welcome as thy master is.—
Support him by the arm. Give me your hand,
And let me all your fortunes understand.   *Exeunt.* 203

❖

3.1

Enter Duke [Frederick], Lords, and Oliver.

DUKE FREDERICK
Not see him since? Sir, sir, that cannot be.   1
But were I not the better part made mercy,   2
I should not seek an absent argument   3
Of my revenge, thou present. But look to it: 4
Find out thy brother, wheresoe'er he is.
Seek him with candle. Bring him dead or living   6
Within this twelvemonth, or turn thou no more   7
To seek a living in our territory.
Thy lands and all things that thou dost call thine
Worth seizure do we seize into our hands,   10
Till thou canst quit thee by thy brother's mouth   11
Of what we think against thee.

---

180 holly (An emblem of Christmastime and holiday cheer, as in "the holly and the ivy.")   **185 nigh** deeply, near (to the heart)   **187 warp** freeze so that the surface of the ice cracks and forces up ridges
194 If that If   **195 faithfully** persuasively and honestly   **196 doth . . . witness** witnesses the likeness of the dead Sir Rowland   **197 limned** painted   **199 The . . . fortune** The rest of your adventure
203 s.d. *Exeunt* (The table must be removed at this point.)
3.1. Location: Duke Frederick's court.
1 Not . . . since? i.e., You mean to tell me you claim not to have seen Orlando since the disappearance of Celia and Rosalind?   **2 were . . . mercy** i.e., if I were not a merciful man. (Literally, if I were not composed mostly of mercy.)   **3–4 I . . . present** i.e., I would seek revenge not on the absent Orlando, but on you, who are right here.   **6 Seek . . . candle** i.e., Look for him everywhere, even in the darkest corners. (See Luke 15:8.)   **7 turn** return   **10 we . . . our** (The royal plural.)
11 quit . . . mouth acquit yourself by the direct testimony of Orlando. (The Duke suspects that Oliver has murdered Orlando.)

---

143 Mewling crying with a catlike noise   **149 bearded . . . pard** having bristling mustaches like the leopard's   **150 Jealous in honor** quick to anger in matters of honor   **153 capon** rooster castrated to make the flesh more tender for eating (and often presented to judges as a bribe)   **155 saws** sayings.   **modern instances** commonplace illustrations   **157 pantaloon** ridiculous, enfeebled old man. (A stock type in Italian *commedia dell'arte*.)   **160 shank** calf   **162 his** its
164 mere oblivion total forgetfulness   **165 Sans** without
173 cousin (A term used by sovereigns to address their nobility.)
179 rude rough.

OLIVER
Oh, that Your Highness knew my heart in this!
I never loved my brother in my life.

DUKE FREDERICK
More villain thou.—Well, push him out of doors,
And let my officers of such a nature
Make an extent upon his house and lands.   16
Do this expediently, and turn him going.   *Exeunt.*   17
                                                            18

❋

3.2

Enter Orlando [with a paper].

ORLANDO
Hang there, my verse, in witness of my love;
    And thou, thrice-crownèd queen of night, survey   2
With thy chaste eye, from thy pale sphere above,
    Thy huntress' name that my full life doth sway.   4
O Rosalind! These trees shall be my books,
    And in their barks my thoughts I'll character,   6
That every eye which in this forest looks
    Shall see thy virtue witnessed everywhere.
Run, run, Orlando, carve on every tree
The fair, the chaste, and unexpressive she.   *Exit.* 10

Enter Corin and [Touchstone the] Clown.

CORIN   And how like you this shepherd's life, Master
Touchstone?

TOUCHSTONE   Truly, shepherd, in respect of itself, it is a   13
good life; but in respect that it is a shepherd's life, it is
naught. In respect that it is solitary, I like it very well;   15
but in respect that it is private, it is a very vile life.
Now in respect it is in the fields, it pleaseth me well;
but in respect it is not in the court, it is tedious. As it
is a spare life, look you, it fits my humor well; but as   19
there is no more plenty in it, it goes much against my
stomach. Hast any philosophy in thee, shepherd?

CORIN   No more but that I know the more one sickens
the worse at ease he is; and that he that wants money,   23
means, and content is without three good friends; that
the property of rain is to wet and fire to burn; that
good pasture makes fat sheep and that a great cause
of the night is lack of the sun; that he that hath learned
no wit by nature nor art may complain of good   28
breeding or comes of a very dull kindred.

TOUCHSTONE   Such a one is a natural philosopher.
Wast ever in court, shepherd?

CORIN   No, truly.

TOUCHSTONE   Then thou art damned.

CORIN   Nay, I hope.   34

TOUCHSTONE   Truly, thou art damned, like an ill-
roasted egg, all on one side.

CORIN   For not being at court? Your reason.

TOUCHSTONE   Why, if thou never wast at court, thou
never saw'st good manners; if thou never saw'st good   39
manners, then thy manners must be wicked; and   40
wickedness is sin, and sin is damnation. Thou art in
a parlous state, shepherd.   42

CORIN   Not a whit, Touchstone. Those that are good
manners at the court are as ridiculous in the country as
the behavior of the country is most mockable at the
court. You told me you salute not at the court but you   46
kiss your hands; that courtesy would be uncleanly, if   47
courtiers were shepherds.

TOUCHSTONE   Instance, briefly; come, instance.   49

CORIN   Why, we are still handling our ewes, and their   50
fells you know are greasy.   51

TOUCHSTONE   Why, do not your courtier's hands sweat?   52
And is not the grease of a mutton as wholesome as the   53
sweat of a man? Shallow, shallow. A better instance, I   54
say. Come.

CORIN   Besides, our hands are hard.

TOUCHSTONE   Your lips will feel them the sooner.
Shallow again. A more sounder instance. Come.

CORIN   And they are often tarred over with the surgery   59
of our sheep; and would you have us kiss tar? The
courtier's hands are perfumed with civet.   61

TOUCHSTONE   Most shallow man! Thou worms'meat, in   62
respect of a good piece of flesh indeed! Learn of the   63
wise, and perpend: civet is of a baser birth than tar,   64
the very uncleanly flux of a cat. Mend the instance,   65
shepherd.

CORIN   You have too courtly a wit for me. I'll rest.

TOUCHSTONE   Wilt thou rest damned? God help thee,
shallow man! God make incision in thee! Thou art   69
raw.   70

CORIN   Sir, I am a true laborer: I earn that I eat, get that   71
I wear, owe no man hate, envy no man's happiness,
glad of other men's good, content with my harm, and   73
the greatest of my pride is to see my ewes graze and
my lambs suck.

TOUCHSTONE   That is another simple sin in you, to bring   76
the ewes and the rams together and to offer to get your   77

---

16 **of such a nature** who attend to such duties   17 **extent** writ of
seizure   18 **expediently** expeditiously.   **turn him going** send him
packing.
3.2. Location: The forest.
2 **thrice-crownèd . . . night** i.e., Diana in the three aspects of her
divinity: as Luna or Cynthia, goddess of the moon; as Diana, goddess
on earth; and as Hecate or Proserpina, goddess in the lower world
4 **Thy huntress'** i.e., Rosalind's, who is here thought of as accompanying Diana, patroness of the hunt and of chastity.   **sway** control.
6 **character** inscribe   10 **unexpressive** inexpressible   13 **in respect of
itself** considered in and for itself   15 **naught** vile, of no social consequence.   19 **spare** frugal.   **humor** temperament   23 **wants** lacks
28 **wit** wisdom.   **art** study.   **complain of** lament the lack of

34 **hope** i.e., hope not.   39 **manners** etiquette   40 **manners** morals
42 **parlous** perilous   46 **salute** greet   46–7 **but . . . hands** without
kissing the other person's hands   49 **Instance** Proof   50 **still** constantly   51 **fells** skins with the wool, or fleeces   52 **your courtier's**
your typical courtier's   53–4 **And . . . man?** (Human sweat was
thought to be fat oozing from the pores.)   59 **tarred over** anointed
with tar on their cuts and sores   61 **civet** a musky perfume derived
from glands in the anal pouch of the civet cat. (As Touchstone points
out.)   62–3 **Thou . . . indeed!** You miserable creature (literally, you
food for worms, subject to the decay of death), if we compare you
with any worthy sample of humankind!   64 **perpend** consider
65 **flux** secretion.   **Mend** Improve   69 **incision** a cut, perhaps for the
purpose of letting blood (here, to let out folly); or for seasoning as
raw meat is scored and salted before cooking   70 **raw** (1) wet behind
the ears (2) uncooked (3) afflicted with a raw wound.   71 **earn . . . eat**
earn my living   73 **content . . . harm** patient with my ill fortune
76 **simple sin** sin arising from simplicity   77 **offer** undertake

living by the copulation of cattle; to be bawd to a bell- 78
wether, and to betray a she-lamb of a twelvemonth to 79
a crooked-pated old cuckoldly ram, out of all reasonable 80
match. If thou be'st not damned for this, the devil him- 81
self will have no shepherds; I cannot see else how thou 82
shouldst scape. 83

CORIN   Here comes young Master Ganymede, my new
mistress's brother.

Enter Rosalind [with a paper, reading].

ROSALIND
"From the east to western Ind, 86
No jewel is like Rosalind.
Her worth, being mounted on the wind,
Through all the world bears Rosalind.
All the pictures fairest lined 90
Are but black to Rosalind. 91
Let no face be kept in mind
But the fair of Rosalind." 93

TOUCHSTONE   I'll rhyme you so eight years together, 94
dinners and suppers and sleeping hours excepted. It 95
is the right butter-women's rank to market. 96

ROSALIND   Out, fool! 97

TOUCHSTONE   For a taste:
If a hart do lack a hind, 99
Let him seek out Rosalind.
If the cat will after kind, 101
So, be sure, will Rosalind.
Wintered garments must be lined, 103
So must slender Rosalind.
They that reap must sheaf and bind; 105
Then to cart with Rosalind. 106
Sweetest nut hath sourest rind;
Such a nut is Rosalind.
He that sweetest rose will find
Must find love's prick and Rosalind. 110

This is the very false gallop of verses. Why do you 111
infect yourself with them?

ROSALIND   Peace, you dull fool! I found them on a tree.

TOUCHSTONE   Truly, the tree yields bad fruit.

ROSALIND   I'll graft it with you, and then I shall graft it 115
with a medlar. Then it will be the earliest fruit i'th' 116
country; for you'll be rotten ere you be half ripe, and
that's the right virtue of the medlar. 118

TOUCHSTONE   You have said; but whether wisely or no,
let the forest judge.

Enter Celia, with a writing.

ROSALIND   Peace! Here comes my sister, reading. Stand
aside.

CELIA [*reads*]
"Why should this a desert be?
For it is unpeopled? No. 124
Tongues I'll hang on every tree,
That shall civil sayings show: 126
Some, how brief the life of man
Runs his erring pilgrimage, 128
That the stretching of a span 129
Buckles in his sum of age; 130
Some, of violated vows
Twixt the souls of friend and friend;
But upon the fairest boughs,
Or at every sentence end,
Will I 'Rosalinda' write,
Teaching all that read to know
The quintessence of every sprite 137
Heaven would in little show. 138
Therefore heaven Nature charged 139
That one body should be filled
With all graces wide-enlarged. 141
Nature presently distilled
Helen's cheek, but not her heart, 143
Cleopatra's majesty,
Atalanta's better part, 145
Sad Lucretia's modesty. 146
Thus Rosalind of many parts
By heavenly synod was devised 148
Of many faces, eyes, and hearts
To have the touches dearest prized. 150
Heaven would that she these gifts should have, 151
And I to live and die her slave." 152

---

78 **cattle** livestock   78–9 **bellwether** the leading male sheep of a flock, wearing a bell   80 **crooked-pated** with crooked horns. **cuckoldly** i.e., horned like a cuckold (husband of an unfaithful wife). **out of** contrary to   81–2 **If . . . shepherds** i.e., Your only possible escape from damnation would be if the devil should find shepherds too objectionable to have in hell under any circumstances   83 **scape** escape.   86 **Ind** Indies   90 **lined** drawn   91 **black to** dark-complexioned and hence ugly compared to   93 **fair** beauty   94 **together** without stop   95–6 **It is . . . market** i.e., The rhymes, all alike, follow each other precisely like a line of butter women or dairy women jogging along to market.   97 **Out** (An exclamation here denoting comic indignation.)   99 **If . . . hind** If a male deer longs for a female deer. (Touchstone wryly suggests in his verses that Rosalind is the responsive object of male desire.)   101 **after kind** follow its natural instinct   103 **Wintered** Old, worn; used in winter.   **lined** (1) given a winter lining (2) stuffed. (The term was sometimes used for the copulating of dogs.)   105 **sheaf and bind** tie in a bundle   106 **to cart** (1) onto the harvest cart (2) onto the cart used to carry prostitutes through the streets, exposing them to public ridicule   110 **prick** thorn. (With bawdy suggestion.)   111 **false gallop** canter

115 **you** (With a pun on "yew.")   116 **medlar** a fruit like a small brown-skinned apple that is eaten when it starts to decay. (With a pun on "meddler.")   118 **right virtue** true quality   124 **For** Because   126 **civil sayings** maxims of civilized life   128 **his erring** its wandering   129–30 **That . . . age** i.e., so that a very brief span encompasses his whole life. (A *span* is a handbreadth. See Psalm 39:5.)   137 **quintessence** highest perfection. (Literally, the fifth essence or element of the medieval alchemists, purer even than fire.)   **sprite** spirit 138 **Heaven . . . show** that heaven wishes to show in one small person, Rosalind (who, in microcosm, embodies the supreme essence of the heavens, or macrocosm).   139 **heaven . . . charged** heaven commanded Nature   141 **wide-enlarged** all-encompassing.   143 **Helen's . . . heart** i.e., the beauty of Helen of Troy but not her false heart 145 **Atalanta's better part** i.e., her beauty or her fleetness of foot, not her scornfulness and greed. (She refused to marry any man who was unable to defeat her in a foot race and, when challenged by Hippomenes, lost to him because Hippomenes dropped in her way three golden apples of the Hesperides.)   146 **Lucretia's** Lucretia was an honorable Roman lady raped by Tarquin (whose story Shakespeare tells in *The Rape of Lucrece*).   148 **synod** assembly   150 **touches** traits 151 **would** decree   152 **And I to** and that I should

ROSALIND   Oh, most gentle Jupiter, what tedious homily 153
of love have you wearied your parishioners withal,
and never cried, "Have patience, good people!"

CELIA   How now? Back, friends. Shepherd, go off a 156
little. [*To Touchstone*] Go with him, sirrah. 157

TOUCHSTONE   Come, shepherd, let us make an honorable retreat, though not with bag and baggage, yet 159
with scrip and scrippage.   *Exit* [*with Corin*]. 160

CELIA   Didst thou hear these verses?

ROSALIND   Oh, yes, I heard them all, and more, too, for
some of them had in them more feet than the verses
would bear.

CELIA   That's no matter. The feet might bear the verses.

ROSALIND   Ay, but the feet were lame and could not
bear themselves without the verse and therefore stood 167
lamely in the verse.

CELIA   But didst thou hear without wondering how thy
name should be hanged and carved upon these trees?

ROSALIND   I was seven of the nine days out of the 171
wonder before you came; for look here what I found 172
on a palm tree. I was never so berhymed since
Pythagoras' time, that I was an Irish rat, which I can 174
hardly remember.

CELIA   Trow you who hath done this? 176

ROSALIND   Is it a man?

CELIA   And a chain that you once wore about his neck. 178
Change you color?

ROSALIND   I prithee, who?

CELIA   Oh, Lord, Lord, it is a hard matter for friends to 181
meet; but mountains may be removed with earth- 182
quakes and so encounter. 183

ROSALIND   Nay, but who is it?

CELIA   Is it possible? 185

ROSALIND   Nay, I prithee now with most petitionary
vehemence, tell me who it is.

CELIA   Oh, wonderful, wonderful, and most wonderful-
wonderful! And yet again wonderful, and after that,
out of all whooping! 190

ROSALIND   Good my complexion! Dost thou think, 191
though I am caparisoned like a man, I have a doublet 192
and hose in my disposition? One inch of delay more 193
is a South Sea of discovery. I prithee, tell me who is it 194
quickly, and speak apace. I would thou couldst stam-

mer, that thou mightst pour this concealed man out of
thy mouth as wine comes out of a narrow-mouthed
bottle, either too much at once or none at all. I prithee,
take the cork out of thy mouth that I may drink thy
tidings.

CELIA   So you may put a man in your belly. 201

ROSALIND   Is he of God's making? What manner of 202
man? Is his head worth a hat, or his chin worth a
beard?

CELIA   Nay, he hath but a little beard.

ROSALIND   Why, God will send more, if the man will be
thankful. Let me stay the growth of his beard, if thou 207
delay me not the knowledge of his chin.

CELIA   It is young Orlando, that tripped up the wrestler's heels and your heart both in an instant.

ROSALIND   Nay, but the devil take mocking. Speak sad 211
brow and true maid. 212

CELIA   I'faith, coz, 'tis he.

ROSALIND   Orlando?

CELIA   Orlando.

ROSALIND   Alas the day, what shall I do with my
doublet and hose? What did he when thou saw'st him?
What said he? How looked he? Wherein went he? 218
What makes he here? Did he ask for me? Where 219
remains he? How parted he with thee? And when 220
shalt thou see him again? Answer me in one word.

CELIA   You must borrow me Gargantua's mouth first; 222
'tis a word too great for any mouth of this age's size.
To say ay and no to these particulars is more than to 224
answer in a catechism. 225

ROSALIND   But doth he know that I am in this forest
and in man's apparel? Looks he as freshly as he did
the day he wrestled?

CELIA   It is as easy to count atomies as to resolve the 229
propositions of a lover. But take a taste of my finding 230
him, and relish it with good observance. I found him 231
under a tree, like a dropped acorn.

ROSALIND   It may well be called Jove's tree, when it 233
drops forth such fruit.

CELIA   Give me audience, good madam. 235

ROSALIND   Proceed.

CELIA   There lay he, stretched along, like a wounded
knight.

ROSALIND   Though it be pity to see such a sight, it well
becomes the ground. 240

CELIA   Cry "holla" to thy tongue, I prithee; it curvets 241
unseasonably. He was furnished like a hunter. 242

---

153 Jupiter (Often emended to "pulpiter.")   **156 Back** i.e., Move back, away. (Addressed to Corin and Touchstone.)   **157 sirrah** a form of address to inferiors (here, Touchstone).   **159 bag and baggage** i.e., equipment appropriate to a retreating army   **160 scrip and scrippage** shepherd's pouch and its contents.   **167 without** (1) without the help of (2) outside   **171–2 seven . . . wonder** (A reference to the common phrase "a nine days' wonder.")   **174 Pythagoras** Greek philosopher credited with the doctrine of the transmigration of souls.   **that** when. **Irish rat** (Refers to a current belief that Irish enchanters could rhyme rats and other animals to death.)   **which** a thing which   **176 Trow you** Have you any idea   **178 And a chain** And with a chain   **181–3 it is . . . encounter** (A playful inversion of the proverb, "Friends may meet, but mountains never greet." Celia appears to be teasing Rosalind's eagerness to meet Orlando.)   **removed with** moved by **185 possible** i.e., possible you don't know.   **190 out . . . whooping** beyond all power to utter.   **191 Good my complexion!** Oh, my (feminine) temperament, my woman's curiosity!   **192 caparisoned** bedecked. (Usually said of a horse.)   **192–3 I have . . . disposition?** i.e., that I have a man's patience?   **194 a South Sea of discovery** i.e., as tedious as a long exploratory voyage to the South Pacific Ocean.

201 belly (1) stomach (2) womb.   **202 of God's making** i.e., a real man, not of a tailor's making.   **207 stay** wait for   **211–12 sad . . . maid** i.e., seriously and truthfully.   **218 Wherein went he?** In what clothes was he dressed?   **219 makes** does   **220 remains** dwells **222 Gargantua's mouth** (Gargantua is the giant of popular literature who, in Rabelais' novel, swallowed five pilgrims in a salad.) **224–5 To . . . catechism** To give even yes and no answers to these questions would take longer than to go through the catechism (i.e., the formal questioning used in the Church to teach the principles of faith).   **229 atomies** motes, specks of dirt   **230 propositions** questions   **231 relish it** heighten its pleasant taste.   **observance** attention.   **233 Jove's tree** the oak   **235 Give me audience** Listen to me **240 becomes** adorns   **241 holla** stop.   **curvets** prances   **242 furnished** equipped, dressed

ROSALIND   Oh, ominous! He comes to kill my heart. 243
CELIA   I would sing my song without a burden. Thou 244
bring'st me out of tune. 245
ROSALIND   Do you not know I am a woman? When I
think, I must speak. Sweet, say on.

Enter Orlando and Jaques.

CELIA   You bring me out.—Soft, comes he not here? 248
ROSALIND   'Tis he. Slink by, and note him.
[*They stand aside and listen.*]
JAQUES   [*to Orlando*]   I thank you for your company,
but, good faith, I had as lief have been myself alone.
ORLANDO   And so had I; but yet, for fashion sake, I 252
thank you too for your society.
JAQUES   God b'wi'you. Let's meet as little as we can. 254
ORLANDO   I do desire we may be better strangers.
JAQUES   I pray you, mar no more trees with writing
love songs in their barks.
ORLANDO   I pray you, mar no more of my verses with
reading them ill-favoredly. 259
JAQUES   Rosalind is your love's name?
ORLANDO   Yes, just. 261
JAQUES   I do not like her name.
ORLANDO   There was no thought of pleasing you when
she was christened.
JAQUES   What stature is she of?
ORLANDO   Just as high as my heart.
JAQUES   You are full of pretty answers. Have you not
been acquainted with goldsmiths' wives, and conned 268
them out of rings? 269
ORLANDO   Not so; but I answer you right painted cloth, 270
from whence you have studied your questions.
JAQUES   You have a nimble wit; I think 'twas made of
Atalanta's heels. Will you sit down with me? And we 273
two will rail against our mistress the world and all our
misery.
ORLANDO   I will chide no breather in the world but 276
myself, against whom I know most faults.
JAQUES   The worst fault you have is to be in love.
ORLANDO   'Tis a fault I will not change for your best
virtue. I am weary of you.
JAQUES   By my troth, I was seeking for a fool when I
found you.
ORLANDO   He is drowned in the brook. Look but in,
and you shall see him.
JAQUES   There I shall see mine own figure. 285
ORLANDO   Which I take to be either a fool or a cipher. 286
JAQUES   I'll tarry no longer with you. Farewell, good
Seigneur Love.

ORLANDO   I am glad of your departure. Adieu, good
Monsieur Melancholy.   [*Exit Jaques.*]
ROSALIND   [*aside to Celia*]   I will speak to him like a
saucy lackey and under that habit play the knave 292
with him.—Do you hear, forester?
ORLANDO   Very well. What would you?
ROSALIND   I pray you, what is't o'clock?
ORLANDO   You should ask me what time o' day.
There's no clock in the forest.
ROSALIND   Then there is no true lover in the forest, else
sighing every minute and groaning every hour would
detect the lazy foot of Time as well as a clock. 300
ORLANDO   And why not the swift foot of Time? Had
not that been as proper?
ROSALIND   By no means, sir. Time travels in divers
paces with divers persons. I'll tell you who Time
ambles withal, who Time trots withal, who Time 305
gallops withal, and who he stands still withal.
ORLANDO   I prithee, who doth he trot withal?
ROSALIND   Marry, he trots hard with a young maid
between the contract of her marriage and the day it is
solemnized. If the interim be but a se'nnight, Time's 310
pace is so hard that it seems the length of seven year.
ORLANDO   Who ambles Time withal?
ROSALIND   With a priest that lacks Latin and a rich man
that hath not the gout, for the one sleeps easily
because he cannot study and the other lives merrily
because he feels no pain, the one lacking the burden of
lean and wasteful learning, the other knowing no 317
burden of heavy tedious penury. These Time ambles
withal.
ORLANDO   Who doth he gallop withal?
ROSALIND   With a thief to the gallows, for though he go
as softly as foot can fall, he thinks himself too soon
there.
ORLANDO   Who stays it still withal?
ROSALIND   With lawyers in the vacation; for they sleep
between term and term, and then they perceive not 326
how Time moves.
ORLANDO   Where dwell you, pretty youth?
ROSALIND   With this shepherdess, my sister, here in the
skirts of the forest, like fringe upon a petticoat.
ORLANDO   Are you native of this place?
ROSALIND   As the coney that you see dwell where she is 332
kindled. 333
ORLANDO   Your accent is something finer than you 334
could purchase in so removed a dwelling. 334
ROSALIND   I have been told so of many. But indeed an
old religious uncle of mine taught me to speak, who 337
was in his youth an inland man, one that knew 338
courtship too well, for there he fell in love. I have 339

---

243 **heart** (With pun on "hart.")   244 **burden** refrain, or bass part.
244–5 **Thou bring'st** You put   248 **Soft** i.e., Wait a minute, or, stop
talking   252 **fashion** fashion's   254 **God b'wi'you** God be with you,
good-bye   259 **ill-favoredly** unsympathetically   261 **just** just so.
268 **conned** memorized   269 **rings** (Verses or "posies" were often
inscribed in rings.)   270 **right painted cloth** in the true spirit of a
painted cloth decorated with commonplace pictures and cliché mot-
toes (frequently mythological or scriptural)   273 **Atalanta's heels**
(See above, the note for line 145.)   276 **breather** living being
285 **figure** reflection. (Narcissus fell in love with his own reflection in
a pool.)   286 **cipher** nonentity, zero.

292 **and under . . . knave** and in that disguise (1) pose as a boy
(2) deal mischievously   300 **detect** reveal   305 **withal** with
310 **se'nnight** week   317 **lean** unremunerative.   **wasteful** making
one waste away   326 **term** court session   332 **coney** rabbit   333 **kindled** littered, born.   334 **something** somewhat   335 **purchase**
acquire.   **removed** remote   337 **religious** i.e., belonging to a religious order   338 **inland** from a center of civilization   339 **courtship**
(1) wooing (2) knowledge of courtly manners

heard him read many lectures against it, and I thank 340
God I am not a woman, to be touched with so many 341
giddy offenses as he hath generally taxed their whole
sex withal.

ORLANDO   Can you remember any of the principal evils
that he laid to the charge of women?

ROSALIND   There were none principal; they were all like
one another as halfpence are, every one fault seeming
monstrous till his fellow fault came to match it.   348

ORLANDO   I prithee, recount some of them.

ROSALIND   No, I will not cast away my physic but on 350
those that are sick. There is a man haunts the forest
that abuses our young plants with carving "Rosalind"
on their barks, hangs odes upon hawthorns and
elegies on brambles, all, forsooth, deifying the name of
Rosalind. If I could meet that fancy-monger, I would 355
give him some good counsel, for he seems to have the
quotidian of love upon him.   357

ORLANDO   I am he that is so love-shaked. I pray you,
tell me your remedy.

ROSALIND   There is none of my uncle's marks upon you.
He taught me how to know a man in love, in which
cage of rushes I am sure you are not prisoner.   362

ORLANDO   What were his marks?

ROSALIND   A lean cheek, which you have not; a blue eye 364
and sunken, which you have not; an unquestionable 365
spirit, which you have not; a beard neglected, which
you have not—but I pardon you for that, for simply 367
your having in beard is a younger brother's revenue. 368
Then your hose should be ungartered, your bonnet un- 369
banded, your sleeve unbuttoned, your shoe untied, 370
and everything about you demonstrating a careless
desolation. But you are no such man. You are rather
point-device in your accoutrements, as loving your- 373
self, than seeming the lover of any other.

ORLANDO   Fair youth, I would I could make thee believe
I love.

ROSALIND   Me believe it? You may as soon make her
that you love believe it, which I warrant she is apter to
do than to confess she does. That is one of the points
in the which women still give the lie to their con- 380
sciences. But in good sooth, are you he that hangs the 381
verses on the trees, wherein Rosalind is so
admired?

ORLANDO   I swear to thee, youth, by the white hand of
Rosalind, I am that he, that unfortunate he.

ROSALIND   But are you so much in love as your rhymes
speak?

ORLANDO   Neither rhyme nor reason can express how
much.

ROSALIND   Love is merely a madness and, I tell you, 390
deserves as well a dark house and a whip as madmen 391
do; and the reason why they are not so punished and
cured is that the lunacy is so ordinary that the
whippers are in love too. Yet I profess curing it by 394
counsel.

ORLANDO   Did you ever cure any so?

ROSALIND   Yes, one, and in this manner. He was to
imagine me his love, his mistress; and I set him every
day to woo me. At which time would I, being but a
moonish youth, grieve, be effeminate, changeable, 400
longing and liking, proud, fantastical, apish, shallow,
inconstant, full of tears, full of smiles; for every passion
something and for no passion truly anything, as boys
and women are for the most part cattle of this color;
would now like him, now loathe him; then entertain 405
him, then forswear him; now weep for him, then spit
at him; that I drave my suitor from his mad humor of 407
love to a living humor of madness, which was to for- 408
swear the full stream of the world and to live in a nook
merely monastic. And thus I cured him; and this way 410
will I take upon me to wash your liver as clean as a 411
sound sheep's heart, that there shall not be one spot of
love in't.

ORLANDO   I would not be cured, youth.

ROSALIND   I would cure you, if you would but call me
Rosalind and come every day to my cote and woo me. 416

ORLANDO   Now by the faith of my love, I will. Tell me
where it is.

ROSALIND   Go with me to it, and I'll show it you; and
by the way you shall tell me where in the forest you 420
live. Will you go?

ORLANDO   With all my heart, good youth.

ROSALIND   Nay, you must call me Rosalind.—Come,
sister, will you go?   *Exeunt.*

❖

3.3

Enter [Touchstone the] Clown, Audrey; and Jaques
[apart].

TOUCHSTONE   Come apace, good Audrey. I will fetch up 1
your goats, Audrey. And how, Audrey, am I the man 2
yet? Doth my simple feature content you?   3

AUDREY   Your features, Lord warrant us! What features? 4

TOUCHSTONE   I am here with thee and thy goats, as the
most capricious poet, honest Ovid, was among the 6
Goths.   7

---

340 **read many lectures** deliver many admonitory speeches
341 **touched** tainted   348 **his** its   350 **physic** medicine   355 **fancy-**
monger love peddler   357 **quotidian** fever recurring daily. (See *love-*
shaked, line 358.)   362 **cage of rushes** i.e., flimsy prison   364 **blue eye**
i.e., having dark circles   365 **unquestionable** unwilling to be conversed with   367–8 **simply . . . revenue** what beard you have is like a
younger brother's inheritance (i.e., small).   369–70 **bonnet**
unbanded hat lacking a band around the crown   373 **point-device**
faultless
380 **still** continually   381 **good sooth** honest truth

390 **merely** utterly   391 **dark . . . whip** (The common treatment of
lunatics.)   394 **profess** am expert in   400 **moonish** changeable
405 **entertain** receive cordially   407 **that** with the result that.   **drave**
drove   407–8 **mad . . . madness** mad fancy of love to a real madness
410 **merely** utterly   411 **liver** (Supposed seat of the emotions, especially love.)   416 **cote** cottage   420 **by** on
3.3. Location: The forest.
1 **apace** quickly   2 **And how** i.e., What do you say   3 **simple feature**
plain appearance. (But Audrey, in her answer, may have her mind on
features as "parts of the body.")   4 **warrant** protect   6 **capricious**
witty, fanciful. (Derived from the Latin *caper*, "male goat"; hence,
"goatish, lascivious.")   7 **Goths** (With pun on "goats"; the two words
were pronounced alike.)

JAQUES [*aside*]   Oh, knowledge ill-inhabited, worse than 8
Jove in a thatched house! 9

TOUCHSTONE   When a man's verses cannot be under- 10
stood, nor a man's good wit seconded with the 11
forward child, understanding, it strikes a man more 12
dead than a great reckoning in a little room. Truly, I 13
would the gods had made thee poetical.

AUDREY   I do not know what "poetical" is. Is it honest
in deed and word? Is it a true thing?

TOUCHSTONE   No, truly; for the truest poetry is the most
feigning, and lovers are given to poetry, and what 18
they swear in poetry may be said as lovers they do 19
feign. 20

AUDREY   Do you wish then that the gods had made me
poetical?

TOUCHSTONE   I do, truly; for thou swear'st to me thou
art honest. Now, if thou wert a poet, I might have 24
some hope thou didst feign. 25

AUDREY   Would you not have me honest?

TOUCHSTONE   No, truly, unless thou wert hard- 27
favored; for honesty coupled to beauty is to have 28
honey a sauce to sugar.

JAQUES [*aside*]   A material fool! 30

AUDREY   Well, I am not fair, and therefore I pray the
gods make me honest.

TOUCHSTONE   Truly, and to cast away honesty upon a
foul slut were to put good meat into an unclean dish. 34

AUDREY   I am not a slut, though I thank the gods I am 35
foul. 36

TOUCHSTONE   Well, praised be the gods for thy foulness!
Sluttishness may come hereafter. But be it as it
may be, I will marry thee, and to that end I have been
with Sir Oliver Mar-text, the vicar of the next village, 40
who hath promised to meet me in this place of the
forest and to couple us.

JAQUES [*aside*]   I would fain see this meeting. 43

AUDREY   Well, the gods give us joy!

TOUCHSTONE   Amen. A man may, if he were of a
fearful heart, stagger in this attempt; for here we have 46
no temple but the wood, no assembly but horn-beasts. 47

But what though? Courage! As horns are odious, they 48
are necessary. It is said, "Many a man knows no end 49
of his goods." Right! Many a man has good horns and 50
knows no end of them. Well, that is the dowry of his 51
wife; 'tis none of his own getting. Horns? Even so. 52
Poor men alone? No, no, the noblest deer hath them 53
as huge as the rascal. Is the single man therefore 54
blessed? No. As a walled town is more worthier than
a village, so is the forehead of a married man more
honorable than the bare brow of a bachelor; and by
how much defense is better than no skill, by so much 58
is a horn more precious than to want. 59

Enter Sir Oliver Mar-text.

Here comes Sir Oliver.—Sir Oliver Mar-text, you are
well met. Will you dispatch us here under this tree, or 61
shall we go with you to your chapel?

SIR OLIVER   Is there none here to give the woman? 63

TOUCHSTONE   I will not take her on gift of any man.

SIR OLIVER   Truly, she must be given, or the marriage is
not lawful.

JAQUES [*advancing*]   Proceed, proceed. I'll give her.

TOUCHSTONE   Good even, good Master What-ye-call-'t. 68
How do you, sir? You are very well met. God 'ild you 69
for your last company. I am very glad to see you. Even 70
a toy in hand here, sir.—Nay, pray be covered. 71

JAQUES   Will you be married, motley?

TOUCHSTONE   As the ox hath his bow, sir, the horse his 73
curb, and the falcon her bells, so man hath his desires; 74
and as pigeons bill, so wedlock would be nibbling. 75

JAQUES   And will you, being a man of your breeding,
be married under a bush like a beggar? Get you to 77
church, and have a good priest that can tell you what 78
marriage is. This fellow will but join you together as 79
they join wainscot; then one of you will prove a
shrunk panel and, like green timber, warp, warp. 81

---

48 what though what though it be so.   **As** Though   **49 necessary**
(1) useful to horned animals (2) unavoidable to cuckolds.
49–50 knows . . . goods is endlessly well provided.   **51 knows . . .
them** i.e., is endlessly supplied with cuckold's horns. (A sardonic
interpretation of the proverb in lines 49–50.)   **dowry** marriage gift
52 getting (1) obtaining (2) begetting (in the sense that his wife's children will not be his).   **Even so** That's just how it is.   **53 deer**
(1) horned animal (2) dear husband   **54 rascal** (1) young deer that are
lean and out of season (2) poor ordinary husband.   **single** unmarried
58 defense (1) fortifications (including a type known as "hornwork")
(2) the art of self-defense   **59 than to want** i.e., than to be without a
horn. (Recalling the "horn of plenty," which is indeed precious.)
61 dispatch us finish off our business   **63 give the woman** give away
the bride; conventionally, the bride's father answered the question,
"Who giveth this woman to be married to this man?"   **68 What-ye-
call-'t** (Probably joking on *Jakes* as "outhouse.")   **69 'ild you** yield
you, reward you   **70 last** most recent   **71 a toy in hand** a trifle to be
attended to, or literally by the hand.   **be covered** put on your hat,
i.e., no need to show respect; or, cover up your bosom. (Said to
Audrey, or perhaps to Jaques, who may have removed his hat in sardonic deference to the ceremony.)   **73 bow** yoke   **74 curb** chain or
strap attached to the horse's bit and used to control it.   **bells**
(Attached to a falcon's leg during training.)   **75 bill** stroke bill with
bill   **77 under a bush** i.e., by a "hedge-priest," an uneducated clergyman   **78–9 tell . . . is** expound the obligations of marriage.   **81 warp**
(1) shrivel and fit badly together (2) stray from the true path.

---

8 ill-inhabited ill-lodged   **9 Jove . . . house!** (An allusion to Ovid's
Metamorphoses 8, containing the story of Jupiter and Mercury lodging
disguised in the humble cottage of Baucis and Philemon.)
10–11 verses . . . understood (Ovid's verses were misunderstood by
the barbaric Goths, among whom he lived in exile, just as Touchstone's wit is misunderstood by Audrey.)   **11–12 nor . . . understanding** (Wisdom, understanding, and memory were thought to occupy
three main ventricles in the brain, and to be interconnected in the
process of thought. *Forward* means "precocious.")   **13 great . . . room**
exorbitant charge for refreshment or lodging in a cramped tavern
room. (Some scholars see in this passage an allusion to the death of
Christopher Marlowe, who was stabbed by Ingram Frysar at an inn
in Deptford in a quarrel over a tavern reckoning, May 30, 1593.)
18 feigning inventive, imaginative. (But Touchstone plays on the
sense of "false, lying.")   **19 may be said** i.e., it may be said   **20 feign**
(With a further play on "desire.")   **24 honest** chaste.   **25 feign**
(1) pretend (2) desire.   **27–8 hard-favored** ugly   **28 honesty** chastity
30 material full of pithy matter   **34 foul** ugly   **35–6 I thank . . . foul**
i.e., my unattractive looks are what destiny has allotted to me.
40 Sir (Courtesy title for a clergyman.)   **43 fain** gladly   **46 stagger**
hesitate   **47 horn-beasts** antlered animals like deer and cattle, and
therefore resembling cuckolded men with their cuckolds' horns.

TOUCHSTONE   I am not in the mind but I were better 82
to be married of him than of another, for he is not 83
like to marry me well; and not being well married, 84
it will be a good excuse for me hereafter to leave my
wife.

JAQUES   Go thou with me, and let me counsel thee.

TOUCHSTONE
Come, sweet Audrey.
We must be married, or we must live in bawdry. 89
Farewell, good Master Oliver; not
        "O sweet Oliver,
        O brave Oliver, 91
    Leave me not behind thee"; 92
but
        "Wind away,
        Begone, I say, 95
    I will not to wedding with thee." 97
            [*Exeunt Jaques, Touchstone, and Audrey.*]

SIR OLIVER   'Tis no matter. Ne'er a fantastical knave of 98
them all shall flout me out of my calling.   *Exit.*

❖

3.4

Enter Rosalind and Celia.

ROSALIND   Never talk to me. I will weep.

CELIA   Do, I prithee, but yet have the grace to consider
that tears do not become a man.

ROSALIND   But have I not cause to weep?

CELIA   As good cause as one would desire; therefore
weep.

ROSALIND   His very hair is of the dissembling color. 7

CELIA   Something browner than Judas's. Marry, his 8
kisses are Judas's own children. 9

ROSALIND   I'faith, his hair is of a good color.

CELIA   An excellent color. Your chestnut was ever the 11
only color. 12

ROSALIND   And his kissing is as full of sanctity as the
touch of holy bread. 14

CELIA   He hath bought a pair of cast lips of Diana. A 15
nun of winter's sisterhood kisses not more religiously; 16
the very ice of chastity is in them.

ROSALIND   But why did he swear he would come this
morning, and comes not?

CELIA   Nay, certainly, there is no truth in him.

ROSALIND   Do you think so?

CELIA   Yes. I think he is not a pickpurse nor a horse-
stealer, but for his verity in love, I do think him as
concave as a covered goblet or a worm-eaten nut. 24

ROSALIND   Not true in love?

CELIA   Yes, when he is in, but I think he is not in.

ROSALIND   You have heard him swear downright he
was.

CELIA   "Was" is not "is." Besides, the oath of a lover is
no stronger than the word of a tapster; they are both
the confirmer of false reckonings. He attends here in 31
the forest on the Duke your father.

ROSALIND   I met the Duke yesterday and had much
question with him. He asked me of what parentage I 34
was. I told him, of as good as he; so he laughed and let
me go. But what talk we of fathers, when there is such 36
a man as Orlando?

CELIA   Oh, that's a brave man! He writes brave verses, 38
speaks brave words, swears brave oaths, and breaks
them bravely, quite traverse, athwart the heart of his 40
lover, as a puny tilter, that spurs his horse but on 41
one side, breaks his staff like a noble goose. But all's 42
brave that youth mounts and folly guides. Who comes 43
here?

Enter Corin.

CORIN
Mistress and master, you have oft inquired
After the shepherd that complained of love,
Who you saw sitting by me on the turf, 46
Praising the proud disdainful shepherdess
That was his mistress.

CELIA   Well, and what of him?

CORIN
If you will see a pageant truly played
Between the pale complexion of true love 51
And the red glow of scorn and proud disdain,
Go hence a little, and I shall conduct you,
If you will mark it.

ROSALIND   Oh, come, let us remove! 54
The sight of lovers feedeth those in love.
Bring us to this sight, and you shall say
I'll prove a busy actor in their play.   *Exeunt.*

❖

---

82 **I am . . . better** I do not know but that it would be better for me.
(Touchstone may be speaking aside here to Jaques.) **83 of** by
84 like likely.   **well** (1) suitably (2) legally   **89 married** i.e., properly
married, as Jaques suggests, not by a hedge-priest. (Having been
found out, Touchstone wryly defers matters for the present.)
91–7 "O . . . thee." (Phrases from a current ballad.)   **92 brave** worthy
95 Wind Wend, go   **98 fantastical** affected
3.4. Location: The forest.
7 the dissembling color i.e., reddish, traditionally the color of Judas's
hair.   **8 Something** Somewhat   **9 Judas's own children** i.e., as false
and betraying as the kiss given by Judas to Jesus when he betrayed
him to the high priests.   **11 Your chestnut** i.e., This chestnut color
that people talk about   **12 only** only fashionable   **14 holy bread**
either the unleavened bread of the Eucharist or ordinary leavened
bread that was blessed after the Eucharist and distributed to those
who had not received communion.   **15 cast** (1) chaste, cold
(2) molded (3) cast off.   **Diana** goddess of chastity.   **16 of winter's
sisterhood** i.e., devoted to barrenness and cold

24 **concave** hollow, i.e., insincere   31 **false reckonings** (Tapsters, or
barkeeps, were notorious for inflating bills.)   34 **question** conversation   36 **what** why   38 **brave** fine, excellent   40 **traverse** across,
awry. (A term from medieval jousting or tilting; hence *tilter*, line 41.)
41 **puny** inexperienced. (Literally, junior.)   **but** only   42 **a noble
goose** i.e., a goose-headed young gallant.   42–3 **But . . . guides** But
everything is admirable that youth undertakes under the influence
of folly. (Said sardonically.)   46 **complained of** uttered a lament
against   51 **pale complexion** (Sighing was believed to draw the
blood from the heart.)   54 **will mark** wish to observe.   **remove**
leave here and go.

3.5

Enter Silvius and Phoebe.

SILVIUS
Sweet Phoebe, do not scorn me, do not, Phoebe!
Say that you love me not, but say not so
In bitterness. The common executioner,
Whose heart th'accustomed sight of death makes
  hard,
Falls not the ax upon the humbled neck   5
But first begs pardon. Will you sterner be   6
Than he that dies and lives by bloody drops?   7

Enter Rosalind, Celia, and Corin [behind].

PHOEBE
I would not be thy executioner;
I fly thee, for I would not injure thee.
Thou tell'st me there is murder in mine eye.
'Tis pretty, sure, and very probable,   11
That eyes, that are the frail'st and softest things,
Who shut their coward gates on atomies,   13
Should be called tyrants, butchers, murderers!
Now I do frown on thee with all my heart,
And if mine eyes can wound, now let them kill thee.
Now counterfeit to swoon; why, now fall down,
Or if thou canst not, oh, for shame, for shame,
Lie not, to say mine eyes are murderers!   19
Now show the wound mine eye hath made in thee.
Scratch thee but with a pin, and there remains
Some scar of it; lean upon a rush,   22
The cicatrice and capable impressure   23
Thy palm some moment keeps; but now mine eyes,   24
Which I have darted at thee, hurt thee not,
Nor, I am sure, there is no force in eyes
That can do hurt.
SILVIUS   O dear Phoebe,
If ever—as that "ever" may be near—
You meet in some fresh cheek the power of fancy,   29
Then shall you know the wounds invisible
That love's keen arrows make.
PHOEBE   But till that time
Come not thou near me; and when that time comes,
Afflict me with thy mocks; pity me not,
As till that time I shall not pity thee.   34
ROSALIND *[advancing]*
And why, I pray you? Who might be your mother,   35
That you insult, exult, and all at once,   36

Over the wretched? What though you have no
  beauty—   37
As, by my faith, I see no more in you   38
Than without candle may go dark to bed—   39
Must you be therefore proud and pitiless?
Why, what means this? Why do you look on me?
I see no more in you than in the ordinary   42
Of nature's sale-work. 'Od's my little life,   43
I think she means to tangle my eyes too!   44
No, faith, proud mistress, hope not after it.
'Tis not your inky brows, your black silk hair,
Your bugle eyeballs, nor your cheek of cream   47
That can entame my spirits to your worship.   48
[To Silvius] You foolish shepherd, wherefore do you
  follow her,
Like foggy south, puffing with wind and rain?   50
You are a thousand times a properer man   51
Than she a woman. 'Tis such fools as you
That makes the world full of ill-favored children.   53
'Tis not her glass, but you, that flatters her,   54
And out of you she sees herself more proper   55
Than any of her lineaments can show her.—   56
But, mistress, know yourself. Down on your knees,
And thank heaven, fasting, for a good man's love!
For I must tell you friendly in your ear,
Sell when you can. You are not for all markets.
Cry the man mercy, love him, take his offer;   61
Foul is most foul, being foul to be a scoffer.—   62
So take her to thee, shepherd. Fare you well.
PHOEBE
Sweet youth, I pray you, chide a year together.   64
I had rather hear you chide than this man woo.
ROSALIND *[to Phoebe]* He's fallen in love with your foul-
  ness, *[to Silvius]* and she'll fall in love with my
  anger. If it be so, as fast as she answers thee with
  frowning looks, I'll sauce her with bitter words. *[To* 69
  Phoebe] Why look you so upon me?
PHOEBE   For no ill will I bear you.
ROSALIND
I pray you, do not fall in love with me,
For I am falser than vows made in wine.   73
Besides, I like you not. *[To Silvius]* If you will know
  my house,
'Tis at the tuft of olives here hard by.—
Will you go, sister?—Shepherd, ply her hard.—   76

3.5. Location: The forest.
5 Falls lets fall **6 But first begs pardon** without first begging pardon
(as executioners did in Elizabethan times).   **7 dies . . . drops** makes
his living by the deaths of others. (Stated as an oxymoron.)   **11 sure**
to be sure **13 coward gates on atomies** i.e., sensitive eyelids to protect against specks of dirt   **19 to say** by saying   **22 a rush** a reed
23–4 The cicatrice . . . keeps the scarlike and perceptible impression
is retained by one's palm for a moment   **29 You . . . fancy** you yourself feel the powerful spell of love for some new face   **34 As** since
35 Who . . . mother (1) What human mother could have produced so
inhuman a daughter (2) From what sort of a mother did you learn
such scorn   **36 insult** exult scornfully.   **all at once** all at the same
time

37 have no beauty are not particularly beautiful   **38–9 I see . . . bed**
i.e., I see nothing in your beauty that might not go entirely unnoticed,
nothing to distinguish you from other young women   **42 ordinary**
common run   **43 sale-work** ready-made products, not of the best
quality, not distinctive.   **'Od's** May God save   **44 tangle** ensnare
47 bugle beadlike, black and glassy   **48 to your worship** (1) to the
worship of you (2) to adore Your Worship (as such beauty deserved
an honorific title).   **50 south** south wind (from which came fog and
rain; hence, Silvius's sighs and tears)   **51 properer** better-looking
(since handsome is as handsome does)   **53 ill-favored** ugly
54 glass mirror   **55 out of you** i.e., with you as her mirror   **56 lineaments** features   **61 Cry . . . mercy** Beg the man's pardon   **62 Foul . . .
scoffer** i.e., unattractive behavior like yours is at its most foul when it
consists of scoffing. (Plays on two meanings of *foul*.)   **64 together**
without intermission.   **69 sauce** rebuke   **73 in wine** while drunk.
76 ply her hard woo her energetically.

Come, sister.—Shepherdess, look on him better,
And be not proud. Though all the world could see,   78
None could be so abused in sight as he.—   79
Come, to our flock.   *Exit [with Celia and Corin].*

PHOEBE
Dead shepherd, now I find thy saw of might,   81
"Who ever loved that loved not at first sight?"   82

SILVIUS
Sweet Phoebe—

PHOEBE   Ha, what say'st thou, Silvius?

SILVIUS   Sweet Phoebe, pity me.

PHOEBE
Why, I am sorry for thee, gentle Silvius.

SILVIUS
Wherever sorrow is, relief would be.   86
If you do sorrow at my grief in love,
By giving love, your sorrow and my grief
Were both extermined.   89

PHOEBE
Thou hast my love. Is not that neighborly?   90

SILVIUS
I would have you.

PHOEBE   Why, that were covetousness.   91
Silvius, the time was that I hated thee,
And yet it is not that I bear thee love;   93
But since that thou canst talk of love so well,   94
Thy company, which erst was irksome to me,   95
I will endure, and I'll employ thee too.
But do not look for further recompense
Than thine own gladness that thou art employed.

SILVIUS
So holy and so perfect is my love,
And I in such a poverty of grace,   100
That I shall think it a most plenteous crop
To glean the broken ears after the man
That the main harvest reaps. Loose now and then
A scattered smile, and that I'll live upon.   104

PHOEBE
Know'st thou the youth that spoke to me erewhile?   105

SILVIUS
Not very well, but I have met him oft,
And he hath bought the cottage and the bounds   107
That the old carlot once was master of.   108

PHOEBE
Think not I love him, though I ask for him.
'Tis but a peevish boy—yet he talks well—
But what care I for words? Yet words do well

When he that speaks them pleases those that hear.
It is a pretty youth—not very pretty—
But sure he's proud—and yet his pride becomes him.
He'll make a proper man. The best thing in him   115
Is his complexion; and faster than his tongue
Did make offense, his eye did heal it up.
He is not very tall—yet for his years he's tall.
His leg is but so-so—and yet 'tis well.
There was a pretty redness in his lip,
A little riper and more lusty red
Than that mixed in his cheek; 'twas just the difference
Betwixt the constant red and mingled damask.   123
There be some women, Silvius, had they marked him
In parcels as I did, would have gone near   125
To fall in love with him; but for my part,   126
I love him not nor hate him not; and yet
I have more cause to hate him than to love him.
For what had he to do to chide at me?   129
He said mine eyes were black and my hair black,
And, now I am remembered, scorned at me.   131
I marvel why I answered not again.   132
But that's all one; omittance is no quittance.   133
I'll write to him a very taunting letter,
And thou shalt bear it. Wilt thou, Silvius?

SILVIUS
Phoebe, with all my heart.

PHOEBE   I'll write it straight;   136
The matter's in my head and in my heart.
I will be bitter with him and passing short.   138
Go with me, Silvius.   *Exeunt.*

❖

4.1

Enter Rosalind and Celia, and Jaques.

JAQUES   I prithee, pretty youth, let me be better acquainted with thee.

ROSALIND   They say you are a melancholy fellow.

JAQUES   I am so. I do love it better than laughing.

ROSALIND   Those that are in extremity of either are   5
abominable fellows and betray themselves to every
modern censure worse than drunkards.   7

JAQUES   Why, 'tis good to be sad and say nothing.

ROSALIND   Why then, 'tis good to be a post.

JAQUES   I have neither the scholar's melancholy, which
is emulation, nor the musician's, which is fantastical,   11
nor the courtier's, which is proud, nor the soldier's,
which is ambitious, nor the lawyer's, which is politic,   13
nor the lady's, which is nice, nor the lover's, which is   14

---

78 **could see** could look at you   79 **abused in sight** deceived through
the eyes   81 **Dead shepherd** i.e., Christopher Marlowe, who died in
1593.   **saw** saying.   **of might** forceful, convincing   82 **Who . . . sight?**
(From Marlowe's *Hero and Leander,* Sestiad 1, 176, first published in
1598.)   86 **Wherever . . . be** Sorrow cries out for relief.   89 **Were both
extermined** would both be exterminated, ended.   90 **Is . . . neighborly?**
i.e., May not I love you in the sense of loving one's neighbor as oneself?
91 **covetousness** (The tenth commandment forbids coveting anything
that is one's neighbor's.)   93 **yet it is not** the time has not yet come
94 **since that** since   95 **erst** formerly   100 **poverty of grace** lack of
reciprocated affection   104 **scattered** thrown negligently, as in the
gleanings of the harvest   105 **erewhile** just now.   107 **bounds** pastures   108 **carlot** churl, countryman. (Perhaps a proper name.)

115 **proper** handsome   123 **mingled damask** mingled red and white,
the color of the damask rose.   125 **In parcels** bit by bit   125–6 **gone . . .
fall** been on the point of falling   129 **what . . . do** what business had
he   131 **am remembered** remember   132 **again** back.   133 **But . . .
quittance** i.e., But just the same, my failure to answer him doesn't
mean I won't do so later.   136 **straight** immediately   138 **passing
short** exceedingly curt.
4.1. Location: The forest.
5 **are . . . of** go to extremes in   7 **modern censure** common judgment
11 **emulation** envy (of the fellow scholar).   **fantastical** extravagantly fanciful
13 **politic** grave and diplomatic, calculated   14 **nice** fastidious

all these; but it is a melancholy of mine own, com- 15
pounded of many simples, extracted from many 16
objects, and indeed the sundry contemplation of my 17
travels, in which my often rumination wraps me in a 18
most humorous sadness. 19

ROSALIND   A traveler! By my faith, you have great
reason to be sad. I fear you have sold your own lands
to see other men's. Then to have seen much and to
have nothing is to have rich eyes and poor hands.

JAQUES   Yes, I have gained my experience.

Enter Orlando.

ROSALIND   And your experience makes you sad. I had
rather have a fool to make me merry than experience
to make me sad—and to travel for it too! 27

ORLANDO   Good day and happiness, dear Rosalind!

JAQUES   Nay, then, God b'wi'you, an you talk in blank 29
verse.

ROSALIND   Farewell, Monsieur Traveler. Look you lisp 31
and wear strange suits, disable all the benefits of your 32
own country, be out of love with your nativity, and 33
almost chide God for making you that countenance
you are, or I will scarce think you have swam in a 35
gondola.   [*Exit Jaques.*] 36
Why, how now, Orlando, where have you been all this
while? You a lover? An you serve me such another
trick, never come in my sight more.

ORLANDO   My fair Rosalind, I come within an hour of
my promise.

ROSALIND   Break an hour's promise in love? He that will
divide a minute into a thousand parts and break but
a part of the thousandth part of a minute in the affairs
of love, it may be said of him that Cupid hath clapped 45
him o'th' shoulder, but I'll warrant him heart-whole. 46

ORLANDO   Pardon me, dear Rosalind.

ROSALIND   Nay, an you be so tardy, come no more in
my sight. I had as lief be wooed of a snail. 49

ORLANDO   Of a snail?

ROSALIND   Ay, of a snail; for though he comes slowly,
he carries his house on his head—a better jointure, I 52
think, than you make a woman. Besides, he brings his 53
destiny with him.

ORLANDO   What's that?

ROSALIND   Why, horns, which such as you are fain to 56
be beholding to your wives for. But he comes armed in 57

his fortune and prevents the slander of his wife. 58

ORLANDO   Virtue is no horn-maker, and my Rosalind is
virtuous.

ROSALIND   And I am your Rosalind.

CELIA   It pleases him to call you so; but he hath a Rosalind of a better leer than you. 63

ROSALIND   Come, woo me, woo me, for now I am in a
holiday humor and like enough to consent. What
would you say to me now, an I were your very, very
Rosalind?

ORLANDO   I would kiss before I spoke.

ROSALIND   Nay, you were better speak first, and when
you were graveled for lack of matter, you might take 70
occasion to kiss. Very good orators, when they are out, 71
they will spit; and for lovers lacking—God warrant 72
us!—matter, the cleanliest shift is to kiss. 73

ORLANDO   How if the kiss be denied?

ROSALIND   Then she puts you to entreaty, and there
begins new matter.

ORLANDO   Who could be out, being before his beloved
mistress?

ROSALIND   Marry, that should you, if I were your
mistress, or I should think my honesty ranker than 80
my wit.

ORLANDO   What, of my suit? 82

ROSALIND   Not out of your apparel, and yet out of your
suit. Am not I your Rosalind?

ORLANDO   I take some joy to say you are, because I
would be talking of her.

ROSALIND   Well, in her person I say I will not have you.

ORLANDO   Then in mine own person, I die.

ROSALIND   No, faith, die by attorney. The poor world is 89
almost six thousand years old, and in all this time 90
there was not any man died in his own person, 91
videlicet, in a love cause. Troilus had his brains 92
dashed out with a Grecian club, yet he did what he 93
could to die before, and he is one of the patterns of
love. Leander, he would have lived many a fair year 95
though Hero had turned nun, if it had not been for a
hot midsummer night; for, good youth, he went but
forth to wash him in the Hellespont and being taken
with the cramp was drowned; and the foolish chron-

15–19 compounded . . . sadness made up of many ingredients,
extracted from the many objects of my observation and, indeed, from
the diversified considerations of my travels, my frequent rumination
upon which wraps me in a most whimsical and moody sadness.
27 travel (Meaning also "travail," labor.)   **29 an** if   **31 Look** Be sure.
(Said ironically.)   **lisp** i.e., affect a foreign accent   **32 disable** disparage
33 nativity country of birth   **35 are** i.e., have   **35–6 swam . . . gondola**
floated in a gondola, i.e., been in Venice, where almost all travelers
go.   **45–6 Cupid . . . heart-whole** Cupid may have tried to arrest him,
but I'm sure his heart remains unengaged. (Arresting officers customarily grasped the culprit by the shoulder.)   **49 lief** willingly.   **of** by
52 jointure marriage settlement   **53 than . . . woman** than you,
Orlando, are able to settle on your prospective wife.
56 horns (1) snails' horns (2) cuckold's horns, signs of an unfaithful
wife.   **fain** obliged   **57 beholding** beholden, indebted

57–8 But . . . fortune The snail comes already provided with the
horns that are his nature and his destiny, thereby forestalling the
scandal that would otherwise attach to his wife. (Since a snail is naturally horned, no scandal can be adduced from them.)   **63 leer**
appearance, color   **70 graveled** stuck. (Literally, run aground on a
shoal.)   **71 out** at a loss through forgetfulness or confusion   **72 warrant** defend   **73 shift** tactic   **80 honesty ranker** chastity more corrupt. (Rosalind would rely on her wit to keep her lover off balance
and thus defend her chastity. She may use Orlando's *out*, line 77, in a
sexual sense of not being admitted.)   **82 of my suit** (Orlando means
"out of my suit," at a loss for words in my wooing; but Rosalind puns
on the meaning "suit of clothes"; to be out of apparel would be to be
undressed.)   **89 attorney** proxy.   **90 six . . . old** (A common figure in
biblical calculation.)   **91 died** who died   **92 videlicet** namely.
Troilus hero of the story of Troilus and Cressida, in which he remains
faithful to her, but she is faithless to him   **92–3 had . . . club** (Troilus
was slain by Achilles with sword or spear in more traditional
accounts. Rosalind's version is calculatedly unromantic.)   **95 Leander** the hero of the story of Hero and Leander, who lost his life swimming the Hellespont to visit his sweetheart. (Rosalind's account of the
cramp again undercuts romantic idealism.)

iclers of that age found it was—Hero of Sestos. But these are all lies. Men have died from time to time, and worms have eaten them, but not for love. 100

ORLANDO   I would not have my right Rosalind of this mind, for I protest her frown might kill me. 103 104

ROSALIND   By this hand, it will not kill a fly. But come, now I will be your Rosalind in a more coming-on disposition; and ask me what you will, I will grant it. 106

ORLANDO   Then love me, Rosalind.

ROSALIND   Yes, faith, will I, Fridays and Saturdays and all.

ORLANDO   And wilt thou have me?

ROSALIND   Ay, and twenty such.

ORLANDO   What sayest thou?

ROSALIND   Are you not good?

ORLANDO   I hope so.

ROSALIND   Why then, can one desire too much of a good thing?—Come, sister, you shall be the priest and marry us.—Give me your hand, Orlando.— What do you say, sister?

ORLANDO   Pray thee, marry us.

CELIA   I cannot say the words.

ROSALIND   You must begin, "Will you, Orlando—"

CELIA   Go to. Will you, Orlando, have to wife this Rosalind? 123

ORLANDO   I will.

ROSALIND   Ay, but when?

ORLANDO   Why now, as fast as she can marry us.

ROSALIND   Then you must say, "I take thee, Rosalind, for wife."

ORLANDO   I take thee, Rosalind, for wife.

ROSALIND   I might ask you for your commission; but I do take thee, Orlando, for my husband. There's a girl goes before the priest, and certainly a woman's thought runs before her actions. 131 133 134

ORLANDO   So do all thoughts; they are winged.

ROSALIND   Now tell me how long you would have her after you have possessed her.

ORLANDO   For ever and a day.

ROSALIND   Say "a day," without the "ever." No, no, Orlando, men are April when they woo, December when they wed. Maids are May when they are maids, but the sky changes when they are wives. I will be more jealous of thee than a Barbary cock-pigeon over his hen, more clamorous than a parrot against rain, more newfangled than an ape, more giddy in my desires than a monkey. I will weep for nothing, like Diana in 143 144 145 146

the fountain, and I will do that when you are disposed to be merry; I will laugh like a hyena, and that when thou art inclined to sleep. 147

ORLANDO   But will my Rosalind do so?

ROSALIND   By my life, she will do as I do.

ORLANDO   Oh, but she is wise.

ROSALIND   Or else she could not have the wit to do this. The wiser, the waywarder. Make the doors upon a woman's wit, and it will out at the casement; shut that, and 'twill out at the keyhole; stop that, 'twill fly with the smoke out at the chimney. 154 155

ORLANDO   A man that had a wife with such a wit, he might say, "Wit, whither wilt?" 159

ROSALIND   Nay, you might keep that check for it till you met your wife's wit going to your neighbor's bed. 160

ORLANDO   And what wit could wit have to excuse that?

ROSALIND   Marry, to say she came to seek you there. You shall never take her without her answer unless you take her without her tongue. Oh, that woman that cannot make her fault her husband's occasion, let her never nurse her child herself, for she will breed it like a fool! 166 167

ORLANDO   For these two hours, Rosalind, I will leave thee.

ROSALIND   Alas, dear love, I cannot lack thee two hours!

ORLANDO   I must attend the Duke at dinner. By two o'clock I will be with thee again.

ROSALIND   Ay, go your ways, go your ways. I knew what you would prove. My friends told me as much, and I thought no less. That flattering tongue of yours won me. 'Tis but one cast away, and so, come, death! Two o'clock is your hour? 177

ORLANDO   Ay, sweet Rosalind.

ROSALIND   By my troth, and in good earnest, and so God mend me, and by all pretty oaths that are not dangerous, if you break one jot of your promise or come one minute behind your hour, I will think you the most pathetical break-promise, and the most hollow lover, and the most unworthy of her you call Rosalind, that may be chosen out of the gross band of the unfaithful. Therefore beware my censure, and keep your promise. 182 184 186

ORLANDO   With no less religion than if thou wert indeed my Rosalind. So adieu. 189

---

100 found it was arrived at the verdict that the cause (of his death) was **103 right** real   **104 protest** insist, proclaim   **106 coming-on** compliant **123 Go to** (An exclamation of mild impatience.)   **131 ask . . . commission** ask you what authority you have for taking her (since no one is here to give the bride away and since she herself has not yet consented) **133 goes . . . priest** who anticipates before the "priest" has even asked the question   **134 runs . . . actions** i.e., goes flightily on, outstripping sane conduct.   **143 Barbary cock-pigeon** an ornamental pigeon actually from the orient, not the Barbary (north) coast of Africa. (Following Pliny, the cock-pigeon's jealousy was often contrasted with the mildness of the hen.)   **144 against** in expectation of   **145 newfangled** infatuated with novelty **146 for nothing** for no apparent reason

146-7 Diana in the fountain (Diana frequently appeared as the centerpiece of fountains. Stow's *Survey of London* describes the setting up of a fountain with a Diana in green marble in the year 1596.) **154 The wiser, the waywarder** i.e., The more experienced in the war of the sexes, the more insisting on her own way.   **Make** Make fast, shut **155 casement** hinged window   **159 Wit, whither wilt?** Wit, where are you going? (A common Elizabethan expression implying that one is talking fantastically, with a wildly wandering wit.)   **160 check** retort **166 make . . . occasion** i.e., turn a defense of her own conduct into an accusation against her husband   **167 breed it** bring it up   **177 but one cast away** only one woman jilted   **182 dangerous** i.e., blasphemous. (Rosalind's oaths are decorous.)   **184 pathetical** awful, miserable **186 gross band** whole troop   **189 religion** strict fidelity

ROSALIND   Well, Time is the old justice that examines all such offenders, and let Time try. Adieu.   192

Exit [Orlando].

CELIA   You have simply misused our sex in your love prate. We must have your doublet and hose plucked over your head and show the world what the bird hath done to her own nest.   193 194 195 196

ROSALIND   Oh, coz, coz, coz, my pretty little coz, that thou didst know how many fathom deep I am in love! But it cannot be sounded; my affection hath an unknown bottom, like the Bay of Portugal.   199

CELIA   Or rather, bottomless, that as fast as you pour affection in, it runs out.   201

ROSALIND   No, that same wicked bastard of Venus, that was begot of thought, conceived of spleen, and born of madness, that blind rascally boy that abuses everyone's eyes because his own are out, let him be judge how deep I am in love. I'll tell thee, Aliena, I cannot be out of the sight of Orlando. I'll go find a shadow and sigh till he come.   203 204 205 206 208

CELIA   And I'll sleep.   *Exeunt.*

❧

4.2

Enter Jaques and Lords [dressed as] foresters.

JAQUES   Which is he that killed the deer?

FIRST LORD   Sir, it was I.

JAQUES   Let's present him to the Duke, like a Roman conqueror, and it would do well to set the deer's horns upon his head for a branch of victory. Have you no song, Forester, for this purpose?   5

SECOND LORD   Yes, sir.

JAQUES   Sing it. 'Tis no matter how it be in tune, so it make noise enough.   *Music.*   8

Song.

SECOND LORD [*sings*]
    What shall he have that killed the deer?
    His leather skin and horns to wear.
    Then sing him home; the rest shall bear   12
        This burden.   13
    Take thou no scorn to wear the horn;   14
    It was a crest ere thou wast born.
        Thy father's father wore it,
        And thy father bore it.
    The horn, the horn, the lusty horn
    Is not a thing to laugh to scorn.   *Exeunt.*

❧

4.3

Enter Rosalind and Celia.

ROSALIND   How say you now? Is it not past two o'clock? And here much Orlando!   2

CELIA   I warrant you, with pure love and troubled brain he hath ta'en his bow and arrows and is gone forth—to sleep.   3

Enter Silvius [with a letter].

    Look who comes here.

SILVIUS [*to Rosalind*]
    My errand is to you, fair youth.
    My gentle Phoebe bid me give you this.

[*He gives the letter.*]

    I know not the contents, but as I guess,
    By the stern brow and waspish action
    Which she did use as she was writing of it,
    It bears an angry tenor. Pardon me;
    I am but as a guiltless messenger.

ROSALIND [*examining the letter*]
    Patience herself would startle at this letter   14
    And play the swaggerer. Bear this, bear all!   15
    She says I am not fair, that I lack manners;
    She calls me proud, and that she could not love me
    Were man as rare as phoenix. 'Od's my will!   18
    Her love is not the hare that I do hunt.
    Why writes she so to me? Well, shepherd, well,
    This is a letter of your own device.

SILVIUS
    No, I protest, I know not the contents.
    Phoebe did write it.

ROSALIND   Come, come, you are a fool,
    And turned into the extremity of love.   24
    I saw her hand; she has a leathern hand,   25
    A freestone-colored hand. I verily did think   26
    That her old gloves were on, but 'twas her hands;
    She has a huswife's hand—but that's no matter.   28
    I say she never did invent this letter;
    This is a man's invention and his hand.

SILVIUS   Sure it is hers.

ROSALIND
    Why, 'tis a boisterous and a cruel style,
    A style for challengers. Why, she defies me,
    Like Turk to Christian. Women's gentle brain
    Could not drop forth such giant-rude invention,

192 **try** determine, judge.   193 **simply misused** absolutely slandered   194–6 **We . . . nest** i.e., We must expose you for what you are, a woman, and show everyone how a woman has defamed her own kind just as a foul bird proverbially fouls its own nest.   199 **sounded** measured for depth   201 **that** so that   203 **bastard of Venus** i.e., Cupid, son of Venus and Mercury (or Zeus) rather than Vulcan, Venus's husband   204 **thought** fancy.   **spleen** i.e., impulse   205 **abuses** deceives   206 **out** blinded   208 **shadow** shady spot
4.2. Location: The forest.
5 **branch** wreath   8 **so** provided that   12–13 **bear This burden** (1) sing this refrain (2) wear the horns that all cuckolds must wear.   14 **Take . . . scorn** Be not ashamed. (Alludes to joke about cuckold's horns.)

4.3. Location: The forest.
2 **much** (Said ironically: A fat lot we see of Orlando!)   3 **warrant** assure   14–15 **Patience . . . all!** Patience herself would be startled into a violent display by this letter. If one were to put up with such a missive, one would have to accept any insult!   18 **phoenix** a fabulous bird of Arabia, the only one of its kind, which lived five hundred years, died in flames, and was reborn of its own ashes.   **'Od's my will!** (An oath: "May God's will be done!")   24 **turned** transformed   25 **leathern** leathery   26 **freestone-colored** sandstone-colored, brownish-yellow   28 **hand** handwriting. (With play on "dishpan hands.")

Such Ethiop words, blacker in their effect   36
Than in their countenance. Will you hear the letter?   37

SILVIUS
So please you, for I never heard it yet;
Yet, heard too much of Phoebe's cruelty.

ROSALIND
She Phoebes me. Mark how the tyrant writes.   40
    (*Read*) "Art thou god to shepherd turned,
    That a maiden's heart hath burned?"
Can a woman rail thus?

SILVIUS   Call you this railing?

ROSALIND
    (*Read*) "Why, thy godhead laid apart,   45
    War'st thou with a woman's heart?"
Did you ever hear such railing?
    "Whiles the eye of man did woo me,
    That could do no vengeance to me."—   49
Meaning me a beast.   50
    "If the scorn of your bright eyne   51
    Have power to raise such love in mine,
    Alack, in me what strange effect
    Would they work in mild aspect!   54
    Whiles you chid me, I did love;   55
    How then might your prayers move!
    He that brings this love to thee
    Little knows this love in me;
    And by him seal up thy mind,   59
    Whether that thy youth and kind   60
    Will the faithful offer take
    Of me and all that I can make,   62
    Or else by him my love deny,
    And then I'll study how to die."

SILVIUS   Call you this chiding?

CELIA   Alas, poor shepherd!

ROSALIND   Do you pity him? No, he deserves no pity.—
Wilt thou love such a woman? What, to make thee an   68
instrument and play false strains upon thee? Not to be   69
endured! Well, go your way to her, for I see love hath
made thee a tame snake, and say this to her: that if she   71
love me, I charge her to love thee; if she will not, I will
never have her unless thou entreat for her. If you be a
true lover, hence, and not a word; for here comes
more company.   *Exit Silvius.*

Enter Oliver.

OLIVER
Good morrow, fair ones. Pray you, if you know,

Where in the purlieus of this forest stands   77
A sheepcote fenced about with olive trees?

CELIA
West of this place, down in the neighbor bottom;   79
The rank of osiers by the murmuring stream   80
Left on your right hand brings you to the place.   81
But at this hour the house doth keep itself;
There's none within.

OLIVER
If that an eye may profit by a tongue,
Then should I know you by description,
Such garments and such years: "The boy is fair,
Of female favor, and bestows himself   87
Like a ripe sister; the woman, low   88
And browner than her brother." Are not you
The owner of the house I did inquire for?

CELIA
It is no boast, being asked, to say we are.

OLIVER
Orlando doth commend him to you both,   92
And to that youth he calls his Rosalind
He sends this bloody napkin. Are not you he?   94
    [*He produces a bloody handkerchief.*]

ROSALIND
I am. What must we understand by this?

OLIVER
Some of my shame, if you will know of me
What man I am, and how, and why, and where
This handkerchief was stained.

CELIA   I pray you, tell it.

OLIVER
When last the young Orlando parted from you
He left a promise to return again
Within an hour, and, pacing through the forest,
Chewing the food of sweet and bitter fancy,   102
Lo, what befell! He threw his eye aside,
And mark what object did present itself:
Under an old oak, whose boughs were mossed with
    age
And high top bald with dry antiquity,
A wretched, ragged man, o'ergrown with hair,
Lay sleeping on his back. About his neck
A green and gilded snake had wreathed itself,
Who with her head, nimble in threats, approached
The opening of his mouth; but suddenly,
Seeing Orlando, it unlinked itself   112
And with indented glides did slip away   113
Into a bush, under which bush's shade
A lioness, with udders all drawn dry,   115
Lay couching, head on ground, with catlike watch,
When that the sleeping man should stir; for 'tis   117

---

36 Ethiop i.e., black   **36–7 blacker ... countenance** even blacker in what they say than in their black appearance on the page.
40 Phoebes me i.e., addresses me in her cruel style.   **45 thy ... apart** having laid aside your godhead (for human shape)   **49 vengeance** mischief, harm   **50 Meaning me** i.e., Implying that I am   **51 eyne** eyes   **54 in mild aspect** i.e., if they looked on me mildly. (Suggests also astrological influence.)   **55 chid** chided   **59 by ... mind** i.e., send your thoughts in a letter via Silvius   **60 Whether ... kind** if your youthful nature   **62 make** make offer of   **68–9 to make ... instrument** to make an instrument (i.e., messenger) of you. (With a suggestion of making a person into a musical instrument; cf. *Hamlet*, 3.2.363, "You would play upon me," etc.)   **69 strains** parts of a piece of music   **71 tame snake** i.e., pathetic wretch

77 purlieus borders, boundaries   **79 neighbor bottom** neighboring dell   **80 rank of osiers** row of willows   **81 Left** left behind, passed   **87 favor** features.   **bestows** comports   **88 ripe** mature or elder   **92 doth commend him** sends his greetings   **94 napkin** handkerchief.   **102 Chewing ... fancy** ruminating on the bittersweet nature of love   **112 unlinked** uncoiled   **113 indented** zigzag   **115 with ... dry** (It would therefore be fierce with hunger.)   **117 When** for the moment

The royal disposition of that beast
To prey on nothing that doth seem as dead.
This seen, Orlando did approach the man
And found it was his brother, his elder brother.

CELIA
Oh, I have heard him speak of that same brother,
And he did render him the most unnatural   123
That lived amongst men.

OLIVER   And well he might so do,
For well I know he was unnatural.

ROSALIND
But to Orlando: did he leave him there,
Food to the sucked and hungry lioness?

OLIVER
Twice did he turn his back and purposed so;
But kindness, nobler ever than revenge,
And nature, stronger than his just occasion,   130
Made him give battle to the lioness,
Who quickly fell before him; in which hurtling   132
From miserable slumber I awaked.

CELIA
Are you his brother?

ROSALIND   Was't you he rescued?

CELIA
Was't you that did so oft contrive to kill him?

OLIVER
'Twas I, but 'tis not I. I do not shame   136
To tell you what I was, since my conversion
So sweetly tastes, being the thing I am.

ROSALIND
But for the bloody napkin?

OLIVER   By and by.   139
When from the first to last betwixt us two
Tears our recounts had most kindly bathed,   141
As how I came into that desert place,
In brief, he led me to the gentle Duke,
Who gave me fresh array and entertainment,   144
Committing me unto my brother's love;
Who led me instantly unto his cave,
There stripped himself, and here upon his arm
The lioness had torn some flesh away,
Which all this while had bled; and now he fainted
And cried, in fainting, upon Rosalind.
Brief, I recovered him, bound up his wound,   151
And after some small space, being strong at heart,
He sent me hither, stranger as I am,
To tell this story, that you might excuse
His broken promise, and to give this napkin
Dyed in his blood unto the shepherd youth
That he in sport doth call his Rosalind.
                                   [Rosalind swoons.]

CELIA
Why, how now, Ganymede, sweet Ganymede!

OLIVER
Many will swoon when they do look on blood.

CELIA
There is more in it.—Cousin Ganymede!

OLIVER   Look, he recovers.

ROSALIND   I would I were at home.

CELIA   We'll lead you thither.—
I pray you, will you take him by the arm?
                            [They help Rosalind up.]

OLIVER   Be of good cheer, youth. You a man? You lack
a man's heart.

ROSALIND   I do so, I confess it. Ah, sirrah, a body would 167
think this was well counterfeited. I pray you, tell my
brother how well I counterfeited. Heigh-ho!

OLIVER   This was not counterfeit. There is too great testimony in your complexion that it was a passion of   171
earnest.   172

ROSALIND   Counterfeit, I assure you.

OLIVER   Well then, take a good heart and counterfeit to
be a man.

ROSALIND   So I do; but, i'faith, I should have been a
woman by right.

CELIA   Come, you look paler and paler. Pray you, draw
homewards.—Good sir, go with us.

OLIVER
That will I, for I must bear answer back
How you excuse my brother, Rosalind.

ROSALIND   I shall devise something. But, I pray you,
commend my counterfeiting to him. Will you go?
                                              Exeunt.

❖

5.1

Enter [Touchstone the] Clown and Audrey.

TOUCHSTONE   We shall find a time, Audrey. Patience,
gentle Audrey.

AUDREY   Faith, the priest was good enough, for all the   3
old gentleman's saying.   4

TOUCHSTONE   A most wicked Sir Oliver, Audrey, a most
vile Mar-text. But Audrey, there is a youth here in the
forest lays claim to you.

AUDREY   Ay, I know who 'tis. He hath no interest in me   8
in the world. Here comes the man you mean.

Enter William.

TOUCHSTONE   It is meat and drink to me to see a clown.   10
By my troth, we that have good wits have much to   11
answer for. We shall be flouting; we cannot hold.   12

WILLIAM   Good even, Audrey.

AUDREY   God gi' good even, William.   14

WILLIAM   And good even to you, sir.
                            [He removes his hat.]

---

123 **render him** describe him as   130 **just occasion** just opportunity
and motive (for revenge)   132 **hurtling** conflict, tumult   136 **do not
shame** am not ashamed   139 **for** as regards   141 **recounts**
relating of events (to one another)   144 **array** attire.   **entertainment**
hospitality, provision   151 **Brief** In brief.   **recovered** revived

167 **a body** anybody   171–2 **a passion of earnest** a genuine swoon.
5.1. Location: The forest.
3–4 **the old gentleman's** i.e., Jaques's   8 **interest in** claim to
10 **clown** i.e., country yokel.   11–12 **we . . . hold** i.e., we professional
fools have much to answer for in providing a model of folly that
yokels like William are too apt to imitate. We fools are always scoffing; we can't restrain ourselves.   14 **God gi' good even** God give you
good evening. (Here, afternoon.)

TOUCHSTONE Good even, gentle friend. Cover thy head, cover thy head. Nay, prithee be covered. How old are you, friend?

WILLIAM Five-and-twenty, sir.

TOUCHSTONE A ripe age. Is thy name William?

WILLIAM William, sir.

TOUCHSTONE A fair name. Wast born i'th' forest here?

WILLIAM Ay, sir, I thank God.

TOUCHSTONE "Thank God"—a good answer. Art rich?

WILLIAM Faith, sir, so-so.

TOUCHSTONE "So-so" is good, very good, very excellent good; and yet it is not, it is but so-so. Art thou wise?

WILLIAM Ay, sir, I have a pretty wit.

TOUCHSTONE Why, thou say'st well. I do now remember a saying, "The fool doth think he is wise, but the wise man knows himself to be a fool." The heathen 32 philosopher, when he had a desire to eat a grape, 33 would open his lips when he put it into his mouth, 34 meaning thereby that grapes were made to eat and 35 lips to open. You do love this maid? 36

WILLIAM I do, sir.

TOUCHSTONE Give me your hand. Art thou learned?

WILLIAM No, sir.

TOUCHSTONE Then learn this of me: to have is to have. For it is a figure in rhetoric that drink, being poured 41 out of a cup into a glass, by filling the one doth empty 42 the other. For all your writers do consent that *ipse* is 43 he. Now, you are not *ipse*, for I am he. 44

WILLIAM Which he, sir?

TOUCHSTONE He, sir, that must marry this woman. Therefore, you clown, abandon—which is in the vulgar "leave"—the society—which in the boorish is "company"—of this female—which in the common is "woman"; which together is, abandon the society of this female, or, clown, thou perishest; or, to thy better understanding, diest; or, to wit, I kill thee, make thee away, translate thy life into death, thy liberty into bondage. I will deal in poison with thee, or in basti- 54 nado, or in steel; I will bandy with thee in faction, I 55 will o'errun thee with policy; I will kill thee a hundred 56 and fifty ways. Therefore tremble, and depart.

AUDREY Do, good William.

WILLIAM God rest you merry, sir. *Exit.* 59

Enter Corin.

CORIN Our master and mistress seeks you. Come, away, away!

TOUCHSTONE Trip, Audrey, trip, Audrey!—I attend, I 62 attend. *Exeunt.*

❋

5.2

Enter Orlando [with his wounded arm in a sling] and Oliver.

ORLANDO Is't possible that on so little acquaintance you should like her? That but seeing, you should love her? And loving, woo? And, wooing, she should grant? And will you persevere to enjoy her?

OLIVER Neither call the giddiness of it in question, the 5 poverty of her, the small acquaintance, my sudden wooing, nor her sudden consenting; but say with me, "I love Aliena"; say with her that she loves me; consent with both that we may enjoy each other. It shall be to your good; for my father's house and all the revenue that was old Sir Rowland's will I estate upon 11 you, and here live and die a shepherd.

Enter Rosalind.

ORLANDO You have my consent. Let your wedding be tomorrow. Thither will I invite the Duke and all 's 14 contented followers. Go you and prepare Aliena; for look you, here comes my Rosalind.

ROSALIND God save you, brother. 17

OLIVER And you, fair sister. [*Exit.*] 18

ROSALIND O my dear Orlando, how it grieves me to see thee wear thy heart in a scarf! 20

ORLANDO It is my arm.

ROSALIND I thought thy heart had been wounded with the claws of a lion.

ORLANDO Wounded it is, but with the eyes of a lady.

ROSALIND Did your brother tell you how I countefeited to swoon when he showed me your handkerchief?

ORLANDO Ay, and greater wonders than that.

ROSALIND Oh, I know where you are. Nay, 'tis true. 28 There was never anything so sudden but the fight of two rams and Caesar's thrasonical brag of "I came, 30 saw, and overcame." For your brother and my sister 31 no sooner met but they looked, no sooner looked but they loved, no sooner loved but they sighed, no sooner sighed but they asked one another the reason, no sooner knew the reason but they sought the remedy; and in these degrees have they made a pair of 36

32–6 The heathen . . . open (This bit of fatuously self-evident wisdom parodies the logical proofs of the ancient philosophers. William, whose mouth is no doubt gaping like a rustic's, is invited to consider the consequences of his desire.) **41 figure** figure of speech, trope **41–3 drink . . . other** i.e., both Touchstone and William cannot possess Audrey. **43–4 For . . . am he** For all the ancient authorities concur that the word *ipse* in Latin means "he." But you are not *ipse*, i.e., the man of the hour, the one destined to win Audrey, for I am that man. **54–5 bastinado** beating with a cudgel **55 bandy** contend. **in faction** factiously **56 o'errun . . . policy** overwhelm you with craft, cunning **59 God . . . merry** (A common salutation at parting.)

62 Trip Go nimbly
5.2. Location: The forest.
5 giddiness sudden speed **11 estate** settle as an estate, bestow **14 all 's** all his **17 brother** i.e., brother-in-law to be. **18 sister** (Rosalind is still dressed as a man, but Oliver evidently adopts the fiction that "Ganymede" is Orlando's Rosalind. See 4.3.92 ff.) **20 scarf** sling. **28 where you are** i.e., what you mean. **30 thrasonical** boastful. (From Thraso, the boaster in Terence's *Eunuchus*.) **30–1 "I came . . . overcame"** (Julius Caesar's famous pronouncement, *Veni, vidi, vici*, on the occasion of his victory over Pharnaces at Zela in 47 B.C.) **36 degrees** (Plays on the original meaning, "steps," and also on the rhetorical figure of climax illustrated by Rosalind's sentence as it moves from one step to the next by linked words, *looked, loved, sighed,* etc.) **pair** flight

stairs to marriage which they will climb incontinent, or 37
else be incontinent before marriage. They are in the
very wrath of love, and they will together. Clubs 39
cannot part them.

ORLANDO   They shall be married tomorrow, and I will
bid the Duke to the nuptial. But oh, how bitter a thing
it is to look into happiness through another man's
eyes! By so much the more shall I tomorrow be at the
height of heart-heaviness, by how much I shall think
my brother happy in having what he wishes for.

ROSALIND   Why, then, tomorrow I cannot serve your
turn for Rosalind?

ORLANDO   I can live no longer by thinking.

ROSALIND   I will weary you then no longer with idle
talking. Know of me then—for now I speak to some
purpose—that I know you are a gentleman of good con- 52
ceit. I speak not this that you should bear a good opin- 53
ion of my knowledge, insomuch I say I know you are; 54
neither do I labor for a greater esteem than may in 55
some little measure draw a belief from you to do 56
yourself good, and not to grace me. Believe then, if you 57
please, that I can do strange things. I have, since I was
three year old, conversed with a magician, most 59
profound in his art and yet not damnable. If you do 60
love Rosalind so near the heart as your gesture cries it 61
out, when your brother marries Aliena shall you 62
marry her. I know into what straits of fortune she is 63
driven; and it is not impossible to me, if it appear not
inconvenient to you, to set her before your eyes 65
tomorrow, human as she is, and without any danger. 66

ORLANDO   Speak'st thou in sober meanings? 67

ROSALIND   By my life, I do, which I tender dearly, 68
though I say I am a magician. Therefore, put you in 69
your best array; bid your friends; for if you will be 70
married tomorrow, you shall, and to Rosalind, if you
will.

Enter Silvius and Phoebe.

Look, here comes a lover of mine and a lover of hers.

PHOEBE [*to Rosalind*]
Youth, you have done me much ungentleness, 74
To show the letter that I writ to you.

ROSALIND
I care not if I have. It is my study 76
To seem despiteful and ungentle to you.
You are there followed by a faithful shepherd.
Look upon him; love him. He worships you.

PHOEBE [*to Silvius*]
Good shepherd, tell this youth what 'tis to love.

SILVIUS
It is to be all made of sighs and tears;
And so am I for Phoebe.

PHOEBE   And I for Ganymede.

ORLANDO   And I for Rosalind.

ROSALIND   And I for no woman.

SILVIUS
It is to be all made of faith and service;
And so am I for Phoebe.

PHOEBE   And I for Ganymede.

ORLANDO   And I for Rosalind.

ROSALIND   And I for no woman.

SILVIUS
It is to be all made of fantasy, 91
All made of passion and all made of wishes,
All adoration, duty, and observance, 93
All humbleness, all patience and impatience,
All purity, all trial, all observance; 95
And so am I for Phoebe.

PHOEBE   And so am I for Ganymede.

ORLANDO   And so am I for Rosalind.

ROSALIND   And so am I for no woman.

PHOEBE [*to Rosalind*]
If this be so, why blame you me to love you? 100

SILVIUS [*to Phoebe*]
If this be so, why blame you me to love you?

ORLANDO
If this be so, why blame you me to love you?

ROSALIND   Why do you speak too, "Why blame you me
to love you?"

ORLANDO   To her that is not here, nor doth not hear.

ROSALIND   Pray you, no more of this; 'tis like the
howling of Irish wolves against the moon. [*To Silvius*]
I will help you, if I can. [*To Phoebe*] I would love you, if
I could.—Tomorrow meet me all together. [*To Phoebe*] I
will marry you, if ever I marry woman, and I'll be
married tomorrow. [*To Orlando*] I will satisfy you, if
ever I satisfied man, and you shall be married
tomorrow. [*To Silvius*] I will content you, if what
pleases you contents you, and you shall be married
tomorrow. [*To Orlando*] As you love Rosalind, meet.
[*To Silvius*] As you love Phoebe, meet. And as I love
no woman, I'll meet. So fare you well. I have left you
commands.

SILVIUS   I'll not fail, if I live.

PHOEBE   Nor I.

ORLANDO   Nor I.   *Exeunt* [*separately*].

---

37 **incontinent** immediately. (Followed by a pun on the meaning
"unchaste or sexually unrestrained.") 39 **wrath** impetuosity, ardor.
Clubs i.e., Physical force, such as that employed by nightwatchmen
armed with clubs 52–3 **conceit** intelligence, understanding. 53 **that**
in order that 54 **insomuch . . . are** from my saying I know you to be
intelligent 55–7 **neither . . . grace me** nor am I interested in winning
approval except insofar as it may, by inspiring your confidence in my
ability, prompt you to do something for your own benefit; it is not
intended to bring favor on myself. 59 **conversed** associated 60 **not
damnable** not a practicer of forbidden or black magic, worthy of execution and damnation. 61 **gesture** bearing 61–2 **cries it out** proclaims 63 **she** Rosalind 65 **inconvenient** inappropriate 66 **human**
i.e., the real Rosalind, not a phantom. **danger** i.e., the danger to the
soul from one's involvement in magic or witchcraft. 67 **in sober
meanings** seriously. 68 **tender dearly** value highly 69 **though . . .
magician** (According to Elizabethan antiwitchcraft statutes, some
forms of witchcraft were punishable by death; Rosalind thus endan-
gers her life by what she has said.) 70 **bid** invite. **friends** family
and friends 74 **ungentleness** discourtesy

76 **study** conscious endeavor 91 **fantasy** fancy, imagination
93 **observance** devotion, respect 95 **observance** (Perhaps a compositor's error, repeated from two lines previous; many editors emend it
to *obedience.*) 100 **to love you** for loving you.

5.3

Enter [Touchstone the] Clown and Audrey.

TOUCHSTONE   Tomorrow is the joyful day, Audrey;
tomorrow will we be married.

AUDREY   I do desire it with all my heart; and I hope it is
no dishonest desire to desire to be a woman of the   4
world. Here come two of the banished Duke's pages.   5

Enter two Pages.

FIRST PAGE   Well met, honest gentleman.   6

TOUCHSTONE   By my troth, well met. Come, sit, sit,
and a song.   [*They sit.*]

SECOND PAGE   We are for you. Sit i'th' middle.   9

FIRST PAGE   Shall we clap into't roundly, without hawk-   10
ing or spitting or saying we are hoarse, which are the   11
only prologues to a bad voice?   12

SECOND PAGE   I'faith, i'faith, and both in a tune, like   13
two gypsies on a horse.   14

Song.

BOTH PAGES

It was a lover and his lass,
    With a hey, and a ho, and a hey-nonny-no,
That o'er the green cornfield did pass   17
    In springtime, the only pretty ring time,   18
When birds do sing, hey ding a ding, ding,
Sweet lovers love the spring.

Between the acres of the rye,   21
    With a hey, and a ho, and a hey-nonny-no,
These pretty country folks would lie
    In springtime, the only pretty ring time,
When birds do sing, hey ding a ding, ding,
Sweet lovers love the spring.

This carol they began that hour,
    With a hey, and a ho, and hey-nonny-no,
How that a life was but a flower
    In springtime, the only pretty ring time,
When birds do sing, hey ding a ding, ding,
Sweet lovers love the spring.

And therefore take the present time,
    With a hey, and a ho, and a hey-nonny-no,
For love is crownèd with the prime   35
    In springtime, the only pretty ring time,
When birds do sing, hey ding a ding, ding,
Sweet lovers love the spring.

TOUCHSTONE   Truly, young gentlemen, though there
was no great matter in the ditty, yet the note was very   40
untunable.   41

5.3. Location: The forest.
4 dishonest immodest   **4–5 woman of the world** married woman;
also, one who advances herself socially.   **6 honest** worthy   **9 We are
for you** i.e., Fine, we're ready.   **10 clap . . . roundly** begin briskly and
with spirit   **10–11 hawking** clearing the throat   **12 only** customary
13 in a tune (1) in unison (2) keeping time   **14 on a** on one   **17 cornfield** field of grain   **18 ring time** time most apt for marriage
21 Between the acres On unplowed strips between the fields
35 prime (1) height of perfection (2) spring   **40 matter** sense, meaning.   **note** music   **41 untunable** discordant.

FIRST PAGE   You are deceived, sir. We kept time, we lost   42
not our time.

TOUCHSTONE   By my troth, yes; I count it but time lost
to hear such a foolish song. God b'wi'you, and God
mend your voices! Come, Audrey. *Exeunt [separately].*

❖

5.4

*Enter Duke Senior, Amiens, Jaques, Orlando,
Oliver, [and] Celia.*

DUKE SENIOR
Dost thou believe, Orlando, that the boy
Can do all this that he hath promisèd?

ORLANDO
I sometimes do believe, and sometimes do not,
As those that fear they hope and know they fear.   4

Enter Rosalind, Silvius, and Phoebe.

ROSALIND
Patience once more, whiles our compact is urged.   5
[*To the Duke*] You say, if I bring in your Rosalind
You will bestow her on Orlando here?

DUKE SENIOR
That would I, had I kingdoms to give with her.

ROSALIND [*to Orlando*]
And you say you will have her when I bring her?

ORLANDO
That would I, were I of all kingdoms king.

ROSALIND [*to Phoebe*]
You say you'll marry me if I be willing?

PHOEBE
That will I, should I die the hour after.

ROSALIND
But if you do refuse to marry me
You'll give yourself to this most faithful shepherd?

PHOEBE   So is the bargain.

ROSALIND [*to Silvius*]
You say that you'll have Phoebe if she will?

SILVIUS
Though to have her and death were both one thing.

ROSALIND
I have promised to make all this matter even.   18
Keep you your word, O Duke, to give your daughter;
You yours, Orlando, to receive his daughter;
Keep you your word, Phoebe, that you'll marry me,
Or else, refusing me, to wed this shepherd;
Keep your word, Silvius, that you'll marry her
If she refuse me; and from hence I go,
To make these doubts all even.

Exeunt Rosalind and Celia.

DUKE SENIOR
I do remember in this shepherd boy
Some lively touches of my daughter's favor.   27

---

42 deceived mistaken
5.4. Location: The forest.
4 they hope i.e., that they merely hope   **5 urged** put forward.
18 make . . . even set all this to rights, square accounts.   **27 lively**
lifelike.   **favor** appearance.

ORLANDO
My lord, the first time that I ever saw him
Methought he was a brother to your daughter.
But, my good lord, this boy is forest-born
And hath been tutored in the rudiments
Of many desperate studies by his uncle,   32
Whom he reports to be a great magician,
Obscurèd in the circle of this forest.   34

Enter [Touchstone the] Clown and Audrey.

JAQUES   There is, sure, another flood toward, and these   35
couples are coming to the ark. Here comes a pair of   36
very strange beasts, which in all tongues are called
fools.

TOUCHSTONE   Salutation and greeting to you all!

JAQUES   [*to the Duke*]   Good my lord, bid him welcome.
This is the motley-minded gentleman that I have so often
met in the forest. He hath been a courtier, he swears.

TOUCHSTONE   If any man doubt that, let him put me to
my purgation. I have trod a measure; I have flattered a   44
lady; I have been politic with my friend, smooth with   45
mine enemy; I have undone three tailors; I have had   46
four quarrels and like to have fought one.   47

JAQUES   And how was that ta'en up?   48

TOUCHSTONE   Faith, we met and found the quarrel was
upon the seventh cause.

JAQUES   How seventh cause?—Good my lord, like this
fellow.

DUKE SENIOR   I like him very well.

TOUCHSTONE   God 'ild you, sir, I desire you of the like.   54
I press in here, sir, amongst the rest of the country   55
copulatives, to swear and to forswear, according as   56
marriage binds and blood breaks. A poor virgin, sir,   57
an ill-favored thing, sir, but mine own; a poor humor   58
of mine, sir, to take that that no man else will. Rich
honesty dwells like a miser, sir, in a poor house, as   60
your pearl in your foul oyster.   61

DUKE SENIOR   By my faith, he is very swift and senten-   62
tious.   63

TOUCHSTONE   According to the fool's bolt, sir, and such   64
dulcet diseases.   65

JAQUES   But for the seventh cause. How did you find
the quarrel on the seventh cause?

TOUCHSTONE   Upon a lie seven times removed—bear
your body more seeming, Audrey—as thus, sir. I did   69
dislike the cut of a certain courtier's beard. He sent me   70
word if I said his beard was not cut well, he was in
the mind it was: this is called the Retort Courteous. If I
sent him word again it was not well cut, he would
send me word he cut it to please himself: this is called
the Quip Modest. If again it was not well cut, he dis-   75
abled my judgment: this is called the Reply Churlish. If   76
again it was not well cut, he would answer I spake
not true: this is called the Reproof Valiant. If again it
was not well cut, he would say I lie: this is called the
Countercheck Quarrelsome. And so to the Lie Cir-   80
cumstantial and the Lie Direct.

JAQUES   And how oft did you say his beard was not well
cut?

TOUCHSTONE   I durst go no further than the Lie Circumstantial, nor he durst not give me the Lie Direct;
and so we measured swords and parted.   86

JAQUES   Can you nominate in order now the degrees of
the lie?

TOUCHSTONE   Oh, sir, we quarrel in print, by the book, as   89
you have books for good manners. I will name you the
degrees. The first, the Retort Courteous; the second,
the Quip Modest; the third, the Reply Churlish; the
fourth, the Reproof Valiant; the fifth, the Countercheck
Quarrelsome; the sixth, the Lie with Circumstance;
the seventh, the Lie Direct. All these you may
avoid but the Lie Direct; and you may avoid that, too,
with an If. I knew when seven justices could not take   97
up a quarrel, but when the parties were met them-   98
selves, one of them thought but of an If, as, "If you
said so, then I said so"; and they shook hands and
swore brothers. Your If is the only peacemaker; much   101
virtue in If.

JAQUES   Is not this a rare fellow, my lord? He's as good
at anything and yet a fool.

DUKE SENIOR   He uses his folly like a stalking-horse,   105
and under the presentation of that he shoots his wit.   106

Enter Hymen, Rosalind, and Celia. Still music.
[Rosalind and Celia are no longer disguised.]

HYMEN
Then is there mirth in heaven,   107
When earthly things made even   108
Atone together.   109
Good Duke, receive thy daughter;
Hymen from heaven brought her,
Yea, brought her hither,

---

32 desperate dangerous   **34 Obscurèd** hidden.   **circle** compass,
boundaries. (With a possible allusion to the magic circle that protected the magician from the devil during incantation.)   **35 toward**
coming on   **36 a pair** (In Genesis 7:2, God commands Noah to take
on board every "clean" beast by sevens, but those that are not clean,
by twos.)   **44 purgation** proof, trial.   **measure** slow, stately dance
45 politic cunning, Machiavellian.   **smooth** insinuating   **46 undone**
bankrupted (by refusing to pay debts owed them)   **47 like** came
close   **48 ta'en up** settled, made up.   **54 'ild** yield, reward.   **I . . .
like** I wish the same to you. (A polite phrase used to reply to a compliment.)   **55–6 country copulatives** country couples about to marry
and with sex on their minds   **57 blood breaks** as desire bursts forth.
58 humor whim   **60 honesty** chastity   **61 your pearl** i.e., the pearl
that one hears about   **62–3 swift and sententious** quick-witted and
good at aphorisms.   **64 fool's bolt** (Alluding to the proverb "A fool's
bolt [arrow] is soon shot.")   **65 dulcet diseases** pleasant afflictions,
entertaining yet sharp. (Touchstone wryly agrees with the Duke's
assessment of the Fool as swift and sententious.)

69 seeming seemly   **70 dislike** express dislike of   **75–6 disabled** dis-
paraged   **80 Countercheck** Rebuff   **86 measured swords** i.e., as in
the mere preliminary to a duel   **89 in . . . book** in a precise way.
(Touchstone is travestying books on the general subject of honor and
arms, which dealt with occasions and circumstances of the duel.)
97–8 take up settle   **101 swore brothers** became sworn brothers.
105 stalking-horse a real or artificial horse under cover of which the
hunter approached his game   **106 presentation** semblance
106.1 Hymen Roman god of faithful marriage.   *Still* Soft   **107 mirth**
joy   **108 made even** set straight   **109 Atone** are at one

That thou mightst join her hand with his
Whose heart within his bosom is.   114

ROSALIND [*to the Duke*]
   To you I give myself, for I am yours.
   [*To Orlando*] To you I give myself, for I am yours.

DUKE SENIOR
   If there be truth in sight, you are my daughter.

ORLANDO
   If there be truth in sight, you are my Rosalind.

PHOEBE
   If sight and shape be true,
   Why then, my love adieu!

ROSALIND [*to the Duke*]
   I'll have no father, if you be not he.
   [*To Orlando*] I'll have no husband, if you be not he.
   [*To Phoebe*] Nor ne'er wed woman, if you be not she.

HYMEN
     Peace, ho! I bar confusion.
     'Tis I must make conclusion
       Of these most strange events.
     Here's eight that must take hands
     To join in Hymen's bands,
       If truth holds true contents.   129
     [*To Orlando and Rosalind*]
     You and you no cross shall part.   130
     [*To Oliver and Celia*]
     You and you are heart in heart.
     [*To Phoebe*]
     You to his love must accord   132
     Or have a woman to your lord.   133
     [*To Touchstone and Audrey*]
     You and you are sure together,   134
     As the winter to foul weather.
     [*To all*]
     Whiles a wedlock hymn we sing,
     Feed yourselves with questioning,   137
     That reason wonder may diminish   138
     How thus we met, and these things finish.

            Song.

     Wedding is great Juno's crown,   140
       O blessèd bond of board and bed!   141
     'Tis Hymen peoples every town;
       High wedlock then be honorèd.   143
     Honor, high honor and renown
     To Hymen, god of every town!

DUKE SENIOR [*to Celia*]
   O my dear niece, welcome thou art to me!
   Even daughter, welcome, in no less degree.   147

PHOEBE [*to Silvius*]
   I will not eat my word, now thou art mine;
   Thy faith my fancy to thee doth combine.   149

     Enter Second Brother [*Jaques de Boys*].

JAQUES DE BOYS
   Let me have audience for a word or two.
   I am the second son of old Sir Rowland,
   That bring these tidings to this fair assembly.
   Duke Frederick, hearing how that every day
   Men of great worth resorted to this forest,
   Addressed a mighty power, which were on foot   155
   In his own conduct, purposely to take   156
   His brother here and put him to the sword;
   And to the skirts of this wild wood he came,
   Where, meeting with an old religious man,
   After some question with him, was converted   160
   Both from his enterprise and from the world,
   His crown bequeathing to his banished brother,
   And all their lands restored to them again
   That were with him exiled. This to be true
   I do engage my life.

DUKE SENIOR   Welcome, young man.   165
   Thou offer'st fairly to thy brothers' wedding: 166
   To one his lands withheld and to the other   167
   A land itself at large, a potent dukedom.   168
   First, in this forest let us do those ends   169
   That here were well begun and well begot;   170
   And after, every of this happy number   171
   That have endured shrewd days and nights with us   172
   Shall share the good of our returnèd fortune
   According to the measure of their states.   174
   Meantime, forget this new-fall'n dignity,   175
   And fall into our rustic revelry.
   Play, music! And you, brides and bridegrooms all,
   With measure heaped in joy, to th' measures fall. 178

JAQUES
   Sir, by your patience.—If I heard you rightly,   179
   The Duke hath put on a religious life
   And thrown into neglect the pompous court.   181

JAQUES DE BOYS   He hath.

JAQUES
   To him will I. Out of these convertites   183
   There is much matter to be heard and learned.   184
   [*To the Duke*] You to your former honor I bequeath;
   Your patience and your virtue well deserves it.
   [*To Orlando*] You to a love that your true faith doth
     merit;

---

114 Whose (Refers to Rosalind.) **129 If . . . contents** if the newly revealed truths are indeed true and bring true contentment.
130 cross vexation, mischance **132 his** i.e., Silvius's. **accord** agree
133 to your lord for your husband. **134 sure** closely united
137 Feed satisfy **138 That . . . diminish** that understanding may lessen your wonder **140 Juno's** (Juno was the Roman queen of the gods, presiding, in the Renaissance view, over faithful wedlock.)
141 board and bed sustenance and lodging; the household.
143 High solemn **147 Even . . . degree** You are as welcome as a daughter.

149 Thy faith . . . combine your faithful love for me ties my love to you. **155 Addressed** prepared. **power** army **156 In . . . conduct** under his own command **160 question** conversation **165 engage** pledge **166 Thou offer'st fairly** You contribute handsomely **167 To one** to Oliver **167–8 to the other . . . large** to Orlando an entire dukedom (since, as husband of Rosalind, Orlando will eventually inherit as duke). **169 do those ends** accomplish those purposes
170 begot conceived **171 every** every one **172 shrewd** hard, trying **174 According . . . states** states according to their degrees. **175 new-fall'n** newly acquired **178 With . . . fall** with an overflowing measure of joy, fall to dancing. (With wordplay on *measure* and *measures*, "dances.") **179 by your patience** by your leave, i.e., let the music wait a moment. **181 pompous** ceremonious **183 convertites** converts **184 matter** sound sense

[*To Oliver*] You to your land and love and great allies; 188
[*To Silvius*] You to a long and well-deservèd bed;
[*To Touchstone*] And you to wrangling, for thy loving
    voyage
Is but for two months victualed. So, to your pleasures. 191
I am for other than for dancing measures.

DUKE SENIOR   Stay, Jaques, stay.

JAQUES
To see no pastime I. What you would have
I'll stay to know at your abandoned cave.   *Exit.*

DUKE SENIOR
Proceed, proceed. We'll begin these rites,
As we do trust they'll end, in true delights.
      [*They dance.*] *Exeunt* [*all but Rosalind*].

❧

[Epilogue]

ROSALIND
It is not the fashion to see the lady the epilogue;
but it is no more unhandsome than to see the 2

188 **allies** kinfolk   191 **victualed** provisioned.
Epilogue
2 **unhandsome** in bad taste

lord the prologue. If it be true that good wine needs 3
no bush, 'tis true that a good play needs no epilogue. 4
Yet to good wine they do use good bushes, and good
plays prove the better by the help of good epilogues.
What a case am I in then, that am neither a good epilogue nor cannot insinuate with you in the behalf of a 8
good play! I am not furnished like a beggar; therefore 9
to beg will not become me. My way is to conjure you, 10
and I'll begin with the women. I charge you, O
women, for the love you bear to men, to like as much
of this play as please you; and I charge you, O men,
for the love you bear to women—as I perceive by your
simpering, none of you hates them—that between
you and the women the play may please. If I were a 16
woman I would kiss as many of you as had beards 17
that pleased me, complexions that liked me, and 18
breaths that I defied not; and I am sure as many as 19
have good beards or good faces or sweet breaths will,
for my kind offer, when I make curtsy, bid me fare- 21
well.   *Exit.* 22

3–4 **good . . . bush** (A proverb derived from the custom of displaying
a piece of ivy or holly at the tavern door to denote that wine was for
sale there.)   8 **insinuate** ingratiate myself   9 **furnished** equipped,
decked out   10 **conjure** adjure, earnestly charge   16–17 **If . . .
woman** (Womens's parts on the Elizabethan stage were played by
boys in feminine costume.)   18 **liked** pleased   19 **defied** rejected,
disdained   21–2 **bid me farewell** i.e., applaud me.

Twelfth Night; or, What You Will

T welfth Night is possibly the latest of the three festive comedies, including *Much Ado About Nothing* and *As You Like It*, with which Shakespeare climaxed his distinctively philosophical and joyous vein of comic writing. Performed on February 2, 1602, at the Middle Temple and written possibly as early as 1599, *Twelfth Night* is usually dated 1600 or 1601. This play is indeed the most festive of the lot. Its keynote is Saturnalian release and the carnival pursuit of love and mirth. Along with such familiar motifs as the plucky heroine disguised as a man (found earlier in *The Two Gentlemen of Verona, As You Like It*, and *The Merchant of Venice*), *Twelfth Night* also returns to the more farcical routines of mistaken identity found in Shakespeare's early comedy. As a witness of the 1602 performance, John Manningham, observes, the play is "much like the *Comedy of Errors*, or *Menaechmi* in Plautus, but most like and near to that in Italian called *Inganni*."

The carnival atmosphere is appropriate to the season designated in the play's title: the twelfth night of Christmas, January 6, the Feast of Epiphany. (The prologue to *Gl'Ingannati*, perhaps the Italian play referred to by Manningham, speaks of "La Notte di Beffania," Epiphany night.) Along with its primary Christian significance as the Feast of the Magi, Epiphany was also in Renaissance times the last day of the Christmas revels. Over a twelve-day period, from Christmas until January 6, noble households sponsored numerous performances of plays, masques, banquets, and every kind of festivity. (Leslie Hotson argues, in fact, that *Twelfth Night* was first performed on twelfth night in early 1601, in the presence of Queen Elizabeth.) Students left schools for vacations, celebrating release from study with plays and revels of their own. The stern rigors of a rule-bound society gave way temporarily to playful inversions of authority. The reign of the Boy Bishop and the Feast of Fools, for example, gave choristers and minor church functionaries the cherished opportunity to boss the hierarchy around, mock the

liturgy with outrageous lampooning, and generally let off steam. Although such customs occasionally got out of hand, the idea was to channel potentially destructive insubordination into playacting and thereby promote harmony. Behind these Elizabethan midwinter customs lies the Roman Saturnalia, with its pagan spirit of gift giving, sensual indulgence, and satirical hostility to those who would curb merriment. Shakespeare's play captures the medieval and Renaissance spirit of Epiphany by its often playful allusions to religious practice: Feste's disguise as "Sir Topas," the priest, Feste's joke about living by the church (3.1.3–7), Sir Toby's defense of "cakes and ale," Feste's swearing by Saint Anne, mother of the Virgin Mary (2.3.115–16), Feste's joking about "clerestories" (4.2.38), and the like. Shakespeare lovingly evokes a tradition of festivals and ceremonies that incorporates self-mockery into its celebration of renewal at Christmas time.

Shakespeare's choice of sources for *Twelfth Night* underscores his commitment to mirth. Renaissance literature offered numerous instances of mistaken identity among twins and of the disguised heroine serving as page to her beloved. Among those in English were the anonymous play *Sir Clyomon and Sir Clamydes* (c. 1570–1583), Sir Philip Sidney's *Arcadia* (1590), and the prose romance *Parismus* by Emmanuel Forde (1598), featuring both a shipwreck and two characters with the names of Olivia and Violetta. Of particular significance, though partly for negative reasons, is Barnabe Riche's tale of "Apollonius and Silla" in *Riche His Farewell to Military Profession* (1581), which was based on François de Belleforest's 1571 French version of Matteo Bandello's *Novelle* (1554). Here we find most of the requisite plot elements: the shipwreck; Silla's disguise as a page in Duke Apollonius's court; her office as ambassador of love from Apollonius to the lady Julina, who thereupon falls in love with Silla; and the arrival of Silla's twin brother Silvio and his consequent success in winning Julina's affection. To Riche, however, this tale is merely a long warning against the enervating power of infatuation. Silvio gets Julina with child and disappears forthwith, making his belated reappearance almost too late to save the wrongly accused Silla. Riche's moralizing puts the blame on the gross and drunken appetite of carnal love. The total mismatching of affection with which the story begins, and the sudden realignments of desire based on mere outward resemblances, are seen as proofs of love's unreasonableness. Shakespeare, of course, retains and capitalizes on the irrational quality of love, as in *A Midsummer Night's Dream*, but in doing so he minimizes the harm done (Olivia is not made pregnant) and repudiates any negative moral judgments. The added subplot, with its rebuking of Malvolio's censoriousness, may have been conceived as a further answer to Riche, Fenton, and their sober school.

Shakespeare's festive spirit owes much, as Manningham observed, to Plautus and the neoclassical Italian comic writers. At least three Italian comedies called *Gl'Inganni* ("The Frauds") employ the motif of mistaken identity, and one of them, by Curzio Gonzaga (1592), supplies Viola's assumed name of "Cesare," or Cesario. Another play with the same title appeared in 1562. More useful is *Gl'Ingannati* ("The Deceived"), performed in 1531 and translated into French in 1543. Besides a plot line generally similar to *Twelfth Night* and the reference to La Notte di Beffania (Epiphany), this play offers the suggestive name *Malevolti*, "evil-faced," and *Fabio* (which resembles "Fabian"). It also contains possible hints for Malvolio, Sir Toby, and company, although the plot of the counterfeit letter is original with Shakespeare. Essentially, Shakespeare combines his own plot with an Italianate novella plot, as he did in *The Taming of the Shrew* and *Much Ado About Nothing*. And it is in the Malvolio story that Shakespeare most pointedly defends merriment. Feste the professional fool, an original stage type for Shakespeare in *Twelfth Night* and in *As You Like It*, also reinforces the theme of seizing the moment of mirth.

This great lesson, of savoring life's pleasures while one is still young, is something that Orsino and Olivia have not yet learned when the play commences. Although suited to one another in rank, wealth, and attractiveness, they are unable to overcome their own willful posturing in the elaborate charade of courtship. Like Silvius in *As You Like It*, Orsino is the conventional wooer trapped in the courtly artifice of love's rules. He opens the play on a cloying note of self-pity. He is fascinated with his own degradation as a rejected suitor and bores his listeners with his changeable moods and fondness for poetical "conceits." He sees himself as a hart pursued by his desires "like fell and cruel hounds," reminding us that enervating lovesickness has, in fact, robbed him of his manly occupation, hunting. He sends ornately contrived messages to Olivia but has not seen her in so long that his passion has become unreal and fantastical, feeding on itself.

Olivia plays the opposite role of chaste, denying womanhood. She explains her retirement from the world as mourning for a dead brother (whose name we never learn), but this withdrawal from life is another unreal vision. Olivia's practice of mourning, whereby she will "water once a day her chamber round / With eye-offending brine" (1.1.28–9), is a lifeless ritual. As others view the matter, she is senselessly wasting her beauty and affection on the dead. "What a plague means my niece to take the death of her brother thus?" Sir Toby expostulates (1.3.1–2). Viola, though she, too, has seemingly lost a brother, is an important foil in this regard, for she continues to hope for her brother's safety, trusts his soul is in heaven if he is dead, and refuses to give up her commitment to life in any case. We suspect that Olivia takes a willful pleasure in self-denial not unlike Orsino's self-congratulatory suffering. She appears to derive satisfaction from the power she holds over Orsino, a power of refusal. And she must know that she looks stunning in black.

Olivia's household reflects, in part, her mood of self-denial. She keeps Malvolio as steward because he, too, dresses somberly, insists on quiet as befits a house in mourning, and maintains order. Yet Olivia also retains a fool, Feste, who is Malvolio's opposite in every way. Hard-pressed to defend his mirthful function in a household so given over to melancholy, Feste must find some way of persuading his mistress that her very gravity is itself the essence of folly. This is a paradox, because sobriety and order appeal to the conventional wisdom of the world. Malvolio, sensing that his devotion to propriety is being challenged by the fool's prating, chides Olivia for taking "delight in such a barren rascal" (1.5.80–1).

Feste must argue for an inversion of appearance and reality whereby many of the world's ordinary pursuits can be seen to be ridiculous. As he observes, in his habitually elliptical manner of speech, "*Cucullus non facit monachum* [the cowl doesn't make the monk]; that's as much to say as I wear not motley in my brain" (1.5.52–4). Feste wins his case by making Olivia laugh at her own illogic in grieving for a brother whose soul she assumes to be in heaven. By extension, Olivia has indeed been a fool for allowing herself to be deprived of happiness in love by her brother's death ("there is no true cuckold but calamity") and for failing to consider the brevity of youth ("beauty's a flower"). Yet, paradoxically, only one who professes to be a fool can point this out, enabled by his detachment and innocence to perceive simple but profound truths denied to supposedly rational persons. This vision of the fool as naturally wise, and of society as self-indulgently insane, fascinated Renaissance writers, from Erasmus's *In Praise of Folly* and Cervantes's *Don Quixote* to Shakespeare's *King Lear*.

Viola, although not dressed in motley, aligns herself with Feste's rejection of self-denial. Refreshingly, even comically, she challenges the staid artifice of Orsino's and Olivia's lives. She is an ocean traveler, like many of Shakespeare's later heroines (Marina in *Pericles*, Perdita in *The Winter's Tale*), arriving on Illyria's shore plucky and determined. On her first embassy to Olivia from Orsino, she exposes with disarming candor the willfully ritualistic quality of Olivia's existence. Viola discards the flowery set speech she had prepared and memorized at Orsino's behest; despite her charmingly conceited assertion that the speech has been "excellently well penned," she senses that its elegant but empty rhetoric is all too familiar to the disdainful Olivia. Instead, Viola departs from her text to urge seizing the moment of happiness. "You do usurp yourself," she lectures Olivia, "for what is yours to bestow is not yours to reserve" (1.5.183–4). Beauty is a gift of nature, and failure to use it is a sin against nature. Or, again, "Lady, you are the cruel'st she alive / If you will lead these graces [Olivia's beauty] to the grave / And leave the world no copy" (lines 236–8). An essential argument in favor of love, as in Shakespeare's sonnets, is the necessity of marriage and childbearing in order to perpetuate beauty. This approach is new to Olivia and catches her wholly by surprise. In part, she reacts, like Phoebe in *As You Like It*, with perverse logic, rejecting a too-willing wooer for one who is hard to get. Yet Olivia is also attracted by a new note of sincerity, prompting her to reenter life and accept maturely both the risks and rewards of romantic involvement. Her longing for "Cesario" is, of course, sexually misdirected, but the appearance of Viola's identical twin, Sebastian, soon puts all to rights.

The motifs of Olivia's attraction for another woman (both actors would have been boys) and of Orsino's deep fondness for a seeming young man ("Cesario"), which matures into sexual love, raise delicate suggestions of love between members of the same sex, as in *As You Like It*. Once again, the ambiguities of disguise point toward the socially constructed nature of sexual difference. Viola as "Cesario" strikes those who meet her as almost sexually indeterminate. Orsino puts the matter well, in conversing with "Cesario," when he observes, "they shall yet belie thy happy years / That say thou art a man. Diana's lip / Is not more smooth and rubious; thy small pipe / Is as the maiden's organ, shrill and sound, / And all is semblative a woman's part" (1.4.30–4). Male adolescence and femininity are seen as virtually indistinguishable—a point that is wittily reinforced in the theater by the fact that a boy actor is playing Viola disguised as "Cesario."

At the same time, this playful confusion of sexual difference becomes the vehicle for a serious exploration of love and friendship. Like Rosalind in *As You Like It*, Viola uses her male attire to win Orsino's pure affection in a friendship nominally devoid of sexual interest, since both seemingly are men. Friendship must come first; the Renaissance generally accorded a higher value to friendship than to erotic passion. Yet Shakespeare also insists, as did many of his contemporaries (including Montaigne), that friendship is not only possible between men and women but also that such a relationship, formalized in marriage, offers the best of all worlds; hence, the importance of Viola's male disguise. As "Cesario," she can teach Orsino about the conventions of love in relaxed and frank conversations that would not be possible if she were known to be a woman. She teaches him to avoid the beguiling but misleading myths of Petrarchan love (named after the Italian sonneteer Francis Petrarch, whose poems embody the idealization of courtly love) and so prepares him for the realities of marriage. Comparing men and women in love, she confides, "We men may say more, swear more, but indeed / Our shows are more than will; for still we prove / Much in our vows, but little in our love" (2.4.116–18). Once she and Orsino have achieved an instinctive rapport—all the more remarkable for their talking so often at cross-purposes—Viola's unmasking can make possible a physical communion as well. Orsino, no longer trapped in the futile worship of a seemingly unapproachable goddess, can come to terms with his sexuality as part of a unified and loving human relationship.

The friendship of Sebastian and Antonio, meanwhile, sorely tested by the mix-ups of the mistaken identity plot, similarly places Sebastian in a love-and-friendship triangle like that involving Bassanio, Portia, and Antonio in *The Merchant of Venice*. Sebastian and Antonio are loving friends, so much so that Antonio willingly risks his life to be with Sebastian in a country where Antonio has many enemies. Antonio's expressions of fondness for Sebastian are extraordinarily warm. "If you will not murder me for my love, let me be your servant," he pleads. "I do adore thee so / That danger shall seem sport, and I will go" (2.1.33–4, 45–6). A desire "More sharp than filèd steel" spurs Antonio to seek out his friend, despite the manifest danger (3.3.4–5). "A witchcraft" draws him to Sebastian (5.1.72). Whether the attachment is homosexual, as it is often played on the modern stage, is debatable; expressions of warmth between men seem to have been more common in Elizabethan times than today, and centuries of intervening time have no doubt altered our understanding of same-sex relationships; the term *homosexual* is of much later date. What remains true for the play is that this portrayal of emotional and loving closeness between two men gives way to the marriage of one of them to a woman (as in *The Merchant of Venice*). The depiction of love and friendship between two men is a repeated motif in the play, embodied most of all in the loving relationship of Orsino and "Cesario." Shakespeare chooses to resolve his plot by defining heterosexual marriage as the completion of relationships begun in friendship and incorporating that friendship in a union that finally offers heterosexual fulfillment as well.

The below-stairs characters of the subplot, Sir Toby and the rest, share with Feste and Viola a commitment to joy. As Sir Toby proclaims in his first speech, "care's an enemy to life" (1.3.2–3). Even the simpleton Sir Andrew, although gulled by Sir Toby into spending his money on a hopeless pursuit of Olivia, seems none the worse for his treatment; he loves to drink in Sir Toby's company and can afford to pay for his entertainment. Sir Toby gives us some of the richly inventive humor of Falstaff, another lovable fat roguish knight. In this subplot, however, the confrontations between merriment and sobriety are more harshly drawn than in the main plot. Whereas the gracious Olivia is won away from her folly, the obdurate Malvolio can only be exposed to ridicule. He is chiefly to blame for the polarization of attitudes, for he insists on rebuking the mirth of others. His name (*Mal-volio*, the "ill-wisher") implies a self-satisfied determination to impose his rigid moral code on others. As Sir Toby taunts him, "Dost thou think, because thou art virtuous, there shall be no more cakes and ale?" (2.3.114–15). Malvolio's inflexible hostility provokes a desire for comic vengeance. The method is satiric: the clever manipulators, Maria and Sir Toby, invent a scheme to entrap Malvolio in his own self-deceit. The punishment fits the crime, for he has long dreamed of himself as "Count Malvolio," rich, powerful, and in a position to demolish Sir Toby and the rest. Without Malvolio's infatuated predisposition to believe that Olivia could actually love him and write such a letter as he finds, Maria's scheme would have no hope of success. He tortures the text to make it yield a suitable meaning, much in the style of Puritan theologizing. His conviction that Jove is

with him (2.5.169) reminds us of the Puritan belief that prosperity of the "elect" is a sign of God's grace.

Indeed, Malvolio in some ways does resemble a Puritan, as Maria observes (2.3.139–47), even though she qualifies the assertion by saying that he is not a religious fanatic but a "time-pleaser." She directs her observation not at a religious group but at all who would be killjoys; if the Puritans are like that, she intimates, so much the worse for them. This uncharacteristic lack of charity gives a sharp tone to the vengeance practiced on Malvolio, evoking from Olivia a protest that "he hath been most notoriously abused" (5.1.379). The belated attempt to make a reconciliation with him seems, however, doomed to failure, in light of his grim resolve to "be revenged on the whole pack of you" (5.1.378). At the height of his discomfiture, he has been tricked into doing the two things he hates most: smiling affably and wearing sportive attire. The appearance of merriment is so grossly unsuited to him that he is declared mad and put into safekeeping. The apostle of sobriety in this play thus comes before us as a declared madman, while the fool Feste offers him sage comment in the guise of a priest. Wisdom and folly have changed places. The upside-down character of the play is epitomized in Malvolio's plaintive remark to Feste (no longer posing as the priest): "I am as well in my wits, Fool, as thou art" (4.2.88). Malvolio's comeuppance is richly deserved, but the severity of vengeance and countervengeance suggests that the triumph of festival will not last long. This brevity is, of course, inherent in the nature of such holiday release from responsibility. As Feste sings, "What's to come is still unsure. / In delay there lies no plenty" (2.3.49–50).

Twelfth Night; or, What You Will

[Dramatis Personae

ORSINO, *Duke (sometimes called Count) of Illyria*
VALENTINE, *gentleman attending on Orsino*
CURIO, *gentleman attending on Orsino*

VIOLA, *a shipwrecked lady, later disguised as Cesario*
SEBASTIAN, *twin brother of Viola*
ANTONIO, *a sea captain, friend to Sebastian*
CAPTAIN *of the shipwrecked vessel*

OLIVIA, *a rich countess of Illyria*
MARIA, *gentlewoman in Olivia's household*

SCENE: *Illyria*]

SIR TOBY BELCH, *Olivia's uncle*
SIR ANDREW AGUECHEEK, *a companion of Sir Toby*
MALVOLIO, *steward of Olivia's household*
FABIAN, *a member of Olivia's household*
FESTE, *a clown, also called* FOOL, *Olivia's jester*

A PRIEST
FIRST OFFICER
SECOND OFFICER

Lords, Sailors, Musicians, and other Attendants

1.1

*Enter Orsino Duke of Illyria, Curio, and other
lords [with musicians].*

ORSINO
If music be the food of love, play on;
Give me excess of it, that surfeiting,
The appetite may sicken and so die.
That strain again! It had a dying fall;   4
Oh, it came o'er my ear like the sweet sound
That breathes upon a bank of violets,
Stealing and giving odor. Enough, no more.
'Tis not so sweet now as it was before.
O spirit of love, how quick and fresh art thou,   9
That, notwithstanding thy capacity
Receiveth as the sea, naught enters there,
Of what validity and pitch soe'er,   12
But falls into abatement and low price   13
Even in a minute! So full of shapes is fancy   14
That it alone is high fantastical.   15

CURIO
Will you go hunt, my lord?
ORSINO   What, Curio?
CURIO   The hart.
ORSINO
Why, so I do, the noblest that I have.   17
Oh, when mine eyes did see Olivia first,
Methought she purged the air of pestilence.
That instant was I turned into a hart,
And my desires, like fell and cruel hounds,   21
E'er since pursue me.

Enter Valentine.

                              How now, what news from her?   22
VALENTINE
So please my lord, I might not be admitted,
But from her handmaid do return this answer:
The element itself, till seven years' heat,   25
Shall not behold her face at ample view;
But like a cloistress she will veilèd walk,   27
And water once a day her chamber round
With eye-offending brine—all this to season   29

A brother's dead love, which she would keep fresh 30
And lasting in her sad remembrance.

ORSINO

Oh, she that hath a heart of that fine frame 32
To pay this debt of love but to a brother,
How will she love, when the rich golden shaft 34
Hath killed the flock of all affections else 35
That live in her; when liver, brain, and heart, 36
These sovereign thrones, are all supplied, and filled 37
Her sweet perfections, with one self king! 38
Away before me to sweet beds of flowers.
Love-thoughts lie rich when canopied with bowers.

                                        Exeunt.

❧

1.2

Enter Viola, a Captain, and sailors.

VIOLA   What country, friends, is this?

CAPTAIN   This is Illyria, lady.

VIOLA

And what should I do in Illyria?
My brother he is in Elysium.
Perchance he is not drowned. What think you, sailors? 4 5

CAPTAIN

It is perchance that you yourself were saved. 6

VIOLA

Oh, my poor brother! And so perchance may he be.

CAPTAIN

True, madam, and to comfort you with chance, 8
Assure yourself, after our ship did split,
When you and those poor number saved with you
Hung on our driving boat, I saw your brother, 11
Most provident in peril, bind himself,
Courage and hope both teaching him the practice,
To a strong mast that lived upon the sea; 14
Where, like Arion on the dolphin's back, 15
I saw him hold acquaintance with the waves
So long as I could see.

VIOLA   For saying so, there's gold.   [*She gives money.*]
Mine own escape unfoldeth to my hope, 19
Whereto thy speech serves for authority, 20
The like of him. Know'st thou this country? 21

CAPTAIN

Ay, madam, well, for I was bred and born
Not three hours' travel from this very place.

VIOLA   Who governs here?

CAPTAIN   A noble duke, in nature as in name.

VIOLA   What is his name?

CAPTAIN   Orsino.

VIOLA

Orsino! I have heard my father name him.
He was a bachelor then.

CAPTAIN

And so is now, or was so very late; 30
For but a month ago I went from hence,
And then 'twas fresh in murmur—as, you know, 32
What great ones do the less will prattle of— 33
That he did seek the love of fair Olivia.

VIOLA   What's she?

CAPTAIN

A virtuous maid, the daughter of a count
That died some twelvemonth since, then leaving her
In the protection of his son, her brother,
Who shortly also died; for whose dear love,
They say, she hath abjured the sight
And company of men.

VIOLA   Oh, that I served that lady,
And might not be delivered to the world 42
Till I had made mine own occasion mellow, 43
What my estate is!

CAPTAIN   That were hard to compass, 44
Because she will admit no kind of suit,
No, not the Duke's. 46

VIOLA

There is a fair behavior in thee, Captain,
And though that nature with a beauteous wall 48
Doth oft close in pollution, yet of thee
I will believe thou hast a mind that suits
With this thy fair and outward character. 51
I prithee, and I'll pay thee bounteously,
Conceal me what I am, and be my aid
For such disguise as haply shall become 54
The form of my intent. I'll serve this duke. 55
Thou shalt present me as an eunuch to him. 56
It may be worth thy pains, for I can sing
And speak to him in many sorts of music
That will allow me very worth his service. 59
What else may hap, to time I will commit;
Only shape thou thy silence to my wit. 61

CAPTAIN

Be you his eunuch, and your mute I'll be; 62
When my tongue blabs, then let mine eyes not see.

VIOLA   I thank thee. Lead me on.   *Exeunt.*

---

30 **A brother's dead love** her love for her dead brother and the memory of his love for her   32 **frame** construction   34 **golden shaft** Cupid's golden-tipped arrow, causing love. (His lead-tipped arrow causes aversion.)   35 **affections else** other feelings   36–8 **when . . . king** i.e., when passion, thought, and feeling all sit in majesty in their proper thrones (liver, brain, and heart), and her sweet perfections are brought to completion by her union with a single lord and husband.
1.2. Location: The seacoast.
4 **Elysium** classical abode of the blessed dead.   5–6 **Perchance . . . perchance** Perhaps . . . by mere chance   8 **chance** i.e., what one may hope that chance will bring about   11 **driving** drifting, driven by the seas   14 **lived** i.e., kept afloat   15 **Arion** a Greek poet who so charmed the dolphins with his lyre that they saved him when he leaped into the sea to escape murderous sailors   19-21 **unfoldeth . . . him** offers a hopeful example that he may have escaped similarly, to which hope your speech provides support.

30 **late** lately   32 **murmur** rumor   33 **less** social inferiors   42 **delivered** revealed, made known. (With suggestion of "born.")   43 **Till . . . mellow** until the time is ripe for my purpose   44 **estate** social rank.   **compass** encompass, bring about   46 **not** not even   48 **though that** though   51 **character** face or features as indicating moral qualities.   54–5 **as haply . . . intent** as may suit the nature of my purpose.   56 **eunuch** castrato, high-voiced singer   59 **allow** prove   61 **wit** plan, invention.   62 **mute** silent attendant. (Sometimes used of nonspeaking actors.)

1.3

Enter Sir Toby [Belch] and Maria.

SIR TOBY   What a plague means my niece to take the death of her brother thus? I am sure care's an enemy to life.

MARIA   By my troth, Sir Toby, you must come in earlier o'nights. Your cousin, my lady, takes great exceptions 5 to your ill hours.

SIR TOBY   Why, let her except before excepted.   7

MARIA   Ay, but you must confine yourself within the modest limits of order.   9

SIR TOBY   Confine? I'll confine myself no finer than I am. 10 These clothes are good enough to drink in, and so be these boots too. An they be not, let them hang them- 12 selves in their own straps.

MARIA   That quaffing and drinking will undo you. I heard my lady talk of it yesterday, and of a foolish knight that you brought in one night here to be her wooer.

SIR TOBY   Who, Sir Andrew Aguecheek?

MARIA   Ay, he.

SIR TOBY   He's as tall a man as any's in Illyria.   20

MARIA   What's that to th' purpose?

SIR TOBY   Why, he has three thousand ducats a year.   22

MARIA   Ay, but he'll have but a year in all these ducats. 23 He's a very fool and a prodigal.

SIR TOBY   Fie, that you'll say so! He plays o'th' viol-de- 25 gamboys, and speaks three or four languages word 26 for word without book, and hath all the good gifts of 27 nature.

MARIA   He hath indeed, almost natural, for, besides that 29 he's a fool, he's a great quarreler, and but that he hath the gift of a coward to allay the gust he hath in quar- 31 reling, 'tis thought among the prudent he would quickly have the gift of a grave.

SIR TOBY   By this hand, they are scoundrels and sub- 34 stractors that say so of him. Who are they?   35

MARIA   They that add, moreover, he's drunk nightly in your company.

SIR TOBY   With drinking healths to my niece. I'll drink to her as long as there is a passage in my throat and drink in Illyria. He's a coward and a coistrel that will 40 not drink to my niece till his brains turn o'th' toe like

a parish top. What, wench? *Castiliano vulgo!* For here 42 comes Sir Andrew Agueface.   43

Enter Sir Andrew [Aguecheek].

SIR ANDREW   Sir Toby Belch! How now, Sir Toby Belch?

SIR TOBY   Sweet Sir Andrew!

SIR ANDREW   *[to Maria]* Bless you, fair shrew.   46

MARIA   And you too, sir.

SIR TOBY   Accost, Sir Andrew, accost.   48

SIR ANDREW   What's that?

SIR TOBY   My niece's chambermaid.   50

SIR ANDREW   Good Mistress Accost, I desire better acquaintance.

MARIA   My name is Mary, sir.

SIR ANDREW   Good Mistress Mary Accost—

SIR TOBY   You mistake, knight. "Accost" is front her, 55 board her, woo her, assail her.   56

SIR ANDREW   By my troth, I would not undertake her in 57 this company. Is that the meaning of "accost"?

MARIA   Fare you well, gentlemen.   *[Going.]*

SIR TOBY   An thou let part so, Sir Andrew, would thou 60 mightst never draw sword again.

SIR ANDREW   An you part so, mistress, I would I might never draw sword again. Fair lady, do you think you have fools in hand?   64

MARIA   Sir, I have not you by th' hand.

SIR ANDREW   Marry, but you shall have, and here's my 66 hand.   *[He gives her his hand.]*

MARIA   Now, sir, thought is free. I pray you, bring your 68 hand to th' buttery-bar, and let it drink.   69

SIR ANDREW   Wherefore, sweetheart? What's your metaphor?

MARIA   It's dry, sir.   72

SIR ANDREW   Why, I think so. I am not such an ass but I can keep my hand dry. But what's your jest?

MARIA   A dry jest, sir.   75

SIR ANDREW   Are you full of them?

MARIA   Ay, sir, I have them at my fingers' ends. Marry, 77 now I let go your hand, I am barren.   78

    [She lets go his hand.] Exit Maria.

1.3. Location: Olivia's house.
5 cousin kinswoman   **7 let . . . excepted** i.e., let her take exception to my conduct all she wants; I don't care. (Plays on the legal phrase *exceptis excipiendis,* "with the exceptions before named.")   **9 modest** moderate   **10 I'll . . . finer** (1) I'll constrain myself no more rigorously (2) I'll dress myself no more finely   **12 An** If   **20 tall** brave. (But Maria pretends to take the word in the common sense.) **22 ducats** coins worth about four or five shillings   **23 he'll . . . ducats** he'll spend all his money within a year.   **25–6 viol-de-gamboys** viola da gamba, leg-viol, bass viol   **27 without book** by heart **29 natural** (With a play on the sense "born idiot.")   **31 gift** natural ability. (But shifted to mean "present" in line 33.)   **allay the gust** moderate the taste   **34–5 substractors** detractors   **40 coistrel** horse-groom, base fellow

42 parish top a large top provided by the parish to be spun by whipping, apparently for exercise.   *Castiliano vulgo!* (Of uncertain meaning. Possibly Sir Toby is saying "Speak of the devil!" Castiliano is the name adopted by a devil in Haughton's *Grim the Collier of Croydon.*) **43 Agueface** (Like *Aguecheek,* this name betokens the thin, pale countenance of one suffering from an ague or fever.)   **46 shrew** i.e., diminutive creature. (But with probably unintended suggestion of shrewishness.)   **48 Accost** Go alongside (a nautical term), i.e., greet her, address her   **50 chambermaid** lady-in-waiting (a gentlewoman, not one who would do menial tasks).   **55 front** confront, come alongside   **56 board** greet, approach (as though preparing to board in a naval encounter)   **57 undertake** have to do with. (Here with unintended sexual suggestion, to which Maria mirthfully replies with her jokes about *dry jests, barren,* and *buttery-bar.*)   **60 An . . . part** If you let her leave   **64 have . . . hand** i.e., have to deal with fools. (But Maria puns on the literal sense.)   **66 Marry** i.e., Indeed. (Originally, "By the Virgin Mary.")   **68 thought is free** i.e., I may think what I like. (Proverbial; replying to *do you think . . . in hand,* above.)   **69 buttery-bar** ledge on top of the half-door to the buttery or the wine cellar. (Maria's language is sexually suggestive, though Sir Andrew seems oblivious to that.)   **72 dry** thirsty; also dried up, a sign of age and sexual debility   **75 dry** (1) ironic (2) dull, barren. (Referring to Sir Andrew.)   **77 at my fingers' ends** (1) at the ready (2) by the hand. **78 barren** i.e., empty of jests and of Sir Andrew's hand.

SIR TOBY   Oh, knight, thou lack'st a cup of canary! When   79
did I see thee so put down?

SIR ANDREW   Never in your life, I think, unless you see
canary put me down. Methinks sometimes I have no   82
more wit than a Christian or an ordinary man has. But
I am a great eater of beef, and I believe that does harm
to my wit.

SIR TOBY   No question.

SIR ANDREW   An I thought that, I'd forswear it. I'll ride
home tomorrow, Sir Toby.

SIR TOBY   *Pourquoi,* my dear knight?   89

SIR ANDREW   What is *"pourquoi"*? Do or not do? I would
I had bestowed that time in the tongues that I   91
have in fencing, dancing, and bearbaiting. Oh, had I   92
but followed the arts!   93

SIR TOBY   Then hadst thou had an excellent head of hair.

SIR ANDREW   Why, would that have mended my hair?   95

SIR TOBY   Past question, for thou see'st it will not curl by
nature.

SIR ANDREW   But it becomes me well enough, does't
not?

SIR TOBY   Excellent. It hangs like flax on a distaff; and I   100
hope to see a huswife take thee between her legs and
spin it off.   102

SIR ANDREW   Faith, I'll home tomorrow, Sir Toby. Your
niece will not be seen, or if she be, it's four to one
she'll none of me. The Count himself here hard by   105
woos her.

SIR TOBY   She'll none o'th' Count. She'll not match
above her degree, neither in estate, years, nor wit; I   108
have heard her swear't. Tut, there's life in't, man.   109

SIR ANDREW   I'll stay a month longer. I am a fellow o'th'
strangest mind i'th' world; I delight in masques and
revels sometimes altogether.

SIR TOBY   Art thou good at these kickshawses, knight?   113

SIR ANDREW   As any man in Illyria, whatsoever he be,
under the degree of my betters, and yet I will not   115
compare with an old man.   116

SIR TOBY   What is thy excellence in a galliard, knight?   117

SIR ANDREW   Faith, I can cut a caper.   118

SIR TOBY   And I can cut the mutton to't.

SIR ANDREW   And I think I have the back-trick simply   120
as strong as any man in Illyria.

SIR TOBY   Wherefore are these things hid? Wherefore
have these gifts a curtain before 'em? Are they like to   123
take dust, like Mistress Mall's picture? Why dost thou   124
not go to church in a galliard and come home in a
coranto? My very walk should be a jig; I would not so   126
much as make water but in a sink-a-pace. What dost   127
thou mean? Is it a world to hide virtues in? I did think,   128
by the excellent constitution of thy leg, it was formed
under the star of a galliard.   130

SIR ANDREW   Ay, 'tis strong, and it does indifferent well   131
in a dun-colored stock. Shall we set about some   132
revels?

SIR TOBY   What shall we do else? Were we not born
under Taurus?   135

SIR ANDREW   Taurus? That's sides and heart.

SIR TOBY   No, sir, it is legs and thighs. Let me see thee
caper. [*Sir Andrew capers.*] Ha, higher! Ha, ha, excel-
lent!   *Exeunt.*

❖

1.4

Enter Valentine, and Viola in man's attire.

VALENTINE   If the Duke continue these favors towards
you, Cesario, you are like to be much advanced. He   2
hath known you but three days, and already you are
no stranger.

VIOLA   You either fear his humor or my negligence,   5
that you call in question the continuance of his love. Is
he inconstant, sir, in his favors?

VALENTINE   No, believe me.

Enter Duke [Orsino], Curio, and attendants.

VIOLA   I thank you. Here comes the Count.

ORSINO   Who saw Cesario, ho?

VIOLA   On your attendance, my lord, here.   11

ORSINO

Stand you awhile aloof. [*The others stand aside.*]
    Cesario,   12
Thou know'st no less but all. I have unclasped
To thee the book even of my secret soul.
Therefore, good youth, address thy gait unto her;   15
Be not denied access, stand at her doors,

---

79 thou . . . canary i.e., you look as if you need a drink. (*Canary* is a sweet wine from the Canary Islands.)   **82 put me down** (1) baffle my wits (2) lay me out flat.   **89 Pourquoi** Why   **91 tongues** languages. (Sir Toby then puns on "tongs," curling irons.)   **92 bearbaiting** the sport of setting dogs on a chained bear.   **93 the arts** the liberal arts, learning. (But Sir Toby plays on the phrase as meaning "artifice," the antithesis of *nature*.)   **95 mended** improved   **100 distaff** a staff for holding the flax, tow, or wool in spinning   **102 spin it off** i.e., (1) treat your flaxen hair as though it were flax on a distaff to be spun (2) cause you to lose hair as a result of venereal disease (3) make you ejaculate. (*Huswife* suggests "hussy," "whore.")   **105 Count** i.e., Duke Orsino, sometimes referred to as Count.   **hard** near   **108 degree** social position.   **estate** fortune, social position   **109 there's life in't** i.e., while there's life there's hope   **113 kickshawses** delicacies, fancy trifles. (From the French, *quelque chose*.)   **115 under . . . betters** excepting those who are above me   **116 old man** i.e., one experienced through age.   **117 galliard** lively dance in triple time   **118 cut a caper** make a lively leap. (But Sir Toby puns on the *caper* used to make a sauce served with mutton. *Mutton,* in turn, suggests "whore.")

120 back-trick backward step in the galliard. (With sexual innuendo; the back was associated with sexual vigor.)   **123–4 like to take** likely to collect   **124 Mistress Mall's picture** i.e., perhaps the portrait of some woman protected from light and dust, as many pictures were, by curtains. (*Mall* is a diminutive of *Mary.*)   **126 coranto** lively running dance.   **127 sink-a-pace** dance like the galliard. (French *cinquepace. Sink* also suggests a cesspool into which one might urinate.)   **128 virtues** talents   **130 under . . . galliard** i.e., under a star favorable to dancing.   **131 indifferent well** well enough. (Said complacently.)   **132 dun-colored stock** mouse-colored stocking.
135 Taurus zodiacal sign. (Sir Andrew is mistaken, since Leo governed sides and hearts in medical astrology. Taurus governed legs and thighs, or, more commonly, neck and throat.)
1.4. Location: Orsino's court.
2 like likely   **5 humor** changeableness   **11 On your attendance**
Ready to do you service   **12 aloof** aside.   **15 address thy gait** go

And tell them, there thy fixèd foot shall grow   17
Till thou have audience.

VIOLA   Sure, my noble lord,
If she be so abandoned to her sorrow
As it is spoke, she never will admit me.

ORSINO
Be clamorous and leap all civil bounds   21
Rather than make unprofited return.

VIOLA
Say I do speak with her, my lord, what then?

ORSINO
Oh, then unfold the passion of my love;
Surprise her with discourse of my dear faith.   25
It shall become thee well to act my woes;   26
She will attend it better in thy youth
Than in a nuncio's of more grave aspect.   28

VIOLA
I think not so, my lord.

ORSINO   Dear lad, believe it;
For they shall yet belie thy happy years
That say thou art a man. Diana's lip
Is not more smooth and rubious; thy small pipe   32
Is as the maiden's organ, shrill and sound,   33
And all is semblative a woman's part.   34
I know thy constellation is right apt   35
For this affair.—Some four or five attend him.
All, if you will, for I myself am best
When least in company.—Prosper well in this,
And thou shalt live as freely as thy lord,
To call his fortunes thine.

VIOLA   I'll do my best
To woo your lady. [Aside] Yet a barful strife!   41
Whoe'er I woo, myself would be his wife.   Exeunt.

❖

1.5

Enter Maria and Clown [Feste].

MARIA   Nay, either tell me where thou hast been, or I
will not open my lips so wide as a bristle may enter in
way of thy excuse. My lady will hang thee for thy
absence.

FESTE   Let her hang me. He that is well hanged in this
world needs to fear no colors.   6

MARIA   Make that good.   7

FESTE   He shall see none to fear.   8

MARIA   A good Lenten answer. I can tell thee where   9
that saying was born, of "I fear no colors."

FESTE   Where, good Mistress Mary?

MARIA   In the wars, and that may you be bold to say in   12
your foolery.   13

FESTE   Well, God give them wisdom that have it; and
those that are fools, let them use their talents.   15

MARIA   Yet you will be hanged for being so long absent;
or to be turned away, is not that as good as a hanging   17
to you?

FESTE   Many a good hanging prevents a bad marriage;   19
and for turning away, let summer bear it out.   20

MARIA   You are resolute, then?

FESTE   Not so, neither, but I am resolved on two
points.   23

MARIA   That if one break, the other will hold; or if both
break, your gaskins fall.   25

FESTE   Apt, in good faith, very apt. Well, go thy way. If
Sir Toby would leave drinking, thou wert as witty a   27
piece of Eve's flesh as any in Illyria.   28

MARIA   Peace, you rogue, no more o' that. Here comes
my lady. Make your excuse wisely, you were best.   30

                          [Exit.]

*Enter Lady Olivia with Malvolio, [and
attendants].*

FESTE   *[aside]*   Wit, an't be thy will, put me into good   31
fooling! Those wits that think they have thee do very
oft prove fools, and I that am sure I lack thee may pass
for a wise man. For what says Quinapalus? "Better a   34
witty fool than a foolish wit."—God bless thee, lady!

OLIVIA   *[to attendants]*   Take the fool away.

FESTE   Do you not hear, fellows? Take away the lady.

OLIVIA   Go to, you're a dry fool. I'll no more of you.   38
Besides, you grow dishonest.

FESTE   Two faults, madonna, that drink and good   40
counsel will amend. For give the dry fool drink, then
is the fool not dry. Bid the dishonest man mend
himself; if he mend, he is no longer dishonest; if he
cannot, let the botcher mend him. Anything that's   44
mended is but patched; virtue that transgresses is but   45
patched with sin, and sin that amends is but patched
with virtue. If that this simple syllogism will serve, so;   47
if it will not, what remedy? As there is no true cuckold   48
but calamity, so beauty's a flower. The lady bade take   49

---

17 **them** i.e., Olivia's servants   21 **civil bounds** bounds of civility
25 **Surprise** Take by storm. (A military term.)   **dear** heartfelt
26 **become** suit   28 **nuncio's** messenger's   32 **rubious** ruby red.
pipe voice, throat   33 **shrill and sound** high and clear, uncracked
34 **semblative** resembling, like   35 **constellation** i.e., nature as determined by your horoscope   41 **barful strife** endeavor full of impediments.
1.5. Location: Olivia's house.
6 **fear no colors** i.e., fear no foe, fear nothing. (With pun on *colors*,
worldly deceptions, and "collars," halters or nooses.)   7 **Make that
good** Explain that.   8 **He . . . fear** i.e., The hanged man will be dead
and unable to see anything.   9 **Lenten** meager, scanty (like Lenten
fare), and morbid

12 **In the wars** (Where *colors* would mean "military standards, enemy
flags"—the literal meaning of the proverb.)   12–13 **that . . . foolery**
that's an answer you may be bold to use in your fool's conundrums.
(*Colors* here refer to military banners and insignia used to align rows
of fighting men in battle.)   15 **talents** abilities. (Also alluding to the
parable of the talents, Matthew 25:14–29, and to "talons," claws.)
17 **turned away** dismissed. (Possibly also meaning "turned off,"
"hanged.")   19 **good hanging** (With possible bawdy pun on "being
well hung.")   20 **for** as for.   **let . . . out** i.e., let mild weather make
dismissal endurable.   23 **points** (Maria plays on the meaning "laces
used to hold up hose or breeches.")   25 **gaskins** wide breeches
27–8 **thou . . . Illyria** (Feste may be hinting ironically that Maria
would be a suitable mate for Sir Toby.)   30 **you were best** it would be
best for you.   31 **an't** if it   34 **Quinapalus** (Feste's invented authority.)   38 **Go to** (An expression of annoyance or expostulation.)   **dry**
dull   40 **madonna** my lady   44 **botcher** mender of old clothes and
shoes. (Playing on two senses of *mend*: "reform" and "repair.")
44–5 **Anything . . . patched** i.e., Life is patched or parti-colored like
the Fool's garment, a mix of good and bad   47 **so** well and good
48–9 **As . . . flower** (Nonsense, yet with a suggestion that Olivia has
wedded calamity but should not be faithful to it, for the natural
course is to seize the moment of youth and beauty before we lose it.)

away the fool; therefore I say again, take her away.

OLIVIA   Sir, I bade them take away you.

FESTE   Misprision in the highest degree! Lady, *cucullus* 52
non facit monachum; that's as much to say as I wear not 53
motley in my brain. Good madonna, give me leave to 54
prove you a fool.

OLIVIA   Can you do it?

FESTE   Dexteriously, good madonna.

OLIVIA   Make your proof.

FESTE   I must catechize you for it, madonna. Good my 59
mouse of virtue, answer me. 60

OLIVIA   Well, sir, for want of other idleness, I'll bide 61
your proof.

FESTE   Good madonna, why mourn'st thou?

OLIVIA   Good fool, for my brother's death.

FESTE   I think his soul is in hell, madonna.

OLIVIA   I know his soul is in heaven, fool.

FESTE   The more fool, madonna, to mourn for your
brother's soul, being in heaven.—Take away the fool,
gentlemen.

OLIVIA   What think you of this fool, Malvolio? Doth he
not mend? 71

MALVOLIO   Yes, and shall do till the pangs of death
shake him. Infirmity, that decays the wise, doth ever
make the better fool.

FESTE   God send you, sir, a speedy infirmity for the
better increasing your folly! Sir Toby will be sworn
that I am no fox, but he will not pass his word for 77
twopence that you are no fool.

OLIVIA   How say you to that, Malvolio?

MALVOLIO   I marvel Your Ladyship takes delight in such
a barren rascal. I saw him put down the other day
with an ordinary fool that has no more brain than a 82
stone. Look you now, he's out of his guard already. 83
Unless you laugh and minister occasion to him, he is 84
gagged. I protest I take these wise men that crow so at 85
these set kind of fools no better than the fools' zanies. 86

OLIVIA   Oh, you are sick of self-love, Malvolio, and taste
with a distempered appetite. To be generous, guiltless, 88
and of free disposition is to take those things for bird- 89
bolts that you deem cannon bullets. There is no slan- 90
der in an allowed fool, though he do nothing but rail; 91
nor no railing in a known discreet man, though he do 92
nothing but reprove. 93

FESTE   Now Mercury endue thee with leasing, for thou 94
speak'st well of fools!

Enter Maria.

MARIA   Madam, there is at the gate a young gentleman
much desires to speak with you.

OLIVIA   From the Count Orsino, is it?

MARIA   I know not, madam. 'Tis a fair young man, and
well attended.

OLIVIA   Who of my people hold him in delay?

MARIA   Sir Toby, madam, your kinsman.

OLIVIA   Fetch him off, I pray you. He speaks nothing
but madman. Fie on him!   [*Exit Maria.*] 104
Go you, Malvolio. If it be a suit from the Count, I am
sick or not at home; what you will, to dismiss it.

Exit Malvolio.

Now you see, sir, how your fooling grows old, and 107
people dislike it.

FESTE   Thou hast spoke for us, madonna, as if thy eldest
son should be a fool; whose skull Jove cram with
brains, for—here he comes—

Enter Sir Toby.

one of thy kin has a most weak *pia mater.* 112

OLIVIA   By mine honor, half drunk.—What is he at the
gate, cousin?

SIR TOBY   A gentleman.

OLIVIA   A gentleman? What gentleman?

SIR TOBY   'Tis a gentleman here—[*He belches.*] A plague
o' these pickle-herring! [*To Feste*] How now, sot? 118

FESTE   Good Sir Toby.

OLIVIA   Cousin, cousin, how have you come so early by 120
this lethargy?

SIR TOBY   Lechery? I defy lechery. There's one at the
gate.

OLIVIA   Ay, marry, what is he?

SIR TOBY   Let him be the devil an he will, I care not.
Give me faith, say I. Well, it's all one.   *Exit.* 126

OLIVIA   What's a drunken man like, Fool?

FESTE   Like a drowned man, a fool, and a madman.
One draft above heat makes him a fool, the second 129
mads him, and a third drowns him.

OLIVIA   Go thou and seek the crowner, and let him sit 131
o' my coz; for he's in the third degree of drink, he's 132
drowned. Go, look after him.

FESTE   He is but mad yet, madonna; and the fool shall
look to the madman.   [*Exit.*]

Enter Malvolio.

MALVOLIO   Madam, yond young fellow swears he will
speak with you. I told him you were sick; he takes on
him to understand so much, and therefore comes to
speak with you. I told him you were asleep; he seems

---

52 Misprision Mistake, misunderstanding. (A legal term meaning a
wrongful action or misdemeanor.)   **52–3** *cucullus . . . monachum* the
cowl does not make the monk   **54 motley** the many-colored garment
of jesters   **59–60 Good . . . virtue** My good, virtuous mouse. (A term
of endearment.)   **61 idleness** pastime.   **bide** endure   **71 mend** i.e.,
improve, grow more amusing. (But Malvolio uses the word to mean
"grow more like a fool.")   **77 pass** give   **82 with** by   **83 out of his
guard** defenseless, unprovided with a witty answer   **84 minister
occasion** provide opportunity (for his fooling)   **85 protest** avow,
declare.   **crow** laugh stridently   **86 set** artificial, stereotyped.
zanies assistants, aping attendants.   **88 distempered** diseased.
generous noble-minded   **89 free** magnanimous   **89–90 bird-bolts**
blunt arrows for shooting small birds   **90–3 There . . . reprove**
Both a licensed fool and a man known for discretion can criticize
freely without being accused of slander in the first instance or railing
in the second. (In rebuking Malvolio here, Olivia implies that he is
not behaving like a "known discreet man.")   **91 allowed** licensed (to
speak freely)

94 Now . . . leasing i.e., May Mercury, the god of deception, make
you a skillful liar   **104 madman** i.e., the words of madness.   **107 old**
stale   **112** *pia mater* i.e., brain. (Actually the soft membrane enclosing the brain.)   **118 sot** (1) fool (2) drunkard.   **120 Cousin** Kinsman.
(Here, uncle.)   **126 Give me faith** i.e., to resist the devil.   **it's all one**
it doesn't matter.   **129 draft above heat** helping of drink raising his
temperature above normal bodily warmth   **131 crowner** coroner
131–2 sit o' my coz hold an inquest on my kinsman (Sir Toby)

to have a foreknowledge of that too, and therefore
comes to speak with you. What is to be said to him,
lady? He's fortified against any denial.

OLIVIA   Tell him he shall not speak with me.

MALVOLIO   He's been told so; and he says he'll stand at
your door like a sheriff's post, and be the supporter to 145
a bench, but he'll speak with you.

OLIVIA   What kind o' man is he?

MALVOLIO   Why, of mankind.

OLIVIA   What manner of man?

MALVOLIO   Of very ill manner. He'll speak with you,
will you or no.

OLIVIA   Of what personage and years is he?

MALVOLIO   Not yet old enough for a man, nor young
enough for a boy; as a squash is before 'tis a peascod, 154
or a codling when 'tis almost an apple. 'Tis with him in 155
standing water between boy and man. He is very 156
well-favored, and he speaks very shrewishly. One 157
would think his mother's milk were scarce out
of him.

OLIVIA   Let him approach. Call in my gentlewoman.

MALVOLIO   Gentlewoman, my lady calls.   *Exit.*

Enter Maria.

OLIVIA
Give me my veil. Come, throw it o'er my face.
We'll once more hear Orsino's embassy. [*Olivia veils.*]

Enter Viola.

VIOLA   The honorable lady of the house, which is she?

OLIVIA   Speak to me; I shall answer for her. Your will?

VIOLA   Most radiant, exquisite, and unmatchable
beauty—I pray you, tell me if this be the lady of the
house, for I never saw her. I would be loath to cast
away my speech; for besides that it is excellently well
penned, I have taken great pains to con it. Good 170
beauties, let me sustain no scorn; I am very comptible, 171
even to the least sinister usage. 172

OLIVIA   Whence came you, sir?

VIOLA   I can say little more than I have studied, and that
question's out of my part. Good gentle one, give
me modest assurance if you be the lady of the house, 176
that I may proceed in my speech.

OLIVIA   Are you a comedian? 178

VIOLA   No, my profound heart; and yet, by the very 179
fangs of malice, I swear I am not that I play. Are you 180
the lady of the house?

OLIVIA   If I do not usurp myself, I am. 182

VIOLA   Most certain, if you are she, you do usurp your- 183
self; for what is yours to bestow is not yours to reserve. 184

But this is from my commission. I will on with my 185
speech in your praise, and then show you the heart of
my message.

OLIVIA   Come to what is important in't. I forgive you 188
the praise.

VIOLA   Alas, I took great pains to study it, and 'tis
poetical.

OLIVIA   It is the more like to be feigned. I pray you,
keep it in. I heard you were saucy at my gates, and
allowed your approach rather to wonder at you than
to hear you. If you be not mad, begone; if you have 195
reason, be brief. 'Tis not that time of moon with me to 196
make one in so skipping a dialogue. 197

MARIA   Will you hoist sail, sir? Here lies your way.

VIOLA   No, good swabber, I am to hull here a little 199
longer.—Some mollification for your giant, sweet 200
lady. Tell me your mind; I am a messenger.

OLIVIA   Sure you have some hideous matter to deliver,
when the courtesy of it is so fearful. Speak your office. 203

VIOLA   It alone concerns your ear. I bring no overture of 204
war, no taxation of homage. I hold the olive in my 205
hand; my words are as full of peace as matter.

OLIVIA   Yet you began rudely. What are you? What 207
would you?

VIOLA   The rudeness that hath appeared in me have I
learned from my entertainment. What I am and what 210
I would are as secret as maidenhead—to your ears, 211
divinity; to any other's, profanation. 212

OLIVIA [*to the others*]   Give us the place here alone. We
will hear this divinity.   [*Exeunt Maria and attendants.*]
Now, sir, what is your text?

VIOLA   Most sweet lady—

OLIVIA   A comfortable doctrine, and much may be said 217
of it. Where lies your text?

VIOLA   In Orsino's bosom.

OLIVIA   In his bosom? In what chapter of his bosom?

VIOLA   To answer by the method, in the first of his 221
heart.

OLIVIA   Oh, I have read it. It is heresy. Have you no
more to say?

VIOLA   Good madam, let me see your face.

OLIVIA   Have you any commission from your lord to
negotiate with my face? You are now out of your text. 227
But we will draw the curtain and show you the

---

145 **sheriff's post** post before the sheriff's door to mark a residence of
authority, often elaborately carved and decorated.   **supporter** prop
154 **squash** unripe pea pod.   **peascod** ripe pea pod. (The image suggests that the boy's testicles have not yet dropped.)   **155 codling**
unripe apple   **155–6 in standing water** at the turn of the tide
157 **well-favored** good-looking.   **shrewishly** sharply.   **170 con**
memorize   **171 comptible** susceptible, sensitive   **172 least sinister**
slightest discourteous   **176 modest** reasonable   **178 comedian** actor.
179 **my profound heart** my most wise lady; or, in all sincerity
179–80 **by . . . I play** (Viola hints at her true identity, which malice
itself might not detect.)   **182 do . . . myself** am not an impostor
183–4 **usurp yourself** i.e., misappropriate yourself, by withholding
yourself from love and marriage

185 **from** outside of   **188 forgive you** excuse you from repeating
195 **not mad** i.e., not altogether mad   **196 reason** sanity.   **moon** (The
moon was thought to affect lunatics according to its changing
phases.)   **197 make one** take part   **199 swabber** one in charge of
washing the decks. (A nautical retort to *hoist sail.*)   **hull** lie with sails
furled   **200 Some . . . for** i.e., Please mollify, pacify.   **giant** i.e., the
diminutive Maria who, like many giants in medieval romances, is
guarding the lady   **203 courtesy** i.e., complimentary, "poetical"
introduction. (Or Olivia may refer to Cesario's importunate manner
at her gate, as reported by Malvolio.)   **office** commission, business.
204 **overture** declaration. (Literally, opening.)   **205 taxation of**
homage demand for tribute.   **olive** olive-branch (signifying peace)
207 **Yet . . . rudely** i.e., Yet you were saucy at my gates.   **210 enter-**
tainment reception.   **211 maidenhead** virginity   **212 divinity** sacred
discourse   **217 comfortable** comforting   **221 To . . . method** i.e., To
continue the metaphor of delivering a sermon, begun with *divinity*
and *what is your text* and continued in *doctrine, heresy,* etc.   **227 out of**
straying from

picture. [*Unveiling.*] Look you, sir, such a one I was 229
this present. Is't not well done?   230

VIOLA   Excellently done, if God did all.

OLIVIA   'Tis in grain, sir; 'twill endure wind and 232
weather.

VIOLA
'Tis beauty truly blent, whose red and white   234
Nature's own sweet and cunning hand laid on.   235
Lady, you are the cruel'st she alive
If you will lead these graces to the grave
And leave the world no copy.   238

OLIVIA   Oh, sir, I will not be so hardhearted. I will give
out divers schedules of my beauty. It shall be invento- 240
ried, and every particle and utensil labeled to my   241
will: as, item, two lips, indifferent red; item, two gray 242
eyes, with lids to them; item, one neck, one chin, and
so forth. Were you sent hither to praise me?   244

VIOLA
I see you what you are: you are too proud.
But, if you were the devil, you are fair.   246
My lord and master loves you. Oh, such love   247
Could be but recompensed, though you were
   crowned   248
The nonpareil of beauty!

OLIVIA   How does he love me? 249

VIOLA
With adorations, fertile tears,   250
With groans that thunder love, with sighs of fire.

OLIVIA
Your lord does know my mind; I cannot love him.
Yet I suppose him virtuous, know him noble,
Of great estate, of fresh and stainless youth,
In voices well divulged, free, learned, and valiant, 255
And in dimension and the shape of nature   256
A gracious person. But yet I cannot love him.   257
He might have took his answer long ago.

VIOLA
If I did love you in my master's flame,   259
With such a suff'ring, such a deadly life,   260
In your denial I would find no sense;
I would not understand it.

OLIVIA   Why, what would you?

VIOLA
Make me a willow cabin at your gate   263
And call upon my soul within the house;   264
Write loyal cantons of contemnèd love   265

And sing them loud even in the dead of night;
Hallow your name to the reverberate hills,   267
And make the babbling gossip of the air   268
Cry out "Olivia!" Oh, you should not rest
Between the elements of air and earth   270
But you should pity me!

OLIVIA   You might do much.
What is your parentage?

VIOLA
Above my fortunes, yet my state is well: 273
I am a gentleman.

OLIVIA   Get you to your lord.
I cannot love him. Let him send no more—
Unless, perchance, you come to me again
To tell me how he takes it. Fare you well.
I thank you for your pains. Spend this for me.
                                    [*She offers a purse.*]

VIOLA
I am no fee'd post, lady. Keep your purse.   279
My master, not myself, lacks recompense.
Love make his heart of flint that you shall love,   281
And let your fervor, like my master's, be
Placed in contempt! Farewell, fair cruelty.   *Exit.*

OLIVIA   "What is your parentage?"
"Above my fortunes, yet my state is well:
I am a gentleman." I'll be sworn thou art!
Thy tongue, thy face, thy limbs, actions, and spirit
Do give thee fivefold blazon. Not too fast! Soft, soft! 288
Unless the master were the man. How now?   289
Even so quickly may one catch the plague?
Methinks I feel this youth's perfections
With an invisible and subtle stealth
To creep in at mine eyes. Well, let it be.—
What ho, Malvolio!

Enter Malvolio.

MALVOLIO   Here, madam, at your service.

OLIVIA
Run after that same peevish messenger,
The County's man. He left this ring behind him,   296
                                    [*giving a ring*]
Would I or not. Tell him I'll none of it.   297
Desire him not to flatter with his lord,   298
Nor hold him up with hopes; I am not for him.
If that the youth will come this way tomorrow,
I'll give him reasons for't. Hie thee, Malvolio.   301

MALVOLIO   Madam, I will.   *Exit.*

OLIVIA
I do I know not what, and fear to find
Mine eye too great a flatterer for my mind.   304

229–30 such . . . present this is a recent portrait of me. (Since it was
customary to hang curtains in front of pictures, Olivia in unveiling
speaks as if she were displaying a picture of herself.)   **232 in grain**
fast dyed   **234 blent** blended   **235 cunning** skillful   **238 copy** i.e., a
child. (But Olivia uses the word to mean "transcript.")   **240 schedules** inventories   **241 utensil** article, item.   **labeled** added as a
codicil   **242 indifferent** somewhat   **244 praise** (With pun on
"appraise.")   **246 if** even if   **247–9 Oh . . . beauty!** i.e., Even if you
were the most beautiful woman alive, that beauty could do no more
than repay my master's love for you!   **250 fertile** copious   **255 In . . .
divulged** well spoken of.   **free** generous   **256 in . . . nature** in his
physical form   **257 gracious** graceful, attractive   **259 flame** passion
260 deadly deathlike   **263 willow cabin** shelter, hut. (Willow was a
symbol of unrequited love.)   **264 my soul** i.e., Olivia   **265 cantons**
songs.   **contemnèd** rejected

267 Hallow (1) halloo (2) bless   **268 babbling . . . air** echo
270 Between . . . air i.e., anywhere   **273 state** social standing
279 fee'd post messenger to be tipped   **281 Love . . . love** May Cupid
make the heart of the man you love as hard as flint   **288 blazon**
heraldic description.   **Soft** Wait a minute   **289 Unless . . . man** i.e.,
Unless Cesario and Orsino changed places.   **296 County's** Count's,
i.e., Duke's   **297 Would I or not** whether I wanted it or not.
298 flatter with encourage   **301 Hie thee** Hasten   **304 Mine . . .
mind** i.e., that my eyes (through which love enters the soul) have
deceived my reason.

Fate, show thy force. Ourselves we do not owe.   305
What is decreed must be; and be this so.   [*Exit.*]

❖

2.1

Enter Antonio and Sebastian.

ANTONIO   Will you stay no longer? Nor will you not   1
that I go with you?

SEBASTIAN   By your patience, no. My stars shine darkly   3
over me. The malignancy of my fate might perhaps   4
distemper yours; therefore I shall crave of you your   5
leave that I may bear my evils alone. It were a bad
recompense for your love to lay any of them on you.

ANTONIO   Let me yet know of you whither you are
bound.

SEBASTIAN   No, sooth, sir; my determinate voyage is   10
mere extravagancy. But I perceive in you so excellent   11
a touch of modesty that you will not extort from me
what I am willing to keep in; therefore it charges me in   13
manners the rather to express myself. You must know   14
of me then, Antonio, my name is Sebastian, which I
called Roderigo. My father was that Sebastian of
Messaline whom I know you have heard of. He left   17
behind him myself and a sister, both born in an hour.   18
If the heavens had been pleased, would we had so
ended! But you, sir, altered that, for some hour before   20
you took me from the breach of the sea was my sister   21
drowned.

ANTONIO   Alas the day!

SEBASTIAN   A lady, sir, though it was said she much resembled me, was yet of many accounted beautiful. But
though I could not with such estimable wonder over-   26
far believe that, yet thus far I will boldly publish her: 27
she bore a mind that envy could not but call fair. She   28
is drowned already, sir, with salt water, though I seem
to drown her remembrance again with more.

ANTONIO   Pardon me, sir, your bad entertainment.   31

SEBASTIAN   O good Antonio, forgive me your trouble.   32

ANTONIO   If you will not murder me for my love, let me   33
be your servant.

SEBASTIAN   If you will not undo what you have done,
that is, kill him whom you have recovered, desire it   36
not. Fare ye well at once. My bosom is full of

kindness, and I am yet so near the manners of my   38
mother that upon the least occasion more mine eyes   39
will tell tales of me. I am bound to the Count Orsino's
court. Farewell.   *Exit.*

ANTONIO
The gentleness of all the gods go with thee!
I have many enemies in Orsino's court,
Else would I very shortly see thee there.
But come what may, I do adore thee so
That danger shall seem sport, and I will go.   *Exit.*

❖

2.2

Enter Viola and Malvolio, at several doors.

MALVOLIO   Were not you ev'n now with the Countess
Olivia?

VIOLA   Even now, sir. On a moderate pace I have since
arrived but hither.

MALVOLIO   She returns this ring to you, sir. You might
have saved me my pains, to have taken it away   6
yourself. She adds, moreover, that you should put
your lord into a desperate assurance she will none of   8
him. And one thing more: that you be never so hardy   9
to come again in his affairs, unless it be to report your   10
lord's taking of this. Receive it so.

VIOLA   She took the ring of me. I'll none of it.   12

MALVOLIO   Come, sir, you peevishly threw it to her,
and her will is it should be so returned. [*He throws
down the ring.*] If it be worth stooping for, there it lies,
in your eye; if not, be it his that finds it.   *Exit.*   16

VIOLA [*picking up the ring*]
I left no ring with her. What means this lady?
Fortune forbid my outside have not charmed her!   18
She made good view of me, indeed so much
That sure methought her eyes had lost her tongue,   20
For she did speak in starts, distractedly.
She loves me, sure! The cunning of her passion
Invites me in this churlish messenger.   23
None of my lord's ring? Why, he sent her none.
I am the man. If it be so—as 'tis—   25
Poor lady, she were better love a dream.
Disguise, I see, thou art a wickedness
Wherein the pregnant enemy does much.   28
How easy is it for the proper false   29
In women's waxen hearts to set their forms!   30
Alas, our frailty is the cause, not we,   31
For such as we are made of, such we be.   32

---

305 owe own, control.
2.1. Location: Somewhere in Illyria.
1 Nor will you not Do you not wish   **3 patience** leave   **4 malignancy** malevolence (of the stars; also in a medical sense)   **5 distemper** infect   **10 sooth** truly.   **determinate** intended, determined upon
11 extravagancy aimless wandering.   **13 am willing . . . in** wish to
keep secret   **13–14 it . . . manners** it is incumbent upon me in all
courtesy   **14 express** reveal   **17 Messaline** possibly Messina, or,
more likely, Massila (the modern Marseilles). In Plautus's *Menaechmi*,
Massilians and Illyrians are mentioned together.   **18 in an hour** in
the same hour.   **20 some hour** about an hour   **21 breach of the sea**
surf   **26 estimable wonder** admiring judgment   **27 publish** proclaim   **28 envy** even malice   **31 Pardon . . . entertainment** i.e., I'm
sorry I cannot offer you better hospitality and comfort.   **32 your
trouble** the trouble I put you to.   **33 murder . . . love** i.e., cause me to
die from lacking your love   **36 recovered** rescued, restored

38 kindness emotion, affection   **38–9 manners of my mother** i.e.,
womanly inclination to weep
2.2. Location: Near Olivia's house.
0.1 *several* different   **6 to have taken** by taking   **8 desperate** without hope   **9–10 so hardy to come** so bold as to come   **12 She . . . it**
(Viola tells a quick and friendly lie to shield Olivia.)   **16 in your eye**
in plain sight   **18 charmed** enchanted   **20 her eyes . . . tongue** i.e.,
the sight of me had deprived her of speech   **23 in** in the person of
25 the man the man of her choice.   **28 the pregnant enemy** the
resourceful enemy (either Satan or Cupid)   **29 the proper false**
deceptively handsome men   **30 waxen** i.e., malleable, impressionable.   **set their forms** stamp their images (as of a seal).   **31–2 our . . .
be** i.e., the fault lies not in us as individuals, but in the frailty of
female nature.

How will this fadge? My master loves her dearly,   33
And I, poor monster, fond as much on him;   34
And she, mistaken, seems to dote on me.
What will become of this? As I am man,
My state is desperate for my master's love;
As I am woman—now, alas the day!—
What thriftless sighs shall poor Olivia breathe!   39
O Time, thou must untangle this, not I;
It is too hard a knot for me t'untie.   [*Exit.*]

�֍

2.3

Enter Sir Toby and Sir Andrew.

SIR TOBY   Approach, Sir Andrew. Not to be abed after
midnight is to be up betimes; and *diluculo surgere*, thou   2
know'st—

SIR ANDREW   Nay, by my troth, I know not, but I know
to be up late is to be up late.

SIR TOBY   A false conclusion. I hate it as an unfilled can.   6
To be up after midnight and to go to bed then, is early;
so that to go to bed after midnight is to go to bed
betimes. Does not our lives consist of the four   9
elements?   10

SIR ANDREW   Faith, so they say, but I think it rather
consists of eating and drinking.

SIR TOBY   Thou'rt a scholar; let us therefore eat and
drink.—Marian, I say, a stoup of wine!   14

Enter Clown [Feste].

SIR ANDREW   Here comes the Fool, i'faith.

FESTE   How now, my hearts! Did you never see the
picture of "we three"?   17

SIR TOBY   Welcome, ass. Now let's have a catch.   18

SIR ANDREW   By my troth, the Fool has an excellent
breast. I had rather than forty shillings I had such a   20
leg, and so sweet a breath to sing, as the Fool has. In   21
sooth, thou wast in very gracious fooling last night,
when thou spok'st of Pigrogromitus, of the Vapians   23
passing the equinoctial of Queubus. 'Twas very good,   24
i'faith. I sent thee sixpence for thy leman. Hadst it?   25

FESTE   I did impeticos thy gratillity; for Malvolio's nose   26
is no whipstock. My lady has a white hand, and the   27
Myrmidons are no bottle-ale houses.   28

SIR ANDREW   Excellent! Why, this is the best fooling,
when all is done. Now, a song.

SIR TOBY   Come on, there is sixpence for you. [*He gives
money.*] Let's have a song.

SIR ANDREW   There's a testril of me too. [*He gives money.*]   33
If one knight give a—

FESTE   Would you have a love song, or a song of good   35
life?   36

SIR TOBY   A love song, a love song.

SIR ANDREW   Ay, ay, I care not for good life.

FESTE (*sings*)
O mistress mine, where are you roaming?
Oh, stay and hear, your true love 's coming,
    That can sing both high and low.
Trip no further, pretty sweeting;
Journeys end in lovers' meeting,
    Every wise man's son doth know.

SIR ANDREW   Excellent good, i'faith.

SIR TOBY   Good, good.

FESTE [*sings*]
What is love? 'Tis not hereafter;
Present mirth hath present laughter;
    What's to come is still unsure.   49
In delay there lies no plenty.
Then come kiss me, sweet and twenty;   51
    Youth's a stuff will not endure.

SIR ANDREW   A mellifluous voice, as I am true knight.

SIR TOBY   A contagious breath.   54

SIR ANDREW   Very sweet and contagious, i'faith.

SIR TOBY   To hear by the nose, it is dulcet in contagion.   56
But shall we make the welkin dance indeed? Shall we   57
rouse the night owl in a catch that will draw three   58
souls out of one weaver? Shall we do that?   59

SIR ANDREW   An you love me, let's do't. I am dog at a   60
catch.   61

FESTE   By'r Lady, sir, and some dogs will catch well.   62

SIR ANDREW   Most certain. Let our catch be "Thou   63
knave."   64

FESTE   "Hold thy peace, thou knave," knight? I shall be   65
constrained in't to call thee knave, knight.   66

SIR ANDREW   'Tis not the first time I have constrained
one to call me knave. Begin, Fool. It begins, "Hold thy
peace."

---

33 fadge turn out   **34 monster** i.e., being both man and woman.
fond dote   **39 thriftless** unprofitable
2.3. Location: Olivia's house.
2 betimes early. **diluculo surgere** (*saluberrimum est*) to rise early is
most healthful. (A sentence from Lilly's *Latin Grammar*.)   **6 can**
tankard.   **9-10 four elements** i.e., fire, air, water, and earth, the elements that were thought to make up all matter.   **14 stoup** drinking
vessel   **17 picture of "we three"** picture of two fools or asses
inscribed "we three," the spectator being the third.   **18 catch** round.
20 breast voice.   **21 leg** (for dancing)   **23-4 Pigrogromitus . . .
Queubus** (Feste's mock erudition.)   **25 leman** sweetheart.
26 impeticos thy gratillity (Suggests "impetticoat, or pocket up, thy
gratuity.")   **27 is no whipstock** is no whip-handle. (More nonsense,
but perhaps suggesting that Malvolio's nose for smelling out faults
does not give him the right to punish, so that he need not be feared.)
has a white hand i.e., is lady-like. (But Feste's speech may be mere
nonsense.)   **28 Myrmidons** followers of Achilles.   **bottle-ale houses**
(Used contemptuously of taverns because they sold low-class drink.)

33 testril tester, a coin worth sixpence   **35-6 good life** virtuous living. (Or perhaps Feste means simply "life's pleasures," but is misunderstood by Sir Andrew to mean "virtuous living.")   **49 still** always
51 sweet and twenty i.e., sweet and twenty times sweet, or twenty
years old   **54 contagious** infectiously delightful   **56 To . . . contagion** i.e., If we were to describe hearing in olfactory terms, we could
say it is sweet in stench.   **57 make . . . dance** i.e., drink till the sky
seems to turn around   **58–9 draw three souls** (Refers to the threefold
nature of the soul—vegetal, sensible, and intellectual—or to the three
singers of the three-part catch; or, just a comic exaggeration.)
59 weaver (Weavers were often associated with psalm singing.)
60 dog at very clever at. (But Feste uses the word literally.)   **61 catch**
round. (But Feste uses it to mean "seize.")   **62 By 'r Lady** (An oath,
originally, "by the Virgin Mary.")   **63–4 "Thou knave"** (This popular
round is arranged so that the three singers repeatedly accost one
another with "Thou knave.")   **65–6 "Hold . . . knight** ("Knight and
knave" is a common antithesis, like "rich and poor.")

FESTE   I shall never begin if I hold my peace.
SIR ANDREW   Good, i'faith. Come, begin.   *Catch sung.*

Enter Maria.

MARIA   What a caterwauling do you keep here! If my 72
lady have not called up her steward Malvolio and bid
him turn you out of doors, never trust me.
SIR TOBY   My lady's a Cataian, we are politicians, 75
Malvolio's a Peg-o'-Ramsey, and [*he sings*] "Three 76
merry men be we." Am not I consanguineous? Am I 77
not of her blood? Tillyvally! Lady! [*He sings.*] "There 78
dwelt a man in Babylon, lady, lady." 79
FESTE   Beshrew me, the knight's in admirable fooling. 80
SIR ANDREW   Ay, he does well enough if he be disposed,
and so do I too. He does it with a better grace,
but I do it more natural. 83
SIR TOBY   [*sings*]
"O' the twelfth day of December"— 84
MARIA   For the love o' God, peace!

Enter Malvolio.

MALVOLIO   My masters, are you mad? Or what are you?
Have you no wit, manners, nor honesty but to gabble 87
like tinkers at this time of night? Do ye make an alehouse of my lady's house, that ye squeak out your coz- 89
iers' catches without any mitigation or remorse of 90
voice? Is there no respect of place, persons, nor time in
you?
SIR TOBY   We did keep time, sir, in our catches. Sneck 93
up! 94
MALVOLIO   Sir Toby, I must be round with you. My 95
lady bade me tell you that though she harbors you as
her kinsman, she's nothing allied to your disorders. If
you can separate yourself and your misdemeanors,
you are welcome to the house; if not, an it would
please you to take leave of her, she is very willing to
bid you farewell.
SIR TOBY   [*sings*]
"Farewell, dear heart, since I must needs be gone." 102
MARIA   Nay, good Sir Toby.
FESTE   [*sings*]
"His eyes do show his days are almost done."
MALVOLIO   Is't even so?
SIR TOBY   [*sings*]
"But I will never die."
FESTE
"Sir Toby, there you lie."

MALVOLIO   This is much credit to you.
SIR TOBY   [*sings*]
"Shall I bid him go?"
FESTE   [*sings*]
"What an if you do?"
SIR TOBY   [*sings*]
"Shall I bid him go, and spare not?"
FESTE   [*sings*]
"Oh, no, no, no, no, you dare not."
SIR TOBY   Out o' tune, sir? Ye lie. Art any more than a 113
steward? Dost thou think, because thou art virtuous,
there shall be no more cakes and ale?
FESTE   Yes, by Saint Anne, and ginger shall be hot i'th' 116
mouth, too.
SIR TOBY   Thou'rt i'the right.—Go, sir, rub your chain 118
with crumbs.—A stoup of wine, Maria! 119
MALVOLIO   Mistress Mary, if you prized my lady's
favor at anything more than contempt, you would not
give means for this uncivil rule. She shall know of it, 122
by this hand.   *Exit.*
MARIA   Go shake your ears. 124
SIR ANDREW   'Twere as good a deed as to drink when a
man's a-hungry to challenge him the field and then to 126
break promise with him and make a fool of him.
SIR TOBY   Do't, knight. I'll write thee a challenge, or I'll
deliver thy indignation to him by word of mouth.
MARIA   Sweet Sir Toby, be patient for tonight. Since the
youth of the Count's was today with my lady, she is
much out of quiet. For Monsieur Malvolio, let me 132
alone with him. If I do not gull him into a nayword 133
and make him a common recreation, do not think I 134
have wit enough to lie straight in my bed. I know I can
do it.
SIR TOBY   Possess us, possess us. Tell us something of 137
him.
MARIA   Marry, sir, sometimes he is a kind of Puritan. 139
SIR ANDREW   Oh, if I thought that, I'd beat him like a
dog.
SIR TOBY   What, for being a Puritan? Thy exquisite
reason, dear knight?
SIR ANDREW   I have no exquisite reason for't, but I
have reason good enough.

---

72 **keep** keep up   75 **Cataian** Cathayan, i.e., Chinese, a trickster or inscrutable; or, just nonsense.   **politicians** schemers, intriguers
76 **Peg-o'-Ramsey** character in a popular song. (Used here contemptuously.)   76–7 **"Three . . . we"** (A snatch of an old song.)   77 **consanguineous** i.e., a blood relative of Olivia.   78 **Tillyvally!** Nonsense, fiddle-faddle!   78–9 **"There . . . lady"** (The first line of a ballad, "The Constancy of Susanna," together with the refrain, "Lady, lady.")
80 **Beshrew** i.e., The devil take. (A mild curse.)   83 **natural** naturally. (But unconsciously suggesting idiocy.)   84 **"O' . . . December!"** (Possibly part of a ballad about the Battle of Musselburgh Field, or Toby's error for the "twelfth day of Christmas," i.e., Twelfth Night.)   87 **wit** common sense.   **honesty** decency   89–90 **coziers'** cobblers'   90 **mitigation or remorse** i.e., considerate lowering   93–4 **Sneck up!** Go hang!   95 **round** blunt   102 **"Farewell . . . gone"** (From the ballad "Corydon's Farewell to Phyllis.")

113 **Out o' tune** (Perhaps a quibbling reply—"We did too keep time in our tune"—to Malvolio's accusation of having no respect for place or time, line 91. Often emended to *Out o' time*, easily misread in secretary hand.)   116 **Saint Anne** mother of the Virgin Mary. (Her cult was derided in the Reformation, much as Puritan reformers also derided the tradition of *cakes and ale* at church feasts.)   **ginger** (Commonly used to spice ale.)   118–19 **rub . . . crumbs** i.e., scour or polish your steward's chain; attend to your own business and remember your station.   122 **give means** i.e., supply drink.   **rule** conduct.
124 **your ears** i.e., your ass's ears.   126 **the field** i.e., to a duel
132 **For** As for   132–3 **let . . . him** leave him to me.   133 **gull** trick.   **nayword** byword. (His name will be synonymous with "dupe.")
134 **recreation** sport   137 **Possess** Inform   139 **puritan** (Maria's point is that Malvolio is sometimes a *kind* of Puritan, insofar as he is precise about moral conduct and censorious of others for immoral conduct, but that he is nothing consistently except a time-server. He is not, then, simply a satirical type of the Puritan sect. The extent of the resemblance is left unstated.)

MARIA   The devil a Puritan that he is, or anything con- 146
stantly, but a time-pleaser; an affectioned ass, that cons 147
state without book and utters it by great swaths; the 148
best persuaded of himself, so crammed, as he thinks, 149
with excellencies, that it is his grounds of faith that all 150
that look on him love him; and on that vice in him
will my revenge find notable cause to work.

SIR TOBY   What wilt thou do?

MARIA   I will drop in his way some obscure epistles of 154
love, wherein by the color of his beard, the shape of
his leg, the manner of his gait, the expressure of his 156
eye, forehead, and complexion, he shall find himself
most feelingly personated. I can write very like my 158
lady your niece; on a forgotten matter we can hardly 159
make distinction of our hands. 160

SIR TOBY   Excellent! I smell a device.

SIR ANDREW   I have't in my nose too.

SIR TOBY   He shall think, by the letters that thou wilt
drop, that they come from my niece, and that she's in
love with him.

MARIA   My purpose is indeed a horse of that color.

SIR ANDREW   And your horse now would make him an
ass.

MARIA   Ass, I doubt not. 169

SIR ANDREW   Oh, 'twill be admirable!

MARIA   Sport royal, I warrant you. I know my physic 171
will work with him. I will plant you two, and let the
Fool make a third, where he shall find the letter. Observe his construction of it. For this night, to bed, 174
and dream on the event. Farewell.   *Exit.* 175

SIR TOBY   Good night, Penthesilea. 176

SIR ANDREW   Before me, she's a good wench. 177

SIR TOBY   She's a beagle true-bred and one that adores 178
me. What o'that?

SIR ANDREW   I was adored once, too.

SIR TOBY   Let's to bed, knight. Thou hadst need send
for more money.

SIR ANDREW   If I cannot recover your niece, I am a foul 183
way out. 184

SIR TOBY   Send for money, knight. If thou hast her not
i'th' end, call me cut. 186

SIR ANDREW   If I do not, never trust me, take it how
you will.

SIR TOBY   Come, come, I'll go burn some sack. 'Tis too 189
late to go to bed now. Come, knight; come, knight. 190
                                                    Exeunt.

❖

2.4

Enter Duke [Orsino], Viola, Curio, and others.

ORSINO
Give me some music. Now, good morrow, friends. 1
Now, good Cesario, but that piece of song, 2
That old and antique song we heard last night. 3
Methought it did relieve my passion much,
More than light airs and recollected terms 5
Of these most brisk and giddy-pacèd times.
Come, but one verse.

CURIO   He is not here, so please Your Lordship, that
should sing it.

ORSINO   Who was it?

CURIO   Feste the jester, my lord, a fool that the Lady
Olivia's father took much delight in. He is about the
house.

ORSINO
Seek him out, and play the tune the while.
                        [*Exit Curio.*] *Music plays.*
[*To Viola*] Come hither, boy. If ever thou shalt love,
In the sweet pangs of it remember me;
For such as I am, all true lovers are,
Unstaid and skittish in all motions else 18
Save in the constant image of the creature
That is beloved. How dost thou like this tune?

VIOLA
It gives a very echo to the seat 21
Where Love is throned.

ORSINO   Thou dost speak masterly.
My life upon't, young though thou art, thine eye
Hath stayed upon some favor that it loves. 24
Hath it not, boy?

VIOLA   A little, by your favor. 25

ORSINO
What kind of woman is't?

VIOLA   Of your complexion.

ORSINO
She is not worth thee, then. What years, i'faith?

VIOLA   About your years, my lord.

ORSINO
Too old, by heaven. Let still the woman take 29
An elder than herself. So wears she to him; 30
So sways she level in her husband's heart. 31
For, boy, however we do praise ourselves,

146–7 constantly consistently   147 time-pleaser time-server, syco-
phant.   affectioned affected   147–8 cons . . . book learns by heart
the phrases and mannerisms of the great   148 by great swaths in
great sweeps, like rows of mown grain   148–9 the best persuaded
having the best opinion   150 grounds of faith creed, belief
154 some obscure epistles an ambiguously worded letter
156 expressure expression   158 personated represented.   159 on a
forgotten matter when we've forgotten which of us wrote something
or what it was about   160 hands handwriting.   169 Ass, I (With a
pun on "as I.")   171 physic medicine   174 construction interpretation   175 event outcome.   176 Penthesilea Queen of the Amazons.
(Another ironical allusion to Maria's diminutive stature.)
177 Before me i.e., On my soul. (A mild oath.)   178 beagle a small,
intelligent hunting dog   183 recover win   183–4 foul way out i.e.,
miserably out of my way and in the mire.)   186 cut A proverbial term of abuse: literally, a horse with a docked
tail; also, a gelding, or the female genital organ.

189 burn some sack warm some Spanish wine.   190.1 *Exeunt* (Feste
may have left earlier; he says nothing after line 117 and is perhaps
referred to without his being present at 172–3.)
2.4. Location: Orsino's court.
1 morrow morning   2 but i.e., I ask only   3 antique old, quaint, fantastic   5 recollected terms studied and artificial expressions   18 all
motions else all other thoughts and emotions   21 the seat i.e., the
heart   24 stayed . . . favor rested upon some face   25 by your favor
if you please. (But also hinting at "like you in feature.")   29 still
always   30 wears she she adapts herself   31 sways she level she
keeps a perfect equipoise and steady affection

Our fancies are more giddy and unfirm,
More longing, wavering, sooner lost and worn, 34
Than women's are.

VIOLA   I think it well, my lord.

ORSINO
Then let thy love be younger than thyself,
Or thy affection cannot hold the bent; 37
For women are as roses, whose fair flower
Being once displayed, doth fall that very hour. 39

VIOLA
And so they are. Alas that they are so,
To die even when they to perfection grow! 41

Enter Curio and Clown [Feste].

ORSINO
Oh, fellow, come, the song we had last night.
Mark it, Cesario, it is old and plain;
The spinsters and the knitters in the sun, 44
And the free maids that weave their thread with
bones, 45
Do use to chant it. It is silly sooth, 46
And dallies with the innocence of love, 47
Like the old age. 48

FESTE   Are you ready, sir?

ORSINO   Ay, prithee, sing.   *Music.*

The Song.

FESTE *[sings]*
Come away, come away, death, 51
    And in sad cypress let me be laid. 52
Fly away, fly away, breath;
    I am slain by a fair cruel maid.
My shroud of white, stuck all with yew, 55
    Oh, prepare it!
My part of death, no one so true 57
    Did share it. 58

Not a flower, not a flower sweet
    On my black coffin let there be strown; 60
Not a friend, not a friend greet
    My poor corpse, where my bones shall be
        thrown.
A thousand thousand sighs to save,
    Lay me, oh, where
Sad true lover never find my grave,
    To weep there!

ORSINO *[offering money]*   There's for thy pains.

FESTE   No pains, sir. I take pleasure in singing, sir.

ORSINO   I'll pay thy pleasure then.

FESTE   Truly, sir, and pleasure will be paid, one time 70
or another. 71

ORSINO   Give me now leave to leave thee. 72

FESTE   Now, the melancholy god protect thee, and the 73
tailor make thy doublet of changeable taffeta, for thy 74
mind is a very opal. I would have men of such con- 75
stancy put to sea, that their business might be every- 76
thing and their intent everywhere, for that's it that 77
always makes a good voyage of nothing. Farewell. 78

Exit.

ORSINO
Let all the rest give place.
                    [Curio and attendants withdraw.]
                    Once more, Cesario, 79
Get thee to yond same sovereign cruelty.
Tell her, my love, more noble than the world,
Prizes not quantity of dirty lands;
The parts that fortune hath bestowed upon her, 83
Tell her, I hold as giddily as fortune; 84
But 'tis that miracle and queen of gems 85
That nature pranks her in attracts my soul. 86

VIOLA   But if she cannot love you, sir?

ORSINO
I cannot be so answered.

VIOLA   Sooth, but you must. 88
Say that some lady—as perhaps there is—
Hath for your love as great a pang of heart
As you have for Olivia. You cannot love her;
You tell her so. Must she not then be answered? 92

ORSINO   There is no woman's sides
Can bide the beating of so strong a passion 94
As love doth give my heart; no woman's heart
So big, to hold so much. They lack retention. 96
Alas, their love may be called appetite,
No motion of the liver, but the palate, 98
That suffer surfeit, cloyment, and revolt; 99
But mine is all as hungry as the sea,
And can digest as much. Make no compare 101
Between that love a woman can bear me
And that I owe Olivia.

VIOLA   Ay, but I know— 103

ORSINO   What dost thou know?

---

34 worn exhausted. (Sometimes emended to *won*.)   **37 hold the bent**
hold steady, keep the intensity (like the tension of a bow)   **39 displayed** full blown   **41 even when** just as   **44 spinsters** spinners
45 free carefree, innocent.   **bones** bobbins on which bone-lace was
made.   **46 Do use** are accustomed.   **silly sooth** simple truth   **47 dallies with** dwells lovingly on, sports with   **48 Like . . . age** as in the
good old times.   **51 Come away** Come hither   **52 cypress** i.e., a coffin of cypress wood, or bier strewn with sprigs of cypress   **55 yew**
yew sprigs. (Emblematic of mourning, like cypress.)   **57–8 My . . . it**
No one died for love so true to love as I.   **60 strown** strewn

70–1 pleasure . . . another sooner or later one must pay for indulgence.   **72 leave to leave** permission to take leave of, dismiss   **73 the
melancholy god** i.e., Saturn, whose planet was thought to control the
melancholy temperament   **74 doublet** close-fitting jacket.
changeable taffeta a silk so woven of various-colored threads that its
color shifts with changing perspective   **75 opal** an iridescent precious stone that changes color when seen from various angles or in
different lights.   **76–7 that . . . everywhere** i.e., so that in the changeableness of the sea their inconstancy could always be exercised
77–8 for . . . nothing because that's the quality that is satisfied with
an aimless voyage.   **79 give place** withdraw.   **83 parts** attributes
such as wealth or rank   **84 I . . . fortune** I esteem as carelessly as I do
fortune, that fickle goddess   **85 that miracle . . . gems** i.e., her beauty
86 pranks adorns.   **attracts** that attracts   **88 Sooth** In truth   **92 be
answered** be satisfied with your answer.   **94 bide** withstand   **96 to
hold** as to contain.   **retention** constancy, the power of retaining.
98 motion impulse.   **liver . . . palate** (Real love is a passion of the
liver, whereas fancy, light love, is born in the eye and nourished in
the palate.)   **99 cloyment** satiety.   **revolt** revulsion   **101 compare**
comparison   **103 owe** have for

VIOLA
Too well what love women to men may owe.
In faith, they are as true of heart as we.
My father had a daughter loved a man
As it might be, perhaps, were I a woman,
I should Your Lordship.

ORSINO   And what's her history?

VIOLA
A blank, my lord. She never told her love,
But let concealment, like a worm i'th' bud,
Feed on her damask cheek. She pined in thought,   112
And with a green and yellow melancholy;   113
She sat like Patience on a monument,   114
Smiling at grief. Was not this love indeed?
We men may say more, swear more, but indeed
Our shows are more than will; for still we prove   117
Much in our vows, but little in our love.

ORSINO
But died thy sister of her love, my boy?

VIOLA
I am all the daughters of my father's house,
And all the brothers too—and yet I know not.
Sir, shall I to this lady?

ORSINO   Ay, that's the theme.
To her in haste; give her this jewel. [*He gives a jewel.*]
    Say
My love can give no place, bide no denay.   124
                            Exeunt [*separately*].

❧

2.5

Enter Sir Toby, Sir Andrew, and Fabian.

SIR TOBY   Come thy ways, Signor Fabian.   1
FABIAN   Nay, I'll come. If I lose a scruple of this sport,   2
    let me be boiled to death with melancholy.   3
SIR TOBY   Wouldst thou not be glad to have the nig-
    gardly rascally sheep-biter come by some notable   5
    shame?
FABIAN   I would exult, man. You know he brought me
    out o'favor with my lady about a bearbaiting here.   8
SIR TOBY   To anger him we'll have the bear again, and
    we will fool him black and blue. Shall we not, Sir An-   10
    drew?
SIR ANDREW   An we do not, it is pity of our lives.   12

    Enter Maria [*with a letter*].

SIR TOBY   Here comes the little villain.—How now, my   13
    metal of India!   14
MARIA   Get ye all three into the boxtree. Malvolio's   15
    coming down this walk. He has been yonder i'the sun
    practicing behavior to his own shadow this half hour.
    Observe him, for the love of mockery, for I know this
    letter will make a contemplative idiot of him. Close, in   19
    the name of jesting! [*The others hide.*] Lie thou there
    [*throwing down a letter*]; for here comes the trout that
    must be caught with tickling.   *Exit.*   22

    Enter Malvolio.

MALVOLIO   'Tis but fortune; all is fortune. Maria once
    told me she did affect me; and I have heard herself   24
    come thus near, that should she fancy, it should be   25
    one of my complexion. Besides, she uses me with a
    more exalted respect than anyone else that follows   27
    her. What should I think on't?
SIR TOBY   Here's an overweening rogue!
FABIAN   Oh, peace! Contemplation makes a rare turkey-   30
    cock of him. How he jets under his advanced plumes!   31
SIR ANDREW   'Slight, I could so beat the rogue!   32
SIR TOBY   Peace, I say.
MALVOLIO   To be Count Malvolio.
SIR TOBY   Ah, rogue!
SIR ANDREW   Pistol him, pistol him.
SIR TOBY   Peace, peace!
MALVOLIO   There is example for't. The lady of the Stra- 38
    chy married the yeoman of the wardrobe.   39
SIR ANDREW   Fie on him, Jezebel!   40
FABIAN   Oh, peace! Now he's deeply in. Look how imag-
    ination blows him.   42
MALVOLIO   Having been three months married to her,
    sitting in my state—   44
SIR TOBY   Oh, for a stone-bow, to hit him in the eye!   45
MALVOLIO   Calling my officers about me, in my
    branched velvet gown; having come from a daybed,   47
    where I have left Olivia sleeping—
SIR TOBY   Fire and brimstone!
FABIAN   Oh, peace, peace!
MALVOLIO   And then to have the humor of state; and   51
    after a demure travel of regard, telling them I know   52
    my place as I would they should do theirs, to ask for
    my kinsman Toby.   54
SIR TOBY   Bolts and shackles!
FABIAN   Oh, peace, peace, peace! Now, now.

---

112 damask pink and white like the damask rose   **113 green and yellow** pale and sallow   **114 on a monument** carved in statuary on a
tomb   **117 shows** displays of passion.   **more than will** greater than
our determination.   **still** always   **124 can . . . denay** cannot yield or
endure denial.
2.5. Location: Olivia's garden.
1 Come thy ways Come along   **2 a scruple** the least bit   **3 boiled**
(With a pun on "biled"; black bile was the "humor" of melancholy
and was thought to be a cold humor.)   **5 sheep-biter** a dog that bites
sheep, i.e., a scoundrel   **8 bearbaiting** (A special target of Puritan
disapproval.)   **10 fool . . . blue** mock him until he is figuratively
black and blue.   **12 An** If.   **pity of our lives** a pity we should live.

13 villain (Here, a term of endearment.)   **14 metal** gold, i.e., priceless
one   **15 boxtree** an evergreen shrub.   **19 contemplative** i.e., from
his musings.   **Close** i.e., Keep close, stay hidden   **22 tickling**
(1) stroking gently about the gills—an actual method of fishing
(2) deception.   **24 she** Olivia.   **affect** have fondness for   **25 fancy**
fall in love   **27 follows** serves   **30 rare** extraordinary   **31 jets** struts.
advanced prominent   **32 'Slight** By His (God's) light   **38 example**
precedent   **38–9 lady of the Strachy** (Apparently a lady who had
married below her station; no certain identification.)   **40 Jezebel** the
proud queen of Ahab, King of Israel.   **42 blows** puffs up   **44 state**
chair of state   **45 stone-bow** crossbow that shoots stones
47 branched adorned with a figured pattern suggesting branched
leaves or flowers.   **daybed** sofa, couch   **51 have . . . state** adopt the
imperious manner of authority   **52 demure . . . regard** grave survey
of the company   **54 Toby** (Malvolio omits the title *Sir*.)

MALVOLIO   Seven of my people, with an obedient start, make out for him. I frown the while, and perchance wind up my watch, or play with my—some rich 59 jewel. Toby approaches; curtsies there to me— 60

SIR TOBY   Shall this fellow live?

FABIAN   Though our silence be drawn from us with 62 cars, yet peace. 63

MALVOLIO   I extend my hand to him thus, quenching my familiar smile with an austere regard of control— 65

SIR TOBY   And does not Toby take you a blow o'the lips 66 then?

MALVOLIO   Saying, "Cousin Toby, my fortunes having cast me on your niece give me this prerogative of speech—"

SIR TOBY   What, what?

MALVOLIO   "You must amend your drunkenness."

SIR TOBY   Out, scab! 73

FABIAN   Nay, patience, or we break the sinews of our 74 plot.

MALVOLIO   "Besides, you waste the treasure of your time with a foolish knight—"

SIR ANDREW   That's me, I warrant you.

MALVOLIO   "One Sir Andrew."

SIR ANDREW   I knew 'twas I, for many do call me fool.

MALVOLIO   What employment have we here? 81
    [*Taking up the letter.*]

FABIAN   Now is the woodcock near the gin. 82

SIR TOBY   Oh, peace, and the spirit of humors intimate 83 reading aloud to him!

MALVOLIO   By my life, this is my lady's hand. These be her very c's, her u's, and her t's; and thus makes she 86 her great P's. It is in contempt of question her hand. 87

SIR ANDREW   Her c's, her u's, and her t's. Why that?

MALVOLIO   [*reads*]   "To the unknown beloved, this, and my good wishes."—Her very phrases! By your 90 leave, wax. Soft! And the impressure her Lucrece, 91 with which she uses to seal. 'Tis my lady. To whom 92 should this be?   [*He opens the letter.*]

FABIAN   This wins him, liver and all. 94

MALVOLIO   [*reads*]
    "Jove knows I love,
        But who?
    Lips, do not move;
        No man must know."
    "No man must know." What follows? The numbers 99 altered! "No man must know." If this should be thee, 100 Malvolio?

SIR TOBY   Marry, hang thee, brock! 102

MALVOLIO   [*reads*]
    "I may command where I adore,
        But silence, like a Lucrece knife,
    With bloodless stroke my heart doth gore;
        M.O.A.I. doth sway my life."

FABIAN   A fustian riddle! 107

SIR TOBY   Excellent wench, say I.

MALVOLIO   "M.O.A.I. doth sway my life." Nay, but first, let me see, let me see, let me see.

FABIAN   What dish o'poison has she dressed him! 111

SIR TOBY   And with what wing the staniel checks 112 at it! 113

MALVOLIO   "I may command where I adore." Why, she may command me; I serve her, she is my lady. Why, this is evident to any formal capacity. There is no 116 obstruction in this. And the end—what should that alphabetical position portend? If I could make that 118 resemble something in me! Softly! "M.O.A.I."—

SIR TOBY   Oh, ay, make up that. He is now at a cold scent. 120

FABIAN   Sowter will cry upon't for all this, though it be 121 as rank as a fox. 122

MALVOLIO   "M"—Malvolio. "M"! Why, that begins my name!

FABIAN   Did not I say he would work it out? The cur is excellent at faults. 126

MALVOLIO   "M"—But then there is no consonancy in the 127 sequel that suffers under probation: "A" should fol- 128 low, but "O" does.

FABIAN   And "O" shall end, I hope. 130

SIR TOBY   Ay, or I'll cudgel him, and make him cry "Oh!"

MALVOLIO   And then "I" comes behind.

FABIAN   Ay, an you had any eye behind you, you 133 might see more detraction at your heels than fortunes 134 before you.

MALVOLIO   "M.O.A.I." This simulation is not as the 136 former. And yet, to crush this a little, it would bow to me, for every one of these letters are in my name. Soft! Here follows prose.

---

59 play with my (Malvolio perhaps means his steward's chain but checks himself in time; as "Count Malvolio," he would not be wearing it. A bawdy meaning of playing with himself is also suggested.) **60 curtsies** bows   **62–3 with cars** with chariots, i.e., pulling apart by force   **65 familiar** (1) customary (2) friendly.   **regard of control** look of authority   **66 take** deliver   **73 scab** scurvy fellow.   **74 break . . . of** hamstring, disable   **81 employment** business   **82 woodcock** (A bird proverbial for its stupidity.)   **gin** snare.   **83 humors** whim, caprice   **86 c's . . . t's** i.e., *cut*, slang for the female pudenda   **87 great** (1) uppercase (2) copious. (*P* suggests "pee.")   **in contempt of** beyond   **90–1 By . . . wax** (Addressed to the seal on the letter.)   **91 Soft** Softly, not so fast.   **impressure** device imprinted on the seal.   **Lucrece** Lucretia, chaste matron who, ravished by Tarquin, committed suicide   **92 uses** is accustomed   **94 liver** i.e., the seat of passion   **99–100 The numbers altered!** More verses, in a different meter!

102 brock badger. (Used contemptuously.)   **107 fustian** bombastic, ridiculously pompous   **111 What** What a.   **dressed** prepared for   **112 wing** speed.   **staniel** kestrel, a sparrow hawk. (The word is used contemptuously because of the uselessness of the staniel for falconry.)   **112–13 checks at it** turns to fly at it.   **116 formal capacity** normal understanding.   **118 position** arrangement   **120 Oh, ay** (Playing on *O.I.* of *M.O.A.I.*)   **make up** work out   **121–2 Sowter . . . fox** The hound Sowter (literally, "Cobbler") will bay triumphantly at picking up this false scent, even though the smell is as rank as a fox. ("M.O.A.I." is a false lead that reeks.)   **126 at faults** i.e., at maneuvering his way past breaks in the line of scent—in this case, on a false trail.   **127–8 no consonancy . . . probation** no pattern in the following letters that stands up under examination. (In fact, the letters "M.O.A.I." represent the first, last, second, and next to last letters of Malvolio's name.)   **130 "O" shall end** (1) "O" ends Malvolio's name (2) *omega* ends the Greek alphabet and is thus a symbol for the ending of the world, *alpha* to *omega* (3) Malvolio's cry of pain will end the matter, as Sir Toby suggests in the next line.   **133 eye** (punning on the "I" of "Oh, ay" and "M.O.A.I.")   **134 detraction . . . heels** defamation pursuing you   **136 simulation** disguise, puzzle

[*He reads.*] "If this fall into thy hand, revolve. In my 140
stars I am above thee, but be not afraid of greatness. 141
Some are born great, some achieve greatness, and
some have greatness thrust upon 'em. Thy Fates open 143
their hands; let thy blood and spirit embrace them; 144
and, to inure thyself to what thou art like to be, cast 145
thy humble slough and appear fresh. Be opposite with 146
a kinsman, surly with servants. Let thy tongue tang 147
arguments of state; put thyself into the trick of 148
singularity. She thus advises thee that sighs for thee. 149
Remember who commended thy yellow stockings,
and wished to see thee ever cross-gartered. I say, 151
remember. Go to, thou art made, if thou desir'st to be 152
so. If not, let me see thee a steward still, the fellow of
servants, and not worthy to touch Fortune's fingers.
Farewell. She that would alter services with thee, 155
                    The Fortunate-Unhappy."
Daylight and champaign discovers not more! This is 157
open. I will be proud, I will read politic authors, I will 158
baffle Sir Toby, I will wash off gross acquaintance, I 159
will be point-devise the very man. I do not now fool 160
myself, to let imagination jade me; for every reason 161
excites to this, that my lady loves me. She did com- 162
mend my yellow stockings of late, she did praise my
leg being cross-gartered; and in this she manifests her- 164
self to my love, and with a kind of injunction drives
me to these habits of her liking. I thank my stars, I am 166
happy. I will be strange, stout, in yellow stockings 167
and cross-gartered, even with the swiftness of putting
on. Jove and my stars be praised! Here is yet a postscript. [*He reads.*] "Thou canst not choose but know who
I am. If thou entertain'st my love, let it appear in thy 171
smiling; thy smiles become thee well. Therefore in my
presence still smile, dear my sweet, I prithee." 173
Jove, I thank thee. I will smile; I will do everything that
thou wilt have me.   *Exit.*

[*Sir Toby, Sir Andrew, and Fabian come from hiding.*]

FABIAN   I will not give my part of this sport for a
pension of thousands to be paid from the Sophy. 177
SIR TOBY   I could marry this wench for this device.
SIR ANDREW   So could I too.
SIR TOBY   And ask no other dowry with her but such
another jest.

        Enter Maria.

SIR ANDREW   Nor I neither.
FABIAN   Here comes my noble gull-catcher.   183
SIR TOBY   Wilt thou set thy foot o' my neck?
SIR ANDREW   Or o' mine either?
SIR TOBY   Shall I play my freedom at tray-trip, and 186
become thy bondslave?
SIR ANDREW   I'faith, or I either?
SIR TOBY   Why, thou hast put him in such a dream that
when the image of it leaves him he must run mad.
MARIA   Nay, but say true, does it work upon him?
SIR TOBY   Like aqua vitae with a midwife.   192
MARIA   If you will then see the fruits of the sport, mark
his first approach before my lady. He will come to her
in yellow stockings, and 'tis a color she abhors, and
cross-gartered, a fashion she detests; and he will smile
upon her, which will now be so unsuitable to her
disposition, being addicted to a melancholy as she is,
that it cannot but turn him into a notable contempt. If 199
you will see it, follow me.
SIR TOBY   To the gates of Tartar, thou most excellent 201
devil of wit!
SIR ANDREW   I'll make one too.   *Exeunt.* 203

3.1

*Enter Viola, and Clown [Feste, playing his pipe
and tabor].*

VIOLA   Save thee, friend, and thy music. Dost thou live 1
by thy tabor?   2
FESTE   No, sir, I live by the church.
VIOLA   Art thou a churchman?
FESTE   No such matter, sir. I do live by the church, for
I do live at my house, and my house doth stand by the
church.
VIOLA   So thou mayst say the king lies by a beggar if 8
a beggar dwell near him, or the church stands by thy 9
tabor if thy tabor stand by the church.   10
FESTE   You have said, sir. To see this age! A sentence is 11
but a cheveril glove to a good wit. How quickly the 12
wrong side may be turned outward!
VIOLA   Nay, that's certain. They that dally nicely with 14
words may quickly make them wanton.   15
FESTE   I would therefore my sister had had no name,
sir.
VIOLA   Why, man?

---

140 **revolve** consider.   141 **stars** fortune   143–4 **open their hands**
offer their bounty   145 **inure** accustom.   **like** likely.   **cast** cast off
146 **slough** skin of a snake; hence, former demeanor of humbleness.
opposite contradictory   147 **tang** sound loud with   148 **state** politics, statecraft   148–9 **trick of singularity** eccentricity of manner.
151 **cross-gartered** wearing garters above and below the knee so as to
cross behind it.   152 **Go to** (An expression of remonstrance.)
155 **alter services** i.e., exchange place of mistress and servant
157 **champaign** open country.   **discovers** discloses   158 **politic** dealing with state affairs   159 **baffle** deride, degrade. (A technical chivalric term used to describe the disgrace of a perjured knight.)   **gross**
base   160 **point-devise** correct to the letter   161 **to let** by letting.
jade me trick me, make me look ridiculous (as an unruly horse might
do)   162 **excites to this** prompts this conclusion   164 **this** this letter
166 **these habits** this attire   167 **happy** fortunate.   **strange, stout**
aloof, haughty   171 **thou entertain'st** you accept   173 **still** continually   177 **Sophy** Shah of Persia.

183 **gull-catcher** tricker of *gulls* or dupes.   186 **play** gamble.   **tray-
trip** a game of dice, success in which depended on throwing a three
(*tray*)   192 **aqua vitae** brandy or other distilled liquor   199 **notable
contempt** notorious object of contempt.   201 **Tartar** Tartarus, the
infernal regions   203 **make one** i.e., tag along
3.1. Location: Olivia's garden.
1 **Save** God save   1–2 **live by** earn your living with. (But Feste uses
the phrase to mean "dwell near.")   2 **tabor** small drum.   8 **lies by**
(1) lies sexually with (2) dwells near   9–10 **stands by . . . stand by**
(1) is maintained by (2) is placed near   11 **You have said** You've
expressed your opinion.   **sentence** maxim, judgment, opinion
12 **cheveril** kidskin   14 **dally nicely** (1) play subtly (2) toy amorously
15 **wanton** (1) equivocal (2) licentious, unchaste. (Feste then "dallies"
with the word in its sexual sense; see line 20.)

FESTE   Why, sir, her name's a word, and to dally with that word might make my sister wanton. But indeed, words are very rascals since bonds disgraced them.   21

VIOLA   Thy reason, man?

FESTE   Troth, sir, I can yield you none without words, and words are grown so false I am loath to prove reason with them.

VIOLA   I warrant thou art a merry fellow and car'st for   26
nothing.   27

FESTE   Not so, sir, I do care for something; but in my conscience, sir, I do not care for you. If that be to care for nothing, sir, I would it would make you invisible.   30

VIOLA   Art not thou the Lady Olivia's fool?

FESTE   No indeed, sir. The Lady Olivia has no folly. She will keep no fool, sir, till she be married, and fools are as like husbands as pilchers are to herrings—the   34
husband's the bigger. I am indeed not her fool but   35
her corrupter of words.

VIOLA   I saw thee late at the Count Orsino's.   37

FESTE   Foolery, sir, does walk about the orb like the   38
sun; it shines everywhere. I would be sorry, sir, but   39
the fool should be as oft with your master as with my   40
mistress. I think I saw Your Wisdom there.   41

VIOLA   Nay, an thou pass upon me, I'll no more with   42
thee. Hold, there's expenses for thee.

[She gives a coin.]

FESTE   Now Jove, in his next commodity of hair, send   44
thee a beard!

VIOLA   By my troth, I'll tell thee, I am almost sick for   46
one—[*aside*] though I would not have it grow on my   47
chin.—Is thy lady within?

FESTE   Would not a pair of these have bred, sir?

VIOLA   Yes, being kept together and put to use.   50

FESTE   I would play Lord Pandarus of Phrygia, sir, to   51
bring a Cressida to this Troilus.

VIOLA   I understand you, sir. 'Tis well begged.

[She gives another coin.]

FESTE   The matter, I hope, is not great, sir, begging   54
but a beggar; Cressida was a beggar. My lady is   55
within, sir. I will conster to them whence you come.   56
Who you are and what you would are out of my
welkin—I might say "element," but the word is   58
overworn.   *Exit.*

---

21 since ... them i.e., since bonds have been needed to make sworn statements good. (Words cannot be relied on since not even contractual promises are reliable.)   **26–7 car'st for nothing** are without any worries. (But Feste puns on *care for* in lines 29–30 in the sense of "like.") **30 invisible** i.e., nothing; absent.   **34 pilchers** pilchards, fish resembling herring but smaller   **35 the bigger** (1) the larger (2) the bigger fool.   **37 late** recently   **38 orb** earth   **39–41 I would ... mistress** (1) I should be sorry not to visit Orsino's house often (2) It would be a shame if folly were no less common there than in Olivia's household. **41 Your Wisdom** i.e., you. (A title of mock courtesy.)   **42 an ... me** if you fence (verbally) with me, pass judgment on me   **44 commodity** supply   **46–7 sick for one** (1) eager to have a beard (2) in love with a bearded man   **50 put to use** put out at interest.   **51 Pandarus** the go-between in the love story of Troilus and Cressida; uncle to Cressida **54–5 begging ... was a beggar** (A reference to Henryson's *Testament of Cresseid* in which Cressida became a leper and a beggar. Feste desires another coin to be the mate of the one he has, just as Cressida, the beggar, was mate to Troilus.)   **56 conster** construe, explain   **58 welkin** sky. **element** (The word can be synonymous with *welkin*, but the common phrase *out of my element* means "beyond my scope.")

VIOLA
This fellow is wise enough to play the fool,
And to do that well craves a kind of wit.
He must observe their mood on whom he jests,
The quality of persons, and the time,   63
Not, like the haggard, check at every feather   64
That comes before his eye. This is a practice   65
As full of labor as a wise man's art;
For folly that he wisely shows is fit,   67
But wise men, folly-fall'n, quite taint their wit.   68

Enter Sir Toby and [Sir] Andrew.

SIR TOBY   Save you, gentleman.

VIOLA   And you, sir.

SIR ANDREW   *Dieu vous garde, monsieur.*   71

VIOLA   *Et vous aussi; votre serviteur.*   72

SIR ANDREW   I hope, sir, you are, and I am yours.

SIR TOBY   Will you encounter the house? My niece is   74
desirous you should enter, if your trade be to her.   75

VIOLA   I am bound to your niece, sir; I mean, she is the   76
list of my voyage.   77

SIR TOBY   Taste your legs, sir. Put them to motion.   78

VIOLA   My legs do better understand me, sir, than I un-   79
derstand what you mean by bidding me taste my legs.

SIR TOBY   I mean, to go, sir, to enter.

VIOLA   I will answer you with gait and entrance.—But   82
we are prevented.   83

Enter Olivia and gentlewoman [Maria].

Most excellent accomplished lady, the heavens rain odors on you!

SIR ANDREW   [*to Sir Toby*]   That youth's a rare courtier. "Rain odors"—well.

VIOLA   [*to Olivia*]   My matter hath no voice, lady, but to   88
your own most pregnant and vouchsafed ear.   89

SIR ANDREW   [*to Sir Toby*]   "Odors," "pregnant," and "vouchsafed." I'll get 'em all three all ready.   91

OLIVIA   Let the garden door be shut, and leave me to my hearing. [*Exeunt Sir Toby, Sir Andrew, and Maria.*] Give me your hand, sir.

VIOLA
My duty, madam, and most humble service.

OLIVIA   What is your name?

VIOLA
Cesario is your servant's name, fair princess.

---

63 quality character, rank   **64 haggard** untrained adult hawk, hence unmanageable   **64–5 check ... eye** strike at every bird it sees, i.e., dart from subject to subject.   **65 practice** exercise of skill   **67–8 For ... wit** for the folly he judiciously displays is appropriate and clever, whereas when wise men fall into folly they utterly infect their own intelligence.   **71 *Dieu ... monsieur*** God keep you, sir.   **72 *Et ... serviteur*** And you, too; (I am) your servant. (Sir Andrew is not quite up to a reply in French.)   **74 encounter** (High-sounding word to express "approach.")   **75 trade** business. (Suggesting also a commercial venture.)   **76 I am bound** (1) I am on a journey. (Continuing Sir Toby's metaphor in *trade*.) (2) I am confined, obligated   **77 list** limit, destination   **78 Taste** Try   **79 understand** stand under, support **82 gait and entrance** going and entering. (With a pun on *gate*: [1] stride [2] entryway.)   **83 prevented** anticipated.   **88 hath no voice** cannot be uttered   **89 pregnant and vouchsafed** receptive and attentive   **91 all ready** committed to memory for future use.

OLIVIA
My servant, sir? 'Twas never merry world   98
Since lowly feigning was called compliment.   99
You're servant to the Count Orsino, youth.

VIOLA
And he is yours, and his must needs be yours;   101
Your servant's servant is your servant, madam.

OLIVIA
For him, I think not on him. For his thoughts,   103
Would they were blanks, rather than filled with me!   104

VIOLA
Madam, I come to whet your gentle thoughts
On his behalf.

OLIVIA   Oh, by your leave, I pray you.   106
I bade you never speak again of him.
But, would you undertake another suit,
I had rather hear you to solicit that
Than music from the spheres.

VIOLA   Dear lady—   110

OLIVIA
Give me leave, beseech you. I did send,
After the last enchantment you did here,
A ring in chase of you; so did I abuse   113
Myself, my servant, and, I fear me, you.
Under your hard construction must I sit,   115
To force that on you in a shameful cunning   116
Which you knew none of yours. What might you
    think?
Have you not set mine honor at the stake   118
And baited it with all th'unmuzzled thoughts   119
That tyrannous heart can think? To one of your
    receiving   120
Enough is shown; a cypress, not a bosom,   121
Hides my heart. So, let me hear you speak.   122

VIOLA
I pity you.

OLIVIA   That's a degree to love.

VIOLA
No, not a grece; for 'tis a vulgar proof   124
That very oft we pity enemies.

OLIVIA
Why then, methinks 'tis time to smile again.   126
Oh, world, how apt the poor are to be proud!   127
If one should be a prey, how much the better

To fall before the lion than the wolf!   *Clock strikes.* 129
The clock upbraids me with the waste of time.
Be not afraid, good youth, I will not have you;
And yet, when wit and youth is come to harvest
Your wife is like to reap a proper man.   133
There lies your way, due west.

VIOLA   Then westward ho!   134
Grace and good disposition attend Your Ladyship.   135
You'll nothing, madam, to my lord by me?

OLIVIA   Stay.
I prithee, tell me what thou think'st of me.

VIOLA
That you do think you are not what you are.   139

OLIVIA
If I think so, I think the same of you.   140

VIOLA
Then think you right. I am not what I am.

OLIVIA
I would you were as I would have you be!

VIOLA
Would it be better, madam, than I am?
I wish it might, for now I am your fool.   144

OLIVIA [*aside*]
Oh, what a deal of scorn looks beautiful
In the contempt and anger of his lip!
A murderous guilt shows not itself more soon
Than love that would seem hid; love's night is noon.—   148
Cesario, by the roses of the spring,
By maidhood, honor, truth, and everything,
I love thee so that, maugre all thy pride,   151
Nor wit nor reason can my passion hide.   152
Do not extort thy reasons from this clause,   153
For that I woo, thou therefore hast no cause,   154
But rather reason thus with reason fetter: 155
Love sought is good, but given unsought is better.

VIOLA
By innocence I swear, and by my youth,
I have one heart, one bosom, and one truth,
And that no woman has, nor never none
Shall mistress be of it save I alone.
And so adieu, good madam. Nevermore
Will I my master's tears to you deplore.   162

OLIVIA
Yet come again, for thou perhaps mayst move
That heart, which now abhors, to like his love.
                      Exeunt [separately].

98–9 'Twas . . . compliment Things have never been the same since affected humility (like calling oneself another's servant) began to be mistaken for courtesy.   **101 is yours** is your servant.   **his** those belonging to him   **103 For** As for   **104 blanks** blank coins ready to be stamped or empty sheets of paper   **106 by your leave** i.e., allow me to interrupt   **110 music from the spheres** (The heavenly bodies were thought to be fixed in hollow concentric spheres that revolved one about the other, producing a harmony too exquisite to be heard by human ears.)   **113 abuse** wrong, mislead   **115 hard construction** harsh interpretation   **116 To force that** for forcing the ring   **118 at the stake** (The figure is from bearbaiting.)   **119 baited** harassed. (Literally, set the unmuzzled dogs on to bite the bear.)   **120 receiving** capacity, intelligence   **121–2 a cypress . . . heart** i.e., I have shown my heart to you, veiled only with thin, gauzelike cypress cloth rather than the opaque flesh of my bosom.   **124 grece** step. (Synonymous with *degree* in the preceding line.)   **vulgar proof** common experience   **126 smile** i.e., cast off love's melancholy   **127 how . . . proud!** how ready the unfortunate and rejected (like myself) are to find something to be proud of in their distress! Or, how apt are persons of comparatively low social station like yourself to show pride in rejecting love!

129 To fall . . . wolf! i.e., to fall before a noble adversary rather than to a person like you who attacks me thus!   **133 like** likely.   **proper** handsome, worthy   **134 westward ho** (The cry of Thames watermen to attract westward-bound passengers.)   **135 Grace . . . Ladyship** May you enjoy God's blessing and a happy frame of mind.   **139 That . . . are** i.e., That you think you are in love with a man, and you are mistaken.   **140 If . . . you** (Olivia may interpret Viola's cryptic statement as suggesting that Olivia "does not know herself," i.e., is distracted with passion; she may also hint at her suspicion that "Cesario" is higher born than he admits.)   **144 fool** butt.   **148 love's . . . noon** i.e., love, despite its attempt to be secret, reveals itself as plain as day.   **151 maugre** in spite of   **152 Nor** neither   **153–4 Do . . . cause** Do not rationalize your indifference along these lines, that because I am the wooer you have no cause to reciprocate.   **155 But . . . fetter** But instead control your reasoning with the following reason   **162 deplore** beweep.

3.2

Enter Sir Toby, Sir Andrew, and Fabian.

SIR ANDREW   No, faith, I'll not stay a jot longer.

SIR TOBY   Thy reason, dear venom, give thy reason. 2

FABIAN   You must needs yield your reason, Sir Andrew.

SIR ANDREW   Marry, I saw your niece do more favors to the Count's servingman than ever she bestowed upon me. I saw't i'th' orchard. 6

SIR TOBY   Did she see thee the while, old boy? Tell me that.

SIR ANDREW   As plain as I see you now.

FABIAN   This was a great argument of love in her toward you. 10

SIR ANDREW   'Slight, will you make an ass o'me? 12

FABIAN   I will prove it legitimate, sir, upon the oaths of judgment and reason. 13

SIR TOBY   And they have been grand-jurymen since before Noah was a sailor.

FABIAN   She did show favor to the youth in your sight only to exasperate you, to awake your dormouse valor, 18 to put fire in your heart and brimstone in your liver. You should then have accosted her, and with some excellent jests, fire-new from the mint, you should 21 have banged the youth into dumbness. This was 22 looked for at your hand, and this was balked. The dou- 23 ble gilt of this opportunity you let time wash off, and 24 you are now sailed into the north of my lady's opinion, 25 where you will hang like an icicle on a Dutchman's 26 beard unless you do redeem it by some laudable at- 27 tempt either of valor or policy. 28

SIR ANDREW   An't be any way, it must be with valor, for policy I hate. I had as lief be a Brownist as a poli- 30 tician. 31

SIR TOBY   Why, then, build me thy fortunes upon the 32 basis of valor. Challenge me the Count's youth to fight 33 with him; hurt him in eleven places. My niece shall take note of it; and assure thyself, there is no love-broker in the world can more prevail in man's 36 commendation with woman than report of valor.

FABIAN   There is no way but this, Sir Andrew.

SIR ANDREW   Will either of you bear me a challenge to him?

SIR TOBY   Go, write it in a martial hand. Be curst and 41 brief; it is no matter how witty, so it be eloquent and full of invention. Taunt him with the license of ink. If 43

thou "thou"-est him some thrice, it shall not be amiss; 44 and as many lies as will lie in thy sheet of paper, 45 although the sheet were big enough for the bed of 46 Ware in England, set 'em down. Go, about it. Let 47 there be gall enough in thy ink, though thou write 48 with a goose pen, no matter. About it. 49

SIR ANDREW   Where shall I find you?

SIR TOBY   We'll call thee at the cubiculo. Go. 51

Exit Sir Andrew.

FABIAN   This is a dear manikin to you, Sir Toby. 52

SIR TOBY   I have been dear to him, lad, some two 53 thousand strong or so.

FABIAN   We shall have a rare letter from him; but you'll 55 not deliver't?

SIR TOBY   Never trust me, then; and by all means stir on the youth to an answer. I think oxen and wainropes 58 cannot hale them together. For Andrew, if he were 59 opened and you find so much blood in his liver as will 60 clog the foot of a flea, I'll eat the rest of th'anatomy. 61

FABIAN   And his opposite, the youth, bears in his 62 visage no great presage of cruelty.

Enter Maria.

SIR TOBY   Look where the youngest wren of nine 64 comes.

MARIA   If you desire the spleen, and will laugh your- 66 selves into stitches, follow me. Yond gull Malvolio is turned heathen, a very renegado; for there is no 68 Christian that means to be saved by believing rightly can ever believe such impossible passages of gross- 70 ness. He's in yellow stockings. 71

SIR TOBY   And cross-gartered?

MARIA   Most villainously, like a pedant that keeps a 73 school i'th' church. I have dogged him like his murderer. He does obey every point of the letter that I dropped to betray him. He does smile his face into more lines than is in the new map with the augmen- 77 tation of the Indies. You have not seen such a thing as 78 'tis. I can hardly forbear hurling things at him. I know my lady will strike him. If she do, he'll smile and take't for a great favor.

SIR TOBY   Come, bring us, bring us where he is.

Exeunt omnes.

44 "thou"-est ("Thou" was used only between friends or to inferiors.) **45 lies** charges of lying   **46–7 bed of Ware** a famous bedstead capable of holding twelve persons, about eleven feet square, said to have been at the Stag Inn in Ware, Hertfordshire   **48 gall** (1) bitterness, rancor (2) a growth found on certain oaks, used as an ingredient of ink **49 goose pen** (1) goose quill (2) foolish style   **51 call thee** call for you. **cubiculo** little chamber, bedchamber.   **52 manikin** puppet   **53 dear** expensive. (Playing on *dear*, "fond," in the previous speech.)   **55 rare** extraordinary   **58 wainropes** wagon ropes   **59 hale** haul.   **For** As for **60 liver** (A pale and bloodless liver was a sign of cowardice.) **61 th'anatomy** the cadaver.   **62 opposite** adversary   **64 youngest ... nine** the last hatched and smallest of a nest of wrens   **66 the spleen** a laughing fit. (The spleen was thought to be the seat of immoderate laughter.)   **68 renegado** renegade, deserter of his religion **70–1 impossible ... grossness** gross impossibilities (i.e., in the letter). **73 villainously** i.e., abominably.   **pedant** schoolmaster   **77–8 the new ... Indies** (Probably a reference to a map made by Emmeric Mollineux in 1599–1600 to be printed in Hakluyt's *Voyages*, showing more of the East indies, including Japan, than had ever been mapped before.)

3.2. Location: Olivia's house.
2 venom i.e., person filled with venomous anger   **6 orchard** garden. **10 argument** proof   **12 'Slight** By his (God's) light   **13 it** my con- tention.   **oaths** i.e., testimony under oath   **18 dormouse** i.e., sleepy and timid   **21 fire-new ... mint** newly coined   **22 banged** struck **23 balked** missed, neglected.   **23–4 double gilt** thick layer of gold, i.e., rare worth   **25 into ... opinion** i.e., out of the warmth and sun- shine of Olivia's favor   **26–7 icicle ... beard** (Alludes to the arctic voyage of William Barents in 1596–1597.)   **28 policy** stratagem. **30 Brownist** (An early name of the Congregationalists, from the name of the founder, Robert Browne.)   **30–1 politician** intriguer. (Sir Andrew misinterprets Fabian's more neutral use of *policy*, "clever stratagem.")   **32–3 build me ... Challenge me** build . . . Challenge. ("Me" is idiomatic.)   **36 love-broker** agent between lovers   **41 curst** fierce   **43 with ... ink** i.e., with all the unfettered eloquence at your disposal as a writer.

3.3

Enter Sebastian and Antonio.

SEBASTIAN
I would not by my will have troubled you,
But since you make your pleasure of your pains,
I will no further chide you.

ANTONIO
I could not stay behind you. My desire,
More sharp than filèd steel, did spur me forth,
And not all love to see you—though so much   6
As might have drawn one to a longer voyage—
But jealousy what might befall your travel,   8
Being skilless in these parts, which to a stranger,   9
Unguided and unfriended, often prove
Rough and unhospitable. My willing love,
The rather by these arguments of fear,   12
Set forth in your pursuit.

SEBASTIAN   My kind Antonio,
I can no other answer make but thanks,
And thanks; and ever oft good turns   15
Are shuffled off with such uncurrent pay.   16
But were my worth, as is my conscience, firm,   17
You should find better dealing. What's to do?   18
Shall we go see the relics of this town?   19

ANTONIO
Tomorrow, sir. Best first go see your lodging.

SEBASTIAN
I am not weary, and 'tis long to night.
I pray you, let us satisfy our eyes
With the memorials and the things of fame
That do renown this city.

ANTONIO   Would you'd pardon me.   24
I do not without danger walk these streets.
Once in a sea fight 'gainst the Count his galleys   26
I did some service, of such note indeed
That were I ta'en here it would scarce be answered.   28

SEBASTIAN
Belike you slew great number of his people?   29

ANTONIO
Th'offense is not of such a bloody nature,
Albeit the quality of the time and quarrel
Might well have given us bloody argument.   32
It might have since been answered in repaying   33
What we took from them, which for traffic's sake   34
Most of our city did. Only myself stood out,
For which, if I be lapsèd in this place,   36
I shall pay dear.

SEBASTIAN   Do not then walk too open.

ANTONIO
It doth not fit me. Hold, sir, here's my purse.
                                    [*He gives his purse.*]
In the south suburbs, at the Elephant,   39
Is best to lodge. I will bespeak our diet,   40
Whiles you beguile the time and feed your knowl-
    edge
With viewing of the town. There shall you have me.   42

SEBASTIAN   Why I your purse?

ANTONIO
Haply your eye shall light upon some toy   44
You have desire to purchase; and your store   45
I think is not for idle markets, sir.   46

SEBASTIAN
I'll be your purse-bearer and leave you
For an hour.

ANTONIO   To th'Elephant.

SEBASTIAN   I do remember.
                                    Exeunt [*separately*].

❧

3.4

Enter Olivia and Maria.

OLIVIA [*aside*]
I have sent after him; he says he'll come.   1
How shall I feast him? What bestow of him?   2
For youth is bought more oft than begged or
    borrowed.
I speak too loud.—
Where's Malvolio? He is sad and civil,   5
And suits well for a servant with my fortunes.
Where is Malvolio?

MARIA   He's coming, madam, but in very strange
manner. He is, sure, possessed, madam.   9

OLIVIA   Why, what's the matter? Does he rave?

MARIA   No, madam, he does nothing but smile. Your
Ladyship were best to have some guard about you if he
come, for sure the man is tainted in's wits.   13

OLIVIA
Go call him hither. [*Maria summons Malvolio.*] I am as
    mad as he,
If sad and merry madness equal be.   15

Enter Malvolio, [*cross-gartered and in yellow
stockings*].

How now, Malvolio?

MALVOLIO   Sweet lady, ho, ho!

OLIVIA   Smil'st thou? I sent for thee upon a sad   18
occasion.

3.3. **Location: A Street.**
6 all only, merely.   **so much** i.e., that was great enough   **8 jealousy**
anxiety   **9 skilless in** unacquainted with   **12 The rather** made all the
more willing   **15 And . . . turns** (This probably corrupt line is usually
made to read, "And thanks and ever thanks; and oft good turns.")
16 shuffled off turned aside.   **uncurrent** worthless (such as mere
thanks)   **17 worth** wealth.   **conscience** i.e., moral inclination to assist
18 dealing treatment, payment.   **19 relics** antiquities   **24 renown**
make famous   **26 Count his** Count's, i.e., Duke's   **28 it . . . answered**
I'd be hard put to offer a defense.   **29 Belike** Perhaps   **32 bloody**
argument cause for bloodshed.   **33 answered** compensated   **34 traf-**
fic's trade's   **36 lapsèd** caught off guard, surprised

---

39 **Elephant** the name of an inn   40 **bespeak our diet** order our food
42 **have** find   44 **Haply** Perhaps.   **toy** trifle   45 **store** store of money
46 **is not . . . markets** cannot afford luxuries
3.4. **Location: Olivia's garden.**
1 **he . . . come** i.e., suppose he says he'll come.   2 **of** on   5 **sad and**
civil sober and decorous   9 **possessed** (1) possessed with an evil
spirit (2) mad   13 **in's** in his   15 **If . . . equal be** i.e., if love melancholy and smiling madness are essentially alike. (Love melancholy
was regarded as a kind of madness.)   18 **sad** serious

MALVOLIO   Sad, lady? I could be sad. This does make 20
some obstruction in the blood, this cross-gartering,
but what of that? If it please the eye of one, it is with
me as the very true sonnet is, "Please one and please 23
all."   24

OLIVIA   Why, how dost thou, man? What is the matter
with thee?

MALVOLIO   Not black in my mind, though yellow in my 27
legs. It did come to his hands, and commands shall be 28
executed. I think we do know the sweet roman hand.   29

OLIVIA   Wilt thou go to bed, Malvolio?   30

MALVOLIO   To bed! "Ay, sweetheart, and I'll come to 31
thee."   32

OLIVIA   God comfort thee! Why dost thou smile so and
kiss thy hand so oft?

MARIA   How do you, Malvolio?

MALVOLIO   At your request? Yes, nightingales answer 36
daws.   37

MARIA   Why appear you with this ridiculous boldness
before my lady?

MALVOLIO   "Be not afraid of greatness." 'Twas well writ.

OLIVIA   What mean'st thou by that, Malvolio?

MALVOLIO   "Some are born great—"

OLIVIA   Ha?

MALVOLIO   "Some achieve greatness—"

OLIVIA   What say'st thou?

MALVOLIO   "And some have greatness thrust upon them."

OLIVIA   Heaven restore thee!

MALVOLIO   "Remember who commended thy yellow
stockings—"

OLIVIA   Thy yellow stockings?

MALVOLIO   "And wished to see thee cross-gartered."

OLIVIA   Cross-gartered?

MALVOLIO   "Go to, thou art made, if thou desir'st to
be so—"

OLIVIA   Am I made?

MALVOLIO   "If not, let me see thee a servant still."

OLIVIA   Why, this is very midsummer madness.   57

Enter Servant.

SERVANT   Madam, the young gentleman of the Count
Orsino's is returned. I could hardly entreat him back.
He attends Your Ladyship's pleasure.

OLIVIA   I'll come to him.   [*Exit Servant.*]
Good Maria, let this fellow be looked to. Where's my
cousin Toby? Let some of my people have a special

care of him. I would not have him miscarry for the half 64
of my dowry.

Exeunt [Olivia and Maria, different ways].

MALVOLIO   Oho, do you come near me now? No worse 66
man than Sir Toby to look to me! This concurs directly
with the letter. She sends him on purpose that I may
appear stubborn to him, for she incites me to that in
the letter. "Cast thy humble slough," says she; "be opposite with a kinsman, surly with servants; let thy
tongue tang with arguments of state; put thyself into
the trick of singularity." And consequently sets down 73
the manner how: as, a sad face, a reverend carriage, a 74
slow tongue, in the habit of some sir of note, and so 75
forth. I have limed her, but it is Jove's doing, and Jove 76
make me thankful! And when she went away now,
"Let this fellow be looked to." "Fellow!" Not "Malvo- 78
lio," nor after my degree, but "fellow." Why, every- 79
thing adheres together, that no dram of a scruple, no 80
scruple of a scruple, no obstacle, no incredulous or un- 81
safe circumstance—what can be said?—nothing that 82
can be can come between me and the full prospect of
my hopes. Well, Jove, not I, is the doer of this, and he
is to be thanked.

Enter [Sir] Toby, Fabian, and Maria.

SIR TOBY   Which way is he, in the name of sanctity? If
all the devils of hell be drawn in little, and Legion him- 87
self possessed him, yet I'll speak to him.

FABIAN   Here he is, here he is.—How is't with you,
sir? How is't with you, man?

MALVOLIO   Go off. I discard you. Let me enjoy my
private. Go off.   92

MARIA   Lo, how hollow the fiend speaks within him!
Did not I tell you? Sir Toby, my lady prays you to have
a care of him.

MALVOLIO   Aha, does she so?

SIR TOBY   Go to, go to! Peace, peace, we must deal
gently with him. Let me alone.—How do you, 98
Malvolio? How is't with you? What, man, defy the 99
devil! Consider, he's an enemy to mankind.

MALVOLIO   Do you know what you say?

MARIA   La you, an you speak ill of the devil, how he 102
takes it at heart! Pray God he be not bewitched!

FABIAN   Carry his water to th' wise woman.   104

MARIA   Marry, and it shall be done tomorrow morning,
if I live. My lady would not lose him for more than
I'll say.

MALVOLIO   How now, mistress?

---

20 **sad** (1) serious (2) melancholy.   23 **sonnet** song, ballad
23–4 **"Please . . . all"** "To please one special person is as good as to
please everybody." (The refain of a ballad.)   27 **black** i.e., melancholic
28 **It** i.e., The letter.   **his** Malvolio's   29 **roman hand** fashionable italic
or Italian style of handwriting rather than English "secretary" handwriting.   30 **go to bed** i.e., try to sleep off your mental distress. (But
Malvolio misinterprets as a sexual invitation.)   31–2 **"Ay . . . thee"**
(Malvolio quotes from a popular song of the day.)   36–7 **nightingales
answer daws** i.e. (to Maria), do you suppose a fine fellow like me
would answer a lowly creature (a *daw*, a "jackdaw") like you?
57 **midsummer madness** (A proverbial phrase; the midsummer
moon was supposed to cause madness.)

64 **miscarry** come to harm   66 **come near** understand, appreciate
73 **consequently** thereafter   74 **sad** serious   75 **habit . . . note** attire
suited to a man of distinction   76 **limed** caught like a bird with
birdlime (a sticky substance spread on branches)   78 **Fellow** (Malvolio takes the basic meaning, "companion.")   79 **after my degree**
according to my position   80 **dram** (Literally, one-eighth of a fluid
ounce.)   **scruple** (Literally, one-third of a dram.)   81 **incredulous**
incredible   81–2 **unsafe** uncertain, unreliable   87 **drawn in little**
(1) portrayed in miniature (2) gathered into a small space.   **Legion**
an unclean spirit. ("My name is Legion, for we are many," Mark 5:9.)
92 **private** privacy.   98 **Let me alone** Leave him to me.   99 **defy**
renounce   102 **La you** Look you   104 **water** urine (for medical
analysis).   **wise woman** sorceress.

MARIA   Oh, Lord!

SIR TOBY   Prithee, hold thy peace; this is not the way. Do you not see you move him? Let me alone with him. 111

FABIAN   No way but gentleness, gently, gently. The fiend is rough, and will not be roughly used.

SIR TOBY   Why, how now, my bawcock! How dost 115 thou, chuck? 116

MALVOLIO   Sir!

SIR TOBY   Ay, biddy, come with me. What, man, 'tis 118 not for gravity to play at cherry-pit with Satan. Hang 119 him, foul collier! 120

MARIA   Get him to say his prayers, good Sir Toby, get him to pray.

MALVOLIO   My prayers, minx?

MARIA   No, I warrant you, he will not hear of godliness.

MALVOLIO   Go hang yourselves all! You are idle, shal- 125 low things; I am not of your element. You shall know 126 more hereafter.   Exit. 127

SIR TOBY   Is't possible?

FABIAN   If this were played upon a stage, now, I could condemn it as an improbable fiction.

SIR TOBY   His very genius hath taken the infection of 131 the device, man.

MARIA   Nay, pursue him now, lest the device take air 133 and taint. 134

FABIAN   Why, we shall make him mad indeed.

MARIA   The house will be the quieter.

SIR TOBY   Come, we'll have him in a dark room and 137 bound. My niece is already in the belief that he's mad. 138 We may carry it thus for our pleasure and his penance 139 till our very pastime, tired out of breath, prompt us to have mercy on him, at which time we will bring the device to the bar and crown thee for a finder of 142 madmen. But see, but see! 143

Enter Sir Andrew [with a letter].

FABIAN   More matter for a May morning. 144

SIR ANDREW   Here's the challenge. Read it. I warrant there's vinegar and pepper in't.

FABIAN   Is't so saucy? 147

SIR ANDREW   Ay, is't, I warrant him. Do but read. 148

SIR TOBY   Give me. [*He reads.*] "Youth, whatsoever thou art, thou art but a scurvy fellow."

FABIAN   Good, and valiant.

SIR TOBY [*reads*]   "Wonder not, nor admire not in thy 152 mind, why I do call thee so, for I will show thee no reason for't."

FABIAN   A good note, that keeps you from the blow of 155 the law.

SIR TOBY [*reads*]   "Thou com'st to the Lady Olivia, and in my sight she uses thee kindly. But thou liest in thy throat; that is not the matter I challenge thee for."

FABIAN   Very brief, and to exceeding good sense—less.

SIR TOBY [*reads*]   "I will waylay thee going home, where if it be thy chance to kill me—"

FABIAN   Good.

SIR TOBY [*reads*]   "Thou kill'st me like a rogue and a villain."

FABIAN   Still you keep o' th' windy side of the law. 166 Good.

SIR TOBY [*reads*]   "Fare thee well, and God have mercy upon one of our souls! He may have mercy upon mine, but my hope is better, and so look to thyself. 170 Thy friend, as thou usest him, and thy sworn enemy,
                        Andrew Aguecheek."
If this letter move him not, his legs cannot. I'll give't 173 him.

MARIA   You may have very fit occasion for't. He is now in some commerce with my lady, and will by and by 176 depart.

SIR TOBY   Go, Sir Andrew. Scout me for him at the 178 corner of the orchard like a bum-baily. So soon as ever 179 thou see'st him, draw, and as thou draw'st, swear hor- 180 rible; for it comes to pass oft that a terrible oath, with 181 a swaggering accent sharply twanged off, gives man- hood more approbation than ever proof itself would 183 have earned him. Away!

SIR ANDREW   Nay, let me alone for swearing.   Exit. 185

SIR TOBY   Now will not I deliver his letter, for the behav- ior of the young gentleman gives him out to be of good capacity and breeding; his employment between his lord and my niece confirms no less. Therefore this letter, being so excellently ignorant, will breed no ter- ror in the youth. He will find it comes from a clodpoll. 191 But, sir, I will deliver his challenge by word of mouth, set upon Aguecheek a notable report of valor, and drive the gentleman—as I know his youth will aptly 194 receive it—into a most hideous opinion of his rage, 195 skill, fury, and impetuosity. This will so fright them both that they will kill one another by the look, like cockatrices. 198

Enter Olivia and Viola.

FABIAN   Here he comes with your niece. Give them way 199 till he take leave, and presently after him. 200

---

111 **move** upset, excite   115 **bawcock** fine fellow. (From the French *beau-coq*.)   116 **chuck** (A form of "chick," term of endearment.) 118 **biddy** chicken   119 **for gravity** suitable for a man of your dig- nity.   **cherry-pit** a children's game consisting of throwing cherry stones into a little hole   120 **collier** i.e., Satan. (Literally, a coal ven- dor.)   125 **idle** foolish   126 **element** sphere.   126–7 **know more** i.e., hear about this   131 **genius** i.e., soul, spirit   133–4 **take . . . taint** become exposed to air (i.e., become known) and thus spoil. 137–8 **have . . . bound** (The standard treatment for insanity at this time.)   139 **carry** manage   142 **bar** i.e., bar of judgment 142–3 **finder of madmen** member of a jury charged with "finding" if the accused is insane.   144 **matter . . . morning** sport for Mayday plays or games.   147 **saucy** (1) spicy (2) insolent.   148 **him** it. 152 **admire** marvel

155 **note** observation, remark   166 **windy** windward, i.e., safe, where one is less likely to be driven onto legal rocks and shoals   170 **my hope is better** (Sir Andrew's comically inept way of saying he hopes to be the survivor; instead, he seems to say, "May I be damned.") 173 **move** (1) stir up (2) set in motion   176 **commerce** transaction 178 **Scout me** Keep watch   179 **bum-baily** minor sheriff's officer employed in making arrests.   180–1 **horrible** horribly   183 **approba- tion** reputation (for courage).   **proof** performance   185 **let . . . swearing** don't worry about my ability in swearing.   191 **clodpoll** blockhead.   194–5 **his . . . it** his inexperience will make him all the more ready to believe it   198 **cockatrices** basilisks, fabulous serpents reputed to be able to kill by a mere look.   199 **Give them way** Stay out of their way   200 **presently** immediately

SIR TOBY   I will meditate the while upon some horrid 201
    message for a challenge.
                    [*Exeunt Sir Toby, Fabian, and Maria.*]
OLIVIA
    I have said too much unto a heart of stone
    And laid mine honor too unchary on't.   204
    There's something in me that reproves my fault,
    But such a headstrong potent fault it is
    That it but mocks reproof.
VIOLA
    With the same havior that your passion bears   208
    Goes on my master's griefs.   209
OLIVIA [*giving a locket*]
    Here, wear this jewel for me. 'Tis my picture.
    Refuse it not; it hath no tongue to vex you.
    And I beseech you come again tomorrow.
    What shall you ask of me that I'll deny,
    That honor, saved, may upon asking give?   214
VIOLA
    Nothing but this: your true love for my master.
OLIVIA
    How with mine honor may I give him that
    Which I have given to you?
VIOLA   I will acquit you.   217
OLIVIA
    Well, come again tomorrow. Fare thee well.
    A fiend like thee might bear my soul to hell.   [*Exit.*] 219

            Enter [Sir] Toby and Fabian.

SIR TOBY   Gentleman, God save thee.
VIOLA   And you, sir.
SIR TOBY   That defense thou hast, betake thee to't. Of 222
    what nature the wrongs are thou hast done him, I
    know not, but thy intercepter, full of despite, bloody 224
    as the hunter, attends thee at the orchard end. 225
    Dismount thy tuck, be yare in thy preparation, for thy 226
    assailant is quick, skillful, and deadly.
VIOLA   You mistake sir. I am sure no man hath any
    quarrel to me. My remembrance is very free and clear 229
    from any image of offense done to any man.
SIR TOBY   You'll find it otherwise, I assure you. There-
    fore, if you hold your life at any price, betake you to
    your guard, for your opposite hath in him what youth, 233
    strength, skill, and wrath can furnish man withal. 234
VIOLA   I pray you, sir, what is he?
SIR TOBY   He is knight, dubbed with unhatched rapier 236

and on carpet consideration, but he is a devil in 237
private brawl. Souls and bodies hath he divorced
three, and his incensement at this moment is so implacable that satisfaction can be none but by pangs of
death and sepulchre. Hob, nob is his word; give't or 241
take't.
VIOLA   I will return again into the house and desire
some conduct of the lady. I am no fighter. I have 244
heard of some kind of men that put quarrels purposely
on others, to taste their valor. Belike this is a 246
man of that quirk.   247
SIR TOBY   Sir, no. His indignation derives itself out of a
very competent injury; therefore, get you on and give 249
him his desire. Back you shall not to the house unless
you undertake that with me which with as much
safety you might answer him. Therefore, on, or strip 252
your sword stark naked; for meddle you must, that's 253
certain, or forswear to wear iron about you.   254
VIOLA   This is as uncivil as strange. I beseech you, do
me this courteous office as to know of the knight what 256
my offense to him is. It is something of my negligence, 257
nothing of my purpose.   258
SIR TOBY   I will do so.—Signor Fabian, stay you by this
gentleman till my return.   *Exit [Sir] Toby.*
VIOLA   Pray you, sir, do you know of this matter?
FABIAN   I know the knight is incensed against you,
even to a mortal arbitrament, but nothing of the 263
circumstance more.
VIOLA   I beseech you, what manner of man is he?
FABIAN   Nothing of that wonderful promise, to read 266
him by his form, as you are like to find him in the 267
proof of his valor. He is, indeed, sir, the most skillful,
bloody, and fatal opposite that you could possibly
have found in any part of Illyria. Will you walk 270
towards him, I will make your peace with him if I can.
VIOLA   I shall be much bound to you for't. I am one
that had rather go with Sir Priest than Sir Knight. I 273
care not who knows so much of my mettle.   *Exeunt.*

            Enter [Sir] Toby and [Sir] Andrew.

SIR TOBY   Why, man, he's a very devil; I have not seen
such a firago. I had a pass with him, rapier, scabbard, 276
and all, and he gives me the stuck-in with such a 277
mortal motion that it is inevitable; and on the answer, 278
he pays you as surely as your feet hits the ground they
step on. They say he has been fencer to the Sophy. 280
SIR ANDREW   Pox on't, I'll not meddle with him.

---

201 horrid terrifying. (Literally, "bristling.")   **204 laid** hazarded.
unchary on't recklessly on it.   **208–9 With . . . griefs** i.e., Orsino's sufferings in love are as reckless and uncontrollable as your feelings.
214 That . . . give? that can be granted without compromising my
honor?   **217 acquit you** release you of your promise.   **219 A fiend . . .
hell** i.e., You are my torment. (*Like thee* means "in your likeness.")
222 That . . . to't Get ready to deploy whatever skill you have in fencing.   **224 intercepter** he who lies in wait.   **despite** defiance, ill will
224–5 bloody as the hunter bloodthirsty as a hunting dog   **226 Dismount thy tuck** Draw your rapier.   **yare** ready, nimble   **229 to** with
233 opposite opponent.   **what** whatsoever   **234 withal** with.
236 unhatched unhacked, unused in battle

237 carpet consideration (A carpet knight was one whose title was
obtained, not in battle, but through connections at court.)   **241 Hob,
nob** Have or have not, i.e., give it or take it, kill or be killed.   **word**
motto   **244 conduct** safe-conduct, escort   **246 taste** test, prove
Belike Probably   **247 quirk** peculiar humor.   **249 competent** sufficient   **252–3 strip . . . naked** draw your sword from its sheath
253 meddle engage (in conflict)   **254 forswear . . . iron** give up your
right to wear a sword   **256 know of** inquire from   **257–8 It is . . .
purpose** It is the result of some oversight, not anything I intended.
263 mortal arbitrament trial to the death   **266–7 read . . . form** judge
him by his appearance   **267 like** likely   **270 Will you** If you will
273 go with associate with.   **Sir Priest** (*Sir* was a courtesy title for
priests.)   **276 firago** virago.   **pass** bout   **277 stuck-in** stoccado, a
thrust in fencing   **278 answer** return hit   **280 to** in the service of

SIR TOBY   Ay, but he will not now be pacified. Fabian can scarce hold him yonder.

SIR ANDREW   Plague on't, an I thought he had been valiant and so cunning in fence, I'd have seen him damned ere I'd have challenged him. Let him let the matter slip and I'll give him my horse, gray Capilet.   287

SIR TOBY   I'll make the motion. Stand here, make a 288 good show on't. This shall end without the perdition 289 of souls. [*Aside, as he crosses to meet Fabian*] Marry, I'll 290 ride your horse as well as I ride you.

Enter Fabian and Viola.

[*Aside to Fabian*] I have his horse to take up the 292 quarrel. I have persuaded him the youth's a devil.

FABIAN   He is as horribly conceited of him, and pants 294 and looks pale as if a bear were at his heels.

SIR TOBY [*to Viola*]   There's no remedy, sir, he will fight with you for's oath's sake. Marry, he hath better bethought him of his quarrel, and he finds that now scarce to be worth talking of. Therefore draw, for the supportance of his vow; he protests he 300 will not hurt you.

VIOLA [*aside*]   Pray God defend me! A little thing 302 would make me tell them how much I lack of a man. 303

FABIAN   Give ground, if you see him furious.

SIR TOBY [*crossing to Sir Andrew*]   Come, Sir Andrew, there's no remedy. The gentleman will, for his honor's sake, have one bout with you. He cannot by the *duello* avoid it. But he has promised me, as he is 308 a gentleman and a soldier, he will not hurt you. Come on, to't.

SIR ANDREW   Pray God he keep his oath!

Enter Antonio.

VIOLA [*to Fabian*]   I do assure you, 'tis against my will.
                                        [*They draw.*]

ANTONIO [*drawing, to Sir Andrew*]
Put up your sword. If this young gentleman
Have done offense, I take the fault on me;
If you offend him, I for him defy you.

SIR TOBY   You, sir? Why, what are you?

ANTONIO
One, sir, that for his love dares yet do more
Than you have heard him brag to you he will.

SIR TOBY [*drawing*]
Nay, if you be an undertaker, I am for you.   319

Enter Officers.

FABIAN   Oh, good Sir Toby, hold! Here come the officers.

SIR TOBY [*to Antonio*]   I'll be with you anon.

VIOLA [*to Sir Andrew*]   Pray, sir, put your sword up, if you please.

SIR ANDREW   Marry, will I, sir; and for that I promised 324 you, I'll be as good as my word. He will bear you 325 easily, and reins well.

FIRST OFFICER   This is the man. Do thy office.

SECOND OFFICER
Antonio, I arrest thee at the suit
Of Count Orsino.

ANTONIO   You do mistake me, sir.

FIRST OFFICER
No, sir, no jot. I know your favor well,   330
Though now you have no sea-cap on your head.—
Take him away. He knows I know him well.

ANTONIO
I must obey. [*To Viola*] This comes with seeking you.
But there's no remedy; I shall answer it.   334
What will you do, now my necessity
Makes me to ask you for my purse? It grieves me
Much more for what I cannot do for you
Than what befalls myself. You stand amazed,
But be of comfort.

SECOND OFFICER   Come, sir, away.

ANTONIO [*to Viola*]
I must entreat of you some of that money.

VIOLA   What money, sir?
For the fair kindness you have showed me here,
And part being prompted by your present trouble,   343
Out of my lean and low ability
I'll lend you something. My having is not much;   345
I'll make division of my present with you.   346
Hold, there's half my coffer.   [*She offers money.*] 347

ANTONIO   Will you deny me now?
Is't possible that my deserts to you   349
Can lack persuasion? Do not tempt my misery,   350
Lest that it make me so unsound a man   351
As to upbraid you with those kindnesses
That I have done for you.

VIOLA   I know of none,
Nor know I you by voice or any feature.
I hate ingratitude more in a man
Than lying, vainness, babbling drunkenness,   356
Or any taint of vice whose strong corruption
Inhabits our frail blood.

ANTONIO   Oh, heavens themselves!

SECOND OFFICER   Come, sir, I pray you, go.

ANTONIO
Let me speak a little. This youth that you see here
I snatched one half out of the jaws of death,
Relieved him with such sanctity of love,   363
And to his image, which methought did promise   364
Most venerable worth, did I devotion.   365

---

287 **Capilet** i.e., "little horse." (From "capel," a nag.)   288 **motion** offer.   289–90 **perdition of souls** i.e., loss of lives.   292 **take up** settle, make up   294 **He . . . him** i.e., Cesario has as horrible a conception of Sir Andrew   300 **supportance** upholding   302–3 **A little . . . man** (With bawdy suggestion of the penis.)   308 **duello** dueling code   319 **undertaker** one who takes upon himself a task or business; here, a challenger.   **for you** ready for you.

324 **for that** as for what   325 **He** i.e., The horse   330 **favor** face   334 **answer it** stand trial and make reparation for it.   343 **part** partly   345 **having** wealth   346 **present** present store   347 **coffer** purse. (Literally, strongbox.)   349–50 **deserts . . . persuasion** claims on you can fail to persuade you to help me.   350 **tempt** try too severely   351 **unsound** morally weak, lacking in self-control   356 **vainness** vaingloriousness   363 **such . . . love** i.e., such veneration as is due to a sacred relic   364 **image** what he appeared to be. (Playing on the idea of a religious icon to be venerated.)   365 **venerable worth** worthiness of being venerated

FIRST OFFICER
What's that to us? The time goes by. Away!

ANTONIO
But, oh, how vile an idol proves this god!
Thou hast, Sebastian, done good feature shame.   368
In nature there's no blemish but the mind;
None can be called deformed but the unkind.   370
Virtue is beauty, but the beauteous evil   371
Are empty trunks o'erflourished by the devil.   372

FIRST OFFICER
The man grows mad. Away with him! Come, come,
sir.

ANTONIO   Lead me on.   *Exit [with Officers].*

VIOLA *[aside]*
Methinks his words do from such passion fly
That he believes himself. So do not I.   376
Prove true, imagination, oh, prove true,
That I, dear brother, be now ta'en for you!

SIR TOBY   Come hither, knight. Come hither, Fabian.
We'll whisper o'er a couplet or two of most sage saws.   380
    [They gather apart from Viola.]

VIOLA
He named Sebastian. I my brother know   381
Yet living in my glass; even such and so   382
In favor was my brother, and he went   383
Still in this fashion, color, ornament,   384
For him I imitate. Oh, if it prove,   385
Tempests are kind, and salt waves fresh in love!
    [Exit.]

SIR TOBY   A very dishonest paltry boy, and more a   387
coward than a hare. His dishonesty appears in leaving   388
his friend here in necessity and denying him; and for   389
his cowardship, ask Fabian.

FABIAN   A coward, a most devout coward, religious in it.   391

SIR ANDREW   'Slid, I'll after him again and beat him.   392

SIR TOBY   Do, cuff him soundly, but never draw thy
sword.

SIR ANDREW   An I do not—   *[Exit.]*

FABIAN   Come, let's see the event.   396

SIR TOBY   I dare lay any money 'twill be nothing yet.   397
    Exeunt.

❖

4.1

Enter Sebastian and Clown [Feste].

FESTE   Will you make me believe that I am not sent for
you?

SEBASTIAN   Go to, go to, thou art a foolish fellow. Let
me be clear of thee.

FESTE   Well held out, i'faith! No, I do not know you,   5
nor I am not sent to you by my lady to bid you come
speak with her, nor your name is not Master Cesario,
nor this is not my nose, neither. Nothing that is so is so.

SEBASTIAN   I prithee, vent thy folly somewhere else.   9
Thou know'st not me.

FESTE   Vent my folly! He has heard that word of some   11
great man, and now applies it to a fool. Vent my folly!
I am afraid this great lubber, the world, will prove a   13
cockney. I prithee now, ungird thy strangeness and   14
tell me what I shall vent to my lady. Shall I vent to her
that thou art coming?

SEBASTIAN   I prithee, foolish Greek, depart from me.   17
There's money for thee. *[He gives money.]* If you tarry
longer, I shall give worse payment.

FESTE   By my troth, thou hast an open hand. These   20
wise men that give fools money get themselves a good
report—after fourteen years' purchase.   22

Enter [Sir] Andrew, [Sir] Toby, and Fabian.

SIR ANDREW   Now, sir, have I met you again? There's
for you!   *[He strikes Sebastian.]*

SEBASTIAN   Why, there's for thee, and there, and there!
    [He beats Sir Andrew with the hilt of his dagger.]
Are all the people mad?

SIR TOBY   Hold, sir, or I'll throw your dagger o'er the
house.

FESTE   This will I tell my lady straight. I would not be in   29
some of your coats for twopence.   *[Exit.]*   30

SIR TOBY   Come on, sir, hold!   *[He grips Sebastian.]*

SIR ANDREW   Nay, let him alone. I'll go another way to
work with him. I'll have an action of battery against   33
him, if there be any law in Illyria. Though I struck him
first, yet it's no matter for that.

SEBASTIAN   Let go thy hand!

SIR TOBY   Come, sir, I will not let you go. Come, my
young soldier, put up your iron. You are well fleshed.   38
Come on.

SEBASTIAN
I will be free from thee. *[He breaks free and draws his
sword.]* What wouldst thou now?
If thou dar'st tempt me further, draw thy sword.   41

SIR TOBY   What, what? Nay, then I must have an ounce
or two of this malapert blood from you.   *[He draws.]*   43

Enter Olivia.

---

368 Thou . . . shame i.e., You have shamed physical beauty by
showing that it does not always reflect inner beauty.   **370 unkind**
ungrateful, unnatural.   **371 beauteous evil** those who are outwardly beautiful but evil within   **372 trunks** (1) chests (2) bodies.
o'erflourished (1) covered with ornamental carvings (2) made outwardly beautiful   **376 So . . . I** i.e., I do not believe myself (in the
hope that has arisen in me).   **380 We'll . . . saws** i.e., Let's converse
privately. (*Saws* are sayings.)   **381–2 I . . . glass** i.e., I know that my
brother's likeness lives in me   **383 favor** appearance   **384 Still**
always   **385 prove** prove true   **387 dishonest** dishonorable
388 dishonesty dishonor   **389 denying** refusing to acknowledge
391 religious in it making a religion of cowardice.   **392 'Slid** By his
(God's) eyelid   **396 event** outcome.   **397 lay** wager.   **yet** nevertheless, after all.
4.1. Location: Before Olivia's house.

5 held out kept up   **9 vent** (1) utter (2) void, excrete, get rid of   **11 of**
from, suited to the diction of; or, with reference to   **13 lubber** lout
14 cockney effeminate or foppish fellow. (Feste comically despairs of
finding common sense anywhere if people start using affected
phrases like those Sebastian uses.   **ungird thy strangeness** put off
your affectation of being a stranger. (Feste apes the kind of high-
flown speech he has just deplored.)   **17 Greek** (1) one who speaks
gibberish (as in "It's all Greek to me") (2) buffoon (as in "merry
Greek")   **20 open** generous. (With money or with blows.)   **22 report**
reputation.   **after . . . purchase** i.e., at great cost and after long
delays. (Land was ordinarily valued at the price of twelve years'
rental; the Fool adds two years to this figure.)   **29 straight** at once.
29–30 in . . . coats i.e., in your shoes   **33 action of battery** lawsuit for
physical assault   **38 fleshed** initiated into battle.   **41 tempt** make
trial of   **43 malapert** saucy, impudent

OLIVIA

Hold, Toby! On thy life I charge thee, hold!

SIR TOBY   Madam—

OLIVIA

Will it be ever thus? Ungracious wretch,
Fit for the mountains and the barbarous caves,
Where manners ne'er were preached! Out of my
    sight!—
Be not offended, dear Cesario.—
Rudesby, begone!

[Exeunt Sir Toby, Sir Andrew, and Fabian.]
                                          I prithee, gentle friend,   50
Let thy fair wisdom, not thy passion, sway
In this uncivil and unjust extent   52
Against thy peace. Go with me to my house,
And hear thou there how many fruitless pranks
This ruffian hath botched up, that thou thereby   55
Mayst smile at this. Thou shalt not choose but go.   56
Do not deny. Beshrew his soul for me!   57
He started one poor heart of mine, in thee.   58

SEBASTIAN [aside]

What relish is in this? How runs the stream?   59
Or I am mad, or else this is a dream.   60
Let fancy still my sense in Lethe steep;   61
If it be thus to dream, still let me sleep!

OLIVIA

Nay, come, I prithee. Would thou'dst be ruled by me!

SEBASTIAN

Madam, I will.

OLIVIA   Oh, say so, and so be!   Exeunt.

❧

4.2

*Enter Maria [carrying a gown and a false
beard], and Clown [Feste].*

MARIA   Nay, I prithee, put on this gown and this beard;
make him believe thou art Sir Topas the curate. Do it
quickly. I'll call Sir Toby the whilst.   [Exit.]   3

FESTE   Well, I'll put it on, and I will dissemble myself   4
in't, and I would I were the first that ever dissembled
in such a gown. [He disguises himself in gown and
beard.] I am not tall enough to become the function   7
well, nor lean enough to be thought a good student;   8

but to be said an honest man and a good housekeeper   9
goes as fairly as to say a careful man and a great   10
scholar. The competitors enter.   11

Enter [Sir] Toby [and Maria].

SIR TOBY   Jove bless thee, Master Parson.

FESTE   *Bonos dies,* Sir Toby. For, as the old hermit of   13
Prague, that never saw pen and ink, very wittily said   14
to a niece of King Gorboduc, "That that is, is"; so I,   15
being Master Parson, am Master Parson; for what is
"that" but "that," and "is" but "is"?

SIR TOBY   To him, Sir Topas.

FESTE   What, ho, I say! Peace in this prison!
                              [He approaches the door
                              behind which Malvolio is confined.]

SIR TOBY   The knave counterfeits well; a good knave.

MALVOLIO *(within)*   Who calls there?

FESTE   Sir Topas the curate, who comes to visit Malvolio
the lunatic.

MALVOLIO   Sir Topas, Sir Topas, good Sir Topas, go to
my lady—

FESTE   Out, hyperbolical fiend! How vexest thou this   26
man! Talkest thou nothing but of ladies?

SIR TOBY   Well said, Master Parson.

MALVOLIO   Sir Topas, never was man thus wronged.
Good Sir Topas, do not think I am mad. They have
laid me here in hideous darkness.

FESTE   Fie, thou dishonest Satan! I call thee by the most
modest terms, for I am one of those gentle ones that   33
will use the devil himself with courtesy. Say'st thou
that house is dark?   35

MALVOLIO   As hell, Sir Topas.

FESTE   Why, it hath bay windows transparent as barri-   37
cadoes, and the clerestories toward the south north   38
are as lustrous as ebony; and yet complainest thou of
obstruction?

MALVOLIO   I am not mad, Sir Topas. I say to you this
house is dark.

FESTE   Madman, thou errest. I say there is no darkness
but ignorance, in which thou art more puzzled than
the Egyptians in their fog.   45

MALVOLIO   I say this house is as dark as ignorance,
though ignorance were as dark as hell; and I say there
was never man thus abused. I am no more mad than
you are. Make the trial of it in any constant question.   49

---

50 **Rudesby** Ruffian   52 **extent** attack   55 **botched up** clumsily contrived   56 **Thou . . . go** I insist on your going with me.   57 **deny**
refuse.   **Beshrew** Curse. (A mild oath.)   **for me** for my part.
58 **He . . . thee** i.e., He alarmed that part of my heart which lies in
your bosom. (To *start* is also to drive an animal such as a *hart* [*heart*]
from its cover.)   59 **What . . . this?** i.e., What am I to make of this?
(*Relish* means "taste.")   60 **Or** Either   61 **Let . . . steep** i.e., Let this
fantasy continue to steep my senses in forgetfulness. (*Lethe* is the river
of forgetfulness in the underworld.)
4.2. Location: Olivia's house.
2 **Sir** (An honorific title for priests.)   **Topas** (A name perhaps derived
from Chaucer's comic knight in the "Rime of Sir Thopas" or from a
similar character in Lyly's *Endymion*. Topaz, a semiprecious stone,
was believed to be a cure for lunacy.)   4 **dissemble** disguise. (With a play
on "feign.")   7 **become the func-
tion** adorn the priestly office   8 **lean** (Scholars were proverbially
sparing of diet.)   **student** scholar (in divinity)

9–11 **to be . . . scholar** to be accounted honest and hospitable is as
good as being known as a painstaking scholar. (Feste suggests that
honesty and charity are found as often in ordinary men as in clerics.)
11 **competitors** associates, partners (in this plot)   13 *Bonos dies* Good
day   13–14 **hermit of Prague** (Probably another invented authority.)
15 **King Gorboduc** a legendary king of ancient Britain, protagonist in
the English tragedy *Gorboduc* (1562)   26 **hyperbolical** vehement,
boisterous.   **fiend** i.e., the devil supposedly possessing Malvolio.
33 **modest** moderate   35 **house** i.e., room   37–8 **barricadoes** barri-
cades. (Which are opaque. Feste speaks comically in impossible paradoxes, but Malvolio seems not to notice.)   38 **clerestories** windows
in an upper wall   45 **Egyptians . . . fog** (Alluding to the darkness
brought upon Egypt by Moses; see Exodus 10:21–3.)   49 **constant
question** problem that requires consecutive reasoning.

FESTE   What is the opinion of Pythagoras concerning   50
wildfowl?   51

MALVOLIO   That the soul of our grandam might haply   52
inhabit a bird.

FESTE   What think'st thou of his opinion?

MALVOLIO   I think nobly of the soul, and no way
approve his opinion.

FESTE   Fare thee well. Remain thou still in darkness.
Thou shalt hold th'opinion of Pythagoras ere I will
allow of thy wits, and fear to kill a woodcock lest thou   59
dispossess the soul of thy grandam. Fare thee well.
    [He moves away from Malvolio's prison.]

MALVOLIO   Sir Topas, Sir Topas!

SIR TOBY   My most exquisite Sir Topas!

FESTE   Nay, I am for all waters.   63

MARIA   Thou mightst have done this without thy beard
and gown. He sees thee not.

SIR TOBY   To him in thine own voice, and bring me
word how thou find'st him.—I would we were well rid
of this knavery. If he may be conveniently delivered, I   68
would he were, for I am now so far in offense with
my niece that I cannot pursue with any safety this
sport to the upshot. Come by and by to my chamber.   71
    Exit [with Maria].

FESTE   [singing as he approaches Malvolio's prison]
    "Hey, Robin, jolly Robin,   72
    Tell me how thy lady does."   73

MALVOLIO   Fool!

FESTE   "My lady is unkind, pardie."   75

MALVOLIO   Fool!

FESTE   "Alas, why is she so?"

MALVOLIO   Fool, I say!

FESTE   "She loves another—" Who calls, ha?

MALVOLIO   Good Fool, as ever thou wilt deserve well at
my hand, help me to a candle, and pen, ink, and
paper. As I am a gentleman, I will live to be thankful
to thee for't.

FESTE   Master Malvolio?

MALVOLIO   Ay, good Fool.

FESTE   Alas, sir, how fell you besides your five wits?   86

MALVOLIO   Fool, there was never man so notoriously   87
abused. I am as well in my wits, Fool, as thou art.   88

FESTE   But as well? Then you are mad indeed, if you be   89
no better in your wits than a fool.

MALVOLIO   They have here propertied me, keep me in   91
darkness, send ministers to me—asses—and do all
they can to face me out of my wits.   93

FESTE   Advise you what you say. The minister is here.   94
[He speaks as Sir Topas.] Malvolio, Malvolio, thy wits
the heavens restore! Endeavor thyself to sleep, and
leave thy vain bibble-babble.

MALVOLIO   Sir Topas!

FESTE   [in Sir Topas's voice]   Maintain no words with
him, good fellow. [In his own voice] Who, I, sir? Not
I, sir. God b'wi'you, good Sir Topas. [In Sir Topas's
voice] Marry, amen. [In his own voice] I will, sir, I will.

MALVOLIO   Fool! Fool! Fool, I say!

FESTE   Alas, sir, be patient. What say you, sir? I am
shent for speaking to you.   105

MALVOLIO   Good Fool, help me to some light and some
paper. I tell thee I am as well in my wits as any man in
Illyria.

FESTE   Welladay that you were, sir!   109

MALVOLIO   By this hand, I am. Good Fool, some ink,
paper, and light; and convey what I will set down to
my lady. It shall advantage thee more than ever the
bearing of letter did.

FESTE   I will help you to't. But tell me true, are you
not mad indeed, or do you but counterfeit?

MALVOLIO   Believe me, I am not. I tell thee true.

FESTE   Nay, I'll ne'er believe a madman till I see his
brains. I will fetch you light and paper and ink.

MALVOLIO   Fool, I'll requite it in the highest degree. I
prithee, begone.

FESTE   [sings]
        I am gone, sir,
        And anon, sir,
    I'll be with you again,
        In a trice,
        Like to the old Vice,   125
    Your need to sustain;

        Who, with dagger of lath,   127
        In his rage and his wrath,
    Cries, "Aha!" to the devil;
        Like a mad lad,
        "Pare thy nails, dad?   131
    Adieu, goodman devil!"   Exit.   132

❖

4.3

Enter Sebastian [with a pearl].

SEBASTIAN
This is the air; that is the glorious sun;

50–1 Pythagoras . . . wildfowl (An opening for the discussion of
transmigration of souls, a doctrine held by Pythagoras.)   52 haply
perhaps   59 allow of thy wits certify your sanity.   woodcock (A
proverbially stupid bird, easily caught.)   63 Nay . . . waters i.e.,
Indeed, I can turn my hand to anything.   68 delivered i.e., delivered
from prison   71 upshot conclusion.   72–3 "Hey, Robin . . . does"
(Another fragment of an old song, a version of which is attributed to
Sir Thomas Wyatt.)   75 pardie i.e., by God, certainly.   86 besides
out of.   five wits The intellectual faculties, usually listed as common
wit, imagination, fantasy, judgment, and memory.   87–8 notoriously
abused egregiously ill treated.   89 But Only   91 propertied me i.e.,
treated me as property and thrown me into the lumber-room
93 face . . . wits brazenly represent me as having lost my wits.

94 Advise you Take care   105 shent scolded, rebuked   109 Welladay Alas, would that   125 Vice comic tempter of the "old" morality
plays   127 dagger of lath comic weapon of the Vice in at least some
morality plays   131 Pare thy nails (This may allude to the belief that
evil spirits could use nail parings to get control of their victims; cf.
Dromio of Syracuse in The Comedy of Errors, 4.3.69, "Some devils ask
but the parings of one's nail," and the Boy's characterization of Pistol
in Henry V, 4.4.72–3, as "this roaring devil i'th' old play, that everyone
may pare his nails with a wooden dagger.")   132 goodman title for a
person of substance but not of gentle birth. (This line could be Feste's
farewell to Malvolio and his "devil.")
4.3. Location: Olivia's garden.

This pearl she gave me, I do feel't and see't;
And though 'tis wonder that enwraps me thus,
Yet 'tis not madness. Where's Antonio, then?
I could not find him at the Elephant;
Yet there he was, and there I found this credit,   6
That he did range the town to seek me out.
His counsel now might do me golden service;
For though my soul disputes well with my sense   9
That this may be some error, but no madness,
Yet doth this accident and flood of fortune   11
So far exceed all instance, all discourse,   12
That I am ready to distrust mine eyes
And wrangle with my reason that persuades me
To any other trust but that I am mad,   15
Or else the lady's mad. Yet if 'twere so,
She could not sway her house, command her
    followers,   17
Take and give back affairs and their dispatch   18
With such a smooth, discreet, and stable bearing
As I perceive she does. There's something in't
That is deceivable. But here the lady comes.   21

Enter Olivia and Priest.

OLIVIA
Blame not this haste of mine. If you mean well,
Now go with me and with this holy man
Into the chantry by. There, before him,   24
And underneath that consecrated roof,
Plight me the full assurance of your faith,
That my most jealous and too doubtful soul   27
May live at peace. He shall conceal it
Whiles you are willing it shall come to note,   29
What time we will our celebration keep   30
According to my birth. What do you say?   31

SEBASTIAN
I'll follow this good man, and go with you,
And having sworn truth, ever will be true.

OLIVIA
Then lead the way, good father, and heavens so shine
That they may fairly note this act of mine!   *Exeunt.*   35

❖

5.1

Enter Clown [Feste] and Fabian.

FABIAN   Now, as thou lov'st me, let me see his letter.
FESTE   Good Master Fabian, grant me another request.
FABIAN   Anything.

FESTE   Do not desire to see this letter.
FABIAN   This is to give a dog and in recompense desire   5
my dog again.   6

Enter Duke [Orsino], Viola, Curio, and lords.

ORSINO   Belong you to the Lady Olivia, friends?
FESTE   Ay, sir, we are some of her trappings.   8
ORSINO   I know thee well. How dost thou, my good fellow?
FESTE   Truly, sir, the better for my foes and the worse   10
for my friends.
ORSINO   Just the contrary—the better for thy friends.
FESTE   No, sir, the worse.
ORSINO   How can that be?
FESTE   Marry, sir, they praise me, and make an ass of   15
me. Now my foes tell me plainly I am an ass, so that   16
by my foes, sir, I profit in the knowledge of myself,
and by my friends I am abused; so that, conclusions to   18
be as kisses, if your four negatives make your two   19
affirmatives, why then the worse for my friends and   20
the better for my foes.
ORSINO   Why, this is excellent.
FESTE   By my troth, sir, no, though it please you to be   23
one of my friends.   24
ORSINO   Thou shalt not be the worse for me. There's gold.
    [He gives a coin.]
FESTE   But that it would be double-dealing, sir, I would   26
you could make it another.
ORSINO   Oh, you give me ill counsel.
FESTE   Put your grace in your pocket, sir, for this once,   29
and let your flesh and blood obey it.   30
ORSINO   Well, I will be so much a sinner to be a   31
double-dealer. There's another. *[He gives another coin.]*
FESTE   *Primo, secundo, tertio,* is a good play, and the old   33
saying is, the third pays for all. The triplex, sir, is a   34
good tripping measure; or the bells of Saint Bennet,   35
sir, may put you in mind—one, two, three.
ORSINO   You can fool no more money out of me at this
throw. If you will let your lady know I am here to   38
speak with her, and bring her along with you, it may
awake my bounty further.
FESTE   Marry, sir, lullaby to your bounty till I come
again. I go, sir, but I would not have you to think that

5–6 This . . . again (Apparently a reference to a well-known reply of
Dr. Bulleyn when Queen Elizabeth asked for his dog and promised a
gift of his choosing in return; he asked to have his dog back.)   8 trappings ornaments, decorations.   10 for because of   15–16 make an
ass of me i.e., flatter me into foolishly thinking well of myself.
18 abused flatteringly deceived   18–20 conclusions . . . affirmatives
i.e., as when a young lady, asked for a kiss, says "no, no" really meaning "yes"; or, as in grammar, two negatives make an affirmative
23 though even though   24 friends i.e., those who, according to
Feste's syllogism, flatter him.   26 But Except for the fact.   double-
dealing (1) giving twice (2) deceit, duplicity   29 Put . . . pocket
(1) Pay no attention to your honor, put it away (2) Reach in your
pocket or purse and show your customary grace or munificence.
(*Your Grace* is also the formal way of addressing a duke.)   30 it i.e.,
my "ill counsel."   31 to be as to be   33 *Primo . . . tertio* Latin ordi-
nals: first, second, third.   play (Perhaps a mathematical game or
game of dice.)   34 The third . . . all the third time is lucky. (Proverbial.)   triplex triple time in music   35 Saint Bennet church of St.
Benedict   38 throw (1) time (2) throw of the dice.

---

6 was was previously.   credit report   9 my soul . . . sense i.e., both
my rational faculties and my physical senses come to the conclusion
11 accident unexpected event   12 instance precedent.   discourse
reason   15 trust belief   17 sway rule   18 Take . . . dispatch receive
reports on matters of household business and see to their execution
21 deceivable deceptive.   24 chantry by private endowed chapel
nearby (where mass would be said for the souls of the dead, including Olivia's brother).   27 jealous anxious, mistrustful.   doubtful
full of doubts   29 Whiles until.   come to note become known
30 What time at which time.   our celebration i.e., the actual marriage. (What they are about to perform is a binding betrothal.)
31 birth social position.   35 fairly note look upon with favor
5.1. Location: Before Olivia's house.

my desire of having is the sin of covetousness. But as
you say, sir, let your bounty take a nap. I will awake
it anon.   *Exit.*

Enter Antonio and Officers.

VIOLA
Here comes the man, sir, that did rescue me.
ORSINO
That face of his I do remember well,
Yet when I saw it last it was besmeared
As black as Vulcan in the smoke of war.   49
A baubling vessel was he captain of,   50
For shallow draft and bulk unprizable,   51
With which such scatheful grapple did he make   52
With the most noble bottom of our fleet   53
That very envy and the tongue of loss   54
Cried fame and honor on him. What's the matter?
FIRST OFFICER
Orsino, this is that Antonio
That took the *Phoenix* and her freight from Candy,   57
And this is he that did the *Tiger* board
When your young nephew Titus lost his leg.
Here in the streets, desperate of shame and state,   60
In private brabble did we apprehend him.   61
VIOLA
He did me kindness, sir, drew on my side,
But in conclusion put strange speech upon me.   63
I know not what 'twas but distraction.   64
ORSINO
Notable pirate, thou saltwater thief,   65
What foolish boldness brought thee to their mercies
Whom thou in terms so bloody and so dear   67
Hast made thine enemies?
ANTONIO   Orsino, noble sir,
Be pleased that I shake off these names you give me.   69
Antonio never yet was thief or pirate,
Though, I confess, on base and ground enough   71
Orsino's enemy. A witchcraft drew me hither.
That most ingrateful boy there by your side
From the rude sea's enragèd and foamy mouth
Did I redeem; a wreck past hope he was.   75
His life I gave him, and did thereto add
My love, without retention or restraint,   77
All his in dedication. For his sake   78
Did I expose myself—pure for his love—   79
Into the danger of this adverse town,   80
Drew to defend him when he was beset;

Where being apprehended, his false cunning,
Not meaning to partake with me in danger,
Taught him to face me out of his acquaintance   84
And grew a twenty years' removèd thing   85
While one would wink; denied me mine own purse,   86
Which I had recommended to his use   87
Not half an hour before.
VIOLA   How can this be?
ORSINO   When came he to this town?
ANTONIO
Today, my lord; and for three months before,
No interim, not a minute's vacancy,
Both day and night did we keep company.

Enter Olivia and attendants.

ORSINO
Here comes the Countess. Now heaven walks on
    earth.
But for thee, fellow—fellow, thy words are madness.   95
Three months this youth hath tended upon me;
But more of that anon.—Take him aside.
OLIVIA [*to Orsino*]
What would my lord—but that he may not have—   98
Wherein Olivia may seem serviceable?—
Cesario, you do not keep promise with me.
VIOLA   Madam?
ORSINO   Gracious Olivia—
OLIVIA
What do you say, Cesario?—Good my lord—   103
VIOLA
My lord would speak. My duty hushes me.
OLIVIA
If it be aught to the old tune, my lord,
It is as fat and fulsome to mine ear   106
As howling after music.
ORSINO   Still so cruel?
OLIVIA   Still so constant, lord.
ORSINO
What, to perverseness? You uncivil lady,
To whose ingrate and unauspicious altars   111
My soul the faithfull'st off'rings have breathed out
That e'er devotion tendered! What shall I do?
OLIVIA
Even what it please my lord that shall become him.   114
ORSINO
Why should I not, had I the heart to do it,
Like to th'Egyptian thief at point of death   116
Kill what I love?—a savage jealousy
That sometime savors nobly. But hear me this: 118

---

49 **Vulcan** Roman god of fire and smith to the other gods; his face
was blackened by the fire   50 **baubling** insignificant, trifling   51 **For**
because of.   **draft** depth of water a ship draws.   **unprizable** of value
too slight to be estimated, not worth taking as a "prize"   52 **scatheful** destructive   53 **bottom** ship   54 **very envy** i.e., even those who
had most reason to hate him, his enemies.   **loss** i.e., the losers
57 **from Candy** on her return from Candia, or Crete   60 **desperate . . .**
state recklessly disregarding the disgrace and danger to himself
61 **brabble** brawl   63 **put . . . me** spoke to me strangely.   64 **but distraction** unless (it was) madness.   65 **Notable** Notorious   67 **in**
terms . . . dear in so bloodthirsty and costly a manner   69 **Be pleased**
that I Allow me to   71 **base and ground** solid grounds   75 **wreck**
shipwrecked person   77 **retention** reservation   78 **All . . . dedication**
devoted wholly to him.   79 **pure** entirely, purely   80 **Into** unto.
adverse hostile

84 **face . . . acquaintance** brazenly deny he knew me   85–6 **grew . . .**
wink in the twinkling of an eye acted as though we had been
estranged for twenty years   87 **recommended** consigned   95 **for** as
for   98 **but . . . have** except that which he may not have—i.e., my
love   103 **Good my lord** (Olivia urges Orsino to listen to Cesario.)
106 **fat and fulsome** gross and offensive   111 **ingrate and unauspicious** thankless and unpropitious   114 **become** suit   116 **th'Egyptian thief** (An allusion to the story of Theagenes and Chariclea in the
Ethiopica, a Greek romance by Heliodorus. The robber chief, Thyamis
of Memphis, having captured Chariclea and fallen in love with her, is
attacked by a larger band of robbers; threatened with death, he
attempts to slay her first.)   118 **savors nobly** is not without nobility.

Since you to nonregardance cast my faith,   119
And that I partly know the instrument   120
That screws me from my true place in your favor,   121
Live you the marble-breasted tyrant still.
But this your minion, whom I know you love,   123
And whom, by heaven I swear, I tender dearly,   124
Him will I tear out of that cruel eye   125
Where he sits crownèd in his master's spite.—   126
Come, boy, with me. My thoughts are ripe in
    mischief.
I'll sacrifice the lamb that I do love,   128
To spite a raven's heart within a dove.   [*Going.*]129

VIOLA
And I, most jocund, apt, and willingly,   130
To do you rest, a thousand deaths would die.   131
                       [*Going.*]

OLIVIA
Where goes Cesario?

VIOLA   After him I love
More than I love these eyes, more than my life,
More by all mores than e'er I shall love wife.   134
If I do feign, you witnesses above
Punish my life for tainting of my love!   136

OLIVIA
Ay me, detested! How am I beguiled!   137

VIOLA
Who does beguile you? Who does do you wrong?

OLIVIA
Hast thou forgot thyself? Is it so long?
Call forth the holy father.   [*Exit an attendant.*]

ORSINO [*to Viola*]   Come, away!

OLIVIA
Whither, my lord?—Cesario, husband, stay.

ORSINO
Husband?

OLIVIA   Ay, husband. Can he that deny?

ORSINO [*to Viola*]
Her husband, sirrah?

VIOLA   No, my lord, not I.   143

OLIVIA
Alas, it is the baseness of thy fear
That makes thee strangle thy propriety.   145
Fear not, Cesario, take thy fortunes up;
Be that thou know'st thou art, and then thou art   147
As great as that thou fear'st.

      Enter Priest.

           Oh, welcome, father!   148
Father, I charge thee by thy reverence

Here to unfold—though lately we intended
To keep in darkness what occasion now   151
Reveals before 'tis ripe—what thou dost know
Hath newly passed between this youth and me.

PRIEST
A contract of eternal bond of love,
Confirmed by mutual joinder of your hands,   155
Attested by the holy close of lips,   156
Strengthened by interchangement of your rings,
And all the ceremony of this compact
Sealed in my function, by my testimony;   159
Since when, my watch hath told me, toward my
    grave
I have traveled but two hours.

ORSINO [*to Viola*]
Oh, thou dissembling cub! What wilt thou be
When time hath sowed a grizzle on thy case?   163
Or will not else thy craft so quickly grow
That thine own trip shall be thine overthrow?   165
Farewell, and take her, but direct thy feet
Where thou and I henceforth may never meet.

VIOLA
My Lord, I do protest—

OLIVIA   Oh, do not swear!
Hold little faith, though thou hast too much fear.   169

      Enter Sir Andrew.

SIR ANDREW   For the love of God, a surgeon! Send one
presently to Sir Toby.   171

OLIVIA   What's the matter?

SIR ANDREW   He's broke my head across, and has given   173
Sir Toby a bloody coxcomb too. For the love of God,   174
your help! I had rather than forty pound I were at
home.

OLIVIA   Who has done this, Sir Andrew?

SIR ANDREW   The Count's gentleman, one Cesario. We
took him for a coward, but he's the very devil
incardinate.   180

ORSINO   My gentleman, Cesario?

SIR ANDREW   'Od's lifelings, here he is!—You broke my   182
head for nothing, and that that I did I was set on to
do't by Sir Toby.

VIOLA
Why do you speak to me? I never hurt you.
You drew your sword upon me without cause,
But I bespake you fair, and hurt you not.   187

SIR ANDREW   If a bloody coxcomb be a hurt, you have
hurt me. I think you set nothing by a bloody cox-   189
comb.

      Enter [Sir] Toby and Clown [Feste].

Here comes Sir Toby, halting. You shall hear more. 191
But if he had not been in drink, he would have tickled
you othergates than he did. 193

ORSINO   How now, gentleman? How is't with you?

SIR TOBY   That's all one. He's hurt me, and there's 195
th'end on't.—Sot, didst see Dick surgeon, sot? 196

FESTE   Oh, he's drunk, Sir Toby, an hour agone; his eyes 197
were set at eight i'th' morning. 198

SIR TOBY   Then he's a rogue, and a passy measures 199
pavane. I hate a drunken rogue. 200

OLIVIA   Away with him! Who hath made this havoc
with them?

SIR ANDREW   I'll help you, Sir Toby, because we'll be 203
dressed together. 204

SIR TOBY   Will you help? An ass-head and a coxcomb
and a knave, a thin-faced knave, a gull!

OLIVIA
Get him to bed, and let his hurt be looked to.
      [Exeunt Feste, Fabian, Sir Toby, and Sir Andrew.]

      Enter Sebastian.

SEBASTIAN
I am sorry, madam, I have hurt your kinsman;
But, had it been the brother of my blood, 209
I must have done no less with wit and safety.— 210
You throw a strange regard upon me, and by that 211
I do perceive it hath offended you.
Pardon me, sweet one, even for the vows
We made each other but so late ago.

ORSINO
One face, one voice, one habit, and two persons, 215
A natural perspective, that is and is not! 216

SEBASTIAN
Antonio, O my dear Antonio!
How have the hours racked and tortured me 218
Since I have lost thee!

ANTONIO   Sebastian are you?

SEBASTIAN   Fear'st thou that, Antonio? 221

ANTONIO
How have you made division of yourself?
An apple cleft in two is not more twin
Than these two creatures. Which is Sebastian?

OLIVIA   Most wonderful!

SEBASTIAN [seeing Viola]
Do I stand there? I never had a brother;
Nor can there be that deity in my nature
Of here and everywhere. I had a sister, 228
Whom the blind waves and surges have devoured. 229
Of charity, what kin are you to me? 230

What countryman? What name? What parentage?

VIOLA
Of Messaline. Sebastian was my father.
Such a Sebastian was my brother, too.
So went he suited to his watery tomb. 234
If spirits can assume both form and suit, 235
You come to fright us.

SEBASTIAN   A spirit I am indeed,
But am in that dimension grossly clad 237
Which from the womb I did participate. 238
Were you a woman, as the rest goes even, 239
I should my tears let fall upon your cheek
And say, "Thrice welcome, drownèd Viola!"

VIOLA
My father had a mole upon his brow.

SEBASTIAN   And so had mine.

VIOLA
And died that day when Viola from her birth
Had numbered thirteen years.

SEBASTIAN
Oh, that record is lively in my soul! 246
He finishèd indeed his mortal act
That day that made my sister thirteen years.

VIOLA
If nothing lets to make us happy both 249
But this my masculine usurped attire,
Do not embrace me till each circumstance
Of place, time, fortune, do cohere and jump 252
That I am Viola—which to confirm
I'll bring you to a captain in this town
Where lie my maiden weeds, by whose gentle help 255
I was preserved to serve this noble count.
All the occurrence of my fortune since
Hath been between this lady and this lord.

SEBASTIAN [to Olivia]
So comes it, lady, you have been mistook.
But nature to her bias drew in that. 260
You would have been contracted to a maid,
Nor are you therein, by my life, deceived.
You are betrothed both to a maid and man. 263

ORSINO [to Olivia]
Be not amazed; right noble is his blood.
If this be so, as yet the glass seems true, 265
I shall have share in this most happy wreck. 266
[To Viola] Boy, thou hast said to me a thousand times
Thou never shouldst love woman like to me. 268

VIOLA
And all those sayings will I over swear, 269
And all those swearings keep as true in soul

191 halting limping.   193 othergates otherwise   195 That's all one
It doesn't matter; never mind.   195–6 there's . . . on't that's all there
is to it.   196 Sot (1) Fool (2) Drunkard   197 agone ago   198 set fixed
or closed   199–200 passy measures pavane passe-measure pavane, a
slow-moving, stately dance. (Suggesting Sir Toby's impatience to
have his wounds dressed.)   203–4 be dressed have our wounds sur-
gically dressed   209 the brother . . . blood my own brother
210 with wit and safety with intelligent concern for my own safety.
211 You . . . me You look strangely at me   215 habit dress   216 A
natural perspective an optical device or illusion created in this
instance by nature   218 Fear'st thou that Do you doubt that   221 Fear'st thou that Do
you doubt that   228 here and everywhere omnipresence.   229 blind
heedless, indiscriminate   230 Of charity (Tell me) in kindness

234 suited dressed; clad in human form   235 form and suit physical
appearance and dress   237 in . . . clad clothed in that fleshly shape
238 participate possess in common with all humanity.   239 as . . . even
since everything else agrees   246 record recollection   249 lets hinders
252 jump coincide, fit exactly   255 weeds clothes   260 nature . . . that
nature followed her bent in that. (The metaphor is from the game of
bowls.)   263 a maid i.e., a virgin man   265 the glass i.e., the natural perspective of line 216   266 wreck shipwreck, accident.   268 like to me as
well as you love me.   269 over swear swear again

As doth that orbèd continent the fire   271
That severs day from night.
ORSINO   Give me thy hand,
And let me see thee in thy woman's weeds.
VIOLA
The captain that did bring me first on shore
Hath my maid's garments. He upon some action   275
Is now in durance, at Malvolio's suit,   276
A gentleman and follower of my lady's.
OLIVIA
He shall enlarge him. Fetch Malvolio hither.   278
And yet, alas, now I remember me,
They say, poor gentleman, he's much distract.

Enter Clown [Feste] with a letter, and Fabian.

A most extracting frenzy of mine own   281
From my remembrance clearly banished his.   282
How does he, sirrah?
FESTE   Truly, madam, he holds Beelzebub at the stave's 284
end as well as a man in his case may do. He's here   285
writ a letter to you; I should have given't you today
morning. But as a madman's epistles are no gospels,   287
so it skills not much when they are delivered.   288
OLIVIA   Open't and read it.
FESTE   Look then to be well edified when the fool
delivers the madman. [*He reads loudly.*] "By the Lord,   291
madam—"
OLIVIA   How now, art thou mad?
FESTE   No, madam, I do but read madness. An Your
Ladyship will have it as it ought to be, you must allow
vox.   296
OLIVIA   Prithee, read i' thy right wits.
FESTE   So I do, madonna; but to read his right wits is to 298
read thus. Therefore perpend, my princess, and give   299
ear.
OLIVIA [*to Fabian*]   Read it you, sirrah.
FABIAN (*reads*)   "By the Lord, madam, you wrong me,
and the world shall know it. Though you have put me
into darkness and given your drunken cousin rule
over me, yet have I the benefit of my senses as well
as Your Ladyship. I have your own letter that induced
me to the semblance I put on, with the which I   307
doubt not but to do myself much right or you much
shame. Think of me as you please. I leave my duty   309
a little unthought of, and speak out of my injury.   310
                    The madly used Malvolio."

OLIVIA   Did he write this?
FESTE   Ay, madam.
ORSINO   This savors not much of distraction.
OLIVIA
See him delivered, Fabian. Bring him hither.   315
                                    [*Exit Fabian.*]
My lord, so please you, these things further thought
on,   316
To think me as well a sister as a wife,   317
One day shall crown th'alliance on't, so please you,   318
Here at my house and at my proper cost.   319
ORSINO
Madam, I am most apt t'embrace your offer.   320
[*To Viola*] Your master quits you; and for your
       service done him,   321
So much against the mettle of your sex,   322
So far beneath your soft and tender breeding,
And since you called me master for so long,
Here is my hand. You shall from this time be
Your master's mistress.
OLIVIA   A sister! You are she.

Enter [Fabian, with] Malvolio.

ORSINO
Is this the madman?
OLIVIA   Ay, my lord, this same.
How now, Malvolio?
MALVOLIO   Madam, you have done me wrong,
Notorious wrong.
OLIVIA   Have I, Malvolio? No.
MALVOLIO [*showing a letter*]
Lady, you have. Pray you, peruse that letter.
You must not now deny it is your hand.
Write from it, if you can, in hand or phrase,   332
Or say 'tis not your seal, not your invention.   333
You can say none of this. Well, grant it then,
And tell me, in the modesty of honor,   335
Why you have given me such clear lights of favor,   336
Bade me come smiling and cross-gartered to you,
To put on yellow stockings, and to frown
Upon Sir Toby and the lighter people?   339
And, acting this in an obedient hope,   340
Why have you suffered me to be imprisoned,
Kept in a dark house, visited by the priest,   342
And made the most notorious geck and gull   343
That e'er invention played on? Tell me why?   344
OLIVIA
Alas, Malvolio, this is not my writing,
Though, I confess, much like the character;   346

---

271 **As . . . fire** i.e., as the sphere of the sun keeps the fire   275 **action**
legal charge   276 **in durance** imprisoned   278 **enlarge** release
281 **extracting** i.e., that obsessed me and drew all thoughts except of
Cesario from my mind   282 **his** i.e., his madness.   284–5 **holds . . .
end** i.e., keeps the devil at a safe distance. (The metaphor is of fighting with quarterstaffs or long poles.)   287 **a madman's . . . gospels**
i.e., there is no truth in a madman's letters. (An allusion to readings
in the church service of selected passages from the epistles and the
gospels.)   288 **skills** matters.   **delivered** (1) delivered to their recipient (2) read aloud.   291 **delivers** speaks the words of   296 **vox** voice,
i.e., an appropriately loud voice.   298 **to read . . . wits** to express his
true state of mind   299 **perpend** consider, attend. (A deliberately
lofty word.)   307 **the which** i.e., the letter   309–10 **I leave . . . injury**
I leave unsaid the expressions of duty with which I would normally
conclude, and convey instead my sense of having been wronged.

315 **delivered** released   316 **so . . . on** if you are pleased on further
consideration of all that has happened   317 **To . . . wife** to regard me
as favorably as a sister-in-law as you had hoped to regard me as a
wife   318 **crown . . . on't** i.e., serve as occasion for two marriages
confirming our new relationships   319 **proper** own   320 **apt** ready
321 **quits** releases   322 **mettle** natural disposition   332 **from it** differently   333 **invention** composition.   335 **in . . . honor** in the name
of all that is decent and honorable   336 **clear lights** evident signs
339 **lighter** lesser   340 **acting . . . hope** i.e., when I acted thus out of obedience to you and in hope of your favor   342 **priest** i.e., Feste
343 **geck** dupe   344 **invention played on** contrivance sported with.
346 **the character** my handwriting

But out of question 'tis Maria's hand.   347
And now I do bethink me, it was she
First told me thou wast mad; then cam'st in smiling,   349
And in such forms which here were presupposed   350
Upon thee in the letter. Prithee, be content.
This practice hath most shrewdly passed upon thee;   352
But when we know the grounds and authors of it,
Thou shalt be both the plaintiff and the judge
Of thine own cause.

FABIAN   Good madam, hear me speak,
And let no quarrel nor no brawl to come   356
Taint the condition of this present hour,   357
Which I have wondered at. In hope it shall not,
Most freely I confess, myself and Toby
Set this device against Malvolio here,
Upon some stubborn and uncourteous parts   361
We had conceived against him. Maria writ   362
The letter at Sir Toby's great importance,   363
In recompense whereof he hath married her.
How with a sportful malice it was followed   365
May rather pluck on laughter than revenge,   366
If that the injuries be justly weighed   367
That have on both sides passed.

OLIVIA [to Malvolio]
Alas, poor fool, how have they baffled thee!   369

FESTE   Why, "Some are born great, some achieve
greatness, and some have greatness thrown upon
them." I was one, sir, in this interlude, one Sir Topas,   372
sir, but that's all one. "By the Lord, fool, I am not   373
mad." But do you remember? "Madam, why laugh
you at such a barren rascal? An you smile not, he's
gagged." And thus the whirligig of time brings in his   376
revenges.

MALVOLIO   I'll be revenged on the whole pack of you!
[Exit.]

OLIVIA
He hath been most notoriously abused.

ORSINO
Pursue him, and entreat him to a peace.
He hath not told us of the captain yet.
When that is known, and golden time convents,   382
A solemn combination shall be made
Of our dear souls. Meantime, sweet sister,
We will not part from hence. Cesario, come—
For so you shall be, while you are a man;
But when in other habits you are seen,   387
Orsino's mistress and his fancy's queen.   388
                                      Exeunt [all, except Feste].

FESTE (sings)
When that I was and a little tiny boy,   389
        With hey, ho, the wind and the rain,
A foolish thing was but a toy,   391
        For the rain it raineth every day.

But when I came to man's estate,
        With hey, ho, the wind and the rain,
'Gainst knaves and thieves men shut their gate,
        For the rain it raineth every day.

But when I came, alas, to wive,
        With hey, ho, the wind and the rain,
By swaggering could I never thrive,
        For the rain it raineth every day.

But when I came unto my beds,   401
        With hey, ho, the wind and the rain,
With tosspots still had drunken heads,   403
        For the rain it raineth every day.

A great while ago the world begun,
        With hey, ho, the wind and the rain,
But that's all one, our play is done,
        And we'll strive to please you every day.
                                                                    [Exit.]

347 **out of** beyond   349 **cam'st** you came   350 **presupposed** specified beforehand   352 **practice** plot.   **shrewdly passed** mischievously
been perpetrated   356 **to come** in the future   357 **condition** (happy)
nature   361 **Upon** on account of.   **parts** qualities, deeds   362 **conceived against him** seen and resented in him.   363 **importance**
importunity   365 **followed** carried out   366 **pluck on** induce
367 **If that** if   369 **baffled** disgraced, quelled   372 **interlude** little play
373 **that's all one** no matter for that.   376 **whirligig** spinning top

382 **convents** (1) summons, calls together (2) suits   387 **habits** attire
388 **fancy's** love's   389 **and a little** a little   391 **toy** trifle   401 **unto
my beds** i.e., (1) drunk to bed, or, perhaps, (2) in the evening of life
403 **tosspots** drunkards

Measure for Measure

"A play Caled Mesur for Mesur" by "Shaxberd" was performed at court, for the new King James I, by "his Maiesties plaiers" on December 26, 1604. Probably it had been composed that same year or in late 1603. The play dates from the very height of Shakespeare's tragic period, three years or so after *Hamlet,* contemporary with *Othello,* shortly before *King Lear* and *Macbeth.* This period includes very little comedy of any sort, and what there is differs markedly from the festive comedy of the 1590s. *Troilus and Cressida* (c. 1601–1602), hovering between satire and tragedy, bleakly portrays a hopeless love affair caught in the toils of a pointless and stalemated war. *All's Well That Ends Well* (c. 1601–1604) resembles *Measure for Measure* in its portrayal of an undeserving protagonist who must be deceived into marriage by the ethically ambiguous trick of substituting one woman for another in the protagonist's bed. *Measure for Measure,* perhaps the last such comedy from the tragic period, illustrates most clearly of all what critics usually mean by "problem comedy" or "problem play."

Its chief concern is not with the triumphs of love, as in the happy comedies, but with moral and social problems: "filthy vices" arising from sexual desire and the abuses of judicial authority. Images of disease abound in this play. We see corruption in Vienna "boil and bubble / Till it o'errun the stew" (5.1.326–7). The protagonist, Angelo, is for most of the play a deeply torn character, abhorring his own perverse sinfulness, compulsively driven to an attempted murder in order to cover up his lust for the heroine, Isabella. His soliloquies are introspective, tortured, focused on the psychological horror of an intelligent mind succumbing to criminal desire. The disguised Duke Vincentio, witnessing this fall into depravity and despair, can offer Angelo's intended victims no better philosophical counsel than Christian renunciation of the world and all its vain hopes. Tragedy is averted only by providential intervention and by the harsh trickery of "Craft against vice" (3.2.270), in which the Duke becomes

involved as chief manipulator and stage manager. Of the concluding marriages, two are foisted on the bridegrooms (Angelo and Lucio) against their wills, whereas that of the Duke and Isabella jars oddly with his stoical teachings and with her previous determination to be a nun. The ending thus seems arbitrary; both justice and romantic happiness are so perilously achieved in this play that they seem inconsistent with the injustice and lechery that have prevailed until the last.

Yet the very improbability of the ending and the sense of tragedy narrowly averted are perhaps intentional. These features are appropriate, not only for problem comedy, but also for tragicomedy or comedy of forgiveness, overlapping genres toward which Shakespeare gravitated in his late romances. Angelo is, like Leontes in *The Winter's Tale* (or like Bertram in *All's Well That Ends Well* and Claudio in *Much Ado About Nothing*), an erring protagonist forgiven in excess of his deserving, spared by a benign, overseeing providence from destroying that which is most precious to him.

That providence is partly ascribed to divine intervention, as when the disguised Duke, at a loss for a means of saving Claudio from imminent death, and learning that a prisoner named Ragozine has just died and is enough like Claudio physically that his head can be substituted for that of Claudio as proof that an execution has taken place, exclaims, "Oh, 'tis an accident that heaven provides!" (4.3.77). Yet most of the "providential" oversight in this play is essentially theatrical and humanly devised. It is engineered by "the old fantastical Duke of dark corners" (4.3.156–7), the resourceful Vincentio. Indeed, this mysterious Duke becomes a kind of embodiment of the manipulations and sleights of hand through which this dark comedy achieves its improbable ends.

The play's title, *Measure for Measure,* introduces a paradox of human justice which this "problem" play cannot wholly resolve. How are fallible humans to judge the sins of their fellow mortals and still obey Christ's injunction of the Sermon on the Mount: "Judge not that ye be not judged"? Three positions emerge from the debate: absolute justice at one extreme, mercy at the other, and equity as a middle ground. Isabella speaks for mercy, and her words ring with biblical authority. Since all humanity would be condemned to eternal darkness were God not merciful as well as just, should not humans also be merciful? The difficulty, however, is that Vienna shows all too clearly the effects of leniency under the indulgent Duke. Vice is rampant; stern measures are needed. Though he has not wished to crack the whip himself, the Duke firmly endorses "strict statutes and most biting laws, / The needful bits and curbs to headstrong steeds" (1.3.19–20). To carry out necessary reform, the Duke has chosen Angelo, spokesman for absolute justice, to represent him. Angelo's position is cold but consistent. Only by a literal and impartial administering of the statutes, he maintains, can the law deter potential offenders. If the judge is found guilty, he must pay the penalty as well. One difficulty here, however, is that literal enforcement of the statute on fornication seems ironically to catch the wrong culprits. Claudio and Juliet, who are about to be married and are already joined by a "true contract" of betrothal, are sentenced to the severest limit of the law, whereas the pimps and whores of Vienna's suburbs manage at first to evade punishment entirely. Angelo's deputy, Escalus, can only shake his head in dismay at this unjust result of strict justice. Angelo has not remembered fully the terms of his commission from the Duke: to practice both "Mortality and mercy" in Vienna, to "enforce or qualify the laws / As to your soul seems good." The attributes of a ruler, like those of God, must include "terror" but also "love" (1.1.20–67).

Escalus's compassionate and pragmatic approach to law illustrates equity or the flexible application of the law to particular cases. Because Claudio is only technically guilty (though still guilty), Escalus would pronounce for him a light sentence. Pompey and Mistress Overdone, on the other hand, require vigorous prosecution. The problem of policing vice is compounded by the law's inefficiency, as well as by erring human nature, which will never be wholly tamed. Constable Elbow, like Dogberry in *Much Ado,* is a pompous user of malapropisms, less clever by far than the criminals he would arrest. His evidence against Pompey is so absurdly circumstantial that Escalus is first obliged to let off this engaging pimp with a stern warning. Yet Escalus patiently and tenaciously attends to such proceedings, unlike Angelo, whose interest in the law is too theoretical. Escalus deals with day-to-day problems effectively. He orders reforms of the system by which constables are selected, instructs Elbow in the rudiments of his office, and so proceeds, ultimately, to an effective arrest. Vice is not eliminated; as Pompey defiantly points out, unless someone plans to "geld and splay all the youth of the city," they "will to't then" (2.1.229–33). Still, vice is held in check. Law can shape the outer person and hope for some inner reform. Even Pompey is taught a trade, albeit a grisly one, as an apprentice hangman. The law must use both "correction" and "instruction."

The solutions arrived at in the comic subplot do not fit the case of Angelo, for he is powerful enough to be above the Viennese law. Indeed, he tries finally to brazen it out, pitting his authority against that of the seemingly friendless Isabella, much like the biblical Elders when justly accused of immorality by the innocent Susannah. Society is on Angelo's side—even the well-meaning Escalus; only a seeming providence can rescue the defenseless. The Duke of Vienna, hovering in the background and seeing all that happens, intervenes just at those points when tragedy threatens to become irreversible. Moreover, the Duke is testing those he observes. As he says to Friar Thomas, explaining why he has delegated his power to Angelo: "Hence shall we see, / If power change purpose, what our seemers be" (1.3.53–4). The Duke obviously expects Angelo to fall. Indeed, he has known all along that Angelo had dishonorably repudiated his solemn contract to Mariana when her marriage dowry disappeared at sea (3.1.215–25). Like an all-seeing deity who keeps a reckoning of humanity's good and evil deeds, the Duke has found out Angelo's great weakness. As Angelo confesses, "I perceive Your Grace, like power divine, / Hath looked upon my passes" (5.1.377–8). Paradoxically, this seemingly tragic story of temptation and fall yields precious benefits of remorse and humility. Angelo is rescued from his self-made nightmare of seduction, murder, and tyranny. Knowing now that he is prone like other mortals to fleshly weakness, he knows also that he needs spiritual assistance and that, as judge, he ought to use mercy. Seen in retrospect, his panic, despair, and humiliation are curative.

The Duke is no less a problematic character than Angelo, Isabella, and the rest. Vienna's deep corruption is, in part, the result of his unwillingness to bear down on vice, and yet, rather than undertake to remedy the failure himself, this strange monarch elects to leave the business to one he suspects will make matters worse. The Duke has a great deal to learn about his own dislike of crowds, his complacent tolerance of human weakness, and his naive supposition that all his subjects speak well of him. He is a highly manipulative character, the one most responsible in the play for the ethically dubious solutions through which craft must be employed against vice. The comforting words of spiritual counsel he offers Claudio, Juliet, and the rest are spoken by a secular ruler fraudulently disguised as a friar. Certainly, the Duke is no allegorized god-figure, for all his omniscience and final role as both punisher and forgiver. As *deux ex machina* of this problem comedy, the Duke is human, frail, and vulnerable—as indeed he ought to be in a play that explores with such rich complexity the ironic distance between divine and human justice.

Yet, for all his manifest and even comic weaknesses, the Duke is finally the authority figure who must attempt to bring order to the imperfect world of Vienna. The devices he employs, including the bed trick, seem morally questionable and yet are palpable comic fictions that unmistakably notify us what genre we are watching. If the Duke's role is more that of artist than ruler or diety, his being so is appropriate to the artistically contrived and theatrical world that Shakespeare presents to us. Within the world of this play, the disguised Duke's chief function is to test the other characters and to mislead them intentionally into expecting the worst, in order to try their resolve. On a comic level, he exposes the amiable but loose-tongued Lucio as a slanderer against the Duke himself and devises for Lucio a suitably satirical exposure and witty punishment. More seriously, as confessor to Juliet, he assures her that her beloved Claudio must die on the morrow. As she ought, she penitentially accepts "shame with joy" and so is cleansed (2.3.37). Because the Duke is not really a friar, he does not have the spiritual authority to do this, and the ruse strikes us as theatrical, employing devices of illusion that actors and dramatists use. Even so, it provides real comfort for Juliet. The very theatricality of the illusion, by reminding us that we are in the theater, enables us to see the Duke as a kind of morally persuasive playwright who can change the lives of his characters for the better.

Similarly, the counsel of Christian renunciation offered to Claudio by the bogus friar (3.1) is at once illusory and comforting. The Duke's poignant reflection on the vanity of human striving is made ironic but not invalid by our awareness that we are viewing a deception with a seemingly benign purpose—that of persuading Claudio to see matters in their true perspective. The Duke characterizes life as a breath, a dreamlike "after-dinner's sleep," a fever of inconstancy in which timorous humans long fretfully for what they do not have and spurn those things they have. Claudio responds as he ought, resolving to "find life" by "seeking death" (3.1.5–43). He achieves this calm, however, in the face of certain execution; ironically, what he must then learn to overmaster is the desperate hope of living by means of his sister's dishonor. Claudio is broken by this test and perversely begs for a few years of guilty life at the cost of eternal shame for himself and Isabella. From this harrowing experience, he emerges at length with a better understanding of his own weakness and a greater compassion toward the weakness of others.

The searing encounter between Claudio and Isabella puts her to the test as well, and her response seems hysterical and no doubt prudish to modern audiences. She has much to learn about the complexities of human behavior. Although she is sincere in protesting that she would lay down her life for her brother and is correct, in the play's terms, to prefer virtue to mere existence, her tone is too strident. Like other major characters, she must be humbled before she can rise. She and Claudio must heed the Duke's essential admonition: "Do not satisfy your resolution with hopes that are fallible" (3.1.170–1). Only then, paradoxically, can Isabella and Claudio go on to achieve earthly happiness.

Isabella and Angelo are paradoxically alike. Both have retreated from the world of carnal pleasure into havens they regard as safe but that turn out not to work in the way they had hoped. Isabella longs for the restraints of the sisterhood into which she is about to enter. Her suspicions about human frailty can be seen in her testing of her brother; she fears he will fail her by begging life at the cost of her eternal shame, and when he does just that, she reacts with shrill condemnation and even hatred. This is a dark moment for Isabella, and she needs the spiritual counsel of the disguised Duke to enable her to forgive not only her brother but also herself. Angelo, meanwhile, has attempted to put down the rebellion of the flesh by suppressing and denying all such feeling in himself. We see him at first as the workaholic official who is not hesitant to condemn in others what he believes he is free of personally. He cherishes restraint as much as Isabella does, and that is why he is so terrified when the apparent absence of his only superior, the Duke, opens up to him the abyss of his own licentiousness. Once his word is law, Angelo perceives that he can play the tyrant and seducer without check. He is horrified to discover not only that he has ungovernable sexual longings within him but also that they perversely direct themselves toward a woman who is virginal and saintly. Why does he yearn to "raze the sanctuary" thus (2.2.178)? The revelation to him of his own innate evil is virtually tragic in the intensity of his self-loathing, and yet, in this strange comedy, this revelation is a first step toward coming to terms with his reprobate self. Until Angelo acknowledges the carnal within, he cannot begin looking for a way to understand and accept this frailty. The Duke's test provides the means of self-discovery that Angelo cannot fashion on his own.

In her final testing, Isabella shows greatness of spirit. Here, Shakespeare significantly alters his chief sources, George Whetstone's *Promos and Cassandra* (1578), Giovanni Baptista Giraldi Cinthio's *Hecatommithi*, and Whetstone's *Heptameron of Civil Discourses*. In all these versions, the character corresponding to Angelo does actually ravish the heroine, and in the *Hecatommithi* he also murders her brother. Shakespeare, by withholding these irreversible acts, not only gives to Angelo a technical innocence, but also allows the Duke, as *deus ex machina*, to practice virtuous deception on Isabella one more time. Can she forgive the supposed murderer of her brother? Her affirmative answer confutes the Old Testament ethic of "An Angelo for Claudio, death for death" whereby "Like doth quit like, and measure still for measure"

(5.1.417–19). Although Angelo concedes that he deserves to die for what he intended, the forfeit need not be paid so long as humanity can reveal itself capable of Isabella's godlike mercy.

With its apparently unsuitable marriages and its improbable plotting, *Measure for Measure* does end by dealing directly with the problems of human nature confronted in the earlier scenes. The bed trick (switching Mariana for Isabella) may seem a legalistic and contrived way to bring Angelo to terms with his own carnality, but it is instructive not only to him but also to Isabella; she, like Angelo, must learn to accept the realities of the human condition. By helping Mariana to achieve her legitimate desire to couple and marry, Isabella sees into her own need. Her begging for Angelo's life is not merely an act of forgiveness to an enemy; it is a gift of continued marriage to Mariana. This realization helps to prepare Isabella herself for a marriage that, although dramatically surprising on stage (and even rejected by her in some modern productions), may be intended to demonstrate her having given up the cloistered life for all that marriage signifies. *Measure for Measure* is thus essentially comic (unlike *Troilus and Cressida*), despite its harrowing scenes of conflict and its awareness of vice everywhere in human nature. The play celebrates the *felix culpa* of human nature, the fall from grace that is an integral part of humanity's rise to happiness and self-knowledge. Throughout, in the play's finest scenes, poignancy is tempered by a wit and humor that are ultimately gracious. The formal and substantive emphasis on marriage stresses not just the benefits of remorse and humility but also the real possibility of psychic and spiritual growth: Isabella can acknowledge that she is a woman, Angelo can be genuinely freed from repression, and Claudio can value life more intensely because he has confronted death. All these recognitions affirm the acceptance and proper use of the physical and sexual side of human nature, and yet they are achieved only through charity and forgiveness. Humanity can learn, however slowly and painfully, that the talents entrusted to it by providence are to be used wisely.

The guardedly hopeful reading of the play offered here is, to be sure, not the only way in which it can be understood. The stage history of *Measure for Measure* highlights much that is problematic and troubling about it. For virtually all of the seventeenth, eighteenth, and

nineteenth centuries, after its initial production, the play disappeared from the theater, other than in a heavily rewritten adaptation of the Restoration period and an even more radically recast nineteenth-century operatic version by Richard Wagner called *Das Liebesverbot* ("Forbidden Love"). The play was, it seems, too disagreeable for audiences in those centuries, too given over to vice and moral ambiguity. Readers were sometimes warned away from it. The twentieth and twenty-first centuries, conversely, have found in *Measure for Measure* a persuasive and even devastating dramatization of human imperfection. In an age that has learned to distrust authority figures, Duke Vincentio can come across as officious and sadistic in his manipulation of human lives, rather than ultimately benign. The director Keith Hack, at Stratford-upon-Avon in 1974, saw the Duke as devious, hypocritical, deeply implicated in the corruption of his city, and bitterly resented by the characters whose lives are intrusively managed by him. Some productions have asked if Lucio is justified in his suspicions that the Duke is really a fleshmonger after all. Isabella's longing for the cloistered life of the convent is sometimes seen today as psychologically driven by a fear of sexuality more than by religious faith. Some stage productions revel in the tawdriness of the bordello world of a corrupted Vienna, as for example in Michael Bogdanov's production at Stratford, Canada, in 1985. To Keith Hack, in 1974, the play was a fable of social impression in the vein of Bertolt Brecht. The marriages with which the play ends are often held up to skeptical scrutiny. Is Angelo chastised by his searing experience into resolving to be a good husband to Mariana, or does he snarl at her when he is led off with her to be married? Most significantly, perhaps, does Isabella accept the surprising offer of marriage from the Duke who has protected her but also deceived her into believing that her brother was dead? Today, beginning with Estelle Kohler in John Barton's production at Stratford-upon-Avon in 1970, actresses and directors get to choose; since Isabella is given no lines indicating her acceptance, the actress may simply be bewildered or may decide, with a gesture of defiance or indifference, to have nothing to do with men. The range of options is extraordinary, and helps demonstrate the way in which Shakespeare provides such an unsettling challenge to actors, directors, and audiences alike.

Measure for Measure

The Names of All the Actors

VINCENTIO, *the Duke*
ANGELO, *the deputy*
ESCALUS, *an ancient lord*
CLAUDIO, *a young gentleman*
LUCIO, *a fantastic*
Two other like GENTLEMEN
PROVOST
THOMAS,⎱
PETER,⎰ *two friars*
[A JUSTICE]
[VARRIUS, *a friend of the Duke*]

ELBOW, *a simple constable*
FROTH, *a foolish gentleman*
CLOWN [*POMPEY, a servant to Mistress Overdone*]

ABHORSON, *an executioner*
BARNARDINE, *a dissolute prisoner*

ISABELLA, *sister to Claudio*
MARIANA, *betrothed to Angelo*
JULIET, *beloved of Claudio*
FRANCISCA, *a nun*
MISTRESS OVERDONE, *a bawd*

[A SERVANT *of Angelo*
BOY *singer*
A MESSENGER *from Angelo*

Lords, Officers, Citizens, Servants, and other Attendants]

THE SCENE: *Vienna*

1.1

Enter Duke, Escalus, lords, [and attendants].

DUKE Escalus.
ESCALUS My lord.
DUKE
  Of government the properties to unfold   3
  Would seem in me t'affect speech and discourse,   4
  Since I am put to know that your own science   5
  Exceeds, in that, the lists of all advice   6
  My strength can give you. Then no more remains   7
  But that to your sufficiency   8
  . . . . as your worth is able,   9
  And let them work. The nature of our people,

Our city's institutions, and the terms   11
For common justice, you're as pregnant in   12
As art and practice hath enrichèd any   13
That we remember. There is our commission,
                    [giving a paper]
From which we would not have you warp.—Call
    hither,   15
I say, bid come before us Angelo.   *[Exit one.]*
What figure of us think you he will bear?   17
For you must know, we have with special soul   18
Elected him our absence to supply,   19
Lent him our terror, dressed him with our love,   20
And given his deputation all the organs   21
Of our own power. What think you of it?
ESCALUS
  If any in Vienna be of worth
  To undergo such ample grace and honor,   24

1.1. Location: Vienna. The court of Duke Vincentio.
3–4 Of . . . discourse For me to deliver an oration on the qualities needed in governing well would make me seem enamored of my own pomposity **5 put to know** obliged to admit. **science** knowledge **6 that** i.e., properties of government (line 3). **lists** limits **7 strength** power of mind **8–9 But . . . able** (The passage appears in the Folio as a single line. Several attempts at emendation have been made, but the most plausible explanation is that something has been deleted or inadvertently omitted.)

11 terms terms of court; or, modes of procedure **12 pregnant** well-informed **13 art** learning, theory **15 warp** deviate. **17 What . . . bear?** i.e., How do you think he will do as my substitute? **18 special soul** all the powers of the mind; whole heart **19 Elected** chosen. **supply** fill, make up for **20 terror** power to inspire awe and fear **21 his deputation** him as deputy. **organs** instruments **24 undergo** bear the weight of

It is Lord Angelo.

Enter Angelo.

DUKE   Look where he comes.
ANGELO
Always obedient to Your Grace's will,
I come to know your pleasure.
DUKE   Angelo,
There is a kind of character in thy life
That to th'observer doth thy history
Fully unfold. Thyself and thy belongings   30
Are not thine own so proper as to waste   31
Thyself upon thy virtues, they on thee.   32
Heaven doth with us as we with torches do,   33
Not light them for themselves; for if our virtues
Did not go forth of us, 'twere all alike   35
As if we had them not. Spirits are not finely touched   36
But to fine issues, nor Nature never lends   37
The smallest scruple of her excellence   38
But, like a thrifty goddess, she determines   39
Herself the glory of a creditor,   40
Both thanks and use. But I do bend my speech   41
To one that can my part in him advertise.   42
Hold, therefore, Angelo:
In our remove be thou at full ourself.   44
Mortality and mercy in Vienna   45
Live in thy tongue and heart. Old Escalus,
Though first in question, is thy secondary.   47
Take thy commission.   [*He gives a paper.*]
ANGELO   Now, good my lord,
Let there be some more test made of my mettle   49
Before so noble and so great a figure
Be stamped upon it.
DUKE   No more evasion.
We have with a leavened and preparèd choice   52
Proceeded to you; therefore take your honors.
Our haste from hence is of so quick condition   54
That it prefers itself and leaves unquestioned   55
Matters of needful value. We shall write to you,
As time and our concernings shall importune,   57
How it goes with us, and do look to know   58

What doth befall you here. So, fare you well.
To th' hopeful execution do I leave you   60
Of your commissions.
ANGELO   Yet give leave, my lord,   61
That we may bring you something on the way.   62
DUKE   My haste may not admit it;   63
Nor need you, on mine honor, have to do   64
With any scruple. Your scope is as mine own,   65
So to enforce or qualify the laws
As to your soul seems good. Give me your hand.
I'll privily away. I love the people   68
But do not like to stage me to their eyes;   69
Though it do well, I do not relish well   70
Their loud applause and "aves" vehement,   71
Nor do I think the man of safe discretion   72
That does affect it. Once more, fare you well.   73
ANGELO
The heavens give safety to your purposes!
ESCALUS
Lead forth and bring you back in happiness!   75
DUKE   I thank you. Fare you well.   *Exit.*
ESCALUS
I shall desire you, sir, to give me leave
To have free speech with you; and it concerns me   78
To look into the bottom of my place.   79
A power I have, but of what strength and nature
I am not yet instructed.
ANGELO
'Tis so with me. Let us withdraw together,
And we may soon our satisfaction have
Touching that point.
ESCALUS   I'll wait upon Your Honor.
         Exeunt.

❖

1.2

Enter Lucio and two other Gentlemen.

LUCIO   If the Duke with the other dukes come not to
composition with the King of Hungary, why then all   2
the dukes fall upon the King.   3
FIRST GENTLEMAN   Heaven grant us its peace, but not
the King of Hungary's!
SECOND GENTLEMAN   Amen.
LUCIO   Thou conclud'st like the sanctimonious pirate
that went to sea with the Ten Commandments but
scraped one out of the table.   9
SECOND GENTLEMAN   "Thou shalt not steal"?
LUCIO   Ay, that he razed.   11

---

30 belongings attributes, endowments   **31 proper** exclusively
31–2 as to . . . thee that you can expend all your efforts developing
your own talents or use them solely for your own advantage.
33 torches (Compare Jesus' command that we not hide our light
under a bushel, Matthew 5:14–16.)   **35 forth of us** out of us and into
the world.   **'twere all alike** it would be exactly the same   **36–7 Spirits . . . issues** Souls are not deeply moved unless for noble purposes
38 scruple bit. (Literally, a small weight.)   **39–41 But . . . use** unless,
like a thrifty goddess, she gathers to herself the glory due to a creditor, gaining both thanks from her debtor and interest on the loan.
41 bend direct   **42 that . . . advertise** who can instruct my role as
duke now vested in him, i.e., who knows already more about governing in my absence than I can tell him.   **44 In . . . ourself** During my
absence be in every respect my deputy. (The royal plural.)   **45 Mortality** The full rigor of the law, the death sentence   **47 first in question** senior and first appointed   **49 mettle** substance, quality. (With
play on "metal," a common variant spelling, continued in the coining
imagery of lines 50–1.)   **52 leavened** i.e., carefully considered (just as
yeast is given time to leaven dough)   **54–5 Our . . . itself** The cause
for my hasty departure is so urgent that it takes precedence over all
other matters   **55 unquestioned** not yet considered   **57 concernings**
affairs.   **importune** urge   **58 look to know** expect to be informed

60 th' hopeful exciting hopes of success.   **execution** carrying out
61 leave permission   **62 bring you something** accompany you for a
short distance   **63 admit** permit   **64–5 have . . . scruple** have the
least doubt or hesitation about what is to be done.   **68 I'll privily
away** I'll go away secretly.   **69 stage me** make a show of myself
70 do well i.e., serves a political purpose   **71 aves** hails of acclamation   **72 safe** sound   **73 affect** desire, court   **75 Lead** May the heavens conduct you   **78 free** frank   **79 the bottom of my place** the
extent of my commission.
1.2. Location: A public place.
2 composition agreement   **3 fall upon** attack   **9 table** tablet.
11 razed scraped out. (The word may also suggest *rased*, "erased.")

FIRST GENTLEMAN   Why, 'twas a commandment to command the captain and all the rest from their function; they put forth to steal. There's not a soldier of us all that, in the thanksgiving before meat, do relish the petition well that prays for peace. 14 15

SECOND GENTLEMAN   I never heard any soldier dislike it.

LUCIO   I believe thee, for I think thou never wast where grace was said.

SECOND GENTLEMAN   No? A dozen times at least.

FIRST GENTLEMAN   What, in meter?

LUCIO   In any proportion or in any language. 22

FIRST GENTLEMAN   I think, or in any religion.

LUCIO   Ay, why not? Grace is grace, despite of all controversy; as, for example, thou thyself art a wicked villain, despite of all grace. 24 25

FIRST GENTLEMAN   Well, there went but a pair of shears between us. 27 28

LUCIO   I grant; as there may between the lists and the velvet. Thou art the list. 29 30

FIRST GENTLEMAN   And thou the velvet. Thou art good velvet; thou'rt a three-piled piece, I warrant thee. I had as lief be a list of an English kersey as be piled, as thou art piled, for a French velvet. Do I speak feelingly now? 32 33 34

LUCIO   I think thou dost, and indeed with most painful feeling of thy speech. I will, out of thine own confession, learn to begin thy health, but, whilst I live, forget to drink after thee. 37 38

FIRST GENTLEMAN   I think I have done myself wrong, have I not? 39

SECOND GENTLEMAN   Yes, that thou hast, whether thou art tainted or free. 42

Enter bawd [Mistress Overdone].

LUCIO   Behold, behold, where Madam Mitigation comes! I have purchased as many diseases under her roof as come to— 43

SECOND GENTLEMAN   To what, I pray?

LUCIO   Judge. 47

SECOND GENTLEMAN   To three thousand dolors a year. 48

FIRST GENTLEMAN   Ay, and more.

LUCIO   A French crown more. 50

FIRST GENTLEMAN   Thou art always figuring diseases in me, but thou art full of error. I am sound. 51

LUCIO   Nay, not, as one would say, healthy, but so sound as things that are hollow. Thy bones are hollow; impiety has made a feast of thee. 54 55

FIRST GENTLEMAN   [*to Mistress Overdone*] How now, which of your hips has the most profound sciatica? 57

MISTRESS OVERDONE   Well, well; there's one yonder arrested and carried to prison was worth five thousand of you all.

SECOND GENTLEMAN   Who's that, I pray thee?

MISTRESS OVERDONE   Marry, sir, that's Claudio, Signor Claudio. 62

FIRST GENTLEMAN   Claudio to prison? 'Tis not so.

MISTRESS OVERDONE   Nay, but I know 'tis so. I saw him arrested, saw him carried away; and, which is more, within these three days his head to be chopped off. 66

LUCIO   But, after all this fooling, I would not have it so. Art thou sure of this? 68

MISTRESS OVERDONE   I am too sure of it; and it is for getting Madam Julietta with child.

LUCIO   Believe me, this may be. He promised to meet me two hours since, and he was ever precise in promise-keeping. 73

SECOND GENTLEMAN   Besides, you know, it draws something near to the speech we had to such a purpose. 75 76 77

FIRST GENTLEMAN   But most of all agreeing with the proclamation.

LUCIO   Away! Let's go learn the truth of it.

Exit [Lucio with the Gentlemen].

MISTRESS OVERDONE   Thus, what with the war, what with the sweat, what with the gallows, and what with poverty, I am custom-shrunk. 82 83

Enter Clown [Pompey].

How now, what's the news with you?

POMPEY   Yonder man is carried to prison.

MISTRESS OVERDONE   Well, what has he done? 86

POMPEY   A woman.

MISTRESS OVERDONE   But what's his offense?

POMPEY   Groping for trouts in a peculiar river. 89

---

14 put forth set out to sea   **15 thanksgiving before meat** saying of grace before a meal. (As in line 19.)   **22 proportion** form **24–5 Grace . . . controversy** (Refers to the Catholic-Protestant *controversy*, line 25, as to whether humanity can be saved by works or by grace alone; with punning on *grace* as "thanks for a meal," line 19, and "gracefulness" or "becomingness," line 26.)   **27–8 there . . . between us** i.e., we're cut from the same cloth.   **29–30 as . . . list** (Lucio jokes that the shears might also cut between, i.e., distinguish between, the mere *lists* or selvages, edges of a woven fabric, and the *velvet* betokening a true gentlemen. Lucio wittily asserts himself to be a true gentleman; the other speaker, not.)   **32 three-piled** having a threefold pile or nap, the best grade. (Velvet patches might be used to conceal syphilitic sores or scars.)   **33 as lief** as soon, rather.   **kersey** a coarse woolen fabric. (The First Gentleman turns the joke on Lucio by saying he would rather be a plain, homespun Englishman than a Frenchified velvet gentleman in decay and threadbare. *Velvet* suggests prostitutes and venereal disease, as in the following notes.)   **be piled** (1) have a cloth nap (2) suffer from hemorrhoids (3) be pilled or peeled, i.e., hairless, bald, as a result of mercury treatment for syphilis (known as the "French disease"; see *French velvet* in the next line and *French crown*, line 50)   **34 feelingly** to the purpose, so as to hit home. (But Lucio's reply quibbles on "painfully," meaning the Gentleman's mouth is affected by the French disease; hence, Lucio will not drink from the same cup after him.)   **37 begin thy health** drink to your health   **37–8 forget . . . thee** take care not to drink from your cup. **39 done myself wrong** i.e., asked for that   **42 tainted** infected **43 Mitigation** (So called because her function is to relieve desire.)

47 Judge Guess.   **48 dolors** (Quibbling on *dollars;* spelled "Dollours" in the Folio.)   **50 French crown** (1) gold coin (2) bald head incurred through syphilis, the "French disease"   **51 figuring** (1) imagining (2) reckoning. (Recalling the monetary puns of lines 48 and 50.) **54 sound** (1) healthy (2) resounding (because of hollow bones caused by syphilis)   **55 impiety** wickedness   **57 sciatica** a disease affecting the sciatic nerve in the hip and thigh, thought to be a symptom of syphilis.   **62 Marry** i.e., By the Virgin Mary   **66 which** what **68 after** notwithstanding   **73 ever** always   **75–6 draws . . . near to** approaches, sounds somewhat like   **76–7 to . . . purpose** on that topic.   **82 sweat** sweating sickness (often fatal), or the plague; also, the sweating tub, a treatment for syphilis   **83 custom-shrunk** having fewer customers.   **86 done** (Pompey quibbles in line 87 on a sexual sense of the word, present also in Mistress Overdone's name.) **89 peculiar** privately owned. (With bawdy suggestion.)

MISTRESS OVERDONE   What? Is there a maid with child
by him?

POMPEY   No, but there's a woman with maid by him.   92
You have not heard of the proclamation, have you?

MISTRESS OVERDONE   What proclamation, man?

POMPEY   All houses in the suburbs of Vienna must be   95
plucked down.

MISTRESS OVERDONE   And what shall become of those
in the city?

POMPEY   They shall stand for seed. They had gone   99
down too, but that a wise burgher put in for them.   100

MISTRESS OVERDONE   But shall all our houses of resort
in the suburbs be pulled down?

POMPEY   To the ground, mistress.

MISTRESS OVERDONE   Why, here's a change indeed in
the commonwealth! What shall become of me?

POMPEY   Come, fear not you. Good counselors lack no   106
clients. Though you change your place, you need not   107
change your trade; I'll be your tapster still. Courage!   108
There will be pity taken on you. You that have worn   109
your eyes almost out in the service, you will be con-   110
sidered.

MISTRESS OVERDONE   What's to do here, Thomas Tapster? Let's withdraw.

POMPEY   Here comes Signor Claudio, led by the Pro-   114
vost to prison; and there's Madam Juliet.   *Exeunt.*   115

*Enter Provost, Claudio, Juliet, Officers; Lucio
and two Gentlemen [follow].*

CLAUDIO   [*to the Provost*]
Fellow, why dost thou show me thus to the world?
Bear me to prison, where I am committed.

PROVOST
I do it not in evil disposition,
But from Lord Angelo by special charge.

CLAUDIO
Thus can the demigod Authority
Make us pay down for our offense, by weight,   121
The words of heaven. On whom it will, it will;   122
On whom it will not, so; yet still 'tis just.   123

LUCIO
Why, how now, Claudio? Whence comes this
restraint?

CLAUDIO
From too much liberty, my Lucio, liberty.

As surfeit is the father of much fast,   126
So every scope, by the immoderate use,   127
Turns to restraint. Our natures do pursue,
Like rats that ravin down their proper bane,   129
A thirsty evil, and when we drink we die.

LUCIO   If I could speak so wisely under an arrest, I   131
would send for certain of my creditors. And yet, to say   132
the truth, I had as lief have the foppery of freedom as   133
the morality of imprisonment. What's thy offense,
Claudio?

CLAUDIO
What but to speak of would offend again.

LUCIO
What, is't murder?

CLAUDIO   No.

LUCIO   Lechery?

CLAUDIO
Call it so.

PROVOST   Away, sir, you must go.

CLAUDIO
One word, good friend.—Lucio, a word with you.

LUCIO
A hundred, if they'll do you any good.
Is lechery so looked after?   141

CLAUDIO
Thus stands it with me: upon a true contract   142
I got possession of Julietta's bed.
You know the lady; she is fast my wife,   144
Save that we do the denunciation lack   145
Of outward order. This we came not to,   146
Only for propagation of a dower   147
Remaining in the coffer of her friends,   148
From whom we thought it meet to hide our love   149
Till time had made them for us. But it chances   150
The stealth of our most mutual entertainment
With character too gross is writ on Juliet.   152

LUCIO
With child, perhaps?

CLAUDIO   Unhappily, even so.
And the new deputy now for the Duke—
Whether it be the fault and glimpse of newness,   155
Or whether that the body public be
A horse whereon the governor doth ride,
Who, newly in the seat, that it may know
He can command, lets it straight feel the spur;   159

---

92 woman with maid (Pompey playfully corrects Mistress Overdone's use of the word "maid," joking that a pregnant woman cannot
be a virgin [maid] though the child she carries is one.)   95 houses i.e.,
brothels.   suburbs (Location of the brothels in Shakespeare's London, as in other walled cities.)   99 for seed to preserve the species.
(With ribald pun.)   100 burgher citizen.   put . . . them interceded on
their behalf, offered to acquire them.   106–7 Good . . . clients Good
lawyers (and, by implication, pimps and bawds) are never at a loss
for clients.   108 tapster one who draws beer in an alehouse
109–10 worn . . . out i.e., worked so hard. (Perhaps with an ironic reference to the traditional image of the blind Cupid, often depicted on
signs hung at the doors of brothels.)   114–15 Provost officer charged
with apprehension, custody, and punishment of offenders
121–2 Make . . . heaven make us pay the full penalty for our offenses
called for in the Bible.   122–3 On whom . . . 'tis just (Compare
Romans 9:18: "Therefore hath he [God] mercy on whom he will have
mercy, and whom he will he hardeneth.")

126 As . . . fast Just as excessive indulgence inevitably leads to revulsion and abstinence   127 scope liberty, license   129 ravin . . . bane
greedily devour what is poisonous to them   131–2 If . . . creditors If
imprisonment would gain me such wisdom, I would send for those
to whom I owe money and thus be arrested for debt.   133 lief willingly.   foppery folly   141 looked after kept under observation.
142 a true contract i.e., one made in the presence of witnesses, though
without a religious ceremony. (Such a precontract was binding but, in
the eyes of the Church, did not confer the right of sexual consummation before the nuptials.)   144 fast my wife i.e., firmly bound by precontract   145 denunciation formal declaration   146 outward order
public ceremony.   147 propagation increase, begetting   148 friends
relatives   149 meet fitting, necessary   150 made . . . us disposed
them in our favor.   152 character too gross writing too evident
155 the fault . . . newness the faulty flashiness of novelty
159 straight at once

Whether the tyranny be in his place,   160
Or in his eminence that fills it up,   161
I stagger in—but this new governor   162
Awakes me all the enrollèd penalties   163
Which have, like unscoured armor, hung by the wall
So long that nineteen zodiacs have gone round   165
And none of them been worn; and for a name   166
Now puts the drowsy and neglected act
Freshly on me. 'Tis surely for a name.

LUCIO   I warrant it is, and thy head stands so tickle on 169
  thy shoulders that a milkmaid, if she be in love, may
  sigh it off. Send after the Duke and appeal to him.

CLAUDIO
I have done so, but he's not to be found.
I prithee, Lucio, do me this kind service:
This day my sister should the cloister enter   174
And there receive her approbation.   175
Acquaint her with the danger of my state;
Implore her, in my voice, that she make friends
To the strict deputy; bid herself assay him.   178
I have great hope in that, for in her youth
There is a prone and speechless dialect   180
Such as move men; beside, she hath prosperous art   181
When she will play with reason and discourse,
And well she can persuade.

LUCIO   I pray she may, as well for the encouragement of 184
  the like, which else would stand under grievous impo-   185
  sition, as for the enjoying of thy life, who I would   186
  be sorry should be thus foolishly lost at a game of tick- 187
  tack. I'll to her.   188

CLAUDIO   I thank you, good friend Lucio.

LUCIO   Within two hours.

CLAUDIO   Come, officer, away!   *Exeunt.*

❧

1.[3]

Enter Duke and Friar Thomas.

DUKE
No, holy Father, throw away that thought;
Believe not that the dribbling dart of love
Can pierce a complete bosom. Why I desire thee   3
To give me secret harbor hath a purpose   4
More grave and wrinkled than the aims and ends   5
Of burning youth.

FRIAR THOMAS   May Your Grace speak of it?

DUKE
My holy sir, none better knows than you
How I have ever loved the life removed   8
And held in idle price to haunt assemblies   9
Where youth and cost witless bravery keeps.   10
I have delivered to Lord Angelo,
A man of stricture and firm abstinence,   12
My absolute power and place here in Vienna,
And he supposes me traveled to Poland;
For so I have strewed it in the common ear,
And so it is received. Now, pious sir,
You will demand of me why I do this.

FRIAR THOMAS   Gladly, my lord.

DUKE
We have strict statutes and most biting laws,
The needful bits and curbs to headstrong steeds,   20
Which for this fourteen years we have let slip,   21
Even like an o'ergrown lion in a cave   22
That goes not out to prey. Now, as fond fathers,   23
Having bound up the threat'ning twigs of birch
Only to stick it in their children's sight
For terror, not to use, in time the rod
Becomes more mocked than feared, so our decrees,
Dead to infliction, to themselves are dead;   28
And liberty plucks justice by the nose,   29
The baby beats the nurse, and quite athwart   30
Goes all decorum.

FRIAR THOMAS   It rested in Your Grace   31
To unloose this tied-up justice when you pleased;
And it in you more dreadful would have seemed
Than in Lord Angelo.

DUKE   I do fear, too dreadful.
Sith 'twas my fault to give the people scope,   35
'Twould be my tyranny to strike and gall them   36
For what I bid them do; for we bid this be done   37
When evil deeds have their permissive pass   38
And not the punishment. Therefore indeed, my father,
I have on Angelo imposed the office,   40
Who may in th'ambush of my name strike home,   41
And yet my nature never in the fight   42
To do in slander. And to behold his sway   43
I will, as 'twere a brother of your order,
Visit both prince and people. Therefore, I prithee,
Supply me with the habit, and instruct me   46
How I may formally in person bear   47

---

160 in his place inherent in the office   **161 his eminence** the eminence of him   **162 I stagger in** I am uncertain   **163 Awakes me** i.e.,
awakes, activates. (*Me* is used colloquially.)   **enrollèd** written on a
roll or deed   **165 zodiacs** i.e., years   **166 for a name** for reputation's
sake   **169 tickle** uncertain, unstable   **174 cloister** i.e., convent
175 approbation novitiate, period of probation.   **178 To** with.   **assay**
try, test   **180 prone** eager, apt, supplicating.   **dialect** language
181 prosperous art skill or ability to gain favorable results   **184–6 as
well . . . life** both for the encouragement of similar sexual activity,
which otherwise would be subject to grave charges or accusations,
and for you to continue to live   **187–8 tick-tack** a form of backgam-
mon in which pegs were fitted into holes. (Here applied bawdily.)
1.3. Location: A friary.
2 dribbling falling short or wide of the mark   **3 complete** perfect,
whole, strong   **4 harbor** shelter   **5 wrinkled** i.e., mature

8 removed retired   **9 in idle price** as little worth. *Idle* means
"unprofitable."   **10 Where . . . keeps** where youth and costly expenditure put themselves foolishly on display.   **12 stricture** strictness
20 steeds (The Folio reading, "weedes," is possible in the sense of
"lawless and uncontrolled impulses.")   **21 fourteen** (Claudio mentions nineteen years at 1.2.165; possibly the compositor confused *xiv*
and *xix*.)   **22 o'ergrown** too old and large   **23 fond** doting   **28 Dead
to infliction** dead in that they are not executed   **29 liberty** license
30 athwart wrongly, awry   **31 decorum** social order.   **It rested . . .
Grace** It lay in your ducal authority, was incumbent on you   **35 Sith**
Since   **36 gall** chafe, injure   **37 we . . . done** i.e., we virtually order a
crime to be committed   **38 pass** sanction   **40 office** duty   **41 Who . . .
home** who may, under cover of my ducal authority, strike to the heart
of the matter   **42 nature** i.e., personal identity (as distinguished from
official capacity)   **43 do in slander** act so as to invite slander (for
being too repressive).   **sway** rule   **46 habit** garment (of a friar)
47 formally in outward appearance.   **bear** bear myself

Like a true friar. More reasons for this action
At our more leisure shall I render you.   49
Only this one: Lord Angelo is precise,   50
Stands at a guard with envy, scarce confesses   51
That his blood flows or that his appetite   52
Is more to bread than stone. Hence shall we see,   53
If power change purpose, what our seemers be.

                                                          Exeunt.

❖

1.[4]

Enter Isabella and Francisca, a nun.

ISABELLA
And have you nuns no farther privileges?
FRANCISCA   Are not these large enough?
ISABELLA
Yes, truly. I speak not as desiring more,
But rather wishing a more strict restraint
Upon the sisterhood, the votarists of Saint Clare.   5
LUCIO   (*within*)
Ho! Peace be in this place!
ISABELLA   Who's that which calls?
FRANCISCA
It is a man's voice. Gentle Isabella,
Turn you the key, and know his business of him.
You may, I may not; you are yet unsworn.   9
When you have vowed, you must not speak with men
But in the presence of the prioress;
Then if you speak you must not show your face,
Or if you show your face you must not speak.
He calls again. I pray you, answer him.   [*Exit.*]
ISABELLA
Peace and prosperity! Who is 't that calls?

              [*She opens the door. Enter Lucio.*]

LUCIO
Hail, virgin, if you be, as those cheek roses   16
Proclaim you are no less. Can you so stead me   17
As bring me to the sight of Isabella,   18
A novice of this place, and the fair sister
To her unhappy brother Claudio?   20
ISABELLA
Why "her unhappy brother"? Let me ask,
The rather for I now must make you know   22
I am that Isabella, and his sister.
LUCIO
Gentle and fair, your brother kindly greets you.
Not to be weary with you, he's in prison.   25

ISABELLA   Woe me! For what?
LUCIO
For that which, if myself might be his judge,
He should receive his punishment in thanks:
He hath got his friend with child.
ISABELLA
Sir, make me not your story.
LUCIO   'Tis true.   30
I would not—though 'tis my familiar sin   31
With maids to seem the lapwing, and to jest,   32
Tongue far from heart—play with all virgins so.
I hold you as a thing enskied and sainted   34
By your renouncement, an immortal spirit
And to be talked with in sincerity
As with a saint.
ISABELLA
You do blaspheme the good in mocking me.   38
LUCIO
Do not believe it. Fewness and truth, 'tis thus: 39
Your brother and his lover have embraced.
As those that feed grow full, as blossoming time   41
That from the seedness the bare fallow brings   42
To teeming foison, even so her plenteous womb   43
Expresseth his full tilth and husbandry.   44
ISABELLA
Someone with child by him? My cousin Juliet?
LUCIO   Is she your cousin?
ISABELLA
Adoptedly, as schoolmaids change their names   47
By vain though apt affection.
LUCIO   She it is.   48
ISABELLA
Oh, let him marry her.
LUCIO   This is the point.
The Duke is very strangely gone from hence;
Bore many gentlemen, myself being one,   51
In hand and hope of action; but we do learn,   52
By those that know the very nerves of state,
His givings-out were of an infinite distance   54
From his true-meant design. Upon his place,   55
And with full line of his authority,   56
Governs Lord Angelo, a man whose blood
Is very snow broth; one who never feels   58
The wanton stings and motions of the sense,   59
But doth rebate and blunt his natural edge   60

---

49 **more** greater   50 **precise** strict, puritanical   51 **Stands . . . envy**
guards himself severely against calumny   52–3 **or . . . stone** or that
he has an appetite for bread (i.e., food or physical pleasure) any more
than if it were stone. (See Matthew 4.3, where the devil tempts Jesus
to turn stone into bread.)
1.4. Location: A convent.
5 votarists of Saint Clare An order founded in 1212 by Saint Francis
of Assisi and Saint Clare; its members were enjoined to a life of
poverty, service, and contemplation.   **9 you . . . unsworn** i.e., you
have not yet taken your formal vows to enter the convent.   **16 cheek
roses** i.e., blushes   **17 stead** help   **18 As** as to   **20 unhappy** unfortunate   **22 The rather for** the more so because   **25 weary** wearisome

30 story subject for mirth.   **31 familiar** customary   **32 lapwing** pee-
wit or plover. (The lapwing runs away from its nest in order to draw
away enemies from its young, much as Lucio throws up smoke-
screens in his seductive talk with young women.)   **34 enskied** placed
in heaven   **38 You . . . me** You blaspheme goodness itself when you
mockingly praise me, unworthy as I am, for saintliness.   **39 it** i.e.,
that I am mocking.   **Fewness and truth** In few words and truly
41–3 As . . . foison Just as the season of blossoming brings the sowing
of the bare untilled land to teeming fruitfulness   **44 Expresseth . . .
husbandry** makes plainly visible Claudio's tilling of the crop, i.e., his
plowing and fertilizing Juliet's body.   **47 change** exchange   **48 vain
though apt** girlish though natural and suitable   **51–2 Bore . . . action**
i.e., he misleadingly kept us in expectation of some military action
54 givings-out public statements   **55 Upon In**   **56 line** extent
58 snow broth melted snow (i.e., ice water)   **59 motions . . . sense**
promptings of sexual desire   **60 But . . . edge** but dulls and blunts
the sharp desire of sexuality

With profits of the mind, study, and fast.
He—to give fear to use and liberty, 62
Which have for long run by the hideous law
As mice by lions—hath picked out an act,
Under whose heavy sense your brother's life 65
Falls into forfeit. He arrests him on it
And follows close the rigor of the statute
To make him an example. All hope is gone,
Unless you have the grace by your fair prayer
To soften Angelo. And that's my pith of business 70
Twixt you and your poor brother.

ISABELLA   Doth he so
Seek his life?

LUCIO   He's censured him already, 72
And, as I hear, the Provost hath a warrant
For 's execution.

ISABELLA   Alas, what poor
Ability's in me to do him good?

LUCIO   Assay the power you have. 76

ISABELLA
My power? Alas, I doubt.

LUCIO   Our doubts are traitors,
And makes us lose the good we oft might win, 78
By fearing to attempt. Go to Lord Angelo,
And let him learn to know, when maidens sue
Men give like gods, but when they weep and kneel,
All their petitions are as freely theirs 82
As they themselves would owe them. 83

ISABELLA   I'll see what I can do.

LUCIO   But speedily.

ISABELLA   I will about it straight,
No longer staying but to give the Mother 87
Notice of my affair. I humbly thank you.
Commend me to my brother. Soon at night 89
I'll send him certain word of my success. 90

LUCIO
I take my leave of you.

ISABELLA   Good sir, adieu.
Exeunt [separately].

❖

2.1

Enter Angelo, Escalus, and servants, [a] Justice.

ANGELO
We must not make a scarecrow of the law,
Setting it up to fear the birds of prey, 2
And let it keep one shape till custom make it
Their perch and not their terror.

ESCALUS   Ay, but yet
Let us be keen and rather cut a little 5

Than fall and bruise to death. Alas, this gentleman 6
Whom I would save had a most noble father!
Let but Your Honor know, 8
Whom I believe to be most strait in virtue, 9
That, in the working of your own affections, 10
Had time cohered with place, or place with wishing,
Or that the resolute acting of your blood 12
Could have attained th'effect of your own purpose, 13
Whether you had not sometime in your life 14
Erred in this point which now you censure him, 15
And pulled the law upon you.

ANGELO
'Tis one thing to be tempted, Escalus,
Another thing to fall. I not deny
The jury, passing on the prisoner's life,
May in the sworn twelve have a thief or two
Guiltier than him they try. What's open made to
    justice,
That justice seizes. What knows the laws 22
That thieves do pass on thieves? 'Tis very pregnant, 23
The jewel that we find, we stoop and take't
Because we see it; but what we do not see
We tread upon and never think of it.
You may not so extenuate his offense
For I have had such faults; but rather tell me, 28
When I that censure him do so offend,
Let mine own judgment pattern out my death 30
And nothing come in partial. Sir, he must die. 31

Enter Provost.

ESCALUS
Be it as your wisdom will.

ANGELO   Where is the Provost?

PROVOST
Here, if it like Your Honor.

ANGELO   See that Claudio 33
Be executed by nine tomorrow morning.
Bring him his confessor; let him be prepared.
For that's the utmost of his pilgrimage. 36
[Exit Provost.]

ESCALUS
Well, heaven forgive him, and forgive us all!
Some rise by sin, and some by virtue fall;
Some run from breaks of ice and answer none, 39
And some condemnèd for a fault alone. 40

Enter Elbow, Froth, Clown [Pompey], officers.

---

62 **use and liberty** habitual licentiousness   65 **heavy sense** severe interpretation   70 **my pith of business** the essence of my business   72 **censured** sentenced   76 **Assay** Try   78 **makes** make   82 **their petitions** i.e., the things the maidens ask for   83 **As . . . them** as they themselves would wish to have them.   87 **but than.** **Mother** Mother Superior, prioress   89 **Soon at night** Early tonight   90 **my success** how I have succeeded.
2.1. Location: A court of justice.
2 **fear** frighten   5 **keen** sharp

6 **fall** let fall heavily.   **bruise** i.e., crush   8 **know** consider   9 **strait** strict   10 **affections** desires   12 **blood** passion   13 **effect** realization   14 **had** would have.   **sometime** on some occasion   15 **censure him** sentence him for   22–3 **What . . . on thieves?** Who knows what laws thieves apply to their fellow thieves?   23 **pregnant** clear   28 **For** because   30–1 **Let . . . partial** let the sentence I have imposed serve as a model in sentencing me if I commit a crime, no partiality or extenuating circumstances being admitted.   33 **like** please   36 **that's . . . pilgrimage** that's the furthest point of his life's journey.   39 **Some . . . none** some break the ice repeatedly (i.e., commit serious infractions of the law) and yet escape punishment. (A famous crux; the Folio reads "brakes of Ice.")   40 **a fault alone** one single infraction.

ELBOW   Come, bring them away. If these be good 41
people in a commonweal that do nothing but use their 42
abuses in common houses, I know no law. Bring them 43
away.

ANGELO   How now, sir, what's your name? And what's
the matter?

ELBOW   If it please Your Honor, I am the poor Duke's 47
constable, and my name is Elbow. I do lean upon 48
justice, sir, and do bring in here before Your good Honor
two notorious benefactors.

ANGELO   Benefactors? Well, what benefactors are they?
Are they not malefactors?

ELBOW   If it please Your Honor, I know not well what
they are; but precise villains they are, that I am sure of, 54
and void of all profanation in the world that good 55
Christians ought to have.

ESCALUS   [to Angelo]   This comes off well. Here's a
wise officer.

ANGELO   Go to. What quality are they of?—Elbow is 59
your name? Why dost thou not speak, Elbow?

POMPEY   He cannot, sir; he's out at elbow. 61

ANGELO   What are you, sir?

ELBOW   He, sir? A tapster, sir, parcel-bawd, one that 63
serves a bad woman, whose house, sir, was, as they
say, plucked down in the suburbs; and now she
professes a hothouse, which I think is a very ill house 66
too.

ESCALUS   How know you that?

ELBOW   My wife, sir, whom I detest before heaven and 69
Your Honor—

ESCALUS   How? Thy wife?

ELBOW   Ay, sir; whom I thank heaven is an honest
woman—

ESCALUS   Dost thou detest her therefore?

ELBOW   I say, sir, I will detest myself also, as well as
she, that this house, if it be not a bawd's house, it is
pity of her life, for it is a naughty house. 77

ESCALUS   How dost thou know that, Constable?

ELBOW   Marry, sir, by my wife, who, if she had been a
woman cardinally given, might have been accused in 80
fornication, adultery, and all uncleanliness there.

ESCALUS   By the woman's means?

ELBOW   Ay, sir, by Mistress Overdone's means; but as
she spit in his face, so she defied him. 84

POMPEY   Sir, if it please Your Honor, this is not so.

ELBOW   Prove it before these varlets here, thou honor- 86
able man, prove it. 87

ESCALUS   [to Angelo]   Do you hear how he misplaces?

POMPEY   Sir, she came in great with child, and longing,
saving Your Honor's reverence, for stewed prunes. Sir, 90
we had but two in the house, which at that very
distant time stood, as it were, in a fruit dish, a 92
dish of some threepence. Your Honors have seen such
dishes; they are not China dishes, but very good
dishes—

ESCALUS   Go to, go to. No matter for the dish, sir.

POMPEY   No, indeed, sir, not of a pin; you are therein 97
in the right. But to the point. As I say, this Mistress
Elbow, being, as I say, with child, and being great-
bellied, and longing, as I said, for prunes; and having
but two in the dish, as I said, Master Froth here, this
very man, having eaten the rest, as I said, and, as I
say, paying for them very honestly—for, as you
know, Master Froth, I could not give you threepence
again. 105

FROTH   No, indeed.

POMPEY   Very well. You being then, if you be
remembered, cracking the stones of the foresaid 108
prunes—

FROTH   Ay, so I did indeed.

POMPEY   Why, very well; I telling you then, if you be
remembered, that such a one and such a one were
past cure of the thing you wot of, unless they kept 113
very good diet, as I told you— 114

FROTH   All this is true.

POMPEY   Why, very well, then—

ESCALUS   Come, you are a tedious fool. To the purpose.
What was done to Elbow's wife, that he hath cause to
complain of? Come me to what was done to her. 119

POMPEY   Sir, Your Honor cannot come to that yet.

ESCALUS   No, sir, nor I mean it not.

POMPEY   Sir, but you shall come to it, by Your Honor's
leave. And, I beseech you, look into Master Froth here,
sir, a man of fourscore pound a year, whose father 124
died at Hallowmas.—Was 't not at Hallowmas, Mas- 125
ter Froth?

FROTH   All-hallond eve. 127

POMPEY   Why, very well. I hope here be truths. He, sir,
sitting, as I say, in a lower chair, sir—'twas in the 129
Bunch of Grapes, where indeed you have a delight to 130
sit, have you not?

---

41 away onward.   **42–3 use . . . houses** practice their vices in bawdy
houses   **47 poor Duke's** i.e., Duke's poor   **48 lean upon** rely on,
appeal to. (With an unintended comic reference to the idea of leaning
on one's elbow.)   **54 precise** complete. (Or perhaps a blunder for "precious." *Precise* unintentionally recalls the description of Angelo as
precise, i.e., strict or puritanical, at 1.3.50.)   **55 profanation** (A blunder
for "profession," or a word meaning "irreverence" where Elbow
intends "reverence." Elbow already has used several malapropisms,
including *lean upon, benefactors,* and *precise.*)   **59 Go to** An expression
of impatience or reproof.   **quality** social standing, occupation   **61 out
at elbow** (1) impoverished, threadbare, hence without any ideas (2)
missing his cue, i.e., at a loss for words after being called by his name.
63 parcel-bawd part-time bawd (and part-time tapster)   **66 professes
a hothouse** professes to run a bathhouse   **69 detest** (For "protest.")
77 pity of her life a great pity.   **naughty** wicked   **80 cardinally** (For
"carnally.")   **given** inclined   **84 she spit . . . face** Elbow's wife spat in
the face of Pompey (who, as pimp, was acting as Mistress Overdone's
means, line 83).

86–7 varlets . . . honorable (Elbow reverses or *misplaces* these epithets.)   **90 saving . . . reverence** i.e., begging your pardon for what
I'm about to say.   **stewed prunes** (Commonly served in houses of
prostitution, or *stews,* and therefore suggesting prostitutes. The dialogue throughout is sexually suggestive.)   **92 distant** (Blunder for
"instant"?)   **97 a pin** i.e., an insignificant trifle   **105 again** back.
108 stones pits. (With suggestion also of "testicles.")   **113 the thing . . .
of** you know what I mean (i.e., venereal disease)   **114 diet** strict regimen prescribed for medical treatment   **119 Come me** i.e., Come. (*Me*
is used colloquially. Pompey makes a vulgar joke on the words *come*
and *done;* see note at line 140.)   **124 of . . . year** i.e., well off   **125 Hallowmas** All Saints' Day, November 1   **127 All-hallond eve** Hal-
loween, October 31.   **129 a lower chair** i.e., an easy chair (?)
130 Bunch of Grapes (It was not uncommon to designate particular
rooms in inns by such names.)

FROTH   I have so, because it is an open room and good 132
for winter.

POMPEY   Why, very well, then. I hope here be truths.

ANGELO
This will last out a night in Russia,
When nights are longest there. I'll take my leave
And leave you to the hearing of the cause,   137
Hoping you'll find good cause to whip them all.

ESCALUS
I think no less. Good morrow to Your Lordship.   139

Exit [Angelo].

Now, sir, come on. What was done to Elbow's wife, 140
once more?

POMPEY   Once, sir? There was nothing done to her
once.   143

ELBOW   I beseech you, sir, ask him what this man did
to my wife.

POMPEY   I beseech Your Honor, ask me.

ESCALUS   Well, sir, what did this gentleman to her?

POMPEY   I beseech you, sir, look in this gentleman's
face. Good Master Froth, look upon His Honor; 'tis for
a good purpose. Doth Your Honor mark his face? 150

ESCALUS   Ay, sir, very well.

POMPEY   Nay, I beseech you, mark it well.

ESCALUS   Well, I do so.

POMPEY   Doth Your Honor see any harm in his face?

ESCALUS   Why, no.

POMPEY   I'll be supposed upon a book, his face is the 156
worst thing about him. Good, then; if his face be the
worst thing about him, how could Master Froth do the
Constable's wife any harm? I would know that of Your
Honor.

ESCALUS   He's in the right, Constable. What say you
to it?

ELBOW   First, an it like you, the house is a respected 163
house; next, this is a respected fellow; and his mistress
is a respected woman.

POMPEY   By this hand, sir, his wife is a more respected
person than any of us all.

ELBOW   Varlet, thou liest! Thou liest, wicked varlet! The
time is yet to come that she was ever respected with
man, woman, or child.

POMPEY   Sir, she was respected with him before he
married with her.

ESCALUS   Which is the wiser here, Justice or Iniquity?— 173
Is this true?

ELBOW   O thou caitiff! O thou varlet! O thou wicked 175
Hannibal! I respected with her before I was married 176
her?—If ever I was respected with her, or she with
me, let not Your Worship think me the poor Duke's

officer.—Prove this, thou wicked Hannibal, or I'll
have mine action of battery on thee.   180

ESCALUS   If he took you a box o'th'ear, you might have 181
your action of slander too.

ELBOW   Marry, I thank Your good Worship for it. What
is't Your Worship's pleasure I shall do with this
wicked caitiff?

ESCALUS   Truly, officer, because he hath some offenses
in him that thou wouldst discover if thou couldst, let 187
him continue in his courses till thou know'st what 188
they are.

ELBOW   Marry, I thank Your Worship for it.—Thou see'st,
thou wicked varlet, now, what's come upon thee: thou
art to continue now, thou varlet, thou art to continue. 192

ESCALUS   *[to Froth]*   Where were you born, friend?

FROTH   Here in Vienna, sir.

ESCALUS   Are you of fourscore pounds a year?   195

FROTH   Yes, an't please you, sir.

ESCALUS   So. *[To Pompey]* What trade are you of, sir?

POMPEY   A tapster, a poor widow's tapster.

ESCALUS   Your mistress' name?

POMPEY   Mistress Overdone.

ESCALUS   Hath she had any more than one husband?

POMPEY   Nine, sir. Overdone by the last.   202

ESCALUS   Nine?—Come hither to me, Master Froth.
Master Froth, I would not have you acquainted with
tapsters. They will draw you, Master Froth, and you 205
will hang them. Get you gone, and let me hear no 206
more of you.

FROTH   I thank Your Worship. For mine own part, I
never come into any room in a taphouse but I am 209
drawn in.   210

ESCALUS   Well, no more of it, Master Froth. Farewell.

[Exit Froth.]

Come you hither to me, Master Tapster. What's your
name, Master Tapster?

POMPEY   Pompey.

ESCALUS   What else?

POMPEY   Bum, sir.

ESCALUS   Troth, and your bum is the greatest thing
about you, so that in the beastliest sense you are Pompey the Great. Pompey, you are partly a bawd, Pompey, howsoever you color it in being a tapster, are you 220
not? Come, tell me true. It shall be the better for you.

POMPEY   Truly, sir, I am a poor fellow that would live.

ESCALUS   How would you live, Pompey? By being a 223
bawd? What do you think of the trade, Pompey? Is it
a lawful trade?

POMPEY   If the law would allow it, sir.

---

132 **open** public   137 **cause** case. (With word play on *cause*, "reason,"
in the next line. See also the play on *leave* in 136–7.)   139 **I . . . less** I
think so, too.   140 **done** (Pompey, in his answer, uses *done* in a sexual
sense.)   143 **once** only once. (Pompey replies wittily to Escalus's *once
more* in 141, meaning "once again.")   150 **mark** observe   156 **supposed** (A malapropism for "deposed," i.e., sworn.)   **book** i.e., Bible
163 **an it like** if it please.   **respected** (For "suspected.")   173 **Justice
or Iniquity** (Personified characters in a morality play.)   175 **caitiff**
knave, villain.   176 **Hannibal** (A blunder for "cannibal," perhaps
also suggested by the fact that Hannibal and Pompey were both
famous generals in the classical world.)

180 **battery** (An error for "slander," as Escalus amusedly points
out.)   181 **took** gave.   **o'** on   187 **discover** (1) detect (2) reveal
188 **courses** courses of action   192 **continue** (Elbow may confuse the
word with its opposite.)   195 **of** possessed of   202 **Overdone . . . last**
(1) Her name, Overdone, was given her by her last husband (2) She
has been worn out (*overdone*) by the last one.   205 **draw** (1) cheat,
take in (2) empty, deplete. (With a pun on the tapster's trade of drawing liquor from a barrel, and on Froth's name.) (3) disembowel, or
drag to execution   206 **will hang them** will be the cause of their
hanging.   209 **taphouse** alehouse   210 **drawn in** enticed. (Still
another meaning of *draw*, line 205.)   220 **color** disguise   223 **live**
make a living

ESCALUS   But the law will not allow it, Pompey; nor it
shall not be allowed in Vienna.

POMPEY   Does Your Worship mean to geld and splay all   229
the youth of the city?

ESCALUS   No, Pompey.

POMPEY   Truly, sir, in my poor opinion they will to't
then. If Your Worship will take order for the drabs and   233
the knaves, you need not to fear the bawds.

ESCALUS   There is pretty orders beginning, I can tell
you. It is but heading and hanging.   236

POMPEY   If you head and hang all that offend that way
but for ten year together, you'll be glad to give out a   238
commission for more heads. If this law hold in Vienna   239
ten year, I'll rent the fairest house in it after threepence   240
a bay. If you live to see this come to pass, say Pompey   241
told you so.

ESCALUS   Thank you, good Pompey. And, in requital of   243
your prophecy, hark you: I advise you let me not find
you before me again upon any complaint whatsoever;
no, not for dwelling where you do. If I do, Pompey, I
shall beat you to your tent and prove a shrewd Caesar   247
to you; in plain dealing, Pompey, I shall have you
whipped. So for this time, Pompey, fare you well.

POMPEY   I thank Your Worship for your good counsel.
[Aside] But I shall follow it as the flesh and fortune
shall better determine.
Whip me? No, no, let carman whip his jade.   253
The valiant heart's not whipped out of his trade.
                                                                    Exit.

ESCALUS   Come hither to me, Master Elbow; come
hither, Master Constable. How long have you been in
this place of constable?

ELBOW   Seven year and a half, sir.

ESCALUS   I thought, by the readiness in the office, you   259
had continued in it some time. You say, seven years
together?

ELBOW   And a half, sir.

ESCALUS   Alas, it hath been great pains to you. They do
you wrong to put you so oft upon't. Are there not
men in your ward sufficient to serve it?   265

ELBOW   Faith, sir, few of any wit in such matters. As
they are chosen, they are glad to choose me for them.   267
I do it for some piece of money and go through with   268
all.   269

ESCALUS   Look you bring me in the names of some six   270
or seven, the most sufficient of your parish.

ELBOW   To Your Worship's house, sir?

ESCALUS   To my house. Fare you well.   [Exit Elbow.]
What's o'clock, think you?

JUSTICE   Eleven, sir.

ESCALUS
I pray you home to dinner with me.   276

JUSTICE   I humbly thank you.

ESCALUS
It grieves me for the death of Claudio;
But there's no remedy.

JUSTICE   Lord Angelo is severe.

ESCALUS   It is but needful.
Mercy is not itself, that oft looks so;   281
Pardon is still the nurse of second woe.   282
But yet—poor Claudio! There is no remedy.
Come, sir.   Exeunt.

❖

2.2

Enter Provost [and a] Servant.

SERVANT
He's hearing of a cause; he will come straight.   1
I'll tell him of you.

PROVOST   Pray you, do.   [Exit Servant.]
                                                            I'll know
His pleasure; maybe he will relent. Alas,
He hath but as offended in a dream!   4
All sects, all ages smack of this vice—and he   5
To die for't!

Enter Angelo.

ANGELO   Now, what's the matter, Provost?

PROVOST
Is it your will Claudio shall die tomorrow?

ANGELO
Did not I tell thee yea? Hadst thou not order?
Why dost thou ask again?

PROVOST   Lest I might be too rash.
Under your good correction, I have seen   11
When, after execution, judgment hath
Repented o'er his doom.   13

ANGELO   Go to; let that be mine.   14
Do you your office, or give up your place,
And you shall well be spared.   16

PROVOST   I crave Your Honor's pardon.
What shall be done, sir, with the groaning Juliet?   18
She's very near her hour.

ANGELO   Dispose of her   19
To some more fitter place, and that with speed.

[Enter a Servant.]

---

229 **splay** spay   233 **take order** take measures.   **drabs** prostitutes
236 **It . . . hanging** Beheading and hanging are the order of the day.
238 **year together** years at a stretch   239 **commission** order.   **hold**
remain in force   240 **after** at the rate of   241 **bay** division of a house
included under one gable.   243 **requital** of return for   247 **shrewd**
harsh, severe.   **Caesar** (Julius Caesar defeated Pompey at Pharsalia
in 48 B.C.)   253 **carman** cart driver.   **jade** broken-down horse.
259 **readiness** proficiency, alacrity   265 **sufficient** able   267 **for them**
i.e., to take their place.   268–9 **go . . . all** i.e., perform my duties thoroughly.   270 **Look** See to it that

276 **dinner** (Dinner was customarily eaten just before midday.)
281 **Mercy . . . so** i.e., What seems merciful may not really be so (since
it may encourage crime and hence lead to more punishment)
282 **Pardon . . . woe** i.e., pardon continually nurtures and encourages
a repetition of offenses and hence of punishment.
**2.2. Location: Adjacent to the court of justice, perhaps at Angelo's
official residence.**
1 **hearing . . . cause** listening to a case.   **straight** immediately.   4 **He . . .
dream** i.e., Claudio offended only as if in a dream.   5 **All sects . . .
smack** All classes of people of all ages (and in all past history) partake   11 **Under . . . correction** i.e., Allow me to say   13 **doom** sentence.   14 **mine** my business.   16 **well be spared** easily be done
without.   18 **groaning** (with labor pains)   19 **hour** time of delivery.

SERVANT
Here is the sister of the man condemned
Desires access to you.

ANGELO   Hath he a sister?   22

PROVOST
Ay, my good lord, a very virtuous maid,
And to be shortly of a sisterhood,
If not already.

ANGELO   Well, let her be admitted.
                                            [*Exit Servant.*]
See you the fornicatress be removed.
Let her have needful but not lavish means.
There shall be order for't.

    Enter Lucio and Isabella.

PROVOST   Save Your Honor!   28

ANGELO [*to Provost*]
Stay a little while. [*To Isabella*] You're welcome.
    What's your will?

ISABELLA
I am a woeful suitor to Your Honor,
Please but Your Honor hear me.

ANGELO   Well, what's your suit?   31

ISABELLA
There is a vice that most I do abhor,
And most desire should meet the blow of justice,
For which I would not plead, but that I must;
For which I must not plead, but that I am
At war twixt will and will not.

ANGELO   Well, the matter?

ISABELLA
I have a brother is condemned to die.
I do beseech you, let it be his fault,   38
And not my brother.

PROVOST [*aside*]   Heaven give thee moving graces!

ANGELO
Condemn the fault, and not the actor of it?
Why, every fault's condemned ere it be done.
Mine were the very cipher of a function,
To fine the faults, whose fine stands in record,   43
And let go by the actor.

ISABELLA   Oh, just but severe law!
I had a brother, then. Heaven keep your honor!

LUCIO [*aside to Isabella*]
Give't not o'er so. To him again, entreat him!   47
Kneel down before him; hang upon his gown.
You are too cold. If you should need a pin,   49
You could not with more tame a tongue desire it.
To him, I say!

ISABELLA [*to Angelo*]
Must he needs die?

ANGELO   Maiden, no remedy.

ISABELLA
Yes, I do think that you might pardon him,
And neither heaven nor man grieve at the mercy.

ANGELO
I will not do't.

ISABELLA   But can you, if you would?

ANGELO
Look what I will not, that I cannot do.   56

ISABELLA
But might you do't, and do the world no wrong,
If so your heart were touched with that remorse   58
As mine is to him?

ANGELO   He's sentenced. 'Tis too late.

LUCIO [*aside to Isabella*]   You are too cold.

ISABELLA
Too late? Why, no; I that do speak a word
May call it back again. Well, believe this:
No ceremony that to great ones 'longs,   64
Not the king's crown, nor the deputed sword,   65
The marshal's truncheon, nor the judge's robe,   66
Become them with one half so good a grace
As mercy does.
If he had been as you, and you as he,
You would have slipped like him; but he, like you, 70
Would not have been so stern.

ANGELO   Pray you, begone.

ISABELLA
I would to heaven I had your potency,
And you were Isabel. Should it then be thus?
No, I would tell what 'twere to be a judge   74
And what a prisoner.

LUCIO [*aside to Isabella*]   Ay, touch him; there's the vein.   75

ANGELO
Your brother is a forfeit of the law,   76
And you but waste your words.

ISABELLA   Alas, alas!
Why, all the souls that were were forfeit once,   78
And He that might the vantage best have took   79
Found out the remedy. How would you be,   80
If He, which is the top of judgment, should   81
But judge you as you are? Oh, think on that,
And mercy then will breathe within your lips,
Like man new-made.

ANGELO   Be you content, fair maid.   84
It is the law, not I, condemn your brother.
Were he my kinsman, brother, or my son,
It should be thus with him. He must die tomorrow.

ISABELLA
Tomorrow! Oh, that's sudden! Spare him, spare him!
He's not prepared for death. Even for our kitchens
We kill the fowl of season. Shall we serve heaven   90
With less respect than we do minister

---

22 Desires who desires   **28 Save** May God save   **31 Please . . . me** if Your Honor will please hear me.   **38 let . . . fault** i.e., let the fault die, be condemned   **43 To fine . . . record** to punish only the faults, for which the penalty stands in the statute books   **47 Give't . . . so** Don't give up so soon.   **49 need a pin** i.e., ask for the smallest trifle

56 Look what Whatever   **58 remorse** pity   **64 'longs** is fitting, belongs   **65 deputed sword** sword of justice entrusted to the ruler   **66 truncheon** staff borne by military officers   **70 like you** in your situation   **74 tell** make known   **75 there's the vein** i.e., that's the right approach. (*Vein* means "lode to be profitably mined," or perhaps "vein for bloodletting.")   **76 a forfeit** one who must incur the penalty   **78–80 Why . . . remedy** (A reference to God's redemption of sinful humanity when He would have been justified in destroying humankind.)   **81 top of judgment** supreme judge   **84 new-made** i.e., created new by salvation, born again.   **90 of season** that is in season and properly mature.

To our gross selves? Good, good my lord, bethink
   you:
Who is it that hath died for this offense?
There's many have committed it.
LUCIO [*aside to Isabella*]   Ay, well said.
ANGELO
The law hath not been dead, though it hath slept.
Those many had not dared to do that evil
If the first that did th'edict infringe
Had answered for his deed. Now 'tis awake,
Takes note of what is done, and like a prophet
Looks in a glass that shows what future evils,   100
Either now, or by remissness new-conceived   101
And so in progress to be hatched and born,   102
Are now to have no successive degrees,   103
But ere they live, to end.
ISABELLA   Yet show some pity.   104
ANGELO
I show it most of all when I show justice;
For then I pity those I do not know,
Which a dismissed offense would after gall,   107
And do him right that, answering one foul wrong,   108
Lives not to act another. Be satisfied;
Your brother dies tomorrow. Be content.
ISABELLA
So you must be the first that gives this sentence,
And he that suffers. Oh, it is excellent
To have a giant's strength, but it is tyrannous
To use it like a giant.
LUCIO [*aside to Isabella*]   That's well said.
ISABELLA   Could great men thunder
As Jove himself does, Jove would never be quiet,   116
For every pelting, petty officer   117
Would use his heaven for thunder,
Nothing but thunder. Merciful heaven,
Thou rather with thy sharp and sulfurous bolt   120
Splits the unwedgeable and gnarlèd oak   121
Than the soft myrtle; but man, proud man,
Dressed in a little brief authority,
Most ignorant of what he's most assured,   124
His glassy essence, like an angry ape   125
Plays such fantastic tricks before high heaven
As makes the angels weep; who, with our spleens,   127
Would all themselves laugh mortal.   128

LUCIO [*aside to Isabella*]
Oh, to him, to him, wench! He will relent.
He's coming, I perceive't.
PROVOST [*aside*]   Pray heaven she win him!   130
ISABELLA
We cannot weigh our brother with ourself.   131
Great men may jest with saints; 'tis wit in them,   132
But in the less, foul profanation.   133
LUCIO [*aside to Isabella*]
Thou'rt i'th' right, girl. More o' that.
ISABELLA
That in the captain's but a choleric word   135
Which in the soldier is flat blasphemy.
LUCIO [*aside to Isabella*]   Art advised o' that? More on't.   137
ANGELO
Why do you put these sayings upon me?   138
ISABELLA
Because authority, though it err like others,   139
Hath yet a kind of medicine in itself   140
That skins the vice o'th' top. Go to your bosom;   141
Knock there, and ask your heart what it doth know
That's like my brother's fault. If it confess
A natural guiltiness such as is his,
Let it not sound a thought upon your tongue
Against my brother's life.
ANGELO [*aside*]   She speaks, and 'tis such sense   147
That my sense breeds with it.—Fare you well.   148
                     [*He starts to go.*]
ISABELLA   Gentle my lord, turn back.   149
ANGELO
I will bethink me. Come again tomorrow.   150
ISABELLA
Hark how I'll bribe you. Good my lord, turn back.
ANGELO   How? Bribe me?
ISABELLA
Ay, with such gifts that heaven shall share with you.   153
LUCIO [*aside to Isabella*]   You had marred all else.   154
ISABELLA
Not with fond sicles of the tested gold,   155
Or stones whose rate are either rich or poor   156
As fancy values them, but with true prayers   157
That shall be up at heaven and enter there
Ere sunrise—prayers from preservèd souls,   159

---

100 glass magic crystal   **101 Either . . . new-conceived** i.e., both evils
already hatched and those that would be encouraged by continued
laxity of enforcement   **102 in progress** in the course of time
103 successive degrees successors or future stages. (Future evils are to
be aborted before they are born and propagate.)   **104 ere they live**
i.e., before they can be committed   **107 Which . . . gall** whom a forgiven offense would give trouble to later on   **108 do . . . answering** do
justice to that person who, by paying the penalty for   **116 be quiet**
(1) have any quiet, or (2) cease thundering   **117 pelting** paltry
120 bolt thunderbolt   **121 unwedgeable** unsplittable   **124–5 Most . . .
essence** i.e., most ignorant of what religion teaches him to know, his
spiritual nature; or, most ignorant of that which is most certainly his
natural frailty   **125 angry ape** i.e., ludicrous buffoon   **127–8 who . . .
mortal** who, if they had the organs of laughter that we have, would
laugh themselves mortal, becoming like us. (The *spleen* was thought to
be the seat of laughter.)

130 coming coming around   **131–3 We . . . profanation** We cannot
judge our fellow mortals by the same standards we use in judging
ourselves. Persons of great authority are allowed liberties that in
lesser persons would be condemned as blasphemies. (Lines 135–6
make much the same point.)   **135 That . . . word** i.e., We treat the
abusive language a commanding officer uses in anger merely as an
outburst; we are indulgent toward the failings of *great men*. (As in
lines 131–3, Isabella's point seems to be that our judgments are biased
by our inordinate regard for authority.)   **137 advised** informed,
aware.   **on't** of it.   **138 put . . . me** apply these sayings to me.
139–41 Because . . . top Because authority, though prone to sinfulness
like all of humankind, has a way of seeming to heal itself by covering
over the boil with a film of skin, leaving the sore unhealed.
147–8 sense . . . sense import . . . sensuality   **149 Gentle my lord** My
noble lord   **150 bethink me** think it over.   **153 that** as   **154 else** otherwise.   **155 Not . . . gold** Not with foolishly valued shekels of pure
gold. (*Shekels* are Hebrew coins.)   **156–7 Or . . . them** or jewels the
value of which is merely subjective and transitory   **159 preservèd
souls** devout religious who have withdrawn from the world

From fasting maids whose minds are dedicate   160
To nothing temporal.

ANGELO   Well, come to me tomorrow.

LUCIO [aside to Isabella]   Go to, 'tis well. Away!

ISABELLA
Heaven keep Your Honor safe!

ANGELO [aside]   Amen!
For I am that way going to temptation,
Where prayers cross.

ISABELLA   At what hour tomorrow   165
Shall I attend Your Lordship?

ANGELO   At any time 'fore noon.

ISABELLA   Save Your Honor!   168
                    [Exeunt Isabella, Lucio, and Provost.]

ANGELO   From thee, even from thy virtue!
What's this, what's this? Is this her fault or mine?
The tempter or the tempted, who sins most, ha?
Not she, nor doth she tempt; but it is I
That, lying by the violet in the sun,
Do, as the carrion does, not as the flower,   174
Corrupt with virtuous season. Can it be   175
That modesty may more betray our sense   176
Than woman's lightness? Having waste ground
  enough,   177
Shall we desire to raze the sanctuary
And pitch our evils there? Oh, fie, fie, fie!   179
What dost thou, or what art thou, Angelo?
Dost thou desire her foully for those things
That make her good? Oh, let her brother live!
Thieves for their robbery have authority
When judges steal themselves. What, do I love her,
That I desire to hear her speak again
And feast upon her eyes? What is't I dream on?
Oh, cunning enemy that, to catch a saint,   187
With saints dost bait thy hook! Most dangerous
Is that temptation that doth goad us on
To sin in loving virtue. Never could the strumpet,
With all her double vigor—art and nature—   191
Once stir my temper; but this virtuous maid   192
Subdues me quite. Ever till now,
When men were fond, I smiled and wondered how.   194
                                            Exit.

❖

2.3

Enter, [meeting,] Duke [disguised as a friar]
and Provost.

DUKE
Hail to you, Provost—so I think you are.

---

160 **fasting maids** i.e., nuns. **dedicate** dedicated   165 **cross** are at
cross purposes.   168 **Save** May God save   174 **carrion** decaying
flesh   175 **Corrupt . . . season** i.e., putrefy while all else flourishes.
(The warmth of flowering time causes the violet, Isabella, to blossom
but causes the carrion lying beside it, Angelo, to rot.)   176 **modesty**
virtue, chastity.   **sense** sensual nature   177 **lightness** immodesty,
lust.   179 **pitch our evils there** i.e., erect a privy, not on *waste ground*
(line 177), but on sanctified ground. (*Evils* also has the more common
meaning of "wickedness.")   187 **enemy** i.e., Satan   191 **double . . .
nature** twofold power (of alluring men) through artifice and a sensu-
ous nature   192 **temper** temperament   194 **fond** foolishly in love
2.3. Location: A prison.

PROVOST
I am the Provost. What's your will, good Friar?

DUKE
Bound by my charity and my blest order,
I come to visit the afflicted spirits
Here in the prison. Do me the common right   5
To let me see them and to make me know
The nature of their crimes, that I may minister
To them accordingly.

PROVOST
I would do more than that, if more were needful.

                    Enter Juliet.

Look, here comes one: a gentlewoman of mine,
Who, falling in the flaws of her own youth,   11
Hath blistered her report. She is with child,   12
And he that got it, sentenced—a young man   13
More fit to do another such offense
Than die for this.

DUKE
When must he die?

PROVOST   As I do think, tomorrow.
[To Juliet] I have provided for you. Stay awhile,   17
And you shall be conducted.   18

DUKE
Repent you, fair one, of the sin you carry?

JULIET
I do, and bear the shame most patiently.

DUKE
I'll teach you how you shall arraign your conscience,   21
And try your penitence, if it be sound   22
Or hollowly put on.   23

JULIET   I'll gladly learn.

DUKE   Love you the man that wronged you?

JULIET
Yes, as I love the woman that wronged him.

DUKE
So then it seems your most offenseful act
Was mutually committed?

JULIET   Mutually.

DUKE
Then was your sin of heavier kind than his.

JULIET
I do confess it and repent it, Father.

DUKE
'Tis meet so, daughter. But lest you do repent   31
As that the sin hath brought you to this shame,   32
Which sorrow is always toward ourselves, not heaven,   33
Showing we would not spare heaven as we love it,   34
But as we stand in fear—

JULIET
I do repent me as it is an evil,

---

5 **common right** i.e., right of all clerics   11 **flaws** (1) weaknesses, fis-
sures (2) sudden gusts (of passion)   12 **blistered her report** marred
her reputation.   13 **got** begot   17 **provided** provided a place to stay
18 **conducted** taken there.   21 **arraign** accuse   22 **try** test   23 **hollowly** falsely   31 **'Tis meet so** It is fitting that you do so   32 **As that**
merely because   33 **toward ourselves** i.e., narrowly self-concerned
rather than loving virtue for its own sake   34 **Showing . . . it** showing that we wish to avoid offending heaven not out of sheer love of
goodness

And take the shame with joy.

DUKE   There rest.   37
Your partner, as I hear, must die tomorrow,
And I am going with instruction to him.
Grace go with you. *Benedicite!*   *Exit.*   40

JULIET
Must die tomorrow? O injurious love,   41
That respites me a life whose very comfort   42
Is still a dying horror!

PROVOST   'Tis pity of him.   *Exeunt.*   43

❖

2.4

Enter Angelo.

ANGELO
When I would pray and think, I think and pray
To several subjects. Heaven hath my empty words,   2
Whilst my invention, hearing not my tongue,   3
Anchors on Isabel; Heaven in my mouth,
As if I did but only chew His name,   5
And in my heart the strong and swelling evil
Of my conception. The state, whereon I studied,   7
Is like a good thing, being often read,
Grown sere and tedious. Yea, my gravity,   9
Wherein—let no man hear me—I take pride,
Could I with boot change for an idle plume,   11
Which the air beats for vain. O place, O form,   12
How often dost thou with thy case, thy habit,   13
Wrench awe from fools and tie the wiser souls   14
To thy false seeming! Blood, thou art blood.   15
Let's write "good angel" on the devil's horn,   16
'Tis not the devil's crest.

Enter Servant.

How now? Who's there?   17
SERVANT
One Isabel, a sister, desires access to you.
ANGELO   Teach her the way.   [*Exit Servant.*]
Oh, heavens!   19
Why does my blood thus muster to my heart,   20

Making both it unable for itself   21
And dispossessing all my other parts
Of necessary fitness?
So play the foolish throngs with one that swoons,   24
Come all to help him, and so stop the air
By which he should revive; and even so
The general subject to a well-wished king   27
Quit their own part and in obsequious fondness   28
Crowd to his presence, where their untaught love   29
Must needs appear offense.

Enter Isabella.

How now, fair maid?   30
ISABELLA   I am come to know your pleasure.
ANGELO
That you might know it would much better please me 32
Than to demand what 'tis. Your brother cannot live. 33
ISABELLA
Even so. Heaven keep Your Honor!   34
[*She turns to leave.*]
ANGELO
Yet may he live awhile; and, it may be,
As long as you or I. Yet he must die.
ISABELLA   Under your sentence?
ANGELO   Yea.
ISABELLA
When, I beseech you? That in his reprieve,
Longer or shorter, he may be so fitted   40
That his soul sicken not.
ANGELO
Ha? Fie, these filthy vices! It were as good   42
To pardon him that hath from nature stolen   43
A man already made, as to remit   44
Their saucy sweetness that do coin heaven's image   45
In stamps that are forbid. 'Tis all as easy   46
Falsely to take away a life true made
As to put metal in restrainèd means   48
To make a false one.
ISABELLA
'Tis set down so in heaven, but not in earth.   50
ANGELO
Say you so? Then I shall pose you quickly: 51
Which had you rather, that the most just law
Now took your brother's life, or, to redeem him,
Give up your body to such sweet uncleanness

---

37 There rest. Hold fast to that truth.   **40 *Benedicite!*** Blessings on you!   **41–3 O . . . horror!** i.e., O sinful pregnancy, that prolongs a life whose greatest comfort will always be a deadly horror! (Pregnancy could save a woman from being executed. However, *love* is sometimes emended to *law*.)   **43 pity of** a pity about
2.4 Location: Angelo's official residence.
2 several separate   **3 invention** imagination   **5 His** i.e., heaven's, God's   **7 conception** thought.   **The state** Statecraft   **9 sere** withered, old   **11–12 Could . . . vain** I could willingly exchange (my gravity) for the frivolity of a pleasure-loving gallant, sporting a feather that seems to beat the air in its vanity (or, perhaps, is beaten by the air in reproof of its vanity).   **12 O place, O form** O authority of high position, O ceremonial dignity of office   **13 thy case . . . habit** your mere outward appearance and garb   **14–15 Wrench . . . seeming** intimidate ordinary foolish men and subjugate even the wise to the seeming virtue of authority.   **15 Blood . . . blood** i.e., No position of authority or birth, no matter how lofty, can protect a person from his own lustful appetites.   **16–17 Let's . . . crest** i.e., No matter how hard we try to disguise evil under the semblance of good, it remains recognizably evil still. (In heraldic terms, the devil is known by his baleful horns; the heraldic crest on his coat of arms does not alter his true identity.)
19 Teach Show   **20 muster to** assemble like soldiers in

21 unable ineffectual   **24 play** behave   **27 general subject** i.e., commoners, subjects.   **well-wished** attended by good wishes   **28 Quit . . . part** abandon their proper function and (politely distant) place
29 untaught ignorant, unmannerly   **30 Must needs** will necessarily
32–3 That . . . 'tis i.e., I wish you could know the nature of my desire without your asking and my having to be explicit. (*Know* suggests carnal knowledge.)   **34 Even so** So be it.   **40 fitted** prepared
42–6 It were . . . forbid One might as well pardon the murderer of a man already alive as pardon the wanton pleasures of those persons who produce illegitimate offspring, like counterfeit coiners.
(*Heaven's image* is humankind, made in God's likeness; Genesis 1:27.)
48 metal i.e., the metal used in coining (lines 45–6), with a play on *mettle*, natural vigor or spirit.   **restrainèd** prohibited, illicit (both in counterfeiting coinage and in begetting illegitimate children)
50 'Tis . . . earth i.e., Equating murder and bastardizing accords with divine law but not with human law, according to which murder is more heinous.   **51 pose you** put a perplexing question to you

As she that he hath stained?

ISABELLA   Sir, believe this,
I had rather give my body than my soul.   56

ANGELO
I talk not of your soul. Our compelled sins   57
Stand more for number than for account.

ISABELLA   How say you?   58

ANGELO
Nay, I'll not warrant that, for I can speak   59
Against the thing I say. Answer to this:
I, now the voice of the recorded law,
Pronounce a sentence on your brother's life;
Might there not be a charity in sin
To save this brother's life?

ISABELLA   Please you to do't,   64
I'll take it as a peril to my soul;   65
It is no sin at all, but charity.

ANGELO
Pleased you to do't at peril of your soul   67
Were equal poise of sin and charity.   68

ISABELLA
That I do beg his life, if it be sin,
Heaven let me bear it! You granting of my suit,
If that be sin, I'll make it my morn prayer
To have it added to the faults of mine,
And nothing of your answer.

ANGELO   Nay, but hear me.   73
Your sense pursues not mine. Either you are ignorant
Or seem so craftily; and that's not good.

ISABELLA
Let me be ignorant, and in nothing good,
But graciously to know I am no better.   77

ANGELO
Thus wisdom wishes to appear most bright
When it doth tax itself, as these black masks   79
Proclaim an enshield beauty ten times louder   80
Than beauty could, displayed. But mark me.
To be receivèd plain, I'll speak more gross: 82
Your brother is to die.

ISABELLA   So.

ANGELO
And his offense is so, as it appears,
Accountant to the law upon that pain.   86

ISABELLA   True.

ANGELO
Admit no other way to save his life—   88
As I subscribe not that, nor any other,   89
But in the loss of question—that you, his sister,   90

Finding yourself desired of such a person   91
Whose credit with the judge, or own great place,
Could fetch your brother from the manacles
Of the all-binding law; and that there were
No earthly means to save him, but that either
You must lay down the treasures of your body
To this supposed, or else to let him suffer.   97
What would you do?

ISABELLA
As much for my poor brother as myself:
That is, were I under the terms of death,   100
Th'impression of keen whips I'd wear as rubies,
And strip myself to death as to a bed
That longing have been sick for, ere I'd yield   103
My body up to shame.

ANGELO   Then must your brother die.

ISABELLA   And 'twere the cheaper way.
Better it were a brother died at once   107
Than that a sister, by redeeming him,
Should die forever.

ANGELO
Were not you then as cruel as the sentence
That you have slandered so?

ISABELLA
Ignomy in ransom and free pardon   112
Are of two houses. Lawful mercy   113
Is nothing kin to foul redemption.   114

ANGELO
You seemed of late to make the law a tyrant,
And rather proved the sliding of your brother   116
A merriment than a vice.

ISABELLA
Oh, pardon me, my lord. It oft falls out,
To have what we would have, we speak not what
   we mean.
I something do excuse the thing I hate   120
For his advantage that I dearly love.

ANGELO
We are all frail.

ISABELLA   Else let my brother die,
If not a fedary but only he   123
Owe and succeed thy weakness.   124

ANGELO   Nay, women are frail too.

ISABELLA
Ay, as the glasses where they view themselves,   126
Which are as easy broke as they make forms.   127

---

56 give i.e., give to death or punishment. (Isabella avoids or does not
understand the drift of the question.)   57–8 Our . . . account Our sins
committed under compulsion are recorded but not charged to our
spiritual account.   59 I'll . . . that i.e., I'm not necessarily endorsing
the view I just expressed   64 Please you If you please   65 take accept
67 Pleased If it pleased   68 Were equal poise there would be equal
balance   73 of your answer to which you will have to answer.
77 graciously through divine grace   79 tax itself accuse itself (of ignorance).   these (Generically referring to any.)   80 enshield shielded,
protected from view behind the black masks   82 receivèd plain
plainly understood.   gross (1) openly (2) offensively   86 Accountant
accountable.   pain penalty.   88 Admit Suppose   89–90 As . . . question since I will admit no alternative possibility in our discussion.
(Loss of question means "forfeiting the terms of our debate.")

91 of by   97 supposed hypothetical person.   him i.e., Claudio
100 terms sentence   103 That . . . for i.e., that I have been sick with
longing for. (Isabella's images are of love, death, and flagellation.)
107 died at once should die once for all, rather than die forever (line
109) in the death of the soul through sin   112–14 Ignomy . . .
redemption Being ransomed under ignominious circumstances and
being released without conditions are two entirely different things.
Mercy under law bears no relation to being spared under foul stipula-
tions.   116 proved argued   120 something to some extent
123 fedary confederate, companion who is equally guilty
124 Owe . . . weakness possess and inherit the weakness you speak
of, or the weakness to which all men as a class are prone. (Isabella
argues that Claudio should die only if he is the only man who is
frail.)   126 glasses mirrors   127 forms (1) images (2) copies of themselves, i.e., children

Women? Help, heaven! Men their creation mar   128
In profiting by them. Nay, call us ten times frail,   129
For we are soft as our complexions are,   130
And credulous to false prints.

ANGELO   I think it well.   131
And from this testimony of your own sex—   132
Since I suppose we are made to be no stronger   133
Than faults may shake our frames—let me be bold.   134
I do arrest your words. Be that you are,   135
That is, a woman; if you be more, you're none.   136
If you be one, as you are well expressed   137
By all external warrants, show it now   138
By putting on the destined livery.   139

ISABELLA
I have no tongue but one. Gentle my lord,   140
Let me entreat you speak the former language.   141

ANGELO   Plainly conceive, I love you.

ISABELLA   My brother did love Juliet,
And you tell me that he shall die for't.

ANGELO
He shall not, Isabel, if you give me love.

ISABELLA
I know your virtue hath a license in't,   146
Which seems a little fouler than it is   147
To pluck on others.

ANGELO   Believe me, on mine honor,   148
My words express my purpose.

ISABELLA
Ha! Little honor to be much believed,
And most pernicious purpose! Seeming, seeming!
I will proclaim thee, Angelo, look for't!
Sign me a present pardon for my brother,   153
Or with an outstretched throat I'll tell the world
  aloud
What man thou art.

ANGELO   Who will believe thee, Isabel?
My unsoiled name, th'austereness of my life,
My vouch against you, and my place i'th' state   157
Will so your accusation overweigh
That you shall stifle in your own report
And smell of calumny. I have begun,   160
And now I give my sensual race the rein.   161
Fit thy consent to my sharp appetite;
Lay by all nicety and prolixious blushes   163
That banish what they sue for. Redeem thy brother   164

By yielding up thy body to my will,
Or else he must not only die the death,   166
But thy unkindness shall his death draw out
To ling'ring sufferance. Answer me tomorrow,   168
Or, by the affection that now guides me most,   169
I'll prove a tyrant to him. As for you,
Say what you can, my false o'erweighs your true.
                                              Exit.

ISABELLA
To whom should I complain? Did I tell this,   172
Who would believe me? O perilous mouths,   173
That bear in them one and the selfsame tongue,   174
Either of condemnation or approof,   175
Bidding the law make curtsy to their will,   176
Hooking both right and wrong to th'appetite,   177
To follow as it draws! I'll to my brother.   178
Though he hath fall'n by prompture of the blood,   179
Yet hath he in him such a mind of honor
That, had he twenty heads to tender down   181
On twenty bloody blocks, he'd yield them up
Before his sister should her body stoop
To such abhorred pollution.
Then, Isabel, live chaste, and, brother, die;
More than our brother is our chastity.
I'll tell him yet of Angelo's request,
And fit his mind to death, for his soul's rest.   Exit.

❖

3.1

*Enter Duke [disguised as before], Claudio, and
Provost.*

DUKE
So then you hope of pardon from Lord Angelo?

CLAUDIO
The miserable have no other medicine
But only hope.
I have hope to live and am prepared to die.

DUKE
Be absolute for death. Either death or life
Shall thereby be the sweeter. Reason thus with life:
If I do lose thee, I do lose a thing
That none but fools would keep. A breath thou art,
Servile to all the skyey influences   9
That dost this habitation where thou keep'st   10
Hourly afflict. Merely, thou art death's fool,   11
For him thou labor'st by thy flight to shun,
And yet run'st toward him still. Thou art not noble,   13

128–9 **Men . . . them** Men mar their creation in God's likeness by taking
advantage of women.   130 **complexions** constitutions, appearance
131 **credulous . . . prints** susceptible to false impressions. (The
metaphor is from the stamping of coins and other metal.)   132 **of**
about   133 **we** i.e., men and women   134 **Than** than that   135 **arrest
your words** take what you have said and hold you to it.   **that** what
136 **if . . . none** i.e., if you insist on remaining a virgin and free of
fleshly desire, you are no woman as we have defined the term—that is,
frail and susceptible.   137–8 **expressed . . . warrants** shown to be by
your physical beauty   139 **putting . . . livery** i.e., assuming the characteristic frailty that all women possess.   140 **tongue** language
141 **speak . . . language** speak to be understood, in the language I
understand.   146–8 **I know . . . others** i.e., I am sure that you, out of
virtuous motives, are speaking licentiously (and with the license of
authority) in order to put me to the test.   153 **present** immediate
157 **vouch** allegation   160 **calumny** slander.   161 **I give . . . rein** I give
free rein to my sensual desires to gallop as they please.   163–4 **Lay . . .
sue for** Set aside all the coyness and time-wasting blushes that make a
pretense of repulsing the embrace they actually beg for.

166 **die the death** be put to death   168 **sufferance** torture.
169 **affection** passion   172 **Did I tell** If I told   173–8 **O perilous . . .
draws!** O dangerous voices of authority, able with one tongue either
to condemn or approve, forcing both right and wrong to obey the
willful appetite!   179 **prompture** prompting, suggestion   181 **tender
down** lay down in payment
3.1. Location: The prison.
9 **skyey influences** influence of the stars   10 **this habitation** i.e., the
earth (and the body as well).   **keep'st** dwell   11 **Merely** Utterly, only
13 **still** always.

For all th'accommodations that thou bear'st   14
Are nursed by baseness. Thou'rt by no means valiant,   15
For thou dost fear the soft and tender fork   16
Of a poor worm. Thy best of rest is sleep,   17
And that thou oft provok'st, yet grossly fear'st   18
Thy death, which is no more. Thou art not thyself,
For thou exists on many a thousand grains
That issue out of dust. Happy thou art not,
For what thou hast not, still thou striv'st to get,
And what thou hast, forget'st. Thou art not certain,   23
For thy complexion shifts to strange effects,   24
After the moon. If thou art rich, thou'rt poor,   25
For, like an ass whose back with ingots bows,
Thou bear'st thy heavy riches but a journey,
And death unloads thee. Friend hast thou none,
For thine own bowels which do call thee sire,   29
The mere effusion of thy proper loins,   30
Do curse the gout, serpigo, and the rheum   31
For ending thee no sooner. Thou hast nor youth
    nor age,   32
But as it were an after-dinner's sleep   33
Dreaming on both, for all thy blessèd youth   34
Becomes as agèd and doth beg the alms   35
Of palsied eld; and, when thou art old and rich,   36
Thou hast neither heat, affection, limb, nor beauty   37
To make thy riches pleasant. What's yet in this
That bears the name of life? Yet in this life
Lie hid more thousand deaths; yet death we fear,
That makes these odds all even.
CLAUDIO   I humbly thank you.   41
To sue to live, I find I seek to die,   42
And, seeking death, find life. Let it come on.

     Enter Isabella.

ISABELLA
What, ho! Peace here; grace and good company!   44
PROVOST
Who's there? Come in. The wish deserves a welcome.
               [He goes to greet her.]
DUKE *[to Claudio]*
Dear sir, ere long I'll visit you again.
CLAUDIO Most holy sir, I thank you.
ISABELLA
My business is a word or two with Claudio.
PROVOST
And very welcome.—Look, signor, here's your sister.
DUKE *[aside to the Provost]* Provost, a word with you.

PROVOST As many as you please.
DUKE
Bring me to hear them speak, where I may be
Concealed.   *[The Duke and the Provost withdraw.]*
CLAUDIO   Now, sister, what's the comfort?
ISABELLA   Why,
As all comforts are: most good, most good indeed.
Lord Angelo, having affairs to heaven,
Intends you for his swift ambassador,
Where you shall be an everlasting leiger.   57
Therefore your best appointment make with speed;   58
Tomorrow you set on.
CLAUDIO   Is there no remedy?   59
ISABELLA
None but such remedy as, to save a head,
To cleave a heart in twain.
CLAUDIO But is there any?
ISABELLA Yes, brother, you may live.
There is a devilish mercy in the judge,
If you'll implore it, that will free your life
But fetter you till death.
CLAUDIO   Perpetual durance?   66
ISABELLA
Ay, just; perpetual durance, a restraint,   67
Though all the world's vastidity you had,   68
To a determined scope.
CLAUDIO   But in what nature?   69
ISABELLA
In such a one as, you consenting to't,
Would bark your honor from that trunk you bear   71
And leave you naked.
CLAUDIO   Let me know the point.
ISABELLA
Oh, I do fear thee, Claudio, and I quake   73
Lest thou a feverous life shouldst entertain,   74
And six or seven winters more respect   75
Than a perpetual honor. Dar'st thou die?
The sense of death is most in apprehension,   77
And the poor beetle that we tread upon
In corporal sufferance finds a pang as great
As when a giant dies.
CLAUDIO Why give you me this shame?
Think you I can a resolution fetch   82
From flow'ry tenderness? If I must die,   83
I will encounter darkness as a bride
And hug it in mine arms.
ISABELLA
There spake my brother! There my father's grave
Did utter forth a voice. Yes, thou must die.
Thou art too noble to conserve a life

---

14 **accommodations** conveniences, civilized comforts 15 **nursed by baseness** nurtured by ignoble means. 16 **fork** forked tongue 17 **worm** (1) snake (2) grave worm. 18 **thou oft provok'st** you often invoke, summon 23 **certain** steadfast 24 **complexion** constitution. **strange effects** new appearances, manifestations 25 **After** in obedience to, under the influence of 29 **bowels** i.e., offspring 30 **mere** very. **proper** own 31 **serpigo** a skin eruption. **rheum** catarrh 32 **nor youth** neither youth 33 **after-dinner's** i.e., afternoon's 34–6 **all . . . eld** your happy youth must decline all too soon into old age and become like a beggar, pleading for the little comfort that palsied infirmity can provide. (Youth is penniless and dependent on the agèd, whereas the old lack the physical capacity of youth.) 37 **heat, affection** vigor, passion 41 **makes . . . even** makes all equal. 42 **To sue** Suing, petitioning 44 **grace** God's grace

---

57 **leiger** resident ambassador. 58 **appointment** preparation 59 **set on** set forward. 66 **durance** imprisonment. 67 **just** just so 67–9 **a restraint . . . scope** a confinement to fixed limits or bounds (i.e., to inescapable guilt and perpetual remorse for the sinful bargain you had struck), even if you had the entire vastness of the world to wander in. 71 **bark** strip off (as one strips bark from a tree *trunk*) 73 **fear** fear for 74 **feverous** feverish. **entertain** maintain, desire 75 **respect** value 77 **apprehension** anticipation 82–3 **Think . . . tenderness?** Do you think I can find the courage to face death in flowery figures of speech?

In base appliances. This outward-sainted deputy,   89
Whose settled visage and deliberate word   90
Nips youth i'th' head, and follies doth enew   91
As falcon doth the fowl, is yet a devil;   92
His filth within being cast, he would appear   93
A pond as deep as hell.

CLAUDIO   The prenzie Angelo?   94

ISABELLA
Oh, 'tis the cunning livery of hell,   95
The damned'st body to invest and cover   96
In prenzie guards! Dost thou think, Claudio: 97
If I would yield him my virginity,
Thou mightst be freed!

CLAUDIO   Oh, heavens, it cannot be.

ISABELLA
Yes, he would give't thee, from this rank offense,   100
So to offend him still. This night's the time   101
That I should do what I abhor to name,
Or else thou diest tomorrow.

CLAUDIO   Thou shalt not do't.

ISABELLA   Oh, were it but my life,
I'd throw it down for your deliverance
As frankly as a pin.

CLAUDIO   Thanks, dear Isabel.   107

ISABELLA
Be ready, Claudio, for your death tomorrow.

CLAUDIO
Yes. Has he affections in him,   109
That thus can make him bite the law by th' nose   110
When he would force it? Sure it is no sin,   111
Or of the deadly seven it is the least.

ISABELLA   Which is the least?

CLAUDIO
If it were damnable, he being so wise,
Why would he for the momentary trick   115
Be perdurably fined? Oh, Isabel!   116

ISABELLA
What says my brother?

CLAUDIO   Death is a fearful thing.

ISABELLA   And shamèd life a hateful.

CLAUDIO
Ay, but to die, and go we know not where,
To lie in cold obstruction and to rot,   120
This sensible warm motion to become   121

A kneaded clod, and the delighted spirit   122
To bathe in fiery floods, or to reside
In thrilling region of thick-ribbèd ice;   124
To be imprisoned in the viewless winds   125
And blown with restless violence round about
The pendent world; or to be worse than worst   127
Of those that lawless and incertain thought   128
Imagine howling—'tis too horrible!
The weariest and most loathèd worldly life
That age, ache, penury, and imprisonment
Can lay on nature is a paradise
To what we fear of death.   133

ISABELLA   Alas, alas!

CLAUDIO   Sweet sister, let me live.
What sin you do to save a brother's life,
Nature dispenses with the deed so far   137
That it becomes a virtue.

ISABELLA   Oh, you beast!
Oh, faithless coward! Oh, dishonest wretch!   139
Wilt thou be made a man out of my vice?
Is't not a kind of incest, to take life
From thine own sister's shame? What should I think?
Heaven shield my mother played my father fair!   143
For such a warpèd slip of wilderness   144
Ne'er issued from his blood. Take my defiance,
Die, perish! Might but my bending down   146
Reprieve thee from thy fate, it should proceed.
I'll pray a thousand prayers for thy death,
No word to save thee.

CLAUDIO
Nay, hear me, Isabel.

ISABELLA   Oh, fie, fie, fie!
Thy sin's not accidental, but a trade.   151
Mercy to thee would prove itself a bawd;   152
'Tis best that thou diest quickly.

CLAUDIO   Oh, hear me, Isabella!

[*The Duke comes forward.*]

DUKE
Vouchsafe a word, young sister, but one word.   155

ISABELLA   What is your will?

DUKE   Might you dispense with your leisure, I would
by and by have some speech with you. The satisfaction I would require is likewise your own benefit.   159

ISABELLA   I have no superfluous leisure—my stay
must be stolen out of other affairs—but I will attend   161
you awhile.   [*She walks apart.*]

DUKE   Son, I have overheard what hath passed between
you and your sister. Angelo had never the purpose to

---

89 **In base appliances** by means of ignoble devices, remedies.
89–92 **This . . . fowl** This outwardly holy deputy, who with composed
features and judiciously chosen words swoops down on youth like a
falcon and drives his prey into covert. (To *enew* is to drive prey down
into the water or into hiding.)   93 **cast** dug out; diagnosed; sounded;
vomited (?)   94, 97 **prenzie** (A word unknown elsewhere, perhaps
meaning "princely" or "precise.")   95–7 **'tis . . . guards** it is the cunning ruse of the devil to clothe and conceal the wickedest man imaginable in decorously proper trimmings.   97 **Dost thou think** i.e.,
Would you believe   100–1 **he would . . . still** he would grant you
license, in return for the committing of this foul crime, to continue
with your fornication.   107 **frankly** freely   109 **affections** passions
110 **bite . . . nose** i.e., flout the law   111 **force** enforce. (Claudio wonders that lust can drive Angelo to make a mockery of the law even
while requiring to enforce it.)   115 **trick** trifle   116 **perdurably**
fined everlastingly punished.   120 **obstruction** cessation of vital
functions   121 **sensible** endowed with feeling.   **motion** organism

122 **kneaded clod** shapeless lump of earth.   **delighted spirit** spirit
that is now attended with delight, or capable of being so
124 **thrilling** piercingly cold   125 **viewless** invisible   127 **pendent**
hanging in space. (A Ptolemaic concept.)   128 **lawless . . . thought**
i.e., wild conjecture   133 **To** compared to   137 **dispenses with**
grants a dispensation for, excuses   139 **dishonest** dishonorable
143 **Heaven . . . fair!** God forbid that my mother was being faithful to
my father when you were sired!   144 **warpèd . . . wilderness** perverse, licentious scion, one that reverts to the original wild stock
146 **but** merely   151 **accidental** casual.   **trade** established habit.
152 **prove . . . bawd** i.e., provide opportunity for sexual license
155 **Vouchsafe** Allow   159 **require** ask   161 **attend** await; listen to

corrupt her; only he hath made an assay of her virtue 165
to practice his judgment with the disposition of na- 166
tures. She, having the truth of honor in her, hath made 167
him that gracious denial which he is most glad to re- 168
ceive. I am confessor to Angelo, and I know this to be
true; therefore prepare yourself to death. Do not satisfy
your resolution with hopes that are fallible. Tomorrow
you must die. Go to your knees and make ready.

CLAUDIO   Let me ask my sister pardon. I am so out of
love with life that I will sue to be rid of it.

DUKE   Hold you there. Farewell.   [*Claudio retires.*] 175
Provost, a word with you.

[*The Provost comes forward.*]

PROVOST   What's your will, Father?

DUKE   That now you are come, you will be gone. Leave
me awhile with the maid. My mind promises with my 179
habit no loss shall touch her by my company.   180

PROVOST   In good time.   *Exit* [*Provost with Claudio*]. 181

[*Isabella comes forward.*]

DUKE   The hand that hath made you fair hath made you
good. The goodness that is cheap in beauty makes 183
beauty brief in goodness; but grace, being the soul of 184
your complexion, shall keep the body of it ever fair. 185
The assault that Angelo hath made to you, fortune
hath conveyed to my understanding; and, but that 187
frailty hath examples for his falling, I should wonder 188
at Angelo. How will you do to content this substitute 189
and to save your brother?

ISABELLA   I am now going to resolve him. I had rather 191
my brother die by the law than my son should be
unlawfully born. But, oh, how much is the good Duke
deceived in Angelo! If ever he return and I can speak
to him, I will open my lips in vain, or discover his 195
government.   196

DUKE   That shall not be much amiss. Yet, as the matter
now stands, he will avoid your accusation; he made 198
trial of you only. Therefore fasten your ear on my
advisings. To the love I have in doing good a remedy
presents itself. I do make myself believe that you may
most uprighteously do a poor wronged lady a merited
benefit, redeem your brother from the angry law, do
no stain to your own gracious person, and much
please the absent Duke, if peradventure he shall ever
return to have hearing of this business.

ISABELLA   Let me hear you speak farther. I have spirit 207
to do anything that appears not foul in the truth of my 208
spirit.   209

DUKE   Virtue is bold, and goodness never fearful. Have
you not heard speak of Mariana, the sister of Frederick, the great soldier who miscarried at sea?

ISABELLA   I have heard of the lady, and good words
went with her name.

DUKE   She should this Angelo have married, was 215
affianced to her by oath, and the nuptial appointed;
between which time of the contract and limit of the 217
solemnity, her brother Frederick was wrecked at sea, 218
having in that perished vessel the dowry of his sister.
But mark how heavily this befell to the poor gentlewoman. There she lost a noble and renowned brother,
in his love toward her ever most kind and natural;
with him, the portion and sinew of her fortune, her 223
marriage dowry; with both, her combinate husband, 224
this well-seeming Angelo.

ISABELLA   Can this be so? Did Angelo so leave her?

DUKE   Left her in her tears, and dried not one of them
with his comfort; swallowed his vows whole, pretend- 228
ing in her discoveries of dishonor; in few, bestowed 229
her on her own lamentation, which she yet wears for 230
his sake; and he, a marble to her tears, is washed with 231
them but relents not.

ISABELLA   What a merit were it in death to take this
poor maid from the world! What corruption in this
life, that it will let this man live! But how out of this can
she avail?   236

DUKE   It is a rupture that you may easily heal, and the
cure of it not only saves your brother but keeps you
from dishonor in doing it.

ISABELLA   Show me how, good Father.

DUKE   This forenamed maid hath yet in her the continuance of her first affection; his unjust unkindness, that
in all reason should have quenched her love, hath, like
an impediment in the current, made it more violent
and unruly. Go you to Angelo; answer his requiring
with a plausible obedience; agree with his demands to 246
the point. Only refer yourself to this advantage: first, 247
that your stay with him may not be long, that the time
may have all shadow and silence in it, and the place 249
answer to convenience. This being granted in
course—and now follows all—we shall advise this
wronged maid to stead up your appointment, go in 252
your place. If the encounter acknowledge itself here- 253
after, it may compel him to her recompense. And here, 254
by this, is your brother saved, your honor untainted,
the poor Mariana advantaged, and the corrupt deputy
scaled. The maid will I frame and make fit for his at- 257

---

165 only he hath he has only.   assay test   166–7 his judgment . . .
natures his ability to judge people's characters.   168 gracious virtuous   175 Hold you there Hold fast to that resolution.
179–80 with my habit as well as my priestly garb (that)   181 In good
time i.e., Very well.   183–84 The goodness . . . in goodness i.e., The
physical attractions that come easily with beauty make beauty soon
cease to be morally good   185 complexion character and appearance
187 but that were it not that   188 examples precedents   189 this
substitute i.e., the deputy, Angelo   191 resolve him set his mind at
rest.   195–6 discover his government expose Angelo's misconduct.
198 avoid evade, refute.   he made i.e., he will say that he made
207 spirit courage   208 truth righteousness   209 spirit soul.

215 She . . . married Angelo was supposed to have married her.
was i.e., he was   217–18 limit . . . solemnity date set for the ceremony   223 the portion and sinew i.e., the mainstay   224 combinate
husband i.e., betrothed   228–9 pretending . . . dishonor falsely alleg-
ing to have found evidence of unchastity in her   229–30 in few . . .
lamentation in short, left her to her grief. (With quibble on *bestowed*,
meaning "gave in marriage.")   230 wears i.e., carries in her heart
231 a marble to i.e., unmoved by   236 avail benefit.   246–7 to the
point precisely.   247 refer . . . advantage obtain these conditions
249 shadow darkness, secrecy   252 stead . . . appointment go in your
stead   253–4 If the . . . hereafter i.e., If she should become pregnant
257 scaled weighed in the scales of justice (and found wanting).
frame prepare

tempt. If you think well to carry this as you may, the doubleness of the benefit defends the deceit from reproof. What think you of it?

ISABELLA   The image of it gives me content already, and I trust it will grow to a most prosperous perfection.

DUKE   It lies much in your holding up. Haste you speed- 264
ily to Angelo. If for this night he entreat you to his bed, give him promise of satisfaction. I will presently to Saint Luke's; there, at the moated grange, resides 267 this dejected Mariana. At that place call upon me; and dispatch with Angelo, that it may be quickly. 269

ISABELLA   I thank you for this comfort. Fare you well, good Father.   *Exit.* [*The Duke remains.*]

❖

[3.2]

Enter [*to the Duke*] *Elbow, Clown* [*Pompey, and*] *officers.*

ELBOW   Nay, if there be no remedy for it but that you will needs buy and sell men and women like beasts, we shall have all the world drink brown and white bastard.   4

DUKE [*aside*]   Oh, heavens, what stuff is here?

POMPEY   'Twas never merry world since, of two usur- 6
ies, the merriest was put down, and the worser al- 7
lowed by order of law a furred gown to keep him 8
warm, and furred with fox on lambskins too, to signify that craft, being richer than innocency, stands 10
for the facing.   11

ELBOW   Come your way, sir.—Bless you, good Father Friar.

DUKE   And you, good Brother Father. What offense hath 14
this man made you, sir?

ELBOW   Marry, sir, he hath offended the law; and, sir, we take him to be a thief too, sir, for we have found upon him, sir, a strange picklock, which we have sent 18
to the deputy.

DUKE [*to Pompey*]
Fie, sirrah, a bawd, a wicked bawd!
The evil that thou causest to be done,
That is thy means to live. Do thou but think
What 'tis to cram a maw or clothe a back 23
From such a filthy vice; say to thyself,
From their abominable and beastly touches 25
I drink, I eat, array myself, and live.

Canst thou believe thy living is a life,
So stinkingly depending? Go mend, go mend.   28

POMPEY   Indeed, it does stink in some sort, sir. But yet, sir, I would prove—   30

DUKE
Nay, if the devil have given thee proofs for sin, 31
Thou wilt prove his.—Take him to prison, officer. 32
Correction and instruction must both work
Ere this rude beast will profit.

ELBOW   He must before the deputy, sir; he has given 35
him warning. The deputy cannot abide a whoremaster. If he be a whoremonger and comes before him, he 37
were as good go a mile on his errand.   38

DUKE
That we were all, as some would seem to be, 39
From our faults, as faults from seeming, free! 40

Enter Lucio.

ELBOW   His neck will come to your waist—a cord, sir. 41

POMPEY   I spy comfort, I cry bail. Here's a gentleman and a friend of mine.

LUCIO   How now, noble Pompey? What, at the wheels of Caesar? Art thou led in triumph? What, is there 45
none of Pygmalion's images, newly made woman, to 46
be had now, for putting the hand in the pocket and extracting it clutched? What reply, ha? What say'st thou 48
to this tune, matter, and method? Is 't not drowned i'th' 49
last rain, ha? What say'st thou, trot? Is the world 50
as it was, man? Which is the way? Is it sad, and few 51
words? Or how? The trick of it?   52

DUKE   Still thus, and thus; still worse!

LUCIO   How doth my dear morsel, thy mistress? Procures she still, ha?

POMPEY   Troth, sir, she hath eaten up all her beef, and 56
she is herself in the tub.   57

LUCIO   Why, 'tis good. It is the right of it, it must be so. Ever your fresh whore and your powdered bawd; an 59
unshunned consequence, it must be so. Art going to 60
prison, Pompey?

---

28 depending supported.   **30 prove** i.e., argue, demonstrate
31 proofs for arguments in defense of   **32 prove** turn out to be
35 must must go.   **deputy** i.e., Angelo. (Though Escalus gave Pompey the warning.)   **37–8 he were . . . errand** i.e., he will have a hard road to travel.   **39 That** Would that   **40 From . . . free** i.e., free from faults, and our faults free from dissembling.   **41 His . . . cord** i.e., He is likely to hang by a cord like that around your waist. (The Duke is habited as a friar.)   **45 Caesar** (Who defeated Pompey at Pharsalia and led his sons in triumph after defeating them at Munda.)   **46 Pygmalion's images** i.e., prostitutes, so called because they "painted" with cosmetics like a painted statue. (Pygmalion was a sculptor, according to legend, whose female statue came to life "newly made.")   **48 clutched** i.e., with money in it. (But also with sexual suggestion.)   **48–50 What say'st . . . rain** i.e., What do you say now to this latest turn of events? Are our prospects a little dampened?   **50 trot** old bawd.   **51–2 Which . . . words?** i.e., What is the latest fashion? Is melancholy now in vogue? (A wry comment on Pompey's silence.)   **52 trick** fashion   **56 eaten . . . beef** (1) consumed all her salt beef, which had been prepared in a powder-tub like that also used to treat venereal disease (2) run through all her prostitutes   **57 in the tub** being treated for venereal disease by the sweating-tub treatment (much as beef was salted down in a tub to preserve it).   **59 Ever . . . bawd** i.e., It is always thus with young whores and old bawds, *powdered* like beef in a tub and caked with cosmetics   **60 unshunned** unshunnable, unavoidable

---

264 holding up ability to carry it off.   **267 moated grange** country house surrounded by a ditch   **269 dispatch** settle, conclude business
3.2. Location: Scene continues. The Duke remains onstage.
4 bastard sweet Spanish wine. (Used quibblingly.)   **6–7 two usuries** i.e., moneylending (the *worser*) and procuring for fornication (the *merriest*), both of which yield increase   **8 furred gown** (Characteristic attire of usurers.)   **10–11 stands . . . facing** represents the outer covering. (Fox symbolizes *craft* or craftiness, lambskin, *innocency*.)
14 Brother Father (The Duke's retort to Elbow's *Father Friar,* i.e., Father Brother.)   **18 picklock** skeleton key, or perhaps a chastity belt in Pompey's possession as pimp; it might seem *strange* to the innocent Elbow   **23 cram . . . back** fill a stomach or provide clothing
25 touches sexual encounters

POMPEY   Yes, faith, sir.

LUCIO   Why, 'tis not amiss, Pompey. Farewell. Go, say I sent thee thither. For debt, Pompey? Or how?

ELBOW   For being a bawd, for being a bawd.

LUCIO   Well, then, imprison him. If imprisonment be the due of a bawd, why, 'tis his right. Bawd is he doubtless, and of antiquity too; bawd-born. Farewell, 68 good Pompey. Commend me to the prison, Pompey. You will turn good husband now, Pompey; you will 70 keep the house. 71

POMPEY   I hope, sir, Your good Worship will be my bail.

LUCIO   No, indeed, will I not, Pompey; it is not the wear. I will pray, Pompey, to increase your bondage. 74 If you take it not patiently, why, your mettle is the 75 more. Adieu, trusty Pompey.—Bless you, Friar. 76

DUKE   And you.

LUCIO   Does Bridget paint still, Pompey, ha? 78

ELBOW   [to Pompey]   Come your ways, sir, come. 79

POMPEY   [to Lucio]   You will not bail me, then, sir?

LUCIO   Then, Pompey, nor now.—What news abroad, 81 Friar? What news?

ELBOW   Come your ways, sir, come.

LUCIO   Go to kennel, Pompey, go.

[Exeunt Elbow, Pompey, and Officers.]
What news, Friar, of the Duke?

DUKE   I know none. Can you tell me of any?

LUCIO   Some say he is with the Emperor of Russia; other 87 some, he is in Rome. But where is he, think you? 88

DUKE   I know not where; but wheresoever, I wish him well.

LUCIO   It was a mad fantastical trick of him to steal from 91 the state and usurp the beggary he was never born to. 92 Lord Angelo dukes it well in his absence; he puts 93 transgression to't. 94

DUKE   He does well in't.

LUCIO   A little more lenity to lechery would do no harm in him. Something too crabbed that way, Friar. 97

DUKE   It is too general a vice, and severity must cure it.

LUCIO   Yes, in good sooth, the vice is of a great kindred; 99 it is well allied. But it is impossible to extirp it quite, 100 Friar, till eating and drinking be put down. They say this Angelo was not made by man and woman after 102 this downright way of creation. Is it true, think you? 103

DUKE   How should he be made, then?

LUCIO   Some report a sea maid spawned him; some, 105 that he was begot between two stockfishes. But it is 106

certain that when he makes water his urine is con-gealed ice; that I know to be true. And he is a motion 108 ungenerative; that's infallible. 109

DUKE   You are pleasant, sir, and speak apace. 110

LUCIO   Why, what a ruthless thing is this in him, for the rebellion of a codpiece to take away the life of a man! 112 Would the Duke that is absent have done this? Ere he would have hanged a man for the getting a hundred bastards, he would have paid for the nursing a thousand. He had some feeling of the sport; he knew the service, and that instructed him to mercy. 117

DUKE   I never heard the absent Duke much detected for 118 women. He was not inclined that way.

LUCIO   Oh, sir, you are deceived.

DUKE   'Tis not possible.

LUCIO   Who, not the Duke? Yes, your beggar of fifty; and his use was to put a ducat in her clack-dish. The 123 Duke had crotchets in him. He would be drunk too, that let me inform you.

DUKE   You do him wrong, surely.

LUCIO   Sir, I was an inward of his. A shy fellow was the 127 Duke, and I believe I know the cause of his with-drawing.

DUKE   What, I prithee, might be the cause?

LUCIO   No, pardon. 'Tis a secret must be locked within the teeth and the lips. But this I can let you understand: the greater file of the subject held the Duke to 133 be wise.

DUKE   Wise? Why, no question but he was.

LUCIO   A very superficial, ignorant, unweighing fellow. 136

DUKE   Either this is envy in you, folly, or mistaking. The 137 very stream of his life and the business he hath helmed 138 must, upon a warranted need, give him a better proc- 139 lamation. Let him be but testimonied in his own 140 bringings-forth, and he shall appear to the envious a 141 scholar, a statesman, and a soldier. Therefore you speak unskillfully; or, if your knowledge be more, it is 143 much darkened in your malice.

LUCIO   Sir, I know him, and I love him.

DUKE   Love talks with better knowledge, and knowl-edge with dearer love.

LUCIO   Come, sir, I know what I know.

DUKE   I can hardly believe that, since you know not what you speak. But if ever the Duke return, as our prayers are he may, let me desire you to make your answer before him. If it be honest you have spoke, you have courage to maintain it. I am bound to call upon you; and, I pray you, your name?

---

68 antiquity long continuance.   **bawd-born** a born bawd and born of a bawd.   **70 good husband** thrifty manager   **71 keep the house** stay indoors. (With pun on the pimp's function as doorkeeper.)   **74 wear** fashion.   **75–6 your . . . more** (1) your spirit is revealed all the more (2) your shackles will be made heavier. (Playing on *mettle/metal*.) **78 paint** use cosmetics   **79 Come your ways** Come along   **81 Then** Neither then.   **abroad** about town   **87–8 other some** some others **91 steal** steal away   **92 beggary** i.e., status of a wanderer or traveler. (With unconscious ironic appropriateness; Lucio clearly does not see through the Duke's disguise as a mendicant friar.)   **93–4 puts . . . to't** puts lawbreaking under severe restraint.   **97 Something too crabbed** Somewhat too harsh   **99 kindred** i.e., family, numerous and well connected   **100 extirp** eradicate   **102 after** in accordance with **103 downright** straightforward, usual   **105 sea maid** mermaid **106 stockfishes** dried codfish.

108–9 motion ungenerative masculine puppet, without sexual potency   **110 pleasant** jocose.   **apace** fast and idly.   **112 codpiece** an appendage to the front of close-fitting hose or breeches worn by men, often ornamented and indelicately conspicuous; hence, slang for "penis"   **117 the service** i.e., prostitution   **118 detected** accused **123 his . . . clack-dish** his custom was to put a coin in her wooden beggar's bowl, with its lid that was "clacked" to attract attention. (Lucio hints that the Duke had sex with her.)   **127 inward** intimate **133 the greater . . . subject** most of his subjects   **136 unweighing** injudicious   **137 envy** malice   **138 helmed** steered   **139 upon . . . need** if a warrant were needed   **139–40 give . . . proclamation** pro-claim him better (than you assert).   **140–1 in . . . bringings-forth** by his own public actions   **141 to the envious** even to the malicious **143 unskillfully** in ignorance

LUCIO   Sir, my name is Lucio, well known to the Duke.

DUKE   He shall know you better, sir, if I may live to report you.

LUCIO   I fear you not.

DUKE   Oh, you hope the Duke will return no more, or you imagine me too unhurtful an opposite. But indeed 160 I can do you little harm; you'll forswear this again. 161

LUCIO   I'll be hanged first. Thou art deceived in me, Friar. But no more of this. Canst thou tell if Claudio die tomorrow or no?

DUKE   Why should he die, sir?

LUCIO   Why? For filling a bottle with a tundish. I would 166 the Duke we talk of were returned again. This ungen- 167 itured agent will unpeople the province with conti- 168 nency. Sparrows must not build in his house eaves, 169 because they are lecherous. The Duke yet would have dark deeds darkly answered; he would never bring 171 them to light. Would he were returned! Marry, this Claudio is condemned for untrussing. Farewell, good 173 Friar. I prithee, pray for me. The Duke, I say to thee again, would eat mutton on Fridays. He's now past it, 175 yet, and I say to thee, he would mouth with a beggar, 176 though she smelt brown bread and garlic. Say that I 177 said so. Farewell.   *Exit.*

DUKE

No might nor greatness in mortality   179
Can censure scape; back-wounding calumny   180
The whitest virtue strikes. What king so strong 181
Can tie the gall up in the slanderous tongue?
But who comes here?

Enter Escalus, Provost, and [officers with] bawd
[Mistress Overdone].

ESCALUS   Go, away with her to prison.

MISTRESS OVERDONE   Good my lord, be good to me. Your Honor is accounted a merciful man. Good my lord.

ESCALUS   Double and treble admonition, and still forfeit 188 in the same kind! This would make mercy swear and 189 play the tyrant.

PROVOST   A bawd of eleven years' continuance, may it please Your Honor.

MISTRESS OVERDONE   My lord, this is one Lucio's infor- 193 mation against me. Mistress Kate Keepdown was with 194 child by him in the Duke's time; he promised her mar-

riage. His child is a year and a quarter old, come Philip 196 and Jacob. I have kept it myself; and see how he goes 197 about to abuse me! 198

ESCALUS   That fellow is a fellow of much license. Let him be called before us. Away with her to prison! Go to, no more words.   [*Exeunt Officers with Mistress Overdone.*]

Provost, my brother Angelo will not be al- 202 tered; Claudio must die tomorrow. Let him be fur- nished with divines and have all charitable 204 preparation. If my brother wrought by my pity, it 205 should not be so with him.

PROVOST   So please you, this friar hath been with him, and advised him for th'entertainment of death.   208

ESCALUS   Good even, good Father.

DUKE   Bliss and goodness on you!

ESCALUS   Of whence are you?

DUKE

Not of this country, though my chance is now
To use it for my time. I am a brother   213
Of gracious order, late come from the See   214
In special business from His Holiness.

ESCALUS   What news abroad i'th' world?

DUKE   None but that there is so great a fever on good- ness that the dissolution of it must cure it. Novelty is 218 only in request, and, as it is, as dangerous to be aged 219 in any kind of course as it is virtuous to be constant 220 in any undertaking. There is scarce truth enough alive 221 to make societies secure, but security enough to make 222 fellowships accursed. Much upon this riddle runs the 223 wisdom of the world. This news is old enough, yet it is every day's news. I pray you, sir, of what disposi- tion was the Duke?

ESCALUS   One that, above all other strifes, contended 227 especially to know himself.

DUKE   What pleasure was he given to?

ESCALUS   Rather rejoicing to see another merry than merry at anything which professed to make him re- 231 joice—a gentleman of all temperance. But leave we him to his events, with a prayer they may prove pros- 233 perous, and let me desire to know how you find Clau- dio prepared. I am made to understand that you have lent him visitation.   236

196–7 Philip and Jacob the Feast of Saint Philip and Saint James (*Jacobus* in Latin), May 1.   **197–8 goes about** busies himself   **202 brother** i.e., fellow officer of state   **204 divines** clergymen   **205 wrought . . . pity** acted in accord with my impulses of pity   **208 th'entertainment** the reception, acceptance   **213 To . . . time** to dwell here for my present purposes.   **214 the See** Rome   **218 the dissolution . . . cure it** i.e., only by dying can goodness be rid of the disease.   **218–19 is only in request** is the only thing people seek   **219–21 as it . . . undertaking** as things currently stand, (it is) as dangerous to be constant in any undertaking as it is virtuous to be thus constant.   **221–3 There . . . accursed** i.e., There is hardly enough integrity extant to establish secure and trusting associations among men, but binding contractual obligations enough to be the curse of friendship. (The Duke thus puns on *security* [1] a sense of trust [2] financial pledge required to borrow money, and on *fellowship* [1] friendship [2] corporations formed for trading ventures.)   **223 upon this riddle** in this riddling fashion   **227 strifes** endeavors   **231 professed** attempted   **233 his events** the outcome of his affairs   **236 lent him visitation** paid him a visit.

160 too . . . opposite too harmless an adversary.   **161 forswear this again** deny another time what you have said under oath.   **166 tundish** funnel. (Here representing the penis.)   **167–8 ungeni- tured agent** sexless deputy   **169 Sparrows** (Proverbially lecherous birds.)   **171 darkly** secretly   **173 untrussing** undressing. (Specifi- cally, untying the points used to fasten hose to doublet.)   **175 eat . . . Fridays** i.e., frequent loose women in flagrant disregard of the law. (Literally, violate religious observance by eating meat on fast days.)   **past it** beyond the age for sex   **176 mouth** kiss   **177 smelt brown bread** smelled of coarse bran bread   **179 mortality** humankind; human life   **180–1 Can . . . strikes** can escape censure; backbiting slander strikes even the purest of virtues.   **181 so** be he never so   **188–9 forfeit . . . kind** guilty of the same offense.   **189 mercy** i.e., even mercy   **193–4 information** accusation

DUKE   He professes to have received no sinister measure 237
from his judge, but most willingly humbles himself to
the determination of justice; yet had he framed to him- 239
self, by the instruction of his frailty, many deceiving 240
promises of life, which I, by my good leisure, have
discredited to him, and now is he resolved to die.

ESCALUS   You have paid the heavens your function, and
the prisoner the very debt of your calling. I have la- 244
bored for the poor gentleman to the extremest shore of 245
my modesty, but my brother justice have I found so 246
severe that he hath forced me to tell him he is indeed
Justice.

DUKE   If his own life answer the straitness of his 249
proceeding, it shall become him well; wherein if he
chance to fail, he hath sentenced himself.

ESCALUS   I am going to visit the prisoner. Fare you well.

DUKE   Peace be with you!

　　　　　　　　　　[Exeunt Escalus and Provost.]

He who the sword of heaven will bear
Should be as holy as severe;
Pattern in himself to know,   256
Grace to stand, and virtue go;   257
More nor less to others paying   258
Than by self-offenses weighing.   259
Shame to him whose cruel striking
Kills for faults of his own liking!
Twice treble shame on Angelo,
To weed my vice and let his grow!   263
Oh, what may man within him hide,
Though angel on the outward side!
How may likeness made in crimes,   266
Making practice on the times,   267
To draw with idle spiders' strings   268
Most ponderous and substantial things!   269
Craft against vice I must apply.
With Angelo tonight shall lie
His old betrothèd but despisèd;
So disguise shall, by the disguisèd,   273
Pay with falsehood false exacting   274
And perform an old contracting.   Exit. 275

---

237 sinister measure unfair treatment meted out to him
239–40 framed to himself formulated in his mind   **240 by ... frailty**
at the prompting of his natural human weakness   **244 the
prisoner ... calling** what your calling as a friar obliges you to give
the prisoner, i.e., the comforts of spiritual counsel.   **245–6 shore ...
modesty** limit of propriety   **249 straitness** strictness   **256–9 Pattern ... weighing** he must know himself and be a pattern for others
to emulate, with the grace to stand firm and the virtue to guide himself in the straight path, judging and punishing others with neither
more nor less severity than he applies to his own offenses.   **263 my
vice** i.e., vice in everyone except Angelo. (The Duke speaks chorically
on behalf of everyone generally.)   **266–9 How ... things!** How may
false seeming of a criminal sort, practicing deception on the world,
make weighty and substantial matters seem as illusory and unsubstantial as spider webs!   **273–5 So ... contracting** so shall disguise,
employed by those in disguise (i.e., Mariana and the Duke himself),
use a kind of (virtuous) falsehood to pay back what was exacted
through deception (by Angelo), and thereby fulfill an old contract.

4.1

Enter Mariana, and Boy singing.

　　　　　　　Song.

BOY
Take, oh, take those lips away,
　That so sweetly were forsworn,
And those eyes, the break of day,
　Lights that do mislead the morn;   4
But my kisses bring again, bring again,   5
Seals of love, but sealed in vain, sealed in vain. 6

Enter Duke [disguised as before].

MARIANA
Break off thy song, and haste thee quick away.
Here comes a man of comfort, whose advice
Hath often stilled my brawling discontent. [*Exit Boy.*] 9
I cry you mercy, sir, and well could wish   10
You had not found me here so musical.
Let me excuse me, and believe me so,
My mirth it much displeased, but pleased my woe.   13

DUKE
'Tis good; though music oft hath such a charm
To make bad good, and good provoke to harm.   15
I pray you, tell me, hath anybody inquired for me here
today? Much upon this time have I promised here   17
to meet.

MARIANA   You have not been inquired after. I have sat
here all day.

Enter Isabella.

DUKE   I do constantly believe you. The time is come 21
even now. I shall crave your forbearance a little. May- 22
be I will call upon you anon, for some advantage to 23
yourself.

MARIANA   I am always bound to you.   *Exit.*

DUKE   Very well met, and welcome.
What is the news from this good deputy?

ISABELLA
He hath a garden circummured with brick,   28
Whose western side is with a vineyard backed;
And to that vineyard is a planchèd gate,   30
That makes his opening with this bigger key.   31
　　　　　　　　　　　　　　　　[*She shows keys.*]

4.1. Location: The moated grange at Saint Luke's.
4 Lights ... morn eyes that mislead the morning (the goddess of
dawn, Eos or Aurora) into taking them for the rising sun   **5 again**
back   **6 Seals** confirmations, pledges   **9 brawling** clamorous
10 cry you mercy beg your pardon   **13 My ... woe** i.e., it suited not a
merry but a melancholy mood.   **15 bad good** i.e., bad seem good,
attractive. (The Duke, echoing Renaissance conceptions of the psychological effects of music, warns that music can sometimes lend a
pleasing aura to sin and lead virtue into harm.)   **17 Much upon**
Pretty nearly about   **21 constantly** confidently   **22 crave ... little**
i.e., ask you to withdraw briefly.   **23 anon** presently   **28 circummured** walled about   **30 planchèd** made of boards, planks
31 his its

This other doth command a little door
Which from the vineyard to the garden leads;
There have I made my promise, upon the   34
Heavy middle of the night, to call upon him.

DUKE
But shall you on your knowledge find this way?

ISABELLA
I have ta'en a due and wary note upon't.
With whispering and most guilty diligence,
In action all of precept, he did show me   39
The way twice o'er.

DUKE   Are there no other tokens
Between you 'greed concerning her observance?   41

ISABELLA
No, none, but only a repair i'th' dark,   42
And that I have possessed him my most stay   43
Can be but brief; for I have made him know
I have a servant comes with me along,
That stays upon me, whose persuasion is   46
I come about my brother.

DUKE   'Tis well borne up.   47
I have not yet made known to Mariana
A word of this.—What, ho, within! Come forth!

            Enter Mariana.

I pray you, be acquainted with this maid;
She comes to do you good.

ISABELLA   I do desire the like.

DUKE
Do you persuade yourself that I respect you?   52

MARIANA
Good Friar, I know you do, and have found it.   53

DUKE
Take then this your companion by the hand,
Who hath a story ready for your ear.
I shall attend your leisure. But make haste;
The vaporous night approaches.

MARIANA   Will't please you walk aside?
                            Exit [with Isabella].

DUKE
O place and greatness! Millions of false eyes
Are stuck upon thee. Volumes of report   60
Run with these false and most contrarious quests   61
Upon thy doings; thousand escapes of wit   62
Make thee the father of their idle dream   63
And rack thee in their fancies.

            Enter Mariana and Isabella.

                            Welcome. How agreed?   64

ISABELLA
She'll take the enterprise upon her, Father,
If you advise it.

DUKE   It is not my consent,   66
But my entreaty too.

ISABELLA   Little have you to say   67
When you depart from him but, soft and low,
"Remember now my brother."

MARIANA   Fear me not.   69

DUKE
Nor, gentle daughter, fear you not at all.
He is your husband on a precontract;   71
To bring you thus together, 'tis no sin,
Sith that the justice of your title to him   73
Doth flourish the deceit. Come, let us go.   74
Our corn's to reap, for yet our tithe's to sow.   *Exeunt.*   75

                            ❖

4.2

            Enter Provost and Clown [Pompey].

PROVOST   Come hither, sirrah. Can you cut off a man's
head?

POMPEY   If the man be a bachelor, sir, I can; but if he be
a married man, he's his wife's head, and I can never   4
cut off a woman's head.   5

PROVOST   Come, sir, leave me your snatches, and yield   6
me a direct answer. Tomorrow morning are to die
Claudio and Barnardine. Here is in our prison a com-   8
mon executioner, who in his office lacks a helper. If   9
you will take it on you to assist him, it shall redeem
you from your gyves; if not, you shall have your full   11
time of imprisonment and your deliverance with an
unpitied whipping, for you have been a notorious
bawd.

POMPEY   Sir, I have been an unlawful bawd time out of
mind, but yet I will be content to be a lawful hangman.
I would be glad to receive some instruction from
my fellow partner.

PROVOST [*calling*]   What, ho, Abhorson! Where's Abhorson, there?

            Enter Abhorson.

ABHORSON   Do you call, sir?

PROVOST   Sirrah, here's a fellow will help you tomorrow
in your execution. If you think it meet, compound   23
with him by the year, and let him abide here with
you; if not, use him for the present and dismiss him.

---

34 **upon** during, at   39 **In action . . . precept** i.e., teaching by demonstration   41 **her observance** what she is supposed to do.   42 **repair**
act of going or coming to a place   43 **possessed** informed.   **my most
stay** my stay at the longest   46 **stays upon** waits for.   **persuasion**
belief   47 **borne up** sustained, carried out.   52 **respect you** are concerned for your welfare.   53 **found it** found it to be true.   60 **stuck**
fastened   60–2 **Volumes . . . doings** Innumerable rumors follow a
false scent and hunt counter in pursuing your activities   62 **escapes**
sallies   63 **Make . . . dream** credit you with being the source of their
fantasies   64 **rack** stretch as on the rack, distort

66 **not** not only   67 **Little . . . say** Say little   69 **Fear me not** i.e., Don't
worry about my carrying out my part.   71 **precontract** legally binding agreement entered into before any church ceremony. (Compare
Claudio's and Juliet's *true contract* at 1.2.142.)   73 **Sith that** since
74 **flourish** adorn, make fair   75 **Our corn's . . . sow** We must first
sow grain before we can expect to reap a harvest; i.e., we must get
started.   **tithe** the grain sown for tithe dues; or, an error for "tilth"
4.2. Location: The prison.
4 **he's . . . head** (Compare Ephesians 5:23: "The husband is the head of
the wife.")   5 **head** (With wordplay on "maidenhead.")   6 **leave . . .
snatches** leave off your quibbles   8–9 **common** public   11 **gyves** fetters, shackles   23 **compound** make an agreement

He cannot plead his estimation with you; he hath   26
been a bawd.

ABHORSON   A bawd, sir? Fie upon him! He will discredit our mystery.   29

PROVOST   Go to, sir, you weigh equally; a feather will
turn the scale.   *Exit.*

POMPEY   Pray, sir, by your good favor—for surely, sir,   32
a good favor you have, but that you have a hanging   33
look—do you call, sir, your occupation a mystery?   34

ABHORSON   Ay, sir, a mystery.

POMPEY   Painting, sir, I have heard say, is a mystery,   36
and your whores, sir, being members of my occupation, using painting, do prove my occupation a
mystery. But what mystery there should be in hanging, if I should be hanged, I cannot imagine.

ABHORSON   Sir, it is a mystery.

POMPEY   Proof?

ABHORSON   Every true man's apparel fits your thief. If it   43
be too little for your thief, your true man thinks it big   44
enough; if it be too big for your thief, your thief thinks   45
it little enough. So every true man's apparel fits your   46
thief.   47

Enter Provost.

PROVOST   Are you agreed?

POMPEY   Sir, I will serve him, for I do find your hangman is a more penitent trade than your bawd: he doth   50
oftener ask forgiveness.   51

PROVOST   You, sirrah, provide your block and your ax
tomorrow four o'clock.

ABHORSON   Come on, bawd. I will instruct thee in my
trade. Follow!

POMPEY   I do desire to learn, sir; and I hope, if you have
occasion to use me for your own turn, you shall find   57
me yare. For truly, sir, for your kindness I owe you a   58
good turn.

PROVOST   Call hither Barnardine and Claudio.

Exit [Pompey, with Abhorson].

Th'one has my pity; not a jot the other,
Being a murderer, though he were my brother.

Enter Claudio.

Look, here's the warrant, Claudio, for thy death.
'Tis now dead midnight, and by eight tomorrow
Thou must be made immortal. Where's Barnardine?   65

CLAUDIO
As fast locked up in sleep as guiltless labor   66
When it lies starkly in the traveler's bones.   67
He will not wake.

PROVOST   Who can do good on him?
Well, go, prepare yourself. [*Knocking within.*] But hark,
what noise?
Heaven give your spirits comfort!   [*Exit Claudio.*]
                              [*calling*] By and by.—
I hope it is some pardon or reprieve
For the most gentle Claudio.

Enter Duke [disguised as before].

                              Welcome, Father.

DUKE
The best and wholesom'st spirits of the night
Envelop you, good Provost! Who called here of late?

PROVOST   None since the curfew rung.

DUKE
Not Isabel?

PROVOST   No.

DUKE   They will, then, ere't be long.

PROVOST   What comfort is for Claudio?

DUKE
There's some in hope.

PROVOST   It is a bitter deputy.

DUKE
Not so, not so. His life is paralleled   79
Even with the stroke and line of his great justice.   80
He doth with holy abstinence subdue
That in himself which he spurs on his power   82
To qualify in others. Were he mealed with that   83
Which he corrects, then were he tyrannous;
But this being so, he's just. [*Knocking within.*] Now
are they come.   [*The Provost goes to the door.*]
This is a gentle provost; seldom when   86
The steelèd jailer is the friend of men.   87
                              [*Knocking within.*]
How now? What noise? That spirit's possessed with
haste
That wounds th'unsisting postern with these strokes.   89

PROVOST [*speaking at the door*]
There he must stay until the officer
Arise to let him in. He is called up.
                              [*He returns to the Duke.*]

DUKE
Have you no countermand for Claudio yet,
But he must die tomorrow?

PROVOST   None, sir, none.

DUKE
As near the dawning, Provost, as it is,

---

26 **plead his estimation** claim any respect on account of his reputation   29 **mystery** craft, occupation.   32 **favor** leave, permission
33 **favor** face   33–4 **hanging look** (1) downcast look (2) look of a
hangman   36 **Painting** (1) Painting of pictures (2) Applying cosmetics   43–7 **Every . . . thief** (Abhorson alludes to the custom of giving
to the hangman the garments of the executed criminal. Like a thief, a
hangman takes from all sorts of men; Death is the great thief. The
hangman's occupation is to settle all scores.)   44–5 **big enough** i.e.,
enough of a loss   46 **little enough** little enough for his efforts.
50–1 **he doth . . . forgiveness** (The executioner perfunctorily asked
forgiveness of those whose lives he was about to take.)   57 **for . . .
turn** (1) as a pimp to provide for your sexual needs (2) as your hangman when it is your turn to be hanged or "turned off" the ladder
58 **yare** ready, alacritous.   65 **made immortal** i.e., executed.

66 **fast** firmly, soundly.   **guiltless labor** (A personification of the
well-earned weariness that tires the innocent laborer.)   67 **starkly**
stiffly.   **traveler's bones** bones of one who travails or labors or journeys.   79–80 **His . . . justice** His life runs parallel and in exact conformity with the straight line and precise execution of the justice he
carries out.   82 **spurs on** encourages, urges   83 **qualify** mitigate.
mealed spotted, stained   86 **seldom when** i.e., it is seldom that
87 **steelèd** hardened   89 **unsisting** unyielding, unresting, or unresist-
ing (?).   **postern** small door

You shall hear more ere morning.
PROVOST   Happily   95
You something know, yet I believe there comes
No countermand. No such example have we;   97
Besides, upon the very siege of justice   98
Lord Angelo hath to the public ear
Professed the contrary.

Enter a Messenger.

                    This is His Lordship's man.
DUKE
And here comes Claudio's pardon.
MESSENGER [*giving a paper*] My lord hath sent you
this note, and by me this further charge, that you
swerve not from the smallest article of it, neither in
time, matter, or other circumstance. Good morrow;
for, as I take it, it is almost day.
PROVOST   I shall obey him.   [*Exit Messenger.*]
DUKE [*aside*]
This is his pardon, purchased by such sin
For which the pardoner himself is in.   109
Hence hath offense his quick celerity,   110
When it is borne in high authority.   111
When vice makes mercy, mercy's so extended   112
That for the fault's love is th'offender friended.—   113
Now, sir, what news?
PROVOST   I told you. Lord Angelo, belike thinking me   115
remiss in mine office, awakens me with this un-   116
wonted putting-on—methinks strangely, for he hath   117
not used it before.
DUKE   Pray you, let's hear.
PROVOST [*reads*] *the letter* "Whatsoever you may hear
to the contrary, let Claudio be executed by four of
the clock, and in the afternoon Barnardine. For my
better satisfaction, let me have Claudio's head sent   123
me by five. Let this be duly performed, with a
thought that more depends on it than we must yet
deliver. Thus fail not to do your office, as you will   126
answer it at your peril." What say you to this, sir?
DUKE   What is that Barnardine who is to be executed in
th'afternoon?
PROVOST   A Bohemian born, but here nursed up and   131
bred; one that is a prisoner nine years old.   132
DUKE   How came it that the absent Duke had not either
delivered him to his liberty or executed him? I have
heard it was ever his manner to do so.
PROVOST   His friends still wrought reprieves for him;
and indeed his fact, till now in the government of Lord   137
Angelo, came not to an undoubtful proof.
DUKE   It is now apparent?

PROVOST   Most manifest, and not denied by himself.
DUKE   Hath he borne himself penitently in prison? How
seems he to be touched?   142
PROVOST   A man that apprehends death no more dread-   143
fully but as a drunken sleep—careless, reckless, and   144
fearless of what's past, present, or to come; insensible   145
of mortality, and desperately mortal.   146
DUKE   He wants advice.   147
PROVOST   He will hear none. He hath evermore had the   148
liberty of the prison; give him leave to escape hence,   149
he would not. Drunk many times a day, if not many
days entirely drunk. We have very oft awaked him, as
if to carry him to execution, and showed him a
seeming warrant for it; it hath not moved him at all.
DUKE   More of him anon. There is written in your brow,
Provost, honesty and constancy; if I read it not truly,
my ancient skill beguiles me, but, in the boldness of   156
my cunning, I will lay myself in hazard. Claudio,   157
whom here you have warrant to execute, is no greater
forfeit to the law than Angelo who hath sentenced him.
To make you understand this in a manifested effect, I   160
crave but four days' respite, for the which you are to
do me both a present and a dangerous courtesy.   162
PROVOST   Pray, sir, in what?
DUKE   In the delaying death.
PROVOST   Alack, how may I do it, having the hour
limited, and an express command, under penalty, to   166
deliver his head in the view of Angelo? I may make
my case as Claudio's, to cross this in the smallest.
DUKE   By the vow of mine order I warrant you, if my
instructions may be your guide. Let this Barnardine
be this morning executed, and his head borne to
Angelo.
PROVOST   Angelo hath seen them both and will discover   173
the favor.   174
DUKE   Oh, death's a great disguiser, and you may add to
it. Shave the head, and tie the beard, and say it was   176
the desire of the penitent to be so bared before his
death. You know the course is common. If anything   178
fall to you upon this more than thanks and good   179
fortune, by the saint whom I profess, I will plead   180
against it with my life.
PROVOST   Pardon me, good Father, it is against my oath.
DUKE   Were you sworn to the Duke or to the deputy?
PROVOST   To him, and to his substitutes.
DUKE   You will think you have made no offense if the
Duke avouch the justice of your dealing?   186
PROVOST   But what likelihood is in that?
DUKE   Not a resemblance, but a certainty. Yet since I see
you fearful, that neither my coat, integrity, nor

---

95 **Happily** Haply, perhaps   97 **example** precedent   98 **siege** seat
109 **in** engaged.   110–11 **Hence . . . authority** Hence it is that criminal
behavior in high places has its (*his*) own quick way of covering its
tracks.   112–13 **When . . . friended** When criminality acts to save a
life, as in this case, mercy is so strangely broadened in definition that
the offender (here, Claudio) is spared for the fault committed by the
person in authority.   115 **belike** perchance   116–17 **unwonted
putting-on** unaccustomed urging   123 **better satisfaction** greater
assurance   126 **deliver** make known.   131 **here** i.e., in Vienna
132 **a prisoner . . . old** nine years a prisoner.   137 **fact** crime

142 **touched** affected, touched by remorse.   143–4 **no more dreadfully but** with no more dread than   145–6 **insensible . . . mortal**
incapable of comprehending the meaning of death, and incorrigible.
147 **wants advice** needs spiritual counsel.   148 **evermore** constantly
148–9 **the liberty . . . prison** freedom to go anywhere within the
prison   156–7 **in the . . . hazard** confident in my knowledge (of
human character), I will put myself at risk.   160 **in . . . effect** by
means of concrete proof   162 **present** immediate   166 **limited** fixed,
set   173–4 **discover the favor** recognize the face.   176 **tie** tie up, tidy
up   178 **course** practice   179 **fall to** befall   180 **the saint . . . profess**
i.e., St. Benedict, whose example I follow   186 **avouch** confirm

persuasion can with ease attempt you, I will go further 190
than I meant, to pluck all fears out of you. Look you,
sir, here is the hand and seal of the Duke. [*He shows a
letter.*] You know the character, I doubt not, and the 193
signet is not strange to you. 194

PROVOST   I know them both.

DUKE   The contents of this is the return of the Duke.
You shall anon overread it at your pleasure, where
you shall find within these two days he will be here.
This is a thing that Angelo knows not, for he this very
day receives letters of strange tenor, perchance of the
Duke's death, perchance entering into some monas- 201
tery, but by chance nothing of what is writ. Look, th'un- 202
folding star calls up the shepherd. Put not yourself 203
into amazement how these things should be; all difficulties are but easy when they are known. Call your
executioner, and off with Barnardine's head. I will
give him a present shrift and advise him for a better 207
place. Yet you are amazed, but this shall absolutely 208
resolve you. Come away; it is almost clear dawn. 209

Exit [with Provost].

❖

4.3

Enter Clown [Pompey].

POMPEY   I am as well acquainted here as I was in our 1
house of profession. One would think it were Mistress
Overdone's own house, for here be many of her old
customers. First, here's young Master Rash; he's in for 4
a commodity of brown paper and old ginger, nine- 5
score and seventeen pounds, of which he made five 6
marks, ready money. Marry, then ginger was not 7
much in request, for the old women were all dead. 8
Then is there here one Master Caper, at the suit of 9
Master Three-pile the mercer, for some four suits of 10
peach-colored satin, which now peaches him a beggar. 11
Then have we here young Dizzy, and young 12
Master Deep-vow, and Master Copper-spur, and 13

---

190 attempt win, tempt   **193 character** handwriting   **194 strange**
unknown   **201 entering** of his entering   **202 writ** i.e., written here.
202-3 unfolding star i.e., morning star, Venus, which bids the shepherd lead his sheep from the fold   **207 present shrift** immediate
absolution for sins (after confession)   **207–8 advise . . . place** counsel
him on the comforts of heaven.   **208 Yet** Still   **209 resolve you** dispel
your uncertainties.
4.3. Location: The prison.
1 well widely   **4 Rash** (All the names mentioned by Pompey apparently glance at contemporary social affectations and defects. *Rash*
means "reckless.")   **5–8 a commodity . . . dead** (To circumvent the
laws against excessive rates of interest, moneylenders often advanced
cheap commodities to gullible borrowers in lieu of cash. Master Rash,
having agreed to a valuation of 197 pounds for such merchandise,
has been able to resell it for only five marks, each mark worth about
two-thirds of a pound, and has been thrown into prison for debt. The
ginger has not fetched a good price, owing to lack of customers, since
the old women who are proverbially fond of ginger are no longer
alive.)   **9 Caper** (To *caper* was to dance or leap gracefully.)
10 Three-pile the thickest nap and most expensive grade of velvet.
mercer cloth merchant.   **suits** (With a play on *suit*, line 9.)
11 peaches him denounces him as. (With a play on *peach*.)   **12 Dizzy**
i.e., giddy, foolish   **13 Deep-vow** one who swears earnestly and
often.   **Copper-spur** (Copper was often used fraudulently to simu-
late gold.)

Master Starve-lackey the rapier and dagger man, and 14
young Drop-heir that killed lusty Pudding, and Mas- 15
ter Forthlight the tilter, and brave Master Shoe-tie the 16
great traveler, and wild Half-can that stabbed Pots, 17
and I think forty more, all great doers in our trade, and
are now "for the Lord's sake." 19

Enter Abhorson.

ABHORSON   Sirrah, bring Barnardine hither.

POMPEY   [*calling*]   Master Barnardine! You must rise and
be hanged, Master Barnardine! 22

ABHORSON   What, ho, Barnardine!

BARNARDINE   (*within*)   A pox o' your throats! Who
makes that noise there? What are you?

POMPEY   Your friends, sir, the hangman. You must be
so good, sir, to rise and be put to death.

BARNARDINE   [*within*]   Away, you rogue, away! I am
sleepy.

ABHORSON   Tell him he must awake, and that quickly,
too.

POMPEY   Pray, Master Barnardine, awake till you are executed, and sleep afterwards.

ABHORSON   Go in to him, and fetch him out.

POMPEY   He is coming, sir, he is coming. I hear his
straw rustle.

Enter Barnardine.

ABHORSON   Is the ax upon the block, sirrah?

POMPEY   Very ready, sir.

BARNARDINE   How now, Abhorson? What's the news
with you?

ABHORSON   Truly, sir, I would desire you to clap into 41
your prayers; for, look you, the warrant's come.

BARNARDINE   You rogue, I have been drinking all night.
I am not fitted for't.

POMPEY   Oh, the better, sir, for he that drinks all night
and is hanged betimes in the morning may sleep the 46
sounder all the next day.

Enter Duke [disguised as before].

ABHORSON   Look you, sir, here comes your ghostly 48
father. Do we jest now, think you?

DUKE   Sir, induced by my charity, and hearing how
hastily you are to depart, I am come to advise you,
comfort you, and pray with you.

BARNARDINE   Friar, not I. I have been drinking hard all
night, and I will have more time to prepare me, or

---

14 Starve-lackey (Spendthrift gallants often virtually starved their
pages.)   **15 Drop-heir** (Perhaps referring to those who disinherited
or preyed on unsuspecting heirs; or else *Drop-hair*, losing hair from
syphilis.)   **lusty** vigorous.   **Pudding** i.e., sausage   **16 Forthlight**
(Unexplained; perhaps an error for *Forthright*, referring to a style of
tilting.)   **tilter** jouster.   **brave** showy, splendidly dressed.   **Shoe-tie**
(Evidently a nickname for travelers and others who affected the foreign fashion of elaborate rosettes on the tie of the shoe.)   **17 Half-can**
i.e., a small drinking tankard.   **Pots** i.e., ale pots   **19 "for . . . sake"**
(The cry of prisoners from jail grates to passers-by to give them food
or alms.)   **22 be hanged** (With a play on the imprecation; compare
"go to the devil.")   **41 clap into** quickly begin   **46 betimes** early
48 ghostly spiritual

they shall beat out my brains with billets. I will not   55
consent to die this day, that's certain.

DUKE
  Oh, sir, you must, and therefore I beseech you
  Look forward on the journey you shall go.

BARNARDINE   I swear I will not die today for any man's
  persuasion.

DUKE   But hear you—

BARNARDINE   Not a word. If you have anything to say
  to me, come to my ward, for thence will not I today.   63
                                                    Exit.

        Enter Provost.

DUKE
  Unfit to live or die. Oh, gravel heart!   64
  After him, fellows. Bring him to the block.
                        [*Exeunt Abhorson and Pompey.*]

PROVOST
  Now, sir, how do you find the prisoner?

DUKE
  A creature unprepared, unmeet for death;   67
  And to transport him in the mind he is   68
  Were damnable.

PROVOST   Here in the prison, Father,
  There died this morning of a cruel fever
  One Ragozine, a most notorious pirate,
  A man of Claudio's years, his beard and head
  Just of his color. What if we do omit   73
  This reprobate till he were well inclined,
  And satisfy the deputy with the visage
  Of Ragozine, more like to Claudio?

DUKE
  Oh, 'tis an accident that heaven provides!
  Dispatch it presently; the hour draws on   78
  Prefixed by Angelo. See this be done,   79
  And sent according to command, whiles I
  Persuade this rude wretch willingly to die.   81

PROVOST
  This shall be done, good Father, presently.
  But Barnardine must die this afternoon.
  And how shall we continue Claudio,   84
  To save me from the danger that might come
  If he were known alive?

DUKE   Let this be done:
  Put them in secret holds, both Barnardine and
  Claudio.   87
  Ere twice the sun hath made his journal greeting   88
  To yond generation, you shall find   89
  Your safety manifested.

PROVOST   I am your free dependent.   91

DUKE
  Quick, dispatch, and send the head to Angelo.
                                        Exit [*Provost*].
  Now will I write letters to Varrius—   93
  The Provost, he shall bear them—whose contents
  Shall witness to him I am near at home,
  And that, by great injunctions, I am bound   96
  To enter publicly. Him I'll desire
  To meet me at the consecrated fount   98
  A league below the city; and from thence,   99
  By cold gradation and well-balanced form,   100
  We shall proceed with Angelo.

        Enter Provost [*with Ragozine's head*].

PROVOST
  Here is the head. I'll carry it myself.

DUKE
  Convenient is it. Make a swift return,   103
  For I would commune with you of such things   104
  That want no ear but yours.

PROVOST   I'll make all speed. *Exit.* 105

ISABELLA (*within*)   Peace, ho, be here!

DUKE
  The tongue of Isabel. She's come to know
  If yet her brother's pardon be come hither.
  But I will keep her ignorant of her good,
  To make her heavenly comforts of despair   110
  When it is least expected.

        Enter Isabella.

ISABELLA   Ho, by your leave!

DUKE
  Good morning to you, fair and gracious daughter.

ISABELLA
  The better, given me by so holy a man.
  Hath yet the deputy sent my brother's pardon?

DUKE
  He hath released him, Isabel, from the world.
  His head is off and sent to Angelo.

ISABELLA
  Nay, but it is not so!

DUKE   It is no other.
  Show your wisdom, daughter, in your close patience. 118

ISABELLA
  Oh, I will to him and pluck out his eyes!

DUKE
  You shall not be admitted to his sight.

ISABELLA
  Unhappy Claudio! Wretched Isabel!
  Injurious world! Most damnèd Angelo!

---

55 billets cudgels, blocks of wood.   63 ward cell   64 gravel stony
67 unmeet unready, unfit   68 transport him i.e., send him to his
doom. he is he is in   73 omit ignore, overlook   78 presently
immediately. (As also in line 82.)   79 Prefixed appointed beforehand,
stipulated   81 rude uncivilized   84 continue preserve
87 holds cells, dungeons   88 journal daily   89 yond i.e., beyond
these walls, outside the perpetually dark prison (?). Sometimes it is
emended to th' under, the people of the Antipodes, on the opposite
side of the earth, or, people under the sun, the human race.   91 free
dependent willing servant.

93 to Varrius (The Folio reads "to Angelo," but see line 99 below and
4.5.12–14; evidently, the Duke's plan is to meet Varrius "a league
below the city" and then proceed to the rendezvous with Angelo.)
96 by great injunctions by powerful precedent or for compelling reasons   98 fount spring   99 league (A measure of varying length but
usually about three miles.)   100 cold . . . form i.e., moving deliberately and with proper observance of all formalities   103 Convenient
Timely, fitting   104 commune converse   105 want require   110 of
from, transformed out of   118 close patience silent enduring.

DUKE
This nor hurts him nor profits you a jot.   123
Forbear it therefore; give your cause to heaven.
Mark what I say, which you shall find
By every syllable a faithful verity.   126
The Duke comes home tomorrow. Nay, dry your eyes;
One of our convent, and his confessor,
Gives me this instance. Already he hath carried   129
Notice to Escalus and Angelo,
Who do prepare to meet him at the gates,
There to give up their pow'r. If you can, pace your
    wisdom   132
In that good path that I would wish it go,
And you shall have your bosom on this wretch,   134
Grace of the Duke, revenges to your heart,   135
And general honor.

ISABELLA   I am directed by you.

DUKE
This letter, then, to Friar Peter give.
                    [*He gives her a letter.*]
'Tis that he sent me of the Duke's return.   138
Say, by this token, I desire his company
At Mariana's house tonight. Her cause and yours
I'll perfect him withal, and he shall bring you   141
Before the Duke, and to the head of Angelo   142
Accuse him home and home. For my poor self,   143
I am combinèd by a sacred vow,   144
And shall be absent. Wend you with this letter.
Command these fretting waters from your eyes   146
With a light heart. Trust not my holy order
If I pervert your course. Who's here?

                    Enter Lucio.

LUCIO   Good even. Friar, where's the Provost?
DUKE   Not within, sir.
LUCIO   Oh, pretty Isabella, I am pale at mine heart to see   151
thine eyes so red. Thou must be patient. I am fain to   152
dine and sup with water and bran; I dare not for my   153
head fill my belly; one fruitful meal would set me   154
to't. But they say the Duke will be here tomorrow.   155
By my troth, Isabel, I loved thy brother. If the old fantastical Duke of dark corners had been at home, he
had lived.   [*Exit Isabella.*]
DUKE   Sir, the Duke is marvelous little beholding to   159
your reports; but the best is, he lives not in them.   160
LUCIO   Friar, thou knowest not the Duke so well as I
do. He's a better woodman than thou tak'st him for.   162

DUKE   Well, you'll answer this one day. Fare ye well.
                    [*He starts to go.*]
LUCIO   Nay, tarry, I'll go along with thee. I can tell thee
pretty tales of the Duke.
DUKE   You have told me too many of him already, sir, if
they be true; if not true, none were enough.
LUCIO   I was once before him for getting a wench with
child.
DUKE   Did you such a thing?
LUCIO   Yes, marry, did I, but I was fain to forswear it.
They would else have married me to the rotten medlar.   172
DUKE   Sir, your company is fairer than honest. Rest you
well.
LUCIO   By my troth, I'll go with thee to the lane's end.
If bawdy talk offend you, we'll have very little of it.
Nay, Friar, I am a kind of burr; I shall stick.   *Exeunt.*

❧

4.4

Enter Angelo and Escalus, [reading letters].

ESCALUS   Every letter he hath writ hath disvouched   1
other.
ANGELO   In most uneven and distracted manner. His
actions show much like to madness. Pray heaven his
wisdom be not tainted! And why meet him at the   5
gates and redeliver our authorities there?
ESCALUS   I guess not.   7
ANGELO   And why should we proclaim it in an hour be-   8
fore his entering, that if any crave redress of injustice,
they should exhibit their petitions in the street?   10
ESCALUS   He shows his reason for that: to have a
dispatch of complaints, and to deliver us from devices   12
hereafter, which shall then have no power to stand
against us.
ANGELO   Well, I beseech you, let it be proclaimed.
Betimes i'th' morn I'll call you at your house. Give   16
notice to such men of sort and suit as are to meet him.   17
ESCALUS   I shall, sir. Fare you well.
ANGELO   Good night.   *Exit [Escalus].*
This deed unshapes me quite, makes me unpregnant   20
And dull to all proceedings. A deflowered maid,
And by an eminent body that enforced   22
The law against it! But that her tender shame   23
Will not proclaim against her maiden loss,
How might she tongue me! Yet reason dares her no,   25
For my authority bears of a credent bulk   26
That no particular scandal once can touch
But it confounds the breather. He should have lived,   28

---

123 **nor hurts** neither hurts   126 **By** with respect to   129 **instance** proof.   132 **pace** teach to move in response to your will, as with a horse   134 **bosom** heart's desire   135 **Grace of** manifestation of favor from.   **to your heart** to your heart's content   138 **that** that which.   **of** concerning   141 **perfect** acquaint completely.   **withal** with   142 **head** i.e., face   143 **home and home** thoroughly.   144 **combinèd** bound   146 **fretting** corroding   151 **pale . . . heart** i.e., pale from sighing (since sighs cost the heart loss of blood)   152 **fain** compelled. (As also in line 171.)   153–4 **for my head** i.e., on my life   154 **fruitful** abundant   154–5 **set me to't** i.e., awaken my lust and thus place me in danger of Angelo's edict.   159 **marvelous** marvelously.   **beholding** beholden   160 **he . . . them** i.e., he is not accurately described by them.   162 **woodman** i.e., hunter (of women)

172 **medlar** a fruit that was eaten after it had begun to rot; here, signifying a prostitute.
4.4. Location: In Vienna.
1 **disvouched** contradicted   5 **tainted** diseased.   7 **guess not** cannot guess.   8 **in an hour** i.e., a full hour   10 **exhibit** present   12 **dispatch** prompt settlement.   **devices** contrived complaints   16 **Betimes** Early   17 **men . . . suit** men of rank with a retinue   20 **unpregnant** unapt   22 **body** person   23 **But that** Were it not that   25 **tongue** i.e., reproach, accuse.   **dares her no** i.e., frightens her to say nothing   26 **bears . . . bulk** bears such a huge credibility   28 **But . . . breather** without its confuting the person who speaks.

Save that his riotous youth, with dangerous sense, 29
Might in the times to come have ta'en revenge
By so receiving a dishonored life 31
With ransom of such shame. Would yet he had lived!
Alack, when once our grace we have forgot,
Nothing goes right; we would, and we would not.

Exit.

❧

4.5

Enter Duke [in his own habit] and Friar Peter.

DUKE
These letters at fit time deliver me.   [*Giving letters.*] 1
The Provost knows our purpose and our plot.
The matter being afoot, keep your instruction, 3
And hold you ever to our special drift, 4
Though sometimes you do blench from this to that 5
As cause doth minister. Go call at Flavius' house, 6
And tell him where I stay. Give the like notice
To Valencius, Rowland, and to Crassus,
And bid them bring the trumpets to the gate; 9
But send me Flavius first.

FRIAR PETER   It shall be speeded well.   [*Exit.*] 11

Enter Varrius.

DUKE
I thank thee, Varrius. Thou hast made good haste.
Come, we will walk. There's other of our friends
Will greet us here anon. My gentle Varrius!   *Exeunt.*

❧

4.6

Enter Isabella and Mariana.

ISABELLA
To speak so indirectly I am loath.
I would say the truth, but to accuse him so,
That is your part. Yet I am advised to do it,
He says, to veil full purpose.

MARIANA   Be ruled by him. 4

ISABELLA
Besides, he tells me that if peradventure 5
He speak against me on the adverse side,
I should not think it strange, for 'tis a physic 7
That's bitter to sweet end.

Enter [Friar] Peter.

MARIANA
I would Friar Peter—

ISABELLA   Oh, peace, the Friar is come.

FRIAR PETER
Come, I have found you out a stand most fit, 10
Where you may have such vantage on the Duke
He shall not pass you. Twice have the trumpets
     sounded.
The generous and gravest citizens 13
Have hent the gates, and very near upon 14
The Duke is entering. Therefore hence, away!

Exeunt.

❧

5.1

*Enter Duke, Varrius, lords, Angelo, Escalus,
Lucio, [Provost, officers, and] citizens at several
doors.*

DUKE
My very worthy cousin, fairly met! 1
Our old and faithful friend, we are glad to see you. 2

ANGELO, ESCALUS
Happy return be to Your royal Grace!

DUKE
Many and hearty thankings to you both.
We have made inquiry of you, and we hear
Such goodness of your justice that our soul
Cannot but yield you forth to public thanks, 7
Forerunning more requital. 8

ANGELO   You make my bonds still greater. 9

DUKE
Oh, your desert speaks loud, and I should wrong it
To lock it in the wards of covert bosom, 11
When it deserves with characters of brass 12
A forted residence 'gainst the tooth of time 13
And razure of oblivion. Give me your hand, 14
And let the subject see, to make them know 15
That outward courtesies would fain proclaim 16
Favors that keep within. Come, Escalus, 17
You must walk by us on our other hand,
And good supporters are you.

Enter [Friar] Peter and Isabella.

FRIAR PETER [*to Isabella*]
Now is your time. Speak loud, and kneel before him.

ISABELLA [*kneeling*]
Justice, O royal Duke! Vail your regard 21
Upon a wronged—I would fain have said a maid.
O worthy prince, dishonor not your eye
By throwing it on any other object
Till you have heard me in my true complaint
And given me justice, justice, justice, justice!

---

29 sense passion, intention   **31 By** for, because of
4.5. Location: Outside the city.
1 me for me   **3 keep** keep to   **4 drift** plot   **5 blench . . . that** swerve
from one expedient to another   **6 minister** prompt, provide occasion.
9 trumpets trumpeters   **11 speeded** accomplished, expedited
4.6. Location: Near the city gate.
4 veil full purpose conceal our plan.   **5 peradventure** perhaps
7 physic remedy

10 stand place to stand   **13 generous** highborn   **14 hent** reached,
occupied.   **very near upon** almost immediately now
5.1. Location: The city gate.
0.2 *several* separate   **1 cousin** fellow nobleman. (Addressed to
Angelo.)   **2 friend** i.e., Escalus   **7 yield . . . to** call you forth to give
you   **8 more requital** further reward.   **9 bonds** obligations   **11 To
lock . . . bosom** i.e., to keep it locked up in my heart   **12 characters**
writing, letters   **13 forted** fortified   **14 razure** effacement   **15 the
subject** those who are subjects   **16–17 That . . . within** that public
ceremonies serve as outward manifestations of the approval my heart
feels for you.   **21 Vail your regard** Look down

DUKE
Relate your wrongs. In what? By whom? Be brief.
Here is Lord Angelo shall give you justice.   28
Reveal yourself to him.

ISABELLA   O worthy Duke,
You bid me seek redemption of the devil.
Hear me yourself; for that which I must speak
Must either punish me, not being believed,   32
Or wring redress from you.
Hear me, oh, hear me, hear!

ANGELO
My lord, her wits, I fear me, are not firm.
She hath been a suitor to me for her brother
Cut off by course of justice.

ISABELLA [standing]   By course of justice!

ANGELO
And she will speak most bitterly and strange.   38

ISABELLA
Most strange, but yet most truly, will I speak.
That Angelo's forsworn, is it not strange?
That Angelo's a murderer, is 't not strange?
That Angelo is an adulterous thief,
An hypocrite, a virgin-violator,
Is it not strange, and strange?

DUKE   Nay, it is ten times strange.

ISABELLA
It is not truer he is Angelo
Than this is all as true as it is strange.
Nay, it is ten times true, for truth is truth   47
To th'end of reck'ning.

DUKE   Away with her! Poor soul,   49
She speaks this in th'infirmity of sense.   50

ISABELLA
O prince, I conjure thee, as thou believ'st
There is another comfort than this world,
That thou neglect me not with that opinion
That I am touched with madness. Make not   53
    impossible   54
That which but seems unlike. 'Tis not impossible   55
But one, the wicked'st caitiff on the ground,   56
May seem as shy, as grave, as just, as absolute   57
As Angelo; even so may Angelo,
In all his dressings, characts, titles, forms,   59
Be an archvillain. Believe it, royal prince,
If he be less, he's nothing; but he's more,   61
Had I more name for badness.

DUKE   By mine honesty,
If she be mad—as I believe no other—
Her madness hath the oddest frame of sense,   64
Such a dependency of thing on thing,   65

As e'er I heard in madness.

ISABELLA   O gracious Duke,
Harp not on that, nor do not banish reason   67
For inequality, but let your reason serve   68
To make the truth appear where it seems hid,
And hide the false seems true.   70

DUKE   Many that are not mad
Have, sure, more lack of reason. What would
    you say?

ISABELLA
I am the sister of one Claudio,
Condemned upon the act of fornication
To lose his head, condemned by Angelo.
I, in probation of a sisterhood,   76
Was sent to by my brother; one Lucio
As then the messenger—

LUCIO   That's I, an't like Your Grace.   78
I came to her from Claudio and desired her
To try her gracious fortune with Lord Angelo
For her poor brother's pardon.

ISABELLA   That's he indeed.

DUKE [to Lucio]
You were not bid to speak.

LUCIO   No, my good lord,
Nor wished to hold my peace.

DUKE   I wish you now, then.
Pray you, take note of it. And when you have
A business for yourself, pray heaven you then
Be perfect.   86

LUCIO   I warrant Your Honor.   87

DUKE
The warrant's for yourself. Take heed to 't.

ISABELLA
This gentleman told somewhat of my tale—

LUCIO   Right.

DUKE
It may be right, but you are i'the wrong
To speak before your time.—Proceed.

ISABELLA   I went
To this pernicious caitiff deputy—

DUKE
That's somewhat madly spoken.

ISABELLA   Pardon it;
The phrase is to the matter.   95

DUKE   Mended again. The matter; proceed.   96

ISABELLA
In brief, to set the needless process by,   97
How I persuaded, how I prayed and kneeled,
How he refelled me, and how I replied—   99
For this was of much length—the vile conclusion

28 shall who shall   **32 not being** if I am not   **38 strange** strangely.
47 Than than that   **49 To . . . reck'ning** to the end of time and Day of
Judgment, always.   **50 in . . . sense** out of a sick mind, out of the
weakness of passion.   **53 with that opinion** out of a supposition
54 Make not Do not consider as   **55 unlike** unlikely.   **56 But** but
that.   **ground** earth   **57 shy** quietly dignified.   **absolute** flawless
59 dressings, characts ceremonial robes, insignia of office   **61 If . . .
nothing** i.e., even if he were less than an archvillain, he would be
worthless   **64 frame of sense** form of reason   **65 dependency . . .
on thing** coherence

67–8 do . . . inequality i.e., do not assume lack of reason on my part
because of the inconsistency between my story and Angelo's refutation, or because of the inequality in our reputations   **70 hide** put out
of sight, remove from consideration.   **seems** that seems   **76 in probation** i.e., a novice   **78 As then** being at that time.   **an't like** if it
please   **86 perfect** prepared.   **87 warrant** assure. (The Duke, however, quibbles in line 88 on the meaning "judicial writ.")   **95 to the
matter** to the purpose.   **96 Mended . . . proceed** That sets things
right. Proceed to the main point.   **97 to set . . . by** not to dwell on
unnecessary details in the story   **99 refelled** refuted, repelled

I now begin with grief and shame to utter.
He would not, but by gift of my chaste body
To his concupiscible intemperate lust, 103
Release my brother; and after much debatement 104
My sisterly remorse confutes mine honor, 105
And I did yield to him. But the next morn betimes, 106
His purpose surfeiting, he sends a warrant 107
For my poor brother's head.

DUKE   This is most likely!

ISABELLA
Oh, that it were as like as it is true! 109

DUKE
By heaven, fond wretch, thou know'st not what thou
    speak'st, 110
Or else thou art suborned against his honor 111
In hateful practice. First, his integrity 112
Stands without blemish. Next, it imports no reason 113
That with such vehemency he should pursue
Faults proper to himself. If he had so offended, 115
He would have weighed thy brother by himself 116
And not have cut him off. Someone hath set you on.
Confess the truth, and say by whose advice
Thou cam'st here to complain.

ISABELLA   And is this all?
Then, O you blessèd ministers above,
Keep me in patience, and with ripened time
Unfold the evil which is here wrapped up 122
In countenance! Heaven shield Your Grace from woe, 123
As I thus wrongèd hence unbelievèd go!
                                    [She starts to leave.]

DUKE
I know you'd fain be gone.—An officer!
To prison with her. Shall we thus permit
A blasting and a scandalous breath to fall 127
On him so near us? This needs must be a practice.
Who knew of your intent and coming hither?

ISABELLA
One that I would were here, Friar Lodowick.

DUKE
A ghostly father, belike. Who knows that Lodowick? 131

LUCIO
My lord, I know him; 'tis a meddling friar.
I do not like the man. Had he been lay, my lord, 133
For certain words he spake against Your Grace
In your retirement, I had swinged him soundly. 135

DUKE
Words against me? This' a good friar, belike! 136
And to set on this wretched woman here

Against our substitute! Let this friar be found.
                        [Exit one or more attendants.]

LUCIO
But yesternight, my lord, she and that friar,
I saw them at the prison. A saucy friar,
A very scurvy fellow.

FRIAR PETER   Blessed be Your royal Grace!
I have stood by, my lord, and I have heard
Your royal ear abused. First, hath this woman
Most wrongfully accused your substitute,
Who is as free from touch or soil with her
As she from one ungot. 147

DUKE   We did believe no less.
Know you that Friar Lodowick that she speaks of?

FRIAR PETER
I know him for a man divine and holy,
Not scurvy, nor a temporary meddler, 151
As he's reported by this gentleman;
And, on my trust, a man that never yet
Did, as he vouches, misreport Your Grace.

LUCIO
My lord, most villainously, believe it.

FRIAR PETER
Well, he in time may come to clear himself;
But at this instant he is sick, my lord,
Of a strange fever. Upon his mere request, 158
Being come to knowledge that there was complaint 159
Intended 'gainst Lord Angelo, came I hither,
To speak, as from his mouth, what he doth know
Is true and false, and what he with his oath
And all probation will make up full clear, 163
Whensoever he's convented. First, for this woman, 164
To justify this worthy nobleman,
So vulgarly and personally accused, 166
Her shall you hear disprovèd to her eyes, 167
Till she herself confess it.   [Exit Isabella, guarded.]

DUKE   Good Friar, let's hear it.
                    [Friar Peter goes to bring in Mariana.]
Do you not smile at this, Lord Angelo?
Oh, heaven, the vanity of wretched fools! 170
Give us some seats.   [Seats are provided.]
                        Come, cousin Angelo,
In this I'll be impartial. Be you judge
Of your own cause.   [The Duke and Angelo sit.]

    Enter Mariana, [veiled, with Friar Peter].

                            Is this the witness, Friar?
First, let her show her face, and after speak.

MARIANA
Pardon, my lord, I will not show my face
Until my husband bid me.

---

103 **concupiscible** lustful   104 **debatement** argument, debate
105 **remorse** pity.   **confutes** confounds, silences   106 **betimes** early
107 **surfeiting** being satiated   109 **like** likely   110 **fond** foolish
111 **suborned** induced to give false testimony   112 **practice** machination, conspiracy.   113 **imports no reason** i.e., makes no sense
115 **proper to himself** of which he himself is guilty.   116 **weighed**
judged   122 **Unfold** disclose   122–3 **wrapped . . . countenance** concealed by the privilege of authority.   127 **blasting** blighting   131 **A**
ghostly . . . belike A cleric, apparently.   133 **lay** not a cleric   135 **In**
your retirement during your absence.   **had swinged** would have
beaten   136 **This'** This is

147 **ungot** unbegotten.   151 **temporary meddler** meddler in temporal
affairs   158 **Upon . . . request** Solely at his request   159 **Being . . .**
knowledge he having learned   163 **probation** proof   164 **convented**
summoned.   166 **vulgarly** publicly   167 **to her eyes** i.e., to her face
168 s.d. **Exit Isbella, guarded** (Isabella seemingly must leave the stage
here or soon afterwards. She is described as "gone" at line 250, and is
summoned at line 278. The phrase "to her eyes" in line 167 may mean
"incontrovertibly.")   170 **vanity** folly

DUKE   What, are you married?

MARIANA   No, my lord.

DUKE   Are you a maid?

MARIANA   No, my lord.

DUKE   A widow, then?

MARIANA   Neither, my lord.

DUKE   Why, you are nothing then, neither maid, widow, nor wife?

LUCIO   My lord, she may be a punk, for many of them   185
are neither maid, widow, nor wife.

DUKE   Silence that fellow. I would he had some cause
To prattle for himself.   188

LUCIO   Well, my lord.

MARIANA
My lord, I do confess I ne'er was married,
And I confess besides I am no maid.
I have known my husband, yet my husband   192
Knows not that ever he knew me.

LUCIO   He was drunk then, my lord; it can be no better.

DUKE   For the benefit of silence, would thou wert so too!

LUCIO   Well, my lord.

DUKE
This is no witness for Lord Angelo.

MARIANA   Now I come to 't, my lord.
She that accuses him of fornication
In selfsame manner doth accuse my husband,
And charges him, my lord, with such a time   201
When, I'll depose, I had him in mine arms   202
With all th'effect of love.   203

ANGELO   Charges she more than me?   204

MARIANA   Not that I know.

DUKE   No? You say your husband?

MARIANA
Why, just, my lord, and that is Angelo,   207
Who thinks he knows that he ne'er knew my body,
But knows he thinks that he knows Isabel's.

ANGELO
This is a strange abuse. Let's see thy face.   210

MARIANA
My husband bids me. Now I will unmask.
                                          [She unveils.]
This is that face, thou cruel Angelo,
Which once thou swor'st was worth the looking on;
This is the hand which, with a vowed contract,
Was fast belocked in thine; this is the body   215
That took away the match from Isabel,   216
And did supply thee at thy garden house
In her imagined person.

DUKE [to Angelo]   Know you this woman?

LUCIO   Carnally, she says.

DUKE   Sirrah, no more!

LUCIO   Enough, my lord.

ANGELO
My lord, I must confess I know this woman,
And five years since there was some speech of
   marriage
Betwixt myself and her, which was broke off,
Partly for that her promisèd proportions   226
Came short of composition, but in chief   227
For that her reputation was disvalued   228
In levity. Since which time of five years   229
I never spake with her, saw her, nor heard from her,
Upon my faith and honor.

MARIANA [kneeling]   Noble prince,
As there comes light from heaven and words from
   breath,
As there is sense in truth and truth in virtue,
I am affianced this man's wife as strongly
As words could make up vows; and, my good lord,
But Tuesday night last gone in's garden house
He knew me as a wife. As this is true,
Let me in safety raise me from my knees,
Or else forever be confixèd here,   239
A marble monument!

ANGELO   I did but smile till now.
Now, good my lord, give me the scope of justice. 242
My patience here is touched. I do perceive   243
These poor informal women are no more   244
But instruments of some more mightier member   245
That sets them on. Let me have way, my lord,
To find this practice out.

DUKE   Ay, with my heart,
And punish them to your height of pleasure.—
Thou foolish friar, and thou pernicious woman,
Compact with her that's gone, think'st thou thy oaths, 250
Though they would swear down each particular saint, 251
Were testimonies against his worth and credit
That's sealed in approbation?—You, Lord Escalus, 253
Sit with my cousin; lend him your kind pains
To find out this abuse, whence 'tis derived.
There is another friar that set them on;
Let him be sent for.
                [The Duke rises; Escalus takes his chair.]

FRIAR PETER
Would he were here, my lord! For he indeed
Hath set the women on to this complaint.
Your Provost knows the place where he abides,
And he may fetch him.

DUKE   Go do it instantly.
                                          [Exit Provost.]
And you, my noble and well-warranted cousin,
Whom it concerns to hear this matter forth,   263
Do with your injuries as seems you best,   264

185 punk harlot   188 To . . . himself to speak in his own defense. (The
Duke hints that there might well be charges pending against Lucio.)
192 known had sexual intercourse with   201 with . . . time with doing
the deed at just the same time   202 depose testify under oath
203 With . . . love i.e., with sexual fulfillment.   204 Charges . . . me?
Does she (Isabella) bring charges against persons besides myself?
207 just just so   210 abuse deception.   215 fast belocked firmly
locked   216 match assignation

226 for that because.   proportions dowry   227 composition agreement   228–9 disvalued In levity discredited for lightness.   239 confixèd firmly fixed   242 scope full authority   243 touched injured,
affected.   244 informal rash, distracted   245 But than   250 Compact . . . gone i.e., in collusion with Isabella   251 swear . . . saint call
down to witness every single saint   253 sealed in approbation ratified by proof, like weights and measures being given a stamp or seal
to attest to their genuineness.   263 forth through   264 Do . . . best
respond to the wrongs done you as seems best to you

In any chastisement. I for a while
Will leave you; but stir not you till you have
Well determined upon these slanderers.   267

ESCALUS   My lord, we'll do it throughly.   *Exit* [*Duke*]. 268
Signor Lucio, did not you say you knew that Friar
Lodowick to be a dishonest person?

LUCIO   *Cucullus non facit monachum*; honest in nothing 271
but in his clothes, and one that hath spoke most
villainous speeches of the Duke.

ESCALUS   We shall entreat you to abide here till he come,
and enforce them against him. We shall find this friar 275
a notable fellow.   276

LUCIO   As any in Vienna, on my word.

ESCALUS   Call that same Isabel here once again. I would
speak with her.   [*Exit an Attendant.*]
Pray you, my lord, give me leave to question. You shall
see how I'll handle her.

LUCIO   Not better than he, by her own report.   282

ESCALUS   Say you?

LUCIO   Marry, sir, I think, if you handled her privately,   284
she would sooner confess; perchance publicly she'll
be ashamed.

ESCALUS   I will go darkly to work with her.   287

LUCIO   That's the way, for women are light at midnight.   288

Enter Duke [*disguised as a friar*], *Provost, Isabella,*
[*and officers*].

ESCALUS   Come on, mistress. Here's a gentlewoman
denies all that you have said.

LUCIO   My lord, here comes the rascal I spoke of, here
with the Provost.

ESCALUS   In very good time. Speak not you to him till
we call upon you.

LUCIO   Mum.

ESCALUS   Come, sir, did you set these women on to
slander Lord Angelo? They have confessed you did.

DUKE   'Tis false.

ESCALUS   How? Know you where you are?

DUKE
Respect to your great place! And let the devil   300
Be sometime honored for his burning throne!   301
Where is the Duke? 'Tis he should hear me speak.

ESCALUS
The Duke's in us, and we will hear you speak.
Look you speak justly.

DUKE
Boldly, at least. But oh, poor souls,
Come you to seek the lamb here of the fox?
Good night to your redress! Is the Duke gone?
Then is your cause gone too. The Duke's unjust,
Thus to retort your manifest appeal,   309

And put your trial in the villain's mouth
Which here you come to accuse.

LUCIO
This is the rascal. This is he I spoke of.

ESCALUS
Why, thou unreverend and unhallowed friar,
Is't not enough thou hast suborned these women
To accuse this worthy man, but, in foul mouth
And in the witness of his proper ear,   316
To call him villain? And then to glance from him
To th'Duke himself, to tax him with injustice?—   318
Take him hence. To th' rack with him!—We'll touse
you   319
Joint by joint, but we will know his purpose.   320
What, "unjust"?

DUKE   Be not so hot. The Duke
Dare no more stretch this finger of mine than he
Dare rack his own. His subject am I not,
Nor here provincial. My business in this state   324
Made me a looker-on here in Vienna,
Where I have seen corruption boil and bubble
Till it o'errun the stew; laws for all faults,   327
But faults so countenanced that the strong statutes   328
Stand like the forfeits in a barber's shop,   329
As much in mock as mark.

ESCALUS   Slander to th' state!   330
Away with him to prison.

ANGELO
What can you vouch against him, Signor Lucio?
Is this the man that you did tell us of?

LUCIO   'Tis he, my lord.—Come hither, Goodman 334
Baldpate. Do you know me?   335

DUKE   I remember you, sir, by the sound of your voice.
I met you at the prison, in the absence of the Duke.

LUCIO   Oh, did you so? And do you remember what you
said of the Duke?

DUKE   Most notedly, sir.   340

LUCIO   Do you so, sir? And was the Duke a fleshmonger, a fool, and a coward, as you then reported him to be?

DUKE   You must, sir, change persons with me ere you 344
make that my report. You indeed spoke so of him, and
much more, much worse.

LUCIO   Oh, thou damnable fellow! Did not I pluck thee by
the nose for thy speeches?

DUKE   I protest I love the Duke as I love myself.

ANGELO   Hark how the villain would close now, after 350
his treasonable abuses!

---

267 determined reached judgment   **268 throughly** thoroughly.
271 Cucullus . . . monachum A cowl doesn't make a monk
275 enforce them forcefully urge your charges   **276 notable** notorious   **282 Not . . . report** (Lucio salaciously turns Escalus's *handle her* into a sexual slur: You, Escalus, will do no better at "handling" Isabella than did Angelo, according to Isabella's testimony.)   **284 if . . . privately** (Lucio continues his sexual joke about "handling.")
287 darkly subtly, slyly   **288 light** wanton, unchaste   **300–1 let . . . throne** i.e., may all authority be respected, even the devil's. (Said sardonically.)   **309 retort** turn back.   **manifest** obviously just

316 in . . . ear within his own hearing   **318 tax him with** accuse him of   **319 touse** tear   **320 but we will** i.e., if necessary to; until we   **324 provincial** subject to the religious authority of this province or state.   **327 stew** (1) stewpot (2) brothel   **328 countenanced** tolerated and protected by corrupt authority   **329 forfeits** cautionary displays, or lists of rules and fines for handling razors, etc., which barbers (who also acted as dentists and surgeons) hung in their shops   **330 As . . . mark** as often flouted as observed.   **334–5 Goodman Baldpate** (Lucio refers to the tonsure that he assumes the Duke must have under his hood, though the Duke is clearly hooded at this point.)   **340 notedly** particularly   **344 change** exchange   **350 close** come to terms, compromise

ESCALUS   Such a fellow is not to be talked withal. Away
with him to prison! Where is the Provost? Away with
him to prison! Lay bolts enough upon him. Let him   354
speak no more. Away with those giglots too, and with   355
the other confederate companion!   356

      [*The Provost lays hands on the Duke.*]

DUKE [*to Provost*]   Stay, sir, stay awhile.

ANGELO   What, resists he? Help him, Lucio.

LUCIO   Come, sir, come, sir, come, sir; foh, sir! Why,
you bald-pated, lying rascal, you must be hooded,
must you? Show your knave's visage, with a pox to
you! Show your sheep-biting face, and be hanged an   362
hour! Will't not off?   363

     [*He pulls off the friar's hood, and discovers*
      the Duke. Angelo and Escalus rise.]

DUKE
Thou art the first knave that e'er mad'st a duke.
First, Provost, let me bail these gentle three.   365
[*To Lucio*] Sneak not away, sir, for the Friar and you
Must have a word anon.—Lay hold on him.

LUCIO   This may prove worse than hanging.

DUKE [*to Escalus*]
What you have spoke I pardon. Sit you down.
We'll borrow place of him. [*To Angelo*] Sir, by your
 leave. [*He takes Angelo's seat. Escalus also sits.*]
Hast thou or word, or wit, or impudence,   371
That yet can do thee office? If thou hast,   372
Rely upon it till my tale be heard,
And hold no longer out.

ANGELO [*kneeling*]   O my dread lord,   374
I should be guiltier than my guiltiness
To think I can be undiscernible,
When I perceive Your Grace, like power divine,
Hath looked upon my passes. Then, good prince,   378
No longer session hold upon my shame,
But let my trial be mine own confession.
Immediate sentence then and sequent death   381
Is all the grace I beg.

DUKE   Come hither, Mariana.—
Say, wast thou e'er contracted to this woman?

ANGELO   I was, my lord.

DUKE
Go take her hence and marry her instantly.
Do you the office, Friar, which consummate,   386
Return him here again. Go with him, Provost.

    Exit [*Angelo, with Mariana, Friar Peter, and*
        Provost].

ESCALUS
My lord, I am more amazed at his dishonor
Than at the strangeness of it.

DUKE   Come hither, Isabel.
Your friar is now your prince. As I was then

Advertising and holy to your business,   391
Not changing heart with habit, I am still
Attorneyed at your service.

ISABELLA   Oh, give me pardon,   393
That I, your vassal, have employed and pained   394
Your unknown sovereignty!

DUKE   You are pardoned, Isabel.
And now, dear maid, be you as free to us.   396
Your brother's death, I know, sits at your heart;
And you may marvel why I obscured myself,
Laboring to save his life, and would not rather
Make rash remonstrance of my hidden power   400
Than let him so be lost. O most kind maid,
It was the swift celerity of his death,
Which I did think with slower foot came on,
That brained my purpose. But peace be with him!   404
That life is better life past fearing death
Than that which lives to fear. Make it your comfort,
So happy is your brother.

  Enter Angelo, Mariana, [*Friar*] *Peter,* [*and*]
  Provost.

ISABELLA   I do, my lord.   407

DUKE
For this new-married man approaching here,
Whose salt imagination yet hath wronged   409
Your well-defended honor, you must pardon
For Mariana's sake. But as he adjudged your
 brother—
Being criminal, in double violation
Of sacred chastity and of promise-breach   413
Thereon dependent, for your brother's life—   414
The very mercy of the law cries out   415
Most audible, even from his proper tongue,   416
"An Angelo for Claudio, death for death!"
Haste still pays haste, and leisure answers leisure;   418
Like doth quit like, and measure still for measure.   419
Then, Angelo, thy fault's thus manifested,
Which, though thou wouldst deny, denies thee
 vantage.   421
We do condemn thee to the very block
Where Claudio stooped to death, and with like haste.
Away with him!

MARIANA   O my most gracious lord,
I hope you will not mock me with a husband!

DUKE
It is your husband mocked you with a husband.
Consenting to the safeguard of your honor,
I thought your marriage fit; else imputation,   428
For that he knew you, might reproach your life   429

---

354 bolts iron fetters **355 giglots** wanton women **356 confederate
companion** i.e., Friar Peter. **362 sheep-biting** knavish. (From the
action of wolves or dogs that prey on sheep.) **362–3 hanged an hour**
(A sardonic way of saying "hanged.") **365 gentle three** i.e., Mariana,
Isabella, and Friar Peter. **371 or word** either word **372 office** service. **374 hold . . . out** then persist no longer. **378 passes** actions,
trespasses. **381 sequent** subsequent **386 Do . . . office** Please perform the service. **consummate** being completed

391 Advertising and holy attentive and wholly dedicated (in my
priestly role) **393 Attorneyed at** serving as agent in **394 pained** put
to trouble **396 as free to us** i.e., as generous in pardoning me.
400 rash remonstrance sudden manifestation **404 brained** dashed,
defeated **407 So** thus **409 salt** lecherous **413–14 promise-breach . . .
dependent** i.e., breaking his promise made in return for the yielding up
of chastity **415 The very . . . law** i.e., even mercy itself **416 his proper**
its own **418 still** always **419 quit** requite **421 though** even if.
vantage i.e., any advantage. (Angelo must suffer the same penalty as
Claudio.) **428 fit** appropriate. **imputation** accusation, slander
429 For that he knew you since he knew you sexually

And choke your good to come. For his possessions,   430
Although by confiscation they are ours,
We do instate and widow you withal,   432
To buy you a better husband.

MARIANA   O my dear lord,
I crave no other, nor no better man.

DUKE
Never crave him; we are definitive.   435

MARIANA [kneeling]
Gentle my liege—

DUKE   You do but lose your labor.—
Away with him to death! [To Lucio] Now, sir, to you.

MARIANA
O my good lord!—Sweet Isabel, take my part!
Lend me your knees, and all my life to come
I'll lend you all my life to do you service.

DUKE
Against all sense you do importune her.
Should she kneel down in mercy of this fact,   442
Her brother's ghost his pavèd bed would break,   443
And take her hence in horror.

MARIANA   Isabel,
Sweet Isabel, do yet but kneel by me!
Hold up your hands, say nothing; I'll speak all.
They say best men are molded out of faults,   447
And, for the most, become much more the better   448
For being a little bad. So may my husband.
O Isabel, will you not lend a knee?

DUKE
He dies for Claudio's death.

ISABELLA [kneeling]   Most bounteous sir,
Look, if it please you, on this man condemned
As if my brother lived. I partly think
A due sincerity governed his deeds,
Till he did look on me. Since it is so,
Let him not die. My brother had but justice,
In that he did the thing for which he died.
For Angelo,
His act did not o'ertake his bad intent,
And must be buried but as an intent   460
That perished by the way. Thoughts are no subjects,   461
Intents but merely thoughts.

MARIANA   Merely, my lord.

DUKE
Your suit's unprofitable. Stand up, I say.
                                    [They stand.]
I have bethought me of another fault.
Provost, how came it Claudio was beheaded
At an unusual hour?

PROVOST   It was commanded so.

DUKE
Had you a special warrant for the deed?

PROVOST
No, my good lord, it was by private message.

DUKE
For which I do discharge you of your office.
Give up your keys.

PROVOST   Pardon me, noble lord.
I thought it was a fault, but knew it not,   472
Yet did repent me after more advice;   473
For testimony whereof, one in the prison,
That should by private order else have died,
I have reserved alive.

DUKE   What's he?

PROVOST   His name is Barnardine.

DUKE
I would thou hadst done so by Claudio.
Go fetch him hither. Let me look upon him.
                                    [Exit Provost.]

ESCALUS
I am sorry one so learnèd and so wise
As you, Lord Angelo, have still appeared,
Should slip so grossly, both in the heat of blood   482
And lack of tempered judgment afterward.

ANGELO
I am sorry that such sorrow I procure,   485
And so deep sticks it in my penitent heart
That I crave death more willingly than mercy.
'Tis my deserving, and I do entreat it.   488

    Enter Barnardine and Provost, Claudio [muffled],
    [and] Juliet.

DUKE
Which is that Barnardine?

PROVOST   This, my lord.

DUKE
There was a friar told me of this man.—
Sirrah, thou art said to have a stubborn soul
That apprehends no further than this world,
And squar'st thy life according. Thou'rt condemned;   493
But, for those earthly faults, I quit them all,   494
And pray thee take this mercy to provide
For better times to come.—Friar, advise him;
I leave him to your hand.—What muffled fellow's
    that?

PROVOST
This is another prisoner that I saved,
Who should have died when Claudio lost his head,
As like almost to Claudio as himself.
                                    [He unmuffles Claudio.]

DUKE [to Isabella]
If he be like your brother, for his sake
Is he pardoned, and for your lovely sake,
Give me your hand and say you will be mine;
He is my brother too. But fitter time for that.
By this Lord Angelo perceives he's safe;
Methinks I see a quick'ning in his eye.
Well, Angelo, your evil quits you well.   507
Look that you love your wife, her worth worth yours.   508

---

430 For As for   432 widow endow with a widow's rights
435 definitive firmly resolved.   442 in . . . fact pleading mercy for
this crime   443 pavèd bed grave covered with a stone slab   447 best
men even the best of men   448 most most part   460 buried i.e., forgotten   461 no subjects i.e., not subject to the state's authority

472 knew it not was not sure   473 advice consideration   482 still always   485 procure cause, prompt   488.1 muffled wrapped up so as to
conceal identity. (As also in line 497.)   493 squar'st regulates   494 for
as for.   quit pardon   507 quits rewards, requites   508 her . . . yours
her worthiness richly deserving your love and worthy of your estate.

I find an apt remission in myself;   509
And yet here's one in place I cannot pardon.   510
[*To Lucio*] You, sirrah, that knew me for a fool, a
   coward,
One all of luxury, an ass, a madman—   512
Wherein have I so deserved of you
That you extol me thus?

LUCIO   Faith, my lord, I spoke it but according to the
trick. If you will hang me for it, you may; but I had   516
rather it would please you I might be whipped.

DUKE
Whipped first, sir, and hanged after.—
Proclaim it, Provost, round about the city,
If any woman wronged by this lewd fellow—
As I have heard him swear himself there's one
Whom he begot with child—let her appear,
And he shall marry her. The nuptial finished,
Let him be whipped and hanged.

LUCIO   I beseech Your Highness, do not marry me to a
whore. Your Highness said even now I made you a   526
duke; good my lord, do not recompense me in making me a cuckold.

DUKE
Upon mine honor, thou shalt marry her.
Thy slanders I forgive and therewithal   530
Remit thy other forfeits.—Take him to prison,   531

And see our pleasure herein executed.   532

LUCIO   Marrying a punk, my lord, is pressing to death,   533
whipping, and hanging.

DUKE
Slandering a prince deserves it.
                               [*Exeunt officers with Lucio.*]
She, Claudio, that you wronged, look you restore.   536
Joy to you, Mariana! Love her, Angelo.
I have confessed her, and I know her virtue.
Thanks, good friend Escalus, for thy much goodness;
There's more behind that is more gratulate.   540
Thanks, Provost, for thy care and secrecy;
We shall employ thee in a worthier place.
Forgive him, Angelo, that brought you home
The head of Ragozine for Claudio's;
Th'offense pardons itself. Dear Isabel,
I have a motion much imports your good,   546
Whereto if you'll a willing ear incline,
What's mine is yours, and what is yours is mine.—
So, bring us to our palace, where we'll show   549
What's yet behind, that's meet you all should know.   550
                               [*Exeunt.*]

---

509 **apt remission** readiness to show mercy   510 **in place** present
512 **luxury** lechery   516 **trick** fashion.   526 **even** just   530–1 **and
therewithal . . . forfeits** i.e., and in addition to that I will not have
you whipped and hanged.

532 **see . . . executed** i.e., see that my order be carried out that Lucio
marry Kate Keepdown (see 3.2.194–6).   533 **pressing to death** i.e., by
having heavy weights placed on the chest. (A standard form of executing those who refused to plead to a felony charge.) Lucio wryly
complains that marrying a whore is as bad as death by torture.
536 **She . . . restore** i.e., See to it that you marry Juliet.   540 **behind** in
store, to come.   **gratulate** gratifying.   546 **motion** proposal (which)
549 **bring** escort   550 **What's yet behind** what is still to be told

The Histories

The Tragedy of King Richard the Third

The fascinating evil ruler for whom *Richard III* is named has already made his appearance in the third part of *Henry VI*, in the four-play sequence that makes up Shakespeare's first foray into English history. In the final installment in this tetralogy, Richard, Duke of Gloucester, stands fully revealed as the evil genius of England's prolonged crisis of civil war. With a bold stroke, Shakespeare opens *Richard III* with his arresting soliloquy; Richard takes over the stage in a way that has held audiences spellbound ever since Richard Burbage first performed the role. Richard announces his determination to "prove a villain," both defying and fulfilling Nature, which made his body deformed. In fact, he has already begun his treacherous course, and we see at once how his plot against Clarence, founded on something so trivial as the letter G, has manipulated the King and has ensnared Clarence. Then, with outrageous hypocrisy, he "comforts" Clarence. Within less than a hundred lines, Shakespeare makes us feel how brilliant, cynical, charming, and dangerous Richard of Gloucester is. Richard proceeds to dominate the other characters—and the whole play—to an extraordinary degree.

By organizing this play firmly around Richard, Shakespeare solved the problems of giving form to his drama and of concluding the series of plays about the dynastic rivalry of York and Lancaster. *Richard III* begins and ends with a peace, yet the recent peace of the Yorkist King Edward is scorned and sabotaged by Richard as soon as it is introduced. It is vulnerable to factions at court and is bitterly denounced by that living embodiment of the cruel and violent past, Queen Margaret. There can be no peace in England while Richard lives to undermine it. Still, as the plot moves through Richard's exhilarating rise to the throne and the events of his tragic fall—when his conscience, the spirits of those he murdered, and the Earl of Richmond punish and defeat him—we see that his career is part of a larger order, a seemingly providential plan of retribution for wickedness and injustice and for reconciling England's divisions. For all its specific reminders of past warfare and atrocity on both Yorkist and Lancastrian sides, *Richard III* dramatizes an archetypal struggle between good and evil, personified in Richard the villain-hero and Richmond his opponent, who plays the role of the righteous agent of divine and poetic justice.

Dramatically, Richmond, like Queen Margaret, is more a symbol than a fully developed character. It is Richard who is the exciting figure as he deceives and manipulates others and finally faces the chillingly isolated condition into which he has brought himself by being so truly a villain. He climbs to power by deceit, and so he is constantly acting a part. Richard's ability as an actor is seemingly limitless. He has already boasted, in *3 Henry VI*, that he can deceive more slyly than Ulysses, Sinon, or Machiavelli and can put on more false shapes than Proteus. To us as audience, he is cynically candid and boastful, setting us up in advance to watch his unbelievable performances. In an instant, before our eyes, he is the concerned younger brother of Clarence, sharing a hatred of Queen Elizabeth and her kindred; he is the jocular uncle of the little princes; or he is the pious recluse studying divinity with his clerical teachers, reluctant to accept the responsibilities of state that are thrust upon him by his importunate subjects (i.e., by Catesby and Buckingham, who are also actors in this staged scene).

None of these bravura performances, however, matches the wooing of Lady Anne. Richard himself sees it as the great test of his powers and is suitably impressed by his victory. The wooing scene, to some critics, challenges credibility. One key to credibility must lie in superb acting. The actor who plays Richard must transform himself from the gloating villain we know in soliloquy to the grief-stricken lover. Richard's argument is, after all, speciously plausible: that he has killed Anne's husband and father-in-law out of desperate love for her. The argument appeals to vanity, that most fatal of human weaknesses.

What power Anne suddenly appears to have over Richard! She can kill him or spare his life. Richard shrewdly judges her as one who is not able to kill, and so he risks offering her his sword. As stage manager, he has altered her role from that of sincere mourner to the stereotype of the proud woman worshiped by her groveling servant in love. With superb irony, Richard has inverted the appearance and the reality of control in this struggle between man and woman, winning mastery by flattering Anne that she has such power over his emotions and his life. From his amazing success, Richard concludes that ordinary men and women can be made to believe anything and to betray their own instincts by "the plain devil and dissembling looks" (1.2.239). Richard is indeed devillike; his role as actor stems in part from that of the Vice in the morality play, brilliantly comic and sinister. Yet even the devil can prevail over his victims only when they acquiesce in evil. The devil can deceive the senses, but acceptance of evil is still an act of the perverted will. Anne is guilty, however much we can appreciate the mesmerizing power of Richard's personality. By the end of the scene, she has violated everything she holds sacred.

The image of Richard as devil or Vice raises questions of motivation and of symbolic meaning, and suggests two seemingly disparate ways of reading the play, one psychological and the other providential. Is Richard a human character, propelled toward the throne by his insatiable ambition, like Macbeth? Is there a clue to his behavior in his ugliness and misanthropy? One might argue that he compensates for his ugliness and unlovability by resolving to domineer. Feeling unwanted, he despises all humans and undertakes to prove them weak and corrupt in order to affirm himself. He expresses a universal human penchant for cruelty and senseless domination. Yet the proposition that Richard is evil *because* he was born ugly logically can be reversed as well: he was born ugly *because* he is evil. In providential terms, Richard can be seen as the result of a divine plan in which evil ironically has a place in a larger scheme of things that is ultimately benign.

This latter concept, owing much to Renaissance notions of platonic correspondence between outer appearances and inner qualities, is grounded on the idea of a vast struggle in the cosmos between the forces of absolute good and the forces of absolute evil, one in which every event in human life has divine meaning and cause. Richard's birth is, according to this theory, a physical manifestation of that divine meaning. Providential destiny, having determined the need for a genius of evil at this point in English history, decrees that Richard shall be born. The teeth and hunched back merely give evidence of what is already predetermined. In the apt words of the choric Queen Margaret, Richard was "sealed in thy nativity / The slave of nature and the son of hell" (1.3.229–30). Though he devotes himself to selfish ambition and evildoing, Richard ultimately serves the righteous purpose of divine Providence in human affairs. He functions, in this interpretation, as a scourge of God, whose tyrannous plotting is permitted in order to bring just retribution upon offenders of the moral law. He is fundamentally unlike Shakespeare's more human villains, such as Macbeth or Claudius, but belongs, instead, to a special group of villains, including Iago in *Othello* and Edmund in *King Lear*. Like them, Richard is driven both by human motivation and by his preexistent evil genius; he displays the "motiveless malignity" ascribed by Coleridge to Iago.

Such a reading is only one approach to an understanding of Richard's character and function; he is also a human being involved in a struggle for power, motivated by ambition and hatred. The two readings, one psychological and the other providential, are complementary and need not contradict each other. The psychological reading seems more intelligible to us today, based as it is on character and motivation. The providential reading, more traditional in its ideology, helps explain not only Richard's delight in evil but also the necessity for so much evil and suffering in England's civil wars. This theory of history owes much to Edward Hall's *Union of the Two Noble and Illustre Families of Lancaster and York* (1542), Shakespeare's chief source, along with Raphael Holinshed's *Chronicles* (1578), for his *Henry VI* plays. Shakespeare's treatment of Richard is ultimately indebted to Polydore Vergil's *Anglica Historia* (1534) and especially to *The History of King Richard the Third*, attributed to Sir Thomas More (published 1557). This latter work, adopted in turn by Edward Hall, Richard Grafton, and Raphael Holinshed, purposefully blackens Richard's character. He becomes a study in the nature of tyranny, an object lesson to future rulers and their subjects. He is, moreover, a result of the curse placed by God on the English people for their sinful disobedience.

Richmond, in this Tudor explanation, becomes God's minister, chosen to destroy the scourge and thereafter to fulfill a new and happy covenant between God and humanity as King Henry VII. Thus, the play hardly touches on the sensitive matter of his somewhat remote Lancastrian claim to the crown. His victory at Bosworth is not one more turn of Fortune's wheel raising or deposing Lancastrian or Yorkist kings, but the end of a long cycle of unnatural violence, and his marriage to the Yorkist Princess Elizabeth is the restoration and the symbol of unity and peace in England's fair land. Although modern historians more impartially regard the defeat of Richard III at Bosworth Field in 1485 as a political overthrow not unlike Henry IV's overthrow of Richard II, and stress that Richard III was a talented administrator guilty of no worse political crimes than those of his more fortunate successor, Elizabethan audiences (under the constant promptings of the Tudor state) could not have found sufficient meaning in such a neutral interpretation. They were taught to see history as revealing God's intention and to view Henry VII's accession not as a parallel to the deposing of Richard II by Henry IV but, instead, as a divinely sanctioned deliverance of the English nation, to which Elizabeth's subjects were the happy heirs. Accordingly, the Tudor myth stressed the tyrannical nature of Richard III's seizure of power and conversely minimized the political and Machiavellian elements in Henry VII's takeover. Bosworth Field was seen as an act of God, a rising up of some irresistible force, and under no circumstances as a precedent for future rebellion.

In the *Henry VI* plays, Shakespeare puts considerable distance between himself and the Tudor orthodox reading of history, allowing the grim realities of civil war to speak for themselves. In *Richard III*, however, the pattern shown in the chronicles provides Shakespeare with an essential structural device. Viewing the civil wars in retrospect, *Richard III* potentially manifests a cohesive sense in which England's suffering has fulfilled a necessary plan of fall from innocence, leading through sin and penitence to regeneration. Evil is seen at last as something through which good triumphs, in English history, as in the story of humankind's fall and a restoration by divine grace.

This providential scheme imposes a double irony on *Richard III*. In the short run, Richard appears to be complete master over his victims. "Your imprisonment shall not be long," Richard assures his brother Clarence. "I will deliver you, or else lie for you" (1.1.114–15). The audience, already let in on the secret, can shiver at the grisly humor of these double entendres. Clarence will indeed soon be delivered—to his death. Richard's henchmen are fond of such jokes, too. When Lord Hastings is on his way to the Tower, where he plans to stay for midday dinner, Buckingham observes aside, "And supper too, although thou know'st it not" (3.2.122). Buckingham, knowing that Hastings is about to be arrested in the Tower and executed for treason, chillingly suggests that Hastings will soon be a feast for worms. Shortly before, Catesby has assured Hastings of Richard's and Buckingham's favor: "The princes both make high account of you—/[*Aside*] For they account his head upon the Bridge" (3.2.69–70). That is to say, Hastings's severed head will soon be raised on a pole on London Bridge as a grim warning to those who run afoul of the new regime. Richard has a phrase for such wit: "Thus, like the formal Vice, Iniquity, /I moralize two meanings in one word" (3.1.82–3). The point of such ironies is always the same: the scheming villain is cleverer than his victims, deceiving them through equivocation and triumphing in their spriritual blindness.

The delayed irony of the play, however, ultimately offers another possible explanation for the seemingly nihilistic conclusions of the early scenes; that is, there may be a larger plan at work, of which Richard is unconscious and in which he plays a role quite unlike the one he creates for himself. In this interpretive view, Shakespeare's Richard fulfills a plan of which he is unaware, as in the chronicles of Edward Hall and others, even in the process of what he gloatingly regards as his own self-aggrandizement.

Providential plans are always complex, inscrutable to the minds of mortals, and understood least by those who unwittingly execute them. In attempting to prove his own contention that human nature is bestial and that a Machiavellian man of utter self-confidence can force his way to the top, flouting all conventions of morality, Richard succeeds in demonstrating the opposite. From the moment he takes the throne, he feels it insecure beneath him; opposition and betrayal spring up from every quarter, and, in his last moments, a mere horse is worth his whole kingdom. With sardonic comedy and poetic justice, Richard becomes the proverbial beguiler who is beguiled.

Even if this is not the only way to interpret Richard's character, the play does offer for our consideration a theory of divine causality in which virtually all of Richard's victims deserve their fate because they have offended God. Prophecies and dreams give structure to the sequence of retributive actions and keep grim score. As the choric Margaret observes, a Yorkist must pay for a Lancastrian, eye for an eye: Edward IV for Henry VI, young Edward V for Henry VI's son Edward. Thus, the Yorkist princes, though guiltless, die for their family's sins. The Yorkist Queen Elizabeth, like the Lancastrian Margaret, must outlive her husband into impotent old age, bewailing her children's cruel deaths. Clarence sees his death as punishment for breaking his oath at the battle of Tewkesbury and for his part in murdering Henry VI's son, Prince Edward. The Queen's kindred have been guilty of ambition, and Lord Hastings, in turn, is vulnerable because he has been willing to plot with Richard against the Queen's kindred. Margaret's curses serve both to warn the characters of their fates (a warning they blindly ignore) and to invite each person to curse himself or herself unwittingly but with ironic appropriateness. Lady Anne wishes unhappiness on any woman so insane as to marry Richard. Buckingham protests in a most sacred oath that whenever he turns again on the Queen's kindred, he will deserve to be punished by the treachery of his dearest friend (i.e., Richard). Dreams serve the same purpose of divine warning, giving Clarence a grotesque intimation of his death by drowning (in a butt of malmsey wine) and warning Hastings (through Stanley's dream) that the boar, Richard, will cut off his head. Thus, the English court punishes itself through Richard. He is the essence of the courtiers' factionalism, able to succeed as he does only because they forswear their most holy vows and conspire to destroy one another. They deserve to be outwitted at their own dismal game. Yet their falls are curative as well; Richard's victims acknowledge the justice of their undoings and penitently implore divine forgiveness. Richard contrastingly finds conscience a torment, rather than a voice of comfort and wisdom.

Richard III is not without its ironies and historical anxieties. Richard's own successful career of evil through much of the play demonstrates how rhetoric and theater can be used to dupe and to corrupt. The political process seems endlessly prone to cynical manipulation, and triumph comes chiefly to those who know how to use rhetoric to calculated effect. The Lord Mayor and his London associates are as pliable as the aristocracy. For all the belated assurances of providential meaning in Richard's rise to power and overthrow, we are allowed to speculate uncomfortably about the pragmatic action of history and its seeming ability to thrust forward into prominence an evil king or a good one, as individual temperament happens to dictate. Finally, there is the question of how Richard is supplanted. Whatever the reasons for Richard's baleful emergence, the process of his overthrow requires human agency and a rebellion against established (even if tyrannical) royal authority. To thoughtful observers in the sixteenth century, including Queen Elizabeth, any such rebellion, no matter how seemingly necessary, established a disturbing precedent and a threat to Tudor monarchical stability. If *Richard III* finds reassuring answers in the victory of Henry Tudor, Earl of Richmond, it does so in the face of pressing and troublesome circumstances.

The pattern of reciprocity and retaliation is much more than a way of demonstrating an ultimate divine purpose in human affairs; it is also a theatrically effective way of structuring a drama so as to make it coherent and entertaining. Shakespeare strikes us as above all a man of the theater, an artist and entertainer who senses masterfully what his audiences want. The shape of *Richard III*, as it moves through the anxieties of Richard's seemingly unstoppable rise to power to an eventual affirmation that brings closure not only to this play but to the entire four-play cycle of the three parts of *Henry VI* and *Richard III*, is immensely satisfying as theatrical experience. Modern audiences, with no ideological commitment to the propagandistic view that God chose Henry VII as the savior of England, can respond warmly to the play's artistic and theatrical depiction of coherence and pattern. That pattern allows us to enjoy Richard's villainies as theatrical performance while perceiving that those villainies are contained and disarmed by a larger structure.

Good eventually triumphs over evil in *Richard III*, if only because some Englishmen have the patience and common sense to endure a presumably deserved punishment and wait for deliverance. As in *3 Henry VI*, the common people have little to do with the action of the play. They are choric spokesmen and bystanders, virtuous in their attitude (except for the two suborned murderers of Clarence). In their plain folk wisdom, they see the folly and evil their betters ignore: "Oh, full of danger is the Duke of Gloucester,/And the Queen's sons and

brothers haught and proud" (2.3.28–9). And, although they accept Richard as ruler, they do so most reluctantly; Buckingham's first attempt to persuade the people to this course meets with apathy and silence. Their wisdom is to "leave it all to God" (line 46). In the fullness of time, this faith in goodness brings its just reward.

Richard III compresses historical time. It begins where *3 Henry VI* has left off, with the return of Edward IV to the throne in 1471, and ends with the defeat of Richard III, the last Yorkist king, at the battle of Bosworth (1485). Because of its close relation in subject to passages in *3 Henry VI* and its similar Senecan style, the play appears to have been written soon after its predecessors, sometime between 1591 and 1594. It greatly condenses events of fourteen years, particularly at the beginning, when King Henry VI's funeral rites (1471), Richard's courtship of Lady Anne (1472), Clarence's murder in the Tower (1478), and Edward's death (1483) are made to take place in rapid succession. Similarly, Buckingham's rebellion (1483), Richmond's thwarted sailing (1483), and his landing at Milford Haven (1485) are also compressed. Queen Margaret's role is a nonhistorical addition to the play, for the widowed Queen never left France after her ransom in 1475 by Louis XI.

Richard III is irresistible in performance. However much Richard reveals himself to be a conscienceless villain, his versatility as a performer and his taking us into his confidence invite a kind of complicity between actor and audience that is the stuff of dramatic excitement. These qualities are brilliantly on display in two film versions, that of Laurence Olivier in 1955 and that of Ian McKellen in 1995. The first shows Richard's protean skills in deception as he soliloquizes candidly to us as his confidants, then transforms himself into the devoted brother of George Clarence (John Gielgud) and then the heartstricken wooer of the Lady Anne (Claire Bloom), seemingly at the mercy of the lady he worships. Ian McKellen transfers the play to the era of an imagined English civil war in the 1930s in which the ruthless, Nazi-like Richard claws his way to the top. His thirst for mayhem is psychotic, but is not without its esthetic dimension as well; he murders with artistry and style, and savors the results by examining photographs of his dead victims. His teamwork with Buckingham (Jim Broadbent) in bamboozling the citizens of London is a thing of beauty. Closeups focus on McKellen's creased visage as he contemplates his next move. Al Pacino's *Looking for Richard* (1996) explores the play in rehearsal with an all-star cast including Winona Ryder, Kevin Spacey, Alec Baldwin, and Aidan Quinn. Many other great actors have excelled in the quintessentially theatrical role of Richard, including Marius Goring, Brian Bedford, Ian Holm, Antony Sher, Kevin Kline, and Simon Russell Beale.

The Tragedy of King Richard the Third

[*Dramatis Personae*

KING EDWARD THE FOURTH
QUEEN ELIZABETH, *wife of King Edward*
EDWARD, PRINCE OF WALES, ⎱ *sons of Edward and*
RICHARD, DUKE OF YORK, ⎰ *Elizabeth*
GEORGE, DUKE OF CLARENCE,
RICHARD, DUKE OF GLOUCESTER,⎱ *brothers of the King*
   later King Richard III
DUCHESS OF YORK, *mother of Edward IV,*
   Clarence, and Richard, Duke of Gloucester
LADY ANNE, *widow of Edward, Prince of Wales*
   (son of Henry VI); later wife of Richard, Duke of
   Gloucester
MARGARET, *widow of King Henry VI*
BOY, *son of Clarence (Edward Plantagenet, Earl of*
   Warwick)
GIRL, *daughter of Clarence (Margaret Plantagenet,*
   Countess of Salisbury)

ANTHONY WOODVILLE, EARL RIVERS, *brother of*
   Queen Elizabeth
MARQUESS OF DORSET,⎱ *sons of Queen*
LORD GREY, ⎰ *Elizabeth*
SIR THOMAS VAUGHAN, *executed with Rivers and*
   Grey

WILLIAM, LORD HASTINGS, *the Lord Chamberlain*
DUKE OF BUCKINGHAM, *Richard's supporter, later*
   in opposition
SIR WILLIAM CATESBY,
SIR RICHARD RATCLIFFE, ⎱ *Richard's supporters*
LORD LOVELL, ⎰ *and henchmen*
SIR JAMES TYRREL,
DUKE OF NORFOLK,⎱ *Richard's generals*
EARL OF SURREY, ⎰

HENRY, EARL OF RICHMOND, *later King Henry VII*

SCENE: *England.*]

LORD STANLEY, EARL OF DERBY,
EARL OF OXFORD,
SIR JAMES BLUNT, ⎱ *supporters of*
SIR WALTER HERBERT, ⎰ *Richmond*
SIR WILLIAM BRANDON,
CHRISTOPHER URSWICK, *a priest,*

CARDINAL BOURCHIER, *Archbishop of Canterbury*
ARCHBISHOP OF YORK (*Thomas Rotherham*)
BISHOP OF ELY (*John Morton*)
GHOSTS *of King Henry VI, Edward Prince of*
   Wales, and others murdered by Richard
   (Clarence, Rivers, Grey, Vaughan, Hastings, the
   two young princes, Anne, and Buckingham)
SIR ROBERT BRACKENBURY, *Lieutenant of the Tower*
TRESSEL,
BERKELEY, ⎱ *attending the*
HALBERDIER,⎰ *Lady Anne*
GENTLEMAN,
Two MURDERERS
KEEPER *in the Tower*
Three CITIZENS
MESSENGER *to Queen Elizabeth*
LORD MAYOR OF LONDON
MESSENGER *to Lord Hastings*
PURSUIVANT
PRIEST
SCRIVENER
Two BISHOPS
PAGE *to Richard III*
Four MESSENGERS *to Richard III*
SHERIFF OF WILTSHIRE

Lords, Attendants, Aldermen, Citizens, Councilors,
   Soldiers

1.1

Enter Richard, Duke of Gloucester, solus.

RICHARD
Now is the winter of our discontent
Made glorious summer by this son of York,   2
And all the clouds that loured upon our house   3
In the deep bosom of the ocean buried.
Now are our brows bound with victorious wreaths,   5
Our bruisèd arms hung up for monuments,   6
Our stern alarums changed to merry meetings,   7
Our dreadful marches to delightful measures.   8
Grim-visaged War hath smoothed his wrinkled
     front;   9
And now, instead of mounting barbèd steeds   10
To fright the souls of fearful adversaries,   11
He capers nimbly in a lady's chamber
To the lascivious pleasing of a lute.
But I, that am not shaped for sportive tricks,   14
Nor made to court an amorous looking glass;
I, that am rudely stamped, and want love's majesty   16
To strut before a wanton ambling nymph;   17
I, that am curtailed of this fair proportion,   18
Cheated of feature by dissembling Nature,   19
Deformed, unfinished, sent before my time
Into this breathing world scarce half made up,
And that so lamely and unfashionable   22
That dogs bark at me as I halt by them—   23
Why, I, in this weak piping time of peace,   24
Have no delight to pass away the time,
Unless to see my shadow in the sun
And descant on mine own deformity.   27
And therefore, since I cannot prove a lover
To entertain these fair well-spoken days,   29
I am determinèd to prove a villain
And hate the idle pleasures of these days.
Plots have I laid, inductions dangerous,   32
By drunken prophecies, libels, and dreams,
To set my brother Clarence and the King
In deadly hate the one against the other;
And if King Edward be as true and just

As I am subtle, false, and treacherous,
This day should Clarence closely be mewed up   38
About a prophecy, which says that G   39
Of Edward's heirs the murderer shall be.
Dive, thoughts, down to my soul; here Clarence
     comes.

     Enter Clarence, guarded, and Brackenbury,
     [Lieutenant of the Tower].

Brother, good day. What means this armèd guard
That waits upon Your Grace?
CLARENCE   His Majesty,   43
Tend'ring my person's safety, hath appointed   44
This conduct to convey me to the Tower.   45
RICHARD
Upon what cause?
CLARENCE   Because my name is George.
RICHARD
Alack, my lord, that fault is none of yours.
He should, for that, commit your godfathers.
Oh, belike His Majesty hath some intent   49
That you should be new christened in the Tower.   50
But what's the matter, Clarence, may I know?   51
CLARENCE
Yea, Richard, when I know; for I protest
As yet I do not. But, as I can learn,
He hearkens after prophecies and dreams,
And from the crossrow plucks the letter G,   55
And says a wizard told him that by G
His issue disinherited should be;   57
And, for my name of George begins with G,   58
It follows in his thought that I am he.
These, as I learn, and suchlike toys as these   60
Hath moved His Highness to commit me now.   61
RICHARD
Why, this it is when men are ruled by women.
'Tis not the King that sends you to the Tower;
My Lady Grey his wife, Clarence, 'tis she   64
That tempers him to this extremity.   65
Was it not she, and that good man of worship,   66
Anthony Woodville, her brother there,   67

1.1. Location: London. Near the Tower.
0.1 *solus* alone. **2 son** Edward IV was the son of Richard, Duke of York. (With a pun on "sun"; Edward IV used the sun on his badge.) **3 loured** looked threateningly **5 brows** foreheads **6 arms** armor. **monuments** trophies **7 alarums** calls to arms, or assaults **8 dreadful** formidable, awe-inspiring. **measures** stately dances. **9 wrinkled front** furrowed forehead **10 barbèd** armored **11 fearful** frightened **14 sportive** amorous **16 rudely stamped** roughly fashioned, coined. **want** lack **17 ambling** walking affectedly, i.e., wantonly **18 curtailed** cut short, denied. **proportion** shape **19 feature** shapeliness of body **22 unfashionable** badly fashioned **23 halt** limp **24 piping time** i.e., a time when the music heard is that of pipes and not fifes and drums **27 descant** compose variations, comment on **29 entertain** pass away pleasurably. **well-spoken** refined, elegant **32 inductions** preparations

38 mewed up confined (like a hawk) **39 prophecy...G** (The prophecy is mentioned in the chronicles; the quibble is that *G* stands for *Gloucester* and not for *George*, the given name of the Duke of Clarence.) **43 waits** attends **44 Tend'ring** having care for **45 conduct** escort **49 belike** probably **50 new christened** (Anticipates, ironically, Clarence's death by drowning in 1.4.) **51 matter** reason, cause **55 crossrow** Christ-crossrow, or alphabet (so called from the cross printed before the alphabet in the hornbook) **57 issue** offspring **58 for** because **60 toys** trifles **61 commit** arrest **64 My Lady Grey** (A disrespectful reference to the Queen, whose maiden name was Elizabeth Woodville and who, when the King married her, was the widow of Sir John Grey.) **65 tempers** governs, directs **66 worship** honor. (Said ironically.) **67 Woodville** i.e., Earl Rivers (whom Richard also disrespectfully refers to by his family name rather than by his recently acquired title)

That made him send Lord Hastings to the Tower,
From whence this present day he is delivered?
We are not safe, Clarence, we are not safe.

CLARENCE
By heaven, I think there is no man secure
But the Queen's kindred and night-walking heralds   72
That trudge betwixt the King and Mistress Shore.   73
Heard you not what an humble suppliant
Lord Hastings was to her for his delivery?   75

RICHARD
Humbly complaining to Her Deity   76
Got my Lord Chamberlain his liberty.   77
I'll tell you what: I think it is our way,   78
If we will keep in favor with the King,
To be her men and wear her livery.   80
The jealous, o'erworn widow and herself,   81
Since that our brother dubbed them gentlewomen,   82
Are mighty gossips in our monarchy.   83

BRACKENBURY
I beseech Your Graces both to pardon me:
His Majesty hath straitly given in charge   85
That no man shall have private conference,
Of what degree soever, with your brother.   87

RICHARD
Even so? An't please Your Worship, Brackenbury,   88
You may partake of anything we say.
We speak no treason, man. We say the King
Is wise and virtuous, and his noble queen
Well struck in years, fair, and not jealous.   92
We say that Shore's wife hath a pretty foot,
A cherry lip, a bonny eye, a passing pleasing tongue;   94
And that the Queen's kindred are made gentlefolks.
How say you, sir? Can you deny all this?

BRACKENBURY
With this, my lord, myself have naught to do.

RICHARD
Naught to do with Mistress Shore? I tell thee, fellow,   98
He that doth naught with her, excepting one,
Were best to do it secretly, alone.

BRACKENBURY   What one, my lord?

RICHARD
Her husband, knave. Wouldst thou betray me?   102

BRACKENBURY
I beseech Your Grace to pardon me, and withal   103
Forbear your conference with the noble Duke.

CLARENCE
We know thy charge, Brackenbury, and will obey.

RICHARD
We are the Queen's abjects, and must obey.   106
Brother, farewell. I will unto the King;
And whatsoe'er you will employ me in,
Were it to call King Edward's widow sister,   109
I will perform it to enfranchise you.   110
Meantime, this deep disgrace in brotherhood
Touches me deeper than you can imagine.   112

CLARENCE
I know it pleaseth neither of us well.

RICHARD
Well, your imprisonment shall not be long;
I will deliver you, or else lie for you.   115
Meantime, have patience.

CLARENCE   I must perforce. Farewell. 116
                Exit Clarence [with Brackenbury and guard].

RICHARD
Go tread the path that thou shalt ne'er return.
Simple, plain Clarence, I do love thee so
That I will shortly send thy soul to heaven,
If heaven will take the present at our hands.
But who comes here? The new-delivered Hastings?   121

                Enter Lord Hastings.

HASTINGS
Good time of day unto my gracious lord.

RICHARD
As much unto my good Lord Chamberlain.
Well are you welcome to the open air.
How hath Your Lordship brooked imprisonment?   125

HASTINGS
With patience, noble lord, as prisoners must.
But I shall live, my lord, to give them thanks   127
That were the cause of my imprisonment.

RICHARD
No doubt, no doubt; and so shall Clarence too,
For they that were your enemies are his,
And have prevailed as much on him as you.

HASTINGS
More pity that the eagles should be mewed,   132
Whiles kites and buzzards prey at liberty.   133

RICHARD   What news abroad?   134

HASTINGS
No news so bad abroad as this at home:

---

72 **night-walking heralds** i.e., secret messengers for an assignation
73 **Mistress Shore** Jane Shore, the King's mistress, and wife of a gold-
smith in Lombard Street. (The title *Mistress* is a respectful form of
address for any woman, married or unmarried.)   75 **her** i.e., Jane
Shore   76 **Her Deity** (A mock title for Jane Shore, suggesting she is
even more elevated than "Her Grace" or "Her Majesty.")   77 **Lord
Chamberlain** i.e., Lord Hastings   78 **our way** i.e., our only way (to
succeed)   80 **men** servants   81 **widow** i.e., Queen Elizabeth. (See the
note for line 64.)   **herself** i.e., Jane Shore   82 **Since that** since.   **gentlewomen** (A sneer at the Queen's family, which was gentle but not
noble until after her marriage with the King; Jane Shore was, of
course, neither gentle nor noble.)   83 **mighty gossips** i.e., influential
busybodies   85 **straitly . . . charge** strictly ordered   87 **degree** rank
88 **An't** If it   92 **Well struck** i.e., well along.   **not jealous** (Implies
there are things she might be jealous about.)   94 **passing** surpassingly   98 **Naught** (Richard quibbles on the meanings "nothing" and
"naughtiness," "the sexual act.")   102 **betray me** i.e., into naming
the King as a person who does "naught" with Mistress Shore.

103 **withal** furthermore   106 **abjects** abjectly servile subjects
109 **King Edward's widow** i.e., the widow whom Edward has made
queen   110 **enfranchise** release from imprisonment   112 **Touches . . .
imagine** (1) distresses me more than can be imagined (2) concerns me
(in my personal ambition) more than you could possibly guess.
115 **lie for you** (1) take your place in prison (2) tell lies about you.
116 **perforce** necessarily.   121 **new-delivered** recently released
125 **brooked** endured   127 **give them thanks** i.e., pay them back.
(Said ironically.)   132 **mewed** caged   133 **kites** scavengers of the
hawk family   134 **abroad** at large, circulating.

The King is sickly, weak, and melancholy,
And his physicians fear him mightily.   137

RICHARD
Now, by Saint John, that news is bad indeed!
Oh, he hath kept an evil diet long   139
And overmuch consumed his royal person.
'Tis very grievous to be thought upon.
Where is he, in his bed?

HASTINGS   He is.

RICHARD
Go you before, and I will follow you.   *Exit Hastings.*
He cannot live, I hope, and must not die
Till George be packed with post-horse up to heaven.   146
I'll in, to urge his hatred more to Clarence
With lies well steeled with weighty arguments;   148
And, if I fail not in my deep intent,
Clarence hath not another day to live.
Which done, God take King Edward to his mercy
And leave the world for me to bustle in!
For then I'll marry Warwick's youngest daughter.   153
What though I killed her husband and her father?   154
The readiest way to make the wench amends
Is to become her husband and her father,
The which will I; not all so much for love
As for another secret close intent   158
By marrying her which I must reach unto.
But yet I run before my horse to market.
Clarence still breathes, Edward still lives and reigns;
When they are gone, then must I count my gains.
                                               Exit.

❖

1.2

Enter the corpse of [King] Henry the Sixth, with
Halberds to guard it; Lady Anne being the
mourner [attended by Tressel and Berkeley].

ANNE
Set down, set down your honorable load—
If honor may be shrouded in a hearse—   2
Whilst I awhile obsequiously lament   3
Th'untimely fall of virtuous Lancaster.
                        [*The bearers set down the coffin.*]
Poor key-cold figure of a holy king,   5
Pale ashes of the house of Lancaster,
Thou bloodless remnant of that royal blood,
Be it lawful that I invocate thy ghost   8
To hear the lamentations of poor Anne,

Wife to thy Edward, to thy slaughtered son,
Stabbed by the selfsame hand that made these wounds!
Lo, in these windows that let forth thy life   12
I pour the helpless balm of my poor eyes.   13
Oh, cursèd be the hand that made these holes!
Cursèd the heart that had the heart to do it!
Cursèd the blood that let this blood from hence!
More direful hap betide that hated wretch   17
That makes us wretched by the death of thee
Than I can wish to wolves, to spiders, toads,
Or any creeping venomed thing that lives!
If ever he have child, abortive be it,   21
Prodigious, and untimely brought to light,   22
Whose ugly and unnatural aspect   23
May fright the hopeful mother at the view,
And that be heir to his unhappiness!   25
If ever he have wife, let her be made
More miserable by the life of him
Than I am made by my young lord and thee!—   28
Come now towards Chertsey with your holy load,   29
Taken from Paul's to be interrèd there.   30
                        [*The bearers take up the hearse.*]
And still as you are weary of this weight,   31
Rest you, whiles I lament King Henry's corpse.

Enter Richard, Duke of Gloucester.

RICHARD
Stay, you that bear the corpse, and set it down.

ANNE
What black magician conjures up this fiend
To stop devoted charitable deeds?   35

RICHARD
Villains, set down the corpse, or, by Saint Paul,
I'll make a corpse of him that disobeys.

HALBERDIER [*advancing with his halberd lowered*]
My lord, stand back, and let the coffin pass.

RICHARD
Unmannered dog, stand thou when I command!   39
Advance thy halberd higher than my breast,   40
Or, by Saint Paul, I'll strike thee to my foot
And spurn upon thee, beggar, for thy boldness.   42
                        [*The bearers set down the hearse.*]

ANNE
What do you tremble? Are you all afraid?   43
Alas, I blame you not, for you are mortal,
And mortal eyes cannot endure the devil.—
Avaunt, thou dreadful minister of hell!   46
Thou hadst but power over his mortal body;
His soul thou canst not have. Therefore, begone.

---

137 fear fear for   **139 diet** course of life, regimen   **146 with post-
horse** by post-horses, i.e., by swiftest possible means   **148 steeled**
reinforced   **153 Warwick's youngest daughter** the Lady Anne
Neville, widow of Edward, Prince of Wales, son of King Henry VI.
154 father i.e., father-in-law (Henry VI).   **158 intent** design (i.e.,
Richard hopes to ally himself with the house of Lancaster to bolster
his claim to the throne)
1.2. Location: London. A street.
0.2 *Halberds* halberdiers, guards with halberds, or long poleaxes
2 hearse (Probably here an open coffin on a bier.)   **3 obsequiously** as
befits a funeral, mournfully   **5 key-cold** extremely cold, cold as a
metal key. (Proverbial.)   **8 Be it** Let it be.   **invocate** invoke

12 windows i.e., wounds   **13 helpless** useless, unavailing
17 hap betide fortune befall   **21 abortive** misshapen, premature
22 Prodigious monstrous, unnatural   **23 aspect** appearance
25 unhappiness evil nature, bad luck.   **28 by . . . thee** i.e., by the
deaths of Prince Edward and King Henry VI.   **29 Chertsey**
monastery in Surrey, near London, where King Henry's body is to be
buried   **30 Paul's** Saint Paul's Cathedral in London   **31 still as** as
often as   **35 devoted** holy   **39 stand** halt   **40 Advance . . . breast**
Raise your halberd upright   **42 spurn** trample   **43 What** Why
46 Avaunt Begone

RICHARD
Sweet saint, for charity, be not so curst.   49

ANNE
Foul devil, for God's sake hence and trouble us not,   50
For thou hast made the happy earth thy hell,
Filled it with cursing cries and deep exclaims.   52
If thou delight to view thy heinous deeds,
Behold this pattern of thy butcheries.   54
[She uncovers the corpse.]
Oh, gentlemen, see, see dead Henry's wounds
Open their congealed mouths and bleed afresh!   56
Blush, blush, thou lump of foul deformity!
For 'tis thy presence that exhales this blood   58
From cold and empty veins where no blood dwells.
Thy deeds inhuman and unnatural
Provokes this deluge most unnatural.
O God, which this blood mad'st, revenge his death!
O earth, which this blood drink'st, revenge his death!
Either heav'n with lightning strike the murd'rer dead,
Or earth gape open wide and eat him quick,   65
As thou dost swallow up this good king's blood,
Which his hell-governed arm hath butcherèd!

RICHARD
Lady, you know no rules of charity,
Which renders good for bad, blessings for curses.

ANNE
Villain, thou know'st nor law of God nor man.   70
No beast so fierce but knows some touch of pity.   71

RICHARD
But I know none, and therefore am no beast.

ANNE
Oh, wonderful, when devils tell the truth!   73

RICHARD
More wonderful, when angels are so angry.
Vouchsafe, divine perfection of a woman,   75
Of these supposèd crimes to give me leave
By circumstance but to acquit myself.   77

ANNE
Vouchsafe, defused infection of a man,   78
Of these known evils but to give me leave
By circumstance t'accuse thy cursèd self.

RICHARD
Fairer than tongue can name thee, let me have
Some patient leisure to excuse myself.

ANNE
Fouler than heart can think thee, thou canst make
No excuse current but to hang thyself.   84

RICHARD
By such despair I should accuse myself.

ANNE
And by despairing shalt thou stand excused
For doing worthy vengeance on thyself
That didst unworthy slaughter upon others.

RICHARD   Say that I slew them not?

ANNE   Then say they were not slain.
But dead they are, and, devilish slave, by thee.

RICHARD   I did not kill your husband.

ANNE   Why, then he is alive.

RICHARD
Nay, he is dead, and slain by Edward's hand.

ANNE
In thy foul throat thou liest! Queen Margaret saw
Thy murd'rous falchion smoking in his blood,   96
The which thou once didst bend against her breast,   97
But that thy brothers beat aside the point.

RICHARD
I was provokèd by her sland'rous tongue,
That laid their guilt upon my guiltless shoulders.   100

ANNE
Thou wast provokèd by thy bloody mind,
That never dream'st on aught but butcheries.   102
Didst thou not kill this king?

RICHARD   I grant ye.

ANNE
Dost grant me, hedgehog? Then God grant me too   104
Thou mayst be damnèd for that wicked deed!
Oh, he was gentle, mild, and virtuous!

RICHARD
The better for the King of Heaven that hath him.

ANNE
He is in heaven, where thou shalt never come.

RICHARD
Let him thank me that holp to send him thither;   109
For he was fitter for that place than earth.

ANNE
And thou unfit for any place but hell.

RICHARD
Yes, one place else, if you will hear me name it.

ANNE   Some dungeon.

RICHARD   Your bedchamber.

ANNE
Ill rest betide the chamber where thou liest!   115

RICHARD
So will it, madam, till I lie with you.

ANNE
I hope so.

RICHARD   I know so. But, gentle Lady Anne,
To leave this keen encounter of our wits
And fall something into a slower method,   119
Is not the causer of the timeless deaths   120
Of these Plantagenets, Henry and Edward,
As blameful as the executioner?

---

49 **curst** spiteful, shrewish.   50 **hence** go hence, depart   52 **exclaims** exclamations.   54 **pattern** example   56 **bleed afresh** (A phenomenon popularly supposed to occur in the presence of the murderer.)   58 **exhales** draws out   65 **quick** alive   70 **nor . . . nor** neither . . . nor   71 **so fierce but knows** is so savage that it has not   73 **Oh . . . truth** (Anne bitterly reinterprets Richard's *am no beast*, "am not beastly," to mean that he is neither man nor beast, but devil.)   75 **Vouchsafe** Deign, consent   77 **circumstance** detailed argument   78 **defused** diffused, disordered, shapeless; *defused infection* means "spreading plague"   84 **current** genuine, acceptable (as in coinage)

96 **falchion** curved sword   97 **bend** direct, aim   100 **their** my brothers'   102 **aught** anything   104 **hedgehog** (Richard's heraldic emblem featured a boar or wild hog.)   109 **holp** helped   115 **betide** befall   119 **something into a** into a somewhat   120 **timeless** untimely

ANNE
Thou wast the cause and most accurst effect.   123

RICHARD
Your beauty was the cause of that effect—   124
Your beauty, that did haunt me in my sleep
To undertake the death of all the world,
So I might live one hour in your sweet bosom.

ANNE
If I thought that, I tell thee, homicide,   128
These nails should rend that beauty from my cheeks.   129

RICHARD
These eyes could not endure that beauty's wrack;   130
You should not blemish it, if I stood by.
As all the world is cheerèd by the sun,
So I by that. It is my day, my life.

ANNE
Black night o'ershade thy day, and death thy life!

RICHARD
Curse not thyself, fair creature—thou art both.

ANNE
I would I were, to be revenged on thee.   136

RICHARD
It is a quarrel most unnatural
To be revenged on him that loveth thee.

ANNE
It is a quarrel just and reasonable
To be revenged on him that killed my husband.

RICHARD
He that bereft thee, lady, of thy husband
Did it to help thee to a better husband.

ANNE
His better doth not breathe upon the earth.

RICHARD
He lives that loves thee better than he could.   144

ANNE
Name him.

RICHARD   Plantagenet.

ANNE   Why, that was he.   145

RICHARD
The selfsame name, but one of better nature.

ANNE
Where is he?

RICHARD   Here.   [*She*] *spits at him.*
Why dost thou spit at me?

ANNE
Would it were mortal poison for thy sake!

RICHARD
Never came poison from so sweet a place.

ANNE
Never hung poison on a fouler toad.   150

Out of my sight! Thou dost infect mine eyes.

RICHARD
Thine eyes, sweet lady, have infected mine.   152

ANNE
Would they were basilisks, to strike thee dead!   153

RICHARD
I would they were, that I might die at once;
For now they kill me with a living death.
Those eyes of thine from mine have drawn salt tears,
Shamed their aspects with store of childish drops;   157
These eyes, which never shed remorseful tear—
No, when my father York and Edward wept
To hear the piteous moan that Rutland made   160
When black-faced Clifford shook his sword at him;   161
Nor when thy warlike father, like a child,   162
Told the sad story of my father's death
And twenty times made pause to sob and weep,
That all the standers-by had wet their cheeks   165
Like trees bedashed with rain—in that sad time
My manly eyes did scorn an humble tear;
And what these sorrows could not thence exhale,   168
Thy beauty hath, and made them blind with weeping.
I never sued to friend nor enemy;   170
My tongue could never learn sweet smoothing words;   171
But now thy beauty is proposed my fee,   172
My proud heart sues and prompts my tongue to speak.
                    She looks scornfully at him.
Teach not thy lip such scorn, for it was made
For kissing, lady, not for such contempt.
If thy revengeful heart cannot forgive,
Lo, here I lend thee this sharp-pointed sword,
Which if thou please to hide in this true breast
And let the soul forth that adoreth thee,
I lay it naked to the deadly stroke
And humbly beg the death upon my knee.   181
        He [*kneels and*] *lays his breast open; she offers at* [*it*]
                                        with his sword.
Nay, do not pause; for I did kill King Henry—
But 'twas thy beauty that provokèd me.
Nay, now dispatch; 'twas I that stabbed young Edward—
But 'twas thy heavenly face that set me on.   185
                    She falls the sword.
Take up the sword again, or take up me.

ANNE
Arise, dissembler. Though I wish thy death,
I will not be thy executioner.

RICHARD [*rising*]
Then bid me kill myself, and I will do it.

---

123 effect fulfillment.   **124 effect** result   **128 homicide** murderer
129 rend tear   **130 wrack** destruction   **136 I would I were** (If Anne
were truly both Richard's day and his life, she could terminate both.)
144 He lives i.e., There is a man.   **he** i.e., Prince Edward   **145 Plantagenet** (Richard's father, the Duke of York, adopted this name when
he made his claim to the English throne—see *1 Henry VI*, 2.4.36—but
the name had been in the family of England's Angevin rulers since
the time of Henry II and thus could also be claimed by Henry VI and
his son, Prince Edward.)   **150 poison . . . toad** (Toads were popularly
regarded as poisonous.)

152 infected i.e., with love (since love was thought to enter through
the eyes)   **153 basilisks** mythical reptiles reputed to kill by their
looks   **157 aspects** appearance   **160 Rutland** second son of Richard,
Duke of York. (See *3 Henry VI*, 1.3, for his death scene.)   **161 black-
faced** i.e., foreboding in appearance   **162 thy warlike father** i.e., the
Earl of Warwick   **165 That** so that   **168 exhale** draw out   **170 sued**
supplicated, appealed   **171 smoothing** flattering   **172 now** now
that.   **proposed my fee** proposed as my reward   **181 the death**
death after sentencing   **181.1 offers** aims   **185.1 falls** lets fall

ANNE
I have already.

RICHARD   That was in thy rage.
Speak it again, and even with the word
This hand, which for thy love did kill thy love,
Shall for thy love kill a far truer love.
To both their deaths shalt thou be accessory.

ANNE   I would I knew thy heart.   195

RICHARD   'Tis figured in my tongue.   196

ANNE   I fear me both are false.

RICHARD   Then never man was true.

ANNE   Well, well, put up your sword.

RICHARD   Say, then, my peace is made.

ANNE   That shalt thou know hereafter.

RICHARD   But shall I live in hope?

ANNE   All men, I hope, live so.

RICHARD   Vouchsafe to wear this ring.   204

ANNE   To take is not to give.   205

[He slips the ring on her finger.]

RICHARD
Look how my ring encompasseth thy finger,   206
Even so thy breast encloseth my poor heart;
Wear both of them, for both of them are thine.
And if thy poor devoted servant may   209
But beg one favor at thy gracious hand,
Thou dost confirm his happiness forever.

ANNE   What is it?

RICHARD
That it may please you leave these sad designs
To him that hath most cause to be a mourner,
And presently repair to Crosby House,   215
Where, after I have solemnly interred
At Chertsey monast'ry this noble king
And wet his grave with my repentant tears,
I will with all expedient duty see you.   219
For divers unknown reasons, I beseech you, 220
Grant me this boon.

ANNE
With all my heart, and much it joys me, too,
To see you are become so penitent.—
Tressel and Berkeley, go along with me.

RICHARD
Bid me farewell.

ANNE   'Tis more than you deserve;
But since you teach me how to flatter you,
Imagine I have said farewell already.
Exeunt two [Tressel and Berkeley] with Anne.

RICHARD
Sirs, take up the corpse.

GENTLEMAN   Towards Chertsey, noble lord?

RICHARD
No, to Whitefriars. There attend my coming.   229
Exeunt [bearers with] corpse.

Was ever woman in this humor wooed?
Was ever woman in this humor won?
I'll have her, but I will not keep her long.
What? I, that killed her husband and his father,
To take her in her heart's extremest hate,
With curses in her mouth, tears in her eyes,
The bleeding witness of my hatred by,
Having God, her conscience, and these bars against me, 237
And I no friends to back my suit withal
But the plain devil and dissembling looks?
And yet to win her! All the world to nothing! 240
Ha!
Hath she forgot already that brave prince,
Edward, her lord, whom I, some three months since,
Stabbed in my angry mood at Tewkesbury?
A sweeter and a lovelier gentleman,
Framed in the prodigality of nature,   246
Young, valiant, wise, and, no doubt, right royal,
The spacious world cannot again afford.   248
And will she yet abase her eyes on me,   249
That cropped the golden prime of this sweet prince 250
And made her widow to a woeful bed?
On me, whose all not equals Edward's moiety? 252
On me, that halts and am misshapen thus?   253
My dukedom to a beggarly denier,   254
I do mistake my person all this while.
Upon my life, she finds, although I cannot,
Myself to be a marv'lous proper man.   257
I'll be at charges for a looking glass,   258
And entertain a score or two of tailors   259
To study fashions to adorn my body.
Since I am crept in favor with myself,
I will maintain it with some little cost.
But first I'll turn yon fellow in his grave,   263
And then return lamenting to my love.
Shine out, fair sun, till I have bought a glass, 265
That I may see my shadow as I pass.   *Exit.*

❖

1.3

Enter the Queen Mother [Elizabeth], Lord Rivers,
[Marquess of Dorset,] and Lord Grey.

RIVERS
Have patience, madam. There's no doubt His Majesty
Will soon recover his accustomed health.

GREY
In that you brook it ill, it makes him worse.   3
Therefore, for God's sake, entertain good comfort, 4
And cheer His Grace with quick and merry eyes.

---

195 **would** wish   196 **figured** portrayed   204 **Vouchsafe** Consent
205 **To take . . . give** i.e., I accept the ring but I make no promises.
206 **Look how** Just as   209 **servant** i.e., male admirer, one whom she
may command   215 **presently repair** go right away.   **Crosby House**
(One of Richard's London dwellings; built originally by Sir John Crosby.)
219 **expedient** expeditious   220 **unknown** secret   229 **Whitefriars**
the Carmelite priory in London.   **attend** await

237 **bars** obstacles   240 **All . . . nothing** i.e., Against infinite odds.
246 **Framed . . . nature** i.e., formed in nature's most lavish mood
248 **afford** (because Nature was so lavish).   249 **abase her eyes** degrade
herself by looking favorably   250 **cropped** cut short.   **prime** springtime, early manhood   252 **Edward's moiety** half of Edward's worth.
253 **halts** limps   254 **denier** small copper coin, the twelfth part of a sou
257 **proper** handsome   258 **be . . . for** undertake the expense of
259 **entertain** retain, employ   263 **in** into   265 **glass** mirror
1.3. Location: London. The royal court.
3 **brook** endure   4 **entertain . . . comfort** cheer up

QUEEN ELIZABETH

    If he were dead, what would betide on me?   6

GREY

    No other harm but loss of such a lord.

QUEEN ELIZABETH

    The loss of such a lord includes all harms.

GREY

    The heavens have blessed you with a goodly son

    To be your comforter when he is gone.

QUEEN ELIZABETH

    Ah, he is young, and his minority

    Is put unto the trust of Richard Gloucester,

    A man that loves not me, nor none of you.

RIVERS

    Is it concluded he shall be Protector?

QUEEN ELIZABETH

    It is determined, not concluded yet;   15

    But so it must be, if the King miscarry.   16

Enter Buckingham and [Lord Stanley Earl of] Derby.

GREY

    Here come the lords of Buckingham and Derby.

BUCKINGHAM

    Good time of day unto Your Royal Grace!

STANLEY

    God make Your Majesty joyful, as you have been!

QUEEN ELIZABETH

    The Countess Richmond, good my lord of Derby,   20

    To your good prayer will scarcely say amen.

    Yet, Derby, notwithstanding she's your wife

    And loves not me, be you, good lord, assured

    I hate not you for her proud arrogance.   24

STANLEY

    I do beseech you, either not believe

    The envious slanders of her false accusers,   26

    Or, if she be accused on true report,

    Bear with her weakness, which I think proceeds

    From wayward sickness and no grounded malice.   29

QUEEN ELIZABETH

    Saw you the King today, my lord of Derby?

STANLEY

    But now the Duke of Buckingham and I   31

    Are come from visiting His Majesty.

QUEEN ELIZABETH

    What likelihood of his amendment, lords?   33

BUCKINGHAM

    Madam, good hope; His Grace speaks cheerfully.

QUEEN ELIZABETH

    God grant him health! Did you confer with him?

BUCKINGHAM

    Ay, madam. He desires to make atonement   36

    Between the Duke of Gloucester and your brothers,   37

    And between them and my Lord Chamberlain,   38

    And sent to warn them to his royal presence.   39

QUEEN ELIZABETH

    Would all were well! But that will never be.

    I fear our happiness is at the height.

Enter Richard [Duke of Gloucester, and Lord Hastings].

RICHARD

    They do me wrong, and I will not endure it!

    Who is it that complains unto the King

    That I, forsooth, am stern and love them not?

    By holy Paul, they love His Grace but lightly

    That fill his ears with such dissentious rumors.   46

    Because I cannot flatter and look fair,   47

    Smile in men's faces, smooth, deceive, and cog,   48

    Duck with French nods and apish courtesy,   49

    I must be held a rancorous enemy.

    Cannot a plain man live and think no harm,

    But thus his simple truth must be abused

    With silken, sly, insinuating Jacks?   53

GREY

    To whom in all this presence speaks Your Grace?   54

RICHARD

    To thee, that hast nor honesty nor grace.   55

    When have I injured thee? When done thee wrong?

    Or thee? Or thee? Or any of your faction?

    A plague upon you all! His Royal Grace—

    Whom God preserve better than you would wish!—

    Cannot be quiet scarce a breathing while   60

    But you must trouble him with lewd complaints.   61

QUEEN ELIZABETH

    Brother of Gloucester, you mistake the matter.

    The King, on his own royal disposition,   63

    And not provoked by any suitor else,

    Aiming, belike, at your interior hatred,   65

    That in your outward action shows itself

    Against my children, brothers, and myself,

    Makes him to send, that he may learn the ground   68

    Of your ill will, and thereby to remove it.

RICHARD

    I cannot tell. The world is grown so bad   70

    That wrens make prey where eagles dare not perch.

---

36 atonement reconciliation   **37 brothers** (Only one brother, Earl Rivers, is mentioned in the play, though historically Elizabeth had others; Shakespeare may be thinking of other kinsmen, including her sons, whom she helped to advance.)   **38 Lord Chamberlain** Hastings **39 warn** summon   **46 dissentious** quarrelsome, discordant   **47 look fair** put on a pleasing appearance   **48 smooth** flatter. **cog** deceive **49 Duck . . . nods** i.e., bow affectedly   **53 With silken** by smooth. **Jacks** lowbred persons.   **54 presence** company   **55 grace** sense of duty or propriety. (Playing upon *Your Grace* in the preceding line.) **60 breathing while** i.e., brief time   **61 lewd** vile, base   **63 disposition** inclination   **65 Aiming** guessing. **belike** probably   **68 Makes him** causes him. (The implied subject is "The King's own disposition.")   **ground** cause   **70 I cannot tell** i.e., I don't know what to think. (Richard plays the role of the exasperated moralist.)

---

6 betide on become of   **15 determined, not concluded** i.e., decided though not officially passed   **16 miscarry** perish.   **20 The Countess Richmond** i.e., Margaret Beaufort (1443–1509), who married, successively, Edmund Tudor (Earl of Richmond), Lord Henry Stafford, and Thomas Lord Stanley (here called the Earl of Derby), to whom she is currently married. By the Earl of Richmond, she was mother of the future Henry VII.   **24 arrogance** i.e., ambition for her son. **26 envious** malicious   **29 wayward** not yielding readily to treatment. **grounded** firmly fixed   **31 But now** Just now   **33 amendment** recovery

Since every Jack became a gentleman,
There's many a gentle person made a Jack.

QUEEN ELIZABETH
Come, come, we know your meaning, brother Gloucester;
You envy my advancement and my friends'. 75
God grant we never may have need of you!

RICHARD
Meantime, God grants that I have need of you.
Our brother is imprisoned by your means, 78
Myself disgraced, and the nobility
Held in contempt, while great promotions
Are daily given to ennoble those
That scarce some two days since were worth a noble. 82

QUEEN ELIZABETH
By Him that raised me to this careful height 83
From that contented hap which I enjoyed, 84
I never did incense His Majesty
Against the Duke of Clarence, but have been
An earnest advocate to plead for him.
My lord, you do me shameful injury
Falsely to draw me in these vile suspects. 89

RICHARD
You may deny that you were not the mean 90
Of my Lord Hastings' late imprisonment.

RIVERS   She may, my lord, for—

RICHARD
She may, Lord Rivers! Why, who knows not so?
She may do more, sir, than denying that:
She may help you to many fair preferments, 95
And then deny her aiding hand therein,
And lay those honors on your high desert. 97
What may she not? She may, ay, marry, may she— 98

RIVERS   What, marry, may she?

RICHARD
What, marry, may she? Marry with a king, 100
A bachelor, and a handsome stripling too! 101
Iwis your grandam had a worser match. 102

QUEEN ELIZABETH
My lord of Gloucester, I have too long borne
Your blunt upbraidings and your bitter scoffs.
By heaven, I will acquaint His Majesty
Of those gross taunts that oft I have endured.
I had rather be a country servant maid
Than a great queen with this condition,
To be so baited, scorned, and stormèd at. 109

Enter old Queen Margaret [behind].

Small joy have I in being England's queen.

QUEEN MARGARET [*aside*]
And lessened be that small, God I beseech him!
Thy honor, state, and seat is due to me. 112

RICHARD
What? Threat you me with telling of the King? 113
Tell him, and spare not. Look what I have said 114
I will avouch 't in presence of the King.
I dare adventure to be sent to the Tower. 116
'Tis time to speak; my pains are quite forgot. 117

QUEEN MARGARET [*aside*]
Out, devil! I do remember them too well: 118
Thou killed'st my husband Henry in the Tower,
And Edward, my poor son, at Tewkesbury.

RICHARD
Ere you were queen, ay, or your husband king,
I was a packhorse in his great affairs, 122
A weeder-out of his proud adversaries,
A liberal rewarder of his friends.
To royalize his blood I spent mine own.

QUEEN MARGARET [*aside*]
Ay, and much better blood than his or thine.

RICHARD
In all which time you and your husband Grey
Were factious for the house of Lancaster; 128
And, Rivers, so were you. Was not your husband 129
In Margaret's battle at Saint Albans slain?
Let me put in your minds, if you forget,
What you have been ere this, and what you are;
Withal, what I have been, and what I am. 133

QUEEN MARGARET [*aside*]
A murd'rous villain, and so still thou art.

RICHARD
Poor Clarence did forsake his father, Warwick, 135
Ay, and forswore himself—which Jesu pardon!—

QUEEN MARGARET [*aside*]   Which God revenge!

RICHARD
To fight on Edward's party for the crown;
And for his meed, poor lord, he is mewed up. 139
I would to God my heart were flint, like Edward's,
Or Edward's soft and pitiful, like mine.
I am too childish-foolish for this world.

QUEEN MARGARET [*aside*]
Hie thee to hell for shame, and leave this world, 143
Thou cacodemon! There thy kingdom is. 144

RIVERS
My lord of Gloucester, in those busy days
Which here you urge to prove us enemies, 146

---

75 friends' i.e., kinsmen's.   **78 Our brother** i.e., Clarence   **82 noble** (1) gold coin worth six shillings eight pence (2) nobleman.   **83 careful** full of cares   **84 hap** fortune   **89 in** into.   **suspects** suspicions.   **90 mean** means   **95 preferments** advantages, promotions   **97 lay . . . desert** attribute these high honors to your rich deservings.   **98 marry** i.e., indeed. (A mild oath, literally, "by the Virgin Mary.")   **100 Marry with** Wed. (Punning on *marry,* indeed, in line 98.)   **101 stripling** young man   **102 Iwis** (1) Certainly (2) *I wis,* I know   **109 baited** harassed, as in bearbaiting   **109.1 Queen Margaret** (Historically, the widow of Henry VI was held prisoner in England for five years following the battle of Tewkesbury in 1471 and then was sent to France; see the note to line 167 below.)

112 state degree, high rank.   **seat** throne   **113 Threat** Threaten   **114 Look what** Whatever   **116 adventure to be** risk being   **117 pains** efforts (in King Edward's behalf)   **118 Out** (An exclamation of anger.)   **122 packhorse** workhorse, beast of burden   **128 Were factious for** fought factiously on the side of   **129 husband** (Queen Elizabeth's first husband, Sir John Grey, fell fighting on the Lancastrian side at Saint Albans.)   **133 Withal** in addition   **135 father** i.e., father-in-law. (See *3 Henry VI,* 4.1, when Clarence deserted his brothers to marry Warwick's daughter Isabella and supported the Lancastrian cause for a time; thereafter, he forswore his oath to Warwick by returning to fight on Edward's *party* [line 138] or side.)   **139 meed** reward. **mewed** caged (like a hawk)   **143 Hie** Hasten   **144 cacodemon** evil spirit.   **146 urge** cite

We followed then our lord, our sovereign king.
So should we you, if you should be our king.

RICHARD
If I should be? I had rather be a peddler.
Far be it from my heart, the thought thereof!

QUEEN ELIZABETH
As little joy, my lord, as you suppose
You should enjoy were you this country's king,
As little joy you may suppose in me
That I enjoy, being the queen thereof.

QUEEN MARGARET [aside]
Ah, little joy enjoys the queen thereof,
For I am she, and altogether joyless.
I can no longer hold me patient.   [Advancing.]
Hear me, you wrangling pirates, that fall out
In sharing that which you have pilled from me!   159
Which of you trembles not that looks on me?
If not, that I am queen, you bow like subjects,   161
Yet that, by you deposed, you quake like rebels?   162
[To Richard] Ah, gentle villain, do not turn away!   163

RICHARD
Foul wrinkled witch, what mak'st thou in my sight?   164

QUEEN MARGARET
But repetition of what thou hast marred;   165
That will I make before I let thee go.   166

RICHARD
Wert thou not banishèd on pain of death?   167

QUEEN MARGARET
I was; but I do find more pain in banishment
Than death can yield me here by my abode.
A husband and a son thou ow'st to me,   170
And thou a kingdom; all of you allegiance.   171
This sorrow that I have by right is yours,
And all the pleasures you usurp are mine.

RICHARD
The curse my noble father laid on thee   174
When thou didst crown his warlike brows with paper
And with thy scorns drew'st rivers from his eyes,
And then, to dry them, gav'st the Duke a clout   177
Steeped in the faultless blood of pretty Rutland—   178
His curses then, from bitterness of soul
Denounced against thee, are all fall'n upon thee;   180
And God, not we, hath plagued thy bloody deed.

QUEEN ELIZABETH
So just is God, to right the innocent.

HASTINGS
Oh, 'twas the foulest deed to slay that babe,   183
And the most merciless, that e'er was heard of!

RIVERS
Tyrants themselves wept when it was reported.   185

DORSET
No man but prophesied revenge for it.   186

BUCKINGHAM
Northumberland, then present, wept to see it.

QUEEN MARGARET
What? Were you snarling all before I came,
Ready to catch each other by the throat,
And turn you all your hatred now on me?
Did York's dread curse prevail so much with heaven
That Henry's death, my lovely Edward's death,
Their kingdom's loss, my woeful banishment,
Should all but answer for that peevish brat?   194
Can curses pierce the clouds and enter heaven?
Why, then, give way, dull clouds, to my quick curses!   196
Though not by war, by surfeit die your king,   197
As ours by murder, to make him a king!
Edward thy son, that now is Prince of Wales,
For Edward our son, that was Prince of Wales,
Die in his youth by like untimely violence!
Thyself a queen, for me that was a queen,
Outlive thy glory, like my wretched self!
Long mayst thou live to wail thy children's death
And see another, as I see thee now,
Decked in thy rights, as thou art stalled in mine!   206
Long die thy happy days before thy death,
And, after many lengthened hours of grief,
Die neither mother, wife, nor England's queen!
Rivers and Dorset, you were standers-by,   210
And so wast thou, Lord Hastings, when my son   211
Was stabbed with bloody daggers: God, I pray him,
That none of you may live his natural age,   213
But by some unlooked accident cut off!   214

RICHARD
Have done thy charm, thou hateful withered hag!   215

QUEEN MARGARET
And leave out thee? Stay, dog, for thou shalt hear me.
If heaven have any grievous plague in store
Exceeding those that I can wish upon thee,
Oh, let them keep it till thy sins be ripe,   219
And then hurl down their indignation
On thee, the troubler of the poor world's peace!
The worm of conscience still begnaw thy soul!   222
Thy friends suspect for traitors while thou liv'st,
And take deep traitors for thy dearest friends!
No sleep close up that deadly eye of thine,
Unless it be while some tormenting dream
Affrights thee with a hell of ugly devils!
Thou elvish-marked, abortive, rooting hog,   228

---

159 pilled pillaged, robbed   **161–2 If . . . rebels** i.e., Even if you do not bow low to me as your queen, you quake as rebels who have deposed me.   **163 gentle** nobly born. *Gentle villain* is an oxymoron, since *villain* can mean "one ignobly born."   **164 mak'st thou** are you doing   **165 But . . . marred** Only reciting your crimes   **166 That** that repetition or recital   **167 banishèd** (Margaret was banished in 1464, returned to England in 1471, and after the Battle of Tewkesbury was confined in the Tower until 1476, when she returned to France, dying there in 1482, one year before the historical time of this scene.)
170 thou i.e., Richard   **171 thou** i.e., Elizabeth   **174 The curse** (See *3 Henry VI*, 1.4.164–6.)   **177 clout** cloth, handkerchief   **178 faultless** innocent   **180 Denounced** proclaimed vengefully   **183 that babe** i.e., Rutland (who historically was an older brother of Richard)

185 Tyrants Even pitiless men   **186 No . . . prophesied** There was no one who did not prophesy   **194 but answer for** merely atone for, equal.   **peevish** silly, senseless   **196 quick** lively, piercing
197 surfeit dissipated living   **206 Decked** dressed.   **stalled** installed
210–11 Rivers, Dorset, Hastings (Not present in Shakespeare's dramatization of the event in *3 Henry VI*, 5.5, but named in the chronicles as having been present.)   **213 natural age** full course of life
214 unlooked unexpected   **215 charm** magic curse, pronounced by a witch   **219 them** i.e., the heavens, heaven   **222 still begnaw** continually gnaw   **228 elvish-marked** marked by elves at birth.   **hog** (Alludes to Richard's badge, the wild boar.)

Thou that wast sealed in thy nativity   229
The slave of nature and the son of hell!   230
Thou slander of thy heavy mother's womb,   231
Thou loathèd issue of thy father's loins,
Thou rag of honor, thou detested—   233

RICHARD
Margaret.

QUEEN MARGARET   Richard!

RICHARD   Ha?

QUEEN MARGARET   I call thee not.

RICHARD
I cry thee mercy then, for I did think   235
That thou hadst called me all these bitter names.

QUEEN MARGARET
Why, so I did, but looked for no reply.
Oh, let me make the period to my curse!   238

RICHARD
'Tis done by me, and ends in "Margaret."

QUEEN ELIZABETH [to Queen Margaret]
Thus have you breathed your curse against yourself.

QUEEN MARGARET
Poor painted queen, vain flourish of my fortune!   241
Why strew'st thou sugar on that bottled spider,   242
Whose deadly web ensnareth thee about?
Fool, fool, thou whet'st a knife to kill thyself.
The day will come that thou shalt wish for me
To help thee curse this poisonous bunch-backed toad.   246

HASTINGS
False-boding woman, end thy frantic curse,   247
Lest to thy harm thou move our patience.

QUEEN MARGARET
Foul shame upon you! You have all moved mine.

RIVERS
Were you well served, you would be taught your duty.   250

QUEEN MARGARET
To serve me well, you all should do me duty,   251
Teach me to be your queen, and you my subjects.   252
Oh, serve me well, and teach yourselves that duty!

DORSET
Dispute not with her. She is lunatic.

QUEEN MARGARET
Peace, Master Marquess, you are malapert.   255
Your fire-new stamp of honor is scarce current.   256
Oh, that your young nobility could judge
What 'twere to lose it and be miserable!
They that stand high have many blasts to shake them,   259
And if they fall, they dash themselves to pieces.

RICHARD
Good counsel, marry! Learn it, learn it, Marquess.

DORSET
It touches you, my lord, as much as me.

RICHARD
Ay, and much more; but I was born so high.   263
Our aerie buildeth in the cedar's top,   264
And dallies with the wind and scorns the sun.

QUEEN MARGARET
And turns the sun to shade; alas, alas!   266
Witness my son, now in the shade of death,
Whose bright outshining beams thy cloudy wrath
Hath in eternal darkness folded up.
Your aerie buildeth in our aerie's nest.
O God, that see'st it, do not suffer it!
As it is won with blood, lost be it so!

BUCKINGHAM
Peace, peace, for shame, if not for charity!

QUEEN MARGARET
Urge neither charity nor shame to me.
                                      [Turning to the others.]
Uncharitably with me have you dealt,
And shamefully my hopes by you are butchered.
My charity is outrage, life my shame,   277
And in that shame still live my sorrow's rage!

BUCKINGHAM   Have done, have done.

QUEEN MARGARET
O princely Buckingham, I'll kiss thy hand
In sign of league and amity with thee.
Now fair befall thee and thy noble house!   282
Thy garments are not spotted with our blood,
Nor thou within the compass of my curse.   284

BUCKINGHAM
Nor no one here; for curses never pass   285
The lips of those that breathe them in the air.

QUEEN MARGARET
I will not think but they ascend the sky   287
And there awake God's gentle-sleeping peace.
O Buckingham, take heed of yonder dog!
Look when he fawns, he bites; and when he bites,   290
His venom tooth will rankle to the death.   291
Have not to do with him, beware of him;
Sin, death, and hell have set their marks on him,
And all their ministers attend on him.

RICHARD
What doth she say, my lord of Buckingham?

BUCKINGHAM
Nothing that I respect, my gracious lord.   296

QUEEN MARGARET
What, dost thou scorn me for my gentle counsel?

---

229 **sealed** stamped   230 **slave of nature** i.e., wretch made by the malignancy of nature (as seen in his deformity)   231 **heavy** (1) sorrowful (2) weighted down in pregnancy   233 **rag** tattered remnant   235 **cry thee mercy** beg your pardon. (Said sarcastically.)   238 **period** conclusion   241 **painted** counterfeit.   **vain . . . fortune** i.e., mere ornament of a position that is mine by right.   242 **bottled** bottle-shaped, swollen   246 **bunch-backed** hunch-backed   247 **False-boding** Falsely prophesying   250 **well served** treated as you deserve. (But Margaret turns the phrase around to mean "served as befitting one of royal rank.")   251 **duty** reverence   252 **Teach me** i.e., show by your obedience what is my role   255 **Master** (A title for a boy of good family, used insultingly here.)   **malapert** impudent.   256 **fire-new** newly coined.   **current** genuine as legal tender.   259 **blasts** strong gusts of wind

263 **born so high** i.e., born noble—unlike you.   264 **aerie** eagle's brood   266 **sun** (With a play on *son* in the next line.)   277 **My . . . shame** i.e., Instead of charity I receive outrage, and the only life given me is one of shame; or, outrage is all the charity I feel, and shame is my only life   282 **fair befall** good luck to   284 **compass** scope, boundary   285 **pass** get any further than   287 **I . . . but** I must believe that   290 **Look when** (1) Whenever (2) Expect that when   291 **venom** envenomed.   **rankle** cause a festering wound   296 **respect** heed

And soothe the devil that I warn thee from? 298
Oh, but remember this another day,
When he shall split thy very heart with sorrow,
And say poor Margaret was a prophetess!
Live each of you the subjects to his hate, 302
And he to yours, and all of you to God's! *Exit.*

BUCKINGHAM
My hair doth stand on end to hear her curses.

RIVERS
And so doth mine. I muse why she's at liberty. 305

RICHARD
I cannot blame her. By God's holy mother,
She hath had too much wrong, and I repent
My part thereof that I have done to her.

QUEEN ELIZABETH
I never did her any, to my knowledge.

RICHARD
Yet you have all the vantage of her wrong. 310
I was too hot to do somebody good 311
That is too cold in thinking of it now. 312
Marry, as for Clarence, he is well repaid;
He is franked up to fatting for his pains— 314
God pardon them that are the cause thereof!

RIVERS
A virtuous and a Christian-like conclusion,
To pray for them that have done scathe to us. 317

RICHARD
So do I ever—(*speaks to himself*) being well advised. 318
For had I cursed now, I had cursed myself.

Enter Catesby.

CATESBY
Madam, His Majesty doth call for you,
And for Your Grace, and yours, my gracious lord.

QUEEN ELIZABETH
Catesby, I come.—Lords, will you go with me?

RIVERS
We wait upon Your Grace. 323
  Exeunt all but [Richard Duke of] Gloucester.

RICHARD
I do the wrong, and first begin to brawl.
The secret mischiefs that I set abroach 325
I lay unto the grievous charge of others. 326
Clarence, who I indeed have cast in darkness,
I do beweep to many simple gulls— 328
Namely, to Derby, Hastings, Buckingham—
And tell them 'tis the Queen and her allies
That stir the King against the Duke my brother.
Now they believe it, and withal whet me 332
To be revenged on Rivers, Dorset, Grey.
But then I sigh and, with a piece of Scripture,

Tell them that God bids us do good for evil. 335
And thus I clothe my naked villainy
With odd old ends stol'n forth of Holy Writ, 337
And seem a saint when most I play the devil.

Enter two Murderers.

But soft! Here come my executioners.— 339
How now, my hardy, stout, resolvèd mates, 340
Are you now going to dispatch this thing?

FIRST MURDERER
We are, my lord, and come to have the warrant
That we may be admitted where he is.

RICHARD
Well thought upon. I have it here about me.
  [*He gives the warrant.*]
When you have done, repair to Crosby Place. 345
But sirs, be sudden in the execution,
Withal obdurate; do not hear him plead; 347
For Clarence is well-spoken, and perhaps
May move your hearts to pity if you mark him. 349

FIRST MURDERER
Tut, tut, my lord, we will not stand to prate; 350
Talkers are no good doers. Be assured
We go to use our hands and not our tongues.

RICHARD
Your eyes drop millstones when fools' eyes fall tears. 353
I like you, lads. About your business straight.
Go, go, dispatch.

FIRST MURDERER We will, my noble lord. [*Exeunt.*]

❖

1.4

Enter Clarence and Keeper.

KEEPER
Why looks Your Grace so heavily today? 1

CLARENCE
Oh, I have passed a miserable night,
So full of fearful dreams, of ugly sights,
That, as I am a Christian faithful man,
I would not spend another such a night
Though 'twere to buy a world of happy days,
So full of dismal terror was the time!

KEEPER
What was your dream, my lord? I pray you, tell me.

CLARENCE
Methoughts that I had broken from the Tower 9
And was embarked to cross to Burgundy, 10
And in my company my brother Gloucester,
Who from my cabin tempted me to walk

---

298 **soothe** flatter 302 **the subjects to** subjugated to 305 **muse** wonder 310 **vantage of her wrong** benefits derived from the wrongs she has suffered. 311 **too hot . . . good** i.e., too eager in helping Edward to the throne 312 **That . . . cold** who is too ungrateful 314 **franked . . . fatting** shut up in a frank or sty to be fattened for slaughter 317 **scathe** harm 318 **well advised** cautious. 323 **wait upon** attend 325 **set abroach** set flowing 326 **lay . . . of** impute as a serious accusation against 328 **gulls** credulous persons 332 **withal** furthermore. **whet** urge, incite

335 **for** in return for 337 **ends** fragments, tags 339 **soft** gently; wait a minute. 340 **stout . . . mates** bold, resolute fellows 345 **repair** betake yourselves 347 **Withal** at the same time 349 **mark** pay attention to 350 **prate** prattle 353 **millstones** heavy stone disks used for grinding. (To *drop millstones* was proverbially to show signs of hardheartedness.) **fall** let fall
1.4. Location: London. The Tower.
1 heavily sad **9 Methoughts** It seemed to me **10 Burgundy** (Clarence and Richard, according to the chronicles, had been sent to Burgundy for protection following their father's death.)

Upon the hatches. Thence we looked toward England 13
And cited up a thousand heavy times, 14
During the wars of York and Lancaster,
That had befall'n us. As we paced along
Upon the giddy footing of the hatches, 17
Methought that Gloucester stumbled, and in falling
Struck me, that thought to stay him, overboard 19
Into the tumbling billows of the main. 20
Oh, Lord, methought what pain it was to drown!
What dreadful noise of waters in my ears!
What sights of ugly death within my eyes!
Methought I saw a thousand fearful wracks; 24
Ten thousand men that fishes gnawed upon;
Wedges of gold, great anchors, heaps of pearl, 26
Inestimable stones, unvalued jewels, 27
All scattered in the bottom of the sea.
Some lay in dead men's skulls, and in the holes
Where eyes did once inhabit there were crept,
As 'twere in scorn of eyes, reflecting gems,
That wooed the slimy bottom of the deep 32
And mocked the dead bones that lay scattered by.

KEEPER
Had you such leisure in the time of death
To gaze upon these secrets of the deep?

CLARENCE
Methought I had, and often did I strive
To yield the ghost; but still the envious flood 37
Stopped in my soul and would not let it forth 38
To seek the empty, vast, and wand'ring air,
But smothered it within my panting bulk, 40
Which almost burst to belch it in the sea.

KEEPER
Awaked you not in this sore agony?

CLARENCE
No, no, my dream was lengthened after life.
Oh, then began the tempest to my soul!
I passed, methought, the melancholy flood, 45
With that sour ferryman which poets write of, 46
Unto the kingdom of perpetual night.
The first that there did greet my stranger soul 48
Was my great father-in-law, renownèd Warwick,
Who spake aloud, "What scourge for perjury
Can this dark monarchy afford false Clarence?"
And so he vanished. Then came wand'ring by
A shadow like an angel, with bright hair 53
Dabbled in blood, and he shrieked out aloud,
"Clarence is come—false, fleeting, perjured Clarence, 55
That stabbed me in the field by Tewkesbury.
Seize on him, Furies, take him unto torment!"
With that, methought, a legion of foul fiends

Environed me and howlèd in mine ears
Such hideous cries that with the very noise
I trembling waked, and for a season after 61
Could not believe but that I was in hell,
Such terrible impression made my dream.

KEEPER
No marvel, my lord, though it affrighted you.
I am afraid, methinks, to hear you tell it.

CLARENCE
Ah, keeper, keeper, I have done these things,
That now give evidence against my soul,
For Edward's sake, and see how he requites me! 68
O God! If my deep prayers cannot appease thee,
But thou wilt be avenged on my misdeeds,
Yet execute thy wrath in me alone!
Oh, spare my guiltless wife and my poor children!
Keeper, I prithee, sit by me awhile.
My soul is heavy, and I fain would sleep. 74

KEEPER
I will, my lord. God give Your Grace good rest!
[Clarence sleeps.]

Enter Brackenbury, the Lieutenant.

BRACKENBURY
Sorrow breaks seasons and reposing hours, 76
Makes the night morning and the noontide night.
Princes have but their titles for their glories,
An outward honor for an inward toil,
And, for unfelt imaginations, 80
They often feel a world of restless cares;
So that between their titles and low name 82
There's nothing differs but the outward fame. 83

Enter two Murderers.

FIRST MURDERER   Ho! Who's here?

BRACKENBURY
What would'st thou, fellow, and how cam'st thou hither?

SECOND MURDERER   I would speak with Clarence, and I
came hither on my legs.

BRACKENBURY   What, so brief?

FIRST MURDERER   'Tis better, sir, than to be tedious.—
Let him see our commission, and talk no more.
[Brackenbury] reads [it].

BRACKENBURY
I am in this commanded to deliver
The noble Duke of Clarence to your hands.
I will not reason what is meant hereby,
Because I will be guiltless from the meaning. 94
There lies the Duke asleep, and there the keys.
[He gives keys.]
I'll to the King and signify to him
That thus I have resigned to you my charge.

13 **hatches** movable planks forming a deck. 14 **cited up** recalled.
heavy difficult   17 **giddy** unsteady   19 **stay** hold, steady   20 **main**
ocean.   24 **wracks** shipwrecked vessels   26 **Wedges** ingots
27 **Inestimable** precious and innumerable.   **unvalued** priceless
32 **wooed** (These lifeless eyes have nothing to flirt with but the
murky depths.)   37 **envious flood** malicious water   38 **Stopped**
held   40 **bulk** body   45 **melancholy flood** i.e., River Styx   46 **ferryman** i.e., Charon, who ferried souls to Hades, *the kingdom of perpetual
night* (line 47)   48 **stranger** i.e., newly arrived   53 **shadow** i.e., ghost of
Edward, Prince of Wales, son of Henry VI   55 **fleeting** fickle, deceitful

61 **season** time   68 **requites** repays   74 **fain** willingly   76 **breaks . . .
hours** disrupts the normal rhythms of life and hours properly
devoted to sleep   80 **for unfelt imaginations** in return for glories
that are merely illusory   82 **low name** i.e., the lowly position of ordinary men   83 **fame** reputation.   94 **will be** wish to be

FIRST MURDERER   You may, sir; 'tis a point of wisdom. Fare you well.   *Exit* [*Brackenbury with Keeper*].

SECOND MURDERER   What, shall I stab him as he sleeps?

FIRST MURDERER   No. He'll say 'twas done cowardly, when he wakes.

SECOND MURDERER   Why, he shall never wake until the great Judgment Day.

FIRST MURDERER   Why, then he'll say we stabbed him sleeping.

SECOND MURDERER   The urging of that word "judgment" hath bred a kind of remorse in me.

FIRST MURDERER   What, art thou afraid?

SECOND MURDERER   Not to kill him, having a warrant, but to be damned for killing him, from the which no warrant can defend me.

FIRST MURDERER   I thought thou hadst been resolute.

SECOND MURDERER   So I am—to let him live.

FIRST MURDERER   I'll back to the Duke of Gloucester and tell him so.

SECOND MURDERER   Nay, I prithee, stay a little. I hope this passionate humor of mine will change. It was   119
wont to hold me but while one tells twenty.   120

FIRST MURDERER   How dost thou feel thyself now?

SECOND MURDERER   Faith, some certain dregs of conscience are yet within me.

FIRST MURDERER   Remember our reward when the deed 's done.

SECOND MURDERER   Zounds, he dies! I had forgot the   126
reward.

FIRST MURDERER   Where's thy conscience now?

SECOND MURDERER   Oh, in the Duke of Gloucester's purse.

FIRST MURDERER   When he opens his purse to give us our reward, thy conscience flies out.

SECOND MURDERER   'Tis no matter; let it go. There's few or none will entertain it.   134

FIRST MURDERER   What if it come to thee again?

SECOND MURDERER   I'll not meddle with it; it makes a man a coward. A man cannot steal but it accuseth him; a man cannot swear but it checks him; a man cannot   138
lie with his neighbor's wife but it detects him. 'Tis a blushing, shamefaced spirit that mutinies in a man's bosom. It fills a man full of obstacles. It made me once restore a purse of gold that by chance I found. It beggars any man that keeps it. It is turned out of towns and cities for a dangerous thing, and every man that means to live well endeavors to trust to himself and live without it.

FIRST MURDERER   Zounds, 'tis even now at my elbow, persuading me not to kill the Duke.

SECOND MURDERER   Take the devil in thy mind, and   149
believe him not. He would insinuate with thee but to   150
make thee sigh.   151

FIRST MURDERER   Tut, I am strong-framed; he cannot prevail with me.

SECOND MURDERER   Spoke like a tall man that respects   154
thy reputation. Come, shall we fall to work?

FIRST MURDERER   Take him on the costard with the hilts   156
of thy sword, and then throw him into the malmsey   157
butt in the next room.   158

SECOND MURDERER   Oh, excellent device! And make a sop   159
of him.

FIRST MURDERER   Soft, he wakes.

SECOND MURDERER   Strike!

FIRST MURDERER   No, we'll reason with him.   163

CLARENCE [*waking*]
Where art thou, keeper? Give me a cup of wine.

SECOND MURDERER
You shall have wine enough, my lord, anon.

CLARENCE   In God's name, what art thou?

FIRST MURDERER   A man, as you are.

CLARENCE   But not, as I am, royal.

FIRST MURDERER   Nor you, as we are, loyal.

CLARENCE
Thy voice is thunder, but thy looks are humble.

FIRST MURDERER
My voice is now the King's, my looks mine own.

CLARENCE
How darkly and how deadly dost thou speak!   172
Your eyes do menace me. Why look you pale?
Who sent you hither? Wherefore do you come?

SECOND MURDERER   To, to, to—

CLARENCE   To murder me?

BOTH   Ay, ay.

CLARENCE
You scarcely have the hearts to tell me so,
And therefore cannot have the hearts to do it.
Wherein, my friends, have I offended you?

FIRST MURDERER
Offended us you have not, but the King.

CLARENCE
I shall be reconciled to him again.

SECOND MURDERER
Never, my lord; therefore prepare to die.

CLARENCE
Are you drawn forth among a world of men   184
To slay the innocent? What is my offense?
Where is the evidence that doth accuse me?
What lawful quest have given their verdict up   187
Unto the frowning judge? Or who pronounced
The bitter sentence of poor Clarence' death
Before I be convict by course of law?   190
To threaten me with death is most unlawful.
I charge you, as you hope to have redemption
By Christ's dear blood shed for our grievous sins,
That you depart and lay no hands on me.
The deed you undertake is damnable.

---

119 passionate humor compassionate mood   120 wont accustomed. tells counts   126 Zounds i.e., By God's (Christ's) wounds   134 entertain it receive it, give it welcome.   138 checks reproves, stops   149–50 Take . . . not i.e., Listen to the devil and pay no heed to conscience.   150–1 He . . . sigh Your conscience would ingratiate itself with you merely for the purpose of making you unhappy.

154 tall brave   156 Take Strike. costard head. (Literally, a kind of apple.)   157–8 malmsey butt wine barrel. (Malmsey is a sweet wine.)   159 sop bread or cake soaked in wine   163 reason talk   172 darkly ominously   184 drawn . . . men especially selected from the whole human race   187 quest inquest, i.e., jury   190 convict convicted

FIRST MURDERER
What we will do, we do upon command.

SECOND MURDERER
And he that hath commanded is our king.

CLARENCE
Erroneous vassals! The great King of kings   198
Hath in the table of His law commanded   199
That thou shalt do no murder. Will you then
Spurn at His edict and fulfill a man's?
Take heed; for He holds vengeance in His hand
To hurl upon their heads that break His law.

SECOND MURDERER
And that same vengeance doth He hurl on thee
For false forswearing and for murder, too.
Thou didst receive the Sacrament to fight   206
In quarrel of the house of Lancaster.

FIRST MURDERER
And, like a traitor to the name of God,
Didst break that vow, and with thy treacherous blade
Unripped'st the bowels of thy sovereign's son.   210

SECOND MURDERER
Whom thou wast sworn to cherish and defend.

FIRST MURDERER
How canst thou urge God's dreadful law to us
When thou hast broke it in such dear degree?   213

CLARENCE
Alas! For whose sake did I that ill deed?
For Edward, for my brother, for his sake.
He sends you not to murder me for this,
For in that sin he is as deep as I.
If God will be avengèd for the deed,
Oh, know you yet he doth it publicly!
Take not the quarrel from His powerful arm.
He needs no indirect or lawless course
To cut off those that have offended Him.

FIRST MURDERER
Who made thee, then, a bloody minister   223
When gallant-springing brave Plantagenet,   224
That princely novice, was struck dead by thee?   225

CLARENCE
My brother's love, the devil, and my rage.   226

FIRST MURDERER
Thy brother's love, our duty, and thy faults
Provoke us hither now to slaughter thee.

CLARENCE
If you do love my brother, hate not me!
I am his brother, and I love him well.
If you are hired for meed, go back again,   231
And I will send you to my brother Gloucester,
Who shall reward you better for my life
Than Edward will for tidings of my death.

SECOND MURDERER
You are deceived. Your brother Gloucester hates you.

CLARENCE
Oh, no, he loves me, and he holds me dear.
Go you to him from me.

FIRST MURDERER   Ay, so we will.

CLARENCE
Tell him, when that our princely father York
Blessed his three sons with his victorious arm
And charged us from his soul to love each other,
He little thought of this divided friendship.
Bid Gloucester think of this, and he will weep.

FIRST MURDERER
Ay, millstones, as he lessoned us to weep.   243

CLARENCE
Oh, do not slander him, for he is kind.

FIRST MURDERER
Right, as snow in harvest. Come, you deceive
    yourself.   245
'Tis he that sends us to destroy you here.

CLARENCE
It cannot be, for he bewept my fortune,
And hugged me in his arms, and swore with sobs
That he would labor my delivery.   249

FIRST MURDERER
Why, so he doth, when he delivers you
From this earth's thralldom to the joys of heaven.   251

SECOND MURDERER
Make peace with God, for you must die, my lord.

CLARENCE
Have you that holy feeling in your souls
To counsel me to make my peace with God,
And are you yet to your own souls so blind
That you will war with God by murd'ring me?
Oh, sirs, consider, they that set you on
To do this deed will hate you for the deed.

SECOND MURDERER [to First Murderer]
What shall we do?

CLARENCE   Relent, and save your souls.
Which of you, if you were a prince's son,
Being pent from liberty, as I am now,   261
If two such murderers as yourselves came to you,
Would not entreat for life?

FIRST MURDERER
Relent? No. 'Tis cowardly and womanish.

CLARENCE
Not to relent is beastly, savage, devilish.
[To Second Murderer] My friend, I spy some pity in thy looks..
Oh, if thine eye be not a flatterer,
Come thou on my side, and entreat for me,
As you would beg, were you in my distress.
A begging prince what beggar pities not?

SECOND MURDERER   Look behind you, my lord.

---

198 Erroneous vassals! Sinful and mistaken wretches!   199 table
tablet (the Ten Commandments)   206 receive the Sacrament i.e.,
swear upon the Sacrament   210 sovereign's son i.e., Prince Edward,
son of Henry VI.   213 dear grievous, costly   223 minister agent of
God   224 gallant-springing i.e., gallant and sprightly, aspiring.
Plantagenet i.e., the Lancastrian Prince Edward, killed in 3 Henry VI,
5.5. (See the note at 1.2.145 on Edward's claim to this name.)
225 novice youth   226 My brother's love i.e., My love for my brother
231 meed financial reward

243 lessoned taught   245 Right . . . harvest i.e., He's just as kind and
natural—that is, both affectionate and with the natural feelings of a
brother—as is snow at harvest time.   249 labor my delivery work for
my release.   251 thralldom bondage, captivity   261 pent shut up

FIRST MURDERER
    Take that, and that! (*Stabs him.*) If all this will not do,
    I'll drown you in the malmsey butt within.
                                            Exit [*with the body*].
SECOND MURDERER
    A bloody deed, and desperately dispatched!
    How fain, like Pilate, would I wash my hands   275
    Of this most grievous murder!

        Enter First Murderer.

FIRST MURDERER
    How now? What mean'st thou that thou help'st me not?
    By heaven, the Duke shall know how slack you
        have been.
SECOND MURDERER
    I would he knew that I had saved his brother!
    Take thou the fee, and tell him what I say,
    For I repent me that the Duke is slain.   *Exit.*
FIRST MURDERER
    So do not I. Go, coward as thou art.—
    Well, I'll go hide his body in some hole
    Till that the Duke give order for his burial;
    And when I have my meed, I will away,
    For this will out, and then I must not stay.   *Exit.* 286

                        ❖

2.1

        Flourish. Enter the King [*Edward*], *sick, the*
        Queen [*Elizabeth*], *Lord Marquess Dorset,* [*Grey,*]
        Rivers, Hastings, Catesby, Buckingham, [*and*
        others].

KING EDWARD
    Why, so. Now have I done a good day's work.
    You peers, continue this united league.
    I every day expect an embassage
    From my Redeemer to redeem me hence;
    And more in peace my soul shall part to heaven,
    Since I have made my friends at peace on earth.
    Rivers and Hastings, take each other's hand;
    Dissemble not your hatred, swear your love.   8
RIVERS [*taking Hastings' hand*]
    By heaven, my soul is purged from grudging hate,
    And with my hand I seal my true heart's love.
HASTINGS
    So thrive I, as I truly swear the like!
KING EDWARD
    Take heed you dally not before your king,   12
    Lest he that is the supreme King of kings
    Confound your hidden falsehood, and award   14
    Either of you to be the other's end.   15

HASTINGS
    So prosper I, as I swear perfect love!
RIVERS
    And I, as I love Hastings with my heart!
KING EDWARD
    Madam, yourself is not exempt from this,
    Nor you, son Dorset, Buckingham, nor you;   19
    You have been factious one against the other.   20
    Wife, love Lord Hastings; let him kiss your hand;
    And what you do, do it unfeignedly.
QUEEN ELIZABETH
    There, Hastings, I will never more remember
    Our former hatred, so thrive I and mine!   24
                            [*Hastings kisses her hand.*]
KING EDWARD
    Dorset, embrace him. Hastings, love Lord Marquess.
DORSET
    This interchange of love, I here protest,   26
    Upon my part shall be inviolable.
HASTINGS   And so swear I.   [*They embrace.*]
KING EDWARD
    Now, princely Buckingham, seal thou this league
    With thy embracements to my wife's allies,
    And make me happy in your unity.
BUCKINGHAM [*to the Queen*]
    Whenever Buckingham doth turn his hate
    Upon Your Grace, but with all duteous love   33
    Doth cherish you and yours, God punish me
    With hate in those where I expect most love!
    When I have most need to employ a friend,
    And most assurèd that he is a friend,
    Deep, hollow, treacherous, and full of guile   38
    Be he unto me! This do I beg of God,
    When I am cold in love to you or yours.
                                    [*They*] *embrace.*
KING EDWARD
    A pleasing cordial, princely Buckingham,   41
    Is this thy vow unto my sickly heart.
    There wanteth now our brother Gloucester here   43
    To make the blessèd period of this peace.   44
BUCKINGHAM   And, in good time,
    Here comes Sir Richard Ratcliffe and the Duke.

        Enter Ratcliffe and [*Richard Duke of*] *Gloucester.*

RICHARD
    Good morrow to my sovereign king and queen;
    And, princely peers, a happy time of day!
KING EDWARD
    Happy, indeed, as we have spent the day.
    Gloucester, we have done deeds of charity,
    Made peace of enmity, fair love of hate,
    Between these swelling wrong-incensèd peers.   52

---

275 **fain** gladly.   **Pilate** The Roman governor of Judaea who ordered
the crucifixion of Jesus at the behest of the chief priests but symboli-
cally washed his hands of the business (Matthew 27:24).   **286 this
will out** ("Murder will out" was a proverbial saying.)
2.1. Location: London. The royal court.
0.1 *Flourish* Trumpet call to announce the arrival of a distinguished
person.   **8 Dissemble** conceal, disguise (under a false appearance of
love)   **12 dally** trifle   **14 Confound** defeat   **15 Either . . . end** each
of you to be the agent of death of the other.

19 **son** stepson   20 **factious** quarrelsome   24 **mine** my family and
children.   26 **protest** declare   33 **but** and does not   38 **Deep** subtle,
crafty   41 **cordial** restorative   43 **wanteth** is lacking   44 **period** conclusion   52 **swelling** i.e., with anger or rivalry

RICHARD
A blessèd labor, my most sovereign lord.
Among this princely heap, if any here,   54
By false intelligence, or wrong surmise,   55
Hold me a foe;
If I unwittingly, or in my rage,
Have aught committed that is hardly borne   58
By any in this presence, I desire
To reconcile me to his friendly peace.
'Tis death to me to be at enmity;
I hate it, and desire all good men's love.
First, madam, I entreat true peace of you,
Which I will purchase with my duteous service;
Of you, my noble cousin Buckingham,
If ever any grudge were lodged between us;
Of you and you, Lord Rivers, and of Dorset,
That all without desert have frowned on me;   68
Dukes, earls, lords, gentlemen—indeed, of all.
I do not know that Englishman alive
With whom my soul is any jot at odds
More than the infant that is born tonight.   72
I thank my God for my humility.

QUEEN ELIZABETH
A holy day shall this be kept hereafter.
I would to God all strifes were well compounded.   75
My sovereign lord, I do beseech Your Highness
To take our brother Clarence to your grace.

RICHARD
Why, madam, have I offered love for this,
To be so flouted in this royal presence?   79
Who knows not that the gentle Duke is dead?   80
                                    They all start.
You do him injury to scorn his corpse.

KING EDWARD
Who knows not he is dead? Who knows he is?

QUEEN ELIZABETH
All-seeing heaven, what a world is this!

BUCKINGHAM
Look I so pale, Lord Dorset, as the rest?

DORSET
Ay, my good lord, and no man in the presence   85
But his red color hath forsook his cheeks.

KING EDWARD
Is Clarence dead? The order was reversed.

RICHARD
But he, poor man, by your first order died,
And that a wingèd Mercury did bear;   89
Some tardy cripple bare the countermand,   90
That came too lag to see him buried.   91

God grant that some, less noble and less loyal,   92
Nearer in bloody thoughts but not in blood,   93
Deserve not worse than wretched Clarence did,   94
And yet go current from suspicion!   95

            Enter [Lord Stanley] Earl of Derby.

STANLEY [kneeling]
A boon, my sovereign, for my service done!   96

KING EDWARD
I prithee, peace. My soul is full of sorrow.

STANLEY
I will not rise unless Your Highness hear me.

KING EDWARD
Then say at once what is it thou requests.

STANLEY
The forfeit, sovereign, of my servant's life,   100
Who slew today a riotous gentleman
Lately attendant on the Duke of Norfolk.

KING EDWARD
Have I a tongue to doom my brother's death,   103
And shall that tongue give pardon to a slave?   104
My brother killed no man; his fault was thought,
And yet his punishment was bitter death.
Who sued to me for him? Who, in my wrath,
Kneeled at my feet, and bid me be advised?   108
Who spoke of brotherhood? Who spoke of love?
Who told me how the poor soul did forsake
The mighty Warwick and did fight for me?
Who told me, in the field at Tewkesbury,
When Oxford had me down, he rescued me   113
And said, "Dear brother, live, and be a king"?
Who told me, when we both lay in the field
Frozen almost to death, how he did lap me   116
Even in his garments, and did give himself,
All thin and naked, to the numb-cold night?   118
All this from my remembrance brutish wrath
Sinfully plucked, and not a man of you
Had so much grace to put it in my mind.
But when your carters or your waiting vassals   122
Have done a drunken slaughter and defaced   123
The precious image of our dear Redeemer,   124
You straight are on your knees for pardon, pardon;   125
And I, unjustly too, must grant it you.

                                        [Stanley rises.]
But for my brother not a man would speak,
Nor I, ungracious, speak unto myself
For him, poor soul. The proudest of you all
Have been beholding to him in his life;   130

92–5 **God . . . suspicion!** i.e., (ironically) Pray God there be not persons who deserve worse than Clarence got, persons less noble or related by blood to the King than he, although closely involved in bloody plots, who yet go undetected! (Richard means the Queen and her kindred.) 95 **go current** are accepted at face value (like legal currency).   **from** free from   96 **A boon** (I crave) a favor   100 **The forfeit** i.e., The remission of the forfeit   103 **doom** decree   104 **slave** servant, wretch. 108 **advised** cautious.   113 **Oxford** (See *3 Henry VI*, 5.5.2; this episode has no historical basis.)   116 **lap** wrap   118 **thin** thinly clad   122 **your carters . . . vassals** your cart drivers or your attendants   123–4 **defaced . . . Redeemer** i.e., killed a man. (God made humanity in his own image; Genesis 1:27.)   125 **straight** at once   130 **beholding** beholden

---

54 **heap** assembly   55 **false intelligence** being misinformed 58 **hardly borne** taken amiss, deeply resented   68 **all without desert** wholly without my having deserved it   72 **More than the infant** i.e., more than is that infant's soul   75 **compounded** settled.   79 **flouted** mocked   80 **gentle** noble   85 **presence** i.e., royal presence   89 **Mercury** messenger of the classical gods   90 **tardy cripple** (Richard privately shares with the audience a jest on his own role in this.)   **bare** bore   91 **lag** late

Yet none of you would once beg for his life.
O God, I fear thy justice will take hold
On me and you, and mine and yours, for this!
Come, Hastings, help me to my closet. Ah, poor Clarence!   134
              Exeunt some with King and Queen.

RICHARD
This is the fruits of rashness. Marked you not
How that the guilty kindred of the Queen
Looked pale when they did hear of Clarence' death?
Oh, they did urge it still unto the King.   138
God will revenge it. Come, lords, will you go
To comfort Edward with our company?
BUCKINGHAM   We wait upon Your Grace.   *Exeunt.*

            ❖

2.2

Enter the old Duchess of York, with the two
children of Clarence, [Edward and Margaret
Plantagenet].

BOY
Good grandam, tell us, is our father dead?
DUCHESS   No, boy.
GIRL
Why do you weep so oft, and beat your breast,
And cry, "O Clarence, my unhappy son"?
BOY
Why do you look on us, and shake your head,
And call us orphans, wretches, castaways,
If that our noble father were alive?   7
DUCHESS
My pretty cousins, you mistake me both.   8
I do lament the sickness of the King,
As loath to lose him, not your father's death;
It were lost sorrow to wail one that's lost.
BOY
Then, you conclude, my grandam, he is dead.
The King mine uncle is to blame for it.
God will revenge it, whom I will importune   14
With earnest prayers all to that effect.
GIRL   And so will I.
DUCHESS
Peace, children, peace! The King doth love you well.
Incapable and shallow innocents,   18
You cannot guess who caused your father's death.
BOY
Grandam, we can; for my good uncle Gloucester
Told me the King, provoked to it by the Queen,
Devised impeachments to imprison him;   22
And when my uncle told me so, he wept,
And pitied me, and kindly kissed my cheek;
Bade me rely on him as on my father,
And he would love me dearly as his child.

DUCHESS
Ah, that deceit should steal such gentle shape,
And with a virtuous visor hide deep vice!   28
He is my son—ay, and therein my shame;
Yet from my dugs he drew not this deceit.   30
BOY
Think you my uncle did dissemble, grandam?
DUCHESS   Ay, boy.
BOY
I cannot think it. Hark, what noise is this?   33

    Enter the Queen [Elizabeth], with her hair about
    her ears; Rivers and Dorset after her.

QUEEN ELIZABETH
Ah, who shall hinder me to wail and weep,
To chide my fortune and torment myself?
I'll join with black despair against my soul,
And to myself become an enemy.
DUCHESS
What means this scene of rude impatience?   38
QUEEN ELIZABETH
To make an act of tragic violence.   39
Edward, my lord, thy son, our king, is dead!   40
Why grow the branches when the root is gone?
Why wither not the leaves that want their sap?
If you will live, lament; if die, be brief,   43
That our swift-wingèd souls may catch the King's,
Or, like obedient subjects, follow him
To his new kingdom of ne'er-changing night.
DUCHESS
Ah, so much interest have I in thy sorrow
As I had title in thy noble husband!   48
I have bewept a worthy husband's death
And lived with looking on his images;   50
But now two mirrors of his princely semblance   51
Are cracked in pieces by malignant death,
And I for comfort have but one false glass,   53
That grieves me when I see my shame in him.   54
Thou art a widow; yet thou art a mother,
And hast the comfort of thy children left;
But death hath snatched my husband from mine arms
And plucked two crutches from my feeble hands,
Clarence and Edward. Oh, what cause have I,   59
Thine being but a moiety of my moan,   60
To overgo thy woes and drown thy cries!   61
BOY
Ah, aunt! You wept not for our father's death.
How can we aid you with our kindred tears?   63

---

134 **closet** private chambers.
2.2. Location: London. The royal court.
7 **If that** if   8 **cousins** kinfolks   14 **importune** solicit, beg
18 **Incapable** Unable to understand   22 **impeachments** accusations

28 **visor** mask   30 **dugs** breasts   33.1–2 *with her . . . ears* (A conventional sign of grief.)   38 **rude impatience** violent unwillingness to accept misfortune.   39 **make** perform. (Continues the theatrical metaphor in the previous line.)   40 **Edward . . . dead** (Clarence's death, February 1478, and Edward IV's death, April 1483, are treated as if they had occurred nearly together.)   43 **brief** quick   48 **title** i.e., as mother of the King   50 **images** likenesses; here, children   51 **two mirrors** i.e., Edward and Clarence. (The Duchess does not count Rutland.)   53 **false glass** i.e., Richard   54 **my . . . him** a son of whom to be ashamed.   59 **what . . . I** what a cause I have   60 **moiety of my moan** half (the cause) of my grief   61 **overgo** exceed   63 **kindred tears** i.e., tears of kinfolks.

GIRL
  Our fatherless distress was left unmoaned;
  Your widow-dolor likewise be unwept!   65
QUEEN ELIZABETH
  Give me no help in lamentation;
  I am not barren to bring forth complaints.   67
  All springs reduce their currents to mine eyes,   68
  That I, being governed by the watery moon,   69
  May send forth plenteous tears to drown the world!
  Ah, for my husband, for my dear lord Edward!
CHILDREN
  Ah, for our father, for our dear lord Clarence!
DUCHESS
  Alas for both, both mine, Edward and Clarence!
QUEEN ELIZABETH
  What stay had I but Edward? And he's gone.   74
CHILDREN
  What stay had we but Clarence? And he's gone.
DUCHESS
  What stays had I but they? And they are gone.
QUEEN ELIZABETH
  Was never widow had so dear a loss!   77
CHILDREN
  Were never orphans had so dear a loss!
DUCHESS
  Was never mother had so dear a loss!
  Alas, I am the mother of these griefs;
  Their woes are parceled, mine is general.   81
  She for an Edward weeps, and so do I;
  I for a Clarence weep, so doth not she.
  These babes for Clarence weep, and so do I;
  I for an Edward weep, so do not they.
  Alas, you three, on me, threefold distressed,
  Pour all your tears! I am your sorrow's nurse,   87
  And I will pamper it with lamentation.   88
DORSET [to Queen Elizabeth]
  Comfort, dear mother. God is much displeased
  That you take with unthankfulness his doing.
  In common worldly things 'tis called ungrateful
  With dull unwillingness to repay a debt   92
  Which with a bounteous hand was kindly lent;
  Much more to be thus opposite with heaven   94
  For it requires the royal debt it lent you.   95
RIVERS
  Madam, bethink you like a careful mother
  Of the young Prince your son. Send straight for him;
  Let him be crowned. In him your comfort lives.
  Drown desperate sorrow in dead Edward's grave

And plant your joys in living Edward's throne.

  Enter Richard [Duke of Gloucester], Buckingham,
  [Lord Stanley Earl of] Derby, Hastings, and
  Ratcliffe.

RICHARD [to Queen Elizabeth]
  Sister, have comfort. All of us have cause
  To wail the dimming of our shining star,
  But none can help our harms by wailing them.—
  Madam, my mother, I do cry you mercy;   104
  I did not see Your Grace. Humbly on my knee
  I crave your blessing.   [He kneels.]
DUCHESS
  God bless thee, and put meekness in thy breast,
  Love, charity, obedience, and true duty!
RICHARD
  Amen! [Aside] And make me die a good old man!
  That is the butt end of a mother's blessing;   110
  I marvel that Her Grace did leave it out.
BUCKINGHAM
  You cloudy princes and heart-sorrowing peers,   112
  That bear this heavy mutual load of moan,   113
  Now cheer each other in each other's love.
  Though we have spent our harvest of this king,
  We are to reap the harvest of his son.
  The broken rancor of your high-swoll'n hates,
  But lately splintered, knit, and joined together,   118
  Must gently be preserved, cherished, and kept.   119
  Me seemeth good that with some little train   120
  Forthwith from Ludlow the young Prince be fet   121
  Hither to London, to be crowned our king.
RIVERS
  Why with some little train, my lord of Buckingham?
BUCKINGHAM
  Marry, my lord, lest by a multitude   124
  The new-healed wound of malice should break out,
  Which would be so much the more dangerous
  By how much the estate is green and yet ungoverned.   127
  Where every horse bears his commanding rein   128
  And may direct his course as please himself,   129
  As well the fear of harm, as harm apparent,   130
  In my opinion, ought to be prevented.
RICHARD
  I hope the King made peace with all of us;
  And the compact is firm and true in me.
RIVERS
  And so in me, and so, I think, in all.
  Yet since it is but green, it should be put
  To no apparent likelihood of breach,

---

65 **widow-dolor** widow's grief   67 **barren to** i.e., unable to. (She is pregnant with grief.)   68 **All . . . eyes** Let all springs be concentrated in my eyes   69 **I . . . moon** (Her grief is now a sea, fed by springs and her tides governed by the moon.)   74 **stay** support   77 **dear** costly, grievous   81 **Their . . . general** the woes of Queen Elizabeth and these children are particular to each of them, mine is all-embracing. 87 **nurse** source of sustenance   88 **pamper** feed luxuriously, nourish 92 **dull** sluggish   94 **opposite with** contrary toward   95 **For it requires** because it calls back

104 **cry you mercy** beg your pardon   110 **butt end** concluding portion. (The *butt* is the end of a spear shaft.)   112 **cloudy** clouded with grief   113 **moan** lamentation   118 **But lately splintered** only recently bound together (as with a splint)   119 **Must . . . preserved** i.e., the recent mending of differences must be preserved   120 **Me seemeth** It seems to me.   **train** entourage   121 **Ludlow** royal castle in Shropshire, near the Welsh border.   **fet** fetched   124 **multitude** i.e., large train or entourage   127 **estate** state, government.   **green** unripe, i.e., newly established   128 **bears . . . rein** controls the reins that ought to control it   129 **as please** as it pleases   130 **As . . . apparent** both the fear of trouble and the actual manifestation of it

Which haply by much company might be urged. 137
Therefore I say with noble Buckingham
That it is meet so few should fetch the Prince. 139

HASTINGS   And so say I.

RICHARD
Then be it so; and go we to determine
Who they shall be that straight shall post to Ludlow. 142
Madam, and you, my sister, will you go
To give your censures in this business? 144

QUEEN ELIZABETH, DUCHESS   With all our hearts. 145

Exeunt. Manent Buckingham and Richard.

BUCKINGHAM
My lord, whoever journeys to the Prince,
For God's sake let not us two stay at home;
For by the way I'll sort occasion, 148
As index to the story we late talked of, 149
To part the Queen's proud kindred from the Prince.

RICHARD
My other self, my counsel's consistory, 151
My oracle, my prophet! My dear cousin,
I, as a child, will go by thy direction.
Toward Ludlow then, for we'll not stay behind.

Exeunt.

❧

2.3

Enter one Citizen at one door, and another at the other.

FIRST CITIZEN
Good morrow, neighbor. Whither away so fast?

SECOND CITIZEN
I promise you, I scarcely know myself. 2
Hear you the news abroad?

FIRST CITIZEN   Yes, that the King is dead.

SECOND CITIZEN
Ill news, by'r Lady; seldom comes the better. 5
I fear, I fear 'twill prove a giddy world. 6

Enter another Citizen.

THIRD CITIZEN
Neighbors, God speed!

FIRST CITIZEN   Give you good morrow, sir.

THIRD CITIZEN
Doth the news hold of good King Edward's death? 8

SECOND CITIZEN
Ay, sir, it is too true, God help the while!

THIRD CITIZEN
Then, masters, look to see a troublous world. 10

FIRST CITIZEN
No, no; by God's good grace his son shall reign.

THIRD CITIZEN
Woe to that land that's governed by a child! 12

SECOND CITIZEN
In him there is a hope of government,
Which in his nonage, council under him, 14
And in his full and ripened years, himself,
No doubt shall then, and till then, govern well.

FIRST CITIZEN
So stood the state when Henry the Sixth
Was crowned in Paris but at nine months old.

THIRD CITIZEN
Stood the state so? No, no, good friends, God wot, 19
For then this land was famously enriched
With politic, grave counsel; then the King 21
Had virtuous uncles to protect His Grace.

FIRST CITIZEN
Why, so hath this, both by his father and mother.

THIRD CITIZEN
Better it were they all came by his father,
Or by his father there were none at all;
For emulation who shall now be nearest 26
Will touch us all too near, if God prevent not.
Oh, full of danger is the Duke of Gloucester,
And the Queen's sons and brothers haught and proud! 29
And were they to be ruled, and not to rule,
This sickly land might solace as before. 31

FIRST CITIZEN
Come, come, we fear the worst. All will be well.

THIRD CITIZEN
When clouds are seen, wise men put on their cloaks;
When great leaves fall, then winter is at hand;
When the sun sets, who doth not look for night?
Untimely storms makes men expect a dearth.
All may be well; but if God sort it so, 37
'Tis more than we deserve or I expect.

SECOND CITIZEN
Truly, the hearts of men are full of fear.
You cannot reason almost with a man 40
That looks not heavily and full of dread. 41

THIRD CITIZEN
Before the days of change, still is it so. 42
By a divine instinct men's minds mistrust 43
Ensuing danger; as, by proof, we see 44
The water swell before a boist'rous storm.
But leave it all to God. Whither away?

SECOND CITIZEN
Marry, we were sent for to the justices.

THIRD CITIZEN
And so was I. I'll bear you company.   *Exeunt.*

❧

---

137 haply perhaps.   **urged** encouraged, provoked.   **139 meet** fitting
142 post hasten   **144 censures** judgments   **145.1 Manent** They
remain onstage   **148 by** on.   **sort** find, contrive   **149 index** prologue.   **late** lately   **151 consistory** council chamber
2.3. Location: London. A street.
2 promise assure   **5 Ill . . . better** Ill news, by Our Lady. Good news
comes seldom; most news is bad news.   **6 giddy** mad   **8 Doth the
news hold** Is the news true   **10 masters** good sirs.   **troublous** troubled, disorderly

12 Woe . . . child! (Compare with Ecclesiastes 10:16: "Woe to thee, O
land, when thy king is a child.")   **14 nonage** minority.   **council
under him** i.e., with the Privy Council governing in his name
19 wot knows   **21 politic** sagacious   **26 emulation** ambitious rivalry
29 haught haughty   **31 solace** be happy, have comfort   **37 sort** dispose   **40 You . . . man** There is scarcely anyone with whom you can
talk   **41 heavily** sad   **42 still** ever   **43 mistrust** suspect, fear
44 proof experience

2.4

Enter [the] Archbishop [of York], [the] young
[Duke of] York, the Queen [Elizabeth], and the
Duchess [of York].

ARCHBISHOP
Last night, I hear, they lay at Stony Stratford,   1
And at Northampton they do rest tonight.   2
Tomorrow, or next day, they will be here.

DUCHESS
I long with all my heart to see the Prince.
I hope he is much grown since last I saw him.

QUEEN ELIZABETH
But I hear, no; they say my son of York
Has almost overta'en him in his growth.

YORK
Ay, mother, but I would not have it so.

DUCHESS
Why, my young cousin? It is good to grow.

YORK
Grandam, one night as we did sit at supper,
My uncle Rivers talked how I did grow
More than my brother. "Ay," quoth my uncle Gloucester,
"Small herbs have grace; great weeds do grow apace."   13
And since, methinks, I would not grow so fast,   14
Because sweet flow'rs are slow and weeds make haste.

DUCHESS
Good faith, good faith, the saying did not hold   16
In him that did object the same to thee.   17
He was the wretched'st thing when he was young,
So long a-growing and so leisurely,
That, if his rule were true, he should be gracious.

ARCHBISHOP
And so no doubt he is, my gracious madam.

DUCHESS
I hope he is, but yet let mothers doubt.

YORK
Now, by my troth, if I had been remembered,   23
I could have given my uncle's Grace a flout   24
To touch his growth nearer than he touched mine.   25

DUCHESS
How, my young York? I prithee, let me hear it.

YORK
Marry, they say my uncle grew so fast
That he could gnaw a crust at two hours old;
'Twas full two years ere I could get a tooth.
Grandam, this would have been a biting jest.   30

2.4. Location: London. The royal court.
1 Stony Stratford village in Buckinghamshire   **2 Northampton** town
in Northamptonshire and hence farther from London than Stony
Stratford. The Prince was taken back to Northampton after the arrest
of Rivers, Grey, and Vaughan. The Archbishop does not yet know of
that arrest, but the Folio version of his speech, followed here, is based
misleadingly on historical information of subsequent events. (The quartos reverse the order in which the two towns are named.)   **13 grace**
virtuous qualities.   **apace** rapidly.   **14 since** ever since   **16–17 the**
saying . . . thee the saying did not at all apply to the person who
applied it to you, i.e., Richard.   **23 troth** truth, faith.   **had been**
remembered had recollected   **24 my . . . flout** His Grace, my uncle, a
mocking gibe   **25 touch . . . nearer** i.e., taunt him about his growth
more tellingly   **30 biting** (With a play on the idea of teething.)

DUCHESS
I prithee, pretty York, who told thee this?

YORK   Grandam, his nurse.

DUCHESS
His nurse? Why, she was dead ere thou wast born.

YORK
If 'twere not she, I cannot tell who told me.

QUEEN ELIZABETH
A parlous boy! Go to, you are too shrewd.   35

DUCHESS
Good madam, be not angry with the child.

QUEEN ELIZABETH   Pitchers have ears.   37

Enter a Messenger.

ARCHBISHOP
Here comes a messenger.—What news?

MESSENGER
Such news, my lord, as grieves me to report.

QUEEN ELIZABETH
How doth the Prince?

MESSENGER   Well, madam, and in health.

DUCHESS   What is thy news?

MESSENGER
Lord Rivers and Lord Grey are sent to Pomfret,   42
And with them Sir Thomas Vaughan, prisoners.

DUCHESS
Who hath committed them?

MESSENGER   The mighty dukes
Gloucester and Buckingham.

ARCHBISHOP   For what offense?

MESSENGER
The sum of all I can, I have disclosed.
Why or for what the nobles were committed
Is all unknown to me, my gracious lord.

QUEEN ELIZABETH
Ay me, I see the ruin of my house!
The tiger now hath seized the gentle hind;   50
Insulting tyranny begins to jut   51
Upon the innocent and aweless throne.   52
Welcome, destruction, blood, and massacre!
I see, as in a map, the end of all.   54

DUCHESS
Accursèd and unquiet wrangling days,
How many of you have mine eyes beheld!
My husband lost his life to get the crown,
And often up and down my sons were tossed   58
For me to joy and weep their gain and loss;
And being seated, and domestic broils   60
Clean overblown, themselves the conquerors   61
Make war upon themselves, brother to brother,
Blood to blood, self against self. O preposterous   63

---

35 parlous cunning, precocious.   **Go to** (An expression of remonstrance.)   **shrewd** sharp-tongued.   **37 Pitchers have ears** Little
pitchers have large ears. (Proverbial.)   **42 Pomfret** the castle at Pontefract in Yorkshire   **50 hind** doe   **51 Insulting** scornfully triumphing.   **jut** encroach   **52 aweless** inspiring no awe (because of the
youth of the King)   **54 map** i.e., of future events   **58 up . . . tossed**
i.e., my sons were raised and then lowered on fortune's wheel
60 seated i.e., on the throne   **61 Clean overblown** entirely finished
63 preposterous monstrous, perverse

And frantic outrage, end thy damnèd spleen, 64
Or let me die, to look on death no more!

QUEEN ELIZABETH
Come, come, my boy, we will to sanctuary. 66
Madam, farewell.

DUCHESS   Stay, I will go with you.

QUEEN ELIZABETH
You have no cause.

ARCHBISHOP [to the Queen]   My gracious lady, go,
And thither bear your treasure and your goods.
For my part, I'll resign unto Your Grace
The seal I keep; and so betide to me 71
As well I tender you and all of yours! 72
Go, I'll conduct you to the sanctuary.   Exeunt.

❖

3.1

*The trumpets sound. Enter [the] young Prince
[Edward], the Dukes of Gloucester and
Buckingham, [Lord] Cardinal [Bourchier, Catesby],
etc.*

BUCKINGHAM
Welcome, sweet Prince, to London, to your chamber. 1

RICHARD
Welcome, dear cousin, my thoughts' sovereign!
The weary way hath made you melancholy.

PRINCE EDWARD
No, uncle, but our crosses on the way 4
Have made it tedious, wearisome, and heavy.
I want more uncles here to welcome me. 6

RICHARD
Sweet Prince, the untainted virtue of your years
Hath not yet dived into the world's deceit.
Nor more can you distinguish of a man
Than of his outward show—which, God he knows,
Seldom or never jumpeth with the heart. 11
Those uncles which you want were dangerous.
Your Grace attended to their sugared words
But looked not on the poison of their hearts.
God keep you from them, and from such false
    friends!

PRINCE EDWARD
God keep me from false friends! But they were none.

RICHARD
My lord, the Mayor of London comes to greet you.

Enter [the] Lord Mayor [and his train].

MAYOR
God bless Your Grace with health and happy days!

PRINCE EDWARD
I thank you, good my lord, and thank you all.
            [*The Mayor and his train stand aside.*]
I thought my mother and my brother York
Would long ere this have met us on the way.
Fie, what a slug is Hastings, that he comes not 22
To tell us whether they will come or no!

Enter Lord Hastings.

BUCKINGHAM
And, in good time, here comes the sweating lord.

PRINCE EDWARD
Welcome, my lord. What, will our mother come?

HASTINGS
On what occasion God he knows, not I, 26
The Queen your mother and your brother York
Have taken sanctuary. The tender Prince
Would fain have come with me to meet Your Grace,
But by his mother was perforce withheld. 30

BUCKINGHAM
Fie, what an indirect and peevish course 31
Is this of hers!—Lord Cardinal, will Your Grace
Persuade the Queen to send the Duke of York
Unto his princely brother presently? 34
If she deny, Lord Hastings, go with him,
And from her jealous arms pluck him perforce. 36

CARDINAL
My lord of Buckingham, if my weak oratory
Can from his mother win the Duke of York,
Anon expect him here; but if she be obdurate 39
To mild entreaties, God in heaven forbid
We should infringe the holy privilege
Of blessèd sanctuary! Not for all this land
Would I be guilty of so deep a sin.

BUCKINGHAM
You are too senseless-obstinate, my lord,
Too ceremonious and traditional. 45
Weigh it but with the grossness of this age, 46
You break not sanctuary in seizing him.
The benefit thereof is always granted
To those whose dealings have deserved the place
And those who have the wit to claim the place.
This prince hath neither claimed it nor deserved it,
And therefore, in mine opinion, cannot have it.
Then, taking him from thence that is not there, 53
You break no privilege nor charter there.
Oft have I heard of sanctuary men,
But sanctuary children never till now.

CARDINAL
My lord, you shall o'errule my mind for once.
Come on, Lord Hastings, will you go with me?

64 spleen i.e., malice, hatred   **66 sanctuary** (Queen Elizabeth, with
her son, daughters, and kinsmen, lodged in the precincts of Westminster
Abbey, which served as a legal refuge for criminals and persons
in danger of their lives.)   **71 seal** seal of office, i.e., the Great Seal of
England. (The Archbishop's giving the Great Seal to Elizabeth is an
unusual and extralegal action.)   **71–2 so . . . you** may my fortunes be
measured by the care I take of you
3.1. Location: London. A street.
1 chamber (London was called the *camera regis*, or King's chamber.)
4 crosses vexations (i.e., the arrests of the Queen's kindred)   **6 want**
(1) lack (2) wish   **11 jumpeth** agrees

22 slug sluggard   **26 On what occasion** For what reason   **30 perforce**
by force   **31 peevish** perverse   **34 presently** at once   **36 jealous**
suspicious   **39 Anon** shortly   **45 ceremonious** bound by
formalities   **46 grossness** lack of moral refinement   **53 taking . . .
there** i.e., taking the Prince from a place that cannot properly be
called a sanctuary in his case

HASTINGS   I go, my lord.

PRINCE EDWARD
Good lords, make all the speedy haste you may.
                    [*Exeunt Cardinal and Hastings.*]
Say, uncle Gloucester, if our brother come,
Where shall we sojourn till our coronation?   62

RICHARD
Where it seems best unto your royal self.
If I may counsel you, some day or two
Your Highness shall repose you at the Tower;   65
Then where you please, and shall be thought most fit
For your best health and recreation.

PRINCE EDWARD
I do not like the Tower, of any place.   68
Did Julius Caesar build that place, my lord?

BUCKINGHAM
He did, my gracious lord, begin that place,
Which, since, succeeding ages have re-edified.   71

PRINCE EDWARD
Is it upon record, or else reported   72
Successively from age to age, he built it?

BUCKINGHAM   Upon record, my gracious lord.

PRINCE EDWARD
But say, my lord, it were not registered,   75
Methinks the truth should live from age to age,
As 'twere retailed to all posterity,   77
Even to the general all-ending day.   78

RICHARD [*aside*]
So wise so young, they say, do never live long.

PRINCE EDWARD   What say you, uncle?

RICHARD
I say, without characters fame lives long.   81
[*Aside*] Thus, like the formal Vice, Iniquity,   82
I moralize two meanings in one word.   83

PRINCE EDWARD
That Julius Caesar was a famous man;
With what his valor did enrich his wit,   85
His wit set down to make his valor live.   86
Death makes no conquest of this conqueror,
For now he lives in fame, though not in life.
I'll tell you what, my cousin Buckingham—

BUCKINGHAM   What, my gracious lord?

PRINCE EDWARD
An if I live until I be a man,   91
I'll win our ancient right in France again
Or die a soldier, as I lived a king.

RICHARD [*aside*]
Short summers lightly have a forward spring.   94

        Enter young York, Hastings, [and the] Cardinal.

BUCKINGHAM
Now, in good time, here comes the Duke of York.

PRINCE EDWARD
Richard of York, how fares our loving brother?   96

YORK
Well, my dread lord—so must I call you now.   97

PRINCE EDWARD
Ay, brother, to our grief, as it is yours.
Too late he died that might have kept that title,   99
Which by his death hath lost much majesty.

RICHARD
How fares our cousin, noble lord of York?

YORK
I thank you, gentle uncle. Oh, my lord,   102
You said that idle weeds are fast in growth;   103
The Prince my brother hath outgrown me far.

RICHARD
He hath, my lord.

YORK   And therefore is he idle?

RICHARD
Oh, my fair cousin, I must not say so.

YORK
Then he is more beholding to you than I.   107

RICHARD
He may command me as my sovereign,
But you have power in me as in a kinsman.

YORK
I pray you, uncle, give me this dagger.

RICHARD
My dagger, little cousin? With all my heart.   111

PRINCE EDWARD   A beggar, brother?

YORK
Of my kind uncle, that I know will give;   113
And being but a toy, which is no grief to give.   114

RICHARD
A greater gift than that I'll give my cousin.

YORK
A greater gift? Oh, that's the sword to it.

RICHARD
Ay, gentle cousin, were it light enough.

YORK
Oh, then I see you will part but with light gifts.   118
In weightier things you'll say a beggar nay.

RICHARD
It is too heavy for Your Grace to wear.

YORK
I weigh it lightly, were it heavier.   121

---

62 sojourn reside   **65 Tower** (Although in the fifteenth century—the historical time this play represents—the Tower of London was a royal palace, by Shakespeare's day it had acquired a sinister reputation.) **68 of any place** of all places.   **71 re-edified** rebuilt.   **72 upon record** in the written record.   **reported** i.e., by oral tradition   **75 say** suppose.   **registered** written down   **77 retailed** repeated, handed down from one to another   **78 general . . . day** Day of Judgment.   **81 without characters** even lacking written records   **82 formal Vice** i.e., the conventional Vice figure of the morality play, a comic tempter to evil, who would habitually *moralize two meanings in one word,* that is, play on double meanings in a single phrase, as Richard does in the phrase *live long*   **83 moralize** interpret, illustrate   **85–6 With . . . live** having improved his understanding through his military achievements, he used his understanding to set down in writing an account (the *Gallic Wars*) that would make his valor immortal.   **91 An if** If

94 lightly commonly, often.   **forward** early. (Alludes to Edward's precociousness.)   **96 our** i.e., my. (The royal "we.")   **97 dread** inspiring reverential fear (as king)   **99 late** lately   **102 gentle** noble   **103 idle** worthless   **107 beholding** beholden   **111 With . . . heart** Willingly. (Richard combines in one phrase an overt generosity and a hidden threat.)   **113 that** who   **114 toy** trifle   **118 light** trivial   **121 I weigh . . . heavier** I consider it a trifle (playing on the literal meanings of "light" and "heavy") and would do so even if it were heavier.

RICHARD
What, would you have my weapon, little lord?

YORK
I would, that I might thank you as you call me.

RICHARD How?

YORK Little.   125

PRINCE EDWARD
My lord of York will still be cross in talk.   126
Uncle, Your Grace knows how to bear with him.

YORK
You mean, to bear me, not to bear with me.
Uncle, my brother mocks both you and me:
Because that I am little, like an ape,
He thinks that you should bear me on your shoulders.   131

BUCKINGHAM [aside to Hastings]
With what a sharp-provided wit he reasons!   132
To mitigate the scorn he gives his uncle,
He prettily and aptly taunts himself.
So cunning and so young is wonderful.

RICHARD [to the Prince]
My lord, will't please you pass along?
Myself and my good cousin Buckingham
Will to your mother, to entreat of her
To meet you at the Tower and welcome you.

YORK [to the Prince]
What, will you go unto the Tower, my lord?

PRINCE EDWARD
My Lord Protector needs will have it so.

YORK
I shall not sleep in quiet at the Tower.

RICHARD Why, what should you fear?

YORK
Marry, my uncle Clarence' angry ghost.
My grandam told me he was murdered there.

PRINCE EDWARD I fear no uncles dead.

RICHARD Nor none that live, I hope.

PRINCE EDWARD
An if they live, I hope I need not fear.   148
But come, my lord; with a heavy heart,
Thinking on them, go I unto the Tower.   150
          [A sennet.] Exeunt Prince, York,
          Hastings, [Cardinal, and others]. Manent
          Richard, Buckingham, [and Catesby].

BUCKINGHAM
Think you, my lord, this little prating York   151
Was not incensèd by his subtle mother   152
To taunt and scorn you thus opprobriously?

RICHARD
No doubt, no doubt. Oh, 'tis a parlous boy,   154
Bold, quick, ingenious, forward, capable.
He is all the mother's, from the top to toe.

BUCKINGHAM
Well, let them rest.—Come hither, Catesby.   157
Thou art sworn as deeply to effect what we intend
As closely to conceal what we impart.
Thou know'st our reasons urged upon the way.   160
What think'st thou? Is it not an easy matter
To make William Lord Hastings of our mind
For the installment of this noble Duke
In the seat royal of this famous isle?

CATESBY
He for his father's sake so loves the Prince   165
That he will not be won to aught against him.

BUCKINGHAM
What think'st thou, then, of Stanley? Will not he?

CATESBY
He will do all in all as Hastings doth.

BUCKINGHAM
Well, then, no more but this: go, gentle Catesby,
And, as it were far off, sound thou Lord Hastings   170
How he doth stand affected to our purpose,   171
And summon him tomorrow to the Tower
To sit about the coronation.   173
If thou dost find him tractable to us,
Encourage him, and tell him all our reasons.
If he be leaden, icy, cold, unwilling,
Be thou so too; and so break off the talk,
And give us notice of his inclination.
For we tomorrow hold divided councils,   179
Wherein thyself shalt highly be employed.

RICHARD
Commend me to Lord William. Tell him, Catesby,   181
His ancient knot of dangerous adversaries   182
Tomorrow are let blood at Pomfret Castle;   183
And bid my lord, for joy of this good news,
Give Mistress Shore one gentle kiss the more.   185

BUCKINGHAM
Good Catesby, go, effect this business soundly.   186

CATESBY
My good lords both, with all the heed I can.   187

RICHARD
Shall we hear from you, Catesby, ere we sleep?

CATESBY You shall, my lord.

RICHARD
At Crosby House, there shall you find us both.
                                    Exit Catesby.

---

125 **Little** (York saucily suggests that he would give little thanks for
such a "light" gift.)   126 **My . . . talk** i.e., My younger brother is always
twisting words in his wittily perverse but annoying way.   131 **bear me
. . . shoulders** (At fairs, the bear commonly carried an ape on his back.
The speech is doubtless an allusion to Richard's hump and puns
triply on *bear with*, "put up with," *bear*, "carry," and *bear*, "an animal.")   132 **sharp-provided** nimble and ready   148 **An if** If.   **they**
i.e., Rivers and Grey. (Grey was, in fact, Edward's stepbrother, not
his uncle. See the note to 1.3.37.)   150.1 *sennet* trumpet call to
announce the approach or departure of processions.   150.2 *Manent*
They remain onstage   151 **prating** chattering, prattling   152 **incensèd** incited

154 **parlous** clever, but also dangerous   157 **let them rest** leave them
for the moment.   160 **the way** i.e., the journey to London from Ludlow.
165 **He . . . sake** i.e., Hastings for King Edward IV's sake   170 **sound**
sound out   171 **doth stand affected** is disposed   173 **sit** sit in council   179 **divided councils** (While the regular Council meets about the
coronation, Richard plans also to have his own private consultation at
Crosby House.)   181 **Lord William** i.e., Hastings.   182 **knot** group
183 **are let blood** will be bled, i.e., executed   185 **Mistress Shore**
(According to Thomas More, Jane Shore had become the mistress of
Hastings after the death of Edward IV.)   186 **soundly** thoroughly.
187 **heed** attention, care

BUCKINGHAM
Now, my lord, what shall we do if we perceive
Lord Hastings will not yield to our complots?   192
RICHARD
Chop off his head. Something we will determine.
And look when I am king, claim thou of me   194
The earldom of Hereford and all the movables   195
Whereof the King my brother was possessed.
BUCKINGHAM
I'll claim that promise at Your Grace's hand.
RICHARD
And look to have it yielded with all kindness.
Come, let us sup betimes, that afterwards   199
We may digest our complots in some form.   *Exeunt.* 200

❖

3.2

Enter a Messenger to the door of Hastings.

MESSENGER   My lord! My lord!
HASTINGS [*within*]   Who knocks?
MESSENGER   One from the Lord Stanley.
HASTINGS [*within*]   What is't o'clock?   4
MESSENGER   Upon the stroke of four.

Enter Lord Hastings.

HASTINGS
Cannot my Lord Stanley sleep these tedious nights?
MESSENGER
So it appears by that I have to say.
First, he commends him to your noble self.
HASTINGS   What then?
MESSENGER
Then certifies Your Lordship that this night   10
He dreamt the boar had razèd off his helm.   11
Besides, he says there are two councils kept,
And that may be determined at the one
Which may make you and him to rue at th'other.   14
Therefore he sends to know Your Lordship's pleasure,
If you will presently take horse with him   16
And with all speed post with him toward the north,
To shun the danger that his soul divines.
HASTINGS
Go, fellow, go, return unto thy lord.
Bid him not fear the separated councils.
His Honor and myself are at the one,   21
And at the other is my good friend Catesby,
Where nothing can proceed that toucheth us
Whereof I shall not have intelligence.   24
Tell him his fears are shallow, without instance.   25

And for his dreams, I wonder he's so simple   26
To trust the mock'ry of unquiet slumbers.
To fly the boar before the boar pursues   28
Were to incense the boar to follow us,
And make pursuit where he did mean no chase.
Go, bid thy master rise and come to me,
And we will both together to the Tower,
Where he shall see the boar will use us kindly.
MESSENGER
I'll go, my lord, and tell him what you say.   *Exit.*

Enter Catesby.

CATESBY
Many good morrows to my noble lord!
HASTINGS
Good morrow, Catesby. You are early stirring.
What news, what news, in this our tott'ring state?
CATESBY
It is a reeling world, indeed, my lord,
And I believe will never stand upright
Till Richard wear the garland of the realm.
HASTINGS
How? Wear the garland? Dost thou mean the crown?
CATESBY   Ay, my good lord.
HASTINGS
I'll have this crown of mine cut from my shoulders   43
Before I'll see the crown so foul misplaced.
But canst thou guess that he doth aim at it?
CATESBY
Ay, on my life, and hopes to find you forward   46
Upon his party for the gain thereof;   47
And thereupon he sends you this good news,
That this same very day your enemies,
The kindred of the Queen, must die at Pomfret.
HASTINGS
Indeed, I am no mourner for that news,
Because they have been still my adversaries.   52
But that I'll give my voice on Richard's side
To bar my master's heirs in true descent,
God knows I will not do it, to the death.   55
CATESBY
God keep Your Lordship in that gracious mind!
HASTINGS
But I shall laugh at this a twelvemonth hence,
That they which brought me in my master's hate,   58
I live to look upon their tragedy.   59
Well, Catesby, ere a fortnight make me older,
I'll send some packing that yet think not on't.
CATESBY
'Tis a vile thing to die, my gracious lord,
When men are unprepared and look not for it.

---

192 **complots** conspiracies.   194 **look when** as soon as   195 **movables**
personal property, other than real estate   199 **betimes** early, soon
200 **digest** arrange, perfect.   **form** good order.
3.2. Location: Before Lord Hastings's house.
4 **What is't o'clock?** What time is it?   10 **certifies** informs   11 **boar**
i.e., Richard.   **razèd** torn, slashed   14 **th'other** i.e., the regular Council meeting in the Tower, in which Hastings and Stanley will participate.   16 **presently** immediately   21 **His Honor** Lord Stanley
24 **intelligence** information.   25 **instance** grounds.

26 **for** as for.   **simple** simpleminded (as)   28 **fly** flee   43 **crown** i.e.,
head. (Recalls Stanley's dream in line 11 and anticipates Hastings's
execution by beheading.)   46 **forward** inclined   47 **Upon his party**
on his side   52 **still** always   55 **to the death** i.e., though I lose my
life. (A common asseveration, but here with ironic meaning.)
58–9 **That . . . tragedy** that I will live to see the fatal end of those who
brought me out of favor with King Edward IV.

HASTINGS
Oh, monstrous, monstrous! And so falls it out   64
With Rivers, Vaughan, Grey; and so 'twill do
With some men else, that think themselves as safe
As thou and I—who, as thou know'st, are dear
To princely Richard and to Buckingham.

CATESBY
The princes both make high account of you—   69
[Aside] For they account his head upon the Bridge.   70

HASTINGS
I know they do, and I have well deserved it.

Enter Lord Stanley [Earl of Derby].

Come on, come on, where is your boar spear, man?
Fear you the boar, and go so unprovided?

STANLEY
My lord, good morrow. Good morrow, Catesby.
You may jest on, but, by the Holy Rood,   75
I do not like these several councils, I.   76

HASTINGS My lord,
I hold my life as dear as you do yours,
And never in my days, I do protest,
Was it so precious to me as 'tis now.
Think you, but that I know our state secure,   81
I would be so triumphant as I am?

STANLEY
The lords at Pomfret, when they rode from London,   83
Were jocund and supposed their states were sure,   84
And they indeed had no cause to mistrust;
But yet you see how soon the day o'ercast.   86
This sudden stab of rancor I misdoubt.   87
Pray God, I say, I prove a needless coward!
What, shall we toward the Tower? The day is spent.   89

HASTINGS
Come, come, have with you. Wot you what, my lord?   90
Today the lords you talk of are beheaded.

STANLEY
They, for their truth, might better wear their heads   92
Than some that have accused them wear their hats.   93
But come, my lord, let's away.   94

Enter a Pursuivant.

HASTINGS
Go on before. I'll talk with this good fellow.
Exit Lord Stanley [Earl of Derby] and Catesby.

How now, sirrah? How goes the world with thee?   96
PURSUIVANT
The better that Your Lordship please to ask.

HASTINGS
I tell thee, man, 'tis better with me now
Than when thou met'st me last where now we meet.
Then was I going prisoner to the Tower,
By the suggestion of the Queen's allies;   101
But now, I tell thee—keep it to thyself—
This day those enemies are put to death,
And I in better state than e'er I was.

PURSUIVANT
God hold it, to Your Honor's good content!   105

HASTINGS
Gramercy, fellow. There, drink that for me.   106
Throws him his purse.
PURSUIVANT   I thank Your Honor.   Exit Pursuivant.

Enter a Priest.

PRIEST
Well met, my lord. I am glad to see Your Honor.

HASTINGS
I thank thee, good Sir John, with all my heart.   109
I am in your debt for your last exercise;   110
Come the next Sabbath, and I will content you.   111
[He whispers in his ear.]
PRIEST   I'll wait upon Your Lordship.

Enter Buckingham.

BUCKINGHAM
What, talking with a priest, Lord Chamberlain?
Your friends at Pomfret, they do need the priest;
Your Honor hath no shriving work in hand.   115

HASTINGS
Good faith, and when I met this holy man,
The men you talk of came into my mind.
What, go you toward the Tower?

BUCKINGHAM
I do, my lord, but long I cannot stay there.
I shall return before Your Lordship thence.

HASTINGS
Nay, like enough, for I stay dinner there.   121

BUCKINGHAM [aside]
And supper too, although thou know'st it not.—   122
Come, will you go?
HASTINGS   I'll wait upon Your Lordship.
Exeunt.

❖

64 so . . . out so it has happened   69 high account great estimation.
(The quibble on high appears in the next line.)   70 account expect,
reckon. (Punning on account in the previous line.)   the Bridge London Bridge, on a tower of which the heads of traitors were exposed.
75 Rood cross   76 several separate   81 our state the positions we
(Stanley and Hastings) occupy   83 London (An error for "Ludlow"?)
84 jocund merry   86 o'ercast became overcast.   87 This . . . misdoubt
This sudden rancorous vengeance (against Rivers, Vaughan, and Grey)
makes me uneasy.   89 spent i.e., well advanced (although the scene
began at 4:00 A.M.)   90 have with you let's go together.   Wot Know
92-3 They . . . hats They, for their honest loyalty (to King Edward and
now his son), might more justly be allowed to keep their heads than
some of their accusers wear their hats of office.   94.1 Pursuivant
attendant on a herald with authority to serve warrants.

96 sirrah (Form of address to inferiors.)   101 suggestion instigation
105 hold it continue it (i.e., the better state)   106 Gramercy Many
thanks   109 Sir (Common title for addressing any priest.)
110 exercise sermon or devotional exercise   111 content compensate
115 shriving work confession and absolution   121 stay stay for
122 And supper . . . not i.e., You won't be leaving as soon as you
think. (Also suggesting that Hastings will be a feast for worms.)

3.3

*Enter Sir Richard Ratcliffe, with Halberds, carrying
the nobles [Rivers, Grey, and Vaughan] to death
at Pomfret.*

RATCLIFFE Come, bring forth the prisoners.

RIVERS
Sir Richard Ratcliffe, let me tell thee this:
Today shalt thou behold a subject die
For truth, for duty, and for loyalty.

GREY
God bless the Prince from all the pack of you! 5
A knot you are of damnèd bloodsuckers. 6

VAUGHAN
You live that shall cry woe for this hereafter.

RATCLIFFE
Dispatch. The limit of your lives is out. 8

RIVERS
O Pomfret, Pomfret! O thou bloody prison,
Fatal and ominous to noble peers!
Within the guilty closure of thy walls 11
Richard the Second here was hacked to death;
And, for more slander to thy dismal seat, 13
We give to thee our guiltless blood to drink.

GREY
Now Margaret's curse is fall'n upon our heads,
When she exclaimed on Hastings, you, and I,
For standing by when Richard stabbed her son.

RIVERS
Then cursed she Richard, then cursed she Buckingham,
Then cursed she Hastings. Oh, remember, God,
To hear her prayer for them, as now for us!
And for my sister and her princely sons,
Be satisfied, dear God, with our true blood,
Which, as thou know'st, unjustly must be spilt.

RATCLIFFE
Make haste. The hour of death is expiate. 24

RIVERS
Come, Grey, come, Vaughan, let us here embrace.
         [They embrace.]
Farewell, until we meet again in heaven. *Exeunt.*

❦

3.4

*Enter Buckingham, [Lord Stanley Earl of] Derby,
Hastings, Bishop of Ely, Norfolk, Ratcliffe, Lovell,
with others, at a table.*

HASTINGS
Now, noble peers, the cause why we are met
Is to determine of the coronation. 2
In God's name, speak. When is the royal day?

BUCKINGHAM
Is all things ready for the royal time?

STANLEY
It is, and wants but nomination. 5

ELY
Tomorrow, then, I judge a happy day. 6

BUCKINGHAM
Who knows the Lord Protector's mind herein?
Who is most inward with the noble Duke? 8

ELY
Your Grace, methinks, should soonest know his mind.

BUCKINGHAM
We know each other's faces; for our hearts, 10
He knows no more of mine than I of yours,
Or I of his, my lord, than you of mine.
Lord Hastings, you and he are near in love.

HASTINGS
I thank His Grace, I know he loves me well;
But, for his purpose in the coronation,
I have not sounded him, nor he delivered
His gracious pleasure any way therein.
But you, my honorable lords, may name the time,
And in the Duke's behalf I'll give my voice, 19
Which I presume he'll take in gentle part. 20

Enter [Richard Duke of] Gloucester.

ELY
In happy time, here comes the Duke himself.

RICHARD
My noble lords and cousins all, good morrow. 22
I have been long a sleeper; but I trust
My absence doth neglect no great design 24
Which by my presence might have been concluded.

BUCKINGHAM
Had you not come upon your cue, my lord,
William Lord Hastings had pronounced your part,
I mean your voice for crowning of the King.

RICHARD
Than my Lord Hastings no man might be bolder.
His Lordship knows me well, and loves me well.—
My lord of Ely, when I was last in Holborn, 31
I saw good strawberries in your garden there.
I do beseech you send for some of them.

ELY
Marry, and will, my lord, with all my heart.
         Exit Bishop.

RICHARD
Cousin of Buckingham, a word with you.
        [Drawing him aside.]
Catesby hath sounded Hastings in our business,
And finds the testy gentleman so hot
That he will lose his head ere give consent
His master's child, as worshipfully he terms it, 39
Shall lose the royalty of England's throne.

3.3. **Location:** Pomfret (Pontefract) Castle.
5 pack gang **6 knot** group **8 Dispatch** Hurry. **is out** has been
reached. **11 closure** enclosure **13 for . . . seat** i.e., to add further to
the evil reputation of this place **24 expiate** fully come.
3.4. **Location:** London. The Tower.
2 determine of decide upon

5 wants but nomination lacks only naming of the day. **6 happy**
favorable **8 inward** intimate **10 for** as for **19 voice** vote
20 in gentle part with gracious acceptance. **22 cousins** i.e., peers
24 neglect cause the neglect of **31 Holborn** (location of the Bishop's
London palace) **39 worshipfully** reverently. (Said contemptuously.)

BUCKINGHAM
Withdraw yourself awhile. I'll go with you.
    Exeunt [Richard and Buckingham].

STANLEY
We have not yet set down this day of triumph.
Tomorrow, in my judgment, is too sudden,
For I myself am not so well provided   44
As else I would be, were the day prolonged.   45

    Enter the Bishop of Ely.

ELY
Where is my lord the Duke of Gloucester?
I have sent for these strawberries.

HASTINGS
His Grace looks cheerfully and smooth this morning;   48
There's some conceit or other likes him well   49
When that he bids good morrow with such spirit.
I think there's never a man in Christendom
Can lesser hide his love or hate than he,
For by his face straight shall you know his heart.

STANLEY
What of his heart perceive you in his face
By any likelihood he showed today?

HASTINGS
Marry, that with no man here he is offended;
For, were he, he had shown it in his looks.

STANLEY   I pray God he be not, I say.

    Enter Richard and Buckingham.

RICHARD
I pray you all, tell me what they deserve
That do conspire my death with devilish plots
Of damnèd witchcraft, and that have prevailed
Upon my body with their hellish charms?

HASTINGS
The tender love I bear Your Grace, my lord,   63
Makes me most forward in this princely presence
To doom th'offenders, whosoe'er they be:
I say, my lord, they have deservèd death.

RICHARD
Then be your eyes the witness of their evil.
                    [He bares his arm.]
Look how I am bewitched! Behold, mine arm
Is like a blasted sapling withered up.   69
And this is Edward's wife, that monstrous witch,
Consorted with that harlot strumpet Shore,   71
That by their witchcraft thus have markèd me.

HASTINGS
If they have done this deed, my noble lord—

RICHARD
If? Thou protector of this damnèd strumpet,
Talk'st thou to me of "ifs"? Thou art a traitor.—
Off with his head! Now, by Saint Paul I swear,
I will not dine until I see the same.
Lovell and Ratcliffe, look that it be done.   78

The rest that love me, rise and follow me.   79
    Exeunt. Manent Lovell and Ratcliffe, with the Lord
                                  Hastings.

HASTINGS
Woe, woe for England! Not a whit for me,
For I, too fond, might have prevented this.   81
Stanley did dream the boar did raze our helms,
And I did scorn it and disdain to fly.
Three times today my footcloth horse did stumble,   84
And started, when he looked upon the Tower,
As loath to bear me to the slaughterhouse.
Oh, now I need the priest that spake to me!
I now repent I told the pursuivant,
As too triumphing, how mine enemies
Today at Pomfret bloodily were butchered,
And I myself secure in grace and favor.
O Margaret, Margaret, now thy heavy curse
Is lighted on poor Hastings' wretched head!

RATCLIFFE
Come, come, dispatch. The Duke would be at
    dinner.
Make a short shrift. He longs to see your head.   95

HASTINGS
Oh, momentary grace of mortal men,   96
Which we more hunt for than the grace of God!
Who builds his hope in air of your good looks   98
Lives like a drunken sailor on a mast,
Ready with every nod to tumble down
Into the fatal bowels of the deep.

LOVELL
Come, come, dispatch. 'Tis bootless to exclaim.   102

HASTINGS
Oh, bloody Richard! Miserable England!
I prophesy the fearful'st time to thee
That ever wretched age hath looked upon.
Come, lead me to the block; bear him my head.
They smile at me who shortly shall be dead.
                                Exeunt.

❖

[3.5]

    Enter Richard [Duke of Gloucester] and
    Buckingham in rotten armor, marvelous
    ill-favored.

RICHARD
Come, cousin, canst thou quake and change thy color,
Murder thy breath in middle of a word,   2
And then again begin, and stop again,
As if thou wert distraught and mad with terror?

79.1 *Manent* They remain onstage   **81 fond** foolish   **84 footcloth**
large, richly ornamented cloth laid over the back of a horse and hanging to the ground on each side.   **stumble** (An omen of misfortune.)
95 shrift confession.   **96 grace** favor, fortune   **98 Who** Anyone who.
in . . . looks on the insubstantial foundation of your favor   **102 boot-**
less useless
3.5. Location: London. The Tower.
0.2 rotten rusty   **0.2–3 marvelous ill-favored** remarkably unattractive.   **2 Murder** i.e., stop, catch

---

44 **provided** equipped   **45 prolonged** postponed.   **48 smooth** pleasant   **49 conceit** fancy, idea.   **likes** pleases   **63 tender** dear
69 blasted shriveled   **71 Consorted** associated   **78 look** see to it

BUCKINGHAM
Tut, I can counterfeit the deep tragedian,
Speak and look back, and pry on every side,   6
Tremble and start at wagging of a straw;
Intending deep suspicion, ghastly looks   8
Are at my service, like enforcèd smiles;
And both are ready in their offices,   10
At any time, to grace my stratagems.
But what, is Catesby gone?

RICHARD
He is; and, see, he brings the Mayor along.

Enter the Mayor and Catesby.

BUCKINGHAM   Lord Mayor—
RICHARD   Look to the drawbridge there!
BUCKINGHAM   Hark, a drum!
RICHARD   Catesby, o'erlook the walls.   [*Exit Catesby.*]   17
BUCKINGHAM
Lord Mayor, the reason we have sent—
RICHARD
Look back, defend thee, here are enemies!
BUCKINGHAM
God and our innocence defend and guard us!

Enter Lovell and Ratcliffe, with Hastings' head.

RICHARD
Be patient. They are friends, Ratcliffe and Lovell.
LOVELL
Here is the head of that ignoble traitor,
The dangerous and unsuspected Hastings.
RICHARD
So dear I loved the man that I must weep.
I took him for the plainest harmless creature
That breathed upon the earth a Christian,
Made him my book wherein my soul recorded   27
The history of all her secret thoughts.
So smooth he daubed his vice with show of virtue
That, his apparent open guilt omitted—   30
I mean, his conversation with Shore's wife—   31
He lived from all attainder of suspects.   32
BUCKINGHAM
Well, well, he was the covert'st sheltered traitor   33
That ever lived. Look ye, my Lord Mayor,
Would you imagine, or almost believe,   35
Were't not that by great preservation   36
We live to tell it, that the subtle traitor
This day had plotted, in the Council House,
To murder me and my good lord of Gloucester?
MAYOR   Had he done so?   40
RICHARD
What, think you we are Turks or infidels?
Or that we would, against the form of law,

Proceed thus rashly in the villain's death,
But that the extreme peril of the case,
The peace of England, and our persons' safety,
Enforced us to this execution?
MAYOR
Now fair befall you! He deserved his death,   47
And Your good Graces both have well proceeded   48
To warn false traitors from the like attempts.
BUCKINGHAM
I never looked for better at his hands
After he once fell in with Mistress Shore.
Yet had we not determined he should die   52
Until Your Lordship came to see his end,
Which now the loving haste of these our friends,
Something against our meanings, have prevented;   55
Because, my lord, we would have had you hear   56
The traitor speak and timorously confess
The manner and the purpose of his treasons,
That you might well have signified the same
Unto the citizens, who haply may   60
Misconster us in him and wail his death.   61
MAYOR
But, my good lord, Your Grace's words shall serve
As well as I had seen and heard him speak.   63
And do not doubt, right noble princes both,
But I'll acquaint our duteous citizens
With all your just proceedings in this cause.
RICHARD
And to that end we wished Your Lordship here,
T'avoid the censures of the carping world.
BUCKINGHAM
Which, since you come too late of our intent,   69
Yet witness what you hear we did intend.   70
And so, my good Lord Mayor, we bid farewell.

Exit Mayor.

RICHARD
Go, after, after, cousin Buckingham.
The Mayor towards Guildhall hies him in all post.   73
There, at your meet'st advantage of the time,   74
Infer the bastardy of Edward's children.   75
Tell them how Edward put to death a citizen
Only for saying he would make his son
Heir to the Crown—meaning indeed his house,   78
Which, by the sign thereof, was termèd so.   79
Moreover, urge his hateful luxury   80

---

6 **back** over my shoulder.   **pry** peer   8 **Intending** pretending
10 **offices** uses, functions   17 **o'erlook** inspect   27 **book** i.e., table
book or diary   30 **his . . . omitted** apart from his manifest open guilt
31 **conversation** sexual intimacy   32 **from . . . suspects** free from all
stain of suspicion.   33 **covert'st sheltered** most secret, hidden
35 **almost** even   36 **great preservation** providential protection
40 **Had he** Would he have

47 **fair** good fortune   48 **Your . . . proceeded** Your Graces (the Dukes
of Gloucester and Buckingham) have done well   52 **had we . . . die**
we had determined he should not die   55 **Something . . . meanings**
somewhat contrary to our intent   56 **we . . . hear** we would have
wished you to have heard   60 **haply** perhaps   61 **Misconster . . . him**
i.e., misconstrue our intentions regarding him   63 **as** as if   69 **of** to
accord with   70 **witness** bear witness to   73 **Guildhall** central hall
for municipal affairs.   **hies . . . post** hurries with all possible speed.
74 **meet'st advantage** most suitable opportunity   75 **Infer** allege,
adduce   78 **the Crown** i.e., a tavern in Cheapside identified by the
sign of the Crown. (King Edward is portrayed as having been so sensitive to possible rivals that he put to death a man merely for naming
his son heir to "the Crown," even though the poor fellow innocently
meant nothing more than his own tavern. The story is from Sir
Thomas More's *History of King Richard III*.)   79 **sign** tavern or shop
sign displayed over the door   80 **luxury** lechery

And bestial appetite in change of lust, 81
Which stretched unto their servants, daughters, wives, 82
Even where his raging eye or savage heart,
Without control, lusted to make a prey.
Nay, for a need, thus far come near my person: 85
Tell them, when that my mother went with child 86
Of that insatiate Edward, noble York 87
My princely father then had wars in France,
And by true computation of the time
Found that the issue was not his begot—
Which well appearèd in his lineaments, 91
Being nothing like the noble duke my father.
Yet touch this sparingly, as 'twere far off,
Because, my lord, you know my mother lives.

BUCKINGHAM
Doubt not, my lord, I'll play the orator
As if the golden fee for which I plead 96
Were for myself. And so, my lord, adieu.

RICHARD
If you thrive well, bring them to Baynard's Castle, 98
Where you shall find me well accompanied
With reverend fathers and well-learnèd bishops.

BUCKINGHAM
I go; and towards three or four o'clock
Look for the news that the Guildhall affords.
Exit Buckingham.

RICHARD
Go, Lovell, with all speed to Doctor Shaw. 103
[*To Ratcliffe*] Go thou to Friar Penker. Bid them both 104
Meet me within this hour at Baynard's Castle.
Exeunt [all but Richard].

Now will I go to take some privy order 106
To draw the brats of Clarence out of sight,
And to give order that no manner person 108
Have any time recourse unto the princes. *Exit.* 109

❖

[3.6]

Enter a Scrivener [with a paper in his hand].

SCRIVENER
Here is the indictment of the good Lord Hastings,
Which in a set hand fairly is engrossed 2
That it may be today read o'er in Paul's. 3
And mark how well the sequel hangs together: 4

Eleven hours I have spent to write it over,
For yesternight by Catesby was it sent me;
The precedent was full as long a-doing. 7
And yet within these five hours Hastings lived,
Untainted, unexamined, free, at liberty. 9
Here's a good world the while! Who is so gross 10
That cannot see this palpable device?
Yet who so bold but says he sees it not?
Bad is the world, and all will come to naught
When such ill dealing must be seen in thought. 14
Exit.

❖

[3.7]

*Enter Richard [Duke of Gloucester] and
Buckingham, at several doors.*

RICHARD
How now, how now, what say the citizens?

BUCKINGHAM
Now, by the holy mother of our Lord,
The citizens are mum, say not a word.

RICHARD
Touched you the bastardy of Edward's children? 4

BUCKINGHAM
I did; with his contract with Lady Lucy 5
And his contract by deputy in France; 6
Th'insatiate greediness of his desire 7
And his enforcement of the city wives; 8
His tyranny for trifles; his own bastardy, 9
As being got, your father then in France, 10
And his resemblance, being not like the Duke.
Withal I did infer your lineaments, 12
Being the right idea of your father 13
Both in your form and nobleness of mind;
Laid open all your victories in Scotland, 15
Your discipline in war, wisdom in peace, 16
Your bounty, virtue, fair humility;
Indeed, left nothing fitting for your purpose
Untouched or slightly handled in discourse.
And when mine oratory drew toward end,
I bid them that did love their country's good
Cry, "God save Richard, England's royal king!"

RICHARD   And did they so?

---

7 **precedent** prepared indictment serving as a first draft   9 **Untainted,
unexamined** not yet accused or interrogated   10 **Here's . . . while!**
Here's a fine state of affairs!   **gross** dull, stupid   14 **seen in thought**
i.e., perceived in silence.
3.7. Location: The courtyard of Baynard's Castle.
0.2 *several* separate   4 **Touched you** Did you deal with, touch upon,
discuss   5 **contract** betrothal.   **Lady Lucy** Elizabeth Lucy (by whom
Edward had a child, though there was no formal contract of
betrothal)   6 **deputy** (See *3 Henry VI*, 3.3.49 ff., where Warwick, as
deputy, contracts with Louis XI of France for the marriage of King
Edward to Lady Bona, sister of the French queen.)   7 **Th'insatiate** the
insatiable   8 **enforcement** forcible seduction   9 **tyranny for trifles**
harsh punishment of minor offenses, or cruel behavior over trifles
10 **got** begot   12 **Withal . . . lineaments** Besides that, I pointed to
your features   13 **right idea** true image   15 **Laid . . . Scotland** I elaborated on your successful expedition against Scotland in 1482
16 **discipline** skill, training

---

81 **in . . . lust** i.e., constantly desiring new mistresses   82 **their** i.e.,
the citizens'   85 **for a need** if necessary   86–7 **when . . . Of** when my
mother was pregnant with   91 **his lineaments** Edward's features
96 **golden fee** i.e., crown   98 **Baynard's Castle** Richard's residence
on the north bank of the Thames. It was founded by Baynard, a
nobleman in the time of the Conquest, and had belonged to Richard's
father.   103, 104 **Doctor Shaw, Friar Penker** (Well-known divines
who delivered sermons in Richard's favor.)   106 **take . . . order** give
some secret instruction   108 **no manner person** no one at all
109 **Have . . . recourse** have access at any time
3.6. Location: London. A street.
2 **in . . . engrossed** is written out in a style of script used for legal documents   3 **read . . . Paul's** posted and read publicly in St. Paul's
Cathedral.   4 **the sequel** what follows

BUCKINGHAM

No, so God help me, they spake not a word,
But, like dumb statues or breathing stones,
Stared each on other and looked deadly pale.
Which when I saw, I reprehended them,
And asked the Mayor what meant this willful silence.
His answer was, the people were not used
To be spoke to but by the Recorder.   30
Then he was urged to tell my tale again:
"Thus saith the Duke, thus hath the Duke inferred"—   32
But nothing spake in warrant from himself.   33
When he had done, some followers of mine own,
At lower end of the hall, hurled up their caps,
And some ten voices cried, "God save King Richard!"
And thus I took the vantage of those few: 37
"Thanks, gentle citizens and friends," quoth I,
"This general applause and cheerful shout
Argues your wisdoms and your love to Richard"—
And even here brake off and came away.   41

RICHARD

What tongueless blocks were they! Would they not speak?

BUCKINGHAM   No, by my troth, my lord.

RICHARD

Will not the Mayor, then, and his brethren come?   44

BUCKINGHAM

The Mayor is here at hand. Intend some fear;   45
Be not you spoke with but by mighty suit.   46
And look you get a prayer book in your hand,
And stand between two churchmen, good my lord,
For on that ground I'll make a holy descant;   49
And be not easily won to our requests.
Play the maid's part: still answer nay and take it.

RICHARD

I go; and if you plead as well for them
As I can say nay to thee for myself,
No doubt we'll bring it to a happy issue.   54

BUCKINGHAM

Go, go, up to the leads. The Lord Mayor knocks.   55

[Exit Richard.]

Enter the Mayor, [aldermen,] and citizens.

Welcome, my lord. I dance attendance here;   56
I think the Duke will not be spoke withal.   57

Enter Catesby.

Now, Catesby, what says your lord to my request?

CATESBY

He doth entreat Your Grace, my noble lord,
To visit him tomorrow or next day.
He is within, with two right reverend fathers,
Divinely bent to meditation,

And in no worldly suits would he be moved
To draw him from his holy exercise.

BUCKINGHAM

Return, good Catesby, to the gracious Duke.
Tell him myself, the Mayor and aldermen,
In deep designs, in matter of great moment,
No less importing than our general good,   68
Are come to have some conference with His Grace.

CATESBY

I'll signify so much unto him straight.   *Exit.*

BUCKINGHAM

Aha, my lord, this prince is not an Edward!
He is not lolling on a lewd love bed
But on his knees at meditation;
Not dallying with a brace of courtesans   74
But meditating with two deep divines;   75
Not sleeping, to engross his idle body,   76
But praying, to enrich his watchful soul.
Happy were England, would this virtuous prince
Take on His Grace the sovereignty thereof;
But sure I fear we shall not win him to it.

MAYOR

Marry, God defend His Grace should say us nay!   81

BUCKINGHAM

I fear he will.—Here Catesby comes again.

Enter Catesby.

Now, Catesby, what says His Grace?

CATESBY   My lord,
He wonders to what end you have assembled
Such troops of citizens to come to him,
His Grace not being warned thereof before.
He fears, my lord, you mean no good to him.

BUCKINGHAM

Sorry I am my noble cousin should
Suspect me that I mean no good to him.
By heaven, we come to him in perfect love,
And so once more return and tell His Grace.

Exit [Catesby].

When holy and devout religious men
Are at their beads, 'tis much to draw them thence,   93
So sweet is zealous contemplation.   94

Enter Richard aloft, between two bishops. [Catesby returns to the main stage.]

MAYOR

See where His Grace stands, 'tween two clergymen!

BUCKINGHAM

Two props of virtue for a Christian prince,
To stay him from the fall of vanity.   97
And, see, a book of prayer in his hand,
True ornaments to know a holy man.—   99
Famous Plantagenet, most gracious prince,

---

30 the Recorder London's chief legal officer.   **32 inferred** alleged, asserted   **33 in . . . himself** on his own authority.   **37 vantage** advantage   **41 brake** broke   **44 brethren** fellow aldermen   **45 Intend** Pretend   **46 mighty suit** importunate entreaty.   **49 ground** the plainsong or melody on which a *descant* or melodious accompaniment is raised   **54 issue** outcome.   **55 leads** flat lead coverings for roof; hence, the roof itself.   **56 dance attendance** i.e., am kept waiting   **57 withal** with.

68 No less importing concerned with nothing less   **74 brace** pair   **75 deep** learned   **76 engross** fatten   **81 defend** forbid   **93 beads** i.e., prayers beads.   **much** hard   **94.1 aloft** i.e., in the gallery above the stage, rear. (The tiring-house facade in this scene is imagined to be the facade of Baynard's Castle.)   **97 stay** steady or keep   **99 ornaments** i.e., the bishops as well as the prayer book

Lend favorable ear to our requests,
And pardon us the interruption
Of thy devotion and right Christian zeal.

RICHARD
My lord, there needs no such apology.
I do beseech Your Grace to pardon me,
Who, earnest in the service of my God,
Deferred the visitation of my friends.
But, leaving this, what is Your Grace's pleasure?

BUCKINGHAM
Even that, I hope, which pleaseth God above,
And all good men of this ungoverned isle.

RICHARD
I do suspect I have done some offense
That seems disgracious in the city's eye,   112
And that you come to reprehend my ignorance.

BUCKINGHAM
You have, my lord. Would it might please Your Grace,
On our entreaties, to amend your fault!

RICHARD
Else wherefore breathe I in a Christian land?   116

BUCKINGHAM
Know then, it is your fault that you resign
The supreme seat, the throne majestical,
The sceptered office of your ancestors,
Your state of fortune and your due of birth,   120
The lineal glory of your royal house,
To the corruption of a blemished stock;   122
While, in the mildness of your sleepy thoughts,   123
Which here we waken to our country's good,
The noble isle doth want her proper limbs;   125
Her face defaced with scars of infamy,
Her royal stock graft with ignoble plants,   127
And almost shouldered in the swallowing gulf   128
Of dark forgetfulness and deep oblivion.
Which to recure, we heartily solicit   130
Your gracious self to take on you the charge
And kingly government of this your land—
Not as protector, steward, substitute,
Or lowly factor for another's gain,   134
But as successively from blood to blood,   135
Your right of birth, your empery, your own.   136
For this, consorted with the citizens,   137
Your very worshipful and loving friends,   138
And by their vehement instigation,
In this just cause come I to move Your Grace.

RICHARD
I cannot tell if to depart in silence
Or bitterly to speak in your reproof

Best fitteth my degree or your condition.   143
If not to answer, you might haply think   144
Tongue-tied ambition, not replying, yielded   145
To bear the golden yoke of sovereignty,
Which fondly you would here impose on me.   147
If to reprove you for this suit of yours,
So seasoned with your faithful love to me,   149
Then on the other side I checked my friends.   150
Therefore, to speak, and to avoid the first,
And then, in speaking, not to incur the last,
Definitively thus I answer you.   153
Your love deserves my thanks, but my desert   154
Unmeritable shuns your high request.   155
First, if all obstacles were cut away,
And that my path were even to the crown   157
As the ripe revenue and due of birth,   158
Yet so much is my poverty of spirit,
So mighty and so many my defects,
That I would rather hide me from my greatness—   161
Being a bark to brook no mighty sea—   162
Than in my greatness covet to be hid   163
And in the vapor of my glory smothered.
But, God be thanked, there is no need of me,
And much I need to help you, were there need.   166
The royal tree hath left us royal fruit,
Which, mellowed by the stealing hours of time,   168
Will well become the seat of majesty
And make, no doubt, us happy by his reign.
On him I lay that you would lay on me,   171
The right and fortune of his happy stars,
Which God defend that I should wring from him!   173

BUCKINGHAM
My lord, this argues conscience in Your Grace;
But the respects thereof are nice and trivial,   175
All circumstances well considerèd.
You say that Edward is your brother's son.
So say we too, but not by Edward's wife;
For first was he contract to Lady Lucy—   179
Your mother lives a witness to his vow—   180
And afterward by substitute betrothed   181
To Bona, sister to the King of France.   182
These both put off, a poor petitioner,
A care-crazed mother to a many sons,

---

112 disgracious unbecoming, displeasing   **116 Else . . . land?** i.e.,
How could I call myself a Christian if I am not prepared to amend my
faults?   **120 state of fortune** position to which fortune entitles you
122 blemished i.e., through bastardy; see lines 177–91 below
123 sleepy passive   **125 want her proper limbs** lack its own limbs, is
crippled   **127 graft** engrafted   **128 shouldered in** jostled into, or
immersed up to the shoulders in   **130 recure** restore, make whole
134 factor agent   **135 successively** in order of succession   **136 empery**
empire   **137 consorted** associated, leagued   **138 worshipful** respectful

---

143 degree rank.   **condition** social status.   **144 haply** perhaps
145 Tongue-tied silent. (Silence gives consent.)   **yielded** consented
147 fondly foolishly   **149 seasoned** i.e., made agreeable or palatable
150 checked rebuked, i.e., would have rebuked   **153 Definitively**
once and for all   **154–5 my desert Unmeritable** my unworthiness
157 even smooth   **158 ripe revenue** possession ready to be inherited
161 my greatness i.e., my claim to the throne   **162 bark** ship.   **brook**
endure   **163 Than . . . hid** than wish to be enveloped in and overwhelmed by my greatness, i.e., the throne   **166 I need** I lack the requisite ability   **168 stealing** stealthily moving   **171 that** what
173 defend forbid   **175 respects thereof** considerations by which
you support your argument.   **nice** overscrupulous   **179 contract**
contracted   **180 Your . . . vow** (According to the chronicles, Richard's
mother, in opposing Edward's intention of marrying Lady Grey because
it was interfering with the negotiations for his marriage to Lady Bona
of Savoy, asserted that Lady Elizabeth Lucy was already Edward's
trothplight wife. Compare with 3.5.75 and 3.7.6.)   **181 substitute**
proxy   **182 sister** i.e., sister-in-law, the Queen's sister

A beauty-waning and distressèd widow,
Even in the afternoon of her best days,
Made prize and purchase of his wanton eye,   187
Seduced the pitch and height of his degree   188
To base declension and loathèd bigamy.   189
By her, in his unlawful bed, he got
This Edward, whom our manners call the Prince.   191
More bitterly could I expostulate,   192
Save that, for reverence to some alive,   193
I give a sparing limit to my tongue.
Then, good my lord, take to your royal self   195
This proffered benefit of dignity,
If not to bless us and the land withal,
Yet to draw forth your noble ancestry   198
From the corruption of abusing times
Unto a lineal true-derivèd course.

MAYOR
Do, good my lord. Your citizens entreat you.

BUCKINGHAM
Refuse not, mighty lord, this proffered love.

CATESBY
Oh, make them joyful. Grant their lawful suit!

RICHARD
Alas, why would you heap this care on me?
I am unfit for state and majesty.
I do beseech you, take it not amiss;
I cannot nor I will not yield to you.

BUCKINGHAM
If you refuse it—as, in love and zeal,   208
Loath to depose the child, your brother's son,
As well we know your tenderness of heart   210
And gentle, kind, effeminate remorse,   211
Which we have noted in you to your kindred
And equally indeed to all estates—   213
Yet know, whe'er you accept our suit or no,   214
Your brother's son shall never reign our king,
But we will plant some other in the throne
To the disgrace and downfall of your house.
And in this resolution here we leave you.—
Come, citizens. Zounds! I'll entreat no more.   219

RICHARD
Oh, do not swear, my lord of Buckingham.

Exeunt [Buckingham,
Mayor, aldermen, and the citizens].

CATESBY
Call him again, sweet prince. Accept their suit.
If you deny them, all the land will rue it.

RICHARD
Will you enforce me to a world of cares?
Call them again. I am not made of stone,
But penetrable to your kind entreaties,
Albeit against my conscience and my soul.

Enter Buckingham and the rest.

Cousin of Buckingham, and sage, grave men,
Since you will buckle fortune on my back,
To bear her burden, whe'er I will or no,
I must have patience to endure the load.
But if black scandal or foul-faced reproach
Attend the sequel of your imposition,   232
Your mere enforcement shall acquittance me   233
From all the impure blots and stains thereof;
For God doth know, and you may partly see,
How far I am from the desire of this.

MAYOR
God bless Your Grace! We see it and will say it.

RICHARD
In saying so, you shall but say the truth.

BUCKINGHAM
Then I salute you with this royal title:
Long live Richard, England's worthy king!

MAYOR AND CITIZENS   Amen.

BUCKINGHAM
Tomorrow may it please you to be crowned?

RICHARD
Even when you please, for you will have it so.

BUCKINGHAM
Tomorrow, then, we will attend Your Grace.
And so most joyfully we take our leave.

RICHARD [*to the Bishops*]
Come, let us to our holy work again.—
Farewell, my cousin. Farewell, gentle friends. *Exeunt.*

❖

4.1

Enter [at one door] the Queen [Elizabeth], the
Duchess of York, and Marquess [of] Dorset; [at
another door] Anne, Duchess of Gloucester,
[leading Lady Margaret Plantagenet, Clarence's
young daughter].

DUCHESS
Who meets us here? My niece Plantagenet   1
Led in the hand of her kind aunt of Gloucester?
Now, for my life, she's wand'ring to the Tower,   3
On pure heart's love to greet the tender Prince.   4
Daughter, well met.

ANNE   God give Your Graces both 5
A happy and a joyful time of day!

QUEEN ELIZABETH
As much to you, good sister. Whither away?   7

---

187 **purchase** booty   188–9 **Seduced . . . declension** i.e., seduced him
away from his high rank to ignoble decline. (*Pitch* is the highest point
in a falcon's flight.)   189 **bigamy** (Edward was not only bound by
previous contracts, as indicated in lines 178–82 above, but also, by
marrying a widow, entered into a union that was widely regarded as
bigamous.)   191 **manners** sense of politeness   192 **expostulate** discuss, dilate   193 **some alive** i.e., the Duchess of York. (See 3.5.93–4.)
195 **good my lord** my good lord   198 **draw forth** rescue, extract
208 **as** from being   210 **As . . . know** since we know well   211 **kind,**
effeminate remorse natural, tender pity   213 **estates** ranks. (Buckingham argues that this virtue of pity is found in Richard's treatment
of everyone.)   214 **whe'er** whether   219 **Zounds!** By His (God's)
wounds!

232 **your imposition** the duty that you lay upon me   233 **Your . . .**
acquittance me the mere fact of your insistence will exonerate me
4.1. Location: London. Before the Tower.
1 **niece** i.e., granddaughter   3 **for** on   4 **On** out of.   **tender** young
5 **Daughter** i.e., Daughter-in-law   7 **sister** i.e., sister-in-law.

ANNE

No farther than the Tower, and, as I guess,
Upon the like devotion as yourselves,   9
To gratulate the gentle princes there.   10

QUEEN ELIZABETH

Kind sister, thanks. We'll enter all together.

Enter [Brackenbury] the Lieutenant.

And, in good time, here the Lieutenant comes.—
Master Lieutenant, pray you, by your leave,
How doth the Prince and my young son of York?

BRACKENBURY

Right well, dear madam. By your patience,
I may not suffer you to visit them;   16
The King hath strictly charged the contrary.

QUEEN ELIZABETH

The King! Who's that?

BRACKENBURY   I mean the Lord Protector.

QUEEN ELIZABETH

The Lord protect him from that kingly title!
Hath he set bounds between their love and me?   20
I am their mother; who shall bar me from them?

DUCHESS

I am their father's mother; I will see them.

ANNE

Their aunt I am in law, in love their mother;
Then bring me to their sights. I'll bear thy blame
And take thy office from thee, on my peril.   25

BRACKENBURY

No, madam, no; I may not leave it so.
I am bound by oath, and therefore pardon me.

Exit Lieutenant.

Enter [Lord] Stanley [Earl of Derby].

STANLEY

Let me but meet you, ladies, one hour hence,
And I'll salute Your Grace of York as mother,   29
And reverend looker-on, of two fair queens.   30
[*To Anne*] Come, madam, you must straight to
    Westminster,
There to be crownèd Richard's royal queen.

QUEEN ELIZABETH   Ah, cut my lace asunder,   33
That my pent heart may have some scope to beat,
Or else I swoon with this dead-killing news!

ANNE

Despiteful tidings! Oh, unpleasing news!

DORSET

Be of good cheer. Mother, how fares Your Grace?

QUEEN ELIZABETH

Oh, Dorset, speak not to me. Get thee gone!
Death and destruction dogs thee at thy heels;
Thy mother's name is ominous to children.
If thou wilt outstrip death, go cross the seas

And live with Richmond, from the reach of hell.   42
Go, hie thee, hie thee from this slaughterhouse,   43
Lest thou increase the number of the dead
And make me die the thrall of Margaret's curse,   45
Nor mother, wife, nor England's counted queen.   46

STANLEY

Full of wise care is this your counsel, madam.
[*To Dorset*] Take all the swift advantage of the hours.
You shall have letters from me to my son   49
In your behalf, to meet you on the way.   50
Be not ta'en tardy by unwise delay.   51

DUCHESS

Oh, ill-dispersing wind of misery!   52
Oh, my accursèd womb, the bed of death!
A cockatrice hast thou hatched to the world,   54
Whose unavoided eye is murderous.

STANLEY [*to Anne*]

Come, madam, come. I in all haste was sent.

ANNE

And I with all unwillingness will go.
Oh, would to God that the inclusive verge   58
Of golden metal that must round my brow
Were red-hot steel, to sear me to the brains!
Anointed let me be with deadly venom   61
And die ere men can say, "God save the Queen!"

QUEEN ELIZABETH

Go, go, poor soul. I envy not thy glory.
To feed my humor, wish thyself no harm.   64

ANNE

No? Why? When he that is my husband now
Came to me, as I followed Henry's corpse,
When scarce the blood was well washed from his hands
Which issued from my other angel husband   68
And that dear saint which then I weeping followed—   69
Oh, when, I say, I looked on Richard's face,
This was my wish: "Be thou," quoth I, "accurst
For making me, so young, so old a widow!   72
And, when thou wed'st, let sorrow haunt thy bed;
And be thy wife—if any be so mad—
More miserable by the life of thee
Than thou hast made me by my dear lord's death!"
Lo, ere I can repeat this curse again,
Within so small a time, my woman's heart
Grossly grew captive to his honey words   79
And proved the subject of mine own soul's curse,

---

42 with Richmond i.e., with Henry Tudor, Earl of Richmond, at this time in Brittany **43 hie** hasten **45 thrall** subject, victim **46 Nor** neither. **counted** accepted, esteemed **49–50 You . . . way** i.e., I will arrange to have a letter catch up with you on your journey, recommending you to my stepson, the Earl of Richmond. (Lord Stanley's own son, George Stanley, may also be involved in this rapid negotiation; see 4.4.494–6 ff. below.) **51 ta'en** taken, caught **52 ill-dispersing** evil-spreading **54 cockatrice** basilisk. (See the note for 1.2.153.) **58 inclusive verge** enclosing circle, i.e., the crown, here likened to an instrument of torture used to punish regicides or other criminals **61 Anointed** (Anne desires to be anointed with poison rather than with holy oil, as in the ceremony of coronation.) **64 To . . . harm** Do not curse yourself (or, possibly, I do not wish you harm) just to satisfy my vengeful mood. **68 angel husband** Edward, son of Henry VI **69 saint** Henry VI **72 so old a widow** i.e., prematurely old as a widow. **79 Grossly** stupidly

---

9 like devotion same devout errand **10 gratulate** greet, salute **16 suffer** permit **20 bounds** barriers **25 take . . . thee** i.e., relieve you of the responsibility **29 mother** i.e., mother-in-law (of Elizabeth as widow of Edward and of Anne as wife of King Richard) **30 looker-on** beholder. **two fair queens** i.e., Elizabeth and Anne, since Anne's husband, Richard, is about to be crowned. **33 lace** cord used to lace the bodice

Which hitherto hath held mine eyes from rest;   81
For never yet one hour in his bed
Did I enjoy the golden dew of sleep,
But with his timorous dreams was still awaked.   84
Besides, he hates me for my father Warwick,
And will, no doubt, shortly be rid of me.

QUEEN ELIZABETH
Poor heart, adieu! I pity thy complaining.

ANNE
No more than with my soul I mourn for yours.

DORSET
Farewell, thou woeful welcomer of glory!   89

ANNE
Adieu, poor soul, that tak'st thy leave of it!

DUCHESS [*to Dorset*]
Go thou to Richmond, and good fortune guide thee!
[*To Anne*] Go thou to Richard, and good angels tend thee!
[*To Queen Elizabeth*] Go thou to sanctuary, and good
    thoughts possess thee!
I to my grave, where peace and rest lie with me!
Eighty-odd years of sorrow have I seen,
And each hour's joy wracked with a week of teen.   96
                        [*They start to go.*]

QUEEN ELIZABETH
Stay, yet look back with me unto the Tower.
Pity, you ancient stones, those tender babes
Whom envy hath immured within your walls—   99
Rough cradle for such little pretty ones!
Rude ragged nurse, old sullen playfellow   101
For tender princes, use my babies well!
So foolish sorrows bids your stones farewell.   *Exeunt.*

4.2

Sound a sennet. Enter Richard, in pomp;
Buckingham, Catesby, Ratcliffe, Lovell, [a Page,
and others].

KING RICHARD
Stand all apart. Cousin of Buckingham!   1
            [*The others stand aside, out of earshot.*]

BUCKINGHAM   My gracious sovereign?

KING RICHARD
Give me thy hand.
            Sound [trumpets. Here he ascends the throne.]
                    Thus high, by thy advice
And thy assistance, is King Richard seated.
But shall we wear these glories for a day?
Or shall they last, and we rejoice in them?

BUCKINGHAM
Still live they, and forever let them last!

KING RICHARD
Ah, Buckingham, now do I play the touch,   8
To try if thou be current gold indeed: 9
Young Edward lives. Think now what I would speak.

BUCKINGHAM   Say on, my loving lord.

KING RICHARD
Why, Buckingham, I say I would be king.

BUCKINGHAM
Why, so you are, my thrice-renownèd lord.

KING RICHARD
Ha! Am I king? 'Tis so. But Edward lives.

BUCKINGHAM
True, noble prince.

KING RICHARD   Oh, bitter consequence,   15
That Edward still should live "true, noble prince"!   16
Cousin, thou wast not wont to be so dull.   17
Shall I be plain? I wish the bastards dead,
And I would have it suddenly performed.   19
What say'st thou now? Speak suddenly; be brief.

BUCKINGHAM   Your Grace may do your pleasure.

KING RICHARD
Tut, tut, thou art all ice; thy kindness freezes.
Say, have I thy consent that they shall die?

BUCKINGHAM
Give me some little breath, some pause, dear lord,
Before I positively speak in this.
I will resolve you herein presently.   *Exit Buckingham.*   26

CATESBY [*to those standing aside*]
The King is angry. See, he gnaws his lip.

KING RICHARD [*aside*]
I will converse with iron-witted fools   28
And unrespective boys. None are for me   29
That look into me with considerate eyes.   30
High-reaching Buckingham grows circumspect.—   31
Boy!

PAGE [*approaching*]   My lord?

KING RICHARD
Know'st thou not any whom corrupting gold
Will tempt unto a close exploit of death?   35

PAGE
My lord, I know a discontented gentleman
Whose humble means match not his haughty spirit.
Gold were as good as twenty orators,
And will, no doubt, tempt him to anything.

KING RICHARD
What is his name?

PAGE   His name, my lord, is Tyrrel.

KING RICHARD
I partly know the man. Go call him hither, boy.
                            Exit [Page].

---

81 **hitherto** until now   84 **timorous** full of fears.   **still** continually
89 **glory** i.e., the rank of queen—*woeful* because it involves marriage
to Richard.   96 **wracked** destroyed, or, *racked*, tortured.   **teen** woe.
99 **envy** malice.   **immured** walled up   101 **Rude** Rough
4.2. Location: London. The royal court.
1 **apart** aside.

8 **play the touch** play the part of a touchstone (to test the quality of
gold)   9 **current** sterling, genuine   15 **bitter consequence** i.e., intolerable answer to my words, and an intolerable fact   16 **"true, noble
prince"** (Richard mockingly repeats Buckingham's evasive reply in
line 15 and applies it to the irritating fact that young Edward still
lives and is a noble prince.)   17 **wast not wont** used not   19 **suddenly** swiftly   26 **resolve** answer   28–31 **I will . . . circumspect** i.e.,
Apparently I have no choice but to communicate my intentions to
dim-witted fools and inattentive boys. I will have nothing more to do
with men who look into my thoughts too searchingly. Ambitious
Buckingham grows wary.   35 **close** secret

[*Aside*] The deep-revolving, witty Buckingham   42
No more shall be the neighbor to my counsels.
Hath he so long held out with me untired,
And stops he now for breath? Well, be it so.

Enter [Lord] Stanley [Earl of Derby].

How now, Lord Stanley? What's the news?
STANLEY   Know, my loving lord,
The Marquess Dorset, as I hear, is fled
To Richmond, in the parts where he abides.
                                   [*He stands apart.*]

KING RICHARD
Come hither, Catesby. Rumor it abroad
That Anne my wife is very grievous sick;
I will take order for her keeping close.   52
Inquire me out some mean poor gentleman,   53
Whom I will marry straight to Clarence' daughter.
The boy is foolish, and I fear not him.   55
Look how thou dream'st! I say again, give out
That Anne my queen is sick and like to die.   57
About it, for it stands me much upon   58
To stop all hopes whose growth may damage me.
                                   [*Exit Catesby.*]
I must be married to my brother's daughter,   60
Or else my kingdom stands on brittle glass.
Murder her brothers, and then marry her—
Uncertain way of gain! But I am in
So far in blood that sin will pluck on sin.   64
Tear-falling pity dwells not in this eye.   65

Enter [Page, with] Tyrrel.

Is thy name Tyrrel?
TYRREL
James Tyrrel, and your most obedient subject.
KING RICHARD
Art thou, indeed?
TYRREL   Prove me, my gracious lord.   68
KING RICHARD
Dar'st thou resolve to kill a friend of mine?
TYRREL   Please you;   70
But I had rather kill two enemies.
KING RICHARD
Why, there thou hast it: two deep enemies,
Foes to my rest and my sweet sleep's disturbers
Are they that I would have thee deal upon—   74
Tyrrel, I mean those bastards in the Tower.
TYRREL
Let me have open means to come to them,   76
And soon I'll rid you from the fear of them.

KING RICHARD
Thou sing'st sweet music. Hark, come hither, Tyrrel.
Go, by this token. [*He gives him a token.*] Rise, and lend
      thine ear.   *Whispers.*
There is no more but so. Say it is done,
And I will love thee and prefer thee for it.   81
TYRREL   I will dispatch it straight.   *Exit.*

Enter Buckingham.

BUCKINGHAM
My lord, I have considered in my mind
The late request that you did sound me in.   84
KING RICHARD
Well, let that rest. Dorset is fled to Richmond.
BUCKINGHAM   I hear the news, my lord.
KING RICHARD
Stanley, he is your wife's son. Well, look to it.   87
BUCKINGHAM
My lord, I claim the gift, my due by promise,
For which your honor and your faith is pawned: 89
Th'earldom of Hereford and the movables
Which you have promisèd I shall possess.
KING RICHARD
Stanley, look to your wife. If she convey
Letters to Richmond, you shall answer it.   93
BUCKINGHAM
What says Your Highness to my just request?
KING RICHARD
I do remember me, Henry the Sixth
Did prophesy that Richmond should be king,
When Richmond was a little peevish boy.
A king! Perhaps, perhaps—
BUCKINGHAM   My lord!
KING RICHARD
How chance the prophet could not at that time   100
Have told me, I being by, that I should kill him?   101
BUCKINGHAM
My lord, your promise for the earldom!
KING RICHARD
Richmond! When last I was at Exeter,
The Mayor in courtesy showed me the castle
And called it Rougemont, at which name I started,   105
Because a bard of Ireland told me once
I should not live long after I saw Richmond.
BUCKINGHAM   My lord!
KING RICHARD   Ay, what's o'clock?   109
BUCKINGHAM
I am thus bold to put Your Grace in mind
Of what you promised me.
KING RICHARD   Well, but what's o'clock?
BUCKINGHAM   Upon the stroke of ten.
KING RICHARD   Well, let it strike.
BUCKINGHAM   Why let it strike?

---

42 deep-revolving deeply scheming. **witty** cunning **52 I will . . . close** I will give orders for her close confinement. **53 mean** of humble station **55 boy** i.e., Clarence's eldest son, Edward Plantagenet, Earl of Warwick **57 like** likely **58 stands . . . upon** is a matter of the utmost importance to me **60 brother's daughter** i.e., Elizabeth of York, daughter to Edward IV, who will, in fact, later become the queen of Henry VII; see 4.5.7–9 and 5.5.29–31 **64 pluck on** draw on **65 Tear-falling** Tear-dropping **68 Prove** Test **70 Please** If it please **74 deal upon** proceed against **76 open** unhampered

81 prefer promote, advance **84 late** recent. **sound me in** ask me about. **87 he** i.e., Richmond **89 pawned** pledged **93 it** for it. **100 the prophet** i.e., Henry VI **101 by** nearby. **him** (The word applies to Richmond and Henry VI.) **105 Rougemont** i.e., Red Hill. (With a play on "Richmond.") **109 what's o'clock?** what time is it?

KING RICHARD
Because that, like a jack, thou keep'st the stroke   116
Betwixt thy begging and my meditation.
I am not in the giving vein today.   118

BUCKINGHAM
May it please you to resolve me in my suit.   119

KING RICHARD
Thou troublest me. I am not in the vein.

Exit [with all but Buckingham].

BUCKINGHAM
And is it thus? Repays he my deep service
With such contempt? Made I him king for this?
Oh, let me think on Hastings, and be gone
To Brecknock, while my fearful head is on!   *Exit.* 124

❖

[4.3]

Enter Tyrrel.

TYRREL
The tyrannous and bloody act is done,
The most arch deed of piteous massacre
That ever yet this land was guilty of.   2
Dighton and Forrest, whom I did suborn   4
To do this piece of ruthless butchery,
Albeit they were fleshed villains, bloody dogs,   6
Melted with tenderness and mild compassion,
Wept like to children in their deaths' sad story.   8
"Oh, thus," quoth Dighton, "lay the gentle babes."
"Thus, thus," quoth Forrest, "girdling one another
Within their alabaster innocent arms.
Their lips were four red roses on a stalk,
Which in their summer beauty kissed each other.
A book of prayers on their pillow lay,
Which once," quoth Forrest, "almost changed my mind;
But oh, the devil!"—there the villain stopped;
When Dighton thus told on: "We smotherèd
The most replenishèd sweet work of Nature   18
That from the prime creation e'er she framed."   19
Hence both are gone; with conscience and remorse   20
They could not speak; and so I left them both,
To bear this tidings to the bloody king.

Enter [King] Richard.

And here he comes.—All health, my sovereign lord!

KING RICHARD
Kind Tyrrel, am I happy in thy news?

TYRREL
If to have done the thing you gave in charge   25
Beget your happiness, be happy then,
For it is done.

KING RICHARD   But didst thou see them dead?

TYRREL
I did, my lord.

KING RICHARD   And buried, gentle Tyrrel?

TYRREL
The chaplain of the Tower hath buried them;
But where, to say the truth, I do not know.

KING RICHARD
Come to me, Tyrrel, soon at after-supper,   31
When thou shalt tell the process of their death.   32
Meantime, but think how I may do thee good,
And be inheritor of thy desire.   34
Farewell till then.

TYRREL   I humbly take my leave.   [*Exit.*]

KING RICHARD
The son of Clarence have I pent up close,   36
His daughter meanly have I matched in marriage,   37
The sons of Edward sleep in Abraham's bosom,   38
And Anne my wife hath bid this world good night.
Now, for I know the Breton Richmond aims   40
At young Elizabeth, my brother's daughter,   41
And by that knot looks proudly on the crown,   42
To her go I, a jolly thriving wooer.

Enter Ratcliffe.

RATCLIFFE   My lord!

KING RICHARD
Good or bad news, that thou com'st in so bluntly?

RATCLIFFE
Bad news, my lord. Morton is fled to Richmond,   46
And Buckingham, backed with the hardy Welshmen,
Is in the field, and still his power increaseth.   48

KING RICHARD
Ely with Richmond troubles me more near   49
Than Buckingham and his rash-levied strength.   50
Come, I have learned that fearful commenting   51
Is leaden servitor to dull delay;   52
Delay leads impotent and snail-paced beggary.   53
Then fiery expedition be my wing,   54
Jove's Mercury, and herald for a king!   55

---

116 jack the figure of a man that strikes the bell on the outside of a clock. (With a play on the meaning "lowbred fellow." Richard's complaint is that Buckingham, like the jack of a clock, being on the point of striking the hour—i.e., speaking his request—breaks the continuity of Richard's reflections.) **118 vein** mood **119 resolve me** give me a final answer **124 Brecknock** i.e., Brecon, Buckingham's family seat in Wales. **fearful** full of fears
4.3. Location: London. The royal court.
2 arch deed i.e., chief or notorious act **4 suborn** bribe **6 fleshed** experienced in bloodshed **8 in their . . . story** in telling the story of their deaths. **18 replenishèd** complete, perfect **19 prime** first **20 gone** undone, unnerved

25 gave in charge ordered, commanded **31 after-supper** dessert after supper **32 process** story **34 be . . . desire** expect to get what you ask. **36 pent up close** strictly confined **37 His . . . marriage** (Margaret Plantagenet was about twelve years old when Richard died. Shakespeare may have confused her with Lady Cicely, a daughter of Edward IV, whom Richard, according to Holinshed, intended to marry to "a man found in a cloud, and of an unknown lineage and family.") **38 Abraham's bosom** (See Luke 16:22.) **40 for** because. **Breton** located in Brittany **41 my brother's** Edward's **42 by that knot** by virtue of that alliance **46 Morton** i.e., John Morton, Bishop of Ely, who had been kept prisoner at Brecknock (or Brecon) Castle; he is the Ely of 3.4 **48 power** army **49 near** deeply **50 rash-levied** hastily recruited **51 fearful commenting** timorous talk **52 leaden servitor** sluggish attendant **53 leads** leads to. **beggary** ruin. **54 expedition** speed **55 Mercury** messenger of the gods

Go muster men. My counsel is my shield; 56
We must be brief when traitors brave the field. 57

Exeunt.

❧

4.[4]

Enter old Queen Margaret.

QUEEN MARGARET

So now prosperity begins to mellow 1
And drop into the rotten mouth of death.
Here in these confines slyly have I lurked 3
To watch the waning of mine enemies.
A dire induction am I witness to, 5
And will to France, hoping the consequence 6
Will prove as bitter, black, and tragical.
Withdraw thee, wretched Margaret. Who comes here?

[She steps aside.]

Enter Duchess [of York] and Queen [Elizabeth].

QUEEN ELIZABETH

Ah, my poor princes! Ah, my tender babes!
My unblown flowers, new-appearing sweets! 10
If yet your gentle souls fly in the air
And be not fixed in doom perpetual, 12
Hover about me with your airy wings
And hear your mother's lamentation!

QUEEN MARGARET *[aside]*

Hover about her; say that right for right 15
Hath dimmed your infant morn to agèd night. 16

DUCHESS

So many miseries have crazed my voice 17
That my woe-wearied tongue is still and mute.
Edward Plantagenet, why art thou dead? 19

QUEEN MARGARET *[aside]*

Plantagenet doth quit Plantagenet. 20
Edward for Edward pays a dying debt. 21

QUEEN ELIZABETH

Wilt thou, O God, fly from such gentle lambs 22
And throw them in the entrails of the wolf?
When didst thou sleep when such a deed was done? 24

QUEEN MARGARET *[aside]*

When holy Harry died, and my sweet son. 25

DUCHESS

Dead life, blind sight, poor mortal-living ghost, 26

Woe's scene, world's shame, grave's due by life usurped, 27
Brief abstract and record of tedious days, 28
Rest thy unrest on England's lawful earth, 29

[sitting down]

Unlawfully made drunk with innocent blood! 30

QUEEN ELIZABETH

Ah, that thou wouldst as soon afford a grave 31
As thou canst yield a melancholy seat!
Then would I hide my bones, not rest them here.
Ah, who hath any cause to mourn but we?

[Sitting down by her.]

QUEEN MARGARET *[coming forward]*

If ancient sorrow be most reverend, 35
Give mine the benefit of seniory 36
And let my griefs frown on the upper hand. 37
If sorrow can admit society, *[sitting down with them]*
Tell o'er your woes again by viewing mine:
I had an Edward, till a Richard killed him: 40
I had a Harry, till a Richard killed him: 41
Thou hadst an Edward, till a Richard killed him; 42
Thou hadst a Richard, till a Richard killed him. 43

DUCHESS

I had a Richard too, and thou didst kill him; 44
I had a Rutland too, thou holp'st to kill him. 45

QUEEN MARGARET

Thou hadst a Clarence too, and Richard killed him.
From forth the kennel of thy womb hath crept
A hellhound that doth hunt us all to death.
That dog, that had his teeth before his eyes 49
To worry lambs and lap their gentle blood, 50
That foul defacer of God's handiwork
That excellent grand tyrant of the earth 52
That reigns in gallèd eyes of weeping souls, 53
Thy womb let loose, to chase us to our graves.
O upright, just, and true-disposing God,
How do I thank thee that this carnal cur 56
Preys on the issue of his mother's body 57
And makes her pew-fellow with others' moan! 58

DUCHESS

O Harry's wife, triumph not in my woes!
God witness with me, I have wept for thine.

QUEEN MARGARET

Bear with me. I am hungry for revenge,
And now I cloy me with beholding it. 62

---

56 My . . . shield i.e., I will take counsel by arming myself and trust no adviser other than my own weapons   **57 brave** challenge
4.4. Location: London. Near the royal court.
1 mellow mature   **3 confines** regions.   **slyly** stealthily   **5 induction** beginning (as of a play)   **6 will** will go.   **the consequence** what follows, the sequel and conclusion (as in a play)   **10 unblown** unopened.   **sweets** flowers.   **12 doom perpetual** eternal destiny **15 right for right** i.e., a just punishment for an offense against justice **16 dimmed . . . night** i.e., brought the youthful promise of your children to ruin and death.   **17 crazed** cracked   **19 Edward Plantagenet** the Duchess's son, the dead King Edward IV; or, his son Edward V   **20 quit** requite   **21 Edward . . . debt** The death of Edward IV (or else Edward V) pays for that of Edward, the son of Margaret and Henry VI. **dying debt** debt paid through death.   **22 fly . . . lambs** i.e., abandon my two sons   **24 When** i.e., Whenever till now   **25 Harry** i.e., Henry VI **26 mortal-living ghost** i.e., a dead person still among the living

27 grave's . . . usurped i.e., one who, by living too long, deprives the grave of its due   **28 abstract** epitome   **29–30 England's . . . drunk** i.e., England's earth, which is unlawfully made drunk   **31 that thou** would that you, England's earth   **35 reverend** worthy of respect **36 seniory** seniority of claim   **37 on . . . hand** i.e., from a place of precedence.   **40 Edward** i.e., my son, the former Prince of Wales **41 Harry** i.e., my husband, King Henry VI   **42 Thou** i.e., Queen Elizabeth.   **Edward** i.e., Edward V   **43 Thou . . . Richard** You, Queen Elizabeth, had a son, the young Duke of York   **44 Richard** i.e., Duke of York, the Duchess's husband and father of Richard III, killed by Margaret's army at the Battle of Wakefield in 1460   **45 Rutland** i.e., Edmund, son of the Duke of York, also killed at Wakefield   **49 teeth** (Richard was supposedly born with teeth.)   **50 worry** bite on the throat, tear to pieces   **52 excellent** unparalleled   **53 gallèd** sore with weeping   **56 carnal** flesh-eating   **57 issue** offspring   **58 pew-fellow** i.e., intimate associate   **62 cloy me** gorge myself

Thy Edward he is dead that killed my Edward; 63
Thy other Edward dead, to quit my Edward; 64
Young York he is but boot, because both they 65
Matched not the high perfection of my loss.
Thy Clarence he is dead that stabbed my Edward;
And the beholders of this frantic play, 68
Th'adulterate Hastings, Rivers, Vaughan, Grey, 69
Untimely smothered in their dusky graves. 70
Richard yet lives, hell's black intelligencer, 71
Only reserved their factor to buy souls 72
And send them thither; but at hand, at hand
Ensues his piteous and unpitied end. 74
Earth gapes, hell burns, fiends roar, saints pray,
To have him suddenly conveyed from hence.
Cancel his bond of life, dear God, I pray,
That I may live and say, "The dog is dead!"

QUEEN ELIZABETH
Oh, thou didst prophesy the time would come
That I should wish for thee to help me curse
That bottled spider, that foul bunch-backed toad! 81

QUEEN MARGARET
I called thee then vain flourish of my fortune; 82
I called thee then poor shadow, painted queen,
The presentation of but what I was, 84
The flattering index of a direful pageant, 85
One heaved a-high to be hurled down below,
A mother only mocked with two fair babes,
A dream of what thou wast, a garish flag 88
To be the aim of every dangerous shot; 89
A sign of dignity, a breath, a bubble, 90
A queen in jest, only to fill the scene.
Where is thy husband now? Where be thy brothers?
Where be thy two sons? Wherein dost thou joy?
Who sues and kneels and says, "God save the Queen"?
Where be the bending peers that flattered thee? 95
Where be the thronging troops that followed thee? 96
Decline all this, and see what now thou art: 97
For happy wife, a most distressèd widow;
For joyful mother, one that wails the name;
For one being sued to, one that humbly sues;
For queen, a very caitiff crowned with care; 101
For she that scorned at me, now scorned of me; 102
For she being feared of all, now fearing one;
For she commanding all, obeyed of none.
Thus hath the course of justice whirled about

And left thee but a very prey to time,
Having no more but thought of what thou wast 107
To torture thee the more, being what thou art.
Thou didst usurp my place, and dost thou not
Usurp the just proportion of my sorrow?
Now thy proud neck bears half my burdened yoke, 111
From which even here I slip my weary head
And leave the burden of it all on thee.
Farewell, York's wife, and queen of sad mischance!
These English woes shall make me smile in France.
[She starts to leave.]

QUEEN ELIZABETH
O thou well skilled in curses, stay awhile,
And teach me how to curse mine enemies!

QUEEN MARGARET
Forbear to sleep the nights, and fast the days;
Compare dead happiness with living woe;
Think that thy babes were sweeter than they were
And he that slew them fouler than he is.
Bett'ring thy loss makes the bad causer worse; 122
Revolving this will teach thee how to curse. 123

QUEEN ELIZABETH
My words are dull. Oh, quicken them with thine! 124

QUEEN MARGARET
Thy woes will make them sharp, and pierce like mine.
Exit Margaret.

DUCHESS
Why should calamity be full of words?

QUEEN ELIZABETH
Windy attorneys to their client's woes, 127
Airy succeeders of intestate joys, 128
Poor breathing orators of miseries, 129
Let them have scope! Though what they will impart
Help nothing else, yet do they ease the heart.

DUCHESS
If so, then be not tongue-tied. Go with me,
And in the breath of bitter words let's smother
My damnèd son that thy two sweet sons smothered.
[Sound trumpet.]
The trumpet sounds. Be copious in exclaims. 135

Enter King Richard and his train [marching, with
drums and trumpets].

KING RICHARD
Who intercepts me in my expedition? 136

DUCHESS
Oh, she that might have intercepted thee,
By strangling thee in her accursèd womb,
From all the slaughters, wretch, that thou hast done!

QUEEN ELIZABETH
Hid'st thou that forehead with a golden crown
Where should be branded, if that right were right,

63 Thy Edward Edward IV. my Edward the son of Henry VI 64 other
Edward Edward V. quit requite 65 Young York Richard, Duke of
York, the younger of the princes murdered in the Tower. but boot
merely into the bargain 68 frantic frenzied, insane 69 Th'adulterate the adulterous 70 smothered buried 71 intelligencer agent,
go-between, spy 72 Only . . . factor chosen above all others as their
(hell's) agent, and sent to earth for no other purpose 74 piteous
deplorable 81 bottled bottle-shaped, swollen (as at 1.3.242).
bunch-backed hunchbacked 82 flourish mere ornament, embellish-
ment. (See 1.3.241.) 84 presentation representation, semblance
85 index argument, preface, prologue. pageant spectacular entertainment 88–9 garish . . . shot i.e., standard-bearer, conspicuous in
appearance, and thus the target of enemy fire 90 sign mere token
95 bending bowing 96 troops supporters, followers 97 Decline
Go through in order. (A grammatical metaphor.) 101 caitiff wretch,
slave 102 of by. (Also in lines 103 and 104.)

107 no . . . thought only the memory 111 burdened burdensome
122 Bett'ring Magnifying 123 Revolving meditating on 124 quicken
put life into 127 Windy . . . woes i.e., Words, which are airy pleaders
on behalf of one who is suffering 128 Airy . . . joys insubstantial
words, all that is left of joys that died unfulfilled. (Literally, having
died without anything to bequeath.) 129 breathing speaking
135 exclaims exclamations. 136 expedition (1) haste (2) military
undertaking.

The slaughter of the prince that owed that crown   142
And the dire death of my poor sons and brothers?
Tell me, thou villain slave, where are my children?

DUCHESS
Thou toad, thou toad, where is thy brother Clarence?
And little Ned Plantagenet, his son?   146

QUEEN ELIZABETH
Where is the gentle Rivers, Vaughan, Grey?

DUCHESS   Where is kind Hastings?

KING RICHARD
A flourish, trumpets! Strike alarum, drums!   149
Let not the heavens hear these telltale women   150
Rail on the Lord's anointed. Strike, I say!
                          Flourish. Alarums.
Either be patient and entreat me fair,   152
Or with the clamorous report of war   153
Thus will I drown your exclamations.

DUCHESS   Art thou my son?

KING RICHARD
Ay, I thank God, my father, and yourself.

DUCHESS
Then patiently hear my impatience.

KING RICHARD
Madam, I have a touch of your condition,   158
That cannot brook the accent of reproof.

DUCHESS
Oh, let me speak!

KING RICHARD   Do then, but I'll not hear.

DUCHESS
I will be mild and gentle in my words.

KING RICHARD
And brief, good mother, for I am in haste.

DUCHESS
Art thou so hasty? I have stayed for thee,   163
God knows, in torment and in agony.   164

KING RICHARD
And came I not at last to comfort you?

DUCHESS
No, by the Holy Rood, thou know'st it well,   166
Thou cam'st on earth to make the earth my hell.
A grievous burden was thy birth to me;
Tetchy and wayward was thy infancy;   169
Thy schooldays frightful, desp'rate, wild, and furious;
Thy prime of manhood daring, bold, and venturous;
Thy age confirmed, proud, subtle, sly, and bloody,   172
More mild, but yet more harmful—kind in hatred.   173
What comfortable hour canst thou name
That ever graced me with thy company?

KING RICHARD
Faith, none, but Humphrey Hour, that called Your Grace   176

To breakfast once forth of my company.   177
If I be so disgracious in your eye,   178
Let me march on and not offend you, madam.—
Strike up the drum.

DUCHESS   I prithee, hear me speak.

KING RICHARD
You speak too bitterly.

DUCHESS   Hear me a word,
For I shall never speak to thee again.

KING RICHARD   So.

DUCHESS
Either thou wilt die by God's just ordinance
Ere from this war thou turn a conqueror,   185
Or I with grief and extreme age shall perish
And nevermore behold thy face again.
Therefore take with thee my most grievous curse,
Which in the day of battle tire thee more
Than all the complete armor that thou wear'st!
My prayers on the adverse party fight,   191
And there the little souls of Edward's children
Whisper the spirits of thine enemies   193
And promise them success and victory!
Bloody thou art, bloody will be thy end;
Shame serves thy life and doth thy death attend.   196
                          Exit.

QUEEN ELIZABETH
Though far more cause, yet much less spirit to curse
Abides in me; I say amen to her.

KING RICHARD
Stay, madam. I must talk a word with you.

QUEEN ELIZABETH
I have no more sons of the royal blood
For thee to slaughter. For my daughters, Richard,   201
They shall be praying nuns, not weeping queens,
And therefore level not to hit their lives.   203

KING RICHARD
You have a daughter called Elizabeth,
Virtuous and fair, royal and gracious.

QUEEN ELIZABETH
And must she die for this? Oh, let her live,
And I'll corrupt her manners, stain her beauty,   207
Slander myself as false to Edward's bed,
Throw over her the veil of infamy;
So she may live unscarred of bleeding slaughter,   210
I will confess she was not Edward's daughter.

KING RICHARD
Wrong not her birth. She is a royal princess.

QUEEN ELIZABETH
To save her life, I'll say she is not so.

KING RICHARD
Her life is safest only in her birth.   214

QUEEN ELIZABETH
And only in that safety died her brothers.

---

142 **owed** owned   146 **Ned Plantagenet** (See 4.3.36.)   149 **flourish** fanfare.   **alarum** call to arms   150 **telltale** tattling, gabbling   152 **entreat me fair** treat me with courtesy   153 **report** noise   158 **condition** disposition   163 **stayed** waited   164 **in agony** i.e., in childbirth.
166 **Holy Rood** Christ's cross   169 **Tetchy** fretful, peevish   172 **age confirmed** riper manhood   173 **kind in hatred** concealing hatred under pretense of kindness.   176 **Humphrey Hour** (To "dine with Duke Humphrey" was to go hungry; hence, Richard flippantly suggests, he was saved from a spare breakfast. The passage is obscure.)

177 **forth of** away from   178 **disgracious** unpleasing, disliked
185 **turn** return   191 **party** side   193 **Whisper** whisper to   196 **serves** accompanies   201 **For my** As for my   203 **level** aim   207 **manners** morals   210 **So** provided.   **of** by   214 **Her . . . birth** Her best guarantee of personal safety is her high birth.

KING RICHARD
Lo, at their birth good stars were opposite. 216
QUEEN ELIZABETH
No, to their lives ill friends were contrary. 217
KING RICHARD
All unavoided is the doom of destiny. 218
QUEEN ELIZABETH
True, when avoided grace makes destiny. 219
My babes were destined to a fairer death,
If grace had blessed thee with a fairer life.
KING RICHARD
You speak as if that I had slain my cousins. 222
QUEEN ELIZABETH
Cousins, indeed, and by their uncle cozened 223
Of comfort, kingdom, kindred, freedom, life.
Whose hand soever lanced their tender hearts, 225
Thy head, all indirectly, gave direction. 226
No doubt the murd'rous knife was dull and blunt
Till it was whetted on thy stone-hard heart,
To revel in the entrails of my lambs.
But that still use of grief makes wild grief tame, 230
My tongue should to thy ears not name my boys
Till that my nails were anchored in thine eyes;
And I, in such a desp'rate bay of death, 233
Like a poor bark of sails and tackling reft, 234
Rush all to pieces on thy rocky bosom.
KING RICHARD
Madam, so thrive I in my enterprise 236
And dangerous success of bloody wars 237
As I intend more good to you and yours
Than ever you or yours by me were harmed!
QUEEN ELIZABETH
What good is covered with the face of heaven,
To be discovered, that can do me good? 240
KING RICHARD
Th'advancement of your children, gentle lady.
QUEEN ELIZABETH
Up to some scaffold, there to lose their heads.
KING RICHARD
Unto the dignity and height of fortune,
The high imperial type of this earth's glory. 245
QUEEN ELIZABETH
Flatter my sorrow with report of it;
Tell me what state, what dignity, what honor,
Canst thou demise to any child of mine? 248
KING RICHARD
Even all I have—ay, and myself and all—
Will I withal endow a child of thine,
So in the Lethe of thy angry soul 251

Thou drown the sad remembrance of those wrongs
Which thou supposest I have done to thee.
QUEEN ELIZABETH
Be brief, lest that the process of thy kindness 254
Last longer telling than thy kindness' date. 255
KING RICHARD
Then know that from my soul I love thy daughter. 256
QUEEN ELIZABETH
My daughter's mother thinks it with her soul.
KING RICHARD   What do you think?
QUEEN ELIZABETH
That thou dost love my daughter from thy soul.
So from thy soul's love didst thou love her brothers, 260
And from my heart's love I do thank thee for it.
KING RICHARD
Be not so hasty to confound my meaning. 262
I mean that with my soul I love thy daughter
And do intend to make her Queen of England.
QUEEN ELIZABETH
Well then, who dost thou mean shall be her king?
KING RICHARD
Even he that makes her queen. Who else should be?
QUEEN ELIZABETH
What, thou?
KING RICHARD   Even so. How think you of it?
QUEEN ELIZABETH
How canst thou woo her?
KING RICHARD   That would I learn of you,
As one being best acquainted with her humor. 269
QUEEN ELIZABETH
And wilt thou learn of me?
KING RICHARD   Madam, with all my heart.
QUEEN ELIZABETH
Send to her, by the man that slew her brothers,
A pair of bleeding hearts; thereon engrave
"Edward" and "York"; then haply will she weep. 273
Therefore present to her—as sometime Margaret 274
Did to thy father, steeped in Rutland's blood— 275
A handkerchief, which, say to her, did drain
The purple sap from her sweet brother's body;
And bid her wipe her weeping eyes withal.
If this inducement move her not to love,
Send her a letter of thy noble deeds.
Tell her thou mad'st away her uncle Clarence,
Her uncle Rivers, ay, and for her sake
Mad'st quick conveyance with her good aunt Anne. 283
KING RICHARD
You mock me, madam. This is not the way
To win your daughter.
QUEEN ELIZABETH   There is no other way,
Unless thou couldst put on some other shape
And not be Richard that hath done all this.

---

216 **opposite** hostile.   217 **contrary** opposed.   218 **unavoided** unavoidable   219 **avoided grace** i.e., Richard, in whom grace is void or lacking   222 **as if that** as if   223 **cozened** cheated   225 **Whose hand soever** Whoever it was whose hand   226 **all indirectly** by indirect means, and wrongly   230 **But . . . of grief** Were it not that constant grieving   233 **bay** (1) inlet (2) position of a hunted animal turning to face the hounds   234 **bark** sailing vessel.   **reft** bereft   236 **so thrive I** May I so thrive   237 **success** sequel, result   240 **covered with** hidden by (and therefore not yet revealed to humanity)   245 **imperial type** symbol of rule   248 **demise** convey, transmit, lease   251 **So** provided that.   **Lethe** river in the underworld, the waters of which produce forgetfulness

254 **process** story   255 **date** duration.   256 **from** with. (But Queen Elizabeth, in lines 259–61, sarcastically uses the word in the sense "apart from," "at variance with.")   260 **So** Just so. (Said ironically.)   262 **confound** deliberately misconstrue   269 **humor** temperament.   273 **haply** perhaps   274 **sometime** once   275 **Rutland's** (See *3 Henry VI*, 1.4.79–83.)   283 **conveyance with** disposal of

KING RICHARD
  Say that I did all this for love of her.
QUEEN ELIZABETH
  Nay, then indeed she cannot choose but hate thee,
  Having bought love with such a bloody spoil.   290
KING RICHARD
  Look what is done cannot be now amended.   291
  Men shall deal unadvisedly sometimes,   292
  Which after-hours gives leisure to repent.
  If I did take the kingdom from your sons,
  To make amends I'll give it to your daughter.
  If I have killed the issue of your womb,
  To quicken your increase I will beget   297
  Mine issue of your blood upon your daughter.
  A grandam's name is little less in love
  Than is the doting title of a mother;
  They are as children but one step below,
  Even of your metal, of your very blood,   302
  Of all one pain, save for a night of groans   303
  Endured of her for whom you bid like sorrow.   304
  Your children were vexation to your youth,
  But mine shall be a comfort to your age.
  The loss you have is but a son being king,
  And by that loss your daughter is made queen.
  I cannot make you what amends I would;
  Therefore accept such kindness as I can.   310
  Dorset your son, that with a fearful soul
  Leads discontented steps in foreign soil,
  This fair alliance quickly shall call home
  To high promotions and great dignity.
  The king that calls your beauteous daughter wife
  Familiarly shall call thy Dorset brother;   316
  Again shall you be mother to a king,
  And all the ruins of distressful times
  Repaired with double riches of content.
  What? We have many goodly days to see.
  The liquid drops of tears that you have shed
  Shall come again, transformed to orient pearl,   322
  Advantaging their love with interest   323
  Of ten times double gain of happiness.
  Go then, my mother, to thy daughter go.
  Make bold her bashful years with your experience;
  Prepare her ears to hear a wooer's tale;
  Put in her tender heart th'aspiring flame
  Of golden sovereignty; acquaint the Princess
  With the sweet silent hours of marriage joys.
  And when this arm of mine hath chastisèd
  The petty rebel, dull-brained Buckingham,
  Bound with triumphant garlands will I come
  And lead thy daughter to a conqueror's bed;
  To whom I will retail my conquest won,   335
  And she shall be sole victoress, Caesar's Caesar.

QUEEN ELIZABETH
  What were I best to say? Her father's brother
  Would be her lord? Or shall I say her uncle?
  Or, he that slew her brothers and her uncles?
  Under what title shall I woo for thee
  That God, the law, my honor, and her love
  Can make seem pleasing to her tender years?
KING RICHARD
  Infer fair England's peace by this alliance.   343
QUEEN ELIZABETH
  Which she shall purchase with still-lasting war.   344
KING RICHARD
  Tell her the King, that may command, entreats.
QUEEN ELIZABETH
  That at her hands which the King's King forbids.   346
KING RICHARD
  Say she shall be a high and mighty queen.
QUEEN ELIZABETH
  To vail the title, as her mother doth.   348
KING RICHARD
  Say I will love her everlastingly.
QUEEN ELIZABETH
  But how long shall that title "ever" last?
KING RICHARD
  Sweetly in force unto her fair life's end.
QUEEN ELIZABETH
  But how long fairly shall her sweet life last?   352
KING RICHARD
  As long as heaven and nature lengthens it.
QUEEN ELIZABETH
  As long as hell and Richard likes of it.
KING RICHARD
  Say I, her sovereign, am her subject low.
QUEEN ELIZABETH
  But she, your subject, loathes such sovereignty.
KING RICHARD
  Be eloquent in my behalf to her.
QUEEN ELIZABETH
  An honest tale speeds best being plainly told.   358
KING RICHARD
  Then plainly to her tell my loving tale.
QUEEN ELIZABETH
  Plain and not honest is too harsh a style.
KING RICHARD
  Your reasons are too shallow and too quick.   361
QUEEN ELIZABETH
  Oh, no, my reasons are too deep and dead—
  Too deep and dead, poor infants, in their graves.
KING RICHARD
  Harp not on that string, madam. That is past.
QUEEN ELIZABETH
  Harp on it still shall I till heartstrings break.

---

290 **spoil** slaughter. (A hunting term.)   291 **Look what** Whatever
292 **shall deal** cannot but act   297 **quicken your increase** give new
life to your progeny   302 **metal** substance. (With a suggestion also of
mettle, "spirit." The Folio reads "mettall.")   303 **pain** labor, effort   304
of by.   **bid** endured, bided   310 **can** am able (to give).   316 **Familiarly** familially   322 **orient** bright, shining   323 **Advantaging their
love** augmenting the love that prompted tears   335 **retail** relate

343 **Infer** Allege, adduce (as a reason)   344 **still-lasting war** i.e., perpetual domestic strife.   346 **forbids** (*The Book of Common Prayer*,
echoing the injunctions of Leviticus 18, prohibits the marriage of a
man with his brother's daughter.)   348 **vail** yield; lower or abase as a
sign of submission   352 **fairly** without foul play   358 **speeds** succeeds   361 **quick** hasty. (With a pun on the meaning "alive," contrasted with *dead* in the next line, just as *shallow* is punningly
contrasted with *deep*.)

KING RICHARD
    Now, by my George, my Garter, and my crown—   366
QUEEN ELIZABETH
    Profaned, dishonored, and the third usurped.
KING RICHARD
    I swear—
QUEEN ELIZABETH   By nothing, for this is no oath.
    Thy George, profaned, hath lost his lordly honor;   369
    Thy Garter, blemished, pawned his knightly virtue;
    Thy crown, usurped, disgraced his kingly glory.
    If something thou wouldst swear to be believed,
    Swear then by something that thou hast not wronged.
KING RICHARD
    Then, by myself—
QUEEN ELIZABETH   Thyself is self-misused.
KING RICHARD
    Now, by the world—
QUEEN ELIZABETH   'Tis full of thy foul wrongs.
KING RICHARD
    My father's death—
QUEEN ELIZABETH   Thy life hath it dishonored.
KING RICHARD
    Why then, by God—
QUEEN ELIZABETH   God's wrong is most of all.
    If thou didst fear to break an oath with Him,
    The unity the King my husband made   379
    Thou hadst not broken, nor my brothers died.
    If thou hadst feared to break an oath by Him,
    Th'imperial metal circling now thy head
    Had graced the tender temples of my child,
    And both the princes had been breathing here,
    Which now, two tender bedfellows for dust,
    Thy broken faith hath made the prey for worms.
    What canst thou swear by now?
KING RICHARD   The time to come.
QUEEN ELIZABETH
    That thou hast wrongèd in the time o'erpast;
    For I myself have many tears to wash
    Hereafter time, for time past wronged by thee.   390
    The children live whose fathers thou hast slaughtered,
    Ungoverned youth, to wail it in their age;   392
    The parents live whose children thou hast butchered,
    Old barren plants, to wail it with their age.
    Swear not by time to come, for that thou hast
    Misused ere used, by times ill-used o'erpast.   396
KING RICHARD
    As I intend to prosper and repent,   397
    So thrive I in my dangerous affairs
    Of hostile arms! Myself myself confound!   399

Heaven and fortune bar me happy hours!
Day, yield me not thy light, nor, night, thy rest!
Be opposite all planets of good luck   402
To my proceeding if, with dear heart's love,
Immaculate devotion, holy thoughts,
I tender not thy beauteous, princely daughter!   405
In her consists my happiness and thine;
Without her follows to myself and thee,
Herself, the land, and many a Christian soul,
Death, desolation, ruin, and decay.
It cannot be avoided but by this;
It will not be avoided but by this.
Therefore, dear mother—I must call you so—
Be the attorney of my love to her.
Plead what I will be, not what I have been,
Not my deserts, but what I will deserve.
Urge the necessity and state of times,   416
And be not peevish-fond in great designs.   417
QUEEN ELIZABETH
    Shall I be tempted of the devil thus?
KING RICHARD
    Ay, if the devil tempt you to do good.
QUEEN ELIZABETH
    Shall I forget myself to be myself?   420
KING RICHARD
    Ay, if yourself's remembrance wrong yourself.   421
QUEEN ELIZABETH
    Yet thou didst kill my children.
KING RICHARD
    But in your daughter's womb I bury them,
    Where in that nest of spicery they will breed   424
    Selves of themselves, to your recomforture.   425
QUEEN ELIZABETH
    Shall I go win my daughter to thy will?
KING RICHARD
    And be a happy mother by the deed.
QUEEN ELIZABETH
    I go. Write to me very shortly,
    And you shall understand from me her mind.
KING RICHARD
    Bear her my true love's kiss; and so, farewell.
                                    Exit Queen [Elizabeth].
Relenting fool, and shallow, changing woman!

        Enter Ratcliffe; [Catesby following].

How now, what news?
RATCLIFFE
    Most mighty sovereign, on the western coast
    Rideth a puissant navy; to our shores   434
    Throng many doubtful, hollow-hearted friends,   435

---

366 **George . . . Garter** (The George, a badge showing Saint George
slaying the dragon, was not added to the insignia of the Order of the
Garter until the reign of Henry VII or Henry VIII.)   **369 his** its (as also
in lines 370, 371)   **379 The unity** i.e., the reconciliation between Queen
Elizabeth and her enemies   **390 Hereafter time** in the future
392 Ungoverned i.e., without a father's guidance or rule
396 Misused . . . o'erpast misused even before it came time to be used,
by your ill use of past times.   **397 As . . . repent** i.e., I swear that as I
hope to thrive and intend to repent   **399 Myself . . . confound!** May I
destroy myself!

402 opposite opposed, adverse   **405 I tender not** I fail to show a tender regard for   **416 state of times** urgent political need   **417 And . . .
designs** and do not stand by, childishly foolish as great plans are
afoot.   **420 Shall . . . myself?** i.e., Shall I, in order to be queen mother,
forget that I am the person you have wronged?   **421 wrong yourself**
i.e., interferes with what is to your advantage.   **424 nest of spicery**
(The fabled phoenix arose anew from the nest of spices, its funeral
pyre.)   **425 recomforture** comfort, consolation.   **434 puissant** powerful   **435 doubtful** apprehensive; not to be trusted

Unarmed and unresolved to beat them back.
'Tis thought that Richmond is their admiral;   437
And there they hull, expecting but the aid   438
Of Buckingham to welcome them ashore.

KING RICHARD
Some light-foot friend post to the Duke of Norfolk: 440
Ratcliffe, thyself, or Catesby; where is he?

CATESBY
Here, my good lord.

KING RICHARD   Catesby, fly to the Duke.

CATESBY
I will, my lord, with all convenient haste.   443

KING RICHARD
Ratcliffe, come hither. Post to Salisbury.
When thou com'st thither—[To Catesby] Dull, unmindful
    villain,
Why stay'st thou here, and go'st not to the Duke?

CATESBY
First, mighty liege, tell me Your Highness' pleasure,
What from Your Grace I shall deliver to him.

KING RICHARD
Oh, true, good Catesby. Bid him levy straight
The greatest strength and power that he can make,   450
And meet me suddenly at Salisbury.   451

CATESBY   I go.   Exit.

RATCLIFFE
What, may it please you, shall I do at Salisbury?

KING RICHARD
Why, what wouldst thou do there before I go?

RATCLIFFE
Your Highness told me I should post before.   455

KING RICHARD
My mind is changed.

Enter Lord Stanley [Earl of Derby].

                Stanley, what news with you?

STANLEY
None good, my liege, to please you with the hearing,
Nor none so bad but well may be reported.

KING RICHARD
Hoyday, a riddle! Neither good nor bad!   459
What need'st thou run so many miles about,
When thou mayst tell thy tale the nearest way?   461
Once more, what news?

STANLEY   Richmond is on the seas.

KING RICHARD
There let him sink, and be the seas on him!
White-livered runagate, what doth he there?   464

STANLEY
I know not, mighty sovereign, but by guess.

KING RICHARD   Well, as you guess?

STANLEY
Stirred up by Dorset, Buckingham, and Morton,

He makes for England, here to claim the crown.

KING RICHARD
Is the chair empty? Is the sword unswayed?   469
Is the King dead? The empire unpossessed?   470
What heir of York is there alive but we?
And who is England's king but great York's heir?
Then tell me, what makes he upon the seas?   473

STANLEY
Unless for that, my liege, I cannot guess.

KING RICHARD
Unless for that he comes to be your liege,
You cannot guess wherefore the Welshman comes.   476
Thou wilt revolt and fly to him, I fear.

STANLEY
No, my good lord; therefore mistrust me not.

KING RICHARD
Where is thy power, then, to beat him back?   479
Where be thy tenants and thy followers?
Are they not now upon the western shore,
Safe-conducting the rebels from their ships?

STANLEY
No, my good lord, my friends are in the north.

KING RICHARD
Cold friends to me! What do they in the north
When they should serve their sovereign in the west?

STANLEY
They have not been commanded, mighty King.
Pleaseth Your Majesty to give me leave,   487
I'll muster up my friends and meet Your Grace
Where and what time Your Majesty shall please.

KING RICHARD
Ay, thou wouldst be gone to join with Richmond.
But I'll not trust thee.

STANLEY   Most mighty sovereign,
You have no cause to hold my friendship doubtful.
I never was nor never will be false.

KING RICHARD
Go then and muster men, but leave behind
Your son, George Stanley. Look your heart be firm,
Or else his head's assurance is but frail.   496

STANLEY
So deal with him as I prove true to you.

                        Exit Stanley [Earl of Derby].

Enter a Messenger.

FIRST MESSENGER
My gracious sovereign, now in Devonshire,
As I by friends am well advertisèd,   499
Sir Edward Courtney and the haughty prelate,
Bishop of Exeter, his elder brother,   501
With many more confederates, are in arms.

Enter another Messenger.

---

437 **their admiral** i.e., of the *puissant navy* named three lines earlier
438 **hull** drift with the sails furled   440 **light-foot** swift-footed.   **post**
hasten   443 **convenient** appropriate, suitable   450 **make** raise
451 **suddenly** swiftly   455 **post** hasten   459 **Hoyday** Heyday.
(Expressing mock wonderment.)   461 **the nearest way** directly, simply.   464 **White-livered runagate** Cowardly renegade, vagabond

469 **chair** throne   470 **empire** kingdom   473 **makes he** is he doing
476 **Welshman** (Richmond was the grandson of Owen Tudor, a
Welshman of Anglesea, who fathered three sons and a daughter by
Katharine of Valois, widow of Henry V.)   479 **power** army
487 **Pleaseth** May it please   496 **assurance** safety   499 **advertisèd**
informed   501 **brother** (Actually, a cousin.)

SECOND MESSENGER
In Kent, my liege, the Guildfords are in arms,
And every hour more competitors   504
Flock to the rebels, and their power grows strong.

Enter another Messenger.

THIRD MESSENGER
My lord, the army of great Buckingham—
KING RICHARD
Out on ye, owls! Nothing but songs of death?   507
                He striketh him.
There, take thou that, till thou bring better news.
THIRD MESSENGER
The news I have to tell Your Majesty
Is that by sudden floods and fall of waters
Buckingham's army is dispersed and scattered,
And he himself wandered away alone,
No man knows whither.
KING RICHARD   I cry thee mercy.   513
There is my purse to cure that blow of thine.
               [*He gives money.*]
Hath any well-advisèd friend proclaimed   515
Reward to him that brings the traitor in?
THIRD MESSENGER
Such proclamation hath been made, my lord.

Enter another Messenger.

FOURTH MESSENGER
Sir Thomas Lovell and Lord Marquess Dorset,   518
'Tis said, my liege, in Yorkshire are in arms.
But this good comfort bring I to Your Highness:
The Breton navy is dispersed by tempest.
Richmond, in Dorsetshire, sent out a boat
Unto the shore, to ask those on the banks
If they were his assistants, yea or no,
Who answered him they came from Buckingham
Upon his party. He, mistrusting them,
Hoised sail and made his course again for Brittany.   527
KING RICHARD
March on, march on, since we are up in arms,
If not to fight with foreign enemies,
Yet to beat down these rebels here at home.

Enter Catesby.

CATESBY
My liege, the Duke of Buckingham is taken!
That is the best news. That the Earl of Richmond
Is with a mighty power landed at Milford   533
Is colder tidings, yet they must be told.
KING RICHARD
Away towards Salisbury! While we reason here,   535

A royal battle might be won and lost.
Someone take order Buckingham be brought
To Salisbury. The rest march on with me.
              Flourish. Exeunt.

❋

4.[5]

*Enter [Lord Stanley Earl of] Derby and Sir
Christopher [Urswick, a priest].*

STANLEY
Sir Christopher, tell Richmond this from me:
That in the sty of the most deadly boar
My son George Stanley is franked up in hold.   3
If I revolt, off goes young George's head;
The fear of that holds off my present aid.
So get thee gone; commend me to thy lord.
Withal say that the Queen hath heartily consented   7
He should espouse Elizabeth her daughter.
But tell me, where is princely Richmond now?
CHRISTOPHER
At Pembroke, or at Ha'rfordwest, in Wales.   10
STANLEY   What men of name resort to him?   11
CHRISTOPHER
Sir Walter Herbert, a renownèd soldier,
Sir Gilbert Talbot, Sir William Stanley,
Oxford, redoubted Pembroke, Sir James Blunt,   14
And Rice ap Thomas, with a valiant crew,
And many other of great name and worth;
And towards London do they bend their power,   17
If by the way they be not fought withal.
STANLEY
Well, hie thee to thy lord; I kiss his hand.   19
My letter will resolve him of my mind.   20
              [*He gives a letter.*]
Farewell.   *Exeunt.*

❋

5.1

*Enter Buckingham, with [Sheriff and] halberds, led
to execution.*

BUCKINGHAM
Will not King Richard let me speak with him?
SHERIFF
No, my good lord. Therefore be patient.
BUCKINGHAM
Hastings, and Edward's children, Grey, and Rivers,
Holy King Henry, and thy fair son Edward,   4
Vaughan, and all that have miscarrièd   5

---

504 competitors confederates   **507 owls** (The cry of the owl was
thought to portend death.)   **513 I cry thee mercy** I beg your pardon.
515 well-advisèd judicious   **518 Sir Thomas Lovell** (Not the Lovell
of 3.4 and 3.5, who was historically Sir Francis Lovell, Richard's Lord
Chamberlain, but perhaps related to him.)   **527 Hoised** hoisted
533 Milford Milford Haven on the coast of Wales in the county of
Pembroke. (A gap of two years is bridged here. Richmond's first fruitless expedition was in October 1483; his landing at Milford was in
August 1485.)   **535 reason** talk

4.5. Location: London. The house of Lord Stanley, Earl of Derby.
0.1 Sir (Honorific title for a clergyman.)   **3 franked up in hold** shut
up in custody, as in a pigpen.   **7 Withal** In addition   **10 Ha'rfordwest** Haverfordwest, in Wales   **11 name** rank   **14 redoubted Pembroke** awe-inspiring Jasper Tudor, Earl of Pembroke (uncle to
Richmond)   **17 bend their power** direct their forces   **19 hie** hasten
20 resolve him of inform him concerning
5.1. Location: Salisbury. An open place.
4 thy i.e., Henry VI's   **5 miscarrièd** perished

By underhand corrupted foul injustice:
If that your moody, discontented souls   7
Do through the clouds behold this present hour,
Even for revenge mock my destruction!
This is All Souls' Day, fellow, is it not?   10
SHERIFF   It is, my lord.
BUCKINGHAM
Why, then All Souls' Day is my body's doomsday.
This is the day which, in King Edward's time,
I wished might fall on me when I was found
False to his children and his wife's allies;
This is the day wherein I wished to fall
By the false faith of him whom most I trusted;
This, this All Souls' Day to my fearful soul
Is the determined respite of my wrongs.   19
That high All-Seer which I dallied with
Hath turned my feignèd prayer on my head
And given in earnest what I begged in jest.
Thus doth He force the swords of wicked men
To turn their own points in their masters' bosoms.
Thus Margaret's curse falls heavy on my neck:
"When he," quoth she, "shall split thy heart with sorrow, 26
Remember Margaret was a prophetess."
Come lead me, officers, to the block of shame.
Wrong hath but wrong, and blame the due of blame.
                    Exeunt Buckingham with officers.

❖

5.2

*Enter Richmond, Oxford, [Sir James] Blunt, [Sir
Walter] Herbert, and others, with drum and
colors.*

RICHMOND
Fellows in arms, and my most loving friends
Bruised underneath the yoke of tyranny,
Thus far into the bowels of the land   3
Have we marched on without impediment;
And here receive we from our father Stanley   5
Lines of fair comfort and encouragement.
The wretched, bloody, and usurping boar,
That spoiled your summer fields and fruitful vines,   8
Swills your warm blood like wash, and makes his trough   9
In your emboweled bosoms, this foul swine   10
Is now even in the center of this isle,
Near to the town of Leicester, as we learn.
From Tamworth thither is but one day's march.
In God's name, cheerly on, courageous friends,   14
To reap the harvest of perpetual peace
By this one bloody trial of sharp war.

OXFORD
Every man's conscience is a thousand swords
To fight against this guilty homicide.
HERBERT
I doubt not but his friends will turn to us.
BLUNT
He hath no friends but what are friends for fear,   20
Which in his dearest need will fly from him.   21
RICHMOND
All for our vantage. Then, in God's name, march!
True hope is swift and flies with swallow's wings;
Kings it makes gods and meaner creatures kings.   24
                    Exeunt omnes.

❖

[5.3]

*Enter King Richard in arms, with Norfolk,
Ratcliffe, and the Earl of Surrey [and others].*

KING RICHARD
Here pitch our tent, even here in Bosworth Field.
My lord of Surrey, why look you so sad?
SURREY
My heart is ten times lighter than my looks.
KING RICHARD
My lord of Norfolk—
NORFOLK   Here, most gracious liege.
KING RICHARD
Norfolk, we must have knocks; ha! Must we not?   5
NORFOLK
We must both give and take, my loving lord.
KING RICHARD
Up with my tent! Here will I lie tonight.
          [*Soldiers begin to set up King Richard's tent.*]
But where tomorrow? Well, all's one for that.   8
Who hath descried the number of the traitors?   9
NORFOLK
Six or seven thousand is their utmost power.
KING RICHARD
Why, our battalia trebles that account.   11
Besides, the King's name is a tower of strength,
Which they upon the adverse faction want.   13
Up with the tent! Come, noble gentlemen,
Let us survey the vantage of the ground.   15
Call for some men of sound direction.   16
Let's lack no discipline, make no delay,
For, lords, tomorrow is a busy day.   *Exeunt.*

*Enter [on the other side of the stage] Richmond,
Sir William Brandon, Oxford, and Dorset, [Blunt,
Herbert, and others. Some of the soldiers pitch
Richmond's tent.]*

---

7 **moody, discontented** angry, vengeance-seeking   10 **All Souls' Day**
November 2, the day on which the Church intercedes for all Christian
souls   19 **the determined . . . wrongs** the ordained date to which
the punishment of my evil practices was respited or postponed.
26 **he** Richard
5.2. Location: A camp near Tamworth.
3 **bowels** interior   5 **father** stepfather, Lord Stanley, Earl of Derby
8 **spoiled** despoiled   9 **Swills** gulps.   **wash** hogwash, swill
10 **emboweled** disemboweled   14 **cheerly** cheerily, heartily

20 **for fear** i.e., out of fearing Richard   21 **dearest** direst   24 **meaner**
of lower degree.   24.1 *omnes* all.
5.3. Location: Bosworth Field.
5 **knocks** blows   8 **all's . . . that** be that as it may.   9 **descried** recon-
noitred   11 **battalia** army   13 **want** lack.   15 **vantage of the ground**
i.e., way in which the field can best be used for tactical advantage.
16 **direction** judgment, military skill.

RICHMOND
　The weary sun hath made a golden set,
　And, by the bright track of his fiery car, 20
　Gives token of a goodly day tomorrow.
　Sir William Brandon, you shall bear my standard. 22
　Give me some ink and paper in my tent.
　I'll draw the form and model of our battle,
　Limit each leader to his several charge, 25
　And part in just proportion our small power. 26
　My lord of Oxford, you, Sir William Brandon,
　And you, Sir Walter Herbert, stay with me.
　The Earl of Pembroke keeps his regiment; 29
　Good Captain Blunt, bear my good-night to him,
　And by the second hour in the morning
　Desire the Earl to see me in my tent.
　Yet one thing more, good Captain, do for me:
　Where is Lord Stanley quartered, do you know?

BLUNT
　Unless I have mista'en his colors much,
　Which well I am assured I have not done,
　His regiment lies half a mile at least
　South from the mighty power of the King. 38

RICHMOND
　If without peril it be possible,
　Sweet Blunt, make some good means to speak with him,
　And give him from me this most needful note.
　　　　　　　　　　　　　　[He gives a letter.]

BLUNT
　Upon my life, my lord, I'll undertake it.
　And so, God give you quiet rest tonight!

RICHMOND
　Good night, good Captain Blunt.　　[Exit Blunt.]
　　　　　　　　　　　Come, gentlemen,
　Let us consult upon tomorrow's business.
　Into my tent; the dew is raw and cold.
　　　　　　　　　They withdraw into the tent.

　　　Enter [to his tent, King] Richard, Ratcliffe,
　　　Norfolk, and Catesby.

KING RICHARD
　What is't o'clock?

CATESBY　　　　　It's suppertime, my lord;
　It's nine o'clock.

KING RICHARD　I will not sup tonight.
　Give me some ink and paper.
　What, is my beaver easier than it was, 50
　And all my armor laid into my tent?

CATESBY
　It is, my liege, and all things are in readiness.

KING RICHARD
　Good Norfolk, hie thee to thy charge.
　Use careful watch; choose trusty sentinels.

NORFOLK　I go, my lord.

KING RICHARD
　Stir with the lark tomorrow, gentle Norfolk.

NORFOLK　I warrant you, my lord.　　　[Exit.] 57

KING RICHARD　Catesby!

CATESBY
　My lord?

KING RICHARD　Send out a pursuivant at arms 59
　To Stanley's regiment. Bid him bring his power 60
　Before sunrising, lest his son George fall
　Into the blind cave of eternal night.　[Exit Catesby.]
　Fill me a bowl of wine. Give me a watch. 63
　Saddle white Surrey for the field tomorrow. 64
　Look that my staves be sound and not too heavy. 65
　Ratcliffe!

RATCLIFFE　My lord?

KING RICHARD
　Saw'st thou the melancholy Lord Northumberland?

RATCLIFFE
　Thomas the Earl of Surrey and himself,
　Much about cockshut time, from troop to troop 70
　Went through the army, cheering up the soldiers.

KING RICHARD
　So, I am satisfied. Give me a bowl of wine.
　I have not that alacrity of spirit
　Nor cheer of mind that I was wont to have. 74
　　　　　　　　　　　　　[Wine is brought.]
　Set it down. Is ink and paper ready?

RATCLIFFE
　It is, my lord.

KING RICHARD　Bid my guard watch. Leave me.
　Ratcliffe, about the mid of night come to my tent
　And help to arm me. Leave me, I say.
　　　　　　　Exit Ratcliffe. [Richard sleeps.]

　　　Enter [Lord Stanley Earl of] Derby, to Richmond
　　　in his tent, [lords and others attending].

STANLEY
　Fortune and victory sit on thy helm! 79

RICHMOND
　All comfort that the dark night can afford
　Be to thy person, noble father-in-law! 81
　Tell me, how fares our loving mother?

STANLEY
　I, by attorney, bless thee from thy mother, 83
　Who prays continually for Richmond's good.
　So much for that. The silent hours steal on,
　And flaky darkness breaks within the east. 86
　In brief—for so the season bids us be— 87
　Prepare thy battle early in the morning, 88
　And put thy fortune to the arbitrament 89

57 warrant guarantee　59 pursuivant at arms junior officer acting as messenger　60 power forces　63 watch watch light, candle marked into equal divisions to show time; or, perhaps, sentinel.　64 white Surrey (The name seems to be Shakespeare's invention. The chroniclers say that Richard was mounted on a "great white courser.")
65 staves lance shafts　70 cockshut time evening twilight; possibly, the time at which the poultry are shut up　74 was wont used　79 helm helmet.　81 father-in-law stepfather.　83 by attorney as proxy　86 flaky streaked with light　87 season time　88 battle troops
89 arbitrament arbitration

20 car chariot (of Phoebus)　22 standard flag.　25 Limit appoint. several charge individual command　26 And . . . power and divide proportionately our small army.　29 keeps i.e., is with　38 power army　50 beaver face-guard or visor of helmet.　easier looser, better fitting

Of bloody strokes and mortal-staring war.   90
I, as I may—that which I would I cannot—   91
With best advantage will deceive the time   92
And aid thee in this doubtful shock of arms.   93
But on thy side I may not be too forward,   94
Lest, being seen, thy brother, tender George,   95
Be executed in his father's sight.
Farewell. The leisure and the fearful time   97
Cuts off the ceremonious vows of love
And ample interchange of sweet discourse
Which so long sundered friends should dwell upon.
God give us leisure for these rites of love!
Once more, adieu. Be valiant, and speed well!   102
RICHMOND
Good lords, conduct him to his regiment.
I'll strive with troubled thoughts to take a nap,
Lest leaden slumber peise me down tomorrow,   105
When I should mount with wings of victory.
Once more, good night, kind lords and gentlemen.
                    Exeunt. [Richmond remains.]
O Thou whose captain I account myself,
Look on my forces with a gracious eye;
Put in their hands Thy bruising irons of wrath,
That they may crush down with a heavy fall
The usurping helmets of our adversaries!
Make us Thy ministers of chastisement,
That we may praise Thee in the victory!
To Thee I do commend my watchful soul
Ere I let fall the windows of mine eyes.   116
Sleeping and waking, oh, defend me still!   117
                         [He sleeps.]

*Enter the Ghost of young Prince Edward, son [of]
Harry the Sixth, to Richard.*

GHOST (*to Richard*)
Let me sit heavy on thy soul tomorrow!   118
Think, how thou stabbed'st me in my prime of youth
At Tewkesbury. Despair therefore and die!
(*To Richmond*) Be cheerful, Richmond, for the wrongèd souls
Of butchered princes fight in thy behalf.
King Henry's issue, Richmond, comforts thee. [*Exit.*]

Enter the Ghost of Henry the Sixth.

GHOST (*to Richard*)
When I was mortal, my anointed body   124
By thee was punchèd full of deadly holes.
Think on the Tower and me. Despair and die!   126
Harry the Sixth bids thee despair and die!
(*To Richmond*) Virtuous and holy, be thou conqueror!

Harry, that prophesied thou shouldst be king,   129
Doth comfort thee in thy sleep. Live and flourish!
                         [Exit.]

Enter the Ghost of Clarence.

GHOST [*to Richard*]
Let me sit heavy in thy soul tomorrow,
I, that was washed to death with fulsome wine,   132
Poor Clarence, by thy guile betrayed to death!
Tomorrow in the battle think on me,
And fall thy edgeless sword. Despair and die!   135
(*To Richmond*) Thou offspring of the house of Lancaster,
The wrongèd heirs of York do pray for thee.
Good angels guard thy battle! Live and flourish!   138
                         [Exit.]

Enter the Ghosts of Rivers, Grey, [and] Vaughan.

GHOST OF RIVERS [*to Richard*]
Let me sit heavy in thy soul tomorrow,
Rivers that died at Pomfret! Despair and die!
GHOST OF GREY [*to Richard*]
Think upon Grey, and let thy soul despair!
GHOST OF VAUGHAN [*to Richard*]
Think upon Vaughan, and, with guilty fear,
Let fall thy lance. Despair and die!
ALL (*to Richmond*)
Awake, and think our wrongs in Richard's bosom
Will conquer him! Awake, and win the day!
                         [Exeunt Ghosts.]

Enter the Ghost of Hastings.

GHOST [*to Richard*]
Bloody and guilty, guiltily awake
And in a bloody battle end thy days!
Think on Lord Hastings. Despair and die!
(*To Richmond*) Quiet untroubled soul, awake, awake!
Arm, fight, and conquer for fair England's sake!
                         [Exit.]

Enter the Ghosts of the two young Princes.

GHOSTS (*to Richard*)
Dream on thy cousins smothered in the Tower.   151
Let us be lead within thy bosom, Richard,
And weigh thee down to ruin, shame, and death!
Thy nephews' souls bid thee despair and die!
(*To Richmond*) Sleep, Richmond, sleep in peace, and
   wake in joy.
Good angels guard thee from the boar's annoy!   156
Live, and beget a happy race of kings!
Edward's unhappy sons do bid thee flourish.
                         [Exeunt Ghosts.]

Enter the Ghost of Lady Anne, his wife.

GHOST [*to Richard*]
Richard, thy wife, that wretched Anne thy wife,
That never slept a quiet hour with thee,

---

90 **mortal-staring** fatal-visaged   91 **that . . . cannot** i.e., I cannot fight
openly on your side, though I want to   92 **With . . . time** as best I can
I will work for your side without seeming to do so   93 **shock**
encounter   94 **forward** zealous   95 **brother** i.e., stepbrother.   **tender**
young, of tender years   97 **leisure** i.e., brief time allowed   102 **speed
well** may you succeed.   105 **peise** weigh   116 **windows** i.e., eyelids
117 **still** continually.   118 **sit heavy on** be oppressive to   124 **anointed**
i.e., with the sacred oil used in the coronation ceremony; compare
with 4.4.151   126 **Tower** (Where Henry VI was supposed to have
been murdered.)

129 **prophesied** (See *3 Henry VI*, 4.6.68 ff.)   132 **washed to death** i.e.,
drowned in a butt of malmsey.   **fulsome** cloying   135 **fall** let fall.
edgeless blunt, useless   138 **battle** troops.   151 **cousins** i.e.,
nephews   156 **the boar's annoy** i.e., Richard's attack.

Now fills thy sleep with perturbations.
Tomorrow in the battle think on me,
And fall thy edgeless sword. Despair and die!
(*To Richmond*) Thou quiet soul, sleep thou a quiet sleep;
Dream of success and happy victory!
Thy adversary's wife doth pray for thee.   [*Exit*.]

Enter the Ghost of Buckingham.

GHOST [*to Richard*]
The first was I that helped thee to the crown;
The last was I that felt thy tyranny.
Oh, in the battle think on Buckingham,
And die in terror of thy guiltiness!
Dream on, dream on of bloody deeds and death;
Fainting, despair; despairing, yield thy breath!   172
(*To Richmond*) I died for hope ere I could lend thee aid,   173
But cheer thy heart, and be thou not dismayed.
God and good angels fight on Richmond's side,
And Richard fall in height of all his pride!   [*Exit*.] 176
          Richard starteth up out of a dream.

KING RICHARD
Give me another horse! Bind up my wounds!
Have mercy, Jesu!—Soft, I did but dream.
O coward conscience, how dost thou afflict me!
The lights burn blue. It is now dead midnight.   180
Cold fearful drops stand on my trembling flesh.
What do I fear? Myself? There's none else by.
Richard loves Richard; that is, I am I.   183
Is there a murderer here? No. Yes, I am.
Then fly. What, from myself? Great reason why: 185
Lest I revenge. What, myself upon myself?
Alack, I love myself. Wherefore? For any good   187
That I myself have done unto myself?
Oh, no! Alas, I rather hate myself
For hateful deeds committed by myself!
I am a villain. Yet I lie, I am not.
Fool, of thyself speak well. Fool, do not flatter.
My conscience hath a thousand several tongues,   193
And every tongue brings in a several tale,
And every tale condemns me for a villain.
Perjury, perjury, in the highest degree,
Murder, stern murder, in the direst degree,
All several sins, all used in each degree,   198
Throng to the bar, crying all, "Guilty! Guilty!"   199
I shall despair. There is no creature loves me,   200
And if I die no soul will pity me.
And wherefore should they, since that I myself
Find in myself no pity to myself?
Methought the souls of all that I had murdered

Came to my tent, and every one did threat
Tomorrow's vengeance on the head of Richard.

Enter Ratcliffe.

RATCLIFFE   My lord!
KING RICHARD   Zounds! Who is there?
RATCLIFFE
My lord, 'tis I. The early village cock
Hath twice done salutation to the morn.
Your friends are up and buckle on their armor.
KING RICHARD
Oh, Ratcliffe, I have dreamed a fearful dream!
What think'st thou, will our friends prove all true?
RATCLIFFE
No doubt, my lord.
KING RICHARD   Oh, Ratcliffe, I fear, I fear!
RATCLIFFE
Nay, good my lord, be not afraid of shadows.
KING RICHARD
By the apostle Paul, shadows tonight
Have struck more terror to the soul of Richard
Than can the substance of ten thousand soldiers
Armèd in proof and led by shallow Richmond.   219
'Tis not yet near day. Come, go with me;
Under our tents I'll play the eavesdropper,
To see if any mean to shrink from me.
          Exeunt [*Richard and Ratcliffe*].

Enter the Lords to Richmond, [sitting in his tent].

LORDS   Good morrow, Richmond!
RICHMOND
Cry mercy, lords and watchful gentlemen,   224
That you have ta'en a tardy sluggard here.
A LORD   How have you slept, my lord?
RICHMOND
The sweetest sleep and fairest-boding dreams
That ever entered in a drowsy head
Have I since your departure had, my lords.
Methought their souls whose bodies Richard murdered
Came to my tent and cried on victory.   231
I promise you, my soul is very jocund   232
In the remembrance of so fair a dream.
How far into the morning is it, lords?
A LORD   Upon the stroke of four.
RICHMOND
Why, then 'tis time to arm and give direction.

His oration to his soldiers.

More than I have said, loving countrymen,   237
The leisure and enforcement of the time   238
Forbids to dwell upon. Yet remember this:
God and our good cause fight upon our side.
The prayers of holy saints and wrongèd souls,
Like high-reared bulwarks, stand before our faces.

---

172 Fainting losing heart   **173 for hope** i.e., for hoping to support
you, or for want of hope, hoping in vain to help   **176 Richard fall**
may Richard fall   **180 lights burn blue** (Superstitiously regarded as
evidence of the presence of ghosts.)   **183 I am I** (A blasphemy of
God's "*ego sum*.")   **185 fly** flee.   **187 Wherefore?** Why?   **193 several**
different, separate   **198 used . . . degree** committed in every degree
of infamy, from bad to worst   **199 bar** i.e., bar of justice   **200 despair**
(Considered the only unforgivable sin.)

219 proof armor   **224 Cry mercy** I beg your pardon   **231 cried on
victory** invoked victory, cried out to it.   **232 promise** assure.
jocund cheerful   **237 have said** have already said before
238 leisure i.e., brief time allowed

Richard except, those whom we fight against 243
Had rather have us win than him they follow.
For what is he they follow? Truly, gentlemen,
A bloody tyrant and a homicide;
One raised in blood, and one in blood established; 247
One that made means to come by what he hath, 248
And slaughtered those that were the means to help him;
A base, foul stone, made precious by the foil 250
Of England's chair, where he is falsely set; 251
One that hath ever been God's enemy.
Then if you fight against God's enemy,
God will in justice ward you as his soldiers; 254
If you do sweat to put a tyrant down,
You sleep in peace, the tyrant being slain;
If you do fight against your country's foes,
Your country's fat shall pay your pains the hire; 258
If you do fight in safeguard of your wives,
Your wives shall welcome home the conquerors;
If you do free your children from the sword,
Your children's children quits it in your age. 262
Then, in the name of God and all these rights,
Advance your standards! Draw your willing swords! 264
For me, the ransom of my bold attempt 265
Shall be this cold corpse on the earth's cold face; 266
But if I thrive, the gain of my attempt
The least of you shall share his part thereof.
Sound drums and trumpets boldly and cheerfully;
God and Saint George! Richmond and victory!
[Exeunt.]

Enter King Richard, Ratcliffe, [attendants and forces].

KING RICHARD
What said Northumberland as touching Richmond?
RATCLIFFE
That he was never trainèd up in arms.
KING RICHARD
He said the truth. And what said Surrey then?
RATCLIFFE
He smiled and said, "The better for our purpose."
KING RICHARD
He was in the right, and so indeed it is.
The clock striketh.
Tell the clock there. Give me a calendar. 276
Who saw the sun today? *[He takes an almanac.]*
RATCLIFFE Not I, my lord.
KING RICHARD
Then he disdains to shine, for by the book 278
He should have braved the east an hour ago. 279
A black day will it be to somebody.

Ratcliffe!
RATCLIFFE
My lord?
KING RICHARD The sun will not be seen today;
The sky doth frown and lour upon our army. 283
I would these dewy tears were from the ground.
Not shine today? Why, what is that to me
More than to Richmond? For the selfsame heaven
That frowns on me looks sadly upon him.

Enter Norfolk.

NORFOLK
Arm, arm, my lord, the foe vaunts in the field! 288
KING RICHARD
Come, bustle, bustle! Caparison my horse. 289
Call up Lord Stanley; bid him bring his power.
I will lead forth my soldiers to the plain,
And thus my battle shall be orderèd: 292
My foreward shall be drawn out all in length, 293
Consisting equally of horse and foot;
Our archers shall be placèd in the midst.
John Duke of Norfolk, Thomas Earl of Surrey,
Shall have the leading of this foot and horse.
They thus directed, we will follow 298
In the main battle, whose puissance on either side 299
Shall be well wingèd with our chiefest horse. 300
This, and Saint George to boot! What think'st thou,
Norfolk? 301
NORFOLK
A good direction, warlike sovereign.
This found I on my tent this morning.
He showeth him a paper.
KING RICHARD *[reads]*
"Jockey of Norfolk, be not so bold, 304
For Dickon thy master is bought and sold." 305
A thing devisèd by the enemy.
Go, gentlemen, every man unto his charge.
Let not our babbling dreams affright our souls;
Conscience is but a word that cowards use,
Devised at first to keep the strong in awe.
Our strong arms be our conscience, swords our law!
March on, join bravely! Let us to it pell-mell; 312
If not to heaven, then hand in hand to hell.

His oration to his army.

What shall I say more than I have inferred? 314
Remember whom you are to cope withal:
A sort of vagabonds, rascals, and runaways, 316
A scum of Bretons and base lackey peasants, 317
Whom their o'ercloyèd country vomits forth 318
To desperate adventures and assured destruction.

---

243 **except** excepted   247 **in blood** by bloodshed   248 **made means** i.e., has taken advantage, created opportunity   250 **foil** a thin leaf of metal placed under a gem to set it off to advantage   251 **chair** throne. **set** (1) seated (2) set like a jewel   254 **ward** protect   258 **Your . . . hire** England's prosperity will reward your efforts   262 **Your . . . age** your grandchildren will requite it when you are old.   264 **Advance** raise   265–6 **the ransom . . . face** i.e., if I fail, there will be no question of ransom, but only death   276 **Tell** Count the strokes of.   **calendar** almanac.   278 **the book** i.e., the almanac   279 **braved** made splendid

283 **lour** look threateningly   288 **vaunts** boasts his strength   289 **Caparison** Put on the battle trappings of   292 **battle** troops   293 **foreward** vanguard   298 **directed** deployed   299 **main battle** main body of troops.   **puissance** strength   300 **wingèd** flanked. **horse** cavalry.   301 **to boot** i.e., to give us aid in addition.   304 **Jockey** i.e., Jack, John   305 **Dickon** i.e., Dick, Richard.   **bought and sold** done for, finished.   312 **join** join battle.   **pell-mell** headlong, hand to hand   314 **inferred** alleged.   316 **sort** gang   317 **lackey** servile   318 **o'ercloyèd** satiated, glutted

You sleeping safe, they bring to you unrest;
You having lands, and blest with beauteous wives,
They would restrain the one, distain the other.   322
And who doth lead them but a paltry fellow,
Long kept in Brittany at our mother's cost?   324
A milksop, one that never in his life
Felt so much cold as over shoes in snow?   326
Let's whip these stragglers o'er the seas again.
Lash hence these overweening rags of France,   328
These famished beggars, weary of their lives,
Who, but for dreaming on this fond exploit,   330
For want of means, poor rats, had hanged themselves.   331
If we be conquered, let men conquer us,
And not these bastard Bretons, whom our fathers
Have in their own land beaten, bobbed, and thumped,   334
And in record left them the heirs of shame.   335
Shall these enjoy our lands? Lie with our wives?
Ravish our daughters? [*Drum afar off.*] Hark! I hear
   their drum.
Fight, gentlemen of England! Fight, bold yeomen!
Draw, archers, draw your arrows to the head!   339
Spur your proud horses hard, and ride in blood;
Amaze the welkin with your broken staves!   341

           [*Enter a Messenger.*]

What says Lord Stanley? Will he bring his power?
MESSENGER   My lord, he doth deny to come.
KING RICHARD   Off with his son George's head!
NORFOLK
   My lord, the enemy is past the marsh.
   After the battle let George Stanley die.
KING RICHARD
   A thousand hearts are great within my bosom.
   Advance our standards! Set upon our foes!   348
   Our ancient word of courage, fair Saint George,   349
   Inspire us with the spleen of fiery dragons!   350
   Upon them! Victory sits on our helms!   *Exeunt.*

                    ❖

[5.4]

   *Alarum. Excursions. [Norfolk and forces continue
   to make forays, entering and exiting.] Enter [in the
   melee] Catesby.*

CATESBY
   Rescue, my lord of Norfolk, rescue, rescue!
   The King enacts more wonders than a man,   2
   Daring an opposite to every danger.   3
   His horse is slain, and all on foot he fights,
   Seeking for Richmond in the throat of death.
   Rescue, fair lord, or else the day is lost!

      [*Alarums.*] *Enter [King] Richard.*

KING RICHARD
   A horse! A horse! My kingdom for a horse!
CATESBY
   Withdraw, my lord. I'll help you to a horse.
KING RICHARD
   Slave, I have set my life upon a cast,   9
   And I will stand the hazard of the die.   10
   I think there be six Richmonds in the field;   11
   Five have I slain today instead of him.
   A horse! A horse! My kingdom for a horse!   [*Exeunt.*]

                    ❖

[5.5]

   *Alarum. Enter Richard and Richmond; they fight.
   Richard is slain. [Exit Richmond.] Then, retreat
   being sounded, [flourish, and] enter Richmond,
   [Lord Stanley Earl of] Derby bearing the crown,
   with other lords, etc.*

RICHMOND
   God and your arms be praised, victorious friends!
   The day is ours; the bloody dog is dead.
STANLEY [*offering him the crown*]
   Courageous Richmond, well hast thou acquit thee.
   Lo, here this long-usurpèd royalty
   From the dead temples of this bloody wretch
   Have I plucked off, to grace thy brows withal.   6
   Wear it, enjoy it, and make much of it.
RICHMOND
   Great God of heaven, say amen to all!
   But, tell me, is young George Stanley living?
STANLEY
   He is, my lord, and safe in Leicester town,
   Whither, if it please you, we may now withdraw us.
RICHMOND
   What men of name are slain on either side?   12
STANLEY
   John Duke of Norfolk, Walter Lord Ferrers,
   Sir Robert Brackenbury, and Sir William Brandon.
RICHMOND
   Inter their bodies as becomes their births.
   Proclaim a pardon to the soldiers fled

322 restrain deprive you of.   **distain** defile, sully   **324 our mother's**
(Richmond's mother was not Richard's. This error occurs in the second
edition of Holinshed's *Chronicles*. The first edition reads "brothers," the
reference being to the fact that Richmond had been supported at the
court of the Duke of Brittany at the cost of Charles, Duke of Burgundy,
Richard's brother-in-law.)   **326 over shoes** i.e., over his shoe-tops
328 rags ragged fellows   **330 fond** foolish   **331 want of means** poverty
334 bobbed thrashed   **335 And . . . shame** and left them with nothing but the promise of a shameful record in history.   **339 to the head**
to the head of the arrow.   **341 Amaze the welkin** frighten the skies
348 Advance our standards! Raise our flags!   **349 word of courage**
battle cry   **350 dragons** (Richard ironically identifies with the dragon
slain by Saint George.)
5.4. Location: Bosworth Field, as before; the action is continuous.
0.1 *Excursions* Sorties.

2 than a man than seems possible for a human being   **3 Daring . . .
danger** boldly facing every danger in battle.   **9 cast** throw of the dice
10 stand the hazard accept the fortune.   **die** (Singular of *dice*.)
11 six Richmonds i.e., Richmond himself and five men dressed like
him as a safety precaution
5.5. Location: Action continues at Bosworth Field.
0.2 *retreat* trumpet signal to withdraw, cease the attack   **6 withal**
with.   **12 of name** of title

That in submission will return to us,
And then, as we have ta'en the Sacrament,   18
We will unite the white rose and the red.
Smile heaven upon this fair conjunction,   20
That long have frowned upon their enmity!
What traitor hears me and says not amen?
England hath long been mad, and scarred herself;
The brother blindly shed the brother's blood,
The father rashly slaughtered his own son,
The son, compelled, been butcher to the sire.
All this divided York and Lancaster,
Divided in their dire division.

Oh, now let Richmond and Elizabeth,
The true succeeders of each royal house,
By God's fair ordinance conjoin together!   31
And let their heirs, God, if thy will be so,
Enrich the time to come with smooth-faced peace,
With smiling plenty, and fair prosperous days!
Abate the edge of traitors, gracious Lord,   35
That would reduce these bloody days again   36
And make poor England weep in streams of blood!
Let them not live to taste this land's increase
That would with treason wound this fair land's peace!
Now civil wounds are stopped, peace lives again.   40
That she may long live here, God say amen! [*Exeunt.*]

18 ta'en the Sacrament sworn a sacred oath on the Sacrament (to marry Princess Elizabeth, daughter of Edward IV, thereby uniting the houses of York and of Lancaster, white rose and red rose) **20 conjunction** union. (An astrological metaphor.)

31 ordinance decree **35 Abate** Blunt, render ineffective **36 reduce** bring back **40 stopped** closed up

The Tragedy of King Richard the Second

R ichard II (c. 1595–1596) is the first play in Shake-speare's great four-play historical saga, or tetralogy, that continues with the two parts of *Henry IV* (c. 1596–1598) and concludes with *Henry V* (1599). In this, his second, tetralogy, Shakespeare dramatizes the beginnings of the great conflict called the Wars of the Roses, having already dramatized the conclusion of that civil war in his earlier tetralogy on Henry VI and Richard III (c. 1589–1594). Both sequences move from an outbreak of civil faction to the eventual triumph of political stability. Together, they comprise the story of England's long century of political turmoil from the 1390s until Henry Tudor's victory over Richard III in 1485. Yet Shakespeare chose to tell the two halves of this chronicle in reverse order. His culminating statement about kingship in *Henry V* focuses on the earlier historical period, on the education and kingly success of Prince Hal.

With *Richard II*, then, Shakespeare turns to the events that had launched England's century of crisis. These events were still fresh and relevant to Elizabethan minds. Richard and Bolingbroke's contest for the English crown provided a sobering example of political wrongdoing and, at least by implication, a rule for political right conduct. One prominent reason for studying history, to an Elizabethan, was to avoid the errors of the past. The relevance of such historical analogy was, in fact, vividly underscored some six years after Shakespeare wrote the play: in 1601, followers of the Earl of Essex commissioned Shakespeare's acting company to perform a revived play about Richard II on the eve of what was to be an abortive rebellion, perhaps with the intention of inciting a riot. Whether the play was Shakespeare's is not certain, but it seems likely. The acting company was ultimately exonerated, but not before Queen Elizabeth concluded that she was being compared to Richard II. When he wrote the play, Shakespeare presumably did not know that it would be used for such a purpose, but he must have known that the overthrow of Richard II was, in any case,

a controversial subject because of its potential use as a precedent for rebellion. The scene of Richard's deposition (4.1) was considered so provocative by Elizabeth's government that it was censored in the printed quartos of Shakespeare's play during the Queen's lifetime.

In view of the startling relevance of this piece of history to Shakespeare's own times, then, what are the rights and wrongs of Richard's deposition, and to what extent can political lessons be drawn from Shakespeare's presentation?

To begin with, we should not underestimate Richard's attractive qualities, as a man and even as a king. Throughout the play, Richard is consistently more impressive and majestic in appearance than his rival, Bolingbroke. Richard fascinates us with his verbal sensitivity, his poetic insight, and his dramatic self-consciousness. He eloquently expounds a sacramental view of kingship, according to which "Not all the water in the rough rude sea / Can wash the balm off from an anointed king" (3.2.54–5). Bolingbroke can depose Richard but can never capture the aura of majesty Richard possesses; Bolingbroke may succeed politically but only at the expense of desecrating an idea. Richard is much more interesting to us as a man than Bolingbroke, more capable of grief, more tender in his personal relationships, and more in need of being understood. Indeed, a major factor in Richard's tragedy is the conflict between his public role (wherein he sees himself as divinely appointed, almost superhuman) and his private role (wherein he is emotionally dependent and easily hurt). He confuses what the medieval and Renaissance world knew as the king's "two bodies," the sacramental body of kingship, which is eternal, and the human body of a single occupant of the throne, whose frail mortal condition is subject to time and fortune. Richard's failure to perceive and to act wisely on this difference is part of his tragic predicament, but his increasing insight, through suffering, into the truth of the distinction is also part of his spiritual growth. His dilemma, however poignantly individual, lies at the heart of kingship. Richard is thus very much a king. Although he sometimes indulges in childish sentimentality, at his best he is superbly refined, perceptive, and poetic.

These qualities notwithstanding, Richard is an incompetent ruler, compared with the man who supplants him. Richard himself confesses to the prodigal expense of "too great a court." In order to raise funds, he has been obliged to "farm our royal realm"; that is, to sell for ready cash the right of collecting taxes to individual courtiers, who are then free to extort what the market will bear (1.4.43–5). Similarly, Richard proposes to issue "blank charters" (line 48) to his minions, who will then be authorized to fill in the amount of tax to be paid by any hapless subject. These abuses were infamous to Elizabethan audiences as symbols of autocratic misgovernment. No less heinous is Richard's seizure of the dukedom of Lancaster from his cousin Bolingbroke. Although Richard does receive the consent of his Council to banish Bolingbroke because of the divisiveness of the quarrel between him and Mowbray, the King violates the very idea of inheritance of property when he takes away Bolingbroke's title and lands. And, as his uncle the Duke of York remonstrates, Richard's own right to the throne depends on that idea of due inheritance. By offending against the most sacred concepts of order and degree, he teaches others to rebel.

Richard's behavior even prior to the commencement of the play arouses suspicion. The nature of his complicity in the death of his uncle Thomas of Woodstock, Duke of Gloucester, is perhaps never entirely clear, and Gloucester may have given provocation. Indeed, one can sympathize with the predicament of a young ruler prematurely thrust into the center of power by the untimely death of his father, the crown prince, now having to cope with an array of worldly-wise, advice-giving uncles. Nevertheless, Richard is unambiguously guilty of murder in the eyes of Gloucester's widow, while her brother-in-law John of Gaunt, Duke of Lancaster, assumes that Richard has caused Gloucester's death, "the which if wrongfully / Let heaven revenge" (1.2.39–40). Apparently, too, Gaunt's son Bolingbroke believes Richard to be a murderer, and he brings accusation against Thomas Mowbray, Duke of Norfolk, partly as a means of embarrassing the King, whom he cannot accuse directly. Mowbray's lot is an unenviable one: he was in command at Calais when Gloucester was executed there, and he hints that Richard ordered the execution (even though Mowbray alleges that he himself did not carry out the order). For his part, Richard is only too glad to banish the man suspected of having been his agent in murder. Mowbray is a convenient scapegoat.

The polished, ceremonial tone of the play's opening is vitiated, then, by our growing awareness of hidden violence and factionalism going on behind the scene. Our first impression of Richard is of a king devoted to the public display of conciliatory even-handedness. He listens to the rival claims of Bolingbroke and Mowbray, and, when he cannot reconcile them peacefully, he orders a trial by combat. This trial (1.3) is replete with ceremonial repetition and ritual. The combatants are duly sworn in the justice of their cause, and God is to decide the quarrel by awarding victory to the champion who speaks the truth. Richard, the presiding officer, assumes the role of God's anointed deputy on earth. Yet it becomes evident in due course that Richard is a major perpetrator of injustice rather than an impartial judge, that Bolingbroke is after greater objectives than he acknowledges even to himself, and that Richard's refusal to let the trial by combat take place and his banishment of the two contenders are his desperate ways of burying a problem he cannot deal with forthrightly. His uncles reluctantly consent to the banishment only because they, too, see that disaffection has reached alarming proportions.

Bolingbroke's motivation in these opening scenes is perhaps even more obscure than Richard's. Our first impression of Bolingbroke is of forthrightness, moral indignation, and patriotic zeal. In fact, we never really question the earnestness of his outrage at Richard's misgovernance, his longing to avenge a family murder (for Gloucester was his uncle, too), or his bitter disappointment at being banished. Yet we are prompted to ask further: what is the essential cause of the enmity between Bolingbroke and Richard? If Mowbray is only a stalking-horse, is not Gloucester's death also the excuse for pursuing a preexistent animosity? Richard, for one, appears to think so. His portrayal of Bolingbroke as a scheming politician, who curries favor with the populace in order to build a widely based alliance against the King himself, is telling and prophetic. Bolingbroke, says Richard, acts "As were our England in reversion his, / And he our subjects' next degree in hope" (1.4.35–6). This unflattering appraisal might be ascribed to malicious envy on Richard's part, were it not proved by subsequent events to be wholly accurate.

Paradoxically, Richard is far the more prescient of the two contenders for the English throne. It is he, in fact, who perceives from the start that the conflict between them is irreconcilable. He banishes Bolingbroke as his chief rival and does not doubt what motives will call Bolingbroke home again. Meanwhile, Bolingbroke disclaims any motive for his return other than love of country and hatred of injustice. Although born with a political canniness that Richard lacks, Bolingbroke does not reflect (out loud, at least) upon the consequences of his own acts. As a man of action, he lives in the present. Richard, conversely, a person of exquisite contemplative powers and poetic imagination, does not deign to cope with the practical. He both envies and despises Bolingbroke's easy way with the commoners. Richard cherishes kingship for the majesty and the royal prerogative it confers, not for the power to govern wisely. Thus it is that, despite his perception of what will follow, Richard habitually indulges his worst instincts, buying a moment of giddy pleasure at the expense of future disaster.

Granted Richard's incompetence as a ruler, is Bolingbroke justified in armed rebellion against him? According to Bolingbroke's uncle, the Duke of York (who later, to be sure, shifts his allegiance), and to the Bishop of Carlisle, Bolingbroke is not justified in the rebellion. The attitude of these men can be summed up by the phrase "passive obedience." And, although Bolingbroke's own father, John of Gaunt, dies before his son returns to England to seize power, Gaunt, too, is opposed to such human defiances of the sacred institution of kingship. "God's is the quarrel," he insists (1.2.37). Because Richard is God's anointed deputy on earth, as Gaunt sees the matter, only God may punish the King's wrongdoing. Gaunt may not question Richard's guilt, but neither does he question God's ability to avenge. Gaunt sees human intervention in God's affair as blasphemous: "for I may never lift / An angry arm against His minister" (1.2.40–1). To be sure, Gaunt does acknowledge a solemn duty to offer frank advice to extremists of both sides, and he does so unsparingly. He consents to the banishment of his son, and he rebukes Richard with his dying breath.

This doctrine of passive obedience was familiar to Elizabethans, for they heard it in church periodically in official homilies against rebellion. It was the Tudor state's answer to those who asserted a right to overthrow reputedly evil kings. The argument was logically ingenious. Why are evil rulers permitted to govern from time to time? Presumably, because God wishes to test a people or to punish them for waywardness. Any king performing such chastisement is a divine scourge. Accordingly, the worst thing a people can do is to rebel against God's scourge, thereby manifesting more waywardness. Instead, they must attempt to remedy the insolence in their hearts, advise the King to mend his ways, and patiently await God's pardon. If they do so, they will not long be disappointed. The doctrine is essentially conservative, defending the status quo. It is reinforced in this play by the Bishop of Carlisle's prophecy that God will avenge through civil war the deposition of his anointed (4.1.126–50); an Elizabethan audience would have appreciated the irony of the prophecy's having come true and having been the subject of Shakespeare's first historical tetralogy. Moreover, in *Richard II* the doctrine of passive obedience is a moderate position between the extremes of tyranny and rebellion, and is expressed by thoughtful, selfless characters. We might be tempted to label it Shakespeare's view if we did not also perceive that the doctrine is continually placed in ironic conflict with harsh political realities. The character who most reflects

the ironies and even ludicrous incongruities of the position is the Duke of York.

York is to an extent a choric character, that is, one who helps direct our viewpoint, because his transfer of loyalties from Richard to Bolingbroke structurally delineates the decline of Richard's fortunes and the concurrent rise of Bolingbroke's. At first York shares his brother Gaunt's unwillingness to act, despite their dismay at Richard's willfulness. It is only when Richard seizes the dukedom of Lancaster that York can no longer hold his tongue. His condemnation is as bitter as that of Gaunt, hinting even at loss of allegiance (2.1.200–8). Still, he accepts the responsibility, so cavalierly bestowed by Richard, of governing England in the King's absence. He musters what force he can to oppose Bolingbroke's advance and lectures against this rebellion with the same vehemence he had used against Richard's despotism. Yet, when faced with Bolingbroke's overwhelming military superiority, he accedes rather than fight on behalf of a lost cause. However much this may resemble cowardice or mere expediency, it also displays a pragmatic logic. Once Bolingbroke has become de facto king, in York's view, he must be acknowledged and obeyed. By a kind of analogy to the doctrine of passive obedience (which more rigorous theorists would never allow), York accepts the status quo as inevitable. He is vigorously ready to defend the new regime, just as he earlier defended Richard's de jure rule. York's inconsistent loyalty helps define the structure of the play.

When, however, this conclusion brings York to the point of turning in his own son, Aumerle, for a traitor and quarreling with his wife as to whether their son shall live, the ironic absurdity is apparent. Bolingbroke, now King Henry, himself is amused, in one of the play's rare lighthearted moments (5.3.79–80). At the same time, the comedy deals with serious issues, especially the conflict between public responsibility urged by York and private or emotional satisfaction urged by his Duchess—a conflict seen earlier, for example, in the debate between Gaunt and his sister-in-law, the widowed Duchess of Gloucester (1.2). When a family and a kingdom are divided against one another, there can be no really satisfactory resolution.

We are never entirely convinced that all the fine old medieval theories surrounding kingship—divine right, passive obedience, trial by combat, and the like—can ever wholly explain or remedy the complex and nasty political situation afflicting England. The one man capable of decisive action, in fact, is he who never theorizes at all: Bolingbroke. As we have seen, his avowed motive for opposing Mowbray—simple patriotic indignation—is uttered with such earnestness that we wonder if indeed Bolingbroke has examined those political ambitions in himself that are so plainly visible to Richard and others. This same discrepancy between surface and depth applies to Bolingbroke's motives in returning to England. We cannot be sure at what time he begins to plot that return; the conspiracy announced by Northumberland (2.1.224–300) follows so closely after Richard's violation of Bolingbroke's hereditary rights and is already so well advanced that we gain the impression of an already existing plot, though some of this impression may be simply owing to Shakespeare's characteristic compression of historic time. When Bolingbroke arrives in England, in any case, he protests to York with seemingly passionate sincerity that he comes only for his dukedom of Lancaster (2.3.113–36). If so, why does he set about executing Richard's followers without legal authority and otherwise establishing his own claim to power? Why does he indulge in homophobic slurs against Richard, insinuating that Richard's favorites have "Broke the possession of a royal bed" (3.1.13), when, as far as we can see from the devotion Richard shows to his queen, the charges are trumped up and untrue? Does Bolingbroke seriously think he can reclaim his dukedom by force and then yield to Richard without either maintaining Richard as a puppet king or placing himself in intolerable jeopardy? And can he suppose that his allies, Northumberland and the rest, who have now openly defied the King, will countenance the return to power of one who would never trust them again? It is in this context that York protests, "Well, well, I see the issue of these arms" (2.3.152). The deposition of Richard and then Richard's death are unavoidable conclusions once Bolingbroke has succeeded in an armed rebellion. There can be no turning back. Yet Bolingbroke simply will not think in these terms. He permits Northumberland to proceed with almost sadistic harshness in the arrest and impeachment of Richard and then admonishes Northumberland in public for acting so harshly; the dirty work goes forward, with Northumberland taking the blame, while Bolingbroke assumes a statesmanlike pose. When the new King Henry discovers—to his surprise, evidently—that Richard's life is now a burden to the state, he ponders aloud, "Have I no friend will rid me of this living fear?" (5.4.2) and then rebukes Exton for proceeding on cue.

Bolingbroke's pragmatic spirit and new mode of governing are the embodiment of de facto rule. Ultimately, the justification for his authority is the very fact of its existence, its functioning. Bolingbroke is the man of the hour. To apply William Butler Yeats's striking contrast, the Lancastrian usurpers, Bolingbroke and his son, are vessels of clay, whereas Richard is a vessel of porcelain. One is durable and utilitarian, yet unattractive; the other is exquisite, fragile, and impractical. The comparison does not force us to prefer one to the other, even though Yeats himself characteristically sided with beauty against politics. Rather, Shakespeare gives us our choice, allowing us to see in ourselves an inclination toward political and social stability or toward artistic temperament.

The paradox may suggest that the qualities of a good administrator are not those of a sensitive, thoughtful man. However hopeless as a king, Richard stands before us increasingly as an introspective and fascinating person. The contradictions of his character are aptly focused in the business of breaking a mirror during his deposition: it is at once symbolic of a narcissistic, shallow concern for appearances and a quest for a deeper, inward truth, so that the smashing of the mirror is an act both of self-destruction and of self-discovery. When Richard's power crumbles, his spirit is enhanced, as though loss of power and royal identity were necessary for the discovery of true values.

In this there is a faint anticipation of King Lear's self-learning, fearfully and preciously bought. The trace is only slight here, because in good part *Richard II* is a political history play rather than a tragedy and because Richard's self-realization is imperfect. Nevertheless, when Richard faces deposition and separation from his queen, and especially when he is alone in prison expecting to die, he strives to understand his life and through it the general condition of humanity. He gains our sympathy in the wonderfully humane interchange between this deposed king and the poor groom of his stable, who once took care of Richard's horse, roan Barbary, now the possession of the new monarch (5.5.67–94). Richard perceives a contradiction in heaven's assurances about salvation: Christ promises to receive all God's children, and yet He also warns that it is as hard for a rich man to enter heaven as for a camel to be threaded through a needle's eye (5.5.16–17). The paradox echoes the Beatitudes: the last shall be first, the meek shall inherit the earth. Richard, now one of the downtrodden, gropes for an understanding of the vanity of human achievement whereby he can aspire to the victory Christ promised. At his death, that victory seems to him assured: his soul will mount to its seat on high "Whilst my gross flesh sinks downward, here to die" (line 112).

In this triumph of spirit over flesh, the long downward motion of Richard's worldly fortune is crucially reversed. By the same token, the worldly success of Bolingbroke is shown to be no more than that: worldly success. His archetype is Cain, the primal murderer of a brother. To the extent that the play is a history, Bolingbroke's de facto success is a matter of political relevance; but, in the belated movement toward Richard's personal tragedy, we experience a profound countermovement that partly achieves a purgative sense of atonement and reassurance. Whatever Richard may have lost, his gain is also great.

Balance and symmetry are unusually important in *Richard II*. The play begins and ends with elaborate ritual obeisance to the concept of social and monarchic order, and yet, in both cases, a note of personal disorder refuses to be subdued by the public ceremonial. Shakespeare keeps our response to both Richard and Bolingbroke ambivalent by clouding their respective responsibilities for murder. Just as Richard's role in Gloucester's death remains unclear, so Bolingbroke's role in the assassination of Richard remains equally unclear. Mowbray and Exton, as scapegoats, are in some respects parallel. Because Richard and Bolingbroke are both implicated in the deaths of near kinsmen, both are associated with Cain's murder of Abel. As Bolingbroke rises in worldly fortune, Richard falls; as Richard finds insight and release through suffering, Bolingbroke finds guilt and remorse through distasteful political necessity. Verbally and structurally, the play explores the rhetorical figure of chiasmus, or the pairing of opposites in an inverted and diagonal pattern whereby one goes down as the other goes up and vice versa. Again and again, the ritual effects of staging and style draw our attention to the balanced conflicts between the two men and within Richard. Symmetry helps to focus these conflicts in visual and aural ways. In particular, the deposition scene, with its spectacle of a coronation in reverse, brings the sacramental and human sides of the central figure into poignant dramatic relationship.

Women play a subsidiary role in this play about male struggles for power, and yet the brief scenes in which women take part—the Duchess of Gloucester with Gaunt (1.2), Richard's queen with his courtiers and gardeners and then with Richard himself (2.2, 3.4, 5.1), the Duchess of York with her husband and son and King Henry (5.2–5.3)—highlight for us important thematic contrasts between the public and private spheres, power and powerlessness, political struggle and humane sensitivity, the state and the family. The women, excluded from roles of practical authority, offer, nonetheless, an invaluable critical perspective on the fateful and often self-consuming political games that men play among themselves. As in *Julius Caesar* and *Troilus and Cressida*, the men of *Richard II* ignore women's warnings and insights to their own peril and to the discomfiting of the body politic.

The imagery of *Richard II* reinforces structure and meaning. The play is unlike the history plays that follow in its extensive use of blank verse and rhyme and in its interwoven sets of recurring images; *Richard II* is, in this respect, more typical of the so-called lyric period (c. 1594–1596) that also produced *Romeo and Juliet* and *A Midsummer Night's Dream*. Image patterns locate the play

in our imaginations as a kind of lost Eden. England is a garden mismanaged by her royal gardener, so that weeds and caterpillars (e.g., Bushy, Bagot, and Green) flourish. The "garden" scene (3.4), located near the center of the play, offering a momentary haven of allegorical reflection on the play's hectic events, is central in the development of the garden metaphor. England is also a sick body, ill-tended by her royal physician, and a family divided against itself, yielding abortive and sterile progeny. Her political ills are attested to by disorders in the cosmos: comets, shooting stars, withered bay trees, and weeping rains. Night owls, associated with death, prevail over the larks of morning. The sun, royally associated at first with Richard, deserts him for Bolingbroke and leaves Richard as the Phaëthon who has mishandled the sun-god's chariot and so scorched the earth. Linked to the sun image is the prevalent leitmotif of ascent and descent. And, touching on all these, a cluster of biblical images sees England as a despoiled garden of Eden witnessing a second fall of humanity. Richard repeatedly brands his enemies and deserters as Judases and Pilates—not always fairly; nonetheless, in his last agony, he finds genuine consolation in Christ's example. For a man so self-absorbed in the drama of his existence, this poetic method is intensely suitable. Language and stage action have combined perfectly to express the conflict between a sensitive but flawed king and his efficient but unlovable successor.

In performance, the play belongs to Richard. However much he ends up the loser, his role calls for a kind of royal charisma that Bolingbroke never achieves. Such was the effect, at any rate, in Brian Bedford's enactment of the role at Stratford, Canada, in 1983; his appearance on the walls of Flint Castle in 3.3, splendidly attired in white robes with gold trim, embodied a regal image of kingship that was then forced to humble itself before Bolingbroke's brute might. John Gielgud, Alec Guinness, Michael Redgrave, Paul Scofield, John Neville, Ian McKellen, Ian Richardson, Richard Pasco, Derek Jacobi, Alan Howard, Jeremy Irons, Ralph Fiennes, the actress Fiona Shaw, and still other leading performers of their day have found the role one in which they could enthrall audiences with the nuanced cadences of Richard's speeches. The role has also afforded a wide range of interpretations; Guinness saw him as unhappily neurotic, Gielgud as kindly, Redgrave as effeminate, Scofield as cerebral and remote, McKellen as one who is convinced of his semi-divine nature. The play has also become a vehicle for spectacle and striking visual effects emphasizing the symmetries of the text's attention to poetic symbolism and social ritual; glittering pageantry and fading splendor vie for our interest and our loyalties.

The Tragedy of King Richard the Second

[*Dramatis Personae*

KING RICHARD THE SECOND
QUEEN, *Richard's wife*
JOHN OF GAUNT, *Duke of Lancaster, King Richard's uncle*
HENRY BOLINGBROKE, *John of Gaunt's son, Duke of Hereford and claimant to his father's dukedom of Lancaster, later King Henry IV*
DUKE OF YORK, *Edmund of Langley, King Richard's uncle*
DUCHESS OF YORK
DUKE OF AUMERLE, *York's son and the Earl of Rutland*
DUCHESS OF GLOUCESTER, *widow of Thomas of Woodstock, Duke of Gloucester (King Richard's uncle)*

THOMAS MOWBRAY, *Duke of Norfolk,*
EARL OF SALISBURY,
LORD BERKELEY,
DUKE OF SURREY,
BISHOP OF CARLISLE,   } *supporters of King Richard*
SIR STEPHEN SCROOP,
ABBOT OF WESTMINSTER,
BUSHY,
BAGOT, } *favorites of King Richard,*
GREEN,
CAPTAIN *of the Welsh Army,*

scene: England and Wales]

EARL OF NORTHUMBERLAND,
HARRY PERCY, *Northumberland's son,*
LORD ROSS,
LORD WILLOUGHBY,   } *supporters of Bolingbroke*
LORD FITZWATER,
SIR PIERCE OF EXTON,
Another LORD,

LORD MARSHAL
Two HERALDS
GARDENER
GARDENER'S MAN
LADY *attending the Queen*
KEEPER *of the prison*
A MAN *attending Exton*

SERVINGMAN *to York*
GROOM *of the stable*

Lords, Officers, Soldiers, Attendants, Ladies attending the Queen

[1.1]

Enter King Richard, John of Gaunt, with other nobles and attendants.

KING RICHARD
Old John of Gaunt, time-honored Lancaster,   1
Hast thou according to thy oath and bond
Brought hither Henry Hereford, thy bold son,
Here to make good the boist'rous late appeal,   4
Which then our leisure would not let us hear,   5
Against the Duke of Norfolk, Thomas Mowbray?
GAUNT   I have, my liege.   7
KING RICHARD
Tell me, moreover, hast thou sounded him   8

1.1. Location: A room of state. (Holinshed's *Chronicles* places this scene at Windsor, in 1398.)
1 Old John of Gaunt (Born in 1340 at Ghent; hence the surname *Gaunt*. In 1398 he was fifty-eight years old.)

4 late recent.   **appeal** accusation, formal challenge or impeachment that the accuser was obliged to maintain in combat   **5 our, us** (The royal plural.)   **leisure** i.e., lack of leisure   **7 liege** i.e., sovereign.
8 sounded inquired of

If he appeal the Duke on ancient malice,   9
Or worthily, as a good subject should,
On some known ground of treachery in him?

GAUNT
As near as I could sift him on that argument,   12
On some apparent danger seen in him   13
Aimed at Your Highness, no inveterate malice.

KING RICHARD
Then call them to our presence.   [*Exit an attendant.*]
                                         Face to face,
And frowning brow to brow, ourselves will hear   16
The accuser and the accusèd freely speak.
High-stomached are they both, and full of ire;   18
In rage, deaf as the sea, hasty as fire.

Enter Bolingbroke and Mowbray.

BOLINGBROKE
Many years of happy days befall
My gracious sovereign, my most loving liege!

MOWBRAY
Each day still better others' happiness,   22
Until the heavens, envying earth's good hap,   23
Add an immortal title to your crown!

KING RICHARD
We thank you both. Yet one but flatters us,
As well appeareth by the cause you come: 26
Namely, to appeal each other of high treason.
Cousin of Hereford, what dost thou object   28
Against the Duke of Norfolk, Thomas Mowbray?

BOLINGBROKE
First—heaven be the record to my speech!—   30
In the devotion of a subject's love,
Tend'ring the precious safety of my prince,   32
And free from other misbegotten hate,
Come I appellant to this princely presence.   34
Now, Thomas Mowbray, do I turn to thee;
And mark my greeting well, for what I speak
My body shall make good upon this earth
Or my divine soul answer it in heaven.   38
Thou art a traitor and a miscreant,   39
Too good to be so and too bad to live,   40
Since the more fair and crystal is the sky,   41
The uglier seem the clouds that in it fly.
Once more, the more to aggravate the note,   43
With a foul traitor's name stuff I thy throat,
And wish, so please my sovereign, ere I move,   45
What my tongue speaks my right-drawn sword may prove.   46

MOWBRAY
Let not my cold words here accuse my zeal.   47
'Tis not the trial of a woman's war,   48
The bitter clamor of two eager tongues,   49
Can arbitrate this cause betwixt us twain;   50
The blood is hot that must be cooled for this.
Yet can I not of such tame patience boast
As to be hushed and naught at all to say.
First, the fair reverence of Your Highness curbs me
From giving reins and spurs to my free speech,
Which else would post until it had returned   56
These terms of treason doubled down his throat.
Setting aside his high blood's royalty,   58
And let him be no kinsman to my liege,   59
I do defy him, and I spit at him,
Call him a slanderous coward and a villain;
Which to maintain I would allow him odds
And meet him, were I tied to run afoot   63
Even to the frozen ridges of the Alps
Or any other ground inhabitable   65
Wherever Englishman durst set his foot.
Meantime, let this defend my loyalty:
By all my hopes, most falsely doth he lie.

BOLINGBROKE [*throwing down his gage*]
Pale trembling coward, there I throw my gage,   69
Disclaiming here the kindred of the King,   70
And lay aside my high blood's royalty,
Which fear, not reverence, makes thee to except.   72
If guilty dread have left thee so much strength
As to take up mine honor's pawn, then stoop.   74
By that, and all the rites of knighthood else,
Will I make good against thee, arm to arm,
What I have spoke or thou canst worse devise.   77

MOWBRAY [*taking up the gage*]
I take it up; and by that sword I swear
Which gently laid my knighthood on my shoulder,
I'll answer thee in any fair degree
Or chivalrous design of knightly trial;
And when I mount, alive may I not light   82
If I be traitor or unjustly fight!

KING RICHARD
What doth our cousin lay to Mowbray's charge?
It must be great that can inherit us   85
So much as of a thought of ill in him.

BOLINGBROKE
Look what I speak, my life shall prove it true: 87
That Mowbray hath received eight thousand nobles   88
In name of lendings for Your Highness' soldiers,   89

---

9 appeal accuse. **on . . . malice** on the grounds of a long-standing enmity   **12 sift** discover by questioning. **argument** subject
13 apparent obvious, manifest   **16 ourselves** I myself. (The royal plural.)   **18 High-stomached** Haughty   **22 Each . . . happiness** May each day improve on the happiness of other past days   **23 hap** fortune   **26 you come** for which you come   **28 what . . . object** what accusation do you bring   **30 record** witness   **32 Tend'ring** watching over, holding dear   **34 appellant** as the accuser   **38 answer** answer for   **39 miscreant** irreligious villain   **40 good** i.e., noble, high-born   **41 crystal** clear. (The image alludes to the crystal spheres in which, according to the Ptolemaic conception of the universe, the heavenly bodies were fixed.)   **43 aggravate the note** emphasize the stigma, i.e., the charge of treason   **45 so please** if it please   **46 right-drawn** justly drawn

47 accuse my zeal cast doubt on my zeal or loyalty.   **48 woman's war** i.e., war of words   **49 eager** sharp, biting   **50 Can** that can   **56 post** ride at high speed (like a messenger riding relays of horses)   **58 Setting . . . royalty** Disregarding Bolingbroke's royal blood (as grandson of Edward III)   **59 let him be** suppose him to be   **63 tied** obliged   **65 inhabitable** uninhabitable   **69 gage** a pledge to combat (usually a glove or gauntlet, i.e., a mailed or armored glove)   **70 Disclaiming** relinquishing.   **kindred** kinship   **72 except** exempt, set aside.
74 pawn i.e., the gage   **77 or . . . devise** or anything worse you can imagine to have been said about you.   **82 light** alight, dismount   **85 inherit us** put me in possession of, make me have   **87 Look what** Whatever   **88 nobles** gold coins worth six shillings eight pence   **89 lendings** advances on pay

The which he hath detained for lewd employments,   90
Like a false traitor and injurious villain.
Besides I say, and will in battle prove
Or here or elsewhere to the furthest verge   93
That ever was surveyed by English eye,
That all the treasons for these eighteen years   95
Complotted and contrivèd in this land   96
Fetch from false Mowbray their first head and
     spring.   97
Further I say, and further will maintain
Upon his bad life to make all this good,
That he did plot the Duke of Gloucester's death,   100
Suggest his soon-believing adversaries,   101
And consequently, like a traitor coward,   102
Sluiced out his innocent soul through streams of
     blood—   103
Which blood, like sacrificing Abel's, cries   104
Even from the tongueless caverns of the earth   105
To me for justice and rough chastisement.
And, by the glorious worth of my descent,
This arm shall do it or this life be spent.

KING RICHARD
How high a pitch his resolution soars!   109
Thomas of Norfolk, what say'st thou to this?

MOWBRAY
Oh, let my sovereign turn away his face
And bid his ears a little while be deaf,
Till I have told this slander of his blood   113
How God and good men hate so foul a liar!

KING RICHARD
Mowbray, impartial are our eyes and ears.
Were he my brother, nay, my kingdom's heir,
As he is but my father's brother's son,
Now, by my scepter's awe I make a vow,   118
Such neighbor nearness to our sacred blood
Should nothing privilege him nor partialize   120
The unstooping firmness of my upright soul.
He is our subject, Mowbray; so art thou.
Free speech and fearless I to thee allow.

MOWBRAY
Then, Bolingbroke, as low as to thy heart
Through the false passage of thy throat thou liest!
Three parts of that receipt I had for Calais   126
Disbursed I duly to His Highness' soldiers;

The other part reserved I by consent,
For that my sovereign liege was in my debt   129
Upon remainder of a dear account   130
Since last I went to France to fetch his queen.   131
Now swallow down that lie. For Gloucester's death,   132
I slew him not, but to my own disgrace   133
Neglected my sworn duty in that case.   134
[*To Gaunt*] For you, my noble lord of Lancaster,
The honorable father to my foe,
Once did I lay an ambush for your life,
A trespass that doth vex my grievèd soul;
But ere I last received the Sacrament
I did confess it, and exactly begged   140
Your Grace's pardon, and I hope I had it.
This is my fault. As for the rest appealed,   142
It issues from the rancor of a villain,
A recreant and most degenerate traitor,   144
Which in myself I boldly will defend,   145
And interchangeably hurl down my gage   146   o
Upon this overweening traitor's foot,   147
To prove myself a loyal gentleman
Even in the best blood chambered in his bosom.   149
          [*He throws down his gage. Bolingbroke picks it up.*]
In haste whereof most heartily I pray   150
Your Highness to assign our trial day.

KING RICHARD
Wrath-kindled gentlemen, be ruled by me;
Let's purge this choler without letting blood.   153
This we prescribe, though no physician;
Deep malice makes too deep incision.
Forget, forgive; conclude and be agreed;   156
Our doctors say this is no month to bleed.—   157
Good uncle, let this end where it begun;
We'll calm the Duke of Norfolk, you your son.

GAUNT
To be a make-peace shall become my age.
Throw down, my son, the Duke of Norfolk's gage.

KING RICHARD
And Norfolk, throw down his.

GAUNT   When, Harry, when?
Obedience bids I should not bid again.

KING RICHARD
Norfolk, throw down, we bid; there is no boot.   164

---

90 **lewd** vile, base   93 **Or** either   95 **these eighteen years** i.e., ever since the Peasants' Revolt of 1381   96 **Complotted** plotted in a conspiracy   97 **Fetch** derive.   **head and spring** (Synonymous words meaning "origin.")   100 **Duke of Gloucester's death** (Thomas of Woodstock, Duke of Gloucester, a younger son of Edward III and brother of John of Gaunt, was murdered at Calais in September 1397, while in Mowbray's custody.)   101 **Suggest . . . adversaries** did prompt Gloucester's easily persuaded enemies (to believe him guilty of treason)   102 **consequently** afterward   103 **Sluiced out** let flow (as by the opening of a sluice, or valve)   104 **Abel's** (For the story of Cain's murder of his brother Abel, the first such murder on earth and the archetype of the killing of a kinsman, see Genesis 4:3–12.)   105 **tongueless** resonant but without articulate speech; echoing   109 **pitch** highest reach of a falcon's flight   113 **this slander . . . blood** this disgrace to the royal family   118 **my scepter's awe** the reverence due my scepter   120 **nothing** not at all.   **partialize** make partial, bias   126 **receipt** money received

129 **For that** because   130 **Upon . . . account** for the balance of a heavy debt   131 **Since . . . queen** (Mowbray went in 1395 to France to negotiate the King's marriage to Isabella, daughter of the French King Charles VI, but Richard himself escorted her to England.)   132–4 **For . . . case** (Mowbray speaks guardedly but seems to imply that he postponed the execution of Gloucester that he was ordered by Richard to carry out.)   132 **For** As for   140 **exactly** (1) explicitly (2) fully   142 **appealed** of which I am charged   144 **recreant** cowardly; or, coward (used as a noun)   145 **Which** which charge.   **in myself** in my own person   146 **interchangeably** in exchange, reciprocally   147 **overweening** arrogant, proud   149 **Even in** by shedding   150 **In haste whereof** To hasten which proof of my innocence   153 **Let's . . . blood** let's treat this wrath (caused by an excess of bile or choler) by purging (vomiting or evacuation) rather than by medical bloodletting. (With a play on "bloodshed in combat.")   156 **conclude** come to a final agreement   157 **no month to bleed** (Learned authorities often differed as to which months or seasons were best for medicinal bloodletting.)   164 **boot** help for it.

MOWBRAY [*kneeling*]
Myself I throw, dread sovereign, at thy foot. 165
My life thou shalt command, but not my shame.
The one my duty owes; but my fair name,
Despite of death that lives upon my grave, 168
To dark dishonor's use thou shalt not have.
I am disgraced, impeached, and baffled here, 170
Pierced to the soul with slander's venomed spear,
The which no balm can cure but his heart-blood
Which breathed this poison.
KING RICHARD   Rage must be withstood. 173
Give me his gage. Lions make leopards tame. 174
MOWBRAY
Yea, but not change his spots. Take but my shame, 175
And I resign my gage. My dear dear lord,
The purest treasure mortal times afford 177
Is spotless reputation; that away,
Men are but gilded loam or painted clay.
A jewel in a ten-times-barred-up chest
Is a bold spirit in a loyal breast.
Mine honor is my life; both grow in one; 182
Take honor from me, and my life is done.
Then, dear my liege, mine honor let me try; 184
In that I live, and for that will I die.
KING RICHARD [*to Bolingbroke*]
Cousin, throw up your gage; do you begin. 186
BOLINGBROKE
Oh, God defend my soul from such deep sin!
Shall I seem crestfallen in my father's sight?
Or with pale beggar-fear impeach my height 189
Before this out-dared dastard? Ere my tongue 190
Shall wound my honor with such feeble wrong, 191
Or sound so base a parle, my teeth shall tear 192
The slavish motive of recanting fear 193
And spit it bleeding in his high disgrace, 194
Where shame doth harbor, even in Mowbray's face. 195
[*Exit Gaunt.*]
KING RICHARD
We were not born to sue but to command;
Which since we cannot do to make you friends,
Be ready, as your lives shall answer it,
At Coventry upon Saint Lambert's day. 199

There shall your swords and lances arbitrate
The swelling difference of your settled hate.
Since we cannot atone you, we shall see 202
Justice design the victor's chivalry. 203
Lord Marshal, command our officers at arms
Be ready to direct these home alarms. 205
Exeunt.

❖

[1.2]

Enter John of Gaunt with the Duchess of Gloucester.

GAUNT
Alas, the part I had in Woodstock's blood 1
Doth more solicit me than your exclaims 2
To stir against the butchers of his life! 3
But since correction lieth in those hands 4
Which made the fault that we cannot correct,
Put we our quarrel to the will of heaven,
Who, when they see the hours ripe on earth,
Will rain hot vengeance on offenders' heads.
DUCHESS
Finds brotherhood in thee no sharper spur?
Hath love in thy old blood no living fire?
Edward's seven sons, whereof thyself art one, 11
Were as seven vials of his sacred blood
Or seven fair branches springing from one root.
Some of those seven are dried by nature's course,
Some of those branches by the Destinies cut;
But Thomas, my dear lord, my life, my Gloucester,
One vial full of Edward's sacred blood,
One flourishing branch of his most royal root,
Is cracked, and all the precious liquor spilt,
Is hacked down, and his summer leaves all faded,
By envy's hand and murder's bloody ax. 21
Ah, Gaunt, his blood was thine! That bed, that womb,
That metal, that self mold that fashioned thee, 23
Made him a man; and though thou livest and
breathest,
Yet art thou slain in him. Thou dost consent 25
In some large measure to thy father's death
In that thou see'st thy wretched brother die,
Who was the model of thy father's life. 28
Call it not patience, Gaunt; it is despair.
In suff'ring thus thy brother to be slaughtered,
Thou showest the naked pathway to thy life, 31

165 Myself I throw i.e., I throw myself, instead of my gage
168 Despite . . . grave that will live in the epitaph on my grave in spite of devouring Death **170 impeached** accused. **baffled** publicly dishonored **173 Which . . . poison** of him who uttered this slander. **174 Lions . . . tame** (The royal arms showed a lion rampant; Mowbray's emblem was a leopard.) **175 spots** (1) leopard spots (2) stains of dishonor. **177 mortal times** our earthly lives **182 in one** inseparably **184 try** put to the test **186 throw . . . gage** i.e., surrender your gage up to me, thereby ending the quarrel. (Richard is probably seated on a raised throne, as in scene 3.) **189 impeach my height** discredit my high rank **190 out-dared** dared down, cowed. **dastard** coward. **191 feeble wrong** dishonorable submission **192 sound . . . parle** trumpet so shameful a negotiation, i.e., consent to ask a truce **192–5 my teeth . . . face** my teeth will bite off my tongue as a craven instrument of cowardly capitulation and spit it out bleeding, to its (the tongue's) great disgrace, into Mowbray's face, where shame abides perpetually. **195.1 Exit Gaunt** (A stage direction from the Folio, adopted by most editors so that Gaunt will not be required to exit at the end of scene 1 and then immediately reenter.) **199 Saint Lambert's day** September 17.

202 atone reconcile **203 design . . . chivalry** designate who is the true chivalric victor. **205 home alarms** domestic conflicts.
1.2. Location: John of Gaunt's house (? No place is specified, and the scene is not in Holinshed.)
1 the part . . . blood my kinship with Thomas of Woodstock, the Duke of Gloucester (i.e., as the older brother) **2 exclaims** exclamations **3 stir** take action **4 those hands** i.e., Richard's (whom Gaunt charges with responsibility for Gloucester's death) **11 Edward's** Edward III's **21 envy's** malice's **23 metal** substance out of which a person or a thing is made. (With a sense too of *mettle*, "temperament, disposition.") **self** selfsame **25 consent** acquiesce **28 model** likeness, copy **31 naked** i.e., undefended

Teaching stern murder how to butcher thee.
That which in mean men we entitle patience 33
Is pale cold cowardice in noble breasts.
What shall I say? To safeguard thine own life
The best way is to venge my Gloucester's death.

GAUNT
God's is the quarrel; for God's substitute, 37
His deputy anointed in His sight,
Hath caused his death; the which if wrongfully 39
Let heaven revenge, for I may never lift
An angry arm against His minister.

DUCHESS
Where then, alas, may I complain myself? 42

GAUNT
To God, the widow's champion and defense.

DUCHESS
Why, then, I will. Farewell, old Gaunt.
Thou goest to Coventry, there to behold
Our cousin Hereford and fell Mowbray fight. 46
Oh, sit my husband's wrongs on Hereford's spear, 47
That it may enter butcher Mowbray's breast!
Or if misfortune miss the first career, 49
Be Mowbray's sins so heavy in his bosom
That they may break his foaming courser's back
And throw the rider headlong in the lists, 52
A caitiff recreant to my cousin Hereford! 53
Farewell, old Gaunt. Thy sometimes brother's wife 54
With her companion, Grief, must end her life.

GAUNT
Sister, farewell. I must to Coventry.
As much good stay with thee as go with me!

DUCHESS
Yet one word more. Grief boundeth where it falls, 58
Not with the empty hollowness, but weight. 59
I take my leave before I have begun, 60
For sorrow ends not when it seemeth done.
Commend me to thy brother, Edmund York. 62
Lo, this is all. Nay, yet depart not so!
Though this be all, do not so quickly go;
I shall remember more. Bid him—ah, what?—
With all good speed at Pleshey visit me. 66
Alack, and what shall good old York there see
But empty lodgings and unfurnished walls, 68
Unpeopled offices, untrodden stones, 69
And what hear there for welcome but my groans?
Therefore commend me; let him not come there

---

33 **mean** lowly   37 **God's substitute** i.e., the King, God's deputy on
earth   39 **his** i.e., Gloucester's   42 **complain myself** lodge a complaint on my own behalf.   46 **cousin** kinsman.   **fell** fierce   47 **sit . . .
wrongs** may my husband's wrongs sit   49 **misfortune** i.e., Mowbray's downfall.   **career** charge of the horse in a tourney or combat
52 **lists** barriers enclosing the tournament area   53 **caitiff** base, cowardly   54 **sometimes** late   58 **boundeth** bounces, rebounds, returns.
(The Duchess apologizes for speaking yet again; her grief, she says,
continues on and on, like a bouncing tennis ball.)   59 **Not . . . weight**
(Grief is not hollow, like a tennis ball, but continues to move because
of its heaviness.)   60 **begun** i.e., begun to grieve   62 **Edmund York**
Edmund of Langley, fifth son of Edward III.   66 **Pleshey** Gloucester's country seat, in Essex   68 **unfurnished** bare   69 **offices** service
quarters, workrooms

To seek out sorrow that dwells everywhere.
Desolate, desolate, will I hence and die.
The last leave of thee takes my weeping eye.   *Exeunt.*

❖

[1.3]

Enter Lord Marshal and the Duke [of] Aumerle.

MARSHAL
My Lord Aumerle, is Harry Hereford armed?

AUMERLE
Yea, at all points, and longs to enter in. 2

MARSHAL
The Duke of Norfolk, sprightfully and bold, 3
Stays but the summons of the appellant's trumpet. 4

AUMERLE
Why then the champions are prepared, and stay
For nothing but His Majesty's approach.

*The trumpets sound, and the King enters with his
nobles [Gaunt, Bushy, Bagot, Green, and others].
When they are set, enter [Mowbray] the Duke of
Norfolk in arms, defendant, [with a herald].*

KING RICHARD
Marshal, demand of yonder champion
The cause of his arrival here in arms.
Ask him his name, and orderly proceed 9
To swear him in the justice of his cause.

MARSHAL [*to Mowbray*]
In God's name and the King's, say who thou art
And why thou comest thus knightly clad in arms,
Against what man thou com'st, and what thy quarrel. 13
Speak truly on thy knighthood and thy oath,
As so defend thee heaven and thy valor!

MOWBRAY
My name is Thomas Mowbray, Duke of Norfolk,
Who hither come engagèd by my oath—
Which God defend a knight should violate!— 18
Both to defend my loyalty and truth
To God, my king, and my succeeding issue
Against the Duke of Hereford that appeals me, 21
And by the grace of God and this mine arm
To prove him, in defending of myself,
A traitor to my God, my king, and me;
And as I truly fight, defend me heaven!

*The trumpets sound. Enter [Bolingbroke,] Duke of
Hereford, appellant, in armor, [with a herald].*

KING RICHARD
Marshal, ask yonder knight in arms

1.3. Location: The lists at Coventry. Scaffolds or raised seats are provided for the King and his nobles, and chairs are provided for the
combatants.
2 **at all points** completely.   **in** i.e., into the lists, the space designed
for combat.   3 **sprightfully** with high spirit   4 **Stays** awaits
9 **orderly** according to the rules   13 **quarrel** complaint.   18 **defend**
forbid   21 **appeals** accuses

Both who he is and why he cometh hither
Thus plated in habiliments of war;   28
And formally, according to our law,
Depose him in the justice of his cause.   30

MARSHAL [to Bolingbroke]
What is thy name? And wherefore com'st thou hither,
Before King Richard in his royal lists?
Against whom comest thou? And what's thy quarrel?
Speak like a true knight, so defend thee heaven!

BOLINGBROKE
Harry of Hereford, Lancaster, and Derby
Am I, who ready here do stand in arms
To prove, by God's grace and my body's valor,
In lists, on Thomas Mowbray, Duke of Norfolk,
That he is a traitor foul and dangerous
To God of heaven, King Richard, and to me;
And as I truly fight, defend me heaven!

MARSHAL
On pain of death, no person be so bold
Or daring-hardy as to touch the lists,   43
Except the Marshal and such officers
Appointed to direct these fair designs.

BOLINGBROKE
Lord Marshal, let me kiss my sovereign's hand
And bow my knee before His Majesty;   47
For Mowbray and myself are like two men
That vow a long and weary pilgrimage.
Then let us take a ceremonious leave
And loving farewell of our several friends.   51

MARSHAL [to King Richard]
The appellant in all duty greets Your Highness
And craves to kiss your hand and take his leave.

KING RICHARD [coming down]
We will descend and fold him in our arms.
                        [He embraces Bolingbroke.]
Cousin of Hereford, as thy cause is right,   55
So be thy fortune in this royal fight!   56
Farewell, my blood—which if today thou shed,
Lament we may, but not revenge thee dead.

BOLINGBROKE
Oh, let no noble eye profane a tear   59
For me if I be gored with Mowbray's spear.   60
As confident as is the falcon's flight
Against a bird do I with Mowbray fight.
[To the King] My loving lord, I take my leave of you;
[To Aumerle] Of you, my noble cousin, Lord Aumerle;
Not sick, although I have to do with death,
But lusty, young, and cheerly drawing breath.   66
Lo, as at English feasts, so I regreet   67
The daintiest last, to make the end most sweet.   68

[To Gaunt] O thou, the earthly author of my blood,
Whose youthful spirit, in me regenerate,   70
Doth with a twofold vigor lift me up   71
To reach at victory above my head,
Add proof unto mine armor with thy prayers,   73
And with thy blessings steel my lance's point
That it may enter Mowbray's waxen coat   75
And furbish new the name of John o' Gaunt   76
Even in the lusty havior of his son.   77

GAUNT
God in thy good cause make thee prosperous!
Be swift like lightning in the execution,
And let thy blows, doubly redoubled,
Fall like amazing thunder on the casque   81
Of thy adverse pernicious enemy.
Rouse up thy youthful blood, be valiant, and live.

BOLINGBROKE
Mine innocence and Saint George to thrive!   84

MOWBRAY
However God or fortune cast my lot,
There lives or dies, true to King Richard's throne,
A loyal, just, and upright gentleman.
Never did captive with a freer heart
Cast off his chains of bondage and embrace
His golden uncontrolled enfranchisement   90
More than my dancing soul doth celebrate
This feast of battle with mine adversary.
Most mighty liege, and my companion peers,
Take from my mouth the wish of happy years.   94
As gentle and as jocund as to jest   95
Go I to fight. Truth hath a quiet breast.   96

KING RICHARD
Farewell, my lord. Securely I espy   97
Virtue with valor couchèd in thine eye.—   98
Order the trial, Marshal, and begin.

MARSHAL
Harry of Hereford, Lancaster, and Derby,
Receive thy lance; and God defend the right!
                        [A lance is given to Bolingbroke.]

BOLINGBROKE
Strong as a tower in hope, I cry "Amen!"   102

MARSHAL [to an officer]
Go bear this lance to Thomas, Duke of Norfolk.
                        [A lance is given to Mowbray.]

FIRST HERALD
Harry of Hereford, Lancaster, and Derby
Stands here for God, his sovereign, and himself,
On pain to be found false and recreant,
To prove the Duke of Norfolk, Thomas Mowbray,

---

28 plated armored. habiliments the attire   30 Depose him take his
sworn deposition   43 daring-hardy daringly bold, reckless. touch
i.e., interfere in   47 bow my knee (Presumably Bolingbroke kneels to
Richard and, at about line 69, to Gaunt.)   51 several various   55 as
insofar as   56 royal fight i.e., a fight taking place in the presence of
the King.   59–60 profane . . . For me misuse tears by weeping for me
66 lusty full of vigor. cheerly cheerfully   67 regreet greet, salute
68 The daintiest i.e., the most tasty, the finest. (Bolingbroke refers to
the custom of ending banquets with a sweet dessert.)

70 regenerate born anew   71 twofold i.e., of father and son   73 proof
invulnerability   75 enter . . . coat pierce Mowbray's armor as though
it were made of wax   76 furbish polish   77 lusty havior vigorous
behavior, deportment   81 amazing bewildering. casque helmet
84 Mine . . . thrive! May my innocence and the protectorship of Saint
George bring me victory!   90 enfranchisement freedom   94 Take . . .
years take from me the wish that you may enjoy many happy years.
95 gentle unperturbed in spirit. to jest i.e., to a play or entertainment   96 quiet calm   97 Securely Confidently   98 couchèd lodged,
expressed, leveled in readiness (as with a lance)   102 Strong . . . hope
(Alludes to Psalm 61:3: "for thou hast been my hope, and a strong
tower for me against the face of the enemy.")

A traitor to his God, his king, and him,   108
And dares him to set forward to the fight.

SECOND HERALD

Here standeth Thomas Mowbray, Duke of Norfolk,
On pain to be found false and recreant,
Both to defend himself and to approve   112
Henry of Hereford, Lancaster, and Derby,
To God, his sovereign, and to him disloyal,   114
Courageously and with a free desire
Attending but the signal to begin.   116

MARSHAL

Sound, trumpets, and set forward, combatants!
                    [*A charge is sounded. Richard throws
                                  down his baton.*]
Stay! The King hath thrown his warder down.   118

KING RICHARD

Let them lay by their helmets and their spears,
And both return back to their chairs again.
[*To his counselors*] Withdraw with us, and let the trumpets
   sound
While we return these dukes what we decree.   122
          [*A long flourish. Richard consults apart with
                                    Gaunt and others.*]
Draw near,
And list what with our council we have done.   124
For that our kingdom's earth should not be soiled   125
With that dear blood which it hath fosterèd;
And for our eyes do hate the dire aspect   127
Of civil wounds plowed up with neighbors' sword;
And for we think the eagle-wingèd pride
Of sky-aspiring and ambitious thoughts,
With rival-hating envy, set on you   131
To wake our peace, which in our country's cradle
Draws the sweet infant breath of gentle sleep,
Which, so roused up with boist'rous untuned drums, 134
With harsh-resounding trumpets' dreadful bray
And grating shock of wrathful iron arms,
Might from our quiet confines fright fair peace
And make us wade even in our kindred's blood:
Therefore we banish you our territories.
You, cousin Hereford, upon pain of life,   140
Till twice five summers have enriched our fields,
Shall not regreet our fair dominions,
But tread the stranger paths of banishment.   143

BOLINGBROKE

Your will be done. This must my comfort be:
That sun that warms you here shall shine on me,
And those his golden beams to you here lent
Shall point on me and gild my banishment.

KING RICHARD

Norfolk, for thee remains a heavier doom,

Which I with some unwillingness pronounce:
The sly slow hours shall not determinate   150
The dateless limit of thy dear exile.   151
The hopeless word of "never to return"
Breathe I against thee, upon pain of life.

MOWBRAY

A heavy sentence, my most sovereign liege,
And all unlooked-for from Your Highness' mouth.
A dearer merit, not so deep a maim   156
As to be cast forth in the common air,
Have I deservèd at Your Highness' hands.
The language I have learned these forty years,
My native English, now I must forgo;
And now my tongue's use is to me no more
Than an unstringèd viol or a harp,   162
Or like a cunning instrument cased up,   163
Or, being open, put into his hands   164
That knows no touch to tune the harmony.
Within my mouth you have enjailed my tongue,
Doubly portcullised with my teeth and lips,   167
And dull unfeeling barren ignorance
Is made my jailer to attend on me.
I am too old to fawn upon a nurse,
Too far in years to be a pupil now.
What is thy sentence then but speechless death,
Which robs my tongue from breathing native breath?   173

KING RICHARD

It boots thee not to be compassionate.   174
After our sentence plaining comes too late.   175

MOWBRAY

Then thus I turn me from my country's light,
To dwell in solemn shades of endless night.
                                        [*He starts to leave.*]

KING RICHARD

Return again, and take an oath with thee.
Lay on our royal sword your banished hands.
             [*They place their hands on Richard's sword.*]
Swear by the duty that you owe to God—
Our part therein we banish with yourselves—   181
To keep the oath that we administer:
You never shall, so help you truth and God,
Embrace each other's love in banishment,
Nor never look upon each other's face,
Nor never write, regreet, nor reconcile
This louring tempest of your homebred hate;   187
Nor never by advisèd purpose meet   188
To plot, contrive, or complot any ill   189
'Gainst us, our state, our subjects, or our land.

BOLINGBROKE   I swear.

---

108 him himself, Bolingbroke. (See line 40.)   **112 approve** prove
114 him i.e., Mowbray. (See line 24.)   **116 Attending** awaiting
118 warder staff or truncheon borne by the King when presiding over
a trial by combat   **122 While we return** until I inform   **122.1 flourish**
fanfare.   **124 list** hear   **125 For that** In order that   **127 for** because
(also in line 129)   **131 envy** enmity.   **set on you** set you on
134 Which i.e., which enmity, disturbance of the peace. (Although, in
literal terms, the antecedent of *Which* is *peace* in line 132.)   **140 life**
i.e., loss of life   **143 stranger** alien

150 sly stealthy.   **determinate** put to an end   **151 dateless limit**
unlimited term.   **dear** grievous   **156 dearer merit** better reward.
maim injury   **162 viol** a six-stringed instrument, related to the modern violin, played with a curved bow   **163 cunning** skillfully made
164 open taken from its case.   **his** that person's   **167 portcullised**
shut in by a portcullis, an iron grating over a gateway that can be
raised and lowered   **173 breathing . . . breath** speaking English.
174 boots avails.   **compassionate** full of laments.   **175 plaining**
complaining   **181 Our part therein** i.e., the duty you owe me as King
187 louring threatening, scowling   **188 advisèd** deliberate, premeditated   **189 complot** plot together

MOWBRAY   And I, to keep all this.

BOLINGBROKE

Norfolk, so far as to mine enemy: 193
By this time, had the King permitted us,
One of our souls had wandered in the air,
Banished this frail sepulchre of our flesh,   196
As now our flesh is banished from this land.
Confess thy treasons ere thou fly the realm.
Since thou hast far to go, bear not along
The clogging burden of a guilty soul.   200

MOWBRAY

No, Bolingbroke. If ever I were traitor,
My name be blotted from the book of life,
And I from heaven banished as from hence!
But what thou art, God, thou, and I do know,
And all too soon, I fear, the King shall rue.—
Farewell, my liege. Now no way can I stray;   206
Save back to England, all the world's my way.   *Exit.*

KING RICHARD [*to Gaunt*]

Uncle, even in the glasses of thine eyes   208
I see thy grievèd heart. Thy sad aspect
Hath from the number of his banished years
Plucked four away. [*To Bolingbroke*] Six frozen winters
    spent,
Return with welcome home from banishment.

BOLINGBROKE

How long a time lies in one little word!
Four lagging winters and four wanton springs   214
End in a word; such is the breath of kings.

GAUNT

I thank my liege that in regard of me
He shortens four years of my son's exile.
But little vantage shall I reap thereby;
For, ere the six years that he hath to spend
Can change their moons and bring their times about,
My oil-dried lamp and time-bewasted light   221
Shall be extinct with age and endless night;
My inch of taper will be burnt and done,   223
And blindfold Death not let me see my son.   224

KING RICHARD

Why, uncle, thou hast many years to live.

GAUNT

But not a minute, King, that thou canst give.
Shorten my days thou canst with sullen sorrow,
And pluck nights from me, but not lend a morrow;
Thou canst help Time to furrow me with age,
But stop no wrinkle in his pilgrimage;   230
Thy word is current with him for my death,   231
But dead, thy kingdom cannot buy my breath.   232

KING RICHARD

Thy son is banished upon good advice,
Whereto thy tongue a party verdict gave.   234
Why at our justice seem'st thou then to lour?

GAUNT

Things sweet to taste prove in digestion sour.
You urged me as a judge, but I had rather
You would have bid me argue like a father.
Oh, had it been a stranger, not my child,
To smooth his fault I should have been more mild.   240
A partial slander sought I to avoid   241
And in the sentence my own life destroyed.
Alas, I looked when some of you should say   243
I was too strict, to make mine own away;   244
But you gave leave to my unwilling tongue
Against my will to do myself this wrong.

KING RICHARD

Cousin, farewell; and, uncle, bid him so.
Six years we banish him, and he shall go.
         [*Flourish. Exit King Richard with his train.*]

AUMERLE [*to Bolingbroke*]

Cousin, farewell. What presence must not know,   249
From where you do remain let paper show.   [*Exit.*] 250

MARSHAL [*to Bolingbroke*]

My lord, no leave take I, for I will ride,   251
As far as land will let me, by your side.
         [*Bolingbroke makes no answer. The Lord Marshal
                                         stands aside.*]

GAUNT [*to Bolingbroke*]

Oh, to what purpose dost thou hoard thy words,
That thou returnest no greeting to thy friends?

BOLINGBROKE

I have too few to take my leave of you,
When the tongue's office should be prodigal   256
To breathe the abundant dolor of the heart.   257

GAUNT

Thy grief is but thy absence for a time.   258

BOLINGBROKE

Joy absent, grief is present for that time.   259

GAUNT

What is six winters? They are quickly gone.

BOLINGBROKE

To men in joy; but grief makes one hour ten.

GAUNT

Call it a travel that thou tak'st for pleasure.   262

BOLINGBROKE

My heart will sigh when I miscall it so,
Which finds it an enforcèd pilgrimage.

GAUNT

The sullen passage of thy weary steps   265

---

193 **so far** let me say this much   196 **sepulchre of our flesh** i.e., body, the temple or tomb of the soul   200 **clogging** (A clog was a wooden block attached to the leg to hinder movement.)   206 **stray** take the wrong road   208 **glasses** mirrors (here glistening with tears)   214 **wanton** luxuriant   221 **oil-dried** empty of oil   223 **taper** candle   224 **blindfold Death** i.e., *blindfold* because *Death* deprives its victims of their sight and because it is often pictured as an eyeless skull   230 **in his pilgrimage** brought about in time's journey   231 **current** i.e., as good as current coin, valid   232 **dead** i.e., once I am dead.   **buy** i.e., restore with a payment

234 **a party verdict** one person's share in a joint verdict   240 **smooth** extenuate   241 **partial slander** accusation of partiality (on behalf of my son)   243 **looked when** expected that, awaited the point at which   244 **to . . . away** in making away with my own (son)   249 **What . . . know** What I cannot learn from you in person   250 **s.d. Exit** (The exit is uncertain; see 1.4.1–4.)   251 **no leave take I** i.e., I will not take my leave of you, my lord; I will not say good-bye   256 **office** function.   **prodigal** lavish   257 **To breathe** in uttering   258 **grief** grievance   259 **grief** unhappiness   262 **travel** (The quarto spelling, "trauaile," suggests an interchangeable meaning of "travel" and "labor.")   265 **sullen** (1) melancholy (2) dull

Esteem as foil wherein thou art to set   266
The precious jewel of thy home return.

BOLINGBROKE

Nay, rather every tedious stride I make
Will but remember me what a deal of world   269
I wander from the jewels that I love.
Must I not serve a long apprenticehood
To foreign passages, and in the end,   272
Having my freedom, boast of nothing else   273
But that I was a journeyman to grief?   274

GAUNT

All places that the eye of heaven visits   275
Are to a wise man ports and happy havens.
Teach thy necessity to reason thus:
There is no virtue like necessity.
Think not the King did banish thee,
But thou the King. Woe doth the heavier sit   280
Where it perceives it is but faintly borne.   281
Go, say I sent thee forth to purchase honor,   282
And not the King exiled thee; or suppose
Devouring pestilence hangs in our air
And thou art flying to a fresher clime.
Look what thy soul holds dear, imagine it   286
To lie that way thou goest, not whence thou com'st.
Suppose the singing birds musicians,
The grass whereon thou tread'st the presence strewed,   289
The flowers fair ladies, and thy steps no more
Than a delightful measure or a dance;   291
For gnarling sorrow hath less power to bite   292
The man that mocks at it and sets it light.   293

BOLINGBROKE

Oh, who can hold a fire in his hand
By thinking on the frosty Caucasus?   295
Or cloy the hungry edge of appetite
By bare imagination of a feast?
Or wallow naked in December snow
By thinking on fantastic summer's heat?   299
Oh, no, the apprehension of the good
Gives but the greater feeling to the worse.
Fell Sorrow's tooth doth never rankle more   302
Than when he bites but lanceth not the sore.   303

GAUNT

Come, come, my son, I'll bring thee on thy way.   304
Had I thy youth and cause, I would not stay.   305

BOLINGBROKE

Then, England's ground, farewell. Sweet soil, adieu,
My mother and my nurse that bears me yet!
Where'er I wander, boast of this I can:
Though banished, yet a trueborn Englishman.

Exeunt.

❖

[1.4]

*Enter the King, with Bagot, [Green,] etc. at one
door, and the Lord Aumerle at another.*

KING RICHARD

We did observe.—Cousin Aumerle,   1
How far brought you high Hereford on his way?

AUMERLE

I brought high Hereford, if you call him so,
But to the next highway, and there I left him.   4

KING RICHARD

And say, what store of parting tears were shed?

AUMERLE

Faith, none for me, except the northeast wind,   6
Which then blew bitterly against our faces,
Awaked the sleeping rheum and so by chance   8
Did grace our hollow parting with a tear.   9

KING RICHARD

What said our cousin when you parted with him?

AUMERLE   "Farewell!"
And, for my heart disdainèd that my tongue   12
Should so profane the word, that taught me craft   13
To counterfeit oppression of such grief
That words seemed buried in my sorrow's grave.
Marry, would the word "farewell" have lengthened
    hours   16
And added years to his short banishment,
He should have had a volume of farewells;
But since it would not, he had none of me.   19

KING RICHARD

He is our cousin, cousin; but 'tis doubt,
When time shall call him home from banishment,
Whether our kinsman come to see his friends.   22
Ourself and Bushy, Bagot here, and Green
Observed his courtship to the common people,
How he did seem to dive into their hearts
With humble and familiar courtesy,
What reverence he did throw away on slaves,
Wooing poor craftsmen with the craft of smiles

---

266 **foil** thin metal leaf set behind gems to show off their luster;
hence, that which sets something off to advantage   269 **remember**
remind.   **a deal of world** a great distance   272 **passages** wanderings, experiences   273 **Having my freedom** (1) having completed my
apprenticeship (2) having been allowed to return home   274 **journeyman** (Literally, one who labors for day wages as a fully qualified
craftsman—with a hint also of one who makes a journey. Bolingbroke
will be proficient only in grief.)   275 **the eye of heaven** the sun
280 **But . . . King** i.e., but suppose that you are banishing the King to
the moral wilderness his crimes deserve.   280–1 **Woe . . . borne** Woe
is all the more oppressive when it perceives that the sufferer is faint-
hearted.   282 **purchase** acquire, win   286 **Look what** Whatever
289 **the presence strewed** the royal presence chamber strewn with
rushes   291 **measure** stately, formal dance   292 **gnarling** snarling,
growling   293 **sets it light** regards it lightly.   295 **Caucasus** mountain range between the Black and Caspian seas.   299 **fantastic** imagined   302 **Fell** Fierce.   **rankle** cause irritation and festering
303 **lanceth not** does not open the wound (to permit the release of the
infection; Bolingbroke's point is that sorrow should be openly confronted, not rationalized or covered over and thus allowed to fester)

304 **bring** escort   305 **stay** linger.
1.4. Location: The court.
1 **We did observe** (The scene begins in the midst of a conversation.)
4 **next** nearest   6 **for me** on my part.   **except** except that   8 **rheum**
watery discharge (i.e., tears)   9 **hollow** insincere   12 **for** because
13 **that** i.e., my disdain. (Aumerle says he pretended to be overcome
by grief in order to avoid saying an insincere "Farewell" to Bolingbroke.)   16 **Marry** Indeed. (From the oath, "by the Virgin Mary.")
19 **of** from   22 **friends** kinsmen, i.e., us, his cousins.

And patient underbearing of his fortune,   29
As 'twere to banish their affects with him.   30
Off goes his bonnet to an oyster wench;
A brace of draymen bid God speed him well   32
And had the tribute of his supple knee,
With "Thanks, my countrymen, my loving friends,"
As were our England in reversion his,   35
And he our subjects' next degree in hope.   36

GREEN
Well, he is gone, and with him go these thoughts.   37
Now for the rebels which stand out in Ireland,   38
Expedient manage must be made, my liege,   39
Ere further leisure yield them further means
For their advantage and Your Highness' loss.

KING RICHARD
We will ourself in person to this war.
And, for our coffers with too great a court   43
And liberal largess are grown somewhat light,   44
We are enforced to farm our royal realm,   45
The revenue whereof shall furnish us
For our affairs in hand. If that come short,
Our substitutes at home shall have blank charters,   48
Whereto, when they shall know what men are rich,
They shall subscribe them for large sums of gold   50
And send them after to supply our wants;   51
For we will make for Ireland presently.   52

Enter Bushy.

Bushy, what news?

BUSHY
Old John of Gaunt is grievous sick, my lord,
Suddenly taken, and hath sent posthaste
To entreat Your Majesty to visit him.

KING RICHARD   Where lies he?

BUSHY   At Ely House.   58

KING RICHARD
Now put it, God, in the physician's mind
To help him to his grave immediately!
The lining of his coffers shall make coats   61
To deck our soldiers for these Irish wars.
Come, gentlemen, let's all go visit him.
Pray God we may make haste and come too late!

ALL   Amen.   *Exeunt.*

[2.1]

Enter John of Gaunt sick, with the Duke of York,
etc.

GAUNT
Will the King come, that I may breathe my last
In wholesome counsel to his unstaid youth?   2

YORK
Vex not yourself, nor strive not with your breath,   3
For all in vain comes counsel to his ear.

GAUNT
Oh, but they say the tongues of dying men
Enforce attention like deep harmony.
Where words are scarce, they are seldom spent in vain,
For they breathe truth that breathe their words in pain.   8
He that no more must say is listened more   9
    Than they whom youth and ease have taught to glose.   10
More are men's ends marked than their lives before.   11
    The setting sun, and music at the close,
As the last taste of sweets, is sweetest last,   13
Writ in remembrance more than things long past.   14
Though Richard my life's counsel would not hear,   15
My death's sad tale may yet undeaf his ear.   16

YORK
No, it is stopped with other, flattering sounds,
As praises, of whose taste the wise are fond;   18
Lascivious meters, to whose venom sound   19
The open ear of youth doth always listen;
Report of fashions in proud Italy,   21
Whose manners still our tardy-apish nation   22
Limps after in base imitation.
Where doth the world thrust forth a vanity—
So it be new, there's no respect how vile—   25
That is not quickly buzzed into his ears?
Then all too late comes counsel to be heard
Where will doth mutiny with wit's regard.   28
Direct not him whose way himself will choose.   29
'Tis breath thou lack'st, and that breath wilt thou lose.

GAUNT
Methinks I am a prophet new inspired,
And thus expiring do foretell of him:
His rash fierce blaze of riot cannot last,   33
For violent fires soon burn out themselves;
Small showers last long, but sudden storms are short;

---

29 underbearing bearing, endurance   **30 banish . . . him** take their
affections with him into banishment.   **32 brace of draymen** pair of
cart drivers   **35 As . . . his** i.e., as if my England were to revert to him
as true owner after my death   **36 our . . . hope** i.e., the heir presumptive to the throne and favorite choice of the people.   **37 go** let go
38 for as for.   **stand out** hold out, resist   **39 Expedient manage**
speedy arrangements   **43 for** because.   **too great a court** i.e., too
great an extravagance at court   **44 liberal largess** extravagant generosity (to courtiers)   **45 farm** lease the right of collecting taxes, for a
present cash payment, to the highest bidder   **48 substitutes** deputies.
blank charters writs authorizing the collection of revenues or forced
loans to the crown, blank spaces being left for the names of the parties and the sums they were to provide   **50 subscribe them** put
down their names   **51 them** i.e., the sums collected   **52 presently** at
once.   **58 Ely House** (Palace of the Bishop of Ely in Holborn, a London district.)   **61 lining** contents. (With pun on lining for coats.)
coats coats of mail, armor

2.1. Location: Ely House.
0.1 *Enter John of Gaunt sick* (Presumably he is carried in by servants in
a chair.)   **2 unstaid** uncontrolled   **3 strive . . . breath** i.e., don't waste
your breath   **8 they** those persons   **9 He . . . listened more** He who
will soon be silenced by death is listened to more   **10 glose** flatter,
deceive in speech.   **11 marked** noticed   **13 is sweetest last** is longest
remembered as sweet   **14 Writ in remembrance** written down in the
memory   **15 my life's counsel** my advice while I lived   **16 My . . . tale**
my grave dying speech   **18 As . . . fond** such as praises, which even
wise men are foolishly inclined to hear   **19 meters** verses. **venom** poisonous   **21 proud Italy** (Roger Ascham, John Lyly, and other sixteenth-century writers complained of the growing influence of Italian
luxury.)   **22 still** always.   **tardy-apish** imitative but behind the times
25 So so long as.   **there's no respect** it makes no difference   **28 Where
. . . regard** where natural inclination rebels against what reason
esteems.   **29 Direct . . . choose** Don't try to offer advice to one who
insists on going his own way.   **33 riot** profligacy

He tires betimes that spurs too fast betimes;   36
With eager feeding food doth choke the feeder;
Light vanity, insatiate cormorant,   38
Consuming means, soon preys upon itself.   39
This royal throne of kings, this sceptered isle,
This earth of majesty, this seat of Mars,   41
This other Eden, demi-paradise,
This fortress built by Nature for herself
Against infection and the hand of war,   44
This happy breed of men, this little world,   45
This precious stone set in the silver sea,
Which serves it in the office of a wall   47
Or as a moat defensive to a house,
Against the envy of less happier lands,
This blessed plot, this earth, this realm, this England,
This nurse, this teeming womb of royal kings,   51
Feared by their breed and famous by their birth,   52
Renownèd for their deeds as far from home
For Christian service and true chivalry
As is the sepulcher in stubborn Jewry   55
Of the world's ransom, blessèd Mary's son,
This land of such dear souls, this dear dear land,
Dear for her reputation through the world,
Is now leased out—I die pronouncing it—
Like to a tenement or pelting farm.   60
England, bound in with the triumphant sea,   61
Whose rocky shore beats back the envious siege
Of wat'ry Neptune, is now bound in with shame,   63
With inky blots and rotten parchment bonds.   64
That England that was wont to conquer others
Hath made a shameful conquest of itself.
Ah, would the scandal vanish with my life,
How happy then were my ensuing death!   68

Enter King [Richard] and Queen, [Aumerle,
Bushy, Green, Bagot, Ross, and Willoughby,] etc.

YORK
The King is come. Deal mildly with his youth,
For young hot colts being reined do rage the more.
QUEEN
How fares our noble uncle Lancaster?
KING RICHARD
What comfort, man? How is't with agèd Gaunt?
GAUNT
Oh, how that name befits my composition!   73
Old Gaunt indeed, and gaunt in being old.
Within me grief hath kept a tedious fast,
And who abstains from meat that is not gaunt?   76
For sleeping England long time have I watched;   77

Watching breeds leanness, leanness is all gaunt.
The pleasure that some fathers feed upon
Is my strict fast—I mean, my children's looks—   80
And, therein fasting, hast thou made me gaunt.   81
Gaunt am I for the grave, gaunt as a grave,
Whose hollow womb inherits naught but bones.   83
KING RICHARD
Can sick men play so nicely with their names?   84
GAUNT
No, misery makes sport to mock itself.   85
Since thou dost seek to kill my name in me,   86
I mock my name, great King, to flatter thee.   87
KING RICHARD
Should dying men flatter with those that live?   88
GAUNT
No, no, men living flatter those that die.   89
KING RICHARD
Thou, now a-dying, sayest thou flatterest me.
GAUNT
Oh, no, thou diest, though I the sicker be.
KING RICHARD
I am in health, I breathe, and see thee ill.
GAUNT
Now He that made me knows I see thee ill;
Ill in myself to see, and in thee seeing ill.   94
Thy deathbed is no lesser than thy land,
Wherein thou liest in reputation sick;
And thou, too careless patient as thou art,
Commit'st thy anointed body to the cure
Of those physicians that first wounded thee.   99
A thousand flatterers sit within thy crown,
Whose compass is no bigger than thy head,   101
And yet, encagèd in so small a verge,   102
The waste is no whit lesser than thy land.   103
Oh, had thy grandsire with a prophet's eye   104
Seen how his son's son should destroy his sons,   105
From forth thy reach he would have laid thy shame,   106
Deposing thee before thou wert possessed,   107
Which art possessed now to depose thyself.   108
Why, cousin, wert thou regent of the world,   109
It were a shame to let this land by lease;

---

36 **betimes** soon, early   38 **Light vanity** frivolous dissipation.
cormorant glutton. (Literally, a voracious seabird.)   39 **means** i.e.,
means of sustenance   41 **earth of majesty** land fit for kings.   **seat of
Mars** residence of the god of war   44 **infection** (1) plague (2) moral
pollution   45 **happy breed** fortunate race   47 **office** function
51 **teeming** fruitful   52 **by their breed** for their ancestral reputation
for prowess   55 **stubborn Jewry** i.e., Judea, called stubborn because
it resisted Christianity   60 **tenement** land or property held by a tenant.   **pelting** paltry   61 **bound in** bordered, surrounded   63 **bound
in** legally constrained   64 **blots . . . bonds** i.e., the blank charters.
68 **ensuing** approaching   73 **composition** constitution.   76 **meat**
food   77 **watched** kept watch at night, been vigilant

80 **Is . . . fast** is something I must forgo   81 **therein fasting** i.e., since I
am starved of that pleasure   83 **inherits** possesses, will receive
84 **nicely** (1) ingeniously (2) triflingly   85 **to mock** of mocking
86–7 **Since . . . thee** Since you seek to destroy my family name (by
banishing my son), I mock my name to please you and flatter your
greatness.   88 **flatter with** try to please   89 **flatter** i.e., are attentive
to, offer comfort to   94 **Ill . . . ill** seeing myself to be physically ill,
and seeing the illness in you of abusing your royal authority.
99 **physicians** i.e., the King's favorites   101 **compass** circle, circumference   102 **verge** (1) circle, ring (2) the compass about the King's
court, which extended for twelve miles   103 **waste** (1) waist, circumference (2) that which is destroyed. (With a quibble on the legal
meaning of *waste*, "damage done to property by a tenant.")   **whit** bit,
speck   104 **grandsire** i.e., Edward III   105 **destroy his sons** (1) destroy
Edward III's sons, Richard's uncles (2) destroy Richard's own heritage   106 **From . . . shame** he would have put the matter you have
shamefully handled out of your reach   107 **Deposing** dispossessing.
possessed put in possession of the crown   108 **Which . . . thyself**
you who are now seized with an obsessive desire to give away your
authority (by leasing the realm to favorites).   109 **cousin** kinsman,
nephew.   **regent** ruler

But, for thy world enjoying but this land,   111
Is it not more than shame to shame it so?
Landlord of England art thou now, not king.   113
Thy state of law is bondslave to the law,   114
And thou—

KING RICHARD   A lunatic lean-witted fool,
Presuming on an ague's privilege,   116
Darest with thy frozen admonition   117
Make pale our cheek, chasing the royal blood
With fury from his native residence.   119
Now, by my seat's right royal majesty,   120
Wert thou not brother to great Edward's son,   121
This tongue that runs so roundly in thy head   122
Should run thy head from thy unreverent shoulders.   123

GAUNT
Oh, spare me not, my brother Edward's son,
For that I was his father Edward's son!   125
That blood already, like the pelican,   126
Hast thou tapped out and drunkenly caroused.   127
My brother Gloucester, plain well-meaning soul—
Whom fair befall in heaven 'mongst happy souls!—   129
May be a precedent and witness good
That thou respect'st not spilling Edward's blood.   131
Join with the present sickness that I have,   132
And thy unkindness be like crooked age   133
To crop at once a too-long-withered flower!—   134
Live in thy shame, but die not shame with thee!   135
These words hereafter thy tormentors be!—
Convey me to my bed, then to my grave.
Love they to live that love and honor have.   138
                        Exit [borne off by his attendants].

KING RICHARD
And let them die that age and sullens have,   139
For both hast thou, and both become the grave.   140

YORK
I do beseech Your Majesty, impute his words
To wayward sickliness and age in him.
He loves you, on my life, and holds you dear
As Harry Duke of Hereford, were he here.   144

KING RICHARD
Right, you say true. As Hereford's love, so his;   145
As theirs, so mine; and all be as it is.

[Enter Northumberland.]

NORTHUMBERLAND
My liege, old Gaunt commends him to Your Majesty.

KING RICHARD
What says he?

NORTHUMBERLAND   Nay, nothing, all is said.
His tongue is now a stringless instrument;
Words, life, and all, old Lancaster hath spent.

YORK
Be York the next that must be bankrupt so!
Though death be poor, it ends a mortal woe.   152

KING RICHARD
The ripest fruit first falls, and so doth he;
His time is spent, our pilgrimage must be.   154
So much for that. Now for our Irish wars:
We must supplant those rough rug-headed kerns,   156
Which live like venom where no venom else   157
But only they have privilege to live.   158
And, for these great affairs do ask some charge,   159
Towards our assistance we do seize to us
The plate, coin, revenues, and movables   161
Whereof our uncle Gaunt did stand possessed.

YORK
How long shall I be patient? Ah, how long
Shall tender duty make me suffer wrong?
Not Gloucester's death, nor Hereford's banishment,
Nor Gaunt's rebukes, nor England's private wrongs,   166
Nor the prevention of poor Bolingbroke   167
About his marriage, nor my own disgrace,   168
Have ever made me sour my patient cheek
Or bend one wrinkle on my sovereign's face.   170
I am the last of noble Edward's sons,
Of whom thy father, Prince of Wales, was first.
In war was never lion raged more fierce,   173
In peace was never gentle lamb more mild,
Than was that young and princely gentleman.
His face thou hast, for even so looked he,
Accomplished with the number of thy hours;   177
But when he frowned, it was against the French
And not against his friends. His noble hand

111 **But . . . land** i.e., but since you enjoy as your domain only this
land of England (rather than the whole world)   113 **Landlord** i.e.,
One who leases out property   114 **Thy . . . to the law** i.e., Your legal
status as King is now subservient to and at the mercy of the law
governing contracts, such as blank charters   116 **an ague's privilege** i.e., a sick person's right to be testy   117 **frozen** (1) chilly
(2) caused by a chill   119 **his** its   120 **seat's** throne's   121 **great
Edward's son** Edward the Black Prince, Richard's father
122–3 **runs . . . run** runs on, talks . . . drive, chase   122 **roundly**
unceremoniously, bluntly   123 **unreverent** irreverent, disrespectful
125 **For that** simply because   126 **pelican** (The pelican was thought
to feed its ungrateful and murderous young with its own blood.)
127 **tapped out** drawn as from a tapped barrel.   **caroused** gulped,
quaffed.   129 **Whom fair befall** to whom may good come   131 **thou
respect'st not** you care nothing about   132–4 **Join . . . flower!** May
your unnatural behavior act in concert with my present illness and
my advanced years to cut down my life like a too-long-withered
flower! (*Unkindness* means both cruelty and behavior contrary to the
natural bond that should exist in blood ties.)   135 **die . . . thee** i.e.,
may your shame live after you.   138 **Love they** Let them desire
139 **sullens** sullenness, melancholy   140 **become** suit   144 **As** i.e., as
he would love. (But see the next note.)

145 **Right . . . his** (Richard deliberately takes the opposite of what
York had intended to say; Richard gibes that Gaunt is as little fond of
the King as is Hereford.)   152 **Though . . . woe** Though death is the
privation of life, it does end the misery of human existence which is
itself a kind of death in life.   154 **our . . . be** i.e., our journey through
life is yet to be completed but will also end.   156–8 **We . . . live** We
must expel these shaggy-haired light-armed Irish foot soldiers, who
live there like poisonous snakes where no others are allowed to exist.
(Richard alludes to the freedom of Ireland from snakes, traditionally
ascribed to Saint Patrick.)   159 **for** because.   **ask some charge** require
some expenditure   161 **movables** personal property   166 **Nor . . .
wrongs** nor the rebukes given to Gaunt, nor wrongs inflicted on private English subjects   167–8 **prevention . . . marriage** (Holinshed's
Chronicles report that Richard had forestalled Bolingbroke's intended
marriage with the Duke de Berri's daughter.)   170 **Or bend . . . face**
or ever frown at the King, or give him reason to frown.   173 **was . . .
fierce** never was there a lion more fiercely enraged   177 **Accomplished . . . hours** i.e., when he was your age

Did win what he did spend, and spent not that
Which his triumphant father's hand had won.
His hands were guilty of no kindred blood,   182
But bloody with the enemies of his kin.
Oh, Richard! York is too far gone with grief,
Or else he never would compare between.   185

KING RICHARD
Why, uncle, what's the matter?

YORK   O my liege,
Pardon me, if you please; if not, I, pleased   187
Not to be pardoned, am content withal.   188
Seek you to seize and grip into your hands
The royalties and rights of banished Hereford?   190
Is not Gaunt dead? And doth not Hereford live?
Was not Gaunt just? And is not Harry true?
Did not the one deserve to have an heir?
Is not his heir a well-deserving son?
Take Hereford's rights away, and take from Time   195
His charters and his customary rights;   196
Let not tomorrow then ensue today;   197
Be not thyself; for how art thou a king
But by fair sequence and succession?
Now, afore God—God forbid I say true!—
If you do wrongfully seize Hereford's rights,
Call in the letters patents that he hath   202
By his attorneys general to sue   203
His livery, and deny his offered homage,   204
You pluck a thousand dangers on your head,
You lose a thousand well-disposèd hearts,
And prick my tender patience to those thoughts   207
Which honor and allegiance cannot think.

KING RICHARD
Think what you will, we seize into our hands
His plate, his goods, his money, and his lands.

YORK
I'll not be by the while. My liege, farewell.   211
What will ensue hereof there's none can tell;
But by bad courses may be understood   213
That their events can never fall out good.   Exit. 214

KING RICHARD
Go, Bushy, to the Earl of Wiltshire straight.   215
Bid him repair to us to Ely House   216
To see this business. Tomorrow next   217
We will for Ireland, and 'tis time, I trow.   218
And we create, in absence of ourself,
Our uncle York Lord Governor of England,
For he is just and always loved us well.—

Come on, our queen. Tomorrow must we part.
Be merry, for our time of stay is short.   223
        [Flourish.] Exeunt King and Queen [with attendants].
        Manet Northumberland [with Willoughby and Ross].

NORTHUMBERLAND
Well, lords, the Duke of Lancaster is dead.

ROSS
And living too, for now his son is duke.

WILLOUGHBY
Barely in title, not in revenues.

NORTHUMBERLAND
Richly in both, if justice had her right.

ROSS
My heart is great, but it must break with silence,   228
Ere't be disburdened with a liberal tongue.   229

NORTHUMBERLAND
Nay, speak thy mind; and let him ne'er speak more   230
That speaks thy words again to do thee harm!

WILLOUGHBY
Tends that thou wouldst speak to the Duke of
        Hereford?   232
If it be so, out with it boldly, man.
Quick is mine ear to hear of good towards him.

ROSS
No good at all that I can do for him,
Unless you call it good to pity him,
Bereft and gelded of his patrimony.   237

NORTHUMBERLAND
Now, afore God, 'tis shame such wrongs are borne
In him, a royal prince, and many more   239
Of noble blood in this declining land.
The King is not himself, but basely led
By flatterers; and what they will inform   242
Merely in hate 'gainst any of us all,   243
That will the King severely prosecute
'Gainst us, our lives, our children, and our heirs.

ROSS
The commons hath he pilled with grievous taxes,   246
And quite lost their hearts; the nobles hath he fined
For ancient quarrels, and quite lost their hearts.

WILLOUGHBY
And daily new exactions are devised,
As blanks, benevolences, and I wot not what.   250
But what i' God's name doth become of this?   251

NORTHUMBERLAND
Wars hath not wasted it, for warred he hath not,
But basely yielded upon compromise
That which his noble ancestors achieved with blows.
More hath he spent in peace than they in wars.

ROSS
The Earl of Wiltshire hath the realm in farm.   256

---

182 kindred blood blood of one's relatives   **185 compare between**
draw comparisons.   **187 pleased** satisfied   **188 withal** with that,
nonetheless.   **190 royalties** privileges granted through the King and
belonging, in this case, to a member of the royal family   **195 Take . . .
and take** i.e., If you take . . . you take   **196 His** Time's   **197 ensue** follow   **202–4 Call . . . livery** i.e., revoke the royal grant giving him the
privilege to sue through his attorneys for possession of his inheritance
204 deny refuse.   **homage** avowal of allegiance (by which ceremony
Bolingbroke would be able legally to secure his inheritance)   **207 prick**
i.e., incite   **211 by** nearby, present   **213 by** concerning. **may** it may
214 events outcomes   **215 Earl of Wiltshire** (The King's Lord Treasurer and one of his notorious favorites.)   **216 repair** come   **217 see**
see to.   **Tomorrow next** Tomorrow   **218 trow** believe.

223.2 Manet He remains onstage   **228 great** i.e., great with sorrow
229 liberal unrestrained, freely speaking   **230 ne'er speak more** i.e.,
die   **232 Tends . . . to** Does what you wish to say concern
237 gelded i.e., deprived. (Literally, castrated.)   **239 In him** his
case, or, by him   **242 inform** charge, report as spies   **243 Merely in
hate** out of pure hatred   **246 pilled** plundered   **250 blanks** blank
charters.   **benevolences** forced loans to the crown (not actually
employed until considerably later, in 1473).   **wot** know   **251 this** i.e.,
this unjustly collected revenue.   **256 in farm** on lease.

WILLOUGHBY
The King's grown bankrupt, like a broken man.   257
NORTHUMBERLAND
Reproach and dissolution hangeth over him.
ROSS
He hath not money for these Irish wars,
His burdenous taxations notwithstanding,
But by the robbing of the banished Duke.
NORTHUMBERLAND
His noble kinsman. Most degenerate king!
But, lords, we hear this fearful tempest sing,
Yet seek no shelter to avoid the storm;
We see the wind sit sore upon our sails,   265
And yet we strike not, but securely perish.   266
ROSS
We see the very wrack that we must suffer,   267
And unavoided is the danger now   268
For suffering so the causes of our wrack.   269
NORTHUMBERLAND
Not so. Even through the hollow eyes of death   270
I spy life peering; but I dare not say
How near the tidings of our comfort is.
WILLOUGHBY
Nay, let us share thy thoughts, as thou dost ours.
ROSS
Be confident to speak, Northumberland.
We three are but thyself, and speaking so
Thy words are but as thoughts. Therefore be bold.
NORTHUMBERLAND
Then thus: I have from Port le Blanc,
A bay in Brittany, received intelligence
That Harry Duke of Hereford, Rainold Lord Cobham,
. . . .   280
That late broke from the Duke of Exeter,   281
His brother, Archbishop late of Canterbury,   282
Sir Thomas Erpingham, Sir John Ramston,
Sir John Norbery, Sir Robert Waterton, and Francis
     Coint,
All these well furnished by the Duke of Brittany
With eight tall ships, three thousand men of war,   286
Are making hither with all due expedience   287
And shortly mean to touch our northern shore.
Perhaps they had ere this, but that they stay   289
The first departing of the King for Ireland.   290
If then we shall shake off our slavish yoke,

Imp out our drooping country's broken wing,   292
Redeem from broking pawn the blemished crown,   293
Wipe off the dust that hides our scepter's gilt,   294
And make high majesty look like itself,
Away with me in post to Ravenspurgh;   296
But if you faint, as fearing to do so,   297
Stay and be secret, and myself will go.
ROSS
To horse, to horse! Urge doubts to them that fear.
WILLOUGHBY
Hold out my horse, and I will first be there.   *Exeunt.*   300

❖

[2.2]

Enter the Queen, Bushy, [and] Bagot.

BUSHY
Madam, Your Majesty is too much sad.
You promised, when you parted with the King,   2
To lay aside life-harming heaviness   3
And entertain a cheerful disposition.   4
QUEEN
To please the King I did; to please myself
I cannot do it. Yet I know no cause
Why I should welcome such a guest as grief,
Save bidding farewell to so sweet a guest
As my sweet Richard. Yet again methinks
Some unborn sorrow ripe in Fortune's womb
Is coming towards me, and my inward soul
With nothing trembles. At something it grieves
More than with parting from my lord the King.
BUSHY
Each substance of a grief hath twenty shadows,   14
Which shows like grief itself but is not so;
For sorrow's eyes, glazèd with blinding tears,
Divides one thing entire to many objects,   17
Like perspectives, which rightly gazed upon   18
Show nothing but confusion, eyed awry   19
Distinguish form. So your sweet Majesty,   20
Looking awry upon your lord's departure,   21
Find shapes of grief more than himself to wail,   22
Which, looked on as it is, is naught but shadows
Of what it is not. Then, thrice-gracious Queen,

292 **Imp out** piece out. (A term from falconry, meaning to attach new feathers to a disabled wing of a bird.)   293 **from broking pawn** from being pledged to pawnbrokers   294 **gilt** gold (with pun on *guilt*)   296 **post** haste.   **Ravenspurgh** on the Yorkshire coast, at the mouth of the Humber River   297 **faint** are fainthearted   300 **Hold . . . and** If my horse holds out
2.2. Location: The court. According to Holinshed, the Queen remained at Windsor Castle when Richard left for Ireland.
2 **with** from   3 **heaviness** melancholy   4 **entertain** put on   14 **Each . . . shadows** i.e., For every real grief there exist twenty imagined ones
17 **thing entire to** complete thing into   18 **perspectives** (In lines 16–17, Bushy seems to have in mind a glass with a multifaceted lens, multiplying images of the object being viewed; in lines 18–20, *perspectives* are pictures of figures made to appear distorted or confused, except when viewed obliquely, *eyed awry*.)   **rightly** directly, straight   19 **awry** obliquely   20 **Distinguish form** make the form distinct and normal.   21 **awry** i.e., mistakenly, distortedly   22 **himself** i.e., the grief itself.   **wail** bewail

257 **broken** financially ruined   265 **sore** sorely, grievously   266 **strike** (1) furl the sails (2) strike blows.   **securely** heedlessly, overconfidently
267 **wrack** ruin   268 **unavoided** unavoidable   269 **suffering** permitting   270 **eyes** eye sockets   280 . . . (A line is probably missing here, perhaps because of censorship. From information contained in Holinshed, it may have read something like "Thomas, son and heir to the Earl of Arundel" or "The son of Richard, Earl of Arundel.")   281 **late broke from** lately escaped from the custody of. (Holinshed records that "the Earl of Arundel's son, named Thomas, which was kept in the Duke of Exeter's house, escaped out of the realm . . . and went to his uncle Thomas Arundel, late Archbishop of Canterbury.")
282 **His** i.e., the Earl of Arundel's.   **late** until recently   286 **tall** stately.
men of war troops   287 **expedience** expedition, speed   289–90 **stay . . . King** wait until the King departs

More than your lord's departure weep not. More is not
  seen,
Or if it be, 'tis with false sorrow's eye,
Which for things true weeps things imaginary.   27

QUEEN
It may be so, but yet my inward soul
Persuades me it is otherwise. Howe'er it be,
I cannot but be sad—so heavy sad
As, though on thinking on no thought I think,   31
Makes me with heavy nothing faint and shrink.   32

BUSHY
'Tis nothing but conceit, my gracious lady.   33

QUEEN
'Tis nothing less. Conceit is still derived   34
From some forefather grief. Mine is not so,
For nothing hath begot my something grief,   36
Or something hath the nothing that I grieve.   37
'Tis in reversion that I do possess;   38
But what it is, that is not yet known what,   39
I cannot name. 'Tis nameless woe, I wot.   40

[Enter Green.]

GREEN
God save Your Majesty! And well met, gentlemen.
I hope the King is not yet shipped for Ireland.

QUEEN
Why hopest thou so? 'Tis better hope he is,
For his designs crave haste, his haste good hope.   44
Then wherefore dost thou hope he is not shipped?

GREEN
That he, our hope, might have retired his power,   46
And driven into despair an enemy's hope,
Who strongly hath set footing in this land.
The banished Bolingbroke repeals himself   49
And with uplifted arms is safe arrived   50
At Ravenspurgh.

QUEEN   Now God in heaven forbid!

GREEN
Ah, madam, 'tis too true; and that is worse,   52
The lord Northumberland, his son young Harry
  Percy,
The lords of Ross, Beaumont, and Willoughby,
With all their powerful friends, are fled to him.

BUSHY
Why have you not proclaimed Northumberland
And all the rest revolted faction traitors?   57

GREEN
We have, whereupon the Earl of Worcester
Hath broken his staff, resigned his stewardship,   59
And all the household servants fled with him
To Bolingbroke.

QUEEN
So, Green, thou art the midwife to my woe,
And Bolingbroke my sorrow's dismal heir.   63
Now hath my soul brought forth her prodigy,   64
And I, a gasping new-delivered mother,
Have woe to woe, sorrow to sorrow joined.

BUSHY
Despair not, madam.

QUEEN   Who shall hinder me?
I will despair, and be at enmity
With cozening hope. He is a flatterer,   69
A parasite, a keeper-back of death
Who gently would dissolve the bonds of life   71
Which false hope lingers in extremity.   72

[Enter York.]

GREEN   Here comes the Duke of York.

QUEEN
With signs of war about his agèd neck.   74
Oh, full of careful business are his looks!   75
Uncle, for God's sake, speak comfortable words.   76

YORK
Should I do so, I should belie my thoughts.
Comfort's in heaven, and we are on the earth,
Where nothing lives but crosses, cares, and grief.   79
Your husband, he is gone to save far off,   80
Whilst others come to make him lose at home.
Here am I left to underprop his land,   82
Who, weak with age, cannot support myself.
Now comes the sick hour that his surfeit made;
Now shall he try his friends that flattered him.   85

[Enter a Servingman.]

SERVINGMAN
My lord, your son was gone before I came.   86

YORK
He was? Why, so. Go all which way it will!
The nobles they are fled, the commons they are cold,
And will, I fear, revolt on Hereford's side.
Sirrah, get thee to Pleshey, to my sister Gloucester;   90
Bid her send me presently a thousand pound.   91
Hold, take my ring.   92

---

27 **for** in place of. **weeps** weeps for   31–2 **As . . . shrink** that,
though I seem to be thinking of nothing, my "nothing" is so *heavy* or
saddening that I faint and fall back under the weight.   33 **conceit**
fancy   34 **'Tis nothing less** i.e., It is anything but that.   **still** always
36 **something** i.e., substantial   37 **something . . . grieve** the unsubstantial grief, the nothing, that I grieve about has something to it,
some substance.   38–40 **'Tis . . . name** i.e., My grief is like a legacy
that will come to me at some future time, but I cannot tell its nature
yet.   40 **wot** know, assume.   44 **For . . . hope** for his plans require
that he proceed expeditiously to Ireland, and that his haste will bring
hope of good success.   46 **retired his power** held back his army (in
order to be able to repulse Bolingbroke's landing)   49 **repeals** recalls
(from exile)   50 **uplifted arms** weapons raised in rebellion   52 **that**
what   57 **rest** rest of the

59 **broken his staff** broken his badge of office (in token of resignation
as Lord High Steward. Worcester is brother of the Earl of Northumberland.)   63 **dismal heir** ill-omened offspring.   64 **prodigy** monstrous birth   69 **cozening** cheating.   **He** i.e., False hope   71 **Who**
i.e., death   72 **lingers** causes to linger   74 **signs of war** i.e., a piece of
armor called the gorget, an iron collar that could be worn with ordinary clothes   75 **careful business** worried preoccupation   76 **comfortable** affording comfort   79 **crosses** obstacles, obstructions
80 **save far off** i.e., defend his rule in Ireland   82 **underprop** prop up,
support   85 **try** test   86 **your son** i.e., the Duke of Aumerle   90 **Sirrah** (Said to inferiors.)   **sister** sister-in-law   91 **presently** immediately   92 **ring** (By which the Duchess will know that the request is
sent by York himself.)

SERVINGMAN
My lord, I had forgot to tell Your Lordship:
Today, as I came by, I callèd there—
But I shall grieve you to report the rest.

YORK What is't, knave?   96

SERVINGMAN
An hour before I came, the Duchess died.

YORK
God for his mercy, what a tide of woes
Comes rushing on this woeful land at once!
I know not what to do. I would to God,
So my untruth had not provoked him to it,   101
The King had cut off my head with my brother's.   102
What, are there no posts dispatched for Ireland?
How shall we do for money for these wars?
Come, sister—cousin, I would say—pray pardon
    me.—
Go, fellow, get thee home. Provide some carts
And bring away the armor that is there.
                   [*Exit Servingman.*]
Gentlemen, will you go muster men?
If I know how or which way to order these affairs
Thus disorderly thrust into my hands,
Never believe me. Both are my kinsmen:
Th'one is my sovereign, whom both my oath
And duty bids defend; t'other again
Is my kinsman, whom the King hath wronged,
Whom conscience and my kindred bids to right.   115
Well, somewhat we must do.—Come, cousin,   116
I'll dispose of you.—Gentlemen,   117
Go, muster up your men, and meet me presently
At Berkeley. I should to Pleshey too,   119
But time will not permit. All is uneven,
And everything is left at six and seven.   121
              Exeunt Duke [*of York*], *Queen.*
              Manent Bushy, [*Bagot,*] *Green.*

BUSHY
The wind sits fair for news to go to Ireland,
But none returns. For us to levy power
Proportionable to the enemy
Is all unpossible.

GREEN
Besides, our nearness to the King in love
Is near the hate of those love not the King.   127

BAGOT
And that is the wavering commons, for their love
Lies in their purses, and whoso empties them
By so much fills their hearts with deadly hate.

BUSHY
Wherein the King stands generally condemned.

BAGOT
If judgment lie in them, then so do we,   132
Because we ever have been near the King.   133

GREEN
Well, I will for refuge straight to Bristol Castle.
The Earl of Wiltshire is already there.

BUSHY
Thither will I with you, for little office   136
Will the hateful commons perform for us,   137
Except like curs to tear us all to pieces.
[*To Bagot*] Will you go along with us?

BAGOT
No, I will to Ireland to His Majesty.
Farewell. If heart's presages be not vain,   141
We three here part that ne'er shall meet again.

BUSHY
That's as York thrives to beat back Bolingbroke.   143

GREEN
Alas, poor duke! The task he undertakes
Is numbering sands and drinking oceans dry.
Where one on his side fights, thousands will fly.
Farewell at once, for once, for all, and ever.

BUSHY
Well, we may meet again.

BAGOT   I fear me, never.
                       [*Exeunt.*]

❖

[2.3]

Enter [*Bolingbroke, Duke of*] *Hereford,* [*and*]
Northumberland [*with forces*].

BOLINGBROKE
How far is it, my lord, to Berkeley now?

NORTHUMBERLAND Believe me, noble lord,
I am a stranger here in Gloucestershire.
These high wild hills and rough uneven ways
Draws out our miles and makes them wearisome;
And yet your fair discourse hath been as sugar,
Making the hard way sweet and delectable.
But I bethink me what a weary way
From Ravenspurgh to Cotswold will be found   9
In Ross and Willoughby, wanting your company,   10
Which, I protest, hath very much beguiled   11
The tediousness and process of my travel.   12
But theirs is sweetened with the hope to have
The present benefit which I possess;
And hope to joy is little less in joy   15
Than hope enjoyed. By this the weary lords   16

---

96 **knave** i.e., fellow.   101 **So my untruth** provided that some disloyalty on my part   102 **brother's** i.e., the Duke of Gloucester's.   115
my . . . right my kinship to him bids that I right his wrong.   116
somewhat something.   **cousin** i.e., the Queen   117 **dispose of** make
arrangements for   119 **Berkeley** a castle near Bristol.   121 **at six and
seven** i.e., in confusion.   121.2 *Manent* They remain onstage   127 **Is
. . . King** makes us enemies of those who oppose the King.

132 **If . . . we** i.e., If the power to pass judgment is given to the wavering commons, then we, too, stand condemned   133 **ever** always
136 **office** service   137 **hateful** full of hate, angry   141 **vain** in
vain   143 **That's . . . thrives** i.e., That depends upon York's efforts
and success
2.3. Location: In Gloucestershire, near Berkeley Castle.
9 **Cotswold** hilly district in Gloucestershire   10 **In** by.   **wanting**
lacking   11 **protest** declare   12 **tediousness and process** tedious
process   15–16 **And hope . . . enjoyed** and the hope of future happiness is only slightly less joyous than happiness already enjoyed.
16 **this** this expectation

Shall make their way seem short, as mine hath done
By sight of what I have: your noble company.

BOLINGBROKE
Of much less value is my company
Than your good words. But who comes here?

Enter Harry Percy.

NORTHUMBERLAND
It is my son, young Harry Percy,
Sent from my brother Worcester whencesoever.—   22
Harry, how fares your uncle?   23

PERCY
I had thought, my lord, to have learned his health of
    you.

NORTHUMBERLAND   Why, is he not with the Queen?

PERCY
No, my good lord. He hath forsook the court,
Broken his staff of office, and dispersed
The household of the King.

NORTHUMBERLAND   What was his reason?
He was not so resolved when last we spake together.

PERCY
Because Your Lordship was proclaimèd traitor.
But he, my lord, is gone to Ravenspurgh,
To offer service to the Duke of Hereford,
And sent me over by Berkeley to discover
What power the Duke of York had levied there,   34
Then with directions to repair to Ravenspurgh.   35

NORTHUMBERLAND
Have you forgot the Duke of Hereford, boy?   36

PERCY
No, my good lord, for that is not forgot
Which ne'er I did remember. To my knowledge
I never in my life did look on him.

NORTHUMBERLAND
Then learn to know him now. This is the Duke.

PERCY
My gracious lord, I tender you my service,   41
Such as it is, being tender, raw, and young,
Which elder days shall ripen and confirm
To more approvèd service and desert.   44

BOLINGBROKE
I thank thee, gentle Percy, and be sure
I count myself in nothing else so happy
As in a soul rememb'ring my good friends;   47
And as my fortune ripens with thy love,   48
It shall be still thy true love's recompense.   49
My heart this covenant makes, my hand thus seals it.
                              [*He offers Percy his hand.*]

NORTHUMBERLAND
How far is it to Berkeley? And what stir   51
Keeps good old York there with his men of war?

PERCY
There stands the castle by yon tuft of trees,
Manned with three hundred men, as I have heard,
And in it are the lords of York, Berkeley, and Seymour,
None else of name and noble estimate.   56

[*Enter Ross and Willoughby.*]

NORTHUMBERLAND
Here come the lords of Ross and Willoughby,
Bloody with spurring, fiery red with haste.   58

BOLINGBROKE
Welcome, my lords. I wot your love pursues   59
A banished traitor. All my treasury
Is yet but unfelt thanks, which, more enriched,   61
Shall be your love and labor's recompense.

ROSS
Your presence makes us rich, most noble lord.

WILLOUGHBY
And far surmounts our labor to attain it.

BOLINGBROKE
Evermore thank's the exchequer of the poor,   65
Which, till my infant fortune comes to years,   66
Stands for my bounty. But who comes here?   67

[*Enter Berkeley.*]

NORTHUMBERLAND
It is my lord of Berkeley, as I guess.

BERKELEY
My lord of Hereford, my message is to you.

BOLINGBROKE
My lord, my answer is—to "Lancaster";   70
And I am come to seek that name in England,
And I must find that title in your tongue
Before I make reply to aught you say.

BERKELEY
Mistake me not, my lord, 'tis not my meaning
To raze one title of your honor out.   75
To you, my lord, I come, what lord you will,   76
From the most gracious regent of this land,
The Duke of York, to know what pricks you on   78
To take advantage of the absent time   79
And fright our native peace with self-borne arms.   80

[*Enter York.*]

---

51 stir action   **56 estimate** rank.   **58 spurring** i.e., hard riding
59 wot am aware that. (Bolingbroke graciously indicates his awareness of the risk they are taking in supporting him.)   **61 unfelt** impal-
pable, expressed in words, not gifts.   **which** i.e., which treasury.
more enriched i.e., with still more thanks added, or, with substantial
gifts at a later date   **65 Evermore . . . poor** "Thank you" is always the
exchequer of the poor, i.e., the only means they have to repay favors
66 comes to years reaches maturity   **67 Stands for** serves in place of
70 "Lancaster" (Bolingbroke will enter into no negotiations unless his
proper title, taken away by Richard, is given him.)   **75 raze** scrape
(or perhaps *rase*, "erase")   **76 what . . . will** whatever title you prefer
to be addressed by. (Said sardonically.)   **78 pricks** spurs   **79 the
absent time** i.e., the time of the King's absence   **80 self-borne** borne
in your own private cause, not the country's welfare. (Also suggesting *self-born*, "originating in the self.")

---

22 whencesoever from wherever he is.   **23 your uncle** i.e., the Earl of
Worcester.   **34 power** troops   **35 directions** instructions.   **repair** go
36 boy (A rebuke for not respectfully greeting Bolingbroke, though
historically Percy was two years Bolingbroke's senior.)   **41 tender**
offer. (With a pun in the next line on the meaning "inexperienced.")
my service (Presumably Percy kneels to Bolingbroke, and so do Ross
and Willoughby when they enter.)   **44 approvèd** proven, demonstrated   **47 in a** in my   **48–9 And . . . recompense** and as my fortunes improve, assisted by your loyalty to me, I will be increasingly
enabled to reward you for that loyalty.

BOLINGBROKE
I shall not need transport my words by you;
Here comes His Grace in person.—My noble uncle!

[*He kneels.*]

YORK
Show me thy humble heart, and not thy knee,
Whose duty is deceivable and false.   84

BOLINGBROKE   My gracious uncle—

YORK   Tut, tut!
Grace me no grace, nor uncle me no uncle.
I am no traitor's uncle; and that word "grace"
In an ungracious mouth is but profane.
Why have those banished and forbidden legs
Dared once to touch a dust of England's ground?   91
But then more "why?" Why have they dared to march
So many miles upon her peaceful bosom,
Frighting her pale-faced villages with war
And ostentation of despisèd arms?   95
Com'st thou because the anointed King is hence?
Why, foolish boy, the King is left behind,
And in my loyal bosom lies his power.
Were I but now the lord of such hot youth
As when brave Gaunt, thy father, and myself
Rescued the Black Prince, that young Mars of men,   101
From forth the ranks of many thousand French,
Oh, then how quickly should this arm of mine,
Now prisoner to the palsy, chastise thee
And minister correction to thy fault!   105

BOLINGBROKE
My gracious uncle, let me know my fault.
On what condition stands it and wherein?   107

YORK
Even in condition of the worst degree:
In gross rebellion and detested treason.
Thou art a banished man, and here art come
Before the expiration of thy time
In braving arms against thy sovereign.   112

BOLINGBROKE [*standing*]
As I was banished, I was banished Hereford;
But as I come, I come for Lancaster.   114
And, noble uncle, I beseech Your Grace
Look on my wrongs with an indifferent eye.   116
You are my father, for methinks in you
I see old Gaunt alive. Oh, then, my father,
Will you permit that I shall stand condemned   119
A wandering vagabond, my rights and royalties   120
Plucked from my arms perforce and given away
To upstart unthrifts? Wherefore was I born?   122
If that my cousin king be King in England,
It must be granted I am Duke of Lancaster.
You have a son, Aumerle, my noble cousin;

Had you first died, and he been thus trod down,   126
He should have found his uncle Gaunt a father
To rouse his wrongs and chase them to the bay.   128
I am denied to sue my livery here,   129
And yet my letters patents give me leave.   130
My father's goods are all distrained and sold,   131
And these, and all, are all amiss employed.
What would you have me do? I am a subject,
And I challenge law. Attorneys are denied me,   134
And therefore personally I lay my claim
To my inheritance of free descent.   136

NORTHUMBERLAND
The noble Duke hath been too much abused.

ROSS
It stands Your Grace upon to do him right.   138

WILLOUGHBY
Base men by his endowments are made great.   139

YORK
My lords of England, let me tell you this:
I have had feeling of my cousin's wrongs   141
And labored all I could to do him right;
But in this kind to come, in braving arms,   143
Be his own carver, and cut out his way   144
To find out right with wrong—it may not be;
And you that do abet him in this kind
Cherish rebellion and are rebels all.

NORTHUMBERLAND
The noble Duke hath sworn his coming is
But for his own, and for the right of that
We all have strongly sworn to give him aid;
And let him never see joy that breaks that oath!   151

YORK
Well, well, I see the issue of these arms.   152
I cannot mend it, I must needs confess,
Because my power is weak and all ill-left;   154
But if I could, by Him that gave me life,
I would attach you all and make you stoop   156
Unto the sovereign mercy of the King.
But since I cannot, be it known unto you
I do remain as neuter. So fare you well—   159
Unless you please to enter in the castle
And there repose you for this night.

BOLINGBROKE
An offer, uncle, that we will accept.
But we must win Your Grace to go with us   163
To Bristol Castle, which they say is held
By Bushy, Bagot, and their complices,   165

---

84 duty gesture of obeisance.   **deceivable** deceitful, deceptive
91 dust particle of dust   **95 ostentation** display.   **despisèd** despicable   **101 the Black Prince** i.e., Edward, the eldest son of Edward III and King Richard's father   **105 minister** administer   **107 condition** defect in me, or provision of the law.   **wherein** in what does it consist.   **112 braving** (1) defiant (2) defiantly. (Also at line 143.)   **114 for Lancaster** i.e., under the title of Lancaster and in order to claim it.   **116 indifferent** impartial   **119 condemned** condemned as   **120 royalties** privileges granted by the King   **122 unthrifts** spendthrifts.

126 first i.e., before Gaunt   **128 rouse** chase from cover, expose.   **the bay** the extremity where the hunted animal turns on its pursuers.
129 I am . . . here I am denied the right to sue for possession of hereditary rights in England. (See 2.1.202–4 and note.)   **130 letters patents** i.e., letters from the King indicating a subject's legal rights
131 distrained seized officially   **134 challenge law** claim my legal rights.   **136 of free descent** by legal succession.   **138 stands . . . upon** is incumbent upon Your Grace   **139 his endowments** i.e., the properties that rightly belong to Bolingbroke   **141 cousin's** nephew's   **143 kind** fashion   **144 Be . . . carver** i.e., act on his own authority, help himself   **151 joy** i.e., the joy of heaven   **152 issue** outcome
154 power army.   **ill-left** left in dismay and with inadequate means
156 attach arrest   **159 as neuter** neutral.   **163 win** persuade
165 Bagot (According to 2.2.140, Bagot had gone to Ireland.)

The caterpillars of the commonwealth,
Which I have sworn to weed and pluck away.

YORK

It may be I will go with you; but yet I'll pause,
For I am loath to break our country's laws.
Nor friends nor foes, to me welcome you are.   170
Things past redress are now with me past care.

                                                    Exeunt.

❖

[2.4]

Enter Earl of Salisbury and a Welsh Captain.

WELSH CAPTAIN

My lord of Salisbury, we have stayed ten days   1
And hardly kept our countrymen together,   2
And yet we hear no tidings from the King.   3
Therefore we will disperse ourselves. Farewell.

SALISBURY

Stay yet another day, thou trusty Welshman.
The King reposeth all his confidence in thee.

WELSH CAPTAIN

'Tis thought the King is dead. We will not stay.
The bay trees in our country are all withered,
And meteors fright the fixèd stars of heaven;
The pale-faced moon looks bloody on the earth,
And lean-looked prophets whisper fearful change;   11
Rich men look sad, and ruffians dance and leap,
The one in fear to lose what they enjoy,
The other to enjoy by rage and war.   14
These signs forerun the death or fall of kings.   15
Farewell. Our countrymen are gone and fled,
As well assured Richard their king is dead.   [*Exit.*]   17

SALISBURY

Ah, Richard! With the eyes of heavy mind
I see thy glory like a shooting star
Fall to the base earth from the firmament.
Thy sun sets weeping in the lowly west,
Witnessing storms to come, woe, and unrest.   22
Thy friends are fled to wait upon thy foes,   23
And crossly to thy good all fortune goes.   [*Exit.*]   24

❖

[3.1]

*Enter [Bolingbroke,] Duke of Hereford, York,
Northumberland, [with] Bushy and Green,
prisoners.*

BOLINGBROKE   Bring forth these men.
Bushy and Green, I will not vex your souls—
Since presently your souls must part your bodies—   3
With too much urging your pernicious lives,   4

For 'twere no charity; yet, to wash your blood
From off my hands, here in the view of men
I will unfold some causes of your deaths.   7
You have misled a prince, a royal king,
A happy gentleman in blood and lineaments,   9
By you unhappied and disfigured clean.   10
You have in manner with your sinful hours   11
Made a divorce betwixt his queen and him,
Broke the possession of a royal bed,
And stained the beauty of a fair queen's cheeks
With tears drawn from her eyes by your foul wrongs.
Myself—a prince by fortune of my birth,
Near to the King in blood, and near in love
Till you did make him misinterpret me—
Have stooped my neck under your injuries
And sighed my English breath in foreign clouds,   20
Eating the bitter bread of banishment,
Whilst you have fed upon my seigniories,   22
Disparked my parks and felled my forest woods,   23
From my own windows torn my household coat,   24
Razed out my imprese, leaving me no sign,   25
Save men's opinions and my living blood,
To show the world I am a gentleman.
This and much more, much more than twice all this,
Condemns you to the death.—See them delivered
    over
To execution and the hand of death.

BUSHY

More welcome is the stroke of death to me
Than Bolingbroke to England. Lords, farewell.

GREEN

My comfort is that heaven will take our souls
And plague injustice with the pains of hell.

BOLINGBROKE

My lord Northumberland, see them dispatched.
    [*Exeunt Northumberland with the prisoners, guarded.*]
Uncle, you say the Queen is at your house.
For God's sake, fairly let her be entreated.   37
Tell her I send to her my kind commends.   38
Take special care my greetings be delivered.

YORK

A gentleman of mine I have dispatched
With letters of your love to her at large.   41

BOLINGBROKE

Thanks, gentle uncle. Come, lords, away,
To fight with Glendower and his complices.   43
Awhile to work, and after holiday.   *Exeunt.*   44

❖

---

7 unfold reveal   **9 happy** fortunate.   **blood and lineaments** birth
and natural characteristics   **10 By . . . clean** by you made wretched
and wholly marred in reputation.   **11 in manner** as it were   **20 foreign clouds** i.e., the air of foreign lands (and adding to the clouds
with sighs)   **22 seigniories** estates   **23 Disparked** thrown open to
uses other than hunting and forestry   **24 household coat** coat of
arms (frequently emblazoned on stained or painted windows)
25 Razed scraped (or perhaps *rased*, "erased").   **imprese** heraldic
device, emblematic design   **37 entreated** treated.   **38 commends**
regards, compliments.   **41 at large** conveyed in full.   **43 Glendower**
(Owen Glendower was not, according to Holinshed's *Chronicles*, at this
time in arms against Bolingbroke. Possibly he is to be identified here
with the Welsh captain of the preceding scene.)   **44 after** afterwards

---

170 Nor Neither as
2.4. Location: A camp in Wales.
1 stayed waited   **2 hardly** with difficulty   **3 yet** still   **11 lean-looked**
lean-looking   **14 to . . . rage** in hopes of possessing by violence
15 forerun anticipate   **17 As** as being   **22 Witnessing** betokening
23 wait upon attend, offer allegiance to   **24 crossly** adversely
3.1. Location: Bristol. The castle.
3 presently immediately   **4 urging** emphasizing as reasons (for your
executions)

[3.2]

[Drums. Flourish and colors.] Enter the King, Aumerle, [the Bishop of] Carlisle, etc. [with soldiers].

KING RICHARD
Barkloughly Castle call they this at hand?   1
AUMERLE
Yea, my lord. How brooks Your Grace the air   2
After your late tossing on the breaking seas?   3
KING RICHARD
Needs must I like it well. I weep for joy   4
To stand upon my kingdom once again.
Dear earth, I do salute thee with my hand,
                        [He bends and touches the ground.]
Though rebels wound thee with their horses' hoofs.
As a long-parted mother with her child   8
Plays fondly with her tears and smiles in meeting,
So, weeping, smiling, greet I thee, my earth,
And do thee favors with my royal hands.
Feed not thy sovereign's foe, my gentle earth,
Nor with thy sweets comfort his ravenous sense,   13
But let thy spiders, that suck up thy venom,   14
And heavy-gaited toads lie in their way,   15
Doing annoyance to the treacherous feet
Which with usurping steps do trample thee.
Yield stinging nettles to mine enemies;
And when they from thy bosom pluck a flower,
Guard it, I pray thee, with a lurking adder,
Whose double tongue may with a mortal touch   21
Throw death upon thy sovereign's enemies.—
Mock not my senseless conjuration, lords.   23
This earth shall have a feeling, and these stones
Prove armèd soldiers, ere her native king   25
Shall falter under foul rebellion's arms.
CARLISLE
Fear not, my lord. That Power that made you king
Hath power to keep you king in spite of all.
The means that heavens yield must be embraced
And not neglected; else heaven would,   30
And we will not. Heaven's offer we refuse,   31
The proffered means of succor and redress.   32
AUMERLE
He means, my lord, that we are too remiss,
Whilst Bolingbroke through our security   34
Grows strong and great in substance and in power.
KING RICHARD
Discomfortable cousin, know'st thou not   36

That when the searching eye of heaven is hid   37
Behind the globe that lights the lower world,   38
Then thieves and robbers range abroad unseen
In murders and in outrage boldly here;
But when from under this terrestrial ball   41
He fires the proud tops of the eastern pines   42
And darts his light through every guilty hole,
Then murders, treasons, and detested sins,
The cloak of night being plucked from off their backs,
Stand bare and naked, trembling at themselves?   46
So when this thief, this traitor, Bolingbroke,
Who all this while hath reveled in the night
Whilst we were wand'ring with the Antipodes,   49
Shall see us rising in our throne, the east,
His treasons will sit blushing in his face,
Not able to endure the sight of day,
But, self-affrighted, tremble at his sin.
Not all the water in the rough rude sea
Can wash the balm off from an anointed king;   55
The breath of worldly men cannot depose   56
The deputy elected by the Lord.   57
For every man that Bolingbroke hath pressed   58
To lift shrewd steel against our golden crown,   59
God for his Richard hath in heavenly pay
A glorious angel. Then, if angels fight,
Weak men must fall, for heaven still guards the right.   62

Enter Salisbury.

Welcome, my lord. How far off lies your power?
SALISBURY
Nor near nor farther off, my gracious lord,   64
Than this weak arm. Discomfort guides my tongue   65
And bids me speak of nothing but despair.
One day too late, I fear me, noble lord,
Hath clouded all thy happy days on earth.
Oh, call back yesterday, bid time return,
And thou shalt have twelve thousand fighting men!
Today, today, unhappy day too late,
O'erthrows thy joys, friends, fortune, and thy state;   72
For all the Welshmen, hearing thou wert dead,
Are gone to Bolingbroke, dispersed, and fled.
AUMERLE
Comfort, my liege. Why looks Your Grace so pale?
KING RICHARD
But now the blood of twenty thousand men   76
   Did triumph in my face, and they are fled;   77
And till so much blood thither come again,
   Have I not reason to look pale and dead?   79

3.2. **Location:** The coast of Wales, near Harlech Castle.
1 **Barkloughly** i.e., Harlech   2 **brooks** enjoys   3 **late** recent   4 **Needs must** Necessarily   8 **a long-parted mother with** a mother long parted from   13 **sweets** i.e., bounty.   **sense** appetite   14 **suck ... venom** (Alludes to the belief that spiders drew their poison from the earth.)   15 **heavy-gaited** lumbering, clumsy   21 **double** forked.   **mortal** deadly   23 **senseless conjuration** solemn entreaty of senseless things; or, one that makes no sense to you, being so fanciful   25 **native** entitled (to the crown) by birth, rightful. (Richard was born at Bordeaux.)   30–1 **else ... not** i.e., otherwise, we spurn heaven's will.   32 **succor and redress** help and remedy.   34 **security** overconfidence   36 **Discomfortable** Disheartening, discouraging

37–8 **when ... world** i.e., when the sun is hid behind the earth, lighting its lower side   41 **this terrestrial ball** the earth   42 **He fires** the sun lights up. (Literally, "sets on fire.")   46 **at themselves** i.e., at being caught in their crimes.   49 **Antipodes** people on the other side of the world; here, the Irish. (A geographical hyperbole.)   55 **balm** consecrated oil used in anointing a king   56 **worldly** earthly   57 **elected** chosen   58 **pressed** impressed, forced into the ranks   59 **shrewd** keen, biting   62 **still** always   64 **Nor near** Neither nearer   65 **Discomfort** Discouragement   72 **state** royal power   76 **But now** Even now.   **twenty** (A seeming discrepancy with *twelve* in line 70; perhaps the result of Richard's hyperbole.)   77 **triumph** i.e., shine forth   79 **pale and dead** deathly pale.

All souls that will be safe, fly from my side,
For time hath set a blot upon my pride.   81

AUMERLE
Comfort, my liege. Remember who you are.

KING RICHARD
I had forgot myself. Am I not king?
Awake, thou coward majesty, thou sleepest!
Is not the king's name twenty thousand names?
Arm, arm, my name! A puny subject strikes
At thy great glory. Look not to the ground,
Ye favorites of a king. Are we not high?
High be our thoughts. I know my uncle York
Hath power enough to serve our turn. But who comes
here?

Enter Scroop.

SCROOP
More health and happiness betide my liege   91
Than can my care-tuned tongue deliver him!   92

KING RICHARD
Mine ear is open and my heart prepared.
The worst is worldly loss thou canst unfold.   94
Say, is my kingdom lost? Why, 'twas my care,   95
And what loss is it to be rid of care?
Strives Bolingbroke to be as great as we?
Greater he shall not be; if he serve God,
We'll serve Him too, and be his fellow so.   99
Revolt our subjects? That we cannot mend;
They break their faith to God as well as us.
Cry woe, destruction, ruin, and decay;
The worst is death, and death will have his day.

SCROOP
Glad am I that Your Highness is so armed   104
To bear the tidings of calamity.
Like an unseasonable stormy day,
Which makes the silver rivers drown their shores
As if the world were all dissolved to tears,
So high above his limits swells the rage   109
Of Bolingbroke, covering your fearful land   110
With hard bright steel and hearts harder than steel.
Whitebeards have armed their thin and hairless scalps 112
Against Thy Majesty; boys with women's voices
Strive to speak big, and clap their female joints   114
In stiff unwieldy arms against thy crown.   115
Thy very beadsmen learn to bend their bows   116
Of double-fatal yew against thy state;   117

Yea, distaff-women manage rusty bills   118
Against thy seat. Both young and old rebel,   119
And all goes worse than I have power to tell.

KING RICHARD
Too well, too well thou tell'st a tale so ill.
Where is the Earl of Wiltshire? Where is Bagot?   122
What is become of Bushy? Where is Green,
That they have let the dangerous enemy
Measure our confines with such peaceful steps?   125
If we prevail, their heads shall pay for it.
I warrant they have made peace with Bolingbroke.

SCROOP
Peace have they made with him indeed, my lord.

KING RICHARD
Oh, villains, vipers, damned without redemption!
Dogs easily won to fawn on any man!
Snakes in my heart-blood warmed, that sting my
heart!
Three Judases, each one thrice worse than Judas!
Would they make peace? Terrible hell
Make war upon their spotted souls for this!   134

SCROOP
Sweet love, I see, changing his property,   135
Turns to the sourest and most deadly hate.
Again uncurse their souls. Their peace is made
With heads and not with hands. Those whom you
curse   138
Have felt the worst of death's destroying wound
And lie full low, graved in the hollow ground.   140

AUMERLE
Is Bushy, Green, and the Earl of Wiltshire dead?

SCROOP
Ay, all of them at Bristol lost their heads.

AUMERLE
Where is the Duke my father with his power?

KING RICHARD
No matter where. Of comfort no man speak!
Let's talk of graves, of worms, and epitaphs,
Make dust our paper, and with rainy eyes
Write sorrow on the bosom of the earth.
Let's choose executors and talk of wills.
And yet not so, for what can we bequeath
Save our deposèd bodies to the ground?   150
Our lands, our lives, and all are Bolingbroke's,
And nothing can we call our own but death
And that small model of the barren earth   153
Which serves as paste and cover to our bones.   154
For God's sake, let us sit upon the ground

---

81 blot stain   **91 More . . . betide** May more health and happiness
befall   **92 care-tuned** i.e., tuned by sorrow and to the key of sorrow.
deliver deliver to   **94 unfold** reveal.   **95 care** trouble   **99 his fellow** his (Bolingbroke's) equal   **104 armed** prepared   **109 his limits**
(1) its banks (2) the limits properly allowed to Bolingbroke's rage
110 fearful full of fears   **112 Whitebeards** Old men.   **thin** sparsely
haired   **114 Strive . . . joints** strive to speak with deep manlike
voices, and thrust their adolescent limbs   **115 arms** armor
116 beadsmen old almsmen or pensioners whose duty it was to pray
for a benefactor; here, for the King   **117 double-fatal** doubly fatal
(since the wood of the yew was used for bows and since its foliage
and berries are poisonous; yews were also commonly planted in
graveyards)

118–19 distaff-women . . . seat spinning women wield unused and
hence rusty pikes (long-handled ax-like weapons) against your throne.
122 Bagot (Although the King names Bagot here, he mentions only *three
Judases* in line 132 and Aumerle does not ask about Bagot in line 141; in
3.4 we learn that Bagot is not executed along with the other three but
reappears instead in 4.1.)   **125 Measure our confines** travel over my
kingdom.   **peaceful** unopposed   **134 spotted** stained with treason
135 his property its distinctive quality   **138 hands** (Used in swearing
oaths, surrendering, etc.)   **140 graved** buried   **150 deposèd**
(1) dethroned, as in 4.1 (2) deprived of those functions carried out by
the body in this transitory life (3) deposited   **153 model** microcosm or
mold, i.e., the body   **154 paste** pastry, pie crust

And tell sad stories of the death of kings—
How some have been deposed, some slain in war,
Some haunted by the ghosts they have deposed,   158
Some poisoned by their wives, some sleeping killed,
All murdered. For within the hollow crown
That rounds the mortal temples of a king   161
Keeps Death his court, and there the antic sits,   162
Scoffing his state and grinning at his pomp,   163
Allowing him a breath, a little scene,   164
To monarchize, be feared, and kill with looks,   165
Infusing him with self and vain conceit,   166
As if this flesh which walls about our life
Were brass impregnable; and humored thus,   168
Comes at the last and with a little pin
Bores through his castle wall, and—farewell, king!
Cover your heads, and mock not flesh and blood   171
With solemn reverence. Throw away respect,
Tradition, form, and ceremonious duty,
For you have but mistook me all this while.
I live with bread like you, feel want,
Taste grief, need friends. Subjected thus,   176
How can you say to me I am a king?

CARLISLE
My lord, wise men ne'er sit and wail their woes,
But presently prevent the ways to wail.   179
To fear the foe, since fear oppresseth strength,   180
Gives in your weakness strength unto your foe,   181
And so your follies fight against yourself.
Fear, and be slain. No worse can come to fight;   183
And fight and die is death destroying death,   184
Where fearing dying pays death servile breath.   185

AUMERLE
My father hath a power. Inquire of him,   186
And learn to make a body of a limb.   187

KING RICHARD
Thou chid'st me well. Proud Bolingbroke, I come
To change blows with thee for our day of doom.   189
This ague fit of fear is overblown;   190
An easy task it is to win our own.   191

Say, Scroop, where lies our uncle with his power?
Speak sweetly, man, although thy looks be sour.
SCROOP
Men judge by the complexion of the sky   194
    The state and inclination of the day.
So may you by my dull and heavy eye;
    My tongue hath but a heavier tale to say.
I play the torturer, by small and small   198
To lengthen out the worst that must be spoken:
Your uncle York is joined with Bolingbroke,
And all your northern castles yielded up,
And all your southern gentlemen in arms   202
Upon his party.
KING RICHARD   Thou hast said enough.   203
[To Aumerle] Beshrew thee, cousin, which didst lead
    me forth   204
Of that sweet way I was in to despair.
What say you now? What comfort have we now?
By heaven, I'll hate him everlastingly
That bids me be of comfort any more.
Go to Flint Castle. There I'll pine away;   209
A king, woe's slave, shall kingly woe obey.
That power I have, discharge, and let them go
To ear the land that hath some hope to grow,   212
For I have none. Let no man speak again
To alter this, for counsel is but vain.
AUMERLE
My liege, one word.
KING RICHARD   He does me double wrong   215
That wounds me with the flatteries of his tongue.
Discharge my followers. Let them hence away,
From Richard's night to Bolingbroke's fair day.
                                               [Exeunt.]

❧

[3.3]

*Enter [with drum and colors] Bolingbroke, York,
Northumberland, [attendants, and forces].*

BOLINGBROKE
So that by this intelligence we learn   1
The Welshmen are dispersed, and Salisbury
Is gone to meet the King, who lately landed
With some few private friends upon this coast.
NORTHUMBERLAND
The news is very fair and good, my lord:
Richard not far from hence hath hid his head.
YORK
It would beseem the Lord Northumberland   7
To say "King Richard." Alack the heavy day
When such a sacred king should hide his head!

---

158 **deposed** deprived of life   161 **rounds** encircles   162 **antic**
grotesque figure, jester   163 **Scoffing his state** scoffing at the King's
regality   164 **breath** breathing space, moment   165 **monarchize** play
the monarch.   **kill with looks** i.e., order someone's death with a mere
glance   166 **self and vain conceit** vain conceit of himself   168 **and
humored thus** and Death, having amused himself at the King's
expense, having led the King on in this humor   171 **Cover your heads**
Replace your hats (which have been removed out of respect for the
King)   176 **Subjected** Made subject to grief, want, etc. (With pun on
"being treated like a subject.")   179 **But . . . wail** but promptly
anticipate and thus prevent the courses that result in lamentation.
180–1 **To fear . . . foe** i.e., To be afraid of the foe is merely a weakness
that, by oppressing your own resolve, gives advantage to the foe
183 **Fear . . . fight** i.e., If you fear, you are sure to be slain, and no
worse fate can come to you if you fight   184–5 **fight . . . breath** to
die fighting is to conquer death in the very act of dying, whereas to
die fearfully pays to death the tribute of servility.   186 **power** army
(as also in line 192).   **of** about, or from   187 **learn . . . limb** i.e., discover how to make a partial force substitute for a complete one.
189 **change** exchange.   **for . . . doom** i.e., in order to settle our fates,
which of us is to die now.   190 **This ague . . . overblown** This parox-
ysm of shivering in fear has blown over   191 **our own** i.e., my own
kingdom.

194 **complexion** appearance   198 **by small and small** little by little
202–3 **And . . . party** and all your men of rank in southern England
are also in arms on Bolingbroke's side.   204 **Beshrew** Confound. (Literally, *curse*.)   **forth** out   209 **Flint Castle** (Near Chester.)   212 **ear**
plow   215 **double wrong** i.e., in deceiving me and in leading me into
false hope once again
3.3. Location: Wales. Before Flint Castle.
1 **intelligence** information   7 **beseem** be appropriate for, be seemly
behavior in

NORTHUMBERLAND
　Your Grace mistakes. Only to be brief
　Left I his title out.
YORK　　　　　　　　The time hath been,
　Would you have been so brief with him, he would
　Have been so brief with you to shorten you, 13
　For taking so the head, your whole head's length. 14
BOLINGBROKE
　Mistake not, uncle, further than you should.
YORK
　Take not, good cousin, further than you should,
　Lest you mistake the heavens are over our heads. 17
BOLINGBROKE
　I know it, uncle, and oppose not myself
　Against their will. But who comes here?

　　　　　Enter Percy.

　Welcome, Harry. What, will not this castle yield?
PERCY
　The castle royally is manned, my lord,
　Against thy entrance.
BOLINGBROKE
　Royally? Why, it contains no king?
PERCY　　Yes, my good lord,
　It doth contain a king. King Richard lies 25
　Within the limits of yon lime and stone,
　And with him are the Lord Aumerle, Lord Salisbury,
　Sir Stephen Scroop, besides a clergyman
　Of holy reverence—who, I cannot learn.
NORTHUMBERLAND
　Oh, belike it is the Bishop of Carlisle. 30
BOLINGBROKE [*to Northumberland*]　Noble lord,
　Go to the rude ribs of that ancient castle; 32
　Through brazen trumpet send the breath of parley 33
　Into his ruined ears, and thus deliver: 34
　Henry Bolingbroke
　On both his knees doth kiss King Richard's hand
　And sends allegiance and true faith of heart
　To his most royal person, hither come
　Even at his feet to lay my arms and power,
　Provided that my banishment repealed 40
　And lands restored again be freely granted. 41
　If not, I'll use the advantage of my power, 42
　And lay the summer's dust with showers of blood
　Rained from the wounds of slaughtered Englishmen—
　The which how far off from the mind of Bolingbroke
　It is such crimson tempest should bedrench 46
　The fresh green lap of fair King Richard's land,
　My stooping duty tenderly shall show. 48

Go, signify as much while here we march
Upon the grassy carpet of this plain.
　[*Northumberland and attendants advance to the castle.*]
Let's march without the noise of threat'ning drum,
That from this castle's tottered battlements 52
Our fair appointments may be well perused. 53
Methinks King Richard and myself should meet
With no less terror than the elements
Of fire and water, when their thund'ring shock 56
At meeting tears the cloudy cheeks of heaven.
Be he the fire, I'll be the yielding water;
The rage be his, whilst on the earth I rain 59
My waters—on the earth, and not on him. 60
March on, and mark King Richard how he looks. 61

　　[*Bolingbroke's forces march about the stage.*] *The*
　　trumpets sound [*a parley without and answer*
　　within, then a flourish. King] *Richard appeareth*
　　on the walls [*with the Bishop of Carlisle, Aumerle,*
　　Scroop, and Salisbury].

See, see, King Richard doth himself appear,
As doth the blushing discontented sun 63
From out the fiery portal of the east
When he perceives the envious clouds are bent 65
To dim his glory and to stain the track
Of his bright passage to the occident. 67
YORK
　Yet looks he like a king. Behold, his eye, 68
　As bright as is the eagle's, lightens forth 69
　Controlling majesty. Alack, alack, for woe,
　That any harm should stain so fair a show!
KING RICHARD [*to Northumberland*]
　We are amazed; and thus long have we stood
　To watch the fearful bending of thy knee, 73
　Because we thought ourself thy lawful king.
　And if we be, how dare thy joints forget
　To pay their awful duty to our presence? 76
　If we be not, show us the hand of God 77
　That hath dismissed us from our stewardship;
　For well we know, no hand of blood and bone 79
　Can grip the sacred handle of our scepter,
　Unless he do profane, steal, or usurp. 81
　And though you think that all, as you have done,
　Have torn their souls by turning them from us, 83
　And we are barren and bereft of friends, 84
　Yet know, my master, God omnipotent, 85
　Is mustering in his clouds on our behalf

---

13 **to** as to　14 **taking so the head** i.e., (1) presumptuously omitting thus his title (2) being headstrong　17 **mistake** fail to perceive that. (Plays on Bolingbroke's use of *mistake,* just as York has punned on *brief* and *head.*)　25 **lies** resides　30 **belike** probably　32 **rude ribs** i.e., rugged walls　33 **brazen** (1) brass (2) bold.　**breath of parley** i.e., call for a conference　34 **his ruined ears** i.e., its (the castle's) ancient and battered loopholes　40 **my banishment repealed** the revocation of my banishment　41 **lands restored again** the restoration of my lands　42 **advantage of my power** superiority of my army　46 **is** is that　48 **stooping duty** submissive kneeling

52 **tottered** in tottering condition, or dilapidated　53 **fair appoint-ments** handsome show of military preparedness　56 **fire and water** i.e., lightning and rain　59–60 **whilst . . . waters** while I moisten the earth with my tears　61.2 *parley* trumpet summons to a negotiation　61.4 *on the walls* i.e., in the gallery of the tiring-house, above, to the rear of the stage　63 **blushing** i.e., turning red with anger　65 **he** i.e., the sun.　**envious** hostile　67 **occident** west.　68 **Yet** Still, or never-theless.　**he** i.e., King Richard　69 **lightens forth** flashes out, like lightning　73 **watch** wait for　76 **awful** reverential, full of awe　77 **hand** signature　79 **no . . . bone** no human hand　81 **Unless he do profane** without committing sacrilege　83 **Have . . . us** have imper-iled their souls by turning traitor to me　84 **And** and that　85 **know** know that

Armies of pestilence; and they shall strike
Your children yet unborn and unbegot,
That lift your vassal hands against my head   89
And threat the glory of my precious crown.   90
Tell Bolingbroke—for yon methinks he stands—
That every stride he makes upon my land
Is dangerous treason. He is come to open   93
The purple testament of bleeding war;   94
But ere the crown he looks for live in peace,
Ten thousand bloody crowns of mothers' sons   96
Shall ill become the flower of England's face,   97
Change the complexion of her maid-pale peace   98
To scarlet indignation, and bedew
Her pastures' grass with faithful English blood.

NORTHUMBERLAND
The King of heaven forbid our lord the King
Should so with civil and uncivil arms   102
Be rushed upon! Thy thrice-noble cousin
Harry Bolingbroke doth humbly kiss thy hand;
And by the honorable tomb he swears
That stands upon your royal grandsire's bones,
And by the royalties of both your bloods,
Currents that spring from one most gracious head,   108
And by the buried hand of warlike Gaunt,
And by the worth and honor of himself,
Comprising all that may be sworn or said,
His coming hither hath no further scope   112
Than for his lineal royalties, and to beg   113
Enfranchisement immediate on his knees;   114
Which on thy royal party granted once,   115
His glittering arms he will commend to rust,   116
His barbèd steeds to stables, and his heart   117
To faithful service of Your Majesty.
This swears he, as he is a prince and just,
And as I am a gentleman I credit him.

KING RICHARD
Northumberland, say thus the King returns: 121
His noble cousin is right welcome hither,
And all the number of his fair demands
Shall be accomplished without contradiction.   124
With all the gracious utterance thou hast
Speak to his gentle hearing kind commends.   126
        [*Northumberland and attendants retire to Bolingbroke
                                        and York.*]
[*To Aumerle*] We do debase ourself, cousin, do we not,
To look so poorly and to speak so fair?   128
Shall we call back Northumberland, and send
Defiance to the traitor, and so die?

AUMERLE
No, good my lord. Let's fight with gentle words
Till time lend friends, and friends their helpful swords.

KING RICHARD
Oh, God, oh, God, that e'er this tongue of mine,
That laid the sentence of dread banishment
On yon proud man, should take it off again
With words of sooth! Oh, that I were as great   136
As is my grief, or lesser than my name!
Or that I could forget what I have been,
Or not remember what I must be now!
Swell'st thou, proud heart? I'll give thee scope to beat, 140
Since foes have scope to beat both thee and me.   141
        [*Northumberland returns to the castle walls.*]

AUMERLE
Northumberland comes back from Bolingbroke.

KING RICHARD
What must the King do now? Must he submit?
The King shall do it. Must he be deposed?
The King shall be contented. Must he lose
The name of king? I' God's name, let it go.
I'll give my jewels for a set of beads,   147
My gorgeous palace for a hermitage,
My gay apparel for an almsman's gown,   149
My figured goblets for a dish of wood,   150
My scepter for a palmer's walking-staff,   151
My subjects for a pair of carvèd saints,
And my large kingdom for a little grave,
A little, little grave, an obscure grave;
Or I'll be buried in the King's highway,
Some way of common trade, where subjects' feet   156
May hourly trample on their sovereign's head;
For on my heart they tread now whilst I live,
And, buried once, why not upon my head?   159
Aumerle, thou weep'st, my tenderhearted cousin.
We'll make foul weather with despisèd tears;
Our sighs and they shall lodge the summer corn   162
And make a dearth in this revolting land.   163
Or shall we play the wantons with our woes   164
And make some pretty match with shedding tears?   165
As thus, to drop them still upon one place,   166
Till they have fretted us a pair of graves   167
Within the earth; and, therein laid, there lies
Two kinsmen digged their graves with weeping eyes.   169
Would not this ill do well? Well, well, I see
I talk but idly, and you laugh at me.—
Most mighty prince, my lord Northumberland,
What says King Bolingbroke? Will His Majesty
Give Richard leave to live till Richard die?
You make a leg, and Bolingbroke says ay.   175

---

89 **That** of you that.   **vassal** subject   90 **threat** threaten   93–4 **open
. . . testament** initiate a bloodstained legacy. (Blood was often said to
be purple.)   96–7 **Ten . . . face** the bloody heads of 10,000 young men
(the flower of England) will disfigure the blossoming face of our
country   98 **maid-pale** i.e., pale like the complexion of a young English maid   102 **civil** used in civil strife.   **uncivil** barbarous, violent
108 **head** source   112 **scope** purpose, aim   113 **lineal royalties**
hereditary rights as one of royal blood   114 **Enfranchisement** freedom (from banishment)   115 **party** part   116 **commend** give over
117 **barbèd** armored   121 **returns** answers   124 **accomplished** fulfilled   126 **commends** regards.   128 **poorly** abject.   **fair** courteously.

136 **sooth** cajolery, flattery.   140 **scope** freedom, space   141 **scope**
capacity, opportunity   147 **set of beads** rosary   149 **almsman's
gown** plain attire of one who lives on alms or charity   150 **figured**
ornamented, embossed   151 **palmer's** pilgrim's   156 **trade** passage
159 **buried once** once I am buried   162 **Our . . . corn** our sighs and
tears will beat down the summer grain fields   163 **revolting**
rebelling   164 **play the wantons** sport, frolic   165 **match** game, contest   166 **still** continually   167 **fretted us** eaten away for us, worn.
(With a play on "complained.")   169 **digged** who dug   175 **a leg** an
obeisance

NORTHUMBERLAND
My lord, in the base court he doth attend   176
To speak with you, may it please you to come down.   177

KING RICHARD
Down, down I come, like glistering Phaëthon,   178
Wanting the manage of unruly jades.   179
In the base court? Base court, where kings grow base,
To come at traitors' calls and do them grace.   181
In the base court? Come down? Down, court! Down,
   king!
For night owls shriek where mounting larks should
   sing.   [Exeunt from above.]

[Northumberland rejoins Bolingbroke.]

BOLINGBROKE
What says His Majesty?

NORTHUMBERLAND   Sorrow and grief of heart
Makes him speak fondly, like a frantic man.   185
Yet he is come.

[Enter King Richard and his attendants below.]

BOLINGBROKE   Stand all apart,   187
And show fair duty to His Majesty.   He kneels down.   188
My gracious lord!

KING RICHARD
Fair cousin, you debase your princely knee   190
To make the base earth proud with kissing it.   191
Me rather had my heart might feel your love   192
Than my unpleased eye see your courtesy.
Up, cousin, up. Your heart is up, I know,
Thus high at least [touching his crown], although your
   knee be low.

BOLINGBROKE [rising]
My gracious lord, I come but for mine own.

KING RICHARD
Your own is yours, and I am yours, and all.

BOLINGBROKE
So far be mine, my most redoubted lord,   198
As my true service shall deserve your love.

KING RICHARD
Well you deserve. They well deserve to have
That know the strong'st and surest way to get.
[To York, who weeps] Uncle, give me your hands. Nay,
   dry your eyes;
Tears show their love, but want their remedies.   203
[To Bolingbroke] Cousin, I am too young to be your
   father,   204

Though you are old enough to be my heir.
What you will have, I'll give, and willing too,
For do we must what force will have us do.
Set on towards London, cousin, is it so?

BOLINGBROKE
Yea, my good lord.

KING RICHARD   Then I must not say no.
                              [Flourish. Exeunt.]

❖

[3.4]

Enter the Queen with [two Ladies,] her attendants.

QUEEN
What sport shall we devise here in this garden,
To drive away the heavy thought of care?

LADY   Madam, we'll play at bowls.   3

QUEEN
'Twill make me think the world is full of rubs,   4
And that my fortune runs against the bias.   5

LADY   Madam, we'll dance.

QUEEN
My legs can keep no measure in delight   7
When my poor heart no measure keeps in grief.   8
Therefore, no dancing, girl; some other sport.

LADY   Madam, we'll tell tales.

QUEEN
Of sorrow or of joy?

LADY   Of either, madam.

QUEEN   Of neither, girl;
For if of joy, being altogether wanting,   13
It doth remember me the more of sorrow;   14
Or if of grief, being altogether had,
It adds more sorrow to my want of joy.
For what I have I need not to repeat,
And what I want it boots not to complain.   18

LADY
Madam, I'll sing.

QUEEN   'Tis well that thou hast cause,
But thou shouldst please me better wouldst thou
   weep.   20

LADY
I could weep, madam, would it do you good.

QUEEN
And I could sing, would weeping do me good,   22
And never borrow any tear of thee.   23

Enter Gardeners [a Master and two Men].

But stay, here come the gardeners.
Let's step into the shadow of these trees.

---

176 **base court** outer or lower court of a castle   177 **may it please you**
if you please   178 **glistering** glistening, glittering.   **Phaëthon** son of
the sun-god, whose chariot he attempted to steer across the sky;
unable to control the horses of the sun, he was hurled from the chariot by Jupiter   179 **Wanting . . . jades** lacking the skill in horsemanship to control unruly nags.   181 **do them grace** (1) bow to them
(2) treat them graciously.   185 **fondly** foolishly.   **frantic** mad
187 **apart** aside   188 **fair duty** respect   190–1 **debase . . . base** (Continues the wordplay on *base* in line 180.)   192 **Me rather had** I had
rather   198 **mine** i.e., my loved lord (changing Richard's meaning of
yours in the previous line).   **redoubted** dread   203 **want their reme-**
dies lack remedies for what caused them.   204 **too young** (Historically, Richard and Bolingbroke were both thirty-three.)

3.4. Location: The Duke of York's garden.
3 bowls lawn bowling. (A common Elizabethan game.)   **4 rubs**
impediments (in the game of bowls)   **5 against the bias** i.e., contrary,
athwart. (Literally, not following the naturally curved path of a bowl,
which was weighted on one side.)   **7 measure** a stately slow dance
8 measure moderation   **13 wanting** lacking   **14 remember** remind
18 boots helps   **20 wouldst thou** if you would   **22 would . . . good**
i.e., if weeping would make me any less unhappy   **23 never borrow**
never need to borrow

My wretchedness unto a row of pins, 26
They will talk of state, for everyone doth so 27
Against a change; woe is forerun with woe. 28
[*The Queen and Ladies stand apart.*]

GARDENER [*to one Man*]
Go bind thou up young dangling apricots
Which, like unruly children, make their sire
Stoop with oppression of their prodigal weight. 31
Give some supportance to the bending twigs.
[*To the other*] Go thou, and like an executioner
Cut off the heads of too-fast-growing sprays
That look too lofty in our commonwealth.
All must be even in our government. 36
You thus employed, I will go root away
The noisome weeds which without profit suck 38
The soil's fertility from wholesome flowers.

MAN
Why should we in the compass of a pale 40
Keep law and form and due proportion,
Showing as in a model our firm estate, 42
When our sea-wallèd garden, the whole land,
Is full of weeds, her fairest flowers choked up,
Her fruit trees all unpruned, her hedges ruined,
Her knots disordered, and her wholesome herbs 46
Swarming with caterpillars?

GARDENER   Hold thy peace.
He that hath suffered this disordered spring 48
Hath now himself met with the fall of leaf. 49
The weeds which his broad-spreading leaves did
    shelter,
That seemed in eating him to hold him up, 51
Are plucked up root and all by Bolingbroke:
I mean the Earl of Wiltshire, Bushy, Green.

MAN
What, are they dead?

GARDENER   They are; and Bolingbroke
Hath seized the wasteful King. Oh, what pity is it
That he had not so trimmed and dressed his land 56
As we this garden! We at time of year 57
Do wound the bark, the skin of our fruit trees,
Lest being overproud in sap and blood 59
With too much riches it confound itself;
Had he done so to great and growing men,
They might have lived to bear and he to taste
Their fruits of duty. Superfluous branches
We lop away, that bearing boughs may live; 64
Had he done so, himself had borne the crown 65
Which waste of idle hours hath quite thrown down.

MAN
What, think you the King shall be deposed?

GARDENER
Depressed he is already, and deposed 68
'Tis doubt he will be. Letters came last night 69
To a dear friend of the good Duke of York's,
That tell black tidings.

QUEEN [*coming forward*] Oh, I am pressed to death 71
Through want of speaking! Thou, old Adam's likeness, 72
Set to dress this garden, how dares 73
Thy harsh rude tongue sound this unpleasing news?
What Eve, what serpent, hath suggested thee 75
To make a second fall of cursèd man?
Why dost thou say King Richard is deposed?
Dar'st thou, thou little better thing than earth,
Divine his downfall? Say where, when, and how 79
Cam'st thou by this ill tidings? Speak, thou wretch.

GARDENER
Pardon me, madam. Little joy have I
To breathe this news, yet what I say is true.
King Richard, he is in the mighty hold
Of Bolingbroke. Their fortunes both are weighed:
In your lord's scale is nothing but himself
And some few vanities that make him light;
But in the balance of great Bolingbroke,
Besides himself, are all the English peers,
And with that odds he weighs King Richard down.
Post you to London and you will find it so; 90
I speak no more than everyone doth know.

QUEEN
Nimble mischance, that art so light of foot,
Doth not thy embassage belong to me, 93
And am I last that knows it? Oh, thou thinkest
To serve me last, that I may longest keep
Thy sorrow in my breast.—Come, ladies, go 96
To meet at London London's king in woe.
What, was I born to this, that my sad look
Should grace the triumph of great Bolingbroke? 99
Gard'ner, for telling me these news of woe,
Pray God the plants thou graft'st may never grow.
                    Exit [*with Ladies*].

GARDENER
Poor queen! So that thy state might be no worse, 102
I would my skill were subject to thy curse.
Here did she fall a tear; here in this place 104
I'll set a bank of rue, sour herb of grace. 105
Rue even for ruth here shortly shall be seen, 106
In the remembrance of a weeping queen. *Exeunt.*

❖

26 My . . . pins i.e., I'd bet my immeasurable grief against the merest trifle 27 state statecraft, politics 28 Against . . . with woe when change is imminent; sad times are heralded by gloomy predictions. 31 prodigal excessive 36 even equal 38 noisome harmful 40 pale enclosure, enclosed garden 42 firm stable 46 knots flower beds laid out in intricate designs 48 suffered allowed 49 fall of leaf i.e., autumn. 51 in eating him i.e., while they were really eating his sustenance 56 dressed put in order 57 at . . . year in the appropriate season 59 overproud in swollen with 64 bearing fruit-bearing 65 crown (1) royal crown (2) crown of a tree

68 Depressed Brought low 69 'Tis doubt there is fear 71 pressed to death (Allusion to the *peine forte et dure,* inflicted by pressure of heavy weights upon the chests of indicted persons who refused to plead and remained silent.) 72 old Adam (In his role as the first gardener.) 73 dress cultivate 75 suggested tempted 79 Divine prophesy 90 Post Hasten. (See the note at 1.1.56.) 93 embassage message. belong to concern 96 Thy sorrow the sorrow that you (mischance) report 99 triumph triumphal procession. Bolingbroke (The original spelling, "Bullingbrooke," indicates the rhyme with *look* in the previous line, pronounced something like "bruke" and "luke.") 102 So that Provided that 104 fall let fall 105 rue "herb of grace," a plant symbolical of repentance, ruth, or sorrow for another's misery 106 ruth pity

[4.1]

Enter Bolingbroke with the Lords [Aumerle,
Northumberland, Harry Percy, Fitzwater, Surrey,
the Bishop of Carlisle, the Abbot of Westminster,
and another Lord, Herald, officers] to Parliament.
[The throne is provided on stage.]

BOLINGBROKE
Call forth Bagot.

Enter [officers with] Bagot.

Now, Bagot, freely speak thy mind,
What thou dost know of noble Gloucester's death,
Who wrought it with the King, and who performed   4
The bloody office of his timeless end.   5

BAGOT
Then set before my face the Lord Aumerle.

BOLINGBROKE [*to Aumerle*]
Cousin, stand forth, and look upon that man.
                          [*Aumerle comes forward.*]

BAGOT
My lord Aumerle, I know your daring tongue
Scorns to unsay what once it hath delivered.   9
In that dead time when Gloucester's death was plotted, 10
I heard you say, "Is not my arm of length,   11
That reacheth from the restful English court   12
As far as Calais, to mine uncle's head?"
Amongst much other talk that very time   14
I heard you say that you had rather refuse
The offer of an hundred thousand crowns
Than Bolingbroke's return to England—   17
Adding withal how blest this land would be   18
In this your cousin's death.

AUMERLE   Princes and noble lords,
What answer shall I make to this base man?
Shall I so much dishonor my fair stars   22
On equal terms to give him chastisement?   23
Either I must, or have mine honor soiled
With the attainder of his slanderous lips.   25
                          [*He throws down his gage.*]
There is my gage, the manual seal of death,   26
That marks thee out for hell. I say thou liest,
And will maintain what thou hast said is false
In thy heart-blood, though being all too base
To stain the temper of my knightly sword.

BOLINGBROKE
Bagot, forbear. Thou shalt not take it up.

AUMERLE
Excepting one, I would he were the best   32
In all this presence that hath moved me so.

FITZWATER [*throwing down a gage*]
If that thy valor stand on sympathy,   34
There is my gage, Aumerle, in gage to thine.   35
By that fair sun which shows me where thou stand'st,
I heard thee say, and vauntingly thou spak'st it, 37
That thou wert cause of noble Gloucester's death.
If thou deny'st it twenty times, thou liest,
And I will turn thy falsehood to thy heart,   40
Where it was forgèd, with my rapier's point.

AUMERLE [*taking up the gage*]
Thou dar'st not, coward, live to see that day.

FITZWATER
Now, by my soul, I would it were this hour.

AUMERLE
Fitzwater, thou art damned to hell for this.

PERCY
Aumerle, thou liest. His honor is as true
In this appeal as thou art all unjust;   46
And that thou art so, there I throw my gage
                          [*throwing down a gage*]
To prove it on thee to the extremest point   48
Of mortal breathing. Seize it if thou dar'st.   49

AUMERLE [*taking up the gage*]
An if I do not, may my hands rot off   50
And never brandish more revengeful steel   51
Over the glittering helmet of my foe!

ANOTHER LORD [*throwing down a gage*]
I task the earth to the like, forsworn Aumerle,   53
And spur thee on with full as many lies   54
As may be holloed in thy treacherous ear
From sun to sun. There is my honor's pawn;   56
Engage it to the trial, if thou darest.   57

AUMERLE [*taking up the gage*]
Who sets me else? By heaven, I'll throw at all!   58
I have a thousand spirits in one breast
To answer twenty thousand such as you.

SURREY
My lord Fitzwater, I do remember well
The very time Aumerle and you did talk.

FITZWATER
'Tis very true. You were in presence then,   63
And you can witness with me this is true.

SURREY   As false, by heaven, as heaven itself is true.

FITZWATER
Surrey, thou liest.

SURREY   Dishonorable boy!
That lie shall lie so heavy on my sword

4.1. Location: Westminster Hall.
4 Who . . . King who prevailed upon the King to have the murder performed   **5 office** function.   **timeless** untimely   **9 unsay** deny, take back.   **delivered** reported.   **10 dead** (1) deadly (2) dark, silent   **11 of length** long   **12 restful** i.e., untroubled by Gloucester   **14 that very time** (An inconsistency; Gloucester's death occurred before Bolingbroke left England.)   **17 Than . . . return** than have Bolingbroke return   **18 withal** in addition   **22 stars** i.e., fortune, rank   **23 On . . . chastisement** as to challenge him as my equal.   **25 attainder** dishonoring accusation   **25.1 gage** usually a glove or a gauntlet (a mailed or armored glove), as at 1.1.69 ff.   **26 manual . . . death** death warrant sealed by my hand

32 one i.e., Bolingbroke.   **best** highest in rank   **34 stand on sympathy** i.e., insists on correspondence of rank in your opponent   **35 in gage** engaged   **37 vauntingly** boastfully   **40 turn** turn back   **46 appeal** accusation. (As also in line 80.)   **all unjust** totally false   **48–9 to . . . breathing** to the point of death.   **50 An if** If   **51 more** any more, ever again   **53 I . . . like** I burden the ground in the same way   **54 lies** accusations of lying   **56 sun to sun** sunrise to sunset.   **honor's pawn** pledge of honor. (Also in line 71.)   **57 Engage . . . trial** take it up as a pledge to combat   **58 Who . . . else?** Who else puts up stakes against me or challenges me to a game?   **throw** (1) throw dice (2) throw down gages   **63 in presence** present

That it shall render vengeance and revenge,   68
Till thou the lie-giver and that lie do lie
In earth as quiet as thy father's skull.
In proof whereof, there is my honor's pawn.
                              [*He throws down a gage.*]
Engage it to the trial if thou dar'st.
FITZWATER [*taking up the gage*]
How fondly dost thou spur a forward horse!   73
If I dare eat, or drink, or breathe, or live,
I dare meet Surrey in a wilderness   75
And spit upon him whilst I say he lies,
And lies, and lies. There is my bond of faith,
To tie thee to my strong correction.
                              [*He throws down a gage.*]
As I intend to thrive in this new world,   79
Aumerle is guilty of my true appeal.   80
Besides, I heard the banished Norfolk say
That thou, Aumerle, didst send two of thy men
To execute the noble Duke at Calais.
AUMERLE
Some honest Christian trust me with a gage.
                    [*He borrows a gage and throws it down.*]
That Norfolk lies, here do I throw down this,
If he may be repealed, to try his honor.   86
BOLINGBROKE
These differences shall all rest under gage   87
Till Norfolk be repealed. Repealed he shall be,
And, though mine enemy, restored again
To all his lands and seigniories. When he is returned,
Against Aumerle we will enforce his trial.
CARLISLE
That honorable day shall never be seen.
Many a time hath banished Norfolk fought
For Jesu Christ in glorious Christian field,
Streaming the ensign of the Christian cross   95
Against black pagans, Turks, and Saracens;
And, toiled with works of war, retired himself   97
To Italy, and there at Venice gave
His body to that pleasant country's earth
And his pure soul unto his captain, Christ,
Under whose colors he had fought so long.
BOLINGBROKE   Why, Bishop, is Norfolk dead?
CARLISLE   As surely as I live, my lord.
BOLINGBROKE
Sweet peace conduct his sweet soul to the bosom   104
Of good old Abraham! Lords appellants,   105
Your differences shall all rest under gage
Till we assign you to your days of trial.   107

    Enter York.

YORK
Great Duke of Lancaster, I come to thee
From plume-plucked Richard, who with willing soul
Adopts thee heir, and his high scepter yields
To the possession of thy royal hand.
Ascend his throne, descending now from him,
And long live Henry, fourth of that name!
BOLINGBROKE
In God's name, I'll ascend the regal throne.
CARLISLE   Marry, God forbid!
Worst in this royal presence may I speak,   116
Yet best beseeming me to speak the truth.   117
Would God that any in this noble presence
Were enough noble to be upright judge
Of noble Richard! Then true noblesse would   120
Learn him forbearance from so foul a wrong.   121
What subject can give sentence on his king?
And who sits here that is not Richard's subject?
Thieves are not judged but they are by to hear,   124
Although apparent guilt be seen in them;   125
And shall the figure of God's majesty,   126
His captain, steward, deputy elect,
Anointed, crownèd, planted many years,
Be judged by subject and inferior breath,
And he himself not present? Oh, forfend it God   130
That in a Christian climate souls refined   131
Should show so heinous, black, obscene a deed!   132
I speak to subjects, and a subject speaks,
Stirred up by God thus boldly for his king.
My lord of Hereford here, whom you call king,   135
Is a foul traitor to proud Hereford's king.
And if you crown him, let me prophesy:
The blood of English shall manure the ground
And future ages groan for this foul act;
Peace shall go sleep with Turks and infidels,
And in this seat of peace tumultuous wars
Shall kin with kin and kind with kind confound;   142
Disorder, horror, fear, and mutiny
Shall here inhabit, and this land be called
The field of Golgotha and dead men's skulls.   145
Oh, if you raise this house against this house,   146
It will the woefullest division prove
That ever fell upon this cursèd earth.
Prevent it, resist it, let it not be so,
Lest child, child's children, cry against you woe!
NORTHUMBERLAND
Well have you argued, sir, and for your pains
Of capital treason we arrest you here.—   152

68 it i.e., my sword   73 fondly foolishly. forward willing   75 in a wilderness i.e., where fighting might go on uninterrupted to the death   79 in . . . world i.e., under the new king   80 appeal accusation.   86 repealed recalled from exile.   try test   87 under gage as challenges   95 Streaming flying   97 toiled wearied   104–5 bosom . . . Abraham i.e., heaven. (See Luke 16:22.)   105 Lords appellants Lords who appear as formal accusers   107.1 Enter York (Probably Richard's scepter, etc., are brought in at line 162, but York here invites Bolingbroke to ascend the throne with the surrendered scepter, and so perhaps the regalia are brought on here.)

116 Worst Least in rank   117 best beseeming me i.e., most befitting to me as a clergyman   120 noblesse nobleness   121 Learn him forbearance teach him to forbear   124 judged . . . by condemned unless they are present   125 apparent manifest   126 figure image   130 forfend forbid   131 souls refined civilized people   132 obscene odious, repulsive   135 My . . . Hereford (Carlisle refuses to refer to Bolingbroke as king or even as Duke of Lancaster, since he lost the latter title at the time of his banishment.)   142 Shall . . . confound will destroy kinsmen by means of kinsmen and fellow countrymen by means of fellow countrymen   145 Golgotha Calvary, the hill outside of Jerusalem called "the place of dead men's skulls" (see Mark 15:22 and John 19:17) where Jesus was crucified   146 this house . . . this house i.e., Lancaster against York. (See Mark 3:25.)   152 Of on a charge of

My lord of Westminster, be it your charge
To keep him safely till his day of trial.
                         [*Carlisle is taken into custody.*]
May it please you, lords, to grant the commons' suit? 155

BOLINGBROKE
Fetch hither Richard, that in common view
He may surrender; so we shall proceed   157
Without suspicion.

YORK   I will be his conduct.   *Exit.* 158

BOLINGBROKE
Lords, you that here are under our arrest,
Procure your sureties for your days of answer.   160
Little are we beholding to your love,   161
And little looked for at your helping hands.   162

        *Enter Richard and York [with Officers bearing
        the crown and regalia].*

KING RICHARD
Alack, why am I sent for to a king,
Before I have shook off the regal thoughts
Wherewith I reigned? I hardly yet have learned
To insinuate, flatter, bow, and bend my knee.
Give sorrow leave awhile to tutor me
To this submission. Yet I well remember
The favors of these men. Were they not mine?   169
Did they not sometime cry, "All hail!" to me?
So Judas did to Christ. But he, in twelve,
Found truth in all but one; I, in twelve thousand, none.
God save the King! Will no man say amen?
Am I both priest and clerk? Well then, amen.   174
God save the King, although I be not he;
And yet, amen, if heaven do think him me.
To do what service am I sent for hither?

YORK
To do that office of thine own good will
Which tired majesty did make thee offer:
The resignation of thy state and crown
To Henry Bolingbroke.

KING RICHARD
Give me the crown. [*He takes the crown.*] Here, cousin,
        seize the crown.
Here, cousin,
On this side my hand, and on that side thine.
Now is this golden crown like a deep well
That owes two buckets, filling one another,   186
The emptier ever dancing in the air,
The other down, unseen, and full of water.

That bucket down and full of tears am I,
Drinking my griefs, whilst you mount up on high.

BOLINGBROKE
I thought you had been willing to resign.

KING RICHARD
My crown I am, but still my griefs are mine.
You may my glories and my state depose,
But not my griefs; still am I king of those.

BOLINGBROKE
Part of your cares you give me with your crown.

KING RICHARD
Your cares set up do not pluck my cares down.   196
My care is loss of care, by old care done;   197
Your care is gain of care, by new care won.   198
The cares I give I have, though given away;   199
They 'tend the crown, yet still with me they stay.   200

BOLINGBROKE
Are you contented to resign the crown?

KING RICHARD
Ay, no; no, ay; for I must nothing be;   202
Therefore no, no, for I resign to thee.   203
Now mark me how I will undo myself: 204
                    [*He yields his crown and scepter.*]
I give this heavy weight from off my head
And this unwieldy scepter from my hand,
The pride of kingly sway from out my heart;
With mine own tears I wash away my balm,
With mine own hands I give away my crown,
With mine own tongue deny my sacred state,
With mine own breath release all duteous oaths.   211
All pomp and majesty I do forswear;
My manors, rents, revenues I forgo;
My acts, decrees, and statutes I deny.
God pardon all oaths that are broke to me!
God keep all vows unbroke are made to thee!   216
Make me, that nothing have, with nothing grieved,   217
And thou with all pleased, that hast all achieved!
Long mayst thou live in Richard's seat to sit,
And soon lie Richard in an earthy pit!
God save King Henry, unkinged Richard says,
And send him many years of sunshine days!—
What more remains?

NORTHUMBERLAND [*presenting a paper*]
                        No more but that you read   223
These accusations and these grievous crimes
Committed by your person and your followers
Against the state and profit of this land;

---

155 the commons' suit request of the commons (i.e., that Richard be formally tried and the causes of his deposition made public. This line begins the abdication passage omitted in early quartos of the play.) 157 surrender i.e., surrender the crown, abdicate 158 conduct escort. 160 sureties persons who will guarantee your appearance. your days of answer the time when you must appear to stand trial. 161 beholding beholden, indebted 162 little . . . hands i.e., I did not expect this from you, thinking you were on our side. 169 favors (1) faces (2) support, good will 174 priest and clerk (In religious services, the clerk or assistant would say "Amen" to the priest's prayers.) 186 owes owns, has. filling one another (The raising of the full bucket lowers the other to be filled in turn.)

196–200 Your . . . stay i.e., Your assuming the cares of office does not assuage my griefs. My grief is loss of kingly responsibility, destroyed by a failure in diligence; your concern is gaining of kingly responsibility, won by zealous effort. The anxieties I transfer to you I also keep for myself, despite my giving them to you; they accompany the crown and yet still remain with me. 202 Ay (1) Yes (2) I. (But, says Richard, I am nothing, and therefore "Ay" is "I" or "nothing," that is, "no.") 203 no, no . . . thee (Richard plays on the logic that a double negative equals a positive; with an aural pun on no/know.) 204 undo (1) divest (2) unmake 211 release . . . oaths release my subjects from their oaths of duty. 216 are that are 217 Make i.e., May God make. with nothing grieved (1) grieved at nothing (2) grieved at having nothing 223 read i.e., read aloud

That, by confessing them, the souls of men
May deem that you are worthily deposed.

KING RICHARD
Must I do so? And must I ravel out   229
My weaved-up follies? Gentle Northumberland,
If thy offenses were upon record,
Would it not shame thee in so fair a troop   232
To read a lecture of them? If thou wouldst,   233
There shouldst thou find one heinous article
Containing the deposing of a king
And cracking the strong warrant of an oath,
Marked with a blot, damned in the book of heaven.   237
Nay, all of you that stand and look upon me,
Whilst that my wretchedness doth bait myself,   239
Though some of you, with Pilate, wash your hands,   240
Showing an outward pity, yet you Pilates
Have here delivered me to my sour cross,   242
And water cannot wash away your sin.

NORTHUMBERLAND
My lord, dispatch. Read o'er these articles.   244

KING RICHARD
Mine eyes are full of tears; I cannot see.
And yet salt water blinds them not so much
But they can see a sort of traitors here.   247
Nay, if I turn mine eyes upon myself,
I find myself a traitor with the rest;
For I have given here my soul's consent
T'undeck the pompous body of a king,   251
Made glory base and sovereignty a slave,
Proud majesty a subject, state a peasant.   253

NORTHUMBERLAND   My lord—

KING RICHARD
No lord of thine, thou haught insulting man,   255
Nor no man's lord. I have no name, no title,
No, not that name was given me at the font,
But 'tis usurped. Alack the heavy day,
That I have worn so many winters out
And know not now what name to call myself!
Oh, that I were a mockery king of snow,
Standing before the sun of Bolingbroke,
To melt myself away in water drops!
Good king, great king, and yet not greatly good,
An if my word be sterling yet in England,   265
Let it command a mirror hither straight,   266
That it may show me what a face I have,
Since it is bankrupt of his majesty.   268

BOLINGBROKE
Go some of you and fetch a looking glass.   269
                        [Exit an Attendant.]

NORTHUMBERLAND
Read o'er this paper while the glass doth come.

KING RICHARD
Fiend, thou torments me ere I come to hell!

BOLINGBROKE
Urge it no more, my lord Northumberland.

NORTHUMBERLAND
The commons will not then be satisfied.

KING RICHARD
They shall be satisfied. I'll read enough
When I do see the very book indeed
Where all my sins are writ, and that's myself.   276

                Enter one with a glass.

Give me that glass, and therein will I read.
                        [He takes the mirror.]
No deeper wrinkles yet? Hath sorrow struck
So many blows upon this face of mine,
And made no deeper wounds? O flattering glass,
Like to my followers in prosperity,   281
Thou dost beguile me! Was this face the face   282
That every day under his household roof
Did keep ten thousand men? Was this the face
That, like the sun, did make beholders wink?   285
Is this the face which faced so many follies,   286
That was at last outfaced by Bolingbroke?   287
A brittle glory shineth in this face—
As brittle as the glory is the face,
                        [He throws down the mirror.]
For there it is, cracked in an hundred shivers.
Mark, silent king, the moral of this sport:
How soon my sorrow hath destroyed my face.

BOLINGBROKE
The shadow of your sorrow hath destroyed   293
The shadow of your face.

KING RICHARD   Say that again.   294
The shadow of my sorrow? Ha! Let's see.
'Tis very true, my grief lies all within;
And these external manners of laments   297
Are merely shadows to the unseen grief   298
That swells with silence in the tortured soul.
There lies the substance; and I thank thee, King,   300
For thy great bounty, that not only giv'st   301
Me cause to wail, but teachest me the way
How to lament the cause. I'll beg one boon,   303
And then be gone and trouble you no more.
Shall I obtain it?

BOLINGBROKE   Name it, fair cousin.

KING RICHARD
"Fair cousin"? I am greater than a king.
For when I was a king, my flatterers
Were then but subjects; being now a subject,

229 **ravel out** unravel   232 **troop** company   233 **read a lecture** give a public reading (as a warning)   237 **Marked . . . damned** (Modifying *article* in line 234)   239 **bait** torment, harass (as in bearbaiting)   240 **wash your hands** (See Matthew 27:24. Richard persistently compares himself to Christ; see also 3.2.132; 4.1.171.)   242 **sour** bitter   244 **dispatch** conclude, be done.   247 **sort** gang   251 **pompous** stately, splendid   253 **state** high rank, stateliness   255 **haught** haughty   265 **An if** if.   **sterling** valid currency   266 **straight** immediately   268 **his** its   269 **some** i.e., someone

276.1 *glass* mirror.   281 **in prosperity** i.e., in my prosperity   282 **Was this face** (An echo of Christopher Marlowe's *Doctor Faustus*, 5.1, in which the protagonist addresses Helen of Troy.)   285 **wink** close the eyes, blink.   286 **faced** countenanced   287 **outfaced** stared down, discountenanced   293 **shadow** outward show, or, overshadowing nature   294 **shadow** reflection (in the mirror)   297 **manners** forms, manifestations   298 **shadows to** shadowings forth or embodiments of   300 **There** i.e., In my soul   301 **that** you who   303 **boon** favor

I have a king here to my flatterer.   309
Being so great, I have no need to beg.

BOLINGBROKE   Yet ask.
KING RICHARD   And shall I have?
BOLINGBROKE   You shall.
KING RICHARD   Then give me leave to go.
BOLINGBROKE   Whither?

KING RICHARD
Whither you will, so I were from your sights.

BOLINGBROKE
Go some of you, convey him to the Tower.   317

KING RICHARD
Oh, good! "Convey"? Conveyers are you all,   318
That rise thus nimbly by a true king's fall.

    [Exeunt King Richard, some lords, and a guard.]

BOLINGBROKE
On Wednesday next we solemnly set down
Our coronation. Lords, prepare yourselves.   321

    *Exeunt. Manent [the Abbot of] Westminster, [the
    Bishop of] Carlisle, Aumerle.*

ABBOT
A woeful pageant have we here beheld.

CARLISLE
The woe's to come, the children yet unborn
Shall feel this day as sharp to them as thorn.   324

AUMERLE
You holy clergymen, is there no plot
To rid the realm of this pernicious blot?

ABBOT   My lord,
Before I freely speak my mind herein,
You shall not only take the Sacrament
To bury mine intents, but also to effect   330
Whatever I shall happen to devise.
I see your brows are full of discontent,
Your hearts of sorrow, and your eyes of tears.
Come home with me to supper; I'll lay
A plot shall show us all a merry day.   *Exeunt.* 335

    ❖

[5.1]

    Enter the Queen with [Ladies,] her attendants.

QUEEN
This way the King will come. This is the way
To Julius Caesar's ill-erected tower,   2
To whose flint bosom my condemnèd lord
Is doomed a prisoner by proud Bolingbroke.
Here let us rest, if this rebellious earth
Have any resting for her true king's queen.

    Enter Richard [and guard].

But soft, but see, or rather do not see
My fair rose wither. Yet look up, behold,

That you in pity may dissolve to dew,
And wash him fresh again with true-love tears.—
Ah, thou, the model where old Troy did stand,   11
Thou map of honor, thou King Richard's tomb,   12
And not King Richard! Thou most beauteous inn,   13
Why should hard-favored grief be lodged in thee   14
When triumph is become an alehouse guest?   15

KING RICHARD
Join not with grief, fair woman, do not so,
To make my end too sudden. Learn, good soul,   17
To think our former state a happy dream,
From which awaked, the truth of what we are
Shows us but this. I am sworn brother, sweet,
To grim Necessity, and he and I
Will keep a league till death. Hie thee to France,   22
And cloister thee in some religious house.   23
Our holy lives must win a new world's crown,   24
Which our profane hours here have thrown down.

QUEEN
What, is my Richard both in shape and mind
Transformed and weakened? Hath Bolingbroke
Deposed thine intellect? Hath he been in thy heart?
The lion dying thrusteth forth his paw
And wounds the earth, if nothing else, with rage
To be o'erpowered; and wilt thou, pupil-like,   31
Take the correction, mildly kiss the rod,
And fawn on rage with base humility,
Which art a lion and the king of beasts?   34

KING RICHARD
A king of beasts, indeed! If aught but beasts,   35
I had been still a happy king of men.
Good sometimes queen, prepare thee hence for France.   37
Think I am dead and that even here thou takest,
As from my deathbed, thy last living leave.
In winter's tedious nights sit by the fire
With good old folks, and let them tell thee tales
Of woeful ages long ago betid;   42
And ere thou bid good night, to quit their griefs   43
Tell thou the lamentable tale of me
And send the hearers weeping to their beds;
Forwhy the senseless brands will sympathize   46
The heavy accent of thy moving tongue,   47
And in compassion weep the fire out;
And some will mourn in ashes, some coal-black,   49
For the deposing of a rightful king.

    Enter Northumberland [attended].

---

309 to as   317 convey escort   318 Convey Steal.   321.1 *Manent*
They remain onstage   324 Shall who will   330 To . . . intents to conceal my plans   335 shall that shall
5.1. Location: London. A street leading to the Tower.
2 Julius . . . tower (The Tower of London, ascribed by tradition to
Julius Caesar, was built by William the Conqueror to hold the city in
subordination.)   ill-erected erected for evil ends or with evil results

11 thou . . . stand i.e., you ruined majesty, pattern of fallen greatness
like the desolate waste where Troy once stood   12 map of honor i.e.,
the mere outline of a once-glorious honor   13 inn residence, house
14 hard-favored unpleasant-looking   15 is . . . guest lodges in such a
vulgar tavern (i.e., in Bolingbroke).   17 To . . . sudden to kill me
quickly with grief.   22 Hie Hasten   23 religious house convent.
24 new world's heaven's   31 To be at being   34 Which art you who
are   35 king of beasts (1) lion (2) ruler over beastly men   37 sometimes former   42 Of . . . betid of woe that happened ages ago
43 quit their griefs requite their tales of woe   46–7 Forwhy . . .
tongue because even the inanimate and unfeeling firebrands will
respond to the doleful tone of your affecting tale   49 And . . . coal-
black and some of the brands will heap ashes on themselves like
grieving mourners and turn black with charring as though dressing
themselves in the black of mourning

NORTHUMBERLAND
My lord, the mind of Bolingbroke is changed;
You must to Pomfret, not unto the Tower. 52
And, madam, there is order ta'en for you: 53
With all swift speed you must away to France.

KING RICHARD
Northumberland, thou ladder wherewithal
The mounting Bolingbroke ascends my throne,
The time shall not be many hours of age
More than it is ere foul sin, gathering head, 58
Shall break into corruption. Thou shalt think, 59
Though he divide the realm and give thee half,
It is too little, helping him to all; 61
He shall think that thou, which knowest the way
To plant unrightful kings, wilt know again,
Being ne'er so little urged another way, 64
To pluck him headlong from the usurpèd throne. 65
The love of wicked men converts to fear, 66
That fear to hate, and hate turns one or both 67
To worthy danger and deservèd death. 68

NORTHUMBERLAND
My guilt be on my head, and there an end. 69
Take leave and part, for you must part forthwith. 70

KING RICHARD
Doubly divorced! Bad men, you violate
A twofold marriage, twixt my crown and me,
And then betwixt me and my married wife.
[To Queen] Let me unkiss the oath twixt thee and me; 74
And yet not so, for with a kiss 'twas made.—
Part us, Northumberland: I towards the north,
Where shivering cold and sickness pines the clime; 77
My wife to France, from whence, set forth in pomp,
She came adornèd hither like sweet May,
Sent back like Hallowmas or short'st of day. 80

QUEEN
And must we be divided? Must we part?

KING RICHARD
Ay, hand from hand, my love, and heart from heart.

QUEEN [to Northumberland]
Banish us both and send the King with me.

NORTHUMBERLAND
That were some love, but little policy. 84

QUEEN
Then whither he goes, thither let me go.

KING RICHARD
So two, together weeping, make one woe.
Weep thou for me in France, I for thee here;
Better far off than, near, be ne'er the near. 88

Go count thy way with sighs, I mine with groans.

QUEEN
So longest way shall have the longest moans. 90

KING RICHARD
Twice for one step I'll groan, the way being short,
And piece the way out with a heavy heart. 92
Come, come, in wooing sorrow let's be brief,
Since, wedding it, there is such length in grief. 94
One kiss shall stop our mouths, and dumbly part; 95
Thus give I mine, and thus take I thy heart.
[They kiss.]

QUEEN
Give me mine own again. 'Twere no good part 97
To take on me to keep and kill thy heart. [They kiss.] 98
So, now I have mine own again, begone,
That I may strive to kill it with a groan.

KING RICHARD
We make woe wanton with this fond delay. 101
Once more, adieu! The rest let sorrow say.
Exeunt [in two separate groups].

❧

[5.2]

Enter Duke of York and the Duchess.

DUCHESS
My lord, you told me you would tell the rest,
When weeping made you break the story off,
Of our two cousins coming into London. 3

YORK
Where did I leave?

DUCHESS   At that sad stop, my lord, 4
Where rude misgoverned hands from windows' tops 5
Threw dust and rubbish on King Richard's head.

YORK
Then, as I said, the Duke, great Bolingbroke,
Mounted upon a hot and fiery steed
Which his aspiring rider seemed to know, 9
With slow but stately pace kept on his course,
Whilst all tongues cried, "God save thee, Bolingbroke!"
You would have thought the very windows spake,
So many greedy looks of young and old
Through casements darted their desiring eyes
Upon his visage, and that all the walls
With painted imagery had said at once, 16
"Jesu preserve thee! Welcome, Bolingbroke!"

---

52 **Pomfret** Pontefract Castle in Yorkshire   53 **order ta'en** arrangement made   58 **gathering head** gathering to a head   59 **corruption** putrid matter, pus.   61 **helping** since you helped   64 **Being . . . way** though scarcely urged at all   65 **To** how to   66 **converts** changes   67 **That fear** i.e., that fear changes.   **one or both** i.e., the new king or his partner, or both   68 **worthy** well-merited   69 **and . . . end** and let the topic be closed on that note.   70 **part . . . part** separate . . . depart   74 **unkiss** annul with a kiss (regarded as the seal of a ceremonial bond)   77 **pines the clime** afflicts the climate   80 **Hallowmas** All Saints' Day (November 1), regarded as the beginning of winter. **short'st of day** the winter solstice.   84 **policy** political practicality. 88 **Better . . . the near** i.e., better to be far apart than near and yet unable to meet. (The second *near* means "nearer.")

90 **So . . . moans** i.e., Then I will have to sigh and groan all the more, since my journey is longer.   92 **piece . . . out** make the journey seem longer   94 **Since . . . grief** i.e., since wedding ourselves to grief, we embark on a sadness that is only beginning. (A wry joke on the commonplace that a brief and romantic courtship is often the prelude to an interminable marriage.)   95 **and dumbly part** and then let us part in silence   97–8 **'Twere . . . me** It would not be wise of me to take it upon myself   101 **We . . . wanton** We sport with our grief. **fond** (1) loving (2) pointless, foolish
5.2. Location: The Duke of York's house.
3 **cousins** kinsmen, i.e., nephews (Richard and Bolingbroke)   4 **leave** leave off.   5 **misgoverned** unruly.   **windows' tops** upper windows 9 **Which . . . know** which seemed to know its ambitious rider
16 **With painted imagery** i.e., showing crowds of people, as on a tapestry or painted cloth, depicting a procession.   **at once** all together

Whilst he, from the one side to the other turning,
Bareheaded, lower than his proud steed's neck,   19
Bespake them thus: "I thank you, countrymen."   20
And thus still doing, thus he passed along.   21

DUCHESS
Alack, poor Richard! Where rode he the whilst?

YORK
As in a theater the eyes of men,
After a well-graced actor leaves the stage,
Are idly bent on him that enters next,   25
Thinking his prattle to be tedious,
Even so, or with much more contempt, men's eyes
Did scowl on gentle Richard. No man cried, "God
    save him!"
No joyful tongue gave him his welcome home,
But dust was thrown upon his sacred head—
Which with such gentle sorrow he shook off,
His face still combating with tears and smiles,
The badges of his grief and patience,   33
That had not God for some strong purpose steeled
The hearts of men, they must perforce have melted,   35
And barbarism itself have pitied him.
But heaven hath a hand in these events,
To whose high will we bound our calm contents.   38
To Bolingbroke are we sworn subjects now,
Whose state and honor I for aye allow.   40

[Enter Aumerle.]

DUCHESS
Here comes my son Aumerle.

YORK   Aumerle that was;   41
But that is lost for being Richard's friend,
And, madam, you must call him Rutland now.
I am in Parliament pledge for his truth   44
And lasting fealty to the new-made king.

DUCHESS
Welcome, my son. Who are the violets now   46
That strew the green lap of the new-come spring?   47

AUMERLE
Madam, I know not, nor I greatly care not.
God knows I had as lief be none as one.   49

YORK
Well, bear you well in this new spring of time,   50
Lest you be cropped before you come to prime.   51
What news from Oxford? Do these jousts and triumphs
    hold?   52

AUMERLE   For aught I know, my lord, they do.

YORK   You will be there, I know.

AUMERLE
If God prevent not, I purpose so.

YORK
What seal is that, that hangs without thy bosom?   56
Yea, look'st thou pale? Let me see the writing.

AUMERLE
My lord, 'tis nothing.

YORK   No matter, then, who see it.
I will be satisfied. Let me see the writing.

AUMERLE
I do beseech Your Grace to pardon me.   60
It is a matter of small consequence,
Which for some reasons I would not have seen.   62

YORK
Which for some reasons, sir, I mean to see.
I fear, I fear—

DUCHESS   What should you fear?
'Tis nothing but some bond that he is entered into
For gay apparel 'gainst the triumph day.   66

YORK
Bound to himself? What doth he with a bond   67
That he is bound to? Wife, thou art a fool.—   68
Boy, let me see the writing.

AUMERLE
I do beseech you, pardon me. I may not show it.

YORK
I will be satisfied. Let me see it, I say.
                    He plucks it out of his bosom and reads it.
Treason! Foul treason! Villain! Traitor! Slave!

DUCHESS   What is the matter, my lord?

YORK [calling offstage]   Ho! Who is within there?

[Enter a Servingman.]

                              Saddle my horse!—
God for his mercy, what treachery is here?   75

DUCHESS   Why, what is it, my lord?

YORK [to the Servingman]
Give me my boots, I say! Saddle my horse!—
                                          [Exit Servingman.]
Now, by mine honor, by my life, my troth,   78
I will appeach the villain.

DUCHESS   What is the matter?   79

YORK
Peace, foolish woman.

DUCHESS
I will not peace. What is the matter, Aumerle?

AUMERLE
Good mother, be content. It is no more
Than my poor life must answer.

DUCHESS   Thy life answer?

19 lower bowing lower   **20 Bespake** addressed   **21 still** continually
25 idly indifferently   **33 badges** insignia, outward signs   **35 perforce** necessarily   **38 we . . . contents** i.e., we bind ourselves to be calmly content.   **40 state** i.e., royal title.   **allow** acknowledge.
41 Aumerle that was (Aumerle, as a member of Richard's party, lost his dukedom, though he remained Earl of Rutland.)   **44 pledge** the guarantor.   **truth** loyalty   **46–7 Who . . . spring** i.e., Who are the favorites of the new king?   **49 I had . . . one** I'd be just as glad to be left out as to be a favorite at court.   **50 bear you** bear yourself
51 cropped plucked, i.e., beheaded   **52 Do . . . hold?** Are those tourneys and pageants going forward? (According to Holinshed, these tourneys at Oxford were part of a conspiracy against Bolingbroke by the Abbot of Westminster and others; the new king was to be invited to attend and there be assassinated.)

56 seal i.e., seal attached to the border of a document   **60 pardon me** i.e., excuse me if I don't comply.   **62 have seen** wish to be seen.
66 'gainst in anticipation of   **67–8 What . . . bound to?** i.e., Why should *he* have the bond instead of the creditor to whom the debt is owed?   **75 God** i.e., I pray God   **78 troth** faith, allegiance
79 appeach inform against, publicly accuse

YORK [*calling*]
    Bring me my boots! I will unto the King.

        His [Serving]man enters with his boots.

DUCHESS
    Strike him, Aumerle. Poor boy, thou art amazed.   85
    [*To the Servingman*] Hence, villain! Never more come
        in my sight.
YORK   Give me my boots, I say.
        [*The Servingman helps him on with his boots, and exit.*]
DUCHESS   Why, York, what wilt thou do?
    Wilt thou not hide the trespass of thine own?
    Have we more sons? Or are we like to have?   90
    Is not my teeming date drunk up with time?   91
    And wilt thou pluck my fair son from mine age
    And rob me of a happy mother's name?
    Is he not like thee? Is he not thine own?
YORK   Thou fond mad woman,   95
    Wilt thou conceal this dark conspiracy?
    A dozen of them here have ta'en the Sacrament,   97
    And interchangeably set down their hands,   98
    To kill the King at Oxford.
DUCHESS   He shall be none;   99
    We'll keep him here. Then what is that to him?   100
YORK
    Away, fond woman! Were he twenty times my son
    I would appeach him.
DUCHESS   Hadst thou groaned for him   102
    As I have done, thou wouldst be more pitiful.   103
    But now I know thy mind. Thou dost suspect
    That I have been disloyal to thy bed,
    And that he is a bastard, not thy son.
    Sweet York, sweet husband, be not of that mind!
    He is as like thee as a man may be,
    Not like to me, or any of my kin,
    And yet I love him.
YORK   Make way, unruly woman!   *Exit.*
DUCHESS
    After, Aumerle! Mount thee upon his horse,   111
    Spur post, and get before him to the King,   112
    And beg thy pardon ere he do accuse thee.
    I'll not be long behind. Though I be old,
    I doubt not but to ride as fast as York.
    And never will I rise up from the ground
    Till Bolingbroke have pardoned thee. Away, begone!
                        [*Exeunt separately.*]

                    ❖

[5.3]

        *Enter [Bolingbroke, now] King [Henry], with his
        nobles [Harry Percy and others].*

KING HENRY
    Can no man tell me of my unthrifty son?   1
    'Tis full three months since I did see him last.
    If any plague hang over us, 'tis he.
    I would to God, my lords, he might be found.
    Inquire at London, 'mongst the taverns there,
    For there, they say, he daily doth frequent
    With unrestrainèd loose companions,
    Even such, they say, as stand in narrow lanes
    And beat our watch, and rob our passengers—   9
    While he, young wanton and effeminate boy,   10
    Takes on the point of honor to support   11
    So dissolute a crew.
PERCY
    My lord, some two days since I saw the Prince,
    And told him of those triumphs held at Oxford.   14
KING HENRY   And what said the gallant?
PERCY
    His answer was, he would unto the stews,   16
    And from the common'st creature pluck a glove,   17
    And wear it as a favor, and with that   18
    He would unhorse the lustiest challenger.   19
KING HENRY
    As dissolute as desperate! Yet through both
    I see some sparks of better hope, which elder years
    May happily bring forth. But who comes here?   22

        Enter Aumerle, amazed.

AUMERLE   Where is the King?
KING HENRY
    What means our cousin, that he stares and looks
        So wildly?
AUMERLE
    God save Your Grace! I do beseech Your Majesty
    To have some conference with Your Grace alone.
KING HENRY [*to his nobles*]
    Withdraw yourselves, and leave us here alone.
                        [*Exeunt Percy and lords.*]
    What is the matter with our cousin now?
AUMERLE [*kneeling*]
    Forever may my knees grow to the earth,
    My tongue cleave to the roof within my mouth,   31
    Unless a pardon ere I rise or speak.
KING HENRY
    Intended or committed was this fault?
    If on the first, how heinous e'er it be,   34

---

85 **Strike him** i.e., Strike the servant.   **amazed** confused, bewildered.
90 **Have we more sons?** (Historically, this Duchess of York was the
Duke's second wife and was not Aumerle's mother; she was, however, the mother of another son, Richard, subsequently Earl of Cambridge.)   91 **teeming date** period of childbearing   95 **fond** foolish
97–9 **A dozen . . . Oxford** ("Hereupon was an indenture sextipartite
made, sealed with their seals and signed with their hands, in the
which each stood bound to other, to do their whole endeavor for the
accomplishing of their purposed exploit." [Holinshed])
100 **that** i.e., the plot   102 **groaned for** i.e., given birth to. (But see
note, line 90.)   103 **pitiful** pitying.   111 **After** Go after him.   **his
horse** i.e., one of York's horses   112 **Spur post** ride as fast as possible

5.3. Location: The court (i.e., Windsor Castle).
1 **unthrifty** profligate   9 **watch** night watchmen.   **passengers**
passers-by, wayfarers   10 **wanton** pampered youth.   **effeminate**
self-indulgent   11 **Takes on** i.e., makes it a   14 **held** i.e., to be
held   16 **stews** brothels   17 **common'st** most promiscuous   18 **with
that** i.e., wearing that as a favor   19 **lustiest** most vigorous and brave
22 **happily** with good fortune   22.1 *amazed* distraught.   31 **My . . .
mouth** (See Psalm 137:6: "If I do not remember thee, let my tongue
cleave to the roof of my mouth.")   34 **If on the first** i.e., If intended
only

To win thy after-love I pardon thee.

AUMERLE [*rising*]
Then give me leave that I may turn the key,
That no man enter till my tale be done.

KING HENRY   Have thy desire.

[*Aumerle locks the door.*] *The Duke of York
knocks at the door and crieth.*

YORK [*within*]
My liege, beware! Look to thyself.
Thou hast a traitor in thy presence there.

KING HENRY [*drawing*]   Villain, I'll make thee safe.   41

AUMERLE
Stay thy revengeful hand. Thou hast no cause to fear.

YORK [*within*]
Open the door, secure, foolhardy King!   43
Shall I for love speak treason to thy face?   44
Open the door, or I will break it open.

[*King Henry unlocks the door.*]

[*Enter York.*]

KING HENRY
What is the matter, uncle? Speak.
Recover breath; tell us how near is danger,
That we may arm us to encounter it.

YORK [*giving letter*]
Peruse this writing here, and thou shalt know
The treason that my haste forbids me show.   50

AUMERLE
Remember, as thou read'st, thy promise passed.
I do repent me. Read not my name there;
My heart is not confederate with my hand.   53

YORK
It was, villain, ere thy hand did set it down.
I tore it from the traitor's bosom, King;
Fear, and not love, begets his penitence.
Forget to pity him, lest thy pity prove   57
A serpent that will sting thee to the heart.

KING HENRY
Oh, heinous, strong, and bold conspiracy!
O loyal father of a treacherous son,
Thou sheer, immaculate, and silver fountain,   61
From whence this stream through muddy passages
Hath held his current and defiled himself,   63
Thy overflow of good converts to bad,   64
And thy abundant goodness shall excuse
This deadly blot in thy digressing son.   66

YORK
So shall my virtue be his vice's bawd,
And he shall spend mine honor with his shame,
As thriftless sons their scraping fathers' gold.   69

Mine honor lives when his dishonor dies,
Or my shamed life in his dishonor lies.   71
Thou kill'st me in his life; giving him breath,   72
The traitor lives, the true man's put to death.

DUCHESS [*within*]
What ho, my liege! For God's sake, let me in.

KING HENRY
What shrill-voiced suppliant makes this eager cry?

DUCHESS [*within*]
A woman, and thy aunt, great King. 'Tis I.
Speak with me, pity me, open the door!
A beggar begs that never begged before.

KING HENRY
Our scene is altered from a serious thing,
And now changed to "The Beggar and the King."   80
My dangerous cousin, let your mother in.
I know she is come to pray for your foul sin.

[*Aumerle opens the door. Enter the Duchess. She
kneels.*]

YORK
If thou do pardon whosoever pray,   83
More sins for this forgiveness prosper may.   84
This festered joint cut off, the rest rest sound;
This let alone will all the rest confound.   86

DUCHESS
O King, believe not this hardhearted man.
Love loving not itself, none other can.   88

YORK
Thou frantic woman, what dost thou make here?   89
Shall thy old dugs once more a traitor rear?   90

DUCHESS
Sweet York, be patient.—Hear me, gentle liege.

KING HENRY
Rise up, good aunt.

DUCHESS   Not yet, I thee beseech.
Forever will I walk upon my knees,
And never see day that the happy sees,   94
Till thou give joy, until thou bid me joy,
By pardoning Rutland, my transgressing boy.

AUMERLE [*kneeling*]
Unto my mother's prayers I bend my knee.   97

YORK [*kneeling*]
Against them both my true joints bended be.
Ill mayst thou thrive, if thou grant any grace!

DUCHESS
Pleads he in earnest? Look upon his face.
His eyes do drop no tears, his prayers are in jest;
His words come from his mouth, ours from our breast.
He prays but faintly and would be denied;

---

41 I'll . . . safe I'll make you harmless (by running you through). **43 secure** unsuspecting, heedless **44 speak . . . face** i.e., speak so disrespectfully as to call you *secure* and *foolhardy*. **50 haste . . . show** i.e., breathlessness prevents me from revealing. **53 hand** signature. **57 Forget** Forget your promise **61 sheer** clear, pure **63 himself** (1) itself (2) himself, Aumerle **64 Thy . . . bad** your excess of goodness atones for what is bad (in Aumerle) **66 digressing** deviating from his proper course, transgressing **69 scraping** parsimonious

71 in . . . lies will be hostage to his dishonorable conduct. **72 in his life** if you permit him to live **80 "The Beggar . . . King"** (Probably one of Shakespeare's many allusions to the ballad of King Cophetua and the Beggar Maid.) **83 whosoever pray** anyone who presents a petition **84 for** because of **86 alone** untreated. **confound** ruin. **88 Love . . . can** i.e., He who does not love himself in his own son can love no one else, not even the King. **89 make** do **90 once . . . rear** i.e., give life again to a traitor by now redeeming Aumerle from death. **94 And . . . sees** and never enjoy the happiness that those who are happy experience **97 Unto** In support of

We pray with heart and soul and all beside.   104
His weary joints would gladly rise, I know;
Our knees still kneel till to the ground they grow.   106
His prayers are full of false hypocrisy,
Ours of true zeal and deep integrity.
Our prayers do outpray his; then let them have
That mercy which true prayer ought to have.

KING HENRY
Good aunt, stand up.

DUCHESS   Nay, do not say "stand up."
Say "pardon" first, and afterwards "stand up."
An if I were thy nurse, thy tongue to teach,   113
"Pardon" should be the first word of thy speech.
I never longed to hear a word till now;
Say "pardon," King; let pity teach thee how.
The word is short, but not so short as sweet;
No word like "pardon" for kings' mouths so meet.

YORK
Speak it in French, King: say "pardonne moy."   119

DUCHESS
Dost thou teach pardon pardon to destroy?
Ah, my sour husband, my hardhearted lord,
That sets the word itself against the word!
Speak "pardon" as 'tis current in our land;
The chopping French we do not understand.   124
Thine eye begins to speak; set thy tongue there,
Or in thy piteous heart plant thou thine ear,
That hearing how our plaints and prayers do pierce,
Pity may move thee "pardon" to rehearse.   128

KING HENRY
Good aunt, stand up.

DUCHESS   I do not sue to stand.
Pardon is all the suit I have in hand.

KING HENRY
I pardon him, as God shall pardon me.

DUCHESS
Oh, happy vantage of a kneeling knee!   132
Yet am I sick for fear. Speak it again;
Twice saying "pardon" doth not pardon twain
But makes one pardon strong.

KING HENRY   With all my heart
I pardon him.   [All rise.]

DUCHESS   A god on earth thou art.

KING HENRY
But for our trusty brother-in-law and the Abbot,   137
With all the rest of that consorted crew,   138
Destruction straight shall dog them at the heels.
Good uncle, help to order several powers   140
To Oxford, or where'er these traitors are.
They shall not live within this world, I swear,
But I will have them, if I once know where.
Uncle, farewell, and, cousin, adieu.

Your mother well hath prayed; and prove you true.   145

DUCHESS
Come, my old son. I pray God make thee new.   146
                    Exeunt [in two groups].

❖

[5.4]

Enter Sir Pierce [of] Exton [and his Men].

EXTON
Didst thou not mark the King, what words he spake,
"Have I no friend will rid me of this living fear?"   2
Was it not so?

MAN   These were his very words.

EXTON
"Have I no friend?" quoth he. He spake it twice,
And urged it twice together, did he not?

MAN   He did.

EXTON
And speaking it, he wishtly looked on me,   7
As who should say, "I would thou wert the man   8
That would divorce this terror from my heart"—
Meaning the King at Pomfret. Come, let's go.
I am the King's friend, and will rid his foe.   11
                    [*Exeunt.*]

❖

[5.5]

Enter Richard alone.

KING RICHARD
I have been studying how I may compare
This prison where I live unto the world;
And, for because the world is populous,   3
And here is not a creature but myself,
I cannot do it. Yet I'll hammer it out.   5
My brain I'll prove the female to my soul,
My soul the father, and these two beget
A generation of still-breeding thoughts;   8
And these same thoughts people this little world,   9
In humors like the people of this world,   10
For no thought is contented. The better sort,
As thoughts of things divine, are intermixed   12
With scruples and do set the word itself   13
Against the word, as thus, "Come, little ones,"   14
And then again,
"It is as hard to come as for a camel
To thread the postern of a small needle's eye."   17

---

145 prove you true may you prove loyal.   146 old unregenerate
5.4. Location: The court. The opening stage direction in the quarto reads *Manet Sir Pierce Exton, etc.,* suggesting continuity of action with the preceding scene.
2 will who will   7 wishtly intently   8 As . . . say as if to say   11 rid rid him of
5.5. Location: Pomfret Castle. A dungeon.
3 for because because   5 hammer i.e., work, puzzle   8 still-breeding constantly breeding   9 this little world myself and this prison as a microcosm of the world   10 humors temperaments, peculiar fancies   12 As such as   13 scruples doubts   13–14 do set . . . word i.e., oppose one scriptural passage against its apparent opposite   14–17 Come . . . eye (See Matthew 19:14, 24.)   17 postern narrow gate

---

104 beside besides.   106 still continually   113 An if If   119 pardonne moy *pardonnez-moi,* excuse me. (An affectedly polite refusal.)   124 chopping logic chopping, changing the sense   128 rehearse pronounce.   132 happy vantage fortunate gain   137 But for But as for.   brother-in-law i.e., John Holland, Earl of Huntingdon and Duke of Exeter, who had married Bolingbroke's sister (see 2.1.281 and note).   Abbot Abbot of Westminster; see 4.1.321–34   138 consorted conspiring, confederate   140 powers forces

Thoughts tending to ambition, they do plot
Unlikely wonders—how these vain weak nails
May tear a passage through the flinty ribs
Of this hard world, my ragged prison walls,   21
And, for they cannot, die in their own pride.   22
Thoughts tending to content flatter themselves   23
That they are not the first of fortune's slaves,
Nor shall not be the last—like seely beggars   25
Who, sitting in the stocks, refuge their shame   26
That many have and others must sit there;
And in this thought they find a kind of ease,
Bearing their own misfortunes on the back
Of such as have before endured the like.
Thus play I in one person many people,
And none contented. Sometimes am I king;
Then treason makes me wish myself a beggar,   33
And so I am. Then crushing penury   34
Persuades me I was better when a king;
Then am I kinged again, and by and by
Think that I am unkinged by Bolingbroke,
And straight am nothing. But whate'er I be,
Nor I, nor any man that but man is,   39
With nothing shall be pleased till he be eased   40
With being nothing. (*The music plays.*) Music do I
    hear?   41
Ha, ha, keep time! How sour sweet music is
When time is broke and no proportion kept!
So is it in the music of men's lives.
And here have I the daintiness of ear
To check time broke in a disordered string,   46
But for the concord of my state and time
Had not an ear to hear my true time broke.
I wasted time, and now doth time waste me;
For now hath Time made me his numb'ring clock.   50
My thoughts are minutes, and with sighs they jar   51
Their watches on unto mine eyes, the outward watch   52
Whereto my finger, like a dial's point,   53
Is pointing still in cleansing them from tears.
Now sir, the sounds that tell what hour it is
Are clamorous groans that strike upon my heart,
Which is the bell. So sighs and tears and groans
Show minutes, hours, and times. But my time   58
Runs posting on in Bolingbroke's proud joy,   59
While I stand fooling here, his jack of the clock.   60
This music mads me. Let it sound no more,   61
For though it have holp madmen to their wits,   62

In me it seems it will make wise men mad.
                    [*The music ceases.*]
Yet blessing on his heart that gives it me!
For 'tis a sign of love; and love to Richard
Is a strange brooch in this all-hating world.   66

Enter a Groom of the stable.

GROOM
   Hail, royal prince!
KING RICHARD   Thanks, noble peer.
   The cheapest of us is ten groats too dear.   68
   What art thou, and how comest thou hither,
   Where no man never comes but that sad dog
   That brings me food to make misfortune live?
GROOM
   I was a poor groom of thy stable, King,
   When thou wert king; who, traveling towards York,
   With much ado at length have gotten leave
   To look upon my sometimes royal master's face.   75
   Oh, how it earned my heart when I beheld   76
   In London streets, that coronation day,
   When Bolingbroke rode on roan Barbary,
   That horse that thou so often hast bestrid,
   That horse that I so carefully have dressed!   80
KING RICHARD
   Rode he on Barbary? Tell me, gentle friend,
   How went he under him?
GROOM
   So proudly as if he disdained the ground.
KING RICHARD
   So proud that Bolingbroke was on his back!
   That jade hath eat bread from my royal hand;   85
   This hand hath made him proud with clapping him.   86
   Would he not stumble? Would he not fall down,
   Since pride must have a fall, and break the neck
   Of that proud man that did usurp his back?
   Forgiveness, horse! Why do I rail on thee,
   Since thou, created to be awed by man,
   Wast born to bear? I was not made a horse,
   And yet I bear a burden like an ass,
   Spurred, galled, and tired by jaucing Bolingbroke.   94

Enter one [a Keeper] to Richard with meat.

KEEPER [*to Groom*]
   Fellow, give place. Here is no longer stay.
KING RICHARD [*to Groom*]
   If thou love me, 'tis time thou wert away.
GROOM
   What my tongue dares not, that my heart shall say.
                             Exit Groom.

---

21 ragged rugged   **22 for** because.   **pride** prime.   **23 content** contentment   **25 seely** simpleminded   **26 refuge their shame** i.e., seek refuge from their disgrace by reflecting   **33 treason** i.e., the thought of treason   **34 penury** poverty   **39–41 Nor . . . nothing** neither I nor any person alive can be fully satisfied with the things of this life until he or she is released by death.   **46 check** rebuke.   **string** stringed instrument   **50 numb'ring clock** i.e., a clock that numbers hours and minutes (not an hourglass).   **51–2 My . . . watch** My sad thoughts, occurring every minute, are parts of an inner clock that, by means of the sighs they provoke, transfer their cares to my eyes, the face of the clock   **53 dial's point** clock hand   **58 times** quarters and halves.   **59 posting** hastening   **60 jack of the clock** manikin that struck the bell on a clock.   **61 mads** maddens   **62 holp** helped

66 strange brooch rare jewel   **68 ten groats too dear** (There is a pun on *royal* and *noble* in the preceding lines. A royal (ten shillings) is worth ten groats (ten times four pence) more than a noble (six shillings, eight pence) is; hence, Richard is saying that he, "the cheapest of us" because he is a prisoner, is worth no more than the groom, whom he greets as his "noble peer.")   **75 sometimes** former **76 earned** grieved   **80 dressed** tended, groomed.   **85 eat** eaten. (Pronounced "et.")   **86 clapping** patting, stroking   **94 galled** made sore. **jaucing** prancing, hard-riding   **94.1 *meat*** food.

KEEPER
My lord, will't please you to fall to?

KING RICHARD
Taste of it first, as thou art wont to do.　99

KEEPER
My lord, I dare not. Sir Pierce of Exton, who
Lately came from the King, commands the contrary.

KING RICHARD
The devil take Henry of Lancaster and thee!
Patience is stale, and I am weary of it.
　　　　　　　　　　　　　　[*He beats the Keeper.*]

KEEPER　Help, help, help!

　　The murderers [*Exton and his men*] *rush in.*

KING RICHARD
How now, what means death in this rude assault?
Villain, thy own hand yields thy death's instrument.
　　　[*He snatches a weapon from a man and kills him.*]
Go thou, and fill another room in hell.　107
　　　[*He kills another.*] *Here Exton strikes him down.*
That hand shall burn in never-quenching fire
That staggers thus my person. Exton, thy fierce hand 109
Hath with the King's blood stained the King's own
　　　land.
Mount, mount, my soul! Thy seat is up on high,
Whilst my gross flesh sinks downward, here to die.
　　　　　　　　　　　　　　　　　[*He dies.*]

EXTON
As full of valor as of royal blood.
Both have I spilled. Oh, would the deed were good!
For now the devil, that told me I did well,
Says that this deed is chronicled in hell.
This dead king to the living king I'll bear.
Take hence the rest, and give them burial here.
　　　　　　　　　　　[*Exeunt, with the bodies.*]

❖

[5.6]

　　[*Flourish.*] *Enter Bolingbroke* [*as King*], *with the
　　Duke of York,* [*other lords, and attendants*].

KING HENRY
Kind uncle York, the latest news we hear
Is that the rebels have consumed with fire
Our town of Ci'cester in Gloucestershire,
But whether they be ta'en or slain we hear not.　3

　　　　Enter Northumberland.

Wecome, my lord. What is the news?

NORTHUMBERLAND
First, to thy sacred state wish I all happiness.
The next news is, I have to London sent

The heads of Salisbury, Spencer, Blunt, and Kent.
The manner of their taking may appear　9
At large discoursèd in this paper here.　10
　　　　　　　　　　　　　　[*He gives a paper.*]

KING HENRY
We thank thee, gentle Percy, for thy pains,
And to thy worth will add right worthy gains.　12

　　　　Enter Lord Fitzwater.

FITZWATER
My lord, I have from Oxford sent to London
The heads of Brocas and Sir Bennet Seely,
Two of the dangerous consorted traitors　15
That sought at Oxford thy dire overthrow.

KING HENRY
Thy pains, Fitzwater, shall not be forgot;
Right noble is thy merit, well I wot.　18

　　　Enter Henry Percy [*with the Bishop of Carlisle,
　　guarded*].

PERCY
The grand conspirator, Abbot of Westminster,　19
With clog of conscience and sour melancholy　20
Hath yielded up his body to the grave;
But here is Carlisle living, to abide　22
Thy kingly doom and sentence of his pride.　23

KING HENRY　Carlisle, this is your doom:
Choose out some secret place, some reverent room,　25
More than thou hast, and with it joy thy life.　26
So as thou liv'st in peace, die free from strife;　27
For though mine enemy thou hast ever been,
High sparks of honor in thee have I seen.

　　　Enter Exton, with [*attendants bearing*] *the coffin.*

EXTON
Great King, within this coffin I present
Thy buried fear. Herein all breathless lies
The mightiest of thy greatest enemies,
Richard of Bordeaux, by me hither brought.

KING HENRY
Exton, I thank thee not, for thou hast wrought
A deed of slander with thy fatal hand　35
Upon my head and all this famous land.

EXTON
From your own mouth, my lord, did I this deed.

KING HENRY
They love not poison that do poison need,
Nor do I thee. Though I did wish him dead,
I hate the murderer, love him murderèd.

---

99 **Taste . . . first** i.e., to ensure that it isn't poisoned　**107 room** place
109 **staggers** causes to stagger
5.6. Location: The court.
3 **Ci'cester** Cirencester

9 **taking** capture　10 **At large discoursèd** related in full　12 **worth**
(1) deserving (2) present wealth　15 **consorted** conspiring　18 **wot**
know.　19 **grand** chief　20 **clog** burden　22 **abide** await　23 **doom**
judgment　25 **reverent room** place suitable for religious retirement
26 **More than thou hast** i.e., larger than your present cell, or more
worthy of reverence.　**joy** enjoy, have the benefit of　27 **So as** Provided that　35 **deed of slander** i.e., a deed sure to arouse slanderous
talk about the new king

The guilt of conscience take thou for thy labor,
But neither my good word nor princely favor.
With Cain go wander through the shades of night,   43
And never show thy head by day nor light.
              [*Exeunt Exton and attendants.*]
Lords, I protest my soul is full of woe
That blood should sprinkle me to make me grow.

Come mourn with me for what I do lament,
And put on sullen black incontinent.   48
I'll make a voyage to the Holy Land
To wash this blood off from my guilty hand.
March sadly after. Grace my mournings here   51
In weeping after this untimely bier.
              [*Exeunt in procession, following the coffin.*]

---

43 Cain murderer of his brother Abel; see 1.1.104

48 incontinent immediately.   **51 Grace** Dignify

The First Part of King Henry the Fourth

The opening of *1 Henry IV* is taut and grave in tone. England is "shaken" and "wan with care." The troubles of *Richard II,* to which this play (c. 1596–1597) is a close sequel, have not been left behind. However much King Henry would prefer to unite his countrymen against a common foreign enemy in a crusade to the Holy Lands, he is prevented from doing so by continuing civil war. The impassioned rhetoric of his opening speech can only end in anticlimax, for the actual purpose of this meeting in council is to receive and assess reports of military action against the throne.

Henry's current troubles are in the far reaches of his kingdom: Scots in the north, Welsh in the west. Fighting for Henry on these two fronts are the nobles of the Percy family who helped him to power: Harry Percy ("Hotspur"), his father (Henry Percy) the Earl of Northumberland, his uncle the Earl of Worcester, and his brother-in-law Edmund Mortimer, the Earl of March. Apparently, they have fought bravely. Yet we soon sense that all is not well between the new King and those who rebelled with him against Richard II. A quarrel breaks out because Hotspur refuses to deliver to Henry some prisoners as required by feudal obedience. The matter of the ransom money is only a technicality; what is really at issue? In part, it is Henry's insistence on being obeyed on principle. Admiring Hotspur inordinately, the King feels he must discipline affectionately this fine young warrior as a father would discipline his son. Even more deeply, however, the issue of the prisoners galls Henry because of the proviso that he ransom Mortimer, captured by the Welsh. Henry does not forget that Mortimer is his chief rival for the English crown, being descended from the Duke of Clarence (elder brother to Henry's father, Gaunt) and having been proclaimed by Richard as heir to the throne. (Shakespeare accentuates the dynastic threat by combining two Edmund Mortimers from his historical sources: one who married Glendower's daughter and another who claimed the English throne; see 1.3.80–5 and

note.) Mortimer is the last person Henry would wish ransomed. Moreover, the King suspects Mortimer of having fought with something less than total zeal against the Welsh Glendower. Mortimer's marriage to Glendower's daughter confirms the King's worst fears. Henry knows Northumberland and Worcester to be expert in treasonous plotting, since they conspired with him to overthrow Richard. Now, Henry believes, these Percys are extending their alliance by a series of calculated marriages in order to seize power once again. This time their claimant is Mortimer.

Shakespeare's sympathies are many sided. The Percy clan is, in fact, organizing against Henry, but not without cause. As they see it, the man they helped to the throne has done little for them since. His manner of disciplining them sounds too much like hostility and ingratitude. Other counselors attend the King constantly while Worcester is banished from court. In such an atmosphere of distrust, suspicion breeds still more suspicion. The situation has deteriorated, surely more than either party originally intended.

Hotspur is the most attractive of the rebels—to us as well as to King Henry. He is outspoken, courageous, witty, and domineering in conversation. Above all, he is a disciple of manliness, loyalty, chivalry, bravery in battle—the attributes of an upstanding and somewhat old-fashioned sense of honor. Yet a fatal defect dwells even in these attractive qualities. Hotspur is impatient, proud, unwilling to tolerate a rival—be it Glendower or Prince Hal (Henry, Prince of Wales). In his first speech, purporting to explain his refusal to deliver the prisoners, he brilliantly satirizes an effete courtier who had come to him from King Henry in the midst of a battle. The satire betrays many harsh qualities in Hotspur: the self-indulgent wrath that returns fully to him even in recollection of the encounter, the pride in his own stoical indifference to suffering, and especially the obsessive nature (revealed in the repetitive pattern of the rhetoric) of his contempt for courtiers generally. Surely his scorn for stay-at-home politicians is directed in part at King Henry himself. To Hotspur, all courtiers are perfume-wearing, affected in mannerism and speech, and scarcely masculine. This preoccupation of Hotspur's makes him extraordinarily prone to one-sided judgments. Like most excessive devotees of chivalry, he divides humanity into two categories: those who are gentlemen, like himself, and those who are beneath contempt. The "vile politician" Bolingbroke and his son, the "sword-and-buckler Prince of Wales" (1.3.240, 229) fall into the latter category.

Prone as he is to such an overly simple view of political behavior, Hotspur can see no good in the King's cause and no evil in his own. He is a poor listener because of his obsession and yet an easy prey to his uncle and father, who require his leadership for their cause. They need only implant the suggestion that King Henry is acting from a political motive in his refusal to ransom Mortimer, and Hotspur is ready to leap incautiously to the defense of their cause. The great irony is that Hotspur fails to see political motives in the machinations of his own relatives. While he fights for bright honor, they maneuver cautiously for position and prove to be uncertain allies when the hour of battle approaches. Most crucially, they betray Hotspur in the prebattle negotiations, at which he is not present. As Worcester explains to Vernon during their return to rebel headquarters (5.2.3–25), they cannot let Hotspur know of the King's offer to settle matters by a general pardon. Although, as they realize, the King could pardon Hotspur's youth, there can be no turning back for themselves. Thus, the honor for which Hotspur fights is at bottom a lie, and the mutual esteem that might have grown between him and a much-reformed Prince of Wales is thwarted by the polarization of attitudes in the two camps. Hotspur's brand of honor is the victim of its own excess and lends some credence to Falstaff's wry conclusion that honor "is a mere scutcheon" (5.1.139–40).

The contrasting of Falstaff and Hotspur on the theme of honor suggests that they are dramatic foils for each other, representing extremes between which Hal must choose. Shakespeare uses this foil device structurally and consciously; for example, he has considerably reduced the age of the Hotspur he found in Raphael Holinshed's *Chronicles* (1578) in order to stress the similarity between Hotspur and Prince Hal. Conversely, to emphasize the contrast between Falstaff and Hotspur, Shakespeare envisages Falstaff as old (nearly sixty, by his own admission), fat, humorous, and without honor. Falstaff's vices are Hotspur's virtues, and the reverse. Whereas Hotspur offers to Hal a model of chivalric striving and attention to duty, Falstaff is a highwayman and a liar. On the other hand, Hotspur is a fanatic, unbending and self-absorbed even in the company of his sprightly wife, Kate, and irritated by music and poetry; Falstaff is the epitome of merriment and joie de vivre. We excuse much in him because he lusts after life with such an appetite and ingratiates himself to others by inviting them to laugh at his expense.

Despite the nearly irresistible attractiveness of Falstaff as a jolly companion and butt of humorous joking, he and Prince Hal are perennially caught up in witty debate as to the importance of Falstaff in Hal's life and whether the young man will have to get rid of Falstaff once Hal is king. The bantering raillery of their first scene (1.2) seems designed to provide diverting entertainment for the Prince and for us, and yet, beneath the word games and oneupmanship, we perceive that Hal and Falstaff are talking about the hanging of thieves and the question of whether or not Hal should give in to sinful temptation. Can the relationship of Hal and Falstaff continue unchanged into the reign of Henry V? Will there be gallows standing and justice for highwaymen? Will "Monsieur Remorse," as Poins calls Falstaff, ever sincerely repent? Will the Prince, for that matter? To allay our fears, Hal soliloquizes at scene's end, vowing his determination to use these scapegrace companions as mere foils for his triumphal reformation at the appropriate time. But this explanation raises an opposite danger in our sympathies: is he callously using his companions merely to create a self-serving myth of Prince Hal, the Politician with the Common Touch? Is Francis the drawer no more to Hal than a butt for his raillery? Since the rejection of Falstaff is, by Hal's own words, already determined, can we credit him with a serious friendship? Where do Shakespeare's sympathies lie—with the need for political order or with the hedonistic spirit of youth? One possible interpretation is that he recognizes the validity of both, and accordingly shows us a prince who is genuinely fond of Falstaff's exuberant company but who also knows that he is a king's son and must sooner or later accept the consequences of that unsought role. Falstaff's gift to him is youthful irresponsibility, which must be cherished (by all of us), even though it cannot last.

This compassionate interpretation is, to be sure, only one of many possibilities. Recent theater history has demonstrated how supple the play is, allowing directors and actors to choose among an array of possibilities. At one extreme, Hal can be played as a matter-of-fact and even cynical young man who knows from the very start exactly where he is going and what use he can make of Falstaff and company—as played, for example, by Richard Burton at Stratford-upon-Avon in 1951 (directed by Anthony Quayle and John Kidd). At the opposite extreme, Hal can be seen as a defiant rebel whose hatred for his unsympathetically cold father makes him reluctant to grow up and accept adult responsibility; this was the line taken, for example, by Gerard Murphy in Trevor Nunn's 1982 production for the Royal Shakespeare Company. Murphy's Hal was an unruly child for whom Falstaff was a nurturing substitute parent. Between these polarities, Hal can be variously seen as an alcoholic or a prudish snob or a playboy or simply a young man who wants to enjoy life. Correspondingly, the role of Falstaff offers widely varying possibilities as a kind of jolly scapegrace older friend, a calculating con artist and jokester who knows how to play for sympathy through self-effacing humor, or a dangerously irresponsible hedonist. King Henry as father can be seen as a sorely tested father burdened with heavy responsibilities and an ungrateful son, a guilt-ridden monarch who fears remorsefully that Hal's waywardness is heaven's punishment for the King's sins, or a hard-bitten politician engaged in a life-and-death struggle for power with aristocrats as Machiavellian as he. An important reason for the play's great success is its openness to interpretation.

In the Gad's Hill robbery, Falstaff reveals that his "cowardice" differs from the natural craven fear of Bardolph and Peto. He fights no longer than he sees "reason," that is, not against unfair odds such as two athletic young men in the dark (or later, at Shrewsbury, against the burly Scots giant, the Douglas). A man could get killed that way. Falstaff's cowardice, then, is philosophic, seen by himself in a humorous perspective. The same is true of his lying about the robbery. However much Hal exults in exposing Falstaff as a fraud, we cannot dismiss the possibility that Falstaff may see through the Prince's scheme, and may then feed Hal the expectedly outlandish lie (two men in buckram become eleven men) as a means of begging for affection. Falstaff's only way of pleading his cause is to tickle the Prince's fancy, in his role as a kind of court fool. What Falstaff most wants is to be loved and retained for what he is, and that, poignantly enough, is the one thing the mature Henry V cannot grant.

Throughout *1 Henry IV,* Shakespeare seems interested in the relationships between fathers and sons. These relationships help structure the comparisons and contrasts among foil characters. Falstaff is a foil, not only for Hotspur, but also for Henry IV; that is, despite all his insistence on youthful irresponsibility, Falstaff acts as a kind of parental figure to Hal. In the tavern scene (2.4), Falstaff and Hal take turns playing king and crown prince, and in both roles Falstaff wittily argues his case as companion and guide to the heir to the throne. Is it better to be old and merry, fat and loved, or to be hated like Pharaoh's lean kine? Falstaff argues against the gravity of council meetings with the same amused fervor that he later directs at the grinning honor of a dead hero. Hal, in his turn as king, questions the propriety of a "devil" haunting the crown prince "in the likeness of an old fat man," a "reverend Vice," a "gray Iniquity," a "father ruffian" (2.4.442–9). For all the good humor in this exchange, both men are asking whether Falstaff or King Henry serves Hal as the better model. Hal anticipates some of the very arguments his father will use against him next day at court, and, indeed, the insistent presence of that sober adult world makes itself felt even in the tavern. When, under the pressure of that looming responsibility, Falstaff's merrymaking turns to something like urgent self-

justification in his moving litany of appeals that Hal "banish not him thy Harry's company—banish plump Jack, and banish all the world," the Prince seems aware that he must face the consequences of his destiny. "I do, I will," he answers (lines 472–6), in a tone that can vary onstage (depending on the actor) from sober resolution to fond regret to awakening as from a dream.

Hotspur, too, is regarded as a son by more than one father. King Henry only half-jokingly wishes it could be proved that some night-tripping fairy had exchanged his Harry in the cradle for Harry Percy (1.1.85–9). Paradoxically, the King admires Hotspur all the more for standing up to him, just as another imperious father figure, Owen Glendower, bestows grudging but real admiration on Hotspur for his outspokenness (3.1.1–185). Hotspur's rebellious ways are cherished because they seem to promise manliness and fame; Hal's rebellious ways are feared and despised because they seem to reject the values of duty and leadership on which King Henry bases his self-respect. In these terms, the play must resolve Hal's coming of age, his acceptance of his role as true son of the King, and his proving his worth to the King. Hal must find his adult self—a self that differs greatly from that of King Henry—but must do so in a way that preserves the integrity of their relationship and the real debt he owes his father.

Prince Hal's uncertain journey toward maturity does not involve him in any significant relationships with women. His task is to fulfill what is expected of him as his father's son in a world of political and military conflict. Women stand on the periphery of affairs, as in *Richard II,* and yet the scenes in which they appear offer important perspectives on male competitiveness and ambition. Hotspur's wife, Kate, must put up with being condescended to and told little about men's doings; yet Hotspur's genuine fondness for her shows the best side of his personality, and her worries about his obsessive ways indicate that she understands him better than he understands himself. Mortimer's Welsh wife, too, introduces into this play an element of tenderness and anxious concern that is notably lacking in the earlier part of 3.1, when Hotspur cannot stop himself from quarreling pointlessly with his senior ally, Glendower. Hotspur's insensitivity to the Welsh lady's beautiful song is perhaps a key to his impending tragedy, for he is never a good listener. On a lower social scale, Mistress Quickly devotedly looks after Falstaff, only to be repaid with misogynistic insults that she does not appear to understand and with mooching that she recognizes all too well. Prince Hal, meantime, plays the role of intelligent observer of the battle of the sexes, even while he postpones his own engagement in that merry war. He must first sort out who he is in terms of male goals of career and success.

These conflicts surrounding Hal reach their climax and resolution at the field of Shrewsbury in Act 5. Hal's worth must be proven at Hotspur's expense. The rivalry between the two has been intense throughout the play, as seen for example in Hal's brilliant mimicking of Hotspur's devotion to bloodshed (2.4.101–8). Aware that his tarnished reputation puts him at a disadvantage, Hal speaks nobly of his rival and impresses even the adversarial camp with his regal bearing (5.1.83–100, 5.2.51–68). He rescues his father in the battle, thereby proving to King Henry that his son does not wish to supplant him, as he had feared. After the battle, Hal frees his Scottish adversary the Douglas in a display of princely magnificence, doing so with a more generous motive than Hotspur had displayed in his earlier release of the Douglas as his prisoner (1.3.259–62). Meantime, Hal has put considerable distance between himself and Falstaff, though sensitive still to the warmth of old memories. When he sees Hotspur and Fal-

staff on the ground together, both seemingly dead, Hal views as in a tableau the contrasting models between which he has shaped his own identity. Yet Falstaff is not dead. He rises to mutilate Hotspur's body and to claim the honor due Hal for Hotspur's death. For all Falstaff's witty commentary at the expense of honor, his own opposite course is unsuited to a time of war or to Hal's new public role. Falstaff's abuse of military conscription, his carrying a bottle of sack in place of a pistol, show him at his wittiest still, but in a world that may not tolerate such pranks. The merry games are out of place and childish. With characteristic generosity and imprudence, Hal gives the credit for Hotspur's death to Falstaff, who claims it so cravenly. Even so, the magic of their association has vanished. The time of adulthood is upon Hal.

The First Part of King Henry The Fourth

[*Dramatis Personae*

KING HENRY THE FOURTH
PRINCE HENRY, *Prince of Wales,* } *sons of the King*
PRINCE JOHN OF LANCASTER,
EARL OF WESTMORLAND
SIR WALTER BLUNT

EARL OF NORTHUMBERLAND, *Henry Percy,*
HARRY PERCY (HOTSPUR), *his son,*
EARL OF WORCESTER, *Northumberland's*
    younger brother,
LORD MORTIMER, *Edmund Mortimer*   *rebels*
    also referred to as the Earl of March,   *against*
OWEN GLENDOWER,   *the King*
EARL OF DOUGLAS, *Archibald Douglas,*
SIR RICHARD VERNON,
ARCHBISHOP OF YORK, *Richard Scroop,*
SIR MICHAEL, *a member of the*
    Archbishop's household,

LADY PERCY, *Hotspur's wife and Mortimer's sister*
LADY MORTIMER, *Mortimer's wife and Glendower's*
    daughter

SIR JOHN FALSTAFF
NED POINS
BARDOLPH
PETO
GADSHILL, *arranger of the highway robbery*
HOSTESS OF THE TAVERN, *Mistress Quickly*
FRANCIS, *a drawer, or tapster*
VINTNER, *or tavern keeper*

FIRST CARRIER
SECOND CARRIER
HOSTLER
CHAMBERLAIN
FIRST TRAVELER
SHERIFF
SERVANT *to Hotspur*
MESSENGER
SECOND MESSENGER

Soldiers, Travelers, Lords, Attendants

SCENE: *England and Wales*]

[1.1]

Enter the King, Lord John of Lancaster, [the] Earl
of Westmorland, [Sir Walter Blunt,] with others.

KING
So shaken as we are, so wan with care,
Find we a time for frighted peace to pant,   2
And breathe short-winded accents of new broils   3
To be commenced in strands afar remote.   4
No more the thirsty entrance of this soil   5
Shall daub her lips with her own children's blood;   6
No more shall trenching war channel her fields   7
Nor bruise her flowerets with the armèd hoofs
Of hostile paces. Those opposèd eyes,   9
Which, like the meteors of a troubled heaven,
All of one nature, of one substance bred,
Did lately meet in the intestine shock   12
And furious close of civil butchery,   13
Shall now in mutual well-beseeming ranks
March all one way and be no more opposed
Against acquaintance, kindred, and allies.
The edge of war, like an ill-sheathèd knife,
No more shall cut his master. Therefore, friends,   18
As far as to the sepulcher of Christ—
Whose soldier now, under whose blessèd cross
We are impressèd and engaged to fight—   21
Forthwith a power of English shall we levy,   22
Whose arms were molded in their mothers' womb   23
To chase these pagans in those holy fields
Over whose acres walked those blessèd feet
Which fourteen hundred years ago were nailed
For our advantage on the bitter cross.
But this our purpose now is twelve month old,
And bootless 'tis to tell you we will go.   29
Therefore we met not now. Then let me hear   30
Of you, my gentle cousin Westmorland,   31
What yesternight our council did decree
In forwarding this dear expedience.   33

WESTMORLAND
My liege, this haste was hot in question,   34
And many limits of the charge set down   35
But yesternight, when all athwart there came   36
A post from Wales loaden with heavy news,   37
Whose worst was that the noble Mortimer,
Leading the men of Herefordshire to fight
Against the irregular and wild Glendower,

Was by the rude hands of that Welshman taken,
A thousand of his people butcherèd—
Upon whose dead corpse there was such misuse,   43
Such beastly shameless transformation,   44
By those Welshwomen done as may not be
Without much shame retold or spoken of.

KING
It seems then that the tidings of this broil
Brake off our business for the Holy Land.

WESTMORLAND
This matched with other did, my gracious lord;   49
For more uneven and unwelcome news   50
Came from the north, and thus it did import:
On Holy Rood Day, the gallant Hotspur there,   52
Young Harry Percy, and brave Archibald,
That ever-valiant and approvèd Scot,   54
At Holmedon met, where they did spend   55
A sad and bloody hour,
As by discharge of their artillery   57
And shape of likelihood the news was told;   58
For he that brought them, in the very heat   59
And pride of their contention did take horse,   60
Uncertain of the issue any way.

KING
Here is a dear, a true industrious friend,   62
Sir Walter Blunt, new lighted from his horse,   63
Stained with the variation of each soil
Betwixt that Holmedon and this seat of ours;
And he hath brought us smooth and welcome news.   66
The Earl of Douglas is discomfited;   67
Ten thousand bold Scots, two-and-twenty knights,
Balked in their own blood, did Sir Walter see   69
On Holmedon's plains. Of prisoners, Hotspur took
Mordake, Earl of Fife and eldest son   71
To beaten Douglas, and the Earl of Atholl,
Of Murray, Angus, and Menteith.
And is not this an honorable spoil?
A gallant prize? Ha, cousin, is it not?

WESTMORLAND
In faith, it is a conquest for a prince to boast of.

KING
Yea, there thou mak'st me sad, and mak'st me sin
In envy that my lord Northumberland
Should be the father to so blest a son—
A son who is the theme of honor's tongue,
Amongst a grove the very straightest plant,   81
Who is sweet Fortune's minion and her pride,   82
Whilst I, by looking on the praise of him,
See riot and dishonor stain the brow   84
Of my young Harry. Oh, that it could be proved

1.1. Location: The royal court.
2 Find we let us find.   **frighted** frightened   **3 breathe short-winded
accents** speak, even though we are out of breath.   **accents** words.
broils battles   **4 strands afar remote** far-off shores, i.e., of the Holy
Land (to which, at the end of *Richard II*, Henry has pledged himself
to a crusade).   **5 thirsty entrance** i.e., parched mouth   **6 daub** coat,
smear   **7 trenching** cutting, plowing   **9 paces** horses' tread.
12 intestine internal   **13 close** hand-to-hand encounter.   **civil** (as in
"civil war")   **18 his** its   **21 impressèd** conscripted   **22 power** army
23 their mother's i.e., England's, but also suggesting *their mothers'*
29 bootless useless   **30 Therefore . . . now** That is not the reason for
our present meeting.   **31 Of** from.   **gentle cousin** noble kinsman
33 dear expedience urgent expedition.   **34 hot in question** being
hotly debated   **35 limits . . . charge** particulars of military responsibility   **36 athwart** at cross purposes, contrarily   **37 post** messenger.
loaden laden

43 corpse corpses   **44 transformation** mutilation   **49 other** other
news   **50 uneven** disconcerting, distressing   **52 Holy Rood Day**
September 14   **54 approvèd** proved by experience   **55 Holmedon**
Humbleton in Northumberland   **57 by** judging from   **58 shape of
likelihood** likely outcome   **59 them** the news   **60 pride** height
62–3 Here . . . Blunt (Whether Blunt enters at the start of the scene,
or now, or possibly not at all, is not certain in the original text.)
66 smooth pleasant   **67 discomfited** defeated   **69 Balked** heaped up
in balks, or ridges   **71 Mordake** i.e., Murdoch, son of the Earl of
Albany   **81 plant** young tree   **82 minion** favorite   **84 riot** debauchery

That some night-tripping fairy had exchanged 86
In cradle clothes our children where they lay,
And called mine Percy, his Plantagenet! 88
Then would I have his Harry, and he mine.
But let him from my thoughts. What think you, coz, 90
Of this young Percy's pride? The prisoners
Which he in this adventure hath surprised 92
To his own use he keeps, and sends me word 93
I shall have none but Mordake, Earl of Fife. 94

WESTMORLAND
This is his uncle's teaching. This is Worcester,
Malevolent to you in all aspects, 96
Which makes him prune himself and bristle up 97
The crest of youth against your dignity.

KING
But I have sent for him to answer this;
And for this cause awhile we must neglect
Our holy purpose to Jerusalem.
Cousin, on Wednesday next our council we
Will hold at Windsor. So inform the lords.
But come yourself with speed to us again,
For more is to be said and to be done
Than out of anger can be utterèd.

WESTMORLAND   I will, my liege.   *Exeunt.*

❖

[1.2]

Enter Prince of Wales and Sir John Falstaff.

FALSTAFF
Now, Hal, what time of day is it, lad?

PRINCE   Thou art so fat-witted with drinking of old sack, 2
and unbuttoning thee after supper, and sleeping upon
benches after noon, that thou hast forgotten to de- 4
mand that truly which thou wouldst truly know. What
a devil hast thou to do with the time of the day? Unless 6
hours were cups of sack, and minutes capons, and
clocks the tongues of bawds, and dials the signs of 8
leaping houses, and the blessèd sun himself a fair hot 9
wench in flame-colored taffeta, I see no reason why 10
thou shouldst be so superfluous to demand the time 11
of the day.

FALSTAFF   Indeed, you come near me now, Hal, for we 13
that take purses go by the moon and the seven stars, 14

and not by Phoebus, "he, that wandering knight so 15
fair." And I prithee, sweet wag, when thou art king, 16
as, God save Thy Grace—Majesty I should say, for 17
grace thou wilt have none—

PRINCE   What, none?

FALSTAFF   No, by my troth, not so much as will serve to 20
be prologue to an egg and butter. 21

PRINCE   Well, how then? Come, roundly, roundly. 22

FALSTAFF   Marry, then, sweet wag, when thou art king, let 23
not us that are squires of the night's body be 24
called thieves of the day's beauty. Let us be Diana's for- 25
esters, gentlemen of the shade, minions of the moon; 26
and let men say we be men of good government, 27
being governed, as the sea is, by our noble and chaste
mistress the moon, under whose countenance we steal. 29

PRINCE   Thou sayest well, and it holds well too, for the 30
fortune of us that are the moon's men doth ebb and
flow like the sea, being governed, as the sea is, by the
moon. As, for proof, now: a purse of gold most
resolutely snatched on Monday night and most disso-
lutely spent on Tuesday morning, got with swearing
"Lay by" and spent with crying "Bring in," now in as 36
low an ebb as the foot of the ladder and by and by in 37
as high a flow as the ridge of the gallows. 38

FALSTAFF   By the Lord, thou say'st true, lad. And is not
my hostess of the tavern a most sweet wench?

PRINCE   As the honey of Hybla, my old lad of the castle. 41
And is not a buff jerkin a most sweet robe of durance? 42

FALSTAFF   How now, how now, mad wag, what, in thy
quips and thy quiddities? What a plague have I to do 44
with a buff jerkin?

PRINCE   Why, what a pox have I to do with my hostess 46
of the tavern?

FALSTAFF   Well, thou hast called her to a reckoning many 48
a time and oft.

PRINCE   Did I ever call for thee to pay thy part?

FALSTAFF   No, I'll give thee thy due, thou hast paid all
there.

PRINCE   Yea, and elsewhere, so far as my coin would
stretch, and where it would not I have used my credit.

---

86 night-tripping i.e., moving nimbly in the night   **88 Plantagenet** (Family name of English royalty since Henry II.)   **90 let him** let him go.   **coz** cousin, i.e., kinsman   **92 surprised** ambushed, captured   **93 To ... use** i.e., to collect ransom for them   **94 none but Mordake** (Since Mordake was of royal blood, being grandson to Robert II of Scotland, Hotspur could not claim him as his prisoner according to the law of arms.)   **96 Malevolent ... aspects** (1) implacably hostile to you (2) in astrological terms, a planet in a disobedient orbit, ominous as seen from every angle   **97 Which ... himself** i.e., which teaching makes Hotspur preen himself (as a falcon preens its feathers).   **1.2. Location: London, perhaps in an apartment of the Prince's.**   **2 sack** a Spanish white wine   **4 forgotten** forgotten how   **6 a devil** in the devil   **8 dials** clocks   **9 leaping houses** houses of prostitution   **10 taffeta** (Commonly worn by prostitutes.)   **11 superfluous** (1) unnecessarily concerned (2) self-indulgent   **13 you ... now** i.e., you've scored a point on me   **14 go by** (1) travel by the light of (2) tell time by.   **the seven stars** the Pleiades

15–16 Phoebus ... fair (Phoebus, god of the sun, is here equated with the wandering knight of a ballad or popular romance.)   **17 Grace** royal highness. (With pun on spiritual *grace* and also on the *grace* or blessing before a meal.)   **20 troth** faith   **21 prologue ... butter** i.e., grace before a brief meal.   **22 roundly** i.e., out with it.   **23 Marry** Indeed. (Literally, "by the Virgin Mary.")   **wag** joker   **24–5 let ... beauty** i.e., let not us who are attendants on the goddess of night, members of her household, be blamed for stealing daylight by sleeping in the daytime.   **25–6 Diana's foresters** (An elegant name for thieves by night; Diana is goddess of the moon and the hunt.)   **26 minions** favorites   **27 government** (1) conduct (2) commonwealth   **29 countenance** (1) face (2) patronage, approval.   **steal** (1) move stealthily (2) rob.   **30 it holds well** the comparison is apt   **36 Lay by** (A cry of highwaymen, like "Hands up!")   **Bring in** (An order given to a waiter in a tavern.)   **37 ladder** (1) pier ladder (2) gallows ladder   **38 ridge** crossbar   **41 Hybla** (A town, famed for its honey, in Sicily near Syracuse.)   **old ... castle** (1) a roisterer (2) the name, Sir John Oldcastle, borne by Falstaff in an earlier version of this play.   **42 buff jerkin** a leather jacket worn by officers of the law.   **durance** (1) imprisonment (2) durability, durable cloth.   **44 quiddities** subtleties of speech.   **46 pox** syphilis. (Here, *what a pox* is used as an expletive, like "what the devil.")   **48 reckoning** settlement of the bill. (With bawdy suggestion that is continued in *pay thy part* and *my coin would stretch*.)

FALSTAFF   Yea, and so used it that, were it not here apparent that thou art heir apparent—But I prithee, sweet wag, shall there be gallows standing in England when thou art king? And resolution thus fubbed as it 58 is with the rusty curb of old father Antic the law? Do 59 not thou, when thou art king, hang a thief.

PRINCE   No, thou shalt.

FALSTAFF   Shall I? Oh, rare! By the Lord, I'll be a brave 62 judge.

PRINCE   Thou judgest false already. I mean, thou shalt have the hanging of the thieves, and so become a rare 65 hangman.

FALSTAFF   Well, Hal, well; and in some sort it jumps 67 with my humor as well as waiting in the court, I can 68 tell you.

PRINCE   For obtaining of suits?   70

FALSTAFF   Yea, for obtaining of suits, whereof the hangman hath no lean wardrobe. 'Sblood, I am as 72 melancholy as a gib cat or a lugged bear.   73

PRINCE   Or an old lion, or a lover's lute.

FALSTAFF   Yea, or the drone of a Lincolnshire bagpipe.

PRINCE   What sayest thou to a hare, or the melancholy 76 of Moorditch?   77

FALSTAFF   Thou hast the most unsavory similes, and art indeed the most comparative, rascalliest, sweet young 79 prince. But Hal, I prithee, trouble me no more with vanity. I would to God thou and I knew where a com- 81 modity of good names were to be bought. An old lord 82 of the council rated me the other day in the street 83 about you, sir, but I marked him not; and yet he talked very wisely, but I regarded him not; and yet he talked wisely, and in the street too.

PRINCE   Thou didst well, for wisdom cries out in the 87 streets and no man regards it.   88

FALSTAFF   Oh, thou hast damnable iteration, and art 89 indeed able to corrupt a saint. Thou hast done much harm upon me, Hal, God forgive thee for it. Before I knew thee, Hal, I knew nothing; and now am I, if a 92 man should speak truly, little better than one of the wicked. I must give over this life, and I will give it over. By the Lord, an I do not I am a villain. I'll be 95 damned for never a king's son in Christendom.

PRINCE   Where shall we take a purse tomorrow, Jack?

FALSTAFF   Zounds, where thou wilt, lad, I'll make one. 98 An I do not, call me villain and baffle me.   99

PRINCE   I see a good amendment of life in thee—from praying to purse taking.

FALSTAFF   Why, Hal, 'tis my vocation, Hal. 'Tis no sin 102 for a man to labor in his vocation.   103

Enter Poins.

Poins! Now shall we know if Gadshill have set a 104 match. Oh, if men were to be saved by merit, what 105 hole in hell were hot enough for him? This is the most omnipotent villain that ever cried "Stand!" to a 107 true man.   108

PRINCE   Good morrow, Ned.

POINS   Good morrow, sweet Hal.—What says Monsieur Remorse? What says Sir John, Sack-and-Sugar Jack? How agrees the devil and thee about thy soul that thou soldest him on Good Friday last for a cup of Madeira and a cold capon's leg?

PRINCE   Sir John stands to his word; the devil shall have 115 his bargain, for he was never yet a breaker of proverbs. He will give the devil his due.

POINS   Then art thou damned for keeping thy word with the devil.

PRINCE   Else he had been damned for cozening the 120 devil.

POINS   But my lads, my lads, tomorrow morning, by four o'clock early, at Gad's Hill, there are pilgrims 123 going to Canterbury with rich offerings and traders riding to London with fat purses. I have vizards for 125 you all; you have horses for yourselves. Gadshill lies 126 tonight in Rochester. I have bespoke supper tomorrow 127 night in Eastcheap. We may do it as secure as sleep. If 128 you will go, I will stuff your purses full of crowns; if 129 you will not, tarry at home and be hanged.

FALSTAFF   Hear ye, Yedward, if I tarry at home and go 131 not, I'll hang you for going.   132

POINS   You will, chops?   133

FALSTAFF   Hal, wilt thou make one?

PRINCE   Who, I rob? I a thief? Not I, by my faith.

FALSTAFF   There's neither honesty, manhood, nor good fellowship in thee, nor thou cam'st not of the blood royal, if thou darest not stand for ten shillings. 138

PRINCE   Well then, once in my days I'll be a madcap.

FALSTAFF   Why, that's well said.

PRINCE   Well, come what will, I'll tarry at home.

FALSTAFF   By the Lord, I'll be a traitor then, when thou art king.

PRINCE   I care not.

POINS   Sir John, I prithee leave the Prince and me alone. I will lay him down such reasons for this adventure that he shall go.

FALSTAFF   Well, God give thee the spirit of persuasion and him the ears of profiting, that what thou speakest may move and what he hears may be believed, that the true prince may, for recreation sake, prove a false thief; for the poor abuses of the time want counte- 152
nance. Farewell. You shall find me in Eastcheap. 153

PRINCE   Farewell, thou latter spring! Farewell, All- 154
hallown summer!   [*Exit Falstaff.*] 155

POINS   Now, my good sweet honey lord, ride with us tomorrow. I have a jest to execute that I cannot manage alone. Falstaff, Peto, Bardolph, and Gadshill shall rob those men that we have already waylaid— 159
yourself and I will not be there—and when they have the booty, if you and I do not rob them, cut this head off from my shoulders.

PRINCE   How shall we part with them in setting forth?

POINS   Why, we will set forth before or after them and appoint them a place of meeting, wherein it is at our pleasure to fail; and then will they adventure upon the 166
exploit themselves, which they shall have no sooner achieved but we'll set upon them.

PRINCE   Yea, but 'tis like that they will know us by our 169
horses, by our habits, and by every other appoint- 170
ment, to be ourselves. 171

POINS   Tut, our horses they shall not see—I'll tie them in the wood; our vizards we will change after we leave them; and, sirrah, I have cases of buckram for the 174
nonce, to immask our noted outward garments. 175

PRINCE   Yea, but I doubt they will be too hard for us. 176

POINS   Well, for two of them, I know them to be as true-bred cowards as ever turned back; and for the 178
third, if he fight longer than he sees reason, I'll for-swear arms. The virtue of this jest will be the incompre- 180
hensible lies that this same fat rogue will tell us when 181
we meet at supper—how thirty at least he fought with, what wards, what blows, what extremities he 183
endured; and in the reproof of this lives the jest. 184

PRINCE   Well, I'll go with thee. Provide us all things necessary and meet me tomorrow night in Eastcheap. There I'll sup. Farewell.

POINS   Farewell, my lord.   *Exit Poins.*

PRINCE
I know you all, and will awhile uphold
The unyoked humor of your idleness. 190
Yet herein will I imitate the sun,
Who doth permit the base contagious clouds 192
To smother up his beauty from the world,
That when he please again to be himself, 194
Being wanted he may be more wondered at 195
By breaking through the foul and ugly mists
Of vapors that did seem to strangle him.
If all the year were playing holidays,
To sport would be as tedious as to work;
But when they seldom come, they wished-for come,
And nothing pleaseth but rare accidents. 201
So when this loose behavior I throw off
And pay the debt I never promisèd,
By how much better than my word I am,
By so much shall I falsify men's hopes; 205
And like bright metal on a sullen ground, 206
My reformation, glitt'ring o'er my fault,
Shall show more goodly and attract more eyes
Than that which hath no foil to set it off. 209
I'll so offend to make offense a skill, 210
Redeeming time when men think least I will.   *Exit.* 211

[1.3]

*Enter the King, Northumberland, Worcester,
Hotspur, Sir Walter Blunt, with others.*

KING
My blood hath been too cold and temperate,
Unapt to stir at these indignities,
And you have found me, for accordingly 3
You tread upon my patience. But be sure
I will from henceforth rather be myself, 5
Mighty and to be feared, than my condition, 6
Which hath been smooth as oil, soft as young down,
And therefore lost that title of respect
Which the proud soul ne'er pays but to the proud.

WORCESTER
Our house, my sovereign liege, little deserves 10
The scourge of greatness to be used on it—
And that same greatness too which our own hands
Have holp to make so portly. 13

NORTHUMBERLAND [*to the King*]   My lord—

KING
Worcester, get thee gone, for I do see

152–3 want countenance lack sponsorship (from men of rank).
154–5 All-hallown summer a season of clement weather around All
Saints' Day, November 1; the *latter spring* or "Indian summer" of Falstaff's old age.   **159 waylaid** set an ambush for   **166 pleasure** choice,
discretion   **169 like** likely   **170 habits** garments   **170–1 appointment** accoutrement   **174 sirrah** (Usually addressed to an inferior;
here, a sign of intimacy.)   **174–5 cases . . . nonce** suits of buckram, a
stiff-finished heavily sized fabric, for the purpose   **175 immask** hide,
disguise.   **noted** known   **176 doubt** fear.   **too hard** too formidable
178 turned back turned their backs and ran away   **180–1 incomprehensible** boundless   **183 wards** parries   **184 reproof** disproof

190 unyoked . . . idleness unbridled inclination of your frivolity.
192 contagious noxious   **194 That** so that   **195 wanted** missed,
lacked   **201 accidents** events.   **205 hopes** expectations   **206 sullen
ground** dark background, like a *foil*. (See line 209.)   **209 foil** metal
sheet laid contrastingly behind a jewel to set off its luster   **210 to** as
to.   **skill** i.e., clever tactic, piece of good policy   **211 Redeeming
time** i.e., making amends for lost time
1.3. Location: London. The court (historically at Windsor).
3 found me found me so   **5 myself** i.e., my royal self   **6 my condition** my natural (mild) disposition   **10 Our house** i.e., The Percy
family   **13 holp** helped.   **portly** majestic, prosperous.

Danger and disobedience in thine eye.
Oh, sir, your presence is too bold and peremptory,
And majesty might never yet endure
The moody frontier of a servant brow.   19
You have good leave to leave us. When we need   20
Your use and counsel, we shall send for you.

                                                        Exit Worcester.
[*To Northumberland*] You were about to speak.

NORTHUMBERLAND   Yea, my good lord.
Those prisoners in Your Highness' name demanded,
Which Harry Percy here at Holmedon took,
Were, as he says, not with such strength denied
As is delivered to Your Majesty.   26
Either envy, therefore, or misprision   27
Is guilty of this fault, and not my son.

HOTSPUR [*to the King*]
My liege, I did deny no prisoners.
But I remember when the fight was done,
When I was dry with rage and extreme toil,
Breathless and faint, leaning upon my sword,
Came there a certain lord, neat and trimly dressed,
Fresh as a bridegroom, and his chin new reaped   34
Showed like a stubble land at harvest home.   35
He was perfumèd like a milliner,   36
And twixt his finger and his thumb he held
A pouncet box, which ever and anon   38
He gave his nose and took't away again,
Who therewith angry, when it next came there,   40
Took it in snuff; and still he smiled and talked,   41
And as the soldiers bore dead bodies by
He called them untaught knaves, unmannerly,
To bring a slovenly unhandsome corpse
Betwixt the wind and his nobility.
With many holiday and lady terms   46
He questioned me, amongst the rest demanded
My prisoners in Your Majesty's behalf.
I then, all smarting with my wounds being cold,
To be so pestered with a popinjay,   50
Out of my grief and my impatience   51
Answered neglectingly I know not what,
He should, or he should not; for he made me mad
To see him shine so brisk, and smell so sweet,
And talk so like a waiting-gentlewoman
Of guns and drums and wounds—God save the
   mark!—   56
And telling me the sovereignest thing on earth   57
Was parmacety for an inward bruise,   58

And that it was great pity, so it was,
This villainous saltpeter should be digged   60
Out of the bowels of the harmless earth,
Which many a good tall fellow had destroyed   62
So cowardly, and but for these vile guns
He would himself have been a soldier.
This bald unjointed chat of his, my lord,   65
I answered indirectly, as I said,   66
And I beseech you, let not his report
Come current for an accusation   68
Betwixt my love and your high majesty.

BLUNT [*to the King*]
The circumstance considered, good my lord,
Whate'er Lord Harry Percy then had said
To such a person and in such a place,
At such a time, with all the rest retold,
May reasonably die, and never rise
To do him wrong or any way impeach   75
What then he said, so he unsay it now.   76

KING
Why, yet he doth deny his prisoners,   77
But with proviso and exception   78
That we at our own charge shall ransom straight   79
His brother-in-law, the foolish Mortimer,   80
Who, on my soul, hath willfully betrayed
The lives of those that he did lead to fight
Against that great magician, damned Glendower,
Whose daughter, as we hear, that Earl of March   84
Hath lately married. Shall our coffers then
Be emptied to redeem a traitor home?
Shall we buy treason and indent with fears   87
When they have lost and forfeited themselves?
No, on the barren mountains let him starve!
For I shall never hold that man my friend
Whose tongue shall ask me for one penny cost
To ransom home revolted Mortimer.   92

HOTSPUR   Revolted Mortimer?
He never did fall off, my sovereign liege,   94
But by the chance of war. To prove that true
Needs no more but one tongue for all those wounds,
Those mouthèd wounds, which valiantly he took, 97
When on the gentle Severn's sedgy bank,   98
In single opposition, hand to hand,

---

19 **moody frontier** i.e., angry brow, frown. (*Frontier* literally means
"outwork" or "fortification.")   20 **good leave** full permission
26 **delivered** reported   27 **envy** malice.   **misprision** misunderstanding   34 **chin new reaped** i.e., with beard freshly barbered according
to the latest fashion, not like a soldier's beard   35 **Showed** looked.
harvest home end of harvest, fields being cut back to stubble.
36 **milliner** dealer in fancy articles, such as gloves and hats
38 **pouncet box** perfume box with perforated lid   40 **Who** i.e., his
nose   41 **Took it in snuff** (1) inhaled it (2) took offense.   **still** continually   46 **holiday and lady** dainty and effeminate   50 **popinjay** parrot   51 **grief** pain   56 **God . . . mark** (Probably originally a formula to
avert evil omen; here, an expression of impatience.)   57 **sovereignest**
most efficacious   58 **parmacety** spermaceti, a fatty substance taken
from the head of the sperm whale, used as a medicinal ointment

60 **saltpeter** potassium nitrate, used to make gunpowder and also
used medicinally   62 **tall** brave   65 **bald** trivial   66 **indirectly** inat-
tentively, offhandedly   68 **Come current** (1) be taken at face value
(2) come rushing in   75 **impeach** discredit   76 **so** provided that
77 **yet** (emphatic) i.e., even now.   **deny** refuse to surrender   78 **proviso and exception** (synonymous terms)   79 **straight** straightway, at
once   80 **Mortimer** (There were two Edmund Mortimers; Shakespeare confuses them and combines their stories. It was the uncle
[1376–1409?] who was captured by Glendower and married Glendower's daughter; it was the nephew [1391–1425], fifth Earl of March,
who was proclaimed heir presumptive to King Richard II after the
death of his father, the fourth earl, whom Richard had named as his
heir. The uncle was brother to the fourth earl and to Hotspur's wife,
Elizabeth, called Kate in this play.)   84 **Earl of March** (The "Mortimer" of line 80; see note there.)   87 **indent with fears** i.e., make a
bargain or come to terms with traitors whom we have reason to fear
92 **revolted** rebellious   94 **fall off** change his allegiance
97 **mouthèd** gaping and eloquent   98 **Severn's** (The Severn River
flows from northern Wales and western England into the Bristol
Channel.)   **sedgy** bordered with reeds

He did confound the best part of an hour　　100
In changing hardiment with great Glendower.　　101
Three times they breathed, and three times did they
　　drink,　　102
Upon agreement, of swift Severn's flood,　　103
Who then, affrighted with their bloody looks,　　104
Ran fearfully among the trembling reeds
And hid his crisp head in the hollow bank,　　106
Bloodstainèd with these valiant combatants.
Never did bare and rotten policy　　108
Color her working with such deadly wounds,　　109
Nor never could the noble Mortimer
Receive so many, and all willingly.
Then let not him be slandered with revolt.　　112

KING
Thou dost belie him, Percy, thou dost belie him.
He never did encounter with Glendower.
I tell thee,
He durst as well have met the devil alone
As Owen Glendower for an enemy.
Art thou not ashamed? But, sirrah, henceforth
Let me not hear you speak of Mortimer.
Send me your prisoners with the speediest means,
Or you shall hear in such a kind from me　　121
As will displease you.—My lord Northumberland,
We license your departure with your son.
Send us your prisoners, or you will hear of it.

　　　　　　Exit King [with Blunt, and train].

HOTSPUR
An if the devil come and roar for them　　125
I will not send them. I will after straight　　126
And tell him so, for I will ease my heart,
Albeit I make a hazard of my head.　　128

NORTHUMBERLAND
What, drunk with choler? Stay and pause awhile.　　129
Here comes your uncle.

　　　　Enter Worcester.

HOTSPUR　　　　　　　　Speak of Mortimer?
Zounds, I will speak of him, and let my soul
Want mercy if I do not join with him!
Yea, on his part I'll empty all these veins,　　132
And shed my dear blood drop by drop in the dust,　　133
But I will lift the downtrod Mortimer
As high in the air as this unthankful king,
As this ingrate and cankered Bolingbroke.　　137

NORTHUMBERLAND
Brother, the King hath made your nephew mad.

WORCESTER
Who struck this heat up after I was gone?

HOTSPUR
He will forsooth have all my prisoners;
And when I urged the ransom once again
Of my wife's brother, then his cheek looked pale,
And on my face he turned an eye of death,　　143
Trembling even at the name of Mortimer.

WORCESTER
I cannot blame him. Was not he proclaimed　　145
By Richard, that dead is, the next of blood?　　146

NORTHUMBERLAND
He was; I heard the proclamation.
And then it was when the unhappy king—　　148
Whose wrongs in us God pardon!—did set forth　　149
Upon his Irish expedition;　　150
From whence he, intercepted, did return　　151
To be deposed and shortly murderèd.

WORCESTER
And for whose death we in the world's wide mouth
Live scandalized and foully spoken of.

HOTSPUR
But, soft, I pray you, did King Richard then　　155
Proclaim my brother Edmund Mortimer　　156
Heir to the crown?

NORTHUMBERLAND　　He did; myself did hear it.

HOTSPUR
Nay, then I cannot blame his cousin king,　　158
That wished him on the barren mountains starve.
But shall it be that you that set the crown
Upon the head of this forgetful man,
And for his sake wear the detested blot
Of murderous subornation—shall it be　　163
That you a world of curses undergo,
Being the agents, or base second means,　　165
The cords, the ladder, or the hangman rather?
Oh, pardon me that I descend so low
To show the line and the predicament　　168
Wherein you range under this subtle king!　　169
Shall it for shame be spoken in these days,
Or fill up chronicles in time to come,
That men of your nobility and power
Did gage them both in an unjust behalf,　　173
As both of you—God pardon it!—have done,
To put down Richard, that sweet lovely rose,
And plant this thorn, this canker, Bolingbroke?　　176
And shall it in more shame be further spoken
That you are fooled, discarded, and shook off
By him for whom these shames ye underwent?
No! Yet time serves wherein you may redeem　　180
Your banished honors and restore yourselves

100 confound consume　**101 changing hardiment** exchanging blows, matching valor　**102 breathed** paused for breath　**103 flood** river **104 Who** i.e., the river　**106 crisp** curly, i.e., rippled　**108 bare** paltry. **policy** cunning　**109 Color** disguise　**112 revolt** i.e., the accusation of rebellion.　**121 kind** manner　**125 An if** If　**126 will after straight** will go after him immediately　**128 Albeit . . . head** even if I risk being beheaded.　**129 choler** anger.　**132 Want mercy** lack mercy, be damned　**133 on his part** i.e., fighting on Mortimer's side **137 cankered** spoiled, malignant.　**Bolingbroke** i.e., King Henry IV. (Hotspur pointedly refuses to acknowledge his royalty.)

143 an eye of death a fearful look　**145 he** i.e., Mortimer　**146 next of blood** heir to the throne.　**148 unhappy** unfortunate　**149 in us** caused by our doings　**150 Irish expedition** (Richard II was putting down a rebellion in Ireland when Bolingbroke returned to England from exile.)　**151 intercepted** interrupted　**155 soft** i.e., wait a minute　**156 brother** brother-in-law　**158 cousin** (With a pun on cozen, "cheat.")　**163 murderous subornation** the suborning of, or inciting to, murder　**165 second means** agents　**168 To . . . predicament** to show the direction things are moving and the danger to you **169 range** (1) are ranked; (2) stray　**173 gage them** engage, pledge themselves　**176 canker** (1) canker rose or dog rose, wild and unfragrant (2) ulcer　**180 Yet** Still

Into the good thoughts of the world again;
Revenge the jeering and disdained contempt 183
Of this proud king, who studies day and night
To answer all the debt he owes to you 185
Even with the bloody payment of your deaths.
Therefore, I say—

WORCESTER   Peace, cousin, say no more. 187
And now I will unclasp a secret book,
And to your quick-conceiving discontents 189
I'll read you matter deep and dangerous,
As full of peril and adventurous spirit
As to o'erwalk a current roaring loud
On the unsteadfast footing of a spear. 193

HOTSPUR
If he fall in, good night, or sink or swim! 194
Send danger from the east unto the west,
So honor cross it from the north to south, 196
And let them grapple. Oh, the blood more stirs
To rouse a lion than to start a hare!

NORTHUMBERLAND [*to Worcester*]
Imagination of some great exploit
Drives him beyond the bounds of patience.

HOTSPUR
By heaven, methinks it were an easy leap
To pluck bright honor from the pale-faced moon,
Or dive into the bottom of the deep,
Where fathom line could never touch the ground, 204
And pluck up drownèd honor by the locks,
So he that doth redeem her thence might wear
Without corrival all her dignities; 207
But out upon this half-faced fellowship! 208

WORCESTER [*to Northumberland*]
He apprehends a world of figures here, 209
But not the form of what he should attend.— 210
Good cousin, give me audience for a while.

HOTSPUR
I cry you mercy.

WORCESTER   Those same noble Scots 212
That are your prisoners—

HOTSPUR   I'll keep them all.
By God, he shall not have a Scot of them, 214
No, if a scot would save his soul, he shall not! 215
I'll keep them, by this hand.

WORCESTER   You start away
And lend no ear unto my purposes.
Those prisoners you shall keep.

HOTSPUR   Nay, I will, that's flat. 218

He said he would not ransom Mortimer,
Forbade my tongue to speak of Mortimer,
But I will find him when he lies asleep,
And in his ear I'll holler "Mortimer!"
Nay, I'll have a starling shall be taught to speak
Nothing but "Mortimer," and give it him
To keep his anger still in motion. 225

WORCESTER   Hear you, cousin, a word.

HOTSPUR
All studies here I solemnly defy, 227
Save how to gall and pinch this Bolingbroke,
And that same sword-and-buckler Prince of Wales. 229
But that I think his father loves him not
And would be glad he met with some mischance,
I would have him poisoned with a pot of ale.

WORCESTER
Farewell, kinsman. I'll talk to you
When you are better tempered to attend.

NORTHUMBERLAND [*to Hotspur*]
Why, what a wasp-stung and impatient fool
Art thou to break into this woman's mood,
Tying thine ear to no tongue but thine own!

HOTSPUR
Why, look you, I am whipped and scourged with rods,
Nettled and stung with pismires, when I hear 239
Of this vile politician, Bolingbroke. 240
In Richard's time—what do you call the place?—
A plague upon it, it is in Gloucestershire;
'Twas where the madcap duke his uncle kept, 243
His uncle York; where I first bowed my knee
Unto this king of smiles, this Bolingbroke—
'Sblood, when you and he came back from
    Ravenspurgh. 246

NORTHUMBERLAND   At Berkeley Castle. 247

HOTSPUR   You say true.
Why, what a candy deal of courtesy 249
This fawning greyhound then did proffer me!
"Look when his infant fortune came to age," 251
And "gentle Harry Percy," and "kind cousin"—
Oh, the devil take such cozeners!—God forgive me! 253
Good uncle, tell your tale; I have done.

WORCESTER
Nay, if you have not, to it again;
We will stay your leisure.

HOTSPUR   I have done, i'faith. 256

WORCESTER
Then once more to your Scottish prisoners.
Deliver them up without their ransom straight, 258
And make the Douglas' son your only mean 259

---

183 Revenge and wherein you may revenge yourself against.
disdained disdainful   **185 answer** satisfy, discharge   **187 cousin**
nephew   **189 quick-conceiving** comprehending quickly   **193 spear**
i.e., spear laid across a stream as a narrow bridge.   **194 If . . . swim** i.e.,
Anyone daring such a thing will face a life-or-death challenge. (Hotspur's imagination is fired by the thought of risking everything on such
an attempt.)   **196 So** provided that. (Also at line 206.)   **204 fathom
line** a weighted line marked at fathom intervals (six feet), used for
measuring the depth of water   **207 corrival** rival, competitor
208 out . . . fellowship! down with this paltry business of sharing glory
with others!   **209 apprehends** snatches at.   **figures** figures of the
imagination, or figures of speech   **210 form** essential nature.   **attend**
give attention to.   **212 cry you mercy** beg your pardon.   **214–15 Scot
. . . scot** Scotsman . . . trifling amount   **218 that's flat** that's for sure.

225 still continually   **227 studies** pursuits.   **defy** renounce
229 sword-and-buckler swashbuckling. (Gentlemen generally preferred
to wear the rapier and the dagger.)   **239 Nettled** stung with nettles.
pismires ants. (From the urinous smell of an anthill.)   **240 politician**
deceitful schemer   **243 kept** dwelled   **246 Ravenspurgh** on the
Yorkshire coast, at the mouth of the Humber River, where Bolingbroke
landed on his return from exile (*Richard II*, 2.1.296).   **247 Berkeley
Castle** castle near Bristol.   **249 candy** sugared, flattering   **251 Look
when** When, as soon as   **253 cozeners** cheats. (With pun on *cousins*.)
256 stay await   **258 Deliver them up** Free them   **259 the Douglas' son**
i.e., Mordake. (See 1.1.71 and note.)   **mean** i.e., agent

For powers in Scotland, which, for divers reasons   260
Which I shall send you written, be assured
Will easily be granted. [*To Northumberland*] You, my
    lord,
Your son in Scotland being thus employed,
Shall secretly into the bosom creep   264
Of that same noble prelate well beloved,
The Archbishop.
HOTSPUR   Of York, is it not?
WORCESTER   True, who bears hard   268
His brother's death at Bristol, the Lord Scroop.
I speak not this in estimation,   270
As what I think might be, but what I know
Is ruminated, plotted, and set down,
And only stays but to behold the face
Of that occasion that shall bring it on.
HOTSPUR
I smell it. Upon my life, it will do well.
NORTHUMBERLAND
Before the game is afoot thou still let'st slip.   276
HOTSPUR
Why, it cannot choose but be a noble plot.   277
And then the power of Scotland and of York   278
To join with Mortimer, ha?
WORCESTER   And so they shall.
HOTSPUR
In faith, it is exceedingly well aimed.   280
WORCESTER
And 'tis no little reason bids us speed,
To save our heads by raising of a head;   282
For, bear ourselves as even as we can,   283
The King will always think him in our debt,   284
And think we think ourselves unsatisfied
Till he hath found a time to pay us home.   286
And see already how he doth begin
To make us strangers to his looks of love.
HOTSPUR
He does, he does. We'll be revenged on him.
WORCESTER
Cousin, farewell. No further go in this
Than I by letters shall direct your course.
When time is ripe, which will be suddenly,   292
I'll steal to Glendower and Lord Mortimer,
Where you and Douglas and our powers at once,   294
As I will fashion it, shall happily meet   295
To bear our fortunes in our own strong arms,   296
Which now we hold at much uncertainty.
NORTHUMBERLAND
Farewell, good brother. We shall thrive, I trust.
HOTSPUR
Uncle, adieu. Oh, let the hours be short
Till fields and blows and groans applaud our sport!   300
                          Exeunt [*in separate groups*].

❦

260 For powers for raising an army   264 secretly . . . creep win the confidence   268 bears hard resents   270 estimation guesswork   276 still let'st slip always let loose the dogs   277 cannot choose but be cannot help being   278 power army   280 aimed designed   282 head army   283 even carefully   284 him himself   286 home (1) fully (2) with a thrust to the heart.   292 suddenly soon   294 at once all together   295 happily fortunately   296 arms (1) limbs (2) military might   300 fields battlefields

[2.1]

Enter a Carrier with a lantern in his hand.

FIRST CARRIER   Heigh-ho! An it be not four by the day,   1
I'll be hanged. Charles's Wain is over the new   2
chimney, and yet our horse not packed. What, hostler!   3
HOSTLER [*within*]   Anon, anon.   4
FIRST CARRIER   I prithee, Tom, beat Cut's saddle, put a   5
few flocks in the point. Poor jade is wrung in the   6
withers out of all cess.   7

Enter another Carrier.

SECOND CARRIER   Peas and beans are as dank here as a   8
dog, and that is the next way to give poor jades the   9
bots. This house is turned upside down since Robin   10
Hostler died.
FIRST CARRIER   Poor fellow never joyed since the price
of oats rose. It was the death of him.
SECOND CARRIER   I think this be the most villainous
house in all London road for fleas. I am stung like a
tench.   16
FIRST CARRIER   Like a tench? By the Mass, there is ne'er
a king Christian could be better bit than I have been   18
since the first cock.   19
SECOND CARRIER   Why, they will allow us ne'er a jordan,   20
and then we leak in your chimney, and your chamber-   21
lye breeds fleas like a loach.   22
FIRST CARRIER [*calling*]   What, Hostler! Come away and   23
be hanged! Come away.
SECOND CARRIER   I have a gammon of bacon and two   25
races of ginger, to be delivered as far as Charing Cross.   26
FIRST CARRIER   God's body, the turkeys in my pannier   27
are quite starved. What, hostler! A plague on thee!
Hast thou never an eye in thy head? Canst not hear?
An 'twere not as good deed as drink to break the pate   30
on thee, I am a very villain. Come, and be hanged!   31
Hast no faith in thee?   32

Enter Gadshill.

2.1. Location: An innyard on the London-Canterbury road.
0.1 *Carrier* one whose trade was conveying goods, usually by packhorses   **1 An** If.   **by the day** in the morning   **2 Charles's Wain** i.e., Charlemagne's wagon; the constellation Ursa Major (the Big Dipper)   **3 horse** horses.   **hostler** groom.   **4 Anon** Right away, coming   **5 beat** soften.   **Cut's saddle** packsaddle of the horse named *Cut*, meaning "bobtailed"   **6 flocks** tufts of wool.   **point** pommel of the saddle.   **jade** nag   **6–7 wrung . . . withers** chafed (by his saddle) on the ridge between his shoulder-blades   **7 cess** measure, estimate.   **8 Peas and beans** i.e., Horse fodder   **8–9 dank . . . dog** i.e., damp as can be   **9 next** nearest, quickest   **10 bots** intestinal maggots.   **house** inn   **16 tench** a spotted fish, whose spots may have been likened to flea bites.   **18 king Christian** Christian king, accustomed to have the best of everything   **19 first cock** i.e., midnight.   **20 jordan** chamberpot   **21 chimney** fireplace   **21–2 chamber-lye** urine   **22 loach** a small freshwater fish, thought to harbor parasites.   **23 Come away** Come along   **25 gammon of bacon** ham   **26 races** roots.   **Charing Cross** a market town lying between London and Westminster.   **27 pannier** basket   **30 An** If   **30–1 An . . . hanged!** i.e., I'll be hanged if it wouldn't be a good idea to smack you on the head. Come along, damn you!   **32 faith** trustworthiness

GADSHILL   Good morrow, carriers. What's o'clock?

FIRST CARRIER   I think it be two o'clock.   34

GADSHILL   I prithee, lend me thy lantern to see my
gelding in the stable.   36

FIRST CARRIER   Nay, by God, soft, I know a trick worth   37
two of that, i'faith.

GADSHILL   [to the Second Carrier]   I pray thee, lend me thine.

SECOND CARRIER   Ay, when, canst tell? Lend me thy   40
lantern, quoth he! Marry, I'll see thee hanged first.   41

GADSHILL   Sirrah carrier, what time do you mean to
come to London?

SECOND CARRIER   Time enough to go to bed with a   44
candle, I warrant thee.—Come, neighbor Mugs, we'll   45
call up the gentlemen. They will along with company,   46
for they have great charge.   Exeunt [Carriers].   47

GADSHILL   What, ho! Chamberlain!   48

Enter Chamberlain.

CHAMBERLAIN   At hand, quoth pickpurse.   49

GADSHILL   That's even as fair as—at hand, quoth the   50
chamberlain; for thou variest no more from picking of   51
purses than giving direction doth from laboring; thou   52
layest the plot how.   53

CHAMBERLAIN   Good morrow, Master Gadshill. It holds   54
current that I told you yesternight: there's a franklin in   55
the Weald of Kent hath brought three hundred marks   56
with him in gold. I heard him tell it to one of his company last night at supper—a kind of auditor, one that
hath abundance of charge too, God knows what. They
are up already, and call for eggs and butter. They will
away presently.   61

GADSHILL   Sirrah, if they meet not with Saint Nicholas'   62
clerks, I'll give thee this neck.   63

CHAMBERLAIN   No, I'll none of it. I pray thee, keep that   64
for the hangman, for I know thou worshipest Saint
Nicholas as truly as a man of falsehood may.

GADSHILL   What talkest thou to me of the hangman? If   67
I hang, I'll make a fat pair of gallows; for if I hang, old
Sir John hangs with me, and thou knowest he is no
starveling. Tut, there are other Trojans that thou   70
dream'st not of, the which for sport sake are content
to do the profession some grace, that would, if matters   72

should be looked into, for their own credit sake   73
make all whole. I am joined with no foot-landrakers,   74
no long-staff sixpenny strikers, none of these mad   75
mustachio purple-hued malt-worms, but with nobility   76
and tranquillity, burgomasters and great oneyers, such   77
as can hold in, such as will strike sooner than speak,   78
and speak sooner than drink, and drink sooner than
pray. And yet, zounds, I lie, for they pray continually
to their saint, the commonwealth, or rather not pray to
her but prey on her, for they ride up and down on her
and make her their boots.   83

CHAMBERLAIN   What, the commonwealth their boots?
Will she hold out water in foul way?   85

GADSHILL   She will, she will. Justice hath liquored her.   86
We steal as in a castle, cocksure. We have the receipt   87
of fern seed; we walk invisible.   88

CHAMBERLAIN   Nay, by my faith, I think you are more
beholding to the night than to fern seed for your   90
walking invisible.

GADSHILL   Give me thy hand. Thou shalt have a share
in our purchase, as I am a true man.   93

CHAMBERLAIN   Nay, rather let me have it as you are a
false thief.

GADSHILL   Go to; *homo* is a common name to all men.   96
Bid the hostler bring my gelding out of the stable. Farewell, you muddy knave.   [Exeunt separately.]   98

❧

[2.2]

Enter Prince, Poins, Peto, and [Bardolph].

POINS   Come, shelter, shelter! I have removed Falstaff's
horse, and he frets like a gummed velvet.   2

PRINCE   Stand close.   [They step aside.]   3

Enter Falstaff.

FALSTAFF   Poins! Poins, and be hanged! Poins!

PRINCE   [coming forward]   Peace, ye fat-kidneyed rascal!
What a brawling dost thou keep!   6

FALSTAFF   Where's Poins, Hal?

---

34 two o'clock (An evasive answer; the First Carrier knows that it is at least four o'clock; see line 1.)   36 gelding castrated male horse   37 soft i.e., wait a minute   40 Ay . . . tell? i.e., You must be joking.   41 quoth he forsooth, indeed.   44–5 Time . . . candle i.e., Soon enough. (Another evasive answer.)   46–7 They . . . charge i.e., They wish to travel in company, because they have lots of valuable cargo.   48 Chamberlain (Male equivalent of a chambermaid. His entrance in the Quarto at line 47 may suggest that he is visible before Gadshill calls for him, giving point to his remark about being "At hand.")   49 At . . . pickpurse i.e., I am right beside you, as the pickpurse said.   50 fair good, apt   51–3 thou variest . . . how i.e., you don't actually do the stealing, but you give directions, like a master workman to his apprentices.   54–5 holds current that holds true what   55 a franklin a yeoman owning his own land   56 Weald wooded region.   marks coins of the value of thirteen shillings four pence   61 presently immediately.   62–3 Saint Nicholas' clerks highwaymen. (Saint Nicholas was popularly supposed the patron of thieves.)   64 I'll none I want none   67 What Why   70 Trojans i.e., jolly fellows, roisterers   72 profession i.e., robbery.   grace credit, favor

73–4 for . . . whole for the sake of their own reputation will make sure that all goes well. (Gadshill hints that they may be joined by some persons of social importance, such as the Prince.)   74 foot-landrakers thieves who travel on foot   75 long-staff six-penny strikers robbers with long staves who would knock down their victims for sixpence   76 mustachio . . . malt-worms purple-faced drunkards with huge mustaches   77 tranquillity those who lead easy lives.   oneyers ones, persons (?)   78 hold in keep a secret; hold fast   83 boots booty. (With pun on boots, "shoes.")   85 Will . . . way? Will she let you go dry in muddy roads? i.e., Will she protect you in tight places?   86 liquored (1) made waterproof by oiling (2) bribed (3) made drunk   87 as in a castle i.e., in complete security.   receipt recipe, formula   88 of fern seed i.e., of becoming invisible (since fern seed, almost invisible itself, was popularly supposed to render its possessor invisible)   90 beholding beholden   93 purchase booty   96 Go to (An expression of impatience.)   homo . . . men the Latin name for man applies to all types; the phrase "true man" applies to me as well as the next man.   98 muddy stupid
2.2. Location: The highway, near Gad's Hill.
2 frets (1) is vexed (2) rubs and frays like *gummed velvet*, velvet made glossy with a stiffening gum   3 close concealed.   6 keep keep up.

PRINCE   He is walked up to the top of the hill. I'll go
seek him.   [*He steps aside.*]
FALSTAFF   I am accursed to rob in that thief's company.
The rascal hath removed my horse and tied him I
know not where. If I travel but four foot by the square   12
further afoot, I shall break my wind. Well, I doubt not
but to die a fair death for all this, if I scape hanging for   14
killing that rogue. I have forsworn his company hourly
any time this two-and-twenty years, and yet I am bewitched with the rogue's company. If the rascal have
not given me medicines to make me love him, I'll be   18
hanged; it could not be else—I have drunk medicines.
Poins! Hal! A plague upon you both! Bardolph! Peto!
I'll starve ere I'll rob a foot further. An 'twere not as   21
good a deed as drink to turn true man and to leave   22
these rogues, I am the veriest varlet that ever chewed   23
with a tooth. Eight yards of uneven ground is three-   24
score-and-ten miles afoot with me, and the stony-
hearted villains know it well enough. A plague upon
it when thieves cannot be true one to another! (*They
whistle.*) Whew! A plague upon you all! Give me my   28
horse, you rogues, give me my horse, and be hanged!
PRINCE   [*coming forward*]   Peace, ye fat-guts! Lie down.
Lay thine ear close to the ground and list if thou   31
canst hear the tread of travelers.
FALSTAFF   Have you any levers to lift me up again, being
down? 'Sblood, I'll not bear mine own flesh so far
afoot again for all the coin in thy father's Exchequer.
What a plague mean ye to colt me thus?   36
PRINCE   Thou liest. Thou art not colted, thou art
uncolted.
FALSTAFF   I prithee, good Prince Hal, help me to my   39
horse, good king's son.   40
PRINCE   Out, ye rogue! Shall I be your hostler?
FALSTAFF   Go hang thyself in thine own heir-apparent
garters! If I be ta'en, I'll peach for this. An I have not   43
ballads made on you all and sung to filthy tunes, let a
cup of sack be my poison. When a jest is so forward,   45
and afoot too! I hate it.   46

Enter Gadshill.

GADSHILL   Stand!   47
FALSTAFF   So I do, against my will.
POINS   [*coming forward with Bardolph and Peto*]   Oh, 'tis our
setter. I know his voice.   50
BARDOLPH   What news?
GADSHILL   Case ye, case ye, on with your vizards!   52

There's money of the King's coming down the hill; 'tis
going to the King's Exchequer.
FALSTAFF   You lie, ye rogue, 'tis going to the King's
Tavern.
GADSHILL   There's enough to make us all.   57
FALSTAFF   To be hanged.
PRINCE   Sirs, you four shall front them in the narrow   59
lane; Ned Poins and I will walk lower. If they scape   60
from your encounter, then they light on us.
PETO   How many be there of them?
GADSHILL   Some eight or ten.
FALSTAFF   Zounds, will they not rob us?
PRINCE   What, a coward, Sir John Paunch?
FALSTAFF   Indeed, I am not John of Gaunt, your   66
grandfather, but yet no coward, Hal.
PRINCE   Well, we leave that to the proof.   68
POINS   Sirrah Jack, thy horse stands behind the hedge.
When thou need'st him, there thou shalt find him.
Farewell, and stand fast.
FALSTAFF   Now cannot I strike him, if I should be   72
hanged.   73
PRINCE   [*to Poins*]   Ned, where are our disguises?
POINS   [*to Prince*]   Here, hard by. Stand close.
                          [*Exeunt Prince and Poins.*]
FALSTAFF   Now, my masters, happy man be his dole,   76
say I. Every man to his business.   [*They stand aside.*]

Enter the Travelers.

FIRST TRAVELER   Come, neighbor. The boy shall lead
our horses down the hill; we'll walk afoot awhile, and
ease our legs.
THIEVES   [*coming forward*]   Stand!
TRAVELERS   Jesus bless us!
FALSTAFF   Strike! Down with them! Cut the villains'
throats! Ah, whoreson caterpillars, bacon-fed knaves!   84
They hate us youth. Down with them, fleece them!
TRAVELERS   Oh, we are undone, both we and ours for-
ever!
FALSTAFF   Hang ye, gorbellied knaves, are ye undone?   88
No, ye fat chuffs; I would your store were here. On,   89
bacons, on! What, ye knaves, young men must live.   90
You are grandjurors, are ye? We'll jure ye, 'faith.   91
          Here they rob them and bind them. Exeunt.

Enter the Prince and Poins [*in buckram*].

PRINCE   The thieves have bound the true men. Now
could thou and I rob the thieves and go merrily to
London, it would be argument for a week, laughter   94
for a month, and a good jest forever.

---

12 square a measuring tool   **14 fair** exemplary.   **for all** despite all
18 medicines love potions   **21–4 An . . . tooth** i.e., If I don't think it's a
good idea to reform and turn informer, I'm the damnedest scoundrel
that ever lived. (Cf. 2.1.30–1 and n.)   **28 Whew** (Perhaps Falstaff tries
to answer the whistling he hears or mocks it.)   **31 list** listen   **36 colt**
trick, cheat. (In lines 37–8, Prince Hal puns on the common meaning.)
39–40 help . . . horse help me to find my horse. (But in line 41, the
Prince comically retorts as though having been asked to hold the stirrup while Falstaff mounted, as a hostler would do.)   **43 peach** inform
on you   **45 so forward** so far advanced   **46 afoot** (1) in progress (2)
on foot, i.e., not on horseback   **47 Stand!** Don't move! (But Falstaff
answers in the sense of "stand on one's feet.")   **50 setter** arranger of
the robbery. (See 1.2.104–5 and note.)   **52 Case ye** Put on your masks

57 make us all make our fortunes (or, as Falstaff sees it, make us be
hanged).   **59 front** confront   **60 lower** further downhill.   **66 John of
Gaunt** Henry IV's father, born at Ghent (and hence giving Falstaff a
chance to pun on *gaunt* as the opposite of his fatness)   **68 proof** test.
72–3 Now . . . hanged (Falstaff wishes he could hit Poins, who is too
quick for him.)   **76 happy . . . dole** may happiness be every man's
portion or lot   **84 Ah . . . knaves!** i.e., Ah, you abominable parasites,
you over-fed rascals!   **88 gorbellied** big-bellied   **89 chuffs** churls,
rich but miserly.   **store** total wealth   **90 bacons** fat men   **91 grandjurors** i.e., men of wealth, able to serve on juries   **94 argument** a subject for conversation

POINS Stand close. I hear them coming.

[They stand aside.]

Enter the thieves again.

FALSTAFF Come, my masters, let us share, and then to 97
horse before day. An the Prince and Poins be not two
arrant cowards, there's no equity stirring. There's no 99
more valor in that Poins than in a wild duck.

[The thieves begin to share the booty.]

PRINCE Your money!

POINS Villains!

*As they are sharing, the Prince and Poins set upon
them. They all run away, and Falstaff, after a blow
or two, runs away too, leaving the booty behind
them.*

PRINCE
Got with much ease. Now merrily to horse.
The thieves are all scattered and possessed with fear
So strongly that they dare not meet each other;
Each takes his fellow for an officer.
Away, good Ned. Falstaff sweats to death
And lards the lean earth as he walks along. 108
Were't not for laughing, I should pity him.

POINS How the fat rogue roared! *Exeunt.*

❖

[2.3]

Enter Hotspur, solus, reading a letter.

HOTSPUR "But, for mine own part, my lord, I could be
well contented to be there, in respect of the love I bear
your house." He could be contented; why is he not, 3
then? In respect of the love he bears our house! He
shows in this he loves his own barn better than he
loves our house. Let me see some more. "The purpose
you undertake is dangerous"—why, that's certain.
'Tis dangerous to take a cold, to sleep, to drink; but I
tell you, my lord fool, out of this nettle, danger, we
pluck this flower, safety. "The purpose you undertake
is dangerous, the friends you have named uncertain,
the time itself unsorted, and your whole plot too light 12
for the counterpoise of so great an opposition." Say 13
you so, say you so? I say unto you again, you are a
shallow, cowardly hind, and you lie. What a lack-brain 15
is this! By the Lord, our plot is a good plot as
ever was laid, our friends true and constant; a good
plot, good friends, and full of expectation; an excellent 18
plot, very good friends. What a frosty-spirited rogue is
this! Why, my lord of York commends the plot and 20

the general course of the action. Zounds, an I were 21
now by this rascal, I could brain him with his lady's 22
fan. Is there not my father, my uncle, and myself? Lord 23
Edmund Mortimer, my lord of York, and Owen Glendower? Is there not besides the Douglas? Have I not all
their letters to meet me in arms by the ninth of the next
month, and are they not some of them set forward
already? What a pagan rascal is this, an infidel! Ha, 28
you shall see now in very sincerity of fear and
cold heart will he to the King and lay open all our
proceedings. Oh, I could divide myself and go to buf- 31
fets for moving such a dish of skim milk with so hon- 32
orable an action! Hang him, let him tell the King, we
are prepared. I will set forward tonight.

Enter his Lady.

How now, Kate? I must leave you within these two
hours.

LADY PERCY
Oh, my good lord, why are you thus alone?
For what offense have I this fortnight been
A banished woman from my Harry's bed?
Tell me, sweet lord, what is't that takes from thee
Thy stomach, pleasure, and thy golden sleep? 41
Why dost thou bend thine eyes upon the earth
And start so often when thou sit'st alone?
Why hast thou lost the fresh blood in thy cheeks
And given my treasures and my rights of thee 45
To thick-eyed musing and curst melancholy? 46
In thy faint slumbers I by thee have watched 47
And heard thee murmur tales of iron wars,
Speak terms of manage to thy bounding steed, 49
Cry, "Courage! To the field!" And thou hast talked
Of sallies and retires, of trenches, tents, 51
Of palisadoes, frontiers, parapets, 52
Of basilisks, of cannon, culverin, 53
Of prisoners' ransom, and of soldiers slain,
And all the currents of a heady fight. 55
Thy spirit within thee hath been so at war,
And thus hath so bestirred thee in thy sleep,
That beads of sweat have stood upon thy brow
Like bubbles in a late-disturbèd stream, 59
And in thy face strange motions have appeared,
Such as we see when men restrain their breath
On some great sudden hest. Oh, what portents are
these? 62
Some heavy business hath my lord in hand,
And I must know it, else he loves me not.

---

97 **masters** good sirs 99 **arrant** notorious, unmitigated. **equity**
judgment, discernment 108 **lards** drips fat on, bastes
2.3. Location: Hotspur's estate (identified historically as Warkworth
Castle in Northumberland).
0.1 solus alone 3 **house** family. (But Hotspur replies derisively in
lines 4–6 as though to the literal sense of a building that one might
compare to a barn.) 12 **unsorted** unsuitable 13 **for . . . of** to counterbalance 15 **hind** menial, peasant 18 **expectation** promise
20 **lord of York** i.e., Archbishop Scroop. (Also in line 24.)

21–2 **an . . . rascal** if I were face to face with this rascal, instead of
reading his letter 22–3 **his lady's fan** his wife's fan—a suitable light
weapon with which to chastise such a milktoast. 28 **pagan** unbelieving 31–2 **divide . . . buffets** i.e., fight with myself 32 **moving** urging 41 **stomach** appetite 45 **And . . . thee** and given the precious
right I have as wife to share your thoughts 46 **thick-eyed** dull-
sighted, vacant, abstracted. **curst** ill-tempered 47 **faint** restless.
watched lain awake 49 **manage** horsemanship 51 **retires** retreats
52–3 **Of . . . culverin** of stakes set in the ground for defense, of ram-
parts, protective walls, of large and smaller cannon 55 **heady** headlong 59 **late-disturbèd** recently stirred up 62 **hest** command;
endeavor.

HOTSPUR [*calling*]
What, ho!

[*Enter a Servant.*]

    Is Gilliams with the packet gone?
SERVANT He is, my lord, an hour ago.
HOTSPUR
Hath Butler brought those horses from the sheriff?   67
SERVANT
One horse, my lord, he brought even now.   68
HOTSPUR
What horse? A roan, a crop-ear, is it not?   69
SERVANT
It is, my lord.
HOTSPUR   That roan shall be my throne.
Well, I will back him straight. Oh, *Esperance!*   71
Bid Butler lead him forth into the park.

[*Exit Servant.*]

LADY PERCY But hear you, my lord.
HOTSPUR What say'st thou, my lady?
LADY PERCY What is it carries you away?   75
HOTSPUR Why, my horse, my love, my horse.
LADY PERCY Out, you mad-headed ape!   77
A weasel hath not such a deal of spleen   78
As you are tossed with. In faith,   79
I'll know your business, Harry, that I will.
I fear my brother Mortimer doth stir
About his title, and hath sent for you   82
To line his enterprise; but if you go—   83
HOTSPUR
So far afoot, I shall be weary, love.
LADY PERCY
Come, come, you paraquito, answer me   85
Directly unto this question that I ask.
In faith, I'll break thy little finger, Harry,
An if thou wilt not tell me all things true.   88
HOTSPUR Away,
Away, you trifler! Love? I love thee not;
I care not for thee, Kate. This is no world
To play with mammets and to tilt with lips.   92
We must have bloody noses and cracked crowns,   93
And pass them current too. Gods me, my horse!   94
What say'st thou, Kate? What wouldst thou have with
me?
LADY PERCY
Do you not love me? Do you not, indeed?
Well, do not, then, for since you love me not

I will not love myself. Do you not love me?
Nay, tell me if you speak in jest or no.
HOTSPUR Come, wilt thou see me ride?
And when I am a-horseback I will swear
I love thee infinitely. But hark you, Kate,
I must not have you henceforth question me
Whither I go, nor reason whereabout.   104
Whither I must, I must; and, to conclude,
This evening must I leave you, gentle Kate.
I know you wise, but yet no farther wise
Than Harry Percy's wife; constant you are,
But yet a woman; and for secrecy,
No lady closer, for I well believe   110
Thou wilt not utter what thou dost not know,
And so far will I trust thee, gentle Kate.
LADY PERCY How, so far?
HOTSPUR
Not an inch further. But hark you, Kate:
Whither I go, thither shall you go too.
Today will I set forth, tomorrow you.
Will this content you, Kate?
LADY PERCY   It must, of force. *Exeunt.* 117

❖

[2.4]

Enter Prince and Poins.

PRINCE Ned, prithee, come out of that fat room, and   1
lend me thy hand to laugh a little.
POINS Where hast been, Hal?
PRINCE With three or four loggerheads amongst three   4
or four score hogsheads. I have sounded the very bass   5
string of humility. Sirrah, I am sworn brother to a
leash of drawers, and can call them all by their Christian   7
names, as Tom, Dick, and Francis. They take it already   8
upon their salvation that, though I be but Prince of   9
Wales, yet I am the king of courtesy, and tell me flatly
I am no proud Jack like Falstaff, but a Corinthian, a lad   11
of mettle, a good boy—by the Lord, so they call me!—
and when I am King of England I shall command all
the good lads in Eastcheap. They call drinking deep   14
"dyeing scarlet"; and when you breathe in your water-   15
ing they cry "hem!" and bid you "play it off." To con-   16
clude, I am so good a proficient in one quarter of an
hour that I can drink with any tinker in his own language during my life. I tell thee, Ned, thou hast lost
much honor that thou wert not with me in this action.

---

67 **sheriff** i.e., bailiff. 68 **even** just 69 **roan** roan-colored, i.e., with white or grey interspersed in the overall color of the coat 71 **back** mount. *Esperance* Hope. (The motto of the Percy family.) 75 **car-ries you away** carries you beyond the bounds of reason and judg-ment. (But Hotspur puns on the literal meaning.) 77 **Out** (An expression of impatience.) 78 **spleen** (The spleen was thought to be the source of impulsive and irritable behavior.) 79 **tossed** tossed about, agitated 82 **title** claim to the throne 83 **line** strengthen 85 **paraquito** little parrot. (A term of endearment.) 88 **An if** if 92 **mammets** dolls. (With a quibble on the Latin *mamma* meaning "breast.") 93 **crowns** (1) heads (2) coins worth five shillings. (Cracked coins would not "pass current," as Hotspur jokes in the next line.) 94 **Gods me** God save me

104 **reason whereabout** ask about what. 110 **closer** more close-mouthed 117 **of force** perforce, of necessity.
2.4. Location: A tavern in Eastcheap, London, usually identified as the Boar's Head. Some tavern furniture, including stools, is pro-vided onstage.
1 **fat** stuffy, or, a vat room 4 **loggerheads** blockheads 5 **hogsheads** wine barrels. **bass** (With a pun on *base*.) 7 **leash of drawers** three waiters 8–9 **take . . . salvation** already maintain it as they hope to be saved 11 **Jack** (1) Jack Falstaff (2) fellow. **Corinthian** i.e., gay blade, good sport. (Corinth was reputed to be licentious.)
14–15 **They . . . scarlet** (Either because excessive drinking causes a red complexion or because urine, produced by *drinking deep*, was some-times used for fixing dyes.) 15–16 **breathe . . . watering** pause for breath in your drinking 16 **play it off** drink it up.

But, sweet Ned—to sweeten which name of Ned, I
give thee this pennyworth of sugar, clapped even now 22
into my hand by an underskinker, one that never 23
spake other English in his life than "Eight shillings
and sixpence," and "You are welcome," with this
shrill addition, "Anon, anon, sir! Score a pint of bas- 26
tard in the Half-Moon," or so. But, Ned, to drive away 27
the time till Falstaff come, I prithee do thou stand in
some by-room while I question my puny drawer to 29
what end he gave me the sugar; and do thou never
leave calling "Francis," that his tale to me may be
nothing but "Anon." Step aside, and I'll show thee a
precedent. [*Exit Poins.*] 33

POINS [*within*] Francis!
PRINCE Thou art perfect.
POINS [*within*] Francis!

Enter [*Francis, a*] drawer.

FRANCIS Anon, anon, sir.—Look down into the Pom- 37
garnet, Ralph. 38
PRINCE Come hither, Francis.
FRANCIS My lord?
PRINCE How long hast thou to serve, Francis? 41
FRANCIS Forsooth, five years, and as much as to—
POINS [*within*] Francis!
FRANCIS [*calling*] Anon, anon, sir.
PRINCE Five year! By'r Lady, a long lease for the 45
clinking of pewter. But Francis, darest thou be so
valiant as to play the coward with thy indenture and 47
show it a fair pair of heels and run from it?
FRANCIS Oh, Lord, sir, I'll be sworn upon all the books in 49
England, I could find in my heart—
POINS [*within*] Francis!
FRANCIS [*calling*] Anon, sir.
PRINCE How old art thou, Francis?
FRANCIS Let me see, about Michaelmas next I shall 54
be—
POINS [*within*] Francis!
FRANCIS [*calling*] Anon, sir. Pray, stay a little, my lord.
PRINCE Nay, but hark you, Francis: for the sugar thou
gavest me, 'twas a pennyworth, was 't not?
FRANCIS Oh, Lord, I would it had been two!
PRINCE I will give thee for it a thousand pound. Ask
me when thou wilt, and thou shalt have it.
POINS [*within*] Francis!
FRANCIS [*calling*] Anon, anon.
PRINCE Anon, Francis? No, Francis; but tomorrow,
Francis, or, Francis, o'Thursday, or indeed, Francis,
when thou wilt. But, Francis—
FRANCIS My lord?

PRINCE Wilt thou rob this leathern-jerkin, crystal- 69
button, not-pated, agate-ring, puke-stocking, caddis- 70
garter, smooth-tongue, Spanish-pouch— 71
FRANCIS Oh, Lord, sir, who do you mean?
PRINCE Why, then, your brown bastard is your only 73
drink; for look you, Francis, your white canvas 74
doublet will sully. In Barbary, sir, it cannot come to so 75
much. 76
FRANCIS What, sir?
POINS [*within*] Francis!
PRINCE Away, you rogue! Dost thou not hear them call? 79
*Here they both call him; the drawer stands
amazed, not knowing which way to go.*

Enter Vintner.

VINTNER What stand'st thou still and hear'st such a 80
calling? Look to the guests within. [*Exit Francis.*]
My lord, old Sir John, with half a dozen more, are at the
door. Shall I let them in?
PRINCE Let them alone awhile, and then open the door.
[*Exit Vintner.*]
[*Calling*] Poins!

Enter Poins.

POINS Anon, anon, sir.
PRINCE Sirrah, Falstaff and the rest of the thieves are at
the door. Shall we be merry?
POINS As merry as crickets, my lad. But hark ye, what
cunning match have you made with this jest of the 90
drawer? Come, what's the issue? 91
PRINCE I am now of all humors that have showed 92
themselves humors since the old days of Goodman 93
Adam to the pupil age of this present twelve o'clock at 94
midnight. 95

[*Enter Francis, hurrying across the stage with
wine.*]

What's o'clock, Francis?
FRANCIS Anon, anon, sir. [*Exit.*]
PRINCE That ever this fellow should have fewer words
than a parrot, and yet the son of a woman! His industry is upstairs and downstairs, his eloquence the parcel 100
of a reckoning. I am not yet of Percy's mind, the Hot- 101
spur of the north, he that kills me some six or seven 102
dozen of Scots at a breakfast, washes his hands, and
says to his wife, "Fie upon this quiet life! I want
work." "Oh, my sweet Harry," says she, "how many

---

22 **sugar** (Used to sweeten wine.)   23 **underskinker** assistant to a
waiter or bartender   26–7 **Anon . . . Half-Moon** Coming, sir!—
Charge a pint of a sweet Spanish wine to the customers in the room
of the inn called "the Half-Moon."   29 **by-room** side-room.   **puny
drawer** inexperienced tapster or bartender   33 **precedent** example.
37–8 **Pomgarnet** Pomegranate. (Another room in the inn.)   41 **serve**
i.e., serve out your apprenticeship   45 **By'r Lady** By Our Lady
47 **indenture** contract of apprenticeship   49 **books** i.e., Bibles
54 **Michaelmas** September 29

69–71 **Wilt . . . Spanish-pouch** i.e., Will you rob your master of your
services by running away, this man with his leather jacket, transparent buttons, cropped hair, a ring with small figures in an agate stone
for a seal, dark woolen stockings, worsted garters, an ingratiating
flattering manner of speech, wallet of Spanish leather   73–6 **Why . . .
much** (The Prince talks seeming nonsense in order to bewilder Francis, but he also implies that Francis should stick to his trade, since he
will not cut much of a figure in the world.)   75 **it** i.e., sugar
79.3 **Vintner** i.e., Innkeeper.   80 **What** Why   90 **match** game, contest
91 **issue** outcome, point.   92–5 **I . . . midnight** i.e., I'm now in a
mood for anything that has happened in the whole history of the
world.   93 **Goodman** (Title for a yeoman.)   94 **pupil** youthful
100–1 **parcel . . . reckoning** items of a bill.   102 **kills me** i.e., kills.
(*Me* is used colloquially.)

hast thou killed today?" "Give my roan horse a
drench," says he, and answers, "Some fourteen," an 107
hour after, "a trifle, a trifle." I prithee, call in Falstaff.
I'll play Percy, and that damned brawn shall play Dame 109
Mortimer his wife. "Rivo!" says the drunkard. Call in 110
ribs, call in tallow. 111

Enter Falstaff, [Gadshill, Bardolph, and Peto;
Francis following with wine].

POINS Welcome, Jack. Where hast thou been?

FALSTAFF A plague of all cowards, I say, and a 113
vengeance too! Marry and amen! Give me a cup of
sack, boy. Ere I lead this life long, I'll sew nether- 115
stocks, and mend them and foot them too. A plague 116
of all cowards! Give me a cup of sack, rogue. Is there
no virtue extant? *He drinketh.*

PRINCE Didst thou never see Titan kiss a dish of butter, 119
pitiful-hearted Titan, that melted at the sweet tale of 120
the sun's? If thou didst, then behold that compound. 121

FALSTAFF You rogue, here's lime in this sack too. There 122
is nothing but roguery to be found in villainous man,
yet a coward is worse than a cup of sack with lime in
it. A villainous coward! Go thy ways, old Jack, die
when thou wilt. If manhood, good manhood, be not
forgot upon the face of the earth, then am I a shotten 127
herring. There lives not three good men unhanged in 128
England, and one of them is fat and grows old, God
help the while! A bad world, I say. I would I were a 130
weaver; I could sing psalms or anything. A plague of 131
all cowards, I say still.

PRINCE How now, woolsack, what mutter you? 133

FALSTAFF A king's son! If I do not beat thee out of thy
kingdom with a dagger of lath, and drive all thy 135
subjects afore thee like a flock of wild geese, I'll never
wear hair on my face more. You, Prince of Wales!

PRINCE Why, you whoreson round man, what's the
matter?

FALSTAFF Are not you a coward? Answer me to that.
And Poins there?

POINS Zounds, ye fat paunch, an ye call me coward, by
the Lord, I'll stab thee.

FALSTAFF I call thee coward? I'll see thee damned ere I
call thee coward, but I would give a thousand pound
I could run as fast as thou canst. You are straight
enough in the shoulders; you care not who sees your
back. Call you that backing of your friends? A plague
upon such backing! Give me them that will face me.

Give me a cup of sack. I am a rogue if I drunk today.

PRINCE Oh, villain, thy lips are scarce wiped since thou
drunk'st last.

FALSTAFF All is one for that. (*He drinketh.*) A plague of 153
all cowards, still say I.

PRINCE What's the matter?

FALSTAFF What's the matter? There be four of us here
have ta'en a thousand pound this day morning. 157

PRINCE Where is it, Jack, where is it?

FALSTAFF Where is it? Taken from us it is. A hundred
upon poor four of us.

PRINCE What, a hundred, man?

FALSTAFF I am a rogue if I were not at half-sword with 162
a dozen of them two hours together. I have scaped by 163
miracle. I am eight times thrust through the doublet, 164
four through the hose, my buckler cut through and 165
through, my sword hacked like a handsaw—*ecce* 166
signum! I never dealt better since I was a man. All 167
would not do. A plague of all cowards! Let them 168
speak. If they speak more or less than truth, they are
villains and the sons of darkness.

PRINCE Speak, sirs, how was it?

GADSHILL We four set upon some dozen—

FALSTAFF Sixteen at least, my lord.

GADSHILL And bound them.

PETO No, no, they were not bound.

FALSTAFF You rogue, they were bound, every man of
them, or I am a Jew else, an Hebrew Jew.

GADSHILL As we were sharing, some six or seven fresh
men set upon us—

FALSTAFF And unbound the rest, and then come in the
other. 181

PRINCE What, fought you with them all?

FALSTAFF All? I know not what you call all, but if I
fought not with fifty of them, I am a bunch of radish.
If there were not two- or three-and-fifty upon poor old
Jack, then am I no two-legged creature.

PRINCE Pray God you have not murdered some of them.

FALSTAFF Nay, that's past praying for. I have peppered
two of them. Two I am sure I have paid, two rogues
in buckram suits. I tell thee what, Hal, if I tell thee a
lie, spit in my face, call me horse. Thou knowest my
old ward. Here I lay, and thus I bore my point. [*He* 192
demonstrates his stance.] Four rogues in buckram let
drive at me—

PRINCE What, four? Thou said'st but two even now. 195

FALSTAFF Four, Hal, I told thee four.

POINS Ay, ay, he said four.

FALSTAFF These four came all afront, and mainly thrust 198
at me. I made me no more ado but took all their seven 199
points in my target, thus. 200

---

107 drench draft (sometimes of medicine).   **says he** i.e., he tells a servant   **109 brawn** fat boar   **110 Rivo** (An exclamation of uncertain
meaning, but related to drinking.)   **111 ribs** rib roast.   **tallow** fat
drippings.   **113 of** on   **115–16 netherstocks** stockings (the sewing or
mending of which is a menial occupation)   **116 foot** make a new foot
for   **119 Titan** i.e., the sun   **120 that** i.e., the butter   **121 compound**
melting butter, i.e., Falstaff.   **122 lime in this sack** i.e., lime added to
make the wine sparkle   **127–8 a shotten herring** a herring that has
cast its roe and is consequently thin.   **130 the while** i.e., in these bad
times.   **131 weaver** (Many psalm-singing Protestant immigrants
from the Low Countries were weavers.)   **133 woolsack** bale of wool
135 dagger of lath (The Vice, a stock comic figure in morality plays,
was so armed.)

153 All . . . that No matter.   **157 this day morning** this morning.
162 at half-sword fighting at close quarters   **163 scaped** escaped
164 doublet Elizabethan upper garment like a jacket   **165 hose** close-
fitting breeches.   **buckler** shield   **166–7 ecce signum** behold the proof.
(Familiar words from the Mass.)   **167–8 All . . . do** All that I did was of
no use.   **181 other** others.   **192 ward** defensive stance, parry.   **lay**
stood   **195 even** just   **198 afront** abreast.   **mainly** powerfully
199 made me made. (*Me* is used colloquially.)   **200 target** shield

PRINCE   Seven? Why, there were but four even now.

FALSTAFF   In buckram?

POINS   Ay, four, in buckram suits.

FALSTAFF   Seven, by these hilts, or I am a villain else.   204

PRINCE [*aside to Poins*]   Prithee, let him alone. We shall have more anon.

FALSTAFF   Dost thou hear me, Hal?

PRINCE   Ay, and mark thee too, Jack.   208

FALSTAFF   Do so, for it is worth the listening to. These nine in buckram that I told thee of—

PRINCE   So, two more already.

FALSTAFF   Their points being broken—   212

POINS   Down fell their hose.

FALSTAFF   Began to give me ground; but I followed me   214
close, came in foot and hand; and with a thought   215
seven of the eleven I paid.

PRINCE   Oh, monstrous! Eleven buckram men grown out of two!

FALSTAFF   But, as the devil would have it, three mis-begotten knaves in Kendal green came at my back   220
and let drive at me; for it was so dark, Hal, that thou couldst not see thy hand.

PRINCE   These lies are like their father that begets them,   223
gross as a mountain, open, palpable. Why, thou claybrained guts, thou knotty-pated fool, thou whore-   225
son, obscene, greasy tallow-keech—   226

FALSTAFF   What, art thou mad? Art thou mad? Is not the truth the truth?

PRINCE   Why, how couldst thou know these men in Kendal green when it was so dark thou couldst not see thy hand? Come, tell us your reason. What sayest thou to this?

POINS   Come, your reason, Jack, your reason.

FALSTAFF   What, upon compulsion? Zounds, an I were at the strappado, or all the racks in the world, I would   235
not tell you on compulsion. Give you a reason on com-pulsion? If reasons were as plentiful as blackberries,   237
I would give no man a reason upon compulsion, I.

PRINCE   I'll be no longer guilty of this sin. This sanguine   239
coward, this bed-presser, this horse-backbreaker, this huge hill of flesh—

FALSTAFF   'Sblood, you starveling, you eel-skin, you dried neat's tongue, you bull's pizzle, you stockfish!   243
Oh, for breath to utter what is like thee! You tailor's yard, you sheath, you bowcase, you vile standing   245
tuck—   246

PRINCE   Well, breathe awhile, and then to it again, and when thou hast tired thyself in base comparisons, hear me speak but this.

POINS   Mark, Jack.

PRINCE   We two saw you four set on four and bound them, and were masters of their wealth. Mark now how a plain tale shall put you down. Then did we two set on you four, and, with a word, outfaced you from   254
your prize, and have it, yea, and can show it you here in the house. And, Falstaff, you carried your guts away as nimbly, with as quick dexterity, and roared for mercy, and still run and roared, as ever I heard bull calf. What a slave art thou, to hack thy sword as thou hast done, and then say it was in fight! What trick, what device, what starting-hole canst thou now find   261
out to hide thee from this open and apparent shame?

POINS   Come, let's hear, Jack. What trick hast thou now?

FALSTAFF   By the Lord, I knew ye as well as he that made ye. Why, hear you, my masters, was it for me to kill the heir apparent? Should I turn upon the true prince? Why, thou knowest I am as valiant as Her-cules, but beware instinct. The lion will not touch the true prince. Instinct is a great matter; I was now a coward on instinct. I shall think the better of myself and thee during my life—I for a valiant lion, and thou for a true prince. But by the Lord, lads, I am glad you have the money. Hostess, clap to the doors! Watch   273
tonight, pray tomorrow. Gallants, lads, boys, hearts   274
of gold, all the titles of good fellowship come to you! What, shall we be merry? Shall we have a play extempore?

PRINCE   Content; and the argument shall be thy run-   278
ning away.

FALSTAFF   Ah, no more of that, Hal, an thou lovest me!

Enter Hostess.

HOSTESS
Oh, Jesu, my lord the Prince!

PRINCE   How now, my lady the hostess, what say'st thou to me?

HOSTESS   Marry, my lord, there is a nobleman of the court at door would speak with you. He says he comes from your father.

PRINCE   Give him as much as will make him a royal   287
man, and send him back again to my mother.   288

FALSTAFF   What manner of man is he?

HOSTESS   An old man.

FALSTAFF   What doth Gravity out of his bed at mid-   291
night? Shall I give him his answer?

PRINCE   Prithee, do, Jack.

FALSTAFF   Faith, and I'll send him packing.   *Exit.*

PRINCE   Now, sirs. By'r Lady, you fought fair; so did you, Peto; so did you, Bardolph. You are lions too, you ran away upon instinct, you will not touch the true prince; no, fie!

BARDOLPH   Faith, I ran when I saw others run.

---

204 **by these hilts** by my sword hilt   208 **mark** (1) pay heed (2) keep count   212 **points** sword points. (But Poins puns on the sense of laces, by which the hose were attached to the doublet.)   214 **followed me** followed   215 **with a thought** quick as a thought   220 **Kendal** a town known for its textiles   223 **their father** (1) Falstaff (2) the devil, proverbially the father of lies   225 **knotty-pated** thickheaded   226 **tallow-keech** lump of tallow   235 **strappado** a kind of torture   237 **reasons . . . blackberries** (Falstaff puns on *raisins*, pronounced nearly like *reasons*.)   239 **sanguine** ruddy   243 **neat's** ox's.   **pizzle** penis.   **stockfish** dried cod.   245 **yard** yardstick   245–6 **standing tuck** rapier standing on its point, or no longer pliant

254 **with a word** (1) in a word (2) with a minimum of speech.   **outfaced** frightened   261 **starting-hole** point of shelter (like a rab-bit's hole)   273 **Watch** (1) Keep watchful vigil. (See Matthew 26:41.) (2) Carouse   274 **pray** (1) pray to God (2) prey   278 **argument** plot of the play   287–8 **Give . . . man** (Prince Hal puns on the value of coins: a *noble* was worth six shillings eight pence; a *royal* was worth ten shillings.)   291 **What doth** Why is

PRINCE   Faith, tell me now in earnest, how came Falstaff's sword so hacked?

PETO   Why, he hacked it with his dagger, and said he would swear truth out of England but he would make 303 you believe it was done in fight, and persuaded us to do the like.

BARDOLPH   Yea, and to tickle our noses with spear grass to make them bleed, and then to beslubber our gar- 307 ments with it and swear it was the blood of true men. I did that I did not this seven year before: I blushed to 309 hear his monstrous devices.

PRINCE   Oh, villain, thou stolest a cup of sack eighteen years ago and wert taken with the manner, and ever 312 since thou hast blushed extempore. Thou hadst fire 313 and sword on thy side, and yet thou ran'st away. What instinct hadst thou for it?

BARDOLPH   My lord, do you see these meteors? Do you 316 behold these exhalations?   [Pointing to his own face.] 317

PRINCE   I do.

BARDOLPH   What think you they portend?   319

PRINCE   Hot livers and cold purses.   320

BARDOLPH   Choler, my lord, if rightly taken.   321

PRINCE   No, if rightly taken, halter.   322

Enter Falstaff.

Here comes lean Jack, here comes bare-bone.—How now, my sweet creature of bombast? How long is't 324 ago, Jack, since thou sawest thine own knee?

FALSTAFF   My own knee? When I was about thy years, Hal, I was not an eagle's talon in the waist; I could have crept into any alderman's thumb ring. A plague of sighing and grief! It blows a man up like a bladder. There's villainous news abroad. Here was Sir John Bracy from your father. You must to the court in the morning. That same mad fellow of the north, Percy, and he of Wales that gave Amamon the bastinado and 333 made Lucifer cuckold and swore the devil his true 334 liegeman upon the cross of a Welsh hook—what a 335 plague call you him?

POINS   Owen Glendower.

FALSTAFF   Owen, Owen, the same; and his son-in-law Mortimer, and old Northumberland, and that

sprightly Scot of Scots, Douglas, that runs a-horseback up a hill perpendicular—

PRINCE   He that rides at high speed, and with his pistol kills a sparrow flying.

FALSTAFF   You have hit it.   344

PRINCE   So did he never the sparrow.

FALSTAFF   Well, that rascal hath good mettle in him; he will not run.   347

PRINCE   Why, what a rascal art thou then to praise him so for running!

FALSTAFF   A-horseback, ye cuckoo; but afoot he will not budge a foot.

PRINCE   Yes, Jack, upon instinct.

FALSTAFF   I grant ye, upon instinct. Well, he is there too, and one Mordake, and a thousand blue-caps more. 354 Worcester is stolen away tonight. Thy father's beard is turned white with the news. You may buy land now as cheap as stinking mackerel.

PRINCE   Why, then, it is like, if there come a hot June 358 and this civil buffeting hold, we shall buy maiden- 359 heads as they buy hobnails, by the hundreds.

FALSTAFF   By the mass, lad, thou sayest true; it is like we shall have good trading that way. But tell me, Hal, art not thou horrible afeard? Thou being heir appar- ent, could the world pick thee out three such enemies again as that fiend Douglas, that spirit Percy, and that devil Glendower? Art thou not horribly afraid? Doth not thy blood thrill at it?

PRINCE   Not a whit, i'faith. I lack some of thy instinct.

FALSTAFF   Well, thou wilt be horribly chid tomorrow 369 when thou comest to thy father. If thou love me, practice an answer.

PRINCE   Do thou stand for my father, and examine me upon the particulars of my life.

FALSTAFF   Shall I? Content. This chair shall be my state, 374 this dagger my scepter, and this cushion my crown. [*Falstaff establishes himself on his "throne."*]

PRINCE   Thy state is taken for a joint stool, thy golden 376 scepter for a leaden dagger, and thy precious rich 377 crown for a pitiful bald crown.

FALSTAFF   Well, an the fire of grace be not quite out of thee, now shalt thou be moved. Give me a cup of sack to make my eyes look red, that it may be thought I have wept; for I must speak in passion, and I will do it in King Cambyses' vein.   383

PRINCE   Well, here is my leg.   [*He bows.*]

FALSTAFF   And here is my speech. Stand aside, nobil- ity.

HOSTESS   Oh, Jesu, this is excellent sport, i'faith!

FALSTAFF

Weep not, sweet queen, for trickling tears are vain.

HOSTESS   Oh, the Father, how he holds his countenance! 389

---

303 **swear . . . would** swear oaths until they go out of fashion if he did not   307 **beslubber** smear, cover   309 **that** something   312 **taken . . . manner** caught with the goods   313 **extempore** without needing any occasion. (Bardolph is red-faced whether he blushes or not.) **fire** i.e., a red nose and complexion caused by heavy drinking 316, 317 **meteors, exhalations** i.e., the red blotches on Bardolph's face. 319 **portend** signify. (Meteors, comets, and other meteorological phe- nomena were widely regarded as omens of disaster.)   320 **Hot . . . purses** i.e., Livers inflamed by drink and purses made empty by spending.   321 **Choler** A choleric or combative temperament.   **taken** understood. (But the Prince, in his next speech, uses the word to mean "arrested.")   322 **halter** hangman's noose. (The Prince plays on Bardolph's *choler,* which he takes as *collar.*)   322.1 (Falstaff's entry in the quarto after line 321 suggests he is visible to the audience while the Prince talks of a hangman's halter.)   324 **bombast** (1) cotton padding (2) fustian speech.   333 **Amamon** (The name of a demon.) **bastinado** beating on the soles of the feet   334 **made . . . cuckold** i.e., gave Lucifer his horns, the sign of cuckoldry   334–5 **and swore . . . liegeman** and made the devil take an oath of allegiance as a true sub- ject   335 **Welsh hook** curved-bladed pike lacking the cross shape of the sword on which such oaths were usually sworn

344 **hit it** described it exactly. (But the Prince takes *hit* literally in the next line.)   347 **run** flee. (But the Prince answers punningly in the sense of "ride at high speed.")   354 **blue-caps** Scottish soldiers 358 **like** likely   359 **hold** continues   369 **chid** chided   374 **state** chair of state, throne   376 **joint stool** a stool made by a joiner or furniture maker   377 **leaden** of soft metal, hence inferior   383 **in . . . vein** i.e., in the ranting and (by Shakespeare's time) old-fashioned style of Thomas Preston's *Cambyses,* an early Elizabethan tragedy.   389 **the Father** i.e., in God's name.   **holds his countenance** keeps a straight face.

FALSTAFF
For God's sake, lords, convey my tristful queen, 390
For tears do stop the floodgates of her eyes. 391
HOSTESS Oh, Jesu, he doth it as like one of these harlotry 392
players as ever I see! 393
FALSTAFF
Peace, good pint pot; peace, good tickle-brain.— 394
Harry, I do not only marvel where thou spendest thy
time, but also how thou art accompanied; for though 396
the camomile, the more it is trodden on the faster it 397
grows, yet youth, the more it is wasted the sooner it 398
wears. That thou art my son I have partly thy mother's 399
word, partly my own opinion, but chiefly a villainous
trick of thine eye and a foolish hanging of thy nether 401
lip that doth warrant me. If then thou be son to me, 402
here lies the point: why, being son to me, art thou so
pointed at? Shall the blessed sun of heaven prove a
micher and eat blackberries? A question not to be 405
asked. Shall the son of England prove a thief and take
purses? A question to be asked. There is a thing, Harry,
which thou hast often heard of, and it is known
to many in our land by the name of pitch. This pitch, 409
as ancient writers do report, doth defile; so doth the 410
company thou keepest. For, Harry, now I do not speak
to thee in drink but in tears, not in pleasure but in
passion, not in words only but in woes also. And yet 413
there is a virtuous man whom I have often noted in
thy company, but I know not his name.
PRINCE What manner of man, an it like Your Majesty? 416
FALSTAFF A goodly portly man, i'faith, and a corpulent; 417
of a cheerful look, a pleasing eye, and a most noble
carriage; and, as I think, his age some fifty, or, by'r
Lady, inclining to threescore; and now I remember me,
his name is Falstaff. If that man should be lewdly 421
given, he deceiveth me; for, Harry, I see virtue in his
looks. If then the tree may be known by the fruit, as the 423
fruit by the tree, then peremptorily I speak it, there is 424
virtue in that Falstaff. Him keep with, the rest banish.
And tell me now, thou naughty varlet, tell me, where
hast thou been this month?
PRINCE Dost thou speak like a king? Do thou stand for
me, and I'll play my father.
FALSTAFF Depose me? If thou dost it half so gravely, so
majestically, both in word and matter, hang me up by
the heels for a rabbit-sucker or a poulter's hare. 432
[*Hal takes Falstaff's place on the "throne."*]

PRINCE Well, here I am set. 433
FALSTAFF And here I stand. Judge, my masters.
PRINCE Now, Harry, whence come you?
FALSTAFF My noble lord, from Eastcheap.
PRINCE The complaints I hear of thee are grievous.
FALSTAFF 'Sblood, my lord, they are false.—Nay, I'll 438
tickle ye for a young prince, i'faith. 439
PRINCE Swearest thou, ungracious boy? Henceforth
ne'er look on me. Thou art violently carried away from
grace. There is a devil haunts thee in the likeness of an
old fat man; a tun of man is thy companion. Why dost 443
thou converse with that trunk of humors, that bolting- 444
hutch of beastliness, that swollen parcel of dropsies, 445
that huge bombard of sack, that stuffed cloak-bag of 446
guts, that roasted Manningtree ox with the pudding in 447
his belly, that reverend Vice, that gray Iniquity, that 448
father ruffian, that vanity in years? Wherein is he good 449
but to taste sack and drink it? Wherein neat and
cleanly but to carve a capon and eat it? Wherein 451
cunning but in craft? Wherein crafty but in villainy? 452
Wherein villainous but in all things? Wherein worthy
but in nothing?
FALSTAFF I would Your Grace would take me with 455
you. Whom means Your Grace? 456
PRINCE That villainous abominable misleader of youth,
Falstaff, that old white-bearded Satan.
FALSTAFF My lord, the man I know.
PRINCE I know thou dost.
FALSTAFF But to say I know more harm in him than in
myself were to say more than I know. That he is old,
the more the pity, his white hairs do witness it; but
that he is, saving your reverence, a whoremaster, that 464
I utterly deny. If sack and sugar be a fault, God help
the wicked! If to be old and merry be a sin, then many
an old host that I know is damned. If to be fat be to be 467
hated, then Pharaoh's lean kine are to be loved. No, 468
my good lord, banish Peto, banish Bardolph, banish
Poins; but for sweet Jack Falstaff, kind Jack Falstaff,
true Jack Falstaff, valiant Jack Falstaff, and therefore
more valiant being as he is old Jack Falstaff, banish not
him thy Harry's company, banish not him thy Harry's
company—banish plump Jack, and banish all the
world.

---

390 **convey** escort away. **tristful** sorrowing   391 **stop** fill   392 **harlotry** scurvy, vagabond   393 **players** actors   394 **tickle-brain** (A slang term for strong liquor, here applied as a nickname for the tavern hostess.)   396–9 **for though . . . wears** (Falstaff parodies the style of John Lyly's *Euphues*, with its elaborate balanced antitheses, alliterative effects, and illustrations drawn from fanciful natural history. *Camomile* is an aromatic creeping herb whose flowers and leaves are used medicinally.)   401 **trick** trait   402 **warrant** assure   405 **micher** truant   409–10 **This . . . defile** (An allusion to the familiar proverb from Ecclesiasticus 13:1 about the defilement of touching pitch.)   **pitch** a sticky, black residue from the distillation of tar, used to seal wood from moisture   413 **passion** sorrow   416 **an it like** if it please   417 **portly** (1) stately (2) corpulent   421 **lewdly** wickedly   423 **If . . . by the fruit** (See Matthew 12:33.)   424 **peremptorily** decisively   432 **rabbit-sucker** unweaned rabbit.   **poulter's** poulterer's

433 **set** seated.   438 **'Sblood** i.e., By Christ's blood   439 **tickle ye for** amuse you in the role of   443 **tun** (1) large barrel (2) ton   444 **converse** associate.   **humors** body fluids, diseases   444–5 **bolting-hutch** large bin   445 **dropsies** accumulations of fluids causing swelling   446 **bombard** leathern drinking vessel.   **cloak-bag** portmanteau   447 **Manningtree ox** (Manningtree, a town in Essex, had noted fairs where, no doubt, oxen were roasted whole.)   **pudding** sausage-like entrails   448 **Vice, Iniquity** (Allegorical names for the chief comic character and tempter in morality plays.)   449 **vanity** person given to worldly desires   451 **cleanly** (1) pure (2) deft.   **a capon** a castrated rooster for the table   452 **cunning** (1) skillful (2) crafty   455–6 **take me with you** let me catch up with your meaning.   464 **saving your reverence** i.e., with my apology for using offensive language   467 **host** innkeeper   468 **Pharaoh's lean kine** (See Genesis 41, where Pharaoh's dream of seven well-fattened cattle being devoured by seven lean ones is interpreted by Joseph as a prophecy of seven years' famine to come.)

PRINCE   I do, I will.   [*A knocking.*
                                  Exeunt Hostess, Francis, and Bardolph.]

    Enter Bardolph, running.

BARDOLPH   Oh, my lord, my lord! The sheriff with a
most monstrous watch is at the door.   478
FALSTAFF   Out, ye rogue! Play out the play. I have
much to say in the behalf of that Falstaff.

    Enter the Hostess.

HOSTESS   Oh, Jesu, my lord, my lord!
PRINCE   Heigh, heigh! The devil rides upon a fiddle- 482
stick. What's the matter?   483
HOSTESS   The sheriff and all the watch are at the door.
They are come to search the house. Shall I let them in?
FALSTAFF   Dost thou hear, Hal? Never call a true piece 486
of gold a counterfeit. Thou art essentially made 487
without seeming so.   488
PRINCE   And thou a natural coward without instinct.
FALSTAFF   I deny your major. If you will deny the 490
sheriff, so; if not, let him enter. If I become not a cart 491
as well as another man, a plague on my bringing up! 492
I hope I shall as soon be strangled with a halter as
another.
PRINCE   Go hide thee behind the arras. The rest walk 495
up above. Now, my masters, for a true face and good 496
conscience.
FALSTAFF   Both which I have had, but their date is out, 498
and therefore I'll hide me.   [*He hides behind the arras.*]
PRINCE   Call in the sheriff.
                              [*Exeunt all except the Prince and Peto.*]

    Enter Sheriff and the Carrier.

Now, Master Sheriff, what is your will with me?
SHERIFF
    First, pardon me, my lord. A hue and cry   502
    Hath followed certain men unto this house.
PRINCE   What men?
SHERIFF
    One of them is well known, my gracious lord,
    A gross, fat man.
CARRIER   As fat as butter.
PRINCE
    The man, I do assure you, is not here,
    For I myself at this time have employed him.
    And, Sheriff, I will engage my word to thee   509
    That I will, by tomorrow dinnertime,   510
    Send him to answer thee, or any man,

    For anything he shall be charged withal;
    And so let me entreat you leave the house.
SHERIFF
    I will, my lord. There are two gentlemen
    Have in this robbery lost three hundred marks.
PRINCE
    It may be so. If he have robbed these men,
    He shall be answerable; and so farewell.
SHERIFF   Good night, my noble lord.
PRINCE
    I think it is good morrow, is it not?   519
SHERIFF
    Indeed, my lord, I think it be two o'clock.
                                          Exit [*with Carrier*].
PRINCE   This oily rascal is known as well as Paul's. Go 521
call him forth.
PETO   [*discovering Falstaff*]   Falstaff—Fast asleep behind
the arras, and snorting like a horse.
PRINCE   Hark, how hard he fetches breath. Search his
pockets. (*He searcheth his pockets, and findeth certain
papers.*) What hast thou found?
PETO   Nothing but papers, my lord.
PRINCE   Let's see what they be. Read them.
PETO   [*reads*]
    Item, A capon,...2s. 2d.
    Item, Sauce,...4d.
    Item, Sack, two gallons, ...5s. 8d.
    Item, Anchovies and sack after
       supper,...2s. 6d.
    Item, Bread,...ob. 534
PRINCE   Oh, monstrous! But one halfpennyworth of
bread to this intolerable deal of sack? What there is
else, keep close; we'll read it at more advantage. There 537
let him sleep till day. I'll to the court in the morning.
We must all to the wars, and thy place shall be
honorable. I'll procure this fat rogue a charge of foot, 540
and I know his death will be a march of twelve score. 541
The money shall be paid back again with advantage. 542
Be with me betimes in the morning; and so, good 543
morrow, Peto.
PETO   Good morrow, good my lord.   545
    Exeunt [*separately. Falstaff is concealed
    once more behind the arras.*]

❖

[3.1]

    *Enter Hotspur, Worcester, Lord Mortimer,
    [and] Owen Glendower.*

---

478 watch posse of constables   **482–3 The . . . fiddlestick** i.e., Here's much ado about nothing.   **486–8 Dost . . . seeming so** (In this difficult passage, Falstaff seems to suggest that he is true gold, not counterfeit, and so should not be betrayed to the watch by the Prince, who, he hopes, is not merely playacting at the tavern but is truly one of its madcap members.)   **490 deny your major** reject your major premise.   **deny** refuse entrance to   **491 become** befit, adorn.   **cart** i.e., hangman's cart   **492 bringing up** (1) upbringing (2) being brought before the authorities to be hanged.   **495 arras** wall hanging or tapestry.   **496 up above** upstairs.   **498 date is out** lease has run out   **502 hue and cry** outcry calling for the pursuit of a felon   **509 engage** pledge   **510 dinnertime** i.e., about noon

519 morrow morning   **521 Paul's** Saint Paul's Cathedral.   **534 ob.** obolus, i.e., halfpenny.   **537 close** hidden.   **advantage** favorable opportunity.   **540 charge of foot** command of a company of infantry   **541 twelve score** i.e., two hundred and forty yards.   **542 advantage** interest.   **543 betimes** early   **545.1–2 Exeunt . . . arras** (Onstage, the arras is evidently arranged so that Falstaff can exit behind it once the scene is over.)
3.1. Location: Wales. Glendower's residence. (Holinshed places a meeting of the rebel deputies at Bangor in the Archdeacon's house, but in this present "unhistorical" scene, as invented by Shakespeare, Glendower is host throughout.) Seats are provided onstage.

MORTIMER
These promises are fair, the parties sure,
And our induction full of prosperous hope.   2
HOTSPUR
Lord Mortimer, and cousin Glendower,
Will you sit down? And uncle Worcester—
A plague upon it, I have forgot the map.
GLENDOWER [*producing a map*]
No, here it is. Sit, cousin Percy,
Sit, good cousin Hotspur—for by that name
As oft as Lancaster doth speak of you   8
His cheek looks pale, and with a rising sigh
He wisheth you in heaven.
HOTSPUR   And you in hell,
As oft as he hears Owen Glendower spoke of.
GLENDOWER
I cannot blame him. At my nativity
The front of heaven was full of fiery shapes,   13
Of burning cressets, and at my birth   14
The frame and huge foundation of the earth
Shaked like a coward.
HOTSPUR   Why, so it would have done
At the same season, if your mother's cat
Had but kittened, though yourself had never been
    born.
GLENDOWER
I say the earth did shake when I was born.
HOTSPUR
And I say the earth was not of my mind,
If you suppose as fearing you it shook.
GLENDOWER
The heavens were all on fire; the earth did tremble.
HOTSPUR
Oh, then the earth shook to see the heavens on fire,
And not in fear of your nativity.
Diseasèd nature oftentimes breaks forth
In strange eruptions; oft the teeming earth
Is with a kind of colic pinched and vexed
By the imprisoning of unruly wind
Within her womb, which, for enlargement striving,   29
Shakes the old beldam earth and topples down   30
Steeples and moss-grown towers. At your birth
Our grandam earth, having this distemp'rature,   32
In passion shook.
GLENDOWER   Cousin, of many men   33
I do not bear these crossings. Give me leave   34
To tell you once again that at my birth
The front of heaven was full of fiery shapes,
The goats ran from the mountains, and the herds
Were strangely clamorous to the frighted fields.
These signs have marked me extraordinary,
And all the courses of my life do show
I am not in the roll of common men.

Where is he living, clipped in with the sea   42
That chides the banks of England, Scotland, Wales,   43
Which calls me pupil or hath read to me?   44
And bring him out that is but woman's son   45
Can trace me in the tedious ways of art   46
And hold me pace in deep experiments.   47
HOTSPUR
I think there's no man speaks better Welsh.   48
I'll to dinner.
MORTIMER
Peace, cousin Percy; you will make him mad.
GLENDOWER
I can call spirits from the vasty deep.   51
HOTSPUR
Why, so can I, or so can any man;
But will they come when you do call for them?
GLENDOWER
Why, I can teach you, cousin, to command the devil.
HOTSPUR
And I can teach thee, coz, to shame the devil
By telling truth. Tell truth and shame the devil.
If thou have power to raise him, bring him hither,
And I'll be sworn I have power to shame him hence.
Oh, while you live, tell truth and shame the devil!
MORTIMER
Come, come, no more of this unprofitable chat.
GLENDOWER
Three times hath Henry Bolingbroke made head   61
Against my power; thrice from the banks of Wye   62
And sandy-bottomed Severn have I sent him
Bootless home and weather-beaten back.   64
HOTSPUR
Home without boots, and in foul weather too!
How scapes he agues, in the devil's name?   66
GLENDOWER
Come, here is the map. Shall we divide our right
According to our threefold order ta'en?   68
MORTIMER
The Archdeacon hath divided it   69
Into three limits very equally: 70
England, from Trent and Severn hitherto,   71
By south and east is to my part assigned;
All westward, Wales beyond the Severn shore,
And all the fertile land within that bound,
To Owen Glendower; and, dear coz, to you   75
The remnant northward, lying off from Trent.

42–4 Where . . . to me? i.e., Where is there anyone in all of sea-walled
Great Britain who can claim to have been my instructor?   **45–7 And . . .
experiments** And I challenge you to produce a single human being
who can follow my tracks in the arcane craft of magic or keep up with
me in occult experiments.   **48 speaks better Welsh** (Hotspur hides
an insult behind the literal meaning, since "to speak Welsh" meant
colloquially both "to boast" and "to speak nonsense.")   **51 call** summon. (But Hotspur sardonically replies in the sense of "call out to,"
whether or not there is any response.)   **vasty deep** lower world.
61 made head raised a force   **62 power** army   **64 Bootless** without
advantage. (But Hotspur quibbles on the sense of "barefoot.")
66 agues fevers   **68 order ta'en** arrangements made.   **69 Archdeacon** i.e., the Archdeacon of Bangor, in whose house, according to
Holinshed, a meeting took place between deputies of the rebel leaders   **70 limits** regions   **71 hitherto** to this point   **75 coz** cousin, i.e.,
brother-in-law

---

2 induction beginning.   **prosperous hope** hope of prospering.
8 Lancaster i.e., King Henry, here demoted to Duke of Lancaster
13 front brow, face. (As also at line 36.)   **14 cressets** lights burning in
metal baskets suspended from the ends of long poles or ceilings;
hence, meteors   **29 enlargement** release   **30 beldam** grandmother
32 distemp'rature disorder   **33 passion** suffering.   **of** from
34 crossings contradictions.

And our indentures tripartite are drawn,   77
Which being sealèd interchangeably—
A business that this night may execute—   79
Tomorrow, cousin Percy, you and I
And my good lord of Worcester will set forth
To meet your father and the Scottish power,
As is appointed us, at Shrewsbury.
My father Glendower is not ready yet,   84
Nor shall we need his help these fourteen days.
[*To Glendower*] Within that space you may have drawn
     together   86
Your tenants, friends, and neighboring gentlemen.

GLENDOWER
A shorter time shall send me to you, lords;
And in my conduct shall your ladies come,   89
From whom you now must steal and take no leave,
For there will be a world of water shed
Upon the parting of your wives and you.

HOTSPUR [*consulting the map*]
Methinks my moiety, north from Burton here,   93
In quantity equals not one of yours.
See how this river comes me cranking in   95
And cuts me from the best of all my land
A huge half-moon, a monstrous cantle, out.   97
I'll have the current in this place dammed up,
And here the smug and silver Trent shall run   99
In a new channel, fair and evenly.
It shall not wind with such a deep indent
To rob me of so rich a bottom here.   102

GLENDOWER
Not wind? It shall, it must. You see it doth.

MORTIMER
Yea, but mark how he bears his course and runs me up   104
With like advantage on the other side,
Gelding the opposèd continent as much   106
As on the other side it takes from you.

WORCESTER
Yea, but a little charge will trench him here   108
And on this north side win this cape of land;
And then he runs straight and even.

HOTSPUR
I'll have it so. A little charge will do it.

GLENDOWER   I'll not have it altered.

HOTSPUR   Will not you?

GLENDOWER   No, nor you shall not.

HOTSPUR   Who shall say me nay?

GLENDOWER   Why, that will I.

HOTSPUR
Let me not understand you, then; speak it in Welsh.

GLENDOWER
I can speak English, lord, as well as you;
For I was trained up in the English court,
Where, being but young, I framèd to the harp   120
Many an English ditty lovely well,
And gave the tongue a helpful ornament—   122
A virtue that was never seen in you.

HOTSPUR
Marry, and I am glad of it with all my heart!
I had rather be a kitten and cry "mew"
Than one of these same meter balladmongers.
I had rather hear a brazen can'stick turned   127
Or a dry wheel grate on the axletree,   128
And that would set my teeth nothing on edge,   129
Nothing so much as mincing poetry.
'Tis like the forced gait of a shuffling nag.   131

GLENDOWER   Come, you shall have Trent turned.

HOTSPUR
I do not care. I'll give thrice so much land
To any well-deserving friend;
But in the way of bargain, mark ye me,
I'll cavil on the ninth part of a hair.   136
Are the indentures drawn? Shall we be gone?   137

GLENDOWER
The moon shines fair; you may away by night.
I'll haste the writer and withal   139
Break with your wives of your departure hence.   140
I am afraid my daughter will run mad,
So much she doteth on her Mortimer.   *Exit.*

MORTIMER
Fie, cousin Percy, how you cross my father!

HOTSPUR
I cannot choose. Sometimes he angers me
With telling me of the moldwarp and the ant,   145
Of the dreamer Merlin and his prophecies,   146
And of a dragon and a finless fish,
A clip-winged griffin and a moulten raven,   148
A couching lion and a ramping cat,   149
And such a deal of skimble-skamble stuff   150
As puts me from my faith. I tell you what: 151
He held me last night at least nine hours
In reckoning up the several devils' names   153

---

77 tripartite i.e., drawn up in triplicate, each document *sealèd interchangeably* (line 78) with the seal of all signatories.   **drawn** drawn up   **79 this night may execute** may be carried out tonight   **84 father** father-in-law   **86 may** will be able to   **89 conduct** escort   **93 moiety** share   **95 comes me cranking in** comes bending in on my share. (The Trent, by turning northward to the North Sea instead of continuing eastward into the Wash, cuts Hotspur off from rich land in Lincolnshire and its vicinity.)   **97 cantle** piece   **99 smug** smooth   **102 bottom** valley   **104 runs me** runs. (*Me* is used colloquially.)   **106 Gelding . . . continent** cutting off from the land which it bounds on the opposite side. (The Trent's southerly loop from Stoke to Burton deprives Mortimer of a piece of land, just as its later northerly course deprives Hotspur.)   **108 charge** expenditure.   **trench** provide a new channel for

120 framèd to the harp set to harp accompaniment   **122 gave . . . ornament** i.e., added to the words a pleasing ornament of music; also, gave to the English tongue the ornament of music and poetry   **127 can'stick turned** candlestick turned on a lathe   **128 axletree** axle   **129 nothing** not at all   **131 shuffling** hobbled   **136 cavil . . . hair** i.e., argue about the most trivial detail.   **137 drawn** drawn up.   **139 writer** i.e., scrivener who would be drawing the indentures.   **withal** also   **140 Break with** inform   **145 moldwarp** mole. (Holinshed tells us that the division was arranged because of a prophecy that represented King Henry as the mole and the others as the dragon, the lion, and the wolf, who should divide the land among them.)   **146 Merlin** the bard, prophet, and magician of Arthurian story, Welsh in origin   **148 griffin** a fabulous beast, half lion, half eagle.   **moulten** having molted   **149 couching** couchant, crouching. (Heraldic term.)   **ramping** rampant, advancing on its hind legs. (Hotspur is ridiculing the heraldic emblems that Glendower holds so dear.)   **150 skimble-skamble** foolish, nonsensical   **151 puts . . . faith** drives me from my (Christian) faith.   **153 several** various

That were his lackeys. I cried "Hum," and "Well, go to," 154
But marked him not a word. Oh, he is as tedious
As a tirèd horse, a railing wife,
Worse than a smoky house. I had rather live
With cheese and garlic in a windmill, far,
Than feed on cates and have him talk to me   159
In any summer house in Christendom.

MORTIMER
In faith, he is a worthy gentleman,
Exceedingly well read, and profited   162
In strange concealments, valiant as a lion   163
And wondrous affable, and as bountiful
As mines of India. Shall I tell you, cousin?
He holds your temper in a high respect   166
And curbs himself even of his natural scope   167
When you come 'cross his humor. Faith, he does.   168
I warrant you that man is not alive
Might so have tempted him as you have done   170
Without the taste of danger and reproof.
But do not use it oft, let me entreat you.

WORCESTER [to Hotspur]
In faith, my lord, you are too willful-blame,   173
And since your coming hither have done enough
To put him quite besides his patience.   175
You must needs learn, lord, to amend this fault.
Though sometimes it show greatness, courage,
    blood—   177
And that's the dearest grace it renders you—   178
Yet oftentimes it doth present harsh rage,   179
Defect of manners, want of government,   180
Pride, haughtiness, opinion, and disdain,   181
The least of which haunting a nobleman
Loseth men's hearts and leaves behind a stain
Upon the beauty of all parts besides,   184
Beguiling them of commendation.   185

HOTSPUR
Well, I am schooled. Good manners be your speed!   186
Here come our wives, and let us take our leave.

        Enter Glendower with the ladies.

MORTIMER
This is the deadly spite that angers me: 188
My wife can speak no English, I no Welsh.

GLENDOWER
My daughter weeps she'll not part with you;
She'll be a soldier too, she'll to the wars.

MORTIMER
Good father, tell her that she and my aunt Percy   192

Shall follow in your conduct speedily.   193
        *Glendower speaks to her in Welsh, and she answers
                                him in the same.*

GLENDOWER
She is desperate here; a peevish self-willed harlotry,   194
One that no persuasion can do good upon.
                        The lady speaks in Welsh.

MORTIMER [to her]
I understand thy looks. That pretty Welsh   196
Which thou pourest down from these swelling heavens 197
I am too perfect in; and, but for shame,   198
In such a parley should I answer thee.   199
                        The lady again in Welsh.
I understand thy kisses and thou mine,
And that's a feeling disputation.   201
But I will never be a truant, love,
Till I have learned thy language; for thy tongue
Makes Welsh as sweet as ditties highly penned,   204
Sung by a fair queen in a summer's bower,
With ravishing division, to her lute.   206

GLENDOWER
Nay, if you melt, then will she run mad.   207
                        The lady speaks again in Welsh.

MORTIMER
Oh, I am ignorance itself in this!

GLENDOWER
She bids you on the wanton rushes lay you down   209
And rest your gentle head upon her lap,
And she will sing the song that pleaseth you
And on your eyelids crown the god of sleep,   212
Charming your blood with pleasing heaviness,   213
Making such difference twixt wake and sleep   214
As is the difference betwixt day and night
The hour before the heavenly-harnessed team   216
Begins his golden progress in the east.

MORTIMER
With all my heart I'll sit and hear her sing.
By that time will our book, I think, be drawn.   219

GLENDOWER   Do so;
And those musicians that shall play to you
Hang in the air a thousand leagues from hence,
And straight they shall be here. Sit, and attend.
                        *[Mortimer reclines with his head
                                in his wife's lap.]*

HOTSPUR   Come, Kate, thou art perfect in lying down;
    come, quick, quick, that I may lay my head in thy lap.

LADY PERCY   Go, ye giddy goose.
                        *[Hotspur lies with his head
                        in Kate's lap.] The music plays.*

---

154 **go to** i.e., you don't say   159 **cates** delicacies   162 **profited** proficient   163 **concealments** occult practices   166 **temper** temperament
167 **scope** freedom of speech   168 **come 'cross** contradict   170 **Might**
who could   173 **too willful-blame** blameworthy for too much self-will
175 **besides** out of   177 **blood** spirit   178 **dearest grace** best (and costli-
est) credit   179 **present** represent   180 **want of government** lack of
self-control   181 **opinion** vanity, arrogance   184 **all parts besides** all
other abilities   185 **Beguiling** depriving   186 **Good . . . speed!** i.e., May
these good manners you praise so bring you success! (Said wryly; Hotspur doubts that good manners count for much in a time of war.)   188
spite vexation   192 **aunt** (Percy's wife, here called Kate, was aunt of
Edmund Mortimer, the fifth Earl of March, but was sister-in-law to the
Sir Edward Mortimer who married Glendower's daughter.)

193 **conduct** safe-conduct, escort   194 **desperate here** adamant on this
point (i.e., her decision to accompany Mortimer).   **peevish self-willed
harlotry** childish, willful, silly wench   196 **That pretty Welsh** i.e., Your
eloquent tears   197 **heavens** i.e., eyes   198 **perfect** proficient
199 **such a parley** i.e., the same language (of weeping)   201 **disputation** conversation, debate.   204 **highly penned** eloquently composed,
in high style   206 **division** variation, passage in which rapid short
notes vary a theme   207 **melt** i.e., weep   209 **wanton rushes** i.e., soft
floor covering   212 **crown . . . sleep** make sleep supreme ruler
213 **heaviness** drowsiness   214 **difference** nearly indistinguishable
difference   216 **the heavenly-harnessed team** i.e., the team of horses
drawing the chariot of the sun   219 **book** document, indentures

HOTSPUR
Now I perceive the devil understands Welsh;
And 'tis no marvel he is so humorous.   228
By'r Lady, he is a good musician.

LADY PERCY   Then should you be nothing but musical,
for you are altogether governed by humors. Lie still,
ye thief, and hear the lady sing in Welsh.   232

HOTSPUR   I had rather hear Lady, my brach, howl in   233
Irish.

LADY PERCY   Wouldst thou have thy head broken?   235

HOTSPUR   No.

LADY PERCY   Then be still.

HOTSPUR   Neither, 'tis a woman's fault.   238

LADY PERCY   Now God help thee!   239

HOTSPUR   To the Welsh lady's bed.

LADY PERCY   What's that?

HOTSPUR   Peace, she sings.

Here the lady sings a Welsh song.

HOTSPUR
Come, Kate, I'll have your song too.

LADY PERCY
Not mine, in good sooth.

HOTSPUR   Not yours, in good sooth! Heart, you swear   245
like a comfit maker's wife. "Not you, in good sooth,"   246
and "as true as I live," and "as God shall mend me,"
and "as sure as day,"
And givest such sarcenet surety for thy oaths   249
As if thou never walk'st further than Finsbury.   250
Swear me, Kate, like a lady as thou art,
A good mouth-filling oath, and leave "in sooth,"
And such protest of pepper-gingerbread,   253
To velvet-guards and Sunday citizens.   254
Come, sing.

LADY PERCY   I will not sing.

HOTSPUR   'Tis the next way to turn tailor, or be redbreast   257
teacher. An the indentures be drawn, I'll away within   258
these two hours; and so, come in when ye will.   *Exit.*

GLENDOWER
Come, come, Lord Mortimer. You are as slow
As hot Lord Percy is on fire to go.
By this our book is drawn; we'll but seal,   262
And then to horse immediately.

MORTIMER   With all my heart.   *Exeunt.*

❧

228 **humorous** whimsical, capricious.   232 **thief** i.e., rascal
233 **brach** bitch hound   235 **broken** i.e., struck so as to break the
skin.   238 **Neither . . . fault** i.e., I won't do that either; it's womanish
to be submissive.   239 **help** amend. (But Hotspur answers in the
sense of "assist with an amour.")   245 **Heart** i.e., By Christ's heart
246 **comfit maker's** confectioner's   249 **sarcenet** soft, flimsy. (From
the soft silken material known as *sarcenet*.)   250 **Finsbury** a field just
outside London frequented by the London citizenry. (Hotspur jokes
with Kate as though she were a citizen's wife, using the pious and
modest oaths of such people.)   253 **protest . . . gingerbread** i.e.,
mealy-mouthed protestations   254 **velvet-guards** i.e., wives who
wear velvet trimming   257–8 **'Tis . . . teacher** i.e., The only use one
might put singing to is to become a tailor (since tailors were noted for
effeminacy and singing at their work) or an instructor to caged song-
birds before they are sold. (Hotspur airily dismisses singing, as he
does poetry.)   262 **By this** By this time.   **but** just

[3.2]

Enter the King, Prince of Wales, and others.

KING
Lords, give us leave. The Prince of Wales and I
Must have some private conference; but be near at
  hand,
For we shall presently have need of you.
                                          Exeunt Lords.
I know not whether God will have it so
For some displeasing service I have done,
That in his secret doom out of my blood   6
He'll breed revengement and a scourge for me;
But thou dost in thy passages of life   8
Make me believe that thou art only marked   9
For the hot vengeance and the rod of heaven   10
To punish my mistreadings. Tell me else,   11
Could such inordinate and low desires,   12
Such poor, such bare, such lewd, such mean attempts,   13
Such barren pleasures, rude society,
As thou art matched withal and grafted to,   15
Accompany the greatness of thy blood
And hold their level with thy princely heart?   17

PRINCE
So please Your Majesty, I would I could
Quit all offenses with as clear excuse   19
As well as I am doubtless I can purge   20
Myself of many I am charged withal.
Yet such extenuation let me beg
As, in reproof of many tales devised,   23
Which oft the ear of greatness needs must hear
By smiling pickthanks and base newsmongers,   25
I may, for some things true, wherein my youth
Hath faulty wandered and irregular,
Find pardon on my true submission.

KING
God pardon thee! Yet let me wonder, Harry,
At thy affections, which do hold a wing   30
Quite from the flight of all thy ancestors.   31
Thy place in Council thou hast rudely lost,   32
Which by thy younger brother is supplied,
And art almost an alien to the hearts
Of all the court and princes of my blood.
The hope and expectation of thy time   36
Is ruined, and the soul of every man
Prophetically do forethink thy fall.

3.2. Location: The royal court (historically, Westminster).
6 **doom** judgment.   **blood** offspring   8 **passages** course, conduct
9–11 **thou . . . mistreadings** (1) you are marked as the means of heaven's
vengeance against me, or (2) you are marked to suffer heaven's
vengeance because of my sins.   11 **else** how otherwise   12 **inordinate** (1) immoderate (2) unworthy of your rank   13 **lewd** low, base.
attempts undertakings   15 **withal** with   17 **hold their level** claim
equality   19 **Quit** acquit myself of   20 **doubtless** certain   23 **in
reproof** upon disproof   25 **By . . . newsmongers** from smiling flatterers and ignoble talebearers   30 **affections** inclinations.   **hold a wing**
fly a course   31 **from** at variance with   32 **rudely** by violence.
(According to an apocryphal story, Prince Hal boxed the ears of the
Lord Chief Justice and was sent to prison for it; see *2 Henry IV*,
1.2.54–5, 192, and 5.2.70–1.)   36 **The hope . . . time** The hopes that
people had for you

Had I so lavish of my presence been,
So common-hackneyed in the eyes of men,   40
So stale and cheap to vulgar company,
Opinion, that did help me to the crown,   42
Had still kept loyal to possession   43
And left me in reputeless banishment,
A fellow of no mark nor likelihood.   45
By being seldom seen, I could not stir
But like a comet I was wondered at,
That men would tell their children, "This is he!"
Others would say, "Where, which is Bolingbroke?"
And then I stole all courtesy from heaven,   50
And dressed myself in such humility
That I did pluck allegiance from men's hearts,
Loud shouts and salutations from their mouths,
Even in the presence of the crownèd King.
Thus did I keep my person fresh and new,
My presence, like a robe pontifical,   56
Ne'er seen but wondered at; and so my state,   57
Seldom but sumptuous, showed like a feast   58
And won by rareness such solemnity.   59
The skipping King, he ambled up and down
With shallow jesters and rash bavin wits,   61
Soon kindled and soon burnt; carded his state,   62
Mingled his royalty with cap'ring fools,
Had his great name profanèd with their scorns,   64
And gave his countenance, against his name,   65
To laugh at gibing boys and stand the push   66
Of every beardless vain comparative;   67
Grew a companion to the common streets,
Enfeoffed himself to popularity,   69
That, being daily swallowed by men's eyes,
They surfeited with honey and began
To loathe the taste of sweetness, whereof a little
More than a little is by much too much.
So when he had occasion to be seen,
He was but as the cuckoo is in June,
Heard, not regarded—seen, but with such eyes
As, sick and blunted with community,   77
Afford no extraordinary gaze,
Such as is bent on sunlike majesty
When it shines seldom in admiring eyes;
But rather drowsed and hung their eyelids down,
Slept in his face, and rendered such aspect   82
As cloudy men use to their adversaries,   83

Being with his presence glutted, gorged, and full.
And in that very line, Harry, standest thou;   85
For thou hast lost thy princely privilege
With vile participation. Not an eye   87
But is aweary of thy common sight,
Save mine, which hath desired to see thee more—
Which now doth that I would not have it do,   90
Make blind itself with foolish tenderness.   91

PRINCE
I shall hereafter, my thrice gracious lord,
Be more myself.

KING   For all the world   93
As thou art to this hour was Richard then
When I from France set foot at Ravenspurgh,
And even as I was then is Percy now.
Now, by my scepter, and my soul to boot,   97
He hath more worthy interest to the state   98
Than thou the shadow of succession.   99
For of no right, nor color like to right,   100
He doth fill fields with harness in the realm,   101
Turns head against the lion's armèd jaws,   102
And, being no more in debt to years than thou,   103
Leads ancient lords and reverend bishops on
To bloody battles and to bruising arms.
What never-dying honor hath he got
Against renownèd Douglas! Whose high deeds,   107
Whose hot incursions and great name in arms
Holds from all soldiers chief majority   109
And military title capital   110
Through all the kingdoms that acknowledge Christ.
Thrice hath this Hotspur, Mars in swaddling clothes,
This infant warrior, in his enterprises
Discomfited great Douglas, ta'en him once,   114
Enlargèd him and made a friend of him,   115
To fill the mouth of deep defiance up   116
And shake the peace and safety of our throne.
And what say you to this? Percy, Northumberland,
The Archbishop's Grace of York, Douglas, Mortimer,   119
Capitulate against us and are up.   120
But wherefore do I tell these news to thee?
Why, Harry, do I tell thee of my foes,
Which art my nearest and dearest enemy?   123
Thou that art like enough, through vassal fear,   124
Base inclination, and the start of spleen,   125
To fight against me under Percy's pay,

---

40 **common-hackneyed** cheapened, vulgarized   42 **Opinion** public opinion   43 **to possession** i.e., to Richard II's sovereignty   45 **mark nor likelihood** importance or likeliness to succeed.   50 **I . . . heaven** i.e., I assumed a bearing of the utmost meekness   56 **pontifical** like that of a pope or archbishop   57–9 **and so . . . solemnity** and so my magnificence on public occasions, infrequent but always sumptuous, looked festive and achieved by this rarity a suitable formal impressiveness.   61 **bavin** brushwood, soon burnt out   62 **carded his state** debased his royal dignity. (To *card* is to stir or mix, hence to adulterate.)   64 **with their scorns** by his favorites' scornful and contemptuous behavior   65–7 **And gave . . . comparative** and lent his authority, to the detriment of his royal dignity and reputation, to find amusement in young scoffers and submit himself to the insolence of every frivolous witcracker   69 **Enfeoffed himself** gave himself up   77 **community** commonness   82–3 **Slept . . . adversaries** dozed off right before his eyes, and looked at the King in the way sullen men look at their adversaries

85 **line** degree, category   87 **vile participation** base association or companionship.   90 **that** that which   91 **tenderness** i.e., tears.   93 **For all the world** In every way   97 **to boot** in addition   98–9 **He . . . succession** i.e., this rebel Hotspur has a better claim to the throne than your merely hereditary claim unsupported by deeds.   100 **of . . . to right** having no rightful claim or even the pretext of one   101 **harness** armor, i.e., men in armor   102 **Turns head** leads an armed insurrection.   **lion's** i.e., King's   103 **being . . . thou** i.e., being no older than you. (Though historically Hotspur was twenty-three years older than the Prince.)   107 **Whose** i.e., Hotspur's   109 **majority** preeminence   110 **capital** chief, principal   114 **Discomfited** defeated   115 **Enlargèd** freed   116 **To . . . up** to swell the roar of deep defiance   119 **The Archbishop's Grace** His Grace the Archbishop   120 **Capitulate** form a league, draw up articles.   **up** up in arms.   123 **dearest** (1) most precious (2) direst   124 **like** likely.   **vassal** slavish   125 **Base . . . spleen** inclination for baseness, and sudden bursts of capricious irascibility

To dog his heels and curtsy at his frowns,
To show how much thou art degenerate.

PRINCE
Do not think so. You shall not find it so.
And God forgive them that so much have swayed
Your Majesty's good thoughts away from me!
I will redeem all this on Percy's head
And in the closing of some glorious day
Be bold to tell you that I am your son,
When I will wear a garment all of blood
And stain my favors in a bloody mask,   136
Which, washed away, shall scour my shame with it.
And that shall be the day, whene'er it lights,   138
That this same child of honor and renown,
This gallant Hotspur, this all-praisèd knight,
And your unthought-of Harry chance to meet.   141
For every honor sitting on his helm,   142
Would they were multitudes, and on my head
My shames redoubled! For the time will come
That I shall make this northern youth exchange
His glorious deeds for my indignities.
Percy is but my factor, good my lord,   147
To engross up glorious deeds on my behalf;   148
And I will call him to so strict account
That he shall render every glory up,
Yea, even the slightest worship of his time,   151
Or I will tear the reckoning from his heart.
This in the name of God I promise here,
The which if He be pleased I shall perform,
I do beseech Your Majesty may salve   155
The long-grown wounds of my intemperance.   156
If not, the end of life cancels all bonds,
And I will die a hundred thousand deaths
Ere break the smallest parcel of this vow.

KING
A hundred thousand rebels die in this!
Thou shalt have charge and sovereign trust herein.   161

Enter Blunt.

How now, good Blunt? Thy looks are full of speed.

BLUNT
So hath the business that I come to speak of.
Lord Mortimer of Scotland hath sent word   164
That Douglas and the English rebels met
The eleventh of this month at Shrewsbury.
A mighty and a fearful head they are,   167
If promises be kept on every hand,
As ever offered foul play in a state.

KING
The Earl of Westmorland set forth today,
With him my son, Lord John of Lancaster;
For this advertisement is five days old.   172
On Wednesday next, Harry, you shall set forward;

On Thursday we ourselves will march. Our meeting   174
Is Bridgnorth. And, Harry, you shall march   175
Through Gloucestershire; by which account,
Our business valuèd, some twelve days hence   177
Our general forces at Bridgnorth shall meet.
Our hands are full of business. Let's away!
Advantage feeds him fat while men delay.   *Exeunt.*   180

[3.3]

Enter Falstaff and Bardolph.

FALSTAFF Bardolph, am I not fallen away vilely since   1
this last action? Do I not bate? Do I not dwindle? Why,   2
my skin hangs about me like an old lady's loose gown;
I am withered like an old applejohn. Well, I'll repent,   4
and that suddenly, while I am in some liking. I shall be   5
out of heart shortly, and then I shall have no strength   6
to repent. An I have not forgotten what the inside of a
church is made of, I am a peppercorn, a brewer's   8
horse. The inside of a church! Company, villainous   9
company, hath been the spoil of me.
BARDOLPH Sir John, you are so fretful you cannot live   11
long.
FALSTAFF Why, there is it. Come sing me a bawdy
song; make me merry. I was as virtuously given as a   14
gentleman need to be, virtuous enough: swore little,
diced not above seven times—a week, went to a
bawdy house not above once in a quarter—of an
hour, paid money that I borrowed—three or four
times, lived well and in good compass; and now I live   19
out of all order, out of all compass.
BARDOLPH Why, you are so fat, Sir John, that you must
needs be out of all compass, out of all reasonable
compass, Sir John.
FALSTAFF Do thou amend thy face, and I'll amend my
life. Thou art our admiral, thou bearest the lantern in   25
the poop, but 'tis in the nose of thee. Thou art the
Knight of the Burning Lamp.   27
BARDOLPH Why, Sir John, my face does you no harm.
FALSTAFF No, I'll be sworn, I make as good use of it as
many a man doth of a death's-head or a *memento mori.*   30
I never see thy face but I think upon hellfire and

---

136 **favors** features 138 **lights** dawns 141 **unthought-of** lightly valued, disregarded 142 **For** As for 147 **factor** agent 148 **engross up** amass, buy up 151 **even . . . time** every smallest honor he has ever won 155 **salve** soothe, heal 156 **intemperance** dissolute living. 161 **charge** command (of troops) 164 **Lord Mortimer of Scotland** (A Scottish nobleman, unrelated to Glendower's son-in-law.) 167 **head** armed force 172 **advertisement** tidings, news

174 **meeting** place of rendezvous 175 **Bridgnorth** a town near Shrewsbury. 177 **Our business valuèd** estimating how long our business will take 180 **Advantage . . . fat** Opportunity (for rebellion) prospers. **him** himself
3.3. Location: A tavern in Eastcheap, as in 2.4.
1 **fallen away** shrunk 2 **action** i.e., the robbery at Gad's Hill. **bate** lose weight. 4 **applejohn** a kind of apple still in good eating condition when shriveled. 5 **liking** (1) good bodily condition (2) inclination. 6 **out of heart** (1) disinclined, disheartened (2) out of condition 8 **peppercorn** unground dried pepper berry 8–9 **brewer's horse** i.e., one that is old, withered, and decrepit. 11 **fretful** (1) anxious (2) fretted, frayed 14 **given** inclined 19 **good compass** reasonable limits; also, in Bardolph's speech, girth, circumference 25 **admiral** flagship. **lantern** i.e., a light for the rest of the fleet to follow; here applied to Bardolph's inflamed nose, red from overdrinking 27 **Knight . . . Lamp** Falstaff parodies the names of heroes in popular chivalric romances. 30 *memento mori* reminder of death, such as a death's-head or a skull engraved on a seal ring.

Dives that lived in purple; for there he is in his robes, 32
burning, burning. If thou wert any way given to
virtue, I would swear by thy face; my oath should be
"By this fire, that's God's angel." But thou art 35
altogether given over, and wert indeed, but for the 36
light in thy face, the son of utter darkness. When thou
ran'st up Gad's Hill in the night to catch my horse, if
I did not think thou hadst been an *ignis fatuus* or a ball 39
of wildfire, there's no purchase in money. Oh, thou art 40
a perpetual triumph, an everlasting bonfire light! 41
Thou hast saved me a thousand marks in links and 42
torches, walking with thee in the night betwixt tavern
and tavern; but the sack that thou hast drunk me
would have bought me lights as good cheap at the 45
dearest chandler's in Europe. I have maintained that 46
salamander of yours with fire any time this two-and- 47
thirty years. God reward me for it!

BARDOLPH   'Sblood, I would my face were in your belly! 49
FALSTAFF   God-a-mercy! So should I be sure to be
heartburned.

Enter Hostess.

How now, Dame Partlet the hen? Have you inquired 52
yet who picked my pocket?
HOSTESS   Why, Sir John, what do you think, Sir John?
Do you think I keep thieves in my house? I have
searched, I have inquired, so has my husband, man
by man, boy by boy, servant by servant. The tithe of a 57
hair was never lost in my house before.
FALSTAFF   Ye lie, hostess. Bardolph was shaved and 59
lost many a hair; and I'll be sworn my pocket was 60
picked. Go to, you are a woman, go.
HOSTESS   Who, I? No, I defy thee! God's light, I was 62
never called so in mine own house before.
FALSTAFF   Go to, I know you well enough.
HOSTESS   No, Sir John, you do not know me, Sir John.
I know you, Sir John. You owe me money, Sir John,
and now you pick a quarrel to beguile me of it. I
bought you a dozen of shirts to your back.
FALSTAFF   Dowlas, filthy dowlas. I have given them 69
away to bakers' wives; they have made bolters of 70
them.
HOSTESS   Now, as I am a true woman, holland of eight 72
shillings an ell. You owe money here besides, Sir 73
John, for your diet and by-drinkings, and money lent 74
you, four-and-twenty pound.

FALSTAFF   He had his part of it. Let him pay. 76
HOSTESS   He? Alas, he is poor, he hath nothing.
FALSTAFF   How, poor? Look upon his face. What call
you rich? Let them coin his nose, let them coin his
cheeks. I'll not pay a denier. What, will you make a 80
younker of me? Shall I not take mine ease in mine inn 81
but I shall have my pocket picked? I have lost a seal
ring of my grandfather's worth forty mark.
HOSTESS   Oh, Jesu, I have heard the Prince tell him, I
know not how oft, that that ring was copper.
FALSTAFF   How? The Prince is a Jack, a sneak-up. 86
'Sblood, an he were here, I would cudgel him like a
dog if he would say so. 88

*Enter the Prince [with Peto], marching, and
Falstaff meets him playing upon his truncheon like
a fife.*

How now, lad, is the wind in that door, i'faith? Must 89
we all march?
BARDOLPH   Yea, two and two, Newgate fashion. 91
HOSTESS   My lord, I pray you, hear me.
PRINCE   What say'st thou, Mistress Quickly? How doth
thy husband? I love him well; he is an honest man.
HOSTESS   Good my lord, hear me.
FALSTAFF   Prithee, let her alone and list to me.
PRINCE   What say'st thou, Jack?
FALSTAFF   The other night I fell asleep here behind the
arras and had my pocket picked. This house is turned 99
bawdy house; they pick pockets.
PRINCE   What didst thou lose, Jack?
FALSTAFF   Wilt thou believe me, Hal? Three or four
bonds of forty pound apiece and a seal ring of my
grandfather's.
PRINCE   A trifle, some eightpenny matter.
HOSTESS   So I told him, my lord, and I said I heard Your
Grace say so; and, my lord, he speaks most vilely of
you, like a foulmouthed man as he is, and said he
would cudgel you.
PRINCE   What, he did not!
HOSTESS   There's neither faith, truth, nor womanhood
in me else.
FALSTAFF   There's no more faith in thee than in a stewed 113
prune, nor no more truth in thee than in a drawn fox; 114
and for womanhood, Maid Marian may be the dep- 115
uty's wife of the ward to thee. Go, you thing, go. 116
HOSTESS   Say, what thing, what thing?
FALSTAFF   What thing? Why, a thing to thank God on. 118
HOSTESS   I am no thing to thank God on, I would thou 119
shouldst know it! I am an honest man's wife, and,

32 Dives the rich man who went to hell, referred to in Luke 16:19–31
35 "By . . . angel" (Psalms 104:4, Hebrews 1:7, and Exodus 3:2
describe angels that appear in flames of fire.)   **36 given over** abandoned to wickedness   **39 *ignis fatuus*** will-o'-the-wisp   **40 wildfire**
fireworks; lightning; will-o'-the-wisp   **41 triumph** procession led by
torches   **42 links** torches, flares   **45 good cheap** cheap   **46 dearest
chandler's** most expensive candle maker's   **47 salamander** lizard
reputed to be able to live in fire   **49 I . . . belly** (A colloquial way of
objecting to an insult. Falstaff responds in the literal sense: A face like
yours would give me massive indigestion.)   **52 Partlet** (Traditional
name of a hen.)   **57 tithe** tenth part   **59 was shaved** (1) had his
beard cut (2) was cheated and robbed   **60 lost many a hair** (1) was
shaved (2) was made bald by syphilis   **62 God's light** (A mild oath.)
69 Dowlas a coarse kind of linen   **70 bolters** cloths for sifting flour
72 holland fine linen   **73 an ell** a measure of forty-five inches.
74 diet meals.   **by-drinkings** drinks between meals

76 He Bardolph   **80 denier** one-twelfth of a French sou; type of very
small coin.   **81 younker** greenhorn   **86 Jack** knave, rascal.   **sneak-
up** sneak.   **88.2 *truncheon*** officer's staff   **89 is . . . door** i.e., is that the
way the wind is blowing   **91 Newgate** a famous city prison in London.
(Prisoners marched two by two.)   **99 arras** curtain   **113–14 stewed
prune** (Customarily associated with bawdy houses.)   **114 drawn fox**
fox driven from cover and wily in getting back   **115–16 Maid . . .
thee** i.e., Maid Marian, a disreputable woman in Robin Hood ballads,
morris dances, and the like, was a model of respectability compared
with you.   **118–19 What thing . . . no thing** (With sexual quibbles.)

setting thy knighthood aside, thou art a knave to call 121
me so.

FALSTAFF   Setting thy womanhood aside, thou art a
beast to say otherwise.

HOSTESS   Say, what beast, thou knave, thou?

FALSTAFF   What beast? Why, an otter.

PRINCE   An otter, Sir John! Why an otter?

FALSTAFF   Why? She's neither fish nor flesh; a man
knows not where to have her.   129

HOSTESS   Thou art an unjust man in saying so. Thou or
any man knows where to have me, thou knave, thou.

PRINCE   Thou say'st true, hostess, and he slanders thee
most grossly.

HOSTESS   So he doth you, my lord, and said this other
day you owed him a thousand pound.

PRINCE   Sirrah, do I owe you a thousand pound?

FALSTAFF   A thousand pound, Hal? A million. Thy love
is worth a million; thou owest me thy love.

HOSTESS   Nay, my lord, he called you Jack and said he
would cudgel you.

FALSTAFF   Did I, Bardolph?

BARDOLPH   Indeed, Sir John, you said so.

FALSTAFF   Yea, if he said my ring was copper.

PRINCE   I say 'tis copper. Darest thou be as good as thy
word now?

FALSTAFF   Why, Hal, thou knowest, as thou art but
man, I dare; but as thou art prince, I fear thee as I fear
the roaring of the lion's whelp.   148

PRINCE   And why not as the lion?

FALSTAFF   The King himself is to be feared as the lion.
Dost thou think I'll fear thee as I fear thy father? Nay,
an I do, I pray God my girdle break.

PRINCE   Oh, if it should, how would thy guts fall about
thy knees! But, sirrah, there's no room for faith, truth,
nor honesty in this bosom of thine; it is all filled up
with guts and midriff. Charge an honest woman with
picking thy pocket? Why, thou whoreson, impudent,
embossed rascal, if there were anything in thy pocket 158
but tavern reckonings, memorandums of bawdy   159
houses, and one poor pennyworth of sugar candy to
make thee long-winded, if thy pocket were enriched
with any other injuries but these, I am a villain. And 162
yet you will stand to it; you will not pocket up wrong! 163
Art thou not ashamed?

FALSTAFF   Dost thou hear, Hal? Thou knowest in the
state of innocency Adam fell; and what should poor
Jack Falstaff do in the days of villainy? Thou see'st I
have more flesh than another man, and therefore
more frailty. You confess then you picked my pocket.

PRINCE   It appears so by the story.

FALSTAFF   Hostess, I forgive thee. Go make ready breakfast. Love thy husband, look to thy servants, cherish
thy guests. Thou shalt find me tractable to any honest
reason; thou see'st I am pacified still. Nay, prithee,   174
begone.   Exit Hostess.
Now, Hal, to the news at court: for the robbery, lad,
how is that answered?

PRINCE   Oh, my sweet beef, I must still be good angel to
thee. The money is paid back again.

FALSTAFF   Oh, I do not like that paying back. 'Tis a
double labor.   181

PRINCE   I am good friends with my father and may do
anything.

FALSTAFF   Rob me the exchequer the first thing thou
dost, and do it with unwashed hands too.   185

BARDOLPH   Do, my lord.

PRINCE   I have procured thee, Jack, a charge of foot.   187

FALSTAFF   I would it had been of horse. Where shall I
find one that can steal well? Oh, for a fine thief, of the 189
age of two-and-twenty or thereabouts! I am heinously
unprovided. Well, God be thanked for these rebels;   191
they offend none but the virtuous. I laud them, I   192
praise them.

PRINCE   Bardolph!

BARDOLPH   My lord?

PRINCE [giving letters]
Go bear this letter to Lord John of Lancaster,
To my brother John; this to my lord of Westmorland.
                                          [Exit Bardolph.]
Go, Peto, to horse, to horse, for thou and I
Have thirty miles to ride yet ere dinnertime.
                                             [Exit Peto.]
Jack, meet me tomorrow in the Temple Hall   200
At two o'clock in the afternoon.
There shalt thou know thy charge, and there receive
Money and order for their furniture.   203
The land is burning. Percy stands on high,
And either we or they must lower lie.   [Exit.]

FALSTAFF
Rare words! Brave world! Hostess, my breakfast, come! 206
Oh, I could wish this tavern were my drum!   [Exit.]   207

❖

[4.1]

[Enter Hotspur, Worcester, and Douglas.]

HOTSPUR
Well said, my noble Scot. If speaking truth

---

121 setting . . . aside (Mistress Quickly means, "without wishing to
offend your rank of knighthood," but Falstaff replies in line 123 with
the meaning, "setting aside your womanhood as of no value or perti-
nence.")   129 have understand. (With a sly suggestion of sexual possession—a meaning that eludes Mistress Quickly.)   148 whelp cub.
158 embossed (1) swollen with fat (2) foaming at the mouth and
exhausted, like a hunted animal.   rascal (1) scoundrel (2) immature
and inferior deer   159 memorandums souvenirs   162 injuries i.e.,
those things you claim to have lost, thereby suffering harm   163 stand
to it make a stand, insist on your supposed rights.   pocket up
endure silently

174 still always.   181 double labor i.e., the taking and the returning.
185 with unwashed hands without further ado   187 charge of foot
command of a company of infantry.   189 one i.e., a companion in
thievery. (Falstaff sees war as the opportunity for stealing and con-
ning.)   191 unprovided ill-equipped.   192 they . . . virtuous i.e., the
rebels, by providing the occasion of war, give dishonest men a chance
to profiteer and hence offend only those who are honest.   200 Temple Hall i.e., at the Inner Temple, one of the Inns of Court   203 furniture equipment, furnishing.   206 Brave Splendid   207 drum
(Possibly Falstaff means that he wishes he could continue to enjoy
this tavern instead of risking his life in battle. He may also be punning on tavern/taborn, i.e., taborin, a kind of drum.)
4.1. Location: The rebel camp near Shrewsbury.

In this fine age were not thought flattery,
Such attribution should the Douglas have   3
As not a soldier of this season's stamp   4
Should go so general current through the world.   5
By God, I cannot flatter; I do defy   6
The tongues of soothers! But a braver place   7
In my heart's love hath no man than yourself.
Nay, task me to my word; approve me, lord.   9

DOUGLAS   Thou art the king of honor.
No man so potent breathes upon the ground   11
But I will beard him.

Enter one [a Messenger] with letters.

HOTSPUR   Do so, and 'tis well.—   12
What letters hast thou there?—I can but thank you.   13

MESSENGER
These letters come from your father.

HOTSPUR
Letters from him? Why comes he not himself?

MESSENGER
He cannot come, my lord. He is grievous sick.

HOTSPUR
Zounds, how has he the leisure to be sick
In such a jostling time? Who leads his power?   18
Under whose government come they along?   19

MESSENGER
His letters bears his mind, not I, my lord.
[*Hotspur reads the letter.*]

WORCESTER
I prithee, tell me, doth he keep his bed?   21

MESSENGER
He did, my lord, four days ere I set forth,
And at the time of my departure thence
He was much feared by his physicians.   24

WORCESTER
I would the state of time had first been whole   25
Ere he by sickness had been visited.
His health was never better worth than now.

HOTSPUR
Sick now? Droop now? This sickness doth infect
The very life-blood of our enterprise;
'Tis catching hither, even to our camp.
He writes me here that inward sickness—
And that his friends by deputation   32
Could not so soon be drawn, nor did he think it meet   33
To lay so dangerous and dear a trust
On any soul removed but on his own.   35
Yet doth he give us bold advertisement   36

That with our small conjunction we should on,   37
To see how fortune is disposed to us;
For, as he writes, there is no quailing now,   39
Because the King is certainly possessed   40
Of all our purposes. What say you to it?

WORCESTER
Your father's sickness is a maim to us.   42

HOTSPUR
A perilous gash, a very limb lopped off.
And yet, in faith, it is not! His present want   44
Seems more than we shall find it. Were it good   45
To set the exact wealth of all our states   46
All at one cast? To set so rich a main   47
On the nice hazard of one doubtful hour?   48
It were not good, for therein should we read   49
The very bottom and the soul of hope,   50
The very list, the very utmost bound   51
Of all our fortunes.

DOUGLAS   Faith, and so we should;
Where now remains a sweet reversion,   53
We may boldly spend upon the hope
Of what is to come in.
A comfort of retirement lives in this.   56

HOTSPUR
A rendezvous, a home to fly unto,
If that the devil and mischance look big   58
Upon the maidenhead of our affairs.   59

WORCESTER
But yet I would your father had been here.
The quality and hair of our attempt   61
Brooks no division. It will be thought   62
By some that know not why he is away
That wisdom, loyalty, and mere dislike   64
Of our proceedings kept the Earl from hence.
And think how such an apprehension   66
May turn the tide of fearful faction   67
And breed a kind of question in our cause.
For well you know we of the off'ring side   69
Must keep aloof from strict arbitrament,   70
And stop all sight-holes, every loop from whence   71
The eye of reason may pry in upon us.
This absence of your father's draws a curtain   73
That shows the ignorant a kind of fear
Before not dreamt of.

HOTSPUR   You strain too far.   75
I rather of his absence make this use:

---

3 attribution praise, tribute   **4–5 As . . . world** that no one coined as a soldier in this current campaign should enjoy such a current reputation. (To *go . . . current* is to be put into circulation, continuing the image of coining in line 4.)   **6 defy** proclaim against   **7 soothers** flatterers.   **braver** better, dearer   **9 task . . . word** challenge me to make good my word.   **approve** test   **11–12 No . . . him** i.e., I am ready to defy anyone alive.   **13 I can . . . you** (Said to Douglas.)   **18 jostling** contending, clashing   **19 government** command   **21 keep** keep to   **24 feared** feared for   **25 time** the times   **32–3 And that . . . drawn** and that his allies could not so soon be assembled by anyone other than himself, any deputy   **33 meet** appropriate   **35 On . . . own** on anyone other than himself.   **36 advertisement** counsel, advice

37 conjunction joint force.   **on** go on   **39 quailing** losing heart   **40 possessed** informed   **42 maim** injury   **44 want** absence   **45 more** more serious   **46 To . . . states** to stake the absolute total of our resources   **47 cast** throw of the dice.   **main** stake in gambling; also, an army   **48 nice** precarious, delicate.   **hazard** (1) game at dice (2) venture   **49–50 should . . . hope** we should discover the utmost foundation and basis of our hopes, the most we could rely on   **51 list** limit   **53 Where . . . reversion** since as things stand we can expect reinforcements. (A *reversion* is literally part of an estate yet to be inherited.)   **56 retirement** something to fall back on   **58 big** threatening   **59 maidenhead** i.e., commencement   **61 hair** kind, nature   **62 Brooks** tolerates   **64 loyalty** i.e., to the crown   **66 apprehension** (1) perception (2) apprehensiveness   **67 fearful faction** timid support   **69 off'ring side** side that attacks   **70 strict arbitrament** just inquiry or investigation   **71 sight-holes** peep-holes. (*Loop* or *loophole* has the same meaning.)   **73 draws** draws aside, opens   **75 strain too far** exaggerate.

It lends a luster and more great opinion,   77
A larger dare to our great enterprise,   78
Than if the Earl were here; for men must think,
If we without his help can make a head   80
To push against a kingdom, with his help
We shall o'erturn it topsy-turvy down.
Yet all goes well, yet all our joints are whole.   83

DOUGLAS
As heart can think. There is not such a word
Spoke of in Scotland as this term of fear.

Enter Sir Richard Vernon.

HOTSPUR
My cousin Vernon, welcome, by my soul.

VERNON
Pray God my news be worth a welcome, lord.
The Earl of Westmorland, seven thousand strong,
Is marching hitherwards; with him Prince John.

HOTSPUR
No harm. What more?

VERNON   And further I have learned
The King himself in person is set forth,
Or hitherwards intended speedily,   92
With strong and mighty preparation.

HOTSPUR
He shall be welcome too. Where is his son,
The nimble-footed madcap Prince of Wales,
And his comrades, that doffed the world aside   96
And bid it pass?

VERNON   All furnished, all in arms   97
All plumed like estridges, that with the wind   98
Bated like eagles having lately bathed,   99
Glittering in golden coats, like images,   100
As full of spirit as the month of May
And gorgeous as the sun at midsummer,
Wanton as youthful goats, wild as young bulls.   103
I saw young Harry, with his beaver on,   104
His cuisses on his thighs, gallantly armed,   105
Rise from the ground like feathered Mercury,
And vaulted with such ease into his seat   107
As if an angel dropped down from the clouds
To turn and wind a fiery Pegasus   109
And witch the world with noble horsemanship.   110

HOTSPUR
No more, no more! Worse than the sun in March   111
This praise doth nourish agues. Let them come.   112
They come like sacrifices in their trim,   113

And to the fire-eyed maid of smoky war   114
All hot and bleeding will we offer them.
The mailèd Mars shall on his altar sit   116
Up to the ears in blood. I am on fire
To hear this rich reprisal is so nigh,   118
And yet not ours. Come, let me taste my horse,   119
Who is to bear me like a thunderbolt
Against the bosom of the Prince of Wales.
Harry to Harry shall, hot horse to horse,
Meet and ne'er part till one drop down a corse.   123
Oh, that Glendower were come!

VERNON   There is more news:
I learned in Worcester, as I rode along,
He cannot draw his power this fourteen days.   126

DOUGLAS
That's the worst tidings that I hear of yet.

WORCESTER
Ay, by my faith, that bears a frosty sound.

HOTSPUR
What may the King's whole battle reach unto?   129

VERNON
To thirty thousand.

HOTSPUR   Forty let it be!
My father and Glendower being both away,
The powers of us may serve so great a day.   132
Come, let us take a muster speedily.
Doomsday is near; die all, die merrily.

DOUGLAS
Talk not of dying. I am out of fear   135
Of death or death's hand for this one half year.
                                        Exeunt.

❦

[4.2]

Enter Falstaff, [and] Bardolph.

FALSTAFF   Bardolph, get thee before to Coventry; fill me
a bottle of sack. Our soldiers shall march through; we'll
to Sutton Coldfield tonight.   3

BARDOLPH   Will you give me money, Captain?

FALSTAFF   Lay out, lay out.   5

BARDOLPH   This bottle makes an angel.   6

FALSTAFF   An if it do, take it for thy labor; an if it make
twenty, take them all; I'll answer the coinage. Bid my   8
lieutenant Peto meet me at town's end.

BARDOLPH   I will, Captain. Farewell.   *Exit.*

FALSTAFF   If I be not ashamed of my soldiers, I am a
soused gurnet. I have misused the King's press dam-   12
nably. I have got, in exchange of a hundred and fifty

---

77 **opinion** renown 78 **dare** daring 80 **make a head** raise an armed
force 83 **Yet** Still. **joints** limbs 92 **intended** on the verge of departure 96–7 **that doffed . . . pass?** i.e., that thumbed their noses at
responsibilities, telling the world to mind its own business? 97 **fur-**
nished equipped 98–9 **All . . . bathed** i.e., all plumed with ostrich
feathers, fluttering their wings in the wind like eagles having just
bathed. (The text may be defective.) 100 **coats** (1) coats of mail
(2) heraldic coats of arms. **images** gilded statues 103 **Wanton**
sportive, frolicsome 104 **beaver** visor; hence, helmet 105 **cuisses**
armor for the thighs 107 **seat** saddle 109 **wind** wheel about.
Pegasus winged horse of Greek mythology 110 **witch** bewitch
111–12 **Worse . . . agues** (The spring sun was believed to give impetus
to chills and fevers, by drawing up vapors. Vernon's speech, says
Hotspur, gives one the shudders.) 113 **sacrifices** beasts for sacrifice.
trim fine apparel, trappings

114 **maid** i.e., Bellona, goddess of war 116 **mailèd** dressed in mail,
armor 118 **reprisal** prize 119 **taste** try, feel under me 123 **corse**
corpse. 126 **draw his power** muster his army 129 **battle** army
132 **The . . . us** our forces 135 **out of** free from
4.2. Location: A public road near Coventry.
3 **Sutton Coldfield** (In Warwickshire near Coventry.) 5 **Lay out** Pay
for it yourself 6 **makes an angel** i.e., makes ten shillings I've spent
for you. (But Falstaff answers as though *makes* means "produces,"
implying that Bardolph can profit from the transaction.) 8 **I'll . . .**
coinage I'll take responsibility for any proceeds. 12 **soused gurnet** a
kind of pickled fish. **King's press** royal warrant for the impressment of troops

soldiers, three hundred and odd pounds. I press me 14
none but good householders, yeomen's sons, inquire 15
me out contracted bachelors, such as had been asked 16
twice on the banns—such a commodity of warm 17
slaves as had as lief hear the devil as a drum, such as 18
fear the report of a caliver worse than a struck fowl or 19
a hurt wild duck. I pressed me none but such toasts- 20
and-butter, with hearts in their bellies no bigger than 21
pins' heads, and they have bought out their services; 22
and now my whole charge consists of ancients, cor- 23
porals, lieutenants, gentlemen of companies—slaves 24
as ragged as Lazarus in the painted cloth, where the 25
glutton's dogs licked his sores, and such as indeed
were never soldiers, but discarded unjust servingmen, 27
younger sons to younger brothers, revolted tapsters, 28
and hostlers trade-fallen, the cankers of a calm world 29
and a long peace, ten times more dishonorable-ragged
than an old feazed ancient. And such have I, to fill up 31
the rooms of them as have bought out their services,
that you would think that I had a hundred and fifty tattered prodigals lately come from swine keeping, from 34
eating draff and husks. A mad fellow met me on the way 35
and told me I had unloaded all the gibbets and pressed 36
the dead bodies. No eye hath seen such scarecrows. I'll
not march through Coventry with them, that's flat. 38
Nay, and the villains march wide betwixt the legs as if
they had gyves on, for indeed I had the most of them 40
out of prison. There's not a shirt and a half in all my
company, and the half shirt is two napkins tacked together and thrown over the shoulders like a herald's
coat without sleeves; and the shirt, to say the truth,
stolen from my host at Saint Albans, or the red-nose 45
innkeeper of Daventry. But that's all one; they'll find 46
linen enough on every hedge. 47

Enter the Prince [and the] Lord of Westmorland.

PRINCE   How now, blown Jack? How now, quilt? 48
FALSTAFF   What, Hal? How now, mad wag? What a
devil dost thou in Warwickshire?—My good lord of

Westmorland, I cry you mercy. I thought Your Honor 51
had already been at Shrewsbury.
WESTMORLAND   Faith, Sir John, 'tis more than time that
I were there, and you too; but my powers are there 54
already. The King, I can tell you, looks for us all. We
must away all night. 56
FALSTAFF   Tut, never fear me. I am as vigilant as a cat to 57
steal cream.
PRINCE   I think, to steal cream indeed, for thy theft hath 59
already made thee butter. But tell me, Jack, whose 60
fellows are these that come after?
FALSTAFF   Mine, Hal, mine.
PRINCE   I did never see such pitiful rascals.
FALSTAFF   Tut, tut, good enough to toss; food for 64
powder, food for powder. They'll fill a pit as well as 65
better. Tush, man, mortal men, mortal men.
WESTMORLAND   Ay, but, Sir John, methinks they are
exceeding poor and bare, too beggarly. 68
FALSTAFF   Faith, for their poverty, I know not where 69
they had that, and for their bareness, I am sure they
never learned that of me.
PRINCE   No, I'll be sworn, unless you call three fingers 72
in the ribs bare. But, sirrah, make haste. Percy is 73
already in the field.   *Exit.*
FALSTAFF   What, is the King encamped?
WESTMORLAND   He is, Sir John. I fear we shall stay too
long.   *[Exit.]*
FALSTAFF   Well,
To the latter end of a fray and the beginning of a feast 79
Fits a dull fighter and a keen guest.   *Exit.* 80

❖

[4.3]

*Enter Hotspur, Worcester, Douglas, [and]
Vernon.*

HOTSPUR
We'll fight with him tonight.
WORCESTER   It may not be.
DOUGLAS
You give him then advantage.
VERNON   Not a whit. 2
HOTSPUR
Why say you so? Looks he not for supply? 3
VERNON
So do we.
HOTSPUR   His is certain; ours is doubtful.

---

14 press me draft, conscript   **15 good** i.e., wealthy.   **yeomen's** small
freeholders'   **16 contracted** engaged to be married   **17 banns** public
announcements, declared on three Sundays in succession, of an intent
to marry.   **warm** i.e., loving their comfort   **18 lief** willingly   **19 caliver**
musket.   **struck** wounded   **20–1 toasts-and-butter** weaklings
22 bought . . . services i.e., paid, bribed, to be released from military
duty   **23 charge** company, troop.   **ancients** ensigns, standard-bear-
ers. (By appointing a disproportionate number of junior officers, Falstaff has made it possible to collect for himself their more substantial
pay.)   **24 gentlemen of companies** a kind of junior officer
25 painted cloth cheap hangings for a room. (For the story of Lazarus
the beggar and Dives the rich man, see Luke 16:19–31.)   **27 unjust**
dishonest   **28 younger sons . . . brothers** (i.e., with no possibility of
inheritance).   **revolted** runaway   **29 trade-fallen** whose business
has fallen away.   **cankers** cankerworms that destroy leaves and
buds. (Used figuratively.)   **31 feazed ancient** frayed flag.   **34 prodigals** spendthrifts. (See Luke 15:15–16.)   **35 draff** hogwash.   **mad**
madcap   **36 gibbets** gallows   **38 that's flat** that's for sure.   **40 gyves**
fetters   **45 my host** the innkeeper   **45, 46 Saint Albans, Daventry**
(Towns north and west of London, on the road to Coventry.)
46 that's all one no matter   **47 hedge** (where wet linen was spread
out to dry and could be easily stolen.)   **48 blown** swollen, inflated;
also, short of wind.   **quilt** thickly padded.

51 cry you mercy beg your pardon.   **54 powers** soldiers   **56 must
away** must march   **57 fear** worry about   **59–60 thy . . . butter** i.e., all
the cream (rich things) you have stolen has been churned into butter-
fat in your barrel-like belly.   **64 toss** toss on a pike   **64–5 food for
powder** cannon fodder   **68 poor and bare** inferior and threadbare.
(But Falstaff puns on the sense of "financially strapped and lean.")
69 for as for   **72–3 three . . . ribs** i.e., Falstaff's fat-covered ribs. (A
finger was a measure of three-fourths of an inch.)   **79–80 To . . . guest**
i.e., Better to be late to a battle and early to a feast. (*Keen* means "with
keen appetite.")
4.3. Location: The rebel camp near Shrewsbury.
2 then i.e., if you wait. (Addressed to Worcester, not Hotspur.)   **3 supply** reinforcements.

WORCESTER
Good cousin, be advised, stir not tonight.

VERNON
Do not, my lord.

DOUGLAS   You do not counsel well.
You speak it out of fear and cold heart.

VERNON
Do me no slander, Douglas. By my life,
And I dare well maintain it with my life,
If well-respected honor bid me on,   10
I hold as little counsel with weak fear   11
As you, my lord, or any Scot that this day lives.
Let it be seen tomorrow in the battle
Which of us fears.

DOUGLAS   Yea, or tonight.

VERNON   Content.

HOTSPUR   Tonight, say I.

VERNON
Come, come, it may not be. I wonder much,
Being men of such great leading as you are,   19
That you foresee not what impediments
Drag back our expedition. Certain horse   21
Of my cousin Vernon's are not yet come up.
Your uncle Worcester's horse came but today,
And now their pride and mettle is asleep,   24
Their courage with hard labor tame and dull,
That not a horse is half the half of himself.

HOTSPUR
So are the horses of the enemy
In general journey-bated and brought low.   28
The better part of ours are full of rest.

WORCESTER
The number of the King exceedeth our.
For God's sake, cousin, stay till all come in.   31
                    The trumpet sounds a parley.

                Enter Sir Walter Blunt.

BLUNT
I come with gracious offers from the King,
If you vouchsafe me hearing and respect.   33

HOTSPUR
Welcome, Sir Walter Blunt; and would to God
You were of our determination!   35
Some of us love you well; and even those some   36
Envy your great deservings and good name
Because you are not of our quality   38
But stand against us like an enemy.

BLUNT
And God defend but still I should stand so,   40
So long as out of limit and true rule   41
You stand against anointed majesty.
But to my charge. The King hath sent to know   43

The nature of your griefs and whereupon   44
You conjure from the breast of civil peace
Such bold hostility, teaching his duteous land
Audacious cruelty. If that the King   47
Have any way your good deserts forgot,
Which he confesseth to be manifold,
He bids you name your griefs, and with all speed
You shall have your desires with interest
And pardon absolute for yourself and these
Herein misled by your suggestion.   53

HOTSPUR
The King is kind; and well we know the King
Knows at what time to promise, when to pay.
My father and my uncle and myself
Did give him that same royalty he wears,
And when he was not six-and-twenty strong,
Sick in the world's regard, wretched and low,
A poor unminded outlaw sneaking home,   60
My father gave him welcome to the shore;
And when he heard him swear and vow to God
He came but to be Duke of Lancaster,
To sue his livery and beg his peace   64
With tears of innocency and terms of zeal,
My father, in kind heart and pity moved,
Swore him assistance, and performed it too.
Now when the lords and barons of the realm
Perceived Northumberland did lean to him,
The more and less came in with cap and knee,   70
Met him in boroughs, cities, villages,
Attended him on bridges, stood in lanes,   72
Laid gifts before him, proffered him their oaths,
Gave him their heirs as pages, followed him   74
Even at the heels in golden multitudes.   75
He presently, as greatness knows itself,   76
Steps me a little higher than his vow   77
Made to my father while his blood was poor   78
Upon the naked shore at Ravenspurgh,
And now, forsooth, takes on him to reform
Some certain edicts and some strait decrees   81
That lie too heavy on the commonwealth,
Cries out upon abuses, seems to weep
Over his country's wrongs; and by this face,   84
This seeming brow of justice, did he win
The hearts of all that he did angle for;
Proceeded further—cut me off the heads   87
Of all the favorites that the absent King
In deputation left behind him here
When he was personal in the Irish war.   90

44 griefs grievances   **47 If that** If   **53 suggestion** instigation.
60 unminded disregarded   **64 To sue . . . peace** to petition to take possession of his rightful inheritance and be reconciled with King Richard II   **70 The more . . . knee** persons of all ranks came to him with cap in hand and with bended knee   **72 Attended** waited for.   **stood in lanes** stood row-deep along the roads   **74 Gave . . . pages** i.e., brought him their heirs to serve as pages and also as hostages to the fathers' loyalty   **75 golden** (1) auspicious, celebrating (2) majestically attired   **76 knows itself** perceives its own strength   **77 Steps me** i.e., steps. (*Me* is used colloquially.)   **vow** i.e., Bolingbroke's vow to seek no more than his inheritance   **78 while . . . poor** i.e., while Bolingbroke's spirits were still humbled and his dynastic claim in question   **81 strait** strict   **84 face** show, pretense   **87 cut me** i.e., cut   **90 personal** in person

10 well-respected well weighed or considered   **11 I hold . . . counsel** I have as little to do   **19 leading** leadership   **21 expedition** speedy progress.   **horse** cavalry. (As also at line 23.)   **24 pride and mettle** spirit   **28 journey-bated** tired from the journey   **31.1 *parley*** trumpet summons to a conference.   **33 respect** attention.   **35 determination** persuasion (in the fight).   **36 even those some** those same persons   **38 Because** only because.   **quality** party   **40 defend** forbid.   **still** always   **41 limit** bounds of allegiance   **43 charge** commission.

BLUNT
    Tut, I came not to hear this.
HOTSPUR   Then to the point.
    In short time after, he deposed the King,
    Soon after that, deprived him of his life,
    And in the neck of that tasked the whole state;   94
    To make that worse, suffered his kinsman March—
    Who is, if every owner were well placed,   96
    Indeed his king—to be engaged in Wales,   97
    There without ransom to lie forfeited;   98
    Disgraced me in my happy victories,   99
    Sought to entrap me by intelligence;   100
    Rated mine uncle from the Council board;   101
    In rage dismissed my father from the court;
    Broke oath on oath, committed wrong on wrong,
    And in conclusion drove us to seek out
    This head of safety, and withal to pry   105
    Into his title, the which we find
    Too indirect for long continuance.
BLUNT
    Shall I return this answer to the King?
HOTSPUR
    Not so, Sir Walter. We'll withdraw awhile.
    Go to the King; and let there be impawned   110
    Some surety for a safe return again,
    And in the morning early shall mine uncle
    Bring him our purposes. And so farewell.   113
BLUNT
    I would you would accept of grace and love.
HOTSPUR
    And maybe so we shall.
BLUNT
                                    Pray God you do. [*Exeunt.*]

❖

[4.4]

Enter [the] Archbishop of York, [and] Sir Michael.

ARCHBISHOP [*giving letters*]
    Hie, good Sir Michael, bear this sealèd brief   1
    With wingèd haste to the Lord Marshal,   2
    This to my cousin Scroop, and all the rest   3
    To whom they are directed. If you knew
    How much they do import, you would make haste.
SIR MICHAEL   My good lord, I guess their tenor.
ARCHBISHOP   Like enough you do.   7
    Tomorrow, good Sir Michael, is a day

Wherein the fortune of ten thousand men
    Must bide the touch; for, sir, at Shrewsbury,   10
    As I am truly given to understand,
    The King with mighty and quick-raisèd power
    Meets with Lord Harry. And I fear, Sir Michael,
    What with the sickness of Northumberland,
    Whose power was in the first proportion,   15
    And what with Owen Glendower's absence thence,
    Who with them was a rated sinew too   17
    And comes not in, o'erruled by prophecies,
    I fear the power of Percy is too weak
    To wage an instant trial with the King.   20
SIR MICHAEL
    Why, my good lord, you need not fear;
    There is Douglas and Lord Mortimer.
ARCHBISHOP   No, Mortimer is not there.
SIR MICHAEL
    But there is Mordake, Vernon, Lord Harry Percy,
    And there is my lord of Worcester, and a head   25
    Of gallant warriors, noble gentlemen.
ARCHBISHOP
    And so there is. But yet the King hath drawn
    The special head of all the land together: 28
    The Prince of Wales, Lord John of Lancaster,
    The noble Westmorland, and warlike Blunt,
    And many more corrivals and dear men   31
    Of estimation and command in arms.   32
SIR MICHAEL
    Doubt not, my lord, they shall be well opposed.
ARCHBISHOP
    I hope no less, yet needful 'tis to fear;
    And, to prevent the worst, Sir Michael, speed.
    For if Lord Percy thrive not, ere the King
    Dismiss his power he means to visit us,   37
    For he hath heard of our confederacy,
    And 'tis but wisdom to make strong against him.
    Therefore make haste. I must go write again
    To other friends; and so farewell, Sir Michael.
                                    Exeunt [separately].

❖

[5.1]

*Enter the King, Prince of Wales, Lord John of
Lancaster, Sir Walter Blunt, [and] Falstaff.*

KING
    How bloodily the sun begins to peer
    Above yon bosky hill! The day looks pale   2
    At his distemperature.
PRINCE   The southern wind   3
    Doth play the trumpet to his purposes,   4

---

94 in . . . that next, immediately after.   tasked laid taxes upon   96 if
. . . placed if every claimant were given his proper place   97 engaged
held as hostage   98 lie forfeited remain prisoner, unreclaimed
99 Disgraced me (by demanding the prisoners; see 1.3.23 ff.)   happy
fortunate   100 intelligence secret information, i.e., from spies
101 Rated scolded   105 head of safety armed force for our protection.
withal also   110 impawned pledged   113 purposes proposals.
4.4. Location: York. The Archbishop's palace.
1 brief letter, dispatch   2 Lord Marshal i.e., Thomas Mowbray, son
of the Duke of Norfolk who is exiled in *Richard II*, and a longtime
enemy of the new King   3 Scroop i.e., perhaps Sir Stephen Scroop
of *Richard II*, 3.2.91–218, or Lord Scroop of Masham of *Henry V*, 2.2
7 Like Likely

10 bide the touch be put to the test (like gold)   15 in . . . proportion
of the largest size   17 rated sinew main strength or support reckoned upon   20 instant immediate   25 head troop   28 special head
notable leaders   31 corrivals partners in the enterprise   32 estimation reputation, importance   37 he i.e., the King
5.1. Location: The King's camp near Shrewsbury.
2 bosky bushy   3 his distemperature i.e., the sun's unhealthy
appearance.   4 trumpet trumpeter.   his its, the sun's

And by his hollow whistling in the leaves
Foretells a tempest and a blust'ring day.

KING
Then with the losers let it sympathize,
For nothing can seem foul to those that win.

The trumpet sounds.

Enter Worcester [and Vernon].

How now, my lord of Worcester? 'Tis not well
That you and I should meet upon such terms
As now we meet. You have deceived our trust
And made us doff our easy robes of peace   12
To crush our old limbs in ungentle steel.
This is not well, my lord, this is not well.
What say you to it? Will you again unknit
This churlish knot of all-abhorrèd war
And move in that obedient orb again   17
Where you did give a fair and natural light,
And be no more an exhaled meteor,   19
A prodigy of fear, and a portent   20
Of broachèd mischief to the unborn times?   21

WORCESTER   Hear me, my liege:
For mine own part, I could be well content
To entertain the lag end of my life   24
With quiet hours, for I protest
I have not sought the day of this dislike.   26

KING
You have not sought it? How comes it, then?

FALSTAFF   Rebellion lay in his way, and he found it.

PRINCE   Peace, chewet, peace!   29

WORCESTER
It pleased Your Majesty to turn your looks
Of favor from myself and all our house;
And yet I must remember you, my lord,   32
We were the first and dearest of your friends.
For you my staff of office did I break
In Richard's time, and posted day and night   35
To meet you on the way, and kiss your hand,
When yet you were in place and in account
Nothing so strong and fortunate as I.   38
It was myself, my brother, and his son
That brought you home and boldly did outdare   40
The dangers of the time. You swore to us,
And you did swear that oath at Doncaster,
That you did nothing purpose 'gainst the state,
Nor claim no further than your new-fall'n right,   44
The seat of Gaunt, dukedom of Lancaster.
To this we swore our aid. But in short space
It rained down fortune show'ring on your head,
And such a flood of greatness fell on you—

What with our help, what with the absent King,
What with the injuries of a wanton time,   50
The seeming sufferances that you had borne,   51
And the contrarious winds that held the King
So long in his unlucky Irish wars
That all in England did repute him dead—
And from this swarm of fair advantages
You took occasion to be quickly wooed   56
To grip the general sway into your hand;
Forgot your oath to us at Doncaster;
And being fed by us, you used us so
As that ungentle gull, the cuckoo's bird,   60
Useth the sparrow; did oppress our nest,
Grew by our feeding to so great a bulk
That even our love durst not come near your sight   63
For fear of swallowing; but with nimble wing
We were enforced, for safety sake, to fly
Out of your sight and raise this present head,   66
Whereby we stand opposèd by such means   67
As you yourself have forged against yourself
By unkind usage, dangerous countenance,   69
And violation of all faith and troth
Sworn to us in your younger enterprise.

KING
These things indeed you have articulate,   72
Proclaimed at market crosses, read in churches,   73
To face the garment of rebellion   74
With some fine color that may please the eye   75
Of fickle changelings and poor discontents,   76
Which gape and rub the elbow at the news   77
Of hurly-burly innovation.   78
And never yet did insurrection want   79
Such water-colors to impaint his cause,   80
Nor moody beggars, starving for a time   81
Of pell-mell havoc and confusion.   82

PRINCE
In both your armies there is many a soul   83
Shall pay full dearly for this encounter,
If once they join in trial. Tell your nephew
The Prince of Wales doth join with all the world
In praise of Henry Percy. By my hopes—   87
This present enterprise set off his head—   88
I do not think a braver gentleman,
More active-valiant or more valiant-young,
More daring or more bold, is now alive
To grace this latter age with noble deeds.

---

12 **easy** comfortable   17 **orb** orbit, sphere of action. (The King's subjects, like planets and stars in the Ptolemaic cosmos, were supposed to revolve around the kingly center, comparable to the earth, in fixed courses.)   19 **exhaled meteor** (Meteors were believed to be vapors drawn up or *exhaled* by the sun and visible as streaks of light; they were regarded as ill omens.)   20 **prodigy of fear** fearful omen   21 **broachèd** set flowing, already begun   24 **entertain** occupy   26 **the . . . dislike** this time of discord.   29 **chewet** chough, jackdaw. (Here, a chatterer.)   32 **remember** remind   35 **posted** rode swiftly   38 **Nothing** not at all   40 **home** back to England from exile   44 **new-fall'n** recently inherited (by the death of John of Gaunt)

50 **injuries** abuses.   **wanton** ill-managed   51 **sufferances** suffering, distress   56 **occasion** the opportunity   60 **ungentle . . . bird** rude nestling, the cuckoo's young offspring. (The cuckoo lays its eggs in other birds' nests.)   63 **our love** we who loved you   66 **head** armed force   67 **opposèd . . . means** goaded into opposition by such factors   69 **dangerous countenance** threatening behavior   72 **articulate** set forth, specified   73 **market crosses** (Christian crosses were often erected in the centers of marketplaces—a good place for public announcements.)   74 **face** trim, adorn   75 **color** (1) hue (2) specious appearance   76 **changelings** turncoats   77 **rub the elbow** i.e., hug themselves with delight   78 **innovation** rebellion.   79 **want** lack   80 **water-colors** i.e., thin excuses. (See *color*, line 75.)   **his** its   81 **moody** sullen, angry   82 **havoc** plundering   83 **both your** i.e., your and our   87 **hopes** i.e., hopes of salvation   88 **This . . . head** i.e., if this present rebellion is taken from his account, not held against him

For my part, I may speak it to my shame,
I have a truant been to chivalry;
And so I hear he doth account me too.
Yet this before my father's majesty:
I am content that he shall take the odds
Of his great name and estimation,   98
And will, to save the blood on either side,
Try fortune with him in a single fight.

KING
And, Prince of Wales, so dare we venture thee,   101
Albeit considerations infinite   102
Do make against it.—No, good Worcester, no.
We love our people well; even those we love
That are misled upon your cousin's part;   105
And, will they take the offer of our grace,   106
Both he and they and you, yea, every man
Shall be my friend again, and I'll be his.
So tell your cousin, and bring me word
What he will do. But if he will not yield,
Rebuke and dread correction wait on us,   111
And they shall do their office. So, begone.
We will not now be troubled with reply.
We offer fair; take it advisedly.

Exit Worcester [with Vernon].

PRINCE
It will not be accepted, on my life.
The Douglas and the Hotspur both together
Are confident against the world in arms.

KING
Hence, therefore, every leader to his charge;
For on their answer will we set on them,
And God befriend us as our cause is just!   120

Exeunt. Manent Prince, Falstaff.

FALSTAFF Hal, if thou see me down in the battle and
bestride me, so; 'tis a point of friendship.   122
PRINCE Nothing but a colossus can do thee that friendship. Say thy prayers, and farewell.
FALSTAFF I would 'twere bedtime, Hal, and all well.
PRINCE Why, thou owest God a death.   [*Exit.*] 126
FALSTAFF Tis not due yet; I would be loath to pay him
before his day. What need I be so forward with him
that calls not on me? Well, 'tis no matter; honor pricks 129
me on. Yea, but how if honor prick me off when I   130
come on? How then? Can honor set to a leg? No. Or   131
an arm? No. Or take away the grief of a wound? No.   132
Honor hath no skill in surgery, then? No. What is
honor? A word. What is in that word "honor"? What is
that "honor"? Air. A trim reckoning! Who hath it? He
that died o' Wednesday. Doth he feel it? No. Doth he
hear it? No. 'Tis insensible, then? Yea, to the dead. But
will it not live with the living? No. Why? Detraction   138

will not suffer it. Therefore I'll none of it. Honor is a   139
mere scutcheon. And so ends my catechism.   140

Exit.

[5.2]

Enter Worcester [and] Sir Richard Vernon.

WORCESTER
Oh, no, my nephew must not know, Sir Richard,
The liberal and kind offer of the King.
VERNON
'Twere best he did.
WORCESTER   Then are we all undone.
It is not possible, it cannot be,
The King should keep his word in loving us;
He will suspect us still and find a time
To punish this offense in other faults.   7
Suspicion all our lives shall be stuck full of eyes;   8
For treason is but trusted like the fox,
Who, never so tame, so cherished, and locked up,   10
Will have a wild trick of his ancestors.   11
Look how we can, or sad or merrily,   12
Interpretation will misquote our looks,
And we shall feed like oxen at a stall,
The better cherished still the nearer death.
My nephew's trespass may be well forgot;
It hath the excuse of youth and heat of blood,
And an adopted name of privilege—   18
A harebrained Hotspur, governed by a spleen.   19
All his offenses live upon my head
And on his father's. We did train him on,   21
And, his corruption being ta'en from us,   22
We as the spring of all shall pay for all.   23
Therefore, good cousin, let not Harry know
In any case the offer of the King.

Enter Hotspur [and Douglas, with soldiers].

VERNON
Deliver what you will; I'll say 'tis so.   26
Here comes your cousin.
HOTSPUR   My uncle is returned.
Deliver up my lord of Westmorland.   28
Uncle, what news?
WORCESTER
The King will bid you battle presently.
DOUGLAS
Defy him by the lord of Westmorland.   31

---

139 suffer allow   **140 scutcheon** heraldic emblem carried in funerals,
displayed on coaches, etc.; it was the lowest form of symbol, having
no pennon or other insignia.   **catechism** the principles of faith given
in the form of question and answer.
5.2. Location: Near the rebel camp.
7 To . . . faults to find other faults in us to punish (as a way of getting
back at us for defying him militarily).   **8 stuck . . . eyes** i.e., provided
with many eyes, suspiciously inquisitive   **10 never so** be he never so
11 trick trait   **12 or sad** either sad   **18 an adopted . . . privilege** i.e., a
nickname, "Hotspur," to justify his rashness   **19 spleen** intemperate
impulse.   **21 train** incite, draw   **22 his . . . us** i.e., since his guilt originated in us   **23 spring** source   **26 Deliver** Report   **28 Deliver up**
Release (as hostage; see 4.3.110–11)   **31 Defy him by** Send back your
defiance with

---

98 estimation reputation   **101 venture** hazard, risk   **102 Albeit**
although it be that. (The subjunctive has the force of "were it not
that.")   **105 cousin's** i.e., nephew's   **106 will they** if they will.
grace pardon   **111 wait on us** are awaiting my royal command
120.1 *Manent* They remain onstage   **122 bestride** stand over in order
to defend.   **so** well and good   **126 thou . . . death** (Proverbial, with a
pun on *debt*.)   **129 pricks** spurs   **130 prick me off** mark me off (as
one dead)   **131 set to** rejoin or set   **132 grief** pain   **138 Detraction**
Slander

HOTSPUR

Lord Douglas, go you and tell him so.

DOUGLAS

Marry, and shall, and very willingly.   *Exit Douglas.*

WORCESTER

There is no seeming mercy in the King.

HOTSPUR

Did you beg any? God forbid!

WORCESTER

I told him gently of our grievances,
Of his oathbreaking, which he mended thus,
By now forswearing that he is forsworn.
He calls us rebels, traitors, and will scourge
With haughty arms this hateful name in us.

Enter Douglas.

DOUGLAS

Arm, gentlemen, to arms! For I have thrown
A brave defiance in King Henry's teeth,   42
And Westmorland, that was engaged, did bear it;   43
Which cannot choose but bring him quickly on.

WORCESTER

The Prince of Wales stepped forth before the King,
And, nephew, challenged you to single fight.

HOTSPUR

Oh, would the quarrel lay upon our heads,
And that no man might draw short breath today
But I and Harry Monmouth! Tell me, tell me,   49
How showed his tasking? Seemed it in contempt?   50

VERNON

No, by my soul. I never in my life
Did hear a challenge urged more modestly,   52
Unless a brother should a brother dare
To gentle exercise and proof of arms.   54
He gave you all the duties of a man,   55
Trimmed up your praises with a princely tongue,   56
Spoke your deservings like a chronicle,
Making you ever better than his praise
By still dispraising praise valued with you;   59
And, which became him like a prince indeed,
He made a blushing cital of himself,   61
And chid his truant youth with such a grace
As if he mastered there a double spirit
Of teaching and of learning instantly.   64
There did he pause. But let me tell the world,
If he outlive the envy of this day,   66
England did never owe so sweet a hope,   67
So much misconstrued in his wantonness.   68

HOTSPUR

Cousin, I think thou art enamorèd
On his follies. Never did I hear
Of any prince so wild a liberty.   71

But be he as he will, yet once ere night
I will embrace him with a soldier's arm,
That he shall shrink under my courtesy.   74
Arm, arm with speed! And, fellows, soldiers, friends,
Better consider what you have to do
Than I, that have not well the gift of tongue,
Can lift your blood up with persuasion.

Enter a Messenger.

FIRST MESSENGER   My lord, here are letters for you.

HOTSPUR   I cannot read them now.
Oh, gentlemen, the time of life is short!
To spend that shortness basely were too long   82
If life did ride upon a dial's point,   83
Still ending at the arrival of an hour.   84
An if we live, we live to tread on kings;
If die, brave death, when princes die with us!   86
Now, for our consciences, the arms are fair   87
When the intent of bearing them is just.

Enter another [Messenger].

SECOND MESSENGER

My lord, prepare. The King comes on apace.

HOTSPUR

I thank him that he cuts me from my tale,
For I profess not talking. Only this—   91
Let each man do his best. And here draw I
A sword, whose temper I intend to stain
With the best blood that I can meet withal
In the adventure of this perilous day.
Now, *Esperance*! Percy! And set on.   96
Sound all the lofty instruments of war,
And by that music let us all embrace;
For, heaven to earth, some of us never shall   99
A second time do such a courtesy.

Here they embrace. The trumpets sound. [Exeunt.]

❧

[5.3]

The King enters with his power [and passes over the stage]. Alarum to the battle. Then enter Douglas, and Sir Walter Blunt [dressed like King Henry].

BLUNT

What is thy name, that in the battle thus
Thou crossest me? What honor dost thou seek
Upon my head?

DOUGLAS   Know then my name is Douglas,
And I do haunt thee in the battle thus
Because some tell me that thou art a king.

---

42 **brave** proud   43 **engaged** held as hostage   49 **Monmouth** (A name for the Prince, taken from the Welsh town where he was born.)   50 **showed his tasking** appeared his giving the challenge.   52 **urged** put forward   54 **gentle** befitting noble birth.   **proof of arms** test of martial skill.   55 **duties** due merits   56 **Trimmed . . . praises** adorned his praise of you   59 **By . . . you** by consistently disparaging praise itself as not sufficient to measure your true worth   61 **cital** account, recital   64 **instantly** simultaneously.   66 **envy** hostility   67 **owe** own   68 **wantonness** playful sportiveness.   71 **liberty** licentiousness.

74 **shrink under my courtesy** (1) be daunted by my greater courtesy (2) fall back before my attack.   82–4 **To . . . hour** Life is too short to spend it basely, even if life were to last only the time needed for the dial (or sundial) to advance a single hour, ending when that hour is up.   86 **brave** glorious   87 **for** as for.   **fair** just   91 **I . . . talking** I have no calling as an orator.   96 **Esperance** (The motto of the Percy family.)   99 **heaven to earth** i.e., I'll wager heaven against earth   **5.3. Location: Shrewsbury field. The scene is virtually continuous.**   0.1 *power* army.   0.2 *Alarum* Trumpet signal to advance

BLUNT   They tell thee true.

DOUGLAS
The lord of Stafford dear today hath bought   7
Thy likeness, for instead of thee, King Harry,   8
This sword hath ended him. So shall it thee,
Unless thou yield thee as my prisoner.

BLUNT
I was not born a yielder, thou proud Scot,
And thou shalt find a king that will revenge
Lord Stafford's death.   *They fight. Douglas kills Blunt.*

    Then enter Hotspur.

HOTSPUR
Oh, Douglas, hadst thou fought at Holmedon thus,
I never had triumphed upon a Scot.

DOUGLAS
All's done, all's won; here breathless lies the King.   16

HOTSPUR   Where?

DOUGLAS   Here.

HOTSPUR
This, Douglas? No. I know this face full well.
A gallant knight he was; his name was Blunt,
Semblably furnished like the King himself.   21

DOUGLAS
A fool go with thy soul, whither it goes!   22
A borrowed title hast thou bought too dear.
Why didst thou tell me that thou wert a king?

HOTSPUR
The King hath many marching in his coats.   25

DOUGLAS
Now, by my sword, I will kill all his coats!
I'll murder all his wardrobe, piece by piece,
Until I meet the King.

HOTSPUR   Up, and away!
Our soldiers stand full fairly for the day.   [*Exeunt.*]   29

    Alarum. Enter Falstaff, solus.

FALSTAFF   Though I could scape shot-free at London, I   30
fear the shot here; here's no scoring but upon the pate.   31
Soft, who are you? Sir Walter Blunt. There's honor for
you. Here's no vanity! I am as hot as molten lead, and   33
as heavy too. God keep lead out of me! I need no more
weight than mine own bowels. I have led my ragamuffins where they are peppered. There's not three of
my hundred and fifty left alive, and they are for the
town's end, to beg during life. But who comes here?   38

    Enter the Prince.

PRINCE
What, stands thou idle here? Lend me thy sword.

---

7 **dear** dearly   7–8 **bought Thy likeness** paid for his resemblance to
you   16 **breathless** i.e., dead   21 **Semblably furnished** similarly
accoutered   22 **A . . . soul** i.e., May the stigma of "fool" accompany
your soul (for having dressed as a decoy of King Henry)   25 **coats**
vests worn over armor embroidered with a coat of arms.   29 **stand . . .
day** i.e., seem in an auspicious position, likely to win the victory.
30 **shot-free** without paying the tavern bill   31 **scoring** (1) cutting
(2) marking up of charges, by notches on a stick or on the inn door
33 **Here's no vanity!** i.e. (ironically), If this doesn't show what I was
saying about honor, then nothing does!   38 **town's end** i.e., city gate,
frequented by beggars

Many a nobleman lies stark and stiff
Under the hoofs of vaunting enemies,
Whose deaths are yet unrevenged. I prithee,
Lend me thy sword.

FALSTAFF   Oh, Hal, I prithee, give me leave to breathe
awhile. Turk Gregory never did such deeds in arms as   45
I have done this day. I have paid Percy, I have made   46
him sure.   47

PRINCE
He is, indeed, and living to kill thee.
I prithee, lend me thy sword.

FALSTAFF   Nay, before God, Hal, if Percy be alive, thou
gets not my sword; but take my pistol, if thou wilt.

PRINCE
Give it me. What, is it in the case?

FALSTAFF   Ay, Hal, 'tis hot, 'tis hot. There's that will   53
sack a city.
        *The Prince draws it out and finds it to be a bottle
                                                of sack.*

PRINCE
What, is it a time to jest and dally now?
                    He throws the bottle at him. Exit.

FALSTAFF   Well, if Percy be alive, I'll pierce him. If he do   56
come in my way, so; if he do not, if I come in his   57
willingly, let him make a carbonado of me. I like not   58
such grinning honor as Sir Walter hath. Give me life,
which if I can save, so; if not, honor comes unlooked
for, and there's an end.   [*Exit.*]   61

    ❋

[5.4]

*Alarum. Excursions. Enter the King, the Prince,
Lord John of Lancaster, [and the] Earl of
Westmorland.*

KING   I prithee,
Harry, withdraw thyself; thou bleedest too much.
Lord John of Lancaster, go you with him.

LANCASTER
Not I, my lord, unless I did bleed too.

PRINCE
I beseech Your Majesty, make up,   5
Lest your retirement do amaze your friends.   6

KING
I will do so. My lord of Westmorland,
Lead him to his tent.

---

45 **Turk Gregory** (*Turk* is an abusive term signifying a tyrant, and
Gregory refers probably to Pope Gregory XIII, who was assumed to
have encouraged the Massacre of Saint Bartholomew [1572], in which
many French Protestants were slain, and to have encouraged plots
against Elizabeth.)   46–7 **made him sure** made sure of him. (But
Prince Hal takes *sure* in a different sense, meaning "safe.")   53 **hot**
(Falstaff implies he has been firing at the enemy.)   56 **Percy . . .
pierce** (Elizabethan pronunciation rendered the pun more obvious
than it is now.)   57 **so** well and good   58 **carbonado** meat scored
across for broiling   61 **there's an end** (1) that concludes the subject of
my catechism (see 5.1.129–40) (2) thus life ends.
5.4. **Location:** Scene continues at Shrewsbury field.
0.1 *Excursions* Sorties. (The fallen body of Blunt may be removed at
some point or may be onstage still at 5.4.77 when Hal kills Hotspur.)
5 **make up** go forward   6 **retirement** retreat.   **amaze** alarm

WESTMORLAND
Come, my lord, I'll lead you to your tent.
PRINCE
Lead me, my lord? I do not need your help.
And God forbid a shallow scratch should drive
The Prince of Wales from such a field as this,
Where stained nobility lies trodden on
And rebels' arms triumph in massacres!
LANCASTER
We breathe too long. Come, cousin Westmorland,   15
Our duty this way lies. For God's sake, come.
              [*Exeunt Prince John and Westmorland.*]
PRINCE
By God, thou hast deceived me, Lancaster!
I did not think thee lord of such a spirit.
Before, I loved thee as a brother, John,
But now I do respect thee as my soul.
KING
I saw him hold Lord Percy at the point   21
With lustier maintenance than I did look for   22
Of such an ungrown warrior.
PRINCE
Oh, this boy lends mettle to us all!   *Exit.*

         [*Enter Douglas.*]

DOUGLAS
Another king? They grow like Hydra's heads.   25
I am the Douglas, fatal to all those
That wear those colors on them. What art thou   27
That counterfeit'st the person of a king?
KING
The King himself, who, Douglas, grieves at heart
So many of his shadows thou hast met   30
And not the very King. I have two boys
Seek Percy and thyself about the field;   32
But, seeing thou fall'st on me so luckily,
I will assay thee; and defend thyself.   34
DOUGLAS
I fear thou art another counterfeit;
And yet, in faith, thou bearest thee like a king.
But mine I am sure thou art, whoe'er thou be,
And thus I win thee.
         They fight; the King being in danger,
                      enter Prince of Wales.
PRINCE
Hold up thy head, vile Scot, or thou art like   39
Never to hold it up again! The spirits
Of valiant Shirley, Stafford, Blunt, are in my arms.
It is the Prince of Wales that threatens thee,
Who never promiseth but he means to pay.   43
                   They fight. Douglas flieth.
Cheerly, my lord. How fares Your Grace?

Sir Nicholas Gawsey hath for succor sent,
And so hath Clifton. I'll to Clifton straight.
KING   Stay and breathe awhile.
Thou hast redeemed thy lost opinion,   48
And showed thou mak'st some tender of my life   49
In this fair rescue thou hast brought to me.
PRINCE
Oh, God, they did me too much injury
That ever said I hearkened for your death.   52
If it were so, I might have let alone
The insulting hand of Douglas over you,   54
Which would have been as speedy in your end
As all the poisonous potions in the world,
And saved the treacherous labor of your son.
KING
Make up to Clifton; I'll to Sir Nicholas Gawsey.   58
                              Exit King.

         Enter Hotspur.

HOTSPUR
If I mistake not, thou art Harry Monmouth.
PRINCE
Thou speak'st as if I would deny my name.
HOTSPUR
My name is Harry Percy.
PRINCE   Why then, I see
A very valiant rebel of the name.
I am the Prince of Wales; and think not, Percy,
To share with me in glory any more.
Two stars keep not their motion in one sphere,
Nor can one England brook a double reign   66
Of Harry Percy and the Prince of Wales.
HOTSPUR
Nor shall it, Harry, for the hour is come
To end the one of us; and would to God
Thy name in arms were now as great as mine!
PRINCE
I'll make it greater ere I part from thee,
And all the budding honors on thy crest
I'll crop to make a garland for my head.   73
HOTSPUR
I can no longer brook thy vanities.   *They fight.* 74

         Enter Falstaff.

FALSTAFF   Well said, Hal! To it, Hal! Nay, you shall find 75
no boy's play here, I can tell you.   76

         Enter Douglas. He fighteth with Falstaff, who falls
         down as if he were dead.   [*Exit Douglas.*]
         The Prince killeth Percy.

HOTSPUR
Oh, Harry, thou hast robbed me of my youth!
I better brook the loss of brittle life
Than those proud titles thou hast won of me;

---

15 breathe rest, pause for breath (as also at line 47)   **21 at the point**
at sword's point   **22 lustier maintenance** more vigorous bearing
25 Hydra's heads (The heads of the Lernaean Hydra grew again as
fast as they were cut off.)   **27 colors** i.e., the colors of the King's
insignia   **30 shadows** having form without substance   **32 Seek** who
seek   **34 assay thee** put you to the test   **39 like** likely   **43 pay**
(1) settle a debt (2) kill.

48 opinion reputation   **49 thou . . . of** you have some care for
52 hearkened listened (as for welcome news)   **54 insulting** exulting
58 Make up Advance   **66 brook** endure   **73 crop** pluck   **74 vanities**
empty boasts.   **75 Well said** Well done   **76.3 killeth** mortally
wounds

They wound my thoughts worse than thy sword my
   flesh.
But thoughts, the slaves of life, and life, time's fool,   81
And time, that takes survey of all the world,
Must have a stop. Oh, I could prophesy,
But that the earthy and cold hand of death
Lies on my tongue. No, Percy, thou art dust,
And food for—   *[He dies.]*

PRINCE
For worms, brave Percy. Fare thee well, great heart.
Ill-weaved ambition, how much art thou shrunk!
When that this body did contain a spirit,
A kingdom for it was too small a bound;
But now two paces of the vilest earth
Is room enough. This earth that bears thee dead
Bears not alive so stout a gentleman.   93
If thou wert sensible of courtesy,   94
I should not make so dear a show of zeal;   95
But let my favors hide thy mangled face,   96
And, even in thy behalf, I'll thank myself
For doing these fair rites of tenderness.
             [He covers Hotspur's face with a scarf
                      or other favor.]
Adieu, and take thy praise with thee to heaven!
Thy ignominy sleep with thee in the grave,
But not remembered in thy epitaph!
           He spieth Falstaff on the ground.
What, old acquaintance, could not all this flesh
Keep in a little life? Poor Jack, farewell!
I could have better spared a better man.
Oh, I should have a heavy miss of thee   105
If I were much in love with vanity.   106
Death hath not struck so fat a deer today,
Though many dearer, in this bloody fray.
Emboweled will I see thee by and by.   109
Till then in blood by noble Percy lie.   *Exit.*
                Falstaff riseth up.

FALSTAFF   Emboweled? If thou embowel me today, I'll
give you leave to powder me and eat me too tomor-   112
row. 'Sblood, 'twas time to counterfeit, or that hot ter-   113
magant Scot had paid me, scot and lot too. Counterfeit?   114
I lie, I am no counterfeit. To die is to be a counterfeit,
for he is but the counterfeit of a man who hath not the
life of a man; but to counterfeit dying, when a man
thereby liveth, is to be no counterfeit but the true and
perfect image of life indeed. The better part of valor is   119
discretion, in the which better part I have saved my
life. Zounds, I am afraid of this gunpowder Percy,
though he be dead. How if he should counterfeit too
and rise? By my faith, I am afraid he would prove the

better counterfeit. Therefore I'll make him sure; yea,
and I'll swear I killed him. Why may not he rise as well
as I? Nothing confutes me but eyes, and nobody sees   126
me. Therefore, sirrah [*stabbing him*], with a new
wound in your thigh, come you along with me.
              He takes up Hotspur on his back.

Enter Prince [and] John of Lancaster.

PRINCE
Come, brother John; full bravely hast thou fleshed   129
Thy maiden sword.
LANCASTER   But soft, whom have we here?
Did you not tell me this fat man was dead?
PRINCE   I did; I saw him dead,
Breathless and bleeding on the ground.—Art thou
   alive?
Or is it fantasy that plays upon our eyesight?
I prithee, speak. We will not trust our eyes
Without our ears. Thou art not what thou seem'st.
FALSTAFF   No, that's certain, I am not a double man; but   137
if I be not Jack Falstaff, then am I a Jack. There is Percy   138
[*throwing the body down*]. If your father will do me
any honor, so; if not, let him kill the next Percy himself. I look to be either earl or duke, I can assure you.
PRINCE
Why, Percy I killed myself and saw thee dead.
FALSTAFF   Didst thou? Lord, Lord, how this world is
given to lying! I grant you I was down and out of
breath, and so was he; but we rose both at an instant   145
and fought a long hour by Shrewsbury clock. If I may
be believed, so; if not, let them that should reward
valor bear the sin upon their own heads. I'll take it   148
upon my death I gave him this wound in the thigh.   149
If the man were alive and would deny it, zounds, I
would make him eat a piece of my sword.
LANCASTER
This is the strangest tale that ever I heard.
PRINCE
This is the strangest fellow, brother John.—
Come, bring your luggage nobly on your back.
For my part, if a lie may do thee grace,   155
I'll gild it with the happiest terms I have.   156
                A retreat is sounded.
The trumpet sounds retreat; the day is our.   157
Come, brother, let us to the highest of the field,   158
To see what friends are living, who are dead.
      Exeunt [Prince of Wales and Lancaster].
FALSTAFF   I'll follow, as they say, for reward. He that re-
wards me, God reward him! If I do grow great, I'll
grow less; for I'll purge, and leave sack, and live   162
cleanly as a nobleman should do.
              Exit [bearing off the body].

---

81 thoughts . . . fool i.e., our mental consciousness, which is dependent on physical existence, and our life itself, which is subject to time
93 stout valiant   **94 sensible of courtesy** able to hear my praise
95 dear handsome, heartfelt.   **zeal** admiration   **96 favors** plume,
scarf, glove, or similar article   **105 heavy** (1) serious (2) corpulent
106 vanity frivolity.   **109 Emboweled** Disemboweled, i.e., for
embalming and burial   **112 powder** salt   **113–14 termagant** violent
and blustering, like the heathen god of the Saracens in medieval and
Renaissance lore   **114 paid** i.e., killed.   **scot and lot** i.e., in full.
(Originally the phrase was the term for a parish tax.)   **119 part** con-
stituent part, quality, role

126 Nothing . . . eyes i.e., Nothing can contradict me but an eyewitness   **129 fleshed** initiated (in battle)   **137 double man** (1) specter
(2) two men   **138 a Jack** a knave.   **145 at an instant** simultaneously
148–9 take . . . death i.e., swear with my eternal soul at risk   **155 a lie**
i.e., this lie of yours.   **grace** credit   **156 happiest** most felicitous
157 our ours.   **158 highest** highest vantage point   **162 purge** (1)
reduce in weight, using laxatives (2) repent

[5.5]

*The trumpets sound. Enter the King, Prince of
Wales, Lord John of Lancaster, Earl of
Westmorland, with Worcester and Vernon
prisoners.*

KING
Thus ever did rebellion find rebuke.
Ill-spirited Worcester! Did not we send grace,
Pardon, and terms of love to all of you?
And wouldst thou turn our offers contrary?
Misuse the tenor of thy kinsman's trust?   5
Three knights upon our party slain today,
A noble earl, and many a creature else
Had been alive this hour,
If like a Christian thou hadst truly borne
Betwixt our armies true intelligence.   10

WORCESTER
What I have done my safety urged me to;
And I embrace this fortune patiently,
Since not to be avoided it falls on me.

KING
Bear Worcester to the death, and Vernon too.
Other offenders we will pause upon.
            [*Exeunt Worcester and Vernon, guarded.*]
How goes the field?

PRINCE
The noble Scot, Lord Douglas, when he saw
The fortune of the day quite turned from him,
The noble Percy slain, and all his men

Upon the foot of fear, fled with the rest;   20
And falling from a hill, he was so bruised
That the pursuers took him. At my tent
The Douglas is; and I beseech Your Grace
I may dispose of him.

KING   With all my heart.

PRINCE
Then, brother John of Lancaster,
To you this honorable bounty shall belong.   26
Go to the Douglas, and deliver him
Up to his pleasure, ransomless and free.
His valors shown upon our crests today   29
Have taught us how to cherish such high deeds
Even in the bosom of our adversaries.

LANCASTER
I thank Your Grace for this high courtesy,
Which I shall give away immediately.   33

KING
Then this remains, that we divide our power.
You, son John, and my cousin Westmorland
Towards York shall bend you with your dearest speed 36
To meet Northumberland and the prelate Scroop,
Who, as we hear, are busily in arms.
Myself and you, son Harry, will towards Wales,
To fight with Glendower and the Earl of March.
Rebellion in this land shall lose his sway,   41
Meeting the check of such another day;   42
And since this business so fair is done,   43
Let us not leave till all our own be won.   *Exeunt.*   44

5.5. Location: The battlefield.
5 Misuse . . . trust? i.e., Would you abuse Hotspur's confidence in
you (by concealing the generosity of my offer, in your role as emissary)?   **10 intelligence** information, report.

---

20 Upon . . . fear fleeing in panic   **26 this honorable bounty** the
honor of this bounteous act   **29 crests** i.e., helmets   **33 give away**
pass along, confer on Douglas   **36 bend you** direct your course.
dearest most urgent   **41 his** its   **42 Meeting . . . day** i.e., when the
rebellion is entirely repulsed at one more battlefield   **43 fair** successfully   **44 leave** leave off

The Life of King Henry the Fifth

enry V (1599) is Shakespeare's culminating statement in the genre of the English history play. Unlike the late and atypical *Henry VIII* (1613), which is separated from the rest of Shakespeare's history plays by some fourteen years, *Henry V* sums up the historical themes with which Shakespeare had been fascinated for an entire decade. The play, first published in a memorially reconstructed and abridged quarto in 1600, must have been written not long after *2 Henry IV,* perhaps as an opening production for the Chamberlain's Men's new Bankside theater, the Globe, in 1599. To be sure, the play does not entirely fulfill the promise made in *2 Henry IV* to "continue the story, with Sir John in it, and make you merry with fair Katharine of France." Falstaff is missing. As before, Shakespeare apparently saw a grand design to his four-play sequence (which had started with *Richard II*) but improvised when he came to the writing of each part. Despite these minor adjustments in the overall plan, however, *Henry V* is clearly intended to bring to fulfillment the education of a politician-prince and to illustrate the arts of political kingship that Prince Hal had derived from his experiences in the earlier plays.

In a sense, too, *Henry V* sums up the achievement of the English history play, not only for Shakespeare, but also for other popular playwrights. The patriotic history play, born in the excitement of the Armada era immediately after 1588, had nearly run its course by 1599 and was soon to be supplanted by other dramatic genres, such as satire and revenge tragedy. Dark and complex political realities were already changing the buoyant mood in which the history play had been born: the aging Queen Elizabeth was near death and without a Protestant heir, while fear of another invasion threatened. In *Henry V*, we sense the approaching end of an era, for the play both celebrates the achievements of the English monarchy and examines its limits.

Henry V has become a controversial play, chiefly because our recent experiences with war have led us to be wary of political leaders who, in the name of patriotism, lay claim to and invade another country. George Bernard Shaw is prominent among those who have deplored Henry as a priggish and complacent warmonger and imperialist. Many historically minded critics, on the other hand, warn of the dangers of reading anachronistically from a modern perspective, and they argue that Henry is an admirable model of conduct according to Renaissance notions of statecraft and military leadership. What is Shakespeare's attitude toward his war hero? Does he sympathize with Henry's condescension toward the French and his order to every soldier to kill his French prisoners? Or is Shakespeare's admiration qualified by ironic reservations? As is usual in Shakespeare's work, the perspective is complex and balanced. The play pulls us in two directions. Although the Chorus, which interprets the play for us, approves of Henry's military posture, the grandiose rhetoric of war is consistently undercut by matter-of-fact revelations of people's self-interested motives. This contrast between rhetorical illusion and political reality extends from the justification of Henry's French campaign to his state marriage with Katharine of France. On the ethical issue of killing the French prisoners, for example, the play offers us contradictory and seemingly irreconcilable impressions. At the end of 4.6, Henry orders that "every soldier" is to "kill his prisoners," evidently because the English are under attack and cannot spare men to guard those who have been captured. In 4.7 (lines 1–10 and 54–5), however, we are told by Gower that the King gave the order in retaliation for the massacre by the cowardly French of the boys guarding the English luggage. Similarly, on the eve of the battle of Agincourt, we are left to draw our own conclusions about King Henry's conversation with his soldiers (4.1. 98–227). Is he evading the question of whether his cause is just by turning to a really very different matter of responsibility for someone else's sins, or is he simply testing his men with hard questions to prepare them for battle? Ironic puzzles such as these probably never amount to open disillusionment in this play, although some modern critics and directors would argue otherwise; the ironies are perhaps, instead, the acknowledgment of a special kind of morality pertaining to kingship.

Skill in rhetoric is a key to Henry's success—in defying the French Dauphin, in preparing troops for battle, or in wooing the French princess for his queen. As the Archbishop of Canterbury notes approvingly, King Henry's versatility as a rhetorician applies to all the vital disciplines of kingship: Henry can "reason in divinity," "debate of commonwealth affairs," "discourse of war," handle "any cause of policy," and in all such matters speak in "sweet and honeyed sentences" (1.1.39–51). Through the arts of language, Henry displays piety, learning, administrative sagacity, political cunning, and military intrepidity. Like the contemporary play *Julius Caesar* (1599), *Henry V* is concerned with techniques of persuasion. (The earlier *Richard III* is also a highly rhetorical play, though chiefly through the negative example of tyrannical behavior.) Yet, however much we may be swayed emotionally by the rhetoric, we realize that the public figure of Henry V is a mask behind which we can perceive little. Only rarely do we glimpse the affable young companion of the *Henry IV* plays. King Henry has accepted the responsibility of playing a political role. It denies him a private and separate identity, even—or especially—in choosing a wife. And it complicates our task of assessing the sincerity of his utterances. Is he genuinely pious, or has he merely learned the usefulness of pious utterance in swaying people's hearts? What especially are his motives for going to war against France?

Shakespeare could have begun this play with the stirring scene (1.2) in which Henry, urged on by his advisers, issues a defiant challenge to the French ambassadors. Instead, Shakespeare treats us to a prior glimpse beneath the patriotic surface. It seems that the Archbishop of Canterbury, threatened with a bill in Parliament designed to take away the better half of the Church's possessions, has resolved to parry with a counterproposal, whereby the Church will give Henry a very substantial sum for his French campaign, provided the offensive tax bill can be conveniently forgotten. The Archbishop has already been negotiating with Henry and surmises that the plan will work. This revelation is not shocking to us; it merely reveals the political process at work. The faint undercurrent of anticlericalism suggests that Henry is to be admired for putting pressure on his clergy with such success; they are rich and can afford to support the war. In any case, the dramatic effect is to show how men's practical motives affect their rhetoric. When, in the subsequent scene, the Archbishop delivers a public lecture on the English claim to France, we know that this learned prelate has a prior and self-interested commitment to the war. His intricate dynastic argument, which he proclaims

to be "as clear as is the summer's sun" (1.2.86), gives to the war a much-needed public justification. Henry's questions indicate not only his genuine concern about the legitimacy of his claim but also his political need for the Church's endorsement of his cause; he has already claimed certain French dukedoms and must have the Church's official approval of those claims before he can proceed. He similarly needs the backing of his nobles, who also have their own reasons for approving the campaign. Henry skillfully orchestrates the scene to produce the desired effect of unanimous and patriotic consent.

Although never directly stated, Henry's own motives for going to war must also combine sincere zeal with calculated self-interest. As king, he longs to recover the French territory that England governed in the great days of Poitiers and Crécy. As a man, he bristles at the contemptuous challenge of the Dauphin; Henry must still strive to overcome his reputation as a wastrel and must prove himself worthy of honorable comparison with his great ancestors. Politically (and this motive remains most hidden), Henry has absorbed his father's sage advice to "busy giddy minds / With foreign quarrels" (*2 Henry IV*, 4.5.213–14), to blunt political opposition at home by uniting English resentment against a foreign scapegoat.

The exigencies of war do indeed provide Henry with an opportunity for proceeding against his political enemies. He arrests the Earl of Cambridge, Lord Scroop, and Sir Thomas Grey at Southampton on charges of conspiring with France. The scene (2.2) is, for Shakespeare, uncharacteristically one-sided. We are never even told that Cambridge is the chief pretender to the English throne, son of the Duke of York, married to Anne Mortimer, and founder of the Yorkist claim in the York-Lancastrian wars—the sort of rival whom Shakespeare elsewhere portrays with understanding. Instead, the rhetoric of the Chorus to Act 2 blatantly warns us to expect "hell and treason" (line 29). These three conspirators, like Judases, says the Chorus, have bargained away their king for gold. (In fact, Cambridge insists that his motive was not financial, though he is not permitted to say what it was.) The playwright does not give them complex motives; they are sinners, so horrified by their own intents that they are actually grateful to be caught. The scene serves, by such rhetorical devices, to strengthen Henry's claim to the English throne as well as to the territories in France. Opposition to his rule during wartime is, in the view of the Chorus, simply treasonous; all persuasive evidences of dynastic rival claims are hidden from our view.

Comedy also contributes to the rhetorical image-making of the hero in *Henry V*. The tavern crew is on hand, though deprived of the now-deceased Falstaff's beguiling company and more distant from Henry than in the earlier history plays. Only briefly and in disguise, on the night before the battle, does the King encounter Pistol. The name of Bardolph comes to Henry as though in recollection of a distant past, when he hears that Bardolph is about to be executed for stealing from French churches. Henry confirms the sentence: "We would have all such offenders so cut off" (3.6.107). Whatever momentary pang Henry may feel, he remains constant to his banishment of Falstaff. And, although Shakespeare pleads for our sympathies in the seriocomic account of Falstaff's death, seen through the childlike naiveté of Mistress Quickly, there is no hope of reconciliation between Henry and his former mates. Pistol, despite his ornamental language, is little more than a boaster, coward, and thief. The tavern revelers are now the opportunists of war, troublemakers such as are found in every army, engaging rascals deserving to be cudgeled by more honorable men.

Pistol gets his comeuppance from Captain Fluellen, who replaces Falstaff as the chief comic figure, both in prominence (his role is second in length to that of Henry) and in proximity to the King. Fluellen is a Welshman, like King Henry, who was born at Monmouth in what was then Wales (hence the appropriateness of his former title as Prince of Wales). Fluellen is proud of this kinship. Because he is loyal and valiant, he is a person worthy to be seen in Henry's company. Yet there is none of the brilliant duel of wits previously linking Henry and Falstaff. Fluellen is a humorous character, identified at once by such comically exaggerated features as his Welsh accent and mannerisms of speech, his old-fashioned and somewhat fanatical sense of military propriety, and his devotion to the ancient rules of military discipline. Fluellen is a caricature, subject to mild satirical laughter, and there is a note of condescension in Henry's habit of playing practical jokes on the captain. We tend to laugh at, rather than with, him. (Henry makes practical jokes at others' expense as well, such as the soldier named Williams, with whom he exchanges gloves.) Unlike Falstaff, Fluellen lacks perspective on his own pomposity. He is a zealot for duty, and one feels Henry is taking unfair advantage when he picks on one who is such an easy mark for laughter. We suspect that Henry is using people again, bolstering his public image as the king with the common touch, borrowing a little Welsh color for myth-making purposes. At the same time, Fluellen is steadfast, upright, and a credit to his countryman Henry. With his fellow captains from Scotland, Ireland, and England, he demonstrates that Britishers can fight together, even if they do antagonize one another with their proud regional customs. Those customs are to be cherished as part of the British character; because Pistol offers gratuitous insult to the Welsh tradition of wearing a leek in the cap on Saint Davy's Day, he must be thrashed.

As with the comic characters and Henry's political enemies, *Henry V* is rhetorically one-sided in its presentation of the French. Patriotism is a raw emotion, and Henry cannot appeal to it without awakening hostility toward the enemy. (Ironically enough, the great film version of *Henry V* by Laurence Olivier was created in 1944 during World War II to arouse national feelings against the Germans rather than against the French, and with complete success. Any enemy will do in such patriotic moods.) The French are portrayed as haughty, vastly superior in numbers, envious of one another, contemptuous of their own leadership (especially the Dauphin), treacherous (attacking the boys with the luggage), and craven. Even their joking is characterized by an unattractively bestial kind of bawdry (3.7.48–68). The British—"we few, we happy few" (4.3.60)—are tired and outnumbered but invincible and seemingly protected by God. Henry's order to kill the French prisoners and his description of the rapes and pillages his soldiers will commit if Harfleur fails to surrender (3.3.1–27) do, to be sure, raise serious questions about the morality of war under the best of kings; the play may be caustic toward the French nobility but does not necessarily exonerate the English. Even here, however, we are led to believe that, because the French are so execrably governed, France will suffer less under English rule. Henry takes care that his soldiers will not despoil the French countryside except under conditions of military "necessity." Only in Montjoy, the Duke of Burgundy, and Katharine of France does Shakespeare offer redeeming portraits of the French character, and in these instances the terms of hierarchical ascendancy seem clear: masculine English dominance, gentle French submissiveness. Katharine becomes "la belle France," depicted in Burgundy's eloquent peacemaking speech as being so much in need of competent management.

Women exist only on the margins of this war play, as in Shakespeare's other historical plays. Mistress Quickly's role is chiefly as a reminder to us that men fight with one another for the possession of women; the ludicrous quarrel of Pistol and Nym over Mistress Quickly anticipates the way in which Katharine of France will be one of the chief spoils of the war itself. Women also wait patiently at home while their men fight, and tend them when they are sick. Mistress Quickly's recollection of the death of Falstaff (2.3.9–25) is masterful in its evocation of tender solicitude, illiterate piety, and unwitting eroticism. Later, in France, Pistol pauses with momentary regret over news of the death of his wife from venereal disease (5.1.80–1). Katharine of France, though vastly better born, finds her role as a woman no less circumscribed. We first see her learning English from Alice, her lady in waiting (3.4). Why is she learning English? The obvious political reason, never explicitly stated, emerges with a kind of violence: the scene of the English lesson follows immediately after King Henry's ultimatum to the citizens of Harfleur to surrender or see their women raped and their children impaled by English weapons (3.3.27–41). Katharine accepts her lot with good grace, as though she had any other choice but to do so. We gather from her scene with Alice that she is a woman of spirit who can be imperious, vain, and curious about sex. Because she also is very French, the wooing scene in Act 5 can play comically on the differences of temperament between her and Henry, who is as English as she is French. These differences make Henry and Katharine potentially compatible through complementarity—male and female, soldier and lady, English and French—but the compact is patently a hierarchical one of conqueror and conquered. (Emma Thompson, in Kenneth Branagh's film version of 1989, brings to the role of Katharine a gracefully and persuasively feminist interpretation of an independent-minded woman who is decidedly skeptical about the courtship to which she is subjected, but even she discovers that she has no choice other than to capitulate to Henry's—i.e., Branagh's—charm and the imperatives of international diplomacy.) Historically, we know that the product of their sexual union, Henry VI, will bring to a dismal end the harmony of discords that presides uncertainly over the end of *Henry V.*

Henry woos Katharine with real flair, despite their unstated mutual recognition that their courtship is, above all, a matter of state, in which they must play predetermined roles. The individual within Henry V gives way to the public personality, but he never loses his style. He manages always to be true to himself, as a wooer or as a soldier. We see him in disguise, hobnobbing with common soldiers of his camp on the eve of battle, earnestly discussing with them the morality of war. We see him, with endearing human inconsistency, coveting all the glory of victory over the French and then adjuring his soldiers to give credit for that victory to God alone. Even if we are at times less attracted to this successful warrior and politician than to the carefree young man of *1 Henry IV,* we can still honor Henry's choice of responsible maturity and see that it is even compassionately self-denying. A king cannot be like other men, and Henry is willing to accept this price of leadership.

The Chorus presents *Henry V* to us as if it were an epic poem as well as a drama. Henry is an epic hero, defined in terms of mythic allusions and abstractions. He is compared to Mars, the god of war, with Famine, Sword, and Fire leashed at his heels, crouched and ready for employment. He is the "mirror of all Christian kings," and his followers are "English Mercurys" (2.0.6–7) with winged heels. Personified Expectation sits in the air, promising crowns and crownets to Henry and his followers. Henry's fleet of ships in the English Channel becomes "A city on th'inconstant billows dancing" (3.0.15). On the eve of battle, amidst his brothers, friends, and countrymen, Henry warms every heart with "cheerful semblance and sweet majesty" and with his "largess universal like the sun" (4.0.40–3). He forbids vainglorious pride and gives credit for his victory "Quite from himself to God" (5.0.22).

The action the Chorus describes is comparably epic, as it moves from England to France and back again, leaping over time, surveying all levels of society in the English nation, portraying famous military encounters seemingly more suited to epic narration (or to film, as both Laurence Olivier's 1944 film and Kenneth Branagh's more recent film version brilliantly demonstrate) than to the stage. The stage's limitation forms, indeed, a major burden of the Chorus's argument. He apologizes to the spectators for the "flat unraisèd spirits" that have dared to bring forth so vast an object "On this unworthy scaffold," in this "cockpit" or "wooden O" (Prologue). The play confines "mighty men" "In little room," "Mangling by starts the full course of their glory" (Epilogue).

This apology sounds like becoming modesty on Shakespeare's part, in conceding the truth of Ben Jonson's objection that a few hired actors with rusty swords can scarcely do justice to England's great wars of the past. *Henry V* is not a Jonsonian neoclassical play. Paradoxically, however, Shakespeare's acknowledgment of the limited means at his disposal to create mimetic spectacle amounts to a defense of his own theater of the imagination. Through the Chorus's repeated urgings that we use our "imaginary forces" to supply what the actors and the theater necessarily lack, Shakespeare invites us as spectators and partners into his world of art. The play becomes a journey of thought, of making "imaginary puissance." When Shakespeare and his acting company talk of horses, we are to "see them / Printing their proud hoofs i'th' receiving earth" (Prologue). This is not to minimize the importance of the theatrical experience but, indeed, quite the opposite, since we are instructed to liberate ourselves through that theatrical experience and to re-create by means of Shakespeare's script an epic vision. Shakespeare's stage, bare of scenery, relying on good actors and the words they speak, becomes through its very flexibility more versatile in creating that vision than the most ornate and mechanically sophisticated illusionistic theater.

Nothing illustrates better the controversial and timely nature of this play than the history of recent productions, on stage and in film and television. Once viewed as a stalwart defense of England's national greatness, so much so that Winston Churchill could invoke Henry's famous speech before the Battle of Agincourt ("We few, we happy few") in celebration of Britain's "finest hour" of defending England against Nazi Germany, *Henry V* was destined to become, in the years of disillusionment following World War II and especially during the Vietnam era, a vehicle for a satirical and dismaying view of war. Directors have sometimes chosen to have the Boy who accompanies Pistol, Bardolph, and Nym to France brutally killed in open view of the audience by French soldiers. (The script does not specify such action.) A production by the Royal Shakespeare Company in 1964, directed by Peter Hall, showed the influence of Bertolt Brecht and Jan Kott (author of *Shakespeare Our Contemporary*) by staging the Battle of Agincourt in terrifying darkness, with reminiscences of the Guernica atrocity of the Spanish Civil War celebrated by Pablo Picasso's famous painting on the subject. In a number of productions, King Henry has been presented as a brazen devotee of imperialistic war, or a calculating politician for whom even the business of wooing is a matter of wearisome diplomatic necessity (as in Ian Holm's portrayal at Stratford-upon-Avon in 1964).

Alternatively, Henry has sometimes been seen as a self-doubting hero, keenly attuned to the absurdity of what it is that destiny has thrust upon him. Some of these remarkable contrasts can be discerned in the differences between Olivier's World War II film production and that of Branagh in 1989, in the wake of Vietnam and the Falklands episode.

The Life of King Henry the Fifth

[Dramatis Personae

CHORUS

KING HENRY THE FIFTH
HUMPHREY, DUKE OF GLOUCESTER,
JOHN, DUKE OF BEDFORD,   *the King's brothers*
DUKE OF CLARENCE,
DUKE OF EXETER, *the King's uncle*
DUKE OF YORK, *the King's cousin*
EARL OF SALISBURY
EARL OF WESTMORLAND
EARL OF WARWICK
EARL OF HUNTINGDON

ARCHBISHOP OF CANTERBURY
BISHOP OF ELY

RICHARD, EARL OF CAMBRIDGE,   *conspirators*
HENRY, LORD SCROOP OF MASHAM,   *against the King*
SIR THOMAS GREY,

SIR THOMAS ERPINGHAM,
CAPTAIN GOWER,
CAPTAIN FLUELLEN,   *officers in the King's army*
CAPTAIN MACMORRIS,
CAPTAIN JAMY,
JOHN BATES,
ALEXANDER COURT,   *soldiers in the King's army*
MICHAEL WILLIAMS,
An English HERALD

PISTOL,
NYM,   *Falstaff's former tavern-mates*
BARDOLPH,
BOY, *formerly Falstaff's page*
HOSTESS, *formerly Mistress Quickly, now married to Pistol*

DUKE OF BURGUNDY

FRENCH KING, *Charles the Sixth*
QUEEN ISABEL *of France*
DAUPHIN, *Lewis*
KATHARINE, *Princess of France*
ALICE, *a lady attending Katharine*
DUKE OF ORLEANS
DUKE OF BERRI
DUKE OF BOURBON
DUKE OF BRITTANY
CONSTABLE OF FRANCE
LORD RAMBURES
LORD GRANDPRÉ
GOVERNOR OF HARFLEUR
MONSIEUR LE FER, *a French soldier*
MONTJOY, *the French herald*
French AMBASSADORS *to England*

Lords, Ladies, Officers, Soldiers, Citizens, Messengers, and Attendants

SCENE: *England, afterwards France*]

Prologue

Enter [Chorus as] Prologue.

CHORUS
Oh, for a Muse of fire, that would ascend	1
The brightest heaven of invention!	2
A kingdom for a stage, princes to act,	
And monarchs to behold the swelling scene!	4
Then should the warlike Harry, like himself,	5
Assume the port of Mars; and at his heels,	6
Leashed in like hounds, should famine, sword, and	
fire	
Crouch for employment. But pardon, gentles all,	8
The flat unraisèd spirits that hath dared	9
On this unworthy scaffold to bring forth	10
So great an object. Can this cockpit hold	11
The vasty fields of France? Or may we cram	12
Within this wooden O the very casques	13
That did affright the air at Agincourt?	
Oh, pardon! Since a crooked figure may	15
Attest in little place a million;	16
And let us, ciphers to this great account,	17
On your imaginary forces work.	18
Suppose within the girdle of these walls	
Are now confined two mighty monarchies,	
Whose high uprearèd and abutting fronts	21
The perilous narrow ocean parts asunder.	22
Piece out our imperfections with your thoughts:	
Into a thousand parts divide one man,	
And make imaginary puissance.	25
Think, when we talk of horses, that you see them	
Printing their proud hoofs i'th' receiving earth.	
For 'tis your thoughts that now must deck our kings,	28
Carry them here and there, jumping o'er times,	
Turning th'accomplishment of many years	
Into an hourglass—for the which supply,	31
Admit me Chorus to this history,	
Who, Prologue-like, your humble patience pray	
Gently to hear, kindly to judge, our play. *Exit.*	

Prologue.
1 Muse of fire (Of the four elements—earth, air, fire, and water—fire is the most sublime and mounting.)   **2 invention** poetic imagination. **4 swelling** splendid, magnificent   **5 like himself** i.e., presented in a fashion worthy of so great a king.   **6 port** bearing   **8 gentles** gentlemen and gentlewomen   **9 flat unraisèd** uninspired, lifeless. **spirits** i.e., actors and playwright.   **hath** (Elizabethan usage often pairs a plural subject with a singular verb.)   **10 scaffold** stage   **11 cockpit** (Elizabethan theaters were shaped rather like arenas for animal fighting.)   **12 vasty** vast, spacious   **13 O** (Refers to a round theater such as the Globe; the play may have been performed at the Curtain Theater.)   **casques** helmets   **15 crooked figure** cipher or zero (which, added to a number, will multiply its value tenfold)   **16 Attest** stand for   **17 account** (1) sum total (continuing the metaphor of *crooked figure*) (2) story   **18 imaginary forces** forces of imagination   **21 abutting** touching, bordering.   **fronts** (1) frontiers, i.e., the cliffs of Dover and Calais (2) foreheads   **22 perilous . . . ocean** i.e., English Channel   **25 puissance** armed might, army.   **28 deck** dress, adorn   **31 the which supply** which service

[1.1]

*Enter the two bishops, [the Archbishop] of
Canterbury and [the Bishop of] Ely.*

CANTERBURY
My lord, I'll tell you. That self bill is urged	1
Which in th'eleventh year of the last king's reign	
Was like, and had indeed against us passed,	3
But that the scambling and unquiet time	4
Did push it out of farther question.	5

ELY
But how, my lord, shall we resist it now?	

CANTERBURY
It must be thought on. If it pass against us,	
We lose the better half of our possession.	
For all the temporal lands which men devout	9
By testament have given to the Church	
Would they strip from us, being valued thus:	
As much as would maintain, to the King's honor,	
Full fifteen earls and fifteen hundred knights,	
Six thousand and two hundred good esquires,	14
And, to relief of lazars and weak age	15
Of indigent faint souls past corporal toil,	16
A hundred almshouses right well supplied;	
And to the coffers of the King beside	
A thousand pounds by th' year. Thus runs the bill.	

ELY   This would drink deep.

CANTERBURY   'Twould drink the cup and all.

ELY   But what prevention?

CANTERBURY
The King is full of grace and fair regard.

ELY
And a true lover of the holy Church.

CANTERBURY
The courses of his youth promised it not.	
The breath no sooner left his father's body	
But that his wildness, mortified in him,	27
Seemed to die too; yea, at that very moment	
Consideration like an angel came	29
And whipped th'offending Adam out of him,	30
Leaving his body as a paradise	
T'envelop and contain celestial spirits.	
Never was such a sudden scholar made;	
Never came reformation in a flood	
With such a heady currance, scouring faults;	35
Nor never Hydra-headed willfulness	36
So soon did lose his seat, and all at once,	37
As in this king.	

ELY   We are blessed in the change.

CANTERBURY
Hear him but reason in divinity,

1.1. Location: England. The royal court.
1 self same   **3 like** likely (to have passed)   **4 scambling** unsettled   **5 question** consideration.   **9 temporal** used for secular purposes   **14 esquires** members of the gentry, ranking just below knights   **15 lazars** lepers   **16 corporal** physical   **27 mortified** killed   **29 Consideration** meditation, reflection   **30 offending Adam** original sin   **35 heady currance** headlong current   **36 Hydra-headed** i.e., many-headed. (Alludes to the Lernaean Hydra, a monster of many heads overcome by Hercules.)   **37 his seat** its throne

And, all-admiring, with an inward wish
You would desire the King were made a prelate.
Hear him debate of commonwealth affairs,
You would say it hath been all in all his study.
List his discourse of war, and you shall hear   44
A fearful battle rendered you in music.   45
Turn him to any cause of policy,   46
The Gordian knot of it he will unloose,   47
Familiar as his garter, that, when he speaks,   48
The air, a chartered libertine, is still,   49
And the mute wonder lurketh in men's ears   50
To steal his sweet and honeyed sentences;   51
So that the art and practic part of life   52
Must be the mistress to this theoric.   53
Which is a wonder how His Grace should glean it,
Since his addiction was to courses vain,   55
His companies unlettered, rude, and shallow,   56
His hours filled up with riots, banquets, sports,   57
And never noted in him any study,
Any retirement, any sequestration
From open haunts and popularity.   60
ELY
The strawberry grows underneath the nettle,
And wholesome berries thrive and ripen best
Neighbored by fruit of baser quality;
And so the Prince obscured his contemplation
Under the veil of wildness, which, no doubt,
Grew like the summer grass, fastest by night,
Unseen, yet crescive in his faculty.   67
CANTERBURY
It must be so, for miracles are ceased.   68
And therefore we must needs admit the means   69
How things are perfected.
ELY   But, my good lord,
How now for mitigation of this bill
Urged by the Commons? Doth His Majesty
Incline to it, or no?
CANTERBURY   He seems indifferent,   73
Or rather swaying more upon our part
Than cherishing th'exhibiters against us;   75
For I have made an offer to His Majesty,
Upon our spiritual convocation   77
And in regard of causes now in hand,   78
Which I have opened to His Grace at large,   79

As touching France, to give a greater sum
Than ever at one time the clergy yet
Did to his predecessors part withal.   82
ELY
How did this offer seem received, my lord?
CANTERBURY
With good acceptance of His Majesty,
Save that there was not time enough to hear,
As I perceived His Grace would fain have done,   86
The severals and unhidden passages   87
Of his true titles to some certain dukedoms,
And generally to the crown and seat of France,   89
Derived from Edward, his great-grandfather.   90
ELY
What was th'impediment that broke this off?
CANTERBURY
The French ambassador upon that instant
Craved audience; and the hour I think is come
To give him hearing. Is it four o'clock?
ELY   It is.
CANTERBURY
Then go we in to know his embassy,   96
Which I could with a ready guess declare
Before the Frenchman speak a word of it.
ELY
I'll wait upon you, and I long to hear it.   *Exeunt.*

❧

[1.2]

Enter the King, Humphrey [Duke of Gloucester],
Bedford, Clarence, Warwick, Westmorland, and
Exeter [with attendants].

KING
Where is my gracious lord of Canterbury?
EXETER
Not here in presence.
KING   Send for him, good uncle.
WESTMORLAND
Shall we call in th'ambassador, my liege?
KING
Not yet, my cousin. We would be resolved,   4
Before we hear him, of some things of weight
That task our thoughts, concerning us and France.   6

Enter two bishops, [the Archbishop of Canter-
bury and the Bishop of Ely].

CANTERBURY
God and his angels guard your sacred throne,
And make you long become it!
KING   Sure we thank you.   8
My learnèd lord, we pray you to proceed,

44 **List** Listen to   45 **rendered** i.e., **music** i.e., eloquently narrated.
46 **cause of policy** matter of statecraft   47 **Gordian knot** i.e., great
difficulty resolved forcefully. (It was foretold that whoever should
untie the Gordian knot would rule Asia. Alexander solved the problem by cutting the knot.)   48 **Familiar** as offhandedly or routinely.
that so that   49 **chartered libertine** free spirit, licensed to roam at
will   50–1 **the mute . . . sentences** i.e., wonder makes men silent,
eagerly listening to hear more of his sweetly profitable wise sayings
52–3 **So . . . theoric** so that experience in practical life must have been
the teacher by which he acquired his theoretical conception.
55 **addiction** inclination   56 **companies** companions.   **rude** coarse
57 **riots** reveling.   **sports** amusements   60 **open . . . popularity**
places of public resort and low company.   67 **crescive . . . faculty** naturally inclined to grow.   68 **miracles are ceased** (Protestants generally believed that no miracles occurred after the revelation of Christ.)
69 **means** i.e., natural causes   73 **indifferent** impartial   75 **exhibiters** those who introduce bills in Parliament   77 **Upon** on behalf of.
convocation formal assembly of the clergy   78 **in hand** under consideration   79 **opened** expounded.   **at large** in full

82 **withal** with.   86 **fain** gladly   87 **severals** details.   **unhidden passages** clear lines of descent   89 **seat** throne   90 **Edward** Edward III
96 **embassy** message
1.2. Location: England. The royal court.
4 **cousin** (A form of address customarily used by royalty in addressing their nobles. In this case, Westmorland is in fact related to the
King by marriage.)   **be resolved** come to a decision   6 **task** engage,
occupy   8 **become** adorn, grace

And justly and religiously unfold
Why the law Salic that they have in France   11
Or should or should not bar us in our claim.   12
And God forbid, my dear and faithful lord,
That you should fashion, wrest, or bow your reading,
Or nicely charge your understanding soul   15
With opening titles miscreate, whose right   16
Suits not in native colors with the truth;   17
For God doth know how many now in health
Shall drop their blood in approbation   19
Of what your reverence shall incite us to.   20
Therefore take heed how you impawn our person,   21
How you awake our sleeping sword of war.
We charge you in the name of God take heed;
For never two such kingdoms did contend
Without much fall of blood, whose guiltless drops
Are every one a woe, a sore complaint   26
'Gainst him whose wrongs gives edge unto the
    swords   27
That makes such waste in brief mortality.   28
Under this conjuration speak, my lord;   29
For we will hear, note, and believe in heart
That what you speak is in your conscience washed
As pure as sin with baptism.

CANTERBURY
Then hear me, gracious sovereign, and you peers,
That owe yourselves, your lives, and services
To this imperial throne. There is no bar
To make against Your Highness' claim to France
But this, which they produce from Pharamond: 37
"In terram Salicam mulieres ne succedant,"
"No woman shall succeed in Salic land."
Which Salic land the French unjustly gloze   40
To be the realm of France, and Pharamond
The founder of this law and female bar.
Yet their own authors faithfully affirm
That the land Salic is in Germany,
Between the floods of Saale and of Elbe;   45
Where, Charles the Great having subdued the Saxons,   46
There left behind and settled certain French,
Who, holding in disdain the German women
For some dishonest manners of their life,   49
Established then this law: to wit, no female
Should be inheritrix in Salic land—
Which Salic, as I said, twixt Elbe and Saale,
Is at this day in Germany called Meissen.
Then doth it well appear the Salic law
Was not devisèd for the realm of France;
Nor did the French possess the Salic land

Until four hundred one-and-twenty years
After defunction of King Pharamond,   58
Idly supposed the founder of this law,   59
Who died within the year of our redemption
Four hundred twenty-six; and Charles the Great
Subdued the Saxons, and did seat the French
Beyond the River Saale, in the year
Eight hundred five. Besides, their writers say,
King Pepin, which deposèd Childeric,   65
Did, as heir general, being descended   66
Of Blithild, which was daughter to King Clothair,
Make claim and title to the crown of France.
Hugh Capet also, who usurped the crown
Of Charles the Duke of Lorraine, sole heir male
Of the true line and stock of Charles the Great,
To find his title with some shows of truth,   72
Though, in pure truth, it was corrupt and naught,
Conveyed himself as th'heir to th' Lady Lingard,   74
Daughter to Charlemagne, who was the son   75
To Lewis the Emperor, and Lewis the son
Of Charles the Great. Also King Lewis the Tenth,   77
Who was sole heir to the usurper Capet,
Could not keep quiet in his conscience,
Wearing the crown of France, till satisfied
That fair Queen Isabel, his grandmother,
Was lineal of the Lady Ermengard,   82
Daughter to Charles the foresaid Duke of Lorraine;
By the which marriage the line of Charles the Great
Was reunited to the crown of France.
So that, as clear as is the summer's sun,
King Pepin's title and Hugh Capet's claim,
King Lewis his satisfaction, all appear   88
To hold in right and title of the female;
So do the kings of France unto this day,
Howbeit they would hold up this Salic law   91
To bar Your Highness claiming from the female,
And rather choose to hide them in a net   93
Than amply to imbar their crooked titles   94
Usurped from you and your progenitors.

KING
May I with right and conscience make this claim?

CANTERBURY
The sin upon my head, dread sovereign!
For in the Book of Numbers is it writ,
When the man dies, let the inheritance   99
Descend unto the daughter. Gracious lord,   100
Stand for your own; unwind your bloody flag!   101
Look back into your mighty ancestors:

---

58 defunction death   **59 Idly** foolishly   **65 which** who. (As also in line 67.)   **66 heir general** heir through male or female line   **72 find** provide   **74 Conveyed himself** passed himself off   **75 Charlemagne** (Holinshed's and Hall's error, followed by Shakespeare, for Charles the Bald or Charles II, emperor of the West; Luitgard [Shakespeare's Lingard] became Charlemagne's wife after the death of Fastrada in 794.)   **77 Lewis the Tenth** (Actually, Louis IX; an error copied from Holinshed.)   **82 lineal of** descended from   **88 Lewis his satisfaction** Lewis's conviction   **91 Howbeit** notwithstanding   **93 hide . . . net** i.e., conceal the weakness of their case in a tangle of contradictions   **94 amply to imbar** frankly to bar claim to   **99–100 When . . . daughter** (This paraphrase leaves out an important phrase. Numbers 27:8 reads, "When a man dies leaving no son, his patrimony shall pass to his daughter.")   **101 unwind** unfurl

---

11 Salic (See explanation at lines 39–45.)   **12 Or** either   **15 nicely charge** subtly and foolishly burden   **16 opening titles miscreate** expounding spurious claims   **17 Suits . . . colors** i.e., does not naturally harmonize   **19 approbation** support, proof   **20 your reverence** (1) an honorific title for an archbishop, Your Reverence (2) your sacred authority   **21 impawn** put under an obligation   **26 woe** grievance.   **sore** severe, grievous   **27 wrongs** wrongdoings   **28 in brief mortality** i.e., among mortal, short-lived men.   **29 conjuration** solemn adjuration   **37 Pharamond** legendary Frankish king   **40 gloze** gloss   **45 floods** rivers   **46 Charles the Great** Charlemagne   **49 dishonest** unchaste

Go, my dread lord, to your great-grandsire's tomb,   103
From whom you claim! Invoke his warlike spirit,
And your great-uncle's, Edward the Black Prince,
Who on the French ground played a tragedy,   106
Making defeat on the full power of France,   107
Whiles his most mighty father on a hill
Stood smiling to behold his lion's whelp
Forage in blood of French nobility.
O noble English, that could entertain   111
With half their forces the full pride of France
And let another half stand laughing by,
All out of work and cold for action!   114

ELY
Awake remembrance of these valiant dead,
And with your puissant arm renew their feats!
You are their heir; you sit upon their throne;
The blood and courage that renownèd them   118
Runs in your veins; and my thrice-puissant liege
Is in the very May morn of his youth,
Ripe for exploits and mighty enterprises.

EXETER
Your brother kings and monarchs of the earth
Do all expect that you should rouse yourself
As did the former lions of your blood.

WESTMORLAND
They know Your Grace hath cause, and means, and
    might;
So hath Your Highness. Never king of England   126
Had nobles richer and more loyal subjects,
Whose hearts have left their bodies here in England
And lie pavilioned in the fields of France.   129

CANTERBURY
Oh, let their bodies follow, my dear liege,
With blood, and sword, and fire to win your right!
In aid whereof we of the spiritualty   132
Will raise Your Highness such a mighty sum
As never did the clergy at one time
Bring in to any of your ancestors.

KING
We must not only arm t'invade the French,
But lay down our proportions to defend   137
Against the Scot, who will make road upon us   138
With all advantages.   139

CANTERBURY
They of those marches, gracious sovereign,   140
Shall be a wall sufficient to defend
Our inland from the pilfering borderers.

KING
We do not mean the coursing snatchers only,   143

But fear the main intendment of the Scot,   144
Who hath been still a giddy neighbor to us.   145
For you shall read that my great-grandfather
Never went with his forces into France
But that the Scot on his unfurnished kingdom   148
Came pouring like the tide into a breach
With ample and brim fullness of his force,   150
Galling the gleanèd land with hot assays,   151
Girding with grievous siege castles and towns;
That England, being empty of defense,
Hath shook and trembled at th'ill neighborhood.   154

CANTERBURY
She hath been then more feared than harmed, my
    liege.   155
For hear her but exampled by herself: 156
When all her chivalry hath been in France   157
And she a mourning widow of her nobles,   158
She hath herself not only well defended
But taken and impounded as a stray   160
The King of Scots, whom she did send to France   161
To fill King Edward's fame with prisoner kings
And make her chronicle as rich with praise
As is the ooze and bottom of the sea
With sunken wrack and sumless treasuries.   165

A LORD
But there's a saying very old and true:
    "If that you will France win,
    Then with Scotland first begin."
For once the eagle England being in prey,   169
To her unguarded nest the weasel Scot
Comes sneaking, and so sucks her princely eggs,
Playing the mouse in absence of the cat,
To 'tame and havoc more than she can eat.   173

EXETER
It follows then the cat must stay at home;
Yet that is but a crushed necessity,   175
Since we have locks to safeguard necessaries
And pretty traps to catch the petty thieves.   177
While that the armèd hand doth fight abroad,   178
Th'advisèd head defends itself at home;   179
For government, though high, and low, and lower,   180
Put into parts, doth keep in one consent,   181

---

103 great-grandsire's i.e., Edward III's. His descent through his mother Isabella from the French King Philip IV is the basis of English claims to the French kingdom—a claim through female inheritance. Hence the importance of lines 39–55.   106 tragedy i.e., the Battle of Crécy, 1346, a major defeat for the French   107 power army   111 entertain engage, encounter   114 for action for want of action.   118 renownèd brought renown to   126 So so indeed   129 pavilioned tented, encamped   132 spiritualty clergy   137 lay . . . proportions allocate our forces   138 road inroad, raid   139 With all advantages whenever a good opportunity presents itself.   140 They . . . marches Our English forces in the territories bordering Scotland   143 coursing snatchers hit-and-run Scottish raiders on fast-galloping horses

144 intendment plan, hostile intent   145 still always.   giddy unstable, fickle   148 unfurnished unprovided with defense   150 brim absolute, complete   151 Galling . . . assays harassing the land stripped of defenders with hot attacks   154 th'ill neighborhood the unneighborliness.   155 feared frightened   156 hear . . . herself i.e., only listen how England can be instructed by an example from her own history   157 chivalry knights   158 And she . . . nobles and she, England, widowlike in being deprived of her nobility while they fight in France   160–1 impounded . . . Scots (King David II of Scotland was captured and imprisoned in 1346 while Edward III was in France.)   161 to France (Historically, David II was imprisoned in London, not sent to France.)   165 wrack wreckage.   sumless inestimable   169 in prey absent in search of prey   173 to 'tame and havoc to attame (i.e., break into) and ravage   175 crushed necessity distorted conclusion   177 pretty ingenious   178 While that While   179 advisèd wise, prudent   180 though . . . lower i.e., though composed of three broad social ranks (corresponding also to three singing voices from treble to bass)   181 Put into parts separated into different functions (and into different parts in part-music).   one consent mutual harmony

Congreeing in a full and natural close,   182
Like music.
CANTERBURY   Therefore doth heaven divide
The state of man in divers functions,
Setting endeavor in continual motion,
To which is fixèd, as an aim or butt,   186
Obedience; for so work the honeybees,
Creatures that by a rule in nature teach
The act of order to a peopled kingdom.
They have a king, and officers of sorts,   190
Where some, like magistrates, correct at home;   191
Others, like merchants, venture trade abroad;
Others, like soldiers, armèd in their stings,
Make boot upon the summer's velvet buds,   194
Which pillage they with merry march bring home
To the tent royal of their emperor,
Who, busied in his majesty, surveys
The singing masons building roofs of gold,
The civil citizens kneading up the honey,
The poor mechanic porters crowding in   200
Their heavy burdens at his narrow gate,
The sad-eyed justice with his surly hum   202
Delivering o'er to executors pale   203
The lazy yawning drone. I this infer,
That many things, having full reference   205
To one consent, may work contrariously.   206
As many arrows loosèd several ways   207
Come to one mark, as many ways meet in one town,   208
As many fresh streams meet in one salt sea,
As many lines close in the dial's center,   210
So may a thousand actions once afoot
End in one purpose, and be all well borne   212
Without defeat. Therefore to France, my liege!
Divide your happy England into four,
Whereof take you one quarter into France,
And you withal shall make all Gallia shake.   216
If we with thrice such powers left at home
Cannot defend our own doors from the dog,
Let us be worried, and our nation lose   219
The name of hardiness and policy.   220
KING
Call in the messengers sent from the Dauphin.   221
    [Exeunt some.]
Now are we well resolved, and by God's help
And yours, the noble sinews of our power,
France being ours, we'll bend it to our awe,   224

Or break it all to pieces. Or there we'll sit,   225
Ruling in large and ample empery   226
O'er France and all her almost kingly dukedoms,
Or lay these bones in an unworthy urn,
Tombless, with no remembrance over them.
Either our history shall with full mouth
Speak freely of our acts, or else our grave,
Like Turkish mute, shall have a tongueless mouth,
Not worshiped with a waxen epitaph.   233

    Enter Ambassadors of France.

Now are we well prepared to know the pleasure
Of our fair cousin Dauphin; for we hear   235
Your greeting is from him, not from the King.
FIRST AMBASSADOR
May't please Your Majesty to give us leave
Freely to render what we have in charge,
Or shall we sparingly show you far off
The Dauphin's meaning and our embassy?
KING
We are no tyrant, but a Christian king,
Unto whose grace our passion is as subject
As is our wretches fettered in our prisons.
Therefore with frank and with uncurbèd plainness
Tell us the Dauphin's mind.
FIRST AMBASSADOR   Thus, then, in few:
Your Highness, lately sending into France,
Did claim some certain dukedoms, in the right
Of your great predecessor, King Edward the Third.
In answer of which claim, the Prince our master
Says that you savor too much of your youth,
And bids you be advised there's naught in France
That can be with a nimble galliard won;   252
You cannot revel into dukedoms there.
He therefore sends you, meeter for your spirit,   254
This tun of treasure, and in lieu of this   255
Desires you let the dukedoms that you claim
Hear no more of you. This the Dauphin speaks.
    [*A casket is presented;*
    Exeter examines its contents.]
KING
What treasure, uncle?
EXETER   Tennis balls, my liege.
KING
We are glad the Dauphin is so pleasant with us.   259
His present and your pains we thank you for.
When we have matched our rackets to these balls,   261
We will in France, by God's grace, play a set
Shall strike his father's crown into the hazard.   263

---

182 Congreeing agreeing together.   **close** musical cadence   **186 aim or butt** target. (All endeavor is to direct itself toward obedience.)   **190 They . . . king** (A common error of early natural history, derived from Aristotle. The simile of the bees appears in Virgil, Sir Thomas Elyot, John Lyly, and others.)   **of sorts** various kinds   **191 correct** administer justice   **194 Make boot** prey   **200 mechanic** engaged in manual labor   **202 sad-eyed** grave-eyed   **203 executors pale** executioners, pale in their terrible sternness   **205–6 having . . . consent** united by a common understanding   **207 As** Just as.   **loosèd several ways** shot from different directions   **208 ways** roads   **210 close** come together.   **dial's** sundial's   **212 borne** carried out, sustained   **216 Gallia** France. (Latin name.)   **219 worried** (1) torn apart or harried, as by dogs (2) made anxious   **220 hardiness and policy** bravery and statesmanship.   **221 Dauphin** heir apparent to the French throne.   **224 ours** i.e., ours by right.   **our awe** submission to us

225 Or there Either there   **226 empery** dominion   **233 Not . . . epitaph** i.e., with not even so much as a wax (as opposed to bronze) epitaph; one easily effaced.   **235 cousin** fellow prince (though Henry does also claim a line of descent in the French royal family)   **252 galliard** a lively dance   **254 meeter** more fitting   **255 tun** cask   **259 pleasant** jocular. (Also in line 281.)   **261 rackets** (1) tennis rackets (2) noisy military assaults   **263 crown** (1) royal crown (2) final point scored, or a coin (worth five shillings in English coinage) staked in the game.   **hazard** (1) in "royal" tennis, an opening in one of the high walls enclosing the court; hitting the ball into such a "hazard" scored a winning point (2) jeopardy.

Tell him he hath made a match with such a wrangler 264
That all the courts of France will be disturbed 265
With chases. And we understand him well, 266
How he comes o'er us with our wilder days, 267
Not measuring what use we made of them.
We never valued this poor seat of England, 269
And therefore, living hence, did give ourself 270
To barbarous license—as 'tis ever common
That men are merriest when they are from home. 272
But tell the Dauphin I will keep my state, 273
Be like a king, and show my sail of greatness 274
When I do rouse me in my throne of France.
For that I have laid by my majesty 276
And plodded like a man for working days, 277
But I will rise there with so full a glory
That I will dazzle all the eyes of France,
Yea, strike the Dauphin blind to look on us.
And tell the pleasant Prince this mock of his
Hath turned his balls to gunstones, and his soul 282
Shall stand sore chargèd for the wasteful vengeance 283
That shall fly with them; for many a thousand
    widows
Shall this his mock mock out of their dear husbands,
Mock mothers from their sons, mock castles down,
And some are yet ungotten and unborn 287
That shall have cause to curse the Dauphin's scorn.
But this lies all within the will of God,
To whom I do appeal, and in whose name
Tell you the Dauphin I am coming on
To venge me as I may, and to put forth
My rightful hand in a well-hallowed cause.
So get you hence in peace; and tell the Dauphin
His jest will savor but of shallow wit
When thousands weep more than did laugh at it.—
Convey them with safe conduct.—Fare you well. 297
        Exeunt Ambassadors.

EXETER   This was a merry message.
KING
We hope to make the sender blush at it.
Therefore, my lords, omit no happy hour 300
That may give furth'rance to our expedition; 301
For we have now no thought in us but France,
Save those to God, that run before our business. 303
Therefore let our proportions for these wars 304
Be soon collected, and all things thought upon
That may with reasonable swiftness add
More feathers to our wings; for, God before, 307

We'll chide this Dauphin at his father's door.
Therefore let every man now task his thought, 309
That this fair action may on foot be brought.
        Flourish. Exeunt.

❖

[2.0]

Enter Chorus.

CHORUS
Now all the youth of England are on fire,
And silken dalliance in the wardrobe lies. 2
Now thrive the armorers, and honor's thought
Reigns solely in the breast of every man.
They sell the pasture now to buy the horse,
Following the mirror of all Christian kings, 6
With wingèd heels, as English Mercurys. 7
For now sits Expectation in the air
And hides a sword from hilts unto the point 9
With crowns imperial, crowns and coronets, 10
Promised to Harry and his followers.
The French, advised by good intelligence 12
Of this most dreadful preparation,
Shake in their fear, and with pale policy 14
Seek to divert the English purposes.
O England! Model to thy inward greatness, 16
Like little body with a mighty heart,
What mightst thou do, that honor would thee do, 18
Were all thy children kind and natural?
But see, thy fault France hath in thee found out,
A nest of hollow bosoms, which he fills
With treacherous crowns; and three corrupted men, 22
One, Richard Earl of Cambridge, and the second,
Henry Lord Scroop of Masham, and the third,
Sir Thomas Grey, knight, of Northumberland,
Have, for the gilt of France—oh, guilt indeed!— 26
Confirmed conspiracy with fearful France, 27
And by their hands this grace of kings must die,
If hell and treason hold their promises,
Ere he take ship for France, and in Southampton.
Linger your patience on, and we'll digest 31
Th'abuse of distance, force a play. 32
The sum is paid, the traitors are agreed,
The King is set from London, and the scene
Is now transported, gentles, to Southampton.
There is the playhouse now, there must you sit,
And thence to France shall we convey you safe,

---

264 **wrangler** adversary, disputant   265 **courts** (1) tennis courts (2) royal courts   266 **chases** (1) returns of the ball (2) chasing after game (3) chasing the enemy.   267 **comes o'er us** taunts me. (*Us* is the royal plural.)   269 **seat** throne   270 **living hence** not frequenting the royal court   272 **from** away from   273 **keep my state** i.e., fulfill the role of king   274 **sail** full swell. (Henry says he has not yet revealed his full majesty in laying claim to France.)   276 **For that** i.e., In anticipation of that great event   277 **for** suited and ready for   282 **gunstones** cannonballs   283 **sore chargèd** sorely burdened with responsibility. **wasteful** destructive   287 **yet ungotten** not yet conceived   297 **Convey** Escort   300 **omit . . . hour** lose no favorable opportunity 301 **expedition** (1) invasion of France (2) haste   303 **that . . . business** that properly come first.   304 **proportions** levies of men   307 **God before** with God leading, helping

309 **task** tax, exercise
2.0. Chorus.
2 **silken . . . lies** i.e., silken apparel and idle pleasure are packed away.   6 **the mirror . . . kings** i.e., the ideal or model to which all other kings should compare themselves   7 **Mercurys** (Mercury, classical messenger of the gods, always wears winged heels.)   9 **hides a sword** i.e., holds up a sword completely impaled with the prizes of war   10 **With . . . coronets** with the crowns of emperors, kings, and nobles   12 **intelligence** information gathering   14 **pale policy** faint-hearted stratagems   16 **Model to** Outward manifestation of 18 **would** would have   22 **crowns** coins, money (as a bribe)   26 **gilt** gold   27 **fearful** frightened, cowardly   31–2 **digest . . . play** compress long distance (and time) into what can be encompassed in a play, an *abuse* of the unities of time and place.

And bring you back, charming the narrow seas
To give you gentle pass; for, if we may,   39
We'll not offend one stomach with our play.   40
But, when the King come forth, and not till then,   41
Unto Southampton do we shift our scene.   *Exit.*   42

❖

[2.1]

Enter Corporal Nym and Lieutenant Bardolph.

BARDOLPH Well met, Corporal Nym.

NYM Good morrow, Lieutenant Bardolph.

BARDOLPH What, are Ancient Pistol and you friends   3
yet?

NYM For my part, I care not. I say little; but when time
shall serve, there shall be smiles—but that shall be as
it may. I dare not fight, but I will wink and hold out   7
mine iron. It is a simple one, but what though? It will   8
toast cheese, and it will endure cold as another man's   9
sword will—and there's an end.   10

BARDOLPH I will bestow a breakfast to make you
friends, and we'll be all three sworn brothers to
France. Let 't be so, good Corporal Nym.

NYM Faith, I will live so long as I may, that's the certain
of it; and when I cannot live any longer, I will do as I
may. That is my rest; that is the rendezvous of it.   16

BARDOLPH It is certain, Corporal, that he is married to
Nell Quickly, and certainly she did you wrong, for
you were trothplight to her.   19

NYM I cannot tell. Things must be as they may. Men
may sleep, and they may have their throats about
them at that time, and some say knives have edges. It
must be as it may. Though Patience be a tired mare,   23
yet she will plod. There must be conclusions. Well, I   24
cannot tell.

Enter Pistol and [Hostess] Quickly.

BARDOLPH Here comes Ancient Pistol and his wife.
Good Corporal, be patient here.

NYM How now, mine host Pistol?

PISTOL
Base tike, call'st thou me host?   29
Now, by this hand, I swear, I scorn the term!
Nor shall my Nell keep lodgers.

HOSTESS No, by my troth, not long; for we cannot lodge
and board a dozen or fourteen gentlewomen that live

honestly by the prick of their needles, but it will be   34
thought we keep a bawdy house straight. [*Nym and
Pistol draw.*] Oh, welladay, Lady! If he be not hewn   36
now, we shall see willful adultery and murder com-   37
itted.

BARDOLPH Good Lieutenant! Good Corporal! Offer   39
nothing here.   40

NYM Pish!

PISTOL
Pish for thee, Iceland dog!   42
Thou prick-eared cur of Iceland!

HOSTESS Good Corporal Nym, show thy valor, and   44
put up your sword.   [*They sheathe their swords.*]

NYM Will you shog off? I would have you solus.   46

PISTOL
Solus, egregious dog? O viper vile!
The solus in thy most mervailous face!   48
The solus in thy teeth, and in thy throat,   49
And in thy hateful lungs, yea, in thy maw, pardie,   50
And, which is worse, within thy nasty mouth!
I do retort the solus in thy bowels;
For I can take, and Pistol's cock is up,   53
And flashing fire will follow.

NYM I am not Barbason; you cannot conjure me. I have   55
an humor to knock you indifferently well. If you grow   56
foul with me, Pistol, I will scour you with my rapier, as 57
I may, in fair terms. If you would walk off, I would   58
prick your guts a little, in good terms, as I may, and
that's the humor of it.   60

PISTOL
O braggart vile and damnèd furious wight!   61
The grave doth gape, and doting death is near.
Therefore exhale!   [*They draw their swords.*] 63

BARDOLPH [*drawing his sword*] Hear me, hear me what
I say. He that strikes the first stroke, I'll run him up to
the hilts, as I am a soldier.

PISTOL
An oath of mickle might, and fury shall abate.   67
[*Pistol and Nym sheathe their swords.*]
[*To Nym*] Give me thy fist, thy forefoot to me give.
Thy spirits are most tall.   69

---

34 prick (With a bawdy double meaning, probably unintended, as also
in *Pistol's cock*, line 53.) **36 welladay** wellaway, alas. **Lady** i.e., by
Our Lady. (An oath.) **hewn** struck down **37 adultery** (Blunder for
"battery"?) **39–40 Offer nothing** Attempt no violence **42 Iceland
dog** a small, shaggy dog often kept as a house pet. (Pistol's humor is
to use extravagant epithets, like this one, tags from current plays, and
scraps of foreign languages.) **44 valor** (She means "calm," "forbearance.") **46 shog off** move along. **solus** alone. (Nym proposes a duel;
see *walk off* in line 58.) **48 mervailous** marvelous, astonishing
49–50 The solus . . . lungs (The most offensive insult possible, as in
Hamlet's "the lie i'th' throat / As deep as to the lungs," 2.2.574–5.)
50 maw belly. **pardie** *par Dieu*, by God **53 take** catch fire. **cock is
up** trigger is cocked. (With bawdy pun.) **55 Barbason** (The name of
a fiend.) **conjure** exorcise. (Nym mocks Pistol's hyperbolic rant as
though it were a conjuration.) **55–6 I have an humor** I'm in the mood.
(*Humor* is a favorite word with Nym, as in lines 60, 71, 97, 116, 121, and
126.) **57 foul** (1) foulmouthed (2) fouled from firing and in need of
scouring **58 in fair terms** i.e., make no mistake about it. (*In good terms*
at line 59 means the same.) **walk off** walk aside (to fight) **60 that's
. . . it** that's my mood. **61 wight** person. **63 exhale** draw (sword, much
as the sun draws forth vapors). **67 mickle** great **69 tall** valiant.

---

39 pass passage **40 offend one stomach** (1) offend anyone's taste by
sudden shifts in scene (2) make anyone seasick **41–2 But . . . scene**
i.e., The scene will be shifted to Southampton after a scene in London.
(These lines sound as though they were added as an afterthought, to
accommodate the inclusion of the comic scene in 2.1.)
2.1. Location: London. A street.
3 Ancient Ensign, standard-bearer **7 wink** shut the eyes **8 iron**
sword. **though** of that. **9 endure cold** i.e., doesn't mind being
drawn from its sheath **10 there's an end** that's all there is to it.
16 rest last stake (in the gambling game of primero). **rendezvous**
last resort **19 trothplight** betrothed **23–4 Though . . . plod** i.e.,
Patient persistence will ultimately achieve its goal. (Nym hints, as
he does elsewhere, at violence toward Pistol.) **24 conclusions** an
end to matters. (Nym hints darkly that the end must come soon.)
29 tike cur

NYM   I will cut thy throat, one time or other, in fair
terms. That is the humor of it.

PISTOL   *Couple a gorge!*   72
That is the word. I thee defy again.
O hound of Crete, think'st thou my spouse to get?   74
No, to the spital go,   75
And from the powdering tub of infamy   76
Fetch forth the lazar kite of Cressid's kind,   77
Doll Tearsheet she by name, and her espouse.
I have, and I will hold, the quondam Quickly   79
For the only she; and—*pauca!* There's enough.   80
Go to.

Enter the Boy.

BOY   Mine host Pistol, you must come to my master,
and you, hostess. He is very sick and would to bed.
Good Bardolph, put thy face between his sheets, and   84
do the office of a warming pan. Faith, he's very ill.

BARDOLPH   Away, you rogue!

HOSTESS   By my troth, he'll yield the crow a pudding   87
one of these days. The King has killed his heart. Good   88
husband, come home presently.   *Exit [with Boy].*   89

BARDOLPH   Come, shall I make you two friends? We
must to France together. Why the devil should we
keep knives to cut one another's throats?

PISTOL
Let floods o'erswell, and fiends for food howl on!

NYM   You'll pay me the eight shillings I won of you at
betting?

PISTOL   Base is the slave that pays.

NYM   That now I will have. That's the humor of it.

PISTOL   As manhood shall compound. Push home.   98
[They] draw.

BARDOLPH   *[drawing]*   By this sword, he that makes
the first thrust, I'll kill him! By this sword, I will.

PISTOL
Sword is an oath, and oaths must have their course.   101
[He sheathes his sword.]

BARDOLPH   Corporal Nym, an thou wilt be friends, be   102
friends; an thou wilt not, why, then, be enemies with
me too. Prithee, put up.   104

NYM   I shall have my eight shillings I won of you at
betting?

PISTOL
A noble shalt thou have, and present pay;   107
And liquor likewise will I give to thee,

And friendship shall combine, and brotherhood.
I'll live by Nym, and Nym shall live by me.   110
Is not this just? For I shall sutler be   111
Unto the camp, and profits will accrue.
Give me thy hand.

NYM   I shall have my noble?

PISTOL   In cash most justly paid.

NYM   Well, then, that's the humor of't.
[Nym and Bardolph sheathe their swords.]

Enter Hostess.

HOSTESS   As ever you come of women, come in quickly 117
to Sir John. Ah, poor heart, he is so shaked of a burning quotidian tertian that it is most lamentable to be-   119
hold. Sweet men, come to him.   *[Exit.]*

NYM   The King hath run bad humors on the knight,   121
that's the even of it.   122

PISTOL   Nym, thou hast spoke the right.
His heart is fracted and corroborate.   124

NYM   The King is a good king, but it must be as it may;
he passes some humors and careers.   126

PISTOL
Let us condole the knight, for, lambkins, we will live.   127
[Exeunt.]

❖

[2.2]

Enter Exeter, Bedford, and Westmorland.

BEDFORD
'Fore God, His Grace is bold to trust these traitors.

EXETER
They shall be apprehended by and by.

WESTMORLAND
How smooth and even they do bear themselves!   3
As if allegiance in their bosoms sat,
Crownèd with faith and constant loyalty.

BEDFORD
The King hath note of all that they intend,
By interception which they dream not of.

EXETER
Nay, but the man that was his bedfellow,   8
Whom he hath dulled and cloyed with gracious
favors—   9

---

72 *Couple a gorge! Couper la gorge!*, "Cut the throat!"   74 **hound of
Crete** (Parallel to *Iceland dog*, line 42.)   75 **spital** hospital   76 **powdering tub** (Originally a tub used for salting beef; here, alluding to a
method of curing venereal disease by sweating.)   77 **lazar . . . kind**
i.e., diseased, leprous whore (a *kite* is a bird of prey) like Cressida,
the fallen woman, who, in Robert Henryson's *Testament of Cresseid*, is
shown as being rejected by Diomede and infected with leprosy
79 **quondam** former   80 **only she** i.e., only woman in the world.
pauca i.e., in brief   84 **face** (Bardolph's face is fiery with drinking.)
87 **he'll** (Refers to the Boy or Falstaff.)   **yield . . . pudding** i.e., be
hanged on the gallows and eaten by carrion birds   88 **his** i.e., Falstaff's   89 **presently** immediately.   98 **As . . . compound** As valor
shall settle the matter (in fight).   101 **Sword is an oath** (Quibbling on
sword as *'s word,* i.e., "God's word.")   102 **an** if   104 **put up** i.e., put
up your sword.   107 **A noble . . . pay** i.e., I'll settle for paying you six
shillings eight pence ready money

110 **Nym** (Quibbles on *nim,* meaning "thief.")   111 **sutler** seller of
liquor and provisions to the soldiers   117 **come of** were born of
119 **quotidian tertian** (A *quotidian* fever was one that came daily; a
tertian fever, one that came on alternate days, though some authorities believed that different fevers might mix and intensify their
effects.)   121 **run bad humors** i.e., vented his displeasure   122 **even**
level truth   124 **fracted** broken.   **corroborate** (Blunder for "broken
to pieces" or "corrupted"? The word means "strengthened, confirmed.")   126 **passes . . . careers** lets pass (i.e., indulges in) some
idiosyncrasies and capers. (A *career* is a full gallop.)   127 **condole**
express our commiseration of or sympathy with.   **lambkins** (A term
of endearment.)
2.2. Location: Southampton, a seaport on England's southern coast.
3 **smooth and even** pleasant and calm   8 **bedfellow** i.e., constant
companion. (Refers to Scroop.)   9 **dulled** dulled the appetite of

That he should, for a foreign purse, so sell
His sovereign's life to death and treachery!

Sound trumpets. Enter the King, Scroop, Cam-
bridge, and Grey, [and attendants].

KING
Now sits the wind fair, and we will aboard.   12
My lord of Cambridge, and my kind lord of Masham,
And you, my gentle knight, give me your thoughts.
Think you not that the pow'rs we bear with us   15
Will cut their passage through the force of France,
Doing the execution and the act
For which we have in head assembled them?   18

SCROOP
No doubt, my liege, if each man do his best.

KING
I doubt not that, since we are well persuaded
We carry not a heart with us from hence
That grows not in a fair consent with ours,   22
Nor leave not one behind that doth not wish
Success and conquest to attend on us.

CAMBRIDGE
Never was monarch better feared and loved
Than is Your Majesty. There's not, I think, a subject
That sits in heart-grief and uneasiness
Under the sweet shade of your government.

GREY
True. Those that were your father's enemies
Have steeped their galls in honey, and do serve you   30
With hearts create of duty and of zeal.   31

KING
We therefore have great cause of thankfulness,
And shall forget the office of our hand   33
Sooner than quittance of desert and merit   34
According to the weight and worthiness.

SCROOP
So service shall with steelèd sinews toil,
And labor shall refresh itself with hope,
To do Your Grace incessant services.

KING
We judge no less.—Uncle of Exeter,
Enlarge the man committed yesterday   40
That railed against our person. We consider
It was excess of wine that set him on,
And on his more advice we pardon him.   43

SCROOP
That's mercy, but too much security.   44
Let him be punished, sovereign, lest example
Breed, by his sufferance, more of such a kind.   46

KING   Oh, let us yet be merciful.

CAMBRIDGE
So may Your Highness, and yet punish too.

GREY
Sir, you show great mercy if you give him life   49
After the taste of much correction.   50

KING
Alas, your too much love and care of me
Are heavy orisons 'gainst this poor wretch!   52
If little faults proceeding on distemper   53
Shall not be winked at, how shall we stretch our eye   54
When capital crimes, chewed, swallowed, and
     digested,   55
Appear before us? We'll yet enlarge that man,   56
Though Cambridge, Scroop, and Grey, in their dear
     care
And tender preservation of our person,
Would have him punished. And now to our French
     causes.
Who are the late commissioners?   60

CAMBRIDGE   I one, my lord.
Your Highness bade me ask for it today.   62

SCROOP   So did you me, my liege.

GREY   And I, my royal sovereign.

KING [*giving them papers*]
Then, Richard Earl of Cambridge, there is yours;
There yours, Lord Scroop of Masham; and sir knight,
Grey of Northumberland, this same is yours.
Read them, and know I know your worthiness.—
My lord of Westmorland, and uncle Exeter,
We will aboard tonight.—Why, how now, gentlemen?
What see you in those papers, that you lose
So much complexion?—Look ye how they change!   72
Their cheeks are paper.—Why, what read you there   73
That have so cowarded and chased your blood
Out of appearance?

CAMBRIDGE   I do confess my fault,   75
And do submit me to Your Highness' mercy.

GREY, SCROOP   To which we all appeal.

KING
The mercy that was quick in us but late   78
By your own counsel is suppressed and killed.
You must not dare, for shame, to talk of mercy,
For your own reasons turn into your bosoms,
As dogs upon their masters, worrying you.—   82
See you, my princes and my noble peers,
These English monsters! My lord of Cambridge here,
You know how apt our love was to accord   85
To furnish him with all appurtenants   86
Belonging to his honor; and this man
Hath for a few light crowns lightly conspired   88
And sworn unto the practices of France   89

---

12 **sits . . . fair** the wind blows from a favorable quarter   15 **pow'rs**
armed forces   18 **in head** as an army   22 **grows . . . consent** does not
act in harmony   30 **galls** i.e., resentment   31 **create** composed
33 **office** use, function   34 **quittance** requital   40 **Enlarge** set free
43 **more advice** explaining and apologizing for what happened
44 **security** overconfidence.   46 **sufferance** being pardoned

49 **give him life** allow him to live   50 **correction** punishment.
52 **heavy orisons** weighty prayers, pleas   53 **proceeding on distem-**
per resulting from unstable condition (caused by excessive drinking)
54 **stretch** open wide, not wink   55 **capital** punishable by death.
chewed . . . digested i.e., premeditated   56 **yet** in spite of what you
say   60 **late** recently appointed (to serve while Henry is in France)
62 **it** i.e., my commission   72 **complexion** color.   73 **paper** i.e., white
as a sheet.   75 **appearance** (1) sight (2) your faces. (Presumably
the traitors kneel at this point.)   78 **quick** alive   82 **worrying you**
tearing at your throat.   85 **accord** consent   86 **appurtenants** appurtenances   88 **light** insignificant.   **lightly** readily, casually
89 **practices** plots

To kill us here in Hampton. To the which
This knight, no less for bounty bound to us   91
Than Cambridge is, hath likewise sworn. But oh,
What shall I say to thee, Lord Scroop, thou cruel,
Ingrateful, savage, and inhuman creature?
Thou that didst bear the key of all my counsels,
That knew'st the very bottom of my soul,
That almost mightst have coined me into gold,
Wouldst thou have practiced on me for thy use?   98
May it be possible that foreign hire
Could out of thee extract one spark of evil
That might annoy my finger? 'Tis so strange   101
That though the truth of it stands off as gross   102
As black and white, my eye will scarcely see it.
Treason and murder ever kept together,
As two yoke-devils sworn to either's purpose,   105
Working so grossly in a natural cause   106
That admiration did not whoop at them.   107
But thou, 'gainst all proportion, didst bring in   108
Wonder to wait on treason and on murder;   109
And whatsoever cunning fiend it was
That wrought upon thee so preposterously   111
Hath got the voice in hell for excellence.   112
All other devils that suggest by treasons   113
Do botch and bungle up damnation   114
With patches, colors, and with forms being fetched   115
From glist'ring semblances of piety;   116
But he that tempered thee bade thee stand up,   117
Gave thee no instance why thou shouldst do treason,   118
Unless to dub thee with the name of traitor.   119
If that same demon that hath gulled thee thus
Should with his lion gait walk the whole world,   121
He might return to vasty Tartar back   122
And tell the legions, "I can never win
A soul so easy as that Englishman's."
Oh, how hast thou with jealousy infected   125
The sweetness of affiance! Show men dutiful?   126
Why, so didst thou. Seem they grave and learnèd?
Why, so didst thou. Come they of noble family?
Why, so didst thou. Seem they religious?
Why, so didst thou. Or are they spare in diet,
Free from gross passion or of mirth or anger,   131
Constant in spirit, not swerving with the blood,   132

Garnished and decked in modest complement,   133
Not working with the eye without the ear,   134
And but in purgèd judgment trusting neither?   135
Such and so finely bolted didst thou seem.
And thus thy fall hath left a kind of blot   137
To mark the full-fraught man and best endued   138
With some suspicion. I will weep for thee;   139
For this revolt of thine, methinks, is like
Another fall of man.—Their faults are open.   141
Arrest them to the answer of the law;   142
And God acquit them of their practices!

EXETER   I arrest thee of high treason, by the name of
Richard Earl of Cambridge.
I arrest thee of high treason, by the name of Henry Lord
Scroop of Masham.
I arrest thee of high treason, by the name of Thomas
Grey, knight, of Northumberland.

SCROOP
Our purposes God justly hath discovered,   150
And I repent my fault more than my death,
Which I beseech Your Highness to forgive,
Although my body pay the price of it.

CAMBRIDGE
For me, the gold of France did not seduce,
Although I did admit it as a motive   155
The sooner to effect what I intended.   156
But God be thankèd for prevention,
Which I in sufferance heartily will rejoice,   158
Beseeching God and you to pardon me.

GREY
Never did faithful subject more rejoice
At the discovery of most dangerous treason
Than I do at this hour joy o'er myself,
Prevented from a damnèd enterprise.
My fault, but not my body, pardon, sovereign.

KING
God quit you in his mercy! Hear your sentence.   165
You have conspired against our royal person,
Joined with an enemy proclaimed, and from his
     coffers
Received the golden earnest of our death,   168
Wherein you would have sold your king to slaughter,
His princes and his peers to servitude,
His subjects to oppression and contempt,
And his whole kingdom into desolation.
Touching our person seek we no revenge,   173

---

91 This knight i.e., Grey   **98 practiced on** plotted against.   **use** profit. (With play on the meaning "interest derived from usury"; Scroop had served as Lord Treasurer.)   **101 annoy** injure   **102 stands . . . gross** appears as obvious   **105 yoke-devils** partners in a diabolical cause   **106–7 Working . . . them** working together so manifestly toward a purpose suited to their evil natures that they provoked no outcry of wonder.   **108 proportion** fitness of things   **109 Wonder** astonishment (that Scroop should be a murderer).   **wait on** attend, accompany   **111 wrought** worked.   **preposterously** unnaturally   **112 voice** vote   **113–16 All . . . piety** All other devils that tempt make at least some effort to dress damnation up in a plausible semblance of piety   **117–19 But . . . traitor** but the devil that tempted you to treason simply ordered you to stand up an unabashed rebel, and gave you no specious justification to do treason other than for the sheer sake of having the name of traitor.   **121 lion gait** (The devil, according to 1 Peter 5:8, strides about the world like a roaring lion, "seeking whom he may devour.")   **122 vasty** vast.   **Tartar** Tartarus, the hell of classical mythology   **125 jealousy** suspicion   **126 affiance** trust.   **Show** Appear   **131 or of** either of   **132 swerving with the blood** sinning through passion

133 decked . . . complement wearing the look of modesty   **134–5 Not . . . neither** trusting neither eye nor ear alone, and not trusting either one except when refined by wisdom and judgment.   **137–9 And . . . suspicion** And thus your fall into sin has been such as to cast some suspicion on even those who seem fully and richly endowed with virtuous qualities.   **141 fall of man** humankind's original disobedience to God in the Garden of Eden.   **open** apparent, obvious.   **142 to the answer of** so that they will be answerable to   **150 discovered** revealed   **155 did . . . motive** i.e., accepted money from France as a means   **156 The . . . intended** (Cambridge's real motive, barely hinted at here, was to assist his brother-in-law Edmund Mortimer, fifth Earl of March, to the throne as the standard-bearer of the Yorkist claim against the Lancastrian Henry.)   **158 sufferance** my suffering and patient endurance   **165 quit** (1) pardon (2) requite, punish   **168 golden earnest** advance payment   **173 Touching our person** As regards my own personal safety

But we our kingdom's safety must so tender,   174
Whose ruin you have sought, that to her laws
We do deliver you. Get you therefore hence,
Poor miserable wretches, to your death,
The taste whereof God of his mercy give
You patience to endure, and true repentance
Of all your dear offenses!—Bear them hence.   180

     Exeunt [Cambridge, Scroop, and Grey, guarded].
Now, lords, for France, the enterprise whereof
Shall be to you, as us, like glorious.   182
We doubt not of a fair and lucky war,
Since God so graciously hath brought to light
This dangerous treason lurking in our way
To hinder our beginnings. We doubt not now
But every rub is smoothèd on our way.   187
Then forth, dear countrymen! Let us deliver
Our puissance into the hand of God,   189
Putting it straight in expedition.   190
Cheerly to sea! The signs of war advance!   191
No king of England, if not king of France!

            Flourish. [Exeunt.]

❖

[2.3]

Enter Pistol, Nym, Bardolph, Boy, and Hostess.

HOSTESS   Prithee, honey-sweet husband, let me bring
thee to Staines.   2
PISTOL   No, for my manly heart doth earn. Bardolph, be   3
blithe; Nym, rouse thy vaunting veins; Boy, bristle thy
courage up; for Falstaff he is dead, and we must earn
therefore.
BARDOLPH   Would I were with him, wheresome'er he is,
either in heaven or in hell!
HOSTESS   Nay, sure he's not in hell. He's in Arthur's   9
bosom, if ever man went to Arthur's bosom. 'A made   10
a finer end, and went away an it had been any   11
christom child. 'A parted ev'n just between twelve   12
and one, ev'n at the turning o'th' tide. For after I saw
him fumble with the sheets, and play with flowers,
and smile upon his finger's end, I knew there was but
one way; for his nose was as sharp as a pen, and 'a   16
babbled of green fields. "How now, Sir John?" quoth I.   17
"What, man? Be o' good cheer." So 'a cried out, "God,
God, God!" three or four times. Now I, to comfort him,
bid him 'a should not think of God; I hoped there was

no need to trouble himself with any such thoughts yet.
So 'a bade me lay more clothes on his feet. I put my
hand into the bed and felt them, and they were as cold
as any stone; then I felt to his knees, and so upward   24
and upward, and all was as cold as any stone.   25
NYM   They say he cried out of sack.   26
HOSTESS   Ay, that 'a did.
BARDOLPH   And of women.
HOSTESS   Nay, that 'a did not.
BOY   Yes, that 'a did, and said they were devils incarnate.
HOSTESS   'A could never abide carnation; 'twas a color
he never liked.
BOY   'A said once the devil would have him about
women.
HOSTESS   'A did in some sort, indeed, handle women;   36
but then he was rheumatic, and talked of the Whore of   37
Babylon.
BOY   Do you not remember, 'a saw a flea stick upon
Bardolph's nose, and 'a said it was a black soul
burning in hell?
BARDOLPH   Well, the fuel is gone that maintained that   42
fire. That's all the riches I got in his service.
NYM   Shall we shog? The King will be gone from South-   44
ampton.
PISTOL
Come, let's away.—My love, give me thy lips.
            [He kisses the Hostess.]
Look to my chattels and my movables.   47
Let senses rule. The word is "Pitch and pay."   48
Trust none,
For oaths are straws, men's faiths are wafer cakes,   50
And Holdfast is the only dog, my duck.   51
Therefore, *caveto* be thy counselor.   52
Go, clear thy crystals.—Yokefellows in arms,   53
Let us to France, like horseleeches, my boys,
To suck, to suck, the very blood to suck!
BOY   And that's but unwholesome food, they say.
PISTOL   Touch her soft mouth, and march.
BARDOLPH   Farewell, hostess.   *[Kissing her.]*
NYM   I cannot kiss, that is the humor of it; but adieu.
PISTOL
Let huswifery appear. Keep close, I thee command.   60
HOSTESS   Farewell! Adieu!   *Exeunt [separately].*

174 tender regard, hold dear   **180 dear** grievous, dire   **182 like** alike, equally   **187 But** but that.   **rub** obstacle. (A bowling term.)   **189 puissance** armed might   **190 straight in expedition** immediately in action.   **191 The signs . . . advance!** Lift high our banners!
2.3. London. A street.
2 Staines town on the road from London to Southampton.   **3 earn** grieve. (But in line 5 there may also be a play on the sense of "find other employment," since Pistol and the others are now on their own.)   **9–10 Arthur's bosom** (Malapropism for "Abraham's bosom"; see Luke 16:22.)   **10 'A** He   **11 an** as if   **12 christom** (Mistress Quickly means "new christened." A *chrisom* is a white robe put on a child at baptism to betoken innocence. Christenings were performed soon after birth because of the high rate of infant mortality.)   **16–17 'a babbled of green fields** (This line contains Theobald's famous emendation. The Folio has "and a Table of greene fields." Mistress Quickly seems unaware that Falstaff was reciting the Twenty-third Psalm.)

24–5 upward . . . stone (The Hostess seems unaware of the sexual implications of her speech. *Stone* can mean "testicle.")   **26 of sack** against sack (a Spanish wine).   **36 handle** discuss. (Though an unintended literal sense is also comically present.)   **37 rheumatic** feverish, or perhaps an error for "lunatic." (Because "Rome" was pronounced "room," *rheumatic* also prepares for the allusion to the Whore of Babylon, i.e., the Church of Rome. See also Revelation 17:4–5.)   **42 fuel** i.e., liquor, supplied by Falstaff, that has given Bardolph his red face   **44 shog** be off. **47 chattels . . . movables** personal property.   **48 Let . . . pay** i.e., Keep your eyes and ears open, and let your motto as hostess be "cash down." **50 wafer cakes** i.e., easily broken   **51 Holdfast . . . dog** i.e., a large clamp or *holdfast* is best at holding things tight, like a tenacious dog. (Compare the proverb, "Brag is a good dog, but Holdfast is better.") Mistress Quickly is bidden to keep a tight hold on things.   **52 caveto** beware. (The correct imperative plural of the Latin is *cavete*.)   **53 clear thy crystals** wipe your eyes.   **Yokefellows** Companions   **60 Let . . . close** i.e., Be a thrifty housekeeper and stay at home

[2.4]

Flourish. Enter the French King, the Dauphin, the Dukes of Berri and Brittany, [the Constable, and others].

FRENCH KING
Thus comes the English with full power upon us,
And more than carefully it us concerns
To answer royally in our defenses.
Therefore the Dukes of Berri and of Brittany,
Of Brabant and of Orleans, shall make forth,   5
And you, Prince Dauphin, with all swift dispatch,
To line and new-repair our towns of war   7
With men of courage and with means defendant;   8
For England his approaches makes as fierce   9
As waters to the sucking of a gulf.   10
It fits us then to be as provident
As fear may teach us, out of late examples   12
Left by the fatal and neglected English   13
Upon our fields.

DAUPHIN   My most redoubted father, 14
It is most meet we arm us 'gainst the foe;   15
For peace itself should not so dull a kingdom,
Though war nor no known quarrel were in question,
But that defenses, musters, preparations,
Should be maintained, assembled, and collected
As were a war in expectation.   20
Therefore, I say 'tis meet we all go forth
To view the sick and feeble parts of France.
And let us do it with no show of fear—
No, with no more than if we heard that England
Were busied with a Whitsun morris dance.   25
For, my good liege, she is so idly kinged,   26
Her scepter so fantastically borne
By a vain, giddy, shallow, humorous youth,   28
That fear attends her not.

CONSTABLE   Oh, peace, Prince Dauphin!
You are too much mistaken in this king.
Question Your Grace the late ambassadors,
With what great state he heard their embassy,   32
How well supplied with noble counselors,
How modest in exception, and withal   34
How terrible in constant resolution,   35
And you shall find his vanities forespent   36
Were but the outside of the Roman Brutus,   37
Covering discretion with a coat of folly,
As gardeners do with ordure hide those roots   39

That shall first spring and be most delicate.

DAUPHIN
Well, 'tis not so, my Lord High Constable;
But though we think it so, it is no matter.
In cases of defense 'tis best to weigh
The enemy more mighty than he seems.
So the proportions of defense are filled,   45
Which of a weak and niggardly projection   46
Doth, like a miser, spoil his coat with scanting
A little cloth.

FRENCH KING   Think we King Harry strong;
And, princes, look you strongly arm to meet him.   49
The kindred of him hath been fleshed upon us;   50
And he is bred out of that bloody strain
That haunted us in our familiar paths.
Witness our too-much-memorable shame
When Crécy battle fatally was struck,   54
And all our princes captived by the hand
Of that black name, Edward, Black Prince of Wales;
Whiles that his mountain sire, on mountain standing,   57
Up in the air, crowned with the golden sun,
Saw his heroical seed and smiled to see him   59
Mangle the work of nature and deface   60
The patterns that by God and by French fathers   61
Had twenty years been made. This is a stem   62
Of that victorious stock; and let us fear
The native mightiness and fate of him.   64

Enter a Messenger.

MESSENGER
Ambassadors from Harry King of England
Do crave admittance to Your Majesty.

FRENCH KING
We'll give them present audience. Go and bring them.
                                        [*Exit Messenger.*]
You see this chase is hotly followed, friends.

DAUPHIN
Turn head and stop pursuit; for coward dogs   69
Most spend their mouths when what they seem to
   threaten   70
Runs far before them. Good my sovereign,
Take up the English short, and let them know
Of what a monarchy you are the head.
Self-love, my liege, is not so vile a sin
As self-neglecting.

Enter Exeter [and others].

FRENCH KING   From our brother of England?   75

2.4. Location: France. The royal court.
5 make forth set forth   **7 line** reinforce   **8 defendant** defensive
9 England the King of England   **10 gulf** whirlpool.   **12 late** recent
13 fatal and neglected fatally underestimated   **14 redoubted** reverenced   **15 meet** appropriate   **20 As were** as if there were   **25 Whitsun morris dance** folk dance often performed during Whitsuntide, in early summer, by persons in fancy costumes and decked with bells.
26 idly frivolously   **28 humorous** capricious   **32 state** dignity
34 exception making objections.   **withal** in addition   **35 terrible** awesome, terrifying   **36 vanities forespent** follies used up and now a thing of the past   **37 Brutus** i.e., the elder Brutus, Lucius Junius Brutus, who pretended to be stupid (*brutus*) as a ruse to allay the suspicions of the tyrant Tarquin until the time for overthrow was ripe
39 ordure manure, mulch

45 So . . . filled In that way an adequate and full defense is provided
46 Which . . . projection which defense, if designed on too small and miserly a scale   **49 look** be sure   **50 kindred** i.e., his great-grandfather Edward III and great-uncle Edward the Black Prince.   **fleshed** initiated in the shedding of blood, with foretaste of further success
54 Crécy French defeat in 1346.   **struck** waged   **57 mountain sire** i.e., Edward III, born in mountainous Wales, and of sturdy proportions   **59–62 Saw . . . made** beheld his heroical son (the Black Prince) and smiled to see him mangle Nature's handiwork in the shape of young Frenchmen, whom, some twenty or so years earlier, God and their French fathers had created and begotten.   **64 fate** what he is destined to do   **69 Turn . . . pursuit** Turn and face the pursuing hounds. (Hunting terms.)   **70 Most . . . mouths** bay the loudest
75 brother fellow monarch

EXETER

From him, and thus he greets Your Majesty:
He wills you, in the name of God Almighty,
That you divest yourself and lay apart   78
The borrowed glories that by gift of heaven,
By law of nature and of nations, 'longs   80
To him and to his heirs, namely, the crown
And all wide-stretchèd honors that pertain   82
By custom and the ordinance of times   83
Unto the crown of France. That you may know
'Tis no sinister nor no awkward claim,   85
Picked from the wormholes of long-vanished days,
Nor from the dust of old oblivion raked,
He sends you this most memorable line,   88
                                [*giving a paper*]
In every branch truly demonstrative,
Willing you overlook this pedigree.   90
And when you find him evenly derived   91
From his most famed of famous ancestors,
Edward the Third, he bids you then resign
Your crown and kingdom, indirectly held   94
From him the native and true challenger.   95

FRENCH KING   Or else what follows?

EXETER

Bloody constraint; for if you hide the crown   97
Even in your hearts, there will he rake for it.
Therefore in fierce tempest is he coming,
In thunder and in earthquake, like a Jove,
That if requiring fail, he will compel;   101
And bids you, in the bowels of the Lord,   102
Deliver up the crown, and to take mercy
On the poor souls for whom this hungry war
Opens his vasty jaws, and on your head   105
Turning the widows' tears, the orphans' cries,   106
The dead men's blood, the privèd maidens' groans, 107
For husbands, fathers, and betrothèd lovers
That shall be swallowed in this controversy.
This is his claim, his threat'ning, and my message—
Unless the Dauphin be in presence here,
To whom expressly I bring greeting too.

FRENCH KING

For us, we will consider of this further.
Tomorrow shall you bear our full intent
Back to our brother of England.

DAUPHIN   For the Dauphin,
I stand here for him. What to him from England?

EXETER

Scorn and defiance, slight regard, contempt,
And anything that may not misbecome   118
The mighty sender, doth he prize you at.   119

Thus says my king, and if your father's Highness
Do not, in grant of all demands at large,   121
Sweeten the bitter mock you sent His Majesty,
He'll call you to so hot an answer of it   123
That caves and womby vaultages of France   124
Shall chide your trespass and return your mock
In second accent of his ordinance.   126

DAUPHIN

Say if my father render fair return   127
It is against my will, for I desire
Nothing but odds with England. To that end,   129
As matching to his youth and vanity,
I did present him with the Paris balls.   131

EXETER

He'll make your Paris Louvre shake for it,   132
Were it the mistress court of mighty Europe.
And be assured, you'll find a diff'rence,
As we his subjects have in wonder found,
Between the promise of his greener days   136
And these he masters now. Now he weighs time
Even to the utmost grain. That you shall read   138
In your own losses, if he stay in France.

FRENCH KING

Tomorrow shall you know our mind at full.   140
                                    Flourish.

EXETER

Dispatch us with all speed, lest that our king
Come here himself to question our delay;
For he is footed in this land already.

FRENCH KING

You shall be soon dispatched with fair conditions.
A night is but small breath and little pause
To answer matters of this consequence.
                            Flourish. Exeunt.

❖

[3.0]

Enter Chorus.

CHORUS

Thus with imagined wing our swift scene flies   1
In motion of no less celerity
Than that of thought. Suppose that you have seen
The well-appointed King at Dover pier   4
Embark his royalty, and his brave fleet   5
With silken streamers the young Phoebus fanning. 6
Play with your fancies, and in them behold

---

78 **apart** aside   80 **'longs** belongs   82 **wide-stretchèd** stretching far
and wide   83 **ordinance of times** decrees of tradition   85 **sinister**
illegitimate.   **awkward** oblique   88 **line** pedigree   90 **Willing you
overlook** desiring that you look over   91 **evenly** directly   94 **indirectly** wrongfully   95 **native** natural (by birthright).   **challenger**
claimant.   97 **constraint** coercion, compulsion   101 **requiring**
requesting   102 **in . . . Lord** in the name of God's compassion. (See
Philippians 1:8).   105–6 **and on . . . tears** and who, poor souls, are
pouring on your head their widows' tears   107 **privèd** deprived (by
loss of loved ones)   118 **misbecome** be inappropriate for   119 **prize**
value, appraise

121 **in grant of** in assenting to.   **at large** in full   123 **of it** for it
124 **womby vaultages** hollow recesses   126 **In . . . ordinance** in loud
echoing of the sound of King Henry's ordnance (cannon).   127 **fair
return** courteous reply   129 **odds** (1) strife (2) betting odds, as in tennis   131 **Paris balls** tennis balls.   132 **Louvre** the French royal palace
136 **greener** younger   138 **grain** grain of sand (in an hourglass).
That . . . read i.e., You will see this new seriousness manifested
140.1 **Flourish** (This trumpet call is sounded as the French King arises
from his throne, thereby dismissing the embassy, but Exeter boldly
insists on speaking further.)
3.0. Chorus.
1 **imagined wing** wings of imagination   4 **well-appointed** well-
equipped.   **Dover** (Seemingly an error for Hampton, i.e., Southampton.)   5 **brave** handsome   6 **the . . . fanning** i.e., fluttering in the
rising sun.

Upon the hempen tackle shipboys climbing;   8
Hear the shrill whistle, which doth order give
To sounds confused; behold the threaden sails,   10
Borne with th'invisible and creeping wind,
Draw the huge bottoms through the furrowed sea,   12
Breasting the lofty surge. Oh, do but think   13
You stand upon the rivage and behold   14
A city on th'inconstant billows dancing;
For so appears this fleet majestical,
Holding due course to Harfleur. Follow, follow!
Grapple your minds to sternage of this navy,   18
And leave your England as dead midnight still,
Guarded with grandsires, babies, and old women,
Either past or not arrived to pith and puissance;   21
For who is he whose chin is but enriched
With one appearing hair that will not follow
These culled and choice-drawn cavaliers to France?   24
Work, work your thoughts, and therein see a siege;
Behold the ordnance on their carriages,
With fatal mouths gaping on girded Harfleur.   27
Suppose th'ambassador from the French comes back,
Tells Harry that the King doth offer him
Katharine his daughter, and with her, to dowry,
Some petty and unprofitable dukedoms.
The offer likes not; and the nimble gunner   32
With linstock now the devilish cannon touches,   33
          Alarum, and chambers go off.
And down goes all before them. Still be kind,
And eke out our performance with your mind.
                                                    Exit.

❖

[3.1]

Enter the King, Exeter, Bedford, and Gloucester.
Alarum, [with soldiers carrying] scaling ladders at
Harfleur.

KING
Once more unto the breach, dear friends, once more,
Or close the wall up with our English dead!
In peace there's nothing so becomes a man
As modest stillness and humility.
But when the blast of war blows in our ears,
Then imitate the action of the tiger:
Stiffen the sinews, conjure up the blood,
Disguise fair nature with hard-favored rage.   8
Then lend the eye a terrible aspect: 9
Let it pry through the portage of the head   10
Like the brass cannon; let the brow o'erwhelm it   11

As fearfully as doth a gallèd rock   12
O'erhang and jutty his confounded base,   13
Swilled with the wild and wasteful ocean.   14
Now set the teeth and stretch the nostril wide,
Hold hard the breath, and bend up every spirit
To his full height. On, on, you noblest English,
Whose blood is fet from fathers of war-proof,   18
Fathers that, like so many Alexanders,   19
Have in these parts from morn till even fought,   20
And sheathed their swords for lack of argument.   21
Dishonor not your mothers; now attest
That those whom you called fathers did beget you.
Be copy now to men of grosser blood,   24
And teach them how to war. And you, good yeomen,
Whose limbs were made in England, show us here
The mettle of your pasture. Let us swear   27
That you are worth your breeding, which I doubt not,
For there is none of you so mean and base
That hath not noble luster in your eyes.
I see you stand like greyhounds in the slips,   31
Straining upon the start. The game's afoot.   32
Follow your spirit, and upon this charge   33
Cry, "God for Harry! England and Saint George!"   34
          Alarum, and chambers go off. [Exeunt.]

❖

[3.2]

Enter Nym, Bardolph, Pistol, and Boy.

BARDOLPH On, on, on, on, on! To the breach, to the
breach!
NYM Pray thee, Corporal, stay. The knocks are too hot,
and for mine own part I have not a case of lives. The   4
humor of it is too hot, that is the very plainsong of it. 5
PISTOL
"The plainsong" is most just; for humors do abound.
Knocks go and come; God's vassals drop and die;   7
[*He sings*] "And sword and shield
        In bloody field
    Doth win immortal fame."
BOY Would I were in an alehouse in London! I would
give all my fame for a pot of ale and safety.
PISTOL And I:
[*He sings*] "If wishes would prevail with me,   14
    My purpose should not fail with me,
        But thither would I hie."   16

BOY [*sings*]

"As duly, but not as truly,
    As bird doth sing on bough."

Enter Fluellen.

FLUELLEN   Up to the breach, you dogs! Avaunt, you cul- 19
lions!   [*Driving them forward.*] 20

PISTOL

Be merciful, great duke, to men of mold. 21
Abate thy rage, abate thy manly rage,
Abate thy rage, great duke!
Good bawcock, bate thy rage! Use lenity, sweet chuck! 24

NYM   These be good humors! Your Honor runs bad 25
humors.   *Exit* [*with all but Boy*]. 26

BOY   As young as I am, I have observed these three
swashers. I am boy to them all three, but all they three, 28
though they would serve me, could not be man to me; 29
for indeed three such antics do not amount to a man. 30
For Bardolph, he is white-livered and red-faced, by the 31
means whereof 'a faces it out but fights not. For Pistol, 32
he hath a killing tongue and a quiet sword, by the
means whereof 'a breaks words and keeps whole 34
weapons. For Nym, he hath heard that men of few
words are the best men, and therefore he scorns to say
his prayers, lest 'a should be thought a coward; but
his few bad words are matched with as few good
deeds, for 'a never broke any man's head but his own,
and that was against a post when he was drunk. They
will steal anything and call it purchase. Bardolph 41
stole a lute case, bore it twelve leagues, and sold it for 42
three halfpence. Nym and Bardolph are sworn brothers in filching, and in Calais they stole a fire shovel. I
knew by that piece of service the men would carry 45
coals. They would have me as familiar with men's 46
pockets as their gloves or their handkerchiefs, which
makes much against my manhood, if I should take 48
from another's pocket to put into mine, for it is plain
pocketing up of wrongs. I must leave them and seek 50
some better service. Their villainy goes against my 51
weak stomach, and therefore I must cast it up.   *Exit.* 52

Enter Gower [*and Fluellen, meeting*].

GOWER   Captain Fluellen, you must come presently to
the mines. The Duke of Gloucester would speak with 54
you.

FLUELLEN   To the mines? Tell you the Duke it is not so
good to come to the mines; for look you, the mines is
not according to the disciplines of the war. The 58
concavities of it is not sufficient. For look you, th'athver- 59
sary, you may discuss unto the Duke, look you, 60
is digt himself four yard under the countermines. By 61
Cheshu, I think 'a will plow up all, if there is not better 62
directions.

GOWER   The Duke of Gloucester, to whom the order of
the siege is given, is altogether directed by an Irish-
man, a very valiant gentleman, i'faith.

FLUELLEN   It is Captain Macmorris, is it not?

GOWER   I think it be.

FLUELLEN   By Cheshu, he is an ass, as in the world! I
will verify as much in his beard. He has no more di- 70
rections in the true disciplines of the wars, look you,
of the Roman disciplines, than is a puppy dog.

Enter Macmorris and Captain Jamy.

GOWER   Here 'a comes, and the Scots captain, Captain
Jamy, with him.

FLUELLEN   Captain Jamy is a marvelous falorous gentleman, that is certain, and of great expedition and 76
knowledge in th'aunchient wars, upon my particular
knowledge of his directions. By Cheshu, he will
maintain his argument as well as any military man in
the world, in the disciplines of the pristine wars of the 80
Romans.

JAMY   I say gud day, Captain Fluellen.

FLUELLEN   Good e'en to Your Worship, good Captain 83
James.

GOWER   How now, Captain Macmorris, have you quit
the mines? Have the pioneers given o'er? 86

MACMORRIS   By Chrish, la, 'tish ill done! The work ish
give over, the trompet sound the retreat. By my hand
I swear, and my father's soul, the work ish ill done; it
ish give over. I would have blowed up the town, so
Chrish save me, la, in an hour. Oh, 'tish ill done, 'tish
ill done! By my hand, 'tish ill done!

FLUELLEN   Captain Macmorris, I beseech you now, will
you voutsafe me, look you, a few disputations with 94
you, as partly touching or concerning the disciplines
of the war, the Roman wars, in the way of argument,

---

19 Avaunt Begone   **19–20 cullions** rascals. (The original meaning
was "testicles.")   **21 duke** leader, commander. (Latin *dux*.) A flattering title for a captain.   **men of mold** mere mortals.   **24 bawcock**
fine fellow. (French *beau coq*.)   **chuck** (A term of endearment.)
25–6 Your . . . humors i.e., (1) You are behaving very idiosyncratically,
Your Honor (2) Your fury is out of control. (Addressed to Fluellen,
who is doubtless threatening or beating Nym, Bardolph, and Pistol to
make them go forward.)   **28 swashers** swashbucklers.   **29 man**
(1) servant (2) a manly, brave person   **30 antics** buffoons, zanies
31 For As for. (Also in lines 32 and 35.)   **white-livered** i.e., cowardly.
(In extreme fear, the blood was thought to sink below the liver, leaving it bloodless.)   **32 'a faces it out** he has the martial-looking face
for it, puts on a brave front   **34 breaks words** (1) misuses language
and fails to keep his word (2) uses words as weapons   **41 purchase**
(1) something paid for (2) thieves' cant for stolen goods.   **42 leagues**
(about three miles each)   **45–6 carry coals** (1) do dirty, hard work,
such as hauling coal (2) put up with insults.   **48 makes** goes
50 pocketing . . . wrongs (1) putting up with insults (2) receiving
stolen goods.   **51–2 goes . . . stomach** (1) goes against my inclination
(2) makes me sick   **52 cast it up** (1) cast it aside (2) vomit it.   **s.d.**
Exit (A scene break may occur here, though it is not marked as such
in most editions. Possibly Fluellen did not leave the stage at line 26.)

54 mines tunnels dug under the walls of the beseiged city to plant
explosives.   **58 disciplines of the war** science of warfare (about
which there were many books from Greek and Roman times down to
the Renaissance; Fluellen's humor involves an obsession with this
study and a preference for traditional methods).   **59 concavities** i.e.,
depth   **59–60 athversary** (Fluellen's pronunciation of *adversary*.)
60 discuss explain   **61 is digt . . . countermines** has dug himself
countermines four yards beneath our mines.   **62 Cheshu** Jesu, Jesus.
plow blow. (In Fluellen's Welsh dialect, *p* is regularly substituted for *b*
and *f* for *v*.)   **70 in his beard** i.e., to his face.   **76 expedition** readiness of argument, quickness of wit   **80 pristine** ancient   **83 Good
e'en** Good afternoon or evening   **86 pioneers** sappers, diggers
94 voutsafe vouchsafe, permit

look you, and friendly communication—partly to satisfy my opinion, and partly for the satisfaction, look
you, of my mind, as touching the direction of the military discipline, that is the point.

JAMY It sall be vary gud, gud feith, gud captens bath, 101
and I sall quite you with gud leve, as I may pick 102
occasion. That sall I, marry. 103

MACMORRIS It is no time to discourse, so Chrish save
me! The day is hot, and the weather, and the wars,
and the King, and the dukes. It is no time to discourse.
The town is beseeched, and the trumpet call us to the 107
breach, and we talk, and, be Chrish, do nothing. 'Tis 108
shame for us all. So God sa' me, 'tis shame to stand
still, it is shame, by my hand! And there is throats to
be cut, and works to be done, and there ish nothing
done, so Chrish sa' me, la! 112

JAMY By the Mess, ere theise eyes of mine take 113
themselves to slomber, ay'll de gud service, or I'll lig i'th' 114
grund for it, ay, or go to death! And I'll pay't as
valorously as I may, that sall I suerly do, that is the
breff and the long. Marry, I wad full fain heard some 117
question 'tween you twae. 118

FLUELLEN Captain Macmorris, I think, look you, under
your correction, there is not many of your nation—

MACMORRIS Of my nation? What ish my nation? Ish a 121
villain, and a bastard, and a knave, and a rascal? What 122
ish my nation? Who talks of my nation?

FLUELLEN Look you, if you take the matter otherwise
than is meant, Captain Macmorris, peradventure I
shall think you do not use me with that affability as in
discretion you ought to use me, look you, being as
good a man as yourself, both in the disciplines of war
and in the derivation of my birth, and in other partic-
ularities.

MACMORRIS I do not know you so good a man as myself. So Chrish save me, I will cut off your head!

GOWER Gentlemen both, you will mistake each other. 133

JAMY Ah, that's a foul fault! *A parley [is sounded].* 134

GOWER The town sounds a parley.

FLUELLEN Captain Macmorris, when there is more better opportunity to be required, look you, I will be so 137
bold as to tell you I know the disciplines of war; and
there is an end. *Exit [with others].*

❖

[3.3]

*[Enter the Governor and some citizens on the
walls.] Enter the King [Henry] and all his train
before the gates.*

KING
How yet resolves the Governor of the town?
This is the latest parle we will admit. 2
Therefore to our best mercy give yourselves,
Or, like to men proud of destruction, 4
Defy us to our worst; for as I am a soldier,
A name that in my thoughts becomes me best,
If I begin the batt'ry once again 7
I will not leave the half-achievèd Harfleur
Till in her ashes she lie burièd.
The gates of mercy shall be all shut up,
And the fleshed soldier, rough and hard of heart, 11
In liberty of bloody hand shall range 12
With conscience wide as hell, mowing like grass 13
Your fresh fair virgins and your flow'ring infants.
What is it then to me if impious War,
Arrayed in flames like to the prince of fiends,
Do with his smirched complexion all fell feats 17
Enlinked to waste and desolation?
What is't to me, when you yourselves are cause,
If your pure maidens fall into the hand
Of hot and forcing violation?
What rein can hold licentious Wickedness
When down the hill he holds his fierce career? 23
We may as bootless spend our vain command 24
Upon th'enragèd soldiers in their spoil
As send precepts to the leviathan 26
To come ashore. Therefore, you men of Harfleur,
Take pity of your town and of your people
Whiles yet my soldiers are in my command,
Whiles yet the cool and temperate wind of grace 30
O'erblows the filthy and contagious clouds 31
Of heady murder, spoil, and villainy, 32
If not, why, in a moment look to see 33
The blind and bloody soldier with foul hand 34
Defile the locks of your shrill-shrieking daughters;
Your fathers taken by the silver beards,
And their most reverend heads dashed to the walls;
Your naked infants spitted upon pikes,

---

101 **bath** both   102 **quite** requite, answer.   **with gud leve** with good
leave, with your kind permission   103 **marry** indeed. (Originally, "by
the Virgin Mary.")   107 **beseeched** besieged   108 **be** by   112 **Chrish
sa' me** Christ save me   113 **Mess** Mass   114 **ay'll de** I'll do.   **lig** lie
117 **breff** brief.   **wad full fain heard** would very willingly have
heard   118 **question** discussion   121 **What ish** i.e., What about
121–2 **Ish a villain** i.e., Is my nation a villain (etc.)?, or Macmorris
may be making a declarative statement, saying that anyone who says
anything against my nation is a villain, etc.   133 **will mistake** (Two
possible meanings: [1] insist on misunderstanding [2] are going to
misunderstand.)   134 **s.d.** *parley* trumpet summons to a negotiation
137 **required** found

3.3. Location: Before the gates of Harfleur, as in the previous scene.
The action is essentially continuous, as it is usually in battle
sequences; possibly some of the captains in 3.2 do not need to exit
here. The gates are represented by the tiring-house facade. Those
who appear *on the walls* are seen in the gallery backstage.
2 **latest parle** last parley   4 **like . . . destruction** i.e., like men elated
at the prospect of slaughter and glorying in destruction   7 **batt'ry**
attack   11 **fleshed** made fierce with the taste of blood   12–13 **In liberty . . . as hell** will range with free license to shed blood and with a
conscience wide and loose enough to sanction anything that hell itself
would justify   17 **smirched** blackened, covered with grime.   **fell**
savage   23 **career** gallop.   24 **bootless** fruitlessly   26 **precepts** written summons.   **leviathan** whale   30 **grace** mercy   31 **O'er blows**
blows away. (Contagion was thought to reside in clouds and mists.)
32 **heady** violent; headstrong   33 **look** expect   34 **blind** i.e., blinded
with lust and rage

Whiles the mad mothers with their howls confused
Do break the clouds, as did the wives of Jewry   40
At Herod's bloody-hunting slaughtermen.   41
What say you? Will you yield, and this avoid,
Or, guilty in defense, be thus destroyed?   43

GOVERNOR
Our expectation hath this day an end.
The Dauphin, whom of succors we entreated,   45
Returns us that his powers are yet not ready   46
To raise so great a siege. Therefore, great King,
We yield our town and lives to thy soft mercy.
Enter our gates, dispose of us and ours,
For we no longer are defensible.

KING
Open your gates.   [*Exit Governor.*]
         Come, uncle Exeter,
Go you and enter Harfleur; there remain,
And fortify it strongly 'gainst the French.
Use mercy to them all. For us, dear uncle,   54
The winter coming on and sickness growing
Upon our soldiers, we will retire to Calais.
Tonight in Harfleur will we be your guest;
Tomorrow for the march are we addressed.   58
             Flourish, and enter the town.

[3.4]

Enter Katharine and [Alice,] an old gentlewoman.

KATHARINE   Alice, tu as été en Angleterre, et tu bien   1
parles le langage.

ALICE   Un peu, madame.

KATHARINE   Je te prie, m'enseignez; il faut que
j'apprenne à parler. Comment appelez-vous la main
en anglais?

ALICE   La main? Elle est appelée de hand.

KATHARINE   De hand. Et les doigts?

ALICE   Les doigts? Ma foi, j'oublie les doigts; mais je me
souviendrai. Les doigts? Je pense qu'ils sont appelés   10
de fingres; oui, de fingres.

KATHARINE   La main, de hand; les doigts, de fingres. Je
pense que je suis le bon écolier; j'ai gagné deux
mots d'anglais vîtement. Comment appelez-vous les
ongles?

ALICE   Les ongles? Nous les appelons de nailes.

KATHARINE   De nailes. Écoutez, dites-moi si je parle
bien: de hand, de fingres, et de nailes.

ALICE   C'est bien dit, madame; il est fort bon anglais.

KATHARINE   Dites-moi l'anglais pour le bras.   20

ALICE   De arm, madame.

KATHARINE   Et le coude?

ALICE   D' elbow.

KATHARINE   D' elbow. Je m'en fais la répétition de tous
les mots que vous m'avez appris dès à présent.

ALICE   Il est trop difficile, madame, comme je pense.

KATHARINE   Excusez-moi, Alice; écoutez: d' hand, de
fingre, de nailes, d' arma, de bilbow.

ALICE   D' elbow, madame.

KATHARINE   Oh, Seigneur Dieu, je m'en oublie! D' elbow.   30
Comment appelez-vous le col?

ALICE   De nick, madame.

KATHARINE   De nick. Et le menton?

ALICE   De chin.

KATHARINE   De sin. Le col, de nick; le menton, de sin.

ALICE   Oui. Sauf votre honneur, en vérité, vous pro-
noncez les mots aussi droit que les natifs d'Angleterre.

KATHARINE   Je ne doute point d'apprendre, par la grâce
de Dieu, et en peu de temps.

ALICE   N'avez-vous pas déjà oublié ce que je vous ai   40
enseigné?

KATHARINE   Non, je réciterai à vous promptement: d'
hand, de fingre, de mailes—

ALICE   De nailes, madame.

KATHARINE   De nailes, de arm, de ilbow.

ALICE   Sauf votre honneur, d' elbow.

KATHARINE   Ainsi dis-je; d' elbow, de nick, et de sin.
Comment appelez-vous le pied et la robe?

---

40 Jewry Judaea   **41 Herod's . . . slaughtermen** (For the account of Herod's slaughter of the innocent children in his attempt to murder the infant Jesus, see Matthew 2:16–18.)   **43 in defense** i.e., by not surrendering   **45 of succors** for help   **46 Returns** replies to   **54 For** As for **58 addressed** prepared.
3.4. Location: The French court at Rouen.

Translation:
KATHARINE   Alice, you have been in England and speak the language well.
ALICE   A little, my lady.
KATHARINE   I pray you teach me; I have to learn to speak it. What do you call *la main* in English?
ALICE   *La main?* It is called de hand.
KATHARINE   De hand. And *les doigts?*
ALICE   *Les doigts?* Dear me, I forget *les doigts;* but I shall remember. I think that they are called de fingres; yes, de fingres.
KATHARINE   *La main,* de hand; *les doigts,* de fingres. I think that I am a clever scholar; I have learned two English words in no time. What do you call *les ongles?*

ALICE   *Les ongles?* We call them de nailes.
KATHARINE   De nailes. Listen; tell me whether or not I speak correctly: de hand, de fingres, and de nailes.
ALICE   That is correct, my lady; it is very good English.
KATHARINE   Tell me the English for *le bras.*
ALICE   De arm, my lady.
KATHARINE   And *le coude?*
ALICE   D' elbow.
KATHARINE   D' elbow. I am going to repeat all the words you have taught me so far.
ALICE   It is too hard, my lady, I fear.
KATHARINE   Pardon me, Alice; listen: d' hand, de fingre, de nailes, d' arma, de bilbow.
ALICE   D' elbow, my lady.
KATHARINE   Oh, Lord, I can't remember! D' elbow. What do you call *le col?*
ALICE   De nick, my lady.
KATHARINE   De nick. And *le menton?*
ALICE   De chin.
KATHARINE   De sin. *Le col,* de nick; *le menton,* de sin.
ALICE   Yes. If I may say so, really you pronounce the words just as correctly as native Englishmen.
KATHARINE   I have no doubt that I shall learn, with God's help, in a very short time.
ALICE   Haven't you already forgotten what I have taught you?
KATHARINE   No. I shall recite to you at once: d' hand, de fingre, de mailes—
ALICE   De nailes, my lady.
KATHARINE   De nailes, de arm, de ilbow.
ALICE   By your leave, d' elbow.
KATHARINE   That's what I said; d' elbow, de nick, and de sin. What do you call *le pied* and *la robe?*

ALICE Le foot, madame, et le count.

KATHARINE Le foot et le count! Oh, Seigneur Dieu! Ils 50
sont les mots de son mauvais, corruptible, gros, et
impudique, et non pour les dames d'honneur d'user.
Je ne voudrais prononcer ces mots devant les seig-
neurs de France pour tout le monde. Foh! Le foot et le
count! Néanmoins, je réciterai une autre fois ma leçon
ensemble: d' hand, de fingre, de nailes, de arm,
d' elbow, de nick, de sin, de foot, le count.

ALICE Excellent, madame!

KATHARINE C'est assez pour une fois. Allons-nous à
dîner. *Exit [with Alice].*

❧

[3.5]

*Enter the King of France, the Dauphin, [the Duke
of Brittany,] the Constable of France, and others.*

FRENCH KING
'Tis certain he hath passed the River Somme.

CONSTABLE
And if he be not fought withal, my lord, 2
Let us not live in France; let us quit all
And give our vineyards to a barbarous people.

DAUPHIN
O Dieu vivant! Shall a few sprays of us, 5
The emptying of our fathers' luxury, 6
Our scions, put in wild and savage stock, 7
Spurt up so suddenly into the clouds 8
And overlook their grafters? 9

BRITTANY
Normans, but bastard Normans, Norman bastards!
Mort de ma vie, if they march along 11
Unfought withal, but I will sell my dukedom 12
To buy a slobbery and a dirty farm 13
In that nook-shotten isle of Albion. 14

CONSTABLE
Dieu de batailles, where have they this mettle? 15
Is not their climate foggy, raw, and dull,

On whom as in despite the sun looks pale, 17
Killing their fruit with frowns? Can sodden water, 18
A drench for sur-reined jades, their barley broth, 19
Decoct their cold blood to such valiant heat? 20
And shall our quick blood, spirited with wine, 21
Seem frosty? Oh, for honor of our land,
Let us not hang like roping icicles 23
Upon our houses' thatch, whiles a more frosty people
Sweat drops of gallant youth in our rich fields!
"Poor" may we call them in their native lords. 26

DAUPHIN By faith and honor,
Our madams mock at us and plainly say 28
Our mettle is bred out, and they will give 29
Their bodies to the lust of English youth
To new-store France with bastard warriors. 31

BRITTANY
They bid us to the English dancing schools 32
And teach lavoltas high and swift corantos, 33
Saying our grace is only in our heels 34
And that we are most lofty runaways. 35

FRENCH KING
Where is Montjoy the herald? Speed him hence. 36
Let him greet England with our sharp defiance.
Up, princes, and with spirit of honor edged 38
More sharper than your swords, hie to the field! 39
Charles Delabreth, High Constable of France,
You Dukes of Orleans, Bourbon, and of Berri,
Alençon, Brabant, Bar, and Burgundy,
Jaques Chatillion, Rambures, Vaudemont,
Beaumont, Grandpré, Roussi, and Faulconbridge,
Foix, Lestrelles, Boucicault, and Charolais,
High dukes, great princes, barons, lords, and knights,
For your great seats now quit you of great shames. 47
Bar Harry England, that sweeps through our land 48
With pennons painted in the blood of Harfleur. 49
Rush on his host, as doth the melted snow 50
Upon the valleys, whose low vassal seat
The Alps doth spit and void his rheum upon. 52
Go down upon him—you have power enough—
And in a captive chariot into Rouen
Bring him our prisoner.

CONSTABLE This becomes the great. 55
Sorry am I his numbers are so few,
His soldiers sick and famished in their march,
For I am sure, when he shall see our army,

ALICE Le foot, my lady, and le count. [As she pronounces them, *foot*
sounds to Katharine like *foutre*, fornicate, and *count* (for *gown*) sounds
like French for the female sexual organ, *cunt* in English.]
KATHARINE Le foot and le count! Oh, Lord! Those are naughty words,
wicked, coarse, and immodest, and are not fit to be used by ladies. I
wouldn't say those words before French gentlemen for the whole
world. Bah! Le foot and le count! Nevertheless, I shall recite my
whole lesson once more: d' hand, de fingre, de nailes, de arm, d'
elbow, de nick, de sin, de foot, le count.
ALICE Excellent, my lady.
KATHARINE That's enough for one time. Let's go to dinner.
3.5. Location: The French court at Rouen.
2 withal with. (As also in line 12.) **5–9 O . . . grafters?** O living God,
shall a few sprigs derived from native French stock, from the pouring
out of our forefathers' lust (during and after the Norman Conquest)
being grafted onto the wild and savage stock (of English Saxons),
sprout up suddenly to lofty heights and domineer over the plants or
trees from which the grafts were taken, i.e., us native French?
11 Mort de ma vie Death to my life **12 but I will** i.e., if I do not
13 slobbery wet and slimy **14 nook-shotten** full of nooks and
angles. (Refers to the coastline.) **isle of Albion** island of England,
Scotland, and Wales. **15 Dieu de batailles** God of battles. **where**
from where

17 as in despite as if despising them, the English **18 sodden water**
boiled water **19 A drench . . . jades** i.e., stuff no better than what
they give their overridden horses to drink. **barley broth** ale
20 Decoct warm up **21 quick** lively **23 roping** hanging down
like a rope **26 "Poor" . . . lords** i.e., Our fields, though rich in themselves, may be called poor in that they are owned by a spiritless
aristocracy. **28 madams** wives, ladies **29 bred out** exhausted by
breeding **31 new-store** newly supply **32 bid us** bid us go
33 lavoltas, corantos fashionable dances **34 in our heels** (1) in dancing gracefully (2) in running away **35 lofty** (1) noble (2) leaping.
runaways cowards. (But referring also to the movements of the
dances.) **36 Montjoy** title of the chief herald of France **38 edged**
given a sharp edge **39 hie** hasten **47 For** in the name of, in defense
of. **seats** positions. **quit you** rid, free yourselves **48 Bar** Stop; bar
the claim of **49 pennons** banners, streamers **50 host** army
52 rheum watery discharge, i.e., streams or avalanches **55 becomes
the great** befits greatness.

He'll drop his heart into the sink of fear   59
And for achievement offer us his ransom.   60

FRENCH KING
Therefore, Lord Constable, haste on Montjoy,
And let him say to England that we send
To know what willing ransom he will give.
Prince Dauphin, you shall stay with us in Rouen.

DAUPHIN
Not so, I do beseech Your Majesty.

FRENCH KING
Be patient, for you shall remain with us.
Now forth, Lord Constable and princes all,
And quickly bring us word of England's fall.   *Exeunt.*

❧

[3.6]

*Enter Captains, English and Welsh: Gower and
Fluellen, [meeting].*

GOWER   How now, Captain Fluellen? Come you from
the bridge?   2

FLUELLEN   I assure you, there is very excellent services   3
committed at the bridge.

GOWER   Is the Duke of Exeter safe?

FLUELLEN   The Duke of Exeter is as magnanimous as
Agamemnon, and a man that I love and honor with   7
my soul, and my heart, and my duty, and my live,   8
and my living, and my uttermost power. He is not—
God be praised and blessed!—any hurt in the world,
but keeps the bridge most valiantly, with excellent discipline. There is an aunchient lieutenant there at the   12
pridge, I think in my very conscience he is as valiant
a man as Mark Antony, and he is a man of no esti-   14
mation in the world, but I did see him do as gallant   15
service.

GOWER   What do you call him?

FLUELLEN   He is called Aunchient Pistol.

GOWER   I know him not.

Enter Pistol.

FLUELLEN   Here is the man.

PISTOL
Captain, I thee beseech to do me favors.
The Duke of Exeter doth love thee well.

FLUELLEN   Ay, I praise God, and I have merited some
love at his hands.

PISTOL
Bardolph, a soldier, firm and sound of heart,
And of buxom valor, hath, by cruel fate   26
And giddy Fortune's furious fickle wheel,

That goddess blind
That stands upon the rolling restless stone—

FLUELLEN   By your patience, Aunchient Pistol. Fortune
is painted blind, with a muffler afore her eyes, to sig-   31
nify to you that Fortune is blind; and she is painted
also with a wheel, to signify to you, which is the moral
of it, that she is turning, and inconstant, and mutabil-
ity, and variation; and her foot, look you, is fixed upon
a spherical stone, which rolls, and rolls, and rolls. In
good truth, the poet is make a most excellent descrip-   37
tion of it. Fortune is an excellent moral.   38

PISTOL
Fortune is Bardolph's foe, and frowns on him;   39
For he hath stol'n a pax,   40
And hangèd must 'a be—a damnèd death!
Let gallows gape for dog; let man go free,
And let not hemp his windpipe suffocate.
But Exeter hath given the doom of death   44
For pax of little price.
Therefore, go speak—the Duke will hear thy voice—
And let not Bardolph's vital thread be cut
With edge of penny cord and vile reproach.   48
Speak, Captain, for his life, and I will thee requite.   49

FLUELLEN   Aunchient Pistol, I do partly understand
your meaning.

PISTOL   Why then rejoice therefor.

FLUELLEN   Certainly, Aunchient, it is not a thing to rejoice at. For if, look you, he were my brother, I would
desire the Duke to use his good pleasure and put him
to execution; for discipline ought to be used.

PISTOL
Die and be damned! And *figo* for thy friendship!   57

FLUELLEN   It is well.

PISTOL   The fig of Spain!   *Exit.*

FLUELLEN   Very good.

GOWER   Why, this is an arrant counterfeit rascal! I
remember him now; a bawd, a cutpurse.

FLUELLEN   I'll assure you, 'a uttered as prave words at
the pridge as you shall see in a summer's day. But it is
very well. What he has spoke to me, that is well, I
warrant you, when time is serve.

GOWER   Why, 'tis a gull, a fool, a rogue, that now and   67
then goes to the wars, to grace himself at his return
into London under the form of a soldier. And such
fellows are perfect in the great commanders' names,   70
and they will learn you by rote where services were   71
done—at such and such a sconce, at such a breach, at   72
such a convoy; who came off bravely, who was shot,
who disgraced, what terms the enemy stood on—and   74
this they con perfectly in the phrase of war, which   75

---

59 sink pit   **60 for achievement** instead of achieving victory, as his
sole accomplishment
3.6. Location: The English camp in northern France.
2 bridge (According to Holinshed, the French were beaten in their
attempt to break down the bridge over the Ternoise. The audience is
not told this, however, and might assume the river to be the Somme,
mentioned in 3.5.1.)   **3 services** exploits. (As also in line 71.)
7 Agamemnon leader of the Greeks against Troy   **8 live** life
12 aunchient lieutenant (Pistol is elsewhere given the rank of
ancient, or ensign.)   **14–15 estimation** fame   **26 buxom** (1) vigorous
(2) compliant, meek

31 muffler blindfold   **37 is make** has made.   **38 moral** emblem.
39 Fortune . . . foe (Probably alludes to the ballad "Fortune, my foe!")
40 pax metal disk with a crucifix stamped on it, kissed by the priest
and communicants during Mass. (But Holinshed describes an incident in which the object stolen is a *pyx*, the vessel containing the consecrated host.)   **44 doom** judgment, sentence   **48 cord** rope
49 requite repay.   **57 *figo*** gesture of contempt made by thrusting the
thumb between the index and middle fingers   **67 gull** simpleton
70 are perfect in i.e., can recite perfectly   **71 learn** teach, recite
72 sconce fortification   **74 terms . . . stood on** conditions the enemy
insisted on   **75 con** learn by heart

they trick up with new-tuned oaths. And what a 76
beard of the General's cut and a horrid suit of the 77
camp will do among foaming bottles and ale-washed 78
wits is wonderful to be thought on. But you must
learn to know such slanders of the age, or else you 80
may be marvelously mistook. 81

FLUELLEN   I tell you what, Captain Gower, I do perceive
he is not the man that he would gladly make show
to the world he is. If I find a hole in his coat, I will tell 84
him my mind. [*Drum heard.*] Hark you, the King is
coming, and I must speak with him from the pridge. 86

Drum and colors. Enter the King and his poor
soldiers [and Gloucester].

God pless Your Majesty!
KING   How now, Fluellen, cam'st thou from the bridge?
FLUELLEN   Ay, so please Your Majesty. The Duke of
Exeter has very gallantly maintained the pridge. The
French is gone off, look you, and there is gallant and
most prave passages. Marry, th'athversary was have 92
possession of the pridge, but he is enforced to retire,
and the Duke of Exeter is master of the pridge. I can
tell Your Majesty, the Duke is a prave man.
KING   What men have you lost, Fluellen?
FLUELLEN   The perdition of th'athversary hath been very 97
great, reasonable great. Marry, for my part, I think the
Duke hath lost never a man, but one that is like to be ex- 99
ecuted for robbing a church, one Bardolph, if Your Majesty know the man. His face is all bubukles, and whelks, 101
and knobs, and flames o' fire, and his lips blows at his
nose, and it is like a coal of fire, sometimes plue and
sometimes red; but his nose is executed, and his fire's
out.
KING   We would have all such offenders so cut off. And we
give express charge that, in our marches through the 107
country, there be nothing compelled from the villages,
nothing taken but paid for, none of the French up-
braided or abused in disdainful language; for when lenity and cruelty play for a kingdom, the gentler gamester 111
is the soonest winner. 112

Tucket. Enter Montjoy.

MONTJOY   You know me by my habit. 113
KING   Well then, I know thee. What shall I know of thee?
MONTJOY   My master's mind.
KING   Unfold it.
MONTJOY   Thus says my King: "Say thou to Harry of
England, though we seemed dead, we did but sleep.
Advantage is a better soldier than rashness. Tell him 119
we could have rebuked him at Harfleur, but that we

thought not good to bruise an injury till it were full 121
ripe. Now we speak upon our cue, and our voice is
imperial. England shall repent his folly, see his 123
weakness, and admire our sufferance. Bid him there- 124
fore consider of his ransom, which must proportion 125
the losses we have borne, the subjects we have lost,
the disgrace we have digested; which in weight to re- 127
answer, his pettiness would bow under. For our losses, 128
his exchequer is too poor; for th'effusion of our blood, 129
the muster of his kingdom too faint a number; and for 130
our disgrace, his own person kneeling at our feet but
a weak and worthless satisfaction. To this add defiance; and tell him, for conclusion, he hath betrayed his
followers, whose condemnation is pronounced." So far 134
my King and master; so much my office.
KING
What is thy name? I know thy quality. 136
MONTJOY   Montjoy.
KING
Thou dost thy office fairly. Turn thee back
And tell thy King I do not seek him now,
But could be willing to march on to Calais
Without impeachment. For, to say the sooth, 141
Though 'tis no wisdom to confess so much
Unto an enemy of craft and vantage, 143
My people are with sickness much enfeebled,
My numbers lessened, and those few I have
Almost no better than so many French,
Who when they were in health, I tell thee, herald,
I thought upon one pair of English legs 148
Did march three Frenchmen. Yet, forgive me, God, 149
That I do brag thus! This your air of France
Hath blown that vice in me. I must repent. 151
Go, therefore, tell thy master here I am;
My ransom is this frail and worthless trunk, 153
My army but a weak and sickly guard.
Yet, God before, tell him we will come on,
Though France himself and such another neighbor
Stand in our way. There's for thy labor, Montjoy.
[*He gives a purse.*]
Go bid thy master well advise himself. 158
If we may pass, we will; if we be hindered,
We shall your tawny ground with your red blood
Discolor. And so, Montjoy, fare you well.
The sum of all our answer is but this:
We would not seek a battle as we are,
Nor, as we are, we say we will not shun it. 164
So tell your master.

<hr>

76 **trick** dress. **new-tuned** i.e., of the latest fashion   77–8 **horrid . . .
camp** fierce battle outfit   80 **slanders of the age** persons who are a
disgrace to the times   81 **mistook** mistaken, deluded.   84 **a hole . . .
coat** i.e., a weak spot in him. (Proverbial.)   86 **from the pridge** with
news concerning the bridge.   86.1 **poor** bedraggled   92 **passages**
deeds of arms.   **was** did   97 **perdition** losses   99 **like** likely
101 **bubukles** carbuncles.   **whelks** boils, pimples   107 **express
charge** explicit orders   111 **gamester** player   112.1 *Tucket* Trumpet
signal, fanfare.   113 **habit** i.e., tabard, herald's coat.   119 **Advantage**
Knowing how to wait for favorable circumstance and position

121 **bruise an injury** squeeze a boil or pimple   123 **England** i.e., King
Henry   124 **admire our sufferance** wonder at our patience.   125 **proportion** be proportional to   127–8 **which . . . under** i.e., to compensate
for which his means are too slender.   129 **exchequer** treasury
130 **muster** roll call   134 **condemnation** death sentence   136 **quality**
rank and profession; ability.   141 **impeachment** impediment.   **sooth**
truth   143 **vantage** superiority in resources
148–9 **upon . . . Frenchman** i.e., an English soldier is worth three
Frenchmen.   151 **blown** swelled; caused to blossom   153 **trunk**
body   158 **advise himself** consider.   164 **as we are** being who we
are. (Playing on the meaning "in the condition we are" in the previous line.)

MONTJOY
I shall deliver so. Thanks to Your Highness.   [*Exit.*]
GLOUCESTER
I hope they will not come upon us now.
KING
We are in God's hand, brother, not in theirs.
March to the bridge. It now draws toward night.
Beyond the river we'll encamp ourselves,
And on tomorrow bid them march away.   *Exeunt.* 171

❖

[3.7]

*Enter the Constable of France, the Lord Rambures,
Orleans, Dauphin, with others.*

CONSTABLE   Tut, I have the best armor of the world.
Would it were day!
ORLEANS   You have an excellent armor; but let my
horse have his due.
CONSTABLE   It is the best horse of Europe.
ORLEANS   Will it never be morning?
DAUPHIN   My lord of Orleans and my Lord High
Constable, you talk of horse and armor?
ORLEANS   You are as well provided of both as any
prince in the world.
DAUPHIN   What a long night is this! I will not change
my horse with any that treads but on four pasterns. 12
Ça, ha! He bounds from the earth as if his entrails 13
were hairs; *le cheval volant*, the Pegasus, *qui a les narines* 14
de feu! When I bestride him, I soar, I am a hawk. He 15
trots the air. The earth sings when he touches it. The
basest horn of his hoof is more musical than the pipe 17
of Hermes. 18
ORLEANS   He's of the color of the nutmeg.
DAUPHIN   And of the heat of the ginger. It is a beast for
Perseus. He is pure air and fire; and the dull elements 21
of earth and water never appear in him, but only in 22
patient stillness while his rider mounts him. He is indeed a horse, and all other jades you may call beasts.
CONSTABLE   Indeed, my lord, it is a most absolute and 25
excellent horse.
DAUPHIN   It is the prince of palfreys. His neigh is like 27
the bidding of a monarch, and his countenance
enforces homage.
ORLEANS   No more, cousin.
DAUPHIN   Nay, the man hath no wit that cannot, from
the rising of the lark to the lodging of the lamb, vary 32

deserved praise on my palfrey. It is a theme as fluent
as the sea; turn the sands into eloquent tongues, and
my horse is argument for them all. 'Tis a subject for a 35
sovereign to reason on, and for a sovereign's sovereign 36
to ride on, and for the world, familiar to us and un- 37
known, to lay apart their particular functions and 38
wonder at him. I once writ a sonnet in his praise, and 39
began thus: "Wonder of nature—"
ORLEANS   I have heard a sonnet begin so to one's
mistress.
DAUPHIN   Then did they imitate that which I composed
to my courser, for my horse is my mistress. 44
ORLEANS   Your mistress bears well.
DAUPHIN   Me well, which is the prescript praise and 46
perfection of a good and particular mistress. 47
CONSTABLE   Nay, for methought yesterday your mis-
tress shrewdly shook your back. 49
DAUPHIN   So perhaps did yours.
CONSTABLE   Mine was not bridled. 51
DAUPHIN   Oh, then belike she was old and gentle, and 52
you rode like a kern of Ireland, your French hose off, 53
and in your strait strossers. 54
CONSTABLE   You have good judgment in horsemanship.
DAUPHIN   Be warned by me, then: they that ride so,
and ride not warily, fall into foul bogs. I had rather
have my horse to my mistress. 58
CONSTABLE   I had as lief have my mistress a jade. 59
DAUPHIN   I tell thee, Constable, my mistress wears his 60
own hair. 61
CONSTABLE   I could make as true a boast as that, if I had
a sow to my mistress.
DAUPHIN   "*Le chien est retourné à son propre vomissement*, 64
et la truie lavée au bourbier." Thou mak'st use of 65
anything.
CONSTABLE   Yet do I not use my horse for my mistress,
or any such proverb so little kin to the purpose. 68
RAMBURES   My Lord Constable, the armor that I saw in
your tent tonight, are those stars or suns upon it?
CONSTABLE   Stars, my lord.
DAUPHIN   Some of them will fall tomorrow, I hope.
CONSTABLE   And yet my sky shall not want. 73
DAUPHIN   That may be, for you bear a many superflu- 74
ously, and 'twere more honor some were away. 75

171 **bid . . . away** bid our army march toward Calais.
3.7. Location: The French camp, near Agincourt.
12 pasterns i.e., hooves. (The *pastern* literally is the part of the horse's
leg just above the hoof.)   **13–14 as . . . hairs** i.e., as if he were a tennis
ball. (Tennis balls were stuffed with hair. Or perhaps *hairs* should
read *hares*.)   **14–15 le cheval . . . feu** the flying horse, Pegasus, with
nostrils breathing fire.   **17 basest horn** (1) lowest part (2) hoofbeat
17–18 pipe of Hermes (Hermes, messenger of the gods, charmed
Argus of the hundred eyes asleep with playing on his pipe.)
21 Perseus (According to some Greek legends and to Ovid, Perseus
rode Pegasus when he rescued Andromeda from the dragon.)
21–2 air . . . water (Of the four elements supposed to make up all matter, water and earth are the heavier, while fire and air ascend.)
25 absolute perfect   **27 palfreys** saddle horses.   **32 lodging** lying
down.   **vary** produce variations of

35 argument subject   **36 reason** discourse   **37–9 for . . . him** for both
the known and unknown worlds to put aside their differences and
join in wondering at him.   **44 horse is my mistress** (Here begins a
series of bawdy double entendres involving human and animal sexuality: *bears, shook your back, rode, foul bogs, doing,* etc.)   **46 prescript**
prescribed   **47 particular** acknowledging only one master
49 shrewdly viciously   **51 Mine . . . bridled** i.e., At least my mistress
was not a horse.   **52 belike** probably   **53 kern** Irish foot soldier.
(Here it is used to mean "rustic" or "boor.")   **French hose** wide
breeches   **54 strait strossers** tight trousers, i.e., bare-legged.   **58 to** as
59 lief happily.   **jade** (1) worn-out horse (2) slut.   **60–1 wears . . .
hair** i.e., is not artificially wigged, like an elegant court lady, and perhaps bald from syphilis.   **64–5 "Le chien . . . bourbier"** The dog is
returned to his own vomit, and the washed sow to the mire. (See 2
Peter 2:22.)   **68 kin** related   **73 sky** i.e., sky of honor.   **want** be lacking (in honor).   **74 a many** many. (Parallel to "a few.")   **75 'twere . . .
away** i.e., it would be more honest and proper if some of your stars
were done away with.

CONSTABLE Even as your horse bears your praises, who would trot as well, were some of your brags dismounted.

DAUPHIN Would I were able to load him with his 79 desert! Will it never be day? I will trot tomorrow a 80 mile, and my way shall be paved with English faces.

CONSTABLE I will not say so, for fear I should be faced 82 out of my way. But I would it were morning, for I 83 would fain be about the ears of the English. 84

RAMBURES Who will go to hazard with me for twenty 85 prisoners?

CONSTABLE You must first go yourself to hazard, ere you have them.

DAUPHIN 'Tis midnight. I'll go arm myself.   Exit.

ORLEANS The Dauphin longs for morning.

RAMBURES He longs to eat the English.

CONSTABLE I think he will eat all he kills.

ORLEANS By the white hand of my lady, he's a gallant prince.

CONSTABLE Swear by her foot, that she may tread out 95 the oath. 96

ORLEANS He is simply the most active gentleman of France.

CONSTABLE Doing is activity, and he will still be doing. 99

ORLEANS He never did harm, that I heard of. 100

CONSTABLE Nor will do none tomorrow. He will keep that good name still.

ORLEANS I know him to be valiant.

CONSTABLE I was told that by one that knows him better than you.

ORLEANS What's he?

CONSTABLE Marry, he told me so himself, and he said he cared not who knew it.

ORLEANS He needs not; it is no hidden virtue in him. 109

CONSTABLE By my faith, sir, but it is. Never anybody 110 saw it but his lackey. 'Tis a hooded valor, and when it 111 appears it will bate. 112

ORLEANS Ill will never said well.

CONSTABLE I will cap that proverb with "There is flattery in friendship."

ORLEANS And I will take up that with "Give the devil 116 his due." 117

CONSTABLE Well placed. There stands your friend for 118 the devil. Have at the very eye of that proverb with "A 119 pox of the devil."

ORLEANS You are the better at proverbs by how much "A fool's bolt is soon shot." 122

CONSTABLE You have shot over. 123

ORLEANS 'Tis not the first time you were overshot. 124

Enter a Messenger.

MESSENGER My Lord High Constable, the English lie within fifteen hundred paces of your tents.

CONSTABLE Who hath measured the ground?

MESSENGER The Lord Grandpré.

CONSTABLE A valiant and most expert gentleman.
          [*Exit Messenger.*]
Would it were day! Alas, poor Harry of England! He longs not for the dawning as we do.

ORLEANS What a wretched and peevish fellow is this King of England, to mope with his fat-brained follow- 133 ers so far out of his knowledge!

CONSTABLE If the English had any apprehension, they 135 would run away.

ORLEANS That they lack; for if their heads had any intellectual armor, they could never wear such heavy headpieces.

RAMBURES That island of England breeds very valiant creatures; their mastiffs are of unmatchable courage.

ORLEANS Foolish curs, that run winking into the mouth 142 of a Russian bear and have their heads crushed like rotten apples. You may as well say "That's a valiant flea that dare eat his breakfast on the lip of a lion."

CONSTABLE Just, just! And the men do sympathize with 146 the mastiffs in robustious and rough coming on, leav- 147 ing their wits with their wives; and then give them great meals of beef and iron and steel, they will eat like wolves and fight like devils.

ORLEANS Ay, but these English are shrewdly out of 151 beef.

CONSTABLE Then shall we find tomorrow they have only stomachs to eat and none to fight. Now is it time 154 to arm. Come, shall we about it?

ORLEANS
It is now two o'clock; but let me see, by ten
We shall have each a hundred Englishmen.   *Exeunt.*

❖

[4.0]

[*Enter*] *Chorus.*

CHORUS
Now entertain conjecture of a time 1
When creeping murmur and the poring dark 2
Fills the wide vessel of the universe.
From camp to camp, through the foul womb of night,
The hum of either army stilly sounds, 5

79–80 Would . . . desert! I wish I could find words to equal his deserving!   **82–3 faced . . . way** braved out of my way, put to shame.   **84 fain** gladly.   **about the ears** buffeting the heads   **85 go to hazard** bet, play at dice. (But the Constable replies in the sense of "encounter danger.")   **95–6 tread . . . oath** (1) fulfill the oath by dancing (2) stamp on, spurn the oath.   **99 Doing** (1) Acting, pretending (2) Copulating.   **still** continually   **100 did harm** i.e., offended. (But the Constable uses it to mean "hurt any enemy.")   **109 He needs not** i.e., There is no need for him to proclaim it himself.   **it** i.e., valor   **110–11 Never . . . lackey** i.e., He shows "valor" only in beating his servant.   **111 hooded valor** (The hawk was kept hooded to prevent it from beating its wings, or "bating.")   **112 bate** (1) beat its wings (2) abate, be downcast.   **116–17 Give . . . due** Give even the devil his due; everyone deserves some praise. (But the Constable turns this proverb against the Dauphin by likening him to the devil.)   **118–19 There . . . devil** i.e., You just called the Dauphin the devil.   **119 Have . . . eye** Shoot straight at the mark. (A sporting term appropriate to this verbal contest of "capping proverbs.")

122 bolt short, blunt arrow   **123 shot over** i.e., shot over the mark.   **124 overshot** i.e., outshot, defeated.   **133 mope** (1) wander about (2) be downcast   **135 apprehension** (1) sense (2) sense of danger   **142 winking** shutting their eyes   **146 Just** Exactly.   **sympathize with** resemble   **147 robustious** violent, boisterous   **151 shrewdly out of** devilishly short of   **154 stomachs** appetites
4.0. Chorus.
1 entertain conjecture of imagine   **2 poring** in which one must strain the eyes to see   **5 stilly** softly

That the fixed sentinels almost receive
The secret whispers of each other's watch.
Fire answers fire, and through their paly flames   8
Each battle sees the other's umbered face.   9
Steed threatens steed, in high and boastful neighs
Piercing the night's dull ear; and from the tents
The armorers, accomplishing the knights,   12
With busy hammers closing rivets up,
Give dreadful note of preparation.
The country cocks do crow, the clocks do toll,
And the third hour of drowsy morning name.
Proud of their numbers and secure in soul,   17
The confident and overlusty French   18
Do the low-rated English play at dice,   19
And chide the cripple tardy-gaited night,
Who like a foul and ugly witch doth limp
So tediously away. The poor condemnèd English,
Like sacrifices, by their watchful fires
Sit patiently and inly ruminate   24
The morning's danger; and their gesture sad,   25
Investing lank-lean cheeks and war-worn coats,   26
Presenteth them unto the gazing moon
So many horrid ghosts. Oh, now, who will behold
The royal captain of this ruined band
Walking from watch to watch, from tent to tent,
Let him cry, "Praise and glory on his head!"
For forth he goes and visits all his host,   32
Bids them good morrow with a modest smile,
And calls them brothers, friends, and countrymen.
Upon his royal face there is no note
How dread an army hath enrounded him.   36
Nor doth he dedicate one jot of color   37
Unto the weary and all-watchèd night,   38
But freshly looks and overbears attaint   39
With cheerful semblance and sweet majesty;
That every wretch, pining and pale before,
Beholding him, plucks comfort from his looks.
A largess universal like the sun
His liberal eye doth give to everyone,
Thawing cold fear, that mean and gentle all   45
Behold, as may unworthiness define,   46
A little touch of Harry in the night.
And so our scene must to the battle fly;
Where—oh, for pity!—we shall much disgrace
With four or five most vile and ragged foils,   50
Right ill-disposed in brawl ridiculous,
The name of Agincourt. Yet sit and see,
Minding true things by what their mockeries be.   53

Exit.

❖

8 **paly** pale   9 **battle** army.   **umbered** shadowed   12 **accomplishing**
equipping   17 **secure** overconfident   18 **overlusty** overly merry
19 **play** gamble for   24 **inly** inwardly   25 **gesture sad** serious bearing
26 **Investing** clothing   32 **host** army   36 **enrounded** surrounded
37 **dedicate** yield up.   **color** i.e., bright color of complexion   38 **all-
watchèd** spent entirely in wakefulness and waiting   39 **overbears
attaint** overcomes the effects of weariness and depression   45 **mean
and gentle** those of low and of high birth   46 **unworthiness** I, who am
unworthy of praising so great an object   50 **foils** blunted fencing swords
53 **Minding** bearing in mind.   **mockeries** inadequate imitations

[4.1]

Enter the King, Bedford, and Gloucester.

KING
Gloucester, 'tis true that we are in great danger;
The greater therefore should our courage be.
Good morrow, brother Bedford. God Almighty!
There is some soul of goodness in things evil,
Would men observingly distill it out;   5
For our bad neighbor makes us early stirrers,
Which is both healthful and good husbandry.   7
Besides, they are our outward consciences,
And preachers to us all, admonishing
That we should dress us fairly for our end.   10
Thus may we gather honey from the weed
And make a moral of the devil himself.

Enter Erpingham.

Good morrow, old Sir Thomas Erpingham.
A good soft pillow for that good white head
Were better than a churlish turf of France.   15
ERPINGHAM
Not so, my liege. This lodging likes me better,   16
Since I may say, "Now lie I like a king."
KING
'Tis good for men to love their present pains
Upon example; so the spirit is eased.   19
And when the mind is quickened, out of doubt
The organs, though defunct and dead before,
Break up their drowsy grave and newly move   22
With casted slough and fresh legerity.   23
Lend me thy cloak, Sir Thomas. [*The King puts on
Erpingham's cloak.*] Brothers both,   24
Commend me to the princes in our camp;   25
Do my good morrow to them, and anon
Desire them all to my pavilion.
GLOUCESTER   We shall, my liege.
ERPINGHAM   Shall I attend Your Grace?
KING   No, my good knight,
Go with my brothers to my lords of England.
I and my bosom must debate awhile,
And then I would no other company.
ERPINGHAM
The Lord in heaven bless thee, noble Harry!
Exeunt [all but the King].
KING
God-a-mercy, old heart! Thou speak'st cheerfully.

Enter Pistol.

PISTOL   *Che vous là?*   36

4.1. **Location:** The English camp at Agincourt.
5 **Would men** if one could   7 **husbandry** economy, thrift.   10 **dress
us fairly** prepare ourselves well   15 **churlish** rough, hard   16 **likes**
pleases   19 **Upon example** i.e., following or considering the example
of persons such as King Henry and Erpingham   22–3 **Break . . . legerity** break out of their lethargy and move nimbly, like a snake having cast off its old skin.   24 **Brothers both** i.e., Bedford and
Gloucester   25 **Commend me** convey my greetings   36 *Che vous là?*
i.e., *Qui va là?* ("Who goes there?") or *Qui vous là?* ("Who are you
there?"). (Pistol's imperfect French.)

KING   A friend.

PISTOL

Discuss unto me: art thou officer,   38
Or art thou base, common, and popular?   39

KING   I am a gentleman of a company.   40

PISTOL   Trail'st thou the puissant pike?   41

KING   Even so. What are you?

PISTOL

As good a gentleman as the Emperor.

KING   Then you are a better than the King.

PISTOL

The King's a bawcock and a heart of gold,   45
A lad of life, an imp of fame,   46
Of parents good, of fist most valiant.
I kiss his dirty shoe, and from heartstring
I love the lovely bully. What is thy name?   49

KING   Harry le Roy.

PISTOL

Le Roy? A Cornish name. Art thou of Cornish crew?

KING   No, I am a Welshman.   52

PISTOL   Know'st thou Fluellen?

KING   Yes.

PISTOL

Tell him I'll knock his leek about his pate   55
Upon Saint Davy's Day.   56

KING   Do not you wear your dagger in your cap that
day, lest he knock that about yours.

PISTOL   Art thou his friend?

KING   And his kinsman too.

PISTOL   The *figo* for thee, then!   61

KING   I thank you. God be with you!

PISTOL   My name is Pistol called.   *Exit.*

KING   It sorts well with your fierceness.   64

Manet King [standing apart].

Enter Fluellen and Gower [meeting].

GOWER   Captain Fluellen!

FLUELLEN   So, in the name of Jesu Christ, speak fewer.   66
It is the greatest admiration in the universal world,   67
when the true and aunchient prerogatifes and laws of
the wars is not kept. If you would take the pains but
to examine the wars of Pompey the Great, you shall   70
find, I warrant you, that there is no tiddle-taddle nor   71
pibble-pabble in Pompey's camp. I warrant you, you   72
shall find the ceremonies of the wars, and the cares of
it, and the forms of it, and the sobriety of it, and the   74
modesty of it, to be otherwise.   75

GOWER   Why, the enemy is loud; you hear him all
night.

FLUELLEN   If the enemy is an ass and a fool and a prating 78
coxcomb, is it meet, think you, that we should also,   79
look you, be an ass and a fool and a prating coxcomb?
In your own conscience, now?

GOWER   I will speak lower.

FLUELLEN   I pray you and beseech you that you will.
Exit [with Gower].

KING

Though it appear a little out of fashion,
There is much care and valor in this Welshman.

*Enter three soldiers, John Bates, Alexander Court,
and Michael Williams.*

COURT   Brother John Bates, is not that the morning
which breaks yonder?

BATES   I think it be. But we have no great cause to
desire the approach of day.

WILLIAMS   We see yonder the beginning of the day, but
I think we shall never see the end of it.—Who goes
there?

KING   A friend.

WILLIAMS   Under what captain serve you?

KING   Under Sir Thomas Erpingham.

WILLIAMS   A good old commander and a most kind
gentleman. I pray you, what thinks he of our estate?   97

KING   Even as men wrecked upon a sand, that look to 98
be washed off the next tide.

BATES   He hath not told his thought to the King?

KING   No, nor it is not meet he should. For, though I 101
speak it to you, I think the King is but a man, as I am.
The violet smells to him as it doth to me; the element 103
shows to him as it doth to me; all his senses have but 104
human conditions. His ceremonies laid by, in his   105
nakedness he appears but a man; and though his
affections are higher mounted than ours, yet when   107
they stoop, they stoop with the like wing. Therefore
when he sees reason of fears, as we do, his fears, out
of doubt, be of the same relish as ours are. Yet, in   110
reason, no man should possess him with any appear-   111
ance of fear, lest he, by showing it, should dishearten
his army.

BATES   He may show what outward courage he will; but
I believe, as cold a night as 'tis, he could wish himself
in Thames up to the neck; and so I would he were,
and I by him, at all adventures, so we were quit here. 117

KING   By my troth, I will speak my conscience of the
King: I think he would not wish himself anywhere but
where he is.

38 Discuss Declare   **39 popular** of low birth.   **40 gentleman of a company** gentleman serving as a volunteer.   **41 Trail'st . . . pike?** i.e., Are you in the infantry?   **45 bawcock** fine fellow. (From the French *beau coq.*)   **46 imp of fame** child or scion of renown   **49 bully** (A term of endearment meaning "fine fellow.")   **52 Welshman** (Henry was born at Monmouth, then considered part of Wales.)   **55–6 leek . . . Day** (On Saint David's Day, March 1, the leek was worn in memory of a Welsh victory over the Saxons in 540 A.D., since Saint David, the Welsh leader, had commanded his followers to wear leeks in their caps on that occasion.)   **61 figo** (A provoking gesture of contempt; see the note for 3.6.57.)   **64 sorts** fits, agrees   **64.1 Manet King** The King remains.   **66 fewer** i.e., calmly, more quietly.   **67 admiration** wonder   **70 Pompey the Great** Roman general defeated by Julius Caesar   **71–2 tiddle-taddle nor pibble-pabble** tittle-tattle nor bibble-babble   **74 sobriety** orderliness, decorum   **75 modesty** propriety

78–9 prating coxcomb chattering fool   **97 estate** situation.   **98 wrecked** shipwrecked   **101 meet** fitting   **103–4 element shows** sky appears   **105 ceremonies** symbols of royalty   **107 affections . . . mounted** desires soar higher. (A falconry metaphor continued in *stoop,* "descend," "swoop down," and *with the like wing,* "similarly.")   **110 relish** taste   **111 possess him with** induce in him   **117 at all adventures** at all events (since the Thames would be less risky under any circumstances than the impending battle).   **quit here** out of this situation.

BATES   Then I would he were here alone. So should he
be sure to be ransomed, and a many poor men's lives
saved.

KING   I dare say you love him not so ill to wish him here
alone, howsoever you speak this to feel other men's 125
minds. Methinks I could not die anywhere so contented as in the King's company, his cause being just
and his quarrel honorable.

WILLIAMS   That's more than we know.

BATES   Ay, or more than we should seek after; for we
know enough if we know we are the King's subjects.
If his cause be wrong, our obedience to the King
wipes the crime of it out of us.

WILLIAMS   But if the cause be not good, the King
himself hath a heavy reckoning to make, when all
those legs and arms and heads, chopped off in a
battle, shall join together at the Latter Day and cry all, 137
"We died at such a place"—some swearing, some
crying for a surgeon, some upon their wives left poor
behind them, some upon the debts they owe, some
upon their children rawly left. I am afeard there are 141
few die well that die in a battle; for how can they
charitably dispose of anything, when blood is their
argument? Now, if these men do not die well, it will
be a black matter for the King that led them to it; who 145
to disobey were against all proportion of subjection. 146

KING   So, if a son that is by his father sent about
merchandise do sinfully miscarry upon the sea, the 148
imputation of his wickedness, by your rule, should be 149
imposed upon his father that sent him; or if a servant,
under his master's command transporting a sum of
money, be assailed by robbers and die in many 152
irreconciled iniquities, you may call the business of the 153
master the author of the servant's damnation. But this
is not so. The King is not bound to answer the par- 155
ticular endings of his soldiers, the father of his son, nor
the master of his servant; for they purpose not their 157
deaths when they propose their services. Besides,
there is no king, be his cause never so spotless, if it 159
come to the arbitrament of swords, can try it out with 160
all unspotted soldiers. Some, peradventure, have on 161
them the guilt of premeditated and contrived murder;
some, of beguiling virgins with the broken seals of 163
perjury; some, making the wars their bulwark, that 164
have before gored the gentle bosom of peace with
pillage and robbery. Now, if these men have defeated 166
the law and outrun native punishment, though they 167
can outstrip men, they have no wings to fly from God.
War is his beadle, war is his vengeance; so that here 169

men are punished for before-breach of the King's laws 170
in now the King's quarrel. Where they feared the 171
death, they have borne life away; and where they 172
would be safe, they perish. Then if they die unpro- 173
vided, no more is the King guilty of their damnation 174
than he was before guilty of those impieties for the
which they are now visited. Every subject's duty is the 176
King's; but every subject's soul is his own. Therefore
should every soldier in the wars do as every sick man
in his bed, wash every mote out of his conscience; and 179
dying so, death is to him advantage, or not dying, the
time was blessedly lost wherein such preparation was
gained. And in him that escapes, it were not sin to
think that, making God so free an offer, He let him
outlive that day to see His greatness and to teach
others how they should prepare.

WILLIAMS   'Tis certain, every man that dies ill, the ill 186
upon his own head, the King is not to answer it.

BATES   I do not desire he should answer for me, and yet
I determine to fight lustily for him.

KING   I myself heard the King say he would not be
ransomed.

WILLIAMS   Ay, he said so, to make us fight cheerfully;
but when our throats are cut, he may be ransomed
and we ne'er the wiser.

KING   If I live to see it, I will never trust his word after.

WILLIAMS   You pay him then! That's a perilous shot out 196
of an elder-gun, that a poor and a private displeasure 197
can do against a monarch. You may as well go about
to turn the sun to ice with fanning in his face with a
peacock's feather. You'll never trust his word after!
Come, 'tis a foolish saying.

KING   Your reproof is something too round. I should be 202
angry with you, if the time were convenient.

WILLIAMS   Let it be a quarrel between us, if you live.

KING   I embrace it.

WILLIAMS   How shall I know thee again?

KING   Give me any gage of thine, and I will wear it in 207
my bonnet. Then if ever thou dar'st acknowledge it, I
will make it my quarrel.

WILLIAMS   Here's my glove. Give me another of thine.

KING   There.   [*They exchange gloves.*]

WILLIAMS   This will I also wear in my cap. If ever thou
come to me and say, after tomorrow, "This is my
glove," by this hand, I will take thee a box on the ear. 214

KING   If ever I live to see it, I will challenge it.

WILLIAMS   Thou dar'st as well be hanged.

KING   Well, I will do it, though I take thee in the King's
company.

WILLIAMS   Keep thy word. Fare thee well.

---

125 feel feel out   **137 Latter Day** last day, Christian Day of Judgment
141 rawly without provision   **145 who** whom   **146 proportion of
subjection** proper duty of a subject.   **148 sinfully miscarry** die in his
sins   **149 imputation . . . wickedness** wickedness imputed to him
152–3 in . . . iniquities with his wicked deeds unabsolved   **155
answer** answer for   **157 purpose** intend   **159–60 if . . . swords** if a
dispute can be settled only by swords   **161 unspotted** innocent
163 broken seals (1) broken promises (2) violated maidenheads
164 bulwark refuge from punishment (for offenses committed)
166 defeated broken   **167 native** at home   **169 beadle** parish officer
responsible for punishing petty offenders

170 before-breach prior violation   **171–3 Where . . . perish** i.e.,
Whereas before they feared execution but escaped punishment, here
where they look for safety they die in battle.   **173–4 unprovided**
spiritually unprepared   **176 visited** i.e., by punishment.   **179 mote**
small impurity   **186 dies ill** dies in sin   **196 You pay him then!** i.e.,
That will really pay him back for his perfidy, won't it? (Said sarcastically.)   **197 elder-gun** popgun made from a branch of elder with the
pith hollowed out   **202 round** direct, brusque.   **207 gage** pledge
214 take give, strike

BATES   Be friends, you English fools, be friends. We
have French quarrels enough, if you could tell how to   221
reckon.

KING   Indeed, the French may lay twenty French crowns   223
to one they will beat us, for they bear them on their
shoulders; but it is no English treason to cut French   225
crowns, and tomorrow the King himself will be a
clipper.   *Exeunt soldiers.*
Upon the King! Let us our lives, our souls,
Our debts, our careful wives,   229
Our children, and our sins lay on the King!
We must bear all. Oh, hard condition,
Twin-born with greatness, subject to the breath   232
Of every fool, whose sense no more can feel   233
But his own wringing! What infinite heartsease   234
Must kings neglect that private men enjoy!
And what have kings that privates have not too,   236
Save ceremony, save general ceremony?
And what art thou, thou idol ceremony?
What kind of god art thou, that suffer'st more
Of mortal griefs than do thy worshipers?
What are thy rents? What are thy comings-in?   241
O ceremony, show me but thy worth!
What is thy soul of adoration?   243
Art thou aught else but place, degree, and form,   244
Creating awe and fear in other men?
Wherein thou art less happy, being feared,
Than they in fearing.
What drink'st thou oft, instead of homage sweet,
But poisoned flattery? Oh, be sick, great greatness,   249
And bid thy ceremony give thee cure!   250
Think'st thou the fiery fever will go out   251
With titles blown from adulation?   252
Will it give place to flexure and low bending?   253
Canst thou, when thou command'st the beggar's
knee,
Command the health of it? No, thou proud dream,
That play'st so subtly with a king's repose.
I am a king that find thee, and I know   257
'Tis not the balm, the scepter, and the ball,   258
The sword, the mace, the crown imperial,   259

The intertissued robe of gold and pearl,   260
The farcèd title running 'fore the king,   261
The throne he sits on, nor the tide of pomp
That beats upon the high shore of this world—
No, not all these, thrice-gorgeous ceremony,
Not all these, laid in bed majestical,
Can sleep so soundly as the wretched slave
Who, with a body filled and vacant mind,
Gets him to rest, crammed with distressful bread;   268
Never sees horrid night, the child of hell,
But like a lackey from the rise to set   270
Sweats in the eye of Phoebus, and all night   271
Sleeps in Elysium; next day after dawn   272
Doth rise and help Hyperion to his horse,   273
And follows so the ever-running year
With profitable labor to his grave.
And but for ceremony, such a wretch,
Winding up days with toil and nights with sleep,
Had the forehand and vantage of a king.   278
The slave, a member of the country's peace,   279
Enjoys it, but in gross brain little wots   280
What watch the King keeps to maintain the peace,   281
Whose hours the peasant best advantages.   282

Enter Erpingham.

ERPINGHAM
My lord, your nobles, jealous of your absence,   283
Seek through your camp to find you.
KING   Good old knight,
Collect them all together at my tent.
I'll be before thee.
ERPINGHAM   I shall do't, my lord.   *Exit.*   286
KING
O God of battles, steel my soldiers' hearts;
Possess them not with fear! Take from them now
The sense of reck'ning, ere th'opposèd numbers   289
Pluck their hearts from them. Not today, O Lord,
Oh, not today, think not upon the fault   291
My father made in compassing the crown!   292
I Richard's body have interrèd new,   293
And on it have bestowed more contrite tears
Than from it issued forcèd drops of blood.
Five hundred poor I have in yearly pay
Who twice a day their withered hands hold up
Toward heaven, to pardon blood; and I have built
Two chantries, where the sad and solemn priests   299
Sing still for Richard's soul. More will I do;   300

---

221 could tell knew   **223 lay** bet. (But also anticipating the meaning
"lay down or lose in battle.")   **crowns** (1) coins (2) heads   **225 English treason** (It was a treasonable offense to clip or "cut" English coins;
it obviously is no offense to slash French heads, and even King Henry
will be such a "clipper.")   **229 careful** full of cares   **232–4 Twin-born
. . . wringing** i.e., inseparable from the condition of being born of
royal rank, a condition that makes a king the subject of the idle gossip
of every fool, even those whose sensibilities pay attention to nothing
other than the rumbling of their own stomachs.   **236 privates** private
persons   **241 comings-in** revenues.   **243 thy soul of adoration** the
essential quality that makes you so much admired.   **244 place** rank
249–50 Oh . . . cure! Learn to cure yourself by being sick, by treating
poisoned flattery and ceremoniousness as a medicine that will purge
you of being in love with your own great greatness.   **251–2 Think'st . . .
adulation?** Do you really think that the fever of vain pride will be
extinguished by speeches breathed by flatterers? (*Blown* also suggests
"inflated.")   **253 Will . . . bending?** i.e., Will the sickness yield to
bowing and scraping?   **257 find thee** i.e., experience greatness and
am able to appraise its worth and limitations   **258 balm** consecrating
oil used to anoint a king in his coronation.   **ball** orb of sovereignty
259 mace ceremonial staff

---

260 intertissued interwoven   **261 farcèd** stuffed (with pompous
phrases)   **268 distressful** earned by hard work   **270 lackey** (1) footman running alongside the chariot of the sun (2) peasant.   **rise to set**
sunrise to sunset   **271 Phoebus** the sun god   **272 Elysium** in Greek
mythology, the abode of the blessed   **273 Hyperion** the father of the
sun, or the sun itself. (The peasant is up before the sun.)   **278 Had**
would have.   **forehand** upper hand   **279 member** sharer   **280 it** i.e.,
peace.   **wots** knows   **281 watch** wakeful guard   **282 the peasant
best advantages** most benefit the peasant.   **283 jealous of** apprehensive because of   **286 be** be there   **289 sense of reck'ning** ability to
reckon up the odds   **291 the fault** i.e., the deposition and murder of
Richard II   **292 compassing** obtaining   **293 new** anew   **299 chantries**
chapels in which masses for the dead were celebrated.   **sad** grave
300 still continually

Though all that I can do is nothing worth,
Since that my penitence comes after all,   302
Imploring pardon.

Enter Gloucester.

GLOUCESTER My liege!
KING My brother Gloucester's voice? Ay;
I know thy errand. I will go with thee.
The day, my friends, and all things stay for me.

Exeunt.

[4.2]

Enter the Dauphin, Orleans, Rambures, and
Beaumont.

ORLEANS
The sun doth gild our armor. Up, my lords!
DAUPHIN *Monte à cheval!* My horse! *Varlet! Lacquais!* Ha!   2
ORLEANS Oh, brave spirit!
DAUPHIN *Via, les eaux et terre!*   4
ORLEANS *Rien puis? L'air et feu?*   5
DAUPHIN *Cieux,* cousin Orleans.   6

Enter Constable.

Now, my Lord Constable?
CONSTABLE
Hark, how our steeds for present service neigh!   8
DAUPHIN
Mount them, and make incision in their hides,   9
That their hot blood may spin in English eyes   10
And dout them with superfluous courage. Ha!   11
RAMBURES
What, will you have them weep our horses' blood?
How shall we then behold their natural tears?

Enter Messenger.

MESSENGER
The English are embattled, you French peers.   14
CONSTABLE
To horse, you gallant princes, straight to horse!
Do but behold yond poor and starvèd band,
And your fair show shall suck away their souls,   17
Leaving them but the shales and husks of men.   18
There is not work enough for all our hands,
Scarce blood enough in all their sickly veins
To give each naked curtal ax a stain   21

That our French gallants shall today draw out
And sheathe for lack of sport. Let us but blow on
    them,
The vapor of our valor will o'erturn them.
'Tis positive against all exceptions, lords,   25
That our superfluous lackeys and our peasants,
Who in unnecessary action swarm
About our squares of battle, were enough   28
To purge this field of such a hilding foe,   29
Though we upon this mountain's basis by   30
Took stand for idle speculation—   31
But that our honors must not. What's to say?   32
A very little little let us do
And all is done. Then let the trumpets sound
The tucket sonance and the note to mount;   35
For our approach shall so much dare the field   36
That England shall couch down in fear and yield.

Enter Grandpré.

GRANDPRÉ
Why do you stay so long, my lords of France?
Yond island carrions, desperate of their bones,   39
Ill-favoredly become the morning field.   40
Their ragged curtains poorly are let loose,   41
And our air shakes them passing scornfully.   42
Big Mars seems bankrupt in their beggared host   43
And faintly through a rusty beaver peeps.   44
The horsemen sit like fixèd candlesticks,
With torch staves in their hand, and their poor jades   46
Lob down their heads, drooping the hides and hips,   47
The gum down-roping from their pale-dead eyes,   48
And in their pale dull mouths the gimmaled bit   49
Lies foul with chewed grass, still and motionless;
And their executors, the knavish crows,   51
Fly o'er them all impatient for their hour.
Description cannot suit itself in words
To demonstrate the life of such a battle   54
In life so lifeless as it shows itself.
CONSTABLE
They have said their prayers, and they stay for death.   56
DAUPHIN
Shall we go send them dinners and fresh suits,
And give their fasting horses provender,   58
And after fight with them?
CONSTABLE
I stay but for my guard. On to the field!   60
I will the banner from a trumpet take,   61

---

302 Since that necessitating that
4.2. Location: The French camp.
0.2 Beaumont (The Folio text mentions Lord Beaumont but does not
give him a speaking part.)   **2 Monte à cheval!** To horse!   **4 Via . . .**
terre! Begone, waters and earth! (The Dauphin imagines himself riding through and over rivers and solid ground.)   **5 Rien . . . feu?**
Nothing more? What about air and fire? (i.e., Why not soar above all
four elements, not just water and earth?)   **6 Cieux** The heavens. (The
Dauphin carries the metaphor one step further to its ultimate height.)
8 present service immediate action   **9 incision** i.e., with spurs
10 spin gush, spatter   **11 And . . . courage** i.e., and put out the English eyes with the horses' superfluous blood, the proof of their excessive courage.   **dout** put out   **14 embattled** arranged in battle order
17 fair show impressive appearance   **18 shales** shells   **21 curtal ax**
cutlass, short sword

25 exceptions objections   **28 squares of battle** four-sided military
formations   **29 hilding** worthless, base   **30 basis** foot.   **by** nearby
31 speculation looking on   **32 But that** except for the fact that
35 tucket sonance trumpet call.   **mount** mount our horses   **36 dare**
(1) defy (2) stupify with fear   **39 carrions** cadavers for the scavenger
birds.   **desperate of** without hope of saving   **40 Ill-favoredly**
become i.e., are an eyesore to   **41 curtains** colors, banners   **42 pass-**
ing exceedingly   **43 Mars** the god of war   **44 beaver** visor   **46 torch**
staves i.e., tapers in place of lances. (The horsemen themselves look
like carved candleholders.)   **47 Lob down** hang down.   **drooping**
letting droop   **48 gum** watery discharge.   **down-roping** hanging
down ropelike   **49 gimmaled** jointed   **51 their executors** the dis-
posers of their remains   **54 battle** army   **56 stay for** await
58 provender fodder   **60 guard** (Including a standard-bearer.)
61 trumpet trumpeter

And use it for my haste. Come, come, away!
The sun is high, and we outwear the day.   *Exeunt.* 63

❖

[4.3]

Enter Gloucester, Bedford, Exeter, Erpingham,
with all his host, Salisbury, and Westmorland.

GLOUCESTER   Where is the King?
BEDFORD
  The King himself is rode to view their battle. 2
WESTMORLAND
  Of fighting men they have full threescore thousand.
EXETER
  There's five to one. Besides, they all are fresh.
SALISBURY
  God's arm strike with us! 'Tis a fearful odds.
  God b'wi' you, princes all; I'll to my charge. 6
  If we no more meet till we meet in heaven,
  Then, joyfully, my noble lord of Bedford,
  My dear lord Gloucester, and my good lord Exeter,
  And my kind kinsman, warriors all, adieu! 10
BEDFORD
  Farewell, good Salisbury, and good luck go with thee!
EXETER
  Farewell, kind lord. Fight valiantly today!
  And yet I do thee wrong to mind thee of it, 13
  For thou art framed of the firm truth of valor. 14
                              [*Exit Salisbury.*]
BEDFORD
  He is as full of valor as of kindness,
  Princely in both.

Enter the King.

WESTMORLAND   Oh, that we now had here
  But one ten thousand of those men in England
  That do no work today!
KING   What's he that wishes so? 18
  My cousin Westmorland? No, my fair cousin.
  If we are marked to die, we are enough 20
  To do our country loss; and if to live, 21
  The fewer men, the greater share of honor.
  God's will, I pray thee, wish not one man more.
  By Jove, I am not covetous for gold,
  Nor care I who doth feed upon my cost; 25
  It yearns me not if men my garments wear; 26
  Such outward things dwell not in my desires.
  But if it be a sin to covet honor
  I am the most offending soul alive.
  No, faith, my coz, wish not a man from England. 30
  God's peace, I would not lose so great an honor
  As one man more, methinks, would share from me 32
  For the best hope I have. Oh, do not wish one more! 33

Rather proclaim it, Westmorland, through my host 34
That he which hath no stomach to this fight, 35
Let him depart; his passport shall be made
And crowns for convoy put into his purse. 37
We would not die in that man's company
That fears his fellowship to die with us. 39
This day is called the Feast of Crispian. 40
He that outlives this day and comes safe home
Will stand a-tiptoe when this day is named
And rouse him at the name of Crispian.
He that shall see this day and live old age 44
Will yearly on the vigil feast his neighbors 45
And say, "Tomorrow is Saint Crispian."
Then will he strip his sleeve and show his scars,
And say, "These wounds I had on Crispin's Day."
Old men forget; yet all shall be forgot, 49
But he'll remember with advantages 50
What feats he did that day. Then shall our names,
Familiar in his mouth as household words—
Harry the King, Bedford and Exeter,
Warwick and Talbot, Salisbury and Gloucester—
Be in their flowing cups freshly remembered.
This story shall the good man teach his son;
And Crispin Crispian shall ne'er go by,
From this day to the ending of the world,
But we in it shall be rememberèd—
We few, we happy few, we band of brothers.
For he today that sheds his blood with me
Shall be my brother; be he ne'er so vile, 62
This day shall gentle his condition. 63
And gentlemen in England now abed
Shall think themselves accurst they were not here,
And hold their manhoods cheap whiles any speaks
That fought with us upon Saint Crispin's Day.

Enter Salisbury.

SALISBURY
  My sovereign lord, bestow yourself with speed. 68
  The French are bravely in their battles set, 69
  And will with all expedience charge on us. 70
KING
  All things are ready, if our minds be so.
WESTMORLAND
  Perish the man whose mind is backward now! 72
KING
  Thou dost not wish more help from England, coz?
WESTMORLAND
  God's will, my liege, would you and I alone,
  Without more help, could fight this royal battle!

---

63 **outwear** waste
4.3. Location: The English camp.
2 **battle** army.   6 **charge** post, command.   10 **kinsman** i.e., Westmorland, whose son had married Salisbury's daughter   13 **mind** remind   14 **framed** made, built   18 **What's** Who is   20–1 **enough . . . loss** enough loss for our country to suffer   25 **upon my cost** at my expense   26 **yearns** grieves   30 **coz** cousin, kinsman   32 **share from me** take from me as his share   33 **For . . . have** i.e., in exchange for my hope of eternal life.

34 **host** army   35 **stomach to** appetite for   37 **crowns for convoy** travel money   39 **That . . . us** who is afraid to risk his life in my company.   40 **Feast of Crispian** Saint Crispin's Day, October 25. (Crispinus and Crispianus were martyrs who fled from Rome in the third century; according to legend, they disguised themselves as shoemakers and afterward became the patron saints of that craft.)   44 **live** live to see   45 **vigil** evening before a feast day   49 **yet** in time   50 **advantages** additions of his own   62 **vile** lowly   63 **gentle his condition** i.e., raise his social status to the equivalent of gentleman in that he is my "brother."   68 **bestow yourself** take up your battle position   69 **bravely . . . set** finely arrayed in their battalions   70 **expedience** speed   72 **backward** reluctant

KING
  Why, now thou hast unwished five thousand men,
  Which likes me better than to wish us one.—   77
  You know your places. God be with you all!

     Tucket. Enter Montjoy.

MONTJOY
  Once more I come to know of thee, King Harry,
  If for thy ransom thou wilt now compound   80
  Before thy most assurèd overthrow;
  For certainly thou art so near the gulf   82
  Thou needs must be englutted. Besides, in mercy   83
  The Constable desires thee thou wilt mind   84
  Thy followers of repentance, that their souls
  May make a peaceful and a sweet retire   86
  From off these fields where, wretches, their poor
     bodies
  Must lie and fester.

KING   Who hath sent thee now?
MONTJOY   The Constable of France.
KING
  I pray thee, bear my former answer back:
  Bid them achieve me, and then sell my bones.   91
  Good God, why should they mock poor fellows thus?
  The man that once did sell the lion's skin
  While the beast lived was killed with hunting him.
  A many of our bodies shall no doubt   95
  Find native graves, upon the which, I trust,   96
  Shall witness live in brass of this day's work.
  And those that leave their valiant bones in France,
  Dying like men, though buried in your dunghills,
  They shall be famed; for there the sun shall greet them
  And draw their honors reeking up to heaven,   101
  Leaving their earthly parts to choke your clime,
  The smell whereof shall breed a plague in France.
  Mark then abounding valor in our English,   104
  That, being dead, like to the bullets crazing   105
  Break out into a second course of mischief,
  Killing in relapse of mortality.   107
  Let me speak proudly. Tell the Constable
  We are but warriors for the working day.   109
  Our gayness and our gilt are all besmirched
  With rainy marching in the painful field.
  There's not a piece of feather in our host—
  Good argument, I hope, we will not fly—
  And time hath worn us into slovenry.   114
  But, by the Mass, our hearts are in the trim!   115
  And my poor soldiers tell me, yet ere night

  They'll be in fresher robes, or they will pluck   117
  The gay new coats o'er the French soldiers' heads   118
  And turn them out of service. If they do this—   119
  As, if God please, they shall—my ransom then
  Will soon be levied. Herald, save thou thy labor.   121
  Come thou no more for ransom, gentle herald.   122
  They shall have none, I swear, but these my joints,
  Which if they have as I will leave 'em them,
  Shall yield them little, tell the Constable.
MONTJOY
  I shall, King Harry. And so fare thee well.
  Thou never shalt hear herald any more.   *Exit.*
KING
  I fear thou wilt once more come again for a ransom.

     Enter York [and kneels].

YORK
  My lord, most humbly on my knee I beg
  The leading of the vaward.   130
KING
  Take it, brave York. Now, soldiers, march away.
  And how thou pleasest, God, dispose the day!
                                 Exeunt.

❖

[4.4]

     Alarum. Excursions. Enter Pistol, French Soldier,
     [and] Boy.

PISTOL   Yield, cur!
FRENCH SOLDIER   *Je pense que vous êtes le gentilhomme de*   2
  bonne qualité.   3
PISTOL
  Qualtitie calmie custure me!   4
  Art thou a gentleman? What is thy name? Discuss.   5
FRENCH SOLDIER   *O Seigneur Dieu!*   6
PISTOL
  Oh, Signieur Dew should be a gentleman.
  Perpend my words, O Signieur Dew, and mark: 8
  O Signieur Dew, thou diest on point of fox,   9
  Except, O signieur, thou do give to me   10
  Egregious ransom.   *[He threatens him with his sword.]*   11
FRENCH SOLDIER   *Oh, prenez miséricorde! Ayez pitié de*   12
  moi!   13
PISTOL
  "Moy" shall not serve. I will have forty moys,   14
  Or I will fetch thy rim out at thy throat   15

---

77 **likes** pleases   80 **compound** make terms   82 **gulf** whirlpool
83 **englutted** swallowed up.   84 **mind** remind   86 **retire** retreat
91 **achieve** capture   95 **A many** Many.   96 **native** in our own land
(i.e., England)   101 **reeking** (1) breathing (2) smelling   104 **abound-**
ing overflowing, abundant   105 **crazing** shattering, with a suggestion also of *grazing*, "ricocheting"   107 **Killing . . . mortality** killing
(their foes) as they (the English) fall back (decompose) into their elements; also, like the bullet, with a deadly ricochet.   109 **for the**
working day to do serious work, not take a holiday.   114 **slovenry**
slovenliness, untidiness.   115 **in the trim** fully rigged, ready for
action.

117–19 **They'll . . . service** they will be more freshly dressed by nightfall, if no other way than by defrocking the French soldiers like incapable servants being dismissed and stripped of their livery. (Soldiers
got to keep such spoils of war from their victims.)   121 **levied** collected.   122 **gentle** noble   130 **vaward** vanguard.
4.4. Location: The field of battle.
0.1 *Excursions* Sorties.   2–3 *Je . . . qualité* I think that you are a gentleman of high rank.   4 *calmie custure me* (These words are perhaps
derived from the refrain of a popular song, supposed to be Irish, "Calen
o custure me.")   5 **Discuss** Speak.   6 *O Seigneur Dieu!* O Lord God!
8 **Perpend** Attend to, consider   9 **fox** sword   10 **Except** unless
11 **Egregious** huge   12–13 *Oh . . . moi!* Oh, have mercy! Take pity on me!
14 **Moy** (Pistol, not understanding, takes *moi* for the name of a coin or
a sum of money, a moiety or half.)   15 **rim** midriff, diaphragm

In drops of crimson blood.

FRENCH SOLDIER   *Est-il impossible d'échapper la force de ton* 17
bras? 18

PISTOL   Brass, cur?
Thou damnèd and luxurious mountain goat, 20
Offer'st me brass?

FRENCH SOLDIER   *Oh, pardonnez-moi!*

PISTOL
Say'st thou me so? Is that a ton of moys?— 23
Come hither, boy. Ask me this slave in French
What is his name.

BOY   *Écoutez: comment êtes-vous appelé?* 26

FRENCH SOLDIER   *Monsieur Le Fer.*

BOY   He says his name is Master Fer.

PISTOL   Master Fer? I'll fer him, and firk him, and ferret 29
him. Discuss the same in French unto him.

BOY   I do not know the French for fer, and ferret, and
firk.

PISTOL
Bid him prepare, for I will cut his throat.

FRENCH SOLDIER   *Que dit-il, monsieur?* 34

BOY   *Il me commande à vous dire que vous faites vous* 35
prêt; car ce soldat ici est disposé tout à cette heure de 36
couper votre gorge. 37

PISTOL
Owy, cuppele gorge, permafoy, 38
Peasant, unless thou give me crowns, brave crowns,
Or mangled shalt thou be by this my sword.

FRENCH SOLDIER   *Oh, je vous supplie, pour l'amour de* 41
Dieu, me pardonner! Je suis le gentilhomme de bonne 42
maison. Gardez ma vie, et je vous donnerai deux cents 43
écus. 44

PISTOL   What are his words?

BOY   He prays you to save his life. He is a gentleman of
a good house, and for his ransom he will give you two 47
hundred crowns.

PISTOL
Tell him my fury shall abate, and I
The crowns will take.

FRENCH SOLDIER   *Petit monsieur, que dit-il?* 51

BOY   *Encore qu'il est contre son jurement de pardonner* 52
aucun prisonnier, néanmoins, pour les écus que vous 53
l'avez promis, il est content à vous donner la liberté, 54
le franchisement. 55

FRENCH SOLDIER   [*kneeling*]   *Sur mes genoux je vous* 56
donne mille remercîments; et je m'estime heureux que 57
j'ai tombé entre les mains d'un chevalier, je pense, 58
le plus brave, vaillant, et très-distingué seigneur 59
d'Angleterre. 60

PISTOL   Expound unto me, boy.

BOY   He gives you, upon his knees, a thousand thanks,
and he esteems himself happy that he hath fallen into
the hands of one, as he thinks, the most brave, valor-
ous, and thrice-worthy signieur of England.

PISTOL
As I suck blood, I will some mercy show.
Follow me!

BOY   *Suivez-vous le grand capitaine.* 68

[*Exeunt Pistol and French Soldier.*]
I did never know so full a voice issue
from so empty a heart! But the saying is true, "The
empty vessel makes the greatest sound." Bardolph and
Nym had ten times more valor than this roaring devil 72
i'th'old play, that everyone may pare his nails with 73
a wooden dagger, and they are both hanged; and so 74
would this be, if he durst steal anything adventur-
ously. I must stay with the lackeys, with the luggage
of our camp. The French might have a good prey of 77
us, if he knew of it, for there is none to guard it but
boys.   *Exit.*

❧

[4.5]

*Enter Constable, Orleans, Bourbon, Dauphin, and
Rambures.*

CONSTABLE   *Oh, diable!* 1

ORLEANS   *Oh, Seigneur! Le jour est perdu, tout est perdu!* 2

DAUPHIN
Mort de ma vie! All is confounded, all. 3
Reproach and everlasting shame
Sits mocking in our plumes.   *A short alarum.*
Oh, méchante fortune! Do not run away. 6

CONSTABLE   Why, all our ranks are broke.

DAUPHIN
Oh, perdurable shame! Let's stab ourselves. 8
Be these the wretches that we played at dice for?

ORLEANS
Is this the king we sent to for his ransom?

BOURBON
Shame and eternal shame, nothing but shame!
Let us die! In once more! Back again!

17–18 *Est-il . . . bras?* Is it impossible to escape the strength of your
arm? (But Pistol takes *bras*, "arm," for *brass*.)   **20 luxurious** lecherous
23 a ton of moys (This is what Pistol phonetically makes out of
pardonnez-moi.)   **26** *Écoutez . . . appelé?* Listen: what is your name?
29 firk trounce.   **ferret** worry (like a ferret)   **34–7** *Que . . . gorge*
What does he say, sir? BOY He bids me tell you that you must prepare
yourself, because this soldier intends to cut your throat immediately.
38 *Owy* Oui, "yes."   **permafoy** *per ma foi*, by my faith   **41–4** *Oh . . .
écus* Oh, I pray you, for the love of God, to pardon me! I am a gentleman of a good house; preserve my life, and I shall give you two hundred crowns.   **47 house** family   **51–5** *Petit . . . franchisement* What
does he say, little sir? BOY Although it is against his oath to pardon
any prisoner, nevertheless, for the sake of the crowns you have
promised, he is willing to give you your liberty, your freedom.

56–60 *Sur . . . d'Angleterre* On my knees, I give you a thousand
thanks, and I consider myself happy that I have fallen into the hands
of a knight, as I think, the bravest, most valiant, and very distinguished gentleman in England.   **68** *Suivez-vous . . . capitaine* Follow
the great captain.   **72–4 this roaring . . . dagger** Shakespeare refers
several times to the devil in the morality play with his dagger of lath;
see *2H6*, 4.2.2 and *Twelfth Night*, 4.2.126. The paring of the devil's nails
was a proverbial act of bravado.   **77 a good prey** i.e., easy pickings
4.5. Location: The field of battle still.
1 *Oh, diable!* Oh, the devil!   **2** *Oh . . . perdu!* Oh, Lord, the day is lost,
all is lost!   **3** *Mort . . . vie!* Death to my life!   **confounded** lost
6 *Oh, méchante fortune!* Oh, malicious fortune!   **8 perdurable** everlasting

And he that will not follow Bourbon now,
Let him go hence, and with his cap in hand,
Like a base pander, hold the chamber door
Whilst by a slave, no gentler than my dog,   16
His fairest daughter is contaminated.

CONSTABLE
Disorder, that hath spoiled us, friend us now!   18
Let us on heaps go offer up our lives.   19

ORLEANS
We are enough yet living in the field
To smother up the English in our throngs,
If any order might be thought upon.

BOURBON
The devil take order now! I'll to the throng.
Let life be short, else shame will be too long.

                     Exeunt.

[4.6]

Alarum. Enter the King and his train, [Exeter,
and others,] with prisoners.

KING
Well have we done, thrice valiant countrymen!
But all's not done; yet keep the French the field.   2

EXETER
The Duke of York commends him to Your Majesty.

KING
Lives he, good uncle? Thrice within this hour
I saw him down, thrice up again and fighting.
From helmet to the spur all blood he was.

EXETER
In which array, brave soldier, doth he lie,
Larding the plain; and by his bloody side,   8
Yokefellow to his honor-owing wounds,   9
The noble Earl of Suffolk also lies.
Suffolk first died; and York, all haggled over,   11
Comes to him, where in gore he lay insteeped,   12
And takes him by the beard, kisses the gashes
That bloodily did yawn upon his face.   14
He cries aloud, "Tarry, my cousin Suffolk!
My soul shall thine keep company to heaven;
Tarry, sweet soul, for mine, then fly abreast,
As in this glorious and well-foughten field
We kept together in our chivalry!"
Upon these words I came and cheered him up.
He smiled me in the face, raught me his hand,
And with a feeble grip says, "Dear my lord,   21
Commend my service to my sovereign."
So did he turn, and over Suffolk's neck
He threw his wounded arm, and kissed his lips,
And so, espoused to death, with blood he sealed

A testament of noble-ending love.
The pretty and sweet manner of it forced
Those waters from me which I would have stopped;   29
But I had not so much of man in me,
And all my mother came into mine eyes   31
And gave me up to tears.

KING   I blame you not;
For, hearing this, I must perforce compound   33
With mistful eyes, or they will issue too.   *Alarum.*   34
But, hark, what new alarum is this same?
The French have reinforced their scattered men.
Then every soldier kill his prisoners!   37
Give the word through.   *Exeunt.*

[4.7]

Enter Fluellen and Gower.

FLUELLEN   Kill the poys and the luggage? 'Tis expressly   1
against the law of arms. 'Tis as arrant a piece of
knavery, mark you now, as can be offert; in your
conscience, now, is it not?

GOWER   'Tis certain there's not a boy left alive; and the
cowardly rascals that ran from the battle ha' done this
slaughter. Besides, they have burned and carried
away all that was in the King's tent, wherefore the
King most worthily hath caused every soldier to cut
his prisoner's throat. Oh, 'tis a gallant king!

FLUELLEN   Ay, he was porn at Monmouth, Captain   11
Gower. What call you the town's name where Alexander the Pig was born?

GOWER   Alexander the Great.

FLUELLEN   Why, I pray you, is not "pig" great? The pig,
or the great, or the mighty, or the huge, or the
magnanimous, are all one reckonings, save the phrase   17
is a little variations.

GOWER   I think Alexander the Great was born in
Macedon. His father was called Philip of Macedon, as
I take it.

FLUELLEN   I think it is e'en Macedon where Alexander is
porn. I tell you, Captain, if you look in the maps of the
'orld, I warrant you sall find, in the comparisons between Macedon and Monmouth, that the situations,
look you, is both alike. There is a river in Macedon,
and there is also moreover a river at Monmouth. It is
called Wye at Monmouth, but it is out of my prains
what is the name of the other river; but 'tis all one, 'tis
alike as my fingers is to my fingers, and there is sal-
mons in both. If you mark Alexander's life well, Harry
of Monmouth's life is come after it indifferent well, for   32
there is figures in all things. Alexander, God knows,   33

---

16 gentler (1) more nobly born (2) tenderer   **18 friend** befriend
19 on in
4.6. Location: The field of battle still.
2 yet . . . field the French are in the field of battle still.   **8 Larding**
fattening, enriching (with his blood)   **9 honor-owing** honor-owning,
honorable   **11 haggled over** mangled, hacked   **12 insteeped**
steeped, soaked   **14 yawn** gape   **21 me in the** in my.   **raught**
reached

---

29 waters i.e., tears   **31 my mother** i.e., the tenderer part of me
33 perforce necessarily.   **compound** come to terms   **34 issue** issue
forth tears   **37 kill his prisoners** (This follows Holinshed, who says
that Henry, alarmed by the outcry of the lackeys and boys of the
camp, feared a new attack and ordered the prisoners killed as a precaution. Gower, 4.7.7–10, attributes the King's action to revenge.)
4.7. Location: The field of battle still.
1 luggage i.e., lackeys guarding the luggage.   **11 Monmouth** (i.e., in
Wales)   **17 are . . . reckonings** come to the same thing   **32 is . . . well**
resembles it fairly well   **33 figures** comparisons, similes

and you know, in his rages, and his furies, and his
wraths, and his cholers, and his moods, and his dis-
pleasures, and his indignations, and also being a little
intoxicates in his prains, did, in his ales and his angers, 37
look you, kill his best friend, Cleitus. 38

GOWER   Our King is not like him in that. He never killed
any of his friends.

FLUELLEN   It is not well done, mark you now, to take
the tales out of my mouth ere it is made and finished.
I speak but in the figures and comparisons of it. As
Alexander killed his friend Cleitus, being in his ales
and his cups, so also Harry Monmouth, being in his
right wits and his good judgments, turned away the
fat knight with the great-belly doublet. He was full of 47
jests, and gipes, and knaveries, and mocks. I have 48
forgot his name.

GOWER   Sir John Falstaff.

FLUELLEN   That is he. I'll tell you there is good men
porn at Monmouth.

GOWER   Here comes His Majesty.

*Alarum. Enter King Harry, [Warwick, Gloucester,
Exeter, and others,] and Bourbon, with [other]
prisoners. Flourish.*

KING
I was not angry since I came to France
Until this instant. Take a trumpet, herald; 55
Ride thou unto the horsemen on yond hill.
If they will fight with us, bid them come down,
Or void the field. They do offend our sight. 58
If they'll do neither, we will come to them,
And make them skirr away as swift as stones 60
Enforcèd from the old Assyrian slings. 61
Besides, we'll cut the throats of those we have,
And not a man of them that we shall take
Shall taste our mercy. Go and tell them so.

Enter Montjoy.

EXETER
Here comes the herald of the French, my liege.

GLOUCESTER
His eyes are humbler than they used to be.

KING
How now, what means this, herald? Know'st thou
not
That I have fined these bones of mine for ransom? 68
Com'st thou again for ransom?

MONTJOY   No, great King.
I come to thee for charitable license,
That we may wander o'er this bloody field
To book our dead and then to bury them, 72
To sort our nobles from our common men.

For many of our princes—woe the while!—
Lie drowned and soaked in mercenary blood; 75
So do our vulgar drench their peasant limbs 76
In blood of princes; and the wounded steeds
Fret fetlock-deep in gore and with wild rage 78
Yerk out their armèd heels at their dead masters, 79
Killing them twice. Oh, give us leave, great King,
To view the field in safety, and dispose
Of their dead bodies!

KING   I tell thee truly, herald,
I know not if the day be ours or no,
For yet a many of your horsemen peer 84
And gallop o'er the field.

MONTJOY   The day is yours.

KING
Praisèd be God, and not our strength, for it!
What is this castle called that stands hard by?

MONTJOY   They call it Agincourt.

KING
Then call we this the field of Agincourt,
Fought on the day of Crispin Crispianus.

FLUELLEN   Your grandfather of famous memory, an't 91
please Your Majesty, and your great-uncle Edward the
Plack Prince of Wales, as I have read in the chronicles,
fought a most prave pattle here in France.

KING   They did, Fluellen.

FLUELLEN   Your Majesty says very true. If Your Majesties is remembered of it, the Welshmen did good
service in a garden where leeks did grow, wearing
leeks in their Monmouth caps, which, Your Majesty 99
know, to this hour is an honorable badge of the
service; and I do believe Your Majesty takes no scorn
to wear the leek upon Saint Tavy's Day. 102

KING
I wear it for a memorable honor,
For I am Welsh, you know, good countryman.

FLUELLEN   All the water in Wye cannot wash Your
Majesty's Welsh plood out of your pody, I can tell you
that. God pless it and preserve it, as long as it pleases
His Grace, and His Majesty too!

KING   Thanks, good my countryman.

FLUELLEN   By Jeshu, I am Your Majesty's countryman.
I care not who know it. I will confess it to all the 'orld.
I need not to be ashamed of Your Majesty, praised be
God, so long as Your Majesty is an honest man.

KING
God keep me so!

Enter Williams [with a glove in his cap].

Our heralds go with him.
Bring me just notice of the numbers dead 115

---

37 **in his ales** i.e., under the influence of ale   38 **Cleitus** a general
and close associate of Alexander, whom Alexander killed in a drinking bout.   47 **great-belly doublet** a man's close-fitting jacket, in
which the lower part was stuffed out with bombast or padding.
48 **gipes** gibes, jokes   55 **trumpet** trumpeter   58 **void** leave
60 **skirr** scurry   61 **Enforcèd** discharged   68 **fined . . . ransom** i.e.,
agreed to pay as a fine or ransom only these bones of mine and no
more.   72 **book** record

75 **mercenary** i.e., of common soldiers, who fought for pay   76 **vulgar** commoners   78 **fetlock-deep** (The *fetlock* is above the hoof, at the
back of the leg.)   79 **Yerk** kick   84 **peer** (1) look about anxiously
(2) appear   91 **grandfather** i.e., great-grandfather, Edward III.   **an't**
if it   99 **Monmouth caps** round and rimless caps with a tapering
crown, commonly worn by the Welsh   102 **Saint Tavy's Day** the festival of Saint David, patron saint of Wales, March 1—an occasion for
the celebration of Welsh traditions, though the wearing of leeks to
commemorate the great victory in 540 against the Saxons did not
begin until well after the setting of this play.   115 **just** exact

On both our parts.
    [*Exeunt Heralds and Gower with Montjoy.*]
    Call yonder fellow hither.

EXETER [*to Williams*]   Soldier, you must come to the King.

KING   Soldier, why wear'st thou that glove in thy cap?

WILLIAMS   An't please Your Majesty, 'tis the gage of
    one that I should fight withal, if he be alive.

KING   An Englishman?

WILLIAMS   An't please Your Majesty, a rascal that swag-
    gered with me last night, who, if 'a live and ever dare
    to challenge this glove, I have sworn to take him a box
    o'th'ear; or if I can see my glove in his cap, which he
    swore, as he was a soldier, he would wear if 'a lived, I
    will strike it out soundly.

KING   What think you, Captain Fluellen, is it fit this
    soldier keep his oath?

FLUELLEN   He is a craven and a villain else, an't please   130
    Your Majesty, in my conscience.

KING   It may be his enemy is a gentleman of great sort,   132
    quite from the answer of his degree.   133

FLUELLEN   Though he be as good a gentleman as the
    devil is, as Lucifer and Beelzebub himself, it is
    necessary, look Your Grace, that he keep his vow and
    his oath. If he be perjured, see you now, his reputation
    is as arrant a villain and a Jack-sauce as ever his   138
    black shoe trod upon God's ground and His earth, in
    my conscience, la!

KING [*to Williams*]   Then keep thy vow, sirrah, when
    thou meet'st the fellow.

WILLIAMS   So I will, my liege, as I live.

KING   Who serv'st thou under?

WILLIAMS   Under Captain Gower, my liege.

FLUELLEN   Gower is a good captain, and is good
    knowledge and literatured in the wars.   147

KING   Call him hither to me, soldier.

WILLIAMS   I will, my liege.   *Exit.*

KING   Here, Fluellen, wear thou this favor for me and
    stick it in thy cap. [*He gives Fluellen Williams's glove.*]
    When Alençon and myself were down together, I
    plucked this glove from his helm. If any man challenge   153
    this, he is a friend to Alençon and an enemy to our
    person. If thou encounter any such, apprehend him,
    an thou dost me love.   156

FLUELLEN [*putting the glove in his cap*]   Your Grace doo's   157
    me as great honors as can be desired in the hearts of
    his subjects. I would fain see the man that   159
    has but two legs that shall find himself aggriefed at
    this glove, that is all. But I would fain see it once, an't   161
    please God of his grace that I might see.

KING   Know'st thou Gower?

FLUELLEN   He is my dear friend, an't please you.

KING   Pray thee, go seek him and bring him to my tent.

FLUELLEN   I will fetch him.   *Exit.*

KING
    My lord of Warwick, and my brother Gloucester,
    Follow Fluellen closely at the heels.
    The glove which I have given him for a favor
    May haply purchase him a box o'th'ear.   170
    It is the soldier's; I by bargain should
    Wear it myself. Follow, good cousin Warwick.
    If that the soldier strike him, as I judge
    By his blunt bearing he will keep his word,
    Some sudden mischief may arise of it;
    For I do know Fluellen valiant
    And touched with choler, hot as gunpowder,   177
    And quickly will return an injury.   178
    Follow, and see there be no harm between them.
    Go you with me, uncle of Exeter.   *Exeunt [separately].*

❖

[4.8]

Enter Gower and Williams.

WILLIAMS   I warrant it is to knight you, Captain.

Enter Fluellen.

FLUELLEN   God's will and his pleasure, Captain, I
    beseech you now, come apace to the King. There is
    more good toward you, peradventure, than is in your
    knowledge to dream of.

WILLIAMS   Sir, know you this glove?

FLUELLEN   Know the glove? I know the glove is a glove.

WILLIAMS   I know this, and thus I challenge it.
                                 Strikes him.

FLUELLEN   'Sblood, an arrant traitor as any 's in the   9
    universal world, or in France, or in England!

GOWER [*to Williams*]   How now, sir? You villain!

WILLIAMS   Do you think I'll be forsworn?

FLUELLEN   Stand away, Captain Gower. I will give
    treason his payment into plows, I warrant you.   14

WILLIAMS   I am no traitor.

FLUELLEN   That's a lie in thy throat.—I charge you in His   16
    Majesty's name, apprehend him. He's a friend of the
    Duke Alençon's.

Enter Warwick and Gloucester.

WARWICK   How now, how now, what's the matter?

FLUELLEN   My lord of Warwick, here is—praised be
    God for it!—a most contagious treason come to light,   21
    look you, as you shall desire in a summer's day.—
    Here is His Majesty.

Enter King [Henry] and Exeter.

KING   How now, what's the matter?

FLUELLEN   My liege, here is a villain and a traitor that,
    look Your Grace, has struck the glove which Your
    Majesty is take out of the helmet of Alençon.

---

130 **craven** coward   132 **sort** rank   133 **quite . . . degree** i.e., too high
in rank to answer the challenge of one so low.   138 **Jack-sauce** saucy
knave   147 **literatured** well read   153 **helm** helmet.   156 **an** if
157 **doo's** does   159 **fain** willingly   161 **an't** if it. (Also in line 164.)

170 **haply** perhaps   177 **touched with choler** hot-tempered
178 **return an injury** repay an insult.
4.8. Location: The English camp.
9 **'Sblood** By His (Christ's) blood   14 **his** its.   **into plows** in blows
16 **lie in thy throat** i.e., inexcusable lie.   21 **contagious** noxious

WILLIAMS   My liege, this was my glove; here is the fellow of it. [*Showing his other glove.*] And he that I gave it
to in change promised to wear it in his cap. I promised   30
to strike him, if he did. I met this man with my glove
in his cap, and I have been as good as my word.

FLUELLEN   Your Majesty hear now, saving Your Majesty's manhood, what an arrant, rascally, beggarly,
lousy knave it is. I hope Your Majesty is pear me   35
testimony and witness, and will avouchment, that this   36
is the glove of Alençon that Your Majesty is give me,
in your conscience, now.

KING   Give me thy glove, soldier. Look, here is the
fellow of it.   [*He shows his other glove.*]
'Twas I indeed thou promised'st to strike,
And thou hast given me most bitter terms.   42

FLUELLEN   An't please Your Majesty, let his neck
answer for it, if there is any martial law in the world.

KING
How canst thou make me satisfaction?

WILLIAMS   All offenses, my lord, come from the heart.
Never came any from mine that might offend Your
Majesty.

KING   It was ourself thou didst abuse.

WILLIAMS   Your Majesty came not like yourself. You
appeared to me but as a common man—witness the
night, your garments, your lowliness. And what Your   52
Highness suffered under that shape, I beseech you take
it for your own fault and not mine; for had you been
as I took you for, I made no offense. Therefore I beseech Your Highness pardon me.

KING
Here, uncle Exeter, fill this glove with crowns,
And give it to this fellow.—Keep it, fellow,
And wear it for an honor in thy cap
Till I do challenge it.—Give him the crowns.
          [*Exeter gives the glove and gold to Williams.*]
And Captain, you must needs be friends with him.

FLUELLEN   By this day and this light, the fellow has
mettle enough in his belly.—Hold, there is twelve-
pence for you. [*He offers Williams a coin.*] And I pray you
to serve God, and keep you out of prawls, and
prabbles, and quarrels, and dissensions, and I warrant   66
you it is the better for you.

WILLIAMS   I will none of your money.

FLUELLEN   It is with a good will. I can tell you, it will
serve you to mend your shoes. Come, wherefore
should you be so pashful? Your shoes is not so good.
'Tis a good silling, I warrant you, or I will change it.

          Enter [*an English*] *Herald.*

KING   Now, herald, are the dead numbered?

HERALD [*giving a paper*]
Here is the number of the slaughtered French.

KING
What prisoners of good sort are taken, uncle?   75

EXETER [*reading*]
Charles Duke of Orleans, nephew to the King;   76
John Duke of Bourbon, and Lord Boucicault;
Of other lords and barons, knights and squires,
Full fifteen hundred, besides common men.

KING
This note doth tell me of ten thousand French
That in the field lie slain. Of princes, in this number,
And nobles bearing banners, there lie dead   82
One hundred twenty-six; added to these,
Of knights, esquires, and gallant gentlemen,
Eight thousand and four hundred, of the which
Five hundred were but yesterday dubbed knights.
So that in these ten thousand they have lost
There are but sixteen hundred mercenaries;
The rest are princes, barons, lords, knights, squires,
And gentlemen of blood and quality.
The names of those their nobles that lie dead:
Charles Delabreth, High Constable of France;
Jaques of Chatillion, Admiral of France;
The Master of the Crossbows, Lord Rambures;
Great-Master of France, the brave Sir Guichard
Dauphin   95
John, Duke of Alençon; Anthony, Duke of Brabant,
The brother to the Duke of Burgundy;
And Edward, Duke of Bar; of lusty earls,   98
Grandpré and Roussi, Faulconbridge and Foix,
Beaumont and Marle, Vaudemont and Lestrelles.
Here was a royal fellowship of death!
Where is the number of our English dead?
                              [*He is given another paper.*]
Edward the Duke of York, the Earl of Suffolk,
Sir Richard Keighley, Davy Gam, esquire;
None else of name, and of all other men   105
But five-and-twenty. O God, thy arm was here!   106
And not to us, but to thy arm alone,
Ascribe we all. When, without stratagem,
But in plain shock and even play of battle,   109
Was ever known so great and little loss
On one part and on th'other? Take it, God,
For it is none but thine.

EXETER   'Tis wonderful.

KING
Come, go we in procession to the village.
And be it death proclaimèd through our host
To boast of this or take that praise from God
Which is his only.

FLUELLEN   Is it not lawful, an't please Your Majesty, to
tell how many is killed?

KING
Yes, Captain, but with this acknowledgment,
That God fought for us.

---

30 **change** exchange   35 **is pear** will bear   36 **avouchment** avouch
42 **terms** words.   52 **lowliness** humble mien.
66 **prabbles** i.e., brabbles, scuffles   75 **good sort** high rank

76–106 **Charles . . . here** (The catalogue of the captured and slain is
from Holinshed.)   82 **bearing banners** i.e., with coats of arms
95 **Great-Master** grandmaster, i.e., the chief officer of the royal household   98 **lusty** vigorous   105 **name** rank, social importance
109 **even** equal

FLUELLEN   Yes, in my conscience, he did us great good.
KING   Do we all holy rites.
    Let there be sung *Non nobis* and *Te Deum*,   123
    The dead with charity enclosed in clay;
    And then to Calais, and to England then,
    Where ne'er from France arrived more happy men.   126
                                                    Exeunt.

❧

5.[0]

    Enter Chorus.

CHORUS
    Vouchsafe to those that have not read the story   1
    That I may prompt them; and of such as have,
    I humbly pray them to admit th'excuse   3
    Of time, of numbers, and due course of things,
    Which cannot in their huge and proper life
    Be here presented. Now we bear the King
    Toward Calais. Grant him there. There seen,
    Heave him away upon your wingèd thoughts
    Athwart the sea. Behold, the English beach   9
    Pales in the flood with men, wives, and boys,   10
    Whose shouts and claps outvoice the deep-mouthed
          sea,
    Which like a mighty whiffler 'fore the King   12
    Seems to prepare his way. So let him land,
    And solemnly see him set on to London.
    So swift a pace hath thought that even now
    You may imagine him upon Blackheath,   16
    Where that his lords desire him to have borne   17
    His bruisèd helmet and his bended sword
    Before him through the city. He forbids it,
    Being free from vainness and self-glorious pride,
    Giving full trophy, signal, and ostent   21
    Quite from himself to God. But now behold,
    In the quick forge and working-house of thought,
    How London doth pour out her citizens!
    The Mayor and all his brethren, in best sort,   25
    Like to the senators of th'antique Rome
    With the plebeians swarming at their heels,
    Go forth and fetch their conquering Caesar in;

    As by a lower but loving likelihood,   29
    Were now the General of our gracious Empress,   30
    As in good time he may, from Ireland coming,
    Bringing rebellion broachèd on his sword,   32
    How many would the peaceful city quit
    To welcome him! Much more, and much more cause,   34
    Did they this Harry. Now in London place him;
    As yet the lamentation of the French   36
    Invites the King of England's stay at home;   37
    The Emperor's coming in behalf of France,   38
    To order peace between them . . . and omit   39
    All the occurrences, whatever chanced,
    Till Harry's back-return again to France.   41
    There must we bring him; and myself have played
    The interim by rememb'ring you 'tis past.   43
    Then brook abridgment, and your eyes advance,   44
    After your thoughts, straight back again to France.
                                                    Exit.

❧

[5.1]

    *Enter Fluellen [with a leek in his cap, and a
    cudgel], and Gower.*

GOWER   Nay, that's right. But why wear you your leek
    today? Saint Davy's Day is past.
FLUELLEN   There is occasions and causes why and
    wherefore in all things. I will tell you asse my friend,   4
    Captain Gower. The rascally, scald, beggarly, lousy,   5
    pragging knave, Pistol, which you and yourself and all
    the world know to be no petter than a fellow, look you
    now, of no merits, he is come to me and prings me
    pread and salt yesterday, look you, and bid me eat my
    leek. It was in a place where I could not breed no con-
    tention with him; but I will be so bold as to wear it in
    my cap till I see him once again, and then I will tell
    him a little piece of my desires.

    Enter Pistol.

GOWER   Why, here he comes, swelling like a turkey-
    cock.
FLUELLEN   'Tis no matter for his swellings nor his
    turkey-cocks.—God pless you, Aunchient Pistol! You
    scurvy, lousy knave, God pless you!
PISTOL
    Ha, art thou bedlam? Dost thou thirst, base Trojan,   19

---

123 *Non nobis* i.e., Psalm 115, beginning, "Not unto us, O Lord,
not unto us, but unto thy name give glory."   *Te Deum* a hymn
of thanksgiving, beginning, "We praise thee O God"   126 **happy**
fortunate
5.0. (Between Acts 4 and 5, there is historically an interval of about
five years during which Henry made a second campaign in France
that brought the French to terms in the Treaty of Troyes, with which
the play ends.)
1 Vouchsafe Permit it   **3 admit th'excuse** excuse our handling
9 Athwart across   **10 Pales in** hems in, surrounds.   **flood** sea
12 whiffler an usher heading the procession to clear the way
16 Blackheath open area just outside London, to the southeast
17 Where that where   **21 Giving . . . ostent** giving every memorial,
token, and display of victory   **25 sort** array

29–34 As . . . him (Seemingly, an allusion to the Earl of Essex, who left
London on his Irish expedition on March 27, 1599, in an attempt to
put down Tyrone's rebellion; he returned unsuccessful and under a
cloud on September 28 of the same year. These lines, therefore, were
probably written between the dates mentioned.)   **29 a . . . likelihood**
a less exalted comparison but one that shows much love   **30 Empress**
i.e., Elizabeth   **32 broachèd** transfixed, spitted   **36–7 As . . . home**
i.e., the French are so dejected that Henry can stay in England without fear of loss in France   **38 Emperor's coming** (The Holy Roman
Emperor, Sigismund, came to England on behalf of France in May
1416.)   **39 them . . . and omit** (Something appears to be left out here.
Possibly it should read, "them, and the death / O' the Dauphin, leap
we over, and omit . . .")   **41 Harry's back-return** i.e., Henry's second
campaign, commencing in 1417   **43 rememb'ring** reminding
44 brook tolerate, excuse
5.1. Location: France. The English camp.
4 asse as   **5 scald** scurvy   **19 bedlam** crazy.   **Trojan** i.e., rascal

To have me fold up Parca's fatal web?   20
Hence, I am qualmish at the smell of leek.   21
FLUELLEN   I peseech you heartily, scurvy, lousy knave,
at my desires, and my requests, and my petitions, to
eat, look you, this leek. [*He offers the leek.*] Because,
look you, you do not love it, nor your affections and
your appetites and your disgestions doo's not agree
with it, I would desire you to eat it.
PISTOL
Not for Cadwallader and all his goats.   28
FLUELLEN   There is one goat for you. (*Strikes him.*) Will
you be so good, scald knave, as eat it?
PISTOL   Base Trojan, thou shalt die.
FLUELLEN   You say very true, scald knave, when God's
will is. I will desire you to live in the meantime and
eat your victuals. Come, there is sauce for it. [*He strikes
him.*] You called me yesterday mountain squire, but I   35
will make you today a squire of low degree. I pray   36
you, fall to. If you can mock a leek, you can eat a leek.
GOWER   Enough, Captain, you have astonished him.   38
FLUELLEN   By Jesu, I will make him eat some part of my
leek, or I will peat his pate four days. Bite, I pray you; 40
it is good for your green wound and your ploody   41
coxcomb.   42
PISTOL   Must I bite?
FLUELLEN   Yes, certainly, and out of doubt and out of
question too, and ambiguities.
PISTOL
By this leek, I will most horribly revenge—
                              [*Fluellen threatens him.*]
I eat and eat—I swear—
FLUELLEN   Eat, I pray you. Will you have some more
sauce to your leek? There is not enough leek to
swear by.
PISTOL
Quiet thy cudgel; thou dost see I eat.
FLUELLEN   Much good do you, scald knave, heartily.
Nay, pray you, throw none away; the skin is good for
your broken coxcomb. When you take occasions to see 54
leeks hereafter, I pray you, mock at 'em, that is all.
PISTOL   Good.
FLUELLEN   Ay, leeks is good. Hold you, there is a groat 57
to heal your pate.   [*He offers a coin.*]
PISTOL   Me, a groat?
FLUELLEN   Yes, verily, and in truth you shall take it, or
I have another leek in my pocket which you shall eat.
PISTOL
I take thy groat in earnest of revenge.   62

FLUELLEN   If I owe you anything, I will pay you in
cudgels. You shall be a woodmonger and buy nothing
of me but cudgels. God b'wi'you, and keep you, and
heal your pate.   *Exit.*
PISTOL   All hell shall stir for this.
GOWER   Go, go, you are a counterfeit cowardly knave.
Will you mock at an ancient tradition, begun upon an
honorable respect and worn as a memorable trophy of 70
predeceased valor, and dare not avouch in your deeds 71
any of your words? I have seen you gleeking and   72
galling at this gentleman twice or thrice. You thought 73
because he could not speak English in the native garb
he could not therefore handle an English cudgel. You
find it otherwise; and henceforth let a Welsh cor-
rection teach you a good English condition. Fare
ye well.   *Exit.*
PISTOL
Doth Fortune play the huswife with me now?   79
News have I that my Doll is dead   80
I'th' spital of a malady of France,   81
And there my rendezvous is quite cut off.
Old I do wax, and from my weary limbs   83
Honor is cudgeled. Well, bawd I'll turn,
And something lean to cutpurse of quick hand.   85
To England will I steal, and there I'll steal;
And patches will I get unto these cudgeled scars,
And swear I got them in the Gallia wars.   *Exit.* 88

[5.2]

Enter, at one door, King Henry, Exeter, Bedford,
[Gloucester, Clarence,] Warwick, [Westmorland,]
and other lords; at another, Queen Isabel, the
[French] King, the Duke of Burgundy, [the
Princess Katharine, Alice,] and other French.

KING HENRY
Peace to this meeting, wherefor we are met!
Unto our brother France and to our sister,
Health and fair time of day; joy and good wishes
To our most fair and princely cousin Katharine;
And, as a branch and member of this royalty,   5
By whom this great assembly is contrived,
We do salute you, Duke of Burgundy;
And princes French, and peers, health to you all!
FRENCH KING
Right joyous are we to behold your face,
Most worthy brother England. Fairly met!
So are you, princes English, every one.

---

20 Parca's (The Parcae, or Fates, spun, drew out, and cut the thread of
destiny.)   **21 qualmish** squeamish, nauseated   **28 Cadwallader** sev-
enth-century Welsh warrior king.   **goats** (Pistol makes the customary
taunt that the Welsh were goatherds.)   **35 mountain squire** i.e., a
squire owning mountainous, poor land   **36 squire of low degree**
(Allusion to a popular medieval romance, *The Squire of Low Degree.*
Fluellen threatens to make Pistol into a lowly, contemptible figure,
towered over by a mountain squire.)   **38 astonished** dazed, terrified
40 pate head   **41 green** raw   **42 coxcomb** fool's cap; here, the scalp.
54 broken bleeding (not "fractured")   **57 groat** fourpenny coin
62 in earnest of as a down payment for

70 respect consideration   **71 predeceased valor** valor of those now
dead   **72–3 gleeking and galling** mocking and scoffing   **79 huswife**
hussy, fickle jade   **80 Doll** (At 2.1.17–18 we learn that Pistol was married to Nell Quickly. The similarity of *Doll* and *Nell* could suggest a
textual error here, or authorial forgetfulness, or a change in the characters' fortunes.)   **81 spital** hospital.   **malady of France** venereal
disease   **83 wax** grow   **85 something lean to** I'll incline somewhat
to   **88 Gallia** French
5.2. Location: The French court.
5 royalty royal family

QUEEN ISABEL
So happy be the issue, brother England,   12
Of this good day and of this gracious meeting,
As we are now glad to behold your eyes—
Your eyes, which hitherto have borne in them
Against the French that met them in their bent   16
The fatal balls of murdering basilisks.   17
The venom of such looks, we fairly hope,
Have lost their quality, and that this day
Shall change all griefs and quarrels into love.   20

KING HENRY
To cry amen to that, thus we appear.

QUEEN ISABEL
You English princes all, I do salute you.

BURGUNDY
My duty to you both, on equal love,
Great Kings of France and England! That I have
labored
With all my wits, my pains, and strong endeavors
To bring your most imperial Majesties
Unto this bar and royal interview,   27
Your mightiness on both parts best can witness.
Since, then, my office hath so far prevailed
That, face to face and royal eye to eye,
You have congreeted, let it not disgrace me   31
If I demand, before this royal view,   32
What rub or what impediment there is   33
Why that the naked, poor, and mangled Peace,
Dear nurse of arts, plenties, and joyful births,
Should not in this best garden of the world,
Our fertile France, put up her lovely visage?   37
Alas, she hath from France too long been chased,
And all her husbandry doth lie on heaps,   39
Corrupting in it own fertility.   40
Her vine, the merry cheerer of the heart,
Unprunèd dies; her hedges even-pleached,   42
Like prisoners wildly overgrown with hair,
Put forth disordered twigs; her fallow leas   44
The darnel, hemlock, and rank fumitory   45
Doth root upon, while that the coulter rusts   46
That should deracinate such savagery.   47
The even mead, that erst brought sweetly forth   48
The freckled cowslip, burnet, and green clover,   49
Wanting the scythe, all uncorrected, rank,   50
Conceives by idleness, and nothing teems   51
But hateful docks, rough thistles, kecksies, burrs,   52
Losing both beauty and utility.
And all our vineyards, fallows, meads, and hedges, 54

Defective in their natures, grow to wildness;   55
Even so our houses and ourselves and children   56
Have lost, or do not learn for want of time,
The sciences that should become our country,   58
But grow like savages—as soldiers will
That nothing but meditate on blood—
To swearing and stern looks, diffused attire,   61
And everything that seems unnatural.
Which to reduce into our former favor   63
You are assembled, and my speech entreats
That I may know the let why gentle Peace   65
Should not expel these inconveniences
And bless us with her former qualities.

KING HENRY
If, Duke of Burgundy, you would the peace,   68
Whose want gives growth to th'imperfections   69
Which you have cited, you must buy that peace
With full accord to all our just demands,
Whose tenors and particular effects   72
You have enscheduled briefly in your hands.   73

BURGUNDY
The King hath heard them, to the which as yet
There is no answer made.

KING HENRY   Well then, the peace,
Which you before so urged, lies in his answer.

FRENCH KING
I have but with a cursitory eye   77
O'erglanced the articles. Pleaseth Your Grace   78
To appoint some of your council presently
To sit with us once more, with better heed
To re-survey them, we will suddenly   81
Pass our accept and peremptory answer.   82

KING HENRY
Brother, we shall.—Go, uncle Exeter,
And brother Clarence, and you, brother Gloucester,
Warwick, and Huntingdon, go with the King,
And take with you free power to ratify,
Augment, or alter, as your wisdoms best
Shall see advantageable for our dignity,   88
Anything in or out of our demands,
And we'll consign thereto.—Will you, fair sister,   90
Go with the princes, or stay here with us?

QUEEN ISABEL
Our gracious brother, I will go with them.
Haply a woman's voice may do some good   93
When articles too nicely urged be stood on.   94

KING HENRY
Yet leave our cousin Katharine here with us.
She is our capital demand, comprised   96
Within the fore-rank of our articles.   97

---

12 **issue** outcome   16 **in their bent** (1) as they were directed (2) in
their glance   17 **fatal balls** (1) cannonballs (2) eyeballs.   **basilisks**
(1) large cannon (2) monsters supposed to kill with their gaze.
20 **griefs** grievances   27 **bar** tribunal   31 **congreeted** greeted each
other   32 **demand** ask   33 **rub** obstacle. (A term from bowls.)
37 **put up** show, lift up   39 **husbandry** harvest, foison   40 **it** its
42 **even-pleached** smoothly intertwined   44 **fallow leas** uncultivated
open fields   45 **darnel . . . fumitory** i.e., weeds that grow in cultivated land   46 **coulter** plow blade   47 **deracinate** root out   48 **even
mead** level meadow.   **erst** formerly   49 **burnet** a herb   50 **Wanting**
lacking   51 **Conceives** gives birth (to weeds).   **teems** flourishes
52 **kecksies** dry stalks   54 **fallows** land plowed and left lying

55 **Defective . . . natures** naturally inclined to wildness   56 **houses**
households   58 **sciences** skills   61 **diffused** disordered   63 **reduce
. . . favor** return to our former good appearance and good graces
65 **let** hindrance   68 **would** wish   69 **want** lack   72 **tenors . . .
effects** general purport and specific details   73 **enscheduled** drawn
up in writing   77 **cursitory** cursory, hasty   78 **Pleaseth** May it please
81 **suddenly** speedily   82 **Pass . . . answer** deliver our agreed-to and
final answer.   88 **advantageable** advantageous   90 **consign** agree,
subscribe   93 **Haply** Perhaps   94 **nicely** punctiliously, with insistence on detail.   **stood on** insisted on.   96 **capital** chief   97 **fore-
rank** first row

QUEEN ISABEL
She hath good leave.
                    Exeunt omnes. Manent King [Henry]
                              and Katharine [with Alice].
KING HENRY   Fair Katharine, and most fair,   98
Will you vouchsafe to teach a soldier terms
Such as will enter at a lady's ear
And plead his love suit to her gentle heart?
KATHARINE   Your Majesty shall mock at me. I cannot
speak your England.
KING HENRY   O fair Katharine, if you will love me
soundly with your French heart, I will be glad to hear
you confess it brokenly with your English tongue. Do
you like me, Kate?
KATHARINE   *Pardonnez-moi,* I cannot tell wat is "like
me."
KING HENRY   An angel is like you, Kate, and you are
like an angel.
KATHARINE   [*to Alice*]   *Que dit-il? Que je suis semblable à*   112
les anges?   113
ALICE   *Oui, vraiment, sauf Votre Grâce, ainsi dit-il.*   114
KING HENRY   I said so, dear Katharine, and I must not
blush to affirm it.
KATHARINE   *Oh, bon Dieu! Les langues des hommes sont*
pleines de tromperies.
KING HENRY   What says she, fair one? That the tongues
of men are full of deceits?
ALICE   *Oui,* dat de tongues of de mans is be full of
deceits. Dat is de Princess.
KING HENRY   The Princess is the better Englishwoman.   123
I'faith, Kate, my wooing is fit for thy understanding.
I am glad thou canst speak no better English, for if
thou couldst, thou wouldst find me such a plain king
that thou wouldst think I had sold my farm to buy my
crown. I know no ways to mince it in love, but directly   128
to say, "I love you." Then if you urge me farther than
to say, "Do you, in faith?" I wear out my suit. Give me   130
your answer, i'faith, do, and so clap hands and a   131
bargain. How say you, lady?
KATHARINE   *Sauf votre honneur,* me understand well.
KING HENRY   Marry, if you would put me to verses or
to dance for your sake, Kate, why, you undid me. For
the one I have neither words nor measure, and for the   136
other I have no strength in measure, yet a reasonable   137
measure in strength. If I could win a lady at leapfrog,   138
or by vaulting into my saddle with my armor on my
back, under the correction of bragging be it spoken, I
should quickly leap into a wife. Or if I might buffet for 141
my love, or bound my horse for her favors, I could lay   142
on like a butcher and sit like a jackanapes, never off.   143
But before God, Kate, I cannot look greenly, nor gasp   144
out my eloquence, nor I have no cunning in protesta-

tion—only downright oaths, which I never use till   146
urged, nor never break for urging. If thou canst love a
fellow of this temper, Kate, whose face is not worth   148
sunburning, that never looks in his glass for love of   149
anything he sees there, let thine eye be thy cook. I   150
speak to thee plain soldier. If thou canst love me for
this, take me. If not, to say to thee that I shall die is
true; but for thy love, by the Lord, no. Yet I love thee
too. And while thou liv'st, dear Kate, take a fellow of
plain and uncoined constancy, for he perforce must   155
do thee right, because he hath not the gift to woo in
other places. For these fellows of infinite tongue that
can rhyme themselves into ladies' favors, they do
always reason themselves out again. What? A speaker
is but a prater, a rhyme is but a ballad. A good leg will
fall, a straight back will stoop, a black beard will turn   161
white, a curled pate will grow bald, a fair face will
wither, a full eye will wax hollow; but a good heart,
Kate, is the sun and the moon—or rather the sun and
not the moon, for it shines bright and never changes,
but keeps his course truly. If thou would have such a
one, take me. And take me, take a soldier; take a
soldier, take a king. And what say'st thou then to my
love? Speak, my fair, and fairly, I pray thee.
KATHARINE   Is it possible dat I sould love de *ennemi* of
France?
KING HENRY   No, it is not possible you should love the
enemy of France, Kate; but in loving me you should
love the friend of France, for I love France so well that
I will not part with a village of it. I will have it all mine.
And, Kate, when France is mine and I am yours, then
yours is France and you are mine.
KATHARINE   I cannot tell wat is dat.
KING HENRY   No, Kate? I will tell thee in French, which
I am sure will hang upon my tongue like a new-
married wife about her husband's neck, hardly to be
shook off. *Je quand sur le possession de France, et quand*   182
vous avez le possession de moi—let me see, what?   183
Saint Denis be my speed!—*donc vôtre est France et vous*   184
êtes mienne. It is as easy for me, Kate, to conquer the   185
kingdom as to speak so much more French. I shall
never move thee in French, unless it be to laugh at
me.
KATHARINE   *Sauf votre honneur, le français que vous parlez,*   189
il est meilleur que l' anglais lequel je parle.   190
KING HENRY   No, faith, is't not, Kate. But thy speaking
of my tongue, and I thine, most truly-falsely, must   192
needs be granted to be much at one. But, Kate, dost   193
thou understand thus much English: Canst thou
love me?

---

98 s.d. *omnes* all.   *Manent* They remain onstage   **112–14** *Que . . .*
ainsi dit-il What does he say? That I am like the angels. ALICE Yes,
truly, save Your Grace, he says so.   **123 is . . . Englishwoman** i.e., is
the better for preferring honesty.   **128 mince it** speak coyly
130 wear out my suit expend all my resources as a wooer.   **131 clap**
clasp   **136 measure** (skill in) meter   **137 measure** dance
138 measure amount, aptitude   **141 buffet** box   **142 bound** make
prance   **143 jackanapes** ape, monkey   **144 greenly** like a lovesick
youth

146 downright straightforward   **148–9 not . . . sunburning** i.e.,
already so tanned that more sun could make it worse. (Tanned and
dark complexions were generally considered unhandsome.)
149 glass mirror   **150 be thy cook** dress up and garnish my plain
looks.   **155 uncoined** (1) not put into circulation (2) unalloyed, fixed,
steady   **161 fall** shrink, lose its shapeliness   **182–5** *Je . . . mienne*
(Henry haltingly translates into French the last sentence of his previous speech.)   **184 Saint Denis** patron saint of France.   **be my speed**
help me.   **189–90** *Sauf . . . parle* Saving your honor, the French that
you speak is better than the English that I speak.   **192 truly-falsely**
true-heartedly but incorrectly   **193 at one** alike.

KATHARINE I cannot tell.

KING HENRY Can any of your neighbors tell, Kate? I'll ask them. Come, I know thou lovest me. And at night, when you come into your closet, you'll question this gentlewoman about me; and I know, Kate, you will to her dispraise those parts in me that you love with your heart. But, good Kate, mock me mercifully, the rather, gentle Princess, because I love thee cruelly. If ever thou be'st mine, Kate, as I have a saving faith within me tells me thou shalt, I get thee with scambling, and thou must therefore needs prove a good soldier-breeder. Shall not thou and I, between Saint Denis and Saint George, compound a boy, half French, half English, that shall go to Constantinople and take the Turk by the beard? Shall we not? What say'st thou, my fair flower-de-luce? 211

KATHARINE I do not know dat.

KING HENRY No; 'tis hereafter to know, but now to promise. Do but now promise, Kate, you will endeavor for your French part of such a boy, and for my English moiety take the word of a king and a bachelor. How answer you, *la plus belle Katharine du monde, mon très cher et devin déesse?* 218

KATHARINE Your Majestee 'ave *fausse* French enough to deceive de most *sage demoiselle* dat is *en France*. 219

KING HENRY Now, fie upon my false French! By mine honor, in true English, I love thee, Kate; by which honor I dare not swear thou lovest me, yet my blood begins to flatter me that thou dost, notwithstanding the poor and untempering effect of my visage. Now beshrew my father's ambition! He was thinking of civil wars when he got me; therefore was I created with a stubborn outside, with an aspect of iron, that when I come to woo ladies I fright them. But in faith, Kate, the elder I wax the better I shall appear. My comfort is that old age, that ill layer-up of beauty, can do no more spoil upon my face. Thou hast me, if thou hast me, at the worst; and thou shalt wear me, if thou wear me, better and better. And therefore tell me, most fair Katharine, will you have me? Put off your maiden blushes; avouch the thoughts of your heart with the looks of an empress; take me by the hand, and say, "Harry of England, I am thine." Which word thou shalt no sooner bless mine ear withal, but I will tell thee aloud, "England is thine, Ireland is thine, France is thine, and Henry Plantagenet is thine"—who, though I speak it before his face, if he be not fellow with the best king, thou shalt find the best king of good fellows. Come, your answer in broken music! For thy voice is music, and thy English broken. Therefore, queen of all, Katharine, break thy mind to me in broken English. Wilt thou have me?

KATHARINE Dat is as it shall please de *roi mon père*. 248

KING HENRY Nay, it will please him well, Kate. It shall please him, Kate.

KATHARINE Den it sall also content me.

KING HENRY Upon that I kiss your hand, and I call you my queen. [*He attempts to kiss her hand.*]

KATHARINE *Laissez, mon seigneur, laissez, laissez! Ma foi, je ne veux point que vous abaissiez votre grandeur en baisant la main d'une—Notre Seigneur!—indigne serviteur. Excusez-moi, je vous supplie, mon très-puissant seigneur.* 258

KING HENRY Then I will kiss your lips, Kate.

KATHARINE *Les dames et demoiselles pour être baisées devant leur noces, il n'est pas la coutume de France.* 261

KING HENRY [*to Alice*] Madam my interpreter, what says she?

ALICE Dat it is not be de fashion *pour les* ladies of France—I cannot tell wat is *baiser* en Anglish.

KING HENRY To kiss.

ALICE Your Majestee *entend* bettre *que moi.* 267

KING HENRY It is not a fashion for the maids in France to kiss before they are married, would she say?

ALICE *Oui, vraiment.* 270

KING HENRY Oh, Kate, nice customs curtsy to great kings. Dear Kate, you and I cannot be confined within the weak list of a country's fashion. We are the makers of manners, Kate; and the liberty that follows our places stops the mouth of all find-faults, as I will do yours, for upholding the nice fashion of your country in denying me a kiss. Therefore, patiently and yielding. [*He kisses her.*] You have witchcraft in your lips, Kate. There is more eloquence in a sugar touch of them than in the tongues of the French council, and they should sooner persuade Harry of England than a general petition of monarchs.—Here comes your father.

Enter the French power and the English lords.

BURGUNDY God save Your Majesty! My royal cousin, teach you our princess English?

KING HENRY I would have her learn, my fair cousin, how perfectly I love her, and that is good English.

BURGUNDY Is she not apt?

KING HENRY Our tongue is rough, coz, and my condition is not smooth; so that, having neither the voice nor the heart of flattery about me, I cannot so conjure up the spirit of love in her that he will appear in his true likeness. 289

---

199 closet private chamber **206 scambling** the scuffles of war **211 flower-de-luce** fleur-de-lis, the emblem of France. **216 moiety** half **217–18 la plus . . . déesse** the most beautiful Katharine in the world, my very dear and divine goddess. **219 fausse** i.e., false (both "incorrect" and "deceptive") **225 untempering** unsettling, unsoftening **226 beshrew** curses on **228 aspect** appearance **236 avouch** vouch for, confirm **243 fellow with** on equal terms with **244 broken music** (Henry quibbles on the term for music composed in parts for different instruments.) **246 break** open

248 de roi mon père the King my father. **254–8 Laissez . . . seigneur** Don't, my lord, don't, don't! By my faith, I do not wish you to lower your greatness by kissing the hand of an—our dear Lord!—unworthy servant; excuse me, I beg you, my most powerful lord. (*Serviteur* is masculine and not appropriately applied to a lady, but the error may be Shakespeare's.) **260–1 Les dames . . . France** It is not customary in France for ladies and young girls to be kissed before their marriage. **267 entend . . . moi** understands better than I. **270 Oui, vraiment** Yes, truly. **271 nice** fastidious **273 list** limit, barrier **274 follows our places** attends our (high) rank **288 Our tongue** (1) Our English language (2) My soldierly speech **288–9 condition** soldierly manner

BURGUNDY   Pardon the frankness of my mirth, if I
answer you for that. If you would conjure in her, you 294
must make a circle; if conjure up love in her in his true
likeness, he must appear naked and blind. Can you 296
blame her then, being a maid yet rosed over with the 297
virgin crimson of modesty, if she deny the appearance 298
of a naked blind boy in her naked seeing self? It were, 299
my lord, a hard condition for a maid to consign to. 300

KING HENRY   Yet they do wink and yield, as love is 301
blind and enforces. 302

BURGUNDY   They are then excused, my lord, when they
see not what they do.

KING HENRY   Then, good my lord, teach your cousin to
consent winking.

BURGUNDY   I will wink on her to consent, my lord, if 307
you will teach her to know my meaning; for maids,
well summered and warm kept, are like flies at Bar- 309
tholomew-tide: blind, though they have their eyes, 310
and then they will endure handling, which before 311
would not abide looking on.

KING HENRY   This moral ties me over to time and a hot 313
summer; and so I shall catch the fly, your cousin, in 314
the latter end, and she must be blind too.

BURGUNDY   As love is, my lord, before it loves. 316

KING HENRY   It is so; and you may, some of you, thank
love for my blindness, who cannot see many a fair 318
French city for one fair French maid that stands in 319
my way. 320

FRENCH KING   Yes, my lord, you see them perspectively, 321
the cities turned into a maid; for they are all girdled
with maiden walls that war hath never entered. 323

KING HENRY   Shall Kate be my wife?

FRENCH KING   So please you.

KING HENRY   I am content, so the maiden cities you talk 326
of may wait on her. So the maid that stood in the way 327
for my wish shall show me the way to my will. 328

FRENCH KING
We have consented to all terms of reason.

KING HENRY   Is't so, my lords of England?

WESTMORLAND
The King hath granted every article:
His daughter first, and then in sequel all
According to their firm proposèd natures.   333

EXETER
Only he hath not yet subscribèd this: 334
Where Your Majesty demands that the King of France,
having any occasion to write for matter of grant, shall 336
name Your Highness in this form and with this ad- 337
dition, in French, *Notre très cher fils Henri, Roi* 338
d'Angleterre, Héritier de France; and thus in Latin, 339
Praeclarissimus filius noster Henricus, Rex Angliae et 340
Haeres Franciae.

FRENCH KING
Nor this I have not, brother, so denied   342
But your request shall make me let it pass.   343

KING HENRY
I pray you then, in love and dear alliance,
Let that one article rank with the rest,
And thereupon give me your daughter.

FRENCH KING
Take her, fair son, and from her blood raise up
Issue to me, that the contending kingdoms
Of France and England, whose very shores look pale
With envy of each other's happiness,
May cease their hatred, and this dear conjunction
Plant neighborhood and Christian-like accord
In their sweet bosoms, that never war advance
His bleeding sword twixt England and fair France.

LORDS   Amen!

KING HENRY
Now, welcome, Kate; and bear me witness all,
That here I kiss her as my sovereign queen.
           [*He kisses her.*] *Flourish.*

QUEEN ISABEL
God, the best maker of all marriages,
Combine your hearts in one, your realms in one!
As man and wife, being two, are one in love,
So be there twixt your kingdoms such a spousal   361
That never may ill office, or fell jealousy,   362
Which troubles oft the bed of blessèd marriage,
Thrust in between the paction of these kingdoms   364
To make divorce of their incorporate league;
That English may as French, French Englishmen,
Receive each other. God speak this "Amen"!

ALL   Amen!

KING HENRY
Prepare we for our marriage, on which day,
My lord of Burgundy, we'll take your oath,
And all the peers', for surety of our leagues.
Then shall I swear to Kate, and you to me;

---

294 conjure in her (with bawdy double meaning of raising up something within her *circle*, line 295)   **296 naked and blind** (as Cupid is conventionally portrayed)   **297 yet rosed over** still blushing **298–9 if . . . self** if she refuses to admit the entry of a naked boy in her sight, or herself being naked?   **300 a hard condition** (Suggesting erection.)   **consign** agree   **301–2 Yet . . . enforces** Yet young maidens do close their eyes and say yes, prompted to do so by their own bashfulness and male importunity.   **307 wink on her** give her an encouraging wink   **309 summered** nurtured   **309–10 Bartholomew-tide** August 24 (when flies, bees, etc., are sluggish)   **311 handling** (1) handling of the beehive (2) sexual handling   **313–14 This moral . . . summer** The lesson of your fable would oblige me to wait for the heat of summer   **316 As . . . loves** (Love is blind before it loves, because it cannot yet see the beloved and because love has not yet opened the lover's eyes.)   **318–20 who . . . my way** i.e., since I am so preoccupied with Katharine that I have forgotten for the moment about all those French towns I want. (He is joking; he gets the French towns, along with her.)   **321 perspectively** i.e., as in an optical device that presents different images when viewed from different angles   **323 maiden** unbreached. (With a sexual metaphor, continued in *entered*.)   **326 so** provided that   **327 wait on her** attend her, go along with her (as part of her dowry).   **328 will** (1) intention of ruling France (2) sexual desire.

333 According . . . natures exactly as specified in the proposals. **334 subscribèd** agreed to, signed to   **336 for . . . grant** in official deeds, granting title to land and the like   **337–8 addition** title **338–9 Notre . . . France** i.e., Our very dear son Henry, King of England, Heir of France   **340 Praeclarissimus** most famous. (Presumably an error for "Praecharissimus" or "Praecarissimus," "most dear." Shakespeare is following Holinshed, who took the error from Hall.)   **342 so** so firmly   **343 But** but that   **361 spousal** marriage   **362 ill office** unfriendly dealings.   **fell** cruel   **364 paction** alliance, compact

And may our oaths well kept and prosperous be!
                              Sennet.   Exeunt.

❖

[Epilogue]

Enter Chorus.

CHORUS
Thus far, with rough and all-unable pen,
  Our bending author hath pursued the story,   2
In little room confining mighty men,
  Mangling by starts the full course of their glory.   4

Small time, but in that small most greatly lived   5
  This star of England. Fortune made his sword,
By which the world's best garden he achieved,   7
  And of it left his son imperial lord.
Henry the Sixth, in infant bands crowned King   9
  Of France and England, did this king succeed;
Whose state so many had the managing
  That they lost France and made his England bleed,
Which oft our stage hath shown; and, for their sake,   13
In your fair minds let this acceptance take.   [*Exit.*]   14

Epilogue.
2 bending i.e., under the weight of his task   **4 by starts** in fits and
starts, in fragments

5 Small time (Henry V ruled for only nine years, dying at the age of
thirty-five.)   **7 best garden** i.e., France   **9 infant bands** swaddling
clothes   **13 Which . . . shown** (Refers to the three parts of *King Henry
VI.*)   **their** i.e., the actors and the author, the presenters on *our stage*
(line 13)   **14 let . . . take** let this play meet with your approval.

The Tragedies

Romeo and Juliet

Though a tragedy, *Romeo and Juliet* is, in some ways, more closely comparable to Shakespeare's romantic comedies and early writings than to his later tragedies. Stylistically belonging to the years 1594–1596, it is in the lyric vein of the sonnets, *A Midsummer Night's Dream, The Merchant of Venice*, and *Richard II*, all of which are from the mid 1590s. Like them, it uses a variety of rhyme schemes (couplets, quatrains, octets, and even sonnets) and revels in punning, metaphor, and wit combat. It is separated in tone and in time from the earliest of the great tragedies, *Julius Caesar* and *Hamlet*, by almost half a decade, and, except for the experimental *Titus Andronicus*, it is the only tragedy (that is not also a history) that Shakespeare wrote in the first decade of his career—a period devoted otherwise to romantic comedy and English history.

Like many comedies, *Romeo and Juliet* is a love story, celebrating the exquisite, brief joy of youthful passion. Even its tragic ending stresses the poignancy of that brief beauty, not the bitter futility of love, as in *Troilus and Cressida* or *Othello*. The tragic ending of *Romeo and Juliet* underscores the observation made by a vexed lover in *A Midsummer Night's Dream* that "The course of true love never did run smooth" (1.1.134). True love in *Romeo and Juliet*, as in *A Midsummer Night's Dream*, is destined to be crossed by differences in blood or family background, differences in age, arbitrary choices of family or friends, or uncontrollable catastrophes, such as war, death, and sickness. Love is thus, as in *A Midsummer Night's Dream*, "momentary as a sound, / Swift as a shadow, short as any dream," swallowed up by darkness; "So quick bright things come to confusion" (1.1.143–9). A dominant pattern of imagery in *Romeo and Juliet* evokes a corresponding sense of suddenness and violence: fire, gunpowder, hot blood, lightning, the inconstant wind, the storm-tossed or shipwrecked vessel. The beauty of a love that is so threatened and so fragile is intensified by the brevity of the experience. A tragic outcome therefore affirms the uniqueness and pristine quality of youthful ecstasy. The flowering and fading of a joy "too rich for use, for earth too dear" (1.5.48), does not so much condemn the unfeeling world as welcome the martyrdom of literally dying for love.

As protagonists, Romeo and Juliet lack tragic stature by any classical definition or in terms of the medieval convention of the Fall of Princes. The lovers are not extraordinary except in their passionate attachment to one another. They belong to prominent merchant families rather than to the nobility. They (especially Juliet) are very young, more so than any other of Shakespeare's tragic protagonists, and are indeed younger than most couples marrying in England at the time the play was written; Juliet is not yet fourteen (1.2.9, 1.3.13). Romeo and Juliet's dilemma of parental opposition is of the domestic sort often found in comedy. In fact, several characters in the play partly resemble the conventional character types of the Latin comic playwright Plautus or of Italian neoclassical comedy: the domineering father who insists that his daughter marry according to his choice, the unwelcome rival wooer, the garrulous and bawdy nurse, and, of course, the lovers. The Italian *novella*, to which Shakespeare often turned for his plots, made use of these same types and paid little attention to the classical precept that protagonists in a tragic story ought to be persons of high rank who are humbled through some inner flaw, or hamartia.

The story of Romeo and Juliet goes back ultimately to the fifth-century A.D. Greek romance of *Ephesiaca*, in which we find the motif of the sleeping potion as a means of escaping an unwelcome marriage. Masuccio of Salerno, in his *Il Novellino*, in 1476, combined the narrative of the heroine's deathlike trance and seeming burial alive with that of the hero's tragic failure to receive news from the friar that she is still alive. Luigi da Porto, in his *novella* (c. 1530), set the scene at Verona, provided the names of Romeo and Giulietta for the hero and heroine, added the account of their feuding families, the Montecchi and Cappelletti, introduced the killing of Tybalt (Theobaldo), and provided other important details. Luigi's version was followed by Matteo Bandello's famous *Novelle* of 1554, which was translated into French by Pierre Boaistuau (1559). The French version became the source for Arthur Brooke's long narrative poem in English, *The Tragical History of Romeus and Juliet* (1562). Brooke mentions having seen a play on the subject, but it is doubtful that Shakespeare knew this old play or, if he did know it, made use of it. Brooke's poem was his chief and probably only source. Shakespeare has condensed Brooke's action from nine months to less than a week, has greatly expanded the role of Mercutio, and has given to the Nurse a warmth and humorous richness not found in the usual Italian duenna, or *balia*. He has also tidied up the Friar's immorality and deleted the antipapal tone. Inheriting from Brooke a cautionary narrative against unruly yielding to sexual passion, in the homiletic vein of Puritan preachers, Shakespeare instead sympathizes with the perils of young lovers whose desires are unappreciated by an unfeeling world. Throughout all these changes, Shakespeare retains Brooke's romantic (rather than classically tragic) conception of love overwhelmed by external obstacles.

Like the romantic comedies, *Romeo and Juliet* is often funny and bawdy. Samson and Gregory in the first scene are slapstick cowards, hiding behind the law and daring to quarrel only when reinforcements arrive. The Nurse delights us with her earthy recollections of the day she weaned Juliet: the child tasting "the wormwood on the nipple / Of my dug" (1.3.31–2), the warm Italian sun, an earthquake, the Nurse's husband telling his lame but often-repeated bawdy joke about women falling on their backs. Mercutio employs his inventive and sardonic humor to twit Romeo for lovesickness and the Nurse for her pomposity. She, in turn, scolds Peter and plagues Juliet (who is breathlessly awaiting news from Romeo) with a history of her back ailments. Mercutio and the Nurse are among Shakespeare's bawdiest characters. Their wry and salacious view of love contrasts with the nobly innocent and yet physically passionate love of Romeo and Juliet. Mercutio and the Nurse cannot take part in the play's denouement; one dies, misinterpreting Romeo's appeasement of Tybalt, and the other proves insensitive to Juliet's depth of feeling. Yet the disappearance of these engaging companions takes from the play some of its vitality and most of its funniness. The death of Tybalt turns the play from comedy to tragedy.

The lovers, too, are at first well suited to Shakespearean romantic comedy. When we meet Romeo, he is not in love with Juliet at all, despite the play's title, but is mooning over a "hardhearted wench" (in Mercutio's words) named Rosaline. This "goddess" appropriately never appears in the play; she is almost a disembodied idea in Romeo's mind, a scornful beauty like Phoebe in *As You Like It*. Romeo's love for her is tedious and self-pitying, like that of the conventional wooer in a sonnet sequence by Francesco Petrarch or one of his imitators. Juliet, although not yet fourteen, must change all this by teaching Romeo the nature of true love. She will have none of his shopworn clichés learned in the service of Rosaline, his flowery protestations and swearing by the moon, lest they prove to be love's perjuries. With her innocent candor, she insists (like many heroines of the romantic comedies) on dispelling the mask of pretense that lovers too often show one another. "Capulet" and "Montague" are mere labels, not the inner self. Although Juliet would have been more coy, she confesses, had she known that Romeo was overhearing her, she will now "prove more true / Than those that have more cunning to be strange" (2.2.100–1). She is more practical than he in assessing danger and making plans. Later she also proves herself remarkably able to bear misfortune.

The comedy of the play's first half is, to be sure, overshadowed by the certainty of disaster. The opening chorus plainly warns us that the lovers will die. They are "star-crossed," and they speak of themselves as such. Romeo fears "Some consequence yet hanging in the stars" when he reluctantly goes to the Capulets' feast (1.4.107); after he has slain Tybalt, he cries, "Oh, I am fortune's fool!" (3.1.135); and, at the news of Juliet's supposed death, he proclaims, "Then I defy you, stars!" (5.1.24). Yet in what sense are Romeo and Juliet "star-crossed"? The concept is deliberately broad in this play, encompassing many factors, such as hatred, bumbling, bad luck, and simple lack of awareness.

The first scene presents feuding as a major cause in the tragedy. The quarrel between the two families is so ancient that the original motives are no longer even discussed. Inspired by the "fiery" Tybalt, factionalism pursues its mindless course, despite the efforts of the Prince to end it. Although the elders of both families talk of peace, they call for their swords quickly enough when a fray begins. Still, this senseless hatred does not lead to tragedy until its effects are fatally complicated through misunderstanding. With poignant irony, good intentions are repeatedly undermined by lack of knowledge. We can see why Juliet does not tell her family of her secret marriage with a presumably hated Montague, but, in fact, Capulet has accepted Romeo as a guest in his house under the terms of chivalric hospitality, praising him as a "virtuous and well governed youth" (1.5.69). For all his dictatorial ways, and the manifest advantages he may see in marrying his daughter to an aristocrat like Paris, Capulet would, of course, never propose the match if he knew his daughter to be married already. Not knowing of Juliet's marriage, he and his wife can only interpret her refusal to marry Paris as caprice. Count Paris himself is victim of this tragedy of unawareness. He is an eminently suitable wooer for Juliet, rich and nobly born, considerate, peace-loving, and deeply fond of Juliet (as he shows by his private and sincere grief at her tomb). Certainly, he would never intentionally woo a married woman. Not knowing, he plays the unattractive role of the rival wooer and dies for it. Similarly, Mercutio cannot understand Romeo's seemingly craven behavior toward Tybalt and so begins the duel that leads to Romeo's banishment. The final scene, with Friar Laurence's retelling of the story, allows us to see the survivors confronted with what they have all unknowingly done.

Chance, or accident, plays a role of importance equal to that of hatred and unawareness. An outbreak of the plague prevents Friar John from conveying Friar Laurence's letter to Romeo at Mantua. Friar Laurence, going hurriedly to the Capulets' tomb, arrives in time for Juliet's awakening but some minutes after Romeo has killed Paris and taken poison. Juliet awakens only moments later. The Watch comes just too late to prevent her suicide. Friar Laurence expresses well the sense of frustration at plans gone awry by such narrow margins: "what an unkind hour / Is guilty of this lamentable chance!" (5.3.145–6). Earlier, Capulet's decision to move the wedding date up one day has crucially affected the timing. Human miscalculation contributes also to the catastrophe: Mercutio is killed under Romeo's arm, and Friar Laurence wonders unhappily if any of his complicated plans "Miscarried by my fault" (5.3.267). Character and human decision play a part in this tragedy, for Romeo should not have dueled with Tybalt, no matter what the provocation. In choosing to kill Tybalt, he has deliberately cast aside as "effeminate" the gentle and forgiving qualities he has learned from his love of Juliet (3.1.113) and thus is guilty of a rash and self-destructive action. To ascribe the cause of the tragedy in Aristotelian fashion to his and Juliet's impulsiveness is, however, to ignore much of the rest of the play.

Instead, the ending of the play brings a pattern out of the seeming welter of mistakes and animosities. "A greater power than we can contradict / Hath thwarted our intents," says Friar Laurence, suggesting that the seeming bad luck of the delayed letter was, in fact, the intent of a mysterious higher intelligence (5.3.153–4). Prince Escalus, too, finds a necessary meaning in the tragic event. "See what a scourge is laid upon your hate," he admonishes the Montagues and Capulets, "That heaven finds means to kill your joys with love." Romeo and Juliet are "Poor sacrifices of our enmity" (lines 292–304). As the Prologue had foretold, their deaths will "bury their parents' strife"; the families' feud is a stub-

born evil force "Which, but their children's end, naught could remove." Order is preciously restored; the price is great, but the sacrifice nonetheless confirms a sense of a larger intention in what had appeared to be simply hatred and misfortune. Throughout the play, love and hate are interrelated opposites, yoked through the rhetorical device of oxymoron, or inherent contradiction. Romeo apostrophizes, "O brawling love, O loving hate" (1.1.176), and Juliet later echoes his words: "My only love sprung from my only hate" (1.5.139). This paradox expresses a conflict in humankind, as in the universe itself. "Two such opposèd kings encamp them still / In man as well as herbs," says Friar Laurence, "grace and rude will" (2.3.27–8). Hatred is a condition of our corrupted wills, of our fall from grace, and it attempts to destroy what is gracious in human beings. In this cosmic strife, love must pay the sacrifice, as Romeo and Juliet do with their lives, but, because their deaths are finally perceived as the cost of so much hatred, the two families come to terms with their collective guilt and resolve henceforth to be worthy of the sacrifice.

Structurally, *Romeo and Juliet* gives considerable prominence to the feuding of the two families. Public scenes occur at key points—at beginning, middle, and end (1.1, 3.1, and 5.3)—and each such scene concerns violence and its consequences. The play begins with a brawl. Tybalt is a baleful presence in 1.1 and 3.1, implacably bent on vengeance. The three public scenes are alike, too, in that they bring into confrontation the entire families of Capulets and Montagues, who call for swords and demand reprisal from the state for what they themselves have set in motion. Prince Escalus dominates these three public scenes. He must offer judgment in each, giving the families fair warning, then exiling Romeo for Tybalt's death, and finally counseling the families on the meaning of their collective tragedy. He is a spokesman for public order and security ("Mercy but murders, pardoning those that kill," 3.1.196), even though he is also unable to prevent the tragedy. He stands above the conflict and yet is affected by it; his own kinsman, Mercutio, is one of the casualties. For all his dignity and impartiality, Escalus's official function is somehow tangential to the central emotional experience of the play. The law does not provide a remedy. Still, it can preside and arbitrate. To Escalus is given the final speech promising both punishment and pardon, and it is he who sums up the paradoxical interdependence of love and hate. Although the morning after the catastrophe brings with it sorrow, it also brings peace, however "glooming." Escalus is master of ceremonies for a restored order through which the families and we are reconciled to what has occurred.

In good part, the public scenes of the play serve to frame the love plot and the increasing isolation of the separated lovers, but these public scenes have a function of their own to the extent that the tragedy has touched and altered everyone. The final tableau is not the kiss of the dying lovers but the handclasp of the reconciled fathers. The long, last public ceremonial is important because, although the private catastrophe of the lovers is unalterably complete, recognition occurs only when the Friar recounts at great length to all the community the story we already know. As we watch the bereaved families responding with shock to the story of Romeo and Juliet's tragedy, we understand the reason for its length: only when it is too late do the families begin to comprehend their own complicity in the disaster that has occurred. This recognition is not that of the protagonists, as in the Aristotelian conception of recognition, nor does it accompany a reversal in the love tragedy; that reversal already has taken place in Romeo's banishment and the lovers' deaths. This lack of correspondence with an Aristotelian definition of tragedy is not, however, a structural flaw; rather, it is a manifestation of the dual focus of the tragedy on the lovers and on all Verona. The city itself is a kind of protagonist, suffering through its own violence and coming at last to the sad comfort that wisdom brings.

The timeless nature of a tragic story about young lovers has resulted in its being an irresistible vehicle for modern updatings in the theater and in film, many of them highly successful in bringing the play into the lives of modern and young audiences. Productions in this vein have raised important questions about the protagonists' attitudes toward love and the nature of the social environment in which their tragedy occurs. The play's vivid bawdry invites an atmosphere of hedonism that can be understood, implicitly at least, in terms of the sexual revolution of the 1960s and afterwards. The boy actor who originally played Juliet on Shakespeare's stage has been replaced by Olivia Hussey, for example, in Franco Zeffirelli's popular film of 1968; Hussey is so gorgeously appealing in her first long night-time conversation with Romeo that his insistent "Oh, wilt thou leave me so unsatisfied?" takes on new urgency. Subsequently, the film briefly shows the lovers in bed,

unclothed. Mercutio is sometimes portrayed as homosexual: mutedly so in the Zeffirelli film, aggressively so in Terry Hands's 1973 production at Stratford-upon-Avon, and flamboyantly so in Baz Luhrmann's immensely successful film, *Romeo + Juliet*, of 1996. In this last version, Mercutio is an African American drag queen, while Friar Laurence is a New Age priest. Juliet's mother in this same film is hilarious as a pill-popping, chain-smoking, and hard-drinking society dame slithering her ectomorphically slim body into a Cleopatra outfit for the huge masked ball that she and her nouveau riche husband are putting on in their tastelessly expensive block-long mansion—just the sort of parents whom one can count on not to understand their daughter. Luhrmann's Nurse is an Hispanic woman bellowing "Huliet! Huliet!" to remind us that the film is set in a southern United States city like Los Angeles or Miami. (It was actually filmed in Mexico City.) The street violence is also Hispanic, with rival gangs setting fire to gas stations and shooting automatic weapons during high-speed car chases. This updating of the violence with which the play begins owes some of its inspiration, presumably, to Leonard Bernstein's *West Side Story* (1957), set in Spanish Harlem.

Such innovations are at their best when they point to the play's insistent dramatization of violence and love in conflict. What responsibility does society bear for youthful tragedy when the models for behavior available to young people are what they are in today's world? How can a young man like Romeo escape the peer pressures of gang loyalties and macho stereotypes? Romeo struggles against these pressures in his crucial moment of decision; knowing that Juliet has taught him a better way, he yet succumbs to the mores of his tribe and to his own need to revenge on Tybalt the death of Mercutio. In these modern productions, as in the play itself, the violent response is too believable. As Friar Laurence says, "grace and rude will" do battle within the human psyche, too often with tragic outcome, and young love must pay the price.

Romeo and Juliet

[*Dramatis Personae*

CHORUS

ESCALUS, *Prince of Verona*
MERCUTIO, *the Prince's kinsman and Romeo's friend*
PARIS, *a young count and kinsman of the Prince*
PAGE *to Count Paris*

MONTAGUE
MONTAGUE'S WIFE
ROMEO, *son of the Montagues*
BENVOLIO, *Montague's nephew and Romeo's friend*
ABRAHAM, *a servant of the Montague household*
BALTHASAR, *a servant of the Montague household
    attending Romeo*

CAPULET
CAPULET'S WIFE
JULIET, *daughter of the Capulets*
NURSE
TYBALT, *nephew of Capulet's Wife*

PETRUCHIO, *Capulet's kinsman*
SECOND CAPULET, *an old man, Capulet's kinsman*
PETER, *a servant of the Capulet household attending the
    Nurse*
SAMSON,
GREGORY,
ANTHONY,
POTPAN,   *servants of the Capulet household*
CLOWN or SERVANT,
Other SERVANTS,

FRIAR LAURENCE,   *Franciscan friars*
FRIAR JOHN,

APOTHECARY
Three MUSICIANS (*Simon Catling, Hugh Rebeck, and James
    Soundpost*)
Three WATCHMEN

Citizens, Maskers, Torchbearers, Guards, Servants, and
    Attendants

SCENE: *Verona; Mantua*]

The Prologue

[Enter Chorus.]

CHORUS
Two households, both alike in dignity,   1
    In fair Verona, where we lay our scene,
From ancient grudge break to new mutiny,   3
    Where civil blood makes civil hands unclean.   4
From forth the fatal loins of these two foes
    A pair of star-crossed lovers take their life;   6
Whose misadventured piteous overthrows   7
Doth with their death bury their parents' strife.
The fearful passage of their death-marked love,   9
    And the continuance of their parents' rage,
Which, but their children's end, naught could remove,
    Is now the two hours' traffic of our stage;   12
The which if you with patient ears attend,
What here shall miss, our toil shall strive to mend.   14
                                                    [Exit.]

❖

Prologue.
1–14 (The Prologue is in the form of a sonnet.)
1 dignity rank, status   **3 mutiny** strife, discord   **4 Where . . .
unclean** where citizens' hands uncivilly are stained in civil strife with
their fellow citizens' blood.   **6 star-crossed** thwarted by destiny, by
adverse stars   **7 misadventured** unlucky

9 passage progress   **12 two hours' traffic** A conventional way of
referring to the length of stage performances in the early modern
period, not to be taken too literally, but indicative of a brisk pace
14 What . . . mend what is defective or inadequate in the short summary I have given you here, the actors' efforts in the following two
hours will amply and fully make clear.

[1.1]

Enter Samson and Gregory, with swords
and bucklers, of the house of Capulet.

SAMSON   Gregory, on my word, we'll not carry coals.   1
GREGORY   No, for then we should be colliers.   2
SAMSON   I mean, an we be in choler, we'll draw.   3
GREGORY   Ay, while you live, draw your neck out of   4
collar.   5
SAMSON   I strike quickly, being moved.   6
GREGORY   But thou art not quickly moved to strike.
SAMSON   A dog of the house of Montague moves me.   8
GREGORY   To move is to stir, and to be valiant is to
stand. Therefore, if thou art moved, thou run'st away.   10
SAMSON   A dog of that house shall move me to stand. I
will take the wall of any man or maid of Montague's.   12
GREGORY   That shows thee a weak slave, for the   13
weakest goes to the wall.   14
SAMSON   'Tis true, and therefore women, being the
weaker vessels, are ever thrust to the wall. Therefore I   16
will push Montague's men from the wall and thrust
his maids to the wall.
GREGORY   The quarrel is between our masters and us   19
their men.   20
SAMSON   'Tis all one. I will show myself a tyrant: when   21
I have fought with the men, I will be civil with the
maids—I will cut off their heads.
GREGORY   The heads of the maids?
SAMSON   Ay, the heads of the maids, or their maidenheads. Take it in what sense thou wilt.   26
GREGORY   They must take it in sense that feel it.   27
SAMSON   Me they shall feel while I am able to stand,   28
and 'tis known I am a pretty piece of flesh.   29
GREGORY   'Tis well thou art not fish; if thou hadst, thou   30
hadst been Poor John. Draw thy tool. Here comes of   31
the house of Montagues.

Enter two other Servingmen
[Abraham and another].

SAMSON   My naked weapon is out. Quarrel, I will back
thee.
GREGORY   How, turn thy back and run?
SAMSON   Fear me not.   36
GREGORY   No, marry. I fear thee!   37
SAMSON   Let us take the law of our side. Let them   38
begin.
GREGORY   I will frown as I pass by, and let them take it
as they list.   41
SAMSON   Nay, as they dare. I will bite my thumb at   42
them, which is disgrace to them if they bear it.
[Samson makes taunting gestures.]
ABRAHAM   Do you bite your thumb at us, sir?
SAMSON   I do bite my thumb, sir.
ABRAHAM   Do you bite your thumb at us, sir?
SAMSON *[aside to Gregory]*   Is the law of our side if I
say ay?
GREGORY *[aside to Samson]*   No.
SAMSON *[to Abraham]*   No, sir, I do not bite my thumb
at you, sir, but I bite my thumb, sir.
GREGORY   Do you quarrel, sir?
ABRAHAM   Quarrel, sir? No, sir.
SAMSON   But if you do, sir, I am for you. I serve as good
a man as you.
ABRAHAM   No better.
SAMSON   Well, sir.

Enter Benvolio.

GREGORY *[to Samson]*   Say "better." Here comes one of   58
my master's kinsmen.   59
SAMSON *[to Abraham]*   Yes, better, sir.
ABRAHAM   You lie.
SAMSON   Draw, if you be men. Gregory, remember thy
washing blow.   *They fight.*   63
BENVOLIO   Part, fools!
Put up your swords. You know not what you do.

Enter Tybalt [with sword drawn].

TYBALT
What, art thou drawn among these heartless hinds?   66
Turn thee, Benvolio. Look upon thy death.
BENVOLIO
I do but keep the peace. Put up thy sword,
Or manage it to part these men with me.   69
TYBALT
What, drawn and talk of peace? I hate the word
As I hate hell, all Montagues, and thee.
Have at thee, coward!   *[They fight.]*   72

Enter three or four Citizens with clubs
or partisans.

1.1. Location: Verona. A public place.
0.2 *bucklers* small shields   **1 carry coals** i.e., endure insults.   **2 colliers**
(Coal carriers were regarded as dirty and of evil repute.)   **3 an** if.
choler anger (produced by one of the four humors).   **draw** draw
swords.   **5 collar** i.e., hangman's noose. (With pun on *colliers* and
choler.)   **6 moved** i.e., to anger. (With pun in next line.)   **8 moves**
incites   **10 stand** i.e., stand one's ground.   **12 take the wall** take the
cleaner side of the walk nearest the wall, thus forcing others out into
the gutter   **13–14 the weakest . . . wall** (A proverb expressing the
idea that the weakest are always forced to give way.)   **16 weaker**
vessels (Saint Paul bids husbands give honor to their wives "as unto
the weaker vessel," 1 Peter 3:7.)   **thrust to the wall** (With suggestion
of amorous assault.)   **19–20 between . . . men** i.e., between the males
of one household and the males of the other household; we have no
quarrel with the women.   **21 one** the same.   **26 what sense** whatever meaning   **27 They . . . feel it** i.e., It is the maids who must
receive by way of physical sensation (*sense*) what I have to offer,
because they are the ones who can feel it.   **28 stand** (With suggestion
of "have an erection," continued in the next few lines in *draw thy tool*
and *my naked weapon is out.*)   **29–30 flesh . . . fish** (Refers to the
proverbial phrase, "neither fish nor flesh.")   **31 Poor John** hake
salted and dried—a poor Lenten kind of food. (Probably with a
bawdy suggestion of sexual insufficiency.)   **comes of** i.e., come
members of

36 Fear Mistrust. (But Gregory deliberately misunderstands in the
next line, saying, in effect, "No indeed, do you think I'd be afraid of
you?")   **37 marry** i.e., indeed. (Originally an oath, "by the Virgin
Mary.")   **38 take the law of** have the law on   **41 list** please.   **42 bite**
my thumb i.e., make an insulting and probably obscene gesture
58–9 one . . . kinsmen i.e., Tybalt, who is approaching. (Not Benvolio,
who has just entered unobserved by the servingmen.)   **63 washing**
slashing with great force   **66 heartless hinds** cowardly menials.
69 manage use   **72 Have at thee** i.e., On guard, here I come
72.2 *partisans* long-handled spears.

CITIZENS
Clubs, bills, and partisans! Strike! Beat them down!   73
Down with the Capulets! Down with the Montagues!   74

Enter old Capulet in his gown, and his Wife.

CAPULET
What noise is this? Give me my long sword, ho!   75

CAPULET'S WIFE
A crutch, a crutch! Why call you for a sword?

CAPULET
My sword, I say! Old Montague is come
And flourishes his blade in spite of me.   78

Enter old Montague and his Wife.

MONTAGUE
Thou villain Capulet!—Hold me not; let me go.

MONTAGUE'S WIFE
Thou shalt not stir one foot to seek a foe.   80

Enter Prince Escalus, with his train.

PRINCE
Rebellious subjects, enemies to peace,
Profaners of this neighbor-stainèd steel—   82
Will they not hear? What, ho! You men, you beasts,
That quench the fire of your pernicious rage
With purple fountains issuing from your veins,   85
On pain of torture, from those bloody hands
Throw your mistempered weapons to the ground   87
And hear the sentence of your movèd prince.   88
Three civil brawls, bred of an airy word,   89
By thee, old Capulet, and Montague,
Have thrice disturbed the quiet of our streets
And made Verona's ancient citizens
Cast by their grave-beseeming ornaments   93
To wield old partisans in hands as old,
Cankered with peace, to part your cankered hate.   95
If ever you disturb our streets again
Your lives shall pay the forfeit of the peace.   97
For this time all the rest depart away.
You, Capulet, shall go along with me,
And Montague, come you this afternoon,
To know our farther pleasure in this case,
To old Freetown, our common judgment-place.   102
Once more, on pain of death, all men depart.
                *Exeunt [all but Montague, Montague's Wife,
                                        and Benvolio].*

MONTAGUE
Who set this ancient quarrel new abroach?   104
Speak, nephew, were you by when it began?   105

BENVOLIO
Here were the servants of your adversary,
And yours, close fighting ere I did approach.
I drew to part them. In the instant came
The fiery Tybalt with his sword prepared,   109
Which, as he breathed defiance to my ears,
He swung about his head and cut the winds
Who, nothing hurt withal, hissed him in scorn.   112
While we were interchanging thrusts and blows,
Came more and more, and fought on part and part   114
Till the Prince came, who parted either part.   115

MONTAGUE'S WIFE
Oh, where is Romeo? Saw you him today?
Right glad I am he was not at this fray.

BENVOLIO
Madam, an hour before the worshiped sun
Peered forth the golden window of the east,   119
A troubled mind drave me to walk abroad,   120
Where, underneath the grove of sycamore
That westward rooteth from this city side,   122
So early walking did I see your son.
Towards him I made, but he was ware of me   124
And stole into the covert of the wood.   125
I, measuring his affections by my own,   126
Which then most sought where most might not be
    found,   127
Being one too many by my weary self,
Pursued my humor, not pursuing his,   129
And gladly shunned who gladly fled from me.   130

MONTAGUE
Many a morning hath he there been seen,
With tears augmenting the fresh morning's dew,
Adding to clouds more clouds with his deep sighs;
But all so soon as the all-cheering sun
Should in the farthest east begin to draw
The shady curtains from Aurora's bed,   136
Away from light steals home my heavy son   137
And private in his chamber pens himself,
Shuts up his windows, locks fair daylight out,
And makes himself an artificial night.
Black and portentous must this humor prove
Unless good counsel may the cause remove.

BENVOLIO
My noble uncle, do you know the cause?

MONTAGUE
I neither know it nor can learn of him.

---

73 Clubs rallying cry, summoning apprentices with their clubs.
bills long-handled spears with hooked blades   **74.1** *gown* nightgown, dressing gown   **75 long sword** heavy, old-fashioned sword
78 spite defiance, despite   **80.1** *train* retinue.   **82 Profaners . . . steel**
you who profane your weapons by staining them with neighbors'
blood   **85 purple** bloody, dark red   **87 mistempered** (1) having been
tempered, or hardened, in hot blood rather than cold water (2) malignant, ill-tempered   **88 movèd** angry   **89 airy** flippant, saucy
93 grave-beseeming ornaments i.e., staffs and other appurtenances
suited to wise old age   **95 Cankered . . . cankered** corroded (from
disuse) . . . malignant   **97 Your . . . peace** death will be the penalty for
breaking the peace.   **102 Freetown** (Brooke's translation, in his poem
Romeus and Juliet, of *Villa Franca*, as found in the Italian story.)
common public

104 set . . . abroach reopened this old quarrel, set it flowing.   **105 by**
near   **109 prepared** drawn, ready   **112 Who . . . withal** which winds,
not at all injured thereby   **114 on part and part** on one side and the
other   **115 either part** both parties.   **119 forth** from forth   **120 drave
. . . abroad** drove me to take a walk   **122 That . . . side** that grows on
the west side of this city   **124 made** moved.   **ware** wary, aware
125 covert cover, hiding place   **126 affections** wishes, inclination
127 Which . . . found which then chiefly desired a place where I
might be alone   **129 humor** mood   **130 who** him who   **136 Aurora**
goddess of dawn   **137 heavy** (1) sad (2) the opposite of *light*.   **son**
(punning on *sun*, line 134)

BENVOLIO

Have you importuned him by any means?   145

MONTAGUE

Both by myself and many other friends.
But he, his own affections' counselor,
Is to himself—I will not say how true,   148
But to himself so secret and so close,   149
So far from sounding and discovery,   150
As is the bud bit with an envious worm   151
Ere he can spread his sweet leaves to the air
Or dedicate his beauty to the sun.
Could we but learn from whence his sorrows grow,
We would as willingly give cure as know.

       Enter Romeo.

BENVOLIO

See where he comes. So please you, step aside.   156
I'll know his grievance or be much denied.

MONTAGUE

I would thou wert so happy by thy stay   158
To hear true shrift.—Come, madam, let's away.   159

      Exeunt [Montague and his Wife].

BENVOLIO

Good morrow, cousin.

ROMEO   Is the day so young?   160

BENVOLIO

But new struck nine.

ROMEO   Ay me! Sad hours seem long.
Was that my father that went hence so fast?

BENVOLIO

It was. What sadness lengthens Romeo's hours?

ROMEO

Not having that which, having, makes them short.

BENVOLIO   In love?

ROMEO   Out—

BENVOLIO   Of love?

ROMEO

Out of her favor where I am in love.

BENVOLIO

Alas, that Love, so gentle in his view,   169
Should be so tyrannous and rough in proof!   170

ROMEO

Alas, that Love, whose view is muffled still,   171
Should without eyes see pathways to his will!   172
Where shall we dine?—Oh, me! What fray was here?
Yet tell me not, for I have heard it all.
Here's much to do with hate, but more with love.
Why, then, O brawling love, O loving hate,
O anything of nothing first create,   177
O heavy lightness, serious vanity,
Misshapen chaos of well-seeming forms,
Feather of lead, bright smoke, cold fire, sick health,

Still-waking sleep, that is not what it is!   181
This love feel I, that feel no love in this.
Dost thou not laugh?

BENVOLIO   No, coz, I rather weep.   183

ROMEO

Good heart, at what?

BENVOLIO   At thy good heart's oppression.

ROMEO

Why, such is love's transgression.
Griefs of mine own lie heavy in my breast,
Which thou wilt propagate, to have it pressed   187
With more of thine. This love that thou hast shown   188
Doth add more grief to too much of mine own.
Love is a smoke made with the fume of sighs;
Being purged, a fire sparkling in lovers' eyes;   191
Being vexed, a sea nourished with lovers' tears.
What is it else? A madness most discreet,   193
A choking gall, and a preserving sweet.
Farewell, my coz.

BENVOLIO   Soft! I will go along.   195
An if you leave me so, you do me wrong.   196

ROMEO

Tut, I have lost myself. I am not here.
This is not Romeo; he's some other where.

BENVOLIO

Tell me in sadness, who is that you love?   199

ROMEO   What, shall I groan and tell thee?

BENVOLIO

Groan? Why, no, but sadly tell me who.   201

ROMEO

Bid a sick man in sadness make his will—
A word ill urged to one that is so ill!   203
In sadness, cousin, I do love a woman.

BENVOLIO

I aimed so near when I supposed you loved.

ROMEO

A right good markman! And she's fair I love.   206

BENVOLIO

A right fair mark, fair coz, is soonest hit.   207

ROMEO

Well, in that hit you miss. She'll not be hit
With Cupid's arrow. She hath Dian's wit,   209
And, in strong proof of chastity well armed,   210
From Love's weak childish bow she lives unharmed.
She will not stay the siege of loving terms,   212
Nor bide th'encounter of assailing eyes,   213
Nor ope her lap to saint-seducing gold.
Oh, she is rich in beauty, only poor
That when she dies, with beauty dies her store.   216

---

181 Still-waking continually awake   **183 coz** cousin, kinsman
187–8 propagate . . . thine increase by having it, i.e., my own grief,
oppressed or made still heavier with your grief on my account.
(The image of propagating and pressing is appropriately sexual.)
191 purged i.e., of smoke   **193 discreet** judicious, prudent   **195 Soft!**
i.e., Wait a moment!   **196 An if** If   **199 sadness** seriousness.   **is that**
is it that   **201 sadly** seriously. (But Romeo plays on the word, and
on *in sadness*, in the sense of "sorrowfully.")   **203 A word** i.e., *sadly*
or *in sadness*—too sad a word, says Romeo, for a melancholy lover
206 fair beautiful   **207 fair mark** clear, distinct target   **209 Dian's**
Diana was huntress and goddess of chastity   **210 proof** armor   **212
stay** submit to   **213 bide** abide, endure   **216 store** wealth. (She will
die without children, and therefore her beauty will die with her.)

---

145 any means every means possible.   **148 true** i.e., wise in counseling himself   **149 close** secretive   **150 sounding** being fathomed (to
discover deep or inner secrets)   **151 envious** malicious   **156 So
please you** If you please   **158 happy** fortunate, successful   **159 To** as
to.   **shrift** confession.   **160 cousin** kinsman.   **169 Love** Cupid.
view appearance   **170 in proof** in reality, in experience.   **171 view . . .
still** sight is blindfolded always. (Love is blind.)   **172 to his will** to
what he wants.   **177 create** created

BENVOLIO
Then she hath sworn that she will still live chaste?   217

ROMEO
She hath, and in that sparing makes huge waste,   218
For beauty starved with her severity   219
Cuts beauty off from all posterity.
She is too fair, too wise, wisely too fair,
To merit bliss by making me despair.   222
She hath forsworn to love, and in that vow   223
Do I live dead, that live to tell it now.

BENVOLIO
Be ruled by me. Forget to think of her.

ROMEO
Oh, teach me how I should forget to think!

BENVOLIO
By giving liberty unto thine eyes:
Examine other beauties.

ROMEO   'Tis the way
To call hers, exquisite, in question more.   229
These happy masks that kiss fair ladies' brows,
Being black, puts us in mind they hide the fair.
He that is strucken blind cannot forget
The precious treasure of his eyesight lost.
Show me a mistress that is passing fair: 234
What doth her beauty serve but as a note
Where I may read who passed that passing fair?   236
Farewell. Thou canst not teach me to forget.

BENVOLIO
I'll pay that doctrine, or else die in debt.   *Exeunt.* 238

❖

[1.2]

Enter Capulet, County Paris, and the Clown
[a Servingman].

CAPULET
But Montague is bound as well as I,   1
In penalty alike, and 'tis not hard, I think,
For men so old as we to keep the peace.

PARIS
Of honorable reckoning are you both,   4
And pity 'tis you lived at odds so long.
But now, my lord, what say you to my suit?

CAPULET
But saying o'er what I have said before: 7
My child is yet a stranger in the world;
She hath not seen the change of fourteen years.
Let two more summers wither in their pride
Ere we may think her ripe to be a bride.

PARIS
Younger than she are happy mothers made.

CAPULET
And too soon marred are those so early made.
The earth hath swallowed all my hopes but she;
She is the hopeful lady of my earth.   15
But woo her, gentle Paris, get her heart;
My will to her consent is but a part;
And, she agreed, within her scope of choice   18
Lies my consent and fair-according voice.   19
This night I hold an old accustomed feast,   20
Whereto I have invited many a guest
Such as I love; and you among the store,   22
One more, most welcome, makes my number more.
At my poor house look to behold this night
Earth-treading stars that make dark heaven light.
Such comfort as do lusty young men feel   26
When well-appareled April on the heel   27
Of limping winter treads, even such delight
Among fresh fennel buds shall you this night   29
Inherit at my house. Hear all, all see,   30
And like her most whose merit most shall be;
Which on more view of many, mine, being one,   32
May stand in number, though in reck'ning none.   33
Come, go with me. [*To the Servingman, giving a paper*]
    Go, sirrah, trudge about   34
Through fair Verona; find those persons out
Whose names are written there, and to them say,
My house and welcome on their pleasure stay.   37
                                    Exit [with Paris].

SERVINGMAN   Find them out whose names are written
here! It is written that the shoemaker should meddle   39
with his yard and the tailor with his last, the fisher   40
with his pencil, and the painter with his nets; but I am   41
sent to find those persons whose names are here writ,   42
and can never find what names the writing person   43
hath here writ. I must to the learned.—In good time!   44

Enter Benvolio and Romeo.

---

217 **still** always   218 **sparing** miserliness   219 **starved with** killed by
222 **To . . . despair** to achieve her own salvation through chaste living
while driving me to the spiritually dangerous state of despair.
223 **forsworn to** renounced, repudiated   229 **in question more** even
more keenly to mind, into consideration.   234 **mistress** i.e., eligible
young woman.   **passing** surpassingly   236 **passed** surpassed
238 **I'll . . . debt** i.e., I'll fulfill my obligation to do that, or feel I have
failed as a friend.
1.2. Location: Verona.
0.1 *County* Count   **1 bound** legally obligated (to keep the peace)
4 reckoning estimation, repute   **7 o'er** again

15 **the hopeful . . . earth** i.e., my heir and hope for posterity. (*Earth*
includes property and lands.)   **18 she** if she be   **19 according** agreeing   **20 old accustomed** traditional   **22 store** group   **26 lusty** lively
27 well-appareled newly clothed in green   **29 fennel** flowering herb
thought to have the power of awakening passion   **30 Inherit** possess
32–3 Which . . . none i.e., when you have looked over many ladies,
my daughter, being one of them, may be numerically counted among
the lot, but you will not think her worth your notice. (Capulet refers
to the proverbial saying, "one is no number.")   **34 sirrah** (Customary
form of address to servants.)   **37 on . . . stay** wait to serve their pleasure.   **39–41 It is . . . nets** i.e., If a shoemaker cannot be expected to
have any skill with a *yard* (a tailor's yardstick) and conversely a tailor
with a *last* (a shoemaker's form), and similarly with a painter's *pencil*
(a paintbrush) in a fisherman's hands or a net in a painter's hands,
why should I, an illiterate servant, be expected to be able to read a
written note of invitation? (*Meddle, yard,* and *pencil* are often slang
expressions for sexual activity and the male sexual organ, but since
last and *nets* don't seem to convey sexual meaning here, the humor is
more directed at comic inappropriateness.)   **42 find** locate   **43 find**
figure out   **44 In good time** i.e., Here comes help.

BENVOLIO

Tut, man, one fire burns out another's burning,
One pain is lessened by another's anguish;   46
Turn giddy, and be holp by backward turning;   47
One desperate grief cures with another's languish.   48
Take thou some new infection to thy eye,
And the rank poison of the old will die.   50

ROMEO

Your plaintain leaf is excellent for that.   51

BENVOLIO

For what, I pray thee?

ROMEO   For your broken shin.

BENVOLIO Why, Romeo, art thou mad?

ROMEO

Not mad, but bound more than a madman is;   54
Shut up in prison, kept without my food,
Whipped and tormented and—Good e'en, good
fellow.   56

SERVINGMAN God gi' good e'en. I pray, sir, can you read?   57

ROMEO

Ay, mine own fortune in my misery.

SERVINGMAN Perhaps you have learned it without   59
book. But, I pray, can you read anything you see?   60

ROMEO

Ay, if I know the letters and the language.

SERVINGMAN Ye say honestly. Rest you merry!   62
                                              [Going.]

ROMEO   Stay, fellow, I can read.   *He reads the letter.*
"Signor Martino and his wife and daughters,
County Anselme and his beauteous sisters,
The lady widow of Vitruvio,
Signor Placentio and his lovely nieces,
Mercutio and his brother Valentine,
Mine uncle Capulet, his wife, and daughters,
My fair niece Rosaline, and Livia,
Signor Valentio and his cousin Tybalt,
Lucio and the lively Helena."
A fair assembly. Whither should they come?

SERVINGMAN Up.

ROMEO   Whither? To supper?

SERVINGMAN To our house.

ROMEO   Whose house?

SERVINGMAN My master's.

ROMEO

Indeed, I should have asked thee that before.

SERVINGMAN Now I'll tell you without asking. My
master is the great rich Capulet; and if you be not of
the house of Montagues, I pray, come and crush a cup   82
of wine. Rest you merry!   *[Exit.]*

---

46 **another's anguish** the anguish of another pain   47 **holp . . . turning** helped by turning in the reverse direction   48 **cures . . . languish**
is cured by the suffering of a second *grief* or pain.   50 **rank** foul
51 **Your . . . that** i.e., (sardonically) Your proverbial nostrums are
about as useful in curing my real grief as is a folk remedy for minor
abrasions such as a *broken shin* (line 52) or surface wound on the leg—
that is, no use at all.   54 **bound** (The usual treatment for madness.)
56 **Good e'en** Good evening. (Used after noon.)   57 **gi'** give you
59–60 **Perhaps . . . book** (1) Perhaps that's some sort of book that
you've committed to memory (2) Misery is something one can learn
without knowing how to read.   62 **Rest you merry** i.e., Farewell.
(The servingman can see he is getting nowhere.)   82 **crush** i.e., drink

BENVOLIO

At this same ancient feast of Capulet's   84
Sups the fair Rosaline whom thou so loves,
With all the admirèd beauties of Verona.
Go thither, and with unattainted eye   87
Compare her face with some that I shall show,
And I will make thee think thy swan a crow.

ROMEO

When the devout religion of mine eye   90
  Maintains such falsehood, then turn tears to fires;   91
And these who, often drowned, could never die,   92
  Transparent heretics, be burnt for liars!   93
One fairer than my love? The all-seeing sun
Ne'er saw her match since first the world begun.

BENVOLIO

Tut, you saw her fair, none else being by,
Herself poised with herself in either eye;   97
But in that crystal scales let there be weighed   98
Your lady's love against some other maid
That I will show you shining at this feast,
And she shall scant show well that now seems best.   101

ROMEO

I'll go along, no such sight to be shown,
But to rejoice in splendor of mine own.   *[Exeunt.]* 103

❖

[1.3]

Enter Capulet's Wife and Nurse.

WIFE

Nurse, where's my daughter? Call her forth to me.

NURSE

Now, by my maidenhead at twelve year old,
I bade her come. What, lamb! What, ladybird!   3
God forbid, where's this girl? What, Juliet!   4

Enter Juliet.

JULIET   How now? Who calls?

NURSE   Your mother.

JULIET

Madam, I am here. What is your will?

WIFE

This is the matter.—Nurse, give leave awhile,   8
We must talk in secret.—Nurse, come back again;
I have remembered me, thou's hear our counsel.   10
Thou knowest my daughter's of a pretty age.

---

84 **ancient** customary   87 **unattainted** unbiased   90–3 **When . . .
liars!** (Romeo, recalling that persons suspected of witchcraft were
sometimes thrown into water to see if they would drown or float, and
that those who did not drown were declared witches and burned at
the stake, protests that whenever he is a heretic in love by looking at
some woman other than Rosaline he should be similarly burned by
having his own tears turn into flames, since he will have shown that
his flood of tears could not drown him, i.e., was insufficient.
Transparent means "manifest," "clear.")   97 **poised** weighed, balanced   98 **crystal scales** i.e., Romeo's eyes   101 **scant** scarcely
103 **mine own** i.e., the sight of my own Rosaline.
1.3. Location: Verona. Capulet's house.
3 **ladybird** (A term of affection.)   4 **God forbid** (A mild oath.)
8 **give leave** leave us   10 **thou's** thou shalt

NURSE
Faith, I can tell her age unto an hour.
WIFE
She's not fourteen.
NURSE   I'll lay fourteen of my teeth—
And yet, to my teen be it spoken, I have but four—   14
She's not fourteen. How long is it now
To Lammastide?
WIFE   A fortnight and odd days.   16
NURSE
Even or odd, of all days in the year,
Come Lammas Eve at night shall she be fourteen.
Susan and she—God rest all Christian souls!—   19
Were of an age. Well, Susan is with God;
She was too good for me. But, as I said,
On Lammas Eve at night shall she be fourteen,
That shall she, marry, I remember it well.   23
'Tis since the earthquake now eleven years,
And she was weaned—I never shall forget it—
Of all the days of the year, upon that day;
For I had then laid wormwood to my dug,   27
Sitting in the sun under the dovehouse wall.
My lord and you were then at Mantua—
Nay, I do bear a brain! But, as I said,   30
When it did taste the wormwood on the nipple
Of my dug and felt it bitter, pretty fool,   32
To see it tetchy and fall out wi'th' dug!   33
"Shake" quoth the dovehouse. 'Twas no need, I trow,   34
To bid me trudge!   35
And since that time it is eleven years,
For then she could stand high-lone; nay, by the rood,   37
She could have run and waddled all about.
For even the day before, she broke her brow,   39
And then my husband—God be with his soul!
'A was a merry man—took up the child.   41
"Yea," quoth he, "dost thou fall upon thy face?
Thou wilt fall backward when thou hast more wit,   43
Wilt thou not, Jule?" and, by my halidom,   44
The pretty wretch left crying and said "Ay."
To see now how a jest shall come about!   46
I warrant, an I should live a thousand years,
I never should forget it. "Wilt thou not, Jule?" quoth
     he,
And, pretty fool, it stinted and said "Ay."   49
WIFE
Enough of this. I pray thee, hold thy peace.

NURSE
Yes, madam. Yet I cannot choose but laugh
To think it should leave crying and say "Ay."
And yet, I warrant, it had upon it brow   53
A bump as big as a young cockerel's stone—   54
A perilous knock—and it cried bitterly.
"Yea," quoth my husband, "fall'st upon thy face?
Thou wilt fall backward when thou comest to age,
Wilt thou not, Jule?" It stinted and said "Ay."
JULIET
And stint thou too, I pray thee, Nurse, say I.   59
NURSE
Peace, I have done. God mark thee to his grace!
Thou wast the prettiest babe that e'er I nursed.
An I might live to see thee married once,   62
I have my wish.
WIFE
Marry, that "marry" is the very theme
I came to talk of. Tell me, daughter Juliet,
How stands your disposition to be married?   66
JULIET
It is an honor that I dream not of.
NURSE
An honor? Were not I thine only nurse,
I would say thou hadst sucked wisdom from thy teat.   69
WIFE
Well, think of marriage now. Younger than you
Here in Verona, ladies of esteem,
Are made already mothers. By my count
I was your mother much upon these years   73
That you are now a maid. Thus then in brief:
The valiant Paris seeks you for his love.
NURSE
A man, young lady! Lady, such a man
As all the world—why, he's a man of wax.   77
WIFE
Verona's summer hath not such a flower.
NURSE
Nay, he's a flower, in faith, a very flower.   79
WIFE
What say you? Can you love the gentleman?
This night you shall behold him at our feast.
Read o'er the volume of young Paris' face,
And find delight writ there with beauty's pen;
Examine every married lineament,   84
And see how one another lends content;   85
And what obscured in this fair volume lies   86
Find written in the margent of his eyes   87
This precious book of love, this unbound lover,   88

---

14 **teen** sorrow. (Playing on *teen* and *four* in *fourteen*.)   16 **Lammas-tide** the days near August 1.   19 **Susan** the Nurse's own child, who has evidently died   23 **marry** i.e., by the Virgin Mary. (A mild oath.)   27 **wormwood** (A bitter-tasting plant used to wean the child from the *dug* or "teat.")   30 **bear a brain** maintain a keen memory.   32 **fool** (A term of endearment here.)   33 **tetchy** peevish, irritable   34 **"Shake" . . . dovehouse** i.e., The dovehouse shook.   **trow** believe, assure you   35 **trudge** be off quickly.   37 **high-lone** on her feet, without help. **rood** cross   39 **broke her brow** bruised her forehead (by falling)   41 **'A** He   43 **wit** understanding   44 **by my halidom** (A mild oath: "by all things holy," but popularly confused with "by my Holy Dame.")   46 **come about** come true.   49 **stinted** ceased

53 **it brow** its brow   54 **cockerel's stone** young rooster's testicle   59 **say I** (With a pun on *said "Ay"* of previous line.)   62 **An** If.   **once** someday   66 **disposition** inclination   69 **thy teat** the teat that nourished you.   73 **much . . . years** at much the same age   77 **a man of wax** as handsome as a figure modeled in wax.   79 **Nay** Indeed   84 **married lineament** harmonized feature   85 **And . . . content** and see how his handsome features enhance one another   86–7 **And what . . . eyes** and whatever you don't fully grasp by seeing his handsome features, find explained in his eyes, as though they were a kind of marginal gloss or commentary found in books.   88 **unbound** i.e., because not bound in marriage. (With a double meaning in the continuing metaphor of an unbound book.)

To beautify him, only lacks a cover. 89
The fish lives in the sea, and 'tis much pride 90
For fair without the fair within to hide. 91
That book in many's eyes doth share the glory, 92
That in gold clasps locks in the golden story; 93
So shall you share all that he doth possess
By having him, making yourself no less.

NURSE
No less? Nay, bigger. Women grow by men. 96

WIFE
Speak briefly, can you like of Paris' love? 97

JULIET
I'll look to like, if looking liking move; 98
But no more deep will I endart mine eye
Than your consent gives strength to make it fly.

Enter Servingman.

SERVINGMAN   Madam, the guests are come, supper
served up, you called, my young lady asked for, the
Nurse cursed in the pantry, and everything in extremity. I must hence to wait. I beseech you, follow straight. 104

WIFE   We follow thee.   [*Exit Servingman.*]
Juliet, the County stays. 105

NURSE
Go, girl, seek happy nights to happy days.   *Exeunt.*

[1.4]

Enter Romeo, Mercutio, Benvolio, with five or
six other masquers; torchbearers.

ROMEO
What, shall this speech be spoke for our excuse? 1
Or shall we on without apology? 2

BENVOLIO
The date is out of such prolixity. 3
We'll have no Cupid hoodwinked with a scarf, 4
Bearing a Tartar's painted bow of lath, 5
Scaring the ladies like a crowkeeper, 6
Nor no without-book prologue, faintly spoke 7
After the prompter, for our entrance;
But let them measure us by what they will, 9
We'll measure them a measure, and be gone. 10

ROMEO
Give me a torch. I am not for this ambling.
Being but heavy, I will bear the light. 12

MERCUTIO
Nay, gentle Romeo, we must have you dance.

ROMEO
Not I, believe me. You have dancing shoes
With nimble soles; I have a soul of lead 15
So stakes me to the ground I cannot move.

MERCUTIO
You are a lover; borrow Cupid's wings,
And soar with them above a common bound. 18

ROMEO
I am too sore enpiercèd with his shaft 19
To soar with his light feathers, and so bound
I cannot bound a pitch above dull woe. 21
Under love's heavy burden do I sink.

MERCUTIO
And, to sink in it, should you burden love— 23
Too great oppression for a tender thing.

ROMEO
Is love a tender thing? It is too rough,
Too rude, too boisterous, and it pricks like thorn.

MERCUTIO
If love be rough with you, be rough with love;
Prick love for pricking, and you beat love down. 28
Give me a case to put my visage in. 29
[*He puts on a mask.*]
A visor for a visor! What care I 30
What curious eye doth quote deformities? 31
Here are the beetle brows shall blush for me.

BENVOLIO
Come, knock and enter, and no sooner in
But every man betake him to his legs. 34

ROMEO
A torch for me. Let wantons light of heart
Tickle the senseless rushes with their heels, 36
For I am proverbed with a grandsire phrase: 37
I'll be a candle-holder and look on. 38
The game was ne'er so fair, and I am done. 39

89 **a cover** i.e., marriage, an embracing wife.   **90–1 The fish . . . hide**
i.e., The fish has its own suitable environment, and similarly in marriage the fair Juliet (here imagined as a beautiful book-cover "binding" Paris) would suitably enhance Paris's worth.   **92–3 That book
. . . story** i.e., In many persons' eyes, a good story is all the more
admirable for being handsomely bound. (*Clasps* means [1] book fas-
tenings [2] embraces.)   **96 bigger** i.e., by pregnancy.   **97 like of** be
pleased with   **98 liking move** may provoke affection   **104 straight**
at once.   **105 County stays** Count (Paris) waits for you.
1.4. Location: Verona. A street.
1 speech (Masquers were customarily preceded by a messenger or
"presenter" with a set speech of compliment.)   **2 on** go on, approach
3 The date . . . prolixity Such windy rhetoric is out of fashion.
4 Cupid i.e., messenger or "presenter," probably a boy, disguised as
Cupid.   **hoodwinked** blindfolded   **5 Tartar's . . . bow** (Tartars'
bows, shorter and more curved than the English longbow, were
thought to have resembled the old Roman bow with which Cupid
was pictured.)   **lath** flimsy wood   **6 crowkeeper** scarecrow
7 without-book memorized   **9 measure** judge   **10 measure . . .
measure** tread a dance for them

12 heavy (1) sad (2) the opposite of *light* (as at 1.1.137)   **15 soul** (Punning on *sole*.)   **18 common bound** (1) ordinary limit (2) normal
dance step.   **19 sore** sorely. (With pun on *soar*.)   **21 bound** leap.
(With wordplay on *bound*, "confined," in the previous line.)   **pitch**
height. (A term from falconry for the highest point of a hawk's flight.)
23 And . . . love i.e., You wouldn't just sink *under* love's heavy burden, you'd sink *into* it and burden it. (Suggesting sexual penetration.)
28 Prick . . . down i.e., If love gets rough, fight back. (But with bawdy
suggestion of *pricking* as a way to satisfy desire and cause detumescence.)   **29 case** mask   **30 A visor . . . visor** i.e., A mask for an ugly
masklike face.   **31 quote** take notice of   **34 to his legs** to dancing.
36 senseless rushes reeds used as floor covering, or insensate green
rushes   **37 proverbed . . . phrase** furnished with an old proverb
38 candle-holder i.e., bystander. (Referring to the proverbial idea that
one who lacks ability himself can hold the candle and thus provide
light for one who is able to act.)   **39 The game . . . done** (Another
proverbial truism, that it is best to quit when one is ahead.)

MERCUTIO
Tut, dun's the mouse, the constable's own word.   40
If thou art dun, we'll draw thee from the mire   41
Of—save your reverence—love, wherein thou stickest   42
Up to the ears. Come, we burn daylight, ho!   43
ROMEO
Nay, that's not so.
MERCUTIO   I mean, sir, in delay
We waste our lights in vain, like lamps by day.
Take our good meaning, for our judgment sits   46
Five times in that ere once in our five wits.   47
ROMEO
And we mean well in going to this masque,
But 'tis no wit to go.
MERCUTIO   Why, may one ask?   49
ROMEO
I dreamt a dream tonight.
MERCUTIO   And so did I.   50
ROMEO
Well, what was yours?
MERCUTIO   That dreamers often lie.   51
ROMEO
In bed asleep, while they do dream things true.
MERCUTIO
Oh, then, I see Queen Mab hath been with you.   53
She is the fairies' midwife, and she comes
In shape no bigger than an agate stone   55
On the forefinger of an alderman,   56
Drawn with a team of little atomi   57
Over men's noses as they lie asleep.
Her chariot is an empty hazelnut,
Made by the joiner squirrel or old grub,   60
Time out o' mind the fairies' coachmakers.
Her wagon spokes made of long spinners' legs,   62
The cover of the wings of grasshoppers,
Her traces of the smallest spider web,
Her collars of the moonshine's wat'ry beams,
Her whip of cricket's bone, the lash of film,   66
Her wagoner a small gray-coated gnat,   67

Not half so big as a round little worm   68
Pricked from the lazy finger of a maid.   69
And in this state she gallops night by night
Through lovers' brains, and then they dream of love;
O'er courtiers' knees, that dream on curtsies straight; 72
O'er lawyers' fingers, who straight dream on fees;
O'er ladies' lips, who straight on kisses dream,
Which oft the angry Mab with blisters plagues
Because their breaths with sweetmeats tainted are.   76
Sometime she gallops o'er a courtier's nose,
And then dreams he of smelling out a suit.   78
And sometime comes she with a tithe-pig's tail   79
Tickling a parson's nose as 'a lies asleep;
Then dreams he of another benefice.   81
Sometime she driveth o'er a soldier's neck,
And then dreams he of cutting foreign throats,
Of breaches, ambuscadoes, Spanish blades,   84
Of healths five fathom deep, and then anon   85
Drums in his ear, at which he starts and wakes,
And being thus frighted swears a prayer or two
And sleeps again. This is that very Mab
That plats the manes of horses in the night,   89
And bakes the elflocks in foul sluttish hairs,   90
Which once untangled much misfortune bodes.   91
This is the hag, when maids lie on their backs,
That presses them and learns them first to bear,   93
Making them women of good carriage.   94
This is she—
ROMEO   Peace, peace, Mercutio, peace!
Thou talk'st of nothing.
MERCUTIO   True, I talk of dreams,
Which are the children of an idle brain,
Begot of nothing but vain fantasy,   98
Which is as thin of substance as the air,
And more inconstant than the wind, who woos
Even now the frozen bosom of the north,
And being angered, puffs away from thence,
Turning his side to the dew-dropping south.
BENVOLIO
This wind you talk of blows us from ourselves.   104
Supper is done, and we shall come too late.
ROMEO
I fear, too early; for my mind misgives   106
Some consequence yet hanging in the stars

---

40 dun's . . . word i.e., "keep still"—just the sort of thing a constable might say. (Matching proverb with proverb, Mercutio answers Romeo's "I am done" by twitting him for being mousy. Constables were much laughed at for inappropriately pompous speech.) **41–3 If . . . ears** (To Mercutio, Romeo's love melancholy recalls the Christmas game called "Dun is in the mire," in which a heavy log, representing a horse named Dun, was hauled out of an imaginary mire by the players. *Save your reverence* is Mercutio's mock apology for speaking of so improper an expression as being mired up to the ears in love.) **43 burn daylight** i.e., waste time. (But Romeo quibbles, protesting that it is not literally daytime.) **46–7 Take . . . wits** Try to understand what I am trying to say (rather than quibbling with phrases like "burn daylight"), for wise judgment is five times more pleased with good meaning than with the ingenious wit of our frail senses. **49 wit** wisdom (playing on *wits* in line 47; *mean* in line 48 plays on *meaning* in line 46) **50 tonight** last night. **51 lie** tell falsehoods. (But Mercutio answers in the sense of "lie down in bed.") **53 Queen Mab** (Possibly a name of Celtic origin for the Fairy Queen.) **55 agate stone** (Precious stone often carved with diminutive figures and set in a ring.) **56 alderman** member of the municipal council **57 atomi** tiny creatures (atoms) **60 joiner** furniture maker. **grub** insect larva (which bores holes in nuts) **62 spinners'** spiders' **66 film** gossamer thread **67 wagoner** chariot driver

68–9 a round . . . maid (Worms proverbially breed in the fingers of the idle.) **72 curtsies** bows, obeisances. **straight** immediately **76 sweetmeats** candies or candied preserves **78 smelling . . . suit** i.e., finding a petitioner from whom will pay for the use of his influence at court. **79 tithe-pig** pig given to the parson in lieu of money as the parishioner's tithing, or granting of a tenth **81 benefice** ecclesiastical living. **84 Of breaches . . . blades** of opening up gaps in fortifications, of ambushes, of swords from Toledo in Spain, where the best swords were made **85 Of healths . . . deep** of toasts drunk deep **89 That plats . . . night** (According to popular superstition, the tangles that persistently turn up in the manes of horses were "witches' stirrups," i.e., footholds for witches as they rode.) **90–1 And bakes . . . bodes** (*Elflocks* or clumps of matted hair were so named because they were imagined to be the work of elves, who would torment anyone so presumptuous as to untangle the elflocks.) **93 learns** teaches **94 good carriage** (1) commendable deportment (2) skill in bearing the weight of men in sexual intercourse (3) able subsequently to carry a child. **98 vain fantasy** delusive imagination **104 from ourselves** from our plans. **106 misgives** fears

Shall bitterly begin his fearful date   108
With this night's revels, and expire the term   109
Of a despisèd life closed in my breast
By some vile forfeit of untimely death.
But He that hath the steerage of my course
Direct my suit! On, lusty gentlemen.   113
BENVOLIO   Strike, drum.   *They march about the stage,*   114
                                and [retire to one side].

❖

[1.5]

Servingmen come forth with napkins.

FIRST SERVINGMAN   Where's Potpan, that he helps not
to take away? He shift a trencher? He scrape a trencher?   2
SECOND SERVINGMAN   When good manners shall lie all
in one or two men's hands, and they unwashed too,
'tis a foul thing.
FIRST SERVINGMAN   Away with the joint stools, remove   6
the court cupboard, look to the plate. Good thou, save   7
me a piece of marchpane, and, as thou loves me, let   8
the porter let in Susan Grindstone and Nell.
                        [Exit Second Servingman.]
Anthony and Potpan!

                [Enter two more Servingmen.]

THIRD SERVINGMAN   Ay, boy, ready.
FIRST SERVINGMAN   You are looked for and called for,
asked for and sought for, in the great chamber.
FOURTH SERVINGMAN   We cannot be here and there
too. Cheerly, boys! Be brisk awhile, and the longest   15
liver take all.   *Exeunt.*   16

        *Enter [Capulet and family and] all the guests
        and gentlewomen to the masquers.*

CAPULET *[to the masquers]*
Welcome, gentlemen! Ladies that have their toes
Unplagued with corns will walk a bout with you.   18
Ah, my mistresses, which of you all
Will now deny to dance? She that makes dainty,   20
She, I'll swear, hath corns. Am I come near ye now?   21
Welcome, gentlemen! I have seen the day
That I have worn a visor and could tell
A whispering tale in a fair lady's ear
Such as would please. 'Tis gone, 'tis gone, 'tis gone.
You are welcome, gentlemen! Come, musicians, play.
                        Music plays, and they dance.

A hall, a hall! Give room! And foot, it, girls.   27
[To Servingmen]   More light, you knaves, and turn the
  tables up,   28
And quench the fire; the room is grown too hot.
[To his cousin]   Ah, sirrah, this unlooked-for sport
  comes well.   30
Nay, sit, nay, sit, good cousin Capulet,   31
For you and I are past our dancing days.
How long is't now since last yourself and I
Were in a mask?
SECOND CAPULET   By'r Lady, thirty years.
CAPULET
What, man? 'Tis not so much, 'tis not so much;
'Tis since the nuptial of Lucentio,
Come Pentecost as quickly as it will,   37
Some five-and-twenty years, and then we masked.
SECOND CAPULET
'Tis more, 'tis more. His son is elder, sir;
His son is thirty.
CAPULET   Will you tell me that?
His son was but a ward two years ago.   41
ROMEO *[to a Servingman]*
What lady's that which doth enrich the hand
Of yonder knight?
SERVINGMAN   I know not, sir.
ROMEO
Oh, she doth teach the torches to burn bright!
It seems she hangs upon the cheek of night
As a rich jewel in an Ethiop's ear—
Beauty too rich for use, for earth too dear!   48
So shows a snowy dove trooping with crows   49
As yonder lady o'er her fellows shows.
The measure done, I'll watch her place of stand,   51
And, touching hers, make blessèd my rude hand.   52
Did my heart love till now? Forswear it, sight!   53
For I ne'er saw true beauty till this night.
TYBALT
This, by his voice, should be a Montague.
Fetch me my rapier, boy. What dares the slave   56
Come hither, covered with an antic face,   57
To fleer and scorn at our solemnity?   58
Now, by the stock and honor of my kin,
To strike him dead I hold it not a sin.
CAPULET
Why, how now, kinsman? Wherefore storm you so?

27 A hall i.e., Clear the hall for dancing   **28 turn . . . up** move the
tables out of the way for the dancing (by taking up the boards and
then removing the supporting trestles)   **30 sirrah** (Normally used in
addressing social inferiors. Perhaps Capulet uses a jesting tone
toward his kinsman or possibly addresses himself.)   **unlooked-for
sport** i.e., arrival of the masquers, providing more men for the dancing   **31 cousin** (*Cousin* often means "kinsman"; at 1.2.69, "Mine
uncle Capulet" is named on the invitation list.)   **37 Pentecost** seventh Sunday after Easter (and never as late as mid-July, two weeks
before Lammas or August 1, when according to 1.3.16, the play takes
place; a seeming inconsistency).   **41 a ward** a minor under guardianship   **48 dear** precious.   **49 shows** appears   **51 The measure done**
When this dance is over.   **her place of stand** where she stands
52 hers her hand.   **rude** rough   **53 Forswear it** Deny any previous
oath   **56 What** How   **57 antic face** grotesque mask   **58 fleer** jeer.
solemnity time-honored festivity.

108 date appointed time   **109 expire** bring to an end   **113 lusty**
lively   **114 drum** drummer.
1.5. Location: The action, continuous from the previous scene, is
now imaginatively transferred to a hall in Capulet's house.
2 take away clear the table.   **trencher** wooden dish or plate.   **6 joint
stools** stools of which the parts are fitted by a joiner or furniture
maker   **7 court cupboard** sideboard.   **plate** silverware.   **8 marchpane** cake made from sugar and almonds, marzipan   **15–16 the
longest . . . all** (A proverb in defense of merriment.)   **18 walk a bout**
dance a turn   **20 makes dainty** seems coyly reluctant (to dance)
21 Am . . . now? Have I hit a sensitive point, struck home?

TYBALT
Uncle, this is a Montague, our foe,
A villain that is hither come in spite 63
To scorn at our solemnity this night.
CAPULET
Young Romeo is it?
TYBALT   'Tis he, that villain Romeo.
CAPULET
Content thee, gentle coz, let him alone.
'A bears him like a portly gentleman, 67
And, to say truth, Verona brags of him
To be a virtuous and well governed youth.
I would not for the wealth of all this town
Here in my house do him disparagement.
Therefore be patient; take no note of him.
It is my will, the which if thou respect,
Show a fair presence and put off these frowns, 74
An ill-beseeming semblance for a feast. 75
TYBALT
It fits when such a villain is a guest.
I'll not endure him.
CAPULET   He shall be endured.
What, goodman boy? I say he shall. Go to! 78
Am I the master here, or you? Go to.
You'll not endure him! God shall mend my soul,
You'll make a mutiny among my guests! 81
You will set cock-a-hoop! You'll be the man! 82
TYBALT
Why, uncle, 'tis a shame.
CAPULET   Go to, go to,
You are a saucy boy. Is't so, indeed?
This trick may chance to scathe you. I know what, 85
You must contrary me. Marry, 'tis time.— 86
Well said, my hearts!—You are a princox, go. 87
Be quiet, or—More light, more light!—For shame!
I'll make you quiet.—What, cheerly, my hearts!
TYBALT
Patience perforce with willful choler meeting 90
Makes my flesh tremble in their different greeting. 91
I will withdraw. But this intrusion shall,
Now seeming sweet, convert to bitt'rest gall. Exit.
ROMEO [to Juliet]
If I profane with my unworthiest hand 94
This holy shrine, the gentle sin is this: 95
My lips, two blushing pilgrims, ready stand
To smooth that rough touch with a tender kiss.
JULIET
Good pilgrim, you do wrong your hand too much,

Which mannerly devotion shows in this;
For saints have hands that pilgrims' hands do touch, 100
And palm to palm is holy palmers' kiss. 101
ROMEO
Have not saints lips, and holy palmers too?
JULIET
Ay, pilgrim, lips that they must use in prayer.
ROMEO
Oh, then, dear saint, let lips do what hands do. 104
They pray; grant thou, lest faith turn to despair.
JULIET
Saints do not move, though grant for prayers' sake. 106
ROMEO
Then move not, while my prayer's effect I take. 107
                    [He kisses her.]
Thus from my lips, by thine, my sin is purged.
JULIET
Then have my lips the sin that they have took.
ROMEO
Sin from my lips? Oh, trespass sweetly urged!
Give me my sin again. [He kisses her.]
JULIET   You kiss by th' book. 111
NURSE [approaching]
Madam, your mother craves a word with you.
                    [Juliet retires.]
ROMEO
What is her mother?
NURSE   Marry, bachelor, 113
Her mother is the lady of the house,
And a good lady, and a wise and virtuous.
I nursed her daughter that you talked withal. 116
I tell you, he that can lay hold of her
Shall have the chinks.
ROMEO [aside]   Is she a Capulet? 118
Oh, dear account! My life is my foe's debt. 119
BENVOLIO [approaching]
Away, begone! The sport is at the best. 120
ROMEO
Ay, so I fear; the more is my unrest.
                    [The masquers prepare to leave.]
CAPULET
Nay, gentlemen, prepare not to be gone.
We have a trifling foolish banquet towards. 123
                    [One whispers in his ear.]
Is it e'en so? Why, then, I thank you all.
I thank you, honest gentlemen. Good night. 125

---

63 spite malice 67 A' He. portly of good deportment 74 presence
demeanor 75 semblance facial expression 78 goodman boy (A
belittling term for Tybalt; goodman applied to one below the rank of
gentleman but still of some substance, like a wealthy farmer.) Go to
(An expression of irritation.) 81 mutiny disturbance 82 You . . .
man! i.e., You'll set mischief abroach (literally, turn the tap and let the
liquor flow)! You'll be the big shot! 85 scathe harm 86 contrary
oppose, thwart. 'tis time i.e., it's time you were taught a lesson.
87 Well said Well done. (Said to the dancers.) princox saucy boy
90–1 Patience . . . greeting The attempt to be patient under duress
when I am so angry causes me to tremble at the contrary meeting of
these two opposite impulses. 94–107 (These lines are in the form of
a Shakespearean sonnet; they are followed by a quatrain.) 95 shrine
i.e., Juliet's hand

100 saints i.e., images of saints that are venerated by pilgrims
101 palmers pilgrims who have been to the Holy Land and have
brought back a palm. (With a pun on the palm of the hand.) 104 let . . .
do let lips touch, just as hands touch. 106 Saints . . . sake Venerated
images and statues of saints remain motionless but nonetheless inter-
cede on behalf of praying pilgrims. 107 move (Romeo quibbles on
Juliet's metaphorical use of the word move to urge that she remain
motionless while he kisses her.) 111 by th' book by the rules, like
an expert. 113 What Who 116 withal with. 118 the chinks plenty
of coins, money. (A slang expression.) 119 dear account heavy reckoning. my foe's debt due to my foe, at his mercy. 120 The sport . . .
best i.e., It is time to leave. (Refers to the proverb, "When play is at
the best, it is time to leave"; compare at 1.4.39.) 123 foolish banquet
towards insignificant light refreshment just ready. 125 honest
honorable

More torches here! Come on then, let's to bed.   126

[*To his cousin*] Ah, sirrah, by my fay, it waxes late.   127
I'll to my rest.

   [*All proceed to leave but Juliet and the Nurse.*]

JULIET
Come hither, Nurse. What is yond gentleman?

NURSE
The son and heir of old Tiberio.

JULIET
What's he that now is going out of door?

NURSE
Marry, that, I think, be young Petruchio.

JULIET
What's he that follows here, that would not dance?

NURSE I know not.

JULIET
Go ask his name. [*The Nurse goes.*] If he be marrièd,
My grave is like to be my wedding bed.   136

NURSE [*returning*]
His name is Romeo, and a Montague,
The only son of your great enemy.

JULIET
My only love sprung from my only hate!
Too early seen unknown, and known too late!
Prodigious birth of love it is to me   141
That I must love a loathèd enemy.

NURSE
What's tis? What's tis?

JULIET   A rhyme I learned even now   143
Of one I danced withal. *One calls within* "Juliet."

NURSE   Anon, anon!   144
Come, let's away. The strangers all are gone. *Exeunt.*

❖

[2.0]

  [*Enter*] *Chorus.*

CHORUS
Now old desire doth in his deathbed lie,   1
 And young affection gapes to be his heir;   2
That fair for which love groaned for and would die,   3
 With tender Juliet matched, is now not fair.   4
Now Romeo is beloved and loves again,
 Alike bewitchèd by the charm of looks;   6
But to his foe supposed he must complain,   7
 And she steal love's sweet bait from fearful hooks.   8
Being held a foe, he may not have access
 To breathe such vows as lovers use to swear;   10
And she as much in love, her means much less
 To meet her new-belovèd anywhere.

But passion lends them power, time means, to meet,   13
Temp'ring extremities with extreme sweet. [*Exit.*]   14

❖

[2.1]

  Enter Romeo alone.

ROMEO
Can I go forward when my heart is here?   1
Turn back, dull earth, and find thy center out.   2

      [*Romeo retires.*]

  Enter Benvolio with Mercutio.

BENVOLIO
Romeo! My cousin Romeo! Romeo!

MERCUTIO He is wise
And, on my life, hath stol'n him home to bed.

BENVOLIO
He ran this way and leapt this orchard wall.
Call, good Mercutio.

MERCUTIO   Nay, I'll conjure too.   7
Romeo! Humors! Madman! Passion! Lover!   8
Appear thou in the likeness of a sigh.
Speak but one rhyme, and I am satisfied;
Cry but "Ay me!" Pronounce but "love" and "dove."
Speak to my gossip Venus one fair word,   12
One nickname for her purblind son and heir,   13
Young Abraham Cupid, he that shot so trim   14
When King Cophetua loved the beggar maid.—   15
He heareth not, he stirreth not, he moveth not;
The ape is dead, and I must conjure him.—   17
I conjure thee by Rosaline's bright eyes,
By her high forehead and her scarlet lip,
By her fine foot, straight leg, and quivering thigh,
And the demesnes that there adjacent lie,   21
That in thy likeness thou appear to us.

BENVOLIO
An if he hear thee, thou wilt anger him.   23

MERCUTIO
This cannot anger him. 'Twould anger him
To raise a spirit in his mistress' circle   25
Of some strange nature, letting it there stand   26

---

126 **torches** i.e., to light the guests as they leave 127 **fay** faith
136 **like** likely 141 **Prodigious** Ominous 143 **tis** this. (Dialect pronunciation.) 144 **Anon** i.e., We're coming
2.0. Chorus.
1–14 (This chorus is a sonnet.) 2 **gapes** waits open-mouthed 3 **fair** beauty, i.e., Rosaline 4 **matched** compared 6 **Alike** i.e., equally with Juliet 7 **foe supposed** i.e., Juliet, a Capulet; also, his opposite number in the war of love. **complain** offer his love plaint 8 **And she . . . hooks** and she must steal moments of happy love from frightening circumstances designed to catch her unawares. 10 **use** are accustomed

13 **time means** time lends them means 14 **Temp'ring extremities** mitigating the hardships. **sweet** sweetness, pleasure.
2.1. Location: Verona. Outside of Capulet's walled orchard.
1 **forward** i.e., away 2 **Turn . . . out** (Romeo bids his own earthbound body find out its *center*, its soul or heart [i.e., Juliet], much as in the Ptolemaic system all earthly things seek out their center, the earth, standing at the center of the universe. His body is *dull* in that, like earth, it is the lowest and heaviest of the four elements, associated with melancholy.) 7 **conjure** raise him with magical incantation 8 **Humors** Moods. 12 **gossip** crony 13 **purblind** dim-sighted
14 **Young Abraham** i.e., one who is young and yet, like the biblical Abraham, old; Cupid was paradoxically the youngest and the oldest of the gods 15 **King Cophetua** (In an old ballad, the King falls in love with a beggar maid and makes her his queen.) 17 **ape** (Used as a term of endearment.) 21 **demesnes** regions. (With bawdy suggestion as to what is adjacent to the thighs; bawdy puns on terms of conjuration continue in *raise, spirit,* i.e., "phallus" or "semen," *circle, stand, laid it, raise up.*) 23 **An if** If 25 **circle** (1) conjuring circle (2) vagina 26 **strange** belonging to another person. (With suggestion of a rival possessing Rosaline sexually.)

Till she had laid it and conjured it down;   27
That were some spite. My invocation   28
Is fair and honest; in his mistress' name
I conjure only but to raise up him.

BENVOLIO
Come, he hath hid himself among these trees
To be consorted with the humorous night.   32
Blind is his love, and best befits the dark.

MERCUTIO
If love be blind, love cannot hit the mark.
Now will he sit under a medlar tree   35
And wish his mistress were that kind of fruit
As maids call medlars when they laugh alone.
Oh, Romeo, that she were, oh, that she were
An open-arse, and thou a pop'ring pear!   39
Romeo, good night. I'll to my truckle bed;   40
This field bed is too cold for me to sleep.   41
Come, shall we go?

BENVOLIO   Go, then, for 'tis in vain
To seek him here that means not to be found.
           Exit [with Mercutio].

❖

[2.2]

ROMEO *[coming forward]*
He jests at scars that never felt a wound.   1
     [A light appears above, as at Juliet's window.]
But soft, what light through yonder window breaks?
It is the east, and Juliet is the sun.
Arise, fair sun, and kill the envious moon,
Who is already sick and pale with grief
That thou her maid art far more fair than she.   6
Be not her maid, since she is envious;   7
Her vestal livery is but sick and green   8
And none but fools do wear it. Cast it off.
     [Juliet appears aloft as at her window.]
It is my lady, oh, it is my love.
Oh, that she knew she were!
She speaks, yet she says nothing. What of that?

Her eye discourses. I will answer it.
I am too bold. 'Tis not to me she speaks.
Two of the fairest stars in all the heaven,
Having some business, do entreat her eyes
To twinkle in their spheres till they return.   17
What if her eyes were there, they in her head?   18
The brightness of her cheek would shame those stars
As daylight doth a lamp; her eyes in heaven
Would through the airy region stream so bright   21
That birds would sing and think it were not night.
See how she leans her cheek upon her hand!
Oh, that I were a glove upon that hand,
That I might touch that cheek!

JULIET   Ay me!

ROMEO *[aside]*   She speaks.
Oh, speak again, bright angel, for thou art
As glorious to this night, being o'er my head,
As is a wingèd messenger of heaven
Unto the white-upturnèd wond'ring eyes   29
Of mortals that fall back to gaze on him
When he bestrides the lazy puffing clouds
And sails upon the bosom of the air.

JULIET *[to herself]*
O Romeo, Romeo, wherefore art thou Romeo?   33
Deny thy father and refuse thy name!
Or, if thou wilt not, be but sworn my love,
And I'll no longer be a Capulet.

ROMEO *[aside]*
Shall I hear more, or shall I speak at this?

JULIET
'Tis but thy name that is my enemy;
Thou art thyself, though not a Montague.   39
What's Montague? It is nor hand, nor foot,   40
Nor arm, nor face, nor any other part
Belonging to a man. Oh, be some other name!
What's in a name? That which we call a rose
By any other word would smell as sweet;
So Romeo would, were he not Romeo called,
Retain that dear perfection which he owes   46
Without that title. Romeo, doff thy name,   47
And for thy name, which is no part of thee,   48
Take all myself.

ROMEO   I take thee at thy word!
Call me but love, and I'll be new baptized;
Henceforth I never will be Romeo.

JULIET
What man art thou that, thus bescreened in night,   52
So stumblest on my counsel?

ROMEO   By a name   53
I know not how to tell thee who I am.
My name, dear saint, is hateful to myself,
Because it is an enemy to thee;
Had I it written, I would tear the word.

---

27 laid it (1) laid the spirit to rest (2) provided sexual satisfaction leading to detumescence   **28 were some spite** would be vexing. **32 consorted** associated.   **humorous** (1) moist, damp (2) well suited to the *humor* of melancholy   **35 medlar** a fruit that was edible only when partly decayed, used as a slang term for women's sexual organs   **39 open-arse** (Another name for the *medlar*, making explicit the sexual metaphor.)   **pop'ring pear** poppering pear (named after Poperinghe in Flanders). A fruit with phallic associations because of its shape and its suggestive name ("pop 'er in").   **40 truckle bed** a bed on casters to be rolled under a standing bed when not in use **41 field bed** i.e., the ground
2.2. Location: The action, continuous from the previous scene, is now imaginatively transferred to inside Capulet's orchard. A rhymed couplet links the two scenes. Romeo has been hiding from his friends as though concealed by the orchard wall. He speaks at once and then turns to observe Juliet's window, which is probably in the gallery above, rear stage.
1.1 *A light appears* (Some editors assume that Juliet is visible at line 1.) **6 maid** i.e., votary of Diana, goddess of the moon and patroness of virgins   **7 her** the moon's, Diana's, as the goddess of chastity. (Addressed to Juliet as the sun; Romeo hopes that she will not be a devotee of chastity.)   **8 Her vestal livery** the uniform of Diana's chaste votaries. **sick and green** (Suggesting the pallor of moonlight, as well as anemia or *greensickness* [see 3.5.156], to which teenage girls were susceptible.)

17 spheres transparent concentric shells supposed to carry the heavenly bodies with them in their revolution around the earth   **18 there** i.e., in the spheres   **21 stream** shine   **29 white-upturnèd** looking upward so that the whites of the eyes are visible   **33 wherefore** why   **39 though not** (1) even if you were not (2) though not in anything essential **40 nor hand** neither hand   **46 owes** owns   **47 doff** cast off   **48 for** in exchange for   **52 bescreened** concealed   **53 counsel** secret thoughts.

JULIET

My ears have yet not drunk a hundred words
Of thy tongue's uttering, yet I know the sound:
Art thou not Romeo and a Montague?

ROMEO

Neither, fair maid, if either thee dislike.   61

JULIET

How camest thou hither, tell me, and wherefore?
The orchard walls are high and hard to climb,
And the place death, considering who thou art,
If any of my kinsmen find thee here.

ROMEO

With love's light wings did I o'erperch these walls,   66
For stony limits cannot hold love out,
And what love can do, that dares love attempt;
Therefore thy kinsmen are no stop to me.

JULIET

If they do see thee, they will murder thee.

ROMEO

Alack, there lies more peril in thine eye
Than twenty of their swords. Look thou but sweet,
And I am proof against their enmity.   73

JULIET

I would not for the world they saw thee here.

ROMEO

I have night's cloak to hide me from their eyes;
And but thou love me, let them find me here.   76
My life were better ended by their hate
Than death proroguèd, wanting of thy love.   78

JULIET

By whose direction found'st thou out this place?

ROMEO

By Love, that first did prompt me to inquire.
He lent me counsel, and I lent him eyes.
I am no pilot; yet, wert thou as far
As that vast shore washed with the farthest sea,
I should adventure for such merchandise.

JULIET

Thou knowest the mask of night is on my face,
Else would a maiden blush bepaint my cheek
For that which thou hast heard me speak tonight.
Fain would I dwell on form—fain, fain deny   88
What I have spoke; but farewell compliment!   89
Dost thou love me? I know thou wilt say "Ay,"
And I will take thy word. Yet if thou swear'st
Thou mayst prove false. At lovers' perjuries,
They say, Jove laughs. O gentle Romeo,
If thou dost love, pronounce it faithfully.
Or if thou thinkest I am too quickly won,
I'll frown and be perverse and say thee nay,
So thou wilt woo, but else not for the world.
In truth, fair Montague, I am too fond,   98
And therefore thou mayst think my havior light.   99
But trust me, gentleman, I'll prove more true
Than those that have more cunning to be strange.   101

I should have been more strange, I must confess,
But that thou overheard'st, ere I was ware,   103
My true-love passion. Therefore pardon me,
And not impute this yielding to light love,
Which the dark night hath so discoverèd.   106

ROMEO

Lady, by yonder blessèd moon I vow,
That tips with silver all these fruit-tree tops—

JULIET

Oh, swear not by the moon, th'inconstant moon,
That monthly changes in her circled orb,   110
Lest that thy love prove likewise variable.

ROMEO

What shall I swear by?

JULIET   Do not swear at all;
Or, if thou wilt, swear by thy gracious self,
Which is the god of my idolatry,
And I'll believe thee.

ROMEO   If my heart's dear love—

JULIET

Well, do not swear. Although I joy in thee,
I have no joy of this contract tonight.   117
It is too rash, too unadvised, too sudden,   118
Too like the lightning, which doth cease to be
Ere one can say it lightens. Sweet, good night!
This bud of love, by summer's ripening breath,
May prove a beauteous flower when next we meet.
Good night, good night! As sweet repose and rest   123
Come to thy heart as that within my breast!

ROMEO

Oh, wilt thou leave me so unsatisfied?

JULIET

What satisfaction canst thou have tonight?

ROMEO

Th'exchange of thy love's faithful vow for mine.

JULIET

I gave thee mine before thou didst request it;
And yet I would it were to give again.

ROMEO

Wouldst thou withdraw it? For what purpose, love?

JULIET

But to be frank and give it thee again.   131
And yet I wish but for the thing I have.
My bounty is as boundless as the sea,
My love as deep; the more I give to thee,
The more I have, for both are infinite.

[The Nurse calls within.]

I hear some noise within. Dear love, adieu!—
Anon, good Nurse!—Sweet Montague, be true.
Stay but a little; I will come again.   [Exit, above.]

ROMEO

Oh, blessèd, blessèd night! I am afeard,
Being in night, all this is but a dream,
Too flattering-sweet to be substantial.

[Enter Juliet, above.]

---

61 thee dislike displeases you.   **66 o'erperch** fly over   **73 proof** protected   **76 but** unless   **78 proroguèd** postponed.   **wanting of** lacking   **88 Fain** Gladly.   **dwell on form** preserve the proper formalities   **89 compliment** etiquette, convention.   **98 fond** infatuated   **99 havior light** behavior frivolous.   **101 strange** reserved, aloof, modest.

103 ware aware   **106 Which** i.e., which yielding.   **discoverèd** revealed.   **110 orb** orbit, sphere   **117 contract** exchanging of vows   **118 unadvised** unconsidered   **123 As** May just as   **131 frank** liberal, bounteous

JULIET
    Three words, dear Romeo, and good night indeed.
    If that thy bent of love be honorable,   143
    Thy purpose marriage, send me word tomorrow,
    By one that I'll procure to come to thee,
    Where and what time thou wilt perform the rite,
    And all my fortunes at thy foot I'll lay
    And follow thee my lord throughout the world.
NURSE [*within*] Madam!
JULIET
    I come, anon.—But if thou meanest not well,
    I do beseech thee—
NURSE [*within*]   Madam!
JULIET   By and by, I come—   151
    To cease thy strife and leave me to my grief.   152
    Tomorrow will I send.
ROMEO   So thrive my soul—
JULIET   A thousand times good night!   [*Exit, above.*]
ROMEO
    A thousand times the worse, to want thy light.
    Love goes toward love as schoolboys from their
        books,
    But love from love, toward school with heavy looks.
              [*He starts to leave.*]

      Enter Juliet [above] again.

JULIET
    Hist! Romeo, hist! Oh, for a falconer's voice,
    To lure this tassel-gentle back again!   160
    Bondage is hoarse and may not speak aloud,   161
    Else would I tear the cave where Echo lies   162
    And make her airy tongue more hoarse than mine
    With repetition of "My Romeo!"
ROMEO
    It is my soul that calls upon my name.
    How silver-sweet sound lovers' tongues by night,
    Like softest music to attending ears!
JULIET
    Romeo!
ROMEO   My nyas?
JULIET   What o'clock tomorrow   168
    Shall I send to thee?
ROMEO   By the hour of nine.
JULIET
    I will not fail. 'Tis twenty year till then.—
    I have forgot why I did call thee back.
ROMEO
    Let me stand here till thou remember it.
JULIET
    I shall forget, to have thee still stand there,   173
    Remembering how I love thy company.

ROMEO
    And I'll still stay, to have thee still forget,
    Forgetting any other home but this.
JULIET
    'Tis almost morning. I would have thee gone—
    And yet no farther than a wanton's bird,   178
    That lets it hop a little from his hand,
    Like a poor prisoner in his twisted gyves,   180
    And with a silken thread plucks it back again,
    So loving-jealous of his liberty.   182
ROMEO
    I would I were thy bird.
JULIET   Sweet, so would I.
    Yet I should kill thee with much cherishing.
    Good night, good night! Parting is such sweet sorrow
    That I shall say good night till it be morrow.
              [*Exit, above.*]
ROMEO
    Sleep dwell upon thine eyes, peace in thy breast!
    Would I were sleep and peace, so sweet to rest!
    Hence will I to my ghostly friar's close cell,   189
    His help to crave, and my dear hap to tell.   *Exit.* 190

❖

[2.3]

    Enter Friar [Laurence] alone, with a basket.

FRIAR LAURENCE
    The gray-eyed morn smiles on the frowning night,
    Check'ring the eastern clouds with streaks of light,
    And fleckled darkness like a drunkard reels   3
    From forth day's path and Titan's fiery wheels.   4
    Now, ere the sun advance his burning eye,   5
    The day to cheer and night's dank dew to dry,
    I must up-fill this osier cage of ours   7
    With baleful weeds and precious-juicèd flowers.   8
    The earth that's nature's mother is her tomb;
    What is her burying grave, that is her womb;
    And from her womb children of divers kind
    We sucking on her natural bosom find,
    Many for many virtues excellent,
    None but for some, and yet all different.   14
    Oh, mickle is the powerful grace that lies   15
    In plants, herbs, stones, and their true qualities.   16
    For naught so vile that on the earth doth live   17
    But to the earth some special good doth give;
    Nor aught so good but, strained from that fair use,   19
    Revolts from true birth, stumbling on abuse.
    Virtue itself turns vice, being misapplied,
    And vice sometime by action dignified.

      Enter Romeo.

---

143 bent purpose, inclination **151 By and by** Immediately
152 strife striving **160 tassel-gentle** tercel gentle, the male of the
goshawk **161 Bondage is hoarse** i.e., In confinement one can speak
only in a loud whisper **162 tear** pierce (with noise). **Echo** (In Book
3 of Ovid's *Metamorphoses*, Echo, rejected by Narcissus, pines away in
lonely caves until only her voice is left.) **168 nyas** eyas, fledgling.
173 still always

178 wanton's spoiled child's **180 gyves** fetters **182 his** its
189 ghostly spiritual. **close** narrow **190 dear hap** good fortune
2.3. Location: Verona. Friar Laurence's monastery garden.
3 fleckled dappled **4 From forth** out of the way of. **Titan's** (Helios,
the sun god, was a descendant of the race of Titans.) **5 advance** raise
7 osier cage willow basket **8 baleful** harmful **14 None but for some**
there are none that are not useful for something **15 mickle** great.
grace beneficent virtue **16 true** proper, inherent **17 For naught so**
vile For there is nothing so vile **19 strained** forced, perverted

Within the infant rind of this weak flower
Poison hath residence and medicine power:
For this, being smelt, with that part cheers each part; 25
Being tasted, stays all senses with the heart. 26
Two such opposèd kings encamp them still 27
In man as well as herbs—grace and rude will;
And where the worser is predominant,
Full soon the canker death eats up that plant. 30

ROMEO
Good morrow, Father.

FRIAR LAURENCE   Benedicite! 31
What early tongue so sweet saluteth me?
Young son, it argues a distempered head 33
So soon to bid good morrow to thy bed.
Care keeps his watch in every old man's eye,
And where care lodges sleep will never lie;
But where unbruisèd youth with unstuffed brain 37
Doth couch his limbs, there golden sleep doth reign.
Therefore thy earliness doth me assure
Thou art uproused with some distemp'rature;
Or if not so, then here I hit it right:
Our Romeo hath not been in bed tonight.

ROMEO
That last is true. The sweeter rest was mine.

FRIAR LAURENCE
God pardon sin! Wast thou with Rosaline?

ROMEO
With Rosaline, my ghostly father? No.
I have forgot that name, and that name's woe.

FRIAR LAURENCE
That's my good son. But where hast thou been, then?

ROMEO
I'll tell thee ere thou ask it me again.
I have been feasting with mine enemy,
Where on a sudden one hath wounded me
That's by me wounded. Both our remedies 51
Within thy help and holy physic lies. 52
I bear no hatred, blessèd man, for, lo,
My intercession likewise steads my foe. 54

FRIAR LAURENCE
Be plain, good son, and homely in thy drift. 55
Riddling confession finds but riddling shrift. 56

ROMEO
Then plainly know my heart's dear love is set
On the fair daughter of rich Capulet.
As mine on hers, so hers is set on mine,
And all combined, save what thou must combine
By holy marriage. When and where and how
We met, we wooed, and made exchange of vow
I'll tell thee as we pass; but this I pray,
That thou consent to marry us today.

FRIAR LAURENCE
Holy Saint Francis, what a change is here!
Is Rosaline, that thou didst love so dear,

So soon forsaken? Young men's love then lies
Not truly in their hearts, but in their eyes.
Jesu Maria, what a deal of brine
Hath washed thy sallow cheeks for Rosaline!
How much salt water thrown away in waste
To season love, that of it doth not taste!
The sun not yet thy sighs from heaven clears,
Thy old groans yet ringing in mine ancient ears.
Lo, here upon thy cheek the stain doth sit
Of an old tear that is not washed off yet.
If e'er thou wast thyself and these woes thine, 77
Thou and these woes were all for Rosaline.
And art thou changed? Pronounce this sentence then: 79
Women may fall, when there's no strength in men.

ROMEO
Thou chid'st me oft for loving Rosaline.

FRIAR LAURENCE
For doting, not for loving, pupil mine.

ROMEO
And bad'st me bury love.

FRIAR LAURENCE   Not in a grave
To lay one in, another out to have.

ROMEO
I pray thee, chide not. She whom I love now
Doth grace for grace and love for love allow. 86
The other did not so.

FRIAR LAURENCE   Oh, she knew well
Thy love did read by rote, that could not spell. 88
But come, young waverer, come, go with me,
In one respect I'll thy assistant be; 90
For this alliance may so happy prove
To turn your households' rancor to pure love. 92

ROMEO
Oh, let us hence! I stand on sudden haste. 93

FRIAR LAURENCE
Wisely and slow. They stumble that run fast.
                                                    Exeunt.

❦

[2.4]

Enter Benvolio and Mercutio.

MERCUTIO
Where the devil should this Romeo be? 1
Came he not home tonight? 2

BENVOLIO
Not to his father's. I spoke with his man.

MERCUTIO
Why, that same pale hardhearted wench, that
     Rosaline,
Torments him so that he will sure run mad.

BENVOLIO
Tybalt, the kinsman to old Capulet,
Hath sent a letter to his father's house.

---

25 **that part** i.e., the odor 26 **stays** halts. **with** together with 27 **them still** themselves always 30 **canker** cankerworm 31 **Benedicite!** A blessing on you! 33 **argues** demonstrates, provides evidence of. **distempered** disturbed, disordered 37 **unstuffed** not overcharged, carefree 51 **Both our remedies** The remedy for both of us 52 **physic** medicine, healing property 54 **intercession** petition. **steads** helps 55 **homely** simple 56 **shrift** absolution.

77 **If . . . thine** If ever you had any proper sense of self and understanding of your love sorrows 79 **sentence** maxim 86 **grace** favor, 88 **did read . . . spell** i.e., was like a schoolboy's exercise, repeating words without understanding. 90 **In one respect** for one reason (at least) 92 **To** as to 93 **stand on** am in need of, insist on
2.4. Location: Verona. A street.
1 **should** can 2 **tonight** last night.

MERCUTIO   A challenge, on my life.

BENVOLIO   Romeo will answer it.   9

MERCUTIO   Any man that can write may answer a letter.

BENVOLIO   Nay, he will answer the letter's master, how
he dares, being dared.

MERCUTIO   Alas poor Romeo! He is already dead,
stabbed with a white wench's black eye, run through
the ear with a love song, the very pin of his heart cleft   15
with the blind bow-boy's butt shaft. And is he a man   16
to encounter Tybalt?

BENVOLIO   Why, what is Tybalt?

MERCUTIO   More than prince of cats. Oh, he's the   19
courageous captain of compliments. He fights as you   20
sing prick song, keeps time, distance, and proportion;   21
he rests his minim rests, one, two, and the third in   22
your bosom. The very butcher of a silk button, a   23
duellist, a duellist, a gentleman of the very first house,   24
of the first and second cause. Ah, the immortal   25
passado! The *punto reverso!* The *hay!*   26

BENVOLIO   The what?

MERCUTIO   The pox of such antic, lisping, affecting phan-   28
tasimes, these new tuners of accent! "By Jesu, a very   29
good blade! A very tall man! A very good whore!"   30
Why, is not this a lamentable thing, grandsire, that we   31
should be thus afflicted with these strange flies, these   32
fashionmongers, these pardon-me's, who stand so   33
much on the new form that they cannot sit at ease on   34
the old bench? Oh, their bones, their bones!   35

Enter Romeo.

BENVOLIO   Here comes Romeo, here comes Romeo.

MERCUTIO   Without his roe, like a dried herring. Oh,   37
flesh, flesh, how art thou fishified! Now is he for the
numbers that Petrarch flowed in. Laura to his lady   39
was but a kitchen wench—marry, she had a better

love to berhyme her—Dido a dowdy, Cleopatra a   41
gypsy, Helen and Hero hildings and harlots, Thisbe a   42
gray eye or so, but not to the purpose. Signor Romeo,   43
bonjour! There's a French salutation to your French   44
slop. You gave us the counterfeit fairly last night.   45

ROMEO   Good morrow to you both. What counterfeit
did I give you?

MERCUTIO   The slip, sir, the slip. Can you not conceive?   48

ROMEO   Pardon, good Mercutio. My business was great,
and in such a case as mine a man may strain courtesy.

MERCUTIO   That's as much as to say, such a case as yours   51
constrains a man to bow in the hams.   52

ROMEO   Meaning, to curtsy.   53

MERCUTIO   Thou hast most kindly hit it.   54

ROMEO   A most courteous exposition.

MERCUTIO   Nay, I am the very pink of courtesy.   56

ROMEO   Pink for flower.

MERCUTIO   Right.

ROMEO   Why then is my pump well flowered.   59

MERCUTIO   Sure wit, follow me this jest now till thou
hast worn out thy pump, that when the single sole of
it is worn, the jest may remain, after the wearing,
solely singular.   63

ROMEO   Oh, single-soled jest, solely singular for the   64
singleness!   65

MERCUTIO   Come between us, good Benvolio. My wits
faints.

ROMEO   Switch and spurs, switch and spurs! Or I'll cry   68
a match.   69

MERCUTIO   Nay, if our wits run the wild-goose chase, I   70
am done, for thou hast more of the wild goose in one
of thy wits than, I am sure, I have in my whole five.
Was I with you there for the goose?   73

ROMEO   Thou wast never with me for anything when
thou wast not there for the goose.   75

MERCUTIO   I will bite thee by the ear for that jest.   76

ROMEO   Nay, good goose, bite not.

MERCUTIO   Thy wit is a very bitter sweeting; it is a most   78
sharp sauce.   79

ROMEO   And is it not, then, well served in to a sweet
goose?

---

9 answer it accept the challenge. (But Mercutio replies in the sense of "write in reply.") **15 pin** peg in the center of a target **16 butt shaft** unbarbed arrow, allotted to children and thus to Cupid. **19 prince of cats** (The name of the king of cats in *Reynard the Fox* was Tybalt or Tybert.) **20 captain of compliments** master of ceremony and dueling etiquette. **21 prick song** music written out. **proportion** rhythm **22 minim rests** short rests in musical notation **23 butcher . . . button** i.e., one able to strike a specific button on his adversary's person **24 first house** best school of fencing **25 first and second cause** causes according to the code of dueling that would oblige one to seek the satisfaction of one's honor. **26 passado** forward thrust. **punto reverso** backhanded stroke. **hay** thrust through. (From the Italian *hai*, meaning "you have [it].") **28 The pox of** Plague take. **antic** grotesque **28–9 phantasimes** coxcombs, fantastically dressed or mannered **29 new tuners of accent** those who introduce new foreign words and slang phrases into their speech. **30 tall** valiant **31 grandsire** i.e., one who disapproves of the new fashion and prefers old custom **32 flies** parasites **33 pardon-me's** i.e., those who affect overly polite manners. **stand** (1) insist (2) the opposite of *sit*, line 34 **34–5 form . . . bench** (*Form* means both "fashion" or "code of manners" and "bench.") **35 bones** French *bon*, "good" (with play on English *bone*) **37 Without his roe** i.e., Looking thin and emaciated, sexually spent. (With a pun on the first syllable of Romeo's name; the remaining syllables, *me-oh*, sound like the expression of a melancholy lover. *Roe* also suggests a female deer or "dear.") **39 numbers** verses. **Laura** the lady to whom the Italian Renaissance poet Petrarch addressed his love poems. (Other romantic heroines are named in the following passage: Dido, Queen of Carthage; Cleopatra; Helen of Troy; Hero, beloved of Leander; and Thisbe, beloved of Pyramus.) **to** in comparison with

41 dowdy homely woman **42 gypsy** Egyptian; whore. **hildings** good-for-nothings **43 not** i.e., that is not **44 to** to match **44–5 French slop** loose trousers of French fashion. **45 fairly** handsomely, effectively **48 slip** (Counterfeit coins were called "slips.") **conceive** i.e., get the joke. **51 case** (1) situation (2) physical condition. (Mercutio also bawdily suggests that Romeo has been in a *case*, i.e., the female genitalia.) **52 bow in the hams** (1) make a low bow (2) show the effects of venereal disease. **53 curtsy** bow, make obeisance. **54 kindly** graciously. (But also suggesting natural and physical explanations.) **56 pink** embodied perfection. (But suggesting also the flower called *pink*, the color, and *pinking* of a shoe; see next note.) **59 pump well flowered** shoe expertly pinked or perforated in ornamental figures suggesting flowers. **63 solely singular** unique. **64 single-soled** i.e., thin, contemptible **65 singleness** feebleness. **68 Switch and spurs** i.e., Keep up the rapid pace of the hunt (in the game of wits) **68–9 cry a match** claim the victory. **70 wild-goose chase** a horse race in which the leading rider dares his competitors to follow him wherever he goes **73 Was . . . goose?** Did I score a point in calling you a goose? **75 for the goose** (1) behaving like a goose (2) looking for a prostitute. **76 bite . . . ear** i.e., give you an affectionate nibble on the ear. (Said ironically, however, and Romeo parries.) **78 sweeting** sweet-flavored variety of apple **79 sharp sauce** (1) "biting" retort (2) tart sauce, of the sort that should be served with cooked goose (as Romeo points out).

MERCUTIO　Oh, here's a wit of cheveril, that stretches 82
　from an inch narrow to an ell broad! 83
ROMEO　I stretch it out for that word "broad," which,
　added to the goose, proves thee far and wide a broad 85
　goose.
MERCUTIO　Why, is not this better now than groaning for
　love? Now art thou sociable, now art thou Romeo;
　now art thou what thou art, by art as well as by nature.
　For this driveling love is like a great natural that runs 90
　lolling up and down to hide his bauble in a hole. 91
BENVOLIO　Stop there, stop there.
MERCUTIO　Thou desirest me to stop in my tale against 93
　the hair. 94
BENVOLIO　Thou wouldst else have made thy tale large.
MERCUTIO　Oh, thou art deceived; I would have made it
　short, for I was come to the whole depth of my tale
　and meant indeed to occupy the argument no longer.
ROMEO　Here's goodly gear! 99

Enter Nurse and her man [Peter].

　A sail, a sail! 100
MERCUTIO　Two, two: a shirt and a smock. 101
NURSE　Peter!
PETER　Anon!
NURSE　My fan, Peter.
MERCUTIO　Good Peter, to hide her face, for her fan's
　the fairer face.
NURSE　God gi' good morrow, gentlemen.
MERCUTIO　God gi' good e'en, fair gentlewoman.
NURSE　Is it good e'en? 109
MERCUTIO　'Tis no less, I tell ye, for the bawdy hand of
　the dial is now upon the prick of noon. 111
NURSE　Out upon you! What a man are you? 112
ROMEO　One, gentlewoman, that God hath made for
　himself to mar. 114
NURSE　By my troth, it is well said. "For himself to mar," 115
　quoth 'a? Gentlemen, can any of you tell me where I 116
　may find the young Romeo?
ROMEO　I can tell you; but young Romeo will be older
　when you have found him than he was when you
　sought him. I am the youngest of that name, for fault 120
　of a worse.
NURSE　You say well.

MERCUTIO　Yea, is the worst well? Very well took, i'faith, 123
　wisely, wisely.
NURSE　If you be he, sir, I desire some confidence with 125
　you.
BENVOLIO　She will indite him to some supper. 127
MERCUTIO　A bawd, a bawd, a bawd! So ho! 128
ROMEO　What hast thou found?
MERCUTIO　No hare, sir, unless a hare, sir, in a lenten 130
　pie, that is something stale and hoar ere it be spent. 131
　　　　　　　　　　　　　　　　　　　[He sings.]
　　　An old hare hoar,
　　　And an old hare hoar,
　　Is very good meat in Lent.
　　　But a hare that is hoar
　　　Is too much for a score, 136
　　When it hoars ere it be spent.
Romeo, will you come to your father's? We'll to din-
　ner thither.
ROMEO　I will follow you.
MERCUTIO　Farewell, ancient lady. Farewell, 　*[singing]*
　"Lady, lady, lady." 　　*Exeunt [Mercutio and Benvolio].* 142
NURSE　I pray you, sir, what saucy merchant was this 143
　that was so full of his ropery? 144
ROMEO　A gentleman, Nurse, that loves to hear himself
　talk, and will speak more in a minute than he will
　stand to in a month. 147
NURSE　An 'a speak anything against me, I'll take him 148
　down, an 'a were lustier than he is, and twenty such 149
　Jacks; and if I cannot, I'll find those that shall. Scurvy 150
　knave! I am none of his flirt-gills. I am none of his 151
　skains-mates. *[To Peter]* And thou must stand by, too, 152
　and suffer every knave to use me at his pleasure!
PETER　I saw no man use you at his pleasure. If I had,
　my weapon should quickly have been out; I warrant 155
　you, I dare draw as soon as another man, if I see
　occasion in a good quarrel, and the law on my side.
NURSE　Now, afore God, I am so vexed that every part 158
　about me quivers. Scurvy knave! Pray you, sir, a 159
　word; and as I told you, my young lady bid me
　inquire you out. What she bid me say, I will keep to
　myself. But first let me tell ye, if ye should lead her
　in a fool's paradise, as they say, it were a very gross
　kind of behavior, as they say. For the gentlewoman
　is young; and therefore if you should deal double

---

82 cheveril kid leather, easily stretched　**83 ell** (forty-five inches)
85 broad large, complete; perhaps also wanton　**90 natural** idiot
91 lolling with his tongue (or bauble) hanging out.　**bauble** (1) jester's
wand (2) phallus　**93 stop in my tale** (1) stop short in my story (2) stuff
in my penis　**93–4 against the hair** against the grain, against my wish.
(With bawdy suggestion of pubic hair. The sexual punning continues
in *large* [erect], *short* [detumescent], *come to the depth of my tale*, *occupy*,
etc.)　**99 goodly gear** matter for mockery. (With suggestion of "ample
sexual apparatus.")　**100 A sail** (To Romeo, the Nurse is an imposing
galleon in full sail.)　**101 a shirt and a smock** i.e., a man and a woman.
109 Is it good e'en? Is it afternoon already?　**111 prick** point on the
dial of a clock. (With bawdy suggestion.)　**112 Out upon you** (Expression of indignation.)　**What** What need　**114 mar** i.e., disfigure
morally through sin. (Humankind, made in God's image, mars that
image sinfully.)　**115 troth** faith　**116 quoth 'a** said he. (A sarcastic
interjection, meaning "forsooth" or "indeed.")　**120 fault** lack

123 took understood　**125 confidence** (The Nurse's mistake for "conference.")　**127 indite** (Benvolio's deliberate malapropism for
"invite.")　**128 So ho** (Cry of hunter sighting game.)　**130 hare**
(Slang word for "prostitute"; similarly, with *stale* and *meat* in the following lines.)　**130–1 a lenten pie** a pie that should contain no meat,
in observance of Lent　**131 hoar** moldy. (With pun on "whore"; *stale*
also can mean "whore.")　**spent** consumed.　**136 for a score** for a
reckoning, to pay good money for　**142 "Lady, lady, lady"** (Refrain
from the ballad *Chaste Susanna*.)　**143 merchant** i.e., fellow　**144 ropery** vulgar humor, knavery.　**147 stand to** carry out, stand in support
of　**148 An 'a** If he　**148–9 take him down** cut him down to size.
(With unintended bawdy suggestion.)　**150 Jacks** knaves　**151 flirt-
gills** loose women.　**152 skains-mates** (Perhaps daggermates, outlaws, or gangster molls.)　**155 weapon** (With bawdy suggestion,
perhaps unrecognized by the speaker, as also in *at his pleasure*.)
158–9 every part . . . quivers (More bawdy suggestion, unrecognized
by the Nurse.)

with her, truly it were an ill thing to be offered to any
gentlewoman, and very weak dealing.   167

ROMEO   Nurse, commend me to thy lady and mistress.
I protest unto thee—   169

NURSE   Good heart, and i'faith I will tell her as much.
Lord, Lord, she will be a joyful woman.

ROMEO   What wilt thou tell her, Nurse? Thou dost not
mark me.   173

NURSE   I will tell her, sir, that you do protest, which, as
I take it, is a gentlemanlike offer.

ROMEO   Bid her devise
Some means to come to shrift this afternoon,   177
And there she shall at Friar Laurence' cell
Be shrived and married. Here is for thy pains.   179
          [He offers money.]

NURSE   No, truly, sir, not a penny.

ROMEO   Go to, I say you shall.

NURSE
This afternoon, sir? Well, she shall be there.

ROMEO
And stay, good Nurse, behind the abbey wall.
Within this hour my man shall be with thee
And bring thee cords made like a tackled stair,   185
Which to the high topgallant of my joy   186
Must be my convoy in the secret night.   187
Farewell. Be trusty, and I'll quit thy pains.   188
Farewell. Commend me to thy mistress.
          [Romeo starts to leave.]

NURSE
Now God in heaven bless thee! Hark you, sir.

ROMEO   What say'st thou, my dear Nurse?

NURSE
Is your man secret? Did you ne'er hear say,   192
"Two may keep counsel, putting one away"?   193

ROMEO
'Warrant thee, my man's as true as steel.

NURSE   Well, sir, my mistress is the sweetest lady—
Lord, Lord! When 'twas a little prating thing—Oh,
there is a nobleman in town, one Paris, that would
fain lay knife aboard; but she, good soul, had as lief   198
see a toad, a very toad, as see him. I anger her
sometimes and tell her that Paris is the properer man,   200
but I'll warrant you, when I say so, she looks as pale
as any clout in the versal world. Doth not rosemary   202
and Romeo begin both with a letter?   203

ROMEO   Ay, Nurse, what of that? Both with an R.

NURSE   Ah, mocker! That's the dog's name; R is for   205
the—No; I know it begins with some other letter; and   206
she hath the prettiest sententious of it, of you and   207
rosemary, that it would do you good to hear it.

ROMEO   Commend me to thy lady.

NURSE   Ay, a thousand times.   [Exit Romeo.]
Peter!

PETER   Anon!

NURSE   Before, and apace.   Exeunt. 212

❖

[2.5]

Enter Juliet.

JULIET
The clock struck nine when I did send the Nurse;
In half an hour she promised to return.
Perchance she cannot meet him. That's not so.
Oh, she is lame! Love's heralds should be thoughts,
Which ten times faster glides than the sun's beams
Driving back shadows over louring hills.   6
Therefore do nimble-pinioned doves draw Love,   7
And therefore hath the wind-swift Cupid wings.
Now is the sun upon the highmost hill
Of this day's journey, and from nine till twelve
Is three long hours, yet she is not come.
Had she affections and warm youthful blood,   12
She would be as swift in motion as a ball;
My words would bandy her to my sweet love,   14
And his to me.
But old folks, many feign as they were dead—   16
Unwieldy, slow, heavy, and pale as lead.

Enter Nurse [and Peter].

Oh, God, she comes!—O honey Nurse, what news?
Hast thou met with him? Send thy man away.

NURSE   Peter, stay at the gate.   [Exit Peter.]

JULIET
Now, good sweet Nurse—Oh, Lord, why lookest thou
sad?
Though news be sad, yet tell them merrily;
If good, thou shamest the music of sweet news
By playing it to me with so sour a face.

NURSE
I am aweary. Give me leave awhile.   25
Fie, how my bones ache! What a jaunce have I had!   26

JULIET
I would thou hadst my bones and I thy news.
Nay, come, I pray thee, speak. Good, good Nurse,
speak.

167 **weak** contemptible   169 **protest** vow. (Romeo may intend only
to protest his good intentions, but the Nurse seemingly takes the
word to mean "propose," as if Romeo is making a *gentlemanlike offer*
[line 175] of marriage that would ensure against Juliet's being led into
a *fool's paradise* [line 163]—i.e., being seduced.)   173 **mark** attend to
177 **shrift** confession and absolution   179 **shrived** absolved
185 **tackled stair** rope ladder   186 **topgallant** highest mast and sail of
a ship, the summit   187 **convoy** conveyance, means of passage
188 **quit** reward, requite   192 **secret** trustworthy.   193 **keep counsel**
keep a secret   198 **fain lay knife aboard** like to assert his claim (just
as a guest at an inn did by bringing his knife to the dinner table; with
sexual suggestion also).   **lief** willingly   200 **properer** handsomer
202 **clout** faded rag.   **versal** universal.   **rosemary** (Associated with
weddings and funerals.)   203 **a letter** one and the same letter.

205 **the dog's name** (The letter *R* was thought to resemble the dog's
growl.)   205–6 **R is for ... letter** (Perhaps the Nurse is about to say
"arse," but has a notion that it begins with some other letter. In any case,
she decides against saying such an indelicate word.)   207 **sententious**
(The Nurse probably means "sentences," maxims.)   212 **Before, and
apace** Go before me quickly.
**2.5. Location: Verona. Outside Capulet's house, perhaps in the
orchard or garden.**
6 **louring** dark, threatening   7 **Love** i.e., Venus, whose chariot was
drawn by swift-winged doves   12 **affections** desires   14 **bandy** toss
to and fro, as in tennis   16 **feign as** act as though   25 **Give me leave**
Let me alone   26 **jaunce** jouncing, jolting

NURSE
Jesu, what haste! Can you not stay awhile?   29
Do you not see that I am out of breath?

JULIET
How art thou out of breath, when thou hast breath
To say to me that thou art out of breath?
The excuse that thou dost make in this delay
Is longer than the tale thou dost excuse.   34
Is thy news good or bad? Answer to that;
Say either, and I'll stay the circumstance.   36
Let me be satisfied: is't good or bad?

NURSE   Well, you have made a simple choice. You know   38
not how to choose a man. Romeo? No, not he. Though
his face be better than any man's, yet his leg excels all
men's; and for a hand, and a foot, and a body, though
they be not to be talked on, yet they are past compare.   42
He is not the flower of courtesy, but, I'll warrant him,
as gentle as a lamb. Go thy ways, wench. Serve God.
What, have you dined at home?

JULIET
No, no; but all this did I know before.
What says he of our marriage? What of that?

NURSE
Lord, how my head aches! What a head have I!
It beats as it would fall in twenty pieces.
My back o' t'other side—ah, my back, my back!   50
Beshrew your heart for sending me about   51
To catch my death with jauncing up and down!

JULIET
I'faith, I am sorry that thou art not well.
Sweet, sweet, sweet Nurse, tell me, what says my
    love?

NURSE
Your love says, like an honest gentleman,
And a courteous, and a kind, and a handsome,
And, I warrant, a virtuous—Where is your mother?

JULIET
Where is my mother? Why, she is within,
Where should she be? How oddly thou repliest!
"Your love says, like an honest gentleman,   60
'Where is your mother?'"

NURSE   O God's Lady dear!
Are you so hot? Marry, come up, I trow.   62
Is this the poultice for my aching bones?
Henceforward do your messages yourself.

JULIET
Here's such a coil! Come, what says Romeo?   65

NURSE
Have you got leave to go to shrift today?

JULIET   I have.

NURSE
Then hie you hence to Friar Laurence' cell;   68
There stays a husband to make you a wife.

Now comes the wanton blood up in your cheeks;
They'll be in scarlet straight at any news.   71
Hie you to church. I must another way,
To fetch a ladder, by the which your love
Must climb a bird's nest soon when it is dark.   74
I am the drudge, and toil in your delight,
But you shall bear the burden soon at night.
Go. I'll to dinner. Hie you to the cell.

JULIET
Hie to high fortune! Honest Nurse, farewell.
                              Exeunt [*separately*].

❖

[2.6]

Enter Friar [*Laurence*] *and Romeo.*

FRIAR LAURENCE
So smile the heavens upon this holy act   1
That after-hours with sorrow chide us not!

ROMEO
Amen, amen! But come what sorrow can,
It cannot countervail the exchange of joy   4
That one short minute gives me in her sight.
Do thou but close our hands with holy words,   6
Then love-devouring death do what he dare;
It is enough I may but call her mine.

FRIAR LAURENCE
These violent delights have violent ends
And in their triumph die, like fire and powder,   10
Which as they kiss consume. The sweetest honey
Is loathsome in his own deliciousness,   12
And in the taste confounds the appetite.   13
Therefore love moderately. Long love doth so;
Too swift arrives as tardy as too slow.

Enter Juliet.

Here comes the lady. Oh, so light a foot
Will ne'er wear out the everlasting flint.
A lover may bestride the gossamers   18
That idles in the wanton summer air,   19
And yet not fall, so light is vanity.   20

JULIET
Good even to my ghostly confessor.   21

FRIAR LAURENCE
Romeo shall thank thee, daughter, for us both.   22

JULIET
As much to him, else is his thanks too much.   23

---

71 **in scarlet straight** i.e., blushing immediately   74 **bird's nest** i.e.,
Juliet's room. (Continues the association of Juliet as a bird, as at 1.3.3,
2.2.168–82, with erotic suggestion. The bawdry is continued in *bear
the burden* two lines later.)
2.6. Location: Verona. Friar Laurence's cell.
1 **So . . . heavens** May the heavens so smile   4 **countervail** outweigh,
counterbalance   6 **close** join   10 **powder** gunpowder   12 **his** its
13 **confounds** destroys   18 **gossamers** filmy cobwebs   19 **wanton**
playful   20 **vanity** transitory human joy.   21 **ghostly** spiritual
22 **thank thee** i.e., give a kiss in thanks for your greeting   23 **As . . .
too much** either (1) Then I must repay him with a kiss, lest I be over-
paid, or (2) My greeting is to Romeo as much as to you; otherwise, his
greeting would exceed mine.

---

29 **stay** wait   34 **excuse** excuse yourself from telling.   36 **stay the circumstance** wait patiently for the details.   38 **simple** foolish   42 **be
not to be talked on** are beneath mention (especially in refined lady-
like company)   50 **o' t'other** on the other   51 **Beshrew** A curse on.
(Used as a mild oath.)   60 **honest** honorable   62 **hot** impatient.
Marry, come up (An expression of impatient reproof.)   65 **coil** turmoil, fuss.   68 **hie** hasten

ROMEO
Ah, Juliet, if the measure of thy joy
Be heaped like mine, and that thy skill be more   25
To blazon it, then sweeten with thy breath   26
This neighbor air, and let rich music's tongue
Unfold the imagined happiness that both   28
Receive in either by this dear encounter.   29

JULIET
Conceit, more rich in matter than in words,   30
Brags of his substance, not of ornament.   31
They are but beggars that can count their worth.
But my true love is grown to such excess
I cannot sum up sum of half my wealth.   34

FRIAR LAURENCE
Come, come with me, and we will make short work;
For, by your leaves, you shall not stay alone
Till Holy Church incorporate two in one.   [*Exeunt.*]

[3.1]

Enter Mercutio, Benvolio, and men.

BENVOLIO
I pray thee, good Mercutio, let's retire.
The day is hot, the Capels are abroad,   2
And if we meet we shall not scape a brawl,
For now, these hot days, is the mad blood stirring.

MERCUTIO   Thou art like one of these fellows that when
he enters the confines of a tavern, claps me his sword   6
upon the table and says, "God send me no need of
thee!" and by the operation of the second cup draws   8
him on the drawer, when indeed there is no need.   9

BENVOLIO   Am I like such a fellow?

MERCUTIO   Come, come, thou art as hot a Jack in thy   11
mood as any in Italy, and as soon moved to be moody,   12
and as soon moody to be moved.   13

BENVOLIO   And what to?

MERCUTIO   Nay, an there were two such, we should   15
have none shortly, for one would kill the other. Thou!
Why, thou wilt quarrel with a man that hath a hair
more or a hair less in his beard than thou hast. Thou
wilt quarrel with a man for cracking nuts, having no
other reason but because thou hast hazel eyes. What
eye but such an eye would spy out such a quarrel? Thy
head is as full of quarrels as an egg is full of meat, and 22
yet thy head hath been beaten as addle as an egg for   23
quarreling. Thou hast quarreled with a man for coughing in the street, because he hath wakened thy dog that

hath lain asleep in the sun. Didst thou not fall out
with a tailor for wearing his new doublet before   27
Easter? With another, for tying his new shoes with old
ribbon? And yet thou wilt tutor me from quarreling!

BENVOLIO   An I were so apt to quarrel as thou art, any
man should buy the fee simple of my life for an hour   31
and a quarter.   32

MERCUTIO   The fee simple! Oh, simple!   33

Enter Tybalt, Petruchio, and others.

BENVOLIO   By my head, here comes the Capulets.

MERCUTIO   By my heel, I care not.

TYBALT [*to his companions*]
Follow me close, for I will speak to them.—
Gentlemen, good e'en. A word with one of you.

MERCUTIO   And but one word with one of us? Couple it
with something: make it a word and a blow.

TYBALT   You shall find me apt enough to that, sir, an
you will give me occasion.

MERCUTIO   Could you not take some occasion without
giving?

TYBALT   Mercutio, thou consortest with Romeo.   44

MERCUTIO   "Consort"? What, dost thou make us minstrels? An thou make minstrels of us, look to hear
nothing but discords. Here's my fiddlestick; here's   47
that shall make you dance. Zounds, "consort"!   48

BENVOLIO
We talk here in the public haunt of men.
Either withdraw unto some private place,
Or reason coldly of your grievances,   51
Or else depart; here all eyes gaze on us.   52

MERCUTIO
Men's eyes were made to look, and let them gaze.
I will not budge for no man's pleasure, I.

Enter Romeo.

TYBALT
Well, peace be with you, sir. Here comes my man.

MERCUTIO
But I'll be hanged, sir, if he wear your livery.   56
Marry, go before to field, he'll be your follower;   57
Your Worship in that sense may call him "man."   58

TYBALT
Romeo, the love I bear thee can afford
No better term than this: thou art a villain.

ROMEO
Tybalt, the reason that I have to love thee
Doth much excuse the appertaining rage   62
To such a greeting. Villain am I none.

---

25 **that** if   26 **blazon** describe, set forth. (A heraldic term.)
28 **Unfold** make known.   **imagined** i.e., unexpressed   29 **in either**
from each other   30–1 **Conceit . . . ornament** True understanding,
more enriched by the actual reality (of love) than by mere words, finds
more worth in the substance of that reality than in outward show.
34 **sum up sum** add up the total
3.1. **Location: Verona. A public place.**
2 **Capels** Capulets   6 **claps me** claps. (*Me* is a now-archaic dative of
reference, used colloquially.)   8–9 **draws . . . drawer** draws his sword
against the tapster or waiter   9 **there is no need** i.e., of his sword.
11 **as hot a Jack** as hot-tempered a fellow   12 **moody** angry   13 **to be
moved** at being provoked.   15 **an** if   22 **meat** i.e., edible matter
23 **addle** addled, confused

27 **doublet** man's jacket   31 **fee simple** outright possession   31–2 **an
hour . . . quarter** i.e., my life would last no longer in such circumstances.
33 **Oh, simple!** Oh, how stupid!   44 **consortest** keep company with.
(But Mercutio quibbles on its musical sense of "accompany" or "play
together.")   47 **fiddlestick** (Mercutio means his sword.)   48 **that** that
which.   **Zounds** By God's (Christ's) wounds   51 **coldly** calmly
52 **depart** go away separately   56 **livery** servant's uniform. (Mercutio
deliberately mistakes Tybalt's phrase *my man* to mean "my servant.")
57 **field** field where a duel might occur   58 **Your Worship** (A title of
honor used here with mock politeness.)   62 **the appertaining rage** the
rage that would ordinarily be appropriate

Therefore, farewell. I see thou knowest me not.

TYBALT

Boy, this shall not excuse the injuries   65
That thou hast done me. Therefore turn and draw.

ROMEO

I do protest I never injured thee,
But love thee better than thou canst devise   68
Till thou shalt know the reason of my love.
And so, good Capulet—which name I tender   70
As dearly as mine own—be satisfied.

MERCUTIO

Oh, calm, dishonorable, vile submission!
Alla stoccata carries it away.   [*He draws.*] 73
Tybalt, you ratcatcher, will you walk?   74

TYBALT   What wouldst thou have with me?

MERCUTIO   Good king of cats, nothing but one of your
nine lives, that I mean to make bold withal, and, as   77
you shall use me hereafter, dry-beat the rest of the   78
eight. Will you pluck your sword out of his pilcher by   79
the ears? Make haste, lest mine be about your ears ere   80
it be out.

TYBALT   I am for you.   [*He draws.*]

ROMEO

Gentle Mercutio, put thy rapier up.

MERCUTIO   Come, sir, your *passado*.   [*They fight.*] 84

ROMEO

Draw, Benvolio, beat down their weapons.
Gentlemen, for shame, forbear this outrage!
Tybalt, Mercutio, the Prince expressly hath
Forbid this bandying in Verona streets.
Hold, Tybalt! Good Mercutio!
        [*Tybalt under Romeo's arm stabs Mercutio.*] *Away*
                        Tybalt [*with his followers*].

MERCUTIO   I am hurt.   89
A plague o' both your houses! I am sped.   90
Is he gone, and hath nothing?

BENVOLIO   What, art thou hurt?

MERCUTIO

Ay, ay, a scratch, a scratch; marry, 'tis enough.
Where is my page? Go, villain, fetch a surgeon.
                                        [*Exit Page.*]

ROMEO

Courage, man, the hurt cannot be much.

MERCUTIO   No, 'tis not so deep as a well, nor so wide as
a church door, but 'tis enough, 'twill serve. Ask for me
tomorrow, and you shall find me a grave man. I am   97
peppered, I warrant, for this world. A plague o' both   98
your houses! Zounds, a dog, a rat, a mouse, a cat, to
scratch a man to death! A braggart, a rogue, a villain,
that fights by the book of arithmetic! Why the devil   101
came you between us? I was hurt under your arm.

ROMEO   I thought all for the best.

MERCUTIO

Help me into some house, Benvolio,
Or I shall faint. A plague o' both your houses!
They have made worm's meat of me. I have it,
And soundly too. Your houses!
                        Exit [*supported by Benvolio*].

ROMEO

This gentleman, the Prince's near ally,   108
My very friend, hath got this mortal hurt   109
In my behalf; my reputation stained
With Tybalt's slander—Tybalt, that an hour
Hath been my cousin! O sweet Juliet,   112
Thy beauty hath made me effeminate,   113
And in my temper softened valor's steel.   114

                    Enter Benvolio.

BENVOLIO

O Romeo, Romeo, brave Mercutio is dead!
That gallant spirit hath aspired the clouds,   116
Which too untimely here did scorn the earth.

ROMEO

This day's black fate on more days doth depend;   118
This but begins the woe others must end.   119

                    [*Enter Tybalt.*]

BENVOLIO

Here comes the furious Tybalt back again.

ROMEO

Alive in triumph, and Mercutio slain!
Away to heaven, respective lenity,   122
And fire-eyed fury be my conduct now!   123
Now, Tybalt, take the "villain" back again
That late thou gavest me, for Mercutio's soul
Is but a little way above our heads,
Staying for thine to keep him company.
Either thou or I, or both, must go with him.

TYBALT

Thou, wretched boy, that didst consort him here,
Shalt with him hence.

ROMEO   This shall determine that.
                        They fight. Tybalt falls.

BENVOLIO   Romeo, away, begone!
The citizens are up, and Tybalt slain.

---

65 **Boy** (A deliberate and grave insult when addressed to a grown
man. Tybalt's use of *thee* and *thou* in lines 59–60 and following is similarly insulting; Romeo's use of this personal form in lines 61–4 and
67–9, on the other hand, is appropriate to a close family tie that he
privately acknowledges but is of course misunderstood by Tybalt and
the bystanders.)   68 **devise** imagine   70 **tender** value   73 *Alla stoccata* . . . **away** i.e. (scornfully), This elegant Italian way of fencing,
and the fancy terminology to go with it, will win the day, I suppose.
(*Alla stoccata* means "at the thrust.")   74 **ratcatcher** (An allusion to
Tybalt as king of cats; see 2.4.19.)   77 **make bold withal** make free
with   78 **dry-beat** beat soundly (without drawing blood)   79–80 **out
. . . ears** out of its scabbard by the handle or hilt.   84 *passado* forward thrust. (Another fancy Italian fencing term of the sort Mercutio
despises.)   89 **s.d.** *Away Tybalt* (Because the phrase is unusual for an
exit stage direction, some editors plausibly assign this as a speech to
Petruchio, who enters at line 33.1 and is otherwise silent.)   90 **sped**
done for.

97 **grave** (Mercutio thus puns with his last breath.)   98 **peppered** finished, done for   101 **by . . . arithmetic** by the numbers, as in a textbook on fencing (as at 2.4.20–3.)   108 **ally** kinsman   109 **very** true
112 **cousin** kinsman.   113 **effeminate** weak   114 **temper** disposition.
(But with a play on the tempering of a steel sword.)   116 **aspired**
ascended to   118 **This day's . . . depend** This day hangs threateningly over the time to come   119 **others** other days to come
122 **respective lenity** considerate gentleness   123 **conduct** guide

Stand not amazed. The Prince will doom thee death   133
If thou art taken. Hence, begone, away!

ROMEO
Oh, I am fortune's fool!

BENVOLIO   Why dost thou stay?   135

Exit Romeo.

Enter Citizens.

FIRST CITIZEN
Which way ran he that killed Mercutio?
Tybalt, that murderer, which way ran he?

BENVOLIO
There lies that Tybalt.

FIRST CITIZEN   Up, sir, go with me.
I charge thee in the Prince's name, obey.

Enter Prince [attended], old Montague,
Capulet, their Wives, and all.

PRINCE
Where are the vile beginners of this fray?

BENVOLIO
O noble Prince, I can discover all   141
The unlucky manage of this fatal brawl.   142
There lies the man, slain by young Romeo,
That slew thy kinsman, brave Mercutio.

CAPULET'S WIFE
Tybalt, my cousin! O my brother's child!
O Prince! O cousin! Husband! Oh, the blood is spilled
Of my dear kinsman! Prince, as thou art true,
For blood of ours shed blood of Montague.
O cousin, cousin!

PRINCE
Benvolio, who began this bloody fray?

BENVOLIO
Tybalt, here slain, whom Romeo's hand did slay.
Romeo, that spoke him fair, bid him bethink   152
How nice the quarrel was, and urged withal   153
Your high displeasure. All this—utterèd
With gentle breath, calm look, knees humbly bowed—
Could not take truce with the unruly spleen   156
Of Tybalt deaf to peace, but that he tilts
With piercing steel at bold Mercutio's breast,
Who, all as hot, turns deadly point to point,
And, with a martial scorn, with one hand beats
Cold death aside and with the other sends
It back to Tybalt, whose dexterity
Retorts it. Romeo he cries aloud,   163
"Hold, friends! Friends, part!" and swifter than his
    tongue
His agile arm beats down their fatal points,
And twixt them rushes; underneath whose arm
An envious thrust from Tybalt hit the life   167
Of stout Mercutio, and then Tybalt fled;   168
But by and by comes back to Romeo,
Who had but newly entertained revenge,   170

And to't they go like lightning, for, ere I
Could draw to part them was stout Tybalt slain,
And, as he fell, did Romeo turn and fly.
This is the truth, or let Benvolio die.

CAPULET'S WIFE
He is a kinsman to the Montague.
Affection makes him false; he speaks not true.   176
Some twenty of them fought in this black strife,
And all those twenty could but kill one life.
I beg for justice, which thou, Prince, must give.
Romeo slew Tybalt; Romeo must not live.

PRINCE
Romeo slew him, he slew Mercutio.
Who now the price of his dear blood doth owe?

MONTAGUE
Not Romeo, Prince, he was Mercutio's friend;
His fault concludes but what the law should end,   184
The life of Tybalt.

PRINCE   And for that offense
Immediately we do exile him hence.
I have an interest in your hate's proceeding;
My blood for your rude brawls doth lie a-bleeding;   188
But I'll amerce you with so strong a fine   189
That you shall all repent the loss of mine.
I will be deaf to pleading and excuses;
Nor tears nor prayers shall purchase out abuses.   192
Therefore use none. Let Romeo hence in haste,   193
Else, when he is found, that hour is his last.   194
Bear hence this body and attend our will.   195
Mercy but murders, pardoning those that kill.   196

Exeunt, [some carrying Tybalt's body].

❋

[3.2]

Enter Juliet alone.

JULIET
Gallop apace, you fiery-footed steeds,   1
Towards Phoebus' lodging! Such a wagoner   2
As Phaëthon would whip you to the west   3
And bring in cloudy night immediately.   4
Spread thy close curtain, love-performing night,   5

---

133 **amazed** dazed.   **doom thee death** sentence you to death
135 **fool** dupe.   141 **discover** reveal   142 **manage** conduct   152 **fair**
civilly.   **bethink** consider   153 **nice** trivial.   **withal** besides
156 **take truce** make peace   163 **Retorts** returns   167 **envious** malicious   168 **stout** brave   170 **entertained** harbored thoughts of

176 **Affection** Partiality   184 **concludes but** only finishes   188 **My
blood** i.e., blood of my kinsman. (Here we learn that Mercutio is kin
to the Prince.)   189 **amerce** penalize   192 **Nor** neither.   **purchase
out abuses** redeem misdeeds.   193 **hence** depart   194 **Else** otherwise   195 **attend our will** be on hand to hear further judgment.
196 **but murders** merely encourages murder by excessive leniency
3.2. Location: Verona. Capulet's house.
1 **apace** quickly.   **steeds** i.e., the horses of the sun god's chariot
2 **Phoebus** (Often equated with Helios, the sun god.)   **lodging** i.e., in
the west, below the horizon.   2–4 **Such . . . immediately** i.e., One
who is impetuously young, as we are, would understand the need to
make the day as short as possible and would quickly bring it to an
end. (The mythical allusion is sadly ironic, for Phaëthon drove the
chariot of the sun so badly that he had to be destroyed by Zeus.)
5 **close** enclosing

That runaways' eyes may wink, and Romeo   6
Leap to these arms, untalked of and unseen.   7
Lovers can see to do their amorous rites
By their own beauties; or, if love be blind,
It best agrees with night. Come, civil night,   10
Thou sober-suited matron all in black,
And learn me how to lose a winning match   12
Played for a pair of stainless maidenhoods.
Hood my unmanned blood, bating in my cheeks,   14
With thy black mantle till strange love grown bold 15
Think true love acted simple modesty.
Come, night. Come, Romeo. Come, thou day in night;
For thou wilt lie upon the wings of night
Whiter than new snow upon a raven's back.
Come, gentle night, come, loving, black-browed night,
Give me my Romeo, and when I shall die   21
Take him and cut him out in little stars,
And he will make the face of heaven so fine
That all the world will be in love with night
And pay no worship to the garish sun.   25
Oh, I have bought the mansion of a love
But not possessed it, and though I am sold,
Not yet enjoyed. So tedious is this day
As is the night before some festival
To an impatient child that hath new robes
And may not wear them. Oh, here comes my nurse, 31

Enter Nurse, with cords.

And she brings news, and every tongue that speaks
But Romeo's name speaks heavenly eloquence.
Now, Nurse, what news? What hast thou there? The
      cords
That Romeo bid thee fetch?

NURSE   Ay, ay, the cords.
                            [*She throws them down.*]
JULIET
Ay me, what news? Why dost thou wring thy hands?
NURSE
Ah, weraday! He's dead, he's dead, he's dead!   37
We are undone, lady, we are undone!
Alack the day, he's gone, he's killed, he's dead!
JULIET
Can heaven be so envious?
NURSE   Romeo can,   40
Though heaven cannot. Oh, Romeo, Romeo!
Who ever would have thought it? Romeo!

JULIET
What devil art thou that dost torment me thus?
This torture should be roared in dismal hell.
Hath Romeo slain himself? Say thou but "Ay,"
And that bare vowel "I" shall poison more   46
Than the death-darting eye of cockatrice.   47
I am not I, if there be such an "Ay,"
Or those eyes shut, that makes thee answer "Ay." 49
If he be slain, say "Ay," or if not, "No."
Brief sounds determine of my weal or woe.   51
NURSE
I saw the wound. I saw it with mine eyes—
God save the mark!—here on his manly breast.   53
A piteous corpse, a bloody piteous corpse;
Pale, pale as ashes, all bedaubed in blood,
All in gore-blood. I swoonèd at the sight.   56
JULIET
Oh, break, my heart! Poor bankrupt, break at once!
To prison, eyes; ne'er look on liberty!
Vile earth, to earth resign; end motion here,   59
And thou and Romeo press one heavy bier!   60
NURSE
O Tybalt, Tybalt, the best friend I had!
O courteous Tybalt! Honest gentleman!   62
That ever I should live to see thee dead!
JULIET
What storm is this that blows so contrary?
Is Romeo slaughtered, and is Tybalt dead?
My dearest cousin, and my dearer lord?
Then, dreadful trumpet, sound the general doom! 67
For who is living, if those two are gone?
NURSE
Tybalt is gone, and Romeo banishèd;
Romeo that killed him, he is banishèd.
JULIET
Oh, God! Did Romeo's hand shed Tybalt's blood?
NURSE
It did, it did. Alas the day it did!
JULIET
O serpent heart, hid with a flow'ring face!   73
Did ever dragon keep so fair a cave?   74
Beautiful tyrant! Fiend angelical!
Dove-feathered raven! Wolvish-ravening lamb!
Despisèd substance of divinest show!   77
Just opposite to what thou justly seem'st,
A damnèd saint, an honorable villain!
O nature, what hadst thou to do in hell
When thou didst bower the spirit of a fiend   81
In mortal paradise of such sweet flesh?
Was ever book containing such vile matter

6–7 That runaways' . . . unseen (Perhaps Juliet is thinking of the elopement that will surely be necessary once she and Romeo secretly marry; they will embrace in the dark of *love-performing night*, untalked of and unseen by others and by each other. A difficult passage that is sometimes interpreted, uncertainly, as referring to the sun's horses as the *runaways*. *Wink* means "close, be shut.") **10 civil** circumspect, somberly attired **12 learn** teach **14 Hood** Cover. (A term in falconry; the hawk's eyes were covered so that it would not *bate* or beat its wings.) **unmanned** untamed (in falconry; with a pun on "not yet sexually possessed") **15 strange** diffident **21 I** (Often emended to *he*, following the fourth quarto, but Juliet may mean that when she is dead she will share Romeo's beauty with the world. Dying may also hint at sexual climax.) **25 garish** dazzling **31.1 cords** ropes (for the ladder). **37 weraday!** welladay, alas! **40 envious** malicious.

46 "I" (Pronounced identically with "Ay.") **47 cockatrice** basilisk, a mythical serpent that could kill by its look. **49 those eyes shut** if Romeo's eyes are shut (in death) **51 weal** welfare, happiness **53 God . . . mark** (An oath registering shock and horror.) **56 gore-blood** clotted blood. **59 Vile . . . here** May my vile body resign itself to burial, ending life itself **60 press** weigh down. **bier** litter for carrying corpses. **62 Honest** Honorable **67 trumpet** i.e., the last trumpet. **general doom** Day of Judgment. **73 hid . . . face** concealed beneath a beautiful face. **74 keep** occupy, guard. **cave** i.e., one with treasure in it. **77 show** appearance. **81 bower** give lodging to

So fairly bound? Oh, that deceit should dwell
In such a gorgeous palace!

NURSE   There's no trust,
No faith, no honesty in men; all perjured,
All forsworn, all naught, all dissemblers.   87
Ah, where's my man? Give me some aqua vitae.   88
These griefs, these woes, these sorrows make me old.
Shame come to Romeo!

JULIET   Blistered be thy tongue
For such a wish! He was not born to shame.
Upon his brow shame is ashamed to sit,
For 'tis a throne where honor may be crowned
Sole monarch of the universal earth.
Oh, what a beast was I to chide at him!

NURSE
Will you speak well of him that killed your cousin?

JULIET
Shall I speak ill of him that is my husband?
Ah, poor my lord, what tongue shall smooth thy name   98
When I, thy three-hours wife, have mangled it?
But wherefore, villain, didst thou kill my cousin?
That villain cousin would have killed my husband.
Back, foolish tears, back to your native spring!
Your tributary drops belong to woe,
Which you, mistaking, offer up to joy.   103
My husband lives, that Tybalt would have slain,   105
And Tybalt's dead, that would have slain my
    husband.
All this is comfort. Wherefore weep I then?
Some word there was, worser than Tybalt's death,
That murdered me. I would forget it fain,   109
But oh, it presses to my memory
Like damnèd guilty deeds to sinners' minds!
"Tybalt is dead, and Romeo—banishèd."
That "banishèd," that one word "banishèd"
Hath slain ten thousand Tybalts. Tybalt's death
Was woe enough, if it had ended there;
Or, if sour woe delights in fellowship
And needly will be ranked with other griefs,   117
Why followed not, when she said "Tybalt's dead,"
"Thy father," or "thy mother," nay, or both,
Which modern lamentation might have moved?   120
But with a rearward following Tybalt's death,   121
"Romeo is banishèd"—to speak that word
Is father, mother, Tybalt, Romeo, Juliet,
All slain, all dead. "Romeo is banishèd!"
There is no end, no limit, measure, bound,
In that word's death; no words can that woe sound. 126
Where is my father and my mother, Nurse?

NURSE
Weeping and wailing over Tybalt's corpse.
Will you go to them? I will bring you thither.

JULIET
Wash they his wounds with tears? Mine shall be spent,
When theirs are dry, for Romeo's banishment.
Take up those cords.—Poor ropes, you are beguiled,
Both you and I, for Romeo is exiled.
He made you for a highway to my bed,
But I, a maid, die maiden-widowèd.
Come, cords, come, Nurse. I'll to my wedding bed,
And death, not Romeo, take my maidenhead.

NURSE [taking up the cords]
Hie to your chamber. I'll find Romeo
To comfort you. I wot well where he is.   139
Hark ye, your Romeo will be here at night.
I'll to him. He is hid at Laurence' cell.

JULIET [giving a ring]
Oh, find him! Give this ring to my true knight,
And bid him come to take his last farewell.
                              Exeunt [separately].

❖

[3.3]

Enter Friar [Laurence].

FRIAR LAURENCE
Romeo, come forth; come forth, thou fearful man.   1
Affliction is enamored of thy parts,   2
And thou art wedded to calamity.

        [Enter] Romeo.

ROMEO
Father, what news? What is the Prince's doom?   4
What sorrow craves acquaintance at my hand
That I yet know not?

FRIAR LAURENCE   Too familiar
Is my dear son with such sour company.
I bring thee tidings of the Prince's doom.

ROMEO
What less than doomsday is the Prince's doom?   9

FRIAR LAURENCE
A gentler judgment vanished from his lips: 10
Not body's death, but body's banishment.

ROMEO
Ha, banishment? Be merciful, say "death";
For exile hath more terror in his look,
Much more than death. Do not say "banishment."

FRIAR LAURENCE
Here from Verona art thou banishèd.
Be patient, for the world is broad and wide.

ROMEO
There is no world without Verona walls   17
But purgatory, torture, hell itself.
Hence "banishèd" is banished from the world,
And world's exile is death. Then "banishèd"   20
Is death mistermed. Calling death "banishèd,"

---

87 **naught** worthless, evil **88 man** servant. **aqua vitae** alcoholic
spirits. **98 poor my lord** my poor lord. **smooth thy name** speak
your name kindly **103 Your . . . woe** You should be shed, offered as
a tribute, on some occasion of real woe **105 that** whom **109 fain**
gladly **117 needly** of necessity. **ranked with** accompanied by
120 Which . . . moved which might have prompted a normal grief-
stricken response. **121 rearward** rearguard, following afterward
126 sound (1) fathom (2) express.

139 **wot** know
3.3. **Location: Verona. Friar Laurence's cell**.
1 **fearful** full of fear **2 parts** qualities **4 doom** judgment.
9 **doomsday** the Day of Judgment, i.e., end of the world
10 **vanished** issued (into air) **17 without** outside of **20 world's
exile** exile from the world

Thou cut'st my head off with a golden ax
And smilest upon the stroke that murders me.

FRIAR LAURENCE
Oh, deadly sin! Oh, rude unthankfulness!
Thy fault our law calls death, but the kind Prince,   25
Taking thy part, hath rushed aside the law   26
And turned that black word "death" to "banishment."
This is dear mercy, and thou see'st it not.

ROMEO
'Tis torture, and not mercy. Heaven is here
Where Juliet lives, and every cat and dog
And little mouse, every unworthy thing,
Live here in heaven and may look on her,
But Romeo may not. More validity,   33
More honorable state, more courtship lives   34
In carrion flies than Romeo. They may seize
On the white wonder of dear Juliet's hand
And steal immortal blessing from her lips,
Who even in pure and vestal modesty   38
Still blush, as thinking their own kisses sin;   39
But Romeo may not, he is banishèd.
Flies may do this, but I from this must fly.
They are free men, but I am banishèd.
And sayest thou yet that exile is not death?
Hadst thou no poison mixed, no sharp-ground knife,
No sudden mean of death, though ne'er so mean,   45
But "banishèd" to kill me? "Banishèd"?
Oh, Friar, the damnèd use that word in hell;
Howling attends it. How hast thou the heart,
Being a divine, a ghostly confessor,
A sin absolver, and my friend professed,
To mangle me with that word "banishèd"?

FRIAR LAURENCE
Thou fond mad man, hear me a little speak.   52

ROMEO
Oh, thou wilt speak again of banishment.

FRIAR LAURENCE
I'll give thee armor to keep off that word,
Adversity's sweet milk, philosophy,
To comfort thee, though thou art banishèd.

ROMEO
Yet "banishèd"? Hang up philosophy!   57
Unless philosophy can make a Juliet,
Displant a town, reverse a prince's doom,   59
It helps not, it prevails not. Talk no more.

FRIAR LAURENCE
Oh, then I see that madmen have no ears.

ROMEO
How should they, when that wise men have no eyes?

FRIAR LAURENCE
Let me dispute with thee of thy estate.   63

ROMEO
Thou canst not speak of that thou dost not feel.   64
Wert thou as young as I, Juliet thy love,
An hour but married, Tybalt murderèd,
Doting like me, and like me banishèd,
Then mightst thou speak, then mightst thou tear thy
    hair,
And fall upon the ground, as I do now,
Taking the measure of an unmade grave.
              [He falls upon the ground.] Knock [within].

FRIAR LAURENCE
Arise. One knocks. Good Romeo, hide thyself.

ROMEO
Not I, unless the breath of heartsick groans,
Mistlike, infold me from the search of eyes.   Knock.

FRIAR LAURENCE
Hark, how they knock!—Who's there?—Romeo, arise.
Thou wilt be taken.—Stay awhile!—Stand up.
                                                 Knock.
Run to my study.—By and by!—God's will,
What simpleness is this?—I come, I come!   Knock.   77
Who knocks so hard? Whence come you? What's your
    will?   [Going to the door.]

NURSE [within]
Let me come in, and you shall know my errand.
I come from Lady Juliet.

FRIAR LAURENCE   Welcome, then.
                                       [He opens the door.]

              Enter Nurse.

NURSE
O holy Friar, oh, tell me, holy Friar,
Where's my lady's lord, where's Romeo?

FRIAR LAURENCE
There on the ground, with his own tears made drunk.

NURSE
Oh, he is even in my mistress' case,   84
Just in her case! Oh, woeful sympathy!   85
Piteous predicament! Even so lies she,
Blubb'ring and weeping, weeping and blubb'ring.—
Stand up, stand up! Stand, an you be a man.
For Juliet's sake, for her sake, rise and stand!
Why should you fall into so deep an O?   90

ROMEO   Nurse!   [He rises.]

NURSE
Ah, sir, ah, sir! Death's the end of all.

ROMEO
Spakest thou of Juliet? How is it with her?
Doth not she think me an old murderer,   94
Now I have stained the childhood of our joy
With blood removed but little from her own?
Where is she? And how doth she? And what says
My concealed lady to our canceled love?   98

---

25 **Thy fault . . . death** For your crime, the law demands a death sentence   26 **rushed** thrust   33 **validity** true worth   34 **courtship** (1) courtliness (2) occasion for wooing   38 **vestal** maidenly   39 **Still . . . sin** continually look red, as though blushing to think that their touching each other is sin   45 **mean . . . mean** means . . . base   52 **fond** foolish, frantic   57 **Yet** Still   59 **Displant** uproot   63 **dispute** reason. **estate** situation.

64 **that** that which   77 **simpleness** foolishness   84 **even** exactly. **case** situation   85 **woeful sympathy** mutuality of grief.   90 **an O** a fit of groaning. (A sexual meaning, unrecognized by the speaker, is suggested by *rise and stand* in the previous line and *case* in lines 84–5.)   94 **old** hardened   98 **concealed** secret.   **canceled** nullified (by the impending exile)

NURSE
Oh, she says nothing, sir, but weeps and weeps,
And now falls on her bed, and then starts up,
And "Tybalt" calls, and then on Romeo cries,
And then down falls again.

ROMEO   As if that name,
Shot from the deadly level of a gun,   103
Did murder her, as that name's cursèd hand
Murdered her kinsman. Oh, tell me, Friar, tell me,
In what vile part of this anatomy
Doth my name lodge? Tell me, that I may sack   107
The hateful mansion.
                    [He draws a weapon, but is restrained.]
FRIAR LAURENCE   Hold thy desperate hand!
Art thou a man? Thy form cries out thou art;
Thy tears are womanish, thy wild acts denote
The unreasonable fury of a beast.
Unseemly woman in a seeming man,
And ill-beseeming beast in seeming both!
Thou hast amazed me. By my holy order,
I thought thy disposition better tempered.   115
Hast thou slain Tybalt? Wilt thou slay thyself,
And slay thy lady, that in thy life lives,
By doing damnèd hate upon thyself?
Why railest thou on thy birth, the heaven, and earth,
Since birth, and heaven, and earth, all three do meet   120
In thee at once, which thou at once wouldst lose?
Fie, fie, thou shamest thy shape, thy love, thy wit,   122
Which, like a usurer, abound'st in all,   123
And usest none in that true use indeed   124
Which should bedeck thy shape, thy love, thy wit.   125
Thy noble shape is but a form of wax,   126
Digressing from the valor of a man;
Thy dear love sworn but hollow perjury,
Killing that love which thou hast vowed to cherish;
Thy wit, that ornament to shape and love,
Misshapen in the conduct of them both,   131
Like powder in a skilless soldier's flask   132
Is set afire by thine own ignorance,
And thou dismembered with thine own defense.   134
What, rouse thee, man! Thy Juliet is alive,
For whose dear sake thou wast but lately dead;   136
There art thou happy. Tybalt would kill thee,   137
But thou slewest Tybalt; there art thou happy.
The law that threatened death becomes thy friend
And turns it to exile; there art thou happy.
A pack of blessings light upon thy back,
Happiness courts thee in her best array,
But like a mishavèd and sullen wench   143
Thou pout'st upon thy fortune and thy love.

Take heed, take heed, for such die miserable.
Go, get thee to thy love, as was decreed.   146
Ascend her chamber; hence and comfort her.
But look thou stay not till the watch be set,   148
For then thou canst not pass to Mantua,
Where thou shalt live till we can find a time
To blaze your marriage, reconcile your friends,   151
Beg pardon of the Prince, and call thee back
With twenty hundred thousand times more joy
Than thou went'st forth in lamentation.
Go before, Nurse. Commend me to thy lady,
And bid her hasten all the house to bed,
Which heavy sorrow makes them apt unto.
Romeo is coming.
NURSE
Oh, Lord, I could have stayed here all the night
To hear good counsel. Oh, what learning is!—
My lord, I'll tell my lady you will come.
ROMEO
Do so, and bid my sweet prepare to chide.
NURSE [giving a ring]
Here, sir, a ring she bid me give you, sir.
Hie you, make haste, for it grows very late.   [Exit.]
ROMEO
How well my comfort is revived by this!
FRIAR LAURENCE
Go hence. Good night. And here stands all your state: 166
Either be gone before the watch be set,
Or by the break of day disguised from hence.
Sojourn in Mantua. I'll find out your man,
And he shall signify from time to time
Every good hap to you that chances here.   171
Give me thy hand. 'Tis late. Farewell, good night.
ROMEO
But that a joy past joy calls out on me,
It were a grief so brief to part with thee.   174
Farewell.   Exeunt [separately].

✤

[3.4]

Enter old Capulet, his Wife, and Paris.

CAPULET
Things have fall'n out, sir, so unluckily,   1
That we have had no time to move our daughter.   2
Look you, she loved her kinsman Tybalt dearly,
And so did I. Well, we were born to die.
'Tis very late. She'll not come down tonight.
I promise you, but for your company   6
I would have been abed an hour ago.
PARIS
These times of woe afford no times to woo.
Madam, good night. Commend me to your daughter.

---

103 **level** aim   107 **sack** destroy   115 **tempered** harmonized, balanced.   120 **birth . . . earth** life, soul, and body   122–5 **thou shamest . . . wit** you shame your physical form, love, and mind (corresponding to life, soul, and body), all of which you have in abundance but which you misuse as a usurer misuses wealth, using improperly the treasure that you should put to proper use.   126 **form of wax** waxwork, mere outer form   131 **conduct** guidance   132 **powder** gunpowder.   **flask** powder horn   134 **dismembered . . . defense** blown to pieces by that which should defend you, i.e., your *wit*, or intellect.   136 **wast . . . dead** i.e., only recently were wishing yourself dead. (See line 70.)   137 **happy** fortunate.   143 **mishavèd** misbehaved

146 **decreed** (1) arranged earlier (2) decreed by heaven for those who have married.   148 **the watch be set** guards are posted (at the city gates)   151 **blaze** publish, divulge.   **friends** relations   166 **here . . . state** your fortune depends on what follows   171 **good hap** fortunate event   174 **brief** quickly
3.4. Location: Verona. Capulet's house.
1 **fall'n out** happened   2 **move** persuade   6 **promise** assure

WIFE

I will, and know her mind early tomorrow.
Tonight she's mewed up to her heaviness.   11

CAPULET

Sir Paris, I will make a desperate tender   12
Of my child's love. I think she will be ruled
In all respects by me; nay, more, I doubt it not.
Wife, go you to her ere you go to bed.
Acquaint her here of my son Paris' love,
And bid her, mark you me, on Wednesday next—   17
But soft, what day is this?

PARIS   Monday, my lord.   18

CAPULET

Monday! Ha, ha! Well, Wednesday is too soon;
O' Thursday let it be. O'Thursday, tell her,
She shall be married to this noble earl.
Will you be ready? Do you like this haste?
We'll keep no great ado—a friend or two;
For hark you, Tybalt being slain so late,   24
It may be thought we held him carelessly,   25
Being our kinsman, if we revel much.
Therefore we'll have some half a dozen friends,
And there an end. But what say you to Thursday?

PARIS

My lord, I would that Thursday were tomorrow.

CAPULET

Well, get you gone. O' Thursday be it, then.
[To his Wife] Go you to Juliet ere you go to bed;
Prepare her, wife, against this wedding day.—   32
Farewell, my lord.—Light to my chamber, ho!—
Afore me, it is so very late   34
That we may call it early by and by.
Good night.   Exeunt.

❖

[3.5]

Enter Romeo and Juliet aloft [at the window].

JULIET

Wilt thou be gone? It is not yet near day.
It was the nightingale, and not the lark,
That pierced the fearful hollow of thine ear;   3
Nightly she sings on yond pomegranate tree.
Believe me, love, it was the nightingale.

ROMEO

It was the lark, the herald of the morn,
No nightingale. Look, love, what envious streaks
Do lace the severing clouds in yonder east.   8
Night's candles are burnt out, and jocund day   9
Stands tiptoe on the misty mountain tops.
I must be gone and live, or stay and die.

JULIET

Yond light is not daylight, I know it, I.
It is some meteor that the sun exhaled   13
To be to thee this night a torchbearer
And light thee on thy way to Mantua.
Therefore stay yet. Thou need'st not to be gone.

ROMEO

Let me be ta'en; let me be put to death.
I am content, so thou wilt have it so.   18
I'll say yon gray is not the morning's eye;
'Tis but the pale reflex of Cynthia's brow.   20
Nor that is not the lark whose notes do beat
The vaulty heaven so high above our heads.
I have more care to stay than will to go.   23
Come, death, and welcome! Juliet wills it so.
How is't, my soul? Let's talk. It is not day.

JULIET

It is, it is. Hie hence, begone, away!   26
It is the lark that sings so out of tune,
Straining harsh discords and unpleasing sharps.   28
Some say the lark makes sweet division;   29
This doth not so, for she divideth us.
Some say the lark and loathèd toad changed eyes;   31
Oh, now I would they had changed voices too,
Since arm from arm that voice doth us affray,   33
Hunting thee hence with hunt's-up to the day.   34
Oh, now begone! More light and light it grows.

ROMEO

More light and light, more dark and dark our woes!

Enter Nurse [hastily].

NURSE   Madam!

JULIET   Nurse?

NURSE

Your lady mother is coming to your chamber.
The day is broke; be wary, look about.   [Exit.]

JULIET

Then window, let day in, and let life out.

ROMEO

Farewell, farewell! One kiss, and I'll descend.
              [They kiss. He climbs down from the window.]

JULIET

Art thou gone so? Love, lord, ay, husband, friend!   43
I must hear from thee every day in the hour,
For in a minute there are many days.
Oh, by this count I shall be much in years   46
Ere I again behold my Romeo!

ROMEO [from below her window]   Farewell!

---

11 mewed up to cooped up with. (A term from falconry, reminiscent of 2.2.159–68.) **heaviness** sorrow. **12 desperate tender** bold offer **17 mark you me** listen to this **18 soft** wait a minute **24 late** recently **25 held him carelessly** did not regard him highly **32 against** in anticipation of **34 Afore me** i.e., By my life. (A mild oath.)
3.5. Location: Verona. Capulet's orchard with Juliet's chamber window above, and, at lines 68 ff., the interior of Juliet's chamber.
3 fearful apprehensive, anxious **8 severing** separating **9 jocund** cheerful

13 exhaled i.e., has drawn out of the ground. (Meteors were thought to be vapors of luminous gas drawn up by the sun.) **18 so** as long as, since **20 reflex** reflection. **Cynthia's** the moon's **23 care** desire, concern **26 Hie hence** Hasten away **28 sharps** notes relatively high in pitch and hence discordant. **29 division** variations on a melody, made by dividing each note into notes of briefer duration **31 changed** exchanged. (A popular saying, to account for the observation that the lark has very ordinary eyes and the toad remarkable ones.) **33 arm from arm** from one another's arms. **affray** frighten **34 hunt's-up** a song or tune originally designed to awaken huntsmen; later, used also to serenade a newly married couple **43 friend** lover. **46 much in years** much older

I will omit no opportunity
That may convey my greetings, love, to thee.

JULIET
Oh, think'st thou we shall ever meet again?

ROMEO
I doubt it not, and all these woes shall serve
For sweet discourses in our times to come.

JULIET
Oh, God, I have an ill-divining soul!   54
Methinks I see thee, now thou art so low,
As one dead in the bottom of a tomb.
Either my eyesight fails or thou lookest pale.

ROMEO
And trust me, love, in my eye so do you.
Dry sorrow drinks our blood. Adieu, adieu!   *Exit.*   59

JULIET
O Fortune, Fortune! All men call thee fickle.
If thou art fickle, what dost thou with him
That is renowned for faith? Be fickle, Fortune.
For then, I hope, thou wilt not keep him long,
But send him back.

                Enter Mother [Capulet's Wife].

WIFE   Ho, daughter, are you up?

JULIET
Who is't that calls? It is my lady mother.
Is she not down so late, or up so early?   66
What unaccustomed cause procures her hither?   67
                [She goeth down from the window.]

WIFE
Why, how now, Juliet?

JULIET   Madam, I am not well.

WIFE
Evermore weeping for your cousin's death?
What, wilt thou wash him from his grave with tears?
An if thou couldst, thou couldst not make him live;
Therefore, have done. Some grief shows much of love,   72
But much of grief shows still some want of wit.   73

JULIET
Yet let me weep for such a feeling loss.   74

WIFE
So shall you feel the loss, but not the friend
Which you weep for.

JULIET   Feeling so the loss,
I cannot choose but ever weep the friend.   77

WIFE
Well, girl, thou weep'st not so much for his death
As that the villain lives which slaughtered him.

JULIET
What villain, madam?

WIFE   That same villain, Romeo.

JULIET *[aside]*
Villain and he be many miles asunder.—
God pardon him! I do, with all my heart;
And yet no man like he doth grieve my heart.   83

WIFE
That is because the traitor murderer lives.

JULIET
Ay, madam, from the reach of these my hands.
Would none but I might venge my cousin's death!

WIFE
We will have vengeance for it, fear thou not.
Then weep no more. I'll send to one in Mantua,
Where that same banished runagate doth live,   89
Shall give him such an unaccustomed dram   90
That he shall soon keep Tybalt company.
And then, I hope, thou wilt be satisfied.

JULIET
Indeed, I never shall be satisfied
With Romeo till I behold him—dead—
Is my poor heart so for a kinsman vexed.
Madam, if you could find out but a man
To bear a poison, I would temper it,   97
That Romeo should, upon receipt thereof,
Soon sleep in quiet. Oh, how my heart abhors
To hear him named, and cannot come to him
To wreak the love I bore my cousin   101
Upon his body that hath slaughtered him!   102

WIFE
Find thou the means, and I'll find such a man.
But now I'll tell thee joyful tidings, girl.

JULIET
And joy comes well in such a needy time.
What are they, beseech Your Ladyship?

WIFE
Well, well, thou hast a careful father, child,   107
One who, to put thee from thy heaviness,   108
Hath sorted out a sudden day of joy   109
That thou expects not, nor I looked not for.

JULIET
Madam, in happy time, what day is that?

WIFE
Marry, my child, early next Thursday morn,   112
The gallant, young, and noble gentleman,
The County Paris, at Saint Peter's Church
Shall happily make thee there a joyful bride.

JULIET
Now, by Saint Peter's Church, and Peter too,
He shall not make me there a joyful bride!

---

54 **ill-divining** prophesying of evil   59 **Dry sorrow** (The heat of the
body in sorrow and despair was thought to descend into the bowels
and dry up the blood.)   66 **down** in bed   67 **procures** induces to
come   67.1 (As indicated by the bracketed stage direction, which is
from the first quarto, Juliet, who has appeared until now at her "window" above the stage, evidently descends quickly to the main stage
and joins her mother for the remainder of the scene. The stage, which
before was to have been imagined as Capulet's orchard, is now
Juliet's chamber. Juliet's mother has entered onto the main stage four
lines earlier.)   72 **have done** cease.   73 **want of wit** lack of intelligence.   74 **feeling** deeply felt   77 **the friend** (Juliet secretly means
"my lover," as at line 43, but, of course, her mother hears it as
"Tybalt.")

83 **no man like he** no man so much as he.   **grieve** (1) anger (2) grieve
with longing. (Juliet speaks to her mother throughout in intentional
ambiguities, at lines 85, 86, 99, 100–2, etc.)   89 **runagate** renegade, fugitive   90 **Shall** who will.   **dram** dose. (Literally, one-eighth of a fluid
ounce.)   97 **temper** (1) mix, concoct (2) alloy, dilute. (In her intended
double meanings about Romeo dead, poisoned, and sleeping in quiet,
Juliet is, of course, unaware of an ironic anticipation of how these things
will be fulfilled.)   101 **wreak** (1) avenge (2) bestow   102 **his body that**
the body of him who   107 **careful** full of care (for you)   108 **heaviness**
sorrow   109 **sorted** chosen   112 **Marry** i.e., By the Virgin Mary

I wonder at this haste, that I must wed
Ere he that should be husband comes to woo.
I pray you, tell my lord and father, madam,
I will not marry yet, and when I do I swear
It shall be Romeo, whom you know I hate,
Rather than Paris. These are news indeed!

WIFE
Here comes your father. Tell him so yourself,
And see how he will take it at your hands.

Enter Capulet and Nurse.

CAPULET
When the sun sets, the earth doth drizzle dew,
But for the sunset of my brother's son
It rains downright.—
How now, a conduit, girl? What, still in tears?   129
Evermore show'ring? In one little body
Thou counterfeits a bark, a sea, a wind;   131
For still thy eyes, which I may call the sea,
Do ebb and flow with tears; the bark thy body is,
Sailing in this salt flood; the winds, thy sighs,
Who, raging with thy tears, and they with them,
Without a sudden calm, will overset   136
Thy tempest-tossèd body.—How now, wife?
Have you delivered to her our decree?

WIFE
Ay, sir, but she will none, she gives you thanks.   139
I would the fool were married to her grave!

CAPULET
Soft, take me with you, take me with you, wife.   141
How? Will she none? Doth she not give us thanks?
Is she not proud? Doth she not count her blest,   143
Unworthy as she is, that we have wrought   144
So worthy a gentleman to be her bride?   145

JULIET
Not proud you have, but thankful that you have.
Proud can I never be of what I hate,
But thankful even for hate that is meant love.   148

CAPULET
How, how, how, how, chopped logic? What is this?
"Proud," and "I thank you," and "I thank you not,"
And yet "not proud"? Mistress minion, you,   151
Thank me no thankings, nor proud me no prouds,
But fettle your joints 'gainst Thursday next   153
To go with Paris to Saint Peter's Church,
Or I will drag thee on a hurdle thither.   155
Out, you greensickness carrion! Out, you baggage!   156
You tallow-face!

WIFE [*to Capulet*]   Fie, fie! What, are you mad?   157

JULIET [*kneeling*]
Good father, I beseech you on my knees,
Hear me with patience but to speak a word.

CAPULET
Hang thee, young baggage, disobedient wretch!
I tell thee what: get thee to church o' Thursday
Or never after look me in the face.
Speak not, reply not, do not answer me!
My fingers itch. Wife, we scarce thought us blest
That God had lent us but this only child;
But now I see this one is one too much,
And that we have a curse in having her.
Out on her, hilding!

NURSE   God in heaven bless her!   168
You are to blame, my lord, to rate her so.   169

CAPULET
And why, my Lady Wisdom? Hold your tongue,
Good Prudence. Smatter with your gossips, go.   171

NURSE
I speak no treason.

CAPULET   Oh, God-i'-good-e'en!   172

NURSE
May not one speak?

CAPULET   Peace, you mumbling fool!
Utter your gravity o'er a gossip's bowl,   174
For here we need it not.

WIFE   You are too hot.

CAPULET   God's bread, it makes me mad!   176
Day, night, hour, tide, time, work, play,   177
Alone, in company, still my care hath been
To have her matched. And having now provided
A gentleman of noble parentage,
Of fair demesnes, youthful, and nobly liened,   181
Stuffed, as they say, with honorable parts,   182
Proportioned as one's thought would wish a man—
And then to have a wretched puling fool,   184
A whining mammet, in her fortune's tender,   185
To answer, "I'll not wed, I cannot love,
I am too young; I pray you, pardon me."
But, an you will not wed, I'll pardon you.   188
Graze where you will, you shall not house with me.
Look to 't, think on 't. I do not use to jest.   190
Thursday is near. Lay hand on heart; advise.   191
An you be mine, I'll give you to my friend;
An you be not, hang, beg, starve, die in the streets,
For, by my soul, I'll ne'er acknowledge thee,
Nor what is mine shall never do thee good.
Trust to 't, bethink you. I'll not be forsworn.   *Exit.* 196

JULIET
Is there no pity sitting in the clouds
That sees into the bottom of my grief?

---

129 **conduit** water pipe, fountain   131 **bark** sailing vessel   136 **Without** unless there is   139 **will ... thanks** says "no thank you," she'll have no part of it.   141 **take ... you** let me understand you   143 **count her** consider herself   144 **wrought** arranged for   145 **bride** bridegroom.   148 **hate ... love** that which is hateful but which was meant lovingly.   151 **minion** spoiled darling, minx   153 **fettle** make ready. **'gainst** in anticipation of   155 **a hurdle** a conveyance on which criminals were dragged to execution   156 **greensickness** (An anemic ailment of young unmarried women; it suggests Juliet's paleness.) **baggage** hussy.   157 **tallow-face** paleface.

168 **hilding** jade, baggage.   169 **rate** berate, scold   171 **Smatter** Chatter. **gossips** gossiping women friends   172 **God-i'-good-e'en** i.e., For God's sake. (Literally, God give you good evening.)   174 **gravity** wisdom. (Said contemptuously.)   176 **God's bread** i.e., By God's (Christ's) Sacrament   177 **tide** season   181 **demesnes** estates. **liened** descended   182 **parts** qualities   184 **puling** whining   185 **mammet** doll. **in ... tender** when an offer of good fortune is made to her   188 **pardon you** i.e., allow you to depart. (Said caustically.)   190 **do not use** am not accustomed   191 **advise** consider carefully.   196 **be forsworn** i.e., go back on my word.

O sweet my mother, cast me not away!
Delay this marriage for a month, a week;
Or if you do not, make the bridal bed
In that dim monument where Tybalt lies.

WIFE
Talk not to me, for I'll not speak a word.
Do as thou wilt, for I have done with thee.   *Exit.*

JULIET   [*rising*]
Oh, God!—O Nurse, how shall this be prevented?
My husband is on earth, my faith in heaven.   206
How shall that faith return again to earth,   207
Unless that husband send it me from heaven   208
By leaving earth? Comfort me, counsel me.   209
Alack, alack, that heaven should practice stratagems
Upon so soft a subject as myself!
What say'st thou? Hast thou not a word of joy?
Some comfort, Nurse.

NURSE   Faith, here it is.
Romeo is banished, and all the world to nothing   214
That he dares ne'er come back to challenge you,   215
Or if he do, it needs must be by stealth.
Then, since the case so stands as now it doth,
I think it best you married with the County.
Oh, he's a lovely gentleman!
Romeo's a dishclout to him. An eagle, madam,   220
Hath not so green, so quick, so fair an eye
As Paris hath. Beshrew my very heart,   222
I think you are happy in this second match,
For it excels your first; or if it did not,
Your first is dead—or 'twere as good he were,
As living here and you no use of him.

JULIET   Speak'st thou from thy heart?

NURSE
And from my soul too. Else beshrew them both.

JULIET   Amen!   229

NURSE   What?

JULIET
Well, thou hast comforted me marvelous much.
Go in, and tell my lady I am gone,
Having displeased my father, to Laurence' cell
To make confession and to be absolved.

NURSE
Marry, I will; and this is wisely done.   [*Exit.*]

JULIET
Ancient damnation! Oh, most wicked fiend!   236
Is it more sin to wish me thus forsworn,   237
Or to dispraise my lord with that same tongue
Which she hath praised him with above compare
So many thousand times? Go, counselor,
Thou and my bosom henceforth shall be twain.   241

---

206 **my faith in heaven** i.e., I am married to Romeo in the sight of
heaven.   207–9 **How . . . leaving earth?** i.e., How can I remarry while
Romeo is still alive?   214 **all . . . nothing** the odds are overwhelming
215 **challenge** lay claim to   220 **dishclout** dishrag   222 **Beshrew** (A
mild oath. Also in line 228.)   229 **Amen** (Juliet says "Amen" as
though to answer the Nurse's prayer that her heart and soul be
cursed. The Nurse does not get the point.)   236 **Ancient damnation!**
Damnable old woman!   237 **forsworn** i.e., false to my marriage vows
241 **bosom** secret thoughts.   **twain** separated.

I'll to the Friar to know his remedy.
If all else fail, myself have power to die.   *Exit.*

❖

[4.1]

Enter Friar [Laurence] and County Paris.

FRIAR LAURENCE
On Thursday, sir? The time is very short.

PARIS
My father Capulet will have it so,
And I am nothing slow to slack his haste.   3

FRIAR LAURENCE
You say you do not know the lady's mind?
Uneven is the course. I like it not.

PARIS
Immoderately she weeps for Tybalt's death,
And therefore have I little talked of love,
For Venus smiles not in a house of tears.   8
Now, sir, her father counts it dangerous
That she do give her sorrow so much sway,
And in his wisdom hastes our marriage
To stop the inundation of her tears,
Which, too much minded by herself alone,   13
May be put from her by society.   14
Now do you know the reason of this haste.

FRIAR LAURENCE   [*aside*]
I would I knew not why it should be slowed.—
Look, sir, here comes the lady toward my cell.

Enter Juliet.

PARIS
Happily met, my lady and my wife!

JULIET
That may be, sir, when I may be a wife.

PARIS
That "may be" must be, love, on Thursday next.

JULIET
What must be shall be.

FRIAR LAURENCE   That's a certain text.

PARIS
Come you to make confession to this father?

JULIET
To answer that, I should confess to you.

PARIS
Do not deny to him that you love me.

JULIET
I will confess to you that I love him.

PARIS
So will ye, I am sure, that you love me.

JULIET
If I do so, it will be of more price,   27
Being spoke behind your back, than to your face.

4.1. **Location: Verona. Friar Laurence's cell.**
3 **nothing . . . haste** not at all reluctant to lessen his haste, i.e., willing to
speed matters along.   8 **Venus . . . tears** (1) amorousness is not appropriate in a house of mourning (2) the planet Venus does not exert a
favorable influence when it is in an inauspicious *house* or constellation
of the zodiac.   13 **too . . . alone** too mind-consuming when she is alone
14 **society** companionship.   27 **more price** greater worth

PARIS
Poor soul, thy face is much abused with tears.

JULIET
The tears have got small victory by that,
For it was bad enough before their spite.   31

PARIS
Thou wrong'st it more than tears with that report.   32

JULIET
That is no slander, sir, which is a truth;
And what I spake, I spake it to my face.   34

PARIS
Thy face is mine, and thou hast slandered it.

JULIET
It may be so, for it is not mine own.—   36
Are you at leisure, holy Father, now,
Or shall I come to you at evening Mass?

FRIAR LAURENCE
My leisure serves me, pensive daughter, now.—   39
My lord, we must entreat the time alone.   40

PARIS
God shield I should disturb devotion!   41
Juliet, on Thursday early will I rouse ye.
Till then, adieu, and keep this holy kiss.   *Exit.*

JULIET
Oh, shut the door! And when thou hast done so,
Come weep with me—past hope, past cure, past help!

FRIAR LAURENCE
Ah, Juliet, I already know thy grief;
It strains me past the compass of my wits.   47
I hear thou must, and nothing may prorogue it,   48
On Thursday next be married to this county.

JULIET
Tell me not, Friar, that thou hearest of this,
Unless thou tell me how I may prevent it.
If in thy wisdom thou canst give no help,
Do thou but call my resolution wise
And with this knife I'll help it presently.   54
                          [*She shows a knife.*]
God joined my heart and Romeo's, thou our hands;
And ere this hand, by thee to Romeo sealed,
Shall be the label to another deed,   57
Or my true heart with treacherous revolt
Turn to another, this shall slay them both.   59
Therefore, out of thy long-experienced time,   60
Give me some present counsel, or, behold,
Twixt my extremes and me this bloody knife   62
Shall play the umpire, arbitrating that
Which the commission of thy years and art   64
Could to no issue of true honor bring.
Be not so long to speak; I long to die   66
If what thou speak'st speak not of remedy.

FRIAR LAURENCE
Hold, daughter. I do spy a kind of hope,
Which craves as desperate an execution
As that is desperate which we would prevent.
If, rather than to marry County Paris,
Thou hast the strength of will to slay thyself,
Then is it likely thou wilt undertake
A thing like death to chide away this shame,
That cop'st with Death himself to scape from it;   75
And if thou darest, I'll give thee remedy.

JULIET
Oh, bid me leap, rather than marry Paris,
From off the battlements of any tower,
Or walk in thievish ways, or bid me lurk   79
Where serpents are; chain me with roaring bears,
Or hide me nightly in a charnel house,   81
O'ercovered quite with dead men's rattling bones,
With reeky shanks and yellow chopless skulls;   83
Or bid me go into a new-made grave
And hide me with a dead man in his tomb—
Things that, to hear them told, have made me
    tremble—
And I will do it without fear or doubt,
To live an unstained wife to my sweet love.

FRIAR LAURENCE
Hold, then. Go home, be merry, give consent
To marry Paris. Wednesday is tomorrow.
Tomorrow night look that thou lie alone;
Let not the Nurse lie with thee in thy chamber.
Take thou this vial, being then in bed,
                          [*showing her a vial*]
And this distilling liquor drink thou off,   94
When presently through all thy veins shall run
A cold and drowsy humor; for no pulse   96
Shall keep his native progress, but surcease;   97
No warmth, no breath shall testify thou livest;
The roses in thy lips and cheeks shall fade
To wanny ashes, thy eyes' windows fall   100
Like death when he shuts up the day of life;
Each part, deprived of supple government,   102
Shall, stiff and stark and cold, appear like death.
And in this borrowed likeness of shrunk death
Thou shalt continue two-and-forty hours,
And then awake as from a pleasant sleep.
Now, when the bridegroom in the morning comes
To rouse thee from thy bed, there art thou dead.
Then, as the manner of our country is,
In thy best robes uncovered on the bier
Thou shalt be borne to that same ancient vault
Where all the kindred of the Capulets lie.
In the meantime, against thou shalt awake,   113
Shall Romeo by my letters know our drift,   114

---

31 **spite** malice.   32 **Thou . . . report** Your apology for your face slanders it more than your tears do.   34 **to my face** (1) openly (2) about my face.   36 **is not mine own** (1) is beyond my control, does not reveal me truly (2) belongs to Romeo.   39 **pensive** sorrowful   40 **entreat . . . alone** ask you to leave us alone.   41 **God shield** God forbid   47 **compass** bounds   48 **prorogue** delay   54 **presently** at once.   57 **label** strip attached to a deed to carry the seal; hence, confirmation, seal   59 **both** i.e., hand and heart.   60 **time** age   62 **extremes** extreme difficulties   64 **commission** authority.   **art** skill   66 **so long** so slow. (With wordplay on *long*, "yearn," later in this same line.)

75 **That . . . himself** either (1) you who are willing to encounter Death by killing yourself, or (2) that simulates Death itself.   **it** this shame   79 **thievish ways** roads frequented by thieves   81 **charnel house** vault for human bones   83 **reeky** reeking, malodorous.   **chopless** without the lower jaw   94 **distilling** infusing the body, or distilled   96 **humor** fluid   97 **his native** its natural.   **surcease** cease   100 **wanny** wan, pale   102 **supple government** control of motion   113 **against** anticipating when   114 **drift** plan

And hither shall he come; and he and I
Will watch thy waking, and that very night   116
Shall Romeo bear thee hence to Mantua.
And this shall free thee from this present shame,
If no inconstant toy nor womanish fear   119
Abate thy valor in the acting it.
JULIET [taking the vial]
Give me, give me! Oh, tell not me of fear!
FRIAR LAURENCE
Hold, get you gone. Be strong and prosperous   122
In this resolve. I'll send a friar with speed
To Mantua, with my letters to thy lord.
JULIET
Love give me strength, and strength shall help afford.   125
Farewell, dear Father!   Exeunt [separately].

❖

[4.2]

Enter Father Capulet, Mother [Capulet's Wife],
Nurse, and Servingmen, two or three.

CAPULET
So many guests invite as here are writ.
                    [Exit one or two Servingmen.]
Sirrah, go hire me twenty cunning cooks.   2
SERVINGMAN You shall have none ill, sir, for I'll try if   3
they can lick their fingers.
CAPULET How canst thou try them so?
SERVINGMAN Marry, sir, 'tis an ill cook that cannot lick
his own fingers; therefore he that cannot lick his
fingers goes not with me.
CAPULET Go, begone.   [Exit Servingman.]
We shall be much unfurnished for this time.   10
What, is my daughter gone to Friar Laurence?
NURSE Ay, forsooth.
CAPULET
Well, he may chance to do some good on her.
A peevish self-willed harlotry it is.   14

Enter Juliet.

NURSE
See where she comes from shrift with merry look.
CAPULET
How now, my headstrong, where have you been
    gadding?
JULIET
Where I have learned me to repent the sin
Of disobedient opposition
To you and your behests, and am enjoined   19
By holy Laurence to fall prostrate here,   [kneeling]
To beg your pardon. Pardon, I beseech you!
Henceforward I am ever ruled by you.
CAPULET
Send for the County! Go tell him of this.
I'll have this knot knit up tomorrow morning.

JULIET
I met the youthful lord at Laurence' cell
And gave him what becomèd love I might,   26
Not stepping o'er the bounds of modesty.
CAPULET
Why, I am glad on't. This is well. Stand up.
                              [Juliet rises.]
This is as 't should be. Let me see the County;
Ay, marry, go, I say, and fetch him hither.
Now, afore God, this reverend holy friar,
All our whole city is much bound to him.   32
JULIET
Nurse, will you go with me into my closet   33
To help me sort such needful ornaments   34
As you think fit to furnish me tomorrow?
WIFE
No, not till Thursday. There is time enough.
CAPULET
Go, Nurse, go with her. We'll to church tomorrow.
                    Exeunt [Juliet and Nurse].
WIFE
We shall be short in our provision.
'Tis now near night.
CAPULET   Tush, I will stir about,
And all things shall be well, I warrant thee, wife.
Go thou to Juliet, help to deck up her.
I'll not to bed tonight. Let me alone.   42
I'll play the huswife for this once.—What, ho!—   43
They are all forth. Well, I will walk myself
To County Paris, to prepare up him
Against tomorrow. My heart is wondrous light,
Since this same wayward girl is so reclaimed.
                                   Exeunt.

❖

[4.3]

Enter Juliet and Nurse.

JULIET
Ay, those attires are best. But, gentle Nurse,
I pray thee, leave me to myself tonight;
For I have need of many orisons   3
To move the heavens to smile upon my state,
Which, well thou knowest, is cross and full of sin. 5

Enter Mother [Capulet's Wife].

WIFE
What, are you busy, ho? Need you my help?
JULIET
No, madam, we have culled such necessaries   7
As are behooveful for our state tomorrow.   8
So please you, let me now be left alone,
And let the Nurse this night sit up with you,

116 watch keep a watch over, be on hand for   119 toy idle fancy
122 prosperous successful   125 help afford provide help.
4.2. Location: Verona. Capulet's house.
2 cunning skilled   3 none ill no bad ones.   try test   10 unfurnished unprovided   14 A peevish . . . is i.e., She's a silly good-for-
nothing.   19 behests commands

26 becomèd befitting   32 bound indebted   33 closet chamber
34 sort choose   42 Let me alone Leave things to me.   43 huswife
housewife
4.3. Location: Verona. Capulet's house; Juliet's bed, enclosed by
bedcurtains, is set up in the discovery space.
3 orisons prayers   5 cross perverse   7 culled picked out
8 behooveful needful.   state ceremony

For I am sure you have your hands full all
In this so sudden business.
WIFE   Good night.
Get thee to bed and rest, for thou hast need.
                    Exeunt [Capulet's Wife and Nurse].

JULIET
Farewell! God knows when we shall meet again.
I have a faint cold fear thrills through my veins   15
That almost freezes up the heat of life.
I'll call them back again to comfort me.—
Nurse!—What should she do here?
My dismal scene I needs must act alone.
Come, vial.   *[She takes out the vial.]*
What if this mixture do not work at all?
Shall I be married then tomorrow morning?
No, no, this shall forbid it. Lie thou there.
                          [She lays down a dagger.]
What if it be a poison, which the Friar
Subtly hath ministered to have me dead,
Lest in this marriage he should be dishonored
Because he married me before to Romeo?
I fear it is; and yet methinks it should not,
For he hath still been tried a holy man.   29
How if, when I am laid into the tomb,
I wake before the time that Romeo
Come to redeem me? There's a fearful point!
Shall I not then be stifled in the vault,
To whose foul mouth no healthsome air breathes in,
And there die strangled ere my Romeo comes?
Or, if I live, is it not very like   36
The horrible conceit of death and night,   37
Together with the terror of the place—
As in a vault, an ancient receptacle,   39
Where for this many hundred years the bones
Of all my buried ancestors are packed;
Where bloody Tybalt, yet but green in earth,   42
Lies fest'ring in his shroud; where, as they say,
At some hours in the night spirits resort—
Alack, alack, is it not like that I,
So early waking, what with loathsome smells,
And shrieks like mandrakes torn out of the earth,   47
That living mortals, hearing them, run mad—   48
Oh, if I wake, shall I not be distraught,
Environèd with all these hideous fears,   50
And madly play with my forefathers' joints,
And pluck the mangled Tybalt from his shroud,
And in this rage, with some great kinsman's bone   53
As with a club dash out my desp'rate brains?
Oh, look! Methinks I see my cousin's ghost
Seeking out Romeo, that did spit his body   56

Upon a rapier's point. Stay, Tybalt, stay!   57
Romeo, Romeo, Romeo! Here's drink—I drink to thee.
                    *[She drinks and falls upon her bed,
                          within the curtains.]*

[4.4]

*Enter Lady of the House [Capulet's Wife]
and Nurse.*

WIFE
Hold, take these keys, and fetch more spices, Nurse.
NURSE
They call for dates and quinces in the pastry.   2

Enter old Capulet.

CAPULET
Come, stir, stir, stir! The second cock hath crowed.
The curfew bell hath rung; 'tis three o'clock.
Look to the baked meats, good Angelica.   5
Spare not for cost.
NURSE   Go, you cotquean, go,   6
Get you to bed. Faith, you'll be sick tomorrow
For this night's watching.   8
CAPULET
No, not a whit. What, I have watched ere now
All night for lesser cause, and ne'er been sick.
WIFE
Ay, you have been a mouse-hunt in your time,   11
But I will watch you from such watching now.   12
                          Exeunt Lady and Nurse.
CAPULET   A jealous hood, a jealous hood!   13

*Enter three or four [Servingmen] with spits and
logs, and baskets.*

Now, fellow, what is there?
FIRST SERVINGMAN
Things for the cook, sir, but I know not what.
CAPULET   Make haste, make haste. *[Exit First Servingman.]*
[To Second Servingman]   Sirrah, fetch drier logs.
Call Peter. He will show thee where they are.
SECOND SERVINGMAN
I have a head, sir, that will find out logs   18
And never trouble Peter for the matter.
CAPULET
Mass, and well said. A merry whoreson, ha!   20

---

57 Stay Stop, wait
4.4. Location: Scene continues. Juliet's bed remains visible.
2 pastry room in which pastry was made.   **5 baked meats** pies, pastry   **6 cotquean** i.e., a man who acts the housewife. (Literally, a cottage housewife.)   **8 watching** being awake.   **11 mouse-hunt** i.e., hunter of women. (Literally, a weasel.)   **12 watch . . . watching** i.e., keep an eye on you to prevent such nighttime activity. (Playing on *watching* in line 8.)   **13 A jealous hood** i.e., You wear the cap of jealousy   **18 I . . . logs** i.e., (1) I have a good head for finding things (2) My wooden head knows all about logs   **20 Mass** By the Mass. **whoreson** i.e., fellow. (An abusive term used familiarly.)

---

15 faint producing faintness.   **thrills** that pierces, shivers   **29 still been tried** always been tried and proven to be   **36 like** likely. (Also at line 45.)   **37 conceit** idea   **39 As** namely   **42 green** new, freshly   **47 mandrakes** (The root of the mandragora or mandrake resembled the human form; the plant was fabled to utter a shriek when torn from the ground.)   **48 That** so that   **50 fears** objects of fear   **53 rage** madness.   **great** i.e., of an earlier generation, as in *great*-grandfather   **56 spit** impale

Thou shalt be loggerhead.   [*Exit Servingman.*]
            Good faith, 'tis day.   21
The County will be here with music straight,   22
For so he said he would.   *Play music* [*within*].
            I hear him near.
Nurse! Wife! What, ho! What, Nurse, I say!

        Enter Nurse.

Go waken Juliet, go and trim her up.
I'll go and chat with Paris. Hie, make haste,
Make haste. The bridegroom he is come already.
Make haste, I say.   [*Exit Capulet.*]

                      ❖

[4.5]

        [*The Nurse goes to the bed.*]

NURSE
Mistress! What, mistress! Juliet!—Fast, I warrant her,
    she.   1
Why, lamb, why, lady! Fie, you slugabed!
Why, love, I say! Madam! Sweetheart! Why, bride!
What, not a word? You take your pennyworths now.   4
Sleep for a week; for the next night, I warrant,
The County Paris hath set up his rest   6
That you shall rest but little. God forgive me,   7
Marry, and amen! How sound is she asleep!   8
I needs must wake her.—Madam, madam, madam!
Ay, let the County take you in your bed;   10
He'll fright you up, i'faith.—Will it not be?
                         [*She opens the bedcurtains.*]
What, dressed, and in your clothes, and down again?
I must needs wake you. Lady, lady, lady!
Alas, alas! Help, help! My lady's dead!
Oh, weraday, that ever I was born!   15
Some aqua vitae, ho! My lord! My lady!   16

        [*Enter Capulet's Wife.*]

WIFE
What noise is here?
NURSE   Oh, lamentable day!
WIFE
What is the matter?
NURSE   Look, look! Oh, heavy day!   18
WIFE
Oh, me, oh, me! My child, my only life!
Revive, look up, or I will die with thee!
Help, help! Call help.

        Enter Father [*Capulet*].

CAPULET
For shame, bring Juliet forth. Her lord is come.

---

21 **loggerhead** (1) put in charge of getting logs (2) a blockhead.
22 **straight** straightway, immediately
4.5. Location: Scene continues. Juliet's bed remains visible.
1 **Fast** Fast asleep   4 **pennyworths** small portions (of sleep)   6 **set . . .
rest** staked his all, resolved to play all out. (From the card game of
primero, here with obviously bawdy meaning.)   7–8 **God . . . amen!**
(The Nurse apologizes amiably for her bawdy talk.)   10 **take . . . bed**
(1) find you still abed (2) possess you sexually   15 **weraday** wellaway,
alas   16 **aqua vitae** strong alcoholic spirits   18 **heavy** sorrowful

---

NURSE
She's dead, deceased. She's dead, alack the day!
WIFE
Alack the day, she's dead, she's dead, she's dead!
CAPULET
Ha! Let me see her. Out, alas! She's cold.
Her blood is settled, and her joints are stiff;   26
Life and these lips have long been separated.
Death lies on her like an untimely frost
Upon the sweetest flower of all the field.
NURSE
Oh, lamentable day!
WIFE   Oh, woeful time!
CAPULET
Death, that hath ta'en her hence to make me wail,
Ties up my tongue and will not let me speak.

        Enter Friar [*Laurence*] *and the County* [*Paris,
        with Musicians*].

FRIAR LAURENCE
Come, is the bride ready to go to church?
CAPULET
Ready to go, but never to return.
Oh, son, the night before thy wedding day
Hath Death lain with thy wife. There she lies,
Flower as she was, deflowered by him.
Death is my son-in-law, Death is my heir;
My daughter he hath wedded. I will die,
And leave him all; life, living, all is Death's.   40
PARIS
Have I thought long to see this morning's face,   41
And doth it give me such a sight as this?
WIFE
Accurst, unhappy, wretched, hateful day!
Most miserable hour that e'er time saw
In lasting labor of his pilgrimage!   45
But one, poor one, one poor and loving child,
But one thing to rejoice and solace in,
And cruel Death hath catched it from my sight!
NURSE
O woe! O woeful, woeful, woeful day!
Most lamentable day, most woeful day
That ever, ever I did yet behold!
O day, O day, O day! O hateful day!
Never was seen so black a day as this.
O woeful day, O woeful day!
PARIS
Beguiled, divorcèd, wrongèd, spited, slain!
Most detestable Death, by thee beguiled,
By cruel, cruel thee quite overthrown!
O love! O life! Not life, but love in death!
CAPULET
Despised, distressèd, hated, martyred, killed!
Uncomfortable time, why cam'st thou now   60

---

26 **settled** congealed   40 **living** means of living, property
41–64 Have . . . burièd (A stage direction in the first quarto, "All at
once cry out and wring their hands," may suggest that the four mourners are to speak simultaneously, a possibility since all have six lines of
text.)   45 **lasting** unceasing   60 **Uncomfortable** Comfortless

To murder, murder our solemnity?   61
O child! O child! My soul, and not my child!
Dead art thou! Alack, my child is dead,
And with my child my joys are buried.   64

FRIAR LAURENCE
Peace, ho, for shame! Confusion's cure lives not   65
In these confusions. Heaven and yourself
Had part in this fair maid; now heaven hath all,
And all the better is it for the maid.
Your part in her you could not keep from death,   69
But heaven keeps his part in eternal life.
The most you sought was her promotion,   71
For 'twas your heaven she should be advanced;   72
And weep ye now, seeing she is advanced
Above the clouds, as high as heaven itself?
Oh, in this love you love your child so ill
That you run mad, seeing that she is well.
She's not well married that lives married long,
But she's best married that dies married young.
Dry up your tears, and stick your rosemary   79
On this fair corpse, and, as the custom is,
And in her best array, bear her to church;
For though fond nature bids us all lament,   82
Yet nature's tears are reason's merriment.   83

CAPULET
All things that we ordainèd festival   84
Turn from their office to black funeral: 85
Our instruments to melancholy bells,
Our wedding cheer to a sad burial feast,
Our solemn hymns to sullen dirges change,   88
Our bridal flowers serve for a buried corpse,
And all things change them to the contrary.   90

FRIAR LAURENCE
Sir, go you in, and, madam, go with him,
And go, Sir Paris. Everyone prepare
To follow this fair corpse unto her grave.
The heavens do lour upon you for some ill;   94
Move them no more by crossing their high will.   95

Exeunt. Manet [Nurse with Musicians].

FIRST MUSICIAN
Faith, we may put up our pipes and be gone.

NURSE
Honest good fellows, ah, put up, put up!
For well you know this is a pitiful case.   [*Exit.*]

FIRST MUSICIAN
Ay, by my troth, the case may be amended.   99

Enter Peter.

PETER   Musicians, oh, musicians, "Heart's ease,"   100
"Heart's ease." Oh, an you will have me live, play
"Heart's ease."

FIRST MUSICIAN   Why "Heart's ease"?

PETER   Oh, musicians, because my heart itself plays "My
heart is full." Oh, play me some merry dump to   105
comfort me.

FIRST MUSICIAN   Not a dump we! 'Tis no time to play
now.

PETER   You will not, then?

FIRST MUSICIAN   No.

PETER   I will then give it you soundly.

FIRST MUSICIAN   What will you give us?

PETER   No money, on my faith, but the gleek; I will give   113
you the minstrel.   114

FIRST MUSICIAN   Then will I give you the serving-   115
creature.   116

PETER   Then will I lay the serving-creature's dagger on   117
your pate. I will carry no crotchets. I'll re you, I'll fa   118
you. Do you note me?   119

FIRST MUSICIAN   An you re us and fa us, you note us.

SECOND MUSICIAN   Pray you, put up your dagger and   121
put out your wit.   122

PETER   Then have at you with my wit! I will dry-beat   123
you with an iron wit, and put up my iron dagger.
Answer me like men:
"When griping griefs the heart doth wound,   126
    And doleful dumps the mind oppress,
    Then music with her silver sound—"   128
Why "silver sound"? Why "music with her silver
sound"? What say you, Simon Catling?   130

FIRST MUSICIAN   Marry, sir, because silver hath a sweet
sound.

PETER   Pretty! What say you, Hugh Rebeck?   133

SECOND MUSICIAN   I say "silver sound" because musicians sound for silver.   135

PETER   Pretty too! What say you, James Soundpost?   136

THIRD MUSICIAN   Faith, I know not what to say.

---

61 solemnity ceremony, festivity.   **65 Confusion's** Calamity's   **69 Your part** i.e., The mortal part you begot   **71 promotion** social advancement   **72 your heaven** i.e., your idea of the greatest good   **79 rosemary** symbol of immortality and enduring love; therefore used at both funerals and weddings   **82 fond nature** foolish human nature   **83 nature's . . . merriment** that which causes human nature to weep is an occasion of joy to reason.   **84 ordainèd festival** intended to be festive   **85 office** function   **88 sullen** mournful   **90 them** themselves   **94 lour . . . ill** frown upon you because of some sinfulness   **95 Move** anger.   **95.1 Manet** She remains on stage   **99 the case . . . amended** things generally could be much better. (With a punning suggestion of an instrument case that is in need of repair.)   **99.1 Peter** (The second quarto has *Enter Will Kemp*, the actor for whom Shakespeare or perhaps the bookkeeper intended this role.)

100 "Heart's ease" (A popular ballad; so too with "My heart is full" in lines 104–5.)   **105 dump** mournful tune or dance   **113 gleek** scornful rebuke   **113–14 I will . . . minstrel** I will insult you by calling you what you are, a minstrel. (Minstrels were widely regarded as vagabonds.)   **115–16 Then . . . serving-creature** Then I'll insult you right back by calling you what you are, a servant.   **117–18 Then . . . crotchets** Then I'll knock you about the head with my dagger. I'll not put up with your whims. (*Crotchets* are also quarter notes, appropriate to the musicians' trade.)   **118–19 I'll re . . . me?** i.e., I'll give you a thrashing, do you hear? (Again using musical terms: *re* and *fa* are the names of notes, and *note* can mean "set to music.")   **121–2 put up . . . wit** sheathe your dagger and stop being a smart aleck. (But *put up* and *put out* can also mean "display." Peter chooses to answer to this meaning.)   **123 have at you** i.e., here I come.   **dry-beat** thrash (without drawing blood)   **126–8 "When . . . sound"** (From Richard Edwards's song, "In Commendation of Music," published in *The Paradise of Dainty Devices*, 1576.)   **130 Catling** (A catling was a small lute-string made of catgut.)   **133 Rebeck** (A rebeck was a fiddle with three strings.)   **135 sound** make music   **136 Soundpost** (A soundpost is the pillar or peg that supports the sounding board of a stringed instrument.)

PETER Oh, I cry you mercy, you are the singer. I will say 138
for you. It is "music with her silver sound" because
musicians have no gold for sounding: 140
     "Then music with her silver sound
          With speedy help doth lend redress." *Exit.*
FIRST MUSICIAN What a pestilent knave is this same!
SECOND MUSICIAN Hang him, Jack! Come, we'll in here,
tarry for the mourners, and stay dinner.   *Exeunt.* 145

❦

[5.1]

Enter Romeo.

ROMEO
If I may trust the flattering truth of sleep,   1
My dreams presage some joyful news at hand.
My bosom's lord sits lightly in his throne,   3
And all this day an unaccustomed spirit
Lifts me above the ground with cheerful thoughts.
I dreamt my lady came and found me dead—
Strange dream, that gives a dead man leave to
     think!—
And breathed such life with kisses in my lips
That I revived and was an emperor.
Ah me, how sweet is love itself possessed   10
When but love's shadows are so rich in joy!   11

Enter Romeo's man [Balthasar, booted].

News from Verona! How now, Balthasar,
Dost thou not bring me letters from the Friar?
How doth my lady? Is my father well?
How fares my Juliet? That I ask again,
For nothing can be ill if she be well.
BALTHASAR
Then she is well, and nothing can be ill.
Her body sleeps in Capels' monument,
And her immortal part with angels lives.
I saw her laid low in her kindred's vault,
And presently took post to tell it you.   21
Oh, pardon me for bringing these ill news,
Since you did leave it for my office, sir.   23
ROMEO
Is it e'en so? Then I defy you, stars!—
Thou knowest my lodging. Get me ink and paper,
And hire post-horses. I will hence tonight.
BALTHASAR
I do beseech you, sir, have patience.
Your looks are pale and wild, and do import   28
Some misadventure.
ROMEO   Tush, thou art deceived.
Leave me, and do the thing I bid thee do.
Hast thou no letters to me from the Friar?

BALTHASAR
No, my good lord.
ROMEO   No matter. Get thee gone,
And hire those horses. I'll be with thee straight.
                              Exit [Balthasar].
Well, Juliet, I will lie with thee tonight.
Let's see for means. O mischief, thou art swift   35
To enter in the thoughts of desperate men!
I do remember an apothecary—   37
And hereabouts 'a dwells—which late I noted   38
In tattered weeds, with overwhelming brows,   39
Culling of simples. Meager were his looks;   40
Sharp misery had worn him to the bones;
And in his needy shop a tortoise hung,
An alligator stuffed, and other skins
Of ill-shaped fishes; and about his shelves
A beggarly account of empty boxes,   45
Green earthen pots, bladders, and musty seeds,
Remnants of packthread, and old cakes of roses   47
Were thinly scattered to make up a show.
Noting this penury, to myself I said,
"An if a man did need a poison now,   50
Whose sale is present death in Mantua,   51
Here lives a caitiff wretch would sell it him."   52
Oh, this same thought did but forerun my need,
And this same needy man must sell it me.
As I remember, this should be the house.
Being holiday, the beggar's shop is shut.—
What, ho! Apothecary!

[Enter Apothecary.]

APOTHECARY   Who calls so loud?
ROMEO
Come hither, man. I see that thou art poor.
Hold, there is forty ducats. [*He shows gold.*] Let me
     have   59
A dram of poison, such soon-speeding gear   60
As will disperse itself through all the veins
That the life-weary taker may fall dead,
And that the trunk may be discharged of breath   63
As violently as hasty powder fired
Doth hurry from the fatal cannon's womb.
APOTHECARY
Such mortal drugs I have, but Mantua's law   66
Is death to any he that utters them.   67
ROMEO
Art thou so bare and full of wretchedness,
And fearest to die? Famine is in thy cheeks,

---

138 **cry you mercy** beg your pardon 140 **have . . . sounding** i.e., (1)
are paid only silver for playing (2) have no gold to jingle in their
pockets 145 **stay** await
5.1. Location: Mantua. A street.
1 **flattering** i.e., telling me what I want to believe 3 **bosom's lord**
i.e., heart 10 **itself possessed** actually enjoyed 11 **love's shadows**
dreams of love 11.1 **booted** wearing riding boots—a conventional
stage sign of traveling. 21 **presently took post** at once started off
with post-horses 23 **for my office** as my duty 28 **import** denote

35 **for means** by what means. 37 **apothecary** druggist 38 **which . . .
noted** whom lately I noticed 39 **weeds** garments. **overwhelming
brows** forehead and eyebrows jutting out over his eyes 40 **simples**
medicinal herbs. **Meager** Impoverished 45 **beggarly account** poor
array 47 **cakes of roses** petals pressed into cakes to be used as perfume 50 **An if** If 51 **present** immediate 52 **caitiff** miserable.
would who would 59 **ducats** gold coins. 60 **soon-speeding gear**
quickly effective stuff 63 **trunk** body 66 **mortal** deadly 67 **any he**
anyone. **utters** issues, sells

Need and oppression starveth in thy eyes,   70
Contempt and beggary hangs upon thy back.
The world is not thy friend, nor the world's law;
The world affords no law to make thee rich.
Then be not poor, but break it, and take this.

APOTHECARY
My poverty but not my will consents.

ROMEO
I pay thy poverty and not thy will.

APOTHECARY [giving poison]
Put this in any liquid thing you will
And drink it off, and if you had the strength
Of twenty men it would dispatch you straight.

ROMEO [giving gold]
There is thy gold—worse poison to men's souls,
Doing more murder in this loathsome world
Than these poor compounds that thou mayst not sell.
I sell thee poison; thou hast sold me none.
Farewell. Buy food, and get thyself in flesh.
     [Exit Apothecary.]
Come, cordial and not poison, go with me   85
To Juliet's grave, for there must I use thee.   Exit.

❧

[5.2]

Enter Friar John to Friar Laurence.

FRIAR JOHN
Holy Franciscan friar! Brother, ho!

Enter [Friar] Laurence.

FRIAR LAURENCE
This same should be the voice of Friar John.
Welcome from Mantua! What says Romeo?
Or if his mind be writ, give me his letter.

FRIAR JOHN
Going to find a barefoot brother out—
One of our order—to associate me   6
Here in this city visiting the sick,
And finding him, the searchers of the town,   8
Suspecting that we both were in a house
Where the infectious pestilence did reign,
Sealed up the doors and would not let us forth,
So that my speed to Mantua there was stayed.   12

FRIAR LAURENCE
Who bare my letter, then, to Romeo?

FRIAR JOHN
I could not send it—here it is again—
Nor get a messenger to bring it thee,
So fearful were they of infection.   [He gives a letter.]

FRIAR LAURENCE
Unhappy fortune! By my brotherhood,
The letter was not nice but full of charge,   18
Of dear import, and the neglecting it   19
May do much danger. Friar John, go hence.
Get me an iron crow and bring it straight   21
Unto my cell.

FRIAR JOHN   Brother, I'll go and bring it thee.   Exit.

FRIAR LAURENCE
Now must I to the monument alone.
Within this three hours will fair Juliet wake.
She will beshrew me much that Romeo   26
Hath had no notice of these accidents;   27
But I will write again to Mantua,
And keep her at my cell till Romeo come—
Poor living corpse, closed in a dead man's tomb!
     Exit.

❧

[5.3]

Enter Paris, and his Page [bearing flowers, perfumed water, and a torch. Juliet, lying in seeming death atop her bier and perhaps concealed at first from the audience's view, is understood to be in the Capulets' burial vault, with Tybalt's body also there.]

PARIS
Give me thy torch, boy. Hence, and stand aloof.   1
Yet put it out, for I would not be seen.
Under yond yew trees lay thee all along,   3
Holding thy ear close to the hollow ground.
So shall no foot upon the churchyard tread,
Being loose, unfirm, with digging up of graves,   6
But thou shalt hear it. Whistle then to me
As signal that thou hearest something approach.
Give me those flowers. Do as I bid thee. Go.

PAGE [aside]
I am almost afraid to stand alone   10
Here in the churchyard, yet I will adventure.
     [He retires.]

PARIS [strewing flowers and perfumed water]
Sweet flower, with flowers thy bridal bed I strew—   12
   Oh, woe! Thy canopy is dust and stones—   13
Which with sweet water nightly I will dew,   14
   Or wanting that, with tears distilled by moans.   15
The obsequies that I for thee will keep   16
Nightly shall be to strew thy grave and weep.
     Whistle Boy.
The boy gives warning something doth approach.
What cursèd foot wanders this way tonight

---

18 nice trivial. charge importance   19 dear precious, urgent   21 crow crowbar   26 beshrew i.e., reprove   27 accidents events
5.3. Location: Verona. A churchyard and the vault or tomb belonging to the Capulets. Juliet's bier may be thrust onstage from the "discovery" space or may be concealed until the tomb is "opened" by Romeo at 83.1, perhaps by the drawing back of curtains.
1 aloof to one side, at a distance.   3 all along at full length   6 Being i.e., the soil being   10 stand stay   12 Sweet flower i.e., Juliet   13 canopy covering   14 sweet perfumed. dew moisten   15 wanting lacking   16 obsequies ceremonies in memory of the dead

70 starveth are revealed by the starving look   85 cordial restorative for the heart
5.2. Location: Verona. Friar Laurence's cell.
6 associate accompany   8 searchers of the town town officials charged with public health (and especially concerned about the pestilence or plague)   12 speed successful journey, progress. stayed stopped.

To cross my obsequies and true love's rite? 20
What, with a torch? Muffle me, night, awhile. 21

[*He retires.*]

Enter Romeo and Balthasar, [with a torch, a mattock, and a crowbar].

ROMEO

Give me that mattock and the wrenching iron. 22

[*He takes the tools.*]

Hold, take this letter. Early in the morning
See thou deliver it to my lord and father.

[*He gives a letter and takes a torch.*]

Give me the light. Upon thy life I charge thee,
Whate'er thou hearest or see'st, stand all aloof
And do not interrupt me in my course. 27
Why I descend into this bed of death
Is partly to behold my lady's face,
But chiefly to take thence from her dead finger
A precious ring—a ring that I must use
In dear employment. Therefore hence, begone. 32
But if thou, jealous, dost return to pry 33
In what I farther shall intend to do,
By heaven, I will tear thee joint by joint
And strew this hungry churchyard with thy limbs. 36
The time and my intents are savage-wild,
More fierce and more inexorable far
Than empty tigers or the roaring sea. 39

BALTHASAR

I will be gone, sir, and not trouble ye.

ROMEO

So shalt thou show me friendship. Take thou that.

[*He gives him money.*]

Live, and be prosperous; and farewell, good fellow.

BALTHASAR [*aside*]

For all this same, I'll hide me hereabout. 43
His looks I fear, and his intents I doubt. [*He retires.*] 44

ROMEO

Thou detestable maw, thou womb of death, 45
Gorged with the dearest morsel of the earth,
Thus I enforce thy rotten jaws to open,
And in despite I'll cram thee with more food. 48

[*He begins to open the tomb.*]

PARIS

This is that banished haughty Montague
That murdered my love's cousin, with which grief
It is supposèd the fair creature died,
And here is come to do some villainous shame
To the dead bodies. I will apprehend him.

[*He comes forward.*]

Stop thy unhallowed toil, vile Montague!
Can vengeance be pursued further than death?

Condemnèd villain, I do apprehend thee.
Obey and go with me, for thou must die.

ROMEO

I must indeed, and therefore came I hither.
Good gentle youth, tempt not a desperate man.
Fly hence and leave me. Think upon these gone; 60
Let them affright thee. I beseech thee, youth,
Put not another sin upon my head
By urging me to fury. Oh, begone!
By heaven, I love thee better than myself,
For I come hither armed against myself.
Stay not, begone. Live, and hereafter say
A madman's mercy bid thee run away.

PARIS

I do defy thy conjuration, 68
And apprehend thee for a felon here.

ROMEO

Wilt thou provoke me? Then have at thee, boy!

[*They fight.*]

PAGE

Oh, Lord, they fight! I will go call the watch. [*Exit.*]

PARIS

Oh, I am slain! [*He falls.*] If thou be merciful,
Open the tomb, lay me with Juliet. [*He dies.*]

ROMEO

In faith, I will. Let me peruse this face.
Mercutio's kinsman, noble County Paris!
What said my man when my betossèd soul
Did not attend him as we rode? I think
He told me Paris should have married Juliet. 78
Said he not so? Or did I dream it so?
Or am I mad, hearing him talk of Juliet,
To think it was so? Oh, give me thy hand,
One writ with me in sour misfortune's book.
I'll bury thee in a triumphant grave.

[*He opens the tomb.*]

A grave? Oh, no! A lantern, slaughtered youth, 84
For here lies Juliet, and her beauty makes
This vault a feasting presence full of light. 86
Death, lie thou there, by a dead man interred.

[*He lays Paris in the tomb.*]

How oft when men are at the point of death
Have they been merry, which their keepers call 89
A lightening before death! Oh, how may I 90
Call this a lightening? O my love, my wife!
Death, that hath sucked the honey of thy breath,
Hath had no power yet upon thy beauty.
Thou art not conquered; beauty's ensign yet 94
Is crimson in thy lips and in thy cheeks,
And death's pale flag is not advancèd there. 96
Tybalt, liest thou there in thy bloody sheet? 97
Oh, what more favor can I do to thee
Than with that hand that cut thy youth in twain
To sunder his that was thine enemy? 100

20 **cross** interrupt 21 **Muffle** Conceal 22 **wrenching iron** crowbar.
27 **course** intended action. 32 **dear employment** important business.
33 **jealous** suspicious 36 **hungry** hungry for corpses 39 **empty**
hungry 43 **For all this same** All the same 44 **fear** distrust. **doubt**
suspect. 45 **womb** belly 48 **in despite** defiantly 48.1 *He . . . tomb*
Whether the tomb is represented by a bier thrust onstage or by a curtained recess (see indication of scene location above at the start of
5.3), Romeo may mime the action here and at line 83.1 of using tools
to open it.

60 **gone** dead 68 **conjuration** solemn entreaty 78 **should have** was
to have 84 **lantern** turret room full of windows 86 **feasting presence** reception chamber for feasting 89 **keepers** attendants, jailers
90 **lightening** exhilaration (supposed to occur just before death)
94 **ensign** banner 96 **advanced** raised 97 **sheet** shroud. 100 **his**
i.e., my (Romeo's) own

Forgive me, cousin!—Ah, dear Juliet,
Why art thou yet so fair? Shall I believe
That unsubstantial Death is amorous,   103
And that the lean abhorrèd monster keeps
Thee here in dark to be his paramour?
For fear of that I still will stay with thee   106
And never from this palace of dim night
Depart again. Here, here will I remain
With worms that are thy chambermaids. Oh, here
Will I set up my everlasting rest   110
And shake the yoke of inauspicious stars
From this world-wearied flesh. Eyes, look your last!
Arms, take your last embrace! And lips, O you
The doors of breath, seal with a righteous kiss
A dateless bargain to engrossing death!   115
                        [*He kisses Juliet.*]
Come, bitter conduct, come, unsavory guide,   116
Thou desperate pilot, now at once run on   117
The dashing rocks thy seasick weary bark!
Here's to my love. [*He drinks.*] O true apothecary!
Thy drugs are quick. Thus with a kiss I die. [*He dies.*]

                *Enter Friar [Laurence] with lantern, crow,
                and spade.*

FRIAR LAURENCE
Saint Francis be my speed! How oft tonight   121
Have my old feet stumbled at graves! Who's there?
BALTHASAR
Here's one, a friend, and one that knows you well.
FRIAR LAURENCE
Bliss be upon you. Tell me, good my friend,
What torch is yond that vainly lends his light   125
To grubs and eyeless skulls? As I discern,   126
It burneth in the Capels' monument.
BALTHASAR
It doth so, holy sir, and there's my master,
One that you love.
FRIAR LAURENCE   Who is it?
BALTHASAR   Romeo.
FRIAR LAURENCE
How long hath he been there?
BALTHASAR   Full half an hour.
FRIAR LAURENCE
Go with me to the vault.
BALTHASAR   I dare not, sir.
My master knows not but I am gone hence,
And fearfully did menace me with death
If I did stay to look on his intents.
FRIAR LAURENCE
Stay, then, I'll go alone. Fear comes upon me.
Oh, much I fear some ill unthrifty thing.   136

BALTHASAR
As I did sleep under this yew tree here
I dreamt my master and another fought,
And that my master slew him.
FRIAR LAURENCE [*advancing to the tomb*]   Romeo!
Alack, alack, what blood is this which stains
The stony entrance of this sepulcher?
What mean these masterless and gory swords
To lie discolored by this place of peace?   143
                        [*He looks in the tomb.*]
Romeo! Oh, pale! Who else? What, Paris too?
And steeped in blood? Ah, what an unkind hour   145
Is guilty of this lamentable chance!
The lady stirs.   [*Juliet wakes.*]
JULIET
O comfortable Friar, where is my lord?   148
I do remember well where I should be,
And there I am. Where is my Romeo?
                        [*A noise within.*]
FRIAR LAURENCE
I hear some noise. Lady, come from that nest
Of death, contagion, and unnatural sleep.
A greater power than we can contradict
Hath thwarted our intents. Come, come away.
Thy husband in thy bosom there lies dead,
And Paris, too. Come, I'll dispose of thee
Among a sisterhood of holy nuns.
Stay not to question, for the watch is coming.
Come, go, good Juliet. [*A noise again.*] I dare no longer
      stay.   *Exit [Friar Laurence].*
JULIET
Go, get thee hence, for I will not away.
What's here? A cup, closed in my true love's hand?
Poison, I see, hath been his timeless end.   162
O churl, drunk all, and left no friendly drop   163
To help me after? I will kiss thy lips;
Haply some poison yet doth hang on them,   165
To make me die with a restorative. [*She kisses him.*]
Thy lips are warm.

                Enter [Paris's] Boy and Watch.

FIRST WATCH   Lead, boy. Which way?
JULIET
Yea, noise? Then I'll be brief. O happy dagger!   169
                        [*She takes Romeo's dagger.*]
This is thy sheath. There rust, and let me die.
                        [*She stabs herself and dies.*]
PAGE
This is the place, there where the torch doth burn.
FIRST WATCH
The ground is bloody. Search about the churchyard.
Go, some of you, whoe'er you find attach.   173
                        [*Exeunt some.*]
Pitiful sight! Here lies the County slain,

---

103 **unsubstantial** lacking material existence   106 **still** always
110 **set . . . rest** (See 4.5.6. The meaning is, "make my final determination," with allusion to the idea of repose.)   115 **dateless bargain**
everlasting contract.   **engrossing** monopolizing, taking all; also,
drawing up the contract   116 **conduct** guide (i.e., the poison)
117 **desperate** reckless, despairing   121 **be my speed** prosper me and
let me arrive in time.   125 **vainly** uselessly   126 **grubs** insect larvae
136 **unthrifty** unfortunate

143.1 *He looks . . . tomb* Whether the Friar is to enter the tomb
depends on staging arrangements.   145 **unkind** unnatural
148 **comfortable** comforting   162 **timeless** (1) untimely (2) everlasting   163 **churl** miser   165 **Haply** perhaps   169 **happy** opportune
173 **attach** arrest, detain.

And Juliet bleeding, warm, and newly dead,
Who here hath lain these two days burièd.
Go tell the Prince. Run to the Capulets.
Raise up the Montagues. Some others search.
                              [*Exeunt others.*]
We see the ground whereon these woes do lie,
But the true ground of all these piteous woes   180
We cannot without circumstance descry.   181

          *Enter [some of the Watch, with] Romeo's
          man [Balthasar].*

SECOND WATCH
Here's Romeo's man. We found him in the
     churchyard.
FIRST WATCH
Hold him in safety till the Prince come hither.   183

          *Enter Friar [Laurence], and another Watchman
          [with tools].*

THIRD WATCH
Here is a friar, that trembles, sighs, and weeps.
We took this mattock and this spade from him
As he was coming from this churchyard's side.
FIRST WATCH
A great suspicion. Stay the Friar, too.   187

          Enter the Prince [and attendants].

PRINCE
What misadventure is so early up
That calls our person from our morning rest?   189

          Enter Capels [Capulet and his Wife].

CAPULET
What should it be that is so shrieked abroad?
CAPULET'S WIFE
Oh, the people in the street cry "Romeo,"
Some "Juliet," and some "Paris," and all run
With open outcry toward our monument.
PRINCE
What fear is this which startles in our ears?   194
FIRST WATCH
Sovereign, here lies the County Paris slain,
And Romeo dead, and Juliet, dead before,
Warm and new killed.
PRINCE
Search, seek, and know how this foul murder comes. 198
FIRST WATCH
Here is a friar, and slaughtered Romeo's man,
With instruments upon them fit to open   200
These dead men's tombs.
CAPULET
O heavens! O wife, look how our daughter bleeds!
This dagger hath mista'en, for lo, his house   203
Is empty on the back of Montague,
And it mis-sheathèd in my daughter's bosom!

CAPULET'S WIFE
Oh, me! This sight of death is as a bell
That warns my old age to a sepulcher.

          Enter Montague.

PRINCE
Come, Montague, for thou art early up
To see thy son and heir more early down.
MONTAGUE
Alas, my liege, my wife is dead tonight;
Grief of my son's exile hath stopped her breath.
What further woe conspires against mine age?
PRINCE   Look, and thou shalt see.
MONTAGUE [*seeing Romeo's body*]
O thou untaught! What manners is in this,   214
To press before thy father to a grave?   215
PRINCE
Seal up the mouth of outrage for a while,   216
Till we can clear these ambiguities
And know their spring, their head, their true descent; 218
And then will I be general of your woes   219
And lead you even to death. Meantime, forbear,   220
And let mischance be slave to patience.   221
Bring forth the parties of suspicion.   222
FRIAR LAURENCE
I am the greatest, able to do least,
Yet most suspected, as the time and place
Doth make against me, of this direful murder;   225
And here I stand, both to impeach and purge   226
Myself condemnèd and myself excused.   227
PRINCE
Then say at once what thou dost know in this.
FRIAR LAURENCE
I will be brief, for my short date of breath   229
Is not so long as is a tedious tale.
Romeo, there dead, was husband to that Juliet,
And she, there dead, that Romeo's faithful wife.
I married them, and their stol'n marriage day
Was Tybalt's doomsday, whose untimely death
Banished the new-made bridegroom from this city,
For whom, and not for Tybalt, Juliet pined.
You, to remove that siege of grief from her,
Betrothed and would have married her perforce   238
To County Paris. Then comes she to me,
And with wild looks bid me devise some means
To rid her from this second marriage,
Or in my cell there would she kill herself.
Then gave I her—so tutored by my art—
A sleeping potion, which so took effect
As I intended, for it wrought on her   245
The form of death. Meantime I writ to Romeo   246

---

180 **ground** basis. (Playing on the meaning "earth" in line 179.) 181
circumstance details 183 **in safety** under guard 187 **Stay** Detain
189 **our person** (The royal "we.") 194 **startles** cries alarmingly
198 **know** learn 200 **instruments** tools 203 **his house** its scabbard

214 **untaught** ill-mannered youth. (Said with affectionate irony.)
215 **press** hasten, go 216 **mouth of outrage** (1) popular outcry (2)
entrance to the tomb 218 **spring, head** (Both words mean "source.")
219 **be . . . woes** be leader in lamentation 220 **even to death** in
lamentation for the dead. 221 **let . . . patience** i.e., let us bear our
misfortune patiently. 222 **of** under 225 **make** conspire, tell
226–7 **to . . . excused** to accuse myself of what is to be condemned in
me and to exonerate myself where I ought to be excused. 229 **date
of breath** time left to live 238 **perforce** by compulsion 245 **wrought**
fashioned 246 **form** appearance

That he should hither come as this dire night 247
To help to take her from her borrowed grave,
Being the time the potion's force should cease.
But he which bore my letter, Friar John,
Was stayed by accident, and yesternight 251
Returned my letter back. Then all alone
At the prefixèd hour of her waking
Came I to take her from her kindred's vault,
Meaning to keep her closely at my cell 255
Till I conveniently could send to Romeo.
But when I came, some minute ere the time
Of her awakening, here untimely lay
The noble Paris and true Romeo dead.
She wakes, and I entreated her come forth
And bear this work of heaven with patience.
But then a noise did scare me from the tomb,
And she, too desperate, would not go with me,
But, as it seems, did violence on herself.
All this I know, and to the marriage
Her nurse is privy; and if aught in this 266
Miscarried by my fault, let my old life
Be sacrificed some hour before his time 268
Unto the rigor of severest law.

PRINCE
We still have known thee for a holy man. 270
Where's Romeo's man? What can he say to this?

BALTHASAR
I brought my master news of Juliet's death,
And then in post he came from Mantua 273
To this same place, to this same monument.
This letter he early bid me give his father, 275
                     [*showing a letter*]
And threatened me with death, going in the vault,
If I departed not and left him there.

PRINCE [*taking the letter*]
Give me the letter. I will look on it.
Where is the County's page, that raised the watch?
Sirrah, what made your master in this place? 280

247 as this this very   **251 stayed** stopped   **255 closely** secretly
266 privy in on the secret   **268 his** its   **270 still** always   **273 post**
haste   **275 This . . . father** He bade me give this letter to his father
early in the morning (5.3.23–4)   **280 made** did

PAGE
He came with flowers to strew his lady's grave,
And bid me stand aloof, and so I did.
Anon comes one with light to ope the tomb,
And by and by my master drew on him,
And then I ran away to call the watch.

PRINCE
This letter doth make good the Friar's words,
Their course of love, the tidings of her death;
And here he writes that he did buy a poison
Of a poor 'pothecary, and therewithal 289
Came to this vault to die, and lie with Juliet.
Where be these enemies? Capulet, Montague,
See what a scourge is laid upon your hate,
That heaven finds means to kill your joys with love. 293
And I, for winking at your discords, too 294
Have lost a brace of kinsmen. All are punished. 295

CAPULET
O brother Montague, give me thy hand.
This is my daughter's jointure, for no more 297
Can I demand.

MONTAGUE   But I can give thee more,
For I will raise her statue in pure gold, 299
That whiles Verona by that name is known
There shall no figure at such rate be set 301
As that of true and faithful Juliet.

CAPULET
As rich shall Romeo's by his lady's lie;
Poor sacrifices of our enmity!

PRINCE
A glooming peace this morning with it brings;
   The sun, for sorrow, will not show his head.
Go hence to have more talk of these sad things.
   Some shall be pardoned, and some punishèd;
For never was a story of more woe
Than this of Juliet and her Romeo.   [*Exeunt.*]

289 therewithal with the poison   **293 kill your joys** (1) destroy your
happiness (2) kill your children. **with** by means of   **294 winking at**
shutting my eyes to   **295 a brace of** two   **297 jointure** marriage
settlement   **299 raise** (The second quarto reading, "raie," is defended
by some editors in the sense of "array," make ready.)   **301 rate** value

Julius Caesar

Julius Caesar stands midway in Shakespeare's dramatic career, at a critical juncture. In some ways, it is an epilogue to his English history plays of the 1590s; in other ways, it introduces the period of the great tragedies. The play evidently was first performed at the new Globe playhouse in the fall of 1599, shortly after *Henry V* (the last of Shakespeare's history plays about medieval England) and around the time of *As You Like It* (one of the last of Shakespeare's happy romantic comedies). It shortly preceded *Hamlet*. It is placed among the tragedies in the Folio of 1623, where it was first published, and is entitled *The Tragedy of Julius Caesar*, but in the table of contents it is listed as *The Life and Death of Julius Caesar* as though it were a history.

Julius Caesar shares with Shakespeare's history plays an absorption in the problems of civil war and popular unrest. Rome, like England, suffers an internal division that is reflected in the perturbed state of the heavens themselves. The commoners, or plebeians, are easily swayed by demagogues. Opportunists prosper in this atmosphere of crisis, although fittingly even they are sometimes undone by their own scheming. Politics seems to require a morality quite apart from that of personal life, posing a tragic dilemma for Brutus, as it did for Richard II or Henry VI. The blending of history and tragedy in *Julius Caesar*, then, is not unlike that found in several English history plays. Rome was a natural subject to which Shakespeare might turn in his continuing depiction of political behavior. Roman culture had recently been elevated to new importance by the classical orientation of the Renaissance. As a model of political organization, it loomed larger in Elizabethan consciousness than it does in ours, because so few other models were available and because Greek culture was less accessible in language and tradition. According to a widely accepted mythology, Elizabethans considered themselves descended from the Romans through another Brutus, the great-grandson of Aeneas.

Yet the differences between Roman and English history are as important as the similarities. Rome's choice during her civil wars lay between a senatorial republican form of government and a strong single ruler. Although the monarchical English might be inclined to be suspicious of republicanism, they had no experience to compare with it—certainly not their various peasants' revolts, such as Jack Cade's rebellion (in *2 Henry VI*). On the other hand, Roman one-man rule as it flourished under Octavius Caesar lacked the English sanctions of divine right. Rome was, after all, a pagan culture, and Shakespeare carefully preserves this non-Christian frame of reference. The gods are frequently invoked and appear to respond with prophetic dreams and auguries, but their ultimate intentions are baffling. Human beings strive blindly; the will of the gods is inscrutable. The outcome of *Julius Caesar* is far different from the restoration of providentially ordained order at the end of *Richard III*. Calm is restored and political authority reestablished, but we are by no means sure that a divine morality has been served. Roman history for Shakespeare is history divested of its divine imperatives and located in a distant political setting, making dispassionate appraisal less difficult.

In Plutarch's *Lives of the Noble Grecians and Romans*, as translated by Sir Thomas North, Shakespeare discovered a rich opportunity for pursuing the ironies of political life to which he had been increasingly attracted in the English histories. In fact, he was drawn throughout his career to Plutarch: to the portrait of Portia in "The Life of Marcus Brutus," not only for Portia in *Julius Caesar*, but also for Lucrece in *The Rape of Lucrece*, Kate in *1 Henry IV*, and Portia in *The Merchant of Venice*; to "The Life of Theseus" for the Duke of *A Midsummer Night's Dream*; and to various lives for *Julius Caesar*, *Coriolanus*, *Antony and Cleopatra*, and *Timon of Athens*. Freed from the orthodoxies of the Elizabethan world view, Shakespeare turned in the Roman or classical plays toward irony or outright satire (as in *Troilus and Cressida*) and toward the personal tragedy of political dilemma (as in *Coriolanus* and *Julius Caesar*). These are to be the dominant motifs of the Roman or classical plays, as distinguished from both the English histories and the great tragedies of evil, in which politics plays a lesser part (*Hamlet, Othello, King Lear, Macbeth*).

Julius Caesar is an ambivalent study of civil conflict. As in *Richard II,* the play is structured around two protagonists rather than one. Caesar and Brutus, men of extraordinary abilities and debilitating weaknesses, are more like one another than either would care to admit. This antithetical balance reflects a dual tradition: the medieval view of Dante and of Geoffrey Chaucer, condemning Brutus and Cassius as conspirators, and the Renaissance view of Sir Philip Sidney and Ben Jonson, condemning Caesar as a tyrant. These opposing views still live on in various twentieth-century productions that seek to enlist the play on the side of conservatism or liberalism. In one famous production by Orson Welles for the Mercury Theatre in 1937, Caesar was made out to resemble Benito Mussolini, Italy's fascist dictator, with reference also to Franco's fascists in Spain when that civil war was at its peak. Welles's subtitle for his production, "Death of a Dictator," left no doubt as to the intended statement. The film version of 1953 by John Houseman and Joseph Maniewicz dyed its khaki military uniforms green to suggest the German Wehrmacht; the music adopted for the production deliberately aped the music that accompanied Nazi marching columns in newsreels in the 1930s. Trevor Nunn, at Stratford-upon-Avon in 1972, similarly drew overt parallels to German fascism. At Stratford, Connecticut, in 1979, director Gerald Freedman presented Caesar as a Latin American dictator; at Ashland, Oregon, in 1982, Jerry Turner likened Caesar to Che Guevara. Such interpretations reflect what the conspirators themselves believe, as they cry "Liberty! Freedom! Tyranny is dead!" but the play itself invites widely varying interpretations. Caesar has sometimes appeared as a great leader and a man of great natural authority despite his manifest weaknesses, involved in a struggle to the death with conspirators whose motives and personalities are as complex as his. Anthony Quayle and Michael Langham sought such a balance in their 1950 production at Stratford-upon-Avon; so did Glen Byam Shaw in 1957. The film version of 1953 by John Houseman and Joseph Mankiewicz achieved a kind of balance, despite its antifascist leanings, by evenly distributing its major roles among various well-known actors and actresses—John Gielgud as Cassius, Marlon Brando as Antony, James Mason as Brutus, Louis Calhern as Caesar, Greer Garson as Calpurnia, Deborah Kerr as Portia—instead of allowing one actor to dominate the play. Most recent criticism similarly has abandoned the fruitless debate as to whether Brutus or Caesar is the tragic protagonist, and whether one or the other of them is to be seen as morally superior, in favor of a multiple perspective.

Caesar is a study in paradox. He is unquestionably a great general, astute in politics, decisive in his judgments, and sharp in his evaluation of men, as, for example, in his distrust of Cassius with his "lean and hungry look" (1.2.194). Yet this mightiest of men, who in Cassius's phrase bestrides the narrow world "like a Colossus" (line 136), is also deaf in one ear, prone to fevers and epilepsy, unable to compete with Cassius by swimming the Tiber fully armed, and afflicted with a sterile marriage. Physical limitations of this sort are common enough, but in Caesar they are constantly juxtaposed with his aspirations to be above mortal weakness. He dies boasting that he is like the "northern star," constant, unique, "Unshaked of motion" (3.1.61–71). He professes to fear nothing and yet is notoriously superstitious. He calmly reflects that "death, a necessary end, / Will come when it will come," and then arrogantly boasts in the next moment that "Danger knows full well / That Caesar is more dangerous than he" (2.2.36–45). As his wife puts it, Caesar's "wisdom is consumed in confidence" (line 49). He willfully betrays his own best instincts and ignores plain warnings through self-deception. He stops a procession to hear a soothsayer and then dismisses the man as "a dreamer" (1.2.24). He commissions his augurers to determine whether he should stay at home on the ides of March and then persuades himself that acting on their advice would be a sign of weakness. Most fatally, he thinks himself above flattery and so is especially vulnerable to it. So wise and powerful a man as this cannot stop the process of his own fate, because his fate and character are interwoven: he is the victim of his own hubris. His insatiable desire for the crown overbalances his judgment; no warnings of the gods can save him. Even his virtues conspire against him, for he regards himself as one who puts public interest ahead of personal affairs, and so he brushes aside the letter of Artemidorus that would have told him of the conspiracy.

Brutus, for all his opposition to Caesar, is also a paradoxical figure. His strengths are quite unlike those of Caesar, but his weaknesses are surprisingly similar. Brutus is a noble Roman from an ancient family whose glory it has been to defend the personal liberties of Rome, the republican tradition. Brutus's virtues are personal virtues. He enjoys an admirable rapport with his courageous and intelligent wife, and is genuinely kind to his servants. In friendship he is trustworthy. He deplores oaths in the conspiracy because his word is his bond. He finds Caesar's ambition for power distasteful and vulgar; his opposition to Caesar is both idealistic and patrician. Brutus's hubris is a pride of family, and on this score he is vulnerable to flattery. As Cassius reminds him, alluding to Brutus's ancestor Lucius Junius Brutus, who founded the Roman Republic in 509 B.C.: "There was a Brutus once that would have brooked / Th'eternal devil to keep his state in Rome / As easily as a king" (1.2.159–61). Should not Marcus Brutus be the savior of his country from a return to tyranny? Is not he a more fit leader for Rome than Caesar? " 'Brutus' and 'Caesar.' What should be in that 'Caesar'? / Why should that name be sounded more than yours?" (lines 142–3). Cassius's strategy is to present to Brutus numerous testimonials "all tending to the great opinion / That Rome holds of his name" (lines 318–19). Cassius plays the role of tempter here, but the notion he suggests is not new to Brutus.

The parallelism of Brutus's pride and Caesar's ambition is strongly underscored by the way in which these great figures appear to us in two adjoining scenes: 2.1 and 2.2. In these two scenes, the protagonists enter alone during the troubled night, call for a servant, receive the conspirators, and dispute the wise caution of their wives. Both men are predisposed to the temptations that are placed before them. Brutus has often thought of himself as the indispensable man for the preservation of Rome's liberties. Despite his good breeding and coolly rational manner, he is as dominating a personality as Caesar and as hard to move once his mind is made up. Indeed, the conspiracy founders on Brutus's repeated insistence on having his own way. He allows no oaths among the conspirators and will not kill Antony along with Caesar. He permits Antony to speak after him at Caesar's funeral. He vetoes Cicero as a fellow conspirator. In each instance, the other conspirators are unanimously opposed to Brutus's choice but yield to him. Brutus cuts off Cassius's objections before hearing them fully, being accustomed to having his way without dispute. His motives are in part noble and idealistic: Brutus wishes to have the conspirators behave generously and openly, as heroes rather than as henchmen. Yet there is something loftily patrician in his desire to have the fruits of conspiracy without any of the dirty work. His willingness to have Antony speak after him betrays a vain confidence in his own oratory and an unjustified faith in the plebeian mob. Moreover, when Brutus overrides Cassius once more in the decision to fight at Philippi and is proved wrong by the event, no idealistic motive can excuse Brutus's insistence on being obeyed; Cassius is the more experienced soldier. Still, Brutus's fatal limitations as leader of a coup d'état are inseparable from his virtues as a private man. The truth is that such a noble man is, by his very nature, unsuited for the stern exigencies of assassination and civil war. Brutus is strong-minded about his ideals, but he cannot be ruthless. The means and the end of revolution drift further and further apart. He cannot supply his troops at Philippi because he will not forage among the peasants of the countryside and will not countenance among his allies the routine corruptions of an army in time of war, though at the same time that he upbraids Cassius for not sending him gold he does not stop to ask where the gold would come from. Even suicide is distasteful for Brutus, obliging him to embarrass his friends by asking their help. Brutus is too high-minded and genteel a man for the troubled times in which he lives.

The times indeed seem to demand ruthless action of the sort Antony and Octavius are all too ready to provide. The greatest irony of Brutus's fall is that the coup he undertakes for Roman liberty yields only further diminutions of that liberty. The plebeians are not ready for the commonwealth Brutus envisages. From the first, they are portrayed as amiable but "saucy" (even in the opinion of their tribunes, Flavius and Marullus). They adulate Caesar at the expense of their previous idol, Pompey. When Brutus successfully appeals for a moment to their changeable loyalties, they cry "Let him be Caesar," and "Caesar's better parts / Shall be crowned in Brutus" (3.2.51–2). If Brutus were not swayed by this hero-worship, he would have good cause to be disillusioned. To his credit, he is not the demagogue the plebeians take him for and so cannot continue to bend them to his will. Cassius, too, for all his villainlike role as tempter to Brutus, his envious motive, and his Epicurean skepticism, reveals a finer nature as the play progresses. Inspired perhaps by Brutus's philosophic idealism, Cassius turns philosopher also and accepts defeat in a noble but ineffectual cause. Yet even his death is futile; Cassius is misinformed about the fate of his friend Titinius and so stabs himself just when the battle is going well for the conspirators.

The ultimate victors are Antony and Octavius. Antony, whatever finer nature he may possess, becomes under the stress of circumstance a cunning bargainer with the conspirators and a masterful rhetorician who characterizes himself to the plebeians as a "plain blunt man" (3.2.219). In sardonic soliloquy at the end of his funeral oration, he observes, "Now let it work. Mischief, thou art afoot. / Take thou what course thou wilt" (lines 261–2). He is, to be sure, stirred by loyalty to Caesar's memory, but to the end of avenging Caesar's death he is prepared to unleash violence at whatever risk to the state. He regards Lepidus contemptuously as a mere creature under his command. Antony is older than Octavius and teaches the younger man about political realities, but an Elizabethan audience would probably savor the irony that Octavius will subsequently beat Antony at his own game. At Philippi, Octavius's refusal to accept Antony's directions in the battle (5.1.16–20) gives us a glimpse of the peremptory manner for which he is to become famous, like his predecessor. Antony and Octavius together are, in any case, a fearsome pair, matter-of-factly noting down the names of those who must die, including their own kinsmen. They cut off the bequests left to the populace in Caesar's will, by which Antony had won the hearts of the plebeians (3.2, 4.1–2). Many innocent persons are sacrificed in the new reign of terror, including Cicero and the poet unluckily named Cinna. In such deaths, art and civilization yield to expediency. Rationality gives way to frenzied rhetoric and to a struggle for power in which Rome's republican tradition is buried forever. Such is the achievement of Brutus's noble revolution.

Appropriately for such a depiction of ambivalent political strife, *Julius Caesar* is written chiefly in the oratorical mode. It resembles its near contemporary, *Henry V,* in devoting so much attention to speeches of public persuasion. The famous orations following Caesar's assassination—one by Brutus in the so-called Laconic style (that is, concise and sententious) and one by Antony in the Asiatic style (that is, more florid, anecdotal, and literary)—are only the most prominent of many public utterances. In the first scene, Marullus rebukes the plebeians for their disloyalty to Pompey and for the moment dissuades them from idolizing Caesar. Decius Brutus changes Caesar's presumably unalterable mind about staying home on the ides of March (2.2). Caesar lectures the Senate on the virtues of constancy. Before Philippi, the contending armies clash with verbal taunts. Antony and Octavius end the play with tributes to the dead Brutus. In less public scenes as well, oratory serves to win Brutus over to the conspirators, to urge unavailingly that Brutus confide in his wife, or to warn the unheeding Caesar of his danger. The decline of the conspirators' cause shows in their descent from rational discourse to private bickering (4.3). The play gives us a range of rhetorical styles, from the deliberative (having to do with careful consideration of choices) to the forensic (analogous to pleading at law, maintaining one side or the other of a given question), to the epideictic (for display, as in set orations). The imagery, suitably public and rhetorical in its function, is of a fixed star in the firmament, a Colossus bestriding the petty world of humans, a tide of fortune in the affairs of humankind, a statue spouting fountains of blood. The city of Rome is a vivid presence in the play, conveyed at times through Elizabethan anachronisms, such as striking clocks, sweaty nightcaps, "towers and windows, yea, . . . chimney tops" (1.1.39), but in an eclectic fusion of native and classical traditions wherein anachronisms become functionally purposeful. Style affords us one more way of considering *Julius Caesar* as a Janus play, looking back to Shakespeare's history plays and forward to his tragedies.

Women are marginalized in *Julius Caesar,* much as in Shakespeare's English history plays. Portia and Calpurnia are alike, not only in their concern for their husbands' welfare, but also in their inability to do anything to ensure their husbands' safety and prosperity. Fittingly in such an unremittingly patriarchal play, Portia and Calpurnia are noble Roman matrons of the type we also see earlier in *The Rape of Lucrece* or *Titus Andronicus* and later in Octavia (*Antony and Cleopatra*) and Volumnia (*Coriolanus*): unassailably virtuous, descended from patrician stock, and submissive to the essentially male values of unflinching duty and stoical reserve. Portia, daughter of the great Cato of Utica who committed suicide rather than submit to Caesar's tyranny, emulates her father's example by taking her own life rather than outlive her husband's shame in defeat. Calpurnia expounds her prophetic dream of Caesar's bleeding statue (2.2.76–9) only to be rebuked for womanly cowardice. These women do what they can to offer their men an alternative perspective on political ambition—one in which caution and attentiveness to family values stand in opposition to the competitive mores of the male-dominated world—but the women are doomed, like Cassandra and Andromache (in *Troilus and Cressida*), to see their quiet wisdom ignored or misinterpreted. Most touching of all is the scene of marital mutuality between Portia and Brutus (2.1.234–310), in which we realize that Portia's concern and sympathy for her husband cannot save Brutus from himself.

A structural pattern to be found in *Julius Caesar,* as noted by John Velz (see bibliography), is the replicating action of rise and fall by which the great men of ancient Rome succeed one another. The process antedates the play itself, for Pompey's faded glory mentioned in Act 1 is a reminder—or should be a reminder—that good fortune lasts but a day. We behold Caesar at the point of his greatest triumph and his imminent decline to death. "O mighty Caesar! Dost thou lie so low?" asks Antony when he sees the prostrate body of the once most powerful man alive. "Are all thy conquests, glories, triumphs, spoils, / Shrunk to this little measure?" (3.1.150–2). Brutus and Cassius step forward into prominence only to be supplanted by Antony and Octavius. Antony is unaware, though presumably the audience is aware, that Antony is to fall at the hands of Octavius. The process of incessant change, reinforced by such metaphors as the tide in the affairs of humans (already noted), offering its mocking comment on Caesar's self-comparison to the fixed northern star, is not simply a meaningless descent on the grand staircase of history, for Octavius's *Pax Romana* lies at the end of the cycle from republic to empire. Still, that resting place is beyond the conclusion of this open-ended play. What we see here again and again is a human blindness to history, through which a succession of protagonists repeat one another's errors without intending to do so. Cassius, like Caesar, goes to his death in the face of unpropitious omens that he now partly believes to be true. The eagles that accompanied Cassius and his army to Philippi desert him as the moment of battle approaches. These omens suggest a balance between character and fate, for, though the leaders of Rome have one by one fallen through their own acts and choices, they have also, it seems, fulfilled a prearranged destiny. Brutus, confronted by the Ghost of Caesar and assured that he will see this spirit of Caesar at Philippi, answers resolutely, "Why, I will see thee at Philippi, then" (4.3.288). Defeated in battle, as he sensed he would be, Brutus takes his own life. Cassius dies on his birthday. *Sic transit gloria mundi.*

Julius Caesar

[*Dramatis Personae*

JULIUS CAESAR
CALPURNIA, *Caesar's wife*
MARK ANTONY,
OCTAVIUS CAESAR,
LEPIDUS,
} *triumvirs after Caesar's death*

MARCUS BRUTUS
PORTIA, *Brutus's wife*
CAIUS CASSIUS,
CASCA,
DECIUS BRUTUS,
CINNA,
METELLUS CIMBER,
TREBONIUS,
CAIUS LIGARIUS,
} *conspirators with Brutus*

CICERO,
PUBLIUS,
POPILIUS LENA,
} *senators*

FLAVIUS,
MARULLUS,
} *tribunes of the people*

SOOTHSAYER
ARTEMIDORUS, *a teacher of rhetoric*
CINNA, *a poet*
Another POET

LUCILIUS,
TITINIUS,
MESSALA,
YOUNG CATO,
VOLUMNIUS,
VARRO,
CLAUDIUS,
CLITUS,
DARDANIUS,
LABEO,
FLAVIUS,
} *officers and soldiers in the army of Brutus and Cassius*

PINDARUS, *Cassius's servant*
LUCIUS,
STRATO,
} *Brutus's servants*

Caesar's SERVANT
Antony's SERVANT
Octavius's SERVANT

CARPENTER
COBBLER
Five PLEBEIANS
Three SOLDIERS *in Brutus' army*
Two SOLDIERS *in Antony's army*
MESSENGER

GHOST *of Caesar*

Senators, Plebeians, Officers, Soldiers, and Attendants

SCENE: *Rome; the neighborhood of Sardis; the neighborhood of Philippi*]

1.1

Enter Flavius, Marullus, and certain commoners over the stage.

FLAVIUS
Hence! Home, you idle creatures, get you home!

Is this a holiday? What, know you not,
Being mechanical, you ought not walk   3
Upon a laboring day without the sign   4
Of your profession?—Speak, what trade art thou?
CARPENTER   Why, sir, a carpenter.
MARULLUS
Where is thy leather apron and thy rule?

1.1. Location: Rome. A street.

3 mechanical of the artisan class   **4 sign** garb and implements

510

What dost thou with thy best apparel on?—
You, sir, what trade are you?

COBBLER   Truly, sir, in respect of a fine workman, I am   10
but, as you would say, a cobbler.   11

MARULLUS
But what trade art thou? Answer me directly.

COBBLER   A trade, sir, that I hope I may use with a safe
conscience, which is indeed, sir, a mender of bad soles.   14

FLAVIUS
What trade, thou knave? Thou naughty knave, what
trade?   15

COBBLER   Nay, I beseech you, sir, be not out with me.   16
Yet if you be out, sir, I can mend you.   17

FLAVIUS
What mean'st thou by that? Mend me, thou saucy
fellow?

COBBLER   Why, sir, cobble you.   19

FLAVIUS   Thou art a cobbler, art thou?

COBBLER   Truly, sir, all that I live by is with the awl. I   21
meddle with no tradesman's matters nor women's   22
matters, but withal I am indeed, sir, a surgeon to old   23
shoes. When they are in great danger, I recover them.   24
As proper men as ever trod upon neat's leather have   25
gone upon my handiwork.

FLAVIUS
But wherefore art not in thy shop today?
Why dost thou lead these men about the streets?

COBBLER   Truly, sir, to wear out their shoes, to get myself
into more work. But indeed, sir, we make holiday
to see Caesar and to rejoice in his triumph.   31

MARULLUS
Wherefore rejoice? What conquest brings he home?
What tributaries follow him to Rome   33
To grace in captive bonds his chariot wheels?
You blocks, you stones, you worse than senseless
things!   35
O you hard hearts, you cruel men of Rome,
Knew you not Pompey? Many a time and oft   37
Have you climbed up to walls and battlements,   38
To towers and windows, yea, to chimney tops,   39
Your infants in your arms, and there have sat
The livelong day, with patient expectation,

To see great Pompey pass the streets of Rome.   42
And when you saw his chariot but appear,
Have you not made an universal shout,
That Tiber trembled underneath her banks   45
To hear the replication of your sounds   46
Made in her concave shores?   47
And do you now put on your best attire?
And do you now cull out a holiday?   49
And do you now strew flowers in his way
That comes in triumph over Pompey's blood?   51
Begone!
Run to your houses, fall upon your knees,
Pray to the gods to intermit the plague   54
That needs must light on this ingratitude.   55

FLAVIUS
Go, go, good countrymen, and for this fault
Assemble all the poor men of your sort;   57
Draw them to Tiber banks, and weep your tears
Into the channel, till the lowest stream   59
Do kiss the most exalted shores of all.   60
                    Exeunt all the commoners.
See whe'er their basest mettle be not moved.   61
They vanish tongue-tied in their guiltiness.
Go you down that way towards the Capitol;
This way will I. Disrobe the images   64
If you do find them decked with ceremonies.   65

MARULLUS   May we do so?
You know it is the Feast of Lupercal.   67

FLAVIUS
It is no matter. Let no images
Be hung with Caesar's trophies. I'll about   69
And drive away the vulgar from the streets;   70
So do you too, where you perceive them thick.
These growing feathers plucked from Caesar's wing
Will make him fly an ordinary pitch,   73
Who else would soar above the view of men   74
And keep us all in servile fearfulness.   *Exeunt.*

10 in . . . workman (1) as far as skilled work is concerned (2) compared with a skilled worker   11 cobbler (1) one who works with
shoes (2) bungler.   14 soles (With pun on "souls.")   15 naughty
good-for-nothing   16 out out of temper   17 out having worn-out
shoes.   mend you (1) cure your bad temper (2) repair your shoes.
19 cobble you mend your shoes. (The meaning "to pelt with stones"
also suggests itself here, though perhaps it was not in general use
until later in the seventeenth century.)   21 awl (Punning on *all*.)
22 meddle with (1) have to do with (2) have sexual intercourse with
23 withal yet. (With pun on *with awl*.)   24 recover (1) resole (2) cure
25 proper fine, handsome.   as . . . leather (Proverbial. *Neat's leather* is
cowhide.)   31 triumph triumphal procession. (Caesar had overthrown the sons of Pompey the Great in Spain at the Battle of Munda,
March 17, 45 B.C. The triumph was held that October.)   33 tributaries
captives who will pay ransom (tribute)   35 senseless insensible like
stone (hence, unfeeling)   37 Pompey (Caesar had overthrown the
great soldier and onetime triumvir at the Battle of Pharsalus in 48 B.C.
Pompey fled to Egypt, where he was murdered.)   38–9 battlements
. . . chimney tops (The details are appropriate to an Elizabethan
cityscape.)

42 great (Alludes to Pompey's epithet, *Magnus*, "great.")   pass pass
through   45 Tiber the Tiber River   46 replication echo   47 concave
hollowed out, overhanging   49 cull pick   51 Pompey's blood (1)
Pompey's offspring (2) the blood of the Pompeys.   54 intermit suspend   55 needs must must necessarily   57 sort rank   59–60 till . . .
all until even at its lowest reach the river is filled to the brim.   61 See
. . . moved See how even their ignoble natures can be appealed to.
(*Mettle* and *metal* are interchangeable, meaning both "temperament"
and the natural substance. A base *metal* is one that is easily changed
or *moved*, unlike gold; compare 1.2.308–10.)   64 images statues (of
Caesar in royal regalia, set up by his followers)   65 ceremonies ceremonial trappings.   67 Feast of Lupercal a feast of purification
(*Februa*, whence *February*) in honor of Pan, celebrated from ancient
times in Rome on February 15 of each year. (Historically, this celebration came some months after Caesar's triumph in October of 45 B.C.
The celebrants, called *Luperci*, raced around the Palatine Hill and the
Circus carrying thongs of goatskin, with which they lightly struck
those who came in their way. Women so touched were suppposed to
be cured of barrenness; hence Caesar's wish that Antony would
strike Calpurnia, 1.2.6–9.)   69 trophies spoils of war hung up as
memorials of victory.   about go around the other way   70 vulgar
commoners, plebeians   73 pitch highest point in flight. (A term from
falconry.)   74 else otherwise

[1.2]

Enter Caesar, Antony for the course, Calpurnia,
Portia, Decius, Cicero, Brutus, Cassius, Casca, a
Soothsayer; after them, Marullus and Flavius;
[citizens following].

CAESAR
Calpurnia!

CASCA   Peace, ho! Caesar speaks.

CAESAR   Calpurnia!

CALPURNIA   Here, my lord.

CAESAR
Stand you directly in Antonio's way   3
When he doth run his course. Antonio!

ANTONY   Caesar, my lord?

CAESAR
Forget not, in your speed, Antonio,
To touch Calpurnia; for our elders say
The barren, touchèd in this holy chase,
Shake off their sterile curse.

ANTONY   I shall remember.   9
When Caesar says "Do this," it is performed.

CAESAR
Set on, and leave no ceremony out.   [*Flourish.*]   11

SOOTHSAYER   Caesar!

CAESAR   Ha? Who calls?

CASCA
Bid every noise be still. Peace yet again!
[*The music ceases.*]

CAESAR
Who is it in the press that calls on me?   15
I hear a tongue shriller than all the music
Cry "Caesar!" Speak. Caesar is turned to hear.

SOOTHSAYER
Beware the ides of March.

CAESAR   What man is that?   18

BRUTUS
A soothsayer bids you beware the ides of March.

CAESAR
Set him before me. Let me see his face.

CASSIUS
Fellow, come from the throng. [*The Soothsayer comes*
forward.] Look upon Caesar.

CAESAR
What say'st thou to me now? Speak once again.

SOOTHSAYER   Beware the ides of March.

CAESAR
He is a dreamer. Let us leave him. Pass.   24
Sennet. Exeunt. Manent Brutus and Cassius.

CASSIUS
Will you go see the order of the course?   25

1.2. Location: A public place or street, perhaps as in the previous
scene.
0.1 *for the course* i.e., stripped for the race, carrying a goatskin thong
3 Antonio's (Here and occasionally elsewhere Shakespeare employs
Italian forms of Latin proper names, perhaps for metrical reasons.)
9 sterile curse curse of barrenness.   **11 Set on** Proceed   **15 press**
throng   **18 ides of March** March 15.   **24.1** *Sennet* trumpet call signaling the arrival or departure of a dignitary.   *Manent* They remain on
stage   **25 order of the course** ritual and progress of the race.

BRUTUS   Not I.

CASSIUS   I pray you, do.

BRUTUS
I am not gamesome. I do lack some part   28
Of that quick spirit that is in Antony.
Let me not hinder, Cassius, your desires;
I'll leave you.

CASSIUS
Brutus, I do observe you now of late.
I have not from your eyes that gentleness
And show of love as I was wont to have.   34
You bear too stubborn and too strange a hand   35
Over your friend that loves you.

BRUTUS   Cassius,
Be not deceived. If I have veiled my look,   37
I turn the trouble of my countenance
Merely upon myself. Vexèd I am   39
Of late with passions of some difference,   40
Conceptions only proper to myself,   41
Which give some soil, perhaps, to my behaviors.   42
But let not therefore my good friends be grieved—
Among which number, Cassius, be you one—
Nor construe any further my neglect
Than that poor Brutus, with himself at war,
Forgets the shows of love to other men.

CASSIUS
Then, Brutus, I have much mistook your passion,
By means whereof this breast of mine hath buried   49
Thoughts of great value, worthy cogitations.   50
Tell me, good Brutus, can you see your face?

BRUTUS
No, Cassius, for the eye sees not itself
But by reflection, by some other things.

CASSIUS   'Tis just.   54
And it is very much lamented, Brutus,
That you have no such mirrors as will turn
Your hidden worthiness into your eye,
That you might see your shadow. I have heard   58
Where many of the best respect in Rome,   59
Except immortal Caesar, speaking of Brutus
And groaning underneath this age's yoke,
Have wished that noble Brutus had his eyes.   62

BRUTUS
Into what dangers would you lead me, Cassius,
That you would have me seek into myself
For that which is not in me?

CASSIUS
Therefore, good Brutus, be prepared to hear;
And since you know you cannot see yourself

28 gamesome fond of sports, merry.   **34 wont** accustomed   **35 You**
. . . hand You behave too stubbornly and in too unfriendly a manner.
(The metaphor is from horsemanship.)   **37 veiled my look** i.e., been
introverted, seemed less friendly   **39 Merely** entirely   **40 passions**
of some difference conflicting emotions   **41 only proper to** relating
only to   **42 soil** blemish   **49–50 By . . . value** because of which misunderstanding (my assuming you were displeased with me) I have
kept to myself important thoughts   **54 just** true.   **58 shadow** image,
reflection.   **59 best respect** highest repute and station   **62 had his**
eyes (1) could see things from the perspective of Caesar's critics, or
(2) could see better with his own eyes.

So well as by reflection, I, your glass, 68
Will modestly discover to yourself 69
That of yourself which you yet know not of.
And be not jealous on me, gentle Brutus. 71
Were I a common laughter, or did use 72
To stale with ordinary oaths my love 73
To every new protester; if you know 74
That I do fawn on men and hug them hard
And after scandal them, or if you know 76
That I profess myself in banqueting 77
To all the rout, then hold me dangerous. 78

Flourish, and shout.

BRUTUS
What means this shouting? I do fear the people
Choose Caesar for their king.

CASSIUS   Ay, do you fear it?
Then must I think you would not have it so.

BRUTUS
I would not, Cassius, yet I love him well.
But wherefore do you hold me here so long?
What is it that you would impart to me?
If it be aught toward the general good,
Set honor in one eye and death i'th'other
And I will look on both indifferently; 87
For let the gods so speed me as I love 88
The name of honor more than I fear death.

CASSIUS
I know that virtue to be in you, Brutus,
As well as I do know your outward favor. 91
Well, honor is the subject of my story.
I cannot tell what you and other men
Think of this life; but, for my single self,
I had as lief not be as live to be 95
In awe of such a thing as I myself. 96
I was born free as Caesar, so were you;
We both have fed as well, and we can both
Endure the winter's cold as well as he.
For once, upon a raw and gusty day,
The troubled Tiber chafing with her shores,
Caesar said to me, "Dar'st thou, Cassius, now
Leap in with me into this angry flood
And swim to yonder point?" Upon the word,
Accoutred as I was, I plungèd in 105
And bade him follow; so indeed he did.
The torrent roared, and we did buffet it
With lusty sinews, throwing it aside 108
And stemming it with hearts of controversy. 109

But ere we could arrive the point proposed,
Caesar cried, "Help me, Cassius, or I sink!"
Ay, as Aeneas, our great ancestor, 112
Did from the flames of Troy upon his shoulder
The old Anchises bear, so from the waves of Tiber
Did I the tirèd Caesar. And this man
Is now become a god, and Cassius is
A wretched creature and must bend his body 117
If Caesar carelessly but nod on him.
He had a fever when he was in Spain,
And when the fit was on him I did mark
How he did shake. 'Tis true, this god did shake.
His coward lips did from their color fly, 122
And that same eye whose bend doth awe the world 123
Did lose his luster. I did hear him groan. 124
Ay, and that tongue of his that bade the Romans
Mark him and write his speeches in their books,
Alas, it cried, "Give me some drink, Titinius,"
As a sick girl. Ye gods, it doth amaze me
A man of such a feeble temper should 129
So get the start of the majestic world 130
And bear the palm alone.   *Shout. Flourish.* 131

BRUTUS   Another general shout!
I do believe that these applauses are
For some new honors that are heaped on Caesar.

CASSIUS
Why, man, he doth bestride the narrow world
Like a Colossus, and we petty men 136
Walk under his huge legs and peep about
To find ourselves dishonorable graves.
Men at some time are masters of their fates.
The fault, dear Brutus, is not in our stars,
But in ourselves, that we are underlings.
"Brutus" and "Caesar." What should be in that
   "Caesar"?
Why should that name be sounded more than yours? 143
Write them together, yours is as fair a name;
Sound them, it doth become the mouth as well;
Weigh them, it is as heavy; conjure with 'em,
"Brutus" will start a spirit as soon as "Caesar." 147
Now, in the names of all the gods at once,
Upon what meat doth this our Caesar feed
That he is grown so great? Age, thou art shamed!
Rome, thou hast lost the breed of noble bloods! 151
When went there by an age since the great flood 152

---

68 glass mirror   **69 modestly discover** reveal without exaggeration **71 jealous on** suspicious of.   **gentle** noble   **72 laughter** laughing-stock, as at 4.3.114; or perhaps *laugher*, a shallow fellow who laughs at every jest.   **did use** were accustomed   **73 stale** cheapen, make common.   **ordinary** (1) commonplace (2) customary (3) tavern   **74 protester** one who protests or declares friendship   **76 after scandal** afterwards slander   **77 profess myself** make declarations of friendship   **78 rout** mob   **78.1** *Flourish* Fanfare for a dignitary   **87 indifferently** impartially   **88 speed me** make me prosper   **91 favor** appearance.   **95 as lief not be** just as soon not exist   **96 such . . . myself** i.e., a fellow mortal.   **105 Accoutred** fully dressed in armor **108 lusty sinews** vigorous might. (Literally, tendons.)   **109 stemming** making headway against.   **hearts of controversy** hearts fired up by rivalry.

112 Aeneas hero of Virgil's *Aeneid*, the legendary founder of Rome (hence *our great ancestor*), who bore his aged father Anchises out of burning Troy as it was falling to the Greeks   **117 bend his body** bow **122 color** (1) i.e., normal healthy hue (2) military colors, flag. (The lips are personified as deserters.)   **123 bend** glance, gaze   **124 his** its **129 temper** constitution   **130 get . . . of** gain ascendancy over **131 palm** victor's prize   **136 Colossus** (A 100-foot-high bronze statue of Helios, the sun god, one of the seven wonders of the ancient world, was commonly supposed to have stood astride the entrance to the harbor of Rhodes.)   **143 be sounded** (1) be spoken and celebrated (2) resound   **147 start** raise. (Perhaps the crowd is heard to shout a third time at this point, or somewhere else in this conversation. At line 226 below, we are told that "They shouted thrice.")   **151 the breed . . . bloods** the bloodline of men of noble stock and valiant spirit.   **152 flood** i.e., the classical analogue of Noah's flood, in which all humanity was destroyed except for Deucalion and his wife Pyrrha

But it was famed with more than with one man? 153
When could they say, till now, that talked of Rome,
That her wide walks encompassed but one man?
Now is it Rome indeed, and room enough, 156
When there is in it but one only man.
Oh, you and I have heard our fathers say
There was a Brutus once that would have brooked 159
Th'eternal devil to keep his state in Rome 160
As easily as a king. 161

BRUTUS
That you do love me, I am nothing jealous. 162
What you would work me to, I have some aim. 163
How I have thought of this and of these times
I shall recount hereafter. For this present,
I would not, so with love I might entreat you, 166
Be any further moved. What you have said 167
I will consider; what you have to say
I will with patience hear and find a time
Both meet to hear and answer such high things. 170
Till then, my noble friend, chew upon this:
Brutus had rather be a villager
Than to repute himself a son of Rome
Under these hard conditions as this time
Is like to lay upon us. 175

CASSIUS   I am glad that my weak words
Have struck but thus much show of fire from Brutus. 177

Enter Caesar and his train. [Brutus and
Cassius continue to confer privately.]

BRUTUS
The games are done, and Caesar is returning.

CASSIUS
As they pass by, pluck Casca by the sleeve,
And he will, after his sour fashion, tell you
What hath proceeded worthy note today.

BRUTUS
I will do so. But look you, Cassius,
The angry spot doth glow on Caesar's brow,
And all the rest look like a chidden train. 184
Calpurnia's cheek is pale, and Cicero
Looks with such ferret and such fiery eyes 186
As we have seen him in the Capitol,
Being crossed in conference by some senators. 188

CASSIUS
Casca will tell us what the matter is.

CAESAR   Antonio!

ANTONY   Caesar?

CAESAR
Let me have men about me that are fat,

Sleek-headed men, and such as sleep o' nights.
Yond Cassius has a lean and hungry look.
He thinks too much. Such men are dangerous.

ANTONY
Fear him not, Caesar, he's not dangerous.
He is a noble Roman, and well given. 197

CAESAR
Would he were fatter! But I fear him not,
Yet if my name were liable to fear,
I do not know the man I should avoid
So soon as that spare Cassius. He reads much,
He is a great observer, and he looks
Quite through the deeds of men. He loves no plays, 203
As thou dost, Antony; he hears no music. 204
Seldom he smiles, and smiles in such a sort 205
As if he mocked himself and scorned his spirit
That could be moved to smile at anything.
Such men as he be never at heart's ease
Whiles they behold a greater than themselves,
And therefore are they very dangerous.
I rather tell thee what is to be feared
Than what I fear, for always I am Caesar.
Come on my right hand, for this ear is deaf,
And tell me truly what thou think'st of him.
Sennet. Exeunt Caesar and his train. [Casca remains
with Brutus and Cassius.]

CASCA   You pulled me by the cloak. Would you speak 215
with me?

BRUTUS
Ay, Casca. Tell us what hath chanced today, 217
That Caesar looks so sad. 218

CASCA   Why, you were with him, were you not?

BRUTUS
I should not then ask Casca what had chanced.

CASCA   Why, there was a crown offered him; and, being
offered him, he put it by with the back of his hand,
thus, and then the people fell a-shouting.

BRUTUS   What was the second noise for?

CASCA   Why, for that too.

CASSIUS
They shouted thrice. What was the last cry for? 226

CASCA   Why, for that too.

BRUTUS   Was the crown offered him thrice?

CASCA   Ay, marry, was't, and he put it by thrice, every 229
time gentler than other, and at every putting-by mine
honest neighbors shouted. 231

CASSIUS   Who offered him the crown?

CASCA   Why, Antony.

BRUTUS
Tell us the manner of it, gentle Casca. 234

CASCA   I can as well be hanged as tell the manner of it.
It was mere foolery; I did not mark it. I saw Mark An-

---

153 **famed with** famous for   156 **Rome, room** (Pronounced alike.)
159 **Brutus** i.e., Lucius Junius Brutus, who expelled the Tarquins and
founded the Roman republic (c. 509 B.C.).   **brooked** tolerated
160 **keep his state** set himself up in majesty   161 **As . . . king** as readily as he would tolerate a king.   162 **nothing jealous** not at all doubtful.   163 **work** persuade.   **aim** inkling.   166 **so . . . you** if I might
entreat you in the name of friendship   167 **moved** urged.   170 **meet**
fitting   175 **like** likely   177.1 **train** retinue. (See 1.2.0.1–4 for the
names of those in the procession.)   184 **a chidden train** scolded followers.   186 **ferret** ferretlike, i.e., small and red   188 **crossed in conference** opposed in debate

197 **given** disposed.   203 **through** i.e., into the motives of   204 **hears
no music** (Regarded as a sign of a morose and treacherous character.)
205 **sort** manner   215 **cloak** (Elizabethan costume; see also *sleeve*, line
179, and *doublet*, line 265. The Roman toga was sleeveless.)
217 **chanced** happened   218 **sad** serious.   226 **thrice** (See note at
1.2.147.)   229 **marry** i.e., indeed. (Originally, "by the Virgin Mary.")
231 **honest** worthy. (Said contemptuously.)   234 **gentle** noble

tony offer him a crown—yet 'twas not a crown neither, 'twas one of these coronets—and, as I told you, 238 he put it by once; but for all that, to my thinking, he would fain have had it. Then he offered it to him again; 240 then he put it by again; but to my thinking he was very loath to lay his fingers off it. And then he offered it the third time. He put it the third time by, and still 243 as he refused it the rabblement hooted and clapped 244 their chapped hands, and threw up their sweaty night- 245 caps, and uttered such a deal of stinking breath be- 246 cause Caesar refused the crown that it had almost choked Caesar, for he swooned and fell down at it. And for mine own part I durst not laugh for fear of opening my lips and receiving the bad air.

CASSIUS
But soft, I pray you. What, did Caesar swoon?   251

CASCA   He fell down in the marketplace, and foamed at mouth, and was speechless.

BRUTUS
'Tis very like. He hath the falling sickness.   254

CASSIUS
No, Caesar hath it not, but you and I,
And honest Casca, we have the falling sickness.

CASCA   I know not what you mean by that, but I am sure Caesar fell down. If the tag-rag people did not 258 clap him and hiss him, according as he pleased and displeased them, as they use to do the players in the 260 theater, I am no true man.   261

BRUTUS
What said he when he came unto himself?

CASCA   Marry, before he fell down, when he perceived the common herd was glad he refused the crown, he plucked me ope his doublet and offered them his throat 265 to cut. An I had been a man of any occupation, if I 266 would not have taken him at a word, I would I might go to hell among the rogues. And so he fell. When he came to himself again, he said if he had done or said anything amiss, he desired Their Worships to think it was his infirmity. Three or four wenches where I stood cried, "Alas, good soul!" and forgave him with all their hearts. But there's no heed to be taken of them; if Caesar had stabbed their mothers they would have done no less.

BRUTUS
And after that, he came thus sad away?   276

CASCA   Ay.

CASSIUS   Did Cicero say anything?

CASCA   Ay, he spoke Greek.

CASSIUS   To what effect?

CASCA   Nay, an I tell you that, I'll ne'er look you i'th' face again. But those that understood him smiled at one another and shook their heads; but, for mine own part, it was Greek to me. I could tell you more news too. Marullus and Flavius, for pulling scarves off Cae- 285 sar's images, are put to silence. Fare you well. There 286 was more foolery yet, if I could remember it.

CASSIUS   Will you sup with me tonight, Casca?

CASCA   No, I am promised forth.   289

CASSIUS   Will you dine with me tomorrow?

CASCA   Ay, if I be alive, and your mind hold, and your dinner worth the eating.

CASSIUS   Good. I will expect you.

CASCA   Do so. Farewell both.   *Exit.*

BRUTUS
What a blunt fellow is this grown to be!
He was quick mettle when he went to school.   296

CASSIUS
So is he now in execution
Of any bold or noble enterprise,
However he puts on this tardy form.   299
This rudeness is a sauce to his good wit,   300
Which gives men stomach to digest his words   301
With better appetite.

BRUTUS
And so it is. For this time I will leave you.
Tomorrow, if you please to speak with me,
I will come home to you; or, if you will,
Come home to me, and I will wait for you.

CASSIUS
I will do so. Till then, think of the world.   307

                                                    Exit Brutus.

Well, Brutus, thou art noble. Yet I see
Thy honorable mettle may be wrought   309
From that it is disposed. Therefore it is meet   310
That noble minds keep ever with their likes;
For who so firm that cannot be seduced?
Caesar doth bear me hard, but he loves Brutus.   313
If I were Brutus now, and he were Cassius,
He should not humor me. I will this night   315
In several hands in at his windows throw,   316
As if they came from several citizens,
Writings, all tending to the great opinion

285 **scarves** decorations, festoons   286 **put to silence** dismissed from office. (So reported in Plutarch. Shakespeare's wording ominously suggests that they were executed.)   289 **promised forth** engaged to dine out.   296 **quick mettle** of a lively temperament   299 **However** however much.   **tardy form** air of ennui and disengagement. 300 **rudeness** rough manner.   **wit** intellect   301 **stomach** appetite, inclination   307 **the world** i.e., the state of the world.   309 **mettle** (As often, the word combines the senses of *mettle,* "temperament," and *metal,* "substance." The latter meaning continues here in the chemical metaphor of metal that is *wrought* or transmuted. As *honorable mettle* [or noble metal], gold cannot be transmuted into base substances, and yet Cassius proposes to do just that with Brutus. Compare this with 1.1.61.)   309–10 **wrought . . . disposed** turned away from its natural disposition.   310 **meet** fitting   313 **doth . . . hard** bears me a grudge and keeps me on a short rein   315 **He . . . humor me** i.e., I wouldn't put up with being cajoled or humored. (*He* could refer to Caesar or Brutus.)   316 **several hands** different handwritings

238 **coronets** chaplets, garlands   240 **fain** gladly   243–4 **still as** whenever   245–6 **nightcaps** (Scornful allusion to the *pilleus,* a felt cap worn by the plebeians on festival days.)   251 **soft** i.e., wait a minute 254 **like** likely.   **falling sickness** epilepsy. (But Cassius takes it to mean "falling into servitude.")   258 **tag-rag** ragtag, riffraff   260 **use are accustomed   261 **true** honest   265 **plucked me ope** pulled open. (*Me* is used colloquially.)   **doublet** Elizabethan upper garment, like a jacket   266 **An** If.   **man . . . occupation** (1) working man (2) man of action   276 **sad** somberly

That Rome holds of his name, wherein obscurely
Caesar's ambition shall be glancèd at.   320
And after this let Caesar seat him sure,   321
For we will shake him, or worse days endure.   *Exit.*

❖

[1.3]

*Thunder and lightning. Enter, [meeting,] Casca
[with his sword drawn] and Cicero.*

CICERO
Good even, Casca. Brought you Caesar home?   1
Why are you breathless? And why stare you so?

CASCA
Are not you moved, when all the sway of earth   3
Shakes like a thing unfirm? Oh, Cicero,
I have seen tempests when the scolding winds
Have rived the knotty oaks, and I have seen   6
Th'ambitious ocean swell and rage and foam
To be exalted with the threat'ning clouds;   8
But never till tonight, never till now,
Did I go through a tempest dropping fire.
Either there is a civil strife in heaven,
Or else the world, too saucy with the gods,   12
Incenses them to send destruction.

CICERO
Why, saw you anything more wonderful?   14

CASCA
A common slave—you know him well by sight—
Held up his left hand, which did flame and burn
Like twenty torches joined, and yet his hand,
Not sensible of fire, remained unscorched.   18
Besides—I ha' not since put up my sword—   19
Against the Capitol I met a lion,   20
Who glazed upon me and went surly by   21
Without annoying me. And there were drawn   22
Upon a heap a hundred ghastly women,   23
Transformèd with their fear, who swore they saw
Men all in fire walk up and down the streets.
And yesterday the bird of night did sit   26
Even at noonday upon the marketplace,
Hooting and shrieking. When these prodigies   28
Do so conjointly meet, let not men say,   29
"These are their reasons, they are natural,"
For I believe they are portentous things
Unto the climate that they point upon.   32

CICERO
Indeed, it is a strange-disposèd time.
But men may construe things after their fashion,   34

Clean from the purpose of the things themselves.   35
Comes Caesar to the Capitol tomorrow?

CASCA
He doth; for he did bid Antonio
Send word to you he would be there tomorrow.

CICERO
Good night then, Casca. This disturbèd sky
Is not to walk in.

CASCA   Farewell, Cicero.   *Exit Cicero.*

Enter Cassius.

CASSIUS
Who's there?

CASCA   A Roman.

CASSIUS   Casca, by your voice.

CASCA
Your ear is good. Cassius, what night is this!   42

CASSIUS
A very pleasing night to honest men.

CASCA
Who ever knew the heavens menace so?

CASSIUS
Those that have known the earth so full of faults.
For my part, I have walked about the streets,
Submitting me unto the perilous night,
And thus unbracèd, Casca, as you see,   48
Have bared my bosom to the thunder-stone;   49
And when the cross blue lightning seemed to open   50
The breast of heaven, I did present myself
Even in the aim and very flash of it.

CASCA
But wherefore did you so much tempt the heavens?
It is the part of men to fear and tremble   54
When the most mighty gods by tokens send   55
Such dreadful heralds to astonish us.   56

CASSIUS
You are dull, Casca, and those sparks of life
That should be in a Roman you do want,   58
Or else you use not. You look pale, and gaze,
And put on fear, and cast yourself in wonder,   60
To see the strange impatience of the heavens.
But if you would consider the true cause
Why all these fires, why all these gliding ghosts,
Why birds and beasts from quality and kind,   64
Why old men, fools, and children calculate,   65
Why all these things change from their ordinance,   66
Their natures, and preformèd faculties,   67
To monstrous quality—why, you shall find   68
That heaven hath infused them with these spirits
To make them instruments of fear and warning
Unto some monstrous state.   71

---

320 **glancèd** hinted   321 **seat him sure** seat himself securely in
power (i.e., watch out)
1.3. Location: A street.
1 **Brought** Escorted   3 **sway** established order   6 **rived** split
8 **exalted with** raised to the level of   12 **saucy** insolent   14 **more
wonderful** else that was wondrous.   18 **Not sensible of** not feeling
19 **put up** sheathed   20 **Against** in front of, opposite   21 **glazed**
stared glassily   22 **annoying** harming   22–3 **drawn . . . heap** huddled together   23 **ghastly** pallid   26 **bird of night** owl, a bird of evil
omen   28 **prodigies** abnormalities, wonders   29 **conjointly meet**
coincide   32 **climate** region   34 **construe** interpret.   **after their
fashion** in their own way

35 **Clean . . . purpose** contrary to the actual import or meaning
42 **what night** what a night   48 **unbracèd** with doublet unfastened
49 **thunder-stone** thunderbolt   50 **cross** forked, jagged   54 **part**
appropriate role   55 **tokens** signs   56 **astonish** stun, terrify
58 **want** lack   60 **put on** adopt, show signs of.   **in wonder** into a
state of wonder   64 **from . . . kind** (behaving) contrary to their true
nature   65 **calculate** reckon, prophesy   66 **ordinance** established
nature   67 **preformèd** innate, congenital   68 **monstrous** unnatural
71 **Unto . . . state** pointing to some disorder in the commonwealth or
state of affairs.

Now could I, Casca, name to thee a man
Most like this dreadful night,
That thunders, lightens, opens graves, and roars
As doth the lion in the Capitol—
A man no mightier than thyself or me
In personal action, yet prodigious grown   77
And fearful, as these strange eruptions are.   78

CASCA

'Tis Caesar that you mean, is it not, Cassius?

CASSIUS

Let it be who it is. For Romans now
Have thews and limbs like to their ancestors';   81
But, woe the while, our fathers' minds are dead,   82
And we are governed with our mothers' spirits.
Our yoke and sufferance show us womanish.   84

CASCA

Indeed, they say the senators tomorrow
Mean to establish Caesar as a king,
And he shall wear his crown by sea and land
In every place save here in Italy.

CASSIUS

I know where I will wear this dagger then;
Cassius from bondage will deliver Cassius.
Therein, ye gods, you make the weak most strong;   91
Therein, ye gods, you tyrants do defeat.
Nor stony tower, nor walls of beaten brass,   93
Nor airless dungeon, nor strong links of iron,
Can be retentive to the strength of spirit;   95
But life, being weary of these worldly bars,   96
Never lacks power to dismiss itself.
If I know this, know all the world besides,   98
That part of tyranny that I do bear
I can shake off at pleasure.   *Thunder still.*

CASCA   So can I.   100
So every bondman in his own hand bears
The power to cancel his captivity.

CASSIUS

And why should Caesar be a tyrant then?
Poor man, I know he would not be a wolf
But that he sees the Romans are but sheep;
He were no lion, were not Romans hinds.   106
Those that with haste will make a mighty fire
Begin it with weak straws. What trash is Rome,
What rubbish and what offal, when it serves   109
For the base matter to illuminate   110
So vile a thing as Caesar! But, O grief,
Where hast thou led me? I perhaps speak this
Before a willing bondman; then I know
My answer must be made. But I am armed,   114
And dangers are to me indifferent.   115

CASCA

You speak to Casca, and to such a man
That is no fleering telltale. Hold. My hand.   117
Be factious for redress of all these griefs,   118
And I will set this foot of mine as far
As who goes farthest.   *[They shake hands.]*

CASSIUS   There's a bargain made.   120
Now know you, Casca, I have moved already   121
Some certain of the noblest-minded Romans
To undergo with me an enterprise
Of honorable dangerous consequence;
And I do know by this they stay for me   125
In Pompey's porch. For now, this fearful night,   126
There is no stir or walking in the streets,
And the complexion of the element   128
In favor 's like the work we have in hand,   129
Most bloody, fiery, and most terrible.

Enter Cinna.

CASCA

Stand close awhile, for here comes one in haste.   131

CASSIUS

'Tis Cinna; I do know him by his gait.
He is a friend.—Cinna, where haste you so?

CINNA

To find out you. Who's that? Metellus Cimber?

CASSIUS

No, it is Casca, one incorporate   135
To our attempts. Am I not stayed for, Cinna?

CINNA

I am glad on't. What a fearful night is this!   137
There's two or three of us have seen strange sights.

CASSIUS   Am I not stayed for? Tell me.

CINNA

Yes, you are. Oh, Cassius, if you could
But win the noble Brutus to our party—

CASSIUS

Be you content. Good Cinna, take this paper,   142
         [giving papers]
And look you lay it in the praetor's chair,   143
Where Brutus may but find it. And throw this   144
In at his window. Set this up with wax
Upon old Brutus' statue. All this done,   146
Repair to Pompey's porch, where you shall find us.   147
Is Decius Brutus and Trebonius there?

CINNA

All but Metellus Cimber, and he's gone

To seek you at your house. Well, I will hie,   150
And so bestow these papers as you bade me.

CASSIUS
That done, repair to Pompey's theater.   *Exit Cinna.*
Come, Casca, you and I will yet ere day
See Brutus at his house. Three parts of him   154
Is ours already, and the man entire
Upon the next encounter yields him ours.

CASCA
Oh, he sits high in all the people's hearts;
And that which would appear offense in us,   158
His countenance, like richest alchemy,   159
Will change to virtue and to worthiness.   160

CASSIUS
Him and his worth, and our great need of him,
You have right well conceited. Let us go,   162
For it is after midnight, and ere day
We will awake him and be sure of him.   *Exeunt.*

❧

2.1

Enter Brutus in his orchard.

BRUTUS   What, Lucius, ho!—
I cannot by the progress of the stars
Give guess how near to day.—Lucius, I say!—
I would it were my fault to sleep so soundly.—
When, Lucius, when? Awake, I say! What, Lucius!   5

Enter Lucius.

LUCIUS   Called you, my lord?
BRUTUS
Get me a taper in my study, Lucius.   7
When it is lighted, come and call me here.
LUCIUS   I will, my lord.   *Exit.*
BRUTUS
It must be by his death. And for my part
I know no personal cause to spurn at him,   11
But for the general. He would be crowned.   12
How that might change his nature, there's the
    question.
It is the bright day that brings forth the adder,
And that craves wary walking. Crown him—that—   15
And then I grant we put a sting in him
That at his will he may do danger with.
Th'abuse of greatness is when it disjoins
Remorse from power. And to speak truth of Caesar,   19

I have not known when his affections swayed   20
More than his reason. But 'tis a common proof   21
That lowliness is young ambition's ladder,   22
Whereto the climber-upward turns his face;
But when he once attains the upmost round   24
He then unto the ladder turns his back,
Looks in the clouds, scorning the base degrees   26
By which he did ascend. So Caesar may.
Then, lest he may, prevent. And since the quarrel
Will bear no color for the thing he is,   29
Fashion it thus: that what he is, augmented,   30
Would run to these and these extremities;
And therefore think him as a serpent's egg
Which, hatched, would, as his kind, grow
    mischievous;   33
And kill him in the shell.

Enter Lucius.

LUCIUS
The taper burneth in your closet, sir.   35
Searching the window for a flint, I found
This paper, thus sealed up, and I am sure
It did not lie there when I went to bed.
                              Gives him the letter.
BRUTUS
Get you to bed again. It is not day.
Is not tomorrow, boy, the ides of March?   40
LUCIUS   I know not, sir.
BRUTUS
Look in the calendar and bring me word.
LUCIUS   I will, sir.   *Exit.*
BRUTUS
The exhalations whizzing in the air   44
Give so much light that I may read by them.
                         Opens the letter and reads.
"Brutus, thou sleep'st. Awake, and see thyself!
Shall Rome, etc. Speak, strike, redress!"
"Brutus, thou sleep'st. Awake!"
Such instigations have been often dropped
Where I have took them up.
"Shall Rome, etc." Thus must I piece it out:
Shall Rome stand under one man's awe? What, Rome?
My ancestors did from the streets of Rome
The Tarquin drive, when he was called a king.
"Speak, strike, redress!" Am I entreated
To speak and strike? O Rome, I make thee promise,
If the redress will follow, thou receivest   57
Thy full petition at the hand of Brutus.   58

Enter Lucius.

LUCIUS   Sir, March is wasted fifteen days.
                                    Knock within.

---

150 hie go quickly   **154 parts** i.e., quarters   **158–60 that which . . .
worthiness** his endorsement and honorable name will convert into
virtue and worthiness those things in our conspiracy that would otherwise seem offensive, just as alchemy is supposed to transform base
metals into richest gold.   **162 conceited** (1) conceived, grasped (2)
expressed in a figure.
2.1. Location: Rome. Brutus' orchard, or garden.
5 When (An exclamation of impatience.)   **7 Get . . . taper** Put a candle for me   **11 spurn** kick   **12 general** general cause, common good.
15 craves requires.   **that** that is the issue   **19 Remorse** scruple, compassion

20 affections swayed passions ruled   **21 proof** experience   **22 lowliness** pretended humbleness   **24 round** rung   **26 base degrees** (1)
lower rungs (2) persons of lower social station   **29 Will . . . is** can
carry no appearance of justice so far as his conduct to date is concerned   **30 Fashion it** put the matter   **33 as his kind** according to its
nature.   **mischievous** harmful   **35 closet** private chamber, study
40 ides fifteenth day   **44 exhalations** meteors   **57 If . . . follow** i.e., if
striking Caesar will lead to the reform of grievances   **58 at** from

BRUTUS
'Tis good. Go to the gate; somebody knocks.
                                    [*Exit Lucius.*]
Since Cassius first did whet me against Caesar,
I have not slept.
Between the acting of a dreadful thing
And the first motion, all the interim is   64
Like a phantasma or a hideous dream.   65
The genius and the mortal instruments   66
Are then in council; and the state of man,   67
Like to a little kingdom, suffers then
The nature of an insurrection.   69

            Enter Lucius.

LUCIUS
Sir, 'tis your brother Cassius at the door,   70
Who doth desire to see you.
BRUTUS   Is he alone?
LUCIUS
No, sir. There are more with him.
BRUTUS   Do you know them?
LUCIUS
No, sir. Their hats are plucked about their ears,
And half their faces buried in their cloaks,
That by no means I may discover them   75
By any mark of favor.
BRUTUS   Let 'em enter.   [*Exit Lucius.*]   76
They are the faction. O conspiracy,
Sham'st thou to show thy dangerous brow by night,
When evils are most free? Oh, then, by day   79
Where wilt thou find a cavern dark enough
To mask thy monstrous visage? Seek none,
       conspiracy!
Hide it in smiles and affability;
For if thou put thy native semblance on,
Not Erebus itself were dim enough   84
To hide thee from prevention.   85

       Enter the conspirators, Cassius, Casca, Decius,
       Cinna, Metellus [Cimber] , and Trebonius.

CASSIUS
I think we are too bold upon your rest.   86
Good morrow, Brutus. Do we trouble you?
BRUTUS
I have been up this hour, awake all night.
Know I these men that come along with you?
CASSIUS
Yes, every man of them, and no man here
But honors you; and every one doth wish
You had but that opinion of yourself

Which every noble Roman bears of you.
This is Trebonius.
BRUTUS   He is welcome hither.
CASSIUS
This, Decius Brutus.
BRUTUS   He is welcome too.
CASSIUS
This, Casca; this, Cinna; and this, Metellus Cimber.
BRUTUS   They are all welcome.
What watchful cares do interpose themselves   98
Betwixt your eyes and night?
CASSIUS   Shall I entreat a word?
            They [Brutus and Cassius] whisper.
DECIUS
Here lies the east. Doth not the day break here?   101
CASCA   No.
CINNA
Oh, pardon, sir, it doth; and yon gray lines
That fret the clouds are messengers of day.   104
CASCA
You shall confess that you are both deceived.   105
Here, as I point my sword, the sun arises,
Which is a great way growing on the south,   107
Weighing the youthful season of the year.   108
Some two months hence, up higher toward the north
He first presents his fire; and the high east   110
Stands, as the Capitol, directly here.
BRUTUS [*coming forward*]
Give me your hands all over, one by one.   112
CASSIUS
And let us swear our resolution.
BRUTUS
No, not an oath. If not the face of men,   114
The sufferance of our souls, the time's abuse—   115
If these be motives weak, break off betimes,   116
And every man hence to his idle bed;   117
So let high-sighted tyranny range on   118
Till each man drop by lottery. But if these,   119
As I am sure they do, bear fire enough
To kindle cowards and to steel with valor   121
The melting spirits of women, then, countrymen,
What need we any spur but our own cause
To prick us to redress? What other bond   124
Than secret Romans that have spoke the word   125
And will not palter? And what other oath   126
Than honesty to honesty engaged   127
That this shall be or we will fall for it?

---

98 watchful cares sleep-preventing worries   **101 Here** (Decius points eastward.)   **104 fret** mark with interlacing lines   **105 deceived** mistaken.   **107 growing** encroaching   **108 Weighing** considering, in consequence of   **110 high** due   **112 all over** one and all   **114–16 If . . . betimes** If the gravely serious faces of Romans, the suffering we feel, the corruptions of the present day are insufficient to move us, we should break off at once   **117 idle** (1) unused (2) in which men are idle   **118 high-sighted** upward-gazing (compare with 2.1.26); or haughty, looking down from on high   **119 by lottery** i.e., as the capricious tyrant chances to pick on him.   **these** i.e., these injustices just cited   **121 cowards** even cowards.   **steel** harden   **124 prick** spur   **125 Than . . . word** than the word of Romans who, having given their word of honor, will remain secret   **126 palter** shift position evasively.   **127 honesty** personal honor

64 motion proposal or impulse   **65 phantasma** hallucination   **66–7 The genius . . . council** The tutelary god or attendant spirit allotted to every person at birth is then intensely at debate with the person's physical faculties and passionate nature   **69 The nature of an** a kind of   **70 brother** i.e., brother-in-law. (Cassius had married a sister of Brutus.)   **75 discover** identify   **76 favor** appearance.   **79 free** free to roam at will.   **84 Erebus** primeval Darkness (sprung, according to Hesiod, from Chaos and his sister Night)   **85 prevention** detection and being forestalled.   **86 upon** in intruding upon

Swear priests and cowards and men cautelous,   129
Old feeble carrions, and such suffering souls   130
That welcome wrongs; unto bad causes swear   131
Such creatures as men doubt. But do not stain   132
The even virtue of our enterprise,   133
Nor th'insuppressive mettle of our spirits,   134
To think that or our cause or our performance   135
Did need an oath, when every drop of blood
That every Roman bears—and nobly bears—
Is guilty of a several bastardy   138
If he do break the smallest particle
Of any promise that hath passed from him.

CASSIUS

But what of Cicero? Shall we sound him?   141
I think he will stand very strong with us.

CASCA

Let us not leave him out.

CINNA   No, by no means.

METELLUS

Oh, let us have him, for his silver hairs
Will purchase us a good opinion   145
And buy men's voices to commend our deeds.
It shall be said his judgment ruled our hands;
Our youths and wildness shall no whit appear,
But all be buried in his gravity.

BRUTUS

Oh, name him not. Let us not break with him,   150
For he will never follow anything
That other men begin.

CASSIUS   Then leave him out.

CASCA   Indeed he is not fit.

DECIUS

Shall no man else be touched but only Caesar?

CASSIUS

Decius, well urged. I think it is not meet   156
Mark Antony, so well beloved of Caesar,
Should outlive Caesar. We shall find of him   158
A shrewd contriver; and you know his means,   159
If he improve them, may well stretch so far   160
As to annoy us all. Which to prevent,   161
Let Antony and Caesar fall together.

BRUTUS

Our course will seem too bloody, Caius Cassius,
To cut the head off and then hack the limbs,
Like wrath in death and envy afterwards;   165
For Antony is but a limb of Caesar.
Let's be sacrificers, but not butchers, Caius.
We all stand up against the spirit of Caesar,
And in the spirit of men there is no blood.

Oh, that we then could come by Caesar's spirit
And not dismember Caesar! But, alas,
Caesar must bleed for it. And, gentle friends,   172
Let's kill him boldly, but not wrathfully;
Let's carve him as a dish fit for the gods,
Not hew him as a carcass fit for hounds.
And let our hearts, as subtle masters do,
Stir up their servants to an act of rage   177
And after seem to chide 'em. This shall make
Our purpose necessary, and not envious;   179
Which so appearing to the common eyes,
We shall be called purgers, not murderers.   181
And for Mark Antony, think not of him;   182
For he can do no more than Caesar's arm
When Caesar's head is off.

CASSIUS   Yet I fear him,
For in the engrafted love he bears to Caesar—   185

BRUTUS

Alas, good Cassius, do not think of him.
If he love Caesar, all that he can do
Is to himself—take thought and die for Caesar.   188
And that were much he should, for he is given   189
To sports, to wildness, and much company.

TREBONIUS

There is no fear in him. Let him not die,   191
For he will live, and laugh at this hereafter.   192
                                          Clock strikes.

BRUTUS

Peace! Count the clock.

CASSIUS   The clock hath stricken three.

TREBONIUS

'Tis time to part.

CASSIUS   But it is doubtful yet
Whether Caesar will come forth today or no;
For he is superstitious grown of late,
Quite from the main opinion he held once
Of fantasy, of dreams, and ceremonies.   198
It may be these apparent prodigies,   199
The unaccustomed terror of this night,
And the persuasion of his augurers   201
May hold him from the Capitol today.

DECIUS

Never fear that. If he be so resolved,
I can o'ersway him; for he loves to hear
That unicorns may be betrayed with trees,   205
And bears with glasses, elephants with holes,   206
Lions with toils, and men with flatterers;   207

129–32 Swear . . . doubt Let priests and cowards and shifty old men tottering on the brink of the grave swear oaths, and long-suffering souls that submit supinely to wrongs; it is contemptible, untrustworthy persons like these who swear oaths to bad causes.   **133 even** steadfast, consistent   **134 insuppressive** indomitable   **135 or . . . or** either . . . or **138 a several bastardy** an individual act unworthy of his parentage **141 sound him** sound him out.   **145 purchase** procure. (Playing on the financial sense of *silver*, line 144.)   **150 break with** confide in **156 meet** fitting   **158 of** in   **159 shrewd** malicious; artful **160 improve** exploit, make good use of   **161 annoy** injure   **165 envy** malice

172 gentle noble   **177 their servants** i.e., our hands   **179 envious** malicious   **181 purgers** those who heal by bleeding the patient **182 for** as for   **185 engrafted** firmly implanted   **188 take thought** give way to melancholy   **189 much he should** more than is to be expected of him, hence unlikely; or, eminently desirable   **191 no fear** nothing to fear   **192.1 Clock strikes** (An anachronism much commented upon; the mechanical clock was not invented until c. 1300.) **198 fantasy** imaginings.   **ceremonies** omens drawn from the performance of some rite.   **199 apparent** manifest, both visible and obvious **201 augurers** augurs, official interpreters of omens   **205 unicorns . . . trees** i.e., by having the unicorn imprison itself by driving its horn into a tree as it charges at the hunter   **206 glasses** mirrors (enabling the hunter to approach the bear while it dazzles itself in the mirror). **holes** pitfalls   **207 toils** nets, snares

But when I tell him he hates flatterers,
He says he does, being then most flattered.
Let me work;
For I can give his humor the true bent,   211
And I will bring him to the Capitol.

CASSIUS
Nay, we will all of us be there to fetch him.

BRUTUS
By the eighth hour. Is that the uttermost?   214

CINNA
Be that the uttermost, and fail not then.

METELLUS
Caius Ligarius doth bear Caesar hard,   216
Who rated him for speaking well of Pompey.   217
I wonder none of you have thought of him.

BRUTUS
Now, good Metellus, go along by him.   219
He loves me well, and I have given him reasons;
Send him but hither, and I'll fashion him.   221

CASSIUS
The morning comes upon 's. We'll leave you, Brutus.
And, friends, disperse yourselves; but all remember
What you have said, and show yourselves true
    Romans.

BRUTUS
Good gentlemen, look fresh and merrily;
Let not our looks put on our purposes,   226
But bear it as our Roman actors do,
With untired spirits and formal constancy.   228
And so good morrow to you every one.   229
                              Exeunt. Manet Brutus.
Boy! Lucius!—Fast asleep? It is no matter.   230
Enjoy the honey-heavy dew of slumber.
Thou hast no figures nor no fantasies   232
Which busy care draws in the brains of men;   233
Therefore thou sleep'st so sound.

            Enter Portia.

PORTIA   Brutus, my lord!
BRUTUS
Portia, what mean you? Wherefore rise you now?
It is not for your health thus to commit
Your weak condition to the raw cold morning.

PORTIA
Nor for yours neither. You've ungently, Brutus,   238
Stole from my bed. And yesternight, at supper,
You suddenly arose, and walked about
Musing and sighing, with your arms across,   241

And when I asked you what the matter was,
You stared upon me with ungentle looks.
I urged you further; then you scratched your head
And too impatiently stamped with your foot.
Yet I insisted, yet you answered not,   246
But with an angry wafture of your hand   247
Gave sign for me to leave you. So I did,
Fearing to strengthen that impatience
Which seemed too much enkindled, and withal   250
Hoping it was but an effect of humor,   251
Which sometime hath his hour with every man.   252
It will not let you eat, nor talk, nor sleep,
And could it work so much upon your shape
As it hath much prevailed on your condition,   255
I should not know you Brutus. Dear my lord,   256
Make me acquainted with your cause of grief.

BRUTUS
I am not well in health, and that is all.

PORTIA
Brutus is wise, and were he not in health
He would embrace the means to come by it.

BRUTUS
Why, so I do. Good Portia, go to bed.   261

PORTIA
Is Brutus sick? And is it physical   262
To walk unbracèd and suck up the humors   263
Of the dank morning? What, is Brutus sick,
And will he steal out of his wholesome bed
To dare the vile contagion of the night,
And tempt the rheumy and unpurgèd air   267
To add unto his sickness? No, my Brutus,
You have some sick offense within your mind,
Which by the right and virtue of my place
I ought to know of. [*She kneels.*] And upon my knees
I charm you, by my once-commended beauty,   272
By all your vows of love, and that great vow
Which did incorporate and make us one,
That you unfold to me, your self, your half,
Why you are heavy, and what men tonight   276
Have had resort to you; for here have been
Some six or seven, who did hide their faces
Even from darkness.

BRUTUS   Kneel not, gentle Portia.
                                    [*He raises her.*]
PORTIA
I should not need if you were gentle Brutus.
Within the bond of marriage, tell me, Brutus,
Is it excepted I should know no secrets   282
That appertain to you? Am I your self
But as it were in sort or limitation,   284

---

211 humor disposition   **214 the eighth hour** i.e., 8 A.M. (The Elizabethan way of reckoning time. By Roman reckoning, the day began at 6 A.M., so that *the eighth hour* would be 2 P.M.)   **uttermost** latest.
216 bear Caesar hard bear a grudge toward Caesar. (See 1.2.313n.)
217 rated rebuked   **219 by him** by way of his house.   **221 fashion** shape (to our purposes)   **226 put on** display, wear in open view
228 formal constancy steadfast appearance, decorum.   **229.1 *Manet*** He remains on stage   **230 Lucius** (Brutus calls to his servant, who is evidently within, asleep, after having admitted the conspirators at line 85; later, at line 310, he is still within when Brutus calls to him.)
232 figures imaginings   **233 care** anxiety   **238 ungently** discourteously, unkindly   **241 across** folded. (A sign of melancholy.)

246 Yet . . . yet Still . . . still   **247 wafture** waving   **250 withal** moreover   **251 humor** imbalance of temperament   **252 his** its   **255 condition** inner state of mind   **256 know you** recognize you as   **261 so I do** (Said with a double meaning not perceived by Portia: I seek through Caesar's death the means to better the health of the state.)
262 physical healthful   **263 unbracèd** with loosened clothing.
humors damps, mists   **267 rheumy and unpurgèd** conducive to illness and not cleansed of its impurities (which night air was thought to contain)   **272 charm** conjure, entreat   **276 heavy** sad   **282 excepted** made an exception that   **284 in . . . limitation** only up to a point. (A legal phrase.)

To keep with you at meals, comfort your bed,   285
And talk to you sometimes? Dwell I but in the suburbs   286
Of your good pleasure? If it be no more,
Portia is Brutus' harlot, not his wife.

BRUTUS
You are my true and honorable wife,
As dear to me as are the ruddy drops
That visit my sad heart.

PORTIA
If this were true, then should I know this secret.
I grant I am a woman, but withal   293
A woman that Lord Brutus took to wife.
I grant I am a woman, but withal
A woman well reputed, Cato's daughter.   296
Think you I am no stronger than my sex,
Being so fathered and so husbanded?
Tell me your counsels, I will not disclose 'em.   299
I have made strong proof of my constancy,
Giving myself a voluntary wound
Here, in the thigh. Can I bear that with patience,
And not my husband's secrets?

BRUTUS   O ye gods,
Render me worthy of this noble wife!
                                        Knock [within].
Hark, hark, one knocks. Portia, go in awhile,
And by and by thy bosom shall partake
The secrets of my heart.
All my engagements I will construe to thee,   308
All the charactery of my sad brows.   309
Leave me with haste.   _Exit Portia._
    [_Calling_]   Lucius, who's that knocks?

        _Enter Lucius and [Caius] Ligarius [wearing a
        kerchief]._

LUCIUS
Here is a sick man that would speak with you.   311

BRUTUS
Caius Ligarius, that Metellus spake of.
Boy, stand aside.   [_Exit Lucius._]
                Caius Ligarius, how?   313

LIGARIUS
Vouchsafe good morrow from a feeble tongue.   314

BRUTUS
Oh, what a time have you chose out, brave Caius,   315
To wear a kerchief! Would you were not sick!

LIGARIUS
I am not sick, if Brutus have in hand
Any exploit worthy the name of honor.

BRUTUS
Such an exploit have I in hand, Ligarius,

Had you a healthful ear to hear of it.

LIGARIUS
By all the gods that Romans bow before,
I here discard my sickness! [_He throws off his kerchief._]
                                Soul of Rome!
Brave son, derived from honorable loins!
Thou like an exorcist hast conjured up
My mortifièd spirit. Now bid me run,   325
And I will strive with things impossible,
Yea, get the better of them. What's to do?

BRUTUS
A piece of work that will make sick men whole.   328

LIGARIUS
But are not some whole that we must make sick?

BRUTUS
That must we also. What it is, my Caius,
I shall unfold to thee as we are going
To whom it must be done.

LIGARIUS   Set on your foot,   332
And with a heart new-fired I follow you
To do I know not what; but it sufficeth
That Brutus leads me on.   _Thunder._

BRUTUS   Follow me, then.   _Exeunt._

                            ❖

[2.2]

        _Thunder and lightning. Enter Julius Caesar, in his
        nightgown._

CAESAR
Nor heaven nor earth have been at peace tonight.   1
Thrice hath Calpurnia in her sleep cried out,
"Help, ho, they murder Caesar!"—Who's within?

        Enter a Servant.

SERVANT   My lord?

CAESAR
Go bid the priests do present sacrifice   5
And bring me their opinions of success.   6

SERVANT   I will, my lord.   _Exit._

        Enter Calpurnia.

CALPURNIA
What mean you, Caesar? Think you to walk forth?
You shall not stir out of your house today.

CAESAR
Caesar shall forth. The things that threatened me
Ne'er looked but on my back. When they shall see
The face of Caesar, they are vanishèd.

CALPURNIA
Caesar, I never stood on ceremonies,   13

---

285 **keep** stay, be   286 **suburbs** periphery. (In Elizabethan London, prostitutes frequented the suburbs.)   293 **withal** in addition
296 **Cato's daughter** (Cato the Younger of Utica was famous for his integrity; he sided with Pompey against Caesar in 48 B.C. and later killed himself rather than submit to Caesar's tyranny. He was Brutus's uncle as well as his father-in-law.)   299 **counsels** secrets   308 **construe** explain fully   309 **charactery** handwriting, i.e., what is figured there   311 **sick man** (In Elizabethan medicine, a poultice was often applied to the forehead of a patient and wrapped in a handkerchief; hence the kerchief in line 316.)   313 **how?** i.e., how are you?   314 **Vouchsafe** Deign (to accept)   315 **brave** noble

325 **mortifièd** deadened   328 **whole** healthy, i.e., free of the disease of tyranny.   332 **To whom** i.e., to him to whom
2.2. Location: Caesar's house.
0.2 **nightgown** housecoat.   1 **Nor** Neither   5 **present sacrifice** immediate examination of the entrails of sacrificed animals for omens
6 **success** the result, what will follow.   13 **stood on ceremonies** attached importance to omens

Yet now they fright me. There is one within,
Besides the things that we have heard and seen,
Recounts most horrid sights seen by the watch.   16
A lioness hath whelpèd in the streets,   17
And graves have yawned and yielded up their dead.   18
Fierce fiery warriors fight upon the clouds
In ranks and squadrons and right form of war,   20
Which drizzled blood upon the Capitol.
The noise of battle hurtled in the air;   22
Horses did neigh, and dying men did groan,
And ghosts did shriek and squeal about the streets.
Oh, Caesar, these things are beyond all use,   25
And I do fear them.
CAESAR   What can be avoided
Whose end is purposed by the mighty gods?
Yet Caesar shall go forth; for these predictions
Are to the world in general as to Caesar.
CALPURNIA
When beggars die there are no comets seen;
The heavens themselves blaze forth the death of
    princes.   31
CAESAR
Cowards die many times before their deaths;
The valiant never taste of death but once.
Of all the wonders that I yet have heard,
It seems to me most strange that men should fear,
Seeing that death, a necessary end,
Will come when it will come.

          Enter a Servant.

                        What say the augurers?
SERVANT
They would not have you to stir forth today.
Plucking the entrails of an offering forth,
They could not find a heart within the beast.
CAESAR
The gods do this in shame of cowardice.
Caesar should be a beast without a heart
If he should stay at home today for fear.
No, Caesar shall not. Danger knows full well
That Caesar is more dangerous than he.
We are two lions littered in one day,
And I the elder and more terrible;
And Caesar shall go forth.
CALPURNIA   Alas, my lord,
Your wisdom is consumed in confidence.   49
Do not go forth today! Call it my fear
That keeps you in the house, and not your own.
We'll send Mark Antony to the Senate House,
And he shall say you are not well today.
Let me, upon my knee, prevail in this.   [*She kneels.*]
CAESAR
Mark Antony shall say I am not well,

And for thy humor I will stay at home.   56
                        [*He raises her.*]

          Enter Decius.

Here's Decius Brutus. He shall tell them so.
DECIUS
Caesar, all hail! Good morrow, worthy Caesar.
I come to fetch you to the Senate House.
CAESAR
And you are come in very happy time   60
To bear my greeting to the senators
And tell them that I will not come today.
Cannot is false, and that I dare not, falser;
I will not come today. Tell them so, Decius.
CALPURNIA
Say he is sick.
CAESAR   Shall Caesar send a lie?
Have I in conquest stretched mine arm so far
To be afeard to tell graybeards the truth?
Decius, go tell them Caesar will not come.
DECIUS
Most mighty Caesar, let me know some cause,
Lest I be laughed at when I tell them so.
CAESAR
The cause is in my will: I will not come.
That is enough to satisfy the Senate.
But for your private satisfaction,
Because I love you, I will let you know.
Calpurnia here, my wife, stays me at home.   75
She dreamt tonight she saw my statue,   76
Which like a fountain with an hundred spouts
Did run pure blood; and many lusty Romans   78
Came smiling and did bathe their hands in it.
And these does she apply for warnings and portents   80
Of evils imminent, and on her knee
Hath begged that I will stay at home today.
DECIUS
This dream is all amiss interpreted;
It was a vision fair and fortunate.
Your statue spouting blood in many pipes,
In which so many smiling Romans bathed,
Signifies that from you great Rome shall suck
Reviving blood, and that great men shall press   88
For tinctures, stains, relics, and cognizance.   89
This by Calpurnia's dream is signified.
CAESAR
And this way have you well expounded it.
DECIUS
I have, when you have heard what I can say;
And know it now. The Senate have concluded
To give this day a crown to mighty Caesar.
If you shall send them word you will not come,

---

16 watch (An anachronism, since there was no *watch*, or "body of
night watchmen," in Caesar's Rome.)   **17 whelpèd** given birth
18 yawned gaped   **20 right form** regular formation   **22 hurtled**
clashed   **25 use** normal experience   **31 blaze forth** proclaim (in
a blaze of light)   **49 consumed in confidence** destroyed by overconfidence.

56 humor whim   **60 happy** opportune   **75 stays** detains
76 tonight last night   **78 lusty** lively, merry   **80 apply for** interpret
as   **88 press** crowd around   **89 tinctures** handkerchiefs dipped in
the blood of martyrs, with healing powers; or colors in a coat of
arms. (*Tinctures, stains,* and *relics* are all venerated properties, as
though Caesar were a saint.)   **cognizance** heraldic emblems worn
by a nobleman's followers.

Their minds may change. Besides, it were a mock   96
Apt to be rendered for someone to say   97
"Break up the Senate till another time
When Caesar's wife shall meet with better dreams."
If Caesar hide himself, shall they not whisper
"Lo, Caesar is afraid"?
Pardon me, Caesar, for my dear dear love
To your proceeding bids me tell you this,   103
And reason to my love is liable.   104

CAESAR
How foolish do your fears seem now, Calpurnia!
I am ashamèd I did yield to them.
Give me my robe, for I will go.

Enter Brutus, Ligarius, Metellus, Casca,
Trebonius, Cinna, and Publius.

And look where Publius is come to fetch me.

PUBLIUS
Good morrow, Caesar.

CAESAR   Welcome, Publius.
What, Brutus, are you stirred so early too?
Good morrow, Casca. Caius Ligarius,
Caesar was ne'er so much your enemy
As that same ague which hath made you lean.   113
What is't o'clock?

BRUTUS   Caesar, 'tis strucken eight.   114

CAESAR
I thank you for your pains and courtesy.

Enter Antony.

See, Antony, that revels long o' nights,
Is notwithstanding up. Good morrow, Antony.

ANTONY   So to most noble Caesar.

CAESAR *[to a Servant]*   Bid them prepare within.   119
[Exit Servant.]
I am to blame to be thus waited for.
Now, Cinna. Now, Metellus. What, Trebonius,
I have an hour's talk in store for you;
Remember that you call on me today.
Be near me, that I may remember you.

TREBONIUS
Caesar, I will. *[Aside]* And so near will I be
That your best friends shall wish I had been further.

CAESAR
Good friends, go in and taste some wine with me,
And we, like friends, will straightway go together.

BRUTUS *[aside]*
That every like is not the same, O Caesar,   129
The heart of Brutus earns to think upon!   *Exeunt.*   130

❧

96–7 mock . . . rendered sarcastic remark apt to be made   **103 proceeding** advantage   **104 reason . . . liable** my reasoning is swayed by my affection.   **113 ague** fever   **114 eight** 8 A.M. (See 2.1.214n on Roman time.)   **119 prepare within** i.e., set out wine in the other room and prepare to leave. (Perhaps addressed to the servant who entered at line 37, or to Calpurnia.) The ritual drinking of wine is a pledge of friendship that should preclude violence; see lines 127–8.
129 That . . . same i.e., That not all those who behave "like friends" (line 128) are actually so. (Proverbial.)   **130 earns** grieves

[2.3]

Enter Artemidorus [reading a paper].

ARTEMIDORUS   "Caesar, beware of Brutus; take heed of
Cassius; come not near Casca; have an eye to Cinna;
trust not Trebonius; mark well Metellus Cimber; Decius Brutus loves thee not; thou hast wronged Caius
Ligarius. There is but one mind in all these men, and
it is bent against Caesar. If thou be'st not immortal,
look about you. Security gives way to conspiracy. The   7
mighty gods defend thee! Thy lover,   8
                                        Artemidorus."
Here will I stand till Caesar pass along,
And as a suitor will I give him this.
My heart laments that virtue cannot live
Out of the teeth of emulation.   13
If thou read this, O Caesar, thou mayest live;
If not, the Fates with traitors do contrive.   *Exit.* 15

[2.4]

Enter Portia and Lucius.

PORTIA
I prithee, boy, run to the Senate House.
Stay not to answer me, but get thee gone.—
Why dost thou stay?

LUCIUS   To know my errand, madam.

PORTIA
I would have had thee there and here again
Ere I can tell thee what thou shouldst do there.
[Aside] O constancy, be strong upon my side;   6
Set a huge mountain 'tween my heart and tongue!
I have a man's mind, but a woman's might.
How hard it is for women to keep counsel!—   9
Art thou here yet?

LUCIUS   Madam, what should I do?
Run to the Capitol, and nothing else?
And so return to you, and nothing else?

PORTIA
Yes, bring me word, boy, if thy lord look well,
For he went sickly forth; and take good note
What Caesar doth, what suitors press to him.
Hark, boy, what noise is that?

LUCIUS   I hear none, madam.

PORTIA   Prithee, listen well.
I heard a bustling rumor, like a fray,   19
And the wind brings it from the Capitol.

LUCIUS   Sooth, madam, I hear nothing.   21

Enter the Soothsayer.

2.3. Location: A street near the Capitol.
7 Security gives way Overconfidence opens a path   **8 lover** friend
13 Out . . . emulation beyond the bite of grudging envy.   **15 contrive** conspire.
2.4. Location: Before the house of Brutus.
6 constancy resolution   **9 counsel** a secret.   **19 bustling rumor** confused sound.   **fray** fight   **21 Sooth** Truly

PORTIA
Come hither, fellow. Which way hast thou been?
SOOTHSAYER   At mine own house, good lady.
PORTIA
What is't o'clock?
SOOTHSAYER   About the ninth hour, lady.   24
PORTIA
Is Caesar yet gone to the Capitol?
SOOTHSAYER
Madam, not yet. I go to take my stand,
To see him pass on to the Capitol.
PORTIA
Thou hast some suit to Caesar, hast thou not?
SOOTHSAYER
That I have, lady, if it will please Caesar
To be so good to Caesar as to hear me:
I shall beseech him to befriend himself.
PORTIA
Why, know'st thou any harm 's intended towards him?
SOOTHSAYER
None that I know will be, much that I fear may chance.
Good morrow to you. Here the street is narrow.
The throng that follows Caesar at the heels,
Of senators, of praetors, common suitors,   36
Will crowd a feeble man almost to death.
I'll get me to a place more void, and there   38
Speak to great Caesar as he comes along.   *Exit.*
PORTIA
I must go in. Ay me, how weak a thing
The heart of woman is! O Brutus,
The heavens speed thee in thine enterprise!—
Sure, the boy heard me.—Brutus hath a suit
That Caesar will not grant.—Oh, I grow faint.—
Run, Lucius, and commend me to my lord;
Say I am merry. Come to me again   46
And bring me word what he doth say to thee.
                                Exeunt [separately].

❖

3.1

*Flourish. Enter Caesar, Brutus, Cassius, Casca,
Decius, Metellus [Cimber], Trebonius, Cinna,
Antony, Lepidus, Artemidorus, Publius, [Popilius
Lena], and the Soothsayer; [others following].*

CAESAR *[to the Soothsayer]*   The ides of March are come.
SOOTHSAYER   Ay, Caesar, but not gone.
ARTEMIDORUS   Hail, Caesar! Read this schedule.   3
DECIUS
Trebonius doth desire you to o'erread,

At your best leisure, this his humble suit.
ARTEMIDORUS
O Caesar, read mine first, for mine's a suit
That touches Caesar nearer. Read it, great Caesar.
CAESAR
What touches us ourself shall be last served.
ARTEMIDORUS
Delay not, Caesar, read it instantly.
CAESAR
What, is the fellow mad?
PUBLIUS   Sirrah, give place.   10
CASSIUS
What, urge you your petitions in the street?
Come to the Capitol.

            *[Caesar goes to the Capitol and takes his place, the
            rest following.]*

POPILIUS *[to Cassius]*
I wish your enterprise today may thrive.
CASSIUS   What enterprise, Popilius?
POPILIUS *[to Cassius]*   Fare you well.
                        [He advances to Caesar.]
BRUTUS   What said Popilius Lena?
CASSIUS
He wished today our enterprise might thrive.
I fear our purpose is discoverèd.
BRUTUS
Look how he makes to Caesar. Mark him.   19
                  [Popilius speaks apart to Caesar.]
CASSIUS
Casca, be sudden, for we fear prevention.
Brutus, what shall be done? If this be known,
Cassius or Caesar never shall turn back,   22
For I will slay myself.
BRUTUS   Cassius, be constant.   23
Popilius Lena speaks not of our purposes;
For look, he smiles, and Caesar doth not change.   25
CASSIUS
Trebonius knows his time, for look you, Brutus,
He draws Mark Antony out of the way.
                        [Exit Trebonius with Antony.]
DECIUS
Where is Metellus Cimber? Let him go
And presently prefer his suit to Caesar.   29
BRUTUS
He is addressed. Press near and second him.   30
CINNA
Casca, you are the first that rears your hand.
                        [They press near Caesar.]
CAESAR
Are we all ready? What is now amiss
That Caesar and his Senate must redress?

---

24 **the ninth hour** i.e., 9 A.M. (In Roman reckoning, the ninth hour
would be 3 P.M.)   36 **praetors** judges   38 **void** empty, uncrowded
46 **merry** cheerful. (Not "mirthful.")
3.1. Location: Before the Capitol, and, following line 12, within the
Capitol.
0.4 *others following* (Citizens may be present, though not certainly
so; see lines 83 and 93–4.)   3 **schedule** document.

10 **Sirrah** Fellow. (A form of address to a social inferior.)   **place** way.
19 **makes to** advances toward   22–3 **Cassius . . . myself** Either Cassius or Caesar will never return from the Capitol alive, for I will commit suicide if this attempt fails.   23 **be constant** hold steady.
25 **change** change expression.   29 **presently prefer** immediately urge
30 **addressed** ready.

METELLUS [*kneeling*]
Most high, most mighty, and most puissant Caesar,   34
Metellus Cimber throws before thy seat
An humble heart—
CAESAR   I must prevent thee, Cimber.   36
These couchings and these lowly courtesies   37
Might fire the blood of ordinary men,   38
And turn preordinance and first decree   39
Into the law of children. Be not fond   40
To think that Caesar bears such rebel blood   41
That will be thawed from the true quality   42
With that which melteth fools—I mean, sweet words,
Low-crookèd curtsies, and base spaniel fawning.   44
Thy brother by decree is banishèd.
If thou dost bend and pray and fawn for him,   46
I spurn thee like a cur out of my way.   47
Know, Caesar doth not wrong, nor without cause
Will he be satisfied.
METELLUS
Is there no voice more worthy than my own
To sound more sweetly in great Caesar's ear
For the repealing of my banished brother?   52
BRUTUS [*kneeling*]
I kiss thy hand, but not in flattery, Caesar,
Desiring thee that Publius Cimber may
Have an immediate freedom of repeal.   55
CAESAR
What, Brutus?
CASSIUS [*kneeling*]   Pardon, Caesar! Caesar, pardon!
As low as to thy foot doth Cassius fall,
To beg enfranchisement for Publius Cimber.   58
CAESAR
I could be well moved, if I were as you;
If I could pray to move, prayers would move me.   60
But I am constant as the northern star,   61
Of whose true-fixed and resting quality   62
There is no fellow in the firmament.   63
The skies are painted with unnumbered sparks;
They are all fire and every one doth shine;
But there's but one in all doth hold his place.
So in the world: 'tis furnished well with men,
And men are flesh and blood, and apprehensive;   68
Yet in the number I do know but one
That unassailable holds on his rank,   70
Unshaked of motion. And that I am he,   71
Let me a little show it even in this:

That I was constant Cimber should be banished,
And constant do remain to keep him so.
CINNA [*kneeling*]
O Caesar—
CAESAR   Hence! Wilt thou lift up Olympus?   75
DECIUS [*kneeling*]
Great Caesar—
CAESAR   Doth not Brutus bootless kneel?   76
CASCA Speak hands for me!
            They stab Caesar, [Casca first, Brutus last].
CAESAR *Et tu, Brutè?* Then fall, Caesar!   *Dies.*   78
CINNA
Liberty! Freedom! Tyranny is dead!
Run hence, proclaim, cry it about the streets.
CASSIUS
Some to the common pulpits, and cry out   81
"Liberty, freedom, and enfranchisement!"   82
BRUTUS
People and senators, be not affrighted.
Fly not; stand still. Ambition's debt is paid.   84
CASCA
Go to the pulpit, Brutus.
DECIUS   And Cassius too.
BRUTUS Where's Publius?   86
CINNA
Here, quite confounded with this mutiny.   87
METELLUS
Stand fast together, lest some friend of Caesar's
Should chance—
BRUTUS
Talk not of standing. Publius, good cheer.   90
There is no harm intended to your person,
Nor to no Roman else. So tell them, Publius.
CASSIUS
And leave us, Publius, lest that the people,
Rushing on us, should do your age some mischief.
BRUTUS
Do so, and let no man abide this deed   95
But we the doers.   [*Exeunt all but the conspirators.*]

        Enter Trebonius.

CASSIUS
Where is Antony?
TREBONIUS   Fled to his house amazed.   97
Men, wives, and children stare, cry out, and run
As it were doomsday.
BRUTUS   Fates, we will know your pleasures.   99
That we shall die, we know; 'tis but the time,   100
And drawing days out, that men stand upon.   101

---

34 **puissant** powerful 36 **prevent** forestall 37 **couchings . . . courtesies** kneelings and submissive bows 38 **fire the blood of** incite 39–40 **And turn . . . children** and turn preordained law into the kinds of childish and flexible rules that children use in their games. 40 **fond** so foolish as 41 **rebel** rebellious against reason 42 **true quality** proper firmness and stability. (The metaphor is from alchemy.) 44 **Low-crookèd curtsies** obsequious bows 46 **bend** bow 47 **spurn** kick 52 **repealing** recall 55 **freedom of repeal** permission to return. 58 **enfranchisement** i.e., restoration of citizenship 60 **pray to move** make petition (as you do) 61 **northern star** polestar 62 **resting** remaining stationary 63 **fellow** equal 68 **apprehensive** capable of perception 70 **rank** place in line or file, position 71 **Unshaked of motion** (1) unswayed by petitions (2) with perfect steadiness.

75 **Olympus** mountain dwelling of the Greek gods 76 **bootless** in vain 78 *Et tu, Brutè?* You too, Brutus? (Literally, "Even thou.") 81 **common pulpits** public platforms or rostra 82 **enfranchisement** restoration of civil rights. (Cf. line 58 above.) 84 **Ambition's debt** What Caesar's ambition deserved 86 **Publius** (An old senator, too confused to flee.) 87 **mutiny** uprising, discord. 90 **standing** making a stand. 95 **abide** (1) suffer the consequences of (2) remain here with 97 **amazed** stupified. 99 **As** as if 100–1 **'tis . . . upon** i.e., it is only the time of our deaths, and how long we have to live, that we are uncertain about, make a question of.

CASCA
  Why, he that cuts off twenty years of life
  Cuts off so many years of fearing death.
BRUTUS
  Grant that, and then is death a benefit.
  So are we Caesar's friends, that have abridged
  His time of fearing death. Stoop, Romans, stoop,
  And let us bathe our hands in Caesar's blood
  Up to the elbows and besmear our swords,
  Then walk we forth even to the marketplace,   109
  And, waving our red weapons o'er our heads,
  Let's all cry "Peace, freedom, and liberty!"
CASSIUS
  Stoop, then, and wash. [*They bathe their hands and*
    weapons.] How many ages hence
  Shall this our lofty scene be acted over
  In states unborn and accents yet unknown!   114
BRUTUS
  How many times shall Caesar bleed in sport,   115
  That now on Pompey's basis lies along   116
  No worthier than the dust!
CASSIUS   So oft as that shall be,
  So often shall the knot of us be called   119
  The men that gave their country liberty.
DECIUS
  What, shall we forth?
CASSIUS   Ay, every man away.
  Brutus shall lead, and we will grace his heels   122
  With the most boldest and best hearts of Rome.

        Enter a Servant.

BRUTUS
  Soft, who comes here? A friend of Antony's.
SERVANT [*kneeling*]
  Thus, Brutus, did my master bid me kneel;
  Thus did Mark Antony bid me fall down,
  And, being prostrate, thus he bade me say:
  "Brutus is noble, wise, valiant, and honest;
  Caesar was mighty, bold, royal, and loving.   128
  Say I love Brutus and I honor him;
  Say I feared Caesar, honored him, and loved him.
  If Brutus will vouchsafe that Antony
  May safely come to him and be resolved   133
  How Caesar hath deserved to lie in death,
  Mark Antony shall not love Caesar dead
  So well as Brutus living, but will follow
  The fortunes and affairs of noble Brutus
  Thorough the hazards of this untrod state   138
  With all true faith." So says my master Antony.
BRUTUS
  Thy master is a wise and valiant Roman;
  I never thought him worse.

  Tell him, so please him come unto this place,   142
  He shall be satisfied and, by my honor,
  Depart untouched.
SERVANT   I'll fetch him presently.   144
             Exit Servant.
BRUTUS
  I know that we shall have him well to friend.   145
CASSIUS
  I wish we may. But yet have I a mind
  That fears him much, and my misgiving still   147
  Falls shrewdly to the purpose.   148

        Enter Antony.

BRUTUS
  But here comes Antony.—Welcome, Mark Antony.
ANTONY
  O mighty Caesar! Dost thou lie so low?
  Are all thy conquests, glories, triumphs, spoils,
  Shrunk to this little measure? Fare thee well.—
  I know not, gentlemen, what you intend,
  Who else must be let blood, who else is rank;   154
  If I myself, there is no hour so fit
  As Caesar's death's hour, nor no instrument
  Of half that worth as those your swords, made rich
  With the most noble blood of all this world.
  I do beseech ye, if you bear me hard,   159
  Now, whilst your purpled hands do reek and smoke, 160
  Fulfill your pleasure. Live a thousand years,   161
  I shall not find myself so apt to die;   162
  No place will please me so, no mean of death,
  As here by Caesar, and by you cut off,
  The choice and master spirits of this age.
BRUTUS
  Oh, Antony, beg not your death of us.
  Though now we must appear bloody and cruel,
  As by our hands and this our present act
  You see we do, yet see you but our hands
  And this the bleeding business they have done.
  Our hearts you see not. They are pitiful;   171
  And pity to the general wrong of Rome—
  As fire drives out fire, so pity pity—   173
  Hath done this deed on Caesar. For your part,
  To you our swords have leaden points, Mark Antony. 175
  Our arms in strength of malice, and our hearts   176
  Of brothers' temper, do receive you in   177
  With all kind love, good thoughts, and reverence.
CASSIUS
  Your voice shall be as strong as any man's   179
  In the disposing of new dignities.   180

---

142 so if it should   **144 presently** immediately.   **145 to friend** for a friend.   **147 fears** distrusts   **148 Falls . . . purpose** is intensely to the point.   **154 let blood** bled (a medical term), i.e., killed.   **rank** swollen, diseased (and hence in need of bleeding)   **159 bear me hard** bear ill will to me   **160 purpled** bloody.   **reek** steam   **161 Live** If I should live   **162 apt** ready   **171 pitiful** full of pity   **173 pity pity** i.e., pity for the general wrong of Rome has driven out pity for Caesar   **175 leaden** i.e., blunt   **176–7 Our . . . temper** i.e., Both our arms, though seeming strong in enmity, and our hearts, full of brotherly feeling   **179 voice** vote, authority   **180 dignities** offices of state.

109 the marketplace i.e., the Forum   **114 accents** languages   **115 in sport** for entertainment   **116 on Pompey's . . . along** lies prostrate on the pedestal of Pompey's statue   **119 knot** group   **122 grace his heels** follow him close at heels (in a triumphal procession; cf. 1.1.34)   **128 honest** honorable   **133 be resolved** receive an explanation   **138 Thorough** through.   **untrod state** still unexplored state of affairs

BRUTUS
Only be patient till we have appeased
The multitude, beside themselves with fear,
And then we will deliver you the cause   183
Why I, that did love Caesar when I struck him,
Have thus proceeded.

ANTONY   I doubt not of your wisdom.
Let each man render me his bloody hand.

[*He shakes hands with the conspirators.*]

First, Marcus Brutus, will I shake with you;
Next, Caius Cassius, do I take your hand;
Now, Decius Brutus, yours; now yours, Metellus;
Yours, Cinna; and, my valiant Casca, yours;
Though last, not least in love, yours, good Trebonius.
Gentlemen all—alas, what shall I say?
My credit now stands on such slippery ground   193
That one of two bad ways you must conceit me,   194
Either a coward or a flatterer.
That I did love thee, Caesar, oh, 'tis true!
If then thy spirit look upon us now,
Shall it not grieve thee dearer than thy death   198
To see thy Antony making his peace,
Shaking the bloody fingers of thy foes—
Most noble—in the presence of thy corpse?
Had I as many eyes as thou hast wounds,
Weeping as fast as they stream forth thy blood,
It would become me better than to close   204
In terms of friendship with thine enemies.
Pardon me, Julius! Here wast thou bayed, brave hart, 206
Here didst thou fall, and here thy hunters stand,
Signed in thy spoil and crimsoned in thy lethe.   208
O world, thou wast the forest to this hart,
And this indeed, O world, the heart of thee!
How like a deer, strucken by many princes,
Dost thou here lie!

CASSIUS
Mark Antony—

ANTONY   Pardon me, Caius Cassius.
The enemies of Caesar shall say this;   214
Then in a friend it is cold modesty.   215

CASSIUS
I blame you not for praising Caesar so,
But what compact mean you to have with us?
Will you be pricked in number of our friends,   218
Or shall we on and not depend on you?

ANTONY
Therefore I took your hands, but was indeed
Swayed from the point by looking down on Caesar.
Friends am I with you all, and love you all,

Upon this hope, that you shall give me reasons
Why and wherein Caesar was dangerous.

BRUTUS
Or else were this a savage spectacle.   225
Our reasons are so full of good regard   226
That were you, Antony, the son of Caesar,
You should be satisfied.

ANTONY   That's all I seek,
And am moreover suitor that I may
Produce his body to the marketplace,   230
And in the pulpit, as becomes a friend,   231
Speak in the order of his funeral.   232

BRUTUS
You shall, Mark Antony.

CASSIUS   Brutus, a word with you.
[*Aside to Brutus*] You know not what you do. Do not
    consent
That Antony speak in his funeral.
Know you how much the people may be moved
By that which he will utter?

BRUTUS [*aside to Cassius*]   By your pardon:
I will myself into the pulpit first
And show the reason of our Caesar's death.
What Antony shall speak, I will protest   240
He speaks by leave and by permission,
And that we are contented Caesar shall
Have all true rites and lawful ceremonies.
It shall advantage more than do us wrong.

CASSIUS [*aside to Brutus*]
I know not what may fall. I like it not.   245

BRUTUS
Mark Antony, here, take you Caesar's body.
You shall not in your funeral speech blame us,
But speak all good you can devise of Caesar,
And say you do't by our permission.
Else shall you not have any hand at all
About his funeral. And you shall speak
In the same pulpit whereto I am going,
After my speech is ended.

ANTONY   Be it so.
I do desire no more.

BRUTUS
Prepare the body then, and follow us.   255

                        Exeunt. Manet Antony.

ANTONY
Oh, pardon me, thou bleeding piece of earth,
That I am meek and gentle with these butchers!
Thou art the ruins of the noblest man
That ever livèd in the tide of times.   259
Woe to the hand that shed this costly blood!   260
Over thy wounds now do I prophesy—
Which, like dumb mouths, do ope their ruby lips

183 **deliver** report to   193 **credit** credibility   194 **conceit** think, judge
198 **dearer** more deeply   204 **close** come to an agreement
206 **bayed** brought to bay.   **hart** stag. (With pun on *heart*.)
208 **Signed . . . spoil** marked with the tokens of your slaughter.
(The *spoil* in hunting is the cutting up of the quarry and distribution
of reward to the hounds.)   **lethe** river of oblivion in the underworld,
here associated with death and blood. (Perhaps fused with Cocytus,
river of blood in the underworld.)   214 **The enemies** Even the
enemies   215 **cold modesty** sober moderation.   218 **pricked** marked
down

225 **else were this** otherwise this would be   226 **regard** account, consideration   230 **Produce** bring forth.   **marketplace** Forum
231 **pulpit** public platform   232 **order** ceremony   240 **protest**
announce, insist   245 **fall** befall, happen.   255.1 *Manet* He remains
onstage   259 **tide of times** course of all history.   260 **costly** (1) valuable (2) fraught with dire consequences

To beg the voice and utterance of my tongue—
A curse shall light upon the limbs of men;
Domestic fury and fierce civil strife
Shall cumber all the parts of Italy;   266
Blood and destruction shall be so in use
And dreadful objects so familiar   268
That mothers shall but smile when they behold
Their infants quartered with the hands of war,   270
All pity choked with custom of fell deeds;   271
And Caesar's spirit, ranging for revenge,   272
With Ate by his side come hot from hell,   273
Shall in these confines with a monarch's voice   274
Cry havoc and let slip the dogs of war,   275
That this foul deed shall smell above the earth
With carrion men, groaning for burial.

       Enter Octavius's Servant.

You serve Octavius Caesar, do you not?
SERVANT   I do, Mark Antony.
ANTONY
Caesar did write for him to come to Rome.
SERVANT
He did receive his letters, and is coming,   281
And bid me say to you by word of mouth—
O Caesar!—   *[Seeing the body.]*
ANTONY
Thy heart is big. Get thee apart and weep.
Passion, I see, is catching, for mine eyes,   285
Seeing those beads of sorrow stand in thine,
Began to water. Is thy master coming?
SERVANT
He lies tonight within seven leagues of Rome.   288
ANTONY
Post back with speed and tell him what hath chanced. 289
Here is a mourning Rome, a dangerous Rome,
No Rome of safety for Octavius yet;   291
Hie hence and tell him so. Yet stay awhile;
Thou shalt not back till I have borne this corpse
Into the marketplace. There shall I try,   294
In my oration, how the people take
The cruel issue of these bloody men,   296
According to the which thou shalt discourse   297
To young Octavius of the state of things.   298
Lend me your hand.   *Exeunt [with Caesar's body].*

           ❖

[3.2]

    Enter Brutus and [presently] goes into the pulpit,
    and Cassius, with the Plebeians.

PLEBEIANS
We will be satisfied! Let us be satisfied!   1
BRUTUS
Then follow me, and give me audience, friends.—
Cassius, go you into the other street
And part the numbers.   4
Those that will hear me speak, let 'em stay here;
Those that will follow Cassius, go with him;
And public reasons shall be renderèd
Of Caesar's death.
FIRST PLEBEIAN   I will hear Brutus speak.
SECOND PLEBEIAN
I will hear Cassius, and compare their reasons
When severally we hear them renderèd.   10
    [Exit Cassius, with some of the Plebeians.]
THIRD PLEBEIAN
The noble Brutus is ascended. Silence!
BRUTUS   Be patient till the last.
  Romans, countrymen, and lovers, hear me for my   13
cause, and be silent that you may hear. Believe me for
mine honor, and have respect to mine honor, that you
may believe. Censure me in your wisdom, and awake   16
your senses, that you may the better judge. If there be   17
any in this assembly, any dear friend of Caesar's, to
him I say that Brutus' love to Caesar was no less than
his. If then that friend demand why Brutus rose
against Caesar, this is my answer: not that I loved Caesar less, but that I loved Rome more. Had you rather
Caesar were living and die all slaves, than that Caesar
were dead, to live all free men? As Caesar loved me, I
weep for him; as he was fortunate, I rejoice at it; as he
was valiant, I honor him; but, as he was ambitious, I
slew him. There is tears for his love; joy for his fortune;
honor for his valor; and death for his ambition.
Who is here so base that would be a bondman? If any,
speak, for him have I offended. Who is here so rude   30
that would not be a Roman? If any, speak, for him
have I offended. Who is here so vile that will not love
his country? If any, speak, for him have I offended. I
pause for a reply.
ALL   None, Brutus, none!
BRUTUS   Then none have I offended. I have done no
more to Caesar than you shall do to Brutus. The ques-   37
tion of his death is enrolled in the Capitol, his glory   38
not extenuated wherein he was worthy, nor his   39

---

266 cumber overwhelm; entangle, burden   **268 objects** sights
270 quartered cut to pieces   **271 custom . . . deeds** the familiarity of
cruel deeds   **272 ranging** roaming up and down in search of prey
273 Ate goddess of discord and moral chaos   **274 confines** regions.
monarch's i.e., authoritative   **275 Cry havoc** give the signal for sack,
pillage, and slaughter, taking no prisoners.   **let slip** unleash
281 letters (Not necessarily plural. The Latin word for letter, *litterae*,
has a plural form.)   **285 Passion** Sorrow   **288 lies** lodges.   **seven
leagues** about twenty miles   **289 Post** Ride.   **chanced** happened.
291 Rome (With pun on "room," as at 1.2.156.)   **294 try** test
296 cruel issue outcome of the cruelty   **297 the which** the outcome of which   **298 young Octavius** (He was eighteen in March
of 44 B.C.)

3.2. Location: The Forum.
1 be satisfied have an explanation.   **4 part** divide   **10 severally** separately   **13 lovers** friends. (This speech by Brutus is in what Plutarch
calls the Lacedemonian or Spartan style, brief and sententious. Its
content is original with Shakespeare.)   **16 Censure** Judge   **17 senses**
intellectual powers   **30 rude** barbarous   **37 than . . . Brutus** (In lines
45–7 below, Brutus offers to die for Rome if his country should ask.)
37–8 The question . . . enrolled The considerations that necessitated
his death are recorded   **39 extenuated** minimized

offenses enforced for which he suffered death.   40

Enter Mark Antony [and others] with Caesar's body.

Here comes his body, mourned by Mark Antony, who, though he had no hand in his death, shall receive the benefit of his dying, a place in the commonwealth, as which of you shall not? With this I depart, that, as I slew my best lover for the good of Rome, I have the   45
same dagger for myself when it shall please my country to need my death.

ALL   Live, Brutus, live, live!   *[Brutus comes down.]*

FIRST PLEBEIAN
Bring him with triumph home unto his house.

SECOND PLEBEIAN
Give him a statue with his ancestors.   50

THIRD PLEBEIAN
Let him be Caesar.

FOURTH PLEBEIAN   Caesar's better parts
Shall be crowned in Brutus.

FIRST PLEBEIAN
We'll bring him to his house with shouts and clamors.

BRUTUS
My countrymen—

SECOND PLEBEIAN   Peace, silence! Brutus speaks.

FIRST PLEBEIAN   Peace, ho!

BRUTUS
Good countrymen, let me depart alone,
And, for my sake, stay here with Antony.
Do grace to Caesar's corpse, and grace his speech   58
Tending to Caesar's glories, which Mark Antony,   59
By our permission, is allowed to make.
I do entreat you, not a man depart,
Save I alone, till Antony have spoke.   *Exit.*

FIRST PLEBEIAN
Stay, ho, and let us hear Mark Antony.

THIRD PLEBEIAN
Let him go up into the public chair.
We'll hear him. Noble Antony, go up.

ANTONY
For Brutus' sake I am beholding to you.   66
   [He goes into the pulpit.]

FOURTH PLEBEIAN   What does he say of Brutus?

THIRD PLEBEIAN   He says, for Brutus' sake
He finds himself beholding to us all.

FOURTH PLEBEIAN
'Twere best he speak no harm of Brutus here.

FIRST PLEBEIAN
This Caesar was a tyrant.

THIRD PLEBEIAN   Nay, that's certain.
We are blest that Rome is rid of him.

SECOND PLEBEIAN
Peace! Let us hear what Antony can say.

ANTONY
You gentle Romans—

ALL   Peace, ho! Let us hear him.

ANTONY
Friends, Romans, countrymen, lend me your ears.   75
I come to bury Caesar, not to praise him.
The evil that men do lives after them;
The good is oft interrèd with their bones.
So let it be with Caesar. The noble Brutus
Hath told you Caesar was ambitious.
If it were so, it was a grievous fault,
And grievously hath Caesar answered it.   82
Here, under leave of Brutus and the rest—   83
For Brutus is an honorable man,
So are they all, all honorable men—
Come I to speak in Caesar's funeral.
He was my friend, faithful and just to me;
But Brutus says he was ambitious,
And Brutus is an honorable man.
He hath brought many captives home to Rome,
Whose ransoms did the general coffers fill.
Did this in Caesar seem ambitious?
When that the poor have cried, Caesar hath wept;   93
Ambition should be made of sterner stuff.
Yet Brutus says he was ambitious,
And Brutus is an honorable man.
You all did see that on the Lupercal   97
I thrice presented him a kingly crown,
Which he did thrice refuse. Was this ambition?
Yet Brutus says he was ambitious,
And sure he is an honorable man.
I speak not to disprove what Brutus spoke,
But here I am to speak what I do know.
You all did love him once, not without cause.
What cause withholds you then to mourn for him?
O judgment! Thou art fled to brutish beasts,
And men have lost their reason. Bear with me;
My heart is in the coffin there with Caesar,
And I must pause till it come back to me.

FIRST PLEBEIAN
Methinks there is much reason in his sayings.

SECOND PLEBEIAN
If thou consider rightly of the matter,
Caesar has had great wrong.

THIRD PLEBEIAN   Has he, masters?   112
I fear there will a worse come in his place.

FOURTH PLEBEIAN
Marked ye his words? He would not take the crown,
Therefore 'tis certain he was not ambitious.

FIRST PLEBEIAN
If it be found so, some will dear abide it.   116

---

40 enforced exaggerated, insisted upon   **45 lover** friend   **50 SECOND PLEBEIAN** (Not the same person who exited at line 10; the numbering here refers to those who stay to hear Brutus.)   **58 Do grace** Show respect.   **grace his speech** listen courteously to Antony's speech   **59 Tending to** relating to, dealing with   **66 beholding** beholden

75 Friends (This speech by Antony is thought to illustrate the Asiatic or "florid" style of speaking. In it Shakespeare gathers various hints from Plutarch ("Marcus Antonius" and "Dion") and Appian, but the speech is Shakespeare's invention.)   **82 answered** paid the penalty for   **83 under leave** by permission   **93 When that** When   **97 Lupercal** (See 1.1.67 and note.)   **112 masters** good sirs.   **116 dear abide it** pay a heavy penalty for it.

SECOND PLEBEIAN
Poor soul, his eyes are red as fire with weeping.

THIRD PLEBEIAN
There's not a nobler man in Rome than Antony.

FOURTH PLEBEIAN
Now mark him. He begins again to speak.

ANTONY
But yesterday the word of Caesar might
Have stood against the world. Now lies he there,
And none so poor to do him reverence.   122
Oh, masters, if I were disposed to stir
Your hearts and minds to mutiny and rage,   124
I should do Brutus wrong, and Cassius wrong,
Who, you all know, are honorable men.
I will not do them wrong; I rather choose
To wrong the dead, to wrong myself and you,
Than I will wrong such honorable men.
But here's a parchment with the seal of Caesar.
I found it in his closet; 'tis his will.   131
                    [*He shows the will.*]
Let but the commons hear this testament—   132
Which, pardon me, I do not mean to read—
And they would go and kiss dead Caesar's wounds
And dip their napkins in his sacred blood,   135
Yea, beg a hair of him for memory,
And dying, mention it within their wills,
Bequeathing it as a rich legacy
Unto their issue.

FOURTH PLEBEIAN
We'll hear the will! Read it, Mark Antony.

ALL
The will, the will! We will hear Caesar's will.

ANTONY
Have patience, gentle friends: I must not read it.
It is not meet you know how Caesar loved you.   143
You are not wood, you are not stones, but men;
And being men, hearing the will of Caesar,
It will inflame you, it will make you mad.
'Tis good you know not that you are his heirs,
For if you should, oh, what would come of it?

FOURTH PLEBEIAN
Read the will! We'll hear it, Antony.
You shall read us the will, Caesar's will.

ANTONY
Will you be patient? Will you stay awhile?
I have o'ershot myself to tell you of it.   152
I fear I wrong the honorable men
Whose daggers have stabbed Caesar; I do fear it.

FOURTH PLEBEIAN
They were traitors. "Honorable men"!

ALL   The will! The testament!

SECOND PLEBEIAN
They were villains, murderers. The will! Read the will!

ANTONY
You will compel me then to read the will?
Then make a ring about the corpse of Caesar
And let me show you him that made the will.
Shall I descend? And will you give me leave?

ALL   Come down.

SECOND PLEBEIAN   Descend.

THIRD PLEBEIAN   You shall have leave.

[*Antony comes down. They gather around Caesar.*]

FOURTH PLEBEIAN   A ring; stand round.

FIRST PLEBEIAN
Stand from the hearse. Stand from the body.   166

SECOND PLEBEIAN
Room for Antony, most noble Antony!

ANTONY
Nay, press not so upon me. Stand farre off.   168

ALL   Stand back! Room! Bear back!

ANTONY
If you have tears, prepare to shed them now.
You all do know this mantle. I remember   171
The first time ever Caesar put it on;
'Twas on a summer's evening in his tent,
That day he overcame the Nervii.   174
Look, in this place ran Cassius' dagger through.
See what a rent the envious Casca made.   176
Through this the well-belovèd Brutus stabbed,
And as he plucked his cursèd steel away,
Mark how the blood of Caesar followed it,
As rushing out of doors to be resolved   180
If Brutus so unkindly knocked or no;   181
For Brutus, as you know, was Caesar's angel.   182
Judge, O you gods, how dearly Caesar loved him!
This was the most unkindest cut of all;   184
For when the noble Caesar saw him stab,
Ingratitude, more strong than traitors' arms,
Quite vanquished him. Then burst his mighty heart,
And in his mantle muffling up his face,
Even at the base of Pompey's statue,
Which all the while ran blood, great Caesar fell.
Oh, what a fall was there, my countrymen!
Then I, and you, and all of us fell down,
Whilst bloody treason flourished over us.   193
Oh, now you weep, and I perceive you feel
The dint of pity. These are gracious drops.   195
Kind souls, what weep you when you but behold   196
Our Caesar's vesture wounded? Look you here,   197
Here is himself, marred as you see with traitors.

                    [*He lifts Caesar's mantle.*]

FIRST PLEBEIAN   Oh, piteous spectacle!

SECOND PLEBEIAN   O noble Caesar!

---

166 hearse bier.   **168 farre** farther   **171 mantle** cloak, toga.   **174 the Nervii** the Belgian tribe whose defeat in 57 B.C. is described in Caesar's *Gallic Wars*, 2.15–28   **176 rent** tear, hole   **envious** malicious, spiteful   **180 be resolved** learn for certain   **181 unkindly** cruelly and unnaturally   **182 angel** (1) daimon or genius, guardian angel (2) best beloved.   **184 unkindest** (1) most cruel (2) most unnatural. (The double superlative was grammatically acceptable in Shakespeare's day.)   **193 flourished** (1) triumphed insolently (2) brandished its sword   **195 dint** impression   **196 what** why, or how much   **197 vesture** clothing

122 And none . . . reverence i.e., and yet no one is below him in fortune now, no one of even the lowest social station to look up to and revere him.   **124 mutiny** riot, tumult   **131 closet** private chamber, study   **132 commons** common people   **135 napkins** handkerchiefs   **143 meet** fitting that   **152 o'ershot myself** gone further than I should

THIRD PLEBEIAN   Oh, woeful day!

FOURTH PLEBEIAN   Oh, traitors, villains!

FIRST PLEBEIAN   Oh, most bloody sight!

SECOND PLEBEIAN   We will be revenged.

ALL   Revenge! About! Seek! Burn! Fire! Kill! Slay! Let   205
not a traitor live!

ANTONY   Stay, countrymen.

FIRST PLEBEIAN   Peace there! Hear the noble Antony.

SECOND PLEBEIAN   We'll hear him, we'll follow him,
we'll die with him!

ANTONY

Good friends, sweet friends, let me not stir you up
To such a sudden flood of mutiny.
They that have done this deed are honorable.
What private griefs they have, alas, I know not,   214
That made them do it. They are wise and honorable,
And will no doubt with reasons answer you.
I come not, friends, to steal away your hearts.
I am no orator, as Brutus is,
But, as you know me all, a plain blunt man
That love my friend, and that they know full well
That gave me public leave to speak of him.   221
For I have neither wit, nor words, nor worth,   222
Action, nor utterance, nor the power of speech   223
To stir men's blood. I only speak right on.
I tell you that which you yourselves do know,
Show you sweet Caesar's wounds, poor poor dumb
    mouths,
And bid them speak for me. But were I Brutus,
And Brutus Antony, there were an Antony
Would ruffle up your spirits and put a tongue   229
In every wound of Caesar that should move
The stones of Rome to rise and mutiny.

ALL

We'll mutiny!

FIRST PLEBEIAN   We'll burn the house of Brutus!

THIRD PLEBEIAN

Away, then! Come, seek the conspirators.

ANTONY

Yet hear me, countrymen. Yet hear me speak.

ALL

Peace, ho! Hear Antony, most noble Antony!

ANTONY

Why, friends, you go to do you know not what.
Wherein hath Caesar thus deserved your loves?
Alas, you know not. I must tell you then:
You have forgot the will I told you of.

ALL

Most true. The will! Let's stay and hear the will.

ANTONY

Here is the will, and under Caesar's seal.
To every Roman citizen he gives,
To every several man, seventy-five drachmas.   243

SECOND PLEBEIAN

Most noble Caesar! We'll revenge his death.

THIRD PLEBEIAN   O royal Caesar!

ANTONY   Hear me with patience.

ALL   Peace, ho!

ANTONY

Moreover, he hath left you all his walks,
His private arbors, and new-planted orchards,
On this side Tiber; he hath left them you,
And to your heirs forever—common pleasures,   251
To walk abroad and recreate yourselves.
Here was a Caesar! When comes such another?

FIRST PLEBEIAN

Never, never! Come, away, away!
We'll burn his body in the holy place
And with the brands fire the traitors' houses.
Take up the body.

SECOND PLEBEIAN   Go fetch fire!

THIRD PLEBEIAN   Pluck down benches!

FOURTH PLEBEIAN   Pluck down forms, windows, any-   259
thing!   *Exeunt Plebeians [with the body].*

ANTONY

Now let it work. Mischief, thou art afoot.
Take thou what course thou wilt.

            Enter [Octavius's] Servant.

                                    How now, fellow?

SERVANT

Sir, Octavius is already come to Rome.

ANTONY   Where is he?

SERVANT

He and Lepidus are at Caesar's house.

ANTONY

And thither will I straight to visit him.   266
He comes upon a wish. Fortune is merry,   267
And in this mood will give us anything.

SERVANT

I heard him say Brutus and Cassius
Are rid like madmen through the gates of Rome.   270

ANTONY

Belike they had some notice of the people,   271
How I had moved them. Bring me to Octavius.
                                    Exeunt.

                    ❖

[3.3]

*Enter Cinna the poet, and after him the Ple-
beians.*

CINNA

I dreamt tonight that I did feast with Caesar,   1

---

205 **About!** To work!   214 **griefs** grievances   221 **public leave** permission to speak publicly   222–3 **neither . . . speech** neither intelligence, vocabulary, moral authority, gesture, rhetorical skill, nor
polished delivery   229 **ruffle up** stir to anger   243 **several** individual.   **drachmas** coins. (This is a substantial bequest.)

251 **common pleasures** public pleasure gardens (in which)
259 **forms, windows** benches, window frames and shutters
266 **straight** straightway, at once   267 **upon a wish** just when
wanted.   **merry** favorably disposed   270 **Are rid** have ridden
271 **Belike** Likely enough.   **of** about; or, from
3.3. Location: A street.
1 **tonight** last night

And things unluckily charge my fantasy.   2
I have no will to wander forth of doors,
Yet something leads me forth.

FIRST PLEBEIAN   What is your name?

SECOND PLEBEIAN   Whither are you going?

THIRD PLEBEIAN   Where do you dwell?

FOURTH PLEBEIAN   Are you a married man or a
bachelor?

SECOND PLEBEIAN   Answer every man directly.

FIRST PLEBEIAN   Ay, and briefly.

FOURTH PLEBEIAN   Ay, and wisely.

THIRD PLEBEIAN   Ay, and truly, you were best.   13

CINNA   What is my name? Whither am I going? Where
do I dwell? Am I a married man or a bachelor? Then
to answer every man directly and briefly, wisely and
truly: wisely I say, I am a bachelor.

SECOND PLEBEIAN   That's as much as to say they are
fools that marry. You'll bear me a bang for that, I fear. 19
Proceed directly.   20

CINNA   Directly, I am going to Caesar's funeral.   21

FIRST PLEBEIAN   As a friend or an enemy?

CINNA   As a friend.

SECOND PLEBEIAN   That matter is answered directly.

FOURTH PLEBEIAN   For your dwelling—briefly.

CINNA   Briefly, I dwell by the Capitol.

THIRD PLEBEIAN   Your name, sir, truly.

CINNA   Truly, my name is Cinna.

FIRST PLEBEIAN   Tear him to pieces! He's a conspirator!

CINNA   I am Cinna the poet, I am Cinna the poet!

FOURTH PLEBEIAN   Tear him for his bad verses, tear him
for his bad verses!

CINNA   I am not Cinna the conspirator.

FOURTH PLEBEIAN   It is no matter, his name's Cinna.
Pluck but his name out of his heart, and turn him   35
going.   36

THIRD PLEBEIAN   Tear him, tear him! Come, brands, ho,
firebrands! To Brutus', to Cassius'; burn all! Some to
Decius' house, and some to Casca's; some to Ligarius'.
Away, go!

Exeunt all the Plebeians, [dragging off Cinna].

❖

4.1

Enter Antony [with a list], Octavius, and Lepidus.

ANTONY
These many, then, shall die. Their names are pricked.   1

OCTAVIUS
Your brother too must die. Consent you, Lepidus?

LEPIDUS
I do consent—

OCTAVIUS   Prick him down, Antony.

LEPIDUS
Upon condition Publius shall not live,
Who is your sister's son, Mark Antony.

ANTONY
He shall not live. Look, with a spot I damn him.   6
But Lepidus, go you to Caesar's house.
Fetch the will hither, and we shall determine   8
How to cut off some charge in legacies.   9

LEPIDUS   What, shall I find you here?

OCTAVIUS   Or here or at the Capitol.   *Exit Lepidus.*   11

ANTONY
This is a slight, unmeritable man,   12
Meet to be sent on errands. Is it fit,
The threefold world divided, he should stand   14
One of the three to share it?

OCTAVIUS   So you thought him,
And took his voice who should be pricked to die   16
In our black sentence and proscription.   17

ANTONY
Octavius, I have seen more days than you;
And though we lay these honors on this man
To ease ourselves of divers sland'rous loads,   20
He shall but bear them as the ass bears gold,
To groan and sweat under the business,
Either led or driven as we point the way;
And having brought our treasure where we will,
Then take we down his load, and turn him off,
Like to the empty ass, to shake his ears   26
And graze in commons.

OCTAVIUS   You may do your will;   27
But he's a tried and valiant soldier.

ANTONY
So is my horse, Octavius, and for that
I do appoint him store of provender.   30
It is a creature that I teach to fight,
To wind, to stop, to run directly on,   32
His corporal motion governed by my spirit.   33
And in some taste is Lepidus but so.   34
He must be taught, and trained, and bid go forth—
A barren-spirited fellow, one that feeds
On objects, arts, and imitations,   37
Which, out of use and staled by other men,   38
Begin his fashion. Do not talk of him   39
But as a property. And now, Octavius,   40

---

6 spot mark (on the list).   **damn** condemn   **8–9 determine . . . lega-cies** find a way to reduce the outlay of Caesar's estate, by altering the will.   **11 Or** Either   **12 slight, unmeritable** insignificant and unde-serving   **14 threefold** i.e., consisting of Europe, Africa, and Asia. The Roman world was divided among the triumvirate, with most of Gaul on both sides of the Alps to Antony, Spain and Old Gaul to Lepidus, and Africa, Sardinia, and Sicily to Octavius.   **16 took his voice** acceded to his opinion (i.e., about Publius)   **17 black sentence** death sentence. **proscription** (Proscription branded a man as an outlaw, confiscated his property, offered a reward for his murder, and prohibited his sons and grandsons from holding public office.)   **20 sland'rous** giving cause for slander   **26 empty** unloaded   **27 commons** public pasture. **30 appoint** assign, provide.   **provender** fodder.   **32 wind** turn. (Horse trainer's term.)   **directly on** straight ahead   **33 corporal** bodily   **34 taste** degree, sense   **37 On . . . imitations** on curiosities, artificial things, and the following of fashion—copied things merely, taken up secondhand   **38 staled** made common or cheap **39 Begin his fashion** are for him the ultimate in fashion.   **40 prop-erty** tool.

---

2 unluckily . . . fantasy oppress my imagination with foreboding. **13 you were best** you'd better.   **19 bear . . . bang** get a beating from me   **20 directly** without evasion.   **21 Directly** (1) Straight there (2) At once   **35–6 turn him going** send him packing. **4.1. Location: Rome. A table is perhaps set out.** **1 pricked** marked down on a list (with a stylus making an impression on a wax tablet, or piercing a sheet of paper).

Listen great things. Brutus and Cassius 41
Are levying powers. We must straight make head. 42
Therefore let our alliance be combined, 43
Our best friends made, our means stretched; 44
And let us presently go sit in council
How covert matters may be best disclosed 46
And open perils surest answerèd. 47

OCTAVIUS
Let us do so, for we are at the stake 48
And bayed about with many enemies; 49
And some that smile have in their hearts, I fear,
Millions of mischiefs.   *Exeunt.* 51

❦

[4.2]

Drum. Enter Brutus, Lucilius, [Lucius,] and the
army. Titinius and Pindarus meet them.

BRUTUS   Stand, ho! 1
LUCILIUS   Give the word, ho, and stand! 2
BRUTUS
What now, Lucilius, is Cassius near?
LUCILIUS
He is at hand, and Pindarus is come
To do you salutation from his master.
BRUTUS
He greets me well. Your master, Pindarus, 6
In his own change, or by ill officers, 7
Hath given me some worthy cause to wish 8
Things done, undone; but if he be at hand
I shall be satisfied.
PINDARUS   I do not doubt 10
But that my noble master will appear
Such as he is, full of regard and honor. 12
BRUTUS
He is not doubted.—A word, Lucilius.
                    [*Brutus and Lucilius speak apart.*]
How he received you let me be resolved. 14
LUCILIUS
With courtesy and with respect enough,
But not with such familiar instances 16
Nor with such free and friendly conference 17
As he hath used of old.
BRUTUS   Thou hast described

A hot friend cooling. Ever note, Lucilius:
When love begins to sicken and decay
It useth an enforcèd ceremony. 21
There are no tricks in plain and simple faith.
But hollow men, like horses hot at hand, 23
Make gallant show and promise of their mettle; 24
                    Low march within.
But when they should endure the bloody spur,
They fall their crests and like deceitful jades 26
Sink in the trial. Comes his army on? 27

LUCILIUS
They mean this night in Sardis to be quartered. 28
The greater part, the horse in general, 29
Are come with Cassius.

Enter Cassius and his powers.

BRUTUS   Hark, he is arrived.
March gently on to meet him. 31
CASSIUS   Stand, ho!
BRUTUS   Stand, ho! Speak the word along.
FIRST SOLDIER   Stand!
SECOND SOLDIER   Stand!
THIRD SOLDIER   Stand!
CASSIUS
Most noble brother, you have done me wrong.
BRUTUS
Judge me, you gods! Wrong I mine enemies?
And if not so, how should I wrong a brother?
CASSIUS
Brutus, this sober form of yours hides wrongs; 40
And when you do them—
BRUTUS   Cassius, be content; 41
Speak your griefs softly. I do know you well. 42
Before the eyes of both our armies here,
Which should perceive nothing but love from us,
Let us not wrangle. Bid them move away.
Then in my tent, Cassius, enlarge your griefs, 46
And I will give you audience.
CASSIUS   Pindarus,
Bid our commanders lead their charges off 48
A little from this ground.
BRUTUS
Lucius, do you the like, and let no man
Come to our tent till we have done our conference.
Let Lucilius and Titinius guard our door. 52
                    Exeunt. Manent Brutus and Cassius.
                    [*Lucilius and Titinius stand guard at the door.*]

❦

---

41 Listen hear   **42 powers** armies.   **straight make head** immediately raise an army.   **43 let . . . combined** let us work as one   **44 made** mustered, made certain.   **stretched** used to fullest advantage, extended to the utmost   **46 How . . . disclosed** (to determine) how hidden dangers may best be discovered   **47 surest answerèd** most safely met.   **48 at the stake** i.e., like a bear in the sport of bear-baiting   **49 bayed about** surrounded as by baying dogs   **51 mischiefs** harms, evils.
4.2. Location: Camp near Sardis, in Asia Minor. Before Brutus's tent. 1–2 Stand . . . stand! Halt! Pass the word!   **6 He . . . well** His greetings are welcome.   **7 In . . . officers** whether from an alteration in his feelings toward me or through the acts of unworthy subordinates   **8 worthy** justifiable   **10 be satisfied** have things explained to my satisfaction.   **12 full . . . honor** deserving all respect and honor.   **14 resolved** informed, put out of doubt.   **16 familiar instances** proofs of intimate friendship   **17 conference** conversation

21 enforcèd constrained   **23 hollow** insincere.   **hot at hand** restless and full of spirit when held in, at the start   **24 mettle** spirit   **26 fall their crests** lower their necks (literally, the ridge or mane of the neck), hang their heads.   **jades** worthless horses   **27 Sink** give way, fail   **28 Sardis** (The capital city of Lydia in Asia Minor.)   **29 the horse in general** all the cavalry   **31 gently** mildly, not hostilely   **40 sober form** dignified manner, appearance   **41 be content** keep calm   **42 griefs** grievances.   **I . . . well** i.e., We've known one another long and can proceed calmly.   **46 enlarge** speak freely   **48 charges** troops   **52 Lucilius** (The Folio reads *Lucius* here and *Lucillius* in line 50, but, when Shakespeare interpolated a passage in the next scene at lines 124–66, he evidently intended to have Lucilius guarding the door.)

[4.3]

CASSIUS

That you have wronged me doth appear in this:
You have condemned and noted Lucius Pella   2
For taking bribes here of the Sardians,
Wherein my letters, praying on his side,   4
Because I knew the man, was slighted off.   5

BRUTUS

You wronged yourself to write in such a case.

CASSIUS

In such a time as this it is not meet   7
That every nice offense should bear his comment.   8

BRUTUS

Let me tell you, Cassius, you yourself
Are much condemned to have an itching palm,   10
To sell and mart your offices for gold   11
To undeservers.

CASSIUS   I an itching palm?
You know that you are Brutus that speaks this,
Or, by the gods, this speech were else your last.   14

BRUTUS

The name of Cassius honors this corruption,   15
And chastisement doth therefore hide his head.   16

CASSIUS   Chastisement?

BRUTUS

Remember March, the ides of March remember.
Did not great Julius bleed for justice' sake?
What villain touched his body that did stab   20
And not for justice? What, shall one of us,   21
That struck the foremost man of all this world
But for supporting robbers, shall we now   23
Contaminate our fingers with base bribes,
And sell the mighty space of our large honors   25
For so much trash as may be graspèd thus?   26
I had rather be a dog and bay the moon   27
Than such a Roman.

CASSIUS   Brutus, bait not me.   28
I'll not endure it. You forget yourself
To hedge me in. I am a soldier, I,   30
Older in practice, abler than yourself
To make conditions.   32

BRUTUS   Go to! You are not, Cassius.

CASSIUS   I am.

BRUTUS   I say you are not.

CASSIUS

Urge me no more; I shall forget myself.   36
Have mind upon your health. Tempt me no farther.   37

BRUTUS   Away, slight man!   38

CASSIUS

Is't possible?

BRUTUS   Hear me, for I will speak.
Must I give way and room to your rash choler?   40
Shall I be frighted when a madman stares?   41

CASSIUS

O ye gods, ye gods! Must I endure all this?

BRUTUS

All this? Ay, more. Fret till your proud heart break.
Go show your slaves how choleric you are,
And make your bondmen tremble. Must I budge?   45
Must I observe you? Must I stand and crouch   46
Under your testy humor? By the gods,   47
You shall digest the venom of your spleen   48
Though it do split you; for, from this day forth,
I'll use you for my mirth, yea, for my laughter,
When you are waspish.

CASSIUS   Is it come to this?   51

BRUTUS

You say you are a better soldier.
Let it appear so; make your vaunting true,   53
And it shall please me well. For mine own part,
I shall be glad to learn of noble men.   55

CASSIUS

You wrong me every way! You wrong me, Brutus.
I said an elder soldier, not a better.
Did I say "better"?

BRUTUS   If you did, I care not.

CASSIUS

When Caesar lived he durst not thus have moved me.   59

BRUTUS

Peace, peace! You durst not so have tempted him.   60

CASSIUS   I durst not?

BRUTUS   No.

CASSIUS

What, durst not tempt him?

BRUTUS   For your life you durst not.

CASSIUS

Do not presume too much upon my love.
I may do that I shall be sorry for.

BRUTUS

You have done that you should be sorry for.
There is no terror, Cassius, in your threats,
For I am armed so strong in honesty
That they pass by me as the idle wind,

4.3. Location: The scene is continuous. Brutus and Cassius remain onstage, which now represents the interior of Brutus's tent.
2 noted publicly disgraced.   **Lucius Pella** a Roman praetor in Sardis
4 letters i.e., letter. (See 3.1.281n.)   **praying** entreating   **5 slighted off** slightingly dismissed.   **7 meet** fitting   **8 nice** trivial.   **bear his comment** be taken note of. (*His* means "its.")   **10 condemned to have** accused of having   **11 mart** traffic in   **14 else** otherwise
15 honors lends the appearance of honor to, countenances   **16 And . . . head** and for that reason those who might rebuke such corruption are reluctant to speak out.   **20–1 What . . . justice?** Which of us was villain enough to stab for any cause other than justice?
23 But only.   **robbers** (According to Plutarch, Caesar "was a favorer and suborner of all of them that did rob and spoil by his countenance and authority.")   **25 the mighty . . . honors** the greatness of our honorable reputations and the high offices we have power to confer   **26 trash** i.e., money (despised in Brutus's stoic philosophy)
27 bay howl at   **28 bait** harass   **30 hedge me in** crowd me, limit my authority.   **32 make conditions** i.e., manage affairs, make decisions about Lucius Pella and other officers.

36 Urge Provoke   **37 Tempt** Provoke   **38 slight** insignificant
40 way and room free course and scope.   **choler** wrathful temperament.   **41 stares** looks wildly at me.   **45 bondmen** (Probably not distinguished from "slaves" in line 44.)   **budge** flinch.   **46 observe** defer to.   **crouch** cringe   **47 humor** temperament.   **48 digest** swallow.   **spleen** i.e., irascibility   **51 waspish** hotheaded.   **53 vaunting** boasting   **55 I shall . . . men** (Said sarcastically: "Wouldn't it be a nice surprise to learn that some men can be noble after all?", or, "I am glad to be corrected by such a noble person as yourself.")   **59 moved** angered   **60 tempted** provoked

Which I respect not. I did send to you 70
For certain sums of gold, which you denied me;
For I can raise no money by vile means. 72
By heaven, I had rather coin my heart
And drop my blood for drachmas than to wring
From the hard hands of peasants their vile trash
By any indirection. I did send 76
To you for gold to pay my legions,
Which you denied me. Was that done like Cassius?
Should I have answered Caius Cassius so?
When Marcus Brutus grows so covetous
To lock such rascal counters from his friends, 81
Be ready, gods, with all your thunderbolts,
Dash him to pieces!

CASSIUS   I denied you not.

BRUTUS
You did.

CASSIUS   I did not. He was but a fool
That brought my answer back. Brutus hath rived my
    heart. 85
A friend should bear his friend's infirmities,
But Brutus makes mine greater than they are.

BRUTUS
I do not, till you practice them on me.

CASSIUS
You love me not.

BRUTUS   I do not like your faults.

CASSIUS
A friendly eye could never see such faults.

BRUTUS
A flatterer's would not, though they do appear
As huge as high Olympus.

CASSIUS
Come, Antony, and young Octavius, come,
Revenge yourselves alone on Cassius;
For Cassius is aweary of the world,
Hated by one he loves, braved by his brother, 96
Checked like a bondman, all his faults observed, 97
Set in a notebook, learned and conned by rote 98
To cast into my teeth. Oh, I could weep
My spirit from mine eyes! There is my dagger,
    [offering his unsheathed dagger]
And here my naked breast; within, a heart
Dearer than Pluto's mine, richer than gold. 102
If that thou be'st a Roman, take it forth.
I, that denied thee gold, will give my heart. 104
Strike, as thou didst at Caesar; for I know,
When thou didst hate him worst, thou loved'st him
    better
Than ever thou loved'st Cassius.

BRUTUS   Sheathe your dagger.
Be angry when you will, it shall have scope; 108

Do what you will, dishonor shall be humor. 109
Oh, Cassius, you are yokèd with a lamb 110
That carries anger as the flint bears fire,
Who, much enforcèd, shows a hasty spark 112
And straight is cold again.

CASSIUS   Hath Cassius lived 113
To be but mirth and laughter to his Brutus
When grief and blood ill-tempered vexeth him? 115

BRUTUS
When I spoke that, I was ill-tempered too.

CASSIUS
Do you confess so much? Give me your hand.

BRUTUS
And my heart too.   [They embrace.]

CASSIUS   Oh, Brutus!

BRUTUS   What's the matter?

CASSIUS
Have not you love enough to bear with me,
When that rash humor which my mother gave me 120
Makes me forgetful?

BRUTUS   Yes, Cassius, and from henceforth,
When you are overearnest with your Brutus,
He'll think your mother chides, and leave you so. 123

    Enter a Poet [followed by Lucilius and Titinius,
    who have been standing guard at the door].

POET
Let me go in to see the generals!
There is some grudge between 'em; 'tis not meet
They be alone.

LUCILIUS   You shall not come to them.

POET   Nothing but death shall stay me.

CASSIUS   How now? What's the matter?

POET
For shame, you generals! What do you mean?
Love and be friends, as two such men should be;
For I have seen more years, I'm sure, than ye.

CASSIUS
Ha, ha, how vilely doth this cynic rhyme! 132

BRUTUS
Get you hence, sirrah. Saucy fellow, hence!

CASSIUS
Bear with him, Brutus. 'Tis his fashion.

BRUTUS
I'll know his humor when he knows his time. 135
What should the wars do with these jigging fools? 136
Companion, hence!

CASSIUS   Away, away, begone!   Exit Poet. 137

BRUTUS
Lucilius and Titinius, bid the commanders

---

70 **respect not** pay no attention to.   72 **can raise no money** i.e., refuse to raise money   76 **indirection** devious or unjust means.   81 **rascal counters** i.e., paltry sums. (*Counters* were uncurrent coins or disks used by shopkeepers as tokens in making reckonings.)   85 **rived** cleft, split   96 **braved** defied   97 **Checked** rebuked   98 **conned by rote** memorized   102 **Dearer** richer.   **Pluto** god of the underworld (fused with Plutus, god of riches)   104 **that denied** i.e., who you insist denied   108 **scope** free rein

109 **dishonor . . . humor** i.e., I'll regard your dishonorable conduct and self-righteous anger as the effects of temperament, something to be humored.   110 **yokèd with** allied with   112 **enforcèd** provoked, struck upon   113 **straight** at once   115 **blood ill-tempered** disposition imbalanced by the humors of the body   120 **that rash humor** i.e., choler, anger   123 **leave you so** let it go at that.   132 **cynic** i.e., rude fellow; also one claiming to be a Cynic philosopher, hence outspoken   135 **I'll . . . time** I'll indulge his eccentric behavior when he knows the proper time for it.   136 **jigging** rhyming in jerky doggerel   137 **Companion** Fellow

Prepare to lodge their companies tonight.

CASSIUS
And come yourselves, and bring Messala with you
Immediately to us.   [*Exeunt Lucilius and Titinius.*]

BRUTUS [*to Lucius within*]   Lucius, a bowl of wine.

CASSIUS
I did not think you could have been so angry.

BRUTUS
Oh, Cassius, I am sick of many griefs.

CASSIUS
Of your philosophy you make no use
If you give place to accidental evils.   145

BRUTUS
No man bears sorrow better. Portia is dead.

CASSIUS   Ha? Portia?

BRUTUS   She is dead.

CASSIUS
How scaped I killing when I crossed you so?   149
Oh, insupportable and touching loss!
Upon what sickness?

BRUTUS   Impatient of my absence,
And grief that young Octavius with Mark Antony
Have made themselves so strong—for with her death   153
That tidings came—with this she fell distract
And, her attendants absent, swallowed fire.   155

CASSIUS
And died so?

BRUTUS   Even so.

CASSIUS   O ye immortal gods!

Enter Boy [*Lucius*] *with wine and tapers.*

BRUTUS
Speak no more of her.—Give me a bowl of wine.—
In this I bury all unkindness, Cassius.   *Drinks.*

CASSIUS
My heart is thirsty for that noble pledge.
Fill, Lucius, till the wine o'erswell the cup;
I cannot drink too much of Brutus' love.   161

                        [*He drinks. Exit Lucius.*]

Enter Titinius and Messala.

BRUTUS
Come in, Titinius. Welcome, good Messala.
Now sit we close about this taper here
And call in question our necessities.   [*They sit.*] 164

CASSIUS
Portia, art thou gone?

BRUTUS   No more, I pray you.
Messala, I have here receivèd letters   166

That young Octavius and Mark Antony
Come down upon us with a mighty power,   168
Bending their expedition toward Philippi.   169
                        [*He shows a letter.*]

MESSALA
Myself have letters of the selfsame tenor.

BRUTUS   With what addition?

MESSALA
That by proscription and bills of outlawry   172
Octavius, Antony, and Lepidus
Have put to death an hundred senators.

BRUTUS
Therein our letters do not well agree;
Mine speak of seventy senators that died
By their proscriptions, Cicero being one.

CASSIUS
Cicero one?

MESSALA   Cicero is dead,
And by that order of proscription.
Had you your letters from your wife, my lord?   180

BRUTUS   No, Messala.

MESSALA
Nor nothing in your letters writ of her?   182

BRUTUS
Nothing, Messala.

MESSALA   That, methinks, is strange.

BRUTUS
Why ask you? Hear you aught of her in yours?

MESSALA   No, my lord.

BRUTUS
Now, as you are a Roman, tell me true.

MESSALA
Then like a Roman bear the truth I tell,
For certain she is dead, and by strange manner.

BRUTUS
Why, farewell, Portia. We must die, Messala.
With meditating that she must die once,   190
I have the patience to endure it now.

MESSALA
Even so great men great losses should endure.   192

CASSIUS
I have as much of this in art as you,   193
But yet my nature could not bear it so.   194

BRUTUS
Well, to our work alive. What do you think   195
Of marching to Philippi presently?

145 **place** way.   **accidental evils** misfortunes caused by chance (which should be a matter of indifference to a philosopher like Brutus).   149 **scaped I killing** did I escape being killed   153 **her death** i.e., news of her death   155 **swallowed fire** (According to Plutarch, as translated by Thomas North, Portia "took hot burning coals and cast them in her mouth, and kept her mouth so close that she choked herself.")   161.2 *Titinius* (Lucilius does not return with Titinius, as he was ordered to do at lines 140–1, probably because he was not in Shakespeare's original version of this scene.)   164 **call in question** consider, discuss   166 **letters** (Probably a single letter. See 3.1.281n and 4.3.4n.)

168 **power** army   169 **Bending** directing.   **expedition** rapid march; warlike enterprise   172 **proscription** (See the note at 4.1.17.)
180–94 **Had . . . so** (This passage is sometimes regarded as contradictory to lines 142–65 and redundant. Perhaps it is the original account of Portia's death, and lines 142–65 are part of a later interpolation, but it is also possible that both are intended, the first being Brutus's intimate revelation of the news to his friend and the second being Brutus's recovery of his stoic reserve now on display for Messala and Titinius.)
182 **nothing . . . her** nothing written about her in the letter or letters you've received.   190 **once** at some time   192 **Even so** In just such a way   193 **art** i.e., the acquired theoretical wisdom of stoical fortitude (as contrasted with the gifts of *nature* in line 194)   195 **alive** concerning us who are alive and dealing with present and future realities.

CASSIUS
  I do not think it good.
BRUTUS   Your reason?
CASSIUS   This it is:
  'Tis better that the enemy seek us.
  So shall he waste his means, weary his soldiers,
  Doing himself offense, whilst we, lying still,   200
  Are full of rest, defense, and nimbleness.
BRUTUS
  Good reasons must of force give place to better.   202
  The people twixt Philippi and this ground
  Do stand but in a forced affection,
  For they have grudged us contribution.
  The enemy, marching along by them,
  By them shall make a fuller number up,
  Come on refreshed, new-added, and encouraged;
  From which advantage shall we cut him off
  If at Philippi we do face him there,
  These people at our back.
CASSIUS   Hear me, good brother—   211
BRUTUS
  Under your pardon. You must note beside   212
  That we have tried the utmost of our friends;
  Our legions are brim full, our cause is ripe.
  The enemy increaseth every day;
  We, at the height, are ready to decline.
  There is a tide in the affairs of men
  Which, taken at the flood, leads on to fortune;
  Omitted, all the voyage of their life
  Is bound in shallows and in miseries.   220
  On such a full sea are we now afloat,
  And we must take the current when it serves
  Or lose our ventures.
CASSIUS   Then, with your will, go on.   223
  We'll along ourselves and meet them at Philippi.
BRUTUS
  The deep of night is crept upon our talk,
  And nature must obey necessity,
  Which we will niggard with a little rest.   227
  There is no more to say.
CASSIUS   No more. Good night.
  Early tomorrow will we rise and hence.   229
BRUTUS
  Lucius!

  Enter Lucius.

       My gown.   [*Exit Lucius.*]
                    Farewell, good Messala.   230
  Good night, Titinius. Noble, noble Cassius,
  Good night and good repose.
CASSIUS   Oh, my dear brother!

This was an ill beginning of the night.
Never come such division 'tween our souls!
Let it not, Brutus.

  Enter Lucius with the gown.

BRUTUS   Everything is well.
CASSIUS   Good night, my lord.
BRUTUS   Good night, good brother.
TITINIUS, MESSALA   Good night, Lord Brutus.
BRUTUS   Farewell, everyone.
                    Exeunt [all but Brutus and Lucius].
  Give me the gown. Where is thy instrument?   241
LUCIUS
  Here in the tent.
BRUTUS   What, thou speak'st drowsily!
  Poor knave, I blame thee not; thou art o'erwatched.   243
  Call Claudius and some other of my men;
  I'll have them sleep on cushions in my tent.
LUCIUS [*calling*]   Varro and Claudius!

  Enter Varro and Claudius.

VARRO   Calls my lord?
BRUTUS
  I pray you, sirs, lie in my tent and sleep.
  It may be I shall raise you by and by   249
  On business to my brother Cassius.
VARRO
  So please you, we will stand and watch your pleasure. 251
BRUTUS
  I will not have it so. Lie down, good sirs.
  It may be I shall otherwise bethink me.   253
                    [*Varro and Claudius lie down.*]
  Look, Lucius, here's the book I sought for so;
  I put it in the pocket of my gown.
LUCIUS
  I was sure Your Lordship did not give it me.
BRUTUS
  Bear with me, good boy, I am much forgetful.
  Canst thou hold up thy heavy eyes awhile
  And touch thy instrument a strain or two?   259
LUCIUS
  Ay, my lord, an't please you.
BRUTUS   It does, my boy.   260
  I trouble thee too much, but thou art willing.
LUCIUS   It is my duty, sir.
BRUTUS
  I should not urge thy duty past thy might;
  I know young bloods look for a time of rest.   264
LUCIUS   I have slept, my lord, already.
BRUTUS
  It was well done, and thou shalt sleep again;
  I will not hold thee long. If I do live,

---

200 **offense** harm   202 **of force** necessarily   211 **These . . . back** i.e., with the people our enemy would otherwise recruit being instead in territory we control.   212 **Under your pardon** i.e., Excuse me, let me continue.   220 **bound in** confined to   223 **ventures** investments (of enterprise at sea).   **with your will** as you wish   227 **niggard** stint (by sleeping only briefly)   229 **hence** depart.   230 **gown** housecoat.

241 **instrument** i.e., perhaps a lute or cittern.   243 **knave** boy. **o'erwatched** tired from lack of sleep.   249 **raise** rouse   251 **watch your pleasure** wakefully await your commands.   253 **otherwise bethink me** change my mind.   259 **touch** i.e., play on.   **strain** tune, musical phrase   260 **an't** if it   264 **young bloods** youthful constitutions

I will be good to thee.
          Music, and a song. [Lucius falls asleep.]
This is a sleepy tune. O murd'rous slumber,   269
Layest thou thy leaden mace upon my boy,   270
That plays thee music? Gentle knave, good night;
I will not do thee so much wrong to wake thee.
If thou dost nod, thou break'st thy instrument;
I'll take it from thee. And, good boy, good night.
          [He removes Lucius's instrument,
                   and begins to read.]
Let me see, let me see; is not the leaf turned down
Where I left reading? Here it is, I think.

      Enter the Ghost of Caesar.

How ill this taper burns! Ha! Who comes here?   277
I think it is the weakness of mine eyes
That shapes this monstrous apparition.
It comes upon me.—Art thou any thing?   280
Art thou some god, some angel, or some devil,
That mak'st my blood cold and my hair to stare?   282
Speak to me what thou art.
GHOST
Thy evil spirit, Brutus.
BRUTUS   Why com'st thou?
GHOST
To tell thee thou shalt see me at Philippi.
BRUTUS   Well; then I shall see thee again?
GHOST   Ay, at Philippi.
BRUTUS
Why, I will see thee at Philippi, then.   *[Exit Ghost.]*
Now I have taken heart, thou vanishest.
Ill spirit, I would hold more talk with thee.—
Boy, Lucius! Varro! Claudius! Sirs, awake!
Claudius!
LUCIUS   The strings, my lord, are false.   292
BRUTUS
He thinks he still is at his instrument.—
Lucius, awake!
LUCIUS   My lord?
BRUTUS
Didst thou dream, Lucius, that thou so cried'st out?
LUCIUS
My lord, I do not know that I did cry.
BRUTUS
Yes, that thou didst. Didst thou see anything?
LUCIUS   Nothing, my lord.
BRUTUS
Sleep again, Lucius. Sirrah Claudius!
[To Varro] Fellow thou, awake!
VARRO   My lord?
CLAUDIUS   My lord?
                   [They get up.]

BRUTUS
Why did you so cry out, sirs, in your sleep?
VARRO, CLAUDIUS
Did we, my lord?
BRUTUS   Ay. Saw you anything?
VARRO
No, my lord, I saw nothing.
CLAUDIUS   Nor I, my lord.
BRUTUS
Go and commend me to my brother Cassius.   305
Bid him set on his powers betimes before,   306
And we will follow.
VARRO, CLAUDIUS   It shall be done, my lord.
                     Exeunt.

          ❖

5.1

      Enter Octavius, Antony, and their army.

OCTAVIUS
Now, Antony, our hopes are answerèd.
You said the enemy would not come down,
But keep the hills and upper regions.   3
It proves not so. Their battles are at hand;   4
They mean to warn us at Philippi here,   5
Answering before we do demand of them.
ANTONY
Tut, I am in their bosoms, and I know   7
Wherefore they do it. They could be content
To visit other places, and come down   9
With fearful bravery, thinking by this face   10
To fasten in our thoughts that they have courage;
But 'tis not so.

      Enter a Messenger.

MESSENGER   Prepare you, generals.   12
The enemy comes on in gallant show.
Their bloody sign of battle is hung out,   14
And something to be done immediately.   15
ANTONY
Octavius, lead your battle softly on   16
Upon the left hand of the even field.
OCTAVIUS
Upon the right hand, I. Keep thou the left.
ANTONY
Why do you cross me in this exigent?   19

---

269 **murd'rous** producing the likeness of death   270 **leaden mace** heavy staff of office (used by a sheriff to touch the shoulder of one being placed under arrest)   277 **How . . . burns!** (Ghostly apparitions were thought to be accompanied by such effects as lights burning low and blue.)   280 **upon** toward   282 **stare** stand on end.   292 **false** out of tune.

305 **commend me** deliver my greetings   306 **set . . . before** march away with his troops early in the morning, before me
5.1. Location: The plains of Philippi, in Macedonia.
3 **keep** remain in   4 **battles** armies   5 **warn** challenge   7 **bosoms** secret councils   9 **visit other places** i.e., be elsewhere   10 **fearful bravery** (1) awesome ostentation (2) a show of bravery to conceal their fear.   **face** pretense (of courage)   12 **'tis not so** (1) their plan cannot deceive us (2) they have no courage.   14 **bloody sign** red flag or crimson coat of arms as battle signal   15 **to be** is to be   16 **softly** warily, with restraint   19 **cross** contradict. **exigent** critical moment.

OCTAVIUS
I do not cross you, but I will do so.   *March.*   20

Drum. Enter Brutus, Cassius, and their army;
[Lucilius, Titinius, Messala, and others].

BRUTUS   They stand and would have parley.
CASSIUS
Stand fast, Titinius. We must out and talk.   22
OCTAVIUS
Mark Antony, shall we give sign of battle?
ANTONY
No, Caesar, we will answer on their charge.   24
Make forth. The generals would have some words.   25
OCTAVIUS [*to his officers*]   Stir not until the signal.
[*The two sides advance toward one another.*]
BRUTUS
Words before blows. Is it so, countrymen?
OCTAVIUS
Not that we love words better, as you do.
BRUTUS
Good words are better than bad strokes, Octavius.
ANTONY
In your bad strokes, Brutus, you give good words.   30
Witness the hole you made in Caesar's heart,
Crying "Long live! Hail, Caesar!"
CASSIUS   Antony,
The posture of your blows are yet unknown;   33
But for your words, they rob the Hybla bees,   34
And leave them honeyless.
ANTONY   Not stingless too?
BRUTUS   Oh, yes, and soundless too.
For you have stol'n their buzzing, Antony,
And very wisely threat before you sting.   39
ANTONY
Villains! You did not so when your vile daggers   40
Hacked one another in the sides of Caesar.
You showed your teeth like apes, and fawned like
hounds,   42
And bowed like bondmen, kissing Caesar's feet,
Whilst damnèd Casca, like a cur, behind,
Struck Caesar on the neck. Oh, you flatterers!
CASSIUS
Flatterers? Now, Brutus, thank yourself!
This tongue had not offended so today
If Cassius might have ruled.   48
OCTAVIUS
Come, come, the cause. If arguing make us sweat,   49
The proof of it will turn to redder drops.   50
Look,   [*He draws.*]

I draw a sword against conspirators.
When think you that the sword goes up again?   53
Never, till Caesar's three-and-thirty wounds   54
Be well avenged, or till another Caesar   55
Have added slaughter to the sword of traitors.   56
BRUTUS
Caesar, thou canst not die by traitors' hands,   57
Unless thou bring'st them with thee.
OCTAVIUS   So I hope.   58
I was not born to die on Brutus' sword.   59
BRUTUS
Oh, if thou wert the noblest of thy strain,   60
Young man, thou couldst not die more honorable.
CASSIUS
A peevish schoolboy, worthless of such honor,   62
Joined with a masker and a reveler!   63
ANTONY
Old Cassius still.
OCTAVIUS   Come, Antony, away!—   64
Defiance, traitors, hurl we in your teeth.
If you dare fight today, come to the field;
If not, when you have stomachs.   67
                    Exeunt Octavius, Antony, and army.
CASSIUS
Why, now, blow wind, swell billow, and swim bark!   68
The storm is up, and all is on the hazard.   69
BRUTUS
Ho, Lucilius! Hark, a word with you.
LUCILIUS (*stands forth*)   My lord?
                    [*Brutus and Lucilius converse apart.*]
CASSIUS   Messala!
MESSALA (*stands forth*)   What says my general?
CASSIUS   Messala,
This is my birthday, as this very day   75
Was Cassius born. Give me thy hand, Messala.
Be thou my witness that against my will,
As Pompey was, am I compelled to set   78
Upon one battle all our liberties.
You know that I held Epicurus strong   80
And his opinion. Now I change my mind
And partly credit things that do presage.   82
Coming from Sardis, on our former ensign   83

53 **up** in its sheath   54 **three-and-thirty** (Plutarch has it three-and-twenty.)   55 **another Caesar** i.e., myself, Octavius   56 **Have . . . to** has also been slaughtered by   57–8 **thou . . . thee** i.e., the only traitors here are in your own army.   58–9 **So . . . sword** i.e. (sardonically), I'm glad to hear that, since you are the traitor I mean, and since you are not in my army, I cannot, according to your assertion, die at your hands.   60 **if** even if.   **strain** lineage   62 **peevish** silly, childish.   **schoolboy** (Octavius was eighteen at the time of Caesar's assassination.)   **worthless** unworthy   63 **a masker . . . reveler** i.e., Antony, noted for his dissipation.   64 **Old . . . still** i.e., Cassius, as envious and ill-willed as ever. (Said sardonically.)   67 **stomachs** appetites (for fighting), courage.   68 **billow** wave.   **swim bark** let the sailing vessel swim for its life.   69 **on the hazard** at stake.   75 **as** inasmuch as   78 **Pompey** (The reference is to the battle of Pharsalus, where Pompey was persuaded to fight Caesar against his own judgment.)   **set** stake   80 **Epicurus** Greek philosopher (341–270 B.C.) who, because he held the gods to be indifferent to human affairs, spurned belief in omens or superstitions   82 **presage** foretell events.   83 **former ensign** foremost standard, the legion's *aquila*, a tall standard surmounted by the image of an eagle

20 **cross you** contradict you perversely.   **do so** do as I said.   22 **out** go out   24 **answer on their charge** respond when they attack. 25 **Make forth** March forward.   30 **In . . . words** i.e., As you deliver cruel blows, Brutus, you use deceiving flattery.   33 **The posture . . . are** how you will strike your blows is   34 **for** as for.   **Hybla** a mountain and a town in ancient Sicily, famous for honey   39 **very wisely** (Said ironically; Brutus suggests that Antony is all bluster and no action.)   **threat** threaten   40 **so** i.e., give warning   42 **showed your teeth** i.e., in smiles   48 **ruled** prevailed (in urging that Antony be killed).   49 **the cause** to our business.   50 **proof** trial

Two mighty eagles fell, and there they perched,   84
Gorging and feeding from our soldiers' hands,
Who to Philippi here consorted us.   86
This morning are they fled away and gone,
And in their steads do ravens, crows, and kites   88
Fly o'er our heads and downward look on us
As we were sickly prey. Their shadows seem   90
A canopy most fatal, under which   91
Our army lies, ready to give up the ghost.

MESSALA
Believe not so.

CASSIUS   I but believe it partly,   93
For I am fresh of spirit and resolved
To meet all perils very constantly.   95

BRUTUS
Even so, Lucilius.   [*He rejoins Cassius.*]

CASSIUS   Now, most noble Brutus,   96
The gods today stand friendly, that we may,   97
Lovers in peace, lead on our days to age!   98
But since the affairs of men rest still incertain,   99
Let's reason with the worst that may befall.   100
If we do lose this battle, then is this
The very last time we shall speak together.
What are you then determinèd to do?

BRUTUS
Even by the rule of that philosophy
By which I did blame Cato for the death   105
Which he did give himself—I know not how,
But I do find it cowardly and vile,
For fear of what might fall, so to prevent   108
The time of life—arming myself with patience   109
To stay the providence of some high powers   110
That govern us below.

CASSIUS   Then, if we lose this battle,
You are contented to be led in triumph
Thorough the streets of Rome?   113

BRUTUS
No, Cassius, no. Think not, thou noble Roman,
That ever Brutus will go bound to Rome;
He bears too great a mind. But this same day
Must end that work the ides of March begun.
And whether we shall meet again I know not;
Therefore our everlasting farewell take.
Forever and forever farewell, Cassius!
If we do meet again, why, we shall smile;
If not, why then this parting was well made.

CASSIUS
Forever and forever farewell, Brutus!
If we do meet again, we'll smile indeed;
If not, 'tis true this parting was well made.

BRUTUS
Why, then, lead on. Oh, that a man might know
The end of this day's business ere it come!   127
But it sufficeth that the day will end,
And then the end is known.—Come, ho, away!
                                                    Exeunt.

❧

[5.2]

Alarum. Enter Brutus and Messala.

BRUTUS
Ride, ride, Messala, ride, and give these bills   1
Unto the legions on the other side.   2
                        [*He hands him written orders.*]
                                                Loud alarum.
Let them set on at once; for I perceive   3
But cold demeanor in Octavio's wing,   4
And sudden push gives them the overthrow.
Ride, ride, Messala! Let them all come down.   6
                                        Exeunt [*separately*].

❧

[5.3]

Alarums. Enter Cassius [*carrying a standard*], *and
Titinius.*

CASSIUS
Oh, look, Titinius, look, the villains fly!   1
Myself have to mine own turned enemy.   2
This ensign here of mine was turning back;   3
I slew the coward and did take it from him.   4

TITINIUS
Oh, Cassius, Brutus gave the word too early,
Who, having some advantage on Octavius,
Took it too eagerly. His soldiers fell to spoil,   7
Whilst we by Antony are all enclosed.   8

Enter Pindarus.

---

84 fell swooped down **86 consorted** accompanied **88 kites** scavenger birds (also raptors) **90 As** as if **91 fatal** presaging death **93 but** only **95 constantly** resolutely. **96 Even so, Lucilius** (This phrase marks the end of Brutus's private conversation apart with Lucilius.) **97 The gods** May the gods **98 Lovers** friends. **age** old age. **99 still** always **100 reason** reckon **105 Cato** i.e., Marcus Porcius Cato, Brutus' father-in-law, who killed himself to avoid submission to Caesar in 46 B.C. (See 2.1.296 and note.) Brutus's condemnation of Cato's suicide out of fear of failure can perhaps be reconciled with lines 114–17 below and with Brutus's own later suicide (5.5.50), since on that occasion Brutus is responding to certain defeat and disgrace. The seeming contradiction may also be owing to an ambiguity in North's Plutarch. **108 fall** befall. **prevent** anticipate the end, cut short **109 time** term, extent **110 stay** await **113 Thorough** through

127 ere before
5.2. Location: The plains of Philippi. The field of battle.
0.1 Alarum (This is seemingly an anticipatory stage direction; the battle actually begins with the *Loud alarum* at line 2. An *alarum* is off stage sounds, signifying a battle.) **1 bills** orders **2 side** wing (i.e., Cassius's wing). **3 set on** attack **4 cold demeanor** faintheartedness **6 come down** i.e., from the hills, where the Republican army has been awaiting the signal to attack. (See 5.1.2–3.)
5.3. Location: The field of battle still.
1 the villains i.e., my own troops **2 mine own** my own men **3 ensign** bearer of the standard. (A legion's *aquila*, or "eagle standard," had great significance and needed to be guarded.) **4 it** i.e., the standard **7 spoil** looting **8 enclosed** surrounded.

PINDARUS
Fly further off, my lord, fly further off!
Mark Antony is in your tents, my lord.
Fly therefore, noble Cassius, fly far off.
CASSIUS
This hill is far enough. Look, look, Titinius:
Are those my tents where I perceive the fire?
TITINIUS
They are, my lord.
CASSIUS   Titinius, if thou lovest me,
Mount thou my horse, and hide thy spurs in him
Till he have brought thee up to yonder troops
And here again, that I may rest assured
Whether yond troops are friend or enemy.
TITINIUS
I will be here again even with a thought.   *Exit.* 19
CASSIUS
Go, Pindarus, get higher on that hill.
My sight was ever thick. Regard Titinius,   21
And tell me what thou not'st about the field.   22
                    [*Pindarus goes up.*]
This day I breathèd first. Time is come round,   23
And where I did begin, there shall I end.
My life is run his compass.—Sirrah, what news?   25
PINDARUS (*above*) Oh, my lord!
CASSIUS What news?
PINDARUS [*above*]
Titinius is enclosèd round about
With horsemen, that make to him on the spur,   29
Yet he spurs on. Now they are almost on him.
Now, Titinius! Now some light. Oh, he   31
Lights too. He's ta'en. (*Shout.*) And hark! They shout
for joy.
CASSIUS Come down, behold no more.
Oh, coward that I am, to live so long
To see my best friend ta'en before my face!   35
                    Enter Pindarus [*from above*].
Come hither, sirrah.
In Parthia did I take thee prisoner,   37
And then I swore thee, saving of thy life,   38
That whatsoever I did bid thee do
Thou shouldst attempt it. Come now, keep thine oath;
Now be a freeman, and with this good sword,
That ran through Caesar's bowels, search this bosom.   42
Stand not to answer. Here, take thou the hilts,   43
And when my face is covered, as 'tis now,
Guide thou the sword. [*Pindarus does so.*] Caesar, thou
art revenged,
Even with the sword that killed thee.   [*He dies.*]

PINDARUS
So, I am free, yet would not so have been,   47
Durst I have done my will. Oh, Cassius!   48
Far from this country Pindarus shall run,
Where never Roman shall take note of him.   [*Exit.*]

        *Enter Titinius [wearing a garland of laurel] and
        Messala.*

MESSALA
It is but change, Titinius; for Octavius   51
Is overthrown by noble Brutus' power,
As Cassius' legions are by Antony.
TITINIUS
These tidings will well comfort Cassius.
MESSALA
Where did you leave him?
TITINIUS   All disconsolate,
With Pindarus his bondman, on this hill.
MESSALA
Is not that he that lies upon the ground?
TITINIUS
He lies not like the living. Oh, my heart!
MESSALA
Is not that he?
TITINIUS   No, this was he, Messala,
But Cassius is no more. O setting sun,
As in thy red rays thou dost sink to night,
So in his red blood Cassius' day is set.
The sun of Rome is set. Our day is gone;   63
Clouds, dews, and dangers come; our deeds are done.
Mistrust of my success hath done this deed.   65
MESSALA
Mistrust of good success hath done this deed.
O hateful Error, Melancholy's child,   67
Why dost thou show to the apt thoughts of men   68
The things that are not? O Error, soon conceived,
Thou never com'st unto a happy birth,
But kill'st the mother that engendered thee.   71
TITINIUS
What, Pindarus! Where art thou, Pindarus?
MESSALA
Seek him, Titinius, whilst I go to meet
The noble Brutus, thrusting this report
Into his ears. I may say "thrusting" it,
For piercing steel and darts envenomèd
Shall be as welcome to the ears of Brutus
As tidings of this sight.
TITINIUS   Hie you, Messala,
And I will seek for Pindarus the while.
                    [*Exit Messala.*]
Why didst thou send me forth, brave Cassius?
Did I not meet thy friends? And did not they
Put on my brows this wreath of victory

---

19 **even . . . thought** as quick as thought.   21 **thick** imperfect, dim.
Regard Observe   22.1 *Pindarus goes up* (Pindarus may climb to the
gallery, or may exit and ascend behind the scenes; see line 35.1 and
note.)   23 **I breathèd first** i.e., it is my birthday.   25 **his compass** its
circuit, circle (as drawn by a geometer's compass).   29 **make . . . spur**
approach him riding rapidly   31 **light** alight, dismount.   35.1 *Enter*
(Pindarus may descend in full view of the audience; see note at 22.1.)
37 **Parthia** (What is now northern Iran.)   38 **swore . . . of** made you
swear, when I spared   42 **search** probe, penetrate   43 **Stand** Delay.
hilts sword hilt

47 **so** in this manner   48 **Durst . . . will** if I had dared do what I
wished.   51 **change** exchange of advantage, quid pro quo   63 **sun**
(With pun on *son*.)   65 **Mistrust** i.e., Cassius's doubt   67 **Melancholy's child** i.e., bred of pessimism   68 **apt** impressionable   71 **the
mother** i.e., the melancholy person who too readily believes the worst

And bid me give it thee? Didst thou not hear their
  shouts?
Alas, thou hast misconstrued everything.
But, hold thee, take this garland on thy brow.   85
       [*He places the garland on Cassius's brow.*]
Thy Brutus bid me give it thee, and I
Will do his bidding. Brutus, come apace   87
And see how I regarded Caius Cassius.
By your leave, gods! This is a Roman's part.
Come, Cassius' sword, and find Titinius' heart.
       [*He stabs himself and*] *dies.*

    Alarum. Enter Brutus, Messala, young Cato,
    Strato, Volumnius, and Lucilius, [Labeo, and
    Flavius].

BRUTUS
Where, where, Messala, doth his body lie?
MESSALA
Lo, yonder, and Titinius mourning it.
BRUTUS
Titinius' face is upward.
CATO   He is slain.
BRUTUS
O Julius Caesar, thou art mighty yet!
Thy spirit walks abroad and turns our swords
In our own proper entrails.   *Low alarums.*
CATO   Brave Titinius!   96
Look whe'er he have not crowned dead Cassius.   97
BRUTUS
Are yet two Romans living such as these?
The last of all the Romans, fare thee well!
It is impossible that ever Rome
Should breed thy fellow. Friends, I owe more tears
To this dead man than you shall see me pay.—
I shall find time, Cassius, I shall find time.—
Come, therefore, and to Thasos send his body.   104
His funerals shall not be in our camp,   105
Lest it discomfort us. Lucilius, come,   106
And come, young Cato, let us to the field.
Labeo and Flavius, set our battles on.   108
'Tis three o'clock, and, Romans, yet ere night   109
We shall try fortune in a second fight.
       Exeunt [with the bodies].

❧

[5.4]

    Alarum. Enter Brutus, Messala, [young] Cato,
    Lucilius, and Flavius.

BRUTUS
Yet, countrymen, oh, yet hold up your heads!
       [*Exit, followed by Messala and Flavius.*]
CATO
What bastard doth not? Who will go with me?   2
I will proclaim my name about the field:
I am the son of Marcus Cato, ho!
A foe to tyrants, and my country's friend.
I am the son of Marcus Cato, ho!

    Enter soldiers, and fight.

LUCILIUS
And I am Brutus, Marcus Brutus I!
Brutus, my country's friend! Know me for Brutus!
      [*Young Cato is slain by Antony's men.*]
O young and noble Cato, art thou down?
Why, now thou diest as bravely as Titinius,
And mayst be honored, being Cato's son.
FIRST SOLDIER [*capturing Lucilius*]
Yield, or thou diest.
LUCILIUS [*offering money*] Only I yield to die.   12
There is so much that thou wilt kill me straight;   13
Kill Brutus, and be honored in his death.
FIRST SOLDIER
We must not. A noble prisoner!
SECOND SOLDIER
Room, ho! Tell Antony, Brutus is ta'en.

    Enter Antony.

FIRST SOLDIER
I'll tell the news. Here comes the General.—
Brutus is ta'en, Brutus is ta'en, my lord.
ANTONY Where is he?
LUCILIUS
Safe, Antony, Brutus is safe enough.
I dare assure thee that no enemy
Shall ever take alive the noble Brutus.
The gods defend him from so great a shame!
When you do find him, or alive or dead,   24
He will be found like Brutus, like himself.
ANTONY [*to First Soldier*]
This is not Brutus, friend, but, I assure you,
A prize no less in worth. Keep this man safe;
Give him all kindness. I had rather have
Such men my friends than enemies.—Go on,
And see whe'er Brutus be alive or dead;   30
And bring us word unto Octavius' tent
How everything is chanced.   32
    Exeunt [separately, some bearing Cato's body].

❧

[5.5]

Enter Brutus, Dardanius, Clitus, Strato, and
Volumnius.

BRUTUS
Come, poor remains of friends, rest on this rock.
                                      [*He sits.*]

CLITUS
Statilius showed the torchlight, but, my lord,   2
He came not back. He is or ta'en or slain.   3

BRUTUS
Sit thee down, Clitus. Slaying is the word.
It is a deed in fashion. Hark thee, Clitus.
                                      [*He whispers.*]

CLITUS
What, I, my lord? No, not for all the world.

BRUTUS
Peace then. No words.

CLITUS   I'll rather kill myself.

BRUTUS
Hark thee, Dardanius.   [*He whispers.*]

DARDANIUS   Shall I do such a deed?
        [*Dardanius and Clitus move away from Brutus.*]

CLITUS Oh, Dardanius!

DARDANIUS   Oh, Clitus!

CLITUS
What ill request did Brutus make to thee?

DARDANIUS
To kill him, Clitus. Look, he meditates.

CLITUS
Now is that noble vessel full of grief,
That it runs over even at his eyes.

BRUTUS
Come hither, good Volumnius. List a word.   15

VOLUMNIUS
What says my lord?

BRUTUS   Why, this, Volumnius:
The ghost of Caesar hath appeared to me
Two several times by night—at Sardis once,   18
And this last night here in Philippi fields.
I know my hour is come.

VOLUMNIUS   Not so, my lord.

BRUTUS
Nay, I am sure it is, Volumnius.
Thou see'st the world, Volumnius, how it goes;
Our enemies have beat us to the pit.   *Low alarums.*   23
It is more worthy to leap in ourselves
Than tarry till they push us. Good Volumnius,
Thou know'st that we two went to school together.
Even for that our love of old, I prithee,   27

Hold thou my sword hilts whilst I run on it.   28

VOLUMNIUS
That's not an office for a friend, my lord.
                                      Alarum still.

CLITUS
Fly, fly, my lord! There is no tarrying here.

BRUTUS
Farewell to you, and you, and you, Volumnius.
Strato, thou hast been all this while asleep;
Farewell to thee too, Strato. Countrymen,
My heart doth joy that yet in all my life
I found no man but he was true to me.
I shall have glory by this losing day
More than Octavius and Mark Antony
By this vile conquest shall attain unto.
So fare you well at once, for Brutus' tongue   39
Hath almost ended his life's history.
Night hangs upon mine eyes; my bones would rest,
That have but labored to attain this hour.   42
            Alarum. Cry within, "Fly, fly, fly!"

CLITUS
Fly, my lord, fly!

BRUTUS   Hence, I will follow.
        [*Exeunt Clitus, Dardanius, and Volumnius.*]
I prithee, Strato, stay thou by thy lord.
Thou art a fellow of a good respect;   45
Thy life hath had some smatch of honor in it.   46
Hold then my sword, and turn away thy face,
While I do run upon it. Wilt thou, Strato?

STRATO
Give me your hand first. Fare you well, my lord.

BRUTUS
Farewell, good Strato. [*He runs on his sword.*] Caesar,
now be still.
I killed not thee with half so good a will.   *Dies.*   51

Alarum. Retreat. Enter Antony, Octavius;
Messala, Lucilius [as prisoners]; and the army.

OCTAVIUS   What man is that?

MESSALA
My master's man. Strato, where is thy master?

STRATO
Free from the bondage you are in, Messala.
The conquerors can but make a fire of him,
For Brutus only overcame himself,   56
And no man else hath honor by his death.

LUCILIUS
So Brutus should be found. I thank thee, Brutus,
That thou hast proved Lucilius' saying true.   59

OCTAVIUS
All that served Brutus, I will entertain them.   60

5.5. Location: The field of battle still.
2–3 Statilius . . . slain (According to Plutarch, a scout named Statilius
has gone through the enemy lines to reconnoitre and to hold up a
torch if all is well at Cassius's camp; he signals back but is then captured and slain.) **3 or ta'en** either taken **15 List** Listen to **18 sev-**
eral separate **23 beat** driven. **pit** trap for wild animals; also, a
grave. **27 that our love** that friendship of ours

28 hilts hilt **39 at once** all together, or without further ado **42 That**
. . . hour that have striven all life long only to achieve this moment
of death. **45 respect** reputation **46 some smatch** some flavor, a
touch **51.1 *Retreat*** signal to retire. **56 Brutus . . . himself** only
Brutus conquered Brutus **59 saying** (See 5.4.21–5.) **60 entertain**
take into service

Fellow, wilt thou bestow thy time with me?

STRATO
Ay, if Messala will prefer me to you.   62

OCTAVIUS   Do so, good Messala.

MESSALA   How died my master, Strato?

STRATO
I held the sword, and he did run on it.

MESSALA
Octavius, then take him to follow thee,   66
That did the latest service to my master.   67

ANTONY
This was the noblest Roman of them all.
All the conspirators save only he
Did that they did in envy of great Caesar;
He only in a general honest thought   71
And common good to all made one of them.

His life was gentle, and the elements   73
So mixed in him that Nature might stand up
And say to all the world, "This was a man!"

OCTAVIUS
According to his virtue let us use him,
With all respect and rites of burial.
Within my tent his bones tonight shall lie,
Most like a soldier, ordered honorably.   79
So call the field to rest, and let's away   80
To part the glories of this happy day.   81

Exeunt omnes [with Brutus's body].

---

62 prefer recommend   **66 follow** serve   **67 latest** last   **71 general** i.e., selfless. (Cf. 2.1.2 n.)

73 gentle noble.   **elements** (Humankind as a microcosm is made up of earth, air, fire, and water, formed into the four humors of phlegm, blood, yellow bile [or choler], and black bile [or melancholy], whose qualities were mingled in Brutus in due proportions.)   **79 ordered** treated, arranged for; accorded solemn rites. (Cf. 1.2.25 n.)   **80 field** army in the field   **81 part** share.   **happy** fortunate   **81.1** *omnes* all

Hamlet, Prince of Denmark

A recurring motif in *Hamlet* is of a seemingly healthy exterior concealing an interior sickness. Mere pretense of virtue, as Hamlet warns his mother, "will but skin and film the ulcerous place, / Whiles rank corruption, mining all within, / Infects unseen" (3.4.154–6). Polonius confesses, when he is about to use his daughter as a decoy for Hamlet, that "with devotion's visage / And pious action we do sugar o'er / The devil himself"; and his observation elicits a more anguished mea culpa from Claudius in an aside: "How smart a lash that speech doth give my conscience! / The harlot's cheek, beautied with plast'ring art, / Is not more ugly to the thing that helps it / Than is my deed to my most painted word" (3.1.47–54).

This motif of concealed evil and disease continually reminds us that, in both a specific and a broader sense, "Something is rotten in the state of Denmark" (1.4.90). The specific source of contamination is a poison: the poison with which Claudius has killed Hamlet's father, the poison in the players' enactment of "The Murder of Gonzago," and the two poisons (envenomed sword and poisoned drink) with which Claudius and Laertes plot to rid themselves of young Hamlet. More generally, the poison is an evil nature seeking to destroy humanity's better self, as in the archetypal murder of Abel by Cain. "Oh, my offense is rank! It smells to heaven," laments Claudius, "It hath the primal eldest curse upon't, / A brother's murder" (3.3.36–8). To Hamlet, his father and Claudius typify what is best and worst in humanity; one is the sun-god Hyperion and the other, a satyr. Claudius is a "serpent" and a "mildewed ear, / Blasting his wholesome brother" (1.5.40; 3.4.65–6). Many a person, in Hamlet's view, is tragically destined to behold his or her better qualities corrupted by "some vicious mole of nature" over which the individual seems to have no control. "His virtues else, be they as pure as grace, / As infinite as man may undergo, / Shall in the general censure take corruption / From that particular fault." The "dram of evil" pollutes "all the noble substance" (1.4.24–37). Thus, poison spreads outward to infect the whole individual, just as bad individuals can infect an entire court or nation.

Hamlet, his mind attuned to philosophical matters, is keenly and poetically aware of humanity's fallen condition. He is, moreover, a shrewd observer of the Danish court, familiar with its ways and at the same time newly returned from abroad, looking at Denmark with a stranger's eyes. What particularly darkens his view of humanity, however, is not the general fact of corrupted human nature but rather Hamlet's knowledge of a dreadful secret. Even before he learns of his father's murder, Hamlet senses that there is something more deeply amiss than his mother's overhasty marriage to her deceased husband's brother. This is serious enough, to be sure, for it violates a taboo (parallel to the marriage of a widower to his deceased wife's sister, long regarded as incestuous by the English) and is thus understandably referred to as "incest" by Hamlet and his father's ghost. The appalling spectacle of Gertrude's "wicked speed, to post / With such dexterity to incestuous sheets" (1.2.156–7) overwhelms Hamlet with revulsion at carnal appetite and intensifies the emotional crisis any son would go through when forced to contemplate his father's death and his mother's remarriage. Still, the Ghost's revelation is of something far worse, something Hamlet has subconsciously feared and suspected. "Oh, my prophetic soul! My uncle!" (1.5.42). Now Hamlet believes he has confirming evidence for his intuition that the world itself is "an unweeded garden / That grows to seed. Things rank and gross in nature / Possess it merely" (1.2.135–7).

Something is indeed rotten in the state of Denmark. The monarch on whom the health and safety of the kingdom depend is a murderer. Yet few persons know his secret: Hamlet, Horatio only belatedly, Claudius himself, and ourselves as audience. Many ironies and misunderstandings within the play cannot be understood without a proper awareness of this gap between Hamlet's knowledge and most others' ignorance of the murder. For, according to their own lights, Polonius and the rest behave as courtiers normally behave, obeying and flattering a king who has been chosen by a constitutional process of "election" and can therefore claim to be their legitimate ruler. They do not know that he is a murderer. Hamlet, for his part, is so obsessed with the secret murder that he overreacts to those around him, rejecting overtures of friendship and becoming embittered, callous, brutal, and even violent. His antisocial behavior gives the others good reason to fear him as a menace to the state. Nevertheless, we share with Hamlet a knowledge of the truth and know that he is right, whereas the others are at best unhappily deceived by their own blind complicity in evil.

Rosencrantz and Guildenstern, for instance, are boyhood friends of Hamlet but are now dependent on the favor of King Claudius. Despite their seeming concern for their one-time comrade and Hamlet's initial pleasure in receiving them, they are faceless courtiers whose very names, like their personalities, are virtually interchangeable. "Thanks, Rosencrantz and gentle Guildenstern," says the King, and "Thanks, Guildenstern and gentle Rosencrantz," echoes the Queen (2.2.33–4). They cannot understand why Hamlet increasingly mocks their overtures of friendship, whereas Hamlet cannot stomach their subservience to the King. The secret murder divides Hamlet from them, since only he knows of it. As the confrontation between Hamlet and Claudius grows more deadly, Rosencrantz and Guildenstern, not knowing the true cause, can only interpret Hamlet's behavior as dangerous madness. The wild display he puts on during the performance of "The Murder of Gonzago" and then the killing of Polonius are evidence of a treasonous threat to the crown, eliciting from them staunch assertions of the divine right of kings. "Most holy and religious fear it is / To keep those many many bodies safe / That live and feed upon Your Majesty," professes Guildenstern, and Rosencrantz reiterates the theme: "The cess of majesty / Dies not alone, but like a gulf doth draw / What's near it with it" (3.3.8–17). These sentiments of Elizabethan orthodoxy, similar to ones frequently heard in Shakespeare's history plays, are here undercut by a devastating irony, since they are spoken unwittingly in defense of a murderer. This irony pursues Rosencrantz and Guildenstern to their graves, for they are killed performing what they see as their duty to convey Hamlet safely to England. They are as ignorant of Claudius's secret orders for the murder of Hamlet in England as they are of Claudius's real reason for wishing to be rid of his stepson. That Hamlet should ingeniously remove the secret commission from Rosencrantz and Guildenstern's packet and substitute an order for their execution is ironically fitting, even though they are guiltless of having plotted Hamlet's death. "Why, man, they did make love to this employment," says Hamlet to Horatio. "They are not near my conscience. Their defeat /

Does by their own insinuation grow" (5.2.57–9). They have condemned themselves, in Hamlet's eyes, by interceding officiously in deadly affairs of which they had no comprehension. Hamlet's judgment of them is harsh, and he himself appears hardened and pitiless in his role as agent in their deaths, but he is right that they have courted their own destiny.

Polonius, too, dies for meddling. It seems an unfair fate, since he wishes no physical harm to Hamlet and is only trying to ingratiate himself with Claudius. Yet Polonius's complicity in jaded court politics is deeper than his fatuous parental sententiousness might lead one to suppose. His famous advice to his son, often quoted out of context as though it were wise counsel, is, in fact, a worldly gospel of self-interest and concern for appearances. Like his son, Laertes, he cynically presumes that Hamlet's affection for Ophelia cannot be serious, since princes are not free to marry ladies of the court; accordingly, Polonius obliges his daughter to return the love letters she so cherishes. Polonius's spies are everywhere, seeking to entrap Polonius's own son in fleshly sin or to discover symptoms of Hamlet's presumed lovesickness. Polonius may cut a ridiculous figure as a prattling busybody, but he is wily and even menacing in his intent. He has actually helped Claudius to the throne and is an essential instrument of royal policy. His ineffectuality and ignorance of the murder do not really excuse his guilty involvement.

Ophelia is more innocent than her father and brother, and more truly affectionate toward Hamlet. She earns our sympathy because she is caught between the conflicting wills of the men who are supremely important to her— her wooer, her father, and her brother. Obedient by instinct and training to patriarchal instruction, she is unprepared to cope with divided authority and so takes refuge in passivity. Nevertheless, her pitiable story suggests that weak-willed acquiescence is poisoned by the evil to which it surrenders. However passively, Ophelia becomes an instrument through which Claudius attempts to spy on Hamlet. She is much like Gertrude, for the Queen has yielded to Claudius's importunity without ever knowing fully what awful price Claudius has paid for her and for the throne. The resemblance between Ophelia and Gertrude confirms Hamlet's tendency to generalize about feminine weakness—"frailty, thy name is woman" (1.2.146)—and prompts his misogynistic outburst against Ophelia when he concludes she, too, is spying on him. His rejection of love and friendship (except for Horatio's) seems paranoid in character and yet is at least partially justified by the fact that so many of the court are in fact conspiring to learn what he is up to.

Their oversimplification of his dilemma and their facile analyses vex Hamlet as much as their meddling. When they presume to diagnose his malady, the courtiers actually reveal more about themselves than about Hamlet— something we as readers and viewers might well bear in mind. Rosencrantz and Guildenstern think in political terms, reflecting their own ambitious natures, and Hamlet takes mordant delight in leading them on. "Sir, I lack advancement," he mockingly answers Rosencrantz's questioning as to the cause of his distemper. Rosencrantz is immediately taken in: "How can that be, when you have the voice of the King himself for your succession in Denmark?" (3.2.338–41). Actually, Hamlet does hold a grudge against Claudius for having "Popped in between th'election and my hopes" (5.2.65), using the Danish custom of "election" by the chief lords of the realm to deprive young Hamlet of the succession that would normally have been his. Nevertheless, it is a gross oversimplification to suppose that political frustration is the key to Hamlet's sorrow, and to speculate thus is presumptuous. "Why, look you now, how unworthy a thing you make of me!" Hamlet protests to Rosencrantz and Guildenstern. "You would play upon me, you would seem to know my stops, you would pluck out the heart of my mystery" (3.2.362–5). An even worse offender in the distortion of complex truth is Polonius, whose facile diagnosis of lovesickness appears to have been inspired by recollections of Polonius's own far-off youth. ("Truly in my youth I suffered much extremity for love, very near this," 2.2.189–91). Polonius's fatuous complacency in his own powers of analysis—"If circumstances lead me, I will find / Where truth is hid, though it were hid indeed / Within the center" (2.2.157–9)—reads like a parody of Hamlet's struggle to discover what is true and what is not.

Thus, although Hamlet may seem to react with excessive bitterness toward those who are set to watch over him, the corruption he decries in Denmark is both real and universal. "The time is out of joint," he laments. "Oh, cursèd spite / That ever I was born to set it right!" (1.5.197–8). How is he to proceed in setting things right? Ever since the nineteenth century, it has been fashionable to discover reasons for Hamlet's delaying his revenge. The basic Romantic approach is to find a defect, or tragic flaw, in Hamlet himself. In Coleridge's words, Hamlet suffers from "an overbalance in the contemplative faculty" and is "one who vacillates from sensibility and procrastinates from thought, and loses the power of action in the energy of resolve." More recent psychological critics, such as Freud's disciple Ernest Jones, still seek answers to the Romantics' question by explaining Hamlet's failure of will. In Jones's interpretation, Hamlet is the victim of an Oedipal trauma: he has longed unconsciously to possess his mother and for that very reason cannot bring himself to punish the hated uncle who has supplanted him in his incestuous and forbidden desire. Such interpretations suggest, among other things, that Hamlet continues to serve as a mirror in which analysts who would pluck out the heart of his mystery see an image of their own concerns—just as Rosencrantz and Guildenstern read politics, and Polonius reads lovesickness, into Hamlet's distress.

We can ask, however, not only whether the explanations for Hamlet's supposed delay are valid but also whether the question they seek to answer is itself valid. Is the delay unnecessary or excessive? The question did not even arise until the nineteenth century. Earlier audiences were evidently satisfied that Hamlet must test the Ghost's credibility, since apparitions can tell half-truths to deceive people, and that, once Hamlet has confirmed the Ghost's word, he proceeds as resolutely as his canny adversary allows. More recent criticism, perhaps reflecting a modern absorption in existentialist philosophy, has proposed that Hamlet's dilemma is a matter, not of personal failure, but of the absurdity of action itself in a corrupt world. Does what Hamlet is asked to do make any sense, given the bestial nature of humanity and the impossibility of knowing what is right? In part, it is a matter of style: Claudius's Denmark is crassly vulgar, and to combat this vulgarity on its own terms seems to require the sort of bad histrionics Hamlet derides in actors who mouth their lines or tear a passion to tatters. Hamlet's dilemma of action can best be studied in the play by comparing him with various characters who are obliged to act in situations similar to his own and who respond in meaningfully different ways.

Three young men—Hamlet, Laertes, and Fortinbras—are called upon to avenge their fathers' violent deaths. Ophelia, too, has lost a father by violent means, and her madness and death are another kind of reaction to such a loss. The responses of Laertes and Fortinbras offer rich parallels to Hamlet, in both cases implying the futility of positive and forceful action. Laertes thinks he has received an unambiguous mandate to take revenge, since Hamlet has undoubtedly slain Polonius and helped to deprive Ophelia of her sanity. Accordingly, Laertes comes back to Denmark in a fury, stirring the rabble with his demagoguery and spouting Senecan rant about dismissing conscience "to the profoundest pit" in his quest for vengeance (4.5.135). When Claudius asks what Laertes would do to Hamlet "To show yourself in deed your father's son / More than in words," Laertes fires back: "To cut his throat i'th' church" (4.7.126–7). This resolution is understandable. The pity is, however, that Laertes has only superficially identified the murderer in the case. He is too easily deceived by Claudius, because he has jumped to easy and fallacious conclusions, and so is doomed to become a pawn in Claudius's sly maneuverings. Too late he sees his error and must die for it, begging and receiving Hamlet's forgiveness. Before we accuse Hamlet of thinking too deliberately before acting, we must consider that Laertes does not think enough.

Fortinbras of Norway, as his name implies ("strong in arms"), is one who believes in decisive action. At the beginning of the play, we learn that his father has been slain in battle by old Hamlet and that Fortinbras has collected an army to win back by force the territory fairly won by the Danes in that encounter. Like Hamlet, young Fortinbras does not succeed his father to the throne but must now contend with an uncle-king. When this uncle, at Claudius's instigation, forbids Fortinbras to march against the Danes and rewards him for his restraint with a huge annual income and a commission to fight the Poles instead, Fortinbras sagaciously welcomes the new opportunity. He pockets the money, marches against Poland, and waits for occasion to deliver Denmark as well into his hands. Clearly this is more of a success story than that of Laertes, and Hamlet does, after all, give his blessing to the "election" of Fortinbras to the Danish throne. Fortinbras is the man of the hour, the representative of a restored political stability. Yet Hamlet's admiration for this man on horseback is qualified by a profound reservation. Hamlet's dying prophecy that the election will light on Fortinbras (5.2.357–8) is suffused with ironies, so much so that the incongruity is sometimes made conscious and deliberate in performance. Earlier in the play, the spectacle of Fortinbras marching against Poland "to gain a little patch of ground / That hath in it no profit but the name" prompts Hamlet to berate himself for inaction, but he cannot ignore the absurdity of the effort. "Two thousand souls and twenty thousand ducats / Will not debate the question of this straw." The soldiers will risk their very lives "Even for an eggshell" (4.4.19–54). It is only one step from this view of the vanity of ambitious striving to the speculation that great Caesar or Alexander, dead and turned to dust, may one day produce the loam or clay with which to stop the bunghole of a beer barrel. Fortinbras epitomizes the ongoing political order after Hamlet's death, but is that order of any consequence to us after we have imagined with Hamlet the futility of most human endeavor?

To ask such a question is to seek passive or self-abnegating answers to the riddle of life, and Hamlet is attuned to such inquiries. Even before he learns of his father's murder, he contemplates suicide, wishing "that the Everlasting had not fixed / His canon 'gainst self-slaughter" (1.2.131–2). As with the alternative of action, other characters serve as foils to Hamlet, revealing both the attractions and perils of withdrawal. Ophelia is destroyed by meekly acquiescing in others' desires. Whether she commits suicide is uncertain, but the very possibility reminds us that Hamlet has twice considered and reluctantly rejected this despairing path as forbidden by Christian teaching—the second such occasion being his "To be, or not to be" soliloquy in 3.1. He has also playacted at the madness to which Ophelia succumbs. Gertrude identifies herself with Ophelia and like her has surrendered her will to male aggressiveness. We suspect she knows little of the actual murder (see 3.4.31) but dares not think how deeply she may be implicated. Although her death is evidently not a suicide (see 5.2.291–7), it is passive and expiatory.

A more attractive alternative to decisive action for Hamlet is acting in the theater, and he is full of exuberant advice to the visiting players. The play they perform before Claudius at Hamlet's request and with some lines added by him—a play consciously archaic in style—offers to the Danish court a kind of heightened reflection of itself, a homiletic artifact, rendering in conventional terms the taut anxieties and terrors of murder for the sake of noble passion. Structurally, the play within the play becomes not an escape for Hamlet into inaction but rather the point on which the whole drama pivots and the scene in which contemplation of past events is largely replaced with stirrings toward action. When Lucianus in the Mousetrap play turns out to be nephew rather than brother to the dead king, the audience finds itself face to face, not with history, but with prophecy. We are not surprised when, in his conversations with the players, Hamlet openly professes his admiration for the way in which art holds "the mirror up to nature, to show virtue her feature, scorn her own image, and the very age and body of the time his form and pressure" (3.2.22–4). Hamlet admires the dramatist's ability to transmute raw human feeling into tragic art, depicting and ordering reality as Shakespeare's play of *Hamlet* does for us. Yet playacting can also be, Hamlet recognizes, a self-indulgent escape for him, a way of unpacking his heart with words and of verbalizing his situation without doing something to remedy it. Acting and talking remind him too much of Polonius, who was an actor in his youth and who continues to be, like Hamlet, an inveterate punster.

Of the passive responses in the play, the stoicism of Horatio is by far the most attractive to Hamlet. "More an antique Roman than a Dane" (5.2.343), Horatio is, as Hamlet praises him, immune to flattering or to opportunities for cheap self-advancement. He is "As one, in suffering all, that suffers nothing, / A man that Fortune's buffets and rewards / Hast ta'en with equal thanks" (3.2.65–7). Such a person has a sure defense against the worst that life can offer. Hamlet can trust and love Horatio as he can no one else. Yet even here there are limits, for Horatio's skeptical and Roman philosophy cuts him off from a Christian and metaphysical overview. "There are more things in heaven and earth, Horatio, / Than are dreamt of in your philosophy" (1.5.175–6). After they have beheld together the skulls of Yorick's graveyard, Horatio seemingly does not share with Hamlet the exulting Christian perception that, although human life is indeed vain, Providence will reveal a pattern transcending human sorrow.

Hamlet's path must lie somewhere between the rash suddenness of Laertes or the canny resoluteness of Fortinbras on the one hand, and the passivity of Ophelia or Gertrude and the stoic resignation of Horatio on the other. At first he alternates between action and inaction, finding neither satisfactory. The Ghost has commanded Hamlet to revenge but has not explained how this is to be done; indeed, Gertrude is to be left passively to heaven and her conscience. If this method will suffice for her (and Christian wisdom taught that such a purgation was as thorough as it was sure), why not for Claudius? If Claudius must be killed, should it be while he is at his sin rather than at his prayers? The play is full of questions, stemming chiefly from the enigmatic commands of the Ghost. "Say, why is this? Wherefore? What should we do?" (1.4.57). Hamlet is not incapable of action. He shows unusual strength and cunning on the pirate ship, in his duel with Laertes ("I shall win at the odds"; 5.2.209), and especially in his slaying of Polonius—an action hardly characterized by "thinking too precisely on th'event" (4.4.42). Here is forthright action of the sort Laertes espouses. Yet, when the corpse behind his mother's arras turns out to be Polonius rather than Claudius, Hamlet concludes from the mistake that he has offended heaven. Even if Polonius deserves what he got, Hamlet believes he has made himself into a cruel "scourge" of Providence who must himself suffer retribution as well as deal it out. Swift action has not accomplished what the Ghost commanded.

The Ghost does not appear to speak for Providence in any case. His message is of revenge, a pagan concept deeply embedded in most societies but at odds with Christian teaching. His wish that Claudius be sent to hell and that Gertrude be more gently treated might, in fact, be the judgment of an impartial deity but here comes wrapped in the passionate involvement of a murdered man's restless spirit. This is not to say that Hamlet is being tempted to perform a damnable act, as he fears is possible, but that the Ghost's command cannot readily be reconciled with a complex and balanced view of justice. If Hamlet were to spring on Claudius in the fullness of his vice and cut his throat, we would pronounce Hamlet a murderer. What Hamlet believes he has learned instead is that he must become the instrument of Providence according to *its* plans, not his own. After his return from England, he senses triumphantly that all will be for the best if he allows an unseen power to decide the time and place for his final act. Under these conditions, rash action will be right. "Rashly, / And praised be rashness for it— let us know / Our indiscretion sometime serves us well / When our deep plots do pall, and that should learn us / There's a divinity that shapes our ends, / Rough-hew them how we will" (5.2.6–11). Passivity, too, is now a proper course, for Hamlet puts himself wholly at the disposal of Providence. What had seemed so impossible when Hamlet tried to formulate his own design proves elementary once he trusts to a divine justice in which he now firmly believes. Rashness and passivity are perfectly fused. Hamlet is revenged without having to commit premeditated murder and is relieved of his painful existence without having to commit suicide.

The circumstances of *Hamlet'* s catastrophe do indeed seem to accomplish all that Hamlet desires, by a route so circuitous that no one could ever have foreseen or devised

it. Polonius's death, as it turns out, was instrumental after all, for it led to Laertes's angry return to Denmark and the challenge to a duel. Every seemingly unrelated event has its place; "There is special providence in the fall of a sparrow" (5.2.217–18). Repeatedly, the characters stress the role of seeming accident leading to just retribution. Even Horatio, for whom the events of the play suggest a pattern of randomness and violence, of "accidental judgments" and "casual slaughters," can see at last, "in this upshot, purposes mistook / Fall'n on th'inventors' heads" (5.2.384–7). In a similar vein, Laertes confesses himself "a woodcock to mine own springe" (line 309). As Hamlet had said earlier, of Rosencrantz and Guildenstern, " 'tis the sport to have the engineer / Hoist with his own petard" (3.4.213–14). Thus, too, Claudius's poisoned cup, intended for Hamlet, kills the Queen for whom Claudius had done such evil in order to acquire her and the throne. The destiny of evil in this play is to overreach itself.

In its final resolution, *Hamlet* incorporates a broader conception of justice than its revenge formula seemed at first to make possible. Yet, in its origins, *Hamlet* is a revenge story, and these traditions have left some residual savagery in the play. In the *Historia Danica* of Saxo Grammaticus, 1180–1208, and in the rather free translation of Saxo into French by François de Belleforest, *Histoires Tragiques* (1576), Hamlet is cunning and bloodily resolute throughout. He kills an eavesdropper without a qualm during the interview with his mother and exchanges letters on his way to England with characteristic shrewdness. Ultimately, he returns to Denmark, sets fire to his uncle's hall, slays its courtly inhabitants, and claims his rightful throne from a grateful people. The Ghost, absent in this account, may well have been derived from Thomas Kyd's *The Spanish Tragedy* (c. 1587) and perhaps a lost *Hamlet* play in existence by 1589. *The Spanish Tragedy* bears many resemblances to our *Hamlet* and suggests what the lost *Hamlet* may well have contained: a sensational murder, a Senecan Ghost demanding revenge, the avenger hampered by court intrigue, his resort to a feigned madness, and his difficulty in authenticating the ghostly vision. A German version of *Hamlet*, called *Der bestrafte Brudermord* (1710), based seemingly on the older *Hamlet*, includes such details as the play within the play, the sparing of the King at his prayers in order to damn his soul, Ophelia's madness, the fencing match with poisoned swords and poisoned drink, and the final catastrophe of vengeance and death. Similarly, the early unauthorized first quarto of *Hamlet* (1603) offers some passages seemingly based on the older play by Kyd.

Although this evidence suggests that Shakespeare received most of the material for the plot intact, his transformation of that material was nonetheless immeasurable. To be sure, Kyd's *The Spanish Tragedy* contains many rhetorical passages on the inadequacy of human justice, but the overall effect is still sensational and the outcome is a triumph for the pagan spirit of revenge. So, too, with the many revenge plays of the 1590s and 1600s that Kyd's dramatic genius had inspired, including Shakespeare's own *Titus Andronicus* (c. 1589–1592). *Hamlet*, written in about 1599–1601 (it is not mentioned by Frances Meres in his *Palladis Tamia: Wit's Treasury*, in 1598, and was entered in the Stationers' Register, the official record book of the London Company of Stationers [booksellers and printers], in 1602), is unparalleled in its philosophical richness. Its ending is truly cathartic, for Hamlet dies, not as a bloodied avenger, but as one who has affirmed the tragic dignity of the human race. His courage and faith, maintained in the face of great odds, atone for the dismal corruption in which Denmark has festered. His resolutely honest inquiries have taken him beyond the revulsion and doubt that express so eloquently, among other matters, the fearful response of Shakespeare's own generation to a seeming breakdown of established political, theological, and cosmological beliefs. Hamlet finally perceives that "if it be not now, yet it will come," and that "The readiness is all" (5.2.219–20). This discovery, this revelation of necessity and meaning in Hamlet's great reversal of fortune, enables him to confront the tragic circumstance of his life with understanding and heroism and to demonstrate the triumph of the human spirit even in the moment of his catastrophe.

Such an assertion of the individual will does not lessen the tragic waste with which *Hamlet* ends. Hamlet is dead, and the great promise of his life is forever lost. Few others have survived. Justice has seemingly been fulfilled in the deaths of Claudius, Gertrude, Rosencrantz and Guildenstern, Polonius, Laertes, and perhaps even Ophelia, but in a wild and extravagant way, as though Justice herself, more vengeful than providential, were unceasingly hungry for victims. Hamlet, the minister of that justice, has likewise grown indifferent to the spilling of blood, even if he submits himself at last to the will of a force he recognizes as providential. Denmark faces the kind of political uncertainty with which the play began. However much Hamlet may admire Fortinbras's resolution, the prince of Norway seems an alien choice for Denmark—even an ironic one. Horatio sees so little point in outliving the catastrophe of this play that he would choose death, were it not that he must draw his breath in pain to ensure that Hamlet's story is truly told. Still, that truth has been rescued from oblivion. Amid the ruin of the final scene, we share the artist's vision, through which we struggle to interpret and give order to the tragedy that proves inseparable from human existence.

The performance history of *Hamlet* is extraordinarily rich. It also attests to a variety of interpetations that is equally textured. Eighteenth-century versions by David Garrick and others often took out or severely reduced the Fortinbras plot; indeed, the play is so long that it almost certainly was not acted in its entirety even in Shake-speare's day. Garrick also deleted the Gravediggers' scene and much besides in Act 5. Pictorial scenery in the nineteenth century tended to favor opulent renditions of the play-within-the-play and Ophelia's mad scenes. Hamlet was portrayed in 1864, at the Lyceum Theater, as a Viking in a primitive medieval decor. Henry Irving, undertaking the role of Hamlet from 1864 to 1885, chose a decor of the fifth or sixth century, with castle battlements set among massive rocks glimmering under the soft light of the moon in the first act. John Gielgud became famous as a leading Hamlet of his day, beginning in 1930 at the Old Vic, emphasizing the pale, introspective, sonorous-voiced Hamlet that Coleridge had imagined. More recently, *Hamlet* has been seen from an existential vantage (by Tyrone Guthrie, 1938, at the Old Vic) in the modern-dress context of a Europe precariously trapped between the first World War and a second about to begin. Laurence Olivier, in his film version of 1948, explored the Freudian dimensions of "a man who could not make up his mind"; influenced by Ernest Jones's *Hamlet and Oedipus*, Olivier allowed the camera eye to linger on the Queen's bedchamber and its bed, where Hamlet encountered his mother in a scene (3.4) heavy with incestuous overtones.

Recent productions on stage, in film, and on television amply demonstrate how Shakespeare's best-known play can lend itself to other kinds of relevance to our modern world. Political interpretations sometimes focus on Claudius as a Machiavel in the school of modern spin-doctoring. At the Wisdom Bridge Theater's Chicago production in the 1970s, for example, directed by Robert Falls with Aiden Quinn as Hamlet, Claudius was the Great Communicator in the style of Ronald Reagan. His first scene (1.2) featured the new king on an array of television sets, blandly explaining to the Danish public the reasons for his rapid assumption of power and marriage with the widow of his dead brother. Claudius and Gertrude never appeared onstage in this scene; the audience saw the king on television, while the stage itself was given over to his zealous public relations team, nattily dressed, preparing a reception for the press representatives, making sure the event went smoothly. Fading posters of the dead king offered contrasting reminders of the regime which Claudius had so astutely supplanted.

More recently, in Michael Almereyda's low-budget film of 2000, the setting throughout is the New York world of privilege and high finance. Claudius (Kyle MacLachlan) is a chief executive officer of a superconglomerate financial empire. Gertrude (Diane Venora) is a suburban wife utterly seduced by the expensive privileges she now enjoys, of stretch limousines, private bathing pools in their high-rise empire, and the surroundings of obsequious flattery that immense wealth can command. Hamlet (Ethan Hawke), conversely, is a rebel with a cause, ostentatiously out of step in his moth-eaten ski cap, his scruffy clothes, his mania for the latest film and computer technology, and his disdain for corrupting privilege. The ghost of Hamlet's father (Sam Shepard) eerily appears on the swank penthouse battlements of New York's concrete skyscrapers, berattling the television monitors of up-to-date security systems. The overall effect is indeed strikingly modern and plausible. Another popular film version is that of Franco Zeffirelli (1990), with Mel Gibson as a matinee idol Hamlet, Alan Bates as a believably sexy Claudius, Glenn Close as a Gertrude who is erotically infatuated with her new husband, and some compellingly handsome scenery. Grigori Kozintsev's Russian film version of 1964, based on a script by Boris Pasternak, is visually eloquent in its recurring images of stone, iron, fire, sea, and earth. Kenneth Branagh's four-hour *Hamlet* (1996) is notable for its intrepedity in offering an essentially uncut version and for

some superb performances, especially that of Derek Jacobi as Claudius. Jacobi had starred earlier as Hamlet onstage (Old Vic, 1979) and in the BBC television series of all the plays beginning in 1979. Richard Burton's memorable stage performance (1964, at New York's Lunt-Fontanne Theater) is available on video. This play is especially fortunate in a rich archive of filmed or televised versions that make possible a comparative study in production by some of the greatest Shakespearean actors of the twentieth and twenty-first centuries. These varied interpretations abundantly show how *Hamlet* and its fascinating protagonist can be satirical, rebellious, mordant, funny, disillusioned, melancholic, introspective, and much more. The play that puzzles and fascinates readers is also immensely disturbing in performance.

Hamlet, Prince of Denmark

[*Dramatis Personae*

GHOST *of Hamlet, the former King of Denmark*
CLAUDIUS, *King of Denmark, the former King's brother*
GERTRUDE, *Queen of Denmark, widow of the former King and now wife of Claudius*
HAMLET, *Prince of Denmark, son of the late King and of Gertrude*

POLONIUS, *councillor to the King*
LAERTES, *his son*
OPHELIA, *his daughter*
REYNALDO, *his servant*

HORATIO, *Hamlet's friend and fellow student*

VOLTIMAND,
CORNELIUS,
ROSENCRANTZ,
GUILDENSTERN, } *members of the Danish court*
OSRIC,
A GENTLEMAN,
A LORD,

SCENE: *Denmark*]

BERNARDO,
FRANCISCO, } *officers and soldiers on watch*
MARCELLUS,

FORTINBRAS, *Prince of Norway*
CAPTAIN *in his army*

Three or Four PLAYERS, *taking the roles of* PROLOGUE, PLAYER KING, PLAYER QUEEN, *and* LUCIANUS
Two MESSENGERS
FIRST SAILOR
Two CLOWNS, *a gravedigger and his companion*
PRIEST
FIRST AMBASSADOR *from England*

Lords, Soldiers, Attendants, Guards, other Players, Followers of Laertes, other Sailors, another Ambassador or Ambassadors from England

[1.1]

Enter Bernardo and Francisco, two sentinels,
[meeting].

BERNARDO   Who's there?

FRANCISCO

Nay, answer me. Stand and unfold yourself.   2

BERNARDO   Long live the King!

FRANCISCO   Bernardo?

BERNARDO   He.

FRANCISCO

You come most carefully upon your hour.

BERNARDO

'Tis now struck twelve. Get thee to bed, Francisco.

FRANCISCO

For this relief much thanks. 'Tis bitter cold,
And I am sick at heart.

BERNARDO   Have you had quiet guard?

FRANCISCO   Not a mouse stirring.

BERNARDO   Well, good night.
If you do meet Horatio and Marcellus,
The rivals of my watch, bid them make haste.   14

Enter Horatio and Marcellus.

FRANCISCO

I think I hear them.—Stand, ho! Who is there?

HORATIO   Friends to this ground.   16

MARCELLUS   And liegemen to the Dane.   17

FRANCISCO   Give you good night.   18

MARCELLUS

Oh, farewell, honest soldier. Who hath relieved you?

FRANCISCO

Bernardo hath my place. Give you good night.
                                                  Exit Francisco.

MARCELLUS   Holla! Bernardo!

BERNARDO   Say, what, is Horatio there?

HORATIO   A piece of him.

BERNARDO

Welcome, Horatio. Welcome, good Marcellus.

HORATIO

What, has this thing appeared again tonight?

BERNARDO   I have seen nothing.

MARCELLUS

Horatio says 'tis but our fantasy,   27
And will not let belief take hold of him
Touching this dreaded sight twice seen of us.
Therefore I have entreated him along   30
With us to watch the minutes of this night,   31
That if again this apparition come
He may approve our eyes and speak to it.   33

HORATIO

Tush, tush, 'twill not appear.

BERNARDO   Sit down awhile

And let us once again assail your ears,
That are so fortified against our story,
What we have two nights seen.

HORATIO   Well, sit we down,
And let us hear Bernardo speak of this.

BERNARDO   Last night of all,   39
When yond same star that's westward from the pole   40
Had made his course t'illume that part of heaven   41
Where now it burns, Marcellus and myself,
The bell then beating one—

Enter Ghost.

MARCELLUS

Peace, break thee off! Look where it comes again!

BERNARDO

In the same figure like the King that's dead.

MARCELLUS

Thou art a scholar. Speak to it, Horatio.   46

BERNARDO

Looks 'a not like the King? Mark it, Horatio.   47

HORATIO

Most like. It harrows me with fear and wonder.

BERNARDO

It would be spoke to.

MARCELLUS   Speak to it, Horatio.   49

HORATIO

What art thou that usurp'st this time of night,   50
Together with that fair and warlike form
In which the majesty of buried Denmark   52
Did sometimes march? By heaven, I charge thee, speak!   53

MARCELLUS

It is offended.

BERNARDO   See, it stalks away.

HORATIO

Stay! Speak, speak! I charge thee, speak!   *Exit Ghost.*

MARCELLUS   'Tis gone and will not answer.

BERNARDO

How now, Horatio? You tremble and look pale.
Is not this something more than fantasy?
What think you on't?   59

HORATIO

Before my God, I might not this believe
Without the sensible and true avouch   61
Of mine own eyes.

MARCELLUS   Is it not like the King?

HORATIO   As thou art to thyself.
Such was the very armor he had on
When he the ambitious Norway combated.   65
So frowned he once when, in an angry parle,   66
He smote the sledded Polacks on the ice.   67
'Tis strange.

1.1. Location: Elsinore castle. A guard platform.
2 me (Francisco emphasizes that *he* is the sentry currently on watch.)
unfold yourself reveal your identity.   **14 rivals** partners   **16 ground**
country, land.   **17 liegemen to the Dane** men sworn to serve the
Danish king.   **18 Give** May God give   **27 fantasy** imagination
30 along to come along   **31 watch** keep watch during   **33 approve**
corroborate

39 Last . . . all i.e., This *very* last night. (Emphatic.)   **40 pole** polestar,
north star   **41 his** its.   **t'illume** to illuminate   **46 scholar** one
learned enough to know how to question a ghost properly.   **47 'a** he
49 It . . . to (It was commonly believed that a ghost could not speak
until spoken to.)   **50 usurp'st** wrongfully takes over   **52 buried**
Denmark the buried King of Denmark   **53 sometimes** formerly
59 on't of it.   **61 sensible** confirmed by the senses.   **avouch** warrant,
evidence   **65 Norway** King of Norway   **66 parle** parley   **67 sledded**
traveling on sleds.   **Polacks** Poles

MARCELLUS

Thus twice before, and jump at this dead hour,   69
With martial stalk hath he gone by our watch.   70

HORATIO

In what particular thought to work I know not,   71
But in the gross and scope of mine opinion   72
This bodes some strange eruption to our state.

MARCELLUS

Good now, sit down, and tell me, he that knows,   74
Why this same strict and most observant watch
So nightly toils the subject of the land,   76
And why such daily cast of brazen cannon   77
And foreign mart for implements of war,   78
Why such impress of shipwrights, whose sore task   79
Does not divide the Sunday from the week.
What might be toward, that this sweaty haste   81
Doth make the night joint-laborer with the day?
Who is't that can inform me?

HORATIO   That can I;
At least, the whisper goes so. Our last king,
Whose image even but now appeared to us,
Was, as you know, by Fortinbras of Norway,
Thereto pricked on by a most emulate pride,   87
Dared to the combat; in which our valiant Hamlet—
For so this side of our known world esteemed him—   89
Did slay this Fortinbras; who by a sealed compact   90
Well ratified by law and heraldry   91
Did forfeit, with his life, all those his lands
Which he stood seized of, to the conqueror;   93
Against the which a moiety competent   94
Was gagèd by our king, which had returned   95
To the inheritance of Fortinbras   96
Had he been vanquisher, as, by the same cov'nant   97
And carriage of the article designed,   98
His fell to Hamlet. Now, sir, young Fortinbras,
Of unimprovèd mettle hot and full,   100
Hath in the skirts of Norway here and there   101
Sharked up a list of lawless resolutes   102
For food and diet to some enterprise   103
That hath a stomach in't, which is no other—   104
As it doth well appear unto our state—
But to recover of us, by strong hand
And terms compulsatory, those foresaid lands
So by his father lost. And this, I take it,
Is the main motive of our preparations,

The source of this our watch, and the chief head   110
Of this posthaste and rummage in the land.   111

BERNARDO

I think it be no other but e'en so.
Well may it sort that this portentous figure   113
Comes armèd through our watch so like the King
That was and is the question of these wars.   115

HORATIO

A mote it is to trouble the mind's eye.   116
In the most high and palmy state of Rome,   117
A little ere the mightiest Julius fell,   118
The graves stood tenantless, and the sheeted dead   119
Did squeak and gibber in the Roman streets;
As stars with trains of fire and dews of blood,   121
Disasters in the sun; and the moist star   122
Upon whose influence Neptune's empire stands   123
Was sick almost to doomsday with eclipse.   124
And even the like precurse of feared events,   125
As harbingers preceding still the fates   126
And prologue to the omen coming on,   127
Have heaven and earth together demonstrated
Unto our climatures and countrymen.   129

Enter Ghost.

But soft, behold! Lo, where it comes again!   130
I'll cross it, though it blast me. (*It spreads his arms.*) Stay,
    illusion!   131
If thou hast any sound or use of voice,
Speak to me!
If there be any good thing to be done
That may to thee do ease and grace to me,
Speak to me!
If thou art privy to thy country's fate,   137
Which, happily, foreknowing may avoid,   138
Oh, speak!
Or if thou hast uphoarded in thy life
Extorted treasure in the womb of earth,
For which, they say, you spirits oft walk in death,
Speak of it! (*The cock crows.*) Stay and speak!—Stop it,
    Marcellus.

MARCELLUS

Shall I strike at it with my partisan?   144

HORATIO   Do, if it will not stand.   [*They strike at it.*]

BERNARDO   'Tis here!   146

HORATIO   'Tis here!   [*Exit Ghost.*]   147

---

69 jump exactly   **70 stalk** stride   **71 to work** i.e., to collect my thoughts and try to understand this   **72 gross and scope** general drift   **74 Good now** (An expression denoting entreaty or expostulation.)   **76 toils** causes to toil.   **subject** subjects   **77 cast** casting   **78 mart** shopping   **79 impress** impressment, conscription   **81 toward** in preparation   **87 Thereto . . . pride** (Refers to old Fortinbras, not the Danish King.)   **pricked on** incited.   **emulate** emulous, ambitious   **89 this . . . world** i.e., all Europe, the Western world   **90 sealed** certified, confirmed   **91 heraldry** chivalry   **93 seized** possessed   **94 Against the** in return for.   **moiety competent** corresponding portion   **95 gagèd** engaged, pledged.   **had returned** would have passed   **96 inheritance** possession   **97 cov'nant** i.e., the *sealed compact* of line 90   **98 carriage . . . designed** purport of the article referred to   **100 unimprovèd mettle** untried, undisciplined spirits   **101 skirts** outlying regions, outskirts   **102–4 Sharked . . . in't** rounded up (as a shark scoops up fish) a troop of lawless desperadoes to feed and supply an enterprise of considerable daring

110 head source   **111 posthaste and rummage** frenetic activity and bustle   **113 Well . . . sort** That would explain why   **115 question** focus of contention   **116 mote** speck of dust   **117 palmy** flourishing   **118 Julius** Julius Caesar   **119 sheeted** shrouded   **121 As** (This abrupt transition suggests that matter is possibly omitted between lines 120 and 121.)   **trains** trails   **122 Disasters** unfavorable signs or aspects.   **moist star** i.e., moon, governing tides   **123 Neptune's . . . stands** the sea depends   **124 Was . . . eclipse** was eclipsed nearly to the cosmic darkness predicted for the second coming of Christ and the ending of the world. (See Matthew 24:29 and Revelation 6:12.)   **125 precurse** heralding, foreshadowing   **126 harbingers** forerunners.   **still** always   **127 omen** calamitous event   **129 climatures** climes, regions   **130 soft** i.e., enough, break off   **131 cross** stand in its path, confront.   **blast** wither, strike with a curse.   **131 s.d. his** its   **137 privy to** in on the secret of   **138 happily** haply, perchance   **144 partisan** long-handled spear.   **146–7 'Tis Here! / 'Tis here!** (Perhaps they attempt to strike at the Ghost, but are baffled by its seeming ability to be here and there and nowhere.)

MARCELLUS   'Tis gone.
We do it wrong, being so majestical,
To offer it the show of violence,
For it is as the air invulnerable,
And our vain blows malicious mockery.

BERNARDO
It was about to speak when the cock crew.

HORATIO
And then it started like a guilty thing
Upon a fearful summons. I have heard
The cock, that is the trumpet to the morn,   156
Doth with his lofty and shrill-sounding throat
Awake the god of day, and at his warning,
Whether in sea or fire, in earth or air,
Th'extravagant and erring spirit hies   160
To his confine; and of the truth herein
This present object made probation.   162

MARCELLUS
It faded on the crowing of the cock.
Some say that ever 'gainst that season comes   164
Wherein our Savior's birth is celebrated,
This bird of dawning singeth all night long,
And then, they say, no spirit dare stir abroad;
The nights are wholesome, then no planets strike,   168
No fairy takes, nor witch hath power to charm,   169
So hallowed and so gracious is that time.   170

HORATIO
So have I heard and do in part believe it.
But, look, the morn in russet mantle clad   172
Walks o'er the dew of yon high eastward hill.
Break we our watch up, and by my advice
Let us impart what we have seen tonight
Unto young Hamlet; for upon my life,
This spirit, dumb to us, will speak to him.
Do you consent we shall acquaint him with it,
As needful in our loves, fitting our duty?

MARCELLUS
Let's do't, I pray, and I this morning know
Where we shall find him most conveniently.

                                    Exeunt.

[1.2]

Flourish. Enter Claudius, King of Denmark,
Gertrude the Queen, [the] Council, as Polonius
and his son Laertes, Hamlet, cum aliis [including
Voltimand and Cornelius].

KING
Though yet of Hamlet our dear brother's death   1
The memory be green, and that it us befitted
To bear our hearts in grief and our whole kingdom
To be contracted in one brow of woe,
Yet so far hath discretion fought with nature
That we with wisest sorrow think on him
Together with remembrance of ourselves.
Therefore our sometime sister, now our queen,   8
Th'imperial jointress to this warlike state,   9
Have we, as 'twere with a defeated joy—
With an auspicious and a dropping eye,   11
With mirth in funeral and with dirge in marriage,
In equal scale weighing delight and dole—   13
Taken to wife. Nor have we herein barred
Your better wisdoms, which have freely gone
With this affair along. For all, our thanks.
Now follows that you know young Fortinbras,   17
Holding a weak supposal of our worth,   18
Or thinking by our late dear brother's death
Our state to be disjoint and out of frame,   20
Co-leaguèd with this dream of his advantage,   21
He hath not failed to pester us with message
Importing the surrender of those lands   23
Lost by his father, with all bonds of law,   24
To our most valiant brother. So much for him.
Now for ourself and for this time of meeting.
Thus much the business is: we have here writ
To Norway, uncle of young Fortinbras—
Who, impotent and bed-rid, scarcely hears   29
Of this his nephew's purpose—to suppress
His further gait herein, in that the levies,   31
The lists, and full proportions are all made   32
Out of his subject; and we here dispatch   33
You, good Cornelius, and you, Voltimand,
For bearers of this greeting to old Norway,
Giving to you no further personal power
To business with the King more than the scope
Of these dilated articles allow.   [*He gives a paper.*] 38
Farewell, and let your haste commend your duty.   39

CORNELIUS, VOLTIMAND
In that, and all things, will we show our duty.

KING
We doubt it nothing. Heartily farewell.   41
                [*Exeunt Voltimand and Cornelius.*]
And now, Laertes, what's the news with you?
You told us of some suit; what is't, Laertes?
You cannot speak of reason to the Dane   44
And lose your voice. What wouldst thou beg, Laertes,   45
That shall not be my offer, not thy asking?
The head is not more native to the heart,   47

---

156 **trumpet** trumpeter   160 **extravagant and erring** wandering
beyond bounds. (The words have similar meaning.)   **hies** hastens
162 **probation** proof.   164 **'gainst** just before   168 **strike** destroy by
evil influence   169 **takes** bewitches.   **charm** cast a spell, control by
enchantment   170 **gracious** full of grace   172 **russet** reddish brown
1.2. Location: The castle.
0.2 *as* i.e., such as, including.   0.3 *cum aliis* with others   1 **our** my.
(The royal "we"; also in the following lines.)

8 **sometime** former   9 **jointress** woman possessing property with
her husband   11 **With . . . eye** with one eye smiling and the other
weeping   13 **dole** grief   17 **Now . . . know** Next, you need to be
informed that   18 **weak supposal** low estimate   20 **disjoint . . .
frame** in a state of total disorder   21 **Co-leaguèd . . . advantage**
joined to his illusory sense of having the advantage over us and to
his vision of future success   23 **Importing** having for its substance
24 **with . . . law** (See 1.1.91, "Well ratified by law and heraldry.")
29 **impotent** helpless   31 **His** i.e., Fortinbras'.   **gait** proceeding
31–3 **in that . . . subject** since the levying of troops and supplies is
drawn entirely from the King of Norway's own subjects   38 **dilated**
set out at length   39 **let . . . duty** let your swift obeying of orders,
rather than mere words, express your dutifulness.   41 **nothing** not
at all.   44 **the Dane** the Danish king   45 **lose your voice** waste your
speech.   47 **native** closely connected, related

The hand more instrumental to the mouth, 48
Than is the throne of Denmark to thy father.
What wouldst thou have, Laertes?

LAERTES   My dread lord,
Your leave and favor to return to France, 51
From whence though willingly I came to Denmark
To show my duty in your coronation,
Yet now I must confess, that duty done,
My thoughts and wishes bend again toward France
And bow them to your gracious leave and pardon. 56

KING
Have you your father's leave? What says Polonius?

POLONIUS
H'ath, my lord, wrung from me my slow leave 58
By laborsome petition, and at last
Upon his will I sealed my hard consent. 60
I do beseech you, give him leave to go.

KING
Take thy fair hour, Laertes. Time be thine, 62
And thy best graces spend it at thy will. 63
But now, my cousin Hamlet, and my son— 64

HAMLET
A little more than kin, and less than kind. 65

KING
How is it that the clouds still hang on you?

HAMLET
Not so, my lord. I am too much in the sun. 67

QUEEN
Good Hamlet, cast thy nighted color off, 68
And let thine eye look like a friend on Denmark. 69
Do not forever with thy vailèd lids 70
Seek for thy noble father in the dust.
Thou know'st 'tis common, all that lives must die, 72
Passing through nature to eternity.

HAMLET
Ay, madam, it is common.

QUEEN   If it be,
Why seems it so particular with thee? 75

HAMLET
Seems, madam? Nay, it is. I know not "seems."
'Tis not alone my inky cloak, good mother,
Nor customary suits of solemn black, 78
Nor windy suspiration of forced breath, 79

No, nor the fruitful river in the eye, 80
Nor the dejected havior of the visage, 81
Together with all forms, moods, shapes of grief, 82
That can denote me truly. These indeed seem,
For they are actions that a man might play.
But I have that within which passes show;
These but the trappings and the suits of woe.

KING
'Tis sweet and commendable in your nature, Hamlet,
To give these mourning duties to your father.
But you must know your father lost a father,
That father lost, lost his, and the survivor bound
In filial obligation for some term
To do obsequious sorrow. But to persever 92
In obstinate condolement is a course 93
Of impious stubbornness. 'Tis unmanly grief.
It shows a will most incorrect to heaven,
A heart unfortified, a mind impatient, 96
An understanding simple and unschooled. 97
For what we know must be and is as common
As any the most vulgar thing to sense, 99
Why should we in our peevish opposition
Take it to heart? Fie, 'tis a fault to heaven,
A fault against the dead, a fault to nature,
To reason most absurd, whose common theme
Is death of fathers, and who still hath cried, 104
From the first corpse till he that died today, 105
"This must be so." We pray you, throw to earth
This unprevailing woe and think of us 107
As of a father; for let the world take note,
You are the most immediate to our throne, 109
And with no less nobility of love
Than that which dearest father bears his son
Do I impart toward you. For your intent 112
In going back to school in Wittenberg, 113
It is most retrograde to our desire, 114
And we beseech you bend you to remain 115
Here in the cheer and comfort of our eye,
Our chiefest courtier, cousin, and our son.

QUEEN
Let not thy mother lose her prayers, Hamlet.
I pray thee, stay with us, go not to Wittenberg.

HAMLET
I shall in all my best obey you, madam. 120

KING
Why, 'tis a loving and a fair reply.
Be as ourself in Denmark. Madam, come.
This gentle and unforced accord of Hamlet
Sits smiling to my heart, in grace whereof 124
No jocund health that Denmark drinks today 125

---

48 instrumental serviceable **51 leave and favor** kind permission
56 bow . . . pardon entreatingly make a deep bow, asking your permission to depart. **58 H'ath** He has **60 sealed** (as if sealing a legal
document). **hard** reluctant **62 Take thy fair hour** Enjoy your time
of youth **63 And . . . will** and may your time be spent in exercising
your best qualities. **64 cousin** any kin not of the immediate family
65 A little . . . kind Too close a blood relation, and yet we are less
than kinsmen in that our relationship lacks affection and is indeed
unnatural. (Hamlet plays on *kind* as [1] kindly [2] belonging to
nature, suggesting that Claudius is not the same kind of being as the
rest of humanity. The line is often delivered as an aside, though it
need not be.) **67 the sun** i.e., the sunshine of the King's royal favor.
(With pun on *son*.) **68 nighted color** (1) mourning garments of black
(2) dark melancholy **69 Denmark** the King of Denmark. **70 vailèd
lids** lowered eyes **72 common** of universal occurrence. (But Hamlet
plays on the sense of "vulgar" in line 74.) **75 particular** personal
78 customary customary to mourning **79 suspiration** sighing

80 fruitful abundant **81 havior** expression **82 moods** outward
expression of feeling **92 obsequious** suited to obsequies or funerals
93 condolement sorrowing **96 unfortified** i.e., against adversity
97 simple ignorant **99 As . . . sense** as the most ordinary experience
104 still always **105 the first corpse** (Abel's) **107 unprevailing**
unavailing, useless **109 most immediate** next in succession
112 impart toward liberally bestow on. **For** As for **113 to school**
i.e., to your studies. **Wittenberg** famous German university where
Luther posted his 95 theses in 1517 **114 retrograde** contrary **115
bend you** incline yourself **120 in all my best** to the best of my ability **124 to** i.e., at. **grace** thanksgiving **125 jocund** merry

But the great cannon to the clouds shall tell,
And the King's rouse the heaven shall bruit again,   127
Respeaking earthly thunder. Come away.   128
Flourish. Exeunt all but Hamlet.

HAMLET
   Oh, that this too too sullied flesh would melt,   129
   Thaw, and resolve itself into a dew!
   Or that the Everlasting had not fixed
   His canon 'gainst self-slaughter! Oh, God, God,   132
   How weary, stale, flat, and unprofitable
   Seem to me all the uses of this world!
   Fie on't, ah, fie! 'Tis an unweeded garden
   That grows to seed. Things rank and gross in nature
   Possess it merely. That it should come to this!   137
   But two months dead—nay, not so much, not two.
   So excellent a king, that was to this   139
   Hyperion to a satyr, so loving to my mother   140
   That he might not beteem the winds of heaven   141
   Visit her face too roughly. Heaven and earth,
   Must I remember? Why, she would hang on him
   As if increase of appetite had grown
   By what it fed on, and yet within a month—
   Let me not think on't; frailty, thy name is woman!—
   A little month, or ere those shoes were old   147
   With which she followed my poor father's body,
   Like Niobe, all tears, why she, even she—   149
   Oh, God, a beast, that wants discourse of reason,   150
   Would have mourned longer—married with my
     uncle,
   My father's brother, but no more like my father
   Than I to Hercules. Within a month,
   Ere yet the salt of most unrighteous tears
   Had left the flushing in her gallèd eyes,   155
   She married. Oh, most wicked speed, to post   156
   With such dexterity to incestuous sheets!   157
   It is not, nor it cannot come to good.
   But break, my heart, for I must hold my tongue.

Enter Horatio, Marcellus, and Bernardo.

HORATIO
   Hail to Your Lordship!
HAMLET   I am glad to see you well.
   Horatio!—or I do forget myself.
HORATIO
   The same, my lord, and your poor servant ever.

HAMLET
   Sir, my good friend; I'll change that name with you.   163
   And what make you from Wittenberg, Horatio?—   164
   Marcellus.
MARCELLUS   My good lord.
HAMLET
   I am very glad to see you. [*To Bernardo*] Good even,
     sir.—
   But what in faith make you from Wittenberg?
HORATIO
   A truant disposition, good my lord.
HAMLET
   I would not hear your enemy say so,
   Nor shall you do my ear that violence
   To make it truster of your own report   172
   Against yourself. I know you are no truant.
   But what is your affair in Elsinore?
   We'll teach you to drink deep ere you depart.
HORATIO
   My lord, I came to see your father's funeral.
HAMLET
   I prithee, do not mock me, fellow student;
   I think it was to see my mother's wedding.
HORATIO
   Indeed, my lord, it followed hard upon.   179
HAMLET
   Thrift, thrift, Horatio! The funeral baked meats   180
   Did coldly furnish forth the marriage tables.   181
   Would I had met my dearest foe in heaven   182
   Or ever I had seen that day, Horatio!   183
   My father!—Methinks I see my father.
HORATIO
   Where, my lord?
HAMLET   In my mind's eye, Horatio.
HORATIO
   I saw him once. 'A was a goodly king.   186
HAMLET
   'A was a man. Take him for all in all,
   I shall not look upon his like again.
HORATIO
   My lord, I think I saw him yesternight.
HAMLET   Saw? Who?
HORATIO   My lord, the King your father.
HAMLET   The King my father?
HORATIO
   Season your admiration for a while   193
   With an attent ear till I may deliver,   194
   Upon the witness of these gentlemen,
   This marvel to you.
HAMLET   For God's love, let me hear!
HORATIO
   Two nights together had these gentlemen,

---

127 rouse drinking of a draft of liquor. **bruit again** loudly echo
128 thunder i.e., of trumpet and kettledrum, sounded when the King
drinks; see 1.4.8–12. **129 sullied** defiled. (The early quartos read
"sallied"; the Folio, "solid.") **132 canon** law **137 merely** completely. **139 to** in comparison to **140 Hyperion** Titan sun-god,
father of Helios. **satyr** a lecherous creature of classical mythology,
half-human but with a goat's legs, tail, ears, and horns **141 beteem**
allow **147 or ere** even before **149 Niobe** Tantalus's daughter,
Queen of Thebes, who boasted that she had more sons and daughters
than Leto; for this, Apollo and Artemis, children of Leto, slew her
fourteen children. She was turned by Zeus into a stone that continually dropped tears. **150 wants . . . reason** lacks the faculty of reason
155 gallèd irritated, inflamed **156 post** hasten **157 incestuous** (In
Shakespeare's day, the marriage of a man like Claudius to his
deceased brother's wife was considered incestuous.)

163 change that name i.e., give and receive reciprocally the name of
"friend" rather than talk of "servant." Or Hamlet may be saying,
"No, I am *your* servant." **164 make you from** are you doing away
from **172 To . . . of** to make it trust **179 hard** close **180 baked
meats** meat pies **181 coldly** i.e., as cold leftovers **182 dearest** closest (and therefore deadliest) **183 Or ever** ere, before **186 'A** He
193 Season your admiration Moderate your astonishment
194 attent attentive

Marcellus and Bernardo, on their watch,
In the dead waste and middle of the night,   199
Been thus encountered. A figure like your father,
Armèd at point exactly, cap-à-pie,   201
Appears before them, and with solemn march
Goes slow and stately by them. Thrice he walked
By their oppressed and fear-surprisèd eyes
Within his truncheon's length, whilst they, distilled   205
Almost to jelly with the act of fear,   206
Stand dumb and speak not to him. This to me
In dreadful secrecy impart they did,   208
And I with them the third night kept the watch,
Where, as they had delivered, both in time,
Form of the thing, each word made true and good,
The apparition comes. I knew your father;
These hands are not more like.

HAMLET   But where was this?
MARCELLUS
My lord, upon the platform where we watch.
HAMLET
Did you not speak to it?
HORATIO   My lord, I did,
But answer made it none. Yet once methought
It lifted up it head and did address   217
Itself to motion, like as it would speak;   218
But even then the morning cock crew loud,   219
And at the sound it shrunk in haste away
And vanished from our sight.
HAMLET   'Tis very strange.
HORATIO
As I do live, my honored lord, 'tis true,
And we did think it writ down in our duty
To let you know of it.
HAMLET
Indeed, indeed, sirs. But this troubles me.
Hold you the watch tonight?
ALL   We do, my lord.
HAMLET   Armed, say you?
ALL   Armed, my lord.
HAMLET   From top to toe?
ALL   My lord, from head to foot.
HAMLET   Then saw you not his face?
HORATIO
Oh, yes, my lord, he wore his beaver up.   232
HAMLET   What looked he, frowningly?   233
HORATIO
A countenance more in sorrow than in anger.
HAMLET   Pale or red?
HORATIO   Nay, very pale.
HAMLET   And fixed his eyes upon you?
HORATIO   Most constantly.
HAMLET   I would I had been there.
HORATIO   It would have much amazed you.
HAMLET   Very like, very like. Stayed it long?

HORATIO
While one with moderate haste might tell a hundred.   242
MARCELLUS, BERNARDO   Longer, longer.
HORATIO   Not when I saw't.
HAMLET   His beard was grizzled—no?
HORATIO
It was, as I have seen it in his life,
A sable silvered.
HAMLET   I will watch tonight.
Perchance 'twill walk again.
HORATIO   I warr'nt it will.
HAMLET
If it assume my noble father's person,
I'll speak to it though hell itself should gape
And bid me hold my peace. I pray you all,
If you have hitherto concealed this sight,
Let it be tenable in your silence still,   253
And whatsomever else shall hap tonight,
Give it an understanding but no tongue.
I will requite your loves. So, fare you well.
Upon the platform twixt eleven and twelve
I'll visit you.
ALL   Our duty to Your Honor.
HAMLET
Your loves, as mine to you. Farewell.   259
                              Exeunt [all but Hamlet].
My father's spirit in arms! All is not well.
I doubt some foul play. Would the night were come!   261
Till then sit still, my soul. Foul deeds will rise,
Though all the earth o'erwhelm them, to men's eyes.
                                                      Exit.

❖

[1.3]

Enter Laertes and Ophelia, his sister.

LAERTES
My necessaries are embarked. Farewell.
And, sister, as the winds give benefit
And convoy is assistant, do not sleep   3
But let me hear from you.
OPHELIA   Do you doubt that?
LAERTES
For Hamlet, and the trifling of his favor,   5
Hold it a fashion and a toy in blood,   6
A violet in the youth of primy nature,   7
Forward, not permanent, sweet, not lasting,   8
The perfume and suppliance of a minute—   9
No more.
OPHELIA   No more but so?
LAERTES   Think it no more.

---

199 **dead waste** desolate stillness   201 **at point** correctly in every
detail.   **cap-à-pie** from head to foot   205 **truncheon** officer's staff.
distilled dissolved   206 **act** action, operation   208 **dreadful** full
of dread   217 **it** its   217–18 **did . . . speak** prepared to move as
though it was about to speak   219 **even then** at that very instant
232 **beaver** visor on the helmet   233 **What** How

242 **tell** count   253 **tenable** held   259 **Your loves** i.e., Say "Your
loves" to me, not just your "duty."   261 **doubt** suspect
1.3. Location: Polonius's chambers.
3 **convoy is assistant** means of conveyance are available   5 **For** As
for   6 **toy in blood** passing amorous fancy   7 **primy** in its prime,
springtime   8 **Forward** precocious   9 **suppliance** pastime, something to fill the time

For nature crescent does not grow alone   11
In thews and bulk, but as this temple waxes   12
The inward service of the mind and soul   13
Grows wide withal. Perhaps he loves you now,   14
And now no soil nor cautel doth besmirch   15
The virtue of his will; but you must fear,   16
His greatness weighed, his will is not his own.   17
For he himself is subject to his birth.
He may not, as unvalued persons do,
Carve for himself, for on his choice depends   20
The safety and health of this whole state,
And therefore must his choice be circumscribed
Unto the voice and yielding of that body   23
Whereof he is the head. Then if he says he loves you,
It fits your wisdom so far to believe it
As he in his particular act and place   26
May give his saying deed, which is no further
Than the main voice of Denmark goes withal.   28
Then weigh what loss your honor may sustain
If with too credent ear you list his songs,   30
Or lose your heart, or your chaste treasure open
To his unmastered importunity.   32
Fear it, Ophelia, fear it, my dear sister,
And keep you in the rear of your affection,   34
Out of the shot and danger of desire.
The chariest maid is prodigal enough   36
If she unmask her beauty to the moon.   37
Virtue itself scapes not calumnious strokes.
The canker galls the infants of the spring   39
Too oft before their buttons be disclosed,   40
And in the morn and liquid dew of youth   41
Contagious blastments are most imminent.   42
Be wary then; best safety lies in fear.
Youth to itself rebels, though none else near.   44

OPHELIA
I shall the effect of this good lesson keep
As watchman to my heart. But, good my brother,
Do not, as some ungracious pastors do,   47
Show me the steep and thorny way to heaven,
Whiles like a puffed and reckless libertine   49
Himself the primrose path of dalliance treads,
And recks not his own rede.

Enter Polonius.

LAERTES   Oh, fear me not.   51

I stay too long. But here my father comes.
A double blessing is a double grace;   53
Occasion smiles upon a second leave.   54
POLONIUS
Yet here, Laertes? Aboard, aboard, for shame!
The wind sits in the shoulder of your sail,
And you are stayed for. There—my blessing with thee!
And these few precepts in thy memory
Look thou character. Give thy thoughts no tongue,   59
Nor any unproportioned thought his act.   60
Be thou familiar, but by no means vulgar.   61
Those friends thou hast, and their adoption tried,   62
Grapple them unto thy soul with hoops of steel,
But do not dull thy palm with entertainment   64
Of each new-hatched, unfledged courage. Beware   65
Of entrance to a quarrel, but being in,
Bear't that th'opposèd may beware of thee.   67
Give every man thy ear, but few thy voice;
Take each man's censure, but reserve thy judgment.   69
Costly thy habit as thy purse can buy,   70
But not expressed in fancy; rich, not gaudy,   71
For the apparel oft proclaims the man,
And they in France of the best rank and station
Are of a most select and generous chief in that.   74
Neither a borrower nor a lender be,
For loan oft loses both itself and friend,
And borrowing dulleth edge of husbandry.   77
This above all: to thine own self be true,
And it must follow, as the night the day,
Thou canst not then be false to any man.
Farewell. My blessing season this in thee!   81
LAERTES
Most humbly do I take my leave, my lord.
POLONIUS
The time invests you. Go, your servants tend.   83
LAERTES
Farewell, Ophelia, and remember well
What I have said to you.
OPHELIA   'Tis in my memory locked,
And you yourself shall keep the key of it.
LAERTES   Farewell.   *Exit Laertes.*
POLONIUS
What is't, Ophelia, he hath said to you?
OPHELIA
So please you, something touching the Lord Hamlet.
POLONIUS   Marry, well bethought.   91
'Tis told me he hath very oft of late
Given private time to you, and you yourself

11–14 For nature ... withal For nature, as it ripens, does not grow only in physical strength, but as the body matures the inner qualities of mind and soul grow along with it. (Laertes warns Ophelia that the mature Hamlet may not cling to his youthful interests.) 15 soil nor cautel blemish nor deceit 16 The ... will the purity of his desire 17 His greatness weighed taking into account his high fortune 20 Carve i.e., choose 23 voice and yielding assent, approval 26 in ... place in his particular restricted circumstances 28 main voice general assent. withal along with. 30 credent credulous. list listen to 32 unmastered uncontrolled 34 keep ... affection don't advance as far as your affection might lead you. (A military metaphor.) 36 chariest most scrupulously modest 37 If she unmask if she does no more than show her beauty. moon (Symbol of chastity.) 39 canker galls cankerworm destroys 40 buttons be disclosed buds be opened 41 liquid dew i.e., time when dew is fresh and bright 42 blastments blights 44 Youth ... rebels Youth yields to the rebellion of the flesh 47 ungracious ungodly 49 puffed bloated, or swollen with pride 51 recks heeds. rede counsel. fear me not don't worry on my account.

53–4 A double ... leave The goddess Occasion or Opportunity smiles on the happy circumstance of being able to say good-bye twice and thus receive a second blessing. 59 Look thou character see to it that you inscribe. 60 unproportioned badly calculated, intemperate. his its 61 familiar sociable. vulgar common. 62 and ... tried and their suitability to be your friends having been put to the test 64 dull thy palm i.e., shake hands so often as to make the gesture meaningless 65 courage swashbuckler. 67 Bear't that manage it so that 69 censure opinion, judgment 70 habit clothing 71 fancy excessive ornament, decadent fashion 74 Are ... that are of a most refined and well-bred preeminence in choosing what to wear. 77 husbandry thrift. 81 season mature 83 invests besieges, presses upon. tend attend, wait. 91 Marry i.e., By the Virgin Mary. (A mild oath.)

Have of your audience been most free and bounteous.
If it be so—as so 'tis put on me,   95
And that in way of caution—I must tell you
You do not understand yourself so clearly
As it behooves my daughter and your honor.   98
What is between you? Give me up the truth.

OPHELIA
He hath, my lord, of late made many tenders   100
Of his affection to me.

POLONIUS
Affection? Pooh! You speak like a green girl,
Unsifted in such perilous circumstance.
Do you believe his tenders, as you call them?   103

OPHELIA
I do not know, my lord, what I should think.

POLONIUS
Marry, I will teach you. Think yourself a baby
That you have ta'en these tenders for true pay
Which are not sterling. Tender yourself more dearly,   108
Or—not to crack the wind of the poor phrase,   109
Running it thus—you'll tender me a fool.   110

OPHELIA
My lord, he hath importuned me with love
In honorable fashion.

POLONIUS
Ay, fashion you may call it. Go to, go to.   113

OPHELIA
And hath given countenance to his speech, my lord,   114
With almost all the holy vows of heaven.

POLONIUS
Ay, springes to catch woodcocks. I do know,   116
When the blood burns, how prodigal the soul   117
Lends the tongue vows. These blazes, daughter,
Giving more light than heat, extinct in both
Even in their promise as it is a-making,   120
You must not take for fire. From this time
Be something scanter of your maiden presence.   122
Set your entreatments at a higher rate   123
Than a command to parle. For Lord Hamlet,   124
Believe so much in him that he is young,   125
And with a larger tether may he walk
Than may be given you. In few, Ophelia,   127
Do not believe his vows, for they are brokers,   128
Not of that dye which their investments show,   129
But mere implorators of unholy suits,   130

Breathing like sanctified and pious bawds,   131
The better to beguile. This is for all: 132
I would not, in plain terms, from this time forth
Have you so slander any moment leisure   134
As to give words or talk with the Lord Hamlet.
Look to't, I charge you. Come your ways.   136

OPHELIA   I shall obey, my lord.   Exeunt.

❖

[1.4]

Enter Hamlet, Horatio, and Marcellus.

HAMLET
The air bites shrewdly; it is very cold.   1

HORATIO
It is a nipping and an eager air.   2

HAMLET
What hour now?

HORATIO   I think it lacks of twelve.   3

MARCELLUS
No, it is struck.

HORATIO   Indeed? I heard it not.
It then draws near the season   5
Wherein the spirit held his wont to walk.   6
          A flourish of trumpets, and two pieces go off
                                                      [*within*].
What does this mean, my lord?

HAMLET
The King doth wake tonight and takes his rouse,   8
Keeps wassail, and the swagg'ring upspring reels;   9
And as he drains his drafts of Rhenish down,   10
The kettledrum and trumpet thus bray out
The triumph of his pledge.

HORATIO   Is it a custom?   12

HAMLET   Ay, marry, is't,
But to my mind, though I am native here
And to the manner born, it is a custom   15
More honored in the breach than the observance.   16
This heavy-headed revel east and west   17
Makes us traduced and taxed of other nations.   18
They clepe us drunkards, and with swinish phrase   19
Soil our addition; and indeed it takes   20
From our achievements, though performed at height,   21
The pith and marrow of our attribute.   22

---

95 put on impressed on, told to   **98 behooves** befits   **100 tenders**
offers   **103 Unsifted** i.e., untried   **108 sterling** legal currency.
Tender . . . dearly (1) Bargain for your favors at a higher rate—i.e.,
hold out for marriage (2) Show greater care of yourself   **109 crack
the wind** i.e., run it until it is broken-winded   **110 tender . . . fool** (1)
make a fool of me (2) present me with a *fool* or baby.   **113 fashion**
mere form, pretense.   **Go to** (An expression of impatience.)
114 countenance credit, confirmation   **116 springes** snares.
woodcocks birds easily caught; here used to connote gullibility.
117 prodigal prodigally   **120 it** i.e., the promise   **122 something**
somewhat   **123–4 Set . . . parle** i.e., As defender of your chastity,
negotiate for something better than a surrender simply because the
besieger requests an interview.   **124 For** As for   **125 so . . . him** this
much concerning him   **127 In few** Briefly   **128 brokers** go-
betweens, procurers   **129 dye** color or sort.   **investments** clothes.
(The vows are not what they seem.)   **130 mere implorators** out-and-
out solicitors

131 Breathing speaking   **132 for all** once for all, in sum   **134 slander**
abuse, misuse.   **moment** moment's   **136 Come your ways** Come
along.
1.4. Location: The guard platform.
1 shrewdly keenly, sharply   **2 eager** biting   **3 lacks of** is just short of
5 season time   **6 held his wont** was accustomed   **6.1** *pieces* i.e., of
ordnance, cannon   **8 wake** stay awake and hold revel.   **takes his
rouse** carouses   **9 Keeps . . . reels** carouses, and riotously dances a
German dance called the upspring   **10 Rhenish** Rhine wine   **12 The
triumph . . . pledge** the celebration of his offering a toast.   **15 manner** custom (of drinking)   **16 More . . . observance** better neglected
than followed.   **17 east and west** i.e., everywhere   **18 taxed of** censured by   **19 clepe** call.   **with swinish phrase** i.e., by calling us
swine   **20 addition** reputation   **21 at height** outstandingly   **22 The
pith . . . attribute** the most essential part of the esteem that should be
attributed to us.

So, oft it chances in particular men,
That for some vicious mole of nature in them,   24
As in their birth—wherein they are not guilty,
Since nature cannot choose his origin—   26
By their o'ergrowth of some complexion,   27
Oft breaking down the pales and forts of reason,   28
Or by some habit that too much o'erleavens   29
The form of plausive manners, that these men,   30
Carrying, I say, the stamp of one defect,
Being nature's livery or fortune's star,   32
His virtues else, be they as pure as grace,   33
As infinite as man may undergo,   34
Shall in the general censure take corruption   35
From that particular fault. The dram of evil   36
Doth all the noble substance often dout   37
To his own scandal.

       Enter Ghost.

HORATIO   Look, my lord, it comes!   38
HAMLET
Angels and ministers of grace defend us!   39
Be thou a spirit of health or goblin damned,   40
Bring with thee airs from heaven or blasts from hell,   41
Be thy intents wicked or charitable,   42
Thou com'st in such a questionable shape   43
That I will speak to thee. I'll call thee Hamlet,
King, father, royal Dane. Oh, answer me!
Let me not burst in ignorance, but tell
Why thy canonized bones, hearsèd in death,   47
Have burst their cerements; why the sepulcher   48
Wherein we saw thee quietly inurned   49
Hath oped his ponderous and marble jaws
To cast thee up again. What may this mean,
That thou, dead corpse, again in complete steel,   52
Revisits thus the glimpses of the moon,   53
Making night hideous, and we fools of nature   54
So horridly to shake our disposition   55
With thoughts beyond the reaches of our souls?
Say, why is this? Wherefore? What should we do?
        [The Ghost] beckons [Hamlet].

HORATIO
It beckons you to go away with it,
As if it some impartment did desire   59
To you alone.
MARCELLUS   Look with what courteous action
It wafts you to a more removèd ground.
But do not go with it.
HORATIO   No, by no means.
HAMLET
It will not speak. Then I will follow it.
HORATIO
Do not, my lord!
HAMLET   Why, what should be the fear?
I do not set my life at a pin's fee,   65
And for my soul, what can it do to that,   66
Being a thing immortal as itself?
It waves me forth again. I'll follow it.
HORATIO
What if it tempt you toward the flood, my lord,   69
Or to the dreadful summit of the cliff
That beetles o'er his base into the sea,   71
And there assume some other horrible form
Which might deprive your sovereignty of reason   73
And draw you into madness? Think of it.
The very place puts toys of desperation,   75
Without more motive, into every brain
That looks so many fathoms to the sea
And hears it roar beneath.
HAMLET
It wafts me still.—Go on, I'll follow thee.
MARCELLUS
You shall not go, my lord.   *[They try to stop him.]*
HAMLET   Hold off your hands!
HORATIO
Be ruled. You shall not go.
HAMLET   My fate cries out,   81
And makes each petty artery in this body   82
As hardy as the Nemean lion's nerve.   83
Still am I called. Unhand me, gentlemen.
By heaven, I'll make a ghost of him that lets me!   85
I say, away!—Go on, I'll follow thee.
        Exeunt Ghost and Hamlet.
HORATIO
He waxes desperate with imagination.
MARCELLUS
Let's follow. 'Tis not fit thus to obey him.
HORATIO
Have after. To what issue will this come?   89
MARCELLUS
Something is rotten in the state of Denmark.

---

24 for . . . mole on account of some natural defect in their constitutions   26 his its   27 their o'ergrowth . . . complexion the excessive growth in individuals of some natural trait   28 pales palings, fences (as of a fortification)   29–30 o'erleavens . . . manners i.e., infects the way we should behave (much as bad yeast spoils the dough). *Plausive* means "pleasing."   32 Being . . . star (that stamp of defect) being a sign identifying one as wearing the livery of, and hence being the servant to, nature (unfortunate inherited qualities) or fortune (mischance)   33 His virtues else i.e., the other qualities of *these men* (line 30)   34 may undergo can sustain   35 in . . . censure in overall appraisal, in people's opinion generally   36-8 The dram . . . scandal i.e., The small drop of evil blots out or works against the noble substance of the whole and brings it into disrepute. (To *dout* is to blot out. A famous crux.)   39 ministers of grace messengers of God   40 Be . . . health Whether you are a good angel   41 Bring whether you bring   42 Be thy intents whether your intentions are   43 questionable inviting question   47 canonized buried according to the canons of the church.   hearsèd coffined   48 cerements grave clothes   49 inurned entombed   52 complete steel full armor   53 the glimpses . . . moon i.e., the sublunary world, all that is beneath the moon   54 fools of nature mere mortals, limited to natural knowledge and subject to nature   55 So . . . disposition to distress our mental composure so violently

59 impartment communication   65 fee value   66 for as for   69 flood sea   71 beetles o'er overhangs threateningly (like bushy eyebrows).   his its   73 deprive . . . reason take away the rule of reason over your mind   75 toys of desperation fancies of desperate acts, i.e., suicide   81 My fate cries out My destiny summons me   82 petty weak.   artery blood vessel system through which the vital spirits were thought to have been conveyed   83 As . . . nerve as a sinew of the huge lion slain by Hercules as the first of his twelve labors.   85 lets hinders   89 Have after Let's go after him.   issue outcome

HORATIO
    Heaven will direct it.
MARCELLUS   Nay, let's follow him.   *Exeunt.* 91

❖

[1.5]

Enter Ghost and Hamlet.

HAMLET
    Whither wilt thou lead me? Speak. I'll go no further.
GHOST
    Mark me.
HAMLET   I will.
GHOST   My hour is almost come,
    When I to sulf'rous and tormenting flames
    Must render up myself.
HAMLET   Alas, poor ghost!
GHOST
    Pity me not, but lend thy serious hearing
    To what I shall unfold.
HAMLET   Speak. I am bound to hear.   7
GHOST
    So art thou to revenge, when thou shalt hear.
HAMLET   What?
GHOST   I am thy father's spirit,
    Doomed for a certain term to walk the night,
    And for the day confined to fast in fires,   12
    Till the foul crimes done in my days of nature   13
    Are burnt and purged away. But that I am forbid   14
    To tell the secrets of my prison house,
    I could a tale unfold whose lightest word
    Would harrow up thy soul, freeze thy young blood,   17
    Make thy two eyes like stars start from their spheres,   18
    Thy knotted and combinèd locks to part,   19
    And each particular hair to stand on end
    Like quills upon the fretful porcupine.
    But this eternal blazon must not be   22
    To ears of flesh and blood. List, list, oh, list!
    If thou didst ever thy dear father love—
HAMLET   Oh, God!
GHOST
    Revenge his foul and most unnatural murder.
HAMLET   Murder?
GHOST
    Murder most foul, as in the best it is,   28
    But this most foul, strange, and unnatural.
HAMLET
    Haste me to know't, that I, with wings as swift
    As meditation or the thoughts of love,
    May sweep to my revenge.
GHOST   I find thee apt;

    And duller shouldst thou be than the fat weed   33
    That roots itself in ease on Lethe wharf,   34
    Wouldst thou not stir in this. Now, Hamlet, hear.
    'Tis given out that, sleeping in my orchard,   36
    A serpent stung me. So the whole ear of Denmark
    Is by a forgèd process of my death   38
    Rankly abused. But know, thou noble youth,   39
    The serpent that did sting thy father's life
    Now wears his crown.
HAMLET   Oh, my prophetic soul! My uncle!
GHOST
    Ay, that incestuous, that adulterate beast,   43
    With witchcraft of his wit, with traitorous gifts—   44
    Oh, wicked wit and gifts, that have the power
    So to seduce!—won to his shameful lust
    The will of my most seeming-virtuous queen.
    Oh, Hamlet, what a falling off was there!
    From me, whose love was of that dignity
    That it went hand in hand even with the vow   50
    I made to her in marriage, and to decline
    Upon a wretch whose natural gifts were poor
    To those of mine!   53
    But virtue, as it never will be moved,   54
    Though lewdness court it in a shape of heaven,   55
    So lust, though to a radiant angel linked,
    Will sate itself in a celestial bed   57
    And prey on garbage.
    But soft, methinks I scent the morning air.
    Brief let me be. Sleeping within my orchard,
    My custom always of the afternoon,
    Upon my secure hour thy uncle stole,   62
    With juice of cursèd hebona in a vial,   63
    And in the porches of my ears did pour   64
    The leprous distillment, whose effect   65
    Holds such an enmity with blood of man
    That swift as quicksilver it courses through
    The natural gates and alleys of the body,   68
    And with a sudden vigor it doth posset   69
    And curd, like eager droppings into milk,   70
    The thin and wholesome blood. So did it mine,
    And a most instant tetter barked about,   72
    Most lazar-like, with vile and loathsome crust,   73
    All my smooth body.
    Thus was I, sleeping, by a brother's hand
    Of life, of crown, of queen at once dispatched,   76

---

91 it i.e., the outcome.
1.5. Location: The battlements of the castle.
7 bound (1) ready (2) obligated by duty and fate. (The Ghost, in line 8, answers in the second sense.) **12 fast** do penance by fasting **13 crimes** sins. **of nature** as a mortal **14 But that** Were it not that **17 harrow up** lacerate, tear **18 spheres** i.e., eye-sockets, here compared to the orbits or transparent revolving spheres in which, according to Ptolemaic astronomy, the heavenly bodies were fixed **19 knotted . . . locks** hair neatly arranged and confined **22 eternal blazon** revelation of the secrets of eternity **28 in the best** even at best

33 shouldst thou be you would have to be. **fat** torpid, lethargic **34 Lethe** the river of forgetfulness in Hades **36 orchard** garden **38 forgèd process** falsified account **39 abused** deceived. **43 adulterate** adulterous **44 gifts** (1) talents (2) presents **50 even with the vow** with the very vow **53 To** compared with **54 virtue, as it** just as virtue **55 shape of heaven** heavenly form **57 sate . . . bed** gratify its lustful appetite to the point of revulsion or ennui, even in a virtuously lawful marriage **62 secure hour** time of being free from worries **63 hebona** a poison. (The word seems to be a form of *ebony*, though it is thought perhaps to be related to *henbane*, a poison, or to *ebenus*, "yew.") **64 porches** gateways **65 leprous distillment** distillation causing leprosylike disfigurement **68 gates** entry ways **69–70 posset . . . curd** coagulate and curdle **70 eager** sour, acid **72 tetter** eruption of scabs. **barked** covered with a rough covering, like bark on a tree **73 lazar-like** leperlike **76 dispatched** suddenly deprived

Cut off even in the blossoms of my sin,
Unhouseled, disappointed, unaneled, 78
No reck'ning made, but sent to my account 79
With all my imperfections on my head.
Oh, horrible! Oh, horrible, most horrible!
If thou hast nature in thee, bear it not. 82
Let not the royal bed of Denmark be
A couch for luxury and damnèd incest. 84
But, howsomever thou pursues this act,
Taint not thy mind nor let thy soul contrive
Against thy mother aught. Leave her to heaven
And to those thorns that in her bosom lodge,
To prick and sting her. Fare thee well at once.
The glowworm shows the matin to be near, 90
And 'gins to pale his uneffectual fire. 91
Adieu, adieu, adieu! Remember me.   [Exit.]

HAMLET
O all you host of heaven! O earth! What else?
And shall I couple hell? Oh, fie! Hold, hold, my heart, 94
And you, my sinews, grow not instant old, 95
But bear me stiffly up. Remember thee?
Ay, thou poor ghost, whiles memory holds a seat
In this distracted globe. Remember thee? 98
Yea, from the table of my memory 99
I'll wipe away all trivial fond records, 100
All saws of books, all forms, all pressures past 101
That youth and observation copied there,
And thy commandment all alone shall live
Within the book and volume of my brain,
Unmixed with baser matter. Yes, by heaven!
Oh, most pernicious woman!
Oh, villain, villain, smiling, damnèd villain!
My tables—meet it is I set it down 108
That one may smile, and smile, and be a villain.
At least I am sure it may be so in Denmark.
So, uncle, there you are. Now to my word: 111
It is "Adieu, adieu! Remember me."
I have sworn't.

Enter Horatio and Marcellus.

HORATIO   My lord, my lord!
MARCELLUS   Lord Hamlet!
HORATIO   Heavens secure him! 116
HAMLET   So be it.
MARCELLUS   Hillo, ho, ho, my lord!
HAMLET   Hillo, ho, ho, boy! Come, bird, come. 119
MARCELLUS   How is't, my noble lord?

HORATIO   What news, my lord?
HAMLET   Oh, wonderful!
HORATIO   Good my lord, tell it.
HAMLET   No, you will reveal it.
HORATIO   Not I, my lord, by heaven.
MARCELLUS   Nor I, my lord.
HAMLET
How say you, then, would heart of man once think it? 127
But you'll be secret?
HORATIO, MARCELLUS   Ay, by heaven, my lord.
HAMLET
There's never a villain dwelling in all Denmark
But he's an arrant knave. 130
HORATIO
There needs no ghost, my lord, come from the grave
To tell us this.
HAMLET   Why, right, you are in the right.
And so, without more circumstance at all, 133
I hold it fit that we shake hands and part,
You as your business and desire shall point you—
For every man hath business and desire,
Such as it is—and for my own poor part,
Look you, I'll go pray.
HORATIO
These are but wild and whirling words, my lord.
HAMLET
I am sorry they offend you, heartily;
Yes, faith, heartily.
HORATIO   There's no offense, my lord.
HAMLET
Yes, by Saint Patrick, but there is, Horatio, 142
And much offense too. Touching this vision here, 143
It is an honest ghost, that let me tell you. 144
For your desire to know what is between us,
O'ermaster't as you may. And now, good friends,
As you are friends, scholars, and soldiers,
Give me one poor request.
HORATIO   What is't, my lord? We will.
HAMLET
Never make known what you have seen tonight.
HORATIO, MARCELLUS   My lord, we will not.
HAMLET   Nay, but swear't.
HORATIO   In faith, my lord, not I. 153
MARCELLUS   Nor I, my lord, in faith.
HAMLET   Upon my sword.   [He holds out his sword.] 155
MARCELLUS   We have sworn, my lord, already. 156
HAMLET   Indeed, upon my sword, indeed.
GHOST (cries under the stage)   Swear.
HAMLET
Ha, ha, boy, say'st thou so? Art thou there, truepenny? 159

78 Unhouseled . . . unaneled without having received the Sacrament or other last rites including confession, absolution, and the holy oil of extreme unction   79 reck'ning settling of accounts   82 nature i.e., the promptings of a son   84 luxury lechery   90 matin morning   91 his its   94 couple add.   Hold Hold together   95 instant instantly   98 globe (1) head (2) world (3) Globe Theater.   99 table tablet, slate   100 fond foolish   101 All . . . past all wise sayings, all shapes or images imprinted on the tablets of my memory, all past impressions   108 My tables . . . down (Editors often specify that Hamlet makes a note in his writing tablet, but he may simply mean that he is making a mental observation of lasting impression.)   111 there you are i.e., there, I've noted that against you.   116 secure him keep him safe.   119 Hillo . . . come (A falconer's call to a hawk in air. Hamlet mocks the hallooing as though it were a part of hawking.)

127 once ever   130 But . . . knave (Hamlet jokingly gives a self-evident answer: every villain is a thoroughgoing knave.)   133 circumstance ceremony, elaboration   142 Saint Patrick the keeper of Purgatory   143 offense (Hamlet deliberately changes Horatio's "no offense taken" to "an offense against all decency.")   144 honest genuine   153 In faith . . . I i.e., I swear not to tell what I have seen. (Horatio is not refusing to swear.)   155 sword i.e., the hilt in the form of a cross.   156 We . . . already i.e., We swore in faith.   159 truepenny honest old fellow.

Come on, you hear this fellow in the cellarage.
Consent to swear.

HORATIO   Propose the oath, my lord.

HAMLET
Never to speak of this that you have seen,
Swear by my sword.

GHOST [*beneath*]   Swear.   [*They swear.*] 164

HAMLET
Hic et ubique? Then we'll shift our ground.   165
                        [*He moves to another spot.*]
Come hither, gentlemen,
And lay your hands again upon my sword.
Swear by my sword
Never to speak of this that you have heard.

GHOST [*beneath*]   Swear by his sword.   [*They swear.*]

HAMLET
Well said, old mole. Canst work i'th'earth so fast?
A worthy pioneer!—Once more remove, good friends. 172
                        [*He moves again.*]

HORATIO
Oh, day and night, but this is wondrous strange!

HAMLET
And therefore as a stranger give it welcome.   174
There are more things in heaven and earth, Horatio,
Than are dreamt of in your philosophy.   176
But come;
Here, as before, never, so help you mercy,   178
How strange or odd some'er I bear myself—
As I perchance hereafter shall think meet
To put an antic disposition on—   181
That you, at such times seeing me, never shall,
With arms encumbered thus, or this headshake,   183
Or by pronouncing of some doubtful phrase
As "Well, we know," or "We could, an if we would,"   185
Or "If we list to speak," or "There be, an if they
    might,"   186
Or such ambiguous giving out, to note   187
That you know aught of me—this do swear,   188
So grace and mercy at your most need help you.

GHOST [*beneath*]   Swear.   [*They swear.*]

HAMLET
Rest, rest, perturbèd spirit!—So, gentlemen,
With all my love I do commend me to you;   192
And what so poor a man as Hamlet is
May do t'express his love and friending to you,   194
God willing, shall not lack. Let us go in together,   195
And still your fingers on your lips, I pray.   196

164 s.d. They swear (Seemingly they swear here, and at lines 170 and
190, as they lay their hands on Hamlet's sword. Triple oaths would
have particular force; these three oaths deal with what they have
seen, what they have heard, and what they promise about Hamlet's
antic disposition.)   **165 Hic et ubique?** Here and everywhere? (Latin.)
172 pioneer foot soldier assigned to dig tunnels and excavations.
174 as a stranger i.e., needing your hospitality   **176 your philosophy**
this subject that is called "natural philosophy" or "science." (*Your* is
not personal.)   **178 so help you mercy** as you hope for God's mercy
when you are judged   **181 antic** grotesque, strange   **183 encumbered** folded   **185 an if** if   **186 list** wished.   **There . . . might** There
are those who could talk if they were at liberty to do so   **187 note**
indicate   **188 aught** anything   **192 commend . . . you** give you my
best wishes   **194 friending** friendliness   **195 lack** be lacking.
196 still always

The time is out of joint. Oh, cursèd spite   197
That ever I was born to set it right!
                        [*They wait for him to leave first.*]
Nay, come, let's go together.   *Exeunt.* 199

✻

[2.1]

Enter old Polonius with his man [*Reynaldo*].

POLONIUS
Give him this money and these notes, Reynaldo.
                        [*He gives money and papers.*]

REYNALDO   I will, my lord.

POLONIUS
You shall do marvelous wisely, good Reynaldo,   3
Before you visit him, to make inquire   4
Of his behavior.

REYNALDO   My lord, I did intend it.

POLONIUS
Marry, well said, very well said. Look you, sir,
Inquire me first what Danskers are in Paris,   7
And how, and who, what means, and where they
    keep,   8
What company, at what expense; and finding
By this encompassment and drift of question   10
That they do know my son, come you more nearer   11
Than your particular demands will touch it.   12
Take you, as 'twere, some distant knowledge of him,   13
As thus, "I know his father and his friends,
And in part him." Do you mark this, Reynaldo?

REYNALDO   Ay, very well, my lord.

POLONIUS
"And in part him, but," you may say, "not well.
But if't be he I mean, he's very wild,
Addicted so and so," and there put on him   19
What forgeries you please—marry, none so rank   20
As may dishonor him, take heed of that,
But, sir, such wanton, wild, and usual slips   22
As are companions noted and most known
To youth and liberty.

REYNALDO   As gaming, my lord.

POLONIUS   Ay, or drinking, fencing, swearing,
Quarreling, drabbing—you may go so far.   27

REYNALDO   My lord, that would dishonor him.

POLONIUS
Faith, no, as you may season it in the charge.   29
You must not put another scandal on him
That he is open to incontinency;   31

197 out of joint in utter disorder.   **199 let's go together** (Probably
they wait for him to leave first, but he refuses this ceremoniousness.)
2.1. Location: Polonius's chambers.
3 marvelous marvelously   **4 inquire** inquiry   **7 Danskers** Danes
8 what means what wealth (they have).   **keep** dwell   **10 encompassment . . . question** roundabout way of questioning   **11-12 come . . .
it** you will find out more this way than by asking pointed questions
(*particular demands*).   **13 Take you** Assume, pretend   **19 put on**
impute to   **20 forgeries** invented tales.   **rank** gross   **22 wanton**
sportive, unrestrained   **27 drabbing** whoring   **29 season** temper,
soften   **31 incontinency** habitual sexual excess

That's not my meaning. But breathe his faults so
  quaintly   32
That they may seem the taints of liberty,   33
The flash and outbreak of a fiery mind,
A savageness in unreclaimèd blood,   35
Of general assault.   36

REYNALDO   But, my good lord—
POLONIUS   Wherefore should you do this?
REYNALDO   Ay, my lord, I would know that.
POLONIUS   Marry, sir, here's my drift,
And I believe it is a fetch of warrant.   41
You laying these slight sullies on my son,
As 'twere a thing a little soiled wi'th' working,   43
Mark you,
Your party in converse, him you would sound,   45
Having ever seen in the prenominate crimes   46
The youth you breathe of guilty, be assured   47
He closes with you in this consequence: 48
"Good sir," or so, or "friend," or "gentleman,"
According to the phrase or the addition   50
Of man and country.
REYNALDO   Very good, my lord.
POLONIUS   And then, sir, does 'a this—'a does—what
was I about to say? By the Mass, I was about to say
something. Where did I leave?
REYNALDO   At "closes in the consequence."
POLONIUS
At "closes in the consequence," ay, marry.
He closes thus: "I know the gentleman,
I saw him yesterday," or "th'other day,"
Or then, or then, with such or such, "and as you say,
There was 'a gaming," "there o'ertook in 's rouse,"   60
"There falling out at tennis," or perchance   61
"I saw him enter such a house of sale,"
Videlicet a brothel, or so forth. See you now,   63
Your bait of falsehood takes this carp of truth;   64
And thus do we of wisdom and of reach,   65
With windlasses and with assays of bias,   66
By indirections find directions out.   67
So by my former lecture and advice   68
Shall you my son. You have me, have you not?   69
REYNALDO
My lord, I have.
POLONIUS   God b'wi'ye; fare ye well.
REYNALDO   Good my lord.

POLONIUS
Observe his inclination in yourself.   72
REYNALDO   I shall, my lord.
POLONIUS   And let him ply his music.
REYNALDO   Well, my lord.
POLONIUS
Farewell.   *Exit Reynaldo.*
      Enter Ophelia.
          How now, Ophelia, what's the matter?
OPHELIA
Oh, my lord, my lord, I have been so affrighted!
POLONIUS   With what, i'th' name of God?
OPHELIA
My lord, as I was sewing in my closet,   79
Lord Hamlet, with his doublet all unbraced,   80
No hat upon his head, his stockings fouled,
Ungartered, and down-gyvèd to his ankle,   82
Pale as his shirt, his knees knocking each other,
And with a look so piteous in purport   84
As if he had been loosèd out of hell
To speak of horrors—he comes before me.
POLONIUS
Mad for thy love?
OPHELIA   My lord, I do not know,
But truly I do fear it.
POLONIUS   What said he?
OPHELIA
He took me by the wrist and held me hard.
Then goes he to the length of all his arm,
And, with his other hand thus o'er his brow
He falls to such perusal of my face
As 'a would draw it. Long stayed he so.   93
At last, a little shaking of mine arm
And thrice his head thus waving up and down,
He raised a sigh so piteous and profound
As it did seem to shatter all his bulk   97
And end his being. That done, he lets me go,
And with his head over his shoulder turned
He seemed to find his way without his eyes,
For out o' doors he went without their helps,
And to the last bended their light on me.
POLONIUS
Come, go with me. I will go seek the King.
This is the very ecstasy of love,   104
Whose violent property fordoes itself   105
And leads the will to desperate undertakings
As oft as any passion under heaven
That does afflict our natures. I am sorry.
What, have you given him any hard words of late?
OPHELIA
No, my good lord, but as you did command
I did repel his letters and denied

---

32 quaintly artfully, subtly **33 taints of liberty** faults resulting from
free living **35-6 A savageness . . . assault** a wildness in untamed
youth that assails all indiscriminately. **41 fetch of warrant** legitimate
trick. **43 wi'th' working** in the process of being made, i.e., in everyday experience **45 Your . . . converse** the person you are conversing
with. **sound** sound out **46 Having ever** if he has ever. **prenominate
crimes** aforenamed offenses **47 breathe** speak **48 closes . . . consequence** takes you into his confidence as follows **50 addition** title
60 o'ertook in 's rouse overcome by drink **61 falling out** quarreling
63 Videlicet namely **64 carp** a fish **65 reach** capacity, ability
66 windlasses i.e., circuitous paths. (Literally, circuits made to head
off the game in hunting.) **assays of bias** attempts through indirection (like the curving path of the bowling ball, which is biased or
weighted to one side) **67 directions** i.e., the way things really are
68 former lecture just-ended set of instructions **69 have** understand

72 in yourself in your own person (as well as by asking questions of
others). **79 closet** private chamber **80 doublet** close-fitting jacket.
unbraced unfastened **82 down-gyvèd** fallen to the ankles (like
gyves or fetters) **84 in purport** in what it expressed **93 As 'a** as if
he **97 As** that. **bulk** body **104 ecstasy** madness **105 property
fordoes** nature destroys

His access to me.

POLONIUS   That hath made him mad.
I am sorry that with better heed and judgment
I had not quoted him. I feared he did but trifle   114
And meant to wrack thee. But beshrew my jealousy!   115
By heaven, it is as proper to our age   116
To cast beyond ourselves in our opinions   117
As it is common for the younger sort
To lack discretion. Come, go we to the King.
This must be known, which, being kept close, might
       move   120
More grief to hide than hate to utter love.   121
Come.   *Exeunt.*

❖

[2.2]

*Flourish. Enter King and Queen, Rosencrantz,
and Guildenstern [with others].*

KING
Welcome, dear Rosencrantz and Guildenstern.
Moreover that we much did long to see you,   2
The need we have to use you did provoke
Our hasty sending. Something have you heard
Of Hamlet's transformation—so call it,
Sith nor th'exterior nor the inward man   6
Resembles that it was. What it should be,   7
More than his father's death, that thus hath put him
So much from th'understanding of himself,
I cannot dream of. I entreat you both
That, being of so young days brought up with him,   11
And sith so neighbored to his youth and havior,   12
That you vouchsafe your rest here in our court   13
Some little time, so by your companies
To draw him on to pleasures, and to gather
So much as from occasion you may glean,   16
Whether aught to us unknown afflicts him thus
That, opened, lies within our remedy.   18

QUEEN
Good gentlemen, he hath much talked of you,
And sure I am two men there is not living
To whom he more adheres. If it will please you
To show us so much gentry and good will   22
As to expend your time with us awhile
For the supply and profit of our hope,   24

Your visitation shall receive such thanks
As fits a kings's remembrance.

ROSENCRANTZ   Both Your Majesties   26
Might, by the sovereign power you have of us,   27
Put your dread pleasures more into command   28
Than to entreaty.

GUILDENSTERN   But we both obey,
And here give up ourselves in the full bent   30
To lay our service freely at your feet,
To be commanded.

KING
Thanks, Rosencrantz and gentle Guildenstern.

QUEEN
Thanks, Guildenstern and gentle Rosencrantz.
And I beseech you instantly to visit
My too much changèd son.—Go, some of you,
And bring these gentlemen where Hamlet is.

GUILDENSTERN
Heavens make our presence and our practices   38
Pleasant and helpful to him!

QUEEN   Ay, amen!
       *Exeunt Rosencrantz and Guildenstern [with some
                                              attendants].*

Enter Polonius.

POLONIUS
Th'ambassadors from Norway, my good lord,
Are joyfully returned.

KING
Thou still hast been the father of good news.   42

POLONIUS
Have I, my lord? I assure my good liege
I hold my duty, as I hold my soul,
Both to my God and to my gracious king;
And I do think, or else this brain of mine
Hunts not the trail of policy so sure   47
As it hath used to do, that I have found
The very cause of Hamlet's lunacy.

KING
Oh, speak of that! That do I long to hear.

POLONIUS
Give first admittance to th'ambassadors.
My news shall be the fruit to that great feast.   52

KING
Thyself do grace to them and bring them in.   53
                                          [Exit Polonius.]
He tells me, my dear Gertrude, he hath found
The head and source of all your son's distemper.

QUEEN
I doubt it is no other but the main,   56
His father's death and our o'erhasty marriage.

*Enter Ambassadors [Voltimand and Cornelius,
with Polonius].*

---

114 quoted observed   **115 wrack** ruin, seduce.   **beshrew my jealousy!** a plague upon my suspicious nature!   **116 proper . . . age** characteristic of us (old) men   **117 cast beyond** overshoot, miscalculate. (A metaphor from hunting.)   **120 known** made known (to the King). **close** secret   **120-1 might . . . love** i.e., might cause more grief (because of what Hamlet might do) by hiding the knowledge of Hamlet's strange behavior to Ophelia than unpleasantness by telling it.
2.2. Location: The castle.
2 Moreover that Besides the fact that   **6 Sith nor** since neither   **7 that** what   **11–12 That . . . havior** that, seeing as you were brought up with him from early youth (see 3.4.209, where Hamlet refers to Rosencrantz and Guildenstern as "my two schoolfellows"), and since you have been intimately acquainted with his youthful ways   **13 vouchsafe your rest** consent to stay   **16 occasion** opportunity   **18 opened** being revealed   **22 gentry** courtesy   **24 supply . . . hope** aid and furtherance of what we hope for

26 As fits . . . remembrance as would be a fitting gift of a king who rewards true service.   **27 of** over   **28 dread** inspiring awe   **30 in . . . bent** to the utmost degree of our capacity. (An archery metaphor.)
38 practices doings   **42 still** always   **47 policy** statecraft   **52 fruit** dessert   **53 grace** honor. (Punning on *grace* said before a *feast,* line 52.)   **56 doubt** fear, suspect

KING
Well, we shall sift him.—Welcome, my good friends! 58
Say, Voltimand, what from our brother Norway? 59
VOLTIMAND
Most fair return of greetings and desires. 60
Upon our first, he sent out to suppress 61
His nephew's levies, which to him appeared
To be a preparation 'gainst the Polack,
But, better looked into, he truly found
It was against Your Highness. Whereat grieved
That so his sickness, age, and impotence 66
Was falsely borne in hand, sends out arrests 67
On Fortinbras, which he, in brief, obeys,
Receives rebuke from Norway, and in fine 69
Makes vow before his uncle never more
To give th'assay of arms against Your Majesty. 71
Whereon old Norway, overcome with joy,
Gives him three thousand crowns in annual fee
And his commission to employ those soldiers,
So levied as before, against the Polack,
With an entreaty, herein further shown, *[giving a paper]*
That it might please you to give quiet pass
Through your dominions for this enterprise
On such regards of safety and allowance 79
As therein are set down.
KING   It likes us well, 80
And at our more considered time we'll read, 81
Answer, and think upon this business.
Meantime we thank you for your well-took labor.
Go to your rest; at night we'll feast together.
Most welcome home!   *Exeunt Ambassadors.*
POLONIUS   This business is well ended.
My liege, and madam, to expostulate 86
What majesty should be, what duty is,
Why day is day, night night, and time is time,
Were nothing but to waste night, day, and time.
Therefore, since brevity is the soul of wit, 90
And tediousness the limbs and outward flourishes,
I will be brief. Your noble son is mad.
Mad call I it, for, to define true madness,
What is't but to be nothing else but mad?
But let that go.
QUEEN   More matter, with less art.
POLONIUS
Madam, I swear I use no art at all.
That he's mad, 'tis true; 'tis true 'tis pity,
And pity 'tis 'tis true—a foolish figure, 98
But farewell it, for I will use no art.
Mad let us grant him, then, and now remains
That we find out the cause of this effect,

Or rather say, the cause of this defect,
For this effect defective comes by cause. 103
Thus it remains, and the remainder thus.
Perpend. 105
I have a daughter—have while she is mine—
Who, in her duty and obedience, mark,
Hath given me this. Now gather and surmise. 108
[He reads the letter.] "To the celestial and my soul's
idol, the most beautified Ophelia"—
That's an ill phrase, a vile phrase; "beautified" is a
vile phrase. But you shall hear. Thus: *[He reads.]*
"In her excellent white bosom, these, etc." 113
QUEEN Came this from Hamlet to her?
POLONIUS
Good madam, stay awhile, I will be faithful. 115
                                           [He reads.]
          "Doubt thou the stars are fire,
               Doubt that the sun doth move,
               Doubt truth to be a liar, 118
               But never doubt I love.
O dear Ophelia, I am ill at these numbers. I have not 120
art to reckon my groans. But that I love thee best, O 121
most best, believe it. Adieu.
               Thine evermore, most dear lady, whilst this
                    machine is to him, Hamlet." 124
This in obedience hath my daughter shown me,
And, more above, hath his solicitings, 126
As they fell out by time, by means, and place, 127
All given to mine ear.
KING   But how hath she 128
Received his love?
POLONIUS   What do you think of me?
KING
As of a man faithful and honorable.
POLONIUS
I would fain prove so. But what might you think, 131
When I had seen this hot love on the wing—
As I perceived it, I must tell you that,
Before my daughter told me—what might you,
Or my dear Majesty your queen here, think,
If I had played the desk or table book, 136
Or given my heart a winking, mute and dumb, 137
Or looked upon this love with idle sight? 138
What might you think? No, I went round to work, 139
And my young mistress thus I did bespeak: 140
"Lord Hamlet is a prince out of thy star; 141
This must not be." And then I prescripts gave her, 142

---

58 sift him question Polonius (or Hamlet) closely. **59 brother** fellow king **60 desires** good wishes. **61 Upon our first** At our first words on the business **66 impotence** weakness **67 borne in hand** deluded, taken advantage of. **arrests** orders to desist **69 in fine** in conclusion **71 give th'assay** make trial of strength, challenge **79 On . . . allowance** i.e., with such considerations for the safety of Denmark and permission for Fortinbras **80 likes** pleases **81 considered** suitable for deliberation **86 expostulate** expound, inquire into **90 wit** sense or judgment **98 figure** figure of speech

103 For . . . cause i.e., for this defective behavior, this madness, must have a cause. **105 Perpend** Consider. **108 gather and surmise** draw your own conclusions. **113 "In . . . etc."** (The letter is poetically addressed to her heart, where a letter would be kept by a young lady.) **115 stay . . . faithful** i.e., hold on, I will do as you wish. **118 Doubt** suspect **120 ill . . . numbers** unskilled at writing verses. **121 reckon** (1) count (2) number metrically, scan **124 machine** i.e., body **126–8 And . . . ear** and moreover she has told me when, how, and where his solicitings of her occurred. **131 fain** gladly **136–7 If . . . dumb** if I had acted as go-between, passing love notes, or if I had refused to let my heart acknowledge what my eyes could see **138 with idle sight** complacently or incomprehendingly **139 round** roundly, plainly **140 bespeak** address **141 out of thy star** above your sphere, position **142 prescripts** orders

That she should lock herself from his resort,
Admit no messengers, receive no tokens.
Which done, she took the fruits of my advice;
And he, repellèd—a short tale to make—
Fell into a sadness, then into a fast,
Thence to a watch, thence into a weakness,   148
Thence to a lightness, and by this declension   149
Into the madness wherein now he raves,
And all we mourn for.

KING [*to the Queen*]   Do you think 'tis this?

QUEEN   It may be, very like.

POLONIUS
Hath there been such a time—I would fain know
    that—
That I have positively said "'Tis so,"
When it proved otherwise?

KING   Not that I know.

POLONIUS
Take this from this, if this be otherwise.   156
If circumstances lead me, I will find
Where truth is hid, though it were hid indeed
Within the center.

KING   How may we try it further?   159

POLONIUS
You know sometimes he walks four hours together
Here in the lobby.

QUEEN   So he does indeed.

POLONIUS
At such a time I'll loose my daughter to him.   162
Be you and I behind an arras then.   163
Mark the encounter. If he love her not
And be not from his reason fall'n thereon,   165
Let me be no assistant for a state,
But keep a farm and carters.

KING   We will try it.   167

Enter Hamlet [reading on a book].

QUEEN
But look where sadly the poor wretch comes reading.

POLONIUS
Away, I do beseech you both, away.
I'll board him presently. Oh, give me leave.   170
        Exeunt King and Queen [with attendants].
How does my good Lord Hamlet?

HAMLET   Well, God-a-mercy.   172

POLONIUS   Do you know me, my lord?

HAMLET   Excellent well. You are a fishmonger.   174

POLONIUS   Not I, my lord.

HAMLET   Then I would you were so honest a man.

POLONIUS   Honest, my lord?

HAMLET   Ay, sir. To be honest, as this world goes, is to
be one man picked out of ten thousand.

POLONIUS   That's very true, my lord.

HAMLET   For if the sun breed maggots in a dead dog,
being a good kissing carrion—Have you a daughter?   182

POLONIUS   I have, my lord.

HAMLET   Let her not walk i'th' sun. Conception is a   184
blessing, but as your daughter may conceive, friend,
look to't.

POLONIUS [*aside*]   How say you by that? Still harping
on my daughter. Yet he knew me not at first; 'a said
I was a fishmonger. 'A is far gone. And truly in my
youth I suffered much extremity for love, very near
this. I'll speak to him again.—What do you read,
my lord?

HAMLET   Words, words, words.

POLONIUS   What is the matter, my lord?   194

HAMLET   Between who?

POLONIUS   I mean, the matter that you read, my lord.

HAMLET   Slanders, sir; for the satirical rogue says here
that old men have gray beards, that their faces are wrinkled, their eyes purging thick amber and plum-tree   199
gum, and that they have a plentiful lack of wit, to-   200
gether with most weak hams. All which, sir, though I
most powerfully and potently believe, yet I hold it not
honesty to have it thus set down, for yourself, sir, shall   203
grow old as I am, if like a crab you could go backward.   204

POLONIUS [*aside*]   Though this be madness, yet there is
method in't.—Will you walk out of the air, my lord?   206

HAMLET   Into my grave.

POLONIUS   Indeed, that's out of the air. [*Aside*] How
pregnant sometimes his replies are! A happiness that   209
often madness hits on, which reason and sanity could
not so prosperously be delivered of. I will leave him   211
and suddenly contrive the means of meeting between   212
him and my daughter.—My honorable lord, I will
most humbly take my leave of you.

HAMLET   You cannot, sir, take from me anything that I
will more willingly part withal—except my life, except   216
my life, except my life.

Enter Guildenstern and Rosencrantz.

POLONIUS   Fare you well, my lord.

HAMLET   These tedious old fools!

POLONIUS   You go to seek the Lord Hamlet. There he is.

ROSENCRANTZ [*to Polonius*]   God save you, sir!
                    [*Exit Polonius.*]

GUILDENSTERN   My honored lord!

---

148 **watch** state of sleeplessness   149 **lightness** lightheadedness.
declension decline, deterioration. (With a pun on the grammatical
sense.)   156 **Take this from this** (The actor probably gestures, indicating that he means his head from his shoulders, or his staff of office
or chain from his hands or neck, or something similar.)   159 **center**
center of the earth, traditionally an extraordinarily inaccessible place.
try test   162 **loose** (As one might release an animal that is being
mated.)   163 **arras** hanging, tapestry   165 **thereon** on that account
167 **carters** wagon drivers.   170 **I'll . . . leave** I'll accost him at once.
Please leave us alone; leave him to me.   172 **God-a-mercy** God have
mercy, i.e., thank you.   174 **fishmonger** fish merchant.

182 **a good kissing carrion** i.e., a good piece of flesh for kissing, or for
the sun to kiss   184 **i'th' sun** in public. (With additional implication
of the sunshine of princely favors.)   **Conception** (1) Understanding
(2) Pregnancy   194 **matter** substance. (But Hamlet plays on the sense
of "basis for a dispute.")   199 **purging** discharging.   **amber** i.e.,
resin, like the resinous *plum-tree gum*   200 **wit** understanding
203 **honesty** decency, decorum   204 **old** as old   206 **out of the air**
(The open air was considered dangerous for sick people.)   209 **pregnant** quick-witted, full of meaning.   **happiness** felicity of expression
211 **prosperously** successfully   212 **suddenly** immediately
216 **withal** with

ROSENCRANTZ   My most dear lord!

HAMLET   My excellent good friends! How dost thou, Guildenstern? Ah, Rosencrantz! Good lads, how do you both?

ROSENCRANTZ
As the indifferent children of the earth.   227

GUILDENSTERN
Happy in that we are not overhappy.
On Fortune's cap we are not the very button.

HAMLET   Nor the soles of her shoe?

ROSENCRANTZ   Neither, my lord.

HAMLET   Then you live about her waist, or in the mid-   232
dle of her favors?   233

GUILDENSTERN   Faith, her privates we.   234

HAMLET   In the secret parts of Fortune? Oh, most true, she is a strumpet. What news?   236

ROSENCRANTZ   None, my lord, but the world's grown honest.

HAMLET   Then is doomsday near. But your news is not true. Let me question more in particular. What have you, my good friends, deserved at the hands of Fortune that she sends you to prison hither?

GUILDENSTERN   Prison, my lord?

HAMLET   Denmark's a prison.

ROSENCRANTZ   Then is the world one.

HAMLET   A goodly one, in which there are many confines, wards, and dungeons, Denmark being one   247 o'th' worst.

ROSENCRANTZ   We think not so, my lord.

HAMLET   Why then 'tis none to you, for there is nothing either good or bad but thinking makes it so. To me it is a prison.

ROSENCRANTZ   Why then, your ambition makes it one. 'Tis too narrow for your mind.

HAMLET   Oh, God, I could be bounded in a nutshell and count myself a king of infinite space, were it not that I have bad dreams.

GUILDENSTERN   Which dreams indeed are ambition, for the very substance of the ambitious is merely the   259 shadow of a dream.

HAMLET   A dream itself is but a shadow.

ROSENCRANTZ   Truly, and I hold ambition of so airy and light a quality that it is but a shadow's shadow.

HAMLET   Then are our beggars bodies, and our mon-   264 archs and outstretched heroes the beggars' shadows.   265 Shall we to th' court? For, by my fay, I cannot reason.   266

ROSENCRANTZ, GUILDENSTERN   We'll wait upon you.   267

HAMLET   No such matter. I will not sort you with the   268 rest of my servants, for, to speak to you like an honest man, I am most dreadfully attended. But, in the   270 beaten way of friendship, what make you at Elsinore?   271

ROSENCRANTZ   To visit you, my lord, no other occasion.

HAMLET   Beggar that I am, I am even poor in thanks; but I thank you, and sure, dear friends, my thanks are too dear a halfpenny. Were you not sent for? Is it your   275 own inclining? Is it a free visitation? Come, come, deal   276 justly with me. Come, come. Nay, speak.

GUILDENSTERN   What should we say, my lord?

HAMLET   Anything but to th' purpose. You were sent   279 for, and there is a kind of confession in your looks which your modesties have not craft enough to color.   281 I know the good King and Queen have sent for you.

ROSENCRANTZ   To what end, my lord?

HAMLET   That you must teach me. But let me conjure   284 you, by the rights of our fellowship, by the consonancy   285 of our youth, by the obligation of our ever-preserved   286 love, and by what more dear a better proposer   287 could charge you withal, be even and direct with me   288 whether you were sent for or no.

ROSENCRANTZ [aside to Guildenstern]   What say you?

HAMLET [aside]   Nay, then, I have an eye of you.—If   291 you love me, hold not off.   292

GUILDENSTERN   My lord, we were sent for.

HAMLET   I will tell you why; so shall my anticipation   294 prevent your discovery, and your secrecy to the King   295 and Queen molt no feather. I have of late—but   296 wherefore I know not—lost all my mirth, forgone all custom of exercises; and indeed it goes so heavily with my disposition that this goodly frame, the earth, seems to me a sterile promontory; this most excellent canopy, the air, look you, this brave o'erhanging   301 firmament, this majestical roof fretted with golden   302 fire, why, it appeareth nothing to me but a foul and pestilent congregation of vapors. What a piece of work   304 is a man! How noble in reason, how infinite in faculties, in form and moving how express and admirable, in   306 action how like an angel, in apprehension how like a   307 god! The beauty of the world, the paragon of animals! And yet, to me, what is this quintessence of dust?   309 Man delights not me—no, nor woman neither, though by your smiling you seem to say so.

---

227 **indifferent** ordinary, at neither extreme of fortune or misfortune 232–3 **the middle . . . favors** i.e., her genitals.   234 **her privates we** (1) we dwell in her privates, her genitals, in the middle of her favors (2) we are her ordinary footsoldiers.   236 **strumpet** (Fortune was proverbially thought of as fickle.)   247 **confines** places of confinement   259 **the very . . . ambitious** that seemingly very substantial thing that the ambitious pursue   264–5 **Then . . . shadows** (Hamlet pursues their argument about ambition to its absurd extreme: if ambition is only a shadow of a shadow, then beggars, who are presumably without ambition, must be real, whereas monarchs and heroes are only their shadows—*outstretched* like elongated shadows, made to look bigger than they are.)   266 **fay** faith   267 **wait upon** accompany, attend. (But Hamlet uses the phrase in the sense of providing menial service.)

268 **sort** class, categorize   270 **dreadfully attended** waited upon in slovenly fashion.   271 **beaten way** familiar path, tried-and-true course.   **make** do   275 **too dear a halfpenny** (1) too expensive at even a halfpenny, i.e., of little worth (2) too expensive by a halfpenny in return for worthless kindness.   276 **free** voluntary   279 **Anything but to th' purpose** Anything except a straightforward answer. (Said ironically.)   281 **color** disguise.   284 **conjure** adjure, entreat 285–6 **the consonancy of our youth** our closeness in our younger days   287 **better** more skillful   288 **charge** urge.   **even** straight, honest   291 **of** on   292 **hold not off** don't hold back.   294–5 **so . . . discovery** in that way my saying it first will spare you from having to reveal the truth   296 **molt no feather** i.e., not diminish in the least. 301 **brave** splendid   302 **fretted** adorned (with fretwork, as in a vaulted ceiling)   304 **congregation** mass.   **piece of work** masterpiece   306 **express** well-framed, exact, expressive   307 **apprehension** power of comprehending   309 **quintessence** very essence. (Literally, the fifth essence beyond earth, water, air, and fire, supposed to be extractable from them.)

ROSENCRANTZ My lord, there was no such stuff in my thoughts.

HAMLET Why did you laugh, then, when I said man delights not me?

ROSENCRANTZ To think, my lord, if you delight not in man, what Lenten entertainment the players shall 317 receive from you. We coted them on the way, and 318 hither are they coming to offer you service.

HAMLET He that plays the king shall be welcome; His Majesty shall have tribute of me. The adventurous 321 knight shall use his foil and target, the lover shall not 322 sigh gratis, the humorous man shall end his part in 323 peace, the clown shall make those laugh whose lungs 324 are tickle o'th' sear, and the lady shall say her mind 325 freely, or the blank verse shall halt for't. What players 326 are they?

ROSENCRANTZ Even those you were wont to take such delight in, the tragedians of the city. 329

HAMLET How chances it they travel? Their residence, 330 both in reputation and profit, was better both ways.

ROSENCRANTZ I think their inhibition comes by the 332 means of the late innovation. 333

HAMLET Do they hold the same estimation they did when I was in the city? Are they so followed?

ROSENCRANTZ No, indeed are they not.

HAMLET How comes it? Do they grow rusty? 337

ROSENCRANTZ Nay, their endeavor keeps in the wonted 338 pace. But there is, sir, an aerie of children, little eyases, 339 that cry out on the top of question and are most tyran- 340 nically clapped for't. These are now the fashion, and 341 so berattle the common stages—so they call them— 342 that many wearing rapiers are afraid of goose quills 343 and dare scarce come thither.

HAMLET What, are they children? Who maintains 'em? How are they escotted? Will they pursue the quality no 346 longer than they can sing? Will they not say after- 347

wards, if they should grow themselves to common 348 players—as it is most like, if their means are no 349 better—their writers do them wrong to make them 350 exclaim against their own succession? 351

ROSENCRANTZ Faith, there has been much to-do on 352 both sides, and the nation holds it no sin to tar them to 353 controversy. There was for a while no money bid for 354 argument unless the poet and the player went to cuffs 355 in the question. 356

HAMLET Is't possible?

GUILDENSTERN Oh, there has been much throwing about of brains.

HAMLET Do the boys carry it away? 360

ROSENCRANTZ Ay, that they do, my lord—Hercules 361 and his load too. 362

HAMLET It is not very strange; for my uncle is King of Denmark, and those that would make mouths at him 364 while my father lived give twenty, forty, fifty, a hundred ducats apiece for his picture in little. 'Sblood, 366 there is something in this more than natural, if philos- ophy could find it out.

A flourish [of trumpets within].

GUILDENSTERN There are the players.

HAMLET Gentlemen, you are welcome to Elsinore. Your hands, come then. Th'appurtenance of welcome is 371 fashion and ceremony. Let me comply with you in this 372 garb, lest my extent to the players, which, I tell you, 373 must show fairly outwards, should more appear like 374 entertainment than yours. You are welcome. But my 375 uncle-father and aunt-mother are deceived.

GUILDENSTERN In what, my dear lord?

HAMLET I am but mad north-north-west. When the 378 wind is southerly I know a hawk from a handsaw. 379

Enter Polonius.

POLONIUS Well be with you, gentlemen!

HAMLET Hark you, Guildenstern, and you too; at each ear a hearer. That great baby you see there is not yet out of his swaddling clouts. 383

ROSENCRANTZ Haply he is the second time come to 384 them, for they say an old man is twice a child.

---

317 Lenten entertainment meager reception (appropriate to Lent) **318 coted** overtook and passed by **321 tribute** (1) applause (2) homage paid in money. **of** from **322 foil and target** sword and shield **323 gratis** for nothing. **humorous man** eccentric character, dominated by one trait or "humor" **323–4 in peace** i.e., with full license **325 tickle o'th' sear** hair trigger, ready to laugh easily. (A *sear* is part of a gun-lock.) **326 halt** limp **329 tragedians** actors **330 residence** remaining in their usual place, i.e., in the city **332 inhibition** formal prohibition (from acting plays in the city) **333 late innovation** i.e., recent new fashion in satirical plays performed by boy actors in the "private" theaters; or the Earl of Essex's abortive rebellion in 1601 against Elizabeth's government. (A much debated passage of seemingly topical reference.) **337 How . . . rusty?** Have they lost their polish, gone out of fashion? (This passage, through line 362, alludes to the rivalry between the children's companies and the adult actors, given strong impetus by the reopening of the Children of the Chapel at the Blackfriars Theater in late 1600.) **338 keeps . . . wonted** continues in the usual **339 aerie** nest. **eyases** young hawks **340 cry . . . question** speak shrilly, dominating the controversy (in decrying the public theaters) **340–1 tyrannically** vehemently **342 berattle . . . stages** clamor against the public theaters **343 many wearing rapiers** i.e., many men of fashion, afraid to patronize the common players for fear of being satirized by the poets writing for the boy actors. **goose quills** i.e., pens of satirists **346 escotted** maintained. **quality** (acting) profession **346–7 no longer . . . sing** i.e., only until their voices change.

348 common regular, adult **349 like** likely **349–50 if . . . better** if they find no better way to support themselves **351 succession** i.e., future careers. **352 to-do** ado **353 tar** incite (as in inciting dogs to attack a chained bear) **354–6 There . . . question** i.e., For a while, no money was offered by the acting companies to playwrights for the plot to a play unless the satirical poets who wrote for the boys and the adult actors came to blows in the play itself. **360 carry it away** i.e., win the day. **361–2 Hercules . . . load** (Thought to be an allusion to the sign of the Globe Theatre, which allegedly was Hercules bearing the world on his shoulders.) **364 mouths** faces **366 ducats** gold coins. **in little** in miniature. **'Sblood** By God's (Christ's) blood **371 Th'appurtenance** The proper accompaniment **372 comply** observe the formalities of courtesy **373 garb** i.e., manner. **my extent** that which I extend, i.e., my polite behavior **374 show fairly outwards** show every evidence of cordiality **375 entertainment** a (warm) reception **378 north-north-west** just off true north, only partly. **379 I . . . handsaw** (Speaking in his mad guise, Hamlet perhaps suggests that he can tell true from false. A *handsaw* may be a *hernshaw* or heron. Still, a supposedly mad disposition might compare hawks and handsaws.) **383 swaddling clouts** cloths in which to wrap a newborn baby. **384 Haply** Perhaps

HAMLET   I will prophesy he comes to tell me of the
players. Mark it.—You say right, sir, o' Monday 387
morning, 'twas then indeed. 388
POLONIUS   My lord, I have news to tell you.
HAMLET   My lord, I have news to tell you. When Roscius 390
was an actor in Rome—
POLONIUS   The actors are come hither, my lord.
HAMLET   Buzz, buzz! 393
POLONIUS   Upon my honor—
HAMLET   Then came each actor on his ass.
POLONIUS   The best actors in the world, either for
tragedy, comedy, history, pastoral, pastoral-comical,
historical-pastoral, tragical-historical, tragical-comical-
historical-pastoral, scene individable, or poem unlim- 399
ited. Seneca cannot be too heavy, nor Plautus too 400
light. For the law of writ and the liberty, these are the 401
only men.
HAMLET   O Jephthah, judge of Israel, what a treasure 403
hadst thou!
POLONIUS   What a treasure had he, my lord?
HAMLET   Why,
    "One fair daughter, and no more,
    The which he lovèd passing well." 408
POLONIUS [aside]   Still on my daughter.
HAMLET   Am I not i'th' right, old Jephthah?
POLONIUS   If you call me Jephthah, my lord, I have a
daughter that I love passing well.
HAMLET   Nay, that follows not. 413
POLONIUS   What follows then, my lord? 414
HAMLET   Why,
    "As by lot, God wot," 416
and then, you know,
    "It came to pass, as most like it was"— 418
the first row of the pious chanson will show you more, 419
for look where my abridgment comes. 420

    Enter the Players.

You are welcome, masters; welcome, all. I am glad to 421
see thee well. Welcome, good friends. Oh, old friend!
Why, thy face is valanced since I saw thee last. Com'st 423
thou to beard me in Denmark? What, my young lady 424

and mistress! By'r Lady, Your Ladyship is nearer to 425
heaven than when I saw you last, by the altitude of a 426
chopine. Pray God your voice, like a piece of uncur- 427
rent gold, be not cracked within the ring. Masters, you 428
are all welcome. We'll e'en to't like French falconers, 429
fly at anything we see. We'll have a speech straight. 430
Come, give us a taste of your quality. Come, a 431
passionate speech.
FIRST PLAYER   What speech, my good lord?
HAMLET   I heard thee speak me a speech once, but it
was never acted, or if it was, not above once, for the
play, I remember, pleased not the million; 'twas cav- 436
iar to the general. But it was—as I received it, and 437
others, whose judgments in such matters cried in the 438
top of mine—an excellent play, well digested in the 439
scenes, set down with as much modesty as cunning. I 440
remember one said there were no sallets in the lines to 441
make the matter savory, nor no matter in the phrase
that might indict the author of affectation, but called it 443
an honest method, as wholesome as sweet, and by very
much more handsome than fine. One speech in't I 445
chiefly loved: 'twas Aeneas' tale to Dido, and there-
about of it especially when he speaks of Priam's 447
slaughter. If it live in your memory, begin at this line: 448
let me see, let me see—
    "The rugged Pyrrhus, like th' Hyrcanian beast"— 450
'Tis not so. It begins with Pyrrhus:
    "The rugged Pyrrhus, he whose sable arms, 452
    Black as his purpose, did the night resemble
    When he lay couchèd in th' ominous horse, 454
    Hath now this dread and black complexion
        smeared
    With heraldry more dismal. Head to foot 456
    Now is he total gules, horridly tricked 457
    With blood of fathers, mothers, daughters, sons,
    Baked and impasted with the parching streets, 459
    That lend a tyrannous and a damnèd light 460

387–8 You say . . . then indeed (Said to impress upon Polonius the idea
that Hamlet is in serious conversation with his friends.)   **390 Roscius** a
famous Roman actor who died in 62 B.C.   **393 Buzz** (An interjection
used to denote stale news.)   **399–400 scene . . . unlimited** plays that
are unclassifiable and all-inclusive. (An absurdly catchall conclusion to
Polonius's pompous list of categories.)   **400 Seneca** writer of Latin
tragedies.   **Plautus** writer of Latin comedies   **401 law . . . liberty** dramatic composition both according to the rules and disregarding the
rules.   **these** i.e., the actors   **403 Jephthah . . . Israel** (Jephthah had to
sacrifice his daughter; see Judges 11. Hamlet goes on to quote from a
ballad on the theme.)   **408 passing** surpassingly   **413 that follows not**
i.e., just because you resemble Jephthah in having a daughter does not
logically prove that you love her.   **414 What . . . lord?** What does follow logically? (But Hamlet, pretending madness, answers with a fragment of a ballad, as if Polonius had asked, "What comes next?" See
419n.)   **416 lot** chance.   **wot** knows   **418 like** likely, probable
419 the first . . . more the first stanza of this biblically based ballad will
satisfy your stated desire to know *what follows* (line 414)   **420 my
abridgment** something that cuts short my conversation; also, a diversion   **421 masters** good sirs   **423 valanced** fringed (with a beard)
424 beard confront, challenge. (With obvious pun.)   **young lady** i.e.,
boy playing women's parts

425 By'r Lady By Our Lady   **425–6 nearer to heaven** i.e., taller
427 chopine thick-soled shoe of Italian fashion.   **427–8 uncurrent** not
passable as lawful coinage   **428 cracked . . . ring** i.e., changed from
adolescent to male voice, no longer suitable for women's roles. (Coins
featured rings enclosing the sovereign's head; if the coin was sufficiently clipped to invade within this ring, it was unfit for currency.)
429 e'en to't go at it   **430 straight** at once.   **431 quality** professional
skill.   **436–7 caviar to the general** i.e., an expensive delicacy not generally palatable to uneducated tastes.   **438–9 cried in the top of** i.e.,
spoke with greater authority than   **439 digested** arranged, ordered
440 modesty moderation, restraint.   **cunning** skill.   **441 sallets** i.e.,
something savory, spicy improprieties   **443 indict** convict
445 handsome well-proportioned.   **fine** elaborately ornamented,
showy.   **447–8 Priam's slaughter** the slaying of the ruler of Troy,
when the Greeks finally took the city.   **450 Pyrrhus** a Greek hero in
the Trojan War, also known as Neoptolemus, son of Achilles—another
avenging son.   **th' Hyrcanian beast** i.e., the tiger. (On the death of
Priam, see Virgil, *Aeneid*, 2.506 ff.; compare the whole speech with
Marlowe's *Dido Queen of Carthage*, 2.1.214 ff. On the *Hyrcanian* tiger,
see *Aeneid*, 4.366–7. Hyrcania is on the Caspian Sea.)   **452 rugged**
shaggy, savage.   **sable** black (for reasons of camouflage during the
episode of the Trojan horse)   **454 couchèd** concealed.   **ominous
horse** fateful Trojan horse, by which the Greeks gained access to Troy
456 dismal calamitous.   **457 total gules** entirely red. (A heraldic
term.)   **tricked** spotted and smeared. (Heraldic.)   **459 Baked . . .
streets** roasted and encrusted, like a thick paste, by the parching heat
of the streets (because of the fires everywhere)   **460 tyrannous** cruel

To their lord's murder. Roasted in wrath and fire,   461
And thus o'ersizèd with coagulate gore,   462
With eyes like carbuncles, the hellish Pyrrhus   463
Old grandsire Priam seeks."
So proceed you.
POLONIUS   'Fore God, my lord, well spoken, with good
accent and good discretion.
FIRST PLAYER   "Anon he finds him
Striking too short at Greeks. His antique sword,   469
Rebellious to his arm, lies where it falls,
Repugnant to command. Unequal matched,   471
Pyrrhus at Priam drives, in rage strikes wide,
But with the whiff and wind of his fell sword   473
Th'unnervèd father falls. Then senseless Ilium,   474
Seeming to feel this blow, with flaming top
Stoops to his base, and with a hideous crash   476
Takes prisoner Pyrrhus' ear. For, lo! His sword,
Which was declining on the milky head   478
Of reverend Priam, seemed i'th'air to stick.
So as a painted tyrant Pyrrhus stood,   480
And, like a neutral to his will and matter,   481
Did nothing.
But as we often see against some storm   483
A silence in the heavens, the rack stand still,   484
The bold winds speechless, and the orb below   485
As hush as death, anon the dreadful thunder
Doth rend the region, so, after Pyrrhus' pause,   487
A rousèd vengeance sets him new a-work,
And never did the Cyclops' hammers fall   489
On Mars's armor forged for proof eterne   490
With less remorse than Pyrrhus' bleeding sword   491
Now falls on Priam.
Out, out, thou strumpet Fortune! All you gods
In general synod take away her power!   494
Break all the spokes and fellies from her wheel,   495
And bowl the round nave down the hill of heaven   496
As low as to the fiends!"
POLONIUS   This is too long.
HAMLET   It shall to the barber's with your beard.—Pri-
thee, say on. He's for a jig or a tale of bawdry, or he   500
sleeps. Say on; come to Hecuba.   501
FIRST PLAYER
"But who, ah woe! had seen the moblèd queen"—   502
HAMLET   "The moblèd queen"?
POLONIUS   That's good. "Moblèd queen" is good.

FIRST PLAYER
"Run barefoot up and down, threat'ning the flames   505
With bisson rheum, a clout upon that head   506
Where late the diadem stood, and, for a robe,   507
About her lank and all o'erteemèd loins   508
A blanket, in the alarm of fear caught up—
Who this had seen, with tongue in venom steeped,
'Gainst Fortune's state would treason have
    pronounced.   511
But if the gods themselves did see her then
When she saw Pyrrhus make malicious sport
In mincing with his sword her husband's limbs,
The instant burst of clamor that she made,
Unless things mortal move them not at all,
Would have made milch the burning eyes of heaven,   517
And passion in the gods."   518
POLONIUS   Look whe'er he has not turned his color and   519
has tears in 's eyes. Prithee, no more.
HAMLET   'Tis well; I'll have thee speak out the rest of
this soon.—Good my lord, will you see the players well
bestowed? Do you hear, let them be well used, for they   523
are the abstract and brief chronicles of the time. After   524
your death you were better have a bad epitaph than
their ill report while you live.
POLONIUS   My lord, I will use them according to their
desert.
HAMLET   God's bodikin, man, much better. Use every   529
man after his desert, and who shall scape whipping?
Use them after your own honor and dignity. The less   531
they deserve, the more merit is in your bounty. Take
them in.
POLONIUS   Come, sirs.   [Exit.]
HAMLET   Follow him, friends. We'll hear a play tomor-
row. [As they start to leave, Hamlet detains the First
Player.] Dost thou hear me, old friend? Can you play
The Murder of Gonzago?
FIRST PLAYER   Ay, my lord.
HAMLET   We'll ha 't tomorrow night. You could, for a   540
need, study a speech of some dozen or sixteen lines   541
which I would set down and insert in't, could you not?
FIRST PLAYER   Ay, my lord.
HAMLET   Very well. Follow that lord, and look you mock
him not.   Exeunt players.
My good friends, I'll leave you till night. You are wel-
come to Elsinore.
ROSENCRANTZ   Good my lord!
                    Exeunt [Rosencrantz and Guildenstern].
HAMLET
Ay, so, goodbye to you.—Now I am alone.
Oh, what a rogue and peasant slave am I!

---

461 **their lord's** i.e., Priam's   462 **o'ersizèd** covered as with size or glue   463 **carbuncles** large fiery-red precious stones thought to emit their own light   469 **antique** ancient, long-used   471 **Repugnant** disobedient, resistant   473 **fell** cruel   474 **Th'unnervèd** the strengthless.   **senseless Ilium** inanimate citadel of Troy   476 **his** its   478 **declining** descending.   **milky** white-haired   480 **painted** motionless, as in a painting   481 **like . . . matter** i.e., as though suspended between his intention and its fulfillment   483 **against** just before   484 **rack** mass of clouds   485 **orb** globe, earth   487 **region** sky   489 **Cyclops'** The Cyclopes were giant armor makers in the smithy of Vulcan.   490 **proof** proven or tested resistance to assault   491 **remorse** pity   494 **synod** assembly   495 **fellies** pieces of wood forming the rim of a wheel   496 **nave** hub.   **hill of heaven** Mount Olympus   500 **jig** comic song and dance often given at the end of a play   501 **Hecuba** wife of Priam.   502 **who . . . had** anyone who had. (Also in line 510.)   **moblèd** muffled

505 **threat'ning the flames** i.e., weeping hard enough to dampen the flames   506 **bisson rheum** blinding tears.   **clout** cloth   507 **late** lately   508 **all o'erteemèd** utterly worn out with bearing children   511 **state** rule, managing.   **pronounced** proclaimed.   517 **milch** milky, moist with tears.   **burning eyes of heaven** i.e., stars, heavenly bodies   518 **passion** overpowering emotion   519 **whe'er** whether   523 **bestowed** lodged.   524 **abstract** summary account   529 **God's bodikin** By God's (Christ's) little body, *bodykin*. (Not to be confused with *bodkin,* "dagger.")   531 **after** according to   540 **ha 't** have it   541 **study** memorize

Is it not monstrous that this player here,
But in a fiction, in a dream of passion,   552
Could force his soul so to his own conceit   553
That from her working all his visage wanned,   554
Tears in his eyes, distraction in his aspect,   555
A broken voice, and his whole function suiting   556
With forms to his conceit? And all for nothing!   557
For Hecuba!
What's Hecuba to him, or he to Hecuba,
That he should weep for her? What would he do
Had he the motive and the cue for passion
That I have? He would drown the stage with tears
And cleave the general ear with horrid speech,   563
Make mad the guilty and appall the free,   564
Confound the ignorant, and amaze indeed   565
The very faculties of eyes and ears. Yet I,
A dull and muddy-mettled rascal, peak   567
Like John-a-dreams, unpregnant of my cause,   568
And can say nothing—no, not for a king
Upon whose property and most dear life   570
A damned defeat was made. Am I a coward?   571
Who calls me villain? Breaks my pate across?   572
Plucks off my beard and blows it in my face?
Tweaks me by the nose? Gives me the lie i'th' throat   574
As deep as to the lungs? Who does me this?
Ha, 'swounds, I should take it; for it cannot be   576
But I am pigeon-livered and lack gall   577
To make oppression bitter, or ere this   578
I should ha' fatted all the region kites   579
With this slave's offal. Bloody, bawdy villain!   580
Remorseless, treacherous, lecherous, kindless villain!   581
Oh, vengeance!
Why, what an ass am I! This is most brave,   583
That I, the son of a dear father murdered,
Prompted to my revenge by heaven and hell,
Must like a whore unpack my heart with words
And fall a-cursing, like a very drab,   587
A scullion! Fie upon't, foh! About, my brains!   588
Hum, I have heard
That guilty creatures sitting at a play
Have by the very cunning of the scene   591
Been struck so to the soul that presently   592

They have proclaimed their malefactions;
For murder, though it have no tongue, will speak
With most miraculous organ. I'll have these players
Play something like the murder of my father
Before mine uncle. I'll observe his looks;
I'll tent him to the quick. If 'a do blench,   598
I know my course. The spirit that I have seen
May be the devil, and the devil hath power
T'assume a pleasing shape; yea, and perhaps,
Out of my weakness and my melancholy,
As he is very potent with such spirits,   603
Abuses me to damn me. I'll have grounds   604
More relative than this. The play's the thing   605
Wherein I'll catch the conscience of the King.   *Exit.*

❧

[3.1]

*Enter King, Queen, Polonius, Ophelia,
Rosencrantz, Guildenstern, lords.*

KING
And can you by no drift of conference   1
Get from him why he puts on this confusion,
Grating so harshly all his days of quiet
With turbulent and dangerous lunacy?
ROSENCRANTZ
He does confess he feels himself distracted,
But from what cause 'a will by no means speak.
GUILDENSTERN
Nor do we find him forward to be sounded,   7
But with a crafty madness keeps aloof
When we would bring him on to some confession
Of his true state.
QUEEN   Did he receive you well?
ROSENCRANTZ   Most like a gentleman.
GUILDENSTERN
But with much forcing of his disposition.   12
ROSENCRANTZ
Niggard of question, but of our demands   13
Most free in his reply.
QUEEN   Did you assay him   14
To any pastime?
ROSENCRANTZ
Madam, it so fell out that certain players
We o'erraught on the way. Of these we told him,   17
And there did seem in him a kind of joy
To hear of it. They are here about the court,
And, as I think, they have already order
This night to play before him.
POLONIUS   'Tis most true,
And he beseeched me to entreat Your Majesties
To hear and see the matter.

---

552 **But** merely   553 **force . . . conceit** bring his innermost being so
entirely into accord with his conception (of the role)   554 **from her
working** as a result of, or in response to, his soul's activity.   **wanned**
grew pale   555 **aspect** look, glance   556–7 **his whole . . . conceit** all
his bodily powers responding with actions to suit his thought.
563 **the general ear** everyone's ear.   **horrid** horrible   564 **appall** (Literally, make pale.)   **free** innocent   565 **Confound the ignorant** i.e.,
dumbfound those who know nothing of the crime that has been
committed.   **amaze** stun   567 **muddy-mettled** dull-spirited
567–8 **peak . . . cause** mope, like a dreaming idler, not quickened by
my cause   570 **property** person and function   571 **damned defeat**
damnable act of destruction   572 **pate** head   574 **Gives . . . throat**
Calls me an out-and-out liar   576 **'swounds** by his (Christ's) wounds
577 **pigeon-livered** (The pigeon or dove was popularly supposed to
be mild because it secreted no gall.)   578 **To . . . bitter** to make things
bitter for oppressors   579 **region kites** kites (birds of prey) of the air
580 **offal** entrails.   581 **Remorseless** Pitiless.   **kindless** unnatural
583 **brave** fine, admirable. (Said ironically.)   587 **drab** whore
588 **scullion** menial kitchen servant. (Apt to be foul-mouthed.)
About About it, to work   591 **cunning** art, skill.   **scene** dramatic
presentation   592 **presently** at once

598 **tent** probe.   **the quick** the tender part of a wound, the core.
blench quail, flinch   603 **spirits** humors (of melancholy)
604 **Abuses** deludes   605 **relative** cogent, pertinent
3.1. Location: The castle.
1 **drift of conference** course of talk   7 **forward** willing.   **sounded**
questioned   12 **disposition** inclination.   13 **Niggard of question**
Laconic.   **demands** questions   14 **assay** try to win   17 **o'erraught**
overtook

KING
  With all my heart, and it doth much content me
  To hear him so inclined.
  Good gentlemen, give him a further edge   26
  And drive his purpose into these delights.
ROSENCRANTZ
  We shall, my lord.
                          Exeunt Rosencrantz and Guildenstern.
KING   Sweet Gertrude, leave us too,
  For we have closely sent for Hamlet hither,   29
  That he, as 'twere by accident, may here
  Affront Ophelia.   31
  Her father and myself, lawful espials,   32
  Will so bestow ourselves that seeing, unseen,
  We may of their encounter frankly judge,
  And gather by him, as he is behaved,
  If 't be th'affliction of his love or no
  That thus he suffers for.
QUEEN   I shall obey you.
  And for your part, Ophelia, I do wish
  That your good beauties be the happy cause
  Of Hamlet's wildness. So shall I hope your virtues
  Will bring him to his wonted way again,
  To both your honors.
OPHELIA   Madam, I wish it may.
                                              [*Exit Queen.*]
POLONIUS
  Ophelia, walk you here.—Gracious, so please you,   43
  We will bestow ourselves. [*To Ophelia*] Read on this
      book,   [*giving her a book*]   44
  That show of such an exercise may color   45
  Your loneliness. We are oft to blame in this—   46
  'Tis too much proved—that with devotion's visage   47
  And pious action we do sugar o'er
  The devil himself.
KING [*aside*] Oh, 'tis too true!
  How smart a lash that speech doth give my
      conscience!
  The harlot's cheek, beautied with plast'ring art,
  Is not more ugly to the thing that helps it   53
  Than is my deed to my most painted word.   54
  Oh, heavy burden!
POLONIUS
  I hear him coming. Let's withdraw, my lord.   56
                          [*The King and Polonius withdraw.*]

      Enter Hamlet. [*Ophelia pretends to read a book.*]

HAMLET
  To be, or not to be, that is the question:
  Whether 'tis nobler in the mind to suffer
  The slings and arrows of outrageous fortune,

  Or to take arms against a sea of troubles
  And by opposing end them. To die, to sleep—
  No more—and by a sleep to say we end
  The heartache and the thousand natural shocks
  That flesh is heir to. 'Tis a consummation
  Devoutly to be wished. To die, to sleep;
  To sleep, perchance to dream. Ay, there's the rub,   66
  For in that sleep of death what dreams may come,
  When we have shuffled off this mortal coil,   68
  Must give us pause. There's the respect   69
  That makes calamity of so long life.   70
  For who would bear the whips and scorns of time,
  Th'oppressor's wrong, the proud man's contumely,   72
  The pangs of disprized love, the law's delay,   73
  The insolence of office, and the spurns   74
  That patient merit of th'unworthy takes,   75
  When he himself might his quietus make   76
  With a bare bodkin? Who would fardels bear,   77
  To grunt and sweat under a weary life,
  But that the dread of something after death,
  The undiscovered country from whose bourn   80
  No traveler returns, puzzles the will,
  And makes us rather bear those ills we have
  Than fly to others that we know not of?
  Thus conscience does make cowards of us all;
  And thus the native hue of resolution   85
  Is sicklied o'er with the pale cast of thought,   86
  And enterprises of great pitch and moment   87
  With this regard their currents turn awry   88
  And lose the name of action.—Soft you now,   89
  The fair Ophelia.—Nymph, in thy orisons   90
  Be all my sins remembered.
OPHELIA   Good my lord,   91
  How does Your Honor for this many a day?
HAMLET
  I humbly thank you; well, well, well.
OPHELIA
  My lord, I have remembrances of yours,
  That I have longèd long to redeliver.
  I pray you, now receive them.   [*She offers tokens.*]
HAMLET
  No, not I, I never gave you aught.
OPHELIA
  My honored lord, you know right well you did,
  And with them words of so sweet breath composed
  As made the things more rich. Their perfume lost,
  Take these again, for to the noble mind

---

26 **edge** incitement   29 **closely** privately   31 **Affront** confront, meet
32 **espials** spies   43 **Gracious** Your Grace (i.e., the King)
44 **bestow** conceal   45 **exercise** religious exercise. (The book she
reads is one of devotion.)   **color** give a plausible appearance to
46 **loneliness** being alone.   47 **too much proved** too often shown to
be true, too often practiced   53 **to . . . helps it** in comparison with the
cosmetic that fashions the cheek's false beauty   54 **painted word**
deceptive utterances.   56.1 *withdraw* (The King and Polonius may
retire behind an arras. The stage directions specify that they "enter"
again near the end of the scene.)

66 **rub** (Literally, an obstacle in the game of bowls.)   68 **shuffled**
sloughed, cast.   **coil** turmoil   69 **respect** consideration   70 **of . . .**
life so long-lived, something we willingly endure for so long. (Also
suggesting that long life is itself a calamity.)   72 **contumely** insolent
abuse   73 **disprized** unvalued   74 **office** officialdom.   **spurns**
insults   75 **of . . . takes** receives from unworthy persons   76 **quietus**
acquittance; here, death   77 **a bare bodkin** a mere dagger,
unsheathed.   **fardels** burdens   80 **bourn** frontier, boundary
85 **native hue** natural color, complexion   86 **cast** tinge, shade of color
87 **pitch** height (as of a falcon's flight).   **moment** importance
88 **regard** respect, consideration.   **currents** courses   89 **Soft you** i.e.,
Wait a minute, gently   90–1 **in . . . remembered** i.e., pray for me, sinner that I am.

Rich gifts wax poor when givers prove unkind.
There, my lord.   [*She gives tokens.*]

HAMLET   Ha, ha! Are you honest?   104

OPHELIA   My lord?

HAMLET   Are you fair?   106

OPHELIA   What means Your Lordship?

HAMLET   That if you be honest and fair, your honesty   108
should admit no discourse to your beauty.   109

OPHELIA   Could beauty, my lord, have better commerce   110
than with honesty?

HAMLET   Ay, truly, for the power of beauty will sooner
transform honesty from what it is to a bawd than the
force of honesty can translate beauty into his likeness.   114
This was sometime a paradox, but now the time gives   115
it proof. I did love you once.   116

OPHELIA   Indeed, my lord, you made me believe so.

HAMLET   You should not have believed me, for virtue   118
cannot so inoculate our old stock but we shall relish of   119
it. I loved you not.   120

OPHELIA   I was the more deceived.

HAMLET   Get thee to a nunnery. Why wouldst thou be a   122
breeder of sinners? I am myself indifferent honest, but   123
yet I could accuse me of such things that it were better
my mother had not borne me: I am very proud,
revengeful, ambitious, with more offenses at my beck   126
than I have thoughts to put them in, imagination to
give them shape, or time to act them in. What should
such fellows as I do crawling between earth and
heaven? We are arrant knaves all; believe none of us.
Go thy ways to a nunnery. Where's your father?

OPHELIA   At home, my lord.

HAMLET   Let the doors be shut upon him, that he may
play the fool nowhere but in 's own house. Farewell.

OPHELIA   Oh, help him, you sweet heavens!

HAMLET   If thou dost marry, I'll give thee this plague for
thy dowry: be thou as chaste as ice, as pure as snow,
thou shalt not escape calumny. Get thee to a nunnery,
farewell. Or, if thou wilt needs marry, marry a fool, for
wise men know well enough what monsters you   140
make of them. To a nunnery, go, and quickly too.
Farewell.

OPHELIA   Heavenly powers, restore him!

HAMLET   I have heard of your paintings too, well   144
enough. God hath given you one face, and you make
yourselves another. You jig, you amble, and you   146
lisp, you nickname God's creatures, and make your   147
wantonness your ignorance. Go to, I'll no more on't;   148

it hath made me mad. I say we will have no more
marriage. Those that are married already—all but
one—shall live. The rest shall keep as they are. To a
nunnery, go.   *Exit.*

OPHELIA
Oh, what a noble mind is here o'erthrown!
The courtier's, soldier's, scholar's, eye, tongue, sword,
Th'expectancy and rose of the fair state,   155
The glass of fashion and the mold of form,   156
Th'observed of all observers, quite, quite down!   157
And I, of ladies most deject and wretched,
That sucked the honey of his music vows,   159
Now see that noble and most sovereign reason
Like sweet bells jangled out of tune and harsh,
That unmatched form and feature of blown youth   162
Blasted with ecstasy. Oh, woe is me,   163
T'have seen what I have seen, see what I see!

Enter King and Polonius.

KING
Love? His affections do not that way tend;   165
Nor what he spake, though it lacked form a little,
Was not like madness. There's something in his soul
O'er which his melancholy sits on brood,   168
And I do doubt the hatch and the disclose   169
Will be some danger; which for to prevent,
I have in quick determination
Thus set it down: he shall with speed to England   172
For the demand of our neglected tribute.
Haply the seas and countries different
With variable objects shall expel   175
This something-settled matter in his heart,   176
Whereon his brains still beating puts him thus   177
From fashion of himself. What think you on't?   178

POLONIUS
It shall do well. But yet do I believe
The origin and commencement of his grief
Sprung from neglected love.—How now, Ophelia?
You need not tell us what Lord Hamlet said;
We heard it all.—My lord, do as you please,
But, if you hold it fit, after the play
Let his queen-mother all alone entreat him
To show his grief. Let her be round with him;   186
And I'll be placed, so please you, in the ear
Of all their conference. If she find him not,   188
To England send him, or confine him where

---

104 **honest** (1) truthful (2) chaste.   106 **fair** (1) beautiful (2) just, honorable.   108 **your honesty** your chastity   109 **discourse to** familiar dealings with   110 **commerce** dealings, intercourse   114 **his** its
115–16 **This . . . proof** This was formerly an unfashionable view, but now the present age confirms how true it is.   118–20 **virtue . . . of it** virtue cannot be grafted onto our sinful condition without our retaining some taste of the old stock.   122 **nunnery** convent. (With an awareness that the word was also used derisively to denote a brothel.)   123 **indifferent honest** reasonably virtuous   126 **beck** command   140 **monsters** (An illusion to the horns of a cuckold.) **you** i.e., you women   144 **paintings** use of cosmetics   146–8 **You jig . . . ignorance** i.e., You prance about frivolously and speak with affected coynesss, you put new labels on God's creatures (by your use of cosmetics), and you excuse your affectations on the grounds of pretended ignorance.   148 **on't** of it

155 **Th'expectancy and rose** the hope and ornament   156 **The glass . . . form** the mirror of true self-fashioning and the pattern of courtly behavior   157 **Th'observed . . . observers** i.e., the center of attention and honor in the court   159 **music** musical, sweetly uttered
162 **blown** blossoming   163 **Blasted with ecstasy** blighted with madness.   165 **affections** emotions, feelings   168 **sits on brood** sits like a bird on a nest, about to *hatch* mischief (line 169)   169 **doubt** suspect, fear.   **disclose** disclosure, hatching   172 **set it down** resolved
175 **variable objects** various sights and surroundings to divert him
176 **This something . . . heart** the strange matter settled in his heart
177 **still** continually   178 **From . . . himself** out of his natural manner.   186 **round** blunt   188 **find him not** fails to discover what is troubling him

Your wisdom best shall think.
KING   It shall be so.
Madness in great ones must not unwatched go.

                                                 Exeunt.

❖

[3.2]

Enter Hamlet and three of the Players.

HAMLET   Speak the speech, I pray you, as I pronounced
it to you, trippingly on the tongue. But if you mouth
it, as many of our players do, I had as lief the town crier   3
spoke my lines. Nor do not saw the air too much with
your hand, thus, but use all gently; for in the very
torrent, tempest, and, as I may say, whirlwind of your
passion, you must acquire and beget a temperance
that may give it smoothness. Oh, it offends me to the
soul to hear a robustious periwig-pated fellow tear a   9
passion to tatters, to very rags, to split the ears of the
groundlings, who for the most part are capable of   11
nothing but inexplicable dumb shows and noise. I   12
would have such a fellow whipped for o'erdoing Ter-   13
magant. It out-Herods Herod. Pray you, avoid it.   14

FIRST PLAYER   I warrant Your Honor.

HAMLET   Be not too tame neither, but let your own
discretion be your tutor. Suit the action to the word,
the word to the action, with this special observance,
that you o'erstep not the modesty of nature. For   19
anything so o'erdone is from the purpose of playing,   20
whose end, both at the first and now, was and is to
hold as 'twere the mirror up to nature, to show virtue
her feature, scorn her own image, and the very age   23
and body of the time his form and pressure. Now this   24
overdone or come tardy off, though it makes the   25
unskillful laugh, cannot but make the judicious grieve,   26
the censure of the which one must in your allowance   27
o'erweigh a whole theater of others. Oh, there be players that I have seen play, and heard others praise, and
that highly, not to speak it profanely, that, neither   30
having th'accent of Christians nor the gait of Chris-   31
tian, pagan, nor man, have so strutted and bellowed   32
that I have thought some of nature's journeymen had   33

made men and not made them well, they imitated
humanity so abominably.   35

FIRST PLAYER   I hope we have reformed that indifferently   36
with us, sir.

HAMLET   Oh, reform it altogether. And let those that play
your clowns speak no more than is set down for them;
for there be of them that will themselves laugh, to set   40
on some quantity of barren spectators to laugh too,   41
though in the meantime some necessary question of
the play be then to be considered. That's villainous,
and shows a most pitiful ambition in the fool that uses
it. Go make you ready.   [*Exeunt Players.*]

Enter Polonius, Guildenstern, and Rosencrantz.

How now, my lord, will the King hear this piece of
work?

POLONIUS   And the Queen too, and that presently.   48

HAMLET   Bid the players make haste.   [*Exit Polonius.*]
Will you two help to hasten them?

ROSENCRANTZ
Ay, my lord.   *Exeunt they two.*

HAMLET   What ho, Horatio!

Enter Horatio.

HORATIO   Here, sweet lord, at your service.
HAMLET
Horatio, thou art e'en as just a man
As e'er my conversation coped withal.   54
HORATIO
Oh, my dear lord—
HAMLET   Nay, do not think I flatter,
For what advancement may I hope from thee
That no revenue hast but thy good spirits
To feed and clothe thee? Why should the poor be
    flattered?
No, let the candied tongue lick absurd pomp,   59
And crook the pregnant hinges of the knee   60
Where thrift may follow fawning. Dost thou hear?   61
Since my dear soul was mistress of her choice
And could of men distinguish her election,   63
Sh' hath sealed thee for herself, for thou hast been   64
As one, in suffering all, that suffers nothing,
A man that Fortune's buffets and rewards
Hast ta'en with equal thanks; and blest are those
Whose blood and judgment are so well commeddled   68
That they are not a pipe for Fortune's finger
To sound what stop she please. Give me that man   70
That is not passion's slave, and I will wear him
In my heart's core, ay, in my heart of heart,
As I do thee.—Something too much of this.—
There is a play tonight before the King.
One scene of it comes near the circumstance
Which I have told thee of my father's death.

3.2 Location: The castle.
3 our players players nowadays.   **I had as lief** I would just as soon
9 robustious violent, boisterous.   **periwig-pated** wearing a wig
11 groundlings spectators who paid least and stood in the yard of the
theater.   **capable of** able to understand   **12 dumb shows and noise**
noisy spectacle (rather than thoughtful drama).   **13–14 Termagant** a
supposed deity of the Mohammedans, not found in any English
medieval play but elsewhere portrayed as violent and blustering.
14 Herod Herod of Jewry. (A character in *The Slaughter of the Innocents*
and other cycle plays. The part was played with great noise and fury.)
19 modesty restraint, moderation   **20 from** contrary to   **23 scorn** i.e.,
something foolish and deserving of scorn   **23–4 and the . . . pressure**
and the present state of affairs its likeness as seen in an impression,
such as wax.   **25 come tardy off** falling short   **25–6 the unskillful**
those lacking in judgment   **27 the censure . . . one** the judgment of
even one of whom.   **your allowance** your scale of values   **30 not . . .
profanely** (Hamlet anticipates his idea in lines 33–4 that some men
were not made by God at all.)   **31 Christians** i.e., ordinary decent
folk   **32 nor man** i.e., nor any human being at all   **33 journeymen**
common workmen

35 abominably (Shakespeare's usual spelling, "abhominably," suggests a literal though etymologically incorrect meaning, "removed
from human nature.")   **36 indifferently** tolerably   **40 of them** some
among them   **41 barren** i.e., of wit   **48 presently** at once.   **54 my . . .
withal** my dealings encountered.   **59 candied** sugared, flattering
60 pregnant compliant   **61 thrift** profit   **63 could . . . election** could
make distinguishing choices among persons   **64 sealed thee** (Literally, as one would seal a legal document to mark possession.)
68 blood passion.   **commeddled** commingled   **70 stop** hole in a
wind instrument for controlling the sound

I prithee, when thou see'st that act afoot,
Even with the very comment of thy soul   78
Observe my uncle. If his occulted guilt   79
Do not itself unkennel in one speech,   80
It is a damnèd ghost that we have seen,
And my imaginations are as foul
As Vulcan's stithy. Give him heedful note,   83
For I mine eyes will rivet to his face,
And after we will both our judgments join
In censure of his seeming.
HORATIO   Well, my lord.   86
If 'a steal aught the whilst this play is playing   87
And scape detecting, I will pay the theft.

> [*Flourish.*] *Enter trumpets and kettledrums, King,*
> *Queen, Polonius, Ophelia, [Rosencrantz,*
> *Guildenstern, and other lords, with guards*
> *carrying torches].*

HAMLET   They are coming to the play. I must be idle.   89
Get you a place.   [*The King, Queen, and courtiers sit.*]
KING   How fares our cousin Hamlet?   91
HAMLET   Excellent, i'faith, of the chameleon's dish: I eat 92
the air, promise-crammed. You cannot feed capons so.   93
KING   I have nothing with this answer, Hamlet. These   94
words are not mine.   95
HAMLET   No, nor mine now. [*To Polonius*] My lord, you   96
played once i'th'university, you say?
POLONIUS   That did I, my lord, and was accounted a
good actor.
HAMLET   What did you enact?
POLONIUS   I did enact Julius Caesar. I was killed i'th' 101
Capitol; Brutus killed me.   102
HAMLET   It was a brute part of him to kill so capital a 103
calf there.—Be the players ready?   104
ROSENCRANTZ   Ay, my lord. They stay upon your   105
patience.
QUEEN   Come hither, my dear Hamlet, sit by me.
HAMLET   No, good mother, here's metal more attractive. 108
POLONIUS [*to the King*]   Oho, do you mark that?
HAMLET   Lady, shall I lie in your lap?   110
> [*Lying down at Ophelia's feet.*]

OPHELIA   No, my lord.
HAMLET   I mean, my head upon your lap?
OPHELIA   Ay, my lord.
HAMLET   Do you think I meant country matters?   114
OPHELIA   I think nothing, my lord.
HAMLET   That's a fair thought to lie between maids'
legs.
OPHELIA   What is, my lord?
HAMLET   Nothing.   119
OPHELIA   You are merry, my lord.
HAMLET   Who, I?
OPHELIA   Ay, my lord.
HAMLET   Oh, God, your only jig maker. What should a   123
man do but be merry? For look you how cheerfully my
mother looks, and my father died within 's two hours.   125
OPHELIA   Nay, 'tis twice two months, my lord.
HAMLET   So long? Nay then, let the devil wear black, for
I'll have a suit of sables. O heavens! Die two months   128
ago, and not forgotten yet? Then there's hope a great
man's memory may outlive his life half a year. But, by'r
Lady, 'a must build churches, then, or else shall 'a
suffer not thinking on, with the hobbyhorse, whose   132
epitaph is "For oh, for oh, the hobbyhorse is forgot."   133

The trumpets sound. Dumb show follows.

Enter a King and a Queen [very lovingly]; the
Queen embracing him, and he her. [She kneels,
and makes show of protestation unto him.] He
takes her up, and declines his head upon her neck.
He lies him down upon a bank of flowers. She,
seeing him asleep, leaves him. Anon comes in
another man, takes off his crown, kisses it, pours
poison in the sleeper's ears, and leaves him. The
Queen returns, finds the King dead, makes
passionate action. The Poisoner with some three or
four come in again, seem to condole with her. The
dead body is carried away. The Poisoner woos the
Queen with gifts; she seems harsh awhile, but in
the end accepts love.

> [*Exeunt players.*]

OPHELIA   What means this, my lord?
HAMLET   Marry, this' miching mallico; it means mis-   135
chief.

---

78 very . . . soul your most penetrating observation and consideration
79 occulted hidden   **80 unkennel** (As one would say of a fox driven
from its lair.)   **83 Vulcan's stithy** the smithy, the place of stiths (anvils)
of the Roman god of fire and metalworking.   **86 censure of his seeming** judgment of his appearance or behavior.   **87 If 'a steal aught** If he
gets away with anything   **89 idle** (1) unoccupied (2) mad.   **91 cousin**
i.e., close relative   **92 chameleon's dish** (Chameleons were supposed
to feed on air. Hamlet deliberately misinterprets the King's *fares* as
"feeds." By his phrase *eat the air* he also plays on the idea of feeding
himself with the promise of succession, of being the *heir*.)   **93 capons**
roosters castrated and *crammed* with feed to make them succulent
94 have . . . with make nothing of, or gain nothing from   **95 are not
mine** do not respond to what I asked.   **96 nor mine now** (Once spoken, words are proverbially no longer the speaker's own—and hence
should be uttered warily.)   **101–2 i'th' Capitol** (where Caesar was
assassinated, according to *Julius Caesar*, 3.1, but see 1.3.126n in that
play)   **103 brute** (The Latin meaning of *brutus*, "stupid," was often
used punningly with the name Brutus.)   **part** (1) deed (2) role
104 calf fool   **105 stay upon** await   **108 metal** substance that is
attractive, i.e., magnetic, but with suggestion also of *mettle*, "disposition"   **110 Lady . . . lap?** Onstage, Hamlet often lies at Ophelia's feet,
but he could instead offer to do this and continue to stand.

114 country matters sexual intercourse. (With a bawdy pun on the
first syllable of *country*.)   **119 Nothing** The figure zero or naught,
suggesting the female sexual anatomy. (*Thing* not infrequently has a
bawdy connotation of male or female anatomy, and the reference here
could be male.)   **123 only jig maker** very best composer of jigs, i.e.,
pointless merriment. (Hamlet replies sardonically to Ophelia's observation that he is merry by saying, "If you're looking for someone who
is really merry, you've come to the right person.")   **125 within 's**
within this (i.e., these)   **128 suit of sables** garments trimmed with
the dark fur of the sable and hence suited for a person in mourning.
132 suffer . . . on undergo oblivion   **133 "For . . . forgot"** (Verse of a
song occurring also in *Love's Labor's Lost*, 3.1.27–8. The hobbyhorse
was a character made up to resemble a horse and rider, appearing in
the morris dance and such May-game sports. This song laments the
disappearance of such customs under pressure from the Puritans.)
133.12 condole with offer sympathy to   **135 this' miching mallico**
this is sneaking mischief

OPHELIA   Belike this show imports the argument of the 137
play.

Enter Prologue.

HAMLET   We shall know by this fellow. The players cannot keep counsel; they'll tell all.   140

OPHELIA   Will 'a tell us what this show meant?

HAMLET   Ay, or any show that you will show him. Be 142
not you ashamed to show, he'll not shame to tell you 143
what it means.

OPHELIA   You are naught, you are naught. I'll mark the 145
play.

PROLOGUE
For us, and for our tragedy,
Here stooping to your clemency,
We beg your hearing patiently.   148   [*Exit.*]

HAMLET   Is this a prologue, or the posy of a ring?   150

OPHELIA   'Tis brief, my lord.

HAMLET   As woman's love.

Enter [two Players as] King and Queen.

PLAYER KING
Full thirty times hath Phoebus' cart gone round   153
Neptune's salt wash and Tellus' orbèd ground,   154
And thirty dozen moons with borrowed sheen   155
About the world have times twelve thirties been,
Since love our hearts and Hymen did our hands   157
Unite commutual in most sacred bands.   158

PLAYER QUEEN
So many journeys may the sun and moon
Make us again count o'er ere love be done!
But, woe is me, you are so sick of late,
So far from cheer and from your former state,
That I distrust you. Yet, though I distrust,   163
Discomfort you, my lord, it nothing must.   164
For women's fear and love hold quantity;   165
In neither aught, or in extremity.   166
Now, what my love is, proof hath made you know,   167
And as my love is sized, my fear is so.
Where love is great, the littlest doubts are fear;   169
Where little fears grow great, great love grows there.

PLAYER KING
Faith, I must leave thee, love, and shortly too;
My operant powers their functions leave to do.   172
And thou shalt live in this fair world behind,   173
Honored, beloved; and haply one as kind
For husband shalt thou—

PLAYER QUEEN   Oh, confound the rest!

Such love must needs be treason in my breast.
In second husband let me be accurst!
None wed the second but who killed the first.   178

HAMLET   Wormwood, wormwood.   179

PLAYER QUEEN
The instances that second marriage move   180
Are base respects of thrift, but none of love.   181
A second time I kill my husband dead
When second husband kisses me in bed.

PLAYER KING
I do believe you think what now you speak,
But what we do determine oft we break.
Purpose is but the slave to memory,   186
Of violent birth, but poor validity,   187
Which now, like fruit unripe, sticks on the tree,   188
But fall unshaken when they mellow be.
Most necessary 'tis that we forget   190
To pay ourselves what to ourselves is debt.   191
What to ourselves in passion we propose,
The passion ending, doth the purpose lose.
The violence of either grief or joy
Their own enactures with themselves destroy.   195
Where joy most revels, grief doth most lament;   196
Grief joys, joy grieves, on slender accident.   197
This world is not for aye, nor 'tis not strange   198
That even our loves should with our fortunes change;
For 'tis a question left us yet to prove,
Whether love lead fortune, or else fortune love.
The great man down, you mark his favorite flies;   202
The poor advanced makes friends of enemies.   203
And hitherto doth love on fortune tend;   204
For who not needs shall never lack a friend,   205
And who in want a hollow friend doth try   206
Directly seasons him his enemy.   207
But, orderly to end where I begun,
Our wills and fates do so contrary run   209
That our devices still are overthrown;   210
Our thoughts are ours, their ends none of our own.   211
So think thou wilt no second husband wed,
But die thy thoughts when thy first lord is dead.

PLAYER QUEEN
Nor earth to me give food, nor heaven light,   214
Sport and repose lock from me day and night,   215

---

137 Belike Probably.   **argument** plot   **140 counsel** secret   **142–3 Be not you** Provided you are not   **145 naught** indecent. (Ophelia is reacting to Hamlet's pointed remarks about not being ashamed to show all.)   **148 stooping** bowing   **150 posy . . . ring** brief motto in verse inscribed in a ring.   **153 Phoebus' cart** the sun-god's chariot, making its yearly cycle   **154 salt wash** the sea.   **Tellus'** Tellus was goddess of the earth, of the *orbèd ground*   **155 borrowed** i.e., reflected   **157 Hymen** god of matrimony   **158 commutual** mutually.   **bands** bonds.   **163 distrust** am anxious about   **164 Discomfort . . . must** it must not distress you at all.   **165 hold quantity** keep proportion with one another   **166 In . . . extremity** (women feel) either no anxiety if they do not love or extreme anxiety if they do love.   **167 proof** experience   **169 the littlest** even the littlest   **172 My . . . to do** my vital functions are shutting down.   **173 behind** after I have gone

178 None (1) Let no woman; or (2) No woman does.   **but who** except the one who   **179 Wormwood** i.e., How bitter. (Literally, a bitter-tasting plant.)   **180 instances** motives.   **move** motivate   **181 base . . . thrift** ignoble considerations of material prosperity   **186 Purpose . . . memory** Our good intentions are subject to forgetfulness   **187 validity** strength, durability   **188 Which** i.e., purpose   **190–1 Most . . . debt** It's inevitable that in time we forget the obligations we have imposed on ourselves.   **195 enactures** fulfillments   **196–7 Where . . . accident** The capacity for extreme joy and grief go together, and often one extreme is instantly changed into its opposite on the slightest provocation.   **198 aye** ever   **202 down** fallen in fortune   **203 The poor . . . enemies** when one of humble station is promoted, you see his enemies suddenly becoming his friends.   **204 hitherto** up to this point in the argument, or, to this extent.   **tend** attend   **205 who not needs** he who is not in need (of wealth)   **206 who in want** he who, being in need.   **try** test (his generosity)   **207 seasons him** ripens him into   **209 Our . . . run** what we want and what we get go so contrarily   **210 devices** intentions.   **still** continually   **211 ends** results   **214 Nor** Let neither   **215 Sport . . . night** may day deny me its pastimes and night its repose

To desperation turn my trust and hope,
An anchor's cheer in prison be my scope!   217
Each opposite that blanks the face of joy   218
Meet what I would have well and it destroy!   219
Both here and hence pursue me lasting strife   220
If, once a widow, ever I be wife!

HAMLET   If she should break it now!

PLAYER KING
'Tis deeply sworn. Sweet, leave me here awhile;
My spirits grow dull, and fain I would beguile   224
The tedious day with sleep.

PLAYER QUEEN   Sleep rock thy brain,
And never come mischance between us twain!
                    [*He sleeps.*] *Exit* [*Player Queen*].

HAMLET   Madam, how like you this play?

QUEEN   The lady doth protest too much, methinks.   228

HAMLET   Oh, but she'll keep her word.

KING   Have you heard the argument? Is there no   230
offense in't?

HAMLET   No, no, they do but jest, poison in jest. No of- 232
fense i'th' world.   233

KING   What do you call the play?

HAMLET   *The Mousetrap*. Marry, how? Tropically.   235
This play is the image of a murder done in Vienna.
Gonzago is the Duke's name, his wife, Baptista. You   237
shall see anon. 'Tis a knavish piece of work, but what
of that? Your Majesty, and we that have free souls, it   239
touches us not. Let the galled jade wince, our withers   240
are unwrung.   241

        Enter Lucianus.

This is one Lucianus, nephew to the King.

OPHELIA   You are as good as a chorus, my lord.   243

HAMLET   I could interpret between you and your love,   244
if I could see the puppets dallying.   245

OPHELIA   You are keen, my lord, you are keen.   246

HAMLET   It would cost you a groaning to take off mine
edge.

OPHELIA   Still better, and worse.   249

HAMLET   So you mis-take your husbands.—Begin, mur-   250
derer; leave thy damnable faces and begin. Come, the
croaking raven doth bellow for revenge.

LUCIANUS
Thoughts black, hands apt, drugs fit, and time
    agreeing,
Confederate season, else no creature seeing,   254
Thou mixture rank, of midnight weeds collected,
With Hecate's ban thrice blasted, thrice infected,   256
Thy natural magic and dire property   257
On wholesome life usurp immediately.
            [*He pours the poison into the sleeper's ear.*]

HAMLET   'A poisons him i'th' garden for his estate. His   259
name's Gonzago. The story is extant, and written in
very choice Italian. You shall see anon how the
murderer gets the love of Gonzago's wife.
                                        [*Claudius rises.*]

OPHELIA   The King rises.

HAMLET   What, frighted with false fire?   264

QUEEN   How fares my lord?

POLONIUS   Give o'er the play.

KING   Give me some light. Away!

POLONIUS   Lights, lights, lights!
            Exeunt all but Hamlet and Horatio.

HAMLET
"Why, let the strucken deer go weep,   269
    The hart ungallèd play.   270
For some must watch, while some must sleep;   271
    Thus runs the world away."   272
Would not this, sir, and a forest of feathers—if the   273
rest of my fortunes turn Turk with me—with two   274
Provincial roses on my razed shoes, get me a fellow-   275
ship in a cry of players?   276

HORATIO   Half a share.

HAMLET   A whole one, I.
"For thou dost know, O Damon dear,   279
    This realm dismantled was   280
Of Jove himself, and now reigns here   281
    A very, very—pajock."   282

---

217 anchor's cheer anchorite's or hermit's fare.   **my scope** the extent of my happiness.   **218–19 Each . . . destroy!** May every adverse thing that causes the face of joy to turn pale meet and destroy everything that I desire to see prosper!   **220 hence** in the life hereafter   **224 spirits** vital spirits   **228 doth . . . much** makes too many promises and protestations   **230 argument** plot.   **232 jest** make believe. **232–3 offense** crime, injury. (Hamlet playfully alters the King's use of the word in line 231 to mean "cause for objection.")   **235 Tropically** Figuratively. (The first quarto reading, "trapically," suggests a pun on *trap* in *Mousetrap*.)   **237 Duke's** i.e., King's. (An inconsistency that may be due to Shakespeare's possible acquaintance with a historical incident, the alleged murder of the Duke of Urbino by Luigi Gonzaga in 1538.)   **239 free** guiltless   **240 galled jade** horse whose hide is rubbed by saddle or harness.   **withers** the part between the horse's shoulder blades   **241 unwrung** not rubbed sore.   **243 chorus** (In many Elizabethan plays, the forthcoming action was explained by an actor known as the "chorus"; at a puppet show, the actor who spoke the dialogue was known as an "interpreter," as indicated by the lines following.)   **244 interpret** (1) ventriloquize the dialogue, as in a puppet show (2) act as pander   **245 puppets dallying** (With suggestion of sexual play, continued in *keen*, "sexually aroused," *groaning*, "moaning in pregnancy," and *edge*, "sexual desire" or "impetuosity.")   **246 keen** sharp, bitter   **249 Still . . . worse** More keen, always *bettering* what other people say with witty wordplay, but at the same time more offensive.

250 So Even thus (in marriage).   **mis-take** take falseheartedly and cheat on. (The marriage vows say "for better, for worse.")   **254 Confederate . . . seeing** the time and occasion conspiring (to assist me), and also no one seeing me   **256 Hecate's ban** the curse of Hecate, the goddess of witchcraft   **257 dire property** baleful quality   **259 estate** i.e., the kingship.   **His** i.e., the King's   **264 false fire** the blank discharge of a gun loaded with powder but no shot.   **269–72 Why . . . away** (Perhaps from an old ballad, with allusion to the popular belief that a wounded deer retires to weep and die; compare with *As You Like It*, 2.1.33–66.)   **270 ungallèd** unafflicted   **271 watch** remain awake   **272 Thus . . . away** Thus the world goes.   **273 this** i.e., this success with the play I have just presented.   **feathers** (Allusion to the plumes that Elizabethan actors were fond of wearing.)   **274 turn Turk with** turn renegade against, go back on   **275 Provincial roses** rosettes of ribbon, named for roses grown in a part of France.   **razed** with ornamental slashing   **275–6 fellowship . . . players** partnership in a theatrical company.   **276 cry** pack (of hounds, etc.)   **279 Damon** the friend of Pythias, as Horatio is friend of Hamlet; or, a traditional pastoral name   **280–2 This realm . . . pajock** i.e., Jove, representing divine authority and justice, has abandoned this realm to its own devices, leaving in his stead only a peacock or vain pretender to virtue (though the rhyme-word expected in place of *pajock* or "peacock" suggests that the realm is now ruled over by an "ass").   **280 dismantled** stripped, divested

HORATIO   You might have rhymed.

HAMLET   Oh, good Horatio, I'll take the ghost's word for a thousand pound. Didst perceive?

HORATIO   Very well, my lord.

HAMLET   Upon the talk of the poisoning?

HORATIO   I did very well note him.

Enter Rosencrantz and Guildenstern.

HAMLET   Aha! Come, some music! Come, the recorders.

"For if the King like not the comedy,
Why then, belike, he likes it not, perdy."   292
Come, some music.

GUILDENSTERN   Good my lord, vouchsafe me a word with you.

HAMLET   Sir, a whole history.

GUILDENSTERN   The King, sir—

HAMLET   Ay, sir, what of him?

GUILDENSTERN   Is in his retirement marvelous distempered.   299 300

HAMLET   With drink, sir?

GUILDENSTERN   No, my lord, with choler.   302

HAMLET   Your wisdom should show itself more richer to signify this to the doctor, for for me to put him to his purgation would perhaps plunge him into more choler.   305

GUILDENSTERN   Good my lord, put your discourse into some frame and start not so wildly from my affair.   308

HAMLET   I am tame, sir. Pronounce.

GUILDENSTERN   The Queen, your mother, in most great affliction of spirit, hath sent me to you.

HAMLET   You are welcome.

GUILDENSTERN   Nay, good my lord, this courtesy is not of the right breed. If it shall please you to make me a wholesome answer, I will do your mother's commandment; if not, your pardon and my return shall be the end of my business.   314 316

HAMLET   Sir, I cannot.

ROSENCRANTZ   What, my lord?

HAMLET   Make you a wholesome answer; my wit's diseased. But, sir, such answer as I can make, you shall command, or rather, as you say, my mother. Therefore no more, but to the matter. My mother, you say—

ROSENCRANTZ   Then thus she says: your behavior hath struck her into amazement and admiration.   325

HAMLET   Oh, wonderful son, that can so 'stonish a mother! But is there no sequel at the heels of this mother's admiration? Impart.

ROSENCRANTZ   She desires to speak with you in her closet ere you go to bed.   330

HAMLET   We shall obey, were she ten times our mother. Have you any further trade with us?

ROSENCRANTZ   My lord, you once did love me.

HAMLET   And do still, by these pickers and stealers.   334

ROSENCRANTZ   Good my lord, what is your cause of distemper? You do surely bar the door upon your own liberty if you deny your griefs to your friend.   337

HAMLET   Sir, I lack advancement.

ROSENCRANTZ   How can that be, when you have the voice of the King himself for your succession in Denmark?

HAMLET   Ay, sir, but "While the grass grows"—the proverb is something musty.   342 343

Enter the Players with recorders.

Oh, the recorders. Let me see one. [*He takes a recorder.*] To withdraw with you: why do you go about to recover the wind of me, as if you would drive me into a toil?   345 346

GUILDENSTERN   Oh, my lord, if my duty be too bold, my love is too unmannerly.   347 348

HAMLET   I do not well understand that. Will you play upon this pipe?   349

GUILDENSTERN   My lord, I cannot.

HAMLET   I pray you.

GUILDENSTERN   Believe me, I cannot.

HAMLET   I do beseech you.

GUILDENSTERN   I know no touch of it, my lord.

HAMLET   It is as easy as lying. Govern these ventages with your fingers and thumb, give it breath with your mouth, and it will discourse most eloquent music. Look you, these are the stops.   356

GUILDENSTERN   But these cannot I command to any utterance of harmony. I have not the skill.

HAMLET   Why, look you now, how unworthy a thing you make of me! You would play upon me, you would seem to know my stops, you would pluck out the heart of my mystery, you would sound me from my lowest note to the top of my compass, and there is much music, excellent voice, in this little organ, yet cannot you make it speak. 'Sblood, do you think I am easier to be played on than a pipe? Call me what instrument you will, though you can fret me, you cannot play upon me.   365 366 367 370

Enter Polonius.

God bless you, sir!

---

292 **perdy** (A corruption of the French *par dieu*, "by God.")
299 **retirement** withdrawal to his chambers   299–300 **distempered** out of humor. (But Hamlet deliberately plays on the wider application to any illness of mind or body, as in lines 335–6, especially to drunkenness.)   302 **choler** anger. (But Hamlet takes the word in its more basic humoral sense of "bilious disorder.")   305 **purgation** (Hamlet hints at something going beyond medical treatment to bloodletting and the extraction of confession.)   308 **frame** order. **start** shy or jump away (like a horse; the opposite of *tame* in line 309) 314 **breed** (1) kind (2) breeding, manners.   316 **pardon** permission to depart   325 **admiration** bewilderment.   330 **closet** private chamber

334 **pickers and stealers** i.e., hands. (So called from the catechism, "to keep my hands from picking and stealing.")   337 **liberty** i.e., being freed from *distemper*, line 336; but perhaps with a veiled threat as well. **deny** refuse to share   342 **"While . . . grows"** (The rest of the proverb is "the silly horse starves"; Hamlet implies that his hopes of succession are distant in time at best.)   343 **something** somewhat   343.1 *Players* actors   345 **withdraw** speak privately   345–6 **recover the wind** get to the windward side (thus allowing the game to scent the hunter and thereby be driven in the opposite direction into the *toil* or net)   346 **toil** snare.   347–8 **if . . . unmannerly** if I am using an unmannerly boldness, it is my love that occasions it.   349 **I . . . that** i.e., I don't understand how genuine love can be unmannerly.   356 **ventages** finger-holes or *stops* (line 359) of the recorder   365 **sound** (1) fathom (2) produce sound in   366 **compass** range (of voice)   367 **organ** musical instrument 370 **fret** irritate. (With a quibble on the *frets* or ridges on the fingerboard of some stringed instruments to regulate the fingering.)

POLONIUS   My lord, the Queen would speak with you,
    and presently.   374
HAMLET   Do you see yonder cloud that's almost in
    shape of a camel?
POLONIUS   By th' Mass, and 'tis, like a camel indeed.
HAMLET   Methinks it is like a weasel.
POLONIUS   It is backed like a weasel.
HAMLET   Or like a whale.
POLONIUS   Very like a whale.
HAMLET   Then I will come to my mother by and by.
    [Aside] They fool me to the top of my bent.—I will   383
    come by and by.
POLONIUS   I will say so.   [Exit.]
HAMLET   "By and by" is easily said. Leave me, friends.
                                            [Exeunt all but Hamlet.]
    'Tis now the very witching time of night,   387
    When churchyards yawn and hell itself breathes out
    Contagion to this world. Now could I drink hot
        blood
    And do such bitter business as the day
    Would quake to look on. Soft, now to my mother.
    O heart, lose not thy nature! Let not ever   392
    The soul of Nero enter this firm bosom.   393
    Let me be cruel, not unnatural;
    I will speak daggers to her, but use none.
    My tongue and soul in this be hypocrites:
    How in my words somever she be shent,   397
    To give them seals never my soul consent!   Exit.   398

                                    ❧

[3.3]

        Enter King, Rosencrantz, and Guildenstern.

KING
    I like him not, nor stands it safe with us   1
    To let his madness range. Therefore prepare you.
    I your commission will forthwith dispatch,   3
    And he to England shall along with you.
    The terms of our estate may not endure   5
    Hazard so near 's as doth hourly grow
    Out of his brows.
GUILDENSTERN   We will ourselves provide.   7
    Most holy and religious fear it is   8
    To keep those many many bodies safe
    That live and feed upon Your Majesty.
ROSENCRANTZ
    The single and peculiar life is bound   11

    With all the strength and armor of the mind
    To keep itself from noyance, but much more   13
    That spirit upon whose weal depends and rests   14
    The lives of many. The cess of majesty   15
    Dies not alone, but like a gulf doth draw   16
    What's near it with it; or it is a massy wheel   17
    Fixed on the summit of the highest mount,
    To whose huge spokes ten thousand lesser things
    Are mortised and adjoined, which, when it falls,   20
    Each small annexment, petty consequence,   21
    Attends the boist'rous ruin. Never alone   22
    Did the King sigh, but with a general groan.
KING
    Arm you, I pray you, to this speedy voyage,   24
    For we will fetters put about this fear,
    Which now goes too free-footed.
ROSENCRANTZ   We will haste us.
        Exeunt gentlemen [Rosencrantz and Guildenstern].

        Enter Polonius.

POLONIUS
    My lord, he's going to his mother's closet.
    Behind the arras I'll convey myself   28
    To hear the process. I'll warrant she'll tax him home,   29
    And, as you said—and wisely was it said—
    'Tis meet that some more audience than a mother,   31
    Since nature makes them partial, should o'erhear
    The speech of vantage. Fare you well, my liege.   33
    I'll call upon you ere you go to bed
    And tell you what I know.
KING   Thanks, dear my lord.
                                        Exit [Polonius].
    Oh, my offense is rank! It smells to heaven.
    It hath the primal eldest curse upon't,   37
    A brother's murder. Pray can I not,
    Though inclination be as sharp as will;   39
    My stronger guilt defeats my strong intent,
    And like a man to double business bound   41
    I stand in pause where I shall first begin,
    And both neglect. What if this cursèd hand
    Were thicker than itself with brother's blood,
    Is there not rain enough in the sweet heavens
    To wash it white as snow? Whereto serves mercy   46
    But to confront the visage of offense?   47
    And what's in prayer but this twofold force,

---

374 presently at once.   **383 They fool . . . bent** They humor my odd
behavior to the limit of my ability or endurance. (Literally, the extent
to which a bow may be bent.)   **387 witching time** time when spells
are cast and evil is abroad   **392 nature** natural feeling.   **393 Nero**
(This infamous Roman emperor put to death his mother, Agrippina,
who had murdered her husband, Claudius.)   **397–8 How . . . consent!** however much she is to be rebuked by my words, may my soul
never consent to ratify those words with deeds of violence!
3.3. Location: The castle.
1 him i.e., his behavior   **3 dispatch** prepare, cause to be drawn up
5 terms of our estate circumstances of my royal position   **7 Out . . .
brows** i.e., from his brain, in the form of plots and threats.   **We . . .
provide** We'll put ourselves in readiness.   **8 religious fear** sacred
concern   **11 single and peculiar** individual and private

13 noyance harm   **14 weal** well-being   **15 cess** decease, cessation
16 gulf whirlpool   **17 massy** massive   **20 mortised** fastened (as with
a fitted joint).   **when it falls** i.e., when it descends, like the wheel of
Fortune, bringing a king down with it   **21 Each . . . consequence** i.e.,
every hanger-on and unimportant person or thing connected with the
King   **22 Attends** participates in   **24 Arm** Provide, prepare
28 arras screen of tapestry placed around the walls of household
apartments. (On the Elizabethan stage, the arras was presumably
over a door or aperture in the tiring-house facade.)   **29 process** proceedings.   **tax him home** reprove him severely   **31 meet** fitting
33 of vantage from an advantageous place, or, in addition.   **37 the
primal eldest curse** the curse of Cain, the first murderer; he killed his
brother Abel   **39 Though . . . will** though my desire is as strong as
my determination   **41 bound** (1) destined (2) obliged. (The King
wants to repent and still enjoy what he has gained.)   **46–7 Whereto . . .
offense?** What function does mercy serve other than to meet sin face
to face?

To be forestallèd ere we come to fall,   49
Or pardoned being down? Then I'll look up.
My fault is past. But oh, what form of prayer
Can serve my turn? "Forgive me my foul murder"?
That cannot be, since I am still possessed
Of those effects for which I did the murder:
My crown, mine own ambition, and my queen.
May one be pardoned and retain th'offense?   56
In the corrupted currents of this world   57
Offense's gilded hand may shove by justice,   58
And oft 'tis seen the wicked prize itself   59
Buys out the law. But 'tis not so above.
There is no shuffling, there the action lies   61
In his true nature, and we ourselves compelled,   62
Even to the teeth and forehead of our faults,   63
To give in evidence. What then? What rests?   64
Try what repentance can. What can it not?
Yet what can it, when one cannot repent?
O wretched state, O bosom black as death,
O limèd soul that, struggling to be free,   68
Art more engaged! Help, angels! Make assay.   69
Bow, stubborn knees, and heart with strings of steel,
Be soft as sinews of the newborn babe!
All may be well.   [*He kneels.*]

              Enter Hamlet.

HAMLET
Now might I do it pat, now 'a is a-praying;   73
And now I'll do't. [*He draws his sword.*] And so 'a goes
   to heaven,
And so am I revenged. That would be scanned: 75
A villain kills my father, and for that,
I, his sole son, do this same villain send
To heaven.
Why, this is hire and salary, not revenge.
'A took my father grossly, full of bread,   80
With all his crimes broad blown, as flush as May;   81
And how his audit stands who knows save heaven?   82
But in our circumstance and course of thought   83
'Tis heavy with him. And am I then revenged,
To take him in the purging of his soul,
When he is fit and seasoned for his passage?   86
No!
Up, sword, and know thou a more horrid hent.   88
                                  [*He puts up his sword.*]

When he is drunk asleep, or in his rage,   89
Or in th'incestuous pleasure of his bed,
At game, a-swearing, or about some act   91
That has no relish of salvation in't—   92
Then trip him, that his heels may kick at heaven,
And that his soul may be as damned and black
As hell, whereto it goes. My mother stays.   95
This physic but prolongs thy sickly days.   *Exit.*   96
KING
My words fly up, my thoughts remain below.
Words without thoughts never to heaven go.   *Exit.*

                         ❖

[3.4]

              Enter [Queen] Gertrude and Polonius.

POLONIUS
'A will come straight. Look you lay home to him.   1
Tell him his pranks have been too broad to bear with,   2
And that Your Grace hath screened and stood
   between
Much heat and him. I'll silence me even here.   4
Pray you, be round with him.   5
HAMLET (*within*) Mother, mother, mother!
QUEEN   I'll warrant you, fear me not.
Withdraw, I hear him coming.
                      [*Polonius hides behind the arras.*]

              Enter Hamlet.

HAMLET   Now, mother, what's the matter?
QUEEN
Hamlet, thou hast thy father much offended.   10
HAMLET
Mother, you have my father much offended.
QUEEN
Come, come, you answer with an idle tongue.   12
HAMLET
Go, go, you question with a wicked tongue.
QUEEN
Why, how now, Hamlet?
HAMLET   What's the matter now?
QUEEN
Have you forgot me?
HAMLET   No, by the rood, not so: 15
You are the Queen, your husband's brother's wife,
And—would it were not so!—you are my mother.
QUEEN
Nay, then, I'll set those to you that can speak.   18

---

49 forestallèd prevented (from sinning)   **56 th'offense** the thing for
which one offended.   **57 currents** courses of events   **58 gilded hand**
hand offering gold as a bribe.   **shove by** thrust aside   **59 wicked
prize** prize won by wickedness   **61 There . . . lies** There in heaven
can be no evasion, there the deed lies exposed to view   **62 his** its
63 to the teeth and forehead face to face, concealing nothing
64 give in provide.   **rests** remains.   **68 limèd** caught as with
birdlime, a sticky substance used to ensnare birds   **69 engaged**
entangled.   **assay** trial. (Said to himself, or to the angels to try him.)
73 pat opportunely   **75 would be scanned** needs to be looked into,
or, would be interpreted as follows   **80 grossly, full of bread** i.e.,
enjoying his worldly pleasures rather than fasting. (See Ezekiel 16:49.)
81 crimes broad blown sins in full bloom.   **flush** vigorous   **82 audit**
account.   **save** except for   **83 in . . . thought** as we see it from our
mortal perspective   **86 seasoned** matured, readied   **88 know . . .
hent** await to be grasped by me on a more horrid occasion. (*Hent*
means "act of seizing.")

89 drunk . . . rage dead drunk, or in a fit of sexual passion   **91 game**
gambling   **92 relish** trace, savor   **95 stays** awaits (me).   **96 physic**
purging (by prayer), or, Hamlet's postponement of the killing
3.4. Location: The Queen's private chamber.
1 lay . . . him reprove him soundly.   **2 broad** unrestrained   **4 Much
heat** i.e., the King's anger.   **I'll silence me** I'll quietly conceal myself.
(Ironic, since it is his crying out at line 24 that leads to his death.
Some editors emend *silence* to "sconce." The first quarto's reading,
"shroud," is attractive.)   **5 round** blunt   **10 thy father** i.e., your stepfather, Claudius   **12 idle** foolish   **15 forgot me** i.e., forgotten that I
am your mother.   **rood** cross of Christ   **18 speak** i.e., speak to someone so rude.

HAMLET
Come, come, and sit you down; you shall not budge.
You go not till I set you up a glass
Where you may see the inmost part of you.

QUEEN
What wilt thou do? Thou wilt not murder me?
Help, ho!

POLONIUS [*behind the arras*]   What ho! Help!

HAMLET [*drawing*]
How now? A rat? Dead for a ducat, dead!   25
       [*He thrusts his rapier through the arras.*]

POLONIUS [*behind the arras*]
Oh, I am slain!   [*He falls and dies.*]

QUEEN   Oh, me, what hast thou done?

HAMLET   Nay, I know not. Is it the King?

QUEEN
Oh, what a rash and bloody deed is this!

HAMLET
A bloody deed—almost as bad, good mother,
As kill a king, and marry with his brother.

QUEEN
As kill a king!

HAMLET   Ay, lady, it was my word.
    [*He parts the arras and discovers Polonius.*]
Thou wretched, rash, intruding fool, farewell!
I took thee for thy better. Take thy fortune.
Thou find'st to be too busy is some danger.—   34
Leave wringing of your hands. Peace, sit you down,
And let me wring your heart, for so I shall,
If it be made of penetrable stuff,
If damnèd custom have not brazed it so   38
That it be proof and bulwark against sense.   39

QUEEN
What have I done, that thou dar'st wag thy tongue
In noise so rude against me?

HAMLET   Such an act
That blurs the grace and blush of modesty,
Calls virtue hypocrite, takes off the rose
From the fair forehead of an innocent love
And sets a blister there, makes marriage vows   45
As false as dicers' oaths. Oh, such a deed
As from the body of contraction plucks   47
The very soul, and sweet religion makes   48
A rhapsody of words. Heaven's face does glow   49
O'er this solidity and compound mass   50
With tristful visage, as against the doom,   51
Is thought-sick at the act.

QUEEN   Ay me, what act,   52
That roars so loud and thunders in the index?   53

HAMLET [*showing her two likenesses*]
Look here upon this picture, and on this,

The counterfeit presentment of two brothers.   55
See what a grace was seated on this brow:
Hyperion's curls, the front of Jove himself,   57
An eye like Mars to threaten and command,   58
A station like the herald Mercury   59
New-lighted on a heaven-kissing hill—   60
A combination and a form indeed
Where every god did seem to set his seal   62
To give the world assurance of a man.
This was your husband. Look you now what follows:
Here is your husband, like a mildewed ear,   65
Blasting his wholesome brother. Have you eyes?   66
Could you on this fair mountain leave to feed   67
And batten on this moor? Ha, have you eyes?   68
You cannot call it love, for at your age
The heyday in the blood is tame, it's humble,   70
And waits upon the judgment, and what judgment
Would step from this to this? Sense, sure, you have,   72
Else could you not have motion, but sure that sense
Is apoplexed, for madness would not err,   74
Nor sense to ecstasy was ne'er so thralled,   75
But it reserved some quantity of choice   76
To serve in such a difference. What devil was't   77
That thus hath cozened you at hoodman-blind?   78
Eyes without feeling, feeling without sight,
Ears without hands or eyes, smelling sans all,   80
Or but a sickly part of one true sense
Could not so mope. O shame, where is thy blush?   82
Rebellious hell,
If thou canst mutine in a matron's bones,   84
To flaming youth let virtue be as wax   85
And melt in her own fire. Proclaim no shame   86
When the compulsive ardor gives the charge,   87
Since frost itself as actively doth burn,   88
And reason panders will.   89

QUEEN   Oh, Hamlet, speak no more!
Thou turn'st mine eyes into my very soul,
And there I see such black and grainèd spots   92

---

25 Dead for a ducat i.e., I bet a ducat he's dead; or, a ducat is his life's fee.   **34 busy** nosey   **38 damnèd custom** habitual wickedness. **brazed** brazened, hardened   **39 proof** impenetrable, like *proof* or tested armor.   **sense** feeling.   **45 sets a blister** i.e., brands as a harlot   **47 contraction** the marriage contract   **48 sweet religion makes** i.e., makes marriage vows   **49 rhapsody** senseless string   **49–52 Heaven's . . . act** Heaven's face blushes at this solid world compounded of the various elements, with sorrowful face as though the day of doom were near, and is sick with horror at the deed (i.e., Gertrude's marriage).   **53 index** table of contents, prelude or preface.

55 counterfeit presentment representation in portraiture   **57 Hyperion's** the sun-god's.   **front** brow   **58 Mars** god of war   **59 station** manner of standing.   **Mercury** winged messenger of the gods   **60 New-lighted** newly alighted.   **heaven-kissing** reaching to the sky   **62 set his seal** i.e., affix his approval   **65 ear** i.e., of grain   **66 Blasting** blighting   **67 leave** cease   **68 batten** gorge.   **moor** barren or marshy ground. (Suggesting also "dark-skinned.")   **70 The heyday . . . blood** (The blood was thought to be the source of sexual desire.)   **72 Sense** Perception through the five senses (the functions of the middle or sensible soul)   **74 apoplexed** paralyzed.   **err** so err   **75–7 Nor . . . difference** nor could your physical senses ever have been so enthralled to *ecstasy* or lunacy that they could not distinguish to some degree between Hamlet Senior and Claudius.   **78 cozened** cheated. **hoodman-blind** blindman's buff. (In this game, says Hamlet, the devil must have pushed Claudius toward Gertrude while she was blindfolded.)   **80 sans** without   **82 mope** be dazed, act aimlessly.   **84 mutine** mutiny   **85–6 To . . . fire** when it comes to sexually passionate youth, let virtue melt like a candle or stick of sealing wax held over a candle flame. (There's no point in hoping for self-restraint among young people when matronly women set such a bad example.)   **86–9 Proclaim . . . will** Call it no shameful business when the compelling ardor of youth delivers the attack, i.e., commits lechery, since the *frost* of advanced age burns with as active a fire of lust and reason perverts itself by fomenting lust rather than restraining it.   **92 grainèd** ingrained, indelible

As will not leave their tinct.
HAMLET   Nay, but to live   93
In the rank sweat of an enseamèd bed,   94
Stewed in corruption, honeying and making love   95
Over the nasty sty!   96
QUEEN   Oh, speak to me no more!
These words like daggers enter in my ears.
No more, sweet Hamlet!
HAMLET   A murderer and a villain,
A slave that is not twentieth part the tithe   100
Of your precedent lord, a vice of kings,   101
A cutpurse of the empire and the rule,
That from a shelf the precious diadem stole
And put it in his pocket!
QUEEN   No more!   105

Enter Ghost [in his nightgown].

HAMLET   A king of shreds and patches—   106
Save me, and hover o'er me with your wings,
You heavenly guards! What would your gracious
    figure?
QUEEN   Alas, he's mad!
HAMLET
Do you not come your tardy son to chide,
That, lapsed in time and passion, lets go by   111
Th'important acting of your dread command?   112
Oh, say!
GHOST
Do not forget. This visitation
Is but to whet thy almost blunted purpose.   115
But look, amazement on thy mother sits.   116
Oh, step between her and her fighting soul!
Conceit in weakest bodies strongest works.   118
Speak to her, Hamlet.
HAMLET   How is it with you, lady?
QUEEN   Alas, how is't with you,
That you do bend your eye on vacancy,
And with th'incorporal air do hold discourse?   122
Forth at your eyes your spirits wildly peep,
And, as the sleeping soldiers in th'alarm,   124
Your bedded hair, like life in excrements,   125
Start up and stand on end. O gentle son,
Upon the heat and flame of thy distemper   127
Sprinkle cool patience. Whereon do you look?

HAMLET
On him, on him! Look you how pale he glares!
His form and cause conjoined, preaching to stones,   130
Would make them capable.—Do not look upon me,   131
Lest with this piteous action you convert   132
My stern effects. Then what I have to do   133
Will want true color—tears perchance for blood.   134
QUEEN   To whom do you speak this?
HAMLET   Do you see nothing there?
QUEEN
Nothing at all, yet all that is I see.
HAMLET   Nor did you nothing hear?
QUEEN   No, nothing but ourselves.
HAMLET
Why, look you there, look how it steals away!
My father, in his habit as he lived!   141
Look where he goes even now out at the portal!
                                        Exit Ghost.
QUEEN
This is the very coinage of your brain.   143
This bodiless creation ecstasy   144
Is very cunning in.   145
HAMLET   Ecstasy?
My pulse as yours doth temperately keep time,
And makes as healthful music. It is not madness
That I have uttered. Bring me to the test,
And I the matter will reword, which madness   150
Would gambol from. Mother, for love of grace,   151
Lay not that flattering unction to your soul   152
That not your trespass but my madness speaks.
It will but skin and film the ulcerous place,   154
Whiles rank corruption, mining all within,   155
Infects unseen. Confess yourself to heaven,
Repent what's past, avoid what is to come,
And do not spread the compost on the weeds   158
To make them ranker. Forgive me this my virtue;   159
For in the fatness of these pursy times   160
Virtue itself of vice must pardon beg,
Yea, curb and woo for leave to do him good.   162
QUEEN
Oh, Hamlet, thou hast cleft my heart in twain.
HAMLET
Oh, throw away the worser part of it,
And live the purer with the other half.
Good night. But go not to my uncle's bed;
Assume a virtue, if you have it not.
That monster, custom, who all sense doth eat,   168
Of habits devil, is angel yet in this,   169

---

93 **leave their tinct** surrender their dark stain.   94 **enseamèd** saturated in the grease and filth of passionate lovemaking   95 **Stewed** soaked, bathed. (With a suggestion of "stew," brothel.)   96 **Over . . . sty** (Like barnyard animals.)   100 **tithe** tenth part   101 **precedent lord** former husband.   **vice** (From the morality plays, a model of iniquity and a buffoon.)   105.1 *nightgown* a robe for indoor wear.   106 **A king . . . patches** i.e., a king whose splendor is all sham; a clown or fool dressed in motley   111 **lapsed . . . passion** having let time and passion slip away   112 **Th'important** the importunate, urgent   115 **whet** sharpen   116 **amazement** distraction   118 **Conceit** Imagination   122 **th'incorporal** the immaterial   124 **as . . . th'alarm** like soldiers called out of sleep by an alarum   125 **bedded** laid flat. **like life in excrements** i.e., as though hair, an outgrowth of the body, had a life of its own. (Hair was thought to be lifeless because it lacks sensation, and so its standing on end would be unnatural and ominous.)   127 **distemper** disorder

130 **His . . . conjoined** His appearance joined to his cause for speaking   131 **capable** capable of feeling, receptive.   132–3 **convert . . . effects** divert me from my stern duty.   134 **want . . . blood** lack plausibility so that (with a play on the normal sense of *color*) I shall shed colorless tears instead of blood.   141 **habit** clothes.   **as** as when   143 **mere**   144–5 **This . . . in** Madness is skillful in creating this kind of hallucination.   150 **reword** repeat word for word   151 **gambol** skip away   152 **unction** ointment   154 **skin** grow a skin over   155 **mining** working under the surface   158 **compost** manure   159 **this my virtue** my virtuous talk in reproving you   160 **fatness** grossness. **pursy** flabby, out of shape   162 **curb** bow, bend the knee.   **leave** permission   168 **who . . . eat** which consumes and overwhelms the physical senses   169 **Of habits devil** devil-like in prompting evil habits

That to the use of actions fair and good
He likewise gives a frock or livery   171
That aptly is put on. Refrain tonight,   172
And that shall lend a kind of easiness
To the next abstinence; the next more easy;
For use almost can change the stamp of nature,   175
And either . . . the devil, or throw him out   176
With wondrous potency. Once more, good night;
And when you are desirous to be blest,   178
I'll blessing beg of you. For this same lord,   179
                 [*pointing to Polonius*]
I do repent; but heaven hath pleased it so
To punish me with this, and this with me,   181
That I must be their scourge and minister.   182
I will bestow him, and will answer well   183
The death I gave him. So, again, good night.
I must be cruel only to be kind.
This bad begins, and worse remains behind.   186
One word more, good lady.
QUEEN   What shall I do?
HAMLET
Not this by no means that I bid you do:
Let the bloat king tempt you again to bed,   189
Pinch wanton on your cheek, call you his mouse,   190
And let him, for a pair of reechy kisses,   191
Or paddling in your neck with his damned fingers,   192
Make you to ravel all this matter out   193
That I essentially am not in madness,
But mad in craft. 'Twere good you let him know,   195
For who that's but a queen, fair, sober, wise,
Would from a paddock, from a bat, a gib,   197
Such dear concernings hide? Who would do so?   198
No, in despite of sense and secrecy,   199
Unpeg the basket on the house's top,   200
Let the birds fly, and like the famous ape,   201
To try conclusions, in the basket creep   202
And break your own neck down.   203
QUEEN
Be thou assured, if words be made of breath,
And breath of life, I have no life to breathe
What thou hast said to me.

HAMLET
I must to England. You know that?
QUEEN   Alack,
I had forgot. 'Tis so concluded on.
HAMLET
There's letters sealed, and my two schoolfellows,
Whom I will trust as I will adders fanged,
They bear the mandate; they must sweep my way   211
And marshal me to knavery. Let it work.   212
For 'tis the sport to have the engineer   213
Hoist with his own petard, and 't shall go hard   214
But I will delve one yard below their mines   215
And blow them at the moon. Oh, 'tis most sweet
When in one line two crafts directly meet.   217
This man shall set me packing.   218
I'll lug the guts into the neighbor room.
Mother, good night indeed. This counselor
Is now most still, most secret, and most grave,
Who was in life a foolish prating knave.—
Come, sir, to draw toward an end with you.—   223
Good night, mother.
        Exeunt [*separately, Hamlet dragging in Polonius*].

[4.1]

        Enter King and Queen, with Rosencrantz and
        Guildenstern.

KING
There's matter in these sighs, these profound heaves.   1
You must translate; 'tis fit we understand them.
Where is your son?
QUEEN
Bestow this place on us a little while.
         [*Exeunt Rosencrantz and Guildenstern.*]
Ah, mine own lord, what have I seen tonight!

---

171 **livery** an outer appearance, a customary garb (and hence a predis-position easily assumed in time of stress)   172 **aptly** readily   175 **use** habit.   **the stamp of nature** our inborn traits   176 **And either** (A defective line, often emended by inserting the word "master" after *either*, following the third quarto and early editors, or some other word such as "shame," "lodge," "curb," or "house.")   178–9 **when . . . you** i.e., when you are ready to be penitent and seek God's blessing, I will ask your blessing as a dutiful son should.   181 **To punish . . . with me** to seek retribution from me for killing Polonius, and from him through my means   182 **their scourge and minister** i.e., agent of heavenly retribution.   183 **bestow** stow, dispose of.   **answer** account or pay for   186 **This** i.e., The killing of Polonius.   **behind** to come.   189 **bloat** bloated   190 **Pinch wanton** i.e., leave his love pinches on your cheeks, branding you as wanton   191 **reechy** dirty, filthy   192 **paddling** fingering amorously   193 **ravel . . . out** unravel, disclose   195 **in craft** by cunning.   **good** (Said sarcastically; also the following eight lines.)   197 **paddock** toad.   **gib** tomcat   198 **dear concernings** important affairs   199 **sense and secrecy** secrecy that common sense requires   200 **Unpeg the basket** open the cage, i.e., let out the secret   201 **famous ape** (In a story now lost.)   202 **try conclusions** test the outcome (in which the ape apparently enters a cage from which birds have been released and then tries to fly out of the cage as they have done, falling to its death)   203 **down** in the fall.

211–12 **sweep . . . knavery** sweep a path before me and conduct me to some *knavery* or treachery prepared for me.   212 **work** proceed. 213 **engineer** maker of *engines* of war   214 **Hoist** with blown up by. **petard** an explosive used to blow in a door or make a breach 214–15 **'t shall . . . will** unless luck is against me, I will   215 **mines** tunnels used in warfare to undermine the enemy's emplacements; Hamlet will countermine by going under their mines   217 **in one line** i.e., mines and countermines on a collision course, or the coun-termines directly below the mines.   **crafts** acts of guile, plots 218 **set me packing** set me to making schemes, and set me to lugging (him), and, also, send me off in a hurry.   223 **draw . . . end** finish up. (With a pun on *draw*, "pull.")
4.1. Location: The castle.
0.1 ***Enter . . . Queen*** (Some editors argue that Gertrude does not in fact exit at the end of 3.4 and that the scene is continuous here. It is true that the Folio ends 3.4 with "*Exit Hamlet tugging in Polonius*," not naming Gertrude, and opens 4.1 with "*Enter King.*" Yet the second quarto concludes 3.4 with a simple "*Exit*," which often stands ambiguously for a single exit or an exeunt in early modern texts, and then starts 4.1 with "*Enter King, and Queene, with Rosencraus and Guyldensterne.*" The King's opening lines in 4.1 suggest that he has had time, during a brief intervening pause, to become aware of Gertrude's highly wrought emotional state. In line 35, the King refers to Gertrude's *closet* as though it were elsewhere. The differences between the second quarto and the Folio offer an alternative staging. In either case, 4.1 follows swiftly upon 3.4.)   1 **matter** significance. **heaves** heavy sighs.

KING
What, Gertrude? How does Hamlet?
QUEEN
Mad as the sea and wind when both contend
Which is the mightier. In his lawless fit,
Behind the arras hearing something stir,
Whips out his rapier, cries, "A rat, a rat!"
And in this brainish apprehension kills   11
The unseen good old man.
KING   Oh, heavy deed!   12
It had been so with us, had we been there.   13
His liberty is full of threats to all—
To you yourself, to us, to everyone.
Alas, how shall this bloody deed be answered?   16
It will be laid to us, whose providence   17
Should have kept short, restrained, and out of haunt   18
This mad young man. But so much was our love,
We would not understand what was most fit,
But, like the owner of a foul disease,
To keep it from divulging, let it feed
Even on the pith of life. Where is he gone?   22
QUEEN
To draw apart the body he hath killed,
O'er whom his very madness, like some ore   25
Among a mineral of metals base,   26
Shows itself pure: 'a weeps for what is done.
KING Oh, Gertrude, come away!
The sun no sooner shall the mountains touch
But we will ship him hence, and this vile deed
We must with all our majesty and skill
Both countenance and excuse.—Ho, Guildenstern!   32

Enter Rosencrantz and Guildenstern.

Friends both, go join you with some further aid.
Hamlet in madness hath Polonius slain,
And from his mother's closet hath he dragged him.
Go seek him out, speak fair, and bring the body
Into the chapel. I pray you, haste in this.   36
           [*Exeunt Rosencrantz and Guildenstern.*]
Come, Gertrude, we'll call up our wisest friends
And let them know both what we mean to do
And what's untimely done   40
Whose whisper o'er the world's diameter,   41
As level as the cannon to his blank,   42
Transports his poisoned shot, may miss our name
And hit the woundless air. Oh, come away!   44
My soul is full of discord and dismay.   *Exeunt.*

❖

[4.2]

Enter Hamlet.

HAMLET Safely stowed.
ROSENCRANTZ, GUILDENSTERN (*within*) Hamlet! Lord
   Hamlet!
HAMLET But soft, what noise? Who calls on Hamlet? Oh,
   here they come.

Enter Rosencrantz and Guildenstern.

ROSENCRANTZ
What have you done, my lord, with the dead body?
HAMLET
Compounded it with dust, whereto 'tis kin.
ROSENCRANTZ
Tell us where 'tis, that we may take it thence
And bear it to the chapel.
HAMLET Do not believe it.
ROSENCRANTZ Believe what?
HAMLET That I can keep your counsel and not mine   12
   own. Besides, to be demanded of a sponge, what rep- 13
   lication should be made by the son of a king?   14
ROSENCRANTZ Take you me for a sponge, my lord?
HAMLET Ay, sir, that soaks up the King's countenance, 16
   his rewards, his authorities. But such officers do the 17
   King best service in the end. He keeps them, like an
   ape, an apple, in the corner of his jaw, first mouthed
   to be last swallowed. When he needs what you have
   gleaned, it is but squeezing you, and, sponge, you
   shall be dry again.
ROSENCRANTZ I understand you not, my lord.
HAMLET I am glad of it. A knavish speech sleeps in a   24
   foolish ear.
ROSENCRANTZ My lord, you must tell us where the
   body is and go with us to the King.
HAMLET The body is with the King, but the King is not 28
   with the body. The King is a thing—   29
GUILDENSTERN A thing, my lord?
HAMLET Of nothing. Bring me to him. Hide fox, and all 31
   after!   *Exeunt* [*running*]. 32

❖

[4.3]

Enter King, and two or three.

4.2. Location: The castle.
12–13 That . . . own i.e., Don't expect me to do as you bid me and not
follow my own counsel. **13 demanded of** questioned by
13–14 replication reply **16 countenance** favor **17 authorities** delegated power, influence. **24 sleeps in** has no meaning to **28–9 The
. . . body** (Perhaps alludes to the legal commonplace of "the king's
two bodies," which drew a distinction between the sacred office of
kingship and the particular mortal who possessed it at any given
time. Hence, although Claudius's body is necessarily a part of him,
true kingship is not contained in it. Similarly, Claudius will have
Polonius's body when it is found, but there is no kingship in this
business either.) **31 Of nothing** (1) Of no account (2) Lacking the
essence of kingship, as in lines 28–9 and note. **31–2 Hide . . . after**
(An old signal cry in the game of hide-and-seek, suggesting that
Hamlet now runs away from them.)
4.3. Location: The castle.

11 brainish apprehension frenzied misapprehension **12 heavy** grievous **13 us** i.e., me. (The royal "we"; also in line 15.) **16 answered**
explained. **17 providence** foresight **18 short** i.e., on a short tether.
out of haunt secluded **22 from divulging** from becoming publicly
known **25 ore** vein of gold **26 mineral** mine **32 countenance** put
the best face on **36 fair** gently, courteously **40 And . . . done** (A
defective line; conjectures as to the missing words include "So, haply,
slander" [Capell and others]; "For, haply, slander" [Theobald and
others]; and "So envious slander" [Jenkins].) **41 diameter** extent
from side to side **42 As level** with as direct aim. **his blank** its target at point-blank range **44 woundless** invulnerable

KING
I have sent to seek him, and to find the body.
How dangerous is it that this man goes loose!
Yet must not we put the strong law on him.
He's loved of the distracted multitude, 4
Who like not in their judgment, but their eyes, 5
And where 'tis so, th'offender's scourge is weighed, 6
But never the offense. To bear all smooth and even, 7
This sudden sending him away must seem
Deliberate pause. Diseases desperate grown 9
By desperate appliance are relieved, 10
Or not at all.

       Enter Rosencrantz, [Guildenstern,]
       and all the rest.

           How now, what hath befall'n?

ROSENCRANTZ
Where the dead body is bestowed, my lord,
We cannot get from him.

KING   But where is he?

ROSENCRANTZ
Without, my lord; guarded, to know your pleasure. 14

KING
Bring him before us.

ROSENCRANTZ *[calling]*   Ho! Bring in the lord.

        They enter [with Hamlet].

KING   Now, Hamlet, where's Polonius?

HAMLET   At supper.

KING   At supper? Where?

HAMLET   Not where he eats, but where 'a is eaten. A
certain convocation of politic worms are e'en at him. 20
Your worm is your only emperor for diet. We fat all 21
creatures else to fat us, and we fat ourselves for maggots. Your fat king and your lean beggar is but
variable service—two dishes, but to one table. That's 24
the end.

KING   Alas, alas!

HAMLET   A man may fish with the worm that hath eat 27
of a king, and eat of the fish that hath fed of that
worm.

KING   What dost thou mean by this?

HAMLET   Nothing but to show you how a king may go
a progress through the guts of a beggar. 32

KING   Where is Polonius?

HAMLET   In heaven. Send thither to see. If your messenger find him not there, seek him i'th'other place yourself. But if indeed you find him not within this month,

you shall nose him as you go up the stairs into the 37
lobby.

KING *[to some attendants]*   Go seek him there.

HAMLET   'A will stay till you come. *[Exeunt attendants.]*

KING
Hamlet, this deed, for thine especial safety—
Which we do tender, as we dearly grieve 42
For that which thou hast done—must send thee hence
With fiery quickness. Therefore prepare thyself.
The bark is ready, and the wind at help, 45
Th'associates tend, and everything is bent 46
For England.

HAMLET   For England!

KING   Ay, Hamlet.

HAMLET   Good.

KING
So is it, if thou knew'st our purposes.

HAMLET   I see a cherub that sees them. But come, for 52
England! Farewell, dear mother.

KING   Thy loving father, Hamlet.

HAMLET   My mother. Father and mother is man and
wife, man and wife is one flesh, and so, my mother.
Come, for England!   *Exit.*

KING
Follow him at foot; tempt him with speed aboard. 58
Delay it not. I'll have him hence tonight.
Away! For everything is sealed and done
That else leans on th'affair. Pray you, make haste. 61
                  [Exeunt all but the King.]
And, England, if my love thou hold'st at aught— 62
As my great power thereof may give thee sense, 63
Since yet thy cicatrice looks raw and red 64
After the Danish sword, and thy free awe 65
Pays homage to us—thou mayst not coldly set 66
Our sovereign process, which imports at full, 67
By letters congruing to that effect, 68
The present death of Hamlet. Do it, England, 69
For like the hectic in my blood he rages, 70
And thou must cure me. Till I know 'tis done,
Howe'er my haps, my joys were ne'er begun.   *Exit.* 72

                 ❖

[4.4]

Enter Fortinbras with his army over the stage.

FORTINBRAS
Go, Captain, from me greet the Danish king.

---

4 of by.   **distracted** fickle, unstable   **5 Who . . . eyes** who choose not
by judgment but by appearance   **6–7 th'offender's . . . offense** i.e.,
the populace often takes umbrage at the severity of a punishment
without taking into account the gravity of the crime.   **7 To . . . even**
To manage the business in an unprovocative way   **9 Deliberate
pause** carefully considered action.   **10 appliance** remedies   **14 Without** Outside   **20 politic worms** crafty worms (suited to a master spy
like Polonius).   **e'en** even now   **21 Your worm** Your average worm.
(Compare *your fat king and your lean beggar* in line 23.)   **diet** food, eating. (With a punning reference to the Diet of Worms, a famous
convocation held in 1521.)   **24 service** food served at table. (Worms
feed on kings and beggars alike.)   **27 eat** eaten. (Pronounced *et*.)
32 progress royal journey of state

37 nose smell   **42 tender** regard, hold dear.   **dearly** intensely
45 bark sailing vessel   **46 tend** wait.   **bent** in readiness   **52 cherub**
(Cherubim are angels of knowledge. Hamlet hints that both he and
heaven are onto Claudius's tricks.)   **58 at foot** close behind, at heel
61 leans on bears upon, is related to   **62 England** i.e., King of England.   **at aught** at any value   **63 As . . . sense** for so my great power
may give you a just appreciation of the importance of valuing my
love   **64 cicatrice** scar   **65 free awe** unconstrained show of respect
66 coldly set regard with indifference   **67 process** command.
imports at full conveys specific directions for   **68 congruing** agreeing   **69 present** immediate   **70 hectic** persistent fever   **72 Howe'er
. . . begun** whatever else happens, I cannot begin to be happy.
4.4. Location: The coast of Denmark.

Tell him that by his license Fortinbras   2
Craves the conveyance of a promised march   3
Over his kingdom. You know the rendezvous.
If that His Majesty would aught with us,
We shall express our duty in his eye;   6
And let him know so.
CAPTAIN   I will do't, my lord.
FORTINBRAS   Go softly on.   [*Exeunt all but the Captain.*]   9

Enter Hamlet, Rosencrantz, [Guildenstern,] etc.

HAMLET   Good sir, whose powers are these?   10
CAPTAIN   They are of Norway, sir.
HAMLET   How purposed, sir, I pray you?
CAPTAIN   Against some part of Poland.
HAMLET   Who commands them, sir?
CAPTAIN
The nephew to old Norway, Fortinbras.
HAMLET
Goes it against the main of Poland, sir,   16
Or for some frontier?
CAPTAIN
Truly to speak, and with no addition,   18
We go to gain a little patch of ground
That hath in it no profit but the name.
To pay five ducats, five, I would not farm it;   21
Nor will it yield to Norway or the Pole
A ranker rate, should it be sold in fee.   23
HAMLET
Why, then the Polack never will defend it.
CAPTAIN
Yes, it is already garrisoned.
HAMLET
Two thousand souls and twenty thousand ducats
Will not debate the question of this straw.   27
This is th'impostume of much wealth and peace,   28
That inward breaks, and shows no cause without   29
Why the man dies. I humbly thank you, sir.
CAPTAIN
God b'wi'you, sir.   [*Exit.*]
ROSENCRANTZ   Will't please you go, my lord?
HAMLET
I'll be with you straight. Go a little before.
                        [*Exeunt all except Hamlet.*]
How all occasions do inform against me   33
And spur my dull revenge! What is a man,
If his chief good and market of his time   35
Be but to sleep and feed? A beast, no more.
Sure he that made us with such large discourse,   37
Looking before and after, gave us not   38
That capability and godlike reason

To fust in us unused. Now, whether it be   40
Bestial oblivion, or some craven scruple   41
Of thinking too precisely on th'event—   42
A thought which, quartered, hath but one part
    wisdom
And ever three parts coward—I do not know
Why yet I live to say "This thing's to do,"
Sith I have cause, and will, and strength, and means   46
To do't. Examples gross as earth exhort me: 47
Witness this army of such mass and charge,   48
Led by a delicate and tender prince,   49
Whose spirit with divine ambition puffed
Makes mouths at the invisible event,   51
Exposing what is mortal and unsure
To all that fortune, death, and danger dare,   53
Even for an eggshell. Rightly to be great   54
Is not to stir without great argument,   55
But greatly to find quarrel in a straw   56
When honor's at the stake. How stand I, then,   57
That have a father killed, a mother stained,
Excitements of my reason and my blood,   59
And let all sleep, while to my shame I see
The imminent death of twenty thousand men
That for a fantasy and trick of fame   62
Go to their graves like beds, fight for a plot   63
Whereon the numbers cannot try the cause,   64
Which is not tomb enough and continent   65
To hide the slain? Oh, from this time forth
My thoughts be bloody or be nothing worth!   *Exit.*

❧

[4.5]

*Enter Horatio, [Queen] Gertrude, and a Gentle-
man.*

QUEEN
I will not speak with her.
GENTLEMAN   She is importunate,
Indeed distract. Her mood will needs be pitied.   2
QUEEN   What would she have?
GENTLEMAN
She speaks much of her father, says she hears
There's tricks i'th' world, and hems, and beats her
    heart,   5
Spurns enviously at straws, speaks things in doubt   6

2 **license** permission   3 **conveyance** unhindered passage   6 **We . . .
eye** I will come pay my respects in person   9 **softly** slowly, circum-
spectly   10 **powers** forces   16 **main** main part   18 **addition** exaggeration   21 **To pay** i.e., For a yearly rental of.   **farm it** take a lease
of it   23 **ranker** higher.   **in fee** fee simple, outright.   27 **debate . . .
straw** argue about this trifling matter.   28 **th'impostume** the abscess
29 **inward breaks** festers within.   **without** externally   33 **inform
against** denounce; take shape against   35 **market of** profit of
37 **discourse** power of reasoning   38 **Looking before and after** able
to review past events and anticipate the future

40 **fust** grow moldy   41 **oblivion** forgetfulness.   **craven** cowardly
42 **precisely** scrupulously.   **th'event** the outcome   46 **Sith** since
47 **gross** obvious   48 **charge** expense   49 **delicate and tender** of fine
and youthful qualities   51 **Makes mouths** makes scornful faces.
invisible event unforeseeable outcome   53 **dare** could do (to him)
54–7 **Rightly . . . stake** True greatness is not a matter of being moved
to action solely by a great cause; rather, it is to respond greatly to an
apparently trivial cause when honor is at the stake.   59 **blood** (The
supposed seat of the passions.)   62 **fantasy** fanciful caprice, illusion.
trick trifle, deceit   63 **plot** plot of ground   64 **Whereon . . . cause** on
which there is insufficient room for the soldiers needed to fight for it
65 **continent** receptacle, container
4.5. Location: The castle.
2 **distract** out of her mind.   5 **tricks** deceptions.   **hems** clears her
throat, makes "hmm" sounds.   **heart** i.e., breast   6 **Spurns . . .
straws** kicks spitefully, takes offense at trifles.   **in doubt** of obscure
meaning

That carry but half sense. Her speech is nothing,
Yet the unshapèd use of it doth move   8
The hearers to collection; they yawn at it,   9
And botch the words up fit to their own thoughts,   10
Which, as her winks and nods and gestures yield
   them,   11
Indeed would make one think there might be thought,   12
Though nothing sure, yet much unhappily.   13

HORATIO
'Twere good she were spoken with, for she may strew
Dangerous conjectures in ill-breeding minds.   15

QUEEN   Let her come in.   *[Exit Gentleman.]*
[*Aside*] To my sick soul, as sin's true nature is,
Each toy seems prologue to some great amiss.   18
So full of artless jealousy is guilt,   19
It spills itself in fearing to be spilt.   20

      Enter Ophelia [distracted].

OPHELIA
Where is the beauteous majesty of Denmark?

QUEEN   How now, Ophelia?

OPHELIA (*she sings*)
   "How should I your true love know
      From another one?
   By his cockle hat and staff,   25
      And his sandal shoon."   26

QUEEN   Alas, sweet lady, what imports this song?

OPHELIA   Say you? Nay, pray you, mark.
   "He is dead and gone, lady,   (*Song.*)
      He is dead and gone;
   At his head a grass-green turf,
      At his heels a stone."
   Oho!   33

QUEEN   Nay, but Ophelia—

OPHELIA   Pray you, mark.
[*Sings*] "White his shroud as the mountain snow"—

      Enter King.

QUEEN   Alas, look here, my lord.

OPHELIA
   "Larded with sweet flowers;   (*Song.*) 38
   Which bewept to the ground did not go
      With true-love showers."   40

KING   How do you, pretty lady?

OPHELIA   Well, God 'ild you! They say the owl was a   42

baker's daughter. Lord, we know what we are, but
know not what we may be. God be at your table!

KING   Conceit upon her father.   45

OPHELIA   Pray let's have no words of this; but when
they ask you what it means, say you this:
   "Tomorrow is Saint Valentine's day,   (*Song.*)
      All in the morning betime,   49
   And I a maid at your window,
      To be your Valentine.
   Then up he rose, and donned his clothes,
      And dupped the chamber door,   53
   Let in the maid, that out a maid
      Never departed more."

KING   Pretty Ophelia—

OPHELIA   Indeed, la, without an oath, I'll make an end
on't:
[*Sings*]   "By Gis and by Saint Charity,   59
      Alack, and fie for shame!
   Young men will do't, if they come to't;
      By Cock, they are to blame.   62
   Quoth she, 'Before you tumbled me,
      You promised me to wed.'"
   He answers:
      "'So would I ha' done, by yonder sun,
      An thou hadst not come to my bed.'"   67

KING   How long hath she been thus?

OPHELIA   I hope all will be well. We must be patient,
but I cannot choose but weep to think they would lay
him i'th' cold ground. My brother shall know of it.
And so I thank you for your good counsel. Come, my
coach! Good night, ladies, good night, sweet ladies,
good night, good night.   *[Exit.]*

KING [*to Horatio*]
Follow her close. Give her good watch, I pray you.
                  [Exit Horatio.]
Oh, this is the poison of deep grief; it springs
All from her father's death—and now behold!
Oh, Gertrude, Gertrude,
When sorrows come, they come not single spies,   79
But in battalions. First, her father slain;
Next, your son gone, and he most violent author
Of his own just remove; the people muddied,   82
Thick and unwholesome in their thoughts and
   whispers
For good Polonius' death—and we have done but
   greenly,   84
In hugger-mugger to inter him; poor Ophelia   85
Divided from herself and her fair judgment,
Without the which we are pictures or mere beasts;
Last, and as much containing as all these,   88
Her brother is in secret come from France,

---

8 unshapèd use incoherent manner   **9 collection** inference, a guess
at some sort of meaning.   **yawn** gape, wonder; grasp. (The Folio
reading, "aim," is possible.)   **10 botch** patch   **11 Which** which
words.   **yield** deliver, represent   **12–13 there might . . . unhappily**
that a great deal could be guessed at of a most unfortunate nature,
even if one couldn't be at all sure.   **15 ill-breeding** prone to suspect
the worst and to make mischief   **18 toy** trifle.   **amiss** calamity.
19–20 So . . . spilt Guilt is so burdened with conscience and guileless
fear of detection that it reveals itself through apprehension of disaster.   **20.1 Enter Ophelia** (In the first quarto, Ophelia enters "*playing
on a lute, and her hair down, singing.*")   **25 cockle hat** hat with cockleshell stuck in it as a sign that the wearer had been a pilgrim to the
shrine of Saint James of Compostella in Spain   **26 shoon** shoes.
33 Oho! (Perhaps a sigh.)   **38 Larded** strewn, bedecked   **40 showers**
i.e., tears.   **42 God 'ild** God yield or reward.   **owl** (Refers to a legend about a baker's daughter who was turned into an owl for being
ungenerous when Jesus begged a loaf of bread.)

45 Conceit Fancy, brooding   **49 betime** early   **53 dupped** did up,
opened   **59 Gis** Jesus   **62 Cock** (A perversion of "God" in oaths;
here also with a quibble on the slang word for penis.)   **67 An** if
79 spies scouts sent in advance of the main force   **82 remove**
removal.   **muddied** stirred up, confused   **84 greenly** foolishly
85 hugger-mugger secret haste   **88 as much containing** as full of
serious matter

Feeds on this wonder, keeps himself in clouds,   90
And wants not buzzers to infect his ear   91
With pestilent speeches of his father's death,
Wherein necessity, of matter beggared,   93
Will nothing stick our person to arraign   94
In ear and ear. Oh, my dear Gertrude, this,   95
Like to a murd'ring piece, in many places   96
Gives me superfluous death.   *A noise within.*   97
QUEEN   Alack, what noise is this?
KING   Attend!   99
Where is my Switzers? Let them guard the door.   100

    Enter a Messenger.

What is the matter?
MESSENGER   Save yourself, my lord!
The ocean, overpeering of his list,   102
Eats not the flats with more impetuous haste   103
Than young Laertes, in a riotous head,   104
O'erbears your officers. The rabble call him lord,
And, as the world were now but to begin,   106
Antiquity forgot, custom not known,   107
The ratifiers and props of every word,   108
They cry, "Choose we! Laertes shall be king!"
Caps, hands, and tongues applaud it to the clouds,   110
"Laertes shall be king, Laertes king!"
QUEEN
How cheerfully on the false trail they cry!
    A noise within.
Oh, this is counter, you false Danish dogs!   113

    Enter Laertes with others.

KING   The doors are broke.
LAERTES
Where is this King?—Sirs, stand you all without.
ALL   No, let's come in.
LAERTES   I pray you, give me leave.
ALL   We will, we will.
LAERTES   I thank you. Keep the door. [*Exeunt followers.*]
    Oh, thou vile king,
Give me my father!
QUEEN [*restraining him*]   Calmly, good Laertes.
LAERTES
That drop of blood that's calm proclaims me bastard,

Cries cuckold to my father, brands the harlot
Even here between the chaste unsmirchèd brow   123
Of my true mother.
KING   What is the cause, Laertes,
That thy rebellion looks so giantlike?   125
Let him go, Gertrude. Do not fear our person.   126
There's such divinity doth hedge a king   127
That treason can but peep to what it would,   128
Acts little of his will. Tell me, Laertes,   129
Why thou art thus incensed. Let him go, Gertrude.
Speak, man.
LAERTES   Where is my father?
KING   Dead.
QUEEN
But not by him.
KING   Let him demand his fill.
LAERTES
How came he dead? I'll not be juggled with.   133
To hell, allegiance! Vows, to the blackest devil!
Conscience and grace, to the profoundest pit!
I dare damnation. To this point I stand,   136
That both the worlds I give to negligence,   137
Let come what comes, only I'll be revenged
Most throughly for my father.   139
KING   Who shall stay you?
LAERTES   My will, not all the world's.   141
And for my means, I'll husband them so well   142
They shall go far with little.
KING   Good Laertes,
If you desire to know the certainty
Of your dear father, is't writ in your revenge
That, swoopstake, you will draw both friend and foe,   146
Winner and loser?
LAERTES   None but his enemies.
KING   Will you know them, then?
LAERTES
To his good friends thus wide I'll ope my arms,
And like the kind life-rendering pelican   151
Repast them with my blood.
KING   Why, now you speak   152
Like a good child and a true gentleman.
That I am guiltless of your father's death,
And am most sensibly in grief for it,   155
It shall as level to your judgment 'pear   156
As day does to your eye.   *A noise within.*

---

90 Feeds . . . clouds feeds his resentment on this whole shocking turn
of events, keeps himself aloof and mysterious   **91 wants** lacks.
buzzers gossipers, informers   **93 necessity** i.e., the need to invent
some plausible explanation.   **of matter beggared** unprovided with
facts   **94–5 Will . . . ear** will not hesitate to accuse my (royal) person
in everybody's ears.   **96 murd'ring piece** cannon loaded so as to
scatter its shot   **97 Gives . . . death** kills me over and over.
99 Attend! Guard me!   **100 Switzers** Swiss guards, mercenaries.
102 overpeering of his list overflowing its shore, boundary   **103 flats**
i.e., flatlands near shore.   **impetuous** violent (perhaps also with the
meaning of *impiteous* ["impitious," Q2], "pitiless")   **104 riotous head**
insurrectional advance   **106–8 And . . . word** and, as if the world
were to be started all over afresh, utterly setting aside all ancient traditional customs that should confirm and underprop our every word
and promise   **110 Caps** (The caps are thrown in the air.)
113 counter (A hunting term, meaning to follow the trail in a direction opposite to that which the game has taken.)

123 between amidst   **125 giantlike** (Recalling the rising of the giants
of Greek mythology against Olympus.)   **126 fear our** fear for my
127 hedge protect, as with a surrounding barrier   **128 can . . . would**
can only peep furtively, as through a barrier, at what it would intend
129 Acts . . . will (but) performs little of what it intends.   **133 juggled
with** cheated, deceived.   **136 To . . . stand** I am resolved in this
137 both . . . negligence i.e., both this world and the next are of no
consequence to me   **139 throughly** thoroughly   **141 My will . . .
world's** I'll stop (*stay*) when my will is accomplished, not for anyone
else's.   **142 for** as for   **146 swoopstake** i.e., indiscriminately. (Literally, taking all stakes on the gambling table at once. *Draw* is also a
gambling term, meaning "take from.")   **151 pelican** (Refers to the
belief that the female pelican fed its young with its own blood.)
152 Repast feed   **155 sensibly** feelingly   **156 level** plain

LAERTES
How now, what noise is that?

Enter Ophelia.

KING   Let her come in.
LAERTES
O heat, dry up my brains! Tears seven times salt
Burn out the sense and virtue of mine eye!   160
By heaven, thy madness shall be paid with weight   161
Till our scale turn the beam. O rose of May!   162
Dear maid, kind sister, sweet Ophelia!
O heavens, is't possible a young maid's wits
Should be as mortal as an old man's life?
Nature is fine in love, and where 'tis fine   166
It sends some precious instance of itself   167
After the thing it loves.   168

OPHELIA
   "They bore him barefaced on the bier,   (*Song.*)
       Hey non nonny, nonny, hey nonny,
       And in his grave rained many a tear—"
Fare you well, my dove!

LAERTES
Hadst thou thy wits and didst persuade revenge,
It could not move thus.

OPHELIA   You must sing "A-down a-down," and you   175
"call him a-down-a." Oh, how the wheel becomes it! It 176
is the false steward that stole his master's daughter. 177

LAERTES   This nothing's more than matter.   178

OPHELIA   There's rosemary, that's for remembrance;   179
pray you, love, remember. And there is pansies; that's 180
for thoughts.

LAERTES   A document in madness, thoughts and re-   182
membrance fitted.

OPHELIA   There's fennel for you, and columbines.   184
There's rue for you, and here's some for me; we may   185
call it herb of grace o' Sundays. You must wear your
rue with a difference. There's a daisy. I would give   187
you some violets, but they withered all when my   188
father died. They say 'a made a good end—

160 **virtue** faculty, power   161 **paid with weight** repaid, avenged
equally or more   162 **beam** crossbar of a balance.   166–8 **Nature . . .**
loves Human nature is exquisitely sensitive in matters of love, and in
cases of sudden loss it sends some precious part of itself after the lost
object of that love. (In this case, Ophelia's sanity deserts her out of
sorrow for her lost father and perhaps too out of her love for Hamlet.)
175–6 **You . . . a-down-a** (Ophelia assigns the singing of refrains, like
her own "Hey non nonny," to others present.)   176 **wheel** spinning
wheel as accompaniment to the song, or refrain   177 **false steward**
(The story is unknown.)   178 **This . . . matter** This seeming nonsense
is more eloquent than sane utterance.   179 **rosemary** (Used as a symbol of remembrance both at weddings and at funerals.)   180 **pansies**
(Emblems of love and courtship; perhaps from French *pensées*,
"thoughts.")   182 **document** instruction, lesson   184 **There's fennel**
. . . columbines (*Fennel* betokens flattery; *columbines*, unchastity or
ingratitude. Throughout, Ophelia addresses her various listeners,
giving one flower to one and another to another, perhaps with particular symbolic significance in each case.)   185 **rue** (Emblem of repentance—a signification that is evident in its popular name, *herb of*
grace.)   187 **with a difference** (A device used in heraldry to distinguish one family from another on the coat of arms, here suggesting
that Ophelia and the others have different causes of sorrow and
repentance; perhaps with a play on *rue* in the sense of "ruth," "pity.")
daisy (Emblem of love's victims and of faithlessness.)   188 **violets**
(Emblems of faithfulness.)

[*Sings*] "For bonny sweet Robin is all my joy."
LAERTES
Thought and affliction, passion, hell itself,   191
She turns to favor and to prettiness.   192

OPHELIA
   "And will 'a not come again?   (*Song.*)
       And will 'a not come again?
       No, no, he is dead.
       Go to thy deathbed,
       He never will come again.

   "His beard was as white as snow,
       All flaxen was his poll.   199
       He is gone, he is gone,
       And we cast away moan.
       God ha' mercy on his soul!"
And of all Christian souls, I pray God. God b'wi'you.
                        [*Exit, followed by Gertrude.*]

LAERTES   Do you see this, O God?
KING
Laertes, I must commune with your grief,
Or you deny me right. Go but apart,
Make choice of whom your wisest friends you will,   207
And they shall hear and judge twixt you and me.
If by direct or by collateral hand   209
They find us touched, we will our kingdom give,   210
Our crown, our life, and all that we call ours
To you in satisfaction; but if not,
Be you content to lend your patience to us,
And we shall jointly labor with your soul
To give it due content.

LAERTES   Let this be so.
His means of death, his obscure funeral—
No trophy, sword, nor hatchment o'er his bones,   217
No noble rite, nor formal ostentation—   218
Cry to be heard, as 'twere from heaven to earth,
That I must call't in question.

KING   So you shall,   220
And where th'offense is, let the great ax fall.
I pray you, go with me.   *Exeunt.*

❖

[4.6]

Enter Horatio and others.

HORATIO
What are they that would speak with me?
GENTLEMAN   Seafaring men, sir. They say they have
letters for you.   3
HORATIO   Let them come in.   [*Exit Gentleman.*]
I do not know from what part of the world

191 **Thought** Melancholy.   **passion** suffering   192 **favor** grace,
beauty   199 **poll** head.   207 **whom** whichever of   209 **collateral**
hand indirect agency   210 **us touched** me implicated   217 **trophy**
memorial.   **hatchment** tablet displaying the armorial bearings of a
deceased person   218 **ostentation** ceremony   220 **That** so that.
call't in question demand an explanation.
4.6. Location: The castle.
3 **letters** a letter

I should be greeted, if not from Lord Hamlet.

Enter Sailors.

FIRST SAILOR   God bless you, sir.

HORATIO   Let him bless thee too.

FIRST SAILOR   'A shall, sir, an't please him. There's a   9
letter for you, sir—it came from th'ambassador that   10
was bound for England—if your name be Horatio, as
I am let to know it is.   [*He gives a letter.*]

HORATIO [*reads*]   "Horatio, when thou shalt have over-   13
looked this, give these fellows some means to the King;   14
they have letters for him. Ere we were two days old at
sea, a pirate of very warlike appointment gave us   16
chase. Finding ourselves too slow of sail, we put on a
compelled valor, and in the grapple I boarded them.
On the instant they got clear of our ship, so I alone
became their prisoner. They have dealt with me like
thieves of mercy, but they knew what they did: I am to   21
do a good turn for them. Let the King have the letters
I have sent, and repair thou to me with as much speed   23
as thou wouldest fly death. I have words to speak in
thine ear will make thee dumb, yet are they much too
light for the bore of the matter. These good fellows will   26
bring thee where I am. Rosencrantz and Guildenstern
hold their course for England. Of them I have much to
tell thee. Farewell.

    He that thou knowest thine, Hamlet."
Come, I will give you way for these your letters,   31
And do't the speedier that you may direct me
To him from whom you brought them.   *Exeunt.*

[4.7]

Enter King and Laertes.

KING
Now must your conscience my acquittance seal,   1
And you must put me in your heart for friend,
Sith you have heard, and with a knowing ear,   3
That he which hath your noble father slain
Pursued my life.

LAERTES   It well appears. But tell me
Why you proceeded not against these feats   6
So crimeful and so capital in nature,   7
As by your safety, greatness, wisdom, all things else,
You mainly were stirred up.   9

KING   Oh, for two special reasons,
Which may to you perhaps seem much unsinewed,   11
But yet to me they're strong. The Queen his mother
Lives almost by his looks, and for myself—
My virtue or my plague, be it either which—

She is so conjunctive to my life and soul   15
That, as the star moves not but in his sphere,   16
I could not but by her. The other motive
Why to a public count I might not go   18
Is the great love the general gender bear him,   19
Who, dipping all his faults in their affection,
Work like the spring that turneth wood to stone,   21
Convert his gyves to graces, so that my arrows,   22
Too slightly timbered for so loud a wind,   23
Would have reverted to my bow again
But not where I had aimed them.

LAERTES
And so have I a noble father lost,
A sister driven into desp'rate terms,   27
Whose worth, if praises may go back again,   28
Stood challenger on mount of all the age   29
For her perfections. But my revenge will come.

KING
Break not your sleeps for that. You must not think
That we are made of stuff so flat and dull
That we can let our beard be shook with danger
And think it pastime. You shortly shall hear more.
I loved your father, and we love ourself;
And that, I hope, will teach you to imagine—

Enter a Messenger with letters.

How now? What news?

MESSENGER   Letters, my lord, from Hamlet:
This to Your Majesty, this to the Queen.
                              [*He gives letters.*]

KING   From Hamlet? Who brought them?

MESSENGER
Sailors, my lord, they say. I saw them not.
They were given me by Claudio. He received them
Of him that brought them.

KING   Laertes, you shall hear them.—
Leave us.   [*Exit Messenger.*]
[*He reads.*] "High and mighty, you shall know I am set
naked on your kingdom. Tomorrow shall I beg leave   45
to see your kingly eyes, when I shall, first asking your
pardon, thereunto recount the occasion of my sudden   47
and more strange return.   Hamlet."
What should this mean? Are all the rest come back?
Or is it some abuse, and no such thing?   50

LAERTES
Know you the hand?

KING   'Tis Hamlet's character. "Naked!"   51
And in a postscript here he says "alone."

9 an't if it   10 th'ambassador (Hamlet's ostensible role; see 3.1.172-3.)
13–14 overlooked looked over   14 means means of access
16 appointment equipage   21 thieves of mercy merciful thieves
23 repair come   26 bore caliber, i.e., importance   31 way means of
access
4.7. Location: The castle.
1 my acquittance seal confirm or acknowledge my innocence   3 Sith
since   6 feats acts   7 capital punishable by death   9 mainly greatly
11 unsinewed weak

15 conjunctive closely united. (An astronomical metaphor.)   16 his
its.   sphere one of the hollow spheres in which, according to Ptolemaic astronomy, the planets were supposed to move   18 count
account, reckoning, indictment   19 general gender common people
21 Work operate, act.   spring i.e., a spring with such a concentration
of lime that it coats a piece of wood with limestone, in effect gilding
and petrifying it   22 gyves fetters (which, gilded by the people's
praise, would look like badges of honor)   23 Too . . . wind with too
light a shaft for so powerful a gust (of popular sentiment)   27 terms
state, condition   28 go back recall what she was   29 on mount set
up on high   45 naked destitute, unarmed, without following
47 pardon (for returning without authorization)   50 abuse deceit.
no such thing not what the letter says.   51 character handwriting.

Can you devise me?

LAERTES
I am lost in it, my lord. But let him come.
It warms the very sickness in my heart
That I shall live and tell him to his teeth,
"Thus didst thou."

KING   If it be so, Laertes—
As how should it be so? How otherwise?—
Will you be ruled by me?

LAERTES   Ay, my lord,
So you will not o'errule me to a peace.

KING
To thine own peace. If he be now returned,
As checking at his voyage, and that he means
No more to undertake it, I will work him
To an exploit, now ripe in my device,
Under the which he shall not choose but fall;
And for his death no wind of blame shall breathe,
But even his mother shall uncharge the practice
And call it accident.

LAERTES   My lord, I will be ruled,
The rather if you could devise it so
That I might be the organ.

KING   It falls right.
You have been talked of since your travel much,
And that in Hamlet's hearing, for a quality
Wherein they say you shine. Your sum of parts
Did not together pluck such envy from him
As did that one, and that, in my regard,
Of the unworthiest siege.

LAERTES   What part is that, my lord?

KING
A very ribbon in the cap of youth,
Yet needful too, for youth no less becomes
The light and careless livery that it wears
Than settled age his sables and his weeds
Importing health and graveness. Two months since
Here was a gentleman of Normandy.
I have seen myself, and served against, the French,
And they can well on horseback, but this gallant
Had witchcraft in't; he grew unto his seat,
And to such wondrous doing brought his horse
As had he been incorpsed and demi-natured
With the brave beast. So far he topped my thought
That I in forgery of shapes and tricks
Come short of what he did.

LAERTES   A Norman was't?

53 KING   A Norman.

LAERTES
Upon my life, Lamord.

KING   The very same.

LAERTES
I know him well. He is the brooch indeed   94
And gem of all the nation.

KING   He made confession of you,   96
And gave you such a masterly report
For art and exercise in your defense,   98
And for your rapier most especial,
That he cried out 'twould be a sight indeed
If one could match you. Th'escrimers of their nation, 101
He swore, had neither motion, guard, nor eye
If you opposed them. Sir, this report of his
Did Hamlet so envenom with his envy
That he could nothing do but wish and beg
Your sudden coming o'er, to play with you.   106
Now, out of this—

LAERTES   What out of this, my lord?

KING
Laertes, was your father dear to you?
Or are you like the painting of a sorrow,
A face without a heart?

LAERTES   Why ask you this?

KING
Not that I think you did not love your father,
But that I know love is begun by time,   112
And that I see, in passages of proof,   113
Time qualifies the spark and fire of it.   114
There lives within the very flame of love
A kind of wick or snuff that will abate it,   116
And nothing is at a like goodness still,   117
For goodness, growing to a pleurisy,   118
Dies in his own too much. That we would do,   119
We should do when we would; for this "would"
  changes
And hath abatements and delays as many   121
As there are tongues, are hands, are accidents,   122
And then this "should" is like a spendthrift sigh, 123
That hurts by easing. But, to the quick o'th'ulcer: 124
Hamlet comes back. What would you undertake
To show yourself in deed your father's son
More than in words?

LAERTES   To cut his throat i'th' church.

53 line numbers: 53, 57, 58, 60, 62, 64, 67, 70, 73, 76, 79, 81, 82, 85, 88, 89, 90

KING
No place, indeed, should murder sanctuarize;   128
Revenge should have no bounds. But good Laertes,
Will you do this, keep close within your chamber.   130
Hamlet returned shall know you are come home.
We'll put on those shall praise your excellence   132
And set a double varnish on the fame
The Frenchman gave you, bring you in fine together,   134
And wager on your heads. He, being remiss,   135
Most generous, and free from all contriving,   136
Will not peruse the foils, so that with ease,
Or with a little shuffling, you may choose
A sword unbated, and in a pass of practice   139
Requite him for your father.

LAERTES   I will do't,
And for that purpose I'll anoint my sword.
I bought an unction of a mountebank   142
So mortal that, but dip a knife in it,
Where it draws blood no cataplasm so rare,   144
Collected from all simples that have virtue   145
Under the moon, can save the thing from death   146
That is but scratched withal. I'll touch my point
With this contagion, that if I gall him slightly,   148
It may be death.

KING   Let's further think of this,
Weigh what convenience both of time and means
May fit us to our shape. If this should fail,   151
And that our drift look through our bad performance,   152
'Twere better not assayed. Therefore this project
Should have a back or second, that might hold
If this did blast in proof. Soft, let me see.   155
We'll make a solemn wager on your cunnings—   156
I ha 't!
When in your motion you are hot and dry—
As make your bouts more violent to that end—   159
And that he calls for drink, I'll have prepared him
A chalice for the nonce, whereon but sipping,   161
If he by chance escape your venomed stuck,   162
Our purpose may hold there. [A cry within.] But stay,
   what noise?

Enter Queen.

QUEEN
One woe doth tread upon another's heel,
So fast they follow. Your sister's drowned, Laertes.

LAERTES   Drowned! Oh, where?

QUEEN
There is a willow grows askant the brook,   167
That shows his hoar leaves in the glassy stream;   168
Therewith fantastic garlands did she make
Of crowflowers, nettles, daisies, and long purples,   170
That liberal shepherds give a grosser name,   171
But our cold maids do dead men's fingers call them.   172
There on the pendent boughs her crownet weeds   173
Clamb'ring to hang, an envious sliver broke,   174
When down her weedy trophies and herself   175
Fell in the weeping brook. Her clothes spread wide,
And mermaidlike awhile they bore her up,
Which time she chanted snatches of old lauds,   178
As one incapable of her own distress,   179
Or like a creature native and endued   180
Unto that element. But long it could not be
Till that her garments, heavy with their drink,
Pulled the poor wretch from her melodious lay   183
To muddy death.

LAERTES   Alas, then she is drowned?

QUEEN   Drowned, drowned.

LAERTES
Too much of water hast thou, poor Ophelia,
And therefore I forbid my tears. But yet
It is our trick; nature her custom holds,   188
Let shame say what it will. [*He weeps.*] When these
   are gone,   189
The woman will be out. Adieu, my lord.   190
I have a speech of fire that fain would blaze,
But that this folly douts it.   *Exit.*

KING   Let's follow, Gertrude.   192
How much I had to do to calm his rage!
Now fear I this will give it start again;
Therefore let's follow.   *Exeunt.*

❖

[5.1]

Enter two Clowns [with spades and mattocks].

FIRST CLOWN   Is she to be buried in Christian burial,
   when she willfully seeks her own salvation?   2

---

128 **sanctuarize** protect from punishment. (Alludes to the right of
sanctuary with which certain religious places were invested.)
130 **Will you do this** if you wish to do this   132 **put on those shall**
arrange for some to   134 **in fine** finally   135 **remiss** negligently
unsuspicious   136 **generous** noble-minded   139 **unbated** not
blunted, having no button.   **pass of practice** treacherous thrust in an
arranged bout   142 **unction** ointment.   **mountebank** quack doctor
144 **cataplasm** plaster or poultice   145 **simples** herbs.   **virtue**
potency   146 **Under the moon** i.e., anywhere (with reference perhaps
to the belief that herbs gathered at night had a special power)
148 **gall** graze, wound   151 **shape** part we propose to act.   152 **drift**
. . . performance intention should be made visible by our bungling
155 **blast in proof** come to grief when put to the test.   156 **cunnings**
respective skills   159 **As** i.e., and you should   161 **nonce** occasion
162 **stuck** thrust. (From *stoccado*, a fencing term.)

167 **askant** aslant   168 **hoar leaves** white or gray undersides of the
leaves   170 **long purples** early purple orchids   171 **liberal** free-spo-
ken.   **a grosser name** (The testicle-resembling tubers of the orchid,
which also in some cases resemble *dead men's fingers*, have earned various slang names like "dogstones" and "cullions.")   172 **cold** chaste
173 **pendent** overhanging.   **crownet** made into a chaplet or coronet
174 **envious sliver** malicious branch   175 **weedy** i.e., of plants
178 **lauds** hymns   179 **incapable of** lacking capacity to apprehend
180 **endued** adapted by nature   183 **lay** ballad, song   188 **It is our**
trick i.e., weeping is our natural way (when sad)   189–90 **When . . .**
out When my tears are all shed, the woman in me will be expended,
satisfied.   192 **douts** extinguishes. (The second quarto reads
"drownes.")
5.1. Location: A churchyard.
0.1 *Clowns* rustics   2 **salvation** (A blunder for "damnation," or perhaps a suggestion that Ophelia was taking her own shortcut to
heaven.)

SECOND CLOWN   I tell thee she is; therefore make her grave straight. The crowner hath sat on her, and finds it Christian burial. 4

FIRST CLOWN   How can that be, unless she drowned herself in her own defense? 5

SECOND CLOWN   Why, 'tis found so. 8

FIRST CLOWN   It must be *se offendendo*, it cannot be else. For here lies the point: if I drown myself wittingly, it argues an act, and an act hath three branches—it is to act, to do, and to perform. Argal, she drowned herself wittingly. 9 12

SECOND CLOWN   Nay, but hear you, goodman delver— 14

FIRST CLOWN   Give me leave. Here lies the water; good. Here stands the man; good. If the man go to this water and drown himself, it is, will he, nill he, he goes, mark you that. But if the water come to him and drown him, he drowns not himself. Argal, he that is not guilty of his own death shortens not his own life. 17

SECOND CLOWN   But is this law?

FIRST CLOWN   Ay, marry, is't—crowner's quest law. 22

SECOND CLOWN   Will you ha' the truth on't? If this had not been a gentlewoman, she should have been buried out o' Christian burial.

FIRST CLOWN   Why, there thou say'st. And the more pity that great folk should have countenance in this world to drown or hang themselves, more than their even-Christian. Come, my spade. There is no ancient gentlemen but gardeners, ditchers, and grave makers. They hold up Adam's profession. 26 27 29 31

SECOND CLOWN   Was he a gentleman?

FIRST CLOWN   'A was the first that ever bore arms. 33

SECOND CLOWN   Why, he had none.

FIRST CLOWN   What, art a heathen? How dost thou understand the Scripture? The Scripture says Adam digged. Could he dig without arms? I'll put another question to thee. If thou answerest me not to the purpose, confess thyself— 37 39

SECOND CLOWN   Go to.

FIRST CLOWN   What is he that builds stronger than either the mason, the shipwright, or the carpenter?

SECOND CLOWN   The gallows maker, for that frame outlives a thousand tenants. 43

FIRST CLOWN   I like thy wit well, in good faith. The gallows does well. But how does it well? It does well to those that do ill. Now thou dost ill to say the gallows 46

is built stronger than the church. Argal, the gallows may do well to thee. To't again, come.

SECOND CLOWN   "Who builds stronger than a mason, a shipwright, or a carpenter?"

FIRST CLOWN   Ay, tell me that, and unyoke. 52

SECOND CLOWN   Marry, now I can tell.

FIRST CLOWN   To't.

SECOND CLOWN   Mass, I cannot tell. 55

Enter Hamlet and Horatio [at a distance].

FIRST CLOWN   Cudgel thy brains no more about it, for your dull ass will not mend his pace with beating; and when you are asked this question next, say "a grave maker." The houses he makes lasts till doomsday. Go get thee in and fetch me a stoup of liquor. 60

[Exit Second Clown. First Clown digs.]
Song.

"In youth, when I did love, did love, 61
    Methought it was very sweet,
To contract—oh—the time for—a—my behove, 63
    Oh, methought there—a—was nothing—a—
        meet." 64

HAMLET   Has this fellow no feeling of his business, 'a sings in grave-making? 65

HORATIO   Custom hath made it in him a property of easiness. 67 68

HAMLET   'Tis e'en so. The hand of little employment hath the daintier sense. 70

FIRST CLOWN   *Song.*

"But age with his stealing steps
    Hath clawed me in his clutch,
And hath shipped me into the land, 73
    As if I had never been such."

[He throws up a skull.]

HAMLET   That skull had a tongue in it and could sing once. How the knave jowls it to the ground, as if 'twere Cain's jawbone, that did the first murder! This might be the pate of a politician, which this ass now o'erreaches, one that would circumvent God, might it not? 76 78 79

HORATIO   It might, my lord.

HAMLET   Or of a courtier, which could say, "Good morrow, sweet lord! How dost thou, sweet lord?" This might be my Lord Such-a-one, that praised my Lord Such-a-one's horse when 'a meant to beg it, might it not?

HORATIO   Ay, my lord.

---

4 straight straightway, immediately. (But with a pun on *strait*, "narrow.")   **crowner** coroner.   **sat on her** conducted an inquest on her case   **4–5 finds it** gives his official verdict that her means of death was consistent with   **8 found so** determined so in the coroner's verdict.   **9 se offendendo** (A comic mistake for *se defendendo*, a term used in verdicts of self-defense.)   **12 Argal** (Corruption of *ergo*, "therefore.")   **14 goodman** (An honorific title often used with the name of a profession or craft.)   **17 will he, nill he** whether he will or no, willy-nilly   **22 quest** inquest   **26 there thou say'st** i.e., that's right.   **27 countenance** privilege   **29 even-Christian** fellow Christians.   **ancient** going back to ancient times   **31 hold up** maintain   **33 bore arms** (To be entitled to bear a coat of arms would make Adam a gentleman, but as one who bore a spade, our common ancestor was an ordinary delver in the earth.)   **37 arms** i.e., the arms of the body.   **39 confess thyself** (The saying continues, "and be hanged.")   **43 frame** (1) gallows (2) structure   **46 does well** (1) is an apt answer (2) does a good turn.

52 unyoke i.e., after this great effort, you may unharness the team of your wits.   **55 Mass** By the Mass   **60 stoup** two-quart measure   **61 In . . . love** (This and the two following stanzas, with nonsensical variations, are from a poem attributed to Lord Vaux and printed in *Tottel's Miscellany*, 1557. The *oh* and *a* [for "ah"] seemingly are the grunts of the digger.)   **63 To contract . . . behove** i.e., to shorten the time for my own advantage. (Perhaps he means to *prolong* it.)   **64 meet** suitable, i.e., more suitable.   **65 'a** that he   **67–8 property of easiness** something he can do easily and indifferently.   **70 daintier sense** more delicate sense of feeling.   **73 into the land** i.e., toward my grave (?) (But note the lack of rhyme in *steps, land*.)   **76 jowls** dashes. (With a pun on *jowl*, "jawbone.")   **78 politician** schemer, plotter   **79 o'erreaches** circumvents, gets the better of

HAMLET   Why, e'en so, and now my Lady Worm's,
chapless, and knocked about the mazard with a sex- 89
ton's spade. Here's fine revolution, an we had the trick 90
to see't. Did these bones cost no more the breeding 91
but to play at loggets with them? Mine ache to think 92
on't.

FIRST CLOWN   *Song.*
         "A pickax and a spade, a spade,
            For and a shrouding sheet; 95
         Oh, a pit of clay for to be made
            For such a guest is meet."
                              [*He throws up another skull.*]

HAMLET   There's another. Why may not that be the skull
of a lawyer? Where be his quiddities now, his quilli- 99
ties, his cases, his tenures, and his tricks? Why does 100
he suffer this mad knave now to knock him about the
sconce with a dirty shovel, and will not tell him of his 102
action of battery? Hum, this fellow might be in 's time 103
a great buyer of land, with his statutes, his recogni- 104
zances, his fines, his double vouchers, his recoveries. 105
Is this the fine of his fines and the recovery of his 106
recoveries, to have his fine pate full of fine dirt? Will 107
his vouchers vouch him no more of his purchases, and 108
double ones too, than the length and breadth of a 109
pair of indentures? The very conveyances of his lands 110
will scarcely lie in this box, and must th'inheritor 111
himself have no more, ha?

HORATIO   Not a jot more, my lord.

HAMLET   Is not parchment made of sheepskins?

HORATIO   Ay, my lord, and of calves' skins too.

HAMLET   They are sheep and calves which seek out as- 116
surance in that. I will speak to this fellow.—Whose 117
grave's this, sirrah? 118

FIRST CLOWN   Mine, sir.
[*Sings*] "Oh, pit of clay for to be made
            For such a guest is meet."

HAMLET   I think it be thine, indeed, for thou liest in't.

FIRST CLOWN   You lie out on't, sir, and therefore 'tis
not yours. For my part, I do not lie in't, yet it is mine.

HAMLET   Thou dost lie in't, to be in't and say it is
thine. 'Tis for the dead, not for the quick; therefore 126
thou liest.

FIRST CLOWN   'Tis a quick lie, sir; 'twill away again
from me to you.

HAMLET   What man dost thou dig it for?

FIRST CLOWN   For no man, sir.

HAMLET   What woman, then?

FIRST CLOWN   For none, neither.

HAMLET   Who is to be buried in't?

FIRST CLOWN   One that was a woman, sir, but, rest her
soul, she's dead.

HAMLET   How absolute the knave is! We must speak by 137
the card, or equivocation will undo us. By the Lord, 138
Horatio, this three years I have took note of it: the age 139
is grown so picked that the toe of the peasant comes so 140
near the heel of the courtier he galls his kibe.—How 141
long hast thou been grave maker?

FIRST CLOWN   Of all the days i'th' year, I came to't that
day that our last king Hamlet overcame Fortinbras.

HAMLET   How long is that since?

FIRST CLOWN   Cannot you tell that? Every fool can tell
that. It was that very day that young Hamlet was
born—he that is mad and sent into England.

HAMLET   Ay, marry, why was he sent into England?

FIRST CLOWN   Why, because 'a was mad. 'A shall
recover his wits there, or if 'a do not, 'tis no great
matter there.

HAMLET   Why?

FIRST CLOWN   'Twill not be seen in him there. There the
men are as mad as he.

HAMLET   How came he mad?

FIRST CLOWN   Very strangely, they say.

HAMLET   How strangely?

FIRST CLOWN   Faith, e'en with losing his wits.

HAMLET   Upon what ground? 160

FIRST CLOWN   Why, here in Denmark. I have been
sexton here, man and boy, thirty years.

HAMLET   How long will a man lie i'th'earth ere he rot?

FIRST CLOWN   Faith, if 'a be not rotten before 'a die—as
we have many pocky corpses nowadays, that will 165
scarce hold the laying in—'a will last you some eight 166
year or nine year. A tanner will last you nine year.

HAMLET   Why he more than another?

FIRST CLOWN   Why, sir, his hide is so tanned with his
trade that 'a will keep out water a great while, and

---

89 chapless having no lower jaw.   **mazard** i.e., head. (Literally, a
drinking vessel.)   **90 revolution** turn of Fortune's wheel, change.
trick knack   **91–2 cost . . . but** involve so little expense and care in
upbringing that we may   **92 loggets** a game in which pieces of hard
wood shaped like Indian clubs or bowling pins are thrown to lie as
near as possible to a stake   **95 For and** and moreover   **99–100 his
quiddities . . . quillities** his subtleties, his legal niceties   **100 tenures**
the holding of a piece of property or office, or the conditions or
period of such holding   **102 sconce** head   **103 action of battery** lawsuit about physical assault.   **104 his statutes** his legal documents
acknowledging obligation of a debt   **104–5 recognizances** bonds
undertaking to repay debts   **105 fines** procedures for converting
entailed estates into "fee simple" or freehold.   **double vouchers**
vouchers signed by two signatories guaranteeing the legality of real
estate titles.   **recoveries** suits to obtain the authority of a court judgment for the holding of land.   **106–7 Is this . . . dirt?** Is this the end of
his legal maneuvers and profitable land deals, to have the skull of his
elegant head filled full of minutely sifted dirt? (With multiple wordplay on *fine* and *fines*.)   **107–10 Will . . . indentures?** Will his vouchers, even double ones, guarantee him no more land than is needed to
bury him in, being no bigger than the deed of conveyance? (An
indenture is literally a legal document drawn up in duplicate on a single sheet and then cut apart on a zigzag line so that each pair was
uniquely matched.)   **111 box** (1) deed box (2) coffin.   **th'inheritor**
the acquirer, owner   **116–17 assurance in that** safety in legal parch-
ments.   **118 sirrah** (A term of address to inferiors.)

126 quick living   **137 absolute** strict, precise   **137–8 by the card** i.e.,
with precision. (Literally, by the mariner's compass-card, on which
the points of the compass were marked.)   **138 equivocation** ambiguity in the use of terms   **139 took** taken   **139–41 the age . . . kibe** i.e.,
the age has grown so finical and mannered that the lower classes ape
their social betters, chafing at their heels. (*Kibes* are chilblains on the
heels.)   **160 ground** cause. (But, in the next line, the gravedigger
takes the word in the sense of "land," "country.")   **165 pocky** rotten,
diseased. (Literally, with the pox, or syphilis.)   **166 hold the laying
in** hold together long enough to be interred.   **last you** last. (*You* is
used colloquially here and in the following lines.)

your water is a sore decayer of your whoreson dead 171
body. [*He picks up a skull.*] Here's a skull now hath
lien you i'th'earth three-and-twenty years. 173

HAMLET   Whose was it?

FIRST CLOWN   A whoreson mad fellow's it was. Whose
do you think it was?

HAMLET   Nay, I know not.

FIRST CLOWN   A pestilence on him for a mad rogue! 'A
poured a flagon of Rhenish on my head once. This 179
same skull, sir, was, sir, Yorick's skull, the King's jester.

HAMLET   This?

FIRST CLOWN   E'en that.

HAMLET   Let me see. [*He takes the skull.*] Alas, poor
Yorick! I knew him, Horatio, a fellow of infinite jest, of
most excellent fancy. He hath bore me on his back a 185
thousand times, and now how abhorred in my
imagination it is! My gorge rises at it. Here hung those 187
lips that I have kissed I know not how oft. Where be
your gibes now? Your gambols, your songs, your 189
flashes of merriment that were wont to set the table on
a roar? Not one now, to mock your own grinning?
Quite chopfallen? Now get you to my lady's chamber 192
and tell her, let her paint an inch thick, to this favor 193
she must come. Make her laugh at that. Prithee,
Horatio, tell me one thing.

HORATIO   What's that, my lord?

HAMLET   Dost thou think Alexander looked o' this
fashion i'th'earth?

HORATIO   E'en so.

HAMLET   And smelt so? Pah! [*He throws down the skull.*]

HORATIO   E'en so, my lord.

HAMLET   To what base uses we may return, Horatio!
Why may not imagination trace the noble dust of
Alexander till 'a find it stopping a bunghole? 204

HORATIO   'Twere to consider too curiously to consider 205
so.

HAMLET   No, faith, not a jot, but to follow him thither
with modesty enough, and likelihood to lead it. As 208
thus: Alexander died, Alexander was buried, Alexander returneth to dust, the dust is earth, of earth we
make loam, and why of that loam whereto he was 211
converted might they not stop a beer barrel?
Imperious Caesar, dead and turned to clay, 213
Might stop a hole to keep the wind away.
Oh, that that earth which kept the world in awe
Should patch a wall t'expel the winter's flaw! 216

Enter King, Queen, Laertes, and the corpse [of
Ophelia, in procession, with Priest, lords, etc.].

But soft, but soft awhile! Here comes the King, 217

The Queen, the courtiers. Who is this they follow?
And with such maimèd rites? This doth betoken 219
The corpse they follow did with desperate hand
Fordo it own life. 'Twas of some estate. 221
Couch we awhile and mark. 222

[*He and Horatio conceal themselves.*
Ophelia's body is taken to the grave.]

LAERTES   What ceremony else?

HAMLET [*to Horatio*]
That is Laertes, a very noble youth. Mark.

LAERTES   What ceremony else?

PRIEST
Her obsequies have been as far enlarged
As we have warranty. Her death was doubtful, 227
And but that great command o'ersways the order 228
She should in ground unsanctified been lodged 229
Till the last trumpet. For charitable prayers, 230
Shards, flints, and pebbles should be thrown on her. 231
Yet here she is allowed her virgin crants, 232
Her maiden strewments, and the bringing home 233
Of bell and burial. 234

LAERTES
Must there no more be done?

PRIEST   No more be done.
We should profane the service of the dead
To sing a requiem and such rest to her 237
As to peace-parted souls.

LAERTES   Lay her i'th'earth, 238
And from her fair and unpolluted flesh
May violets spring! I tell thee, churlish priest, 240
A ministering angel shall my sister be
When thou liest howling.

HAMLET [*to Horatio*]   What, the fair Ophelia! 242

QUEEN [*scattering flowers*]   Sweets to the sweet! Farewell.
I hoped thou shouldst have been my Hamlet's wife.
I thought thy bride-bed to have decked, sweet maid,
And not t' have strewed thy grave.

LAERTES   Oh, treble woe
Fall ten times treble on that cursèd head
Whose wicked deed thy most ingenious sense 248
Deprived thee of! Hold off the earth awhile,
Till I have caught her once more in mine arms.

[*He leaps into the grave and embraces Ophelia.*]
Now pile your dust upon the quick and dead,
Till of this flat a mountain you have made
T' o'ertop old Pelion or the skyish head 253
Of blue Olympus.

---

219 maimèd mutilated, incomplete   **221 Fordo it** destroy its.   **estate**
rank.   **222 Couch we** Let's hide, lie low   **227 warranty** i.e., ecclesiastical authority.   **228 order** (1) prescribed practice (2) religious order
of clerics   **229 She should . . . lodged** she should have been buried in
unsanctified ground   **230 For** In place of   **231 Shards** broken bits of
pottery   **232 crants** garlands betokening maidenhood   **233 strew-**
ments flowers strewn on a coffin   **233–4 bringing . . . burial** laying
the body to rest, to the sound of the bell.   **237 such rest** i.e., to pray
for such rest   **238 peace-parted souls** those who have died at peace
with God.   **240 violets** (See 4.5.188 and note.)   **242 howling** i.e., in
hell.   **248 ingenious sense** a mind that is quick, alert, of fine qualities
253 Pelion a mountain in northern Thessaly; compare *Olympus* and
Ossa in lines 254 and 286. (In their rebellion against the Olympian
gods, the giants attempted to heap Ossa on Pelion in order to scale
Olympus.)

---

171 sore keen, veritable.   **whoreson** (An expression of contemptuous
familiarity.)   **173 lien you** lain. (See the note at line 166.)   **179 Rhen-**
ish Rhine wine   **185 bore** borne   **187 My gorge rises** i.e., I feel nauseated   **189 gibes** taunts   **192 chopfallen** (1) lacking the lower jaw
(2) dejected.   **193 favor** aspect, appearance   **204 bunghole** hole for
filling or emptying a cask.   **205 curiously** minutely   **208 with . . .**
lead it with moderation and plausibility.   **211 loam** a mixture of clay,
straw, sand, etc. used to mold bricks, or, in this case, bungs for a beer
barrel   **213 Imperious** Imperial   **216 flaw** gust of wind.   **217 soft**
i.e., wait, be careful

HAMLET [*coming forward*] What is he whose grief
  Bears such an emphasis, whose phrase of sorrow 255
  Conjures the wandering stars and makes them stand 256
  Like wonder-wounded hearers? This is I, 257
  Hamlet the Dane. 258

LAERTES [*grappling with him*] The devil take thy soul! 259

HAMLET Thou pray'st not well.
  I prithee, take thy fingers from my throat,
  For though I am not splenitive and rash,
  Yet have I in me something dangerous, 262
  Which let thy wisdom fear. Hold off thy hand.

KING Pluck them asunder.

QUEEN Hamlet, Hamlet!

ALL Gentlemen!

HORATIO Good my lord, be quiet.

       [*Hamlet and Laertes are parted.*]

HAMLET
  Why, I will fight with him upon this theme
  Until my eyelids will no longer wag. 270

QUEEN Oh, my son, what theme?

HAMLET
  I loved Ophelia. Forty thousand brothers
  Could not with all their quantity of love
  Make up my sum. What wilt thou do for her?

KING Oh, he is mad, Laertes.

QUEEN For love of God, forbear him. 276

HAMLET
  'Swounds, show me what thou'lt do. 277
  Woo't weep? Woo't fight? Woo't fast? Woo't tear
    thyself? 278
  Woo't drink up eisel? Eat a crocodile? 279
  I'll do't. Dost come here to whine?
  To outface me with leaping in her grave?
  Be buried quick with her, and so will I. 282
  And if thou prate of mountains, let them throw
  Millions of acres on us, till our ground,
  Singeing his pate against the burning zone, 285
  Make Ossa like a wart! Nay, an thou'lt mouth, 286
  I'll rant as well as thou.

QUEEN This is mere madness, 287
  And thus awhile the fit will work on him;
  Anon, as patient as the female dove

  When that her golden couplets are disclosed, 290
  His silence will sit drooping.

HAMLET Hear you, sir.
  What is the reason that you use me thus?
  I loved you ever. But it is no matter.
  Let Hercules himself do what he may, 294
  The cat will mew, and dog will have his day. 295

              Exit Hamlet.

KING
  I pray thee, good Horatio, wait upon him.

             [*Exit*] *Horatio.*

  [*To Laertes*] Strengthen your patience in our last
    night's speech; 297
  We'll put the matter to the present push.— 298
  Good Gertrude, set some watch over your son.—
  This grave shall have a living monument. 300
  An hour of quiet shortly shall we see; 301
  Till then, in patience our proceeding be. *Exeunt.*

            ❖

[5.2]

Enter Hamlet and Horatio.

HAMLET
  So much for this, sir; now shall you see the other. 1
  You do remember all the circumstance?

HORATIO Remember it, my lord!

HAMLET
  Sir, in my heart there was a kind of fighting
  That would not let me sleep. Methought I lay
  Worse than the mutines in the bilboes. Rashly, 6
  And praised be rashness for it—let us know 7
  Our indiscretion sometime serves us well 8
  When our deep plots do pall, and that should learn us 9
  There's a divinity that shapes our ends,
  Rough-hew them how we will—

HORATIO That is most certain. 11

HAMLET Up from my cabin,
  My sea-gown scarfed about me, in the dark 13
  Groped I to find out them, had my desire, 14
  Fingered their packet, and in fine withdrew 15
  To mine own room again, making so bold,
  My fears forgetting manners, to unseal
  Their grand commission; where I found, Horatio—
  Ah, royal knavery!—an exact command,

---

255 emphasis i.e., rhetorical and florid emphasis. (*Phrase* has a similar rhetorical connotation.) **256 wandering stars** planets **257 wonder-wounded** struck with amazement **258 the Dane** (This title normally signifies the King; see 1.1.17 and note.) **259 s.d. grappling with him** The testimony of the first quarto that *"Hamlet leaps in after Laertes"* and of the ballad "Elegy on Burbage," published in *Gentleman's Magazine* in 1825 ("Oft have I seen him leap into a grave") seem to indicate one way in which this fight was staged; however, the difficulty of fitting two contenders and Ophelia's body into a confined space (probably the trapdoor) suggests to many editors the alternative, that Laertes jumps out of the grave to attack Hamlet.) **262 splenitive** quick-tempered **270 wag** move. (A fluttering eyelid is a conventional sign that life has not yet gone.) **276 forbear him** leave him alone. **277 'Swounds** By His (Christ's) wounds **278 Woo't** Wilt thou **279 Woo't . . . eisel?** Will you drink up a whole draft of vinegar? (An extremely self-punishing task as a way of expressing grief.) **crocodile** (Crocodiles were tough and dangerous, and were supposed to shed crocodile tears.) **282 quick** alive **285 his pate** its head, i.e., top. **burning zone** zone in the celestial sphere containing the sun's orbit, between the tropics of Cancer and Capricorn **286 Ossa** (See 253n.) **an thou'lt mouth** if you want to rant **287 mere** utter

290 golden couplets two baby pigeons, covered with yellow down. **disclosed** hatched **294–5 Let . . . day** i.e., (1) Even Hercules couldn't stop Laertes's theatrical rant (2) I, too, will have my turn; i.e., despite any blustering attempts at interference, every person will sooner or later do what he or she must do. **297 in** i.e., by recalling **298 present push** immediate test. **300 living** lasting. (For Laertes' private understanding, Claudius also hints that Hamlet's death will serve as such a monument.) **301 hour of quiet** time free of conflict
5.2. Location: The castle.
1 see the other hear the other news. (See 4.6.24–6.) **6 mutines** mutineers. **bilboes** shackles. **(2)** I, too, will have my turn. (This adverb goes with lines 12 ff.) **7 know** acknowledge **8 indiscretion** lack of foresight and judgment (not an indiscreet act) **9 pall** fail, falter, go stale. **learn** teach **11 Rough-hew** shape roughly **13 sea-gown** seaman's coat. **scarfed** loosely wrapped **14 them** i.e., Rosencrantz and Guildenstern **15 Fingered** pilfered, pinched. **in fine** finally, in conclusion

Larded with many several sorts of reasons   20
Importing Denmark's health and England's too,   21
With, ho! such bugs and goblins in my life,   22
That on the supervise, no leisure bated,   23
No, not to stay the grinding of the ax,   24
My head should be struck off.

HORATIO   Is't possible?

HAMLET [*giving a document*]
Here's the commission. Read it at more leisure.
But wilt thou hear now how I did proceed?

HORATIO   I beseech you.

HAMLET
Being thus benetted round with villainies—
Ere I could make a prologue to my brains,   30
They had begun the play—I sat me down,   31
Devised a new commission, wrote it fair.   32
I once did hold it, as our statists do,   33
A baseness to write fair, and labored much   34
How to forget that learning, but, sir, now
It did me yeoman's service. Wilt thou know
Th'effect of what I wrote?

HORATIO   Ay, good my lord.

HAMLET
An earnest conjuration from the King,   38
As England was his faithful tributary,
As love between them like the palm might flourish,   40
As peace should still her wheaten garland wear   41
And stand a comma 'tween their amities,   42
And many suchlike "as"es of great charge,   43
That on the view and knowing of these contents,
Without debatement further more or less,
He should those bearers put to sudden death,
Not shriving time allowed.

HORATIO   How was this sealed?   47

HAMLET
Why, even in that was heaven ordinant.   48
I had my father's signet in my purse,   49
Which was the model of that Danish seal;   50
Folded the writ up in the form of th'other,   51
Subscribed it, gave't th'impression, placed it safely,   52
The changeling never known. Now, the next day   53
Was our sea fight, and what to this was sequent   54
Thou knowest already.

HORATIO
So Guildenstern and Rosencrantz go to't.

HAMLET
Why, man, they did make love to this employment.
They are not near my conscience. Their defeat   58
Does by their own insinuation grow.   59
'Tis dangerous when the baser nature comes   60
Between the pass and fell incensèd points   61
Of mighty opposites.

HORATIO   Why, what a king is this!   62

HAMLET
Does it not, think thee, stand me now upon—   63
He that hath killed my king and whored my mother,
Popped in between th'election and my hopes,   65
Thrown out his angle for my proper life,   66
And with such coz'nage—is't not perfect conscience   67
To quit him with this arm? And is't not to be damned   68
To let this canker of our nature come   69
In further evil?   70

HORATIO
It must be shortly known to him from England
What is the issue of the business there.

HAMLET
It will be short. The interim is mine,
And a man's life's no more than to say "one."   74
But I am very sorry, good Horatio,
That to Laertes I forgot myself,
For by the image of my cause I see
The portraiture of his. I'll court his favors.
But, sure, the bravery of his grief did put me   79
Into a tow'ring passion.

HORATIO   Peace, who comes here?

Enter a Courtier [Osric].

OSRIC   Your Lordship is right welcome back to Denmark.

HAMLET   I humbly thank you, sir. [*To Horatio*] Dost
know this water fly?

HORATIO   No, my good lord.

HAMLET   Thy state is the more gracious, for 'tis a vice to
know him. He hath much land, and fertile. Let a beast   86
be lord of beasts, and his crib shall stand at the King's   87
mess. 'Tis a chuff, but, as I say, spacious in the   88
possession of dirt.

OSRIC   Sweet lord, if Your Lordship were at leisure, I
should impart a thing to you from His Majesty.

HAMLET   I will receive it, sir, with all diligence of spirit.
Put your bonnet to his right use; 'tis for the head.   93

---

20 Larded garnished. **several** different   **21 Importing** relating to
22 With . . . life i.e., with all sorts of warnings of imaginary dangers if
I were allowed to continue living. (*Bugs* are bugbears, hobgoblins.)
23 That . . . bated that on the reading of this commission, no delay
being allowed   **24 stay** await   **30–1 Ere . . . play** before I could consciously turn my brain to the matter, it had started working on a plan
32 fair in a clear hand.   **33 statists** politicians, men of public affairs
34 A baseness beneath my dignity   **38 conjuration** entreaty
40 palm (An image of health; see Psalm 92:12.)   **41 still** always.
wheaten garland (Symbolic of fruitful agriculture, of peace and
plenty.)   **42 comma** (Indicating continuity, link.)   **43 "as"es** (1) the
"whereases" of a formal document (2) asses.   **charge** (1) import (2)
burden (appropriate to asses)   **47 shriving time** time for confession
and absolution   **48 ordinant** directing.   **49 signet** small seal
50 model replica   **51 writ** writing   **52 Subscribed** signed (with
forged signature).   **impression** i.e., with a wax seal   **53 changeling**
i.e., substituted letter. (Literally, a fairy child substituted for a human
one.)   **54 was sequent** followed

58 defeat destruction   **59 insinuation** intrusive intervention, sticking
their noses in my business   **60 baser** of lower social station   **61 pass**
thrust.   **fell** fierce   **62 opposites** antagonists.   **63 stand me now
upon** become incumbent on me now   **65 th'election** (The Danish
monarch was "elected" by a small number of high-ranking electors.)
66 angle fishhook.   **proper** very   **67 coz'nage** trickery   **68 quit**
requite, pay back   **69 canker** ulcer   **69–70 come In** grow into
74 a man's . . . "one" one's whole life occupies such a short time, only
as long as it takes to count to 1.   **79 bravery** bravado   **86–8 Let . . .
mess** i.e., If a man, no matter how beastlike, is as rich in livestock and
possessions as Osric, he may eat at the King's table.   **87 crib** manger
88 chuff boor, churl. (The second quarto spelling, "chough," is a variant spelling that also suggests the meaning here of "chattering jackdaw.")   **93 bonnet** any kind of cap or hat.   **his** its

OSRIC   I thank Your Lordship, it is very hot.

HAMLET   No, believe me, 'tis very cold. The wind is northerly.

OSRIC   It is indifferent cold, my lord, indeed.   97

HAMLET   But yet methinks it is very sultry and hot for my complexion.   99

OSRIC   Exceedingly, my lord. It is very sultry, as 'twere—I cannot tell how. My lord, His Majesty bade me signify to you that 'a has laid a great wager on your head. Sir, this is the matter—

HAMLET   I beseech you, remember.

[Hamlet moves him to put on his hat.]

OSRIC   Nay, good my lord; for my ease, in good faith.   105
Sir, here is newly come to court Laertes—believe me, an absolute gentleman, full of most excellent differ-   107
ences, of very soft society and great showing. Indeed,   108
to speak feelingly of him, he is the card or calendar of   109
gentry, for you shall find in him the continent of what   110
part a gentleman would see.   111

HAMLET   Sir, his definement suffers no perdition in   112
you, though I know to divide him inventorially would   113
dozy th'arithmetic of memory, and yet but yaw   114
neither in respect of his quick sail. But, in the verity of   115
extolment, I take him to be a soul of great article, and   116
his infusion of such dearth and rareness as, to make   117
true diction of him, his semblable is his mirror and   118
who else would trace him his umbrage, nothing   119
more.   120

OSRIC   Your Lordship speaks most infallibly of him.

HAMLET   The concernancy, sir? Why do we wrap the   122
gentleman in our more rawer breath?   123

OSRIC   Sir?

HORATIO   Is't not possible to understand in another   125
tongue? You will do't, sir, really.   126

HAMLET   What imports the nomination of this gentle-   127
man?

OSRIC   Of Laertes?

HORATIO   *[to Hamlet]*   His purse is empty already; all 's golden words are spent.

HAMLET   Of him, sir.

OSRIC   I know you are not ignorant—

HAMLET   I would you did, sir. Yet in faith if you did,   134
it would not much approve me. Well, sir?   135

OSRIC   You are not ignorant of what excellence Laertes is—

HAMLET   I dare not confess that, lest I should compare   138
with him in excellence. But to know a man well were   139
to know himself.   140

OSRIC   I mean, sir, for his weapon; but in the imputation   141
laid on him by them, in his meed he's unfellowed.   142

HAMLET   What's his weapon?

OSRIC   Rapier and dagger.

HAMLET   That's two of his weapons—but well.   145

OSRIC   The King, sir, hath wagered with him six Barbary horses, against the which he has impawned, as I take   147
it, six French rapiers and poniards, with their assigns,   148
as girdle, hangers, and so. Three of the carriages, in   149
faith, are very dear to fancy, very responsive to the   150
hilts, most delicate carriages, and of very liberal con-   151
ceit.   152

HAMLET   What call you the carriages?   153

HORATIO   *[to Hamlet]*   I knew you must be edified by the margent ere you had done.   155

OSRIC   The carriages, sir, are the hangers.

HAMLET   The phrase would be more germane to the matter if we could carry a cannon by our sides; I would it might be hangers till then. But, on: six Barbary horses against six French swords, their assigns, and three lib-eral-conceited carriages; that's the French bet against the Danish. Why is this impawned, as you call it?

OSRIC   The King, sir, hath laid, sir, that in a dozen   163
passes between yourself and him, he shall not exceed   164
you three hits. He hath laid on twelve for nine, and it would come to immediate trial, if Your Lordship would vouchsafe the answer.   167

HAMLET   How if I answer no?

---

97 indifferent somewhat   **99 complexion** constitution.   **105 for my ease** (A conventional reply declining the invitation to put the hat back on.)   **107 absolute** perfect   **107–8 differences** special qualities **108 soft society** agreeable manners.   **great showing** distinguished appearance.   **109 feelingly** with just perception   **109–10 the card . . . gentry** the model or paradigm (literally, a chart or directory) of good breeding   **110–11 the continent . . . see** one who contains in himself all the qualities a gentleman would like to see. (A *continent* is that which contains.)   **112–15 his definement . . . sail** the task of defining Laertes's excellences suffers no diminution in your description of him, though I know that to enumerate all his graces would stupify one's powers of memory, and even so could do no more than veer unsteadily off course in a vain attempt to keep up with his rapid for-ward motion. (Hamlet mocks Osric by parodying his jargon-filled speeches.)   **115–20 But . . . more** But, in true praise of him, I take him to be a person of remarkable value, and his essence of such rarity and excellence as, to speak truly of him, none can compare with him other than his own mirror; anyone following in his footsteps can only hope to be the shadow to his substance, nothing more.   **122 concernancy** import, relevance   **123 rawer breath** unrefined speech that can only come short in praising him.   **125–6 Is't . . . tongue?** i.e., Is it not pos-sible for you, Osric, to understand and communicate in any other tongue than the overblown rhetoric you have used? (Alternatively, Horatio could be asking Hamlet to speak more plainly.)   **126 You will do't** i.e., You can if you try, or, you may well have to try (to speak plainly).   **127 nomination** naming

134–5 I would . . . approve me (Responding to Osric's incompleted sentence as though it were a complete statement, Hamlet says, with mock politeness, "I wish you did know me to be not ignorant [i.e., to be knowledgeable] about matters," and then turns this into an insult: "But if you did, your recommendation of me would be of little value in any case.")   **138–40 I dare . . . himself** I dare not boast of knowing Laertes's excellence lest I seem to imply a comparable excellence in myself. Certainly, to know another person well, one must know one-self.   **141–2 I mean . . . unfellowed** I mean his excellence with his rapier, not his general excellence; in the reputation he enjoys for use of his weapons, his merit is unequaled.   **145 but well** but never mind.   **147 he** i.e., Laertes.   **impawned** staked, wagered **148 poniards** daggers.   **assigns** appurtenances   **149 hangers** straps on the sword belt (*girdle*), from which the sword hung.   **and so** and so on.   **149–52 Three . . . conceit** Three of the hangers, truly, are very pleasing to the fancy, decoratively matched with the hilts, delicate in workmanship, and made with elaborate ingenuity.   **153 What call you** What do you refer to when you say   **155 margent** margin of a book, place for explanatory notes   **163 laid** wagered   **164 passes** bouts. (The odds of the betting are hard to explain. Possibly the King bets that Hamlet will win at least five out of twelve, at which point Laertes raises the odds against himself by betting he will win nine.)   **167 vouchsafe the answer** be so good as to accept the challenge. (Hamlet deliberately takes the phrase in its literal sense of replying.)

OSRIC   I mean, my lord, the opposition of your person in trial.

HAMLET   Sir, I will walk here in the hall. If it please His Majesty, it is the breathing time of day with me. Let 172 the foils be brought, the gentleman willing, and the King hold his purpose, I will win for him an I can; if not, I will gain nothing but my shame and the odd hits.

OSRIC   Shall I deliver you so?   177

HAMLET   To this effect, sir—after what flourish your nature will.

OSRIC   I commend my duty to Your Lordship.   180

HAMLET   Yours, yours.   [Exit Osric.]
'A does well to commend it himself; there are no tongues else for 's turn.   183

HORATIO   This lapwing runs away with the shell on his 184 head.

HAMLET   'A did comply with his dug before 'a sucked 186 it. Thus has he—and many more of the same breed 187 that I know the drossy age dotes on—only got the 188 tune of the time, and, out of an habit of encounter, a 189 kind of yeasty collection, which carries them through 190 and through the most fanned and winnowed opin- 191 ions; and do but blow them to their trial, the bubbles 192 are out.   193

Enter a Lord.

LORD   My lord, His Majesty commended him to you by young Osric, who brings back to him that you attend him in the hall. He sends to know if your pleasure hold to play with Laertes, or that you will take longer 197 time.

HAMLET   I am constant to my purposes; they follow the King's pleasure. If his fitness speaks, mine is ready; 200 now or whensoever, provided I be so able as now.

LORD   The King and Queen and all are coming down.

HAMLET   In happy time.   203

LORD   The Queen desires you to use some gentle enter- 204 tainment to Laertes before you fall to play.   205

HAMLET   She well instructs me.   [Exit Lord.]

HORATIO   You will lose, my lord.

HAMLET   I do not think so. Since he went into France, I have been in continual practice; I shall win at the odds.

But thou wouldst not think how ill all's here about my heart; but it is no matter.

HORATIO   Nay, good my lord—

HAMLET   It is but foolery, but it is such a kind of gain- 213 giving as would perhaps trouble a woman.   214

HORATIO   If your mind dislike anything, obey it. I will forestall their repair hither and say you are not fit.   216

HAMLET   Not a whit, we defy augury. There is special 217 providence in the fall of a sparrow. If it be now, 'tis not to come; if it be not to come, it will be now; if it be not now; yet it will come. The readiness is all. Since 220 no man of aught he leaves knows, what is't to leave 221 betimes? Let be.   222

A table prepared. [Enter] trumpets, drums, and officers with cushions; King, Queen, [Osric,] and all the state; foils, daggers, [and wine borne in;] and Laertes.

KING
    Come, Hamlet, come and take this hand from me.
        [The King puts Laertes's hand into Hamlet's.]

HAMLET [to Laertes]
    Give me your pardon, sir. I have done you wrong,
    But pardon't as you are a gentleman.
    This presence knows,   226
    And you must needs have heard, how I am punished 227
    With a sore distraction. What I have done
    That might your nature, honor, and exception   229
    Roughly awake, I here proclaim was madness.
    Was't Hamlet wronged Laertes? Never Hamlet.
    If Hamlet from himself be ta'en away,
    And when he's not himself does wrong Laertes,
    Then Hamlet does it not, Hamlet denies it.
    Who does it, then? His madness. If't be so,
    Hamlet is of the faction that is wronged;   236
    His madness is poor Hamlet's enemy.
    Sir, in this audience
    Let my disclaiming from a purposed evil
    Free me so far in your most generous thoughts
    That I have shot my arrow o'er the house
    And hurt my brother.

LAERTES   I am satisfied in nature,   242
    Whose motive in this case should stir me most   243
    To my revenge. But in my terms of honor
    I stand aloof, and will no reconcilement
    Till by some elder masters of known honor
    I have a voice and precedent of peace   247
    To keep my name ungored. But till that time   248
    I do receive your offered love like love,

172 **breathing time** exercise period.   **Let** i.e., If   177 **deliver you** report what you say   180 **commend** commit to your favor. (A conventional salutation, but Hamlet wryly uses a more literal meaning, "recommend," "praise," in line 182.)   183 **for 's turn** for his purposes, i.e., to do it for him.   184 **lapwing** (A proverbial type of youthful forwardness. Also, a bird that draws intruders away from its nest and was thought to run about with its head in the shell when newly hatched; a seeming reference to Osric's hat.)   186 **comply . . . dug** observe ceremonious formality toward his nurse's or mother's teat   187–93 **Thus . . . are out** Thus has he—and many like him of the sort our frivolous age dotes on—acquired the trendy manner of speech of the time, and, out of habitual conversation with courtiers of their own kind, have collected together a kind of frothy medley of current phrases, which enables such gallants to hold their own among persons of the most select and well-sifted views; and yet do but test them by merely blowing on them, and their bubbles burst.   197 **play** fence.   **that if**   200 **If . . . ready** If he declares his readiness, my convenience waits on his   203 **In happy time** (A phrase of courtesy indicating that the time is convenient.)   204–5 **entertainment** greeting

213–14 **gaingiving** misgiving   216 **repair** coming   217 **augury** the attempt to read signs of future events in order to avoid predicted trouble.   220–2 **Since . . . Let be** Since no one has knowledge of what he is leaving behind, what does an early death matter after all? Enough; forbear.   222.1 **trumpets, drums** trumpeters, drummers   222.3 **all the state** the entire court   226 **presence** royal assembly   227 **punished** afflicted   229 **exception** disapproval   236 **faction** party   242 **in nature** i.e., as to my personal feelings   243 **motive** prompting   247 **voice** authoritative pronouncement.   **of peace** for reconciliation   248 **name ungored** reputation unwounded.

And will not wrong it.

HAMLET   I embrace it freely,
And will this brothers' wager frankly play.—   251
Give us the foils. Come on.

LAERTES   Come, one for me.

HAMLET
I'll be your foil, Laertes. In mine ignorance   253
Your skill shall, like a star i'th' darkest night,
Stick fiery off indeed.

LAERTES   You mock me, sir.   255

HAMLET   No, by this hand.

KING
Give them the foils, young Osric. Cousin Hamlet,
You know the wager?

HAMLET   Very well, my lord.
Your Grace has laid the odds o'th' weaker side.   259

KING
I do not fear it; I have seen you both.
But since he is bettered, we have therefore odds.   261

LAERTES
This is too heavy. Let me see another.
                    [He exchanges his foil for another.]

HAMLET
This likes me well. These foils have all a length?   263
                    [They prepare to fence.]

OSRIC   Ay, my good lord.

KING
Set me the stoups of wine upon that table.
If Hamlet give the first or second hit,
Or quit in answer of the third exchange,   267
Let all the battlements their ordnance fire.
The King shall drink to Hamlet's better breath,   269
And in the cup an union shall he throw   270
Richer than that which four successive kings
In Denmark's crown have worn. Give me the cups,
And let the kettle to the trumpet speak,   273
The trumpet to the cannoneer without,
The cannons to the heavens, the heaven to earth,
"Now the King drinks to Hamlet." Come, begin.
                    Trumpets the while.
And you, the judges, bear a wary eye.

HAMLET   Come on, sir.

LAERTES   Come, my lord. [They fence. Hamlet scores a hit.]

HAMLET   One.

LAERTES   No.

HAMLET   Judgment.

OSRIC   A hit, a very palpable hit.   282
                    Drum, trumpets, and shot. Flourish.
                    A piece goes off.

LAERTES   Well, again.

KING
Stay, give me drink. Hamlet, this pearl is thine.
                    [He drinks, and throws a pearl in Hamlet's cup.]
Here's to thy health. Give him the cup.

HAMLET
I'll play this bout first. Set it by awhile.
Come. [They fence.] Another hit; what say you?

LAERTES   A touch, a touch, I do confess't.

KING
Our son shall win.

QUEEN   He's fat and scant of breath.   289
Here, Hamlet, take my napkin, rub thy brows.   290
The Queen carouses to thy fortune, Hamlet.   291

HAMLET   Good madam!

KING   Gertrude, do not drink.

QUEEN
I will, my lord, I pray you pardon me.   [She drinks.]

KING [aside]
It is the poisoned cup. It is too late.

HAMLET
I dare not drink yet, madam; by and by.

QUEEN   Come, let me wipe thy face.

LAERTES [aside to the King]
My lord, I'll hit him now.

KING   I do not think't.

LAERTES [aside]
And yet it is almost against my conscience.

HAMLET
Come, for the third, Laertes. You do but dally.
I pray you, pass with your best violence;   301
I am afeard you make a wanton of me.   302

LAERTES   Say you so? Come on.   [They fence.]

OSRIC   Nothing neither way.

LAERTES
Have at you now!   305
                    [Laertes wounds Hamlet; then, in scuffling,
                    they change rapiers, and Hamlet wounds Laertes.]

KING   Part them! They are incensed.

HAMLET
Nay, come, again.   [The Queen falls.]

OSRIC   Look to the Queen there, ho!

HORATIO
They bleed on both sides. How is it, my lord?

OSRIC   How is't, Laertes?

LAERTES
Why, as a woodcock to mine own springe, Osric;   309
I am justly killed with mine own treachery.

HAMLET
How does the Queen?

KING   She swoons to see them bleed.

---

251 **frankly** without ill feeling or the burden of rancor   253 **foil** thin metal background which sets a jewel off. (With pun on the blunted rapier for fencing.)   255 **Stick fiery off** stand out brilliantly   259 **laid . . . side** backed the weaker side.   261 **is bettered** is the odds-on favorite. (Laertes's handicap is the "three hits" specified in line 165.)   263 **likes** pleases   267 **Or . . . exchange** or draws even with Laertes by winning the third exchange   269 **better breath** improved vigor   270 **union** pearl. (So called, according to Pliny's *Natural History*, 9, because pearls are *unique*, never identical.)   273 **kettle** kettledrum   282.2 *A piece* A cannon

289 **fat** not physically fit, out of training   290 **napkin** handkerchief   291 **carouses** drinks a toast   301 **pass** thrust   302 **make . . . me** i.e., treat me like a spoiled child, trifle with me.   305.1–2 *in scuffling, they change rapiers* (This stage direction occurs in the Folio. According to a widespread stage tradition, Hamlet receives a scratch, realizes that Laertes's sword is unbated, and accordingly forces an exchange.)   309 **woodcock** a bird, a type of stupidity or as a decoy.   **springe** trap, snare

QUEEN
No, no, the drink, the drink—Oh, my dear Hamlet—
The drink, the drink! I am poisoned.   [*She dies.*]

HAMLET
Oh, villainy! Ho, let the door be locked!
Treachery! Seek it out.   [*Laertes falls. Exit Osric.*]

LAERTES
It is here, Hamlet. Hamlet, thou art slain.
No med'cine in the world can do thee good;
In thee there is not half an hour's life.
The treacherous instrument is in thy hand,
Unbated and envenomed. The foul practice   320
Hath turned itself on me. Lo, here I lie,
Never to rise again. Thy mother's poisoned.
I can no more. The King, the King's to blame.

HAMLET
The point envenomed too? Then, venom, to thy work.
     [*He stabs the King.*]

ALL   Treason! Treason!

KING
Oh, yet defend me, friends! I am but hurt.

HAMLET [*forcing the King to drink*]
Here, thou incestuous, murderous, damnèd Dane,
Drink off this potion. Is thy union here?   328
Follow my mother.   [*The King dies.*]

LAERTES   He is justly served.
It is a poison tempered by himself.   330
Exchange forgiveness with me, noble Hamlet.
Mine and my father's death come not upon thee,
Nor thine on me!   [*He dies.*]

HAMLET
Heaven make thee free of it! I follow thee.
I am dead, Horatio. Wretched Queen, adieu!
You that look pale and tremble at this chance,   336
That are but mutes or audience to this act,   337
Had I but time—as this fell sergeant, Death,   338
Is strict in his arrest—oh, I could tell you—   339
But let it be. Horatio, I am dead;
Thou livest. Report me and my cause aright
To the unsatisfied.

HORATIO   Never believe it.
I am more an antique Roman than a Dane.   343
Here's yet some liquor left.
     [*He attempts to drink from the poisoned cup.*
       Hamlet prevents him.]

HAMLET   As thou'rt a man,
Give me the cup! Let go! By heaven, I'll ha 't.
Oh, God, Horatio, what a wounded name,
Things standing thus unknown, shall I leave behind
   me!
If thou didst ever hold me in thy heart,
Absent thee from felicity awhile,

And in this harsh world draw thy breath in pain
To tell my story. *A march afar off* [*and a volley within*].
What warlike noise is this?

     Enter Osric.

OSRIC
Young Fortinbras, with conquest come from Poland,
To th'ambassadors of England gives
This warlike volley.

HAMLET   Oh, I die, Horatio!
The potent poison quite o'ercrows my spirit.   355
I cannot live to hear the news from England,
But I do prophesy th'election lights
On Fortinbras. He has my dying voice.   358
So tell him, with th'occurrents more and less   359
Which have solicited. The rest is silence.   [*He dies.*] 360

HORATIO
Now cracks a noble heart. Good night, sweet prince,
And flights of angels sing thee to thy rest!
     [*March within.*]
Why does the drum come hither?

     Enter Fortinbras, with the [*English*] *Ambassadors*
     [*with drum, colors, and attendants*].

FORTINBRAS
Where is this sight?

HORATIO   What is it you would see?
If aught of woe or wonder, cease your search.

FORTINBRAS
This quarry cries on havoc. O proud Death,   366
What feast is toward in thine eternal cell,   367
That thou so many princes at a shot
So bloodily hast struck?

FIRST AMBASSADOR   The sight is dismal,
And our affairs from England come too late.
The ears are senseless that should give us hearing,
To tell him his commandment is fulfilled,
That Rosencrantz and Guildenstern are dead.
Where should we have our thanks?

HORATIO   Not from his mouth, 374
Had it th'ability of life to thank you.
He never gave commandment for their death.
But since, so jump upon this bloody question,   377
You from the Polack wars and you from England
Are here arrived, give order that these bodies
High on a stage be placèd to the view,   380
And let me speak to th' yet unknowing world
How these things came about. So shall you hear
Of carnal, bloody, and unnatural acts,
Of accidental judgments, casual slaughters,   384

---

320 Unbated not blunted with a button.   **practice** plot   **328 union** pearl. (See line 270; with grim puns on the word's other meanings: marriage, shared death.)   **330 tempered** mixed   **336 chance** mischance   **337 mutes** silent observers. (Literally, actors with nonspeaking parts.)   **338 fell sergeant** remorseless arresting officer   **339 strict** (1) severely just (2) unavoidable.   **arrest** (1) taking into custody (2) stopping my speech   **343 Roman** (Suicide was an honorable choice for many Romans as an alternative to a dishonorable life.)

355 o'ercrows triumphs over (like the winner in a cockfight) **358 voice** vote.   **359 th'occurrents** the events, incidents **360 solicited** moved, urged. (Hamlet doesn't finish saying what the events have prompted—presumably, his acts of vengeance, or his reporting of those events to Fortinbras.)   **366 This . . . havoc** This heap of dead bodies loudly proclaims a general slaughter.   **367 feast** i.e., Death feasting on those who have fallen.   **toward** in preparation **374 his** Claudius's   **377 so jump . . . question** so hard on the heels of this bloody business   **380 stage** platform   **384 judgments** retributions.   **casual** occurring by chance

Of deaths put on by cunning and forced cause,   385
And, in this upshot, purposes mistook
Fall'n on th'inventors' heads. All this can I
Truly deliver.
FORTINBRAS   Let us haste to hear it,
And call the noblest to the audience.
For me, with sorrow I embrace my fortune.
I have some rights of memory in this kingdom,   391
Which now to claim my vantage doth invite me.   392
HORATIO
Of that I shall have also cause to speak,
And from his mouth whose voice will draw on more.   394
But let this same be presently performed,   395

Even while men's minds are wild, lest more
    mischance
On plots and errors happen.
FORTINBRAS   Let four captains   397
Bear Hamlet, like a soldier, to the stage,
For he was likely, had he been put on,   399
To have proved most royal; and for his passage,   400
The soldiers' music and the rite of war
Speak loudly for him.   402
Take up the bodies. Such a sight as this
Becomes the field, but here shows much amiss.   404
Go bid the soldiers shoot.
        *Exeunt [marching, bearing off the dead bodies;
                     a peal of ordnance is shot off].*

385 put on instigated. **forced cause** contrivance **391 of memory** traditional, remembered, unforgotten **392 vantage** favorable opportunity **394 voice . . . more** vote will influence still others. **395 presently** immediately

397 On on top of **399 put on** i.e., invested in royal office and so put to the test **400 for his passage** to mark his passing **402 Speak** (let them) speak **404 Becomes the field** suits the field of battle

Othello, the Moor of Venice

Othello differs in several respects from the other three major Shakespearean tragedies with which it is usually ranked. Written seemingly about the time of its performance at court by the King's Men (Shakespeare's acting company) on November 1, 1604, after *Hamlet* (c. 1599–1601) and before *King Lear* (1605–1606) and *Macbeth* (c. 1606–1607), *Othello* shares with these other plays a fascination with evil in its most virulent and universal aspect. These plays study the devastating effects of ambitious pride, ingratitude, wrath, jealousy, and vengeful hate—the deadly sins of the spirit—with only a passing interest in the political strife to which Shakespeare's Roman or classical tragedies are generally devoted. Of the four, *Othello* is the most concentrated upon one particular evil. The action concerns sexual jealousy, and, although human sinfulness is such that jealousy ceaselessly touches on other forms of depravity, the center of interest always returns in *Othello* to the destruction of a love through jealousy. *Othello* is a tragic portrait of a marriage. The protagonist is not a king or a prince, as in the tragedies already mentioned, but a general recently married. There are no supernatural visitations, as in *Hamlet* and *Macbeth*. Ideas of divine justice, while essential to *Othello*'s portrayal of a battle between good and evil for the allegiance of the protagonist, do not encompass the wide sweep of *King Lear*, nor do we find here the same broad indictment of humanity. Social order is not seriously shaken by Othello's tragedy. The fairminded Duke of Venice remains firmly in control, and his deputy Lodovico oversees a just conclusion on Cyprus.

By the same token, *Othello* does not offer the remorseless questioning about humanity's relationship to the cosmos that we find in *King Lear, Hamlet,* and *Macbeth*. The battle of good and evil is, of course, cosmic, but in *Othello* that battle is realized through a taut narrative of jealousy and murder. Its poetic images are accordingly focused to a large extent on the natural world. One cluster of images is domestic and animal, having to do with goats, mon-

keys, wolves, baboons, guinea hens, wildcats, spiders, flies, asses, dogs, copulating horses and sheep, serpents, and toads; other images, more wide-ranging in scope, include green-eyed monsters, devils, poisons, money purses, tarnished jewels, music untuned, and light extinguished. The story is immediate and direct, retaining the sensational atmosphere of its Italian prose source by Giovanni Baptista Giraldi Cinthio, in his *Hecatommithi* of 1565 (translated into French in 1584). Events move even more swiftly than in Cinthio's work, for Shakespeare has compressed the story into two or three nights and days (albeit with an intervening sea journey and with an elastic use of stage time to allow for the maturing of long-term plans, as when we learn that Iago has begged Emilia "a hundred times" to steal Desdemona's handkerchief, 3.3.308, or that Iago has accused Cassio of making love to Desdemona "A thousand times," 5.2.219). *Othello* does not have a fully developed double plot, as in *King Lear,* or a comparatively large group of characters serving as foils to the protagonist, as in *Hamlet. Othello*'s cast is small, and the plot is concentrated to an unusual degree on Othello, Desdemona, and Iago. What *Othello* may lose in breadth it gains in dramatic intensity.

Daringly, Shakespeare opens this tragedy of love, not with a direct and sympathetic portrayal of the lovers themselves, but with a scene of vicious insinuation about their marriage. The images employed by Iago to describe the coupling of Othello and Desdemona are revoltingly animalistic, sodomistic. "Even now, now, very now, an old black ram / Is tupping your white ewe," he taunts Desdemona's father, Brabantio. (Tupping is a word used specifically for the copulating of sheep.) "You'll have your daughter covered with a Barbary horse; you'll have your nephews neigh to you"; "your daughter and the Moor are now making the beast with two backs"; "the devil will make a grandsire of you" (1.1.90–3, 113–20). This degraded view reduces the marriage to one of utter carnality, with repeated emphasis on the word "gross": Desdemona has yielded "to the gross clasps of a lascivious Moor" and has made "a gross revolt" against her family and society (lines 129, 137). Iago's second theme, one that is habitual with him, is money. "What ho, Brabantio! Thieves, thieves, thieves! / Look to your house, your daughter, and your bags" (lines 81–2). The implication is of a sinister bond between thievery in sex and thievery in gold. Sex and money are both commodities to be protected by watchful fathers against libidinous and opportunistic children.

We as audience make plentiful allowance for Iago's bias in all this, since he has admitted to Roderigo his knavery and resentment of Othello. Even so, the carnal vision of love we confront is calculatedly disturbing, because it seems so equated with a pejorative image of blackness. Othello is unquestionably a black man, referred to disparagingly by his detractors as the "thick-lips," with a "sooty bosom" (1.1.68; 1.2.71); Elizabethan usage applied the term "Moor" without attempting to distinguish between Arabian and African peoples. From the ugly start of the play, Othello and Desdemona have to prove the worth of their love in the face of preset attitudes against miscegenation. Brabantio takes refuge in the thought that Othello must have bewitched Desdemona. His basic assumption—one to be echoed later by Iago and when Othello's confidence is undermined by Othello himself—is that miscegenation is unnatural by definition. In confronting and accusing Othello, he repeatedly appeals "to all things of sense" (that is, to common sense) and asks if it is not "gross in sense" (self-evident) that Othello has practiced magic on her, since nothing else could prompt human nature so to leave its natural path. "For nature so preposterously to err, / Being not deficient, blind, or lame of sense, / Sans witchcraft could not" (1.2.65, 73; 1.3.64–6). We as audience can perceive the racial bias in Brabantio's view and can recognize also in him the type of imperious father who conventionally opposes romantic love. It is sadly ironic that he should now prefer Roderigo as a son-in-law, evidently concluding that any white Venetian would be preferable to the prince of blacks. Still, Brabantio has been hospitable to the Moor and trusting of his daughter. He is a sorrowful rather than ridiculous figure, and the charge he levels at the married pair, however much it is based on a priori assumptions of what is "natural" in human behavior, remains to be answered.

After all, we find ourselves wondering, what did attract Othello and Desdemona to one another? Even though he certainly did not use witchcraft, may Othello not have employed a subtler kind of enchantment in the exotic character of his travels among "the Cannibals that each other eat, / The Anthropophagi, and men whose heads / Do grow beneath their shoulders" (1.3.145–7)? These "passing strange" events fascinate Desdemona as they do everyone, including the Duke of Venice ("I think this tale would win my daughter too"). Othello has not practiced unfairly on her—"This only is the witchcraft I have used" (lines 162, 171–3). Yet may he not represent for Desdemona a radical novelty, being a man at once less devious and more interesting than the dissolute Venetian swaggerers, such as Roderigo and the "wealthy curlèd darlings of our nation" (1.2.69), who follow her about? Was her deceiving of her father by means of the elopement a protest, an escape from conventionality? Why has she been attracted to a man older than herself? For his part, Othello gives the impression of being inexperienced with women, at least of Desdemona's rank and complexion, and is both intrigued and flattered by her attentions. "She loved me for the dangers I had passed, / And I loved her that she did pity them" (1.3.169–70). Desdemona fulfills a place in Othello's view of himself. Does she also represent status for him in Venetian society, where he has been employed as a military commander but treated nonetheless as something of an alien?

These subtle but impertinent ways of doubting the motivations of Othello and Desdemona, adding to the difficulties that are inherent in an attempt to understand the mysteries of attraction in any relationship, are thrust upon us by the play's opening and are later crucial to Iago's strategy of breeding mistrust. Just as importantly, however, these insinuations are refuted by Othello and especially by Desdemona. Whatever others may think, she never gives the slightest indication of regarding her husband as different because he is black and old. In fact, the images of blackness and age are significantly reversed during the play's early scenes. Othello has already embraced the Christian faith, whereas Iago, a white Italian in a Christian culture, emerges as innately evil from the very start of the play. Othello's first appearance onstage, when he confronts a party of torch-bearing men coming to arrest him and bids his followers sheathe their swords (1.2.60), is perhaps reminiscent of Christ's arrest in the Garden of Gethsemane; if so, it suggests a fleeting comparison between Othello and the Christian God whose charity and forbearance he seeks to emulate. Othello's blackness may be used in part as an emblem of fallen humanity, but so are we all fallen. His age similarly strengthens our impression of his wisdom, restraint, and leadership. Any suggestions of comic sexual infidelity in the marriage of an older man and an attractive young bride are confuted by what we see in Desdemona's chaste yet sensual regard for the good man she has chosen.

Desdemona is devoted to Othello, admiring, and faithful. We believe her when she says that she does not even know what it means to be unfaithful; the word *whore* is not in her vocabulary. She is defenseless against the charges brought against her because she does not even comprehend them and cannot believe that anyone would imagine such things. Her love, both erotic and chaste, is of that transcendent wholesomeness common to several late Shakespearean heroines, such as Cordelia in *King Lear* and Hermione in *The Winter's Tale.* Her "preferring" Othello to her father, like Cordelia's placing her duty to a husband before that to a father, is not ungrateful but natural and proper. And Othello, however much he may regard Desdemona in terms of his own identity (he calls her "my fair warrior"), does cherish Desdemona as she deserves. "I cannot speak enough of this content," he exclaims when he rejoins her on Cyprus. "It stops me here; it is too much of joy" (2.1.182, 196–7). The passionate intensity of his love prepares the way for his tragedy; he speaks more truly than he knows in saying, "when I love thee not, / Chaos is come again" (3.3.99–100). Iago speaks truly also when he observes that Othello "Is of a constant, loving, noble nature" (2.1.290). Othello's tragedy is not that he is easily duped, but that his strong faith can be destroyed at such terrible cost. Othello never forgets how much he is losing. The threat to his love is not an initial lack of his being happily married, but rather the insidious assumption that Desdemona cannot love him because such a love might be unnatural. The fear of being unlovable exists in Othello's mind, but the human instrument of this vicious gospel is Iago.

Iago belongs to a select group of villains in Shakespeare who, while plausibly motivated in human terms, also take delight in evil for its own sake: Aaron the Moor in *Titus Andronicus*, Richard III, Don John in *Much Ado About Nothing*, and Edmund in *King Lear.* They are not, like Macbeth or like Claudius in *Hamlet,* men driven by ambition to commit crimes they clearly recognize to be wrong. Although Edmund does belatedly try to make amends, these villains are essentially conscienceless, sinister, and amused by their own cunning. They are related to one another by a stage metaphor of personified evil derived from the Vice of the morality play, whose typical role is to win the Mankind figure away from virtue and to corrupt him with worldly enticements. Like that engaging tempter, Shakespeare's villains in these plays take the audience into their confidence, boast in soliloquy of their cleverness, exult in the triumph of evil, and improvise plans with daring and resourcefulness. They are all superb actors, deceiving virtually every character onstage until late in the action with their protean and hypocritical display. They take pleasure in this "sport" and amaze us by their virtuosity. The role is paradoxically comic in its use of ingenious and resourceful deception— the grim and ironic comedy of vice. We know that we are to condemn morally even while we applaud the skill.

This theatrical tradition of the Vice may best explain a puzzling feature of Iago, noted long ago and memorably phrased by Samuel Taylor Coleridge as "the motive hunting of a motiveless malignity." To be sure, Iago does offer plausible motives for what he does. Despite his resemblance to the morality Vice, he is no allegorized abstraction but an ensign in the army, a junior field officer who hates being out-ranked by a theoretician or staff officer. As an old-school professional, he also resents that he has not been promoted on the basis of seniority, the "old gradation" (1.1.38). Even his efforts at using influence with Othello have come to naught, and Iago can scarcely be blamed for supposing that Cassio's friendship with Othello has won him special favor. Thus, Iago has reason to plot against Cassio as well as Othello. Nevertheless a further dimension is needed to explain Iago's gloating, his utter lack of moral reflection, his concentration on destroying Desdemona (who has not wronged Iago), his absorption in ingenious methods of plotting, his finesse and style. Hatred precedes any plausible motive in Iago and ultimately does not depend on psychological causality. Probably the tradition of the stage Machiavel (another type of gloating villain based on stereotyped attitudes toward the heretical political ideas of Niccolò Machiavelli), as in Marlowe's *The Jew of Malta,* contributes to the portraiture; this tradition was readily assimilated with that of the Vice.

Iago's machinations yield him both "sport" and "profit" (1.3.387); that is, he enjoys his evildoing, although he is also driven by a motive. This Vice-like behavior in human garb creates a restless sense of a destructive metaphysical reality lying behind his visible exterior. Even his stated motives do not always make sense. When in an outburst of hatred he soliloquizes that "I hate the Moor; / And it is thought abroad that twixt my sheets / He's done my office," Iago goes on to concede the unlikelihood of this charge. "I know not if't be true; / But I, for mere suspicion in that kind, / Will do as if for surety" (lines 387–91). The charge is so absurd, in fact, that we have to look into Iago himself for the origin of this jealous paranoia. The answer may be partly emblematic: as the embodiment and genius of sexual jealousy, Iago suffers with ironic appropriateness from the evil he preaches, and without external cause. Emilia understands that jealousy is not a rational affliction but a self-induced disease of the mind. Jealous persons, she tells Desdemona, "are not ever jealous for the cause, / But jealous for they're jealous. It is a monster / Begot upon itself, born on itself" (3.4.161–3). Iago's own testimonial bears this out, for his jealousy is at once wholly irrational and agonizingly self-destructive. "I do suspect the lusty Moor / Hath leaped into my seat, the thought whereof / Doth, like a poisonous mineral, gnaw my innards" (2.1.296–8). In light of this nightmare, we can see that even his seemingly plausible resentment of Cassio's promotion is jealous envy. The "daily beauty" in Cassio's life makes Iago feel "ugly" by comparison (5.1.19–20), engendering in Iago a profound sense of lack of worth from which he can temporarily find relief only by reducing Othello and others to his own miserable condition. He is adept at provoking self-hatred in others because he suffers from it himself. His declaration to Othello that "I am your own forever"

(3.3.495) is, of course, cynical, but it also signals the extent to which Iago has succeeded in wooing Othello away from Desdemona and Cassio into a murderous union between two women-hating men. The Iago who thus dedicates himself as partner in the fulfillment of Othello's homicidal fantasies is, we learn, capable of fantasizing a bizarre amorous encounter between himself and Cassio (lines 429–41).

Othello comes at last to regard Iago as a "demi-devil" who has tempted Othello to damn himself "beneath all depth in hell"; Lodovico speaks of Iago in the closing lines of the play as a "hellish villain" (5.2.142, 309, 379); and Iago himself boasts that "When devils will the blackest sins put on, / They do suggest at first with heavenly shows, / As I do now" (2.3.345–7). Iago thus bears some affinity to both the Vice and the devil, suggesting his relationship both to Othello's inner temptation and to a pre-existent evil force in the universe itself. Conversely, Desdemona is in Emilia's words an "angel," purely chaste; "So come my soul to bliss as I speak true" (5.2.134, 259). When Desdemona lands on Cyprus, she is greeted in words that echo the *Ave Maria:* "Hail to thee, lady! And the grace of heaven . . . Enwheel thee round" (2.1.87–9). These images introduce metaphorically a conflict of good and evil in which Othello, typical of fallen humanity, has chosen evil and destroyed the good at the prompting of a diabolical counselor. Again we see the heritage of the morality play, especially of the later morality play in which the Mankind figure was sometimes damned rather than saved. Even so, to allegorize *Othello* is to obscure and misread its clash of human passion. In fact, we see that the impulse to reduce human complexity to simplistic moral absolutes is a fatal weakness in Othello; by insisting on viewing Desdemona as a type or abstraction, he loses sight of her wonderful humanity. The theological issue of salvation or damnation is not relevant in dramatic terms; the play is not a homily on the dangers of jealousy. The metaphysical dimensions of a homiletic tradition are transmuted into human drama. Acknowledging these limitations, we can notwithstanding see a spiritual analogy in Iago's devil-like method of undoing his victims.

His trick resembles that of the similarly mischief-making Don John in *Much Ado About Nothing:* an optical illusion by which the blameless heroine is impugned as an adulteress. The concealed Othello must watch Cassio boasting of sexual triumphs and believe he is talking about Desdemona. Like the devil, Iago is given power over people's frail senses, especially the eyes. He can create illusions to induce Othello to see what Iago wants him to see, as Don John does with Claudio, but Othello's acceptance of the lie must be his own responsibility, a failure of his corrupted will. Iago practices on Othello with an a priori logic used before on Brabantio and Roderigo, urging the proneness of all mortals to sin and the alleged unnaturalness of a black-white marriage. All women have appetites; Desdemona is a woman; hence, Desdemona has appetites. "The wine she drinks is made of grapes," he scoffs to Roderigo. "If she had been blessed, she would never have loved the Moor" (2.1.253–5). She is a Venetian, and "In Venice they do let God see the pranks / They dare not show their husbands" (3.3.216–17). Therefore, she, too, is a hypocrite; "She did deceive her father" (line 220). Most of all, it stands to reason that she must long for a man of her own race. Iago succeeds in getting Othello to concur: "And yet, how nature erring from itself—" (line 243). This proposition that Nature teaches all persons, including Desdemona, to seek a harmonious matching of "clime, complexion, and degree" strikes a responsive chord in Othello, since he knows that even though he has authority as a general serving his adopted city he is also black and in some senses a foreigner, an alien. "Haply, for I am black / And have not those soft parts of conversation / That chamberers have." Then, too, he is sensitive that he is older than she, "declined / Into the vale of years" (lines 246, 279–82), "the young affects / In me defunct" (1.3.266–7). And so, if one must conclude from the preceding that Desdemona will seek a lover, the only question is who. "This granted—as it is a most pregnant and unforced position—who stands so eminent in the degree of this fortune as Cassio does?" (2.1.236–9). Once Othello has accepted this syllogistic sequence of proofs, specious not through any lapse in logic but because the axiomatic assumptions about human nature are degraded and do not apply to Desdemona, Othello has arrived at an unshakable conclusion to which all subsequent evidence must be applied. "Villain, be sure thou prove my love a whore," he commissions Iago (3.3.375). Desdemona's innocent pleading for Cassio only makes things look worse. Cassio's reputed muttering while asleep, like the handkerchief seen in his possession or his giddy talk about his mistress Bianca, "speaks against her [Desdemona] with the other proofs" (line 456).

How has Othello fallen so far? His bliss with Desdemona as they are rejoined on Cyprus knows no limit. These two persons represent married love at its very best, erotic and spiritual, she enhancing his manliness, he cherishing her beauty and virtue. His blackness and age are positive images in him, despite earlier insinuations to the contrary. Indeed, we have no reason to suppose that Othello is what we would call "old," despite his worries about being "declined / Into the vale of years" and having lost the "young effects" of sexual desire; he appears to be middle-aged and vigorous, so much so that Desdemona is attracted to him sexually as well as in other ways. He is a man of public worthiness, of command, of self-assurance. Desdemona is the most domestic of Shakespeare's tragic heroines, even while she is also representative of so much that is transcendent. Husband and wife are bound happily in one of Shakespeare's few detailed portraits of serious commitment in marriage. Othello initially has the wisdom to know that Desdemona's feminine attractiveness ought not to be threatening to him: he need not be jealous because she is beautiful, "free of speech," and loves dancing and music, since "Where virtue is, these are more virtuous." Nor does he see any reason at first to fear her "revolt" simply because he is black and older than his wife; "she had eyes, and chose me" (3.3.197–203). Othello's self-assurance through the love he perceives in Desdemona is the strongest sign of his happiness in marriage.

What then gives way? We look at Iago for one important insight, but ultimately the cause must be in Othello himself. Arthur Kirsch has argued persuasively (in *Shakespeare and the Experience of Love*, 1981) that Othello's most grave failing is an insufficient regard for himself. It is in part an inability to counter the effects on him of a culture that regards him as an outsider; he is at last persuaded to see himself with the eyes of Venice, not just of Iago, but of Brabantio (who gladly entertains Othello until he has the presumption to elope with Brabantio's white daughter) and others. The resulting destruction of self-regard is devastating. Othello's jealousy stems from a profound suspicion that others cannot love him because he does not deem himself lovable.

Othello has loved Desdemona as an extention of himself, and, in his moments of greatest contentedness, his marriage is sustained by an idealized vision of himself serving as the object of his exalted romantic passion. When he destroys Desdemona, as he realizes with a terrible clarity, Othello destroys himself; the act is a prelude to his actual suicide. Iago's means of temptation, then, is to persuade Othello to regard himself with the eyes of Venice, to accept the view that Othello is himself alien and that any woman who loves him does so perversely. In Othello's tainted state of mind, Desdemona's very sexuality becomes an unbearable threat to him, her warmth and devotion a "proof" of disloyalty. Othello's most tortured speeches (3.4.57–77, 4.2.49–66) reveal the extent to which he equates the seemingly betraying woman, whom he has so depended on for happiness, with his own mother, who was given a handkerchief by an Egyptian sorceress and was warned that, if she should lose it, she would lose her husband's affection. Othello has briefly learned and then forgotten the precious art of harmonizing erotic passion and spiritual love, and, as these two great aims of love are driven apart in him, he comes to loathe and fear the sexuality that puts him so much in mind of his physical frailty and dependence on woman. The horror and pity of *Othello* rests, above all, in the spectacle of a love that was once so whole and noble made filthy by self-hatred. The tragic flaw thus lies in Othello's maleness, in his fear of betrayal by the innocent woman he loves, and his apparent need to degrade her for the very thing he finds desirable in her—a tendency so common among men that Freud, in the early twentieth century, could declare it to be "the most prevalent form of degradation in erotic life" (in Freud's *Sammlung*, volume 4).

The increasing surrender of Othello's judgment to passion can be measured in three successive trial scenes in the play: the entirely fair trial of Othello himself by the Venetian Senate concerning the elopement, Othello's trial of Cassio for drinking and rioting (when, ominously, Othello's "blood begins my safer guides to rule," 2.3.199), and finally the prejudged sentencing of Desdemona without providing her any opportunity to defend herself. In a corollary decline, Othello falls from the Christian compassion of the opening scenes (he customarily confesses to heaven "the vices of my blood," 1.3.125) to the pagan savagery of his vengeful and ritualistic execution of his wife. "My heart is turned to stone" (4.1.184–5), he vows, and at the play's end he grievingly characterizes himself as a "base Indian" who "threw a pearl away / Richer than all his tribe" (5.2.357–8). Iago knows that he must persuade Othello to sentence and to execute Desdemona himself, for only by active commitment to evil will Othello damn himself. In nothing does Iago so resemble the devil as in his wish to see Othello destroy the innocence and goodness on which his happiness depends.

The fate of some of the lesser characters echoes that of Othello, for Iago's evil intent is to "enmesh them all" (2.3.356). Cassio, in particular, is, like Othello, an attractive man with a single, vulnerable weakness—in his case, a fleshly appetite for wine and women. For him, alternately idolizing and depreciating women as he does, the gap between spiritual and sensual love remains vast, but he is essentially good-natured and trustworthy. His seemingly genial flaws lead to disaster, because they put him at the mercy of a remorseless enemy. Iago is, with fitting irony, the apostle of absolute self-control: "Our bodies are our gardens, to the which our wills are gardeners" (1.3.323–4). Thus, Cassio's tragedy is anything but a straightforward homily on the virtues of temperance. Similarly, Bianca is undone, not through any simple cause-and-effect punishment of her sexual conduct—she is, after all, fond of Cassio and loyal to him, even if he will not marry her—but because Iago is able to turn appearances against her. With his usual appeal to a priori logic, he builds a case that she and Cassio are in cahoots: "I do suspect this trash / To be a party in this injury . . . This is the fruits of whoring" (5.1.86–7, 118). Roderigo is another of Iago's victims, a contemptible one, led by the nose because he, too, has surrendered reason to passion. Emilia cannot escape Iago's evil influence and steals the handkerchief for him, despite knowing its value for Desdemona. Flaws are magnified into disasters by a remorseless evil intelligence. Men and women both must be ceaselessly circumspect; a good reputation is sooner lost than recovered. Emilia is a conventionally decent enough woman—she jests to Desdemona that she would be faithless in marriage only for a very high price—and yet her one small compromise with her conscience contributes to the murder of her mistress. Like Othello, she offers atonement too late, by denouncing her husband in a gesture of defiance toward male authority that says much about the tragic consequences of male mistrust of women. Desdemona is the only person in the play too good to be struck down through some inner flaw, which may explain why Iago is so intent on destroying her along with Othello and Cassio.

As a tragic hero, Othello obtains self-knowledge at a terrible price. He knows finally that what he has destroyed was ineffably good. The discovery is too late for him to make amends, and he dies by his own hand as atonement. The deaths of Othello and Desdemona are, in their separate ways, equally devastating: he is in part the victim of racism, though he nobly refuses to deny his own culpability, and she is the victim of sexism, lapsing sadly into the stereotypical role of passive and silent sufferer that the Venetian world expects of women. Despite the loss, however, Othello's reaffirmation of faith in Desdemona's goodness undoes what the devil-like Iago had most hoped to achieve: the separation of Othello from his loving trust in one who is good. In this important sense, Othello's self-knowledge is cathartic and a compensation for the terrible price he has paid. The very existence of a person as good as Desdemona gives the lie to Iago's creed that everyone has his or her price. She is the sacrificial victim who must die for Othello's loss of faith and, by dying, rekindle that faith. ("My life upon her faith!" Othello prophetically affirms, in response to her father's warning that she may deceive [1.3.297].) She cannot restore him to himself, for self-hatred has done its ugly work, but she is the means by which he understands at last the chimerical and wantonly destructive nature of his jealousy. His greatness appears in his acknowledgment of this truth and in the heroic struggle with which he has confronted an inner darkness we all share.

Onstage and in film and television, *Othello* proves itself to be jarringly relevant to modern concerns about racial conflict and about men's mistreatment of women. Janet Suzman chose to produce the play onstage and subsequently for educational television in Johannesburg,

South Africa, at a time when apartheid was soon to be dismantled, even though that surprising if inevitable event was not yet discernible. A racially mixed audience came to see a racially mixed cast, with John Kani, a well-known South African Black actor, as Othello, and a very fair-haired South African actress as Desdemona. Iago unmistakably represented the mindset of a state police officer obsessed with preserving the purity of the White race and therefore venemous in his racial hatred of Othello for his miscegenated marriage with a White woman. The explosively powerful emotions of that production carry over into a memorable film version. Orson Welles's 1951 film version, recently remastered, featured Othello in blackface as the protagonist; so did Laurence Olivier's film of 1965, based on a National Theatre stage production of 1964 with Frank Finlay as Iago and Maggie Smith as Desdemona. Indeed, most Othellos onstage over the centuries have been White actors (including Edmund Kean, John Philip Kemble, Edwin Booth, Charles Macready, Edwin Forrest, Henry Irving, Tommaso Salvini, and Paul Scofield, many of whom also played Iago), with notable exceptions that include Ira Aldridge, Earle Hyman, and Paul Robeson. Robeson's galvanizing performances at the Savoy Theatre in 1930 with Peggy Ashcroft as Desdemona, and then in Margaret Webster's New York production of 1943–1945 with Uta Hagen as Desdemona and José Ferrer as Iago, helped establish the role of Othello as one that great Black actors could perform. Today racially mixed casting allows for all sorts of permutations, though Kenneth Branagh's recent film chooses the more recognizable pattern with Branagh himself as Iago and Laurence Fishburne as Othello. In another recent development, Emilia has stood out in several productions as the raisonneur and heroic figure in the play, speaking as she does on behalf of maltreated women, urging Desdemona to stand up for her rights. One recent Chicago production went so far as to rewrite the ending: Othello and Iago both survive unpunished for what they have done, while Desdemona and Emilia lie dead as their innocent victims. This deliberate and provocative overstatement might seem extreme to some viewers, but unquestionably did signal the direction of recent performance history of this profoundly disturbing play.

Othello, the Moor of Venice

The Names of the Actors

OTHELLO, *the Moor*
BRABANTIO, [*a senator,*] *father to Desdemona*
CASSIO, *an honorable lieutenant* [*to Othello*]
IAGO, [*Othello's ancient,*] *a villain*
RODERIGO, *a gulled gentleman*
DUKE OF VENICE
SENATORS [*of Venice*]
MONTANO, *Governor of Cyprus*
GENTLEMEN *of Cyprus*
LODOVICO *and* GRATIANO, [*kinsmen to Brabantio,*] *two*
  noble Venetians
SAILORS
CLOWN

DESDEMONA, [*daughter to Brabantio and*] *wife to*
  Othello
EMILIA, *wife to Iago*
BIANCA, *a courtesan* [*and mistress to Cassio*]

[A MESSENGER
A HERALD
A MUSICIAN

Servants, Attendants, Officers, Senators,
Musicians, Gentlemen

SCENE: *Venice; a seaport in Cyprus*]

1.1

Enter Roderigo and Iago.

RODERIGO
Tush, never tell me! I take it much unkindly   1
That thou, Iago, who hast had my purse
As if the strings were thine, shouldst know of this.   3

IAGO 'Sblood, but you'll not hear me.   4
If ever I did dream of such a matter,
Abhor me.

RODERIGO
Thou told'st me thou didst hold him in thy hate.   7

IAGO Despise me
If I do not. Three great ones of the city,
In personal suit to make me his lieutenant,
Off-capped to him; and by the faith of man,
I know my price, I am worth no worse a place.
But he, as loving his own pride and purposes,
Evades them with a bombast circumstance   14

Horribly stuffed with epithets of war,   15
And, in conclusion,
Nonsuits my mediators. For, "Certes," says he,   17
"I have already chose my officer."
And what was he?
Forsooth, a great arithmetician,   20
One Michael Cassio, a Florentine,
A fellow almost damned in a fair wife,   22
That never set a squadron in the field
Nor the division of a battle knows   24
More than a spinster—unless the bookish theoric,   25
Wherein the togaed consuls can propose   26
As masterly as he. Mere prattle without practice
Is all his soldiership. But he, sir, had th'election;
And I, of whom his eyes had seen the proof   29
At Rhodes, at Cyprus, and on other grounds

---

15 epithets of war military expressions   **17 Nonsuits** rejects the petition of.   **Certes** Certainly   **20 arithmetician** i.e., a man whose military knowledge is merely theoretical, based on books of tactics   **22 A . . . wife** (Cassio does not seem to be married, but his counterpart in Shakespeare's source does have a woman in his house. See also 4.1.131.)   **24 division of a battle** disposition of a military unit   **25 a spinster** i.e., a housewife, one whose regular occupation is spinning.   **theoric** theory   **26 togaed consuls** toga-wearing counselors or senators.   **propose** discuss   **29 his** Othello's

---

1.1. Location: Venice. A street.
1 never tell me (An expression of incredulity, like "tell me another one.")   **3 this** i.e., Desdemona's elopement.   **4 'Sblood** By His (Christ's) blood   **7 him** Othello   **14 bombast circumstance** wordy evasion. (*Bombast* is cotton padding.)

Christened and heathen, must be beleed and calmed   31
By debitor and creditor. This countercaster,   32
He, in good time, must his lieutenant be,   33
And I—God bless the mark!—His Moorship's ancient.   34

RODERIGO
By heaven, I rather would have been his hangman.   35

IAGO
Why, there's no remedy. 'Tis the curse of service;
Preferment goes by letter and affection,   37
And not by old gradation, where each second   38
Stood heir to th' first. Now, sir, be judge yourself
Whether I in any just term am affined   40
To love the Moor.

RODERIGO   I would not follow him then.

IAGO   Oh, sir, content you.   43
I follow him to serve my turn upon him.
We cannot all be masters, nor all masters
Cannot be truly followed. You shall mark   46
Many a duteous and knee-crooking knave
That, doting on his own obsequious bondage,
Wears out his time, much like his master's ass,
For naught but provender, and when he's old,
   cashiered.   50
Whip me such honest knaves. Others there are   51
Who, trimmed in forms and visages of duty,   52
Keep yet their hearts attending on themselves,
And, throwing but shows of service on their lords,
Do well thrive by them, and when they have lined
   their coats,   55
Do themselves homage. These fellows have some
   soul,   56
And such a one do I profess myself. For, sir,
It is as sure as you are Roderigo,
Were I the Moor I would not be Iago.   59
In following him, I follow but myself—
Heaven is my judge, not I for love and duty,
But seeming so for my peculiar end.   62
For when my outward action doth demonstrate
The native act and figure of my heart   64
In compliment extern, 'tis not long after   65

But I will wear my heart upon my sleeve
For daws to peck at. I am not what I am.   67

RODERIGO
What a full fortune does the thick-lips owe   68
If he can carry't thus!

IAGO   Call up her father.   69
Rouse him, make after him, poison his delight,
Proclaim him in the streets; incense her kinsmen,
And, though he in a fertile climate dwell,   72
Plague him with flies. Though that his joy be joy,   73
Yet throw such changes of vexation on't   74
As it may lose some color.   75

RODERIGO
Here is her father's house. I'll call aloud.

IAGO
Do, with like timorous accent and dire yell   77
As when, by night and negligence, the fire   78
Is spied in populous cities.

RODERIGO
What ho, Brabantio! Signor Brabantio, ho!

IAGO
Awake! What ho, Brabantio! Thieves, thieves, thieves!
Look to your house, your daughter, and your bags!
Thieves, thieves!   83

        Brabantio [enters] above [at a window].

BRABANTIO
What is the reason of this terrible summons?
What is the matter there?

RODERIGO
Signor, is all your family within?

IAGO
Are your doors locked?

BRABANTIO   Why, wherefore ask you this?

IAGO
Zounds, sir, you're robbed. For shame, put on your
   gown!   88
Your heart is burst; you have lost half your soul.
Even now, now, very now, an old black ram
Is tupping your white ewe. Arise, arise!   91
Awake the snorting citizens with the bell,   92
Or else the devil will make a grandsire of you.   93
Arise, I say!

BRABANTIO   What, have you lost your wits?

RODERIGO
Most reverend signor, do you know my voice?

---

31 beleed and calmed left to leeward without wind, becalmed. (A sailing metaphor.)   **32 debitor and creditor** (A name for a system of bookkeeping, here used as a contemptuous nickname for Cassio.) **countercaster** i.e., bookkeeper, one who tallies with *counters*, or "metal disks." (Said contemptuously.)   **33 in good time** opportunely, i.e., forsooth   **34 God bless the mark** (Perhaps originally a formula to ward off evil; here an expression of impatience.)   **ancient** standard-bearer, ensign.   **35 his hangman** the executioner of him. **37 Preferment** promotion.   **letter and affection** personal influence and favoritism   **38 old gradation** step-by-step seniority, the traditional way   **40 term** respect.   **affined** bound   **43 content you** don't you worry about that.   **46 truly** faithfully   **50 cashiered** dismissed from service.   **51 Whip me** Whip, as far as I'm concerned **52 trimmed . . . duty** dressed up in the mere form and show of dutifulness   **55 lined their coats** i.e., stuffed their purses   **56 Do themselves homage** i.e., attend to self-interest solely.   **59 Were . . . Iago** i.e., if I were able to assume command, I certainly would not choose to remain a subordinate, or, I would keep a suspicious eye on a flattering subordinate.   **62 peculiar** particular, personal   **64 native** innate.   **figure** shape, intent   **65 compliment extern** outward show (conforming in this case to the inner workings and intention of the heart)

67 daws small crowlike birds, proverbially stupid and avaricious. **I am not what I am** i.e., I am not one who wears his heart on his sleeve.   **68 full** swelling.   **thick-lips** (Elizabethans often applied the term "Moor" to Negroes.)   **owe** own   **69 carry't thus** carry this off. **72–3 though . . . flies** though he seems prosperous and happy now, vex him with misery.   **73 Though . . . be joy** Although he seems fortunate and happy. (Repeats the idea of line 72.)   **74 changes of vexation** vexing changes   **75 As . . . color** that may cause it to lose some of its first gloss.   **77 timorous** frightening   **78 As . . . fire** as when a fire, having gained hold by negligence at night   **83.1 *at a window*** (This stage direction, from the Quarto, probably calls for an appearance on the gallery above and rearstage.)   **88 Zounds** By His (Christ's) wounds   **91 tupping** covering, copulating with. (Said of sheep.)   **92 snorting** snoring   **93 the devil** (The devil was conventionally pictured as black.)

BRABANTIO   Not I. What are you?

RODERIGO   My name is Roderigo.

BRABANTIO   The worser welcome.
I have charged thee not to haunt about my doors.
In honest plainness thou hast heard me say
My daughter is not for thee; and now, in madness,
Being full of supper and distemp'ring drafts,   102
Upon malicious bravery dost thou come   103
To start my quiet.   104

RODERIGO
Sir, sir, sir—

BRABANTIO   But thou must needs be sure
My spirits and my place have in their power   106
To make this bitter to thee.

RODERIGO   Patience, good sir.

BRABANTIO
What tell'st thou me of robbing? This is Venice;
My house is not a grange.

RODERIGO   Most grave Brabantio,   109
In simple and pure soul I come to you.   110

IAGO   Zounds, sir, you are one of those that will not
serve God if the devil bid you. Because we come to do
you service and you think we are ruffians, you'll have
your daughter covered with a Barbary horse; you'll   114
have your nephews neigh to you; you'll have coursers   115
for cousins and jennets for germans.   116

BRABANTIO   What profane wretch art thou?

IAGO   I am one, sir, that comes to tell you your daughter
and the Moor are now making the beast with two
backs.

BRABANTIO
Thou art a villain.

IAGO   You are—a senator.   121

BRABANTIO
This thou shalt answer. I know thee, Roderigo.   122

RODERIGO
Sir, I will answer anything. But I beseech you,
If't be your pleasure and most wise consent—   124
As partly I find it is—that your fair daughter,
At this odd-even and dull watch o'th' night,   126
Transported with no worse nor better guard   127
But with a knave of common hire, a gondolier,   128
To the gross clasps of a lascivious Moor—
If this be known to you and your allowance   130
We then have done you bold and saucy wrongs.   131
But if you know not this, my manners tell me
We have your wrong rebuke. Do not believe

That, from the sense of all civility,   134
I thus would play and trifle with your reverence.   135
Your daughter, if you have not given her leave,
I say again, hath made a gross revolt,
Tying her duty, beauty, wit, and fortunes   138
In an extravagant and wheeling stranger   139
Of here and everywhere. Straight satisfy yourself.   140
If she be in her chamber or your house,
Let loose on me the justice of the state
For thus deluding you.

BRABANTIO [calling]   Strike on the tinder, ho!   144
Give me a taper! Call up all my people!
This accident is not unlike my dream.   146
Belief of it oppresses me already.
Light, I say, light!   Exit [above].

IAGO   Farewell, for I must leave you.
It seems not meet nor wholesome to my place   149
To be produced—as, if I stay, I shall—   150
Against the Moor. For I do know the state,
However this may gall him with some check,   152
Cannot with safety cast him, for he's embarked   153
With such loud reason to the Cyprus wars,   154
Which even now stands in act, that, for their souls,   155
Another of his fathom they have none   156
To lead their business; in which regard,   157
Though I do hate him as I do hell pains,
Yet for necessity of present life   159
I must show out a flag and sign of love,
Which is indeed but sign. That you shall surely find
him,
Lead to the Sagittary the raisèd search,   162
And there will I be with him. So farewell.   Exit.   163

*Enter [below] Brabantio [in his nightgown] with
servants and torches.*

BRABANTIO
It is too true an evil. Gone she is;
And what's to come of my despisèd time   165
Is naught but bitterness. Now, Roderigo,
Where didst thou see her?—Oh, unhappy girl!—
With the Moor, say'st thou?—Who would be a father!—
How didst thou know 'twas she?—Oh, she deceives
me
Past thought!—What said she to you?—Get more
tapers.
Raise all my kindred.—Are they married, think you?

---

102 **distemp'ring** intoxicating   103 **Upon malicious bravery** with
hostile intent to defy me   104 **start** startle, disrupt   106 **My . . .
power** my temperament and my authority of office have it in their
power   109 **grange** isolated country house.   110 **simple** sincere
114 **Barbary** from northern Africa (and hence associated with Othello)   115 **nephews** i.e., grandsons   115–16 **you'll . . . germans**
you'll consent to have powerful horses for kinfolks and small Spanish horses for near relatives.   121 **a senator** (Said with mock politeness, as though the word itself were an insult.)   122 **answer** be held
accountable for.   124 **wise** well-informed   126 **At . . . night** at this
hour that is between day and night, neither the one nor the other
127 **with** by   128 **But with a knave** than by a low fellow, a servant
130 **and your allowance** and has your permission   131 **saucy**
insolent

134 **from** contrary to.   **civility** good manners, decency   135 **your
reverence** (1) the respect due to you (2) Your Reverence.   138 **wit**
intelligence   139–40 **In . . . everywhere** to a wandering and
vagabond foreigner of uncertain origins.   140 **Straight** Straightaway
144 **tinder** charred linen ignited by a spark from flint and steel, used
to light torches or *tapers* (lines 145, 170)   146 **accident** occurrence,
event   149 **meet** fitting.   **place** position (as ensign)   150 **produced**
produced (as a witness)   152 **gall** rub; oppress.   **check** rebuke
153 **cast** dismiss.   **embarked** engaged   154 **loud** urgent   155 **stands
in act** have started.   **for their souls** to save their souls   156 **fathom**
i.e., ability, depth of experience   157 **in which regard** out of regard
for which   159 **life** livelihood   162 **Sagittary** (An inn or house
where Othello and Desdemona are staying, named for its sign of
Sagittarius, or Centaur.)   **raisèd search** search party roused out of
sleep.   163.1 *nightgown* dressing gown. (This costuming is specified
in the Quarto text.)   165 **time** i.e., remainder of life

RODERIGO   Truly, I think they are.

BRABANTIO

Oh, heaven! How got she out? Oh, treason of the
    blood!
Fathers, from hence trust not your daughters' minds
By what you see them act. Is there not charms   175
By which the property of youth and maidhood   176
May be abused? Have you not read, Roderigo,   177
Of some such thing?

RODERIGO   Yes, sir, I have indeed.

BRABANTIO

Call up my brother.—Oh, would you had had her!—
Some one way, some another.—Do you know
Where we may apprehend her and the Moor?

RODERIGO

I think I can discover him, if you please   182
To get good guard and go along with me.

BRABANTIO

Pray you, lead on. At every house I'll call;
I may command at most.—Get weapons, ho!   185
And raise some special officers of night.—
On, good Roderigo. I will deserve your pains.   187

                                        Exeunt.

❋

1.2

Enter Othello, Iago, attendants with torches.

IAGO

Though in the trade of war I have slain men,
Yet do I hold it very stuff o'th' conscience
To do no contrived murder. I lack iniquity   2
Sometimes to do me service. Nine or ten times   3
I had thought t'have yerked him here under the ribs.   5

OTHELLO

'Tis better as it is.

IAGO   Nay, but he prated,
And spoke such scurvy and provoking terms
Against your honor
That, with the little godliness I have,
I did full hard forbear him. But, I pray you, sir,   10
Are you fast married? Be assured of this,
That the magnifico is much beloved,   12
And hath in his effect a voice potential   13
As double as the Duke's. He will divorce you,
Or put upon you what restraint or grievance
The law, with all his might to enforce it on,
Will give him cable.

OTHELLO   Let him do his spite.   17
My services which I have done the seigniory   18

Shall out-tongue his complaints. 'Tis yet to know—   19
Which, when I know that boasting is an honor,
I shall promulgate—I fetch my life and being
From men of royal siege, and my demerits   22
May speak unbonneted to as proud a fortune   23
As this that I have reached. For know, Iago,
But that I love the gentle Desdemona,
I would not my unhousèd free condition   26
Put into circumscription and confine   27
For the seas' worth. But look, what lights come yond?   28

Enter Cassio [and officers] with torches.

IAGO

Those are the raisèd father and his friends.
You were best go in.

OTHELLO   Not I. I must be found.
My parts, my title, and my perfect soul   31
Shall manifest me rightly. Is it they?

IAGO   By Janus, I think no.   33

OTHELLO

The servants of the Duke? And my lieutenant?
The goodness of the night upon you, friends!
What is the news?

CASSIO   The Duke does greet you, General,
And he requires your haste-post-haste appearance
Even on the instant.

OTHELLO   What is the matter, think you?

CASSIO

Something from Cyprus, as I may divine.   39
It is a business of some heat. The galleys   40
Have sent a dozen sequent messengers   41
This very night at one another's heels,
And many of the consuls, raised and met,   43
Are at the Duke's already. You have been hotly called
    for;
When, being not at your lodging to be found,
The Senate hath sent about three several quests   46
To search you out.

OTHELLO   'Tis well I am found by you.
I will but spend a word here in the house
And go with you.   [*Exit.*]

CASSIO   Ancient, what makes he here?   49

IAGO

Faith, he tonight hath boarded a land carrack.   50
If it prove lawful prize, he's made forever.   51

---

175 charms spells **176 property** special quality, nature **177 abused**
deceived. **182 discover** reveal, uncover **185 command** demand
assistance **187 deserve** show gratitude for
1.2. Location: Venice. Another street, before Othello's lodgings.
2 very stuff essence, basic material. (Continuing the metaphor of
trade from line 1.) **3 contrived** premeditated **5 yerked** stabbed.
him i.e., Roderigo **10 I . . . him** I restrained myself with great difficulty from assaulting him. **12 magnifico** Venetian grandee, i.e., Brabantio **13 in his effect** at his command. **potential** powerful
17 cable i.e., scope. **18 seigniory** Venetian government

19 yet to know not yet widely known **22 siege** i.e., rank. (Literally, a
seat used by a person of distinction.) **demerits** deserts **23 unbonneted** without removing the hat, i.e., on equal terms. (? Or "with hat
off," "in all due modesty.") **26 unhousèd** unconfined, undomesti-
cated **27 circumscription and confine** restriction and confinement
28 the seas' worth all the riches at the bottom of the sea. **28.1** *officers*
(The quarto text specifies, "*Enter Cassio with lights, Officers, and
torches.*") **31 My . . . soul** My natural gifts, my position or reputation, and my unflawed conscience **33 Janus** Roman two-faced god
of beginnings **39 divine** guess. **40 heat** urgency. **41 sequent** successive **43 consuls** senators **46 about** all over the city. **several**
separate **49 makes** does **50 boarded** gone aboard and seized as an
act of piracy. (With sexual suggestion.) **carrack** large merchant ship.
51 prize booty

CASSIO
  I do not understand.

IAGO   He's married.

CASSIO   To who?

  [*Enter Othello.*]

IAGO
  Marry, to—Come, Captain, will you go?   53

OTHELLO   Have with you.   54

CASSIO
  Here comes another troop to seek for you.   55

  Enter Brabantio, Roderigo, with officers and
  torches.

IAGO
  It is Brabantio. General, be advised.   56
  He comes to bad intent.

OTHELLO   Holla! Stand there!

RODERIGO
  Signor, it is the Moor.

BRABANTIO   Down with him, thief!
  [*They draw on both sides.*]

IAGO
  You, Roderigo! Come, sir, I am for you.

OTHELLO
  Keep up your bright swords, for the dew will rust
    them.   60
  Good signor, you shall more command with years
  Than with your weapons.

BRABANTIO
  O thou foul thief, where hast thou stowed my
    daughter?
  Damned as thou art, thou hast enchanted her!
  For I'll refer me to all things of sense,   65
  If she in chains of magic were not bound
  Whether a maid so tender, fair, and happy,
  So opposite to marriage that she shunned
  The wealthy curlèd darlings of our nation,
  Would ever have, t'incur a general mock,
  Run from her guardage to the sooty bosom   71
  Of such a thing as thou—to fear, not to delight.
  Judge me the world if 'tis not gross in sense   73
  That thou hast practiced on her with foul charms,
  Abused her delicate youth with drugs or minerals   75
  That weakens motion. I'll have't disputed on;   76
  'Tis probable and palpable to thinking.
  I therefore apprehend and do attach thee   78
  For an abuser of the world, a practicer   79
  Of arts inhibited and out of warrant.—   80
  Lay hold upon him! If he do resist,

Subdue him at his peril.

OTHELLO   Hold your hands,
  Both you of my inclining and the rest.   83
  Were it my cue to fight, I should have known it
  Without a prompter.—Whither will you that I go
  To answer this your charge?

BRABANTIO   To prison, till fit time
  Of law and course of direct session   88
  Call thee to answer.

OTHELLO   What if I do obey?
  How may the Duke be therewith satisfied,
  Whose messengers are here about my side
  Upon some present business of the state
  To bring me to him?

OFFICER   'Tis true, most worthy signor.
  The Duke's in council, and your noble self,
  I am sure, is sent for.

BRABANTIO   How? The Duke in council?
  In this time of the night? Bring him away.   96
  Mine's not an idle cause. The Duke himself,   97
  Or any of my brothers of the state,
  Cannot but feel this wrong as 'twere their own;
  For if such actions may have passage free,   100
  Bondslaves and pagans shall our statesmen be.
                                                    Exeunt.

❖

1.3

Enter Duke [and] Senators [and sit at a table, with
lights], and Officers. [The Duke and Senators
are reading dispatches.]

DUKE
  There is no composition in these news   1
  That gives them credit.

FIRST SENATOR   Indeed, they are disproportioned.   3
  My letters say a hundred and seven galleys.

DUKE
  And mine, a hundred forty.

SECOND SENATOR   And mine, two hundred.
  But though they jump not on a just account—   6
  As in these cases, where the aim reports   7
  'Tis oft with difference—yet do they all confirm
  A Turkish fleet, and bearing up to Cyprus.

DUKE
  Nay, it is possible enough to judgment.
  I do not so secure me in the error   11
  But the main article I do approve   12
  In fearful sense.

---

53 Marry (An oath, originally "by the Virgin Mary"; here used
with wordplay on *married*.)   **54 Have with you** i.e., Let's go.
55.1–2 officers and torches (The quarto text calls for "*others with lights*
and weapons.")   **56 be advised** be on your guard.   **60 Keep up** Keep
in the sheath   **65 I'll . . . sense** I'll submit my case to one and all
71 guardage guardianship   **73 gross in sense** obvious
75 minerals i.e., poisons   **76 weakens motion** impair the vital faculties.   **disputed on** argued in court by professional counsel, debated
by experts   **78 attach** arrest   **79 abuser** deceiver   **80 arts inhibited**
prohibited arts, black magic.   **out of warrant** illegal.

83 inclining following, party   **88 course of direct session** regular or
specially convened legal proceedings   **96 away** right along.   **97 idle**
trifling   **100 may . . . free** are allowed to go unchecked
1.3. Location: Venice. A council chamber.
0.1–2 Enter . . . Officers (The quarto text calls for the Duke and senators to "*set at a Table with lights and Attendants.*")   **1 composition** consistency   **3 disproportioned** inconsistent.   **6 jump** agree.   **just** exact
7 the aim conjecture   **11–12 I do not . . . approve** I do not take such
(false) comfort in the discrepancies that I fail to perceive the main
point, i.e., that the Turkish fleet is threatening

SAILOR (*within*)   What ho, what ho, what ho!

Enter Sailor.

OFFICER   A messenger from the galleys.

DUKE   Now, what's the business?

SAILOR
The Turkish preparation makes for Rhodes.   16
So was I bid report here to the state
By Signor Angelo.

DUKE
How say you by this change?

FIRST SENATOR   This cannot be   19
By no assay of reason. 'Tis a pageant   20
To keep us in false gaze. When we consider   21
Th'importancy of Cyprus to the Turk,
And let ourselves again but understand
That, as it more concerns the Turk than Rhodes,
So may he with more facile question bear it,   25
For that it stands not in such warlike brace,   26
But altogether lacks th'abilities   27
That Rhodes is dressed in—if we make thought of this,   28
We must not think the Turk is so unskillful   29
To leave that latest which concerns him first,   30
Neglecting an attempt of ease and gain
To wake and wage a danger profitless.   32

DUKE
Nay, in all confidence, he's not for Rhodes.

OFFICER   Here is more news.

Enter a Messenger.

MESSENGER
The Ottomites, reverend and gracious,
Steering with due course toward the isle of Rhodes,
Have there injointed them with an after fleet.   37

FIRST SENATOR
Ay, so I thought. How many, as you guess?

MESSENGER
Of thirty sail; and now they do restem   39
Their backward course, bearing with frank
appearance   40
Their purposes toward Cyprus. Signor Montano,
Your trusty and most valiant servitor,   42
With his free duty recommends you thus,   43
And prays you to believe him.

DUKE   'Tis certain then for Cyprus.
Marcus Luccicos, is not he in town?

FIRST SENATOR   He's now in Florence.

DUKE
Write from us to him, post-post-haste. Dispatch.

FIRST SENATOR
Here comes Brabantio and the valiant Moor.

*Enter Brabantio, Othello, Cassio, Iago,
Roderigo, and officers.*

DUKE
Valiant Othello, we must straight employ you   50
Against the general enemy Ottoman.   51
[*To Brabantio*] I did not see you; welcome, gentle
signor.   52
We lacked your counsel and your help tonight.

BRABANTIO
So did I yours. Good Your Grace, pardon me;
Neither my place nor aught I heard of business   55
Hath raised me from my bed, nor doth the general
care
Take hold on me, for my particular grief   57
Is of so floodgate and o'erbearing nature   58
That it engluts and swallows other sorrows   59
And it is still itself.

DUKE   Why, what's the matter?   60

BRABANTIO
My daughter! Oh, my daughter!

DUKE AND SENATORS   Dead?

BRABANTIO   Ay, to me.
She is abused, stol'n from me, and corrupted   62
By spells and medicines bought of mountebanks;
For nature so preposterously to err,
Being not deficient, blind, or lame of sense,   65
Sans witchcraft could not.   66

DUKE
Whoe'er he be that in this foul proceeding
Hath thus beguiled your daughter of herself,
And you of her, the bloody book of law
You shall yourself read in the bitter letter
After your own sense—yea, though our proper son   71
Stood in your action.

BRABANTIO   Humbly I thank Your Grace.   72
Here is the man, this Moor, whom now it seems
Your special mandate for the state affairs
Hath hither brought.

ALL   We are very sorry for't.

DUKE [*to Othello*]
What, in your own part, can you say to this?

BRABANTIO   Nothing, but this is so.

OTHELLO
Most potent, grave, and reverend signors,
My very noble and approved good masters: 79
That I have ta'en away this old man's daughter,
It is most true; true, I have married her.
The very head and front of my offending   82

---

16 preparation fleet prepared for battle   19 by about   20 assay test.
pageant mere show   21 in false gaze looking the wrong way.   25 So
may . . . it so also he (the Turk) can more easily capture it (Cyprus)
26 For that since.   brace state of defense   27 th'abilities the means
of self-defense   28 dressed in equipped with   29 unskillful deficient in judgment   30 latest last   32 wake and wage stir up and risk
37 injointed them joined themselves.   after second, following
39–40 restem . . . course retrace their original course   40 frank
appearance undisguised intent   42 servitor officer under your command   43 free duty freely given and loyal service.   recommends
commends himself and reports to

50 straight straightaway   51 general enemy universal enemy to all
Christendom   52 gentle noble   55 place official position   57 particular personal   58 floodgate i.e., overwhelming (as when floodgates
are opened)   59 engluts engulfs   60 is still itself remains undiminished.   62 abused deceived   65 deficient defective.   lame of sense
deficient in sensory perception   66 Sans without   71 After . . .
sense according to your own interpretation.   our proper my own
72 Stood . . . action were under your accusation.   79 approved
proved, esteemed   82 head and front height and breadth, entire
extent

Hath this extent, no more. Rude am I in my speech,   83
And little blessed with the soft phrase of peace;
For since these arms of mine had seven years' pith,   85
Till now some nine moons wasted, they have used   86
Their dearest action in the tented field;   87
And little of this great world can I speak
More than pertains to feats of broils and battle,
And therefore little shall I grace my cause
In speaking for myself. Yet, by your gracious patience,
I will a round unvarnished tale deliver   92
Of my whole course of love—what drugs, what
    charms,
What conjuration, and what mighty magic,
For such proceeding I am charged withal,   95
I won his daughter.

BRABANTIO   A maiden never bold;
Of spirit so still and quiet that her motion   97
Blushed at herself; and she, in spite of nature,   98
Of years, of country, credit, everything,   99
To fall in love with what she feared to look on!
It is a judgment maimed and most imperfect
That will confess perfection so could err   102
Against all rules of nature, and must be driven
To find out practices of cunning hell   104
Why this should be. I therefore vouch again   105
That with some mixtures powerful o'er the blood,   106
Or with some dram conjured to this effect,   107
He wrought upon her.

DUKE   To vouch this is no proof,
Without more wider and more overt test   109
Than these thin habits and poor likelihoods   110
Of modern seeming do prefer against him.   111

FIRST SENATOR   But Othello, speak.
Did you by indirect and forcèd courses   113
Subdue and poison this young maid's affections?
Or came it by request and such fair question   115
As soul to soul affordeth?

OTHELLO   I do beseech you,
Send for the lady to the Sagittary
And let her speak of me before her father.
If you do find me foul in her report,
The trust, the office I do hold of you
Not only take away, but let your sentence
Even fall upon my life.

DUKE   Fetch Desdemona hither.

OTHELLO [to Iago]
Ancient, conduct them. You best know the place.
                                        [Exeunt Iago and attendants.]

And, till she come, as truly as to heaven
I do confess the vices of my blood,   125
So justly to your grave ears I'll present   126
How I did thrive in this fair lady's love,
And she in mine.

DUKE   Say it, Othello.

OTHELLO
Her father loved me, oft invited me,
Still questioned me the story of my life   131
From year to year—the battles, sieges, fortunes
That I have passed.
I ran it through, even from my boyish days
To th' very moment that he bade me tell it,
Wherein I spoke of most disastrous chances,
Of moving accidents by flood and field,   137
Of hairbreadth scapes i'th'imminent deadly breach,   138
Of being taken by the insolent foe
And sold to slavery, of my redemption thence,
And portance in my travels' history,   141
Wherein of antres vast and deserts idle,   142
Rough quarries, rocks, and hills whose heads touch
    heaven,   143
It was my hint to speak—such was my process—   144
And of the Cannibals that each other eat,
The Anthropophagi, and men whose heads   146
Do grow beneath their shoulders. These things to hear
Would Desdemona seriously incline;
But still the house affairs would draw her thence,
Which ever as she could with haste dispatch
She'd come again, and with a greedy ear
Devour up my discourse. Which I, observing,
Took once a pliant hour, and found good means   153
To draw from her a prayer of earnest heart
That I would all my pilgrimage dilate,   155
Whereof by parcels she had something heard,   156
But not intentively. I did consent,   157
And often did beguile her of her tears,
When I did speak of some distressful stroke
That my youth suffered. My story being done,
She gave me for my pains a world of sighs.
She swore, in faith, 'twas strange, 'twas passing
    strange,   162
'Twas pitiful, 'twas wondrous pitiful.
She wished she had not heard it, yet she wished
That heaven had made her such a man. She thanked
    me,   165
And bade me, if I had a friend that loved her,
I should but teach him how to tell my story,
And that would woo her. Upon this hint I spake.   168
She loved me for the dangers I had passed,

---

83 **Rude** Unpolished   85 **since . . . pith** i.e., since I was seven. (*Pith* means "strength, vigor.")   86 **Till . . . wasted** until some nine months ago (since when Othello has evidently not been on active duty, but in Venice)   87 **dearest** most valuable   92 **round** plain   95 **withal** with   97–8 **her . . . herself** i.e., she blushed easily at herself. (*Motion* can suggest the impulse of the soul or of the emotions, or physical movement.)   99 **years** i.e., difference in age.   **credit** virtuous reputation   102 **confess** concede (that)   104 **practices** plots   105 **vouch** assert   106 **blood** passions   107 **dram . . . effect** dose made by magical spells to have this effect   109 **more wider** fuller.   **test** testimony   110 **habits** garments, i.e., appearances.   **poor likelihoods** weak inferences   111 **modern seeming** commonplace assumption.   **prefer** bring forth   113 **forcèd courses** means used against her will   115 **question** conversation

125 **blood** passions, human nature   126 **justly** truthfully, accurately   131 **Still** continually   137 **moving accidents** stirring happenings   138 **i'th'imminent . . . breach** in death-threatening gaps made in a fortification   141 **portance** conduct   142 **antres** caverns.   **idle** barren, desolate   143 **Rough quarries** rugged rock formations   144 **hint** occasion, opportunity   146 **Anthropophagi** man-eaters. (A term from Pliny's *Natural History*.)   153 **pliant** well-suiting   155 **dilate** relate in detail   156 **by parcels** piecemeal   157 **intentively** with full attention, continuously.   162 **passing** exceedingly   165 **made her** (1) created her to be (2) made for her   168 **hint** (1) opportunity (2) hint (in the modern sense)

And I loved her that she did pity them.
This only is the witchcraft I have used.
Here comes the lady. Let her witness it.

Enter Desdemona, Iago, [and] attendants.

DUKE
I think this tale would win my daughter too.
Good Brabantio,
Take up this mangled matter at the best.   175
Men do their broken weapons rather use
Than their bare hands.

BRABANTIO   I pray you, hear her speak.
If she confess that she was half the wooer,
Destruction on my head if my bad blame
Light on the man!—Come hither, gentle mistress.
Do you perceive in all this noble company
Where most you owe obedience?

DESDEMONA   My noble father,
I do perceive here a divided duty.
To you I am bound for life and education;   184
My life and education both do learn me   185
How to respect you. You are the lord of duty;   186
I am hitherto your daughter. But here's my husband,
And so much duty as my mother showed
To you, preferring you before her father,
So much I challenge that I may profess   190
Due to the Moor my lord.

BRABANTIO   God be with you! I have done.
Please it Your Grace, on to the state affairs.
I had rather to adopt a child than get it.   194
Come hither, Moor.   [*He joins the hands of Othello
and Desdemona.*]
I here do give thee that with all my heart   196
Which, but thou hast already, with all my heart   197
I would keep from thee.—For your sake, jewel,   198
I am glad at soul I have no other child,
For thy escape would teach me tyranny,   200
To hang clogs on them.—I have done, my lord.   201

DUKE
Let me speak like yourself, and lay a sentence   202
Which, as a grece or step, may help these lovers   203
Into your favor.
When remedies are past, the griefs are ended   205
By seeing the worst, which late on hopes depended.   206
To mourn a mischief that is past and gone   207
Is the next way to draw new mischief on.   208
What cannot be preserved when fortune takes,   209
Patience her injury a mock'ry makes.   210

The robbed that smiles steals something from the thief;
He robs himself that spends a bootless grief.   212

BRABANTIO
So let the Turk of Cyprus us beguile,
We lose it not, so long as we can smile.
He bears the sentence well that nothing bears   215
But the free comfort which from thence he hears,   216
But he bears both the sentence and the sorrow   217
That, to pay grief, must of poor patience borrow.   218
These sentences, to sugar or to gall,   219
Being strong on both sides, are equivocal.   220
But words are words. I never yet did hear
That the bruised heart was piercèd through the ear.   222
I humbly beseech you, proceed to th'affairs of state.

DUKE   The Turk with a most mighty preparation makes
for Cyprus. Othello, the fortitude of the place is best 225
known to you; and though we have there a substitute   226
of most allowed sufficiency, yet opinion, a sovereign   227
mistress of effects, throws a more safer voice on you.   228
You must therefore be content to slubber the gloss of   229
your new fortunes with this more stubborn and   230
boisterous expedition.   231

OTHELLO
The tyrant custom, most grave senators,
Hath made the flinty and steel couch of war
My thrice-driven bed of down. I do agnize   234
A natural and prompt alacrity
I find in hardness, and do undertake   236
These present wars against the Ottomites.
Most humbly therefore bending to your state,   238
I crave fit disposition for my wife,
Due reference of place and exhibition,   240
With such accommodation and besort   241
As levels with her breeding.   242

DUKE
Why, at her father's.

BRABANTIO   I will not have it so.

OTHELLO
Nor I.

DESDEMONA   Nor I. I would not there reside,
To put my father in impatient thoughts
By being in his eye. Most gracious Duke,
To my unfolding lend your prosperous ear,   247

212 spends a bootless grief indulges in unavailing grief.   **215–18 He
bears . . . borrow** A person can easily be comforted by your maxim
that enjoys its platitudinous comfort without having to experience
the misfortune that occasions sorrow, but anyone whose grief bank-
rupts his poor patience is left with your saying and his sorrow, too.
(*Bears the sentence* also plays on the meaning, "receives judicial sentence.")   **219–20 These . . . equivocal** These fine maxims are equivocal, being equally appropriate to happiness or bitterness.
222 piercèd . . . ear relieved by mere words reaching it through the
ear.   **225 fortitude** strength   **226 substitute** deputy   **227 allowed**
acknowledged   **227–8 opinion . . . on you** general opinion, an important determiner of affairs, chooses you as the best man.   **229 slubber**
soil, sully   **230–1 stubborn . . . expedition** rough and violent expedition, for which haste is needed.   **234 thrice-driven** thrice sifted, winnowed.   **agnize** know in myself, acknowledge   **236 hardness**
hardship   **238 bending . . . state** bowing or kneeling to your authority   **240–2 Due . . . breeding** proper respect for her place (as my
wife) and maintenance, with such suitable provision and attendance
as befits her upbringing.   **247 my unfolding** what I shall unfold or
say.   **prosperous** favorable

175 Take . . . best make the best of a bad bargain.   **184 education**
upbringing   **185 learn** teach   **186 of duty** to whom duty is due
190 challenge claim   **194 get** beget   **196 with all my heart** wherein
my whole affection has been engaged   **197 with all my heart** willingly, gladly   **198 For your sake** Because of you   **200 escape** elopement   **201 clogs** (Literally, blocks of wood fastened to the legs of
criminals or animals to inhibit escape.)   **202 like yourself** i.e., as you
would, in your proper temper.   **lay a sentence** apply a maxim
203 grece step   **205–6 When . . . depended** When all hope of remedy
is past, our sorrows are ended by realizing that the worst has already
happened which lately we hoped would not happen.   **207 mischief**
misfortune, injury   **208 next** nearest   **209–10 What . . . makes** When
fortune takes away what cannot be saved, patience makes a mockery
of fortune's wrongdoing.

And let me find a charter in your voice,   248
T'assist my simpleness.

DUKE   What would you, Desdemona?

DESDEMONA
That I did love the Moor to live with him,
My downright violence and storm of fortunes   252
May trumpet to the world. My heart's subdued
Even to the very quality of my lord.   254
I saw Othello's visage in his mind,
And to his honors and his valiant parts   256
Did I my soul and fortunes consecrate.
So that, dear lords, if I be left behind
A moth of peace, and he go to the war,   259
The rites for why I love him are bereft me,   260
And I a heavy interim shall support   261
By his dear absence. Let me go with him.   262

OTHELLO   Let her have your voice.   263
Vouch with me, heaven, I therefor beg it not
To please the palate of my appetite,
Nor to comply with heat—the young affects   266
In me defunct—and proper satisfaction,   267
But to be free and bounteous to her mind.   268
And heaven defend your good souls that you think   269
I will your serious and great business scant
When she is with me. No, when light-winged toys
Of feathered Cupid seel with wanton dullness   272
My speculative and officed instruments,   273
That my disports corrupt and taint my business,   274
Let huswives make a skillet of my helm,
And all indign and base adversities   276
Make head against my estimation!   277

DUKE
Be it as you shall privately determine,
Either for her stay or going. Th'affair cries haste,
And speed must answer it.

A SENATOR   You must away tonight.

DESDEMONA
Tonight, my lord?

DUKE   This night.

OTHELLO   With all my heart.

DUKE
At nine i'th' morning here we'll meet again.
Othello, leave some officer behind,
And he shall our commission bring to you,
With such things else of quality and respect   285
As doth import you.

OTHELLO   So please Your Grace, my ancient; 286

A man he is of honesty and trust.
To his conveyance I assign my wife,
With what else needful Your Good Grace shall think
To be sent after me.

DUKE   Let it be so.
Good night to everyone. [To Brabantio] And, noble
    signor,
If virtue no delighted beauty lack,   292
Your son-in-law is far more fair than black.

FIRST SENATOR
Adieu, brave Moor. Use Desdemona well.

BRABANTIO
Look to her, Moor, if thou hast eyes to see.
She has deceived her father, and may thee.
        Exeunt [Duke, Brabantio, Cassio, Senators, and
                                                  officers].

OTHELLO
My life upon her faith!—Honest Iago,
My Desdemona must I leave to thee.
I prithee, let thy wife attend on her,
And bring them after in the best advantage.   300
Come, Desdemona. I have but an hour
Of love, of worldly matters and direction,   302
To spend with thee. We must obey the time.   303
            Exit [with Desdemona].

RODERIGO   Iago—

IAGO   What say'st thou, noble heart?

RODERIGO   What will I do, think'st thou?

IAGO   Why, go to bed and sleep.

RODERIGO   I will incontinently drown myself.   308

IAGO   If thou dost, I shall never love thee after. Why,
    thou silly gentleman?

RODERIGO   It is silliness to live when to live is torment;
    and then have we a prescription to die when death is 312
    our physician.

IAGO   Oh, villainous! I have looked upon the world for 314
    four times seven years, and, since I could distinguish
    betwixt a benefit and an injury, I never found man
    that knew how to love himself. Ere I would say I
    would drown myself for the love of a guinea hen, I   318
    would change my humanity with a baboon.   319

RODERIGO   What should I do? I confess it is my shame
    to be so fond, but it is not in my virtue to amend it. 321

IAGO   Virtue? A fig! 'Tis in ourselves that we are thus or 322
    thus. Our bodies are our gardens, to the which our
    wills are gardeners; so that if we will plant nettles or
    sow lettuce, set hyssop and weed up thyme, supply it 325
    with one gender of herbs or distract it with many,   326
    either to have it sterile with idleness or manured with 327

industry—why, the power and corrigible authority of 328
this lies in our wills. If the beam of our lives had not 329
one scale of reason to poise another of sensuality, the 330
blood and baseness of our natures would conduct us 331
to most preposterous conclusions. But we have reason
to cool our raging motions, our carnal stings, our 333
unbitted lusts, whereof I take this that you call love to 334
be a sect or scion. 335

RODERIGO   It cannot be.

IAGO   It is merely a lust of the blood and a permission
of the will. Come, be a man. Drown thyself? Drown
cats and blind puppies. I have professed me thy friend, 339
and I confess me knit to thy deserving with cables of
perdurable toughness. I could never better stead thee 341
than now. Put money in thy purse. Follow thou the
wars; defeat thy favor with an usurped beard. I say, 343
put money in thy purse. It cannot be long that Desdemona should continue her love to the Moor—put
money in thy purse—nor he his to her. It was a violent commencement in her, and thou shalt see an an- 347
swerable sequestration—put but money in thy purse. 348
These Moors are changeable in their wills—fill thy 349
purse with money. The food that to him now is as
luscious as locusts shall be to him shortly as bitter as 351
coloquintida. She must change for youth; when she is 352
sated with his body, she will find the error of her
choice. She must have change, she must. Therefore
put money in thy purse. If thou wilt needs damn thyself, do it a more delicate way than drowning. Make 356
all the money thou canst. If sanctimony and a frail vow 357
betwixt an erring barbarian and a supersubtle Vene- 358
tian be not too hard for my wits and all the tribe of
hell, thou shalt enjoy her. Therefore make money. A
pox of drowning thyself! It is clean out of the way. 361
Seek thou rather to be hanged in compassing thy joy 362
than to be drowned and go without her.

RODERIGO   Wilt thou be fast to my hopes if I depend on 364
the issue? 365

IAGO   Thou art sure of me. Go, make money. I have
told thee often, and I retell thee again and again, I hate
the Moor. My cause is hearted; thine hath no less rea- 368
son. Let us be conjunctive in our revenge against him. 369
If thou canst cuckold him, thou dost thyself a pleasure,
me a sport. There are many events in the womb of
time which will be delivered. Traverse, go, provide thy 372
money. We will have more of this tomorrow. Adieu.

RODERIGO   Where shall we meet i'th' morning?

IAGO   At my lodging.

RODERIGO   I'll be with thee betimes. [*He starts to leave.*] 376

IAGO   Go to, farewell.—Do you hear, Roderigo? 377

RODERIGO   What say you?

IAGO   No more of drowning, do you hear?

RODERIGO   I am changed.

IAGO   Go to, farewell. Put money enough in your
purse.

RODERIGO   I'll sell all my land.   *Exit.*

IAGO
Thus do I ever make my fool my purse;
For I mine own gained knowledge should profane
If I would time expend with such a snipe   386
But for my sport and profit. I hate the Moor;
And it is thought abroad that twixt my sheets   388
He's done my office. I know not if't be true;   389
But I, for mere suspicion in that kind,
Will do as if for surety. He holds me well;   391
The better shall my purpose work on him.
Cassio's a proper man. Let me see now: 393
To get his place and to plume up my will   394
In double knavery—How, how?—Let's see:
After some time, to abuse Othello's ear   396
That he is too familiar with his wife.   397
He hath a person and a smooth dispose   398
To be suspected, framed to make women false.   399
The Moor is of a free and open nature,   400
That thinks men honest that but seem to be so,
And will as tenderly be led by the nose   402
As asses are.
I have't. It is engendered. Hell and night
Must bring this monstrous birth to the world's light.
                                              [*Exit.*]

❖

2.1

Enter Montano and two Gentlemen.

MONTANO
What from the cape can you discern at sea?

FIRST GENTLEMAN
Nothing at all. It is a high-wrought flood.   2
I cannot, twixt the heaven and the main,   3
Descry a sail.

MONTANO
Methinks the wind hath spoke aloud at land;
A fuller blast ne'er shook our battlements.
If it hath ruffianed so upon the sea,   7

---

328 corrigible authority power to correct   **329 beam** balance
330 poise counterbalance   **331 blood** natural passions   **333 motions**
appetites   **334 unbitted** unbridled, uncontrolled   **335 sect or scion**
cutting or offshoot.   **339 blind** i.e., newborn and helpless   **341 perdurable** very durable.   **stead** assist   **343 defeat thy favor** disguise
your face.   **usurped** (The suggestion is that Roderigo is not man
enough to have a beard of his own.)   **347–8 an answerable sequestration** a corresponding cutting off or estrangement   **349 wills** carnal
appetites   **351 locusts** fruit of the carob tree (see Matthew 3:4), or
perhaps honeysuckle   **352 coloquintida** colocynth or bitter apple, a
purgative.   **356 Make** Raise, collect   **357 sanctimony** (1) an aura of
goodness (2) love-worship   **358 erring** wandering, vagabond,
unsteady   **361 clean . . . way** entirely unsuitable as a course of action.
362 compassing encompassing, embracing   **364 fast** true   **365 issue**
(successful) outcome.   **368 hearted** fixed in the heart, heartfelt
369 conjunctive united   **372 Traverse** (A military marching term.)

376 betimes early.   **377 Go to** (An expression of impatience or jolly-
ing along others.)   **386 snipe** woodcock, i.e., fool   **388 it is thought
abroad** it is rumored   **389 my office** i.e., my sexual function as husband.   **391 do . . . surety** act as if on certain knowledge.   **holds me
well** regards me favorably   **393 proper** handsome   **394 plume up**
put a feather in the cap of, i.e., glorify, gratify   **396 abuse** deceive
397 he Cassio.   **his** Othello's   **398 dispose** disposition   **399 framed**
formed, made   **400 free and open** frank and unsuspecting   **402 tenderly** readily
2.1. Location: A seaport in Cyprus. An open place near the quay.
2 high-wrought flood very agitated sea.   **3 main** ocean. (Also at line
41.)   **7 ruffianed** raged

What ribs of oak, when mountains melt on them,   8
Can hold the mortise? What shall we hear of this?   9

SECOND GENTLEMAN
A segregation of the Turkish fleet.   10
For do but stand upon the foaming shore,
The chidden billow seems to pelt the clouds;   12
The wind-shaked surge, with high and monstrous
  mane,
Seems to cast water on the burning Bear   13
And quench the guards of th'ever-fixèd pole.   14
I never did like molestation view   16
On the enchafèd flood.   17

MONTANO   If that the Turkish fleet   18
Be not ensheltered and embayed, they are drowned;   19
It is impossible to bear it out.   20

Enter a [Third] Gentleman.

THIRD GENTLEMAN   News, lads! Our wars are done.
The desperate tempest hath so banged the Turks
That their designment halts. A noble ship of Venice   23
Hath seen a grievous wreck and sufferance   24
On most part of their fleet.

MONTANO   How? Is this true?

THIRD GENTLEMAN   The ship is here put in,
A Veronesa; Michael Cassio,   28
Lieutenant to the warlike Moor Othello,
Is come on shore; the Moor himself at sea,
And is in full commission here for Cyprus.

MONTANO
I am glad on't. 'Tis a worthy governor.

THIRD GENTLEMAN
But this same Cassio, though he speak of comfort
Touching the Turkish loss, yet he looks sadly   34
And prays the Moor be safe, for they were parted
With foul and violent tempest.

MONTANO   Pray heaven he be,
For I have served him, and the man commands
Like a full soldier. Let's to the seaside, ho!   38
As well to see the vessel that's come in
As to throw out our eyes for brave Othello,
Even till we make the main and th'aerial blue   41
An indistinct regard.

THIRD GENTLEMAN   Come, let's do so,   42
For every minute is expectancy   43

Of more arrivance.   44

Enter Cassio.

CASSIO
Thanks, you the valiant of this warlike isle,
That so approve the Moor! Oh, let the heavens   46
Give him defense against the elements,
For I have lost him on a dangerous sea.

MONTANO   Is he well shipped?

CASSIO
His bark is stoutly timbered, and his pilot
Of very expert and approved allowance;   51
Therefore my hopes, not surfeited to death,   52
Stand in bold cure.
              [A cry] within: "A sail, a sail, a sail!"   53

CASSIO   What noise?

A GENTLEMAN
The town is empty. On the brow o'th' sea   55
Stand ranks of people, and they cry "A sail!"

CASSIO
My hopes do shape him for the governor.   57
                                    [A shot within.]

SECOND GENTLEMAN
They do discharge their shot of courtesy;   58
Our friends at least.

CASSIO   I pray you, sir, go forth,
And give us truth who 'tis that is arrived.

SECOND GENTLEMAN   I shall.   *Exit.*

MONTANO
But, good Lieutenant, is your general wived?

CASSIO
Most fortunately. He hath achieved a maid
That paragons description and wild fame,   64
One that excels the quirks of blazoning pens,   65
And in th'essential vesture of creation   66
Does tire the engineer.

Enter [Second] Gentleman.

                              How now? Who has put in?   67

SECOND GENTLEMAN
'Tis one Iago, ancient to the General.

CASSIO
He's had most favorable and happy speed.
Tempests themselves, high seas, and howling winds,
The guttered rocks and congregated sands—   71
Traitors ensteeped to clog the guiltless keel—   72
As having sense of beauty, do omit   73
Their mortal natures, letting go safely by   74

---

8 **mountains** i.e., of water   9 **hold the mortise** hold their joints
together. (A *mortise* is the socket hollowed out in fitting timbers.)
10 **segregation** dispersal   12 **chidden** i.e., rebuked, repelled (by the
shore), and thus shot into the air   13 **monstrous mane** (The surf is
like the mane of a wild beast.)   14 **the burning Bear** i.e., the constellation Ursa Minor or the Little Bear, which includes the polestar (and
hence regarded as the *guards of th'ever-fixèd pole* in the next line; sometimes the term *guards* is applied to the two "pointers" of the Big Bear
or Dipper, which may be intended here.)   16 **like molestation** comparable disturbance   17 **enchafèd** angry   18 **If that** If   19 **embayed**
sheltered by a bay   20 **bear it out** survive, weather the storm.
23 **designment halts** enterprise is crippled. (Literally, "is lame.")
24 **wreck** shipwreck.   **sufferance** damage, disaster   28 **Veronesa**
from Verona (and perhaps in service with Venice)   34 **sadly** gravely
38 **full** perfect   41 **the main . . . blue** the sea and the sky   42 **An
indistinct regard** indistinguishable in our view.   43 **is expectancy**
gives expectation

44 **arrivance** arrival.   46 **approve** admire, honor   51 **approved
allowance** tested reputation   52–3 **not . . . cure** not worn thin
through repeated application or delayed fulfillment, strongly persist.
55 **brow o'th' sea** cliff-edge   57 **My . . . governor** I hope and imagine
this ship to be Othello's.   58 **discharge . . . courtesy** fire a salute in
token of respect and courtesy   64 **paragons** surpasses.   **wild fame**
extravagant report   65 **quirks** witty conceits.   **blazoning** setting
forth as though in heraldic language   66–7 **And in . . . engineer** and
in her real, God-given, beauty, (she) defeats any attempt to praise her.
(An *engineer* is one who devises, here a poet.)   67 **put in** i.e., to harbor.   71 **guttered** jagged, trenched   72 **ensteeped** lying under water
73 **As** as if.   **omit** forbear to exercise   74 **mortal** deadly

The divine Desdemona.

MONTANO   What is she?

CASSIO

She that I spake of, our great captain's captain,
Left in the conduct of the bold Iago,
Whose footing here anticipates our thoughts   78
A sennight's speed. Great Jove, Othello guard,   79
And swell his sail with thine own powerful breath,
That he may bless this bay with his tall ship,   81
Make love's quick pants in Desdemona's arms,
Give renewed fire to our extinced spirits,
And bring all Cyprus comfort!

Enter Desdemona, Iago, Roderigo, and Emilia.

                              Oh, behold,
The riches of the ship is come on shore!
You men of Cyprus, let her have your knees.
          [*The gentlemen make curtsy to Desdemona.*]
Hail to thee, lady! And the grace of heaven
Before, behind thee, and on every hand
Enwheel thee round!

DESDEMONA   I thank you, valiant Cassio.
What tidings can you tell me of my lord?

CASSIO

He is not yet arrived, nor know I aught
But that he's well and will be shortly here.

DESDEMONA

Oh, but I fear—How lost you company?

CASSIO

The great contention of the sea and skies
Parted our fellowship.

                    (*Within*) "A sail, a sail!" [*A shot.*]
                              But hark. A sail!

SECOND GENTLEMAN

They give their greeting to the citadel.
This likewise is a friend.

CASSIO   See for the news.
                    [*Exit Second Gentleman.*]
Good Ancient, you are welcome. [*Kissing Emilia.*]
    Welcome, mistress.
Let it not gall your patience, good Iago,
That I extend my manners; 'tis my breeding   100
That gives me this bold show of courtesy.

IAGO

Sir, would she give you so much of her lips
As of her tongue she oft bestows on me,
You would have enough.

DESDEMONA   Alas, she has no speech!   105

IAGO   In faith, too much.
I find it still, when I have list to sleep.   107
Marry, before Your Ladyship, I grant,
She puts her tongue a little in her heart
And chides with thinking.

EMILIA   You have little cause to say so. 110

IAGO

Come on, come on. You are pictures out of doors,   111
Bells in your parlors, wildcats in your kitchens,   112
Saints in your injuries, devils being offended,   113
Players in your huswifery, and huswives in your beds. 114

DESDEMONA   Oh, fie upon thee, slanderer!

IAGO

Nay, it is true, or else I am a Turk.   116
You rise to play, and go to bed to work.

EMILIA

You shall not write my praise.

IAGO   No, let me not.

DESDEMONA

What wouldst write of me, if thou shouldst praise me?

IAGO

Oh, gentle lady, do not put me to't,
For I am nothing if not critical.   121

DESDEMONA

Come on, essay.—There's one gone to the harbor?   122

IAGO   Ay, madam.

DESDEMONA

I am not merry, but I do beguile
The thing I am by seeming otherwise.   125
Come, how wouldst thou praise me?

IAGO

I am about it, but indeed my invention
Comes from my pate as birdlime does from frieze—   128
It plucks out brains and all. But my Muse labors,   129
And thus she is delivered:
If she be fair and wise, fairness and wit,
The one's for use, the other useth it.   132

DESDEMONA

Well praised! How if she be black and witty?   133

IAGO

If she be black, and thereto have a wit,
She'll find a white that shall her blackness fit.   135

DESDEMONA

Worse and worse.

EMILIA   How if fair and foolish?

IAGO

She never yet was foolish that was fair,
For even her folly helped her to an heir.   138

DESDEMONA   These are old fond paradoxes to make fools 139

78–9 **Whose . . . speed** whose arrival here has happened a week
sooner than we expected.   81 **tall** tall-masted   100 **extend** give scope
to.   **breeding** training in the niceties of etiquette   105 **she has no
speech** i.e., she's not a chatterbox, as you allege.   107 **still** always.
list desire   110 **with thinking** i.e., in her thoughts only.

111 **pictures out of doors** i.e., as pretty as pictures, and silently well-
behaved in public   112 **Bells** i.e., jangling, noisy, and brazen.   **in
your kitchens** i.e., in domestic affairs. (Ladies would not do the cooking.)   113 **Saints . . . injuries** i.e., putting on airs of sanctity and innocence when wronged by others   114 **Players . . . beds** play-actors at
domesticity and truly energetic only as lovers in bed.   116 **a Turk** an
infidel, not to be believed.   121 **critical** censorious.   122 **essay** try.
125 **The thing I am** i.e., my anxious self   128 **birdlime** sticky substance used to catch small birds.   **frieze** coarse woolen cloth
129 **labors** (1) exerts herself (2) prepares to deliver a child. (With a following pun on *delivered* in line 130.)   132 **The one's . . . it** i.e., her
cleverness will make use of her beauty.   133 **black** dark-complexioned, brunette   135 **She'll . . . fit** she will find a fair-complexioned
mate suited to her dark complexion. (Punning on *wight*, person, and
contrasting *white* and *black*, with suggestion of sexual coupling.)
138 **folly** (With added meaning of "lechery, wantonness.")   **to an
heir** i.e., to bear a child.   139 **fond** foolish

laugh i'th'alehouse. What miserable praise hast thou
for her that's foul and foolish?   141

IAGO
There's none so foul and foolish thereunto,   142
But does foul pranks which fair and wise ones do.   143

DESDEMONA Oh, heavy ignorance! Thou praisest the worst
best. But what praise couldst thou bestow on a deserving woman indeed, one that, in the authority of her mer-
it, did justly put on the vouch of very malice itself?   147

IAGO
She that was ever fair, and never proud,
Had tongue at will, and yet was never loud,   149
Never lacked gold and yet went never gay,   150
Fled from her wish, and yet said, "Now I may,"   151
She that being angered, her revenge being nigh,
Bade her wrong stay and her displeasure fly,   153
She that in wisdom never was so frail
To change the cod's head for the salmon's tail,   155
She that could think and ne'er disclose her mind,
See suitors following and not look behind,
She was a wight, if ever such wight were—

DESDEMONA To do what?

IAGO
To suckle fools and chronicle small beer.   160

DESDEMONA Oh, most lame and impotent conclusion! Do
not learn of him, Emilia, though he be thy husband.
How say you, Cassio? Is he not a most profane and   163
liberal counselor?   164

CASSIO He speaks home, madam. You may relish him   165
more in the soldier than in the scholar.   166

[*Cassio and Desdemona stand together,
conversing intimately.*]

IAGO [*aside*] He takes her by the palm. Ay, well said,   167
whisper. With as little a web as this will I ensnare as
great a fly as Cassio. Ay, smile upon her, do; I will
gyve thee in thine own courtship. You say true; 'tis so,   170
indeed. If such tricks as these strip you out of your
lieutenantry, it had been better you had not kissed
your three fingers so oft, which now again you are
most apt to play the sir in. Very good; well kissed! An   174
excellent courtesy! 'Tis so, indeed. Yet again your fingers to your lips? Would they were clyster pipes for   176
your sake! [*Trumpet within.*] The Moor! I know his
trumpet.

CASSIO 'Tis truly so.

DESDEMONA   Let's meet him and receive him.

CASSIO Lo, where he comes!

Enter Othello and attendants.

OTHELLO
Oh, my fair warrior!

DESDEMONA   My dear Othello!

OTHELLO
It gives me wonder great as my content
To see you here before me. O my soul's joy,
If after every tempest come such calms,
May the winds blow till they have wakened death,
And let the laboring bark climb hills of seas
Olympus-high, and duck again as low
As hell's from heaven! If it were now to die,
'Twere now to be most happy, for I fear
My soul hath her content so absolute
That not another comfort like to this
Succeeds in unknown fate.

DESDEMONA   The heavens forbid   193
But that our loves and comforts should increase
Even as our days do grow!

OTHELLO Amen to that, sweet powers!
I cannot speak enough of this content.
It stops me here; it is too much of joy.
And this, and this, the greatest discords be   199
                                [*They kiss.*]
That e'er our hearts shall make!

IAGO [*aside*] Oh, you are well tuned now!
But I'll set down the pegs that make this music,   202
As honest as I am.   203

OTHELLO   Come, let us to the castle.
News, friends! Our wars are done, the Turks are
drowned.
How does my old acquaintance of this isle?—
Honey, you shall be well desired in Cyprus;   207
I have found great love amongst them. Oh, my sweet,
I prattle out of fashion, and I dote   209
In mine own comforts.—I prithee, good Iago,
Go to the bay and disembark my coffers.   211
Bring thou the master to the citadel;   212
He is a good one, and his worthiness
Does challenge much respect.—Come, Desdemona.—   214
Once more, well met at Cyprus!
                *Exeunt Othello and Desdemona [and all
                                but Iago and Roderigo].*

IAGO [*to a departing attendant*] Do thou meet me presently at
the harbor. [*To Roderigo*] Come hither. If thou be'st
valiant—as, they say, base men being in love have   218
then a nobility in their natures more than is native to
them—list me. The Lieutenant tonight watches on   220
the court of guard. First, I must tell thee this: 221
Desdemona is directly in love with him.

---

141 foul ugly   **142 thereunto** in addition   **143 foul** sluttish   **147 put
. . . vouch** compel the approval   **149 Had . . . will** was never at a loss
for words   **150 gay** extravagantly clothed   **151 Fled . . . may** avoided
temptation where the choice was hers   **153 Bade . . . stay** i.e.,
resolved to put up with her injury and bade her anger to cease
155 To . . . tail i.e., to be selfishly demanding and ambitious. (The
fish's lower body, below the rib cage, has fewest bones and is generally the succulent portion. With sexual implication as well: *cod's head*
can be slang for "penis," and *tail* for "pudendum.")   **160 To . . . beer**
i.e., To breastfeed babies and keep petty household accounts.
163–4 profane and liberal irreverent and licentious   **165 home** right
to the target. (A term from fencing.)   **relish** appreciate   **166 in** in the
character of   **167 well said** well done   **170 gyve** fetter, shackle.
courtship courtesy, show of courtly manners.   **You say true** i.e.,
That's right, go ahead   **174 the sir** i.e., the fine gentleman
176 clyster pipes tubes used for enemas and douches

193 Succeeds . . . fate i.e., can follow in the unknown future.
199.1 They kiss (The direction is from the quarto.)   **202 set down**
loosen (and hence untune the instrument)   **203 As . . . I am** for all my
supposed honesty.   **207 desired** sought after   **209 out of fashion**
indecorously, incoherently   **211 coffers** chests, baggage.   **212 master**
ship's captain   **214 challenge** lay claim to, deserve   **218 base men**
even ignoble men   **220 list** listen to   **221 court of guard** guardhouse.
(Cassio is in charge of the watch.)

RODERIGO   With him? Why, 'tis not possible.

IAGO   Lay thy finger thus, and let thy soul be instructed. 224
Mark me with what violence she first loved the Moor,
but for bragging and telling her fantastical lies. To love 226
him still for prating? Let not thy discreet heart think it.
Her eye must be fed; and what delight shall she have
to look on the devil? When the blood is made dull with
the act of sport, there should be, again to inflame it 230
and to give satiety a fresh appetite, loveliness in favor, 231
sympathy in years, manners, and beauties—all which 232
the Moor is defective in. Now, for want of these
required conveniences, her delicate tenderness will 234
find itself abused, begin to heave the gorge, disrelish 235
and abhor the Moor. Very nature will instruct her in it 236
and compel her to some second choice. Now, sir, this
granted—as it is a most pregnant and unforced 238
position—who stands so eminent in the degree of this 239
fortune as Cassio does? A knave very voluble, no 240
further conscionable than in putting on the mere form 241
of civil and humane seeming for the better compass- 242
ing of his salt and most hidden loose affection. Why, 243
none, why, none. A slipper and subtle knave, a finder 244
out of occasions, that has an eye can stamp and 245
counterfeit advantages, though true advantage never 246
present itself; a devilish knave. Besides, the knave is
handsome, young, and hath all those requisites in him
that folly and green minds look after. A pestilent 249
complete knave, and the woman hath found him 250
already.

RODERIGO   I cannot believe that in her. She's full of
most blessed condition.   253

IAGO   Blessed fig's end! The wine she drinks is made of 254
grapes. If she had been blessed, she would never have
loved the Moor. Blessed pudding! Didst thou not see 256
her paddle with the palm of his hand? Didst not mark
that?

RODERIGO   Yes, that I did; but that was but courtesy.

IAGO   Lechery, by this hand. An index and obscure pro- 260
logue to the history of lust and foul thoughts. They
met so near with their lips that their breaths embraced
together. Villainous thoughts, Roderigo! When these
mutualities so marshal the way, hard at hand comes 264
the master and main exercise, th'incorporate conclu- 265
sion. Pish! But, sir, be you ruled by me. I have brought

you from Venice. Watch you tonight; for the com- 267
mand, I'll lay't upon you. Cassio knows you not. I'll 268
not be far from you. Do you find some occasion to
anger Cassio, either by speaking too loud, or tainting 270
his discipline, or from what other course you please,
which the time shall more favorably minister.   272

RODERIGO   Well.

IAGO   Sir, he's rash and very sudden in choler, and haply 274
may strike at you. Provoke him that he may, for
even out of that will I cause these of Cyprus to mutiny, 276
whose qualification shall come into no true taste again 277
but by the displanting of Cassio. So shall you have a
shorter journey to your desires by the means I shall
then have to prefer them, and the impediment most 280
profitably removed, without the which there were no
expectation of our prosperity.

RODERIGO   I will do this, if you can bring it to any
opportunity.

IAGO   I warrant thee. Meet me by and by at the citadel. 285
I must fetch his necessaries ashore. Farewell.

RODERIGO   Adieu.   Exit.

IAGO
That Cassio loves her, I do well believe't;
That she loves him, 'tis apt and of great credit.   289
The Moor, howbeit that I endure him not,
Is of a constant, loving, noble nature,
And I dare think he'll prove to Desdemona
A most dear husband. Now, I do love her too,
Not out of absolute lust—though peradventure
I stand accountant for as great a sin—   295
But partly led to diet my revenge   296
For that I do suspect the lusty Moor
Hath leaped into my seat, the thought whereof
Doth, like a poisonous mineral, gnaw my innards;
And nothing can or shall content my soul
Till I am evened with him, wife for wife,
Or failing so, yet that I put the Moor
At least into a jealousy so strong
That judgment cannot cure. Which thing to do,
If this poor trash of Venice, whom I trace   305
For his quick hunting, stand the putting on,   306
I'll have our Michael Cassio on the hip,   307
Abuse him to the Moor in the rank garb—   308
For I fear Cassio with my nightcap too—   309
Make the Moor thank me, love me, and reward me
For making him egregiously an ass
And practicing upon his peace and quiet   312

224 **thus** i.e., on your lips   226 **but** only   230 **the act of sport** sex
231 **favor** appearance   232 **sympathy** correspondence, similarity
234 **required conveniences** things conducive to sexual compatibility
235 **abused** cheated, revolted.   **heave the gorge** experience nausea
236 **Very nature** Her very instincts   238 **pregnant** evident, cogent
239 **in . . . of** as next in line for   240 **voluble** facile, glib   241 **conscionable** conscientious, conscience-bound   242 **humane** polite,
courteous   243 **salt** licentious.   **affection** passion.   244 **slipper** slippery   245 **an eye can stamp** an eye that can coin, create   246 **advantages** favorable opportunities   249 **folly** wantonness.   **green**
immature   250 **found him** sized him up, perceived his intent
253 **condition** disposition.   254 **fig's end** (See 1.3.322 for the vulgar
gesture of the fig.)   256 **pudding** sausage.   260 **index** table of contents.   **obscure** veiled, hidden   264 **mutualities** exchanges, intima-
cies.   **hard at hand** closely following   265 **th'incorporate** the carnal

267 **Watch you** Stand watch   267–8 **for . . . you** I'll arrange for you to
be appointed, given orders; or, I'll put you in charge.   270 **tainting**
disparaging   272 **minister** provide.   274 **choler** wrath.   **haply** perhaps   276 **mutiny** riot   277 **qualification** pacification.   **true taste**
i.e., acceptable state   280 **prefer** advance   285 **warrant** assure.
by and by immediately   289 **apt** probable.   **credit** credibility.
295 **accountant** accountable   296 **diet** feed   305 **trace** i.e., pursue,
dog; or, keep hungry (?) or perhaps *trash*, a hunting term, meaning to
put weights on a hunting dog in order to slow him down   306 **For** to
make more eager for.   **stand . . . on** responds properly when I incite
him to quarrel   307 **on the hip** at my mercy, where I can throw him.
(A wrestling term.)   308 **Abuse** slander.   **rank garb** coarse manner,
gross fashion   309 **with my nightcap** i.e., as a rival in my bed, as one
who gives me cuckold's horns   312 **practicing upon** plotting against

Even to madness. 'Tis here, but yet confused.
Knavery's plain face is never seen till used.   *Exit.*

❧

2.2

Enter Othello's Herald with a proclamation.

HERALD   It is Othello's pleasure, our noble and valiant
general, that, upon certain tidings now arrived, importing the mere perdition of the Turkish fleet, every   3
man put himself into triumph: some to dance, some to   4
make bonfires, each man to what sport and revels his
addiction leads him. For, besides these beneficial   6
news, it is the celebration of his nuptial. So much was
his pleasure should be proclaimed. All offices are open,   8
and there is full liberty of feasting from this present
hour of five till the bell have told eleven. Heaven bless
the isle of Cyprus and our noble general Othello!
                                                      Exit.

❧

[2.3]

*Enter Othello, Desdemona, Cassio, and
attendants.*

OTHELLO
Good Michael, look you to the guard tonight.
Let's teach ourselves that honorable stop   2
Not to outsport discretion.   3
CASSIO
Iago hath direction what to do,
But notwithstanding, with my personal eye
Will I look to't.
OTHELLO   Iago is most honest.
Michael, good night. Tomorrow with your earliest   7
Let me have speech with you. [*To Desdemona*] Come,
  my dear love,
The purchase made, the fruits are to ensue;   9
That profit's yet to come 'tween me and you.—   10
Good night.
          Exit [*Othello, with Desdemona and attendants*].
          Enter Iago.

CASSIO   Welcome, Iago. We must to the watch.
IAGO   Not this hour, Lieutenant; 'tis not yet ten o'th'   13
clock. Our general cast us thus early for the love of his   14
Desdemona; who let us not therefore blame. He hath   15
not yet made wanton the night with her, and she is
sport for Jove.
CASSIO   She's a most exquisite lady.
IAGO   And, I'll warrant her, full of game.

CASSIO   Indeed, she's a most fresh and delicate creature.
IAGO   What an eye she has! Methinks it sounds a parley   21
to provocation.
CASSIO   An inviting eye, and yet methinks right modest.
IAGO   And when she speaks, is it not an alarum to love?   24
CASSIO   She is indeed perfection.
IAGO   Well, happiness to their sheets! Come, Lieutenant,
I have a stoup of wine, and here without are a brace of   27
Cyprus gallants that would fain have a measure to the   28
health of black Othello.
CASSIO   Not tonight, good Iago. I have very poor and
unhappy brains for drinking. I could well wish cour-
tesy would invent some other custom of entertain-
ment.
IAGO   Oh, they are our friends. But one cup! I'll drink for   34
you.   35
CASSIO   I have drunk but one cup tonight, and that was
craftily qualified too, and behold what innovation it   37
makes here. I am unfortunate in the infirmity and   38
dare not task my weakness with any more.
IAGO   What, man? 'Tis a night of revels. The gallants
desire it.
CASSIO   Where are they?
IAGO   Here at the door. I pray you, call them in.
CASSIO   I'll do't, but it dislikes me.   *Exit.*   44
IAGO
If I can fasten but one cup upon him,
With that which he hath drunk tonight already,
He'll be as full of quarrel and offense   47
As my young mistress' dog. Now, my sick fool
  Roderigo,
Whom love hath turned almost the wrong side out,
To Desdemona hath tonight caroused   50
Potations pottle-deep; and he's to watch.   51
Three lads of Cyprus—noble swelling spirits,   52
That hold their honors in a wary distance,   53
The very elements of this warlike isle—   54
Have I tonight flustered with flowing cups,
And they watch too. Now, 'mongst this flock of
  drunkards   56
Am I to put our Cassio in some action
That may offend the isle.—But here they come.

          Enter Cassio, Montano, and gentlemen; [*servants
          following with wine*].

If consequence do but approve my dream,   59
My boat sails freely both with wind and stream.   60
CASSIO   'Fore God, they have given me a rouse already.   61

2.2. **Location: Cyprus.**
3 **mere perdition** complete destruction   4 **triumph** public celebration
6 **addiction** inclination   8 **offices** rooms where food and drink are kept
2.3. **Location: Cyprus. The citadel.**
2 **stop** restraint   3 **outsport** celebrate beyond the bounds of   7 **with
your earliest** at your earliest convenience   9–10 **The purchase . . .
you** i.e., though married, we haven't yet consummated our love.
(Possibly, too, Othello is referring to pregnancy. At all events, his
desire for sexual union is manifest.)   13 **Not this hour** Not for an
hour yet   14 **cast** dismissed   15 **who** i.e., Othello

21 **sounds a parley** calls for a conference, issues an invitation
24 **alarum** signal calling men to arms. (Continuing the military
metaphor of *parley*, line 21.)   27 **stoup** measure of liquor, two quarts.
without outside.   **brace** pair   28 **fain have a measure** gladly drink a
toast   34–5 **for you** in your place. (Iago will do the steady drinking
to keep the gallants company while Cassio has only one cup.)
37 **qualified** diluted.   **innovation** disturbance, insurrection   38 **here**
i.e., in my head.   44 **it dislikes me** i.e., I'm reluctant.   47 **offense**
readiness to give or take offense   50 **caroused** drunk off   51 **pottle-
deep** to the bottom of the tankard.   **watch** stand watch.
52 **swelling** proud   53 **hold . . . distance** i.e., are extremely sensitive
of their honor   54 **elements** lifeblood   56 **watch** are members of the
guard   59 **If . . . dream** If subsequent events will only confirm my
dreams and hopes   60 **stream** current.   61 **rouse** full draft of liquor

MONTANO   Good faith, a little one; not past a pint, as I
am a soldier.

IAGO   Some wine, ho!

[*He sings.*]   "And let me the cannikin clink, clink,   65
And let me the cannikin clink.
A soldier's a man,
Oh, man's life's but a span;   68
Why, then, let a soldier drink."
Some wine, boys!

CASSIO   'Fore God, an excellent song.

IAGO   I learned it in England, where indeed they are
most potent in potting. Your Dane, your German, and   73
your swag-bellied Hollander—drink, ho!—are nothing to your English.

CASSIO   Is your Englishman so exquisite in his drinking?

IAGO   Why, he drinks you, with facility, your Dane   77
dead drunk; he sweats not to overthrow your Almain;   78
he gives your Hollander a vomit ere the next pottle can
be filled.

CASSIO   To the health of our general!

MONTANO   I am for it, Lieutenant, and I'll do you justice.   82

IAGO   O sweet England! [*He sings.*]

"King Stephen was and-a worthy peer,
His breeches cost him but a crown;
He held them sixpence all too dear,
With that he called the tailor lown.   87

He was a wight of high renown,
And thou art but of low degree.
'Tis pride that pulls the country down;   90
Then take thy auld cloak about thee."   91

Some wine, ho!

CASSIO   'Fore God, this is a more exquisite song than
the other.

IAGO   Will you hear't again?

CASSIO   No, for I hold him to be unworthy of his place
that does those things. Well, God's above all; and
there be souls must be saved, and there be souls must
not be saved.

IAGO   It's true, good Lieutenant.

CASSIO   For mine own part—no offense to the General,
nor any man of quality—I hope to be saved.   102

IAGO   And so do I too, Lieutenant.

CASSIO   Ay, but, by your leave, not before me; the lieutenant is to be saved before the ancient. Let's have no
more of this; let's to our affairs.—God forgive us our
sins!—Gentlemen, let's look to our business. Do not
think, gentlemen, I am drunk. This is my ancient; this
is my right hand, and this is my left. I am not drunk
now. I can stand well enough, and speak well enough.

GENTLEMEN   Excellent well.

CASSIO   Why, very well then; you must not think then
that I am drunk.   *Exit.*

MONTANO   To th' platform, masters. Come, let's set the watch.   114
[*Exeunt Gentlemen.*]

IAGO
You see this fellow that is gone before.
He's a soldier fit to stand by Caesar
And give direction; and do but see his vice.
'Tis to his virtue a just equinox,   118
The one as long as th'other. 'Tis pity of him.
I fear the trust Othello puts him in,
On some odd time of his infirmity,
Will shake this island.

MONTANO   But is he often thus?

IAGO
'Tis evermore the prologue to his sleep.
He'll watch the horologe a double set,   124
If drink rock not his cradle.

MONTANO   It were well
The General were put in mind of it.
Perhaps he sees it not, or his good nature
Prizes the virtue that appears in Cassio
And looks not on his evils. Is not this true?

Enter Roderigo.

IAGO [*aside to him*]   How now, Roderigo?
I pray you, after the Lieutenant; go.   [*Exit Roderigo.*]

MONTANO
And 'tis great pity that the noble Moor
Should hazard such a place as his own second   133
With one of an engraffed infirmity.   134
It were an honest action to say so
To the Moor.

IAGO   Not I, for this fair island.
I do love Cassio well and would do much
To cure him of this evil.   [*Cry within:* "Help! Help!"]
                But, hark! What noise?   138

Enter Cassio, pursuing Roderigo.

CASSIO   Zounds, you rogue! You rascal!

MONTANO   What's the matter, Lieutenant?

CASSIO   A knave teach me my duty? I'll beat the knave
into a twiggen bottle.   142

RODERIGO   Beat me?

CASSIO   Dost thou prate, rogue?   [*He strikes Roderigo.*]

MONTANO   Nay, good Lieutenant. [*Restraining him.*] I
pray you, sir, hold your hand.

CASSIO   Let me go, sir, or I'll knock you o'er the
mazard.   148

---

65 **cannikin** small drinking vessel   68 **span** brief span of time. (Compare Psalm 39:5 as rendered in the Book of Common Prayer: "Thou
hast made my days as it were a span long.")   73 **potting** drinking.
77 **drinks you** drinks.   **your Dane** your typical Dane   78 **sweats not**
i.e., need not exert himself.   **Almain** German   82 **I'll . . . justice** i.e.,
I'll drink as much as you.   87 **lown** lout, rascal.   90 **pride** i.e.,
extravagance in dress   91 **auld** old   102 **quality** rank

114 **set the watch** mount the guard.   118 **just equinox** exact counterpart. (*Equinox* is an equal length of days and nights.)   124 **watch . . .
set** stay awake twice around the clock or *horologe*   133–4 **hazard . . .
With** risk giving such an important position as his second in command to   134 **engraffed** engrafted, inveterate   138.1 *pursuing* (The
quarto text reads, "*driuing in.*")   142 **twiggen** wicker-covered. (Cassio vows to assail Roderigo until his skin resembles wickerwork or
until he has driven Roderigo through the holes in a wickerwork.)
148 **mazard** i.e., head. (Literally, a drinking vessel.)

MONTANO   Come, come, you're drunk.

CASSIO   Drunk?   [They fight.]

IAGO [aside to Roderigo]
Away, I say. Go out and cry a mutiny.   151
    [Exit Roderigo.]
Nay, good Lieutenant—God's will, gentlemen—
Help, ho!—Lieutenant—sir—Montano—sir—
Help, masters!—Here's a goodly watch indeed!   154
    [A bell rings.]
Who's that which rings the bell?—Diablo, ho!   155
The town will rise. God's will, Lieutenant, hold!   156
You'll be ashamed forever.

    Enter Othello and attendants [with weapons].

OTHELLO
What is the matter here?

MONTANO   Zounds, I bleed still.
I am hurt to th' death. He dies!   [He thrusts at Cassio.]

OTHELLO   Hold, for your lives!

IAGO
Hold, ho! Lieutenant—sir—Montano—gentlemen—
Have you forgot all sense of place and duty?
Hold! The General speaks to you. Hold, for shame!

OTHELLO
Why, how now, ho! From whence ariseth this?
Are we turned Turks, and to ourselves do that   164
Which heaven hath forbid the Ottomites?   165
For Christian shame, put by this barbarous brawl!
He that stirs next to carve for his own rage   167
Holds his soul light; he dies upon his motion.   168
Silence that dreadful bell. It frights the isle
From her propriety. What is the matter, masters?   170
Honest Iago, that looks dead with grieving,
Speak. Who began this? On thy love, I charge thee.

IAGO
I do not know. Friends all but now, even now,
In quarter and in terms like bride and groom   174
Devesting them for bed; and then, but now—   175
As if some planet had unwitted men—
Swords out, and tilting one at others' breasts
In opposition bloody. I cannot speak   178
Any beginning to this peevish odds;   179
And would in action glorious I had lost
Those legs that brought me to a part of it!

OTHELLO
How comes it, Michael, you are thus forgot?   182

CASSIO
I pray you, pardon me. I cannot speak.

OTHELLO
Worthy Montano, you were wont be civil;   184
The gravity and stillness of your youth   185
The world hath noted, and your name is great
In mouths of wisest censure. What's the matter   187
That you unlace your reputation thus   188
And spend your rich opinion for the name   189
Of a night-brawler? Give me answer to it.

MONTANO
Worthy Othello, I am hurt to danger.
Your officer, Iago, can inform you—
While I spare speech, which something now offends
    me—   193
Of all that I do know; nor know I aught
By me that's said or done amiss this night,
Unless self-charity be sometimes a vice,
And to defend ourselves it be a sin
When violence assails us.

OTHELLO   Now, by heaven,
My blood begins my safer guides to rule,   199
And passion, having my best judgment collied,   200
Essays to lead the way. Zounds, if I stir   201
Or do but lift this arm, the best of you
Shall sink in my rebuke. Give me to know
How this foul rout began, who set it on;   204
And he that is approved in this offense,   205
Though he had twinned with me, both at a birth,
Shall lose me. What? In a town of war   207
Yet wild, the people's hearts brim full of fear,
To manage private and domestic quarrel?   209
In night, and on the court and guard of safety?   210
'Tis monstrous. Iago, who began't?

MONTANO [to Iago]
If partially affined, or leagued in office,   212
Thou dost deliver more or less than truth,
Thou art no soldier.

IAGO   Touch me not so near.
I had rather have this tongue cut from my mouth
Than it should do offense to Michael Cassio;
Yet, I persuade myself, to speak the truth
Shall nothing wrong him. Thus it is, General:
Montano and myself being in speech,
There comes a fellow crying out for help,
And Cassio following him with determined sword
To execute upon him. Sir, this gentleman   222
    [indicating Montano]
Steps in to Cassio and entreats his pause.   223
Myself the crying fellow did pursue,
Lest by his clamor—as it so fell out—
The town might fall in fright. He, swift of foot,

---

151 mutiny riot.   154 masters sirs.   154.1 A bell rings (This direction
is from the quarto, as are Exit Roderigo at line 131, They fight at line
150, and with weapons at line 157.1.)   155 Diablo The devil   156 rise
grow riotous.   164–5 to ourselves . . . Ottomites inflict on ourselves
the harm that heaven has prevented the Turks from doing (by
destroying their fleet).   167 carve for i.e., indulge, satisfy with his
sword   168 Holds . . . light i.e., places little value on his life. upon
his motion if he moves.   170 propriety proper state or condition.
174 In quarter . . . terms in conduct and speech   175 Devesting them
undressing themselves   178 speak explain   179 peevish odds childish quarrel   182 are thus forgot have forgotten yourself thus.

184 wont be accustomed to be   185 stillness sobriety   187 censure
judgment.   188 unlace undo, lay open (as one might loose the strings
of a purse containing reputation)   189 opinion reputation
193 something somewhat. offends pains   199 blood passion (of
anger). guides i.e., reason   200 collied darkened   201 Essays
undertakes   204 rout riot   205 approved in found guilty of
207 town of town garrisoned for   209 manage undertake   210 on . . .
safety at the main guardhouse or headquarters and on watch.
212 If . . . office If made partial by personal relationship or by your
being fellow officers   222 execute upon him (1) proceed violently
against him (2) execute him.   223 his pause him to stop.

Outran my purpose, and I returned, the rather   227
For that I heard the clink and fall of swords
And Cassio high in oath, which till tonight
I ne'er might say before. When I came back—
For this was brief—I found them close together
At blow and thrust, even as again they were
When you yourself did part them.
More of this matter cannot I report.
But men are men; the best sometimes forget.   235
Though Cassio did some little wrong to him,
As men in rage strike those that wish them best,   237
Yet surely Cassio, I believe, received
From him that fled some strange indignity,
Which patience could not pass.

OTHELLO   I know, Iago,   240
Thy honesty and love doth mince this matter,
Making it light to Cassio. Cassio, I love thee,
But nevermore be officer of mine.

Enter Desdemona, attended.

Look if my gentle love be not raised up.
I'll make thee an example.

DESDEMONA
What is the matter, dear?

OTHELLO   All's well now, sweeting;
Come away to bed. [*To Montano*] Sir, for your hurts,
Myself will be your surgeon.—Lead him off.   248
                    [*Montano is led off.*]
Iago, look with care about the town
And silence those whom this vile brawl distracted.
Come, Desdemona. 'Tis the soldiers' life
To have their balmy slumbers waked with strife.
                    Exit [*with all but Iago and Cassio*].

IAGO   What, are you hurt, Lieutenant?

CASSIO   Ay, past all surgery.

IAGO   Marry, God forbid!

CASSIO   Reputation, reputation, reputation! Oh, I have
lost my reputation! I have lost the immortal part of
myself, and what remains is bestial. My reputation,
Iago, my reputation!

IAGO   As I am an honest man, I thought you had
received some bodily wound; there is more sense in
that than in reputation. Reputation is an idle and most
false imposition, oft got without merit and lost with-   263
out deserving. You have lost no reputation at all,
unless you repute yourself such a loser. What, man,
there are more ways to recover the General again. You   266
are but now cast in his mood—a punishment more in   267
policy than in malice, even so as one would beat his   268
offenseless dog to affright an imperious lion. Sue to   269
him again and he's yours.

CASSIO   I will rather sue to be despised than to deceive
so good a commander with so slight, so drunken, and   272
so indiscreet an officer. Drunk? And speak parrot?   273
And squabble? Swagger? Swear? And discourse fustian with one's own shadow? O thou invisible spirit
of wine, if thou hast no name to be known by, let us
call thee devil!

IAGO   What was he that you followed with your sword?
What had he done to you?

CASSIO   I know not.

IAGO   Is't possible?

CASSIO   I remember a mass of things, but nothing
distinctly; a quarrel, but nothing wherefore. Oh, God,   283
that men should put an enemy in their mouths to steal
away their brains! That we should, with joy, pleas-
ance, revel, and applause transform ourselves into   286
beasts!

IAGO   Why, but you are now well enough. How came
you thus recovered?

CASSIO   It hath pleased the devil drunkenness to give
place to the devil wrath. One unperfectness shows me
another, to make me frankly despise myself.

IAGO   Come, you are too severe a moraler. As the time,   293
the place, and the condition of this country stands, I
could heartily wish this had not befallen; but since it is
as it is, mend it for your own good.

CASSIO   I will ask him for my place again; he shall tell
me I am a drunkard. Had I as many mouths as Hydra,   298
such an answer would stop them all. To be now a
sensible man, by and by a fool, and presently a beast!
Oh, strange! Every inordinate cup is unblessed, and the   301
ingredient is a devil.

IAGO   Come, come, good wine is a good familiar
creature, if it be well used. Exclaim no more against it.
And, good Lieutenant, I think you think I love you.

CASSIO   I have well approved it, sir. I drunk!   306

IAGO   You or any man living may be drunk at a time,   307
man. I'll tell you what you shall do. Our general's wife
is now the general—I may say so in this respect, for   309
that he hath devoted and given up himself to the   310
contemplation, mark, and denotement of her parts   311
and graces. Confess yourself freely to her; importune
her help to put you in your place again. She is of so
free, so kind, so apt, so blessed a disposition, she   314
holds it a vice in her goodness not to do more than she
is requested. This broken joint between you and her
husband entreat her to splinter; and, my fortunes   317
against any lay worth naming, this crack of your love   318
shall grow stronger than it was before.

CASSIO   You advise me well.

---

227 **rather** sooner   235 **forget** forget themselves.   237 **those . . . best**
i.e., even those who are well disposed toward them   240 **pass** pass
over, overlook.   248 **be your surgeon** i.e., make sure you receive
medical attention.   263 **false imposition** thing artificially imposed
and of no real value   266 **recover** regain favor with   267 **cast in his
mood** dismissed in a moment of anger   267–8 **in policy** done for
expediency's sake and as a public gesture   268–9 **would . . . lion** i.e.,
would make an example of a minor offender in order to deter more
important and dangerous offenders.   269 **Sue** Petition

272 **slight** worthless   273 **speak parrot** talk nonsense, rant. (*Discourse
fustian*, lines 274–5, has much the same meaning.)   283 **wherefore**
why.   286 **applause** desire for applause   293 **moraler** moralizer.
298 **Hydra** the Lernaean Hydra, a monster with many heads and the
ability to grow two heads when one was cut off, slain by Hercules
as the second of his twelve labors   301 **inordinate** immoderate
306 **approved** proved by experience   307 **at a time** at one time or
another   309–10 **for that** that   311 **mark, and denotement** (Both
words mean "observation.")   **parts** qualities   314 **free** generous
317 **splinter** bind with splints   318 **lay** stake, wager

IAGO   I protest, in the sincerity of love and honest 321
kindness.

CASSIO   I think it freely; and betimes in the morning I 323
will beseech the virtuous Desdemona to undertake for
me. I am desperate of my fortunes if they check me 325
here.

IAGO   You are in the right. Good night, Lieutenant. I
must to the watch.

CASSIO   Good night, honest Iago.   *Exit Cassio.*

IAGO
And what's he then that says I play the villain,
When this advice is free I give, and honest,   331
Probal to thinking, and indeed the course   332
To win the Moor again? For 'tis most easy
Th'inclining Desdemona to subdue   334
In any honest suit; she's framed as fruitful   335
As the free elements. And then for her   336
To win the Moor—were't to renounce his baptism,
All seals and symbols of redeemèd sin—   338
His soul is so enfettered to her love
That she may make, unmake, do what she list,
Even as her appetite shall play the god   341
With his weak function. How am I then a villain,   342
To counsel Cassio to this parallel course   343
Directly to his good? Divinity of hell!   344
When devils will the blackest sins put on,   345
They do suggest at first with heavenly shows,   346
As I do now. For whiles this honest fool
Plies Desdemona to repair his fortune,
And she for him pleads strongly to the Moor,
I'll pour this pestilence into his ear,
That she repeals him for her body's lust;   351
And by how much she strives to do him good,
She shall undo her credit with the Moor.
So will I turn her virtue into pitch,   354
And out of her own goodness make the net
That shall enmesh them all.

Enter Roderigo.

How now, Roderigo?

RODERIGO   I do follow here in the chase, not like a
hound that hunts, but one that fills up the cry. My 358
money is almost spent; I have been tonight exceedingly well cudgeled; and I think the issue will be I shall 360
have so much experience for my pains, and so, 361
with no money at all and a little more wit, return again
to Venice.

IAGO
How poor are they that have not patience!
What wound did ever heal but by degrees?
Thou know'st we work by wit, and not by witchcraft,
And wit depends on dilatory time.
Does't not go well? Cassio hath beaten thee,
And thou, by that small hurt, hast cashiered Cassio.   369
Though other things grow fair against the sun,   370
Yet fruits that blossom first will first be ripe.   371
Content thyself awhile. By the Mass, 'tis morning!
Pleasure and action make the hours seem short.
Retire thee; go where thou art billeted.
Away, I say! Thou shalt know more hereafter.
Nay, get thee gone.   *Exit Roderigo.*
            Two things are to be done.
My wife must move for Cassio to her mistress;   377
I'll set her on;
Myself the while to draw the Moor apart
And bring him jump when he may Cassio find   380
Soliciting his wife. Ay, that's the way.
Dull not device by coldness and delay.   *Exit.* 382

❖

3.1

Enter Cassio [and] Musicians.

CASSIO
Masters, play here—I will content your pains—   1
Something that's brief, and bid "Good morrow,
    General."   [*They play.*]

[*Enter*] *Clown.*

CLOWN   Why, masters, have your instruments been in
Naples, that they speak i'th' nose thus?   4

A MUSICIAN   How, sir, how?

CLOWN   Are these, I pray you, wind instruments?

A MUSICIAN   Ay, marry, are they, sir.

CLOWN   Oh, thereby hangs a tail.

A MUSICIAN   Whereby hangs a tale, sir?

CLOWN   Marry, sir, by many a wind instrument that I 10
know. But, masters, here's money for you. [*He gives
money.*] And the General so likes your music that he
desires you, for love's sake, to make no more noise
with it.

A MUSICIAN   Well, sir, we will not.

CLOWN   If you have any music that may not be heard, 16
to't again; but, as they say, to hear music the General
does not greatly care.

A MUSICIAN   We have none such, sir.

---

321 protest insist, declare   **323 freely** unreservedly   **325 check**
repulse   **331 free** (1) free from guile (2) freely given   **332 Probal**
probable, reasonable   **334 Th'inclining** the favorably disposed.
subdue persuade   **335 framed as fruitful** created as generous
336 free elements i.e., earth, air, fire, and water, unrestrained and
spontaneous.   **338 seals** tokens   **341 her appetite** her desire, or, perhaps, his desire for her   **342 function** exercise of faculties (weakened
by his fondness for her).   **343 parallel** i.e., seemingly in his best interests but at the same time threatening   **344 Divinity of hell!** Inverted
theology of hell (which seduces the soul to its damnation)!   **345 put
on** further, instigate   **346 suggest** tempt   **351 repeals him** attempts
to get him restored   **354 pitch** i.e., (1) foul blackness (2) a snaring
substance   **358 fills up the cry** merely takes part as one of the pack.
360 issue outcome   **361 so much** just so much and no more

369 cashiered dismissed from service   **370–1 Though . . . ripe** i.e.,
Plans that are well prepared and set expeditiously in motion will
soonest ripen into success.   **377 move** plead   **380 jump** precisely
382 device plot.   **coldness** lack of zeal
3.1. Location: Before the chamber of Othello and Desdemona.
1 Masters Good sirs.   **content your pains** reward your efforts
4 speak i'th' nose (1) sound nasal (2) sound like one whose nose has
been attacked by syphilis. (Naples was popularly supposed to have a
high incidence of venereal disease.)   **10 wind instrument** (With a
joke on flatulence. The *tail*, line 8, that hangs nearby the *wind instrument* suggests the penis.)   **16 may not** cannot

CLOWN   Then put up your pipes in your bag, for I'll
away. Go, vanish into air, away!   *Exeunt Musicians.*

CASSIO   Dost thou hear, mine honest friend?

CLOWN   No, I hear not your honest friend; I hear you.

CASSIO   Prithee, keep up thy quillets. There's a poor   24
piece of gold for thee. [*He gives money.*] If the gentlewoman that attends the General's wife be stirring, tell
her there's one Cassio entreats her a little favor of   27
speech. Wilt thou do this?   28

CLOWN   She is stirring, sir. If she will stir hither, I shall   29
seem to notify unto her.   30

CASSIO
Do, good my friend.   *Exit Clown.*

Enter Iago.

In happy time, Iago.   31

IAGO   You have not been abed, then?

CASSIO   Why, no. The day had broke
Before we parted. I have made bold, Iago,
To send in to your wife. My suit to her
Is that she will to virtuous Desdemona
Procure me some access.

IAGO   I'll send her to you presently;
And I'll devise a mean to draw the Moor
Out of the way, that your converse and business
May be more free.

CASSIO
I humbly thank you for't.   *Exit [Iago].*
I never knew
A Florentine more kind and honest.   43

Enter Emilia.

EMILIA
Good morrow, good Lieutenant. I am sorry
For your displeasure; but all will sure be well.   45
The General and his wife are talking of it,
And she speaks for you stoutly. The Moor replies   47
That he you hurt is of great fame in Cyprus   48
And great affinity, and that in wholesome wisdom   49
He might not but refuse you; but he protests he loves
you   50
And needs no other suitor but his likings
To take the safest occasion by the front   52
To bring you in again.

CASSIO   Yet I beseech you,
If you think fit, or that it may be done,
Give me advantage of some brief discourse
With Desdemon alone.

EMILIA   Pray you, come in.
I will bestow you where you shall have time
To speak your bosom freely.   58

CASSIO   I am much bound to you.   [*Exeunt.*]

❖

3.2

Enter Othello, Iago, and Gentlemen.

OTHELLO [*giving letters*]
These letters give, Iago, to the pilot,
And by him do my duties to the Senate.   2
That done, I will be walking on the works;   3
Repair there to me.

IAGO   Well, my good lord, I'll do't.   4

OTHELLO
This fortification, gentlemen, shall we see't?

GENTLEMEN   We'll wait upon Your Lordship.   *Exeunt.*   6

❖

3.3

Enter Desdemona, Cassio, and Emilia.

DESDEMONA
Be thou assured, good Cassio, I will do
All my abilities in thy behalf.

EMILIA
Good madam, do. I warrant it grieves my husband
As if the cause were his.

DESDEMONA
Oh, that's an honest fellow. Do not doubt, Cassio,
But I will have my lord and you again
As friendly as you were.

CASSIO   Bounteous madam,
Whatever shall become of Michael Cassio,
He's never anything but your true servant.

DESDEMONA
I know't. I thank you. You do love my lord;
You have known him long, and be you well assured
He shall in strangeness stand no farther off   12
Than in a politic distance.

CASSIO   Ay, but, lady,   13
That policy may either last so long,
Or feed upon such nice and waterish diet,   15
Or breed itself so out of circumstance,   16
That, I being absent and my place supplied,   17
My general will forget my love and service.

DESDEMONA
Do not doubt that. Before Emilia here   19
I give thee warrant of thy place. Assure thee,   20
If I do vow a friendship I'll perform it
To the last article. My lord shall never rest.
I'll watch him tame and talk him out of patience;   23

---

24 **keep . . . quillets** refrain from quibbling.   27–8 **a little . . . speech**
the favor of a brief talk.   29 **stir** bestir herself. (With a play on
stirring, "rousing herself from rest.")   30 **seem** deem it good, think fit
31 **In happy time** i.e., Well met   43 **Florentine** i.e., even a fellow Florentine. (Iago is a Venetian; Cassio is a Florentine.)   45 **displeasure**
fall from favor   47 **stoutly** spiritedly.   48 **fame** reputation, importance   49 **affinity** kindred, family connection   50 **protests** insists
52 **occasion . . . front** opportunity by the forelock   58 **bosom** inmost
thoughts

3.2. Location: The citadel.
2 **do my duties** convey my respects   3 **works** breastworks, fortifications   4 **Repair** return, come   6 **wait upon** attend
3.3. Location: The citadel.
12 **strangeness** aloofness   13 **politic** required by wise policy
15 **Or . . . diet** or sustain itself at length upon such trivial and meager
technicalities   16 **breed . . . circumstance** continually renew itself so
out of chance events, or yield so few chances for my being pardoned
17 **supplied** filled by another person   19 **doubt** fear   20 **warrant**
guarantee   23 **watch him tame** tame him by keeping him from sleeping. (A term from falconry.)   **out of patience** past his endurance

His bed shall seem a school, his board a shrift;   24
I'll intermingle everything he does
With Cassio's suit. Therefore be merry, Cassio,
For thy solicitor shall rather die   27
Than give thy cause away.   28

Enter Othello and Iago [at a distance].

EMILIA Madam, here comes my lord.
CASSIO Madam, I'll take my leave.
DESDEMONA Why, stay, and hear me speak.
CASSIO
Madam, not now. I am very ill at ease,
Unfit for mine own purposes.
DESDEMONA Well, do your discretion. *Exit Cassio.* 34
IAGO Ha? I like not that.
OTHELLO What dost thou say?
IAGO
Nothing, my lord; or if—I know not what.
OTHELLO
Was not that Cassio parted from my wife?
IAGO
Cassio, my lord? No, sure, I cannot think it,
That he would steal away so guiltylike,
Seeing you coming.
OTHELLO I do believe 'twas he.
DESDEMONA *[joining them]* How now, my lord?
I have been talking with a suitor here,
A man that languishes in your displeasure.
OTHELLO Who is't you mean?
DESDEMONA
Why, your lieutenant, Cassio. Good my lord,
If I have any grace or power to move you,
His present reconciliation take;   49
For if he be not one that truly loves you,
That errs in ignorance and not in cunning,   51
I have no judgment in an honest face.
I prithee, call him back.
OTHELLO Went he hence now?
DESDEMONA Yes, faith, so humbled
That he hath left part of his grief with me
To suffer with him. Good love, call him back.
OTHELLO
Not now, sweet Desdemon. Some other time.
DESDEMONA But shall't be shortly?
OTHELLO The sooner, sweet, for you.
DESDEMONA Shall't be tonight at supper?
OTHELLO No, not tonight.
DESDEMONA Tomorrow dinner, then?   63
OTHELLO I shall not dine at home.
I meet the captains at the citadel.
DESDEMONA
Why, then, tomorrow night, or Tuesday morn,
On Tuesday noon, or night, on Wednesday morn.
I prithee, name the time, but let it not
Exceed three days. In faith, he's penitent;

And yet his trespass, in our common reason—   70
Save that, they say, the wars must make example   71
Out of her best—is not almost a fault   72
T'incur a private check. When shall he come?   73
Tell me, Othello. I wonder in my soul
What you would ask me that I should deny,
Or stand so mamm'ring on. What? Michael Cassio,   76
That came a-wooing with you, and so many a time,
When I have spoke of you dispraisingly,
Hath ta'en your part—to have so much to do
To bring him in! By'r Lady, I could do much—   80
OTHELLO
Prithee, no more. Let him come when he will;
I will deny thee nothing.
DESDEMONA Why, this is not a boon.
'Tis as I should entreat you wear your gloves,
Or feed on nourishing dishes, or keep you warm,
Or sue to you to do a peculiar profit   86
To your own person. Nay, when I have a suit
Wherein I mean to touch your love indeed,   88
It shall be full of poise and difficult weight,   89
And fearful to be granted.
OTHELLO I will deny thee nothing.
Whereon, I do beseech thee, grant me this,   92
To leave me but a little to myself.
DESDEMONA
Shall I deny you? No. Farewell, my lord.
OTHELLO
Farewell, my Desdemona. I'll come to thee straight.   95
DESDEMONA
Emilia, come.—Be as your fancies teach you;   96
Whate'er you be, I am obedient. *Exit [with Emilia].*
OTHELLO
Excellent wretch! Perdition catch my soul   98
But I do love thee! And when I love thee not,   99
Chaos is come again.   100
IAGO My noble lord—
OTHELLO What dost thou say, Iago?
IAGO
Did Michael Cassio, when you wooed my lady,
Know of your love?
OTHELLO
He did, from first to last. Why dost thou ask?
IAGO
But for a satisfaction of my thought;
No further harm.
OTHELLO Why of thy thought, Iago?

---

70 common reason everyday judgments **71–2 Save . . . best** were it not that, as the saying goes, military discipline requires making an example of the very best men. (*Her* refers to wars as a singular concept.) **72 not almost** scarcely **73 a private check** even a private reprimand. **76 mamm'ring on** wavering or muttering about. **80 bring him in** restore him to favor. **86 peculiar** particular, personal **88 touch** test **89 poise . . . weight** delicacy and weightiness **92 Whereon** In return for which **95 straight** straightaway. **96 fancies** inclinations **98 wretch** (A term of affectionate endearment.) **99–100 And . . . again** i.e., My love for you will last forever, until the end of time when chaos will return. (But with an unconscious, ironic suggestion that, if anything should induce Othello to cease loving Desdemona, the result would be chaos.)

---

24 board dining table. **shrift** confessional **27 solicitor** advocate **28 away** up. **34 do your discretion** do as you think fit. **49 His . . . take** let him be reconciled to you right away **51 in cunning** wittingly **63 dinner** (The noontime meal.)

IAGO

I did not think he had been acquainted with her.

OTHELLO

Oh, yes, and went between us very oft.

IAGO   Indeed?

OTHELLO

Indeed? Ay, indeed. Discern'st thou aught in that?
Is he not honest?

IAGO   Honest, my lord?

OTHELLO   Honest. Ay, honest.

IAGO   My lord, for aught I know.

OTHELLO   What dost thou think?

IAGO   Think, my lord?

OTHELLO

"Think, my lord?" By heaven, thou echo'st me,
As if there were some monster in thy thought
Too hideous to be shown. Thou dost mean something.
I heard thee say even now, thou lik'st not that,
When Cassio left my wife. What didst not like?
And when I told thee he was of my counsel   123
In my whole course of wooing, thou cried'st "Indeed?"
And didst contract and purse thy brow together   125
As if thou then hadst shut up in thy brain
Some horrible conceit. If thou dost love me,   127
Show me thy thought.

IAGO   My lord, you know I love you.

OTHELLO   I think thou dost;
And, for I know thou'rt full of love and honesty,   131
And weigh'st thy words before thou giv'st them
  breath,
Therefore these stops of thine fright me the more; 133
For such things in a false disloyal knave
Are tricks of custom, but in a man that's just   135
They're close dilations, working from the heart   136
That passion cannot rule.

IAGO   For Michael Cassio,   137
I dare be sworn I think that he is honest.

OTHELLO

I think so too.

IAGO   Men should be what they seem;
Or those that be not, would they might seem none!   140

OTHELLO

Certain, men should be what they seem.

IAGO

Why, then, I think Cassio's an honest man.

OTHELLO   Nay, yet there's more in this.
I prithee, speak to me as to thy thinkings,
As thou dost ruminate, and give thy worst of thoughts
The worst of words.

IAGO   Good my lord, pardon me.
Though I am bound to every act of duty,
I am not bound to that all slaves are free to.   148
Utter my thoughts? Why, say they are vile and false,
As where's that palace whereinto foul things

Sometimes intrude not? Who has that breast so pure
But some uncleanly apprehensions
Keep leets and law days, and in sessions sit   153
With meditations lawful?   154

OTHELLO

Thou dost conspire against thy friend, Iago,   155
If thou but think'st him wronged and mak'st his ear
A stranger to thy thoughts.

IAGO   I do beseech you,
Though I perchance am vicious in my guess—   158
As I confess it is my nature's plague
To spy into abuses, and oft my jealousy   160
Shapes faults that are not—that your wisdom then,
From one that so imperfectly conceits,   162
Would take no notice, nor build yourself a trouble
Out of his scattering and unsure observance.   164
It were not for your quiet nor your good,
Nor for my manhood, honesty, and wisdom,
To let you know my thoughts.

OTHELLO   What dost thou mean?

IAGO

Good name in man and woman, dear my lord,
Is the immediate jewel of their souls.   169
Who steals my purse steals trash; 'tis something,
  nothing;
'Twas mine, 'tis his, and has been slave to thousands;
But he that filches from me my good name
Robs me of that which not enriches him
And makes me poor indeed.

OTHELLO   By heaven, I'll know thy thoughts.

IAGO

You cannot, if my heart were in your hand,   176
Nor shall not, whilst 'tis in my custody.

OTHELLO   Ha?

IAGO   Oh, beware, my lord, of jealousy.
It is the green-eyed monster, which doth mock   179
The meat it feeds on. That cuckold lives in bliss   180
Who, certain of his fate, loves not his wronger;   181
But oh, what damnèd minutes tells he o'er   182
Who dotes, yet doubts, suspects, yet fondly loves!

OTHELLO   Oh, misery!

IAGO

Poor and content is rich, and rich enough,   185
But riches fineless is as poor as winter   186
To him that ever fears he shall be poor.

123 **of my counsel** in my confidence   125 **purse** knit   127 **conceit**
fancy.   131 **for** because   133 **stops** pauses   135 **of custom** customary   136–7 **They're . . . rule** they are secret or involuntary expressions of feeling that are too strong to be kept back.   137 **For** As for
140 **seem none** not seem at all, not seem to be honest.   148 **that** that
which.   **free to** free with respect to.

153 **Keep leets and law days** i.e., hold court, set up their authority in
one's heart. (*Leets* are a kind of manor court; *law days* are the days
courts sit in session, or those sessions.)   153–4 **and . . . lawful** i.e.,
and coexist in a kind of spiritual conflict with virtuous thoughts.
155 **thy friend** i.e., Othello   158 **vicious** wrong   160 **jealousy** suspicious nature   162 **one** i.e., myself, Iago.   **conceits** judges, conjectures
164 **scattering** random   169 **immediate** essential, most precious
176 **if** even if   179–80 **which . . . feeds on** (Jealousy mocks both itself
and the sufferer of jealousy; it is self-devouring and is its own punishment.)   180–1 **That . . . wronger** A cuckolded husband who
knows his wife to be unfaithful can at least take comfort in knowing
the truth, so that he will not continue to love her or to befriend her
lover. (Othello echoes this sentiment in lines 204–6, when he vows
that he would end uncertainty and cease to love an unfaithful wife.)
182 **tells** counts   185 **Poor . . . enough** To be content with what little
one has is the greatest wealth of all. (Proverbial.)   186 **fineless**
boundless

Good God, the souls of all my tribe defend
From jealousy!
OTHELLO   Why, why is this?
Think'st thou I'd make a life of jealousy,
To follow still the changes of the moon   192
With fresh suspicions? No! To be once in doubt   193
Is once to be resolved. Exchange me for a goat   194
When I shall turn the business of my soul
To such exsufflicate and blown surmises   196
Matching thy inference. 'Tis not to make me jealous   197
To say my wife is fair, feeds well, loves company,
Is free of speech, sings, plays, and dances well;
Where virtue is, these are more virtuous.
Nor from mine own weak merits will I draw
The smallest fear or doubt of her revolt,   202
For she had eyes, and chose me. No, Iago,
I'll see before I doubt; when I doubt, prove;
And on the proof, there is no more but this—
Away at once with love or jealousy.
IAGO
I am glad of this, for now I shall have reason
To show the love and duty that I bear you
With franker spirit. Therefore, as I am bound,
Receive it from me. I speak not yet of proof.
Look to your wife; observe her well with Cassio.
Wear your eyes thus, not jealous nor secure.   212
I would not have your free and noble nature,
Out of self-bounty, be abused. Look to't.   214
I know our country disposition well;
In Venice they do let God see the pranks
They dare not show their husbands; their best
    conscience
Is not to leave't undone, but keep't unknown.
OTHELLO   Dost thou say so?
IAGO
She did deceive her father, marrying you;
And when she seemed to shake and fear your looks,
She loved them most.
OTHELLO   And so she did.
IAGO   Why, go to, then! 222
She that, so young, could give out such a seeming,   223
To seel her father's eyes up close as oak,   224
He thought 'twas witchcraft! But I am much to blame.
I humbly do beseech you of your pardon
For too much loving you.
OTHELLO   I am bound to thee forever.   228
IAGO
I see this hath a little dashed your spirits.

OTHELLO
Not a jot, not a jot.
IAGO   I'faith, I fear it has.
I hope you will consider what is spoke
Comes from my love. But I do see you're moved.
I am to pray you not to strain my speech
To grosser issues nor to larger reach   234
Than to suspicion.
OTHELLO   I will not.
IAGO   Should you do so, my lord,
My speech should fall into such vile success   238
Which my thoughts aimed not. Cassio's my worthy
    friend.
My lord, I see you're moved.
OTHELLO   No, not much moved.
I do not think but Desdemona's honest.   241
IAGO
Long live she so! And long live you to think so!
OTHELLO
And yet, how nature erring from itself—
IAGO
Ay, there's the point! As—to be bold with you—
Not to affect many proposèd matches   245
Of her own clime, complexion, and degree,   246
Whereto we see in all things nature tends—
Foh! One may smell in such a will most rank,   248
Foul disproportion, thoughts unnatural.   249
But pardon me. I do not in position   250
Distinctly speak of her, though I may fear
Her will, recoiling to her better judgment,   252
May fall to match you with her country forms   253
And happily repent.
OTHELLO   Farewell, farewell!   254
If more thou dost perceive, let me know more.
Set on thy wife to observe. Leave me, Iago.
IAGO [going] My lord, I take my leave.
OTHELLO
Why did I marry? This honest creature doubtless
Sees and knows more, much more, than he unfolds.
IAGO [returning]
My lord, I would I might entreat Your Honor
To scan this thing no farther. Leave it to time.   261
Although 'tis fit that Cassio have his place—
For, sure, he fills it up with great ability—
Yet, if you please to hold him off awhile,
You shall by that perceive him and his means.   265
Note if your lady strain his entertainment   266
With any strong or vehement importunity;
Much will be seen in that. In the meantime,
Let me be thought too busy in my fears—   269

192–3 **To follow . . . suspicions?** to be constantly imagining new causes for suspicion, changing incessantly like the moon? **194 once** once and for all.   **resolved** free of doubt, having settled the matter. **196 exsufflicate and blown** inflated and blown up or flyblown, hence, loathsome, disgusting **197 inference** description or allegation. **202 doubt . . . revolt** fear of her unfaithfulness **212 not** neither.   **secure** free from uncertainty. **214 self-bounty** inherent or natural goodness and generosity.   **abused** deceived. **222 go to** (An expression of impatience.) **223 seeming** false appearance **224 seel** blind. (A term from falconry.)   **oak** (A close-grained wood.) **228 bound** indebted. (But perhaps with ironic sense of "tied.")

234 **issues** significances.   **reach** meaning, scope   **238 success** effect, result **241 honest** chaste. **245 affect** prefer, desire **246 clime . . . degree** country, temperament or skin color, and social position **248 will** sensuality, appetite   **249 disproportion** abnormality **250 in position** in making this argument or proposition **252 recoiling** reverting.   **better** i.e., more natural and reconsidered **253 fall . . . forms** undertake to compare you with Venetian norms of handsomeness **254 happily repent** haply repent her marriage.   **261 scan** scrutinize **265 his means** the method he uses (to regain his post). **266 strain his entertainment** urge his reinstatement **269 busy** officious

As worthy cause I have to fear I am—
And hold her free, I do beseech Your Honor.   271

OTHELLO   Fear not my government.   272

IAGO   I once more take my leave.   *Exit.*

OTHELLO
This fellow's of exceeding honesty,
And knows all qualities, with a learnèd spirit,   275
Of human dealings. If I do prove her haggard,   276
Though that her jesses were my dear heartstrings,   277
I'd whistle her off and let her down the wind   278
To prey at fortune. Haply, for I am black   279
And have not those soft parts of conversation   280
That chamberers have, or for I am declined   281
Into the vale of years—yet that's not much—
She's gone. I am abused, and my relief   283
Must be to loathe her. Oh, curse of marriage,
That we can call these delicate creatures ours
And not their appetites! I had rather be a toad
And live upon the vapor of a dungeon
Than keep a corner in the thing I love
For others' uses. Yet, 'tis the plague of great ones;
Prerogatived are they less than the base.   290
'Tis destiny unshunnable, like death.
Even then this forkèd plague is fated to us   292
When we do quicken. Look where she comes.   293

Enter Desdemona and Emilia.

If she be false, oh, then heaven mocks itself!
I'll not believe't.

DESDEMONA   How now, my dear Othello?
Your dinner, and the generous islanders   296
By you invited do attend your presence.   297

OTHELLO
I am to blame.

DESDEMONA   Why do you speak so faintly?
Are you not well?

OTHELLO
I have a pain upon my forehead here.

DESDEMONA
Faith, that's with watching. 'Twill away again.   301
              [*She offers her handkerchief.*]
Let me but bind it hard, within this hour
It will be well.

OTHELLO   Your napkin is too little.   303
Let it alone. Come, I'll go in with you.   304
              [*He puts the handkerchief from him, and it drops.*]

DESDEMONA
I am very sorry that you are not well.

              Exit [with Othello].

EMILIA [*picking up the handkerchief*]
I am glad I have found this napkin.
This was her first remembrance from the Moor.
My wayward husband hath a hundred times   308
Wooed me to steal it, but she so loves the token—
For he conjured her she should ever keep it—
That she reserves it evermore about her
To kiss and talk to. I'll have the work ta'en out,   312
And give't Iago. What he will do with it
Heaven knows, not I;
I nothing but to please his fantasy.   315

Enter Iago.

IAGO
How now? What do you here alone?

EMILIA
Do not you chide. I have a thing for you.

IAGO
You have a thing for me? It is a common thing—   318

EMILIA   Ha?

IAGO   To have a foolish wife.

EMILIA
Oh, is that all? What will you give me now
For that same handkerchief?

IAGO   What handkerchief?

EMILIA   What handkerchief?
Why, that the Moor first gave to Desdemona;
That which so often you did bid me steal.

IAGO   Hast stolen it from her?

EMILIA
No, faith. She let it drop by negligence,
And to th'advantage I, being here, took't up.   329
Look, here 'tis.

IAGO   A good wench! Give it me.

EMILIA
What will you do with't, that you have been so earnest
To have me filch it?

IAGO [*snatching it*]   Why, what is that to you?

EMILIA
If it be not for some purpose of import,
Give't me again. Poor lady, she'll run mad
When she shall lack it.

IAGO   Be not acknown on't.   335
I have use for it. Go, leave me.   *Exit Emilia.*
I will in Cassio's lodging lose this napkin   337
And let him find it. Trifles light as air
Are to the jealous confirmations strong
As proofs of Holy Writ. This may do something.
The Moor already changes with my poison.

271 **hold her free** regard her as innocent   272 **government** self-control, conduct.   275 **qualities** natures, types   276 **haggard** wild (like a wild female hawk)   277 **jesses** straps fastened around the legs of a trained hawk   278 **I'd . . . wind** i.e., I'd let her go forever. (To release a hawk downwind was to turn it loose.)   279 **prey at fortune** fend for herself in the wild.   **Haply, for** Perhaps because   280 **soft . . . conversation** pleasing social graces   281 **chamberers** drawing-room gallants   283 **abused** deceived   290 **Prerogatived** privileged (to have honest wives).   **the base** ordinary citizens. (Socially prominent men are especially prone to the common destiny of being cuckolded and to the public shame that goes with it.)   292 **forkèd** (An allusion to the horns of the cuckold.)   293 **quicken** receive life. (*Quicken* may also mean to swarm with maggots as the body festers, as in 4.2.69, in which case lines 292–3 suggest that *even then*, in death, we are cuckolded by *forkèd* worms.)   296 **generous** noble   297 **attend** await   301 **watching** too little sleep.   303 **napkin** handkerchief   304 **Let it alone** i.e., Never mind.

308 **wayward** capricious   312 **work ta'en out** design of the embroidery copied   315 **fantasy** whim.   318 **common thing** (With bawdy suggestion; *common* suggests coarseness and availability to all comers, and *thing* is a slang term for the pudendum.)   329 **to th'advantage** taking the opportunity   335 **lack** miss.   **Be . . . on't** Do not confess knowledge of it; keep out of this.   337 **lose** (The Folio spelling, "loose," is a normal spelling for "lose," but it may also contain the idea of "let go," "release.")

Dangerous conceits are in their natures poisons,   342
Which at the first are scarce found to distaste,   343
But with a little act upon the blood   344
Burn like the mines of sulfur.

Enter Othello.

                                  I did say so.
Look where he comes! Not poppy nor mandragora   346
Nor all the drowsy syrups of the world
Shall ever medicine thee to that sweet sleep
Which thou owed'st yesterday.

OTHELLO   Ha, ha, false to me?   349

IAGO
Why, how now, General? No more of that.

OTHELLO
Avaunt! Begone! Thou hast set me on the rack.
I swear 'tis better to be much abused
Than but to know't a little.

IAGO   How now, my lord?

OTHELLO
What sense had I of her stolen hours of lust?
I saw't not, thought it not, it harmed not me.
I slept the next night well, fed well, was free and
    merry;   356
I found not Cassio's kisses on her lips.
He that is robbed, not wanting what is stolen,   358
Let him not know't and he's not robbed at all.

IAGO   I am sorry to hear this.

OTHELLO
I had been happy if the general camp,
Pioneers and all, had tasted her sweet body,   362
So I had nothing known. Oh, now, forever   363
Farewell the tranquil mind! Farewell content!
Farewell the plumèd troops and the big wars   365
That makes ambition virtue! Oh, farewell!
Farewell the neighing steed and the shrill trump,
The spirit-stirring drum, th'ear-piercing fife,
The royal banner, and all quality,   369
Pride, pomp, and circumstance of glorious war!   370
And O you mortal engines, whose rude throats   371
Th'immortal Jove's dread clamors counterfeit,   372
Farewell! Othello's occupation's gone.

IAGO   Is't possible, my lord?

OTHELLO
Villain, be sure thou prove my love a whore!
Be sure of it. Give me the ocular proof,
Or, by the worth of mine eternal soul,
Thou hadst been better have been born a dog
Than answer my waked wrath!

IAGO   Is't come to this?

OTHELLO
Make me to see't, or at the least so prove it

That the probation bear no hinge nor loop   381
To hang a doubt on, or woe upon thy life!

IAGO   My noble lord—

OTHELLO
If thou dost slander her and torture me,
Never pray more; abandon all remorse;   385
On horror's head horrors accumulate;   386
Do deeds to make heaven weep, all earth amazed;   387
For nothing canst thou to damnation add
Greater than that.

IAGO   O grace! O heaven forgive me!
Are you a man? Have you a soul or sense?
God b'wi'you; take mine office. O wretched fool,   391
That lov'st to make thine honesty a vice!   392
O monstrous world! Take note, take note, O world,
To be direct and honest is not safe.
I thank you for this profit, and from hence   395
I'll love no friend, sith love breeds such offense.   396

OTHELLO   Nay, stay. Thou shouldst be honest.   397

IAGO
I should be wise, for honesty's a fool
And loses that it works for.

OTHELLO   By the world,   399
I think my wife be honest and think she is not;
I think that thou art just and think thou art not.
I'll have some proof. My name, that was as fresh
As Dian's visage, is now begrimed and black   403
As mine own face. If there be cords, or knives,
Poison, or fire, or suffocating streams,
I'll not endure it. Would I were satisfied!

IAGO
I see, sir, you are eaten up with passion.
I do repent me that I put it to you.
You would be satisfied?

OTHELLO   Would? Nay, and I will.

IAGO
And may; but how? How satisfied, my lord?
Would you, the supervisor, grossly gape on?   411
Behold her topped?

OTHELLO   Death and damnation! Oh!

IAGO
It were a tedious difficulty, I think,
To bring them to that prospect. Damn them then,   414
If ever mortal eyes do see them bolster   415
More than their own. What then? How then?   416
What shall I say? Where's satisfaction?
It is impossible you should see this,
Were they as prime as goats, as hot as monkeys,   419

---

342 **conceits** fancies, ideas   343 **distaste** be distasteful   344 **act** action, working   346 **mandragora** an opiate made of the mandrake root   349 **thou owed'st** you did own   356 **free** carefree   358 **wanting** missing   362 **Pioneers** diggers of mines, the lowest grade of soldiers   363 **So** provided   365 **big** mighty   369 **quality** character, essential nature   370 **Pride** rich display. **circumstance** pageantry   371 **mortal engines** i.e., cannon. (*Mortal* means "deadly.")   372 **Jove's dread clamors** i.e., thunder

381 **probation** proof   385 **remorse** pity, penitent hope for salvation   386 **horrors accumulate** add still more horrors   387 **amazed** confounded with horror   391 **O wretched fool** (Iago addresses himself as a fool for having carried honesty too far.)   392 **vice** failing, something overdone.   395 **profit** profitable instruction. **hence** henceforth   396 **sith** since. **offense** i.e., harm to the one who offers help and friendship.   397 **Thou shouldst be** It appears that you are. (But Iago replies in the sense of "ought to be.")   399 **that** what   403 **Dian** Diana, goddess of the moon and of chastity   411 **supervisor** onlooker   414 **Damn them then** i.e., They would have to be really incorrigible   415 **bolster** go to bed together, share a bolster   416 **More** other. **own** own eyes.   419 **prime** lustful

As salt as wolves in pride, and fools as gross   420
As ignorance made drunk. But yet I say,
If imputation and strong circumstances   422
Which lead directly to the door of truth
Will give you satisfaction, you might have't.

OTHELLO
Give me a living reason she's disloyal.

IAGO   I do not like the office.
But sith I am entered in this cause so far,   427
Pricked to't by foolish honesty and love,   428
I will go on. I lay with Cassio lately,
And being troubled with a raging tooth
I could not sleep. There are a kind of men
So loose of soul that in their sleeps will mutter
Their affairs. One of this kind is Cassio.
In sleep I heard him say, "Sweet Desdemona,
Let us be wary, let us hide our loves!"
And then, sir, would he grip and wring my hand,
Cry "O sweet creature!", then kiss me hard,
As if he plucked up kisses by the roots
That grew upon my lips; then laid his leg
Over my thigh, and sighed, and kissed, and then
Cried, "Cursèd fate that gave thee to the Moor!"

OTHELLO
Oh, monstrous! Monstrous!

IAGO   Nay, this was but his dream.

OTHELLO
But this denoted a foregone conclusion.   443
'Tis a shrewd doubt, though it be but a dream.   444

IAGO
And this may help to thicken other proofs
That do demonstrate thinly.

OTHELLO   I'll tear her all to pieces.

IAGO
Nay, but be wise. Yet we see nothing done;
She may be honest yet. Tell me but this:
Have you not sometimes seen a handkerchief
Spotted with strawberries in your wife's hand?   450

OTHELLO
I gave her such a one. 'Twas my first gift.

IAGO
I know not that; but such a handkerchief—
I am sure it was your wife's—did I today
See Cassio wipe his beard with.

OTHELLO   If it be that—

IAGO
If it be that, or any that was hers,
It speaks against her with the other proofs.

OTHELLO
Oh, that the slave had forty thousand lives!   457
One is too poor, too weak for my revenge.
Now do I see 'tis true. Look here, Iago,
All my fond love thus do I blow to heaven.   460

'Tis gone.
Arise, black vengeance, from the hollow hell!
Yield up, O love, thy crown and hearted throne   463
To tyrannous hate! Swell, bosom, with thy freight,   464
For 'tis of aspics' tongues!   465

IAGO   Yet be content.   466

OTHELLO   Oh, blood, blood, blood!

IAGO
Patience, I say. Your mind perhaps may change.

OTHELLO
Never, Iago. Like to the Pontic Sea,   469
Whose icy current and compulsive course
Ne'er feels retiring ebb, but keeps due on
To the Propontic and the Hellespont,   472
Even so my bloody thoughts with violent pace
Shall ne'er look back, ne'er ebb to humble love,
Till that a capable and wide revenge   475
Swallow them up. Now, by yond marble heaven,   476
[Kneeling] In the due reverence of a sacred vow
I here engage my words.

IAGO   Do not rise yet.
[He kneels.] Witness, you ever-burning lights above,   479
You elements that clip us round about,   480
Witness that here Iago doth give up
The execution of his wit, hands, heart,   482
To wrongèd Othello's service. Let him command,
And to obey shall be in me remorse,   484
What bloody business ever.   [They rise.]

OTHELLO   I greet thy love,   485
Not with vain thanks, but with acceptance bounteous,
And will upon the instant put thee to't.   487
Within these three days let me hear thee say
That Cassio's not alive.

IAGO   My friend is dead;
'Tis done at your request. But let her live.

OTHELLO
Damn her, lewd minx! Oh, damn her, damn her!   491
Come, go with me apart. I will withdraw
To furnish me with some swift means of death
For the fair devil. Now art thou my lieutenant.

IAGO   I am your own forever.   Exeunt.

❖

3.4

Enter Desdemona, Emilia, and Clown.

DESDEMONA   Do you know, sirrah, where Lieutenant   1
Cassio lies?   2

---

420 **salt** wanton, sensual.   **pride** heat   **422 imputation . . . circum-**
stances strong circumstantial evidence   **427 sith** since   **428 Pricked**
spurred   **443 foregone conclusion** previous experience or action.
444 shrewd doubt suspicious circumstance   **450 Spotted with straw-**
berries embroidered with a strawberry pattern   **457 the slave** i.e.,
Cassio   **460 fond** foolish. (But also suggesting "affectionate.")

463 **hearted** fixed in the heart   **464 freight** burden   **465 aspics'**
venomous serpents'   **466 content** calm.   **469 Pontic Sea** Black Sea
472 Propontic Sea of Marmora, between the Black Sea and the
Aegean.   **Hellespont** Dardanelles, straits where the Sea of Marmora
joins with the Aegean   **475 capable** ample, comprehensive
476 marble i.e., gleaming, polished, and indifferent to human suffering   **479 s.d.** *He kneels* (In the quarto text, Iago kneels here after Othello has knelt at line 477.)   **480 clip** encompass   **482 execution**
exercise, action.   **wit** mind   **484 remorse** pity (for Othello's wrongs)
485 ever soever.   **487 to't** to the proof.   **491 minx** wanton.
3.4. Location: Before the citadel.
1 sirrah (A form of address to an inferior.)   **2 lies** lodges. (But the
Clown makes the obvious pun.)

CLOWN   I dare not say he lies anywhere.

DESDEMONA   Why, man?

CLOWN   He's a soldier, and for me to say a soldier lies, 'tis stabbing.

DESDEMONA   Go to. Where lodges he?

CLOWN   To tell you where he lodges is to tell you where I lie.

DESDEMONA   Can anything be made of this?

CLOWN   I know not where he lodges, and for me to devise a lodging and say he lies here, or he lies there, were to lie in mine own throat.   13

DESDEMONA   Can you inquire him out, and be edified by report?

CLOWN   I will catechize the world for him; that is, make questions, and by them answer.

DESDEMONA   Seek him, bid him come hither. Tell him I have moved my lord on his behalf and hope all will be   19 well.

CLOWN   To do this is within the compass of man's wit, and therefore I will attempt the doing it.   *Exit Clown.*

DESDEMONA   Where should I lose that handkerchief, Emilia?

EMILIA   I know not, madam.

DESDEMONA   Believe me, I had rather have lost my purse Full of crusadoes; and but my noble Moor   26 Is true of mind and made of no such baseness As jealous creatures are, it were enough To put him to ill thinking.

EMILIA   Is he not jealous?

DESDEMONA   Who, he? I think the sun where he was born Drew all such humors from him.

EMILIA   Look where he comes.   31

Enter Othello.

DESDEMONA   I will not leave him now till Cassio Be called to him.—How is't with you, my lord?

OTHELLO   Well, my good lady. [*Aside*] Oh, hardness to dissemble!— How do you, Desdemona?

DESDEMONA   Well, my good lord.

OTHELLO   Give me your hand. [*She gives her hand.*] This hand is moist, my lady.

DESDEMONA   It yet hath felt no age nor known no sorrow.

OTHELLO   This argues fruitfulness and liberal heart.   38 Hot, hot, and moist. This hand of yours requires A sequester from liberty, fasting and prayer,   40

Much castigation, exercise devout;   41 For here's a young and sweating devil here That commonly rebels. 'Tis a good hand, A frank one.

DESDEMONA   You may indeed say so,   44 For 'twas that hand that gave away my heart.

OTHELLO   A liberal hand. The hearts of old gave hands,   46 But our new heraldry is hands, not hearts.   47

DESDEMONA   I cannot speak of this. Come now, your promise.

OTHELLO   What promise, chuck?   49

DESDEMONA   I have sent to bid Cassio come speak with you.

OTHELLO   I have a salt and sorry rheum offends me;   51 Lend me thy handkerchief.

DESDEMONA   Here, my lord.   [*She offers a handkerchief.*]

OTHELLO   That which I gave you.

DESDEMONA   I have it not about me.

OTHELLO   Not?

DESDEMONA   No, faith, my lord.

OTHELLO   That's a fault. That handkerchief Did an Egyptian to my mother give. She was a charmer, and could almost read   59 The thoughts of people. She told her, while she kept it 'Twould make her amiable and subdue my father   61 Entirely to her love, but if she lost it Or made a gift of it, my father's eye Should hold her loathèd and his spirits should hunt After new fancies. She, dying, gave it me,   65 And bid me, when my fate would have me wived, To give it her. I did so; and take heed on't;   67 Make it a darling like your precious eye. To lose't or give't away were such perdition   69 As nothing else could match.

DESDEMONA   Is't possible?

OTHELLO   'Tis true. There's magic in the web of it.   71 A sibyl, that had numbered in the world The sun to course two hundred compasses,   73 In her prophetic fury sewed the work;   74 The worms were hallowed that did breed the silk, And it was dyed in mummy which the skillful   76 Conserved of maidens' hearts.

DESDEMONA   I'faith! Is't true?   77

---

13 **lie . . . throat** lie egregiously and deliberately.   **19 moved my lord** petitioned Othello   **26 crusadoes** Portuguese gold coins   **31 humors** (Refers to the four bodily fluids thought to determine temperament.)   **38 argues** gives evidence of.   **fruitfulness** generosity, amorousness, and fecundity.   **liberal** generous and sexually free   **40 sequester** sequestration

41 castigation corrective discipline.   **exercise devout** i.e., prayer, religious meditation, etc.   **44 frank** generous, open. (With sexual suggestion.)   **46–7 The hearts . . . hearts** i.e., In former times, people would give their hearts when they gave their hands to something, but in our dedacent present age the joining of hands no longer has that spiritual sense.   **49 chuck** (A term of endearment.)   **51 salt . . . rheum** distressful head cold or watering of the eyes   **59 charmer** sorceress   **61 amiable** desirable   **65 fancies** loves.   **67 her** i.e., to my wife.   **69 perdition** loss   **71 web** fabric, weaving   **73 compasses** annual circlings. (The *sibyl*, or prophetess, was two hundred years old.)   **74 prophetic fury** frenzy of prophetic inspiration.   **work** embroidered pattern   **76 mummy** medicinal or magical preparation drained from mummified bodies   **77 Conserved of** prepared or preserved out of

OTHELLO
  Most veritable. Therefore look to't well.

DESDEMONA
  Then would to God that I had never seen't!

OTHELLO Ha? Wherefore?

DESDEMONA
  Why do you speak so startingly and rash?   81

OTHELLO
  Is't lost? Is't gone? Speak, is't out o'th' way?   82

DESDEMONA Heaven bless us!

OTHELLO Say you?

DESDEMONA
  It is not lost; but what an if it were?   85

OTHELLO How?

DESDEMONA
  I say it is not lost.

OTHELLO   Fetch't, let me see't.

DESDEMONA
  Why, so I can, sir, but I will not now.
  This is a trick to put me from my suit.
  Pray you, let Cassio be received again.

OTHELLO
  Fetch me the handkerchief! My mind misgives.

DESDEMONA Come, come,
  You'll never meet a more sufficient man.   93

OTHELLO
  The handkerchief!

DESDEMONA   I pray, talk me of Cassio.   94

OTHELLO
  The handkerchief!

DESDEMONA   A man that all his time   95
  Hath founded his good fortunes on your love,   96
  Shared dangers with you—

OTHELLO   The handkerchief!

DESDEMONA I'faith, you are to blame.

OTHELLO Zounds!   *Exit Othello.*

EMILIA Is not this man jealous?

DESDEMONA I ne'er saw this before.
  Sure, there's some wonder in this handkerchief.
  I am most unhappy in the loss of it.   104

EMILIA
  'Tis not a year or two shows us a man.   105
  They are all but stomachs, and we all but food;   106
  They eat us hungerly, and when they are full   107
  They belch us.

      Enter Iago and Cassio.

      Look you, Cassio and my husband.

IAGO [*to Cassio*]
  There is no other way; 'tis she must do't.
  And, lo, the happiness! Go and importune her.   110

DESDEMONA
  How now, good Cassio? What's the news with you?

CASSIO
  Madam, my former suit. I do beseech you
  That by your virtuous means I may again   113
  Exist and be a member of his love
  Whom I, with all the office of my heart,   115
  Entirely honor. I would not be delayed.
  If my offense be of such mortal kind   117
  That nor my service past, nor present sorrows,   118
  Nor purposed merit in futurity
  Can ransom me into his love again,
  But to know so must be my benefit;   121
  So shall I clothe me in a forced content,
  And shut myself up in some other course,   123
  To fortune's alms.

DESDEMONA   Alas, thrice-gentle Cassio,   124
  My advocation is not now in tune.   125
  My lord is not my lord; nor should I know him,
  Were he in favor as in humor altered.   127
  So help me every spirit sanctified   128
  As I have spoken for you all my best
  And stood within the blank of his displeasure   130
  For my free speech! You must awhile be patient.   131
  What I can do I will, and more I will
  Than for myself I dare. Let that suffice you.

IAGO
  Is my lord angry?

EMILIA   He went hence but now,
  And certainly in strange unquietness.

IAGO
  Can he be angry? I have seen the cannon
  When it hath blown his ranks into the air,
  And like the devil from his very arm
  Puffed his own brother—and is he angry?
  Something of moment then. I will go meet him.   140
  There's matter in't indeed, if he be angry.

DESDEMONA
  I prithee, do so.   *Exit [Iago].*
         Something, sure, of state,   142
  Either from Venice, or some unhatched practice   143
  Made demonstrable here in Cyprus to him,
  Hath puddled his clear spirit; and in such cases   145
  Men's natures wrangle with inferior things,
  Though great ones are their object. 'Tis even so;
  For let our finger ache, and it indues   148
  Our other, healthful members even to a sense
  Of pain. Nay, we must think men are not gods,

---

81 startingly and rash disjointedly and impetuously, excitedly.
82 out o'th' way lost, misplaced. **85 an if** if **93 sufficient** able, complete **94 talk** talk to **95–6 A man . . . love** A man who throughout his career has relied on your favor for his advancement
104 unhappy (1) unfortunate (2) sad **105 'Tis . . . man** A year or two is not enough time for us women to know what men really are.
106 but nothing but **107 hungerly** hungrily **110 the happiness** in happy time, fortunately met.

113 virtuous (1) efficacious (2) morally good **115 office** loyal service
117 mortal fatal **118 nor . . . nor** neither . . . nor **121 But . . . benefit** merely to know that my case is hopeless will have to content me (and will be better than uncertainty) **123 shut . . . in** commit myself to
124 To fortune's alms throwing myself on the mercy of fortune. **125 advocation** advocacy **127 favor** appearance. **humor** mood **128 So . . . sanctified** So help me all the heavenly host **130 within the blank** within point-blank range. (The *blank* is the center of the target.)
131 free frank **140 of moment** of immediate importance, momentous **142 of state** concerning state affairs **143 unhatched practice** as yet unexecuted or undiscovered plot **145 puddled** muddied
148 indues endows, brings to the same condition

Nor of them look for such observancy　　　　151
As fits the bridal. Beshrew me much, Emilia,　　152
I was, unhandsome warrior as I am,　　153
Arraigning his unkindness with my soul;　　154
But now I find I had suborned the witness,　　155
And he's indicted falsely.

EMILIA　　　　　　　Pray heaven it be
State matters, as you think, and no conception
Nor no jealous toy concerning you.　　158

DESDEMONA
Alas the day! I never gave him cause.

EMILIA
But jealous souls will not be answered so;
They are not ever jealous for the cause,
But jealous for they're jealous. It is a monster　　162
Begot upon itself, born on itself.　　163

DESDEMONA
Heaven keep that monster from Othello's mind!

EMILIA　Lady, amen.

DESDEMONA
I will go seek him. Cassio, walk hereabout.
If I do find him fit, I'll move your suit
And seek to effect it to my uttermost.

CASSIO
I humbly thank Your Ladyship.

Exit [Desdemona with Emilia].

Enter Bianca.

BIANCA
Save you, friend Cassio!

CASSIO　　　　　　　What make you from home?　170
How is't with you, my most fair Bianca?
I' faith, sweet love, I was coming to your house.

BIANCA
And I was going to your lodging, Cassio.
What, keep a week away? Seven days and nights?
Eightscore-eight hours? And lovers' absent hours　175
More tedious than the dial eightscore times?　176
Oh, weary reck'ning!

CASSIO　　　　　　　Pardon me, Bianca.
I have this while with leaden thoughts been pressed;
But I shall, in a more continuate time,　179
Strike off this score of absence. Sweet Bianca,　180
[giving her Desdemona's handkerchief]
Take me this work out.

BIANCA　　　　　Oh, Cassio, whence came this?　181
This is some token from a newer friend.　182
To the felt absence now I feel a cause.
Is't come to this? Well, well.

CASSIO　　　　　　　Go to, woman!
Throw your vile guesses in the devil's teeth,

From whence you have them. You are jealous now
That this is from some mistress, some remembrance.
No, by my faith, Bianca.

BIANCA　　　　　　Why, whose is it?

CASSIO
I know not, neither. I found it in my chamber.
I like the work well. Ere it be demanded—　190
As like enough it will—I would have it copied.　191
Take it and do't, and leave me for this time.

BIANCA　Leave you? Wherefore?

CASSIO
I do attend here on the General,
And think it no addition, nor my wish,　195
To have him see me womaned.

BIANCA　Why, I pray you?

CASSIO　Not that I love you not.

BIANCA　　　　But that you do not love me.
I pray you, bring me on the way a little,　200
And say if I shall see you soon at night.

CASSIO
'Tis but a little way that I can bring you,
For I attend here; but I'll see you soon.

BIANCA
'Tis very good. I must be circumstanced.　204

Exeunt omnes.

❖

4.1

Enter Othello and Iago.

IAGO
Will you think so?

OTHELLO　　　　　Think so, Iago?

IAGO　　　　　　　　　　　What,
To kiss in private?

OTHELLO　　　　　An unauthorized kiss!

IAGO
Or to be naked with her friend in bed
An hour or more, not meaning any harm?

OTHELLO
Naked in bed, Iago, and not mean harm?
It is hypocrisy against the devil.
They that mean virtuously and yet do so,
The devil their virtue tempts, and they tempt heaven.

IAGO
If they do nothing, 'tis a venial slip.　9
But if I give my wife a handkerchief—

OTHELLO　What then?

IAGO
Why then, 'tis hers, my lord, and being hers,
She may, I think, bestow't on any man.

OTHELLO
She is protectress of her honor too.
May she give that?

---

151 observancy attentiveness　**152 bridal** wedding (when a bride-groom is newly attentive to his bride).　**Beshrew me** (A mild oath.)
153 unhandsome insufficient, unskillful　**154 with** before the bar of
155 suborned the witness induced the witness to give false testimony
158 toy fancy　**162 for** because　**163 Begot upon itself** generated
solely from itself　**170 Save** God save.　**make** do　**175 Eightscore-eight** one hundred sixty-eight, the number of hours in a week
176 the dial a complete revolution of the clock　**179 continuate** unin-terrupted　**180 Strike . . . score** settle this account　**181 Take . . . out**
copy this embroidery for me.　**182 friend** mistress.

190 demanded inquired for　**191 like** likely　**195 addition** i.e., addi-tion to my reputation　**200 bring** accompany　**204 be circumstanced**
be governed by circumstance, yield to your conditions.
4.1. Location: Before the citadel.
9 venial pardonable

IAGO
    Her honor is an essence that's not seen;
    They have it very oft that have it not.   17
    But, for the handkerchief—
OTHELLO
    By heaven, I would most gladly have forgot it.
    Thou said'st—Oh, it comes o'er my memory
    As doth the raven o'er the infectious house,   21
    Boding to all—he had my handkerchief.
IAGO
    Ay, what of that?
OTHELLO   That's not so good now.
IAGO   What
    If I had said I had seen him do you wrong?
    Or heard him say—as knaves be such abroad,   25
    Who having, by their own importunate suit,   26
    Or voluntary dotage of some mistress,   27
    Convincèd or supplied them, cannot choose   28
    But they must blab—
OTHELLO   Hath he said anything?   29
IAGO
    He hath, my lord; but, be you well assured,
    No more than he'll unswear.
OTHELLO   What hath he said?
IAGO
    Faith, that he did—I know not what he did.
OTHELLO   What? What?
IAGO
    Lie—
OTHELLO   With her?
IAGO   With her, on her; what you will.
OTHELLO   Lie with her? Lie on her? We say "lie on her"
    when they belie her. Lie with her? Zounds, that's ful-   36
    some.—Handkerchief—confessions—handkerchief!   37
    —To confess and be hanged for his labor—first to be   38
    hanged and then to confess.—I tremble at it. Nature   39
    would not invest herself in such shadowing passion   40
    without some instruction. It is not words that shakes   41
    me thus. Pish! Noses, ears, and lips.—Is't possible?
    —Confess—handkerchief!—O devil!
                                 Falls in a trance.
IAGO   Work on,
    My medicine, work! Thus credulous fools are caught,
    And many worthy and chaste dames even thus,
    All guiltless, meet reproach.—What, ho! My lord!
    My lord, I say! Othello!

        Enter Cassio.

        How now, Cassio?

CASSIO   What's the matter?
IAGO
    My lord is fall'n into an epilepsy.
    This is his second fit. He had one yesterday.
CASSIO
    Rub him about the temples.
IAGO   No, forbear.
    The lethargy must have his quiet course.   53
    If not, he foams at mouth, and by and by
    Breaks out to savage madness. Look, he stirs.
    Do you withdraw yourself a little while.
    He will recover straight. When he is gone,
    I would on great occasion speak with you.   58
                             [*Exit Cassio.*]
    How is it, General? Have you not hurt your head?
OTHELLO
    Dost thou mock me?
IAGO   I mock you not, by heaven.   60
    Would you would bear your fortune like a man!
OTHELLO
    A hornèd man's a monster and a beast.
IAGO
    There's many a beast then in a populous city,
    And many a civil monster.   64
OTHELLO   Did he confess it?
IAGO   Good sir, be a man.
    Think every bearded fellow that's but yoked   67
    May draw with you. There's millions now alive   68
    That nightly lie in those unproper beds   69
    Which they dare swear peculiar. Your case is better.   70
    Oh, 'tis the spite of hell, the fiend's arch-mock,
    To lip a wanton in a secure couch   72
    And to suppose her chaste! No, let me know,
    And knowing what I am, I know what she shall be.   74
OTHELLO   Oh, thou art wise. 'Tis certain.
IAGO   Stand you awhile apart;
    Confine yourself but in a patient list.   77
    Whilst you were here o'erwhelmèd with your grief—
    A passion most unsuiting such a man—
    Cassio came hither. I shifted him away,   80
    And laid good 'scuse upon your ecstasy,   81
    Bade him anon return and here speak with me,
    The which he promised. Do but encave yourself   83
    And mark the fleers, the gibes, and notable scorns   84
    That dwell in every region of his face;
    For I will make him tell the tale anew,
    Where, how, how oft, how long ago, and when
    He hath and is again to cope your wife.   88

---

17 They have it i.e., They enjoy a reputation for it   **21 raven . . . house** (Allusion to the belief that the raven hovered over a house of sickness or infection, such as one visited by the plague.)   **25–9 as . . . blab**— since there are rascals enough who, having seduced a woman either through their own importunity or through the woman's willing infatuation, cannot keep quiet about it—   **36 belie** slander   **36–7 fulsome** foul.   **38–9 first . . . to confess** (Othello reverses the proverbial *confess and be hanged*; Cassio is to be given no time to confess before he dies.)   **39–41 Nature . . . instruction** i.e., Without some foundation in fact, nature would not have dressed herself in such an overwhelming passion that comes over me now and fills my mind with images, or in such a lifelike fantasy as Cassio had in his dream of lying with Desdemona.   **41 words** mere words

53 lethargy coma. **his** its **58 on great occasion** on a matter of great importance **60 mock me** (Othello takes Iago's question about hurting his head to be a mocking reference to the cuckold's horns.) **64 civil** i.e., dwelling in a city **67 yoked** (1) married (2) put into the yoke of infamy and cuckoldry **68 draw with you** pull as you do, like oxen who are yoked, i.e., share your fate as cuckold. **69 unproper** not exclusively their own **70 peculiar** private, their own. **better** i.e., because you know the truth. **72 lip** kiss. **secure** free from suspicion **74 And . . . shall be** and, knowing myself to be a cuckold, I'll know for certain that she's a whore. **77 in . . . list** within the bounds of patience. **80–1 I shifted . . . ecstasy** I got him out of the way, using your fit as my excuse for doing so **83 encave** conceal **84 fleers** sneers **88 cope** encounter with, have sex with

I say, but mark his gesture. Marry, patience!
Or I shall say you're all-in-all in spleen, 90
And nothing of a man.

OTHELLO　　　　　　　　　Dost thou hear, Iago?
I will be found most cunning in my patience;
But—dost thou hear?—most bloody.

IAGO　　　　　　　　　　　　That's not amiss;
But yet keep time in all. Will you withdraw? 94

[Othello stands apart.]

Now will I question Cassio of Bianca,
A huswife that by selling her desires 96
Buys herself bread and clothes. It is a creature
That dotes on Cassio—as 'tis the strumpet's plague
To beguile many and be beguiled by one.
He, when he hears of her, cannot restrain 100
From the excess of laughter. Here he comes.

　　Enter Cassio.

As he shall smile, Othello shall go mad;
And his unbookish jealousy must conster 103
Poor Cassio's smiles, gestures, and light behaviors
Quite in the wrong.—How do you now, Lieutenant?

CASSIO
The worser that you give me the addition 106
Whose want even kills me. 107

IAGO
Ply Desdemona well and you are sure on't.
[Speaking lower] Now, if this suit lay in Bianca's power,
How quickly should you speed!

CASSIO *[laughing]*　Alas, poor caitiff! 111

OTHELLO *[aside]*　Look how he laughs already!

IAGO
I never knew a woman love man so.

CASSIO
Alas, poor rogue! I think, i'faith, she loves me.

OTHELLO *[aside]*
Now he denies it faintly, and laughs it out.

IAGO
Do you hear, Cassio?

OTHELLO *[aside]*　　　Now he importunes him
To tell it o'er. Go to! Well said, well said. 117

IAGO
She gives it out that you shall marry her.
Do you intend it?

CASSIO　Ha, ha, ha!

OTHELLO *[aside]*
Do you triumph, Roman? Do you triumph? 121

CASSIO　I marry her? What? A customer? Prithee, bear 122
some charity to my wit; do not think it so unwhole- 123
some. Ha, ha, ha!

OTHELLO *[aside]*　So, so, so, so! They laugh that win. 125

IAGO　Faith, the cry goes that you shall marry her. 126

CASSIO　Prithee, say true.

IAGO　I am a very villain else. 128

OTHELLO *[aside]*　Have you scored me? Well. 129

CASSIO　This is the monkey's own giving out. She is
persuaded I will marry her out of her own love and
flattery, not out of my promise. 132

OTHELLO *[aside]*　Iago beckons me. Now he begins the 133
story.

CASSIO　She was here even now; she haunts me in every
place. I was the other day talking on the seabank with 136
certain Venetians, and thither comes the bauble, and, 137
by this hand, she falls me thus about my neck— 138

　　　　　　　[He embraces Iago.]

OTHELLO *[aside]*　Crying, "Oh, dear Cassio!" as it were; his
gesture imports it.

CASSIO　So hangs and lolls and weeps upon me, so
shakes and pulls me. Ha, ha, ha!

OTHELLO *[aside]*　Now he tells how she plucked him to my
chamber. Oh, I see that nose of yours, but not that dog 144
I shall throw it to. 145

CASSIO　Well, I must leave her company.

IAGO　Before me, look where she comes. 147

　　Enter Bianca [with Desdemona's handkerchief].

CASSIO　'Tis such another fitchew! Marry, a perfumed 148
one.—What do you mean by this haunting of me?

BIANCA　Let the devil and his dam haunt you! What did 150
you mean by that same handkerchief you gave me
even now? I was a fine fool to take it. I must take out
the work? A likely piece of work, that you should find 153
it in your chamber and know not who left it there!
This is some minx's token, and I must take out the
work? There; give it your hobbyhorse. *[She gives him* 156
the handkerchief.] Wheresoever you had it, I'll take out
no work on't.

CASSIO　How now, my sweet Bianca? How now? How
now?

OTHELLO *[aside]*　By heaven, that should be my hand- 161
kerchief!

BIANCA　If you'll come to supper tonight, you may; if
you will not, come when you are next prepared for. 164

IAGO　After her, after her. 　　　　　　　　　　　*Exit.*

CASSIO　Faith, I must. She'll rail in the streets else.

IAGO　Will you sup there?

CASSIO　Faith, I intend so.

IAGO　Well, I may chance to see you, for I would very
fain speak with you.

---

90 all-in-all in spleen utterly governed by passionate impulses
94 keep time keep yourself steady (as in music)　**96 huswife** hussy
100 restrain refrain　**103 his unbookish** Othello's uninstructed.
conster construe　**106 addition** title　**107 Whose want** the lack of
which　**111 caitiff** wretch.　**117 Go to** (An expression of remonstrance.)　**Well said** Well done. (Sarcastic.)　**121 Roman** (The
Romans were noted for their *triumphs* or triumphal processions.)
122 A customer? Who, I, the whore's customer? (Or, *customer* could
mean "prostitute.")　**122–3 bear . . . wit** be more charitable to my
judgment

125 They . . . win i.e., They that laugh last laugh best.　**126 cry** rumor
128 I . . . else Call me a complete rogue if I'm not telling the truth.
129 scored me scored off me, beaten me, made up my reckoning,
branded me.　**132 flattery** self-flattery, self-deception　**133 beckons**
signals to　**136 seabank** seashore　**137 bauble** plaything　**138 by
this hand** I make my vow　**144–5 not . . . to** (Othello imagines himself cutting off Cassio's nose and throwing it to a dog.)　**147 Before
me** i.e., On my soul　**148 'Tis . . . fitchew!** What a whore she is! Just
like all the others. (*Fitchew* or "polecat" was a common term of contempt for a courtesan or prostitute.)　**150 dam** mother　**153 A likely
. . . work** A fine story　**156 hobbyhorse** harlot.　**161 should be** must
be　**164 when . . . for** when I'm ready for you (i.e., never).

CASSIO   Prithee, come. Will you?

IAGO   Go to. Say no more.   [*Exit Cassio.*] 172

OTHELLO [*advancing*]   How shall I murder him, Iago?

IAGO   Did you perceive how he laughed at his vice?

OTHELLO   Oh, Iago!

IAGO   And did you see the handkerchief?

OTHELLO   Was that mine?

IAGO   Yours, by this hand. And to see how he prizes
the foolish woman your wife! She gave it him, and he
hath given it his whore.

OTHELLO   I would have him nine years a-killing. A fine
woman! A fair woman! A sweet woman!

IAGO   Nay, you must forget that.

OTHELLO   Ay, let her rot and perish, and be damned
tonight, for she shall not live. No, my heart is turned
to stone; I strike it, and it hurts my hand. Oh, the world
hath not a sweeter creature! She might lie by an emperor's side and command him tasks.

IAGO   Nay, that's not your way.   189

OTHELLO   Hang her! I do but say what she is. So delicate
with her needle! An admirable musician! Oh, she will
sing the savageness out of a bear. Of so high and plenteous wit and invention!   193

IAGO   She's the worse for all this.

OTHELLO   Oh, a thousand, a thousand times! And then,
of so gentle a condition!   196

IAGO   Ay, too gentle.   197

OTHELLO   Nay, that's certain. But yet the pity of it, Iago!
Oh, Iago, the pity of it, Iago!

IAGO   If you are so fond over her iniquity, give her patent 200
to offend, for if it touch not you it comes near nobody.

OTHELLO   I will chop her into messes. Cuckold me?   202

IAGO   Oh, 'tis foul in her.

OTHELLO   With mine officer?

IAGO   That's fouler.

OTHELLO   Get me some poison, Iago, this night. I'll not
expostulate with her, lest her body and beauty unpro- 207
vide my mind again. This night, Iago.   208

IAGO   Do it not with poison. Strangle her in her bed,
even the bed she hath contaminated.

OTHELLO   Good, good! The justice of it pleases. Very good.

IAGO   And for Cassio, let me be his undertaker. You 212
shall hear more by midnight.

OTHELLO
Excellent good. [*A trumpet within.*] What trumpet is
that same?

IAGO   I warrant, something from Venice.

Enter Lodovico, Desdemona, and attendants.

'Tis Lodovico. This comes from the Duke.
See, your wife's with him.

LODOVICO
God save you, worthy General!

OTHELLO   With all my heart, sir. 218

LODOVICO [*giving him a letter*]
The Duke and the senators of Venice greet you.

OTHELLO
I kiss the instrument of their pleasures.
                    [*He opens the letter, and reads.*]

DESDEMONA
And what's the news, good cousin Lodovico?

IAGO
I am very glad to see you, signor.
Welcome to Cyprus.

LODOVICO
I thank you. How does Lieutenant Cassio?

IAGO   Lives, sir.

DESDEMONA
Cousin, there's fall'n between him and my lord
An unkind breach; but you shall make all well.   227

OTHELLO   Are you sure of that?

DESDEMONA   My lord?

OTHELLO [*reads*]   "This fail you not to do, as you will—"

LODOVICO
He did not call; he's busy in the paper.
Is there division twixt my lord and Cassio?

DESDEMONA
A most unhappy one. I would do much
T'atone them, for the love I bear to Cassio.   234

OTHELLO   Fire and brimstone!

DESDEMONA   My lord?

OTHELLO   Are you wise?

DESDEMONA
What, is he angry?

LODOVICO   Maybe the letter moved him;
For, as I think, they do command him home,
Deputing Cassio in his government.   240

DESDEMONA   By my troth, I am glad on't.   241

OTHELLO   Indeed?

DESDEMONA   My lord?

OTHELLO   I am glad to see you mad.   244

DESDEMONA   Why, sweet Othello—

OTHELLO [*striking her*]   Devil!

DESDEMONA   I have not deserved this.

LODOVICO
My lord, this would not be believed in Venice,
Though I should swear I saw't. 'Tis very much.   249
Make her amends; she weeps.

OTHELLO   Oh, devil, devil!
If that the earth could teem with woman's tears,   251
Each drop she falls would prove a crocodile.   252
Out of my sight!

DESDEMONA   I will not stay to offend you. [*Going.*]

---

172 **Go to** (An expression of remonstrance.)   189 **your way** i.e., the
way you should think of her.   193 **invention** imagination.   196 **gentle a condition** wellborn and well-bred.   197 **gentle** generous, yielding (to other men).   200 **fond** foolish.   **patent** license   202 **messes**
portions of meat, i.e., bits.   207–8 **unprovide** weaken, disarm
212 **be his undertaker** undertake to dispatch him.

218 **With all my heart** i.e., I thank you most heartily   227 **unkind**
unnatural, contrary to their natures; hurtful   234 **T'atone** to reconcile
240 **government** office.   241 **on't** of it.   244 **I am . . . mad** i.e., I am
glad to see that you are insane enough to rejoice in Cassio's promotion. (? Othello bitterly plays on Desdemona's *I am glad*.)   249 **very**
much too much, outrageous.   251 **teem** breed, be impregnated
252 **falls** lets fall.   **crocodile** (Crocodiles were supposed to weep
hypocritical tears for their victims.)

LODOVICO   Truly, an obedient lady.
I do beseech Your Lordship, call her back.
OTHELLO [*calling*]   Mistress!
DESDEMONA [*returning*]   My lord?
OTHELLO   What would you with her, sir?   258
LODOVICO   Who, I, my lord?
OTHELLO
Ay, you did wish that I would make her turn.
Sir, she can turn, and turn, and yet go on
And turn again; and she can weep, sir, weep;
And she's obedient, as you say, obedient,   263
Very obedient.—Proceed you in your tears.—
Concerning this, sir—Oh, well-painted passion!—   265
I am commanded home.—Get you away;
I'll send for you anon.—Sir, I obey the mandate
And will return to Venice.—Hence, avaunt!
                              [*Exit Desdemona.*]
Cassio shall have my place. And, sir, tonight
I do entreat that we may sup together.
You are welcome, sir, to Cyprus.—Goats and
    monkeys!   *Exit.* 271
LODOVICO
Is this the noble Moor whom our full Senate
Call all in all sufficient? Is this the nature
Whom passion could not shake? Whose solid virtue
The shot of accident nor dart of chance
Could neither graze nor pierce?
IAGO   He is much changed.
LODOVICO
Are his wits safe? Is he not light of brain?
IAGO
He's that he is. I may not breathe my censure   278
What he might be. If what he might he is not,   279
I would to heaven he were!
LODOVICO   What, strike his wife?   280
IAGO
Faith, that was not so well; yet would I knew
That stroke would prove the worst!
LODOVICO   Is it his use?   282
Or did the letters work upon his blood   283
And new-create his fault?
IAGO   Alas, alas!
It is not honesty in me to speak
What I have seen and known. You shall observe him,
And his own courses will denote him so   287
That I may save my speech. Do but go after,
And mark how he continues.
LODOVICO
I am sorry that I am deceived in him.   *Exeunt.*

❧

4.2

Enter Othello and Emilia.

OTHELLO   You have seen nothing, then?
EMILIA
Nor ever heard, nor ever did suspect.
OTHELLO
Yes, you have seen Cassio and she together.
EMILIA
But then I saw no harm, and then I heard
Each syllable that breath made up between them.
OTHELLO   What, did they never whisper?
EMILIA   Never, my lord.
OTHELLO   Nor send you out o'th' way?
EMILIA   Never.
OTHELLO
To fetch her fan, her gloves, her mask, nor nothing?
EMILIA   Never, my lord.
OTHELLO   That's strange.
EMILIA
I durst, my lord, to wager she is honest,
Lay down my soul at stake. If you think other,   14
Remove your thought; it doth abuse your bosom.   15
If any wretch have put this in your head,
Let heaven requite it with the serpent's curse!   17
For if she be not honest, chaste, and true,
There's no man happy; the purest of their wives
Is foul as slander.
OTHELLO   Bid her come hither. Go.
                          Exit Emilia.   21
She says enough; yet she's a simple bawd   21
That cannot say as much. This is a subtle whore,   22
A closet lock and key of villainous secrets.   23
And yet she'll kneel and pray; I have seen her do't.

Enter Desdemona and Emilia.

DESDEMONA   My lord, what is your will?
OTHELLO   Pray you, chuck, come hither.
DESDEMONA
What is your pleasure?
OTHELLO   Let me see your eyes.
Look in my face.
DESDEMONA   What horrible fancy's this?
OTHELLO [*to Emilia*]   Some of your function, mistress.   29
Leave procreants alone and shut the door;   30
Cough or cry "hem" if anybody come.
Your mystery, your mystery! Nay, dispatch.   32
                          Exit Emilia.
DESDEMONA [*kneeling*]
Upon my knees, what doth your speech import?

258 What . . . sir? (Othello implies that Desdemona is pliant and will do a *turn* sexually with any man.)   263 obedient (With much the same sexual connotation as *turn* in lines 260–2.)   265 passion i.e., grief.   271 Goats and monkeys (See 3.3.419.)   278–80 I may . . . were! I dare not venture an opinion as to whether he's of unsound mind, as you suggest, but, if he isn't, then it might be better to wish he were in fact insane, since only that could excuse his wild behavior!   282 use custom.   283 blood passions   287 courses will denote actions will reveal

4.2. Location: The citadel.
14 at stake as the wager.   15 abuse your bosom deceive your breast, your heart.   17 the serpent's curse the curse pronounced by God on the serpent for deceiving Eve, just as some man has done to Othello and Desdemona. (See Genesis 3:14.)   21–2 she's . . . much i.e., any procuress or go-between who couldn't make up as plausible a story as Emilia's would have to be pretty stupid.   22 This i.e., Desdemona   23 closet lock and key i.e., concealer   29 Some . . . function i.e., Practice your chosen profession, that of bawd (by guarding the door)   30 procreants mating couples   32 mystery trade, occupation

I understand a fury in your words,
But not the words.

OTHELLO
Why, what art thou?

DESDEMONA   Your wife, my lord, your true
And loyal wife.

OTHELLO   Come, swear it, damn thyself,
Lest, being like one of heaven, the devils themselves   38
Should fear to seize thee. Therefore be double
    damned:
Swear thou art honest.

DESDEMONA   Heaven doth truly know it.

OTHELLO
Heaven truly knows that thou art false as hell.

DESDEMONA
To whom, my lord? With whom? How am I false?

OTHELLO [weeping]
Ah, Desdemon! Away, away, away!

DESDEMONA
Alas the heavy day! Why do you weep?
Am I the motive of these tears, my lord?   45
If haply you my father do suspect
An instrument of this your calling back,
Lay not your blame on me. If you have lost him,
I have lost him too.

OTHELLO   Had it pleased heaven
To try me with affliction, had they rained   50
All kinds of sores and shames on my bare head,
Steeped me in poverty to the very lips,
Given to captivity me and my utmost hopes,
I should have found in some place of my soul
A drop of patience. But, alas, to make me
A fixèd figure for the time of scorn   56
To point his slow and moving finger at!   57
Yet could I bear that too, well, very well.
But there where I have garnered up my heart,   59
Where either I must live or bear no life,
The fountain from the which my current runs   61
Or else dries up—to be discarded thence!
Or keep it as a cistern for foul toads   63
To knot and gender in! Turn thy complexion there,   64
Patience, thou young and rose-lipped cherubin—   65
Ay, there look grim as hell!   66

DESDEMONA
I hope my noble lord esteems me honest.   67

OTHELLO
Oh, ay, as summer flies are in the shambles,   68
That quicken even with blowing. O thou weed,   69
Who art so lovely fair and smell'st so sweet
That the sense aches at thee, would thou hadst ne'er
    been born!

DESDEMONA
Alas, what ignorant sin have I committed?   72

OTHELLO
Was this fair paper, this most goodly book,
Made to write "whore" upon? What committed?
Committed? Oh, thou public commoner!   75
I should make very forges of my cheeks,
That would to cinders burn up modesty,
Did I but speak thy deeds. What committed?
Heaven stops the nose at it and the moon winks;   79
The bawdy wind, that kisses all it meets,   80
Is hushed within the hollow mine of earth   81
And will not hear't. What committed?
Impudent strumpet!

DESDEMONA   By heaven, you do me wrong.

OTHELLO
Are not you a strumpet?

DESDEMONA   No, as I am a Christian.
If to preserve this vessel for my lord   86
From any other foul unlawful touch
Be not to be a strumpet, I am none.

OTHELLO   What, not a whore?

DESDEMONA   No, as I shall be saved.

OTHELLO   Is't possible?

DESDEMONA
Oh, heaven forgive us!

OTHELLO   I cry you mercy, then.   92
I took you for that cunning whore of Venice
That married with Othello. [Calling out] You, mistress,
That have the office opposite to Saint Peter
And keep the gate of hell!

        Enter Emilia.

                    You, you, ay, you!
We have done our course. There's money for your
    pains.   [He gives money.]   97
I pray you, turn the key and keep our counsel.   Exit.

EMILIA
Alas, what does this gentleman conceive?   99
How do you, madam? How do you, my good lady?

DESDEMONA   Faith, half asleep.   101

EMILIA
Good madam, what's the matter with my lord?

DESDEMONA   With who?

EMILIA   Why, with my lord, madam.

DESDEMONA
Who is thy lord?

EMILIA   He that is yours, sweet lady.

DESDEMONA
I have none. Do not talk to me, Emilia.
I cannot weep, nor answers have I none
But what should go by water. Prithee, tonight   108

38 being . . . heaven looking like an angel   **45 motive** cause   **50 they** the heavenly powers   **56–7 A fixèd . . . finger at** a figure of ridicule to be pointed at scornfully for all of eternity by the slowly moving finger of Time.   **59 garnered** stored   **61 fountain** spring   **63 cistern** cesspool   **64 To . . . gender in** to couple sexually and conceive in.   **64–6 Turn . . . hell!** Direct your gaze there, Patience, and your youthful and rosy cherubic countenance will turn grim and pale at this hellish spectacle!   **67 honest** chaste.   **68 shambles** slaughterhouse   **69 That . . . blowing** that come to life with the puffing up of the rotten meat on which the flies and their maggots are breeding.

72 ignorant sin sin in ignorance   **75 commoner** prostitute.   **79 winks** closes her eyes. (The moon symbolizes chastity.)   **80 bawdy** kissing one and all   **81 mine** cave (where the winds were thought to dwell)   **86 vessel** body   **92 cry you mercy** beg your pardon. (Sarcastic.)   **97 course** business. (With an indecent suggestion of "trick," turn at sex.)   **99 conceive** suppose, think.   **101 half asleep** i.e., dazed.   **108 go by water** be conveyed by tears.

Lay on my bed my wedding sheets, remember;
And call thy husband hither.
EMILIA   Here's a change indeed!   *Exit.*
DESDEMONA
'Tis meet I should be used so, very meet.   112
How have I been behaved, that he might stick   113
The small'st opinion on my least misuse?   114

Enter Iago and Emilia.

IAGO
What is your pleasure, madam? How is't with you?
DESDEMONA
I cannot tell. Those that do teach young babes
Do it with gentle means and easy tasks.
He might have chid me so, for, in good faith,
I am a child to chiding.
IAGO   What is the matter, lady?
EMILIA
Alas, Iago, my lord hath so bewhored her,
Thrown such despite and heavy terms upon her,
That true hearts cannot bear it.
DESDEMONA   Am I that name, Iago?
IAGO   What name, fair lady?
DESDEMONA
Such as she said my lord did say I was.
EMILIA
He called her whore. A beggar in his drink
Could not have laid such terms upon his callet.   128
IAGO   Why did he so?
DESDEMONA   [*weeping*]
I do not know. I am sure I am none such.
IAGO   Do not weep, do not weep. Alas the day!
EMILIA
Hath she forsook so many noble matches,
Her father and her country and her friends,
To be called whore? Would it not make one weep?
DESDEMONA
It is my wretched fortune.
IAGO   Beshrew him for't!   135
How comes this trick upon him?
DESDEMONA   Nay, heaven doth know. 136
EMILIA
I will be hanged if some eternal villain,   137
Some busy and insinuating rogue,   138
Some cogging, cozening slave, to get some office,   139
Have not devised this slander. I will be hanged else.
IAGO
Fie, there is no such man. It is impossible.
DESDEMONA
If any such there be, heaven pardon him!
EMILIA
A halter pardon him! And hell gnaw his bones!   143

Why should he call her whore? Who keeps her
   company?
What place? What time? What form? What
   likelihood?   145
The Moor's abused by some most villainous knave,
Some base notorious knave, some scurvy fellow.
Oh, heavens, that such companions thou'dst unfold, 148
And put in every honest hand a whip
To lash the rascals naked through the world
Even from the east to th' west!
IAGO   Speak within door.   151
EMILIA
Oh, fie upon them! Some such squire he was   152
That turned your wit the seamy side without   153
And made you to suspect me with the Moor.
IAGO
You are a fool. Go to.
DESDEMONA   Oh, God, Iago,   155
What shall I do to win my lord again?
Good friend, go to him; for, by this light of heaven,
I know not how I lost him. Here I kneel. [*She kneels.*]
If e'er my will did trespass 'gainst his love,
Either in discourse of thought or actual deed,   160
Or that mine eyes, mine ears, or any sense   161
Delighted them in any other form;   162
Or that I do not yet, and ever did,   163
And ever will—though he do shake me off
To beggarly divorcement—love him dearly,
Comfort forswear me! Unkindness may do much,   166
And his unkindness may defeat my life,   167
But never taint my love. I cannot say "whore."
It does abhor me now I speak the word;   169
To do the act that might the addition earn   170
Not the world's mass of vanity could make me.   171
                                               [*She rises.*]
IAGO
I pray you, be content. 'Tis but his humor.   172
The business of the state does him offense,
And he does chide with you.
DESDEMONA   If 'twere no other—
IAGO   It is but so, I warrant.   [*Trumpets within.*]
Hark, how these instruments summon you to supper!
The messengers of Venice stays the meat.   178
Go in, and weep not. All things shall be well.
                        Exeunt Desdemona and Emilia.

Enter Roderigo.

How now, Roderigo?
RODERIGO   I do not find that thou deal'st justly with me.
IAGO   What in the contrary?

---

112 **'Tis . . . very meet** i.e., It must be I somehow have deserved this.
113–14 How . . . misuse? What have I done that prompts Othello to
attach even the slightest censure to whatever little fault I may have
committed?   **128 callet** whore.   **135 Beshrew** May evil befall. (An
oath.)   **136 trick** strange behavior, delusion   **137 eternal** inveterate
138 insinuating ingratiating, fawning, wheedling   **139 cogging, cozening** cheating, defrauding   **143 halter** hangman's noose

145 form manner, circumstance.   **148 that . . . unfold** would that you
would expose such fellows   **151 within door** i.e., not so loud.
152 squire fellow   **153 seamy side without** wrong side out   **155 Go
to** i.e., That's enough.   **160 discourse of thought** process of thinking
161 that if. (Also in line 163.)   **162 Delighted them** took delight
163 yet still   **166 Comfort forswear** may heavenly comfort forsake
167 defeat destroy   **169 abhor** (1) fill me with abhorrence (2) make
me whorelike   **170 addition** title   **171 vanity** showy splendor
172 humor mood.   **178 stays the meat** are waiting to dine.

RODERIGO   Every day thou daff'st me with some device, 183
Iago, and rather, as it seems to me now, keep'st
from me all conveniency than suppliest me with the 185
least advantage of hope. I will indeed no longer 186
endure it, nor am I yet persuaded to put up in peace 187
what already I have foolishly suffered.

IAGO   Will you hear me, Roderigo?

RODERIGO   Faith, I have heard too much, for your words
and performances are no kin together.

IAGO   You charge me most unjustly.

RODERIGO   With naught but truth. I have wasted myself
out of my means. The jewels you have had from me to
deliver Desdemona would half have corrupted a vo- 195
tarist. You have told me she hath received them and 196
returned me expectations and comforts of sudden re- 197
spect and acquaintance, but I find none. 198

IAGO   Well, go to, very well.

RODERIGO   "Very well"! "Go to"! I cannot go to, man, 200
nor 'tis not very well. By this hand, I think it is scurvy,
and begin to find myself fopped in it. 202

IAGO   Very well.

RODERIGO   I tell you 'tis not very well. I will make myself 204
known to Desdemona. If she will return me my jewels,
I will give over my suit and repent my unlawful solicitation; if not, assure yourself I will seek satisfaction 207
of you.

IAGO   You have said now? 209

RODERIGO   Ay, and said nothing but what I protest 210
intendment of doing. 211

IAGO   Why, now I see there's mettle in thee, and even
from this instant do build on thee a better opinion
than ever before. Give me thy hand, Roderigo. Thou
hast taken against me a most just exception; but yet I
protest I have dealt most directly in thy affair.

RODERIGO   It hath not appeared.

IAGO   I grant indeed it hath not appeared, and your
suspicion is not without wit and judgment. But,
Roderigo, if thou hast that in thee indeed which I have
greater reason to believe now than ever—I mean
purpose, courage, and valor—this night show it. If
thou the next night following enjoy not Desdemona,
take me from this world with treachery and devise
engines for my life. 225

RODERIGO   Well, what is it? Is it within reason and
compass?

IAGO   Sir, there is especial commission come from
Venice to depute Cassio in Othello's place.

RODERIGO   Is that true? Why, then Othello and Desdemona return again to Venice.

IAGO   Oh, no; he goes into Mauritania and takes away
with him the fair Desdemona, unless his abode be
lingered here by some accident; wherein none can be
so determinate as the removing of Cassio. 235

RODERIGO   How do you mean, removing of him?

IAGO   Why, by making him uncapable of Othello's
place—knocking out his brains.

RODERIGO   And that you would have me to do?

IAGO   Ay, if you dare do yourself a profit and a right.
He sups tonight with a harlotry, and thither will I go to 241
him. He knows not yet of his honorable fortune. If
you will watch his going thence, which I will fashion
to fall out between twelve and one, you may take him 244
at your pleasure. I will be near to second your attempt,
and he shall fall between us. Come, stand not amazed
at it, but go along with me. I will show you such a
necessity in his death that you shall think yourself
bound to put it on him. It is now high suppertime, 249
and the night grows to waste. About it. 250

RODERIGO   I will hear further reason for this.

IAGO   And you shall be satisfied.   *Exeunt.*

4.3

*Enter Othello, Lodovico, Desdemona, Emilia, and
attendants.*

LODOVICO
I do beseech you, sir, trouble yourself no further.

OTHELLO
Oh, pardon me; 'twill do me good to walk.

LODOVICO
Madam, good night. I humbly thank Your Ladyship.

DESDEMONA
Your Honor is most welcome.

OTHELLO   Will you walk, sir?
Oh, Desdemona!

DESDEMONA   My lord?

OTHELLO   Get you to bed on th'instant. I will be returned forthwith. Dismiss your attendant there. Look't
be done.

DESDEMONA   I will, my lord.
        Exit [Othello, with Lodovico and attendants].

EMILIA   How goes it now? He looks gentler than he did.

DESDEMONA
He says he will return incontinent, 12
And hath commanded me to go to bed,
And bid me to dismiss you.

EMILIA   Dismiss me?

DESDEMONA
It was his bidding. Therefore, good Emilia,
Give me my nightly wearing, and adieu.
We must not now displease him.

EMILIA   I would you had never seen him!

---

183 **thou daff'st me** you put me off.   **device** excuse, trick
185 **conveniency** advantage, opportunity   186 **advantage** increase
187 **put up** submit to, tolerate   195 **deliver** deliver to   195–6 **votarist**
nun.   197-8 **sudden respect** immediate consideration   200 **I cannot
go to** (Roderigo changes Iago's *go to,* an expression urging patience,
to *I cannot go to,* "I have no opportunity for success in wooing.")
202 **fopped** fooled, duped   204 **not very well** (Roderigo changes
Iago's *Very well,* "All right, then," to *not very well,* "not at all good.")
207 **satisfaction** repayment. (The term normally means settling of
accounts in a duel.)   209 **You . . . now?** Have you finished?
210–11 **protest intendment** avow my intention   225 **engines** plots,
snares

235 **determinate** conclusive, instrumental   241 **harlotry** slut
244 **fall out** occur   249 **high** fully   250 **grows to waste** wastes away.
4.3. Location: The citadel.
12 **incontinent** immediately

DESDEMONA

So would not I. My love doth so approve him
That even his stubbornness, his checks, his frowns— 21
Prithee, unpin me—have grace and favor in them.

[Emilia prepares Desdemona for bed.]

EMILIA   I have laid those sheets you bade me on the
bed.

DESDEMONA

All's one. Good faith, how foolish are our minds! 25
If I do die before thee, prithee shroud me
In one of these same sheets.

EMILIA   Come, come, you talk. 27

DESDEMONA

My mother had a maid called Barbary.
She was in love, and he she loved proved mad 29
And did forsake her. She had a song of "Willow."
An old thing 'twas, but it expressed her fortune,
And she died singing it. That song tonight
Will not go from my mind; I have much to do 33
But to go hang my head all at one side 34
And sing it like poor Barbary. Prithee, dispatch.

EMILIA   Shall I go fetch your nightgown? 36

DESDEMONA   No, unpin me here.
This Lodovico is a proper man. 38

EMILIA   A very handsome man.

DESDEMONA   He speaks well.

EMILIA   I know a lady in Venice would have walked
barefoot to Palestine for a touch of his nether lip.

DESDEMONA *[singing]*

"The poor soul sat sighing by a sycamore tree,
    Sing all a green willow; 44
Her hand on her bosom, her head on her knee,
    Sing willow, willow, willow.
The fresh streams ran by her and murmured her
    moans;
    Sing willow, willow, willow;
Her salt tears fell from her, and softened the
    stones—"
Lay by these.
[Singing] "Sing willow, willow, willow—"
Prithee, hie thee. He'll come anon. 52
[Singing] "Sing all a green willow must be my garland.
    Let nobody blame him; his scorn I approve—"
Nay, that's not next.—Hark! Who is't that knocks?

EMILIA   It's the wind.

DESDEMONA *[singing]*

"I called my love false love; but what said he
    then?
    Sing willow, willow, willow;
If I court more women, you'll couch with more
    men."
So, get thee gone. Good night. Mine eyes do itch;
Doth that bode weeping?

EMILIA   'Tis neither here nor there.

DESDEMONA

I have heard it said so. Oh, these men, these men!
Dost thou in conscience think—tell me, Emilia—
That there be women do abuse their husbands 64
In such gross kind?

EMILIA   There be some such, no question.

DESDEMONA

Wouldst thou do such a deed for all the world?

EMILIA

Why, would not you?

DESDEMONA   No, by this heavenly light!

EMILIA

Nor I neither by this heavenly light;
I might do't as well i'th' dark.

DESDEMONA

Wouldst thou do such a deed for all the world?

EMILIA

The world's a huge thing. It is a great price
For a small vice.

DESDEMONA

Good troth, I think thou wouldst not.

EMILIA   By my troth, I think I should, and undo't when
I had done. Marry, I would not do such a thing for a
joint ring, nor for measures of lawn, nor for gowns, 76
petticoats, nor caps, nor any petty exhibition. But for 77
all the whole world! Uds pity, who would not make 78
her husband a cuckold to make him a monarch? I
should venture Purgatory for't.

DESDEMONA

Beshrew me if I would do such a wrong
For the whole world.

EMILIA   Why, the wrong is but a wrong i'th' world, and
having the world for your labor, 'tis a wrong in your
own world, and you might quickly make it right.

DESDEMONA

I do not think there is any such woman.

EMILIA   Yes, a dozen, and as many 87
To th' vantage as would store the world they played
    for. 88
But I do think it is their husbands' faults
If wives do fall. Say that they slack their duties 90
And pour our treasures into foreign laps, 91
Or else break out in peevish jealousies,
Throwing restraint upon us? Or say they strike us, 93
Or scant our former having in despite? 94
Why, we have galls, and though we have some grace, 95
Yet have we some revenge. Let husbands know
Their wives have sense like them. They see, and smell, 97
And have their palates both for sweet and sour,
As husbands have. What is it that they do 99

---

21 **stubbornness** roughness.   **checks** rebukes   25 **All's one** All
right. It doesn't really matter.   27 **talk** i.e., prattle.   29 **mad** wild,
lunatic   33-4 **I . . . hang** I can scarcely keep myself from hanging
36 **nightgown** dressing gown.   38 **proper** handsome   44 **willow**
(A conventional emblem of disappointed love.)   52 **hie thee** hurry.
anon right away.

64 **abuse** deceive   76 **joint ring** a ring made in separate halves.
lawn fine linen   77 **exhibition** gift.   78 **Uds** God's   87–8 **and . . .
played for** and enough additionally to stock the world men have
gambled and sported sexually for.   90 **they** our husbands.   **duties**
marital duties   91 **pour . . . laps** i.e., are unfaithful, give what is
rightfully ours (semen) to other women   93 **Throwing . . . us** jeal-
ously restricting our freedom.   94 **Or . . . despite** or spitefully take
away from us whatever we enjoyed before.   95 **have galls** i.e., are
capable of resenting injury and insult.   **grace** inclination to be merciful   97 **sense** sensory perception and appetite   99 **they** husbands

When they change us for others? Is it sport?   100
I think it is. And doth affection breed it?   101
I think it doth. Is't frailty that thus errs?
It is so, too. And have not we affections,
Desires for sport, and frailty, as men have?
Then let them use us well; else let them know,
The ills we do, their ills instruct us so.

DESDEMONA
Good night, good night. God me such uses send   107
Not to pick bad from bad, but by bad mend!   108

Exeunt.

❦

5.1

Enter Iago and Roderigo.

IAGO
Here stand behind this bulk. Straight will he come.   1
Wear thy good rapier bare, and put it home.   2
Quick, quick! Fear nothing. I'll be at thy elbow.
It makes us or it mars us. Think on that,
And fix most firm thy resolution.

RODERIGO
Be near at hand. I may miscarry in't.

IAGO
Here, at thy hand. Be bold, and take thy stand.
[*Iago stands aside, Roderigo conceals himself.*]

RODERIGO
I have no great devotion to the deed;
And yet he hath given me satisfying reasons.
'Tis but a man gone. Forth, my sword! He dies.
[*He draws.*]

IAGO
I have rubbed this young quat almost to the sense,   11
And he grows angry. Now, whether he kill Cassio
Or Cassio him, or each do kill the other,
Every way makes my gain. Live Roderigo,   14
He calls me to a restitution large
Of gold and jewels that I bobbed from him   16
As gifts to Desdemona.
It must not be. If Cassio do remain,
He hath a daily beauty in his life
That makes me ugly; and besides, the Moor
May unfold me to him; there stand I in much peril.   21
No, he must die. Be't so. I hear him coming.

Enter Cassio.

RODERIGO [*coming forth*]
I know his gait, 'tis he.—Villain, thou diest!
[*He attacks Cassio.*]

CASSIO
That thrust had been mine enemy indeed,
But that my coat is better than thou know'st.   25
I will make proof of thine.
[*He draws, and wounds Roderigo.*]

RODERIGO   Oh, I am slain!   [*He falls.*   26
*Iago, from behind, wounds Cassio
in the leg, and exit.*]

CASSIO
I am maimed forever. Help, ho! Murder! Murder!

Enter Othello.

OTHELLO   The voice of Cassio! Iago keeps his word.
RODERIGO   Oh, villain that I am!
OTHELLO   It is even so.
CASSIO   Oh, help, ho! Light! A surgeon!
OTHELLO
'Tis he. O brave Iago, honest and just,
That hast such noble sense of thy friend's wrong!
Thou teachest me.—Minion, your dear lies dead,   34
And your unblest fate hies. Strumpet, I come.   35
Forth of my heart those charms, thine eyes, are blotted;   36
Thy bed, lust-stained, shall with lust's blood be
spotted.   *Exit Othello.*

Enter Lodovico and Gratiano.

CASSIO
What ho! No watch? No passage? Murder! Murder!   38
GRATIANO
'Tis some mischance. The voice is very direful.
CASSIO   Oh, help!
LODOVICO   Hark!
RODERIGO   Oh, wretched villain!
LODOVICO
Two or three groan. 'Tis heavy night;   43
These may be counterfeits. Let's think't unsafe
To come in to the cry without more help.   45
[*They remain near the entrance.*]

RODERIGO
Nobody come? Then shall I bleed to death.

Enter Iago [in his shirtsleeves, with a light].

LODOVICO   Hark!
GRATIANO
Here's one comes in his shirt, with light and weapons.
IAGO
Who's there? Whose noise is this that cries on murder?   49
LODOVICO
We do not know.
IAGO   Did not you hear a cry?
CASSIO
Here, here! For heaven's sake, help me!
IAGO   What's the matter?
[*He moves toward Cassio.*]

---

100 change exchange.   **sport** sexual pastime.   **101 affection** passion
107 uses habit, practice   **108 Not . . . mend** i.e., not to learn bad conduct from others' badness (as Emilia has suggested women learn
from men), but to mend my ways by perceiving what badness is,
making spiritual benefit out of evil and adversity.
5.1. Location: A street in Cyprus.
1 bulk framework projecting from the front of a shop.   **2 bare**
unsheathed.   **home** all the way into the target.   **11 quat** pimple,
pustule.   **to the sense** to the quick   **14 Live Roderigo** If Roderigo
lives   **16 bobbed** swindled   **21 unfold** expose

25 coat (Possibly a garment of mail under the outer clothing, or simply a tougher coat than Roderigo expected.)   **26 proof** a test
34 Minion Hussy (i.e., Desdemona)   **35 hies** hastens on.   **36 Forth
of** From out   **38 passage** people passing by.   **43 heavy** thick, dark
45 come in to approach   **49 cries** cries out

GRATIANO [to Lodovico]
 This is Othello's ancient, as I take it.

LODOVICO [to Gratiano]
 The same indeed, a very valiant fellow.

IAGO [to Cassio]
 What are you here that cry so grievously?   54

CASSIO
 Iago? Oh, I am spoiled, undone by villains!   55
 Give me some help.

IAGO
 Oh, me, Lieutenant! What villains have done this?

CASSIO
 I think that one of them is hereabout,
 And cannot make away.

IAGO   Oh, treacherous villains!   59
 [To Lodovico and Gratiano] What are you there? Come
   in, and give some help.   [They advance.]

RODERIGO   Oh, help me there!

CASSIO
 That's one of them.

IAGO   Oh, murderous slave! Oh, villain!
                                [He stabs Roderigo.]

RODERIGO
 Oh, damned Iago! Oh, inhuman dog!

IAGO
 Kill men i'th' dark?—Where be these bloody thieves?—
 How silent is this town!—Ho! Murder, murder!—
 [To Lodovico and Gratiano] What may you be? Are you
   of good or evil?

LODOVICO   As you shall prove us, praise us.   67

IAGO   Signor Lodovico?

LODOVICO   He, sir.

IAGO
 I cry you mercy. Here's Cassio hurt by villains.   70

GRATIANO   Cassio?

IAGO   How is't, brother?

CASSIO   My leg is cut in two.

IAGO   Marry, heaven forbid!
 Light, gentlemen! I'll bind it with my shirt.
       [He hands them the light, and tends to Cassio's
                                              wound.]

       Enter Bianca.

BIANCA
 What is the matter, ho? Who is't that cried?

IAGO   Who is't that cried?

BIANCA   Oh, my dear Cassio!
 My sweet Cassio! Oh, Cassio, Cassio, Cassio!

IAGO
 Oh, notable strumpet! Cassio, may you suspect
 Who they should be that have thus mangled you?

CASSIO   No.

GRATIANO
 I am sorry to find you thus. I have been to seek you.

IAGO
 Lend me a garter. [He applies a tourniquet.] So.—Oh, for
   a chair,   83
 To bear him easily hence!

BIANCA
 Alas, he faints! Oh, Cassio, Cassio, Cassio!

IAGO
 Gentlemen all, I do suspect this trash
 To be a party in this injury.—
 Patience awhile, good Cassio.—Come, come;
 Lend me a light. [He shines the light on Roderigo.] Know
   we this face or no?
 Alas, my friend and my dear countryman
 Roderigo! No.—Yes, sure.—Oh, heaven! Roderigo!

GRATIANO   What, of Venice?

IAGO   Even he, sir. Did you know him?

GRATIANO   Know him? Ay.

IAGO
 Signor Gratiano? I cry your gentle pardon.   95
 These bloody accidents must excuse my manners   96
 That so neglected you.

GRATIANO   I am glad to see you.

IAGO
 How do you, Cassio?—Oh, a chair, a chair!

GRATIANO   Roderigo!

IAGO
 He, he, 'tis he. [A litter is brought in.] Oh, that's well
   said; the chair.   100
 Some good man bear him carefully from hence;
 I'll fetch the General's surgeon. [To Bianca] For you,
   mistress,   102
 Save you your labor.—He that lies slain here, Cassio,   103
 Was my dear friend. What malice was between you?   104

CASSIO
 None in the world, nor do I know the man.

IAGO [to Bianca]
 What, look you pale?—Oh, bear him out o'th'air.   106
                    [Cassio and Roderigo are borne off.]
 Stay you, good gentlemen.—Look you pale,
   mistress?—   107
 Do you perceive the gastness of her eye?—   108
 Nay, if you stare, we shall hear more anon.—   109
 Behold her well; I pray you, look upon her.
 Do you see, gentlemen? Nay, guiltiness
 Will speak, though tongues were out of use.

       [Enter Emilia.]

EMILIA
 'Las, what's the matter? What's the matter, husand?

IAGO
 Cassio hath here been set on in the dark
 By Roderigo and fellows that are scaped.
 He's almost slain, and Roderigo dead.

---

54 **What** Who. (Also at lines 60 and 66.)   55 **spoiled** ruined, done for
59 **make** get   67 **prove us** prove us to be.   **praise** appraise   70 **I cry
you mercy** I beg your pardon.

83 **chair** litter   95 **gentle** noble   96 **accidents** sudden events
100 **well said** well done   102 **For** As for   103 **Save ... labor** i.e.,
never you mind tending Cassio.   104 **malice** enmity   106 **bear ...
air** (Fresh air was thought to be dangerous for a wound.)   107 **Stay
you** (Lodovico and Gratiano are evidently about to leave.)   108 **gastness** terror   109 **stare** (Iago pretends to interpret Bianca's wild looks
as an involuntary confession of guilt.)

EMILIA
Alas, good gentleman! Alas, good Cassio!
IAGO
This is the fruits of whoring. Prithee, Emilia,
Go know of Cassio where he supped tonight.   119
[*To Bianca*] What, do you shake at that?
BIANCA
He supped at my house, but I therefore shake not.
IAGO
Oh, did he so? I charge you go with me.
EMILIA   Oh, fie upon thee, strumpet!
BIANCA
I am no strumpet, but of life as honest   124
As you that thus abuse me.
EMILIA   As I? Faugh! Fie upon thee!
IAGO
Kind gentlemen, let's go see poor Cassio dressed.— 127
Come, mistress, you must tell 's another tale.—
Emilia, run you to the citadel
And tell my lord and lady what hath happed.—
Will you go on afore? [*Aside*] This is the night
That either makes me or fordoes me quite.   *Exeunt.* 132

❖

5.2

*Enter Othello [with a light], and Desdemona in
her bed.*

OTHELLO
It is the cause, it is the cause, my soul.   1
Let me not name it to you, you chaste stars!
It is the cause. Yet I'll not shed her blood,
Nor scar that whiter skin of hers than snow,
And smooth as monumental alabaster.   5
Yet she must die, else she'll betray more men.
Put out the light, and then put out the light.   7
If I quench thee, thou flaming minister,   8
I can again thy former light restore,
Should I repent me; but once put out thy light,   10
Thou cunning'st pattern of excelling nature,   11
I know not where is that Promethean heat   12
That can thy light relume. When I have plucked thy
     rose,   13
I cannot give it vital growth again;
It needs must wither. I'll smell thee on the tree.
                              [*He kisses her.*]
Oh, balmy breath, that dost almost persuade
Justice to break her sword! One more, one more.

119 **know** learn   124 **honest** chaste   127 **Cassio dressed** Cassio's
wounds dressed.   132 **fordoes** undoes, ruins
5.2. Location: A bedchamber in the citadel.
0.1–2 *in her bed* (Either the curtains are drawn back to reveal the bed
in a recessed area backstage, or the bed is "thrust out" onstage as the
scene begins.)   1 **cause** i.e., cause of justice, the offense itself, which
must be corrected in the name of justice   5 **monumental** i.e., used in
making tombs and funeral monuments   7 **the light . . . light** the
torch or lamp . . . Desdemona's life.   8 **minister** servant   10 **repent
me** change my mind   11 **Thou . . . pattern** you skillfully wrought
perfect example   12 **Promethean heat** (Alludes to two myths: that of
Prometheus stealing fire from heaven for humanity, and that of his
creating humankind.)   13 **relume** rekindle.

Be thus when thou art dead, and I will kill thee,
And love thee after. One more, and that's the last.
                              [*He kisses her.*]
So sweet was ne'er so fatal. I must weep,
But they are cruel tears. This sorrow's heavenly; 21
It strikes where it doth love. She wakes.   22
DESDEMONA   Who's there? Othello?
OTHELLO   Ay, Desdemona.
DESDEMONA   Will you come to bed, my lord?
OTHELLO   Have you prayed tonight, Desdemon?
DESDEMONA   Ay, my lord.
OTHELLO
If you bethink yourself of any crime   28
Unreconciled as yet to heaven and grace,
Solicit for it straight.   30
DESDEMONA
Alack, my lord, what may you mean by that?
OTHELLO
Well, do it, and be brief. I will walk by.
I would not kill thy unpreparèd spirit.
No, heaven forfend! I would not kill thy soul.   34
DESDEMONA
Talk you of killing?
OTHELLO   Ay, I do.
DESDEMONA   Then heaven
Have mercy on me!
OTHELLO   Amen, with all my heart!
DESDEMONA
If you say so, I hope you will not kill me.
OTHELLO   Humh!
DESDEMONA
And yet I fear you; for you're fatal then
When your eyes roll so. Why I should fear I know not,
Since guiltiness I know not; but yet I feel I fear.
OTHELLO
Think on thy sins.
DESDEMONA   They are loves I bear to you.   42
OTHELLO   Ay, and for that thou diest.
DESDEMONA
That death's unnatural that kills for loving.
Alas, why gnaw you so your nether lip?
Some bloody passion shakes your very frame.
These are portents; but yet I hope, I hope,
They do not point on me.
OTHELLO   Peace, and be still!
DESDEMONA   I will so. What's the matter?
OTHELLO
That handkerchief which I so loved and gave thee
Thou gav'st to Cassio.
DESDEMONA   No, by my life and soul!
Send for the man and ask him.
OTHELLO
Sweet soul, take heed, take heed of perjury.
Thou art on thy deathbed.

21 **they are cruel tears** these tears betoken a sorrowful cruelty, regrettable but just.   22 **It . . . love** (Compare Hebrews 12:6: "For whom the
Lord loveth he chasteneth.")   28 **crime** sin   30 **Solicit** petition, pray.
straight immediately.   34 **forfend** forbid.   42 **They . . . you** i.e., My
only sins are my idolatry of loving you too much.

DESDEMONA
Ay, but not yet to die.

OTHELLO   Yes, presently.   56
Therefore confess thee freely of thy sin;
For to deny each article with oath
Cannot remove nor choke the strong conception   59
That I do groan withal. Thou art to die.   60

DESDEMONA
Then Lord have mercy on me!

OTHELLO   I say, amen.

DESDEMONA
And have you mercy too! I never did
Offend you in my life; never loved Cassio
But with such general warranty of heaven   64
As I might love. I never gave him token.

OTHELLO
By heaven, I saw my handkerchief in 's hand.
Oh, perjured woman! Thou dost stone my heart,   67
And makes me call what I intend to do
A murder, which I thought a sacrifice.
I saw the handkerchief.

DESDEMONA   He found it, then.
I never gave it him. Send for him hither;
Let him confess a truth.

OTHELLO   He hath confessed.

DESDEMONA   What, my lord?

OTHELLO
That he hath used thee.

DESDEMONA   How? Unlawfully?

OTHELLO   Ay.

DESDEMONA
He will not say so.

OTHELLO   No, his mouth is stopped;
Honest Iago hath ta'en order for 't.   76

DESDEMONA
Oh, my fear interprets. What, is he dead?

OTHELLO
Had all his hairs been lives, my great revenge
Had stomach for them all.

DESDEMONA
Alas, he is betrayed and I undone!   [*She weeps.*]

OTHELLO
Out, strumpet! Weep'st thou for him to my face?

DESDEMONA
Oh, banish me, my lord, but kill me not!

OTHELLO   Down, strumpet!

DESDEMONA
Kill me tomorrow; let me live tonight!

OTHELLO   Nay, if you strive—

DESDEMONA
But half an hour!

OTHELLO   Being done, there is no pause.   86

DESDEMONA
But while I say one prayer!

OTHELLO   It is too late.
                       Smothers her.

EMILIA (*at the door*)
My lord, my lord! What, ho! My lord, my lord!

OTHELLO
What noise is this? Not dead? Not yet quite dead?
I that am cruel am yet merciful;
I would not have thee linger in thy pain.
                    [*He dispatches her.*]
So, so.

EMILIA (*within*)   What, ho! My lord, my lord!

OTHELLO   Who's there?

EMILIA [*within*]
Oh, good my lord, I would speak a word with you!

OTHELLO
Yes, 'tis Emilia.—By and by.—She's dead.
'Tis like she comes to speak of Cassio's death.—   95
The noise was here. Ha! No more moving?   96
Still as the grave. Shall she come in? Were 't good?—
I think she stirs again. No. What's best to do?
If she come in, she'll sure speak to my wife.
My wife! My wife! What wife? I have no wife.
Oh, insupportable! Oh, heavy hour!
Methinks it should be now a huge eclipse
Of sun and moon, and that th'affrighted globe
Should yawn at alteration.

EMILIA [*within*]   I do beseech you   104
That I may speak with you, O good my lord!

OTHELLO
I had forgot thee. Oh, come in, Emilia.—
Soft, by and by. Let me the curtains draw.—   107
   [*He closes the bedcurtains and opens the door.*]
Where art thou?

           Enter Emilia.

             What's the matter with thee now?

EMILIA
Oh, my good lord, yonder's foul murders done!

OTHELLO   What, now?

EMILIA   But now, my lord.

OTHELLO
It is the very error of the moon;   112
She comes more nearer earth than she was wont,   113
And makes men mad.   114

EMILIA
Cassio, my lord, hath killed a young Venetian
Called Roderigo.

OTHELLO   Roderigo killed?

---

56 presently immediately.   **59 conception** (1) belief in your guilt
(2) plan in my mind   **60 groan withal** (1) groan at in sorrow
(2) groan as in giving birth.   **64 warranty** sanction   **67 stone** turn to
stone, harden   **76 ta'en order** taken measures   **86 Being done** i.e.,
Since justice has begun its relentless course

95 like likely that   **96 here** (The Folio's "high" is possible, suggesting
that the commotion of the attack on Cassio was loud.)   **104 Should . . .
alteration** should gape wide in an earthquake, as if expressing
amazement at an eclipse. (According to Pliny, earthquakes often happen during eclipses. The cataclismic event here is especially terrifying
in that it imagines the impossible concurrence of a solar and lunar
eclipse—an apocalyptic scenario befitting the horror of Desdemona's
death.)   **107 Soft** Wait a minute   **112 error** aberration, irregularity
113 She Luna, the moon goddess   **114 mad** i.e., "lunatic."

And Cassio killed?

EMILIA   No, Cassio is not killed.

OTHELLO
Not Cassio killed? Then murder's out of tune,
And sweet revenge grows harsh.

DESDEMONA   Oh, falsely, falsely murdered!

EMILIA   Oh, Lord, what cry is that?

OTHELLO   That? What?

EMILIA
Out and alas, that was my lady's voice.   123
                    [*She opens the bedcurtains.*]
Help, help, ho, help! O lady, speak again!
Sweet Desdemona! O sweet mistress, speak!

DESDEMONA   A guiltless death I die.

EMILIA   Oh, who hath done this deed?

DESDEMONA   Nobody; I myself. Farewell.
Commend me to my kind lord. Oh, farewell! [*She dies.*]

OTHELLO
Why, how should she be murdered?

EMILIA   Alas, who knows?

OTHELLO
You heard her say herself it was not I.

EMILIA
She said so. I must needs report the truth.

OTHELLO
She's like a liar gone to burning hell!
'Twas I that killed her.

EMILIA   Oh, the more angel she,
And you the blacker devil!

OTHELLO
She turned to folly, and she was a whore.   136

EMILIA
Thou dost belie her, and thou art a devil.   137

OTHELLO   She was false as water.

EMILIA   Thou art rash as fire to say
That she was false. Oh, she was heavenly true!

OTHELLO
Cassio did top her. Ask thy husband else.   141
Oh, I were damned beneath all depth in hell
But that I did proceed upon just grounds
To this extremity. Thy husband knew it all.

EMILIA   My husband?

OTHELLO   Thy husband.

EMILIA   That she was false to wedlock?

OTHELLO
Ay, with Cassio. Nay, had she been true,
If heaven would make me such another world
Of one entire and perfect chrysolite,   150
I'd not have sold her for it.

EMILIA   My husband?

OTHELLO
Ay, 'twas he that told me on her first.
An honest man he is, and hates the slime
That sticks on filthy deeds.

EMILIA   My husband?

OTHELLO
What needs this iterance, woman? I say thy husband. 157

EMILIA
Oh, mistress, villainy hath made mocks with love!   158
My husband say she was false?

OTHELLO   He, woman;
I say thy husband. Dost understand the word?
My friend, thy husband, honest, honest Iago.

EMILIA
If he say so, may his pernicious soul
Rot half a grain a day! He lies to th' heart.
She was too fond of her most filthy bargain.

OTHELLO   Ha?   [*He draws.*]

EMILIA   Do thy worst!
This deed of thine is no more worthy heaven
Than thou wast worthy her.

OTHELLO   Peace, you were best.   168

EMILIA
Thou hast not half that power to do me harm
As I have to be hurt. O gull! O dolt!   170
As ignorant as dirt! Thou hast done a deed—
I care not for thy sword; I'll make thee known,
Though I lost twenty lives.—Help! Help, ho, help!
The Moor hath killed my mistress! Murder, murder!

Enter Montano, Gratiano, and Iago.

MONTANO
What is the matter? How now, General?

EMILIA
Oh, are you come, Iago? You have done well,
That men must lay their murders on your neck.   177

GRATIANO   What is the matter?

EMILIA [*to Iago*]
Disprove this villain, if thou be'st a man.
He says thou told'st him that his wife was false.
I know thou didst not; thou'rt not such a villain.   181
Speak, for my heart is full.

IAGO
I told him what I thought, and told no more
Than what he found himself was apt and true.   184

EMILIA
But did you ever tell him she was false?

IAGO   I did.

EMILIA
You told a lie, an odious, damnèd lie!
Upon my soul, a lie, a wicked lie.
She false with Cassio? Did you say with Cassio?

IAGO
With Cassio, mistress. Go to, charm your tongue.   190

EMILIA
I will not charm my tongue; I am bound to speak.
My mistress here lies murdered in her bed—

ALL   Oh, heavens forfend!

EMILIA
And your reports have set the murder on.

123 Out (A cry of dismay, intensifying *alas*.) **136 folly** i.e., wantonness, fleshly sin **137 belie** slander **141 else** i.e., if you don't believe me. **150 chrysolite** precious topaz **157 iterance** iteration, repetition **158 made mocks with** made a mockery of **168 Peace . . . best** You'd better be quiet. **170 to be hurt** i.e., to endure hurt. **gull** dupe. **177 on your neck** to your charge. **181 such a villain** such a villain as all that. **184 apt** plausible **190 charm** control

OTHELLO
Nay, stare not, masters. It is true indeed.
GRATIANO   'Tis a strange truth.
MONTANO
Oh, monstrous act!
EMILIA   Villainy, villainy, villainy!
I think upon't—I think I smell't! Oh, villainy!
I thought so then—I'll kill myself for grief—   199
Oh, villainy, villainy!
IAGO
What, are you mad? I charge you, get you home.
EMILIA
Good gentlemen, let me have leave to speak.
'Tis proper I obey him, but not now.
Perchance, Iago, I will ne'er go home.
OTHELLO
Oh! Oh! Oh!   [Othello falls on the bed.]
EMILIA   Nay, lay thee down and roar,   205
For thou hast killed the sweetest innocent
That e'er did lift up eye.
OTHELLO [rising]   Oh, she was foul!   207
I scarce did know you, uncle. There lies your niece,
Whose breath indeed these hands have newly
    stopped.
I know this act shows horrible and grim.   210
GRATIANO
Poor Desdemon! I am glad thy father's dead.
Thy match was mortal to him, and pure grief
Shore his old thread in twain. Did he live now,   213
This sight would make him do a desperate turn,   214
Yea, curse his better angel from his side,
And fall to reprobance.   216
OTHELLO
'Tis pitiful. But yet Iago knows
That she with Cassio hath the act of shame
A thousand times committed. Cassio confessed it;
And she did gratify his amorous works   220
With that recognizance and pledge of love   221
Which I first gave her. I saw it in his hand;
It was a handkerchief, an antique token
My father gave my mother.
EMILIA   Oh, God! Oh, heavenly God!
IAGO
Zounds, hold your peace.
EMILIA   'Twill out, 'twill out! I peace?
No, I will speak as liberal as the north.   227
Let heaven and men and devils, let them all,
All, all, cry shame against me, yet I'll speak.
IAGO
Be wise, and get you home.
EMILIA   I will not.
                            [Iago threatens Emilia.]
GRATIANO   Fie,

Your sword upon a woman?
EMILIA
Oh, thou dull Moor! That handkerchief thou speak'st of
I found by fortune and did give my husband;
For often, with a solemn earnestness,
More than indeed belonged to such a trifle,   235
He begged of me to steal't.
IAGO   Villainous whore!
EMILIA
She give it Cassio? No, alas! I found it,
And I did give't my husband.
IAGO   Filth, thou liest!
EMILIA
By heaven, I do not, I do not, gentlemen.
Oh, murderous coxcomb! What should such a fool   240
Do with so good a wife?
OTHELLO   Are there no stones in heaven   242
But what serves for the thunder?—Precious villain!   243
    [He runs at Iago; Montano disarms Othello. Iago,
                        from behind, stabs Emilia.]
GRATIANO
The woman falls! Sure he hath killed his wife.
EMILIA
Ay, ay. Oh, lay me by my mistress' side.
                            [Exit Iago.]
GRATIANO   He's gone, but his wife's killed.
MONTANO
'Tis a notorious villain. Take you this weapon,
Which I have here recovered from the Moor.
Come, guard the door without. Let him not pass,
But kill him rather. I'll after that same villain,
For 'tis a damnèd slave.
                    Exit [with all but Othello and Emilia,
                        who has been laid by Desdemona's side].
OTHELLO   I am not valiant neither,
But every puny whipster gets my sword.   253
But why should honor outlive honesty?   254
Let it go all.
EMILIA   What did thy song bode, lady?
Hark, canst thou hear me? I will play the swan,   256
And die in music. [She sings] "Willow, willow, willow."
Moor, she was chaste. She loved thee, cruel Moor.
So come my soul to bliss as I speak true.
So speaking as I think, alas, I die.   [She dies.]
OTHELLO
I have another weapon in this chamber;
It was a sword of Spain, the ice-brook's temper—   262
Oh, here it is. [He finds a sword.] Uncle, I must come
    forth.
GRATIANO [within]
If thou attempt it, it will cost thee dear.

---

235 belonged was appropriate   **240 coxcomb** fool. (Addressed to Othello.)   **242 stones** bolts, such as those used for thunderbolts   **243 Precious** i.e., Arrant, utter   **243.1–2 He . . . Emilia** (The quarto text reads, "The Moore runnes at Iago. Iago kils his wife." The quarto also specifies the exit of Iago at line 245 and the death of Emilia at line 260.)   **253 every . . . sword** every whipper-snapper can get the better of me and my sword.   **254 why . . . honesty?** why should a soldier's reputation for bravery outlive true integrity?   **256 play the swan** (The swan was fabled to sing only at its death.)   **262 the icebrook's temper** tempered in ice-cold water

---

199 then (Perhaps at 3.3.331–2 and 4.2.137–54.)   **205 s.d. Othello . . . bed** (This direction is from the quarto, as also He kisses her at line 19 and She dies at line 129.)   **207 lift up eye** i.e., lift her eyes to heaven.   **210 shows** looks   **213 Shore . . . thread** sheared the thread of his old age (as Atropos, one of the three Fates, was thought to do)   **214 turn** deed   **216 reprobance** damnation, i.e., suicide.   **220 gratify** reward   **221 recognizance** token   **227 liberal as the north** freely as the north wind (blows).

Thou hast no weapon, and perforce must suffer.

OTHELLO
Look in upon me then and speak with me,
Or, naked as I am, I will assault thee.   267

[Enter Gratiano.]

GRATIANO
What is the matter?

OTHELLO   Behold, I have a weapon;
A better never did itself sustain
Upon a soldier's thigh. I have seen the day
That, with this little arm and this good sword,
I have made my way through more impediments
Than twenty times your stop. But oh, vain boast!   273
Who can control his fate? 'Tis not so now.
Be not afraid, though you do see me weaponed;
Here is my journey's end, here is my butt   276
And very seamark of my utmost sail.   277

[Gratiano steps back.]

Do you go back dismayed? 'Tis a lost fear;   278
Man but a rush against Othello's breast   279
And he retires. Where should Othello go?

[He turns to Desdemona.]

Now, how dost thou look now? Oh, ill-starred wench!
Pale as thy smock! When we shall meet at compt,   282
This look of thine will hurl my soul from heaven,
And fiends will snatch at it. Cold, cold, my girl?
Even like thy chastity. Oh, cursèd, cursèd slave!   285
Whip me, ye devils,
From the possession of this heavenly sight!
Blow me about in winds! Roast me in sulfur!
Wash me in steep-down gulfs of liquid fire!
Oh, Desdemon! Dead, Desdemon! Dead! Oh! Oh!   290

Enter Lodovico, Cassio [carried in a litter],
Montano, and Iago [prisoner], with officers.

LODOVICO
Where is this rash and most unfortunate man?

OTHELLO
That's he that was Othello. Here I am.

LODOVICO
Where is that viper? Bring the villain forth.

[Iago is led forward.]

OTHELLO
I look down towards his feet; but that's a fable.   294
If that thou be'st a devil, I cannot kill thee.

[He wounds Iago.]

LODOVICO
Wrench his sword from him.   [Othello is disarmed.]

IAGO   I bleed, sir, but not killed.

OTHELLO
I am not sorry neither. I'd have thee live,

For in my sense 'tis happiness to die.   298

LODOVICO
O thou Othello, that was once so good,
Fall'n in the practice of a cursèd slave,   300
What shall be said to thee?

OTHELLO   Why, anything.
An honorable murderer, if you will,
For naught I did in hate, but all in honor.

LODOVICO
This wretch hath part confessed his villainy.
Did you and he consent in Cassio's death?   305

OTHELLO   Ay.

CASSIO
Dear General, I never gave you cause.

OTHELLO
I do believe it, and I ask your pardon.
Will you, I pray, demand that demi-devil
Why he hath thus ensnared my soul and body?

IAGO
Demand me nothing. What you know, you know.
From this time forth I never will speak word.

LODOVICO   What, not to pray?

GRATIANO   Torments will ope your lips.   314

OTHELLO   Well, thou dost best.   315

LODOVICO
Sir, you shall understand what hath befall'n,
Which, as I think, you know not. Here is a letter
Found in the pocket of the slain Roderigo;
And here another. [He produces letters.] The one of them
     imports
The death of Cassio, to be undertook
By Roderigo.

OTHELLO
Oh, villain!

CASSIO   Most heathenish and most gross!   322

LODOVICO [showing another paper]
Now here's another discontented paper   323
Found in his pocket too. And this, it seems,
Roderigo meant t'have sent this damnèd villain;
But that belike Iago in the interim   326
Came in and satisfied him.   327

OTHELLO [to Iago]   Oh, thou pernicious caitiff!—
How came you, Cassio, by that handkerchief
That was my wife's?

CASSIO   I found it in my chamber;
And he himself confessed but even now
That there he dropped it for a special purpose
Which wrought to his desire.

OTHELLO   Oh, fool, fool, fool!   333

CASSIO
There is besides in Roderigo's letter
How he upbraids Iago, that he made him

---

267 **naked** unarmed   273 **your stop** the obstruction you present.
276 **butt** goal, limit. (An archery term.)   277 **seamark** beacon (marking his destination or limit)   278 **lost** groundless   279 **Man . . . rush** wield no more than a reed   282 **compt** account, judgment day   285 **slave** i.e., Othello himself.   290.1 *in a litter* (The quarto specifies that Cassio is *"in a Chaire."*)   294 **towards his feet** i.e., to see if they are cloven, as the devil's are fabled to be

298 **in my sense** to one who feels as I do   300 **in the practice** through the plotting, into the snare.   **slave** villain   305 **consent** agree
314 **Torments** Torture   315 **thou dost best** you (Iago) do best not to talk.   322 **gross** monstrous.   323 **discontented** full of discontent
326 **belike** most likely   327 **Came . . . him** interposed and gave him satisfactory explanation.   333 **wrought . . . desire** worked out as he wished, fitted in with his plan.

Brave me upon the watch, whereon it came   336
That I was cast; and even but now he spake,   337
After long seeming dead, Iago hurt him,
Iago set him on.

LODOVICO [*to Othello*]
You must forsake this room and go with us.
Your power and your command is taken off,   341
And Cassio rules in Cyprus. For this slave,
If there be any cunning cruelty
That can torment him much and hold him long,   344
It shall be his. You shall close prisoner rest   345
Till that the nature of your fault be known
To the Venetian state.—Come, bring away.

OTHELLO
Soft you; a word or two before you go.   348
I have done the state some service, and they know't.
No more of that. I pray you, in your letters,
When you shall these unlucky deeds relate,   351
Speak of me as I am; nothing extenuate,
Nor set down aught in malice. Then must you speak
Of one that loved not wisely but too well;
Of one not easily jealous but, being wrought,   355
Perplexed in the extreme; of one whose hand,   356
Like the base Indian, threw a pearl away   357
Richer than all his tribe; of one whose subdued eyes,   358
Albeit unusèd to the melting mood,
Drops tears as fast as the Arabian trees

336 Brave defy. **whereon it came** whereof it came about   **337 cast** dismissed   **341 taken off** taken away   **344 hold him long** keep him alive a long time (during his torture)   **345 rest** remain   **348 Soft you** One moment   **351 unlucky** unfortunate   **355 wrought** worked upon, worked into a frenzy   **356 Perplexed** distraught   **357 Indian** (This reading from the quarto pictures an ignorant savage who cannot recognize the value of a precious jewel. The Folio reading, "Iudean," i.e., infidel or disbeliever, may refer to Herod, who slew Miriamne in a fit of jealousy, or to Judas Iscariot, the betrayer of Christ.)   **358 subdued** i.e., overcome by grief

Their medicinable gum. Set you down this;   361
And say besides that in Aleppo once,
Where a malignant and a turbaned Turk
Beat a Venetian and traduced the state,
I took by th' throat the circumcisèd dog
And smote him, thus.   [*He stabs himself.*]   366

LODOVICO   Oh, bloody period!   367

GRATIANO   All that is spoke is marred.

OTHELLO
I kissed thee ere I killed thee. No way but this,
Killing myself, to die upon a kiss.
       [*He kisses Desdemona and*] *dies.*

CASSIO
This did I fear, but thought he had no weapon;
For he was great of heart.

LODOVICO [*to Iago*]   O Spartan dog,   372
More fell than anguish, hunger, or the sea!   373
Look on the tragic loading of this bed.
This is thy work. The object poisons sight;
Let it be hid. Gratiano, keep the house,   376
       [*The bedcurtains are drawn.*]
And seize upon the fortunes of the Moor,   377
For they succeed on you. [*To Cassio*] To you, Lord
   Governor,   378
Remains the censure of this hellish villain,   379
The time, the place, the torture. Oh, enforce it!
Myself will straight aboard, and to the state
This heavy act with heavy heart relate.   *Exeunt.*

361 gum i.e., myrrh.   **366 s.d.** *He stabs himself* (This direction is in the quarto text.)   **367 period** termination, conclusion.   **372 Spartan dog** (Spartan dogs were noted for their savagery and silence.)   **373 fell** cruel   **376 Let it be hid** i.e., draw the bedcurtains. (No stage direction specifies that the dead are to be carried offstage at the end of the play.)   **keep** guard   **377 seize upon** take legal possession of   **378 succeed on** pass as though by inheritance to   **379 censure** sentencing

King Lear

In *King Lear*, Shakespeare pushes to its limit the hypothesis of a malign or at least indifferent universe in which human life is meaningless and brutal. Few plays other than *Hamlet* and *Macbeth* approach *King Lear* in evoking the wretchedness of human existence, and even they cannot match the devastating spectacle of the Earl of Gloucester blinded or Cordelia dead in Lear's arms. The responses of the chief characters are correspondingly searing. "Is man no more than this?" rages Lear. "Unaccommodated man is no more but such a poor, bare, forked animal as thou art" (3.4.101–7). Life he calls a "great stage of fools," an endless torment: "the first time that we smell the air / We wawl and cry" (4.6.179–83). Gloucester's despair takes the form of accusing the gods of gleeful malice toward humanity: "As flies to wanton boys are we to th' gods; / They kill us for their sport" (4.1.36–7). Gloucester's ministering son Edgar can offer him no greater consolation than stoic resolve: "Men must endure / Their going hence, even as their coming hither; / Ripeness is all" (5.2.9–11). These statements need not be read as choric expressions of meaning for the play as a whole, but they do attest to the depth of suffering. In no other Shakespearean play does injustice appear to triumph so ferociously, for so long, and with such impunity. Will the heavens countenance this reign of injustice on earth? Retribution is late in coming and is not certainly the work of the heavens themselves. For, at the last, we must confront the wanton death of the innocent Cordelia—a death no longer willed even by the villain who arranged her execution. "Is this the promised end?" (5.3.268) asks the Earl of Kent, stressing the unparalleled horror of the catastrophe.

Throughout its earlier history, the ancient story of King Lear had always ended happily. In the popular folktale of Cinderella, to which the legend of Lear's daughters bears a significant resemblance, the youngest and virtuous daughter triumphs over her two older wicked sisters and is married to her princely wooer. Geoffrey of Monmouth's *Historia Regum Britanniae* (c. 1136), the earliest known version of the Lear story, records that, after Lear is overthrown by his sons-in-law (more than by his daughters), he is restored to his throne by the intervention of the French King and is allowed to enjoy his kingdom and Cordelia's love until his natural death. (Cordelia, as his successor, is later dethroned and murdered by her wicked nephews, but that is another story.) Sixteenth-century Tudor versions of the Lear story with which Shakespeare was familiar—John Higgins's account in *The First Part of the Mirror for Magistrates* (1574), Raphael Holinshed's *Chronicles* (1587), Edmund Spenser's *The Faerie Queene*, 2.10.27–32, and a play called *The True Chronicle History of King Leir* (by 1594, published 1605)—all retain the happy ending. The tragic pattern may have been suggested instead by Shakespeare's probable source for the Gloucester-Edgar-Edmund plot, Sir Philip Sidney's *Arcadia*, 2.10, in which the Paphlagonian King is the victim of filial ingratitude and deceit.

Yet even Shakespeare's authority was not sufficient to put down the craving for a happy resolution. Nahum Tate's adaptation (1681), which banished the Fool as indecorous for a tragedy and united Edgar and Cordelia in marriage, placing Lear once again on his throne, held the English stage for about 150 years. David Garrick restored some of Shakespeare's lines, and Edmund Kean restored the tragic ending, but it was not until 1838 that *King Lear* was again performed more or less as the dramatist wrote it. One of Shakespeare's editors, Dr. Samuel Johnson, evidently spoke for most eighteenth-century audiences when he confessed that he could hardly bring himself to read Shakespeare's text. Cordelia's slaughter violated that age's longing for "poetic justice." Her death implied a wanton universe and so counseled philosophic despair. Today, Shakespeare's relentless honesty and refusal to accept easy answers convince us that he was right to defy the conventions of his source, though no doubt we, too, distort the play to conform with our supposed toughness of vision.

Shakespeare evidently wrote *King Lear* some time before it was performed at court in December of 1606, probably in 1605 and certainly no earlier than 1603–1604; Edgar's speeches as Tom o' Bedlam contain references to Samuel Harsnett's *Declaration of Egregious Popish Impostures*, which was registered for publication in March of 1603. Thus, *King Lear* was probably written between *Othello* (c. 1603–1604) and *Macbeth* (c. 1606–1607), when Shakespeare was at the height of his literary power in the writing of tragedies.

When we look at the play in formal terms, we are apt to be struck first by its complex double plot. Nowhere else in Shakespearean tragedy do we find anything approaching the rich orchestration of the double plotting in *King Lear*. The links and parallels between the two plots are established on a narrative level early in the play and continue to the end. King Lear misjudges his children and disinherits his loving daughter Cordelia in favor of her duplicitous sisters, whereas Gloucester falls prey to Edmund's deceptions and disinherits his loyal son Edgar; Lear is turned out into the storm by his false daughters, while Gloucester is branded as a traitor by Edmund and deprived of his eyesight; Lear in his madness realizes his fault against Cordelia, while the blind Gloucester "sees" at last the truth about Edgar; and both fathers are cared for by their loving children and are belatedly reconciled to them, but then die brokenhearted. As recent criticism has noted, these narrative parallels are not especially significant in themselves; we are moved, not by the mere repetition of events, but by the enlargement of tragic vision that results from the counterpointing of two such actions. When we see juxtaposed to each other two scenes of trial, Lear's mad arraignment of the absent Goneril and Regan and then the cruel imposition of the mere "form of justice" on the pinioned Gloucester (3.6 and 3.7), we begin to measure the extent to which justice and injustice are inverted by cruelty. When at last the two old men come together, during the storm scenes and especially at Dover, the sad comfort they derive from sharing the wreckage of their lives calls forth piercing eloquence against the stench of mortality. The sight is "most pitiful in the meanest wretch, / Past speaking of in a king" (4.6.204–5).

The play's double structure suggests another duality central to *King Lear*: an opposition of parable and realism, in which "divided and distinguished worlds" are bound together for instructive contrast. (These terms are Maynard Mack's, in his *King Lear in Our Time*, 1965.) To a remarkable degree, this play derives its story from folklore and legend, with many of the wondrous and implausible circumstances of popular romance. A prose rendition might almost begin, "Once upon a time there was a king who had three daughters . . . ." Yet Shakespeare arouses romantic expectation only to crush it by aborting the conventional happy ending, setting up a dramatic tension between an idealized world of make-

believe and the actual world of disappointed hopes. We are aware of artifice and convention, and yet are deeply moved by the "truth" of suffering, love, and hatred. The characters pull us two ways at once; we regard them as types with universalized characteristics—a king and father, his cruel daughters, his loving daughter, and the like—and yet we scrutinize them for psychological motivation because they seem so real and individual.

This duality appears in both the central and the secondary characters. The King of France is in part a hero out of romance, who makes selfless choices and rescues the heroine Cordelia from her distress; yet his motive must also be appraised in the context of a bitter struggle for power. Why does he leave the English court "in choler," and why does he return to England with an army? Is it only to aid his wife and her beleaguered father, or is he negotiating for military advantage? Certainly, a French invasion of England on behalf of Lear complicates the issues of loyalty for the well-meaning Duke of Albany (and perhaps as well for an English Renaissance audience, with its habitual mistrust of the French). The dual focus of the play invites conflicting interpretation. Similarly, Edgar is presented to us on the one hand as the traduced victim in a starkly pessimistic story, dominated by his rationalistic brother, Edmund, who scoffs at religion and undertakes to manipulate those around him for personal gain; on the other hand, Edgar's story grows increasingly improbable as he undertakes a series of disguises and emerges finally as an anonymous champion of chivalry, challenging his brother in the lists like a knight-errant out of Arthurian romance. Edgar's motives are hard to follow. Is he the hero of a fabulous story whose disguises and contriving of illusions for his father are simply part of that storytelling tradition, or is he, in more realistic terms, a man whose disguises are a defensive mask and whose elaborate contrivances defeat themselves? Edmund, his brother, is no less complex. Onstage today he is usually interpreted as smooth and plausible, well-motivated by his father's condescending attitude and by the arbitrariness of the law that has excluded him from legitimacy and inheritance. Yet parable elevates Edmund into something monstrous. He becomes an embodiment of gleeful villainy, like Iago in *Othello*, malignantly evil simply because the evil that is in the universe must find a human form through which to express itself. Edmund's belated attempt to do some good adds to our difficulties in appraising his character, but the restless power of the dual conception supplies a vitality not to be found in pure fable or in realistic literature.

What we see then in Edmund and in others is the union of the universal and the particular, making *King Lear* at once parable and compellingly real. The parable or folktale element is prominent at the beginning of the play and focuses attention on the archetypal situations with which the story is concerned: rivalry between siblings, fear of parental rejection, and, at the same time, parental fear of children's callousness. The "unrealistic" contrast between Cordelia and her wicked sisters, or between Edgar and Edmund, is something we accept as a convention of storytelling, because it expresses vividly the psychic truth of rivalry between brothers and sisters. We identify with Cordelia and Edgar as virtuous children whose worth is misjudged, and who are losing to wicked siblings the contest for parental approval. (In folklore, the rejecting parent is usually a stepparent, which signifies our conviction that he or she is not a true parent at all.) Similarly, we accept as a meaningful convention of storytelling the equally "unrealistic" device by which Lear tests the love of his daughters. Like any parent, he wishes to be loved and appreciated in response to the kindnesses he has performed. The tension between fathers and their marriageable daughters is a recurrent pattern in Shakespeare's late plays, as in *Othello* (in which Brabantio accuses Desdemona of deceiving and deserting him), in *Pericles, Cymbeline,* and *The Winter's Tale,* and in *The Tempest,* in which the pattern is best resolved. In *King Lear,* Shakespeare explores the inherently explosive situation of an imperious father who, having provided for his children and having grown old, assumes he has a right to expect that those children will express their love and gratitude by looking after him.

The difficulty is that the parable of Lear and his children presents two contrasting viewpoints—that of the unappreciated child and that of the unwanted aging parent. Tragic misunderstanding is inevitable, and it outweighs the question of assessing blame. From Lear's point of view, Cordelia's silence is a truculent scanting of obedience. What he has devised is, after all, only a prearranged formality, with Cordelia to receive the richest third of England. Cannot such a ceremony be answered with the conventional hyperbole of courtly language, to which the King's ear is attuned? Don't parents have a right to be verbally reassured of their children's love? How can children be so laconic about such a precious matter? For her part, however, Cordelia senses that Lear is demanding love as payment for his parental kindliness, quid pro quo. Genuine love ought rather to be selfless, as the King of France tells the Duke of Burgundy: "Love's not love / When it is mingled with regards that stands / Aloof from th'entire point" (1.1.242–4). Is Cordelia being asked to prefer Lear before her own husband-to-be? Is this the price she must pay for her upbringing? Lear's ego seems fully capable of demanding this sacrifice from his daughters, especially from his favorite, Cordelia; he has given them his whole kingdom, now let them care for him as befits his royal rank and patriarchal role. The "second childishness" of his old age brings with it a self-centered longing to monopolize the lives of his children and to be a child again. Besides, as king, Lear has long grown accustomed to flattery and absolute obedience. Goneril

and Regan are content to flatter and promise obedience, knowing they will turn him out once he has relinquished his authority. Cordelia refuses to lie in this fashion, but she also will not yield to Lear's implicit request for her undivided affection. Part of her must be loyal to her own husband and her children, in the natural cycle of the generations. "When I shall wed, / That lord whose hand must take my plight shall carry / Half my love with him, half my care and duty" (1.1.100–2). Marriage will not prevent her from obeying, loving, and honoring her father as is fit but will establish for her a new priority. To Lear, as to other fathers contemplating a daughter's marriage in late Shakespearean plays, this savors of desertion.

Lear is sadly deficient in self-knowledge. As Regan dryly observes, "he hath ever but slenderly known himself" (1.1.296–7) and has grown ever more changeable and imperious with age. By dividing his kingdom in three, ostensibly so that "future strife / May be prevented now" (lines 44–5), he instead sets in motion a civil war and French invasion. His intention of putting aside his regal authority while still retaining "The name and all th'addition to a king" (line 136) perhaps betrays a lack of comprehension of the realities of power, although Lear may also have plausible political reasons for what he does, in view of the restive ambitions of the Dukes of Cornwall, Albany, and Burgundy. In any case, he welcomes poisoned flattery but interprets well-intended criticism, whether from Cordelia or Kent, as treason. These failures in no sense justify what Lear's ungrateful children do to him; as he later says, just before going mad, "I am a man / More sinned against than sinning" (3.2.59–60). His failures are, however, tokens of his worldly insolence, for which he must fall. The process is a painful one, but, since it brings self-discovery, it is not without its compensations. Indeed, a central paradox of the play is that by no other way could Lear have learned what human suffering and need are all about.

Lear's Fool is instrumental in elucidating this paradox. The Fool offers Lear advice in palatable form as mere foolery or entertainment and thus obtains a hearing when Kent and Cordelia have been angrily dismissed. Beneath his seemingly innocent jibes, however, are plain warnings of the looming disaster Lear blindly refuses to acknowledge. The Fool knows, as indeed any fool could tell, that Goneril and Regan are remorseless and unnatural. The real fool, therefore, is Lear himself, for having placed himself in their power. In a paradox familiar to Renaissance audiences—as in Erasmus's *In Praise of Folly,* Cervantes's *Don Quixote,* and Shakespeare's own earlier *As You Like It* and *Twelfth Night*—folly and wisdom exchange places. By a similar inversion of logic, the Fool offers his coxcomb to the Earl of Kent for siding with Lear in his exile, "for taking one's part that's out of favor" (1.4.97). Worldly wisdom suggests that we serve those whose fortunes are on the rise, as the obsequious and servile Oswald does.

Indeed, the sinister progress of the first half of the play seems to confirm the Fool's contention that kindness and love are a sure way to exile and poverty. "Let go thy hold when a great wheel runs down a hill lest it break thy neck with following; but the great one that goes upward, let him draw thee after" (2.4.70–3). Yet the Fool resolves to ignore his own sardonic advice; "I would have none but knaves follow it, since a fool gives it" (lines 74–5). Beneath his mocking, the Fool expresses the deeper truth that it is better to be a "fool" and suffer than to win on the cynical world's terms. The greatest fools truly are those who prosper through cruelty and become hardened in sin. As the Fool puts it, deriving a seemingly contrary lesson from Lear's rejection of Cordelia: "Why, this fellow has banished two on 's daughters and did the third a blessing against his will" (1.4.99–101).

These inversions find a parallel in Christian teaching, although the play is nominally pagan in setting. (The lack of explicit Christian reference may be in part the result of a parliamentary order in 1606 banning references to "God" onstage as blasphemous.) Christianity does not hold a monopoly on the idea that one must lose the world in order to win a better world, but its expressions of that idea were plentifully available to Shakespeare: "Blessed are the meek, for they shall inherit the earth" (the Sermon on the Mount); "Go and sell that thou hast, and give to the poor, and thou shalt have treasure in heaven" (Matthew 19:21); "He hath put down the mighty from their seats, and exalted them of low degree" (Luke 1:52). Cordelia's vision of genuine love is of this exalted spiritual order. She is, as the King of France extols her, "most rich being poor, / Most choice, forsaken, and most loved, despised" (1.1.254–5). This is the sense in which Lear has bestowed on her an unintended blessing, by exiling her from a worldly prosperity that is inherently pernicious. Now, with poetic fitness, Lear must learn the same lesson himself. He does so, paradoxically, at the very moment he goes mad, parting ways with the conventional truths of the corrupted world. "My wits begin to turn," he says (3.2.67), and then speaks his first kind words to the Fool, who is his companion in the storm. Lear senses companionship with a fellow mortal who is cold and outcast as he is. In his madness, he perceives both the worth of this insight and the need for suffering to attain it: "The art of our necessities is strange, / And can make vile things precious" (lines 70–1). Misery teaches Lear things he never could know as king about other "Poor naked wretches" who "bide the pelting of this pitiless storm." How are such poor persons to be fed and clothed? "Oh, I have ta'en / Too little care of this! Take physic, pomp; / Expose thyself to feel what wretches feel, / That thou mayst shake the superflux to them / And show the heavens more just" (3.4.28–36). This vision of perfect justice is visionary and utopian, utterly mad, in fact, but it is also spiritual wisdom dearly bought.

Gloucester learns a similar truth and expresses it in much the same way. Like Lear, he has driven into exile a virtuous child and has placed himself in the power of the wicked. Enlightenment comes only through suffering. Just as Lear achieves spiritual wisdom when he goes mad, Gloucester achieves spiritual vision when he is physically blinded. His eyes having been ground out by the heel of Cornwall's boot, Gloucester asks for Edmund only to learn that Edmund has betrayed him in return for siding with Lear in the approaching civil war. Gloucester's response, however, is not to accuse Edmund of treachery but to beg forgiveness of the wronged Edgar. No longer does Gloucester need eyes to see this truth: "I stumbled when I saw." Although the discovery is shattering, Gloucester perceives, as does Lear, that adversity is paradoxically of some benefit, since prosperity had previously caused him to be so spiritually blind. "Full oft 'tis seen / Our means secure us, and our mere defects / Prove our commodities" (4.1.19–21). And this realization leads him, as it does Lear, to express a longing for utopian social justice in which arrogant men will be humbled and the poor raised up by redistributed wealth. "Heavens, deal so still! / Let the superfluous and lust-dieted man, / That slaves your ordinance, that will not see / Because he does not feel, feel your pow'r quickly! / So distribution should undo excess / And each man have enough" (lines 65–70).

To say that Lear and Gloucester learn something precious is not, however, to deny that they are also devastated and broken by their savage humiliation. Indeed, Gloucester is driven to a despairing attempt at suicide, and Lear remains obsessed with the rotten stench of his own mortality, "bound / Upon a wheel of fire" (4.7.47–8). Every decent value that we like to associate with civilization is grotesquely inverted during the storm scenes. Justice, for example, is portrayed in two sharply contrasting scenes: the mere "form of justice" by which Cornwall condemns Gloucester for treason (3.7.26) and the earnestly playacted trial by which the mad Lear arraigns Goneril and Regan of filial ingratitude (3.6). The appearance and the reality of justice have exchanged places, as have folly and wisdom or blindness and seeing. The trial of Gloucester is outwardly correct, for Cornwall possesses the legal authority to try his subjects and at least goes through the motions of interrogating his prisoner. The outcome is, however, cruelly predetermined. In the playacting trial concurrently taking place in a wretched hovel, the outward appearance of justice is pathetically absurd. Here, justice on earth is personified by a madman (Lear), Edgar disguised as another madman (Tom o' Bedlam), and a Fool, of whom the latter two are addressed by Lear as "Thou robèd man of justice" and "thou, his yokefellow of equity" (lines 36–7). They are caught up in a pastime of illusion, using a footstool to represent Lear's ungrateful daughters. Yet true justice is here and not inside the manor house.

Similar contrasts invert the values of loyalty, obedience, and family bonds. Edmund becomes, in the language of the villains, the "loyal" son whose loyalty is demonstrated by turning on his own "traitorous" father. Cornwall becomes a new father to Edmund ("thou shalt find a dearer father in my love," 3.5.25–6). Conversely, a servant who tries to restrain Cornwall from blinding Gloucester is, in Regan's eyes, monstrously insubordinate. "A peasant stand up thus?" (3.7.83). Personal and sexual relationships betray signs of the universal malaise. The explicitly sexual ties in the play, notably those of Goneril, Regan, and Edmund, are grossly carnal and lead to jealousy and murder, while in Cordelia's wifely role the sensual is underplayed. The relationships we are invited to cherish—those of Cordelia, Kent, the Fool, and Gloucester to King Lear, and Edgar to Gloucester—are filial or are characterized by loyal service, both of which are pointedly nonsexual. Nowhere do we find an embodiment of love that is both sensual and spiritual, as in Desdemona in *Othello* or Hermione in *The Winter's Tale*. The Fool's and Tom o' Bedlam's (i.e., Edgar's) gibes about codpieces and plackets (3.2.27–40, 3.4.96) anticipate Lear's towering indictment of carnality, in which his fear of woman's insatiable appetite and his revulsion at her body "Down from the waist" ("there is the sulfurous pit, burning, scalding, stench, consumption. Fie, fie, fie! Pah, pah!") combine with a destructive self-hatred (4.6.124–30).

All these inversions and polarizations are subsumed in the inversion of the word "natural." Edmund is the "natural" son of Gloucester, meaning literally that he is illegitimate. Figuratively, he therefore represents a violation of traditional moral order. In appearance he is smooth and plausible, but in reality he is an archdeceiver like the Vice in a morality play, a superb actor who boasts to the audience in soliloquy of his protean villainy. "Nature" is Edmund's goddess, and by this he means something like a naturalistic universe in which the race goes to the swiftest and in which conscience, morality, and religion are empty myths. Whereas Lear invokes Nature as a goddess who will punish ungrateful daughters and defend rejected fathers (1.4.274–88) and whereas Gloucester believes in a cosmic correspondence between eclipses of the moon or sun and mutinous discords among people (1.2.106–17), Edmund scoffs at all such metaphysical speculations. He spurns, in other words, the Boethian conception of a divine harmony uniting the cosmos and humankind, with humankind at the center of the universe. As a rationalist, Edmund echoes Jacobean disruptions of the older world order in politics and religion as well as in science. He is Machiavellian, an atheist, and Epicurean—everything inimical to traditional Elizabethan ideals of order. To him, "natural" means precisely what Lear and Gloucester call "unnatural."

His creed provides the play with its supreme test. Which definition of "natural" is true? Does heaven exist, and will it let Edmund and the other villainous persons get away with their evil? The question is frequently asked, but the answers are ambiguous. "If you do love old men," Lear implores the gods, "if your sweet sway / Allow obedience, if you yourselves are old, / Make it your cause" (2.4.191–3). His exhortations mount into frenzied rant, until finally the heavens do send down a terrible storm—on Lear himself. Witnesses agree that the absence of divine order in the universe would have the gravest consequences. "If that the heavens do not their visible spirits / Send quickly down to tame these vile offenses," says Albany of Lear's ordeal, "It will come, / Humanity must perforce prey on itself, / Like monsters of the deep" (4.2.47–51). And Cornwall's servants (in a passage missing from the Folio text) have perceived earlier the dire implications of their masters' evil deeds. "I'll never care what wickedness I do, / If this man come to good," says one, and his fellow agrees: "If she [Regan] live long, / And in the end meet the old course of death, / Women will all turn monsters" (3.7.102–5). Yet these servants do, in fact, obey their own best instincts, turning on Cornwall and ministering to Gloucester despite danger to themselves. Similarly, Albany abandons his mild attempts to conciliate his domineering wife and instead uses his power for good. Cordelia's ability to forgive and cherish her father, and Edgar's comparable ministering to Gloucester, give the lie to Edmund's "natural" or amoral view of humanity; a few people, at least, are capable of charity, even when it does not serve their own material self-interest. Conversely, the play suggests that villainy will at last destroy itself, and not simply because the gods are just; Albany's hopeful insistence that "This shows you are above, / You justicers" (4.2.79–80) may be a little more than wishful thinking, to be undercut by some fresh disaster, but at least the insatiable ambitions of Edmund, Goneril, Regan, Cornwall, and Oswald do lead to their violent deaths. Edmund's belated attempt to save the life of Cordelia, though unsuccessful, suggests that this intelligent villain has at last begun to understand the great flaw in his naturalistic creed and to see that, like Goneril and Regan, he has been consumed by his own lust.

Even with such reassurances that villainy will eventually undo itself, the devastation at the end of *King Lear* is so appalling that our questions about justice remain finally unanswered. To ask the question "Who must pay for Lear's self-knowledge?" is to remind ourselves that women must often die in Shakespeare's tragedies so that men may learn, and to perceive even further that, in the absurdist world of *Lear*, the Cartesian logic of cause and effect and poetic justice simply will not account for all that we long to understand. As Roland Barthes well expresses the matter in an essay on Racine, "tragedy is only a means of reclaiming human unhappiness, of subsuming it, thus justifying it under the form of necessity, or wisdom, or purification." Tragedy cannot explain away the death of

Cordelia and the heartbreak of her father. The last tableau is a vision of doomsday, with Cordelia strangled, Lear broken and dying, and the "gored state" in such disarray that we cannot be sure what restoration can occur. The very question of political order is dwarfed by the enormity of the personal disaster of Lear and Cordelia. No one wishes longer life for the King: "He hates him / That would upon the rack of this tough world / Stretch him out longer." He is dead; "The wonder is he hath endured so long" (5.3.319–26). Lear's view of life's terrible corruption, pronounced in his madness, seems confirmed in his end. Perhaps the only way in which this tragedy can reclaim so much unhappiness is to suggest that, given the incurable badness of the world, we can at least choose whether to attempt to be like Cordelia and Edgar (knowing what the price may be for such courage) or to settle for being our worst selves, like Edmund, Goneril, and Regan. Overwhelmed as we are by the testimonial before us of humankind's vicious capacity for self-destruction, we are stirred nonetheless by the ability of some men and women to confront their fearful destiny with probity and stoic renunciation, adhering to what they believe to be good and expecting Fortune to give them absolutely nothing. The power of love, though learned too late to avert catastrophe, is at last discovered in its very defeat.

King Lear has become a fable for our times, on stage, in film and television, and in fictional adaptations in novel form. The role of Lear has been a compelling one for so many great Shakespearean actors, including Philip Kemble, Henry Irving, Edwin Forrest, John Gielgud, Donald Wolfit, Donald Sinden, Brian Cox, Michael Gambon, Robert Stephens, and John Wood. Peter Brook's film version of 1970, based on a stage production of 1962, with Paul Scofield as Lear, did much to equate the play's bleak vision with that of our modern existential world. Stimulated by Jan Kott's *Shakespeare Our Contemporary* (translated 1964), a post–World War II apocalyptic interpretation of Shakespeare from the perspective of an ideologically embattled eastern Europe, Brook unfolds a narrative of unrelieved disillusionment. The medium of film enables him to show what it would be like, for example, to have a hundred knights and all their followers descend on Albany's castle at the same time, demanding to be fed and quarreling with the servants of Goneril and Albany; the din and confusion are overwhelming, to such an extent that one can see Goneril's point in wanting to cut back on the King's retinue. A barren, wintry landscape adds visual reinforcement to the savage energies of family and dynastic conflict. Grigori Kozintsev's film of 1971, the work of a great Soviet director, sees the larger movements of the play in Marxist terms as the dialectical imperatives of political and social history; again, the medium of film makes it possible for Kozintsev to do what the stage can-

not do, deploy huge casts of anonymous soldiers and workers as both victims and movers of social change. Laurence Olivier's performance of Lear for Grenada Television (directed by Michael Elliott, 1983, Granada Video, 1984) came at the very end of Olivier's life, as his climactic and final role; his interpretation is deeply enhanced by one's perception that the actor is literally dying of cancer. Olivier, weakened but determined, had to be helped through the rigors of the screening, with the result that his Lear is tender, vulnerable, frail, though capable of the outbursts of rage that often come with advanced age. His *King Lear* is about the approach of death. Akira Kurosawa, in his epic *Ran* (1985), chose a more radical adaptation, that of telling a story of a Japanese warlord and his three sons, one of them (like Cordelia) dear but misunderstood, the others treacherous. One of their wives (the Lady Kaede) turns out to be another Edmund, Goneril, Regan, and Lady Macbeth all combined in one, fiercely and murderously determined that her husband succeed by whatever means possible. Kurosawa's vision of evil in the human heart is meant to be terrifying, and it is. The Royal National Theatre production of *King Lear* won several awards for Best Actor (Ian Holm as Lear) and Best Director (Richard Eyre), and is available on video from the BBC and Mobil Masterpiece Theatre (1998). In fiction, Jane Smiley's *A Thousand Acres* (1991) features a similar transposition, in this case to a midwestern American farm run by an aging farmer who transfers his land to his daughters and then sinks into alcoholism and insanity as two daughters squabble over their inheritance and end up losing everything, including their husbands, while their sister Caroline (Cordelia), unwilling to take part in the dividing of the farm, tries unsuccessfully as a lawyer to have the property restored to her father. Edward Bond's stage play called *Lear* (1971) accentuated *King Lear*'s already formidable bleakness by adding to its cruelty and violence; in it, war became a never-ending cycle of repression and escalating oppression. In these varied reworkings, we see the remarkable malleability of *King Lear* as an endlessly fascinating subject for new historicist, cultural materialist, deconstructive, and feminist readings that open up topics of misogyny and patriarchy, political ideologies, and philosophical pessimism.

King Lear exists in two early texts, the quarto of 1608 and the considerably changed Folio version of 1623. Similar disparities appear in *Hamlet, Othello, Troilus and Cressida, Henry IV Part II*, and a number of other plays, but the problem is especially acute in *King Lear*. Shakespeare must have had a hand in the revisions that led to the Folio text. It contains new material. At the same time, the quarto text contains passages not found in the Folio. The revisions may have resulted from a number of circumstances: cutting for performance (the play as it stands in either version is too long to have been produced in its entirety on the Jacobean stage), censorship, errors in transcription, and still more. The Folio version does alter some matters especially having to do with the French invasion; characters like Albany appear in a different light. The very ending is changed as to which characters speak the concluding lines.

Given these factors, many editions today present two or even three texts for the reader, or mark the text with brackets and other indicators of textual variation. This edition does not do so, though the textual notes do indicate the differences that occur. The reasons for choosing to present here the more traditional composite or eclectic text are these: *King Lear*'s textual variations between quarto and Folio are more extensive than in some other plays, but are not always different in kind, so that it is a distortion to treat this play alone as a multiple-text play.

To choose either quarto or Folio is to lose important material that is unquestionably Shakespeare's. To print two or even three versions is to add pages to an already weighty collection. And the presentation of multiple texts, or of a single text that is flagged with bracketed markers, also imposes on the reader a task of sorting out a complex and uncertain textual history that, however important ultimately in studying Shakespeare as a writer and as a reviser, is perhaps best left to subsequent investigation in a full-scale critical edition after one has absorbed the greatness of this play as a piece of writing for the theater. The present composite *King Lear*, based on the Folio text but including the 300 or so lines found only in the first quarto along with some quarto readings where the Folio version seems less textually reliable, is in a sense a compromise, but it is one that seems well suited to the purposes of this present edition.

King Lear

[*Dramatis Personae*

KING LEAR
GONERIL, }
REGAN,   } *Lear's daughters*
CORDELIA, }
DUKE OF ALBANY, *Goneril's husband*
DUKE OF CORNWALL, *Regan's husband*
KING OF FRANCE, *Cordelia's suitor and husband*
DUKE OF BURGUNDY, *suitor to Cordelia*

EARL OF KENT, *later disguised as Caius*
EARL OF GLOUCESTER
EDGAR, *Gloucester's son and heir, later disguised as
    poor Tom*
EDMUND, *Gloucester's bastard son*

SCENE: *Britain*]

OSWALD, *Goneril's steward*
A KNIGHT *serving King Lear*
Lear's FOOL
CURAN, *in Gloucester's household*
GENTLEMEN
Three SERVANTS
OLD MAN, *a tenant of Gloucester*
Three MESSENGERS
A GENTLEMAN *attending Cordelia as a Doctor*
Two CAPTAINS
HERALD

*Knights, Gentlemen, Attendants, Servants, Officers,
    Soldiers, Trumpeters*

1.1

Enter Kent, Gloucester, and Edmund.

KENT　I thought the King had more affected the Duke of 　1
　Albany than Cornwall.　2

GLOUCESTER　It did always seem so to us; but now in
　the division of the kingdom it appears not which of
　the dukes he values most, for equalities are so weighed 　5
　that curiosity in neither can make choice of either's 　6
　moiety.　7

KENT　Is not this your son, my lord?

GLOUCESTER　His breeding, sir, hath been at my charge. 　9
　I have so often blushed to acknowledge him that now
　I am brazed to't.　11

KENT　I cannot conceive you.　12

GLOUCESTER　Sir, this young fellow's mother could;
　whereupon she grew round-wombed and had indeed,
　sir, a son for her cradle ere she had a husband
　for her bed. Do you smell a fault?　16

KENT　I cannot wish the fault undone, the issue of it 　17
　being so proper.　18

GLOUCESTER　But I have a son, sir, by order of law, some 　19
　year elder than this, who yet is no dearer in my ac- 　20
　count. Though this knave came something saucily to 　21
　the world before he was sent for, yet was his mother
　fair, there was good sport at his making, and the
　whoreson must be acknowledged.—Do you know this 　24
　noble gentleman, Edmund?

EDMUND　No, my lord.

GLOUCESTER　My lord of Kent. Remember him hereafter
　as my honorable friend.

EDMUND　My services to Your Lordship.　29

KENT　I must love you, and sue to know you better.　30

EDMUND　Sir, I shall study deserving.　31

GLOUCESTER　He hath been out nine years, and away 　32
　he shall again. The King is coming.　33

Sennet. Enter [one bearing a coronet, then] King
Lear, Cornwall, Albany, Goneril, Regan, Cordelia,
and attendants.

LEAR
　Attend the lords of France and Burgundy, Gloucester. 　34

GLOUCESTER　I shall, my liege.　　　　　　*Exit.*

1.1. **Location: King Lear's palace.**
1 affected favored　**2 Albany** i.e., Scotland　**5–7 equalities . . .**
moiety the shares balance so equally that close scrutiny cannot find
advantage in either's portion.　**9 breeding** raising, care.　**charge**
expense.　**11 brazed** hardened　**12 conceive** understand. (But
Gloucester puns in the sense of "become pregnant.")　**16 fault** (1) sin
(2) loss of scent by the hounds.　**17 issue** (1) result (2) offspring
18 proper (1) excellent (2) handsome.　**19 by order of law** legitimate
19–20 some year about a year　**20–1 account** estimation.　**21 knave**
young fellow. (Not said disapprovingly, though the word is ironic.)
something somewhat　**24 whoreson** low fellow; suggesting bastardy, but (like *knave* above) used with affectionate condescension
29 services duty　**30 sue** petition, beg　**31 study deserving** strive to
be worthy (of your esteem).　**32 out** i.e., abroad, absent　**33.1** *Sennet*
trumpet signal heralding a procession.　*one . . . then* (This direction
is from the quarto. The *coronet* is perhaps intended for Cordelia or her
betrothed. A coronet signifies nobility below the rank of king.)　**34**
Attend Wait upon, usher ceremoniously

LEAR
　Meantime we shall express our darker purpose.　36
　Give me the map there. [*He takes a map.*] Know that we
　　have divided
　In three our kingdom; and 'tis our fast intent　38
　To shake all cares and business from our age,
　Conferring them on younger strengths while we
　Unburdened crawl toward death. Our son of
　　Cornwall,
　And you, our no less loving son of Albany,
　We have this hour a constant will to publish　43
　Our daughters' several dowers, that future strife　44
　May be prevented now. The princes, France and
　　Burgundy,
　Great rivals in our youngest daughter's love,
　Long in our court have made their amorous sojourn
　And here are to be answered. Tell me, my
　　daughters—
　Since now we will divest us both of rule,
　Interest of territory, cares of state—　50
　Which of you shall we say doth love us most,
　That we our largest bounty may extend
　Where nature doth with merit challenge? Goneril,　53
　Our eldest born, speak first.

GONERIL
　Sir, I love you more than words can wield the matter,
　Dearer than eyesight, space, and liberty,　56
　Beyond what can be valued, rich or rare,
　No less than life, with grace, health, beauty, honor;
　As much as child e'er loved, or father found;　59
　A love that makes breath poor and speech unable.　60
　Beyond all manner of so much I love you.

CORDELIA　[*aside*]
　What shall Cordelia speak? Love and be silent.

LEAR　[*indicating on map*]
　Of all these bounds, even from this line to this,
　With shadowy forests and with champains riched,　64
　With plenteous rivers and wide-skirted meads,　65
　We make thee lady. To thine and Albany's issue
　Be this perpetual.—What says our second daughter,
　Our dearest Regan, wife of Cornwall? Speak.

REGAN
　I am made of that self mettle as my sister,　69
　And prize me at her worth. In my true heart　70
　I find she names my very deed of love;　71
　Only she comes too short, that I profess　72
　Myself an enemy to all other joys
　Which the most precious square of sense possesses,　74

---

36 we, our (The royal plural; also in lines 37–44, etc.)　**darker pur-**
pose undeclared intention.　**38 fast** firm　**43 constant . . . publish**
firm resolve to proclaim　**44 several** individual　**50 Interest of** right
or title to, possession of　**53 Where . . . challenge** where both natural
affection and merit claim our bounty as its due.　**56 space, and lib-**
erty possession of land, and freedom of action　**59 found** i.e., found
himself to be loved　**60 breath . . . unable** utterance impoverished
and speech inadequate.　**64 shadowy** shady.　**champains riched** fertile plains　**65 plenteous . . . meads** abundant rivers bordered with
wide meadows　**69 that self mettle** that same spirited temperament
70 prize . . . worth value myself as her equal (in love for you). (*Prize*
suggests "price.")　**71 names . . . love** describes my love in action
72 that in that　**74 Which . . . possesses** which the most delicately
sensitive part of my nature can enjoy

And find I am alone felicitate   75
In your dear Highness' love.

CORDELIA *[aside]*   Then poor Cordelia!
And yet not so, since I am sure my love's
More ponderous than my tongue.   78

LEAR
To thee and thine hereditary ever
Remain this ample third of our fair kingdom,
No less in space, validity, and pleasure   81
Than that conferred on Goneril.—Now, our joy,
Although our last and least, to whose young love   83
The vines of France and milk of Burgundy   84
Strive to be interested, what can you say to draw   85
A third more opulent than your sisters'? Speak.

CORDELIA   Nothing, my lord.

LEAR   Nothing?

CORDELIA   Nothing.

LEAR
Nothing will come of nothing. Speak again.

CORDELIA
Unhappy that I am, I cannot heave
My heart into my mouth. I love Your Majesty
According to my bond, no more nor less.   93

LEAR
How, how, Cordelia? Mend your speech a little,
Lest you may mar your fortunes.

CORDELIA   Good my lord,
You have begot me, bred me, loved me. I
Return those duties back as are right fit,   97
Obey you, love you, and most honor you.
Why have my sisters husbands if they say
They love you all? Haply, when I shall wed,   100
That lord whose hand must take my plight shall carry 101
Half my love with him, half my care and duty.
Sure I shall never marry like my sisters,
To love my father all.

LEAR
But goes thy heart with this?

CORDELIA   Ay, my good lord.

LEAR   So young, and so untender?

CORDELIA   So young, my lord, and true.

LEAR
Let it be so! Thy truth then be thy dower!
For, by the sacred radiance of the sun,
The mysteries of Hecate and the night,   110
By all the operation of the orbs   111
From whom we do exist and cease to be,   112
Here I disclaim all my paternal care,
Propinquity, and property of blood,   114
And as a stranger to my heart and me

Hold thee from this forever. The barbarous Scythian, 116
Or he that makes his generation messes   117
To gorge his appetite, shall to my bosom
Be as well neighbored, pitied, and relieved   119
As thou my sometime daughter.

KENT   Good my liege—   120

LEAR   Peace, Kent!
Come not between the dragon and his wrath.
I loved her most, and thought to set my rest   123
On her kind nursery. *[To Cordelia]* Hence, and avoid
   my sight!—   124
So be my grave my peace, as here I give   125
Her father's heart from her. Call France. Who stirs? 126
Call Burgundy.   *[Exit one.]*
                     Cornwall and Albany,
With my two daughters' dowers digest the third.   128
Let pride, which she calls plainness, marry her.   129
I do invest you jointly with my power,
Preeminence, and all the large effects   131
That troop with majesty. Ourself by monthly course, 132
With reservation of an hundred knights   133
By you to be sustained, shall our abode
Make with you by due turns. Only we shall retain
The name and all th'addition to a king.   136
The sway, revenue, execution of the rest,   137
Belovèd sons, be yours, which to confirm,
This coronet part between you.

KENT   Royal Lear,   139
Whom I have ever honored as my king,
Loved as my father, as my master followed,
As my great patron thought on in my prayers—

LEAR
The bow is bent and drawn. Make from the shaft.   143

KENT
Let it fall rather, though the fork invade   144
The region of my heart. Be Kent unmannerly
When Lear is mad. What wouldst thou do, old man?
Think'st thou that duty shall have dread to speak
When power to flattery bows?
To plainness honor's bound   149
When majesty falls to folly. Reserve thy state,   150
And in thy best consideration check   151
This hideous rashness. Answer my life my judgment, 152

---

75 felicitate made happy   **78 ponderous** weighty   **81 validity** value.
pleasure pleasing features   **83 least** youngest   **84 vines** vineyards.
milk pastures (?)   **85 be interested** be affiliated, establish a claim, be
admitted as to a privilege.   **draw** win   **93 bond** filial obligation
97 right fit proper and fitting   **100 all** exclusively, and with all of
themselves.   **Haply** Perhaps, with luck   **101 plight** pledge in marriage   **110 mysteries** secret rites.   **Hecate** goddess of witchcraft and
the moon   **111 operation** influence.   **orbs** planets and stars
112 From whom under whose influence   **114 Propinquity . . . blood**
close kinship, and rights and duties entailed in blood ties

116 this this time forth.   **Scythian** (Scythians were famous in antiquity for savagery.)   **117 makes . . . messes** makes meals of his children or parents   **119 neighbored** helped in a neighborly way
120 sometime former   **123 set my rest** rely wholly. (A phrase from a
game of cards, meaning "to stake all.")   **124 nursery** nursing, care.
avoid get out of   **125 So . . . peace, as** As I hope to rest peacefully in
my grave   **126 Who stirs?** i.e., Jump to it; don't just stand there.
128 digest assimilate, incorporate   **129 Let . . . her** Let pride, which
she calls plain speaking, be her dowry and get her a husband.
131 effects outward shows   **132 troop with** accompany, serve.
Ourself (The royal "we.")   **133 With reservation of** reserving to
myself the right to be attended by   **136 th'addition** the honors and
prerogatives   **137 sway** sovereign authority   **139 coronet** (Perhaps
Lear gestures toward this coronet that was to have symbolized
Cordelia's dowry and marriage, hands it to his sons-in-law, or actually attempts to divide it.)   **143 Make from** Get out of the way of
144 fall strike.   **fork** barbed head of an arrow   **149 To . . . bound**
Loyalty demands frankness   **150 Reserve thy state** Retain your royal
authority   **151 And . . . check** and with wise deliberation restrain
152 Answer . . . judgment I wager my life on my judgment that

Thy youngest daughter does not love thee least,
Nor are those emptyhearted whose low sounds
Reverb no hollowness.

LEAR   Kent, on thy life, no more.   155

KENT
My life I never held but as a pawn   156
To wage against thine enemies, nor fear to lose it,   157
Thy safety being motive.

LEAR   Out of my sight!   158

KENT
See better, Lear, and let me still remain
The true blank of thine eye.   160

LEAR   Now, by Apollo—

KENT   Now, by Apollo, King,
Thou swear'st thy gods in vain.

LEAR   Oh, vassal! Miscreant!   164

[Laying his hand on his sword.]

ALBANY, CORNWALL   Dear sir, forbear.

KENT
Kill thy physician, and the fee bestow
Upon the foul disease. Revoke thy gift,
Or whilst I can vent clamor from my throat
I'll tell thee thou dost evil.

LEAR
Hear me, recreant, on thine allegiance hear me!   170
That thou hast sought to make us break our vows,   171
Which we durst never yet, and with strained pride   172
To come betwixt our sentence and our power,   173
Which nor our nature nor our place can bear,   174
Our potency made good, take thy reward.   175
Five days we do allot thee for provision
To shield thee from disasters of the world,
And on the sixth to turn thy hated back
Upon our kingdom. If on the tenth day following
Thy banished trunk be found in our dominions,   180
The moment is thy death. Away! By Jupiter,
This shall not be revoked.

KENT
Fare thee well, King. Sith thus thou wilt appear,   183
Freedom lives hence and banishment is here.
[To Cordelia] The gods to their dear shelter take thee,
    maid,
That justly think'st and hast most rightly said!
[To Regan and Goneril] And your large speeches may
    your deeds approve,   187
That good effects may spring from words of love.
Thus Kent, O princes, bids you all adieu.

He'll shape his old course in a country new.   Exit.   190

Flourish. Enter Gloucester, with France and
Burgundy; attendants.

GLOUCESTER
Here's France and Burgundy, my noble lord.

LEAR   My lord of Burgundy,
We first address toward you, who with this king   193
Hath rivaled for our daughter. What in the least   194
Will you require in present dower with her
Or cease your quest of love?

BURGUNDY   Most royal Majesty,
I crave no more than hath Your Highness offered,
Nor will you tender less.

LEAR   Right noble Burgundy,   198
When she was dear to us we did hold her so,   199
But now her price is fallen. Sir, there she stands.
If aught within that little-seeming substance,   201
Or all of it, with our displeasure pieced,   202
And nothing more, may fitly like Your Grace,   203
She's there, and she is yours.

BURGUNDY   I know no answer.

LEAR
Will you, with those infirmities she owes,   205
Unfriended, new-adopted to our hate,
Dowered with our curse and strangered with our
    oath,   207
Take her, or leave her?

BURGUNDY   Pardon me, royal sir.
Election makes not up in such conditions.   209

LEAR
Then leave her, sir, for by the power that made me,
I tell you all her wealth. [To France] For you, great King,   211
I would not from your love make such a stray   212
To match you where I hate; therefore beseech you   213
T'avert your liking a more worthier way   214
Than on a wretch whom Nature is ashamed
Almost t'acknowledge hers.

FRANCE   This is most strange,
That she whom even but now was your best object,
The argument of your praise, balm of your age,   218
The best, the dearest, should in this trice of time   219
Commit a thing so monstrous to dismantle   220
So many folds of favor. Sure her offense
Must be of such unnatural degree
That monsters it, or your forevouched affection   223
Fall into taint, which to believe of her   224

---

155 **Reverb no hollowness** do not reverberate like a hollow drum, insincerely.   **156–7 My . . . wage** I never regarded my life other than as a pledge to hazard in warfare   **158 motive** that which prompts me to act.   **160 The true . . . eye** i.e., the means to enable you to see better. (*Blank* means "the white center of the target," or, "the true direct aim," as in "point-blank," traveling in a straight line.)   **164 vassal** i.e., wretch.   **Miscreant** (Literally, infidel, heretic; hence, villain, rascal.)   **170 recreant** traitor   **171 That** In that, since   **172 strained** excessive   **173 To . . . power** i.e., to block my power to command and judge   **174 Which . . . place** which neither my temperament nor my office as king   **175 Our . . . good** my power enacted, demonstrated   **180 trunk** body   **183 Sith** Since   **187 your . . . approve** may your deeds confirm your speeches with their vast claims

190 shape . . . course follow his traditional plainspoken ways   **190.1 Flourish** trumpet fanfare used for the entrance or exit of important persons   **193 address** address myself   **194 rivaled** competed. **in the least** at the lowest   **198 tender** offer   **199 so** i.e., *dear*, beloved and valued at a high price   **201 little-seeming substance** one who seems substantial but whose substance is, in fact, little, or, one who refuses to flatter   **202 pieced** added, joined   **203 like** please   **205 owes** owns   **207 strangered** disowned   **209 Election . . . conditions** No choice is possible under such conditions.   **211 tell you** (1) inform you of (2) enumerate for you.   **For** As for   **212 make such a stray** stray so far   **213 To** as to.   **beseech** I beseech   **214 T'avert your liking** to turn your affections   **218 argument** theme   **219 trice** moment   **220 to** as to   **223 monsters it** makes it monstrous   **223–4 or . . . taint** or else the affection for her you have hitherto affirmed must fall into suspicion

Must be a faith that reason without miracle
Should never plant in me.

CORDELIA　I yet beseech Your Majesty—
If for I want that glib and oily art　228
To speak and purpose not, since what I well intend　229
I'll do't before I speak—that you make known
It is no vicious blot, murder, or foulness,　231
No unchaste action or dishonored step
That hath deprived me of your grace and favor,
But even for want of that for which I am richer:　234
A still-soliciting eye and such a tongue　235
That I am glad I have not, though not to have it
Hath lost me in your liking.

LEAR　　　　　　　　　　　Better thou
Hadst not been born than not t'have pleased me better.

FRANCE
Is it but this? A tardiness in nature
Which often leaves the history unspoke　240
That it intends to do?—My lord of Burgundy,
What say you to the lady? Love's not love
When it is mingled with regards that stands　243
Aloof from th'entire point. Will you have her?　244
She is herself a dowry.

BURGUNDY [to Lear]　　　　Royal King,
Give but that portion which yourself proposed,
And here I take Cordelia by the hand,
Duchess of Burgundy.

LEAR
Nothing. I have sworn. I am firm.

BURGUNDY [to Cordelia]
I am sorry, then, you have so lost a father
That you must lose a husband.

CORDELIA　　　　　　　　Peace be with Burgundy!
Since that respects of fortune are his love,　252
I shall not be his wife.

FRANCE
Fairest Cordelia, that art most rich being poor,
Most choice, forsaken, and most loved, despised,
Thee and thy virtues here I seize upon,
Be it lawful I take up what's cast away.　257
　　　　　　　　　　　　　　[He takes her hand.]
Gods, gods! 'Tis strange that from their cold'st neglect　258
My love should kindle to inflamed respect.—　259
Thy dowerless daughter, King, thrown to my chance,　260
Is queen of us, of ours, and our fair France.
Not all the dukes of wat'rish Burgundy　262
Can buy this unprized precious maid of me.—　263
Bid them farewell, Cordelia, though unkind.　264
Thou losest here, a better where to find.　265

LEAR
Thou hast her, France. Let her be thine, for we
Have no such daughter, nor shall ever see
That face of hers again. Therefore begone
Without our grace, our love, our benison.　269
Come, noble Burgundy.
　　　　Flourish. Exeunt [all but France, Goneril, Regan,
　　　　　　　　　　　　　　　　and Cordelia].

FRANCE　Bid farewell to your sisters.

CORDELIA
Ye jewels of our father, with washed eyes　272
Cordelia leaves you. I know you what you are,
And like a sister am most loath to call　274
Your faults as they are named. Love well our father.　275
To your professèd bosoms I commit him.　276
But yet, alas, stood I within his grace,
I would prefer him to a better place.　278
So, farewell to you both.

REGAN
Prescribe not us our duty.

GONERIL　　　　　　　　Let your study
Be to content your lord, who hath received you
At Fortune's alms. You have obedience scanted,　282
And well are worth the want that you have wanted.　283

CORDELIA
Time shall unfold what plighted cunning hides;　284
Who covers faults, at last shame them derides.　285
Well may you prosper!

FRANCE　　　　　　　　Come, my fair Cordelia.
　　　　　　　　　　　Exeunt France and Cordelia.

GONERIL　Sister, it is not little I have to say of what most
nearly appertains to us both. I think our father will
hence tonight.

REGAN　That's most certain, and with you; next month
with us.

GONERIL　You see how full of changes his age is; the
observation we have made of it hath not been little.
He always loved our sister most, and with what poor
judgment he hath now cast her off appears too grossly.　295

REGAN　'Tis the infirmity of his age. Yet he hath ever
but slenderly known himself.

GONERIL　The best and soundest of his time hath been　298
but rash. Then must we look from his age to receive　299
not alone the imperfections of long-ingraffed condi-　300
tion, but therewithal the unruly waywardness that in-　301
firm and choleric years bring with them.

REGAN　Such unconstant starts are we like to have from　303
him as this of Kent's banishment.

---

228 for I want because I lack　**229 purpose not** not intend to do what
I say　**231 foulness** immorality　**234 for which** for lack of which
235 still-soliciting ever begging　**240 history** tale, narrative
243–4 regards . . . point irrelevant considerations.　**252 Since . . . fortune** Since concern for wealth and position　**257 Be it lawful** if it be
lawful that　**258 from . . . neglect** out of the cold neglect of the gods
259 inflamed respect ardent regard.　**260 chance** lot　**262 wat'rish**
(1) well-watered with rivers (2) feeble, watery　**263 unprized** not
appreciated. (With perhaps a sense also of "priceless.")　**264 though
unkind** though they have behaved unnaturally.　**265 here** this place.
where place elsewhere

269 benison blessing.　**272 washed** tear-washed　**274 like a sister** i.e.,
because I am your sister　**275 as . . . named** by their true names.
276 professèd bosoms publicly avowed love　**278 prefer** advance,
recommend　**282 At . . . alms** as a pittance or dole from Fortune.
283 And well . . . wanted i.e., and well deserve to be without the
dowry and the parental affection that you have both lacked and
flouted.　**284–5 Time . . . derides** Time will bring to light what cunning attempts to conceal as if in the folds of a cloak; those who hide
their faults may do so for a while, but in time they will be shamed and
derided.　**295 grossly** obviously.　**298–9 The best . . . rash** Even in the
prime of his life, he was stormy and unpredictable.　**300–1 long-
ingraffed condition** long-implanted habit　**301 therewithal** added
thereto　**303 unconstant starts** impulsive outbursts.　**like** likely

GONERIL　There is further compliment of leave-taking 305
between France and him. Pray you, let us hit together. 306
If our father carry authority with such disposition as 307
he bears, this last surrender of his will but offend us. 308
REGAN　We shall further think of it.
GONERIL　We must do something, and i'th' heat. 310

Exeunt.

❧

1.2

Enter Bastard [Edmund, with a letter].

EDMUND
Thou, Nature, art my goddess; to thy law 1
My services are bound. Wherefore should I
Stand in the plague of custom and permit 3
The curiosity of nations to deprive me, 4
For that I am some twelve or fourteen moonshines 5
Lag of a brother? Why bastard? Wherefore base? 6
When my dimensions are as well compact, 7
My mind as generous, and my shape as true, 8
As honest madam's issue? Why brand they us 9
With base? With baseness? Bastardy? Base, base?
Who in the lusty stealth of nature take 11
More composition and fierce quality 12
Than doth within a dull, stale, tirèd bed
Go to th' creating a whole tribe of fops 14
Got 'tween asleep and wake? Well, then, 15
Legitimate Edgar, I must have your land.
Our father's love is to the bastard Edmund
As to th' legitimate. Fine word, "legitimate"!
Well, my legitimate, if this letter speed 19
And my invention thrive, Edmund the base 20
Shall top th' legitimate. I grow, I prosper.
Now, gods, stand up for bastards!

Enter Gloucester.

GLOUCESTER
Kent banished thus? And France in choler parted?
And the King gone tonight? Prescribed his power, 24
Confined to exhibition? All this done 25
Upon the gad? Edmund, how now? What news? 26
EDMUND　So please Your Lordship, none.

[Putting up the letter.]

GLOUCESTER　Why so earnestly seek you to put up that
letter?
EDMUND　I know no news, my lord.
GLOUCESTER　What paper were you reading?
EDMUND　Nothing, my lord.
GLOUCESTER　No? What needed then that terrible dis- 33
patch of it into your pocket? The quality of nothing 34
hath not such need to hide itself. Let's see. Come, if it
be nothing I shall not need spectacles.
EDMUND　I beseech you, sir, pardon me. It is a letter
from my brother, that I have not all o'erread; and for 38
so much as I have perused, I find it not fit for your
o'erlooking. 40
GLOUCESTER　Give me the letter, sir.
EDMUND　I shall offend either to detain or give it. The
contents, as in part I understand them, are to blame. 43
GLOUCESTER　Let's see, let's see.

[Edmund gives the letter.]

EDMUND　I hope for my brother's justification he wrote
this but as an essay or taste of my virtue. 46
GLOUCESTER (*reads*)　"This policy and reverence of age 47
makes the world bitter to the best of our times, keeps 48
our fortunes from us till our oldness cannot relish
them. I begin to find an idle and fond bondage in the 50
oppression of aged tyranny, who sways not as it hath 51
power but as it is suffered. Come to me, that of this I 52
may speak more. If our father would sleep till I waked
him, you should enjoy half his revenue forever and live
the beloved of your brother,　　　　　　　　　Edgar."
Hum! Conspiracy! "Sleep till I waked him, you should
enjoy half his revenue." My son Edgar! Had he
a hand to write this? A heart and brain to breed it
in? When came you to this? Who brought it? 59
EDMUND　It was not brought me, my lord; there's the
cunning of it. I found it thrown in at the casement of 61
my closet. 62
GLOUCESTER　You know the character to be your 63
brother's?
EDMUND　If the matter were good, my lord, I durst 65
swear it were his; but in respect of that I would fain 66
think it were not.
GLOUCESTER　It is his.
EDMUND　It is his hand, my lord, but I hope his heart is
not in the contents.
GLOUCESTER　Has he never before sounded you in this
business?
EDMUND　Never, my lord. But I have heard him oft
maintain it to be fit that, sons at perfect age and fathers 74
declined, the father should be as ward to the son, and 75
the son manage his revenue.

---

305 **compliment** ceremony　306 **hit** agree　307–8 **If . . . offend us** If
our father continues to boss us around with his accustomed imperi-
ousness, this most recent display of willfulness will do us nothing but
harm.　310 **i'th' heat** i.e., while the iron is hot.
1.2. Location: The Earl of Gloucester's house.
1 **Nature** i.e., the sanction that governs the material world through
mechanical amoral forces　3 **Stand . . . custom** submit to the vexa-
tious injustice of convention　4 **The curiosity of nations** arbitrary
social gradations　5 **For that** because.　**moonshines** months
6 **Lag of** lagging behind　7 **dimensions** proportions.　**compact** knit
together, fitted　8 **generous** noble, refined　9 **honest** chaste
11–12 **Who . . . quality** Whose begetting in the sexual act both
requires and engenders a fuller mixture and more energetic force
14 **fops** fools　15 **Got** begotten　19 **speed** succeed, prosper
20 **invention thrive** scheme prosper　24 **tonight** last night.
Prescribed Limited　25 **exhibition** an allowance, pension.
26 **Upon the gad** suddenly, as if pricked by a gad or spur.

33–4 **terrible dispatch** fearful quick disposal　38 **for** as for　40 **o'erlooking** perusal.　43 **to blame** (The Folio reading, "too blame," "too
blameworthy to be shown," may be correct.)　46 **essay or taste** assay,
test　47 **policy and reverence of** policy of reverencing　48 **the best . . .
times** the best years of our lives, i.e., our youth　50 **idle and fond**
useless and foolish　51 **who sways** which rules　52 **suffered** permitted.　59 **to this** upon this (letter).　61 **casement** window　62 **closet**
private room.　63 **character** handwriting　65 **matter** contents　66 **in
. . . that** considering what the contents are.　**fain** gladly　74 **fit** fitting, appropriate.　**perfect age** full maturity　75 **declined** having
become feeble

GLOUCESTER   Oh, villain, villain! His very opinion in the 77
letter! Abhorred villain! Unnatural, detested, brutish 78
villain! Worse than brutish! Go, sirrah, seek him. I'll 79
apprehend him. Abominable villain! Where is he?

EDMUND   I do not well know, my lord. If it shall please
you to suspend your indignation against my brother
till you can derive from him better testimony of his
intent, you should run a certain course; where, if you 84
violently proceed against him, mistaking his purpose,
it would make a great gap in your own honor and
shake in pieces the heart of his obedience. I dare pawn 87
down my life for him that he hath writ this to feel my 88
affection to Your Honor, and to no other pretense of 89
danger.   90

GLOUCESTER   Think you so?

EDMUND   If Your Honor judge it meet, I will place you 92
where you shall hear us confer of this, and by an 93
auricular assurance have your satisfaction, and that 94
without any further delay than this very evening.

GLOUCESTER   He cannot be such a monster—

EDMUND   Nor is not, sure.

GLOUCESTER   To his father, that so tenderly and entirely loves him. Heaven and earth! Edmund, seek
him out; wind me into him, I pray you. Frame the 100
business after your own wisdom. I would unstate 101
myself to be in a due resolution.   102

EDMUND   I will seek him, sir, presently, convey the 103
business as I shall find means, and acquaint you
withal.   105

GLOUCESTER   These late eclipses in the sun and moon 106
portend no good to us. Though the wisdom of nature 107
can reason it thus and thus, yet nature finds itself
scourged by the sequent effects. Love cools, friend- 109
ship falls off, brothers divide; in cities, mutinies; in
countries, discord; in palaces, treason; and the bond
cracked twixt son and father. This villain of mine
comes under the prediction; there's son against father.
The King falls from bias of nature; there's father 114
against child. We have seen the best of our time.
Machinations, hollowness, treachery, and all ruinous
disorders follow us disquietly to our graves. Find out
this villain, Edmund; it shall lose thee nothing. Do it 118
carefully. And the noble and truehearted Kent banished! His offense, honesty! 'Tis strange.   *Exit.*

EDMUND   This is the excellent foppery of the world, that 121
when we are sick in fortune—often the surfeits of our 122
own behavior—we make guilty of our disasters the 123
sun, the moon, and stars, as if we were villains on 124
necessity, fools by heavenly compulsion, knaves,
thieves, and treachers by spherical predominance, 126
drunkards, liars, and adulterers by an enforced obedience of planetary influence, and all that we are evil
in, by a divine thrusting on. An admirable evasion of 129
whoremaster man, to lay his goatish disposition on 130
the charge of a star! My father compounded with my 131
mother under the Dragon's tail and my nativity was 132
under Ursa Major, so that it follows I am rough and 133
lecherous. Fut, I should have been that I am, had the 134
maidenliest star in the firmament twinkled on my
bastardizing. Edgar—

Enter Edgar.

and pat he comes like the catastrophe of the old 137
comedy. My cue is villainous melancholy, with a sigh
like Tom o' Bedlam.—Oh, these eclipses do portend 139
these divisions! Fa, sol, la, mi.   140

EDGAR   How now, brother Edmund, what serious
contemplation are you in?

EDMUND   I am thinking, brother, of a prediction I read
this other day, what should follow these eclipses.   144

EDGAR   Do you busy yourself with that?

EDMUND   I promise you, the effects he writes of succeed 146
unhappily, as of unnaturalness between the child and 147
the parent, death, dearth, dissolutions of ancient amities, divisions in state, menaces and maledictions
against king and nobles, needless diffidences, banish- 150
ment of friends, dissipation of cohorts, nuptial 151
breaches, and I know not what.

EDGAR   How long have you been a sectary astronom- 153
ical?   154

EDMUND   Come, come, when saw you my father last?

EDGAR   The night gone by.

EDMUND   Spake you with him?

EDGAR   Ay, two hours together.

EDMUND   Parted you in good terms? Found you no
displeasure in him by word nor countenance?   160

EDGAR   None at all.

---

77 **villain** vile wretch, diabolical schemer   78 **Abhorred** Abhorrent.
detested hated and hateful   79 **sirrah** (Form of address used to inferiors or children.)   84 **run a certain course** proceed with safety and
certainty.   **where** whereas   87–8 **pawn down** stake   88 **feel** feel out
89–90 **pretense of danger** dangerous purpose.   92 **meet** fitting,
proper   93–4 **by an ... satisfaction** satisfy yourself as to the truth by
what you hear   100 **wind me into him** insinuate yourself into his
confidence. (*Me* is used colloquially.)   **Frame** Arrange   101 **after
your own wisdom** as you think best.   101–2 **I would ... resolution** I
would give up my wealth and rank to know the truth, have my
doubts resolved.   103 **presently** immediately.   **convey** manage
105 **withal** therewith.   106 **late** recent   107 **the wisdom of nature**
natural science   109 **sequent effects** i.e., devastating consequences.
114 **bias of nature** natural inclination   118 **lose thee nothing** i.e.,
earn you a reward.   121 **foppery** foolishness

122–3 **surfeits ... behavior** consequences of our own overindulgence
124 **on** by   126 **treachers** traitors.   **spherical predominance** astrological determinism, because a certain planet was ascendant at the
hour of our birth   129 **divine** supernatural   130 **goatish** lecherous
130–1 **on the charge** to the responsibility   131–2 **compounded ...
Dragon's tail** had sex with my mother under the constellation Draco
(not one of the regular signs of the zodiac), or under the descending
point at which the moon's orbit intersects with the ecliptic or apparent orbit of the sun (when an eclipse might occur)   133 **Ursa Major**
the big bear or dipper—not one of the regular signs of the zodiac
134 **Fut** i.e., 'Sfoot, by Christ's foot.   **that** what   137 **pat** on cue.
catastrophe conclusion, resolution (of a play)   139 **Tom o' Bedlam** a
lunatic patient of Bethlehem Hospital in London turned out to beg for
his bread.   140 **divisions** social and family conflicts. (But with a
musical sense also of florid variations on a theme, thus prompting
Edmund's singing.)   144 **this other day** the other day   146 **promise**
assure   146–7 **succeed unhappily** follow unluckily   150 **needless
diffidences** groundless distrust of others   151 **dissipation of cohorts**
breaking up of military companies, large-scale desertions   153–4 **sectary astronomical** believer in astrology.   160 **countenance** demeanor.

EDMUND   Bethink yourself wherein you may have offended him, and at my entreaty forbear his presence 163
until some little time hath qualified the heat of his 164
displeasure, which at this instant so rageth in him that
with the mischief of your person it would scarcely 166
allay.   167

EDGAR   Some villain hath done me wrong.

EDMUND   That's my fear. I pray you, have a continent 169
forbearance till the speed of his rage goes slower; and, 170
as I say, retire with me to my lodging, from whence I
will fitly bring you to hear my lord speak. Pray ye, go! 172
There's my key. [*He gives a key.*] If you do stir abroad,
go armed.

EDGAR   Armed, brother?

EDMUND   Brother, I advise you to the best. I am no honest man if there be any good meaning toward you. I 177
have told you what I have seen and heard, but faintly, 178
nothing like the image and horror of it. Pray you, 179
away.

EDGAR   Shall I hear from you anon?

EDMUND
I do serve you in this business.   *Exit* [*Edgar*].
A credulous father and a brother noble,
Whose nature is so far from doing harms
That he suspects none; on whose foolish honesty
My practices ride easy. I see the business.   186
Let me, if not by birth, have lands by wit.   187
All with me's meet that I can fashion fit.   *Exit.* 188

❖

1.3

Enter Goneril, and [*Oswald, her*] *steward.*

GONERIL   Did my father strike my gentleman for chiding of his fool?

OSWALD   Ay, madam.

GONERIL   By day and night he wrongs me! Every hour
He flashes into one gross crime or other   5
That sets us all at odds. I'll not endure it.
His knights grow riotous, and himself upbraids us
On every trifle. When he returns from hunting
I will not speak with him. Say I am sick.
If you come slack of former services   10
You shall do well; the fault of it I'll answer.   11
                                   [*Horns within.*]

OSWALD   He's coming, madam. I hear him.

GONERIL
Put on what weary negligence you please,
You and your fellows. I'd have it come to question.   14
If he distaste it, let him to my sister,   15

Whose mind and mine, I know, in that are one,
Not to be overruled. Idle old man,   17
That still would manage those authorities   18
That he hath given away! Now, by my life,
Old fools are babes again, and must be used
With checks as flatteries, when they are seen abused.   21
Remember what I have said.

OSWALD   Well, madam.

GONERIL
And let his knights have colder looks among you.
What grows of it, no matter. Advise your fellows so.
I would breed from hence occasions, and I shall,   26
That I may speak. I'll write straight to my sister   27
To hold my very course. Prepare for dinner.   *Exeunt.*

❖

1.4

Enter Kent [*disguised*].

KENT
If but as well I other accents borrow   1
That can my speech diffuse, my good intent   2
May carry through itself to that full issue   3
For which I razed my likeness. Now, banished Kent,   4
If thou canst serve where thou dost stand condemned,
So may it come thy master, whom thou lov'st,   6
Shall find thee full of labors.

Horns within. Enter Lear, [*Knights,*] *and
attendants.*

LEAR   Let me not stay a jot for dinner. Go get it ready. 8
                            [*Exit an Attendant.*]
[*To Kent*] How now, what art thou?

KENT   A man, sir.

LEAR   What dost thou profess? What wouldst thou with 11
us?

KENT   I do profess to be no less than I seem: to serve
him truly that will put me in trust, to love him that is
honest, to converse with him that is wise and says 15
little, to fear judgment, to fight when I cannot choose, 16
and to eat no fish.   17

LEAR   What art thou?

KENT   A very honest-hearted fellow, and as poor as the
King.

---

17 Idle Foolish   **18 manage those authorities** exercise those prerogatives   **21 With . . . abused** with rebukes in place of flattering attentiveness, when such flattery is seen to be taken advantage of.
26 occasions opportunities for taking offense   **27 speak** speak
bluntly.   **straight** immediately
**1.4. Location: The Duke of Albany's palace still. The sense of time
is virtually continuous.**
1 as well i.e., as well as I have disguised myself by means of costume
2 diffuse render confused or indistinct   **3–4 May . . . likeness** may
achieve the desired result for which I scraped off my beard and
erased my outward appearance.   **6 come** come to pass that   **8 stay**
wait   **8.1 *Attendant*** (This attendant may be a knight; certainly the
one who speaks at line 50 is a knight.)   **11 What . . . profess?** What is
your special calling? (But Kent puns in his answer on *profess* meaning
to "claim.")   **15 honest** honorable.   **converse** associate   **16 judgment** i.e., God's judgment.   **choose** i.e., choose but to fight   **17 eat
no fish** i.e., eat a manly diet (?), be a good Protestant (?).

---

163 forbear his presence avoid meeting him   **164 qualified** moder-
ated   **166 with . . . person** with the harmful effect of your presence;
or, even if there were injury done to you   **167 allay** be allayed.
169–70 have . . . forbearance keep a wary distance   **172 fitly** at a fit
time.   **my lord** our father   **177 meaning** intention   **178 but faintly**
only with a faint impression   **179 image and horror** horrid reality
186 practices plots.   **the business** i.e., how my plots should proceed.
187 wit cleverness.   **188 meet** justifiable.   **fit to my purpose.**
1.3. Location: The Duke of Albany's palace.
5 crime offense   **10 come slack** fall short   **11 answer** be answerable
for.   **14 come to question** be made an issue.   **15 distaste** dislike

LEAR   If thou be'st as poor for a subject as he's for a
king, thou'rt poor enough. What wouldst thou?

KENT   Service.

LEAR   Who wouldst thou serve?

KENT   You.

LEAR   Dost thou know me, fellow?

KENT   No, sir, but you have that in your countenance   27
which I would fain call master.

LEAR   What's that?

KENT   Authority.

LEAR   What services canst do?

KENT   I can keep honest counsel, ride, run, mar a curi-   32
ous tale in telling it, and deliver a plain message   33
bluntly. That which ordinary men are fit for I am
qualified in, and the best of me is diligence.

LEAR   How old art thou?

KENT   Not so young, sir, to love a woman for singing,   37
nor so old to dote on her for anything. I have years on
my back forty-eight.

LEAR   Follow me; thou shalt serve me. If I like thee no
worse after dinner, I will not part from thee yet.—
Dinner, ho, dinner! Where's my knave, my fool? Go
you and call my fool hither.   [Exit one.]

        Enter steward [Oswald].

You! You, sirrah, where's my daughter?

OSWALD   So please you—   Exit.

LEAR   What says the fellow there? Call the clodpoll   46
back.   [Exit a knight.]
Where's my fool, ho? I think the world's asleep.

        [Enter Knight.]

How now? Where's that mongrel?

KNIGHT   He says, my lord, your daughter is not well.

LEAR   Why came not the slave back to me when I called
him?

KNIGHT   Sir, he answered me in the roundest manner,   53
he would not.

LEAR   He would not?

KNIGHT   My lord, I know not what the matter is, but to
my judgment Your Highness is not entertained with   57
that ceremonious affection as you were wont. There's
a great abatement of kindness appears as well in the
general dependents as in the Duke himself also and   60
your daughter.

LEAR   Ha? Say'st thou so?

KNIGHT   I beseech you, pardon me, my lord, if I be
mistaken, for my duty cannot be silent when I think
Your Highness wronged.

LEAR   Thou but rememberest me of mine own concep-   66
tion. I have perceived a most faint neglect of late,   67
which I have rather blamed as mine own jealous   68

curiosity than as a very pretense and purpose of   69
unkindness. I will look further into't. But where's my
fool? I have not seen him this two days.   71

KNIGHT   Since my young lady's going into France, sir,
the Fool hath much pined away.

LEAR   No more of that. I have noted it well. Go you and
tell my daughter I would speak with her. [Exit one.]
Go you call hither my fool.   [Exit one.]

        Enter steward [Oswald].

Oh, you, sir, you, come you hither, sir. Who am I, sir?

OSWALD   My lady's father.

LEAR   "My lady's father"? My lord's knave! You whoreson dog, you slave, you cur!

OSWALD   I am none of these, my lord, I beseech your
pardon.

LEAR   Do you bandy looks with me, you rascal?   83
                                    [He strikes Oswald.]

OSWALD   I'll not be strucken, my lord.   84

KENT   Nor tripped neither, you base football player.   85
                                    [He trips up Oswald's heels.]

LEAR   I thank thee, fellow. Thou serv'st me, and I'll love
thee.

KENT   Come, sir, arise, away! I'll teach you differences.   88
Away, away! If you will measure your lubber's length   89
again, tarry; but away! Go to. Have you wisdom? So.   90
                                    [He pushes Oswald out.]

LEAR   Now, my friendly knave, I thank thee. There's
earnest of thy service.   [He gives Kent money.]   92

        Enter Fool.

FOOL   Let me hire him too. Here's my coxcomb.   93
                                    [Offering Kent his cap.]

LEAR   How now, my pretty knave, how dost thou?

FOOL   [to Kent] Sirrah, you were best take my coxcomb.   95

KENT   Why, Fool?

FOOL   Why? For taking one's part that's out of favor.
Nay, an thou canst not smile as the wind sits, thou'lt   98
catch cold shortly. There, take my coxcomb. Why, this   99
fellow has banished two on 's daughters and did the   100
third a blessing against my will. If thou follow him, thou   101
must needs wear my coxcomb.—How now, nuncle?   102
Would I had two coxcombs and two daughters.

LEAR   Why, my boy?

69 very pretense true intention   71 this these   83 bandy looks
exchange glances (in such a way as to imply that Oswald and Lear
are social equals)   84 strucken struck   85 football (A raucous street
game played by the lower classes.)   88 differences distinctions in
rank.   89–90 If . . . again i.e., If you want to be laid out flat again, you
clumsy ox   90 Go to (An expression of impatience or anger.)   Have
you wisdom? i.e., Wise up.   92 earnest of a first payment for
93 coxcomb fool's cap, crested with a red comb.   95 you were best
you had better   98–9 an . . . shortly i.e., if you can't play along with
those in power, you'll find yourself out in the cold.   100 banished
(Paradoxically, by giving Goneril and Regan his kingdom, Lear has
lost them, given them power over him.)   on 's of his   101 blessing
i.e., bestowing Cordelia on France and saving her from the curse of
insolent prosperity   102 nuncle (Contraction of "mine uncle," the
Fool's way of addressing Lear.)

27 countenance face and bearing   32 keep honest counsel respect
confidences   32–3 curious ornate, elaborate   37 to love as to love
46 clodpoll blockhead   53 roundest bluntest   57 entertained treated
60 general dependents servants generally   66 rememberest remind
66–7 conception idea, thought.   67 faint halfhearted   68–9 jealous
curiosity overscrupulous regard for matters of etiquette

FOOL   If I gave them all my living, I'd keep my 105
coxcombs myself. There's mine; beg another of thy 106
daughters. 107

LEAR   Take heed, sirrah—the whip.

FOOL   Truth's a dog must to kennel. He must be
whipped out, when the Lady Brach may stand by th' 110
fire and stink.

LEAR   A pestilent gall to me! 112

FOOL   Sirrah, I'll teach thee a speech.

LEAR   Do.

FOOL   Mark it, nuncle:
    Have more than thou showest, 116
    Speak less than thou knowest,
    Lend less than thou owest, 118
    Ride more than thou goest, 119
    Learn more than thou trowest, 120
    Set less than thou throwest; 121
    Leave thy drink and thy whore,
    And keep in-a-door, 123
    And thou shalt have more 124
    Than two tens to a score. 125

KENT   This is nothing, Fool.

FOOL   Then 'tis like the breath of an unfee'd lawyer; you 127
gave me nothing for't. Can you make no use of nothing, nuncle?

LEAR   Why, no, boy. Nothing can be made out of
nothing.

FOOL   [to Kent]   Prithee, tell him; so much the rent of his 132
land comes to. He will not believe a fool. 133

LEAR   A bitter fool! 134

FOOL   Dost know the difference, my boy, between a
bitter fool and a sweet one?

LEAR   No, lad. Teach me.

FOOL
    That lord that counseled thee
        To give away thy land,
    Come place him here by me;
        Do thou for him stand. 141
    The sweet and bitter fool
        Will presently appear: 143
    The one in motley here, 144
    The other found out there. 145

105 living property   105–6 keep my coxcombs (as proof of my folly)
106–7 beg . . . daughters i.e., beg for the coxcomb that you deserve for
dealing with your daughters as you did.   110 Brach bitch hound
(here likened to Goneril and Regan, who have been given favored
places despite their reeking of dishonest flattery)   112 gall irritation,
bitterness—literally, a painful swelling, or bile. (Lear is stung by the
Fool's gibe because it is so true.)   116 Have . . . showest don't display your wealth ostentatiously   118 owest own   119 goest i.e., on
foot. (Travel unostentatiously on horseback, not afoot.)   120 Learn
i.e., listen to.   trowest believe   121 Set . . . throwest don't stake
everything on a single throw   123 in-a-door indoors, at home
124–5 And . . . score and you will do better than break even (since a
score equals two tens, or twenty).   127 'tis . . . lawyer i.e., it is free—
and useless—advice. (Lawyers, being proverbially mercenary, would
not give good advice unless paid well.)   132–3 so . . . to (Because
Lear has given away his land, he can collect no rent.)   134 bitter
satirical   141 Do . . . stand take his place.   143 presently immediately   144 motley the parti-colored dress of the professional fool.
(The Fool identifies himself as the sweet fool, Lear as the bitter fool
who counseled himself to give away his kingdom.)   145 found out
there discovered there. (The Fool points at Lear.)

LEAR   Dost thou call me fool, boy?

FOOL   All thy other titles thou hast given away; that
thou wast born with.

KENT   This is not altogether fool, my lord.

FOOL   No, faith, lords and great men will not let me; if 150
I had a monopoly out, they would have part on't. And 151
ladies too, they will not let me have all the fool to myself; they'll be snatching. Nuncle, give me an egg and 153
I'll give thee two crowns.

LEAR   What two crowns shall they be?

FOOL   Why, after I have cut the egg i'th' middle and eat 156
up the meat, the two crowns of the egg. When thou 157
clovest thy crown i'th' middle and gav'st away both
parts, thou bor'st thine ass on thy back o'er the dirt. 159
Thou hadst little wit in thy bald crown when thou
gav'st thy golden one away. If I speak like myself in 161
this, let him be whipped that first finds it so. 162
    [Sings.]   "Fools had ne'er less grace in a year, 163
        For wise men are grown foppish 164
    And know not how their wits to wear, 165
        Their manners are so apish." 166

LEAR   When were you wont to be so full of songs,
sirrah?

FOOL   I have used it, nuncle, e'er since thou mad'st thy 169
daughters thy mothers; for when thou gav'st them the
rod and putt'st down thine own breeches,
    [Sings]   "Then they for sudden joy did weep,
        And I for sorrow sung,
    That such a king should play bo-peep 174
        And go the fools among."
Prithee, nuncle, keep a schoolmaster that can teach
thy fool to lie. I would fain learn to lie.

LEAR   An you lie, sirrah, we'll have you whipped. 178

FOOL   I marvel what kin thou and thy daughters are.
They'll have me whipped for speaking true, thou'lt
have me whipped for lying, and sometimes I am
whipped for holding my peace. I had rather be any
kind o' thing than a fool. And yet I would not be thee,
nuncle. Thou hast pared thy wit o' both sides and left
nothing i'th' middle. Here comes one o' th' parings.

Enter Goneril.

LEAR
How now, daughter? What makes that frontlet on? 186
You are too much of late i'th' frown.

150 No . . . let me i.e., Great persons at court will not let me monopolize folly; I am not *altogether fool* in the sense of being "all the fool
there is"   151 a monopoly out a corner on the market. (The granting
of monopolies was a common abuse under King James and Queen
Elizabeth.)   on't of it.   153 snatching seizing their share (including
sexual pleasure).   156–7 and eat . . . meat and have eaten the edible
part   159 bor'st . . . dirt i.e., bore the ass instead of letting the ass
bear you.   161–2 If . . . so If I speak like a fool in saying this, let the
first person to discover the truth of this be whipped (since in this corrupt world those who speak truth are punished for doing so).
163–6 "Fools . . . apish" "Fools have never been so out of favor, for
wise men foppishly trade places with the fools and no longer know
how to show off their wit to advantage, they have grown so foolish
in their manners."   169 used practiced   174 bo-peep (A child's
game.)   178 An If   186 What . . . on? What is that frown doing on
your forehead?

FOOL   Thou wast a pretty fellow when thou hadst no
need to care for her frowning; now thou art an O with-   189
out a figure. I am better than thou art now; I am a fool,   190
thou art nothing. [*To Goneril*] Yes, forsooth, I will
hold my tongue; so your face bids me, though you say
nothing.
     Mum, mum,
     He that keeps nor crust nor crumb,   195
     Weary of all, shall want some.   196
[*Pointing to Lear*] That's a shelled peascod.   197

GONERIL
     Not only, sir, this your all-licensed fool,   198
     But other of your insolent retinue
     Do hourly carp and quarrel, breaking forth   200
     In rank and not-to-be-endurèd riots. Sir,   201
     I had thought by making this well known unto you
     To have found a safe redress, but now grow fearful,   203
     By what yourself too late have spoke and done,   204
     That you protect this course and put it on   205
     By your allowance; which if you should, the fault   206
     Would not scape censure, nor the redresses sleep   207
     Which in the tender of a wholesome weal   208
     Might in their working do you that offense,   209
     Which else were shame, that then necessity   210
     Will call discreet proceeding.   211

FOOL   For you know, nuncle,
     "The hedge sparrow fed the cuckoo so long   213
     That it had it head bit off by it young."   214
So, out went the candle, and we were left darkling.   215

LEAR [*to Goneril*]   Are you our daughter?

GONERIL
     I would you would make use of your good wisdom,
     Whereof I know you are fraught, and put away   218
     These dispositions which of late transport you   219
     From what you rightly are.

FOOL   May not an ass know when the cart draws the   221
horse? Whoop, Jug! I love thee.   222

LEAR
     Does any here know me? This is not Lear.
     Does Lear walk thus, speak thus? Where are his eyes?
     Either his notion weakens, or his discernings   225
     Are lethargied—Ha! Waking? 'Tis not so.   226
     Who is it that can tell me who I am?

FOOL   Lear's shadow.

LEAR
     I would learn that; for, by the marks of sovereignty,   229
     Knowledge, and reason, I should be false persuaded   230
     I had daughters.   231

FOOL   Which they will make an obedient father.   232

LEAR   Your name, fair gentlewoman?

GONERIL
     This admiration, sir, is much o'th' savor   234
     Of other your new pranks. I do beseech you   235
     To understand my purposes aright.
     As you are old and reverend, should be wise.   237
     Here do you keep a hundred knights and squires,
     Men so disordered, so debauched and bold   239
     That this our court, infected with their manners,
     Shows like a riotous inn. Epicurism and lust   241
     Makes it more like a tavern or a brothel
     Than a graced palace. The shame itself doth speak   243
     For instant remedy. Be then desired,   244
     By her that else will take the thing she begs,
     A little to disquantity your train,   246
     And the remainders that shall still depend   247
     To be such men as may besort your age,   248
     Which know themselves and you.

LEAR   Darkness and devils!   249
     Saddle my horses! Call my train together! [*Exit one.*]   250
     Degenerate bastard, I'll not trouble thee.
     Yet have I left a daughter.

GONERIL
     You strike my people, and your disordered rabble
     Make servants of their betters.

     Enter Albany.

LEAR
     Woe, that too late repents!—Oh, sir, are you come?   255
     Is it your will? Speak, sir.—Prepare my horses.
                                        [*Exit one.*]
     Ingratitude, thou marble-hearted fiend,
     More hideous when thou show'st thee in a child
     Than the sea monster!

ALBANY   Pray, sir, be patient.

LEAR [*to Goneril*]   Detested kite, thou liest!   261
     My train are men of choice and rarest parts,   262
     That all particulars of duty know
     And in the most exact regard support   264
     The worships of their name. Oh, most small fault,   265

189–90 O without a figure zero, cipher of no value unless preceded by
a digit.   **195–6 He . . . some** i.e., That person who, having grown weary
of his possessions, gives all away, will find himself in need of part of
what is gone.   **196 want** lack   **197 shelled peascod** shelled pea pod,
empty of its contents.   **198 all-licensed** allowed to speak or act as he
pleases   **200 carp** find fault   **201 rank** gross, excessive   **203 safe** certain   **204 too late** all too recently   **205 put it on** encourage it
206 allowance approval   **207–11 nor . . . proceeding** nor would the
punishments lie dormant which, out of care for the common welfare,
might prove unpleasant to you—proceedings that the stern necessity of
the times will regard as prudent even if under normal circumstances
they might seem shameful.   **213 cuckoo** a bird that lays its eggs in
other birds' nests   **214 it head** its head.   **it young** i.e., the young
cuckoo. (A cautionary fable about ungrateful children.)   **215 darkling**
in the dark.   **218 fraught** freighted, provided   **219 dispositions** inclinations, moods   **221–2 May . . . horse?** i.e., May not even a fool see
that matters are backwards when a daughter lectures her father?
222 Jug i.e., Joan. (The origin of this phrase is uncertain.)   **225 notion**
intellectual power   **225–6 or his . . . lethargied** or his faculties are
asleep   **226 Waking?** i.e., Am I really awake?

229 that i.e., who I am.   **marks of sovereignty** outward and visible
evidence of being king   **230–1 I should . . . daughters** i.e., all these
outward signs of sanity and status would seem to suggest (falsely)
that I am the king who had obedient daughters.   **232 Which** Whom
234 admiration (guise of) wonderment   **235 other** other of
237 should i.e., you should   **239 Men . . . bold** men so disorderly, so
depraved and impudent   **241 Shows** appears.   **Epicurism** Excess,
hedonism   **243 graced** dignified   **244 desired** requested   **246 dis-
quantity your train** diminish the number of your attendants   **247 the
remainders . . . depend** those who remain to attend you   **248 besort**
befit   **249 Which . . . you** servants who have proper self-knowledge
and an awareness of how they should serve you.   **250 train** retinue
255 Woe, that Woe to the person who   **261 kite** bird of prey
262 parts qualities   **264–5 And . . . name** and with utter scrupulous-
ness may uphold the honor of their reputation.

How ugly didst thou in Cordelia show!
Which, like an engine, wrenched my frame of nature 267
From the fixed place, drew from my heart all love, 268
And added to the gall. Oh, Lear, Lear, Lear! 269
Beat at this gate [*striking his head*] that let thy folly in
And thy dear judgment out!—Go, go, my people. 271

[Exeunt some.]

ALBANY
My lord, I am guiltless as I am ignorant
Of what hath moved you.
LEAR   It may be so, my lord.—
Hear, Nature, hear! Dear goddess, hear!
Suspend thy purpose if thou didst intend
To make this creature fruitful!
Into her womb convey sterility;
Dry up in her the organs of increase,
And from her derogate body never spring 279
A babe to honor her! If she must teem, 280
Create her child of spleen, that it may live 281
And be a thwart disnatured torment to her! 282
Let it stamp wrinkles in her brow of youth,
With cadent tears fret channels in her cheeks, 284
Turn all her mother's pains and benefits 285
To laughter and contempt, that she may feel
How sharper than a serpent's tooth it is
To have a thankless child! Away, away!

Exit [with Kent and the rest of Lear's followers].

ALBANY
Now, gods that we adore, whereof comes this?
GONERIL
Never afflict yourself to know more of it, 290
But let his disposition have that scope 291
As dotage gives it. 292

Enter Lear.

LEAR
What, fifty of my followers at a clap?
Within a fortnight?
ALBANY   What's the matter, sir?
LEAR
I'll tell thee. [*To Goneril*] Life and death! I am ashamed
That thou hast power to shake my manhood thus,
That these hot tears, which break from me perforce,
Should make thee worth them. Blasts and fogs upon
    thee! 298
Th'untented woundings of a father's curse 299
Pierce every sense about thee! Old fond eyes, 300
Beweep this cause again, I'll pluck ye out 301
And cast you, with the waters that you loose, 302

To temper clay. Yea, is't come to this? 303
Ha! Let it be so. I have another daughter,
Who, I am sure, is kind and comfortable. 305
When she shall hear this of thee, with her nails
She'll flay thy wolvish visage. Thou shalt find
That I'll resume the shape which thou dost think 308
I have cast off forever.   *Exit.*
GONERIL [*to Albany*]   Do you mark that? 309
ALBANY
I cannot be so partial, Goneril,
To the great love I bear you— 311
GONERIL
Pray you, content.—What, Oswald, ho!
[*To the Fool*] You, sir, more knave than fool, after your
    master.
FOOL   Nuncle Lear, nuncle Lear! Tarry, take the Fool 314
    with thee. 315
        A fox, when one has caught her,
        And such a daughter
        Should sure to the slaughter, 318
        If my cap would buy a halter. 319
        So the Fool follows after.   *Exit.*
GONERIL
This man hath had good counsel. A hundred knights? 321
'Tis politic and safe to let him keep 322
At point a hundred knights—yes, that on every
    dream, 323
Each buzz, each fancy, each complaint, dislike, 324
He may enguard his dotage with their powers 325
And hold our lives in mercy.—Oswald, I say! 326
ALBANY   Well, you may fear too far. 327
GONERIL   Safer than trust too far.
Let me still take away the harms I fear, 329
Not fear still to be taken. I know his heart. 330
What he hath uttered I have writ my sister.
If she sustain him and his hundred knights
When I have showed th'unfitness—

Enter steward [Oswald].

                                How now, Oswald?
What, have you writ that letter to my sister?
OSWALD   Ay, madam.
GONERIL
Take you some company and away to horse.
Inform her full of my particular fear,
And thereto add such reasons of your own
As may compact it more. Get you gone, 339

267–8 Which . . . place which, like a powerful mechanical contrivance, wrenched my natural affection away from where it belonged   **269 gall** bitterness.   **271 dear** precious   **279 derogate** debased   **280 teem** produce offspring   **281 spleen** violent ill nature   **282 thwart disnatured** obstinate, perverse, and unnatural, unfilial   **284 cadent** cascading.   **fret** wear away   **285 benefits** pleasures of motherhood   **290 Never . . . know** Don't distress yourself by seeking to know   **291 disposition** humor, mood   **292 As** that   **298 Should . . . them** should seem to suggest that you are worth a king's tears.   **Blasts and fogs** Infectious blights and disease-bearing fogs   **299 untented** too deep to be probed and cleansed   **300 fond** foolish   **301 Beweep** if you weep for   **302 loose** let loose (in tears)

303 To temper clay to mix with earth. (Lear threatens to cast both his eyes and their tears to the ground.)   **305 comfortable** comforting.   **308 the shape** i.e., the kingship   **309 Do . . . that?** i.e., Did you hear his threat to resume royal power?   **311 To** because of   **314–15 take . . . thee** (1) take me with you (2) take the name "fool" with you. (A stock phrase of taunting farewell.)   **318 Should sure** should certainly be sent   **319 halter** (1) rope for leading an animal (2) hangman's noose.   **321 This . . . counsel** (Said sarcastically.)   **322 politic** prudent. (Said ironically.)   **323 At point** armed and ready.   **dream** i.e., imagined wrong   **324 buzz** idle rumor   **325 enguard** protect   **326 in mercy** at his mercy.   **327 fear too far** overestimate the danger.   **329 still take away** always remove   **330 Not . . . taken** rather than dwell continually in the fear of being taken prisoner by such harms.   **339 compact** confirm

And hasten your return.   [*Exit Oswald.*]
                              No, no, my lord,
This milky gentleness and course of yours   341
Though I condemn not, yet, under pardon,   342
You're much more attasked for want of wisdom   343
Than praised for harmful mildness.   344

ALBANY
How far your eyes may pierce I cannot tell.   345
Striving to better, oft we mar what's well.

GONERIL   Nay, then—
ALBANY   Well, well, th'event.   *Exeunt.* 348

❖

1.5

Enter Lear, Kent [disguised as Caius], and Fool.

LEAR   [*giving a letter to Kent*]   Go you before to Gloucester   1
with these letters. Acquaint my daughter no further   2
with anything you know than comes from her demand   3
out of the letter. If your diligence be not speedy, I shall   4
be there afore you.

KENT   I will not sleep, my lord, till I have delivered your
letter.   *Exit.*

FOOL   If a man's brains were in 's heels, were't not in   8
danger of kibes?   9

LEAR   Ay, boy.

FOOL   Then, I prithee, be merry. Thy wit shall not go   11
slipshod.   12

LEAR   Ha, ha, ha!

FOOL   Shalt see thy other daughter will use thee kindly,   14
for though she's as like this as a crab's like an apple,   15
yet I can tell what I can tell.

LEAR   What canst tell, boy?

FOOL   She will taste as like this as a crab does to a crab.
Thou canst tell why one's nose stands i'th' middle
on 's face?   20

LEAR   No.

FOOL   Why, to keep one's eyes of either side 's nose,   22
that what a man cannot smell out he may spy into.

LEAR   I did her wrong.   24

FOOL   Canst tell how an oyster makes his shell?

LEAR   No.

FOOL   Nor I neither. But I can tell why a snail has a
house.

LEAR   Why?

FOOL   Why, to put 's head in, not to give it away to his   30
daughters and leave his horns without a case.   31

LEAR   I will forget my nature. So kind a father!—Be my   32
horses ready?

FOOL   Thy asses are gone about 'em. The reason why   34
the seven stars are no more than seven is a pretty   35
reason.

LEAR   Because they are not eight.

FOOL   Yes, indeed. Thou wouldst make a good fool.

LEAR   To take't again perforce! Monster ingratitude!   39

FOOL   If thou wert my fool, nuncle, I'd have thee beaten
for being old before thy time.

LEAR   How's that?

FOOL   Thou shouldst not have been old till thou hadst
been wise.

LEAR
Oh, let me not be mad, not mad, sweet heaven!
Keep me in temper; I would not be mad!   46

[*Enter Gentleman.*]

How now, are the horses ready?

GENTLEMAN   Ready, my lord.

LEAR   Come, boy.   [*Exeunt Lear and Gentleman.*]

FOOL
She that's a maid now, and laughs at my departure,
Shall not be a maid long, unless things be cut
shorter.   *Exit.* 51

❖

2.1

Enter Bastard [Edmund] and Curan, severally.

EDMUND   Save thee, Curan.   1

CURAN   And you, sir. I have been with your father and
given him notice that the Duke of Cornwall and Regan
his duchess will be here with him this night.

EDMUND   How comes that?

CURAN   Nay, I know not. You have heard of the news
abroad—I mean the whispered ones, for they are yet   7
but ear-kissing arguments?   8

EDMUND   Not I. Pray you, what are they?

CURAN   Have you heard of no likely wars toward twixt   10
the Dukes of Cornwall and Albany?

EDMUND   Not a word.

CURAN   You may do, then, in time. Fare you well, sir.
                                         Exit.

341 **milky . . . course** effeminate and gentle way   342 **under pardon**
if you'll excuse my saying so   343 **attasked** taken to task for, blamed
344 **harmful mildness** mildness that causes harm.   345 **pierce** i.e.,
see into matters   348 **th'event** i.e., time will tell.
1.5. Location: Before Albany's palace.
1 **Gloucester** i.e., the place in Gloucestershire   2 **these letters** this letter.   3 **demand** inquiry   4 **out of** prompted by   8–9 **were't . . .**
kibes? wouldn't his brains be in danger of that common affliction of
the heel called chilblains?   11–12 **Thy wit . . . slipshod** i.e., Your
brains would have no need for slippers to avoid chafing the
chilblains, since you have no brains. (Anyone who journeys to Regan
in hopes of kind treatment is utterly brainless.)   14 **Shalt** Thou shalt.
kindly (1) with filial kindness (2) according to her own nature
15 **crab** crab apple   20 **on 's** of his   22 **of either side 's** on either side
of his   24 **her** i.e., Cordelia

30–1 **Why, to . . . case** i.e., The snail's head and horns are unendan-
gered with its *case* or shell; Lear, conversely, has given away his
crown to his daughters, leaving his brows unadorned and vulnerable.
(With a suggestion too of the cuckold's horned head, as though
Lear's victimization had a sexual dimension.)   32 **nature** natural
affection. (Compare line 14 and note.)   34 **Thy . . . 'em** i.e., Your servants (who labor like asses in your service) have gone about readying
the horses.   35 **seven stars** Pleiades   39 **To take't . . . perforce!** i.e.,
To think that Goneril would forcibly take back again the privileges
guaranteed to me! (Or perhaps Lear is meditating an armed restoration of his monarchy.)   46 **temper** mental equilibrium
51 **things** i.e., penises.   **cut shorter** (A bawdy joke addressed to the
audience.)
2.1. Location: The Earl of Gloucester's house.
0.1 *severally* separately.   1 **Save** God save   7 **abroad** going the
rounds.   **ones** i.e., the news, regarded as plural   8 **ear-kissing argu-**
ments lightly whispered topics.   10 **toward** impending

EDMUND
The Duke be here tonight? The better! Best!   14
This weaves itself perforce into my business.
My father hath set guard to take my brother,
And I have one thing, of a queasy question,   17
Which I must act. Briefness and fortune, work!—   18
Brother, a word. Descend. Brother, I say!

Enter Edgar.

My father watches. Oh, sir, fly this place!
Intelligence is given where you are hid.
You have now the good advantage of the night.
Have you not spoken 'gainst the Duke of Cornwall?
He's coming hither, now, i'th' night, i'th' haste,   24
And Regan with him. Have you nothing said
Upon his party 'gainst the Duke of Albany?   26
Advise yourself.

EDGAR   I am sure on't, not a word.   27
EDMUND
I hear my father coming. Pardon me;
In cunning I must draw my sword upon you.
Draw. Seem to defend yourself. Now, quit you well.—
                                    [*They draw.*]   30
Yield! Come before my father!—Light, ho, here!—   31
Fly, brother.—Torches, torches!—So, farewell.   32
                                    Exit Edgar.
Some blood drawn on me would beget opinion   33
Of my more fierce endeavor. I have seen drunkards   34
Do more than this in sport. [*He wounds himself in the
arm.*] Father, father!
Stop, stop! No help?

Enter Gloucester, and servants with torches.

GLOUCESTER   Now, Edmund, where's the villain?
EDMUND
Here stood he in the dark, his sharp sword out,
Mumbling of wicked charms, conjuring the moon
To stand 's auspicious mistress.
GLOUCESTER   But where is he?   39
EDMUND
Look, sir, I bleed.
GLOUCESTER   Where is the villain, Edmund?
EDMUND
Fled this way, sir. When by no means he could—
GLOUCESTER   Pursue him, ho! Go after.
                            [*Exeunt some servants.*]
                            By no means what?
EDMUND
Persuade me to the murder of Your Lordship,
But that I told him the revenging gods   44

'Gainst parricides did all the thunder bend,   45
Spoke with how manifold and strong a bond
The child was bound to th' father; sir, in fine,   47
Seeing how loathly opposite I stood   48
To his unnatural purpose, in fell motion   49
With his preparèd sword he charges home   50
My unprovided body, latched mine arm;   51
And when he saw my best alarumed spirits,   52
Bold in the quarrel's right, roused to th'encounter, 53
Or whether ghasted by the noise I made,   54
Full suddenly he fled.
GLOUCESTER   Let him fly far.   55
Not in this land shall he remain uncaught;
And found—dispatch. The noble Duke my master,   57
My worthy arch and patron, comes tonight.   58
By his authority I will proclaim it
That he which finds him shall deserve our thanks,
Bringing the murderous coward to the stake;   61
He that conceals him, death.
EDMUND
When I dissuaded him from his intent
And found him pight to do it, with curst speech   64
I threatened to discover him. He replied,   65
"Thou unpossessing bastard, dost thou think,   66
If I would stand against thee, would the reposal   67
Of any trust, virtue, or worth in thee
Make thy words faithed? No. What I should deny—   69
As this I would, ay, though thou didst produce
My very character—I'd turn it all   71
To thy suggestion, plot, and damnèd practice;   72
And thou must make a dullard of the world   73
If they not thought the profits of my death   74
Were very pregnant and potential spirits   75
To make thee seek it."
GLOUCESTER   Oh, strange and fastened villain! 76
Would he deny his letter, said he?
I never got him.   *Tucket within.* 78
Hark, the Duke's trumpets! I know not why he comes.
All ports I'll bar; the villain shall not scape.   80
The Duke must grant me that. Besides, his picture   81
I will send far and near, that all the kingdom
May have due note of him; and of my land,

---

45 bend aim **47 in fine** in conclusion **48 loathly opposite**
loathingly opposed **49 fell motion** deadly thrust **50 preparèd**
unsheathed and ready. **home** to the very heart **51 unprovided**
unprotected. **latched** nicked, lanced **52 best alarumed** thoroughly
aroused to action, as by a trumpet **53 quarrel's right** justice of the
cause **54 ghasted** frightened **55 Let him fly far** i.e., Any fleeing, no
matter how far, will be in vain. **57 dispatch** i.e., that will be the end
for him. **58 arch and patron** chief patron **61 to the stake** i.e., to
reckoning **64 pight** determined. **curst** angry **65 discover** expose
66 unpossessing unable to inherit, beggarly **67 reposal** placing
69 faithed believed. **What** That which, whatever **71 character**
written testimony, handwriting. **turn** attribute **72 suggestion** instigation. **practice** scheming **73–6 And . . . seek it** and you must
think everyone slow-witted indeed not to suppose that they would
see how the profits to be gained by my death would be fertile and
potent tempters to make you seek my death. **76 strange and fastened** unnatural and hardened **78 got** begot. **s.d. Tucket** series of
notes on the trumpet, here indicating Cornwall's arrival **80 ports**
seaports, or gateways **81 picture** description

---

14 The better! Best! So much the better; in fact, the best that could
happen! **17 queasy question** matter not for queasy stomachs
18 Briefness and fortune Expeditious dispatch and good luck
24 i'th' haste in great haste **26 Upon his party** i.e., recklessly on
Cornwall's behalf (? It would be dangerous to speak on either side.)
27 Advise yourself Consider your situation. **on't of it 30 quit you**
defend, acquit yourself **31–2 Yield . . . farewell** (Edmund speaks
loudly as though trying to arrest Edgar, calls for others to help, and
privately bids Edgar to flee.) **33–4 beget . . . endeavor** create an
impression of my having fought fiercely. **39 stand 's** stand his, act as
his **44 that** when

Loyal and natural boy, I'll work the means   84
To make thee capable.   85

Enter Cornwall, Regan, and attendants.

CORNWALL
How now, my noble friend? Since I came hither,
Which I can call but now, I have heard strange news.
REGAN
If it be true, all vengeance comes too short
Which can pursue th'offender. How dost, my lord?
GLOUCESTER
Oh madam, my old heart is cracked, it's cracked!
REGAN
What, did my father's godson seek your life?
He whom my father named? Your Edgar?
GLOUCESTER
Oh, lady, lady, shame would have it hid!
REGAN
Was he not companion with the riotous knights
That tended upon my father?
GLOUCESTER
I know not, madam. 'Tis too bad, too bad.
EDMUND
Yes, madam, he was of that consort.   97
REGAN
No marvel, then, though he were ill affected.   98
'Tis they have put him on the old man's death,   99
To have th'expense and spoil of his revenues.   100
I have this present evening from my sister
Been well informed of them, and with such cautions
That if they come to sojourn at my house
I'll not be there.
CORNWALL   Nor I, assure thee, Regan.
Edmund, I hear that you have shown your father
A childlike office.
EDMUND   It was my duty, sir.   106
GLOUCESTER [*to Cornwall*]
He did bewray his practice, and received   107
This hurt you see striving to apprehend him.   108
CORNWALL   Is he pursued?
GLOUCESTER   Ay, my good lord.
CORNWALL
If he be taken, he shall never more
Be feared of doing harm. Make your own purpose,   112
How in my strength you please. For you, Edmund,   113
Whose virtue and obedience doth this instant
So much commend itself, you shall be ours.
Natures of such deep trust we shall much need;
You we first seize on.
EDMUND   I shall serve you, sir,
Truly, however else.   118
GLOUCESTER   For him I thank Your Grace.

CORNWALL
You know not why we came to visit you—
REGAN
—Thus out of season, threading dark-eyed night:
Occasions, noble Gloucester, of some poise,   122
Wherein we must have use of your advice.
Our father he hath writ, so hath our sister,
Of differences, which I least thought it fit   125
To answer from our home. The several messengers   126
From hence attend dispatch. Our good old friend,   127
Lay comforts to your bosom, and bestow
Your needful counsel to our businesses,
Which craves the instant use.
GLOUCESTER   I serve you, madam.   130
Your Graces are right welcome.   *Flourish. Exeunt.*

❖

2.2

*Enter Kent [disguised as Caius] and steward
[Oswald], severally.*

OSWALD   Good dawning to thee, friend. Art of this   1
house?
KENT   Ay.
OSWALD   Where may we set our horses?
KENT   I'th' mire.
OSWALD   Prithee, if thou lov'st me, tell me.   6
KENT   I love thee not.
OSWALD   Why then, I care not for thee.
KENT   If I had thee in Lipsbury pinfold, I would make   9
thee care for me.   10
OSWALD   Why dost thou use me thus? I know thee not.
KENT   Fellow, I know thee.   12
OSWALD   What dost thou know me for?
KENT   A knave, a rascal, an eater of broken meats;   14
a base, proud, shallow, beggarly, three-suited,   15
hundred-pound, filthy worsted-stocking knave; a   16
lily-livered, action-taking, whoreson, glass-gazing,   17
superserviceable, finical rogue; one-trunk-inheriting   18
slave; one that wouldst be a bawd in way of good ser-   19
vice, and art nothing but the composition of a knave,   20
beggar, coward, pander, and the son and heir of a

---

122 poise weight   **125 differences** quarrels.   **which** which letters
126 from our home while still at our palace in Cornwall.   **127 attend
dispatch** wait to be dispatched.   **130 the instant use** immediate
attention.
2.2. Location: Before Gloucester's house.
0.2 *severally* at separate doors.   **1 dawning** (It is not yet day.)   **6 if
thou lov'st me** i.e., if you bear good will toward me. (But Kent deliberately takes the phrase in its literal, not courtly, sense.)   **9 in Lipsbury pinfold** i.e., within the pinfold of the lips, between my teeth. (A
pinfold is a pound for stray animals.)   **10 care for** i.e., be wary of.
(Playing on *care not for*, "do not like," in line 8.)   **12 I know thee** i.e., I
know you for what you are. (Playing on *know thee not*, "am unacquainted with you," in line 11.)   **14 broken meats** scraps of food
(such as were passed out to the most lowly)   **15–16 three-suited . . .
knave** i.e., a steward of a household, with an allowance of three suits
a year and a comfortable income of one hundred pounds, dressed in
dirty wool stockings appropriate to the servant class   **16–19 a lily-
livered . . . slave** a cowardly, litigious, insufferable, self-infatuated,
officious, foppish rogue, whose personal property all fits into one
trunk   **19–20 bawd . . . service** i.e., pimp or pander as a way of providing whatever is wanted   **20 composition** compound

---

84 natural (1) prompted by natural feelings of loyalty and affection
(2) bastard   **85 capable** legally able to become the inheritor.   **97 consort** crew.   **98 though** if.   **ill affected** ill-disposed, disloyal.   **99 put
him on** incited him to   **100 th'expense and spoil** the squandering
106 childlike filial   **107 bewray his practice** expose his (Edgar's)
plot   **108 apprehend** arrest   **112–13 Make . . . please** Go about
achieving your purpose, making free use of my authority and
resources.   **113 For** As for   **118 however else** above all else.

mongrel bitch; one whom I will beat into clamorous whining if thou deny'st the least syllable of thy addi- 23
tion. 24

OSWALD   Why, what a monstrous fellow art thou thus to rail on one that is neither known of thee nor knows thee!

KENT   What a brazen-faced varlet art thou to deny thou knowest me! Is it two days since I tripped up thy heels and beat thee before the King? Draw, you rogue, for though it be night, yet the moon shines. I'll make a sop o'th' moonshine of you, you whoreson, cullionly 32
barbermonger. Draw!   [He brandishes his sword.] 33

OSWALD   Away! I have nothing to do with thee.

KENT   Draw, you rascal! You come with letters against the King, and take Vanity the puppet's part against 36
the royalty of her father. Draw, you rogue, or I'll so carbonado your shanks—draw, you rascal! Come 38
your ways. 39

OSWALD   Help, ho! Murder! Help!

KENT   Strike, you slave! Stand, rogue, stand, you neat 41
slave, strike!   [He beats him.]

OSWALD   Help, ho! Murder! Murder!

Enter Bastard [Edmund, with his rapier drawn], Cornwall, Regan, Gloucester, servants.

EDMUND   How now, what's the matter? Part! 44

KENT   With you, goodman boy, an you please! Come, 45
I'll flesh ye. Come on, young master. 46

GLOUCESTER   Weapons? Arms? What's the matter here?

CORNWALL   Keep peace, upon your lives! [Kent and Oswald are parted.] He dies that strikes again. What is the matter?

REGAN   The messengers from our sister and the King.

CORNWALL   What's your difference? Speak. 52

OSWALD   I am scarce in breath, my lord.

KENT   No marvel, you have so bestirred your valor. You cowardly rascal, nature disclaims in thee. A tailor 55
made thee.

CORNWALL   Thou art a strange fellow. A tailor make a man?

KENT   A tailor, sir. A stonecutter or a painter could not have made him so ill, though they had been but two years o'th' trade.

CORNWALL   Speak yet, how grew your quarrel?

OSWALD   This ancient ruffian, sir, whose life I have spared at suit of his gray beard—

KENT   Thou whoreson zed! Thou unnecessary letter!— 65
My lord, if you'll give me leave, I will tread this un- 66
bolted villain into mortar and daub the wall of a jakes 67
with him.—Spare my gray beard, you wagtail? 68

CORNWALL   Peace, sirrah!
You beastly knave, know you no reverence?

KENT
Yes, sir, but anger hath a privilege.

CORNWALL   Why art thou angry?

KENT
That such a slave as this should wear a sword,
Who wears no honesty. Such smiling rogues as these,
Like rats, oft bite the holy cords atwain 75
Which are too intrinse t'unloose; smooth every passion 76
That in the natures of their lords rebel, 77
Bring oil to fire, snow to their colder moods, 78
Renege, affirm, and turn their halcyon beaks 79
With every gale and vary of their masters, 80
Knowing naught, like dogs, but following.— 81
A plague upon your epileptic visage! 82
Smile you my speeches, as I were a fool? 83
Goose, an I had you upon Sarum plain, 84
I'd drive ye cackling home to Camelot. 85

CORNWALL   What, art thou mad, old fellow?

GLOUCESTER   How fell you out? Say that.

KENT
No contraries hold more antipathy
Than I and such a knave.

CORNWALL
Why dost thou call him knave? What is his fault?

KENT   His countenance likes me not. 91

CORNWALL
No more, perchance, does mine, nor his, nor hers.

KENT
Sir, 'tis my occupation to be plain:
I have seen better faces in my time
Than stands on any shoulder that I see
Before me at this instant.

CORNWALL   This is some fellow
Who, having been praised for bluntness, doth affect 97

---

65 zed the letter z (regarded as unnecessary and often not included in dictionaries of the time); hence, coarse **66–7 unbolted** unsifted; hence, coarse **67 daub** plaster.   **jakes** privy   **68 wagtail** i.e., bird wagging its tail feathers in pert obsequiousness.   **75 holy cords** sacred bonds of loyalty and order   **76 intrinse** intricate, tightly knotted.   **smooth** flatter, humor   **77 rebel** rebel against reason   **78 Bring . . . moods** flatteringly fuel the flame of their masters' angry passions, while similarly exacerbating their downward mood swings   **79 Renege, affirm** naysay one moment (when their lords are in a denying mood) and serve as yes-men the next.   **halcyon beaks** (The halcyon, or kingfisher, if hung up, would supposedly turn its beak into the wind.)   **80 gale and vary** shifting wind   **81 following** fawning and flattery.   **82 epileptic** i.e., trembling and pale with fright and distorted with a grin **83 Smile you** Do you smile at.   **as** as if   **84–5 Goose . . . Camelot** (The reference is obscure, but the general sense is that Kent, if given space and opportunity, would send Oswald packing like a cackling goose. Camelot, the legendary seat of King Arthur and his Knights of the Round Table, was thought to have been in the general vicinity of Salisbury, Sarum, and Gloucester.)   **91 likes** pleases **97 affect** adopt the style of

---

23–4 thy addition the titles I've given you.   **32 sop o'th' moonshine** something so perforated that it will soak up moonshine as a sop (floating piece of toast) soaks up liquor   **32–3 cullionly barbermonger** base frequenter of barber shops, fop. (*Cullion* originally meant "testicle.")   **36 Vanity . . . part** i.e., the part of Goneril (here personified as a character in a morality play)   **38 carbonado** cut crosswise, like meat for broiling   **38–9 Come your ways** Come on.   **41 neat** (1) foppish (2) calflike. (*Neat* means "horned cattle.")   **44 matter** i.e., trouble. (But Kent takes the meaning "cause for quarrel.")   **45 With you** I'll fight with you; my quarrel is with you.   **goodman boy** (A contemptuous epithet, a title of mock respect, addressed seemingly to Edmund.)   **an if**   **46 flesh** initiate into combat   **52 difference** quarrel.   **55 disclaims in** disowns

A saucy roughness, and constrains the garb 98
Quite from his nature. He cannot flatter, he; 99
An honest mind and plain, he must speak truth!
An they will take't, so; if not, he's plain. 101
These kind of knaves I know, which in this plainness
Harbor more craft and more corrupter ends
Than twenty silly-ducking observants 104
That stretch their duties nicely. 105

KENT
Sir, in good faith, in sincere verity, 106
Under th'allowance of your great aspect, 107
Whose influence, like the wreath of radiant fire 108
On flickering Phoebus' front—

CORNWALL   What mean'st by this? 109

KENT To go out of my dialect, which you discommend
so much. I know, sir, I am no flatterer. He that be- 111
guiled you in a plain accent was a plain knave, which 112
for my part I will not be, though I should win your 113
displeasure to entreat me to't. 114

CORNWALL [to Oswald] What was th'offense you gave him?

OSWALD I never gave him any.
It pleased the King his master very late 117
To strike at me, upon his misconstruction; 118
When he, compact, and flattering his displeasure, 119
Tripped me behind; being down, insulted, railed, 120
And put upon him such a deal of man 121
That worthied him, got praises of the King 122
For him attempting who was self-subdued; 123
And, in the fleshment of this dread exploit, 124
Drew on me here again.

KENT None of these rogues and cowards 126
But Ajax is their fool.

CORNWALL   Fetch forth the stocks! 127

98–9 constrains . . . nature i.e., distorts plainness quite from its true purpose so that it becomes instead a way of deceiving the listener. **99 He . . . he** He professes to be one who abhors the use of flattering speech. (Said sardonically.) **101 An . . . plain** If people will take his rudeness, fine; if not, his excuse is that he speaks plain truth. **104–5 Than . . . nicely** than twenty foolishly bowing, obsequious courtiers who outdo themselves in the punctilious performance of their courtly duties. **106 Sir, in good faith** (Kent assumes the wordy mannerisms of courtly flattery.) **107 th'allowance** the approval. **aspect** (1) countenance (2) astrological position **108 influence** astrological power **109 Phoebus' front** i.e., the sun's forehead **111–14 He . . . to't** The man who used plain speech to you craftily (see lines 102–5) and thereby taught you to suspect plain speakers of being deceitful was in fact a plain rascal, which part I will not play, much as it would please me to incur your displeasure if speaking thus would have that effect. (Kent would prefer to displease Cornwall, since Cornwall is pleased only by flatterers, and Kent has assumed until now that plain speech was the best way to offend, but he now argues mockingly that he can no longer speak plainly, since his honest utterance would be interpreted as duplicity.) **117 late** recently **118 upon his misconstruction** as a result of the King's misunderstanding (me) **119 When . . . displeasure** whereupon Kent, in cahoots with the King and his party, and wishing to gratify the King's anger at me **120 being down, insulted** when I was down, he exulted over me **121–2 And put . . . him** and acted with a bravado that earned him an accolade **123 For . . . self-subdued** for assailing one (i.e., myself) who chose not to resist **124 And . . . exploit** and, in the excitement of his first success in this fearless deed. (Said ironically.) **126–7 None . . . fool** i.e., You never find any rogues and cowards of this sort who do not outdo the blustering Ajax in their boasting.

You stubborn, ancient knave, you reverend braggart, 128
We'll teach you.

KENT   Sir, I am too old to learn.
Call not your stocks for me. I serve the King,
On whose employment I was sent to you.
You shall do small respect, show too bold malice
Against the grace and person of my master, 133
Stocking his messenger.

CORNWALL
Fetch forth the stocks! As I have life and honor,
There shall he sit till noon.

REGAN
Till noon? Till night, my lord, and all night too.

KENT
Why, madam, if I were your father's dog
You should not use me so. 139

REGAN   Sir, being his knave, I will. 140

CORNWALL
This is a fellow of the selfsame color 141
Our sister speaks of.—Come, bring away the stocks! 142
                                          Stocks brought out.

GLOUCESTER
Let me beseech Your Grace not to do so.
His fault is much, and the good King his master
Will check him for't. Your purposed low correction 145
Is such as basest and contemned'st wretches 146
For pilferings and most common trespasses
Are punished with. The King must take it ill
That he, so slightly valued in his messenger,
Should have him thus restrained.

CORNWALL   I'll answer that. 150

REGAN
My sister may receive it much more worse
To have her gentleman abused, assaulted,
For following her affairs. Put in his legs.
                                          [Kent is put in the stocks.]
Come, my good lord, away.
                                          Exeunt [all but Gloucester and Kent].

GLOUCESTER
I am sorry for thee, friend. 'Tis the Duke's pleasure,
Whose disposition, all the world well knows,
Will not be rubbed nor stopped. I'll entreat for thee. 157

KENT
Pray, do not, sir. I have watched and traveled hard. 158
Some time I shall sleep out; the rest I'll whistle.
A good man's fortune may grow out at heels. 160
Give you good morrow! 161

GLOUCESTER
The Duke's to blame in this. 'Twill be ill taken. Exit.

---

128 reverend (because old) **133 grace** sovereignty, royal grace **139 should** would **140 being** since you are **141 color** complexion, character **142 away** along **145 check** rebuke, correct **146 contemned'st** most despised **150 answer** be answerable for **157 rubbed** hindered, obstructed. (A term from bowls.) **158 watched** gone sleepless **160 A . . . heels** i.e., Even good men suffer decline in fortune at times. (To be out at heels is literally to be threadbare, coming through one's stockings.) **161 Give you** i.e., God give you

KENT
Good King, that must approve the common saw,   163
Thou out of heaven's benediction com'st
To the warm sun!   [*He takes out a letter.*]
Approach, thou beacon to this under globe,   166
That by thy comfortable beams I may   167
Peruse this letter. Nothing almost sees miracles   168
But misery. I know 'tis from Cordelia,   169
Who hath most fortunately been informed
Of my obscurèd course, "and shall find time   171
From this enormous state, seeking to give   172
Losses their remedies." All weary and o'erwatched,   173
Take vantage, heavy eyes, not to behold   174
This shameful lodging.   175
Fortune, good night. Smile once more; turn thy wheel!   176
    [*He sleeps.*]

❖

[2.3]

Enter Edgar.

EDGAR   I heard myself proclaimed,
And by the happy hollow of a tree   2
Escaped the hunt. No port is free, no place   3
That guard and most unusual vigilance   4
Does not attend my taking. Whiles I may scape   5
I will preserve myself, and am bethought   6
To take the basest and most poorest shape
That ever penury, in contempt of man,   8
Brought near to beast. My face I'll grime with filth,
Blanket my loins, elf all my hairs in knots,   10
And with presented nakedness outface   11
The winds and persecutions of the sky.
The country gives me proof and precedent   13
Of Bedlam beggars who with roaring voices   14
Strike in their numbed and mortifièd arms   15
Pins, wooden pricks, nails, sprigs of rosemary;   16
And with this horrible object, from low farms,   17

Poor pelting villages, sheepcotes, and mills,   18
Sometimes with lunatic bans, sometimes with prayers,   19
Enforce their charity. Poor Turlygod! Poor Tom!   20
That's something yet. Edgar I nothing am.   *Exit.*   21

❖

[2.4]

Enter Lear, Fool, and Gentleman.

LEAR
'Tis strange that they should so depart from home   1
And not send back my messenger.
GENTLEMAN   As I learned,
The night before there was no purpose in them
Of this remove.
KENT   Hail to thee, noble master!   4
LEAR   Ha?
Mak'st thou this shame thy pastime?
KENT   No, my lord.
FOOL   Ha, ha, he wears cruel garters. Horses are tied by   7
the heads, dogs and bears by th' neck, monkeys by
th' loins, and men by th' legs. When a man's over-   9
lusty at legs, then he wears wooden netherstocks.   10
LEAR
What's he that hath so much thy place mistook
To set thee here?
KENT   It is both he and she: 12
Your son and daughter.
LEAR   No.
KENT   Yes.
LEAR   No, I say.
KENT   I say yea.
LEAR   No, no, they would not.
KENT   Yes, they have.
LEAR   By Jupiter, I swear no.
KENT   By Juno, I swear ay.
LEAR   They durst not do't!
They could not, would not do't. 'Tis worse than
    murder
To do upon respect such violent outrage.   23
Resolve me with all modest haste which way   24
Thou mightst deserve, or they impose, this usage,
Coming from us.

---

163 approve prove true.   **saw** proverb (i.e., "To run out of God's blessing into the warm sun," meaning "to go from better to worse," from a state of bliss into the pitiless world. Kent sees Lear as heading for trouble.)   **166 beacon ... globe** i.e., the sun. (Daylight is coming soon.)   **167 comfortable** comforting   **168–9 Nothing ... misery** Scarcely anything can make one appreciate miracles like being in a state of misery; to the miserable, any relief seems miraculous.   **171 obscurèd** disguised   **171–3 "and shall ... remedies"** i.e., "and who, in the fullness of time, will bring relief from the monstrous state of affairs under which we suffer, seeking to remedy what has been destroyed." (The passage may be corrupt. Kent may be reading from his letter.)   **173 o'erwatched** exhausted with staying awake   **174 vantage** advantage (of sleep)   **175 lodging** i.e., the stocks.   **176 wheel** (Since Kent is at the bottom of Fortune's wheel, any turning should improve his situation.)   **2.3. Location: Scene continues. Kent is dozing in the stocks.**   **2 happy** luckily found   **3 port** (See 2.1.80 and note.)   **4 That** in which   **5 attend my taking** lie in wait to capture me.   **6 bethought** resolved   **8 in ... man** in order to show how contemptible humankind is   **10 elf** tangle into elflocks   **11 presented** exposed to view, displayed   **13 proof** example   **14 Bedlam** (See the note to 1.2.139.)   **15 Strike** stick.   **mortifièd** deadened   **16 wooden pricks** skewers   **17 object** spectacle.   **low** lowly

18 pelting paltry   **19 bans** curses   **20 Enforce their charity** manage to beg something.   **Poor ... Tom** (Edgar practices the begging role he is about to adopt. Beggars were known as "poor Toms.")   **Turlygod** (Meaning unknown.)   **21 That's ... am** There's some kind of existence for me as poor Tom. I am Edgar no longer.   **2.4. Location: Scene continues before Gloucester's house. Kent still dozing in the stocks.**   **1 they** Cornwall and Regan   **4 remove** change of residence.   **7 cruel** (1) unkind (2) crewel (compare the quarto spelling, "crewell"), a thin yarn of which hose were made   **9–10 overlusty at legs** given to running away, or overly active sexually   **10 netherstocks** stockings.   **12 To** as to   **23 upon respect** i.e., against my officers (who deserve respect)   **24 Resolve** Enlighten.   **modest** moderate

KENT   My lord, when at their home   26
I did commend Your Highness' letters to them,   27
Ere I was risen from the place that showed   28
My duty kneeling, came there a reeking post,   29
Stewed in his haste, half breathless, panting forth   30
From Goneril his mistress salutations;
Delivered letters, spite of intermission,   32
Which presently they read; on whose contents   33
They summoned up their meiny, straight took horse,   34
Commanded me to follow and attend
The leisure of their answer, gave me cold looks;
And meeting here the other messenger,
Whose welcome, I perceived, had poisoned mine—
Being the very fellow which of late
Displayed so saucily against Your Highness—   40
Having more man than wit about me, drew.   41
He raised the house with loud and coward cries.
Your son and daughter found this trespass worth
The shame which here it suffers.
FOOL   Winter's not gone yet if the wild geese fly that   45
way.   46
         Fathers that wear rags
              Do make their children blind,   48
         But fathers that bear bags   49
              Shall see their children kind.
         Fortune, that arrant whore,
              Ne'er turns the key to th' poor.   52
But, for all this, thou shalt have as many dolors for thy   53
daughters as thou canst tell in a year.   54
LEAR
Oh, how this mother swells up toward my heart!   55
Hysterica passio, down, thou climbing sorrow!   56
Thy element's below.—Where is this daughter?   57
KENT   With the Earl, sir, here within.
LEAR   Follow me not. Stay here.   *Exit.*
GENTLEMAN
Made you no more offense but what you speak of?
KENT   None.
How chance the King comes with so small a number?   62
FOOL   An thou hadst been set i'th' stocks for that ques-   63
tion, thou'dst well deserved it.
KENT   Why, Fool?

FOOL   We'll set thee to school to an ant to teach thee   66
there's no laboring i'th' winter. All that follow their   67
noses are led by their eyes but blind men, and there's   68
not a nose among twenty but can smell him that's   69
stinking. Let go thy hold when a great wheel runs   70
down a hill lest it break thy neck with following; but
the great one that goes upward, let him draw thee after. When a wise man gives thee better counsel, give
me mine again. I would have none but knaves follow
it, since a fool gives it.
         That sir which serves and seeks for gain,
              And follows but for form,
         Will pack when it begins to rain   78
              And leave thee in the storm.
         But I will tarry; the fool will stay,
              And let the wise man fly.
         The knave turns fool that runs away;   82
              The fool no knave, pardie.   83

Enter Lear and Gloucester.

KENT   Where learned you this, Fool?
FOOL   Not i'th' stocks, fool.
LEAR
Deny to speak with me? They are sick? They are
   weary?
They have traveled all the night? Mere fetches,   87
The images of revolt and flying off.   88
Fetch me a better answer.
GLOUCESTER   My dear lord,
You know the fiery quality of the Duke,
How unremovable and fixed he is
In his own course.
LEAR
Vengeance! Plague! Death! Confusion!   93
Fiery? What quality? Why, Gloucester, Gloucester,
I'd speak with the Duke of Cornwall and his wife.
GLOUCESTER
Well, my good lord, I have informed them so.
LEAR
Informed them? Dost thou understand me, man?
GLOUCESTER   Ay, my good lord.
LEAR
The King would speak with Cornwall. The dear father
Would with his daughter speak, commands, tends
   service.   100
Are they informed of this? My breath and blood!   101
Fiery? The fiery Duke? Tell the hot Duke that—
No, but not yet. Maybe he is not well.
Infirmity doth still neglect all office   104
Whereto our health is bound; we are not ourselves   105

26 their home (Kent and Oswald went first to Cornwall's palace after leaving Albany's palace.)   **27 commend** deliver   **28–9 from . . . kneeling** from the kneeling posture that showed my duty   **29 reeking** steaming (with heat of travel)   **30 Stewed** i.e., thoroughly heated, soaked   **32 spite of intermission** in disregard of interrupting me, or, in spite of the interruptions caused by his being out of breath   **33 presently** instantly.   **on** on the basis of   **34 meiny** retinue of servants, household   **40 Displayed so saucily** behaved so insolently   **41 more man than wit** more courage than good sense   **45–6 Winter's . . . way** i.e., The signs still point to continued and worsening fortune; the wild geese are still flying south.   **48 blind** i.e., indifferent to their father's needs   **49 bags** i.e., of gold   **52 turns the key** opens the door   **53 dolors** griefs. (With pun on "dollars," English word for an Austrian or Spanish coin.)   **for** (1) on account of (2) in exchange for   **54 tell** (1) relate (2) count   **55, 56 mother, *Hysterica passio*** i.e., hysteria, giving the sensation of choking or suffocating   **57 element's** proper place is. (Hysteria, from the Greek *hystera*, womb, was thought to be produced by vapors ascending from the uterus or abdomen.)   **62 chance** chances it   **63 An** If

66–7 We'll . . . winter i.e., Just as the ant knows not to labor in the winter, the wise man knows not to labor for one whose fortunes are fallen.   **67–70 All . . . stinking** i.e., One who is out of favor can be easily detected (he smells of misfortune) and so is easily avoided by timeservers.   **78 pack** be off   **82 The knave . . . away** i.e., Deserting one's master is the greatest folly   **83 pardie** *par Dieu* (French), "by God."   **87 fetches** pretexts, dodges   **88 images** signs.   **flying off** desertion.   **93 Confusion!** Destruction!   **100 tends** attends, waits for   **101 My . . . blood!** i.e., By my very life. (An oath.)   **104–5 Infirmity . . . bound** Sickness always prompts us to neglect all duties which in good health we are bound to perform

When nature, being oppressed, commands the mind
To suffer with the body. I'll forbear,
And am fallen out with my more headier will,   108
To take the indisposed and sickly fit   109
For the sound man. [*Looking at Kent*] Death on my
    state! Wherefore   110
Should he sit here? This act persuades me
That this remotion of the Duke and her   112
Is practice only. Give me my servant forth.   113
Go tell the Duke and 's wife I'd speak with them,
Now, presently. Bid them come forth and hear me,   115
Or at their chamber door I'll beat the drum
Till it cry sleep to death.   117

GLOUCESTER   I would have all well betwixt you.   *Exit.*

LEAR
Oh, me, my heart, my rising heart! But down!

FOOL   Cry to it, nuncle, as the cockney did to the eels   120
when she put 'em i'th' paste alive. She knapped 'em   121
o'th' coxcombs with a stick and cried, "Down, wan-   122
tons, down!" 'Twas her brother that, in pure kindness   123
to his horse, buttered his hay.   124

*Enter Cornwall, Regan, Gloucester, [and]
servants.*

LEAR   Good morrow to you both.
CORNWALL   Hail to Your Grace!
                        Kent here set at liberty.
REGAN   I am glad to see Your Highness.
LEAR
Regan, I think you are. I know what reason
I have to think so. If thou shouldst not be glad,
I would divorce me from thy mother's tomb,   130
Sepulch'ring an adultress. [*To Kent*] Oh, are you free?   131
Some other time for that.—Belovèd Regan,
Thy sister's naught. Oh, Regan, she hath tied   133
Sharp-toothed unkindness, like a vulture, here.
               [*He lays his hand on his heart.*]
I can scarce speak to thee. Thou'lt not believe
With how depraved a quality—Oh, Regan!   136

REGAN
I pray you, sir, take patience. I have hope   137
You less know how to value her desert   138
Than she to scant her duty.
LEAR   Say? How is that?   139
REGAN
I cannot think my sister in the least
Would fail her obligation. If, sir, perchance
She have restrained the riots of your followers,
'Tis on such ground and to such wholesome end
As clears her from all blame.
LEAR   My curses on her!
REGAN   Oh, sir, you are old;
Nature in you stands on the very verge   147
Of his confine. You should be ruled and led   148
By some discretion that discerns your state   149
Better than you yourself. Therefore, I pray you,
That to our sister you do make return.
Say you have wronged her.
LEAR   Ask her forgiveness?
Do you but mark how this becomes the house: 153
[*Kneeling*] "Dear daughter, I confess that I am old;
Age is unnecessary. On my knees I beg
That you'll vouchsafe me raiment, bed, and food."
REGAN
Good sir, no more. These are unsightly tricks.
Return you to my sister.
LEAR [*rising*]   Never, Regan.
She hath abated me of half my train,   159
Looked black upon me, struck me with her tongue
Most serpentlike upon the very heart.
All the stored vengeances of heaven fall
On her ingrateful top! Strike her young bones,   163
You taking airs, with lameness!
CORNWALL   Fie, sir, fie!   164
LEAR
You nimble lightnings, dart your blinding flames
Into her scornful eyes! Infect her beauty,
You fen-sucked fogs drawn by the powerful sun   167
To fall and blister!   168
REGAN
O the blest gods! So will you wish on me
When the rash mood is on.
LEAR
No, Regan, thou shalt never have my curse.
Thy tender-hafted nature shall not give   172
Thee o'er to harshness. Her eyes are fierce, but thine
Do comfort and not burn. 'Tis not in thee
To grudge my pleasures, to cut off my train,

108–10 And . . . man and now disapprove of my more impetuous will in having rashly supposed that those who are indisposed and sickly were in sound health.   **110 Death . . . state!** (A common oath, here ironically appropriate to a king whose royal authority is dying.) **112 remotion** removal, inaccessibility   **113 practice** deception. **forth** out of the stocks.   **115 presently** at once.   **117 cry sleep to death** i.e., puts an end to sleep by the noise.   **120 cockney** i.e., a Londoner, ignorant of ways of cooking eels   **121 paste** pastry pie. **knapped** rapped   **122 coxcombs** heads   **122–3 wantons** playful creatures, sexy rogues. (A term of affectionate abuse. The cockney wife is trying to coax and wheedle the eels into laying down their lives for the making of the pastry pie—a plea that is about as ineffectual as Lear's imploring his rising heart to subside.)   **123–4 'Twas . . . hay** (Another city ignorance; the act is well intended, but horses do not like greasy hay. As with Lear, good intentions are not enough. The *brother* is related to the cockney wife in that they are both misguidedly tenderhearted.)   **130–1 I would . . . adultress** i.e., I would cease to honor your dead mother's tomb, since it would surely contain the dead body of an adultress. (Only such a fantasy of illegitimacy could explain to Lear filial ingratitude of the monstrous sort that now confronts him.)   **133 naught** wicked. **136 quality** disposition

137–9 I have . . . duty I trust this is more a matter of your undervaluing her merit than of her falling slack in her duty to you.   **139 Say? Come again?   147–8 Nature . . . confine** i.e., Your life has almost completed its allotted scope.   **149 By . . . state** by some discreet person who understands your situation and condition   **153 becomes the house** suits domestic decorum and the royal family line. (Said with bitter irony.)   **159 abated** deprived   **163 ingrateful top** ungrateful head.   **164 taking** infectious   **167 fen-sucked** (It was supposed that the sun sucked up poisons from fens or marshes.)   **168 To fall and blister** to fall upon her and blister her beauty.   **172 tender-hafted** gentle. (Literally, set in a tender *haft*, i.e., handle or frame.)

To bandy hasty words, to scant my sizes,   176
And, in conclusion, to oppose the bolt   177
Against my coming in. Thou better know'st
The offices of nature, bond of childhood,   179
Effects of courtesy, dues of gratitude.   180
Thy half o'th' kingdom hast thou not forgot,
Wherein I thee endowed.
REGAN   Good sir, to th' purpose.   182
LEAR
Who put my man i'th' stocks?   *Tucket within.*
CORNWALL   What trumpet's that?
REGAN
I know't—my sister's. This approves her letter,   184
That she would soon be here.

       Enter steward [Oswald].

               Is your lady come?
LEAR
This is a slave, whose easy-borrowed pride   186
Dwells in the fickle grace of her he follows.—   187
Out, varlet, from my sight!
CORNWALL   What means Your Grace?   188
LEAR
Who stocked my servant? Regan, I have good hope
Thou didst not know on't.

       Enter Goneril.

          Who comes here? O heavens,
If you do love old men, if your sweet sway
Allow obedience, if you yourselves are old,   192
Make it your cause; send down, and take my part!
[*To Goneril*] Art not ashamed to look upon this beard?
             [*Goneril and Regan join hands.*] 194
Oh, Regan, will you take her by the hand?
GONERIL
Why not by th' hand, sir? How have I offended?
All's not offense that indiscretion finds   197
And dotage terms so.
LEAR   O sides, you are too tough!   198
Will you yet hold?—How came my man i'th' stocks?
CORNWALL
I set him there, sir; but his own disorders
Deserved much less advancement.
LEAR   You? Did you?   201
REGAN
I pray you, father, being weak, seem so.   202
If till the expiration of your month
You will return and sojourn with my sister,
Dismissing half your train, come then to me.

I am now from home, and out of that provision   206
Which shall be needful for your entertainment.   207
LEAR
Return to her? And fifty men dismissed?
No! Rather I abjure all roofs, and choose
To wage against the enmity o'th'air,   210
To be a comrade with the wolf and owl—
Necessity's sharp pinch. Return with her?
Why, the hot-blooded France, that dowerless took   213
Our youngest born—I could as well be brought
To knee his throne and, squirelike, pension beg   215
To keep base life afoot. Return with her?
Persuade me rather to be slave and sumpter   217
To this detested groom.   [*He points to Oswald.*]
GONERIL   At your choice, sir.
LEAR
I prithee, daughter, do not make me mad.
I will not trouble thee, my child. Farewell.
We'll no more meet, no more see one another.
But yet thou art my flesh, my blood, my daughter—
Or rather a disease that's in my flesh,
Which I must needs call mine. Thou art a boil,
A plague-sore, or embossèd carbuncle   225
In my corrupted blood. But I'll not chide thee;
Let shame come when it will, I do not call it.   227
I do not bid the thunder-bearer shoot,   228
Nor tell tales of thee to high-judging Jove.   229
Mend when thou canst; be better at thy leisure.
I can be patient. I can stay with Regan,
I and my hundred knights.
REGAN   Not altogether so.
I looked not for you yet, nor am provided   234
For your fit welcome. Give ear, sir, to my sister;
For those that mingle reason with your passion   236
Must be content to think you old, and so—   237
But she knows what she does.
LEAR   Is this well spoken?
REGAN
I dare avouch it, sir. What, fifty followers?   239
Is it not well? What should you need of more?
Yea, or so many, sith that both charge and danger   241
Speak 'gainst so great a number? How in one house
Should many people under two commands
Hold amity? 'Tis hard, almost impossible.
GONERIL
Why might not you, my lord, receive attendance
From those that she calls servants, or from mine?
REGAN
Why not, my lord? If then they chanced to slack ye,   247
We could control them. If you will come to me—   248
For now I spy a danger—I entreat you

176 **bandy** volley, exchange. **scant my sizes** diminish my
allowances 177 **oppose the bolt** lock the door 179 **The offices . . .**
childhood the natural duties and filial obligations due to parents
180 **Effects** outward manifestations 182 **to th' purpose** get to the
point. 184 **approves** confirms 186 **easy-borrowed** easily put on
187 **grace** favor 188 **varlet** worthless fellow 192 **Allow** approve,
sanction 194 **beard** (A sign of age and presumed entitlement to
respect.) 197–8 **All's . . . so** Not everything that the poor judgment
and dotage of old age deem offensive is actually so. 198 **sides** i.e.,
sides of the chest (stretched by the swelling heart) 201 **much less**
advancement far less honor, i.e., far worse treatment. 202 **seem so**
i.e., don't act as if you were strong.

206 **from** away from 207 **entertainment** proper reception.
210 **wage** wage war 213 **hot-blooded** spirited, youthful; choleric
215 **knee** fall on my knees before 217 **sumpter** packhorse; hence,
drudge 225 **embossèd** swollen, tumid 227 **call** summon 228 **the**
thunder-bearer i.e., Jove 229 **high-judging** judging from on high
234 **looked not for** did not expect 236–7 **For . . . old** for those who
dispassionately consider your intemperate outbursts must conclude
that you are old 239 **avouch** vouch for 241 **sith that** since. **charge**
expense 247 **slack** neglect 248 **control** correct

To bring but five-and-twenty. To no more
Will I give place or notice.   251

LEAR
I gave you all—

REGAN   And in good time you gave it.

LEAR
Made you my guardians, my depositaries,   253
But kept a reservation to be followed   254
With such a number. What, must I come to you
With five-and-twenty? Regan, said you so?

REGAN
And speak't again, my lord. No more with me.

LEAR
Those wicked creatures yet do look well-favored   258
When others are more wicked; not being the worst
Stands in some rank of praise. [*To Goneril*] I'll go with
   thee.   260
Thy fifty yet doth double five-and-twenty,
And thou art twice her love.

GONERIL   Hear me, my lord:
What need you five-and-twenty, ten, or five,
To follow in a house where twice so many   264
Have a command to tend you?

REGAN   What need one?

LEAR
Oh, reason not the need! Our basest beggars   266
Are in the poorest thing superfluous.   267
Allow not nature more than nature needs,   268
Man's life is cheap as beast's. Thou art a lady;
If only to go warm were gorgeous,   270
Why, nature needs not what thou gorgeous wear'st,   271
Which scarcely keeps thee warm. But, for true need—   272
You heavens, give me that patience, patience I need!
You see me here, you gods, a poor old man,
As full of grief as age, wretched in both.
If it be you that stirs these daughters' hearts
Against their father, fool me not so much   277
To bear it tamely; touch me with noble anger,   278
And let not women's weapons, water drops,
Stain my man's cheeks. No, you unnatural hags,
I will have such revenges on you both
That all the world shall—I will do such things—
What they are yet I know not, but they shall be
The terrors of the earth. You think I'll weep;
No, I'll not weep.   *Storm and tempest.*
I have full cause of weeping; but this heart
Shall break into a hundred thousand flaws   287

Or ere I'll weep. Oh, Fool, I shall go mad!   288
   Exeunt [Lear, Gloucester, Kent, Gentleman,
                                                 and Fool].

CORNWALL
Let us withdraw. 'Twill be a storm.

REGAN
This house is little. The old man and 's people
Cannot be well bestowed.   291

GONERIL
'Tis his own blame hath put himself from rest,   292
And must needs taste his folly.   293

REGAN
For his particular, I'll receive him gladly,   294
But not one follower.

GONERIL
So am I purposed. Where is my lord of Gloucester?

CORNWALL
Followed the old man forth.

   Enter Gloucester.

                          He is returned.

GLOUCESTER
The King is in high rage.

CORNWALL   Whither is he going?

GLOUCESTER
He calls to horse, but will I know not whither.

CORNWALL
'Tis best to give him way. He leads himself.   300

GONERIL [*to Gloucester*]
My lord, entreat him by no means to stay.   301

GLOUCESTER
Alack, the night comes on, and the bleak winds
Do sorely ruffle. For many miles about   303
There's scarce a bush.

REGAN   Oh, sir, to willful men
The injuries that they themselves procure
Must be their schoolmasters. Shut up your doors.
He is attended with a desperate train,
And what they may incense him to, being apt   308
To have his ear abused, wisdom bids fear.   309

CORNWALL
Shut up your doors, my lord; 'tis a wild night.
My Regan counsels well. Come out o'th' storm.
                                                                          Exeunt.

                                  ❈

3.1

   Storm still. Enter Kent [disguised as Caius]
         and a Gentleman, severally.

KENT   Who's there, besides foul weather?

---

251 **place or notice** houseroom or recognition.   253 **depositaries**
trustees   254 **kept a reservation** reserved a right   258 **well-favored**
attractive, fair of feature   260 **Stands . . . praise** achieves, by necessity, some relative deserving of praise.   264 **follow** be your attendants   266 **reason not** do not dispassionately analyze   266–7 **Our . . .**
superfluous Even our most destitute beggars have some wretched
possessions beyond what they absolutely need.   268 **Allow not** If
you do not allow.   **needs** i.e., to survive   270–2 **If . . . warm** If fashions in clothes were determined only by the need for warmth, this
natural standard wouldn't justify the rich robes you wear to be gorgeous—which don't serve well for warmth in any case.   277–8 **fool**
. . . To do not make me so foolish as to   287 **flaws** fragments

288 **Or ere** before   291 **bestowed** lodged.   292 **blame** fault.   **hath**
that he has, or, that has.   **from rest** i.e., out of the house; also, lacking
peace of mind   293 **taste** experience   294 **For his particular** As for
him individually   300 **give . . . himself** give him his own way. He is
guided only by his own willfulness.   301 **entreat . . . means** by no
means entreat him   303 **ruffle** bluster.   308–9 **being . . . abused** (he)
being inclined to hearken to harken to hearken to counsel
3.1. Location: An open place in Gloucestershire.
0.2 *severally* at separate doors.

GENTLEMAN
One minded like the weather, most unquietly.
KENT   I know you. Where's the King?
GENTLEMAN
Contending with the fretful elements;
Bids the wind blow the earth into the sea
Or swell the curlèd waters 'bove the main,   6
That things might change or cease; tears his white hair,   7
Which the impetuous blasts with eyeless rage
Catch in their fury and make nothing of;   9
Strives in his little world of man to outstorm   10
The to-and-fro-conflicting wind and rain.
This night, wherein the cub-drawn bear would couch,   12
The lion and the belly-pinchèd wolf
Keep their fur dry, unbonneted he runs
And bids what will take all.
KENT   But who is with him?   15
GENTLEMAN
None but the Fool, who labors to outjest   16
His heart-struck injuries.
KENT   Sir, I do know you,   17
And dare upon the warrant of my note   18
Commend a dear thing to you. There is division,   19
Although as yet the face of it is covered
With mutual cunning, twixt Albany and Cornwall;
Who have—as who have not, that their great stars   22
Throned and set high?—servants, who seem no less,   23
Which are to France the spies and speculations   24
Intelligent of our state. What hath been seen,   25
Either in snuffs and packings of the dukes,   26
Or the hard rein which both of them hath borne   27
Against the old kind King, or something deeper,   28
Whereof perchance these are but furnishings—   29
But true it is, from France there comes a power   30
Into this scattered kingdom, who already,   31
Wise in our negligence, have secret feet   32
In some of our best ports and are at point   33
To show their open banner. Now to you:
If on my credit you dare build so far   35
To make your speed to Dover, you shall find
Some that will thank you, making just report   37
Of how unnatural and bemadding sorrow
The King hath cause to plain.   39
I am a gentleman of blood and breeding,   40

And from some knowledge and assurance offer   41
This office to you.   42
GENTLEMAN
I will talk further with you.
KENT   No, do not.
For confirmation that I am much more
Than my outwall, open this purse and take   45
What it contains. [*He gives a purse and a ring.*] If you
shall see Cordelia—
As fear not but you shall—show her this ring,   47
And she will tell you who that fellow is   48
That yet you do not know. Fie on this storm!
I will go seek the King.
GENTLEMAN
Give me your hand. Have you no more to say?
KENT
Few words, but, to effect, more than all yet: 52
That when we have found the King—in which your
pain   53
That way, I'll this—he that first lights on him   54
Holla the other.   *Exeunt* [*separately*].

❖

3.2

Storm still. Enter Lear and Fool.

LEAR
Blow, winds, and crack your cheeks! Rage, blow!
You cataracts and hurricanoes, spout   2
Till you have drenched our steeples, drowned the
cocks!   3
You sulfurous and thought-executing fires,   4
Vaunt-couriers of oak-cleaving thunderbolts,   5
Singe my white head! And thou, all-shaking thunder,
Strike flat the thick rotundity o'th' world!
Crack nature's molds, all germens spill at once   8
That makes ingrateful man!
FOOL   Oh, nuncle, court holy water in a dry house is bet-   10
ter than this rainwater out o'door. Good nuncle, in,
ask thy daughters blessing. Here's a night pities   12
neither wise men nor fools.
LEAR
Rumble thy bellyful! Spit, fire! Spout, rain!
Nor rain, wind, thunder, fire are my daughters.   15
I tax not you, you elements, with unkindness;   16
I never gave you kingdom, called you children.
You owe me no subscription. Then let fall   18

6 main mainland   **7 things** all things   **9 make nothing of** blow about contemptuously   **10 little world of man** i.e., microcosm, which is an epitome of the macrocosm or universe   **12 cub-drawn** famished, with udders sucked dry (and hence ravenous).   **couch** lie close in its den   **15 bids . . . all** (A cry of desperate defiance; "take all" is the cry of a gambler in staking his last.)   **16 outjest** exorcise or relieve by jesting   **17 heart-struck injuries** injuries that strike to the very heart.   **18–19 And . . . to you** and dare, on the strength of what I know about you, entrust a precious undertaking to you.   **22–3 as . . . high** as who does not, among those whom a mighty destiny has enthroned on high   **23 no less** i.e., no other than servants   **24 speculations** scouts, spies   **25 Intelligent of** supplying intelligence pertinent to   **26 snuffs and packings** resentments and intrigues   **27–8 Or . . . King** or the harsh reining in they both have inflicted on King Lear   **29 furnishings** outward shows   **30 power** army   **31 scattered** divided   **32 Wise in** taking advantage of.   **feet** footholds   **33 at point** ready   **35 credit** trustworthiness.   **so far** so far as   **37 making just report** for making an accurate report   **39 plain** complain.   **40 blood and breeding** good family and education

41 assurance confidence, certainty   **42 office** assignment   **45 outwall** exterior appearance   **47 fear not but** be assured that   **48 fellow** i.e., Kent   **52 to effect** in its effect   **53–4 in which . . . this** in which task, you search in that direction while I go this way
3.2. Location: An open place, as before.
2 hurricanoes waterspouts   **3 drenched** drowned.   **cocks** weathercocks.   **4 thought-executing fires** lightning that acts with the quickness of thought   **5 Vaunt-couriers** forerunners   **8 Crack . . . at once** Crack the molds in which nature makes all life; destroy all seeds at once   **10 court holy water** flattery   **12 ask . . . blessing** (For Lear to do so would be to acknowledge their authority.)   **15 Nor** Neither   **16 tax** accuse.   **with** of   **18 subscription** allegiance.

Your horrible pleasure. Here I stand your slave,
A poor, infirm, weak, and despised old man.
But yet I call you servile ministers, 21
That will with two pernicious daughters join
Your high-engendered battles 'gainst a head 23
So old and white as this. Oho! 'Tis foul.

FOOL He that has a house to put 's head in has a good
headpiece. 26
    The codpiece that will house 27
      Before the head has any, 28
    The head and he shall louse; 29
      So beggars marry many. 30
    The man that makes his toe 31
      What he his heart should make 32
    Shall of a corn cry woe, 33
      And turn his sleep to wake. 34
For there was never yet fair woman but she made 35
mouths in a glass. 36

LEAR
No, I will be the pattern of all patience;
I will say nothing.

Enter Kent, [disguised as Caius].

KENT Who's there?

FOOL Marry, here's grace and a codpiece; that's a wise 40
man and a fool.

KENT
Alas, sir, are you here? Things that love night
Love not such nights as these. The wrathful skies
Gallow the very wanderers of the dark 44
And make them keep their caves. Since I was man, 45
Such sheets of fire, such bursts of horrid thunder,
Such groans of roaring wind and rain I never
Remember to have heard. Man's nature cannot carry 48
Th'affliction nor the fear.

LEAR   Let the great gods, 49
That keep this dreadful pother o'er our heads, 50
Find out their enemies now. Tremble, thou wretch,
That hast within thee undivulgèd crimes
Unwhipped of justice! Hide thee, thou bloody hand,
Thou perjured, and thou simular of virtue 54
That art incestuous! Caitiff, to pieces shake, 55
That under covert and convenient seeming 56

Has practiced on man's life! Close pent-up guilts, 57
Rive your concealing continents and cry 58
These dreadful summoners grace! I am a man 59
More sinned against than sinning.

KENT   Alack, bareheaded?
Gracious my lord, hard by here is a hovel;
Some friendship will it lend you 'gainst the tempest.
Repose you there while I to this hard house—
More harder than the stones whereof 'tis raised,
Which even but now, demanding after you, 65
Denied me to come in—return and force
Their scanted courtesy.

LEAR   My wits begin to turn. 67
Come on, my boy. How dost, my boy? Art cold?
I am cold myself.—Where is this straw, my fellow?
The art of our necessities is strange,
And can make vile things precious. Come, your
    hovel.—
Poor fool and knave, I have one part in my heart
That's sorry yet for thee.

FOOL *[sings]*
  "He that has and a little tiny wit, 74
    With heigh-ho, the wind and the rain,
  Must make content with his fortunes fit,
    Though the rain it raineth every day." 77

LEAR
True, boy.—Come, bring us to this hovel.
                 Exit [with Kent].

FOOL This is a brave night to cool a courtesan. I'll speak 79
a prophecy ere I go:

  When priests are more in word than matter; 81
  When brewers mar their malt with water; 82
  When nobles are their tailors' tutors, 83
  No heretics burned but wenches' suitors, 84
  Then shall the realm of Albion 85
  Come to great confusion.

  When every case in law is right, 87
  No squire in debt, nor no poor knight;
  When slanders do not live in tongues, 89
  Nor cutpurses come not to throngs;

---

21 **ministers** agents 23 **high-engendered battles** battalions engendered in the heavens 26 **headpiece** (1) helmetlike covering for the head (2) head for common sense. 27–30 **The codpiece . . . many** i.e., A man who houses his genitals in a sexual embrace before he has a roof over his head can expect the lice-infested penury of a penniless marriage. (The *codpiece* is a covering for the genitals worn by men with their close-fitting hose; here representing the genitals themselves.) 31–4 **The man . . . wake** i.e., Anyone who unwisely places his affection on base things will be afflicted with sorrow and sleeplessness. (The *corn* is a bunion on the toe.) 35–6 **made . . . glass** practiced making attractive faces in a mirror. 40 **Marry** (An oath, originally "by the Virgin Mary.") **grace** royal grace. **codpiece** (Often prominent in the Fool's costume.) 44 **Gallow . . . dark** frighten the very wild beasts of the night 45 **keep** occupy, remain inside 48 **carry** endure 49 **Th'affliction** the physical affliction 50 **pother** hubbub, turmoil 54 **simular** pretender 55 **Caitiff** Wretch 56 **convenient seeming** deception fitted to the purpose

57 **practiced on** plotted against 57–9 **Close . . . grace!** O you secret and buried consciousnesses of guilt, burst open the hiding places that conceal you, and pray for mercy! (*Summoners* are the officers who cited offenders to appear before ecclesiastical courts.) 65 **Which** i.e., the occupants of which. **demanding** I inquiring 67 **scanted** stinted 74–7 **"He . . . day"** (Derived from the popular song that Feste sings in *Twelfth Night*, 5.1.389 ff.) 79 **This . . . courtesan** i.e., This night is stormy enough to cool even the lust of a courtesan. (*Brave* means "fine, excellent.") 81 **When priests . . . matter** i.e., When priests do not practice what they preach. (This and the next three lines satirize the present state of affairs.) 82 **mar** adulterate 83 **are . . . tutors** can instruct their own tailors about fashion 84 **No heretics . . . suitors** i.e., when the prevailing heresy is lechery (a heresy, in other words, against love rather than against true religion), punished by burning not at the stake but by means of venereal infection 85 **realm of Albion** kingdom of England. (The Fool is parodying a pseudo-Chaucerian prophetic verse.) 87 **right** just. (This and the next five lines offer a utopian vision of justice and charity that will never be realized in this corrupted world.) 89 **When slanders . . . tongues** when no tongues speak slanders

When usurers tell their gold i'th' field,   91
And bawds and whores do churches build,
Then comes the time, who lives to see't,   93
That going shall be used with feet.   94

This prophecy Merlin shall make, for I live before his   95
time.   *Exit.*

❖

3.3

Enter Gloucester and Edmund [with lights].

GLOUCESTER Alack, alack, Edmund, I like not this unnatural dealing. When I desired their leave that I might
pity him, they took from me the use of mine own   3
house, charged me on pain of perpetual displeasure
neither to speak of him, entreat for him, or any way
sustain him.

EDMUND Most savage and unnatural!

GLOUCESTER Go to; say you nothing. There is division   8
between the dukes, and a worse matter than that. I
have received a letter this night; 'tis dangerous to be
spoken; I have locked the letter in my closet. These in- 11
juries the King now bears will be revenged home;   12
there is part of a power already footed. We must in-   13
cline to the King. I will look him and privily relieve   14
him. Go you and maintain talk with the Duke, that
my charity be not of him perceived. If he ask for me,   16
I am ill and gone to bed. If I die for't, as no less is
threatened me, the King my old master must be relieved. There is strange things toward, Edmund. Pray   19
you, be careful.   *Exit.*

EDMUND
This courtesy forbid thee shall the Duke   21
Instantly know, and of that letter too.
This seems a fair deserving, and must draw me   23
That which my father loses—no less than all.   24
The younger rises when the old doth fall.   *Exit.*

❖

3.4

Enter Lear, Kent [disguised as Caius], and Fool.

KENT
Here is the place, my lord. Good my lord, enter.

The tyranny of the open night's too rough
For nature to endure.   *Storm still.*
LEAR   Let me alone.   3
KENT
Good my lord, enter here.
LEAR   Wilt break my heart?   4
KENT
I had rather break mine own. Good my lord, enter.
LEAR
Thou think'st 'tis much that this contentious storm
Invades us to the skin. So 'tis to thee,
But where the greater malady is fixed   8
The lesser is scarce felt. Thou'dst shun a bear,
But if thy flight lay toward the roaring sea
Thou'dst meet the bear i'th' mouth. When the mind's
free,   11
The body's delicate. This tempest in my mind   12
Doth from my senses take all feeling else
Save what beats there. Filial ingratitude!
Is it not as this mouth should tear this hand   15
For lifting food to't? But I will punish home.   16
No, I will weep no more. In such a night
To shut me out? Pour on; I will endure.
In such a night as this? Oh, Regan, Goneril,
Your old kind father, whose frank heart gave all—   20
Oh, that way madness lies; let me shun that!
No more of that.
KENT   Good my lord, enter here.
LEAR
Prithee, go in thyself; seek thine own ease.
This tempest will not give me leave to ponder   24
On things would hurt me more. But I'll go in.   25
[*To the Fool*] In, boy; go first. You houseless poverty—
Nay, get thee in. I'll pray, and then I'll sleep.
                              Exit [Fool into the hovel].
Poor naked wretches, wheresoe'er you are,
That bide the pelting of this pitiless storm,   29
How shall your houseless heads and unfed sides,   30
Your looped and windowed raggedness, defend you   31
From seasons such as these? Oh, I have ta'en
Too little care of this! Take physic, pomp;   33
Expose thyself to feel what wretches feel,
That thou mayst shake the superflux to them   35
And show the heavens more just.
EDGAR [*within*] Fathom and half, fathom and half!   37
Poor Tom!

Enter Fool [from the hovel].

---

91 **tell** count. **i'th' field** i.e., openly, without fear 93 **who** whoever
94 **That . . . feet** that walking will be done on foot. (A comical anticlimax: Nothing will have been changed; don't expect these utopian
dreams to have materialized.) 95 **Merlin** (A great wizard of the
court of King Arthur, who came after Lear. The Fool's comical inversion ends his song on a note of paradox and impossibility.)
3.3. Location: Gloucester's house.
3 **pity** be merciful to, relieve 8 **Go to** i.e., No more of that 11 **closet**
private chamber. 12 **home** thoroughly 13 **power** armed force.
footed landed. 13–14 **incline to** side with 14 **look** look for
16 **of** by 19 **toward** impending 21 **courtesy forbid thee** kindess
(to Lear) which you were forbidden to show 23–4 **This . . . all** i.e.,
This betraying by me of my father is something he has brought on
himself, and will surely confer upon me the earldom of Gloucester
and all his wealth.
3.4. Location: An open place. Before a hovel.

3 **nature** human nature 4 **Wilt . . . heart?** i.e., Do you want to relieve
my physical wants and thereby force me to remember my daughters'
ingratitude? 8 **fixed** lodged, implanted 11 **i'th' mouth** i.e., head-
on. **free** free of anxiety 12 **The body's delicate** i.e., the body's
importunate needs can assert themselves. 15 **as** as if 16 **home**
fully. 20 **frank** liberal 24 **will . . . leave** i.e., keeps me too preoccupied 25 **things would** things (such as filial ingratitude) that would
29 **bide** endure 30 **unfed sides** i.e., lean ribs 31 **looped and windowed** full of openings like windows and loopholes 33 **Take
physic, pomp** Cure yourself, O distempered great ones 35 **superflux** superfluity. (With suggestion of *flux*, "bodily discharge," introduced by *physic*, "purgative," in line 33.) 37 **Fathom and half** (A
sailor's cry while taking soundings, hence appropriate to a deluge.)

FOOL Come not in here, nuncle; here's a spirit. Help
me, help me!

KENT Give me thy hand. Who's there?

FOOL A spirit, a spirit! He says his name's poor Tom.

KENT
What art thou that dost grumble there i'th' straw?   43
Come forth.

Enter Edgar [disguised as a madman].

EDGAR Away! The foul fiend follows me! Through the   45
sharp hawthorn blows the cold wind. Hum! Go to thy   46
bed and warm thee.

LEAR Didst thou give all to thy daughters? And art
thou come to this?

EDGAR Who gives anything to poor Tom? Whom the
foul fiend hath led through fire and through flame,
through ford and whirlpool, o'er bog and quagmire;
that hath laid knives under his pillow and halters in   53
his pew, set ratsbane by his porridge, made him   54
proud of heart to ride on a bay trotting horse over   55
four-inched bridges to course his own shadow for a   56
traitor. Bless thy five wits! Tom's a-cold. Oh, do de,   57
do de, do de. Bless thee from whirlwinds, star-blast-   58
ing, and taking! Do poor Tom some charity, whom the   59
foul fiend vexes. There could I have him now—and   60
there—and there again—and there.   *Storm still.*

LEAR
Has his daughters brought him to this pass?—   62
Couldst thou save nothing? Wouldst thou give 'em
all?

FOOL Nay, he reserved a blanket, else we had been all   64
shamed.

LEAR
Now, all the plagues that in the pendulous air   66
Hang fated o'er men's faults light on thy daughters!   67

KENT He hath no daughters, sir.

LEAR
Death, traitor! Nothing could have subdued nature
To such a lowness but his unkind daughters.
Is it the fashion that discarded fathers
Should have thus little mercy on their flesh?   72
Judicious punishment! 'Twas this flesh begot   73
Those pelican daughters.   74

EDGAR Pillicock sat on Pillicock Hill. Alow, alow, loo,   75
loo!

FOOL This cold night will turn us all to fools and madmen.

EDGAR Take heed o'th' foul fiend. Obey thy parents;
keep thy word's justice; swear not; commit not with   80
man's sworn spouse; set not thy sweet heart on proud
array. Tom's a-cold.

LEAR What hast thou been?

EDGAR A servingman, proud in heart and mind, that   84
curled my hair, wore gloves in my cap, served the lust   85
of my mistress' heart, and did the act of darkness with
her; swore as many oaths as I spake words, and broke
them in the sweet face of heaven. One that slept in the
contriving of lust and waked to do it. Wine loved I
deeply, dice dearly, and in woman out-paramoured   90
the Turk. False of heart, light of ear, bloody of hand;   91
hog in sloth, fox in stealth, wolf in greediness, dog in
madness, lion in prey. Let not the creaking of shoes   93
nor the rustling of silks betray thy poor heart to   94
woman. Keep thy foot out of brothels, thy hand out of
plackets, thy pen from lenders' books, and defy the   96
foul fiend. Still through the hawthorn blows the cold
wind; says suum, mun, nonny. Dolphin my boy, boy,   98
sessa! Let him trot by.   *Storm still.*   99

LEAR Thou wert better in a grave than to answer with
thy uncovered body this extremity of the skies. Is man
no more than this? Consider him well. Thou ow'st the   102
worm no silk, the beast no hide, the sheep no wool,   103
the cat no perfume. Ha! Here's three on 's are sophis-   104
ticated; thou art the thing itself. Unaccommodated   105
man is no more but such a poor, bare, forked animal
as thou art. Off, off, you lendings! Come, unbutton
here.   *[Tearing off his clothes.]*

FOOL Prithee, nuncle, be contented; 'tis a naughty night   109
to swim in. Now a little fire in a wild field were like   110
an old lecher's heart—a small spark, all the rest on 's   111
body cold.

Enter Gloucester, with a torch.

Look, here comes a walking fire.

---

43 **grumble** mutter, mumble   45 **Away!** Keep away!   45–6 **Through . . .
wind** (Possibly a line from a ballad.)   53–4 **that hath . . . porridge** (The
fiend has laid in poor Tom's way tempting means to despairing suicide,
the most damnable of sins: knives under his pillow when he is asleep,
nooses in his church pew when he should be at prayer, and rat poison
set beside his soup when he should eat.)   54–7 **made him . . . traitor**
(The next temptation is a prideful act of great bravado that would be
impossible without the devil's aid: riding a horse over bridges only four
inches wide in pursuit of one's own shadow.)   57 **five wits** (Either the
five physical senses—sight, hearing, etc.—or the five faculties of the
mind: common wit, imagination, fantasy, estimation, and memory.)
58–9 **star-blasting** being blighted by influence of the stars   59 **taking**
infection, evil influence, enchantment.   60 **There** (Perhaps he slaps at
lice and other vermin as if they were devils.)   62 **pass** miserable plight.
64 **reserved a blanket** kept a wrap (for his nakedness)   66 **pendulous**
suspended, overhanging   67 **fated** having the power of fate   72 **have . . .
flesh** i.e., punish themselves, as Edgar has done (probably with pins
and thorns stuck in his flesh).   73 **Judicious** Appropriate to the crime
74 **pelican** greedy. (Young pelicans supposedly smote their parents and
fed on the blood of their mothers' breasts.)

75 **Pillicock** (From an old rhyme, suggested by the sound of *pelican*.
Pillicock in nursery rhyme seems to have been a euphemism for penis;
Pillicock Hill, for the Mount of Venus.)   80 **justice** integrity.   **commit
not** i.e., do not commit adultery. (Edgar's mad homily contains fragments of the Ten Commandments.)   84 **servingman** either a "servant" in the language of courtly love or an ambitious servant in a
household   85 **gloves** i.e., my mistress's favors   90–1 **out-
paramoured the Turk** outdid the Sultan in keeping mistresses.
91 **light of ear** i.e., listening intently for information that can be used
criminally   93 **prey** preying.   93–4 **creaking . . . silks** (Telltale noises
of lovers in a secret assignation.)   96 **plackets** slits in skirts or petticoats.   **thy pen . . . books** i.e., do not sign a contract for a loan
98 **suum . . . nonny** (Imitative of the wind?)   **Dolphin my boy** (A
slang phrase or bit of song?)   99 **sessa** i.e., away, cease (?).
102–4 **Thou . . . perfume** Stripped of your finery, you are not indebted
to the silkworm for silk, cattle for hide, the sheep for wool, or the civet
cat for the perfume derived from its anal pouch.   104–5 **Here . . .
itself** The three of us here (Kent, the Fool, and Lear) are decked out in
the sophistication of supposedly civilized society; you (Edgar) are the
unadorned, natural essence, the natural man.   105 **Unaccommodated**
Unfurnished with the trappings of civilization, such as clothing
109 **naughty** bad, nasty   110 **wild** barren, uncultivated   111 **on 's**
of his

EDGAR   This is the foul fiend Flibbertigibbet! He begins   114
at curfew and walks till the first cock; he gives the web   115
and the pin, squinnies the eye and makes the harelip,   116
mildews the white wheat, and hurts the poor creature   117
of earth.
        Swithold footed thrice the 'old;   119
        He met the nightmare and her ninefold;   120
            Bid her alight,
            And her troth plight,
        And aroint thee, witch, aroint thee!   123
KENT   How fares Your Grace?
LEAR   What's he?
KENT   Who's there? What is't you seek?
GLOUCESTER   What are you there? Your names?
EDGAR   Poor Tom, that eats the swimming frog, the
toad, the tadpole, the wall newt and the water; that in   129
the fury of his heart, when the foul fiend rages, eats
cow dung for salads, swallows the old rat and the
ditch-dog, drinks the green mantle of the standing   132
pool; who is whipped from tithing to tithing and   133
stock-punished and imprisoned; who hath had three   134
suits to his back, six shirts to his body,   135
        Horse to ride, and weapon to wear;
        But mice and rats and such small deer   137
        Have been Tom's food for seven long year.
Beware my follower. Peace, Smulkin! Peace, thou fiend!   139
GLOUCESTER
    What, hath Your Grace no better company?
EDGAR   The Prince of Darkness is a gentleman. Modo   141
he's called, and Mahu.
GLOUCESTER [to Lear]
    Our flesh and blood, my lord, is grown so vile   143
    That it doth hate what gets it.   144
EDGAR   Poor Tom's a-cold.
GLOUCESTER
    Go in with me. My duty cannot suffer   146
    T'obey in all your daughters' hard commands.   147
    Though their injunction be to bar my doors
    And let this tyrannous night take hold upon you,

Yet have I ventured to come seek you out
And bring you where both fire and food is ready.
LEAR
    First let me talk with this philosopher.
    [To Edgar] What is the cause of thunder?
KENT   Good my lord,
    Take his offer. Go into th' house.
LEAR
    I'll talk a word with this same learnèd Theban.   155
    [To Edgar] What is your study?   156
EDGAR   How to prevent the fiend, and to kill vermin.   157
LEAR   Let me ask you one word in private.
                            [Lear and Edgar talk apart.]
KENT [to Gloucester]
    Importune him once more to go, my lord.
    His wits begin t'unsettle.
GLOUCESTER   Canst thou blame him?
                                            Storm still.
    His daughters seek his death. Ah, that good Kent!
    He said it would be thus, poor banished man.
    Thou sayest the King grows mad; I'll tell thee, friend,
    I am almost mad myself. I had a son,
    Now outlawed from my blood; he sought my life   165
    But lately, very late. I loved him, friend,
    No father his son dearer. True to tell thee,
    The grief hath crazed my wits. What a night's this!—
    I do beseech Your Grace—
LEAR   Oh, cry you mercy, sir.   170
    [To Edgar] Noble philosopher, your company.
EDGAR   Tom's a-cold.
GLOUCESTER [to Edgar]
    In, fellow, there, in th' hovel. Keep thee warm.
LEAR [starting toward the hovel]
    Come, let's in all.
KENT   This way, my lord.
LEAR   With him!
    I will keep still with my philosopher.
KENT [to Gloucester]
    Good my lord, soothe him. Let him take the fellow.   176
GLOUCESTER [to Kent]   Take you him on.   177
KENT [to Edgar]
    Sirrah, come on. Go along with us.
LEAR   Come, good Athenian.   179
GLOUCESTER   No words, no words! Hush.
EDGAR
    Child Rowland to the dark tower came;   181
    His word was still, "Fie, foh, and fum,   182
    I smell the blood of a British man."   Exeunt.   183

❧

114 Flibbertigibbet (A devil from Elizabethan folklore whose name appears in Samuel Harsnett's *Declaration of Egregious Popish Impostures*, 1603, and elsewhere.)   **114–15 He . . . cock** He walks from nightfall till dawn   **115–16 web and the pin** cataract of the eye   **116 squinnies** squints   **117 white** ripening, ready for harvest   **119 Swithold** Saint Withold, an Anglo-Saxon exorcist, who here provides defense against the *nightmare*, or demon thought to afflict sleepers, by commanding the nightmare to *alight*, i.e., stop riding over the sleeper, and *plight* her *troth*, i.e., vow true faith, promise to do no harm. (Or, an error for *Swithin*.)   **footed . . . 'old** thrice traversed the wold (tract of hilly upland)   **120 ninefold** nine offspring. (With possible pun on *fold, foal*.)   **123 aroint thee** begone   **129 water** water newt   **132 ditch-dog** dead dog in a ditch.   **mantle** scum.   **standing** stagnant   **133 from . . . to tithing** from one ward or parish to another   **134 stock-punished** placed in the stocks   **134–5 three suits** (Like the menial servant at 2.2.15.)   **137 deer** animals   **139 follower** familiar, attendant devil.   **Smulkin** a devil's name (in Samuel Harsnet's *Declaration*, as are *Modo* and *Mahu* in lines 141–2).   **141 The Prince of Darkness** The devil   **143–4 Our . . . gets it** (1) Children have become so hardened in sin that they hate their parents (2) Life is so intolerable that humans cry out at having been born.   **146 suffer** permit me   **147 in all** in all matters

155 Theban i.e., one deeply versed in "philosophy" or natural science.   **156 study** special competence.   **157 prevent** thwart   **165 outlawed . . . blood** disowned, disinherited, and legally outlawed   **170 cry you mercy** I beg your pardon   **176 soothe** humor   **177 Take . . . on** i.e., Go on ahead with Edgar.   **179 Athenian** i.e., philosopher.   **181 Child Rowland**, etc. (Probably a fragment of a ballad about the hero of the Charlemagne legends. A *child* is a candidate for knighthood.)   **182 word** watchword   **182–3 "Fie . . . man"** (This is essentially what the Giant says in "Jack, the Giant Killer.")

3.5

Enter Cornwall and Edmund [with a letter].

CORNWALL　I will have my revenge ere I depart his house.

EDMUND　How, my lord, I may be censured, that nature 3
thus gives way to loyalty, something fears me to 4
think of.

CORNWALL　I now perceive it was not altogether your
brother's evil disposition made him seek his death, 7
but a provoking merit set awork by a reprovable 8
badness in himself. 9

EDMUND　How malicious is my fortune, that I must 10
repent to be just! This is the letter he spoke of, which 11
approves him an intelligent party to the advantages 12
of France. Oh, heavens! That this treason were not, or 13
not I the detector!

CORNWALL　Go with me to the Duchess.

EDMUND　If the matter of this paper be certain, you have
mighty business in hand.

CORNWALL　True or false, it hath made thee Earl of
Gloucester. Seek out where thy father is, that he may
be ready for our apprehension. 20

EDMUND　*[aside]*　If I find him comforting the King, it 21
will stuff his suspicion more fully.—I will persevere 22
in my course of loyalty, though the conflict be sore
between that and my blood. 24

CORNWALL　I will lay trust upon thee, and thou shalt
find a dearer father in my love.　　　　　*Exeunt.*

3.6

*Enter Kent [disguised as Caius] and
Gloucester.*

GLOUCESTER　Here is better than the open air; take it
thankfully. I will piece out the comfort with what 2
addition I can. I will not be long from you.

KENT　All the power of his wits have given way to his
impatience. The gods reward your kindness! 5
　　　　　　　　　　　　　　　　　Exit [Gloucester].

Enter Lear, Edgar [as poor Tom], and Fool.

EDGAR　Franeretto calls me, and tells me Nero is an 6
angler in the lake of darkness. Pray, innocent, and 7
beware the foul fiend.

FOOL　Prithee, nuncle, tell me whether a madman be a
gentleman or a yeoman? 10

LEAR　A king, a king!

FOOL　No, he's a yeoman that has a gentleman to his
son; for he's a mad yeoman that sees his son a
gentleman before him.

LEAR
To have a thousand with red burning spits
Come hizzing in upon 'em— 16

EDGAR　The foul fiend bites my back. 17

FOOL　He's mad that trusts in the tameness of a wolf, a 18
horse's health, a boy's love, or a whore's oath. 19

LEAR
It shall be done; I will arraign them straight. 20
[To Edgar] Come, sit thou here, most learnèd justicer. 21
[To the Fool] Thou, sapient sir, sit here. Now, you she-
foxes! 22

EDGAR　Look where he stands and glares! Want'st thou 23
eyes at trial, madam? 24
[Sings.] "Come o'er the burn, Bessy, to me—" 25

FOOL *[sings]*
　　　Her boat hath a leak,
　　　And she must not speak
　　Why she dares not come over to thee.

EDGAR　The foul fiend haunts poor Tom in the voice of a
nightingale. Hoppedance cries in Tom's belly for two 30
white herring. Croak not, black angel; I have no food 31
for thee.

KENT *[to Lear]*
How do you, sir? Stand you not so amazed. 33
Will you lie down and rest upon the cushions?

LEAR
I'll see their trial first. Bring in their evidence. 35
[To Edgar] Thou robèd man of justice, take thy place; 36
[To the Fool] And thou, his yokefellow of equity, 37

3.5. Location: Gloucester's house.
3 censured judged.　**nature** attachment to family　**4 something
fears** somewhat frightens　**7 his** his father's　**8–9 but . . . himself**
but the promptings of self-worth stimulated by the reprehensible
badness of the Earl of Gloucester.　**10–11 How . . . just!** i.e., How
cruel of fate to oblige me to be upright and loyal by betraying my
own father!　**11–13 which . . . France** which proves him to be a spy
on behalf of the French.　**20 for our apprehension** for our arresting
of him.　**21 If . . . comforting** If I find Gloucester giving aid and comfort to　**22 his suspicion** suspicion of him　**24 blood** family loyalty,
filial instincts.
3.6. Location: Within a building on Gloucester's estate, near or
adjoining his house, or part of the house itself. See 3.4.146–54.
Cushions are provided, and stools.
2 piece eke　**5 impatience** rage, inability to endure more.

6 Franeretto (Another of the fiends from Harsnett.)　**6–7 Nero is an
angler** (Chaucer's "Monk's Tale," lines 2474–5, tells how Nero fished
in the Tiber with nets of gold thread; in Rabelais, 2.30, Nero is
described as a hurdy-gurdy player and Trajan an angler for frogs in
the underworld.)　**7 innocent** simpleton, fool (i.e., the Fool)　**10 yeoman** property owner below the rank of gentleman. (The Fool's bitter
jest in lines 12–14 is that such a man might go mad to see his son
advanced over him.)　**16 hizzing** hissing. (Lear imagines his wicked
daughters suffering torments in hell or being attacked by enemies.)
17 bites (i.e., in the shape of a louse.)　**18–19 tameness . . . health**
(Wolves are untamable, and horses are prone to disease.)　**20 arraign
them** (Lear now imagines the trial of his cruel daughters.)　**21 justicer** judge, justice.　**22 sapient** wise　**23 he** (Probably one of Edgar's
devils, or, Lear.)　**23–4 Want'st . . . trial** Do you lack spectators at
your trial? or, Can't you see who's looking at you?　**25 "Come . . .
me"** (First line of a ballad by William Birche, 1558. A *burn* is a brook.
The Fool makes a ribald reply, in which the *leaky boat* suggests the
woman's easy virtue or perhaps her menstrual period.)　**30 nightingale** (Edgar pretends to take the Fool's singing for that of a fiend disguised as a nightingale.)　**Hoppedance** (Harsnett mentions
"Hoberdidance.")　**31 white** unsmoked (contrasted with *black angel*,
a demon).　**Croak** (Refers to the rumbling in Edgar's stomach,
denoting hunger.)　**33 amazed** bewildered.　**35 their evidence** the
witnesses against them.　**36 robèd man** i.e., Edgar, with his blanket
37 yokefellow of equity partner in the law

Bench by his side. [*To Kent*] You are o'th' commission;   38
Sit you, too.   [*They sit.*]

EDGAR   Let us deal justly.   [*He sings.*]
Sleepest or wakest thou, jolly shepherd?
    Thy sheep be in the corn;   42
And for one blast of thy minikin mouth,   43
    Thy sheep shall take no harm.   44
Purr the cat is gray.   45

LEAR   Arraign her first; 'tis Goneril, I here take my oath
before this honorable assembly, kicked the poor King   47
her father.

FOOL   Come hither, mistress. Is your name Goneril?

LEAR   She cannot deny it.

FOOL   Cry you mercy, I took you for a joint stool.   51

LEAR
And here's another, whose warped looks proclaim   52
What store her heart is made on. Stop her there!   53
Arms, arms, sword, fire! Corruption in the place!   54
False justicer, why hast thou let her scape?

EDGAR   Bless thy five wits!

KENT
Oh, pity! Sir, where is the patience now
That you so oft have boasted to retain?

EDGAR [*aside*]
My tears begin to take his part so much
They mar my counterfeiting.

LEAR   The little dogs and all,
Tray, Blanch, and Sweetheart, see, they bark at me.

EDGAR   Tom will throw his head at them.—Avaunt, you   63
curs!
    Be thy mouth or black or white,   65
    Tooth that poisons if it bite,
    Mastiff, greyhound, mongrel grim,
    Hound or spaniel, brach or lym,   68
    Bobtail tike or trundle-tail,   69
    Tom will make him weep and wail;
    For, with throwing thus my head,
    Dogs leap the hatch, and all are fled.   72
Do de, de, de. Sessa! Come, march to wakes and fairs   73
and market towns. Poor Tom, thy horn is dry.   74

LEAR   Then let them anatomize Regan; see what breeds   75
about her heart. Is there any cause in nature that makes
these hard hearts? [*To Edgar*] You, sir, I entertain   77

---

38 **Bench** take your place on the bench.   **o'th' commission** one commissioned to be a justice   42 **corn** grainfield   43–4 **And . . . harm** i.e., one shout from your dainty (*minikin*) mouth can recall the sheep from the grainfield and thus save them from dangerous overeating.
45 **Purr the cat** (A devil or familiar from Harsnett; see the note for 3.4.114. *Purr* may be the sound the familiar makes.)   47 **kicked** who kicked   51 **joint stool** low stool made by a joiner, or maker of furniture with joined parts. (Proverbially, the phrase "I took . . . stool" meant "I beg your pardon for failing to notice you." The reference is also presumably to a real stool onstage.)   52 **another** i.e., Regan   53 **store** abundance, material.   **on** of.   54 **Corruption in the place!** i.e., There is iniquity or bribery in this court!   63 **throw his head at** i.e., threaten   65 **or black** either black   68 **brach or lym** bitch-hound or bloodhound   69 **Bobtail . . . trundle-tail** mongrel dog with a docked or bobbed tail, or one that is curly-tailed   72 **hatch** lower half of a divided door   73 **Sessa** i.e., Away, cease.   **wakes** parish festivals   74 **horn** horn-bottle, used by beggars to drink from and to beg for alms   75 **anatomize** dissect   77 **entertain** take into my service

---

for one of my hundred; only I do not like the fashion of
your garments. You will say they are Persian; but let   79
them be changed.

KENT
Now, good my lord, lie here and rest awhile.

LEAR [*lying on cushions*]   Make no noise, make no
noise. Draw the curtains. So, so. We'll go to supper   83
i'th' morning.   [*He sleeps.*]

FOOL   And I'll go to bed at noon.

    Enter Gloucester.

GLOUCESTER [*to Kent*]
Come hither, friend. Where is the King my master?

KENT
Here, sir, but trouble him not; his wits are gone.

GLOUCESTER
Good friend, I prithee, take him in thy arms.
I have o'erheard a plot of death upon him.   89
There is a litter ready; lay him in't
And drive toward Dover, friend, where thou shalt
    meet
Both welcome and protection. Take up thy master.
If thou shouldst dally half an hour, his life,
With thine and all that offer to defend him,
Stand in assurèd loss. Take up, take up,   95
And follow me, that will to some provision   96
Give thee quick conduct.

KENT   Oppressèd nature sleeps.   97
This rest might yet have balmed thy broken sinews,   98
Which, if convenience will not allow,   99
Stand in hard cure. [*To the Fool*] Come, help to bear thy
    master.   100
Thou must not stay behind.   [*They pick up Lear.*]

GLOUCESTER   Come, come, away!
    Exeunt [all but Edgar].

EDGAR
When we our betters see bearing our woes,   102
We scarcely think our miseries our foes.   103
Who alone suffers suffers most i'th' mind,   104
Leaving free things and happy shows behind;   105
But then the mind much sufferance doth o'erskip   106
When grief hath mates, and bearing fellowship.   107
How light and portable my pain seems now,   108
When that which makes me bend makes the King
    bow—
He childed as I fathered. Tom, away!   110

---

79 **Persian** (Lear madly asks if Edgar's wretched blanket is a rich Persian fabric.)   83 **curtains** bedcurtains. (They presumably exist only in Lear's mad imagination.)   89 **upon** against   95 **Stand . . . loss** will assuredly be lost.   96 **provision** supplies, or, means of providing for safety   97 **conduct** guidance.   98 **balmed** soothed, healed.   **sinews** nerves   99 **convenience** circumstances   100 **Stand . . . cure** will be hard to cure.   102 **our woes** woes like ours   103 **We . . . foes** we almost forget our own miseries (since we see how human suffering afflicts even the great).   104–7 **Who . . . fellowship** Anyone who has no companionship in suffering undergoes the mental anguish of forgetting entirely the carefree ways and happy scenes that were once enjoyed, whereas fellowship in grief enables the mind to rise above such suffering. (I.e., Misery loves company.)   108 **portable** bearable, endurable   110 **He . . . fathered** he suffering cruelty from his children as I from my father.

Mark the high noises, and thyself bewray   111
When false opinion, whose wrong thoughts defile
   thee,   112
In thy just proof repeals and reconciles thee.   113
What will hap more tonight, safe scape the King!   114
Lurk, lurk.   [*Exit.*] 115

❖

3.7

Enter Cornwall, Regan, Goneril, Bastard
[Edmund], and Servants.

CORNWALL [*to Goneril*] Post speedily to my lord your hus- 1
band; show him this letter. [*He gives a letter.*] The army
of France is landed.—Seek out the traitor Gloucester.
                 [*Exeunt some Servants.*]
REGAN Hang him instantly.
GONERIL Pluck out his eyes.
CORNWALL Leave him to my displeasure. Edmund,
keep you our sister company. The revenges we are   7
bound to take upon your traitorous father are not fit   8
for your beholding. Advise the Duke, where you are   9
going, to a most festinate preparation; we are bound   10
to the like. Our posts shall be swift and intelligent   11
betwixt us. Farewell, dear sister; farewell, my lord of   12
Gloucester.   13

Enter steward [Oswald].

How now? Where's the King?
OSWALD
My lord of Gloucester hath conveyed him hence.
Some five- or six-and-thirty of his knights,   16
Hot questrists after him, met him at gate,   17
Who, with some other of the lord's dependents,   18
Are gone with him toward Dover, where they boast
To have well-armèd friends.
CORNWALL Get horses for your mistress. [*Exit Oswald.*]
GONERIL Farewell, sweet lord, and sister.
CORNWALL
   Edmund, farewell.   *Exeunt [Goneril and Edmund].*
       Go seek the traitor Gloucester.
Pinion him like a thief; bring him before us.
              [*Exeunt Servants.*]
Though well we may not pass upon his life   25
Without the form of justice, yet our power

Shall do a court'sy to our wrath, which men   27
May blame but not control.

Enter Gloucester, and Servants [leading him].

               Who's there? The traitor?
REGAN Ingrateful fox! 'Tis he.
CORNWALL Bind fast his corky arms.   30
GLOUCESTER
What means Your Graces? Good my friends, consider
You are my guests. Do me no foul play, friends.
CORNWALL
Bind him, I say.   [*Servants bind him.*]
REGAN   Hard, hard. Oh, filthy traitor!
GLOUCESTER
Unmerciful lady as you are, I'm none.
CORNWALL
To this chair bind him.—Villain, thou shalt find—
          [*Regan plucks Gloucester's beard.*]
GLOUCESTER
By the kind gods, 'tis most ignobly done
To pluck me by the beard.
REGAN
So white, and such a traitor?
GLOUCESTER   Naughty lady,   38
These hairs which thou dost ravish from my chin
Will quicken and accuse thee. I am your host.   40
With robbers' hands my hospitable favors   41
You should not ruffle thus. What will you do?   42
CORNWALL
Come, sir, what letters had you late from France?   43
REGAN
Be simple-answered, for we know the truth.   44
CORNWALL
And what confederacy have you with the traitors
Late footed in the kingdom?
REGAN   To whose hands   46
You have sent the lunatic King. Speak.
GLOUCESTER
I have a letter guessingly set down,   48
Which came from one that's of a neutral heart,
And not from one opposed.
CORNWALL Cunning.
REGAN And false.
CORNWALL Where hast thou sent the King?
GLOUCESTER To Dover.
REGAN
Wherefore to Dover? Wast thou not charged at peril—   55
CORNWALL
Wherefore to Dover? Let him answer that.
GLOUCESTER
I am tied to th' stake, and I must stand the course.   57

111–13 Mark . . . thee Observe what is being said about those in high places or about great events, and reveal your identity only when the general opinion that now slanders you, at length establishing your innocence, recalls you from banishment and restores you to favor.
114 What . . . King! Whatever else happens tonight, may the King escape safely!   **115 Lurk** Keep out of sight
3.7. Location: Gloucester's house.
1 Post speedily Hurry   **7 sister** sister-in-law, Goneril   **8 bound** intending; obliged   **9 the Duke** Albany   **10 festinate** hasty.   **are bound** intend, are committed   **11 posts** messengers.   **intelligent** serviceable in bearing information, knowledgeable   **12–13 my . . . Gloucester** i.e., Edmund, the recipient now of his father's forfeited estate and title. (Two lines later, Oswald uses the same title to refer to Edmund's father.)   **16 his** Lear's   **17 questrists after him** searchers for Lear   **18 the lord's** i.e., Gloucester's   **25 pass upon his life** pass the death sentence upon him

27 do a court'sy i.e., bow before, yield precedence   **30 corky** withered with age   **38 white** white-haired, venerable.   **Naughty** Wicked   **40 quicken** come to life   **41–2 With . . . thus** You should not roughly handle my welcoming face with your hands as though you were robbers.   **43 late** lately   **44 simple-answered** straightforward in your answers   **46 Late footed** recently landed   **48 guessingly set down** conjecturally written   **55 charged at peril** commanded on peril of your life   **57 tied to th' stake** i.e., like a bear to be baited with dogs.   **the course** the dogs' attack.

REGAN   Wherefore to Dover?

GLOUCESTER
Because I would not see thy cruel nails
Pluck out his poor old eyes, nor thy fierce sister
In his anointed flesh rash boarish fangs.   61
The sea, with such a storm as his bare head
In hell-black night endured, would have buoyed up   63
And quenched the stellèd fires;   64
Yet, poor old heart, he holp the heavens to rain.   65
If wolves had at thy gate howled that dern time,   66
Thou shouldst have said, "Good porter, turn the key."   67
All cruels else subscribe. But I shall see   68
The wingèd Vengeance overtake such children.   69

CORNWALL
See't shalt thou never.—Fellows, hold the chair.
Upon these eyes of thine I'll set my foot.

GLOUCESTER
He that will think to live till he be old,   72
Give me some help!
                [*Servants hold the chair as Cornwall grinds
                out one of Gloucester's eyes with his boot.*]
                                    Oh, cruel! O you gods!

REGAN
One side will mock another. Th'other too.

CORNWALL [*to Gloucester*]
If you see Vengeance—

FIRST SERVANT   Hold your hand, my lord!
I have served you ever since I was a child;
But better service have I never done you
Than now to bid you hold.

REGAN   How now, you dog?

FIRST SERVANT [*to Regan*]
If you did wear a beard upon your chin,
I'd shake it on this quarrel.—What do you mean?   80

CORNWALL   My villain?   [*He draws his sword.*]   81

FIRST SERVANT [*drawing*]
Nay, then, come on, and take the chance of anger.   82
                [*They fight. Cornwall is wounded.*]

REGAN [*to another Servant*]
Give me thy sword. A peasant stand up thus?   83
                [*She takes a sword and runs at him behind.*]

FIRST SERVANT
Oh, I am slain! My lord, you have one eye left
To see some mischief on him. Oh!   [*He dies.*]   85

CORNWALL
Lest it see more, prevent it. Out, vile jelly!
                [*He puts out Gloucester's other eye.*]

Where is thy luster now?

GLOUCESTER
All dark and comfortless. Where's my son Edmund?
Edmund, enkindle all the sparks of nature   89
To quit this horrid act.

REGAN   Out, treacherous villain!   90
Thou call'st on him that hates thee. It was he
That made the overture of thy treasons to us,   92
Who is too good to pity thee.

GLOUCESTER
Oh, my follies! Then Edgar was abused.   94
Kind gods, forgive me that, and prosper him!

REGAN [*to a Servant*]
Go thrust him out at gates and let him smell
His way to Dover.   *Exit* [*a Servant*] *with Gloucester.*
                How is't, my lord? How look you?   97

CORNWALL
I have received a hurt. Follow me, lady.—
Turn out that eyeless villain. Throw this slave
Upon the dunghill.—Regan, I bleed apace.
Untimely comes this hurt. Give me your arm.
                Exeunt [*Cornwall, supported by Regan.*]

SECOND SERVANT
I'll never care what wickedness I do,
If this man come to good.

THIRD SERVANT   If she live long,
And in the end meet the old course of death,   104
Women will all turn monsters.

SECOND SERVANT
Let's follow the old Earl, and get the Bedlam   106
To lead him where he would. His roguish madness   107
Allows itself to anything.   108

THIRD SERVANT
Go thou. I'll fetch some flax and whites of eggs
To apply to his bleeding face. Now, heaven help him! 110
                Exeunt [*with the body.*]

❧

4.1

Enter Edgar [*as poor Tom*].

EDGAR
Yet better thus, and known to be contemned,   1
Than still contemned and flattered. To be worst,   2
The lowest and most dejected thing of fortune,   3
Stands still in esperance, lives not in fear.   4

---

61 **anointed** consecrated with holy oil.   **rash** slash, stick
63–4 would . . . fires would have swelled high enough, like a wave-lifted buoy, to quench the stars. (*Stellèd* means "starry" or "fixed.")
65 holp helped   **66 dern** dire, dread   **67 turn the key** i.e., let them in.   **68 All . . . subscribe** All other cruel creatures would show forgiveness except you; this cruelty is unparalleled.   **69 The wingèd Vengeance** the swift vengeance of the avenging angel of divine wrath
72 will think hopes   **80 I'd . . . quarrel** i.e., I'd pull your beard in vehement defiance in this cause.   **What do you mean?** i.e., What are you thinking of, what do you think you're doing? (Said perhaps to Cornwall.)   **81 villain** servant, bondman. (Cornwall's question implies, "How dare you do such a thing?")   **82 the chance of anger** the risks of an angry encounter.   **83.1 She . . . behind** (This stage direction appears in the quarto.)   **85 mischief** injury

89 nature i.e., filial love   **90 quit** requite.   **Out** (An exclamation of anger or impatience.)   **92 overture** disclosure   **94 abused** wronged.
97 How look you? How is it with you?   **104 old** customary, natural
106 Bedlam i.e., lunatic discharged from the insane asylum and licensed to beg   **107–8 His . . . anything** His being a madman and derelict allows him to do anything we ask.   **110.1 Exeunt** (At some point after lines 99–100, the body of the slain First Servant must be removed.)
4.1. Location: An open place.
1–2 Yet . . . flattered It is better to be openly despised as a beggar than continually despised behind one's back and flattered to one's face.
3 dejected cast down   **4 Stands . . . fear** gives one some cause for hope, having nothing to fear (since everything is already lost).

The lamentable change is from the best;
The worst returns to laughter. Welcome, then,
Thou unsubstantial air that I embrace!
The wretch that thou hast blown unto the worst
Owes nothing to thy blasts.

Enter Gloucester, and an Old Man [leading him].

                          But who comes here?   9
My father, poorly led? World, world, O world!
But that thy strange mutations make us hate thee,   11
Life would not yield to age.   12

OLD MAN
Oh, my good lord, I have been your tenant
And your father's tenant these fourscore years.

GLOUCESTER
Away, get thee away! Good friend, begone.
Thy comforts can do me no good at all;
Thee they may hurt.

OLD MAN   You cannot see your way.

GLOUCESTER
I have no way and therefore want no eyes;
I stumbled when I saw. Full oft 'tis seen
Our means secure us, and our mere defects   20
Prove our commodities. O dear son Edgar,   21
The food of thy abusèd father's wrath!   22
Might I but live to see thee in my touch,   23
I'd say I had eyes again!

OLD MAN   How now? Who's there?

EDGAR [aside]
O gods! Who is't can say, "I am at the worst"?
I am worse than e'er I was.

OLD MAN   'Tis poor mad Tom.

EDGAR [aside]
And worse I may be yet. The worst is not   27
So long as we can say, "This is the worst."   28

OLD MAN [to Edgar]
Fellow, where goest?

GLOUCESTER   Is it a beggar-man?

OLD MAN   Madman and beggar too.

GLOUCESTER
He has some reason, else he could not beg.   31
I'th' last night's storm I such a fellow saw,
Which made me think a man a worm. My son
Came then into my mind, and yet my mind
Was then scarce friends with him. I have heard more
    since.
As flies to wanton boys are we to th' gods;   36

They kill us for their sport.   5

EDGAR [aside]   How should this be?   37
Bad is the trade that must play fool to sorrow,   38
Ang'ring itself and others.—Bless thee, master!   39

GLOUCESTER
Is that the naked fellow?

OLD MAN   Ay, my lord.

GLOUCESTER
Then, prithee, get thee gone. If for my sake
Thou wilt o'ertake us hence a mile or twain   42
I'th' way toward Dover, do it for ancient love,   43
And bring some covering for this naked soul,
Which I'll entreat to lead me.

OLD MAN   Alack, sir, he is mad.

GLOUCESTER
'Tis the time's plague, when madmen lead the blind.   46
Do as I bid thee, or rather do thy pleasure;
Above the rest, begone.   48

OLD MAN
I'll bring him the best 'parel that I have,
Come on't what will.   *Exit.*

GLOUCESTER   Sirrah, naked fellow—   50

EDGAR
Poor Tom's a-cold. [Aside] I cannot daub it further.   51

GLOUCESTER   Come hither, fellow.

EDGAR [aside]
And yet I must.—Bless thy sweet eyes, they bleed.

GLOUCESTER   Know'st thou the way to Dover?

EDGAR   Both stile and gate, horseway and footpath.
Poor Tom hath been scared out of his good wits. Bless
thee, good man's son, from the foul fiend! Five fiends
have been in poor Tom at once: of lust, as Obidicut;   58
Hobbididance, prince of dumbness; Mahu, of stealing;   59
Modo, of murder; Flibbertigibbet, of mopping   60
and mowing, who since possesses chambermaids and   61
waiting women. So, bless thee, master!

GLOUCESTER [giving a purse]
Here, take this purse, thou whom the heavens'
    plagues
Have humbled to all strokes. That I am wretched   64
Makes thee the happier. Heavens, deal so still!
Let the superfluous and lust-dieted man,   66

5–6 The lamentable . . . laughter Any change from the best is grievous, just as any change from the worst is bound to be for the better.
9 Owes nothing can pay no more, is free of obligation   11–12 But . . .
age If it were not for your hateful inconstancy, we would never be
reconciled to old age and death.   20–1 Our . . . commodities Our
prosperity makes us proudly overconfident, whereas the sheer afflictions we suffer prove beneficial (by teaching us humility.   22 The . . .
wrath on whom thy deceived father's wrath fed, the object of his
anger.   23 in by means of   27–8 The worst . . . worst So long as we
can speak and act and delude ourselves with false hopes, our fortunes can, in fact, grow worse.   31 reason sanity   36 wanton childishly cruel

37 How . . . be? i.e., How can he have suffered so much, changed so
much?   38–9 Bad . . . others It's a bad business to have to play the
fool to my sorrowing father, vexing myself and others (with this
delay in revealing my true identity).   42 o'ertake us catch up to us
(after you have found clothing for Tom o' Bedlam)   43 ancient love
i.e., the mutually trusting relationship of master and tenant that you
and I have long enjoyed   46 'Tis the time's plague It well expresses
the spreading sickness of our present state   48 the rest all   50 Come
. . . will whatever comes of this as regards myself.   51 I . . . further
i.e., I cannot keep up this pretense any longer. (Literally, "I cannot
plaster up the wall.")   58–60 Obidicut . . . Flibbertigibbet (Fiends
borrowed, as before in 3.4.114 and 139–42, from Harsnett.)
60–1 mopping and mowing making grimaces and mouths   61 since
ever since then   64 Have . . . strokes have brought so low as to bear
every blow of Fortune.   66 superfluous and lust-dieted immoderately gluttonous and luxuriously fed

That slaves your ordinance, that will not see 67
Because he does not feel, feel your pow'r quickly! 68
So distribution should undo excess
And each man have enough. Dost thou know Dover?

EDGAR Ay, master.

GLOUCESTER
There is a cliff, whose high and bending head 72
Looks fearfully in the confinèd deep. 73
Bring me but to the very brim of it
And I'll repair the misery thou dost bear
With something rich about me. From that place 76
I shall no leading need.

EDGAR   Give me thy arm.
Poor Tom shall lead thee.   *Exeunt.*

❧

4.2

Enter Goneril [and] Bastard [Edmund].

GONERIL
Welcome, my lord. I marvel our mild husband 1
Not met us on the way.

        [Enter] steward [Oswald].

                              Now, where's your master? 2

OSWALD
Madam, within, but never man so changed.
I told him of the army that was landed;
He smiled at it. I told him you were coming;
His answer was "The worse." Of Gloucester's
    treachery
And of the loyal service of his son
When I informed him, then he called me sot 8
And told me I had turned the wrong side out.
What most he should dislike seems pleasant to him;
What like, offensive.

GONERIL [*to Edmund*] Then shall you go no further.
It is the cowish terror of his spirit, 12
That dares not undertake. He'll not feel wrongs 13
Which tie him to an answer. Our wishes on the way 14
May prove effects. Back, Edmund, to my brother; 15
Hasten his musters and conduct his powers. 16
I must change names at home and give the distaff 17

Into my husband's hands. This trusty servant
Shall pass between us. Ere long you are like to hear, 19
If you dare venture in your own behalf,
A mistress's command. Wear this; spare speech. 21
                    [She gives him a favor.]
Decline your head. [*She kisses him.*] This kiss, if it durst
    speak,
Would stretch thy spirits up into the air.
Conceive, and fare thee well. 24

EDMUND
Yours in the ranks of death.   *Exit.*

GONERIL   My most dear Gloucester!
Oh, the difference of man and man!
To thee a woman's services are due;
My fool usurps my body. 28

OSWALD Madam, here comes my lord.   [*Exit.*] 29

        Enter Albany.

GONERIL
I have been worth the whistling.

ALBANY   Oh, Goneril, 30
You are not worth the dust which the rude wind
Blows in your face. I fear your disposition; 32
That nature which contemns its origin 33
Cannot be bordered certain in itself. 34
She that herself will sliver and disbranch 35
From her material sap perforce must wither 36
And come to deadly use. 37

GONERIL No more. The text is foolish. 38

ALBANY
Wisdom and goodness to the vile seem vile;
Filths savor but themselves. What have you done? 40
Tigers, not daughters, what have you performed?
A father, and a gracious agèd man,
Whose reverence even the head-lugged bear would
    lick, 43
Most barbarous, most degenerate, have you madded. 44
Could my good brother suffer you to do it? 45
A man, a prince, by him so benefited?
If that the heavens do not their visible spirits 47
Send quickly down to tame these vile offenses,
It will come,
Humanity must perforce prey on itself,
Like monsters of the deep.

GONERIL   Milk-livered man, 51

---

67 That . . . ordinance who enslaves your divine ordinances to his
own corrupt will   67–8 that . . . feel who is resistant to spiritual
insight because, not having suffered himself, he lacks the sympathy
of fellow feeling   72 bending overhanging   73 in . . . deep i.e., into
the sea below, which is confined by its shores.   76 about me on my
person.
4.2. Location: Before the Duke of Albany's palace.
1 Welcome (Goneril, who has just arrived home from Gloucestershire
escorted by Edmund, bids him brief welcome before he must return.)
2 Not met has not met   8 sot fool   12 cowish cowardly   13 undertake venture.   13–14 He'll . . . answer He will ignore insults that, if
he took notice, would oblige him to respond, to fight.   14–15 Our . . .
effects The hopes we discussed on our journey here (presumably
concerning the supplanting of Albany by Edmund) may come to
pass.   15 brother brother-in-law, Cornwall   16 musters assembling
of troops.   powers armed forces.   17 change names i.e., exchange
the roles of master and mistress of the household, and exchange the
insignia of man and woman: the sword and the *distaff.*   distaff spinning staff, symbolizing the wife's role

19 like likely   21 mistress's (With sexual double meaning.)   24 Conceive Understand, take my meaning. (With sexual double entendre,
continuing from *stretch thy spirits* in the previous line and continued in
death, line 25, and *a woman's services,* line 27.)   28 My fool . . . body i.e.,
my husband claims possession of me but is unfitted to do so.   29 s.d.
Exit (Oswald could exit later with Goneril, at line 88.)   30 worth the
whistling i.e., worth the attentions of men. (Alludes to the proverb, "it
is a poor dog that is not worth the whistling.")   32 fear your disposition mistrust your nature   33 contemns spurns   34 bordered certain
safely restrained, kept within bounds   35 sliver tear off   36 material
sap nourishing substance, the stock from which she grew   37 to
deadly use to a bad end, to a destructive purpose.   38 The text i.e., on
which you have been preaching   40 savor but themselves hunger
only for that which is filthy.   43 head-lugged dragged by the head (or
by the ring in its nose) and infuriated   44 madded driven mad.
45 brother brother-in-law (Cornwall)   47 If that If.   visible manifested   51 Milk-livered White-livered, cowardly

That bear'st a cheek for blows, a head for wrongs,
Who hast not in thy brows an eye discerning　53
Thine honor from thy suffering, that not know'st　54
Fools do those villains pity who are punished　55
Ere they have done their mischief. Where's thy drum?　56
France spreads his banners in our noiseless land,　57
With plumèd helm thy state begins to threat,　58
Whilst thou, a moral fool, sits still and cries,　59
"Alack, why does he so?"

ALBANY　　　　　　　　　See thyself, devil!　60
Proper deformity shows not in the fiend　61
So horrid as in woman.

GONERIL　　　　　　　　Oh, vain fool!　62

ALBANY
Thou changèd and self-covered thing, for shame,　63
Bemonster not thy feature. Were't my fitness　64
To let these hands obey my blood,　65
They are apt enough to dislocate and tear　66
Thy flesh and bones. Howe'er thou art a fiend,　67
A woman's shape doth shield thee.　68

GONERIL　Marry, your manhood! Mew!　69

Enter a Messenger.

ALBANY　What news?

MESSENGER
Oh, my good lord, the Duke of Cornwall's dead,
Slain by his servant, going to put out
The other eye of Gloucester.

ALBANY　　　　　　　　Gloucester's eyes!

MESSENGER
A servant that he bred, thrilled with remorse,　74
Opposed against the act, bending his sword　75
To his great master, who, thereat enraged,　76
Flew on him and amongst them felled him dead,　77
But not without that harmful stroke which since
Hath plucked him after.

ALBANY　　　　　　　This shows you are above,　79

You justicers, that these our nether crimes　80
So speedily can venge! But, oh, poor Gloucester!
Lost he his other eye?

MESSENGER　　　　　Both, both, my lord.—
This letter, madam, craves a speedy answer;
'Tis from your sister.　　　[*He gives her a letter.*]

GONERIL [*aside*]　　　One way I like this well;　84
But being widow, and my Gloucester with her,　85
May all the building in my fancy pluck　86
Upon my hateful life. Another way　87
The news is not so tart.—I'll read, and answer.　88
　　　　　　　　　　　　　　　[*Exit.*]

ALBANY
Where was his son when they did take his eyes?　89

MESSENGER
Come with my lady hither.

ALBANY　　　　　　　He is not here.

MESSENGER
No, my good lord. I met him back again.　91

ALBANY　Knows he the wickedness?

MESSENGER
Ay, my good lord. 'Twas he informed against him,
And quit the house on purpose that their punishment
Might have the freer course.

ALBANY　　　　　　　Gloucester, I live　95
To thank thee for the love thou show'dst the King
And to revenge thine eyes.—Come hither, friend.
Tell me what more thou know'st.　　　*Exeunt.*

❖

4.[3]

Enter Kent [disguised] and a Gentleman.

KENT　Why the King of France is so suddenly gone back
　know you no reason?

GENTLEMAN　Something he left imperfect in the state,　3
　which since his coming forth is thought of, which im-　4
　ports to the kingdom so much fear and danger that his　5
　personal return was most required and necessary.

KENT
Who hath he left behind him general?

GENTLEMAN
The Marshal of France, Monsieur la Far.

KENT　Did your letters pierce the Queen to any demon-
　stration of grief?

GENTLEMAN
Ay, sir. She took them, read them in my presence,
And now and then an ample tear trilled down　12
Her delicate cheek. It seemed she was a queen

53–4 **discerning . . . suffering** able to tell the difference between an insult to your honor and something you should tolerate　54–6 **that not . . . mischief** you who fail to understand that only fools like yourself are so tenderhearted as to pity villains (like Gloucester, Lear, and Cordelia) who are apprehended and punished before they have committed a crime.　56 **Where's thy drum?** Where is your military preparedness?　57 **noiseless** peaceful, unprepared for war　58 **thy state . . . threat** (France) begins to threaten your kingdom　59 **moral** moralizing　60 **"Alack . . . so?"** (An utterly ineffectual response to invasion.)　61–2 **Proper . . . woman** The deformity that is appropriate in a fiend's features is even uglier in a woman's (since it is so at variance with her nominally feminine appearance).　63–4 **Thou . . . feature** i.e., You creature whose transformation into a fiend now overwhelms your womanliness, do not, however evil you are, take on the outward form of a monster or fiend.　64 **Were't my fitness** If it were suitable for me　65 **blood** passion　66 **apt** ready　67 **Howe'er . . . fiend** However much you may be a fiend in reality　68 **shield** (Since I, as a gentleman, cannot lay violent hands on a lady.)　69 **Mew** (An exclamation of disgust, a derisive catcall: You speak of manhood in shielding me as a woman. Some manhood!)　74 **bred** kept in his household.　**thrilled with remorse** deeply moved with pity　75 **Opposed** opposed himself　75–6 **bending . . . To** directing his sword against　77 **amongst them** together with the others (?) in their midst (?) out of their number (?)　79 **after** along (to death).

80 **justicers** (heavenly) judges.　**nether** i.e., committed here below, on earth　84 **One way** (i.e., because Edmund is now Duke of Gloucester, and Cornwall, a dangerous rival for the throne, is dead)　85–7 **But . . . life** but she being now a widow, and Edmund in her company, may pull down my imagined happiness (of having the entire kingdom with Edmund), leaving my hopes in ruins.　88 **tart** bitter, sour. (See line 84 and note.)　89 **his son** Edmund.　**his** Gloucester's.　91 **back again** on the way back (from Albany's palace).　95 **Gloucester** The old Earl of Gloucester
4.3. Location: The French camp near Dover.
3 **imperfect in the state** unsettled in state affairs　4–5 **imports** portends　12 **trilled** trickled

Over her passion, who, most rebel-like,   14
Sought to be king o'er her.
KENT   Oh, then it moved her?
GENTLEMAN
Not to a rage. Patience and sorrow strove
Who should express her goodliest. You have seen   17
Sunshine and rain at once. Her smiles and tears
Were like a better way; those happy smilets   19
That played on her ripe lip seemed not to know   20
What guests were in her eyes, which parted thence   21
As pearls from diamonds dropped. In brief,
Sorrow would be a rarity most beloved   23
If all could so become it.   24
KENT   Made she no verbal question?   25
GENTLEMAN
Faith, once or twice she heaved the name of "father"   26
Pantingly forth, as if it pressed her heart;
Cried, "Sisters, sisters! Shame of ladies, sisters!
Kent! Father! Sisters! What, i'th' storm, i'th' night?
Let pity not be believed!" There she shook   30
The holy water from her heavenly eyes,
And, clamor-moistened, then away she started   32
To deal with grief alone.
KENT   It is the stars,
The stars above us, govern our conditions,   34
Else one self mate and make could not beget   35
Such different issues. You spoke not with her since?   36
GENTLEMAN   No.
KENT
Was this before the King returned?
GENTLEMAN   No, since.   38
KENT
Well, sir, the poor distressèd Lear's i'th' town,
Who sometime in his better tune remembers   40
What we are come about, and by no means
Will yield to see his daughter.
GENTLEMAN   Why, good sir? 42
KENT
A sovereign shame so elbows him—his own
    unkindness   43
That stripped her from his benediction, turned her   44
To foreign casualties, gave her dear rights   45
To his dog-hearted daughters—these things sting
His mind so venomously that burning shame
Detains him from Cordelia.   48

GENTLEMAN   Alack, poor gentleman!
KENT
Of Albany's and Cornwall's powers you heard not?   50
GENTLEMAN   'Tis so. They are afoot.   51
KENT
Well, sir, I'll bring you to our master Lear
And leave you to attend him. Some dear cause   53
Will in concealment wrap me up awhile.
When I am known aright, you shall not grieve   55
Lending me this acquaintance. I pray you, go   56
Along with me.   *Exeunt.*

❖

4.[4]

Enter, with drum and colors, Cordelia,
Gentleman, and soldiers.

CORDELIA
Alack, 'tis he! Why, he was met even now
As mad as the vexed sea, singing aloud,
Crowned with rank fumiter and furrow weeds,   3
With hardocks, hemlock, nettles, cuckooflowers,   4
Darnel, and all the idle weeds that grow   5
In our sustaining corn. A century send forth!   6
Search every acre in the high-grown field
And bring him to our eye.   [*Exit a soldier or soldiers.*]
                                    What can man's wisdom   8
In the restoring his bereavèd sense,
He that helps him take all my outward worth.   10
GENTLEMAN   There is means, madam.
Our foster nurse of nature is repose,
The which he lacks. That to provoke in him   13
Are many simples operative, whose power   14
Will close the eye of anguish.
CORDELIA   All blest secrets,
All you unpublished virtues of the earth,   16
Spring with my tears! Be aidant and remediate   17
In the good man's distress! Seek, seek for him,
Lest his ungoverned rage dissolve the life   19
That wants the means to lead it.

Enter Messenger.

MESSENGER   News, madam.   20
The British powers are marching hitherward.   21

---

14 who which   **17 Who . . . goodliest** which of the two could portray
her best.   **19 like a better way** better than that, though similar
20–1 seemed . . . eyes seemed oblivious of her tears   **23 a rarity** i.e., a
precious thing, like a jewel   **24 If . . . it** i.e., if all persons were as
attractive in sorrow as she.   **25 verbal** i.e., as distinguished from her
tears and looks   **26 heaved** breathed out with difficulty   **30 Let . . .
believed!** i.e., Let no show of pity be trusted (since they are proved to
be so false)!   **32 clamor-moistened** i.e., her outcry of grief assuaged
by tears.   **started** i.e., went   **34 conditions** characters   **35 Else . . .
make** otherwise, one couple (husband and wife)   **36 issues** offspring.   **38 before . . . returned** before the King of France returned to
his kingdom.   **40 better tune** more composed state of mind
42 yield consent   **43 sovereign** overruling.   **elbows him** i.e., prods
his memory, jostles him, thrusts him back   **44 turned her** turned her
out   **45 foreign casualties** chances of fortune abroad   **48 Detains
him from** holds him back from seeing

50 powers troops, armies   **51 afoot** on the march.   **53 dear cause**
important purpose   **55–6 grieve . . . acquaintance** regret having
made my acquaintance.
4.4. Location: The French camp.
0.2 Gentleman (The quarto specifies "Doctor" here and at line 11.)
3 fumiter fumitory, a weed or herb.   **furrow weeds** weeds growing
in plowed furrows   **4 hardocks** probably burdock, a coarse weedy
plant.   **cuckooflowers** flowers of late spring, when the cuckoo is
heard   **5 Darnel** weed of the grass kind.   **idle** worthless   **6 sustaining corn** sustenance-giving grain.   **A century** (Literally, a troop of
one hundred men.)   **8 What . . . wisdom** i.e., What medical knowledge can accomplish   **10 outward** material   **13 That to provoke** To
induce that   **14 Are . . . operative** many herbal remedies are efficacious; or, there are many effective remedies. (*Simples* are prepared
from a single herb.)   **16 unpublished virtues** little-known benign
herbs   **17 Spring** grow.   **aidant and remediate** helpful and remedial
19 rage frenzy   **20 That . . . lead it** that lacks the means to live sanely.
21 powers armies

CORDELIA
'Tis known before. Our preparation stands
In expectation of them. O dear father,
It is thy business that I go about;
Therefore great France
My mourning and importuned tears hath pitied.   26
No blown ambition doth our arms incite,   27
But love, dear love, and our aged father's right.
Soon may I hear and see him!   *Exeunt.*

❖

4.[5]

Enter Regan and steward [Oswald].

REGAN   But are my brother's powers set forth?   1
OSWALD   Ay, madam.
REGAN   Himself in person there?
OSWALD   Madam, with much ado.   4
  Your sister is the better soldier.
REGAN
  Lord Edmund spake not with your lord at home?
OSWALD   No, madam.
REGAN
  What might import my sister's letters to him?   8
OSWALD   I know not, lady.
REGAN
  Faith, he is posted hence on serious matter.   10
  It was great ignorance, Gloucester's eyes being out,   11
  To let him live. Where he arrives he moves
  All hearts against us. Edmund, I think, is gone,
  In pity of his misery, to dispatch   14
  His nighted life; moreover to descry   15
  The strength o'th'enemy.
OSWALD
  I must needs after him, madam, with my letter.
REGAN
  Our troops set forth tomorrow. Stay with us;
  The ways are dangerous.
OSWALD   I may not, madam.
  My lady charged my duty in this business.   20
REGAN
  Why should she write to Edmund? Might not you
  Transport her purposes by word? Belike   22
  Something—I know not what. I'll love thee much;
  Let me unseal the letter.
OSWALD   Madam, I had rather—
REGAN
  I know your lady does not love her husband,
  I am sure of that; and at her late being here   26
  She gave strange oeillades and most speaking looks   27
  To noble Edmund. I know you are of her bosom.   28
OSWALD   I, madam?

REGAN
I speak in understanding; y'are, I know't.   30
Therefore I do advise you, take this note: 31
My lord is dead; Edmund and I have talked,   32
And more convenient is he for my hand   33
Than for your lady's. You may gather more.   34
If you do find him, pray you, give him this;   35
And when your mistress hears thus much from you,   36
I pray, desire her call her wisdom to her.   37
So, fare you well.
If you do chance to hear of that blind traitor,
Preferment falls on him that cuts him off.   40
OSWALD
Would I could meet him, madam! I should show
What party I do follow.
REGAN   Fare thee well.
    Exeunt [separately].

❖

4.[6]

Enter Gloucester, and Edgar [in peasant's clothes, leading his father].

GLOUCESTER
When shall I come to th' top of that same hill?   1
EDGAR
You do climb up it now. Look how we labor.
GLOUCESTER
Methinks the ground is even.
EDGAR   Horrible steep.
Hark, do you hear the sea?
GLOUCESTER   No, truly.
EDGAR
Why, then, your other senses grow imperfect
By your eyes' anguish.
GLOUCESTER   So may it be, indeed.
Methinks thy voice is altered, and thou speak'st
In better phrase and matter than thou didst.
EDGAR
You're much deceived. In nothing am I changed
But in my garments.
GLOUCESTER   Methinks you're better spoken.
EDGAR
Come on, sir, here's the place. Stand still. How fearful
And dizzy 'tis to cast one's eyes so low!
The crows and choughs that wing the midway air   13
Show scarce so gross as beetles. Halfway down   14
Hangs one that gathers samphire—dreadful trade!   15
Methinks he seems no bigger than his head.
The fishermen that walk upon the beach

---

26 **importuned** importunate   27 **blown** swollen
4.5. Location; Gloucester's house.
1 **my brother's powers** Albany's forces   4 **with much ado** after much fuss and persuasion.   8 **import** bear as their purport, express   10 **is posted** has hurried   11 **ignorance** error, folly   14 **his** Gloucester's   15 **nighted** benighted, blinded.   **descry** spy out   20 **charged my duty** laid great stress on my obedience   22 **Belike** It may be   26 **late** recently   27 **oeillades** amorous glances   28 **of her bosom** in her confidence.

30 **y'are** you are   31 **take this note** take note of this   32 **have talked** have come to an understanding   33 **convenient** fitting   34 **gather more** infer what I am trying to suggest.   35 **this** i.e., this information, or a love token, or possibly a letter (though only one letter, Goneril's, is found on his dead body at 4.6.262)   36 **thus much** what I have told you   37 **call . . . to her** recall herself to her senses.   40 **Preferment** advancement
4.6. Location: Open place near Dover.
1 **that same hill** i.e., the cliff we talked about (4.1.72–4).   13 **choughs** jackdaws.   **midway** halfway down   14 **gross** large   15 **samphire** (A herb used in pickling.)

Appear like mice, and yond tall anchoring bark   18
Diminished to her cock; her cock, a buoy   19
Almost too small for sight. The murmuring surge,
That on th'unnumbered idle pebble chafes,   21
Cannot be heard so high. I'll look no more,
Lest my brain turn, and the deficient sight   23
Topple down headlong.
GLOUCESTER   Set me where you stand.   24
EDGAR
Give me your hand. You are now within a foot
Of th'extreme verge. For all beneath the moon   26
Would I not leap upright.
GLOUCESTER   Let go my hand.   27
Here, friend, 's another purse; in it a jewel
Well worth a poor man's taking.   [*He gives a purse.*]
Fairies and gods   29
Prosper it with thee! Go thou further off.   30
Bid me farewell, and let me hear thee going.
EDGAR [*moving away*]
Now fare ye well, good sir.
GLOUCESTER   With all my heart.
EDGAR [*aside*]
Why I do trifle thus with his despair
Is done to cure it.
GLOUCESTER [*kneeling*]   O you mighty gods!
This world I do renounce, and in your sights
Shake patiently my great affliction off.
If I could bear it longer and not fall
To quarrel with your great opposeless wills,   38
My snuff and loathèd part of nature should   39
Burn itself out. If Edgar live, oh, bless him!
Now, fellow, fare thee well.   [*He falls forward.*]
EDGAR   Gone, sir. Farewell.—
And yet I know not how conceit may rob   42
The treasury of life, when life itself
Yields to the theft. Had he been where he thought,   44
By this had thought been past. Alive or dead?—   45
Ho, you, sir! Friend! Hear you, sir! Speak!—
Thus might he pass indeed; yet he revives.—   47
What are you, sir?
GLOUCESTER   Away, and let me die.   48
EDGAR
Hadst thou been aught but gossamer, feathers, air,
So many fathom down precipitating,
Thou'dst shivered like an egg; but thou dost breathe,
Hast heavy substance, bleed'st not, speak'st, art
sound.   52

Ten masts at each make not the altitude   53
Which thou hast perpendicularly fell.
Thy life's a miracle. Speak yet again.
GLOUCESTER   But have I fall'n or no?
EDGAR
From the dread summit of this chalky bourn.   57
Look up aheight; the shrill-gorged lark so far   58
Cannot be seen or heard. Do but look up.
GLOUCESTER   Alack, I have no eyes.
Is wretchedness deprived that benefit
To end itself by death? 'Twas yet some comfort
When misery could beguile the tyrant's rage   63
And frustrate his proud will.
EDGAR   Give me your arm.
[*He lifts him up.*]
Up—so. How is't? Feel you your legs? You stand.
GLOUCESTER
Too well, too well.
EDGAR   This is above all strangeness.
Upon the crown o'th' cliff what thing was that
Which parted from you?
GLOUCESTER   A poor unfortunate beggar.
EDGAR
As I stood here below, methought his eyes
Were two full moons; he had a thousand noses,
Horns whelked and waved like the enridgèd sea.   71
It was some fiend. Therefore, thou happy father,   72
Think that the clearest gods, who make them honors   73
Of men's impossibilities, have preserved thee.   74
GLOUCESTER
I do remember now. Henceforth I'll bear
Affliction till it do cry out itself   76
"Enough, enough," and die. That thing you speak of,   77
I took it for a man; often 'twould say
"The fiend, the fiend." He led me to that place.
EDGAR
Bear free and patient thoughts.

Enter Lear [*mad, fantastically dressed with wild*
flowers].

But who comes here?   80
The safer sense will ne'er accommodate   81
His master thus.   82
LEAR   No, they cannot touch me for coining. I am the   83
King himself.   84
EDGAR   Oh, thou side-piercing sight!   85

---

18 **bark** small sailing vessel   19 **Diminished . . . cock** reduced to the size of her cockboat, small ship's boat   21 **th'unnumbered idle pebble** innumerable, randomly shifting, pebbles   23–4 **Lest . . . head-long** lest I become dizzy, and my failing sight topple me headlong. 26 **For . . . moon** i.e., For the whole world   27 **upright** i.e., up and down, much less forward.   29–30 **Fairies . . . thee!** May the fairies and gods cause this to multiply in your possession!   38 **To quarrel with** into rebellion against.   **opposeless** irresistible   39 **snuff** i.e., useless residue. (Literally, the smoking wick of a candle.)   **of nature** i.e., of my life   42 **conceit** imagination   44 **Yields** consents   45 **By this** by this time   47 **pass** die   48 **What** Who. (Edgar now speaks in a new voice, differing from that of "poor Tom" and also from the "altered" voice he used at the start of this scene; see lines 7–10.)
52 **heavy substance** the substance of the flesh

53 **at each** end to end   57 **bourn** limit, boundary (i.e., the edge of the sea).   58 **aheight** on high.   **shrill-gorged** shrill-throated   63 **beguile** outwit   71 **whelked** twisted, convoluted.   **enridgèd** furrowed (by the wind)   72 **happy father** lucky old man   73 **clearest** purest, most righteous   73–4 **who . . . impossibilities** who win our awe and reverence by doing things impossible to men   76–7 **till . . . die** i.e., until affliction itself has had enough, or until I die.   80 **free** i.e., free from despair   81–2 **The safer . . . thus** i.e., A person in his right senses would never dress himself in such a fashion. (*His master* is the owner of the *safer sense* or sane mind. *His* means "its.")   83–4 **they . . . himself** they cannot prosecute me for minting coins. As king, I enjoy the exclusive royal prerogative for doing so. (Lear goes on to discuss his need for money to pay his imaginary soldiers.)   85 **side-piercing** heartrending. (With a suggestion of Christ's suffering on the cross.)

LEAR   Nature's above art in that respect. There's your 86
press money. That fellow handles his bow like a crow- 87
keeper. Draw me a clothier's yard. Look, look, a 88
mouse! Peace, peace; this piece of toasted cheese will
do't. There's my gauntlet; I'll prove it on a giant. Bring 90
up the brown bills. Oh, well flown, bird! I'th' clout, 91
i'th' clout—hewgh! Give the word. 92

EDGAR   Sweet marjoram. 93

LEAR   Pass.

GLOUCESTER   I know that voice.

LEAR   Ha! Goneril with a white beard? They flattered
me like a dog and told me I had white hairs in my 97
beard ere the black ones were there. To say ay and 98
no to everything that I said ay and no to was 99
no good divinity. When the rain came to wet me 100
once and the wind to make me chatter, when the 101
thunder would not peace at my bidding, there I found 102
'em, there I smelt 'em out. Go to, they are not men o' 103
their words. They told me I was everything. 'Tis a
lie. I am not ague-proof. 105

GLOUCESTER
The trick of that voice I do well remember. 106
Is't not the King?

LEAR   Ay, every inch a king.
When I do stare, see how the subject quakes.
I pardon that man's life. What was thy cause? 109
Adultery?
Thou shalt not die. Die for adultery? No.
The wren goes to't, and the small gilded fly
Does lecher in my sight.
Let copulation thrive; for Gloucester's bastard son
Was kinder to his father than my daughters
Got 'tween the lawful sheets.
To't, luxury, pell-mell, for I lack soldiers. 117
Behold yond simpering dame,
Whose face between her forks presages snow, 119
That minces virtue and does shake the head 120
To hear of pleasure's name; 121
The fitchew nor the soilèd horse goes to't 122

With a more riotous appetite.
Down from the waist they're centaurs, 124
Though women all above.
But to the girdle do the gods inherit; 126
Beneath is all the fiends'.
There's hell, there's darkness, there is the sulfurous pit,
burning, scalding, stench, consumption. Fie, fie, fie!
Pah, pah! Give me an ounce of civet, good apothecary, 130
sweeten my imagination. There's money for thee.

GLOUCESTER   Oh, let me kiss that hand!

LEAR   Let me wipe it first; it smells of mortality.

GLOUCESTER
Oh, ruined piece of nature! This great world 134
Shall so wear out to naught. Dost thou know me? 135

LEAR   I remember thine eyes well enough. Dost thou
squinny at me? No, do thy worst, blind Cupid; I'll not 137
love. Read thou this challenge. Mark but the penning
of it.

GLOUCESTER
Were all thy letters suns, I could not see.

EDGAR [aside]
I would not take this from report. It is, 141
And my heart breaks at it.

LEAR   Read.

GLOUCESTER   What, with the case of eyes? 144

LEAR   Oho, are you there with me? No eyes in your 145
head, nor no money in your purse? Your eyes are in a
heavy case, your purse in a light, yet you see how this 147
world goes.

GLOUCESTER   I see it feelingly. 149

LEAR   What, art mad? A man may see how this world
goes with no eyes. Look with thine ears. See how
yond justice rails upon yond simple thief. Hark in 152
thine ear: change places and, handy-dandy, which is 153
the justice, which is the thief? Thou hast seen a
farmer's dog bark at a beggar?

GLOUCESTER   Ay, sir.

LEAR   And the creature run from the cur? There thou 157
mightst behold the great image of authority: a dog's 158
obeyed in office. 159
Thou rascal beadle, hold thy bloody hand! 160
Why dost thou lash that whore? Strip thine own back;
Thou hotly lusts to use her in that kind 162
For which thou whipp'st her. The usurer hangs the
cozener. 163

---

86 Nature's . . . respect Real life can offer more heart-piercing examples than art.   **87 press money** enlistment bonus.   **87–8 crowkeeper** laborer hired to scare away the crows.   **88 Draw . . . yard** i.e., Draw your bow to the full length of the arrow, a cloth-yard long.   **90 do't** i.e., capture the mouse, an imagined enemy.   **gauntlet** armored glove thrown down as a challenge.   **prove it on** maintain it against **91 brown bills** soldiers carrying pikes (painted brown), or the pikes themselves.   **well flown, bird** (Lear uses the language of hawking to describe the flight of an arrow.)   **clout** target, bull's-eye   **92 hewgh** (The arrow's noise.)   **word** password.   **93 Sweet marjoram** (A herb used to cure madness.)   **97 like a dog** as a dog fawns   **97–8 told . . . there** i.e., told me I had the white-haired wisdom of old age before I had even attained the manliness of a beard.   **98–100 To . . . divinity** i.e., To agree flatteringly with everything I said was not good theology, since the Bible teaches us to "let your yea be yea and your nay, nay" (James 5:12; see also Matthew 5:37 and 2 Cor. 1:18).   **100–3 When . . . out** i.e., Suffering wet, cold, and storm have taught me about the frailty of the human condition.   **103 Go to** (An expression of impatience.)   **105 ague-proof** immune against illness (literally, fever).   **106 trick** peculiar characteristic   **109 cause** offense.   **117 luxury** lechery   **119 Whose . . . snow** whose frosty countenance seems to suggest frigidity between her legs   **120 minces** affects, mimics   **121 of pleasure's name** the very name of pleasure   **122 The fitchew . . . to't** neither the polecat nor the well-pastured horse indulges in sexual pleasure

124 centaurs fabulous creatures with the head, trunk, and arms of a man joined to the body and legs of a horse   **126 But** Only.   **girdle** waist.   **inherit** have possession   **130 civet** musk perfume **134 piece** (1) fragment (2) masterpiece   **134–5 This . . . naught** Even so will the whole universe come to an apocalyptic end.   **137 squinny** squint   **141 take** believe, credit.   **It is** It is taking place, incredibly enough   **144 case** mere sockets   **145 are . . . me?** is that your meaning, the point you are making?   **147 heavy case** sad plight. (With pun on *case* in line 144.)   **149 feelingly** (1) by touch (2) keenly, painfully. **152 simple** of humble station   **153 handy-dandy** take your choice of hands (as in a well-known child's game)   **157 creature** poor fellow **158–9 a dog's . . . office** i.e., even currish power commands submission.   **160 beadle** parish officer, responsible for giving whippings **162 kind** way   **163 The usurer . . . cozener** The moneylender (who can buy out justice) hangs the con man.

Through tattered clothes small vices do appear; 164
Robes and furred gowns hide all. Plate sin with gold, 165
And the strong lance of justice hurtless breaks; 166
Arm it in rags, a pygmy's straw does pierce it.
None does offend, none, I say, none. I'll able 'em. 168
Take that of me, my friend, who have the power 169
To seal th'accuser's lips. Get thee glass eyes, 170
And like a scurvy politician seem 171
To see the things thou dost not. Now, now, now, now! 172
Pull off my boots. Harder, harder! So.

EDGAR [aside]
Oh, matter and impertinency mixed, 174
Reason in madness!

LEAR
If thou wilt weep my fortunes, take my eyes.
I know thee well enough; thy name is Gloucester.
Thou must be patient. We came crying hither.
Thou know'st the first time that we smell the air
We wawl and cry. I will preach to thee. Mark.

GLOUCESTER   Alack, alack the day!

LEAR
When we are born, we cry that we are come
To this great stage of fools.—This' a good block. 183
It were a delicate stratagem to shoe 184
A troop of horse with felt. I'll put 't in proof, 185
And when I have stol'n upon these son-in-laws,
Then, kill, kill, kill, kill, kill, kill!

Enter a Gentleman [with attendants].

GENTLEMAN
Oh, here he is. Lay hand upon him.—Sir,
Your most dear daughter—

LEAR
No rescue? What, a prisoner? I am even
The natural fool of fortune. Use me well; 191
You shall have ransom. Let me have surgeons;
I am cut to th' brains.

GENTLEMAN   You shall have anything. 193

LEAR   No seconds? All myself? 194
Why, this would make a man a man of salt 195
To use his eyes for garden waterpots,
Ay, and laying autumn's dust.
I will die bravely, like a smug bridegroom. What? 198

I will be jovial. Come, come, I am a king, 199
Masters, know you that? 200

GENTLEMAN
You are a royal one, and we obey you.

LEAR   Then there's life in't. Come, an you get it, you 202
shall get it by running. Sa, sa, sa, sa. 203
            Exit [running, followed by attendants].

GENTLEMAN
A sight most pitiful in the meanest wretch,
Past speaking of in a king! Thou hast one daughter
Who redeems nature from the general curse 206
Which twain have brought her to. 207

EDGAR   Hail, gentle sir. 208

GENTLEMAN   Sir, speed you. What's your will? 209

EDGAR
Do you hear aught, sir, of a battle toward? 210

GENTLEMAN
Most sure and vulgar. Everyone hears that 211
Which can distinguish sound.

EDGAR   But, by your favor, 212
How near's the other army?

GENTLEMAN
Near and on speedy foot. The main descry 214
Stands on the hourly thought. 215

EDGAR   I thank you, sir; that's all.

GENTLEMAN
Though that the Queen on special cause is here, 217
Her army is moved on.

EDGAR   I thank you, sir.
                        Exit [Gentleman].

GLOUCESTER
You ever-gentle gods, take my breath from me;
Let not my worser spirit tempt me again 220
To die before you please!

EDGAR   Well pray you, father. 222

GLOUCESTER   Now, good sir, what are you? 223

EDGAR
A most poor man, made tame to fortune's blows, 224
Who, by the art of known and feeling sorrows, 225
Am pregnant to good pity. Give me your hand. 226
I'll lead you to some biding.   [He offers his arm.]

GLOUCESTER   Hearty thanks. 227

164–5 Through . . . all i.e., Beggars' small vices are apparent for all to see; rich folk, in expensive clothes, succeed in hiding a great deal. 165 Plate Arm in plate armor   166 hurtless breaks splinters harmlessly   168 able empower, give warrant to   169 Take . . . me (1) Learn that from me (2) Take that protection from me   170–2 Get . . . dost not If Gloucester were to fit himself out with spectacles (or perhaps with glass eyeballs, though they are not mentioned elsewhere until later in the seventeenth century), he would look wise like a hypocritical politician.   174 matter and impertinency sense and nonsense   183 This' This is.   block mold for a felt hat. (Lear may refer to the weeds strewn in his hair, which he removes as though doffing a hat before preaching a sermon.)   184 delicate subtle   185 felt i.e., padding to deaden the sound of the footfall.   in proof to the test   191 natural fool born plaything   193 cut wounded   194 seconds supporters.   195 of salt of salt tears   198 bravely (1) courageously (2) splendidly attired.   smug trimly dressed. (Bridegroom continues the punning sexual suggestion of die bravely, "have sex successfully.")

199 jovial (1) Jovelike, majestic (2) jolly.   200 Masters good sirs 202 life i.e., hope still.   an if   203 Sa . . . sa (A hunting cry.) 206 general curse fallen condition of the human race   207 twain (1) Goneril and Regan (2) Adam and Eve   208 gentle noble   209 speed you Godspeed, may God prosper you.   210 toward imminent. 211 vulgar in everyone's mouth, generally known.   212 Which who 214–15 The main . . . thought The full view of the main body is expected any hour now.   217 Though that Although.   on special cause for a special reason, i.e., to minister to Lear   220 worser spirit bad angel, or ill thoughts   222 father (A term of respect to older men, as also in lines 72, 259, and 290, though with ironic double meaning throughout the scene.)   223 what who. (Again, Edgar alters his voice to personate a new stranger assisting Gloucester. See line 48, above, and note.)   224 tame submissive   225 known and feeling personally experienced and heartfelt   226 pregnant prone   227 biding abode.

The bounty and the benison of heaven   228
To boot, and boot!

Enter steward [Oswald].

OSWALD   A proclaimed prize! Most happy!   229
                [He draws his sword.]
That eyeless head of thine was first framed flesh   230
To raise my fortunes. Thou old unhappy traitor,
Briefly thyself remember. The sword is out   232
That must destroy thee.
GLOUCESTER   Now let thy friendly hand   233
Put strength enough to't.   *[Edgar intervenes.]*
OSWALD   Wherefore, bold peasant,
Durst thou support a published traitor? Hence,   235
Lest that th'infection of his fortune take   236
Like hold on thee. Let go his arm.   237
EDGAR   'Chill not let go, zir, without vurther 'cagion.   238
OSWALD   Let go, slave, or thou diest!
EDGAR   Good gentleman, go your gait, and let poor volk   240
pass. An 'chud ha' bin zwaggered out of my life,   241
'twould not ha' bin zo long as 'tis by a vortnight. Nay,   242
come not near th' old man; keep out, 'che vor ye, or   243
Ise try whether your costard or my ballow be the   244
harder. 'Chill be plain with you.
OSWALD   Out, dunghill!
EDGAR   'Chill pick your teeth, zir. Come, no matter vor
your foins. *[They fight. Edgar fells him with his cudgel.]*   248
OSWALD
Slave, thou hast slain me. Villain, take my purse.   249
If ever thou wilt thrive, bury my body
And give the letters which thou find'st about me   251
To Edmund, Earl of Gloucester. Seek him out
Upon the English party. Oh, untimely death!   253
Death!   *[He dies.]*
EDGAR
I know thee well: a serviceable villain,   255
As duteous to the vices of thy mistress
As badness would desire.
GLOUCESTER   What, is he dead?
EDGAR   Sit you down, father. Rest you. *[Gloucester sits.]*
Let's see these pockets; the letters that he speaks of
May be my friends. He's dead; I am only sorry
He had no other deathsman. Let us see.   262
            [He finds a letter and opens it.]
Leave, gentle wax, and, manners, blame us not.   263

To know our enemies' minds we rip their hearts;
Their papers is more lawful.   *(Reads the letter.)*
"Let our reciprocal vows be remembered. You have
many opportunities to cut him off; if your will want   267
not, time and place will be fruitfully offered. There is   268
nothing done if he return the conqueror. Then am I   269
the prisoner, and his bed my jail, from the loathed
warmth whereof deliver me and supply the place for   271
your labor.   272
Your—wife, so I would say—affectionate servant,
     and for you her own for venture, Goneril."   274
Oh, indistinguished space of woman's will!   275
A plot upon her virtuous husband's life,
And the exchange my brother! Here in the sands
Thee I'll rake up, the post unsanctified   278
Of murderous lechers; and in the mature time   279
With this ungracious paper strike the sight   280
Of the death-practiced Duke. For him 'tis well   281
That of thy death and business I can tell.
            [Exit with the body.]
GLOUCESTER
The King is mad. How stiff is my vile sense,   283
That I stand up and have ingenious feeling   284
Of my huge sorrows! Better I were distract;   285
So should my thoughts be severed from my griefs,
And woes by wrong imaginations lose   287
The knowledge of themselves.   *Drum afar off.*

[Enter Edgar.]

EDGAR   Give me your hand.
Far off, methinks, I hear the beaten drum.
Come, father, I'll bestow you with a friend.   290
          Exeunt, [Edgar leading his father].

❖

4.7

Enter Cordelia, Kent [dressed still in his disguise costume], and Gentleman.

CORDELIA
O thou good Kent, how shall I live and work
To match thy goodness? My life will be too short,
And every measure fail me.   3

228–9 The bounty . . . and boot! In addition to my thanks, I wish you the bounty and blessings of heaven.   **229 proclaimed prize** one with a price on his head.   **happy** fortunate.   **230 framed flesh** born **232 thyself remember** i.e., say your prayers.   **233 friendly** i.e., welcome, since I desire death   **235 published** proclaimed   **236 Lest that** lest   **237 Like** similar   **238 'Chill** I will. (Literally, a contraction of *Ich will.* Edgar adopts Somerset dialect, a stage convention regularly used for peasants.)   **vurther 'cagion** further occasion.   **240 go your gait** go your own way   **241 An 'chud** If I could.   **zwaggered** swaggered, bullied   **242 'twould . . . vortnight** it (my life) wouldn't have lasted a fortnight.   **243 'che vor ye** I warrant you   **244 Ise** I shall. **costard** head. (Literally, an apple.)   **ballow** cudgel   **248 foins** thrusts.   **249 Villain** Serf   **251 letters** letter. (See 4.5.35 and note.) **about me** upon my person   **253 Upon** on.   **party** side.   **255 serviceable** officious   **262 deathsman** executioner.   **263 Leave** By your leave.   **wax** wax seal on the letter

267 him Albany   **267–8 want not** is not lacking   **268 fruitfully** plentifully and with results   **268–9 There is nothing done** i.e., We will have accomplished nothing   **271 supply** fill   **271–2 for your labor** (1) as recompense for your efforts (2) as a place for your amorous labors.   **274 and for . . . venture** and one ready to venture her own fortunes for your sake   **275 indistinguished . . . will** limitless and incalculable expanse of woman's appetite.   **278 rake up** cover up. **post unsanctified** unholy messenger   **279 in . . . time** when the time is ripe   **280 ungracious** wicked.   **strike** blast   **281 Of . . . well** of Albany, whose death is plotted. It's a good thing for him   **283 How . . . sense** How obstinate is my deplorable sanity and power of sensation **284 ingenious** conscious. (Gloucester laments that he remains sane and hence fully conscious of his troubles, unlike Lear.)   **285 distract** distracted, crazy   **287 wrong imaginations** delusions   **290 bestow** lodge. (At the scene's end, Edgar leads off Gloucester; presumably, at line 282 or else here, he must also dispose of Oswald's body in the trapdoor or by lugging it offstage.)
4.7. Location: The French camp.
0.2 Gentleman ("*Doctor*" in Q.)   **3 every . . . me** every attempt (to match your goodness) will fall short.

KENT
To be acknowledged, madam, is o'erpaid.
All my reports go with the modest truth,   5
Nor more nor clipped, but so.
CORDELIA   Be better suited.   6
These weeds are memories of those worser hours;   7
I prithee, put them off.
KENT   Pardon, dear madam;
Yet to be known shortens my made intent.   9
My boon I make it that you know me not   10
Till time and I think meet.   11
CORDELIA
Then be't so, my good lord. [*To the Gentleman*] How
does the King?
GENTLEMAN   Madam, sleeps still.
CORDELIA   O you kind gods,
Cure this great breach in his abusèd nature!
Th'untuned and jarring senses, oh, wind up   16
Of this child-changèd father!   17
GENTLEMAN   So please Your Majesty
That we may wake the King? He hath slept long.
CORDELIA
Be governed by your knowledge, and proceed
I'th' sway of your own will.—Is he arrayed?   21

Enter Lear in a chair carried by servants.

GENTLEMAN
Ay, madam. In the heaviness of sleep
We put fresh garments on him.
Be by, good madam, when we do awake him.
I doubt not of his temperance.
CORDELIA   Very well.   [*Music.*]   25
GENTLEMAN
Please you, draw near.—Louder the music there!
CORDELIA [*kissing him*]
O my dear father! Restoration hang
Thy medicine on my lips, and let this kiss
Repair those violent harms that my two sisters
Have in thy reverence made!
KENT   Kind and dear princess!   30
CORDELIA
Had you not been their father, these white flakes   31
Did challenge pity of them. Was this a face   32
To be opposed against the warring winds?
To stand against the deep dread-bolted thunder   34
In the most terrible and nimble stroke

Of quick cross lightning? To watch—poor perdu!—   36
With this thin helm? Mine enemy's dog,   37
Though he had bit me, should have stood that night
Against my fire; and wast thou fain, poor father,   39
To hovel thee with swine and rogues forlorn   40
In short and musty straw? Alack, alack!   41
'Tis wonder that thy life and wits at once
Had not concluded all.—He wakes! Speak to him.   43
GENTLEMAN   Madam, do you; 'tis fittest.
CORDELIA
How does my royal lord? How fares Your Majesty?
LEAR
You do me wrong to take me out o'th' grave.
Thou art a soul in bliss; but I am bound
Upon a wheel of fire, that mine own tears   48
Do scald like molten lead.
CORDELIA   Sir, do you know me?
LEAR
You are a spirit, I know. Where did you die?
CORDELIA   Still, still, far wide!   51
GENTLEMAN
He's scarce awake. Let him alone awhile.
LEAR
Where have I been? Where am I? Fair daylight?
I am mightily abused. I should ev'n die with pity   54
To see another thus. I know not what to say.   55
I will not swear these are my hands. Let's see;
I feel this pinprick. Would I were assured
Of my condition!
CORDELIA [*kneeling*]   Oh, look upon me, sir,
And hold your hands in benediction o'er me.
                                   [*He attempts to kneel.*]
No, sir, you must not kneel.
LEAR   Pray, do not mock me.
I am a very foolish fond old man,   61
Fourscore and upward, not an hour more nor less;
And, to deal plainly,
I fear I am not in my perfect mind.
Methinks I should know you, and know this man,
Yet I am doubtful; for I am mainly ignorant   66
What place this is, and all the skill I have
Remembers not these garments, nor I know not
Where I did lodge last night. Do not laugh at me,
For, as I am a man, I think this lady
To be my child Cordelia.
CORDELIA [*weeping*]   And so I am, I am.
LEAR
Be your tears wet? Yes, faith. I pray, weep not.
If you have poison for me I will drink it.
I know you do not love me, for your sisters
Have, as I do remember, done me wrong.
You have some cause, they have not.

---

5 **All my reports go** All my reports (of my service as Caius to Lear)
conform   6 **Nor . . . clipped** i.e., neither more nor less.   **suited**
dressed.   7 **weeds** garments.   **memories** remembrances   9 **Yet . . .
intent** to reveal my true identity now would alter my carefully made
plan.   10 **My . . . it** The favor I seek is.   **know** acknowledge
11 **meet** appropriate.   16 **wind up** tune (as by tightening the slack-
ened string of an instrument)   17 **child-changèd** changed by children's cruelty   21 **I'th' sway** under the direction   25 **temperance**
self-control, calm behavior.   30 **reverence** venerable condition
31 **Had you** Even if you had.   **flakes** locks of hair   32 **Did challenge**
would have demanded   34 **deep** bass-voiced.   **dread-bolted** furnished with the dreadful thunderbolt

36 **cross** zigzag.   **watch** stay awake (like a sentry on duty).   **perdu**
lost one; a sentinel placed in a position of peculiar danger.   37 **helm**
helmet, i.e., scanty hair.   39 **Against** before, in front of.   **fain**
constrained   40 **rogues forlorn** abandoned vagabonds
41 **short** broken up and hence uncomfortable   43 **concluded all** come
to an end altogether.   48 **wheel of fire** (A hellish torment for the eternally damned.)   **that** so that   51 **wide** wide of the mark, wandering.
54 **abused** confused, deluded.   55 **thus** i.e., thus confused, bewildered.   61 **fond** in my dotage   66 **mainly** entirely

CORDELIA   No cause, no cause.

LEAR   Am I in France?

KENT   In your own kingdom, sir.

LEAR   Do not abuse me.   81

GENTLEMAN
Be comforted, good madam. The great rage,   82
You see, is killed in him, and yet it is danger
To make him even o'er the time he has lost.   84
Desire him to go in. Trouble him no more
Till further settling.   86

CORDELIA   Will't please Your Highness walk?   87

LEAR   You must bear with me.
Pray you now, forget and forgive.
I am old and foolish.

                    Exeunt [all but Kent and Gentleman].

GENTLEMAN   Holds it true, sir, that the Duke of Corn-   91
wall was so slain?

KENT   Most certain, sir.

GENTLEMAN   Who is conductor of his people?   94

KENT   As 'tis said, the bastard son of Gloucester.

GENTLEMAN   They say Edgar, his banished son, is with
the Earl of Kent in Germany.

KENT   Report is changeable. 'Tis time to look about; the   98
powers of the kingdom approach apace.   99

GENTLEMAN   The arbitrament is like to be bloody. Fare   100
you well, sir.   *[Exit.]*

KENT
My point and period will be throughly wrought,   102
Or well or ill, as this day's battle's fought.   *Exit.*   103

                                   ❖

5.1

Enter, with drum and colors, Edmund, Regan,
Gentlemen, and soldiers.

EDMUND   *[to a Gentleman]*
Know of the Duke if his last purpose hold,   1
Or whether since he is advised by aught   2
To change the course. He's full of alteration   3
And self-reproving. Bring his constant pleasure.   4
                              [Exit Gentleman.]

REGAN
Our sister's man is certainly miscarried.   5

EDMUND
'Tis to be doubted, madam.

REGAN   Now, sweet lord,   6
You know the goodness I intend upon you.   7
Tell me, but truly—but then speak the truth—
Do you not love my sister?

EDMUND   In honored love.   9

REGAN
But have you never found my brother's way
To the forfended place?   11

EDMUND   That thought abuses you.   12

REGAN
I am doubtful that you have been conjunct   13
And bosomed with her, as far as we call hers.   14

EDMUND   No, by mine honor, madam.

REGAN
I never shall endure her. Dear my lord,
Be not familiar with her.   17

EDMUND
Fear me not.—She and the Duke her husband!   18

          Enter, with drum and colors, Albany, Goneril,
          [and] soldiers.

GONERIL   *[aside]*
I had rather lose the battle than that sister
Should loosen him and me.

ALBANY   *[to Regan]*
Our very loving sister, well bemet.   21
[To Edmund] Sir, this I heard: the King is come to his
          daughter,
With others whom the rigor of our state   23
Forced to cry out. Where I could not be honest,   24
I never yet was valiant. For this business,   25
It touches us as France invades our land,   26
Not bolds the King, with others whom, I fear,   27
Most just and heavy causes make oppose.   28

EDMUND   Sir, you speak nobly.

REGAN   Why is this reasoned?   30

GONERIL
Combine together 'gainst the enemy;
For these domestic and particular broils   32
Are not the question here.

ALBANY   Let's then determine
With th'ancient of war on our proceeding.   34

EDMUND
I shall attend you presently at your tent.

REGAN   Sister, you'll go with us?

GONERIL   No.

---

81 abuse deceive. (Or perhaps Lear feels hurt by the reminder of his having divided the kingdom.)   **82 rage** frenzy   **84 even o'er** fill in, go over in his mind   **86 settling** composing of his mind.   **87 walk** withdraw.   **91 Holds it true** Is it still held to be true   **94 conductor** leader, general   **98 look about** be wary, take stock of the situation   **99 powers of the kingdom** British armies (marching against the French invaders)   **100 arbitrament** decision by arms, decisive encounter   **102 My . . . wrought** i.e., The conclusion of my destiny (literally, the full stop at the end of my life's sentence) will be thoroughly shaped   **103 Or** either.   **as** according as
5.1. Location: The British camp near Dover.
1 Know Inquire.   **last purpose hold** most recent intention (to fight) remains firm   **2 since** since then.   **advised by aught** persuaded by any consideration   **3 alteration** vacillation   **4 constant pleasure** settled decision.   **5 man** i.e., Oswald.   **miscarried** lost, perished.

6 doubted feared   **7 intend** intend to confer   **9 honored** honorable
11 forfended forbidden (by the commandment against adultery)
12 abuses degrades, wrongs   **13–14 I . . . hers** I fear that you have been sexually intimate with her to the fullest extent possible.
17 familiar intimate   **18 Fear me not** Don't worry about me on that score.   **21 bemet** met.   **23 rigor of our state** harshness of our rule
24 cry out rebel.   **Where** In a case where.   **honest** honorable
25 For As for   **26 touches us as** concerns us insofar as   **27–8 Not . . . oppose** not because the matter emboldens the King and others who, I fear, are driven into opposition by just and weighty grievances.
30 Why . . . reasoned? i.e., Why are we arguing about reasons for fighting, instead of fighting?   **32 particular broils** private quarrels
34 th'ancient of war the veteran officers

REGAN
  'Tis most convenient. Pray, go with us.   38
GONERIL [*aside*]
  Oho, I know the riddle.—I will go.   39

       [*As they are going out,*] *enter Edgar* [*disguised*].

EDGAR [*to Albany*]
  If e'er Your Grace had speech with man so poor,
  Hear me one word.
ALBANY [*to the others*]   I'll overtake you.
                                  Exeunt both the armies.
                                  Speak.
EDGAR [*giving a letter*]
  Before you fight the battle, ope this letter.   42
  If you have victory, let the trumpet sound   43
  For him that brought it. Wretched though I seem,
  I can produce a champion that will prove   45
  What is avouchèd there. If you miscarry,   46
  Your business of the world hath so an end,
  And machination ceases. Fortune love you!   48
ALBANY   Stay till I have read the letter.
EDGAR   I was forbid it.
  When time shall serve, let but the herald cry
  And I'll appear again.   *Exit* [*Edgar*].
ALBANY
  Why, fare thee well. I will o'erlook thy paper.   53

       Enter Edmund.

EDMUND
  The enemy's in view. Draw up your powers.
                            [*He offers Albany a paper.*]
  Here is the guess of their true strength and forces   55
  By diligent discovery; but your haste   56
  Is now urged on you.
ALBANY   We will greet the time.   *Exit.*   57
EDMUND
  To both these sisters have I sworn my love,
  Each jealous of the other as the stung   59
  Are of the adder. Which of them shall I take?
  Both? One? Or neither? Neither can be enjoyed
  If both remain alive. To take the widow
  Exasperates, makes mad her sister Goneril,
  And hardly shall I carry out my side,   64
  Her husband being alive. Now then, we'll use
  His countenance for the battle, which being done,   66
  Let her who would be rid of him devise
  His speedy taking off. As for the mercy   68
  Which he intends to Lear and to Cordelia,
  The battle done and they within our power,

  Shall never see his pardon, for my state   71
  Stands on me to defend, not to debate.   72
                                  Exit.

                        ❖

5.2

  Alarum within. Enter, with drum and colors, Lear,
  Cordelia, and soldiers, over the stage; and exeunt.

  Enter Edgar and Gloucester.

EDGAR
  Here, father, take the shadow of this tree   1
  For your good host. Pray that the right may thrive.   2
  If ever I return to you again,
  I'll bring you comfort.
GLOUCESTER   Grace go with you, sir!   4
                            Exit [*Edgar*].

  Alarum and retreat within. Enter Edgar.

EDGAR
  Away, old man! Give me thy hand. Away!
  King Lear hath lost, he and his daughter ta'en.
  Give me thy hand. Come on.
GLOUCESTER
  No further, sir. A man may rot even here.
EDGAR
  What, in ill thoughts again? Men must endure
  Their going hence, even as their coming hither;
  Ripeness is all. Come on.
GLOUCESTER   And that's true too.   11
                                  Exeunt.

                        ❖

5.3

  Enter, in conquest, with drum and colors, Edmund;
  Lear and Cordelia, as prisoners; soldiers, Captain.

EDMUND
  Some officers take them away. Good guard   1
  Until their greater pleasures first be known   2
  That are to censure them.
CORDELIA [*to Lear*]   We are not the first   3
  Who with best meaning have incurred the worst.   4
  For thee, oppressèd King, I am cast down;
  Myself could else outfrown false Fortune's frown.
  Shall we not see these daughters and these sisters?   7

38 convenient proper, fitting.   **39 I know the riddle** i.e., I understand the reason for Regan's enigmatic demand that I accompany her, which is that she wants to keep me away from Edmund.   **42 this letter** i.e., Goneril's letter to Edmund found on Oswald's body.
43 sound sound a summons   **45 prove** i.e., in trial by combat
46 avouchèd affirmed.   **miscarry** lose the battle and die   **48 machination** plotting (against your life)   **53 o'erlook** peruse   **55 guess** estimate   **56 discovery** reconnoitering   **57 We . . . time** We will be ready for whatever happens.   **59 jealous** suspicious   **64 carry . . . side** carry out my end of the bargain in our *reciprocal vows* (4.6.266)
66 countenance backing, authority of his name   **68 taking off** killing.

71 Shall they shall   **71–2 my state . . . debate** my position depends upon maintenance by forceful action, not by talk.
5.2. Location: The battlefield.
0.1 *Alarum* trumpet call to arms   **1 father** i.e., reverend old man
2 host shelterer.   **4.2** *retreat* trumpet signal for withdrawal
11 Ripeness (Humans shouldn't die before their time, just as fruit doesn't fall until it's ripe.)
5.3. Location: The British camp.
1 Good guard Guard them well   **2 their greater pleasures** the wishes of those in command   **3 censure** judge   **4 meaning** intentions
7 Shall . . . sisters? i.e., Aren't we even allowed to speak to Goneril and Regan before they order to prison their own father and sister?

LEAR

No, no, no, no! Come, let's away to prison.
We two alone will sing like birds i' th' cage.
When thou dost ask me blessing, I'll kneel down
And ask of thee forgiveness. So we'll live,
And pray, and sing, and tell old tales, and laugh
At gilded butterflies, and hear poor rogues   13
Talk of court news; and we'll talk with them too—
Who loses and who wins; who's in, who's out—
And take upon 's the mystery of things,   16
As if we were God's spies; and we'll wear out,   17
In a walled prison, packs and sects of great ones,   18
That ebb and flow by th' moon.

EDMUND   Take them away.   19

LEAR

Upon such sacrifices, my Cordelia,
The gods themselves throw incense. Have I caught
    thee?   21
He that parts us shall bring a brand from heaven   22
And fire us hence like foxes. Wipe thine eyes;   23
The good years shall devour them, flesh and fell,   24
Ere they shall make us weep. We'll see 'em starved
    first.   25
Come.   *Exit [with Cordelia, guarded].*

EDMUND   Come hither, Captain. Hark.
Take thou this note. [*He gives a paper.*] Go follow them
    to prison.
One step I have advanced thee; if thou dost
As this instructs thee, thou dost make thy way
To noble fortunes. Know thou this: that men
Are as the time is. To be tender-minded   32
Does not become a sword. Thy great employment   33
Will not bear question; either say thou'lt do't   34
Or thrive by other means.

CAPTAIN   I'll do't, my lord.

EDMUND   About it, and write "happy" when th' hast done.   36
Mark, I say, instantly, and carry it so   37
As I have set it down.

CAPTAIN

I cannot draw a cart, nor eat dried oats;
If it be man's work, I'll do't.   *Exit Captain.*

*Flourish. Enter Albany, Goneril, Regan, [another
Captain, and] soldiers.*

ALBANY

Sir, you have showed today your valiant strain,
And fortune led you well. You have the captives
Who were the opposites of this day's strife;   43
I do require them of you, so to use them
As we shall find their merits and our safety
May equally determine.

EDMUND   Sir, I thought it fit
To send the old and miserable King
To some retention and appointed guard,   49
Whose age had charms in it, whose title more,   50
To pluck the common bosom on his side   51
And turn our impressed lances in our eyes   52
Which do command them. With him I sent the Queen,   53
My reason all the same; and they are ready
Tomorrow, or at further space, t'appear   55
Where you shall hold your session. At this time
We sweat and bleed; the friend hath lost his friend,
And the best quarrels in the heat are cursed   58
By those that feel their sharpness.   59
The question of Cordelia and her father
Requires a fitter place.

ALBANY   Sir, by your patience,   61
I hold you but a subject of this war,   62
Not as a brother.

REGAN   That's as we list to grace him.   63
Methinks our pleasure might have been demanded   64
Ere you had spoke so far. He led our powers,
Bore the commission of my place and person,
The which immediacy may well stand up   67
And call itself your brother.

GONERIL   Not so hot!
In his own grace he doth exalt himself
More than in your addition.

REGAN   In my rights,   70
By me invested, he compeers the best.   71

GONERIL

That were the most if he should husband you.   72

REGAN

Jesters do oft prove prophets.

GONERIL   Holla, holla!   73
That eye that told you so looked but asquint.   74

REGAN

Lady, I am not well, else I should answer
From a full-flowing stomach. [*To Edmund*] General,   76

---

13 **gilded butterflies** i.e., gaily dressed courtiers and other ephemeral types, or perhaps actual butterflies   16 **take upon 's** assume the burden of, or profess to understand   17 **God's spies** i.e., detached observers surveying the deeds of humanity from an eternal vantage point.   **wear out** outlast   18–19 **packs . . . moon** i.e., followers and cliques attached to persons of high station, whose fortunes change erratically and constantly.   21 **The gods . . . incense** (The gods make offerings to Cordelia instead of receiving them.)   22–3 **He . . . foxes** i.e., Nothing short of a firebrand from heaven will ever part us again. (Firebrands were used to smoke foxes from their lairs; compare also Samson's use of firebrands tied to the tails of foxes in order to punish the Philistines for denying him his wife, in Judges 15:4–5.)   24–5 **The good . . . weep** i.e., the years will be good to us and will utterly foil our enemies' attempts to make us sorrowful as long as we are together (?).   32 **Are . . . is** i.e., must adapt themselves to stern exigencies.   33 **become a sword** i.e., suit a warrior.   34 **bear question** admit of discussion   36 **write "happy"** call yourself fortunate. **th'** thou   37 **carry it** carry it out

43 **opposites** enemies   49 **retention** confinement   50–3 **Whose . . . them** whose advanced age had magic in it, and whose title as king had even more, to win the sympathy of the commoners and turn against us the weapons of those very troops whom we impressed into service. (*In our eyes* may suggest retaliation for the blinding of Gloucester.)   55 **space** interval of time   58–9 **And . . . sharpness** and even the best of causes, at this moment when the passions of battle have not cooled, are viewed with hatred by those who have suffered the painful consequences. (Edmund pretends to worry that Lear and Cordelia would not receive a fair trial.)   61 **by your patience** if you please   62 **subject of** subordinate in   63 **list** please   64 **pleasure** wish.   **demanded** asked about   67 **immediacy** nearness of connection   70 **your addition** the titles you confer.   71 **compeers** is equal with   72 **That . . . most** That investiture would be most complete   73 **prove** turn out to be   74 **asquint** (Jealousy proverbially makes the eye look *asquint*, "furtively, suspiciously.")   76 **full-flowing stomach** full tide of angry rejoinder.

Take thou my soldiers, prisoners, patrimony; 77
Dispose of them, of me; the walls is thine. 78
Witness the world that I create thee here
My lord and master.

GONERIL   Mean you to enjoy him?

ALBANY
The let-alone lies not in your good will. 81

EDMUND
Nor in thine, lord.

ALBANY   Half-blooded fellow, yes. 82

REGAN [to Edmund]
Let the drum strike and prove my title thine.

ALBANY
Stay yet; hear reason. Edmund, I arrest thee
On capital treason; and, in thy attaint 85
This gilded serpent. [Pointing to Goneril] For your
    claim, fair sister,
I bar it in the interest of my wife;
'Tis she is subcontracted to this lord,
And I, her husband, contradict your banns. 89
If you will marry, make your loves to me; 90
My lady is bespoke.

GONERIL   An interlude! 91

ALBANY
Thou art armed, Gloucester. Let the trumpet sound.
If none appear to prove upon thy person
Thy heinous, manifest, and many treasons,
There is my pledge. [He throws down a glove.] I'll make
    it on thy heart, 95
Ere I taste bread, thou art in nothing less 96
Than I have here proclaimed thee.

REGAN   Sick, oh, sick!

GONERIL [aside]   If not, I'll ne'er trust medicine. 99

EDMUND [throwing down a glove]
There's my exchange. What in the world he is 100
That names me traitor, villain-like he lies.
Call by the trumpet. He that dares approach,
On him, on you—who not?—I will maintain
My truth and honor firmly.

ALBANY
A herald, ho!

EDMUND   A herald, ho, a herald!

        Enter a Herald.

ALBANY [to Edmund]
Trust to thy single virtue; for thy soldiers, 106
All levied in my name, have in my name
Took their discharge.

REGAN   My sickness grows upon me.

ALBANY [to Soldiers]
She is not well. Convey her to my tent.
                        [Exit Regan, supported.]
Come hither, herald. Let the trumpet sound,
And read out this.   [He gives a paper.]

CAPTAIN   Sound, trumpet!   A trumpet sounds.

HERALD (reads)   "If any man of quality or degree within 113
    the lists of the army will maintain upon Edmund, sup- 114
    posed Earl of Gloucester, that he is a manifold traitor,
    let him appear by the third sound of the trumpet. He
    is bold in his defense."

EDMUND   Sound!   First trumpet.

HERALD   Again!   Second trumpet.

HERALD   Again!   Third trumpet.
                        Trumpet answers within.

    Enter Edgar, armed, [with a trumpeter before
    him].

ALBANY
Ask him his purposes, why he appears
Upon this call o'th' trumpet.

HERALD   What are you? 122
Your name, your quality, and why you answer
This present summons?

EDGAR   Know my name is lost,
By treason's tooth bare-gnawn and canker-bit. 125
Yet am I noble as the adversary
I come to cope.

ALBANY   Which is that adversary? 127

EDGAR
What's he that speaks for Edmund, Earl of
    Gloucester?

EDMUND
Himself. What say'st thou to him?

EDGAR   Draw thy sword,
That, if my speech offend a noble heart,
Thy arm may do thee justice. Here is mine.
                        [He draws his sword.]
Behold, it is the privilege of mine honors, 132
My oath, and my profession. I protest, 133
Maugre thy strength, place, youth, and eminence, 134
Despite thy victor sword and fire-new fortune, 135
Thy valor, and thy heart, thou art a traitor— 136
False to thy gods, thy brother, and thy father,
Conspirant 'gainst this high-illustrious prince,
And from th'extremest upward of thy head 139
To the descent and dust below thy foot 140
A most toad-spotted traitor. Say thou no, 141
This sword, this arm, and my best spirits are bent 142
To prove upon thy heart, whereto I speak,
Thou liest.

---

77 **patrimony** inheritance   78 **the walls is thine** i.e., the citadel of my
heart and body surrenders completely to you.   81 **let-alone** preventing, denying   82 **Half-blooded** Only partly of noble blood, bastard
85 **in thy attaint** i.e., as partner in your corruption and as one who
has (unwittingly) provided the *attaint* or impeachment against you
89 **banns** public announcement of a proposed marriage.   90 **make . . .
me** i.e., sue to me for permission   91 **An interlude!** A play; i.e., you
are being melodramatic, or, what a farce this is!   95 **make** prove
96 **in nothing less** in no respect less guilty   99 **medicine** i.e., poison.
100 **What** Whoever   106 **single virtue** unaided prowess

113 **quality or degree** noble birth or rank. (Also in line 123.)
114 **lists** roster   122 **What** Who   125 **canker-bit** eaten as by the
caterpillar.   127 **cope** encounter.   132 **of mine honors** i.e., of my
knighthood   133 **profession** i.e., knighthood.   134 **Maugre** in spite
of   135 **victor** victorious.   **fire-new** newly minted   136 **heart**
courage   139 **upward** top   140 **descent** lowest extreme   141 **toad-
spotted** venomous, or having spots of infamy.   **Say thou** If you say
142 **bent** prepared

EDMUND   In wisdom I should ask thy name.   144
But since thy outside looks so fair and warlike,
And that thy tongue some say of breeding breathes,   146
What safe and nicely I might well delay   147
By rule of knighthood, I disdain and spurn,   148
Back do I toss those treasons to thy head,   149
With the hell-hated lie o'erwhelm thy heart,   150
Which—for they yet glance by and scarcely bruise—   151
This sword of mine shall give them instant way,   152
Where they shall rest forever.—Trumpets, speak!   153
     [*He draws.*] *Alarums. Fight.* [*Edmund falls.*]
ALBANY [*to Edgar*]
Save him, save him!
GONERIL   This is practice, Gloucester.   154
By th' law of arms thou wast not bound to answer
An unknown opposite. Thou art not vanquished,
But cozened and beguiled.
ALBANY   Shut your mouth, dame,   157
Or with this paper shall I stopple it.—Hold, sir.   158
Thou worse than any name, read thine own evil.
       [*He shows the letter.*]
[*To Goneril*] No tearing, lady; I perceive you know it.
GONERIL
Say if I do, the laws are mine, not thine.
Who can arraign me for't?
ALBANY   Most monstrous! Oh!
Know'st thou this paper?
GONERIL   Ask me not what I know.
       Exit.
ALBANY
Go after her. She's desperate; govern her.   164
       [*Exit a soldier.*]
EDMUND
What you have charged me with, that have I done,
And more, much more. The time will bring it out.
'Tis past, and so am I. But what art thou
That hast this fortune on me? If thou'rt noble,   168
I do forgive thee.
EDGAR   Let's exchange charity.   169
I am no less in blood than thou art, Edmund;
If more, the more th' hast wronged me.   171
My name is Edgar, and thy father's son.
The gods are just, and of our pleasant vices   173
Make instruments to plague us.
The dark and vicious place where thee he got   175

Cost him his eyes.
EDMUND   Th' hast spoken right. 'Tis true.
The wheel is come full circle; I am here.   177
ALBANY [*to Edgar*]
Methought thy very gait did prophesy
A royal nobleness. I must embrace thee.
       [*They embrace.*]
Let sorrow split my heart if ever I
Did hate thee or thy father!
EDGAR   Worthy prince, I know't.
ALBANY   Where have you hid yourself?
How have you known the miseries of your father?
EDGAR
By nursing them, my lord. List a brief tale,   185
And when 'tis told, oh, that my heart would burst!
The bloody proclamation to escape   187
That followed me so near—oh, our lives' sweetness,   188
That we the pain of death would hourly die   189
Rather than die at once!—taught me to shift   190
Into a madman's rags, t'assume a semblance
That very dogs disdained; and in this habit   192
Met I my father with his bleeding rings,   193
Their precious stones new lost; became his guide,   194
Led him, begged for him, saved him from despair;
Never—oh, fault!—revealed myself unto him
Until some half hour past, when I was armed.
Not sure, though hoping, of this good success,   198
I asked his blessing, and from first to last
Told him our pilgrimage. But his flawed heart—   200
Alack, too weak the conflict to support—
Twixt two extremes of passion, joy and grief,
Burst smilingly.
EDMUND   This speech of yours hath moved me,
And shall perchance do good. But speak you on;
You look as you had something more to say.
ALBANY
If there be more, more woeful, hold it in,
For I am almost ready to dissolve,   207
Hearing of this.
EDGAR   This would have seemed a period   208
To such as love not sorrow; but another,   209
To amplify too much, would make much more   210
And top extremity. Whilst I   211
Was big in clamor, came there in a man   212
Who, having seen me in my worst estate,
Shunned my abhorred society; but then, finding
Who 'twas that so endured, with his strong arms
He fastened on my neck and bellowed out

---

144 wisdom prudence   **146 say** smack, taste, indication   **147 safe and nicely** prudently and punctiliously   **148 I . . . spurn** i.e., I disdain to insist on my right to refuse combat with one of lower rank. **149 treasons . . . head** i.e., accusations of treason in your teeth **150 hell-hated** hated as hell is hated   **151 Which . . . bruise** i.e., which charges of treason—since as yet they merely glance off my armor and do no harm   **152 give . . . way** provide them an immediate pathway (to your heart)   **153 Where . . . forever** i.e., my victory in trial by combat will prove forever that the charges of treason apply to you.   **154 Save** Spare. (Albany wishes to spare Edmund's life so that he may confess and be found guilty.)   **practice** trickery, or (said sardonically) astute management   **157 cozened** tricked   **158 stopple** stop up.   **Hold, sir** (Addressed to Edgar or, more probably, Edmund.) **164 govern** restrain   **168 fortune on** victory over   **169 charity** forgiveness (for Edmund's wickedness toward Edgar and Edgar's having slain Edmund).   **171 th' hast** thou hast   **173 pleasant** pleasurable   **175 got** begot

177 The wheel . . . here (Alludes both to the wheel of fortune and to the idea of a completed circle whereby crime meets its appropriate punishment. Edmund sees that everything has at last come around to where it began.)   **185 List** Listen to   **187 The . . . escape** In order to escape the death-threatening proclamation   **188–90 oh . . . at once!** oh, the perversity of our attachment to our lives' sweetness, that we prefer to suffer continually the fear of death rather than die at once and be done with it!   **192 habit** garb   **193 rings** sockets   **194 stones** i.e., eyeballs   **198 success** outcome   **200 flawed** cracked   **207 dissolve** i.e., in tears   **208 a period** the limit   **209–11 but . . . extremity** i.e., but another sorrowful circumstance, adding to what is already too much, would increase it and exceed the limit.   **212 big in clamor** loud in my lamenting

As he'd burst heaven, threw him on my father,
Told the most piteous tale of Lear and him
That ever ear received, which in recounting
His grief grew puissant, and the strings of life
Began to crack. Twice then the trumpets sounded,
And there I left him tranced.

ALBANY   But who was this?

EDGAR
Kent, sir, the banished Kent, who in disguise
Followed his enemy king and did him service
Improper for a slave.

Enter a Gentleman [with a bloody knife].

GENTLEMAN
Help, help, oh, help!

EDGAR   What kind of help?

ALBANY   Speak, man.

EDGAR
What means this bloody knife?

GENTLEMAN   'Tis hot, it smokes.
It came even from the heart of—Oh, she's dead!

ALBANY   Who dead? Speak, man.

GENTLEMAN
Your lady, sir, your lady! And her sister
By her is poisoned; she confesses it.

EDMUND
I was contracted to them both. All three
Now marry in an instant.

EDGAR   Here comes Kent.

Enter Kent.

ALBANY
Produce the bodies, be they alive or dead.
                                  [Exit Gentleman.]
This judgment of the heavens, that makes us tremble,
Touches us not with pity.—Oh, is this he?
[To Kent] The time will not allow the compliment
Which very manners urges.

KENT   I am come
To bid my king and master aye good night.
Is he not here?

ALBANY   Great thing of us forgot!
Speak, Edmund, where's the King? And where's
   Cordelia?
          Goneril and Regan's bodies [are] brought out.
See'st thou this object, Kent?

KENT   Alack, why thus?

EDMUND   Yet Edmund was beloved.
The one the other poisoned for my sake
And after slew herself.

ALBANY   Even so. Cover their faces.

217
220
222
224
227
237
238
239
242

EDMUND
I pant for life. Some good I mean to do,
Despite of mine own nature. Quickly send—
Be brief in it—to th' castle, for my writ
Is on the life of Lear and on Cordelia.
Nay, send in time.

ALBANY   Run, run, oh, run!

EDGAR
To who, my lord? Who has the office? *[To Edmund]*
Send
Thy token of reprieve.

EDMUND   Well thought on. Take my sword. The captain!
Give it the Captain.

EDGAR   Haste thee, for thy life.
          [Exit one with Edmund's sword.]

EDMUND
He hath commission from thy wife and me
To hang Cordelia in the prison and
To lay the blame upon her own despair,
That she fordid herself.

ALBANY
The gods defend her! Bear him hence awhile.
          [Edmund is borne off.]

Enter Lear, with Cordelia in his arms; [Captain].

LEAR
Howl, howl, howl! Oh, you are men of stones!
Had I your tongues and eyes, I'd use them so
That heaven's vault should crack. She's gone forever.
I know when one is dead and when one lives;
She's dead as earth. Lend me a looking glass;
If that her breath will mist or stain the stone,
Why, then she lives.

KENT   Is this the promised end?

EDGAR
Or image of that horror?

ALBANY   Fall and cease!

LEAR
This feather stirs; she lives! If it be so,
It is a chance which does redeem all sorrows
That ever I have felt.

KENT *[kneeling]*   O my good master!

LEAR
Prithee, away.

EDGAR   'Tis noble Kent, your friend.

LEAR
A plague upon you, murderers, traitors all!
I might have saved her; now she's gone forever!
Cordelia, Cordelia! Stay a little. Ha?
What is't thou say'st? Her voice was ever soft,
Gentle, and low, an excellent thing in woman.
I killed the slave that was a-hanging thee.

CAPTAIN
'Tis true, my lords, he did.

LEAR   Did I not, fellow?

253
260
267
268
269

217 **As** as if. **threw ... father** threw himself on my father's body 220 **His** i.e., Kent's. **puissant** powerful. **strings of life** heartstrings 222 **tranced** entranced, senseless. 224 **his enemy king** i.e., the king who had rejected and banished him 227 **smokes** steams. 237 **compliment** ceremony 238 **Which ... urges** which common courtesy requires. 239 **aye good night** farewell forever. (Kent believes he himself is near death, his heartstrings having begun to crack.) 242 **object** sight

253 **office** commission. 260 **fordid** destroyed 267 **stone** crystal or polished stone of which the mirror is made 268 **Is ... end?** (Kent may mean "Is this what all our hopes have come to?" Edgar replies by invoking the Last Judgment.) 269 **image** representation. **Fall and cease!** i.e., Let all things cease to be!

I have seen the day, with my good biting falchion　281
I would have made them skip. I am old now,
And these same crosses spoil me.—Who are you?　283
Mine eyes are not o'th' best; I'll tell you straight.　284

KENT
If Fortune brag of two she loved and hated,　285
One of them we behold.　286

LEAR
This is a dull sight. Are you not Kent?

KENT　　　　　　　　　　　　　　　　　　The same,　287
Your servant Kent. Where is your servant Caius?　288

LEAR
He's a good fellow, I can tell you that;
He'll strike, and quickly too. He's dead and rotten.

KENT
No, my good lord, I am the very man—

LEAR　I'll see that straight.　292

KENT
That from your first of difference and decay　293
Have followed your sad steps—

LEAR　　　　　　　　　　　　　You are welcome hither.

KENT
Nor no man else. All's cheerless, dark, and deadly.　295
Your eldest daughters have fordone themselves,　296
And desperately are dead.

LEAR　　　　　　　　　　　　　Ay, so I think.　297

ALBANY
He knows not what he says, and vain is it
That we present us to him.

EDGAR　　　　　　　　　　　　　Very bootless.　299

Enter a Messenger.

MESSENGER　Edmund is dead, my lord.

ALBANY　That's but a trifle here.
You lords and noble friends, know our intent:
What comfort to this great decay may come　303

---

281 **falchion** light sword　283 **crosses spoil me** adversities take away
my strength.　284 **I'll . . . straight** I'll recognize you in a moment.
285–6 **If . . . behold** If Fortune were to brag of two persons whom she
has subjected to the greatest fall from her favor into her hatred, Lear
would have to be one of them.　287 **This . . . sight** i.e., My vision is
clouding, or, this is a dismal spectacle.　288 **Caius** (Kent's disguise
name.)　292 **see that straight** attend to that in a moment.　293 **from
. . . decay** from the beginning of your quarrel (with Cordelia) to your
decline of fortune　295 **Nor . . . else** No, not I nor anyone else, or, I
am the *very man* (line 291), him and no one else.　296 **fordone**
destroyed　297 **desperately** in despair　299 **bootless** in vain.
303 **What . . . come** i.e., whatever means of comforting this ruined
king and state of affairs may present themselves

Shall be applied. For us, we will resign,　304
During the life of this old majesty,
To him our absolute power; [*to Edgar and Kent*] you, to
　your rights,
With boot and such addition as your honors　307
Have more than merited. All friends shall taste
The wages of their virtue, and all foes
The cup of their deservings.—Oh, see, see!

LEAR
And my poor fool is hanged! No, no, no life?　311
Why should a dog, a horse, a rat have life,
And thou no breath at all? Thou'lt come no more,
Never, never, never, never, never!
Pray you, undo this button. Thank you, sir.
Do you see this? Look on her, look, her lips,
Look there, look there!　　　　　　　　　　　*He dies.*

EDGAR　　　　　　　　He faints.—My lord, my lord!

KENT
Break, heart, I prithee, break!

EDGAR　　　　　　　　　　　　　Look up, my lord.

KENT
Vex not his ghost. Oh, let him pass! He hates him　319
That would upon the rack of this tough world　320
Stretch him out longer.

EDGAR　　　　　　　　　　　He is gone indeed.

KENT
The wonder is he hath endured so long.
He but usurped his life.

ALBANY
Bear them from hence. Our present business
Is general woe. [*To Kent and Edgar*] Friends of my soul,
　you twain
Rule in this realm, and the gored state sustain.

KENT
I have a journey, sir, shortly to go.　327
My master calls me; I must not say no.

EDGAR
The weight of this sad time we must obey;
Speak what we feel, not what we ought to say.
The oldest hath borne most; we that are young
Shall never see so much nor live so long.　332
　　　　　　　　　　Exeunt, with a dead march.

---

304 **For** As for　307 **With . . . honors** with advantage and such further distinctions or titles as your honorable conduct in this war
311 **poor fool** i.e., Cordelia. (*Fool* is here a term of endearment.)
319 **ghost** departing spirit.　320 **rack** torture rack. (With suggestion,
in the Folio and quarto spelling, "wracke," of shipwreck, disaster.)
327 **journey** i.e., to another world, to death　332.1 *Exeunt* (Presumably the dead bodies are borne out in procession.)

Macbeth

Macbeth is seemingly the last of four great Shakespearean tragedies—*Hamlet* (c. 1599–1601), *Othello* (c. 1603–1604), *King Lear* (1605–1606), and *Macbeth* (c. 1606–1607)—that examine the dimensions of spiritual evil, as distinguished from the political strife of Roman tragedies such as *Julius Caesar, Antony* and *Cleopatra,* and *Coriolanus.* Whether or not Shakespeare intended *Macbeth* as a culmination of a series of tragedies on evil, the play does offer a particularly terse and gloomy view of humanity's encounter with the powers of darkness. Macbeth, more consciously than any other of Shakespeare's major tragic protagonists, has to face the temptation of committing what he knows to be a monstrous crime. Like Doctor Faustus in Christopher Marlowe's play, *The Tragedy of Doctor Faustus* (c. 1588), and to a lesser extent like Adam in John Milton's *Paradise Lost* (1667), Macbeth understands the reasons for resisting evil and yet goes ahead with his disastrous plan. His awareness and sensitivity to moral issues, together with his conscious choice of evil, produce an unnerving account of human failure, all the more distressing because Macbeth is so representatively human. He seems to possess freedom of will and accepts personal responsibility for his fate, and yet his tragic doom seems unavoidable. Nor is there eventual salvation to be hoped for, as there is in *Paradise Lost,* since Macbeth's crime is too heinous and his heart too hardened. He is more like Doctor Faustus—damned and in despair.

To an extent not found in the other tragedies, the issue is stated in terms of salvation versus damnation. Macbeth knows before he acts that King Duncan's virtues "Will plead like angels, trumpet-tongued, against / The deep damnation of his taking-off" (1.7.19–20). After the murder, he is equally aware that he has "Put rancors in the vessel of my peace . . . and mine eternal jewel / Given to the common enemy of man" (3.1.68–70). His enemies later describe him as a devil and a "hellhound" (5.8.3). He, like Marlowe's Doctor Faustus before him, has knowingly sold his soul for gain. And, although as a mortal he still has time to repent his crimes, horrible as they are,

Macbeth cannot find the words to be penitent. "Wherefore could not I pronounce 'Amen'?" he implores his wife after they have committed the murder. "I had most need of blessing, and 'Amen' / Stuck in my throat" (2.2.35–7). Macbeth's own answer seems to be that he has committed himself so inexorably to evil that he cannot turn back. Sentence has been pronounced: "Glamis hath murdered sleep, and therefore Cawdor / Shall sleep no more; Macbeth shall sleep no more" (lines 46–7).

Macbeth is not a conventional morality play (even less so than *Doctor Faustus*) and is not concerned primarily with preaching against sinfulness or demonstrating that Macbeth is finally damned for what he does. A tradition of moral and religious drama has been transformed into an intensely human study of the psychological effects of evil on a particular man and, to a lesser extent, on his wife. That moral tradition nevertheless provides as its legacy a perspective on the operation of evil in human affairs. A perverse ambition seemingly inborn in Macbeth himself is abetted by dark forces dwelling in the universe, waiting to catch him off guard. Among Shakespeare's tragedies, indeed, *Macbeth* is remarkable for its focus on evil in the protagonist and on his relationship to the sinister forces tempting him. In no other Shakespearean play is the audience asked to identify to such an extent with the evildoer himself. *Richard III* also focuses on an evil protagonist, but in that play the spectators are distanced by the character's gloating and are not partakers in the introspective soliloquies of a man confronting his own ambition. Macbeth is more representatively human. If he betrays an inclination toward brutality, he also humanely attempts to resist that urge. We witness and struggle to understand his downfall through two phases: the spiritual struggle before he actually commits the crime and the despairing aftermath, with its vain quest for security through continued violence. Evil is thus presented in two aspects: first as an insidious suggestion leading Macbeth on toward an illusory promise of gain and then as a frenzied addiction to the hated thing by which he is possessed.

In the first phase, before the commission of the crime, we wonder to what extent the powers of darkness are a determining factor in what Macbeth does. Can he avoid the fate the witches proclaim? Evidently, he and Lady Macbeth have previously considered murdering Duncan; the witches appear after the thought, not before. Lady Macbeth reminds her wavering husband that he was the first to "break this enterprise" to her, on some previous occasion when "Nor time nor place / Did then adhere, and yet you would make both" (1.7.49–53). Elizabethans would probably understand that evil spirits such as witches appear when summoned, whether by our conscious or unconscious minds. Macbeth is ripe for their insinuations: a mind free of taint would see no sinister invitation in their prophecy of greatness to come. And, in a saner moment, Macbeth knows that his restless desire to interfere with destiny is arrogant and useless. "If chance will have me king, why, chance may crown me / Without my stir" (1.3.145–6). Banquo, his companion, serves as his dramatic opposite by consistently displaying a more stoical attitude toward the witches. "Speak then to me," he addresses them, "who neither beg nor fear / Your favors nor your hate" (lines 60–1). Like Horatio in *Hamlet*, Banquo strongly resists the blandishments of fortune as well as its buffets, though not without an agonizing night of moral struggle. Indeed, promises of success are often more ruinous than setbacks—as in the seemingly paradoxical instance of the farmer, cited by Macbeth's porter, who "hanged himself on th'expectation of plenty" (2.3.4–5). It is by showing Macbeth that he is two-thirds of his way to the throne that the witches tempt him to seize the last third at whatever cost. "Glamis, and Thane of Cawdor! / The greatest is behind" (1.3.116–17).

Banquo comprehends the nature of temptation. "To win us to our harm," he observes, "The instruments of darkness tell us truths, / Win us with honest trifles, to betray's / In deepest consequence" (1.3.123–6). The devil can speak true, and his strategy is to invite us into a trap we help prepare. Without our active consent in evil (as Othello also learns), we cannot fall. Yet in what sense are the witches trifling with Macbeth or prevaricating? When they address him as one "that shalt be king hereafter" (line 50), they are stating a certainty, for they can "look into the seeds of time / And say which grain will grow and which will not," as Banquo says (lines 58–9). They know that Banquo will be "Lesser than Macbeth, and greater. / Not so happy, yet much happier" (lines 65–6), since Banquo will beget a race of kings and Macbeth will not. How then do they know that Macbeth will be king? If we consider the hypothetical question, what if Macbeth does *not* murder Duncan, we can gain some understanding of the relationship between character and fate; for the only valid answer is that the question remains hypothetical—Macbeth *does* kill Duncan, the witches are right in their prediction. It is idle to speculate that Providence would have found another way to make Macbeth king, for the witches' prophecy is self-fulfilling in the very way they foresee. Character is fate; they know Macbeth's fatal weakness and know they can "enkindle" him to seize the crown by laying irresistible temptations before him. This does not mean that they determine his choice but, rather, that Macbeth's choice is predictable and therefore unvoidable, even though not preordained. He has free choice, but that choice will, in fact, go only one way—as with Adam and Eve in Milton's *Paradise Lost* and in the medieval tradition from which this poem was derived.

Although the powers of evil cannot determine Macbeth's choice, they can influence the external conditions affecting that choice. By a series of apparently circumstantial events, well timed in their effect, they can repeatedly assail him just when he is about to rally to the call of conscience. The witches, armed with supernatural knowledge, inform Macbeth of his new title shortly before the King's ambassadors confirm that he is to be the Thane of Cawdor. Duncan chooses this night to lodge under Macbeth's roof. And, just when Macbeth resolves to abandon even this unparalleled opportunity, his wife intervenes on the side of the witches. Macbeth commits the murder in part to keep his word to her and to prove he is no coward (like Donwald, the slayer of King Duff in one of Shakespeare's chief sources, Raphael Holinshed's *Chronicles*). Not only the opportunities presented to Macbeth, but also the obstacles put in his way are cannily timed to overwhelm his conscience. When King Duncan announces that his son Malcolm is now Prince of Cumberland and official heir to the throne (1.4.36–42), the unintended threat deflects Macbeth's mood from one of gratitude and acceptance to one of hostility. These are mitigating circumstances that affect our judgment of Macbeth, and, even though they cannot excuse him, they certainly increase our sympathetic identification.

We are moved, too, by the poetic intensity of Macbeth's moral vision. His soliloquies are memorable as poetry, not merely because Shakespeare wrote them, but because Macbeth is sensitive and aware. The horror, indeed, of his crime is that his cultivated self is revolted by what he cannot prevent himself from doing. He understands with a terrible clarity, not only the moral wrong of what he is about to do, but also the inescapably destructive consequences for himself. He is as reluctant as we to see the crime committed, and yet he goes to it with a sad and rational deliberateness rather than in a self-blinding fury. For Macbeth, there is no seeming loss of perspective, and yet there is total alienation of the act from his moral consciousness. The arguments for and against murdering Duncan, as Macbeth pictures them in his acutely visual imagination, when weighed, are overwhelmingly opposed to the deed. Duncan is his king and his guest, deserving Macbeth's duty and hospitality. The King is virtuous and able. He has shown every favor to

Macbeth, thereby removing any sane motive for striving after further promotion. All human history shows that murders of this sort "return / To plague th'inventor" (1.7.9–10), that is, provide only guilt and punishment rather than satisfaction. Finally, judgment in "the life to come" includes the prospect of eternal torment. On the other side of the argument is nothing but Macbeth's "Vaulting ambition, which o'erleaps itself" (line 27)—a perverse refusal to be content with his present good fortune because there is more that beckons. Who could weigh the issues so dispassionately and still choose the wrong? Yet the failure is, in fact, predictable; Macbeth is presented to us as typically human, both in his understanding and in his perverse ambition.

Macbeth's clarity of moral imagination is contrasted with his wife's imperceptiveness. He is always seeing visions or hearing voices—a dagger in the air, the ghost of Banquo, a voice crying "Sleep no more!"—and she is always denying them. "The sleeping and the dead / Are but as pictures," she insists. He knows that "all great Neptune's ocean" cannot wash the blood from his hands; "No, this my hand will rather / The multitudinous seas incarnadine, / Making the green one red." To Lady Macbeth, contrastingly, "A little water clears us of this deed. / How easy is it, then!" (2.2.57–72). Macbeth knows that the murder of Duncan is but the beginning: "We have scorched the snake, not killed it." Lady Macbeth would prefer to believe that "What's done is done" (3.2.14–15). Ironically, it is she, finally, who must endure visions of the most agonizing sort, sleepwalking in her distress and trying to rub away the "damned spot" that before seemed so easy to remove. "All the perfumes of Arabia will not sweeten this little hand," she laments (5.1.33–52). This relationship between Macbeth and Lady Macbeth owes much to traditional contrasts between male and female principles. As in the pairing of Adam and Eve, the man is putatively the more rational of the two but knowingly shares his wife's sin through fondness for her. She has failed to foresee the long-range consequences of sinful ambition and so becomes a temptress to her husband. The fall of man and woman into the bondage of sin takes place in an incongruous atmosphere of domestic intimacy and mutual concern; Lady Macbeth is motivated by ambition for her husband in much the same way that he sins to win her approbation.

The fatal disharmony flawing this domestic accord is conveyed through images of sexual inversion. Lady Macbeth prepares for her ordeal with the incantation, "Come, you spirits / That tend on mortal thoughts, unsex me here . . . Come to my woman's breasts / And take my milk for gall" (1.5.40–8). When she accuses her husband of unmanly cowardice and vows she would dash out the brains of her own infant for such effeminacy as he has displayed, he extols her with "Bring forth men-children only! / For thy undaunted mettle should compose / Nothing but males" (1.7.73–5). She takes the initiative,

devising and then carrying out the plan to drug Duncan's chamber-guards with wine. This assumption of the dominant male role by the woman might well remind Elizabethan spectators of numerous biblical, medieval, and classical parallels deploring the ascendancy of passion over reason: Eve choosing for Adam, Noah's wife taking command of the ark, the Wife of Bath dominating her husbands, Venus emasculating Mars, and others.

In *Macbeth*, sexual inversion also allies Lady Macbeth with the witches or weird sisters, the bearded women. Their unnaturalness betokens disorder in nature, for they can sail in a sieve and "look not like th'inhabitants o'th'earth / And yet are on't" (1.3.41–2). Characteristically, they speak in paradoxes: "When the battle's lost and won," "Fair is foul, and foul is fair" (1.1.4,11). Shakespeare probably drew on numerous sources to depict the witches: Holinshed's *Chronicles* (from which he conflated two accounts, one of Duncan and Macbeth, and the other of King Duff slain by Donwald with the help of his wife), King James's writings on witchcraft, Samuel Harsnett's *Declaration of Egregious Popish Impostures* (used also for *King Lear*), and the accounts of the Scottish witch trials published around 1590. In the last, particularly, Shakespeare could have found mention of witches raising storms and sailing in sieves to endanger vessels at sea, performing threefold rituals blaspheming the Trinity, and brewing witches' broth. Holinshed's *Chronicles* refer to the Weird Sisters as "goddesses of destiny," associating them with the three fates, Clotho, Lachesis, and Atropos, who hold the spinning distaff, draw off the thread of life, and cut it. In *Macbeth*, the Weird Sisters' power to control fortune is curtailed, and they are portrayed as witches according to popular contemporary understanding, rather than as goddesses of destiny; nonetheless, witches were thought to be servants of the devil (Banquo wonders if the devil can speak true in their utterances, 1.3.107), and through them Macbeth has made an ominous pact with evil itself. His visit to their seething cauldron in 4.1 brings him to the witches' masters, those unknown powers that know his very thought and who tempt him with those equivocations of which Banquo has warned Macbeth. The popularity of witchlore tempted Shakespeare's acting company to expand the witches' scenes with spectacles of song and dance; even the Folio text we have evidently contains interpolations derived in part from Thomas Middleton's *The Witch* (see especially 3.5 and part of 4.1, containing mention of Middleton's songs "Come away" and "Black spirits"). Nevertheless, Shakespeare's original theme of a disharmony in nature remains clearly visible.

The disharmonies of gender relations in *Macbeth* suggest another disturbing dimension of this tragedy. The play is filled with what Janet Adelman (in *Cannibals, Witches, and Divorce*, edited by Marjorie Garber, 1985) aptly calls fantasies of maternal power. Macbeth, like many males, attempts to cope with his imaginings of a destructive maternal power and his fantasies of escape into a world fashioned and controlled solely by himself. Initially, he submits to his wife's idea of manliness and commits murder in order to win her approval, destroying in the process a fatherly figure whose manhood is nonetheless ambivalently presented to us: Duncan is to be sure a nurturing father-king, but he is also too soft and trusting for his own good. Macbeth chooses to side with his masculinized wife against the gentler side of human nature, lauding her as a woman who should "Bring forth men-children only," since her "undaunted mettle should compose / Nothing but males" (1.7.73–5), but, in the longer term, Macbeth finds himself desiccated by his own vulnerability to this masculinized mother. He turns unsuccessfully to the witches for the power he needs to make him author of himself; in the process of attempting to make himself wholly "masculine," he manages instead to strip away from himself "honor, love, obedience, troops of friends," and all the graces that should "accompany old age" (5.3.24–5). His nemesis is appropriately one who was not, in the normal sense, "of woman born," since Macduff "was from his mother's womb / Untimely ripped" (5.8.13–16). Macduff represents, in other words, the self-creating and invulnerable masculinity that Macbeth cannot fashion for himself. The ending of the play is distressingly absolute in its consolidation of male power—a reestablishment of control that seems necessary in view of the virulence of the maternal power the play has dared to unleash.

Patterns of imagery throughout the play point similarly to disorders in nature and in human relationships. The murder of Duncan, like that of Caesar in *Julius Caesar*, is accompanied by signs of the heavens' anger. Various observers report that chimneys blow down during the unruly night, that owls clamor and attack falcons, that the earth shakes, and that Duncan's horses devour each other. (Some of these portents are from Holinshed.) Banquo's ghost returns from the dead to haunt his murderer, prompting Macbeth to speak in metaphors of charnel houses and graves that send back their dead and of birds of prey that devour the corpses. The drunken porter who opens the gate to Macduff and Lennox after the murder (2.3) invokes images of judgment and everlasting bonfire, through which the scene takes on the semblance of hell gate and the Harrowing of Hell. Owls appear repeatedly in the imagery, along with other creatures associated with nighttime and horror: wolves, serpents, scorpions, bats, toads, beetles, crows, rooks. Darkness itself assumes tangible and menacing shapes of hidden stars or extinguished candles, a thick blanket shrouded "in the dunnest smoke of hell" (1.5.51), an entombment of the earth in place of "living light" (2.4.10), a scarf to hoodwink the eye of "pitiful day" (3.2.50), and a "bloody and invisible hand" to tear to pieces the lives of the virtuous (3.2.51–2). Sleep is transformed from "great nature's second course" and a "nourisher" of life that "knits up the raveled sleave of

care" (2.2.41–4) into "death's counterfeit" (2.3.77) and a living hell for Lady Macbeth. Life becomes sterile for Macbeth, a denial of harvest, the lees or dregs of the wine and "the sere, the yellow leaf" (5.3.23). In a theatrical metaphor, life becomes for him unreal, "a walking shadow, a poor player / That struts and frets his hour upon the stage / And then is heard no more" (5.5.24–6). This theme of empty illusion carries over into the recurring image of borrowed or ill-fitting garments that belie the wearer. Macbeth is an actor, a hypocrite, whose "False face must hide what the false heart doth know" (1.7.83) and who must "Look like th'innocent flower, / But be the serpent under't" (1.5.65–6). Even the show of grief is an assumed mask whereby evildoers deceive the virtuous, so much so that Malcolm, Donalbain, and Macduff learn to conceal their true feelings rather than be thought to "show an unfelt sorrow" (2.3.138).

Blood is not only a literal sign of disorder but an emblem of Macbeth's remorseless butchery, a "damned spot" on the conscience, and a promise of divine vengeance: "It will have blood, they say; blood will have blood" (3.4.123). The emphasis on corrupted blood also suggests disease, in which Macbeth's tyranny is a sickness to his country as well as to himself. Scotland bleeds (4.3.32), needing a physician; Macduff and his allies call themselves "the med'cine of the sickly weal" (5.2.27). Lady Macbeth's disease is incurable, something spiritually corrupt wherein "the patient / Must minister to himself" (5.3.47–8). Conversely, the English King Edward is renowned for his divine gift of curing what was called the king's evil, or scrofula (4.3.147–8). These images are generally paternalistic in their invocation of kings and fathers who heal and unite.

Throughout, the defenders of righteousness are associated with positive images of natural order and with patriarchal control. Duncan rewards his subjects by saying, "I have begun to plant thee, and will labor / To make thee full of growing" (1.4.28–9). His arrival at Inverness Castle is heralded by signs of summer, sweet air, and "the temple-haunting martlet" (1.6.4). He is a fatherly figure, so much so that even Lady Macbeth balks at an act so like patricide. Macduff, too, is a father and husband whose family is butchered. The forest of Birnam marching to confront Macbeth, although rationally explainable as a device of camouflage for Macduff's army, is emblematic of the natural order itself rising up against the monstrosity of Macbeth's crimes. Banquo is, above all, a patriarchal figure, ancestor of the royal line governing Scotland and England at the time the play was written. These harmonies are to an extent restorative. Even the witches' riddling prophecies, "th'equivocation of the fiend" (5.5.43), luring Macbeth into further atrocities with the vain promise of security, anticipate a just retribution.

Nonetheless, the play's vision of evil shakes us deeply. Scotland's peace has been violated, so much so that "to do harm / Is often laudable, to do good sometime /

Accounted dangerous folly" (4.2.76–8). Macduff has been forced to deny his proper manly role of protecting his wife and family; Lady Macduff and her son, along with young Siward, have had to pay with their innocent lives the terrible price of Scotland's tyranny. In his frenzied attempt to prevent the fulfillment of the prophecy about Banquo's lineage inheriting the kingdom, Macbeth has, like King Herod, slaughtered much of the younger generation on whom the future depends. We can only hope that the stability to which Scotland returns after his death will be lasting. Banquo's line is to rule eventually and to produce a line of kings reaching down to the royal occupant to whom Shakespeare will present his play, but, when *Macbeth* ends, it is Malcolm who is king. The killing of a traitor (Macbeth) and the placing of his head on a pole replicate the play's beginning in the treason and beheading of the Thane of Cawdor—a gentleman on whom Duncan built "An absolute trust" (1.4.14). Most troublingly, the humanly representative nature of Macbeth's crime leaves us with little assurance that we could resist his temptation. The most that can be said is that wise and good persons such as Banquo and Macduff have learned to know the evil in themselves and to resist it as nobly as they can.

Along with its timeless interest in murder and the human conscience, *Macbeth* is an intensely political play. It surely was viewed as such when it was first produced in 1606–1607. The drunken porter in 2.3 seemingly refers to the infamous attempt to blow up the houses of Parliament known as the Gunpowder Plot of 1605, and to the subsequent trial of the Jesuit Henry Garnet, the notorious "equivocator," for his part in the conspiracy (2.3.8). Banquo fulfills a historical role as progenitor of the dynastic line that would lead eventually to James VI of Scotland, who had become James I of England in 1603. The pageant of *"eight Kings and Banquo last"* that Macbeth must witness on the occasion of his final visit to the Weird Sisters (4.1.111.1) ends with a *glass* or magic mirror showing many more kings bearing the appurtenances of royal office, including the "twofold balls and treble sceptres" (4.1.121) that seemingly refer to James's double coronation in 1603 as King of England and Scotland. James was keenly interested in witchcraft. Scotland was a constant worry on England's northern border, aligning itself with France, marauding across the English border, tearing itself apart through clan violence, and, from an English point of view, manifesting the kind of tyranny that the English especially feared. The Scotland of this play thus helps to define, largely by contrast, what is thought to be truly English. The English King who is described as doing "A most miraculous work" in curing "the evil," or scrofula, by his touch (4.3.147–8) suggests a flattering reference to James, who claimed this power of curing. This unnamed English king lends his support to the military attack against Macbeth through which the tyrant is finally overthrown. The play simultaneously incorporates an uneasy attitude of hostility toward Scotland along with a vision of union between the two countries that is brought about by the subjugation of Scotland to her southern neighbor. A rough kind of harmony is achieved out of disharmony. Macbeth's act of murderous regicide is answered by another regicide in the name of English law. The quandaries of such a resolution may point to the ambivalence that many English people felt about their odd ruler from the north, the man who came to be known as "the wisest fool in Christendom."

Macbeth is a difficult play to present on stage, at least according to stage tradition: ever since the early twentieth century, actors have referred to it superstitiously as "the Scottish play" as a way of avoiding bad luck that otherwise can hover menacingly over the acting company. Presumably this is a theatrical response to the play's dark probing of irrational magic, fatal determinism, and human frailty. Not coincidentally, perhaps, some of the greatest successes in performance have been on film. Akira Kurosawa's *Throne of Blood* (1957) retells the story of Macbeth, in black and white, as a devastating exploration of ambitious strife among Japanese warlords. Although the dialogue and characters' names of Shakespeare's play are altered throughout, this version captures magnificently the mysterious and malign intent of the prophetic figure Macbeth encounters in a forest, tempting him to evil by the ambiguous promises of future greatness. The forest itself is a striking presence in this film, invested as it is with supernatural terror in the midst of a thunderstorm. The Lady Asaji, wife to Washizu (the Macbeth figure), is horrifyingly obsessed with ambition for her husband; her seeming role as an obedient and decorously aristocratic Japanese wife accentuates the contrast between the surfaces of civilized behavior and the dark inner promptings of competitive self-assertion. A film version with Ian McKellen and Judi Dench as Macbeth and his wife, based on a stage version directed by Trevor Nunn (1976–1978) at Stratford-upon-Avon, London, and Newcastle-upon-Tyne, emphasizes the demonic in such a way as to give the Weird Sisters a real power that is both psychologically plausible and frighteningly irrational. Roman Polanski's film version (1971), though faulted for its sponsorship by Playboy Productions and its consequent flaunting of some grotesque nakedness, does successfully portray Macbeth and Lady Macbeth as a vitally young couple for whom sexuality is integral to their ambition. And of course there have been great stage productions, despite the shibboleth of the bad-luck legend, notably Glen Byam Shaw's production at Stratford-upon-Avon in 1955 starring Laurence Olivier and Vivien Leigh that invited admiration for husband and wife as magnificent, courageous, loyal, and of genuinely tragic stature even if fatally flawed by their hearkening to the voice of evil.

Macbeth

[*Dramatis Personae*

DUNCAN, *King of Scotland*
MALCOLM, } *his sons*
DONALBAIN,

MACBETH, *Thane of Glamis, later of Cawdor, later King of Scotland*
LADY MACBETH

BANQUO, *a thane of Scotland*
FLEANCE, *his son*
MACDUFF, *Thane of Fife*
LADY MACDUFF
SON *of Macduff and Lady Macduff*

LENNOX, }
ROSS,
MENTEITH, } *thanes and noblemen of Scotland*
ANGUS,
CAITHNESS,

SIWARD, *Earl of Northumberland*
YOUNG SIWARD, *his son*

SEYTON, *an officer attending Macbeth*
Another LORD
ENGLISH DOCTOR
SCOTTISH DOCTOR
GENTLEWOMAN *attending Lady Macbeth*
CAPTAIN *serving Duncan*
PORTER
OLD MAN
Three MURDERERS *of Banquo*
FIRST MURDERER *at Macduff's castle*
MESSENGER *to Lady Macbeth*
MESSENGER *to Lady Macduff*
SERVANT *to Macbeth*
SERVANT *to Lady Macbeth*
Three WITCHES *or* WEIRD SISTERS
HECATE
Three APPARITIONS

Lords, Gentlemen, Officers, Soldiers, Murderers, and Attendants

SCENE: *Scotland; England*]

1.1

Thunder and lightning. Enter three Witches.

FIRST WITCH
    When shall we three meet again?
    In thunder, lightning, or in rain?
SECOND WITCH
    When the hurlyburly's done,
    When the battle's lost and won.   3
THIRD WITCH
    That will be ere the set of sun.

1.1. Location: An open place.
3 hurlyburly's tumult's

FIRST WITCH
    Where the place?
SECOND WITCH   Upon the heath.
THIRD WITCH
    There to meet with Macbeth.
FIRST WITCH   I come, Grimalkin!
SECOND WITCH   Paddock calls.   8 9
THIRD WITCH   Anon.   10

8 **Grimalkin** i.e., gray cat, name of the witch's familiar—a demon or evil spirit supposed to answer a witch's call and to allow him or her to perform black magic.   9 **Paddock** toad; also a familiar   10 **Anon** At once, right away.

ALL
> Fair is foul, and foul is fair.
> Hover through the fog and filthy air.   *Exeunt.*

❖

1.2

Alarum within. Enter King [Duncan], Malcolm,
Donalbain, Lennox, with attendants, meeting a
bleeding Captain.

DUNCAN
> What bloody man is that? He can report,
> As seemeth by his plight, of the revolt
> The newest state.

MALCOLM   This is the sergeant   3
> Who like a good and hardy soldier fought
> 'Gainst my captivity.—Hail, brave friend!
> Say to the King the knowledge of the broil   6
> As thou didst leave it.

CAPTAIN   Doubtful it stood,
> As two spent swimmers that do cling together   8
> And choke their art. The merciless Macdonwald—   9
> Worthy to be a rebel, for to that   10
> The multiplying villainies of nature   11
> Do swarm upon him—from the Western Isles   12
> Of kerns and gallowglasses is supplied;   13
> And Fortune, on his damnèd quarrel smiling,   14
> Showed like a rebel's whore. But all's too weak;   15
> For brave Macbeth—well he deserves that name—   16
> Disdaining Fortune, with his brandished steel,
> Which smoked with bloody execution,
> Like valor's minion carved out his passage   19
> Till he faced the slave,   20
> Which ne'er shook hands nor bade farewell to him   21
> Till he unseamed him from the nave to th' chops,   22
> And fixed his head upon our battlements.

DUNCAN
> Oh, valiant cousin, worthy gentleman!   24

CAPTAIN
> As whence the sun 'gins his reflection   25
> Shipwrecking storms and direful thunders break,   26
> So from that spring whence comfort seemed to come   27
> Discomfort swells. Mark, King of Scotland, mark.   28
> No sooner justice had, with valor armed,
> Compelled these skipping kerns to trust their heels   30
> But the Norweyan lord, surveying vantage,   31
> With furbished arms and new supplies of men,
> Began a fresh assault.

DUNCAN
> Dismayed not this our captains, Macbeth and
> Banquo?

CAPTAIN
> Yes, as sparrows eagles, or the hare the lion.   35
> If I say sooth, I must report they were   36
> As cannons overcharged with double cracks,   37
> So they doubly redoubled strokes upon the foe.
> Except they meant to bathe in reeking wounds   39
> Or memorize another Golgotha,   40
> I cannot tell.
> But I am faint. My gashes cry for help.

DUNCAN
> So well thy words become thee as thy wounds;
> They smack of honor both.—Go get him surgeons.
> > [*Exit Captain, attended.*]

Enter Ross and Angus.

> Who comes here?

MALCOLM   The worthy Thane of Ross.   45

LENNOX   What a haste looks through his eyes!
> So should he look that seems to speak things strange.   47

ROSS   God save the King!

DUNCAN   Whence cam'st thou, worthy thane?

ROSS   From Fife, great King,
> Where the Norweyan banners flout the sky   51
> And fan our people cold.   52
> Norway himself, with terrible numbers,   53
> Assisted by that most disloyal traitor,
> The Thane of Cawdor, began a dismal conflict,   55
> Till that Bellona's bridegroom, lapped in proof,   56
> Confronted him with self-comparisons,   57

1.2. Location: A camp near Forres.
0.1 *Alarum* trumpet call to arms   **3 newest state** latest news.
sergeant i.e., staff officer. (There may be no inconsistency with his
rank of "captain" in the stage direction and speech prefixes in the
Folio.)   **6 broil** battle   **8 spent** tired out   **9 choke their art** render
their skill in swimming useless.   **9–13 The merciless . . . supplied**
The merciless Macdonwald—worthy of the hated name of rebel, for
in the cause of rebellion an ever-increasing number of villainous persons and unnatural qualities swarm about him like vermin—is joined
by light-armed Irish footsoldiers and ax-armed horsemen from the
western islands of Scotland (the Hebrides and perhaps Ireland)
14–15 And Fortune . . . whore i.e., Fortune, proverbially a false
strumpet, smiles at first on Macdonwald's damned rebellion but
deserts him in his hour of need.   **16 well . . . name** well he deserves a
name that is synonymous with "brave"   **19 minion** darling. (Macbeth is Valor's darling, not Fortune's.)   **20 the slave** i.e., Macdonwald   **21 Which . . . to him** i.e., Macbeth paused for no ceremonious
greeting or farewell to Macdonwald   **22 nave** navel.   **chops** jaws
24 cousin kinsman

25–8 As . . . swells Just as terrible storms at sea arise out of the east,
from the place where the sun first shows itself in the seeming comfort
of the dawn, even thus did a new military threat come on the heels of
the seeming good news of Macdonwald's execution.   **30 skipping**
(1) lightly armed, quick at maneuvering (2) skittish   **31 surveying
vantage** seeing an opportunity   **35 Yes . . . eagles** Yes, about as much
as sparrows terrify eagles. (Said ironically.)   **36 say sooth** tell the
truth   **37 cracks** charges of explosive   **39 Except** Unless   **40 memorize** make memorable or famous.   **Golgotha** "place of a skull,"
where Christ was crucified. (Mark 15:22.)   **45 Thane** Scottish title of
honor, roughly equivalent to "Earl"   **47 seems to** seems about to
51 flout mock, insult   **52 fan . . . cold** fan cold fear into our troops.
53 Norway The King of Norway.   **terrible numbers** terrifying numbers of troops   **55 dismal** ominous   **56 Till . . . proof** i.e., until Macbeth, clad in well-tested armor. (Bellona was the Roman goddess of
war.)   **57 him** i.e., the King of Norway.   **self-comparisons** i.e.,
matching counterthrusts

Point against point, rebellious arm 'gainst arm,
Curbing his lavish spirit; and to conclude,
The victory fell on us.

DUNCAN   Great happiness!

ROSS   That now
Sweno, the Norways' king, craves composition;   62
Nor would we deign him burial of his men
Till he disbursèd at Saint Colme's Inch   64
Ten thousand dollars to our general use.   65

DUNCAN
No more that Thane of Cawdor shall deceive
Our bosom interest. Go pronounce his present death,   67
And with his former title greet Macbeth.

ROSS   I'll see it done.

DUNCAN
What he hath lost noble Macbeth hath won.
                                               Exeunt.

❖

1.3

Thunder. Enter the three Witches.

FIRST WITCH   Where hast thou been, sister?
SECOND WITCH   Killing swine.
THIRD WITCH   Sister, where thou?
FIRST WITCH
A sailor's wife had chestnuts in her lap,
And munched, and munched, and munched. "Give
   me," quoth I.
"Aroint thee, witch!" the rump-fed runnion cries.   6
Her husband's to Aleppo gone, master o'th' *Tiger*;   7
But in a sieve I'll thither sail,
And like a rat without a tail   9
I'll do, I'll do, and I'll do.   10
SECOND WITCH
I'll give thee a wind.
FIRST WITCH
Thou'rt kind.
THIRD WITCH
And I another.
FIRST WITCH
I myself have all the other,   14
And the very ports they blow,   15
All the quarters that they know   16
I'th' shipman's card.   17
I'll drain him dry as hay.   18

Sleep shall neither night nor day
Hang upon his penthouse lid.   20
He shall live a man forbid.   21
Weary sev'nnights nine times nine   22
Shall he dwindle, peak, and pine.   23
Though his bark cannot be lost,
Yet it shall be tempest-tossed.
Look what I have.
SECOND WITCH   Show me, show me.
FIRST WITCH
Here I have a pilot's thumb,
Wrecked as homeward he did come.   *Drum within.*
THIRD WITCH
A drum, a drum!
Macbeth doth come.
ALL [*dancing in a circle*]
The Weird Sisters, hand in hand,   32
Posters of the sea and land,   33
Thus do go about, about,
Thrice to thine, and thrice to mine,
And thrice again, to make up nine.
Peace! The charm's wound up.

Enter Macbeth and Banquo.

MACBETH
So foul and fair a day I have not seen.
BANQUO
How far is't called to Forres?—What are these,   39
So withered and so wild in their attire,
That look not like th'inhabitants o'th'earth
And yet are on't?—Live you? Or are you aught
That man may question? You seem to understand me
By each at once her choppy finger laying   44
Upon her skinny lips. You should be women,
And yet your beards forbid me to interpret
That you are so.
MACBETH   Speak, if you can. What are you?
FIRST WITCH
All hail, Macbeth! Hail to thee, Thane of Glamis!
SECOND WITCH
All hail, Macbeth! Hail to thee, Thane of Cawdor!
THIRD WITCH
All hail, Macbeth, that shalt be king hereafter!
BANQUO
Good sir, why do you start and seem to fear
Things that do sound so fair?—I'th' name of truth,
Are ye fantastical or that indeed   53
Which outwardly ye show? My noble partner   54
You greet with present grace and great prediction   55
Of noble having and of royal hope,
That he seems rapt withal. To me you speak not.   57
If you can look into the seeds of time

---

62 Norways' Norwegians'.   **composition** agreement, treaty of peace
64 Saint Colme's Inch Inchcolm, the Isle of St. Columba in the Firth
of Forth   **65 dollars** Spanish or Dutch coins   **67 Our** (The royal
"we.")   **bosom** close and intimate.   **present** immediate
1.3. Location: A heath near Forres.
6 Aroint thee Begone.   **rump-fed runnion** fat-rumped baggage
7 Tiger (A ship's name.)   **9–10 like . . . do** (Suggestive of the witches'
deformity and sexual insatiability. Witches were thought to seduce
men sexually. *Do* means [1] act [2] perform sexually.)   **14–17 I . . .
card** I can summon all other winds, wherever they blow and from
whatever *quarter* in the shipman's compass card.   **18 I'll . . . hay**
(With a suggestion of sexually draining the seaman's semen.)

20 penthouse lid i.e., eyelid (which projects out over the eye like a
penthouse or slope-roofed structure).   **21 forbid** accursed.   **22 sev'n-
nights** weeks   **23 peak** grow peaked or thin   **32 Weird Sisters**
women connected with fate or destiny; also women having a mysterious or unearthly, uncanny appearance   **33 Posters of** swift travelers
over   **39 is't called** is it said to be   **44 choppy** chapped   **53 fantastical** creatures of fantasy or imagination   **54 show** appear.   **55 grace**
honor   **57 rapt withal** entranced.

And say which grain will grow and which will not,
Speak then to me, who neither beg nor fear   60
Your favors nor your hate.   61

FIRST WITCH   Hail!

SECOND WITCH   Hail!

THIRD WITCH   Hail!

FIRST WITCH
Lesser than Macbeth, and greater.

SECOND WITCH
Not so happy, yet much happier.   66

THIRD WITCH
Thou shalt get kings, though thou be none.   67
So all hail, Macbeth and Banquo!

FIRST WITCH
Banquo and Macbeth, all hail!

MACBETH
Stay, you imperfect speakers, tell me more!   70
By Sinel's death I know I am Thane of Glamis,   71
But how of Cawdor? The Thane of Cawdor lives
A prosperous gentleman; and to be king
Stands not within the prospect of belief,
No more than to be Cawdor. Say from whence   75
You owe this strange intelligence, or why   76
Upon this blasted heath you stop our way   77
With such prophetic greeting? Speak, I charge you.
                                        Witches vanish.

BANQUO
The earth hath bubbles, as the water has,
And these are of them. Whither are they vanished?

MACBETH
Into the air; and what seemed corporal melted,   81
As breath into the wind. Would they had stayed!

BANQUO
Were such things here as we do speak about?
Or have we eaten on the insane root   84
That takes the reason prisoner?

MACBETH
Your children shall be kings.

BANQUO   You shall be king.

MACBETH
And Thane of Cawdor too. Went it not so?

BANQUO
To th' selfsame tune and words.—Who's here?

Enter Ross and Angus.

ROSS
The King hath happily received, Macbeth,
The news of thy success; and when he reads   90
Thy personal venture in the rebels' fight,   91
His wonders and his praises do contend   92
Which should be thine or his. Silenced with that,   93
In viewing o'er the rest o' th' selfsame day

He finds thee in the stout Norweyan ranks,   95
Nothing afeard of what thyself didst make,   96
Strange images of death. As thick as tale   97
Came post with post, and every one did bear   98
Thy praises in his kingdom's great defense,
And poured them down before him.

ANGUS   We are sent
To give thee from our royal master thanks,
Only to herald thee into his sight,
Not pay thee.

ROSS
And, for an earnest of a greater honor,   104
He bade me, from him, call thee Thane of Cawdor;
In which addition, hail, most worthy thane,   106
For it is thine.

BANQUO   What, can the devil speak true?

MACBETH
The Thane of Cawdor lives. Why do you dress me
In borrowed robes?

ANGUS   Who was the thane lives yet,   109
But under heavy judgment bears that life
Which he deserves to lose. Whether he was combined 111
With those of Norway, or did line the rebel   112
With hidden help and vantage, or that with both
He labored in his country's wrack, I know not;   114
But treasons capital, confessed and proved,   115
Have overthrown him.

MACBETH [*aside*]   Glamis, and Thane of Cawdor!
The greatest is behind. [*To Ross and Angus*] Thanks for
   your pains.   117
[*Aside to Banquo*] Do you not hope your children shall
   be kings
When those that gave the Thane of Cawdor to me
Promised no less to them?

BANQUO [*to Macbeth*]   That, trusted home,   120
Might yet enkindle you unto the crown,
Besides the Thane of Cawdor. But 'tis strange;
And oftentimes to win us to our harm
The instruments of darkness tell us truths,
Win us with honest trifles, to betray 's
In deepest consequence.—   126
Cousins, a word, I pray you.   127
                 [*He converses apart with Ross and Angus.*]

MACBETH [*aside*]   Two truths are told,
As happy prologues to the swelling act   129
Of the imperial theme.—I thank you, gentlemen.
[*Aside*] This supernatural soliciting   131
Cannot be ill, cannot be good. If ill,
Why hath it given me earnest of success

60–1 beg . . . hate beg your favors nor fear your hate.   66 happy fortunate   67 get beget   70 imperfect cryptic   71 Sinel's (Sinel was Macbeth's father.)   75–6 Say . . . intelligence Say from what source you have this disturbing information   77 blasted blighted   81 corporal corporeal   84 on of.   insane root root causing insanity; variously identified   90–3 and when . . . his and when he reads of your extraordinary valor in fighting the rebels, he concludes that your wondrous deeds outdo any praise he could offer.

95 stout haughty, determined, valiant   96 Nothing not at all   97–8 As . . . with post As fast as could be told, i.e., counted, came messenger after messenger. (Unless the text should be amended to "As thick as hail.")   104 earnest token payment   106 addition title   109 Who He who   111 combined confederate   112 line the rebel reinforce Macdonwald   114 in . . . wrack to bring about his country's ruin   115 capital deserving death   117 The greatest is behind either (1) Two of the three prophecies (and thus the greatest number of them) have already been fulfilled, or (2) The greatest one, the kingship, is still to come.   120 home all the way   126 In deepest consequence in the profoundly important sequel.   127 Cousins i.e., Fellow lords   129 swelling act stately drama   131 soliciting tempting

Commencing in a truth? I am Thane of Cawdor.
If good, why do I yield to that suggestion
Whose horrid image doth unfix my hair   136
And make my seated heart knock at my ribs,
Against the use of nature? Present fears   138
Are less than horrible imaginings.
My thought, whose murder yet is but fantastical,   140
Shakes so my single state of man   141
That function is smothered in surmise,   142
And nothing is but what is not.   143

BANQUO   Look how our partner's rapt.

MACBETH [aside]
If chance will have me king, why, chance may crown
    me
Without my stir.

BANQUO   New honors come upon him,   146
Like our strange garments, cleave not to their mold   147
But with the aid of use.

MACBETH [aside]   Come what come may,   148
Time and the hour runs through the roughest day.   149

BANQUO
Worthy Macbeth, we stay upon your leisure.   150

MACBETH
Give me your favor. My dull brain was wrought   151
With things forgotten. Kind gentlemen, your pains
Are registered where every day I turn   153
The leaf to read them. Let us toward the King.
[Aside to Banquo]   Think upon what hath chanced,
    and at more time,   155
The interim having weighed it, let us speak   156
Our free hearts each to other.   157

BANQUO [to Macbeth]   Very gladly.

MACBETH [to Banquo]   Till then, enough.—Come, friends.
                                              Exeunt.

❖

1.4

*Flourish. Enter King [Duncan], Lennox, Malcolm,
Donalbain, and attendants.*

DUNCAN
Is execution done on Cawdor? Are not
Those in commission yet returned?

MALCOLM   My liege,   2
They are not yet come back. But I have spoke

With one that saw him die, who did report
That very frankly he confessed his treasons,
Implored Your Highness' pardon, and set forth
A deep repentance. Nothing in his life
Became him like the leaving it. He died   8
As one that had been studied in his death   9
To throw away the dearest thing he owed   10
As 'twere a careless trifle.

DUNCAN   There's no art   11
To find the mind's construction in the face.
He was a gentleman on whom I built
An absolute trust.

          Enter Macbeth, Banquo, Ross, and Angus.

                         O worthiest cousin!
The sin of my ingratitude even now
Was heavy on me. Thou art so far before   16
That swiftest wing of recompense is slow
To overtake thee. Would thou hadst less deserved,
That the proportion both of thanks and payment   19
Might have been mine! Only I have left to say,   20
More is thy due than more than all can pay.

MACBETH
The service and the loyalty I owe,
In doing it, pays itself. Your Highness' part
Is to receive our duties; and our duties
Are to your throne and state children and servants,   25
Which do but what they should by doing everything
Safe toward your love and honor.

DUNCAN   Welcome hither!   27
I have begun to plant thee, and will labor
To make thee full of growing. Noble Banquo,
That hast no less deserved, nor must be known
No less to have done so, let me infold thee
And hold thee to my heart.

BANQUO   There if I grow,
The harvest is your own.

DUNCAN   My plenteous joys,
Wanton in fullness, seek to hide themselves   34
In drops of sorrow.—Sons, kinsmen, thanes,
And you whose places are the nearest, know
We will establish our estate upon   37
Our eldest, Malcolm, whom we name hereafter
The Prince of Cumberland; which honor must   39
Not unaccompanied invest him only,   40
But signs of nobleness, like stars, shall shine
On all deservers.—From hence to Inverness,   42
And bind us further to you.   43

---

136 **unfix my hair** make my hair stand on end   138 **use** custom.
fears things feared   140 **whose . . . fantastical** in which the conception of murder is merely imaginary at this point   141 **single . . . man**
weak human condition   142 **function** normal power of action.
surmise speculation, imaginings   143 **And . . . not** and everything
seems unreal.   146 **stir** bestirring (myself).   **come** i.e., which have
come   147–8 **cleave . . . use** do not take the shape of the wearer until
often worn. (Macbeth is often connected in the text with clothes that
don't really fit him.)   149 **Time . . . day** time moves relentlessly on,
no matter what else happens.   150 **stay** wait
151 **favor** pardon.   **wrought** shaped, preoccupied   153 **registered**
recorded (in my memory)   155 **at more time** at a time of greater
leisure   156 **weighed it** given opportunity for reflection on its meaning   157 **Our free hearts** our hearts freely
1.4. Location: Forres. The palace.
2 **in commission** having warrant (to see to the execution of Cawdor)

8 **Became** graced, befitted   9 **been studied** made it his study
10 **owed** owned   11 **careless** uncared for   16 **before** ahead (in
deserving)   19–20 **That . . . mine** that I might have thanked and
rewarded you in ample proportion to your worth.   25 **Are . . . servants** are like children and servants in relation to your throne and
dignity, existing only to serve you   27 **Safe . . . honor** to safeguard
you whom we love and honor.   34 **Wanton** unrestrained   37 **We**
(The royal "we.")   **establish our estate** fix the succession of our state
39 **Prince of Cumberland** title of the heir apparent to the Scottish
throne   40 **Not . . . only** not be bestowed on Malcolm alone; other
deserving nobles are to share honors   42 **Inverness** the seat or location of Macbeth's castle, Dunsinane   43 **bind . . . you** put me further
in your (Macbeth's) obligation by your hospitality.

MACBETH
　The rest is labor which is not used for you.   44
　I'll be myself the harbinger and make joyful   45
　The hearing of my wife with your approach;
　So humbly take my leave.
DUNCAN   My worthy Cawdor!
MACBETH [aside]
　The Prince of Cumberland! That is a step
　On which I must fall down or else o'erleap,
　For in my way it lies. Stars, hide your fires;   50
　Let not light see my black and deep desires.
　The eye wink at the hand; yet let that be   52
　Which the eye fears, when it is done, to see.   Exit.   53
DUNCAN
　True, worthy Banquo. He is full so valiant,   54
　And in his commendations I am fed;   55
　It is a banquet to me. Let's after him,
　Whose care is gone before to bid us welcome.
　It is a peerless kinsman.   Flourish. Exeunt.

❖

1.5

Enter Macbeth's Wife, alone, with a letter.

LADY MACBETH [reads] "They met me in the day of success; and I have learned by the perfect'st report they   2
have more in them than mortal knowledge. When I
burnt in desire to question them further, they made
themselves air, into which they vanished. Whiles I
stood rapt in the wonder of it came missives from the   6
King, who all-hailed me 'Thane of Cawdor,' by which
title, before, these Weird Sisters saluted me, and referred me to the coming on of time with 'Hail, king
that shalt be!' This have I thought good to deliver thee,   10
my dearest partner of greatness, that thou mightst not
lose the dues of rejoicing by being ignorant of what
greatness is promised thee. Lay it to thy heart, and
farewell."
　Glamis thou art, and Cawdor, and shalt be
What thou art promised. Yet do I fear thy nature;   16
It is too full o'th' milk of human kindness
To catch the nearest way. Thou wouldst be great,
Art not without ambition, but without
The illness should attend it. What thou wouldst
　highly,   20
That wouldst thou holily; wouldst not play false,

And yet wouldst wrongly win. Thou'dst have, great
　Glamis,
That which cries "Thus thou must do," if thou have it,   23
And that which rather thou dost fear to do   24
Than wishest should be undone. Hie thee hither,   25
That I may pour my spirits in thine ear
And chastise with the valor of my tongue
All that impedes thee from the golden round   28
Which fate and metaphysical aid doth seem   29
To have thee crowned withal.

Enter [a servant as] Messenger.

　　　　　　　　　　　　　　　　　What is your tidings?   30
MESSENGER
　The King comes here tonight.
LADY MACBETH   Thou'rt mad to say it!
　Is not thy master with him, who, were't so,
　Would have informed for preparation?   33
MESSENGER
　So please you, it is true. Our thane is coming.
　One of my fellows had the speed of him,   35
　Who, almost dead for breath, had scarcely more
　Than would make up his message.
LADY MACBETH   Give him tending;   37
　He brings great news.   *Exit Messenger.*
　　　　　　　　　　　　　The raven himself is hoarse
That croaks the fatal entrance of Duncan
Under my battlements. Come, you spirits
That tend on mortal thoughts, unsex me here   41
And fill me from the crown to the toe top-full
Of direst cruelty! Make thick my blood;
Stop up th'access and passage to remorse,   44
That no compunctious visitings of nature   45
Shake my fell purpose, nor keep peace between   46
Th'effect and it! Come to my woman's breasts   47
And take my milk for gall, you murd'ring ministers,   48
Wherever in your sightless substances   49
You wait on nature's mischief! Come, thick night,   50
And pall thee in the dunnest smoke of hell,   51
That my keen knife see not the wound it makes,
Nor heaven peep through the blanket of the dark
To cry "Hold, hold!"

Enter Macbeth.

　　　　　　　　　　　Great Glamis! Worthy Cawdor!   54
Greater than both by the all-hail hereafter!
Thy letters have transported me beyond   56

---

44 The rest . . . you All activity not devoted to serving you is mere
tediousness and hard work.   45 harbinger forerunner, messenger
50 in my way it lies (The monarchy was not hereditary, and Macbeth
had a right to believe that he himself might be chosen as Duncan's
successor; he here questions whether he will interfere with the
course of events.)   52–3 The eye . . . see Let the eye shut itself and
not see the hand's deed; yet when the deed is done, let it be fearful to
behold.   54 full so valiant fully as valiant as you say. (Apparently,
Duncan and Banquo have been conversing privately on this subject
during Macbeth's soliloquy.)   55 in . . . fed it nourishes me to hear
him praised
1.5. Location: Inverness. Macbeth's castle.
2 perfect'st most accurate   6 missives messengers   10 deliver thee
inform you of   16 do I fear I mistrust   20 illness evil (that).
highly greatly

23 have are to have, want to have   24–5 And that . . . undone i.e.,
and the thing you ambitiously crave frightens you more in terms of
the means needed to achieve it than in the idea of having it; if you
could have it without those means, you certainly wouldn't wish it
undone.   25 Hie Hasten   28 round crown   29 metaphysical supernatural   30 withal with.   33 informed for preparation i.e., sent me
word so that I might get things ready.   35 had . . . of outstripped
37 Give him tending Tend to his needs   41 tend . . . thoughts attend
on, act as the instruments of, deadly or murderous thoughts
44 remorse pity   45 nature natural feelings   46 fell fierce, cruel
46–7 nor . . . and it nor intervene between my *fell purpose* and its
accomplishment.   48 for gall in exchange for gall, or perhaps *as* gall.
ministers agents   49 sightless invisible   50 You . . . mischief you
aid and abet the wickedness of human nature.   51 pall envelop.
dunnest darkest   54 Hold Stop   56 letters have i.e., letter has

This ignorant present, and I feel now
The future in the instant.

MACBETH   My dearest love,
Duncan comes here tonight.

LADY MACBETH   And when goes hence?

MACBETH
Tomorrow, as he purposes.

LADY MACBETH   Oh, never
Shall sun that morrow see!
Your face, my thane, is as a book where men
May read strange matters. To beguile the time,   63
Look like the time; bear welcome in your eye,   64
Your hand, your tongue. Look like th'innocent flower,
But be the serpent under't. He that's coming
Must be provided for; and you shall put
This night's great business into my dispatch,   68
Which shall to all our nights and days to come
Give solely sovereign sway and masterdom.

MACBETH
We will speak further.

LADY MACBETH   Only look up clear.   71
To alter favor ever is to fear.   72
Leave all the rest to me.   *Exeunt.*

❖

1.6

Hautboys and torches. Enter King [Duncan],
Malcolm, Donalbain, Banquo, Lennox, Macduff,
Ross, Angus, and attendants.

DUNCAN
This castle hath a pleasant seat. The air   1
Nimbly and sweetly recommends itself
Unto our gentle senses.

BANQUO   This guest of summer,   3
The temple-haunting martlet, does approve   4
By his loved mansionry that the heaven's breath   5
Smells wooingly here. No jutty, frieze,   6
Buttress, nor coign of vantage but this bird   7
Hath made his pendent bed and procreant cradle.   8
Where they most breed and haunt, I have observed
The air is delicate.

Enter Lady [Macbeth].

DUNCAN   See, see, our honored hostess!
The love that follows us sometime is our trouble,   11
Which still we thank as love. Herein I teach you   12

How you shall bid God 'ild us for your pains,   13
And thank us for your trouble.

LADY MACBETH   All our service
In every point twice done, and then done double,
Were poor and single business to contend   16
Against those honors deep and broad wherewith   17
Your Majesty loads our house. For those of old,   18
And the late dignities heaped up to them,   19
We rest your hermits.

DUNCAN   Where's the Thane of Cawdor?   20
We coursed him at the heels, and had a purpose   21
To be his purveyor; but he rides well,   22
And his great love, sharp as his spur, hath holp him   23
To his home before us. Fair and noble hostess,
We are your guest tonight.

LADY MACBETH   Your servants ever   25
Have theirs, themselves, and what is theirs in compt   26
To make their audit at Your Highness' pleasure,   27
Still to return your own.

DUNCAN   Give me your hand.   28
Conduct me to mine host. We love him highly,
And shall continue our graces towards him.
By your leave, hostess.   *Exeunt.*

❖

1.7

Hautboys. Torches. Enter a sewer, and divers
servants with dishes and service, [and pass] over
the stage. Then enter Macbeth.

MACBETH
If it were done when 'tis done, then 'twere well
It were done quickly. If th'assassination   2
Could trammel up the consequence, and catch   3
With his surcease success—that but this blow   4
Might be the be-all and the end-all!—here,   5
But here, upon this bank and shoal of time,
We'd jump the life to come. But in these cases   7

63–4 To beguile . . . time To deceive everyone, look the way people
expect you to look   **68 dispatch** management   **71–2 Only . . . fear**
Whatever else you do, keep a cheerful countenance. To alter one's
countenance is to betray a guilty conscience.
1.6. Location: Before Macbeth's castle.
0.1 *Hautboys* oboelike instruments   **1 seat** site.   **3 gentle** (1) noble
(2) refined (by the delicate air)   **4–5 The . . . mansionry** The house
martin, that loves to nest in churches, proves by his devoted nest
building   **6 jutty** projection of wall or building   **7 coign of vantage**
convenient corner, i.e., for nesting   **8 pendent** hanging, suspended.
procreant for breeding   **11–12 The love . . . love** The love that sometimes forces itself inconveniently upon us we still appreciate, since it
is meant as love. (Duncan is graciously suggesting that his visit is a
bother, but, he hopes, a welcome one.)

13 bid . . . pains ask God to reward me for the trouble I'm giving you.
(This is said in the same gently jocose spirit as lines 11–12.)   **'ild**
yield, repay   **16–17 Were . . . Against** would be poor and small when
compared with   **18–20 For . . . hermits** In gratitude for the dignities
heaped upon us in former days and still others more recently added
to them, we are your thankful worshipers who pray for you like hermits or beadsmen.   **21 coursed** followed (as in a hunt)   **22 purveyor**
an officer sent ahead to provide for entertainment; here, forerunner
23 holp helped   **25 We** (the royal "we," also in lines 13–14 and 29)
25–8 Your . . . own Those who serve you hold their own servants,
themselves, and all their possessions in trust from you, and can render an account whenever you wish, ready always to render back to
you what is yours. (A feudal concept of obligation.)
1.7. Location: Macbeth's castle; an inner courtyard.
0.1 *sewer* chief waiter, butler   **2–4 If . . . success** i.e., If only the assassination of Duncan could proceed without further consequences and
end the matter with the completion of the deed itself. (To *trammel* is to
bind up or entangle in a net; *surcease* means "cessation"; *success*
means "what succeeds or follows.")   **4 that but** so that only   **5 here**
in this world   **7 jump** risk. (But imaging the physical act is characteristic of Macbeth; compare this with line 27.)

We still have judgment here, that we but teach 8
Bloody instructions, which, being taught, return 9
To plague th'inventor. This evenhanded justice 10
Commends th'ingredience of our poisoned chalice 11
To our own lips. He's here in double trust:
First, as I am his kinsman and his subject,
Strong both against the deed; then, as his host,
Who should against his murderer shut the door,
Not bear the knife myself. Besides, this Duncan
Hath borne his faculties so meek, hath been 17
So clear in his great office, that his virtues 18
Will plead like angels, trumpet-tongued, against
The deep damnation of his taking-off; 20
And Pity, like a naked newborn babe
Striding the blast, or heaven's cherubin, horsed 22
Upon the sightless couriers of the air, 23
Shall blow the horrid deed in every eye,
That tears shall drown the wind. I have no spur 25
To prick the sides of my intent, but only
Vaulting ambition, which o'erleaps itself
And falls on th'other— 28

Enter Lady [Macbeth].

How now, what news?

LADY MACBETH
He has almost supped. Why have you left the
chamber?

MACBETH
Hath he asked for me?

LADY MACBETH   Know you not he has?

MACBETH
We will proceed no further in this business.
He hath honored me of late, and I have bought 33
Golden opinions from all sorts of people,
Which would be worn now in their newest gloss, 35
Not cast aside so soon.

LADY MACBETH   Was the hope drunk
Wherein you dressed yourself? Hath it slept since?
And wakes it now, to look so green and pale 38
At what it did so freely? From this time
Such I account thy love. Art thou afeard
To be the same in thine own act and valor
As thou art in desire? Wouldst thou have that
Which thou esteem'st the ornament of life, 43
And live a coward in thine own esteem,
Letting "I dare not" wait upon "I would," 45

Like the poor cat i'th' adage?

MACBETH   Prithee, peace! 46
I dare do all that may become a man;
Who dares do more is none.

LADY MACBETH   What beast was't, then,
That made you break this enterprise to me? 49
When you durst do it, then you were a man;
And, to be more than what you were, you would
Be so much more the man. Nor time nor place 52
Did then adhere, and yet you would make both. 53
They have made themselves, and that their fitness
now 54
Does unmake you. I have given suck, and know
How tender 'tis to love the babe that milks me;
I would, while it was smiling in my face,
Have plucked my nipple from his boneless gums
And dashed the brains out, had I so sworn as you
Have done to this.

MACBETH   If we should fail?

LADY MACBETH   We fail?
But screw your courage to the sticking place 61
And we'll not fail. When Duncan is asleep—
Whereto the rather shall his day's hard journey
Soundly invite him—his two chamberlains 64
Will I with wine and wassail so convince 65
That memory, the warder of the brain, 66
Shall be a fume, and the receipt of reason 67
A limbeck only. When in swinish sleep 68
Their drenchèd natures lies as in a death, 69
What cannot you and I perform upon
Th'unguarded Duncan? What not put upon
His spongy officers, who shall bear the guilt 72
Of our great quell?

MACBETH   Bring forth men-children only! 73
For thy undaunted mettle should compose 74
Nothing but males. Will it not be received, 75
When we have marked with blood those sleepy two
Of his own chamber and used their very daggers,
That they have done't?

LADY MACBETH   Who dares receive it other, 78
As we shall make our griefs and clamor roar 79
Upon his death?

MACBETH   I am settled, and bend up 80
Each corporal agent to this terrible feat. 81

8–10 We . . . th'inventor i.e., we still have punishment for crime in this world, whereby our bloody acts establish guilty precedents and thereby invite the just reciprocity of punishing blood with blood. **11 Commends** presents. **th'ingredience** the contents of a mixture **17 faculties** powers of office **18 clear** free of taint **20 taking-off** murder **22 Striding the blast** bestriding the tempest. (Putti and cherubs are often portrayed this way in Renaissance graphic arts.) **23 sightless couriers** invisible steeds or runners, i.e., the winds **25 tears . . . wind** (Showers of rain were popularly supposed to still the wind.) **28 th'other** the other side. (The image is of a horseman vaulting into his saddle and ignominiously falling on the opposite side.) **33 bought** acquired (by bravery in battle) **35 would** ought to, should **38 green** sickly **43 the ornament of life** i.e., the crown **45 wait upon** accompany, always follow

46 adage (i.e., "The cat would eat fish but she will not wet her feet.") **49 break** broach **52 Nor** Neither **53 adhere** agree, suit. **would** wanted to **54 that their fitness** that very suitability of time and place **61 But** Only. **the sticking place** the notch into which is fitted the string of a crossbow cranked taut for shooting **64 chamberlains** attendants on the bedchamber **65 wassail** carousal, drink. **convince** overpower **66–8 warder . . . only** (The brain was thought to be divided into three ventricles: imagination in front, memory at the back, and between them the seat of reason. The fumes of wine, arising from the stomach, would deaden memory and judgment.) **67 receipt** receptacle, ventricle **68 limbeck** device for distilling liquids **69 drenchèd** drowned (in wine) **72 spongy** soaked, drunken **73 quell** murder. **74 mettle** (the same word as *metal*): substance, temperament **75 received** i.e., as truth **78 other** otherwise **79 As** inasmuch as **80–1 bend up . . . agent** harness and direct every part of me

Away, and mock the time with fairest show.   82
False face must hide what the false heart doth know.
                                                              Exeunt.

❖

2.1

Enter Banquo, and Fleance, with a torch before him.

BANQUO   How goes the night, boy?

FLEANCE
The moon is down. I have not heard the clock.

BANQUO
And she goes down at twelve.

FLEANCE   I take't, 'tis later, sir.

BANQUO
Hold, take my sword. [*He gives him his sword.*] There's
   husbandry in heaven;   4
Their candles are all out. Take thee that too.
                        [*He gives him his belt and dagger.*]
A heavy summons lies like lead upon me,   6
And yet I would not sleep. Merciful powers,   7
Restrain in me the cursèd thoughts that nature
Gives way to in repose!

Enter Macbeth, and a Servant with a torch.

Give me my sword. Who's there? [*He takes his sword.*]

MACBETH   A friend.

BANQUO
What, sir, not yet at rest? The King's abed.
He hath been in unusual pleasure,
And sent forth great largess to your offices.   14
This diamond he greets your wife withal,
By the name of most kind hostess, and shut up   16
In measureless content.   [*He gives a diamond.*]

MACBETH   Being unprepared,   17
Our will became the servant to defect,   18
Which else should free have wrought.   19

BANQUO   All's well.
I dreamt last night of the three Weird Sisters.
To you they have showed some truth.

MACBETH   I think not of them.
Yet, when we can entreat an hour to serve,
We would spend it in some words upon that business,
If you would grant the time.

BANQUO   At your kind'st leisure.

MACBETH
If you shall cleave to my consent when 'tis,   26
It shall make honor for you.

BANQUO   So I lose none   27
In seeking to augment it, but still keep
My bosom franchised and allegiance clear,   29
I shall be counseled.

MACBETH   Good repose the while!   30

BANQUO   Thanks, sir. The like to you.
                                Exit Banquo [with Fleance].

MACBETH [*to Servant*]
Go bid thy mistress, when my drink is ready,   32
She strike upon the bell. Get thee to bed.
                                          Exit [Servant].
Is this a dagger which I see before me,
The handle toward my hand? Come, let me clutch
   thee.
I have thee not, and yet I see thee still.
Art thou not, fatal vision, sensible   37
To feeling as to sight? Or art thou but
A dagger of the mind, a false creation,
Proceeding from the heat-oppressèd brain?   40
I see thee yet, in form as palpable
As this which now I draw.   [*He draws a dagger.*]
Thou marshall'st me the way that I was going,   43
And such an instrument I was to use.
Mine eyes are made the fools o'th'other senses,
Or else worth all the rest. I see thee still,
And on thy blade and dudgeon gouts of blood,   47
Which was not so before. There's no such thing.
It is the bloody business which informs
Thus to mine eyes. Now o'er the one half world
Nature seems dead, and wicked dreams abuse   51
The curtained sleep. Witchcraft celebrates   52
Pale Hecate's offerings, and withered Murder,   53
Alarumed by his sentinel, the wolf,   54
Whose howl's his watch, thus with his stealthy pace,   55
With Tarquin's ravishing strides, towards his design   56
Moves like a ghost. Thou sure and firm-set earth,
Hear not my steps which way they walk, for fear
Thy very stones prate of my whereabout
And take the present horror from the time   60
Which now suits with it. Whiles I threat, he lives;   61

Words to the heat of deeds too cold breath gives. 62
A bell rings.

I go, and it is done. The bell invites me.
Hear it not, Duncan, for it is a knell
That summons thee to heaven or to hell. *Exit.*

❖

2.2

Enter Lady [Macbeth].

LADY MACBETH
That which hath made them drunk hath made me
    bold;
What hath quenched them hath given me fire. Hark!
    Peace!
It was the owl that shrieked, the fatal bellman, 3
Which gives the stern'st good-night. He is about it. 4
The doors are open; and the surfeited grooms 5
Do mock their charge with snores. I have drugged
    their possets, 6
That death and nature do contend about them
Whether they live or die.

MACBETH [*within*]   Who's there? What, ho!

LADY MACBETH
Alack, I am afraid they have awaked,
And 'tis not done. Th'attempt and not the deed
Confounds us. Hark! I laid their daggers ready; 11
He could not miss 'em. Had he not resembled
My father as he slept, I had done't.

Enter Macbeth, [bearing bloody daggers].

My husband!

MACBETH
I have done the deed. Didst thou not hear a noise?

LADY MACBETH
I heard the owl scream and the crickets cry. 16
Did not you speak?

MACBETH When?

LADY MACBETH Now.

MACBETH As I descended?

LADY MACBETH Ay.

MACBETH Hark! Who lies i'th' second chamber?

LADY MACBETH Donalbain.

MACBETH [*looking at his hands*] This is a sorry sight.

LADY MACBETH
A foolish thought, to say a sorry sight.

MACBETH
There's one did laugh in 's sleep, and one cried
    "Murder!"
That they did wake each other. I stood and heard
    them.

But they did say their prayers, and addressed them 28
Again to sleep.

LADY MACBETH   There are two lodged together.

MACBETH
One cried "God bless us!" and "Amen!" the other,
As they had seen me with these hangman's hands. 31
List'ning their fear, I could not say "Amen"
When they did say "God bless us!"

LADY MACBETH   Consider it not so deeply.

MACBETH
But wherefore could not I pronounce "Amen"?
I had most need of blessing, and "Amen"
Stuck in my throat.

LADY MACBETH   These deeds must not be thought 37
After these ways; so, it will make us mad. 38

MACBETH
Methought I heard a voice cry "Sleep no more!
Macbeth does murder sleep," the innocent sleep,
Sleep that knits up the raveled sleave of care, 41
The death of each day's life, sore labor's bath, 42
Balm of hurt minds, great nature's second course, 43
Chief nourisher in life's feast—

LADY MACBETH   What do you mean?

MACBETH
Still it cried "Sleep no more!" to all the house;
"Glamis hath murdered sleep, and therefore Cawdor
Shall sleep no more; Macbeth shall sleep no more."

LADY MACBETH
Who was it that thus cried? Why, worthy thane,
You do unbend your noble strength to think 49
So brainsickly of things. Go get some water
And wash this filthy witness from your hand. 51
Why did you bring these daggers from the place?
They must lie there. Go, carry them and smear
The sleepy grooms with blood.

MACBETH   I'll go no more.
I am afraid to think what I have done;
Look on't again I dare not.

LADY MACBETH   Infirm of purpose!
Give me the daggers. The sleeping and the dead
Are but as pictures. 'Tis the eye of childhood
That fears a painted devil. If he do bleed,
I'll gild the faces of the grooms withal, 60
For it must seem their guilt.
          [*She takes the daggers, and] exit. Knock within.*

MACBETH   Whence is that knocking?
How is't with me, when every noise appalls me?
What hands are here? Ha! They pluck out mine eyes.
Will all great Neptune's ocean wash this blood
Clean from my hand? No, this my hand will rather
The multitudinous seas incarnadine, 66

---

62 **Words . . . gives** Words give only lifeless expression to live deeds,
are no substitute for deeds.
2.2. Location: Scene continues.
3 **bellman** one who rings a bell to announce a death or to mark the
hours of the night   4 **Which . . . good-night** i.e., that announces the
last good-night, death.   5 **grooms** servants   6 **mock their charge**
make a mockery of their guard duty.   **possets** hot bedtime drinks (as
in 2.1.32)   11 **Confounds** ruins   16 **owl, crickets** (The sounds of
both could be ominous and prophetic of death.)

28 **addressed them** settled themselves   31 **As** as if.   **hangman's
hands** bloody hands of the executioner.   37 **thought** thought about
38 **so** if we do so   41 **raveled sleave** tangled skein   42 **bath** i.e., to
relieve the soreness   43 **second course** (Ordinary feasts had two
courses, of which the second was the *chief nourisher;* here, sleep is
seen as following eating in a restorative process.)   49 **unbend**
slacken (as one would a bow; contrast with "bend up" in 1.7.80)
51 **witness** evidence   60 **gild** smear, coat, as if with a thin layer of
gold. (Gold was ordinarily spoken of as red.)   66 **multitudinous**
numerous and teeming.   **incarnadine** stain red

Making the green one red.   67

Enter Lady [Macbeth].

LADY MACBETH
My hands are of your color, but I shame
To wear a heart so white. (*Knock.*) I hear a knocking
At the south entry. Retire we to our chamber.
A little water clears us of this deed.
How easy is it, then! Your constancy   72
Hath left you unattended. (*Knock.*) Hark! More
  knocking.   73
Get on your nightgown, lest occasion call us   74
And show us to be watchers. Be not lost   75
So poorly in your thoughts.

MACBETH
To know my deed, 'twere best not know myself.   77
                                                   Knock.
Wake Duncan with thy knocking! I would thou
  couldst!   *Exeunt.*

❖

2.3

Knocking within. Enter a Porter.

PORTER   Here's a knocking indeed! If a man were porter
of hell gate, he should have old turning the key.   2
(*Knock.*) Knock, knock, knock! Who's there, i'th'
name of Beelzebub? Here's a farmer that hanged   4
himself on th'expectation of plenty. Come in time!   5
Have napkins enough about you; here you'll sweat for't.   6
(*Knock.*) Knock, knock! Who's there, in th'other
devil's name? Faith, here's an equivocator, that could   8
swear in both the scales against either scale, who
committed treason enough for God's sake, yet could
not equivocate to heaven. Oh, come in, equivocator.
(*Knock.*) Knock, knock, knock! Who's there? Faith,
here's an English tailor come hither for stealing out of 13
a French hose. Come in, tailor. Here you may roast   14
your goose. (*Knock.*) Knock, knock! Never at quiet!   15

---

67 **one red** one all-pervading red.   72–3 **Your . . . unattended** Your
preoccupation with yourself has left you inattentive to other matters.
74 **nightgown** dressing gown   75 **to be watchers** to have been awake
and not abed.   77 **To know . . . myself** To come to terms with what I
have done, I would do best to shut out the horror entirely and deny
who I am.
2.3. **Location: Scene continues.** The knocking at the door has
already been heard in 2.2. It is not necessary to assume literally,
however, that Macbeth and Lady Macbeth have been talking near
the *south entry* (2.2.70) where the knocking is heard.
2 **old** plenty of   4 **Beelzebub** a devil.   4–5 **Here's . . . plenty** i.e., Here's
a farmer who has hoarded in anticipation of a scarcity and will be justly
punished by a crop surplus and low prices.   5 **Come in time!** i.e., You
have come in good time!   6 **napkins** handkerchiefs or towels (to mop
up the sweat)   8 **equivocator** (This is regarded by many editors as an
allusion to the trial of the Jesuit Henry Garnet for treason in the spring of
1606 and to the doctrine of equivocation said to have been presented in
his defense; according to this doctrine, a lie was not a lie if the utterer
had in his mind a different meaning in which the utterance was true.)
13–14 **for stealing . . . hose** (French fashions, much in demand by style-
conscious courtiers, no doubt provided opportunities for tailors to skimp
in the making of garments while charging customers the full amount.)
14–15 **roast your goose** heat your tailor's smoothing iron—something
easily done in the flames of hell. (With a pun on the sense, "cook your
goose." A *goose* could also be a long-handled iron, or a prostitute.)

What are you? But this place is too cold for hell. I'll
devil-porter it no further. I had thought to have let in
some of all professions that go the primrose way to
th'everlasting bonfire. (*Knock.*) Anon, anon! [*He opens the
gate.*] I pray you, remember the porter.

Enter Macduff and Lennox.

MACDUFF
Was it so late, friend, ere you went to bed,
That you do lie so late?

PORTER   Faith, sir, we were carousing till the second   23
cock; and drink, sir, is a great provoker of three things. 24

MACDUFF   What three things does drink especially
provoke?

PORTER   Marry, sir, nose-painting, sleep, and urine.   27
Lechery, sir, it provokes and unprovokes: it provokes
the desire but it takes away the performance. Therefore much drink may be said to be an equivocator
with lechery: it makes him and it mars him; it sets him
on and it takes him off; it persuades him and dis-
heartens him, makes him stand to and not stand to;   33
in conclusion, equivocates him in a sleep and, giving   34
him the lie, leaves him.   35

MACDUFF   I believe drink gave thee the lie last night. 36

PORTER   That it did, sir, i'the very throat on me. But I 37
requited him for his lie, and, I think, being too strong
for him, though he took up my legs sometimes, yet I   39
made a shift to cast him.   40

MACDUFF   Is thy master stirring?

Enter Macbeth.

Our knocking has awaked him. Here he comes.
                                          [*Exit Porter.*]

LENNOX
Good morrow, noble sir.

MACBETH   Good morrow, both.

MACDUFF
Is the King stirring, worthy thane?

MACBETH   Not yet.

MACDUFF
He did command me to call timely on him.   45
I have almost slipped the hour.

MACBETH   I'll bring you to him.   46

MACDUFF
I know this is a joyful trouble to you,
But yet 'tis one.

23–4 **second cock** second crowing of the cock before dawn   27 **Marry**
(Originally, an oath, "by the Virgin Mary.")   **nose-painting** i.e., red-
dening of the nose through drink   33 **makes . . . not stand to** arouses
him sexually but then takes away the ability to perform sexually.
(Repeating the idea of the previous phrases about how it *makes him
and mars him*, etc.)   34 **equivocates . . . sleep** (1) lulls him asleep
(2) gives him an erotic experience in dream only   34–5 **giving him
the lie** (1) deceiving him (2) laying him out flat   35 **leaves him**
(1) dissipates as intoxication (2) is passed off as urine.   36 **gave thee
the lie** (1) called you a liar (2) made you unable to stand and put you
to sleep   37 **i'the . . . me** (1) giving me the deepest insult imaginable
(2) literally, going down my throat. (*On* means "of.")   39 **took . . .
legs** made me unable to stand and threw me to the ground as a
wrestler might do   40 **made a shift** managed.   **cast** (1) throw, as in
wrestling (2) vomit   45 **timely** betimes, early   46 **slipped** let slip

MACBETH
  The labor we delight in physics pain.   49
  This is the door.
MACDUFF   I'll make so bold to call,
  For 'tis my limited service.   *Exit Macduff.*   51
LENNOX   Goes the King hence today?
MACBETH   He does; he did appoint so.
LENNOX
  The night has been unruly. Where we lay,
  Our chimneys were blown down, and, as they say,
  Lamentings heard i'th'air, strange screams of death,
  And prophesying with accents terrible   57
  Of dire combustion and confused events   58
  New hatched to the woeful time. The obscure bird   59
  Clamored the livelong night. Some say the earth
  Was feverous and did shake.
MACBETH   'Twas a rough night.
LENNOX
  My young remembrance cannot parallel
  A fellow to it.

          Enter Macduff.

MACDUFF   Oh, horror, horror, horror!
  Tongue nor heart cannot conceive nor name thee!
MACBETH AND LENNOX   What's the matter?
MACDUFF
  Confusion now hath made his masterpiece!   66
  Most sacrilegious murder hath broke ope
  The Lord's anointed temple and stole thence
  The life o'th' building!
MACBETH   What is't you say? The life?
LENNOX   Mean you His Majesty?
MACDUFF
  Approach the chamber and destroy your sight
  With a new Gorgon. Do not bid me speak;   73
  See, and then speak yourselves.
                    Exeunt Macbeth and Lennox.
                          Awake, awake!
  Ring the alarum bell. Murder and treason!
  Banquo and Donalbain, Malcolm, awake!
  Shake off this downy sleep, death's counterfeit,   77
  And look on death itself! Up, up, and see
  The great doom's image! Malcolm, Banquo,   79
  As from your graves rise up and walk like sprites   80
  To countenance this horror! Ring the bell.   *Bell rings.*   81

          Enter Lady [*Macbeth*].

LADY MACBETH   What's the business,
  That such a hideous trumpet calls to parley   83

---

49 physics pain i.e., cures that labor of its troublesome aspect.
51 limited appointed   **57 accents terrible** terrifying utterances
58 combustion tumult   **59 New . . . time** newly born to accompany
the woeful nature of the time.   **obscure bird** owl, the bird of darkness
66 Confusion Destruction   **73 Gorgon** one of three monsters with
hideous faces (Medusa was a Gorgon), whose look turned the beholders to stone.   **77 downy** feathery, unsubstantial   **79 great doom's
image** simulacrum of the Last Judgment, of Doomsday.   **80 As . . .
rise up** (At the Last Judgment, the dead will rise from their graves to
be judged.)   **sprites** souls, ghosts   **81 countenance** (1) be in keeping
with (2) witness   **83 trumpet** (Another metaphorical suggestion of
the Last Judgment; the *trumpet* here is the shouting and the bell.)

  The sleepers of the house? Speak, speak!
MACDUFF   Oh, gentle lady,
  'Tis not for you to hear what I can speak.
  The repetition in a woman's ear   87
  Would murder as it fell.

          Enter Banquo.

                          Oh, Banquo, Banquo,
  Our royal master's murdered!
LADY MACBETH   Woe, alas!
  What, in our house?
BANQUO   Too cruel anywhere.
  Dear Duff, I prithee, contradict thyself
  And say it is not so.

          Enter Macbeth, Lennox, and Ross.

MACBETH
  Had I but died an hour before this chance   93
  I had lived a blessèd time; for from this instant
  There's nothing serious in mortality.   95
  All is but toys. Renown and grace is dead;   96
  The wine of life is drawn, and the mere lees   97
  Is left this vault to brag of.   98

          Enter Malcolm and Donalbain.

DONALBAIN
  What is amiss?
MACBETH   You are, and do not know't.
  The spring, the head, the fountain of your blood
  Is stopped, the very source of it is stopped.
MACDUFF
  Your royal father's murdered.
MALCOLM   Oh, by whom?
LENNOX
  Those of his chamber, as it seemed, had done't.
  Their hands and faces were all badged with blood;   104
  So were their daggers, which unwiped we found
  Upon their pillows. They stared and were distracted;
  No man's life was to be trusted with them.
MACBETH
  Oh, yet I do repent me of my fury,
  That I did kill them.
MACDUFF   Wherefore did you so?
MACBETH
  Who can be wise, amazed, temp'rate and furious,   110
  Loyal and neutral, in a moment? No man.
  Th'expedition of my violent love   112
  Outran the pauser, reason. Here lay Duncan,
  His silver skin laced with his golden blood,   114
  And his gashed stabs looked like a breach in nature   115
  For ruin's wasteful entrance; there the murderers,   116
  Steeped in the colors of their trade, their daggers

---

87 repetition recital, report   **93 chance** occurrence   **95 serious in
mortality** worthwhile in mortal life.   **96 toys** trifles.   **97 lees** dregs
98 vault (1) wine-vault (2) earth, with its vaulted sky   **104 badged**
marked, as with a badge or emblem   **110 amazed** bewildered
112 Th'expedition The haste   **114 golden** (See the note for 2.2.60.)
115 breach in nature gap in the defenses of life. (A metaphor of military siege.)   **116 wasteful** destructive

Unmannerly breeched with gore. Who could refrain 118
That had a heart to love, and in that heart
Courage to make 's love known?
LADY MACBETH [*fainting*]   Help me hence, ho! 120
MACDUFF
Look to the lady.
MALCOLM [*aside to Donalbain*]
            Why do we hold our tongues,
That most may claim this argument for ours? 122
DONALBAIN [*aside to Malcolm*]
What should be spoken here, where our fate,
Hid in an auger hole, may rush and seize us? 124
Let's away. Our tears are not yet brewed. 125
MALCOLM [*aside to Donalbain*]
Nor our strong sorrow upon the foot of motion. 126
BANQUO   Look to the lady.
            [*Lady Macbeth is helped out.*]
And when we have our naked frailties hid, 128
That suffer in exposure, let us meet
And question this most bloody piece of work 130
To know it further. Fears and scruples shake us. 131
In the great hand of God I stand, and thence 132
Against the undivulged pretense I fight 133
Of treasonous malice.
MACDUFF   And so do I.
ALL   So all. 134
MACBETH
Let's briefly put on manly readiness 135
And meet i'th' hall together.
ALL   Well contented.
            Exeunt [all but Malcolm and Donalbain].
MALCOLM
What will you do? Let's not consort with them. 137
To show an unfelt sorrow is an office
Which the false man does easy. I'll to England. 139
DONALBAIN
To Ireland, I. Our separated fortune
Shall keep us both the safer. Where we are,
There's daggers in men's smiles; the nea'er in blood, 142
The nearer bloody.
MALCOLM   This murderous shaft that's shot 143
Hath not yet lighted, and our safest way 144
Is to avoid the aim. Therefore to horse,
And let us not be dainty of leave-taking, 146
But shift away. There's warrant in that theft 147

118 **breeched with gore** covered (as with breeches) to the hilts with gore. 120 **make 's love known** make manifest his love. 122 **That . . . ours** we to whom this business matters most. 124 **in an auger hole** i.e., in some hiding place, in ambush. (An *auger* is a hole-drilling tool.) 125 **Our . . . brewed** i.e., Our real sorrow has not yet ripened. 126 **upon . . . motion** yet prepared to express itself fully. 128 **our naked frailties hid** clothed our poor, shivering bodies (which remind us of our human frailty) 130 **question** discuss 131 **scruples** doubts, suspicions 132–4 **thence . . . malice** with God's help, I will fight against the as-yet-unknown purpose that prompted this treason. 133 **pretense** design 134 **malice** enmity. 135 **briefly** quickly. **manly readiness** men's clothing and resolute purpose 137 **consort** keep company, associate 139 **easy** easily. 142–3 **the nea'er . . . bloody** the closer the relationship, the greater the danger to be feared of bloody intent. 144 **lighted** alighted, descended 146 **dainty of** tediously ceremonious in 147 **shift away** disappear by stealth. **warrant** justification

Which steals itself when there's no mercy left.
            Exeunt.

❖

2.4

            Enter Ross with an Old Man.

OLD MAN
Threescore and ten I can remember well,
Within the volume of which time I have seen
Hours dreadful and things strange, but this sore night 3
Hath trifled former knowings.
ROSS   Ha, good father, 4
Thou see'st the heavens, as troubled with man's act, 5
Threatens his bloody stage. By th' clock 'tis day, 6
And yet dark night strangles the traveling lamp. 7
Is't night's predominance or the day's shame
That darkness does the face of earth entomb
When living light should kiss it?
OLD MAN   'Tis unnatural,
Even like the deed that's done. On Tuesday last
A falcon, tow'ring in her pride of place, 12
Was by a mousing owl hawked at and killed. 13
ROSS
And Duncan's horses—a thing most strange and
            certain—
Beauteous and swift, the minions of their race, 15
Turned wild in nature, broke their stalls, flung out,
Contending 'gainst obedience, as they would 17
Make war with mankind.
OLD MAN   'Tis said they eat each other. 18
ROSS
They did so, to th'amazement of mine eyes
That looked upon't.
            Enter Macduff.
                        Here comes the good Macduff.—
How goes the world, sir, now?
MACDUFF   Why, see you not?
ROSS
Is't known who did this more than bloody deed?
MACDUFF
Those that Macbeth hath slain.
ROSS   Alas the day,
What good could they pretend?
MACDUFF   They were suborned. 24
Malcolm and Donalbain, the King's two sons,
Are stol'n away and fled, which puts upon them
Suspicion of the deed.
ROSS   'Gainst nature still!

2.4. Location: Outside Macbeth's castle of Inverness.
3 **sore** dreadful, grievous 4 **trifled former knowings** made trivial all former experiences. **father** old man 5–6 **the heavens . . . stage** a solar eclipse threatens disapprovingly our human scene of murder. (With a theatrical metaphor in *heavens* [the decorated roof over the stage], *act*, and *stage*.) 7 **traveling lamp** i.e., sun. 12 **tow'ring** circling higher and higher. (A term in falconry.) **place** pitch, highest point in the falcon's flight 13 **mousing** i.e., ordinarily preying on mice 15 **minions** darlings 17 **as** as if 18 **eat** ate. (Pronounced "et.") 24 **What . . . pretend?** i.e., what could they hope to gain by it? **suborned** bribed, hired.

Thriftless ambition, that will ravin up   28
Thine own life's means! Then 'tis most like   29
The sovereignty will fall upon Macbeth.

MACDUFF
He is already named and gone to Scone   31
To be invested.

ROSS   Where is Duncan's body?

MACDUFF   Carried to Colmekill,   33
The sacred storehouse of his predecessors
And guardian of their bones.

ROSS   Will you to Scone?

MACDUFF
No, cousin, I'll to Fife.

ROSS   Well, I will thither.   36

MACDUFF
Well, may you see things well done there. Adieu,
Lest our old robes sit easier than our new!

ROSS   Farewell, father.

OLD MAN
God's benison go with you, and with those   40
That would make good of bad, and friends of foes!
                                    Exeunt omnes.

❖

3.1

Enter Banquo.

BANQUO
Thou hast it now—King, Cawdor, Glamis, all
As the weird women promised, and I fear
Thou played'st most foully for't. Yet it was said
It should not stand in thy posterity,   4
But that myself should be the root and father
Of many kings. If there come truth from them—
As upon thee, Macbeth, their speeches shine—   7
Why, by the verities on thee made good,
May they not be my oracles as well
And set me up in hope? But hush, no more.   10

        Sennet sounded. Enter Macbeth as King, Lady
        [Macbeth], Lennox, Ross, lords, and attendants.

MACBETH
Here's our chief guest.

LADY MACBETH   If he had been forgotten,
It had been as a gap in our great feast
And all-thing unbecoming.   13

MACBETH
Tonight we hold a solemn supper, sir,   14
And I'll request your presence.

BANQUO   Let Your Highness
Command upon me, to the which my duties   16

Are with a most indissoluble tie
Forever knit.

MACBETH   Ride you this afternoon?

BANQUO   Ay, my good lord.

MACBETH
We should have else desired your good advice,
Which still hath been both grave and prosperous,   22
In this day's council; but we'll take tomorrow.
Is't far you ride?

BANQUO
As far, my lord, as will fill up the time
Twixt this and supper. Go not my horse the better,   26
I must become a borrower of the night
For a dark hour or twain.

MACBETH   Fail not our feast.

BANQUO   My lord, I will not.

MACBETH
We hear our bloody cousins are bestowed   31
In England and in Ireland, not confessing
Their cruel parricide, filling their hearers
With strange invention. But of that tomorrow,   34
When therewithal we shall have cause of state   35
Craving us jointly. Hie you to horse. Adieu,   36
Till you return at night. Goes Fleance with you?

BANQUO
Ay, my good lord. Our time does call upon 's.

MACBETH
I wish your horses swift and sure of foot,
And so I do commend you to their backs.   40
Farewell.   *Exit Banquo.*
Let every man be master of his time
Till seven at night. To make society
The sweeter welcome, we will keep ourself   44
Till suppertime alone. While then, God be with you!   45
        Exeunt Lords [and all but Macbeth and a Servant].
Sirrah, a word with you. Attend those men   46
Our pleasure?

SERVANT
They are, my lord, without the palace gate.

MACBETH
Bring them before us.   *Exit Servant.*
                        To be thus is nothing,   49
But to be safely thus.—Our fears in Banquo   50
Stick deep, and in his royalty of nature   51
Reigns that which would be feared. 'Tis much he
    dares;   52
And to that dauntless temper of his mind   53
He hath a wisdom that doth guide his valor
To act in safety. There is none but he
Whose being I do fear; and under him
My genius is rebuked, as it is said   57

---

28 Thriftless Spendthrift.   **ravin up** devour ravenously   **29 like**
likely   **31 named** chosen. (See the note for 1.4.50.)   **Scone** ancient
royal city of Scotland near Perth   **33 Colmekill** Icolmkill, i.e., Cell of
St. Columba, the barren islet of Iona in the Western Islands, a sacred
spot where the kings were buried; here, called a *storehouse*   **36 Fife**
(Of which Macduff is Thane.)   **40 bension** blessing
3.1. Location: Forres. The palace.
4 stand stay, remain   **7 shine** beam favorably   **10.1** *Sennet* trumpet
call   **13 all-thing** in every way   **14 solemn** ceremonious   **16 Com-**
mand lay your command

22 still always.   **grave and prosperous** weighty and profitable
26 this this present moment.   **Go . . . better** Unless my horse makes
better time than I expect   **31 bestowed** lodged   **34 invention** falsehood.   **35 therewithal** besides that   **35–6 cause . . . jointly** questions
of state occupying our joint attention.   **40 commend** commit, entrust
44 we . . . ourself I will keep to myself   **45 While** Till   **46 Sirrah** (A
form of address to a social inferior.)   **49 thus** i.e., king   **50 But**
unless.   **in** concerning   **51 royalty of nature** natural kingly bearing
52 would be deserves to be   **53 to** added to   **57 My genius is**
rebuked my guardian spirit is daunted or abashed

Mark Antony's was by Caesar. He chid the sisters   58
When first they put the name of king upon me,
And bade them speak to him. Then, prophetlike,
They hailed him father to a line of kings.
Upon my head they placed a fruitless crown
And put a barren scepter in my grip,
Thence to be wrenched with an unlineal hand,   64
No son of mine succeeding. If't be so,
For Banquo's issue have I filed my mind;   66
For them the gracious Duncan have I murdered,
Put rancors in the vessel of my peace   68
Only for them, and mine eternal jewel   69
Given to the common enemy of man   70
To make them kings, the seeds of Banquo kings.
Rather than so, come fate into the list,   72
And champion me to th'utterance!—Who's there?   73

Enter Servant and two Murderers.

Now go to the door, and stay there till we call.
                                                    Exit Servant.
Was it not yesterday we spoke together?
MURDERERS
    It was, so please Your Highness.
MACBETH   Well then, now
    Have you considered of my speeches? Know
    That it was he in the times past which held you
    So under fortune, which you thought had been   79
    Our innocent self. This I made good to you
    In our last conference, passed in probation with you   81
    How you were borne in hand, how crossed, the
        instruments,   82
    Who wrought with them, and all things else that
        might   83
    To half a soul and to a notion crazed   84
    Say, "Thus did Banquo."
FIRST MURDERER   You made it known to us.
MACBETH
    I did so, and went further, which is now
    Our point of second meeting. Do you find
    Your patience so predominant in your nature
    That you can let this go? Are you so gospeled   89
    To pray for this good man and for his issue,
    Whose heavy hand hath bowed you to the grave
    And beggared yours forever?
FIRST MURDERER   We are men, my liege.   92
MACBETH
    Ay, in the catalogue ye go for men,   93
    As hounds and greyhounds, mongrels, spaniels, curs,

Shoughs, water-rugs, and demi-wolves are clept   95
All by the name of dogs. The valued file   96
Distinguishes the swift, the slow, the subtle,
The housekeeper, the hunter, every one   98
According to the gift which bounteous nature
Hath in him closed, whereby he does receive   100
Particular addition from the bill   101
That writes them all alike; and so of men.   102
Now, if you have a station in the file,   103
Not i'th' worst rank of manhood, say't,   104
And I will put that business in your bosoms
Whose execution takes your enemy off,   106
Grapples you to the heart and love of us,
Who wear our health but sickly in his life,   108
Which in his death were perfect.
SECOND MURDERER   I am one, my liege,
    Whom the vile blows and buffets of the world
    Hath so incensed that I am reckless what
    I do to spite the world.
FIRST MURDERER   And I another,
    So weary with disasters, tugged with fortune,   113
    That I would set my life on any chance   114
    To mend it or be rid on't.
MACBETH   Both of you
    Know Banquo was your enemy.
BOTH MURDERERS   True, my lord.
MACBETH
    So is he mine, and in such bloody distance   117
    That every minute of his being thrusts   118
    Against my near'st of life. And though I could   119
    With barefaced power sweep him from my sight   120
    And bid my will avouch it, yet I must not,   121
    For certain friends that are both his and mine,   122
    Whose loves I may not drop, but wail his fall   123
    Who I myself struck down. And thence it is   124
    That I to your assistance do make love,   125
    Masking the business from the common eye
    For sundry weighty reasons.
SECOND MURDERER   We shall, my lord,
    Perform what you command us.
FIRST MURDERER   Though our lives—
MACBETH
    Your spirits shine through you. Within this hour at
        most   129
    I will advise you where to plant yourselves,

---

58 **Caesar** Octavius Caesar. 64 **with** by. **unlineal** not of lineal descent from me 66 **filed** defiled 68 **rancors** malignant enemies (here visualized as a poison added to a vessel full of wholesome drink) 69 **eternal jewel** i.e., soul 70 **common . . . man** i.e., devil 72 **list** lists, place of combat 73 **champion me** fight with me in single combat. **to th'utterance** to the last extremity (French, *à l'outrance*). 79 **under fortune** down in your fortunes 81–3 **passed . . . with them** went over the proof with you how you were deceived by false promises, how you were thwarted, who the agents were, who directed their activities 84 **To . . . crazed** even to a half-wit of unsound mind 89 **gospeled** imbued with the gospel spirit 92 **yours** your family 93 **go for** pass for, are entered for

95 **Shoughs . . . clept** shaggy lap-dogs, long-haired water dogs, and dogs that have been crossbred with wolves are called 96 **valued file** list classified according to value 98 **housekeeper** watchdog 100 **in him closed** enclosed in him 101–2 **Particular . . . alike** particular qualification apart from the catalog that lists them all indiscriminately 103–4 **if . . . manhood** if you occupy not the worst of places in the *rank and file* of men 106 **Whose execution** the doing of which 108 **in his life** while he lives 113 **tugged with** pulled about by (as in wrestling) 114 **set** risk, stake 117 **distance** (1) hostility, enmity (2) interval of distance between fencers 118–19 **thrusts . . . life** stabs me to the heart. 120 **With barefaced power** by open use of my supreme royal authority 121 **And . . . avouch it** and use my mere wish as my justification 122 **For** because of, for the sake of 123–4 **wail . . . Who** I must bewail the death of him whom 125 **That . . . love** that I woo your aid 129 **Your . . . you** i.e., Enough; I can see your determination in your faces.

Acquaint you with the perfect spy o'th' time,   131
The moment on't, for't must be done tonight,   132
And something from the palace; always thought   133
That I require a clearness. And with him—   134
To leave no rubs nor botches in the work—   135
Fleance his son, that keeps him company,
Whose absence is no less material to me
Than is his father's, must embrace the fate
Of that dark hour. Resolve yourselves apart;   139
I'll come to you anon.
BOTH MURDERERS   We are resolved, my lord.
MACBETH
I'll call upon you straight. Abide within.

                                            Exeunt [Murderers].
It is concluded. Banquo, thy soul's flight,
If it find heaven, must find it out tonight.   [*Exit.*]

❖

3.2

Enter Macbeth's Lady and a Servant.

LADY MACBETH   Is Banquo gone from court?
SERVANT
Ay, madam, but returns again tonight.
LADY MACBETH
Say to the King I would attend his leisure
For a few words.
SERVANT   Madam, I will.   *Exit.*
LADY MACBETH   Naught's had, all's spent,
Where our desire is got without content.   7
'Tis safer to be that which we destroy
Than by destruction dwell in doubtful joy.   9

        Enter Macbeth.

How now, my lord? Why do you keep alone,
Of sorriest fancies your companions making,   11
Using those thoughts which should indeed have died   12
With them they think on? Things without all remedy
Should be without regard. What's done is done.   14
MACBETH
We have scorched the snake, not killed it.   15
She'll close and be herself, whilst our poor malice   16
Remains in danger of her former tooth.   17
But let the frame of things disjoint, both the worlds
    suffer,   18
Ere we will eat our meal in fear and sleep
In the affliction of these terrible dreams

That shake us nightly. Better be with the dead,
Whom we, to gain our peace, have sent to peace,   22
Than on the torture of the mind to lie   23
In restless ecstasy. Duncan is in his grave;   24
After life's fitful fever he sleeps well.
Treason has done his worst; nor steel, nor poison,   26
Malice domestic, foreign levy, nothing   27
Can touch him further.
LADY MACBETH   Come on,
Gentle my lord, sleek o'er your rugged looks.   30
Be bright and jovial among your guests tonight.
MACBETH
So shall I, love, and so, I pray, be you.
Let your remembrance apply to Banquo;   33
Present him eminence, both with eye and tongue—   34
Unsafe the while, that we   35
Must lave our honors in these flattering streams   36
And make our faces vizards to our hearts,   37
Disguising what they are.
LADY MACBETH   You must leave this.
MACBETH
Oh, full of scorpions is my mind, dear wife!
Thou know'st that Banquo and his Fleance lives.
LADY MACBETH
But in them nature's copy's not eterne.   41
MACBETH
There's comfort yet; they are assailable.
Then be thou jocund. Ere the bat hath flown
His cloistered flight, ere to black Hecate's summons   44
The shard-borne beetle with his drowsy hums   45
Hath rung night's yawning peal, there shall be done   46
A deed of dreadful note.
LADY MACBETH   What's to be done?
MACBETH
Be innocent of the knowledge, dearest chuck,   48
Till thou applaud the deed. Come, seeling night,   49
Scarf up the tender eye of pitiful day,   50
And with thy bloody and invisible hand
Cancel and tear to pieces that great bond   52
Which keeps me pale! Light thickens,   53
And the crow makes wing to th' rooky wood;   54
Good things of day begin to droop and drowse,

131–2 **with . . . on't** with full and precise instructions as to when it is
to be done. (*Spy* means "espial, observation.") **133 something from**
some distance removed from. **thought** being borne in mind
134 clearness freedom from suspicion. **135 rubs** defects, rough
spots **139 Resolve yourselves apart** Make up your minds in private
conference
3.2. Location: The palace.
7 content contentedness. **9 Than . . . joy** than by destroying achieve
only an apprehensive joy. **11 sorriest** most despicable or wretched
12 Using keeping company with, entertaining **14 without regard**
not pondered upon. **15 scorched** slashed, cut **16 close** heal, close
up again. **poor malice** feeble hostility **17 her former tooth** her
fang, just as before. **18 let . . . suffer** let the universe itself fall apart,
both heaven and earth perish

22 to gain . . . to peace to gain contentedness through satisfied ambition, have sent to eternal rest **23 torture** rack **24 ecstasy** frenzy.
26 nor steel neither steel **27 Malice domestic** civil war. **foreign
levy** the levying of troops abroad (against Scotland) **30 Gentle . . .
looks** my noble lord, smooth over your rough looks. **33 Let . . .
apply** Remember to pay special attention **34 eminence** favor
35–6 Unsafe . . . streams we being unsafe at present, we must put on
a show of flattering cordiality to make clean our honor. (To *lave* is to
wash.) **37 vizards** masks **41 nature's . . . eterne** nature's pattern
will not continue forever. **44 cloistered** secluded. **Hecate** goddess
of night and witchcraft, as in 2.1.53 **45 shard-borne** borne on shards,
or horny wing cases, or, *shard-born*, bred in cow-droppings (shards)
46 yawning drowsy **48 chuck** (A term of endearment.) **49 seeling**
eye-closing. (Night is pictured here as a falconer sewing up the eyes
of day lest it should struggle against the deed that is to be done.)
50 Scarf up blindfold. **pitiful** compassionate **52 that . . . bond** i.e.,
the bond of natural and moral law (here associated with the full light
of day) **53 pale** sickly, pallid (like moonlight, contrasted with the
full light of day); also, pallid from fear. **Light thickens** Darkness is
coming on **54 crow** rook. **rooky** full of rooks

Whiles night's black agents to their preys do rouse.   56
Thou marvel'st at my words, but hold thee still.
Things bad begun make strong themselves by ill.
So, prithee, go with me.   *Exeunt.*

❦

3.3

Enter three Murderers.

FIRST MURDERER [*to the Third Murderer*]
But who did bid thee join with us?

THIRD MURDERER   Macbeth.

SECOND MURDERER [*to the First Murderer*]
He needs not our mistrust, since he delivers   2
Our offices and what we have to do   3
To the direction just.

FIRST MURDERER   Then stand with us.   4
The west yet glimmers with some streaks of day.
Now spurs the lated traveler apace   6
To gain the timely inn, and near approaches   7
The subject of our watch.

THIRD MURDERER   Hark, I hear horses.

BANQUO (*within*) Give us a light there, ho!

SECOND MURDERER   Then 'tis he. The rest
That are within the note of expectation   12
Already are i'th' court.

FIRST MURDERER   His horses go about.   14

THIRD MURDERER
Almost a mile; but he does usually—
So all men do—from hence to th' palace gate
Make it their walk.

Enter Banquo and Fleance, with a torch.

SECOND MURDERER   A light, a light!

THIRD MURDERER   'Tis he.

FIRST MURDERER   Stand to't.

BANQUO   It will be rain tonight.

FIRST MURDERER   Let it come down!
                              [*They attack Banquo.*]

BANQUO
Oh, treachery! Fly, good Fleance, fly, fly, fly!
Thou mayst revenge.—Oh, slave!
                        [*He dies. Fleance escapes.*]

THIRD MURDERER
Who did strike out the light?

FIRST MURDERER   Was't not the way?   25

THIRD MURDERER
There's but one down; the son is fled.

SECOND MURDERER
We have lost best half of our affair.

FIRST MURDERER
Well, let's away and say how much is done.   28
                                        Exeunt.

❦

3.4

*Banquet prepared. Enter Macbeth, Lady
[Macbeth], Ross, Lennox, Lords, and attendants.*

MACBETH
You know your own degrees; sit down. At first   1
And last, the hearty welcome.   [*They sit.*]

LORDS   Thanks to Your Majesty. 2

MACBETH
Ourself will mingle with society   3
And play the humble host.
Our hostess keeps her state, but in best time   5
We will require her welcome.   6

LADY MACBETH
Pronounce it for me, sir, to all our friends,
For my heart speaks they are welcome.

Enter First Murderer [to the door].

MACBETH
See, they encounter thee with their hearts' thanks.   9
Both sides are even. Here I'll sit i'th' midst. 10
Be large in mirth; anon we'll drink a measure   11
The table round. [*He goes to the Murderer.*] There's
        blood upon thy face.

MURDERER   'Tis Banquo's, then.

MACBETH
'Tis better thee without than he within.   14
Is he dispatched?

MURDERER
My lord, his throat is cut. That I did for him.

MACBETH   Thou art the best o'th' cutthroats.
Yet he's good that did the like for Fleance;
If thou didst it, thou art the nonpareil.   19

MURDERER   Most royal sir, Fleance is scaped.

MACBETH
Then comes my fit again. I had else been perfect,
Whole as the marble, founded as the rock,   22
As broad and general as the casing air.   23
But now I am cabined, cribbed, confined, bound in 24
To saucy doubts and fears. But Banquo's safe?   25

---

56 to . . . rouse bestir themselves to hunt their prey.
3.3. Location: A park near the palace.
2–4 He . . . just We need not mistrust this man, since the instructions
he brings from Macbeth are so precise.   **6 lated** belated   **7 timely**
arrived at in good time   **12 within . . . expectation** in the list of those
expected   **14 go about** i.e., can be heard as servants take the horses
to the stables (while Banquo and Fleance, provided with a torch, walk
from the palace gate to the castle).   **25 way** i.e., thing to do.

28.1 Exeunt (Presumably, the murderers drag the body of Banquo offstage as they go.)
3.4. Location: A room of state in the palace.
1 degrees ranks (as a determinant of seating)   **1–2 At . . . last** Once
for all   **3 mingle with society** i.e., leave the chair of state and circulate among the guests   **5 keeps her state** remains in her canopied
chair of state.   **in best time** when it is most appropriate   **6 require
her welcome** call upon her to give the welcome.   **9 encounter**
respond to   **10 even** full, with equal numbers on both sides.
11 large liberal, free.   **measure** i.e., cup filled to the brim for a toast
14 'Tis . . . within It is better to have his blood on you than he to have
it within him.   **19 the nonpareil** without equal.   **22 founded** firmly
established   **23 broad and general** unconfined.   **casing** encasing,
enveloping   **24 cribbed** shut in   **25 saucy** sharp, impudent, importunate

MURDERER
Ay, my good lord. Safe in a ditch he bides,
With twenty trenchèd gashes on his head,
The least a death to nature.

MACBETH   Thanks for that.
There the grown serpent lies; the worm that's fled   29
Hath nature that in time will venom breed,
No teeth for th' present. Get thee gone. Tomorrow
We'll hear ourselves again.   *Exit Murderer.*

LADY MACBETH   My royal lord,   32
You do not give the cheer. The feast is sold   33
That is not often vouched, while 'tis a-making,   34
'Tis given with welcome. To feed were best at home;   35
From thence, the sauce to meat is ceremony;   36
Meeting were bare without it.

>   *Enter the Ghost of Banquo, and sits in Macbeth's*
>   *place.*

MACBETH   Sweet remembrancer!   37
Now, good digestion wait on appetite,   38
And health on both!

LENNOX   May't please Your Highness sit?

MACBETH
Here had we now our country's honor roofed   40
Were the gracèd person of our Banquo present,
Who may I rather challenge for unkindness   42
Than pity for mischance.

ROSS   His absence, sir,
Lays blame upon his promise. Please't Your Highness
To grace us with your royal company?

MACBETH [*seeing his place occupied*]
The table's full.

LENNOX   Here is a place reserved, sir.

MACBETH   Where?

LENNOX
Here, my good lord. What is't that moves Your
   Highness?

MACBETH
Which of you have done this?

LORDS   What, my good lord?

MACBETH
Thou canst not say I did it. Never shake
Thy gory locks at me.

ROSS
Gentlemen, rise. His Highness is not well.
                          [*They start to rise.*]

LADY MACBETH
Sit, worthy friends. My lord is often thus,
And hath been from his youth. Pray you, keep seat.
The fit is momentary; upon a thought   55
He will again be well. If much you note him

You shall offend him and extend his passion.   57
Feed, and regard him not.—[*She confers apart with*
   Macbeth.] Are you a man?

MACBETH
Ay, and a bold one, that dare look on that
Which might appall the devil.

LADY MACBETH   Oh, proper stuff!   60
This is the very painting of your fear.
This is the air-drawn dagger which, you said,   62
Led you to Duncan. Oh, these flaws and starts,   63
Impostors to true fear, would well become   64
A woman's story at a winter's fire,
Authorized by her grandam. Shame itself!   66
Why do you make such faces? When all's done,
You look but on a stool.

MACBETH   Prithee, see there!
Behold, look! Lo, how say you?—
Why, what care I? If thou canst nod, speak too.   70
If charnel houses and our graves must send   71
Those that we bury back, our monuments   72
Shall be the maws of kites.   [*Exit Ghost.*]   73

LADY MACBETH   What, quite unmanned in folly?

MACBETH
If I stand here, I saw him.

LADY MACBETH   Fie, for shame!

MACBETH
Blood hath been shed ere now, i'th' olden time,
Ere humane statute purged the gentle weal;   77
Ay, and since too, murders have been performed
Too terrible for the ear. The time has been
That, when the brains were out, the man would die,
And there an end; but now they rise again
With twenty mortal murders on their crowns,   82
And push us from our stools. This is more strange
Than such a murder is.

LADY MACBETH   My worthy lord,
Your noble friends do lack you.

MACBETH   I do forget.
Do not muse at me, my most worthy friends;
I have a strange infirmity, which is nothing
To those that know me. Come, love and health to all!
Then I'll sit down. Give me some wine. Fill full.
                          [*He is given wine.*]

>   *Enter Ghost.*

I drink to th' general joy o'th' whole table,
And to our dear friend Banquo, whom we miss.
Would he were here! To all, and him, we thirst,   92

---

29 worm small serpent   **32 hear ourselves** personally confer
33 give the cheer welcome your guests.   **33–5 The feast . . . welcome**
A feast seems grudgingly and mercenarily given unless it is repeatedly graced with assurances of welcome.   **35–7 To feed . . . without**
it Plain eating is best done in one's own domestic setting; on more
social occasions, the spice to a feast is ceremony; gatherings are too
unadorned without it.   **38 wait on** attend   **40 roofed** under one roof
42 Who . . . unkindness whom I hope I may sooner reprove for negligence   **55 upon a thought** in a moment

57 offend him make him worse   **60 Oh, proper stuff!** Oh, stuff and
nonsense!   **62 air-drawn** made of thin air, or floating disembodied in
space   **63 flaws** gusts, outbursts   **64 to** compared with.   **become**
befit   **66 Authorized by** told on the authority of   **70 thou** Banquo
71 charnel houses depositories for bones or bodies   **72–3 our . . .**
kites i.e., we will have to leave the unburied bodies to scavenging
birds of prey.   **77 Ere . . . weal** before the institution of law cleansed
the commonwealth of violence and made it civilized. (*Humane,* interchangeable with *human,* means both "appertaining to humankind"
and "benevolent, civilizing.")   **82 mortal murders** deadly wounds.
crowns heads   **92 thirst** desire to drink

And all to all.

LORDS   Our duties and the pledge.   93
[*They drink.*]

MACBETH [*seeing the Ghost*]
Avaunt, and quit my sight! Let the earth hide thee!
Thy bones are marrowless, thy blood is cold;
Thou hast no speculation in those eyes   96
Which thou dost glare with!

LADY MACBETH   Think of this, good peers,
But as a thing of custom. 'Tis no other;
Only it spoils the pleasure of the time.

MACBETH   What man dare, I dare.
Approach thou like the rugged Russian bear,
The armed rhinoceros, or th' Hyrcan tiger;   102
Take any shape but that, and my firm nerves   103
Shall never tremble. Or be alive again
And dare me to the desert with thy sword.   105
If trembling I inhabit then, protest me   106
The baby of a girl. Hence, horrible shadow!   107
Unreal mockery, hence!   [*Exit Ghost.*]
                      Why, so; being gone,
I am a man again. Pray you, sit still.

LADY MACBETH
You have displaced the mirth, broke the good meeting
With most admired disorder.

MACBETH   Can such things be,   111
And overcome us like a summer's cloud,   112
Without our special wonder? You make me strange   113
Even to the disposition that I owe,   114
When now I think you can behold such sights
And keep the natural ruby of your cheeks
When mine is blanched with fear.

ROSS   What sights, my lord?

LADY MACBETH
I pray you, speak not. He grows worse and worse;
Question enrages him. At once, good night.   119
Stand not upon the order of your going,   120
But go at once.

LENNOX   Good night, and better health
Attend His Majesty!

LADY MACBETH   A kind good night to all!
                      Exeunt Lords [*and attendants*].

MACBETH
It will have blood, they say; blood will have blood.
Stones have been known to move, and trees to speak;   124
Augurs and understood relations have   125
By maggotpies and choughs and rooks brought forth   126
The secret'st man of blood. What is the night?   127

LADY MACBETH
Almost at odds with morning, which is which.

MACBETH
How say'st thou, that Macduff denies his person   129
At our great bidding?

LADY MACBETH   Did you send to him, sir?

MACBETH
I hear it by the way; but I will send.   131
There's not a one of them but in his house   132
I keep a servant fee'd. I will tomorrow—   133
And betimes I will—to the Weird Sisters.   134
More shall they speak, for now I am bent to know   135
By the worst means the worst. For mine own good
All causes shall give way. I am in blood   137
Stepped in so far that, should I wade no more,   138
Returning were as tedious as go o'er.   139
Strange things I have in head, that will to hand,
Which must be acted ere they may be scanned.   141

LADY MACBETH
You lack the season of all natures, sleep.   142

MACBETH
Come, we'll to sleep. My strange and self-abuse   143
Is the initiate fear that wants hard use.   144
We are yet but young in deed.   *Exeunt.*

❖

3.5

*Thunder. Enter the three Witches, meeting
Hecate.*

FIRST WITCH
Why, how now, Hecate? You look angerly.   1

HECATE
Have I not reason, beldams as you are?   2
Saucy and overbold, how did you dare
To trade and traffic with Macbeth
In riddles and affairs of death,
And I, the mistress of your charms,
The close contriver of all harms,   7
Was never called to bear my part
Or show the glory of our art?
And, which is worse, all you have done
Hath been but for a wayward son,
Spiteful and wrathful, who, as others do,
Loves for his own ends, not for you.
But make amends now. Get you gone,
And at the pit of Acheron   15

93 **all to all** all good wishes to all, or, let all drink to everyone else.
96 **speculation** power of sight   102 **armed** armor-plated.   **Hyrcan** of
Hyrcania, in ancient times a region near the Caspian Sea   103 **nerves**
sinews   105 **the desert** some solitary place   106–7 **If . . . girl** If then I
tremble, proclaim me a baby girl, or a girl's doll.   111 **admired disorder**
wondered-at lack of self-control.   112 **overcome** come over   113–14 **You
make . . . owe** You cause me to feel I do not know my own nature (which
I had presumed to be that of a brave man)   119 **At once** To you all; now
120 **Stand . . . going** Do not take the time to leave in ceremonious order
of rank, as you entered   124 **Stones . . . speak** i.e., Even inanimate
nature speaks in such a way as to reveal the unnatural act of murder
125–7 **Augurs . . . blood** Prophets versed in the interpretation of occult
mysteries have, by reading the signs of magpies and jackdaws, revealed
secret murderers.   127 **the night** i.e., the time of night.

129 **How say'st thou** What do you say to the fact   131 **by the way**
indirectly   132 **them** my Scottish nobles   133 **fee'd** i.e., paid to spy.
134 **betimes** (1) early (2) while there is still time   135 **bent** determined   137 **All causes** all other considerations   138 **should . . . more**
even if I were to wade no farther   139 **were** would be.   **go o'er** to
proceed.   141 **acted . . . scanned** put into performance even before
there is time to scrutinize them.   142 **season** preservative   143–4 **My
. . . use** My strange self-punishing fear is that felt by a novice who
lacks toughening experience.
3.5. Location: A heath. (This scene is probably by another author.)
1 **angerly** angrily, angry.   2 **beldams** hags   7 **close** secret
15 **Acheron** the river of sorrows in Hades; here, hell itself

Meet me i'th' morning. Thither he
Will come to know his destiny.
Your vessels and your spells provide,
Your charms and everything beside.
I am for th'air. This night I'll spend
Unto a dismal and a fatal end.   21
Great business must be wrought ere noon.
Upon the corner of the moon
There hangs a vap'rous drop profound;   24
I'll catch it ere it come to ground,
And that, distilled by magic sleights,
Shall raise such artificial sprites   27
As by the strength of their illusion
Shall draw him on to his confusion.   29
He shall spurn fate, scorn death, and bear
His hopes 'bove wisdom, grace, and fear.
And you all know, security   32
Is mortals' chiefest enemy.   *Music and a song.*
Hark! I am called. My little spirit, see,
Sits in a foggy cloud and stays for me.   [*Exit.*]   35
        Sing within, "Come away, come away," *etc.*
FIRST WITCH
Come, let's make haste. She'll soon be back again.
                                                  Exeunt.

❖

3.6

Enter Lennox and another Lord.

LENNOX
My former speeches have but hit your thoughts,   1
Which can interpret farther. Only I say   2
Things have been strangely borne. The gracious
    Duncan   3
Was pitied of Macbeth; marry, he was dead.   4
And the right valiant Banquo walked too late,
Whom you may say, if't please you, Fleance killed,
For Fleance fled. Men must not walk too late.
Who cannot want the thought how monstrous   8
It was for Malcolm and for Donalbain
To kill their gracious father? Damnèd fact!   10
How it did grieve Macbeth! Did he not straight   11
In pious rage the two delinquents tear
That were the slaves of drink and thralls of sleep?   13
Was not that nobly done? Ay, and wisely too;
For 'twould have angered any heart alive
To hear the men deny't. So that I say

He has borne all things well; and I do think   17
That had he Duncan's sons under his key—
As, an't please heaven, he shall not—they should find   19
What 'twere to kill a father. So should Fleance.
But peace! For from broad words, and 'cause he failed   21
His presence at the tyrant's feast, I hear   22
Macduff lives in disgrace. Sir, can you tell
Where he bestows himself?
LORD   The son of Duncan,   24
From whom this tyrant holds the due of birth,   25
Lives in the English court, and is received
Of the most pious Edward with such grace   27
That the malevolence of fortune nothing
Takes from his high respect. Thither Macduff   29
Is gone to pray the holy king, upon his aid,   30
To wake Northumberland and warlike Siward,   31
That by the help of these—with Him above
To ratify the work—we may again
Give to our tables meat, sleep to our nights,   34
Free from our feasts and banquets bloody knives,   35
Do faithful homage, and receive free honors—   36
All which we pine for now. And this report
Hath so exasperate the King that he   38
Prepares for some attempt of war.
LENNOX   Sent he to Macduff?
LORD
He did; and with an absolute "Sir, not I,"   41
The cloudy messenger turns me his back   42
And hums, as who should say, "You'll rue the time   43
That clogs me with this answer."
LENNOX   And that well might   44
Advise him to a caution, t' hold what distance   45
His wisdom can provide. Some holy angel   46
Fly to the court of England and unfold
His message ere he come, that a swift blessing   48
May soon return to this our suffering country   49
Under a hand accursed!   50
LORD   I'll send my prayers with him.   *Exeunt.*

❖

---

17 borne all things well managed everything cleverly   **19 an't** if it.
should would be sure to   **21 from broad words** on account of plain
speech   **22 His presence** i.e., to be present   **24 bestows himself** is
quartered, has taken refuge. **The son of Duncan** Malcolm
25 holds . . . birth withholds the birthright (i.e., the Scottish crown)
27 Of by.   **Edward** Edward the Confessor, King of England   **29 his
high respect** the high respect paid to him. (Being out of fortune has
not lessened the dignity with which Malcolm is received in England.)
30 upon his aid in aid of Malcolm   **31 wake Northumberland** rouse
the people of Northumberland   **34 meat** food   **35 Free . . . banquets**
free our feasts and banquets from   **36 free** freely bestowed, or, pertaining to freemen   **38 exasperate the King** exasperated Macbeth
41 with . . . I i.e., when Macduff answered the messenger curtly with
a refusal   **42 cloudy** louring, scowling.   **turns me** i.e., turns. (*Me* is
used colloquially for emphasis.)   **43 hums . . . say** says "umph!" as if
to say   **44 clogs** encumbers, loads   **45–6 Advise . . . provide** warn
him (Macduff) to keep what safe distance he can (from Macbeth).
48 His message i.e., the request for aid against Scotland that Macduff
is going to present to King Edward (see lines 29 ff.)   **49–50 suffering
country Under** country suffering under

21 dismal disastrous, ill-omened   **24 profound** i.e., heavily pendent,
ready to drop off   **27 artificial sprites** spirits produced by magical
arts   **29 confusion** ruin.   **32 security** overconfidence   **35.1 "Come
away," etc.** (The song occurs in Thomas Middleton's *The Witch.*)
3.6. Location: Somewhere in Scotland.
1–2 My . . . farther What I've just said has coincided with your own
thought. I needn't say more; you can surmise the rest.   **3 borne** carried on.   **3–4 The gracious . . . dead** (Lennox ironically implies that
Macbeth's show of sorrow was hypocritical and came only after the
murder.)   **8 cannot . . . thought** can help thinking   **10 fact** deed,
crime.   **11 straight** straightaway, at once   **13 thralls** slaves

4.1

[A cauldron.] Thunder. Enter the three Witches.

FIRST WITCH
    Thrice the brinded cat hath mewed.   1
SECOND WITCH
    Thrice, and once the hedgepig whined.   2
THIRD WITCH
    Harpier cries. 'Tis time, 'tis time!   3
FIRST WITCH
    Round about the cauldron go;
    In the poisoned entrails throw.
    Toad, that under cold stone
    Days and nights has thirty-one   7
    Sweltered venom sleeping got,   8
    Boil thou first i'th' charmèd pot.
ALL *[as they dance round the cauldron]*
    Double, double, toil and trouble;
    Fire burn, and cauldron bubble.
SECOND WITCH
    Fillet of a fenny snake,   12
    In the cauldron boil and bake;
    Eye of newt and toe of frog,
    Wool of bat and tongue of dog,
    Adder's fork and blindworm's sting,   16
    Lizard's leg and owlet's wing,
    For a charm of powerful trouble,
    Like a hell-broth boil and bubble.
ALL
    Double, double, toil and trouble;
    Fire burn, and cauldron bubble.
THIRD WITCH
    Scale of dragon, tooth of wolf,
    Witches' mummy, maw and gulf   23
    Of the ravined salt-sea shark,   24
    Root of hemlock digged i'th' dark,
    Liver of blaspheming Jew,
    Gall of goat, and slips of yew   27
    Slivered in the moon's eclipse,   28
    Nose of Turk and Tartar's lips,
    Finger of birth-strangled babe
    Ditch-delivered by a drab,   31
    Make the gruel thick and slab.   32
    Add thereto a tiger's chaudron   33
    For th'ingredience of our cauldron.   34

ALL
    Double, double, toil and trouble;
    Fire burn, and cauldron bubble.
SECOND WITCH
    Cool it with a baboon's blood,
    Then the charm is firm and good.   38

Enter Hecate to the other three Witches.

HECATE
    Oh, well done! I commend your pains,   39
    And everyone shall share i'th' gains.
    And now about the cauldron sing
    Like elves and fairies in a ring,
    Enchanting all that you put in.   43
         Music and a song: "Black spirits," etc.
         [Exit Hecate.]
SECOND WITCH
    By the pricking of my thumbs,
    Something wicked this way comes.
        Open, locks,
        Whoever knocks!

    Enter Macbeth.

MACBETH
    How now, you secret, black, and midnight hags?   48
    What is't you do?
ALL   A deed without a name.
MACBETH
    I conjure you, by that which you profess,
    Howe'er you come to know it, answer me.
    Though you untie the winds and let them fight
    Against the churches, though the yeasty waves   53
    Confound and swallow navigation up,   54
    Though bladed corn be lodged and trees blown down, 55
    Though castles topple on their warders' heads,   56
    Though palaces and pyramids do slope   57
    Their heads to their foundations, though the treasure
    Of nature's germens tumble all together   59
    Even till destruction sicken, answer me   60
    To what I ask you.
FIRST WITCH   Speak.
SECOND WITCH   Demand.
THIRD WITCH   We'll answer.
FIRST WITCH
    Say if thou'dst rather hear it from our mouths
    Or from our masters?
MACBETH   Call 'em. Let me see 'em.
FIRST WITCH
    Pour in sow's blood, that hath eaten
    Her nine farrow; grease that's sweaten   65

4.1. Location: A cavern (see 3.5.15). In the middle, a boiling cauldron (provided presumably by means of the trapdoor; see 4.1.106. The trapdoor must also be used in this scene for the apparitions.) 1 brinded marked by streaks (as by fire), brindled **2 hedgepig** hedgehog **3 Harpier** (The name of a familiar spirit; probably derived from *harpy*.) **cries** i.e., gives the signal to begin **7–8 Days . . . got** for thirty-one days and nights has exuded venom formed during sleep **12 Fillet** Slice. **fenny** inhabiting fens or swamps **16 fork** forked tongue. **blindworm's** A blindworm is a slowworm, a harmless burrowing lizard. **23 mummy** mummified flesh made into a magical potion. **maw and gulf** gullet and stomach **24 ravined** ravenous, or glutted with prey (?) **27 Gall** gall bladder. **slips** cuttings for grafting or planting. **yew** (A tree often planted in churchyards and associated with mourning.) **28 Slivered** broken off (as a branch) **31 Ditch . . . drab** born in a ditch of a harlot **32 slab** viscous. **33 chaudron** entrails **34 th'ingredience** the ingredients

38.1 other (Said because Hecate is a witch, too, not because more witches enter.) **39–43 Oh . . . in** (These lines are universally regarded as non-Shakespearean.) **43.1 "Black spirits,"** *etc.* (This song is found in Middleton's *The Witch*.) **48 black** i.e., dealing in black magic **53 yeasty** foamy **54 Confound** destroy **55 Though . . . lodged** though unripe grain be laid flat **56 warders'** guardsmen's **57 slope** bend **59 nature's germens** seed or elements from which all nature operates **60 sicken** be surfeited with its own excess **65 nine farrow** litter of nine. **sweaten** sweated

From the murderer's gibbet throw   66
Into the flame.
ALL   Come high or low,   67
Thyself and office deftly show!   68

Thunder. First Apparition, an armed Head.

MACBETH
Tell me, thou unknown power—
FIRST WITCH   He knows thy thought.
Hear his speech, but say thou naught.
FIRST APPARITION
Macbeth! Macbeth! Macbeth! Beware Macduff,
Beware the Thane of Fife. Dismiss me. Enough.   72
                              He descends.

MACBETH
Whate'er thou art, for thy good caution, thanks;
Thou hast harped my fear aright. But one word
  more—   74
FIRST WITCH
He will not be commanded. Here's another,
More potent than the first.   76

Thunder. Second Apparition, a bloody Child.

SECOND APPARITION   Macbeth! Macbeth! Macbeth!
MACBETH   Had I three ears, I'd hear thee.
SECOND APPARITION
Be bloody, bold, and resolute; laugh to scorn
The power of man, for none of woman born
Shall harm Macbeth.   *Descends.*
MACBETH
Then live, Macduff; what need I fear of thee?
But yet I'll make assurance double sure,
And take a bond of fate. Thou shalt not live,   84
That I may tell pale-hearted fear it lies,
And sleep in spite of thunder.   86

*Thunder. Third Apparition, a Child crowned, with
a tree in his hand.*

                    What is this
That rises like the issue of a king   87
And wears upon his baby brow the round   88
And top of sovereignty?
ALL   Listen, but speak not to't.   89
THIRD APPARITION
Be lion-mettled, proud, and take no care
Who chafes, who frets, or where conspirers are.
Macbeth shall never vanquished be until

Great Birnam Wood to high Dunsinane Hill
Shall come against him.   *Descends.*
MACBETH   That will never be.
Who can impress the forest, bid the tree   95
Unfix his earthbound root? Sweet bodements, good! 96
Rebellious dead, rise never till the wood   97
Of Birnam rise, and our high-placed Macbeth   98
Shall live the lease of nature, pay his breath   99
To time and mortal custom. Yet my heart   100
Throbs to know one thing. Tell me, if your art
Can tell so much: shall Banquo's issue ever
Reign in this kingdom?
ALL   Seek to know no more.
MACBETH
I will be satisfied. Deny me this,
And an eternal curse fall on you! Let me know.   105
          [*The cauldron descends.*] *Hautboys.*
Why sinks that cauldron? And what noise is this?   106
FIRST WITCH   Show!
SECOND WITCH   Show!
THIRD WITCH   Show!
ALL
Show his eyes, and grieve his heart;
Come like shadows, so depart!   111

*A show of eight kings and Banquo last; [the eighth
King] with a glass in his hand.*

MACBETH
Thou art too like the spirit of Banquo. Down!
Thy crown does sear mine eyeballs. And thy hair,
Thou other gold-bound brow, is like the first.   114
A third is like the former. Filthy hags,
Why do you show me this? A fourth? Start, eyes!   116
What, will the line stretch out to th' crack of doom? 117
Another yet? A seventh? I'll see no more.
And yet the eighth appears, who bears a glass
Which shows me many more; and some I see
That twofold balls and treble scepters carry.   121
Horrible sight! Now I see 'tis true,
For the blood-boltered Banquo smiles upon me   123
And points at them for his. [*The apparitions vanish.*]
    What, is this so?   124

66 **gibbet** gallows   67 **high or low** of the upper or lower air, from under the earth or in hell; or, one and all   68 **office** function **68.1 armed Head** (Perhaps symbolizes the head of Macbeth cut off by Macduff and presented by him to Malcolm, or else the head of Macduff, armed in rebellion against Macbeth.)   72.1 **He descends** (i.e., by means of the trapdoor).   74 **harped** hit, touched (as in touching a harp to make it sound)   76.1 **bloody Child** (Symbolizes Macduff untimely ripped from his mother's womb; see 5.8.15–16.)   84 **take a bond of** get a guarantee from (i.e., by killing Macduff, to make doubly sure he can do no harm)   86.1-2 **Child . . . hand** (Symbolizes Malcolm, the royal child; the tree anticipates the cutting of boughs in Birnam Wood, 5.4.)   87 **like** in the likeness of   88–9 **round And top** crown

95 **impress** press into service, like soldiers   96 **bodements** prophecies   97–8 **Rebellious . . . rise** i.e., May the souls of those I have murdered (Banquo, Duncan) never rise again, since trees themself cannot rise. (An image of the Day of Judgment, when bodies are prophesied to rise again; see *Henry V*, 4.1.135–8.)   99–100 **Shall . . . custom** will live out his full life span until it is time for him to expire (*pay his breath*) in the way of all mortals.   105.1 **Hautboys** oboelike instruments.   106 **noise** music   111.1 **eight kings** (Banquo was the supposed ancestor of the Stuart dynasty, leading forward to King James VI of Scotland and James I of England, the *eighth King* here.)   111.2 *glass* (magic) mirror (also in line 119)   114 **other** i.e., second   116 **Start** Bulge from their sockets   117 **th' crack of doom** the thunder-peal of Doomsday at the end of time.   121 **twofold balls** (A probable reference to the double coronation of James at Scone and Westminster, as King of England and Scotland.)   **treble scepters** (Probably refers to James' assumed title as King of Great Britain, France, and Ireland.)   123 **blood-boltered** having his hair matted with blood   124 **for his** as his descendants.

FIRST WITCH

> Ay, sir, all this is so. But why   125
> Stands Macbeth thus amazedly?   126
> Come, sisters, cheer we up his sprites   127
> And show the best of our delights.
> I'll charm the air to give a sound,
> While you perform your antic round,   130
> That this great king may kindly say
> Our duties did his welcome pay.   132

> > *Music. The Witches dance, and vanish.*

MACBETH

> Where are they? Gone? Let this pernicious hour
> Stand aye accursèd in the calendar!
> Come in, without there!

> > *Enter Lennox.*

LENNOX   What's Your Grace's will?

MACBETH

> Saw you the Weird Sisters?

LENNOX   No, my lord.

MACBETH

> Came they not by you?

LENNOX   No, indeed, my lord.

MACBETH

> Infected be the air whereon they ride,
> And damned all those that trust them! I did hear
> The galloping of horse. Who was't came by?   140

LENNOX

> 'Tis two or three, my lord, that bring you word
> Macduff is fled to England.

MACBETH   Fled to England!

LENNOX

> Ay, my good lord.

MACBETH *[aside]*

> Time, thou anticipat'st my dread exploits.   144
> The flighty purpose never is o'ertook   145
> Unless the deed go with it. From this moment   146
> The very firstlings of my heart shall be   147
> The firstlings of my hand. And even now,   148
> To crown my thoughts with acts, be it thought and
> > done:
> The castle of Macduff I will surprise,   150
> Seize upon Fife, give to th'edge o'th' sword
> His wife, his babes, and all unfortunate souls
> That trace him in his line. No boasting like a fool;   153
> This deed I'll do before this purpose cool.
> But no more sights!—Where are these gentlemen?
> Come, bring me where they are.   *Exeunt.*

> > ❖

125–32 Ay . . . pay (These lines are assumed to have been written by
someone other than Shakespeare.)   126 amazedly stunned.
127 sprites spirits   130 antic round grotesque dance in a circle
132 pay repay.   140 horse horses.   144 thou anticipat'st you forestall
145 flighty fleeting   146 Unless . . . it unless the execution of the
deed accompanies the conception of it immediately.   147–8 The
very . . . hand the firstborn promptings of my heart will become my
first of deeds.   150 surprise attack without warning   153 trace . . .
line follow him in the line of inheritance.

4.2

> *Enter Macduff's Wife, her Son, and Ross.*

LADY MACDUFF

> What had he done to make him fly the land?

ROSS

> You must have patience, madam.

LADY MACDUFF   He had none.

> His flight was madness. When our actions do not,   3
> Our fears do make us traitors.

ROSS   You know not   4

> Whether it was his wisdom or his fear.

LADY MACDUFF

> Wisdom? To leave his wife, to leave his babes,
> His mansion, and his titles in a place   7
> From whence himself does fly? He loves us not,
> He wants the natural touch; for the poor wren,   9
> The most diminutive of birds, will fight,
> Her young ones in her nest, against the owl.   11
> All is the fear and nothing is the love,
> As little is the wisdom, where the flight
> So runs against all reason.

ROSS   My dearest coz,   14

> I pray you, school yourself. But, for your husband,   15
> He is noble, wise, judicious, and best knows
> The fits o'th' season. I dare not speak much further,   17
> But cruel are the times when we are traitors   18
> And do not know ourselves, when we hold rumor   19
> From what we fear, yet know not what we fear,   20
> But float upon a wild and violent sea
> Each way and none. I take my leave of you;   22
> Shall not be long but I'll be here again.   23
> Things at the worst will cease, or else climb upward
> To what they were before.—My pretty cousin,
> Blessing upon you!

LADY MACDUFF

> Fathered he is, and yet he's fatherless.

ROSS

> I am so much a fool, should I stay longer
> It would be my disgrace and your discomfort.   29
> I take my leave at once.   *Exit Ross.*

LADY MACDUFF   Sirrah, your father's dead;   31

> And what will you do now? How will you live?

SON

> As birds do, mother.

LADY MACDUFF   What, with worms and flies?

SON

> With what I get, I mean; and so do they.

4.2. Location: Fife. Macduff's castle.
3–4 When . . . traitors Even when we have committed no treasonous
act, our fearful responses make us look guilty.   **7 titles** possessions to
which he has title   **9 wants . . . touch** lacks the natural instinct to protect his family   **11 Her . . . nest** when her young ones are in the nest
14 coz kinswoman   **15 school** control.   **for** as for   **17 fits o'th' season** violent convulsions of the time.   **18–19 are traitors . . . ourselves**
are alienated from one another by a climate of fear and suspected
treason   **19–20 hold . . . From what we fear** believe every fearful
rumor on the basis of what we fear might be   **22 Each . . . none** this
way and that.   **23 Shall** it shall.   **but** before   **29 It . . . discomfort** I
should disgrace my manhood by weeping and cause you distress.
31 Sirrah (Here, an affectionate form of address to a child.)

LADY MACDUFF   Poor bird! Thou'dst never fear   35
The net nor lime, the pitfall nor the gin.   36

SON
Why should I, mother? Poor birds they are not set for.   37
My father is not dead, for all your saying.

LADY MACDUFF
Yes, he is dead. How wilt thou do for a father?

SON   Nay, how will you do for a husband?

LADY MACDUFF   Why, I can buy me twenty at any
market.

SON   Then you'll buy 'em to sell again.

LADY MACDUFF
Thou speak'st with all thy wit,
And yet, i'faith, with wit enough for thee.

SON   Was my father a traitor, mother?

LADY MACDUFF   Ay, that he was.

SON   What is a traitor?

LADY MACDUFF   Why, one that swears and lies.

SON   And be all traitors that do so?

LADY MACDUFF
Every one that does so is a traitor,
And must be hanged.

SON
And must they all be hanged that swear and lie?

LADY MACDUFF   Every one.

SON   Who must hang them?

LADY MACDUFF   Why, the honest men.

SON   Then the liars and swearers are fools, for there are
liars and swearers enough to beat the honest men and
hang up them.

LADY MACDUFF   Now, God help thee, poor monkey!
But how wilt thou do for a father?

SON   If he were dead, you'd weep for him; if you would
not, it were a good sign that I should quickly have a
new father.

LADY MACDUFF   Poor prattler, how thou talk'st!

Enter a Messenger.

MESSENGER
Bless you, fair dame! I am not to you known,
Though in your state of honor I am perfect.   67
I doubt some danger does approach you nearly.   68
If you will take a homely man's advice,   69
Be not found here. Hence with your little ones!
To fright you thus, methinks, I am too savage;
To do worse to you were fell cruelty,   72
Which is too nigh your person. Heaven preserve you!   73
I dare abide no longer.   *Exit Messenger.*

LADY MACDUFF   Whither should I fly?
I have done no harm. But I remember now
I am in this earthly world, where to do harm
Is often laudable, to do good sometime
Accounted dangerous folly. Why then, alas,

Do I put up that womanly defense
To say I have done no harm?

Enter Murderers.

What are these faces?

FIRST MURDERER   Where is your husband?

LADY MACDUFF
I hope in no place so unsanctified
Where such as thou mayst find him.

FIRST MURDERER   He's a traitor.

SON
Thou liest, thou shag-haired villain!

FIRST MURDERER   What, you egg?
[*He stabs him.*]
Young fry of treachery!

SON   He has killed me, mother.   85
Run away, I pray you!   [*He dies.*]
*Exit [Lady Macduff] crying "Murder!"
[followed by the Murderers with the Son's body].*

❖

4.3

Enter Malcolm and Macduff.

MALCOLM
Let us seek out some desolate shade, and there
Weep our sad bosoms empty.

MACDUFF   Let us rather
Hold fast the mortal sword, and like good men   3
Bestride our downfall'n birthdom. Each new morn   4
New widows howl, new orphans cry, new sorrows
Strike heaven on the face, that it resounds   6
As if it felt with Scotland and yelled out   7
Like syllable of dolor.

MALCOLM   What I believe, I'll wail;   8
What know, believe; and what I can redress,   9
As I shall find the time to friend, I will.   10
What you have spoke it may be so, perchance.
This tyrant, whose sole name blisters our tongues,   12
Was once thought honest. You have loved him well;
He hath not touched you yet. I am young; but
something   14
You may deserve of him through me, and wisdom   15
To offer up a weak, poor, innocent lamb
T'appease an angry god.

MACDUFF   I am not treacherous.

MALCOLM   But Macbeth is.

---

35 **Thou'dst never fear** You are too innocent to be prudently wary of
36 **lime** birdlime (a sticky substance put on branches to snare birds).
gin snare.   37 **Poor . . . for** i.e., Traps are not set for *poor* birds, as you
call me.   67 **Though . . . perfect** though I am perfectly acquainted
with your honorable state.   68 **doubt** fear   69 **homely** plain
72–3 **To . . . person** to frighten you still further would be savage cruelty, which cruelty is all too near at hand.

85 **fry** spawn, progeny
4.3. Location: England. Before King Edward the Confessor's palace.
3 **mortal** deadly   4 **Bestride** stand over in defense.   **birthdom** native
land.   6 **that it resounds** so that it echoes   7–8 **As . . . dolor** as if
heaven, feeling itself the blow delivered to Scotland, cried out with a
similar cry of pain.   8–9 **What . . . believe** i.e., What I believe to be
amiss in Scotland I will grieve for, and anything I am certain to be
true I will believe. (But one must be cautious in these duplicitous
times.)   10 **to friend** opportune, congenial   12 **sole** mere   14 **He . . .
yet** i.e., the fact that Macbeth hasn't hurt you yet makes me suspicious of your loyalties.   **young** i.e., inexperienced   14–15 **something
. . . me** i.e., you may win favor with Macbeth by delivering me to him
15 **wisdom** i.e., it would be worldly-wise

A good and virtuous nature may recoil   20
In an imperial charge. But I shall crave your pardon.   21
That which you are my thoughts cannot transpose;   22
Angels are bright still, though the brightest fell.   23
Though all things foul would wear the brows of grace,   24
Yet grace must still look so.
MACDUFF   I have lost my hopes.   25
MALCOLM
Perchance even there where I did find my doubts.   26
Why in that rawness left you wife and child,   27
Those precious motives, those strong knots of love,
Without leave-taking? I pray you,
Let not my jealousies be your dishonors,   30
But mine own safeties. You may be rightly just,   31
Whatever I shall think.
MACDUFF   Bleed, bleed, poor country!
Great tyranny, lay thou thy basis sure,   33
For goodness dare not check thee; wear thou thy
    wrongs,   34
The title is affeered! Fare thee well, lord.   35
I would not be the villain that thou think'st
For the whole space that's in the tyrant's grasp,
And the rich East to boot.
MALCOLM   Be not offended.   38
I speak not as in absolute fear of you.   39
I think our country sinks beneath the yoke;
It weeps, it bleeds, and each new day a gash
Is added to her wounds. I think withal   42
There would be hands uplifted in my right;   43
And here from gracious England have I offer   44
Of goodly thousands. But, for all this,
When I shall tread upon the tyrant's head,
Or wear it on my sword, yet my poor country
Shall have more vices than it had before,
More suffer, and more sundry ways than ever,   49
By him that shall succeed.
MACDUFF   What should he be?   50
MALCOLM
It is myself I mean, in whom I know

All the particulars of vice so grafted   52
That, when they shall be opened, black Macbeth   53
Will seem as pure as snow, and the poor state
Esteem him as a lamb, being compared
With my confineless harms.
MACDUFF   Not in the legions   56
Of horrid hell can come a devil more damned
In evils to top Macbeth.
MALCOLM   I grant him bloody,   58
Luxurious, avaricious, false, deceitful,   59
Sudden, malicious, smacking of every sin   60
That has a name. But there's no bottom, none,
In my voluptuousness. Your wives, your daughters,
Your matrons, and your maids could not fill up
The cistern of my lust, and my desire
All continent impediments would o'erbear   65
That did oppose my will. Better Macbeth   66
Than such an one to reign.
MACDUFF   Boundless intemperance
In nature is a tyranny; it hath been   68
Th'untimely emptying of the happy throne
And fall of many kings. But fear not yet   70
To take upon you what is yours. You may
Convey your pleasures in a spacious plenty,   72
And yet seem cold; the time you may so hoodwink.   73
We have willing dames enough. There cannot be
That vulture in you to devour so many
As will to greatness dedicate themselves,
Finding it so inclined.
MALCOLM   With this there grows
In my most ill-composed affection such   78
A stanchless avarice that, were I king,   79
I should cut off the nobles for their lands,
Desire his jewels and this other's house,   81
And my more-having would be as a sauce
To make me hunger more, that I should forge   83
Quarrels unjust against the good and loyal,
Destroying them for wealth.
MACDUFF   This avarice
Sticks deeper, grows with more pernicious root
Than summer-seeming lust, and it hath been   87
The sword of our slain kings. Yet do not fear;   88
Scotland hath foisons to fill up your will   89
Of your mere own. All these are portable,   90
With other graces weighed.   91
MALCOLM
But I have none. The king-becoming graces,
As justice, verity, temperance, stableness,

20–1 A good . . . charge i.e., Even as good a virtuous nature as you have, Macduff, may give way to the insinuations of a royal command from Macbeth. (With wordplay on the *recoil* of a firearm that is *charged* with power and shot.)   **22 That . . . transpose** My suspicious thoughts cannot change you from what you are, cannot make you evil   **23 the brightest** i.e., Lucifer   **24–5 Though . . . so** Even though evil puts on the appearance of good so often as to cast that appearance into deep suspicion, yet goodness must go on looking and acting like itself.   **25 hopes** i.e., hopes of persuading Malcolm to lead the cause against Macbeth.   **26 Perchance even there** i.e., Perhaps in that same mistrustful frame of mind.   **doubts** i.e., fears such as that Macduff may covertly be on Macbeth's side.   **27 rawness** unprotected condition. (Malcolm suggests that Macduff's leaving his family unprotected could be construed as more evidence of his not having anything to fear from Macbeth.)   **30–1 Let . . . safeties** may it be true that my suspicions of your lack of honor are founded only in my own wariness.   **33 basis** foundation   **34 check** rebuke, call to account. **wear . . . wrongs** continue to enjoy your wrongfully gained powers **35 affeered** confirmed, certified.   **38 to boot** in addition. **39 absolute fear** complete mistrust   **42 withal** in addition   **43 right** cause   **44 England** the King of England   **49 More . . . ways** suffer more grievously and in more varied ways   **50 What . . . be?** Whom could you possibly mean?

52 grafted (1) engrafted, indissolubly mixed (2) grafted like a plant that will then *open* or unfold   **53 opened** unfolded (like a bud) **56 confineless** limitless   **58 top** surpass   **59 Luxurious** lecherous **60 Sudden** violent, impetuous   **65 continent** (1) chaste (2) restraining, containing   **66 will** lust. (Also in line 89.)   **68 nature** human nature   **70 yet** nevertheless   **72 Convey** manage with secrecy **73 cold** chaste.   **the time . . . hoodwink** you may thus deceive the age.   **78 ill-composed affection** evil disposition   **79 stanchless** insatiable   **81 his** one man's.   **this other's** another's   **83 that** so that **87 summer-seeming** appropriate to youth (and lessening in later years)   **88 sword** i.e., cause of overthrow   **89 foisons** resources, plenty   **90 Of . . . own** out of your own royal estates alone. **portable** bearable   **91 weighed** counterbalanced.

Bounty, perseverance, mercy, lowliness,   94
Devotion, patience, courage, fortitude,
I have no relish of them, but abound   96
In the division of each several crime,   97
Acting it many ways. Nay, had I power, I should
Pour the sweet milk of concord into hell,
Uproar the universal peace, confound   100
All unity on earth.
MACDUFF   O Scotland, Scotland!
MALCOLM
If such a one be fit to govern, speak.
I am as I have spoken.
MACDUFF   Fit to govern?
No, not to live. O nation miserable,
With an untitled tyrant bloody-sceptered,   105
When shalt thou see thy wholesome days again,
Since that the truest issue of thy throne
By his own interdiction stands accurst   108
And does blaspheme his breed? Thy royal father   109
Was a most sainted king; the queen that bore thee,
Oft'ner upon her knees than on her feet,
Died every day she lived. Fare thee well.   112
These evils thou repeat'st upon thyself
Hath banished me from Scotland. O my breast,   114
Thy hope ends here!
MALCOLM   Macduff, this noble passion,
Child of integrity, hath from my soul   116
Wiped the black scruples, reconciled my thoughts
To thy good truth and honor. Devilish Macbeth
By many of these trains hath sought to win me   119
Into his power, and modest wisdom plucks me   120
From overcredulous haste. But God above
Deal between thee and me! For even now
I put myself to thy direction and
Unspeak mine own detraction, here abjure   124
The taints and blames I laid upon myself
For strangers to my nature. I am yet   126
Unknown to woman, never was forsworn,   127
Scarcely have coveted what was mine own,
At no time broke my faith, would not betray
The devil to his fellow, and delight
No less in truth than life. My first false speaking
Was this upon myself. What I am truly   132
Is thine and my poor country's to command—
Whither indeed, before thy here-approach,
Old Siward with ten thousand warlike men,
Already at a point, was setting forth.   136

Now we'll together; and the chance of goodness   137
Be like our warranted quarrel!—Why are you silent?   138
MACDUFF
Such welcome and unwelcome things at once
'Tis hard to reconcile.

Enter a Doctor.

MALCOLM
Well, more anon.—Comes the King forth, I pray you?
DOCTOR
Ay, sir. There are a crew of wretched souls
That stay his cure. Their malady convinces   143
The great essay of art; but at his touch—   144
Such sanctity hath heaven given his hand—
They presently amend.
MALCOLM   I thank you, Doctor.   146
Exit [Doctor].
MACDUFF
What's the disease he means?
MALCOLM   'Tis called the evil.   147
A most miraculous work in this good king,
Which often, since my here-remain in England,   149
I have seen him do. How he solicits heaven   150
Himself best knows; but strangely-visited people,   151
All swoll'n and ulcerous, pitiful to the eye,
The mere despair of surgery, he cures,   153
Hanging a golden stamp about their necks   154
Put on with holy prayers; and 'tis spoken,   155
To the succeeding royalty he leaves   156
The healing benediction. With this strange virtue   157
He hath a heavenly gift of prophecy,
And sundry blessings hang about his throne
That speak him full of grace.

Enter Ross.

MACDUFF   See who comes here.
MALCOLM
My countryman, but yet I know him not.   161
MACDUFF
My ever-gentle cousin, welcome hither.   162
MALCOLM
I know him now. Good God betimes remove   163
The means that makes us strangers!
ROSS   Sir, amen.
MACDUFF
Stands Scotland where it did?
ROSS   Alas, poor country,
Almost afraid to know itself. It cannot

---

94 lowliness humility   **96 relish** flavor or trace   **97 division** subdi-
visions, various possible forms.   **several** separate   **100 Uproar**
throw into an uproar   **105 untitled** lacking rightful title, usurping
108 interdiction debarring of self   **109 does blaspheme his breed**
defames his breeding, i.e., is a disgrace to his royal lineage.
112 Died . . . lived lived a life of daily mortification.   **114 breast**
heart   **116 Child of integrity** a product of your integrity of spirit;
or, you person of perfect integrity   **119 trains** plots, artifices
120 modest . . . me wise prudence holds me back   **124 Unspeak . . .**
detraction take back all I said in detraction of myself   **126 For** as
127 Unknown to woman a virgin   **132 upon** against   **136 at**
a point prepared

137–8 the chance . . . quarrel may our chance of success be propor-
tionate to the justice of our cause.   **143 stay** wait for.   **convinces**
conquers   **144 essay of art** efforts of medical skill   **146 presently**
immediately   **147 evil** i.e., scrofula, supposedly cured by the royal
touch; James I claimed this power.   **149 here-remain** stay   **150 solic-**
its prevails by prayer with   **151 strangely-visited** afflicted by strange
diseases   **153 mere** utter   **154 stamp** minted coin   **155–7 and 'tis . . .**
benediction it is said that he bequeaths this healing blessedness to
his royal progeny.   **157 virtue** healing power   **161 My countryman**
(So identified by his dress.)   **know** recognize   **162 gentle** noble
163 betimes speedily

Be called our mother, but our grave; where nothing 167
But who knows nothing is once seen to smile; 168
Where sighs and groans and shrieks that rend the air
Are made, not marked; where violent sorrow seems 170
A modern ecstasy. The dead man's knell 171
Is there scarce asked for who, and good men's lives
Expire before the flowers in their caps, 173
Dying or ere they sicken.

MACDUFF   Oh, relation 174
Too nice, and yet too true!

MALCOLM   What's the newest grief? 175

ROSS
That of an hour's age doth hiss the speaker; 176
Each minute teems a new one.

MACDUFF   How does my wife? 177

ROSS
Why, well.

MACDUFF And all my children?

ROSS   Well too. 178

MACDUFF
The tyrant has not battered at their peace?

ROSS
No, they were well at peace when I did leave 'em.

MACDUFF
Be not a niggard of your speech. How goes 't?

ROSS
When I came hither to transport the tidings
Which I have heavily borne, there ran a rumor 183
Of many worthy fellows that were out, 184
Which was to my belief witnessed the rather 185
For that I saw the tyrant's power afoot. 186
Now is the time of help. [*To Malcolm*] Your eye in
  Scotland
Would create soldiers, make our women fight, 188
To doff their dire distresses.

MALCOLM   Be 't their comfort 189
We are coming thither. Gracious England hath 190
Lent us good Siward and ten thousand men;
An older and a better soldier none 192
That Christendom gives out.

ROSS   Would I could answer 193
This comfort with the like! But I have words
That would be howled out in the desert air, 195
Where hearing should not latch them.

MACDUFF   What concern they? 196

The general cause? Or is it a fee-grief 197
Due to some single breast?

ROSS   No mind that's honest 198
But in it shares some woe, though the main part
Pertains to you alone.

MACDUFF If it be mine,
Keep it not from me; quickly let me have it.

ROSS
Let not your ears despise my tongue forever,
Which shall possess them with the heaviest sound 203
That ever yet they heard.

MACDUFF   Hum! I guess at it.

ROSS
Your castle is surprised, your wife and babes
Savagely slaughtered. To relate the manner
Were, on the quarry of these murdered deer, 207
To add the death of you.

MALCOLM   Merciful heaven!
What, man, ne'er pull your hat upon your brows; 209
Give sorrow words. The grief that does not speak
Whispers the o'erfraught heart and bids it break. 211

MACDUFF
My children too?

ROSS   Wife, children, servants, all
That could be found.

MACDUFF   And I must be from thence! 213
My wife killed too?

ROSS   I have said.

MALCOLM   Be comforted.
Let's make us med'cines of our great revenge
To cure this deadly grief.

MACDUFF
He has no children. All my pretty ones? 217
Did you say all? O hell-kite! All? 218
What, all my pretty chickens and their dam
At one fell swoop? 220

MALCOLM Dispute it like a man. 221

MACDUFF I shall do so;
But I must also feel it as a man.
I cannot but remember such things were,
That were most precious to me. Did heaven look on
And would not take their part? Sinful Macduff,
They were all struck for thee! Naught that I am, 227
Not for their own demerits, but for mine,
Fell slaughter on their souls. Heaven rest them now!

MALCOLM
Be this the whetstone of your sword. Let grief
Convert to anger; blunt not the heart, enrage it.

167–8 nothing But who nobody except a person who   **168 once** ever **170 marked** noticed (because they are so common)   **171 modern ecstasy** commonplace emotion.   **173 flowers** (Often worn in Elizabethan caps.)   **174 or ere they sicken** before they have had time to fall ill.   **relation** report   **175 nice** minutely accurate, elaborately phrased   **176 That . . . speaker** The speaker of news that is scarcely an hour old is hissed at for reporting stale news   **177 teems** teems with, yields   **178 well** (Ross quibbles, in his reluctance to tell the bad news. "The dead are well" means they are at rest.)   **183 heavily** sadly   **184–6 Of . . . afoot** about many worthy Scots who have been driven into exile and armed rebellion, which rumor was strengthened all the more when I saw Macbeth's army on the move (in anticipation of being attacked).   **188 our women** even our women   **189 doff** put off, get rid of   **190 Gracious England** i.e., Edward the Confessor **192 none** there is none   **193 gives out** tells of, proclaims.   **195 would** should   **196 latch** catch (the sound of)

197 fee-grief a grief with an individual owner, having absolute ownership   **198 Due to** i.e., owned by   **203 possess them with** put them in possession of   **207 quarry** heap of slaughtered deer at a hunt. (With a pun on *dear, deer*.)   **209 pull your hat** (A conventional gesture of grief.)   **211 Whispers** whispers to.   **o'erfraught** overburdened **213 must** had to   **217 He has no children** (Referring either to Macbeth, who must not be a father if he can do such a thing, or, to Malcolm, who speaks comfortingly without knowing what such a loss feels like to a father.)   **218 hell-kite** (The *kite* is a rapacious bird of prey; a term of disdain and dislike.)   **220 fell** cruel   **221 Dispute** Strive against, debate   **227 for thee** i.e., as divine punishment for your sins.   **Naught** Wicked

MACDUFF
Oh, I could play the woman with mine eyes
And braggart with my tongue! But, gentle heavens,
Cut short all intermission. Front to front   234
Bring thou this fiend of Scotland and myself;
Within my sword's length set him. If he scape,   236
Heaven forgive him too!

MALCOLM   This tune goes manly.   237
Come, go we to the King. Our power is ready;   238
Our lack is nothing but our leave. Macbeth   239
Is ripe for shaking, and the powers above
Put on their instruments. Receive what cheer you may.   241
The night is long that never finds the day.   *Exeunt.*

❖

5.1

Enter a Doctor of Physic and a Waiting-
Gentlewoman.

DOCTOR   I have two nights watched with you, but can
perceive no truth in your report. When was it she last
walked?

GENTLEWOMAN   Since His Majesty went into the field, I
have seen her rise from her bed, throw her nightgown
upon her, unlock her closet, take forth paper, fold it,   6
write upon't, read it, afterwards seal it, and again
return to bed; yet all this while in a most fast sleep.

DOCTOR   A great perturbation in nature, to receive at
once the benefit of sleep and do the effects of   10
watching! In this slumbery agitation, besides her   11
walking and other actual performances, what, at any
time, have you heard her say?

GENTLEWOMAN   That, sir, which I will not report after her.

DOCTOR   You may to me, and 'tis most meet you should.   16

GENTLEWOMAN   Neither to you nor anyone, having no
witness to confirm my speech.

Enter Lady [Macbeth], with a taper.

Lo you, here she comes! This is her very guise, and,
upon my life, fast asleep. Observe her. Stand close.   20
[They stand aside.]

DOCTOR   How came she by that light?

GENTLEWOMAN   Why, it stood by her. She has light by
her continually. 'Tis her command.

DOCTOR   You see her eyes are open.

GENTLEWOMAN   Ay, but their sense are shut.

DOCTOR   What is it she does now? Look how she rubs
her hands.

GENTLEWOMAN   It is an accustomed action with her to
seem thus washing her hands. I have known her
continue in this a quarter of an hour.

---

234 **intermission** delay, interval.   **Front to front** Face to face
236–7 **If . . . too!** If I let him escape, may he find forgiveness not only
from me but from heaven itself! (This is a condition that Macduff will
not allow to happen.)   238 **power** army   239 **Our . . . leave** we need
only to take our leave (of the English King).   241 **Put . . . instruments**
set us on as their agents, or, arm themselves.
5.1. Location: Dunsinane. Macbeth's castle.
0.1 *Physic* medicine   6 **closet** chest or cabinet   10–11 **do . . . watch-**
ing act as though awake.   16 **meet** suitable   20 **close** concealed.

LADY MACBETH   Yet here's a spot.

DOCTOR   Hark, she speaks. I will set down what comes
from her, to satisfy my remembrance the more   33
strongly.

LADY MACBETH   Out, damned spot! Out, I say! One—
two—why then, 'tis time to do't. Hell is murky.—
Fie, my lord, fie, a soldier, and afeard? What need we
fear who knows it, when none can call our power to
account? Yet who would have thought the old man to
have had so much blood in him?

DOCTOR   Do you mark that?

LADY MACBETH   The Thane of Fife had a wife. Where is
she now?—What, will these hands ne'er be
clean?—No more o'that, my lord, no more o' that;
you mar all with this starting.   45

DOCTOR   Go to, go to. You have known what you   46
should not.

GENTLEWOMAN   She has spoke what she should not, I
am sure of that. Heaven knows what she has known!

LADY MACBETH   Here's the smell of the blood still. All
the perfumes of Arabia will not sweeten this little
hand. Oh, oh, oh!

DOCTOR   What a sigh is there! The heart is sorely   53
charged.   54

GENTLEWOMAN   I would not have such a heart in my
bosom for the dignity of the whole body.   56

DOCTOR   Well, well, well.

GENTLEWOMAN   Pray God it be, sir.   58

DOCTOR   This disease is beyond my practice. Yet I have
known those which have walked in their sleep who
have died holily in their beds.

LADY MACBETH   Wash your hands, put on your nightgown; look not so pale! I tell you yet again, Banquo's
buried. He cannot come out on 's grave.   64

DOCTOR   Even so?

LADY MACBETH   To bed, to bed! There's knocking at the
gate. Come, come, come, come, give me your hand.
What's done cannot be undone. To bed, to bed,
to bed!   *Exit Lady.*

DOCTOR   Will she go now to bed?

GENTLEWOMAN   Directly.

DOCTOR
Foul whisperings are abroad. Unnatural deeds
Do breed unnatural troubles. Infected minds
To their deaf pillows will discharge their secrets.
More needs she the divine than the physician.
God, God forgive us all! Look after her;
Remove from her the means of all annoyance,   77
And still keep eyes upon her. So, good night.   78
My mind she has mated, and amazed my sight.   79
I think, but dare not speak.

GENTLEWOMAN   Good night, good Doctor.
Exeunt.

---

33 **satisfy** confirm, support   45 **this starting** these startled movements.
46 **Go to** (An exclamation of reproof, directed at Lady Macbeth.)
53–4 **sorely charged** heavily burdened.   56 **dignity** worth, value   58 **Pray**
. . . sir Pray God it will turn out well, as you say, sir. (Playing on the
Doctor's "Well, well," i.e., "Dear, dear.")   64 **on 's** of his   77 **annoyance**
i.e., harming herself   78 **still** constantly   79 **mated** bewildered, stupefied

5.2

Drum and colors. Enter Menteith, Caithness,
Angus, Lennox, [and] soldiers.

MENTEITH
  The English power is near, led on by Malcolm,
  His uncle Siward, and the good Macduff.
  Revenges burn in them, for their dear causes   3
  Would to the bleeding and the grim alarm   4
  Excite the mortified man.
ANGUS   Near Birnam Wood   5
  Shall we well meet them; that way are they coming.   6
CAITHNESS
  Who knows if Donalbain be with his brother?
LENNOX
  For certain, sir, he is not. I have a file   8
  Of all the gentry. There is Siward's son,
  And many unrough youths that even now   10
  Protest their first of manhood.
MENTEITH   What does the tyrant?   11
CAITHNESS
  Great Dunsinane he strongly fortifies.
  Some say he's mad, others that lesser hate him
  Do call it valiant fury; but for certain
  He cannot buckle his distempered cause   15
  Within the belt of rule.
ANGUS   Now does he feel
  His secret murders sticking on his hands;
  Now minutely revolts upbraid his faith-breach.   18
  Those he commands move only in command,   19
  Nothing in love. Now does he feel his title
  Hang loose about him, like a giant's robe
  Upon a dwarfish thief.
MENTEITH   Who then shall blame
  His pestered senses to recoil and start,   23
  When all that is within him does condemn
  Itself for being there?
CAITHNESS   Well, march we on
  To give obedience where 'tis truly owed.
  Meet we the med'cine of the sickly weal,   27
  And with him pour we in our country's purge   28
  Each drop of us.
LENNOX   Or so much as it needs   29
  To dew the sovereign flower and drown the weeds.   30
  Make we our march towards Birnam.
                         Exeunt, marching.

❧

5.3

Enter Macbeth, Doctor, and attendants.

MACBETH
  Bring me no more reports. Let them fly all!   1
  Till Birnam Wood remove to Dunsinane,
  I cannot taint with fear. What's the boy Malcolm?   3
  Was he not born of woman? The spirits that know
  All mortal consequences have pronounced me thus: 5
  "Fear not, Macbeth. No man that's born of woman
  Shall e'er have power upon thee." Then fly, false
       thanes,
  And mingle with the English epicures!   8
  The mind I sway by and the heart I bear   9
  Shall never sag with doubt nor shake with fear.

            Enter Servant.

  The devil damn thee black, thou cream-faced loon!   11
  Where got'st thou that goose look?
SERVANT
  There is ten thousand—
MACBETH   Geese, villain?
SERVANT   Soldiers, sir.
MACBETH
  Go prick thy face and over-red thy fear,   14
  Thou lily-livered boy. What soldiers, patch?   15
  Death of thy soul! Those linen cheeks of thine   16
  Are counselors to fear. What soldiers, whey-face?   17
SERVANT   The English force, so please you.
MACBETH   Take thy face hence.   *[Exit Servant.]*
         [Calling] Seyton!—I am sick at heart
  When I behold—Seyton, I say!—This push   20
  Will cheer me ever, or disseat me now.   21
  I have lived long enough. My way of life   22
  Is fall'n into the sere, the yellow leaf,   23
  And that which should accompany old age,
  As honor, love, obedience, troops of friends,   25
  I must not look to have, but in their stead
  Curses, not loud but deep, mouth-honor, breath
  Which the poor heart would fain deny and dare not.
  Seyton!

            Enter Seyton.

SEYTON
  What's your gracious pleasure?
MACBETH   What news more?

5.2. Location: The country near Dunsinane.
3–5 their . . . man their grievous wrongs would awaken even the dead to answer the bloody and grim call to battle. **6 well** conveniently   **8 file** list, roster   **10 unrough** beardless   **11 Protest** assert publicly   **15 distempered** disease-swollen, dropsical   **18 Now . . . faith-breach** every minute now, revolts upbraid him for his violation of all trust and sacred vows.   **19 in command** under orders   **23 pestered** troubled, tormented   **27 Meet we . . . weal** i.e., Let us join forces with Malcolm, the physician of our sick land   **28–9 pour . . . of us** i.e., let us shed all our blood as a bloodletting or *purge* of our country.   **30 dew** bedew, water.   **sovereign** (1) royal (2) medically efficacious

5.3. Location: Dunsinane. Macbeth's castle.
1 Let . . . all! Let all the thanes desert!   **3 taint with** become imbued or infected with, weakened by   **5 All . . . consequences** all that happens in this mortal life   **8 English epicures** luxury-loving Englishmen.   **9 sway** rule myself   **14 Go . . . fear** i.e., Go prick or pinch your pale cheeks to bring some color into them. (Current medical theory held that fear caused a retreat of the blood to the abdominal organs, leaving the countenance pale or *lily-livered,* line 15.)   **15 patch** domestic fool.   **16 Death . . . soul!** May your soul die an eternal death! (An oath.)   **linen** i.e., pale, white   **17 Are . . . fear** (The fear is contagious to the rest of the body and to other observers.)   **20 behold** (Macbeth does not finish this thought.) **push** effort, crisis   **21 cheer** (With a suggestion of "chair.")   **disseat** dethrone   **22 way** course   **23 sere** dry and withered   **25 As** such as

SEYTON
    All is confirmed, my lord, which was reported.
MACBETH
    I'll fight till from my bones my flesh be hacked.
    Give me my armor.
SEYTON   'Tis not needed yet.
MACBETH   I'll put it on.
    Send out more horses. Skirr the country round.   36
    Hang those that talk of fear. Give me mine armor.
    How does your patient, Doctor?
DOCTOR   Not so sick, my lord,
    As she is troubled with thick-coming fancies
    That keep her from her rest.
MACBETH   Cure her of that.
    Canst thou not minister to a mind diseased,
    Pluck from the memory a rooted sorrow,
    Raze out the written troubles of the brain,   44
    And with some sweet oblivious antidote   45
    Cleanse the stuffed bosom of that perilous stuff
    Which weighs upon the heart?
DOCTOR   Therein the patient
    Must minister to himself.
MACBETH
    Throw physic to the dogs! I'll none of it.   49
    Come, put mine armor on. Give me my staff.   50
                  [*Attendants arm him.*]
    Seyton, send out. Doctor, the thanes fly from me.—
    Come, sir, dispatch.—If thou couldst, Doctor, cast   52
    The water of my land, find her disease,   53
    And purge it to a sound and pristine health,
    I would applaud thee to the very echo,
    That should applaud again.—Pull't off, I say.—   56
    What rhubarb, senna, or what purgative drug   57
    Would scour these English hence? Hear'st thou of
      them?   58
DOCTOR
    Ay, my good lord. Your royal preparation
    Makes us hear something.
MACBETH   Bring it after me.—   60
    I will not be afraid of death and bane   61
    Till Birnam Forest come to Dunsinane.
                Exeunt [*all but the Doctor*].
DOCTOR
    Were I from Dunsinane away and clear,
    Profit again should hardly draw me here.   [*Exit.*]

❧

5.4

    Drum and colors. Enter Malcolm, Siward,
    Macduff, Siward's Son, Menteith, Caithness,
    Angus, [Lennox, Ross,] and soldiers, marching.

MALCOLM
    Cousins, I hope the days are near at hand   1
    That chambers will be safe.
MENTEITH   We doubt it nothing.   2
SIWARD
    What wood is this before us?
MENTEITH   The wood of Birnam.
MALCOLM
    Let every soldier hew him down a bough
    And bear't before him. Thereby shall we shadow
    The numbers of our host and make discovery   6
    Err in report of us.
SOLDIERS   It shall be done.
SIWARD
    We learn no other but the confident tyrant   8
    Keeps still in Dunsinane and will endure   9
    Our setting down before't.
MALCOLM   'Tis his main hope;   10
    For where there is advantage to be given,   11
    Both more and less have given him the revolt,   12
    And none serve with him but constrainèd things
    Whose hearts are absent too.
MACDUFF   Let our just censures   14
    Attend the true event, and put we on   15
    Industrious soldiership.
SIWARD   The time approaches
    That will with due decision make us know
    What we shall say we have and what we owe.   18
    Thoughts speculative their unsure hopes relate,   19
    But certain issue strokes must arbitrate—   20
    Towards which advance the war.   *Exeunt, marching.*   21

❧

5.5

    Enter Macbeth, Seyton, and soldiers, with drum
    and colors.

MACBETH
    Hang out our banners on the outward walls.
    The cry is still, "They come!" Our castle's strength
    Will laugh a siege to scorn. Here let them lie
    Till famine and the ague eat them up.   4
    Were they not forced with those that should be ours,   5
    We might have met them dareful, beard to beard,   6

---

36 Skirr Scour   **44 Raze** scrape; erase.   **written troubles of** troubles recorded in   **45 oblivious** causing forgetfulness   **49 physic** medicine **50 staff** lance or baton of office.   **52 dispatch** hurry.   **52–3 cast The water** diagnose disease by the inspection of urine   **56 Pull't off** (Refers to some part of the armor not properly put on.)   **57 senna** a purgative drug   **58 scour** purge, cleanse, rid   **60 it** i.e., the armor not yet put on   **61 bane** ruin
5.4. Location: Country near Birnam Wood.

1 Cousins Kinsmen, peers   **2 chambers . . . safe** i.e., we may sleep safely in our bedchambers.   **nothing** not at all.   **6 discovery** scouting reports   **8 no other but** no other news but that   **9 Keeps** remains.   **endure** allow, not attempt to prevent   **10 setting down before't** laying siege to it.   **11 advantage** opportunity (i.e., in military operations outside Macbeth's castle in which it is possible for would-be deserters to slip away; in a siege, his forces will be more confined to the castle and under his watchful eye)   **12 more and less** high and low   **14–15 Let . . . event** Let us postpone judgment about these uncertain matters until we've achieved our goal   **18 What . . . owe** what we only claim to have, as distinguished from what we actually have. (*Owe* can mean "own.")   **19–20 Thoughts . . . arbitrate** Speculating can only convey our sense of hope; blows must decide the actual outcome   **21 war** army.
5.5. Location: Dunsinane. Macbeth's castle.
4 the ague fever, disease   **5 forced** reinforced   **6 dareful** boldly, in open battle

And beat them backward home.

A cry within of women.
What is that noise?

SEYTON

It is the cry of women, my good lord.

[He goes to the door.]

MACBETH

I have almost forgot the taste of fears.
The time has been my senses would have cooled   10
To hear a night-shriek, and my fell of hair   11
Would at a dismal treatise rouse and stir   12
As life were in't. I have supped full with horrors;   13
Direness, familiar to my slaughterous thoughts,
Cannot once start me.

[Seyton returns.]

Wherefore was that cry?   15

SEYTON   The Queen, my lord, is dead.

MACBETH   She should have died hereafter;   17
There would have been a time for such a word.
Tomorrow, and tomorrow, and tomorrow   19
Creeps in this petty pace from day to day   20
To the last syllable of recorded time,
And all our yesterdays have lighted fools   22
The way to dusty death. Out, out, brief candle!   23
Life's but a walking shadow, a poor player
That struts and frets his hour upon the stage
And then is heard no more. It is a tale
Told by an idiot, full of sound and fury,
Signifying nothing.   28

Enter a Messenger.

Thou com'st to use thy tongue; thy story quickly.

MESSENGER   Gracious my lord,
I should report that which I say I saw,
But know not how to do't.

MACBETH   Well, say, sir.

MESSENGER

As I did stand my watch upon the hill,
I looked toward Birnam, and anon, methought,
The wood began to move.

MACBETH   Liar and slave!

MESSENGER

Let me endure your wrath if't be not so.
Within this three mile may you see it coming;
I say, a moving grove.

MACBETH   If thou speak'st false,
Upon the next tree shall thou hang alive
Till famine cling thee. If thy speech be sooth,   40
I care not if thou dost for me as much.

I pull in resolution, and begin   42
To doubt th'equivocation of the fiend
That lies like truth. "Fear not, till Birnam Wood
Do come to Dunsinane," and now a wood
Comes toward Dunsinane. Arm, arm, and out!
If this which he avouches does appear,
There is nor flying hence nor tarrying here.
I 'gin to be aweary of the sun,
And wish th'estate o'th' world were now undone.   50
Ring the alarum bell! Blow wind, come wrack,   51
At least we'll die with harness on our back.   *Exeunt.*   52

❖

5.6

*Drum and colors. Enter Malcolm, Siward,
Macduff, and their army, with boughs.*

MALCOLM

Now near enough. Your leafy screens throw down,
And show like those you are. You, worthy uncle,   2
Shall with my cousin, your right noble son,
Lead our first battle. Worthy Macduff and we   4
Shall take upon 's what else remains to do,
According to our order.

SIWARD   Fare you well.   6
Do we but find the tyrant's power tonight,   7
Let us be beaten, if we cannot fight.

MACDUFF

Make all our trumpets speak! Give them all breath,
Those clamorous harbingers of blood and death!   10

Exeunt. Alarums continued.

❖

5.7

Enter Macbeth.

MACBETH

They have tied me to a stake. I cannot fly,
But bearlike I must fight the course. What's he   2
That was not born of woman? Such a one
Am I to fear, or none.

Enter young Siward.

YOUNG SIWARD   What is thy name?

MACBETH   Thou'lt be afraid to hear it.

YOUNG SIWARD

No, though thou call'st thyself a hotter name
Than any is in hell.

MACBETH   My name's Macbeth.

---

10 cooled felt the chill of terror   **11 my fell of hair** the hair of my scalp   **12 dismal treatise** sad story   **13 As** as if   **15 start me** make me start.   **17 She . . . hereafter** She would have died someday, or, she should have died at some more appropriate time, freed from the relentless pressures of the moment   **19–28 Tomorrow . . . nothing** (For biblical echoes in this speech, see Psalms 18:28, 22:15, 90:9; Job 8:9, 14:1–2, 18:6.)   **20 in this** at this   **22 lighted** (The metaphor is of a candle used to light one to bed, just as life is a brief transit for wretched mortals to their deathbeds.)   **23 dusty** (Since life, made out of dust, returns to dust.)   **40 cling** cause to shrivel.   **sooth** truth

42 pull in resolution can no longer give free rein to my self-confident determination   **50 th'estate** the settled order   **51 wrack** ruin   **52 harness** armor
5.6. Location: Dunsinane. Before Macbeth's castle.
2 show appear.   **uncle** i.e., Siward   **4 battle** battalion.   **6 order** plan of battle.   **7 Do we** If we do.   **power** army   **10 harbingers** forerunners
5.7. Location: Before Macbeth's castle; the battle action is continuous here.
2 course bout or round of bearbaiting, in which the bear was tied to a stake and dogs were set upon him.

YOUNG SIWARD
The devil himself could not pronounce a title
More hateful to mine ear.
MACBETH   No, nor more fearful.
YOUNG SIWARD
Thou liest, abhorrèd tyrant! With my sword
I'll prove the lie thou speak'st.
                         Fight, and young Siward slain.
MACBETH   Thou wast born of woman.   12
But swords I smile at, weapons laugh to scorn,
Brandished by man that's of a woman born.   *Exit.*

    Alarums. Enter Macduff.

MACDUFF
That way the noise is. Tyrant, show thy face!
If thou be'st slain, and with no stroke of mine,
My wife and children's ghosts will haunt me still.
I cannot strike at wretched kerns, whose arms   18
Are hired to bear their staves. Either thou, Macbeth,   19
Or else my sword with an unbattered edge
I sheathe again undeeded. There thou shouldst be;   21
By this great clatter one of greatest note
Seems bruited. Let me find him, Fortune,   23
And more I beg not.   *Exit. Alarums.*

    Enter Malcolm and Siward.

SIWARD
This way, my lord. The castle's gently rendered: 25
The tyrant's people on both sides do fight,
The noble thanes do bravely in the war,
The day almost itself professes yours,   28
And little is to do.
MALCOLM   We have met with foes
That strike beside us.
SIWARD   Enter, sir, the castle.   30
                         Exeunt. Alarum.

❧

[5.8]

    Enter Macbeth.

MACBETH
Why should I play the Roman fool and die   1
On mine own sword? Whiles I see lives, the gashes   2

Do better upon them.

    Enter Macduff.

MACDUFF   Turn, hellhound, turn!
MACBETH
Of all men else I have avoided thee.
But get thee back! My soul is too much charged
With blood of thine already.
MACDUFF   I have no words;
My voice is in my sword, thou bloodier villain
Than terms can give thee out!   *Fight. Alarum.*
MACBETH   Thou losest labor.   8
As easy mayst thou the intrenchant air   9
With thy keen sword impress as make me bleed.   10
Let fall thy blade on vulnerable crests;
I bear a charmèd life, which must not yield
To one of woman born.
MACDUFF   Despair thy charm,   13
And let the angel whom thou still hast served   14
Tell thee, Macduff was from his mother's womb
Untimely ripped.   16
MACBETH
Accursèd be that tongue that tells me so,
For it hath cowed my better part of man!   18
And be these juggling fiends no more believed   19
That palter with us in a double sense,   20
That keep the word of promise to our ear   21
And break it to our hope. I'll not fight with thee.   22
MACDUFF   Then yield thee, coward,
And live to be the show and gaze o'th' time!   24
We'll have thee, as our rarer monsters are,
Painted upon a pole, and underwrit,   26
"Here may you see the tyrant."
MACBETH   I will not yield
To kiss the ground before young Malcolm's feet
And to be baited with the rabble's curse.
Though Birnam Wood be come to Dunsinane,
And thou opposed, being of no woman born,
Yet I will try the last. Before my body   32
I throw my warlike shield. Lay on, Macduff,
And damned be him that first cries, "Hold, enough!"   34
                         Exeunt, fighting. Alarums.

    Enter fighting, and Macbeth slain. [Exit Macduff
    with Macbeth's body.] Retreat, and flourish. Enter,
    with drum and colors, Malcolm, Siward, Ross,
    thanes, and soldiers.

---

12 s.d. *young Siward slain* (In some unspecified way, young Siward's body must be removed from the stage; his own father enters at line 24.1 and perceives nothing amiss, and in 5.8.38 young Siward is reported *missing* in action. Perhaps Macbeth drags off the body, or perhaps it is removed by soldiers during the alarums.) **18 kerns** (Properly, Irish foot soldiers; here, applied contemptuously to the rank and file.) **19 staves** spears. **Either thou** i.e., Either I find you and sheathe my sword in you **21 undeeded** having seen no action. **shouldst be** ought to be (judging by the noise) **23 bruited** announced. **25 gently rendered** surrendered without fighting **28 professes** declares itself **30 strike beside us** fight on our side, or miss us deliberately. **5.8. Location: Before Macbeth's castle, as the battle continues; after line 34, within the castle.** **1 Roman fool** i.e., suicide, like Brutus, Mark Antony, and others **2 Whiles . . . lives** i.e., As long as I see any enemy living

8 give thee out name you, describe you. **9 intrenchant** that cannot be cut, indivisible **10 impress** make an impression on **13 Despair** Despair of **14 angel** evil angel, Macbeth's genius. **still** always **16 Untimely** prematurely, i.e., by Caesarian delivery **18 better . . . man** i.e., courage. **19 juggling** deceiving **20 palter . . . sense** equivocate with us **21–2 That . . . hope** that make promises we hear (and think we understand) but then break promise with what we hoped and expected. **24 gaze o'th' time** spectacle or sideshow of the age. **26 Painted . . . pole** i.e., painted on a board or cloth and suspended on a pole **32 the last** i.e., my last resort: my own strength and resolution. **34.3 *Retreat*** a trumpet call ordering an end to the fighting. **34.3–4 *Enter, with drum and colors*, etc.** (The remainder of the play is perhaps imagined as taking place in Macbeth's castle and could be marked as a separate scene. In Shakespeare's theater, however, the shift is so nonrepresentational and without scenic alteration that the action is virtually continuous.)

MALCOLM

I would the friends we miss were safe arrived.

SIWARD

Some must go off; and yet, by these I see   36
So great a day as this is cheaply bought.

MALCOLM

Macduff is missing, and your noble son.

ROSS [to Siward]

Your son, my lord, has paid a soldier's debt.
He only lived but till he was a man,
The which no sooner had his prowess confirmed
In the unshrinking station where he fought,   42
But like a man he died.

SIWARD   Then he is dead?

ROSS

Ay, and brought off the field. Your cause of sorrow
Must not be measured by his worth, for then
It hath no end.

SIWARD   Had he his hurts before?

ROSS

Ay, on the front.

SIWARD   Why then, God's soldier be he!
Had I as many sons as I have hairs
I would not wish them to a fairer death.
And so, his knell is knolled.

MALCOLM   He's worth more sorrow,
And that I'll spend for him.

SIWARD   He's worth no more.
They say he parted well and paid his score,   52
And so, God be with him! Here comes newer comfort.

Enter Macduff, with Macbeth's head.

36 go off die. **by these** to judge by these (assembled) **42 unshrinking station** post from which he did not shrink **52 parted** departed,
died. **score** reckoning

MACDUFF

Hail, King! For so thou art. Behold where stands   54
Th'usurper's cursèd head. The time is free.   55
I see thee compassed with thy kingdom's pearl,   56
That speak my salutation in their minds,
Whose voices I desire aloud with mine:
Hail, King of Scotland!

ALL   Hail, King of Scotland!   *Flourish.*

MALCOLM

We shall not spend a large expense of time
Before we reckon with your several loves   62
And make us even with you. My thanes and kinsmen, 63
Henceforth be earls, the first that ever Scotland
In such an honor named. What's more to do
Which would be planted newly with the time,   66
As calling home our exiled friends abroad
That fled the snares of watchful tyranny,
Producing forth the cruel ministers   69
Of this dead butcher and his fiendlike queen—
Who, as 'tis thought, by self and violent hands   71
Took off her life—this, and what needful else
That calls upon us, by the grace of Grace
We will perform in measure, time, and place.
So, thanks to all at once and to each one,
Whom we invite to see us crowned at Scone.   76

                                Flourish. Exeunt omnes.

54 stands i.e., on a pole **55 free** released from tyranny. **56 compassed . . . pearl** surrounded by the nobles of your kingdom
(literally, the pearls encircling a crown) **62 reckon** come to a
reckoning. **several** individual **63 make . . . you** repay your worthiness. **66 would . . . time** should be established at the commencement of this new era **69 Producing forth** bringing forward to
trial. **ministers** agents **71 self and violent** her own violent
76.1 *omnes* all.

Antony and Cleopatra

Shakespeare probably wrote *Antony and Cleopatra* in 1606 or 1607; it was registered for publication on May 20, 1608, and apparently influenced a revision of Samuel Daniel's *Cleopatra* that was published "newly altered" in 1607. *Antony and Cleopatra* was thus roughly contemporary with *King Lear* and *Macbeth*. Yet the contrast between those two tragedies and *Antony and Cleopatra* is immense. Unlike *Macbeth,* with its taut focus on a murderer and his wife, *Antony and Cleopatra* moves back and forth across the Mediterranean in its epic survey of characters and events, bringing together the fates of Pompey, Octavius Caesar, Octavia, and Lepidus with those of the protagonists. *King Lear* gives proper names to fourteen characters, *Macbeth* to eighteen, *Antony and Cleopatra* to thirty-one. The Roman play requires no fewer than forty-two separate scenes, of which most occur in what modern editors label Acts 3 and 4, although no play is less suited to the classical rigors of five-act structure, and these divisions are not found in the reliable Folio text of 1623. Indeed, it is as though Shakespeare resolved at the height of his career to show that he could dispense entirely with the classical "rules," which had never taken serious hold of the English popular stage in any case. The flouting of the unities is so extreme that John Dryden, in his *All for Love, or The World Well Lost* (1678), undertook not so much to revise Shakespeare as to start afresh on the same subject. Dryden's play is restricted to the last few hours of the protagonists' lives, at Cleopatra's tomb in Alexandria, with a severely limited cast of characters and much of the narrative revealed through recollection. Although a substantial achievement in its own right, *All for Love* surely demonstrates that Shakespeare knew what he was doing, for Dryden has excised a good deal of the panorama, the excitement, and the "infinite variety" (2.2.246).

Shakespeare departs also from the somber tone of his tragedies of evil. He creates, instead, a world that bears affinities to the ambiguous conflicts of the other Roman plays, to the varying humorous perspectives of the comedies, and to the imaginative reconstructions of the late romances. As protagonists, Antony and Cleopatra lack tragic stature, or so it first appears: she is a tawny gypsy temptress and he a "strumpet's fool," a once-great general now bound in "strong Egyptian fetters" and lost in "dotage" (1.1.13; 1.2.122–3). Several scenes, especially those set in Egypt, are comic and delightfully bawdy: Charmian learning her fortune from the soothsayer, Cleopatra practicing her charms in vain to keep Antony from leaving Egypt or raunchily daydreaming of being Antony's horse "to bear the weight of Antony" (1.5.22), Cleopatra flying into a magnificent rage at the news of Antony's marriage to Octavia and then consoling herself with catty reflections on Octavia's reported low voice and shortness of stature ("I think so, Charmian. Dull of tongue, and dwarfish," 3.3.17). In its comic texture, the play somewhat resembles *Romeo and Juliet*, an earlier play about a younger pair of lovers, although there the bawdry is used chiefly to characterize the lovers' companions and confidants, whereas in *Antony and Cleopatra* it is central to our vision of Cleopatra especially. In any case, the later play is a tragedy about lovers who, despite their quarrels and uncertainties and betrayals of self, are reconciled in a vision of the greatness of their love. In its depiction of two contrasting worlds, also, *Antony and Cleopatra* recalls the movement of several earlier comedies from the realistic world of political conniving to a dreamworld of the romantic and the unexpected. We can endorse neither world fully in *Antony and Cleopatra,* and, accordingly, the vision of life presented is often ambivalent and ironic as much as it is tragic. The contrast of values separating Egypt and Rome underscores the paradox of humanity's quest for seemingly irreconcilable goals. The ending is neither a triumph nor a defeat for the lovers but something of both. If Antony and Cleopatra seem in one way too small to be tragic protagonists, in another way they seem too large, creating imaginative visions of themselves and their union that escape the realm of tragedy altogether. Our attention is focused less on the way in which the protagonists come to understand some meaningful relationship between their character and the fate required of them by a tragic universe than on the almost comic way in which the absurdities of Roman worldly striving and Egyptian dissipation are transfigured in the world of the imagination.

The Roman point of view opens the play and never entirely loses its force. At first, it may seem superior to that of Egypt. Demetrius and Philo, who invite us to view the play's first encounter between Antony and Cleopatra (1.1) from the perspective of the professional Roman soldier, lament the decline of Antony into Circean enslavement. Their tragic concept is of the Fall of Princes, all the more soberly edifying because of the height from which Antony has toppled. "You shall see in him / The triple pillar of the world transformed / Into a strumpet's fool" (1.1.11–13). Egypt is enchanting but clearly enervating—a bizarre assemblage of soothsayers, eunuchs, and waiting-gentlewomen who wish to be "married to three kings in a forenoon and widow them all" (1.2.28–9). Their mirth is all bawdry, tinged with practices, such as transvestitism, that Roman custom views as licentious. The prevailing images are of procreation in various shapes, sleep (mandragora, Lethe), the oriental opulence of Cleopatra's barge (a golden poop, purple sails, silver oars, divers-colored fans), Epicurean feasting, and drinking. As Enobarbus says, "Mine, and most of our fortunes tonight, shall be—drunk to bed" (1.2.47–8).

Antony, for all his reckless defiance of Rome, agrees in his more reflective moments with what Demetrius and Philo have said. "A Roman thought hath struck him," Cleopatra observantly remarks, and Antony has indeed determined that "I must from this enchanting queen break off" (1.2.88, 135). His later return to Cleopatra is at least in part a surrender, a betrayal of his marriage vows to Octavia and his political assurances to Caesar. In the ensuing battles, Antony submits himself dangerously to Cleopatra's governance, and this inversion of dominance in sexual roles, as conventionally understood by the Roman patriarchal world, is emblematic of a deeper disorder within Antony. As Enobarbus concludes bitterly, Antony "would make his will / Lord of his reason" and so has subverted his "judgment" (3.13.3–4, 37) to passion.

From the beginning, Cleopatra has sought dominance over Antony in the war of the sexes. When Antony first came to her on the River Cydnus, we learn, he was so overcome in all his senses that he was "barbered ten times o'er" (2.2.234). Cleopatra boasts that she "angled" for Antony on many occasions, catching him the way fishermen "betray" fish, and that, when she had "drunk him to his bed," she "put my tires and mantles on him, whilst / I wore his sword Philippan" (2.5.10–23). Caesar, affronted by such transvestite debauchery, charges that Antony "is not more manlike / Than Cleopatra, nor the queen of

Ptolemy / More womanly than he" (1.4.5–7). During the battle scenes, Antony's followers complain that "Photinus, an eunuch" (probably Mardian), and Cleopatra's maids manage the war: "So our leader's led, / And we are women's men" (3.7.14–15, 70–1). Antony confesses too late that they were right. He becomes a "doting mallard," one whose heart is "tied by th' strings" to Cleopatra's rudder when her ships retreat in the first naval engagement (3.10.20, 3.11.56). In the mythic images used to raise their relationship to heroic proportions, Antony is like Mars to Cleopatra's Venus (1.5.19), in both a positive and a negative sense. The image has positive connotations of the way in which, as Milton puts it, the "two great sexes animate the world," the masterful soldier and his attractive consort complementing one another in a right relationship of martial prowess and beauty, bravery and love, reason and will; however, to the Renaissance, the myth of Mars and Venus could also be read in a destructive sense, as an adulterous relationship in which reason is subverted to appetite. In another mythic comparison, Antony is like Hercules, not in his prime, but with the shirt of Nessus on his back—a poisoned shirt given to Hercules by his wife in a mistaken hope of thereby assuring his love for her (4.12.43). Antony's soldiers understandably believe that the god Hercules has deserted his reputed descendant and onetime champion (4.3.21–2).

Despite Antony's shameful violation of manhood, honor, attention to duty, self-knowledge, and all that Rome stands for, however, the end of his story is anything but a one-sided endorsement for the Roman point of view. The actual Rome, disfigured by political conniving, falls far short of the ideal. Antony has a point when he protests that "Kingdoms are clay" (1.1.37). Alliances are unstable and are governed by mere political expediency. At first, Antony's wife Fulvia and his brother Lucius have fought one another until forced to unite against the greater threat of Octavius Caesar. Similarly, Antony and Caesar come together only because Pompey has become dangerously powerful at sea and has won the favor of the fickle mob, "Our slippery people" (1.2.192). This detente is not meant to last. As Enobarbus bluntly puts it, "if you borrow one another's love for the instant, you may, when you hear no more words of Pompey, return it again" (2.2.109–11). Enobarbus is rebuked for his unstatesmanlike tone, but no one denies the validity of what he says. In this cynical negotiation, Octavia is a pawn between husband and brother, shabbily treated by both. Caesar coldly bargains away the happiness of the one person of whom he protests that "no brother / Did ever love so dearly" (2.2.159–60). Antony, although hating false promises and resolving to be loyal to Octavia, knows within himself that it won't work. To make matters worse for the fair-minded Antony, he has received great favors from Pompey that he must now uncharitably repudiate in the interests of politics. Pompey does not miss the opportunity to remind Antony of his ingratitude, but the prevailing mood is not so much of bitterness as of ironic futility. Old friendships must be sacrificed; no one seems wholly to blame, and no one can stop the game. Pompey is as much in the wrong as anyone and as powerless. Despite his idealistic hope of restoring republican government to Rome, he has had to ally himself with pirates who offer him sinister temptations. He could be "lord of all the world" (2.7.62) if he would only murder on occasion, but Pompey is destined to be trapped between lofty ends and ignoble means. Lepidus is still another dismaying victim of political callousness, used condescendingly by Caesar and permitted to drink himself into oblivion, until he is cashiered on a trumped-up charge and imprisoned for life.

Octavius Caesar embodies most of all the ironic limits of political ambition. He has avoided enslavement to passion at the very real cost of enslaving himself to his public career as general, triumvir, and future emperor. His ideal warrior is one who, driven by military necessity, would "drink / The stale [urine] of horses and the gilded puddle / Which beasts would cough at" (1.4.62–4). As a general, he is Antony's opposite in every way. He attacks only when he has the advantage and places those who have deserted Antony in his own front lines so "That Antony may seem to spend his fury / Upon himself" (4.6.10–11). He controls his supplies cannily, believing it a "waste" to feast his army (4.1.17). He, of course, declines Antony's offers of single combat. Antony meantime recklessly accepts Caesar's challenge to fight at sea, feasts debauchingly in one "gaudy night" after another (3.13.186), and generously refuses to blame or penalize those who leave him. His sending Enobarbus's belongings after him into Caesar's camp convinces that honest soldier he has made a fatal error, for, however imprudent Antony's chivalry may be, it is unquestionably noble and great-hearted. Caesar is a superb general and political genius, but he is also a military automaton, a logistical reckoner, a Machiavellian pragmatist. In his personal life, he is no less austere and puritanical. He deplores loosening his tongue with alcohol. About women, he is deeply cynical, believing that "want will perjure / The ne'er-touched vestal" (3.12.30–1). Between him and Cleopatra, there is a profound antipathy, based in part on his revulsion at her earlier affair with his namesake and adoptive father, Julius Caesar (3.6.6). Cleopatra may entertain briefly the notion of trying to seduce this new Caesar (3.13.46 ff.), for like Charmian she loves long life "better than figs"(1.2.34), but, if so, she soon discovers that she and Caesar are not compatible. All that he represents she must instead grandly repudiate, choosing death and the fantasy of an eternity with Antony as her way to "call great Caesar ass / Unpolicied" (5.2.307–8).

Cleopatra is a "lass unparalleled" (5.2.316), whose greatness is elusive and all the more enthralling because it is so mysterious. She rises above her counterpart in Shakespeare's source, Plutarch's *Lives of the Noble Grecians and Romans,* in which she is an impressive queenly woman but still essentially a temptress causing the lamentable fall of the hero. Shakespeare's Cleopatra is that but is also something indefinable that can be gotten at only through paradox. Her very character is the essence of contradiction: she knows how "to chide, to laugh, / To weep" (1.1.51–2), to be sullen or violent, like a skillful actor keeping Antony continually off guard. Dispassionately examined, she is a woman no longer young who abuses messengers like an oriental despot, who sends Antony a false report of her death out of fear for her own safety, who will not risk leaving her monument even when Antony lies outside mortally wounded, and who lies about her wealth when captured by Caesar (what is she planning to do with that wealth, anyway?). We cannot be sure that she would not have "packed cards with Caesar" (4.14.19) if she had found him susceptible to her charms. Yet we are not invited to see her dispassionately. Her charm is eternal, and so are the myths surrounding that charm. Observers evoking her splendor do not describe her person directly but, rather, her effects and surroundings: Enobarbus says simply that "For her own person, / It beggared all description" and goes on to catalogue her cloth-of-gold pavilion and her mermaidlike attendants. Most of all, she is a paradox: she makes defect perfection, age cannot wither her, and "vilest things / Become themselves in her, that the holy priests / Bless her when she is riggish" (2.2.207–50). She is both a whore and the Lucretian Venus; both sluttish and holy.

Inspired by Cleopatra, Antony shows himself ready to break down conventional barriers between the sexes and to explore new emotional territory by giving up part of his self-protective masculinity. Antony's embracing of an attractive but sexually dangerous woman is all the more remarkable in a play that follows the harrowing depictions of sexual conflict in *Hamlet, Othello,* and *Lear* and the degrading portrait of erotic enslavement in the "Dark Lady" sonnets, for here the relationship of the lovers, though doomed, is also triumphant. Shakespeare takes a look at something like midlife crisis, conceding freely how ridiculous the male appears to himself and to others in his compulsive tendency to polarize women into saints and whores. Yet Shakespeare also explores ways in which the man and the woman attempt to become increasingly like each other, enabling the man to participate in a vision of union with the feminine principle of generative, erotic, fertile, life-giving vitality, and enabling the woman to join her "husband" in the noble resolve of a Roman suicide.

In Cleopatra, "fancy" exceeds "nature"; the fertility of her Egypt overflows the measure, exceeding the sterility of Rome as her own imaginative fertility exceeds reality itself. When she protests that she will not go to Rome to behold herself in a wretched play and thus see "Some squeaking Cleopatra boy my greatness / I'th' posture of a whore" (5.2.220–1), we realize that Shakespeare is calling attention to his own art as well, pointing out how Elizabethan boy actors on a bare stage can transform reality into a dream that we believe. Cleopatra's mystery is like that of poetry itself. The "real" world pales into insignificance of a "little O, the earth," something "No better than a sty," full of illusory shadows that "mock our eyes with air" (5.2.80, 4.15.64, 4.14.7); and Caesar's triumph vanishes with it. In its place, Antony and Cleopatra raise up a vision of themselves as lovers who, through art, have indeed become eternal. Together they will overpicture Venus and Mars, and will be so renowned that "Dido and her Aeneas shall want troops, / And all the haunt be ours" (4.14.53–4). They are virtually husband and wife—"Husband, I come!" exclaims Cleopatra just before she dies (5.2.287)—united at last in a re-creative vision almost appropriate to comedy; and in their marriage they find a kind of redemption for the defeat that history can inflict. Antony is no longer dying Hercules but the god of Cleopatra's dream whose "legs bestrid the ocean; his reared arm / Crested the world; his voice was propertied / As all the tunèd spheres" (lines 81–3). Through Cleopatra's vision, we realize how all the characteristics that made Antony at once so noble and so sure to fall before Caesar—his generosity amounting to imprudence, his spontaneity, his impatience with the ordinary, his staking his all on love when he hears of Cleopatra's supposed death—have not deserted him. His death serves to reaffirm the magnificence of the very qualities that have brought him down. His essential nobility is confirmed, even if it must be defined in non-Roman ways. He and Cleopatra share the "immortal longings" for which she goes willingly to her death, dressed in her "best attires" like a queen (lines 281, 228), for neither lover will accept anything less than greatness.

Antony and Cleopatra is a daunting play to stage, because the main characters take on a mythic character that seems larger than life, larger than art itself. Michael Goldman imagines what it would be like for an actor to try out for the part of Antony only to be instructed by the casting director, "Now, stand there and be a triple pillar of the world." How can an actor convey the charisma of a man whose very name is legendary? The problem in acting Cleopatra is even more acute. The great actresses who have taken on the assignment have all been praised for many things but also faulted for lacking other dimensions of this amazing character. Vivien Leigh, playing opposite Laurence Olivier's Antony at the St. James Theatre, London, in 1951, was applauded by the critics for her coquettish sexiness and magnetism but perhaps deficient in animal heat and duskiness. Peggy Ashcroft, in Glen Byam Shaw's production at Stratford-upon-Avon in 1953, was lauded as impressively intelligent and capable of huge emotional variation, but was seen as physically small and not as sexually glamorous as Leigh. Margaret Whiting, at the Old Vic in 1957, was regarded by most viewers as simply too young for the part. Vanessa Redgrave, at the Bankside Globe Playhouse in 1973, threw cola bottles at her servants in her fits of temper, and somehow lacked dignity for the final scenes. Glenda Jackson, playing Cleopatra in Peter Brook's deromanticized version at Stratford-upon-Avon in 1978, was brilliant for her iciness of tone and angularity in wit combat, but at the expense of tenderness and erotic feeling. The role has attracted the greatest of talent, from Janet Suzman to Helen Mirren to Judi Dench, with similar praise and qualifications. These limits are a tribute to the play itself but a thorny problem for those who are producing the play. Film versions have tended to succumb to the temptations of visual splendor, in the style of Cecil B. DeMille, thus missing the point of the play's verbal and theatrical invocation of the ineffable. One singularly successful production is that on audiotape with Michael Redgrave as Antony and Peggy Ashcroft as Cleopatra; here the listener can imagine the lovers to be as toweringly great as the play's language suggests, magnificently assisted by the voices of two great actors. This is not to say that *Antony and Cleopatra* is unplayable; to the contrary, it shows Shakespeare at the very height of his powers as a professional writer for the theater. At the same time, few plays have ever posed a greater challenge for an acting ensemble.

Antony and Cleopatra

Dramatis Personae

MARK ANTONY,
OCTAVIUS CAESAR, } *triumvirs*
LEPIDUS,

CLEOPATRA,
CHARMIAN,
IRAS,
ALEXAS,
MARDIAN, *a eunuch*,
DIOMEDES,
SELEUCUS, *Cleopatra's treasurer*,
} *Cleopatra's attendants*

OCTAVIA, *sister of Octavius Caesar and wife of
   Antony*

DEMETRIUS,
PHILO,
DOMITIUS ENOBARBUS,
VENTIDIUS,
SILIUS,
EROS,
CANIDIUS,
SCARUS,
DERCETUS,
} *Antony's friends and followers*

A SCHOOLMASTER, *Antony's* AMBASSADOR *to Caesar*

MAECENAS,
AGRIPPA,
TAURUS,
THIDIAS,
DOLABELLA,
GALLUS,
PROCULEIUS,
} *Octavius Caesar's friends and followers*

SEXTUS POMPEIUS *or* POMPEY
MENAS,
MENECRATES,
VARRIUS,
} *Pompey's friends*

MESSENGERS *to Antony, Octavius, Caesar, and Cleopatra*
A SOOTHSAYER
Two SERVANTS *of Pompey*
SERVANTS *of Antony and Cleopatra*
A BOY
SOLDIERS, SENTRIES, GUARDSMEN *of Antony
   and Octavius Caesar*
A CAPTAIN *in Antony's army*
An EGYPTIAN
A CLOWN *with figs*

Ladies attending Cleopatra, Eunuchs, Servants, Soldiers, Captains, Officers, silent named characters
   (Rannius, Lucillius, Lamprius)

SCENE: *In several parts of the Roman Empire*]

1.1

Enter Demetrius and Philo.

PHILO
  Nay, but this dotage of our general's   1
  O'erflows the measure. Those his goodly eyes,   2

  That o'er the files and musters of the war   3
  Have glowed like plated Mars, now bend, now turn   4
  The office and devotion of their view   5
  Upon a tawny front. His captain's heart,   6
  Which in the scuffles of great fights hath burst
  The buckles on his breast, renges all temper   8

1.1. Location: Alexandria. Cleopatra's palace.
1 dotage foolish affection, sometimes associated with old age
2 O'erflows the measure exceeds moderation, exceeds the means of
measuring it.

3 files and musters orderly formations   **4 plated** clothed in armor
5 office function   **6 tawny front** dark face. (Literally, forehead.)
8 renges all temper renounces all moderation

And is become the bellows and the fan
To cool a gypsy's lust.

Flourish. Enter Antony, Cleopatra, her ladies, the
train, with eunuchs fanning her.

               Look, where they come.   10
Take but good note, and you shall see in him
The triple pillar of the world transformed   12
Into a strumpet's fool. Behold and see.   13

CLEOPATRA
If it be love indeed, tell me how much.

ANTONY
There's beggary in the love that can be reckoned.   15

CLEOPATRA
I'll set a bourn how far to be beloved.   16

ANTONY
Then must thou needs find out new heaven, new
    earth.   17

Enter a Messenger.

MESSENGER   News, my good lord, from Rome.
ANTONY   Grates me! The sum.   19
CLEOPATRA   Nay, hear them, Antony.   20
Fulvia perchance is angry, or who knows   21
If the scarce-bearded Caesar have not sent   22
His powerful mandate to you, "Do this, or this;
Take in that kingdom, and enfranchise that;   24
Perform't, or else we damn thee."   25
ANTONY   How, my love?   26
CLEOPATRA   Perchance? Nay, and most like.   27
You must not stay here longer; your dismission   28
Is come from Caesar. Therefore hear it, Antony.
Where's Fulvia's process? Caesar's, I would say. Both?   30
Call in the messengers. As I am Egypt's queen,
Thou blushest, Antony, and that blood of thine
Is Caesar's homager; else so thy cheek pays shame   33
When shrill-tongued Fulvia scolds. The messengers!

ANTONY
Let Rome in Tiber melt and the wide arch
Of the ranged empire fall! Here is my space.   36
Kingdoms are clay; our dungy earth alike
Feeds beast as man. The nobleness of life

Is to do thus; when such a mutual pair   39
And such a twain can do't, in which I bind,   40
On pain of punishment, the world to weet   41
We stand up peerless.
CLEOPATRA   Excellent falsehood!   42
Why did he marry Fulvia, and not love her?   43
I'll seem the fool I am not. Antony   44
Will be himself.
ANTONY   But stirred by Cleopatra.   45
Now, for the love of Love and her soft hours,
Let's not confound the time with conference harsh.   47
There's not a minute of our lives should stretch   48
Without some pleasure now. What sport tonight?

CLEOPATRA
Hear the ambassadors.

ANTONY   Fie, wrangling queen!
Whom everything becomes—to chide, to laugh,
To weep; whose every passion fully strives
To make itself, in thee, fair and admired!
No messenger but thine; and all alone
Tonight we'll wander through the streets and note
The qualities of people. Come, my queen,
Last night you did desire it.—Speak not to us.
     Exeunt [Antony and Cleopatra] with the train.

DEMETRIUS
Is Caesar with Antonius prized so slight?   58
PHILO
Sir, sometimes when he is not Antony
He comes too short of that great property   60
Which still should go with Antony.
DEMETRIUS   I am full sorry   61
That he approves the common liar, who   62
Thus speaks of him at Rome; but I will hope
Of better deeds tomorrow. Rest you happy!   *Exeunt.*   64

❖

[1.2]

Enter Enobarbus, Lamprius, a Soothsayer, Ran-
nius, Lucillius, Charmian, Iras, Mardian the
eunuch, and Alexas.

CHARMIAN   Lord Alexas, sweet Alexas, most anything
Alexas, almost most absolute Alexas, where's the   2
soothsayer that you praised so to th' Queen? Oh, that

---

10 **gypsy's** (Gypsies were widely believed to have come from Egypt, to enjoy magical powers, and to be lustful and cunning.)   **s.d.** *Flourish* trumpet fanfare announcing the arrival or departure of an important person.   *train* retinue   **12 triple** one of three. (Alludes to the triumvirate of Antony, Lepidus, and Octavius Caesar; also to tripartite division of the world into Asia, Africa, and Europe.)   **13 fool** plaything.   **15 There's . . . reckoned** i.e., Love that can be quantified is paltry; ours is infinite.   **16 bourn** boundary, limit   **17 Then . . . earth** i.e., Only in some new universe could you find a limit to my love. (The language echoes Revelation 21:1 and other biblical passages.)   **19 Grates . . . sum** It annoys me! Be brief.   **20 them** i.e., the news   **21 Fulvia** Antony's wife   **22 scarce-bearded Caesar** (Octavius Caesar was twenty-three in 40 B.C., at the time of the play's opening. Antony was forty-three.)   **24 Take in** conquer.   **enfranchise** set free   **25 damn** condemn to death   **26 How** i.e., What's that you say?   **27 Perchance** (Cleopatra reconsiders what she has said in line 21.) **like** likely.   **28 dismission** order to depart   **30 process** writ to appear in court.   **33 Is . . . shame** is Caesar's vassal, doing homage to him; or else your blushing pays the tribute of shame   **36 ranged** well-ordered and far-extending

39 **thus** (May indicate an embrace, or Antony may refer more generally to their way of life.)   **40–2 in which . . . peerless** with respect to which I insist that the world, under penalty of punishment if it fails to do so, acknowledge us to be peerless.   **43 and not** if he did not **44 I'll . . . not** i.e., I'll pretend to be gullible and believe him, though I know better.   **45 be himself** i.e., be the Roman Antony, be the fool and deceiver he always is, etc.   **stirred** (1) prompted to noble deeds (2) moved to folly (3) sexually stirred   **47 confound** ruin, waste. **conference** conversation   **48 should stretch** that should be prolonged   **58 prized** valued   **60 property** quality, distinction   **61 still** always   **62 approves** corroborates   **64 Of** for **1.2. Location: Alexandria. Cleopatra's palace.** **0.1–2 Lamprius . . . Lucillius** (Lamprius may possibly be the soothsayer, but Rannius and Lucillius have no speaking parts here and do not appear again in the play. Mardian is mute here but does speak in later scenes.)   **2 absolute** perfect

I knew this husband, which, you say, must charge his 4
horns with garlands! 5

ALEXAS   Soothsayer!

SOOTHSAYER   Your will?

CHARMIAN
Is this the man?—Is't you, sir, that know things?

SOOTHSAYER
In nature's infinite book of secrecy
A little I can read.

ALEXAS [to Charmian]   Show him your hand.

ENOBARBUS [to servants within]
Bring in the banquet quickly; wine enough 12
Cleopatra's health to drink.

CHARMIAN [giving her hand to the Soothsayer]   Good sir,
give me good fortune.

SOOTHSAYER   I make not, but foresee.

CHARMIAN   Pray, then, foresee me one.

SOOTHSAYER
You shall be yet far fairer than you are.

CHARMIAN   He means in flesh. 19

IRAS   No, you shall paint when you are old. 20

CHARMIAN   Wrinkles forbid!

ALEXAS   Vex not his prescience. Be attentive.

CHARMIAN   Hush!

SOOTHSAYER
You shall be more beloving than beloved.

CHARMIAN   I had rather heat my liver with drinking. 25

ALEXAS   Nay, hear him.

CHARMIAN   Good now, some excellent fortune! Let me 27
be married to three kings in a forenoon and widow
them all. Let me have a child at fifty, to whom Herod 29
of Jewry may do homage. Find me to marry me with 30
Octavius Caesar, and companion me with my mis- 31
tress. 32

SOOTHSAYER
You shall outlive the lady whom you serve.

CHARMIAN   Oh, excellent! I love long life better than figs. 34

SOOTHSAYER
You have seen and proved a fairer former fortune 35
Than that which is to approach.

CHARMIAN   Then belike my children shall have no 37
names. Prithee, how many boys and wenches must I 38
have? 39

SOOTHSAYER
If every of your wishes had a womb,
And fertile every wish, a million.

CHARMIAN   Out, fool! I forgive thee for a witch. 42

ALEXAS   You think none but your sheets are privy to 43
your wishes.

CHARMIAN   Nay, come, tell Iras hers.

ALEXAS   We'll know all our fortunes.

ENOBARBUS   Mine, and most of our fortunes tonight,
shall be—drunk to bed.

IRAS [giving her hand to the Soothsayer]   There's a palm
presages chastity, if nothing else.

CHARMIAN   E'en as the o'erflowing Nilus presageth 51
famine. 52

IRAS   Go, you wild bedfellow, you cannot soothsay. 53

CHARMIAN   Nay, if an oily palm be not a fruitful prog- 54
nostication, I cannot scratch mine ear. Prithee, tell her 55
but a workaday fortune. 56

SOOTHSAYER   Your fortunes are alike.

IRAS   But how, but how? Give me particulars.

SOOTHSAYER   I have said. 59

IRAS   Am I not an inch of fortune better than she?

CHARMIAN   Well, if you were but an inch of fortune better than I, where would you choose it?

IRAS   Not in my husband's nose. 63

CHARMIAN   Our worser thoughts heavens mend! Al- 64
exas—come, his fortune, his fortune! Oh, let him marry
a woman that cannot go, sweet Isis, I beseech thee, 66
and let her die too, and give him a worse, and let
worse follow worse till the worst of all follow him
laughing to his grave, fiftyfold a cuckold! Good Isis,
hear me this prayer, though thou deny me a matter of 70
more weight; good Isis, I beseech thee!

IRAS   Amen, dear goddess, hear that prayer of the people! For, as it is a heart-breaking to see a handsome
man loose-wived, so it is a deadly sorrow to behold a 74
foul knave uncuckolded. Therefore, dear Isis, keep de- 75
corum, and fortune him accordingly! 76

CHARMIAN   Amen.

ALEXAS   Lo now, if it lay in their hands to make me a
cuckold, they would make themselves whores but 79
they'd do't. 80

Enter Cleopatra.

ENOBARBUS
Hush! Here comes Antony.

CHARMIAN   Not he. The Queen.

CLEOPATRA [to Enobarbus]   Saw you my lord?

---

4 this husband (Evidently Alexas has told Charmian that the Soothsayer will prophesy a husband for her.)   4–5 must . . . garlands i.e.,
must decorate his cuckold's horns with a garland of flowers, like a
sacrificial beast. (Cuckolded men were derisively thought of as growing horns, as a badge of their infamy.)   12 banquet light repast,
dessert   19 in flesh i.e., by putting on weight.   20 paint i.e., use
makeup   25 heat . . . drinking i.e., heat my liver with wine rather
than with unrequited love. (The liver was believed to be the seat of
sexual desire.)   27 Good now Come on, now   29–30 Herod of Jewry
i.e., even the blustering tyrant who massacred the children of Judea
30 Find me i.e., Find in my palm   31–2 companion . . . mistress give
me equal fortune with Cleopatra; or, perhaps, let Cleopatra become
my "companion" or attendant.   34 better than figs (Probably a
proverbial expression; with genital suggestion.)   35 proved experienced   37 belike probably   37–8 have no names be illegitimate.
38 wenches girls   38–9 must I have am I to have.

42 Out . . . witch (Charmian jokingly says that, since soothsayers, like
fools, are allowed to speak freely without penalty, she will forgive
him for slander.)   43 privy to in on the secret of   51–2 E'en . . .
famine (Charmian speaks ironically; the overflowing Nile presages
abundance. See 2.7.17–23.)   53 wild wanton   54 oily palm sweaty or
moist palm (indicating a sensual disposition)   54–5 fruitful prognostication omen of fertility   56 workaday ordinary   59 I have said I
have no more to say.   63 Not . . . nose (Iras bawdily hints at some
place other than in the nose where she would prefer to see her husband well endowed.)   64 Our . . . mend! (Charmian pretends to be
shocked: May heaven improve our dirty minds!)   66 cannot go (1) is
lame (2) cannot make love satisfactorily or cannot bear children.   Isis
Egyptian goddess usually identified with fertility and the moon
70 hear me hear (on my behalf)   74 loose-wived with an unfaithful
wife   75 foul ugly   75–6 keep decorum deal suitably with the case
76 fortune him grant him fortune   79–80 they . . . do't i.e., they
would stop at nothing, even becoming whores, to cuckold me.

ENOBARBUS   No, lady.

CLEOPATRA [to Charmian]   Was he not here?

CHARMIAN   No, madam.

CLEOPATRA

He was disposed to mirth, but on the sudden
A Roman thought hath struck him. Enobarbus!

ENOBARBUS   Madam?

CLEOPATRA

Seek him and bring him hither. Where's Alexas?

ALEXAS

Here at your service.—My lord approaches.

Enter Antony with a Messenger.

CLEOPATRA

We will not look upon him. Go with us.
            Exeunt [all but Antony and the Messenger].

FIRST MESSENGER

Fulvia thy wife first came into the field.   93

ANTONY   Against my brother Lucius?

FIRST MESSENGER   Ay.

But soon that war had end, and the time's state   96
Made friends of them, jointing their force 'gainst
            Caesar,   97
Whose better issue in the war from Italy   98
Upon the first encounter drave them.   99

ANTONY   Well, what worst?

FIRST MESSENGER

The nature of bad news infects the teller.   101

ANTONY

When it concerns the fool or coward. On.
Things that are past are done with me. 'Tis thus:
Who tells me true, though in his tale lie death,
I hear him as he flattered.

FIRST MESSENGER   Labienus—   105
This is stiff news—hath with his Parthian force
Extended Asia; from Euphrates   107
His conquering banner shook, from Syria
To Lydia and to Ionia,
Whilst—

ANTONY   Antony, thou wouldst say.

FIRST MESSENGER   Oh, my lord!

ANTONY

Speak to me home; mince not the general tongue.   111
Name Cleopatra as she is called in Rome;
Rail thou in Fulvia's phrase, and taunt my faults   113
With such full license as both truth and malice
Have power to utter. Oh, then we bring forth weeds
When our quick minds lie still, and our ills told us   116
Is as our earing. Fare thee well awhile.   117

FIRST MESSENGER   At your noble pleasure.
                        Exit [First] Messenger.

Enter another Messenger.

ANTONY

From Sicyon, ho, the news! Speak there.

SECOND MESSENGER

The man from Sicyon—is there such an one?   120

THIRD MESSENGER [at the door]

He stays upon your will.

ANTONY   Let him appear.—   121
            [Exeunt Second and Third Messengers.]
These strong Egyptian fetters I must break,
Or lose myself in dotage.

Enter another Messenger, with a letter.

                        What are you?

FOURTH MESSENGER   Fulvia thy wife is dead.

ANTONY   Where died she?

FOURTH MESSENGER   In Sicyon.

Her length of sickness, with what else more serious
Importeth thee to know, this bears. [He gives a letter.]

ANTONY   Forbear me.   128
                        [Exit Fourth Messenger.]
There's a great spirit gone! Thus did I desire it.
What our contempts doth often hurl from us
We wish it ours again. The present pleasure,
By revolution lowering, does become   132
The opposite of itself. She's good, being gone;
The hand could pluck her back that shoved her on.   134
I must from this enchanting queen break off.
Ten thousand harms more than the ills I know
My idleness doth hatch.—How now, Enobarbus!

Enter Enobarbus.

ENOBARBUS   What's your pleasure, sir?

ANTONY   I must with haste from hence.

ENOBARBUS   Why, then, we kill all our women. We see
how mortal an unkindness is to them; if they suffer
our departure, death's the word.

ANTONY   I must be gone.

ENOBARBUS   Under a compelling occasion, let women
die. It were pity to cast them away for nothing, though
between them and a great cause they should be esteemed nothing. Cleopatra, catching but the least noise   147
of this, dies instantly; I have seen her die twenty times   148
upon far poorer moment. I do think there is mettle in   149

---

93 field battlefield.   **96 time's state** circumstances prevailing at the moment   **97 jointing** uniting   **98–9 Whose . . . them** whose better military success drove them from Italy upon the very first encounter.   **101 infects the teller** i.e., makes the teller seem unwelcome.   **105 as** as if.   **Labienus** (Brutus and Cassius [see *Julius Caesar*] had sent Quintus Labienus to Orodes, King of Parthia, to seek aid against Antony and Octavius Caesar; with a force thus obtained, he is now overrunning the Roman provinces in the Middle East.)   **107 Extended** seized upon. (A legal phrase.)   **111 Speak . . . tongue** Speak bluntly; don't minimize the common report.   **113 Rail . . . phrase** Scold me as Fulvia would   **116 quick** alive, inventive   **116–17 our ills . . . earing** hearing our faults told to us improves us, as plowing (*earing*) improves land by rooting out the weeds.

120 The man from Sicyon (The messenger who has just entered, not being from Sicyon, realizes in some confusion that Antony wants to hear the news from Sicyon. This second messenger therefore calls out to ask if the messenger from Sicyon is to be found. Another messenger at the door replies that such a man is indeed waiting, and in a moment that messenger from Sicyon enters with his report. Some editors change the second and third messengers into attendants.) *Sicyon* is an ancient city in Greece, where Antony left Fulvia.   **121 stays upon** awaits   **128 Importeth** concerns.   **Forbear** Leave   **132 By revolution lowering** sinking in our estimation in the course of time and Fortune's turning wheel   **134 could** would be willing to   **147 noise** hint, rumor   **148 die** (Playing on a common second meaning of "achieve sexual orgasm.")   **149 poorer moment** lesser cause. **mettle** i.e., sexual vigor

death, which commits some loving act upon her, she
hath such a celerity in dying.

ANTONY   She is cunning past man's thought.

ENOBARBUS   Alack, sir, no, her passions are made of
nothing but the finest part of pure love. We cannot call
her winds and waters sighs and tears; they are greater 155
storms and tempests than almanacs can report. This
cannot be cunning in her; if it be, she makes a shower
of rain as well as Jove.

ANTONY   Would I had never seen her!

ENOBARBUS   Oh, sir, you had then left unseen a wonderful piece of work, which not to have been blessed
withal would have discredited your travel.

ANTONY   Fulvia is dead.

ENOBARBUS   Sir?

ANTONY   Fulvia is dead.

ENOBARBUS   Fulvia?

ANTONY   Dead.

ENOBARBUS   Why, sir, give the gods a thankful sacrifice.
When it pleaseth their deities to take the wife of a man
from him, it shows to man the tailors of the earth; 170
comforting therein, that when old robes are worn out,
there are members to make new. If there were no more 172
women but Fulvia, then had you indeed a cut, and the
case to be lamented. This grief is crowned with consolation; your old smock brings forth a new petticoat, 175
and indeed the tears live in an onion that should water 176
this sorrow. 177

ANTONY
The business she hath broachèd in the state 178
Cannot endure my absence.

ENOBARBUS   And the business you have broached here
cannot be without you, especially that of Cleopatra's,
which wholly depends on your abode. 182

ANTONY
No more light answers. Let our officers 183
Have notice what we purpose. I shall break 184
The cause of our expedience to the Queen 185
And get her leave to part. For not alone 186
The death of Fulvia, with more urgent touches, 187
Do strongly speak to us, but the letters too
Of many our contriving friends in Rome 189
Petition us at home. Sextus Pompeius 190
Hath given the dare to Caesar and commands
The empire of the sea. Our slippery people, 192

Whose love is never linked to the deserver
Till his deserts are past, begin to throw 194
Pompey the Great and all his dignities 195
Upon his son, who—high in name and power,
Higher than both in blood and life—stands up 197
For the main soldier; whose quality, going on, 198
The sides o'th' world may danger. Much is breeding, 199
Which, like the courser's hair, hath yet but life, 200
And not a serpent's poison. Say our pleasure, 201
To such whose place is under us, requires 202
Our quick remove from hence. 203

ENOBARBUS   I shall do't.   [Exeunt separately.]

❖

[1.3]

Enter Cleopatra, Charmian, Alexas, and Iras.

CLEOPATRA
Where is he?

CHARMIAN   I did not see him since. 1

CLEOPATRA [to Alexas]
See where he is, who's with him, what he does.
I did not send you. If you find him sad, 3
Say I am dancing; if in mirth, report
That I am sudden sick. Quick, and return. 5
                                        [Exit Alexas.]

CHARMIAN
Madam, methinks, if you did love him dearly,
You do not hold the method to enforce 7
The like from him.

CLEOPATRA   What should I do I do not? 8

CHARMIAN
In each thing give him way. Cross him in nothing.

CLEOPATRA
Thou teachest like a fool: the way to lose him.

CHARMIAN
Tempt him not so too far. I wish, forbear; 11
In time we hate that which we often fear.

Enter Antony.

But here comes Antony.

CLEOPATRA   I am sick and sullen. 13

ANTONY
I am sorry to give breathing to my purpose— 14

---

155 **sighs** i.e., mere sighs   170 **tailors** (The gods can fashion a new
wife for a man, much as a tailor can mend or replace a worn-out garment.)   172 **members** (The word has a bawdy suggestion, pursued
in lines 173–4 and 180 in *cut, case, business,* and *broached; cut* and *case*
suggest the female sexual organs; *broached* suggests something that is
stabbed, pricked, opened.)   175 **smock** undergarment. (Also used
defamatorily of women.)   176–7 **the tears . . . sorrow** i.e., only an
onion could produce tears on this occasion of Fulvia's death.
178 **broachèd** opened up. (But see the note for line 172.)   182 **abode**
staying.   183 **light** frivolous, indelicate   184 **break** i.e., break the
news of   185 **expedience** haste   186 **leave** consent   187 **urgent
touches** pressing matters   189 **Of . . . friends** from many friends
working in our interest   190 **at home** to come home.   **Sextus Pompeius** son of Pompey the Great, who, though outlawed, has been able
to exploit the division between Antony and Octavius and thereby
gain command of Sicily and the sea; he appears in Act 2
192 **slippery** fickle

194 **throw** bestow   195 **Pompey the Great** i.e., the title and honored
status of "Pompey the Great"   197 **blood and life** mettle and vitality
197–8 **stands . . . soldier** lays claim to being the greatest soldier
198–9 **whose . . . danger** whose aspiring character and situation, if
allowed to continue unchecked, may endanger the frame of the
Roman world.   200 **like . . . hair** (Allusion to the popular belief that a
horsehair put into water would turn to a snake.)   200–1 **hath . . .
poison** is alive at this point but not yet a poisonous full-grown serpent.   201–3 **Say . . . hence** Tell those who serve me that my wish is
to depart quickly.
1.3. Location: Alexandria. Cleopatra's palace.
1 **since** lately.   3 **I did . . . you** i.e., Do not let him know I sent you.
sad serious   5 **sudden** suddenly taken   7 **hold the method** follow
the right course   8 **I do not** that I am not doing.   11 **Tempt** Try.
I wish I wish you would   13 **sullen** depressed, melancholy.
14 **breathing** utterance

CLEOPATRA
Help me away, dear Charmian! I shall fall.
It cannot be thus long; the sides of nature   16
Will not sustain it.

ANTONY   Now, my dearest queen—

CLEOPATRA
Pray you, stand farther from me.

ANTONY   What's the matter?   18

CLEOPATRA
I know by that same eye there's some good news.
What, says the married woman you may go?   20
Would she had never given you leave to come!
Let her not say 'tis I that keep you here.
I have no power upon you; hers you are.

ANTONY
The gods best know—

CLEOPATRA   Oh, never was there queen
So mightily betrayed! Yet at the first
I saw the treasons planted.

ANTONY   Cleopatra—

CLEOPATRA
Why should I think you can be mine, and true—
Though you in swearing shake the thronèd gods—
Who have been false to Fulvia? Riotous madness,   29
To be entangled with those mouth-made vows   30
Which break themselves in swearing!

ANTONY   Most sweet queen—   31

CLEOPATRA
Nay, pray you, seek no color for your going,   32
But bid farewell and go. When you sued staying,   33
Then was the time for words. No going then.
Eternity was in our lips and eyes,   35
Bliss in our brows' bent; none our parts so poor   36
But was a race of heaven. They are so still,   37
Or thou, the greatest soldier of the world,
Art turned the greatest liar.

ANTONY   How now, lady?

CLEOPATRA
I would I had thy inches. Thou shouldst know   40
There were a heart in Egypt.

ANTONY   Hear me, Queen: 41
The strong necessity of time commands
Our services awhile, but my full heart
Remains in use with you. Our Italy   44
Shines o'er with civil swords; Sextus Pompeius   45
Makes his approaches to the port of Rome;

Equality of two domestic powers   47
Breed scrupulous faction; the hated, grown to
  strength,   48
Are newly grown to love; the condemned Pompey,   49
Rich in his father's honor, creeps apace   50
Into the hearts of such as have not thrived
Upon the present state, whose numbers threaten;   52
And quietness, grown sick of rest, would purge   53
By any desperate change. My more particular,   54
And that which most with you should safe my going,   55
Is Fulvia's death.

CLEOPATRA
Though age from folly could not give me freedom,
It does from childishness. Can Fulvia die?

ANTONY   She's dead, my queen.   [He offers letters.]
Look here, and at thy sovereign leisure read
The garboils she awaked; at the last, best,   61
See when and where she died.

CLEOPATRA   Oh, most false love!
Where be the sacred vials thou shouldst fill   63
With sorrowful water? Now I see, I see,
In Fulvia's death how mine received shall be.

ANTONY
Quarrel no more, but be prepared to know
The purposes I bear, which are or cease   67
As you shall give th'advice. By the fire   68
That quickens Nilus' slime, I go from hence   69
Thy soldier, servant, making peace or war
As thou affects.

CLEOPATRA   Cut my lace, Charmian, come!   71
But let it be; I am quickly ill, and well,
So Antony loves.

ANTONY   My precious queen, forbear,   73
And give true evidence to his love which stands   74
An honorable trial.

CLEOPATRA   So Fulvia told me.   75
I prithee, turn aside and weep for her;
Then bid adieu to me, and say the tears
Belong to Egypt. Good now, play one scene   78

---

16 It . . . long I can't last long at this rate.   sides of nature human body, frame 18 stand farther from me give me air. 20 the married woman Fulvia 29 Who you who. Riotous madness What folly on my part 30 mouth-made insincerely spoken 31 in swearing even while they are being sworn. 32 color pretext 33 sued staying begged to stay 35 our i.e., my. (The royal plural.) 36 bent arch, curve. none . . . poor none of my features, however poor 37 race of heaven of heavenly origin, or, possibly, of the flavor of heaven. 40 inches (1) height (2) manly strength. (With perhaps a bawdy suggestion.) 41 a heart in Egypt a mighty courage in the Queen of Egypt. 44 in use with you for your use. 45 Shines . . . swords glitters everywhere with weapons of civil war

47–8 Equality . . . faction the equal splitting of domestic power between two (Antony and Caesar) breeds petty bickering 48–9 the hated . . . love those (like Pompey) who were out of favor, being now strong, have recently come back into popular favor 49–50 Pompey . . . apace i.e., Sextus Pompeius, richly inheriting the honor once accorded Pompey the Great, quickly insinuates himself 52 state government (of the triumvirate). whose i.e., those supporting Pompey 53–4 And quietness . . . change and peace, bored with its own long continuance, longs to purge itself by the violence of war (medically speaking, by vomiting, bowel evacuation, or bloodletting). 54 particular personal concern 55 safe make safe 61 garboils disturbances, commotions. best i.e., best of all 63 sacred vials (Alludes to the supposed Roman custom of putting bottles filled with tears in the tombs of the departed.) 67 which are which will proceed 68 fire i.e., sun 69 quickens . . . slime brings to life the mud left by the overflow of the Nile 71 thou affects you desire. lace cord or laces fastening the bodice. (Cleopatra pretends she is fainting.) 73 So provided that, or, possibly, "in the same way, with changes as sudden as my own" 74–5 And . . . trial and bear true witness to the love of one who withstands any honorable test. 75 So . . . me i.e., So Fulvia would have said, no doubt. (Said as a taunt.) 78 Belong to Egypt are shed for the Queen of Egypt. Good now (An expression of entreaty.)

Of excellent dissembling, and let it look
Like perfect honor.

ANTONY   You'll heat my blood. No more.   80

CLEOPATRA
You can do better yet; but this is meetly.   81

ANTONY
Now, by my sword—

CLEOPATRA   And target. Still he mends.   82
But this is not the best. Look, prithee, Charmian,
How this Herculean Roman does become   84
The carriage of his chafe.   85

ANTONY   I'll leave you, lady.

CLEOPATRA   Courteous lord, one word.
Sir, you and I must part, but that's not it;
Sir, you and I have loved, but there's not it;
That you know well. Something it is I would—   90
Oh, my oblivion is a very Antony,   91
And I am all forgotten.

ANTONY   But that your royalty   92
Holds idleness your subject, I should take you   93
For idleness itself.

CLEOPATRA   'Tis sweating labor   94
To bear such idleness so near the heart   95
As Cleopatra this. But sir, forgive me,   96
Since my becomings kill me when they do not   97
Eye well to you. Your honor calls you hence;   98
Therefore be deaf to my unpitied folly,
And all the gods go with you! Upon your sword
Sit laurel victory, and smooth success   101
Be strewed before your feet!

ANTONY   Let us go. Come;
Our separation so abides and flies   103
That thou, residing here, goes yet with me,
And I, hence fleeting, here remain with thee.
Away!   Exeunt.

❖

[1.4]

Enter Octavius [Caesar], reading a letter, Lepidus,
and their train.

CAESAR
You may see, Lepidus, and henceforth know,
It is not Caesar's natural vice to hate

Our great competitor. From Alexandria   3
This is the news: he fishes, drinks, and wastes
The lamps of night in revel; is not more manlike
Than Cleopatra, nor the queen of Ptolemy   6
More womanly than he; hardly gave audience, or   7
Vouchsafed to think he had partners. You shall find
there
A man who is the abstract of all faults   9
That all men follow.

LEPIDUS   I must not think there are
Evils enough to darken all his goodness.
His faults in him seem as the spots of heaven,   12
More fiery by night's blackness, hereditary   13
Rather than purchased, what he cannot change   14
Than what he chooses.

CAESAR
You are too indulgent. Let's grant it is not   16
Amiss to tumble on the bed of Ptolemy,
To give a kingdom for a mirth, to sit   18
And keep the turn of tippling with a slave,   19
To reel the streets at noon, and stand the buffet   20
With knaves that smells of sweat. Say this becomes
him—
As his composure must be rare indeed   22
Whom these things cannot blemish—yet must Antony
No way excuse his foils when we do bear   24
So great weight in his lightness. If he filled   25
His vacancy with his voluptuousness,   26
Full surfeits and the dryness of his bones   27
Call on him for't. But to confound such time   28
That drums him from his sport and speaks as loud   29
As his own state and ours, 'tis to be chid   30
As we rate boys who, being mature in knowledge,   31
Pawn their experience to their present pleasure   32
And so rebel to judgment.

Enter a Messenger.

LEPIDUS   Here's more news.   33

FIRST MESSENGER
Thy biddings have been done, and every hour,
Most noble Caesar, shalt thou have report
How 'tis abroad. Pompey is strong at sea,

---

80 heat my blood i.e., anger me.   **81 meetly** i.e., fairly well acted.
(Said mockingly.)   **82 target** shield.   **mends** improves (in his "scene
/ Of excellent dissembling").   **84–5 How . . . chafe** i.e., how Antony,
who claims descent from Hercules, plays the role of his enraged
ancestor well. (Hercules had become a stock figure of the enraged
hero or tyrant.)   **chafe** rage.   **90 would** wished to say   **91 my . . .
Antony** my forgetful memory is like Antony (who is now leaving and
thus forgetting me)   **92 I . . . forgotten** (1) I have forgotten what I
was going to say (2) I am entirely forgotten (by Antony).   **92–4 But . . .
itself** Since you are a queen, your frivolousness must be your subject
(i.e., ruled by you); otherwise, I'd think you were frivolousness itself.
94–6 'Tis . . . this i.e., I am not being frivolous; this is hard for me to
bear. (*Sweating, labor,* and *bear* are all associated with pregnancy.)
97 my becomings (1) those qualities that become me (2) the various
roles that I adopt   **98 Eye** appear   **101 laurel** wreathed with laurel
103 so abides and flies mingles remaining and going in such a paradoxical fashion
1.4. Location: Rome.

3 competitor partner. (With a suggestion also of "rival.")   **6 Ptolemy**
(Cleopatra's royal brother, to whom she had been married according
to Egyptian custom.)   **7 gave audience** i.e., received messengers
9 abstract epitome   **12–13 His . . . blackness** His faults are enhanced
by contrast with his virtues, just as the stars in the sky stand out from
the darkness   **14 purchased** acquired   **16 Let's grant** Even if we
were to grant   **18 mirth** jest, diversion   **19 keep . . . of** take turns
20 stand the buffet exchange blows   **22 As his composure** and a
man's composition or temperament   **24 foils** blemishes   **24–5 when
. . . lightness** when we have to carry the heavy burden imposed by
his levity.   **26 His vacancy** his leisure time   **27–8 Full . . . for't** the
physical disabilities resulting from such voluptuousness (such as
venereal disease) would call him to account and would be adequate
punishment.   **28 confound** waste   **29 drums** summons (as by a military drum).   **sport** amorous pastime   **29–30 speaks . . . ours** summons him urgently in view of his political position and ours as well
30 chid chided, reprimanded   **31 rate** berate.   **mature in knowledge**
old enough to know better   **32 Pawn . . . pleasure** risk for the sake of
immediate gratification what experience tells them will be ultimately
painful   **33 to judgment** against better judgment.

And it appears he is beloved of those   37
That only have feared Caesar. To the ports   38
The discontents repair, and men's reports   39
Give him much wronged.   [*Exit.*]
CAESAR   I should have known no less.   40
It hath been taught us from the primal state   41
That he which is was wished until he were;   42
And the ebbed man, ne'er loved till ne'er worth love,   43
Comes deared by being lacked. This common body,   44
Like to a vagabond flag upon the stream,   45
Goes to and back, lackeying the varying tide   46
To rot itself with motion.

[Enter a Second Messenger.]

SECOND MESSENGER   Caesar, I bring thee word
Menecrates and Menas, famous pirates,   49
Makes the sea serve them, which they ear and wound   50
With keels of every kind. Many hot inroads
They make in Italy. The borders maritime   52
Lack blood to think on't, and flush youth revolt.   53
No vessel can peep forth but 'tis as soon
Taken as seen; for Pompey's name strikes more   55
Than could his war resisted.   [*Exit.*]
CAESAR   Antony,   56
Leave thy lascivious wassails. When thou once   57
Was beaten from Modena, where thou slew'st
Hirtius and Pansa, consuls, at thy heel
Did famine follow, whom thou fought'st against,   60
Though daintily brought up, with patience more
Than savages could suffer. Thou didst drink   62
The stale of horses and the gilded puddle   63
Which beasts would cough at. Thy palate then did
deign   64
The roughest berry on the rudest hedge.
Yea, like the stag, when snow the pasture sheets,   66
The barks of trees thou browsèd. On the Alps   67
It is reported thou didst eat strange flesh,
Which some did die to look on. And all this—
It wounds thine honor that I speak it now—
Was borne so like a soldier that thy cheek
So much as lanked not.   72
LEPIDUS   'Tis pity of him.   73
CAESAR   Let his shames quickly
Drive him to Rome. 'Tis time we twain
Did show ourselves i'th' field, and to that end

Assemble we immediate council. Pompey
Thrives in our idleness.
LEPIDUS   Tomorrow, Caesar,
I shall be furnished to inform you rightly
Both what by sea and land I can be able   80
To front this present time.
CAESAR   Till which encounter   81
It is my business too. Farewell.
LEPIDUS
Farewell, my lord. What you shall know meantime
Of stirs abroad, I shall beseech you, sir,   84
To let me be partaker.
CAESAR
Doubt not, sir, I knew it for my bond.   86
Exeunt [separately].

❖

[1.5]

Enter Cleopatra, Charmian, Iras, and Mardian.

CLEOPATRA   Charmian!
CHARMIAN   Madam?
CLEOPATRA
Ha, ha! Give me to drink mandragora.   3
CHARMIAN   Why, madam?
CLEOPATRA
That I might sleep out this great gap of time
My Antony is away.
CHARMIAN   You think of him too much.
CLEOPATRA
Oh, 'tis treason!
CHARMIAN   Madam, I trust not so.
CLEOPATRA
Thou, eunuch Mardian!
MARDIAN   What's Your Highness' pleasure?
CLEOPATRA
Not now to hear thee sing. I take no pleasure
In aught an eunuch has. 'Tis well for thee   11
That, being unseminared, thy freer thoughts   12
May not fly forth of Egypt. Hast thou affections?   13
MARDIAN   Yes, gracious madam.
CLEOPATRA   Indeed?
MARDIAN
Not in deed, madam, for I can do nothing   16
But what indeed is honest to be done.   17
Yet have I fierce affections, and think
What Venus did with Mars.
CLEOPATRA   Oh, Charmian,
Where think'st thou he is now? Stands he or sits he?
Or does he walk? Or is he on his horse?
Oh, happy horse, to bear the weight of Antony!

---

37 of by   **38 That . . . Caesar** that have obeyed Caesar only through fear.   **39 discontents** discontented. (See 1.3.48–52.)   **40 Give him** represent him as   **41–4 It . . . lacked** It is an ironic lesson of history from the earliest times that the man currently in the public eye is avidly sought after only until he becomes ruler, whereas the public figure whose fortunes have decayed, sought after only when he is no longer worthy of love, becomes loved once he is gone.   **44 common body** populace   **45 vagabond flag** shifting and undependable weeds   **46 lackeying** following in servile fashion, like a lackey   **49 famous** notorious   **50 ear** plow   **52 borders maritime** coastal territories   **53 Lack blood** turn pale.   **flush** vigorous; flushed, ruddy (contrasted with those who *Lack blood*)   **55–6 strikes . . . resisted** inflicts more damage than his forces could against our resistance.   **57 wassails** carousals.   **60 whom** i.e., famine   **62 suffer** show in suffering.   **63 stale** urine.   **gilded** covered with iridescent slime   **64 deign** not disdain   **66 sheets** covers   **67 browsèd** fed upon.   **72 lanked not** did not become thin.   **73 of** about

80 be able be capable of mustering   **81 front** confront, deal with   **84 stirs** commotions   **86 knew** already knew.   **bond** duty, obligation.
1.5. Location: Egypt. Cleopatra's palace.
3 mandragora juice of the mandrake (a narcotic).   **11 aught** (With bawdy suggestion.)   **12 unseminared** castrated   **13 of** from. **affections** passions.   **16 Not in deed** (Mardian punningly takes the *deed* of *Indeed* in line 15 to mean "physical act.")   **do** (With suggestion of sexual intercourse.)   **17 honest** chaste

Do bravely, horse, for wot'st thou whom thou mov'st?   23
The demi-Atlas of this earth, the arm   24
And burgonet of men. He's speaking now,   25
Or murmuring, "Where's my serpent of old Nile?"
For so he calls me. Now I feed myself
With most delicious poison. Think on me,   28
That am with Phoebus' amorous pinches black   29
And wrinkled deep in time. Broad-fronted Caesar,   30
When thou wast here above the ground, I was
A morsel for a monarch. And great Pompey   32
Would stand and make his eyes grow in my brow;   33
There would he anchor his aspect, and die   34
With looking on his life.   35

       Enter Alexas.

ALEXAS   Sovereign of Egypt, hail!
CLEOPATRA
How much unlike art thou Mark Antony!
Yet, coming from him, that great med'cine hath   38
With his tinct gilded thee.   39
How goes it with my brave Mark Antony?   40
ALEXAS   Last thing he did, dear Queen,
He kissed—the last of many doubled kisses—
This orient pearl. [*He gives a pearl.*] His speech sticks in
    my heart.   43
CLEOPATRA
Mine ear must pluck it thence.
ALEXAS   "Good friend," quoth he,
"Say the firm Roman to great Egypt sends   45
This treasure of an oyster; at whose foot,
To mend the petty present, I will piece   47
Her opulent throne with kingdoms. All the East,
Say thou, shall call her mistress." So he nodded,
And soberly did mount an arm-gaunt steed,   50
Who neighed so high that what I would have spoke
Was beastly dumbed by him.   52
CLEOPATRA   What, was he sad, or merry?
ALEXAS
Like to the time o'th' year between the extremes
Of hot and cold, he was nor sad nor merry.   55

CLEOPATRA
Oh, well-divided disposition! Note him,   56
Note him, good Charmian, 'tis the man; but note him.   57
He was not sad, for he would shine on those   58
That make their looks by his; he was not merry,   59
Which seemed to tell them his remembrance lay
In Egypt with his joy; but between both.
Oh, heavenly mingle! Be'st thou sad or merry,
The violence of either thee becomes,   63
So does it no man else.—Met'st thou my posts?   64
ALEXAS
Ay, madam, twenty several messengers.   65
Why do you send so thick?
CLEOPATRA   Who's born that day   66
When I forget to send to Antony
Shall die a beggar. Ink and paper, Charmian.   68
Welcome, my good Alexas. Did I, Charmian,
Ever love Caesar so?
CHARMIAN   Oh, that brave Caesar!
CLEOPATRA
Be choked with such another emphasis!   71
Say, "the brave Antony."
CHARMIAN   The valiant Caesar!
CLEOPATRA
By Isis, I will give thee bloody teeth
If thou with Caesar paragon again   74
My man of men.
CHARMIAN   By your most gracious pardon,
I sing but after you.
CLEOPATRA   My salad days,
When I was green in judgment, cold in blood,   77
To say as I said then. But, come, away,
Get me ink and paper.
He shall have every day a several greeting,
Or I'll unpeople Egypt.   *Exeunt.* 81

      ❖

[2.1]

*Enter Pompey, Menecrates, and Menas, in war-
like manner.*

POMPEY
If the great gods be just, they shall assist
The deeds of justest men.
MENAS   Know, worthy Pompey,   2
That what they do delay they not deny.   3

23 **Do** (With sexual suggestion, as in line 16.)   **wot'st thou** do you
know   24 **demi-Atlas** one who (together with Caesar) supports the
weight of the whole world, as Atlas did. (Cleopatra disregards Lepidus as a triumvir.)   **arm** strong right arm or weapon   25 **burgonet**
light helmet or steel cap, i.e., protector   28–30 **Think . . . time**
(Cleopatra reflects on her ability to attract Antony, given the fact that
she is dark-skinned [as from the amorous pinches of her lover, the
sun] and increasingly wrinkled with age.)   29 **Phoebus'** the sun's
30 **Broad-fronted Caesar** Broad-foreheaded Julius Caesar   32 **great
Pompey** Gnaeus Pompey, oldest son of Pompey the Great. (Shakespeare may conflate the two.)   33 **make . . . brow** i.e., rivet his eyes
on my face   34 **aspect** look, gaze.   **die** i.e., suffer the extremity of
love. (And with suggestion of orgasm, as at 1.2.148.)   35 **his life** that
which he lived for.   38 **great med'cine** the philosopher's stone, the
supposed substance by which alchemists hoped to turn all baser metals into gold   39 **his tinct** its alchemical potency; also, its color
40 **brave** splendid   43 **orient** shining, bright. (The best pearls were
from the East or Orient.)   45 **firm** constant, true.   **Egypt** the Queen
of Egypt   47 **piece** augment   50 **arm-gaunt** made trim and hard by
warlike service, or hungry for battle   52 **dumbed** drowned out,
made inaudible   55 **nor sad** neither sad

56 **well-divided disposition** well-balanced temperament.   57 **the
man** i.e., perfectly characteristic of him.   **but** do but, only   58 **would**
wished to   59 **make . . . his** model their demeanor on his look
63 **thee becomes** is becoming to you   64 **posts** messengers.   65 **several** separate, distinct. (Also in line 80.)   66 **Who's** Anyone who is
68 **Shall . . . beggar** (since that day, sure never to come, would be ill-
omened)   71 **emphasis** emphatic expression.   74 **paragon** match or
compare   77 **green** immature   81 **Or . . . Egypt** Or I will send so
many messengers that Egypt will be unpeopled. (Perhaps too with a
darker threat of violence.)
2.1. Location: Pompey's camp, probably at Messina, Sicily.
2 MENAS (The Folio assigns the speeches in this scene to "*Mene.*";
some could be for Menecrates, but Pompey ignores him entirely at
lines 33–53, and Menecrates never reappears in the play.)   3 **not
deny** i.e., do not necessarily deny.

The ne'er-lust-wearied Antony.

POMPEY
    Whiles we are suitors to their throne, decays   4
    The thing we sue for.

MENAS   We, ignorant of ourselves,   5
    Beg often our own harms, which the wise powers
    Deny us for our good; so find we profit
    By losing of our prayers.

POMPEY   I shall do well.
    The people love me, and the sea is mine;
    My powers are crescent, and my auguring hope   10
    Says it will come to th' full. Mark Antony   11
    In Egypt sits at dinner, and will make
    No wars without doors. Caesar gets money where   13
    He loses hearts. Lepidus flatters both,
    Of both is flattered; but he neither loves,   15
    Nor either cares for him.

MENAS   Caesar and Lepidus
    Are in the field. A mighty strength they carry.   17

POMPEY
    Where have you this? 'Tis false.

MENAS   From Silvius, sir.

POMPEY
    He dreams. I know they are in Rome together
    Looking for Antony. But all the charms of love,   20
    Salt Cleopatra, soften thy waned lip!   21
    Let witchcraft joined with beauty, lust with both,
    Tie up the libertine in a field of feasts,   23
    Keep his brain fuming. Epicurean cooks,   24
    Sharpen with cloyless sauce his appetite,   25
    That sleep and feeding may prorogue his honor   26
    Even till a Lethe'd dullness—

Enter Varrius.

                  How now, Varrius?   27

VARRIUS
    This is most certain that I shall deliver: 28
    Mark Antony is every hour in Rome
    Expected. Since he went from Egypt 'tis
    A space for further travel.   31

POMPEY   I could have given less matter   32
    A better ear. Menas, I did not think
    This amorous surfeiter would have donned his helm   34
    For such a petty war. His soldiership
    Is twice the other twain. But let us rear   36
    The higher our opinion, that our stirring   37
    Can from the lap of Egypt's widow pluck   38

MENAS   I cannot hope   39
    Caesar and Antony shall well greet together.   40
    His wife that's dead did trespasses to Caesar;   41
    His brother warred upon him, although, I think,   42
    Not moved by Antony.

POMPEY   I know not, Menas,   43
    How lesser enmities may give way to greater.
    Were't not that we stand up against them all,
    'Twere pregnant they should square between
        themselves,   46
    For they have entertainèd cause enough   47
    To draw their swords. But how the fear of us
    May cement their divisions and bind up
    The petty difference, we yet not know.
    Be't as our gods will have't! It only stands   51
    Our lives upon to use our strongest hands.   52
    Come, Menas.   *Exeunt.*

❖

[2.2]

Enter Enobarbus and Lepidus.

LEPIDUS
    Good Enobarbus, 'tis a worthy deed,
    And shall become you well, to entreat your captain
    To soft and gentle speech.

ENOBARBUS   I shall entreat him
    To answer like himself. If Caesar move him,   4
    Let Antony look over Caesar's head   5
    And speak as loud as Mars. By Jupiter,
    Were I the wearer of Antonio's beard,
    I would not shave't today.   8

LEPIDUS
    'Tis not a time for private stomaching.

ENOBARBUS   Every time   9
    Serves for the matter that is then born in't.

LEPIDUS
    But small to greater matters must give way.

ENOBARBUS
    Not if the small come first.

LEPIDUS   Your speech is passion;
    But pray you stir no embers up. Here comes
    The noble Antony.

Enter Antony and Ventidius [in conversation].

ENOBARBUS   And yonder, Caesar.

*Enter Caesar, Maecenas, and Agrippa, [also in
conversation, by another door].*

4–5 Whiles . . . for While we are praying, that for which we pray is being destroyed. **10 My . . . crescent** My armed forces are on the increase. **auguring** prophesying **11 it** i.e., my powers or fortune (seen as a crescent moon, becoming full) **13 without doors** outdoors, i.e., in the battlefield, rather than in the bedroom. **15 Of** by. **neither loves** loves neither **17 A . . . carry** They command a mighty army. **20 Looking for** awaiting. **charms** spells **21 Salt** lustful. **waned** faded, withered **23 Tie . . . feasts** i.e., tether him like an animal in a rich pasture **24 Epicurean** Let epicurean **25 cloyless** i.e., which will not satiate **26 prorogue** defer the operation of **27 Lethe'd** oblivious. (From the river of the underworld whose waters cause forgetfulness in those who drink.) **28 deliver** report **31 space . . . travel** time enough for an even longer journey and labor (travail). **32 less** less important **34 helm** helmet **36 rear** raise **37 opinion** i.e., of ourselves **38 Egypt's widow** i.e., Cleopatra, widow of the young King Ptolemy

39 hope expect **40 well greet** greet one another kindly **41 did trespasses to** wronged **42 brother** i.e., Lucius Antonius. (See 1.2.94 ff.) **43 moved** provoked, incited **46 pregnant** clear, obvious. **square** quarrel **47 entertainèd** maintained **51–2 It . . . hands** Our very lives depend upon our using our greatest strength.
2.2. Location: Rome. Furniture is put out on which Antony and Caesar are to sit.
4 like himself i.e., in a way befitting his greatness. **move him** i.e., to anger **5 look . . . head** i.e., condescend to Caesar as a smaller man **8 I . . . shave't** i.e., I would continue to wear it and thereby dare Caesar to pluck it (in a symbolic gesture for starting a fight) **9 private stomaching** personal resentment.

ANTONY
If we compose well here, to Parthia.   15
Hark, Ventidius.   [*They confer apart.*]

CAESAR
I do not know, Maecenas, ask Agrippa.

LEPIDUS Noble friends,
That which combined us was most great, and let not
A leaner action rend us. What's amiss,   20
May it be gently heard. When we debate
Our trivial difference loud, we do commit
Murder in healing wounds. Then, noble partners,   23
The rather for I earnestly beseech,   24
Touch you the sourest points with sweetest terms,
Nor curstness grow to th' matter.

ANTONY   'Tis spoken well.   26
Were we before our armies, and to fight,   27
I should do thus.   *Flourish.*

CAESAR Welcome to Rome.

ANTONY Thank you.

CAESAR Sit.

ANTONY Sit, sir.

CAESAR Nay, then.   [*They sit.*]

ANTONY
I learn you take things ill which are not so,
Or being, concern you not.

CAESAR   I must be laughed at   35
If, or for nothing or a little, I   36
Should say myself offended, and with you
Chiefly i'th' world; more laughed at that I should   38
Once name you derogately, when to sound your name   39
It not concerned me.   40

ANTONY
My being in Egypt, Caesar, what was't to you?

CAESAR
No more than my residing here at Rome
Might be to you in Egypt. Yet if you there
Did practice on my state, your being in Egypt   44
Might be my question.

ANTONY   How intend you "practiced"?   45

CAESAR
You may be pleased to catch at mine intent   46
By what did here befall me. Your wife and brother
Made wars upon me, and their contestation
Was theme for you. You were the word of war.   49

ANTONY
You do mistake your business. My brother never
Did urge me in his act. I did inquire it,   51
And have my learning from some true reports   52

That drew their swords with you. Did he not rather   53
Discredit my authority with yours,   54
And make the wars alike against my stomach,   55
Having alike your cause? Of this my letters   56
Before did satisfy you. If you'll patch a quarrel,   57
As matter whole you have to make it with,   58
It must not be with this.

CAESAR   You praise yourself   59
By laying defects of judgment to me, but
You patched up your excuses.

ANTONY   Not so, not so.
I know you could not lack—I am certain on't—   62
Very necessity of this thought, that I,   63
Your partner in the cause 'gainst which he fought,   64
Could not with graceful eyes attend those wars   65
Which fronted mine own peace. As for my wife,   66
I would you had her spirit in such another.   67
The third o'th' world is yours, which with a snaffle   68
You may pace easy, but not such a wife.   69

ENOBARBUS Would we had all such wives, that the men
might go to wars with the women!

ANTONY
So much uncurbable, her garboils, Caesar,   72
Made out of her impatience—which not wanted   73
Shrewdness of policy too—I grieving grant   74
Did you too much disquiet. For that you must   75
But say I could not help it.

CAESAR   I wrote to you   76
When rioting in Alexandria; you   77
Did pocket up my letters and with taunts
Did gibe my missive out of audience.

ANTONY   Sir,   79
He fell upon me ere admitted, then.   80
Three kings I had newly feasted, and did want   81
Of what I was i'th' morning. But next day   82
I told him of myself, which was as much   83
As to have asked him pardon. Let this fellow
Be nothing of our strife; if we contend,   85
Out of our question wipe him.

CAESAR   You have broken   86
The article of your oath, which you shall never   87
Have tongue to charge me with.

LEPIDUS Soft, Caesar!   89

ANTONY No, Lepidus, let him speak.

---

15 compose come to an agreement **20 leaner** lesser, more trivial. **rend** divide. **What's** Whatever is **23 healing** i.e., attempting to heal **24 The rather for** all the more because **26 Nor . . . grow** nor let ill humor be added **27 to** about to **35 being** being so, i.e., even if they are amiss **36 or . . .** or either . . . or **38 i'th' world** of all people **39 Once** under any circumstances. **derogately** disparagingly **39–40 when . . . concerned me** i.e., if, as you say, it were none of my business. **44 practice on my state** plot against my position **45 question** business. **How intend you** What do you mean **46 catch at** infer **49 Was . . . war** had you for its theme. They made war in your name. (*Word* here means "watchword.") **51 urge . . . act** claim that he was fighting in my behalf. **inquire** inquire into **52 reports** reporters

53 That . . . you that fought in your army. **54 Discredit** injure. **with** along with **55 stomach** desire **56 Having . . . cause** i.e., I having just as much reason as you to deplore Lucius's action. **57–9 If . . . this** If you insist on manufacturing a quarrel out of shreds and patches, as if you had substantial material to make it with, you've chosen a weak matter to use. **62–3 I know . . . thought** I'm certain you must have realized **64 he** i.e., Lucius **65 with . . . attend** regard favorably **66 fronted** confronted, opposed **67 her . . . another** i.e., a wife such as she was. **68 snaffle** bridle bit **69 pace** put through its paces, manage **72–5 So . . . disquiet** I unhappily concede that her unmanageable commotions, caused by her impatience (at my being in Egypt) but not lacking in keenness of stratagem, did much to disquiet you, Caesar. **76 But say** concede that **77 When** while you were **79 Did . . . audience** taunted my messenger out of your presence. **80 fell** burst in **81–2 did want . . . morning** was not at my best as I had been earlier in the day. **83 of myself** i.e., of my having had a lot to drink **85 Be . . . of** have no part in **86 question** contention **87 article** terms **89 Soft** Gently, go easy

The honor is sacred which he talks on now,
Supposing that I lacked it. But, on, Caesar: 92
The article of my oath—

CAESAR
To lend me arms and aid when I required them,   94
The which you both denied.

ANTONY   Neglected, rather;
And then when poisoned hours had bound me up
From mine own knowledge. As nearly as I may   97
I'll play the penitent to you, but mine honesty   98
Shall not make poor my greatness, nor my power   99
Work without it. Truth is that Fulvia,   100
To have me out of Egypt, made wars here,
For which myself, the ignorant motive, do   102
So far ask pardon as befits mine honor
To stoop in such a case.

LEPIDUS   'Tis noble spoken.   104

MAECENAS
If it might please you to enforce no further
The griefs between ye; to forget them quite   106
Were to remember that the present need
Speaks to atone you.

LEPIDUS   Worthily spoken, Maecenas.   108

ENOBARBUS   Or, if you borrow one another's love for the
instant, you may, when you hear no more words of
Pompey, return it again. You shall have time to wrangle in when you have nothing else to do.

ANTONY
Thou art a soldier only. Speak no more.

ENOBARBUS   That truth should be silent I had almost
forgot.

ANTONY
You wrong this presence. Therefore speak no more.   116

ENOBARBUS   Go to, then; your considerate stone.   117

CAESAR
I do not much dislike the matter, but
The manner of his speech; for't cannot be
We shall remain in friendship, our conditions   120
So diff'ring in their acts. Yet, if I knew
What hoop should hold us staunch, from edge to edge   122
O'th' world I would pursue it.

AGRIPPA   Give me leave, Caesar.

CAESAR   Speak, Agrippa.

AGRIPPA
Thou hast a sister by the mother's side,
Admired Octavia. Great Mark Antony
Is now a widower.

CAESAR   Say not so, Agrippa.
If Cleopatra heard you, your reproof
Were well deserved of rashness.   130

ANTONY
I am not married, Caesar. Let me hear
Agrippa further speak.

AGRIPPA
To hold you in perpetual amity,
To make you brothers, and to knit your hearts
With an unslipping knot, take Antony
Octavia to his wife, whose beauty claims
No worse a husband than the best of men,
Whose virtue and whose general graces speak   138
That which none else can utter. By this marriage   139
All little jealousies, which now seem great,   140
And all great fears, which now import their dangers,   141
Would then be nothing. Truths would be tales,   142
Where now half tales be truths. Her love to both   143
Would each to other and all loves to both
Draw after her. Pardon what I have spoke,
For 'tis a studied, not a present thought,
By duty ruminated.

ANTONY   Will Caesar speak?

CAESAR
Not till he hears how Antony is touched   148
With what is spoke already.   149

ANTONY   What power is in Agrippa
If I would say, "Agrippa, be it so,"
To make this good?

CAESAR   The power of Caesar and
His power unto Octavia.

ANTONY   May I never   153
To this good purpose, that so fairly shows,   154
Dream of impediment! Let me have thy hand
Further this act of grace, and from this hour   156
The heart of brothers govern in our loves
And sway our great designs!

CAESAR   There's my hand.
                       [*They clasp hands.*]
A sister I bequeath you whom no brother
Did ever love so dearly. Let her live
To join our kingdoms and our hearts; and never   161
Fly off our loves again!

LEPIDUS   Happily, amen!   162

ANTONY
I did not think to draw my sword 'gainst Pompey,
For he hath laid strange courtesies and great   164
Of late upon me. I must thank him only,   165
Lest my remembrance suffer ill report;   166
At heel of that, defy him.

LEPIDUS   Time calls upon 's.   167
Of us must Pompey presently be sought,   168
Or else he seeks out us.

---

92 Supposing implying   **94 required** requested   **97 From . . . knowledge** from knowing myself.   **98–100 mine . . . it** my honesty (in admitting my overindulgence) will not go so far as to dishonor my greatness, nor, conversely, will my authority be used in a dishonorable way.   **102 motive** moving or inciting cause   **104 noble** nobly **106 griefs** grievances   **108 atone** reconcile   **116 presence** company. **117 Go . . . stone** i.e., All right, all right. I'll keep my thoughts to myself.   **120 conditions** temperaments, dispositions   **122 hoop** barrel hoop.   **staunch** firm, watertight   **130 Were . . . rashness** would richly deserve the rebuke it would get for such rashness.

138–9 Whose . . . utter whose virtues declare themselves better than any words about them could do.   **140 jealousies** misunderstandings, suspicions   **141 import** imply; carry with them   **142–3 Truths . . . truths** True reports (no matter how distressing) would then be discounted as mere rumors, whereas at present half-true reports are taken for the whole truth.   **148–9 touched With** affected by **153 unto** over   **154 so fairly shows** looks so promising   **156 Further** in furtherance of   **161–2 never . . . again** may our amity never desert us again.   **164 strange** remarkable   **165 only** at least   **166 Lest . . . report** lest I be accused of ingratitude   **167 At heel of** immediately after   **168 Of** By.   **presently** at once

ANTONY Where lies he?

CAESAR
About the mount Misena.

ANTONY   What is his strength 171
By land?

CAESAR Great and increasing; but by sea
He is an absolute master.

ANTONY   So is the fame. 173
Would we had spoke together! Haste we for it. 174
Yet, ere we put ourselves in arms, dispatch we
The business we have talked of.

CAESAR   With most gladness, 176
And do invite you to my sister's view, 177
Whither straight I'll lead you. 178

ANTONY
Let us, Lepidus, not lack your company.

LEPIDUS
Noble Antony, not sickness should detain me. 180
Flourish. Exeunt. Manent Enobarbus, Agrippa,
Maecenas.

MAECENAS Welcome from Egypt, sir.

ENOBARBUS Half the heart of Caesar, worthy Maecenas! 182
My honorable friend, Agrippa!

AGRIPPA Good Enobarbus!

MAECENAS We have cause to be glad that matters are so
well digested. You stayed well by't in Egypt. 186

ENOBARBUS Ay, sir, we did sleep day out of counte- 187
nance and made the night light with drinking. 188

MAECENAS Eight wild boars roasted whole at a breakfast, and but twelve persons there; is this true?

ENOBARBUS This was but as a fly by an eagle. We had 191
much more monstrous matter of feast, which worthily
deserved noting.

MAECENAS She's a most triumphant lady, if report be 194
square to her. 195

ENOBARBUS When she first met Mark Antony, she
pursed up his heart upon the river of Cydnus. 197

AGRIPPA There she appeared indeed, or my reporter de- 198
vised well for her. 199

ENOBARBUS I will tell you.
The barge she sat in, like a burnished throne 201
Burnt on the water. The poop was beaten gold; 202
Purple the sails, and so perfumèd that
The winds were lovesick with them. The oars were
   silver,
Which to the tune of flutes kept stroke, and made
The water which they beat to follow faster,

As amorous of their strokes. For her own person, 207
It beggared all description: she did lie
In her pavilion—cloth-of-gold of tissue— 209
O'erpicturing that Venus where we see
The fancy outwork nature. On each side her 211
Stood pretty dimpled boys, like smiling Cupids,
With divers-colored fans, whose wind did seem 213
To glow the delicate cheeks which they did cool, 214
And what they undid did.

AGRIPPA   Oh, rare for Antony!

ENOBARBUS
Her gentlewomen, like the Nereides, 216
So many mermaids, tended her i'th'eyes 217
And made their bends adornings. At the helm 218
A seeming mermaid steers. The silken tackle
Swell with the touches of those flower-soft hands,
That yarely frame the office. From the barge 221
A strange invisible perfume hits the sense
Of the adjacent wharfs. The city cast 223
Her people out upon her; and Antony,
Enthroned i'th' marketplace, did sit alone,
Whistling to th'air, which, but for vacancy, 226
Had gone to gaze on Cleopatra too,
And made a gap in nature.

AGRIPPA   Rare Egyptian!

ENOBARBUS
Upon her landing, Antony sent to her,
Invited her to supper. She replied
It should be better he became her guest,
Which she entreated. Our courteous Antony,
Whom ne'er the word of "No" woman heard speak,
Being barbered ten times o'er, goes to the feast,
And for his ordinary pays his heart 235
For what his eyes eat only.

AGRIPPA   Royal wench! 236
She made great Caesar lay his sword to bed; 237
He plowed her, and she cropped.

ENOBARBUS   I saw her once 238
Hop forty paces through the public street,
And having lost her breath, she spoke and panted,
That she did make defect perfection, 241
And, breathless, power breathe forth.

MAECENAS
Now Antony must leave her utterly.

ENOBARBUS Never. He will not.
Age cannot wither her, nor custom stale 245
Her infinite variety. Other women cloy
The appetites they feed, but she makes hungry

---

171 Misena i.e., Misenum, in southern Italy. (Not in Sicily, where 2.1 perhaps takes place.) **173 So is the fame** So it is reported.
174 Would . . . together! Would that we had had a chance to parley before battle! **176 most** the greatest **177 to my sister's view** to see my sister **178 straight** straightway **180.1 Manent** They remain onstage **182 Half . . . Caesar** You who are very close to Caesar, one of his closest advisers **186 digested** disposed. **stayed well by't** kept at it **187–8 we . . . countenance** we insulted day by sleeping right through it **188 light** (1) brightly lit (2) debauched and giddy **191 This . . . eagle** i.e., This was nothing compared with greater feasting. **194 triumphant** magnificent **195 square** just **197 pursed up** pocketed up, put in her purse **198–9 devised** invented **201 burnished** lustrous, shiny **202 poop** a short deck built over the main deck at the stern of the vessel

207 As as if. **For** As for **209 cloth-of-gold of tissue** cloth made of gold thread and silk woven together **211 fancy** imagination **213 divers-colored** multicolored **214 glow** cause to glow **216 Nereides** sea nymphs **217 So . . . i'th'eyes** as if they were so many mermaids, attended to her every glance or nod **218 made . . . adornings** made their graceful bowings beautiful. **221 yarely . . . office** nimbly perform their function. **223 wharfs** banks. **226 but for vacancy** except that it would have created a vacuum **235 ordinary** meal, supper (such as one might obtain at a public table in a tavern) **236 eat** ate. (Pronounced *et*.) **237 Caesar** i.e., Julius Caesar, by whom Cleopatra had a son named Caesarion **238 cropped** bore fruit (a son). **241 That** so that **245 custom stale** repeated experience make stale

Where most she satisfies; for vilest things
Become themselves in her, that the holy priests   249
Bless her when she is riggish.   250

MAECENAS
If beauty, wisdom, modesty can settle
The heart of Antony, Octavia is
A blessèd lottery to him.

AGRIPPA   Let us go.   253
Good Enobarbus, make yourself my guest
Whilst you abide here.

ENOBARBUS   Humbly, sir, I thank you.
          Exeunt.

❖

[2.3]

          Enter Antony, Caesar, Octavia between them.

ANTONY
The world and my great office will sometimes
Divide me from your bosom.

OCTAVIA   All which time
Before the gods my knee shall bow my prayers
To them for you.

ANTONY   Good night, sir. My Octavia,
Read not my blemishes in the world's report.   5
I have not kept my square, but that to come   6
Shall all be done by th' rule. Good night, dear lady.
Good night, sir.

CAESAR   Good night.   *Exit [with Octavia].*

          Enter Soothsayer.

ANTONY
Now, sirrah: you do wish yourself in Egypt?   10

SOOTHSAYER   Would I had never come from thence,
nor you thither!   12

ANTONY   If you can, your reason?

SOOTHSAYER   I see it in my motion, have it not in my   14
tongue; but yet hie you to Egypt again.   15

ANTONY
Say to me, whose fortunes shall rise higher,
Caesar's or mine?

SOOTHSAYER   Caesar's.
Therefore, O Antony, stay not by his side.
Thy daemon—that thy spirit which keeps thee—is   20
Noble, courageous, high unmatchable,   21
Where Caesar's is not; but near him thy angel   22
Becomes afeard, as being o'erpowered. Therefore
Make space enough between you.

ANTONY   Speak this no more.

SOOTHSAYER
To none but thee; no more but when to thee.   25
If thou dost play with him at any game,
Thou art sure to lose; and of that natural luck   27
He beats thee 'gainst the odds. Thy luster thickens   28
When he shines by. I say again, thy spirit   29
Is all afraid to govern thee near him;
But, he away, 'tis noble.

ANTONY   Get thee gone.
Say to Ventidius I would speak with him.
          Exit [Soothsayer].
He shall to Parthia.—Be it art or hap,   33
He hath spoken true. The very dice obey him,
And in our sports my better cunning faints   35
Under his chance. If we draw lots, he speeds;   36
His cocks do win the battle still of mine   37
When it is all to naught, and his quails ever   38
Beat mine, inhooped, at odds. I will to Egypt;   39
And though I make this marriage for my peace,
I'th'East my pleasure lies.

          Enter Ventidius.

          Oh, come, Ventidius.
You must to Parthia. Your commission's ready;
Follow me, and receive't.   *Exeunt.*

❖

[2.4]

          Enter Lepidus, Maecenas, and Agrippa.

LEPIDUS
Trouble yourselves no further. Pray you, hasten
Your generals after.

AGRIPPA   Sir, Mark Antony   2
Will e'en but kiss Octavia, and we'll follow.   3

LEPIDUS
Till I shall see you in your soldier's dress,   4
Which will become you both, farewell.

MAECENAS   We shall,   5
As I conceive the journey, be at th' Mount   6
Before you, Lepidus.

LEPIDUS   Your way is shorter;
My purposes do draw me much about.   8
You'll win two days upon me.

MAECENAS, AGRIPPA   Sir, good success!

LEPIDUS   Farewell.   *Exeunt.*

❖

---

249 **Become themselves** are becoming, attractive.   **that** so that
250 **riggish** lustful.   253 **lottery** prize, gift of fortune
2.3. Location: Rome.
5 **Read** interpret.   **in** according to   6 **kept my square** kept to a
straight course (as guided by a carpenter's square; with pun on *rule*,
"ruler" in next line).   **that that which is**   10 **sirrah** (A form of
address to a social inferior.)   12 **thither** to that place.   14 **in my
motion** intuitively, by inward prompting   15 **hie** hasten   20 **Thy . . .
thee** Your guardian spirit, the spirit that protects you   21 **high
unmatchable** unmatchable in the extreme   22 **Where . . . not** wherever Caesar's spirit is not present (to daunt yours)

25 **no more but when** only when   27 **of** by   28 **thickens** grows dim
29 **by** nearby.   33 **art or hap** skill or luck   35 **cunning** skill
36 **chance** luck.   **speeds** wins   37 **still of** always from   38 **When . . .
naught** when the odds are everything to nothing (in my favor)
39 **inhooped** (The birds were enclosed in hoops to make them fight.)
at odds against the odds.
2.4. Location: Rome.
2 **Your generals after** after your generals.   3 **e'en but** only, just
4 **dress** garb, apparel   5 **become** suit   6 **conceive** understand.
th' Mount i.e., Mount Misenum   8 **about** roundabout.

[2.5]

Enter Cleopatra, Charmian, Iras, and Alexas.

CLEOPATRA
Give me some music; music, moody food
Of us that trade in love.

ALL   The music, ho!

Enter Mardian the eunuch.

CLEOPATRA
Let it alone. Let's to billiards. Come, Charmian.

CHARMIAN
My arm is sore. Best play with Mardian.

CLEOPATRA
As well a woman with an eunuch played
As with a woman. Come, you'll play with me, sir?

MARDIAN   As well as I can, madam.

CLEOPATRA
And when good will is showed, though't come too
    short,   8
The actor may plead pardon. I'll none now.   9
Give me mine angle; we'll to th' river. There,   10
My music playing far off, I will betray
Tawny-finned fishes. My bended hook shall pierce
Their slimy jaws, and as I draw them up
I'll think them every one an Antony,
And say, "Aha! You're caught."

CHARMIAN   'Twas merry when
You wagered on your angling, when your diver
Did hang a salt fish on his hook, which he   17
With fervency drew up.

CLEOPATRA   That time—oh, times!—
I laughed him out of patience; and that night
I laughed him into patience. And next morn,
Ere the ninth hour, I drunk him to his bed,   21
Then put my tires and mantles on him, whilst   22
I wore his sword Philippan.

Enter a Messenger.

                              Oh, from Italy!   23
Ram thou thy fruitful tidings in mine ears,
That long time have been barren.

MESSENGER   Madam, madam—

CLEOPATRA
Antonio's dead! If thou say so, villain,
Thou kill'st thy mistress; but well and free,
If thou so yield him, there is gold, and here   28
My bluest veins to kiss—a hand that kings
Have lipped, and trembled kissing.
              [*She offers him gold, and her hand to kiss.*]

MESSENGER   First, madam, he is well.

CLEOPATRA
Why, there's more gold. But, sirrah, mark, we use
To say the dead are well. Bring it to that,   33
The gold I give thee will I melt and pour
Down thy ill-uttering throat.

MESSENGER   Good madam, hear me.

CLEOPATRA   Well, go to, I will.   37
But there's no goodness in thy face, if Antony
Be free and healthful—so tart a favor   39
To trumpet such good tidings! If not well,
Thou shouldst come like a Fury crowned with snakes, 41
Not like a formal man.

MESSENGER   Will't please you hear me? 42

CLEOPATRA
I have a mind to strike thee ere thou speak'st.
Yet, if thou say Antony lives, is well,
Or friends with Caesar, or not captive to him,
I'll set thee in a shower of gold and hail
Rich pearls upon thee.

MESSENGER   Madam, he's well.

CLEOPATRA   Well said.

MESSENGER
And friends with Caesar.

CLEOPATRA   Thou'rt an honest man. 48

MESSENGER
Caesar and he are greater friends than ever.

CLEOPATRA
Make thee a fortune from me.

MESSENGER   But yet, madam—

CLEOPATRA
I do not like "But yet"; it does allay   51
The good precedence. Fie upon "But yet"!   52
"But yet" is as a jailer to bring forth
Some monstrous malefactor. Prithee, friend,
Pour out the pack of matter to mine ear,   55
The good and bad together. He's friends with Caesar,
In state of health, thou say'st, and, thou say'st, free.

MESSENGER
Free, madam? No, I made no such report.
He's bound unto Octavia.

CLEOPATRA   For what good turn?   59

MESSENGER
For the best turn i'th' bed.

CLEOPATRA   I am pale, Charmian.

MESSENGER
Madam, he's married to Octavia.

CLEOPATRA
The most infectious pestilence upon thee!
                                    Strikes him down.

MESSENGER
Good madam, patience.

CLEOPATRA   What say you?   *Strikes him.*
                                          Hence,

2.5 **Location:** Alexandria. Cleopatra's palace.
8 **too short** (A bawdy joke on Mardian's being castrated; *will* suggests
"sexual desire"; *come* suggests "reach orgasm.")   9 **I'll none now** i.e.,
I won't play billiards after all.   10 **angle** rod and line   17 **salt** dried,
preserved in salt   21 **ninth hour** i.e., 9 A.M.   **drunk** drank   22 **tires**
headdresses, or perhaps attire.   **mantles** garments   23 **Philippan**
(Named for Antony's victory over Brutus and Cassius at Philippi.)
28 **yield** (1) grant (2) report

33 **well** i.e., well out of it, in heaven.   **Bring it to that** If that is your
meaning   37 **go to** i.e., all right, then. (Said remonstratingly.)   39 **tart
a favor** sour a face   41 **Fury** avenging goddess of classical mythology
42 **like . . . man** in ordinary human form.   48 **honest** worthy
51–2 **allay . . . precedence** annul the good news that preceded it.
55 **pack of matter** entire contents (as of a peddler's pack)   59 **turn**
favor, purpose. (But the Messenger replies in the sense of "feat, bout,"
with sexual suggestion.)

Horrible villain, or I'll spurn thine eyes   64
Like balls before me! I'll unhair thy head!   65
               She hales him up and down.
Thou shalt be whipped with wire and stewed in brine,
Smarting in ling'ring pickle!
MESSENGER   Gracious madam,   67
I that do bring the news made not the match.
CLEOPATRA
Say 'tis not so, a province I will give thee
And make thy fortunes proud. The blow thou hadst
Shall make thy peace for moving me to rage,   71
And I will boot thee with what gift beside   72
Thy modesty can beg.
MESSENGER   He's married, madam.   73
CLEOPATRA
Rogue, thou hast lived too long!   *Draw a knife.*
MESSENGER   Nay then, I'll run.
What mean you, madam? I have made no fault. *Exit.*
CHARMIAN
Good madam, keep yourself within yourself.   76
The man is innocent.
CLEOPATRA
Some innocents scape not the thunderbolt.
Melt Egypt into Nile, and kindly creatures   79
Turn all to serpents! Call the slave again.
Though I am mad, I will not bite him. Call!   81
CHARMIAN
He is afeard to come.
CLEOPATRA   I will not hurt him.
                [The Messenger is sent for.]
These hands do lack nobility, that they strike
A meaner than myself, since I myself   84
Have given myself the cause.

       Enter the Messenger again.

                Come hither, sir.   85
Though it be honest, it is never good
To bring bad news. Give to a gracious message
An host of tongues, but let ill tidings tell   88
Themselves when they be felt.   89
MESSENGER   I have done my duty.
CLEOPATRA   Is he married?
I cannot hate thee worser than I do
If thou again say "Yes."
MESSENGER   He's married, madam.
CLEOPATRA
The gods confound thee! Dost thou hold there still?   94
MESSENGER
Should I lie, madam?
CLEOPATRA   Oh, I would thou didst,

So half my Egypt were submerged and made   96
A cistern for scaled snakes! Go, get thee hence.   97
Hadst thou Narcissus in thy face, to me   98
Thou wouldst appear most ugly. He is married?
MESSENGER
I crave Your Highness' pardon.
CLEOPATRA   He is married?
MESSENGER
Take no offense that I would not offend you.   101
To punish me for what you make me do
Seems much unequal. He's married to Octavia.   103
CLEOPATRA
Oh, that his fault should make a knave of thee,   104
That art not what thou'rt sure of! Get thee hence.   105
The merchandise which thou hast brought from
    Rome
Are all too dear for me. Lie they upon thy hand,   107
And be undone by 'em!   *[Exit Messenger.]*
CHARMIAN   Good Your Highness, patience.   108
CLEOPATRA
In praising Antony, I have dispraised Caesar.
CHARMIAN   Many times, madam.
CLEOPATRA
I am paid for't now. Lead me from hence;
I faint. Oh, Iras, Charmian! 'Tis no matter.
Go to the fellow, good Alexas. Bid him
Report the feature of Octavia: her years,
Her inclination. Let him not leave out
The color of her hair. Bring me word quickly.   115
                  [Exit Alexas.]
Let him forever go!—Let him not, Charmian.   117
Though he be painted one way like a Gorgon,   118
The other way's a Mars. *[To Mardian]* Bid you Alexas   119
Bring me word how tall she is.—Pity me, Charmian,
But do not speak to me. Lead me to my chamber.
                     Exeunt.

❖

[2.6]

Flourish. Enter Pompey [and] Menas at one door, with drum and trumpet; at another, Caesar, Lepidus, Antony, Enobarbus, Maecenas, Agrippa, with soldiers marching.

96 **So** even if   97 **cistern** tank.   **scaled** scaly   98 **Narcissus** beautiful youth of Greek mythology who fell in love with his own reflected image   101 **Take . . . offend you** Don't be offended that I hesitate to offend you (by telling bad news), or, don't interpret as offense what is not meant to offend.   103 **much unequal** most unjust.   104–5 **Oh, that . . . sure of!** How regrettable that Antony's fault puts you in the wrong, you who are not yourself hateful even if you have had to report hateful news as a certain fact!   107 **dear** (1) expensive (2) emotionally precious   107–8 **Lie . . . by 'em** May they remain in your possession unsold, and may you be bankrupt, financially ruined! (i.e., May you never profit from your bad tidings!)   115 **inclination** disposition.   117 **him** Antony   118–19 **Though . . . Mars** (Alludes to a type of picture known as a perspective, which shows different images when looked at from different angles of vision. A *Gorgon* is a female monster with serpents in her hair, capable of turning to stone anything that meets her gaze.)
2.6. Location: Near Misenum, in southern Italy near modern Naples. (But 2.1 perhaps took place in Messina, Sicily.)

64 **spurn** kick   65.1 *hales* drags   67 **pickle** pickling solution.
71 **make thy peace** compensate, mollify me   72 **boot thee with** give you into the bargain, or, make amends with.   **what** whatever
73 **Thy modesty** one of your modest expectations   76 **keep . . . yourself** i.e., control yourself.   79 **kindly** endowed with innately good qualities   81 **mad** (1) angry (2) insane, and so apt to bite
84 **A meaner** one of lower social station   84–5 **since . . . cause** since I am the one I ought to blame.   85 **the cause** i.e., by loving Antony.
88 **host** multitude   89 **when . . . felt** i.e., by being felt rather than spoken aloud. Let bad tidings announce themselves.   94 **confound** destroy.   **hold there still** stick to your story.

POMPEY
  Your hostages I have, so have you mine,
  And we shall talk before we fight.
CAESAR   Most meet   2
  That first we come to words; and therefore have we
  Our written purposes before us sent,   4
  Which if thou hast considered, let us know
  If 'twill tie up thy discontented sword   6
  And carry back to Sicily much tall youth   7
  That else must perish here.
POMPEY   To you all three,
  The senators alone of this great world,   9
  Chief factors for the gods: I do not know   10
  Wherefore my father should revengers want,   11
  Having a son and friends, since Julius Caesar,   12
  Who at Philippi the good Brutus ghosted,   13
  There saw you laboring for him. What was't   14
  That moved pale Cassius to conspire? And what
  Made th'all-honored, honest Roman Brutus,   16
  With the armed rest, courtiers of beauteous freedom, 17
  To drench the Capitol, but that they would   18
  Have one man but a man? And that is it   19
  Hath made me rig my navy, at whose burden
  The angered ocean foams, with which I meant
  To scourge th'ingratitude that despiteful Rome
  Cast on my noble father.
CAESAR   Take your time.
ANTONY
  Thou canst not fear us, Pompey, with thy sails;   24
  We'll speak with thee at sea. At land thou know'st 25
  How much we do o'ercount thee.
POMPEY   At land indeed   26
  Thou dost o'ercount me of my father's house;
  But since the cuckoo builds not for himself,   28
  Remain in't as thou mayst.
LEPIDUS   Be pleased to tell us— 29
  For this is from the present—how you take   30
  The offers we have sent you.
CAESAR   There's the point.

ANTONY
  Which do not be entreated to, but weigh   32
  What it is worth embraced.
CAESAR   And what may follow,   33
  To try a larger fortune.
POMPEY   You have made me offer   34
  Of Sicily, Sardinia; and I must
  Rid all the sea of pirates; then, to send   36
  Measures of wheat to Rome. This 'greed upon,
  To part with unhacked edges and bear back   38
  Our targes undinted.
CAESAR, ANTONY, LEPIDUS   That's our offer.
POMPEY   Know then   39
  I came before you here a man prepared
  To take this offer, but Mark Antony
  Put me to some impatience. Though I lose   42
  The praise of it by telling, you must know,   43
  When Caesar and your brother were at blows,
  Your mother came to Sicily and did find
  Her welcome friendly.
ANTONY   I have heard it, Pompey,
  And am well studied for a liberal thanks   47
  Which I do owe you.
POMPEY   Let me have your hand.
                    [They shake hands.]
  I did not think, sir, to have met you here.
ANTONY
  The beds i'th'East are soft; and thanks to you,
  That called me timelier than my purpose hither,   51
  For I have gained by't.
CAESAR   Since I saw you last
  There's a change upon you.
POMPEY   Well, I know not
  What counts harsh Fortune casts upon my face,   54
  But in my bosom shall she never come
  To make my heart her vassal.
LEPIDUS   Well met here.
POMPEY
  I hope so, Lepidus. Thus we are agreed.
  I crave our composition may be written   58
  And sealed between us.
CAESAR   That's the next to do.   59
POMPEY
  We'll feast each other ere we part, and let's
  Draw lots who shall begin.
ANTONY   That will I, Pompey.   61
POMPEY
  No, Antony, take the lot. But, first or last,   62

2 meet fitting   4 purposes propositions   6 tie . . . sword i.e., satisfy your concerns and allow you to forgo a fight   7 tall brave   9 senators alone i.e., sole rulers of the state (who have thus supplanted the Senate)   10 factors agents   10–14 I do . . . for him (Julius Caesar defeated Pompey's father, Pompey the Great, and was subsequently assassinated by Brutus and Cassius, among others. Caesar's ghost appeared to Brutus at Philippi, where the combined forces of Antony, Octavius, and Lepidus defeated Brutus and Cassius. [See Julius Caesar.] Since Antony, Octavius, and Lepidus thus defeated the avengers of Pompey the Great's death, Pompey the Great's sons and friends should become his avengers by continuing to war on Antony, Octavius, and Lepidus.)   11 want lack   13 ghosted haunted   16 honest honorable   17 the armed rest i.e., the rest of those who were armed.   courtiers . . . freedom those who serve freedom only   18 drench bathe in blood   19 Have . . . a man (The republican conspirators acted to keep Julius Caesar from accepting the crown.)   24 fear frighten   25 speak with confront   26 o'ercount outnumber. (But Pompey's use of the word in the next line implies that Antony has cheated him. Plutarch informs us that Antony bought the elder Pompey's house at auction and later refused to pay for it.)   28 cuckoo a bird that builds no nest for itself but lays its eggs in other birds' nests   29 as thou mayst as long as you can, or, since you can.   30 from the present digressing from the business at hand

32 do . . . to i.e., do not accept merely because we ask   33 embraced if accepted by you.   34 To . . . fortune i.e., if you decide to risk war with the triumvirs, or, if you join with us to share a greater fortune.   36 to send I am to send   38 To part we are to part company.   edges swords   39 targes shields   42–3 Though . . . telling i.e., Though I forfeit praise from others by praising myself   47 well studied for well prepared to deliver   51 timelier earlier   54 counts tally marks. (From the practice of casting accounts or reckonings by means of marks or notches on tallies.)   casts calculates   58 composition agreement   59 sealed between us stamped with the official seal of each co-signer.   61 That will I I will begin   62 take the lot draw lots with the rest of us, accept the results of the lottery.   first or last whether you win the lottery to go first or last

Your fine Egyptian cookery shall have
The fame. I have heard that Julius Caesar
Grew fat with feasting there.

ANTONY   You have heard much.

POMPEY   I have fair meanings, sir.   67

ANTONY   And fair words to them.   68

POMPEY   Then so much have I heard.   69
And I have heard Apollodorus carried—   70

ENOBARBUS
No more of that. He did so.

POMPEY   What, I pray you?   71

ENOBARBUS
A certain queen to Caesar in a mattress.   72

POMPEY
I know thee now. How far'st thou, soldier?

ENOBARBUS   Well,
And well am like to do, for I perceive   74
Four feasts are toward.

POMPEY   Let me shake thy hand.   75
[_They shake hands._]
I never hated thee. I have seen thee fight
When I have envied thy behavior.

ENOBARBUS   Sir,
I never loved you much, but I ha' praised ye
When you have well deserved ten times as much
As I have said you did.

POMPEY   Enjoy thy plainness;   80
It nothing ill becomes thee.   81
Aboard my galley I invite you all.
Will you lead, lords?

CAESAR, ANTONY, LEPIDUS   Show 's the way, sir.

POMPEY   Come.   83
Exeunt. Manent Enobarbus and Menas.

MENAS [_aside_] Thy father, Pompey, would ne'er have
made this treaty.—You and I have known, sir.   85

ENOBARBUS   At sea, I think.

MENAS   We have, sir.

ENOBARBUS   You have done well by water.

MENAS   And you by land.

ENOBARBUS   I will praise any man that will praise me,
though it cannot be denied what I have done by land.

MENAS   Nor what I have done by water.

ENOBARBUS   Yes, something you can deny for your own
safety: you have been a great thief by sea.

MENAS   And you by land.

ENOBARBUS   There I deny my land service. But give me   96
your hand, Menas. [_They shake hands._] If our eyes had
authority, here they might take two thieves kissing.   98

MENAS   All men's faces are true, whatsome'er their hands
are.

ENOBARBUS   But there is never a fair woman has a true   101
face.

MENAS   No slander; they steal hearts.   103

ENOBARBUS   We came hither to fight with you.

MENAS   For my part, I am sorry it is turned to a drinking.   105
Pompey doth this day laugh away his fortune.

ENOBARBUS   If he do, sure he cannot weep't back
again.

MENAS   You've said, sir. We looked not for Mark   109
Antony here. Pray you, is he married to Cleopatra?

ENOBARBUS   Caesar's sister is called Octavia.

MENAS   True, sir. She was the wife of Caius Marcellus.

ENOBARBUS   But she is now the wife of Marcus Antonius.

MENAS   Pray ye, sir?   115

ENOBARBUS   'Tis true.

MENAS   Then is Caesar and he forever knit together.

ENOBARBUS   If I were bound to divine of this unity, I   118
would not prophesy so.

MENAS   I think the policy of that purpose made more in   120
the marriage than the love of the parties.

ENOBARBUS   I think so too. But you shall find the band
that seems to tie their friendship together will be
the very strangler of their amity. Octavia is of a holy, cold,
and still conversation.   125

MENAS   Who would not have his wife so?

ENOBARBUS   Not he that himself is not so, which is
Mark Antony. He will to his Egyptian dish again.
Then shall the sighs of Octavia blow the fire up in
Caesar, and, as I said before, that which is the strength
of their amity shall prove the immediate author of   131
their variance. Antony will use his affection where it   132
is; he married but his occasion here.   133

MENAS   And thus it may be. Come, sir, will you
aboard? I have a health for you.   135

ENOBARBUS   I shall take it, sir. We have used our
throats in Egypt.

MENAS   Come, let's away.   _Exeunt._

❧

[2.7]

_Music plays. Enter two or three Servants with a
banquet._

FIRST SERVANT   Here they'll be, man. Some o' their
plants are ill-rooted already; the least wind i'th' world   2
will blow them down.

---

67 fair i.e., friendly   **68 fair** i.e., well-chosen   **69 Then . . . heard** i.e.,
I am not implying more about Antony in Egypt than my words hon-
estly mean.   **70–2 Apollodorus . . . mattress** (Alludes to a tale told by
Plutarch according to which Cleopatra had herself rolled up in a mattress and carried secretly by Apollodorus to meet Julius Caesar.)
74 like likely   **75 toward** coming up.   **80 Enjoy thy plainness** Give
free rein to your bluntness   **81 nothing . . . thee** suits you not at all
badly.   **83.1 Manent** They remain onstage   **85 known** known each
other   **96 There** In respect to that   **98 authority** i.e., to make arrests,
like a constable.   **take** arrest.   **two thieves kissing** (1) our two thieving hands shaking (2) two thieves greeting each other.

101 true honest (because women use cosmetic art to conceal defects)
103 No . . . hearts i.e., You speak true, since women in their own way are
thieves, stealing men's affections.   **105 a drinking** an occasion for drinking.   **109 You've said** You've spoken truly   **115 Pray ye, sir?** Are you in
earnest?   **118 divine of** prophesy about   **120 made more** played more
of a role   **125 conversation** demeanor.   **131–2 author . . . variance** cause
of their falling out.   **132–3 use . . . it is** i.e., satisfy his passion in Egypt
133 his occasion what his interests demanded   **135 health** toast
2.7. Location: On board Pompey's galley, off Misenum in southern
Italy. A table and stools are brought on.
0.2 banquet a course of the feast, probably dessert.   **2 plants**
(1) planted trees (2) soles of the feet

SECOND SERVANT   Lepidus is high-colored.   4

FIRST SERVANT   They have made him drink alms-drink.   5

SECOND SERVANT   As they pinch one another by the   6
disposition, he cries out, "No more," reconciles them   7
to his entreaty, and himself to th' drink.   8

FIRST SERVANT   But it raises the greater war between
him and his discretion.

SECOND SERVANT   Why, this it is to have a name in   11
great men's fellowship. I had as lief have a reed that   12
will do me no service as a partisan I could not heave.   13

FIRST SERVANT   To be called into a huge sphere,   14
and not to be seen to move in't, are the holes where   15
eyes should be, which pitifully disaster the cheeks.   16

A sennet sounded. Enter Caesar, Antony,
Pompey, Lepidus, Agrippa, Maecenas, Enobarbus,
Menas, with other captains [and a Boy].

ANTONY
Thus do they, sir: they take the flow o'th' Nile   17
By certain scales i'th' pyramid. They know   18
By th' height, the lowness, or the mean if dearth   19
Or foison follow. The higher Nilus swells   20
The more it promises; as it ebbs, the seedsman
Upon the slime and ooze scatters his grain,
And shortly comes to harvest.

LEPIDUS   You've strange serpents there.

ANTONY   Ay, Lepidus.

LEPIDUS   Your serpent of Egypt is bred now of your   26
mud by the operation of your sun; so is your crocodile.

ANTONY   They are so.

POMPEY   Sit—and some wine. A health to Lepidus!   29
[They sit and drink.]

LEPIDUS   I am not so well as I should be, but I'll   30
ne'er out.   31

ENOBARBUS   Not till you have slept; I fear me you'll be
in till then.   33

LEPIDUS   Nay, certainly, I have heard the Ptolemies'
pyramises are very goodly things; without contradic-   35
tion I have heard that.

MENAS   *[aside to Pompey]*   Pompey, a word.

POMPEY   *[to Menas]*   Say in mine ear. What is't?

MENAS   *(whispers in 's ear)*
Forsake thy seat, I do beseech thee, captain,
And hear me speak a word.

POMPEY   *[to Menas]*
Forbear me till anon.—This wine for Lepidus!   41

LEPIDUS   What manner o' thing is your crocodile?

ANTONY   It is shaped, sir, like itself, and it is as broad as
it hath breadth. It is just so high as it is, and moves
with it own organs. It lives by that which nourisheth   45
it, and, the elements once out of it, it transmigrates.   46

LEPIDUS   What color is it of?

ANTONY   Of it own color too.

LEPIDUS   'Tis a strange serpent.

ANTONY   'Tis so. And the tears of it are wet.   50

CAESAR   Will this description satisfy him?

ANTONY   With the health that Pompey gives him, else
he is a very epicure.   *[Menas whispers again.]*   53

POMPEY   *[aside to Menas]*
Go hang, sir, hang! Tell me of that? Away!
Do as I bid you.—Where's this cup I called for?

MENAS   *[aside to Pompey]*
If for the sake of merit thou wilt hear me,   56
Rise from thy stool.

POMPEY   *[rising]*   I think thou'rt mad. The matter?
[They walk aside.]

MENAS
I have ever held my cap off to thy fortunes.   58

POMPEY
Thou hast served me with much faith. What's else to
say?—   59
Be jolly, lords.

ANTONY   These quicksands, Lepidus,
Keep off them, for you sink.
[Menas and Pompey speak aside.]

MENAS
Wilt thou be lord of all the world?

POMPEY   What say'st thou?

MENAS
Wilt thou be lord of the whole world? That's twice.

POMPEY
How should that be?

MENAS   But entertain it,   64
And, though thou think me poor, I am the man
Will give thee all the world.

POMPEY   Hast thou drunk well?

MENAS
No, Pompey, I have kept me from the cup.
Thou art, if thou dar'st be, the earthly Jove.

---

4 high-colored flushed.   **5 alms-drink** i.e., drink charitably consumed in the furtherance of reconciliation. (See next speech and note.)   **6–8 As . . . drink** As they chafe one another, prompted by their various temperaments, Lepidus entreats them to stop quarreling, and reconciles himself to the peacemaking business of downing one drink after another in response to their toasts.   **11 a name** a name only   **12 had as lief** would just as soon   **13 partisan** long-bladed spear. (Here, metaphorically, too large a weapon for Lepidus to wield.)   **14–16 To . . . cheeks** To be summoned by fortune to greatness and yet not be able to fulfill the role greatly is like having eye sockets with no eyes in them, a defect that will disfigure (*disaster*) the cheeks. (The underlying image is of a heavenly body that cannot move properly in its sphere, causing *disaster*, meaning both disfigurement and the evil effects of unfavorable aspect of a planet.)
16.1 *sennet* trumpet call signaling the approach of a procession
17 sir (Usually thought to refer to Caesar, but the matter is uncertain.)
take measure   **18 scales** graduated markings   **19 mean** middle
20 foison plenty   **26 Your serpent** i.e., This serpent that people talk about. (The colloquial indefinite *your*.)   **29 health** toast. (Lepidus is obliged to drink up every time a toast is proposed to him.)   **30–1 I'll ne'er out** i.e., I'll never refuse a toast, never quit.   **33 in** in drink, in your cups. (With a play of antitheses between *in* and *out* in line 31.)
35 pyramises (Lepidus's drunken error for *pyramides*, plural of *pyramis* or *pyramid*.)

41 Forbear . . . anon Excuse me for a moment.   **45 it own** its own. (Also in line 48.)   **46 elements** vital elements   **50 tears** (Alludes to the ancient belief that the crocodile wept insincere "crocodile tears" over its victim before devouring it.)   **53 epicure** (1) glutton (2) atheist. (The Epicureans did not believe in an afterlife. Antony's jesting point is that only an atheist or epicure would be skeptical of such a satisfying description as Antony has just given of the crocodile.)
56 merit i.e., my merits as a loyal follower, or, the merit of my ideas
58 held . . . off i.e., been a respectful and faithful servant   **59 faith** faithfulness.   **64 But entertain it** Only accept the possibility

Whate'er the ocean pales or sky inclips   69
Is thine, if thou wilt ha 't.
POMPEY   Show me which way.
MENAS
These three world-sharers, these competitors,   71
Are in thy vessel. Let me cut the cable,
And, when we are put off, fall to their throats.   73
All there is thine.
POMPEY   Ah, this thou shouldst have done
And not have spoke on't! In me 'tis villainy;   75
In thee 't had been good service. Thou must know,   76
'Tis not my profit that does lead mine honor;
Mine honor, it. Repent that e'er thy tongue   78
Hath so betrayed thine act. Being done unknown,   79
I should have found it afterwards well done,
But must condemn it now. Desist, and drink.
                              [He returns to the feast.]
MENAS [aside]   For this,
I'll never follow thy palled fortunes more.   83
Who seeks and will not take when once 'tis offered   84
Shall never find it more.
POMPEY   This health to Lepidus!
ANTONY
Bear him ashore. I'll pledge it for him, Pompey.   86
ENOBARBUS
Here's to thee, Menas!   [They drink.]
MENAS   Enobarbus, welcome!
POMPEY   Fill till the cup be hid.
ENOBARBUS   There's a strong fellow, Menas.
              [Pointing to one who carries off Lepidus.]
MENAS   Why?
ENOBARBUS   'A bears the third part of the world, man; 91
see'st not?
MENAS
The third part, then, is drunk. Would it were all,
That it might go on wheels!   94
ENOBARBUS   Drink thou; increase the reels.   95
MENAS   Come.
POMPEY
This is not yet an Alexandrian feast.
ANTONY
It ripens towards it. Strike the vessels, ho!   98
Here's to Caesar!
CAESAR   I could well forbear 't.
It's monstrous labor when I wash my brain
And it grows fouler.
ANTONY   Be a child o'th' time.
CAESAR   Possess it, I'll make answer.   102
But I had rather fast from all four days   103

Than drink so much in one.
ENOBARBUS [to Antony]   Ha, my brave emperor!   104
Shall we dance now the Egyptian Bacchanals   105
And celebrate our drink?   106
POMPEY   Let's ha 't, good soldier.
ANTONY   Come, let's all take hands
Till that the conquering wine hath steeped our sense 109
In soft and delicate Lethe.
ENOBARBUS   All take hands.   110
Make battery to our ears with the loud music,   111
The while I'll place you; then the boy shall sing.
The holding every man shall bear as loud   113
As his strong sides can volley.   114
         Music plays. Enobarbus places them hand in hand.

                    The Song.

BOY [sings]
Come, thou monarch of the vine,
Plumpy Bacchus with pink eyne!   116
In thy fats our cares be drowned,   117
With thy grapes our hairs be crowned.
ALL   Cup us till the world go round,   119
Cup us till the world go round!
CAESAR
What would you more? Pompey, good night.—Good
brother,
Let me request you off. Our graver business   122
Frowns at this levity. Gentle lords, let's part;
You see we have burnt our cheeks. Strong Enobarb   124
Is weaker than the wine, and mine own tongue
Splits what it speaks. The wild disguise hath almost 126
Anticked us all. What needs more words? Good night. 127
Good Antony, your hand.
POMPEY   I'll try you on the shore. 128
ANTONY
And shall, sir. Give 's your hand.
POMPEY   Oh, Antony,
You have my father's house. But what? We are
friends.
Come down into the boat.
ENOBARBUS   Take heed you fall not. 131
              [Exeunt all but Enobarbus and Menas.]
Menas, I'll not on shore.
MENAS   No, to my cabin.
These drums, these trumpets, flutes! What!
Let Neptune hear we bid a loud farewell
To these great fellows. Sound and be hanged, sound
out!   Sound a flourish, with drums.

69 pales impales, fences in. inclips embraces 71 competitors partners. (With secondary sense of "rivals.") 73 are put off have put to sea 75 on't of it. 76 Thou must know I must inform you that 78 Mine honor, it i.e., my honor comes before my personal profit. Repent Regret 79 unknown i.e., without my knowledge 83 palled decayed, darkened 84 Who He who 86 pledge it i.e., drink the toast (since Lepidus is too far gone to drink) 91 'A He 94 go on wheels go fast or easily. (Proverbial.) 95 reels (1) revels (2) reeling and whirling of drunkenness. 98 Strike the vessels Broach or tap the casks 102 Possess . . . answer My answer is, be master of the time; or, possibly, Drink it off, I'll drink in return. 103 all all nourishment

104 brave splendid 105 Bacchanals drunken dance to Bacchus, god of wine 106 celebrate consecrate with observances 109 Till that until 110 Lethe i.e., forgetfulness. (Literally, the river of oblivion in Hades.) 111 Make battery to Assault 113 holding refrain. bear carry, sing 114 volley sing in return, answering the stanza with the refrain. 116 pink eyne i.e., eyes half-shut, from drinking. 117 fats vats, vessels 119 Cup Intoxicate 122 off to disembark. 124 we . . . cheeks our complexions are flushed with drinking. 126 disguise (1) masque (2) transforming drunkenness 127 Anticked us (1) made dancers of us in a masque (2) made buffoons or fools of us 128 try you i.e., take you on in a drinking contest 131 boat small boat for taking the party ashore.

ENOBARBUS   Hoo! says 'a. There's my cap.
                        [*He flings it in the air.*]
MENAS   Hoo! Noble captain, come.   *Exeunt.*

❖

[3.1]

Enter Ventidius as it were in triumph [with Silius,
and other Romans, officers, and soldiers], the dead
body of Pacorus borne before him.

VENTIDIUS
  Now, darting Parthia, art thou struck, and now   1
  Pleased fortune does of Marcus Crassus' death   2
  Make me revenger. Bear the King's son's body
  Before our army. Thy Pacorus, Orodes,   4
  Pays this for Marcus Crassus.
SILIUS   Noble Ventidius,
  Whilst yet with Parthian blood thy sword is warm,
  The fugitive Parthians follow. Spur through Media,   7
  Mesopotamia, and the shelters whither
  The routed fly. So thy grand captain, Antony,
  Shall set thee on triumphant chariots and   10
  Put garlands on thy head.
VENTIDIUS   Oh, Silius, Silius,
  I have done enough. A lower place, note well,   12
  May make too great an act. For learn this, Silius:
  Better to leave undone than by our deed
  Acquire too high a fame when him we serve's away.
  Caesar and Antony have ever won
  More in their officer than person. Sossius,   17
  One of my place in Syria, his lieutenant,   18
  For quick accumulation of renown,
  Which he achieved by th' minute, lost his favor.   20
  Who does i'th' wars more than his captain can   21
  Becomes his captain's captain; and ambition,
  The soldier's virtue, rather makes choice of loss   23
  Than gain which darkens him.   24
  I could do more to do Antonius good,
  But 'twould offend him, and in his offense   26
  Should my performance perish.
SILIUS   Thou hast, Ventidius, that   28
  Without the which a soldier and his sword   29
  Grants scarce distinction. Thou wilt write to Antony? 30
VENTIDIUS
  I'll humbly signify what in his name,

That magical word of war, we have effected: 32
How with his banners and his well-paid ranks
The ne'er-yet-beaten horse of Parthia   34
We have jaded out o'th' field.
SILIUS   Where is he now?   35
VENTIDIUS
  He purposeth to Athens, whither, with what haste
  The weight we must convey with 's will permit,   37
  We shall appear before him.—On, there. Pass along!
                                                Exeunt.

❖

[3.2]

Enter Agrippa at one door, Enobarbus at another.

AGRIPPA   What, are the brothers parted?   1
ENOBARBUS
  They have dispatched with Pompey; he is gone.   2
  The other three are sealing. Octavia weeps   3
  To part from Rome; Caesar is sad; and Lepidus,   4
  Since Pompey's feast, as Menas says, is troubled
  With the greensickness.
AGRIPPA   'Tis a noble Lepidus.   6
ENOBARBUS
  A very fine one. Oh, how he loves Caesar!   7
AGRIPPA
  Nay, but how dearly he adores Mark Antony!
ENOBARBUS
  Caesar? Why, he's the Jupiter of men.
AGRIPPA
  What's Antony? The god of Jupiter.
ENOBARBUS
  Spake you of Caesar? How, the nonpareil!
AGRIPPA
  O Antony, O thou Arabian bird!   12
ENOBARBUS
  Would you praise Caesar, say "Caesar"; go no further.
AGRIPPA
  Indeed, he plied them both with excellent praises.
ENOBARBUS
  But he loves Caesar best; yet he loves Antony.
  Hoo! Hearts, tongues, figures, scribes, bards, poets,
    cannot   16
  Think, speak, cast, write, sing, number, hoo!   17
  His love to Antony. But as for Caesar,
  Kneel down, kneel down, and wonder.
AGRIPPA   Both he loves.

3.1. Location: The Middle East.
1 darting (The Parthians were famous for archery and for the Parthian
dart which they discharged as they fled.) **Parthia** i.e., Orodes, King
of Parthia **2 Crassus' death** (Crassus, member of the first triumvirate with Pompey the Great and Julius Caesar, was overthrown and
treacherously murdered by Orodes in 53 B.C.) **4 Pacorus, Orodes**
(Pacorus was the son of Orodes.) **7 The . . . follow** follow the fleeing
Parthians. **10 triumphant** triumphal **12 A lower place** One of
lower rank **17 More . . . person** more through the actions of their
lieutenants than by their own efforts. **18 of my place** of the same
rank as I. **his lieutenant** i.e., the commanding officer acting for
Antony **20 by th' minute** minute by minute, continually **21 Who**
He who **23–4 rather . . . him** prefers to lose rather than gain in such
a way as to darken his reputation. **26 offense** taking offense
28–30 that . . . distinction i.e., discretion, without which a soldier can
scarcely be distinguished from the sword he uses.

32 word watchword. **effected** achieved **34 horse** cavalry **35 jaded**
driven exhausted like jades, inferior horses **37 with 's** with us
3.2. Location: Rome.
1 brothers parted brothers-in-law departed. **2 dispatched** concluded the business **3 sealing** affixing seals to their agreements, settling matters. **4 sad** sober **6 greensickness** a kind of anemia
supposed to affect young women, especially those afflicted with love-
longing. (Used ironically here to refer to Lepidus's hangover and to
his love for Antony and Caesar.) **7 fine** (*Lepidus* in Latin means
"fine," "elegant.") **12 Arabian bird** i.e., the fabled phoenix. (Only
one existed at a time; it re-created itself by arising from its ashes.)
16 figures figures of speech **17 cast** calculate. **number** write verses

ENOBARBUS
They are his shards, and he their beetle. [*Trumpets within.*] So;   20
This is to horse. Adieu, noble Agrippa.   21

AGRIPPA
Good fortune, worthy soldier, and farewell.

Enter Caesar, Antony, Lepidus, and Octavia.

ANTONY   No further, sir.   23

CAESAR
You take from me a great part of myself;
Use me well in't.—Sister, prove such a wife
As my thoughts make thee, and as my farthest bond   26
Shall pass on thy approof.—Most noble Antony,   27
Let not the piece of virtue which is set   28
Betwixt us as the cement of our love
To keep it builded be the ram to batter
The fortress of it; for better might we
Have loved without this mean, if on both parts   32
This be not cherished.

ANTONY   Make me not offended
In your distrust.

CAESAR   I have said.

ANTONY   You shall not find,   34
Though you be therein curious, the least cause   35
For what you seem to fear. So the gods keep you,
And make the hearts of Romans serve your ends!
We will here part.

CAESAR
Farewell, my dearest sister, fare thee well.
The elements be kind to thee, and make
Thy spirits all of comfort! Fare thee well.   40

OCTAVIA [*weeping*]   My noble brother!

ANTONY
The April's in her eyes; it is love's spring,
And these the showers to bring it on.—Be cheerful.

OCTAVIA [*to Caesar*]
Sir, look well to my husband's house; and—   45

CAESAR
What, Octavia?

OCTAVIA   I'll tell you in your ear.
[*She whisper to Caesar.*]

ANTONY
Her tongue will not obey her heart, nor can   47
Her heart inform her tongue—the swan's down feather,   48
That stands upon the swell at full of tide,   49
And neither way inclines.   50

ENOBARBUS [*aside to Agrippa*]   Will Caesar weep?

AGRIPPA [*aside to Enobarbus*]   He has a cloud in 's face.

ENOBARBUS [*aside to Agrippa*]
He were the worse for that, were he a horse;   53
So is he, being a man.

AGRIPPA [*aside to Enobarbus*]   Why, Enobarbus,
When Antony found Julius Caesar dead,
He cried almost to roaring; and he wept
When at Philippi he found Brutus slain.

ENOBARBUS [*aside to Agrippa*]
That year indeed he was troubled with a rheum.   58
What willingly he did confound he wailed,   59
Believe't, till I wept too.

CAESAR   No, sweet Octavia,
You shall hear from me still. The time shall not   61
Outgo my thinking on you.

ANTONY   Come, sir, come,   62
I'll wrestle with you in my strength of love.
Look, here I have you [*embracing him*]; thus I let you go,
And give you to the gods.

CAESAR   Adieu. Be happy!

LEPIDUS
Let all the number of the stars give light
To thy fair way!

CAESAR   Farewell, farewell!   *Kisses Octavia.*

ANTONY   Farewell!
Trumpets sound. Exeunt [in separate groups].

❖

[3.3]

Enter Cleopatra, Charmian, Iras, and Alexas.

CLEOPATRA
Where is the fellow?

ALEXAS   Half afeard to come.

CLEOPATRA
Go to, go to.

Enter the Messenger as before.

Come hither, sir.

ALEXAS   Good Majesty,   2
Herod of Jewry dare not look upon you   3
But when you are well pleased.

CLEOPATRA   That Herod's head
I'll have; but how, when Antony is gone,
Through whom I might command it?—Come thou near.

MESSENGER   Most gracious Majesty!

CLEOPATRA   Didst thou behold Octavia?

---

20 **shards** patches of dung, or, perhaps, wings or wing-cases, i.e., protectors, patrons 21 **This is to horse** i.e., The trumpet call gives the signal to depart. 23 **No further** i.e., You need not go on urging your point, or, you need accompany me no further 26–7 **as . . . approof** such that my utmost bond shall be justified in certifying what you will prove to be. 28 **piece** masterpiece 32 **mean** intermediary, or means 34 **In** by. **I have said** i.e., I stand by what I've said. 35 **curious** overly inquisitive or touchy 40 **elements** heavens 45 **husband's house** i.e., Antony's house, as at 2.7.130, though Octavia is also a widow; see 3.3.29 47–50 **Her . . . inclines** i.e., Her conflicting emotions make her unable to speak aloud, like a swan's down feather floating at full tide, moving neither up nor down stream.

53 **He . . . horse** (Alludes to the belief that a horse with a dark spot on its face was apt to be bad-tempered.) 58 **rheum** i.e., running at the eyes. (Said of any discharge of secretion from the head.) 59 **What . . . wailed** He bewailed what he intentionally destroyed 61 **still** regularly. 61–2 **The time . . . you** Time itself will not outlast my thinking of you.

3.3. **Location: Alexandria. Cleopatra's palace.**
2 **Go to** (An expression of impatience.) 3 **Herod of Jewry** i.e., Even the famous tyrant who slaughtered the children. (See 1.2.29–30.)

MESSENGER
Ay, dread Queen.

CLEOPATRA   Where?

MESSENGER   Madam, in Rome.
I looked her in the face, and saw her led
Between her brother and Mark Antony.

CLEOPATRA
Is she as tall as me?

MESSENGER   She is not, madam.

CLEOPATRA
Didst hear her speak? Is she shrill-tongued or low?

MESSENGER
Madam, I heard her speak. She is low-voiced.

CLEOPATRA
That's not so good. He cannot like her long.   15

CHARMIAN
Like her! Oh, Isis, 'tis impossible.

CLEOPATRA
I think so, Charmian. Dull of tongue, and dwarfish.—
What majesty is in her gait? Remember,
If e'er thou looked'st on majesty.

MESSENGER   She creeps:
Her motion and her station are as one.   20
She shows a body rather than a life,   21
A statue than a breather.

CLEOPATRA   Is this certain?   22

MESSENGER
Or I have no observance.

CHARMIAN   Three in Egypt   23
Cannot make better note.

CLEOPATRA   He's very knowing,   24
I do perceive't. There's nothing in her yet.
The fellow has good judgment.

CHARMIAN   Excellent.

CLEOPATRA   Guess at her years, I prithee.

MESSENGER   Madam,
She was a widow—

CLEOPATRA   Widow? Charmian, hark.

MESSENGER   And I do think she's thirty.

CLEOPATRA
Bear'st thou her face in mind? Is't long or round?

MESSENGER   Round, even to faultiness.

CLEOPATRA
For the most part, too, they are foolish that are so.—
Her hair, what color?

MESSENGER   Brown, madam; and her forehead
As low as she would wish it.   36

CLEOPATRA [giving money]   There's gold for thee.
Thou must not take my former sharpness ill.
I will employ thee back again; I find thee   39
Most fit for business. Go make thee ready;

Our letters are prepared.   [Exit Messenger.]

CHARMIAN   A proper man.   41

CLEOPATRA
Indeed, he is so. I repent me much
That so I harried him. Why, methinks, by him,   43
This creature's no such thing.

CHARMIAN   Nothing, madam.   44

CLEOPATRA
The man hath seen some majesty, and should know.

CHARMIAN
Hath he seen majesty? Isis else defend,   46
And serving you so long!   47

CLEOPATRA
I have one thing more to ask him yet, good
     Charmian—
But 'tis no matter; thou shalt bring him to me
Where I will write. All may be well enough

CHARMIAN   I warrant you, madam.   Exeunt.   51

✿

[3.4]

Enter Antony and Octavia.

ANTONY
Nay, nay, Octavia, not only that—
That were excusable, that and thousands more
Of semblable import—but he hath waged   3
New wars 'gainst Pompey; made his will, and read it 4
To public ear;
Spoke scantly of me; when perforce he could not   6
But pay me terms of honor, cold and sickly
He vented them, most narrow measure lent me;   8
When the best hint was given him, he not took't,   9
Or did it from his teeth.

OCTAVIA   Oh, my good lord,   10
Believe not all, or, if you must believe,
Stomach not all. A more unhappy lady,   12
If this division chance, ne'er stood between,   13
Praying for both parts.
The good gods will mock me presently
When I shall pray, "Oh, bless my lord and husband!"
Undo that prayer by crying out as loud,   17
"Oh, bless my brother!" Husband win, win brother,
Prays and destroys the prayer; no midway
Twixt these extremes at all.

ANTONY   Gentle Octavia,
Let your best love draw to that point which seeks   21
Best to preserve it. If I lose mine honor,   22

---

15 **not so good** i.e., not so good for her.   20 **Her . . . one** i.e., she
moves with so little animation that it's all the same whether she's
moving or standing.   21 **shows** appears as   22 **breather** living
being.   23–4 **Three . . . note** There are not three people in Egypt who
are better observers.   36 **As . . . it** i.e., such that she wouldn't wish it
to be any lower. (A colloquial way of suggesting she is ugly; high
foreheads were thought more beautiful.)   39 **employ . . . again** send
you back with a message

41 **proper** good   43 **harried** maltreated.   **by** according to   44 **no such
thing** nothing much.   46 **else defend** forbid that it be otherwise. (An
interjection.)   47 **serving** i.e., he having served   51 **warrant** assure
3.4. Location: Athens.
3 **semblable** similar   4 **read it** (In order to win the populace by
showing them what benefits they might expect from him.)   6 **scantly**
slightingly   8 **vented** gave vent to, expressed.   **narrow measure lent
me** gave me minimal praise   9 **hint** occasion (to praise Antony)
10 **from his teeth** i.e., between clenched teeth, not from the heart.
12 **Stomach** resent   13 **chance** occur   17 **Undo** i.e., and then undo,
or, I shall undo   21–2 **Let . . . it** let your warmest love be given to that
one of us who seeks to preserve it (your love) best.

I lose myself; better I were not yours
Than yours so branchless. But, as you requested, 24
Yourself shall go between 's. The meantime, lady, 25
I'll raise the preparation of a war 26
Shall stain your brother. Make your soonest haste; 27
So your desires are yours.

OCTAVIA   Thanks to my lord. 28
The Jove of power make me, most weak, most weak,
Your reconciler! Wars twixt you twain would be
As if the world should cleave, and that slain men 31
Should solder up the rift. 32

ANTONY
When it appears to you where this begins, 33
Turn your displeasure that way, for our faults 34
Can never be so equal that your love 35
Can equally move with them. Provide your going; 36
Choose your own company and command what cost
Your heart has mind to.   *Exeunt.*

❖

[3.5]

Enter Enobarbus and Eros, [meeting].

ENOBARBUS   How now, friend Eros?
EROS   There's strange news come, sir.
ENOBARBUS   What, man?
EROS   Caesar and Lepidus have made wars upon Pompey.
ENOBARBUS   This is old. What is the success? 6
EROS   Caesar, having made use of him in the wars 7
'gainst Pompey, presently denied him rivality, would 8
not let him partake in the glory of the action; and, not
resting here, accuses him of letters he had formerly 10
wrote to Pompey; upon his own appeal seizes him. 11
So the poor third is up, till death enlarge his confine. 12

ENOBARBUS
Then, world, thou hast a pair of chops, no more; 13
And throw between them all the food thou hast,
They'll grind the one the other. Where's Antony? 15

EROS
He's walking in the garden—thus, and spurns 16
The rush that lies before him; cries, "Fool Lepidus!" 17

---

24 **branchless** pruned (of honor).   25 **The meantime** In the meantime   26–7 **I'll . . . brother** I'll raise an army that will deprive your brother of his luster.   28 **So . . . yours** i.e., thus you have obtained your desire (to go). (Or, *so* may mean "as long as.")   31 **cleave** split   32 **Should** would be needed to   33 **where this begins** who started this quarrel   34 **our** i.e., Caesar's and my   34–6 **our faults . . . them** i.e., you will have to judge between our faults and choose.   36 **Provide** Make arrangements for   **3.5. Location:** Athens.   6 **success** outcome, result.   7 **him** i.e., Lepidus   8 **presently** immediately.   **rivality** rights of a partner. (Caesar and Lepidus have newly gone to war against Pompey and have defeated him.)   10 **resting here** stopping with this insult   11 **his own appeal** Caesar's own accusation   12 **up** shut up (in prison).   **enlarge his confine** set him free.   13 **a pair . . . more** a single pair of jaws, with no third partner   15 **They'll . . . other** the jaws will still grind against each other, grind each other down.   16 **thus** (Eros imitates Antony's angry walk.)   **spurns** kicks   17 **rush** strewn rushes

---

And threats the throat of that his officer 18
That murdered Pompey.

ENOBARBUS   Our great navy's rigged. 19

EROS
For Italy and Caesar. More, Domitius: 20
My lord desires you presently. My news 21
I might have told hereafter.

ENOBARBUS   'Twill be naught,
But let it be. Bring me to Antony.

EROS   Come, sir.   *Exeunt.*

❖

[3.6]

Enter Agrippa, Maecenas, and Caesar.

CAESAR
Contemning Rome, he has done all this and more 1
In Alexandria. Here's the manner of 't:
I'th' marketplace, on a tribunal silvered, 3
Cleopatra and himself in chairs of gold
Were publicly enthroned. At the feet sat
Caesarion, whom they call my father's son, 6
And all the unlawful issue that their lust
Since then hath made between them. Unto her
He gave the stablishment of Egypt, made her 9
Of lower Syria, Cyprus, Lydia,
Absolute queen.

MAECENAS   This in the public eye?

CAESAR
I'th' common showplace, where they exercise. 12
His sons he there proclaimed the kings of kings:
Great Media, Parthia, and Armenia
He gave to Alexander; to Ptolemy he assigned
Syria, Cilicia, and Phoenicia. She
In th' habiliments of the goddess Isis 17
That day appeared, and oft before gave audience,
As 'tis reported, so.

MAECENAS   Let Rome be thus informed.

AGRIPPA   Who, queasy with his insolence already, 21
Will their good thoughts call from him. 22

CAESAR
The people knows it, and have now received
His accusations.

AGRIPPA   Who does he accuse?

CAESAR
Caesar, and that, having in Sicily
Sextus Pompeius spoiled, we had not rated him 26
His part o'th'isle. Then does he say he lent me 27

---

18 **And . . . officer** and threatens the life of the officer of his   19 **Pompey** (After his defeat by Caesar and Lepidus, Pompey was murdered—perhaps, according to history, on Antony's orders, but here Antony blames his officer.)   20 **More** I have more to say   21 **presently** immediately.   **3.6. Location:** Rome.   1 **Contemning** Disdaining   3 **tribunal** seat of state, dais   6 **my father's** i.e., Julius Caesar's. (Julius Caesar had adopted his grandnephew Octavius as his son.)   9 **stablishment** settled possession   12 **exercise** put on entertainments and sports.   17 **habiliments** attire   21 **queasy** nauseated, "fed up." (Refers to the Roman people.)   22 **call** withdraw   26 **spoiled** despoiled, plundered.   **rated him** allotted to Antony   27 **th'isle** i.e., Sicily.

Some shipping, unrestored. Lastly, he frets 28
That Lepidus of the triumvirate 29
Should be deposed, and, being, that we detain 30
All his revenue.

AGRIPPA   Sir, this should be answered.

CAESAR
'Tis done already, and the messenger gone.
I have told him Lepidus was grown too cruel,
That he his high authority abused
And did deserve his change. For what I have
    conquered, 35
I grant him part; but then in his Armenia,
And other of his conquered kingdoms, I
Demand the like.

MAECENAS   He'll never yield to that.

CAESAR
Nor must not then be yielded to in this.

Enter Octavia with her train.

OCTAVIA
Hail, Caesar, and my lord! Hail, most dear Caesar!

CAESAR
That ever I should call thee castaway!

OCTAVIA
You have not called me so, nor have you cause.

CAESAR
Why have you stol'n upon us thus? You come not
Like Caesar's sister. The wife of Antony
Should have an army for an usher and
The neighs of horse to tell of her approach 46
Long ere she did appear. The trees by th' way 47
Should have borne men, and expectation fainted,
Longing for what it had not. Nay, the dust
Should have ascended to the roof of heaven,
Raised by your populous troops. But you are come
A market maid to Rome, and have prevented 52
The ostentation of our love, which, left unshown, 53
Is often left unloved. We should have met you 54
By sea and land, supplying every stage 55
With an augmented greeting.

OCTAVIA   Good my lord,
To come thus was I not constrained, but did it
On my free will. My lord, Mark Antony,
Hearing that you prepared for war, acquainted
My grievèd ear withal, whereon I begged
His pardon for return.

CAESAR   Which soon he granted, 61
Being an obstruct 'tween his lust and him. 62

OCTAVIA
Do not say so, my lord.

CAESAR   I have eyes upon him,
And his affairs come to me on the wind.
Where is he now?

OCTAVIA   My lord, in Athens.

CAESAR
No, my most wrongèd sister. Cleopatra
Hath nodded him to her. He hath given his empire
Up to a whore; who now are levying 69
The kings o'th' earth for war. He hath assembled
Bocchus, the King of Libya; Archelaus,
Of Cappadocia; Philadelphos, King
Of Paphlagonia; the Thracian king, Adallas;
King Manchus of Arabia; King of Pont;
Herod of Jewry; Mithridates, King
Of Comagene; Polemon and Amyntas,
The Kings of Mede and Lycaonia,
With a more larger list of scepters. 78

OCTAVIA   Ay me, most wretched,
That have my heart parted betwixt two friends
That does afflict each other!

CAESAR   Welcome hither.
Your letters did withhold our breaking forth 82
Till we perceived both how you were wrong led 83
And we in negligent danger. Cheer your heart. 84
Be you not troubled with the time, which drives 85
O'er your content these strong necessities, 86
But let determined things to destiny 87
Hold unbewailed their way. Welcome to Rome, 88
Nothing more dear to me. You are abused 89
Beyond the mark of thought, and the high gods, 90
To do you justice, makes his ministers 91
Of us and those that love you. Best of comfort, 92
And ever welcome to us.

AGRIPPA   Welcome, lady.

MAECENAS   Welcome, dear madam.
Each heart in Rome does love and pity you.
Only th'adulterous Antony, most large 97
In his abominations, turns you off 98
And gives his potent regiment to a trull 99
That noises it against us.

OCTAVIA   Is it so, sir? 100

CAESAR
Most certain. Sister, welcome. Pray you
Be ever known to patience. My dear'st sister! *Exeunt.* 102

[3.7]

Enter Cleopatra and Enobarbus.

---

28 **unrestored** that I did not return to him.   29 **of** from   30 **being** having been deposed   35 **For** As for   46 **horse** horses   47 **by** along   52 **prevented** forestalled (by your unannounced arrival)   53 **ostentation** ceremonial display   53–4 **which . . . unloved** which, if not made manifest through ceremonious display, often remains unappreciated or ceases to exist.   55 **stage** stage of your journey   61 **pardon** permission   62 **Being . . . him** i.e., since your return to Rome removed the obstacle between him and the gratification of his desires.

69 **who** i.e., and they   78 **a more larger** an even longer   82 **withhold . . . forth** restrain my advancing to battle   83 **wrong led** wronged, abused   84 **negligent danger** danger through neglect of taking necessary action.   85 **the time** the present state of affairs   85–6 **which . . . necessities** i.e., which tramples your happiness underfoot like a team of animals pulling a wagon   87–8 **let . . . way** allow inevitable events to go unbewailed to their destined conclusion.   89 **Nothing . . . me** i.e., you who are more dear to me than anything.   90 **mark** reach   90–2 **the high . . . you** i.e., the high gods (here treated as a singular subject of the verb "makes," and referred to as "his" in line 91) make us and those that love you their ministers of justice in your cause.   97 **large** unrestrained   98 **turns you off** rejects you   99 **regiment** government, rule.   **trull** prostitute   100 **noises it** is clamorous   102 **Be . . . patience** be patient.

3.7. Location: Near Actium, on the northwestern coast of Greece. Antony's camp.

CLEOPATRA

I will be even with thee, doubt it not.

ENOBARBUS But why, why, why?

CLEOPATRA

Thou hast forspoke my being in these wars, 3
And say'st it is not fit.

ENOBARBUS Well, is it, is it? 4

CLEOPATRA

If not denounced against us, why should not we 5
Be there in person?

ENOBARBUS [aside] Well, I could reply.
If we should serve with horse and mares together, 7
The horse were merely lost; the mares would bear 8
A soldier and his horse.

CLEOPATRA What is't you say? 9

ENOBARBUS

Your presence needs must puzzle Antony, 10
Take from his heart, take from his brain, from's time
What should not then be spared. He is already
Traduced for levity, and 'tis said in Rome 13
That Photinus, an eunuch, and your maids 14
Manage this war.

CLEOPATRA Sink Rome, and their tongues rot
That speak against us! A charge we bear i'th' war, 16
And as the president of my kingdom will 17
Appear there for a man. Speak not against it. 18
I will not stay behind.

Enter Antony and Canidius.

ENOBARBUS Nay, I have done.
Here comes the Emperor.

ANTONY Is it not strange, Canidius,
That from Tarentum and Brundusium
He could so quickly cut the Ionian sea 22
And take in Toryne?—You have heard on't, sweet? 23

CLEOPATRA

Celerity is never more admired 24
Than by the negligent.

ANTONY A good rebuke,
Which might have well becomed the best of men, 26
To taunt at slackness. Canidius, we
Will fight with him by sea.

CLEOPATRA By sea, what else?

CANIDIUS Why will my lord do so?

ANTONY For that he dares us to't. 30

ENOBARBUS

So hath my lord dared him to single fight.

CANIDIUS

Ay, and to wage this battle at Pharsalia,
Where Caesar fought with Pompey. But these offers,
Which serve not for his vantage, he shakes off,
And so should you.

ENOBARBUS Your ships are not well manned;
Your mariners are muleteers, reapers, people 36
Engrossed by swift impress. In Caesar's fleet 37
Are those that often have 'gainst Pompey fought;
Their ships are yare, yours heavy. No disgrace 39
Shall fall you for refusing him at sea, 40
Being prepared for land.

ANTONY By sea, by sea.

ENOBARBUS

Most worthy sir, you therein throw away
The absolute soldiership you have by land,
Distract your army, which doth most consist 44
Of war-marked footmen, leave unexecuted 45
Your own renownèd knowledge, quite forgo
The way which promises assurance, and
Give up yourself merely to chance and hazard 48
From firm security.

ANTONY I'll fight at sea.

CLEOPATRA

I have sixty sails, Caesar none better.

ANTONY

Our overplus of shipping will we burn,
And with the rest full-manned, from th' head of
Actium 52
Beat th'approaching Caesar. But if we fail,
We then can do't at land.

Enter a Messenger.

Thy business?

MESSENGER

The news is true, my lord; he is descried. 55
Caesar has taken Toryne.

ANTONY

Can he be there in person? 'Tis impossible;
Strange that his power should be. Canidius, 58
Our nineteen legions thou shalt hold by land,
And our twelve thousand horse. We'll to our ship.
Away, my Thetis!

Enter a Soldier.

How now, worthy soldier? 61

SOLDIER

O noble Emperor, do not fight by sea;
Trust not to rotten planks. Do you misdoubt
This sword and these my wounds? Let th'Egyptians
And the Phoenicians go a-ducking; we 65

---

3 **forspoke** spoken against   4 **fit** appropriate.   5 **If . . . us** i.e., Even if the war were not declared against me (which it is)   7 **horse** stallions 8 **merely** utterly   8–9 **bear . . . horse** be mounted by a rider and a stallion.   10 **puzzle** bewilder   13 **Traduced** criticized, censured 14 **an eunuch** (Probably Mardian. In North's Plutarch, Caesar complains that "Mardian the eunuch, Photinus, and Iras . . . and Charmian . . . ruled the affairs of Antonius' empire." But Photinus [or Pothinus] was a eunuch, too.)   16 **charge** responsibility, cost 17 **president** ruler   18 **for** in the capacity of   22 **Ionian** (Often applied to the Aegean, but here the Adriatic. Tarentum and Brundusium or Brundisium are in the "heel" of Italy, across the Adriatic from Actium and Toryne.)   23 **take in** conquer   24 **Celerity** Swiftness.   **admired** wondered at   26 **becomed** become, suited   30 **For that** Because

36 **muleteers** mule-drivers, peasants   37 **Engrossed** collected wholesale.   **impress** impressment, conscription.   39 **yare** quick, maneuverable   40 **fall** befall   44 **Distract** divide, divert.   **most** for the most part   45 **footmen** foot soldiers.   **unexecuted** unused 48 **merely** entirely   52 **head** promontory   55 **he is descried** he has been sighted.   58 **his power** i.e., his army, let alone himself 61 **Thetis** sea goddess, the mother of Achilles.   65 **go a-ducking** (1) get drenched (2) cringe

Have used to conquer standing on the earth   66
And fighting foot to foot.
ANTONY   Well, well, away!
     Exeunt Antony, Cleopatra, and Enobarbus.
SOLDIER
By Hercules, I think I am i'th' right.
CANIDIUS
Soldier, thou art; but his whole action grows   69
Not in the power on't. So our leader's led,   70
And we are women's men.
SOLDIER   You keep by land   71
The legions and the horse whole, do you not?   72
CANIDIUS
Marcus Octavius, Marcus Justeius,
Publicola, and Caelius are for sea;
But we keep whole by land. This speed of Caesar's
Carries beyond belief.   76
SOLDIER   While he was yet in Rome
His power went out in such distractions as   78
Beguiled all spies.
CANIDIUS   Who's his lieutenant, hear you?
SOLDIER
They say, one Taurus.
CANIDIUS   Well I know the man.

    Enter a Messenger.

MESSENGER   The Emperor calls Canidius.
CANIDIUS
With news the time's in labor, and throws forth   82
Each minute some.   *Exeunt.*   83

❧

[3.8]

    Enter Caesar [and Taurus] with his army,
    marching.

CAESAR   Taurus!
TAURUS   My lord?
CAESAR
Strike not by land; keep whole. Provoke not battle
Till we have done at sea. Do not exceed
The prescript of this scroll. [*He gives a scroll.*] Our
    fortune lies   5
Upon this jump.   *Exeunt.*   6

❧

[3.9]

    Enter Antony and Enobarbus.

ANTONY
Set we our squadrons on yond side o'th' hill,
In eye of Caesar's battle, from which place   2
We may the number of the ships behold
And so proceed accordingly.   *Exeunt.*

❧

[3.10]

    Canidius marcheth with his land army one way
    over the stage, and Taurus, the lieutenant of
    Caesar, the other way. After their going in is heard
    the noise of a sea fight.

    Alarum. Enter Enobarbus.

ENOBARBUS
Naught, naught, all naught! I can behold no longer.   1
Th'*Antoniad,* the Egyptian admiral,   2
With all their sixty, fly and turn the rudder.
To see't mine eyes are blasted.

    Enter Scarus.

SCARUS   Gods and goddesses,
All the whole synod of them!
ENOBARBUS   What's thy passion?   5
SCARUS
The greater cantle of the world is lost   6
With very ignorance; we have kissed away   7
Kingdoms and provinces.
ENOBARBUS   How appears the fight?
SCARUS
On our side like the tokened pestilence,   9
Where death is sure. Yon ribaudred nag of Egypt—   10
Whom leprosy o'ertake!—i'th' midst o'th' fight,
When vantage like a pair of twins appeared   12
Both as the same, or rather ours the elder,   13
The breeze upon her, like a cow in June,   14
Hoists sails and flies.
ENOBARBUS   That I beheld.
Mine eyes did sicken at the sight, and could not
Endure a further view.
SCARUS   She once being loofed,   18
The noble ruin of her magic, Antony,   19
Claps on his sea wing and, like a doting mallard,   20
Leaving the fight in height, flies after her.   21
I never saw an action of such shame.
Experience, manhood, honor, ne'er before

---

66 **Have used** are accustomed. **standing on the earth** (1) fighting on land (2) standing upright, not *ducking,* or "cringing" **69–70 his . . . on't** his whole strategy has been developed without regard to where his power really lies. **71 men** servingmen. **72 horse** cavalry. **whole** undivided, held in reserve **76 Carries** surpasses (like an arrow in archery) **78 distractions** detachments, divisions **82–3 With . . . some** More news is born each minute. (*Throws forth* means "gives birth.") **3.8. Location: A field near Actium, as before.** **5 prescript** orders **6 jump** chance, hazard. **3.9. Location: A field near Actium, as before.**

2 **eye** sight. **battle** battle line
3.10. Location: A field near Actium, as before.
1 **Naught** All has come to naught **2 admiral** flagship **5 synod** assembly **6 cantle** corner; hence, piece or part **7 With very ignorance** through utter stupidity **9 tokened pestilence** (Certain red spots appeared on the bodies of the plague-smitten, called tokens.) **10 ribaudred** foul, obscene **12–13 When . . . same** i.e., when the advantage was equal on either side **13 elder** i.e., more advanced, more likely to inherit **14 breeze** (1) gadfly (2) light wind **18 loofed** luffed, with ship's head brought close to the wind. (With a pun on *aloofed,* "becoming distant.") **19 ruin of** object ruined by **20 Claps . . . sea wing** i.e., hoists sail, preparing for flight like a water bird. **mallard** drake **21 in** at its

Did violate so itself.

ENOBARBUS   Alack, alack!

Enter Canidius.

CANIDIUS
Our fortune on the sea is out of breath,
And sinks most lamentably. Had our general
Been what he knew himself, it had gone well.
Oh, he has given example for our flight
Most grossly by his own!

ENOBARBUS
Ay, are you thereabouts? Why then, good night
indeed.   30

CANIDIUS
Toward Peloponnesus are they fled.   31

SCARUS
'Tis easy to't, and there I will attend   32
What further comes.

CANIDIUS   To Caesar will I render   33
My legions and my horse. Six kings already   34
Show me the way of yielding.

ENOBARBUS   I'll yet follow
The wounded chance of Antony, though my reason   36
Sits in the wind against me.   *[Exeunt separately.]*   37

❖

[3.11]

Enter Antony with attendants.

ANTONY
Hark! The land bids me tread no more upon't;
It is ashamed to bear me. Friends, come hither.
I am so lated in the world that I   3
Have lost my way forever. I have a ship
Laden with gold. Take that, divide it; fly,   5
And make your peace with Caesar.

ALL   Fly? Not we.

ANTONY
I have fled myself, and have instructed cowards
To run and show their shoulders. Friends, begone.   8
I have myself resolved upon a course
Which has no need of you. Begone.
My treasure's in the harbor. Take it. Oh,
I followed that I blush to look upon!   12
My very hairs do mutiny, for the white   13
Reprove the brown for rashness, and they them   14

For fear and doting. Friends, begone. You shall
Have letters from me to some friends that will
Sweep your way for you. Pray you, look not sad,   17
Nor make replies of loathness. Take the hint   18
Which my despair proclaims. Let that be left   19
Which leaves itself. To the seaside straightway!   20
I will possess you of that ship and treasure.
Leave me, I pray, a little. Pray you now,
Nay, do so, for indeed I have lost command.   23
Therefore I pray you. I'll see you by and by.   24
[Exeunt attendants. Antony] sits down.

Enter Cleopatra led by Charmian, [Iras,] and Eros.

EROS
Nay, gentle madam, to him, comfort him.

IRAS   Do, most dear Queen.

CHARMIAN   Do; why, what else?

CLEOPATRA   Let me sit down. O Juno!

ANTONY   No, no, no, no, no.

EROS   See you here, sir?

ANTONY   Oh, fie, fie, fie!

CHARMIAN   Madam!

IRAS   Madam, O good Empress!

EROS   Sir, sir!

ANTONY
Yes, my lord, yes. He at Philippi kept   35
His sword e'en like a dancer, while I struck   36
The lean and wrinkled Cassius, and 'twas I
That the mad Brutus ended. He alone   38
Dealt on lieutenantry, and no practice had   39
In the brave squares of war; yet now—no matter. 40

CLEOPATRA
Ah, stand by.

EROS   The Queen, my lord, the Queen.   41

IRAS
Go to him, madam, speak to him.
He's unqualitied with very shame.   43

CLEOPATRA   Well then, sustain me. Oh!

EROS
Most noble sir, arise. The Queen approaches.
Her head's declined, and death will seize her but   46
Your comfort makes the rescue.

ANTONY
I have offended reputation,
A most unnoble swerving.

EROS   Sir, the Queen.   49

---

30 **thereabouts** i.e., of that mind, thinking of desertion.   **good night indeed** i.e., it's all over.   31 **Peloponnesus** southern Greece (from which Antony then crosses the Mediterranean to Egypt)   32 **to't** to get to it.   **attend** await   33 **render** surrender   34 **horse** cavalry.   36 **wounded chance** broken fortunes   37 **Sits . . . me** i.e., is on my downwind side, tracking me and hunting me down.
3.11. **Location: Historically, events such as dispatching the Schoolmaster to Caesar took place in Egypt; however, the dramatic impression of this scene is that it occurs soon after the battle.**
3 **lated** belated, like a traveler still journeying when night falls   5 **fly** flee   8 **shoulders** i.e., backs.   12 **that** that which   13 **mutiny** contend among themselves   14 **they them** i.e., the brown hairs reprove the white

17 **Sweep your way** clear your way (to Caesar)   18 **loathness** unwillingness.   **hint** opportunity   19 **that** i.e., Antony and his cause   20 **leaves** is untrue to, deserts   23 **lost command** i.e., of myself and of my authority.   24 **pray** entreat (as opposed to "command")   35 **Yes . . . yes** (Antony is absorbed in his own bitter thoughts, as also in lines 29 and 31.)   **He** i.e., Octavius.   **kept** kept in its sheath   36 **e'en . . . dancer** i.e., as though for ornament only, in a dance   38 **ended** i.e., defeated. (Not *killed;* Brutus and Cassius committed suicide.)   **He alone** Caesar merely   39 **Dealt on lieutenantry** let his subordinates do the fighting   40 **brave squares** splendid squadrons, bodies of troops drawn up in square formation   41 **stand by** (Cleopatra indicates she is about to faint and needs assistance.)   43 **unqualitied** dispossessed of his own nature, i.e., not himself   46 **but** unless   49 **swerving** lapse, transgression.

ANTONY
　　Oh, whither hast thou led me, Egypt? See   50
　　How I convey my shame out of thine eyes   51
　　By looking back what I have left behind   52
　　'Stroyed in dishonor.
CLEOPATRA   Oh, my lord, my lord,   53
　　Forgive my fearful sails! I little thought   54
　　You would have followed.
ANTONY   Egypt, thou knew'st too well
　　My heart was to thy rudder tied by th' strings,   56
　　And thou shouldst tow me after. O'er my spirit
　　Thy full supremacy thou knew'st, and that
　　Thy beck might from the bidding of the gods   59
　　Command me.
CLEOPATRA   Oh, my pardon!
ANTONY   Now I must   60
　　To the young man send humble treaties, dodge   61
　　And palter in the shifts of lowness, who   62
　　With half the bulk o'th' world played as I pleased,
　　Making and marring fortunes. You did know
　　How much you were my conqueror, and that
　　My sword, made weak by my affection, would   66
　　Obey it on all cause.
CLEOPATRA   Pardon, pardon!   67
ANTONY
　　Fall not a tear, I say; one of them rates   68
　　All that is won and lost. Give me a kiss.   [They kiss.]
　　Even this repays me.—We sent our schoolmaster;   70
　　Is 'a come back?—Love, I am full of lead.—
　　Some wine, within there, and our viands! Fortune
　　knows   72
　　We scorn her most when most she offers blows.
　　　　　　　　　　　　　　　　　　　　　　　　　　　Exeunt.

❧

[3.12]

Enter Caesar, Agrippa, [Thidias,] and Dolabella,
with others.

CAESAR
　　Let him appear that's come from Antony.
　　Know you him?
DOLABELLA   Caesar, 'tis his schoolmaster—
　　An argument that he is plucked, when hither   3
　　He sends so poor a pinion of his wing,   4
　　Which had superfluous kings for messengers   5

Not many moons gone by.
　　　　　　Enter Ambassador from Antony.
CAESAR   Approach and speak.
AMBASSADOR
　　Such as I am, I come from Antony.
　　I was of late as petty to his ends   8
　　As is the morn-dew on the myrtle leaf
　　To his grand sea.
CAESAR   Be't so. Declare thine office.   10
AMBASSADOR
　　Lord of his fortunes he salutes thee, and
　　Requires to live in Egypt; which not granted,   12
　　He lessens his requests, and to thee sues   13
　　To let him breathe between the heavens and earth   14
　　A private man in Athens. This for him.
　　Next, Cleopatra does confess thy greatness,
　　Submits her to thy might, and of thee craves
　　The circle of the Ptolemies for her heirs,   18
　　Now hazarded to thy grace.
CAESAR   For Antony,   19
　　I have no ears to his request. The Queen
　　Of audience nor desire shall fail, so she   21
　　From Egypt drive her all-disgracèd friend
　　Or take his life there. This if she perform
　　She shall not sue unheard. So to them both.
AMBASSADOR
　　Fortune pursue thee!
CAESAR   Bring him through the bands.   25
　　　　　　　　　　　　[Exit Ambassador, attended.]
　　[To Thidias] To try thy eloquence now 'tis time.
　　　　Dispatch.
　　From Antony win Cleopatra. Promise,
　　And in our name, what she requires; add more,   28
　　From thine invention, offers. Women are not   29
　　In their best fortunes strong, but want will perjure   30
　　The ne'er-touched vestal. Try thy cunning, Thidias.   31
　　Make thine own edict for thy pains, which we   32
　　Will answer as a law.
THIDIAS   Caesar, I go.   33
CAESAR
　　Observe how Antony becomes his flaw,   34
　　And what thou think'st his very action speaks   35
　　In every power that moves.
THIDIAS   Caesar, I shall.   *Exeunt.*   36

❧

50–3 See . . . dishonor i.e., See how ashamed I am to have you see me like this, looking back on what I have left behind dishonorably destroyed. **54 fearful** timorous　**56 th' strings** (1) the heartstrings (2) towing cable　**59–60 Thy . . . Command me** your mere beckoning would command me away from doing the bidding of the gods themselves.　**61 treaties** entreaties, propositions for settlement.　**dodge** shuffle, cringe　**62 palter** use trickery, prevaricate, equivocate.　**shifts of lowness** pitiful evasions used by those lacking power　**66 affection** passion　**67 on all cause** whatever the reason.　**68 Fall** Let fall.　**rates** equals　**70 Even this** This by itself.　**schoolmaster** (Identified in Plutarch as Euphronius, tutor to Antony's children by Cleopatra.)　**72 viands** food.
3.12. Location: Egypt. Caesar's camp.
3 An argument an indication　**4 pinion** i.e., pinion-feather, outer feather　**5 Which** who

8 petty to insignificant in terms of　**10 To . . . sea** compared to its, the dewdrop's, great source, the sea.　**thine office** your official business.　**12 Requires** asks.　**which not granted** and if that request is not granted　**13 sues** petitions　**14 breathe** i.e., live　**18 circle** crown　**19 hazarded . . . grace** dependent on your favor.　**For** As for　**21 Of audience** neither of hearing.　**so** provided that　**25 Bring** Escort.　**bands** troops on guard, military lines.　**28 requires** asks　**28–9 add . . . offers** add ideas of your own.　**29–31 Women . . . vestal** Women are not strong even at the height of their good fortune, but need will cause even an untouched vestal virgin to break her vows.　**31 cunning** skill　**32 Make . . . edict** Decree your own reward　**33 answer as a law** confirm as if it were a law.　**34 becomes his flaw** bears his misfortune and disgrace　**35–6 And . . . moves** and what you think his gestures signify in every move he makes.

[3.13]

Enter Cleopatra, Enobarbus, Charmian, and Iras.

CLEOPATRA
What shall we do, Enobarbus?

ENOBARBUS   Think, and die.   1

CLEOPATRA
Is Antony or we in fault for this?   2

ENOBARBUS
Antony only, that would make his will   3
Lord of his reason. What though you fled
From that great face of war, whose several ranges   5
Frighted each other? Why should he follow?
The itch of his affection should not then   7
Have nicked his captainship, at such a point,   8
When half to half the world opposed, he being   9
The merèd question. 'Twas a shame no less   10
Than was his loss, to course your flying flags   11
And leave his navy gazing.

CLEOPATRA   Prithee, peace.

Enter the Ambassador with Antony.

ANTONY   Is that his answer?

AMBASSADOR   Ay, my lord.

ANTONY
The Queen shall then have courtesy, so she   15
Will yield us up.

AMBASSADOR   He says so.

ANTONY   Let her know't.—
To the boy Caesar send this grizzled head,
And he will fill thy wishes to the brim
With principalities.

CLEOPATRA   That head, my lord?

ANTONY [*to the Ambassador*]
To him again. Tell him he wears the rose
Of youth upon him, from which the world should
  note
Something particular. His coin, ships, legions,   22
May be a coward's, whose ministers would prevail   23
Under the service of a child as soon
As i'th' command of Caesar. I dare him therefore
To lay his gay caparisons apart   26
And answer me declined, sword against sword,   27
Ourselves alone. I'll write it. Follow me.

[*Exeunt Antony and Ambassador.*]

ENOBARBUS [*aside*]
Yes, like enough, high-battled Caesar will   29

Unstate his happiness and be staged to th' show   30
Against a sworder! I see men's judgments are   31
A parcel of their fortunes, and things outward   32
Do draw the inward quality after them   33
To suffer all alike. That he should dream,   34
Knowing all measures, the full Caesar will   35
Answer his emptiness! Caesar, thou hast subdued   36
His judgment too.

Enter a Servant.

SERVANT   A messenger from Caesar.

CLEOPATRA
What, no more ceremony? See, my women,
Against the blown rose may they stop their nose   39
That kneeled unto the buds.—Admit him, sir.

[*Exit Servant.*]

ENOBARBUS [*aside*]
Mine honesty and I begin to square.   41
The loyalty well held to fools does make   42
Our faith mere folly; yet he that can endure   43
To follow with allegiance a fall'n lord
Does conquer him that did his master conquer   45
And earns a place i'th' story.

Enter Thidias.

CLEOPATRA   Caesar's will?

THIDIAS
Hear it apart.

CLEOPATRA   None but friends. Say boldly.   47

THIDIAS
So haply are they friends to Antony.   48

ENOBARBUS
He needs as many, sir, as Caesar has,
Or needs not us. If Caesar please, our master   50
Will leap to be his friend. For us, you know   51
Whose he is we are, and that is Caesar's.

THIDIAS   So.   52
Thus then, thou most renowned: Caesar entreats
Not to consider in what case thou stand'st   54
Further than he is Caesar.

CLEOPATRA   Go on: right royal.   55

3.13. Location: Alexandria. Cleopatra's palace.
1 Think, and die Think despondently, and die of melancholy or by
suicide.   **2 we** I   **3 will** desire (especially sexual)   **5 ranges** ranks,
lines (of ships)   **7 affection** sexual passion   **8 nicked** cut short or
maimed, or got the better of.   **point** crisis   **9–10 When . . . question**
when the two halves of the world found themselves in conflict,
Antony being the sole ground of the quarrel.   **11 course** pursue (as in
hunting)   **15 so** provided that   **22 Something particular** some
exceptional exploit.   **23 May be** could as well be.   **ministers** agents,
subordinates   **26 gay caparisons** resplendent trappings   **27 answer
me declined** meet me as I am, lowered in fortune and advanced in
years   **29 like** likely.   **high-battled** provided with a mighty army

30–1 Unstate . . . sworder set aside his advantageous fortune and be
exhibited publicly in a sword-fight contest with a mere gladiator.
31–4 I see . . . alike I see that men's judgments are inextricably linked
to their fortunes, whereby outward circumstances draw after them
inward qualities of character in such a way that both suffer at the
same time.   **35 Knowing all measures** i.e., having experienced every
degree of fortune.   **full** at full fortune   **36 Answer** (1) meet man to
man with (2) correspond with   **39 blown** overblown, starting to
decay   **41 honesty** (With meaning also of "honor.")   **square** quarrel.
42–3 The . . . folly A stubborn loyalty bestowed on fools is folly itself
45 Does . . . conquer i.e., achieves a moral victory over the very fortune or the person that subdued one's own master   **47 apart** in private.   **48 haply** perhaps   **50 Or . . . us** i.e., or else he doesn't need
even us, his case being hopeless.   **51 For** As for   **52 Whose . . .
Caesar's** i.e., we are Antony's friends, and he is Caesar's, so that we,
too, are Caesar's.   **54–5 Not . . . Caesar** i.e., not to worry about your
situation other than to consider that you are dealing with Caesar, the
embodiment of magnanimity.   **55 right royal** i.e., that is very magnanimous.

THIDIAS
He knows that you embrace not Antony
As you did love, but as you feared him.

CLEOPATRA   Oh!

THIDIAS
The scars upon your honor therefore he
Does pity as constrainèd blemishes,
Not as deserved.

CLEOPATRA   He is a god and knows
What is most right. Mine honor was not yielded,   61
But conquered merely.

ENOBARBUS [aside]   To be sure of that,   62
I will ask Antony. Sir, sir, thou art so leaky
That we must leave thee to thy sinking, for
Thy dearest quit thee.   Exit Enobarbus.

THIDIAS   Shall I say to Caesar
What you require of him? For he partly begs   66
To be desired to give. It much would please him
That of his fortunes you should make a staff
To lean upon; but it would warm his spirits
To hear from me you had left Antony
And put yourself under his shroud,   71
The universal landlord.

CLEOPATRA   What's your name?

THIDIAS
My name is Thidias.

CLEOPATRA   Most kind messenger,
Say to great Caesar this in deputation: 74
I kiss his conquering hand. Tell him I am prompt   75
To lay my crown at 's feet, and there to kneel
Till from his all-obeying breath I hear   77
The doom of Egypt.

THIDIAS   'Tis your noblest course.   78
Wisdom and fortune combating together,   79
If that the former dare but what it can,   80
No chance may shake it. Give me grace to lay   81
My duty on your hand.   [He kisses her hand.]

CLEOPATRA   Your Caesar's father oft,   83
When he hath mused of taking kingdoms in,   84
Bestowed his lips on that unworthy place,
As it rained kisses.

Enter Antony and Enobarbus.

ANTONY   Favors? By Jove that thunders!   86
What art thou, fellow?

THIDIAS   One that but performs
The bidding of the fullest man, and worthiest   88
To have command obeyed.

ENOBARBUS [aside]   You will be whipped.

ANTONY [calling for Servants]
Approach, there!—Ah, you kite!—Now, gods and
    devils!   90
Authority melts from me of late. When I cried "Ho!",
Like boys unto a muss kings would start forth   92
And cry, "Your will?"—Have you no ears? I am
Antony yet.

Enter a Servant [followed by others].

                    Take hence this jack and whip him.   94

ENOBARBUS [aside]
'Tis better playing with a lion's whelp   95
Than with an old one dying.

ANTONY   Moon and stars!
Whip him. Were't twenty of the greatest tributaries   97
That do acknowledge Caesar, should I find them
So saucy with the hand of she here—what's her name
Since she was Cleopatra? Whip him, fellows,
Till like a boy you see him cringe his face   101
And whine aloud for mercy. Take him hence.

THIDIAS
Mark Antony—

ANTONY   Tug him away! Being whipped,
Bring him again. This jack of Caesar's shall
Bear us an errand to him.

                    Exeunt [Servants] with Thidias.
[To Cleopatra] You were half blasted ere I knew you.
    Ha?   106
Have I my pillow left unpressed in Rome,
Forborne the getting of a lawful race,   108
And by a gem of women, to be abused   109
By one that looks on feeders?   110

CLEOPATRA   Good my lord—

ANTONY   You have been a boggler ever.   112
But when we in our viciousness grow hard—
Oh, misery on't!—the wise gods seel our eyes,   114
In our own filth drop our clear judgments, make us
Adore our errors, laugh at 's while we strut
To our confusion.

CLEOPATRA   Oh, is't come to this?   117

ANTONY
I found you as a morsel cold upon
Dead Caesar's trencher; nay, you were a fragment   119
Of Gnaeus Pompey's, besides what hotter hours,   120
Unregistered in vulgar fame, you have   121
Luxuriously picked out. For I am sure,   122
Though you can guess what temperance should be,

---

61 right true. **62 merely** utterly. **66 require** ask. **partly** i.e., as commensurate with his dignity **71 shroud** shelter. (With suggestion too of a burial cloth.) **74 in deputation** by you as deputy **75 prompt** ready **77 all-obeying** obeyed by all **78 The doom of Egypt** i.e., my fate. **79–81 Wisdom . . . shake it** When wisdom and fortune are at odds, if the wise person will have the resolution to desire only what fortune will allow, then fortune cannot shake that wisdom. **83 Your Caesar's father** i.e., Julius Caesar, actually Octavius' great-uncle. (See note at 3.6.6.) **84 mused . . . in** thought about conquering kingdoms **86 As** as if **88 fullest** most fortunate, best

90 kite a rapacious bird of prey that feeds on ignoble objects, and a slang word for "whore." (Said of Cleopatra.) **92 muss** game in which small objects are thrown down to be scrambled for **94 jack** fellow. (Contemptuous.) **95 whelp** cub **97 tributaries** rulers paying tribute **101 cringe** contract in pain **106 blasted** withered, blighted **108 getting** begetting. **lawful** legitimate **109 abused** deceived, betrayed **110 feeders** servants. **112 boggler** waverer, shifty person. (Often used of shying horses.) **114 seel** blind. (A term in falconry for sewing shut the eyes of wild hawks in order to tame them.) **117 confusion** destruction. **119 trencher** wooden plate. **fragment** leftover **120 Gnaeus Pompey's** (See 1.5.32 and note.) **121 vulgar fame** common gossip **122 Luxuriously** lustfully

You know not what it is.

CLEOPATRA   Wherefore is this?   124

ANTONY
To let a fellow that will take rewards
And say "God quit you!" be familiar with   126
My playfellow, your hand, this kingly seal
And plighter of high hearts! Oh, that I were   128
Upon the hill of Basan, to outroar   129
The hornèd herd! For I have savage cause,   130
And to proclaim it civilly were like
A haltered neck which does the hangman thank
For being yare about him.

Enter a Servant with Thidias.

                              Is he whipped?   133

SERVANT   Soundly, my lord.

ANTONY   Cried he? And begged 'a pardon?

SERVANT   He did ask favor.

ANTONY [*to Thidias*]
If that thy father live, let him repent
Thou wast not made his daughter; and be thou sorry
To follow Caesar in his triumph, since
Thou hast been whipped for following him.
   Henceforth
The white hand of a lady fever thee;   141
Shake thou to look on't. Get thee back to Caesar.
Tell him thy entertainment. Look thou say   143
He makes me angry with him; for he seems
Proud and disdainful, harping on what I am,
Not what he knew I was. He makes me angry,
And at this time most easy 'tis to do't,
When my good stars, that were my former guides,
Have empty left their orbs and shot their fires   149
Into th'abysm of hell. If he mislike   150
My speech and what is done, tell him he has
Hipparchus, my enfranchèd bondman, whom   152
He may at pleasure whip, or hang, or torture,
As he shall like, to quit me. Urge it thou.—   154
Hence with thy stripes, begone!

Exit [Servant with] Thidias.

CLEOPATRA   Have you done yet?

ANTONY
Alack, our terrene moon is now eclipsed,   156
And it portends alone the fall of Antony.

CLEOPATRA   I must stay his time.   158

ANTONY
To flatter Caesar, would you mingle eyes

With one that ties his points?

CLEOPATRA   Not know me yet?   160

ANTONY
Coldhearted toward me?

CLEOPATRA   Ah, dear, if I be so,
From my cold heart let heaven engender hail,
And poison it in the source, and the first stone
Drop in my neck; as it determines, so   164
Dissolve my life! The next Caesarion smite,
Till by degrees the memory of my womb,   166
Together with my brave Egyptians all,   167
By the discandying of this pelleted storm   168
Lie graveless till the flies and gnats of Nile
Have buried them for prey!

ANTONY   I am satisfied.   170
Caesar sits down in Alexandria, where   171
I will oppose his fate. Our force by land   172
Hath nobly held; our severed navy too
Have knit again, and fleet, threat'ning most sealike.   174
Where hast thou been, my heart? Dost thou hear,
   lady?   175
If from the field I shall return once more
To kiss these lips, I will appear in blood;   177
I and my sword will earn our chronicle.   178
There's hope in't yet.

CLEOPATRA   That's my brave lord!

ANTONY
I will be treble-sinewed, hearted, breathed,   181
And fight maliciously. For when mine hours   182
Were nice and lucky, men did ransom lives   183
Of me for jests; but now I'll set my teeth   184
And send to darkness all that stop me. Come,   185
Let's have one other gaudy night. Call to me   186
All my sad captains. Fill our bowls once more;
Let's mock the midnight bell.

CLEOPATRA   It is my birthday.
I had thought t'have held it poor; but since my lord   189
Is Antony again, I will be Cleopatra.

ANTONY   We will yet do well.

CLEOPATRA [*to attendants*]
Call all his noble captains to my lord.

ANTONY
Do so. We'll speak to them, and tonight I'll force
The wine peep through their scars. Come on, my
   queen,
There's sap in't yet. The next time I do fight   195

---

124 **Wherefore is this?** i.e., What brought this on?   126 **quit** reward. (*God quit you* is said obsequiously to acknowledge a tip.)   128 **plighter** pledger   129–30 **hill of Basan . . . The hornèd herd** (Allusion to the strong bulls of Bashan, Psalms 22:12 and 68:15. Antony imagines himself as the greatest horned beast, i.e., cuckold, of that herd.)   133 **yare** deft, quick   141 **fever thee** make you shiver   143 **entertainment** reception.   **Look** Be sure that   149 **orbs** spheres   150 **th'abysm** the abyss   152 **Hipparchus** (According to Plutarch, the man was a deserter to Caesar's side.)   **enfranchèd** enfranchised, freed   154 **quit** requite, pay back   156 **our . . . eclipsed** i.e., (1) the moon in eclipse portends disaster (2) the waning of the love of Cleopatra (equated with Isis, the moon goddess) spells the end for me   158 **stay his time** i.e., be patient until his fury has subsided.

160 **ties his points** i.e., helps Caesar as a valet with the metal-tipped laces used to fasten articles of clothing.   164 **neck** throat or head.   **determines** comes to an end, dissolves. (See line 168.)   166 **memory of my womb** i.e., my offspring   167 **brave** splendid. (Also in line 180.)   168 **discandying** melting.   **pelleted** falling in pellets   170 **for prey** i.e., by eating them.   171 **sits down** lays siege to   172 **oppose his fate** confront his (seemingly irresistible) fortune.   174 **fleet** float   175 **heart** courage.   177 **in blood** (1) bloody from battle (2) full-spirited   178 **chronicle** place in history.   181 **treble-sinewed . . . breathed** thrice myself in strength, courage, and endurance   182 **maliciously** violently, fiercely.   183 **nice** delicate, refined   183–4 **men . . . jests** I allowed enemies to be ransomed for trifles or as a magnanimous gesture   185 **to darkness** i.e., to death, the underworld   186 **gaudy** festive   189 **held it poor** celebrated it simply   195 **sap in't** i.e., life in our enterprise

I'll make Death love me, for I will contend   196
Even with his pestilent scythe.   197
                        Exeunt [all but Enobarbus].

ENOBARBUS
Now he'll outstare the lightning. To be furious   198
Is to be frighted out of fear, and in that mood
The dove will peck the estridge; and I see still   200
A diminution in our captain's brain
Restores his heart. When valor preys on reason,   202
It eats the sword it fights with. I will seek   203
Some way to leave him.   *Exit.*

❧

[4.1]

*Enter Caesar, Agrippa, and Maecenas, with his
army, Caesar reading a letter.*

CAESAR
He calls me boy, and chides as he had power   1
To beat me out of Egypt. My messenger
He hath whipped with rods, dares me to personal
    combat,
Caesar to Antony. Let the old ruffian know
I have many other ways to die, meantime
Laugh at his challenge.
MAECENAS   Caesar must think,
When one so great begins to rage, he's hunted   8
Even to falling. Give him no breath, but now   9
Make boot of his distraction. Never anger   10
Made good guard for itself.
CAESAR   Let our best heads   11
Know that tomorrow the last of many battles
We mean to fight. Within our files there are,   13
Of those that served Mark Antony but late,   14
Enough to fetch him in. See it done,   15
And feast the army; we have store to do't,   16
And they have earned the waste. Poor Antony!   17
                                           Exeunt.

❧

[4.2]

*Enter Antony, Cleopatra, Enobarbus,
Charmian, Iras, Alexas, with others.*

ANTONY
He will not fight with me, Domitius?

ENOBARBUS   No.
ANTONY   Why should he not?
ENOBARBUS
He thinks, being twenty times of better fortune,
He is twenty men to one.
ANTONY   Tomorrow, soldier,
By sea and land I'll fight. Or I will live   6
Or bathe my dying honor in the blood
Shall make it live again. Woo't thou fight well?   8
ENOBARBUS
I'll strike, and cry, "Take all."
ANTONY   Well said. Come on!   9
Call forth my household servants. Let's tonight   10

            Enter three or four servitors.

Be bounteous at our meal.—Give me thy hand.
Thou hast been rightly honest—so hast thou—   12
Thou—and thou—and thou. You have served me
    well,
And kings have been your fellows.
CLEOPATRA *[aside to Enobarbus]*   What means this?   14
ENOBARBUS *[aside to Cleopatra]*
'Tis one of those odd tricks which sorrow shoots
Out of the mind.
ANTONY   And thou art honest too.
I wish I could be made so many men,   17
And all of you clapped up together in   18
An Antony, that I might do you service
So good as you have done.
ALL   The gods forbid!
ANTONY
Well, my good fellows, wait on me tonight:
Scant not my cups, and make as much of me   22
As when mine empire was your fellow too,   23
And suffered my command.
CLEOPATRA *[aside to Enobarbus]*   What does he mean?   24
ENOBARBUS *[aside to Cleopatra]*
To make his followers weep.
ANTONY   Tend me tonight;
May be it is the period of your duty.   26
Haply you shall not see me more, or if,   27
A mangled shadow. Perchance tomorrow   28
You'll serve another master. I look on you
As one that takes his leave. Mine honest friends,
I turn you not away, but, like a master
Married to your good service, stay till death.
Tend me tonight two hours, I ask no more,
And the gods yield you for't!
ENOBARBUS   What mean you, sir,   34
To give them this discomfort? Look, they weep,

196–7 I will . . . scythe i.e., I will outdo even Death himself and his
scythe of *pestilence* or plague.   **198 outstare** stare down.   **furious**
frenzied   **200 estridge** ostrich, or, a kind of hawk.   **still** constantly
202–3 When . . . with When valor turns to unreasonable fury, it
destroys the very quality of reasonableness that valor depends on in
battle.
4.1. Location: Before Alexandria. Caesar's camp.
1 as as if   **8 rage** rave   **9 breath** breathing space   **10 boot** advantage.
distraction frenzy.   **11 best heads** commanding officers   **13 files** (As
in "rank and file.")   **14 late** lately   **15 fetch him in** surround, capture him.   **16 store** provisions   **17 waste** lavish expenditure.
4.2. Location: Alexandria. Cleopatra's palace.

6 Or Either   **8 Shall** that will.   **Woo't** Wilt   **9 strike . . . Take all**
(1) fight to the finish, crying, "Winner take all" (2) strike sail and surrender.   **10.1 *servitors*** attendants.   **12 honest** true, loyal   **14 fellows** i.e., fellow servants of me.   **17 made . . . men** divided into as
many men as you are   **18 clapped up** combined   **22 Scant not my
cups** i.e., Provide generously   **23 fellow** i.e., fellow servant   **24 suffered** acknowledged, submitted to   **26 period** end   **27 Haply** Perhaps.   **if** if you do   **28 shadow** ghost.   **34 yield** reward

And I, an ass, am onion-eyed. For shame,
Transform us not to women.
ANTONY   Ho, ho, ho!
Now the witch take me if I meant it thus!   38
Grace grow where those drops fall! My hearty friends,   39
You take me in too dolorous a sense,
For I spake to you for your comfort, did desire you
To burn this night with torches. Know, my hearts,   42
I hope well of tomorrow, and will lead you
Where rather I'll expect victorious life
Than death and honor. Let's to supper, come,
And drown consideration.   *Exeunt.* 46

❖

[4.3]

Enter a company of Soldiers.

FIRST SOLDIER
Brother, good night. Tomorrow is the day.
SECOND SOLDIER
It will determine one way. Fare you well.   2
Heard you of nothing strange about the streets?   3
FIRST SOLDIER   Nothing. What news?
SECOND SOLDIER
Belike 'tis but a rumor. Good night to you.   5
FIRST SOLDIER   Well, sir, good night.

They meet other Soldiers.

SECOND SOLDIER   Soldiers, have careful watch.
THIRD SOLDIER   And you. Good night, good night.
          They place themselves in every corner of the stage.
SECOND SOLDIER   Here we. And if tomorrow   9
Our navy thrive, I have an absolute hope
Our landmen will stand up.
FIRST SOLDIER   'Tis a brave army, and full of purpose. 12
          Music of the hautboys is under the stage.
SECOND SOLDIER   Peace! What noise?
FIRST SOLDIER   List, list!   14
SECOND SOLDIER   Hark!
FIRST SOLDIER   Music i'th'air.
THIRD SOLDIER   Under the earth.
FOURTH SOLDIER   It signs well, does it not?   18
THIRD SOLDIER   No.
FIRST SOLDIER   Peace, I say! What should this mean?
SECOND SOLDIER
'Tis the god Hercules, whom Antony loved,
Now leaves him.
FIRST SOLDIER   Walk; let's see if other watchmen
Do hear what we do.
          [They advance toward their fellow watchmen.]
SECOND SOLDIER   How now, masters?   24

ALL *[speak together]*   How now? How now? Do you
hear this?
FIRST SOLDIER   Ay. Is't not strange?
THIRD SOLDIER   Do you hear, masters? Do you hear?
FIRST SOLDIER
Follow the noise so far as we have quarter;   29
Let's see how it will give off.   30
ALL   Content. 'Tis strange.   *Exeunt.*

❖

[4.4]

*Enter Antony and Cleopatra, with [Charmian and]
others [attending].*

ANTONY
Eros! Mine armor, Eros!
CLEOPATRA   Sleep a little.
ANTONY
No, my chuck.—Eros, come, mine armor, Eros!   2

Enter Eros [with armor].

Come, good fellow, put thine iron on.   3
If fortune be not ours today, it is
Because we brave her. Come.
CLEOPATRA   Nay, I'll help too.   5
What's this for?   *[She helps to arm him.]*
ANTONY   Ah, let be, let be! Thou art
The armorer of my heart. False, false; this, this.   7
CLEOPATRA
Sooth, la, I'll help. Thus it must be.
ANTONY   Well, well,   8
We shall thrive now. See'st thou, my good fellow?
Go, put on thy defenses.
EROS   Briefly, sir.   10
CLEOPATRA
Is not this buckled well?
ANTONY   Rarely, rarely.   11
He that unbuckles this, till we do please   12
To doff't for our repose, shall hear a storm.   13
Thou fumblest, Eros, and my queen's a squire   14
More tight at this than thou. Dispatch. O love,   15
That thou couldst see my wars today, and knew'st   16
The royal occupation! Thou shouldst see   17
A workman in't.

Enter an armed Soldier.

                    Good morrow to thee. Welcome.   18
Thou look'st like him that knows a warlike charge.   19

4.4. Location: Alexandria. The palace.
2 chuck (A term of endearment.)   **3 thine iron** i.e., my armor that
you have there. (Or perhaps he is telling Eros to arm.)   **5 brave** defy
7 False You're putting it on wrong   **8 Sooth** In truth   **10 defenses**
armor.   **Briefly** In a moment   **11 Rarely** Excellently   **12–13 He . . .
storm** i.e., Anyone who attempts to burst my armor in the fight,
before I choose myself to unarm and rest, will be greeted by a storm
of blows.   **14 squire** armor-bearer of a knight   **15 tight** deft, skillful.
Dispatch Finish up.   **16–17 knew'st . . . occupation** (would that) you
could appreciate how excellently I carry out the royal art of warfare.
18 workman craftsman, professional   **19 charge** duty, responsibility.

---

38 the witch take me may I be bewitched   **39 Grace grow** (1) May
rue or herb of grace grow (2) May gracious fortune flourish.   **hearty**
loving   **42 burn . . . torches** i.e., revel through the night.   **46 drown
consideration** drown brooding thought in our wine cups.
4.3. Location: Alexandria. Before the palace.
2 determine one way be decided, come to an end one way or the
other.   **3 about** in   **5 Belike** Probably   **9 Here we** Here's our station.   **12 brave** splendid, gallant   **12.1 hautboys** oboelike instruments   **14 List** Listen   **18 signs well** is a good sign   **24 masters**
good sirs. (Also in line 28.)

To business that we love we rise betimes 20
And go to't with delight.

SOLDIER   A thousand, sir,
Early though 't be, have on their riveted trim 22
And at the port expect you. *Shout. Trumpets flourish.* 23

Enter Captains and soldiers.

CAPTAIN
The morn is fair. Good morrow, General.

ALL
Good morrow, General.

ANTONY   'Tis well blown, lads. 25
This morning, like the spirit of a youth
That means to be of note, begins betimes.
So, so. Come, give me that. This way. Well said. 28
Fare thee well, dame. Whate'er becomes of me,
This is a soldier's kiss. [*He kisses her.*] Rebukable,
And worthy shameful check it were, to stand 31
On more mechanic compliment. I'll leave thee 32
Now like a man of steel.—You that will fight,
Follow me close. I'll bring you to't. Adieu.
        Exeunt [Antony, Eros, Captains, and soldiers].

CHARMIAN
Please you, retire to your chamber?

CLEOPATRA   Lead me.
He goes forth gallantly. That he and Caesar might
Determine this great war in single fight!
Then Antony—but now—Well, on.   *Exeunt.*

❖

[4.5]

Trumpets sound. Enter Antony and Eros; [a Soldier meeting them].

SOLDIER
The gods make this a happy day to Antony! 1

ANTONY
Would thou and those thy scars had once prevailed 2
To make me fight at land!

SOLDIER   Hadst thou done so,
The kings that have revolted, and the soldier 4
That has this morning left thee, would have still
Followed thy heels.

ANTONY   Who's gone this morning?

SOLDIER   Who?
One ever near thee. Call for Enobarbus,
He shall not hear thee, or from Caesar's camp
Say, "I am none of thine."

ANTONY   What sayest thou?

SOLDIER   Sir,
He is with Caesar.

EROS   Sir, his chests and treasure

He has not with him.

ANTONY   Is he gone?

SOLDIER   Most certain.

ANTONY
Go, Eros, send his treasure after. Do it.
Detain no jot, I charge thee. Write to him—
I will subscribe—gentle adieus and greetings. 14
Say that I wish he never find more cause
To change a master. Oh, my fortunes have
Corrupted honest men! Dispatch.—Enobarbus! 17
                              Exeunt.

❖

[4.6]

Flourish. Enter Agrippa, Caesar, with Enobarbus, and Dolabella.

CAESAR
Go forth, Agrippa, and begin the fight.
Our will is Antony be took alive;
Make it so known.

AGRIPPA Caesar, I shall.   [*Exit.*]

CAESAR
The time of universal peace is near. 5
Prove this a prosp'rous day, the three-nooked world 6
Shall bear the olive freely.

Enter a Messenger.

MESSENGER   Antony 7
Is come into the field.

CAESAR   Go charge Agrippa 8
Plant those that have revolted in the van, 9
That Antony may seem to spend his fury
Upon himself.   *Exeunt [all but Enobarbus].*

ENOBARBUS
Alexas did revolt and went to Jewry on 12
Affairs of Antony, there did dissuade 13
Great Herod to incline himself to Caesar
And leave his master Antony. For this pains,
Caesar hath hanged him. Canidius and the rest
That fell away have entertainment but 17
No honorable trust. I have done ill,
Of which I do accuse myself so sorely 19
That I will joy no more.

Enter a Soldier of Caesar's.

SOLDIER   Enobarbus, Antony
Hath after thee sent all thy treasure, with
His bounty overplus. The messenger 22

---

14 **subscribe** sign   17 **Dispatch** Make haste, get on with it.
4.6. Location: Before Alexandria. Caesar's camp.
5 **The . . . near** (The Renaissance identified Octavius Caesar, or the Emperor Augustus as he was subsequently titled, with this *Pax Romana*, peace under the Roman Empire.)   6 **Prove this** If this prove to be. **three-nooked** three-cornered. (Refers to Asia, Europe, and Africa.)   7 **bear** (1) bring forth (2) wear as a triumphal garland. **olive** symbol of peace   8 **charge Agrippa** order Agrippa to   9 **van** vanguard, front lines   12 **Jewry** Judaea   13 **dissuade** i.e., from following Antony   17 **entertainment** employment, maintenance   19 **sorely** heavily   22 **overplus** in addition.

---

20 **betimes** early   22 **riveted trim** i.e., armor riveted into place
23 **port** gate   25 **'Tis well blown** i.e., The morning begins well. (Or, refers to trumpets in line 23 s.d.)   28 **Well said** Well done.   31 **check** reproof   31–2 **stand . . . compliment** insist on vulgar and routine ceremonies of leavetaking.
4.5. Location: Before Alexandria. Antony's camp.
1 **happy** fortunate   2 **once** formerly   4 **revolted** deserted

Came on my guard, and at thy tent is now   23
Unloading of his mules.

ENOBARBUS   I give it you.

SOLDIER   Mock not, Enobarbus,
I tell you true. Best you safed the bringer   27
Out of the host. I must attend mine office,   28
Or would have done't myself. Your emperor
Continues still a Jove.   *Exit.*

ENOBARBUS
I am alone the villain of the earth,   31
And feel I am so most. O Antony,   32
Thou mine of bounty, how wouldst thou have paid   33
My better service, when my turpitude
Thou dost so crown with gold! This blows my heart.   35
If swift thought break it not, a swifter mean   36
Shall outstrike thought; but thought will do't, I feel.   37
I fight against thee? No, I will go seek
Some ditch wherein to die. The foul'st best fits
My latter part of life.   *Exit.*

❧

[4.7]

Alarum. Drums and trumpets. Enter Agrippa
[and others].

AGRIPPA
Retire! We have engaged ourselves too far.
Caesar himself has work, and our oppression   2
Exceeds what we expected.   *Exeunt.*   3

Alarums. Enter Antony, and Scarus wounded.

SCARUS
O my brave Emperor, this is fought indeed!
Had we done so at first, we had droven them home   5
With clouts about their heads.

ANTONY   Thou bleed'st apace.   6

SCARUS
I had a wound here that was like a T,
But now 'tis made an H.   *[Sound retreat] far off.*

ANTONY   They do retire.   8

SCARUS
We'll beat 'em into bench holes. I have yet   9
Room for six scotches more.   10

Enter Eros.

EROS
They are beaten, sir, and our advantage serves   11
For a fair victory.

SCARUS   Let us score their backs   12
And snatch 'em up, as we take hares, behind!
'Tis sport to maul a runner.

ANTONY   I will reward thee   14
Once for thy spritely comfort and tenfold
For thy good valor. Come thee on.

SCARUS   I'll halt after.   *Exeunt.*   17

❧

[4.8]

Alarum. Enter Antony again in a march; Scarus,
with others.

ANTONY
We have beat him to his camp. Run one before   1
And let the Queen know of our gests. [*Exit a Soldier.*]
                                   Tomorrow,   2
Before the sun shall see 's, we'll spill the blood
That has today escaped. I thank you all,
For doughty-handed are you, and have fought   5
Not as you served the cause, but as't had been   6
Each man's like mine; you have shown all Hectors.   7
Enter the city, clip your wives, your friends,   8
Tell them your feats, whilst they with joyful tears
Wash the congealment from your wounds and kiss
The honored gashes whole.

Enter Cleopatra [attended].

                   [*To Scarus*] Give me thy hand;
To this great fairy I'll commend thy acts,   12
Make her thanks bless thee. [*To Cleopatra*] O thou day
   o'th' world,   13
Chain mine armed neck; leap thou, attire and all,   14
Through proof of harness to my heart, and there   15
Ride on the pants triumphing!   [*They embrace.*]

CLEOPATRA   Lord of lords,   16
O infinite virtue, com'st thou smiling from   17
The world's great snare uncaught?

ANTONY   My nightingale,
We have beat them to their beds. What, girl, though
   gray
Do something mingle with our younger brown, yet
   ha' we   20
A brain that nourishes our nerves and can   21

---

23 **on my guard** while I was standing guard   27 **Best you safed** You
would do well to provide safe-conduct for   28 **host** army.   **attend
mine office** see to my duties   31 **alone the** the only, the greatest
32 **And . . . most** and am the one who feels it most.   33 **mine** abundant store   35 **blows** causes to swell to the bursting point   36 **mean**
i.e., suicide   37 **thought** melancholy.   **do't** i.e., break my heart
4.7. Location: Field of battle between the camps.
2 **has work** is hard pressed.   **our oppression** the heavy attacks
against us   3 **s.d. Exeunt** (The cleared stage technically marks a new
scene, although the alarums provide a sense of continuous action.)
5 **droven** driven   6 **clouts** (1) bandages (2) blows and knocks
8 **H** i.e., the bottom of the T has been cut across to make an H lying
on its side. (There is a pun on *ache*, pronounced *aitch*.)   9 **bench
holes** the holes of privies, i.e., any desperate place to hide.
10 **scotches** cuts

11–12 **our . . . victory** i.e., we are in such a favorable position that a
complete victory seems in prospect.   12 **score** mark by cuts from a
whip   14 **a runner** one in retreat.   17 **halt** limp
4.8. Location: Before Alexandria. The action is virtually continuous.
1 **beat** driven.   **Run one** Let someone run   2 **gests** deeds.
5 **doughty-handed** valiant   6–7 **Not . . . mine** not as if you were
merely serving the general cause, but as if it were your cause personally   7 **shown** shown yourselves   8 **clip** embrace   12 **fairy**
enchantress, dispenser of good fortune   13 **day** light   14 **Chain . . .
neck** hang around my neck in an embrace like a medal on a chain
15 **proof of harness** proof-armor, tested armor   16 **pants** heartbeats
17 **virtue** valor   20 **something** somewhat   21 **nerves** sinews, tendons

Get goal for goal of youth. Behold this man;   22
Commend unto his lips thy favoring hand.—   23
Kiss it, my warrior. [*Scarus kisses Cleopatra's hand.*] He
   hath fought today
As if a god, in hate of mankind, had
Destroyed in such a shape.

CLEOPATRA   I'll give thee, friend,
An armor all of gold; it was a king's.

ANTONY
He has deserved it, were it carbuncled   28
Like holy Phoebus' car. Give me thy hand.   29
Through Alexandria make a jolly march;
Bear our hacked targets like the men that owe them.   31
Had our great palace the capacity
To camp this host, we all would sup together   33
And drink carouses to the next day's fate,   34
Which promises royal peril. Trumpeters,   35
With brazen din blast you the city's ear;
Make mingle with our rattling taborins,   37
That heaven and earth may strike their sounds
   together,   38
Applauding our approach. [*Trumpets sound.*] *Exeunt.*

❖

[4.9]

Enter a Sentry and his company. Enobarbus
follows.

SENTRY
If we be not relieved within this hour,
We must return to th' court of guard. The night   2
Is shiny, and they say we shall embattle   3
By the second hour i'th' morn.

FIRST WATCH   This last day was a shrewd one to 's.   5

ENOBARBUS   Oh, bear me witness, night—

SECOND WATCH
What man is this?

FIRST WATCH   Stand close, and list him.   8
               [*They stand aside.*]

ENOBARBUS
Be witness to me, O thou blessèd moon,
When men revolted shall upon record   10
Bear hateful memory: poor Enobarbus did
Before thy face repent.

SENTRY   Enobarbus?

SECOND WATCH   Peace! Hark further.

ENOBARBUS
O sovereign mistress of true melancholy,   15
The poisonous damp of night disponge upon me,   16
That life, a very rebel to my will,
May hang no longer on me. Throw my heart
Against the flint and hardness of my fault,
Which, being dried with grief, will break to powder   20
And finish all foul thoughts. O Antony,
Nobler than my revolt is infamous,
Forgive me in thine own particular,   23
But let the world rank me in register   24
A master-leaver and a fugitive.   25
O Antony! O Antony!   [*He dies.*]

FIRST WATCH   Let's speak to him.

SENTRY
Let's hear him, for the things he speaks
May concern Caesar.

SECOND WATCH   Let's do so. But he sleeps.

SENTRY
Swoons rather, for so bad a prayer as his
Was never yet for sleep.

FIRST WATCH   Go we to him.   31
            [*They approach Enobarbus.*]

SECOND WATCH   Awake, sir, awake. Speak to us.

FIRST WATCH   Hear you, sir?

SENTRY   The hand of death hath raught him.   34
                  Drums afar off.
Hark, the drums demurely wake the sleepers.   35
Let us bear him to th' court of guard;
He is of note. Our hour is fully out.   37

SECOND WATCH
Come on, then. He may recover yet.
               Exeunt [*with the body*].

❖

[4.10]

Enter Antony and Scarus, with their army.

ANTONY
Their preparation is today by sea;
We please them not by land.

SCARUS   For both, my lord.

ANTONY
I would they'd fight i'th' fire or i'th'air;   3
We'd fight there too. But this it is: our foot   4
Upon the hills adjoining to the city
Shall stay with us—order for sea is given;   6

---

22 Get . . . of i.e., stay competitively equal with.   **this man** i.e., Scarus
23 Commend entrust, commit   **28 carbuncled** set with jewels
29 Phoebus' car the chariot of the sun.   **31 Bear . . . them** bear our
hacked shields, well suited to the warriors who, like their shields,
have sustained blows. (*Owe* means "own.")   **33 camp this host**
accommodate this army   **34 carouses** toasts   **35 royal peril** i.e., war,
the sport of monarchs.   **37 taborins** drums   **38 That . . . together** i.e.,
that the heavens may echo and augment the loud noise of the drums
4.9. Location: Caesar's camp.
2 court of guard guardroom.   **3 shiny** bright, moonlit.   **embattle**
assemble for the combat   **5 shrewd** unlucky   **8 close** concealed.
list listen to   **10 revolted** who have broken their allegiance.   **upon**
record in the record of history

15 mistress . . . melancholy i.e., the moon, so addressed because of
her supposed influence in causing lunacy   **16 disponge** pour down
(as from a squeezed sponge)   **20 Which** i.e., the heart.   **dried with**
grief (Cold and melancholy blood was thought to strangle and dry
up the heart.)   **23 in . . . particular** in your own person   **24 rank me**
in register put me down in its records   **25 master-leaver** (1) one who
deserts his master (2) nonpareil of deserters.   **fugitive** deserter.
31 for a prelude to   **34 raught** reached   **35 demurely** with solemn
sound   **37 of note** of rank.
4.10. Location: The field of battle.
3 fire . . . air (Along with earth and water, where Antony is already
prepared, fire and air make up the traditional four elements of all
matter.)   **4 foot** foot soldiers   **6 for sea** to fight at sea

They have put forth the haven— 7
Where their appointment we may best discover 8
And look on their endeavor.   *Exeunt.*

❖

[4.11]

Enter Caesar and his army.

CAESAR
But being charged, we will be still by land, 1
Which, as I take't, we shall; for his best force 2
Is forth to man his galleys. To the vales, 3
And hold our best advantage.   *Exeunt.* 4

❖

[4.12]

Enter Antony and Scarus.

ANTONY
Yet they are not joined. Where yond pine does stand,
I shall discover all. I'll bring thee word
Straight how 'tis like to go.   *Exit.*
Alarum afar off, as at a sea fight.
SCARUS   Swallows have built 3
In Cleopatra's sails their nests. The augurers 4
Say they know not, they cannot tell, look grimly,
And dare not speak their knowledge. Antony
Is valiant, and dejected, and by starts
His fretted fortunes give him hope and fear 8
Of what he has and has not.

Enter Antony.

ANTONY   All is lost!
This foul Egyptian hath betrayèd me.
My fleet hath yielded to the foe, and yonder
They cast their caps up and carouse together
Like friends long lost. Triple-turned whore! 'Tis thou 13
Hast sold me to this novice, and my heart
Makes only wars on thee. Bid them all fly;
For when I am revenged upon my charm, 16
I have done all. Bid them all fly. Begone!
                            [*Exit Scarus.*]
O sun, thy uprise shall I see no more.
Fortune and Antony part here; even here
Do we shake hands. All come to this? The hearts 20
That spanieled me at heels, to whom I gave 21
Their wishes, do discandy, melt their sweets 22

On blossoming Caesar; and this pine is barked 23
That overtopped them all. Betrayed I am.
Oh, this false soul of Egypt! This grave charm, 25
Whose eye becked forth my wars and called them
    home, 26
Whose bosom was my crownet, my chief end, 27
Like a right gypsy hath at fast and loose 28
Beguiled me to the very heart of loss. 29
[*Calling*] What, Eros, Eros!

Enter Cleopatra.

                        Ah, thou spell! Avaunt! 30
CLEOPATRA
Why is my lord enraged against his love?
ANTONY
Vanish, or I shall give thee thy deserving
And blemish Caesar's triumph. Let him take thee 33
And hoist thee up to the shouting plebeians!
Follow his chariot, like the greatest spot 35
Of all thy sex; most monsterlike be shown 36
For poor'st diminutives, for dolts, and let 37
Patient Octavia plow thy visage up
With her preparèd nails!   *Exit Cleopatra.*
                        'Tis well thou'rt gone,
If it be well to live; but better 'twere
Thou fell'st into my fury, for one death 41
Might have prevented many.—Eros, ho!— 42
The shirt of Nessus is upon me. Teach me, 43
Alcides, thou mine ancestor, thy rage. 44
Let me lodge Lichas on the horns o'th' moon, 45
And with those hands, that grasped the heaviest club,
Subdue my worthiest self. The witch shall die.
To the young Roman boy she hath sold me, and I fall
Under this plot. She dies for't.—Eros, ho!   *Exit.*

❖

[4.13]

Enter Cleopatra, Charmian, Iras, [and] Mardian.

CLEOPATRA
Help me, my women! Oh, he's more mad

---

7 **forth** forth from   8 **appointment** disposition of forces, equipment. **discover** descry
4.11. Location: The field of battle.
1 **But being** Unless we are.   **still** inactive   2 **we shall** i.e., we will be left undisturbed   3 **Is forth** has gone forth.   **vales** valleys   4 **hold . . . advantage** take the most advantageous position.
4.12. Location: The field of battle at first, though by scene's end the action appears to be located in Alexandria.
3 **Straight** immediately.   **like** likely   4 **augurers** augurs, soothsayers   8 **fretted** worn away, vexed, checkered   13 **Triple-turned** Three times faithless (to Julius Caesar, Gnaeus Pompey, and now Antony)
16 **charm** practicer of charms or spells   20 **shake hands** i.e., in parting.   **hearts** good fellows   21 **spanieled** fawned upon like a spaniel
22 **Their wishes** whatever they wished.   **discandy** melt, dissolve

23 **this pine** i.e., Antony.   **barked** stripped of its bark and thus killed
25 **This grave charm** i.e., This sorceress who casts fatal spells
26 **becked** beckoned   27 **Whose . . . end** whose embraces were the crown of my achievement and my goal   28 **right** veritable.   **fast and loose** a cheating game in which the victim bets that he can make fast a knot in an ingeniously coiled rope, whereupon the knot is pulled loose   29 **loss** ruin.   30 **spell** enchantment.   **Avaunt!** Begone!
33 **blemish Caesar's triumph** i.e., mutilate you and thereby frustrate Caesar's plan to display you in his triumphal procession into Rome.
35 **spot** blemish, disgrace   36 **shown** exhibited   37 **diminutives** underlings, i.e., the populace   41 **Thou fell'st into** you had fallen a victim to   42 **many** i.e., many other deaths resulting from my rage.
43–5 **Nessus . . . Lichas** (When Hercules or *Alcides* had fatally wounded the centaur *Nessus* for trying to rape Hercules's wife Deianira, Nessus vengefully gave his blood-soaked shirt to Deianira as a supposed love charm for her husband. The poison gave Hercules such agony that he cast his page *Lichas* into the air.)
4.13. Location: Alexandria. This scene appears to follow scene 12 closely. The sense of location is very fluid, and it is not clear where the end of scene 12 takes place.

Than Telamon for his shield; the boar of Thessaly　2
Was never so embossed.

CHARMIAN　　　　　　　　To th' monument!　3
There lock yourself and send him word you are dead.
The soul and body rive not more in parting　5
Than greatness going off.

CLEOPATRA　　　　　　　　To th' monument!　6
Mardian, go tell him I have slain myself.
Say that the last I spoke was "Antony,"
And word it, prithee, piteously. Hence, Mardian,
And bring me how he takes my death. To th'
monument!　　　　　　　　　　　　　　　*Exeunt.*

❧

[4.14]

Enter Antony and Eros.

ANTONY
Eros, thou yet behold'st me?

EROS　　　　　　　　　　　　Ay, noble lord.

ANTONY
Sometime we see a cloud that's dragonish,　2
A vapor sometime like a bear or lion,
A towered citadel, a pendant rock,　4
A forkèd mountain, or blue promontory
With trees upon't that nod unto the world
And mock our eyes with air. Thou hast seen these
signs;
They are black vesper's pageants.

EROS　　　　　　　　　　　Ay, my lord.　8

ANTONY
That which is now a horse, even with a thought
The rack dislimns and makes it indistinct　10
As water is in water.

EROS　　　　　　　　It does, my lord.

ANTONY
My good knave Eros, now thy captain is　12
Even such a body. Here I am Antony,
Yet cannot hold this visible shape, my knave.
I made these wars for Egypt, and the Queen,
Whose heart I thought I had, for she had mine—
Which whilst it was mine had annexed unto't
A million more, now lost—she, Eros, has
Packed cards with Caesar and false-played my glory　19
Unto an enemy's triumph.　20

Nay, weep not, gentle Eros. There is left us
Ourselves to end ourselves.

Enter Mardian.

　　　　　　　　　　　　　　Oh, thy vile lady!
She has robbed me of my sword.

MARDIAN　　　　　　　　　　No, Antony,　23
My mistress loved thee, and her fortunes mingled
With thine entirely.

ANTONY　　　　　Hence, saucy eunuch, peace!
She hath betrayed me and shall die the death.　26

MARDIAN
Death of one person can be paid but once,　27
And that she has discharged. What thou wouldst do　28
Is done unto thy hand. The last she spake　29
Was, "Antony, most noble Antony!"
Then in the midst a tearing groan did break
The name of Antony; it was divided　32
Between her heart and lips. She rendered life　33
Thy name so buried in her.

ANTONY　　　　　　　　Dead, then?

MARDIAN　　　　　　　　　　　Dead.　34

ANTONY
Unarm, Eros. The long day's task is done,
And we must sleep. [*To Mardian*] That thou depart'st
hence safe
Does pay thy labor richly; go.　　*Exit Mardian.*
　　　　　　　　Off, pluck off! [*Eros unarms him.*]
The sevenfold shield of Ajax cannot keep　38
The battery from my heart. Oh, cleave, my sides!　39
Heart, once be stronger than thy continent;　40
Crack thy frail case! Apace, Eros, apace.　41
No more a soldier. Bruisèd pieces, go;
You have been nobly borne.—From me awhile.　43
　　　　　　　　　　　　　　　　Exit Eros.
I will o'ertake thee, Cleopatra, and
Weep for my pardon. So it must be, for now
All length is torture; since the torch is out,　46
Lie down, and stray no farther. Now all labor
Mars what it does; yea, very force entangles　48
Itself with strength. Seal then, and all is done.　49
Eros!—I come, my queen.—Eros!—Stay for me.　50
Where souls do couch on flowers, we'll hand in hand,　51
And with our sprightly port make the ghosts gaze.　52

---

2 Telamon Ajax Telamon, who after the capture of Troy went mad and slew himself when he was not awarded the shield and armor of Achilles.　**the boar of Thessaly** the boar sent by Diana or Artemis to ravage the fields of Calydon, slain by Meleager　**3 embossed** foaming at the mouth from rage and exhaustion.　**monument** tomb presumably built to house Cleopatra's royal remains after her death, like the pyramids.　**5 rive** split, sever　**6 going off** i.e., bidding farewell to its glory.
4.14. Location: Alexandria. (See location of scene 13; again, the sense of time is immediate and the place is fluid.)
2 dragonish shaped like a dragon　**4 pendant** overhanging　**8 black . . . pageants** i.e., the evanescent splendor of a sunset heralding the approach of night.　**10 The rack dislimns** the mass of cloud changes its shape　**12 knave** lad　**19 Packed cards** i.e., stacked the deck. **false-played** falsely played away　**20 triumph** (1) victory (2) trump card.

23 sword i.e., prowess as a soldier, masculinity.　**26 die the death** be put to death.　**27 of** by　**28 discharged** paid.　**29 unto thy hand** for you, without your having to lift a finger.　**32–3 it . . . lips** i.e., she groaned out half of Antony's name and then died with the unspoken part in her heart only.　**33–4 She . . . in her** She gave back to Nature that part of your name thus buried in her heart.　**38 sevenfold** with seven thicknesses. (The shield of Ajax was of brass reinforced with seven thicknesses of oxhide.)　**39 battery** battering　**40 thy continent** that which contains you　**41 Apace** Quickly　**43 From** Go from　**46 length** prolongation of life.　**the torch** i.e., the life of Cleopatra　**48 very force** any resolute action　**49 with strength** i.e., with its own strength.　**Seal** Finish the business (as in sealing a letter)　**50 Eros** (The meaning of Eros's name, erotic love, is especially apt here.)　**51 couch** lie (here, in the Elysian fields)　**52 sprightly** (1) high-spirited (2) spiritlike, ghostly.　**port** bearing

Dido and her Aeneas shall want troops,   53
And all the haunt be ours.—Come, Eros, Eros!   54

Enter Eros.

EROS
What would my lord?
ANTONY   Since Cleopatra died
I have lived in such dishonor that the gods
Detest my baseness. I, that with my sword
Quartered the world, and o'er green Neptune's back   58
With ships made cities, condemn myself to lack   59
The courage of a woman—less noble mind
Than she which by her death our Caesar tells
"I am conqueror of myself." Thou art sworn, Eros,
That when the exigent should come which now   63
Is come indeed, when I should see behind me
Th'inevitable prosecution of   65
Disgrace and horror, that on my command
Thou then wouldst kill me. Do't. The time is come.
Thou strik'st not me, 'tis Caesar thou defeat'st.
Put color in thy cheek.
EROS   The gods withhold me!   69
Shall I do that which all the Parthian darts,
Though enemy, lost aim and could not?
ANTONY   Eros,
Wouldst thou be windowed in great Rome and see   72
Thy master thus with pleached arms, bending down   73
His corrigible neck, his face subdued   74
To penetrative shame, whilst the wheeled seat   75
Of fortunate Caesar, drawn before him, branded   76
His baseness that ensued?
EROS   I would not see't.   77
ANTONY
Come, then, for with a wound I must be cured.
Draw that thy honest sword, which thou hast worn   79
Most useful for thy country.
EROS   Oh, sir, pardon me!   80
ANTONY
When I did make thee free, swor'st thou not then
To do this when I bade thee? Do it at once,
Or thy precedent services are all   83
But accidents unpurposed. Draw, and come.   84
EROS
Turn from me then that noble countenance

53 **Dido ... troops** We will be the most distinguished lovers in the
Elysian fields, outshining even the Queen of Carthage and her
famous lover. (In the *Aeneid*, Aeneas deserts Dido in order to found
Rome, putting public good ahead of private passion as Antony does
not. Dido scorns Aeneas when they meet in the underworld; Antony
here imagines himself and Cleopatra in the Elysian fields.)   **want
troops** lack followers   54 **all ... ours** i.e., we shall be the objects of
everyone's attention.   58–9 **Quartered ... cities** divided and conquered the world, and at sea assembled flotillas as dense and populous as cities   59 **to lack** for lacking   63 **exigent** exigency, time of
compelling need   65 **prosecution** consequence   69 **The gods withhold me!** i.e., God forbid!   72 **windowed** placed as in a window
73 **pleached** folded or bound   74 **corrigible** submissive to correction
75 **penetrative** penetrating.   **wheeled seat** chariot   76–7 **branded ...
ensued** stigmatized, as by a brand, the shame of him that followed.
79 **honest** honorable   80 **pardon me!** excuse me from doing this!
83 **precedent** former   84 **accidents unpurposed** events leading to no
purpose.

Wherein the worship of the whole world lies.   86
ANTONY   Lo thee!   [*He turns away.*]
EROS [*drawing his sword*]
My sword is drawn.
ANTONY   Then let it do at once
That thing why thou hast drawn it.
EROS   My dear master,
My captain, and my emperor, let me say,
Before I strike this bloody stroke, farewell.
ANTONY   'Tis said, man, and farewell.
EROS
Farewell, great chief. Shall I strike now?
ANTONY   Now, Eros.
EROS (*kills himself*)
Why, there then! Thus I do escape the sorrow
Of Antony's death.   [*He dies.*]
ANTONY   Thrice nobler than myself!
Thou teachest me, O valiant Eros, what
I should, and thou couldst not. My queen and Eros   97
Have by their brave instruction got upon me   98
A nobleness in record. But I will be   99
A bridegroom in my death, and run into't
As to a lover's bed. Come, then, and Eros,
Thy master dies thy scholar. To do thus
I learned of thee.   [*He falls on his sword.*]
                 How, not dead? Not dead?
The guard, ho! Oh, dispatch me!   104

Enter [Dercetus and others of] a Guard.

FIRST GUARD   What's the noise?
ANTONY   I have done my work ill, friends.
Oh, make an end of what I have begun!
SECOND GUARD   The star is fallen.
FIRST GUARD   And time is at his period.   109
ALL   Alas, and woe!
ANTONY   Let him that loves me strike me dead.
FIRST GUARD   Not I.
SECOND GUARD   Nor I.
THIRD GUARD   Nor anyone.   *Exeunt [Guard].*
DERCETUS
Thy death and fortunes bid thy followers fly.
This sword but shown to Caesar, with this tidings,
Shall enter me with him. [*He takes up Antony's sword.*] 117

Enter Diomedes.

DIOMEDES   Where's Antony?
DERCETUS   There, Diomed, there.
DIOMEDES
Lives he? Wilt thou not answer, man? [*Exit Dercetus.*]
ANTONY
Art thou there, Diomed? Draw thy sword and give me
Sufficing strokes for death.
DIOMEDES   Most absolute lord,
My mistress Cleopatra sent me to thee.

86 **worship** honor, worth   97 **I should ... not** I should have done for
myself and you couldn't do for me.   98–9 **got ... record** won a noble
place in history before I have.   104 **dispatch** finish   109 **his period**
its end.   117 **enter ... him** admit me to his service, put me in his
good graces.

ANTONY
When did she send thee?
DIOMEDES   Now, my lord.
ANTONY   Where is she?
DIOMEDES
Locked in her monument. She had a prophesying fear
Of what hath come to pass. For when she saw—
Which never shall be found—you did suspect   127
She had disposed with Caesar, and that your rage 128
Would not be purged, she sent you word she was
    dead;
But, fearing since how it might work, hath sent
Me to proclaim the truth, and I am come,
I dread, too late.
ANTONY
Too late, good Diomed. Call my guard, I prithee.
DIOMEDES [*calling*]
What ho, the Emperor's guard! The guard, what ho!
Come, your lord calls.

        Enter four or five of the Guard of Antony.

ANTONY
Bear me, good friends, where Cleopatra bides.   136
'Tis the last service that I shall command you.
FIRST GUARD
Woe, woe are we, sir, you may not live to wear   138
All your true followers out.
ALL   Most heavy day!   139
ANTONY
Nay, good my fellows, do not please sharp fate
To grace it with your sorrows. Bid that welcome   141
Which comes to punish us, and we punish it,
Seeming to bear it lightly. Take me up.
I have led you oft; carry me now, good friends,
And have my thanks for all.
            Exeunt, bearing Antony [and Eros].

[4.15]

        *Enter Cleopatra and her maids aloft, with
        Charmian and Iras.*

CLEOPATRA
Oh, Charmian, I will never go from hence.
CHARMIAN
Be comforted, dear madam.
CLEOPATRA   No, I will not.
All strange and terrible events are welcome,
But comforts we despise. Our size of sorrow,
Proportioned to our cause, must be as great
As that which makes it.

        Enter [below] Diomedes.

                    How now? Is he dead?

DIOMEDES
His death's upon him, but not dead.
Look out o'th'other side your monument;
His guard have brought him thither.

        *Enter [below] Antony, and the Guard
        [bearing him].*

CLEOPATRA   O sun,
Burn the great sphere thou mov'st in; darkling stand   11
The varying shore o'th' world! O Antony,
Antony, Antony! Help, Charmian, help, Iras, help!
Help, friends below! Let's draw him hither.
ANTONY   Peace!
Not Caesar's valor hath o'erthrown Antony,
But Antony's hath triumphed on itself.
CLEOPATRA
So it should be, that none but Antony
Should conquer Antony; but woe 'tis so!
ANTONY
I am dying, Egypt, dying. Only
I here importune death awhile, until   20
Of many thousand kisses the poor last
I lay upon thy lips.
CLEOPATRA   I dare not, dear—   22
Dear my lord, pardon—I dare not,
Lest I be taken. Not th'imperious show   24
Of the full-fortuned Caesar ever shall
Be brooched with me. If knife, drugs, serpents, have 26
Edge, sting, or operation, I am safe.   27
Your wife Octavia, with her modest eyes
And still conclusion, shall acquire no honor   29
Demuring upon me. But come, come, Antony—   30
Help me, my women—we must draw thee up.
Assist, good friends.
ANTONY   Oh, quick, or I am gone.
                    [*They begin lifting.*]
CLEOPATRA
Here's sport indeed! How heavy weighs my lord!
Our strength is all gone into heaviness,   34
That makes the weight. Had I great Juno's power,
The strong-winged Mercury should fetch thee up
And set thee by Jove's side. Yet come a little;
Wishers were ever fools. Oh, come, come, come!   38
            They heave Antony aloft to Cleopatra.
And welcome, welcome! Die when thou hast lived;   39
Quicken with kissing. Had my lips that power,   40
Thus would I wear them out.   [*She kisses him.*]   42
ALL   A heavy sight!
ANTONY   I am dying, Egypt, dying.
Give me some wine, and let me speak a little.

---

127 **found** found true   128 **disposed with** come to terms with
136 **bides** abides, dwells.   138–9 **live . . . out** outlive those that serve
you.   141 **To grace** by gracing or honoring
4.15. Location: Alexandria. Cleopatra's monument.
0.1 *aloft* in the gallery above the main stage

11 **sphere** concentric sphere in which, according to Ptolemaic astronomy, the sun moved about the earth, as did the planets and stars.
darkling in darkness   20 **importune** i.e., beg a delay of   22 **I dare
not** i.e., I dare not come down   24 **th'imperious show** the imperial
triumphal procession   26 **brooched** adorned (as with a brooch)
27 **operation** power, efficacy   29 **still conclusion** silent judgment
30 **Demuring** looking demurely   34 **heaviness** (1) sadness (2) weight
38 **Wishers . . . fools** Those who wish for things are always fools.
39 **Die . . . lived** i.e., Die after living intensely. (With a pun on *die* suggesting sexual consummation; hence *Quicken* in line 40.)   40 **Quicken**
revive   42 **heavy** doleful

CLEOPATRA
No, let me speak, and let me rail so high
That the false huswife Fortune break her wheel,   46
Provoked by my offense.
ANTONY   One word, sweet Queen: 47
Of Caesar seek your honor, with your safety. Oh!   48
CLEOPATRA
They do not go together.
ANTONY   Gentle, hear me.
None about Caesar trust but Proculeius.
CLEOPATRA
My resolution and my hands I'll trust,
None about Caesar.
ANTONY
The miserable change now at my end
Lament nor sorrow at, but please your thoughts   54
In feeding them with those my former fortunes,
Wherein I lived the greatest prince o'th' world,
The noblest; and do now not basely die,
Not cowardly put off my helmet to
My countryman—a Roman by a Roman
Valiantly vanquished. Now my spirit is going;
I can no more.
CLEOPATRA   Noblest of men, woo't die?   61
Hast thou no care of me? Shall I abide
In this dull world, which in thy absence is
No better than a sty? [Antony dies.] Oh, see, my
     women,
The crown o'th'earth doth melt. My lord!
Oh, withered is the garland of the war;
The soldier's pole is fall'n! Young boys and girls   67
Are level now with men. The odds is gone,   68
And there is nothing left remarkable
Beneath the visiting moon.   [She faints.]
CHARMIAN   Oh, quietness, lady!
IRAS   She's dead too, our sovereign.
CHARMIAN   Lady!
IRAS   Madam!
CHARMIAN   Oh, madam, madam, madam!
IRAS   Royal Egypt, Empress!   [Cleopatra stirs.]
CHARMIAN   Peace, peace, Iras.
CLEOPATRA
No more but e'en a woman, and commanded
By such poor passion as the maid that milks
And does the meanest chares. It were for me   80
To throw my scepter at the injurious gods,
To tell them that this world did equal theirs
Till they had stol'n our jewel. All's but naught;
Patience is sottish, and impatience does   84
Become a dog that's mad. Then is it sin   85
To rush into the secret house of death
Ere death dare come to us? How do you, women?

What, what, good cheer! Why, how now, Charmian?
My noble girls! Ah, women, women! Look,
Our lamp is spent, it's out. Good sirs, take heart.   90
We'll bury him; and then, what's brave, what's noble,   91
Let's do't after the high Roman fashion
And make death proud to take us. Come, away.
This case of that huge spirit now is cold.
Ah, women, women! Come. We have no friend
But resolution, and the briefest end.   96
           Exeunt, [those above] bearing off Antony's body.

❖

[5.1]

Enter Caesar, Agrippa, Dolabella, Maecenas,
[Gallus, Proculeius,] with his council of war.

CAESAR
Go to him, Dolabella, bid him yield;
Being so frustrate, tell him, he mocks   2
The pauses that he makes.
DOLABELLA   Caesar, I shall.   [Exit.]   3

Enter Dercetus, with the sword of Antony.

CAESAR
Wherefore is that? And what art thou that dar'st
Appear thus to us?
DERCETUS   I am called Dercetus.
Mark Antony I served, who best was worthy
Best to be served. Whilst he stood up and spoke
He was my master, and I wore my life
To spend upon his haters. If thou please   9
To take me to thee, as I was to him
I'll be to Caesar; if thou pleasest not,
I yield thee up my life.
CAESAR   What is't thou say'st?
DERCETUS
I say, O Caesar, Antony is dead.
CAESAR
The breaking of so great a thing should make   14
A greater crack. The round world   15
Should have shook lions into civil streets   16
And citizens to their dens. The death of Antony   17
Is not a single doom; in the name lay   18
A moiety of the world.
DERCETUS   He is dead, Caesar,   19
Not by a public minister of justice,
Nor by a hirèd knife; but that self hand   21
Which writ his honor in the acts it did
Hath, with the courage which the heart did lend it,

90 **Good sirs** (Addressed to the women.)   91 **brave** fine   96 **briefest**
swiftest
5.1. Location: Alexandria. Caesar's camp.
2 **frustrate** helpless, baffled   2–3 **mocks . . . makes** makes himself
ridiculous by his delays (in yielding).   9 **spend** expend   14 **break-**
ing (1) destruction (2) disclosure   15 **crack** (1) cracking apart (2) loud
report.   16 **civil** city   17 **their** i.e., the lions', or else, the citizens
scurry to safety indoors, in their own "dens." (In either case, nature is
inverted in a kind of disorder that earlier accompanied the death of
Julius Caesar.)   18 **Is . . . doom** i.e., signifies the death and destruction of much more than a single man   19 **moiety** half   21 **self** same

46 **false huswife** treacherous hussy   47 **offense** offensive speech.
48 **Of** from   54 **Lament** i.e., neither lament   61 **woo't** wilt thou
67 **pole** polestar or battle standard. (Probably with a suggestion of a
sexual potency now withered and fallen through death.)   68 **The**
odds is gone The distinction between great and small has disappeared   80 **chares** chores, drudgery.   **were** would be fitting
84–5 **Patience . . . mad** i.e., Patience is for fools, and impatience is for
the mad; both are useless here.

Splitted the heart. This is his sword.

[*He offers the sword.*]

I robbed his wound of it. Behold it stained
With his most noble blood.

CAESAR   Look you sad, friends?
The gods rebuke me, but it is tidings   27
To wash the eyes of kings.

AGRIPPA   And strange it is
That nature must compel us to lament
Our most persisted deeds.

MAECENAS   His taints and honors   30
Waged equal with him.

AGRIPPA   A rarer spirit never   31
Did steer humanity; but you gods will give us   32
Some faults to make us men. Caesar is touched.

MAECENAS
When such a spacious mirror's set before him,
He needs must see himself.

CAESAR   O Antony,
I have followed thee to this; but we do launch   36
Diseases in our bodies. I must perforce   37
Have shown to thee such a declining day,   38
Or look on thine; we could not stall together   39
In the whole world. But yet let me lament
With tears as sovereign as the blood of hearts   41
That thou, my brother, my competitor   42
In top of all design, my mate in empire,   43
Friend and companion in the front of war,   44
The arm of mine own body, and the heart   45
Where mine his thoughts did kindle—that our stars,   46
Unreconcilable, should divide   47
Our equalness to this. Hear me, good friends—   48

Enter an Egyptian.

But I will tell you at some meeter season.   49
The business of this man looks out of him;   50
We'll hear him what he says.—Whence are you?   51

EGYPTIAN
A poor Egyptian yet, the Queen my mistress,   52
Confined in all she has, her monument,
Of thy intents desires instruction,
That she preparedly may frame herself   55
To th' way she's forced to.

CAESAR   Bid her have good heart.
She soon shall know of us, by some of ours,   57

How honorable and how kindly we
Determine for her; for Caesar cannot live
To be ungentle.

EGYPTIAN   So the gods preserve thee!   *Exit.*

CAESAR
Come hither, Proculeius. Go and say
We purpose her no shame. Give her what comforts   62
The quality of her passion shall require,   63
Lest, in her greatness, by some mortal stroke   64
She do defeat us; for her life in Rome   65
Would be eternal in our triumph. Go,   66
And with your speediest bring us what she says   67
And how you find of her.

PROCULEIUS   Caesar, I shall.   68

Exit Proculeius.

CAESAR   Gallus, go you along.   [*Exit Gallus.*]
     Where's Dolabella,
To second Proculeius?

ALL   Dolabella!

CAESAR
Let him alone, for I remember now   71
How he's employed. He shall in time be ready.
Go with me to my tent, where you shall see
How hardly I was drawn into this war,   74
How calm and gentle I proceeded still   75
In all my writings. Go with me and see   76
What I can show in this.   *Exeunt.*

❖

[5.2]

Enter Cleopatra, Charmian, Iras, and Mardian.

CLEOPATRA
My desolation does begin to make
A better life. 'Tis paltry to be Caesar;   2
Not being Fortune, he's but Fortune's knave,   3
A minister of her will. And it is great
To do that thing that ends all other deeds,   5
Which shackles accidents and bolts up change,   6
Which sleeps and never palates more the dung,   7
The beggar's nurse and Caesar's.   8

Enter [to the gates of the monument] Proculeius.

PROCULEIUS
Caesar sends greeting to the Queen of Egypt,
And bids thee study on what fair demands   10
Thou mean'st to have him grant thee.

CLEOPATRA   What's thy name?

---

27 **but it is** if it is not   30 **persisted** persistently desired or pursued
31 **Waged equal with** battled equally in   32 **steer humanity** govern
any individual.   **will give** insist on giving   36 **followed** pursued
36–7 **but . . . bodies** i.e., I have hurt you to cure myself, as men lance
diseases in their own bodies.   37 **perforce** necessarily   38 **shown to
thee** i.e., suffered myself at your hands   39 **stall** dwell   41 **as sovereign . . . hearts** as precious or efficacious as heart's blood   42 **competitor** associate, partner (and rival)   43 **In . . . design** at the head of
every grand enterprise   44 **front** forehead, face   45–6 **the heart . . .
kindle** the brave heart where my heart kindled its (*his*) thoughts of
courage   47–8 **should . . . this** should divide our equal partnership to
this extreme.   49 **meeter season** more suitable time.   50 **looks . . .
him** reveals itself in his expression   51 **Whence are you?** Where do
you come from?   52 **A . . . yet** i.e., Egyptian Cleopatra, still reduced
in circumstance (and awaiting your will), or, I am a poor Egyptian
still, though subject to Rome's authority   55 **frame herself** shape her
course of action   57 **ours** my people

62 **purpose** intend   63 **passion** grief   64 **greatness** greatness of spirit
65 **life in Rome** presence in Rome alive   66 **eternal in our triumph**
an eternal glory in my triumphal procession.   67 **with your speediest** as quickly as you can   68 **of** concerning   71 **Let him alone** Don't
bother about him now   74 **hardly** reluctantly   75 **still** always
76 **writings** i.e., letters to Antony.
5.2. Location: Alexandria. Cleopatra's monument.
2 **better** i.e., rising above the vicissitudes of fortune   3 **knave** servant
5–8 **To do . . . Caesar's** i.e., to commit suicide, a sleep that arrests accident and change, and in which the sleeper relishes no more the
dungy earth that sustains both Caesar and the beggar.   10 **study on**
consider carefully

PROCULEIUS
My name is Proculeius.

CLEOPATRA   Antony
Did tell me of you, bade me trust you; but
I do not greatly care to be deceived,   14
That have no use for trusting. If your master   15
Would have a queen his beggar, you must tell him
That majesty, to keep decorum, must
No less beg than a kingdom. If he please
To give me conquered Egypt for my son,
He gives me so much of mine own as I   20
Will kneel to him with thanks.

PROCULEIUS   Be of good cheer;
You're fall'n into a princely hand. Fear nothing.
Make your full reference freely to my lord,   23
Who is so full of grace that it flows over
On all that need. Let me report to him
Your sweet dependency, and you shall find   26
A conqueror that will pray in aid for kindness   27
Where he for grace is kneeled to.

CLEOPATRA   Pray you, tell him
I am his fortune's vassal, and I send him   29
The greatness he has got. I hourly learn   30
A doctrine of obedience, and would gladly
Look him i'th' face.

PROCULEIUS   This I'll report, dear lady.
Have comfort, for I know your plight is pitied
Of him that caused it.   34
               [*Roman soldiers enter from
              behind Cleopatra and take her prisoner.*]
You see how easily she may be surprised.
[*To the soldiers*] Guard her till Caesar come.

IRAS   Royal Queen!

CHARMIAN
Oh, Cleopatra! Thou art taken, Queen.

CLEOPATRA [*drawing a dagger*]
Quick, quick, good hands.

PROCULEIUS   Hold, worthy lady, hold!
                      [*He disarms her.*]
Do not yourself such wrong, who are in this
Relieved, but not betrayed.

CLEOPATRA   What, of death too,   40
That rids our dogs of languish?

PROCULEIUS   Cleopatra,   41
Do not abuse my master's bounty by
Th'undoing of yourself. Let the world see
His nobleness well acted, which your death   44
Will never let come forth.

CLEOPATRA   Where art thou, Death?   45
Come hither, come! Come, come, and take a queen

Worth many babes and beggars!

PROCULEIUS   Oh, temperance, lady!   47

CLEOPATRA
Sir, I will eat no meat, I'll not drink, sir;
If idle talk will once be necessary,   49
I'll not sleep, neither. This mortal house I'll ruin,
Do Caesar what he can. Know, sir, that I
Will not wait pinioned at your master's court,   52
Nor once be chastised with the sober eye
Of dull Octavia. Shall they hoist me up
And show me to the shouting varletry   55
Of censuring Rome? Rather a ditch in Egypt
Be gentle grave unto me! Rather on Nilus' mud
Lay me stark nak'd and let the waterflies
Blow me into abhorring! Rather make   59
My country's high pyramides my gibbet   60
And hang me up in chains!

PROCULEIUS   You do extend
These thoughts of horror further than you shall
Find cause in Caesar.

             Enter Dolabella.

DOLABELLA   Proculeius,
What thou hast done thy master Caesar knows,
And he hath sent for thee. For the Queen,   65
I'll take her to my guard.

PROCULEIUS   So, Dolabella,
It shall content me best. Be gentle to her.
[*To Cleopatra*] To Caesar I will speak what you shall
   please,   68
If you'll employ me to him.

CLEOPATRA   Say I would die.
           Exit Proculeius [*with soldiers*].

DOLABELLA
Most noble Empress, you have heard of me?

CLEOPATRA
I cannot tell.

DOLABELLA   Assuredly you know me.

CLEOPATRA
No matter, sir, what I have heard or known.
You laugh when boys or women tell their dreams;
Is't not your trick?

DOLABELLA   I understand not, madam.   74

CLEOPATRA
I dreamt there was an emperor Antony.
Oh, such another sleep, that I might see
But such another man!

DOLABELLA   If it might please ye—

CLEOPATRA
His face was as the heavens, and therein stuck   78
A sun and moon, which kept their course and lighted

---

14 do . . . to be am wary of being   **15 That** since I   **20 as that**
23 Make . . . reference Refer your case   **26 dependency** submissiveness   **27 pray . . . kindness** beg your assistance to ensure that he may
omit no kindness   **29–30 I send . . . got** i.e., I acknowledge his superiority over all he has won, including myself.   **34 Of** by.   **34.1** *Roman
soldiers* (Perhaps led by Gallus; see 5.1.69. Possibly some speech for
him has been omitted.)   **40 Relieved** rescued.   **of death too** i.e.,
(1) am I *relieved* or deprived even of death (2) am I *betrayed* even of the
right to die   **41 our dogs of languish** even our dogs of lingering disease.   **44 acted** accomplished   **45 let come forth** allow to be displayed.

47 babes and beggars i.e., those whom death takes easily and often.
49 If . . . necessary even if on occasion I must resort to idle talk (to
keep myself awake)   **52 wait pinioned** wait in attendance, like a bird
with clipped wings, unable to fly   **55 varletry** rabble   **59 Blow . . .
abhorring** cause me to swell abhorrently with maggots, or, deposit
their eggs on me until I become abhorrent.   **60 gibbet** gallows
65 For As for   **68 what** whatever   **74 trick** manner, way.   **78 stuck**
were set

The little O, the earth.

DOLABELLA　　　　　　Most sovereign creature—

CLEOPATRA　His legs bestrid the ocean; his reared arm 81
Crested the world; his voice was propertied 82
As all the tunèd spheres, and that to friends; 83
But when he meant to quail and shake the orb, 84
He was as rattling thunder. For his bounty, 85
There was no winter in't; an autumn 'twas
That grew the more by reaping. His delights 87
Were dolphinlike; they showed his back above 88
The element they lived in. In his livery 89
Walked crowns and crownets; realms and islands
were 90
As plates dropped from his pocket.

DOLABELLA　　　　　　　　　Cleopatra— 91

CLEOPATRA
Think you there was or might be such a man
As this I dreamt of?

DOLABELLA　　　　　Gentle madam, no.

CLEOPATRA
You lie, up to the hearing of the gods.
But if there be nor ever were one such, 95
It's past the size of dreaming. Nature wants stuff 96
To vie strange forms with fancy; yet t'imagine 97
An Antony were nature's piece 'gainst fancy, 98
Condemning shadows quite.

DOLABELLA　　　　　　Hear me, good madam: 99
Your loss is as yourself, great; and you bear it
As answering to the weight. Would I might never 101
O'ertake pursued success but I do feel, 102
By the rebound of yours, a grief that smites
My very heart at root.

CLEOPATRA　　　　　I thank you, sir.
Know you what Caesar means to do with me?

DOLABELLA
I am loath to tell you what I would you knew.

CLEOPATRA
Nay, pray you, sir.

DOLABELLA　　　　　Though he be honorable—

CLEOPATRA　He'll lead me, then, in triumph.

DOLABELLA　Madam, he will, I know't.　　　　Flourish.

*Enter Proculeius, Caesar, Gallus, Maecenas,
and others of his train.*

ALL　Make way there! Caesar!

CAESAR　Which is the Queen of Egypt?

DOLABELLA　It is the Emperor, madam.

　　　　　　　　　　　　　　Cleopatra kneels.

CAESAR　Arise, you shall not kneel. I pray you, rise.
Rise, Egypt.

CLEOPATRA [*rising*] Sir, the gods will have it thus;
My master and my lord I must obey.

CAESAR　Take to you no hard thoughts. 116
The record of what injuries you did us,
Though written in our flesh, we shall remember
As things but done by chance.

CLEOPATRA　　　　　Sole sir o'th' world, 119
I cannot project mine own cause so well 120
To make it clear, but do confess I have 121
Been laden with like frailties which before
Have often shamed our sex.

CAESAR　　　　　Cleopatra, know
We will extenuate rather than enforce. 124
If you apply yourself to our intents, 125
Which towards you are most gentle, you shall find
A benefit in this change; but if you seek
To lay on me a cruelty by taking 128
Antony's course, you shall bereave yourself 129
Of my good purposes and put your children
To that destruction which I'll guard them from
If thereon you rely. I'll take my leave.

CLEOPATRA
And may, through all the world! 'Tis yours, and we, 133
Your scutcheons and your signs of conquest, shall 134
Hang in what place you please. Here, my good lord. 135
　　　　　　　　　　　　[*She gives him a scroll.*]

CAESAR
You shall advise me in all for Cleopatra. 136

CLEOPATRA
This is the brief of money, plate, and jewels 137
I am possessed of. 'Tis exactly valued,
Not petty things admitted. Where's Seleucus? 139

　　　　　　[*Enter Seleucus.*]

SELEUCUS　Here, madam.

CLEOPATRA
This is my treasurer. Let him speak, my lord,
Upon his peril, that I have reserved
To myself nothing.—Speak the truth, Seleucus.

SELEUCUS
Madam, I had rather seal my lips
Than to my peril speak that which is not.

CLEOPATRA　What have I kept back?

SELEUCUS
Enough to purchase what you have made known.

---

81 bestrid straddled (like the Colossus of Rhodes)　**82 Crested** surmounted　**82–3 propertied . . . friends** endowed with qualities which, when he spoke to friends, recalled the harmony of the heavenly bodies in their spheres　**84 quail** make quail, overawe.　**orb** world　**85 For** As for　**87–9 His . . . in** i.e., Like the dolphin sportfully rising up out of the sea, his pleasures arose out of the element in which he lived, both glorying in and transcending that element. **89–90 In . . . crownets** i.e., Among his retainers (those who would wear his livery) were kings and princes　**91 plates** coins　**95 nor ever were** or if there never existed　**96 It's . . . dreaming** no dream can come up to it, my image of him.　**96–9 Nature . . . quite** Nature lacks material to equal the remarkable forms produced by fancy or imagination; yet an Antony such as I have pictured forth would himself be a work of nature, in fact would be Nature's masterpiece in competition with the imagination.　**101 As . . . weight** commensurate with the weightiness of the loss.　**101–2 Would . . . feel** May I never succeed at what I desire if I do not feel

116 Take . . . thoughts Don't torment yourself with reproaches. **119 sir** master　**120 project** set forth　**121 clear** free of blame **124 enforce** press home.　**125 If . . . intents** If you comply with my plans　**128 lay . . . cruelty** force me to be cruel　**129 bereave** rob **133 And may** i.e., (1) You may leave when you choose (2) You may have your will in anything　**134 scutcheons** shields showing armorial bearings; hence, shields hung up as monuments of victory **135 Hang** be hung up in display as your trophies. (But with a hidden suggestion of "be hanged as your captives.")　**136 in all for Cleopatra** i.e., in all matters pertaining to yourself.　**137 brief** list　**139 Not . . . admitted** petty things omitted.

CAESAR
    Nay, blush not, Cleopatra. I approve
    Your wisdom in the deed.
CLEOPATRA   See, Caesar! Oh, behold
    How pomp is followed! Mine will now be yours,   150
    And, should we shift estates, yours would be mine.   151
    The ingratitude of this Seleucus does
    Even make me wild.—Oh, slave, of no more trust
    Than love that's hired! [*Seleucus retreats from her.*]
        What, goest thou back? Thou shalt   154
    Go back, I warrant thee! But I'll catch thine eyes,
    Though they had wings. Slave, soulless villain, dog!
    Oh, rarely base!
CAESAR   Good Queen, let us entreat you.   157
CLEOPATRA
    Oh, Caesar, what a wounding shame is this,
    That thou vouchsafing here to visit me,   159
    Doing the honor of thy lordliness
    To one so meek, that mine own servant should
    Parcel the sum of my disgraces by   162
    Addition of his envy! Say, good Caesar,   163
    That I some lady trifles have reserved,   164
    Immoment toys, things of such dignity   165
    As we greet modern friends withal, and say   166
    Some nobler token I have kept apart
    For Livia and Octavia, to induce   168
    Their mediation; must I be unfolded   169
    With one that I have bred? The gods! It smites me   170
    Beneath the fall I have. [*To Seleucus*] Prithee, go hence,
    Or I shall show the cinders of my spirits   172
    Through th'ashes of my chance. Wert thou a man,   173
    Thou wouldst have mercy on me.
CAESAR   Forbear, Seleucus.   [*Exit Seleucus.*]   175
CLEOPATRA
    Be it known that we, the greatest, are misthought   176
    For things that others do; and when we fall
    We answer others' merits in our name,   178
    Are therefore to be pitied.
CAESAR   Cleopatra,
    Not what you have reserved nor what acknowledged
    Put we i'th' roll of conquest. Still be't yours;
    Bestow it at your pleasure, and believe   182
    Caesar's no merchant, to make prize with you   183
    Of things that merchants sold. Therefore be cheered.
    Make not your thoughts your prisons. No, dear
        Queen,   185
    For we intend so to dispose you as   186

    Yourself shall give us counsel. Feed and sleep.
    Our care and pity is so much upon you
    That we remain your friend; and so adieu.
CLEOPATRA
    My master, and my lord!
CAESAR   Not so. Adieu.
                    Flourish. Exeunt Caesar and his train.
CLEOPATRA
    He words me, girls, he words me, that I should not   191
    Be noble to myself. But hark thee, Charmian.   192
                    [*She whispers to Charmian.*]
IRAS
    Finish, good lady. The bright day is done,
    And we are for the dark.
CLEOPATRA [*to Charmian*]   Hie thee again.   194
    I have spoke already, and it is provided;   195
    Go put it to the haste.
CHARMIAN   Madam, I will.

                    Enter Dolabella.

DOLABELLA
    Where's the Queen?
CHARMIAN   Behold, sir.   [*Exit.*]
CLEOPATRA   Dolabella!
DOLABELLA
    Madam, as thereto sworn by your command,
    Which my love makes religion to obey,
    I tell you this: Caesar through Syria
    Intends his journey, and within three days
    You with your children will he send before.
    Make your best use of this. I have performed
    Your pleasure and my promise.
CLEOPATRA   Dolabella,
    I shall remain your debtor.
DOLABELLA   I your servant.
    Adieu, good Queen. I must attend on Caesar.
CLEOPATRA
    Farewell, and thanks.   *Exit* [*Dolabella*].
                    Now, Iras, what think'st thou?
    Thou an Egyptian puppet shall be shown
    In Rome as well as I. Mechanic slaves   209
    With greasy aprons, rules, and hammers shall   210
    Uplift us to the view. In their thick breaths,
    Rank of gross diet, shall we be enclouded   212
    And forced to drink their vapor.
IRAS   The gods forbid!   213
CLEOPATRA
    Nay, 'tis most certain, Iras. Saucy lictors   214
    Will catch at us like strumpets, and scald rhymers   215
    Ballad us out o' tune. The quick comedians   216
    Extemporally will stage us and present   217

---

150 **How . . . followed!** how greatness is served! **Mine** All the pomp
and following that attends me   151 **shift estates** reverse fortunes,
exchange places   154 **hired** paid for.   157 **rarely** exceptionally
159 **vouchsafing** deigning to come   162 **Parcel** particularize
163 **envy** malice.   164 **lady** ladylike, feminine   165 **Immoment toys**
trifles of no moment or importance   166 **modern** common.   **withal**
with   168 **Livia** Octavius Caesar's wife   169–70 **unfolded . . . bred**
exposed by one of my household.   172 **cinders** smoldering hot coals
173 **chance** (fallen) fortune.   175 **Forbear** Withdraw   176 **mis-
thought** misjudged   178 **We . . . name** we are accountable for the
deeds of others done in our name   182 **Bestow** use   183 **make prize**
haggle   185 **Make . . . prisons** i.e., Don't imprison yourself in your
thoughts by misconceiving of your situation.   186 **dispose** dispose of

191–2 **he words . . . myself** he tries to deceive me with mere words to
keep me from suicide.   194 **Hie thee again** Return quickly.   195
spoke given orders (for the means of suicide)   209 **Mechanic slaves**
Common laborers   210 **rules** straight-edged measuring sticks
212 **Rank . . . diet** reeking of coarse food   213 **drink** drink in, breathe
deeply   214 **lictors** minor officials in attendance on Roman magistrates   215 **scald** scurvy   216 **Ballad us** sing ballads about us.
quick quick-witted   217 **Extemporally** in improvised performance

Our Alexandrian revels; Antony
Shall be brought drunken forth, and I shall see
Some squeaking Cleopatra boy my greatness   220
I'th' posture of a whore.

IRAS   O the good gods!

CLEOPATRA   Nay, that's certain.

IRAS

I'll never see't! For I am sure my nails
Are stronger than mine eyes.

CLEOPATRA   Why, that's the way
To fool their preparation and to conquer
Their most absurd intents.

        Enter Charmian.

                            Now, Charmian!
Show me, my women, like a queen. Go fetch   227
My best attires. I am again for Cydnus,
To meet Mark Antony. Sirrah Iras, go—   229
Now, noble Charmian, we'll dispatch indeed—   230
And when thou hast done this chare I'll give thee
    leave   231
To play till doomsday. Bring our crown and all.   232
        [Exit Iras.] A noise within.
Wherefore's this noise?

        Enter a Guardsman.

GUARDSMAN   Here is a rural fellow
That will not be denied Your Highness' presence.
He brings you figs.

CLEOPATRA
Let him come in.   *Exit Guardsman.*
            What poor an instrument   236
May do a noble deed! He brings me liberty.
My resolution's placed, and I have nothing   238
Of woman in me. Now from head to foot
I am marble-constant; now the fleeting moon   240
No planet is of mine.

        *Enter Guardsman, and Clown [bringing in a
        basket].*

GUARDSMAN   This is the man.   241

CLEOPATRA   Avoid, and leave him.   *Exit Guardsman.*   242
Hast thou the pretty worm of Nilus there,   243
That kills and pains not?

CLOWN   Truly, I have him, but I would not be the party
that should desire you to touch him, for his biting is
immortal. Those that do die of it do seldom or never   247
recover.

CLEOPATRA   Remember'st thou any that have died on't?

CLOWN   Very many, men and women too. I heard of   250
one of them no longer than yesterday—a very honest
woman, but something given to lie, as a woman   252
should not do but in the way of honesty—how she
died of the biting of it, what pain she felt. Truly, she
makes a very good report o'th' worm. But he that will
believe all that they say shall never be saved by half   256
that they do. But this is most falliable, the worm's an   257
odd worm.

CLEOPATRA   Get thee hence, farewell.

CLOWN   I wish you all joy of the worm.
        [He sets down his basket.]

CLEOPATRA   Farewell.

CLOWN   You must think this, look you, that the worm
will do his kind.   263

CLEOPATRA   Ay, ay; farewell.

CLOWN   Look you, the worm is not to be trusted but in
the keeping of wise people, for indeed there is no
goodness in the worm.

CLEOPATRA   Take thou no care; it shall be heeded.   268

CLOWN   Very good. Give it nothing, I pray you, for it is
not worth the feeding.

CLEOPATRA   Will it eat me?

CLOWN   You must not think I am so simple but I know
the devil himself will not eat a woman. I know that a
woman is a dish for the gods, if the devil dress her   274
not. But truly, these same whoreson devils do the   275
gods great harm in their women, for in every ten that
they make, the devils mar five.

CLEOPATRA   Well, get thee gone. Farewell.

CLOWN   Yes, forsooth. I wish you joy o'th' worm.
                                    Exit.

        [Enter Iras with royal attire.]

CLEOPATRA
Give me my robe. Put on my crown. I have
Immortal longings in me. Now no more   281
The juice of Egypt's grape shall moist this lip.
        [The women dress her.]
Yare, yare, good Iras; quick. Methinks I hear   283
Antony call; I see him rouse himself
To praise my noble act. I hear him mock
The luck of Caesar, which the gods give men   286
To excuse their after wrath. Husband, I come!   287
Now to that name my courage prove my title!   288
I am fire and air; my other elements   289

---

250 **heard of** heard from   252 **to lie** (With sexual second meaning hinted at also in *honest*, i.e., "chaste," *die*, i.e., "reach orgasm," and *worm*.)   256 **all . . . half** (The Clown comically reverses the sensible order of these two words.)   257 **falliable** (Blunder for "infallible.")   263 **his kind** its natural function.   268 **Take thou no care** Don't worry   274 **dress** prepare, as in cooking. (With a suggestion also of dressing in alluring clothes.)   275 **whoreson** i.e., rascally, abominable. (A slang expression.)   281 **Immortal longings** longings for immortality   283 **Yare** Quickly   286–7 **which . . . wrath** the luck that the gods give men when they intend to mock and punish them subsequently for their hubris.   288 **to . . . title!** may my courage prove my right to call myself Antony's wife!   289 **other elements** i.e., earth and water, the heavier elements

220 **boy** (Allusion to the practice of having women's parts acted by boys on the Elizabethan stage.)   227 **Show** Display   229 **Sirrah** (Compare *sirs*, addressed to the women, in 4.15.90.)   230 **dispatch** (1) finish (2) hasten   231 **chare** task, chore   232.1 *Exit Iras* (It is possible that Charmian leaves, too.)   236 **What** How   238 **placed** fixed   240 **fleeting** inconstant, changing   241 **s.d.** *Clown* rustic   242 **Avoid** Withdraw   243 **worm** snake, serpent. (But elsewhere in this scene with the added connotations of "the male sexual organ" and "earthworm.")   247 **immortal** (Blunder for "mortal.")

I give to baser life. So, have you done?
Come then, and take the last warmth of my lips.
Farewell, kind Charmian. Iras, long farewell.
> [*She kisses them. Iras falls and dies.*]

Have I the aspic in my lips? Dost fall?   293
If thou and nature can so gently part,
The stroke of death is as a lover's pinch,
Which hurts, and is desired. Dost thou lie still?
If thus thou vanishest, thou tell'st the world
It is not worth leave-taking.   298

CHARMIAN
Dissolve, thick cloud, and rain, that I may say
The gods themselves do weep!

CLEOPATRA   This proves me base.
If she first meet the curlèd Antony,   301
He'll make demand of her, and spend that kiss   302
Which is my heaven to have. [*To an asp*] Come, thou
    mortal wretch,   303
With thy sharp teeth this knot intrinsicate   304
Of life at once untie. Poor venomous fool,
Be angry, and dispatch. Oh, couldst thou speak,
That I might hear thee call great Caesar ass
Unpolicied!

CHARMIAN   O eastern star!

CLEOPATRA   Peace, peace!   308
Dost thou not see my baby at my breast,
That sucks the nurse asleep?

CHARMIAN   Oh, break! Oh, break!

CLEOPATRA
As sweet as balm, as soft as air, as gentle—
O Antony!—Nay, I will take thee too.
> [*Applying another asp to her arm.*]

What should I stay—   *Dies.* 313

CHARMIAN
In this wild world? So, fare thee well.   314
Now boast thee, Death, in thy possession lies
A lass unparalleled. Downy windows, close;   316
And golden Phoebus never be beheld
Of eyes again so royal! Your crown's awry;   318
I'll mend it, and then play—   319

> *Enter the Guard, rustling in.*

FIRST GUARD
Where's the Queen?

CHARMIAN   Speak softly. Wake her not.

FIRST GUARD
Caesar hath sent—

CHARMIAN   Too slow a messenger.
> [*She applies an asp to herself.*]

Oh, come apace, dispatch! I partly feel thee.

FIRST GUARD
Approach, ho! All's not well. Caesar's beguiled.   323

SECOND GUARD
There's Dolabella sent from Caesar. Call him.
> [*Exit a guard.*]

FIRST GUARD
What work is here, Charmian? Is this well done?

CHARMIAN
It is well done, and fitting for a princess
Descended of so many royal kings.
Ah, soldier!   *Charmian dies.*

> *Enter Dolabella.*

DOLABELLA
How goes it here?

SECOND GUARD   All dead.

DOLABELLA   Caesar, thy thoughts
Touch their effects in this. Thyself art coming   330
To see performed the dreaded act which thou
So sought'st to hinder.

> *Enter Caesar and all his train, marching.*

ALL   A way there, a way for Caesar!   333

DOLABELLA
Oh, sir, you are too sure an augurer;
That you did fear is done.

CAESAR   Bravest at the last,   335
She leveled at our purposes and, being royal,   336
Took her own way. The manner of their deaths?
I do not see them bleed.

DOLABELLA   Who was last with them?

FIRST GUARD
A simple countryman, that brought her figs.   339
This was his basket.

CAESAR   Poisoned, then.

FIRST GUARD   Oh, Caesar,
This Charmian lived but now; she stood and spake.
I found her trimming up the diadem
On her dead mistress; tremblingly she stood,
And on the sudden dropped.

CAESAR   Oh, noble weakness!
If they had swallowed poison, 'twould appear
By external swelling; but she looks like sleep,   346
As she would catch another Antony   347
In her strong toil of grace.

DOLABELLA   Here on her breast   348
There is a vent of blood and something blown;   349
The like is on her arm.

---

293 **aspic** asp   298 **is . . . leave-taking** does not deserve a ceremonious farewell.   301 **curlèd** with curled hair   302 **make demand**
(1) ask questions (2) ask pleasure.   **spend that kiss** expend his desire
on her   303 **mortal** deadly.   **wretch** (An affectionate term of abuse,
like *fool* in line 305.)   304 **intrinsicate** intricate   308 **Unpolicied** outwitted.   **eastern star** i.e., Venus, the morning star.   313 **What** Why
314 **wild** savage. (Sometimes emended to *vild*, "vile.")   316 **Downy
windows** i.e., Soft eyelids   318 **Of** by   319 **mend** fix, straighten

323 **beguiled** cheated, tricked.   330 **Touch their effects** meet with
realization   333 **A way** Make a path   335 **That** that which   336 **leveled at** aimed at, guessed   339 **simple** humbly born   346 **like sleep**
as if asleep   347 **As** as if   348 **toil** net   349 **vent** discharge.   **blown**
deposited, or, swollen

FIRST GUARD
  This is an aspic's trail, and these fig leaves
  Have slime upon them, such as th'aspic leaves
  Upon the caves of Nile.
CAESAR   Most probable
  That so she died; for her physician tells me
  She hath pursued conclusions infinite   355
  Of easy ways to die. Take up her bed,
  And bear her women from the monument.
  She shall be buried by her Antony.
  No grave upon the earth shall clip in it   359

355 **conclusions** experiments   359 **clip** embrace, clasp

  A pair so famous. High events as these
  Strike those that make them; and their story is   361
  No less in pity than his glory which   362
  Brought them to be lamented. Our army shall   363
  In solemn show attend this funeral,
  And then to Rome. Come, Dolabella, see
  High order in this great solemnity.   366
              Exeunt omnes, [bearing the dead bodies].

361 Strike . . . them touch with sorrow those who brought about
these deeds   **361–3 their story . . . lamented** the story of these
famous lovers is no less pitiable than the fame of him who brought
them low is glorious.   **366.1** *omnes* all

The Romances

The Winter's Tale *The Tempest*

The Winter's Tale

The Winter's Tale (c. 1609–1611), with its almost symmetrical division into two halves of bleak tragedy and comic romance, illustrates perhaps more clearly than any other Shakespearean play the genre of tragicomedy. To be sure, all the late romances feature journeys of separation, apparent deaths, and tearful reconciliations. Marina and Thaisa in *Pericles*, Imogen in *Cymbeline*, and Ferdinand in *The Tempest*, all supposed irrecoverably lost, are brought back to life by apparently miraculous devices. Of the four late romances, however, *The Winter's Tale* uses the most formal structure to evoke the antithesis of tragedy and romance. It is sharply divided into contrasting halves by a gap of sixteen years. The tragic first half takes place almost entirely in Sicilia, whereas the action of the second half is limited for the most part to Bohemia. At the court of Sicilia, we see tyrannical jealousy producing a spiritual climate of "winter / In storm perpetual"; in Bohemia, we witness a pastoral landscape and a sheepshearing evoking "the sweet o'th' year," "When daffodils begin to peer" (3.2.212–13; 4.3.1–3). Paradoxically, the contrast between the two halves is intensified by parallels between the two: both begin with Camillo onstage and proceed to scenes of confrontation and jealousy in which, ironically, the innocent cause of jealousy in the first half, Polixenes, becomes the jealous tyrant of the second half. The mirroring reminds us of the cyclical nature of time and the hope it brings of renewal as we move from tragedy to romantic comedy.

Although this motif of a renewing journey from jaded court to idealized countryside reminds us of *As You Like It* and other early comedies, we sense in the late romances and especially in *The Winter's Tale* a new preoccupation with humanity's tragic folly. The vision of human depravity is world-weary and pessimistic, as though infected by the gloomy spirit of the great tragedies. And because humanity is so bent on destroying itself, the restoration is at once more urgently needed and more miraculous than in the "festive" world of early comedy. Renewal is mythically associated with the seasonal cycle from winter to summer.

King Leontes's tragedy seems at first irreversible and terrifying, like that of Shakespeare's greatest tragic protagonists. He suffers from irrational jealousy, as does Othello, and attempts to destroy the person on whom all his happiness depends. As with Othello, his jealousy stems from a characteristically male fear of inadequacy and rejection. Unlike Othello, however, Leontes needs no diabolical tempter such as Iago to poison his mind against Queen Hermione. Leontes is undone by his own fantasies. No differences in race or age can explain Leontes's fears of estrangement from Hermione. She is not imprudent in her conduct, like her counterpart in Robert Greene's *Pandosto* (1588), the prose romance from which Shakespeare drew his narrative. Although Hermione is graciously fond of Leontes's dear friend Polixenes and urges him to stay longer in Sicilia, she does so only with a hospitable warmth demanded by the occasion and encouraged by her husband. In every way, then, Shakespeare strips away from Leontes the motive and the occasion for plausible doubting of his wife. All observers in the Sicilian court are incredulous and shocked at the King's accusations. Even so, Leontes is neither an unsympathetic nor an unbelievable character. Like Othello, Leontes cherishes his wife and perceives with a horrifying intensity what a fearful cost they both must pay for his suspicions. Not only his marriage, but also his lifelong friendship with Polixenes, his sense of pride in his children, and his enjoyment of his subjects' warm regard, all must be sacrificed to a single overwhelming compulsion.

Whatever may be the psychological cause of this obsession, it manifests itself as a revulsion against all sexual behavior. Like mad Lear, Leontes imagines lechery to be the unavoidable fact of the cosmos and of the human condition, the lowest common denominator to which all persons (including Hermione) must stoop. He is persuaded that "It is a bawdy planet," in which cuckolded man has "his pond fished by his next neighbor, by / Sir Smile, his neighbor" (1.2.195–201). Leontes's tortured soliloquies are laden with sexual images, of unattended "gates" letting in and out the enemy "With bag and baggage," and of a "dagger" that must be "muzzled / Lest it should bite its master" (lines 197, 206, 156–7). As in *King Lear*, order is inverted to disorder, sanity to madness, legitimacy to illegitimacy. Sexual misconduct is emblematic of a universal malaise: "Why, then the world and all that's in't is nothing, / The covering sky is nothing, Bohemia nothing, / My wife is nothing" (lines 292–4). Other characters, too, see the trial of Hermione as a testing of humanity's worth: if Hermione proves false, Antigonus promises, he will treat his own wife as a stable horse and will "geld" his three daughters (2.1.148). Prevailing images are of spiders, venom, infection, sterility, and the "dungy earth" (line 158).

Cosmic order is never really challenged, however, even though the human suffering is very real and the injustice to women especially apparent. Leontes's fantasies of universal disorder are chimerical. His wife is, in fact, chaste, Polixenes true, and the King's courtiers loyal. Camillo refuses to carry out Leontes's order to murder Polixenes, not only because he knows murder to be wrong, but also because history offers not one example of a man "that had struck anointed kings / And flourished after" (1.2.357–8). The cosmos of this play is one in which crimes are invariably and swiftly punished. The Delphic oracle vindicates Hermione and gives Leontes stern warning. When Leontes persists in his madness, his son Mamillius's death follows as an immediate consequence. As Leontes at once perceives, "Apollo's angry, and the heavens themselves / Do strike at my injustice" (3.2.146–7). Leontes paradoxically welcomes the lengthy contrition he must undergo, for it confirms a pattern in the universe of just cause and effect. Although as tragic protagonist he has discovered the truth about Hermione moments too late and so must pay richly for his error, Leontes has at least recovered faith in Hermione's transcendent goodness. His nightmare now over, he accepts and embraces suffering as a necessary atonement.

The transition to romance is therefore anticipated to an extent by the play's first half, even though the tone of the last two acts is strikingly different. The old Shepherd signals a momentous change when he speaks to his son of a cataclysmic storm and a ravenous bear set in opposition to the miraculous discovery of a child: "Now bless thyself. Thou met'st with things dying, I with things newborn" (3.3.110–11). Time comes onstage as Chorus, like Gower in *Pericles*, to remind us of the conscious artifice of the dramatist. He can "o'erthrow law" and carry us over sixteen years as if we had merely dreamed out the interim (4.1). Shakespeare flaunts the improbability

of his story by giving Bohemia a seacoast (much to the distress of Ben Jonson) and by bringing onstage either a live bear or an actor costumed as one ("*Exit, pursued by a bear,*" 3.3.57 s.d.). The narrative uses many typical devices of romance: a babe abandoned to the elements, a princess brought up by shepherds, a prince disguised as a swain, a sea voyage, and a recognition scene. Love is threatened, not by the internal psychic obstacle of jealousy, but by the external obstacles of parental opposition and a seeming disparity of social rank between the lovers. Comedy easily finds solutions for such difficulties by the unraveling of illusion. This comic world also properly includes clownish shepherds, coy shepherdesses, and Autolycus, the roguish peddler, whose machinations contribute in an unforeseen manner to the working out of the love plot. Autolycus is in many ways the presiding genius of the play's second half, as dominant a character as Leontes in the first half and one whose delightful function is to do good "against my will" (5.2.125). In this paradox of knavery converted surprisingly to benign ends, we see how the comic providence of Shakespeare's tragicomic world makes use of the most implausible and outrageous happenings in pursuit of its own inscrutable design.

The conventional romantic ending is infused, however, with a sadness and a mystery that take the play well beyond what is usual in comedy. Mamillius and Antigonus are really dead, and that irredeemable fact is not forgotten in the play's final happy moments. Hermione, although vindicated by the gods, has suffered public shame, the death of one child, separation from her other child, and prolonged isolation from her husband; like Imogen in *Cymbeline*, she has had to endure the consequences of male frailty and thereby redeem her husband through her suffering. Her husband, having thrown her aside, must, like Pericles, rediscover and learn to cherish the woman he once chose who now has aged; he must reconfirm his marriage to her, even as he learns to accept the marriage of his daughter to a younger man. All of these crucial turnings hinge upon Shakespeare's most notable departure from his source, Greene's *Pandosto*: Hermione is brought back to life. All observers regard this event, and the rediscovery of Perdita, as grossly implausible, "so like an old tale that the verity of it is in strong suspicion" (5.2.29–30). The play's very title, *The Winter's Tale*, reinforces this sense of naive improbability. Why does Shakespeare stress this riddling paradox of an unbelievable reality, and why does he deliberately mislead his audience into believing that Hermione has, in fact, died (3.3.15–45), using a kind of theatrical trickery found in no other Shakespearean play? The answer may well be that, in Paulina's words, we must awake our faith, accepting a narrative of death and return to life that cannot ultimately be comprehended by reason. On the rational level, we are told that Hermione has been kept in hiding for sixteen years, in order to fulfill the condition of the oracle that Leontes is to live without an heir (and hence without a wife) until Perdita is found. Such an explanation seems psychologically incomprehensible, however, for it demands that Hermione live in extended isolation and that Paulina serve as the King's conscience for such a long period of time without any way for the participants to know when their suffering will end. Instead, we are drawn toward an emblematic interpretation, bearing in mind that it is more an evocative hint than a complete truth. Throughout the play, Hermione has been repeatedly associated with "Grace" and with the goddess Proserpina, whose return from the underworld, after "Three crabbèd months had soured themselves to death" (1.2.102), signals the coming of spring. Perdita, also associated with Proserpina (4.4.116), is welcomed by her father "As is the spring to th' earth" (5.1.152). The emphasis on the bond of father and daughter, so characteristic of Shakespeare's late plays and especially his romances, goes importantly beyond the patriarchalism of Shakespeare's earlier history plays in its exploration of family relationships. Paulina has a similarly emblematic role, that of Conscience, patiently guiding the King to a divinely appointed renewal of his joy. Paulina speaks of herself as an artist figure, like Prospero in *The Tempest*, performing wonders of illusion, though she rejects the assistance of wicked powers. These emblematic hints do not rob the story of its human drama, but they do lend a transcendent signifi-cance to Leontes's bittersweet story of sinful error, affliction, and an unexpected second happiness.

On stage in recent decades, the play has shown its remarkable dramaturgic effectiveness, especially in the restoration of Hermione to her husband as a living and breathing statue. Peter Brook, at the Phoenix Theatre in London, 1951, chose a permanent set to underscore the play's malleable swift action and its need for the audience to participate imaginatively in the fashioning of theatrical illusion. Trevor Nunn's set at Stratford-upon-Avon in 1969 was a three-sided white box in which nothing was realistically represented. Nunn and John Barton, at Stratford-upon-Avon in 1976, visualized bears everywhere: in motifs of wall hangings and carpets, in a bearskin draped on a couch. The violent irrationality of Ian McKellen's Leontes seemed plausible in such a symbolic and mythic landscape. In Terry Hands's 1986 production also at Stratford-upon-Avon, a huge bear rug on the cool marble floor of Leontes's Regency palace during the play's first half became, in Bohemia, the live bear that tore into the shoulder of Antigonus. Above all, the apparent bringing back to life of Hermione's statue in the final scene has proven again and again to be a masterly *coup de théâtre*. What we see in the theater is of course an illusion, but at what level? Are we to understand that a statue comes to life? Much depends on the actress's skill in appearing motionless and then warm to her husband's touch. The moment is indeed one calculated to awaken our faith in the miracle of renewal and in the power of art to confound illusion and reality. We are led to ponder deeply the mysteries of our own uncertain existence.

The Winter's Tale

The Names of the Actors

LEONTES, *King of Sicilia*
MAMILLIUS, *young prince of Sicilia*
CAMILLO,
ANTIGONUS,
CLEOMENES, } *four Lords of Sicilia*
DION,

HERMIONE, *Queen to Leontes*
PERDITA, *daughter to Leontes and Hermione*
PAULINA, *wife to Antigonus*
EMILIA, *a lady [attending on Hermione]*

POLIXENES, *King of Bohemia*
FLORIZEL, *Prince of Bohemia*
ARCHIDAMUS, *a lord of Bohemia*
Old SHEPHERD, *reputed father of Perdita*
CLOWN, *his son*
AUTOLYCUS, *a rogue*

[SCENE: *Sicilia, and Bohemia*]

[MOPSA,
[DORCAS, } *Shepherdesses*]

[A MARINER
A JAILER
Two LADIES *attending Hermione*
Two SERVANTS *attending Leontes*
One or more LORDS *attending Leontes*
An OFFICER *of the court*
A GENTLEMAN *attending Leontes*
Three GENTLEMEN *of the court of Sicilia*
A SERVANT *of the Old Shepherd*

TIME, *as Chorus*]

Other Lords and Gentlemen, [Ladies, Officers,] and
Servants; Shepherds and Shepherdesses; [Twelve
Countrymen disguised as Satyrs]

1.1

Enter Camillo and Archidamus.

ARCHIDAMUS If you shall chance, Camillo, to visit Bohemia on the like occasion whereon my services are ²
now on foot, you shall see, as I have said, great ³
difference betwixt our Bohemia and your Sicilia.

CAMILLO I think this coming summer the King of Sicilia
means to pay Bohemia the visitation which he justly ⁶
owes him.

ARCHIDAMUS Wherein our entertainment shall shame ⁸
us, we will be justified in our loves; for indeed— ⁹

CAMILLO Beseech you—

ARCHIDAMUS Verily, I speak it in the freedom of my ¹¹
knowledge. We cannot with such magnificence—in ¹²
so rare—I know not what to say. We will give you
sleepy drinks, that your senses, unintelligent of our ¹⁴
insufficience, may, though they cannot praise us, as
little accuse us.

CAMILLO You pay a great deal too dear for what's
given freely.

ARCHIDAMUS Believe me, I speak as my understanding
instructs me and as mine honesty puts it to utterance.

CAMILLO Sicilia cannot show himself overkind to Bo- ²¹
hemia. They were trained together in their childhoods,
and there rooted betwixt them then such an affection
which cannot choose but branch now. Since their ²⁴
more mature dignities and royal necessities made
separation of their society, their encounters, though ²⁶

1.1. Location: Sicilia. The court of Leontes.
2–3 on the . . . foot on an occasion like this one that I am engaged in
(attending on King Polixenes)   **6 Bohemia** the King of Bohemia.
(Also at lines 21–2.)   **8–9 Wherein . . . loves** In whatever way our
attempts to entertain you will shame us by falling short, we will
make up for by our affection

11–12 in . . . knowledge as my knowledge entitles me to speak.
14 sleepy sleep-inducing.   **unintelligent** unaware   **21 Sicilia** The
King of Sicilia   **24 branch** put forth new growth, flourish. (Also perhaps with opposite and unconscious suggestion of "divide.")
26 their society their being together

805

not personal, hath been royally attorneyed with 27
interchange of gifts, letters, loving embassies, that
they have seemed to be together though absent,
shook hands as over a vast, and embraced as it were 30
from the ends of opposed winds. The heavens con- 31
tinue their loves!

ARCHIDAMUS   I think there is not in the world either
malice or matter to alter it. You have an unspeakable
comfort of your young prince Mamillius. It is a 35
gentleman of the greatest promise that ever came into
my note. 37

CAMILLO   I very well agree with you in the hopes of
him. It is a gallant child, one that indeed physics the 39
subject, makes old hearts fresh. They that went on 40
crutches ere he was born desire yet their life to see him 41
a man.

ARCHIDAMUS   Would they else be content to die?

CAMILLO   Yes, if there were no other excuse why they
should desire to live.

ARCHIDAMUS   If the King had no son, they would desire 46
to live on crutches till he had one.   *Exeunt.* 47

1.2

Enter Leontes, Hermione, Mamillius, Polixenes,
Camillo.

POLIXENES
Nine changes of the wat'ry star hath been   1
The shepherd's note since we have left our throne   2
Without a burden. Time as long again   3
Would be filled up, my brother, with our thanks,
And yet we should for perpetuity   5
Go hence in debt. And therefore, like a cipher,   6
Yet standing in rich place, I multiply   7
With one "We thank you" many thousands more
That go before it.

LEONTES   Stay your thanks awhile
And pay them when you part.

POLIXENES   Sir, that's tomorrow.
I am questioned by my fears of what may chance   11
Or breed upon our absence, that may blow   12
No sneaping winds at home to make us say,   13
"This is put forth too truly." Besides, I have stayed 14

To tire your royalty.

LEONTES   We are tougher, brother,
Than you can put us to't.

POLIXENES   No longer stay.   16

LEONTES
One sev'nnight longer.

POLIXENES   Very sooth, tomorrow.   17

LEONTES
We'll part the time between 's, then, and in that   18
I'll no gainsaying.

POLIXENES   Press me not, beseech you, so. 19
There is no tongue that moves, none, none i' th' world
So soon as yours could win me. So it should now,
Were there necessity in your request, although
'Twere needful I denied it. My affairs
Do even drag me homeward, which to hinder
Were in your love a whip to me, my stay   25
To you a charge and trouble. To save both,   26
Farewell, our brother.

LEONTES   Tongue-tied, our Queen? Speak you.

HERMIONE
I had thought, sir, to have held my peace until   28
You had drawn oaths from him not to stay. You, sir, 29
Charge him too coldly. Tell him you are sure
All in Bohemia's well; this satisfaction   31
The bygone day proclaimed. Say this to him,   32
He's beat from his best ward.

LEONTES   Well said, Hermione.   33

HERMIONE
To tell he longs to see his son were strong.   34
But let him say so then, and let him go.
But let him swear so and he shall not stay;   36
We'll thwack him hence with distaffs.   37
[*To Polixenes*] Yet of your royal presence I'll adventure 38
The borrow of a week. When at Bohemia   39
You take my lord, I'll give him my commission
To let him there a month behind the gest   41
Prefixed for 's parting.—Yet, good deed, Leontes,   42
I love thee not a jar o' th' clock behind   43
What lady she her lord.—You'll stay?

POLIXENES   No, madam.   44

HERMIONE
Nay, but you will?

POLIXENES   I may not, verily.

HERMIONE   Verily?

16 Than . . . to't than anything you can do to try me.   **17 sev'nnight**
week.   **Very sooth** Truly   **18 part the time** split the difference, i.e.,
divide a week in two   **19 I'll no gainsaying** I won't take "no" for an
answer.   **25 Were . . . to me** would be a punishment to me, though
done through love   **26 charge** expense, burden   **28–9 I . . . to stay**
i.e., I almost thought that you were going to get him to swear he *won't*
stay, before I got a chance to say anything.   **31–2 this . . . proclaimed**
yesterday brought news to satisfy on that score.   **32 Say** If you say
33 ward defensive posture. (A fencing term.)   **34 tell** tell us that.
strong a strong argument.   **36 he shall not stay** i.e., we wouldn't let
him stay even if he wanted to   **37 distaffs** sticks used in spinning,
here employed as a domestic kind of weapon.   **38 adventure** risk
39 borrow borrowing   **41–2 To . . . parting** to let him stay there a
month longer than the originally agreed-upon time for his departure.
42 good deed indeed   **43–4 I love . . . lord** I love you not even a tiny
bit (literally, a tick of the clock) less than any noble lady loves her
husband.

You put me off with limber vows; but I, 47
Though you would seek t'unsphere the stars with
  oaths,
Should yet say, "Sir, no going." Verily,
You shall not go. A lady's "verily" is
As potent as a lord's. Will you go yet?
Force me to keep you as a prisoner,
Not like a guest: so you shall pay your fees 53
When you depart, and save your thanks. How say
  you?
My prisoner or my guest? By your dread "verily,"
One of them you shall be.

POLIXENES   Your guest, then, madam.
To be your prisoner should import offending, 57
Which is for me less easy to commit
Than you to punish.

HERMIONE   Not your jailer, then,
But your kind hostess. Come, I'll question you
Of my lord's tricks and yours when you were boys.
You were pretty lordings then?

POLIXENES   We were, fair Queen,
Two lads that thought there was no more behind 63
But such a day tomorrow as today,
And to be boy eternal.

HERMIONE   Was not my lord
The verier wag o'th' two? 66

POLIXENES
We were as twinned lambs that did frisk i'th' sun
And bleat the one at th'other. What we changed 68
Was innocence for innocence; we knew not
The doctrine of ill-doing, nor dreamed
That any did. Had we pursued that life,
And our weak spirits ne'er been higher reared
With stronger blood, we should have answered
  heaven 73
Boldly "Not guilty," the imposition cleared 74
Hereditary ours.

HERMIONE   By this we gather 75
You have tripped since.

POLIXENES   Oh, my most sacred lady,
Temptations have since then been born to 's, for
In those unfledged days was my wife a girl; 78
Your precious self had then not crossed the eyes
Of my young playfellow.

HERMIONE   Grace to boot! 80
Of this make no conclusion, lest you say 81
Your queen and I are devils. Yet go on.
Th'offenses we have made you do we'll answer,
If you first sinned with us, and that with us
You did continue fault, and that you slipped not

With any but with us. 86

LEONTES   Is he won yet?

HERMIONE
He'll stay, my lord.

LEONTES   At my request he would not.
Hermione, my dearest, thou never spok'st
To better purpose.

HERMIONE   Never?

LEONTES   Never but once.

HERMIONE
What? Have I twice said well? When was 't before?
I prithee, tell me. Cram 's with praise and make 's
As fat as tame things. One good deed dying
  tongueless 92
Slaughters a thousand waiting upon that. 93
Our praises are our wages. You may ride 's
With one soft kiss a thousand furlongs ere
With spur we heat an acre. But to th' goal: 96
My last good deed was to entreat his stay.
What was my first? It has an elder sister,
Or I mistake you. Oh, would her name were Grace!
But once before I spoke to the purpose. When?
Nay, let me have't; I long.

LEONTES   Why, that was when
Three crabbèd months had soured themselves to
  death
Ere I could make thee open thy white hand
And clap thyself my love. Then didst thou utter, 104
"I am yours forever."

HERMIONE   'Tis grace indeed.
Why, lo you now, I have spoke to th' purpose twice:
The one forever earned a royal husband,
Th'other for some while a friend.
                    [She gives her hand to Polixenes.]

LEONTES [aside]   Too hot, too hot!
To mingle friendship far is mingling bloods. 109
I have *tremor cordis* on me. My heart dances, 110
But not for joy, not joy. This entertainment 111
May a free face put on, derive a liberty 112
From heartiness, from bounty, fertile bosom, 113
And well become the agent. 'T may, I grant. 114
But to be paddling palms and pinching fingers,
As now they are, and making practiced smiles
As in a looking glass, and then to sigh, as 'twere
The mort o'th' deer; oh, that is entertainment 118
My bosom likes not, nor my brows.—Mamillius, 119
Art thou my boy?

MAMILLIUS   Ay, my good lord.

LEONTES   I'fecks, 120

47 limber limp   **53 fees** payments demanded by jailers of prisoners
at the time of their release   **57 import offending** imply my having
offended   **63 behind** still to come   **66 The verier wag** truly the more
mischievous   **68 changed** exchanged   **73 stronger blood** mature
sexual passions   **74–5 the imposition . . . ours** i.e., being freed from
original sin itself (if we had continued in that state); or, excepting of
course the original sin that is the common condition of all mortals.
78 unfledged not yet feathered, i.e., immature   **80 Grace to boot!**
Heaven help me!   **81 Of . . . conclusion** Don't follow your implied
line of reasoning to its logical conclusion

86 Is he won yet? (Leontes has been out of hearing for much of their
conversation.)   **92 tongueless** unpraised, unsung   **93 Slaughters . . .
that** i.e., will inhibit many other good deeds that would have been
inspired by that praise.   **96 heat** traverse as in a race.   **to th' goal** to
come to the point   **104 clap** clasp hands, pledge   **109 mingling
bloods** (Sexual intercourse was thought to produce a mingling of
bloods.)   **110 tremor cordis** fluttering of the heart   **111 entertainment** i.e., of Polixenes by Hermione   **112 free face** innocent appearance   **113 fertile bosom** i.e., generous affection   **114 well . . . agent**
do credit to the doer.   **118 mort** note sounded on a horn at the death
of the hunted deer   **119 brows** (Alludes to cuckolds' horns, the supposed badge of men whose wives are unfaithful.)   **120 I'fecks** In
faith

Why, that's my bawcock. What, hast smutched thy
  nose?   121
They say it is a copy out of mine. Come, captain,
We must be neat; not neat, but cleanly, captain.   123
And yet the steer, the heifer, and the calf
Are all called neat.—Still virginaling   125
Upon his palm?—How now, you wanton calf?   126
Art thou my calf?
MAMILLIUS   Yes, if you will, my lord.
LEONTES
Thou want'st a rough pash and the shoots that I have   128
To be full like me. Yet they say we are   129
Almost as like as eggs. Women say so,
That will say anything. But were they false
As o'erdyed blacks, as wind, as waters, false   132
As dice are to be wished by one that fixes   133
No bourn twixt his and mine, yet were it true   134
To say this boy were like me. Come, sir page,
Look on me with your welkin eye. Sweet villain!   136
Most dear'st! My collop! Can thy dam?—may't be?—   137
Affection, thy intention stabs the center.   138
Thou dost make possible things not so held,   139
Communicat'st with dreams—how can this be?—   140
With what's unreal thou coactive art,   141
And fellow'st nothing. Then 'tis very credent   142
Thou mayst cojoin with something; and thou dost,   143
And that beyond commission, and I find it,   144
And that to the infection of my brains
And hard'ning of my brows.
POLIXENES   What means Sicilia?   146
HERMIONE
He something seems unsettled.
POLIXENES   How, my lord?   147
What cheer? How is't with you, best brother?
HERMIONE   You look
As if you held a brow of much distraction.
Are you moved, my lord?
LEONTES   No, in good earnest.   150
How sometimes nature will betray its folly,   151
Its tenderness, and make itself a pastime   152
To harder bosoms! Looking on the lines   153

Of my boy's face, methoughts I did recoil   154
Twenty-three years, and saw myself unbreeched,   155
In my green velvet coat, my dagger muzzled   156
Lest it should bite its master and so prove,
As ornaments oft do, too dangerous.
How like, methought, I then was to this kernel,
This squash, this gentleman.—Mine honest friend,   160
Will you take eggs for money?   161
MAMILLIUS   No, my lord, I'll fight.
LEONTES
You will? Why, happy man be 's dole!—My brother,   163
Are you so fond of your young prince as we
Do seem to be of ours?
POLIXENES   If at home, sir,
He's all my exercise, my mirth, my matter,   166
Now my sworn friend and then mine enemy,
My parasite, my soldier, statesman, all.
He makes a July's day short as December,
And with his varying childness cures in me   170
Thoughts that would thick my blood.
LEONTES   So stands this squire   171
Officed with me. We two will walk, my lord,   172
And leave you to your graver steps. Hermione,
How thou lov'st us, show in our brother's welcome.   174
Let what is dear in Sicily be cheap.   175
Next to thyself and my young rover, he's
Apparent to my heart.
HERMIONE   If you would seek us,   177
We are yours i'th' garden. Shall 's attend you there?   178
LEONTES
To your own bents dispose you. You'll be found,   179
Be you beneath the sky. [Aside] I am angling now,
Though you perceive me not how I give line.   181
Go to, go to!   182
How she holds up the neb, the bill to him,   183
And arms her with the boldness of a wife   184
To her allowing husband!
              [Exeunt Polixenes and Hermione.]
              Gone already!   185
Inch thick, knee-deep, o'er head and ears a forked
  one!—   186
Go play, boy, play. Thy mother plays, and I   187
Play too, but so disgraced a part, whose issue   188

---

121 **bawcock** i.e., fine fellow. (French *beau coq*.)   123 **not . . . cleanly**
(Leontes changes the word because *neat* also means "cattle" and hence
reminds him of cuckolds' horns.)   125 **virginaling** touching hands, as
in playing on the virginals, a keyboard instrument   126 **wanton** frisky
128 **Thou . . . have** You lack a shaggy head and the horns that I have.
(Again alluding to cuckolds' horns.)   129 **full** fully   132 **o'erdyed
blacks** black garments, or ones that have been weakened by too
much dye or that have been dyed over another color (thereby betraying a falseness in the mourner)   132–4 **false . . . mine** as false as dice
are wished false by one who intends to cheat me, and who respects
no boundary between what is his and mine   136 **welkin** sky-blue
137 **collop** small piece of meat; i.e., of my own flesh.   **dam** mother
138–43 **Affection . . . something** Strong passion, your intense power
pierces to the very center, the soul. You make possible things normally considered fantastic, partaking as you do of the nature of
dreams. How can this be? You collaborate with unreality and imagined fantasies. It's all the likelier, then, that such imaginings may also
fasten on a real object   144 **commission** what is lawful   146 **What
means Sicilia?** Why is the King of Sicily looking so distracted?
147 **something** somewhat   150 **moved** angry   151 **nature** i.e., affectionate feeling between parent and child   152 **pastime** occasion for
amusement   153 **To harder bosoms** for persons who are less tenderhearted.

154 **methoughts** it seemed to me.   **recoil** i.e., go back in memory
155 **unbreeched** not yet wearing breeches   156 **muzzled** i.e., sheathed.
(With phallic suggestion.)   160 **squash** unripe peascod or pea pod.
honest worthy   161 **take eggs for money** i.e., be imposed upon, taken
advantage of, cheated. (Proverbial.)   163 **happy . . . dole** may good
fortune be his lot. (Proverbial.)   166 **matter** concern   170 **childness**
childlike ways   171 **thick my blood** (Melancholy thoughts were supposed to thicken the blood.)   172 **Officed** placed in particular function
174–5 **How . . . cheap** (A hidden second meaning in these lines may be
intentional: show just how much you love me by the way you encourage Polixenes's attentions and thereby cheapen the most precious thing
in Sicily.)   177 **Apparent** heir apparent (perhaps with a suggestion too
of "evident, revealed")   178 **Shall 's** Shall we   179 **To . . . dispose you**
Act according to your inclinations. (With more bitter double meaning,
continued in *You'll be found*, i.e., found out.)   181 **give line** pay out line
(to let the fish hook itself well).   182 **Go to** (An expression of remonstrance.)   183 **neb** beak, i.e., nose, mouth   184 **arms her with** assumes
185 **allowing** approving   186 **forked** horned   187 **play** play games.
plays i.e., in a sexual liaison   188 **Play** play a role.   **issue** outcome.
(With a pun on the sense of "offspring" and "theatrical exit.")

Will hiss me to my grave. Contempt and clamor
Will be my knell. Go play, boy, play. There have been,
Or I am much deceived, cuckolds ere now;
And many a man there is, even at this present,
Now while I speak this, holds his wife by th' arm,
That little thinks she has been sluiced in 's absence   194
And his pond fished by his next neighbor, by
Sir Smile, his neighbor. Nay, there's comfort in 't
Whiles other men have gates and those gates opened,   197
As mine, against their will. Should all despair
That have revolted wives, the tenth of mankind   199
Would hang themselves. Physic for 't there's none.   200
It is a bawdy planet, that will strike   201
Where 'tis predominant; and 'tis powerful, think it,   202
From east, west, north, and south. Be it concluded,
No barricado for a belly. Know 't,   204
It will let in and out the enemy
With bag and baggage. Many thousand on 's   206
Have the disease and feel 't not.—How now, boy?

MAMILLIUS
I am like you, they say.

LEONTES   Why, that's some comfort.
What, Camillo there?

CAMILLO [coming forward]   Ay, my good lord.

LEONTES
Go play, Mamillius; thou'rt an honest man.
                                                    [Exit Mamillius.]
Camillo, this great sir will yet stay longer.

CAMILLO
You had much ado to make his anchor hold.
When you cast out, it still came home.

LEONTES   Didst note it?   213

CAMILLO
He would not stay at your petitions, made
His business more material.

LEONTES   Didst perceive it?   215
[Aside] They're here with me already, whisp'ring,
    rounding,   216
"Sicilia is a so-forth." 'Tis far gone   217
When I shall gust it last.—How came 't, Camillo,   218
That he did stay?

CAMILLO   At the good Queen's entreaty.

LEONTES
"At the Queen's" be 't. "Good" should be pertinent,   220
But so it is, it is not. Was this taken   221
By any understanding pate but thine?

For thy conceit is soaking, will draw in   223
More than the common blocks. Not noted, is 't,   224
But of the finer natures? By some severals   225
Of headpiece extraordinary? Lower messes   226
Perchance are to this business purblind? Say.   227

CAMILLO
Business, my lord? I think most understand
Bohemia stays here longer.

LEONTES
Ha?

CAMILLO   Stays here longer.

LEONTES   Ay, but why?

CAMILLO
To satisfy Your Highness and the entreaties
Of our most gracious mistress.

LEONTES   Satisfy?   232
Th'entreaties of your mistress? Satisfy?
Let that suffice. I have trusted thee, Camillo,
With all the nearest things to my heart, as well   235
My chamber councils, wherein, priestlike, thou   236
Hast cleansed my bosom. I from thee departed
Thy penitent reformed. But we have been
Deceived in thy integrity, deceived
In that which seems so.

CAMILLO   Be it forbid, my lord!   240

LEONTES
To bide upon 't, thou art not honest; or,   241
If thou inclin'st that way, thou art a coward,   242
Which hoxes honesty behind, restraining   243
From course required; or else thou must be counted 244
A servant grafted in my serious trust   245
And therein negligent; or else a fool
That see'st a game played home, the rich stake drawn, 247
And tak'st it all for jest.

CAMILLO   My gracious lord,
I may be negligent, foolish, and fearful;
In every one of these no man is free
But that his negligence, his folly, fear,
Among the infinite doings of the world
Sometime puts forth. In your affairs, my lord,   253
If ever I were willful-negligent,
It was my folly; if industriously   255
I played the fool, it was my negligence,
Not weighing well the end; if ever fearful
To do a thing where I the issue doubted,   258

Whereof the execution did cry out   259
Against the nonperformance, 'twas a fear   260
Which oft infects the wisest. These, my lord,
Are such allowed infirmities that honesty   262
Is never free of. But, beseech Your Grace,
Be plainer with me. Let me know my trespass
By its own visage. If I then deny it,   265
'Tis none of mine.

LEONTES   Ha' not you seen, Camillo—
But that's past doubt; you have, or your eyeglass   267
Is thicker than a cuckold's horn—or heard—   268
For to a vision so apparent, rumor   269
Cannot be mute—or thought—for cogitation
Resides not in that man that does not think—   271
My wife is slippery? If thou wilt confess,
Or else be impudently negative   273
To have nor eyes nor ears nor thought, then say   274
My wife's a hobbyhorse, deserves a name   275
As rank as any flax-wench that puts to   276
Before her trothplight. Say't and justify't.   277

CAMILLO
I would not be a stander-by to hear
My sovereign mistress clouded so without
My present vengeance taken. 'Shrew my heart,   280
You never spoke what did become you less
Than this, which to reiterate were sin   282
As deep as that, though true.

LEONTES   Is whispering nothing?   283
Is leaning cheek to cheek? Is meeting noses?
Kissing with inside lip? Stopping the career   285
Of laughter with a sigh—a note infallible
Of breaking honesty? Horsing foot on foot?   287
Skulking in corners? Wishing clocks more swift,
Hours minutes, noon midnight? And all eyes   289
Blind with the pin and web but theirs, theirs only,   290
That would unseen be wicked? Is this nothing?
Why, then the world and all that's in't is nothing,
The covering sky is nothing, Bohemia nothing,
My wife is nothing, nor nothing have these nothings,
If this be nothing.

CAMILLO   Good my lord, be cured
Of this diseased opinion, and betimes,   296
For 'tis most dangerous.

LEONTES   Say it be, 'tis true.   297

259–60 Whereof . . . nonperformance in which the completion of the
task showed how wrong I was in being reluctant to undertake it
262 allowed acknowledged.   that as   265 visage face, i.e., plain
appearance.   267 eyeglass lens of the eye   268 cuckold's horn (A
thin sheet of horn can be seen through like a lens, though a cuckold's
horn is another matter.)   269 to a vision so apparent about something so plainly visible   271 think i.e., think so   273–4 Or . . . eyes
or, as the only possible alternative, insist impudently that you have
neither eyes   275 hobbyhorse wanton woman   276 flax-wench
common slut.   puts to engages in sex   277 justify't affirm it.
280 present immediate.   'Shrew Beshrew, curse   282–3 which . . .
true i.e., to repeat which accusation would be to sin as deeply as her
supposed adultery, even if it were true (which it isn't).   285 career
full gallop   287 honesty chastity.   Horsing foot on foot Placing
one's foot on that of another person and then moving the feet up and
down together.   289 Hours minutes wishing hours were minutes
290 pin and web cataract of the eye. (The lovers wish to think themselves unobserved.)   296 betimes quickly   297 Say it be Even if it is
dangerous

CAMILLO
No, no, my lord.

LEONTES   It is. You lie, you lie!
I say thou liest, Camillo, and I hate thee,
Pronounce thee a gross lout, a mindless slave,
Or else a hovering temporizer, that   301
Canst with thine eyes at once see good and evil,
Inclining to them both. Were my wife's liver   303
Infected as her life, she would not live   304
The running of one glass.

CAMILLO   Who does infect her?   305

LEONTES
Why, he that wears her like her medal, hanging   306
About his neck, Bohemia—who, if I
Had servants true about me, that bare eyes   308
To see alike mine honor as their profits,
Their own particular thrifts, they would do that   310
Which should undo more doing. Ay, and thou,   311
His cupbearer—whom I from meaner form   312
Have benched and reared to worship, who mayst see   313
Plainly as heaven sees earth and earth sees heaven
How I am galled—mightst bespice a cup   315
To give mine enemy a lasting wink,   316
Which draft to me were cordial.

CAMILLO   Sir, my lord,   317
I could do this, and that with no rash potion,   318
But with a ling'ring dram that should not work
Maliciously like poison. But I cannot   320
Believe this crack to be in my dread mistress,   321
So sovereignly being honorable.   322
I have loved thee—

LEONTES   Make that thy question, and go rot!   323
Dost think I am so muddy, so unsettled,   324
To appoint myself in this vexation, sully   325
The purity and whiteness of my sheets—
Which to preserve is sleep, which being spotted
Is goads, thorns, nettles, tails of wasps—
Give scandal to the blood o' th' prince my son,
Who I do think is mine and love as mine,
Without ripe moving to't? Would I do this?   331
Could man so blench?

CAMILLO   I must believe you, sir.   332
I do, and will fetch off Bohemia for't;   333
Provided that, when he's removed, Your Highness
Will take again your queen as yours at first,

301 hovering wavering   303 Inclining . . . both being tolerant of evil
along with the good.   304 Infected as her life as full of disease as is
her moral conduct   305 glass hourglass.   306 like her medal like a
miniature portrait of her, worn in a locket   308 bare bore, had
310 thrifts gains   311 undo prevent   312 meaner form humbler station   313 benched placed on the bench of authority.   worship dignity, honor   315 galled rubbed, chafed   316 lasting wink
everlasting closing of the eyes (in death)   317 were cordial would be
restorative.   318 rash quick-acting (and therefore easily detected)
320 Maliciously virulently   321 crack flaw.   dread worthy of awe
322 sovereignly supremely   323 Make . . . rot! i.e., If you're going to
question my accusations, may you rot in hell!   324 muddy muddle-
headed   325 To . . . vexation to give myself this vexation   331 ripe
ample, urgent   332 blench swerve (from sensible conduct).
333 fetch off do away with; or, with deliberate ambiguity, rescue. (As
also in removed in the next line.)

Even for your son's sake, and thereby for sealing   336
The injury of tongues in courts and kingdoms
Known and allied to yours.

LEONTES   Thou dost advise me
Even so as I mine own course have set down.
I'll give no blemish to her honor, none.

CAMILLO   My lord,
Go then, and with a countenance as clear
As friendship wears at feasts, keep with Bohemia   343
And with your queen. I am his cupbearer.
If from me he have wholesome beverage,
Account me not your servant.

LEONTES   This is all.
Do't and thou hast the one half of my heart;
Do't not, thou splitt'st thine own.

CAMILLO   I'll do't, my lord.

LEONTES
I will seem friendly, as thou hast advised me.   *Exit.*

CAMILLO
Oh, miserable lady! But, for me,
What case stand I in? I must be the poisoner
Of good Polixenes, and my ground to do't
Is the obedience to a master, one
Who in rebellion with himself will have
All that are his so too. To do this deed,   355
Promotion follows. If I could find example   356
Of thousands that had struck anointed kings
And flourished after, I'd not do't; but since   358
Nor brass, nor stone, nor parchment bears not one,   359
Let villainy itself forswear't. I must
Forsake the court. To do't or no is certain   361
To me a breakneck. Happy star reign now!   362
Here comes Bohemia.

Enter Polixenes.

POLIXENES [*to himself*]   This is strange. Methinks
My favor here begins to warp. Not speak?—   364
Good day, Camillo.

CAMILLO   Hail, most royal sir!

POLIXENES
What is the news i'th' court?

CAMILLO   None rare, my lord.   366

POLIXENES
The King hath on him such a countenance
As he had lost some province and a region   368
Loved as he loves himself. Even now I met him
With customary compliment, when he,
Wafting his eyes to th' contrary and falling   371
A lip of much contempt, speeds from me, and

So leaves me to consider what is breeding   373
That changeth thus his manners.

CAMILLO   I dare not know, my lord.

POLIXENES
How, dare not? Do not? Do you know, and dare not?   376
Be intelligent to me. 'Tis thereabouts,   377
For to yourself what you do know you must,   378
And cannot say you dare not. Good Camillo,   379
Your changed complexions are to me a mirror
Which shows me mine changed too; for I must be   381
A party in this alteration, finding   382
Myself thus altered with't.

CAMILLO   There is a sickness
Which puts some of us in distemper, but
I cannot name the disease; and it is caught
Of you that yet are well.

POLIXENES   How? Caught of me?   386
Make me not sighted like the basilisk.   387
I have looked on thousands who have sped the better 388
By my regard, but killed none so. Camillo,   389
As you are certainly a gentleman, thereto   390
Clerklike experienced, which no less adorns   391
Our gentry than our parents' noble names,   392
In whose success we are gentle, I beseech you,   393
If you know aught which does behoove my
        knowledge
Thereof to be informed, imprison't not
In ignorant concealment.

CAMILLO   I may not answer.   396

POLIXENES
A sickness caught of me, and yet I well?
I must be answered. Dost thou hear, Camillo?
I conjure thee, by all the parts of man   399
Which honor does acknowledge, whereof the least   400
Is not this suit of mine, that thou declare   401
What incidency thou dost guess of harm   402
Is creeping toward me; how far off, how near;
Which way to be prevented, if to be;   404
If not, how best to bear it.

CAMILLO   Sir, I will tell you,
Since I am charged in honor and by him   406
That I think honorable. Therefore mark my counsel,
Which must be even as swiftly followed as
I mean to utter it, or both yourself and me

---

336 **for sealing** for the sake of silencing. (Some editors prefer
forsealing, sealing up tight.)   343 **keep** remain in company   355 **All
. . . too** i.e., all his followers like him in rebelling against the best in
themselves and in obeying his worst self.   **To do** If I do   356 **If** Even
if   358–9 **but . . . one** but since recorded history shows no instances
of persons who have killed a king and prospered afterwards   361 **To
do 't or no** i.e., Either to kill Polixenes or not to kill him   362 **breakneck** destruction, ruin.   **Happy** Propitious, favorable   364 **warp**
change, shrivel, grow askew (as wood warps).   **Not speak?** (Leontes
has just passed by Polixenes without speaking.)   366 **rare** noteworthy   368 **As** as if   371 **Wafting . . . contrary** averting his eyes.
falling letting fall

373 **breeding** hatching   376 **Do not?** i.e., Or do you mean you don't
know?   377 **intelligent** intelligible.   **'Tis thereabouts** It must be
something of this sort, i.e., that you know and dare not tell
378–9 **For . . . dare not** i.e., for in your heart, whatever it is you know,
you must in fact know, and can't claim it's a matter of not daring to
know.   381–2 **for . . . alteration** i.e., for my looks must have changed,
too, reflecting this change in my position   386 **Of** from   387 **sighted**
provided with a gaze.   **basilisk** a fabled serpent whose gaze was
fatal.   388 **sped** prospered   389 **regard** look   390–3 **thereto . . . gentle** in addition to which you are a cultivated and educated person—
something that graces our gentlemanlike condition no less than the
worthy name of our ancestors, by succession from whom we are
made noble   396 **ignorant concealment** concealment that would
keep me ignorant or that would proceed from pretended ignorance
on your part.   399 **parts** obligations   400–1 **whereof . . . not** not the
least of which is (to answer)   402 **incidency** likely incident   404 **if to
be** if it can be (prevented)   406 **by him** i.e., by you yourself

Cry lost, and so good night!

POLIXENES   On, good Camillo.   410

CAMILLO
I am appointed him to murder you.   411

POLIXENES
By whom, Camillo?

CAMILLO   By the King.

POLIXENES   For what?

CAMILLO
He thinks, nay, with all confidence he swears,
As he had seen't or been an instrument
To vice you to't, that you have touched his queen   415
Forbiddenly.

POLIXENES   Oh, then my best blood turn
To an infected jelly, and my name
Be yoked with his that did betray the Best!   418
Turn then my freshest reputation to
A savor that may strike the dullest nostril   420
Where I arrive, and my approach be shunned,
Nay, hated too, worse than the great'st infection
That e'er was heard or read!

CAMILLO   Swear his thought over   423
By each particular star in heaven and
By all their influences, you may as well
Forbid the sea for to obey the moon   426
As or by oath remove or counsel shake   427
The fabric of his folly, whose foundation   428
Is piled upon his faith and will continue   429
The standing of his body.

POLIXENES   How should this grow?   430

CAMILLO
I know not. But I am sure 'tis safer to
Avoid what's grown than question how 'tis born.
If therefore you dare trust my honesty,
That lies enclosèd in this trunk which you   434
Shall bear along impawned, away tonight!   435
Your followers I will whisper to the business,   436
And will by twos and threes at several posterns   437
Clear them o'th' city. For myself, I'll put
My fortunes to your service, which are here
By this discovery lost. Be not uncertain,   440
For, by the honor of my parents, I
Have uttered truth, which if you seek to prove,   442
I dare not stand by; nor shall you be safer   443
Than one condemned by the King's own mouth,
      thereon
His execution sworn.

POLIXENES   I do believe thee;

I saw his heart in 's face. Give me thy hand.
Be pilot to me, and thy places shall   447
Still neighbor mine. My ships are ready, and   448
My people did expect my hence departure
Two days ago. This jealousy
Is for a precious creature. As she's rare,
Must it be great; and as his person's mighty,
Must it be violent; and as he does conceive
He is dishonored by a man which ever
Professed to him, why, his revenges must   455
In that be made more bitter. Fear o'ershades me.
Good expedition be my friend, and comfort   457
The gracious Queen, part of his theme, but nothing   458
Of his ill-ta'en suspicion! Come, Camillo,   459
I will respect thee as a father if
Thou bear'st my life off. Hence! Let us avoid.   461

CAMILLO
It is in mine authority to command
The keys of all the posterns. Please Your Highness
To take the urgent hour. Come, sir, away.   *Exeunt.*

❖

2.1

Enter Hermione, Mamillius, [and] Ladies.

HERMIONE
Take the boy to you. He so troubles me,
'Tis past enduring.

FIRST LADY [*taking Mamillius from the Queen*]
                          Come, my gracious lord,
Shall I be your playfellow?

MAMILLIUS
No, I'll none of you.

FIRST LADY   Why, my sweet lord?   4

MAMILLIUS
You'll kiss me hard and speak to me as if
I were a baby still.—I love you better.

SECOND LADY
And why so, my lord?

MAMILLIUS   Not for because   7
Your brows are blacker; yet black brows, they say,
Become some women best, so that there be not   9
Too much hair there, but in a semicircle,
Or a half-moon made with a pen.

SECOND LADY   Who taught' this?   11

MAMILLIUS
I learned it out of women's faces. Pray now,
What color are your eyebrows?

FIRST LADY   Blue, my lord.

MAMILLIUS
Nay, that's a mock. I have seen a lady's nose

---

410 good night i.e., this is the end.   **411 him** by him (Leontes), or, the one   **415 vice** force, as with a carpenter's tool, or, impel, tempt. (The *Vice* was a tempter in the morality play.)   **418 his . . . Best** the name of him (Judas) who betrayed Christ.   **420 savor** stench   **423 Swear . . . over** i.e., Even if you should deny his suspicion with oaths   **426 for to** to   **427 or . . . or** either . . . or   **428 fabric** edifice   **428–30 whose . . . body** the foundation of which is built upon an unshaken conviction and which will last as long as his body exists.   **430 How . . . grow?** How could this suspicion have arisen?   **434 trunk** body. (With a suggestion too of a traveling trunk.)   **435 impawned** i.e., as a pledge of good faith   **436 whisper to** secretly inform of and urge   **437 posterns** rear gates   **440 discovery** revelation, disclosure   **442 prove** test   **443 stand by** affirm publicly; stay

447–8 thy . . . mine your official position will always be near to me. **455 Professed** openly professed friendship   **457–9 Good . . . suspicion!** May good speed befriend me, and may my quick departure ease the predicament of the gracious Queen, who is the object of the King's suspicions but who is guiltless of them!   **461 bear'st my life off** can get me out of this alive.   **avoid** depart.
2.1. Location: Sicilia. The royal court.
4 none of you have nothing to do with you.   **7 for because** because
9 so provided   **11 taught'** taught you

That has been blue, but not her eyebrows.

FIRST LADY   Hark ye,
The Queen your mother rounds apace. We shall
Present our services to a fine new prince
One of these days, and then you'd wanton with us, 18
If we would have you.

SECOND LADY   She is spread of late
Into a goodly bulk. Good time encounter her!   20

HERMIONE *[calling to her women]*
What wisdom stirs amongst you?—Come, sir, now
I am for you again. Pray you, sit by us   22
And tell 's a tale.

MAMILLIUS   Merry or sad shall 't be?

HERMIONE   As merry as you will.

MAMILLIUS
A sad tale's best for winter. I have one
Of sprites and goblins.

HERMIONE   Let's have that, good sir.
Come on, sit down. Come on, and do your best
To fright me with your sprites. You're powerful at it.

MAMILLIUS
There was a man—

HERMIONE   Nay, come sit down, then on.
                                        [Mamillius sits.]

MAMILLIUS
Dwelt by a churchyard. I will tell it softly;
Yond crickets shall not hear it.   31

HERMIONE
Come on, then, and give 't me in mine ear.
                              [They converse privately.]

[Enter] Leontes, Antigonus, Lords, *[and others]*.

LEONTES
Was he met there? His train? Camillo with him?

A LORD
Behind the tuft of pines I met them. Never
Saw I men scour so on their way. I eyed them   35
Even to their ships.

LEONTES   How blest am I
In my just censure, in my true opinion!   37
Alack, for lesser knowledge! How accurst   38
In being so blest! There may be in the cup   39
A spider steeped, and one may drink, depart,   40
And yet partake no venom, for his knowledge
Is not infected; but if one present
Th'abhorred ingredient to his eye, make known
How he hath drunk, he cracks his gorge, his sides, 44
With violent hefts. I have drunk, and seen the spider. 45
Camillo was his help in this, his pander.
There is a plot against my life, my crown.
All's true that is mistrusted. That false villain 48

Whom I employed was pre-employed by him.
He has discovered my design, and I   50
Remain a pinched thing, yea, a very trick   51
For them to play at will. How came the posterns   52
So easily open?

A LORD   By his great authority,
Which often hath no less prevailed than so
On your command.

LEONTES   I know't too well.
[To Hermione] Give me the boy. I am glad you did not
nurse him.
Though he does bear some signs of me, yet you
Have too much blood in him.

HERMIONE   What is this? Sport?   59

LEONTES *[to a Lord]*
Bear the boy hence; he shall not come about her.
Away with him! And let her sport herself
With that she's big with, *[to Hermione]* for 'tis Polixenes
Has made thee swell thus.   *[Mamillius is led out.]*

HERMIONE   But I'd say he had not,   63
And I'll be sworn you would believe my saying,
Howe'er you lean to th' nayward.

LEONTES   You, my lords,   65
Look on her, mark her well. Be but about
To say "She is a goodly lady," and   67
The justice of your hearts will thereto add
"'Tis pity she's not honest, honorable."   69
Praise her but for this her without-door form,   70
Which on my faith deserves high speech, and straight 71
The shrug, the hum or ha, these petty brands   72
That calumny doth use—oh, I am out,   73
That mercy does, for calumny will sear   74
Virtue itself—these shrugs, these hums and ha's,
When you have said she's goodly, come between   76
Ere you can say she's honest. But be't known,
From him that has most cause to grieve it should be,
She's an adulteress.

HERMIONE   Should a villain say so,
The most replenished villain in the world,   80
He were as much more villain. You, my lord,   81
Do but mistake.

LEONTES   You have mistook, my lady, 82
Polixenes for Leontes. Oh, thou thing!
Which I'll not call a creature of thy place,   84
Lest barbarism, making me the precedent,
Should a like language use to all degrees   86
And mannerly distinguishment leave out   87

---

18 **wanton** sport, play   20 **Good . . . her!** May she have a happy
issue!   22 **for you** ready for you   31 **crickets** i.e., the court ladies, tit-
tering and laughing   35 **scour** scurry   37 **censure** judgment
38 **Alack . . . knowledge!** Would that there were less for me to know!
39 **blest** i.e., with knowledge (that causes unhappiness).   40 **A spider**
(The superstition referred to here is that the drinker is not poisoned
by the spider in the cup unless the spider is known to be there.)
44 **gorge** throat   45 **hefts** heavings, retchings.   48 **mistrusted**
suspected.

50 **discovered** disclosed   51 **pinched** tortured, ridiculous.   **trick**
plaything   52 **play** play with.   **posterns** gates   59 **Sport?** A joke?
63 **I'd** I need only   65 **th' nayward** the contrary.   67 **goodly** attractive   69 **honest** chaste   70 **without-door** outward, external
71 **straight** straightaway, at once   72 **brands** i.e., signs, stigmas
73 **out** wrong, in error   74 **does** uses. (Leontes's point is that no one
commits calumny by suggesting with a shrug that Hermione is
unchaste; calumny attacks *virtue itself*, whereas Hermione has only the
false appearance of virtue.)   76 **come between** interrupt   80 **replenished** complete   81 **He . . . villain** his saying so would double his villainy.   82 **mistook** taken wrongfully. (Playing bitterly on *mistake*,
"misapprehend.")   84 **Which . . . place** whose exalted rank I will not
desecrate by calling you what you really are   86 **like** similar.   **degrees**
social ranks   87 **And . . . out** and leave out proper distinctions

Betwixt the prince and beggar. I have said
She's an adult'ress; I have said with whom.
More, she's a traitor, and Camillo is
A fedarie with her, and one that knows   91
What she should shame to know herself   92
But with her most vile principal, that she's   93
A bed-swerver, even as bad as those   94
That vulgars give bold'st titles, ay, and privy   95
To this their late escape.

HERMIONE   No, by my life,   96
Privy to none of this. How will this grieve you,
When you shall come to clearer knowledge, that
You thus have published me! Gentle my lord,   99
You scarce can right me throughly than to say   100
You did mistake.

LEONTES   No. If I mistake
In those foundations which I build upon,
The center is not big enough to bear   103
A schoolboy's top.—Away with her to prison!
He who shall speak for her is afar off guilty   105
But that he speaks.

HERMIONE   There's some ill planet reigns.   106
I must be patient till the heavens look
With an aspect more favorable. Good my lords,
I am not prone to weeping, as our sex
Commonly are, the want of which vain dew   110
Perchance shall dry your pities; but I have
That honorable grief lodged here which burns
Worse than tears drown. Beseech you all, my lords,
With thoughts so qualified as your charities   114
Shall best instruct you, measure me; and so   115
The King's will be performed!

LEONTES   Shall I be heard?   116

HERMIONE
Who is't that goes with me? Beseech Your Highness
My women may be with me, for you see
My plight requires it.—Do not weep, good fools;   119
There is no cause. When you shall know your mistress
Has deserved prison, then abound in tears
As I come out. This action I now go on   122
Is for my better grace.—Adieu, my lord.   123
I never wished to see you sorry; now
I trust I shall. My women, come, you have leave.   125

LEONTES   Go, do our bidding. Hence!
                    [Exit Queen, guarded, with Ladies.]

A LORD
Beseech Your Highness, call the Queen again.

ANTIGONUS
Be certain what you do, sir, lest your justice

Prove violence, in the which three great ones suffer:
Yourself, your queen, your son.

A LORD   For her, my lord,
I dare my life lay down and will do't, sir,
Please you t'accept it, that the Queen is spotless
I'th'eyes of heaven and to you—I mean
In this which you accuse her.

ANTIGONUS   If it prove
She's otherwise, I'll keep my stables where   135
I lodge my wife. I'll go in couples with her;   136
Than when I feel and see her no farther trust her. 137
For every inch of woman in the world,
Ay, every dram of woman's flesh is false,
If she be.

LEONTES   Hold your peaces.

A LORD   Good my lord—   140

ANTIGONUS
It is for you we speak, not for ourselves.
You are abused, and by some putter-on   142
That will be damned for't. Would I knew the villain;
I would land-damn him. Be she honor-flawed,   144
I have three daughters—the eldest is eleven,
The second and the third, nine and some five—   146
If this prove true, they'll pay for't. By mine honor,
I'll geld 'em all! Fourteen they shall not see   148
To bring false generations. They are co-heirs,   149
And I had rather glib myself than they   150
Should not produce fair issue.

LEONTES   Cease, no more!   151
You smell this business with a sense as cold
As is a dead man's nose; but I do see't and feel't
As you feel doing thus, and see withal   154
The instruments that feel.

ANTIGONUS   If it be so,   155
We need no grave to bury honesty;
There's not a grain of it the face to sweeten
Of the whole dungy earth.

LEONTES   What? Lack I credit?   158

A LORD
I had rather you did lack than I, my lord,
Upon this ground; and more it would content me   160
To have her honor true than your suspicion,
Be blamed for't how you might.

LEONTES   Why, what need we   162
Commune with you of this, but rather follow

91 fedarie confederate   92–3 to know . . . principal to acknowledge
privately even with her contemptible partner   94 bed-swerver adulteress   95 That . . . titles that common people call by the rudest
names.   privy in on the secret   96 late recent   99 published proclaimed.   Gentle my My noble   100 You . . . say you scarcely can do
me full justice then merely by saying   103 center earth   105 afar off
indirectly   106 But . . . speaks merely by speaking.   110 want lack
114 qualified tempered   115 measure judge   116 heard i.e., obeyed.
119 fools (Here, a term of endearment.)   122 come out am released
from prison.   122–3 The action . . . grace What I now must undergo
will ultimately make me seem more gracious in others' eyes and
ennoble me by suffering.   125 leave permission (to attend me).

135–6 I'll . . . wife (If Hermione is an adulteress, says Antigonus,
then all women are no better than animals, to be penned up and
guarded suspiciously.)   136 in couples i.e., like two hounds leashed
together and hence inseparable   137 Than . . . trust her trust her no
further than I can feel her next to me and actually see her.   140 she
i.e., Hermione   142 abused deceived.   putter-on instigator
144 land-damn lambaste (? Meaning uncertain.)   146 some about
148 geld sterilize, de-sex   149 bring false generations have illegitimate children.   They are co-heirs i.e., They will share my inheritance (since I have no son to inherit all)   150 glib castrate, geld
151 fair issue legitimate offspring.   154 thus (Leontes presumably
grasps Antigonus by the arm or pinches him or tweaks his nose.)
154–5 and see . . . feel i.e., just as you and I see these fingers that
pinch, I see in my mind's eye the amorous touching of Hermione and
Polixenes. (Withal means "in addition.")   158 credit credibility.
160 Upon this ground in this matter   162 we I. (The royal "we.")

Our forceful instigation? Our prerogative   164
Calls not your counsels, but our natural goodness   165
Imparts this; which if you—or stupefied   166
Or seeming so in skill—cannot or will not   167
Relish a truth like us, inform yourselves   168
We need no more of your advice. The matter,
The loss, the gain, the ordering on't, is all   170
Properly ours.

ANTIGONUS   And I wish, my liege,
You had only in your silent judgment tried it,
Without more overture.

LEONTES   How could that be?   173
Either thou art most ignorant by age,   174
Or thou wert born a fool. Camillo's flight,
Added to their familiarity—
Which was as gross as ever touched conjecture,   177
That lacked sight only, naught for approbation   178
But only seeing, all other circumstances
Made up to th' deed—doth push on this proceeding.   180
Yet, for a greater confirmation—
For in an act of this importance 'twere
Most piteous to be wild—I have dispatched in post   183
To sacred Delphos, to Apollo's temple,   184
Cleomenes and Dion, whom you know
Of stuffed sufficiency. Now from the oracle   186
They will bring all, whose spiritual counsel had   187
Shall stop or spur me. Have I done well?

A LORD   Well done, my lord.

LEONTES
Though I am satisfied, and need no more
Than what I know, yet shall the oracle
Give rest to th' minds of others, such as he   192
Whose ignorant credulity will not
Come up to th' truth. So have we thought it good   194
From our free person she should be confined,   195
Lest that the treachery of the two fled hence
Be left her to perform. Come, follow us.
We are to speak in public, for this business
Will raise us all.

ANTIGONUS [aside]   To laughter, as I take it,   199
If the good truth were known.   Exeunt.

❖

2.2

Enter Paulina, a Gentleman, [and attendants].

PAULINA
The keeper of the prison, call to him.
Let him have knowledge who I am.
                          [*The Gentleman goes to the door.*]
                                        Good lady,   2
No court in Europe is too good for thee;
What dost thou then in prison?

                          [*Enter*] *Jailer.*

                                        Now, good sir,
You know me, do you not?

JAILER   For a worthy lady
And one who much I honor.

PAULINA   Pray you then,
Conduct me to the Queen.

JAILER   I may not, madam.
To the contrary I have express commandment.

PAULINA
Here's ado, to lock up honesty and honor from
Th'access of gentle visitors! Is't lawful, pray you,
To see her women? Any of them? Emilia?

JAILER   So please you, madam,
To put apart these your attendants, I   13
Shall bring Emilia forth.

PAULINA   I pray now, call her.—
Withdraw yourselves.
                          [*Gentleman and attendants withdraw.*]

JAILER   And, madam,
I must be present at your conference.

PAULINA   Well, be't so, prithee.   [*Exit Jailer.*]
Here's such ado, to make no stain a stain   19
As passes coloring.

                          [*Enter Jailer, with*] *Emilia.*

                                        Dear gentlewoman,   20
How fares our gracious lady?

EMILIA
As well as one so great and so forlorn
May hold together. On her frights and griefs—   23
Which never tender lady hath borne greater—   24
She is something before her time delivered.   25

PAULINA
A boy?

EMILIA   A daughter, and a goodly babe,
Lusty and like to live. The Queen receives   27
Much comfort in't, says, "My poor prisoner,
I am innocent as you."   I dare be sworn.
PAULINA
These dangerous unsafe lunes i'th' King, beshrew
them!   30
He must be told on't, and he shall. The office   31
Becomes a woman best; I'll take't upon me.   32

---

164 Our . . . instigation my own strong inclination.   **164–6 Our prerogative . . . this** My royal prerogative is under no obligation to consult you, but rather out of natural generosity I inform you of the matter   **166 or** either   **167 Or . . . skill** or pretending to be stupefied out of cunning   **168 Relish** savor, appreciate   **170 on't** of it   **173 overture** public disclosure.   **174 by age** through the folly of old age   **177 as gross . . . conjecture** as palpably evident as any conjecture ever touched upon and verified   **178 approbation** proof   **180 Made up** added up.   **push on** urge onward   **183 wild** rash.   **post** haste   **184 Delphos** (See note at 3.1.2.)   **186 Of stuffed sufficiency** abundantly qualified and trustworthy.   **187 all** the whole truth.   **had** having been obtained   **192 he** any person (such as Antigonus)   **194 Come up to** face   **195 From** away from.   **free** accessible   **199 raise** rouse
2.2. Location: Sicilia. A prison.

2 Good lady (Addressed to the absent Hermione.)   **13 put apart** dismiss   **19–20 to make . . . coloring** to make out of no stain at all a besmirching of honor that surpasses any justification. (Expressed in a metaphor of dyeing and painting.)   **23 On** In consequence of   **24 Which** than which   **25 something** somewhat. (Also in line 55.)   **27 Lusty** vigorous.   **like** likely   **30 lunes** fits of lunacy   **31 on't** of it   **32 Becomes** suits

If I prove honeymouthed, let my tongue blister 33
And never to my red-looked anger be 34
The trumpet any more. Pray you, Emilia,
Commend my best obedience to the Queen. 36
If she dares trust me with her little babe,
I'll show't the King and undertake to be
Her advocate to th' loud'st. We do not know 39
How he may soften at the sight o'th' child.
The silence often of pure innocence
Persuades when speaking fails.

EMILIA   Most worthy madam,
Your honor and your goodness is so evident
That your free undertaking cannot miss 44
A thriving issue. There is no lady living 45
So meet for this great errand. Please Your Ladyship 46
To visit the next room, I'll presently 47
Acquaint the Queen of your most noble offer,
Who but today hammered of this design, 49
But durst not tempt a minister of honor 50
Lest she should be denied.

PAULINA   Tell her, Emilia,
I'll use that tongue I have. If wit flow from't 52
As boldness from my bosom, let 't not be doubted
I shall do good.

EMILIA   Now be you blest for it!
I'll to the Queen.—Please you, come something nearer. 55

JAILER
Madam, if't please the Queen to send the babe,
I know not what I shall incur to pass it, 57
Having no warrant.

PAULINA   You need not fear it, sir.
This child was prisoner to the womb and is
By law and process of great Nature thence
Freed and enfranchised, not a party to
The anger of the King, nor guilty of—
If any be—the trespass of the Queen.

JAILER   I do believe it.

PAULINA
Do not you fear. Upon mine honor, I
Will stand betwixt you and danger.   *Exeunt.*

❖

2.3

Enter Leontes.

LEONTES
Nor night nor day, no rest! It is but weakness
To bear the matter thus, mere weakness. If
The cause were not in being—part o'th' cause, 3
She th'adulteress, for the harlot King 4

Is quite beyond mine arm, out of the blank 5
And level of my brain, plot-proof, but she 6
I can hook to me—say that she were gone, 7
Given to the fire, a moiety of my rest 8
Might come to me again.—Who's there?

[Enter a] Servant.

SERVANT   My lord?
LEONTES   How does the boy?
SERVANT
He took good rest tonight; 'tis hoped 11
His sickness is discharged.

LEONTES   To see his nobleness!
Conceiving the dishonor of his mother, 13
He straight declined, drooped, took it deeply, 14
Fastened and fixed the shame on't in himself, 15
Threw off his spirit, his appetite, his sleep,
And downright languished.—Leave me solely. Go, 17
See how he fares.   *[Exit Servant.]*
            Fie, fie! No thought of him. 18
The very thought of my revenges that way
Recoil upon me—in himself too mighty,
And in his parties, his alliance. Let him be, 21
Until a time may serve. For present vengeance,
Take it on her. Camillo and Polixenes
Laugh at me, make their pastime at my sorrow.
They should not laugh if I could reach them, nor
Shall she, within my power.

Enter Paulina [with a baby]; Antigonus and Lords [trying to hold her back].

A LORD   You must not enter.
PAULINA
Nay, rather, good my lords, be second to me. 27
Fear you his tryannous passion more, alas,
Than the Queen's life? A gracious innocent soul,
More free than he is jealous.

ANTIGONUS   That's enough. 30
SERVANT
Madam, he hath not slept tonight, commanded
None should come at him.

PAULINA   Not so hot, good sir.
I come to bring him sleep. 'Tis such as you,
That creep like shadows by him and do sigh
At each his needless heavings, such as you 35
Nourish the cause of his awaking. I 36
Do come with words as medicinal as true,
Honest as either, to purge him of that humor 38
That presses him from sleep.

LEONTES   What noise there, ho?

---

33 blister (It was popularly supposed that lying blistered the tongue.)
34 red-looked red-faced   **36 Commend** deliver   **39 to th' loud'st** as loudly as I can.   **44 free** generous   **45 thriving issue** successful outcome.   **46 meet** suited.   **Please** If it please   **47 presently** at once
49 hammered of mused upon   **50 tempt** solicit (to serve as ambassador in such a case)   **52 wit** wisdom   **55 come . . . nearer** i.e., come into the next room (as in lines 46–7).   **57 to pass it** if I let it pass
2.3. Location: Sicilia. The royal court.
3 not in being dead   **4 harlot** lewd. (Originally applied to either sex.)

5–6 out . . . level beyond the range. (Archery terms: *blank* is the center of the target or the close range needed for a direct shot at it, as in "point-blank"; *level* is the action of aiming.)   **7 hook** (As with grappling hooks.)   **8 Given to the fire** burned at the stake (as a traitor conspiring against the King).   **moiety** portion   **11 tonight** last night
13 Conceiving Grasping the enormity of   **14 straight** immediately
15 on't of it   **17 solely** alone.   **18 him** i.e., Polixenes.   **21 his parties . . . alliance** his supporters and allies.   **27 be second to** aid, second
30 free innocent   **35 heavings** sighs or groans   **36 awaking** inability to sleep.   **38 humor** distemper

PAULINA
No noise, my lord, but needful conference
About some gossips for Your Highness.

LEONTES   How?   41
Away with that audacious lady! Antigonus,
I charged thee that she should not come about me.
I knew she would.

ANTIGONUS   I told her so, my lord,
On your displeasure's peril and on mine,
She should not visit you.

LEONTES   What, canst not rule her?

PAULINA
From all dishonesty he can. In this,
Unless he take the course that you have done—
Commit me for committing honor—trust it,   49
He shall not rule me.

ANTIGONUS   La you now, you hear!   50
When she will take the rein I let her run,
But she'll not stumble.

PAULINA   Good my liege, I come—
And, I beseech you hear me, who professes
Myself your loyal servant, your physician,
Your most obedient counselor, yet that dares
Less appear so in comforting your evils   56
Than such as most seem yours—I say, I come   57
From your good queen.

LEONTES Good queen?

PAULINA
Good queen, my lord, good queen, I say good queen,
And would by combat make her good, so were I   61
A man, the worst about you.

LEONTES [to Lords]   Force her hence.   62

PAULINA
Let him that makes but trifles of his eyes
First hand me. On mine own accord I'll off,
But first I'll do my errand. The good Queen,
For she is good, hath brought you forth a daughter—
Here 'tis—commends it to your blessing.
                              [She lays down the baby.]

LEONTES   Out!
A mankind witch! Hence with her, out o' door!   68
A most intelligencing bawd!

PAULINA   Not so.   69
I am as ignorant in that as you
In so entitling me, and no less honest
Than you are mad; which is enough, I'll warrant,
As this world goes, to pass for honest.

LEONTES [to Lords]   Traitors!
Will you not push her out? [To Antigonus] Give her the
  bastard.
Thou dotard, thou art woman-tired, unroosted   75

By thy Dame Partlet here. Take up the bastard!   76
Take't up, I say. Give't to thy crone.

PAULINA [to Antigonus]   Forever
Unvenerable be thy hands if thou
Tak'st up the Princess by that forcèd baseness   79
Which he has put upon't!

LEONTES   He dreads his wife.

PAULINA
So I would you did. Then 'twere past all doubt
You'd call your children yours.

LEONTES   A nest of traitors!

ANTIGONUS
I am none, by this good light.

PAULINA   Nor I, nor any   83
But one that's here, and that's himself; for he
The sacred honor of himself, his queen's,
His hopeful son's, his babe's, betrays to slander,
Whose sting is sharper than the sword's; and will
  not—
For, as the case now stands, it is a curse   88
He cannot be compelled to't—once remove   89
The root of his opinion, which is rotten   90
As ever oak or stone was sound.

LEONTES   A callet   91
Of boundless tongue, who late hath beat her husband   92
And now baits me! This brat is none of mine;   93
It is the issue of Polixenes.
Hence with it, and together with the dam
Commit them to the fire!

PAULINA   It is yours;
And, might we lay th'old proverb to your charge,
So like you, 'tis the worse. Behold, my lords,   98
Although the print be little, the whole matter
And copy of the father—eye, nose, lip,
The trick of 's frown, his forehead, nay, the valley,   101
The pretty dimples of his chin and cheek, his smiles,
The very mold and frame of hand, nail, finger.
And thou, good goddess Nature, which hast made it
So like to him that got it, if thou hast   105
The ordering of the mind too, 'mongst all colors
No yellow in't, lest she suspect, as he does,   107
Her children not her husband's!

LEONTES   A gross hag!
And, lozel, thou art worthy to be hanged,   109
That wilt not stay her tongue.

ANTIGONUS   Hang all the husbands   110
That cannot do that feat, you'll leave yourself

41 gossips godparents for the baby at its baptism 49 Commit i.e., to
prison 50 La . . . hear! i.e., There now, you hear how she will go on
talking! 56–7 in comforting . . . yours when it comes to encouraging
your evil courses than those flatterers who seem to be your most loyal
servants 61 by combat by trial by combat. make prove 62 worst
least manly, or, lowest in rank 68 mankind masculine, behaving like
a man 69 intelligencing bawd acting as go-between and spy (for
the Queen and Polixenes). 75 woman-tired henpecked. (From tire in
falconry, meaning "tear with the beak.") unroosted driven from
perch

76 Partlet or Pertilote, a common name for a hen (as in Reynard the
Fox and in Chaucer's "Nun's Priest's Tale") 79 by that forcèd baseness under that wrongfully imposed name of bastard 83 by this
good light by the light of day. (A common oath.) 88–90 as . . . opinion i.e., since he is King, he regrettably can't be compelled to change
his deeply rooted opinion 91 callet scold 92 late recently 93 baits
(With a pun on beat in the previous line, pronounced "bate.") 98 So . . .
worse she's so like you that she fares the worse for it. 101 trick characteristic expression. valley cleft above the upper lip 105 got begot
107 No yellow let there be no yellow, i.e., the color of jealousy. (A
chaste woman could hardly expect that her own children are illegitimate, but Paulina may be hyperbolically ridiculing Leontes's suspicions.) 109 lozel worthless person, scoundrel. (Addressed to
Antigonus.) 110 stay restrain

Hardly one subject.

LEONTES   Once more, take her hence.

PAULINA
A most unworthy and unnatural lord
Can do no more.

LEONTES   I'll ha' thee burnt.

PAULINA   I care not.
It is an heretic that makes the fire,   115
Not she which burns in't. I'll not call you tyrant;   116
But this most cruel usage of your queen,
Not able to produce more accusation   118
Than your own weak-hinged fancy, something savors
Of tyranny and will ignoble make you,
Yea, scandalous to the world.

LEONTES [to Antigonus]   On your allegiance,
Out of the chamber with her! Were I a tyrant,
Where were her life? She durst not call me so   123
If she did know me one. Away with her!

PAULINA
I pray you, do not push me; I'll be gone.
Look to your babe, my lord; 'tis yours. Jove send her
A better guiding spirit!—What needs these hands?   127
You that are thus so tender o'er his follies
Will never do him good, not one of you.
So, so. Farewell, we are gone.   Exit.

LEONTES [to Antigonus]
Thou, traitor, hast set on thy wife to this.
My child? Away with't! Even thou, that hast
A heart so tender o'er it, take it hence
And see it instantly consumed with fire;
Even thou and none but thou. Take it up straight.
Within this hour bring me word 'tis done,
And by good testimony, or I'll seize thy life,
With what thou else call'st thine. If thou refuse
And wilt encounter with my wrath, say so;
The bastard brains with these my proper hands   140
Shall I dash out. Go, take it to the fire,
For thou set'st on thy wife.

ANTIGONUS   I did not, sir.
These lords, my noble fellows, if they please,
Can clear me in't.

LORDS   We can. My royal liege,
He is not guilty of her coming hither.

LEONTES   You're liars all.

A LORD
Beseech Your Highness, give us better credit.   147
We have always truly served you, and beseech'   148
So to esteem of us; and on our knees we beg,
As recompense of our dear services   150
Past and to come, that you do change this purpose,
Which being so horrible, so bloody, must
Lead on to some foul issue. We all kneel.

115–16 It is . . . in 't i.e., In burning me, you who would be making or
building the fire are the heretic, not me (since loss of faith in innocence is a kind of heresy), or, you can burn a woman if you like, but
it's a heretic's fire only if she is, in fact, a heretic.   118 Not able you
not being able   123 Where . . . life? how could she escape execution
at my command?   127 What . . . hands? What need is there to push
me?   140 proper own   147 credit belief.   148 beseech' beseech you
150 dear loyal, heartfelt

LEONTES
I am a feather for each wind that blows.
Shall I live on to see this bastard kneel
And call it father? Better burn it now
Than curse it then. But be it; let it live.
It shall not neither. [To Antigonus] You, sir, come you
    hither,
You that have been so tenderly officious
With Lady Margery, your midwife there,   160
To save this bastard's life—for 'tis a bastard,
So sure as this beard's gray. What will you adventure   162
To save this brat's life?

ANTIGONUS   Anything, my lord,
That my ability may undergo
And nobleness impose. At least thus much:
I'll pawn the little blood which I have left
To save the innocent—anything possible.

LEONTES [holding his sword]
It shall be possible. Swear by this sword
Thou wilt perform my bidding.

ANTIGONUS [his hand on the hilt]   I will, my lord.

LEONTES
Mark and perform it, see'st thou; for the fail   170
Of any point in't shall not only be
Death to thyself but to thy lewd-tongued wife,
Whom for this time we pardon. We enjoin thee,
As thou art liegeman to us, that thou carry   174
This female bastard hence, and that thou bear it
To some remote and desert place quite out
Of our dominions, and that there thou leave it,
Without more mercy, to it own protection   178
And favor of the climate. As by strange fortune
It came to us, I do in justice charge thee,
On thy soul's peril and thy body's torture,
That thou commend it strangely to some place   182
Where chance may nurse or end it. Take it up.

ANTIGONUS [taking up the baby]
I swear to do this, though a present death
Had been more merciful.—Come on, poor babe.
Some powerful spirit instruct the kites and ravens
To be thy nurses! Wolves and bears, they say,
Casting their savageness aside, have done
Like offices of pity.—Sir, be prosperous
In more than this deed does require!—And blessing   190
Against this cruelty fight on thy side,
Poor thing, condemned to loss!   Exit [with the baby].

LEONTES   No, I'll not rear   192
Another's issue.

                Enter a Servant.

SERVANT   Please Your Highness, posts   193
From those you sent to th'oracle are come
An hour since. Cleomenes and Dion,

160 Margery (A derisive term, evidently equivalent to Partlet in line
76.)   162 this beard's (Probably Antigonus's.)   170 see'st thou i.e.,
do you hear.   fail failure   174 liegeman loyal subject   178 it its
182 commend . . . place commit it to some foreign place   190 more
i.e., more ways, more extent.   require deserve.   192 loss destruction.   193 posts messengers

Being well arrived from Delphos, are both landed,
Hasting to th' court.

A LORD　　　　　　　　　So please you, sir, their speed
Hath been beyond account.

LEONTES　　　　　　　Twenty-three days　198
They have been absent. 'Tis good speed, foretells
The great Apollo suddenly will have　200
The truth of this appear. Prepare you, lords.
Summon a session, that we may arraign　202
Our most disloyal lady; for, as she hath
Been publicly accused, so shall she have
A just and open trial. While she lives
My heart will be a burden to me. Leave me,
And think upon my bidding.　　　*Exeunt [separately].*

❖

3.1

Enter Cleomenes and Dion.

CLEOMENES
The climate's delicate, the air most sweet,
Fertile the isle, the temple much surpassing　2
The common praise it bears.

DION　　　　　　　　　I shall report,
For most it caught me, the celestial habits—　4
Methinks I so should term them—and the reverence
Of the grave wearers. Oh, the sacrifice!
How ceremonious, solemn, and unearthly
It was i'th'offering!

CLEOMENES　　　　　But of all, the burst
And the ear-deaf'ning voice o'th'oracle,
Kin to Jove's thunder, so surprised my sense　10
That I was nothing.

DION　　　　　　　　If th'event o'th' journey　11
Prove as successful to the Queen—Oh, be't so!—
As it hath been to us rare, pleasant, speedy,
The time is worth the use on't.

CLEOMENES　　　　　　　Great Apollo　14
Turn all to th' best! These proclamations,
So forcing faults upon Hermione,
I little like.

DION　　　　　The violent carriage of it　17
Will clear or end the business. When the oracle,
Thus by Apollo's great divine sealed up,　19
Shall the contents discover, something rare　20
Even then will rush to knowledge. Go. Fresh horses!
And gracious be the issue!　　　　　　*Exeunt.*

3.2

Enter Leontes, Lords, [and] Officers.

LEONTES
This sessions, to our great grief we pronounce,
Even pushes 'gainst our heart: the party tried
The daughter of a king, our wife, and one
Of us too much beloved. Let us be cleared　4
Of being tyrannous, since we so openly
Proceed in justice, which shall have due course
Even to the guilt or the purgation.　7
Produce the prisoner.

OFFICER
It is His Highness' pleasure that the Queen
Appear in person here in court. Silence!

[Enter] Hermione, as to her trial, [Paulina, and] Ladies.

LEONTES　　Read the indictment.

OFFICER [*reads*]　"Hermione, Queen to the worthy
Leontes, King of Sicilia, thou art here accused and ar-
raigned of high treason, in committing adultery with
Polixenes, King of Bohemia, and conspiring with
Camillo to take away the life of our sovereign lord the
King, thy royal husband; the pretense whereof being　17
by circumstances partly laid open, thou, Hermione,
contrary to the faith and allegiance of a true subject,
didst counsel and aid them, for their better safety, to
fly away by night."

HERMIONE
Since what I am to say must be but that
Which contradicts my accusation, and
The testimony on my part no other
But what comes from myself, it shall scarce boot me　25
To say "not guilty." Mine integrity,
Being counted falsehood, shall, as I express it,
Be so received. But thus: if powers divine
Behold our human actions, as they do,
I doubt not then but innocence shall make
False accusation blush and tyranny
Tremble at patience. You, my lord, best know,
Who least will seem to do so, my past life
Hath been as continent, as chaste, as true
As I am now unhappy; which is more
Than history can pattern, though devised　36
And played to take spectators. For behold me—　37
A fellow of the royal bed, which owe　38
A moiety of the throne, a great king's daughter,　39
The mother to a hopeful prince—here standing
To prate and talk for life and honor 'fore

---

198 **beyond account** unprecedented, or, beyond explanation.
200 suddenly at once　**202 session** trial
3.1. Location: Sicilia. On the way to Leontes's court.
2 isle (Shakespeare follows Greene's *Pandosto* in fictitiously placing
Delphi on an island. Delphi, sometimes known as Delphos [see
2.1.184, 2.3.196, and 3.2.126], was often confused with Delos, the
island birthplace of Apollo and location also of an oracle.)　**4 habits**
vestments　**10 surprised** overwhelmed　**11 th'event** the outcome
14 is worth . . . on't has been well employed.　**17 carriage** execution,
management　**19 great divine** chief priest　**20 discover** reveal

3.2. Location: Sicilia. A place of justice, probably at court.
4 Of us by me　**7 purgation** acquittal.　**17 pretense** purpose, design
25 boot avail　**36 history** story, drama.　**pattern** show a similar
example for　**37 take** please, charm　**38 which owe** who owns
39 moiety share

Who please to come and hear. For life, I prize it   42
As I weigh grief, which I would spare. For honor,   43
'Tis a derivative from me to mine,   44
And only that I stand for. I appeal   45
To your own conscience, sir, before Polixenes   46
Came to your court, how I was in your grace,
How merited to be so; since he came,
With what encounter so uncurrent I   49
Have strained t'appear thus; if one jot beyond   50
The bound of honor, or in act or will
That way inclining, hardened be the hearts   52
Of all that hear me, and my near'st of kin
Cry "Fie" upon my grave!

LEONTES   I ne'er heard yet
That any of these bolder vices wanted   55
Less impudence to gainsay what they did   56
Than to perform it first.

HERMIONE   That's true enough,
Though 'tis a saying, sir, not due to me.   58

LEONTES
You will not own it.

HERMIONE   More than mistress of   59
Which comes to me in name of fault, I must not   60
At all acknowledge. For Polixenes,   61
With whom I am accused, I do confess
I loved him as in honor he required;   63
With such a kind of love as might become
A lady like me; with a love even such,
So, and no other, as yourself commanded;
Which not to have done I think had been in me
Both disobedience and ingratitude
To you and toward your friend, whose love had
    spoke,   69
Even since it could speak, from an infant, freely   70
That it was yours. Now, for conspiracy,   71
I know not how it tastes, though it be dished   72
For me to try how. All I know of it
Is that Camillo was an honest man;
And why he left your court, the gods themselves,
Wotting no more than I, are ignorant.   76

LEONTES
You knew of his departure, as you know
What you have underta'en to do in 's absence.

HERMIONE   Sir,
You speak a language that I understand not.
My life stands in the level of your dreams,   81

Which I'll lay down.

LEONTES   Your actions are my dreams.   82
You had a bastard by Polixenes,
And I but dreamed it. As you were past all shame—
Those of your fact are so—so past all truth,   85
Which to deny concerns more than avails; for as   86
Thy brat hath been cast out, like to itself,   87
No father owning it—which is indeed
More criminal in thee than it—so thou
Shalt feel our justice, in whose easiest passage   90
Look for no less than death.

HERMIONE   Sir, spare your threats.   91
The bug which you would fright me with I seek.   92
To me can life be no commodity.   93
The crown and comfort of my life, your favor,
I do give lost, for I do feel it gone,   95
But know not how it went. My second joy
And firstfruits of my body, from his presence
I am barred, like one infectious. My third comfort,
Starred most unluckily, is from my breast,   99
The innocent milk in it most innocent mouth,   100
Haled out to murder; myself on every post   101
Proclaimed a strumpet; with immodest hatred   102
The childbed privilege denied, which longs   103
To women of all fashion; lastly, hurried   104
Here to this place, i'th'open air, before
I have got strength of limit. Now, my liege,   106
Tell me what blessings I have here alive
That I should fear to die? Therefore proceed.
But yet hear this; mistake me not. No life,   109
I prize it not a straw. But for mine honor,
Which I would free, if I shall be condemned   111
Upon surmises, all proofs sleeping else
But what your jealousies awake, I tell you
'Tis rigor and not law. Your Honors all,   114
I do refer me to the oracle.
Apollo be my judge!

A LORD   This your request
Is altogether just. Therefore bring forth,
And in Apollo's name, his oracle.

[*Exeunt certain Officers.*]

HERMIONE
The Emperor of Russia was my father.
Oh, that he were alive and here beholding
His daughter's trial! That he did but see

---

42 Who please whoever chooses   **42–5 For . . . stand for** As for life, I value it as I value grief, and would as willingly do without; as for honor, it is transmitted from me to my descendants, and that only I make a stand for.   **46 conscience** consideration, inward knowledge   **49–50 With . . . thus** (I ask) by what behavior so unacceptable I have transgressed so that I appear thus (in disgrace and on trial)   **52 hardened** hardened against me   **55–6 wanted Less** were more lacking in   **58 due** applicable   **59–61 More . . . acknowledge** I must not acknowledge more faults than I actually have.   **61 For** As for   **63 required** deserved   **69–71 your friend . . . yours** i.e., Polixenes, who professed love for you from earliest childhood (as you for him).   **71 for** as for   **72 though . . . dished** even if it were to be served up   **76 Wotting** supposing they know   **81 level** aim, range

82 Which i.e., my life.   **Your . . . dreams** i.e., You have performed what I have fantasized, and what you have done preys on my mind.   **85 Those of your fact** All those who do what you did   **86 Which . . . avails** your denial of which is understandable, but it won't do you any good   **87 like to itself** as an outcast, fatherless brat ought to be   **90–1 in whose . . . death** i.e., which will impose the death sentence at least, perhaps torture also.   **92 bug** bugbear, bogey, imaginary object of terror   **93 commodity** asset.   **95 give** reckon as, or give up for   **99 Starred most unluckily** born under a most unlucky star   **100 it** its   **101 post** posting place for public notices   **102 immodest** immoderate   **103 The childbed . . . longs** denied the privilege of bedrest after giving birth, something that is the right   **104 all fashion** every rank   **106 got . . . limit** regained my strength after having borne a child.   **109 No life** i.e., I do not ask for life   **111 free** vindicate   **114 rigor** tyranny

The flatness of my misery, yet with eyes 122
Of pity, not revenge!

[*Enter Officers, with*] Cleomenes [*and*] Dion.

OFFICER [*holding a sword*]
You here shall swear upon this sword of justice
That you, Cleomenes and Dion, have
Been both at Delphos, and from thence have brought
This sealed-up oracle, by the hand delivered
Of great Apollo's priest, and that since then
You have not dared to break the holy seal
Nor read the secrets in't.

CLEOMENES, DION   All this we swear.

LEONTES
Break up the seals and read. 131

OFFICER [*reads*]   "Hermione is chaste, Polixenes blameless, Camillo a true subject, Leontes a jealous tyrant,
his innocent babe truly begotten, and the King shall
live without an heir if that which is lost be not
found."

LORDS
Now blessèd be the great Apollo!

HERMIONE   Praised!

LEONTES
Hast thou read truth?

OFFICER   Ay, my lord, even so
As it is here set down.

LEONTES
There is no truth at all i'th'oracle.
The sessions shall proceed. This is mere falsehood.

[*Enter a Servant.*]

SERVANT
My lord the King, the King!

LEONTES   What is the business?

SERVANT
Oh, sir, I shall be hated to report it! 143
The Prince your son, with mere conceit and fear 144
Of the Queen's speed, is gone.

LEONTES   How? Gone?

SERVANT   Is dead. 145

LEONTES
Apollo's angry, and the heavens themselves
Do strike at my injustice. [*Hermione swoons.*] How now
there?

PAULINA
This news is mortal to the Queen. Look down
And see what death is doing.

LEONTES   Take her hence.
Her heart is but o'ercharged; she will recover.
I have too much believed mine own suspicion.
Beseech you, tenderly apply to her
Some remedies for life.

[*Exeunt Paulina and Ladies, with Hermione.*]
Apollo, pardon
My great profaneness 'gainst thine oracle!
I'll reconcile me to Polixenes,

New woo my queen, recall the good Camillo,
Whom I proclaim a man of truth, of mercy;
For, being transported by my jealousies
To bloody thoughts and to revenge, I chose
Camillo for the minister to poison
My friend Polixenes; which had been done,
But that the good mind of Camillo tardied 162
My swift command, though I with death and with
Reward did threaten and encourage him,
Not doing it and being done. He, most humane 165
And filled with honor, to my kingly guest
Unclasped my practice, quit his fortunes here, 167
Which you knew great, and to the hazard
Of all incertainties himself commended, 169
No richer than his honor. How he glisters 170
Through my rust! And how his piety 171
Does my deeds make the blacker!

[*Enter Paulina.*]

PAULINA   Woe the while!
Oh, cut my lace, lest my heart, cracking it, 173
Break too!

A LORD   What fit is this, good lady?

PAULINA
What studied torments, tyrant, hast for me? 175
What wheels, racks, fires? What flaying, boiling 176
In leads or oils? What old or newer torture
Must I receive, whose every word deserves 178
To taste of thy most worst? Thy tyranny, 179
Together working with thy jealousies—
Fancies too weak for boys, too green and idle 181
For girls of nine—oh, think what they have done,
And then run mad indeed, stark mad! For all
Thy bygone fooleries were but spices of it. 184
That thou betrayed'st Polixenes, 'twas nothing;
That did but show thee, of a fool, inconstant 186
And damnable ingrateful. Nor was 't much
Thou wouldst have poisoned good Camillo's honor,
To have him kill a king—poor trespasses, 189
More monstrous standing by; whereof I reckon 190
The casting forth to crows thy baby daughter 191
To be or none or little, though a devil 192
Would have shed water out of fire ere done't. 193
Nor is't directly laid to thee, the death
Of the young Prince, whose honorable thoughts,
Thoughts high for one so tender, cleft the heart 196
That could conceive a gross and foolish sire 197

---

122 flatness boundlessness   **131 up** open   **143 to report** for reporting
144 conceit and fear i.e., anxious concern   **145 speed** fate, fortune

162 tardied delayed   **165 Not . . . done** i.e., death if he did not do it
and reward if he did.   **167 Unclasped my practice** disclosed my plot
169 himself commended entrusted himself   **170 No richer than** with
no riches except   **170–1 How . . . rust!** How he shines in contrast with
my fault!   **173 my lace** the lace of my stays   **175 studied** ingeniously
devised   **176 wheels . . . flaying** (Various methods of torture: being
stretched on a wheel or rack until the bones are broken or pulled
apart at the joints, being burned or skinned alive.)   **178–9 whose . . .
worst?** I, whose every word seems to invite your severest punishment?   **181 idle** foolish   **184 spices** foretastes, samples   **186 of** for
189 To have by having.   **poor** slight   **190 More . . . by** when more
monstrous sins are at hand for comparison   **191 crows** carrion birds
192 or none either none   **193 shed . . . fire** wept from his fiery eyes or
while surrounded by hellfire   **196 tender** young   **197 conceive**
apprehend that

Blemished his gracious dam. This is not, no,   198
Laid to thy answer. But the last—Oh, lords,   199
When I have said, cry woe! The Queen, the Queen,   200
The sweet'st, dear'st creature's dead, and vengeance
    for't
Not dropped down yet.

A LORD   The higher powers forbid!

PAULINA
I say she's dead. I'll swear't. If word nor oath
Prevail not, go and see. If you can bring
Tincture or luster in her lip, her eye,   205
Heat outwardly or breath within, I'll serve you
As I would do the gods. But, O thou tyrant!
Do not repent these things, for they are heavier
Than all thy woes can stir. Therefore betake thee   209
To nothing but despair. A thousand knees
Ten thousand years together, naked, fasting,
Upon a barren mountain, and still winter   212
In storm perpetual, could not move the gods
To look that way thou wert.

LEONTES   Go on, go on.   214
Thou canst not speak too much. I have deserved
All tongues to talk their bitt'rest.

A LORD [to Paulina]   Say no more.
Howe'er the business goes, you have made fault
I'th' boldness of your speech.

PAULINA   I am sorry for't.
All faults I make, when I shall come to know them,   219
I do repent. Alas, I have showed too much
The rashness of a woman! He is touched
To th' noble heart. What's gone and what's past help
Should be past grief.—Do not receive affliction   223
At my petition. I beseech you, rather   224
Let me be punished, that have minded you   225
Of what you should forget. Now, good my liege,
Sir, royal sir, forgive a foolish woman.
The love I bore your queen—lo, fool again!
I'll speak of her no more, nor of your children;
I'll not remember you of my own lord,   230
Who is lost too. Take your patience to you,   231
And I'll say nothing.

LEONTES   Thou didst speak but well
When most the truth, which I receive much better
Than to be pitied of thee. Prithee, bring me
To the dead bodies of my queen and son.
One grave shall be for both. Upon them shall
The causes of their death appear, unto
Our shame perpetual. Once a day I'll visit
The chapel where they lie, and tears shed there
Shall be my recreation. So long as nature   240
Will bear up with this exercise, so long

I daily vow to use it. Come and lead me
To these sorrows.   *Exeunt.*

❖

3.3

Enter Antigonus [and] a Mariner, [with a] babe.

ANTIGONUS
Thou art perfect then, our ship hath touched upon   1
The deserts of Bohemia?

MARINER   Ay, my lord, and fear   2
We have landed in ill time. The skies look grimly
And threaten present blusters. In my conscience,   4
The heavens with that we have in hand are angry
And frown upon 's.

ANTIGONUS   Their sacred wills be done! Go, get aboard;
Look to thy bark. I'll not be long before   8
I call upon thee.

MARINER   Make your best haste, and go not
Too far i'th' land. 'Tis like to be loud weather.   10
Besides, this place is famous for the creatures
Of prey that keep upon't.

ANTIGONUS   Go thou away.   12
I'll follow instantly.

MARINER   I am glad at heart
To be so rid o'th' business.   *Exit.*

ANTIGONUS   Come, poor babe.
I have heard, but not believed, the spirits o'th' dead
May walk again. If such thing be, thy mother
Appeared to me last night, for ne'er was dream
So like a waking. To me comes a creature,
Sometimes her head on one side, some another;   19
I never saw a vessel of like sorrow,
So filled and so becoming. In pure white robes,   21
Like very sanctity, she did approach
My cabin where I lay, thrice bowed before me,
And, gasping to begin some speech, her eyes
Became two spouts. The fury spent, anon
Did this break from her: "Good Antigonus,
Since fate, against thy better disposition,
Hath made thy person for the thrower-out
Of my poor babe, according to thine oath,
Places remote enough are in Bohemia;
There weep and leave it crying. And, for the babe   31
Is counted lost forever, Perdita,   32
I prithee, call't. For this ungentle business   33
Put on thee by my lord, thou ne'er shalt see
Thy wife Paulina more." And so, with shrieks,
She melted into air. Affrighted much,
I did in time collect myself and thought
This was so and no slumber. Dreams are toys;   38

198 dam mother.   199 Laid . . . answer presented as a charge that
you must answer.   200 said finished speaking   205 Tincture color
209 woes can stir penance can remove.   212 still always   214 To look
. . . wert to regard you.   219 I make that I make   223–4 Do . . . petition Do not afflict yourself with remorse at my urging.   225 minded
you put you in mind   230 remember remind   231 Take . . . you Arm
yourself with patience   240 my recreation (1) my sole diversion (2) my
spiritual regeneration.   nature my physical being

3.3. Location: Bohemia. The seacoast.
1 perfect certain   2 deserts of Bohemia i.e., deserted region on the
coast. (Shakespeare follows Greene's *Pandosto* in giving Bohemia a
seacoast.)   4 present immediate.   conscience opinion   8 bark ship.
10 like likely.   loud stormy   12 keep upon't inhabit it.   19 some
another sometimes the other   21 So . . . becoming i.e., so filled with
sorrow and able to bear it so gracefully.   31 for because   32 Perdita
i.e., the lost one   33 ungentle ignoble   38 toys trifles

Yet for this once, yea, superstitiously,
I will be squared by this. I do believe   40
Hermione hath suffered death, and that
Apollo would, this being indeed the issue
Of King Polixenes, it should here be laid,
Either for life or death, upon the earth
Of its right father. Blossom, speed thee well!
                                    [*He lays down the baby.*]
There lie, and there thy character; there these,   46
        [*He places a box and a fardel beside the baby.*]
Which may, if fortune please, both breed thee, pretty,   47
And still rest thine. [*Thunder.*] The storm begins. Poor
    wretch,   48
That for thy mother's fault art thus exposed
To loss and what may follow! Weep I cannot,   50
But my heart bleeds; and most accurst am I
To be by oath enjoined to this. Farewell!
The day frowns more and more. Thou'rt like to have
A lullaby too rough. I never saw
The heavens so dim by day. A savage clamor!
Well may I get aboard! This is the chase.
I am gone forever!   *Exit, pursued by a bear.*

        [*Enter a*] Shepherd.

SHEPHERD   I would there were no age between ten and
three-and-twenty, or that youth would sleep out the
rest, for there is nothing in the between but getting
wenches with child, wronging the ancientry, stealing,   61
fighting—Hark you now, would any but these boiled   62
brains of nineteen and two-and-twenty hunt this   63
weather? They have scared away two of my best sheep,
which I fear the wolf will sooner find than the master.
If anywhere I have them, 'tis by the seaside, browsing
of ivy. Good luck, an't be thy will! [*Seeing the child*]. 67
What have we here? Mercy on 's, a bairn, a very pretty   68
bairn! A boy or a child, I wonder? A pretty one, a very   69
pretty one. Sure some scape. Though I am not bookish,   70
yet I can read waiting-gentlewoman in the scape.
This has been some stair-work, some trunk-work,   72
some behind-door-work. They were warmer that got   73
this than the poor thing is here. I'll take it up for pity.
Yet I'll tarry till my son come; he hallooed but even
now.—Whoa, ho, hoa!   76

        Enter Clown.

CLOWN   Hilloa, loa!

SHEPHERD   What, art so near? If thou'lt see a thing to
talk on when thou art dead and rotten, come hither.
What ail'st thou, man?
CLOWN   I have seen two such sights, by sea and by
land! But I am not to say it is a sea, for it is now the sky;
betwixt the firmament and it you cannot thrust a
bodkin's point.   84
SHEPHERD   Why, boy, how is it?
CLOWN   I would you did but see how it chafes, how it
rages, how it takes up the shore! But that's not to the   87
point. Oh, the most piteous cry of the poor souls! Sometimes to see 'em, and not to see 'em; now the ship
boring the moon with her mainmast, and anon swallowed with yeast and froth, as you'd thrust a cork into   91
a hogshead. And then for the land service, to see how   92
the bear tore out his shoulder bone; how he cried to
me for help and said his name was Antigonus, a nobleman. But to make an end of the ship: to see how
the sea flapdragoned it! But first, how the poor souls   96
roared and the sea mocked them, and how the poor
gentleman roared and the bear mocked him, both
roaring louder than the sea or weather.
SHEPHERD   Name of mercy, when was this, boy?
CLOWN   Now, now. I have not winked since I saw these   101
sights. The men are not yet cold under water, nor the
bear half dined on the gentleman. He's at it now.
SHEPHERD   Would I had been by, to have helped the
old man!
CLOWN   I would you had been by the ship side, to have
helped her. There your charity would have lacked
footing.   108
SHEPHERD   Heavy matters, heavy matters! But look thee
here, boy. Now bless thyself. Thou met'st with things
dying, I with things newborn. Here's a sight for thee;
look thee, a bearing cloth for a squire's child! Look   112
thee here; take up, take up, boy. Open't. So, let's see.
It was told me I should be rich by the fairies. This is
some changeling. Open't. What's within, boy?   115
                        [*The Clown opens the box.*]
CLOWN   You're a made old man. If the sins of your
youth are forgiven you, you're well to live. Gold, all   117
gold!
SHEPHERD   This is fairy gold, boy, and 'twill prove so.
Up with't, keep it close. Home, home, the next way.   120
We are lucky, boy, and to be so still requires nothing   121
but secrecy. Let my sheep go. Come, good boy, the   122
next way home.

---

40 squared directed in my course   **46 thy character** the written
account of you (i.e., the one that subsequently will serve to identify
Perdita).   **these** i.e., the gold and jewels found by the Shepherd, also
later used to identify her.   **46.1 box, fardel** (The box, containing gold
and jewels, is later produced by the old Shepherd and the Clown; see
4.4.758–9. They also have a *fardel*, or "bundle," consisting evidently of
the bearing cloth [3.3.112] and/or mantle [5.2.34] in which the babe
was found.)   **47 breed thee** keep you, pay for your support.   **pretty
pretty one   48 And still rest thine** i.e., and still provide a heritage with
what is unspent.   **50 Weep I cannot** i.e., I cannot weep as the Queen
instructed me (line 31)   **61 ancientry** old people   **62–3 boiled brains**
addlepated youths   **67 Good . . . will!** i.e., May God grant me good
luck in finding my sheep!   **68 bairn** child   **69 child** i.e., female infant
70 scape sexual escapade.   **72–3 stair-work . . . behind-door-work** i.e.,
sexual liaisons under or behind the stairs or using a room or a trunk for
concealment.   **73 got** begot   **76.1 Clown** country fellow, rustic.

84 bodkin's needle's. (A *bodkin* can also be a dagger, awl, etc.)   **87 takes
up** (1) contends with, rebukes (2) swallows   **91 yeast** foam   **92 hogshead**
large barrel. (The image is of a cork swimming in a turbulent expanse
of frothing liquid.)   **land service** (1) dish of food served on land
(2) military service on land (as distinguished from naval service);
here, the doings on land   **96 flapdragoned** swallowed as one would
a flapdragon, i.e., a raisin or the like swallowed out of burning brandy
in the game of snapdragon   **101 winked** blinked an eye   **108 footing** (1) foothold (2) establishment of a charitable foundation, one that
would provide *charity* (line 107).   **112 bearing cloth** rich cloth or
mantle in which a child was carried to its baptism   **115 changeling**
child left or taken by fairies.   **117 well to live** well-to-do.   **120 close**
secret.   **next** nearest   **121–2 to be . . . secrecy** (To talk about fairy
gifts would be to insure bad luck.)   **121 still** on a continuing basis

CLOWN   Go you the next way with your findings. I'll go
see if the bear be gone from the gentleman, and how
much he hath eaten. They are never curst but when 126
they are hungry. If there be any of him left, I'll bury it.

SHEPHERD   That's a good deed. If thou mayest discern
by that which is left of him what he is, fetch me to th' 129
sight of him.

CLOWN   Marry, will I; and you shall help to put him i'th' 131
ground.

SHEPHERD   'Tis a lucky day, boy, and we'll do good
deeds on't.   Exeunt.

❖

4.1

Enter Time, the Chorus.

TIME
I, that please some, try all, both joy and terror   1
Of good and bad, that makes and unfolds error,   2
Now take upon me, in the name of Time,
To use my wings. Impute it not a crime
To me or my swift passage that I slide
O'er sixteen years and leave the growth untried   6
Of that wide gap, since it is in my power
To o'erthrow law and in one self-born hour   8
To plant and o'erwhelm custom. Let me pass   9
The same I am ere ancient'st order was   10
Or what is now received. I witness to   11
The times that brought them in; so shall I do   12
To th' freshest things now reigning, and make stale
The glistering of this present as my tale   14
Now seems to it. Your patience this allowing,   15
I turn my glass and give my scene such growing   16
As you had slept between. Leontes leaving   17
Th'effects of his fond jealousies, so grieving   18
That he shuts up himself, imagine me,
Gentle spectators, that I now may be
In fair Bohemia. And remember well
I mentioned a son o'th' King's, which Florizel
I now name to you; and with speed so pace   23
To speak of Perdita, now grown in grace   24
Equal with wond'ring. What of her ensues   25
I list not prophesy; but let Time's news   26
Be known when 'tis brought forth. A shepherd's
daughter,

And what to her adheres, which follows after,   28
Is th'argument of Time. Of this allow,   29
If ever you have spent time worse ere now;
If never, yet that Time himself doth say   31
He wishes earnestly you never may.   *Exit.*

❖

4.2

Enter Polixenes and Camillo.

POLIXENES   I pray thee, good Camillo, be no more
importunate. 'Tis a sickness denying thee anything, a
death to grant this.

CAMILLO   It is fifteen years since I saw my country.   4
Though I have for the most part been aired abroad, I   5
desire to lay my bones there. Besides, the penitent
King, my master, hath sent for me, to whose feeling   7
sorrows I might be some allay—or I o'erween to think   8
so—which is another spur to my departure.

POLIXENES   As thou lov'st me, Camillo, wipe not out the
rest of thy services by leaving me now. The need I
have of thee thine own goodness hath made. Better
not to have had thee than thus to want thee. Thou,   13
having made me businesses which none without thee
can sufficiently manage, must either stay to execute
them thyself or take away with thee the very services
thou hast done; which if I have not enough
considered—as too much I cannot—to be more thank-   18
ful to thee shall be my study, and my profit therein
the heaping friendships. Of that fatal country, Sicilia, 20
prithee, speak no more, whose very naming punishes
me with the remembrance of that penitent, as thou
call'st him, and reconciled King, my brother, whose
loss of his most precious queen and children are even
now to be afresh lamented. Say to me, when saw'st
thou the Prince Florizel, my son? Kings are no less
unhappy, their issue not being gracious, than they are 27
in losing them when they have approved their virtues.   28

CAMILLO   Sir, it is three days since I saw the Prince.
What his happier affairs may be are to me unknown;
but I have missingly noted he is of late much retired   31
from court and is less frequent to his princely exercises 32
than formerly he hath appeared.

POLIXENES   I have considered so much, Camillo, and   34
with some care, so far that I have eyes under my ser-   35
vice which look upon his removedness; from whom I   36
have this intelligence, that he is seldom from the   37
house of a most homely shepherd—a man, they say,   38

---

126 curst mean, fierce   **129 what he is** what is his identity or rank
131 Marry i.e., Indeed. (Originally an oath, "by the Virgin Mary.")
4.1.
1 try test   **2 that . . . error** i.e., I who make error, thus bringing joy to
the bad and terror to the good, and then at last unfold or disclose error,
thus bringing joy to the good and terror to the bad   **6 growth untried**
developments unexplored   **8 law** any established order (including the
rule of the unity of time in a dramatic performance, conventionally
limiting the action to twenty-four hours).   **self-born** selfsame, or born
of myself (since hours are the creations of Time)   **9–11 Let . . . received**
Let me continue as I have been from before the beginning of time to the
present.   **12 them** i.e., law and custom   **14 glistering** glittering shine
15 seems to it seems (stale) when compared with the present.
16 glass hourglass   **17 As** as if   **18 fond** foolish   **23 pace** proceed
24–5 now . . . wondering now grown so gracious (and graceful) as to
inspire wonderment.   **26 list not** do not care to

28 to her adheres concerns her   **29 th'argument** the subject matter
31 yet that i.e., yet allow that
4.2. Location: Bohemia. The court of Polixenes.
4 fifteen (Compare "sixteen" at 4.1.6.)   **5 been aired abroad** lived
abroad   **7 feeling** heartfelt   **8 allay** means of abatement.   **o'erween**
am presumptuous enough   **13 want** lack   **18 considered** rewarded
20 heaping friendships accumulation of your kind services and our
mutual affection.   **27 their . . . gracious** if their children behave ungra-
ciously   **28 approved** proved   **31 missingly** being aware that he is
missing   **32 frequent to** devoted to   **34 so much** as much   **35–6 eyes
. . . removedness** spies who keep an eye on him in his absence
37 intelligence news.   **from** away from   **38 homely** simple

that from very nothing, and beyond the imagination
of his neighbors, is grown into an unspeakable estate. 40

CAMILLO I have heard, sir, of such a man, who hath a
daughter of most rare note. The report of her is 42
extended more than can be thought to begin from
such a cottage.

POLIXENES That's likewise part of my intelligence; but,
I fear, the angle that plucks our son thither. Thou shalt 46
accompany us to the place, where we will, not appearing what we are, have some question with the shep- 48
herd; from whose simplicity I think it not uneasy to 49
get the cause of my son's resort thither. Prithee, be my
present partner in this business, and lay aside the
thoughts of Sicilia.

CAMILLO I willingly obey your command.

POLIXENES My best Camillo! We must disguise ourselves.   *Exit [with Camillo].*

4.3

Enter Autolycus, singing.

AUTOLYCUS
When daffodils begin to peer,   1
    With heigh, the doxy over the dale!   2
Why, then comes in the sweet o'the year,
    For the red blood reigns in the winter's pale.   4

The white sheet bleaching on the hedge,
    With heigh, the sweet birds, oh, how they
        sing!
Doth set my pugging tooth on edge,   7
    For a quart of ale is a dish for a king.   8

The lark, that tirralirra chants,
    With heigh, with heigh, the thrush and the jay!
Are summer songs for me and my aunts,   11
    While we lie tumbling in the hay.

I have served Prince Florizel and in my time wore
three-pile, but now I am out of service.   14

But shall I go mourn for that, my dear?   15
    The pale moon shines by night,
And when I wander here and there,   17
    I then do most go right.   18

If tinkers may have leave to live,   19
    And bear the sow-skin budget,   20

Then my account I well may give,   21
    And in the stocks avouch it.   22

My traffic is sheets; when the kite builds, look to lesser 23
linen. My father named me Autolycus, who, being, as 24
I am, littered under Mercury, was likewise a snap- 25
per-up of unconsidered trifles. With die and drab I 26
purchased this caparison, and my revenue is the silly 27
cheat. Gallows and knock are too powerful on the 28
highway; beating and hanging are terrors to me. For 29
the life to come, I sleep out the thought of it. A prize, 30
a prize!

Enter Clown.

CLOWN Let me see: every 'leven wether tods; every tod 32
yields pound and odd shilling; fifteen hundred shorn,
what comes the wool to?

AUTOLYCUS [*aside*] If the springe hold, the cock's mine. 35

CLOWN I cannot do't without counters. Let me see; 36
what am I to buy for our sheepshearing feast? Three
pound of sugar, five pound of currants, rice—what
will this sister of mine do with rice? But my father hath
made her mistress of the feast, and she lays it on. She
hath made me four-and-twenty nosegays for the shear- 41
ers—three-man-song men all, and very good ones; 42
but they are most of them means and basses, but one 43
Puritan amongst them, and he sings psalms to horn- 44
pipes. I must have saffron to color the warden pies; 45
mace; dates?—none, that's out of my note; nutmegs, 46
seven; a race or two of ginger, but that I may beg; four 47
pound of prunes, and as many of raisins o'th' sun. 48

AUTOLYCUS Oh, that ever I was born! [*He grovels on the
ground.*]

CLOWN I'th' name of me!   50

AUTOLYCUS Oh, help me, help me! Pluck but off these
rags, and then death, death!

---

40 unspeakable beyond description   **42 note** distinction.   **46 angle**
baited fishhook.   **our** (The royal plural; also in *us*, line 47.)   **48 question** talk   **49 uneasy** difficult
4.3. Location: Bohemia. A road near the Shepherd's cottage.
1 peer peep out, appear   **2 doxy** beggar's wench   **4 pale** (1) paleness
(2) domain, region of authority. (The image is of red blood restoring
vitality to a pale complexion.)   **7 set . . . on edge** i.e., whets the
appetite of my thieving tooth, my taste for thieving. (To *pug* is to
"pull, tug.")   **8 quart of ale** (To be paid for perhaps with profits from
theft of sheets.)   **11 aunts** i.e., whores   **14 three-pile** velvet having
very rich pile or nap   **15 for that** i.e., for being out of service
17 wander (i.e., as a thief)   **18 most go right** i.e., live the life that is
meant for me.   **19 leave to live** permission to practice their trade
20 budget tool bag

21 my account an account of myself   **22 in . . . avouch it** i.e., affirm
that I am a tinker if I find myself sitting in the stocks, where vagabonds
often end up. (Autolycus passes himself off as a tinker to mask his real
calling of thief.)   **23–4 when . . . linen** (The kite, a bird of prey, was
thought to carry off small pieces of linen with which to construct its
nest, whereas Autolycus makes off with larger linen or sheets hung out
to dry.)   **24 Autolycus** (Like his namesake, Ulysses's grandfather, the
son of Mercury, this Autolycus is an expert thief.)   **who** (Refers
ambiguously to Autolycus and "My father"; see next note.)   **25 littered under Mercury** (1) sired by Mercury, the god of thieves (2) born
when the planet Mercury was in the ascendant   **26 unconsidered** left
unattended, not worth thinking about   **26–8 With . . . cheat** Gambling
and whoring have brought me to the wearing of these tattered rags,
and my source of income is petty trickery used to cheat simpletons.
28–9 Gallows . . . to me i.e., Hanging and being beaten, the ordinary
hazards of being a highwayman, are too much for me; I'll stick to being
a petty thief.   **29 For** As for   **30 sleep . . . it** i.e., don't give a thought to
punishment in the next world.   **prize** booty   **32 every . . . tods** every
eleven sheep yield a *tod*, i.e., a bulk of wool weighing twenty-eight
pounds   **35 springe** snare.   **cock** woodcock. (A proverbially stupid
bird.)   **36 counters** metal disks used in reckoning.   **41 made me**
made. (*Me* is used colloquially.)   **nosegays** bouquets   **42 three-man-
song men** singers of songs for three male voices: bass, tenor, and treble
43 means tenors   **43–5 but . . . hornpipes** (Puritans were often laughed
at for their pious singing; this Puritan is imagined as singing hymns
even to the sounds of raucous merriment at a fair.)   **45 warden** made
of the warden pear   **46 out of my note** not on my list   **47 race** root
48 o'th' sun dried in the sun.   **50 I'th' name of me!** (An unusual and
perhaps comic oath.)

CLOWN   Alack, poor soul! Thou hast need of more rags
to lay on thee, rather than have these off.

AUTOLYCUS   Oh, sir, the loathsomeness of them offend
me more than the stripes I have received, which are
mighty ones and millions.

CLOWN   Alas, poor man! A million of beating may come
to a great matter.

AUTOLYCUS   I am robbed, sir, and beaten; my money
and apparel ta'en from me, and these detestable things
put upon me.

CLOWN   What, by a horseman or a footman?   63

AUTOLYCUS   A footman, sweet sir, a footman.

CLOWN   Indeed, he should be a footman by the garments he has left with thee. If this be a horseman's
coat, it hath seen very hot service. Lend me thy hand;
I'll help thee. Come, lend me thy hand. [*He helps him
up.*]

AUTOLYCUS   Oh, good sir, tenderly. Oh!

CLOWN   Alas, poor soul!

AUTOLYCUS   Oh, good sir, softly, good sir! I fear, sir, my
shoulder blade is out.

CLOWN   How now? Canst stand?

AUTOLYCUS   [*picking his pocket*] Softly, dear sir; good
sir, softly. You ha' done me a charitable office.

CLOWN   [*reaching for his purse*] Dost lack any money? I   76
have a little money for thee.   77

AUTOLYCUS   No, good sweet sir; no, I beseech you, sir.
I have a kinsman not past three quarters of a mile
hence, unto whom I was going; I shall there have
money or anything I want. Offer me no money, I pray
you. That kills my heart.

CLOWN   What manner of fellow was he that robbed
you?

AUTOLYCUS   A fellow, sir, that I have known to go about
with troll-my-dames. I knew him once a servant of the   85
Prince. I cannot tell, good sir, for which of his virtues
it was, but he was certainly whipped out of the court.

CLOWN   His vices, you would say. There's no virtue
whipped out of the court. They cherish it to make it
stay there; and yet it will no more but abide.   90

AUTOLYCUS   Vices, I would say, sir. I know this man
well. He hath been since an ape bearer, then a process   92
server, a bailiff. Then he compassed a motion of   93
the Prodigal Son and married a tinker's wife within a
mile where my land and living lies, and, having flown   95
over many knavish professions, he settled only in
rogue. Some call him Autolycus.

CLOWN   Out upon him! Prig, for my life, prig! He   98
haunts wakes, fairs, and bearbaitings.   99

AUTOLYCUS   Very true, sir. He, sir, he. That's the rogue
that put me into this apparel.

CLOWN   Not a more cowardly rogue in all Bohemia. If
you had but looked big and spit at him, he'd have
run.

AUTOLYCUS   I must confess to you, sir, I am no fighter.
I am false of heart that way, and that he knew, I   106
warrant him.

CLOWN   How do you now?

AUTOLYCUS   Sweet sir, much better than I was. I can
stand and walk. I will even take my leave of you and
pace softly towards my kinsman's.   111

CLOWN   Shall I bring thee on the way?   112

AUTOLYCUS   No, good-faced sir, no, sweet sir.

CLOWN   Then fare thee well. I must go buy spices for
our sheep-shearing.   *Exit.*

AUTOLYCUS   Prosper you, sweet sir! Your purse is not   116
hot enough to purchase your spice. I'll be with you at   117
your sheep-shearing too. If I make not this cheat bring 118
out another, and the shearers prove sheep, let me be   119
unrolled and my name put in the book of virtue!   120

Song.

Jog on, jog on, the footpath way,
        And merrily hent the stile-a;   122
A merry heart goes all the day,
        Your sad tires in a mile-a.   *Exit.*

❖

4.4

*Enter Florizel [in shepherd's garb, and] Perdita [in
holiday attire].*

FLORIZEL
These your unusual weeds to each part of you   1
Does give a life; no shepherdess, but Flora   2
Peering in April's front. This your sheepshearing   3
Is as a meeting of the petty gods,   4
And you the queen on't.

PERDITA   Sir, my gracious lord,
To chide at your extremes it not becomes me.   6
Oh, pardon that I name them! Your high self,
The gracious mark o'th' land, you have obscured   8
With a swain's wearing, and me, poor lowly maid,   9

---

63 horseman highwayman. **footman** footpad. (As the Clown
observes in line 65, a common robber on foot would have poorer
clothes than a mounted highwayman.) **76–7 I have . . . thee** (The
Clown reaches for his money and might have discovered the robbery
if Autolycus had not quickly begged him not to bother.) **85 troll-
my-dames** or troll-madams (from the French *trou-madame*), a game in
which the object was to *troll* balls through arches set on a board.
(Autolycus uses the word to suggest women who *troll* or saunter
about.) **90 no more but abide** make only a temporary or unwilling
stay. **92 ape bearer** one who carries a trained monkey about for
exhibition **92–3 process server** sheriff's officer who serves processes
or summonses **93 compassed a motion** devised a puppet show
95 living property

98 Prig Thief **99 wakes** village festivals **106 false** cowardly
111 softly slowly **112 bring . . . way** go part of the way with you.
116 Prosper . . . sir! (Said to the departing Clown.) **116–17 Your . . .
spice** i.e., You'll find but a cold purse to pay for your hot spices; an
empty purse is a cold one. (Said after the Clown's departure.)
118–19 cheat bring out swindle lead to **120 unrolled** taken off the
roll (of rogues and vagabonds) **122 hent** take hold of (as a means of
leaping over)
4.4. Location: Bohemia. The Shepherd's cottage. (See lines 181–2,
187, etc.)
1 unusual weeds special, holiday attire **2 Flora** goddess of flowers
3 Peering . . . front peeping forth in early April, or, in April's countenance or garb. **4 petty** minor **6 extremes** extravagant statements
8 mark o'th' land one who is noted and used as a model by everyone
9 wearing garb

Most goddesslike pranked up. But that our feasts 10
In every mess have folly, and the feeders 11
Digest it with a custom, I should blush 12
To see you so attired, swoon, I think,
To show myself a glass.
FLORIZEL   I bless the time 14
When my good falcon made her flight across
Thy father's ground.
PERDITA   Now Jove afford you cause! 16
To me the difference forges dread; your greatness 17
Hath not been used to fear. Even now I tremble
To think your father by some accident
Should pass this way as you did. Oh, the Fates!
How would he look to see his work, so noble, 21
Vilely bound up? What would he say? Or how 22
Should I, in these my borrowed flaunts, behold 23
The sternness of his presence?
FLORIZEL   Apprehend
Nothing but jollity. The gods themselves,
Humbling their deities to love, have taken
The shapes of beasts upon them. Jupiter 27
Became a bull, and bellowed; the green Neptune 28
A ram, and bleated; and the fire-robed god, 29
Golden Apollo, a poor humble swain, 30
As I seem now. Their transformations
Were never for a piece of beauty rarer,
Nor in a way so chaste, since my desires 33
Run not before mine honor, nor my lusts
Burn hotter than my faith.
PERDITA   Oh, but sir,
Your resolution cannot hold when 'tis
Opposed, as it must be, by th' power of the King.
One of these two must be necessities,
Which then will speak: that you must change this
     purpose
Or I my life.
FLORIZEL   Thou dearest Perdita, 40
With these forced thoughts, I prithee, darken not 41
The mirth o'th' feast. Or I'll be thine, my fair, 42
Or not my father's. For I cannot be
Mine own, nor anything to any, if
I be not thine. To this I am most constant,
Though destiny say no. Be merry, gentle! 46
Strangle such thoughts as these with anything 47
That you behold the while. Your guests are coming. 48

Lift up your countenance as it were the day 49
Of celebration of that nuptial which
We two have sworn shall come.
PERDITA   O Lady Fortune,
Stand you auspicious!
FLORIZEL   See, your guests approach.
Address yourself to entertain them sprightly, 53
And let's be red with mirth.

     [Enter] Shepherd, Clown; Polixenes, Camillo
     [disguised]; Mopsa, Dorcas; servants.

SHEPHERD
Fie, daughter! When my old wife lived, upon
This day she was both pantler, butler, cook, 56
Both dame and servant; welcomed all, served all; 57
Would sing her song and dance her turn; now here,
At upper end o'th' table, now i'th' middle;
On his shoulder, and his; her face afire 60
With labor, and the thing she took to quench it 61
She would to each one sip. You are retired, 62
As if you were a feasted one and not
The hostess of the meeting. Pray you, bid
These unknown friends to 's welcome, for it is 65
A way to make us better friends, more known. 66
Come, quench your blushes and present yourself
That which you are, mistress o'th' feast. Come on,
And bid us welcome to your sheepshearing,
As your good flock shall prosper.
PERDITA [to Polixenes]   Sir, welcome.
It is my father's will I should take on me
The hostess-ship o'th' day. [To Camillo] You're
     welcome, sir.—
Give me those flowers there, Dorcas.—Reverend sirs,
For you there's rosemary and rue; these keep
Seeming and savor all the winter long. 75
Grace and remembrance be to you both, 76
And welcome to our shearing! [Giving them flowers.]
POLIXENES   Shepherdess—
A fair one are you—well you fit our ages
With flowers of winter.
PERDITA   Sir, the year growing ancient, 79
Not yet on summer's death nor on the birth
Of trembling winter, the fairest flow'rs o'th' season
Are our carnations and streaked gillyvors, 82
Which some call nature's bastards. Of that kind 83
Our rustic garden's barren, and I care not
To get slips of them.
POLIXENES   Wherefore, gentle maiden, 85
Do you neglect them?
PERDITA   For I have heard it said 86

10 pranked up bedecked. 10–12 But . . . custom Were it not that when-ever folks gather for merry feasting one encounters some folly, which the guests take in their stride as to be expected 14 To show . . . glass if I were to see myself in a mirror. 16 Jove . . . cause! May Jove grant that you have good reason to be thankful! 17 To me . . . dread To me, the difference in our social rank is a source of dread 21–2 How . . . bound up? What would he think to see the nobly-born son he created so vilely outfitted? (The work, Florizel, is metaphorically a piece of writing, and his garments are the binding of the book.) 23 flaunts finery 27–30 Jupiter . . . swain (Jupiter in the guise of a bull wooed Europa, Neptune disguised as a ram deceived Bisaltes or Theophane [Ovid, Metamorphoses, 6.117], and Apollo took the guise of a humble shepherd to enable Admetus to woo Alcestis.) 33 in a way i.e., pursuing a pur-pose 40 Or I my life i.e., or I will be threatened with loss of life (as Polixenes indeed threatens at lines 436–43). 41 forced farfetched, unnatural 42 Or Either 46 gentle i.e., my gentle love. 47–8 Strangle . . . while i.e., Put down such thoughts by attending to matters at hand.

49 as as if 53 Address Prepare 56 pantler pantry servant 57 dame mistress of the household 60 On his . . . his at one person's . . . another's 61–2 and . . . sip and she would toast each one with the drink she took to quench the fire of her labor. 65 to 's each to his 66 more known better acquainted. 75 Seeming outward appear-ance, color 76 Grace and remembrance Divine grace and remem-brance after death. (Equated respectively with rue and rosemary.) 79 the year . . . ancient i.e., when autumn arrives 82 gillyvors gillyflowers, a kind of carnation 83 nature's bastards i.e., the result of artificial breeding. (See lines 86–8.) 85 slips cuttings 86 For Because

There is an art which in their piedness shares   87
With great creating nature.

POLIXENES   Say there be;
Yet nature is made better by no mean   89
But nature makes that mean. So, over that art   90
Which you say adds to nature is an art
That nature makes. You see, sweet maid, we marry
A gentler scion to the wildest stock,   93
And make conceive a bark of baser kind
By bud of nobler race. This is an art
Which does mend nature—change it, rather—but
The art itself is nature.

PERDITA   So it is.

POLIXENES
Then make your garden rich in gillyvors,
And do not call them bastards.

PERDITA   I'll not put
The dibble in earth to set one slip of them,   100
No more than, were I painted, I would wish   101
This youth should say 'twere well, and only therefore
Desire to breed by me. Here's flowers for you:
                              [giving them flowers]
Hot lavender, mints, savory, marjoram,   104
The marigold, that goes to bed wi'th' sun
And with him rises weeping. These are flowers
Of middle summer, and I think they are given   107
To men of middle age. You're very welcome.

CAMILLO
I should leave grazing, were I of your flock,
And only live by gazing.

PERDITA   Out, alas!   110
You'd be so lean that blasts of January
Would blow you through and through. [To Florizel]
    Now, my fair'st friend,
I would I had some flow'rs o'th' spring that might
Become your time of day; [to the Shepherdesses] and
    yours, and yours,
That wear upon your virgin branches yet
Your maidenheads growing. O Proserpina,   116
For the flow'rs now that, frighted, thou let'st fall
From Dis's wagon! Daffodils,
That come before the swallow dares, and take   119
The winds of March with beauty; violets dim,   120
But sweeter than the lids of Juno's eyes
Or Cytherea's breath; pale primroses,   122
That die unmarried ere they can behold

Bright Phoebus in his strength—a malady   124
Most incident to maids; bold oxlips and   125
The crown imperial; lilies of all kinds,   126
The flower-de-luce being one. Oh, these I lack   127
To make you garlands of, and my sweet friend,   128
To strew him o'er and o'er!

FLORIZEL   What, like a corpse?

PERDITA
No, like a bank for Love to lie and play on,   130
Not like a corpse; or if, not to be buried,   131
But quick and in mine arms. Come, take your flowers.   132
                              [Giving flowers.]
Methinks I play as I have seen them do
In Whitsun pastorals. Sure this robe of mine   134
Does change my disposition.

FLORIZEL   What you do
Still betters what is done. When you speak, sweet,   136
I'd have you do it ever. When you sing,
I'd have you buy and sell so, so give alms,
Pray so; and, for the ord'ring your affairs,
To sing them too. When you do dance, I wish you
A wave o'th' sea, that you might ever do
Nothing but that—move still, still so,
And own no other function. Each your doing,   143
So singular in each particular,   144
Crowns what you are doing in the present deeds,   145
That all your acts are queens.

PERDITA   Oh, Doricles,   146
Your praises are too large. But that your youth,   147
And the true blood which peeps fairly through 't
Do plainly give you out an unstained shepherd,   149
With wisdom I might fear, my Doricles,
You wooed me the false way.

FLORIZEL   I think you have
As little skill to fear as I have purpose   152
To put you to't. But come, our dance, I pray.   153
Your hand, my Perdita. So turtles pair,   154
That never mean to part.

PERDITA   I'll swear for 'em.   155
                              [They speak apart.]

POLIXENES [to Camillo]
This is the prettiest lowborn lass that ever

---

87 **art** i.e., of crossbreeding.   **piedness** particolored appearance.
(Perdita disclaims the art of crossbreeding, since it infringes on what
nature itself does so well.)   **89 mean** means   **90 But** unless. (Polixenes's point is that the art of improving on nature is itself natural.)
93 **gentler** nobler, more cultivated   **100 dibble** trowel   **101 painted**
made artificially beautiful by cosmetics   **104 Hot** eager, ardent, aromatic (?) (Spices were classified as hot or cold.)   **107 middle summer**
(Having no autumn flowers in any case [lines 79–82], since it is too
early in the season, Perdita flatters her older guests by giving them
flowers appropriate to *middle age*.)   **110 Out** (An exclamation of dismay.)   **116 Proserpina** daughter of Ceres, stolen away by Pluto
(*Dis*) and taken to Hades when, according to Ovid, she was gathering
flowers   **119 take** charm   **120 dim** with hanging heads
122 Cytherea's Venus's

124 Phoebus the sun-god   **124–5 a malady . . . maids** (Young maids,
suffering from greensickness, a kind of anemia, are pale like the primrose.)   **126 crown imperial** flower from the Levant, cultivated in
English gardens   **127 flower-de-luce** fleur-de-lis.   **I lack** (Because
the season is too late for them.)   **128 To . . . friend** to make garlands
of them for you (Polixenes and Camillo) and for my sweet friend
(Florizel)   **130 like . . . play on** as if one were strewing a bank where
Cupid himself might lie in amorous play   **131 or if** or if like a corpse,
that is, a living body   **132 quick** alive   **134 Whitsun pastorals** plays
(including Robin Hood plays) and English morris dances often performed at Whitsuntide, seven Sundays after Easter. (The part of
Maid Marian strikes Perdita as immodest for her usual behavior.)
136 Still . . . done gets better and better.   **143 Each your doing** Each
thing you do and how you do it   **144 singular** unique and peerless
145 Crowns . . . deeds makes whatever you are doing at the moment
seem supremely wonderful   **146 Doricles** (Florizel's disguise name.)
147 large lavish.   **But that** Were it not that   **149 give you out** proclaim you to be   **152 skill** reason   **153 To . . . to't** i.e., to woo you
"the false way," with intent to seduce you.   **154 turtles** turtledoves,
as symbols of faithful love   **155 I'll swear for 'em** i.e., I'll be sworn
they do.

Ran on the greensward. Nothing she does or seems 157
But smacks of something greater than herself,
Too noble for this place.

CAMILLO   He tells her something
That makes her blood look out. Good sooth, she is 160
The queen of curds and cream.

CLOWN   Come on, strike up!

DORCAS
Mopsa must be your mistress. Marry, garlic, 162
To mend her kissing with!

MOPSA   Now, in good time! 163

CLOWN
Not a word, a word. We stand upon our manners. 164
Come, strike up! 165

[*Music.*] *Here a dance of shepherds and*
shepherdesses.

POLIXENES
Pray, good shepherd, what fair swain is this
Which dances with your daughter?

SHEPHERD
They call him Doricles, and boasts himself 168
To have a worthy feeding; but I have it 169
Upon his own report and I believe it.
He looks like sooth. He says he loves my daughter. 171
I think so too, for never gazed the moon
Upon the water as he'll stand and read,
As 'twere, my daughter's eyes; and, to be plain,
I think there is not half a kiss to choose
Who loves another best.

POLIXENES   She dances featly. 176

SHEPHERD
So she does anything—though I report it
That should be silent. If young Doricles
Do light upon her, she shall bring him that 179
Which he not dreams of.

Enter Servant.

SERVANT   Oh, master, if you did but hear the peddler at
the door, you would never dance again after a tabor 182
and pipe; no, the bagpipe could not move you. He
sings several tunes faster than you'll tell money. He 184
utters them as he had eaten ballads and all men's ears 185
grew to his tunes.

CLOWN   He could never come better. He shall come in. 187
I love a ballad but even too well, if it be doleful matter 188
merrily set down, or a very pleasant thing indeed and 189
sung lamentably. 190

SERVANT   He hath songs for man or woman, of all sizes. 191
No milliner can so fit his customers with gloves. He 192

has the prettiest love songs for maids, so without
bawdry, which is strange, with such delicate burdens 194
of dildos and fadings, "Jump her and thump her"; and 195
where some stretchmouthed rascal would, as it were, 196
mean mischief and break a foul gap into the matter, 197
he makes the maid to answer, "Whoop, do me no
harm, good man"; puts him off, slights him, with
"Whoop, do me no harm, good man."

POLIXENES   This is a brave fellow. 201

CLOWN   Believe me, thou talkest of an admirable con- 202
ceited fellow. Has he any unbraided wares? 203

SERVANT   He hath ribbons of all the colors i'th'
rainbow; points more than all the lawyers in Bohemia 205
can learnedly handle, though they come to him by th'
gross; inkles, caddisses, cambrics, lawns. Why, he 207
sings 'em over as they were gods or goddesses; you
would think a smock were a she-angel, he so chants to 209
the sleevehand and the work about the square on't. 210

CLOWN   Prithee, bring him in, and let him approach
singing.

PERDITA   Forewarn him that he use no scurrilous words
in 's tunes.   [*The Servant goes to the door.*]

CLOWN   You have of these peddlers that have more in 215
them than you'd think, sister.

PERDITA   Ay, good brother, or go about to think. 217

Enter Autolycus, singing.

AUTOLYCUS
Lawn as white as driven snow,
Cyprus black as e'er was crow, 219
Gloves as sweet as damask roses, 220
Masks for faces and for noses,
Bugle bracelet, necklace amber, 222
Perfume for a lady's chamber,
Golden coifs and stomachers, 224
For my lads to give their dears,
Pins and poking-sticks of steel, 226
What maids lack from head to heel,
Come buy of me, come. Come buy, come buy.
Buy, lads, or else your lasses cry.
Come buy.

CLOWN   If I were not in love with Mopsa, thou shouldst

---

157 greensward grassy turf.   **160 makes . . . out** makes her blush.
162 mistress i.e., partner in the dance.   **163 kissing** i.e., bad breath.
(Dorcas jests that even garlic would improve Mopsa's breath.)   **in**
good time (An expression of indignation.)   **164 stand upon** set store
by   **165.1 dance** (Probably a morris dance.)   **168 and** i.e., and they
say he   **169 feeding** pasturage, lands   **171 He . . . sooth** He appears
to be honest.   **176 another** the other.   **featly** gracefully.   **179 light**
upon choose   **182 tabor** small drum   **184 several** various.   **tell**
count   **185 as** as if. (Also in line 208.)   **187 better** at a better time.
188 but even too well all too well   **189 pleasant** merry   **190 lamen-**
tably mournfully.   **191 sizes** sorts.   **192 milliner** vendor of fancy
ware and apparel, including gloves, ribbons, and bonnets

194 burdens refrains   **195 dildos and fadings** words used as part of
the refrains of ballads. (But with bawdy double meaning unperceived
by the servant, as also in *jump her, thump her, do me no harm*, etc.)
196 stretchmouthed widemouthed, foulmouthed   **197 break . . .**
matter insert some gross obscenity into the song, or, act in a suggestive way   **201 brave** excellent   **202–3 admirable conceited** wonderfully witty and clever   **203 unbraided** not shopworn, new
205 points (1) laces for fastening clothes (2) headings in an argument
207 inkles . . . lawns linen tapes, worsted tape used for garters, fine
heavy linen fabrics, fine sheer linens.   **209 smock** petticoat
210 sleevehand wristband.   **square on't** embroidered bosom or yoke
of the garment.   **215 You . . . peddlers** You'll find peddlers   **217 go**
about intend, wish   **217.1 Enter Autolycus** (Apparently he is wearing a false beard; later in this scene, he removes it to impersonate a
courtier to the Clown and Shepherd.)   **219 Cyprus** crepe   **220 sweet**
i.e., perfumed. (Also in line 249.)   **222 Bugle bracelet** bracelet of
black glossy beads   **224 coifs** close-fitting caps.   **stomachers**
embroidered fronts for ladies' dresses   **226 poking-sticks** rods used
for ironing and stiffening the plaits of ruffs. (With bawdy suggestion.)

take no money of me, but being enthralled as I am, it 232
will also be the bondage of certain ribbons and gloves. 233

MOPSA   I was promised them against the feast, but they 234
come not too late now.

DORCAS   He hath promised you more than that, or 236
there be liars. 237

MOPSA   He hath paid you all he promised you. Maybe
he has paid you more, which will shame you to give 239
him again. 240

CLOWN   Is there no manners left among maids? Will 241
they wear their plackets where they should bear their 242
faces? Is there not milking time, when you are going to 243
bed, or kilnhole, to whistle of these secrets, but you 244
must be tittle-tattling before all our guests? 'Tis well
they are whisp'ring. Clamor your tongues, and not a 246
word more.

MOPSA   I have done. Come, you promised me a tawdry 248
lace and a pair of sweet gloves. 249

CLOWN   Have I not told thee how I was cozened by the 250
way and lost all my money?

AUTOLYCUS   And indeed, sir, there are cozeners abroad;
therefore it behooves men to be wary.

CLOWN   Fear not thou, man, thou shalt lose nothing
here.

AUTOLYCUS   I hope so, sir, for I have about me many
parcels of charge. 257

CLOWN   What hast here? Ballads?

MOPSA   Pray now, buy some. I love a ballad in print
alife, for then we are sure they are true. 260

AUTOLYCUS   Here's one to a very doleful tune, how a
usurer's wife was brought to bed of twenty moneybags at a burden, and how she longed to eat adders' 263
heads and toads carbonadoed. 264

MOPSA   Is it true, think you?

AUTOLYCUS   Very true, and but a month old.

DORCAS   Bless me from marrying a usurer! 267

AUTOLYCUS   Here's the midwife's name to't, one
Mistress Taleporter, and five or six honest wives that 269
were present. Why should I carry lies abroad?

MOPSA   Pray you now, buy it.

CLOWN   Come on, lay it by, and let's first see more
ballads. We'll buy the other things anon.

AUTOLYCUS   Here's another ballad, of a fish that appeared upon the coast on Wednesday the fourscore of 275
April, forty thousand fathom above water, and sung 276
this ballad against the hard hearts of maids. It was

thought she was a woman and was turned into a cold
fish for she would not exchange flesh with one that 279
loved her. The ballad is very pitiful and as true.

DORCAS   Is it true too, think you?

AUTOLYCUS   Five justices' hands at it, and witnesses 282
more than my pack will hold.

CLOWN   Lay it by too. Another.

AUTOLYCUS   This is a merry ballad, but a very pretty
one.

MOPSA   Let's have some merry ones.

AUTOLYCUS   Why, this is a passing merry one and goes 288
to the tune of "Two Maids Wooing a Man." There's
scarce a maid westward but she sings it. 'Tis in 290
request, I can tell you.

MOPSA   We can both sing it. If thou'lt bear a part, thou
shalt hear; 'tis in three parts.

DORCAS   We had the tune on't a month ago. 294

AUTOLYCUS   I can bear my part; you must know 'tis my
occupation. Have at it with you. 296

Song.

AUTOLYCUS
Get you hence, for I must go
Where it fits not you to know.

DORCAS
            Whither?

MOPSA   Oh, whither?

DORCAS   Whither?

MOPSA
It becomes thy oath full well,
Thou to me thy secrets tell.

DORCAS
Me too. Let me go thither.

MOPSA
Or thou goest to th' grange or mill. 303

DORCAS
If to either, thou dost ill.

AUTOLYCUS
Neither.

DORCAS   What, neither?

AUTOLYCUS   Neither.

DORCAS
Thou hast sworn my love to be.

MOPSA
Thou hast sworn it more to me.
Then whither goest? Say, whither?

CLOWN   We'll have this song out anon by ourselves. 309
My father and the gentlemen are in sad talk, and we'll 310
not trouble them. Come, bring away thy pack after
me. Wenches, I'll buy for you both. Peddler, let's have
the first choice. Follow me, girls.

                              [*Exit with Dorcas and Mopsa.*]

AUTOLYCUS   And you shall pay well for 'em.

                              [*He follows singing.*]

232–3 it will . . . bondage it will mean the taking into custody (by
means of purchase and tying up into a parcel)   **234 against** in anticipation of, in time for   **236–7 He . . . liars** i.e., He promised to marry
you, too, or else rumor is a liar.   **239 paid you more** i.e., made you
pregnant   **239–40 which . . . again** i.e., which will shame you by giving birth to his child.   **241–3 Will . . . faces?** i.e., Will they always be
talking and revealing personal secrets?   **plackets** slits in petticoats.
(With bawdy suggestion of the pudendum, as in line 613.)   **244 kilnhole** fire hole of a baking oven (where maids might gossip).   **whistle**
whisper   **246 Clamor** i.e., Silence   **248–9 tawdry lace** cheap and
showy lace, or, neckerchief. (So called from St. Audrey's Fair.)
250 cozened cheated   **257 parcels of charge** valuable items.
260 alife on my life   **263 at a burden** in one childbirth   **264 carbonadoed** scored across and grilled.   **267 Bless** God protect, keep
269 Taleporter i.e., talebearer, gossip   **275 fourscore** eightieth (!)
276 forty thousand fathom 240,000 feet

279 exchange flesh have sex   **282 hands at it** signatures on it
288 passing surpassingly   **290 westward** in the West Country
294 on't of it   **296 Have at it** Here goes   **303 Or Either.   grange**
farm   **309 have this song out** finish this song   **310 sad** serious

Song.

Will you buy any tape,
Or lace for your cape,
My dainty duck, my dear-a?
Any silk, any thread,
And toys for your head,   319
Of the new'st and fin'st, fin'st wear-a?
Come to the peddler;
Money's a meddler,   322
That doth utter all men's ware-a.   *Exit.* 323

[*Enter a Servant.*]

SERVANT Master, there is three carters, three shep- 324
herds, three neatherds, three swineherds, that have 325
made themselves all men of hair. They call themselves 326
saultiers, and they have a dance which the wenches say 327
is a gallimaufry of gambols, because they are not in't; 328
but they themselves are o'th' mind, if it be not too
rough for some that know little but bowling, it will 330
please plentifully.

SHEPHERD Away! We'll none on't. Here has been too
much homely foolery already.—I know, sir, we 333
weary you.

POLIXENES You weary those that refresh us. Pray, let's
see these four threes of herdsmen.

SERVANT One three of them, by their own report, sir, 337
hath danced before the King, and not the worst of the
three but jumps twelve foot and a half by the square. 339

SHEPHERD Leave your prating. Since these good men 340
are pleased, let them come in; but quickly now.

SERVANT Why, they stay at door, sir.

[*He goes to the door.*]

Here a dance of twelve Satyrs.

POLIXENES [*to the Shepherd*]
Oh, father, you'll know more of that hereafter. 343
[*To Camillo*] Is it not too far gone? 'Tis time to part
them.
He's simple and tells much. [*To Florizel*] How now, fair
shepherd? 345
Your heart is full of something that does take
Your mind from feasting. Sooth, when I was young
And handed love as you do, I was wont 348
To load my she with knacks. I would have ransacked
The peddler's silken treasury and have poured it
To her acceptance; you have let him go, 351
And nothing marted with him. If your lass 352

Interpretation should abuse and call this 353
Your lack of love or bounty, you were straited 354
For a reply, at least if you make a care
Of happy holding her.
FLORIZEL   Old sir, I know 356
She prizes not such trifles as these are.
The gifts she looks from me are packed and locked 358
Up in my heart, which I have given already,
But not delivered. [*To Perdita*] Oh, hear me breathe my
life 360
Before this ancient sir, who, it should seem, 361
Hath sometime loved! I take thy hand, this hand,
As soft as dove's down and as white as it,
Or Ethiopian's tooth, or the fanned snow that's bolted 364
By th' northern blasts twice o'er.   [*He takes her hand.*]
POLIXENES   What follows this?
How prettily the young swain seems to wash
The hand was fair before! I have put you out. 367
But to your protestation; let me hear 368
What you profess.
FLORIZEL   Do, and be witness to't.
POLIXENES
And this my neighbor too?
FLORIZEL   And he, and more
Than he, and men—the earth, the heavens, and all:
That, were I crowned the most imperial monarch,
Thereof most worthy, were I the fairest youth 373
That ever made eye swerve, had force and knowledge 374
More than was ever man's, I would not prize them
Without her love; for her employ them all,
Commend them and condemn them to her service 377
Or to their own perdition.
POLIXENES   Fairly offered. 378
CAMILLO
This shows a sound affection.
SHEPHERD   But, my daughter,
Say you the like to him?
PERDITA   I cannot speak
So well, nothing so well; no, nor mean better.
By th' pattern of mine own thoughts I cut out 382
The purity of his.
SHEPHERD   Take hands, a bargain! 383
And, friends unknown, you shall bear witness to't:
I give my daughter to him and will make
Her portion equal his.
FLORIZEL   Oh, that must be
I'th' virtue of your daughter. One being dead, 387

319 **toys** trifles   322 **meddler** i.e., go-between in commercial transactions   323 **utter** put on the market   324 **carters** cart drivers
325 **neatherds** cowherds   326 **of hair** dressed in skins.   327 **saultiers** leapers or vaulters. (With perhaps a play on *Saltiers* as a blunder for "satyrs.")   328 **gallimaufry** jumble   330 **bowling** (A more gentle sport than the vigorous satyr dancing.)   333 **homely** unpolished
337 **three** threesome   339 **by the square** precisely.   340 **Leave** Leave off   343 **Oh, ... hereafter** (Polixenes completes the conversation he has been having with the old Shepherd during the dance. *Father* is a respectful term of address for older men.)   345 **He's simple** The old Shepherd is guileless   348 **handed** handled, dealt in   351 **To her acceptance** for her to choose   352 **nothing marted with** have done no business with

353 **Interpretation should abuse** should interpret wrongly   354 **were straited** would be hard-pressed   356 **happy holding her** keeping her happy.   358 **looks** looks for   360 **But not delivered** i.e., but I have not confirmed it by a solemn vow before witnesses, making binding the contract.   **breathe my life** i.e., pronounce eternal vows   361 **this ancient sir** Polixenes   364 **fanned** blown.   **bolted** sifted   367 **was** that was.   **put you out** interrupted what you were saying.   368 **to your protestation** on with your public affirmation   373 **Thereof most worthy** the most worthy of monarchs   374 **swerve** turn in my direction (out of awe and respect)   377–8 **Commend . . . perdition** either commend them to her service, or, failing that, condemn them to deserved destruction.   382–3 **By . . . of his** By the purity of my own thoughts I can define the purity of his. (A metaphor of clothes-making; Perdita has formed her own thoughts on the model of his.)   387 **One being dead** When a certain person dies

I shall have more than you can dream of yet;
Enough then for your wonder. But come on: 389
Contract us 'fore these witnesses.

SHEPHERD   Come, your hand;
And, daughter, yours.

POLIXENES   Soft, swain, awhile, beseech you.   391
Have you a father?

FLORIZEL   I have, but what of him?

POLIXENES   Knows he of this?

FLORIZEL   He neither does nor shall.

POLIXENES   Methinks a father
Is at the nuptial of his son a guest
That best becomes the table. Pray you, once more,
Is not your father grown incapable
Of reasonable affairs? Is he not stupid   400
With age and altering rheums? Can he speak? Hear?   401
Know man from man? Dispute his own estate?   402
Lies he not bedrid, and again does nothing
But what he did being childish?

FLORIZEL   No, good sir,   404
He has his health and ampler strength indeed
Than most have of his age.

POLIXENES   By my white beard,
You offer him, if this be so, a wrong
Something unfilial. Reason my son   408
Should choose himself a wife, but as good reason
The father, all whose joy is nothing else
But fair posterity, should hold some counsel   411
In such a business.

FLORIZEL   I yield all this;   412
But for some other reasons, my grave sir,
Which 'tis not fit you know, I not acquaint
My father of this business.

POLIXENES   Let him know't.

FLORIZEL
He shall not.

POLIXENES   Prithee, let him.

FLORIZEL   No, he must not.

SHEPHERD
Let him, my son. He shall not need to grieve
At knowing of thy choice.

FLORIZEL   Come, come, he must not.
Mark our contract.

POLIXENES [discovering himself]   Mark your divorce,
     young sir,
Whom son I dare not call. Thou art too base
To be acknowledged. Thou a scepter's heir,
That thus affects a sheephook?—Thou old traitor,   422
I am sorry that by hanging thee I can
But shorten thy life one week.—And thou, fresh piece

Of excellent witchcraft, who of force must know   425
The royal fool thou cop'st with—

SHEPHERD   Oh, my heart!   426

POLIXENES
I'll have thy beauty scratched with briers and made
More homely than thy state.—For thee, fond boy,   428
If I may ever know thou dost but sigh
That thou no more shalt see this knack—as never   430
I mean thou shalt—we'll bar thee from succession,
Not hold thee of our blood, no, not our kin,
Farre than Deucalion off. Mark thou my words.   433
Follow us to the court.—Thou churl, for this time,   434
Though full of our displeasure, yet we free thee
From the dead blow of it.—And you, enchantment,   436
Worthy enough a herdsman—yea, him too,   437
That makes himself, but for our honor therein,   438
Unworthy thee—if ever henceforth thou   439
These rural latches to his entrance open,
Or hoop his body more with thy embraces,
I will devise a death as cruel for thee
As thou art tender to't.   Exit.

PERDITA   Even here undone!
I was not much afeard; for once or twice
I was about to speak and tell him plainly
The selfsame sun that shines upon his court
Hides not his visage from our cottage, but
Looks on alike. Will't please you, sir, begone?   448
I told you what would come of this. Beseech you,
Of your own state take care. This dream of mine—
Being now awake, I'll queen it no inch farther,
But milk my ewes and weep.

CAMILLO   Why, how now, father?
Speak ere thou diest.

SHEPHERD   I cannot speak, nor think,   453
Nor dare to know that which I know. [To Florizel] Oh,
     sir,
You have undone a man of fourscore three,
That thought to fill his grave in quiet, yea,
To die upon the bed my father died,   457
To lie close by his honest bones; but now
Some hangman must put on my shroud and lay me
Where no priest shovels in dust. [To Perdita] Oh,
     cursed wretch,
That knew'st this was the Prince, and wouldst adven-
     ture
To mingle faith with him! Undone, undone!   462
If I might die within this hour, I have lived
To die when I desire.   Exit.

FLORIZEL [to Perdita]   Why look you so upon me?

---

389 Enough . . . wonder there will be enough then for you to wonder
at.   **391 Soft** Wait a minute   **400 reasonable affairs** matters requiring the use of reason.   **401 altering rheums** weakening catarrhs or
other diseases.   **402 Dispute** Discuss.   **estate** affairs, condition.
404 being childish when he was a child.   **408 Something** somewhat.
Reason my son It is reasonable that my son. (The disguised Polixenes
purports to be speaking hypothetically, using himself as an example,
but of course the application to Florizel is direct.)   **411 hold some
counsel** be consulted   **412 yield** concede   **422 affects** desires, shows
inclination for

425 of force of necessity   **426 thou cop'st** you deal   **428 homely**
(1) unattractive (2) humble.   **fond** foolish   **430 knack** trifle, schemer
433 Farre . . . off farther in kinship than Deucalion (the Noah of classical legend and hence the primal, distant ancestor of the whole human
race).   **434 churl** i.e., the Shepherd   **436 dead** deadly.   **enchantment**
i.e., Perdita   **437–9 him too . . . thee** worthy indeed of him (Florizel)
whose behavior renders him unworthy even of you, if we were to set
aside for the moment the question of the dignity of our royal house
448 alike both alike.   **453 ere thou diest** before you die of grief (?).
(Although Polixenes has relented of his threat to hang the Shepherd,
the Shepherd is gloomily sure it will come to a hanging, lines 459–60.)
457 died died on   **462 mingle faith** exchange pledges

I am but sorry, not afeard; delayed,
But nothing altered. What I was, I am,
More straining on for plucking back, not following   468
My leash unwillingly.
CAMILLO   Gracious my lord,
You know your father's temper. At this time
He will allow no speech, which I do guess
You do not purpose to him; and as hardly
Will he endure your sight as yet, I fear.
Then, till the fury of His Highness settle,
Come not before him.
FLORIZEL   I not purpose it.
I think Camillo?
CAMILLO   Even he, my lord.
PERDITA
How often have I told you 'twould be thus?
How often said my dignity would last   478
But till 'twere known?
FLORIZEL   It cannot fail but by
The violation of my faith; and then   480
Let nature crush the sides o'th'earth together
And mar the seeds within! Lift up thy looks.   482
From my succession wipe me, father; I   483
Am heir to my affection.
CAMILLO   Be advised.   484
FLORIZEL
I am, and by my fancy. If my reason   485
Will thereto be obedient, I have reason;   486
If not, my senses, better pleased with madness,
Do bid it welcome.
CAMILLO   This is desperate, sir.
FLORIZEL
So call it, but it does fulfill my vow;
I needs must think it honesty. Camillo,
Not for Bohemia nor the pomp that may
Be thereat gleaned, for all the sun sees or
The close earth wombs or the profound seas hides   493
In unknown fathoms, will I break my oath
To this my fair beloved. Therefore, I pray you,
As you have ever been my father's honored friend,
When he shall miss me—as, in faith, I mean not
To see him any more—cast your good counsels
Upon his passion. Let myself and fortune   499
Tug for the time to come. This you may know   500
And so deliver: I am put to sea   501
With her who here I cannot hold on shore;   502
And most opportune to our need I have
A vessel rides fast by, but not prepared   504

For this design. What course I mean to hold
Shall nothing benefit your knowledge nor   506
Concern me the reporting.
CAMILLO   Oh, my lord,   507
I would your spirit were easier for advice,   508
Or stronger for your need.
FLORIZEL   Hark, Perdita.
[To Camillo] I'll hear you by and by.
                         [He draws Perdita aside.]
CAMILLO [aside]   He's irremovable,   510
Resolved for flight. Now were I happy if
His going I could frame to serve my turn,   512
Save him from danger, do him love and honor,
Purchase the sight again of dear Sicilia
And that unhappy king, my master, whom
I so much thirst to see.
FLORIZEL   Now, good Camillo,
I am so fraught with curious business that   517
I leave out ceremony.
CAMILLO   Sir, I think   518
You have heard of my poor services i'th' love
That I have borne your father?
FLORIZEL   Very nobly
Have you deserved. It is my father's music
To speak your deeds, not little of his care
To have them recompensed as thought on.
CAMILLO   Well, my lord,   523
If you may please to think I love the King
And through him what's nearest to him, which is
Your gracious self, embrace but my direction,   526
If your more ponderous and settled project   527
May suffer alteration. On mine honor,   528
I'll point you where you shall have such receiving
As shall become Your Highness, where you may   530
Enjoy your mistress—from the whom I see
There's no disjunction to be made but by,
As heavens forfend, your ruin—marry her,   533
And, with my best endeavors in your absence   534
Your discontenting father strive to qualify   535
And bring him up to liking.
FLORIZEL   How, Camillo,   536
May this, almost a miracle, be done,
That I may call thee something more than man,
And after that trust to thee?
CAMILLO   Have you thought on   539
A place whereto you'll go?
FLORIZEL   Not any yet.
But as th'unthought-on accident is guilty   541
To what we wildly do, so we profess   542

---

468 **More . . . back** i.e., like a hound on the leash, all the more eager to go forward for being restrained   478 **my dignity** i.e., the new status this marriage would have offered   480 **then** when that happens   482 **mar the seeds within** i.e., destroy the very sources of life on earth (since all material life was thought to be derived from *seeds*).   483 **From . . . father** (Florizel apostrophizes the absent Polixenes.)   483–4 **I . . . affection** i.e., I will be content with my passionate love for Perdita in place of my inheritance.   484 **Be advised** Think carefully, be receptive to wise advice.   485 **fancy** love.   486 **have reason** (1) will be reasonable (2) will be sane   493 **wombs** encloses, conceals   499 **passion** anger.   500 **Tug** contend   501 **deliver** report   502 **who** whom   504 **rides** that rides at anchor.   **but** though

506–7 **Shall . . . reporting** would not behoove you to know nor me to report.   508 **easier for** more open to   510 **irremovable** immovable   512 **frame** shape   517 **curious** demanding care   518 **I . . . ceremony** (Florizel apologizes for failing to observe proper ceremony toward Camillo under the pressures of the present crisis.)   523 **as thought on** as deservingly as they merit.   526 **embrace . . . direction** simply follow my advice   527 **ponderous** weighty   528 **suffer** permit   530 **become Your Highness** suit your royal rank, suit Your Highness   533 **forfend** forbid   534 **with** together with   535 **discontenting** discontented, displeased.   **qualify** appease, pacify   536 **bring . . . liking** get him to the point of approval.   539 **after** ever after   541–2 **as . . . wildly do** just as the unexpected happening (e.g., of our being discovered by the King) is responsible for what we rashly do at this point

Ourselves to be the slaves of chance and flies   543
Of every wind that blows.

CAMILLO   Then list to me.
This follows, if you will not change your purpose
But undergo this flight: make for Sicilia,
And there present yourself and your fair princess—
For so I see she must be—'fore Leontes.
She shall be habited as it becomes   549
The partner of your bed. Methinks I see
Leontes opening his free arms and weeping   551
His welcomes forth; asks thee there "Son,
    forgiveness!"
As 'twere i'th' father's person; kisses the hands
Of your fresh princess; o'er and o'er divides him   554
Twixt his unkindness and his kindness. Th'one   555
He chides to hell, and bids the other grow
Faster than thought or time.

FLORIZEL   Worthy Camillo,   557
What color for my visitation shall I   558
Hold up before him?

CAMILLO   Sent by the King your father   559
To greet him and to give him comforts. Sir,
The manner of your bearing towards him, with
What you, as from your father, shall deliver—   562
Things known betwixt us three—I'll write you down,
The which shall point you forth at every sitting   564
What you must say, that he shall not perceive
But that you have your father's bosom there   566
And speak his very heart.

FLORIZEL   I am bound to you.
There is some sap in this.

CAMILLO   A course more promising
Than a wild dedication of yourselves
To unpathed waters, undreamed shores, most certain
To miseries enough; no hope to help you,
But as you shake off one to take another;   572
Nothing so certain as your anchors, who   573
Do their best office if they can but stay you   574
Where you'll be loath to be. Besides, you know   575
Prosperity's the very bond of love,   576
Whose fresh complexion and whose heart together   577
Affliction alters.

PERDITA   One of these is true: 578
I think affliction may subdue the cheek,   579
But not take in the mind.

CAMILLO   Yea, say you so?   580

There shall not at your father's house these seven
    years   581
Be born another such.

FLORIZEL   My good Camillo,
She's as forward of her breeding as she is   583
I'th' rear 'our birth.   584

CAMILLO   I cannot say 'tis pity
She lacks instructions, for she seems a mistress   585
To most that teach.

PERDITA   Your pardon, sir; for this
I'll blush you thanks.

FLORIZEL   My prettiest Perdita!
But oh, the thorns we stand upon! Camillo,
Preserver of my father, now of me,
The medicine of our house, how shall we do?
We are not furnished like Bohemia's son,
Nor shall appear so in Sicilia.

CAMILLO   My lord,
Fear none of this. I think you know my fortunes
Do all lie there. It shall be so my care
To have you royally appointed as if   595
The scene you play were mine. For instance, sir,
That you may know you shall not want, one word.
    [They talk aside.]

    Enter Autolycus.

AUTOLYCUS   Ha, ha, what a fool Honesty is! And Trust,
his sworn brother, a very simple gentleman! I have
sold all my trumpery; not a counterfeit stone, not a
ribbon, glass, pomander, brooch, table book, ballad,   601
knife, tape, glove, shoe tie, bracelet, horn ring, to
keep my pack from fasting. They throng who should   603
buy first, as if my trinkets had been hallowed and   604
brought a benediction to the buyer; by which means
I saw whose purse was best in picture, and what I   606
saw, to my good use I remembered. My clown, who
wants but something to be a reasonable man, grew so   608
in love with the wenches' song that he would not stir
his pettitoes till he had both tune and words, which   610
so drew the rest of the herd to me that all their other
senses stuck in ears. You might have pinched a   612
placket, it was senseless. 'Twas nothing to geld a cod-   613
piece of a purse. I could have filed keys off that hung   614
in chains. No hearing, no feeling, but my sir's song,   615
and admiring the nothing of it. So that in this time of   616
lethargy I picked and cut most of their festival purses;
and had not the old man come in with hubbub

---

543 flies i.e., insignificant insects, blown about by the winds of chance
549 habited (richly) dressed   551 free generous, noble   554 fresh
young and beautiful   554–5 divides . . . kindness divides his speech
between his former unkindness (which he condemns) and his present
intention of kindness.   557 Faster firmer; also, more swiftly
558 color excuse, pretext   559 Hold up before present to.   Sent i.e.,
Say you are sent   562 deliver say   564 point you forth indicate to
you.   sitting conference   566 bosom inmost thoughts   572 one one
misery, one misfortune.   take encounter   573 Nothing not at all.
573–5 who . . . to be which are doing as well as can be hoped if they
simply hold you in some undesirable place (rather than allowing you
to proceed on toward even greater disaster).   576–8 Prosperity's . . .
alters i.e., young love flourishes while things are going well but loses
its fresh complexion and strength of feeling under the test of adversity.   579 subdue the cheek make the complexion look pale and
wasted   580 take in overcome

581 your father's (Said either to Florizel or Perdita.)   these seven
years i.e., for a long time to come. (Camillo's point is that she is a
nonpareil.)   583 forward . . . breeding far in advance of her lowly
upbringing   584 I'th' rear 'our below me in   585 instructions formal
schooling.   a mistress a teacher   595 appointed equipped, outfitted
601 pomander scent-ball.   table book notebook   603 from fasting
i.e., from being empty.   604 hallowed made sacred, like relics
606 best in picture i.e., best to look at, most promising   608 wants
but something lacks one thing only (i.e., intelligence)   610 pettitoes
pig's toes; here, toes   612 stuck in ears were occupied with hearing.
613 placket (Literally, slit in a petticoat; with bawdy suggestion.)
senseless insensible.   613–14 geld . . . purse cut a purse loose from
the pouch worn at the front of a man's breeches.   615 my sir's i.e.,
the Clown's   616 nothing (1) vacuity (2) noting, tune. (Nothing and
noting were sounded alike in Elizabethan English.)

against his daughter and the King's son and scared my
choughs from the chaff, I had not left a purse alive in 620
the whole army.

[*Camillo, Florizel, and Perdita come forward.*]

CAMILLO
Nay, but my letters, by this means being there
So soon as you arrive, shall clear that doubt.

FLORIZEL
And those that you'll procure from King Leontes—

CAMILLO
Shall satisfy your father.

PERDITA   Happy be you!
All that you speak shows fair.

CAMILLO [*seeing Autolycus*]   Who have we here?
We'll make an instrument of this, omit
Nothing may give us aid.   628

AUTOLYCUS [*aside*] If they have overheard me now,
why, hanging.

CAMILLO How now, good fellow? Why shak'st thou so?
Fear not, man, here's no harm intended to thee.

AUTOLYCUS I am a poor fellow, sir.

CAMILLO Why, be so still. Here's nobody will steal that
from thee. Yet for the outside of thy poverty we must 635
make an exchange. Therefore discase thee instantly— 636
thou must think there's a necessity in't—and change 637
garments with this gentleman. Though the penny- 638
worth on his side be the worst, yet hold thee, there's 639
some boot.   [*He gives money.*] 640

AUTOLYCUS I am a poor fellow, sir. [*Aside*] I know ye
well enough.

CAMILLO Nay, prithee, dispatch. The gentleman is half 643
flayed already.   644

AUTOLYCUS Are you in earnest, sir? [*Aside*] I smell the
trick on't.

FLORIZEL Dispatch, I prithee.

AUTOLYCUS Indeed, I have had earnest, but I cannot 648
with conscience take it.

CAMILLO Unbuckle, unbuckle.

[*Florizel and Autolycus exchange garments.*]
Fortunate mistress—let my prophecy   651
Come home to ye!—you must retire yourself   652
Into some covert. Take your sweetheart's hat   653
And pluck it o'er your brows, muffle your face,
Dismantle you, and, as you can, disliken   655
The truth of your own seeming, that you may—   656
For I do fear eyes—over to shipboard   657
Get undescried.

PERDITA   I see the play so lies
That I must bear a part.

CAMILLO   No remedy.—

Have you done there?

FLORIZEL   Should I now meet my father,
He would not call me son.

CAMILLO Nay, you shall have no hat.
                              [*He gives it to Perdita.*]
Come, lady, come. Farewell, my friend.

AUTOLYCUS   Adieu, sir.

FLORIZEL
Oh, Perdita, what have we twain forgot?
Pray you, a word.   [*They speak aside.*]

CAMILLO [*aside*]
What I do next shall be to tell the King
Of this escape and whither they are bound;
Wherein my hope is I shall so prevail
To force him after, in whose company
I shall re-view Sicilia, for whose sight   670
I have a woman's longing.

FLORIZEL   Fortune speed us!
Thus we set on, Camillo, to th' seaside.

CAMILLO The swifter speed the better.
                        Exit [*with Florizel and Perdita*].

AUTOLYCUS I understand the business; I hear it. To
have an open ear, a quick eye, and a nimble hand is
necessary for a cutpurse; a good nose is requisite also,
to smell out work for th'other senses. I see this is the
time that the unjust man doth thrive. What an
exchange had this been without boot! What a boot is 679
here with this exchange! Sure the gods do this year
connive at us, and we may do anything extempore. 681
The Prince himself is about a piece of iniquity, stealing 682
away from his father with his clog at his heels. If I 683
thought it were a piece of honesty to acquaint the King
withal, I would not do't. I hold it the more knavery to 685
conceal it; and therein am I constant to my profession.

Enter Clown and Shepherd [*carrying a bundle and
a box*].

Aside, aside! Here is more matter for a hot brain.
Every lane's end, every shop, church, session, hang- 688
ing, yields a careful man work.   [*He stands aside.*]

CLOWN See, see, what a man you are now! There is no
other way but to tell the King she's a changeling and 691
none of your flesh and blood.

SHEPHERD Nay, but hear me.

CLOWN Nay, but hear me.

SHEPHERD Go to, then.   695

CLOWN She being none of your flesh and blood, your
flesh and blood has not offended the King, and so
your flesh and blood is not to be punished by him.
Show those things you found about her, those secret
things, all but what she has with her. This being done,
let the law go whistle, I warrant you.

SHEPHERD I will tell the King all, every word, yea, and
his son's pranks too; who, I may say, is no honest

620 choughs jackdaws   628 Nothing nothing that   635 the outside . . .
poverty i.e., your ragged clothing   636 discase undress   637 think
understand   638–9 pennyworth i.e., value of the bargain   640 some
boot something in addition.   643 dispatch hurry. (Also in line 647.)
644 flayed skinned, i.e., undressed   648 earnest advance payment.
(Playing on in earnest in line 645.)   651–2 let . . . to ye! i.e., let my
prophecy that you, Perdita, will be fortunate be fulfilled for you!
653 covert hidden place.   655–6 as you . . . seeming as much as you
can, disguise your outward appearance   657 eyes spying eyes

670 re-view see again   679 without boot i.e., even without added
payment.   What a boot What a profit   681 connive at look indul-
gently at   682 about engaged in   683 clog encumbrance (i.e.,
Perdita)   685 withal with it   688 session court session   691
changeling child left by the fairies   695 Go to Go ahead. (Or, an
expression of impatience.)

man, neither to his father nor to me, to go about to 704
make me the King's brother-in-law.

CLOWN   Indeed, brother-in-law was the farthest off you
could have been to him, and then your blood had
been the dearer by I know not how much an ounce.

AUTOLYCUS [aside]   Very wisely, puppies!

SHEPHERD   Well, let us to the King. There is that in this
fardel will make him scratch his beard.   711

AUTOLYCUS [aside]   I know not what impediment this
complaint may be to the flight of my master.   713

CLOWN   Pray heartily he be at' palace.   714

AUTOLYCUS [aside]   Though I am not naturally honest,
I am so sometimes by chance. Let me pocket up my
peddler's excrement. [He takes off his false beard.] How 717
now, rustics, whither are you bound?

SHEPHERD   To the palace, an it like Your Worship.   719

AUTOLYCUS   Your affairs there, what, with whom, the
condition of that fardel, the place of your dwelling, 721
your names, your ages, of what having, breeding, and 722
anything that is fitting to be known, discover.   723

CLOWN   We are but plain fellows, sir.   724

AUTOLYCUS   A lie; you are rough and hairy. Let me have
no lying. It becomes none but tradesmen, and they
often give us soldiers the lie, but we pay them for it 727
with stamped coin, not stabbing steel; therefore they
do not give us the lie.   729

CLOWN   Your Worship had like to have given us one, if 730
you had not taken yourself with the manner.   731

SHEPHERD   Are you a courtier, an' like you, sir?

AUTOLYCUS   Whether it like me or no, I am a courtier.
See'st thou not the air of the court in these enfoldings? 734
Hath not my gait in it the measure of the court? Re- 735
ceives not thy nose court odor from me? Reflect I not
on thy baseness court contempt? Think'st thou, for 737
that I insinuate to toze from thee thy business, I am 738
therefore no courtier? I am courtier cap-à-pie, and one 739
that will either push on or pluck back thy business
there. Whereupon I command thee to open thy affair. 741

SHEPHERD   My business, sir, is to the King.

AUTOLYCUS   What advocate hast thou to him?

SHEPHERD   I know not, an' like you.

CLOWN [aside to Shepherd]   "Advocate" 's the court
word for a pheasant. Say you have none.   746

SHEPHERD   None, sir. I have no pheasant, cock nor hen.

AUTOLYCUS [aside]
How blessed are we that are not simple men!
Yet nature might have made me as these are;
Therefore I will not disdain.

CLOWN [to Shepherd]   This cannot be but a great cour- 751
tier.

SHEPHERD   His garments are rich, but he wears them
not handsomely.

CLOWN   He seems to be the more noble in being fantas- 755
tical. A great man, I'll warrant. I know by the picking 756
on's teeth.   757

AUTOLYCUS   The fardel there? What's i'th' fardel?
Wherefore that box?

SHEPHERD   Sir, there lies such secrets in this fardel and
box which none must know but the King, and which
he shall know within this hour if I may come to the
speech of him.

AUTOLYCUS   Age, thou hast lost thy labor.   764

SHEPHERD   Why, sir?

AUTOLYCUS   The King is not at the palace. He is gone
aboard a new ship to purge melancholy and air
himself; for, if thou be'st capable of things serious, 768
thou must know the King is full of grief.

SHEPHERD   So 'tis said, sir; about his son, that should
have married a shepherd's daughter.

AUTOLYCUS   If that shepherd be not in handfast, let him 772
fly. The curses he shall have, the tortures he shall feel,
will break the back of man, the heart of monster.

CLOWN   Think you so, sir?

AUTOLYCUS   Not he alone shall suffer what wit can make 776
heavy and vengeance bitter, but those that are ger- 777
mane to him, though removed fifty times, shall all 778
come under the hangman—which, though it be great
pity, yet it is necessary. An old sheep-whistling rogue, 780
a ram tender, to offer to have his daughter come into 781
grace? Some say he shall be stoned; but that death is 782
too soft for him, say I. Draw our throne into a sheep- 783
cote? All deaths are too few, the sharpest too easy.   784

CLOWN   Has the old man e'er a son, sir, do you hear,
an' like you, sir?

AUTOLYCUS   He has a son, who shall be flayed alive; then,
'nointed over with honey, set on the head of a wasp's
nest; then stand till he be three-quarters and a dram 789
dead; then recovered again with aqua vitae or some 790
other hot infusion; then, raw as he is, and in the hot-
test day prognostication proclaims, shall he be set 792
against a brick wall, the sun looking with a southward
eye upon him, where he is to behold him with flies 794
blown to death. But what talk we of these traitorly ras- 795
cals, whose miseries are to be smiled at, their offenses

704 go about make it his object   **711 fardel** bundle   **713 my master**
i.e., Florizel. (See 4.3.13.)   **714 at'** at the   **717 excrement** outgrowth of
hair, beard.   **719 an it like** if it please   **721 condition** nature
722 having property   **723 discover** reveal.   **724 plain** simple. (But
Autolycus plays on the meaning "smooth.")   **727 give . . . lie** i.e.,
cheat us. (But *giving the lie* also means to accuse a person to his face of
lying, an affront which a soldier would repay with *stabbing steel*.)
729 give (Autolycus punningly observes that, since soldiers pay
tradesmen for their wares, the tradesmen cannot be said to have *given*
the lie, and so a duel is avoided.)   **730 had like** was about   **731 taken
. . . manner** i.e., caught yourself in the act, stopped short. (The Clown
observes that Autolycus has once again avoided the "giving of the lie"
and its consequences in a duel by his clever equivocation. Compare
with Touchstone in *As You Like It*, 5.4.)   **734 enfoldings** clothes.   **735
measure** stately tread   **737–8 for that . . . business** because I undertake to pry out of you what your business may be   **739 cap-à-pie**
from head to foot   **741 open** reveal   **746 pheasant** (The rustics suppose that Autolycus has asked them what gift they propose to present
as a bribe, as one might do to a judge in a court of law.)

751 be but be anyone but   **755–6 fantastical** eccentric.   **756–7 picking
on's teeth** (A stylish affectation in Shakespeare's time.)   **764 Age** Old
man   **768 be'st capable of** know anything about   **772 handfast** custody. (With a play on "betrothal.")   **776 wit** ingenuity (in devising tortures)   **777–8 germane** related   **780 sheep-whistling** tending sheep by
whistling after them   **781 offer** dare   **782 grace** favor.   **783–4 sheepcote** pen for sheep.   **789 a dram** i.e., a small amount, a fraction
790 aqua vitae brandy   **792 prognostication** forecasting (in the
almanac)   **794 he** i.e., the sun   **795 blown** swollen.   **what** i.e., why

being so capital? Tell me, for you seem to be honest
plain men, what you have to the King. Being some- ⁷⁹⁸
thing gently considered, I'll bring you where he is ⁷⁹⁹
aboard, tender your persons to his presence, whisper ⁸⁰⁰
him in your behalfs; and if it be in man besides the
King to effect your suits, here is man shall do it.

CLOWN [*to Shepherd*] He seems to be of great authority.
Close with him, give him gold; and though authority ⁸⁰⁴
be a stubborn bear, yet he is oft led by the nose
with gold. Show the inside of your purse to the outside of his hand, and no more ado. Remember—
"stoned," and "flayed alive."

SHEPHERD An't please you, sir, to undertake the
business for us, here is that gold I have. [*He offers
money.*] I'll make it as much more and leave this young
man in pawn till I bring it you.   ⁸¹²

AUTOLYCUS After I have done what I promised?

SHEPHERD Ay, sir.

AUTOLYCUS [*taking the money*] Well, give me the moiety. ⁸¹⁵
[*To the Clown*] Are you a party in this business?

CLOWN In some sort, sir. But, though my case be a piti- ⁸¹⁷
ful one, I hope I shall not be flayed out of it.

AUTOLYCUS Oh, that's the case of the shepherd's son.
Hang him, he'll be made an example.

CLOWN [*to Shepherd*] Comfort, good comfort! We must
to the King and show our strange sights. He must
know 'tis none of your daughter nor my sister; we are
gone else.—Sir, I will give you as much as this old ⁸²⁴
man does when the business is performed, and
remain, as he says, your pawn till it be brought you.

AUTOLYCUS I will trust you. Walk before toward the
seaside; go on the right hand. I will but look upon the ⁸²⁸
hedge and follow you.   ⁸²⁹

CLOWN [*to Shepherd*] We are blessed in this man, as I
may say, even blessed.

SHEPHERD Let's before, as he bids us. He was provided
to do us good.   *Exeunt* [*Shepherd and Clown*].

AUTOLYCUS If I had a mind to be honest, I see Fortune
would not suffer me; she drops booties in my mouth.
I am courted now with a double occasion: gold, and a ⁸³⁶
means to do the Prince my master good, which who
knows how that may turn back to my advancement? I ⁸³⁸
will bring these two moles, these blind ones, aboard ⁸³⁹
him. If he think it fit to shore them again and that the ⁸⁴⁰
complaint they have to the King concerns him noth- ⁸⁴¹
ing, let him call me rogue for being so far officious, for ⁸⁴²
I am proof against that title and what shame else ⁸⁴³
belongs to't. To him will I present them. There may be
matter in it.   [*Exit.*]

❖

5.1

*Enter Leontes, Cleomenes, Dion, Paulina, [and]
servants.*

CLEOMENES
Sir, you have done enough, and have performed
A saintlike sorrow. No fault could you make
Which you have not redeemed—indeed, paid down
More penitence than done trespass. At the last,
Do as the heavens have done: forget your evil.
With them, forgive yourself.

LEONTES   Whilst I remember
Her and her virtues, I cannot forget
My blemishes in them, and so still think of   ⁸
The wrong I did myself, which was so much
That heirless it hath made my kingdom and
Destroyed the sweet'st companion that e'er man
Bred his hopes out of. True?

PAULINA   Too true, my lord.
If one by one you wedded all the world,
Or from the all that are took something good   ¹⁴
To make a perfect woman, she you killed
Would be unparalleled.

LEONTES   I think so. Killed?
She I killed? I did so, but thou strik'st me
Sorely to say I did. It is as bitter
Upon thy tongue as in my thought. Now, good now, ¹⁹
Say so but seldom.

CLEOMENES   Not at all, good lady.
You might have spoken a thousand things that would
Have done the time more benefit and graced
Your kindness better.

PAULINA   You are one of those
Would have him wed again.

DION   If you would not so,
You pity not the state nor the remembrance   ²⁵
Of his most sovereign name, consider little   ²⁶
What dangers by His Highness' fail of issue   ²⁷
May drop upon his kingdom and devour
Incertain lookers-on. What were more holy   ²⁹
Than to rejoice the former queen is well?   ³⁰
What holier than, for royalty's repair,
For present comfort and for future good,
To bless the bed of majesty again
With a sweet fellow to't?

PAULINA   There is none worthy,
Respecting her that's gone. Besides, the gods   ³⁵
Will have fulfilled their secret purposes;   ³⁶
For has not the divine Apollo said,
Is't not the tenor of his oracle,
That King Leontes shall not have an heir

798 what you have to what business you have with   **798–9 Being . . .
considered** i.e., (1) Being a gentleman of some influence (2) If I receive
a gentlemanly consideration, a bribe   **800 tender your persons** introduce you   **804 Close with him** Accept his offer   **812 in pawn** as
security   **815 moiety** half.   **817 case** (1) cause (2) skin   **824 gone
else** undone otherwise.   **828–9 look . . . hedge** i.e., relieve myself
836 occasion opportunity   **838 turn back** redound   **839–40 aboard
him** i.e., to him (Prince Florizel) aboard his ship.   **840 shore** put
ashore   **841–2 nothing** not at all   **843 proof against** invulnerable to

5.1. Location: Sicilia. The royal court.
8 in them in comparison with them   **14 the all that are** all the women
that there are   **19 good now** i.e., if you please   **25 nor the remembrance** i.e., nor give consideration to the perpetuation (through bearing a child and heir)   **26 consider** you consider   **27 fail of issue**
failure to produce an heir   **29 Incertain** not knowing what to think or
do (about the royal succession)   **30 well** happy, at rest (in heaven).
35 Respecting in comparison with   **36 Will . . . purposes** are determined to have their secret purposes fulfilled

Till his lost child be found? Which that it shall
Is all as monstrous to our human reason
As my Antigonus to break his grave   42
And come again to me, who, on my life,
Did perish with the infant. 'Tis your counsel   44
My lord should to the heavens be contrary,
Oppose against their wills. [*To Leontes*] Care not for
   issue.   46
The crown will find an heir. Great Alexander
Left his to th' worthiest; so his successor   48
Was like to be the best.

LEONTES   Good Paulina,
Who hast the memory of Hermione,
I know, in honor, oh, that ever I
Had squared me to thy counsel! Then even now   52
I might have looked upon my queen's full eyes,
Have taken treasure from her lips—

PAULINA   And left them
More rich for what they yielded.

LEONTES   Thou speak'st truth.
No more such wives, therefore no wife. One worse,   56
And better used, would make her sainted spirit   57
Again possess her corpse, and on this stage,   58
Where we're offenders now, appear soul-vexed,
And begin, "Why to me?"

PAULINA   Had she such power,   60
She had just cause.

LEONTES   She had, and would incense me   61
To murder her I married.

PAULINA   I should so.   62
Were I the ghost that walked, I'd bid you mark
Her eye and tell me for what dull part in't
You chose her. Then I'd shriek, that even your ears
Should rift to hear me, and the words that followed   66
Should be, "Remember mine."

LEONTES   Stars, stars,   67
And all eyes else dead coals! Fear thou no wife;   68
I'll have no wife, Paulina.

PAULINA   Will you swear
Never to marry but by my free leave?

LEONTES
Never, Paulina, so be blest my spirit!

PAULINA
Then, good my lords, bear witness to his oath.

CLEOMENES
You tempt him overmuch.

PAULINA   Unless another,   73
As like Hermione as is her picture,

Affront his eye.

CLEOMENES   Good madam—

PAULINA   I have done.   75
Yet if my lord will marry—if you will, sir,
No remedy, but you will—give me the office
To choose you a queen. She shall not be so young
As was your former, but she shall be such
As, walked your first queen's ghost, it should take joy   80
To see her in your arms.

LEONTES   My true Paulina,
We shall not marry till thou bidd'st us.

PAULINA   That
Shall be when your first queen's again in breath;
Never till then.   84

Enter a Gentleman.

GENTLEMAN
One that gives out himself Prince Florizel,   85
Son of Polixenes, with his princess—she
The fairest I have yet beheld—desires access
To your high presence.

LEONTES   What with him? He comes not   88
Like to his father's greatness. His approach,   89
So out of circumstance and sudden, tells us   90
'Tis not a visitation framed, but forced   91
By need and accident. What train?

GENTLEMAN   But few,   92
And those but mean.

LEONTES   His princess, say you, with him?   93

GENTLEMAN
Ay, the most peerless piece of earth, I think,
That e'er the sun shone bright on.

PAULINA   Oh, Hermione,
As every present time doth boast itself   96
Above a better gone, so must thy grave   97
Give way to what's seen now! [*To the Gentleman*] Sir,
   you yourself   98
Have said and writ so, but your writing now
Is colder than that theme. She had not been   100
Nor was not to be equaled—thus your verse   101
Flowed with her beauty once. 'Tis shrewdly ebbed   102
To say you have seen a better.

GENTLEMAN   Pardon, madam.
The one I have almost forgot—your pardon!
The other, when she has obtained your eye,
Will have your tongue too. This is a creature,   106
Would she begin a sect, might quench the zeal
Of all professors else, make proselytes   108

---

42 As as for   **44 'Tis your counsel** It's your advice that   **46 Oppose** oppose himself.   **Care not for** Do not be anxious about   **48 Left . . . worthiest** (When Alexander the Great died in 323 B.C., his son Alexander was yet unborn, necessitating the choice of an heir.) **52 squared me** adjusted or regulated myself   **56–7 One . . . used** i.e., If I took a new, less excellent wife and treated her better   **57 her** Hermione's   **58 possess her corpse** i.e., return to earth (*this stage*) in Hermione's human shape   **60 Why to me?** Why this offense to me? **61 had** would have.   **incense** stir up, incite   **62 should** so would similarly incite you.   **66 rift** rive, split   **67 mine** my eyes.   **Stars** i.e., Her eyes were stars   **68 all eyes else** all other eyes   **73 tempt** bear down on

75 Affront confront   **80 walked . . . ghost** if your first queen's ghost were to walk.   **take joy** be overjoyed   **84.1 *Enter a Gentleman*** (He is called a "Servant" in the Folio text, but his writing poetry in lines 100–4 is more consistent with his being a courtier. Any such person at court is a servant of the king.)   **85 gives out himself** reports himself to be   **88 What** What retinue   **89 Like to** in a manner consistent with   **90 out of circumstance** without ceremony   **91 framed** planned **92 train** retinue.   **93 mean** lowly.   **96–8 As . . . now!** As every present age boasts its superiority to past times that were in point of fact better, so you, long dead, must give way to present fashion!   **100 that theme** i.e., Hermione, the subject of your verses.   **100–1 She . . . equaled** (Presumably, the poet wrote "She has not been nor is not to be equaled.")   **102 'Tis shrewdly ebbed** i.e., You've egregiously gone back on your word   **106 tongue** i.e., approval   **108 professors else** believers in other sects or deities

Of who she but bid follow.

PAULINA   How? Not women!   109

GENTLEMAN

Women will love her that she is a woman
More worth than any man; men, that she is
The rarest of all women.

LEONTES   Go, Cleomenes.
Yourself, assisted with your honored friends,
Bring them to our embracement.

        Exit [Cleomenes with others].

            Still, 'tis strange
He thus should steal upon us.

PAULINA   Had our prince,
Jewel of children, seen this hour, he had paired
Well with this lord. There was not full a month
Between their births.

LEONTES   Prithee, no more, cease. Thou know'st
He dies to me again when talked of. Sure,
When I shall see this gentleman, thy speeches
Will bring me to consider that which may
Unfurnish me of reason. They are come.   123

     Enter Florizel, Perdita, Cleomenes, and others.

Your mother was most true to wedlock, Prince,
For she did print your royal father off,
Conceiving you. Were I but twenty-one,
Your father's image is so hit in you,   127
His very air, that I should call you brother,
As I did him, and speak of something wildly
By us performed before. Most dearly welcome!
And your fair princess—goddess! Oh! Alas,
I lost a couple that twixt heaven and earth
Might thus have stood begetting wonder as
You, gracious couple, do. And then I lost—
All mine own folly—the society,
Amity too, of your brave father, whom,   136
Though bearing misery, I desire my life   137
Once more to look on him.

FLORIZEL   By his command   138
Have I here touched Sicilia, and from him
Give you all greetings that a king, at friend,   140
Can send his brother; and but infirmity,   141
Which waits upon worn times, hath something seized   142
His wished ability, he had himself   143
The lands and waters twixt your throne and his
Measured to look upon you, whom he loves—   145
He bade me say so—more than all the scepters
And those that bear them living.

LEONTES   O my brother!   147
Good gentleman, the wrongs I have done thee stir
Afresh within me, and these thy offices,   149

So rarely kind, are as interpreters   150
Of my behindhand slackness. Welcome hither,   151
As is the spring to th'earth. And hath he too
Exposed this paragon to th' fearful usage—
At least ungentle—of the dreadful Neptune,   154
To greet a man not worth her pains, much less
Th'adventure of her person?   156

FLORIZEL   Good my lord,
She came from Libya.

LEONTES   Where the warlike Smalus,
That noble honored lord, is feared and loved?

FLORIZEL

Most royal sir, from thence, from him, whose daughter   159
His tears proclaimed his, parting with her. Thence,   160
A prosperous south wind friendly, we have crossed,
To execute the charge my father gave me
For visiting Your Highness. My best train
I have from your Sicilian shores dismissed,
Who for Bohemia bend, to signify   165
Not only my success in Libya, sir,
But my arrival and my wife's in safety
Here where we are.

LEONTES   The blessèd gods
Purge all infection from our air whilst you
Do climate here! You have a holy father,   170
A graceful gentleman, against whose person,   171
So sacred as it is, I have done sin,
For which the heavens, taking angry note,
Have left me issueless; and your father's blest,
As he from heaven merits it, with you,
Worthy his goodness. What might I have been,
Might I a son and daughter now have looked on,
Such goodly things as you?

        Enter a Lord.

LORD   Most noble sir,
That which I shall report will bear no credit
Were not the proof so nigh. Please you, great sir,
Bohemia greets you from himself by me;
Desires you to attach his son, who has—   182
His dignity and duty both cast off—   183
Fled from his father, from his hopes, and with
A shepherd's daughter.

LEONTES   Where's Bohemia? Speak.

LORD

Here in your city. I now came from him.
I speak amazedly, and it becomes   187
My marvel and my message. To your court   188
Whiles he was hast'ning—in the chase, it seems,
Of this fair couple—meets he on the way
The father of this seeming lady and

---

109 Of . . . follow of all those whom she merely told to follow her.
How? Not women! What do you mean? Surely women wouldn't
become converts! **123 Unfurnish** deprive, divest **127 hit** exactly
reproduced **136 brave** noble **137 my life** i.e., to live long enough
138 him (Redundant in modern syntax.) **140 at friend** in friendship
141 but were it not that **142 waits . . . times** attends old age **142–3
something . . . ability** to some extent taken away his ability (to travel)
as he wishes **145 Measured** traversed **147 those . . . living** those
living kings who bear scepters. **149 offices** messages of good will,
courteous attentions

150 rarely exceptionally **150–1 are . . . slackness** are like commentators on my slowness in greeting you. **154 Neptune** god of the sea
156 Th'adventure the hazard **159–60 whose . . . her** whose tears, as
he parted with her, proclaimed her to be his daughter. **165 bend**
direct their course **170 climate** dwell, reside (in this clime) **171
graceful** full of grace, gracious **182 attach** arrest **183 dignity and
duty** princely dignity and filial duty **187–8 I . . . message** i.e., I
speak perplexedly as befits my perplexity and my astonishing news.

Her brother, having both their country quitted
With this young prince.

FLORIZEL   Camillo has betrayed me,
Whose honor and whose honesty till now
Endured all weathers.

LORD   Lay't so to his charge.   195
He's with the King your father.

LEONTES   Who? Camillo?

LORD
Camillo, sir. I spake with him, who now
Has these poor men in question. Never saw I   198
Wretches so quake. They kneel, they kiss the earth,
Forswear themselves as often as they speak.
Bohemia stops his ears and threatens them
With divers deaths in death.

PERDITA   Oh, my poor father!   202
The heaven sets spies upon us, will not have
Our contract celebrated.

LEONTES   You are married?

FLORIZEL
We are not, sir, nor are we like to be.   205
The stars, I see, will kiss the valleys first;
The odds for high and low's alike.

LEONTES   My lord,   207
Is this the daughter of a king?

FLORIZEL   She is,
When once she is my wife.

LEONTES
That "once," I see, by your good father's speed
Will come on very slowly. I am sorry,
Most sorry, you have broken from his liking
Where you were tied in duty, and as sorry
Your choice is not so rich in worth as beauty,   214
That you might well enjoy her.

FLORIZEL [to Perdita]   Dear, look up.
Though Fortune, visible an enemy,   216
Should chase us with my father, power no jot   217
Hath she to change our loves.—Beseech you, sir,
Remember since you owed no more to time   219
Than I do now. With thought of such affections,   220
Step forth mine advocate. At your request
My father will grant precious things as trifles.

LEONTES
Would he do so, I'd beg your precious mistress,
Which he counts but a trifle.

PAULINA   Sir, my liege,
Your eye hath too much youth in't. Not a month
'Fore your queen died, she was more worth such
   gazes
Than what you look on now.

LEONTES   I thought of her
Even in these looks I made. [To Florizel] But your
   petition

Is yet unanswered. I will to your father.
Your honor not o'erthrown by your desires,   230
I am friend to them and you. Upon which errand
I now go toward him. Therefore follow me,
And mark what way I make. Come, good my lord.   233
                                   Exeunt.

❖

5.2

Enter Autolycus and a Gentleman.

AUTOLYCUS   Beseech you, sir, were you present at this
   relation?   2

FIRST GENTLEMAN   I was by at the opening of the fardel,
   heard the old shepherd deliver the manner how he   4
   found it; whereupon, after a little amazedness, we
   were all commanded out of the chamber. Only this,
   methought, I heard the shepherd say he found the
   child.

AUTOLYCUS   I would most gladly know the issue of it.   9

FIRST GENTLEMAN   I make a broken delivery of the busi-   10
   ness, but the changes I perceived in the King and Camillo were very notes of admiration. They seemed al-   12
   most, with staring on one another, to tear the cases of 13
   their eyes. There was speech in their dumbness, lan-   14
   guage in their very gesture. They looked as they had   15
   heard of a world ransomed, or one destroyed. A notable
   passion of wonder appeared in them, but the wisest
   beholder, that knew no more but seeing, could not say   18
   if th'importance were joy or sorrow; but in the ex-   19
   tremity of the one it must needs be.   20

Enter another Gentleman.

Here comes a gentleman that haply knows more.—   21
The news, Rogero?

SECOND GENTLEMAN   Nothing but bonfires. The oracle
   is fulfilled; the King's daughter is found. Such a deal of 24
   wonder is broken out within this hour that ballad
   makers cannot be able to express it.

Enter another Gentleman.

Here comes the Lady Paulina's steward. He can deliver
you more.—How goes it now, sir? This news which is
called true is so like an old tale that the verity of it is in
strong suspicion. Has the King found his heir?

THIRD GENTLEMAN   Most true, if ever truth were preg-   31
   nant by circumstance. That which you hear you'll   32
   swear you see, there is such unity in the proofs. The
   mantle of Queen Hermione's, her jewel about the neck

---

195 Lay't . . . charge Confront him with it directly.   198 in question
under interrogation.   202 deaths i.e., tortures   205 like likely   207
The odds . . . alike Fortune treats high and low alike.   214 worth
rank   216–17 Though . . . father Though the goddess Fortune herself
were to manifest herself as our enemy and join my father in chasing
us   219–20 since . . . now when you were no older than I am now.
220 With . . . affections Recalling what it was to be in love at that age

230 Your . . . desires If your chaste honor has not been overcome by
sexual desire, or, if what you want in this match is compatible with
your royal honor   233 way progress
5.2. Location: Sicilia. At court.
2 relation narrative, account.   4 deliver report   9 issue outcome
10 broken disjointed, fragmented   12 very notes of admiration veritable marks of wonderment.   13–14 cases of their eyes eyelids.   15 as
as if   18 no . . . seeing nothing except what he could see   19 th'importance the import, meaning   20 of the one of one or the other
21 haply perhaps   24 deal huge quantity   31–2 pregnant by circumstance made apparent by circumstantial evidence.

of it, the letters of Antigonus found with it which they
know to be his character, the majesty of the creature in   36
resemblance of the mother, the affection of nobleness   37
which nature shows above her breeding, and many   38
other evidences proclaim her with all certainty to be
the King's daughter. Did you see the meeting of the
two kings?

SECOND GENTLEMAN   No.

THIRD GENTLEMAN   Then have you lost a sight which
was to be seen, cannot be spoken of. There might you
have beheld one joy crown another, so and in such
manner that it seemed Sorrow wept to take leave of
them, for their joy waded in tears. There was casting
up of eyes, holding up of hands, with countenance of   48
such distraction that they were to be known by
garment, not by favor. Our king, being ready to leap   50
out of himself for joy of his found daughter, as if that
joy were now become a loss, cries, "Oh, thy mother,
thy mother!" then asks Bohemia forgiveness; then
embraces his son-in-law; then again worries he his   54
daughter with clipping her; now he thanks the old   55
shepherd, which stands by like a weather-bitten con-   56
duit of many kings' reigns. I never heard of such   57
another encounter, which lames report to follow it and   58
undoes description to do it.   59

SECOND GENTLEMAN   What, pray you, became of Antigonus, that carried hence the child?

THIRD GENTLEMAN   Like an old tale still, which will have
matter to rehearse though credit be asleep and not an   63
ear open. He was torn to pieces with a bear. This   64
avouches the shepherd's son, who has not only his   65
innocence, which seems much, to justify him, but a   66
handkerchief and rings of his that Paulina knows.   67

FIRST GENTLEMAN   What became of his bark and his
followers?

THIRD GENTLEMAN   Wrecked the same instant of their
master's death and in the view of the shepherd; so that
all the instruments which aided to expose the child
were even then lost when it was found. But oh, the
noble combat that twixt joy and sorrow was fought in
Paulina! She had one eye declined for the loss of her   75
husband, another elevated that the oracle was fulfilled.   76
She lifted the Princess from the earth, and so locks her
in embracing as if she would pin her to her heart, that
she might no more be in danger of losing.   79

FIRST GENTLEMAN   The dignity of this act was worth
the audience of kings and princes, for by such was it
acted.

THIRD GENTLEMAN   One of the prettiest touches of all,
and that which angled for mine eyes—caught the

water, though not the fish—was when, at the relation
of the Queen's death, with the manner how she came
to't bravely confessed and lamented by the King,
how attentiveness wounded his daughter; till, from   88
one sign of dolor to another, she did, with an "Alas!" I   89
would fain say, bleed tears, for I am sure my heart
wept blood. Who was most marble there changed   91
color; some swooned, all sorrowed. If all the world
could have seen't, the woe had been universal.

FIRST GENTLEMAN   Are they returned to the court?

THIRD GENTLEMAN   No. The Princess hearing of her
mother's statue, which is in the keeping of Paulina—a
piece many years in doing and now newly performed   97
by that rare Italian master, Julio Romano, who, had he   98
himself eternity and could put breath into his work,
would beguile Nature of her custom, so perfectly he is   100
her ape; he so near to Hermione hath done Hermione   101
that they say one would speak to her and stand in
hope of answer—thither with all greediness of affec-   103
tion are they gone, and there they intend to sup.   104

SECOND GENTLEMAN   I thought she had some great matter there in hand, for she hath privately twice or thrice
a day, ever since the death of Hermione, visited that
removed house. Shall we thither and with our com-   108
pany piece the rejoicing?   109

FIRST GENTLEMAN   Who would be thence that has the
benefit of access? Every wink of an eye some new
grace will be born. Our absence makes us unthrifty to   112
our knowledge. Let's along.   *Exeunt* [*Gentlemen*].

AUTOLYCUS   Now, had I not the dash of my former life   114
in me, would preferment drop on my head. I brought   115
the old man and his son aboard the Prince, told him I   116
heard them talk of a fardel and I know not what. But
he at that time overfond of the shepherd's daughter—so he then took her to be—who began to be
much seasick, and himself little better, extremity of
weather continuing, this mystery remained undiscovered. But 'tis all one to me, for had I been the finder   122
out of this secret, it would not have relished among   123
my other discredits.

Enter Shepherd and Clown, [*dressed in finery*].

Here come those I have done good to against my will,
and already appearing in the blossoms of their fortune.

SHEPHERD   Come, boy. I am past more children, but
thy sons and daughters will be all gentlemen born.

CLOWN [*to Autolycus*]   You are well met, sir. You denied to fight
with me this other day because I was no gentleman   131

36 character handwriting   **37 affection of** natural disposition to
38 breeding rearing   **48 countenance** bearing, demeanor   **50 favor**
features.   **54 worries he** he pesters   **55 clipping** embracing
56–7 which . . . reigns who stands by weeping like a weather-beaten
fountain that has stood there over the course of many kings' reigns.
58–9 which . . . do it which makes any account of it seem inadequate
and beggars the powers of description in an attempt to do justice to
it.   **63 rehearse** relate.   **credit** belief   **64 with** by   **65 avouches** confirms, corroborates   **66 innocence** simplemindedness (such that he
would seem unable to invent such a story)   **67 his** Antigonus's
75–6 She . . . fulfilled i.e., She wept and laughed at the same time.
79 losing being lost.

88 attentiveness listening to it   **89 dolor** grief   **91 Who . . . marble**
Even the most hardhearted   **97 performed** completed   **98 Julio**
Romano Italian painter and sculptor of the sixteenth century, better
known as a painter (and an anachronism in this play)   **100 beguile**
deprive, cheat.   **custom** trade   **101 ape** imitator   **103–4 greediness**
of affection eagerness born of love   **104 sup** i.e., feed their hungry
eyes (?) or, perhaps, have a commemorative banquet (?).
108 removed sequestered   **109 piece** add to, augment   **112 unthrifty**
to passing up an opportunity to increase   **114–15 had I . . . head** if it
weren't for the lingering aura of petty thievery that hangs about me,
royal favor would be sure to fall to my lot.   **116 the Prince** the
Prince's ship   **122 'tis all one** it's all the same   **123 relished** tasted
well, suited   **131 this other** the other

born. See you these clothes? Say you see them not and
think me still no gentleman born. You were best say
these robes are not gentlemen born. Give me the lie,   134
do, and try whether I am not now a gentleman born.

AUTOLYCUS   I know you are now, sir, a gentleman born.

CLOWN   Ay, and have been so any time these four
hours.

SHEPHERD   And so have I, boy.

CLOWN   So you have. But I was a gentleman born before
my father; for the King's son took me by the hand
and called me brother; and then the two kings called
my father brother; and then the Prince my brother and
the Princess my sister called my father father; and so
we wept, and there was the first gentlemanlike tears
that ever we shed.

SHEPHERD   We may live, son, to shed many more.

CLOWN   Ay, or else 'twere hard luck, being in so pre-   148
posterous estate as we are.   149

AUTOLYCUS   I humbly beseech you, sir, to pardon me
all the faults I have committed to Your Worship, and to
give me your good report to the Prince my master.   152

SHEPHERD   Prithee, son, do; for we must be gentle, now   153
we are gentlemen.

CLOWN   [to Autolycus]   Thou wilt amend thy life?

AUTOLYCUS   Ay, an it like Your good Worship.   156

CLOWN   Give me thy hand. I will swear to the Prince
thou art as honest a true fellow as any is in Bohemia.   158

SHEPHERD   You may say it, but not swear it.

CLOWN   Not swear it, now I am a gentleman? Let boors   160
and franklins say it; I'll swear it.   161

SHEPHERD   How if it be false, son?

CLOWN   If it be ne'er so false, a true gentleman may
swear it in the behalf of his friend.—And I'll swear to
the Prince thou art a tall fellow of thy hands and that   165
thou wilt not be drunk; but I know thou art no tall
fellow of thy hands and that thou wilt be drunk. But
I'll swear it, and I would thou wouldst be a tall fellow
of thy hands.

AUTOLYCUS   I will prove so, sir, to my power.   170

CLOWN   Ay, by any means prove a tall fellow. If I do not
wonder how thou dar'st venture to be drunk, not
being a tall fellow, trust me not. Hark, the kings and
the princes, our kindred, are going to see the Queen's
picture. Come, follow us. We'll be thy good masters.   175

                                                    Exeunt.

❧

5.3

Enter Leontes, Polixenes, Florizel, Perdita,

Camillo, Paulina, lords, etc.

LEONTES
O grave and good Paulina, the great comfort
That I have had of thee!

PAULINA   What, sovereign sir,   2
I did not well, I meant well. All my services
You have paid home. But that you have vouchsafed,   4
With your crowned brother and these your contracted
Heirs of your kingdoms, my poor house to visit,
It is a surplus of your grace which never   7
My life may last to answer.

LEONTES   O Paulina,   8
We honor you with trouble. But we came   9
To see the statue of our queen. Your gallery
Have we passed through, not without much content
In many singularities; but we saw not   12
That which my daughter came to look upon,
The statue of her mother.

PAULINA   As she lived peerless,
So her dead likeness, I do well believe,
Excels whatever yet you looked upon
Or hand of man hath done. Therefore I keep it
Lonely, apart. But here it is. Prepare   18
To see the life as lively mocked as ever   19
Still sleep mocked death. Behold, and say 'tis well.   20
        [*Paulina draws a curtain, and discovers*]
                Hermione [*standing*] *like a statue.*
I like your silence; it the more shows off
Your wonder. But yet speak; first, you, my liege.
Comes it not something near?

LEONTES   Her natural posture!   23
Chide me, dear stone, that I may say indeed
Thou art Hermione; or rather, thou art she
In thy not chiding, for she was as tender
As infancy and grace. But yet, Paulina,
Hermione was not as much wrinkled, nothing   28
So agèd as this seems.

POLIXENES   Oh, not by much.

PAULINA
So much the more our carver's excellence,
Which lets go by some sixteen years and makes her
As she lived now.

LEONTES   As now she might have done,   32
So much to my good comfort as it is
Now piercing to my soul. Oh, thus she stood,
Even with such life of majesty—warm life,
As now it coldly stands—when first I wooed her!
I am ashamed. Does not the stone rebuke me
For being more stone than it? O royal piece!   38
There's magic in thy majesty, which has
My evils conjured to remembrance and
From thy admiring daughter took the spirits,   41

5.3. Location: Sicilia. Paulina's house.
2 What Whatever   **4 home** fully.   **7–8 which . . . answer** which I can
never live long enough to be able to repay.   **9 We . . . trouble** i.e., we
trouble you with the demands of hospitality, though you are kind
enough to call it an honor.   **12 singularities** rarities, curiosities
18 Lonely isolated   **19 as lively mocked** as realistically counterfeited
20 Still motionless   **23 something** somewhat   **28 nothing** not at all
32 As she as if she   **38 piece** work of art.   **41 admiring** filled with
wonder.   **spirits** vital spirits

---

134 Give me the lie Accuse me to my face of lying (an insult that
requires a challenge to a duel)   **148–9 preposterous** (Blunder for
"prosperous.")   **152 me** on my behalf   **153 gentle** nobly generous
156 an it like if it please   **158 honest a true** worthy an honest   **160
boors** peasants   **161 franklins** farmers owning their own small
farms   **165 tall . . . hands** brave fellow   **170 my power** the best of my
ability. (Autolycus slyly promises to use his hands well—in picking
pockets.)   **175 picture** i.e., likeness, painted statue.

Standing like stone with thee.

PERDITA   And give me leave,
And do not say 'tis superstition, that
I kneel and then implore her blessing. Lady,
                                        [kneeling]
Dear Queen, that ended when I but began,
Give me that hand of yours to kiss.

PAULINA   Oh, patience!
The statue is but newly fixed; the color's   47
Not dry.

CAMILLO
My lord, your sorrow was too sore laid on,   49
Which sixteen winters cannot blow away,
So many summers dry. Scarce any joy   51
Did ever so long live; no sorrow
But killed itself much sooner.

POLIXENES   Dear my brother,
Let him that was the cause of this have power   54
To take off so much grief from you as he
Will piece up in himself.

PAULINA   Indeed, my lord,   56
If I had thought the sight of my poor image
Would thus have wrought you—for the stone is
    mine—   58
I'd not have showed it.

LEONTES   Do not draw the curtain.

PAULINA
No longer shall you gaze on't, lest your fancy
May think anon it moves.

LEONTES   Let be, let be.
Would I were dead but that methinks already—
What was he that did make it? See, my lord,
Would you not deem it breathed? And that those veins
Did verily bear blood?

POLIXENES   Masterly done.
The very life seems warm upon her lip.

LEONTES
The fixture of her eye has motion in't,   67
As we are mocked with art.

PAULINA   I'll draw the curtain.   68
My lord's almost so far transported that
He'll think anon it lives.

LEONTES   Oh, sweet Paulina,
Make me to think so twenty years together!
No settled senses of the world can match   72
The pleasure of that madness. Let't alone.

PAULINA
I am sorry, sir, I have thus far stirred you; but
I could afflict you farther.

LEONTES   Do, Paulina;
For this affliction has a taste as sweet

As any cordial comfort. Still methinks   77
There is an air comes from her. What fine chisel
Could ever yet cut breath? Let no man mock me,
For I will kiss her.

PAULINA   Good my lord, forbear.
The ruddiness upon her lip is wet;
You'll mar it if you kiss it, stain your own
With oily painting. Shall I draw the curtain?   83

LEONTES
No, not these twenty years.

PERDITA   So long could I
Stand by, a looker on.

PAULINA   Either forbear,
Quit presently the chapel, or resolve you   86
For more amazement. If you can behold it,
I'll make the statue move indeed, descend
And take you by the hand. But then you'll think—
Which I protest against—I am assisted
By wicked powers.

LEONTES   What you can make her do
I am content to look on, what to speak
I am content to hear; for 'tis as easy
To make her speak as move.

PAULINA   It is required
You do awake your faith. Then all stand still.
On; those that think it is unlawful business   96
I am about, let them depart.

LEONTES   Proceed.
No foot shall stir.

PAULINA   Music, awake her; strike!   [Music.]   98
'Tis time. Descend. Be stone no more. Approach.
Strike all that look upon with marvel. Come,   100
I'll fill your grave up. Stir, nay, come away,
Bequeath to death your numbness, for from him   102
Dear life redeems you.—You perceive she stirs.
                        [Hermione comes down.]
Start not. Her actions shall be holy as
You hear my spell is lawful. Do not shun her   105
Until you see her die again, for then   106
You kill her double. Nay, present your hand.   107
When she was young you wooed her. Now in age
Is she become the suitor?   [Leontes touches her.]

LEONTES   Oh, she's warm!
If this be magic, let it be an art
Lawful as eating.

POLIXENES   She embraces him.

CAMILLO   She hangs about his neck.
If she pertain to life, let her speak too.   114

POLIXENES
Ay, and make it manifest where she has lived,
Or how stol'n from the dead.

PAULINA   That she is living,
Were it but told you, should be hooted at
Like an old tale; but it appears she lives,
Though yet she speak not. Mark a little while.

---

47 **fixed** made fast in its color   49 **sore** heavily   51 **So ... dry** i.e.,
and sixteen summers cannot dry up. (Camillo tells the King that he
has imposed too heavy a sorrow on himself if even sixteen years'
time cannot end it.)   54 **him** i.e., myself (as an innocent cause, but
still a cause)   56 **piece up in himself** add to his own burden.   58
wrought affected   67 **The fixture ... in't** i.e., Her eye, though
motionless, gives the appearance of motion   68 **As ... art** in such a
way that we are fooled by artistic illusion.   72 **No settled ... world**
No calm mind in the world

---

77 **cordial** restorative, heartwarming   83 **painting** paint.
86 **presently** immediately   96 **On; those** (Often emended to *Or
those.*)   98 **strike** strike up.   100 **upon** on   102 **him** i.e., death
105–7 **Do ... double** i.e., If you ever shun her during the rest of her
life, you will kill her again.   114 **pertain to life** be truly alive

[*To Perdita*] Please you to interpose, fair madam. Kneel,   120
And pray your mother's blessing.—Turn, good lady;
Our Perdita is found.

HERMIONE   You gods, look down
And from your sacred vials pour your graces
Upon my daughter's head!—Tell me, mine own,
Where hast thou been preserved? Where lived? How
    found
Thy father's court? For thou shalt hear that I,
Knowing by Paulina that the oracle
Gave hope thou wast in being, have preserved
Myself to see the issue.   129

PAULINA   There's time enough for that,
Lest they desire upon this push to trouble   131
Your joys with like relation. Go together,   132
You precious winners all; your exultation
Partake to everyone. I, an old turtle,   134
Will wing me to some withered bough and there
My mate, that's never to be found again,   136
Lament till I am lost.

LEONTES   Oh, peace, Paulina!   137

Thou shouldst a husband take by my consent,
As I by thine a wife. This is a match,
And made between 's by vows. Thou hast found
    mine,
But how is to be questioned, for I saw her,
As I thought, dead, and have in vain said many
A prayer upon her grave. I'll not seek far—
For him, I partly know his mind—to find thee   144
An honorable husband. Come, Camillo,
And take her by the hand, whose worth and honesty   146
Is richly noted and here justified   147
By us, a pair of kings. Let's from this place.
[*To Hermione*] What? Look upon my brother. Both your
    pardons,
That e'er I put between your holy looks
My ill suspicion. This' your son-in-law   151
And son unto the King, whom, heavens directing,
Is trothplight to your daughter. Good Paulina,   153
Lead us from hence, where we may leisurely
Each one demand and answer to his part
Performed in this wide gap of time since first
We were dissevered. Hastily lead away.   *Exeunt.*

120 **madam** (Addressed to Perdita as Princess and affianced to be married.)   129 **the issue** (1) the outcome (2) my child.   131–2 **Lest . . . relation** lest they (bystanders) insist, at this critical juncture, on interrupting this moment of joy with your relating of your story or with their telling what has happened to them.   134 **Partake to** share with, communicate to.   **turtle** turtledove   136–7 **My mate . . . lost** grieve for my lost mate until I die.

144 **For** as for   146 **whose** i.e., Camillo's   147 **richly noted** abundantly acknowledged.   **justified** avouched   151 **This'** This is   153 **trothplight** betrothed

The Tempest

Shakespeare creates in *The Tempest* a world of the imagination, a place of conflict and ultimately of magical rejuvenation, like the forests of *A Midsummer Night's Dream* and *As You Like It*. The journey to Shakespeare's island is to a realm of art where everything is controlled by the artist-figure. Yet the journey is no escape from reality, for the island shows people what they are, as well as what they ought to be. Even its location juxtaposes the "real" world with an idealized landscape: like Plato's New Atlantis or Thomas More's Utopia, Shakespeare's island is to be found both somewhere and nowhere. On the narrative level, it is located in the Mediterranean Sea. Yet there are overtones of the New World, the Western Hemisphere, where Thomas More had situated his island of Utopia. Ariel fetches dew at Prospero's command from the "Bermudas" (1.2.230). Caliban when prostrate reminds Trinculo of a "dead Indian" (2.2.33) who might be displayed before gullible crowds eager to see such a prodigious creature from across the seas, and Caliban's god, Setebos, was, according to Richard Eden's account of Magellan's circumnavigation of the globe (in *History of Travel*, 1577), worshiped by South American natives. An inspiration for Shakespeare's story (for which no direct literary source is known) may well have been various accounts of the shipwreck in the Bermudas in 1609 of the *Sea Venture*, which was carrying settlers to the new Virginian colony. Shakespeare borrowed details from Sylvester Jourdain's *A Discovery of the Bermudas, Otherwise Called the Isle of Devils*, published in 1610, and from William Strachey's *A True Reportory of the Wreck and Redemption . . . from the Islands of the Bermudas*, which Shakespeare must have seen in manuscript since it was not published until after his death. He wrote the play shortly after reading these works, for *The Tempest* was acted at court in 1611. He may also have known or heard of various accounts of Magellan's circumnavigation of the world in 1519–1522 (including Richard Eden's shortened English version, as part of his *History of Travel*,

of an Italian narrative by Antonio Pigafetta), Francis Fletcher's journal of Sir Francis Drake's circumnavigation in 1577–1580, Richard Rich's *News from Virginia* (1610), and still other potential sources of information. Shakespeare's fascination with the Western Hemisphere gave him, not the actual location of his story, which remains Mediterranean, but a state of mind associated with newness and the unfamiliar. From this strange and unknown place, we gain a radical perspective on the old world of European culture. Miranda sees on the island a "new world" in which humankind appears "brave" (5.1.185), and, although her wonder must be tempered by Prospero's rejoinder that "'Tis new to thee" (line 186) and by Aldous Huxley's still more ironic use of her phrase in the title of his satirical novel *Brave New World*, the island endures as a restorative vision. Even though we experience it fleetingly, as in a dream, this nonexistent realm assumes a permanence enjoyed by all great works of art.

Prospero rules autocratically as artist-king and patriarch over this imaginary world, conjuring up trials and visions to test people's intentions and awaken their consciences. To the island come an assortment of persons who, because they require varied ordeals, are separated by Prospero and Ariel into three groups: King Alonso and those accompanying him; Alonso's son, Ferdinand; and Stephano and Trinculo. Prospero's authority over them, though strong, has limits. As Duke of Milan, he was bookishly inattentive to political matters and thus vulnerable to the Machiavellian conniving of his younger brother, Antonio. Only in this world apart, the artist's world, do his powers derived from learning find their proper sphere. Because he cannot control the world beyond his isle, he must wait for "strange, bountiful Fortune, / Now my dear lady" (1.2.179–80) to bring his enemies near his shore. He eschews, moreover, the black arts of diabolism. His is a white magic, devoted ultimately to what he considers moral ends: rescuing Ariel from the spell of the witch Sycorax, curbing the appetite of Caliban, spying on Antonio and Sebastian in the role of Conscience. He thus comes to see Fortune's gift of delivering his enemies into his hands as an opportunity for him to forgive and restore them, not be revenged.

Such an assumption of godlike power is close to arrogance, even blasphemy, for Prospero is no god. His chief power, learned from books and exercised through Ariel, is to control the elements so as to create illusion—of separation, of death, of the gods' blessing. Yet, since he is human, even this power is an immense burden and temptation. Prospero has much to learn, like those whom he controls. He must subdue his anger, his self-pity, his readiness to blame others, and his domineering over Miranda. He must overcome the vengeful impulse he experiences toward those who have wronged him, and he must conquer the longing many a father feels to hold on to his daughter when she is desired by another man. He struggles with these problems through his art, devising games and shows in which his angry self-pity and jealousy are transmuted into playacting scenes of divine warning and forgiveness toward his enemies and watchful parental austerity toward Miranda and Ferdinand. Prospero's responsibilities cause him to behave magisterially and to be resented by the spirits of the isle. His authority is problematic to us because he seems so patriarchal, colonialist, even sexist and racist in his arrogating to himself the right and responsibility to control others in the name of values they may not share. Ariel longs to be free of this authority. Perhaps our sympathy for Prospero is greatest when we perceive that he, too, with mixed feelings of genuine relief and melancholy, is ready to lay aside his demanding and self-important role as creative moral intelligence.

Alonso and his court party variously illustrate the unregenerate world left behind in Naples and Milan. We first see them on shipboard, panicky and desperate, their titles and finery mocked by roaring waves. Futile ambition seems destined for a watery demise. Yet death by water in this play is a transfiguration rather than an end, a mystical rebirth, as in the regenerative cycle of the seasons from winter to summer. Ariel suggests as much in his song about a drowned father: "Those are pearls that were his eyes. / Nothing of him that doth fade / But doth suffer a sea change / Into something rich and strange" (1.2.402–5). Still, this miracle is not apparent at first to those who are caught in the illusion of death. As in T. S. Eliot's *The Waste Land*, which repeatedly alludes to *The Tempest*, self-blinded human beings fear a disaster that is ironically the prelude to reawakening.

The illusions created on the island serve to test these imperfect men and to make them reveal their true selves. Only Gonzalo, who long ago aided Prospero and Miranda when they were banished from Milan, responds affirmatively to illusion. In his eyes, their having been saved from drowning is a miracle: they breathe fresh air, the grass is green on the island, and their very garments appear not to have been stained by the salt water. His ideal commonwealth (2.1.150–71), which Shakespeare drew in part from an essay by Montaigne, postulates a natural goodness in humanity and makes no allowance for the darker propensities of human behavior, but at least Gonzalo's cheerfulness is in refreshing contrast to the jaded sneers of some of his companions. Sebastian and Antonio react to the magic isle, as to Gonzalo's commonwealth, by cynically refusing to believe in miracles. They scoff at Gonzalo for insistently looking on the bright side; if he were to examine his supposedly unstained clothes more carefully, they jest, he would discover that his pockets are filled with mud. Confident that they are unobserved, they seize the opportunity afforded by Alonso's being asleep to plot a murder and political coup. This attempt is not only despicable but also madly ludicrous, for they are all shipwrecked and no longer have kingdoms over which to quarrel. Even more ironically, Sebastian and Antonio, despite their insolent belief in their self-sufficiency, are being observed. The villains must be taught that an unseen power keeps track of their misdeeds. However presumptuous Prospero may be to assume through Ariel's means the role of godlike observer, he does awaken conscience and prevent murder. The villains may revert to type when returned to their usual habitat, but even they are at least briefly moved to an awareness of the unseen (3.3.21–7). Alonso, more worthy than they, though burdened, too, with sin, responds to his situation with guilt and despair, for he assumes that his son Ferdinand's death is the just punishment of the gods for Alonso's part in the earlier overthrow of Prospero. Alonso must be led, by means of curative illusions, through the purgative experience of contrition to the reward he thinks impossible and undeserved: reunion with his lost son.

Alonso is thus, like Posthumus in *Cymbeline* or Leontes in *The Winter's Tale*, a tragicomic figure—sinful, contrite, forgiven. Alonso's son Ferdinand must also undergo ordeals and visions devised by Prospero to test his worth, but more on the level of romantic comedy. Ferdinand is young, innocent, and hopeful, well matched to Miranda. From the start, Prospero obviously approves of his prospective son-in-law. Yet even Prospero, needing to prepare himself for a life in which Miranda will no longer be solely his, is not ready to lay aside at least the comic fiction of parental opposition. He invents difficulties, imposes tasks of logbearing (like those assigned Caliban), and issues stern warnings against premarital sex. In the comic mode, parents are expected to cross their children in matters of the heart. Prospero is so convincing in his role of overbearing parent, insisting on absolute unthinking obedience from his daughter, that we remain unsure whether he is truly like that or whether we are meant to sense in his performance a grappling with his own deepest feelings of possessiveness and autocratic authority, tempered finally by his awareness of the arbitrariness of such a role and his readiness to let Miranda decide for herself. As a teacher of youth, moreover, Prospero is convinced by long experience that prizes too easily won are too lightly esteemed. Manifold are the temptations urging Ferdinand to surrender to the natural rhythms of the isle as Caliban would. In place of ceremonies conducted in civilized societies by the church, Prospero must create the illusion of ceremony by his art. The betrothal of Ferdinand and Miranda accordingly unites the best of both worlds: the natural innocence of the island, which teaches them to avoid the corruptions of civilization at its worst, and the higher law of nature achieved through moral wisdom at its best. To this marriage, the goddesses Iris, Ceres, and Juno bring promises of bounteous harvest, "refreshing showers," celestial harmony, and a springtime brought back to the earth by Proserpina's return from Hades (4.1.76–117). In Ferdinand and Miranda, "nurture" is wedded to "nature." This bond unites spirit and flesh, legitimizing erotic pleasure by incorporating it within Prospero's vision of a cosmic moral order.

At the lowest level of this traditional cosmic and moral framework, in Prospero's view, are Stephano and Trinculo. Their comic scenes juxtapose them with Caliban, for he represents untutored Nature, whereas they represent the unnatural depths to which human beings brought up in civilized society can fall. In this they resemble Sebastian and Antonio, who have learned in supposedly civilized Italy arts of intrigue and political murder. The antics of Stephano and Trinculo burlesque the conduct of their presumed betters, thereby exposing to ridicule the self-deceptions of ambitious men. The clowns desire to exploit the natural wonders of the isle by taking Caliban back to civilization to be shown in carnivals or by plying him with strong drink and whetting his resentment against authority. These plottings are in vain, however, for, like Sebastian and Antonio, the clowns are being watched. The clowns teach Caliban to cry out for "freedom" (2.2.184), by which they mean license to do as one pleases, but are foiled by Ariel as comic nemesis. Because they are degenerate buffoons, Prospero as satirist devises for them an exposure that is appropriately humiliating and satirical.

In contrast with them, Caliban is in many ways a sympathetic character. His sensitivity to natural beauty, as in his descriptions of the "nimble marmoset" or the dreaming music he so often hears (2.2.168; 3.2.137–45), is entirely appropriate to this child of nature. He is, to be sure, the child of a witch and is called many harsh names by Miranda and Prospero, such as "Abhorrèd slave" and "a born devil, on whose nature / Nurture can never stick" (1.2.354; 4.1.188–9). Yet he protests with some justification that the island was his in the first place and that Prospero and Miranda are interlopers. His very existence calls radically into question the value of civilization, which has shown itself capable of limitless depravity. What profit has

Caliban derived from learning Prospero's language other than, as he puts it, to "know how to curse" (1.2.367)? With instinctive cunning, he senses that books are his chief enemy and plots to destroy them first in his attempt at rebellion. The unspoiled natural world does indeed offer civilization a unique perspective on itself. In this it resembles Gonzalo's ideal commonwealth, which, no matter how laughably implausible from the cynic's point of view, does at least question some assumptions—economic, political, and social—common in western societies.

Radical perspectives of this kind invite consideration of many unsettling questions about exploration, colonialist empire building, and sexual imperialism. The fleeting comparison of Caliban to an indigenous native (2.2.33), although ignored in stage productions of the play until the late nineteenth century, suggests a discourse on colonialism in *The Tempest* that anticipates to a remarkable degree a doleful history of exploitation, of providing rum and guns to the natives, and of taking away land through violent expropriation in the name of bringing civilization and God to the New World. Stephano and Trinculo, pouring wine down Caliban's throat and thus reducing him to a worshiping slave, show exploitation at its worst, but surely the play allows us to wonder also if Prospero's enslavement of Caliban, however high-minded in its claims of preventing disorder and rape, is not tainted by the same imperatives of possession and control. The issue is wonderfully complex. Caliban is a projection of both the naturally depraved savage described in many explorers' accounts and the nobly innocent savage described by Montaigne. By dramatizing the conflict without taking sides, Shakespeare leaves open a debate about the worth of Prospero's endeavor to contain Caliban's otherness and produces an ambivalent result in which the apparent victory of colonialism and censorship does not entirely conceal the contradictory struggle through which those values are imposed. The play's many open-ended questions apply not only to the New World but also, nearer at hand, to Ireland—an island on the margins of Britain that was regarded as both savage and threatening.

The play's discourse also raises issues of class and political justice. The battle between Prospero and Caliban is one of "master" and "man" (2.2.183); even if Caliban's cry of "freedom" leads him only into further enslavement by Stephano and Trinculo (who are themselves masterless men), the play does not resolve the conflict by simply reimposing social hierarchy. Caliban, Stephano, and Trinculo are all taught a lesson and are satirically punished for their rebellious behavior, but Caliban at least is pardoned and is left behind on the island at the play's end where presumably he will no longer be a slave. In political terms, Prospero resolves the long-standing hostilities between Milan and Naples by his astute arranging of the betrothal of Miranda to Ferdinand. However much it is idealized as a romantic match presided over harmoniously by the gods, it is also a political union aimed at bringing together the ruling families of those two city-states. Prospero's masque, his ultimate vision of the triumph of civilization, transforms the myth of the rape of a daughter (Proserpina) in such a way as to preserve the daughter's chaste honor in a union that will repair the political and social damage done by the ouster of Prospero from his dukedom of Milan. For these reasons, the betrothal of Ferdinand and Miranda must have seemed politically relevant to Shakespeare's audience when *The Tempest* was performed before King James at Whitehall in November of 1611 and then again at court in 1613 in celebration of the marriage of James's daughter Elizabeth to Frederick, the Elector Palatine.

The play's ending is far from perfectly stable. Antonio never repents, and we cannot be sure what the island will be like once Prospero has disappeared from the scene. Since Prospero's occupation of the island replicates in a sense the process by which he himself was overthrown, we cannot know when the cycle of revolution will ever cease. We cannot even be sure of the extent to which Shakespeare is master of his own colonial debate in *The Tempest* or, conversely, the extent to which today we should feel ourselves free to relativize, ironize, or in other ways criticize this play for apparent or probable prejudices. Not even a great author like Shakespeare can escape the limits of his own time, any more than we can escape the limits of our own. Perhaps we can nonetheless project ourselves, as spectators and readers, into Shakespeare's attempt to celebrate humanity's highest achievement in the union of the island with the civilized world. Miranda and Ferdinand have bright hopes for the future, even if those hopes must be qualified by Prospero's melancholic observation that the "brave new world" with "such people in't" is only "new to thee," to those who are young and not yet experienced in the world's vexations. Even Caliban may be at last reconciled to Prospero's insistent idea of a harmony between will and reason, no matter how perilously and delicately achieved. Prospero speaks of Caliban as a "thing of darkness I / Acknowledge mine," and Caliban vows to "be wise hereafter / And seek for grace" (5.1.278–9, 298–9). Prospero's view is that the natural human within is more contented, better understood, and more truly free when harmonized with reason.

Caliban is a part of humanity; Ariel is not. Ariel can comprehend what compassion and forgiveness would be like, "were I human" (5.1.20), and can take good-natured part in Prospero's designs to castigate or reform his fellow mortals, but Ariel longs to be free in quite another sense from that meant by Caliban. Ariel takes no part in the final integration of human society. This spirit belongs to a magic world of song, music, and illusion that the artist borrows for his use but that exists eternally outside of him. Like the elements of air, earth, fire, and water in

which it mysteriously dwells, this spirit is morally neutral but incredibly vital. From it the artist achieves powers of imagination, enabling him to bedim the noontide sun or call forth the dead from their graves. These visions are illusory in the profound sense that all life is illusory, an "insubstantial pageant" melted into thin air (4.1.150–5). Prospero the artist cherishes his own humanity, as a promise of surcease from his labors. Yet the artifact created by the artist endures, existing apart from time and place, as does Ariel: "Then to the elements / Be free, and fare thou well!" (5.1.321–2). No doubt it is a romantic fiction to associate the dramatist Shakespeare with Prospero's farewell to his art, but it is an almost irresistible idea, because we are so moved by the sense of completion and yet humility, the exultation and yet the calm contained in this leave-taking.

As though to demonstrate the summation of his artistry as magician-poet in what he may indeed have designed as his farewell to the stage, Shakespeare puts on a dazzling display of the verbal artistry for which he had already become famous. His command of blank verse is, by this time, more flexible and protean than ever before, with a marked increase in run-on lines, caesuras in mid line, the sharing of blank verse lines between two or more speakers, feminine endings, and other features of the late Shakespearean style. (See General Introduction, pp. lxxxiii–lxxxiv). The play is notable for its bravura passages, such as those that begin "Our revels now are ended" (4.1.148–58) and "Ye elves of hills" (5.1.33–57). With its opening storm scene and its solemn shows and masques—the *"several strange shapes"* bringing in a banquet and the appearance of Ariel *"like a harpy"* in 3.3, the masque of Iris, Ceres, and Juno in 4.1, and Prospero's confining the Neapolitans to a charmed circle in 5.1—*The Tempest* presents itself as a tour de force of spectacle and grandeur in which all of these dazzling events are also astutely interrupted by the resurgence of human appetite and by satiric correction. At every turn the drama manifests a deft compression of time and event. The tone is masterfully assured, in prose as in verse. Images of a dreamlike world come together in a remarkable amalgam whereby the characters participate in a fluid world that moves through them even as they move through it, becoming one with the tempest of time.

In performance, *The Tempest* reveals an extraordinary range of interpretive possibilities. Caliban, in nineteenth-century stage versions, was apt to be a grotesque specimen of Darwinian evolution, outfitted with gills, fishy scales, and long fingernails for prying shellfish out of rocks (the long fingernails are in fact mentioned, at 2.2.166). Herbert Beerbohm Tree, in 1904, saw Caliban as hairy from head to foot, with unkempt beard, pointed ears, sinister eyes, and long fingernails. To Frank Benson, at Stratford-upon-Avon in 1891, Caliban (played by Benson himself) was the missing link in an evolutionary chain of monkeys, baboons, and other presumably human ancestors; the Caliban of this production climbed a tree on stage, hung upside down, and gibbered. More recently, in accord with critical interest in the play as a potential critique of colonialism, Caliban has often been seen as a Caribbean native, physically imposing and even handsome, restive under his slavery, a man of immense human dignity. An example is that of David Suchet in Clifford Williams's 1987 production for the Royal Shakespeare Company; Suchet's Caliban, a sympathetic victim of imperialism, evoked unmistakable echoes of third-world exploited populations from the West Indies and sub-Saharan Africa. Prospero has undergone no less of a sea change, from the benign authorial stand-in of traditional nineteenth-century productions to a man who can be tyrannical, arbitrary, menacing, close to violence, deeply angry, as in Derek Jarman's 1980 film. Interpretations of Ariel have varied from saccharine sweetness to the punk-haired and drug-inebriated, as in Mark Rylance's Ariel in Ron Daniels's 1982 RSC production. Underlying sexual tensions are evident on all sides in recent productions. Some of the most remarkable versions of the play have abandoned Shakespeare's script to varying degrees, as in Peter Brook's Round House production of 1968 featuring an enormous Sycorax giving birth to Caliban, a takeover of the island and capture of Prospero by Caliban, and a wild orgy. Derek Jarman's film version of 1980 saw the play as dominantly gay, with Caliban as an aging "queen." Giorgio Strehler's *La Tempesta*, Milan, 1977, pictured Ariel as a commedia dell'arte Pierrot attached to a wire, soaring through the air and landing as though on Prospero's raised finger. Peter Greenaway's 1991 film called *Prospero's Books* presented the entire play through Prospero's eyes; John Gielgud, as Prospero, spoke virtually all the lines. The extraordinary range of theatrical innovations that has been brought to this play testifies to the script's own remarkable theatrical self-consciousness and its delight in magic and illusion.

The Tempest

Names of the Actors

ALONSO, *King of Naples*
SEBASTIAN, *his brother*
PROSPERO, *the right Duke of Milan*
ANTONIO, *his brother, the usurping Duke of Milan*
FERDINAND, *son to the King of Naples*
GONZALO, *an honest old counselor*
ADRIAN *and* }
FRANCISCO, } *lords*
CALIBAN, *a savage and deformed slave*
TRINCULO, *a jester*
STEPHANO, *a drunken butler*
MASTER *of a ship*

BOATSWAIN
MARINERS

MIRANDA, *daughter to Prospero*

ARIEL, *an airy spirit*
IRIS,
CERES,
JUNO, } *[presented by] spirits*
NYMPHS,
REAPERS,

[*Other Spirits attending on Prospero*]

THE SCENE: *An uninhabited island*

1.1

A tempestuous noise of thunder and lightning heard. Enter a Shipmaster and a Boatswain.

MASTER Boatswain!

BOATSWAIN Here, Master. What cheer?

MASTER Good, speak to th' mariners. Fall to't yarely, or we run ourselves aground. Bestir, bestir! *Exit.* 3

Enter Mariners.

BOATSWAIN Heigh, my hearts! Cheerly, cheerly, my hearts! Yare, yare! Take in the topsail. Tend to th' Master's whistle.—Blow till thou burst thy wind, if room enough! 6 / 7 / 8

Enter Alonso, Sebastian, Antonio, Ferdinand, Gonzalo, and others.

ALONSO Good Boatswain, have care. Where's the Master? Play the men. 10

BOATSWAIN I pray now, keep below.

ANTONIO Where is the Master, Boatswain?

BOATSWAIN Do you not hear him? You mar our labor. Keep your cabins! You do assist the storm. 14

GONZALO Nay, good, be patient. 15

BOATSWAIN When the sea is. Hence! What cares these roarers for the name of king? To cabin! Silence! Trouble us not. 17

GONZALO Good, yet remember whom thou hast aboard.

BOATSWAIN None that I more love than myself. You are a councillor; if you can command these elements to silence and work the peace of the present, we will not hand a rope more. Use your authority. If you cannot, give thanks you have lived so long and make yourself ready in your cabin for the mischance of the hour, if it so hap.—Cheerly, good hearts!—Out of our way, I say. *Exit.* 23 / 24 / 27

GONZALO I have great comfort from this fellow. Methinks he hath no drowning mark upon him; his complexion is perfect gallows. Stand fast, good Fate, to his hanging! Make the rope of his destiny our cable, for our own doth little advantage. If he be not born to be 30 / 31 / 33

---

hanged, our case is miserable. *Exeunt [courtiers].* 34

Enter Boatswain.

BOATSWAIN Down with the topmast! Yare! Lower, lower! Bring her to try wi'th' main course. (*A cry within.*) A plague upon this howling! They are louder than the weather or our office. 36 / 38

Enter Sebastian, Antonio, and Gonzalo.

Yet again? What do you here? Shall we give o'er and drown? Have you a mind to sink? 39

SEBASTIAN A pox o'your throat, you bawling, blasphemous, incharitable dog!

BOATSWAIN Work you, then.

ANTONIO Hang, cur! Hang, you whoreson, insolent noisemaker! We are less afraid to be drowned than thou art.

GONZALO I'll warrant him for drowning, though the ship were no stronger than a nutshell and as leaky as an unstanched wench. 47 / 49

BOATSWAIN Lay her ahold, ahold! Set her two courses. Off to sea again! Lay her off! 50

Enter Mariners, wet.

MARINERS All lost! To prayers, to prayers! All lost!
[*The Mariners run about in confusion, exiting at random.*]

BOATSWAIN What, must our mouths be cold? 53

GONZALO
The King and Prince at prayers! Let's assist them,
For our case is as theirs.

SEBASTIAN   I am out of patience.

ANTONIO
We are merely cheated of our lives by drunkards. 56
This wide-chapped rascal! Would thou mightst lie drowning 57
The washing of ten tides!

GONZALO   He'll be hanged yet, 58
Though every drop of water swear against it
And gape at wid'st to glut him.
(*A confused noise within:*)   "Mercy on us!"— 60
"We split, we split!"—"Farewell my wife and children!"— 61
"Farewell, brother!"—"We split, we split, we split!"
[*Exit Boatswain.*]

ANTONIO Let's all sink wi'th' King.

SEBASTIAN Let's take leave of him.

Exit [with Antonio].

GONZALO Now would I give a thousand furlongs of sea

Names of the Actors This list appears at the end of the play in the First Folio, in this order, with Miranda's name below that of the men, as was conventional in lists of the period. **PROSPERO, *the right*** the rightful **CALIBAN . . . *slave*** The Folio reads "*saluage,*" a common alternative spelling of *savage* but perhaps also with a resonance of being salvaged from shipwreck. *Slave* has a range of meanings: wretch, rascal, servile creature, one who is owned by another person, one who is divested of freedom and personal rights.
1.1. Location: On board ship, off the island's coast.
3 Good i.e., It's good you've come, or, my good fellow. **yarely** nimbly **6 Tend** Attend **7 Blow** (Addressed to the wind.) **7–8 if room enough** as long as we have sea room enough. **10 Play the men** Act like men, with spirit. **14 Keep** Remain in **15 good** good fellow **17 roarers** waves or winds, or both; spoken to as though they were "bullies" or "blusterers" **23 work . . . present** bring calm to our present circumstances **24 hand** handle **27 hap** happens. **30–1 complexion . . . gallows** appearance shows he was born to be hanged (and therefore, according to the proverb, in no danger of drowning). **33 our . . . advantage** our own cable is of little benefit.

34 case is miserable circumstances are desperate. **36 Bring . . . course** Sail her close to the wind by means of the mainsail. **38 our office** i.e., the noise we make at our work. **39 give o'er** give up **47 warrant him for drowning** guarantee that he will never be drowned **49 unstanched** insatiable, loose, unrestrained. (Suggesting also "incontinent" and "menstrual.") **50 ahold** ahull, close to the wind. **courses** sails, i.e., foresail as well as mainsail, set in an attempt to get the ship back out into open water. **53 must . . . cold?** i.e., must we drown in the cold sea? **56 merely** utterly **57 wide-chapped** big-mouthed **57–8 Would . . . tides!** (Pirates were hanged on the shore and left until three tides had come in.) **60 at wid'st** wide open. **glut** swallow **61 split** break apart.

for an acre of barren ground: long heath, brown furze,   66
anything. The wills above be done! But I would fain   67
die a dry death.   *Exit.*

❧

1.2

Enter Prospero [in his magic cloak] and Miranda.

MIRANDA
If by your art, my dearest father, you have   1
Put the wild waters in this roar, allay them.   2
The sky, it seems, would pour down stinking pitch,
But that the sea, mounting to th' welkin's cheek,   4
Dashes the fire out. Oh, I have suffered
With those that I saw suffer! A brave vessel,   6
Who had, no doubt, some noble creature in her,
Dashed all to pieces. Oh, the cry did knock
Against my very heart! Poor souls, they perished.
Had I been any god of power, I would
Have sunk the sea within the earth or ere   11
It should the good ship so have swallowed and
The freighting souls within her.
PROSPERO   Be collected.   13
No more amazement. Tell your piteous heart   14
There's no harm done.
MIRANDA   Oh, woe the day!
PROSPERO   No harm.
I have done nothing but in care of thee,   16
Of thee, my dear one, thee, my daughter, who
Art ignorant of what thou art, naught knowing
Of whence I am, nor that I am more better   19
Than Prospero, master of a full poor cell,   20
And thy no greater father.
MIRANDA   More to know
Did never meddle with my thoughts.
PROSPERO   'Tis time   22
I should inform thee farther. Lend thy hand
And pluck my magic garment from me. So,
          [*laying down his magic cloak and staff*]
Lie there, my art.—Wipe thou thine eyes. Have
    comfort.
The direful spectacle of the wreck, which touched   26
The very virtue of compassion in thee,   27
I have with such provision in mine art
So safely ordered that there is no soul—
No, not so much perdition as an hair   30
Betid to any creature in the vessel   31
Which thou heard'st cry, which thou saw'st sink. Sit
    down,   32

For thou must now know farther.
MIRANDA [*sitting*]   You have often
Begun to tell me what I am, but stopped
And left me to a bootless inquisition,
Concluding, "Stay, not yet."   35
PROSPERO   The hour's now come;
The very minute bids thee ope thine ear.
Obey, and be attentive. Canst thou remember
A time before we came unto this cell?
I do not think thou canst, for then thou wast not
Out three years old.
MIRANDA   Certainly, sir, I can.   41
PROSPERO
By what? By any other house or person?
Of anything the image, tell me, that
Hath kept with thy remembrance.
MIRANDA   'Tis far off,
And rather like a dream than an assurance   45
That my remembrance warrants. Had I not   46
Four or five women once that tended me?
PROSPERO
Thou hadst, and more, Miranda. But how is it
That this lives in thy mind? What see'st thou else
In the dark backward and abysm of time?   50
If thou rememb'rest aught ere thou cam'st here,   51
How thou cam'st here thou mayst.
MIRANDA   But that I do not.
PROSPERO
Twelve year since, Miranda, twelve year since,
Thy father was the Duke of Milan and
A prince of power.
MIRANDA   Sir, are not you my father?
PROSPERO
Thy mother was a piece of virtue, and   56
She said thou wast my daughter; and thy father
Was Duke of Milan, and his only heir
And princess no worse issued.
MIRANDA   Oh, the heavens!   59
What foul play had we, that we came from thence?
Or blessèd was't we did?
PROSPERO   Both, both, my girl.
By foul play, as thou say'st, were we heaved thence,
But blessedly holp hither.
MIRANDA   Oh, my heart bleeds   63
To think o'th' teen that I have turned you to,   64
Which is from my remembrance! Please you, farther.   65
PROSPERO
My brother and thy uncle, called Antonio—
I pray thee mark me—that a brother should
Be so perfidious!—he whom next thyself   68
Of all the world I loved, and to him put
The manage of my state, as at that time   70
Through all the seigniories it was the first,   71

---

66 **heath** heather.   **furze** gorse, a weed growing on wasteland
67 **fain** rather
1.2. Location: The island, near Prospero's cell. On the Elizabethan
stage, this cell is implicitly at hand throughout the play, although
in some scenes the convention of flexible distance allows us to
imagine characters in other parts of the island.
1 **art** magic   2 **allay** pacify   4 **welkin's cheek** sky's face   6 **brave**
gallant, splendid   11 **or ere** before   13 **freighting souls** cargo of
souls.   **collected** calm, composed.   14 **amazement** consternation.
piteous pitying   16 **but** except   19 **more better** of higher rank
20 **full** very   22 **meddle** mingle   26 **wreck** shipwreck   27 **virtue**
essence   30 **perdition** loss   31 **Betid** happened   32 **Which** whom

35 **bootless inquisition** profitless inquiry   41 **Out** fully   45–6 **assurance . . . warrants** certainty that my memory guarantees.   50 **backward
. . . time** abyss of the past.   51 **aught** anything   56 **piece** masterpiece,
exemplar   59 **no worse issued** no less nobly born, descended.   63 **holp**
helped   64 **teen . . . to** trouble I've caused you to remember, or put you
to   65 **from** out of   68 **next** next to   70 **manage** management, administration   71 **seigniories** i.e., city-states of northern Italy

And Prospero the prime duke, being so reputed   72
In dignity, and for the liberal arts
Without a parallel; those being all my study,
The government I cast upon my brother
And to my state grew stranger, being transported   76
And rapt in secret studies. Thy false uncle—
Dost thou attend me?

MIRANDA   Sir, most heedfully.

PROSPERO
Being once perfected how to grant suits,   79
How to deny them, who t'advance and who
To trash for overtopping, new created   81
The creatures that were mine, I say, or changed 'em,   82
Or else new formed 'em; having both the key   83
Of officer and office, set all hearts i'th' state   84
To what tune pleased his ear, that now he was   85
The ivy which had hid my princely trunk
And sucked my verdure out on't. Thou attend'st not.   87

MIRANDA
Oh, good sir, I do.

PROSPERO   I pray thee, mark me.
I, thus neglecting worldly ends, all dedicated
To closeness and the bettering of my mind   90
With that which, but by being so retired,   91
O'erprized all popular rate, in my false brother   92
Awaked an evil nature; and my trust,
Like a good parent, did beget of him   94
A falsehood in its contrary as great
As my trust was, which had indeed no limit,
A confidence sans bound. He being thus lorded   97
Not only with what my revenue yielded
But what my power might else exact, like one   99
Who, having into truth by telling of it,   100
Made such a sinner of his memory   101
To credit his own lie, he did believe   102
He was indeed the Duke, out o'th' substitution   103
And executing th'outward face of royalty   104
With all prerogative. Hence his ambition growing—   105
Dost thou hear?

MIRANDA   Your tale, sir, would cure deafness.

PROSPERO
To have no screen between this part he played   107
And him he played it for, he needs will be   108
Absolute Milan. Me, poor man, my library   109
Was dukedom large enough. Of temporal royalties   110
He thinks me now incapable; confederates—   111
So dry he was for sway—wi'th' King of Naples   112
To give him annual tribute, do him homage,   113
Subject his coronet to his crown, and bend   114
The dukedom yet unbowed—alas, poor Milan!—   115
To most ignoble stooping.

MIRANDA   O the heavens!

PROSPERO
Mark his condition and th'event, then tell me   117
If this might be a brother.

MIRANDA   I should sin
To think but nobly of my grandmother.   119
Good wombs have borne bad sons.

PROSPERO   Now the condition.
This King of Naples, being an enemy
To me inveterate, hearkens my brother's suit,   122
Which was that he, in lieu o'th' premises   123
Of homage and I know not how much tribute,
Should presently extirpate me and mine   125
Out of the dukedom and confer fair Milan,
With all the honors, on my brother. Whereon,
A treacherous army levied, one midnight
Fated to th' purpose did Antonio open
The gates of Milan, and, i'th' dead of darkness,
The ministers for th' purpose hurried thence   131
Me and thy crying self.

MIRANDA   Alack, for pity!
I, not remembering how I cried out then,
Will cry it o'er again. It is a hint   134
That wrings mine eyes to 't.

PROSPERO   Hear a little further,   135
And then I'll bring thee to the present business
Which now 's upon 's, without the which this story
Were most impertinent.

MIRANDA   Wherefore did they not   138
That hour destroy us?

PROSPERO   Well demanded, wench.   139
My tale provokes that question. Dear, they durst
   not,
So dear the love my people bore me, nor set   141
A mark so bloody on the business, but   142

---

72 **prime** first in rank and importance   76 **to . . . stranger** i.e., withdrew
from my responsibilities as duke.   **transported** carried away   79 **perfected** grown skillful   81 **trash** check a hound by tying a cord or weight
to its neck.   **overtopping** running too far ahead of the pack; surmount-
ing, exceeding one's authority   81–3 **new . . . formed 'em** won the loyalty of my officers by appointing them to new posts, or replaced them
with others who would be loyal to Antonio, or else redefined the positions and their occupants   83–5 **having . . . ear** having now under his
control both the officers and the positions, he set a tone for his rule
according to his own inclination. (*Key* is also a metaphor for tuning
stringed instruments.)   87 **verdure** vitality.   **on't** of it.   90 **closeness**
retirement, seclusion   91–2 **but . . . rate** i.e., were it not that its private
nature caused me to neglect my public responsibilities, had a value far
beyond what public opinion could appreciate, or, simply because it was
done in such seclusion, had a value not appreciated by popular opinion
94 **good parent** (Alludes to the proverb that good parents often bear
bad children; see also line 120.)   **of** in   97 **sans** without.   **lorded**
raised to lordship, with power and wealth   99 **else** otherwise, additionally   100–2 **Who . . . lie** i.e., who, by repeatedly telling the lie (that he
was indeed Duke of Milan), made his memory such a confirmed sinner
against truth that he began to believe his own lie   103–5 **out . . . prerogative** as a result of his making himself my substitute and carrying out
all the visible functions of royalty with all its rights and privileges.

107–9 **To have . . . Milan** In order to eliminate all separation between
his role and himself, he insisted on becoming the Duke of Milan in
name as well as in fact.   110 **temporal royalties** practical prerogatives and responsibilities of a sovereign   111 **confederates** conspires,
allies himself   112 **dry** thirsty.   **sway** power   113 **him** i.e., the King
of Naples   114 **his . . . his** Antonio's . . . the King of Naples's.   **bend**
make bow down   115 **yet** hitherto   117 **condition** pact.   **th'event**
the outcome   119 **but** other than   122 **hearkens** listens to   123 **he**
the King of Naples.   **in . . . premises** in return for the stipulation
125 **presently extirpate** at once remove   131 **ministers . . . purpose**
agents employed to do this.   **thence** from there   134 **hint** prompting
135 **wrings** (1) constrains (2) wrings tears from   138 **impertinent**
irrelevant.   **Wherefore** Why   139 **demanded** asked.   **wench** (Here
a term of endearment.)   141–2 **set . . . bloody** i.e., make obvious their
murderous intent. (From the practice of marking with the blood of
the prey those who have participated in a successful hunt.)

With colors fairer painted their foul ends.   143
In few, they hurried us aboard a bark,   144
Bore us some leagues to sea, where they prepared
A rotten carcass of a butt, not rigged,   146
Nor tackle, sail, nor mast; the very rats   147
Instinctively have quit it. There they hoist us,   148
To cry to th' sea that roared to us, to sigh
To th' winds whose pity, sighing back again,
Did us but loving wrong.

MIRANDA   Alack, what trouble   151
Was I then to you!

PROSPERO   Oh, a cherubin
Thou wast that did preserve me. Thou didst smile,
Infusèd with a fortitude from heaven,   154
When I have decked the sea with drops full salt,   155
Under my burden groaned, which raised in me   156
An undergoing stomach, to bear up   157
Against what should ensue.

MIRANDA   How came we ashore?

PROSPERO   By Providence divine.
Some food we had, and some fresh water, that
A noble Neapolitan, Gonzalo,
Out of his charity, who being then appointed
Master of this design, did give us, with
Rich garments, linens, stuffs, and necessaries,   165
Which since have steaded much. So, of his
  gentleness,   166
Knowing I loved my books, he furnished me
From mine own library with volumes that
I prize above my dukedom.

MIRANDA   Would I might   169
But ever see that man!

PROSPERO   Now I arise.   170
[He puts on his magic cloak.]
Sit still, and hear the last of our sea sorrow.   171
Here in this island we arrived; and here
Have I, thy schoolmaster, made thee more profit   173
Than other princes can, that have more time   174
For vainer hours and tutors not so careful.   175

MIRANDA
Heavens thank you for't! And now, I pray you, sir—
For still 'tis beating in my mind—your reason
For raising this sea storm?

PROSPERO   Know thus far forth:
By accident most strange, bountiful Fortune,
Now my dear lady, hath mine enemies   180
Brought to this shore; and by my prescience
I find my zenith doth depend upon   182

A most auspicious star, whose influence   183
If now I court not, but omit, my fortunes   184
Will ever after droop. Here cease more questions.
Thou art inclined to sleep. 'Tis a good dullness,   186
And give it way. I know thou canst not choose.   187
[Miranda sleeps.]
Come away, servant, come! I am ready now.   188
Approach, my Ariel, come.

Enter Ariel.

ARIEL
All hail, great master, grave sir, hail! I come
To answer thy best pleasure; be't to fly,
To swim, to dive into the fire, to ride
On the curled clouds, to thy strong bidding task   193
Ariel and all his quality.

PROSPERO   Hast thou, spirit,   194
Performed to point the tempest that I bade thee?   195

ARIEL   To every article.
I boarded the King's ship. Now on the beak,   197
Now in the waist, the deck, in every cabin,   198
I flamed amazement. Sometime I'd divide   199
And burn in many places; on the topmast,
The yards, and bowsprit would I flame distinctly,   201
Then meet and join. Jove's lightning, the precursors
O'th' dreadful thunderclaps, more momentary
And sight-outrunning were not. The fire and cracks   204
Of sulfurous roaring the most mighty Neptune   205
Seem to besiege and make his bold waves tremble,
Yea, his dread trident shake.

PROSPERO   My brave spirit!   207
Who was so firm, so constant, that this coil   208
Would not infect his reason?

ARIEL   Not a soul
But felt a fever of the mad and played   210
Some tricks of desperation. All but mariners
Plunged in the foaming brine and quit the vessel,
Then all afire with me. The King's son, Ferdinand,
With hair up-staring—then like reeds, not hair—   214
Was the first man that leapt; cried, "Hell is empty,
And all the devils are here!"

PROSPERO   Why, that's my spirit!
But was not this nigh shore?

ARIEL   Close by, my master.

PROSPERO
But are they, Ariel, safe?

ARIEL   Not a hair perished.
On their sustaining garments not a blemish,   219
But fresher than before; and, as thou bad'st me,   220

---

143 **fairer** apparently more attractive   144 **few** few words.   **bark**
ship   146 **butt** cask, tub   147 **Nor tackle** neither rigging   148 **quit**
abandoned   151 **Did . . . wrong** i.e., pitied us even as they drove us
on.   154 **Infusèd** filled, suffused   155 **decked** covered (with salt
tears); adorned   156 **which** i.e., the smile   157 **undergoing stomach**
courage to go on   165 **stuffs** supplies   166 **steaded much** been of
much use.   **So, of** Similarly, out of   169 **Would** I wish   170 **But ever**
i.e., someday   171 **sea sorrow** sorrowful adventure at sea.
173–4 **made . . . can** provided a more valuable education than other
royal children (of either sex) can enjoy   175 **vainer** more foolishly
spent   180 **my dear lady** (Refers to Fortune, not Miranda.)
182 **zenith** height of fortune. (Astrological term.)

183 **influence** astrological power   184 **but omit** but ignore instead
186 **dullness** drowsiness   187 **give it way** let it happen (i.e., don't
fight it).   188 **Come away** Come   193 **task** make demands upon
194 **quality** (1) fellow spirits (2) abilities.   195 **to point** to the smallest
detail   197 **beak** prow   198 **waist** midships.   **deck** poop deck at the
stern   199 **flamed amazement** struck terror in the guise of fire, i.e.,
Saint Elmo's fire.   201 **distinctly** in different places   204 **sight-outrunning** swifter than sight.   **were not** could not have been.
205 **Neptune** Roman god of the sea   207 **trident** three-pronged
weapon   208 **coil** tumult   210 **of the mad** such as madmen feel
214 **up-staring** standing on end   219 **sustaining** protecting
220 **bad'st** ordered

In troops I have dispersed them 'bout the isle.   221
The King's son have I landed by himself,
Whom I left cooling of the air with sighs   223
In an odd angle of the isle, and sitting,   224
His arms in this sad knot.   [*He folds his arms.*]

PROSPERO   Of the King's ship,   225
The mariners, say how thou hast disposed,
And all the rest o'th' fleet.

ARIEL   Safely in harbor
Is the King's ship; in the deep nook where once   228
Thou called'st me up at midnight to fetch dew   229
From the still-vexed Bermudas, there she's hid;   230
The mariners all under hatches stowed,
Who, with a charm joined to their suffered labor,   232
I have left asleep. And for the rest o'th' fleet,
Which I dispersed, they all have met again
And are upon the Mediterranean float   235
Bound sadly home for Naples,
Supposing that they saw the King's ship wrecked
And his great person perish.

PROSPERO   Ariel, thy charge
Exactly is performed. But there's more work.
What is the time o'th' day?

ARIEL   Past the mid season.   240

PROSPERO
At least two glasses. The time twixt six and now   241
Must by us both be spent most preciously.

ARIEL
Is there more toil? Since thou dost give me pains,   243
Let me remember thee what thou hast promised,   244
Which is not yet performed me.

PROSPERO   How now? Moody?
What is't thou canst demand?

ARIEL   My liberty.

PROSPERO
Before the time be out? No more!

ARIEL   I prithee,
Remember I have done thee worthy service,
Told thee no lies, made thee no mistakings, served
Without or grudge or grumblings. Thou did promise
To bate me a full year.

PROSPERO   Dost thou forget   251
From what a torment I did free thee?

ARIEL   No.

PROSPERO
Thou dost, and think'st it much to tread the ooze
Of the salt deep,
To run upon the sharp wind of the north,
To do me business in the veins o'th' earth   256

When it is baked with frost.

ARIEL   I do not, sir.   257

PROSPERO
Thou liest, malignant thing! Hast thou forgot
The foul witch Sycorax, who with age and envy   259
Was grown into a hoop? Hast thou forgot her?   260

ARIEL   No, sir.

PROSPERO
Thou hast. Where was she born? Speak. Tell me.

ARIEL
Sir, in Argier.

PROSPERO   Oh, was she so? I must   263
Once in a month recount what thou hast been,
Which thou forget'st. This damned witch Sycorax,
For mischiefs manifold and sorceries terrible
To enter human hearing, from Argier,
Thou know'st, was banished. For one thing she did   268
They would not take her life. Is not this true?

ARIEL   Ay, sir.

PROSPERO
This blue-eyed hag was hither brought with child   271
And here was left by th' sailors. Thou, my slave,
As thou report'st thyself, was then her servant;
And, for thou wast a spirit too delicate   274
To act her earthy and abhorred commands,
Refusing her grand hests, she did confine thee,   276
By help of her more potent ministers
And in her most unmitigable rage,
Into a cloven pine, within which rift
Imprisoned thou didst painfully remain
A dozen years; within which space she died
And left thee there, where thou didst vent thy
        groans
As fast as mill wheels strike. Then was this island—   283
Save for the son that she did litter here,   284
A freckled whelp, hag-born—not honored with   285
A human shape.

ARIEL   Yes, Caliban her son.   286

PROSPERO
Dull thing, I say so: he, that Caliban   287
Whom now I keep in service. Thou best know'st
What torment I did find thee in. Thy groans
Did make wolves howl, and penetrate the breasts
Of ever-angry bears. It was a torment
To lay upon the damned, which Sycorax
Could not again undo. It was mine art,
When I arrived and heard thee, that made gape   294
The pine and let thee out.

ARIEL   I thank thee, master.

221 troops groups   **223 cooling of** cooling   **224 angle** corner
225 sad knot (Folded arms are indicative of melancholy.)   **228 nook**
bay   **229 dew** (Collected at midnight for magical purposes; compare
with line 324.)   **230 still-vexed Bermudas** ever stormy Bermudas.
(Perhaps refers to the then recent Bermuda shipwreck; see play Introduction. The Folio text reads "*Bermoothes*.")   **232 with . . . labor** by
means of a spell added to all the labor they have undergone
235 float sea   **240 mid season** noon.   **241 glasses** hourglasses.
243 pains labors   **244 remember** remind   **251 bate** remit, deduct
256 do me do for me.   **veins** veins of minerals, or, underground
streams, thought to be analogous to the veins of the human body

257 baked hardened   **259 envy** malice   **260 grown into a hoop** i.e.,
so bent over with age as to resemble a hoop.   **263 Argier** Algiers.
268 one . . . did (Perhaps a reference to her pregnancy, for which her
life would be spared.)   **271 blue-eyed** with dark circles under the
eyes or with blue eyelids, implying pregnancy.   **with child** pregnant
274 for because   **276 hests** commands   **283 as mill wheels strike** as
the blades of a mill wheel strike the water.   **284 Save** except.   **litter**
give birth to   **285 whelp** offspring. (Used of animals.)   **hag-born**
born of a female demon   **286 Yes . . . son** (Ariel is probably concur-
ring with Prospero's comment about a "freckled whelp," not contradicting the point about "A human shape.")   **287 Dull . . . so** i.e.,
Exactly, that's what I said, you dullard   **294 gape** open wide

PROSPERO

If thou more murmur'st, I will rend an oak
And peg thee in his knotty entrails till   297
Thou hast howled away twelve winters.

ARIEL   Pardon, master.
I will be correspondent to command   299
And do my spriting gently.   300

PROSPERO   Do so, and after two days
I will discharge thee.

ARIEL   That's my noble master!
What shall I do? Say what? What shall I do?

PROSPERO

Go make thyself like a nymph o'th' sea. Be subject
To no sight but thine and mine, invisible
To every eyeball else. Go take this shape
And hither come in't. Go, hence with diligence!
                                                Exit [Ariel].
[To Miranda] Awake, dear heart, awake! Thou hast
    slept well.
Awake!

MIRANDA   The strangeness of your story put
Heaviness in me.

PROSPERO   Shake it off. Come on,   310
We'll visit Caliban, my slave, who never
Yields us kind answer.

MIRANDA   'Tis a villain, sir,
I do not love to look on.

PROSPERO   But, as 'tis,
We cannot miss him. He does make our fire,   314
Fetch in our wood, and serves in offices   315
That profit us.—What ho! Slave! Caliban!
Thou earth, thou! Speak.

CALIBAN (within)   There's wood enough within.

PROSPERO

Come forth, I say! There's other business for thee.
Come, thou tortoise! When?   319

        Enter Ariel like a water nymph.

Fine apparition! My quaint Ariel,   320
Hark in thine ear.   [He whispers.]

ARIEL   My lord, it shall be done.   Exit.

PROSPERO

Thou poisonous slave, got by the devil himself   322
Upon thy wicked dam, come forth!   323

        Enter Caliban.

CALIBAN

As wicked dew as e'er my mother brushed   324
With raven's feather from unwholesome fen   325
Drop on you both! A southwest blow on ye   326
And blister you all o'er!

PROSPERO

For this, be sure, tonight thou shalt have cramps,

Side-stitches that shall pen thy breath up. Urchins   329
Shall forth at vast of night that they may work   330
All exercise on thee. Thou shalt be pinched
As thick as honeycomb, each pinch more stinging   332
Than bees that made 'em.

CALIBAN   I must eat my dinner.   333
This island's mine, by Sycorax my mother,
Which thou tak'st from me. When thou cam'st first,
Thou strok'st me and made much of me, wouldst give
    me
Water with berries in't, and teach me how
To name the bigger light, and how the less,   338
That burn by day and night. And then I loved thee
And showed thee all the qualities o'th'isle,
The fresh springs, brine pits, barren place and fertile.
Cursed be I that did so! All the charms   342
Of Sycorax, toads, beetles, bats, light on you!
For I am all the subjects that you have,
Which first was mine own king; and here you sty me 345
In this hard rock, whiles you do keep from me
The rest o'th'island.

PROSPERO   Thou most lying slave,
Whom stripes may move, not kindness! I have used
    thee,   348
Filth as thou art, with humane care, and lodged thee 349
In mine own cell, till thou didst seek to violate
The honor of my child.

CALIBAN

Oho, oho! Would't had been done!
Thou didst prevent me; I had peopled else   353
This isle with Calibans.

MIRANDA   Abhorrèd slave,   354
Which any print of goodness wilt not take,   355
Being capable of all ill! I pitied thee,
Took pains to make thee speak, taught thee each hour
One thing or other. When thou didst not, savage,
Know thine own meaning, but wouldst gabble like
A thing most brutish, I endowed thy purposes   360
With words that made them known. But thy vile race, 361
Though thou didst learn, had that in't which good
    natures
Could not abide to be with; therefore wast thou
Deservedly confined into this rock,
Who hadst deserved more than a prison.   365

CALIBAN

You taught me language, and my profit on't
Is I know how to curse. The red plague rid you   367

297 his its   299 correspondent responsive, submissive   300 spriting
gently duties as a spirit willingly.   310 Heaviness drowsiness
314 miss do without   315 offices functions, duties   319 When (An
exclamation of impatience.)   320 quaint ingenious   322 got begotten, sired   323 dam mother. (Used of animals.)   324 wicked mischievous, harmful   325 fen marsh, bog   326 southwest i.e., wind
thought to bring disease

329 Urchins Hedgehogs; here, suggesting goblins in the guise of
hedgehogs   330 vast lengthy, desolate time. (Malignant spirits were
thought to be restricted to the hours of darkness.)   332 as honeycomb i.e., as a honeycomb full of bees   333 'em i.e., the honeycomb.
338 the bigger . . . less i.e., the sun and the moon. (See Genesis 1:16:
"God then made two great lights: the greater light to rule the day, and
the less light to rule the night.")   342 charms spells   345 sty confine
as in a sty   348 stripes lashes   349 humane (Not distinguished as a
word from human.)   353 peopled else otherwise populated   354–65
Abhorrèd . . . prison (Sometimes assigned by editors to Prospero.)
355 print imprint, impression   360 purposes meanings, desires
361 race natural disposition; species, nature   367 red plague plague
characterized by red sores and evacuation of blood.   rid destroy

For learning me your language!

PROSPERO   Hagseed, hence!   368
Fetch us in fuel, and be quick, thou'rt best,   369
To answer other business. Shrugg'st thou, malice?   370
If thou neglect'st or dost unwillingly
What I command, I'll rack thee with old cramps,   372
Fill all thy bones with aches, make thee roar   373
That beasts shall tremble at thy din.

CALIBAN   No, pray thee.
[Aside]   I must obey. His art is of such power
It would control my dam's god, Setebos,   376
And make a vassal of him.

PROSPERO   So, slave, hence!   377
                                    Exit Caliban.

Enter Ferdinand; and Ariel, invisible, playing and
singing. [Ferdinand does not see Prospero and
Miranda.]

Ariel's Song.

ARIEL
Come unto these yellow sands,
    And then take hands;
Curtsied when you have, and kissed   380
    The wild waves whist;   381
Foot it featly here and there,   382
    And, sweet sprites, bear   383
The burden. Hark, hark!   384
        Burden, dispersedly [within].Bow-wow.   385
The watchdogs bark.
        [Burden, dispersedly within.] Bow-wow.
Hark, hark! I hear
The strain of strutting chanticleer
    Cry Cock-a-diddle-dow.

FERDINAND
Where should this music be? I'th'air or th'earth?
It sounds no more; and sure it waits upon   392
Some god o'th'island. Sitting on a bank,   393
Weeping again the King my father's wreck,
This music crept by me upon the waters,
Allaying both their fury and my passion   396
With its sweet air. Thence I have followed it,   397
Or it hath drawn me rather. But 'tis gone.
No, it begins again.

Ariel's Song.

ARIEL
Full fathom five thy father lies.
Of his bones are coral made.

Those are pearls that were his eyes.
    Nothing of him that doth fade
But doth suffer a sea change
Into something rich and strange.
Sea nymphs hourly ring his knell.   406
            Burden [within]. Ding dong.
Hark, now I hear them, ding dong bell.

FERDINAND
The ditty does remember my drowned father.   409
This is no mortal business, nor no sound
That the earth owes. I hear it now above me.   411

PROSPERO [to Miranda]
The fringèd curtains of thine eye advance   412
And say what thou see'st yond.

MIRANDA   What is't? A spirit?
Lord, how it looks about! Believe me, sir,
It carries a brave form. But 'tis a spirit.   415

PROSPERO
No, wench, it eats and sleeps and hath such senses
As we have, such. This gallant which thou see'st
Was in the wreck; and, but he's something stained   418
With grief, that's beauty's canker, thou mightst
    call him   419
A goodly person. He hath lost his fellows
And strays about to find 'em.

MIRANDA   I might call him
A thing divine, for nothing natural
I ever saw so noble.

PROSPERO [aside]   It goes on, I see,
As my soul prompts it.—Spirit, fine spirit, I'll free thee
Within two days for this.

FERDINAND [seeing Miranda]   Most sure, the goddess
On whom these airs attend!—Vouchsafe my prayer   426
May know if you remain upon this island,   427
And that you will some good instruction give
How I may bear me here. My prime request,   429
Which I do last pronounce, is—O you wonder!—   430
If you be maid or no?

MIRANDA   No wonder, sir,   431
But certainly a maid.

FERDINAND   My language? Heavens!
I am the best of them that speak this speech,   433
Were I but where 'tis spoken.

PROSPERO [coming forward]   How? The best?
What wert thou if the King of Naples heard thee?

FERDINAND
A single thing, as I am now, that wonders   436
To hear thee speak of Naples. He does hear me,   437

368 learning teaching. Hagseed Offspring of a female demon
369 thou'rt best you'd be well advised   370 answer other business
perform other tasks.   372 old such as old people suffer, or, plenty of
373 aches (Pronounced "aitches.")   376 Setebos (A god of the Patago-
nians, named in Richard Eden's History of Travel, 1577.)   377.2 Ariel,
invisible (Ariel wears a garment that by convention indicates he is invisible to Ferdinand and Miranda.)   380 Curtsied . . . have when you have
curtsied   380–1 kissed . . . whist kissed the waves into silence, or, kissed
while the waves are being hushed   382 Foot it featly dance nimbly
383 sprites spirits   384 burden refrain, undersong.   385 s.d. dispersedly i.e., from all directions, not in unison   392 waits upon serves,
attends   393 bank sandbank   396 passion grief   397 Thence i.e.,
From the bank on which I sat

406 knell announcement of a death by the tolling of a bell.
409 remember commemorate   411 owes owns.   412 advance raise
415 brave excellent   418 but . . . stained were it not that his luster is
somewhat darkened   419 canker cankerworm (feeding on buds and
leaves)   426 airs songs. Vouchsafe Grant   427 remain dwell
429 bear me conduct myself.   prime chief   430 wonder (Miranda's
name means "to be wondered at.")   431 maid (1) a human maiden as
opposed to a goddess (2) unmarried (3) a virgin   433 best i.e., in
birth   436 A single . . . now (1) A single figure who combines into
one person both self and King of Naples (since Ferdinand believes he
has inherited the kingship) (2) A lonely shipwrecked figure
437 Naples the King of Naples. He . . . me I who hear my own
words am the King of Naples

And that he does I weep. Myself am Naples, 438
Who with mine eyes, never since at ebb, beheld 439
The King my father wrecked.

MIRANDA   Alack, for mercy!

FERDINAND
Yes, faith, and all his lords, the Duke of Milan
And his brave son being twain.

PROSPERO [aside]   The Duke of Milan 442
And his more braver daughter could control thee, 443
If now 'twere fit to do't. At the first sight
They have changed eyes.—Delicate Ariel, 445
I'll set thee free for this. [To Ferdinand] A word, good
   sir.
I fear you have done yourself some wrong. A word! 447

MIRANDA [aside]
Why speaks my father so ungently? This
Is the third man that e'er I saw, the first
That e'er I sighed for. Pity move my father
To be inclined my way!

FERDINAND [to Miranda]   Oh, if a virgin,
And your affection not gone forth, I'll make you
The Queen of Naples.

PROSPERO   Soft, sir! One word more.
[Aside] They are both in either's powers; but this swift
   business 454
I must uneasy make, lest too light winning 455
Make the prize light. [To Ferdinand] One word more: I
   charge thee 456
That thou attend me. Thou dost here usurp 457
The name thou ow'st not, and hast put thyself 458
Upon this island as a spy, to win it
From me, the lord on't.

FERDINAND   No, as I am a man. 460

MIRANDA
There's nothing ill can dwell in such a temple.
If the ill spirit have so fair a house,
Good things will strive to dwell with't.

PROSPERO   Follow me.— 463
Speak not you for him; he's a traitor.—Come,
I'll manacle thy neck and feet together.
Seawater shalt thou drink; thy food shall be
The fresh-brook mussels, withered roots, and husks
Wherein the acorn cradled. Follow.

FERDINAND   No!
I will resist such entertainment till 469
Mine enemy has more pow'r.
                    He draws, and is charmed from moving.

MIRANDA   O dear father, 470
Make not too rash a trial of him, for 471

He's gentle, and not fearful.

PROSPERO   What, I say, 472
My foot my tutor?—Put thy sword up, traitor, 473
Who mak'st a show but dar'st not strike, thy
   conscience
Is so possessed with guilt. Come from thy ward, 475
For I can here disarm thee with this stick
And make thy weapon drop. [He brandishes his staff.]

MIRANDA [trying to hinder him]   Beseech you, father!

PROSPERO
Hence! Hang not on my garments.

MIRANDA   Sir, have pity!
I'll be his surety.

PROSPERO   Silence! One word more 479
Shall make me chide thee, if not hate thee. What,
An advocate for an impostor? Hush!
Thou think'st there is no more such shapes as he,
Having seen but him and Caliban. Foolish wench,
To th' most of men this is a Caliban, 484
And they to him are angels.

MIRANDA   My affections
Are then most humble; I have no ambition
To see a goodlier man.

PROSPERO [to Ferdinand]   Come on, obey.
Thy nerves are in their infancy again 488
And have no vigor in them.

FERDINAND   So they are.
My spirits, as in a dream, are all bound up. 490
My father's loss, the weakness which I feel,
The wreck of all my friends, nor this man's threats
To whom I am subdued, are but light to me, 493
Might I but through my prison once a day
Behold this maid. All corners else o'th'earth 495
Let liberty make use of; space enough
Have I in such a prison.

PROSPERO [aside]   It works. [To Ferdinand] Come on.—
Thou hast done well, fine Ariel! [To Ferdinand] Follow
   me.
[To Ariel] Hark what thou else shalt do me.

MIRANDA [to Ferdinand]   Be of comfort. 499
My father's of a better nature, sir,
Than he appears by speech. This is unwonted 501
Which now came from him.

PROSPERO [to Ariel]   Thou shalt be as free
As mountain winds; but then exactly do 503
All points of my command.

ARIEL   To th' syllable.

PROSPERO [to Ferdinand]
Come, follow. [To Miranda] Speak not for him.
                                        Exeunt.

❦

438 And . . . weep i.e., and I weep at this reminder that my father is
seemingly dead, leaving me heir.   **439 never . . . ebb** never dry, continually weeping   **442 son** (The only reference in the play to a son of
Antonio.)   **443 more braver** more splendid.   **control** refute
445 changed eyes exchanged amorous glances.   **447 done . . . wrong**
i.e., spoken falsely.   **454 both in either's** each in the other's
455 uneasy difficult   **456 light** cheap. (Playing on *light*, "easy," in
455.)   **457 attend** follow, obey   **458 ow'st** ownest   **460 on't** of it.
463 strive . . . with't i.e., expel the evil and occupy the *temple,* the
body.   **469 entertainment** treatment   **470 s.d.** *charmed* magically
prevented   **471 rash** harsh

472 gentle (1) wellborn (2) easily managed.   **fearful** frightening,
dangerous.   **473 My . . . tutor?** i.e., Do you, as my daughter and thus
bound to me by obedience, dare presume to teach me what to do?
475 ward defensive posture (in fencing)   **479 surety** guarantee.
484 To compared with   **488 nerves** sinews   **490 spirits** vital powers
493 light unimportant   **495 corners else** other corners, regions
499 me for me.   **501 unwonted** unusual   **503 then** if so, then

2.1

Enter Alonso, Sebastian, Antonio, Gonzalo,
Adrian, Francisco, and others.

GONZALO [*to Alonso*]
Beseech you, sir, be merry. You have cause,
So have we all, of joy, for our escape
Is much beyond our loss. Our hint of woe   3
Is common; every day some sailor's wife,
The masters of some merchant, and the merchant,   5
Have just our theme of woe. But for the miracle,   6
I mean our preservation, few in millions
Can speak like us. Then wisely, good sir, weigh   8
Our sorrow with our comfort.
ALONSO   Prithee, peace.   9
SEBASTIAN [*aside to Antonio*]   He receives comfort like
cold porridge.   11
ANTONIO [*aside to Sebastian*]   The visitor will not give   12
him o'er so.   13
SEBASTIAN   Look, he's winding up the watch of his wit;
by and by it will strike.
GONZALO [*to Alonso*]   Sir—
SEBASTIAN [*aside to Antonio*]   One. Tell.   17
GONZALO   When every grief is entertained   18
That's offered, comes to th'entertainer—   19
SEBASTIAN   A dollar.   20
GONZALO   Dolor comes to him, indeed. You have spo-
ken truer than you purposed.
SEBASTIAN   You have taken it wiselier than I meant you
should.
GONZALO [*to Alonso*]   Therefore, my lord—
ANTONIO   Fie, what a spendthrift is he of his tongue!
ALONSO [*to Gonzalo*]   I prithee, spare.   27
GONZALO   Well, I have done. But yet—
SEBASTIAN [*aside to Antonio*]   He will be talking.
ANTONIO [*aside to Sebastian*]   Which, of he or Adrian,   30
for a good wager, first begins to crow?   31
SEBASTIAN   The old cock.   32
ANTONIO   The cockerel.   33
SEBASTIAN   Done. The wager?
ANTONIO   A laughter.   35

SEBASTIAN   A match!   36
ADRIAN   Though this island seem to be desert—   37
ANTONIO   Ha, ha, ha!
SEBASTIAN   So, you're paid.   39
ADRIAN   Uninhabitable and almost inaccessible—
SEBASTIAN   Yet—
ADRIAN   Yet—
ANTONIO   He could not miss't.   43
ADRIAN   It must needs be of subtle, tender, and delicate   44
temperance.   45
ANTONIO   Temperance was a delicate wench.   46
SEBASTIAN   Ay, and a subtle, as he most learnedly   47
delivered.   48
ADRIAN   The air breathes upon us here most sweetly.
SEBASTIAN   As if it had lungs, and rotten ones.
ANTONIO   Or as 'twere perfumed by a fen.   51
GONZALO   Here is everything advantageous to life.
ANTONIO   True, save means to live.   53
SEBASTIAN   Of that there's none, or little.
GONZALO   How lush and lusty the grass looks! How   55
green!
ANTONIO   The ground indeed is tawny.   57
SEBASTIAN   With an eye of green in't.   58
ANTONIO   He misses not much.
SEBASTIAN   No. He doth but mistake the truth totally.   60
GONZALO   But the rarity of it is—which is indeed
almost beyond credit—
SEBASTIAN   As many vouched rarities are.   63
GONZALO   That our garments, being, as they were,
drenched in the sea, hold notwithstanding their fresh-
ness and glosses, being rather new-dyed than stained
with salt water.
ANTONIO   If but one of his pockets could speak, would   68
it not say he lies?   69
SEBASTIAN   Ay, or very falsely pocket up his report.   70
GONZALO   Methinks our garments are now as fresh as
when we put them on first in Afric, at the marriage of
the King's fair daughter Claribel to the King of Tunis.
SEBASTIAN   'Twas a sweet marriage, and we prosper
well in our return.
ADRIAN   Tunis was never graced before with such a
paragon to their queen.   77

2.1. Location: Another part of the island.
3 hint occasion   **5 The masters . . . the merchant** the officers or owners of some merchant vessel and the merchant who owns the cargo
6 for as for   **8–9 weigh . . . comfort** balance our sorrow against our
comfort.   **11 porridge** (Punningly suggested by *peace*, i.e., "peas" or
"pease," a common ingredient of porridge.)   **12 visitor** one bringing
nourishment and comfort to the sick, as Gonzalo is doing   **12–13 give
him o'er** abandon him   **17 Tell** Keep count.   **18–19 When . . . entertainer** When every sorrow that presents itself is accepted without
resistance, there comes to the recipient   **20 dollar** widely circulated
coin, the German thaler and the Spanish piece of eight. (Sebastian
puns on *entertainer* in the sense of paid performer or innkeeper; to
Gonzalo, *dollar* suggests "dolor," grief.)   **27 spare** forbear, cease.
30–1 Which . . . crow? Which of the two, Gonzalo or Adrian, do you
bet will speak (crow) first?   **32 The old cock** Gonzalo.   **33 The cockerel** Adrian.   **35 laughter** (1) burst of laughter (2) sitting of eggs.
(When Adrian, the *cockerel*, begins to speak two lines later, Sebastian
loses the bet. The Folio speech prefixes in lines 38–9 are here reversed
so that Antonio enjoys his laugh as the prize for winning, as in the
proverb "He who laughs last laughs best" or "He laughs that wins."
The Folio assignment can work in the theater, however, if Sebastian
pays for losing with a sardonic laugh of concession.)

36 A match! A bargain; agreed!   **37 desert** uninhabited   **39 you're
paid** i.e., you've had your laugh.   **43 miss't** (1) avoid saying "Yet"
(2) miss the island.   **44 must needs be** has to be   **45 temperance**
mildness of climate.   **46 Temperance** a girl's name.   **delicate** (Here
it means "given to pleasure, voluptuous"; in line 44, "pleasant."
Antonio is evidently suggesting that *tender, and delicate temperance*
sounds like a Puritan phrase, which Antonio then mocks by applying
the words to a woman rather than an island. He began this bawdy
comparison with a double entendre on *inaccessible*, line 40.)   **47 subtle** (Here it means "tricky, sexually crafty"; in line 44, "delicate.")
48 delivered uttered. (Sebastian joins Antonio in baiting the Puritans
with his use of the pious cant phrase *learnedly delivered*.)   **51 fen** evil-
smelling marshland.   **53 save** except   **55 lusty** healthy   **57 tawny**
dull brown, yellowish.   **58 eye** tinge, or spot. (Sebastian is mocking
Gonzalo's optimism by saying there's precious little green to see anywhere. Antonio echoes him in line 59 with similar sarcasm.)   **60 He
. . . totally** i.e., He's only a tiny 100% wrong. (Sarcastic.)   **63 As . . . are**
(More sarcasm: Just as many alleged strange sights are doubtful,
including this one.)   **68–70 If . . . report** (More wisecracking: Gonzalo's mud-filled pockets would surely give the lie to his talk of clean
fresh garments, thereby *pocketing up* or tabling the *report*.)   **77 to** for

GONZALO   Not since widow Dido's time.   78

ANTONIO   [aside to Sebastian]   Widow? A pox o' that!
How came that "widow" in? Widow Dido!

SEBASTIAN   What if he had said "widower Aeneas"
too? Good Lord, how you take it!   82

ADRIAN   [to Gonzalo]   "Widow Dido" said you? You make
me study of that. She was of Carthage, not of Tunis.   84

GONZALO   This Tunis, sir, was Carthage.

ADRIAN   Carthage?

GONZALO   I assure you, Carthage.

ANTONIO   His word is more than the miraculous harp.   88

SEBASTIAN   He hath raised the wall, and houses too.

ANTONIO   What impossible matter will he make easy
next?

SEBASTIAN   I think he will carry this island home in his
pocket and give it his son for an apple.

ANTONIO   And, sowing the kernels of it in the sea,   94
bring forth more islands.

GONZALO   Ay.   96

ANTONIO   Why, in good time.   97

GONZALO   [to Alonso]   Sir, we were talking that our garments seem now as fresh as when we were at Tunis
at the marriage of your daughter, who is now queen.

ANTONIO   And the rarest that e'er came there.   101

SEBASTIAN   Bate, I beseech you, widow Dido.   102

ANTONIO   Oh, widow Dido? Ay, widow Dido.

GONZALO   Is not, sir, my doublet as fresh as the first   104
day I wore it? I mean, in a sort.   105

ANTONIO   That "sort" was well fished for.   106

GONZALO   When I wore it at your daughter's marriage.

ALONSO
You cram these words into mine ears against
The stomach of my sense. Would I had never   109
Married my daughter there! For, coming thence,   110
My son is lost and, in my rate, she too,   111
Who is so far from Italy removed
I ne'er again shall see her. O thou mine heir
Of Naples and of Milan, what strange fish
Hath made his meal on thee?

FRANCISCO   Sir, he may live.
I saw him beat the surges under him   116
And ride upon their backs. He trod the water,

Whose enmity he flung aside, and breasted
The surge most swoll'n that met him. His bold head
'Bove the contentious waves he kept, and oared   120
Himself with his good arms in lusty stroke   121
To th' shore, that o'er his wave-worn basis bowed,   122
As stooping to relieve him. I not doubt   123
He came alive to land.

ALONSO   No, no, he's gone.

SEBASTIAN   [to Alonso]
Sir, you may thank yourself for this great loss,
That would not bless our Europe with your daughter,   126
But rather loose her to an African,   127
Where she at least is banished from your eye,   128
Who hath cause to wet the grief on't.

ALONSO   Prithee, peace.   129

SEBASTIAN
You were kneeled to and importuned otherwise   130
By all of us, and the fair soul herself   131
Weighed between loathness and obedience at   132
Which end o'th' beam should bow. We have lost your
son,   133
I fear, forever. Milan and Naples have
More widows in them of this business' making   135
Than we bring men to comfort them.
The fault's your own.

ALONSO   So is the dear'st o'th' loss.   138

GONZALO   My lord Sebastian,
The truth you speak doth lack some gentleness
And time to speak it in. You rub the sore   141
When you should bring the plaster.

SEBASTIAN   Very well.   142

ANTONIO   And most chirurgeonly.   143

GONZALO   [to Alonso]
It is foul weather in us all, good sir,
When you are cloudy.

SEBASTIAN   [to Antonio]   Fowl weather?

ANTONIO   [to Sebastian]   Very foul.   145

GONZALO
Had I plantation of this isle, my lord—   146

ANTONIO   [to Sebastian]
He'd sow 't with nettle seed.

SEBASTIAN   Or docks, or mallows.   147

GONZALO
And were the king on't, what would I do?

---

78 widow Dido's Queen of Carthage, deserted by Aeneas. (She was, in fact, a widow when Aeneas, a widower, met her, but Antonio may be amused at Gonzalo's prudish use of the term "widow" to describe a woman deserted by her lover.)   **82 take** understand, respond to, interpret   **84 study of** think about   **88 miraculous harp** (Alludes to Amphion's harp, with which he raised the walls of Thebes; Gonzalo has exceeded that deed by recreating ancient Carthage—*wall and houses*—mistakenly on the site of modern-day Tunis. Some Renaissance commentators believed, like Gonzalo, that the two sites were near each other.)   **94 kernels** seeds   **96 Ay** (Gonzalo may be reasserting his point about Carthage, or he may be responding ironically to Antonio, who, in turn, answers sarcastically.)   **97 in good time** (An expression of ironical acquiescence or amazement, i.e., "sure, right away.")   **101 rarest** most remarkable, beautiful   **102 Bate** Abate, except, leave out. (Sebastian says sardonically, surely you should allow widow Dido to be an exception.)   **104 doublet** close-fitting jacket   **105 in a sort** in a way.   **106 sort** (Antonio plays on the idea of drawing lots and on "fishing" for something to say.)   **109 The stomach ... sense** my appetite for hearing them.   **110 Married** given in marriage   **111 rate** estimation, opinion   **116 surges** waves

120 oared propelled as by an oar   **121 lusty** vigorous   **122 that ... bowed** that projected out over its (*his*) surf-eroded base, bending down toward the sea   **123 As** as if   **126 That** you who   **127 But ... her** but would rather turn her loose (or, "lose her")   **128–9 Where ... on't** where at least she is not a constant reproach in your eye, which has good reason to weep sorrowfully for this unhappy development.   **130 importuned** urged, implored   **131–3 the fair ... bow** Claribel herself was poised uncertainly, as in a balancing scale, between being unwilling to marry and yet wishing to obey her father.   **135 of ... making** on account of this marriage and subsequent shipwreck   **138 dear'st** heaviest, most costly   **141 time** appropriate time   **142 plaster** (A medical application.)   **143 chirurgeonly** like a skilled surgeon. (Antonio mocks Gonzalo's medical analogy of a *plaster* applied curatively to a wound.)   **145 Fowl** (With a pun on *foul*, returning to the imagery of lines 30–5.)   **146 plantation** colonial settlement. (With subsequent wordplay on the literal meaning, "planting.")   **147 docks ... mallows** (Weeds; the first was used as an antidote for nettle stings.)

SEBASTIAN   Scape being drunk for want of wine.   149
GONZALO
    I'th' commonwealth I would by contraries   150
    Execute all things; for no kind of traffic   151
    Would I admit; no name of magistrate;
    Letters should not be known; riches, poverty,   153
    And use of service, none; contract, succession,   154
    Bourn, bound of land, tilth, vineyard, none;   155
    No use of metal, corn, or wine, or oil;   156
    No occupation; all men idle, all,
    And women too, but innocent and pure;
    No sovereignty—
SEBASTIAN   Yet he would be king on't.
ANTONIO   The latter end of his commonwealth forgets
    the beginning.
GONZALO
    All things in common nature should produce
    Without sweat or endeavor. Treason, felony,
    Sword, pike, knife, gun, or need of any engine   164
    Would I not have; but nature should bring forth,
    Of it own kind, all foison, all abundance,   166
    To feed my innocent people.
SEBASTIAN   No marrying 'mong his subjects?
ANTONIO   None, man, all idle—whores and knaves.
GONZALO
    I would with such perfection govern, sir,
    T'excel the Golden Age.
SEBASTIAN   'Save His Majesty!   171
ANTONIO
    Long live Gonzalo!
GONZALO   And—do you mark me, sir?
ALONSO
    Prithee, no more. Thou dost talk nothing to me.
GONZALO   I do well believe Your Highness, and did it
    to minister occasion to these gentlemen, who are of   175
    such sensible and nimble lungs that they always use   176
    to laugh at nothing.
ANTONIO   'Twas you we laughed at.
GONZALO   Who in this kind of merry fooling am nothing
    to you; so you may continue, and laugh at nothing still.
ANTONIO   What a blow was there given!
SEBASTIAN   An it had not fallen flat-long.   182
GONZALO   You are gentlemen of brave mettle; you   183
    would lift the moon out of her sphere if she would   184

continue in it five weeks without changing.

Enter Ariel [invisible] playing solemn music.

SEBASTIAN   We would so, and then go a-batfowling.   186
ANTONIO   Nay, good my lord, be not angry.
GONZALO   No, I warrant you, I will not adventure my   188
    discretion so weakly. Will you laugh me asleep? For I 189
    am very heavy.   190
ANTONIO   Go sleep, and hear us.   191
    [*All sleep except Alonso, Sebastian, and Antonio.*]
ALONSO
    What, all so soon asleep? I wish mine eyes
    Would, with themselves, shut up my thoughts. I find 193
    They are inclined to do so.
SEBASTIAN   Please you, sir,
    Do not omit the heavy offer of it.   195
    It seldom visits sorrow; when it doth,
    It is a comforter.
ANTONIO   We two, my lord,
    Will guard your person while you take your rest,
    And watch your safety.
ALONSO   Thank you. Wondrous heavy.
    [*Alonso sleeps. Exit Ariel.*]
SEBASTIAN
    What a strange drowsiness possesses them!
ANTONIO
    It is the quality o'th' climate.
SEBASTIAN   Why
    Doth it not then our eyelids sink? I find not
    Myself disposed to sleep.
ANTONIO   Nor I. My spirits are nimble.
    They fell together all, as by consent;   204
    They dropped, as by a thunderstroke. What might,
    Worthy Sebastian, oh, what might—? No more.
    And yet methinks I see it in thy face
    What thou shouldst be. Th'occasion speaks thee, and 208
    My strong imagination sees a crown
    Dropping upon thy head.
SEBASTIAN   What, art thou waking?
ANTONIO
    Do you not hear me speak?
SEBASTIAN   I do, and surely
    It is a sleepy language, and thou speak'st   212
    Out of thy sleep. What is it thou didst say?
    This is a strange repose, to be asleep
    With eyes wide open—standing, speaking, moving—
    And yet so fast asleep.
ANTONIO   Noble Sebastian,
    Thou let'st thy fortune sleep—die, rather; wink'st   217

---

149 **Scape** Escape.   **want** lack. (Sebastian jokes sarcastically that this hypothetical ruler would be saved from dissipation only by the barrenness of the island.)   150 **by contraries** by what is directly opposite to usual custom   151 **traffic** trade   153 **Letters** learning   154 **use of service** custom of employing servants.   **succession** holding of property by right of inheritance   155 **Bourn . . . tilth** boundaries, property limits, tillage of soil   156 **corn** grain   164 **pike** lance. **engine** instrument of warfare   166 **it** its.   **foison** plenty   171 **the Golden Age** an age of prelapsarian abundance and peace; the first of four "ages" of human history, followed by silver, bronze, and lead. **'Save** God save   175 **minister occasion** furnish opportunity (for laughter)   176 **sensible** sensitive.   **use** are accustomed   182 **An** If. **flat-long** with the flat of the sword, i.e., ineffectually.   183 **mettle** temperament, courage. (The sense of *metal*, indistinguishable as a form from *mettle*, continues the metaphor of the sword. F reads "mettal.")   184 **sphere** orbit. (Literally, one of the concentric zones occupied by planets in Ptolemaic astronomy.)

186 **a-batfowling** hunting birds at night with lantern and *bat*, or "stick"; also, gulling a simpleton. (Gonzalo is the simpleton, or fowl, and Sebastian will use the moon as his lantern.)   188–9 **adventure . . . weakly** risk my reputation for discretion for so trivial a cause (by getting angry).   190 **heavy** sleepy.   191 **Go . . . us** i.e., Get ready for sleep, and we'll do our part by laughing.   193 **Would . . . thoughts** would shut off my melancholy brooding when they (my eyes) close themselves in sleep.   195 **Do . . . it** do not decline the invitation to drowsiness.   204 **They . . . consent** The others all fell asleep simultaneously, as if by common agreement   208 **Th' occasion . . . thee** The opportunity of the moment calls upon you   212 **sleepy** dreamlike, fantastic   217 **wink'st** (you) shut your eyes

Whiles thou art waking.

SEBASTIAN   Thou dost snore distinctly;   218
There's meaning in thy snores.

ANTONIO
I am more serious than my custom. You
Must be so too if heed me, which to do   221
Trebles thee o'er.

SEBASTIAN   Well, I am standing water.   222

ANTONIO
I'll teach you how to flow.

SEBASTIAN   Do so. To ebb   223
Hereditary sloth instructs me.

ANTONIO   Oh,   224
If you but knew how you the purpose cherish   225
Whiles thus you mock it! How, in stripping it,   226
You more invest it! Ebbing men, indeed,   227
Most often do so near the bottom run   228
By their own fear or sloth.

SEBASTIAN   Prithee, say on.
The setting of thine eye and cheek proclaim   230
A matter from thee, and a birth indeed   231
Which throes thee much to yield.

ANTONIO   Thus, sir: 232
Although this lord of weak remembrance, this   233
Who shall be of as little memory   234
When he is earthed, hath here almost persuaded—   235
For he's a spirit of persuasion, only   236
Professes to persuade—the King his son's alive,   237
'Tis as impossible that he's undrowned
As he that sleeps here swims.

SEBASTIAN   I have no hope
That he's undrowned.

ANTONIO   Oh, out of that "no hope"
What great hope have you! No hope that way is   241
Another way so high a hope that even   242
Ambition cannot pierce a wink beyond,   243
But doubt discovery there. Will you grant with me   244
That Ferdinand is drowned?

SEBASTIAN   He's gone.

ANTONIO   Then tell me,
Who's the next heir of Naples?

SEBASTIAN   Claribel.

ANTONIO
She that is Queen of Tunis; she that dwells
Ten leagues beyond man's life; she that from Naples   248
Can have no note, unless the sun were post—   249
The Man i'th' Moon's too slow—till newborn chins
Be rough and razorable; she that from whom   251
We all were sea-swallowed, though some cast again,   252
And by that destiny to perform an act
Whereof what's past is prologue, what to come
In yours and my discharge.   255

SEBASTIAN   What stuff is this? How say you?
'Tis true my brother's daughter's Queen of Tunis,
So is she heir of Naples, twixt which regions
There is some space.

ANTONIO   A space whose ev'ry cubit   259
Seems to cry out, "How shall that Claribel
Measure us back to Naples? Keep in Tunis,   261
And let Sebastian wake." Say this were death   262
That now hath seized them, why, they were no worse
Than now they are. There be that can rule Naples   264
As well as he that sleeps, lords that can prate   265
As amply and unnecessarily
As this Gonzalo. I myself could make   267
A chough of as deep chat. Oh, that you bore   268
The mind that I do! What a sleep were this
For your advancement! Do you understand me?

SEBASTIAN
Methinks I do.

ANTONIO   And how does your content   271
Tender your own good fortune?

SEBASTIAN   I remember   272
You did supplant your brother Prospero.

ANTONIO   True.
And look how well my garments sit upon me,
Much feater than before. My brother's servants   275
Were then my fellows. Now they are my men.

SEBASTIAN But, for your conscience?   277

ANTONIO
Ay, sir, where lies that? If 'twere a kibe,   278
'Twould put me to my slipper; but I feel not   279
This deity in my bosom. Twenty consciences   280
That stand twixt me and Milan, candied be they   281
And melt ere they molest! Here lies your brother,   282
No better than the earth he lies upon,
If he were that which now he's like—that's dead,
Whom I, with this obedient steel, three inches of it,

218 distinctly articulately 221 if heed if you heed 222 Trebles thee
o'er makes you three times as great and rich. standing water water
that neither ebbs nor flows, at a standstill. 223 ebb recede, decline
224 Hereditary sloth i.e., natural laziness and the position of younger
brother, one who cannot inherit 225–6 If . . . mock it! If you only
knew how much you secretly cherish ambition even while your words
mock it! 226–7 How . . . invest it! How the more you speak flippantly
of ambition, the more you, in effect, affirm it, clothing what you have
stripped! 228 the bottom i.e., on which unadventurous men may go
aground and miss the tide of fortune 230 setting set expression (of
earnestness) 231 matter matter of importance 232 throes causes
pain, as in giving birth. yield give forth, speak about. 233–7
Although . . . alive although this owner of weak memory, he who will
be only weakly remembered when he is dead, has nearly persuaded—
since he's a mind or soul devoted solely to persuade—King Alonso
that Ferdinand lives 241 that way i.e., in regard to Ferdinand's being
saved 242–4 that . . . there i.e., that even ambition for high status cannot
see anything higher, and even there it doubts the reality of what it sees
(because the place is so supremely high). (What then follows is Antonio's analysis of why although they can proceed without fear.)

248 Ten . . . life i.e., further than the journey of a lifetime 249 note
news, intimation. post messenger 251 razorable ready for shaving.
from on our voyage from 252 cast were disgorged, cast ashore. (With
a pun on casting of parts for a play.) 255 discharge part to play. 259
cubit ancient measure of length of about twenty inches 261 Measure
us retrace our journey. Keep You, Claribel, stay 262 wake i.e., to
his good fortune. 264 There be There are those 265 prate speak
foolishly 267–8 I . . . chat I could teach a jackdaw to talk as wisely,
or, be such a garrulous talker myself. 271–2 And . . . fortune? And
how does your contentment with what I've just said further your
good fortune? 275 feater more becomingly, fittingly 277 for as for
278 kibe chilblain, here a sore on the heel 279 put me to oblige me
to wear 280–2 Twenty . . . molest! Even if there were twenty consciences between me and the dukedom of Milan, may they be
lumped together or crystallized like candy and then melted down
before I'd let them interfere!

Can lay to bed forever; whiles you, doing thus,   286
To the perpetual wink for aye might put   287
This ancient morsel, this Sir Prudence, who
Should not upbraid our course. For all the rest,   289
They'll take suggestion as a cat laps milk;   290
They'll tell the clock to any business that   291
We say befits the hour.

SEBASTIAN   Thy case, dear friend,
Shall be my precedent. As thou got'st Milan,
I'll come by Naples. Draw thy sword. One stroke
Shall free thee from the tribute which thou payest,   295
And I the king shall love thee.

ANTONIO   Draw together;
And when I rear my hand, do you the like
To fall it on Gonzalo.   [*They draw.*]

SEBASTIAN   Oh, but one word.   298
                              [*They talk apart.*]

Enter Ariel [*invisible*], *with music and song.*

ARIEL [*to Gonzalo*]
My master through his art foresees the danger
That you, his friend, are in, and sends me forth—
For else his project dies—to keep them living.
                         Sings in Gonzalo's ear.
    While you here do snoring lie,
    Open-eyed conspiracy
        His time doth take.   304
    If of life you keep a care,
    Shake off slumber, and beware.
        Awake, awake!

ANTONIO   Then let us both be sudden.

GONZALO [*waking*]   Now, good angels preserve the King!
                              [*The others wake.*]

ALONSO
Why, how now, ho, awake? Why are you drawn?
Wherefore this ghastly looking?

GONZALO   What's the matter?

SEBASTIAN
Whiles we stood here securing your repose,   312
Even now, we heard a hollow burst of bellowing
Like bulls, or rather lions. Did 't not wake you?
It struck mine ear most terribly.

ALONSO   I heard nothing.

ANTONIO
Oh, 'twas a din to fright a monster's ear,
To make an earthquake! Sure it was the roar
Of a whole herd of lions.

ALONSO   Heard you this, Gonzalo?

GONZALO
Upon mine honor, sir, I heard a humming,
And that a strange one too, which did awake me.
I shaked you, sir, and cried. As mine eyes opened,   321
I saw their weapons drawn. There was a noise,

That's verily. 'Tis best we stand upon our guard,   323
Or that we quit this place. Let's draw our weapons.

ALONSO
Lead off this ground, and let's make further search
For my poor son.

GONZALO   Heavens keep him from these beasts!
For he is, sure, i'th'island.

ALONSO   Lead away.

ARIEL [*aside*]
Prospero my lord shall know what I have done.
So, King, go safely on to seek thy son.
                              Exeunt [*separately*].

❖

2.2

*Enter Caliban with a burden of wood. A noise of
thunder heard.*

CALIBAN
All the infections that the sun sucks up
From bogs, fens, flats, on Prosper fall, and make him   2
By inchmeal a disease! His spirits hear me,   3
And yet I needs must curse. But they'll nor pinch,   4
Fright me with urchin shows, pitch me i'th' mire,   5
Nor lead me, like a firebrand, in the dark   6
Out of my way, unless he bid 'em. But
For every trifle are they set upon me,
Sometimes like apes, that mow and chatter at me   9
And after bite me; then like hedgehogs, which
Lie tumbling in my barefoot way and mount
Their pricks at my footfall. Sometime am I
All wound with adders, who with cloven tongues   13
Do hiss me into madness.

Enter Trinculo.

                          Lo, now, lo!
Here comes a spirit of his, and to torment me
For bringing wood in slowly. I'll fall flat.
Perchance he will not mind me.   [*He lies down.*]   17

TRINCULO   Here's neither bush nor shrub to bear off   18
any weather at all. And another storm brewing; I hear
it sing i'th' wind. Yond same black cloud, yond huge
one, looks like a foul bombard that would shed his   21
liquor. If it should thunder as it did before, I know not
where to hide my head. Yond same cloud cannot
choose but fall by pailfuls. [*Seeing Caliban*] What have
we here, a man or a fish? Dead or alive? A fish, he
smells like a fish; a very ancient and fishlike smell; a
kind of not-of-the-newest Poor John. A strange fish!   27
Were I in England now, as once I was, and had but
this fish painted, not a holiday fool there but would   29

---

286 thus similarly. (The actor makes a stabbing gesture.)   287 wink
sleep, closing of eyes.   aye ever   289 Should not must not be
allowed to   290 take suggestion respond to prompting   291 tell the
clock i.e., agree, answer appropriately, chime   295 tribute (See
1.2.113–24.)   298 fall it let it fall   304 time opportunity   312 securing standing guard over   321 cried called out.

323 verily true.
2.2. Location: Another part of the island.
2 flats swamps   3 By inchmeal inch by inch   4 needs must have to.
nor neither   5 urchin shows elvish apparitions shaped like hedgehogs   6 like a firebrand they in the guise of a will-o'-the-wisp
9 mow make faces   13 wound with entwined by   17 mind notice
18 bear off keep off   21 foul bombard dirty leather jug.   his its
27 Poor John salted fish, type of poor fare.   29 painted i.e., painted
on a sign set up outside a booth or tent at a fair

give a piece of silver. There would this monster make 30
a man. Any strange beast there makes a man. When 31
they will not give a doit to relieve a lame beggar, they 32
will lay out ten to see a dead Indian. Legged like a
man, and his fins like arms! Warm, o' my troth! I do 34
now let loose my opinion, hold it no longer: this is no 35
fish, but an islander, that hath lately suffered by a
thunderbolt. [*Thunder.*] Alas, the storm is come again!
My best way is to creep under his gaberdine. There is 38
no other shelter hereabout. Misery acquaints a man
with strange bedfellows. I will here shroud till the 40
dregs of the storm be past. 41

                  [*He creeps under Caliban's garment.*]

Enter Stephano, singing, [a bottle in his hand].

STEPHANO
   I shall no more to sea, to sea,
      Here shall I die ashore—
This is a very scurvy tune to sing at a man's funeral.
Well, here's my comfort.   *Drinks.*
(*Sings.*)
     The master, the swabber, the boatswain, and I, 46
       The gunner and his mate,
     Loved Mall, Meg, and Marian, and Margery,
       But none of us cared for Kate.
     For she had a tongue with a tang,
     Would cry to a sailor, 'Go hang!' 50
     She loved not the savor of tar nor of pitch,
     Yet a tailor might scratch her where'er she did itch. 53
     Then to sea, boys, and let her go hang!
This is a scurvy tune too. But here's my comfort.
                           Drinks.
CALIBAN   Do not torment me! Oh! 56
STEPHANO   What's the matter? Have we devils here? Do 57
you put tricks upon 's with savages and men of Ind, 58
ha? I have not scaped drowning to be afeard now of
your four legs. For it hath been said, "As proper a man 60
as ever went on four legs cannot make him give 61
ground"; and it shall be said so again while Stephano
breathes at' nostrils. 63
CALIBAN   This spirit torments me! Oh!
STEPHANO   This is some monster of the isle with four
legs, who hath got, as I take it, an ague. Where the 66
devil should he learn our language? I will give him 67
some relief, if it be but for that. If I can recover him 68
and keep him tame and get to Naples with him, he's

a present for any emperor that ever trod on neat's 70
leather. 71
CALIBAN   Do not torment me, prithee. I'll bring my
wood home faster.
STEPHANO   He's in his fit now and does not talk after 74
the wisest. He shall taste of my bottle. If he have never 75
drunk wine afore, it will go near to remove his fit. If I 76
can recover him and keep him tame, I will not take too 77
much for him. He shall pay for him that hath him, and 78
that soundly.
CALIBAN   Thou dost me yet but little hurt; thou wilt
anon, I know it by thy trembling. Now Prosper works
upon thee.
STEPHANO   Come on your ways. Open your mouth. Here
is that which will give language to you, cat. Open your 84
mouth. This will shake your shaking, I can tell you, 85
and that soundly. [*Giving Caliban a drink.*] You cannot 86
tell who's your friend. Open your chaps again. 87
TRINCULO   I should know that voice. It should be—but
he is drowned, and these are devils. Oh, defend me!
STEPHANO   Four legs and two voices—a most delicate 90
monster! His forward voice now is to speak well of his
friend; his backward voice is to utter foul speeches and 92
to detract. If all the wine in my bottle will recover him, 93
I will help his ague. Come. [*Giving a drink.*] Amen! I
will pour some in thy other mouth.
TRINCULO   Stephano!
STEPHANO   Doth thy other mouth call me? Mercy,
mercy! This is a devil, and no monster. I will leave
him. I have no long spoon. 99
TRINCULO   Stephano! If thou be'st Stephano, touch me
and speak to me, for I am Trinculo—be not afeard—
thy good friend Trinculo.
STEPHANO   If thou be'st Trinculo, come forth. I'll pull
thee by the lesser legs. If any be Trinculo's legs, these
are they. [*Pulling him out.*] Thou art very Trinculo
indeed! How cam'st thou to be the siege of this 106
mooncalf? Can he vent Trinculos? 107
TRINCULO   I took him to be killed with a thunderstroke.
But art thou not drowned, Stephano? I hope now thou
art not drowned. Is the storm overblown? I hid me 110
under the dead mooncalf's gaberdine for fear of the
storm. And art thou living, Stephano? Oh, Stephano,
two Neapolitans scaped!   [*He capers with Stephano.*]

30–1 make a man (1) make a man's fortune (2) pass for a human
being.   **32 doit** small coin   **34 o' my troth** by my faith.   **35 hold it**
hold it in   **38 gaberdine** cloak, loose upper garment.   **40 shroud**
take shelter   **41 dregs** i.e., last remains (as in a *bombard* or jug, line 21)
46 swabber crew member whose job is to wash the decks   **50 tang**
sting   **53 tailor . . . itch** (A dig at tailors for their supposed effeminacy and a bawdy suggestion of satisfying a sexual craving.)   **56 Do**
. . . me! (Caliban assumes that one of Prospero's spirits has come to
punish him.)   **57 What's the matter?** What's going on here?   **58 put**
tricks upon 's trick us with conjuring shows.   **Ind** India   **60 proper**
handsome   **61 four legs** (The conventional phrase would supply *two*
legs, but the creature Stephano thinks he sees has four.)   **63 at'** at the
66 ague fever. (Probably both Caliban and Trinculo are quaking; see
lines 56 and 81.)   **67 should he learn** could he have learned   **68 for**
that i.e., for knowing our language.   **recover** revive. (Also in line 77.)

70–1 neat's leather cowhide.   **74–5 after the wisest** in the wisest
fashion.   **76 afore** before.   **go near** to be in a fair way to   **77 recover**
restore   **77–8 I will . . . much** i.e., no sum can be too much   **78 He**
shall . . . hath him Anyone who wants him will have to pay dearly
for him   **84–5 cat . . . mouth** (Allusion to the proverb "Good liquor
will make a cat speak.")   **85 shake** shake off   **86–7 You . . . friend**
i.e., You can't tell who's your friend until someone like me provides
you with a drink.   **87 chaps** jaws   **90 delicate** ingenious   **92 back-**
ward voice (Trinculo and Caliban are facing in opposite directions.
Stephano supposes the monster to have a rear end that can emit *foul*
speeches or foul-smelling wind at the monster's *other mouth*, line 95.)
93 If . . . him Even if it takes all the wine in my bottle to cure him
99 long spoon (Allusion to the proverb "He that sups with the devil
has need of a long spoon.")   **106 siege** excrement   **107 mooncalf**
monstrous or misshapen creature (whose deformity is caused by the
malignant influence of the moon).   **vent** excrete, defecate
110 overblown blown over.

STEPHANO   Prithee, do not turn me about. My stomach
is not constant.   115

CALIBAN
These be fine things, an if they be not spirits.   116
That's a brave god, and bears celestial liquor.   117
I will kneel to him.

STEPHANO   How didst thou scape? How cam'st thou
hither? Swear by this bottle how thou cam'st hither. I
escaped upon a butt of sack which the sailors heaved   121
o'erboard—by this bottle, which I made of the bark of   122
a tree with mine own hands since I was cast ashore.

CALIBAN   [*kneeling*]   I'll swear upon that bottle to be
thy true subject, for the liquor is not earthly.

STEPHANO   Here. Swear then how thou escaped'st.

TRINCULO   Swum ashore, man, like a duck. I can swim
like a duck, I'll be sworn.

STEPHANO   Here, kiss the book. Though thou canst   129
swim like a duck, thou art made like a goose.
                                   [*Giving him a drink.*]

TRINCULO   Oh, Stephano, hast any more of this?

STEPHANO   The whole butt, man. My cellar is in a rock
by th' seaside, where my wine is hid.—How now,
mooncalf? How does thine ague?

CALIBAN   Hast thou not dropped from heaven?

STEPHANO   Out o'th' moon, I do assure thee. I was the
man i'th' moon when time was.   137

CALIBAN
I have seen thee in her, and I do adore thee.
My mistress showed me thee, and thy dog, and thy
bush.   139

STEPHANO   Come, swear to that. Kiss the book. I will
furnish it anon with new contents. Swear.
                                   [*Giving him a drink.*]

TRINCULO   By this good light, this is a very shallow   142
monster! I afeard of him? A very weak monster! The
man i'th' moon? A most poor credulous monster!
Well drawn, monster, in good sooth!   145

CALIBAN   [*to Stephano*]
I'll show thee every fertile inch o'th'island,
And I will kiss thy foot. I prithee, be my god.

TRINCULO   By this light, a most perfidious and drunken
monster! When 's god's asleep, he'll rob his bottle.   149

CALIBAN
I'll kiss thy foot. I'll swear myself thy subject.

STEPHANO   Come on then. Down, and swear.
                                       [*Caliban kneels.*]

TRINCULO   I shall laugh myself to death at this puppy-
headed monster. A most scurvy monster! I could find
in my heart to beat him—

STEPHANO   Come, kiss.

TRINCULO   But that the poor monster's in drink. An   156
abominable monster!

CALIBAN
I'll show thee the best springs. I'll pluck thee berries.
I'll fish for thee and get thee wood enough.
A plague upon the tyrant that I serve!
I'll bear him no more sticks, but follow thee,
Thou wondrous man.

TRINCULO   A most ridiculous monster, to make a
wonder of a poor drunkard!

CALIBAN
I prithee, let me bring thee where crabs grow,   165
And I with my long nails will dig thee pignuts,   166
Show thee a jay's nest, and instruct thee how
To snare the nimble marmoset. I'll bring thee   168
To clust'ring filberts, and sometimes I'll get thee
Young scamels from the rock. Wilt thou go with me?   170

STEPHANO   I prithee now, lead the way without any
more talking.—Trinculo, the King and all our com-   172
pany else being drowned, we will inherit here.—   173
Here, bear my bottle.—Fellow Trinculo, we'll fill him
by and by again.

CALIBAN   (*sings drunkenly*)
Farewell, master, farewell, farewell!

TRINCULO   A howling monster; a drunken monster!

CALIBAN
No more dams I'll make for fish,
   Nor fetch in firing   179
      At requiring,
   Nor scrape trenchering, nor wash dish.   181
      'Ban, 'Ban, Ca–Caliban
      Has a new master. Get a new man!   183
Freedom, high-day! High-day, freedom! Freedom,   184
high-day, freedom!

STEPHANO   O brave monster! Lead the way.   *Exeunt.*

❖

3.1

Enter Ferdinand, bearing a log.

FERDINAND
There be some sports are painful, and their labor   1
Delight in them sets off. Some kinds of baseness   2
Are nobly undergone, and most poor matters   3
Point to rich ends. This my mean task   4
Would be as heavy to me as odious, but   5

---

115 **constant** steady.   116 **an if** if   117 **brave** fine, magnificent
121 **butt of sack** barrel of Canary wine   122 **by this bottle** i.e., I swear
by this bottle   129 **book** i.e., bottle. (But with ironic reference to the
practice of kissing the Bible in swearing an oath; see *I'll be sworn* in line
128.)   137 **when time was** once upon a time.   139 **dog . . . bush** (The
man in the moon was popularly imagined to have with him a dog and
a bush of thorn.)   142 **By . . . light** By God's light, by this good light
from heaven   145 **Well . . . sooth!** Well pulled on the bottle, truly!
149 **When . . . bottle** i.e., Caliban wouldn't even stop at robbing his
god (i.e., Stephano) of his bottle if he could catch him asleep.

156 **But that** were it not that.   **in drink** drunk.   165 **crabs** crab apples,
or crabs   166 **pignuts** earthnuts, edible tuberous roots   168 **marmoset** small monkey.   170 **scamels** (Possibly *seamews*, mentioned in
Strachey's letter, or shellfish, or perhaps from *squamelle*, "furnished
with little scales." Contemporary French and Italian travel accounts
report that the natives of Patagonia in South America ate small fish
described as *fort scameux* and *squame*.)   172–3 **all . . . else** all the rest
of our shipboard companions   173 **inherit** take possession   179 **firing** firewood   181 **trenchering** trenchers, wooden plates   183 **Get a
new man** (Addressed to Prospero.)   184 **high-day** holiday.
3.1. Location: Before Prospero's cell.
1–2 **There . . . sets off** Some pastimes are laborious, but the pleasure
we get from them compensates for the effort. (Pleasure is *set off* by
labor as a jewel is set off by its foil.)   2 **baseness** menial activity
3 **undergone** undertaken.   **most poor** poorest   4 **mean** lowly   5 **but**
were it not that

The mistress which I serve quickens what's dead 6
And makes my labors pleasures. Oh, she is
Ten times more gentle than her father's crabbed,
And he's composed of harshness. I must remove
Some thousands of these logs and pile them up,
Upon a sore injunction. My sweet mistress 11
Weeps when she sees me work and says such baseness
Had never like executor. I forget; 13
But these sweet thoughts do even refresh my labors,
Most busy lest when I do it.

Enter Miranda; and Prospero [at a distance, unseen].

MIRANDA   Alas now, pray you, 15
Work not so hard. I would the lightning had
Burnt up those logs that you are enjoined to pile! 17
Pray, set it down and rest you. When this burns, 18
'Twill weep for having wearied you. My father 19
Is hard at study. Pray now, rest yourself.
He's safe for these three hours.
FERDINAND   O most dear mistress, 21
The sun will set before I shall discharge 22
What I must strive to do.
MIRANDA   If you'll sit down,
I'll bear your logs the while. Pray, give me that.
I'll carry it to the pile.
FERDINAND   No, precious creature,
I had rather crack my sinews, break my back,
Than you should such dishonor undergo
While I sit lazy by.
MIRANDA   It would become me
As well as it does you; and I should do it
With much more ease, for my good will is to it,
And yours it is against.
PROSPERO [aside]   Poor worm, thou art infected!
This visitation shows it.
MIRANDA   You look wearily. 32
FERDINAND
No, noble mistress, 'tis fresh morning with me
When you are by at night. I do beseech you— 34
Chiefly that I might set it in my prayers—
What is your name?
MIRANDA   Miranda.—O my father,
I have broke your hest to say so.
FERDINAND   Admired Miranda! 37
Indeed the top of admiration, worth
What's dearest to the world! Full many a lady 39
I have eyed with best regard, and many a time 40
The harmony of their tongues hath into bondage

Brought my too diligent ear. For several virtues 42
Have I liked several women, never any
With so full soul but some defect in her
Did quarrel with the noblest grace she owed 45
And put it to the foil. But you, O you, 46
So perfect and so peerless, are created
Of every creature's best!
MIRANDA   I do not know 48
One of my sex; no woman's face remember,
Save, from my glass, mine own. Nor have I seen
More that I may call men than you, good friend,
And my dear father. How features are abroad 52
I am skilless of; but, by my modesty, 53
The jewel in my dower, I would not wish
Any companion in the world but you;
Nor can imagination form a shape,
Besides yourself, to like of. But I prattle 57
Something too wildly, and my father's precepts 58
I therein do forget.
FERDINAND   I am in my condition 59
A prince, Miranda; I do think, a king—
I would, not so!—and would no more endure 61
This wooden slavery than to suffer 62
The flesh-fly blow my mouth. Hear my soul speak: 63
The very instant that I saw you did
My heart fly to your service, there resides
To make me slave to it, and for your sake
Am I this patient log-man.
MIRANDA   Do you love me?
FERDINAND
O heaven, O earth, bear witness to this sound,
And crown what I profess with kind event 69
If I speak true! If hollowly, invert 70
What best is boded me to mischief! I 71
Beyond all limit of what else i'th' world 72
Do love, prize, honor you.
MIRANDA [weeping]   I am a fool
To weep at what I am glad of.
PROSPERO [aside]   Fair encounter
Of two most rare affections! Heavens rain grace
On that which breeds between 'em!
FERDINAND   Wherefore weep you?
MIRANDA
At mine unworthiness, that dare not offer
What I desire to give, and much less take
What I shall die to want. But this is trifling, 79
And all the more it seeks to hide itself
The bigger bulk it shows. Hence, bashful cunning, 81

---

6 **quickens** gives life to   11 **sore injunction** severe command.
13 **Had . . . executor** was never before undertaken by so noble a
being.   **I forget** i.e., I forget that I'm supposed to be working
15 **Most . . . do it** (Ferdinand seems to say that the busier he is, the
less likely he is to forget the sweet thoughts that make his labors
pleasant. The line may be in need of emendation.)   17 **enjoined** commanded   18 **this** i.e., the log   19 **weep** i.e., exude resin   21 **these** the
next   22 **discharge** complete   32 **visitation** (1) Miranda's visit to
Ferdinand (2) visitation of the plague, i.e., infection of love   34 **by**
nearby   37 **hest** command.   **Admired Miranda** (Her name means
"to be admired or wondered at.")   39 **dearest** most treasured
40 **best regard** thoughtful and approving attention

42 **diligent** attentive.   **several** various. (Also in line 43.)   45 **owed**
owned   46 **put . . . foil** (1) overthrew it (as in fencing or wrestling)
(2) served as a *foil*, or "contrast," to set it off.   48 **Of** out of   52 **How . . .**
abroad What people look like in other places   53 **skilless** ignorant.
modesty virginity   57 **like of** be pleased with, be fond of.   58 **Some-**
thing somewhat   59 **condition** rank   61 **I would** I wish it were
62 **wooden slavery** being compelled to carry wood   62–3 **than . . .**
mouth than I would allow flying insects to deposit their eggs in my
mouth as if in decaying flesh.   69 **kind event** favorable outcome
70 **hollowly** insincerely, falsely.   **invert** turn   71 **boded** in store for.
mischief harm.   72 **what** whatever   79 **die** (Probably with an
unconscious sexual meaning that underlies all of lines 77–81.)   **to**
want through lacking.   81 **bashful cunning** coyness

And prompt me, plain and holy innocence!
I am your wife, if you will marry me;
If not, I'll die your maid. To be your fellow   84
You may deny me, but I'll be your servant
Whether you will or no.

FERDINAND   My mistress, dearest,   86
And I thus humble ever.

MIRANDA   My husband, then?

FERDINAND   Ay, with a heart as willing   89
As bondage e'er of freedom. Here's my hand.

MIRANDA [*clasping his hand*]
And mine, with my heart in't. And now farewell
Till half an hour hence.

FERDINAND   A thousand thousand!   92
        Exeunt [Ferdinand and Miranda, separately].

PROSPERO
So glad of this as they I cannot be,
Who are surprised with all; but my rejoicing   94
At nothing can be more. I'll to my book,
For yet ere suppertime must I perform
Much business appertaining.   *Exit.*   97

❖

3.2

Enter Caliban, Stephano, and Trinculo.

STEPHANO   Tell not me. When the butt is out, we will   1
drink water, not a drop before. Therefore bear up and   2
board 'em. Servant monster, drink to me.   3

TRINCULO   Servant monster? The folly of this island!   4
They say there's but five upon this isle. We are three
of them; if th'other two be brained like us, the state   6
totters.

STEPHANO   Drink, servant monster, when I bid thee.
Thy eyes are almost set in thy head.   [*Giving a drink.*]   9

TRINCULO   Where should they be set else? He were a   10
brave monster indeed if they were set in his tail.   11

STEPHANO   My man-monster hath drowned his tongue
in sack. For my part, the sea cannot drown me. I   13
swam, ere I could recover the shore, five and thirty   14
leagues off and on. By this light, thou shalt be my   15
lieutenant, monster, or my standard.   16

TRINCULO   Your lieutenant, if you list; he's no standard.   17

STEPHANO   We'll not run, Monsieur Monster.   18

TRINCULO   Nor go neither, but you'll lie like dogs and   19
yet say nothing neither.

STEPHANO   Mooncalf, speak once in thy life, if thou
be'st a good mooncalf.

CALIBAN
How does Thy Honor? Let me lick thy shoe.
I'll not serve him. He is not valiant.

TRINCULO   Thou liest, most ignorant monster, I am in   25
case to jostle a constable. Why, thou deboshed fish,   26
thou, was there ever man a coward that hath drunk so   27
much sack as I today? Wilt thou tell a monstrous lie,
being but half a fish and half a monster?

CALIBAN
Lo, how he mocks me! Wilt thou let him, my lord?

TRINCULO   "Lord," quoth he? That a monster should be
such a natural!   32

CALIBAN
Lo, lo, again! Bite him to death, I prithee.

STEPHANO   Trinculo, keep a good tongue in your head.
If you prove a mutineer—the next tree! The poor mon-   35
ster's my subject, and he shall not suffer indignity.

CALIBAN
I thank my noble lord. Wilt thou be pleased
To hearken once again to the suit I made to thee?

STEPHANO   Marry, will I. Kneel and repeat it. I will   39
stand, and so shall Trinculo.   [*Caliban kneels.*]   40

Enter Ariel, invisible.

CALIBAN
As I told thee before, I am subject to a tyrant,
A sorcerer, that by his cunning hath
Cheated me of the island.

ARIEL [*mimicking Trinculo*]
Thou liest.

CALIBAN   Thou liest, thou jesting monkey, thou!
I would my valiant master would destroy thee.
I do not lie.

STEPHANO   Trinculo, if you trouble him any more in 's
tale, by this hand, I will supplant some of your teeth.   48

TRINCULO   Why, I said nothing.

STEPHANO   Mum, then, and no more.—Proceed.

CALIBAN
I say by sorcery he got this isle;
From me he got it. If Thy Greatness will
Revenge it on him—for I know thou dar'st,
But this thing dare not—   54

STEPHANO   That's most certain.

CALIBAN
Thou shalt be lord of it, and I'll serve thee.

---

84 maid handmaiden, servant. **fellow** mate   **86 will** desire it.   **My mistress** i.e., The woman I adore and serve (not an illicit sexual partner)   **89 willing** desirous   **92 A thousand thousand!** A thousand thousand farewells!   **94 with al** by everything that has happened, or, *withal*, "by it"   **97 appertaining** related to this.
3.2. Location: Another part of the island.
1 out empty   **2–3 bear . . . 'em** (Stephano uses the terminology of maneuvering at sea and boarding a vessel under attack as a way of urging an assault on the liquor supply.)   **4 folly of** i.e., stupidity found on   **6 be brained** are endowed with intelligence   **9 set . . . head** fixed in a drunken stare. (But Trinculo answers in a literal sense.)   **10 set** placed   **11 brave** fine, splendid   **13 sack** a Spanish white wine. (Also in line 28.)   **14 recover** gain, reach   **14–15 five . . . on** i.e., a little over a hundred miles, give or take, or, off and on, intermittently. (A drunken hyperbole.)   **15 By this light** (An oath: By the light of the sun.)   **16 standard** standard-bearer, ensign. (But Trinculo answers in the literal sense: Caliban is *no standard*, not able to stand up because he's so drunk.)   **17 list** prefer

18 run run away, retreat (as a standard-bearer should not do)   **19 Nor . . . dogs** i.e., You won't even walk, much less run; you'll lie down in the field like the proverbial cowardly dog. (With a play on *lie*, tell falsehoods.)   **25–6 in case** ready, valiant enough   **26 deboshed** debauched, drunken   **27 ever . . . coward** ever a coward. (Trinculo appeals to his gargantuan drinking as refutation of the charge that he is *not valiant*, line 24.   **32 natural** fool, idiot.   **35 the next tree** i.e., you'll hang.   **39 Marry** i.e., Indeed. (Originally an oath, "by the Virgin Mary.")   **40.1 invisible** i.e., wearing a garment to connote invisibility, as at 1.2.377.2.   **48 supplant** uproot, displace   **54 this thing** i.e., Trinculo

STEPHANO   How now shall this be compassed? Canst   57
thou bring me to the party?

CALIBAN
Yea, yea, my lord. I'll yield him thee asleep,
Where thou mayst knock a nail into his head.

ARIEL [*mimicking Trinculo*]   Thou liest; thou canst not.

CALIBAN
What a pied ninny's this! Thou scurvy patch!—   62
I do beseech Thy Greatness, give him blows
And take his bottle from him. When that's gone
He shall drink naught but brine, for I'll not show
him
Where the quick freshes are.   66

STEPHANO   Trinculo, run into no further danger. Interrupt the monster one word further and, by this hand,
I'll turn my mercy out o' doors and make a stockfish of   69
thee.

TRINCULO   Why, what did I? I did nothing. I'll go farther
off.

STEPHANO   Didst thou not say he lied?

ARIEL [*mimicking Trinculo*]   Thou liest.

STEPHANO   Do I so? Take thou that. [*He beats Trinculo.*]
As you like this, give me the lie another time.   76

TRINCULO   I did not give the lie. Out o' your wits and
hearing too? A pox o' your bottle! This can sack and   78
drinking do. A murrain on your monster, and the   79
devil take your fingers!

CALIBAN   Ha, ha, ha!

STEPHANO   Now, forward with your tale.
[*To Trinculo*] Prithee, stand further off.

CALIBAN
Beat him enough. After a little time
I'll beat him too.

STEPHANO   Stand farther.—Come, proceed.

CALIBAN
Why, as I told thee, 'tis a custom with him
I'th'afternoon to sleep. There thou mayst brain him,
Having first seized his books; or with a log
Batter his skull, or paunch him with a stake,   90
Or cut his weasand with thy knife. Remember   91
First to possess his books, for without them
He's but a sot, as I am, nor hath not   93
One spirit to command. They all do hate him
As rootedly as I. Burn but his books.
He has brave utensils—for so he calls them—   96
Which, when he has a house, he'll deck withal.   97
And that most deeply to consider is
The beauty of his daughter. He himself
Calls her a nonpareil. I never saw a woman
But only Sycorax my dam and she;
But she as far surpasseth Sycorax
As great'st does least.

STEPHANO   Is it so brave a lass?   103

CALIBAN
Ay, lord. She will become thy bed, I warrant,   104
And bring thee forth brave brood.

STEPHANO   Monster, I will kill this man. His daughter
and I will be king and queen—save Our Graces!—and
Trinculo and thyself shall be viceroys. Dost thou like
the plot, Trinculo?

TRINCULO   Excellent.

STEPHANO   Give me thy hand. I am sorry I beat thee;
but, while thou liv'st, keep a good tongue in thy head.

CALIBAN
Within this half hour will he be asleep.
Wilt thou destroy him then?

STEPHANO   Ay, on mine honor.

ARIEL [*aside*]   This will I tell my master.

CALIBAN
Thou mak'st me merry; I am full of pleasure.
Let us be jocund. Will you troll the catch   118
You taught me but whilere?   119

STEPHANO   At thy request, monster, I will do reason,   120
any reason.—Come on, Trinculo, let us sing.   *Sings.*   121
Flout 'em and scout 'em   122
And scout 'em and flout 'em!
Thought is free.

CALIBAN   That's not the tune.   125
Ariel plays the tune on a tabor and pipe.

STEPHANO   What is this same?

TRINCULO   This is the tune of our catch, played by the
picture of Nobody.   128

STEPHANO   If thou be'st a man, show thyself in thy
likeness. If thou be'st a devil, take't as thou list.   130

TRINCULO   Oh, forgive me my sins!

STEPHANO   He that dies pays all debts. I defy thee.   132
Mercy upon us!

CALIBAN   Art thou afeard?

STEPHANO   No, monster, not I.

CALIBAN
Be not afeard. The isle is full of noises,
Sounds, and sweet airs, that give delight and hurt not.
Sometimes a thousand twangling instruments
Will hum about mine ears, and sometimes voices
That, if I then had waked after long sleep,
Will make me sleep again; and then, in dreaming,
The clouds methought would open and show riches
Ready to drop upon me, that when I waked
I cried to dream again.   144

STEPHANO   This will prove a brave kingdom to me,
where I shall have my music for nothing.

CALIBAN   When Prospero is destroyed.

---

57 compassed achieved.   **62 pied ninny** fool in motley.   **patch** fool.
66 quick freshes running springs   **69 turn . . . o' doors** banish all
merciful feelings.   **stockfish** dried cod beaten before cooking
76 give me the lie call me a liar to my face   **78 A pox** i.e., A plague.
(A curse.)   **79 murrain** plague. (Literally, a cattle disease.)   **90 paunch**
stab in the belly   **91 weasand** windpipe   **93 sot** fool   **96 brave utensils** fine furnishings   **97 deck withal** furnish it with.

103 brave splendid, attractive   **104 become** suit (sexually)   **118 jocund**
jovial, merry.   **troll the catch** sing the round   **119 but whilere** only a
short time ago.   **120–1 reason, any reason** anything reasonable.
122 Flout Scoff at.   **scout** deride   **125.1 tabor** small drum   **128 picture of Nobody** (Refers to a familiar figure with head, arms, and legs
but no trunk.)   **130 take't . . . list** (A proverbial formula of bravado
and defiance, as in *Romeo and Juliet*, 1.1.40–1.)   **132 He . . . debts**
(Another proverbial swagger: Death settles all scores, I'm not afraid
to fight.)   **144 to dream** desirous of dreaming

STEPHANO   That shall be by and by. I remember the 148
story.

TRINCULO   The sound is going away. Let's follow it,
and after do our work.

STEPHANO   Lead, monster; we'll follow. I would I could
see this taborer! He lays it on.   153

TRINCULO   Wilt come? I'll follow, Stephano.

Exeunt [following Ariel's music].

❧

3.3

*Enter Alonso, Sebastian, Antonio, Gonzalo,
Adrian, Francisco, etc.*

GONZALO
By'r lakin, I can go no further, sir.   1
My old bones aches. Here's a maze trod indeed
Through forthrights and meanders! By your patience,   3
I needs must rest me.

ALONSO   Old lord, I cannot blame thee,
Who am myself attached with weariness,   5
To th' dulling of my spirits. Sit down and rest.   6
Even here I will put off my hope, and keep it
No longer for my flatterer. He is drowned
Whom thus we stray to find, and the sea mocks
Our frustrate search on land. Well, let him go.   10
[Alonso and Gonzalo sit.]

ANTONIO *[aside to Sebastian]*
I am right glad that he's so out of hope.
Do not, for one repulse, forgo the purpose   12
That you resolved t'effect.

SEBASTIAN *[to Antonio]*   The next advantage
Will we take throughly.

ANTONIO *[to Sebastian]*   Let it be tonight,   14
For, now they are oppressed with travel, they   15
Will not, nor cannot, use such vigilance   16
As when they are fresh.

SEBASTIAN *[to Antonio]*   I say tonight. No more.   17

*Solemn and strange music; and Prospero on
the top, invisible.*

ALONSO
What harmony is this? My good friends, hark!

GONZALO   Marvelous sweet music!

*Enter several strange shapes, bringing in a ban-
quet, and dance about it with gentle actions of
salutations; and, inviting the King, etc., to eat,
they depart.*

ALONSO
Give us kind keepers, heavens! What were these?   20

SEBASTIAN
A living drollery. Now I will believe   21
That there are unicorns; that in Arabia
There is one tree, the phoenix' throne, one phoenix   23
At this hour reigning there.

ANTONIO   I'll believe both;
And what does else want credit, come to me   25
And I'll be sworn 'tis true. Travelers ne'er did lie,
Though fools at home condemn 'em.

GONZALO   If in Naples
I should report this now, would they believe me
If I should say I saw such islanders?
For, certes, these are people of the island,   30
Who, though they are of monstrous shape, yet note,
Their manners are more gentle, kind, than of
Our human generation you shall find
Many, nay, almost any.

PROSPERO *[aside]*   Honest lord,
Thou hast said well, for some of you there present
Are worse than devils.

ALONSO   I cannot too much muse   36
Such shapes, such gesture, and such sound,
expressing—
Although they want the use of tongue—a kind   38
Of excellent dumb discourse.

PROSPERO *[aside]*   Praise in departing.   39

FRANCISCO
They vanished strangely.

SEBASTIAN   No matter, since
They have left their viands behind, for we have
stomachs.   41
Will 't please you taste of what is here?

ALONSO   Not I.

GONZALO
Faith, sir, you need not fear. When we were boys,
Who would believe that there were mountaineers   44
Dewlapped like bulls, whose throats had hanging at
'em   45
Wallets of flesh? Or that there were such men   46
Whose heads stood in their breasts? Which now we
find   47
Each putter-out of five for one will bring us   48
Good warrant of.

ALONSO   I will stand to and feed,   49

---

148 **by and by** very soon.   153 **lays it on** i.e., plays the drum vigorously.
3.3. Location: Another part of the island.
1 **By'r lakin** By our Ladykin, by our Lady   3 **forthrights and meanders** paths straight and crooked.   5 **attached with** seized by   6 **To . . .
spirits** to the point of being dull-spirited.   10 **frustrate** frustrated
12 **for** because of   14 **throughly** thoroughly.   15 **now** now that.
travel (Spelled "trauaile" in the Folio and carrying the sense of labor
as well as traveling.)   16 **use such vigilance** be as vigilant   17.1–2 *on
the top* at some high point of the tiring-house or the theater, on a
third level above the gallery

20 **kind keepers** guardian angels   21 **living drollery** comic entertainment, caricature, or puppet show put on by live actors.   23 **phoenix'**
The phoenix was a mythical bird consumed to ashes every five hundred to six hundred years, only to be renewed into another cycle.
25 **want credit** lack credibility   30 **certes** certainly   36 **muse** wonder
at   38 **want** lack   39 **Praise in departing** i.e., Save your praise until
the end of the performance. (Proverbial.)   41 **viands** provisions.
stomachs appetites.   44 **mountaineers** mountain dwellers
45 **Dewlapped** having a dewlap, or fold of skin hanging from the
neck, like cattle   46 **Wallets** pendent folds of skin, wattles   47 **in
their breasts** (i.e., like the Anthropophagi described in *Othello,*
1.3.146.)   48 **putter-out . . . one** one who invests money or gambles
on the risks of travel on the condition that the traveler who returns
safely is to receive five times the amount deposited; hence, any traveler   49 **Good warrant** assurance.   **stand to** come forward, fall to.
(Also in line 52.)

Although my last—no matter, since I feel 50
The best is past. Brother, my lord the Duke, 51
Stand to, and do as we.   [*They approach the table.*] 52

Thunder and lightning. Enter Ariel, like a harpy,
claps his wings upon the table, and with a quaint
device the banquet vanishes.

ARIEL
You are three men of sin, whom Destiny— 53
That hath to instrument this lower world 54
And what is in't—the never-surfeited sea 55
Hath caused to belch up you, and on this island 56
Where man doth not inhabit, you 'mongst men
Being most unfit to live. I have made you mad;
And even with suchlike valor men hang and drown 59
Their proper selves.   [*Alonso, Sebastian, and Antonio*
draw their swords.]
You fools! I and my fellows 60
Are ministers of Fate. The elements
Of whom your swords are tempered may as well 62
Wound the loud winds, or with bemocked-at stabs 63
Kill the still-closing waters, as diminish 64
One dowl that's in my plume. My fellow ministers 65
Are like invulnerable. If you could hurt, 66
Your swords are now too massy for your strengths 67
And will not be uplifted. But remember—
For that's my business to you—that you three
From Milan did supplant good Prospero;
Exposed unto the sea, which hath requit it, 71
Him and his innocent child; for which foul deed
The powers, delaying, not forgetting, have
Incensed the seas and shores, yea, all the creatures,
Against your peace. Thee of thy son, Alonso,
They have bereft; and do pronounce by me
Ling'ring perdition, worse than any death 77
Can be at once, shall step by step attend
You and your ways; whose wraths to guard you
    from— 79
Which here, in this most desolate isle, else falls 80
Upon your heads—is nothing but heart's sorrow 81
And a clear life ensuing. 82

He vanishes in thunder; then, to soft music,
enter the shapes again, and dance, with mocks
and mows, and carrying out the table.

PROSPERO
Bravely the figure of this harpy hast thou 83
Performed, my Ariel; a grace it had devouring. 84
Of my instruction hast thou nothing bated 85
In what thou hadst to say. So, with good life 86
And observation strange, my meaner ministers 87
Their several kinds have done. My high charms work, 88
And these mine enemies are all knit up
In their distractions. They now are in my power; 90
And in these fits I leave them, while I visit
Young Ferdinand, whom they suppose is drowned,
And his and mine loved darling.   [*Exit above.*]
GONZALO
I'th' name of something holy, sir, why stand you 94
In this strange stare?
ALONSO   Oh, it is monstrous, monstrous! 95
Methought the billows spoke and told me of it; 96
The winds did sing it to me, and the thunder,
That deep and dreadful organ pipe, pronounced
The name of Prosper; it did bass my trespass. 99
Therefor my son i'th'ooze is bedded; and
I'll seek him deeper than e'er plummet sounded, 101
And with him there lie mudded.   *Exit.*
SEBASTIAN   But one fiend at a time, 103
I'll fight their legions o'er.
ANTONIO   I'll be thy second. 104
    Exeunt [Sebastian and Antonio].
GONZALO
All three of them are desperate. Their great guilt, 105
Like poison given to work a great time after, 106
Now 'gins to bite the spirits. I do beseech you, 107
That are of suppler joints, follow them swiftly 108
And hinder them from what this ecstasy 109
May now provoke them to.
ADRIAN   Follow, I pray you.
    Exeunt omnes.

♣

4.1

Enter Prospero, Ferdinand, and Miranda.

PROSPERO
If I have too austerely punished you,
Your compensation makes amends, for I

---

50 Although my last even if this were to be my last meal   **51 best** best part of life   **52.1 harpy** a fabulous monster with a woman's face and breasts and a vulture's body, supposed to be a minister of divine vengeance   **52.2–3 with . . . vanishes** by means of some ingenious stage contrivance, the food vanishes. (The table remains until line 82.)   **53–6 whom . . . up** you whom Destiny, acting through this sublunary world as its instrument, has caused the ever-hungry sea to belch up   **59 suchlike valor** i.e., the reckless valor derived from madness   **60 proper** own   **62 whom** which.   **tempered** made hard   **63 bemocked-at** scorned   **64 still-closing** always closing again when parted   **65 dowl** soft, fine feather   **66 like** likewise, similarly.   **If** Even if   **67 massy** heavy   **71 requit** requited, avenged   **77 perdition** ruin, destruction   **79 whose . . . from** to guard you from which heavenly wrath   **80 else** otherwise   **81 is nothing** there is no way   **82 clear** unspotted, innocent   **82.2–3 mocks and mows** mocking gestures and grimaces

83 Bravely Finely, dashingly   **84 a grace . . . devouring** your impersonation displayed a ravishing grace. (With a punning suggestion of having caused the banquet to disappear as if by consuming it.)   **85 bated** abated, omitted   **86–8 So . . . done** Similarly, my lesser spirits assisting you have done their various tasks with observant care and attention to detail.   **90 distractions** trancelike state.   **94–5 why . . . stare?** (Gonzalo was not addressed in Ariel's speech to the *three men of sin*, line 53, and is not, as they are, in a maddened state; see lines 105–7.)   **95 it** i.e., my sin. (Also in line 96.)   **96 billows** waves   **99 bass my trespass** proclaim my trespass like a bass note in the music.   **101 than . . . sounded** than ever a lead weight attached to a line tested the depth   **103–4 But . . . o'er** If the demons come at me one at a time, I'll fight them all.   **105 desperate** despairing and reckless.   **106 Like . . . after** like poison, starting to work long after it has been administered   **107 bite the spirits** sap their vital powers through anguish.   **107–8 you . . . joints** Adrian, Francisco, and others not under Ariel's numbing spell   **109 ecstasy** mad frenzy   **4.1. Location: Before Prospero's cell.**

Have given you here a third of mine own life,   3
Or that for which I live; who once again
I tender to thy hand. All thy vexations   5
Were but my trials of thy love, and thou
Hast strangely stood the test. Here, afore heaven,   7
I ratify this my rich gift. O Ferdinand,
Do not smile at me that I boast her off,   9
For thou shalt find she will outstrip all praise
And make it halt behind her.

FERDINAND   I do believe it   11
Against an oracle.   12

PROSPERO
Then, as my gift and thine own acquisition
Worthily purchased, take my daughter. But
If thou dost break her virgin-knot before
All sanctimonious ceremonies may   16
With full and holy rite be ministered,
No sweet aspersion shall the heavens let fall   18
To make this contract grow; but barren hate,
Sour-eyed disdain, and discord shall bestrew
The union of your bed with weeds so loathly   21
That you shall hate it both. Therefore take heed,
As Hymen's lamps shall light you.

FERDINAND   As I hope   23
For quiet days, fair issue, and long life,   24
With such love as 'tis now, the murkiest den,
The most opportune place, the strong'st suggestion   26
Our worser genius can, shall never melt   27
Mine honor into lust, to take away   28
The edge of that day's celebration   29
When I shall think or Phoebus' steeds are foundered   30
Or Night kept chained below.

PROSPERO   Fairly spoke.
Sit then and talk with her. She is thine own.
    [Ferdinand and Miranda sit and talk together.]
What, Ariel! My industrious servant, Ariel!   33

    Enter Ariel.

ARIEL
What would my potent master? Here I am.

PROSPERO
Thou and thy meaner fellows your last service   35
Did worthily perform, and I must use you
In such another trick. Go bring the rabble,   37

O'er whom I give thee power, here to this place.
Incite them to quick motion, for I must
Bestow upon the eyes of this young couple
Some vanity of mine art. It is my promise,   41
And they expect it from me.

ARIEL   Presently?   42

PROSPERO   Ay, with a twink.   43

ARIEL
Before you can say "Come" and "Go,"
And breathe twice, and cry "So, so,"
Each one, tripping on his toe,
Will be here with mop and mow.   47
Do you love me, master? No?

PROSPERO
Dearly, my delicate Ariel. Do not approach
Till thou dost hear me call.

ARIEL   Well; I conceive.   Exit. 50

PROSPERO
Look thou be true; do not give dalliance   51
Too much the rein. The strongest oaths are straw
To th' fire i'th' blood. Be more abstemious,
Or else good night your vow!

FERDINAND   I warrant you, sir,   54
The white cold virgin snow upon my heart   55
Abates the ardor of my liver.

PROSPERO   Well.   56
Now come, my Ariel! Bring a corollary,   57
Rather than want a spirit. Appear, and pertly!—   58
No tongue! All eyes! Be silent.   Soft music.   59

    Enter Iris.

IRIS
Ceres, most bounteous lady, thy rich leas   60
Of wheat, rye, barley, vetches, oats, and peas;   61
Thy turfy mountains, where live nibbling sheep,
And flat meads thatched with stover, them to keep;   63
Thy banks with pionèd and twillèd brims,   64
Which spongy April at thy hest betrims   65
To make cold nymphs chaste crowns; and thy
    broom groves,   66
Whose shadow the dismissèd bachelor loves,   67
Being lass-lorn; thy poll-clipped vineyard;   68
And thy sea marge, sterile and rocky hard,   69
Where thou thyself dost air: the queen o'th' sky,   70

---

3 a third i.e., Miranda, into whose education I have put a third of my life, or (less precisely) who represents a large part of what I have cared about, along with my dukedom and my magical art   **5 tender** offer   **7 strangely** exceptionally   **9 boast her off** i.e., praise her so, or, perhaps an error for "boast of her"; the Folio reads "boast her of"   **11 halt** limp   **12 Against an oracle** even if an oracle should declare otherwise.   **16 sanctimonious** sacred   **18 aspersion** dew, shower   **21 weeds** (In place of the flowers customarily strewn on the marriage bed.)   **23 As . . . you** i.e., as you long for happiness and concord in your marriage. (Hymen was the Greek and Roman god of marriage; his symbolic torches, the wedding torches, were supposed to burn brightly for a happy marriage and smokily for a troubled one.)   **24 issue** offspring   **26–7 the strong'st . . . can** the strongest temptation that the evil spirit within us can propose   **28 to** so as to   **29 edge** keen enjoyment, sexual ardor   **30 or . . . foundered** either that the horses of the sun's chariot have gone lame (thus delaying the night for which I will be so eager)   **33 What** Now then   **35 meaner fellows** subordinates   **37 trick** device.   **rabble** band, i.e., the *meaner fellows* of line 35

41 vanity (1) illusion (2) trifle (3) desire for admiration, conceit   **42 Presently?** Immediately?   **43 with a twink** in the twinkling of an eye.   **47 mop and mow** grimaces.   **50 conceive** understand.   **51 true** true to your promise   **54 good night** i.e., say good-bye to.   **warrant** guarantee   **55 The white . . . heart** i.e., the chaste ideal to which my heart is devoted   **56 liver** (The presumed seat of the passions.)   **57 corollary** surplus, extra supply   **58 want** lack.   **pertly** briskly.   **59 No tongue!** Quiet, everyone!   **59.1 Iris** goddess of the rainbow and Juno's messenger.   **60 Ceres** goddess of the generative power of nature.   **leas** meadows   **61 vetches** plants for forage, fodder   **63 meads** meadows.   **stover** winter fodder for cattle   **64 pionèd and twillèd** undercut by the swift current and protected by roots and branches that tangle to form a barricade   **65 spongy** wet.   **hest** command   **66 broom groves** clumps of broom, gorse, yellow-flowered shrub   **67 dismissèd bachelor** rejected male lover   **68 poll-clipped** pruned, lopped at the top, or *pole-clipped*, "hedged in with poles"   **69 sea marge** shore   **70 thou . . . air** you take the air, go for walks.   **queen o'th' sky** i.e., Juno

Whose wat'ry arch and messenger am I,　　　　　　71
Bids thee leave these, and with her sovereign grace,　72
　　　　　　Juno descends [slowly in her car].
Here on this grass plot, in this very place,
To come and sport. Her peacocks fly amain.　　　　74
Approach, rich Ceres, her to entertain.　　　　　　75

　　　Enter Ceres.

CERES
Hail, many-colored messenger, that ne'er
Dost disobey the wife of Jupiter,
Who with thy saffron wings upon my flowers　　　　78
Diffusest honeydrops, refreshing showers,
And with each end of thy blue bow dost crown　　　80
My bosky acres and my unshrubbed down,　　　　　81
Rich scarf to my proud earth. Why hath thy queen　82
Summoned me hither to this short-grassed green?

IRIS
A contract of true love to celebrate,
And some donation freely to estate　　　　　　　85
On the blest lovers.

CERES　　　　　　　Tell me, heavenly bow,
If Venus or her son, as thou dost know,　　　　　87
Do now attend the Queen? Since they did plot　　　88
The means that dusky Dis my daughter got,　　　　89
Her and her blind boy's scandaled company　　　　90
I have forsworn.

IRIS　　　　　　　Of her society　　　　　91
Be not afraid. I met Her Deity　　　　　　　　92
Cutting the clouds towards Paphos, and her son　　93
Dove-drawn with her. Here thought they to have
　　done　　　　　　　　　　　　　　　　　94
Some wanton charm upon this man and maid,　　　95
Whose vows are that no bed-right shall be paid　　96
Till Hymen's torch be lighted; but in vain.
Mars's hot minion is returned again;　　　　　　98
Her waspish-headed son has broke his arrows,　　　99
Swears he will shoot no more, but play with
　　sparrows　　　　　　　　　　　　　　　100
And be a boy right out.

　　　[Juno alights.]

CERES　　　　　　　Highest Queen of state,　101
Great Juno, comes; I know her by her gait.　　　102

JUNO
How does my bounteous sister? Go with me　　　103
To bless this twain, that they may prosperous be,
And honored in their issue.　　　　*They sing:* 105

JUNO
Honor, riches, marriage blessing,
Long continuance, and increasing,
Hourly joys be still upon you!　　　　　　　108
Juno sings her blessings on you.

CERES
Earth's increase, foison plenty,　　　　　　　110
Barns and garners never empty,　　　　　　　111
Vines with clust'ring bunches growing,
Plants with goodly burden bowing;

Spring come to you at the farthest
In the very end of harvest!　　　　　　　　115
Scarcity and want shall shun you;
Ceres' blessing so is on you.

FERDINAND
This is a most majestic vision, and
Harmonious charmingly. May I be bold　　　　119
To think these spirits?

PROSPERO　　　　　　Spirits, which by mine art
I have from their confines called to enact
My present fancies.

FERDINAND　　　　　Let me live here ever!
So rare a wondered father and a wise　　　　　123
Makes this place Paradise.

　　　　Juno and Ceres whisper, and send
　　　　　Iris on employment.

PROSPERO　　　　　　Sweet now, silence!
Juno and Ceres whisper seriously;
There's something else to do. Hush and be mute,
Or else our spell is marred.

IRIS *[calling offstage]*
You nymphs, called naiads, of the windring brooks,　128
With your sedged crowns and ever-harmless looks,　129
Leave your crisp channels, and on this green land　130
Answer your summons; Juno does command.
Come, temperate nymphs, and help to celebrate　132
A contract of true love. Be not too late.

　　　Enter certain nymphs.

You sunburned sicklemen, of August weary,　　　134
Come hither from the furrow and be merry.　　　135

---

71 wat'ry arch rainbow　**72.1** *Juno descends* i.e., starts her descent from the "heavens" above the stage　**74 peacocks** birds sacred to Juno and used to pull her chariot.　**amain** with full speed.　**75 entertain** receive.　**78 saffron** yellow　**80 bow** rainbow　**81 bosky** wooded.　**unshrubbed down** open upland　**82 scarf** (The rainbow is like a colored silk band adorning the earth.)　**85 estate** bestow　**87 son** i.e., Cupid.　**as** as far as　**88–91 Since . . . forsworn** Since Venus and her blind son Cupid plotted the means by which Dis (Pluto) carried off my daughter Proserpina to be his bride in Hades, I have forsworn their scandalous company.　**92 Her Deity** i.e., Her Highness　**93 Paphos** place on the island of Cyprus, sacred to Venus　**94 Dove-drawn** (Venus's chariot was drawn by doves.)　**94–5 done . . . charm** inflicted some lustful spell　**96 that . . . paid** that their union will not be sexually consummated　**98 Mars's hot minion** i.e., Venus, the beloved of Mars.　**returned** i.e., returned to Paphos　**99 waspish-headed** hotheaded, peevish　**100 sparrows** (Supposed lustful, and sacred to Venus.)　**101 right out** outright.　**Highest . . . state** Most majestic Queen　**102 gait** i.e., majestic bearing.

103 sister i.e., fellow goddess.　**105 issue** offspring.　**108 still** always　**110 foison plenty** plentiful harvest　**111 garners** granaries　**115 In . . . harvest** i.e., with no winter in between.　**119 charmingly** enchantingly.　**123 wondered** wonder-performing, wondrous.　**wise** (The Folio appears to read "wise" here, but with a tall "s" that resembles an "f," leading to much dispute over this reading. In some copies of the Folio the "s" looks like an "f," perhaps damaged, but evidently as the result of an inkblot, so that the true reading is "s." Even so, an error in transmission would be easy, so that the author's intention is uncertain. The matter bears importantly on whether or not Ferdinand includes Miranda in his vision of paradise.)　**128 naiads** nymphs of springs, rivers, or lakes.　**windring** wandering, winding (?)　**129 sedged** made of reeds.　**ever-harmless** ever innocent　**130 crisp** curled, rippled　**132 temperate** chaste　**134 sicklemen** harvesters, field workers who cut down grain and grass.　**of August weary** i.e., weary of the hard work of the harvest　**135 furrow** i.e., plowed fields

Make holiday; your rye-straw hats put on,
And these fresh nymphs encounter every one   137
In country footing.   138

*Enter certain reapers, properly habited. They join
with the nymphs in a graceful dance, towards the
end whereof Prospero starts suddenly, and speaks;
after which, to a strange, hollow, and confused
noise, they heavily vanish.*

PROSPERO *[aside]*
I had forgot that foul conspiracy
Of the beast Caliban and his confederates
Against my life. The minute of their plot
Is almost come. *[To the Spirits]* Well done! Avoid; no
    more!   142
FERDINAND *[to Miranda]*
This is strange. Your father's in some passion
That works him strongly.
MIRANDA   Never till this day   144
Saw I him touched with anger so distempered.
PROSPERO
You do look, my son, in a moved sort,   146
As if you were dismayed. Be cheerful, sir.
Our revels now are ended. These our actors,   148
As I foretold you, were all spirits and
Are melted into air, into thin air;
And, like the baseless fabric of this vision,   151
The cloud-capped towers, the gorgeous palaces,
The solemn temples, the great globe itself,   153
Yea, all which it inherit, shall dissolve,   154
And, like this insubstantial pageant faded,
Leave not a rack behind. We are such stuff   156
As dreams are made on, and our little life   157
Is rounded with a sleep. Sir, I am vexed.   158
Bear with my weakness. My old brain is troubled.
Be not disturbed with my infirmity.   160
If you be pleased, retire into my cell   161
And there repose. A turn or two I'll walk
To still my beating mind.
FERDINAND, MIRANDA   We wish your peace.   163
        Exeunt [Ferdinand and Miranda].
PROSPERO
Come with a thought! I thank thee, Ariel. Come.   164

        Enter Ariel.

ARIEL
Thy thoughts I cleave to. What's thy pleasure?   165
PROSPERO   Spirit,
We must prepare to meet with Caliban.

ARIEL
Ay, my commander. When I presented Ceres,   167
I thought to have told thee of it, but I feared
Lest I might anger thee.
PROSPERO
Say again, where didst thou leave these varlets?
ARIEL
I told you, sir, they were red-hot with drinking;
So full of valor that they smote the air
For breathing in their faces, beat the ground
For kissing of their feet; yet always bending   174
Towards their project. Then I beat my tabor,
At which, like unbacked colts, they pricked their ears, 176
Advanced their eyelids, lifted up their noses   177
As they smelt music. So I charmed their ears   178
That calflike they my lowing followed through   179
Toothed briers, sharp furzes, pricking gorse, and
    thorns,   180
Which entered their frail shins. At last I left them
I'th' filthy-mantled pool beyond your cell,   182
There dancing up to th' chins, that the foul lake
O'erstunk their feet.
PROSPERO   This was well done, my bird.   184
Thy shape invisible retain thou still.
The trumpery in my house, go bring it hither,   186
For stale to catch these thieves.
ARIEL   I go, I go.   *Exit.* 187
PROSPERO
A devil, a born devil, on whose nature
Nurture can never stick; on whom my pains,
Humanely taken, all, all lost, quite lost!
And as with age his body uglier grows,
So his mind cankers. I will plague them all,   192
Even to roaring.

        Enter Ariel, loaden with glistering apparel, etc.

            Come, hang them on this line.   193

        *[Ariel hangs up the showy finery; Prospero and
        Ariel remain, invisible.] Enter Caliban, Stephano,
        and Trinculo, all wet.*

CALIBAN
Pray you, tread softly, that the blind mole may
Not hear a foot fall. We now are near his cell.
STEPHANO Monster, your fairy, which you say is a
harmless fairy, has done little better than played the
jack with us.   198

---

137 encounter join   **138 country footing** country dancing.
138.1 *properly* suitably   **138.5** *heavily* slowly, dejectedly   **142 Avoid**
Withdraw   **144 works** affects, agitates   **146 moved sort** troubled
state, condition   **148 revels** entertainment, pageant   **151 baseless
fabric** unsubstantial theatrical edifice or contrivance   **153 great
globe** (With a glance at the Globe Theatre.)   **154 which it inherit**
who subsequently occupy it   **156 rack** wisp of cloud   **157 on** of
158 rounded surrounded (before birth and after death), or crowned,
rounded off   **160 with** by   **161 retire** withdraw, go   **163 beating**
agitated   **164 with a thought** i.e., on the instant, or, summoned by
my thought, no sooner thought of than here.   **165 cleave** cling,
adhere

167 presented acted the part of, or, introduced   **174 bending** aiming
176 unbacked unbroken, unridden   **177 Advanced** lifted up   **178 As**
as if   **179 lowing** mooing   **180 furzes . . . gorse** prickly shrubs
182 filthy-mantled covered with a slimy coating   **184 O'erstunk**
smelled worse than, or, caused to stink terribly   **186 trumpery** cheap
goods, the *glistering apparel* mentioned in the following stage direction   **187 stale** (1) decoy (2) out-of-fashion garments. (With possible
further suggestions of "horse piss," as in line 199, and "steal," pronounced like *stale. For stale* could also mean "fit for a prostitute.")
192 cankers festers, grows malignant.   **193 line** lime tree or linden.
193.1–2 *Prospero and Ariel remain* (The staging is uncertain. They
may instead exit here and return with the spirits at line 256.)
198 jack (1) knave (2) will-o'-the-wisp

TRINCULO   Monster, I do smell all horse piss, at which
my nose is in great indignation.
STEPHANO   So is mine. Do you hear, monster? If I
should take a displeasure against you, look you—
TRINCULO   Thou wert but a lost monster.
CALIBAN
Good my lord, give me thy favor still.
Be patient, for the prize I'll bring thee to
Shall hoodwink this mischance. Therefore speak
    softly.   206
All's hushed as midnight yet.
TRINCULO   Ay, but to lose our bottles in the pool—
STEPHANO   There is not only disgrace and dishonor in
that, monster, but an infinite loss.
TRINCULO   That's more to me than my wetting. Yet this
is your harmless fairy, monster!
STEPHANO   I will fetch off my bottle, though I be o'er   213
ears for my labor.   214
CALIBAN
Prithee, my king, be quiet. See'st thou here,
This is the mouth o'th' cell. No noise, and enter.
Do that good mischief which may make this island
Thine own forever, and I thy Caliban
For aye thy footlicker.
STEPHANO   Give me thy hand. I do begin to have bloody
thoughts.
TRINCULO   [seeing the finery] O King Stephano! O peer!   222
O worthy Stephano! Look what a wardrobe here is
for thee!
CALIBAN
Let it alone, thou fool, it is but trash.
TRINCULO   Oho, monster! We know what belongs to a
frippery. O King Stephano!   [He puts on a gown.]   227
STEPHANO   Put off that gown, Trinculo. By this hand,
I'll have that gown.
TRINCULO   Thy Grace shall have it.
CALIBAN
The dropsy drown this fool! What do you mean   231
To dote thus on such luggage? Let 't alone   232
And do the murder first. If he awake,
From toe to crown he'll fill our skins with pinches,   234
Make us strange stuff.
STEPHANO   Be you quiet, monster.—Mistress line, is   236
not this my jerkin? [He takes it down.] Now is the jerkin 237
under the line. Now, jerkin, you are like to lose your   238
hair and prove a bald jerkin.   239

TRINCULO   Do, do! We steal by line and level, an't like 240
Your Grace.
STEPHANO   I thank thee for that jest. Here's a garment
for't. [He gives a garment.] Wit shall not go unrewarded
while I am king of this country. "Steal by line and
level" is an excellent pass of pate. There's another 245
garment for't.
TRINCULO   Monster, come, put some lime upon your 247
fingers, and away with the rest.
CALIBAN
I will have none on't. We shall lose our time,
And all be turned to barnacles, or to apes   250
With foreheads villainous low.   251
STEPHANO   Monster, lay to your fingers. Help to bear 252
this away where my hogshead of wine is, or I'll turn 253
you out of my kingdom. Go to, carry this.   254
TRINCULO   And this.
STEPHANO   Ay, and this.
    [They load Caliban with more and more garments.]

A noise of hunters heard. Enter divers spirits, in
shape of dogs and hounds, hunting them about,
Prospero and Ariel setting them on.

PROSPERO   Hey, Mountain, hey!
ARIEL   Silver! There it goes, Silver!
PROSPERO   Fury, Fury! There, Tyrant, there! Hark! Hark!
    [Caliban, Stephano, and Trinculo are driven out.]
Go, charge my goblins that they grind their joints
With dry convulsions, shorten up their sinews   261
With agèd cramps, and more pinch-spotted make
    them   262
Than pard or cat o' mountain.
ARIEL   Hark, they roar!   263
PROSPERO
Let them be hunted soundly. At this hour   264
Lies at my mercy all mine enemies.
Shortly shall all my labors end, and thou
Shalt have the air at freedom. For a little   267
Follow, and do me service.   Exeunt.

❖

5.1

Enter Prospero in his magic robes, [with his
staff,] and Ariel.

---

206 **hoodwink this mischance** cover up (literally, blindfold) this mistake.   **213–14 o'er ears** over my ears in the filthy horse pond (line 182)   **222 King . . . peer** (Alludes to the old ballad beginning, "King Stephen was a worthy peer.")   **227 frippery** second-hand-clothing shop. (Trinculo knows that what they have just found is much finer.) **231 The dropsy drown** (An oath. *Dropsy* is a disease characterized by the accumulation of fluid in the connective tissue of the body.) **232 luggage** cumbersome trash.   **234 crown** head   **236 Mistress line** (Addressed to the linden or lime tree upon which, at line 193, Ariel hung the *glistering apparel*.)   **237 jerkin** jacket made of leather **238 under the line** under the lime tree. (With punning sense of being south of the equinoctial line or equator; sailors on long voyages to the southern regions were popularly supposed to lose their hair from scurvy or other diseases. Stephano also quibbles bawdily on losing hair through syphilis, and puns in *Mistress* and *jerkin*.)   **like** likely **239 bald** (1) hairless, napless (2) meager

240 **Do, do!** i.e., Bravo! (Said in response to the jesting or to the taking of the jerkin, or both.)   **steal . . . level** i.e., steal by means of plumb line and carpenter's level, methodically. (With pun on *line*, "lime tree," line 238, and *steal*, pronounced like *stale*, i.e., prostitute, continuing Stephano's bawdy quibble.)   **an't like** if it please   **245 pass of pate** sally of wit. (The metaphor is from fencing.)   **247 lime** birdlime, sticky substance (to give Caliban sticky fingers)   **250 barnacles** barnacle geese, formerly supposed to be hatched from barnacles attached to trees or to rotting timber; here, evidently used, like *apes*, as types of simpletons   **251 villainous** vilely   **252 lay to** start using **253 this** i.e., the *glistering apparel*.   **hogshead** large cask   **254 Go to** (An expression of exhortation or remonstrance.)   **261 dry convulsions** racking cramps   **262 agèd** characteristic of old age   **263 pard** panther or leopard.   **cat o' mountain** wildcat.   **264 soundly** severely.   **267 little** little while longer
5.1. Location: Before Prospero's cell.

PROSPERO
Now does my project gather to a head.
My charms crack not, my spirits obey, and Time   2
Goes upright with his carriage. How's the day?   3

ARIEL
On the sixth hour, at which time, my lord,   4
You said our work should cease.

PROSPERO   I did say so,
When first I raised the tempest. Say, my spirit,
How fares the King and 's followers?

ARIEL   Confined together
In the same fashion as you gave in charge,
Just as you left them; all prisoners, sir,
In the line grove which weather-fends your cell.   10
They cannot budge till your release. The King,   11
His brother, and yours abide all three distracted,   12
And the remainder mourning over them,
Brim full of sorrow and dismay; but chiefly
Him that you termed, sir, the good old lord,
    Gonzalo.
His tears run down his beard like winter's drops
From eaves of reeds. Your charm so strongly works
    'em   17
That if you now beheld them your affections   18
Would become tender.

PROSPERO   Dost thou think so, spirit?

ARIEL
Mine would, sir, were I human.

PROSPERO   And mine shall.
Hast thou, which art but air, a touch, a feeling   21
Of their afflictions, and shall not myself,
One of their kind, that relish all as sharply   23
Passion as they, be kindlier moved than thou art?   24
Though with their high wrongs I am struck to th'
    quick,
Yet with my nobler reason 'gainst my fury
Do I take part. The rarer action is   27
In virtue than in vengeance. They being penitent,
The sole drift of my purpose doth extend
Not a frown further. Go release them, Ariel.
My charms I'll break, their senses I'll restore,
And they shall be themselves.

ARIEL   I'll fetch them, sir.
                                                         Exit.
    [*Prospero traces a charmed circle with his staff.*]

PROSPERO
Ye elves of hills, brooks, standing lakes, and groves,   33
And ye that on the sands with printless foot
Do chase the ebbing Neptune, and do fly him

When he comes back; you demi-puppets that   36
By moonshine do the green sour ringlets make,   37
Whereof the ewe not bites; and you whose pastime
Is to make midnight mushrooms, that rejoice   39
To hear the solemn curfew; by whose aid,   40
Weak masters though ye be, I have bedimmed   41
The noontide sun, called forth the mutinous winds,
And twixt the green sea and the azured vault   43
Set roaring war; to the dread rattling thunder   44
Have I given fire, and rifted Jove's stout oak   45
With his own bolt; the strong-based promontory   46
Have I made shake, and by the spurs plucked up   47
The pine and cedar; graves at my command
Have waked their sleepers, oped, and let 'em forth
By my so potent art. But this rough magic   50
I here abjure, and when I have required   51
Some heavenly music—which even now I do—
To work mine end upon their senses that   53
This airy charm is for, I'll break my staff,
Bury it certain fathoms in the earth,
And deeper than did ever plummet sound
I'll drown my book.   *Solemn music.*

    *Here enters Ariel before; then Alonso, with a
    frantic gesture, attended by Gonzalo; Sebastian and
    Antonio in like manner, attended by Adrian and
    Francisco. They all enter the circle which Prospero
    had made, and there stand charmed; which
    Prospero observing, speaks:*

[*To Alonso*] A solemn air, and the best comforter   58
To an unsettled fancy, cure thy brains,   59
Now useless, boiled within thy skull! [*To Sebastian
    and Antonio*] There stand,   60
For you are spell-stopped.—
Holy Gonzalo, honorable man,
Mine eyes, e'en sociable to the show of thine,   63
Fall fellowly drops. [*Aside*] The charm dissolves
    apace,   64
And as the morning steals upon the night,
Melting the darkness, so their rising senses
Begin to chase the ignorant fumes that mantle   67
Their clearer reason.—O good Gonzalo,   68
My true preserver, and a loyal sir
To him thou follow'st! I will pay thy graces   70
Home both in word and deed.—Most cruelly   71
Didst thou, Alonso, use me and my daughter.
Thy brother was a furtherer in the act.—   73

---

2 **crack** collapse, fail. (The metaphor is probably alchemical, as in *project* and *gather to a head*, line 1.)   3 **his carriage** its burden. (Time is no longer heavily burdened and so can go *upright*, standing straight and unimpeded.)   4 **On** Approaching   10 **line grove** grove of lime trees.   **weather-fends** protects from the weather   11 **your release** you release them.   12 **distracted** out of their wits   17 **eaves of reeds** thatched roofs.   18 **affections** disposition, feelings   21 **touch** sense, apprehension   23–4 **that . . . they** I who experience human passions as acutely as they   24 **kindlier** (1) more sympathetically (2) more naturally, humanly   27 **rarer** nobler   33 **Ye . . . groves** (This passage, down through line 50, is an embellished paraphrase of Golding's translation of Ovid's *Metamorphoses*, 7.197–219.)

36 **demi-puppets** puppets of half size, i.e., elves and fairies   37 **green sour ringlets** fairy rings, circles in grass (actually produced by mushrooms)   39 **midnight mushrooms** mushrooms appearing overnight   40 **curfew** evening bell, usually rung at nine o'clock, ushering in the time when spirits are abroad   41 **Weak masters** i.e., subordinate spirits, as in 4.1.35   43 **the azured vault** i.e., the sky   44–5 **to . . . fire** I have discharged the dread rattling thunderbolt   45 **rifted** riven, split.   **oak** a tree that was sacred to Jove   46 **bolt** thunderbolt   47 **spurs** roots   50 **rough** violent   51 **required** demanded   53 **their senses that** the senses of those whom   58 **air** song.   **and** i.e., which is   59 **fancy** imagination   60 **boiled** i.e., extremely agitated   63 **sociable** sympathetic. **show** appearance   64 **Fall** let fall   67 **ignorant fumes** fumes that render them incapable of comprehension.   **mantle** envelop   68 **clearer** growing clearer   70 **pay thy graces** requite your favors and virtues   71 **Home** fully   73 **furtherer** accomplice

Thou art pinched for't now, Sebastian. [*To Antonio*]
        Flesh and blood,   74
You, brother mine, that entertained ambition,
Expelled remorse and nature, whom, with Sebastian,   76
Whose inward pinches therefore are most strong,
Would here have killed your king, I do forgive thee,
Unnatural though thou art.—Their understanding
Begins to swell, and the approaching tide
Will shortly fill the reasonable shore   81
That now lies foul and muddy. Not one of them
That yet looks on me, or would know me.—Ariel,
Fetch me the hat and rapier in my cell.
        [*Ariel goes to the cell and returns immediately.*]
I will discase me and myself present   85
As I was sometime Milan. Quickly, spirit!   86
Thou shalt ere long be free.
                Ariel sings and helps to attire him.

ARIEL
        Where the bee sucks, there suck I.
        In a cowslip's bell I lie;
        There I couch when owls do cry.   90
        On the bat's back I do fly
        After summer merrily.   92
        Merrily, merrily shall I live now
        Under the blossom that hangs on the bough.

PROSPERO
        Why, that's my dainty Ariel! I shall miss thee,
        But yet thou shalt have freedom. So, so, so.   96
        To the King's ship, invisible as thou art!
        There shalt thou find the mariners asleep
        Under the hatches. The Master and the Boatswain
        Being awake, enforce them to this place,
        And presently, I prithee.   101

ARIEL
        I drink the air before me, and return
        Or ere your pulse twice beat.   *Exit.* 103

GONZALO
        All torment, trouble, wonder, and amazement
        Inhabits here. Some heavenly power guide us
        Out of this fearful country!

PROSPERO   Behold, sir King,   106
        The wrongèd Duke of Milan, Prospero.
        For more assurance that a living prince
        Does now speak to thee, I embrace thy body;
        And to thee and thy company I bid
        A hearty welcome.   [*Embracing him.*]

ALONSO   Whe'er thou be'st he or no,
        Or some enchanted trifle to abuse me,   112
        As late I have been, I not know. Thy pulse   113
        Beats as of flesh and blood; and, since I saw thee,
        Th'affliction of my mind amends, with which

I fear a madness held me. This must crave—   116
An if this be at all—a most strange story.   117
Thy dukedom I resign, and do entreat   118
Thou pardon me my wrongs. But how should
        Prospero   119
Be living, and be here?

PROSPERO [*to Gonzalo*]   First, noble friend,
        Let me embrace thine age, whose honor cannot   121
        Be measured or confined.   [*Embracing him.*]

GONZALO   Whether this be
        Or be not, I'll not swear.

PROSPERO   You do yet taste
        Some subtleties o'th'isle, that will not let you   124
        Believe things certain. Welcome, my friends all!
        [*Aside to Sebastian and Antonio*] But you, my brace of
                lords, were I so minded,   126
        I here could pluck His Highness' frown upon you
        And justify you traitors. At this time   128
        I will tell no tales.

SEBASTIAN   The devil speaks in him.

PROSPERO   No.
        [*To Antonio*] For you, most wicked sir, whom to call
                brother
        Would even infect my mouth, I do forgive
        Thy rankest fault—all of them; and require
        My dukedom of thee, which perforce I know
        Thou must restore.

ALONSO   If thou be'st Prospero,
        Give us particulars of thy preservation,
        How thou hast met us here, whom three hours since   136
        Were wrecked upon this shore; where I have lost—
        How sharp the point of this remembrance is!—
        My dear son Ferdinand.

PROSPERO   I am woe for't, sir.   139

ALONSO
        Irreparable is the loss, and Patience
        Says it is past her cure.

PROSPERO   I rather think
        You have not sought her help, of whose soft grace
        For the like loss I have her sovereign aid   143
        And rest myself content.

ALONSO   You the like loss?

PROSPERO
        As great to me as late, and supportable   145
        To make the dear loss, have I means much weaker   146
        Than you may call to comfort you; for I   147
        Have lost my daughter.

ALONSO   A daughter?
        O heavens, that they were living both in Naples,

---

74 pinched punished, afflicted   **76 remorse and nature** pity and natural feeling.   **whom** you who   **81 reasonable shore** shores of reason, i.e., minds. (Their reason returns, like the incoming tide.)
85 discase disrobe   **86 As . . . Milan** in my former appearance as
Duke of Milan.   **90 couch** lie   **92 After summer** following summer
as it moves to various parts of the world   **96 So, so, so** (Expresses
approval of Ariel's help as valet.)   **101 presently** immediately
103 Or ere before   **106 fearful** frightening   **112 trifle** trick of magic.
abuse deceive   **113 late** lately

116 crave require   **117 An . . . all** if this is actually happening.   **story**
i.e., explanation.   **118 Thy . . . resign** (Alonso made arrangement
with Antonio at the time of Prospero's banishment for Milan to pay
tribute to Naples; see 1.2.113–27.)   **119 wrongs** wrongdoings.
121 thine age your venerable self   **124 subtleties** illusions, magical
powers. (Playing on the idea of "pastries, concoctions.")   **126 brace**
pair   **128 justify you** prove you to be   **136 whom** we who   **139 woe**
sorry   **143 sovereign** efficacious   **145 late** recent   **145–7 and supportable . . . you** and I have much weaker means to make my loss
supportable than you can call upon to comfort you

The king and queen there! That they were, I wish 151
Myself were mudded in that oozy bed 152
Where my son lies. When did you lose your daughter? 153
PROSPERO
In this last tempest. I perceive these lords
At this encounter do so much admire 155
That they devour their reason and scarce think 156
Their eyes do offices of truth, their words 157
Are natural breath. But, howsoever you have 158
Been jostled from your senses, know for certain
That I am Prospero and that very duke
Which was thrust forth of Milan, who most strangely 161
Upon this shore, where you were wrecked, was
  landed
To be the lord on't. No more yet of this,
For 'tis a chronicle of day by day, 164
Not a relation for a breakfast nor
Befitting this first meeting. Welcome, sir.
This cell's my court. Here have I few attendants,
And subjects none abroad. Pray you, look in. 168
My dukedom since you have given me again,
I will requite you with as good a thing, 170
At least bring forth a wonder to content ye
As much as me my dukedom. 172

Here Prospero discovers Ferdinand and Miranda,
playing at chess.

MIRANDA   Sweet lord, you play me false. 173
FERDINAND   No, my dearest love,
I would not for the world.
MIRANDA
Yes, for a score of kingdoms you should wrangle, 176
And I would call it fair play.
ALONSO   If this prove 177
A vision of the island, one dear son 178
Shall I twice lose.
SEBASTIAN   A most high miracle!
FERDINAND [*approaching his father*]
Though the seas threaten, they are merciful;
I have cursed them without cause.   [*He kneels.*]
ALONSO   Now all the blessings
Of a glad father compass thee about! 182
Arise, and say how thou cam'st here.
                            [*Ferdinand rises.*]
MIRANDA   Oh, wonder!
How many goodly creatures are there here!
How beauteous mankind is! Oh, brave new world 185

That has such people in't!
PROSPERO   'Tis new to thee.
ALONSO
What is this maid with whom thou wast at play?
Your eld'st acquaintance cannot be three hours. 188
Is she the goddess that hath severed us,
And brought us thus together?
FERDINAND   Sir, she is mortal;
But by immortal Providence she's mine.
I chose her when I could not ask my father
For his advice, nor thought I had one. She
Is daughter to this famous Duke of Milan,
Of whom so often I have heard renown,
But never saw before; of whom I have
Received a second life; and second father
This lady makes him to me.
ALONSO   I am hers.
But oh, how oddly will it sound that I
Must ask my child forgiveness!
PROSPERO   There, sir, stop.
Let us not burden our remembrances with
A heaviness that's gone.
GONZALO   I have inly wept, 202
Or should have spoke ere this. Look down, you gods,
And on this couple drop a blessèd crown!
For it is you that have chalked forth the way 205
Which brought us hither.
ALONSO   I say amen, Gonzalo!
GONZALO
Was Milan thrust from Milan, that his issue 207
Should become kings of Naples? Oh, rejoice
Beyond a common joy, and set it down
With gold on lasting pillars: in one voyage
Did Claribel her husband find at Tunis,
And Ferdinand, her brother, found a wife
Where he himself was lost; Prospero his dukedom
In a poor isle; and all of us ourselves 214
When no man was his own.
ALONSO [*to Ferdinand and Miranda*] Give me your hands. 215
Let grief and sorrow still embrace his heart 216
That doth not wish you joy!
GONZALO   Be it so! Amen!

Enter Ariel, with the Master and Boatswain
amazedly following.

Oh, look, sir, look, sir! Here is more of us.
I prophesied, if a gallows were on land,
This fellow could not drown.—Now, blasphemy, 220
That swear'st grace o'erboard, not an oath on shore? 221
Hast thou no mouth by land? What is the news?
BOATSWAIN
The best news is that we have safely found

151–3 **That . . . lies** I would wish myself buried in that muddy bed where my son's body lies drowned if that would somehow make them alive and reigning in Naples.   155 **admire** wonder   156 **devour their reason** i.e., are openmouthed, dumbfounded   156–8 **and scarce . . . breath** and scarcely can believe their eyes or their own words.   161 **of** from   164 **of day by day** requiring days to tell, or covering a long span of time   168 **abroad** anywhere else.   170 **requite** repay   172.1 *discovers* i.e., by opening a curtain, presumably rearstage   173 **play me false** cheat.   176–7 **Yes . . . play** i.e., Yes, even if we were playing for twenty kingdoms, something less than the whole world, you would still press your advantage against me, and I would lovingly let you do it as though it were fair play.   178 **vision** illusion   182 **compass** encompass, embrace   185 **brave** splendid, gorgeously appareled, handsome

188 **eld'st** longest   202 **heaviness** sadness.   **inly** inwardly   205 **chalked . . . way** marked as with a piece of chalk the pathway   207 **Was Milan** Was the Duke of Milan.   **issue** offspring   214–15 **all . . . own** all of us have found ourselves and our sanity when we all had lost our senses.   216 **still** always.   **his** that person's   220 **blasphemy** i.e., blasphemer   221 **That swear'st grace o'erboard** i.e., you who expel heavenly grace from the ship by your blasphemies.   **not an oath** aren't you going to swear an oath

Our King and company; the next, our ship—
Which, but three glasses since, we gave out split— 225
Is tight and yare and bravely rigged as when 226
We first put out to sea.
ARIEL [*aside to Prospero*]   Sir, all this service
Have I done since I went.
PROSPERO [*aside to Ariel*]   My tricksy spirit! 228
ALONSO
These are not natural events; they strengthen 229
From strange to stranger. Say, how came you hither?
BOATSWAIN
If I did think, sir, I were well awake,
I'd strive to tell you. We were dead of sleep, 232
And—how we know not—all clapped under hatches,
Where but even now, with strange and several noises 234
Of roaring, shrieking, howling, jingling chains,
And more diversity of sounds, all horrible,
We were awaked; straightway at liberty;
Where we, in all her trim, freshly beheld
Our royal, good, and gallant ship, our Master
Cap'ring to eye her. On a trice, so please you, 240
Even in a dream, were we divided from them 241
And were brought moping hither.
ARIEL [*aside to Prospero*]   Was't well done? 242
PROSPERO [*aside to Ariel*]
Bravely, my diligence. Thou shalt be free.
ALONSO
This is as strange a maze as e'er men trod,
And there is in this business more than nature
Was ever conduct of. Some oracle 246
Must rectify our knowledge.
PROSPERO   Sir, my liege,
Do not infest your mind with beating on 248
The strangeness of this business. At picked leisure, 249
Which shall be shortly, single I'll resolve you, 250
Which to you shall seem probable, of every 251
These happened accidents; till when, be cheerful 252
And think of each thing well. [*Aside to Ariel*] Come
hither, spirit. 253
Set Caliban and his companions free.
Untie the spell.   [*Exit Ariel.*]
[*To Alonso*]   How fares my gracious sir?
There are yet missing of your company
Some few odd lads that you remember not. 257

Enter Ariel, driving in Caliban, Stephano, and
Trinculo, in their stolen apparel.

STEPHANO   Every man shift for all the rest, and let no 258
man take care for himself; for all is but fortune. *Corag-* 259

gio, bully monster, *coraggio!* 260
TRINCULO   If these be true spies which I wear in my 261
head, here's a goodly sight.
CALIBAN
O Setebos, these be brave spirits indeed! 263
How fine my master is! I am afraid 264
He will chastise me.
SEBASTIAN   Ha, ha!
What things are these, my lord Antonio?
Will money buy 'em?
ANTONIO   Very like. One of them
Is a plain fish, and no doubt marketable.
PROSPERO
Mark but the badges of these men, my lords, 270
Then say if they be true. This misshapen knave, 271
His mother was a witch, and one so strong
That could control the moon, make flows and ebbs,
And deal in her command without her power. 274
These three have robbed me, and this demidevil—
For he's a bastard one—had plotted with them 276
To take my life. Two of these fellows you
Must know and own. This thing of darkness I 278
Acknowledge mine.
CALIBAN   I shall be pinched to death.
ALONSO
Is not this Stephano, my drunken butler?
SEBASTIAN   He is drunk now. Where had he wine?
ALONSO
And Trinculo is reeling ripe. Where should they 282
Find this grand liquor that hath gilded 'em? 283
[*To Trinculo*] How cam'st thou in this pickle? 284
TRINCULO   I have been in such a pickle since I saw you
last that, I fear me, will never out of my bones. I shall
not fear flyblowing. 287
SEBASTIAN   Why, how now, Stephano?
STEPHANO   Oh, touch me not! I am not Stephano, but a
cramp.
PROSPERO   You'd be king o'the isle, sirrah? 291
STEPHANO   I should have been a sore one, then. 292
ALONSO [*pointing to Caliban*]
This is a strange thing as e'er I looked on.
PROSPERO
He is as disproportioned in his manners
As in his shape.—Go, sirrah, to my cell.
Take with you your companions. As you look
To have my pardon, trim it handsomely. 297

225 glasses hourglasses. gave out split reported shipwrecked, gave up for lost 226 yare ready. bravely splendidly 228 tricksy ingenious, sportive 229 strengthen increase 232 dead of sleep deep in sleep 234 several diverse 240 Cap'ring to eye dancing for joy to see. On a trice In an instant 241 them i.e., the other crew members 242 moping in a daze 246 conduct director 248 infest harass, disturb. beating on worrying about 249 picked chosen, convenient 250 single privately. resolve satisfy, explain to 251 probable plausible 251–2 of every These about every one of these 252 accidents occurrences 253 well favorably. 257 odd unaccounted for 258–9 Every . . . himself (Stephano drunkenly inverts the saying "Every man for himself.")

259–60 Coraggio . . . monster Have courage, gallant monster 261 true spies accurate observers (i.e., sharp eyes) 263 brave handsome 264 fine splendidly attired 270 badges emblems worn by servants to indicate whom they serve 271 say . . . true say if they are worthy and loyal servants. 274 And . . . power and usurp the moon's command (over tides) without her authority. (Sycorax could control the moon and hence the tides.) 276 bastard counterfeit 278 own acknowledge. 282 reeling ripe staggeringly drunk. 283 gilded 'em flushed their complexion (from the drink), giving them a ruddy or gilded appearance. 284 pickle (1) fix, predicament (2) pickling brine (in this case, horse urine). 287 flyblowing i.e., being fouled by fly eggs (from which he is saved by being pickled). 291 sirrah (Standard form of address to an inferior, here expressing reprimand.) 292 sore (1) tyrannical (2) sorry, inept (3) wracked by pain 297 trim prepare, decorate

CALIBAN
Ay, that I will; and I'll be wise hereafter
And seek for grace. What a thrice-double ass   299
Was I to take this drunkard for a god
And worship this dull fool!

PROSPERO   Go to. Away!

ALONSO
Hence, and bestow your luggage where you found it.

SEBASTIAN   Or stole it, rather.

                [*Exeunt Caliban, Stephano, and Trinculo.*]

PROSPERO
Sir, I invite Your Highness and your train
To my poor cell, where you shall take your rest
For this one night; which, part of it, I'll waste   306
With such discourse as, I not doubt, shall make it
Go quick away: the story of my life,
And the particular accidents gone by   309
Since I came to this isle. And in the morn
I'll bring you to your ship, and so to Naples,
Where I have hope to see the nuptial
Of these our dear-belovèd solemnized;
And thence retire me to my Milan, where
Every third thought shall be my grave.

ALONSO   I long
To hear the story of your life, which must
Take the ear strangely.

PROSPERO   I'll deliver all;   317
And promise you calm seas, auspicious gales,
And sail so expeditious that shall catch   319
Your royal fleet far off. [*Aside to Ariel*] My Ariel, chick,   320

299 **grace** pardon, favor.   306 **waste** spend   309 **accidents** occurrences   317 **Take** take effect upon, enchant.   **deliver** declare, relate   319–20 **catch . . . far off** enable you to catch up with the main part of your royal fleet, now afar off en route to Naples. (See 1.2.235–6.)

That is thy charge. Then to the elements
Be free, and fare thou well!
                [*To the others*] Please you, draw near. 322
                Exeunt omnes [*except Prospero*].

Epilogue   *Spoken by* PROSPERO.

Now my charms are all o'erthrown,
And what strength I have 's mine own,
Which is most faint. Now, 'tis true,
I must be here confined by you
Or sent to Naples. Let me not,
Since I have my dukedom got
And pardoned the deceiver, dwell
In this bare island by your spell,
But release me from my bands   9
With the help of your good hands.   10
Gentle breath of yours my sails   11
Must fill, or else my project fails,
Which was to please. Now I want   13
Spirits to enforce, art to enchant,
And my ending is despair,
Unless I be relieved by prayer,   16
Which pierces so that it assaults   17
Mercy itself, and frees all faults.   18
As you from crimes would pardoned be,   19
Let your indulgence set me free.   *Exit.* 20

322 **draw near** i.e., enter my cell.
Epilogue.
9 **bands** bonds   10 **hands** i.e., applause (the noise of which could break a charm).   11 **Gentle breath** Favorable breeze (produced by hands clapping or favorable comment)   13 **want** lack   16 **prayer** i.e., Prospero's petition to the audience   17 **assaults** penetrates the heart of   18 **frees** obtains forgiveness for   19 **crimes** sins   20 **indulgence** (1) humoring, lenient approval (2) remission of punishment for sin

The Poems

Sonnets

Sonnets

Shakespeare seems to have cared more about his reputation as a lyric poet than as a dramatist. He contributed to the major nondramatic genres of his day: to amatory Ovidian narrative in *Venus and Adonis*, to the Complaint in *The Rape of Lucrece*, to philosophical poetry in "The Phoenix and Turtle." He cooperated in the publication of his first two important poems, dedicating them to the young Earl of Southampton with a plea to him for sponsorship. To write poetry in this vein was more fashionable than to write plays, which one did mainly for money.

A poet with ambitions of this sort simply had to write a sonnet sequence. Sonneteering was the rage in England in the early and mid 1590s. Based on the sonneteering tradition of Francesco Petrarch, Sir Thomas Wyatt, and others, and gaining new momentum in 1591 with the publication of Sir Philip Sidney's *Astrophel and Stella*, the vogue ended almost as suddenly as it began, in 1596 or 1597. The sonnet sequences of this brief period bear the names of most well-known and minor poets of the day: *Amoretti* by Edmund Spenser (1595), *Delia* by Samuel Daniel (1591 and 1592), *Caelica* by Fulke Greville (not published until 1633), *Idea's Mirror* by Michael Drayton (1594), *Diana* by Henry Constable (1592), *Phyllis* by Thomas Lodge (1593), and the more imitative sequences of Barnabe Barnes, Giles Fletcher, William Percy, Bartholomew Griffin, William Smith, and Robert Tofte.

Shakespeare wrote sonnets during the heyday of the genre, for in 1598 Francis Meres, in his *Palladis Tamia: Wit's Treasury*, praised Shakespeare's "sugared sonnets among his private friends." Even though they were not printed at the time, we know from Meres's remark that they were circulated in manuscript among the cognoscenti and commanded respect. Shakespeare may actually have preferred to delay the publication of his sonnets, not through indifference to their literary worth, but through a desire not to seem too professional. The "courtly makers" of the English Renaissance, those gentlemen whose chivalric accomplishments were supposed to include versifying, looked on the writing of poetry as an avocation designed to amuse one's peers or to court a lady. Publication was not quite genteel, and many such authors affected dismay when their verses were pirated into print. The young wits about London of the 1590s, whether aristocratic or not, sometimes imitated this fashion. Like young John Donne, they sought the favorable verdict of their fellow wits at the Inns of Court (where young men studied law) and professed not to care about wider recognition. Whether Shakespeare was motivated in this way we do not know, but, in any event, his much-sought-after sonnet sequence was not published until 1609, long after the vogue had passed. The publisher, Thomas Thorpe, seems not to have obtained Shakespeare's authorization. Two sonnets, numbers 138 and 144, had been pirated ten years earlier by William Jaggard in *The Passionate Pilgrim*, 1599, a little anthology with some poems by Shakespeare and some wrongly attributed to him. The sonnets were not reprinted until 1640, either because the sonnet vogue had passed or because Thorpe's edition had been suppressed.

The unexplained circumstances of publication have given rise to a host of vexing and apparently unanswerable questions. Probably no puzzle in all English literature has provoked so much speculation and produced so little agreement. To whom are the sonnets addressed? Do they tell a consistent story, and, if so, do they tell us anything about Shakespeare's life? The basic difficulty is that we cannot be sure that the order in which Thorpe published the sonnets represents Shakespeare's intention, nor can we assume that Thorpe spoke for Shakespeare when he dedicated the sonnets to "Mr. W. H." As they stand, most of the first 126 sonnets appear to be addressed in warm friendship to a handsome young aristocrat, whereas sonnets 127–52 mostly speak of the poet's dark-haired mistress. Yet the last two sonnets, 153–4, seem unrelated to anything previous and cast some doubt on the reliability of the ordering. Within each large grouping of the sonnets, moreover, we find evident inconsistencies: jealousies disappear and suddenly reappear, the poet bewails his absolute rejection by the friend and then speaks a few sonnets later of harmonious affection as though nothing had happened, and so on. Some sonnets are closely linked to their predecessors; some are apparently disconnected (although even here we must allow for the real possibility that Shakespeare intends juxtaposition and contrast). We cannot be sure if the friend of sonnets 1–126 is really one person or several. We can only speculate that the unhappy love triangle described in sonnets 40–2, in which the friend has usurped the poet's mistress, can be identified with the love triangle of the "Dark Lady" sonnets, 127–52. Most readers sense a narrative continuity of the whole yet find blocks of sonnets stubbornly out of place. The temptation to rearrange the order has proved irresistible, but no alternative order has ever won acceptance. The consensus is that Thorpe's order is at times suspect but may have more rationale than at first appears. It is, in any case, the only authoritative order we have.

No less frustrating is Thorpe's dedication "To the Only Begetter of These Ensuing Sonnets, Mr. W. H." Given the late and unauthorized publication, we cannot assume that Thorpe speaks for Shakespeare. Quite possibly he is only thanking the person who obtained the sonnets for him, making publication possible. Mundanely enough, Mr. W. H. could be William Hall, an associate of Thorpe's in the publishing business. Yet Elizabethan usage affords few instances of "begetter" in this sense of "obtainer." Donald Foster has offered new and persuasive arguments for the idea that "Mr. W. H." is only a typographical error of a common sort and that Thorpe meant to say "Mr. W. S.," Master William Shakespeare. In this case, "begetter" would mean simply "creator." This solution has a wonderful neatness about it, but other readers have wondered if it answers the seeming contradiction when Thorpe speaks of "Mr. W. H." and "our ever-living poet" in the dedication as though they are two people. Thorpe offers to Mr. W. H. "that eternity promised by our ever-living poet," as though Mr. W. H. were the very subject of those sonnets whom Shakespeare vows to immortalize.

This interpretation of "begetter" as "inspirer" has prompted many enthusiasts to search for a Mr. W. H. in Shakespeare's life, a nobleman who befriended him. The chief candidates are two. First is the young Earl of Southampton, to whom Shakespeare had dedicated *Venus and Adonis* and *The Rape of Lucrece*. The dedication to the second of these poems bespeaks a warmth and gratitude that had been less evident in the first. The Earl's name, Henry Wriothesley, yields initials that are the reverse of W. H. If this correspondence seems unconvincing, W. H. could stand for Sir William Harvey, third husband of Mary, Lady Southampton, the young Earl's

mother. Some researchers would have us believe that Shakespeare wrote the sonnets for Lady Southampton, especially those urging a young man (her son) to marry and procreate. This entire case is speculative, however, and we have no evidence that Shakespeare had any dealings with Southampton after *The Rape of Lucrece*. The plain ascription "Mr. W. H." seems an oddly uncivil way for Thorpe to have addressed an earl. If meant for Southampton, the sonnets must have been written fairly early in the 1590s, for they give no hint of Southampton's later career: his courtship of Elizabeth Vernon, her pregnancy and their secret marriage in 1598, and his later involvement in Essex's Irish campaign and abortive uprising against Queen Elizabeth. Those literary sleuths who stress similarities to the Southampton relationship are too willing to overlook dissimilarities.

The next chief candidate for Mr. W. H. is William Herbert, third Earl of Pembroke, to whom, along with his brother, Shakespeare's colleagues dedicated the First Folio of 1623. In 1595, Pembroke's parents were attempting to arrange his marriage with Lady Elizabeth Carey, granddaughter of the first Lord Hunsdon, who was Lord Chamberlain and patron of Shakespeare's company. In 1597, another alliance was attempted with Bridget Vere, granddaughter of Lord Burghley. In both negotiations, young Pembroke objected to the girl in question. This hypothesis requires, however, an uncomfortably late date for the sonnets and postulates a gap in age between Shakespeare and Pembroke that would have afforded little opportunity for genuine friendship. Pembroke was only fifteen in 1595; Shakespeare was thirty-one. Besides, no evidence supports the claim other than historical coincidence. The common initials W. H. can be made to produce other candidates as well, such as the Lincolnshire lawyer named William Hatcliffe proposed (to no one's satisfaction) by Leslie Hotson. Hotson wants to date most of the sonnets before 1589, since Hatcliffe came to London in 1587–1588. When such speculations are constructed on the single enigmatic testimonial of the dedication by Thomas Thorpe, who may well have had no connection with Shakespeare, we are left with a case that would not be worth describing had it not captured the imagination of so many researchers.

Biographical identifications have also been proposed for the various personages in the sonnet sequence, predictably with no better success. The rival poet, with "the proud full sail of his great verse" (sonnet 86), has been linked to Christopher Marlowe (who died in 1593), George Chapman, and others. The sequence gives us little to go on, other than that the rival poet possesses a considerable enough talent to intimidate the author of the sonnets and to ingratiate himself with the author's aristocratic friend. No biographical circumstances resembling this rivalry have come to light. Various candidates have also been found for the "Dark Lady." One is Mary

Fitton, a lady-in-waiting at court who bore a child by Pembroke in 1601. Again, we have no evidence that Shakespeare knew her, nor is he likely to have carried on an affair with one of such high rank. A. L. Rowse has proposed Emilia Lanier, wife of Alfonso Lanier and daughter of a court musician named Bassano, a woman of suitably dark complexion perhaps but whose presumed connection with Shakespeare rests only on the reported rumor that she was a mistress of Lord Hunsdon. We are left finally without knowing who any of these people were, or whether indeed Shakespeare was attempting to be biographical at all.

The same irresolution afflicts the dating of the sonnets. Do they give hints of a personal chronicle extending over some years, following Thorpe's arrangement of the sonnets or some alternative order? Sonnet 104 speaks of three years having elapsed since the poet met his friend. Are there other signposts that relate to contemporary events? A line in sonnet 107 ("The mortal moon hath her eclipse endured") is usually linked to the death of Queen Elizabeth (known as Diana or Cynthia) in 1603, though Leslie Hotson prefers to see in it an allusion to the Spanish Armada, shaped for sea battle in a moonlike crescent when it met defeat in 1588. The newly built pyramids in sonnet 123 remind Hotson of the obelisks built by Pope Sixtus V in Rome, 1586–1589; other researchers have discovered pyramids erected on London's streets in 1603 to celebrate the coronation of James I. As these illustrations suggest, speculative dating can be used to support a hypothesis of early or late composition. The wary consensus of most scholars is that the sonnets were written over a number of years; a large number, certainly, before 1598, but some perhaps later and even up to the date of publication in 1609.

However fruitless this quest for nonexistent certainties, it does at least direct us to a meaningful critical question: should we expect sonnets of this "personal" nature to be at least partly autobiographical? Shakespeare's sonnets have struck many readers as cries from the heart, voicing at times fears of rejection, self-hatred, and humiliation, and at other times a serene gratitude for reciprocated affection. This power of expression may, however, be a tribute to Shakespeare's dramatic gift rather than evidence of personal involvement. Earlier sonnet sequences, both Elizabethan and pre-Elizabethan, had established a variety of artistic conventions that tended to displace biography. Petrarch's famous *Rime*, or sonnets, later collected in his *Canzoniere*, though addressed to Laura in two sequences (during her life and after her death), idealized her into the unapproachable lady worshiped by the self-abasing and miserable lover. Petrarch's imitators—Serafino Aquilano, Pietro Bembo, Ludovico Ariosto, and Torquato Tasso among the Italians, Clement Marot, Joachim du Bellay, Pierre de Ronsard, and Philippe Desportes among the French Pléiade—reworked these

conventions in countless variations. In England, the fashion was taken up by Sir Thomas Wyatt, the Earl of Surrey, George Gascoigne, Thomas Watson, and others. Spenser's *Amoretti* and Sidney's *Astrophel and Stella*, though inspired at least in part by real women in the poets' lives, are also deeply concerned with theories of writing poetry. Rejection of the stereotyped attitudes and relationships that had come to dominate the typical Petrarchan sonnet sequence is evidence not of biographical literalism in art but of a new insistence on lifelike emotion in art; as Sidney's muse urges him, "look in thy heart and write." Thus, both the Petrarchan and the anti-Petrarchan schools avoid biographical writing for its own sake. This is essentially true of all Elizabethan sonneteering, from Drayton's serious pursuit of platonic abstraction in his *Idea's Mirror* to the facile chorusing of lesser sonnet writers about Diana, Phyllis, Zepheria, or Fidessa.

The "story" connecting the individual poems of an Elizabethan sonnet sequence is never very important or consistent, even when we can be sure of the order in which the sonnets were written. Dante had used prose links in his *La Vita Nuova* (c. 1282) to stress narrative continuity, and so had Petrarch, but this sturdy framework had been abandoned by the late sixteenth century. Rather than telling a chronological story, the typical Elizabethan sonnet sequence offers a thematically connected series of lyrical meditations, chiefly on love but also on poetic theory, the adversities of fortune, death, or what have you. The narrative events mentioned from time to time are not the substance of the sequence but the occasion for meditative reflection. Attitudes need not be consistent throughout, and the characters need not be consistently motivated like dramatis personae in a play.

Shakespeare's sonnet sequence retains these conventions of Elizabethan sonneteering and employs many archetypal situations and themes that had been explored by his predecessors and contemporaries. His emphasis on friendship seems new, for no other sequence addressed a majority of its sonnets to a friend rather than to a mistress, but even here the anti-Petrarchan quest for spontaneity and candor is in the best Elizabethan tradition of Sidney and Spenser. Besides, the exaltation of friendship over love was itself a widespread Neoplatonic commonplace recently popularized in the writings of John Lyly. Shakespeare's sequence makes use of the structural design found in contemporary models. Even though we cannot reconstruct a rigorously consistent chronological narrative from the sonnets, we can discern overall patterns out of which the poet's emotional crises arise and upon which he constructs his meditative lyrics. Certain groupings, such as the sonnets addressed to the "Dark Lady," 127–52, in which individually they comment on one another through reinforcement or antithetical design and are thus enhanced by their context, achieve a plausible cohesion; a case can be made, in other words, for the order of the poems as Thorpe printed them. Even the last two sonnets, 153 and 154, have their defenders (see Michael J. B. Allen's essay in *Shakespeare Survey*, 1978). Juxtaposition is a favorite technique in Shakespeare's plays, and we must remember that he alone among the major Elizabethan sonneteers wrote for the stage.

Taking note of such considerations, we can account for most of the situations portrayed in Shakespeare's sonnets by postulating four figures: the poet-speaker himself, his friend, his mistress, and a rival poet. The order of events in this tangled relationship is not what the poet wishes to describe; instead, he touches upon this situation from time to time as he explores his own reaction to love in its various aspects.

The poet's relationship to his friend is a vulnerable one. This friend to whom he writes is aristocratic, handsome, and younger than he is. The poet is beholden to this friend as a sponsor and must consider himself as subservient, no matter how deep their mutual affection. Even at its happiest, their relationship is hierarchical. The poet abases himself in order to extol his friend's beauty and virtues (sonnets 52–4, 105–6). He confesses that his love would be idolatry, except that the friend's goodness excels all poetic hyperbole. As the older of the two, the poet sententiously urges his young friend to marry and eternize his beauty through the engendering of children (sonnets 1–17). Such a course, he argues, is the surest way to conquer devouring Time, the enemy of all earthly beauty and love. Yet elsewhere the poet exalts his own art as the surest defense against Time (sonnets 55, 60, 63–5, etc.). These conclusions are nominally contradictory, offering procreation in one instance and poetry in another as the best hope for immortality, but thematically the two are obviously related. In even the happiest of the sonnets, such as those giving thanks for "the marriage of true minds" (116, 123), the consciousness of devouring Time is inescapable. If love and celebratory poetry can sometimes triumph over Time, the victory is all the more precious because it is achieved in the face of such odds.

Love and perfect friendship are a refuge for the poet faced with hostile fortune and an indifferent world. He is too often "in disgrace with fortune and men's eyes" (sonnet 29), oppressed by his own failings, saddened by the facile success of opportunists (sonnets 66–8), ashamed of having sold himself cheap in his own profession (sonnets 110–11). If taken biographically, this could mean that Shakespeare was not happy about his career as actor and playwright, but the motif makes complete sense in the sonnet sequence without resort to biography. A biographical reading also raises the question of homosexual attraction, as urged by Joseph Pequigney in his *Such Is My Love* (University of Chicago Press, 1985). The bawdy reference in sonnet 20.12 to the friend's possession of "one thing to my purpose nothing" would seem to militate against the idea of a consummated homosexual relation-

ship, while conversely many sonnets (such as 138) do point to the poet's consummation with his mistress. Still, the bond between poet and friend is extraordinarily strong, and certainly there is a danger that traditional scholarship has minimized the erotic bond between the poet and his friend out of a distaste for the idea. Occasional absences torture the poet with the physical separation, even though he realizes that pure love of the spirit ought not to be hampered by distance or time (sonnets 43–51). The absence is especially painful when the poet must confess his own disloyalty (sonnets 117–18). The chronology of these absences cannot be worked out satisfactorily, but the haunting theme of separation is incessant and overwhelming. By extension, it includes the fear of separation through death (sonnets 71–3, 126). The concern with absence is closely related to the poet's obsession with devouring Time.

All the poet's misfortunes would be bearable if love were constant, but his dependency on the aristocratic friend leaves him at the mercy of that friend's changeable moods. The poet must not complain when his wellborn friend entertains a rival poet (sonnets 78–86) or forms other emotional attachments, even with the poet's own mistress (sonnets 40–2). These disloyalties evoke outbursts of jealousy. The poet vacillates between forgiveness and recrimination. Sometimes even his forgiveness is self-loathing, in which the poet confesses he would take back the friend on any terms (sonnets 93–5). At times the poet grovels, conceding that he deserves no better treatment (sonnets 57–8), but at other times his stored-up resentment bursts forth (sonnets 93–5). The poet's fears, though presented in no clear chronological order, run the gamut from a fatalistic sense that rejection will come one day (sonnet 49) to an abject and bitter final farewell (sonnet 87). Sometimes he is tormented by jealousy (sonnet 61) and sometimes by self-hate (sonnets 88–9).

The sonnets addressed to the poet's mistress, the "Dark Lady," similarly convey fear, self-abasement, and a panicky awareness of loss of self-control. In rare moments of happiness, the poet praises her dark features as proof of her being a real woman, not a Petrarchan goddess (sonnet 130). Too often, however, her lack of ideal beauty reminds the poet of his irrational enchantment (sonnets 148–50). She is tyrannous, disdainful, spiteful, disloyal, a "female evil" (sonnet 144) who has tempted away from the poet his better self, his friend. The poet is distressed not so much by her perfidy as by his own self-betrayal; he sees bitterly that he offends his nobler reason by his attachment to the rebellious flesh. He worships what others abhor and perjures himself by swearing to what he knows to be false (sonnets 150–2). His only hope for escape is to punish his flesh and renounce the vanity of all worldly striving (sonnet 146), but this solution evades him as he plunges helplessly back into the perverse enslavement of a sickened appetite.

This sketch of only some themes of the sequence may suggest the range and yet the interconnection of Shakespeare's meditations on love, friendship, and poetry. Patterns are visible, even if the exact chronology (never important in the Elizabethan sonnet sequence) cannot be determined. The pattern suggests a pivotal role for the sonnets in Shakespeare's development, as Richard Wheeler has urged in his *Shakespeare's Development* (University of California Press, 1981): the early sonnets about love and marriage pursue relationships central to the comedies, whereas subsequent sonnets move with increasing intensity toward the portrayal of promiscuity and degradation in erotic love and toward new assaults upon the binding power of friendship in such a way as to anticipate the darker vision of the tragedies. The playful and unthreatening heroine of the comedies gives way to a dark lady who inspires in the poet a compulsive and humiliating self-hatred; mutuality in friendship finds itself threatened by a one-sided relationship in which the abasement of the poet is answered by the indifference and infidelity of the friend. It is as though in the sonnets Shakespeare opened the Pandora's box of hazardous erotic entanglements he was to dramatize in his late plays.

Shakespeare's concern with patterning is equally evident in matters of versification and imagery. The sonnets are written throughout in the "Shakespearean" or English form, *abab cdcd efef gg.* (Sonnet 126, written entirely in couplets, is an exception, perhaps because it was intended as the envoi to the series addressed to the poet's friend.) This familiar sonnet form, introduced by Wyatt and developed by Sidney, differs markedly from the octave-sestet division of the Petrarchan, or Italian, sonnet. The English form of three quatrains and a concluding couplet lends itself to a step-by-step development of idea and image, culminating in an epigrammatic two-line conclusion that may summarize the thought of the preceding twelve lines or give a sententious interpretation of the images developed up to this point. Sonnet 7 pursues the image of the sun at morning, noon, and evening through three quatrains, one for each phase of the day, and then in the couplet "applies" the image to the friend's unwillingness to beget children. Sonnet 29 moves from resentment of misfortune to a rejoicing in the friend's love and rhetorically mirrors this sudden elevation of mood in the image of the lark "at break of day arising / From sullen earth." Shakespeare's rhetorical and imagistic devices exploit the sonnet structure he inherited and perfected, and remind us again of the strong element of convention and artifice in these supremely "personal" sonnets. The recurring images—the canker on the rose, the pleading of a case at law, the seasonal rhythms of summer and winter, the alternations of day and night, the harmonies and dissonances of music—also testify to the artistic unity of the whole and to the artist's extraordinary discipline in evoking a sense of helpless loss of self-control.

Sonnets

To the Only Begetter of These Ensuing Sonnets

Mr. W. H.

All Happiness and That Eternity Promised
   by Our Ever-living Poet
Wisheth the Well-wishing Adventurer in
   Setting Forth

                          T. T.

1

From fairest creatures we desire increase,   1
That thereby beauty's rose might never die,
But as the riper should by time decease,   3
His tender heir might bear his memory;   4
But thou, contracted to thine own bright eyes,   5
Feed'st thy light's flame with self-substantial fuel,   6
Making a famine where abundance lies,
Thyself thy foe, to thy sweet self too cruel.
Thou that art now the world's fresh ornament
And only herald to the gaudy spring,   10
Within thine own bud buriest thy content,   11
And, tender churl, mak'st waste in niggarding.   12
    Pity the world, or else this glutton be:
    To eat the world's due, by the grave and thee.   14

2

When forty winters shall besiege thy brow
And dig deep trenches in thy beauty's field,   2

Thy youth's proud livery, so gazed on now,   3
Will be a tattered weed, of small worth held.   4
Then being asked where all thy beauty lies,
Where all the treasure of thy lusty days,   6
To say within thine own deep-sunken eyes
Were an all-eating shame and thriftless praise.   8
How much more praise deserved thy beauty's use   9
If thou couldst answer, "This fair child of mine
Shall sum my count and make my old excuse,"   11
Proving his beauty by succession thine.   12
    This were to be new made when thou art old,   13
    And see thy blood warm when thou feel'st it cold.

3

Look in thy glass, and tell the face thou viewest   1
Now is the time that face should form another,
Whose fresh repair if now thou not renewest   3
Thou dost beguile the world, unbless some mother.   4
For where is she so fair whose uneared womb   5
Disdains the tillage of thy husbandry?   6
Or who is he so fond will be the tomb   7
Of his self-love, to stop posterity?
Thou art thy mother's glass, and she in thee   9
Calls back the lovely April of her prime;
So thou through windows of thine age shalt see,   11
Despite of wrinkles, this thy golden time.   12
    But if thou live remembered not to be,   13
    Die single, and thine image dies with thee.

---

3 proud livery handsome garments **4 weed** garment. (With a play
on a *weed* growing in *beauty's field*, line 2.) **6 lusty** (1) vigorous
(2) lustful **8 Were . . . praise** would be a shameful admission of
gluttony and praise of idle extravagance. **9 deserved . . . use** would
the proper investment and employment of your beauty deserve
11 Shall . . . excuse will balance my account and make amends in my
old age **12 thine** derived from you. **13 were** would be
3.1 glass mirror **3 fresh repair** youthful condition **4 beguile** cheat.
unbless some mother withhold the happiness of childbearing from
some woman. **5 uneared** untilled, uncultivated **6 husbandry** cultivation. (With obvious suggestion of "playing the husband.") **7 fond**
foolish, (self-)loving. **will be** i.e., that he is willing to be **9 thy
mother's glass** the image of your mother **11–12 So . . . time** in just
the same way, you, looking through eyes dimmed by advancing
years, and despite your own wrinkles of age, will see in your child an
image of your own happy youth. **13 remembered not to be** in such
a way as not to be remembered, without children

1.1 increase procreation **3 as** just as, while **4 His** its, the ripening
creation (including the young man). **bear his memory** i.e., immortalize it by bearing its features **5 contracted** (1) engaged, espoused
(2) shrunk **6 self-substantial** of your own substance **10 only herald to** principal or unique messenger of **11 thy content** (1) that
which is contained in you; potential fatherhood (2) your contentment
12 mak'st . . . niggarding squander your substance by being miserly.
(An oxymoron, like *tender churl*, "youthful old miser.") **14 the
world's due** i.e., the offspring you owe to posterity. **by . . . thee**
(consumed) by death and by your willfully remaining childless.
2.2 trenches i.e., wrinkles. **field** (1) meadow (2) battlefield
(3) heraldic background

4

Unthrifty loveliness, why dost thou spend 1
Upon thyself thy beauty's legacy? 2
Nature's bequest gives nothing, but doth lend,
And being frank she lends to those are free. 4
Then, beauteous niggard, why dost thou abuse
The bounteous largess given thee to give?
Profitless usurer, why dost thou use 7
So great a sum of sums, yet canst not live? 8
For having traffic with thyself alone, 9
Thou of thyself thy sweet self dost deceive. 10
Then how, when Nature calls thee to be gone,
What acceptable audit canst thou leave?
   Thy unused beauty must be tombed with thee, 13
   Which, usèd, lives th'executor to be. 14

5

Those hours, that with gentle work did frame 1
The lovely gaze where every eye doth dwell, 2
Will play the tyrants to the very same 3
And that unfair which fairly doth excel; 4
For never-resting Time leads summer on 5
To hideous winter and confounds him there, 6
Sap checked with frost and lusty leaves quite gone, 7
Beauty o'ersnowed and bareness everywhere.
Then, were not summer's distillation left 9
A liquid prisoner pent in walls of glass, 10
Beauty's effect with beauty were bereft, 11
Nor it nor no remembrance what it was. 12
   But flowers distilled, though they with winter meet,
   Leese but their show; their substance still lives sweet. 14

6

Then let not winter's ragged hand deface 1
In thee thy summer ere thou be distilled.
Make sweet some vial; treasure thou some place 3
With beauty's treasure ere it be self-killed.
That use is not forbidden usury 5
Which happies those that pay the willing loan; 6
That's for thyself to breed another thee, 7

Or ten times happier, be it ten for one. 8
Ten times thyself were happier than thou art, 9
If ten of thine ten times refigured thee; 10
Then what could death do, if thou shouldst depart,
Leaving thee living in posterity?
   Be not self-willed, for thou art much too fair 13
   To be death's conquest and make worms thine heir.

7

Lo, in the orient when the gracious light 1
Lifts up his burning head, each under eye 2
Doth homage to his new-appearing sight,
Serving with looks his sacred majesty;
And having climbed the steep-up heavenly hill,
Resembling strong youth in his middle age,
Yet mortal looks adore his beauty still,
Attending on his golden pilgrimage;
But when from highmost pitch, with weary car, 9
Like feeble age, he reeleth from the day,
The eyes, 'fore duteous, now converted are 11
From his low tract and look another way. 12
   So thou, thyself outgoing in thy noon,
   Unlooked on diest, unless thou get a son. 14

8

Music to hear, why hear'st thou music sadly? 1
Sweets with sweets war not, joy delights in joy. 2
Why lov'st thou that which thou receiv'st not gladly, 3
Or else receiv'st with pleasure thine annoy? 4
If the true concord of well-tunèd sounds,
By unions married, do offend thine ear, 6
They do but sweetly chide thee, who confounds 7
In singleness the parts that thou shouldst bear. 8
Mark how one string, sweet husband to another, 9
Strikes each in each by mutual ordering, 10
Resembling sire and child and happy mother
Who, all in one, one pleasing note do sing;
   Whose speechless song, being many, seeming one, 13
   Sings this to thee: "Thou single wilt prove none." 14

4.1 Unthrifty (1) Prodigal (2) Unavailing   **2 thy beauty's legacy** the beauty you inherited (and should pass on to your children).   **4 frank** liberal, bounteous.   **are free** who are generous.   **7 use** (1) use up (2) fail to invest for profit. (See sonnet 6.5 and note.)   **8 live** (1) have a livelihood (2) live in your posterity.   **9 traffic** commerce. (The commercial and financial metaphor hints at sexual self-fascination.) **10 deceive** cheat.   **13 unused** (1) unemployed (2) not invested for profit   **14 lives** would live (in your son)
5.1 frame make   **2 gaze** object of gazes   **3 play . . . to** oppress **4 that unfair** make that unlovely.   **fairly** (1) in beauty (2) truly, honestly   **5 leads summer on** (1) guides the steps of summer (2) lures summer   **6 confounds** destroys   **7 lusty** vigorous   **9 summer's distillation** distilled perfume of flowers   **10 walls of glass** glass containers   **11 with . . . bereft** would be lost along with beauty itself **12 Nor it nor no** (leaving behind) neither it (beauty) nor any   **14 Leese** lose.   **still** (1) notwithstanding (2) always
6.1 ragged rough   **3 vial** (With suggestion of a womb.)   **treasure** enrich **5 use** lending money at interest   **6 happies** makes happy.   **pay . . . loan** willingly borrow on these terms and repay the loan   **7 That's . . . thee** i.e., such would be the case if you were to sire a child like you

8 Or . . . one i.e., or indeed the happy mother (of line 6) would be ten times happier were she to bear you ten children instead of one. (*Ten for one* alludes to the highest legal rate of interest, one for ten.) **9 Ten . . . art** i.e., Ten children of yours would be a tenfold blessing and would make you happier   **10 refigured** duplicated, copied (producing one hundred grandchildren)   **13 self-willed** (1) obstinate (2) bequeathed to self
7.1 orient east.   **light** i.e., sun   **2 under** earthly   **9 pitch** highest point (as of a falcon's flight before it attacks)   **car** chariot (of the sun-god)   **11 converted** turned away   **12 tract** course   **14 get** beget **8.1 Music to hear** i.e., You whom it is music to hear.   **2 Sweets** Sweet things   **3–4 Why . . . annoy?** Why do you not gladly love the sweet things you hear, or find irksome that which is pleasurable?   **6 By unions married** perfectly blended in harmonious chords   **7–8 who . . . bear** you who destroy, by playing a single part only, the harmony (i.e., marriage) that you should sustain.   **9 sweet husband** i.e., paired, as on the double strings of the lute, one string vibrating sympathetically to the other   **10 each in each** i.e., with double resonance, sounding mutually   **13 Whose** i.e., the strings'.   **being . . . one** i.e., making harmony out of several voices   **14 Thou . . . none** (Alludes to the proverb, "One is no number." The single person who dies without posterity leaves nothing of himself behind.)

9

Is it for fear to wet a widow's eye   1
That thou consum'st thyself in single life?
Ah, if thou issueless shalt hap to die,   3
The world will wail thee like a makeless wife.   4
The world will be thy widow and still weep   5
That thou no form of thee hast left behind,
When every private widow well may keep,   7
By children's eyes, her husband's shape in mind.   8
Look what an unthrift in the world doth spend   9
Shifts but his place, for still the world enjoys it;   10
But beauty's waste hath in the world an end,
And, kept unused, the user so destroys it.   12
    No love toward others in that bosom sits
    That on himself such murd'rous shame commits.

10

For shame, deny that thou bear'st love to any,
Who for thyself art so unprovident!
Grant, if thou wilt, thou art beloved of many,
But that thou none lov'st is most evident;
For thou art so possessed with murd'rous hate
That 'gainst thyself thou stick'st not to conspire,   6
Seeking that beauteous roof to ruinate   7
Which to repair should be thy chief desire.
Oh, change thy thought, that I may change my mind!   9
Shall hate be fairer lodged than gentle love?
Be, as thy presence is, gracious and kind,   11
Or to thyself at least kindhearted prove:
    Make thee another self, for love of me,
    That beauty still may live in thine or thee.

11

As fast as thou shalt wane, so fast thou grow'st   1
In one of thine from that which thou departest;   2
And that fresh blood which youngly thou bestow'st   3
Thou mayst call thine when thou from youth convertest.   4
Herein lives wisdom, beauty, and increase;
Without this, folly, age, and cold decay.
If all were minded so, the times should cease   7
And threescore year would make the world away.   8
Let those whom Nature hath not made for store,   9
Harsh, featureless, and rude, barrenly perish;   10

Look whom she best endowed she gave the more,   11
Which bounteous gift thou shouldst in bounty cherish.
    She carved thee for her seal, and meant thereby   13
    Thou shouldst print more, not let that copy die.

12

When I do count the clock that tells the time,   1
And see the brave day sunk in hideous night;   2
When I behold the violet past prime,
And sable curls all silvered o'er with white;   4
When lofty trees I see barren of leaves
Which erst from heat did canopy the herd,   6
And summer's green, all girded up in sheaves,   7
Borne on the bier with white and bristly beard,   8
Then of thy beauty do I question make   9
That thou among the wastes of time must go,
Since sweets and beauties do themselves forsake
And die as fast as they see others grow;
    And nothing 'gainst Time's scythe can make defense
    Save breed, to brave him when he takes thee hence.   14

13

Oh, that you were yourself! But, love, you are   1
No longer yours than you yourself here live.   2
Against this coming end you should prepare,   3
And your sweet semblance to some other give.
So should that beauty which you hold in lease
Find no determination; then you were   6
Yourself again after yourself's decease,
When your sweet issue your sweet form should bear.
Who lets so fair a house fall to decay,
Which husbandry in honor might uphold   10
Against the stormy gusts of winter's day
And barren rage of death's eternal cold?
    Oh, none but unthrifts! Dear my love, you know
    You had a father; let your son say so.

14

Not from the stars do I my judgment pluck,   1
And yet methinks I have astronomy—   2
But not to tell of good or evil luck,
Of plagues, of dearths, or seasons' quality;   4
Nor can I fortune to brief minutes tell,   5
'Pointing to each his thunder, rain, and wind,   6

9.1 **Is . . . eye** Is it for fear of eventually leaving some woman a grieving widow when you die   3 **issueless** without offspring   4 **makeless** mateless, widowed   5 **still** constantly, always   7 **private** individual, as distinguished from the whole world   8 **By** by means of   9 **Look what** Whatever.   **unthrift** spendthrift   10 **his** its.   **enjoys** uses, keeps in circulation   12 **user** i.e., he who should use it. (With a suggestion of a *usurer* who is miserly.)
10.6 **thou stick'st** you scruple   7 **that . . . roof** i.e., your aristocratic family   9 **thought** intention.   **my mind** my opinion.   11 **presence** appearance, bearing
11.1–2 **thou grow'st . . . departest** i.e., you survive in a child of your own, though you leave the world behind   3 **youngly** in youth   4 **thou . . . convertest** you change from youth (to old age).   7 **minded so** sharing your intention (to have no children).   **times** succeeding generations   8 **year** years   9 **for store** for breeding   10 **Harsh . . . rude** ugly, lacking attractive features or appearance, and rudely fashioned

11 **Look . . . more** to whomever Nature endowed with the greatest gifts, she gave even more   13 **seal** stamp of authority, stamp from which impressions are made
12.1 **tells** (1) announces (2) counts   2 **brave** splendid   4 **sable** black   6 **erst** formerly   7 **girded** bundled   8 **bier** i.e., harvest cart. (But with suggestion of funeral bier.)   **beard** i.e., the tufted grain. (But suggesting also a dead man laid out for burial.)   9 **do . . . make** I discuss with myself   14 **breed** begetting offspring.   **brave him** defy Time
13.1 **yourself** i.e., your eternal self, not vulnerable to Time's decay.   2 **here** i.e., here on earth   3 **Against** In anticipation of   6 **determination** end   10 **husbandry** careful management. (With a pun on "being a husband.")
14.1 **my judgment pluck** derive my conclusions   2 **have astronomy** am skilled in astrology   4 **seasons' quality** what the weather of the seasons will be like   5 **fortune . . . tell** foretell events to the precise minute   6 **'Pointing** appointing, assigning.   **each** each minute.   **his** its

Or say with princes if it shall go well   7
By oft predict that I in heaven find.   8
But from thine eyes my knowledge I derive,
And, constant stars, in them I read such art   10
As truth and beauty shall together thrive   11
If from thyself to store thou wouldst convert.   12
  Or else of thee this I prognosticate:
  Thy end is truth's and beauty's doom and date.   14

15

When I consider every thing that grows
Holds in perfection but a little moment,   2
That this huge stage presenteth naught but shows   3
Whereon the stars in secret influence comment;
When I perceive that men as plants increase,   5
Cheerèd and checked even by the selfsame sky,   6
Vaunt in their youthful sap, at height decrease,   7
And wear their brave state out of memory;   8
Then the conceit of this inconstant stay   9
Sets you most rich in youth before my sight,
Where wasteful Time debateth with Decay   11
To change your day of youth to sullied night;
  And, all in war with Time for love of you,   13
  As he takes from you I engraft you new.   14

16

But wherefore do not you a mightier way
Make war upon this bloody tyrant, Time,
And fortify yourself in your decay
With means more blessèd than my barren rhyme?   4
Now stand you on the top of happy hours,
And many maiden gardens yet unset   6
With virtuous wish would bear your living flowers,   7
Much liker than your painted counterfeit.   8
So should the lines of life that life repair   9
Which this time's pencil, or my pupil pen,   10
Neither in inward worth nor outward fair   11
Can make you live yourself in eyes of men.   12
  To give away yourself keeps yourself still,   13
  And you must live, drawn by your own sweet skill.   14

17

Who will believe my verse in time to come
If it were filled with your most high deserts?
Though yet, heaven knows, it is but as a tomb   3
Which hides your life and shows not half your parts.   4
If I could write the beauty of your eyes
And in fresh numbers number all your graces,   6
The age to come would say, "This poet lies;
Such heavenly touches ne'er touched earthly faces."
So should my papers, yellowed with their age,
Be scorned like old men of less truth than tongue,   10
And your true rights be termed a poet's rage   11
And stretchèd meter of an antique song.   12
  But were some child of yours alive that time,
  You should live twice, in it and in my rhyme.

18

Shall I compare thee to a summer's day?
Thou art more lovely and more temperate.
Rough winds do shake the darling buds of May,
And summer's lease hath all too short a date.   4
Sometime too hot the eye of heaven shines,   5
And often is his gold complexion dimmed;
And every fair from fair sometimes declines,   7
By chance or nature's changing course untrimmed.   8
But thy eternal summer shall not fade
Nor lose possession of that fair thou ow'st;   10
Nor shall Death brag thou wand'r'st in his shade,
When in eternal lines to time thou grow'st.   12
  So long as men can breathe or eyes can see,
  So long lives this, and this gives life to thee.   14

19

Devouring Time, blunt thou the lion's paws,
And make the earth devour her own sweet brood;
Pluck the keen teeth from the fierce tiger's jaws,
And burn the long-lived phoenix in her blood;   4
Make glad and sorry seasons as thou fleet'st,   5
And do whate'er thou wilt, swift-footed Time,
To the wide world and all her fading sweets.
But I forbid thee one most heinous crime:
Oh, carve not with thy hours my love's fair brow,
Nor draw no lines there with thine antique pen;   10
Him in thy course untainted do allow   11
For beauty's pattern to succeeding men.

---

7 Or . . . well or say if things will go well for certain rulers   **8 oft predict** frequent predictions   **10–11 read . . . As** gather such learning as, in effect, that   **12 store** replenishment (through the begetting of children). **convert** turn.   **14 doom and date** limit of duration, destruction.
15.2 Holds in perfection maintains its prime   **3 stage** i.e., the world   **5 as** like   **6 Cheerèd and checked** (1) urged on, nourished, and held back, starved (2) applauded and hissed   **7 Vaunt** boast, exult.   **sap** vigor.   **at height decrease** i.e., no sooner reach full maturity but they (humans) start to decline   **8 brave** splendid.   **out of memory** until forgotten   **9 conceit** notion.   **inconstant stay** mutable brief time (on earth)   **11 debateth** competes   **13 all in war** I, fighting with might and main   **14 engraft you new** renew you by grafting, infusing new life into you (by means of my verse).
16.4 barren (1) unable to produce offspring (2) poetically sterile   **6 unset** (1) unplanted (2) unimpregnated   **7 virtuous wish** desire that is still chaste   **8 liker** more resembling you.   **painted** rendered by art (including poetry), artificial.   **counterfeit** portrait.   **9 lines of life** lineage, i.e., children (whose lineaments are more lifelike than lines of verse or of a portrait)   **10 this time's pencil** a portraiture done in this present age. **pupil** apprenticed, inexpert   **11 fair** beauty   **12 live** survive as   **13 give away yourself** i.e., marry and beget children.   **keeps** preserves   **14 skill** i.e., artistry in reproducing yourself, mightier than the poet's pen.

17.3 yet as yet   **4 parts** qualities.   **6 numbers** verses   **10 of . . . tongue** more garrulous than truthful   **11 rage** exaggerated inspiration   **12 stretchèd meter** overstrained poetry, poetic license
18.4 lease allotted time.   **date** duration.   **5 eye** i.e., sun   **7 fair from fair** beautiful thing from beauty   **8 untrimmed** stripped of ornament and beauty.   **10 fair thou ow'st** beauty you own   **12 lines** i.e., of poetry.   **to . . . grow'st** you become incorporated into time, engrafted upon it.   **14 this** i.e., this sonnet
19.4 phoenix legendary bird reputed to live for hundreds of years and then to be consumed alive (*in her blood*) in its own ashes, from which it is then reborn   **5 sorry** i.e., miserable, uncomfortable.   **thou fleet'st** you fleet, hurry   **10 antique** (1) old (2) antic, capricious, fantastic   **11 untainted** unsullied; uninjured

Yet, do thy worst, old Time. Despite thy wrong,
My love shall in my verse ever live young.   14

20

A woman's face with Nature's own hand painted   1
Hast thou, the master-mistress of my passion;   2
A woman's gentle heart, but not acquainted
With shifting change, as is false women's fashion;   4
An eye more bright than theirs, less false in rolling,   5
Gilding the object whereupon it gazeth;   6
A man in hue, all hues in his controlling,   7
Which steals men's eyes and women's souls amazeth.
And for a woman wert thou first created,
Till Nature, as she wrought thee, fell a-doting,   10
And by addition me of thee defeated,   11
By adding one thing to my purpose nothing.   12
    But since she pricked thee out for women's pleasure,   13
    Mine be thy love and thy love's use their treasure.   14

21

So is it not with me as with that muse,   1
Stirred by a painted beauty to his verse,   2
Who heaven itself for ornament doth use   3
And every fair with his fair doth rehearse,   4
Making a couplement of proud compare   5
With sun and moon, with earth and sea's rich gems,
With April's firstborn flowers, and all things rare
That heaven's air in this huge rondure hems.   8
Oh, let me, true in love, but truly write,
And then, believe me, my love is as fair
As any mother's child, though not so bright
As those gold candles fixed in heaven's air.   12
    Let them say more that like of hearsay well;   13
    I will not praise that purpose not to sell.   14

22

My glass shall not persuade me I am old   1
So long as youth and thou are of one date;   2
But when in thee Time's furrows I behold,
Then look I death my days should expiate.   4
For all that beauty that doth cover thee   5
Is but the seemly raiment of my heart,   6
Which in thy breast doth live, as thine in me.   7
How can I then be elder than thou art?
Oh, therefore, love, be of thyself so wary
As I, not for myself, but for thee will,   10
Bearing thy heart, which I will keep so chary   11
As tender nurse her babe from faring ill.
    Presume not on thy heart when mine is slain;   13
    Thou gav'st me thine, not to give back again.

23

As an unperfect actor on the stage   1
Who with his fear is put beside his part,   2
Or some fierce thing replete with too much rage,   3
Whose strength's abundance weakens his own heart,   4
So I, for fear of trust, forget to say   5
The perfect ceremony of love's rite,
And in mine own love's strength seem to decay,
O'ercharged with burden of mine own love's might.
Oh, let my books be then the eloquence   9
And dumb presagers of my speaking breast,   10
Who plead for love and look for recompense
More than that tongue that more hath more expressed.   12
    Oh, learn to read what silent love hath writ.
    To hear with eyes belongs to love's fine wit.   14

24

Mine eye hath played the painter and hath stelled   1
Thy beauty's form in table of my heart;   2
My body is the frame wherein 'tis held,
And perspective it is best painter's art.   4
For through the painter must you see his skill   5

---

14 My love (1) my beloved friend (2) my affection for him
20.1 with ... hand i.e., naturally beautiful   **2 master-mistress** i.e., both master and mistress, male and female.   **passion** love   **4 as ... fashion** as is the way with women, who are false by nature   **5 rolling** i.e., roving   **6 Gilding** causing to shine brightly   **7 A man ... controlling** one who has a manly appearance surpassing all other forms. (Suggesting, too, that he captivates all beholders and that his *hue* is womanly as well as manly.)   **10 fell a-doting** fell infatuatedly in love with you and so went mildly crazy   **11 defeated** defrauded, deprived   **12 to my purpose nothing** out of line with my wishes.   **13 pricked** designated. (With bawdy suggestion; the *thing* in line 12 is a phallus.)   **for women's pleasure** to give (sexual) pleasure to women   **14 Mine ... treasure** I will have your love in the truest sense, while women will enjoy you sexually and bear you children. (Expressed as a metaphor of financial capital or principal, which belongs to the poet, versus the *use* or interest, which belongs to women.)
21.1 muse i.e., poet   **2 Stirred** inspired.   **painted** artificial, created by cosmetics   **3 Who ... use** who does not scruple to invoke heaven itself as an ornament of praise for his mistress   **4 every ... rehearse** compares his lady fair with every lovely thing   **5 Making ... compare** joining (her) in proud comparison   **8 rondure** sphere.   **hems** encloses, encircles.   **12 gold candles** i.e., stars. (The trite and exaggerated metaphor is of the sort the poet hopes to eschew.)   **13 like ... well** like to deal in secondhand or trite expressions   **14 I will ... sell** I, who do not intend to sell as a merchant might, will accordingly not indulge in extravagant and empty praise.

22.1 glass mirror   **2 of one date** of an age, i.e., young   **4 look I** I foresee that.   **expiate** end.   **5–7 For ... me** Since my heart dwells in your breast (and yours in me), your beauty is in effect a becoming cover for my heart.   **10 will** i.e., will take wary care of myself for your sake   **11 Bearing** since I bear.   **chary** carefully   **13 Presume ... slain** Do not expect to receive back your heart when mine is slain (as would happen if you were to stop loving me)
23.1 unperfect one who has not learned his lines sufficiently   **2 is ... part** forgets his lines   **3 Or ... rage** i.e., or some wild creature overfilled with ungovernable rage   **4 Whose ... heart** whose excess of emotion collapses on itself   **5 for ... trust** mistrusting myself and fearful of not being trusted.   **forget** forget how   **9 books** (Possibly refers to the sonnets or to *Venus and Adonis* and *The Rape of Lucrece* or, more generally, the works of the persona poet.)   **10 dumb presagers** silent messengers or presenters   **12 that tongue** the tongue of some rival speaker.   **more hath more expressed** has more often or more fully said more.   **14 fine wit** sharp intelligence.
24.1 played acted the part of.   **stelled** fixed, installed; or perhaps steeled, i.e., engraved. (The quarto reads "steeld.")   **2 table** tablet, wooden panel used for painting   **3 frame** (1) picture frame (2) bodily frame   **4 perspective** an artist's method of producing a distorted picture that looks right only from an oblique point of view; or, a painter's technique used to produce the illusion of reality; or, the science of optics   **5 For ... skill** i.e., You must look through the eyes of me, the skillful painter

To find where your true image pictured lies,
Which in my bosom's shop is hanging still,   7
That hath his windows glazèd with thine eyes.   8
Now see what good turns eyes for eyes have done:
Mine eyes have drawn thy shape, and thine for me
Are windows to my breast, wherethrough the sun
Delights to peep, to gaze therein on thee.
        Yet eyes this cunning want to grace their art: 13
        They draw but what they see, know not the heart.   14

25

Let those who are in favor with their stars
Of public honor and proud titles boast,
Whilst I, whom fortune of such triumph bars,   3
Unlooked for joy in that I honor most.   4
Great princes' favorites their fair leaves spread   5
But as the marigold at the sun's eye,   6
And in themselves their pride lies burièd,   7
For at a frown they in their glory die.   8
The painful warrior famousèd for fight,   9
After a thousand victories once foiled,
Is from the book of honor rasèd quite,   11
And all the rest forgot for which he toiled.   12
        Then happy I, that love and am beloved
        Where I may not remove nor be removed.   14

26

Lord of my love, to whom in vassalage   1
Thy merit hath my duty strongly knit,
To thee I send this written embassage
To witness duty, not to show my wit—   4
Duty so great, which wit so poor as mine   5
May make seem bare, in wanting words to show it,   6
But that I hope some good conceit of thine   7
In thy soul's thought, all naked, will bestow it;   8
Till whatsoever star that guides my moving   9
Points on me graciously with fair aspect,   10
And puts apparel on my tattered loving
To show me worthy of thy sweet respect.
        Then may I dare to boast how I do love thee;
        Till then not show my head where thou mayst prove   14
        me.

27

Weary with toil, I haste me to my bed,
The dear repose for limbs with travel tirèd;   2
But then begins a journey in my head,
To work my mind when body's work's expirèd.
For then my thoughts, from far where I abide,   5
Intend a zealous pilgrimage to thee,   6
And keep my drooping eyelids open wide,
Looking on darkness which the blind do see;   8
Save that my soul's imaginary sight   9
Presents thy shadow to my sightless view,   10
Which, like a jewel hung in ghastly night,
Makes black night beauteous and her old face new.
        Lo, thus by day my limbs, by night my mind,
        For thee and for myself no quiet find.   14

28

How can I then return in happy plight
That am debarred the benefit of rest?
When day's oppression is not eased by night,
But day by night, and night by day, oppressed?   4
And each, though enemies to either's reign,
Do in consent shake hands to torture me,   6
The one by toil, the other to complain   7
How far I toil, still farther off from thee.
I tell the day, to please him, thou art bright
And dost him grace when clouds do blot the heaven;   10
So flatter I the swart-complexioned night,   11
When sparkling stars twire not, thou gild'st th' even.   12
        But day doth daily draw my sorrows longer,
        And night doth nightly make grief's strength seem
        stronger.

29

When, in disgrace with fortune and men's eyes,
I all alone beweep my outcast state,
And trouble deaf heaven with my bootless cries,   3
And look upon myself and curse my fate,   4
Wishing me like to one more rich in hope,   5
Featured like him, like him with friends possessed,   6
Desiring this man's art and that man's scope,   7

7 **bosom's shop** i.e., heart   **8 his** its.   **glazèd** fitted with glass, paned. (The friend, looking into the poet's eyes where his own eyes are reflected, sees into the poet's heart.)   **13 this cunning want** lack this skill.   **grace** enhance   **14 know not** do not perceive the thoughts of
25.3 of from   **4 Unlooked for** (1) unexpectedly (2) out of the public eye.   **that** that which   **5 their . . . spread** i.e., flourish, blossom, prosper   **6 But** only   **7 lies burièd** i.e., will die with the ending of their brief glory   **8 a frown** (1) a prince's frown (2) a cloud obscuring the sun   **9 painful** enduring much, striving.   **famousèd** renowned.   **fight** (Reads "worth" in the 1609 quarto; some editors retain and emend "quite" in line 11 to "forth." Other editors prefer "might.")   **11 rasèd** erased (or *razèd*, scraped out)   **12 the rest** i.e., his *thousand victories*   **14 remove** i.e., be unfaithful.   **removed** i.e., removed from favor.
26.1 vassalage allegiance   **4 witness** bear witness to.   **wit** skill, literary ingenuity   **5 wit** intelligence and skill   **6 wanting** lacking
7 good conceit good conception, favorable opinion   **8 all naked** i.e., poor verse though it is.   **bestow** give lodging to   **9 moving** life and deeds   **10 Points on** directs its rays at.   **aspect** influence (as of a star)   **14 prove** test

27.2 travel (With connotation also of *travail*; spelled "trauaill" in the quarto.)   **5 from far** i.e., far away from you   **6 Intend** (1) set out upon (2) have purposefully in mind   **8 Looking . . . see** while my thoughts try to peer (toward you) through the darkness, like the blind, who see only darkness   **9 Save** except   **10 thy shadow** the image of you   **14 For** on account of
28.4 But . . . oppressed i.e., but experiencing sleeplessness at night and fatigue during the day.   **6 in . . . hands** i.e., come to a mutual agreement   **7 the other to complain** i.e., the night by causing me to complain   **10 And . . . heaven** i.e., and that you shine in place of the sun when the sun is overclouded   **11 So flatter I** similarly I gratify.   **swart** dark   **12 When . . . even** i.e., by saying that, when sparkling stars do not twinkle or peep out, you make bright the evening.
29.3 bootless useless   **4 look upon myself** consider my predicament   **5 more rich in hope** with better prospects of success
6 Featured formed, i.e., having good looks.   **like him, like him** like a second man, like a third   **7 art** literary skill, learning.   **scope** range of powers

With what I most enjoy contented least;   8
Yet in these thoughts myself almost despising,
Haply I think on thee, and then my state,   10
Like to the lark at break of day arising
From sullen earth, sings hymns at heaven's gate;
    For thy sweet love remembered such wealth brings
    That then I scorn to change my state with kings.   14

30

When to the sessions of sweet silent thought   1
I summon up remembrance of things past,
I sigh the lack of many a thing I sought,   3
And with old woes new wail my dear time's waste.   4
Then can I drown an eye, unused to flow,   5
For precious friends hid in death's dateless night,   6
And weep afresh love's long-since-canceled woe,   7
And moan th'expense of many a vanished sight.   8
Then can I grieve at grievances foregone,   9
And heavily from woe to woe tell o'er   10
The sad account of fore-bemoanèd moan,   11
Which I new pay as if not paid before.
    But if the while I think on thee, dear friend,
    All losses are restored and sorrows end.

31

Thy bosom is endearèd with all hearts   1
Which I by lacking have supposèd dead,   2
And there reigns love and all love's loving parts,   3
And all those friends which I thought buried.
How many a holy and obsequious tear   5
Hath dear religious love stol'n from mine eye
As interest of the dead, which now appear   7
But things removed that hidden in thee lie!   8
Thou art the grave where buried love doth live,
Hung with the trophies of my lovers gone,   10
Who all their parts of me to thee did give;   11
That due of many now is thine alone.   12
    Their images I loved I view in thee,   13
    And thou, all they, hast all the all of me.   14

32

If thou survive my well-contented day   1
When that churl Death my bones with dust shall cover,
And shalt by fortune once more re-survey   3
These poor rude lines of thy deceasèd lover,   4
Compare them with the bett'ring of the time,   5
And though they be outstripped by every pen,
Reserve them for my love, not for their rhyme,   7
Exceeded by the height of happier men.   8
Oh, then vouchsafe me but this loving thought: 9
"Had my friend's Muse grown with this growing age,
A dearer birth than this his love had brought   11
To march in ranks of better equipage;   12
    But since he died and poets better prove,   13
    Theirs for their style I'll read, his for his love."

33

Full many a glorious morning have I seen   1
Flatter the mountaintops with sovereign eye,   2
Kissing with golden face the meadows green,
Gilding pale streams with heavenly alchemy;
Anon permit the basest clouds to ride   5
With ugly rack on his celestial face,   6
And from the forlorn world his visage hide,
Stealing unseen to west with this disgrace.
Even so my sun one early morn did shine
With all-triumphant splendor on my brow.
But out, alack! He was but one hour mine;   11
The region cloud hath masked him from me now.   12
    Yet him for this my love no whit disdaineth;
    Suns of the world may stain when heaven's sun
      staineth.   14

34

Why didst thou promise such a beauteous day
And make me travel forth without my cloak,
To let base clouds o'ertake me in my way,   3
Hiding thy brav'ry in their rotten smoke?   4
'Tis not enough that through the cloud thou break,
To dry the rain on my storm-beaten face,
For no man well of such a salve can speak
That heals the wound and cures not the disgrace.   8

---

8 most enjoy possess most securely and take greatest pleasure in
10 Haply perchance; happily.   **state** state of mind. (Suggesting also
"fortunes.")   **14 change** exchange
30.1 sessions (The metaphor is that of a court of law, continued in
summon up, line 2.)   **3 sigh** sigh for   **4 new ... waste** lament anew
the wasting of precious time or time's erosion of those things held
precious.   **5 unused to flow** not prone to weep   **6 dateless** endless
7 canceled paid in full (by grieving)   **8 th'expense** the loss, expenditure   **9 grievances foregone** sorrows past   **10 heavily** sadly.   **tell**
count   **11 account** (1) narrative (2) financial reckoning.   **fore-
bemoanèd moan** previously uttered laments
31.1 endearèd with all hearts (1) beloved by all (2) made dear to me
by representing and including those I have loved   **2 lacking** not having   **3 parts** attributes   **5 obsequious** suitable to mourning   **6 religious** dutiful, reverent   **7 interest of** that which is rightfully due to.
which who   **8 But ... lie** i.e., no more than absent persons (now
dead), whose best qualities are to be found buried in you.
10 Hung ... gone festooned with symbolic memorials of my past triumphs in being loved by many   **11 parts** shares   **12 That due of
many** that which was both owed by, and paid to, many   **13 I loved**
which I loved   **14 all they** (you) who comprise all of them

32.1 my ... day i.e., the day of my death, which will content me well
3 And ... fortune and if by chance you happen   **4 rude** unpolished.
lover friend   **5 bett'ring** i.e., improved writing, greater cultural
sophistication   **7 Reserve** preserve.   **for my love** (1) out of love for
me (2) for the sake of my love for you.   **rhyme** i.e., poetic skill
8 height superiority, highest achievement.   **happier** more gifted or
fortunate   **9 vouchsafe me but** deign to bestow on me just   **11 dearer
birth** i.e., better poem, better artistic creation   **12 better equipage** i.e.,
more finely wrought verse   **13 better prove** turn out to be superior
33.1 Full Very   **2 sovereign eye** i.e., morning sunlight   **5 Anon** soon
afterward.   **basest** darkest   **6 rack** mass of cloud scudding before
the wind   **11 out, alack!** (An expression of dismay.)   **12 region** of the
upper air   **14 Suns** i.e., great men. (With a pun on *sons of the world*,
"mortal men.")   **stain** grow dim, be obscured, soiled.   **staineth** is
clouded over.
34.3 To only to   **4 brav'ry** finery.   **rotten smoke** foul vapors.   **8 disgrace** i.e., the scar, the disfigurement caused by his friend's neglect or
harsh treatment; the *loss* mentioned in line 10.

Nor can thy shame give physic to my grief;   9
Though thou repent, yet I have still the loss.
Th'offender's sorrow lends but weak relief
To him that bears the strong offense's cross.   12
    Ah, but those tears are pearl which thy love sheds,
    And they are rich, and ransom all ill deeds.   14

35

No more be grieved at that which thou hast done.
Roses have thorns, and silver fountains mud,
Clouds and eclipses stain both moon and sun,   3
And loathsome canker lives in sweetest bud.   4
All men make faults, and even I in this,
Authorizing thy trespass with compare,   6
Myself corrupting, salving thy amiss,   7
Excusing thy sins more than thy sins are.   8
For to thy sensual fault I bring in sense—   9
Thy adverse party is thy advocate—   10
And 'gainst myself a lawful plea commence.
Such civil war is in my love and hate
    That I an accessary needs must be   13
    To that sweet thief which sourly robs from me.

36

Let me confess that we two must be twain,   1
Although our undivided loves are one;
So shall those blots that do with me remain,   3
Without thy help, by me be borne alone.
In our two loves there is but one respect,   5
Though in our lives a separable spite,   6
Which, though it alter not love's sole effect,   7
Yet doth it steal sweet hours from love's delight.
I may not evermore acknowledge thee,   9
Lest my bewailèd guilt should do thee shame,
Nor thou with public kindness honor me
Unless thou take that honor from thy name.   12
    But do not so; I love thee in such sort   13
    As, thou being mine, mine is thy good report.   14

37

As a decrepit father takes delight
To see his active child do deeds of youth,

So I, made lame by Fortune's dearest spite,   3
Take all my comfort of thy worth and truth.   4
For whether beauty, birth, or wealth, or wit,   5
Or any of these all, or all, or more,
Entitled in thy parts do crownèd sit,   7
I make my love engrafted to this store.   8
So then I am not lame, poor, nor despised,
Whilst that this shadow doth such substance give   10
That I in thy abundance am sufficed
And by a part of all thy glory live.
    Look what is best, that best I wish in thee.   13
    This wish I have; then ten times happy me!

38

How can my Muse want subject to invent   1
While thou dost breathe, that pour'st into my verse   2
Thine own sweet argument, too excellent   3
For every vulgar paper to rehearse?   4
Oh, give thyself the thanks, if aught in me   5
Worthy perusal stand against thy sight,   6
For who's so dumb that cannot write to thee,   7
When thou thyself dost give invention light?   8
Be thou the tenth Muse, ten times more in worth
Than those old nine which rhymers invocate;
And he that calls on thee, let him bring forth
Eternal numbers to outlive long date.   12
    If my slight Muse do please these curious days,   13
    The pain be mine, but thine shall be the praise.   14

39

Oh, how thy worth with manners may I sing,   1
When thou art all the better part of me?
What can mine own praise to mine own self bring?   3
And what is't but mine own when I praise thee?   4
Even for this let us divided live,   5
And our dear love lose name of single one,
That by this separation I may give
That due to thee which thou deserv'st alone.
O absence, what a torment wouldst thou prove,
Were it not thy sour leisure gave sweet leave   10
To entertain the time with thoughts of love,   11
Which time and thoughts so sweetly doth deceive,   12

---

9 **shame** repentance for the wrong done.   **physic** remedy   **12 cross** affliction.   **14 ransom** atone for
35.3 stain dim, obscure   **4 canker** cankerworm   **6 Authorizing** sanctioning, justifying.   **compare** comparisons (as in this sonnet)
7 Myself . . . amiss excusing your misdeed, thereby bringing blame on myself   **8 Excusing . . . are** going further to excuse your sins than they warrant, or, excusing you for even worse sins than you have actually committed.   **9 For . . . sense** I reason away your fleshly offenses   **10 Thy . . . advocate** I who profess to be your accuser find myself, instead, pleading your case   **13 That . . . be** that I am compelled (by my love) to be a guilty accomplice
36.1 twain parted   **3 blots** defects, stains of dishonor   **5 but one respect** a mutual regard, singleness of attitude   **6 separable spite** vexing separation   **7 sole effect** unique effect (of making the two of us into one)   **9 not evermore acknowledge** nevermore admit my acquaintance with   **12 Unless . . . from** without consequent loss of honor to   **13 in such sort** in such a way   **14 As . . . report** that since you are mine, your good reputation sustains me also.

37.3 made lame handicapped in life.   **dearest** most bitter   **4 of** in, from   **5 wit** intelligence   **7 Entitled . . . sit** sit enthroned among your qualities   **8 I make . . . store** I add my love to this abundance (and thereby flourish by drawing on their strength).   **10 shadow** idea (in the platonic sense).   **substance** actuality   **13 Look what** Whatever
38.1 want . . . invent lack something to write about   **2 that** you who   **3 Thine . . . argument** yourself as subject   **4 vulgar paper** common piece of writing.   **rehearse** recite, repeat.   **5–6 if . . . sight** if any of my writing strikes you as worthy of perusal   **7 dumb** silent, lacking in subject   **8 When . . . light** when you bring such a light of invention to yourself as poetic subject.   **12 numbers** verses.   **long date** even a very distant limit in time.   **13 curious** finicky   **14 pain** labor
39.1 with manners decently, becomingly   **3–4 What . . . thee?** i.e., Since my better self is entirely yours, what can I gain from praising you but a kind of vainglorious self-praise?   **5 Even for** Precisely because of   **10 not** not that   **11 entertain** pass, occupy   **12 Which . . . deceive** (thoughts of love), which sweetly beguile away time and (sad) thoughts

And that thou teachest how to make one twain
By praising him here who doth hence remain!   14

40

Take all my loves, my love, yea, take them all;   1
What hast thou then more than thou hadst before?
No love, my love, that thou mayst true love call;   3
All mine was thine before thou hadst this more.
Then if for my love thou my love receivest,   5
I cannot blame thee for my love thou usest;   6
But yet be blamed if thou this self deceivest   7
By willful taste of what thyself refusest.   8
I do forgive thy robb'ry, gentle thief,
Although thou steal thee all my poverty;   10
And yet love knows it is a greater grief
To bear love's wrong than hate's known injury.   12
    Lascivious grace, in whom all ill well shows,   13
    Kill me with spites; yet we must not be foes.

41

Those pretty wrongs that liberty commits   1
When I am sometime absent from thy heart,
Thy beauty and thy years full well befits,   3
For still temptation follows where thou art.   4
Gentle thou art, and therefore to be won;
Beauteous thou art, therefore to be assailed;
And when a woman woos, what woman's son   7
Will sourly leave her till he have prevailed?   8
Ay me, but yet thou mightst my seat forbear,   9
And chide thy beauty and thy straying youth,
Who lead thee in their riot even there   11
Where thou art forced to break a twofold truth: 12
    Hers, by thy beauty tempting her to thee,
    Thine, by thy beauty being false to me.

42

That thou hast her, it is not all my grief,
And yet it may be said I loved her dearly;
That she hath thee is of my wailing chief,   3
A loss in love that touches me more nearly.
Loving offenders, thus I will excuse ye:

Thou dost love her because thou know'st I love her,
And for my sake even so doth she abuse me,   7
Suff'ring my friend for my sake to approve her.   8
If I lose thee, my loss is my love's gain,   9
And, losing her, my friend hath found that loss;   10
Both find each other, and I lose both twain,
And both for my sake lay on me this cross.   12
    But here's the joy: my friend and I are one.
    Sweet flattery! Then she loves but me alone.   14

43

When most I wink, then do mine eyes best see,   1
For all the day they view things unrespected;   2
But when I sleep, in dreams they look on thee,
And, darkly bright, are bright in dark directed.   4
Then thou, whose shadow shadows doth make bright,   5
How would thy shadow's form form happy show   6
To the clear day with thy much clearer light,
When to unseeing eyes thy shade shines so!   8
How would, I say, mine eyes be blessèd made
By looking on thee in the living day,
When in dead night thy fair imperfect shade   11
Through heavy sleep on sightless eyes doth stay!   12
    All days are nights to see till I see thee,   13
    And nights bright days when dreams do show thee
    me.   14

44

If the dull substance of my flesh were thought,   1
Injurious distance should not stop my way;
For then despite of space I would be brought,
From limits far remote, where thou dost stay.   4
No matter then although my foot did stand
Upon the farthest earth removed from thee;   6
For nimble thought can jump both sea and land
As soon as think the place where he would be.   8
But, ah, thought kills me that I am not thought,   9
To leap large lengths of miles when thou art gone,
But that, so much of earth and water wrought,   11
I must attend time's leisure with my moan,   12

14 here (1) here where I am (2) here in this poem
40.1 all my loves (1) all those whom I love (2) all the love I have. (The young man addressed has taken away the poet's mistress.)   3 No . . . call i.e., Any love more than you had already—my complete affection—cannot be called true love   5 my love . . . my love love of me . . . her whom I love   6 for because.   thou usest you enjoy (sexually)
7 this self i.e., me, your other love. (Often emended to "thyself.")
8 By . . . refusest i.e., by tasting sexual pleasures that your best self would refuse.   10 steal . . . poverty take for your own the poor little that I have   12 To . . . injury to endure injuries arising out of a loving relationship than those stemming from calculated hatred.   13 Lascivious grace i.e., You who are gracious even in your lasciviousness
41.1 pretty graciously committed, sportive.   liberty licentiousness
3 befits (The subject is wrongs, line 1.)   4 still constantly   7–8 And . . . prevailed i.e., When a woman woos, what man can resist until he has scored? (He is sometimes emended to "she.")   9 seat place, that which belongs to me (i.e., my mistress)   11 Who which.   riot debauchery   12 twofold truth i.e., her plighted love to me and your plighted friendship to me
42.3 is . . . chief is chief cause of my lamentation

7 abuse betray, wrong   8 Suff'ring allowing.   approve try, test (in a sexual sense)   9 my love's hers whom I love, my mistress's   10 losing her i.e., I losing her   12 for my sake as though out of love for me.
cross torment.   14 flattery gratifying deception.
43.1 wink close my eyes in sleep   2 unrespected unnoticed, unregarded; not deserving notice   4 And . . . directed and, able to see in the darkness (though still shut), are directed toward your brightness in the dark.   5 whose . . . bright whose image makes darkness bright   6 thy shadow's . . . show the substance of the shadow, i.e., your presence, make a gladdening sight   8 unseeing eyes i.e., closed eyes of the dreamer   11 imperfect unsubstantial, indistinct as in a dream   12 stay linger, dwell.   13 All . . . to see All days are gloomy to behold   14 thee me you to me. (But also suggesting "me to you.")
44.1 dull heavy   4 limits regions, bounds.   where to the place where   6 farthest earth removed that part of the earth farthest removed   8 he thought   9 ah, thought ah, the thought   11 so . . . wrought i.e., I, compounded to such an extent of the heavier elements, earth and water. (The lighter elements are fire and air.)
12 attend time's leisure i.e., wait until time has leisure to reunite us

Receiving naught by elements so slow   13
But heavy tears, badges of either's woe.   14

45

The other two, slight air and purging fire,   1
Are both with thee, wherever I abide;
The first my thought, the other my desire,
These present-absent with swift motion slide.   4
For when these quicker elements are gone
In tender embassy of love to thee,
My life, being made of four, with two alone   7
Sinks down to death, oppressed with melancholy;   8
Until life's composition be recured   9
By those swift messengers returned from thee,   10
Who even but now come back again, assured
Of thy fair health, recounting it to me.
   This told, I joy; but then no longer glad,
   I send them back again and straight grow sad.   14

46

Mine eye and heart are at a mortal war   1
How to divide the conquest of thy sight;   2
Mine eye my heart thy picture's sight would bar,   3
My heart mine eye the freedom of that right.   4
My heart doth plead that thou in him dost lie—
A closet never pierced with crystal eyes—   6
But the defendant doth that plea deny   7
And says in him thy fair appearance lies.
To 'cide this title is impanelèd   9
A quest of thoughts, all tenants to the heart,   10
And by their verdict is determinèd
The clear eye's moiety and the dear heart's part,   12
   As thus: mine eye's due is thy outward part,   13
   And my heart's right thy inward love of heart.

47

Betwixt mine eye and heart a league is took,   1
And each doth good turns now unto the other.
When that mine eye is famished for a look,   3
Or heart in love with sighs himself doth smother,   4

With my love's picture then my eye doth feast   5
And to the painted banquet bids my heart;   6
Another time mine eye is my heart's guest
And in his thoughts of love doth share a part.
So, either by thy picture or my love,
Thyself, away, are present still with me;
For thou no farther than my thoughts canst move,
And I am still with them and they with thee;   12
   Or, if they sleep, thy picture in my sight
   Awakes my heart to heart's and eye's delight.

48

How careful was I, when I took my way,   1
Each trifle under truest bars to thrust,   2
That to my use it might unusèd stay   3
From hands of falsehood, in sure wards of trust!   4
But thou, to whom my jewels trifles are,   5
Most worthy comfort, now my greatest grief,   6
Thou best of dearest and mine only care,
Art left the prey of every vulgar thief.   8
Thee have I not locked up in any chest,
Save where thou art not—though I feel thou art—
Within the gentle closure of my breast,
From whence at pleasure thou mayst come and part;   12
   And even thence thou wilt be stol'n, I fear,
   For truth proves thievish for a prize so dear.   14

49

Against that time, if ever that time come,   1
When I shall see thee frown on my defects,
Whenas thy love hath cast his utmost sum,   3
Called to that audit by advised respects;   4
Against that time when thou shalt strangely pass   5
And scarcely greet me with that sun, thine eye,
When love, converted from the thing it was,
Shall reasons find of settled gravity—   8
Against that time do I ensconce me here   9
Within the knowledge of mine own desart,   10
And this my hand against myself uprear,   11
To guard the lawful reasons on thy part.   12
   To leave poor me thou hast the strength of laws,
   Since why to love I can allege no cause.   14

13 **by** from   14 **badges** signs, tokens.   **either's** (1) both earth's and
water's, because the earth is heavy and the sea is salt and wet like
tears (2) both your and my
45.1 **other two** (i.e., of the four elements discussed in sonnet 44).
slight insubstantial.   **purging** purifying   4 **present-absent** (1) now
here and immediately gone (2) simultaneously both present and
absent   7 **two alone** i.e., earth and water   8 **melancholy** a humor
thought to be induced by an excess of earth and water   9 **composition** proper balance among the four elements.   **recured** restored
10 **swift messengers** i.e., fire and air, thought and desire   14 **straight**
straightaway
46.1 **mortal** deadly   2 **How . . . sight** how to divide the spoils of war,
namely, the sight of you   3–4 **Mine . . . right** my eye wishes to bar
my heart from seeing your image (perhaps a painting), and conversely my heart would like to deny my eye the free enjoyment of
that right.   6 **closet** (1) small private room (2) cabinet   7 **the defendant** the eye   9 **'cide** decide   10 **quest** inquest, jury   12 **moiety** portion   13 **mine . . . part** i.e., the eye gets the outward appearance of
you. (The jury, composed entirely of those who are loyal to the heart,
being its *tenants,* awards true love to the heart.)
47.1 **a league is took** an agreement is reached   3 **When that** When
4 **Or heart** or when my heart.   **himself** itself

5 **With** i.e., on   6 **painted banquet** i.e., visual feast, perhaps an actual
picture of the friend   12 **still** constantly
48.1 **took my way** set out on my journey   2 **truest** most trusty   3 **to
my use** for my own use and profit   3–4 **stay . . . falsehood** remain
out of the hands of thieves   5 **to** compared to   6 **worthy** valuable.
grief anxiety, cause of sorrow (i.e., because of your absence and likelihood of being stolen from me)   8 **vulgar** common   12 **part** depart
14 **truth** i.e., even honesty itself
49.1 **Against** In anticipation of   3 **Whenas** when.   **cast . . . sum**
added up the sum total. (The metaphor is from closing accounts on a
dissolution of partnership.)   4 **advised respects** careful consideration
5 **strangely** as a stranger   8 **of settled gravity** (1) for a dignified
reserve or continued coldness (2) of sufficient weight   9 **ensconce**
fortify, shelter   10 **desart** i.e., deserving, such as it is. (This quarto
spelling of desert, "desart," indicates the rhyme with *part.*)   11 **this . . .
uprear** I raise my own hand (as a witness) against my own interest
12 **To . . . part** i.e., to testify in behalf of the lawful reasons on your
side of the case.   14 **Since . . . cause** since I can urge no lawful cause
why you should love me.

50

How heavy do I journey on the way, 1
When what I seek, my weary travel's end, 2
Doth teach that ease and that repose to say, 3
"Thus far the miles are measured from thy friend!" 4
The beast that bears me, tirèd with my woe,
Plods dully on, to bear that weight in me,
As if by some instinct the wretch did know
His rider loved not speed being made from thee.
The bloody spur cannot provoke him on
That sometimes anger thrusts into his hide,
Which heavily he answers with a groan,
More sharp to me than spurring to his side;
    For that same groan doth put this in my mind:
    My grief lies onward and my joy behind.

51

Thus can my love excuse the slow offense 1
Of my dull bearer when from thee I speed: 2
From where thou art why should I haste me thence?
Till I return, of posting is no need. 4
Oh, what excuse will my poor beast then find
When swift extremity can seem but slow? 6
Then should I spur, though mounted on the wind;
In wingéd speed no motion shall I know. 8
Then can no horse with my desire keep pace;
Therefore desire, of perfect'st love being made,
Shall neigh—no dull flesh—in his fiery race. 11
But love, for love, thus shall excuse my jade: 12
    Since from thee going he went willful slow,
    Towards thee I'll run, and give him leave to go.

52

So am I as the rich whose blessèd key 1
Can bring him to his sweet up-lockèd treasure,
The which he will not ev'ry hour survey,
For blunting the fine point of seldom pleasure. 4
Therefore are feasts so solemn and so rare, 5
Since, seldom coming, in the long year set,
Like stones of worth they thinly placèd are,
Or captain jewels in the carcanet. 8
So is the time that keeps you as my chest, 9
Or as the wardrobe which the robe doth hide,
To make some special instant special blest

By new unfolding his imprisoned pride. 12
Blessèd are you whose worthiness gives scope, 13
Being had, to triumph; being lacked, to hope. 14

53

What is your substance, whereof are you made,
That millions of strange shadows on you tend? 2
Since everyone hath, every one, one shade,
And you, but one, can every shadow lend. 4
Describe Adonis, and the counterfeit 5
Is poorly imitated after you;
On Helen's cheek all art of beauty set, 7
And you in Grecian tires are painted new. 8
Speak of the spring and foison of the year; 9
The one doth shadow of your beauty show,
The other as your bounty doth appear,
And you in every blessèd shape we know. 12
    In all external grace you have some part,
    But you like none, none you, for constant heart. 14

54

Oh, how much more doth beauty beauteous seem
By that sweet ornament which truth doth give! 2
The rose looks fair, but fairer we it deem
For that sweet odor which doth in it live.
The canker blooms have full as deep a dye 5
As the perfumèd tincture of the roses,
Hang on such thorns, and play as wantonly 7
When summer's breath their maskèd buds discloses; 8
But, for their virtue only is their show, 9
They live unwooed and unrespected fade, 10
Die to themselves. Sweet roses do not so; 11
Of their sweet deaths are sweetest odors made. 12
    And so of you, beauteous and lovely youth, 13
    When that shall vade, by verse distills your truth. 14

55

Not marble nor the gilded monuments
Of princes shall outlive this powerful rhyme,

12 his its. **pride** splendor, proud treasure. **13–14 gives . . . hope** gives me opportunity, when you are with me, to rejoice, and when you are away from me, to hope for reunion.
53.2 strange (1) exotic (2) not belonging to you. **tend** attend. **3 shade** shadow (as cast by the sun) **4 And . . . lend** and yet you, being only one person, can cast all sorts of shadowy images or reflections (such as Adonis, Helen, etc.). **5 Adonis** beautiful youth beloved of Venus. **counterfeit** likeness, portrait **7–8 On . . . new** set forth the entire art used to beautify the cheek of Helen of Troy, and the result will be a portrait of you in Grecian attire or headdress. **9 foison** abundance, i.e., autumn **12 you . . . know** we recognize you in every beautiful image. **14 But . . . heart** but in the matter of constancy you resemble no one and no one can resemble you.
54.2 By by means of. **truth** (1) constancy (2) substance, integrity **5 canker blooms** dog roses (outwardly attractive but not as sweetly scented as the damask rose). **dye** tincture **7 wantonly** sportively **8 discloses** causes to open **9 for** because. **their show** in their appearance **10 unrespected** unregarded **11 to themselves** i.e., without profit to others. **12 Of . . . made** i.e., perfumes are made from the crushed petals of these roses. **13 of you** (1) distilled from you (2) with regard to you. **lovely** (1) lovable (2) handsome **14 When . . . truth** when your physical beauty fades, your true substance will be distilled and preserved by (my) verse. (See sonnet 5.) **vade** (1) fade (2) go away

50.1 heavy sadly and slowly **2–4 When . . . friend** when the ease and repose I seek at journey's end will merely remind me that I have gone so many miles from my friend.
51.1 slow offense offense consisting in slowness **2 my dull bearer** i.e., the horse **4 posting** riding swiftly **6 swift extremity** extreme swiftness (in returning to you) **8 In . . . know** even at the speed of flight I won't perceive the motion at all, won't feel as though I'm moving. **11 Shall . . . race** i.e., will neigh proudly in its fire-swift race, since it, composed like fire of a lighter element, is not held back by the heavy flesh. (See sonnet 45.) **12 for love** for love's sake. **jade** nag **14 go** travel on at his own pace.
52.1 as the rich like the rich man **4 For . . . pleasure** lest he blunt the delicacy of pleasure sparingly enjoyed. **5 feasts** feast days. **solemn** ceremonious, festive. **rare** excellent; uncommon **8 captain** principal. **carcanet** necklace of jewels. **9 keeps you** (1) watches over you (2) keeps you from me. **as** like

But you shall shine more bright in these contents 3
Than unswept stone besmeared with sluttish time. 4
When wasteful war shall statues overturn, 5
And broils root out the work of masonry, 6
Nor Mars his sword nor war's quick fire shall burn 7
The living record of your memory.
'Gainst death and all-oblivious enmity 9
Shall you pace forth; your praise shall still find room
Even in the eyes of all posterity
That wear this world out to the ending doom. 12
    So, till the judgment that yourself arise, 13
    You live in this, and dwell in lovers' eyes.

56

Sweet love, renew thy force! Be it not said 1
Thy edge should blunter be than appetite, 2
Which but today by feeding is allayed, 3
Tomorrow sharpened in his former might. 4
So, love, be thou; although today thou fill
Thy hungry eyes even till they wink with fullness, 6
Tomorrow see again, and do not kill
The spirit of love with a perpetual dullness.
Let this sad interim like the ocean be 9
Which parts the shore where two contracted new 10
Come daily to the banks, that, when they see 11
Return of love, more blest may be the view; 12
    As call it winter, which being full of care 13
    Makes summer's welcome thrice more wished, more
    rare.

57

Being your slave, what should I do but tend 1
Upon the hours and times of your desire?
I have no precious time at all to spend,
Nor services to do, till you require.
Nor dare I chide the world-without-end hour 5
Whilst I, my sovereign, watch the clock for you, 6
Nor think the bitterness of absence sour 7
When you have bid your servant once adieu.
Nor dare I question with my jealous thought 9
Where you may be, or your affairs suppose, 10

But, like a sad slave, stay and think of naught
Save where you are how happy you make those.
    So true a fool is love that in your will, 13
    Though you do anything, he thinks no ill.

58

That god forbid, that made me first your slave,
I should in thought control your times of pleasure,
Or at your hand th'account of hours to crave, 3
Being your vassal, bound to stay your leisure! 4
Oh, let me suffer, being at your beck,
Th'imprisoned absence of your liberty, 6
And, patience-tame to sufferance, bide each check, 7
Without accusing you of injury.
Be where you list, your charter is so strong 9
That you yourself may privilege your time 10
To what you will; to you it doth belong
Yourself to pardon of self-doing crime. 12
    I am to wait, though waiting so be hell, 13
    Not blame your pleasure, be it ill or well.

59

If there be nothing new, but that which is 1
Hath been before, how are our brains beguiled,
Which, laboring for invention, bear amiss 3
The second burden of a former child! 4
Oh, that record could with a backward look, 5
Even of five hundred courses of the sun, 6
Show me your image in some antique book,
Since mind at first in character was done! 8
That I might see what the old world could say
To this composèd wonder of your frame; 10
Whether we are mended, or whe'er better they, 11
Or whether revolution be the same. 12
    Oh, sure I am the wits of former days 13
    To subjects worse have given admiring praise.

60

Like as the waves make towards the pebbled shore, 1
So do our minutes hasten to their end,
Each changing place with that which goes before, 3

55.3 these contents i.e., the contents of my poems written in praise of you   **4 Than unswept stone** than in a memorial stone that has been left unswept, unattended.   **sluttish** neglectful, slovenly, whorish   **5 wasteful** laying waste   **6 broils** uprisings, battles   **7 Nor Mars his sword** Neither Mars's sword (shall destroy)   **9 all-oblivious enmity** oblivion, at enmity with everything   **12 That . . . doom** that will last from now till doomsday. (*That* may refer to *eyes, praise,* or *posterity*.)   **13 till . . . arise** until the Judgment Day, when you will arise from the dead
56.1 love i.e., the spirit of love. (The friend is not directly mentioned in this sonnet.)   **1–2 Be . . . appetite** Let no one attempt to argue that true love should be any less sharp-edged in desire than sexual appetite   **3 but** only for   **4 his** its   **6 wink** shut   **9 sad interim** a period of love's abatement or absence   **10 parts the shore** separates the shores.   **contracted new** newly betrothed   **11 banks** shores   **12 love** the loved one   **13 As** just as appropriately
57.1 tend attend   **5 world-without-end** interminable   **6 Whilst . . . you** while I count the minutes, my sovereign, waiting for your command   **7 Nor think** nor dare I think   **9 question with** (1) debate with (2) seek to know by means of   **10 suppose** make conjectures about

13 true (1) constant (2) utter.   **in your will** with regard to your desire (with perhaps an allusion to "Will Shakespeare"; "will" is capitalized in the 1609 quarto, as in sonnet 135)
58.3 th'account . . . crave should crave an accounting of how you spend your time   **4 stay** await   **6 Th'imprisoned . . . liberty** the lack of freedom I suffer in being absent from you, arising from (*of*) your freedom and licentious behavior   **7 And . . . check** and, trained to endure any suffering, let me put up with each rebuke   **9 list** please.   **charter** privilege   **10 privilege** authorize   **12 self-doing** committed by yourself   **13 am to** must
59.1 that everything   **3–4 laboring . . . child** striving to give birth to a new creation, merely miscarry with the repetition of something created before.   **5 record** memory, especially memory preserved in writing   **6 courses . . . sun** years   **8 Since . . . done** since thought was first expressed in writing.   **10 composèd wonder** wonderful composition   **11 mended** improved.   **whe'er** whether   **12 revolution . . . same** the revolving of the ages brings only repetition.   **13 wits** discerning persons; poets
60.1 Like . . . shore Just as waves move up the shingle beach
3 changing place with replacing

In sequent toil all forwards do contend. 4
Nativity, once in the main of light, 5
Crawls to maturity, wherewith being crowned,
Crookèd eclipses 'gainst his glory fight, 7
And Time that gave doth now his gift confound. 8
Time doth transfix the flourish set on youth 9
And delves the parallels in beauty's brow, 10
Feeds on the rarities of nature's truth, 11
And nothing stands but for his scythe to mow. 12
      And yet to times in hope my verse shall stand, 13
      Praising thy worth despite his cruel hand.

61

Is it thy will thy image should keep open
My heavy eyelids to the weary night?
Dost thou desire my slumbers should be broken
While shadows like to thee do mock my sight? 4
Is it thy spirit that thou send'st from thee
So far from home into my deeds to pry,
To find out shames and idle hours in me,
The scope and tenor of thy jealousy? 8
Oh, no, thy love, though much, is not so great;
It is my love that keeps mine eye awake,
Mine own true love that doth my rest defeat,
To play the watchman ever for thy sake.
      For thee watch I whilst thou dost wake elsewhere, 13
      From me far off, with others all too near.

62

Sin of self-love possesseth all mine eye,
And all my soul, and all my every part;
And for this sin there is no remedy,
It is so grounded inward in my heart.
Methinks no face so gracious is as mine, 5
No shape so true, no truth of such account,
And for myself mine own worth do define 7
As I all other in all worths surmount. 8
But when my glass shows me myself indeed, 9
Beated and chapped with tanned antiquity, 10
Mine own self-love quite contrary I read;
Self so self-loving were iniquity. 12
      'Tis thee, my self, that for myself I praise, 13
      Painting my age with beauty of thy days. 14

63

Against my love shall be, as I am now, 1
With Time's injurious hand crushed and o'erworn; 2
When hours have drained his blood and filled his brow
With lines and wrinkles; when his youthful morn
Hath traveled on to age's steepy night, 5
And all those beauties whereof now he's king
Are vanishing or vanished out of sight,
Stealing away the treasure of his spring;
For such a time do I now fortify 9
Against confounding age's cruel knife,
That he shall never cut from memory 11
My sweet love's beauty, though my lover's life. 12
      His beauty shall in these black lines be seen, 13
      And they shall live, and he in them still green. 14

64

When I have seen by Time's fell hand defaced 1
The rich proud cost of outworn buried age; 2
When sometime lofty towers I see down-razed 3
And brass eternal slave to mortal rage; 4
When I have seen the hungry ocean gain
Advantage on the kingdom of the shore,
And the firm soil win of the wat'ry main, 7
Increasing store with loss and loss with store; 8
When I have seen such interchange of state, 9
Or state itself confounded to decay, 10
Ruin hath taught me thus to ruminate
That Time will come and take my love away. 12
      This thought is as a death, which cannot choose 13
      But weep to have that which it fears to lose. 14

65

Since brass, nor stone, nor earth, nor boundless sea 1
But sad mortality o'ersways their power,
How with this rage shall beauty hold a plea, 3
Whose action is no stronger than a flower? 4
Oh, how shall summer's honey breath hold out
Against the wrackful siege of batt'ring days, 6

4 In . . . contend one after another, all struggle onward. 5 Nativity . . . light The newborn infant, no sooner born into the broad expanse of this world and the light of day 7 Crookèd perverse, malignant 8 doth . . . confound now destroys what it gave. 9 doth . . . flourish pierces through and destroys the ornament, i.e., the physical beauty 10 delves the parallels digs the wrinkles, furrows 11 Feeds . . . truth consumes the most precious things created by the fidelity of nature 12 but . . . mow that can escape the mowing of Time's scythe. 13 times in hope times to come
61.4 shadows images. (But also suggesting spirits.) 8 The scope . . . jealousy the aim and purport of your suspicion. (Probably in apposition to shames and idle hours.) 13 watch stay awake. wake revel
62.5 Methinks It seems to me 7 for myself (1) by my own reckoning (2) for my own pleasure 8 As as if. other others 9 glass mirror. indeed as I actually am 10 Beated battered, weather-beaten. tanned antiquity i.e., leathery old age 12 Self . . . iniquity it would be wicked for the self to love such an aged and unattractive self. 13 thee, my self you, with whom I identify myself. for as 14 days i.e., youth.

63.1 Against my love Anticipating the time when my beloved friend 2 crushed and o'erworn creased and worn threadbare (like a long-used garment) 5 traveled (1) journeyed (2) labored. steepy precipitous, i.e., descending swiftly toward death 9 For such a time (Parallel in construction with Against in line 1.) fortify raise works of defense 10 confounding destroying 11 That so that 12 though i.e., though he cut 13 black (1) inscribed in ink (2) the opposite of fair or beautiful 14 still (1) even in death (2) forever. green i.e., as in springtime and youth.
64.1 fell cruel 2 The rich . . . age i.e., those monuments that were the product of proud wealth and magnificent outlay in times now past and forgotten 3 sometime formerly 4 brass . . . rage i.e., seemingly indestructible brass subdued by the destructive power of decay 7 of . . . main at the expense of the ocean 8 Increasing . . . store one gaining as the other loses, and losing as the other gains 9 state condition 10 state pomp, greatness; condition in the abstract. confounded to decay destroyed to the point of being in ruins 12 love beloved friend 13 which cannot choose (Modifies thought.) 14 to have at having
65.1 Since i.e., Since there is neither 3 How . . . plea how against this destructive force can beauty hope to make its case 4 action (1) efficacy (2) case (in law) 6 wrackful destructive

When rocks impregnable are not so stout, 7
Nor gates of steel so strong, but Time decays? 8
Oh, fearful meditation! Where, alack, 9
Shall Time's best jewel from Time's chest lie hid? 10
Or what strong hand can hold his swift foot back?
Or who his spoil of beauty can forbid? 12
    Oh, none, unless this miracle have might,
    That in black ink my love may still shine bright. 14

66

Tired with all these, for restful death I cry: 1
As, to behold desert a beggar born, 2
And needy nothing trimmed in jollity, 3
And purest faith unhappily forsworn, 4
And gilded honor shamefully misplaced, 5
And maiden virtue rudely strumpeted, 6
And right perfection wrongfully disgraced, 7
And strength by limping sway disablèd, 8
And art made tongue-tied by authority, 9
And folly doctorlike controlling skill, 10
And simple truth miscalled simplicity, 11
And captive good attending captain ill. 12
    Tired with all these, from these would I be gone,
    Save that, to die, I leave my love alone. 14

67

Ah, wherefore with infection should he live, 1
And with his presence grace impiety,
That sin by him advantage should achieve 3
And lace itself with his society? 4
Why should false painting imitate his cheek
And steal dead seeming of his living hue? 6
Why should poor beauty indirectly seek 7
Roses of shadow, since his rose is true? 8

Why should he live, now Nature bankrupt is, 9
Beggared of blood to blush through lively veins, 10
For she hath no exchequer now but his, 11
And, proud of many, lives upon his gains? 12
    Oh, him she stores, to show what wealth she had 13
    In days long since, before these last so bad. 14

68

Thus is his cheek the map of days outworn, 1
When beauty lived and died as flowers do now,
Before these bastard signs of fair were born, 3
Or durst inhabit on a living brow; 4
Before the golden tresses of the dead, 5
The right of sepulchers, were shorn away 6
To live a second life on second head; 7
Ere beauty's dead fleece made another gay. 8
In him those holy antique hours are seen 9
Without all ornament, itself and true, 10
Making no summer of another's green,
Robbing no old to dress his beauty new;
    And him as for a map doth Nature store, 13
    To show false art what beauty was of yore.

69

Those parts of thee that the world's eye doth view
Want nothing that the thought of hearts can mend; 2
All tongues, the voice of souls, give thee that due, 3
Utt'ring bare truth, even so as foes commend. 4
Thy outward thus with outward praise is crowned, 5
But those same tongues that give thee so thine own 6
In other accents do this praise confound 7
By seeing farther than the eye hath shown.
They look into the beauty of thy mind,
And that, in guess, they measure by thy deeds; 10
Then, churls, their thoughts, although their eyes were kind,
To thy fair flower add the rank smell of weeds. 12

7 stout sturdy, impregnable **8 decays** brings about their decay.
9–10 Where . . . hid? Where, alas, shall the youth and beauty of my friend (*Time's best jewel*) be hidden away from being deposited by Time in its repository of forgetfulness? **12 spoil** despoliation, ravaging **14 my love** (1) my beloved friend (2) the love I feel for him
66.1 all these i.e., the following **2 As** for instance, namely. **desert** one who is deserving **3 And needy . . . jollity** and empty worthlessness adorned in finery **4 unhappily forsworn** wretchedly and evilly betrayed **5 gilded** golden, splendid. (Not here suggesting mere appearance of splendor.) **6 strumpeted** accused of profligacy, or violated **7 right** true. **disgraced** banished from favor **8 limping sway** halting leadership **9 And art . . . authority** and literature and learning stifled by censorship **10 doctorlike** assuming a learned bearing. **controlling** dominating, curbing **11 miscalled simplicity** slandered as foolishness, naivetè **12 attending** waiting on, subordinated to **14 to die** in dying
67.1 wherefore why. **with infection** i.e., with the world's ills, as enumerated in the preceding sonnet. **he** i.e., the poet's friend **3 That . . . achieve** with the result that sin should flourish by being associated with him **4 lace . . . society** (1) adorn itself with his company (2) weave its way into his company. **6 dead seeming of** lifeless appearance from **7 poor** inferior. **indirectly** imitatively, or, falsely **8 Roses of shadow** i.e., painted roses, cosmetically applied. **since** (1) just because (2) since after all

9–12 Why . . . gains? Why should he continue to live in this bad world, seeing that Nature has now squandered all her resources of beauty on him, with no genuine way left to produce a natural blush on the cheek, since she has no treasury of natural beauty other than what is vested in him, and, though (falsely) taking pride in her abundance (of offspring), lives solely on the wealth (of beauty) that he provides? **13 stores** preserves, keeps in store **14 last** i.e., recent days, the present
68.1 map embodiment, image **3 bastard . . . fair** i.e., cosmetics. **born** (Suggesting also *borne*, "worn.") **4 inhabit** dwell **5–7 Before . . . head** i.e., before the deplorable current fad of making wigs out of dead persons' hair **8 gay** lovely, gaudy **9 holy antique hours** blessed ancient times **10 all** any **13 store** stock (with beauty) and preserve
69.2 Want lack. **mend** improve upon **3–4 the voice . . . commend** i.e., uttering heartfelt conviction, allow that as your due, thus saying what even your enemies would concede to be the bare truth. **5 outward praise** the kind of praise suited to mere outward qualities **6 thine own** your due **7 In other accents** in other terms and with another emphasis. **confound** confute, destroy **10 in guess** at a guess **12 To . . . weeds** i.e., to the flower of your outward beauty, they contrastingly suggest something putrid within.

But why thy odor matcheth not thy show, 13
The soil is this, that thou dost common grow. 14

70

That thou art blamed shall not be thy defect, 1
For slander's mark was ever yet the fair; 2
The ornament of beauty is suspect, 3
A crow that flies in heaven's sweetest air. 4
So thou be good, slander doth but approve 5
Thy worth the greater, being wooed of time, 6
For canker vice the sweetest buds doth love, 7
And thou present'st a pure unstainèd prime. 8
Thou hast passed by the ambush of young days, 9
Either not assailed, or victor being charged; 10
Yet this thy praise cannot be so thy praise 11
To tie up envy, evermore enlarged. 12
　If some suspect of ill masked not thy show, 13
　Then thou alone kingdoms of hearts shouldst owe. 14

71

No longer mourn for me when I am dead
Than you shall hear the surly sullen bell 2
Give warning to the world that I am fled
From this vile world, with vilest worms to dwell.
Nay, if you read this line, remember not
The hand that writ it, for I love you so
That I in your sweet thoughts would be forgot
If thinking on me then should make you woe. 8
Oh, if, I say, you look upon this verse
When I perhaps compounded am with clay, 10
Do not so much as my poor name rehearse, 11
But let your love even with my life decay, 12
　Lest the wise world should look into your moan 13
　And mock you with me after I am gone. 14

72

Oh, lest the world should task you to recite 1
What merit lived in me that you should love,

After my death, dear love, forget me quite;
For you in me can nothing worthy prove—
Unless you would devise some virtuous lie
To do more for me than mine own desert,
And hang more praise upon deceasèd I 7
Than niggard truth would willingly impart.
Oh, lest your true love may seem false in this,
That you for love speak well of me untrue, 10
My name be buried where my body is, 11
And live no more to shame nor me nor you. 12
　For I am shamed by that which I bring forth, 13
　And so should you, to love things nothing worth. 14

73

That time of year thou mayst in me behold
When yellow leaves, or none, or few, do hang
Upon those boughs which shake against the cold,
Bare ruined choirs where late the sweet birds sang. 4
In me thou see'st the twilight of such day
As after sunset fadeth in the west,
Which by and by black night doth take away,
Death's second self, that seals up all in rest. 8
In me thou see'st the glowing of such fire
That on the ashes of his youth doth lie 10
As the deathbed whereon it must expire,
Consumed with that which it was nourished by. 12
　This thou perceiv'st, which makes thy love more strong,
　To love that well which thou must leave ere long. 14

74

But be contented when that fell arrest 1
Without all bail shall carry me away; 2
My life hath in this line some interest, 3
Which for memorial still with thee shall stay. 4
When thou reviewest this, thou dost review 5
The very part was consecrate to thee. 6
The earth can have but earth, which is his due; 7
My spirit is thine, the better part of me.

---

13 odor i.e., reputation　**14 soil** (1) blemish, fault (2) origin, source, ground.　**common** cheapened by being too familiar and available to all, inferior (like a weed)
70.1 defect fault　**2 mark** target　**3 The . . . suspect** i.e., Beauty is always attended by suspicion (*suspect*), as though suspicion were a necessary ornament to beauty　**5 So** Provided that.　**approve** prove
6 being . . . time i.e., since it shows you are courted by the world
7 canker vice i.e., slander, that is like the cankerworm　**8 unstainèd prime** unspoiled youth (like the pure, unspoiled flower that attracts the cankerworm)　**9 ambush . . . days** temptations of youth
10 being charged when you were assailed　**11–12 Yet . . . enlarged** yet the praise you receive cannot be enough to silence malice, which is always at liberty to do its worst.　**13 If . . . show** If some suspicion (*suspect*) of ill doing did not partly obscure your outward attractiveness　**14 owe** own.
71.2 bell a passing bell for one who has died, rung once for each year of that person's life　**8 on** of, about.　**make you woe** cause you woe or make you woeful.　**10 compounded** mingled　**11 rehearse** repeat
12 even with at the same time as　**13 look . . . moan** investigate the cause of your sorrow　**14 with** because of; for loving; along with
72.1 recite tell

7 hang (as in hanging trophies on a funeral monument)　**10 of me untrue** (1) about me untruly (2) about me, flawed and inconstant as I am　**11 My name be** let my name be　**12 nor . . . nor** neither . . . nor　**13 that . . . forth** (Perhaps a deprecatory reference to the author's acting and writing of plays, but more probably his verse or his written work generally.)　**14 should you** i.e., you ought to be ashamed
73.4 Bare . . . sang (In their arched shape, the bare trees resemble the church choir where the service is sung; with a hint of *quires*, gatherings of *leaves* [see line 2] in a book or manuscript, and evoking memories of church buildings left in ruins by the dissolution of the monasteries in the English Reformation. *Late* means "lately.")　**8 seals** closes　**10 his** its　**12 with** (1) by (2) along with　**14 that** (1) me, your beloved friend (2) youth and life itself.　**leave** i.e., lose by the speaker's death
74.1 be contented . . . arrest do not be distressed when that cruel arrest (carried out by Death)　**3 line** verse.　**interest** legal concern, right, or title　**4 still** (1) always (2) despite death　**5 reviewest this** see this again (and view it with a critical eye)　**6 part was consecrate** part (of me) that was dedicated solemnly (as in a religious service)
7 his its

So then thou hast but lost the dregs of life,
The prey of worms, my body being dead,
The coward conquest of a wretch's knife,   11
Too base of thee to be rememberèd.   12
    The worth of that is that which it contains,   13
    And that is this, and this with thee remains.   14

75

So are you to my thoughts as food to life,   1
Or as sweet-seasoned showers are to the ground.   2
And for the peace of you I hold such strife   3
As twixt a miser and his wealth is found:
Now proud as an enjoyer, and anon
Doubting the filching age will steal his treasure;   6
Now counting best to be with you alone,   7
Then bettered that the world may see my pleasure;   8
Sometime all full with feasting on your sight,
And by and by clean starvèd for a look;   10
Possessing or pursuing no delight
Save what is had or must from you be took.   12
    Thus do I pine and surfeit day by day,   13
    Or gluttoning on all, or all away.   14

76

Why is my verse so barren of new pride?   1
So far from variation or quick change?   2
Why with the time do I not glance aside   3
To newfound methods and to compounds strange?   4
Why write I still all one, ever the same,   5
And keep invention in a noted weed,   6
That every word doth almost tell my name,
Showing their birth and where they did proceed?   8
Oh, know, sweet love, I always write of you,
And you and love are still my argument;   10
So all my best is dressing old words new,
Spending again what is already spent.
    For as the sun is daily new and old,
    So is my love still telling what is told.   14

77

Thy glass will show thee how thy beauties wear,   1
Thy dial how thy precious minutes waste;   2
The vacant leaves thy mind's imprint will bear,   3
And of this book this learning mayst thou taste: 4
The wrinkles which thy glass will truly show
Of mouthèd graves will give thee memory;   6
Thou by thy dial's shady stealth mayst know   7
Time's thievish progress to eternity.
Look what thy memory cannot contain   9
Commit to these waste blanks, and thou shalt find   10
Those children nursed, delivered from thy brain,   11
To take a new acquaintance of thy mind.   12
    These offices, so oft as thou wilt look,   13
    Shall profit thee and much enrich thy book.   14

78

So oft have I invoked thee for my Muse
And found such fair assistance in my verse   2
As every alien pen hath got my use   3
And under thee their poesy disperse.   4
Thine eyes, that taught the dumb on high to sing   5
And heavy ignorance aloft to fly,
Have added feathers to the learnèd's wing   7
And given grace a double majesty.   8
Yet be most proud of that which I compile,   9
Whose influence is thine and born of thee.   10
In others' works thou dost but mend the style,   11
And arts with thy sweet graces gracèd be;   12
    But thou art all my art, and dost advance   13
    As high as learning my rude ignorance.

79

Whilst I alone did call upon thy aid,
My verse alone had all thy gentle grace,
But now my gracious numbers are decayed,   3
And my sick Muse doth give another place.   4

77.1 glass mirror. **wear** wear away   **2 dial** sundial   **3 vacant leaves** blank pages. (Apparently these lines accompanied the gift of a book of blank pages, a memorandum book.)   **thy mind's imprint** i.e., your reflections and ideas, to be set down in the memorandum book **4 this learning** i.e., mental profit derived from reflecting and keeping a journal, as explained in lines 9 ff.   **6 mouthèd** all-devouring, gaping.   **memory** reminder   **7 shady stealth** stealthy shadow   **9 Look what** Whatever   **10 waste blanks** blank pages   **10–12 thou . . . mind** you will see those thoughts, the children of your brain, nursed to maturity and ready to be newly reencountered by your mind. **13 offices** duties (of meditation and reflection)   **14 thy book** i.e., the memorandum book, where these reflections are to be set down. **78.2 fair** favorable   **3 As** that.   **alien** belonging to others.   **got my use** adopted my practice   **4 under thee** i.e., with you as their muse or patron; under your influence.   **disperse** circulate.   **5 on high** aloud. (Also anticipating *aloft*.)   **7 added . . . wing** i.e., enabled learned poets to fly higher still. (A falconry metaphor; birds could be given extra wing feathers.)   **8 And . . . majesty** and have added to the majesty of poets already capable of it.   **9 compile** compose, write **10 influence** inspiration. (With suggestion of astrological meaning.) **11 mend the style** correct or improve the style. (Also with a suggestion of repairing the point of a writing quill or stylus, continuing the metaphor of *pen* and *feathers*.)   **12 arts** learning, literary culture **13 advance** lift up
79.3 numbers verse   **4 doth . . . place** yields place to another.

11 The coward . . . knife i.e., the cowardly conquest that even such a poor wretch as Mortality, or Death, can make with his scythe   **12 of . . . rememberèd** to be remembered by you.   **13–14 The worth . . . remains** The only worth of my body is the spirit it contains, i.e., this verse, which will remain with you and endure through you.
75.1 as food to life what food is to life   **2 sweet-seasoned** of the sweet season, i.e., spring   **3 of you** to be found in loving you   **6 Doubting** suspecting, fearing that.   **filching** thieving   **7 counting** (1) thinking it (2) reckoning, like a miser   **8 bettered** made happier, better pleased. **see my pleasure** i.e., see me with you, enjoying your company **10 clean** completely, absolutely.   **a look** (1) a glimpse of you (2) an exchange of glances   **12 Save . . . took** except what is had or must be received from you alone.   **13 pine and surfeit** starve and overeat **14 Or . . . or** either . . . or.   **all away** i.e., all food being taken away. **76.1 pride** ornament.   **2 quick change** fashionable innovation. **3 time** way of the world, fashion   **4 compounds strange** literary inventions, or perhaps, compound words, neologisms.   **5 still all one** continually one way   **6 invention** literary creation.   **noted weed** familiar garment   **8 where** whence   **10 still** always. **argument** subject, theme   **14 telling** (1) retelling (2) counting over. (Continuing the financial wordplay of *Spending* and *spent* in line 12, and *counting* in 75.7.)

I grant, sweet love, thy lovely argument   5
Deserves the travail of a worthier pen,
Yet what of thee thy poet doth invent   7
He robs thee of and pays it thee again.   8
He lends thee virtue, and he stole that word
From thy behavior; beauty doth he give,
And found it in thy cheek; he can afford   11
No praise to thee but what in thee doth live.
    Then thank him not for that which he doth say,
    Since what he owes thee thou thyself dost pay.

80

Oh, how I faint when I of you do write,   1
Knowing a better spirit doth use your name,   2
And in the praise thereof spends all his might
To make me tongue-tied, speaking of your fame!
But since your worth, wide as the ocean is,   5
The humble as the proudest sail doth bear,   6
My saucy bark, inferior far to his,
On your broad main doth willfully appear.   8
Your shallowest help will hold me up afloat,   9
Whilst he upon your soundless deep doth ride;   10
Or, being wrecked, I am a worthless boat,   11
He of tall building and of goodly pride.   12
    Then if he thrive and I be cast away,   13
    The worst was this: my love was my decay.   14

81

Or I shall live your epitaph to make,   1
Or you survive when I in earth am rotten,
From hence your memory death cannot take,   3
Although in me each part will be forgotten.   4
Your name from hence immortal life shall have,   5
Though I, once gone, to all the world must die;
The earth can yield me but a common grave,
When you entombèd in men's eyes shall lie.
Your momument shall be my gentle verse,
Which eyes not yet created shall o'erread,
And tongues to be your being shall rehearse   11
When all the breathers of this world are dead.   12
    You still shall live—such virtue hath my pen—   13
    Where breath most breathes, even in the mouths of
      men.   14

82

I grant thou wert not married to my Muse,
And therefore mayst without attaint o'erlook   2
The dedicated words which writers use   3
Of their fair subject, blessing every book.   4
Thou art as fair in knowledge as in hue,   5
Finding thy worth a limit past my praise,   6
And therefore art enforced to seek anew
Some fresher stamp of these time-bettering days.   8
And do so, love; yet when they have devised
What strainèd touches rhetoric can lend,
Thou, truly fair, wert truly sympathized   11
In true plain words by thy true-telling friend;
    And their gross painting might be better used   13
    Where cheeks need blood; in thee it is abused.   14

83

I never saw that you did painting need,   1
And therefore to your fair no painting set;   2
I found, or thought I found, you did exceed
The barren tender of a poet's debt;   4
And therefore have I slept in your report,   5
That you yourself, being extant, well might show   6
How far a modern quill doth come too short,   7
Speaking of worth, what worth in you doth grow.   8
This silence for my sin you did impute,   9
Which shall be most my glory, being dumb;   10
For I impair not beauty, being mute,   11
When others would give life and bring a tomb.   12
    There lives more life in one of your fair eyes
    Than both your poets can in praise devise.   14

84

Who is it that says most which can say more   1
Than this rich praise: that you alone are you,   2
In whose confine immurèd is the store   3
Which should example where your equal grew?   4

5 thy lovely argument the theme of your lovable qualities   **6 travail** labor   **7–8 Yet . . . again** yet whatever a poet under your patronage discovers as a literary subject concerning you he merely robs from you and gives you back your own again.   **11 afford** furnish, extend   **80.1 faint** grow weak, falter   **2 better spirit** i.e., rival poet, whom the speaker admires   **5 wide . . . is** as wide as is the ocean   **6 as** as well as   **8 main** ocean.   **willfully** perversely, audaciously   **9 Your . . . afloat** i.e., My genius is so slight that I derive only minimal benefit from the greatness of you as my subject   **10 soundless** unfathomable   **11 wrecked** shipwrecked   **12 tall building** i.e., sturdy construction.   **pride** splendor.   **13 cast away** (1) shipwrecked (2) abandoned   **14 my love** (1) my love for you, which led me to be so reckless in my inferior boat (2) you, my beloved friend.   **decay** ruin.   **81.1 Or** Whether   **3 hence** (1) this poetry (2) the world   **4 in . . . part** every quality of mine (as distinguished from the poetry)   **5 from hence** (1) from this poetry (2) henceforth   **11 to be** i.e., of persons yet unborn.   **rehearse** recite   **12 breathers** living people.   **this world** this present time   **13 virtue** power   **14 even in the** in the very

82.2 attaint blame, discredit.   **o'erlook** look at, peruse   **3 dedicated** devoted. (With suggestion of "dedicatory.")   **writers** i.e., other writers   **4 blessing every book** i.e., you bestowing favor thus on the writings presented to you, or, writers commending their own work.   **5 hue** complexion, appearance   **6 a limit . . . praise** an area extending beyond the capacities of my praise   **8 Some . . . days** some more recently issued imprint, i.e., more up-to-date literary product of this culturally sophisticated age.   **11 wert truly sympathized** would be faithfully matched and described   **13 gross painting** flattery that is heavily laid on, like a cosmetic   **14 abused** misused, misapplied.   **83.1 painting** i.e., artificial enhancement of beauty   **2 fair** beauty.   **set** applied   **4 The barren . . . debt** the worthless homage that a poet can offer you   **5 slept . . . report** been neglectful in writing praisingly of you   **6 That** because, so that.   **extant** still alive and much in the public eye   **7 modern** (1) commonplace (2) up-to-date   **7–8 doth come . . . grow** comes too short, in describing your worth, of the actual worth that flourishes in you.   **9–10 This . . . dumb** You imputed my silence to willful failure when, in fact, it will prove most to my credit   **11 being mute** (Modifies *I*.)   **12 bring a tomb** i.e., instead, they bring an inadequate monument that conceals lifelessly rather than enhances.   **14 both your poets** i.e., (probably,) I and the rival poet   **84.1–2 Who . . . praise** What extravagant writer of praise can say more than this in way of praise   **3–4 In . . . grew** in whose person are contained all those rich qualities that would be needed as a model to produce again your equal in beauty.

Lean penury within that pen doth dwell 5
That to his subject lends not some small glory; 6
But he that writes of you, if he can tell
That you are you, so dignifies his story. 8
Let him but copy what in you is writ,
Not making worse what nature made so clear, 10
And such a counterpart shall fame his wit, 11
Making his style admirèd everywhere.
　　You to your beauteous blessings add a curse, 13
　　Being fond on praise, which makes your praises 14
　　　worse.

85

My tongue-tied Muse in manners holds her still, 1
While comments of your praise, richly compiled, 2
Reserve thy character with golden quill 3
And precious phrase by all the Muses filed. 4
I think good thoughts whilst other write good words, 5
And like unlettered clerk still cry "Amen" 6
To every hymn that able spirit affords 7
In polished form of well-refinèd pen.
Hearing you praised, I say "'Tis so, 'tis true,"
And to the most of praise add something more; 10
But that is in my thought, whose love to you, 11
Though words come hindmost, holds his rank before. 12
　　Then others for the breath of words respect, 13
　　Me for my dumb thoughts, speaking in effect. 14

86

Was it the proud full sail of his great verse, 1
Bound for the prize of all-too-precious you, 2
That did my ripe thoughts in my brain inhearse, 3
Making their tomb the womb wherein they grew?
Was it his spirit, by spirits taught to write 5
Above a mortal pitch, that struck me dead? 6
No, neither he, nor his compeers by night 7
Giving him aid, my verse astonishèd. 8
He, nor that affable familiar ghost 9

Which nightly gulls him with intelligence, 10
Deceives the rivals of my silence cannot boast;
I was not sick of any fear from thence. 12
　　But when your countenance filled up his line, 13
　　Then lacked I matter; that enfeebled mine. 14

87

Farewell! Thou art too dear for my possessing, 1
And like enough thou know'st thy estimate. 2
The charter of thy worth gives thee releasing; 3
My bonds in thee are all determinate. 4
For how do I hold thee but by thy granting,
And for that riches where is my deserving?
The cause of this fair gift in me is wanting,
And so my patent back again is swerving. 8
Thyself thou gav'st, thy own worth then not knowing,
Or me, to whom thou gav'st it, else mistaking; 10
So thy great gift, upon misprision growing, 11
Comes home again, on better judgment making. 12
　　Thus have I had thee as a dream doth flatter,
　　In sleep a king, but waking no such matter.

88

When thou shalt be disposed to set me light 1
And place my merit in the eye of scorn,
Upon thy side against myself I'll fight 3
And prove thee virtuous, though thou art forsworn.
With mine own weakness being best acquainted,
Upon thy part I can set down a story
Of faults concealed, wherein I am attainted, 7
That thou in losing me shall win much glory. 8
And I by this will be a gainer too;
For, bending all my loving thoughts on thee,
The injuries that to myself I do,
Doing thee vantage, double-vantage me. 12
　　Such is my love, to thee I so belong,
　　That for thy right myself will bear all wrong.

89

Say that thou didst forsake me for some fault, 1
And I will comment upon that offense; 2
Speak of my lameness, and I straight will halt, 3

5–6 **Lean . . . glory** It is a poor piece of writing indeed that does not confer at least some glory on its subject　8 **so** sufficiently, thus
10 **clear** glorious, shining　11 **counterpart** copy, likeness.　**fame** endow with fame　13 **curse** (1) defect in character (2) burden for those seeking to praise you　14 **Being fond** doting.　**which . . . worse** (1) which encourages false flattery (2) which makes all praise seem inadequate in comparison to you.
85.1 **in . . . still** politely remains silent　2 **comments . . . compiled** eulogies of you composed in fine language　3 **Reserve thy character** store up praise of you in their writings.　**golden** aureate, affected
4 **precious** affected.　**filed** polished.　5 **other** others　6–7 **like . . . affords** like an illiterate assistant to a priest continually give my approval to every praising verse that the rival poet (and others like him) provides　10 **most** highmost　11 **that . . . thought** that which I add is added silently　12 **holds . . . before** is second to none in love.
13 **Then . . . respect** Then take notice of others for what they say
14 **speaking in effect** conveying what speech would say.
86.1 **his** i.e., an unidentified rival poet's　2 **prize** capture, booty (as in a seized cargo vessel)　3 **inhearse** coffin up　5 **spirits** i.e., literary ancestors or contemporaries. (With a suggestion also of *daemons*, attendant spirits.)　6 **pitch** height. (A term from falconry.)　**dead** i.e., dumb, silent.　7 **compeers by night** spirits (see line 5) visiting and aiding the poet in his dreams or nighttime reading　8 **astonishèd** struck dumb.　9 **ghost** spirit (as in lines 5 and 7)

10 **gulls** misleads.　**intelligence** information, ideas　12 **of** with
13 **countenance filled up** (1) approval repaired any defect in
(2) beauty served as subject for　14 **lacked I matter** I had nothing left to write about
87.1 **dear** precious　2 **like** likely, probably.　**estimate** value.　3 **charter of** privilege derived from.　**releasing** i.e., release from obligations of love　4 **determinate** ended, expired. (A legal term, as throughout this sonnet.)　8 **my . . . swerving** my rights of possession revert to you.
10 **mistaking** i.e., overvaluing　11 **upon misprision growing** arising out of error　12 **on . . . making** on your forming a more accurate judgment.
88.1 **set me light** make light of me, value me slightingly　3 **Upon thy side** supporting your case. (Also *Upon thy part* in line 6.)　7 **concealed** not publicly known.　**attainted** dishonored　8 **That** so that.
losing i.e., separating from. (With a suggestion of "loosing," "setting free," the quarto spelling.)　12 **vantage** advantage
89.1 **Say** Assert, claim　2 **comment** enlarge　3 **Speak . . . halt** i.e., if you ascribe to me any kind of handicap, I immediately will limp to show that you are right. (*Halt* also has the suggestion of ceasing to object, remaining silent.)

Against thy reasons making no defense. 4
Thou canst not, love, disgrace me half so ill, 5
To set a form upon desirèd change, 6
As I'll myself disgrace, knowing thy will. 7
I will acquaintance strangle and look strange, 8
Be absent from thy walks, and in my tongue 9
Thy sweet belovèd name no more shall dwell,
Lest I, too much profane, should do it wrong
And haply of our old acquaintance tell. 12
　For thee against myself I'll vow debate, 13
　For I must ne'er love him whom thou dost hate.

90

Then hate me when thou wilt; if ever, now;
Now, while the world is bent my deeds to cross, 2
Join with the spite of fortune, make me bow,
And do not drop in for an after-loss. 4
Ah, do not, when my heart hath scaped this sorrow, 5
Come in the rearward of a conquered woe; 6
Give not a windy night a rainy morrow, 7
To linger out a purposed overthrow. 8
If thou wilt leave me, do not leave me last,
When other petty griefs have done their spite,
But in the onset come; so shall I taste 11
At first the very worst of fortune's might,
　And other strains of woe, which now seem woe, 13
　Compared with loss of thee will not seem so.

91

Some glory in their birth, some in their skill,
Some in their wealth, some in their body's force,
Some in their garments, though newfangled ill, 3
Some in their hawks and hounds, some in their horse; 4
And every humor hath his adjunct pleasure, 5
Wherein it finds a joy above the rest.
But these particulars are not my measure; 7
All these I better in one general best. 8
Thy love is better than high birth to me,
Richer than wealth, prouder than garments' cost, 10
Of more delight than hawks or horses be;
And having thee, of all men's pride I boast— 12
　Wretched in this alone, that thou mayst take
　All this away and me most wretched make.

92

But do thy worst to steal thyself away, 1
For term of life thou art assurèd mine,
And life no longer than thy love will stay, 2
For it depends upon that love of thine.
Then need I not to fear the worst of wrongs, 5
When in the least of them my life hath end; 6
I see a better state to me belongs 7
Than that which on thy humor doth depend. 8
Thou canst not vex me with inconstant mind,
Since that my life on thy revolt doth lie. 10
Oh, what a happy title do I find, 11
Happy to have thy love, happy to die!
　But what's so blessèd-fair that fears no blot? 13
　Thou mayst be false, and yet I know it not. 14

93

So shall I live, supposing thou art true, 1
Like a deceivèd husband; so love's face 2
May still seem love to me, though altered new, 3
Thy looks with me, thy heart in other place.
For there can live no hatred in thine eye, 5
Therefore in that I cannot know thy change. 6
In many's looks the false heart's history
Is writ in moods and frowns and wrinkles strange, 8
But heaven in thy creation did decree
That in thy face sweet love should ever dwell;
Whate'er thy thoughts or thy heart's workings be,
Thy looks should nothing thence but sweetness tell.
　How like Eve's apple doth thy beauty grow,
　If thy sweet virtue answer not thy show! 14

94

They that have power to hurt and will do none, 1
That do not do the thing they most do show, 2
Who, moving others, are themselves as stone,
Unmovèd, cold, and to temptation slow, 4
They rightly do inherit heaven's graces 5
And husband nature's riches from expense; 6

---

4 reasons charges, arguments **5 disgrace** discredit **6 To . . . change** to provide a pretext for (in the interest of justifying) your change of affection and to set it in proper order **7 As . . . disgrace** as I will disfigure and depreciate myself **8 acquaintance strangle** put an end to familiarity (with you). **strange** like a stranger **9 walks** haunts **12 haply** perchance **13 vow debate** declare hostility, quarrel **90.2 bent** determined. **cross** thwart **4 drop . . . after-loss** crushingly add to my sorrow. **5–6 do not . . . woe** do not, when I have just recovered from my present grief, attack me from the rear **7 windy, rainy** (Suggestive of sighs and tears.) **8 linger out** protract. **purposed** intended, inevitable **11 in the onset** at the outset **13 strains** (1) kinds (2) stresses **91.3 newfangled ill** fashionably unattractive **4 horse** horses **5 humor** disposition, temperament. **his adjunct** its corresponding **7 measure** standard (of happiness); lot in life **8 better** surpass, improve upon **10 prouder** more splendid **12 of . . . boast** I boast of having the equivalent of all that is a source of pride in other men

92.1 But do i.e., But even if you do **2 term of life** i.e., my lifetime **5–6 Then . . . end** I need not fear what most people would call the worst of misfortunes, since the seemingly lesser misfortune—loss of your friendship—would prove fatal to me **7–8 I see . . . depend** i.e., I see that I am happier than most people whose happiness ends when they are cast from favor, since my very existence will cease when I am cast from favor and thus will end my misery. **humor** whim, fancy **10 Since . . . lie** since if you desert me it will cost me my life. **11 happy title** right to be thought happy; fortunate legal right of ownership **13 that fears** as to fear **14 Thou . . . not** i.e., My worst fate would be to lose your affection without knowing it and thereby live on in an unloved state, unreleased by the death that certainty of your desertion would bring. **93.1 So** (Continues the thought of sonnet 92.) **supposing** I supposing (incorrectly) **2 face** appearance **3 new** to something new **5 For** Since **6 in . . . change** I won't be able to detect your changed affection from your eyes. **8 moods** moody looks. **strange** unfriendly **14 answer . . . show** does not conform with your outward appearance. **94.1 and . . . none** and do not willfully try to do hurt **2 show** i.e., show themselves capable of, or, seem to do **4 cold** dispassionate **5 inherit** (1) receive through inheritance (2) enjoy, make use of **6 husband** carefully manage, preserve. **expense** waste, expenditure

They are the lords and owners of their faces,   7
Others but stewards of their excellence.   8
The summer's flower is to the summer sweet,   9
Though to itself it only live and die,   10
But if that flower with base infection meet,
The basest weed outbraves his dignity.   12
　　For sweetest things turn sourest by their deeds;
　　Lilies that fester smell far worse than weeds.   14

95

How sweet and lovely dost thou make the shame
Which, like a canker in the fragrant rose,   2
Doth spot the beauty of thy budding name!   3
Oh, in what sweets dost thou thy sins enclose!
That tongue that tells the story of thy days,
Making lascivious comments on thy sport,   6
Cannot dispraise, but, in a kind of praise,
Naming thy name, blesses an ill report.   8
Oh, what a mansion have those vices got
Which for their habitation chose out thee,
Where beauty's veil doth cover every blot,
And all things turns to fair that eyes can see!   12
　　Take heed, dear heart, of this large privilege;   13
　　The hardest knife ill used doth lose his edge.   14

96

Some say thy fault is youth, some wantonness;   1
Some say thy grace is youth and gentle sport;   2
Both grace and faults are loved of more and less;   3
Thou mak'st faults graces that to thee resort.   4
As on the finger of a thronèd queen
The basest jewel will be well esteemed,
So are those errors that in thee are seen
To truths translated and for true things deemed.   8
How many lambs might the stern wolf betray,   9
If like a lamb he could his looks translate!   10
How many gazers mightst thou lead away,   11
If thou wouldst use the strength of all thy state!   12
　　But do not so; I love thee in such sort   13
　　As, thou being mine, mine is thy good report.   14

97

How like a winter hath my absence been
From thee, the pleasure of the fleeting year!
What freezings have I felt, what dark days seen!
What old December's bareness everywhere!
And yet this time removed was summer's time,   5
The teeming autumn, big with rich increase,   6
Bearing the wanton burden of the prime,   7
Like widowed wombs after their lords' decease.
Yet this abundant issue seemed to me   9
But hope of orphans and unfathered fruit,   10
For summer and his pleasures wait on thee,   11
And, thou away, the very birds are mute;
　　Or, if they sing, 'tis with so dull a cheer   13
　　That leaves look pale, dreading the winter's near.

98

From you have I been absent in the spring,
When proud-pied April, dressed in all his trim,   2
Hath put a spirit of youth in everything,
That heavy Saturn laughed and leapt with him.   4
Yet nor the lays of birds nor the sweet smell   5
Of different flowers in odor and in hue   6
Could make me any summer's story tell,   7
Or from their proud lap pluck them where they grew.   8
Nor did I wonder at the lily's white,
Nor praise the deep vermilion in the rose;
They were but sweet, but figures of delight   11
Drawn after you, you pattern of all those.   12
　　Yet seemed it winter still, and, you away,
　　As with your shadow I with these did play.   14

99

The forward violet thus did I chide: 1
"Sweet thief, whence didst thou steal thy sweet that
　　smells,   2
If not from my love's breath? The purple pride   3
Which on thy soft cheek for complexion dwells
In my love's veins thou hast too grossly dyed."   5
The lily I condemnèd for thy hand,   6
And buds of marjoram had stol'n thy hair;   7
The roses fearfully on thorns did stand,   8

7 They . . . faces they are completely masters of themselves and of the qualities that appear in them   8 but stewards are merely custodians or dispensers   9–10 The . . . die i.e., Such self-contained persons may seem like flowers that live and die unto themselves, though having much sweetness and beauty to bestow   12 outbraves his dignity surpasses in show its worth.   14 Lilies . . . weeds (This line appears in the anonymous play *Edward III*, usually dated before 1595 and attributed in part by some editors to Shakespeare.)
95.2 canker cankerworm that destroys buds and leaves   3 name reputation.   6 sport amours   8 blesses graces   12 all . . . fair makes everything deceptively beautiful   13 large unlimited, licentious   14 his its
96.1 wantonness (1) exuberance (2) lechery   2 gentle sport gentlemanlike amorousness   3 of more and less by high and low   4 Thou . . . resort you convert into graces the faults that attend you.   8 translated transformed   9 stern cruel   10 like i.e., unto those of   11 away astray   12 the strength . . . state the full power at your command, i.e., your wealth, charm, and social rank.   13–14 But . . . report (The same couplet ends sonnet 36.)   report reputation.

97.5 time removed time of separation   6 big pregnant   7 the wanton . . . prime the fruit or offspring of wanton spring, i.e., the crops planted in springtime   9 issue offspring   10 hope of orphans orphaned hope   11 his its.   wait on thee attend on you, are at your disposal   13 with . . . cheer in so melancholy a fashion
98.2 proud-pied gorgeously multicolored.   trim finery   4 That so that.   Saturn (A planet associated with melancholy, *heavy*.)   5 nor the lays neither the songs   6 different flowers flowers differing   7 any summer's story i.e., any pleasant story   8 proud lap i.e., the earth   11 but sweet . . . delight mere sweetness, mere delightful forms or emblems   12 after resembling   14 shadow image, portrait.   these i.e., the flowers
99.1 forward early and presumptuous. (This sonnet has fifteen lines, the first being introductory.)   2 thy sweet your scent   3 pride splendor   5 grossly obviously and heavily   6 for thy hand i.e., because it has stolen its whiteness from your hand   7 And . . . hair i.e., and I condemned the buds of marjoram for having stolen your hair.   buds of marjoram (These are dark purple-red or auburn, and it may be that the reference is to color, although marjoram is noted for its sweet scent.)   8 on thorns did stand grew on thorny stems. (With a suggestion of being apprehensive.)

One blushing shame, another white despair; 9
A third, nor red nor white, had stol'n of both 10
And to his robbery had annexed thy breath, 11
But, for his theft, in pride of all his growth 12
A vengeful canker ate him up to death. 13
  More flowers I noted, yet I none could see
  But sweet or color it had stol'n from thee. 15

100

Where art thou, Muse, that thou forget'st so long
To speak of that which gives thee all thy might?
Spend'st thou thy fury on some worthless song, 3
Dark'ning thy pow'r to lend base subjects light? 4
Return, forgetful Muse, and straight redeem 5
In gentle numbers time so idly spent; 6
Sing to the ear that doth thy lays esteem 7
And gives thy pen both skill and argument. 8
Rise, resty Muse, my love's sweet face survey 9
If Time have any wrinkle graven there; 10
If any, be a satire to decay, 11
And make Time's spoils despisèd everywhere. 12
  Give my love fame faster than Time wastes life; 13
  So thou prevent'st his scythe and crooked knife. 14

101

O truant Muse, what shall be thy amends 1
For thy neglect of truth in beauty dyed? 2
Both truth and beauty on my love depends; 3
So dost thou too, and therein dignified. 4
Make answer, Muse. Wilt thou not haply say, 5
"Truth needs no color with his color fixed, 6
Beauty no pencil, beauty's truth to lay, 7
But best is best, if never intermixed"? 8
Because he needs no praise, wilt thou be dumb? 9
Excuse not silence so, for't lies in thee
To make him much outlive a gilded tomb
And to be praised of ages yet to be. 12
  Then do thy office, Muse; I teach thee how 13
  To make him seem, long hence, as he shows now. 14

102

My love is strengthened, though more weak in seeming; 1
I love not less, though less the show appear.
That love is merchandized whose rich esteeming 3
The owner's tongue doth publish everywhere. 4
Our love was new and then but in the spring 5
When I was wont to greet it with my lays, 6
As Philomel in summer's front doth sing 7
And stops her pipe in growth of riper days— 8
Not that the summer is less pleasant now
Than when her mournful hymns did hush the night,
But that wild music burdens every bough 11
And sweets grown common lose their dear delight.
  Therefore like her I sometime hold my tongue,
  Because I would not dull you with my song. 14

103

Alack, what poverty my Muse brings forth, 1
That, having such a scope to show her pride, 2
The argument all bare is of more worth 3
Than when it hath my added praise beside.
Oh, blame me not if I no more can write! 5
Look in your glass, and there appears a face 6
That overgoes my blunt invention quite, 7
Dulling my lines and doing me disgrace. 8
Were it not sinful then, striving to mend,
To mar the subject that before was well?
For to no other pass my verses tend 11
Than of your graces and your gifts to tell;
  And more, much more, than in my verse can sit 13
  Your own glass shows you when you look in it.

104

To me, fair friend, you never can be old,
For, as you were when first your eye I eyed,
Such seems your beauty still. Three winters cold
Have from the forests shook three summers' pride, 4
Three beauteous springs to yellow autumn turned
In process of the seasons have I seen, 6
Three April perfumes in three hot Junes burned
Since first I saw you fresh, which yet are green. 8

9 shame i.e., red for shame   **10 nor red** neither (purely) red   **11 to . . . annexed** to this robbery had added the robbery of   **12 But, for** although, in punishment for.   **in pride . . . growth** in his prime   **13 canker** cankerworm   **15 But** except.   **sweet** scent (as in line 2)   **100.3 fury** poetic inspiration   **4 Dark'ning** debasing   **5 straight** straightaway   **6 gentle numbers** noble verses.   **idly** foolishly   **7 lays** songs   **8 argument** subject.   **9 resty** inactive, lazy   **10 If to** see if   **11 If any** if there are any.   **satire to** satirist of, here one composing a satire on Time as a despoiler   **12 spoils** acts of destruction, ravages   **13 faster** (1) more quickly (2) more firmly   **14 thou prevent'st** you forestall, thwart.   **crooked knife** curved blade.   **101.1 what . . . amends** what reparation will you make   **2 truth . . . dyed** truth made integrally a part of the beauty which it inhabits.   **3–4 Both . . . dignified** i.e., Both faith and beauty depend on my love for their proper appreciation and recognition, and you, my Muse, depend for your very office and dignity on that same function.   **5 haply** perhaps   **6 no . . . fixed** no artificial color (with suggestion of *pretense*) added to its natural and permanent color or hue   **7 pencil** paintbrush.   **lay** apply color to, as with a brush   **8 intermixed** adulterated.   **9 dumb** silent.   **12 of** by   **13 office** function   **14 long hence** long in the future.   **shows** appears

102.1 seeming outward appearance   **3 merchandized** degraded by being treated as a thing of sale.   **esteeming** valuation   **4 publish** announce, advertise   **5 in the spring** only just beginning   **6 wont . . . lays** accustomed to salute it (our love) with my song   **7 Philomel** the nightingale.   **front** forehead, beginning   **8 stops her pipe** stops singing.   **riper** i.e., those of late summer and autumn   **11 But . . . music** i.e., but because a profusion of wild birds' singing. (Refers to other poets.)   **burdens** weighs down. (But with a musical sense as well; a *burden* is a chorus.)   **14 dull** surfeit   **103.1 poverty** poor stuff   **2 pride** splendor   **3 argument all bare** subject alone, unadorned   **5 no more can write** i.e., (1) am silent (2) cannot go beyond what you yourself are, cannot excel my own poverty of invention.   **6 glass** mirror   **7 overgoes** surpasses; overwhelms.   **blunt invention** unpolished style, writing   **8 Dulling** i.e., making dull by comparison   **11 pass** purpose, issue   **13 sit** reside   **104.4 pride** splendor   **6 process** the progression   **8 which yet** who still

Ah, yet doth beauty, like a dial hand, 9
Steal from his figure and no pace perceived. 10
So your sweet hue, which methinks still doth stand, 11
Hath motion, and mine eye may be deceived,
　　For fear of which, hear this, thou age unbred: 13
　　Ere you were born was beauty's summer dead.

105

Let not my love be called idolatry,
Nor my belovèd as an idol show, 2
Since all alike my songs and praises be
To one, of one, still such, and ever so. 4
Kind is my love today, tomorrow kind,
Still constant in a wondrous excellence;
Therefore my verse, to constancy confined,
One thing expressing, leaves out difference. 8
"Fair, kind, and true" is all my argument,
"Fair, kind, and true" varying to other words;
And in this change is my invention spent, 11
Three themes in one, which wondrous scope affords.
　　Fair, kind, and true have often lived alone, 13
　　Which three till now never kept seat in one. 14

106

When in the chronicle of wasted time 1
I see descriptions of the fairest wights, 2
And beauty making beautiful old rhyme 3
In praise of ladies dead and lovely knights,
Then, in the blazon of sweet beauty's best, 5
Of hand, of foot, of lip, of eye, of brow,
I see their antique pen would have expressed
Even such a beauty as you master now. 8
So all their praises are but prophecies
Of this our time, all you prefiguring;
And, for they looked but with divining eyes, 11
They had not skill enough your worth to sing.
　　For we, which now behold these present days, 13
　　Have eyes to wonder, but lack tongues to praise. 14

107

Not mine own fears nor the prophetic soul 1
Of the wide world dreaming on things to come 2
Can yet the lease of my true love control, 3
Supposed as forfeit to a confined doom. 4
The mortal moon hath her eclipse endured, 5
And the sad augurs mock their own presage; 6
Incertainties now crown themselves assured, 7
And peace proclaims olives of endless age. 8
Now with the drops of this most balmy time 9
My love looks fresh, and Death to me subscribes, 10
Since, spite of him, I'll live in this poor rhyme,
While he insults o'er dull and speechless tribes; 12
　　And thou in this shalt find thy monument,
　　When tyrants' crests and tombs of brass are spent. 14

108

What's in the brain that ink may character 1
Which hath not figured to thee my true spirit? 2
What's new to speak, what now to register, 3
That may express my love or thy dear merit?
Nothing, sweet boy; but yet, like prayers divine,
I must each day say o'er the very same,
Counting no old thing old—thou mine, I thine— 7
Even as when first I hallowed thy fair name. 8
So that eternal love in love's fresh case 9
Weighs not the dust and injury of age, 10
Nor gives to necessary wrinkles place,
But makes antiquity for aye his page, 12
　　Finding the first conceit of love there bred 13
　　Where time and outward form would show it dead. 14

109

Oh, never say that I was false of heart,
Though absence seemed my flame to qualify. 2

9–10 yet . . . perceived yet beauty slips almost imperceptibly away, like the dial hand of a watch making its stealthy progress away from number to number on the dial face. 11 hue appearance, complexion. still doth stand remains seemingly unaltered 13 unbred not yet born
105.2 show appear 4 To . . . so (The poet loves his friend in phrases that recall the paradoxical and mysterious duality of two in one, as in "The Phoenix and Turtle." Such sacred love, by analogy, cannot be idolatry.) 8 difference diversity of theme and the seeming diversity of two persons (the poet and his friend) who are essentially one; also the seeming diversity of "Fair, kind, and true" which is also a variation on a single theme. 11 this change variations on this theme. invention inventiveness. spent expended 13 alone separately (in different people) 14 kept seat resided; sat enthroned
106.1 wasted past, used up 2 wights persons 3 beauty (1) beauty of style and language (2) beauty of the persons described 5 blazon i.e., glorification, cataloguing of qualities. (A heraldic metaphor.) 8 master possess, control 11 for because. divining guessing or predicting as to the future 13 For we For even we 14 praise i.e., praise you worthily, sufficiently.

107.1–2 soul . . . world collective consciousness of humanity 3–4 Can . . . doom can set a limit to the time allotted to me to love you, though imagined to be destined to expire after a limited term. 5 mortal moon (Probably a reference to Queen Elizabeth, ill or deceased, most probably to her death in 1603; she was known as Diana, Cynthia, etc.) 6 And . . . presage and the solemn prophets of disaster now mock their earlier predictions 7 Incertainties . . . assured uncertainties have triumphantly given way to certainties. (Probably a reference to the accession and coronation of King James VI of Scotland and I of England.) 8 olives (Conventionally associated with peace and probably pointing here to King James I's resolutions of war with Spain and strife in Ireland.) of endless age without foreseen end. 9 with the drops i.e., healed as though by a balmy dew. (Balm was employed in the coronation ceremony for James in 1603, as in all such coronations.) 10 subscribes yields 12 insults . . . tribes triumphs scornfully over endless generations of dead who have no poet to celebrate them 14 crests trophies adorning a tomb. spent expended, wasted away.
108.1 character write 2 figured revealed, represented. true constant 3 register record 7 Counting . . . thine dismissing no old truth as out of date or shopworn, such as the truth that you are mine and I yours 8 hallowed (As in "hallowed be thy name" from the Lord's Prayer.) 9 fresh case new exterior and circumstance 10 Weighs not is unconcerned about 11 place consideration, primacy 12–14 But . . . dead Love makes age serve its grand purposes, finding in age and antiquity the first stirrings of love, in a place where conventionally one would suppose it to be dead.
109.2 flame passion. qualify temper, moderate.

As easy might I from myself depart
As from my soul, which in thy breast doth lie.
That is my home of love; if I have ranged, 5
Like him that travels I return again,
Just to the time, not with the time exchanged, 7
So that myself bring water for my stain. 8
Never believe, though in my nature reigned
All frailties that besiege all kinds of blood, 10
That it could so preposterously be stained
To leave for nothing all thy sum of good; 12
    For nothing this wide universe I call
    Save thou, my rose; in it thou art my all.

110

Alas, 'tis true, I have gone here and there
And made myself a motley to the view, 2
Gored mine own thoughts, sold cheap what is most dear, 3
Made old offenses of affections new; 4
Most true it is that I have looked on truth 5
Askance and strangely. But, by all above, 6
These blenches gave my heart another youth, 7
And worse essays proved thee my best of love. 8
Now all is done, have what shall have no end. 9
Mine appetite I never more will grind 10
On newer proof, to try an older friend, 11
A god in love, to whom I am confined.
    Then give me welcome, next my heaven the best, 13
    Even to thy pure and most most loving breast.

111

Oh, for my sake do you with Fortune chide, 1
The guilty goddess of my harmful deeds, 2
That did not better for my life provide 3
Than public means which public manners breeds. 4
Thence comes it that my name receives a brand, 5
And almost thence my nature is subdued
To what it works in, like the dyer's hand. 7
Pity me then, and wish I were renewed, 8
Whilst, like a willing patient, I will drink

Potions of eisel 'gainst my strong infection; 10
No bitterness that I will bitter think, 11
Nor double penance, to correct correction. 12
    Pity me then, dear friend, and I assure ye
    Even that your pity is enough to cure me. 14

112

Your love and pity doth th'impression fill 1
Which vulgar scandal stamped upon my brow; 2
For what care I who calls me well or ill,
So you o'ergreen my bad, my good allow? 4
You are my all the world, and I must strive 5
To know my shames and praises from your tongue;
None else to me, nor I to none alive, 7
That my steeled sense or changes, right or wrong. 8
In so profound abysm I throw all care 9
Of others' voices that my adder's sense 10
To critic and to flatterer stoppèd are. 11
Mark how with my neglect I do dispense: 12
    You are so strongly in my purpose bred 13
    That all the world besides, methinks, are dead.

113

Since I left you, mine eye is in my mind, 1
And that which governs me to go about 2
Doth part his function and is partly blind, 3
Seems seeing, but effectually is out; 4
For it no form delivers to the heart
Of bird, of flower, or shape, which it doth latch; 6
Of his quick objects hath the mind no part, 7
Nor his own vision holds what it doth catch; 8
For if it see the rud'st or gentlest sight, 9
The most sweet-favor or deformd'st creature, 10
The mountain or the sea, the day or night,
The crow or dove, it shapes them to your feature. 12

10 **eisel** vinegar, used as an antiseptic against the plague and also as an agent for removing stains   11 **No bitterness** there is no bitterness   12 **Nor . . . correction** nor will I think it bitter to undertake a twofold penance in order to correct what must be doubly corrected.   14 **Even that your pity** that very pity of yours
112.1 **doth th'impression fill** effaces the scar   2 **vulgar scandal** notoriety (for being an actor?)   4 **So you o'ergreen** provided that you cover as with green growth.   **allow** approve.   5 **my all the world** everything to me   7–8 **None . . . wrong** no one else but you affects my fixed and hardened sensibilities, whether for better or for worse. 9–11 **In . . . are** Into so deep an abyss do I throw all concern as to what others may think that, adderlike, my ears are deaf to critic and flatterer alike. (Adders were popularly supposed to have no sense of hearing.)   12 **Mark . . . dispense** See how I justify my disregard of the opinion of others   13 **You . . . bred** you are so nurtured in my thoughts and are such a powerful influence over my intentions
113.1 **mine . . . mind** i.e., I'm guided by my mind's eye   2 **that . . . about** i.e., my physical sight   3 **part** (1) divide (2) abandon.   **his** its, i.e., the physical eye's. (Also in lines 7 and 8.)   4 **Seems . . . out** seems to be seeing, but in reality is blind   5 **heart** (Here portrayed as capable of receiving sense impressions and of consciousness, as in sonnet 47.)   6 **latch** catch or receive the sight of   7 **Of . . . part** i.e., the mind, attuned to its inner eye, takes no part in the fleeting and lively (*quick*) things seen by the physical sight   8 **Nor . . . holds** nor does the eye itself retain.   **catch** see glimpsingly   9 **For . . . sight** for whether it see the most uncouth or most gracious sight   10 **sweet-favor** sweet-featured   12 **shapes . . . feature** makes them resemble you.

5 **ranged** traveled, wandered   7 **Just . . . exchanged** punctual to the minute, not changed by the period of separation   8 **water for my stain** i.e., repentant tears, to wash away the stain of my offense. 10 **blood** temperament, sensual nature   12 **for** in exchange for 110.2 **motley** jester, fool.   **to the view** in the eyes of the audience 3 **Gored** wounded   4 **Made . . . new** i.e., repeated old offenses or made offense against old friendship in forming new attachments 5 **truth** constancy   6 **Askance and strangely** disdainfully, obliquely and at a distance.   **by all above** by heaven   7 **blenches** swervings. **another youth** i.e., a renewal of true friendship   8 **essays** experiments (in friendship)   9 **Now all** Now that all that.   **have what . . . end** take what is eternal (my friendship).   10 **grind** whet, sharpen 11 **newer proof** further experiment, experience.   **try** test   13 **next my heaven** you, who are to me second only to heaven itself 111.1 **do you** (A command: "Do")   2 **guilty goddess of** goddess responsible for   3 **life** livelihood   4 **Than . . . breeds** than providing me a means of livelihood that depends on catering to the public. (A probable reference to Shakespeare's career as an actor.)   5 **receives a brand** is disgraced (through prejudice against my occupation) 7 **like the dyer's hand** (The dyer's hand is stained by the dye it handles, just as the dramatist's or actor's nature is almost overpowered by the medium in which he works—the theater.)   8 **renewed** restored to what I was by nature, cleansed

Incapable of more, replete with you,
My most true mind thus maketh mine eye untrue.

114

Or whether doth my mind, being crowned with you,	1
Drink up the monarch's plague, this flattery?	2
Or whether shall I say mine eye saith true,	3
And that your love taught it this alchemy,	4
To make of monsters and things indigest	5
Such cherubins as your sweet self resemble,	6
Creating every bad a perfect best	7
As fast as objects to his beams assemble?	8
Oh, 'tis the first, 'tis flatt'ry in my seeing,	9
And my great mind most kingly drinks it up;	
Mine eye well knows what with his gust is greeing,	11
And to his palate doth prepare the cup.	12
If it be poisoned, 'tis the lesser sin	13
That mine eye loves it and doth first begin.	14

115

Those lines that I before have writ do lie,
Even those that said I could not love you dearer;
Yet then my judgment knew no reason why
My most full flame should afterwards burn clearer.
But reckoning Time, whose millioned accidents   5
Creep in twixt vows and change decrees of kings,   6
Tan sacred beauty, blunt the sharp'st intents,   7
Divert strong minds to th' course of alt'ring things—   8
Alas, why, fearing of Time's tyranny,   9
Might I not then say, "Now I love you best,"   10
When I was certain o'er incertainty,   11
Crowning the present, doubting of the rest?   12
    Love is a babe; then might I not say so,   13
    To give full growth to that which still doth grow.   14

116

Let me not to the marriage of true minds
Admit impediments. Love is not love   2

Which alters when it alteration finds,   3
Or bends with the remover to remove.   4
Oh, no, it is an ever-fixèd mark   5
That looks on tempests and is never shaken;
It is the star to every wand'ring bark,   7
Whose worth's unknown, although his height be taken.   8
Love's not Time's fool, though rosy lips and cheeks   9
Within his bending sickle's compass come;   10
Love alters not with his brief hours and weeks,
But bears it out even to the edge of doom.   12
    If this be error and upon me proved,
    I never writ, nor no man ever loved.

117

Accuse me thus: that I have scanted all   1
Wherein I should your great deserts repay,
Forgot upon your dearest love to call,   3
Whereto all bonds do tie me day by day;
That I have frequent been with unknown minds,   5
And given to time your own dear-purchased right;   6
That I have hoisted sail to all the winds
Which should transport me farthest from your sight.   8
Book both my willfulness and errors down,   9
And on just proof surmise accumulate;   10
Bring me within the level of your frown,   11
But shoot not at me in your wakened hate,
    Since my appeal says I did strive to prove   13
    The constancy and virtue of your love.

118

Like as to make our appetites more keen   1
With eager compounds we our palate urge;   2
As to prevent our maladies unseen   3
We sicken to shun sickness when we purge: 4
Even so, being full of your ne'er-cloying sweetness,   5
To bitter sauces did I frame my feeding   6
And, sick of welfare, found a kind of meetness   7

114.1, 3 **Or whether** (Indicates alternative possibilities.)   **1 crowned with you** elevated by possession of you   **2 the monarch's . . . flattery** this pleasing delusion to which all monarchs are prone.   **4 your love** my love of you.   **alchemy** science of transmuting base metals   **5 indigest** chaotic, formless   **6 cherubins** angelic forms (suggesting the youth and beauty of the friend)   **7 Creating** creating out of **8 his beams** its (the eye's) gaze   **9 'tis flatt'ry . . . seeing** my eye is flattering my mind (see lines 1–2)   **11 what . . . greeing** what agrees with the mind's taste   **12 to** to suit   **13–14 'tis . . . begin** it extenuates the eye's sinful deed (of misleading the mind) that it tastes of the poison first, like an official taster sampling food before it is given to the king.
115.5 **reckoning Time** (1) Time, which we reckon up (2) Time, which demands a reckoning and settles all accounts.   **millioned accidents** multitudinous unforeseen occurrences   **6 twixt vows** i.e., between the making of vows and their fulfillment   **7 Tan** darken, i.e., coarsen **8 Divert . . . things** divert the most resolute of intentions into the current of changing circumstances   **9 fearing of** fearing   **10 Might . . . say** i.e., wasn't it understandable for me to say then, when I wrote *Those lines* (line 1)   **11 certain o'er incertainty** i.e., certain of my love's perfection then, as contrasted with the uncertainty of the future **12 Crowning** exalting.   **doubting of** fearing   **13 then might . . . so** i.e., therefore it was wrong of me to say, "Now I love you best" (line 10)   **14 To give** thereby giving
116.2 **Admit** concede that there might be, allow consideration of. (An echo of the marriage service.)

3 alteration i.e., in age, beauty, affection, health, circumstance   **4 Or . . . remove** or changes simply because there is change (by ill health, mental deterioration, death, absence, or inconstancy) in the person loved.   **5 mark** seamark, conspicuous object distinguishable at sea as an aid to navigation   **7 wand'ring bark** lost ship   **8 Whose . . . taken** whose value is beyond estimation, although its altitude above the horizon can be determined (for purposes of navigation).   **9 fool** plaything, laughingstock   **10 his** i.e., Time's. (Also in line 11.) **bending** curved.   **compass** range   **12 bears . . . doom** endures or holds out to the very Day of Judgment.
117.1 **scanted** come short in   **3 Forgot . . . call** forgot to invoke or call upon your most precious love   **5 frequent** familiar.   **unknown minds** strangers of no consequence   **6 And . . . right** and wasted time that should have been devoted to you, to which you had every right   **8 should** were likely to   **9 Book . . . down** Record both my willful faults and errors   **10 on . . . accumulate** to sure proof add surmise, suspicion   **11 level** point-blank range, aim   **13 appeal** legal appealing of the case.   **I . . . prove** my intention was to test
118.1 **Like as** Just as   **2 eager compounds** pungent, bitter concoctions.   **urge** stimulate   **3 As** just as.   **prevent** anticipate, forestall **4 We . . . purge** we induce a kind of sickness through purging (i.e., evacuation of stomach or bowel), in order to ward off greater sickness **5 Even so** in just the same way   **6 bitter sauces** i.e., other loves, undesirable in comparison with you.   **frame** adapt, direct   **7 sick of welfare** surfeited by health and happiness (in love).   **meetness** suitability

To be diseased ere that there was true needing.   8
Thus policy in love, t'anticipate   9
The ills that were not, grew to faults assured,   10
And brought to medicine a healthful state   11
Which, rank of goodness, would by ill be cured.   12
　　But thence I learn, and find the lesson true:
　　Drugs poison him that so fell sick of you.   14

119

What potions have I drunk of siren tears,   1
Distilled from limbecks foul as hell within,   2
Applying fears to hopes and hopes to fears,   3
Still losing when I saw myself to win!   4
What wretched errors hath my heart committed,
Whilst it hath thought itself so blessèd never!   6
How have mine eyes out of their spheres been fitted   7
In the distraction of this madding fever!   8
Oh, benefit of ill! Now I find true
That better is by evil still made better;
And ruined love, when it is built anew,
Grows fairer than at first, more strong, far greater.
　　So I return rebuked to my content,
　　And gain by ills thrice more than I have spent.

120

That you were once unkind befriends me now,   1
And for that sorrow which I then did feel   2
Needs must I under my transgression bow,   3
Unless my nerves were brass or hammered steel.   4
For if you were by my unkindness shaken
As I by yours, you've passed a hell of time,   6
And I, a tyrant, have no leisure taken   7
To weigh how once I suffered in your crime.   8
Oh, that our night of woe might have remembered   9
My deepest sense how hard true sorrow hits,   10
And soon to you, as you to me then, tendered   11

The humble salve which wounded bosoms fits!   12
　　But that your trespass now becomes a fee;   13
　　Mine ransoms yours, and yours must ransom me.   14

121

'Tis better to be vile than vile esteemed   1
When not to be receives reproach of being,   2
And the just pleasure lost which is so deemed   3
Not by our feeling but by others' seeing.   4
For why should others' false adulterate eyes   5
Give salutation to my sportive blood?   6
Or on my frailties why are frailer spies,   7
Which in their wills count bad what I think good?   8
No, I am that I am, and they that level   9
At my abuses reckon up their own.   10
I may be straight though they themselves be bevel.   11
By their rank thoughts my deeds must not be shown,   12
　　Unless this general evil they maintain:
　　All men are bad, and in their badness reign.   14

122

Thy gift, thy tables, are within my brain   1
Full charactered with lasting memory,   2
Which shall above that idle rank remain   3
Beyond all date, even to eternity—
Or at the least, so long as brain and heart
Have faculty by nature to subsist;   6
Till each to razed oblivion yield his part   7
Of thee, thy record never can be missed.   8
That poor retention could not so much hold,   9
Nor need I tallies thy dear love to score;   10
Therefore to give them from me was I bold,   11

---

12 humble salve i.e., apology and remorse.   **which . . . fits** which is just what wounded hearts need.   **13 that your trespass** that unkindness of yours.   **fee** payment, compensation   **14 ransoms** redeems, excuses   **121.1 vile esteemed** (to be) considered vile   **2 When . . . being** when not to be vile receives the reproach of vileness. (It's even worse to be unjustly accused of wickedness than to be reproved when one's conduct is truly vile.)   **3–4 And . . . seeing** and to lose justifiable pleasure because its justification has to depend not on our feelings but on the censorious attitudes of others.   **5 false adulterate eyes** i.e., the eyes of those whose own wickedness prompts them to misconstrue my innocent love   **6 Give . . . blood** i.e., greet me, in my lusty merriment, with familiarity and with a knowing wink of the eye.   **7 Or . . . spies** Or why should there be persons more faulty than I spying on my fleshly indulgences   **8 Which in their wills** who by the measure of their prurient, licentious minds   **9 am that** am what.   **level** (1) aim (2) guess   **10 abuses** misdoings.   **reckon up their own** i.e., merely enumerate their own misdeeds.   **11 bevel** out of square, crooked.   **12 rank** ugly, foul.   **shown** viewed, interpreted   **14 reign** i.e., prosper. (Only a cynic would interpret my success in love as a paradoxical proof of my sharing in general human depravity.)
122.1 tables writing tablet, memorandum book   **2 charactered with** written by   **3 that idle rank** i.e., the relative unimportance of that memorandum book (as compared with the memory itself)   **6 faculty . . . subsist** natural power to survive   **7–8 Till . . . missed** until both heart and brain have given up their memory of you to the ravages of time, what you have written never can be lost. (Hence the memorandum book itself, which the poet has given away, is not essential.)   **9 retention** i.e., the book, an instrument for retaining memoranda.   **so much** i.e., as much as is in my memory   **10 tallies** sticks notched to serve for reckoning. (The notebook is such a mere *tally*.)   **score** reckon   **11 to . . . me** i.e., to give away the writing tablet.   **bold** i.e., bold in taking the liberty

---

8 ere . . . needing before there was any real necessity for it.   **9 policy** shortsighted calculation.   **t'anticipate** to forestall   **10 assured** actual   **11 to medicine** into a state of needing medical care   **12 rank of goodness** gorged and sickened by good health   **14 Drugs . . . you** a rash and unnecessary course of treatment inflicted true sickness on one (myself) who had thought himself weary of your company.
119.1 siren i.e., deceitful. (The poet seems to speak of an affair.)   **2 limbecks** vessels used in distillation.   **foul as hell within** i.e., possessing an inner ugliness and evil contrasted with a beautiful and seductive appearance   **3 Applying . . . fears** trying vainly to control my wild hopes with a sense of fear and to assuage my fears with hope   **4 Still** always.   **saw myself** vainly expected   **6 so blessèd never** never before so fortunate.   **7 How . . . fitted** How my eyes have popped out in convulsive fit   **8 distraction** frenzy.   **madding fever** fever that drives me mad.
120.1 befriends benefits (by giving me perspective on what I now need to do)   **2–3 for . . . bow** i.e., realizing the sorrow I felt from your unkindness, I must now acknowledge my own guilt in being unkind to you   **4 nerves** sinews   **6 hell of** hellish   **7 have . . . taken** have not taken the opportunity   **8 weigh** consider.   **in your crime** i.e., from your unkindness; or, from erring as you did. (If I suffered so, I should realize you've suffered, too, from my unkindness.)   **9 that our night of woe** would that the dark and woeful time of our earlier estrangement.   **remembered** reminded   **10 sense** consciousness, apprehension   **11 And . . . tendered** i.e., and would that I had quickly offered to you, as you did to me

To trust those tables that receive thee more.   12
    To keep an adjunct to remember thee   13
    Were to import forgetfulness in me.   14

123

No, Time, thou shalt not boast that I do change.
Thy pyramids built up with newer might   2
To me are nothing novel, nothing strange;   3
They are but dressings of a former sight.   4
Our dates are brief, and therefore we admire   5
What thou dost foist upon us that is old,
And rather make them born to our desire   7
Than think that we before have heard them told.   8
Thy registers and thee I both defy,   9
Not wond'ring at the present nor the past,   10
For thy records and what we see doth lie,   11
Made more or less by thy continual haste.   12
    This I do vow and this shall ever be:
    I will be true, despite thy scythe and thee.

124

If my dear love were but the child of state,   1
It might for Fortune's bastard be unfathered,   2
As subject to Time's love or to Time's hate,
Weeds among weeds, or flowers with flowers gathered.   4
No, it was builded far from accident;   5
It suffers not in smiling pomp, nor falls   6
Under the blow of thrallèd discontent,   7
Whereto th'inviting time our fashion calls.   8
It fears not Policy, that heretic,   9
Which works on leases of short-numbered hours,   10
But all alone stands hugely politic,   11
That it nor grows with heat nor drowns with showers.   12
    To this I witness call the fools of Time,   13
    Which die for goodness, who have lived for crime.   14

125

Were't aught to me I bore the canopy,   1
With my extern the outward honoring,
Or laid great bases for eternity   3
Which proves more short than waste or ruining?   4
Have I not seen dwellers on form and favor   5
Lose all, and more, by paying too much rent,   6
For compound sweet forgoing simple savor,   7
Pitiful thrivers, in their gazing spent?   8
No, let me be obsequious in thy heart,   9
And take thou my oblation, poor but free,   10
Which is not mixed with seconds, knows no art   11
But mutual render, only me for thee.   12
    Hence, thou suborned informer! A true soul   13
    When most impeached stands least in thy control.   14

126

O thou, my lovely boy, who in thy power   1
Dost hold Time's fickle glass, his sickle hour;   2
Who hast by waning grown, and therein show'st   3
Thy lovers withering as thy sweet self grow'st;   4
If Nature, sovereign mistress over wrack,   5
As thou goest onwards, still will pluck thee back,   6
She keeps thee to this purpose, that her skill   7
May Time disgrace and wretched minutes kill.   8
Yet fear her, O thou minion of her pleasure!   9
She may detain, but not still keep, her treasure.   10
Her audit, though delayed, answered must be,   11
And her quietus is to render thee.   12

12 those tables i.e., those of memory. **receive thee more** retain more of you. **13 adjunct** aid **14 Were** would be. **import** imply, impute **123.2 pyramids** (May refer to obelisks or other structures erected in Rome in 1586 or in London in 1603.) **3 nothing** not at all **4 dressings . . . sight** reconstructions in new form of things from the past. **5 dates** life spans **7 make . . . desire** consider them newly created to our liking and reinvented by us **8 told** reckoned, told about. **9 registers** visual records, monuments **10 wond'ring** marveling **11 doth lie** deceives us **12 Made . . . haste** i.e., raised one minute and ruined the next (by Time), and alternately overvalued and undervalued by us. **124.1–2 If . . . unfathered** If my love for you were merely the product of circumstances and your high position, we might disavow it as nothing but the bastard child of Fortune **4 Weeds . . . gathered** either despised as worthless like a weed or cherished like a flower as Fortune dictates. **5 accident** chance, fortune **6–8 It . . . calls** it does not grow acquiescent to the dictates of pomp and finery, nor does it weaken under the blows of slavish adversity, both of which the insidious mores of our present age tempt us to regard as fashionable. **9 Policy, that heretic** cunning expediency, false to the spirit of love **10 Which . . . hours** which thinks only shortsightedly of short-term gain and makes only short-term commitments **11 hugely politic** prudent in a long-term sense **12 That . . . showers** so that it neither pins its hopes unrealistically on rising fortunes nor grows desperate in times of adversity. **13–14 To . . . crime** I call as witnesses those creatures of Time who succumb to the moral weaknesses described in this sonnet, and who repent their evil ways only after having lived corruptly.

125.1–4 Were't . . . ruining? Would it mean anything to me if I did public homage to great persons by carrying over their heads a cloth of state as they go in procession, thereby honoring what is external by means of a purely external action, or if I laid foundations for supposedly eternal monuments which then prove to last no longer than the forces of decay and ruin allow? **5 dwellers . . . favor** those who depend on court etiquette and influence peddling; also, in figure and face **6 by paying . . . rent** i.e., by overdoing flattery and depending too much on hopes of obtaining favor **7 For . . . savor** i.e., foregoing wholesome sincerity for the sake of obsequious flattery **8 Pitiful . . . spent** pitiful in their unsuccessful attempts, their means consumed in their ineffectual fawning on greatness. **9 obsequious** (1) courtly (2) devoted **10 oblation** offering. **free** freely offered **11 seconds** inferior matter, adulterants. **art** artifice **12 render** exchange **13 suborned informer** perjured witness, the envious one who has charged the poet with self-interested flattery. **14 impeached** accused **126.1** (This sonnet is made up of six couplets.) **2 Time's . . . hour** Time's treacherous and inexorable hourglass, his reaping time **3 Who . . . grown** you who have grown more youthfully beautiful as you have aged. **show'st** show by way of contrast with yourself **4 Thy lovers** (including the poet) **5 wrack** ruin. (Nature is mistress over decay in that she decays and renews.) **6 onwards** i.e., in life's journey **7 to** for **8 May . . . kill** may put Time to shame and render powerless the passing of the minutes. **9 Yet . . . pleasure!** Yet fear Nature too, you who as her darling are subject to her will! **10 She . . . treasure** i.e., Nature may keep and restore you for a time, but Time will ultimately triumph. **11 Her audit** i.e., The proverbial paying of one's debt to Nature through death; also, Nature's account to Time. **answered** paid **12 quietus** discharge, quittance. **render** surrender

127

In the old age black was not counted fair,   1
Or if it were, it bore not beauty's name;   2
But now is black beauty's successive heir,   3
And beauty slandered with a bastard shame.   4
For since each hand hath put on nature's power,   5
Fairing the foul with art's false borrowed face,   6
Sweet beauty hath no name, no holy bower,   7
But is profaned, if not lives in disgrace.   8
Therefore my mistress' eyes are raven black,
Her brows so suited, and they mourners seem   10
At such who, not born fair, no beauty lack,   11
Sland'ring creation with a false esteem.   12
    Yet so they mourn, becoming of their woe,   13
    That every tongue says beauty should look so.

128

How oft, when thou, my music, music play'st
Upon that blessèd wood whose motion sounds   2
With thy sweet fingers when thou gently sway'st   3
The wiry concord that mine ear confounds,   4
Do I envy those jacks that nimble leap   5
To kiss the tender inward of thy hand,
Whilst my poor lips, which should that harvest reap,
At the wood's boldness by thee blushing stand!   8
To be so tickled, they would change their state   9
And situation with those dancing chips
O'er whom thy fingers walk with gentle gait,
Making dead wood more blest than living lips.
    Since saucy jacks so happy are in this,   13
    Give them thy fingers, me thy lips to kiss.

129

Th'expense of spirit in a waste of shame   1
Is lust in action; and, till action, lust   2

Is perjured, murd'rous, bloody, full of blame,   3
Savage, extreme, rude, cruel, not to trust,   4
Enjoyed no sooner but despisèd straight,   5
Past reason hunted, and no sooner had   6
Past reason hated, as a swallowed bait
On purpose laid to make the taker mad;
Mad in pursuit, and in possession so;
Had, having, and in quest to have, extreme;
A bliss in proof, and proved, a very woe;   11
Before, a joy proposed; behind, a dream.   12
    All this the world well knows; yet none knows well
    To shun the heaven that leads men to this hell.   14

130

My mistress' eyes are nothing like the sun;   1
Coral is far more red than her lips' red;
If snow be white, why then her breasts are dun;   3
If hairs be wires, black wires grow on her head.
I have seen roses damasked, red and white,   5
But no such roses see I in her cheeks;
And in some perfumes is there more delight
Than in the breath that from my mistress reeks.   8
I love to hear her speak, yet well I know
That music hath a far more pleasing sound.
I grant I never saw a goddess go;   11
My mistress, when she walks, treads on the ground.
    And yet, by heaven, I think my love as rare   13
    As any she belied with false compare.   14

131

Thou art as tyrannous, so as thou art,   1
As those whose beauties proudly make them cruel;
For well thou know'st to my dear doting heart   3
Thou art the fairest and most precious jewel.
Yet, in good faith, some say that thee behold
Thy face hath not the power to make love groan;
To say they err I dare not be so bold,
Although I swear it to myself alone.
And, to be sure that is not false I swear,   9
A thousand groans, but thinking on thy face,   10
One on another's neck, do witness bear   11
Thy black is fairest in my judgment's place.   12
    In nothing art thou black save in thy deeds,
    And thence this slander, as I think, proceeds.   14

127.1 **old age** olden times.   **black** darkness of hair and eyes.   **fair**
(1) beautiful (2) light-complexioned   **2 it bore . . . name** i.e., it was not
called beautiful   **3 now . . . heir** nowadays black has been named lawful successor to the title of beauty   **4 beauty . . . shame** i.e., blonde
beauty is declared illegitimate, created artificially by cosmetics.   **5 put on**
assumed   **6 Fairing the foul** making the ugly beautiful.   **borrowed**
face i.e., cosmetics   **7 no name . . . bower** no reputation or pride of family, and no sacred abode   **8 if not** or even   **10 so suited** decked out in
the same color and for the same reason   **11 At** for.   **no beauty lack** i.e.,
nonetheless make themselves attractive   **12 Sland'ring . . . esteem** i.e.,
dishonoring nature by blurring the distinction between real and false
beauty.   **13 they** i.e., my mistress' eyes.   **becoming of** gracing or being
graced by
128.2 **wood** keys of the spinet or virginal.   **motion** mechanism
3 thou gently sway'st you gently control   **4 wiry concord** harmony
produced by strings.   **confounds** i.e., pleasurably overwhelms
5 jacks (Literally, upright pieces of wood fixed to the key lever and
fitted with a quill that plucks the strings of the virginal; here used of
the keys and with a pun on *jacks* in the sense of "common fellows," as
in line 13.)   **8 by** beside, or, with. (The poet stands beside the lady as
she plays, blushing to his very lips; he blushes in vexation at the *jacks'*
boldness with her hand.)   **9 they** i.e., my lips   **13 jacks** (With a pun
on "knaves, fellows," as in line 5.)
129.1–2 **Th'expense . . . action** Lust being consummated is the expenditure or dissipation of vital energy in an orgy of shameful extravagance and guilt. (*Spirit* also suggests "sperm.")   **2 till action** until it
achieves consummation

3 blame (1) guilt (2) recrimination   **4 rude** brutal.   **to trust** to be
trusted   **5 straight** immediately   **6 Past reason** madly, intemperately
11 in proof while experienced.   **proved** i.e., afterward   **12 Before** in
prospect   **14 the heaven** the seeming bliss of sexual consumation.
hell (Often equated imagistically with the vagina.)
130.1 **nothing** not at all   **3 dun** dull grayish brown, mouse-colored
5 damasked mingled red and white   **8 reeks** emanates.   **11 go** walk
13 rare extraordinary and unique   **14 As . . . compare** as any woman
misrepresented with false comparison.
131.1 **tyrannous** pitiless and domineering.   **so as thou art** just as you
are (dark, not considered handsome)   **3 dear** fond   **9 to be sure** as
proof.   **false I** false that I   **10 but thinking on** when I do no more
than think of   **11 One . . . neck** one rapidly after another   **12 black**
dark complexion.   **my judgment's place** my opinion.   **14 this slan-**
der (See lines 5–6.)   **proceeds** originates.

132

Thine eyes I love, and they, as pitying me,   1
Knowing thy heart torment me with disdain,   2
Have put on black, and loving mourners be,
Looking with pretty ruth upon my pain.   4
And truly not the morning sun of heaven
Better becomes the gray cheeks of the east,   6
Nor that full star that ushers in the even   7
Doth half that glory to the sober west   8
As those two mourning eyes become thy face.
Oh, let it then as well beseem thy heart   10
To mourn for me, since mourning doth thee grace,   11
And suit thy pity like in every part.   12
    Then will I swear beauty herself is black,
    And all they foul that thy complexion lack.   14

133

Beshrew that heart that makes my heart to groan   1
For that deep wound it gives my friend and me!
Is't not enough to torture me alone,
But slave to slavery my sweet'st friend must be?   4
Me from myself thy cruel eye hath taken,
And my next self thou harder hast engrossed.   6
Of him, myself, and thee I am forsaken—
A torment thrice threefold thus to be crossed.   8
Prison my heart in thy steel bosom's ward,   9
But then my friend's heart let my poor heart bail;   10
Whoe'er keeps me, let my heart be his guard;
Thou canst not then use rigor in my jail.   12
    And yet thou wilt; for I, being pent in thee,   13
    Perforce am thine, and all that is in me.   14

134

So, now I have confessed that he is thine,   1
And I myself am mortgaged to thy will,   2
Myself I'll forfeit, so that other mine   3
Thou wilt restore to be my comfort still.
But thou wilt not, nor he will not be free,   5
For thou art covetous and he is kind;

He learned but surety-like to write for me   7
Under that bond that him as fast doth bind.   8
The statute of thy beauty thou wilt take,   9
Thou usurer, that put'st forth all to use,   10
And sue a friend came debtor for my sake;   11
So him I lose through my unkind abuse.   12
    Him have I lost; thou hast both him and me;
    He pays the whole, and yet am I not free.   14

135

Whoever hath her wish, thou hast thy Will,   1
And Will to boot, and Will in overplus;
More than enough am I that vex thee still,   3
To thy sweet will making addition thus.
Wilt thou, whose will is large and spacious,
Not once vouchsafe to hide my will in thine?   6
Shall will in others seem right gracious,   7
And in my will no fair acceptance shine?
The sea, all water, yet receives rain still
And in abundance addeth to his store;   10
So thou, being rich in Will, add to thy Will
One will of mine, to make thy large Will more.
    Let no unkind no fair beseechers kill;   13
    Think all but one, and me in that one Will.   14

136

If thy soul check thee that I come so near,   1
Swear to thy blind soul that I was thy Will,   2
And will, thy soul knows, is admitted there;
Thus far for love my love suit, sweet, fulfill.   4
Will will fulfill the treasure of thy love,   5
Ay, fill it full with wills, and my will one.   6
In things of great receipt with ease we prove   7
Among a number one is reckoned none.   8
Then in the number let me pass untold,   9

132.1 **as** as if   2 **Knowing ... torment** knowing that your heart torments   4 **ruth** pity   6 **becomes** adorns.   **cheeks** i.e., clouds   7 **that full star** the evening star, Hesperus, i.e., Venus.   **even** evening   8 **Doth** i.e., lends.   **sober** somber, subdued in color   9 **mourning** black. (Spelled "morning" in the quarto, suggesting a pun on line 5.)   10 **beseem** suit   11 **since ... grace** since you look very attractive in mourning black   12 **And suit ... part** and dress your pity similarly, in your heart and eyes.   14 **And ... that** and that all those are ugly who
133.1 **Beshrew** i.e., A plague upon   4 **slave to slavery** utterly enslaved   6 **And ... engrossed** i.e., and you have put my dearest friend, my other self, under even greater restraint.   **engrossed** (1) driven into obsession (2) bought up wholesale.   8 **crossed** thwarted, afflicted.   9 **Prison** Imprison   **thy ... ward** the prison cell of your hard heart   10 **bail** set free by taking its place   11 **keeps** has custody of.   **his guard** my friend's guardhouse   12 **rigor** harshness.   **my jail** i.e., my heart, where my friend is kept (and where I can protect him from your harsh authority).   13 **pent** shut up   14 **and all** along with everything (including my friend's heart)
134.1 **now** now that   2 **will** (1) wishes (2) fleshly desire   3 **so ... mine** provided that my other self, my friend   5 **will not** does not wish to, won't

7 **surety-like** as security, as guarantor.   **write** sign the bond, endorse (suggesting that the friend has taken the poet's place with the mistress)   8 **Under ... bind** under that mortgage or bond (of sexual enslavement) that now binds him as securely as it does me.   9 **statute** a usurer's security or amount of money secured under his bond.   **take** call in, invoke. (The lady will exact the full forfeiture specified in the mortgage as the amount to which her beauty entitles her.)   10 **use** (1) usury (2) sexual pleasure   11 **sue** (With suggestion also of "woo.")   **came** i.e., who became   12 **my unkind abuse** your ill usage and unkind deceiving (of me).   14 **pays** (With sexual suggestion.)
135.1 **Will** (This and the following sonnet and sonnet 143 ring changes on the word *will*—sexual desire, temper, passion, and the poet's name; possibly also the friend's name. The word can also suggest the sexual organs, male and female.)   3 **vex** (by unwelcome wooing).   **still** continually   6 **hide ... thine** (With sexual suggestion.)   7 **will in others** others' wills   10 **his** its   13 **Let ... kill** Let no unkind word kill any who seek your favors, or, do not kill your wooers with the word *no*   14 **Think ... Will** i.e., think all your wooers and their wills to be but one, all comprised in me.
136.1 **check** rebuke.   **come so near** i.e., come so near the truth about you (in my previous sonnet); with suggestion of physical nearness also   2 **blind** unperceptive; shut up in the body without sensory organs   4 **fulfill** grant.   5 **fulfill the treasure** fill full the treasury. (With suggestion of sexual entry.)   6 **my will** (Suggesting "my penis.")   **one** one of them.   7 **receipt** capacity. (Suggesting profligacy.)   8 **one ... none** (A variant of the common saying "one is no number.")   9 **untold** uncounted

Though in thy store's account I one must be; 10
For nothing hold me, so it please thee hold 11
That nothing me, a something, sweet, to thee. 12
    Make but my name thy love, and love that still, 13
    And then thou lovest me for my name is Will. 14

137

Thou blind fool, Love, what dost thou to mine eyes 1
That they behold and see not what they see? 2
They know what beauty is, see where it lies, 3
Yet what the best is take the worst to be. 4
If eyes corrupt by overpartial looks 5
Be anchored in the bay where all men ride, 6
Why of eyes' falsehood hast thou forgèd hooks, 7
Whereto the judgment of my heart is tied? 8
Why should my heart think that a several plot 9
Which my heart knows the wide world's common place? 10
Or mine eyes seeing this, say this is not, 11
To put fair truth upon so foul a face? 12
    In things right true my heart and eyes have erred,
    And to this false plague are they now transferred. 14

138

When my love swears that she is made of truth 1
I do believe her, though I know she lies, 2
That she might think me some untutored youth, 3
Unlearnèd in the world's false subtleties. 4
Thus vainly thinking that she thinks me young, 5
Although she knows my days are past the best, 6
Simply I credit her false-speaking tongue; 7
On both sides thus is simple truth suppressed. 8
But wherefore says she not she is unjust? 9
And wherefore say not I that I am old? 10
Oh, love's best habit is in seeming trust, 11
And age in love loves not to have years told. 12

Therefore I lie with her, and she with me, 13
And in our faults by lies we flattered be. 14

139

Oh, call not me to justify the wrong 1
That thy unkindness lays upon my heart; 2
Wound me not with thine eye but with thy tongue; 3
Use power with power, and slay me not by art. 4
Tell me thou lov'st elsewhere, but in my sight, 5
Dear heart, forbear to glance thine eye aside; 6
What need'st thou wound with cunning when thy might 7
Is more than my o'erpressed defense can bide? 8
Let me excuse thee: "Ah, my love well knows 9
Her pretty looks have been mine enemies, 10
And therefore from my face she turns my foes, 11
That they elsewhere might dart their injuries." 12
    Yet do not so; but since I am near slain, 13
    Kill me outright with looks and rid my pain. 14

140

Be wise as thou art cruel; do not press 1
My tongue-tied patience with too much disdain, 2
Lest sorrow lend me words, and words express 3
The manner of my pity-wanting pain. 4
If I might teach thee wit, better it were, 5
Though not to love, yet, love, to tell me so, 6
As testy sick men, when their deaths be near, 7
No news but health from their physicians know. 8
For if I should despair, I should grow mad, 9
And in my madness might speak ill of thee. 10
Now this ill-wresting world is grown so bad, 11
Mad slanderers by mad ears believèd be. 12
    That I may not be so, nor thou belied, 13
    Bear thine eyes straight, though thy proud heart go
    wide. 14

141

In faith, I do not love thee with mine eyes, 1
For they in thee a thousand errors note; 2
But 'tis my heart that loves what they despise, 3
Who in despite of view is pleased to dote. 4
Nor are mine ears with thy tongue's tune delighted,

10 in . . . account in your (huge) inventory (of lovers) 11–12 For . . . thee i.e., consider me too insignificant to think of, provided that you deign to hold insignificant me to you, my sweet, thereby making me something of worth. (*Something* is sexually suggestive of "some thing.") 13 my name i.e., "will," that is, desire. still continually 14 for because
137.1 Love Cupid, portrayed as blind 2 see not do not comprehend 3 lies resides (and deceives through false appearance) 4 Yet . . . be yet take the worst for the best. 5 corrupt by overpartial looks corrupted by doting and frankly prejudiced gazing 6 Be . . . ride seek harbor where all men do so, i.e., *ride* in the arms of promiscuous women 7 Why . . . hooks why have you, Love, fashioned snares out of my eyes' delusion 9 think . . . plot think that to be a private field, i.e., that woman to be the exclusive property of one man 10 knows knows to be. common place (1) a commons, a common pasture (2) a woman's body that is open, promiscuous. 11 Or Or why should. not not so 14 false plague (1) plague of judging falsely (2) false woman
138.1 (A version of this sonnet appears in *The Passionate Pilgrim*.) truth fidelity, constancy 2 believe i.e., pretend to believe 5 vainly thinking acting as though I thought 7 Simply (1) pretending to be foolish (2) unconditionally. credit give credence to 9 unjust unfaithful, deceitful. 11 habit demeanor. (With, however, a suggestion of *garb*, i.e., "something put on.") seeming trust apparent fidelity 12 age in love an aging person in love, or, in matters of love. told (1) counted (2) divulged.

13 lie with (1) deceive (2) have sex with 14 And . . . be and so by lies we flatteringly deceive ourselves about our moral lapses.
139.1 call ask. justify the wrong i.e., condone something actually taking place under my eyes 2 unkindness i.e., flagrant infidelity 3 with thine eye i.e., with a roving eye. (See lines 5–6.) 4 with power i.e., candidly, directly. art artifice, cunning. 7 What why 8 bide abide, withstand. 11 foes i.e., the *pretty looks*, the beauty and wanton glances of line 10 13 near nearly 14 rid end. (*Rid my pain* also suggests "satiate my craving.")
140.4 pity-wanting (1) unpitied by you (2) pity-craving 5 wit wisdom, prudence 5–6 better . . . so (I would teach you that) even though you don't love me, yet, dear friend, it would be better to tell me that you do 8 know i.e., hear. 11 ill-wresting misinterpreting in an evil sense. bad bad (that) 13 so i.e., a *mad slanderer* who is *believèd*. belied slandered 14 Bear . . . straight keep your eyes on me. wide astray.
141.2 errors flaws in beauty 4 Who . . . view which (i.e., the heart), in spite of what the eyes see

Nor tender feeling to base touches prone,   6
Nor taste, nor smell, desire to be invited
To any sensual feast with thee alone.
But my five wits nor my five senses can   9
Dissuade one foolish heart from serving thee,
Who leaves unswayed the likeness of a man,   11
Thy proud heart's slave and vassal wretch to be.
   Only my plague thus far I count my gain,   13
   That she that makes me sin awards me pain.   14

142

Love is my sin, and thy dear virtue hate,   1
Hate of my sin, grounded on sinful loving.   2
Oh, but with mine compare thou thine own state,
And thou shalt find it merits not reproving;   4
Or, if it do, not from those lips of thine
That have profaned their scarlet ornaments   6
And sealed false bonds of love as oft as mine,   7
Robbed others' beds' revenues of their rents.   8
Be it lawful I love thee as thou lov'st those   9
Whom thine eyes woo as mine importune thee.   10
Root pity in thy heart, that when it grows
Thy pity may deserve to pitied be.   12
   If thou dost seek to have what thou dost hide,   13
   By self-example mayst thou be denied.

143

Lo, as a careful huswife runs to catch
One of her feathered creatures broke away,   2
Sets down her babe and makes all swift dispatch
In pursuit of the thing she would have stay,
Whilst her neglected child holds her in chase,   5
Cries to catch her whose busy care is bent
To follow that which flies before her face,   7

Not prizing her poor infant's discontent: 8
So run'st thou after that which flies from thee,
Whilst I, thy babe, chase thee afar behind;
But if thou catch thy hope, turn back to me,
And play the mother's part: kiss me, be kind.
   So will I pray that thou mayst have thy Will,   13
   If thou turn back and my loud crying still.   14

144

Two loves I have, of comfort and despair,   1
Which like two spirits do suggest me still: 2
The better angel is a man right fair,   3
The worser spirit a woman colored ill.   4
To win me soon to hell, my female evil
Tempteth my better angel from my side,
And would corrupt my saint to be a devil,
Wooing his purity with her foul pride.
And whether that my angel be turned fiend
Suspect I may, yet not directly tell;
But being both from me, both to each friend,   11
I guess one angel in another's hell.   12
   Yet this shall I ne'er know, but live in doubt
   Till my bad angel fire my good one out.   14

145

Those lips that Love's own hand did make   1
Breathed forth the sound that said "I hate"
To me that languished for her sake;
But when she saw my woeful state,
Straight in her heart did mercy come,   5
Chiding that tongue that ever sweet
Was used in giving gentle doom,   7
And taught it thus anew to greet:
"I hate" she altered with an end,
That followed it as gentle day
Doth follow night, who like a fiend
From heaven to hell is flown away.
   "I hate" from hate away she threw,   13
   And saved my life, saying "not you."   14

6 Nor . . . prone nor (is) my delicate sense of touch inclined toward carnal contact (with you)   **9 my five wits** (neither) my five intellectual senses, i.e., the common sense, imagination, fancy, estimation (judgment), and memory   **11 Who . . . man** i.e., which heart abandons the proper government of my person, leaving me the mere likeness of a man   **13 thus far** to the following extent   **14 That . . . pain** i.e., that the sin brings with it its own punishment and contrition, thus presumably shortening my torment after death. (With a suggestion in *pain* of "sexual pleasure"; see sonnet 139.)
142.1–2 Love . . . loving My sin is to love you, and your best virtue is to hate—hate that sin in me, but also because of your uncontrolled sexual longing for other men. (The bitter paradox here is that hatred of sin must be virtue, and yet the lady is herself deeply implicated in this sin; her hatred is more a disdainful rejection of the poet's love than a noble virtue.)   **4 it** i.e., my state   **6–7 That . . . mine** i.e., that have forsworn themselves in love as often as my lips have. (The *scarlet ornaments* are lips and also red wax used to seal documents; they *seal* with a kiss.)   **8 Robbed . . . rents** i.e., and committed adultery with other women's husbands. (The metaphor is of income-yielding estates, *revenues*, whose *rents* or payments made by tenants are not properly paid; the husband does not pay what is owed to the wife in terms of marital affection and the producing of children.)   **9–10 Be . . . thee** i.e., I am as justified in loving you and imploring you with my eyes as you are in pursuing other men. (*Be it lawful* is a legal phrase meaning "Let it be considered lawful that.")   **12 deserve** make you deserving   **13 what . . . hide** what you withhold, i.e., pity   **143.1 careful** distressed, full of cares, busy.   **huswife** housewife   **2 feathered . . . away** domestic fowl which has broken away from the flock   **5 holds her in chase** chases after her   **7 flies** flees

8 Not prizing disregarding   **13 Will** (See sonnets 135, 136.)   **14 still** hush, make quiet.
144.1 (This sonnet appears, somewhat altered, in *The Passionate Pilgrim*.)   **2 suggest** urge, offer counsel, tempt.   **still** continually   **3 right fair** very handsome and blond   **4 ill** i.e., dark of complexion.   **11 from me** away from me. (The poet suspects they are together.)   **both . . . friend** friends to each other   **12 I . . . hell** I suspect that she (the evil angel) has him in her power (i.e., her sexual embracement; *hell* is slang for the pudenda).   **14 fire . . . out** drive out my good angel, stop seeing him. (With the suggestion of driving him out of the lady's sexual body as one would use fire and smoke to drive an animal out of its burrow, and with the further suggestion that the *fire* is venereal disease. *Bad angel* also hints at bad coinage driving out good money.)
145.1 (This sonnet is in eight-syllable meter.)   **5 Straight** at once   **7 used . . . doom** accustomed to passing a mild sentence   **13 "I hate" . . . threw** i.e., She separated the phrase "I hate" from the hatred I feared it expressed, from hateful meaning   **13–14 hate away . . . And** (Punning perhaps on the name of Shakespeare's wife, Anne Hathaway.)

146

Poor soul, the center of my sinful earth, 1
Thrall to these rebel powers that thee array, 2
Why dost thou pine within and suffer dearth, 3
Painting thy outward walls so costly gay? 4
Why so large cost, having so short a lease, 5
Dost thou upon thy fading mansion spend? 6
Shall worms, inheritors of this excess,
Eat up thy charge? Is this thy body's end? 8
Then, soul, live thou upon thy servant's loss, 9
And let that pine to aggravate thy store; 10
Buy terms divine in selling hours of dross; 11
Within be fed, without be rich no more.
    So shalt thou feed on Death, that feeds on men,
    And Death once dead, there's no more dying then.

147

My love is as a fever, longing still 1
For that which longer nurseth the disease, 2
Feeding on that which doth preserve the ill, 3
Th'uncertain sickly appetite to please. 4
My reason, the physician to my love,
Angry that his prescriptions are not kept,
Hath left me, and I desperate now approve 7
Desire is death, which physic did except. 8
Past cure I am, now reason is past care, 9
And frantic-mad with evermore unrest; 10
My thoughts and my discourse as madmen's are,
At random from the truth vainly expressed; 12
    For I have sworn thee fair and thought thee bright,
    Who art as black as hell, as dark as night.

148

Oh, me, what eyes hath love put in my head,
Which have no correspondence with true sight!
Or, if they have, where is my judgment fled,
That censures falsely what they see aright? 4
If that be fair whereon my false eyes dote,
What means the world to say it is not so?

If it be not, then love doth well denote 7
Love's eye is not so true as all men's "no." 8
How can it? Oh, how can love's eye be true,
That is so vexed with watching and with tears? 10
No marvel then though I mistake my view; 11
The sun itself sees not till heaven clears.
    O cunning love, with tears thou keep'st me blind,
    Lest eyes well-seeing thy foul faults should find.

149

Canst thou, O cruel, say I love thee not,
When I against myself with thee partake? 2
Do I not think on thee when I forgot 3
Am of myself, all tyrant for thy sake? 4
Who hateth thee that I do call my friend?
On whom frown'st thou that I do fawn upon?
Nay, if thou lour'st on me, do I not spend 7
Revenge upon myself with present moan? 8
What merit do I in myself respect 9
That is so proud thy service to despise, 10
When all my best doth worship thy defect, 11
Commanded by the motion of thine eyes?
    But, love, hate on, for now I know thy mind:
    Those that can see thou lov'st, and I am blind. 14

150

Oh, from what power hast thou this powerful might
With insufficiency my heart to sway? 2
To make me give the lie to my true sight 3
And swear that brightness doth not grace the day? 4
Whence hast thou this becoming of things ill, 5
That in the very refuse of thy deeds 6
There is such strength and warrantise of skill 7
That, in my mind, thy worst all best exceeds? 8
Who taught thee how to make me love thee more,
The more I hear and see just cause of hate?
Oh, though I love what others do abhor,
With others thou shouldst not abhor my state. 12
    If thy unworthiness raised love in me,
    More worthy I to be beloved of thee.

146.1 sinful earth body **2 Thrall . . . array** made captive by the rebellious flesh that decks you in finery and lines you up in battle array. ("Thrall to" is one of several conjectures; the quarto repeats "My sinful earth" from line 1.) **4 outward walls** i.e., the body, decked out in finery, cosmetics, etc. **5 having . . . lease** having so brief a period of residence in this world **6 mansion** dwelling, i.e., the body **8 charge** expense, outlay. **Is . . . end?** Is this what your body was intended to be used for? **9 thy servant's** i.e., the body's **10 let that . . . store** let the body starve to increase your stock of spiritual riches **11 Buy . . . dross** i.e., purchase eternal life in return for giving up (selling) mere hours of wasteful pleasure; secure *terms* that only God can provide
147.1 still always **2 nurseth** nourishes **3 preserve the ill** sustain the illness **4 Th'uncertain** the finicky **7–8 and I . . . except** and I now, desperately sick and in desperation, discover by experience that desire, which rejected medicine (or, which medical advice warned against), is fatal. **9 care** medical care. (The line is an inversion of the proverb, "things past cure are past care," i.e., don't worry about what can't be helped. Reason, the physician, has ceased to care for his patient.) **10 evermore** constant and increasing **12 vainly** to no sensible purpose
148.4 censures judges

7 love i.e., the self-deceiving nature of my love. **denote** indicate, demonstrate (that) **8 eye** (With a pun on "ay," yes.) **10 vexed** troubled. **watching** remaining awake **11 I** (Punning on "eye.") **mistake my view** err in what I see
149.2 partake take part (against myself). **3–4 Do . . . sake?** Do I not put consideration of you foremost when I am tyrannously neglectful of, or oblivious of, myself and my best interests on your behalf?
7 spend vent **8 present moan** immediate suffering and lamentation.
9 respect value **10 thy . . . despise** as to think it demeaning to serve you **11 all my best** all that is best in me. **defect** flaws **14 Those . . . blind** i.e., you scorn one who loves you in a blind passion, in defiance of reason, and are drawn instead to those who know you for what you are.
150.2 With insufficiency by means of all your shortcomings. **sway** rule. **3 give the lie to** accuse flatly of lying **4 And . . . day** i.e., and swear that what is so is not so, that what is fair and beautiful is not fair and beautiful, since you are dark. **5 becoming . . . ill** i.e., ability to show ill things in a becoming light **6 in . . . deeds** in the most debased of your actions **7 warrantise of skill** warrant or assurance of expertise **12 state** i.e., condition of being helplessly in love.

151

Love is too young to know what conscience is;   1
Yet who knows not conscience is born of love?   2
Then, gentle cheater, urge not my amiss,   3
Lest guilty of my faults thy sweet self prove.
For, thou betraying me, I do betray   5
My nobler part to my gross body's treason.
My soul doth tell my body that he may   7
Triumph in love; flesh stays no farther reason,   8
But, rising at thy name, doth point out thee   9
As his triumphant prize. Proud of this pride,   10
He is contented thy poor drudge to be,
To stand in thy affairs, fall by thy side.   12
    No want of conscience hold it that I call   13
    Her "love" for whose dear love I rise and fall.

152

In loving thee thou know'st I am forsworn,   1
But thou art twice forsworn, to me love swearing:
In act thy bed-vow broke, and new faith torn   3
In vowing new hate after new love bearing.   4
But why of two oaths' breach do I accuse thee,
When I break twenty? I am perjured most,
For all my vows are oaths but to misuse thee,   7
And all my honest faith in thee is lost.   8
For I have sworn deep oaths of thy deep kindness,
Oaths of thy love, thy truth, thy constancy,
And, to enlighten thee, gave eyes to blindness,   11
Or made them swear against the thing they see;

For I have sworn thee fair. More perjured eye,   13
To swear against the truth so foul a lie!

153

Cupid laid by his brand and fell asleep.   1
A maid of Dian's this advantage found,   2
And his love-kindling fire did quickly steep
In a cold valley-fountain of that ground,   4
Which borrowed from this holy fire of Love
A dateless lively heat, still to endure,
And grew a seething bath, which yet men prove   7
Against strange maladies a sovereign cure.   8
But at my mistress' eye Love's brand new-fired,   9
The boy for trial needs would touch my breast;   10
I, sick withal, the help of bath desired,   11
And thither hied, a sad distempered guest,   12
    But found no cure. The bath for my help lies
    Where Cupid got new fire—my mistress' eyes.

154

The little love god lying once asleep
Laid by his side his heart-inflaming brand,
Whilst many nymphs that vowed chaste life to keep
Came tripping by; but in her maiden hand
The fairest votary took up that fire
Which many legions of true hearts had warmed,
And so the general of hot desire   7
Was, sleeping, by a virgin hand disarmed.
This brand she quenchèd in a cool well by,   9
Which from Love's fire took heat perpetual,
Growing a bath and healthful remedy   11
For men diseased; but I, my mistress' thrall,   12
    Came there for cure, and this by that I prove: 13
    Love's fire heats water, water cools not love.

151.1 **too young** (Love is personified as the young Cupid.) **2 con-science** guilty knowing, carnal knowledge. (Playing on *conscience*, "moral sense," in line 1.) **3 urge** stress, invoke. **amiss** sin **5 betray-ing** (1) cheating on (2) leading into temptation **6 nobler part** i.e., soul **7–8 that . . . in love** that he, the soul, may triumph in virtuous love. (But ambiguously misinterpretable as urging the flesh to triumph carnally.) **8 flesh . . . reason** my flesh waits no longer to hear reason's lecture **9 rising** (With bawdy suggestion of erection, continued in *point, Proud, stand, fall.* Metaphors of conjuration and of the compass needle's point are also invoked.) **10 triumphant prize** spoils to be enjoyed in victory. **Proud of** Swelling with. **pride** splendor; erection **12 stand** (1) serve, undertake business (2) be erect. **fall** (as in battle; with sexual sugges-tion of detumescence) **13 want** lack

152.1 **forsworn** i.e., faithless to my vows of love (perhaps marriage vows) **3 act** sexual act. **bed-vow** marriage vows to your husband **3–4 In . . . bearing** i.e., a new contract of fidelity is torn up by your swearing hatred toward me, to whom you have only recently pro-fessed love. (Or the *new faith* that is torn up may be that which the lady has sworn to the friend.) **7 but to misuse** merely to deceive **8 And . . . lost** i.e., and all my professions of honesty are belied when I perjure myself by praising you for loving constancy. **11 And . . . blindness** i.e., and, to invest you with brightness, I made my eyes tes-tify to things they did not see

13 eye (With a pun on "I.")
153 (This sonnet and the following seemingly have no direct connec-tion with those preceding. They are derived ultimately, through Renaissance adaptations, from an epigram by the fifth-century Byzan-tine poet Marianus Scholasticus in the Greek Anthology.) **1 brand** torch. (With phallic suggestion.) **2 maid** attendant virgin, votaress. **Dian** Diana, goddess of chastity **4 of that ground** i.e., nearby. (*Valley-fountain* suggests the female sexual anatomy; compare with 154.9.) **6 dateless** endless, eternal. **still** always **7–8 And grew . . . cure** and became a spring of hot medicinal waters, which even today men dis-cover to be an efficacious cure against strange maladies. (Syphilis was conventionally treated with hot medicinal baths.) **9 new-fired** having been reignited **10 for trial** by way of test **11 withal** from it **12 hied** hastened. **distempered** sick. (The bath is suggestive again of the sweating cure for venereal disease.)
154.7 general inspirer and commander, i.e., Cupid **9 by** nearby **11 Growing** becoming **12 thrall** slave, bondman **13 cure** (With sug-gestion of treatment for venereal disease, as in 153.7–14.) **this** i.e., the following proposition. **that** i.e., my coming, which failed to cure me

Appendix 1

⟨❧⟩

Canon, Dates,
and Early Texts

By "canon" we mean a listing of plays that can be ascribed to Shakespeare on the basis of reliable evidence. Such evidence is either "internal," derived from matters of style or poetics in the plays themselves (see General Introduction), or "external," derived from outside the play. The latter includes any reference by Shakespeare's contemporaries to his plays, any allusions in the plays themselves to contemporary events, the entering of Shakespeare's plays for publication in the Stationers' Register (S. R.), actual publication of the plays, and records of early performances. These matters of external evidence are also essential in attempting to date the plays.

The greatest single source of information is the First Folio text of Shakespeare's plays, sponsored by Shakespeare's fellow actors John Heminges and Henry Condell and published in 1623. It contains all the plays included in this present edition of Shakespeare except *Pericles* and *The Two Noble Kinsmen* and offers strong presumptive evidence of being a complete and accurate compilation of Shakespeare's work by men who knew him and cherished his memory. It provides the only texts we have for these eighteen plays: *The Comedy of Errors, The Two Gentlemen of Verona, The Taming of the Shrew, 1 Henry VI, King John, As You Like It, Twelfth Night, Julius Caesar, All's Well That Ends Well, Measure for Measure, Timon of Athens, Macbeth, Antony and Cleopatra, Coriolanus, Cymbeline, The Winter's Tale, The Tempest*, and *Henry VIII*. This includes nearly half the known canon of Shakespeare's plays. Our debt to the First Folio is incalculable and confirms our impression of its reliability.

The information of the First Folio is further confirmed by contemporary references. In 1598, a cleric and minor writer of the period named Francis Meres wrote in his *Palladis Tamia, Wit's Treasury*:

As the soul of Euphorbus was thought to live in Pythagoras, so the sweet, witty soul of Ovid lives in mellifluous and honey-tongued Shakespeare: witness his *Venus and Adonis*, his *Lucrece*, his sugared sonnets among his private friends, etc.

As Plautus and Seneca are accounted the best for comedy and tragedy among the Latins, so Shakespeare among the English is the most excellent in both kinds for the stage; for comedy, witness his *Gentlemen of Verona*, his *Errors*, his *Love's Labor's Lost*, his *Love's Labor's Won*, his *Midsummer's Night Dream*, and his *Merchant of Venice*; for tragedy his *Richard the II, Richard the III, Henry the IV, King John, Titus Andronicus* and his *Romeo and Juliet*.

Though this list was meant to offer praise, not to be an exhaustive catalogue, it is remarkably full. If the tantalizing *Love's Labor's Won* refers to *The Taming of the Shrew*, Meres's list of comedies is substantially complete down almost to 1598. It does not include the comedies that Shakespeare appears to have written around that date or soon afterward: *Much Ado About Nothing, The Merry Wives of Windsor, As You Like It*, and *Twelfth Night*. Meres correctly names all of Shakespeare's history plays except the *Henry VI* trilogy and of course the later histories, *Henry V* (1599) and *Henry VIII* (1613). He names both of Shakespeare's early tragedies that are not based on English history: *Titus Andronicus* and *Romeo and Juliet*. He tells us about the important nondramatic poems, which did not appear in the First Folio, since that volume is devoted exclusively to plays. Not much can be made of the order in which Meres names the plays, however, for we learn from other sources that *Richard III* clearly precedes *Richard II* in date of composition and that *King John* precedes the *Henry IV* plays.

Other writers of the 1590s add further confirming evidence. John Weever, in an epigram "*Ad Gulielmum Shakespeare*," published in 1599, refers to "Rose-cheeked Adonis" and "Fair fire-hot Venus," to "Chaste Lucretia" and "Proud lust-stung Tarquin," and to "*Romeo, Richard*—more whose names I know not." Richard Barnfield, in

Poems in Divers Humors (1598), praises Shakespeare for "*Venus*" and "*Lucrece.*" Both Thomas Nashe and Robert Greene seemingly refer to the *Henry VI* plays, missing from Meres's list. Nashe, in his *Pierce Penniless* (1592), speculates how it would "have joyed brave Talbot (the terror of the French) to think that after he had lain two hundred years in his tomb, he should triumph again on the stage." Talbot is the hero of *1 Henry VI*, and we know of no other play on the subject. Greene, in his *Greene's Groats-worth of Wit* (1592), lashes out at an "upstart crow, beautified with our feathers, that with his '*Tiger's heart wrapped in a player's hide*' supposes he is as well able to bombast out a blank verse as the best of you, and, being an absolute *Johannes Factotum*, is in his own conceit the only Shake-scene in a country." The line about "Tiger's heart" is deliberately misquoted from *3 Henry VI*, 1.4.137. (It is possible that this famous attack on Shakespeare was actually written not by Greene himself but by Henry Chettle, his literary executor.)

The Taming of the Shrew (c. 1590–1593)

The Taming of the Shrew was not printed until the First Folio of 1623. Francis Meres does not mention the play in 1598 in his *Palladis Tamia*, unless it is the mysterious "*Loue labours wonne*" on his list. (Meres is not totally accurate, for he omits *Henry VI* from the history plays.) The play must have existed prior to 1598, however, for its style is comparable with that of *The Two Gentlemen of Verona* and other early comedies. Moreover, a play called *The Taming of a Shrew* appeared in print in 1594 (Stationers' Register, 1594). Four theories can be adduced to explain the problematic relationship of *A Shrew* to Shakespeare's play. The two least plausible theories are that Shakespeare, for some reason, reworked someone else's play shortly after its first performance or else wrote *A Shrew* himself as an early version. The third theory is that *A Shrew* represents an imitation of Shakespeare's play by some rival dramatist, who relied chiefly on his memory and who changed characters' names and the location to make the play seem his. Fourth and most plausibly, *A Shrew* may be a somewhat uncharacteristic kind of reported or memorially reconstructed quarto, "improved" upon by a writer who also borrowed admiringly from Christopher Marlowe and other Elizabethan dramatists. In either of the latter two scenarios, Shakespeare's play would have to be dated earlier than May 1594.

The title page of *A Shrew* proclaims that "it was sundry times acted by the *Right honorable the Earle of Pembrook his seruants.*" Quite possibly this derivative version was merely trying to capitalize on the original's stage success and was, in fact, describing performances of Shakespeare's play. Theater owner and manager Philip Henslowe's record of a performance of "*the Tamynge of A Shrowe*" in 1594 at Newington Butts, a mile south of London Bridge, may also refer to Shakespeare's play; certainly, the minute distinction between "A Shrew" and "The Shrew" is one that the official records of the time would overlook. The Admiral's Men and the Lord Chamberlain's Men, acting companies, were playing at Newington Butts at the time, either jointly or alternatingly. Since Shakespeare's company, the Lord Chamberlain's, later owned *The Shrew*, they may well have owned and acted it on this occasion in 1594, having obtained it from the Earl of Pembroke's Men when that company disbanded in 1593. Many of Pembroke's leading players joined the Lord Chamberlain's, Shakespeare being quite possibly among them. (The possibility that he came to the Lord Chamberlain's from Lord Strange's men seems less certain today than it once did.) Several echoes of Shakespeare's play in other plays of the early 1590s tend to confirm a date in or before 1593. It is entirely possible, then, that *The Shrew* was acted by Pembroke's men in 1592–1593 and subsequently passed along to the Lord Chamberlain's.

The Folio text of this play is now generally thought to have been printed from Shakespeare's working manuscript or possibly from a transcript of his papers, with perhaps some theatrical annotations as well. Some signs of revision are discernible.

A Midsummer Night's Dream (c. 1595)

A Midsummer Night's Dream was entered on the Stationers' Register, the official record book of the London Company of Stationers (booksellers and printers), by Thomas Fisher on October 8, 1600, and published by Richard Bradock that same year in quarto:

A Midsommer nights dreame. As it hath beene sundry times pub*lickely acted, by the Right honoura*ble, the Lord Chamberlaine his *seruants. Written by William Shakespeare.* Imprinted at London, for *Thomas Fisher*, and are to be soulde at his shoppe, at the Signe of the White Hart, in *Fleetestreete*. 1600.

This text appears to have been set from Shakespeare's working manuscript. Its inconsistencies in time scheme and other irregularities may reflect some revision, although the inconsistencies are not noticeable in performance. A second quarto appeared in 1619, though falsely dated 1600; it was a reprint of the first quarto, with some minor corrections and many new errors. A copy of this second quarto, evidently with some added stage directions and other minor changes from a theatrical manuscript in the company's possession, served as the basis for the First Folio text of 1623. Changes of speech assignment in the Folio text, especially in Act 5, may reflect a late revival over which Shakespeare had no control. Essentially, the first quarto remains the authoritative text.

Other than Francis Meres's listing of the play in 1598 in his *Palladis Tamia*, external clues as to date are elusive. Possibly the worry that a lion in a play might frighten the ladies (3.1.24–31) echoes published accounts of a baptismal feast at court in August 1594, when a blackamoor was chosen to draw in a chariot in place of a lion for fear of alarming nearby spectators. The description of unruly weather (2.1.88–114) has been related to the bad summer of 1594, but complaints about the weather are perennial. On the assumption that the play celebrates some noble wedding of the period, scholars have come up with a number of suitable marriages. Chief are those of Sir Thomas Heneage to Mary, Countess of Southampton, in 1594; of William Stanley, Earl of Derby, to Elizabeth Vere, daughter of the Earl of Oxford, in 1595; and of Thomas, son of Lord Berkeley, to Elizabeth, daughter of Lord Carey, in 1596. The Countess of Southampton was the widowed mother of the young Earl of Southampton, to whom Shakespeare had dedicated his *Venus and Adonis* and *The Rape of Lucrece*. No one has ever proved convincingly, however, that the play was written for any occasion other than commercial public performance. The play makes sense for a general audience and does not need to depend on references to a private marriage. Shakespeare was, after all, in the business of writing plays for his fellow actors, who earned their livelihood chiefly by public acting before large paying audiences. In any event, the search for a court marriage is a circular argument in terms of dating; suitable court marriages can be found for any year of the decade. In the last analysis, the play has to be dated on the basis of its stylistic affinity to plays like *Romeo and Juliet* and *Richard II*, works of the "lyric" mid-1590s. The "Pyramus and Thisbe" performance in *A Midsummer Night's Dream* would seem to bear an obvious relation to *Romeo and Juliet*, although no one can say for sure which came first.

The Merchant of Venice (c. 1596–1597)

The Stationers' Register, the official record book of the London Company of Stationers (booksellers and printers), for July 22, 1598, contains an entry on behalf of the printer James Roberts for "a booke of the Marchaunt of Venyce, or otherwise called the Iewe of Venyce, Prouided, that yt bee not prynted by the said James Robertes or anye other whatsoeuer without lycence first had from the Right honorable the lord Chamberlen." Roberts evidently enjoyed a close connection with the Chamberlain's men (Shakespeare's acting company) and seemingly was granted the special favor of registering the play at this time, even though the company did not wish to see the play published until later (or until they were paid). In 1600, at any rate, Roberts trans-

ferred his rights as publisher to Thomas Heyes and printed the volume for him with the following title:

The most excellent Historie of the *Merchant of Venice*. VVith the extreame crueltie of *Shylocke* the Iewe towards the sayd Merchant, in cutting a iust pound of his flesh: and the obtayning of *Portia* by the choyse of three chests. *As it hath beene diuers times acted by the Lord Chamberlaine his Seruants*. Written by William Shakespeare. AT LONDON, Printed by *I. R.* [James Roberts] for Thomas Heyes, and are to be sold in Paules Church-yard, at the signe of the Greene Dragon. 1600.

The text of this 1600 quarto is generally a good one, based seemingly on an accurate copy of Shakespeare's papers by the dramatist himself or some reliable transcriber. It served as copy for the second quarto of 1619 (printed by William Jaggard for Thomas Pavier and fraudulently dated 1600) and for the First Folio of 1623. Although some theatrical manuscript seems also to have been consulted in preparation for the Folio text, the Folio variations appear to have little authority.

Francis Meres mentions the play in 1598 in his *Palladis Tamia*. Establishing an earlier limit for dating has proven not so easy. Many scholars have urged a connection with the Roderigo Lopez affair of 1594 (see the Introduction to the play). The supposed allusion to Lopez in the lines about "a wolf, who, hanged for human slaughter" (4.1.134) may simply indicate, however, that wolves were actually hanged for attacking men in Shakespeare's day (as dogs were for killing sheep). Besides, the Lopez case remained so notorious throughout the 1590s that even a proven allusion to it in *The Merchant* would not limit the play to 1594 or 1595. Christopher Marlowe's play, *The Jew of Malta*, was revived in 1594 to exploit anti-Lopez sentiment but was also revived in 1596. There may be, moreover, an allusion in 1.1.27 to the *St. Andrew*, a Spanish ship captured at Cadiz in 1596, and Shylock's allusion to Jacob and Laban (1.3.69–88) may well echo Miles Mosse's *The Arraignment and Conviction of Usury*, 1595. If so, the likeliest date is 1596–1597.

Much Ado About Nothing (1598–1599)

"The Commedie of muche A doo about nothing a booke" was entered in the Stationers' Register, the official record book of the London Company of Stationers (booksellers and printers), on August 4, 1600, along with *As You Like It, Henry V*, and Ben Jonson's *Every Man in His Humor*, all marked as plays of "My lord chamberlens men" (Shakespeare's acting company) and all "to be staied"—that is, not published without further permission. Earlier in the same memorandum, written on a spare page in the Register, occurs the name of the printer James Roberts, whose registration of *The Merchant of Venice* in 1598 was similarly stayed, pending further permission to publish.

Evidently, the Chamberlain's Men were attempting to ensure that they were paid for any plays printed or else to prevent unauthorized publication of these very popular plays. If the latter was their motive, they were too late to forestall the appearance of an unauthorized quarto of *Henry V* in August 1600, but they did manage to control release of the others. *Much Ado About Nothing* appeared later that same year in a seemingly authorized version:

Much adoe about Nothing. *As it hath been sundrie times publikely* acted by the right honourable, the Lord Chamberlaine his seruants. *Written by William Shakespeare.* LONDON Printed by V. S. [Valentine Sims] for Andrew Wise, and William Aspley. 1600.

Once thought to have been set up from a theatrical playbook and then used itself in the theater as a playbook before serving as copy for the First Folio of 1623, this 1600 quarto text is now generally regarded as having been set from Shakespeare's own manuscript. The names of the actors Will Kempe and Richard Cowley appear among the speech prefixes in 4.2, indicating that Shakespeare had them in mind as he wrote; other irregularities in speech prefixes and scene headings (including "ghost" characters, such as Leonato's wife Innogen) read more like a manuscript in the last stages of revision than a playbook for a finished production. The Folio text was based on this 1600 quarto, lightly annotated with reference to the playbook but providing little in the way of new readings other than the correction of obvious error.

Francis Meres does not mention the play in September 1598 in his *Palladis Tamia*, unless (and this seems unlikely) it is his "*Loue labours wonne.*" Will Kempe, who played Dogberry, left the Chamberlain's Men early in 1599. The likeliest date, then, is the winter of 1598–1599, though publication was not until 1600.

As You Like It (1598–1600)

"As you like yt, a booke" was entered in the Stationers' Register, the official record book of the London Company of Stationers (booksellers and printers), on August 4, 1600, along with *Much Ado About Nothing, Henry V*, and Ben Jonson's *Every Man in His Humor*, all labeled as "My lord chamberlens mens plaies" and all ordered "to be staied" from publication until further notice. Evidently, the Chamberlain's Men (Shakespeare's acting company) were anxious to ensure payment or otherwise protect their rights to these very popular plays. Despite their efforts, *Henry V* appeared in an unauthorized quarto that same month. *As You Like It* did not appear in print, however, until the First Folio of 1623. The Folio text is a good one, based seemingly on the theatrical playbook that still retained certain authorial features (conceivably, because an autograph fair copy served as the basis for it) or on a literary transcript either of the playbook or of an authorial manuscript.

Francis Meres does not mention the play in September 1598 in his *Palladis Tamia*. However, the play contains an unusually clear allusion to Christopher Marlowe's *Hero and Leander* ("Who ever loved that loved not at first sight?" 3.5.82), of which the first extant edition appeared in 1598, although Shakespeare may well have known it earlier in manuscript or in some lost edition. Even so, other possible allusions, to the burning of satirical books in June 1599 (see 1.2.85–6) and to the new Globe Theater ("All the world's a stage," 2.7.138), point to a date between late 1598 and the summer of 1600, probably after *Much Ado About Nothing*.

Twelfth Night (1600–1602)

Twelfth Night was registered with the London Company of Stationers (booksellers and printers) in 1623 and was first published in the First Folio of that year in a good text set up from what may have been a scribal transcript of Shakespeare's draft manuscript or possibly the playbook (assuming that the scribe might omit theatrical notations). There was a brief delay in printing *Twelfth Night* in the First Folio, possibly because a transcript was being prepared. The play was first mentioned, however, in the *Diary* of a Middle Temple law student or barrister named John Manningham, who describes the festivities for Candlemas Day, February 2, 1602, as follows:

At our feast wee had a play called "Twelue Night, or What you Will," much like the Commedy of Errores, or Menechmi in Plautus, but most like and neere to that in Italian called *Inganni*. A good practise in it to make the Steward beleeue his Lady widdowe was in love with him, by couterfeyting a letter as from his Lady in generall termes, telling him what shee liked best in him, and prescribing his gesture in smiling, his apparaile, & c., and then when he came to practise making him beleeue they tooke him to be mad.

This entry was once suspected to be a forgery perpetrated by John Payne Collier, who published the *Diary* in 1831, but its authenticity is now generally accepted. The date accords with several possible allusions in the play itself. When Fabian jokes about "a pension of thousands to be paid from the Sophy" (2.5.176–7), he seems to be recalling Sir Anthony Shirley's reception by the Shah of Persia (the Sophy) between the summer of 1598 and late 1601. An account of this visit was entered in the Stationers' Register in November 1601. Viola's description of Feste as "wise enough to play the fool" (3.1.60) may recall a poem beginning "True it is, he plays the fool indeed," published in 1600–1601 by Robert Armin (who had played the role of Feste). Maria's comparison of Malvolio's smiling face to "the new map with the augmentation of the Indies" (3.2.77–8) refers to new maps published in 1599 in which more was shown of the East Indies, including Japan, than had been mapped before. Fabian's reference to sailing north and to the icicle on a Dutchman's beard (3.2.25–6) sounds like an allusion to William Barentz's Arctic expedition, first described in English in an account entered in the Stationers' Register on June 13, 1598, though no edition survives before 1609. Leslie Hotson (*The First Night of Twelfth Night*, 1954) has argued for a first performance at court on Twelfth Night in January 1601, when Queen Elizabeth entertained Don Virginio Orsino, Duke of Bracciandy, but this hypothesis has not gained general acceptance, partly because the role of Orsino in the play would scarcely flatter such a noble visitor and partly because there is no proof that any of Shakespeare's plays were originally commissioned for private performance. Nevertheless, the episode may have suggested to Shakespeare the name Orsino. All in all, a date between 1600 and early 1602 seems most likely. Francis Meres does not mention the play in 1598 in his *Palladis Tamia*.

Measure for Measure (1603–1604)

Measure for Measure first appeared in the First Folio of 1623. The text was evidently set from scrivener Ralph Crane's copy, possibly of Shakespeare's own draft; the usual inconsistencies of composition have not yet been smoothed away by use in the theater. On the other hand, spellings tend to suggest that Crane was copying a transcript. A recent and controversial hypothesis is that Crane based his copy on a playbook in use after Shakespeare's death, which incorporated some theatrical adaptation by Thomas Middleton and some other reviser, including a song (4.1.1–6) that could have originated in *Rollo, Duke of Normandy* (c. 1617) by John Fletcher and others.

The first recorded performance (according to a Revels account document) was on December 26, 1604, St. Stephen's Night, when "a play Caled Mesur for Mesur" by "Shaxberd" was acted in the banqueting hall at Whitehall "by his Maiesties plaiers." Shakespeare's acting company, previously the Lord Chamberlain's Men, had become the King's Men after the accession to the throne of James I in 1603. Several allusions in the play seem to point to the summer of 1604, when the theaters, having been closed for a year because of the plague, were reopened. A reference to the King of Hungary (1.2.1–5) may reflect anxieties in England over James's negotiations for a settlement with Spain; censorship would forbid a direct mentioning of Spain. Mistress Overdone's complaint about the war, the "sweat" (plague), the "gallows" (public executions), and poverty (1.2.81–3) are all suggestive of events in 1603–1604, when war with Spain and the plague were still very much in evidence. Duke Vincentio's reticent habits have been seen as a flattering reference to James's well-known dislike of crowds. Stylistically, the play is clearly later than *Twelfth Night* (1600–1602), so that a date close to the first recorded performance in 1604 is a necessity, even if we cannot be positive about all the supposed allusions to King James.

Richard III (c. 1592–1594)

A quarto edition of *Richard III*, registered by Andrew Wise on October 20, 1597, appeared later that same year with the following title:

THE TRAGEDY of King Richard the third. Containing, His treacherous Plots against his brother Clarence: the pittiefull murther of his iunocent nephewes: his tyrannicall vsurpation: with the whole course of his detested life, and most deserued death. As it hath beene lately Acted by the Right honourable the Lord Chamberlaine his seruants. AT LONDON Printed by Valentine Sims, for Andrew Wise, dwelling in Paules Chu[r]ch-yard, at the Signe of the Angell. 1597.

This text, one of the most perplexing in all Shakespeare, is sometimes regarded as one that was created when the acting company banded together to reconstruct a play of which the copy was missing. The reconstructed version may have been cut, perhaps for provincial performance. This defective text was the basis of the 1597 quarto, which was reprinted in 1598, 1602, 1605, 1612, 1622, 1629, and 1634, each of which was successively more error-laden than the previous one. The First Folio text of 1623 seems to have been set mainly from copies of the third and sixth quartos (1602 and 1622), which had been sporadically but heavily corrected against an independent manuscript—possibly Shakespeare's own working manuscript or a copy of it. This manuscript source, some of which may have been interleaved into the printers' copy, represents a generally superior authority to that of the first quarto. Parts of the Folio text, however, were set from an uncorrected copy of the third quarto (1602), and for those passages (3.1.1–158 and 5.3.48 to end of play) the first quarto, from which the third quarto was derived, must serve as copy text. Otherwise, the Folio text is the most authoritative, though it must be approached with caution.

The situation is indeed fraught with unusual uncertainty, since there are many opportunities for the Folio to have perpetuated errors of the earlier quartos; moreover, its "improvements" over the readings of those quartos could in some instances be editorial sophistications. The first quarto offers some readings that demand serious attention. Especially when the Folio's reading differs from those of the first quarto and is instead derived from quartos two through six, the first quarto should be preferred unless it is manifestly wrong. At the same time, however, since the first quarto may reflect adaptation of the original acting text, its changes may not represent

Shakespeare's artistic intention either. For these reasons, one must be wary of the first quarto's assignment of speeches when they vary from the Folio's assignments and also of the first quarto's cuts, some of which are substantial.

The play is mentioned by Francis Meres in 1598 in his *Palladis Tamia*. John Weever names a *"Richard"* in his *Epigrams*, published in 1599. Most scholars date *Richard III* as 1592–1594, on the basis of its style and its close affinity to the *Henry VI* series (completed probably in 1591–1592). The play may have been influenced by the anonymous *The True Tragedy of Richard III*, registered in June 1594 but probably written in 1590–1592 or even earlier. Shakespeare's play may also have been influenced by Thomas Kyd's *The Spanish Tragedy* (c. 1587) and by Christopher Marlowe's dramas (he died in 1593).

Richard II (c. 1595–1596)

On August 29, 1597, "The Tragedye of Richard the Second" was entered in the Stationers' Register, the official record book of the London Company of Stationers (booksellers and printers), by Andrew Wise, and was published by him later that same year:

THE Tragedie of King Richard the second. *As it hath beene publikely acted by the right Honourable the Lorde Chamberlaine his Seruants.* LONDON Printed by Valentine Simmes for Androw Wise, and are to be sold at his shop in Paules church yard at the signe of the Angel. 1597.

This is a good text, printed evidently from the author's papers or a nontheatrical transcript of them. Wise issued two more quartos of this popular play in 1598, each set from the previous quarto, and then in 1603 transferred his rights to the play to Matthew Law. This publisher issued in 1608 a fourth quarto "With new additions of the Parliament Sceane, and the deposing of King Richard" (according to the title page in some copies). The deposition scene has indeed been omitted from the earlier quartos, probably through censorship. A fifth quarto appeared in 1615, based on the fourth quarto. All the quartos after the first attribute the play to Shakespeare. The added deposition scene in quartos 4 and 5 seems to have been memorially reconstructed. The First Folio text of 1623 gives a better version of the deposition scene, seemingly because the printers of the Folio had access to the manuscript playbook for this portion of the text. (Some scholars maintain that the Folio text was derived from an earlier quarto or quartos that had been marked up and used as a playbook, but that case has been weakened by recent research.) Most of the Folio text was probably set from an annotated copy of the third quarto, and perhaps a leaf in Act 5 from the fifth quarto. The annotation was evidently quite uneven, and so the most authoritative text for all

but the deposition scene remains the first quarto; nevertheless, at certain points (especially the first 900 lines, part of 3.2, and much of Act 5), the annotation with reference to the playbook seems to have been more thorough. At such points, the Folio readings deserve serious attention, and the stage directions are often illuminating.

Francis Meres mentions the play in 1598 in his *Palladis Tamia*. Clearly it had been written and performed prior to the Stationers' Register entry in August 1597. Its earliest probable date is 1595, since the play seemingly is indebted to Samuel Daniel's poem, *The First Four Books of the Civil Wars*, published in that year. Shakespeare follows Daniel, for example, in increasing the Queen's age from eleven (according to the chronicles) to maturity, and in other significant details. On December 7, 1595, Sir Edward Hoby invited Sir Robert Cecil to his house in Cannon Row, "where as late as it shall please you a gate for your supper shall be open, and King Richard present himself to your view." Although it is by no means certain that this passage refers to a private performance of Shakespeare's play, stylistic considerations favor a date around 1595 rather than 1597. If, as some scholars contend, Daniel's *Civil Wars* was written after Shakespeare's play rather than before it, the date of *Richard II* might be as early as 1594.

Henry IV, Part I (1596–1597)

On February 25, 1598, "The historye of Henry the IIIJth with his battaile of Shrewsburye against Henry Hottspurre of the Northe with the conceipted mirthe of Sir John Ffalstoff" was entered in the Stationers' Register, the official record book of the London Company of Stationers (booksellers and printers), by Andrew Wise. Later that year appeared the following quarto:

THE HISTORY OF HENRIE THE FOVRTH; With the battell at Shrewsburie, *betweene the King and Lord* Henry Percy, surnamed Henrie Hotspur of the North. *With the humorous conceits of Sir* Iohn Falstalffe. AT LONDON, Printed by P. S. [Peter Short] for *Andrew Wise,* dwelling in Paules Churchyard, at the signe of the Angell. 1598.

Actually this was not the first quarto, for an earlier fragment of eight pages has survived, part of a text that served as copy for the first complete extant quarto. Together, these quartos make up an excellent authoritative text, based seemingly on the author's papers or, more probably, a scribal transcript of them. Four more quartos appeared before the First Folio of 1623, each based on the previous quarto. The Folio itself was based on the last of these, perhaps with reference also to some kind of manuscript, although the number of authoritative readings that can be claimed for the Folio is small.

1 Henry IV shows signs of revision in the use of characters' names, most notably that of Falstaff. Plainly, the original version of the play called him Sir John Oldcastle, after one of the prince's companions in the anonymous *Famous Victories of Henry the Fifth* (c. 1588). The name "Oldcastle" was originally intended for *2 Henry IV* as well. The speech prefix "Old." is left standing at 1.2.119 in the quarto of *2 Henry IV*, one or two lines of verse in *1 Henry IV* are one syllable short, evidently because "Oldcastle" has been altered to "Falstaff," and Falstaff is jokingly referred to as "my old lad of the castle" (*1 Henry IV*, 1.2.41). Moreover, there are several contemporary allusions to a play about a fat knight named Oldcastle. Apparently, Henry Brooke, Lord Cobham, a living descendant of the Lollard martyr Oldcastle of Henry V's reign, took umbrage at the profane use Shakespeare had made of this revered name, whereupon Shakespeare's acting company shifted to another less controversial name from the chronicles, Sir John Fastolfe or Falstaff (called "Falstaffe" in the Folio text of Shakespeare's *1 Henry VI* and assigned a cowardly role in the French wars of that play). The revision also changed the names of Oldcastle's cronies from Harvey and Russell to Peto and Bardolph. This edition retains the name "Falstaff," since Shakespeare clearly accepted it as the new name of the character in all his "Falstaff" plays.

Cobham was Lord Chamberlain from July 1596 until his death in March 1597, during which interval Shakespeare's company bore the name of Lord Hunsdon's men. Quite possibly, the difficulty over the name "Oldcastle" erupted during that period, for *1 Henry IV* seems to have been written and performed in late 1596 and early 1597, not long after Shakespeare had finished *Richard II* (c. 1595–1596).

Francis Meres, in his *Palladis Tamia*, 1598, refers to "*Henry the IV*" without specifying one or two parts. Publication of *1 Henry IV* in 1598 confirmed to the Elizabethan public that the changes in names to Falstaff, Peto, and Bardolph had taken place.

Henry V (1599)

An entry in the Stationers' Register, the official record book of the London Company of Stationers (booksellers and printers), for August 4, 1600, provides that "Henry the fift" and three other plays belonging to the Lord Chamberlain's Men (Shakespeare's acting company) are "to be staied" from publication until further permission is granted. Evidently, the Chamberlain's Men were anxious to ensure they were paid or to prevent unauthorized publication. They did not succeed, in any event, in preventing the appearance of an unauthorized text of *Henry V*. An entry in the Stationers' Register for August 14 assigns to Thomas Pavier an already published work entitled "The historye of Henry the Vth with the battell of Agencourt." The quarto volume to which this entry refers is the following:

THE CHRONICLE History of Henry the fift, With his battell fought at *Agin Court* in *France*. Togither with *Auntient Pistoll*. *As it hath bene sundry times playd by the Right honorable the Lord Chamberlaine his seruants*. LONDON Printed by *Thomas Creede*, for Tho. Millington, and Iohn Busby. And are to be sold at his house in Carter Lane, next the Powle head. 1600.

The text of this play is manifestly corrupt. It is considerably shorter than the First Folio version and completely omits the choruses and three entire scenes (1.1, 3.1, and 4.2). The remainder seems to have been put together by memorial reconstruction. This unauthorized quarto served as the basis for a second quarto printed by Thomas Creed for Thomas Pavier in 1602 and a third printed by William Jaggard for Thomas Pavier in 1619 but fraudulently dated 1608. The Folio text was printed seemingly from an authorial manuscript, perhaps with occasional reference to the third quarto (which contains some potentially troublesome contamination). The Folio text is thus the most reliable version, though the first quarto is also an interesting witness, especially for visual effects recorded in its stage directions, for a few readings in the text, and for verse lineation of Pistol's speeches.

Francis Meres does not mention the play in 1598 in his *Palladis Tamia*, though he does mention "*Henry the IV*." The epilogue to *2 Henry IV* (written probably in 1597) promises that "our humble author will continue the story, with Sir John in it, and make you merry with fair Katharine of France"; since the prediction is not really accurate regarding Falstaff, we can be reasonably certain that Shakespeare had not yet begun *Henry V* in 1597. An allusion in the Chorus of Act 5 to "the General of our gracious Empress," who may in good time come home from Ireland with "rebellion broachèd on his sword," has been taken by virtually all editors to refer to the Earl of Essex, who left in March 1599 to quell the Irish rebellion headed by Tyrone. Although Essex returned on September 28 of that same year, having failed utterly in his assignment, the departure of such a charismatic figure could have inspired Shakespeare's praising remark. A minority view holds that the choruses (which do not appear in the unauthorized quarto of 1600) could have been written later in 1601 for Essex's far more victorious successor, Lord Mountjoy (see Warren D. Smith on *Henry V* in *JEGP*, 1954). Still, Essex was more prominent during those exciting years, more likely to have been the subject of adulation. In any case, the play itself must have been written before August 1600, most probably in 1599. The reference to "this wooden O" in the Chorus of Act 1 is often thought to be Shakespeare's compliment to the company's new theater, the Globe, which was ready for their use probably in 1599; but the play may have been produced at the Curtain instead.

Romeo and Juliet (1594–1596)

A corrupt and unregistered quarto of *Romeo and Juliet* appeared in 1597 with the following title:

AN excellent conceited Tragedie OF Romeo and Iuliet, As it hath been often (with great applause) plaid publiquely, by the right Honourable the L. of *Hunsdon* his Seruants. LONDON, Printed by Iohn Danter. 1597.

This edition, intended no doubt to capitalize on the play's great popularity, seems to have been memorially reconstructed by two or more actors (probably those playing Romeo and Paris), and possibly thereafter to have been used as a playbook. Its appearance seems to have caused the issuance two years later of a clearly authoritative version:

THE MOST EXcellent and lamentable Tragedie, of Romeo and *Iuliet. Newly corrected, augmented, and amended*: As it hath bene sundry times publiquely acted, by the right Honourable the Lord Chamberlaine his Seruants. LONDON Printed by Thomas Creede, for Cuthbert Burby, and are to be sold at his shop neare the Exchange. 1599.

This text is some 800 lines longer than the first and corrects errors in that earlier version. It seems at one point, however, to have been contaminated by the first quarto, as though the manuscript source for the second quarto (probably the author's rough draft) was defective at some point. A passage from 1.2.53 to 1.3.34 was apparently set directly from the first quarto. (On this matter, see George W. Williams's old-spelling edition of the play, Duke Univ. Press, 1964.) Q1 may also have influenced Q2 in some other isolated instances. Despite this contamination, however, the second quarto is the authoritative text, except for the passage of direct indebtedness to Q1. Q2 served as the basis for the third quarto (1609), which in turn served as copy for the fourth quarto (undated, but placed in 1622) and the First Folio of 1623. A fifth quarto appeared in 1637. The Folio text may embody a few authoritative readings of its own, perhaps by way of reference to a theatrical manuscript.

Francis Meres, in his *Palladis Tamia*, 1598, assigns the play to Shakespeare. So does John Weever in his *Epigrams* of 1599. Internal evidence on dating is not reliable. The Nurse observes that "'Tis since the earthquake now eleven years" (1.3.24); however, it has been discovered that suitable earthquakes occurred in 1580, 1583, 1584, and 1585, giving us a wide choice of dates even if we accept the dubious proposition that the Nurse is speaking accurately. Astronomical reckoning of the position of the moon at the time the play purportedly takes place ("A fortnight and odd days" before Lammastide, August 1, 1.3.16) indicates

the year 1596; again, however, we have no reason to assume Shakespeare cared about this sort of internal accuracy. More suggestive perhaps is the argument that Danter's unauthorized publication in 1597 was seeking to exploit a popular new play—one the acting company certainly did not yet wish to see published, since it was a moneymaker. Danter assigns the play to Lord Hunsdon's servants, a name that Shakespeare's company could have used only from July 22, 1596 (when the old Lord Chamberlain, Henry Carey, first Lord Hunsdon, died) to March 17, 1597 (when George Carey, second Lord Hunsdon, was appointed to his father's erstwhile position as Lord Chamberlain). Danter could simply have been using the name of the company at the time he obtained the play, but he may also have indicated performance in late 1596. Danter printed only the first four sheets, but he must have done so by February–March 1597, when his presses were seized. Stylistically, the play is clearly of the "lyric" period of *A Midsummer Night's Dream* and *Richard II*. There are also stylistic affinities to the sonnets and to the narrative poems of 1593–1594. A date between 1594 and 1596 is likely, especially toward the latter end of this period. Whether the play comes before or after *A Midsummer Night's Dream* is, however, a matter of conjecture.

Julius Caesar (1599)

Julius Caesar was first published in the First Folio of 1623. The text is an excellent one, based evidently on a theater playbook or a transcript of it; some theatrical features, such as a provision for the doubling of Cassius and Caius Ligarius, appear to represent a staging configuration that Shakespeare had not anticipated. On the other hand, some stage directions sound authorial, as though Shakespeare's own words had survived into the playbook. Some confusions have survived as well, notably in the handling of Lucilius, Lucius, Titinius, and Pindarus in 4.2. In the Folio, the play is included among the tragedies and entitled *The Tragedy of Julius Caesar*, although the table of contents lists it as *The Life and death of Julius Caesar*.

The play's first performance must have occurred in 1599 or slightly earlier. On September 21, 1599, a Swiss visitor named Thomas Platter crossed the River Thames after lunch with a company of spectators to see "the tragedy of the first Emperor Julius Caesar" performed in a thatched-roofed building. The description fits the Globe, the Rose, and the Swan theaters, but the last of these was not in regular use. The Admiral's Men at the Rose are not known to have had a Caesar play, whereas the Chamberlain's Men certainly had Shakespeare's play about this time. They had only recently moved from their Theatre in the northeast suburbs of London to the Globe south of the river, and *Julius Caesar* was probably a new play for the occasion.

John Weever, in *The Mirror of Martyrs* (1601), is surely referring to Shakespeare's play when he describes "the many-headed multitude" listening first to "Brutus' speech, that Caesar was ambitious" and then to "eloquent Mark Antony." (The dedication to Weever's book claims he wrote it "some two years ago," in 1599; however, since this book has been shown to be heavily indebted to a work that first appeared in 1600, Weever's allusion is not as helpful in limiting the date as was once thought.) Ben Jonson's *Every Man in His Humor*, acted in 1599, may also contain allusions to Shakespeare's play. Francis Meres does not mention it in 1598 in his *Palladis Tamia*.

Hamlet (c. 1600–1601)

Like everything else about *Hamlet*, the textual problem is complicated. On July 26, 1602, James Roberts entered in the Stationers' Register, the official record book of the London Company of Stationers (booksellers and printers), "A booke called the Revenge of Hamlett Prince Denmarke as yt was latelie Acted by the Lord Chamberleyne his servantes." For some reason, however, Roberts did not print his copy of *Hamlet* until 1604, by which time the following unauthorized edition had appeared:

THE Tragicall Historie of HAMLET *Prince of Denmarke* By William Shake-speare. As it hath beene diuerse times acted by his Highnesse seruants in the Cittie of London: as also in the two Vniuersities of Cambridge and Oxford, and else-where. At London printed for N. L. [Nicholas Ling] and Iohn Trundell. 1603.

This edition, the first quarto of *Hamlet*, seems to have been memorially reconstructed by actors who toured the provinces (note the references to Cambridge, Oxford, and so on), with some recollection of an earlier *Hamlet* play (the *Ur-Hamlet*) written before 1589 and acted during the 1590s. The actors seemingly had no recourse to an authoritative manuscript. One of these actors may have played Marcellus and possibly Lucianus and Voltimand. Their version appears to have been based on an adaptation of the company's original playbook, which itself stood once removed from Shakespeare's working papers by way of an intermediate manuscript. The resulting text is very corrupt, and yet it seems to have affected the more authentic text, because the compositors of the second quarto made use of it, especially when they typeset the first act.

The authorized quarto of *Hamlet* appeared in 1604. Roberts, the printer, seems to have reached some agreement with Ling, one of the publishers of the first quarto, for their initials are now paired on the title page:

THE Tragicall Historie of HAMLET, *Prince of Denmarke*. By William Shakespeare. Newly imprinted and enlarged to almost as much againe as it was, according to the true and perfect Coppie. AT LONDON, Printed by I. R. [James Roberts] for N. L. [Nicholas Ling] and are to be sold at his shoppe vnder Saint Dunstons Church in Fleetstreete. 1604.

Some copies of this edition are dated 1605. This text was based seemingly on Shakespeare's own papers, with the bookkeeper's annotations, but is marred by printing errors and is at times contaminated by the first quarto—presumably, when the printers found Shakespeare's manuscript unreadable. This second quarto served as copy for a third quarto in 1611, Ling having meanwhile transferred his rights in the play to John Smethwick. A fourth quarto, undated but before 1623, was based on the third.

The First Folio text of 1623 omits more than two hundred lines found in the second quarto, yet it supplies some clearly authentic passages. It seems to derive from a transcript of Shakespeare's draft, in which cuts made by the author were observed—cuts made by Shakespeare quite possibly because he knew the draft to be too long for performance and which had either not been marked in the second quarto copy or had been ignored there by the compositors. The Folio also incorporates other alterations seemingly made for clarity or in anticipation of performance. To this theatrically motivated transcript, Shakespeare apparently contributed some revisions. Subsequently, this version evidently was copied again by a careless scribe who took many liberties with the text. Typesetting from this inferior manuscript, the Folio compositors occasionally consulted the fourth quarto, but not often enough. Thus, even though the Folio supplies some genuine readings, as does the first quarto when both the Folio and the second quarto are wrong, the second quarto remains the most authentic version of the text.

Since the text of the second quarto is too long to be accommodated in the two hours' traffic of the stage and since it becomes even longer when the words found only in the Folio are added, Shakespeare must have known it would have to be cut for performance and probably marked at least some omissions himself. Since he may have consented to such cuts primarily because of the constraints of time, however, this present edition holds to the view that the passages in question should not be excised from the text we read. The *Hamlet* presented here is doubtless longer than any version ever acted in Shakespeare's day and thus does not represent a script for any actual performance, but it may well represent the play as Shakespeare wrote it and then expanded it somewhat while also including passages that he may reluctantly have consented to cut for performance. It is also possible that some cuts were artistically intended, but, in the face of real uncertainty in this matter, an editorial policy of inclusion gives to the reader those passages that would otherwise have to be excised or put in an appendix on questionable grounds of authorial "intent."

Hamlet must have been produced before the Stationers' Register entry of July 26, 1602. Francis Meres does not mention the play in 1598 in his *Palladis Tamia*. Gabriel Harvey attributes the "tragedy of Hamlet, Prince of Denmark" to Shakespeare in a marginal note in Harvey's copy of Speght's Chaucer; Harvey acquired the book in 1598, but he could have written the note any time between then and 1601, or even 1603. More helpful in dating is *Hamlet*'s clear reference to the so-called War of the Theaters, the rivalry between the adult actors and the boy actors whose companies had newly revived in 1598–1599 after nearly a decade of inactivity (see 2.2.337–62). The Children of the Chapel Royal began acting at Blackfriars in 1598 and provided such keen competition in 1599–1601 that the adult actors were at times forced to tour the provinces (see *Hamlet*, 2.2.332–62). *Hamlet*'s reference to the rivalry appears, however, only in the Folio text and could represent a late addition. The reference to an "inhibition" imposed on acting companies "by the means of the late innovation" (2.2.332–3), printed in the 1604 quarto, may possibly refer to the abortive uprising of the Earl of Essex on February 8, 1601, or to a decree issued by the Privy Council on June 22, 1600, restricting London companies to two performances a week in each of two playhouses. Revenge tragedy was also in fashion during these years: John Marston's *Antonio's Revenge*, for example, dates from 1599–1601, and *The Malcontent* is from about the same time or slightly later, though it is hard to tell who influenced whom. *Hamlet*'s apparent indebtedness to John Florio's translation of Montaigne suggests that Shakespeare had access to that work in manuscript before its publication in 1603; the Florio had been registered for publication in 1595 and 1600.

Othello (c. 1603–1604)

On October 6, 1621, Thomas Walkley entered in the Stationers' Register, the official record book of the London Company of Stationers (booksellers and printers), "The Tragedie of Othello, the moore of Venice," and published the play in the following year:

THE Tragoedy of Othello, The Moore of Venice. *As it hath beene diuerse times acted at the* Globe, *and at the Black-Friers, by his Maiesties Seruants. Written by* VVilliam Shakespeare. LONDON, Printed by N. O. [Nicholas Okes] for *Thomas Walkley*, and are to be sold at his shop, at the Eagle and Child, in Brittans Bursse. 1622.

This text of this quarto is a good one, based probably on a scribal transcript of Shakespeare's working manuscript, although it is some one hundred and sixty lines shorter than the Folio text of 1623, mostly in scattered small omissions. The Folio text may have been derived (via an intermediate transcript) from a revision of the original authorial manuscript, in which Shakespeare himself copied over his work and made a large number of synonymous or nearly synonymous changes as he

did so. These papers, edited by someone else to remove profanity as required by law and introducing other stylistic changes in the process, seemingly became the basis of the playbook and also of the Folio text. E. A. J. Honigmann (*The Texts of "Othello" and Shakespearian Revision*, 1996) proposes that Ralph Crane prepared a transcript to serve as copy for the Folio text, though not all scholars have agreed.

The textual situation is thus complex. The Folio text appears to contain a significant number of authorial changes, but it was also worked on by one or more sophisticating scribes and by compositors whose changes are sometimes hard to distinguish from those of Shakespeare. The quarto text was printed by a printing establishment that was not known for careful work but does stand close in some ways to a Shakespearean original. Editorially, then, the Folio is the copy text, and its readings are to be preferred when the quarto is not clearly correct and especially when the Folio gives us genuinely new words, but the quarto's readings demand careful consideration when the Folio text may be suspected of mechanical error (e.g., the shortening of words in full lines) or compositorial substitution of alternative forms, normalizations, and easy adjustments of meter. There are times when the Folio's compositor may have been misled by nearby words or letters in his copy. And, because the Folio's stage directions are probably scribal, attention should be paid to those in the quarto.

According to a Revels account that was suspected of being a forgery soon after its publication in 1842 but is now generally accepted, the earliest mention of the play is on "Hallamas Day, being the first of Nouembar," 1604, when "the Kings Maiesties plaiers" performed "A Play in the Banketinge house att Whit Hall Called The Moor of Venis." Possible echoes of *Othello* in *The Honest Whore, Part I*, by Thomas Dekker and Thomas Middleton (1604) and in Richard Knolles's *History of the Turks* (1603) help fix a forward date of composition. Francis Meres does not list the play in 1598. On stylistic grounds, the play is usually dated in 1603 or 1604, although arguments are sometimes presented for a date as early as 1601 or 1602.

King Lear (c. 1605–1606)

On November 26, 1607, Nathaniel Butter and John Busby entered in the Stationers' Register, the official record book of the London Company of Stationers (booksellers and printers), "A booke called. Master William Shakespeare his historye of Kinge Lear, as yt was played before the Kinges maiestie at Whitehall vppon Sainct Stephens night at Christmas Last, by his maiesties servantes playinge vsually at the Globe on the Banksyde." Next year appeared the following quarto:

M. William Shak-speare: HIS True Chronicle Historie of the life and death of King LEAR and his three Daughters. *With the vnfortunate life* of Edgar, *sonne* and heire to the Earle of Gloster, and his sullen and assumed humor of Tom of Bedlam: *As it was played before the Kings Maiestie at Whitehall vpon S.* Stephans *night in Christmas Hollidayes.* By his Maiesties seruants playing vsually at the Gloabe on the Bancke-side. *LONDON*, Printed for *Nathaniel Butter*, and are to be sold at his shop in *Pauls* Church-yard at the signe of the Pide Bull neere St. *Austins* Gate. 1608.

This quarto is often called the "Pied Bull" quarto in reference to its place of sale. Twelve copies exist today, in ten different "states," because proofreading was being carried on while the sheets were being run off in the press; the copies variously combine corrected and uncorrected sheets. A second quarto, printed in 1619 by William Jaggard for Thomas Pavier with the fraudulent date of 1608, was based on a copy of the first quarto, combining corrected and uncorrected sheets.

The First Folio text of 1623 may have been typeset from a playbook cut for performance or from a transcript of such a manuscript, and the playbook in its turn appears to have been based on Shakespeare's fair copy (with revisions) of his first draft. The Folio compositors also almost certainly consulted a copy of the second quarto from time to time or may have typeset directly from this quarto as annotated with reference to Shakespeare's fair copy. In writing the fair copy, Shakespeare may have marked some three hundred lines for deletion, but it is possible that he did so chiefly to shorten the time of performance. He also seems to have added some one hundred lines, an apparent contradiction in view of the need for cutting, but possibly dictated by Shakespeare's developing sense of his play. It is also possible that the cuts were carried out by someone else in the preparation of the playbook.

The first quarto, on the other hand, appears to have been printed from Shakespeare's unrevised and evidently untidy working papers. It is often corrupt, owing in part to type shortages, compositorial uncertainties with the manuscript, and other difficulties in Nicholas Okes's shop. Still, in some matters—especially variants indifferent in meaning (such as *an/if* or *thine/thy*)— the first quarto may be closer to Shakespeare's preferences than the Folio, behind which are several stages of transmission.

This edition agrees with most recent students of the *Lear* text that the Folio represents a theatrical revision, in which the cuts were devised for performance by Shakespeare's company and quite possibly by Shakespeare himself as a member of that company. The case for artistic preference in the making of those cuts, on the other hand, is less certain and may have been overstated. Many of the cuts have the effect of shortening scenes, especially in the latter half of the play. Some scenes, like 3.6, show open gaps as a result of the cutting: Lear's "Then let them anatomize Regan" (line 75) implies the trial of Goneril as it is dramatized in the first quarto but cut from the Folio.

Other omissions also read like expedients, although they can also be explained by a hypothesis of literary and theatrical rewriting; if Shakespeare himself undertook the cutting, he would presumably do so as expertly as possible. The fact that the Folio text gives almost no rewritten speeches may suggest that the large cuts were motivated by the need for shortening. This edition holds to the principle that it is unwise to omit the material cut from the Folio text, since we cannot be sure that Shakespeare would have shortened the text had there been no external constraints. At the same time, the added material in the Folio is clearly his and belongs in his conception of the play. The resulting text is a conflation, but one that avoids cutting material that Shakespeare may well have regretted having to excise.

The Stationers' Register entry for November 26, 1607, describes a performance at court on the previous St. Stephen's night, December 26, 1606. The title page of the first quarto confirms this performance on St. Stephen's night. Such a performance at court was not likely to have been the first, however. Shakespeare's repeated use of Samuel Harsnett's *Declaration of Egregious Popish Impostures*, registered on March 16, 1603, sets an early limit for composition of the play. Other circumstances point to composition of the quarto text in 1605 or 1606. In May 1605, an old play called *The True Chronicle History of King Leir* was entered in the Stationers' Register as a "Tragecall historie," a phrase possibly suggesting the influence of Shakespeare's play, since the old *King Leir* does not end tragically. Moreover, the title page of the old *King Leir*, issued in 1605, proclaims the text to be "as it hath bene diuers and sundry times lately acted." In view of the unlikelihood that such an old play (written before 1594) would be revived in 1605, scholars have suggested that the title page was the publisher's way of trying to capitalize on the recent popularity of Shakespeare's play. In this case, the likeliest date for the composition of Shakespeare's *King Lear* would be in the winter of 1604–1605. Shakespeare certainly used the old *King Leir* as a chief source, but he need not have waited for its publication in 1605 if, as seems perfectly plausible, his company owned the playbook. This hypothesis of the publication of the old *King Leir* after performances of Shakespeare's play must do battle, however, with indications that Shakespeare did not write *King Lear* until late 1605 or 1606. Gloucester's mentioning of "These late eclipses in the sun and moon" (1.2.106) seems to refer to an eclipse of the moon in September and of the sun in October 1605.

There may be echoes in the first quarto of *King Lear* of *Eastward Ho!* by George Chapman, Ben Jonson, and John Marston, written in early 1605, and *Miseries of Enforced Marriage*, written by mid-1605. *King Lear* may allude to concerns at court about the King's frequent absences for hunting, about monopolies, the giving away of knighthoods, the King's need of money, and the like, all of which would have seemed pertinent in 1605–1606. The Folio revisions may date from some time around 1610, according to the editors of the Oxford Shakespeare.

Macbeth (c. 1606–1607)

Macbeth was first printed in the First Folio of 1623. It was set up from a playbook or a transcript of one. The text is unusually short and seems to have been cut for reasons of censorship or for some special performance. Moreover, all of 3.5 and parts of 4.1 (39–43, 125–32) appear to be interpolations, containing songs from Thomas Middleton's *The Witch* (c.1609–1616). Middleton may have been responsible for other alterations and additions.

Simon Forman, in his manuscript *The Book of Plays and Notes thereof per Formans for Common Policy*, records the first known performance of *Macbeth* on April 20, 1611, at the Globe Theatre. The play must have been in existence by 1607, however, for allusions to it seemingly occur in *Lingua* and *The Puritan* (both published in 1607) and in *The Knight of the Burning Pestle* (probably acted in 1607). On the other hand, the play itself seemingly alludes to James I's royal succession in 1603, to his touching for "the king's evil" (see 4.3.147), and to the trial of the notorious Gunpowder Plot conspirators in March 1606. The interpolations from Middleton's *The Witch* are probably from a later date, perhaps after 1613.

Antony and Cleopatra (1606–1607)

On May 20, 1608, Edward Blount entered in the Stationers' Register, the official record book of the London Company of Stationers (booksellers and printers), "A booke Called. Anthony. and Cleopatra," along with "A booke called. The booke of Pericles prynce of Tyre." Blount was friendly with Shakespeare's company, and his entry may have been a "staying entry" designed to forestall unauthorized publication of these texts. If so, the tactic did not succeed with *Pericles*, issued in 1609 by another publisher, but it did succeed with *Antony and Cleopatra*. The play was first printed in the First Folio of 1623. It is a good text, set evidently from Shakespeare's own draft in a more finished state than most of his working papers, or possibly from a transcript of those papers, though not yet prepared to be a playbook.

The year 1608 is thus the latest possible date for *Antony and Cleopatra*. Evidently, it was written in 1606–1607, however, for a "newly altered" edition in 1607 of Samuel Daniel's play *Cleopatra* seems to have been influenced by Shakespeare's play. Shakespeare himself had probably consulted the original edition of *Cleopatra*, published in 1594, or the slightly revised edition of 1599, but Daniel's more thorough revision in 1607

shows signs of his having seen Shakespeare's play in the interim. Also, a play by Barnabe Barnes called *The Devil's Charter* (1607) may contain a parody of Cleopatra's death by asps. Although the printed text of this play advertises corrections and augmentations that could postdate a court performance in February 1607, recent scholarship favors the likelihood that Barnes saw *Antony and Cleopatra* before that—perhaps in late 1606.

The Winter's Tale (c. 1609–1611)

The Winter's Tale was first printed in the First Folio of 1623. Its text is a good one, taken evidently from Ralph Crane's transcript of Shakespeare's own well-finished draft or possibly the playbook. As in most other Crane transcriptions, the stage directions are sparse, and the characters' names are grouped at the beginning of each scene. The first recorded performance was on May 15, 1611, when Simon Forman saw the play at the Globe Theater and recorded a summary of it in his commonplace book. Another performance that year at court, on November 5, is recorded in the *Revels Account*, and still another during the winter of 1612–1613. Quite possibly the play was new at the time Forman saw it. It apparently contains an allusion to the dance of ten or twelve satyrs in Ben Jonson's *Masque of Oberon*, performed at court on January 1, 1611. A 1623 entry in the *Office book* of Sir Henry Herbert, Master of the Revels, refers to *The Winter's Tale* as "an old play . . . formerly allowed of by Sir George Bucke." Bucke (or Buc) was first appointed Master of the Revels in 1610 but had occasionally licensed plays before that date during his predecessor's illness, so that the backward limit of 1610 cannot be considered absolute. Still, matters of style confirm the likelihood that Forman was seeing a new play in 1611.

The Tempest (c. 1611)

The Tempest was first printed in the First Folio of 1623. It occupies first place in the volume and is a scrupulously prepared text from a transcript by Ralph Crane of a theater playbook or of Shakespeare's draft after it had been annotated for production; or, Crane may have provided some of the elaboration of stage directions. Shakespeare's colleagues may have placed *The Tempest* first in the Folio because they considered it his most recent complete play. The first recorded performance was at court on November 1, 1611: "Hallomas nyght was presented att Whithall before yᵉ kinges Maiestie a play Called the Tempest." The actors were "the Kings players" (*Revels Account*). The play was again presented at court during the winter of 1612–1613, this time "before the Princes Highnes the Lady Elizabeth and the Prince Pallatyne Elector." The festivities for this important betrothal and wedding were sumptuous and included at least thirteen other plays. Various arguments have been put forward that Shakespeare composed parts of *The Tempest*, especially the masque, for this occasion, but there is absolutely no evidence that the play was singled out for special prominence among the many plays presented, and the masque is integral to the play as it stands. Probably the 1611 production was of a fairly new play. Simon Forman, who saw *Cymbeline* and *The Winter's Tale* in 1611, does not mention *The Tempest*. He died in September 1611. According to every stylistic test, such as run-on and hypermetric lines, the play is very late. Shakespeare probably knew Sylvester Jourdain's *A Discovery of the Bermudas*, published in 1610, and William Strachey's *A True Reportory of the Wreck and Redemption*, dated July 1610, although not published until 1625.

The Sonnets (c. 1593–1603)

On May 20, 1609, "Thomas Thorpe Entred for his copie vnder thandes of master Wilson and master Lownes Warden a Booke called Shakespeares sonnettes." In the same year appeared the following volume:

SHAKE-SPEARES SONNETS. Neuer before Imprinted. AT LONDON By *G. Eld* for *T. T.* [Thomas Thorpe] and are to be solde by *Iohn Wright*, dwelling at Christ Church gate. 1609.

Some copies of this same edition are marked to be sold by William Aspley rather than John Wright; evidently, Thorpe had set up two sellers to distribute the volume. The sonnets were not reprinted until John Benson's rearranged edition of 1640, possibly because the first edition had been suppressed or because sonnets were no longer in vogue. The 1609 edition may rest on a transcript of Shakespeare's sonnets by someone other than the author, and the edition itself is marred by misprints, though Thorpe was a reputable printer. Clearly, the collection was not supervised through the press as were *Venus and Adonis* and *The Rape of Lucrece*. All the evidence suggests that it was obtained without Shakespeare's permission from a manuscript that had been in private circulation (as we know from Francis Meres's 1598 allusion, in his *Palladis Tamia*, to Shakespeare's "sugared sonnets among his private friends"). Two sonnets, 138 and 144, had appeared in 1599 in *The Passionate Pilgrim*. On questions of dating and order of the sonnets, see the Introduction to *The Sonnets* in this volume.

Appendix 2

Sources

The Taming of the Shrew

Scholars do not agree on the relationship of *The Taming of the Shrew* to the play called *The Taming of a Shrew,* published in 1594. *A Shrew* has been argued to be an earlier version of Shakespeare's play, or a memorial reconstruction of it, or derived from a common original. Some recent critics argue that the two versions should be treated as distinct texts. An often-held view is that *A Shrew* is derived from a now-lost earlier version of Shakespeare's play, to which the compiler added original material and borrowed or even plagiarized from other literary sources as well. If so, *A Shrew* would not appear to be a source for Shakespeare's play, as Geoffrey Bullough has argued in his *Narrative and Dramatic Sources of Shakespeare.* Apart from this question, all critics agree that Shakespeare's play consists of three elements, each with its own source: the romantic love plot of Lucentio and Bianca, the wife-taming plot of Petruchio and Kate, and the framing plot, or induction, of Christopher Sly.

The romantic love plot is derived from George Gascoigne's *Supposes,* a neoclassical comedy performed at Gray's Inn (one of the Inns of Court, where young men studied law in London) in 1566. Gascoigne's play was a rather close translation of Ludovico Ariosto's *I Suppositi* (1509), which in turn was based on two classical plays, Terence's *Eunuchus* and Plautus's *Captivi.* The heroine of Gascoigne's version (as of Ariosto's) is Polynesta, the resourceful daughter of Damon, a widower of Ferrara. Two suitors vie for Polynesta's hand: Dr. Cleander, an aged and miserly lawyer, and Erostrato, a Sicilian gentleman who has purportedly come to Ferrara to study. In fact, however, this "Erostrato" is the servant Dulippo in disguise, having changed places with his master. (These disguisings are the "supposes"

of the title.) As a servant in Damon's household, "Dulippo" has secretly become the lover of Polynesta and has made her pregnant. Balia, the nurse or duenna, is their go-between. Meanwhile, "Erostrato" takes great delight in outwitting Dr. Cleander and his unattractive parasite, Pasiphilo. The counterfeit Erostrato's ruse is to produce a rich father who will guarantee a handsome dowry and thereby outbid Cleander in the contest for Polynesta's hand. The "father" he produces, however, is actually an old Sienese stranger, who is persuaded that he is in danger in Ferrara unless he cloaks his identity. Complications arise when Damon learns of his daughter's affair and throws the lover, "Dulippo," into a dungeon. The crafty Pasiphilo overhears this compromising information and resolves to cause mischief for all the principals. Moreover, when Erostrato's real father, Philogano, arrives in Ferrara, he is barred from his son's house by the counterfeit Philogano and resolves to get help. His clever servant, Litio, suggests employing the famous lawyer, Cleander. All is happily resolved when the real Dulippo proves to be the son of Dr. Cleander and the real Erostrato is revealed to be rich and socially eligible for Polynesta's hand in marriage. Cleander is even reconciled to his parasite, Pasiphilo.

Shakespeare, in his play, has almost entirely eliminated the satire of the law that is in his source. Gremio is aged and wealthy, but no shyster. The lover is not imprisoned in a dungeon. The parasite is gone, as also in *The Comedy of Errors.* Bianca does not consummate her affair with Lucentio, as does Polynesta, and hence has no need for a go-between like Balia. Shakespeare adapts a sophisticated neoclassical comedy, racy and cosmopolitan, to the moral standards of his public theater. The witless

Hortensio, the tutoring in Latin, and the music lesson are Shakespeare's inventions.

The wife-taming plot of Petruchio and Kate reflects an ancient comic misogynistic tradition, still extant today in the Scottish folksong "The Cooper of Fife" or "The Wife Wrapped in Wether's Skin" (Francis James Child, *The English and Scottish Popular Ballads* [1888–1898], 5:104). Richard Hosley has argued (in *Huntington Library Quarterly, 27*, 1964) that Shakespeare's likeliest source was *A Merry Jest of a Shrewd and Curst Wife Lapped in Morel's Skin, for her Good Behavior* (printed c. 1550). In this version, the husband beats his shrewish wife with birch rods until she bleeds and faints, whereupon he wraps her in the raw salted skin of an old plow-horse named Morel. Like Kate, this shrewish wife has a gentle younger sister who is their father's favorite. This father warns the man who proposes to marry his older daughter that she is shrewish, but the suitor goes ahead and subsequently tames his wife with Morel's skin. Thereafter, at a celebratory dinner, everyone is impressed by the thoroughness of the taming.

Shakespeare avoids the misogynistic extremes of this story, despite the similarity of the narrative. Instead, he seems to have had in mind the more humanistic spirit of Erasmus's *A Merry Dialogue Declaring the Properties of Shrewd Shrews and Honest Wives* (translated 1557) and Juan Luis Vives's *The Office and Duty of an Husband* (translated 1555). Specific elements of the wife-taming plot have been traced to other possible sources. The scolding of a tailor occurs in Gerard Legh's *Accidence of Armory* (1562); a wife agrees with her husband's assertion of a patent falsehood in Don Juan Manuel's *El Conde Lucanor* (1335); and three husbands wager on the obedience of their wives in *The Book of the Knight of La Tour-Landry* (printed 1484).

The induction story, of the beggar duped into believing himself a rich lord, is an old tale occurring in the *Arabian Nights*. An interesting analogue occurs in P. Heuterus's *De Rebus Burgundicis* (1584), translated into the French of S. Goulart (1606?) and thence into the English of Edward Crimeston (1607). According to Heuterus, in 1440, Philip the Good of Burgundy actually entertained a drunken beggar in his palace "to make trial of the vanity of our life," plying him with fine clothes, bed, a feast, and the performance of "a pleasant comedy."

A Midsummer Night's Dream

No single source has been discovered that unites the various elements that we find in *A Midsummer Night's Dream*, but the four main strands of action can be individually discussed in terms of sources. The four strands are: (1) the marriage of Theseus (Duke of Athens) and Queen Hippolyta, (2) the romantic tribulations and triumphs of the four young lovers, (3) the quarrel of King Oberon and Queen Titania, together with the fairies' manipulations of human affairs, and (4) the "rude mechanicals" and their play of "Pyramus and Thisbe."

For his conception of Theseus, Shakespeare went chiefly to Geoffrey Chaucer's "The Knight's Tale" and to Thomas North's 1579 translation of "The Life of Theseus" in Plutarch's *Lives of the Noble Grecians and Romans*. Chaucer's Theseus is a duke of "wisdom" and "chivalrye," renowned for his conquest of the Amazons and his marriage to Hippolyta. Plutarch provides information concerning Theseus's other conquests (to which Oberon alludes in 2.1.77 ff.), including that of Antiopa. Shakespeare could have learned more about Theseus from Chaucer's *The Legend of Good Women* and from Ovid's *Metamorphoses*. He seems to have blended all or some of these impressions together with his own notion of a noble yet popular Renaissance ruler.

The romantic narrative of the four lovers appears to be original with Shakespeare, although one can find many analogous situations of misunderstanding and rivalry in love. Chaucer's "The Knight's Tale" tells of two friends battling over one woman. Shakespeare's own *The Two Gentlemen of Verona* gives us four lovers, properly matched at first until one of the men shifts his attentions to his friend's ladylove; eventually, all is righted when the false lover recovers his senses. Parallel situations arise in Sir Philip Sidney's *Arcadia* (1590) and in Jorge de Montemayor's *Diana Enamorada* (c. 1559), a source for *The Two Gentlemen*. What Shakespeare adds in *A Midsummer* is the intervention of the fairies in human love affairs.

Shakespeare's knowledge of fairy lore must have been extensive and is hard to trace exactly. Doubtless, much of it was from oral traditions about leprechauns, gremlins, and elves, who were thought to cause such mischief as spoiling fermentation or preventing milk from churning into butter; Puck's tricks mentioned in 2.1.34 ff. are derived from such lore. Some of the oral tales circulating about Robin Goodfellow later reached print, probably somewhat modified, in the prose pamphlet *Robin Good Fellow, His Mad Pranks and Merry Jests* (London, 1628) and a ballad, "The Mad Merry Pranks of Robbin Good-fellow" (c. 1600) in Roxburghe Ballads, vol. 2, ed. William Chappell (Hertford: Stephen Austin for the Ballad Society, 1872), p. 83. Shakespeare seems to have consulted literary sources as well. In Chaucer's "The Merchant's Tale," Pluto and Proserpina as King and Queen of the fairies intervene in the affairs of old January, his young wife May, and her lover Damyan. Fairies appear on stage in John Lyly's *Endymion* (1588), protecting true lovers and tormenting those who are morally tainted. Shakespeare later reflects this tradition in *The Merry Wives of Windsor* (1597–1601). The name Oberon probably comes from the French romance *Huon of Bordeaux* (translated by Lord Berners by about 1540), where Oberon is a dwarfish fairy King from the mysterious East who practices enchantment in a haunted wood. In Edmund Spenser's *The Faerie Queene*, Oberon is the Elfin father of Queen Gloriana (2.10. 75–6). Robert Greene's *James IV* (c. 1591) also features Oberon as the fairy King, and a lost play called *Huon of Bordeaux* was performed by Sussex's Men, an acting company, at about this same time. The name "Titania" comes from Ovid's *Metamorphoses*, where it is used as a synonym for both the enchantress Circe and the chaste goddess Diana. The name "Titania" does not appear in Arthur Golding's translation (1567), suggesting that Shakespeare found it in the original. Puck, or Robin Goodfellow, is essentially the product of oral tradition, although Reginald Scot's *The Discovery of Witchcraft* (1584) discusses Robin in pejorative terms as an incubus or hobgoblin in whom intelligent people no longer believe.

Scot also reports the story of a man who finds an ass's head placed on his shoulders by enchantment. Similar legends of transformation occur in Apuleius's *The Golden Ass* (translated by William Adlington, 1566) and in the well-known story of the ass's ears bestowed by Phoebus Apollo on King Midas for his presumption. Perhaps the most suggestive possible source for Shakespeare's clownish actors, however, is Anthony Munday's play *John a Kent and John a Cumber* (c. 1587–1590). In it a group of rude artisans, led by the intrepid Turnop, stage a ludicrous interlude written by their churchwarden in praise of his millhorse. Turnop's prologue is a medley of lofty comparisons. The entertainment is presented before noble spectators, who are graciously amused. *John a Kent* also features a lot of magic trickery, a boy named Shrimp whose role is comparable to that of Puck, and a multiple love plot.

"Pyramus and Thisbe" itself is based on the *Metamorphoses* (4.55 ff.). Other versions that Shakespeare may have known include Chaucer's *The Legend of Good Women*, a poem by William Griffith in 1562, George Pettie's *A Petite Palace of Pettie His Pleasure* (1576), *A Gorgeous Gallery of Gallant Inventions* (1578), and "A New Sonnet of Pyramus and Thisbe" from Clement Robinson's *A Handful of Pleasant Delights* (1584). Several of these, especially the last three, are bad enough to have given Shakespeare materials to lampoon, though the sweep of his parody goes beyond the particular story of Pyramus and Thisbe. The occasionally stilted phraseology of Golding's translation of the *Metamorphoses* contributed to the fun. According to Kenneth Muir (*Shakespeare's Sources*, 1957), Shakespeare must also have known Thomas Mouffet's *Of the Silkworms and Their Flies* (published 1599, but possibly circulated earlier in manuscript), which contains perhaps the most ridiculous of all versions of the Pyramus and Thisbe story. Shakespeare also appears to have been spoofing the inept dramatic style and lame verse of English dramas of the 1560s, 1570s, and 1580s, especially in their treatment of tragic sentiment and high emotion; *Cambises, Damon and Pythias*, and *Appius and Virginia* are examples.

The Merchant of Venice

Shakespeare's probable chief source for *The Merchant of Venice* was the first story of the fourth day of *Il Pecorone (The Dunce)*, by Ser Giovanni Fiorentino. This collection of tales dates from the late fourteenth century but was first published in 1558 at Milan and was not published in English translation in Shakespeare's time. If Shakespeare was unable to read it in Italian, he may conceivably have consulted a translation in some now-lost manuscript; such translations did sometimes circulate. Behind Ser Giovanni's story lies an old tradition of a bond given for human flesh, as found in Persia, India, and the Twelve Tables of Roman Law. This legend first appears in English in the thirteenth-century *Cursor Mundi*, with a Jew as the creditor. A thirteenth-century version of the *Gesta Romanorum* (a popular collection of stories in Latin) adds a romantic love plot; the evil moneylender in this story is not Jewish. The hero pawns his own flesh to a merchant in order to win a lady. He succeeds on his third attempt, having learned to avoid a magic spell that had previously put him to sleep and cost him a large number of florins. When he goes to pay his forfeit, the lady follows him disguised as a knight, and foils the evil merchant by pointing out a quibbling distinction between flesh and blood.

Il Pecorone provided Shakespeare with a number of essential elements, although not all that he has included. Ser Giovanni's story tells of Giannetto, the adventurous youngest son of a Florentine merchant, who goes to live with his father's dearest friend, Ansaldo, in Venice. This worthy merchant gives him money to seek his fortune at sea. Unbeknownst to Ansaldo, Giannetto twice risks everything to woo the lady of Belmont: if he can succeed in sleeping with her, he will win her and her country, but, if he fails, he loses all his wealth. Twice Giannetto is given a sleeping medicine and has to forfeit everything. Returning destitute to Venice twice, he is reunited each time with Ansaldo and given the means to seek his fortune again. For the third such voyage, however, Ansaldo is driven to borrow ten thousand florins from a Jew, using the forfeiture of a pound of flesh as a guarantee. This time, one of the lady's maids warns Giannetto not to drink his wine, and he finally possesses the lady as his wife. Sometime later, remembering that the day of Ansaldo's forfeiture has arrived, Giannetto explains the predicament to his wife and is sent by her to Venice with a hundred thousand florins, but he arrives after the forfeiture has fallen due. The lady, however, following after him in the disguise of a doctor of laws, decrees that the Jew may have no blood and must take no more or no less than one pound of flesh. The Jew is jeered at and receives no money. The "doctor of laws" refuses any payment other than the ring Giannetto was given by his lady. Giving it up unwillingly, he returns to Belmont, where his lady vexes him about the ring but finally relents and tells him all. Shakespeare could thus have found in one source the wooing, the borrowing from a Jewish moneylender, the pound of flesh, the trial, and the business of the rings. The story provides no casket episode, courtship of Nerissa by Gratiano, elopement of Jessica, or clowning of Lancelot Gobbo. The Jew's motive is not prompted by the way he has been treated.

Shakespeare may also have known "The Ballad of Gernutus," a popular English work that seems to be older than the play. It has no love plot but dwells on the unnatural cruelty of a Jewish Venetian usurer who takes a bond of flesh for "a merry jest." Anthony Munday's prose *Zelauto* (1580), though its villain is a Christian rather than a Jewish moneylender, also features a bond of this sort, taken purportedly as a mere sport but with hidden malice. Truculento, the villain, takes the bond of two young men, Rodolfo and his friend Strabino, as surety for a loan. If they forfeit the loan, the young men are to lose their lands and their right eyes as well. The villain has a daughter, Brisana, whom he permits to marry Rodolfo, since Truculento expects to marry Rodolfo's sister Cornelia himself. When Cornelia instead marries Strabino, Truculento angrily takes the young men to court to demand his bond. The two brides disguise themselves as scholars and go to court, where they appeal for mercy and then foil Truculento by means of the legal quibble about blood.

Another possible source for the courtroom scene is *The Orator*, translated into English in 1596 from the French of Alexandre Sylvain. An oration, entitled "Of a Jew, who would for his debt have a pound of the flesh of a Christian," uses many specious arguments also employed by Shylock, and is forthrightly confuted in "The Christian's Answer."

Shylock's relationship to his daughter finds obvious earlier parallels in *Zelauto* and in Christopher Marlowe's play, *The Jew of Malta* (c. 1589), in which Barabas's daughter Abigail loves a Christian and ultimately renounces her faith. The actual elopement, however, is closer to the fourteenth story in Masuccio of Salerno's fifteenth-century *Il Novellino* (not published in English translation in Shakespeare's day).

The casket-choosing episode, not found in *Il Pecorone*, was a widespread legend, occurring, for example, in the story of *Barlaam and Josophat* (ninth-century Greek, translated into Latin by the thirteenth century), in Vincent of Beauvais's *Speculum Historiale*, in the *Legenda Aurea*, in Giovanni Boccaccio's *Decameron* (Day 10, Story 1), in John Gower's *Confessio Amantis*, and—closest to Shakespeare—in the *Gesta Romanorum* (translated into English

in 1577 by Richard Robinson and "bettered" by him in 1595). In this last account, the choice is between a gold, silver, and lead casket, each with its own inscription. The first two inscriptions are like Shakespeare's; the third reads, "Thei that chese me, shulle fynde [in] me that God hathe disposid." The chooser, however, is a maiden, and she is not preceded by other contestants.

An old play called *The Jew* is referred to by Stephen Gosson in 1579 as containing "the greediness of worldly choosers, and bloody minds of usurers." Scholars have speculated that this was a source play for Shakespeare, but actually we have too little to go on to make a reliable judgment. Gosson was surely not referring to Robert Wilson's *The Three Ladies of London* (c. 1581) in any case, even though it is sometimes suggested as an analogue to *The Merchant of Venice*, for its Jewish figure, named Gerontus (compare Gernutus in the ballad), is an exemplary person. Besides, the probable date of this play is later than Gosson's remark.

Much Ado About Nothing

Shakespeare's probable chief source for the Hero-Claudio plot of *Much Ado* was the twenty-second story from the *Novelle* of Matteo Bandello (Lucca, 1554). A French translation by François de Belleforest, in his *Histoires Tragiques* (1569 edition), was available to Shakespeare, as was the Italian original. The story of the maiden falsely accused was, however, much older than the story by Bandello. Perhaps the earliest version that has been found is the Greek romance *Chaereas and Callirrhoe*, fourth or fifth century A.D., in which the hero Chaereas, warned by envious rivals of his wife's purported infidelity, watches at dusk while an elegantly attired stranger is admitted by the maid to the house where Callirrhoe lives. Chaereas rushes in and strikes mistakenly at his wife in the dark but is acquitted of murder when the maid confesses her part in a conspiracy to delude Chaereas. Callirrhoe is buried in a deathlike trance but awakens in time to be carried off by pirates. The story reappears in a fifteenth-century Spanish romance, *Tirante el Blanco*, in which the princess Blanche is courted seemingly by a repulsive black man. This Spanish version probably inspired the account in Canto 5 of Ludovico Ariosto's *Orlando Furioso* (1516), to which all subsequent Renaissance versions are ultimately indebted.

In Ariosto's account, as translated into English by Sir John Harington (1591), the narrator is Dalinda, maid to the virtuous Scottish princess Genevra. Dalinda tells how she has fallen guiltily in love with Polynesso, Duke of Albany, an evil man who often makes love to Dalinda in her mistress's rooms but who longs in fact to marry Genevra. Consequently, Polynesso arranges for Genevra's noble Italian suitor, Ariodante, and Ariodante's brother Lurcanio, to witness the Duke's ascent to Genevra's window by a rope ladder. The woman who admits the Duke is, of course, not Genevra but Dalinda disguised as her mistress, having been duped into believing that the Duke merely wishes to satisfy his craving for Genevra by making love to her image. Lurcanio publicly accuses the innocent Genevra and offers to fight anyone who defends her cause (compare Claudio's quarrel with Leonato). The evil Duke tries to get rid of Dalinda, but all is finally put to rights by Rinaldo (the hero of *Orlando Furioso*) and Ariodante. This account gives an unusually vivid motivation for the maid and the villain—a clearer motivation than in Shakespeare's play. A lost dramatic version, *Ariodante and Genevora*, was performed at the English court in 1583.

Shakespeare probably consulted not only Ariosto but also Edmund Spenser's *The Faerie Queene* (2.4), based on Ariosto. Spenser's emphasis is on the blind rage of Phedon, a young squire in love with Claribell. Phedon is tricked by his erstwhile friend Philemon and by Claribell's maid Pryene into believing Claribell false. Pryene's motive in dressing up as Claribell is to prove she is as beautiful as her mistress. When, after having slain Claribell for her supposed perfidy, Phedon learns the truth, he poisons Philemon and furiously pursues Pryene until he is utterly possessed by a mad frenzy.

Shakespeare's greatest debt is, however, to Bandello's story. In a number of details, the story is closer to Shakespeare's play than are those already discussed. Several names are substantially the same as in Shakespeare: the location is Messina, the father of the slandered bride is Lionato di' Lionati (compare Shakespeare's Leonato), and her lover is in the service of King Piero of Aragon (compare Don Pedro of Aragon). As in Shakespeare, a young knight (named Sir Timbreo) seeks the hand in marriage of his beloved (Fenicia) through the matchmaking offices of a noble emissary. The complication of this wooing is somewhat different in that Timbreo's friend Girondo also falls in love with Fenicia, but Girondo then plots with a mischief-loving courtier (resembling Shakespeare's Don John) to poison Timbreo's mind against Fenicia, and Girondo thereupon escorts Timbreo to a garden, where they see Girondo's servant, elegantly dressed, enter Fenicia's window. No maid takes part in the ruse, however, nor indeed is any woman seen at the window. When Fenicia is wrongly accused, she falls into a deathlike trance and is pronounced dead by a doctor, but she is revived. Her father, believing in her innocence, sends her off to a country retreat and circulates the report that she is, in fact, dead. Soon both Timbreo and Girondo are stricken with remorse, Timbreo magnanimously spares his friend's life, and both confess the truth to Fenicia's family. A year later, Timbreo marries a wife chosen for him by Lionato who turns out, of course, to be Fenicia. Girondo marries her sister Belfiore. This account does not provide any equivalent for Beatrice and Benedick. Shakespeare enhances the Friar's role and provides a brother

for Leonato. Claudio and Leonato are of comparable social station in Shakespeare, whereas Bandello makes a point of Timbreo's superior social rank.

A lost play, *Panecia* (1574–1575), may have been based on Bandello's work. One other version Shakespeare may have known is George Whetstone's *The Rock of Regard* (1576), based on Ariosto and Bandello. It contains a suggestive parallel to Claudio's rejection of Hero in church. Various Italian plays in the tradition of Luigi Pasqualigo's *Il Fedele* (1579), and also a version perhaps by Anthony Munday, *Fedele and Fortunio* (published 1585), are analogous in situation, though Shakespeare need not have known any of them.

For the Beatrice-Benedick plot, no source has been discovered, apart from Shakespeare's own earlier fascination with wit-combat and candid wooing in *Love's Labor's Lost* and *The Taming of the Shrew*. Nor has a plausible source been found for Dogberry and the watch.

As You Like It

Shakespeare's chief source for *As You Like It* was Thomas Lodge's graceful pastoral romance, *Rosalynde: Euphues' Golden Legacy* (1590). Lodge was indebted in turn to *The Tale of Gamelyn*, a fourteenth-century poem wrongly included by some medieval scribes as "The Cook's Tale" in Chaucer's *Canterbury Tales*. *Gamelyn* was not printed until 1721, but Lodge clearly had access to a manuscript of it. Although Shakespeare may not have known *Gamelyn* directly, his play still retains the hearty spirit of this Robin Hood legend. (In later Robin Hood ballads, Gamelyn or Gandelyn is identified with Will Scarlet, a member of Robin Hood's band.)

Even a brief account of *Gamelyn* suggests how greatly the original tale is inspired by Robin Hood legends of outlaws valiantly defying the corrupt social order presided over by the Sheriff and his henchmen. Gamelyn, the youngest of three brothers, is denied his inheritance by his churlish eldest brother John. When Gamelyn demands his rights, John orders his men to beat Gamelyn, but the young man arms himself with a pestle and proves to be a formidable fighter. After defeating the champion wrestler in a local wrestling match (a lower-class sport befitting the social milieu of this story), Gamelyn returns home to find himself locked out by his brother. He kills the porter, flings the man's body down a well, and feasts his companions day and night for a week. John feigns a reconciliation and slyly asks if he can bind Gamelyn hand and foot merely to satisfy an oath he has sworn over the death of the porter. Gamelyn trustingly agrees and is made prisoner. After his bonds have been secretly loosed by Adam the Spencer (the steward), Gamelyn pretends to remain bound until the propitious moment for revenge and escape. The moment arrives during a feast of monks who churlishly refuse to help Gamelyn. With

Adam's help, he fells many of them, ties up his brother, and escapes to the woods, where he and Adam are rescued from hunger by a band of merry outlaws. As their chief, Gamelyn becomes a champion of the poor and an enemy of rich churchmen. His brother, now sheriff, brands Gamelyn an outlaw and manages to imprison him, but Gamelyn's second brother, Sir Ote, stands bail for him. On the day of the trial, Gamelyn frees Sir Ote and hangs the sheriff and the jury. Gamelyn finally obtains his inheritance and becomes chief officer of the King's royal forests. This story is uninfluenced by the pastoral tradition and contains no love plot. Its Robin Hood traditions are very much present, nonetheless, in Shakespeare's contrasting portrayal of a tyrannical court and of a just society in banishment.

Lodge retains the primitive vigor of *Gamelyn* but adds generous infusions of pastoral sentiment in the manner of Sir Philip Sidney's *Arcadia* (1590) and sententious moralizing in the manner of John Lyly's *Euphues* (1578). The pastoralism is presented in conventional terms, with none of the genial self-reflexive satire we find in Shakespeare. Psychological motive is intricate, often more so than in Shakespeare's play. The style is also heavily influenced by Lyly's exquisitely balanced, antithetical, and ornamented prose. For his pastoralism, Lodge was indebted not only to Sidney but also to the ancient pastoral tradition that included the Greek Theocritus and the Roman Virgil, the Italian Sannazaro (*Arcadia*), and the Portuguese Jorge de Montemayor (*Diana*). Pastoralism by Lodge's time had become thoroughly imbued with artificial conventions: abject lovers writing sonnets to their disdainful mistresses, princes and princesses in shepherds' disguise, idealized landscapes, stylized debate as to the relative merits of love and friendship, youth and age, city life and country life, and so on. Some of these conventions were derived also from the vogue of sonneteering pioneered by Francesco Petrarch and can thus be described as the stereotypes of "Petrarchism." Lodge accepts these conventions and gives us typical pastoral lovers even in his hero and heroine, although the elements he derived from *Gamelyn* certainly add a contrasting note of violence and danger.

Lodge's account begins much like that of *Gamelyn*. Saladyne, the envious eldest brother, bribes the champion wrestler to do away with Rosader (Orlando) in the wrestling match. Rosader succeeds instead in killing the wrestler and in winning the heart of Rosalynde, daughter of the banished King Gerismond. When she sends him a jewel, Rosader is not at all at a loss for words; indeed, he composes a Petrarchan sonnet on the spot. The usurping King Torismond (no relation to Gerismond), despite his evil nature, is impressed by Rosader's grace and martial prowess. Rosader returns home with friends, breaks open the door, and feasts his company. The wily Saladyne overwhelms Rosader in his sleep and binds him to a post,

but Rosader is untied by Adam and makes havoc among the eldest brother's guests, as in *Gamelyn*. In this case, however, the guests are Saladyne's kindred and allies, all of whom have refused to help Rosader. The sheriff tries to arrest Rosader and Adam, but they make good their escape to the Forest of Arden in France. They are saved from starvation by the kindly King Gerismond and his exiled followers. Rosalynde and King Torismond's daughter Alinda meanwhile have been banished from court and have taken abode in the forest under the names of Ganymede and Aliena. They befriend old Corydon (Corin) and young Montanus (Silvius), who is hopelessly in love with the haughty Phoebe. "Ganymede" poses as a woman to test Rosader in his wooing, and they are joined in a mock marriage. Saladyne, now repenting of his evil deeds, comes to the forest, is saved by his brother from a lion, and falls in love with Alinda (whom he helps to rescue from ruffians). The denouement is as in Shakespeare, although the triumphant return to society is more complete: King Torismond is slain, Gerismond is restored to his throne, Rosader is named heir-apparent, and all the friends are appropriately rewarded.

Despite Shakespeare's extensive indebtedness to this charming romance, there is a crucial difference: Lodge's pastoral world is never subjected to a wry or satirical exploration. Lodge offers no equivalent for Touchstone, the fool who sees the absurdity of both country and city; Jaques, the malcontent traveler; William and Audrey, the clownishly simple peasants; or Sir Oliver Martext, the ridiculous hedge-priest. Nor does Lodge tell of Le Beau, the court butterfly. Hymen is a Shakespearean addition, and the conversion of Duke Frederick by a hermit instead of his being overthrown and killed is a characteristically Shakespearean softening touch. Shakespeare's added characters are virtually all foils to the conventional pastoral vision he found in his source.

Twelfth Night

John Manningham's description of a performance of *Twelfth Night* on February 2, 1602, at the Middle Temple (one of the Inns of Court, where young men studied law in London), compares the play to Plautus's *Menaechmi* and to an Italian play called *Inganni*. The comment offers a helpful hint on sources. The *Menaechmi* had been the chief source for Shakespeare's earlier play, *The Comedy of Errors*, and that farce of mistaken identity clearly resembles *Twelfth Night* in the hilarious mix-ups resulting from the confusion of two look-alike twins. Shakespeare certainly profited from his earlier experimenting with this sort of comedy. *Twelfth Night* is not necessarily directly indebted to the *Menaechmi*, however, for Renaissance Italian comedy offered many imitations of Plautus from which Shakespeare could have taken his *Twelfth Night* plot. These include *Gl'Inganni* (1562) by Nicolò Secchi, another *Gl'Inganni* (1592) by Curzio Gonzaga, and, most important, an anonymous *Gl'Ingannati* (published 1537). This last play was translated into French by Charles Estienne as *Les Abusés* (1543) and adapted into Spanish by Lope de Rueda in *Los Engaños* (1567). A Latin version, *Laelia*, based on the French, was performed at Cambridge in the 1590s but never printed. Obviously, *Gl'Ingannati* was widely known, and Manningham was probably referring to it in his diary. To trace Shakespeare's own reading in this matter is difficult, owing to the large number of versions available to him, but we can note the suggestive points of comparison in each.

Both *Inganni* plays feature a brother and a sister mistaken for one another. In the later play (by Gonzaga), the sister uses the disguise name of "Cesare." In Secchi's *Inganni*, the disguised sister is in love with her master, who is told that a woman the exact age of his supposed page is secretly in love with him. Another play by Secchi, *L'Interesse* (1581), has a comic duel involving a disguised heroine. Of the Italian plays considered here, however, *Gl'Ingannati* is closest to Shakespeare's play. A short prefatory entertainment included with it in most editions features the name Malevolti. In the play itself, the heroine, Lelia, disguises herself as a page in the service of Flaminio, whom she secretly loves, and is sent on embassies to Flaminio's disdainful mistress Isabella. This lady falls in love with "Fabio," as Lelia calls herself. Lelia's father, Virginio, learning of her disguise and resolving to marry her to old Gherardo (Isabella's father), seeks out Lelia but instead mistakenly arrests her longlost twin brother, Fabrizio, who has just arrived in Modena. Fabrizio is locked up as a madman in Isabella's room, whereupon Isabella takes the opportunity to betroth herself to the person she mistakes for "Fabio." A recognition scene clears up everything and leads to the marriages of Fabrizio to Isabella and Flaminio to Lelia. This story lacks the subplot of Malvolio, Sir Toby, *et al*. Nor is there a shipwreck.

Matteo Bandello based one of the stories in his *Novelle* (1554) on *Gl'Ingannati*, and this prose version was then translated into French by François de Belleforest in his *Histoires Tragiques* (1579 edition). Shakespeare may well have read both, for he consulted these collections of stories in writing *Much Ado About Nothing*. His most direct source, however, seems to have been the story of "Apollonius and Silla" by Barnabe Riche (an English soldier and fiction writer), in *Riche His Farewell to Military Profession* (1581), which was derived from Belleforest. Riche involves his characters in more serious moral predicaments than Shakespeare allows in his festive comedy. The plot situation is much the same: Silla (the equivalent of Shakespeare's Viola) is washed ashore near Constantinople, where, disguised as "Silvio," she takes service with a duke, Apollonius (Shakespeare's Orsino), and goes on embassies to the wealthy widow Julina (Shakespeare's Olivia), who proceeds at once to fall in love with "Silvio." When Silla's twin brother, the real Silvio, arrives, he is mistaken by Julina for his twin and is invited to a rendezvous, like Shakespeare's Sebastian. The differences at this point are marked, however, for Silvio becomes Julina's lover and leaves her pregnant when he departs the next day on his quest for Silla. Apollonius is understandably furious to learn of "Silvio's" apparent success with Julina and throws his page into prison. Julina is no less distressed when she learns that the supposed father of her child is in actuality a woman. Only Silvio's eventual return to marry Julina resolves these complications. Shakespeare eschews the pregnancy, the desertion, the imprisonment, and all of Riche's stern moralizing about the bestiality of lust that accompanies this lurid tale. Moreover, he adds the plot of Malvolio, for which Riche provides little suggestion. Shakespeare changes the location to Illyria, with its hint of delirium and illusion, and provides an English flavor in the comic scenes that intensifies the festive character of the play.

Shakespeare's reading may also have included the anonymous play *Sir Clyomon and Sir Clamydes* (c. 1570–1583), Sir Philip Sidney's *Arcadia* (1590), and Emmanuel Forde's prose romance *Parismus* (1598), in which one "Violetta" borrows the disguise of a page. Scholars have suggested that the Malvolio plot may reflect an incident at Queen Elizabeth's court in which the Comptroller of the Household, Sir William Knollys, interrupted a noisy late-night party dressed in only his nightshirt and a pair of spectacles, with a copy of the Italian pornographic writer Aretino's work in his hand. A similar confrontation between revelry and sobriety occurred in 1598: Ambrose Willoughby quieted a disturbance after the Queen had gone to bed and was afterward thanked by her for doing his duty. Such incidents were no doubt common, however, and there is no compelling reason to suppose Shakespeare was sketching from current court gossip.

Measure for Measure

Stories about corrupt magistrates are ancient and universal, but Shakespeare's particular story in *Measure for Measure* seems to go back to an actual incident in the sixteenth-century Italian court of Don Ferdinando de Gonzaga. A Hungarian student named Joseph Macarius, writing from Vienna, tells about an Italian citizen accused of murder whose wife submitted to the embraces of the magistrate in hopes of saving her husband. When the magistrate executed her husband despite her having fulfilled her bargain, she appealed to the Duke, who ordered the magistrate to give her a dowry and marry her. Thereafter, the Duke ordered the magistrate to be executed. This incident seems to have inspired a Senecan drama by Claude

Rouillet called *Philanira* (1556), a French translation of this play (1563), a novella in the *Hecatommithi* of G. B. Giraldi Cinthio (1565), and a play by Cinthio called *Epitia* (posthumously published in 1583). Shakespeare may have known both the prose and the dramatic versions by Cinthio.

In Cinthio's story, the wise Emperor Maximian appoints his friend Juriste to govern Innsbruck, warning him to rule justly or expect no mercy from the Emperor. Juriste rules long and well, to the satisfaction of his master and the people of Innsbruck. When a young man named Vico is brought before him for ravishing a virgin, Juriste assigns the mandatory sentence of death. Vico's sister, Epitia, an extraordinarily beautiful virgin of eighteen, pleads for Vico's life, urging that his deed was one of passion and that he stands ready to marry the girl he forced. The judge, secretly inflamed with lust for Epitia, promises to consider the matter carefully. She reports this seemingly encouraging news to Vico, who urges her to persevere. When, however, the judge proposes to take her chastity in return for her brother's life, Epitia is mortified and refuses unless Juriste will marry her. During another interim in these negotiations, Vico begs his sister to save his life at any cost. She then submits to Juriste on the condition that he will both marry her and spare Vico. Next morning, however, the jailer brings her the body of her decapitated brother. She lays her complaint before the Emperor, who confronts Juriste with his guilt. Conscience-stricken, Juriste confesses and begs for mercy. At first, Epitia demands strict justice, but when the Emperor compels Juriste to marry her and then be beheaded, she reveals "her natural kindness" and begs successfully for the life of her wronger. There are several important differences between this account and Shakespeare's play: Vico is actually killed, unlike Claudio, and Epitia sleeps with Juriste and then is married to him. No equivalent to Mariana appears, or to Lucio, Pompey, Mistress Overdone, Elbow, and other characters in the comic scenes of Shakespeare's play. No duke oversees the career of Juriste and ensures that no fatal wrong will occur.

Shakespeare may also have consulted Cinthio's play *Epitia*, but his chief source was George Whetstone's two-part play *Promos and Cassandra* (1578) and a novella on the same subject. In the English play, the corrupt judge is Promos, administrator of the city of Julio under the King of Hungary. The law forbidding adultery has lain in abeyance for some years when a young gentleman named Andrugio is arrested and condemned for "incontinency." His sister Cassandra, like Epitia in Cinthio's play, lays down her precious chastity to Promos in response to her brother's piteous entreaties. Promos gives his assurance that he will marry her and save Andrugio's life. When Promos instead treacherously orders the execution of Andrugio, the jailer secretly substitutes the head

of a felon, newly executed and so mutilated as to be unrecognizable even by Cassandra. (This rescue is seen as an intervention "by the providence of God.") The King sentences Promos, just as the Emperor sentences Juriste in Cinthio's play, but in Whetstone's play the King refuses Cassandra's pleas for the life of her new husband until Andrugio reveals himself to be still alive and offers to die for Promos. The King forgives Andrugio on condition that he marry Polina, whom he has wronged. The play also features a courtesan named Lamia and her man, Rosko, who ingratiate themselves with the corrupt officer (Phallax) in charge of investigating their case. Phallax is ultimately caught and dismissed from office while Lamia is publicly humiliated.

Whetstone wrote a prose novella of this same story in the *Heptameron of Civil Discourses* (1582). Shakespeare appears to have consulted it as well as the play, for the prose version mentions the names of Isabella (as the narrator of the story) and Crassus (compare *Measure for Measure*, 4.5.8), and the King's awarding of measure for measure in his sentencing of Promos—"You shall be measured with the grace you bestowed on Andrugio"—may have given Shakespeare an idea for the title of his play. Shakespeare was also indebted for a few details to a version in Thomas Lupton's *Too Good to Be True* (1581).

Even though Shakespeare's play is closely related to Whetstone's play and novella, Shakespeare has changed much. He adds the motif of the Duke's mysterious disguise. (A not very compelling analogue to this motif occurs in Sir Thomas Elyot's *The Image of Governance*, 1541.) Shakespeare introduces the use of the bed trick, found also in his presumably earlier play *All's Well That Ends Well*. Most important, Shakespeare stresses the moral and legal complexity of his story. Isabella is about to renounce the world by entering a convent. By contrast, Lucio, a Shakespearean addition, is an engaging cynic, hedonist, and slanderer. Claudio, although guilty of fornication, is only technically in violation of the laws against sexual license. Isabella does not surrender her chastity. Her breakdown in the scene with Claudio intensifies her emotional crisis and renders all the more triumphant her final ability to forgive Angelo. Angelo himself is made puritanical in temperament and is spared the actual consequences of his worst intentions so that he can be worthy of being forgiven. Isabella need not marry Angelo, since he has not actually seduced her; she is thus free to marry the Duke. No felon need be executed in Claudio's stead, for Providence provides a natural death in the prison. In the subplot, going well beyond the merest hints in Whetstone, Pompey is a brilliantly original innovation, Elbow a characteristically Shakespearean clown modeled on the earlier Dogberry of *Much Ado About Nothing*, and Escalus a significant spokesman for a moderate and practical course of equity in the law.

Richard III

Richard III, like the *Henry VI* series, is based on Edward Hall's *The Union of the Two Noble and Illustre Families of Lancaster and York* (1542) and on the 1587 edition of Raphael Holinshed's *The Chronicles of England, Scotland, and Ireland*. Both of these historical compilations were deeply indebted for their hostile view of Richard III to Polydore Vergil and Thomas More. Vergil, a papal tax collector who came to England in 1501, spent many years under the patronage of Henry VII writing in Latin his *Anglica Historia* (first published in Basel, 1534). This work portrayed Richard negatively in order to glorify the claim of the Tudor monarch who had deposed Richard in 1485. Vergil argued that England's suffering was a divinely sent scourge, intended to cleanse England of rebelliousness and to prepare the English people for the providential reward of Tudor rule.

Thomas More's *The History of King Richard III*, left unfinished in 1513, was published in two slightly different versions: one in English (1557) and one in Latin (1566). Thomas More obtained much information and possibly an early draft of his narrative from Cardinal Morton, in whose household More lived as a youth. Morton had figured in the struggles of Richard III's reign—he was the Bishop of Ely from whom Richard requested the strawberries (3.4.32–3)—and had become a bitter enemy of the Yorkist king. Thomas More's own purpose in writing the life of Richard III was surely not to glorify Henry VII, with whom More had a strained relationship, but to characterize the evil of political opportunism. His portrait of Richard becomes that of the generic tyrant, behaving as such tyrants behaved in the various literary models from Renaissance Italy with which More was doubtless familiar. The result was, in any case, one-sided. The historical Richard seems to have been no worse than many another late medieval ruler and had indeed some admirable ideas on efficiency in government. More's blackened portrait, because it served the purposes of the Tudor state, became part of the legend and was available to Shakespeare in many versions. Holinshed incorporated verbatim a good deal of More's account.

Apart from Hall's and Holinshed's chronicles, those of Robert Fabyan (first published in 1516) and the *Annals* of John Stow (1580, 1592) may have provided Shakespeare with further details. Another possible source is *A Mirror for Magistrates* (first published in 1559), in which, for example, in "The Complaint of George, Duke of Clarence," we find the riddling prophecy about the letter *G* (see 1.1.39). A second edition of the *Mirror* (1563) contains the Complaints of Edward IV, Anthony Woodville (Lord Rivers), Hastings, Buckingham, Shore's wife, and others. Shakespeare's particular indebtedness to the *Mirror* is not great, though he certainly was familiar with it. The same is probably true of the Latin tragedy *Richardus Tertius* by Thomas Legge (1579) at Cambridge, which contains an interesting scene of Richard's wooing of the Lady Anne not reported in the chronicles. The anonymous *The True Tragedy of Richard III* (published 1594, written c. 1590–1592) may have been useful in its fusing of Senecan revenge motifs with English history and in its focus on the single figure of Richard. The Richard of this anonymous play is an overreacher, a worshiper of Fortune who meets his nemesis in the devoutly Christian Earl of Richmond. Opinion is divided as to whether Shakespeare actually used the play, chiefly because by 1590 he could have found the legend of Richard III set forth in so many works.

Richard II

Shakespeare's primary source for *Richard II* was the 1587 edition of Raphael Holinshed's *Chronicles* covering the years 1398 to 1400. As in his earlier *Henry VI* plays and *Richard III*, Shakespeare departs from historical accuracy in the interests of artistic design. Queen Isabel's part is almost wholly invented, for historically she was a child of eleven at the time the events in this play occurred. Her "Garden Scene" (3.4) is a fine piece of invention, bringing together images of order and disorder that are found in the rest of the play. The Duchess of York's role is entirely original; Holinshed reports the scene in which York's son Aumerle (the Earl of Rutland) rides to the new king and begs for mercy while his father simultaneously denounces him as a traitor, but the Duchess is never mentioned. Shakespeare has added the poignant conflict between husband and wife. Northumberland's role as conspirator against Richard and as hatchet man for Bolingbroke is greatly enlarged; for example, Holinshed never names the persons who engage in the original plotting against Richard. Shakespeare's Bolingbroke returns to England on his own initiative, whereas in Holinshed he does so at the barons' invitation, a change that accentuates the puzzle of Bolingbroke's motive. Another invention is the meeting between John of Gaunt and the Duchess of Gloucester (1.2). In fact, most of Gaunt's character and behavior has no basis in Holinshed at all. Shakespeare creates him to fill the role of thoughtfully conservative statesman, agonized by his son's banishment but doggedly obedient to his monarch. Finally, and most important, Shakespeare has greatly enlarged the role and the poetic nature of King Richard, especially in the final two acts.

Many of these alterations are Shakespeare's own; others derive from his reading in other sources. Samuel Daniel's *The First Four Books of the Civil Wars* (1595) may have had an important influence. Although we cannot discount the possibility that Shakespeare's play may have been written first, the consensus today is that he knew Daniel's poem. It gave him the idea of the Queen's maturity and grief (although not the Garden Scene), and the final meeting of King and Queen. Daniel's Hotspur is unhistorically a young man, as in 2.3 of Shakespeare's play. Like Shakespeare, Daniel sees York as a man of "a mild temperateness." Daniel's Richard and Bolingbroke ride together into London, not separately as in Holinshed. In Daniel's poem, Bolingbroke's indirect manner of insinuating his desire for Richard's death ("And wished that some would so his life esteem/As rid him of these fears wherein he stood") is verbally close to Shakespeare's depiction of this scene. Richard's final soliloquies in these two works show an unmistakable similarity to one another.

Richard II's reign was a controversial subject in the 1590s and produced other plays of varying political coloration that Shakespeare must have known. *The Life and Death of Jack Straw* (anonymous, 1590–1593) distorts history in its friendly portrayal of Richard's role in the Peasants' Revolt of 1381 and whitewashes government policy. In contrast, the anonymous play *Thomas of Woodstock*, sometimes known as *1 Richard II* (1591–1595), is almost a call for open rebellion against tyranny. Many verbal similarities link this latter play with Shakespeare's *Richard II*, and, although scholars have difficulty in determining which was written first, the wary consensus is that Shakespeare borrowed from *Woodstock*. Such a hypothesis would explain some of the mysterious references to Woodstock's death in the first act of *Richard II*, since the anonymous play deals with historical events preceding those of Shakespeare's play. Shakespeare's debt to *Jack Straw*, on the other hand, is slight, even though he probably knew the play. Christopher Marlowe's *Edward II* (c. 1592), although dealing with another reign, probably taught Shakespeare much about constructing a play in which a weak king gains sympathy in his suffering, while his successor becomes morally tainted by the act of deposition.

Other sources have been proposed—so many, in fact, that Shakespeare's task of writing the play has been compared to that of a historical researcher. More probably he assimilated his wide and varied reading without any formal program of study. He had certainly read Edward Hall's *Union of the Two Noble and Illustre Families of Lancaster and York* (1542), a chief source for his earlier history plays, but in *Richard II* he seems to have recalled little more than its overall thematic pattern. Shakespeare must have known the Complaints of Mowbray and Richard in *A Mirror for Magistrates*, but the verbal echoes are slight in this case. The same is essentially true of *The Chronicles of England* by Jean Froissart, translated by Lord Berners (1525), and two French eyewitness accounts available to Shakespeare only in manuscript: the anonymous *Chronique de la Traïson et Mort de Richard Deux Roi d'Angleterre* and Jean Créton's *Histoire du Roi d'Angleterre Richard*. The Froissart *Chronicles* perhaps gave some hints

for Gaunt's refusal to avenge Gloucester's death, for Richard's insensitivity at Gaunt's death, and for Northumberland's role as conspirator. The *Traïson* is notably sympathetic to Richard in his decline, although Shakespeare might also have found this sympathy in Daniel's *Civil Wars*.

Shakespeare's second series of English history plays (*Richard II*, *1* and *2 Henry IV*, *Henry V*) is even freer of the Tudor providential view of history than his first. The second series does not lead forward by any direct link to the reign of the Tudors, as does the first. Henry A. Kelly has shown (*Divine Providence in the England of Shakespeare's Histories*, 1970) that Shakespeare does not follow a single "Tudor myth" but allows spokesmen for both Richard II and his opponents to repeat arguments found in the various chronicles. This practice is especially evident in *Richard II*, in which some spokesmen eloquently warn of the disasters that will follow Bolingbroke's assumption of the throne, while other spokesmen are sympathetic to Bolingbroke's takeover as a political necessity.

Henry IV, Part I

Shakespeare's chief historical source for *1 Henry IV* was the 1587 edition of Raphael Holinshed's *Chronicles*, but he also took some important ideas from Samuel Daniel's *The First Four Books of the Civil Wars* (1595). Following Daniel, Shakespeare readjusts the age of Hotspur (who was historically older than Henry IV) to match that of Prince Hal. Daniel's Hotspur is, like Shakespeare's, dauntless and stubborn, a turbulent yet noble spirit. The theme of a nemesis of rebellion afflicting Henry IV for his usurpation, only touched upon in Shakespeare's play, owes something to Daniel's presentation, although the idea of nemesis is to be found also in Holinshed. Both Holinshed and Daniel err in confusing the Edmund Mortimer whom Glendower captured with his nephew Edmund Mortimer, claimant to the throne; Shakespeare perpetuates this error. Hal's killing of Hotspur is unhistorical, since both Holinshed and Daniel report only that Hal bravely helped rescue his father from attack and that Hotspur was killed in the melee. Daniel does give prominence to Prince Henry in the battle, however, and implies that he and Hotspur will meet face-to-face. Shakespeare invents the scenes in which we see Mortimer as a devoted husband and Hotspur as a fond combatant in wit with his wife Kate; Holinshed merely informs us that these two men were married. Shakespeare greatly expands Glendower's fascination with magic and poetry, changing him from a ruthless barbarian (in Holinshed) into a cranky but charismatic Welshman. Hotspur, despite hints from Daniel and Holinshed, is chiefly Shakespeare's creation.

The most impressive transformations are those of Hal and Falstaff. Shakespeare knew many legends of Hal's wild youth: some from John Stow's *The Chronicles of England* (1580) and *The Annals of England* (1592); others from oral tradition. Many of these stories were also available in Holinshed. Shakespeare's readiest source, however, was a rowdy and chauvinistic play called *The Famous Victories of Henry the Fifth*, registered 1594 but usually ascribed to Richard Tarlton or Samuel Rowley around 1587 or 1588. This play covers all the events of the *Henry IV* plays and *Henry V* in one chaotic sequence. Prince Hal has three companions, Sir John Oldcastle, Tom, and Ned (cf. Ned Poins), in whose company he robs the King's receivers of 1,000 pounds, visits the old tavern in Eastcheap, vexes his father, and strikes the Lord Chief Justice. A crucial difference is that this Hal is truly unregenerate. He not only chases after women and robs, but encourages his companions to look forward to unrestricted license when he is king. Hal seems consciously to desire his father's death. Yet he does reform and banishes his companions beyond a ten-mile limit with a promise to assist them if they amend their conduct. Although Hal's reform is crude and sudden, his popularity aids him when he goes to war against the French. He is followed by a comic crew of London artisans and thieves, who prove invincible against the effete enemy.

Shakespeare owes much to this unsophisticated, vibrant account of Hal's riotous youth, but he has transformed it to his own use. He limits himself in *1 Henry IV* to the action leading up to the Battle of Shrewsbury in order to focus on the coming of age of Prince Henry and the pairing and contrasting of Hotspur, Falstaff, and King Henry IV as alternative models for Hal's behavior. He invents unforgettable comic characters, such as Mistress Quickly, Francis, and Bardolph. Most of all, Shakespeare's portrayal of Falstaff is essentially his own. Sir John Oldcastle of the anonymous play is a minor character, not Hal's closest companion. Falstaff owes something to the tradition of the guileful and inventive Vice of the Tudor morality play (especially when Falstaff is called jestingly "that reverend Vice, that gray Iniquity," 2.4.448), but the influence of the morality play is general rather than specific. To label Falstaff a "Vice" is to reduce him to comic tempter and villain. Falstaff is in part an allowed fool, a parasite, and a *miles gloriosus* or braggart soldier, but he transcends all these conventionalized types with his own unique vitality.

1 Henry IV suggests some acquaintance with the anonymous play *Thomas of Woodstock* (c. 1591–1595), which Shakespeare may also have used for *Richard II*, and with the Complaints of Owen Glendower and Northumberland in *A Mirror for Magistrates* (1559). In neither case is the debt extensive. More suggestive as possible sources are events and social conditions in Shakespeare's England: the Northern Rebellion of 1569 against Queen Elizabeth's government, abuses of military authority by unscrupulous officers, the dangerous state of the high-ways, the raucous vitality of tavern life in Eastcheap, and the like.

Henry V

Shakespeare's principal historical source for *Henry V*, as for *Richard II* and the *Henry IV* plays, was the 1587 edition of Raphael Holinshed's *Chronicles*. Holinshed's account of Henry V, however, depended so heavily on Edward Hall's *The Union of the Two Noble and Illustre Families of Lancaster and York* (1542) that we sometimes have difficulty knowing whether Shakespeare consulted Holinshed or Hall. He was certainly familiar with both. Shakespeare's sources all acclaim Henry V a hero-king. Samuel Daniel's *The First Four Books of the Civil Wars* (1595), which Shakespeare may have used for his account of the treasonous plot against Henry (2.2), also praises the King in encomiastic terms.

Shakespeare follows the order of events laid down in Holinshed and Hall: the personal rivalry between Henry and the French Dauphin, Henry's request for reassurance from the clergy as to the legitimacy of the war, the maneuvering of the clergy to forestall a bill in Parliament threatening to seize Church land, the foiling of a plot against Henry's life, the siege of Harfleur, and the glorious victory at Agincourt. Both Holinshed and Hall offer Shakespeare many particulars about the English claim to France: in both accounts, the Archbishop quotes the law—*In terram Salicam mulieres ne succedant*—and goes on at length about King Pharamond, the rivers Elbe and Saale, King Pepin, Hugh Capet, the Book of Numbers, and the rest. On the other hand, Shakespeare omits a three-year campaign that historically intervened between Agincourt and the peace treaty of Troyes. He passes over the Lollard controversy in England, with the execution of Sir John Oldcastle. And, of course, he adds unforgettable characters whom we do not find in the chronicles—Welshmen, Irishmen, Scots, common soldiers, thieves—who show the unity of the British nation under King Henry's charismatic leadership.

For many of his additions to the chronicles, Shakespeare was indebted to the anonymous *The Famous Victories of Henry the Fifth* (c. 1588), a work to which he had turned earlier in writing *1* and *2 Henry IV*. This old play, not registered until 1594 and not printed until 1598, exists today only in a corrupt text; quite possibly Shakespeare knew a fuller and more authentic version that would have given him still more material. Other plays may have existed on the subject, for the Admiral's Men (a rival acting company) acted a "harey the v" in 1595 and 1596 that may or may not have been *The Famous Victories*. In any event, the relationship between *Henry V* and *Famous Victories* is at times close. *Famous Victories* omits Henry's long campaign between Agincourt and the final peace treaty, as does Shakespeare's play. The Archbishop of *Famous*

Victories discusses the French claim just before the arrival of the French Ambassador with the tennis balls. (In Holinshed, the tennis-ball incident occurs first, at Kenilworth, whereas the Archbishop's lecture occurs sometime later at a meeting of Parliament in Leicester.) Henry assures the French ambassador that he has "free liberty and license to speak." To the Dauphin's insolent gift, taunting Henry about his wild youth, the King suavely replies that "My lord prince Dauphin is very pleasant with me" and promises to repay the insult with balls of brass and iron. (Holinshed mentions this apparently non-historical legend only briefly.) When the French noblemen assembled at the French court hear of Henry's arrival on their shores, they tremble with fear, even though the Dauphin recklessly scoffs at so young and prodigal a king. Henry is accompanied to France by a ludicrous assortment of London artisans and thieves, such as John Cobbler, who bids farewell to his wife in a comic scene similar to Pistol's parting from the Hostess, and Derick, who turns the tables on a French soldier much as Pistol deals with Monsieur le Fer. When King Henry woos Katharine of France, he protests to her that he cannot speak flatteringly because he is a plain soldier. She asks in return: "How should I love him, that hath dealt so hardly / With my father?" Despite these resemblances, however, Shakespeare's *Henry V* is incomparably superior to the old play and contains many original scenes and characters, such as King Henry's touring of his camp incognito, the quarrel between Henry and Williams, and above all the scenes involving Fluellen and his fellow captains.

Other possible sources include the *Henrici Quinti Angliae Regis Gesta*, written by a chaplain in Henry V's army; the *Vita et Gesta Henrici Quinti*, erroneously ascribed to Thomas Elmham; the *Vita Henrici Quinti* by "Titus Livius," translated in 1513 (in which the French brag about their horses and armor); a ballad called "The Battle of Agincourt" (c. 1530); and *The Annals of Cornelius Tacitus*, translated in 1598 (in which Germanicus walks disguised through his camp at night "to sound the soldiers' mind," and hears his leadership praised).

Romeo and Juliet

Shakespeare's chief source for *Romeo and Juliet* was a long narrative poem by Arthur Brooke called *The Tragical History of Romeus and Juliet, written first in Italian by Bandell and now in English by Ar. Br.* (1562). Other English versions of this popular legend were available to Shakespeare, in particular William Painter's *The Palace of Pleasure* (1566), but Shakespeare shows only a passing indebtedness to it. Brooke mentions having seen (prior to 1562) a play about the two lovers, but such an old play is not likely to have been of much service to Shakespeare. Nor does he appear to have extensively consulted the various continental versions that lay behind Brooke's poem. Still, these versions help explain the genesis of the story.

The use of a sleeping potion to escape an unwelcome marriage goes back at least to the *Ephesiaca* of Xenophon of Ephesus (by the fifth century A.D.). Masuccio of Salemo, in his *Il Novellino* (1476), seems to have been the first to combine this sleeping potion story with an ironic aftermath of misunderstanding and suicide (as found in the Pyramus and Thisbe story of Ovid's *Metamorphoses*). In Masuccio's account, the lovers Mariotto and Giannozza of Siena are secretly married by a friar. When Mariotto kills a prominent citizen of Siena in a quarrel, he is banished to Alexandria. Giannozza, to avoid marriage with a suitor of her father's choosing, takes a sleeping potion given her by the friar and is buried as though dead. She is thereupon taken from the tomb by the friar and sent on her way to Alexandria. Mariotto, however, having failed to hear from her because the messenger is intercepted by pirates, returns in disguise to her tomb where he is discovered and executed. Giannozza, hearing this sad news, retires to a Sienese convent and dies of a broken heart.

In Luigi da Porto's *Historia novellamente ritrovata di due Nobili Amanti* (published c. 1530), based on Masuccio's account, the scene shifts to Verona. Despite the feuding of their two families, the Montecchi and the Cappelletti, Romeo and Guilietta meet and fall in love at a carnival ball. Romeo at once forgets his unrequited passion for a scornful lady. Friar Lorenzo, an experimenter in magic, secretly marries the lovers. Romeo tries to avoid brawling with the Cappelletti, but when some of his own kinsmen suffer defeat, he kills Theobaldo Cappelletti. After Romeo's departure for Mantua, Guilietta's family arranges a match for her with the Count of Lodrone. Friar Lorenzo gives Guilietta a sleeping potion and sends a letter to Romeo by a fellow friar, but this messenger is unable to find Romeo in Mantua. Romeo, hearing of Guilietta's supposed death from her servant Peter, returns to Verona with a poison he already possesses. Guilietta awakens in time to converse with Romeo before he dies. Then, refusing the Friar's advice to retire to a convent, she dies by stopping her own breath. This story provides no equivalents for Mercutio and the Nurse, although a young man named Marcuccio appears briefly at the Cappelletti's ball.

Da Porto's version inspired that of Matteo Bandello in his *Novelle* of 1554. Some details are added: Romeo goes to the ball in a vizard (mask), he has a servant named Pietro, a rope ladder is given to the Nurse enabling Romeo to visit Julietta's chamber before their marriage, Romeo obtains a poison from one Spolentino, and so on. The young man at the ball, Marcuccio, is now named Mercutio but is still a minor figure. This Bandello version was translated into French by Pierre Boaistuau in his *Histoires Tragiques* (1559); Boaistuau adds the Apothecary (who is racked and hanged for his part in the tragedy) and has Romeo die before Juliet awakens and slays herself with Romeo's dagger.

Despite Arthur Brooke's implication on the title page that his version is based on Bandello, the narrative poem *Romeus and Juliet* is taken from Boaistuau. Brooke's poem is a severely pious work written in "Poulter's Measure," couplets with alternating lines of six and seven feet. Brooke openly disapproves of the lovers' carnality and haste, although fortunately the story itself remains sympathetic to Romeus and Juliet. Brooke stresses starcrossed fortune and the antithesis of love and hate. He reduces Juliet's age from eighteen (as in Bandello) to sixteen. (Shakespeare further reduces her age to less than fourteen.) Brooke's narrative is generally close to Shakespeare's, though with important exceptions. Shakespeare compresses time from some nine months to a few days. In Brooke, for example, some two weeks elapse between the masked ball and Romeus's encounter with Juliet in her garden, and about two months elapse between the marriage and Tybalt's death. Shakespeare also unifies his play by such devices as introducing Tybalt and Paris early in the story; in Brooke's poem, Tybalt appears only at the time he is slain, and Juliet's proposed marriage to Count Paris emerges as a threat only after Romeus's banishment. Shakespeare's greatest transformation is of the characters. Brooke's Juliet is scheming. His Mercutio remains a shadowy figure, as in Bandello *et al.* Brooke's Nurse is unattractive, although she does occasionally hint at comic greatness: for example, she garrulously confides to Romeus the details of Juliet's infancy and then keeps Juliet on tenterhooks while she prates about Romeus's fine qualities (lines 631–714). Even if Shakespeare's play is incomparably superior to Brooke's drably versified poem, the indebtedness is extensive.

Julius Caesar

Julius Caesar represents Shakespeare's first extensive use of the work of the first-century Greek biographer Plutarch, in Thomas North's translation (based on the French of Jacques Amyot) of *The Lives of the Noble Grecians and Romans* (1579 and 1595). Plutarch was to become Shakespeare's most often used source in the 1600s; prior to 1599 he had consulted it briefly on a number of other occasions. In *Julius Caesar*, he borrows details from three lives: Caesar, Brutus, and Antonius. He uses particular traits of character, such as Caesar's belief that it is "better to die once than always to be afraid of death," Brutus's determination to "frame his manners of life by the rules of virtue and study of philosophy," Cassius's choleric disposition and his "hating Caesar privately more than he did the tyranny openly," and Antonius's inclination to "rioting and banqueting."

The events of the play are substantially present in Plutarch, especially in "The Life of Julius Caesar."

Antonius runs the course on the Feast of Lupercal to cure barrenness and offers the diadem to Caesar. Flavius and Marullus despoil the images of Caesar. Caesar observes that he mistrusts pale and lean men such as Brutus and Cassius. Papers are thrown by the conspirators where Brutus can find them, proclaiming "Thou sleepest, Brutus, and art not Brutus indeed." Caesar's death is preceded by prodigies: a slave's hand burns but is unconsumed, a sacrificial beast is found to contain no heart. When Caesar encounters the soothsayer who previously had warned him of his fate and boasts that "the ides of March be come," the soothsayer has the last word: "So they be, but yet are they not past." Brutus's wife Portia complains to him of being treated "like a harlot," not like a partner. Brutus commits what Plutarch calls two serious errors when he forbids his fellow conspirators to kill Antonius and when he permits Antonius to speak at Caesar's funeral. Cinna the Poet is slain by an angry crowd mistaking him for Cinna the conspirator. A ghost appears to Brutus shortly before the last battle saying, "I am thy ill angel, Brutus, and thou shalt see me by the city of Phillippes," to which Brutus replies, "Well, I shall see thee then." Antonius says of the vanquished conspirators that "there was none but Brutus only that was moved to do it, as thinking the act commendable of itself: but that all the other conspirators did conspire his death for some private malice or envy." Shakespeare's debt to Plutarch is greater than these few examples can indicate.

Of course, Shakespeare reshapes and selects, as in his history plays. He compresses into one day Caesar's triumphant procession, the disrobing of the images, and the offer of the crown to Caesar on the Lupercal, when, in fact, these events were chronologically separate. Casca is by and large an invented character, and Octavius's role is considerably enlarged. Brutus's servant Lucius is a minor but effective addition, illustrating Brutus's capacity for warmth and humanity. Brutus's two speeches after the assassination (as mentioned by Plutarch) become one, and Antonius's speech is made to follow immediately after. (In Plutarch, Antonius speaks the following day, after the reading of the will.) Shakespeare accentuates the irrationality and vacillation of the mob, for in Plutarch the people are never much swayed by Brutus's rhetoric, even though they respectfully allow him to speak. The unforgettable speeches of both Brutus and Antonius are not set down at all in Plutarch. More compression of time occurs after the assassination: in Plutarch, Octavius does not arrive in Rome until some six weeks afterward and does not agree to the formation of the Triumvirate until more than a year of quarreling has taken place. The inexorable buildup of tension in Shakespeare's play is the result of careful selection from a vast amount of material. Shakespeare's borrowing from "The Life of Marcus Brutus" is no less extensive and is at the same time reshaped and given new emphasis.

Although Shakespeare depended heavily on Plutarch, he was also aware of later and conflicting traditions about Caesar. On the one hand, Dante's *Divine Comedy* (c. 1310–1321) consigns Brutus and Cassius to the lowest circle of hell, along with Judas Iscariot and other betrayers of their masters. Geoffrey Chaucer's "The Monk's Tale," from the *Canterbury Tales*, similarly portrays Caesar as the manly and uncorruptible victim of envious attackers. On the other hand, Montaigne stresses the hubris of Caesar in aspiring to divinity. (Shakespeare could have read Montaigne in the French original or, if he had access to a manuscript, in John Florio's English translation, published in 1603.) A pro-Brutus view could also be found in the Latin *Julius Caesar* of Marc-Antoine Muret (1553) and the French *César* of Jacques Grévin (1561). That Shakespeare knew these works is unlikely, but they kept alive a tradition with which he was certainly familiar. Possibly he knew such Roman works as Lucan's account of Caesar in the *Pharsalia* and Cicero's letters and orations, which were republican in tenor. Other possible sources include the *Chronicle of the Romans' Wars* by Appian of Alexandria (translated 1578), the anonymous play *Caesar's Revenge* (published 1606–1607, performed in the early 1590s at Oxford), and Thomas Kyd's *Cornelia* (translated from the French Senecan tragedy by Garnier). *Il Cesare* by Orlando Pescetti (1594) is now almost universally rejected as a possible source. The result of Shakespeare's acquaintance with both pro- and anti-Caesar traditions is that he subordinates his own political vision to a balanced presentation of history, showing the significant strengths and disabling weaknesses in both Caesar and the conspirators.

Hamlet

The ultimate source of the *Hamlet* story is Saxo Grammaticus's *Historia Danica* (1180–1208), the saga of one Amlothi or (as Saxo calls him) Amlethus. The outline of the story is essentially that of Shakespeare's play, even though the emphasis of the Danish saga is overwhelmingly on cunning, brutality, and bloody revenge. Amlethus's father is Horwendil, a Governor of Jutland, who bravely kills the King of Norway in single combat and thereby wins the hand in marriage of Gerutha, daughter of the King of Denmark. This good fortune goads the envious Feng into slaying his brother Horwendil and marrying Gerutha, "capping unnatural murder with incest." Though the deed is known to everyone, Feng invents excuses and soon wins the approbation of the fawning courtiers. Young Amlethus vows revenge but, perceiving his uncle's cunning, feigns madness. His mingled words of craft and candor awaken suspicions that he may be playing a game of deception.

Two attempts are made to lure Amlethus into revealing that he is actually sane. The first plan is to tempt him into lechery, on the theory that one who lusts for women cannot be truly insane. Feng causes an attractive woman to be placed in a forest where Amlethus will meet her as though by chance; but Amlethus, secretly warned of the trap by a kindly foster brother, spirits the young lady off to a hideaway where they can make love unobserved by Feng's agents. She confesses the plot to Amlethus. In a second stratagem, a courtier who is reported to be "gifted with more assurance than judgment" hides himself under some straw in the Queen's chamber in order to overhear her private conversations with Amlethus. The hero, suspecting just such a trap, feigns madness and begins crowing like a noisy rooster, bouncing up and down on the straw until he finds the eavesdropper. Amlethus stabs the man to death, drags him forth, cuts the body into morsels, boils them, and flings the bits "through the mouth of an open sewer for the swine to eat." Thereupon he returns to his mother to accuse her of being an infamous harlot. He wins her over to repentant virtue and even cooperation. When Feng, returning from a journey, looks around for his counselor, Amlethus jestingly (but in part truly) suggests that the man went to the sewer and fell in.

Feng now sends Amlethus to the King of Britain with secret orders for his execution. However, Amlethus finds the letter to the British King in the coffers of the two unnamed retainers accompanying him on the journey and substitutes a new letter ordering their execution instead. The new letter, purportedly written and signed by Feng, goes on to urge that the King of Britain marry his daughter to a young Dane being sent from the Danish court. By this means, Amlethus gains an English wife and rids himself of the escorts. A year later Amlethus returns to Jutland, gets the entire court drunk, flings a tapestry (knitted for him by his mother) over the prostrate courtiers, secures the tapestry with stakes, and then sets fire to the palace. Feng escapes this holocaust, but Amlethus cuts him down with the King's own sword. (Amlethus exchanges swords because his own has been nailed fast into its scabbard by his enemies.) Subsequently, Amlethus convinces the people of the justice of his cause and is chosen King of Jutland. After ruling for several years, he returns to Britain, bigamously marries a Scottish Queen, fights a battle with his first father-in-law, is betrayed by his second wife, and is finally killed in battle.

In Saxo's account, we thus find the prototypes of Hamlet, Claudius, Gertrude, Polonius, Ophelia, Rosencrantz, and Guildenstern. Several episodes are close in narrative detail to Shakespeare's play: the original murder and incestuous marriage, the feigned madness, the woman used as a decoy, the eavesdropping counselor, and especially the trip to England. A translation of Saxo into French by François de Belleforest, in *Histoires Tragiques* (1576 edition), adds a few details, such as Gertrude's adultery before the murder and Hamlet's melancholy. Belleforest's version is longer than Saxo's, with more psychological and moral observation and more dialogue. Shakespeare probably consulted it.

Shakespeare need not have depended extensively on these older versions of his story, however. His main source was almost certainly an old play of *Hamlet*. Much evidence testifies to the existence of such a play. The *Diary* of Philip Henslowe, a theater owner and manager, records a performance, not marked as "new," of a *Hamlet* at Newington Butts on June 11, 1594, by "my Lord Admiral's Men" or "my Lord Chamberlain's Men," probably the latter. Thomas Lodge's pamphlet, *Wit's Misery, and the World's Madness* (1596), refers to "the visard of the ghost which cried so miserably at the theater, like an oyster wife, 'Hamlet, revenge!'" And Thomas Nashe, in his *Epistle* prefixed to Robert Greene's romance *Menaphon* (1589), offers the following observation:

It is a common practice nowadays amongst a sort of shifting companions, that run through every art and thrive by none, to leave the trade of noverint, whereto they were born, and busy themselves with the endeavors of art, that could scarcely Latinize their neck verse if they should have need; yet English Seneca read by candlelight yields many good sentences, as "Blood is a beggar," and so forth; and if you entreat him fair in a frosty morning, he will afford you whole *Hamlets*, I should say handfuls, of tragical speeches. But O grief! *Tempus edax rerum*, what's that will last always? The sea exhaled by drops will in continuance be dry, and Seneca, let blood line by line and page by page, at length must needs die to our stage; which makes his famished followers to imitate the Kid in Aesop, who, enamored with the Fox's newfangles, forsook all hopes of life to leap into a new occupation; and these men, renouncing all possibilities of credit or estimation, to intermeddle with Italian translations . . .

Nashe's testimonial describes a *Hamlet* play, written in the Senecan style by some person born to the trade of "noverint," or scrivener, who has turned to hack writing and translation. The description has often been fitted to Thomas Kyd, though this identification is not certain. (Nashe could be punning on Kyd's name when he refers to "the Kid in Aesop.") Certainly Thomas Kyd's *The Spanish Tragedy* (c. 1587) shows many affinities with Shakespeare's play and provides many Senecan ingredients missing from Saxo and Belleforest: the ghost, the difficulty in ascertaining whether the ghost's words are believable, the resulting need for delay and a feigning of madness, the moral perplexities afflicting a sensitive man called upon to revenge, the play within the play, the clever reversals and ironically caused deaths in the catastrophe, the rhetoric of tragic passion. Whether or not Kyd, in fact, wrote the *Ur-Hamlet*, his extant play enables us to see more clearly what that lost play must have contained. The unauthorized first quarto of *Hamlet* (1603) also offers a few seemingly authentic details that are not found in the authoritative second quarto but are found in the

earlier sources and may have been a part of the *Ur-Hamlet*. For example, after Hamlet has killed Corambis (corresponding to Polonius), the Queen vows to assist Hamlet in his strategies against the King; later, when Hamlet has returned to England, the Queen sends him a message by Horatio warning him to be careful.

One last document sheds light on the *Ur-Hamlet*. A German play, *Der bestrafte Brudermord (Fratricide Punished)*, from a now-lost manuscript dated 1710, seems to have been based on a text used by English actors traveling in Germany in 1586 and afterward. Though changed by translation and manuscript transmission, and too entirely different from Shakespeare's play to have been based on it, this German version may well have been based on Shakespeare's source-play. Polonius's name in this text, Corambus, is the Corambis of the first quarto of 1603. (The name may mean "cabbage cooked twice," from *coramblebis*, a proverbially dull dish.)

Der bestrafte Brudermord begins with a prologue in the Senecan manner, followed by the appearance of the ghost to Francisco, Horatio, and sentinels of the watch. Within the palace, meanwhile, the King carouses. Hamlet joins the watch, confiding to Horatio that he is "sick at heart" over his father's death and his mother's hasty remarriage. The ghost appears to Hamlet, tells him how the juice of hebona was poured into his ear, and urges revenge. When Hamlet swears Horatio and Francisco to silence, the ghost (now invisible) says several times "We swear," his voice following the men as they move from place to place. Hamlet reveals to Horatio the entire circumstance of the murder. Later, in a formal session of the court, the new King speaks hypocritically of his brother's death and explains the reasons for his marriage to the Queen. Hamlet is forbidden to return to Wittenberg, though Corambus's son Leonhardus has already set out for France.

Some time afterward, Corambus reports the news of Hamlet's madness to the King and Queen, and presumes on the basis of his own youthful passions to diagnose Hamlet's malady as lovesickness. Concealed, he and the King overhear Hamlet tell Ophelia to "go to a nunnery." When players arrive from Germany, Hamlet instructs them in the natural style of acting and then requests them to perform a play before the King about the murder of King Pyrrus by his brother. (Death is again inflicted by hebona poured in the ear.) After the King's guilty reaction to the play, Hamlet finds him alone at prayers but postpones the killing lest the King's soul be sent to heaven. Hamlet kills Corambus behind the tapestry in the Queen's chamber and is visited again by the ghost (who says nothing, however). Ophelia, her mind deranged, thinks herself in love with a court butterfly named Phantasmo. (This creature is also involved in a comic action to help the clown Jens with a tax problem.)

The King sends Hamlet to England with two unnamed courtiers who are instructed to kill Hamlet after

SOURCES A-29

their arrival. A contrary wind takes them instead to an island near Dover, where Hamlet foils his two enemies by kneeling between them and asking them to shoot him on signal; at the proper moment, he ducks and they shoot one another. He finishes them off with their own swords and discovers a letter on their persons ordering Hamlet's execution by the English King if the original plot should fail. When Hamlet returns to Denmark, the King arranges a duel between him and Corambus's son Leonhardus. If Leonhardus's poisoned dagger misses its mark, a beaker of wine containing finely ground oriental diamond dust is to do the rest. Hamlet is informed of the impending duel by Phantasmo (compare Osric), whom Hamlet taunts condescendingly and calls "Signora Phantasmo." Shortly before the duel takes place, Ophelia is reported to have thrown herself off a hill to her death. The other deaths occur much as in Shakespeare's play. The dying Hamlet bids that the crown be conveyed to his cousin, Duke Fortempras of Norway, of whom we have not heard earlier.

From the extensive similarities between *Hamlet* and this German play, we can see that Shakespeare inherited his narrative material almost intact, though in a jumble and so pitifully mangled that the modern reader can only laugh at the contrast. No source study in Shakespeare reveals so clearly the extent of Shakespeare's wholesale borrowing of plot and the incredible transformation he achieved in reordering his materials.

Othello

Shakespeare's main source for *Othello* was the seventh story from the third decade of G. B. Giraldi Cinthio's *Hecatommithi* (1565). Cinthio was available in French but not in English translation during Shakespeare's lifetime. The verbal echoes in Shakespeare's play are usually closer to the Italian original than to Gabriel Chappuys's French version of 1584. Cinthio's account may have been based on an actual incident occurring in Venice around 1508.

Shakespeare is considerably indebted to Cinthio's story for the essentials of the narrative: the marriage of a Moorish captain to a Venetian lady, Disdemona, whose relatives wish her to marry someone else, the mutual attraction to noble qualities of mind in both husband and wife, their happiness together at first, the dispatching of the Moor to Cyprus to take charge of the garrison there, Disdemona's insistence on accompanying her husband through whatever dangers may occur (though the sea voyage, as it turns out, is a very calm one), the ensign's treachery and resolve to destroy the Moor's happiness with Disdemona, her begging her husband to reinstate the squadron leader whom the Moor has demoted for fighting on guard duty (although no mention is made of drunkenness or of the ensign's role in starting the trou-

ble), the ensign's insinuations to the Moor that his wife is cuckolding him because she is becoming weary of her marriage with a black man, the ensign's difficulty in providing ocular proof, his planting of Disdemona's handkerchief in the squadron leader's quarters and his showing the Moor that the handkerchief is now in the squadron leader's possession, his arranging for the Moor to witness at a distance a conversation between the ensign and squadron leader that is, in fact, not about Disdemona, Disdemona's confusion when she is asked to produce the handkerchief, the attack on the squadron leader in the dark, the murder of Disdemona in her bed, the Moor's deep regret at the loss of his wife, the eventual punishment of both the Moor and and the ensign, and the telling of the story publicly by the ensign's wife, who has heretofore kept silent because of her fear of her husband.

Although these correspondences in the story are many, Shakespeare has changed a great deal. He provides Desdemona with a caring and saddened father, Brabantio, out of Cinthio's brief suggestion of family opposition to her marriage, and adds the entire opening scene in which Iago arouses the prejudices of Brabantio. Roderigo is a brilliantly invented character used to reveal Iago's skill in manipulation. Cinthio's ensign, though thoroughly wicked, never expresses a resentment for the squadron leader's promotion and favored treatment by the Moor; instead, the ensign lusts for Disdemona and turns against her and the Moor only when his passion is unrequited. In his complex portrayal of a consuming and irrational jealousy in Iago, Shakespeare goes far beyond his source, making use as well of the inventive villainy of the Vice in the English late medieval morality play. In Cinthio's account, the ensign filches the handkerchief from Disdemona while she is hugging the ensign's three-year-old daughter; the ensign's wife is uninvolved in this mischief, though she does unwillingly learn of her husband's villainy (since he has an idea of using her in his plot) and later feels constrained to hold her tongue when Disdemona asks her if she knows why the Moor is behaving so strangely. (As is usual in prose narrative, the passage of time is much more extended than in Shakespeare's play.)

In the later portions of the story, the changes are more marked. Cinthio relates an episode in which the squadron leader, finding the handkerchief in his room, takes it back to Disdemona while the Moor is out but is interrupted by the Moor's unexpected return home; Shakespeare instead has Cassio approach Desdemona (earlier in the story) to beg her assistance in persuading Othello to reinstate him. Cinthio tells of a woman in the squadron leader's household who copies the embroidery of the handkerchief before it is returned and is seen with it at a window by the Moor; here, Shakespeare finds a suggestion for Bianca, but her role is considerably augmented, partly with the help of a passing remark in Cinthio's account that the squadron leader is attacked and wounded as he leaves the house of a courtesan with whom he occasionally takes his pleasure. In the absence of any character corresponding to Roderigo, the Cinthio narrative assigns to the ensign himself the role of wounding the squadron leader. The manner in which Disdemona is murdered is strikingly different. Cinthio has nothing equivalent to the tender scene between Desdemona and Emilia as Desdemona prepares to go to bed. Cinthio's Moor hides the ensign in a dressing room next to his bedroom and commissions the ensign to bludgeon her to death with a sand-filled stocking, after which the two murderers cause the ceiling of the room to collapse on her and create the impression that a rafter has smashed her skull.

Cinthio also treats the aftermath of the murder in a very different way. The Moor, distracted with grief, turns on the ensign and demotes him, whereupon the ensign persuades the squadron commander to take vengeance on the Moor as his attacker (according to the lying ensign) and killer of Disdemona. When the squadron commander accuses the Moor before the Seigniory, the Moor keeps silent but is banished and eventually killed by Disdemona's relatives. The ensign, returning to his own country, gets in trouble by making a false accusation and dies as the result of torture. Cinthio sees this as God's retribution. The ensign's wife lives to tell her story, unlike Shakespeare's Emilia.

The changed ending is essential to Shakespeare's play. Emilia becomes a more complex figure than the ensign's wife: Shakespeare implicates her in the stealing of the handkerchief but also accentuates her love for Desdemona and her brave denunciation of her husband when at last she knows the full truth. Othello's ritual slaying of Desdemona avoids the appalling butchery of the source story. Shakespeare's ending is more unified, and brings both Othello and Iago to account for the deeds they have committed in this play. Most important, Shakespeare transforms a sensational murder story into a moving tragedy of love.

King Lear

The story of Lear goes back into ancient legend. The motif of two wicked sisters and a virtuous youngest sister reminds us of Cinderella. Lear himself appears to come from Celtic mythology. Geoffrey of Monmouth, a Welshman in close contact with Celtic legend, included a Lear or Leir as one of the pseudo-historical Kings in his *Historia Regum Britanniae* (c. 1136). This fanciful mixture of history and legend traces a supposed line of descent from Brut, great-grandson of Aeneas of Troy, through Locrine, Bladud, Leir, Gorboduc, Ferrex and Porrex, Lud, Cymbeline, Bonduca, Vortigern, Arthur, and so forth, to the historical Kings of England. The Tudor monarchs made much of their purported claim to such an ancient dynasty,

and in Shakespeare's day this mythology had a quasi-official status demanding a certain reverential suspension of disbelief.

King Leir, according to Geoffrey, is the father of three daughters, Gonorilla, Regan, and Cordeilla, among whom he intends to divide his kingdom. To determine who deserves most, he asks them who loves him most. The two eldest sisters protest undying devotion, but Cordeilla, perceiving how the others flatter and deceive him, renounces hyperbole and promises only to love him as a daughter should love a father. Furious, the King denies Cordeilla her third of the kingdom but permits her to marry Aganippus, King of the Franks, without dowry. Thereafter, Leir bestows his two eldest daughters on the Dukes of Albania and Cornubia (Albany and Cornwall), together with half the island during his lifetime and the possession of the remainder after his death. In due course, his two sons-in-law rebel against Leir and seize his power. Thereafter Maglaunus, Duke of Albania, agrees to maintain Leir with sixty retainers, but, after two years of chafing at this arrangement, Gonorilla insists that the number be reduced to thirty. Angrily, the King goes to Henvin, Duke of Cornubia, where all goes well for a time; within a year, however, Regan demands that Leir reduce his retinue to five knights. When Gonorilla refuses to take him back with more than one retainer, Leir crosses into France and is generously received by Cordeilla and Aganippus. An invasion restores Leir to his throne. Three years later, he and Aganippus die, after which Cordeilla rules successfully for five years until overthrown by the sons of Maglaunus and Henvin. In prison she commits suicide.

This story, as part of England's mythic genealogy, was repeated in various Tudor versions, such as *The First Part of the Mirror for Magistrates* (1574), William Warner's *Albion's England* (1586), and Raphael Holinshed's *Chronicles* (second edition, 1587). Warner refers to the King's sons-in-law as "the Prince of Albany" and "the Cornish prince"; Holinshed refers to them as "the Duke of Albania" and "the Duke of Cornwall" but reports that it is Cornwall who marries the eldest daughter Gonorilla. *The Mirror*, closer to Shakespeare in these details, speaks of "Gonorell" as married to "Albany" and of "Cordila" as married to "the King of France." Edmund Spenser's *The Faerie Queene* (2.10.27–32) reports that "Cordeill" or "Cordelia" ends her life by hanging herself. Other retellings appear in Gerard Legh's *Accidence of Armory* and William Camden's *Remains*. All of these accounts leave the story virtually unchanged.

Shakespeare's immediate source for *King Lear* was an old play called *The True Chronicle History of King Leir*. It was published in 1605 but plainly is much earlier in style. The Stationers' Register, the official record of the London Company of Stationers (booksellers and printers), for May 14, 1594, lists "A booke called the Tragecall historie of Kinge Leir and his Three Daughters &c.," and a short time earlier Philip Henslowe's *Diary* records the performance of a "Kinge Leare" at the Rose Theatre on April 6 and 8, 1594. The actors were either the Queen's or the Earl of Sussex's Men (two acting companies), though probably the Queen's. The play may have been written as early as 1588. George Peele, Robert Greene, Thomas Lodge, and Thomas Kyd have all been suggested as possible authors. Shakespeare probably knew the play before its publication in 1605.

This play of *Leir* ends happily, with the restoration of Leir to his throne. Essentially, the play is a legendary history with a strong element of romance. The two wicked sisters are warned of the King's plans for dividing his kingdom by an obsequious courtier named Skalliger (compare Oswald). It is Skalliger, in fact, who proposes the idea of apportioning the Kingdom in accord with the lovingness of the daughters' responses. Cordella receives the ineffectual support of an honest courtier, Perillus (compare Kent) but is disinherited by her angry father. Trusting herself to God's mercy and setting forth alone to live by her own labor, Cordella is found by the Gallian King and his bluff companion Mumford, who have come to England disguised as palmers to see if the English King's daughters are as beautiful as reported. The King hears Cordella's sad story, falls in love with her, and woos her (still wearing his disguise) in the name of the Gallian King. When she virtuously suggests the palmer woo for himself, he throws off his disguise and marries her forthwith.

Meanwhile the other sons-in-law, Cornwall and Combria (compare Albany), draw lots for their shares of the kingdom. Leir announces that he will sojourn with Cornwall and Gonorill first. Cornwall treats the King with genuine solicitude, but Gonorill, abetted by Skalliger, tauntingly drives her father away. The King acknowledges to his loyal companion Perillus that he has wronged Cordella. Regan, who rules her mild husband as she pleases, receives the King with seeming tenderness but secretly hires an assassin to end his life. (Gonorill is partner in this plot.) The suborned agent, frightened into remorse by a providentially sent thunderstorm, shows his intended victim the letter ordering the assassination.

The Gallian King and Cordella, who have previously sent ambassadors to Leir urging him to come to France, now decide to journey with Mumford into Britain disguised as countryfolk. Before they can do so, however, Leir and Perillus arrive in France, in mariners' garb, where they encounter Cordella and her party dressed as country folk. Cordella recognizes Leir's voice, and father and daughter are tearfully reunited. The Gallian King invades England and restores Leir to his throne.

Shakespeare has changed much in the narrative of his source. He discards not only the happy ending but also the attempted assassination and the numerous romance-like uses of disguise (although Tom o' Bedlam, in an added plot, repeatedly uses disguise). Shakespeare eliminates the humorous Mumford and replaces Perillus with both Kent and the Fool. He turns Cornwall into a villain and Albany into a belated champion of justice. He creates the storm scene out of a mere suggestion of such an event, serving a very different purpose, in his source.

Most of all, he adds the parallel plot of Gloucester, Edgar, and Edmund. Here Shakespeare derived some of his material from Sir Philip Sidney's *Arcadia* (1590). In Book 2, chapter 10 of this greatest of Elizabethan prose romances, the two heroes, Pyrocles and Musidorus, encounter a son leading his blind old father. The old man tells his pitiful tale. He is the deposed King of Paphlagonia, father of a bastard son named Plexirtus who, he now bitterly realizes, turned the King against his true son Leonatus—the very son who is now his guide and guardian. The true son, having managed to escape his father's order of execution, has been forced to live poorly as a soldier, while the bastard son has proceeded to usurp his father's throne. In his wretchedness, the King has been succored by his forgiving true son and has been prevented from casting himself off the top of a hill. At the conclusion of this narrative, the villain Plexirtus arrives and attacks Leonatus; reinforcements arrive on both sides, but eventually Plexirtus is driven off, enabling the King to return to his court and bestow the crown on Leonatus. The old King thereupon dies, his heart having been stretched beyond the limits of endurance.

Other parts of the *Arcadia* may have given Shakespeare further suggestions; for example, the disguises adopted by Kent and Edgar are like those of Zelmane and Pyrocles in Sidney's prose work, and Albany's speeches about anarchy and the monstrosity that results from assaults on the rule of law recall one of Sidney's deepest concerns. Edmund is decidedly indebted to the allegorical Vice figure of the late medieval morality play tradition. For Tom o' Bedlam's mad language, Shakespeare consulted Samuel Harsnett's *Declaration of Egregious Popish Impostures*, 1603. (See Kenneth Muir's Arden edition of *King Lear*, pp. 253–6, for an extensive comparison.)

Macbeth

Shakespeare's chief source for *Macbeth* was Raphael Holinshed's *Chronicles* (1587 edition). Holinshed had gone for most of his material to Hector Boece, *Scotorum Historiae* (1526–1527), who in turn was indebted to a fourteenth-century priest named John of Fordun and to a fifteenth-century chronicler, Andrew of Wyntoun. By the time Holinshed found it, the story of Macbeth had become more fiction than fact. The historical Macbeth, who ruled from 1040 to 1057, did take the throne by killing Duncan, but in a civil conflict between two clans contending for the kingship. Contemporary observers credit him with having been a good ruler. Although he was defeated by the Earl of Northumbria (the Siward of Shakespeare's play) at Birnam Wood in 1054, the Earl was forced by his own losses to retire, and Macbeth ruled three years longer before being slain by Duncan's son Malcolm. Banquo and Fleance are fictional characters apparently invented by Boece.

In Holinshed's telling of the story, Duncan is a King with a soft and gentle nature, negligent in punishing his enemies and thereby an unwitting encourager of sedition. It falls to his cousin, Macbeth, a critic of this soft line, and to Banquo, the Thane of Lochaber, to defend Scotland against her enemies: first against Macdowald (Macdonwald in Shakespeare), with his Irish kerns and gallowglasses, and then against Sueno, King of Norway. (Shakespeare fuses these battles into one.) Shortly thereafter, Macbeth and Banquo encounter "three women in strange and wild apparel, resembling creatures of elder world," who predict their futures as in the play. Although Macbeth and Banquo jest about the matter, common opinion later maintains that "these women were either the Weird Sisters, that is (as ye would say), the goddesses of destiny, or else some nymphs or fairies, endued with knowledge of prophecy." Certainly Macbeth soon becomes the Thane of Cawdor, whereupon, jestingly reminded of the three sisters' promise by Banquo, he resolves to seek the throne. His way is blocked, however, by Duncan's naming of his eldest but still underage son Malcolm to be Prince of Cumberland and heir to the throne. Macbeth's resentment at this is understandable, since Scottish law provides that, until the King's son is of age, the "next of blood unto him"—that is, Macbeth himself, as Duncan's cousin—should reign. Accordingly, Macbeth begins to plot with his associates how to usurp the kingdom by force. His "very ambitious" wife urges him on because of her "unquenchable desire" to be Queen. Banquo is one among many trusted friends with whose support Macbeth slays the King at Inverness or at Bothgowanan. (No mention is made of a visit to Macbeth's castle.) Malcolm and Donald Bane, the dead King's sons, fly for their safety to Cumberland, where Malcolm is well received by Edward the Confessor of England; Donald Bane proceeds on to Ireland.

Holinshed's Macbeth is at first no brutal tyrant, as in Shakespeare. For some ten years he rules well, using great liberality and correcting the laxity of his predecessor's reign. (Holinshed does suggest, to be sure, that his justice is only contrived to court popularity among his subjects.) Inevitably, however, the Weird Sisters' promise of a posterity to Banquo goads Macbeth into ordering the murder of his onetime companion. Fleance escapes Macbeth's henchmen in the dark and afterward founds the lineage of the Stuart Kings. (This genealogy is fictitious.) Macbeth's vain quest for absolute power further causes him to build Dunsinane fortress. When Macduff refuses to help, the King turns against him and would kill him except that "a certain witch, whom he had in great trust," tells the King he need never fear a man born of woman nor any vanquishment till Birnam Wood come to Dunsinane. Macduff flees for his safety into England and joins Malcolm, whereupon Macbeth's agents slaughter Macduff's wife and children at Fife. Malcolm, fearing that Macduff may be an agent of Macbeth, dissemblingly professes to be a voluptuary, miser, and tyrant, but, when Macduff responds as he should in righteous sorrow at Scotland's evil condition, Malcolm reveals his steadfast commitment to the cause of right. These leaders return to Scotland and defeat Macbeth at Birnam Wood, with their soldiers carrying branches before them. Macduff, proclaiming that he is a man born of no woman since he was "ripped out" of his mother's womb, slays Macbeth.

Despite extensive similarities, Shakespeare has made some significant changes. Duncan is no longer an ineffectual king. Macbeth can no longer justify his claim to the throne. Most important, Banquo is no longer partner in a broadly based though secret conspiracy against Duncan. Banquo is, after all, ancestor of James I (at least according to this legendary history), and so his hands must be kept scrupulously clean; King James disapproved of all tyrannicides, whatever the circumstances. Macbeth is no longer a just lawgiver. The return of Banquo's ghost to Macbeth's banqueting table is an added scene. Macbeth hears the prophecy about Birnam Wood and Macduff from the Weird Sisters, not, as in Holinshed, from some witch. Lady Macbeth's role is considerably enhanced, and her sleepwalking scene is original. Shakespeare compresses time, as he usually does.

In making some of these alterations, Shakespeare turned to another story in Holinshed's chronicle of Scotland: the murder of King Duff by Donwald. King Duff, never suspecting any treachery in Donwald, often spends time at the castle of Forres, where Donwald is captain of the castle. On one occasion, Donwald's wife, bearing great malice toward the King, shows Donwald (who already bears a grudge against Duff) "the means whereby he might soonest accomplish" the murder. The husband and wife ply Duff's few chamberlains with much to eat and drink. Donwald abhors the act "greatly in heart" but perseveres "through instigation of his wife." Four of Donwald's servants actually commit the murder under his instruction. Next morning, Donwald breaks into the King's chamber and slays the chamberlains, as though believing them guilty. Donwald is so overzealous in his investigation of the murder that many lords begin to suspect him of having done it. For six months afterward, the sun refuses to appear by day and the moon by night.

The chronicle accounts in Holinshed of Malcolm and Edward the Confessor supplied Shakespeare with further details. A more important supplementary source may have been George Buchanan's *Rerum Scoticarum Historia* (1582), a Latin history not translated in Shakespeare's lifetime, presenting a more complex psychological portrait of the protagonist than in Holinshed. Finally, Shakespeare may have used King James I's *Daemonology* (1597), John Studley's early-seventeenth-century version of Seneca's *Medea*, Samuel Harsnett's *Declaration of Egregious Popish Impostures* (1603), and accounts of the Scottish witch trials published around 1590.

Antony and Cleopatra

In writing *Antony* and *Cleopatra*, Shakespeare relied to an unusual extent on his chief source, "The Life of Marcus Antonius" in the first-century Greek biographer Plutarch's *The Lives of the Noble Grecians and Romans* (in an English version by Sir Thomas North, 1579). Perhaps the best-known example in all Shakespeare of his skillful use of source material is in 2.2.201–36, when Enobarbus describes the first meeting of Antony and Cleopatra on the river Cydnus. Plutarch reports the event as follows:

She disdained to set forward otherwise but to take her barge in the river of Cydnus, the poop whereof was of gold, the sails of purple, and the oars of silver, which kept stroke in rowing after the sound of the music of flutes, hautboys, citterns, viols, and such other instruments as they played upon in the barge. And now for the person of herself: she was laid under a pavilion of cloth of gold of tissue, appareled and attired like the goddess Venus, commonly drawn in picture; and hard by her, on either hand of her, pretty fair boys appareled as painters do set forth god Cupid, with little fans in their hands with the which they fanned wind upon her. Her ladies and gentlewomen also, the fairest of them, were appareled like the nymphs Nereides (which are the mermaids of the waters) and like the Graces, some steering the helm, others tending the tackle and ropes of the barge, out of the which there came a wonderful passing sweet savor of perfumes that perfumed the wharf's side, pestered with innumerable multitudes of people. Some of them followed the barge all alongst the river's side; others also ran out of the city to see her coming in. So that in the end, there ran such multitudes of people one after another to see her that Antonius was left post alone in the marketplace, in his imperial seat, to give audience.

Shakespeare retains virtually every detail describing Cleopatra's barge: the poop of gold, the sails of purple, the oars of silver, the flutes, the boys with fans, the gentlewomen like the Nereides, and so on. He borrows phrases and images virtually intact from North, as in the account of Cleopatra's own person. Yet Shakespeare also transforms this scene by putting the description in the mouth of Enobarbus, a largely invented character. Enobarbus's sardonic view derived from military experience, his wry but genuine admiration for Cleopatra, and the prurient curiosity of his Roman listeners—all combine to produce the paradox of cloying appetite and insatiable hunger that helps to define the unforgettable greatness of Cleopatra as a character.

Shakespeare turns to Plutarch for other fabulous stories as well: eight wild boars roasted whole for only twelve guests (2.2.189–90), Cleopatra teasing Antony by causing an old dried salt fish to be placed on his fishing line (2.5.15–18), Menas the pirate suggesting to Pompey that they cut the anchor cable with all their noble guests still aboard (2.7.62–85), Cleopatra's sudden changes from weeping to laughing, and her willingness to be flattered by those who tell her Antony has married Octavia solely out of necessity (3.3), Octavius's tenderness for his sister, the ill-omened nesting of swallows in Cleopatra's sails (4.12.3–4), Antony's disregarding the advice of a valiant captain not to fight at sea (3.7.62–71), Cleopatra's study of swift means of death (5.2.353–6), Antony's jealous reaction to the embassy of the young Thyreus, or Thidias (3.13.86–170), the suicide of Antony's servant Eros (4.14.85–97), Cleopatra's difficulty in lifting Antony up to her tomb or monument (4.15.30–8), his warning that she should trust none but Proculeius (4.15.50), Cleopatra's deception of Caesar through persuading him that she desires to live (5.2.110–90), the countryman with the basket of figs (5.2.233–5), Cleopatra's death "attired and arrayed in her royal robes" attended by Charmian and Iras, and much more.

Despite these extensive and detailed borrowings, Shakespeare is highly innovative in his use of his sources. He compresses time in order to give a sense of dramatic momentum to the events of many years. He creates vibrant characters like Enobarbus, Charmian, Iras, Mardian, the Soothsayer, Menas, Thidias, Dollabella, and many others for whom the historical sources provide only a sketchy impression or no information at all. In his characterization of the main figures as well, Shakespeare is not content to rely on Plutarch's estimate. To Plutarch, Antony is the tragic victim of infatuation. For all Cleopatra's cultivation and fascination—she knows several languages and rules her country with royal bearing—she is the source of Antony's downfall. Plutarch's attitude is, like Enobarbus's, admiring but ironic. "In the end," he writes, "the horse of the mind, as Plato termeth it, that is so hard of rein (I mean the unreined lust of concupiscence) did put out of Antonius's head all honest and commendable thoughts." This "Roman" view is present in *Antony and Cleopatra*, to be sure, but is counterbalanced by the "Egyptian" view that finds greatness in Antony and Cleopatra's capacity for love. Shakespeare's play sets up a debate among conflicting traditions, as found in various medieval and Renaissance treatments of this famous story. The moralistic perspective condemning vice was popular in medieval texts, such as *De Casibus Virorum Illustrium* and its continuation, John Lydgate's *The Fall of Princes*. The interpretation of Cleopatra as love's martyr was to be found in Geoffrey Chaucer's *The Legend of Good Women*.

And, finally, the view of Antony and Cleopatra as heroic protagonists rising above their guilt found expression in several neo-Senecan dramas of the later sixteenth century. Most important for Shakespeare were *The Tragedy of Antony*, translated from Robert Garnier's *Marc Antoine* by Mary Herbert, Countess of Pembroke, in about 1590 (published 1592 and 1595), and *The Tragedy of Cleopatra* by Samuel Daniel (1594), a companion play dealing mainly with the end of Cleopatra's life. Garnier's play had been based on Étienne Jodelle's *Cléopâtre Captive* (1552), the first regular French tragedy. Shakespeare certainly gained from such works as these a sense of tragic greatness in his protagonists. He seems also to have been aware of favorable and unfavorable historical appraisals of Octavius Caesar as both a great ruler and a ruthless and even treacherous politician. One influential work on the more critical side may have been the *Chronicle of the Romans' Wars* by Appian of Alexandria (translated 1578). Virgil's *Aeneid* gave Shakespeare a model for a drama of passion set in the context of Roman history.

The Winter's Tale

Shakespeare based *The Winter's Tale* on Robert Greene's romantic novella called *Pandosto: The Triumph of Time* (1588), or *The History of Dorastus and Fawnia* in its running title. Shakespeare changes the names, reverses the two kingdoms of Sicilia and Bohemia, and alters the unhappy ending that afflicts King Pandosto and Queen Bellaria of Bohemia (Leontes and Hermione of Sicilia). Otherwise, the narrative outline remains intact. The story begins with the state visit of King Egistus of Sicilia (Polixenes of Bohemia) to his boyhood companion, King Pandosto of Bohemia. Queen Bellaria entertains their guest with such warmth, "oftentimes coming herself into his bedchamber to see that nothing should be amiss to mislike him," that Pandosto grows jealous. He commands his cupbearer Franion (Camillo) to murder Egistus, and the latter seems to agree but instead warns his victim to flee with him. Their hasty departure appears to confirm Pandosto's worst suspicions. He sends the guard to arrest Bellaria as she plays with her young son Garinter (Mamillius). When the Queen gives birth to a daughter in prison, the King orders the child destroyed, but he relents upon the insistence of his courtiers and causes the infant to be set adrift in a small boat. The Queen nobly defends herself at her trial (in language that Shakespeare has copied in some detail). She herself requests that the oracle at Delphos be consulted. The oracle replies in words that Shakespeare has altered only slightly: "Bellaria is chaste, Egistus blameless, Franion a true subject, Pandosto treacherous, his babe an innocent; and the King shall live without an heir if that which is lost be not found." Pandosto is immediately stricken with remorse, and, when Queen Bellaria

collapses at the news of her son Garinter's death, she is truly and irrecoverably dead.

A similarly close parallel in the narrative, along with telling changes in a number of details, characterizes the story's second half. The babe is conveyed by a tempest to the coast of Sicilia and is discovered by an impoverished shepherd named Porrus. He and his wife Mopsa adopt the child, naming her Fawnia. By the age of sixteen, Fawnia's natural beauty rivals that of the goddess Flora. At a meeting of the farmers' daughters of Sicilia, where she is chosen mistress of the feast, Fawnia is seen by the King's son Dorastus on his way home from hawking. She counters his importunate suit with the argument that she is too lowly a match for him, but he replies that the gods themselves sometimes take earthly lovers. Her foster father, distressed by the Prince's repeated visits (though he comes in shepherd's costume), resolves to carry the jewels he found with Fawnia to the King and reveal her story, thereby escaping blame for the goings-on. Dorastus escapes with Fawnia to a ship, aided by his servant Capnio (compare Camillo). Capnio also fulfills a role given by Shakespeare to Autolycus, for he manages to trick the shepherd Porrus into thinking he can see the King if he comes aboard Dorastus's ship. A storm drives these voyagers to Bohemia where, because of the ancient enmity between Egistus and Pandosto, they disguise themselves. Pandosto, happening to hear of Fawnia's beauty, orders her and the others to be arrested as spies and summoned to court, whereupon he falls incestuously in love with the disguised Fawnia. He promises to free the young man (who has taken the name of Meleagrus to conceal his identity) only if he will relinquish his claim to Fawnia. King Egistus meanwhile has discovered his son's whereabouts and sends ambassadors to Bohemia demanding the return of Dorastus and the execution of Fawnia, Capnio, and Porrus. Pandosto, his love for Fawnia having turned to hate, is about to comply when Porrus reveals the circumstances of Fawnia's infancy. Overjoyed to rediscover his daughter, Pandosto permits her to marry Dorastus but then falls into a melancholy fit and commits suicide.

Shakespeare has almost entirely created some characters, such as Paulina, Antigonus, the clownish shepherd's son, and Autolycus, though Capnio does perform one of Autolycus's functions by inveigling the old shepherd aboard ship. Antigonus's journey to the seacoast of Bohemia with the infant Perdita and his fatal exit *"pursued by a bear"* are Shakespearean additions. The character of Time is also added, and the shift in tone from tragedy to tragicomedy averts the catastrophe in Greene's novella (in which Pandosto commits suicide). The shepherdesses at the sheepshearing are Shakespearean. The old shepherd has a more substantial and comic role; Camillo is a stronger person than Capnio. Greene's Mopsa, the shrewish wife of old Porrus, disappears from the play. Shakespeare omits the incestuous love of Pandosto for his daughter and brings Hermione back to life. (For this motif of a statue made to breathe, he may well have recalled Ovid's account of Pygmalion in Ovid's *Metamorphoses*, Book 10.) Shakespeare's Leontes is more irrationally jealous than in Greene's account. Leontes's purgative sorrow is more intense and also more restorative than in the source; he is a truly noble and tragicomic figure, the center of a play about forgiveness and renewal.

Shakespeare may also have known Francis Sabie's *The Fisherman's Tale* (1595) and its continuation, *Flora's Fortune* (1595). From Greene's pamphlets, describing in vividly colloquial detail the life of London's underworld, Shakespeare probably derived many of Autolycus's tricks.

The Tempest

No direct literary source for the whole of *The Tempest* has been found. Shakespeare does seem to have drawn material from various accounts of the shipwreck of the *Sea Venture* in the Bermudas, in 1609, although the importance of these materials should not be overstated. Several of the survivors wrote narratives of the shipwreck itself and of their life on the islands for some nine months. Sylvester Jourdain, in *A Discovery of the Bermudas*, published 1610, speaks of miraculous preservation despite the island's reputation for being "a most prodigious and enchanted place." William Strachey's letter, written in July of 1610 and published much later (1625) as *A True Reportory of the Wreck and Redemption . . . from the Islands of the Bermudas*, describes the panic among the passengers and crew, the much feared reputation of the island as the habitation of devils and wicked spirits, the actual beauty and fertility of the place with its abundance of wild life (compare Caliban's descriptions), and the treachery of the Indians they later encounter in Virginia. Shakespeare seems to have read Strachey's letter in manuscript and may have been acquainted with him. The storm scene in Chapter 4 of Laurence Twine's *The Pattern of Painful Adventures*, a major source for *Pericles*, may also have given Shakespeare material for the first scene of *The Tempest*. Shakespeare also kept up with travel accounts of Sir Walter Ralegh and Thomas Harriot, and knew various classical evocations of a New World. The name "Setebos" came from Richard Eden's *History of Travel* (1577), translated from Peter Martyr's *De Novo Orbe* and from other travel accounts of the period. (See the Introduction to *The Tempest* for the potential relevance of various journals of the circumnavigation of the globe.) All these hints are indeed suggestive, but they are scattered and relate more to the setting and general circumstance of Shakespeare's play than to the plot.

Shakespeare certainly consulted Michel de Montaigne's essay "Of the Cannibals," as translated by John Florio in 1603. Gonzalo's reverie on an ideal commonwealth (2.1.150–71) contains many verbal echoes of the essay. Montaigne's point is that supposedly civilized men who condemn as barbarous any society not conforming with their own are simply refusing to examine their own shortcomings. A supposedly primitive society may well embody perfect religion, justice, and harmony; civilized art can never rival the achievements of nature. The ideal commonwealth has no need of magistrates, riches, poverty, and contracts, all of which breed dissimulation and covetousness. The significance of these ideas for *The Tempest* extends well beyond the particular passage in which they are found. And Caliban himself, whose name is an anagram of "cannibal," illustrates (even though he is not an eater of human flesh) the truth of Montaigne's observation apropos of the intense and wanton cruelty he finds so widespread in so-called Western civilization: "I think there is more barbarism in eating men alive than to feed upon them being dead."

Prospero's famous valedictory speech to "Ye elves of hills, brooks, standing lakes, and groves" (5.1.33–57) owes its origin to Medea's similar invocation in Ovid's *Metamorphoses* (Book 7), which Shakespeare knew both in the Latin original and in Golding's translation: "Ye airs and winds, ye elves of hills, of brooks, of woods alone, / Of standing lakes . . . " Medea also anticipates Shakespeare's Sycorax. Medea thus provides material for the representation of both black and white magic in *The Tempest*, so carefully differentiated by Shakespeare. Ariel is part English fairy, like Puck, and part daemon. The pastoral situation in *The Tempest* is perhaps derived from Edmund Spenser's *The Faerie Queene*, Book 6 (with its distinctions between savage lust and true courtesy, between nature and art). Italian pastoral drama as practiced by Guarini and (in England) by John Fletcher may also have been an influence. The masque element in *The Tempest*, prominent as in much late Shakespeare, bears the imprint of the courtly masque tradition of Ben Jonson, Francis Beaumont, and John Fletcher. Virgil's *Aeneid* may have provided Shakespeare with a more indirect source, with its story of wandering in the Mediterranean and storm at sea, love in Carthage, the intervention of the gods, and the fulfillment of destiny in Italy. Donna Hamilton (*Virgil and "The Tempest,"* 1990) contends that Shakespeare "imitated" Virgil so as to argue for a politics of retrenchment.

A German play, *Die Schöne Sidea* by Jacob Ayrer, written before 1605, was once thought to have been based on an earlier version of *The Tempest* as performed by English players traveling in Germany. Today, the similarities between the two plays are generally attributed to conventions found everywhere in romance.

The Sonnets

See the Introduction to *The Sonnets* for a discussion of the sonnet vogue in England of the 1590s, and the previous history of the sonnet in England and on the Continent.

Appendix 3

❦

Shakespeare in Performance

Lois Potter, University of Delaware

Although we know a good deal about the conditions of performance at the time Shakespeare's plays were first produced, much of this information (summarized in the Introduction, pp. xlvi–xlviii) raises as many questions as it answers. We know, for example, that Shakespeare wrote most of his plays for the Lord Chamberlain's Men, first formed in 1594 after a period of plague and theater closures, and that the company (officially servants of the courtier whose duties included supervising court entertainments) was honored with the title of the King's Men at the accession of James I. Elizabethan acting companies were all male, with boys or young men playing women's roles, but we know almost nothing about how they acted, or who played which parts. We know that the stages of the public, partially roofed playhouses jutted into the yard where the audience stood on three sides, looking up at the actors; the rest of the spectators sat in covered galleries looking down on them. But we are not sure whether the gallery above the stage, pictured in the contemporary illustration of the Swan Theatre interior shown on page xlvii, was meant for musicians, spectators, or both. (And of course we do not know how much the Globe's interior resembled the Swan's.) If, as appears from the illustrations of theater interiors on pages xlvii and lxv, some spectators normally watched the action from behind the stage, the actors would have had to move a great deal during a scene, as in modern theater-in-the-round productions, to make sure that they were visible and audible to all parts of their audience.

However much information we have, we still cannot know if aspects of the theater that were common then but unusual in our eyes were taken for granted by the spectators who watched the plays in the reigns of Elizabeth and James I. Did they think of the boy actresses as boys or believe in them as women? Those who had traveled to France and Italy would have known that women played women's parts in those countries and were often as famous as the male actors. What was the acting style for love scenes between a man and a cross-dressed boy, and what was the range of responses to it? The players in the open theaters performed by day (normally beginning at 2 P.M.), but used torches and candles to indicate when the action was supposed to be taking place at night. Did audiences find it difficult to accept a convention by which actors, fully visible to the audience, declare that they are unable to see anything? There is probably no single answer. It is likely that then, as always, audience members differed in the extent to which they preferred to believe in the performance or feel superior to it.

To the audiences of Shakespeare's time, the theaters were sumptuous and impressive buildings. Their wooden interiors were painted to look like marble, and the ceiling of the Globe was apparently decorated with the signs of the zodiac (perhaps, when Hamlet and Othello addressed the heavens, they looked at both a real and an artificial sky). Visitors from abroad were taken to see plays; actors traveled with them as far as Prague; versions of them were being translated into German as early as 1618. All this indicates how much English plays and players were respected. By about 1597, the company for which Shakespeare wrote was the one most frequently invited to perform at court, evidence that it was considered the best in London.

The theater in fact offered a great deal of visual and musical pleasure even for those who could not understand the language. Vast sums of money were spent on costumes. The most valuable surviving evidence, an account book of Philip Henslowe, manager of the Rose playhouse, shows that their bright or striking colors (often red and black, with silver and gold) allowed them to stand out on a stage that depended on daylight for most of its illumination. These were not "costumes" but clothes, sometimes bought in secondhand shops and sometimes donated or sold by gentlemen patrons. Characters normally wore contemporary dress, but with some indications of historical costume, like togas for classical characters (see the contemporary drawing, usually taken to be an illustration of *Titus Andronicus*, on p. lxii). Costumes and wigs, as well as false beards, were obviously important for a theater in which twelve to fourteen actors frequently doubled in as many as thirty roles. Music was frequently used in productions and a number of writers, including Shakespeare, incorporated popular contemporary songs into their plays. Robert Johnson, who is credited with the songs to a number of Jacobean plays, may have been the company's in-house composer. Some plays may have had as much music as a modern musical comedy, though very little of it has been identified.

Shakespeare's plays were designed to show off the actors' talents: singing, playing an instrument, dancing, and fencing. Most of his most popular plays end with either a dance or a fight, and nearly all of his tragic heroes (with the interesting exceptions of Othello and Antony) have at least one heroic fight scene. Since memorization and oratory were part of every grammar school education, audiences could recognize the superior memories of the actors who learned the long and complicated speeches that Shakespeare wrote for them. The combination of great actors and a dramatist who wrote great roles for them was attractive to other playwrights, and helped to ensure the company's continuing preeminence.

Shakespeare's practice of writing plays dominated by one very large starring role probably followed Richard Burbage's rise to stardom. Many contemporary references identify him with Richard III (see the anecdote on p. lxxv), and he is also known to have played Romeo, Hamlet, Othello, and Lear. John Lowin, who joined the company in 1602–1603, seems to have partnered Burbage in plays with two substantial roles. Shakespeare was unusual in that he wrote equally well for tragic and comic actors, and for the company clown, a type of performer traditionally famous for his ad-libs. Will Kempe, the most famous comedian of his day, certainly created the role of Dogberry—his name accidentally replaces the character's in one quarto of the play. It is not absolutely certain that he played Falstaff, but his departure from the Lord Chamberlain's Men in 1599 is often linked with Shakespeare's writing the character out of *Henry V* after having apparently promised (at the end of *2 Henry IV*) to include him in the sequel. Those who think that Shakespeare was in agreement with Hamlet's advice to the players ("Let those that play your clowns speak no more than is set down for them") wonder whether Kempe's inability to refrain from "speaking" led to friction with his leading playwright.

Kempe's successor was Robert Armin, and it is often said that the more literary quality of Shakespeare's later fools resulted from their being tailored for the new actor.

Little is known about the other chief sharers in the company, though attempts have been made to identify them with, for example, references to exceptionally thin or exceptionally fat actors. It is not known whether any particular young actor inspired Shakespeare to write his best female roles, but many boys seem to have been good enough to have a personal following. A spectator who saw *Othello* in Oxford in 1610 mentions how moved the spectators were at the sight of Desdemona after her death.

It has often been suggested that Hamlet's insistence on naturalness, and the First Player's modest claim to have "reformed" the practice of overacting at least to some extent, reflect a perceived difference between the actors for whom Shakespeare wrote and the more melodramatic ones in the company led by Philip Henslowe and its leading actor Edward Alleyn. Yet Alleyn, who created the major Marlowe roles, was no less intelligent and talented than Burbage. It was Alleyn who retired early to live the life of a gentleman (in 1597, when he was only 31), with one brief comeback in 1601–1604. Burbage, on the other hand, went on acting up to his death at the age of 46, a fact that suggests a more theatrical personality than Alleyn's. If there was a movement toward greater naturalism in the 1590s, it probably resulted from greater professionalization and better training of actors, along with greater sophistication of the audiences themselves.

As the Lord Chamberlain's Men grew more successful, they looked for a more select location. In 1597 James Burbage, Richard's father, purchased part of the disused monastic site of Blackfriars in the City of London. Protests from the local residents forced him to rent out the building to boys' companies (which performed less frequently) until, early in the reign of James I, times became more favorable. Finally moving into the new premises some time after 1607, the company was able to restrict its public to those who could afford the higher admission prices. In the indoor theaters, all the spectators were seated. Comfortable spectators cause less trouble than uncomfortable ones. The smaller size may have allowed for a more "realistic" style of playing. At the same time, the company continued to use the Globe throughout the period, as well as acting at court and elsewhere, so the actors must have been able to adapt their style to circumstances. In many ways, Shakespeare's last plays are his least "realistic," since they often involve magic, but the technology available in the Blackfriars playhouse may have made the magic convincing.

Besides, if realistic acting means acting that makes one forget that one is watching a play, it is unlikely that the drama was ever truly realistic. Other dramatists' allusions to Shakespeare are obviously meant to break the dramatic illusion: "What, Hamlet, are you mad?" asks a character in *Eastward Ho!* (1605), speaking to a servant who is named Hamlet only so that someone can ask him that question. Shakespeare himself also refers to his own plays. It is likely that the lovers' suicides in "Pyramus and Thisbe," performed at the end of *A Midsummer Night's Dream*, are meant as an absurd version of the end of *Romeo and Juliet*; Malvolio's madness, in *Twelfth Night*, probably parodies Hamlet's. Perhaps a comedy can make jokes about a tragedy without destroying the atmosphere, but *Hamlet* does the same thing. When Polonius tells Hamlet about playing Julius Caesar "at the university," and being killed by Brutus, many of their audience would remember that, not long before, the two actors speaking these lines had played Caesar and Brutus, respectively, in *Julius Caesar*.

The deaths of Shakespeare in 1616 and of Burbage in 1619 may have temporarily affected Shakespeare's theatrical popularity. Burbage was so much identified with the major roles that, according to one elegy, these characters seemed to have died with him. The Earl of Pembroke may have been typical when, in a letter, he expresses reluctance to go to the theater again. Joseph Taylor, who replaced Burbage in 1619, inherited a number of his roles. He and Lowin led the company for the next twenty years, with first John Fletcher and then Philip Massinger as their leading dramatist. The company had been called the King's Men since 1603, but the name was even more appropriate under Charles I than under his father, since the actors were much closer to the court. Taylor even served as acting coach to Queen Henrietta Maria and her ladies when they put on a pastoral tragicomedy in 1633.

Though not all Puritans or parliamentarians were hostile to the theater, and not all of Charles I's courtiers approved of it, the English civil war created a further association between theater and crown. Parliament closed the theaters at the start of the war in 1642, refusing to reopen them even when hostilities had ended. Performances continued nevertheless: professionals acted illegally in the theater buildings that were still usable, or, like amateurs, legally in private houses and inns. Some also went abroad and acted for English royalists in exile. Since the prohibition applied only to plays, scenes involving popular characters (Hamlet and the gravediggers, Falstaff, Bottom) were adapted and disguised as "drolls"—comic sketches—that could be performed in a mixed program of music, dance, and drama. The 1662 frontispiece to a collection of these drolls (p. lxv) shows how Falstaff and Mrs. Quickly were probably costumed in this period.

The Restoration and the Eighteenth Century (1660–1776)

At the Restoration of 1660, one of Charles II's first acts was to establish two licensed acting companies, one patronized by him, the other by his brother the Duke of York. Each company was assigned a selection of plays from the prewar period. Shakespeare's were among the first to be revived; indeed, actors were already playing them in London before the new theaters had opened. Although one of the speakers in Dryden's dialogue on drama (*An Essay of Dramatic Poesy*, 1665) says that Beaumont and Fletcher's plays were more popular than Shakespeare's or Jonson's, the evidence indicates that Shakespeare went on being a frequently acted dramatist throughout this period. Since the King's company seems to have received preferential treatment, it is likely that the plays awarded to them—*1 Henry IV*, *The Merry Wives of Windsor*, and *Othello*—were the most popular of Shakespeare's works in 1660.

It was natural that Shakespeare's works would need updating; nearly fifty years after their author's death, their language, grammar, and jokes were already becoming obsolete. Audiences saw themselves as too refined for plays with clowns and devils. Both theater managers (Thomas Killigrew and William Davenant) had been playwrights before the war, and both produced the prewar drama with extensive alterations. *The Taming of the Shrew*, as produced in 1667 by the King's company under Killigrew, was called, improbably, *Sauny the Scot*, after the new comic servant who replaced Grumio; the actor John Lacy wrote the title role for himself, exploiting the anti-Scots feeling that had been exacerbated by the Civil War. "Scenes," or scenery, the norm in the theaters of France and Italy, had already been used in prewar masques, and in the 1630s Davenant had already been planning to open a theater equipped to use it for plays. As manager of the Duke's company, he set about revising old plays to create more possibilities for spectacle. His *The Law Against Lovers* (1662) conflated *Measure for Measure* and *Much Ado About Nothing*, neither of which was well known at the period. The result was an emphasis on the romantic part of both plays, as opposed to their low comedy. He added more music and scenery in his adaptations of *Macbeth* (1664) and *The Tempest* (1667); in later revivals, these two works became almost operatic. The new theaters were rather small, and actors still played at the front of the stage, with the wings and backdrop of the new scenery stretching away behind them. Scene changes could be made quickly by rolling away one sliding backdrop to reveal another one behind it, sometimes with a new set of characters already in place. The same painted wings and backdrop were expected to serve for a number of plays, acting as a kind of shorthand to distinguish indoor from outdoor settings. The idea that each play belonged to its own particular visual world did not gain currency until well into the nineteenth century.

Charles II had insisted, in his patent for the new theaters, that the custom of boy actors—unique to England—must end. Most of the women who became actresses during the early years of the Restoration were, inevitably, untrained. The famous Nell Gwyn, mistress of Charles II, was a star of the King's company. She was considered delightful in contemporary comedies, some of which were written especially for her; however, Pepys always insisted that she was disastrous in serious roles, and there is no record of her playing Shakespeare. The new actresses could exploit their natural gifts, their beauty, and their novelty, but no one wanted to see them in character parts, especially those of elderly women. As a result, roles like the witches in *Macbeth* were taken by men, often the company's low comedians, a practice that continued for centuries. The small number of parts for attractive young women in Shakespeare now became a problem. Davenant was skillful at multiplying them. He expanded the part of Lady Macduff; Miranda, no longer the only woman in *The Tempest*, acquired a naïve younger sister, while Caliban and Ariel were likewise paired off with a female monster and spirit respectively.

Some of these changes also had a moral purpose. Davenant balanced the wickedness of Macbeth and his Lady by developing the virtuous Macduffs as foils to them. He also gave Macbeth a death speech (only one line long) to show that the dying man recognized the vanity of his ambition. Later adaptations were still more concerned with "poetic justice." This term meant simply that art ought to reward virtue and punish vice, not because this is what happens in the real world, but because art's duty is to offer virtuous models whenever possible. John Dryden, who had worked with Davenant on *The Tempest*, later wrote free adaptations of both *Antony and Cleopatra* and *Troilus and Cressida*, in which the lovers, far from being unfaithful, are only sympathetic victims of misunderstanding. His version of *Antony and Cleopatra*, called *All for Love, or, the World Well Lost* (1675–1677), largely replaced its model for much of the next century, and was often played under Shakespeare's title. Though Dryden claimed that he had made Antony's wife Octavia a virtuous foil to Cleopatra, the play's success was due less to its superior morality (indeed, its most popular scene was one in which the two women insult each other) than to its simplification of the structure, which subordinated political history to the love story. Shadwell's *Timon of Athens* (1678) provided a faithful woman as well as a faithful steward, to contrast with the mercenary friends and mistress who desert the hero. Thomas Otway's *Caius Marius* (1679) made the suicides of Romeo and Juliet more acceptable by locating them in a classical world. One of Otway's other innovations—letting the heroine revive in time to converse with the hero before they die—was to outlast the adaptation itself. Nahum Tate's *King Lear* (1681) made the virtuous Cordelia a large and dramatic role, worthy of a star actress. He also added a love interest between her and Edgar, and provided a happy ending in which Lear is restored to his throne. The adaptation remained in the repertory for 150 years, and Samuel Johnson defended it in 1765 on the grounds that,

although the unjust tragic ending might be more true to life, "all reasonable beings naturally love justice." Tate's omission of the Fool, a character associated with old-fashioned theater, was not even noticed.

After 1679, the Popish Plot and uncertainty over the royal succession led to Shakespearean adaptations designed to score political points. In 1680, John Crowne wrote *The Miseries of Civil War* (1680), the first of two adaptations based on the *Henry VI* plays, while Tate's *The Sicilian Usurper*, adapted from *Richard II*, fell foul of the censor, even though its deposed ruler was more sympathetic than Shakespeare's. In the following year, Tate reversed the order of scenes in *King Lear*, beginning with Edmund's first soliloquy: a bastard son claiming his right to inherit was bound to be topical in the reign of a king who had no legitimate children and whose next heir was a Roman Catholic brother. The turbulent political climate kept audiences away, and the two companies amalgamated in 1682. Very few plays of any kind survive from the last years of Charles II's reign and the three years of James II's leading to the revolution of 1688. In the reign of William and Mary (James's daughter), *King Lear* was once again so topical that it could not be staged. Mary and her sister Anne looked all too much like Lear's daughters, especially since Tate's version ends with the king's abdication in favor of his daughter and son-in-law.

Colley Cibber's *Richard III* (1699), the most successful of all adaptations, benefited from the fact that a number of Shakespeare's history plays had dropped out of the repertory by the end of the century, thus providing a quarry from which the adapter could borrow. Feeling that he had a free hand, Cibber removed Queen Margaret and, since he intended to play Richard himself, gave him some good lines from other histories, including (from *2 Henry IV*) the death speech that Shakespeare had neglected to write for his hero. This Richard, literally an actor's dream, was more theatrically popular than Shakespeare's had been, a fact that kept the version alive well into the twentieth century (the Olivier film, which also cut Margaret's role, used two recognizable Cibber lines). Cibber had some difficulties with the licenser just before the first performance because it was feared that his opening scene, showing the deposed Henry VI in the Tower, would remind its audiences of the deposed James II. He made sure to show his loyalty in his next adaptation—*King John*, under the title *Papal Tyranny*, coincided with the threatened invasion, in 1715, of James II's exiled Catholic son. As one of the managers of Drury Lane, and as poet laureate (from 1730), Cibber became a popular target for satire, and he is best remembered for Pope's attacks on him in *The Dunciad* (1743). But his entertaining autobiography, *An Apology for the Life of Colley Cibber, Comedian* (1740), is still the best source of information on the early eighteenth-century theater.

Indeed, without Cibber's book, it would be difficult to say much about Shakespearean acting at the turn of the

eighteenth century. Though Thomas Betterton was recognized as the greatest actor of his age from the first years
of the Restoration, those, like Samuel Pepys, who saw
him at this time, praised him highly but in vague terms.
Because of the division of the theatrical repertory, Betterton acquired some major Shakespearean roles, like Othello, only after the unification of the two companies in
1682, when senior actors of the King's company took the
opportunity to retire. After this, he had virtually a
monopoly, and went on playing a much-acclaimed Hamlet until he was seventy, as well as taking the role of Falstaff in what seems to have been his own adaptation of
the *Henry IV* plays. Cibber's description of Betterton's
Hamlet reacting to the first sight of his father's ghost
became a point of comparison for later Hamlets well into
the nineteenth century. It is clear that his effects had to do
with "presence" rather than with movement—though, of
course, Cibber was describing him in his last years, when
he was presumably less active.

The early female performers are still more shadowy
figures. Women had appeared on stage as singers, or
singing actresses, in "operas" performed in the 1650s, and
one of these, perhaps Margaret Hughes, may have been
the first to play a Shakespearean role (probably Desdemona). Mary Sanderson, who became Mrs. Betterton,
was the first Lady Macbeth. Her successor, Elizabeth
Barry, was primarily a tragic actress. She is said to have
owed her initial success to careful instruction by her
lover, the Earl of Rochester, who recognized the importance of constant repetition and, like a modern director,
insisted that she should rehearse in the dress that she was
going to wear in performance. The best-loved comic
actress of Cibber's youth, Anne Bracegirdle, played several Shakespearean comedy heroines alongside the Congreve roles for which she was famous. The popularity of
The Merry Wives of Windsor may have been due not only
to Betterton's playing of Falstaff but also to its two excellent roles for actresses past their first youth, probably the
only women in the company experienced enough to do
justice to Shakespearean comedy.

Though the history of Shakespeare editing begins in
the early eighteenth century, the plays still belonged
essentially to the theater; hence, the publication of acting
editions, which allowed audiences to read what they
were actually going to see in the theater, usually heavily
cut and partially modernized. Even so, the first half of the
century saw a steady return to original versions, as one
role after another was suddenly revealed to be a superb
vehicle for a particular actor. Shylock, for instance, had
been a not-very-interesting comic miser in a not-very-
interesting romantic comedy, often replaced by George
Granville's adaptation, *The Jew of Venice* (1701). When
Shakespeare's original was revived in 1741, Charles
Macklin astonished his fellow-actors as much as the audience by emphasizing Shylock's terrifying malevolence.

Although later actors would play the character more
sympathetically, Macklin made him what he has been
ever since: a disturbing character who cannot be assimilated into a comic structure. Something of a theorist on
acting, Macklin, in teaching other actors, insisted on clear
and intelligent diction. Perhaps for that reason, his Iago
was the most convincing of the period.

Richard III, in Cibber's version, was the role in which
David Garrick made his London debut in 1741. The actor
became famous almost instantly and went on to manage
the Drury Lane Theatre from 1747 to 1776. Garrick was a
self-proclaimed idolater of Shakespeare whose "Jubilee"
at Stratford-upon-Avon in 1769 not only inaugurated the
practice of celebrations and festivals but also led contemporaries to regard him as almost equal in importance
with his author. Despite his reputation for restoring
Shakespeare, Garrick was as much of an adapter as his
famous predecessors, turning *The Taming of the Shrew* and
the last part of *The Winter's Tale* into short three-act plays
and making operas out of *A Midsummer Night's Dream*
and *The Tempest*. His *Macbeth* had a death speech, much
more dramatic and pathetic than the one-line moral that
Davenant had given him. His *Romeo and Juliet* had a
pathetic farewell scene based on the one in Otway's *Caius
Marius*. In response to French criticisms, he even directed a *Hamlet* in 1771 with the low comedy of the gravediggers omitted. Yet he also revived many plays not seen in
their Shakespearean form since the Restoration, showing
by his acting what superb roles they contained. He was
equally gifted at comedy and tragedy. Two of his most
popular roles were Benedick and (Tate's) King Lear. *Julius
Caesar* and *Othello,* plays in which Betterton had been
particularly successful, were better acted by Garrick's
chief rival, Spranger Barry, a tall and handsome actor
with a beautiful voice. Garrick, shorter and less romantic in appearance, was famous for his mobile and expressive features that allowed him to delineate the transitions
between the "passions." It was this grasp of human psychology that he praised in Shakespeare and that others
praised in him. His most significant leading lady, Hannah Pritchard, must have been equally versatile, since
she was famous both as Rosalind and as Lady Macbeth.
It was, however, characteristic of Garrick that he was able
to form an excellent company around himself, including
a number of fine actresses and low comedians. Without
these conditions, it would have been impossible to revive
so many of the comedies.

The Romantic Period (1776–1850)

Between Garrick's retirement in 1776 and the end of the
century, the theaters changed to the point where a rapid,
subtle style like Garrick's was becoming almost impossible. The Licensing Act of 1737 had limited spoken

drama to Drury Lane and Covent Garden, the descendents of the two London theaters licensed in 1660 by Charles II. The late eighteenth century saw the rapid growth of a London population in search of entertainment. The two theaters responded by increasing their audience capacity until, at the end of the century, Covent Garden held over 3,000 spectators, and Drury Lane 3,600. When much of the audience was too far from the stage to see facial expressions or hear the softer tones of an actor's voice, the most successful performers were those who could establish themselves through their volume or through visual effects. Two tall and statuesque actors, John Philip Kemble and his more gifted sister, Sarah Siddons, dominated the theater of this period. Siddons's Lady Macbeth was probably the finest performance of the age: when she said that she could smell blood, at least one contemporary spectator declared that he could smell it too. Her other finest Shakespearean roles were Isabella in *Measure for Measure* and Hermione in *The Winter's Tale*, both of them strong women whose sublime moral grandeur dwarfed everyone else. Kemble's attempt to impose greater discipline and unity on theatrical productions, with more historically "correct" sets and costumes, resulted in what must have been the most genuinely classical theater yet seen in Britain. *Coriolanus*, with Kemble in the title role and Siddons as a heroically obsessed Volumnia, was the triumph of their approach. It was ironic that it should have come in an age dominated by the spirit of revolution and of the complex attitudes that are summed up as Romanticism.

It was to this spirit that Edmund Kean appealed. Those who saw him make his famous London debut as Shylock in 1814, wearing a black wig instead of the traditional red one, would have realized at once that he was going to play, not a tragic villain, but a tragic victim. He had been a singer, dancer, and Harlequin before taking London by storm, and his acting benefited from these other skills. Unlike Kemble, who expressed authority and aristocratic dignity, he excelled as Shakespeare's outsiders and outlaws: the hunchbacked Richard III (still in Cibber's softened version), the Moor Othello, and the melancholy Hamlet. Knowing his gift for pathos, he starred in an adaptation of *3 Henry VI* (where York sobs over his murdered son) and attempted to bring back the original ending of *King Lear* (where Lear grieves over the dead Cordelia), but audiences were not yet ready for either. Those who saw him at his best never forgot his haunting delivery of Richard III's forebodings before Bosworth and Othello's farewell to arms, which provided the kind of appreciative, poetic commentary on Shakespeare that characterized the best contemporary criticism.

Kean's career was short, wrecked by drink and scandal. In 1833, just as he had reached his miserable end, another actor, using the stage name of Keane, made his Covent Garden debut in the role of Othello. Ira Aldridge, a black American, may have hoped to announce himself as Kean's successor, but racial prejudice in England prevented him from being accepted as a leading tragedian. He would, however, play Othello all over Europe, and especially in Russia, in bilingual productions with local casts. Like Kean, he sought out the roles of victims and social outcasts: Aaron in his own adaptation of *Titus Andronicus*, as well as (in white make-up) Macbeth, Shylock, and King Lear; like Kean, he was also capable of singing songs in dialect or even a Russian folksong. The excitement that German and Russian spectators felt at the sight of a black actor playing a black character would become an important part of theatrical experience a century later; at this point, it was a novelty. In the 1860s Aldridge finally acted in major London theaters and might have returned to the United States after the Civil War if he had not died unexpectedly while on tour in Poland.

Meanwhile, both of the unruly London theaters were managed, in turn, by William Macready, who, as his diary makes clear, took seriously his responsibility to a dramatist he worshipped. Still more than Kemble, he behaved like a modern director, with a vision of the production as a whole. His revivals of the history plays showed the possibilities of historical reconstruction. He is best known for restoring the Fool to *King Lear* in 1838, though he gave the role to a young woman to ensure that it would be played for pathos rather than low comic effects that might distract from his own scenes. A number of fine actresses played opposite him: Helen Faucit, young, fragile, refined, who would later write a perceptive if sentimental account of her approach to acting some of Shakespeare's female characters; Fanny Kemble, a member of the famous Kemble family, whose memoirs indicate the struggle involved for women in a star-dominated theater; Charlotte Cushman, a powerful visitor from America who sometimes played male roles. The plays were still heavily cut and showed the influence of earlier adaptations, but by the end of his career, Macready could fairly claim to have restored a good deal of Shakespeare's text and to have made the theater more respectable. The repeal of the Licensing Act in 1843, which allowed smaller theaters to cater to different publics, also encouraged gentrification. Samuel Phelps, who managed the working-class Sadler's Wells Theatre from 1844 to 1869, did even more than Macready had, performing thirty-four of Shakespeare's plays; he even restored the original *Richard III*, though other actors continued to prefer the Cibber version. Charles Kean (son of Edmund), at the Princess's Theatre from 1850 to 1859, carried the historicizing process still further; his "archaeological" productions were likely to be accompanied by notes explaining the reason for the choice of period, costumes, and props.

Still, it was only rarely that anyone had the opportunity to impose a concept of Shakespearean production on an acting company in his own theater. Star actors tended to spend much of their time on tour, both in England and America, performing their favorite roles after perhaps one rehearsal with the resident company. Far from seeking new ways to interpret a play, these actors had to rely on standardized stage business (when Mr. Wopsle plays Hamlet in Dickens's *Great Expectations*, an unsympathetic audience comments loudly on each theatrical cliché as it occurs). They naturally tended to conceive of their characters in isolation and to favor tragedy over comedy, which requires ensemble playing. (Similarly, nineteenth-century critics usually focus on the analysis of individual characters.) A common practice was the pitting of one actor against another in a famous role, arguing over which one was the "true" Hamlet or Lear. In one case, the rivalry developed a nationalistic dimension. Macready's visit to America, in 1849, is notorious for the riot at Astor Place in New York, when soldiers fired on and killed some of the crowd outside the theater. The rioters had been trying to drown out Macready's performance of *Macbeth* out of a mistaken loyalty to the American tragedian, Edwin Forrest. On a visit to Britain, Forrest had hissed Macready for some foppish business with a handkerchief that the actor, as Hamlet, had used to illustrate the phrase "I must be idle." Now his personal hostility became a quarrel about effete English acting versus the manly American tradition. In fact, the distinction was largely meaningless: many well-known American actors had begun their careers in England or Ireland. While some American Shakespeareans might have seen themselves as part of the Forrest tradition, and some (like the touring performers depicted by Mark Twain in *Huckleberry Finn*) were of no tradition at all, most American actors continued to look to Europe for models.

The Victorian Era and the Early Twentieth Century (1850–1912)

The greatest American actor of the next generation, Edwin Booth, was a refined and melancholy figure whose readings of the great Shakespearean roles were psychological and poetic. Booth was the son of Junius Brutus Booth, who had acted in London opposite Edmund Kean, and the brother of John Wilkes Booth, the assassin of Abraham Lincoln. (Ironically, all three members of this acting family had once performed together in the great assassination play, *Julius Caesar*.) Though Booth briefly attempted theater management, he spent much of his time in the exhausting business of touring. He clearly thought deeply about his own roles, and about the moments when other characters interacted with him. His correspondence with the New Variorum Shakespeare

editor, H.H. Furness, is quoted in many notes of that edition—an early example of successful communication between the theater and the scholarly world. Yet when Booth was alternating the two leading roles of *Othello* with Henry Irving in 1881, he sent his servant to take notes at rehearsal for him. Nothing in his experience had prepared him for a theater in which the actor-manager expected everyone to fit into a total artistic conception.

It was Irving, the first actor to be knighted, who dominated English Shakespearean acting in the late Victorian era. His pictorial sense was even stronger than that of the actor-managers who preceded him, and the technical means at his disposal in the Lyceum Theatre, which he began to manage in 1878, were much better. The old system of sliding screens in grooves, flanked by a series of wings, had been replaced by the "box set," which was built like a piece of architecture, creating a complete environment. Electric lighting, introduced in the 1880s, provided new, subtle visual effects. The elaborate and beautiful sets often required interminable scene changes and, sometimes, rearrangement of the plays to accommodate them. Irving's own performances were usually controversial. His Malvolio, like his Shylock, was a tragic figure, while his Iago was so witty and likeable that, playing opposite Booth's Othello, he stole all the sympathy from the hero. His theater offered a beautiful dream for the spectator to share: if it also disturbed the spectator, it was through its revelation of the psychological depths of character, never through its comments on social and political issues. Irving's leading lady, Ellen Terry, was both beautiful and brilliant; in most productions she was allowed to be only the former. Bernard Shaw, longing for her to appear in plays about "grownup" topics, by himself or Henrik Ibsen, resented her imprisonment in Irving's world. For Shaw and other modern thinkers, Shakespeare was becoming synonymous with nostalgia and with the moralistic and idealistic thinking that the new drama regarded as a vice. The early twentieth-century theater was finally affected by these critical attempts to reform it, but two kinds of production coexisted for some time. At His Majesty's Theatre, Herbert Beerbohm Tree, like Irving, offered psychologically based character acting in a beautiful scenic environment, recreating Cleopatra's Egypt and Henry VIII's England; having seen his lavish production of *Macbeth*, one critic commented that "Nature put up a pretty feeble imitation of what several barrels of stones and a few sheets of tin could do in His Majesty's." At the Savoy, on the other hand, Harley Granville Barker, a disciple of Bernard Shaw, developed a decorative visual style that was not tied to a specific historical period.

Meanwhile, a more experimental approach to acting was being developed in Germany. The country's unusual political structure, with small dukedoms and cities sponsoring their own theaters, made it possible for the

Duke of Saxe-Meiningen to sponsor his own company of players, sixty-six in all. His leading actors were unremarkable but, when he took them on tour in the 1880s, audiences were impressed by his handling of large groups. The Duke insisted that those who played major roles in one production should be walk-ons in another, so that crowds could be properly rehearsed instead of being assembled from those gathered around the stage door and drilled by the stage manager immediately before each performance.

Frank Benson, a young Oxford graduate, saw the Saxe-Meiningen company at Drury Lane in 1881, and was inspired to develop his own touring company— though, unlike the Duke, he acted in his own productions and consequently shaped them from a star's point of view. From 1886 on, the Bensonians became regular visitors at Stratford-upon-Avon. Shakespeare's birthplace had been briefly famous in 1769, the year of Garrick's Jubilee, but it was only in 1879, when the first Memorial Theatre was built, that tourists had any reason to visit for more than a few hours. Benson essentially created the first Stratford company, though it used the theater only during a short "Festival" season. Having a regular venue and a devoted audience enabled him to revive unusual works, if often drastically cut. In 1901 he inaugurated the new century with a "Grand Cycle" of Shakespeare's histories—the first English production of the plays as a group.

The desire to return to fuller texts and something like the original conditions of Shakespearean performance was initially associated with Germany and then with outsiders like William Poel, who founded the English Stage Society in 1894. Previously, Poel had given an experimental matinee of the first quarto *Hamlet* at St. George's Hall in 1881. More surprisingly (though his friendship with Bernard Shaw in part explains it), the popular London actor Johnston Forbes-Robertson played an unusually full text of *Hamlet* in 1897, with characters like Reynaldo and Fortinbras appearing for the first time in centuries. Then Benson's company played an uncut *Hamlet* in 1899 and 1900. Poel, who often worked with amateurs, using all-purpose curtains rather than scenery on what was meant to be an Elizabethan stage, revived works previously considered unperformable, by Shakespeare's contemporaries as well as by Shakespeare. For example, he gave the first important *Troilus and Cressida* to be seen in London since 1734, dressing it in Elizabethan rather than classical costume. It was 1912. He had discovered the play's antiwar potential.

The Twentieth Century

World War I drastically curtailed many Shakespearean projects, including those for a gigantic celebration of the anniversary of his death in 1916, which at one point was intended to include the opening of a National Theatre. Although this theater did not come into existence until nearly 100 years after Irving had first suggested it, other developments were creating the conditions that would make Shakespeare plays, with their large casts, commercially viable.

One was the rise of repertory theaters, which could support a large company and a varied range of plays. The most famous of these was London's Royal Victoria, or "Old Vic," founded in 1914. Under a number of gifted directors (notably Robert Atkins, who had directed all the plays in the 1623 Folio by 1923, Harcourt Williams, and Tyrone Guthrie), it was the home to many legendary productions, including John Gielgud's first *Hamlet* (1929) and Olivier's first *Hamlet* (1937). At the Birmingham Repertory Theatre, Barry Jackson had already directed a modern-dress *Hamlet* in 1925. Modern dress had been common practice until the nineteenth century; it now seemed eccentric, but would by the end of the century become almost the norm. The Memorial Theatre at Stratford, after struggling to find its identity, saw some brilliant productions by Peter Brook in the 1940s and 1950s, including three plays traditionally considered minor: *Love's Labor's Lost* (1946), *Measure for Measure* (1948), and a *Titus Andronicus* (1955), starring Olivier, at which audience members regularly fainted at what was then unusual stage violence: the amputation of the hero's hand and the cutting of the villains' throats. Stratford and the Old Vic were becoming rival Shakespeare companies and in the 1960s each achieved a new status. The Memorial Theatre was renamed the Royal Shakespeare Theatre in 1960, with Peter Hall as director, whereas the Old Vic was designated the National Theatre in 1963. Olivier directed its opening production of *Hamlet*, with Peter O'Toole in the title role, and played a famous Othello in 1964. The National Theatre eventually moved into new premises in an arts complex, with three stages, on the South Bank of the Thames.

In the United States, the most exciting Shakespeare productions also occurred during a period of government subsidy: it was depression-era financing that enabled Orson Welles to direct Shakespeare on radio, and, for the Mercury Theatre, his "voodoo" *Macbeth* (1938) with an all-black cast, his anti-Fascist *Julius Caesar* (1937), and his condensation of the major history plays, *Five Kings*, which, although unsuccessful, later influenced his Falstaff film, *Chimes at Midnight* (1966). The other significant development in North America was the growth of summer Shakespeare festivals at outdoor Elizabethan-style theaters, beginning with the Elizabethan Stage at Ashland, Oregon (founded 1935), and the Guthrie-designed Festival Theatre at Stratford, Ontario (1953). Festival seasons allowed juxtapositions of related plays and the yearly performance of successive plays in a history cycle.

It was the English Stratford-upon-Avon, however, that fully seized on the history plays, performing the *Richard II–Henry V* group in 1951, during the Festival of Britain that celebrated the country's emergence from wartime and postwar rationing. For the rest of the century, the "cycle" of history plays would be recognized as a national epic, to be performed for special occasions. For the new Royal Shakespeare Company, Peter Hall and John Barton produced the *Henry VI–Richard III* group of plays—rewritten, reduced to three plays, and called *The Wars of the Roses*. They revived these, along with the other *Henry* plays, for the Shakespeare quatercentenary in 1964. The histories were produced again in 1975 by Terry Hands, with Alan Howard playing all the kings except Henry IV; in 1982 the *Henry IV* plays opened the company's new London theater at the Barbican under Trevor Nunn; and the company, now under Adrian Noble, marked the arrival of the millennium with a freshly conceived production of the *Richard II–Richard III* sequence. Just as the 1951 production showed the influence of Tillyard's essays on the histories as a unified cycle, the plays of the year 2000, deliberately disparate in style and even venue, were the product of a critical movement that emphasized discontinuity and diversity.

Contemporary Critical Approaches

By now, productions might require as much interpretation as plays. In the last half of the twentieth century, the spread of school and university education had created a substantial population that had studied at least one Shakespeare play and a smaller population, including some theater practitioners, that had read not only the plays but also the criticism. Stratford's John Barton, a former Cambridge don, directed *Twelfth Night* (1969) as if it were by Chekhov, encouraging the audience to imagine the unspoken feelings of the characters—not only Viola (Judi Dench), smiling through heartbreak, but Maria, in her apparently hopeless love for Sir Toby, and Sir Andrew in his even more hopeless love for Olivia. This attention to character, often created out of masses of tiny realistic details, informed some of the theater's most highly praised productions. Barton's *Richard II* (1973) worked very differently, externalizing the play's images in ways that were clearly independent of the characters' awareness: for instance, a glimpse of a melting snowman echoed Richard's wish that he were "a mockery king of snow" and linked the fall and rise of kings to a natural cycle of dissolution and renewal.

Other major critical approaches, easier to categorize, quickly found their way onto the stage. Political readings, often influenced by a Brechtian production style, dominated the 1960s and 1970s. These were usually Marxist and anti-authority: lines in which characters expressed high moral sentiments might be juxtaposed (legitimately) with those in which they showed themselves less noble, or (illegitimately) by setting them in a context that undermined them, as when, in Peter Zadek's *Held Henry* (Hero Henry), Henry V delivers the St. Crispin's Day speech to his bored mistress. Even before its first English publication in 1964, *Shakespeare Our Contemporary*, by the Polish critic Jan Kott, had powerfully influenced theater with his comparison of *Hamlet* and the histories to life under a totalitarian regime, *King Lear* to Theater of the Absurd, and the comedies to a Freudian nightmare. Both Brecht and Kott could be recognized behind Peter Brook's *King Lear* (1962), which, in place of the traditional sympathy with the king (a frighteningly harsh Paul Scofield), emphasized his and his followers' brutality toward Goneril's servants, and ruthlessly cut anything that might be cathartic; the Dover cliff meeting between Lear and Gloucester frankly drew on the stage imagery of Samuel Beckett's *Waiting for Godot*. Brook's *A Midsummer Night's Dream* (1970), which based its erotic treatment of Titania and Bottom on Kott's work, found a purely theatrical language for the critical commonplaces about the play's metatheatricality. Without makeup, under bright light, in a white-walled gymnasium that replaced the traditional moonlit forest, Oberon and Puck sat on trapezes and passed the aphrodisiac "flower," a metal plate, from one spinning metallic wand to another. The fact that this operation could, and occasionally did, go wrong was the point: it reminded the audience that the real magic lay in its own willingness to trust the actors. Even the "Pyramus and Thisbe" actors in the final scene were treated as serious artists, representatives of working-class culture who deserved respect. For many of his later productions, Peter Brook went abroad in search of a multilingual, multiethnic cast, searching for ways of escaping the "easy" assumptions about Shakespeare.

It was in fact race and gender rather than class that dominated Shakespeare production in the last quarter of the century. The concern with race began with the great American theatrical event of the 1940s, Margaret Webster's production of *Othello* with the charismatic Paul Robeson in the title role. After the longest run of any Shakespeare play on Broadway, it was taken on tour all over America in 1945, playing only in desegregated theaters. Although Robeson had already played Othello in London (1930), and would do so again at Stratford-upon-Avon, England, in 1959, his long period of disgrace in the politically polarized United States of the 1950s delayed the movement toward race-based casting as a norm. After initial embarrassment about racist language in Shakespeare, the theater began deliberately to explore its implications, as race became a subject for academic study. The range of *Othello* videos available by the 1990s indicates the play's performance history: besides Orson

Welles's film from 1952, these include the National Theatre production of 1964 starring Laurence Olivier and the BBC one with Antony Hopkins (1981), both with white actors in the title role; Trevor Nunn's Chekhovian version originally staged in 1989; the historic South African production by Janet Suzman, a political act at a time when apartheid still existed; and Oliver Parker's 1994 version, with Laurence Fishburne (opposite Kenneth Branagh's convincingly ordinary Iago), consciously conveying the concentrated power and sensuality associated with blackness. Confusion between "color-blind casting" (when the audience is supposed to ignore the race of both actor and character) and "race-based casting" (when the audience is being told something about race through the casting) was deliberately cultivated in Jude Kelly's Othello (Washington, D.C., 1997). This production enabled Patrick Stewart to achieve his otherwise unrealizable ambition of playing the title role by surrounding a white Othello with African American and Hispanic actors, yet with the play's racial references unaltered.

Just as some critics of racism felt that Othello and The Merchant of Venice had become theatrically unacceptable, some feminist responses to Shakespeare argued the same about The Taming of the Shrew, in which a female character is made to acquiesce in her humiliation by a husband who uses patriarchal arguments to justify his behavior. The play had usually been directed to soften its final moral, either by making it clear that the protagonists have fallen in love at first sight or by emphasizing its nature as a play within a play, safely distant from real life. A famous production by Michael Bogdanov (Royal Shakespeare Theatre, 1978) doubled the drunken tinker Sly with Petruchio and showed Kate being brutalized into a dazed submission that horrified even her husband. Obviously, the play in this version was no longer a comedy. A less obvious effect of feminism has been the increasing attention paid to Shakespeare's female characters. They tend now to be on stage more than the text directs, as when Ophelia stands appalled while her father reads Hamlet's love letters to the court or Gertrude enters in time to hear Claudius and Laertes plan to poison Hamlet, so that her decision to drink from the cup is recognized as a heroic device to save her son's life. The young Elizabeth of York, who does not appear in the text of Richard III although she is important to its plot, has frequently been seen and even heard in stage versions, as in the 1995 film by Richard Loncraine. The fact that women are often denied speech at crucial moments can be turned to an advantage, as when John Barton and a number of subsequent directors of Measure for Measure in the 1980s made Isabella silently refuse the Duke's proposal, which earlier actors and directors had assumed she would eagerly accept.

Still more important, in a theater in which women are far more likely than men to be underemployed, were devices that increased the number of Shakespearean roles for women. Cross-dressed performances, parallel to the productions focused on race, hovered between gender based and gender blind. Deborah Warner's Richard II in 1995, with Fiona Shaw as the title character (National Theatre, London), suggested a troubled and potentially erotic relationship between Richard and Bolingbroke without defining it further. In the all-male Cheek-by-Jowl production of As You Like It (1995), the audience was never certain whether it was meant to be thinking of Rosalind (Adrian Lester) as male or female. A similar confusion was exploited when Michael Kahn's King Lear (Washington, D.C., 1999) cast Cordelia as a deaf-mute, signing her lines, which were then interpreted by the Fool. This decision, which would have been meaningless if the audience had not known that the actress (Monique Holt) really was a deaf-mute, might be seen either as a return to the self-conscious theatricality of the Renaissance stage or as an example of identity politics.

Shakespeare on Film

Of course, the sense of identity between actor and role is strongest in the cinema, where physical appearance matters more and where audiences are particularly likely to bring with them recollections of an actor's previous roles. Films of Shakespeare plays are as old as film itself. Their transfer to videotape and then laserdisc and DVD, a process that began in the 1970s, has given them a much wider circulation and canonized some performances: Olivier's Richard III, for instance, now has much the same iconic status that Cibber gave to Betterton's Hamlet. Orson Welles's film versions of Macbeth (1947) and Othello (1952), visually remarkable as they were, have benefited from remastering to make their soundtracks more intelligible. The BBC made-for-TV versions of Shakespeare, 1979–1985, often disappointed both film and Shakespeare enthusiasts, though for different reasons, but have been widely used in schools. Kenneth Branagh's films, including a remarkable four-hour uncut Hamlet (1996), have been surprisingly successful in making the plays accessible to a popular audience. His Henry V (1989) was unfairly praised for being more "real" than Olivier's; both films were star-centered, with Olivier playing a more controlled king, Branagh a more vulnerable one. Whereas Olivier began his film with a view of an idealized Elizabethan London, then of a playhouse viewed from a superior perspective as old-fashioned and in some ways comic, Branagh introduced his Chorus (Derek Jacobi) in a room full of movie cameras, though he later allowed him to move among the actors in the film. As often in films, the moments most remembered were visual: Henry's (Branagh's) grief when, in order to enforce proper discipline, he is obliged to order the hanging of Bardolph, or the long shot, after the Battle of Agincourt, that shows Henry carrying the dead boy in a procession of English soldiers singing *Non nobis Domine.*

Branagh's youth was an asset in bringing Shakespeare to a young audience. Later filmmakers have aimed at a still younger group. *William Shakespeare's Romeo + Juliet* (directed by Baz Luhrmann, 1996), filled as it was with icons of contemporary youth culture, is perhaps the first of these, though it retains Shakespeare's language, juxtaposing it with contradictory images, so that it can be understood either as a complex visual-verbal experience or as a rather simple visual one. The *Hamlet* directed by Michael Almereyda (2000) represents its young characters as college students obsessed with modern technology: Hamlet (Ethan Hawke) is an amateur filmmaker and Ophelia is a photographer; "To be or not to be" is spoken in a video store against a background of videos labeled "Action." For students of the new field of Shakespeare in Popular Culture, Teenage Shakespeare, with the stories rewritten in contemporary language and settings, is becoming a genre in its own right. *10 Things I Hate About You* (directed by Gil Junger, 1999) and *O* (directed by Tim Blake Nelson, 2001) retell *The Taming of the Shrew* and *Othello* in American high school settings. *The Children's Midsummer Night's Dream* (directed by Christine Edzard, 2001) has a cast of primary school children.

International Contexts and Contemporary Adaptations

Not only have the plays been adapted for every age group, they have turned out to speak an international language. This had not always been true, though English and French actors had visited each other's countries since the seventeenth century: in 1629 French actresses were booed by English audiences, still accustomed to an all-male stage; one group of English actors was booed in the Paris of 1818, but another visiting company in 1827 inspired French writers and actors to try to understand Shakespeare. English and American audiences saw *Othello* with new eyes when the Italian actor Tommaso Salvini, followed by several other famous Italians, performed on tour in the late nineteenth century. Along with the visit of the Berliner Ensemble to London in 1956, the most important influences in the late twentieth century came from Asian, especially Japanese, theater and from central and eastern Europe. Kurosawa's films, *Throne of Blood* (*Macbeth*, 1957) and *Ran* (*King Lear*, 1986), transpose Shakespearean plots into Japanese culture and images. Successful Russian films have ranged from the visually stunning colors of Yan Fried's *Twelfth Night* and Sergei Yutkevitch's *Othello* (both 1955) to Grigori Kozintsev's black-and-white *Hamlet* (1964) and *King Lear* (1971).

The opening up of contacts with central and eastern Europe after 1989 has resulted in visits from theater companies of the former eastern bloc countries. When London audiences in 1990 saw *Hamlet* by the Bulandra Theatre of Romania (directed by Alexander Tocilescu), they discovered that plays often regarded in Britain and America as "conservative" tools of the "establishment" had elsewhere been a powerful vehicle for the expression of political dissent. When first produced in 1985, Tocilescu's *Hamlet* was clearly understood to be equating the rottenness of Elsinore with the world created by Nicolae Ceaucescu, the dictator executed in 1989; Ion Caramitru, the actor who played Hamlet, had been one of the leaders of the revolution. In Czech productions of Shakespeare, similarly, actors and audience had gathered in a deliberate act of misreading directed at the occupying Russians: in *Love's Labor's Lost*, of all plays, the princess's suggestion that the courtiers disguised as Muscovites should "be gone" was the high point of the evening.

Western directors have sometimes attempted to deal with a difficult text by interpreting it as "Other," particularly as Japanese: the samurai warrior culture was the background to Barry Kyle's *The Two Noble Kinsmen* (Swan Theatre, Stratford, 1986) and to David Farr's *Coriolanus* (Royal Shakespeare Theatre, 2002), whereas Ron Daniels's *Timon of Athens* (The Other Place, Stratford, 1980) drew on the concept of a society based on gift-giving. Conversely, Yukio Ninagawa's Japanese Shakespeare productions have combined Japanese costumes with a soundtrack of European music (*Macbeth*) and interpreted *The Tempest* through the story of the famous Japanese exile, Shunkan. Such cross-cultural borrowings have sometimes been denigrated as "cultural tourism," by which critics seem to mean that it is illegitimate to appropriate the merely visual aspects of a culture to which one does not belong.

Similarly, the reconstructed "Shakespeare's Globe" in London, which opened in 1997, was accused of attempting to appropriate the emotions of another historical period. Perhaps because the opening production was *Henry V,* the "groundlings" who stood in the yard for only £5 apiece seemed to be modeling themselves on their counterparts in the Globe sequence of Olivier's film, who boo when they hear that Falstaff has been banished. Their willingness to boo the French (and, in the next season, Shylock) at first shocked the critics, and it was suggested that this theater might be suited only to comedies and histories demanding a presentational style, but productions of *Hamlet* (2000) and *King Lear* (2001) showed that it was possible to control audience response to the tragedies. Mark Rylance's *Hamlet* skillfully played his line about groundlings "capable of nothing but inexplicable dumbshow," so that he could respond to their laughter by adding "*and* noise." Whether or not the theater can really tell anyone anything about Elizabethan stage conventions and audience response, it has given considerable pleasure. Other Globes, more and less historically based, now can be found in several countries (the United States, Japan, Poland, and the Czech Republic, among others), while the open stage of Stratford, Canada, remains one of the most successful modifications of the Elizabethan model. In a reversal of the search for authenticity, the Shakespeare Theatre in Washington, D.C., has abandoned its home in the reconstructed Fortune Theatre at the Folger Shakespeare Library for a purpose-built modern auditorium. In fact, the two kinds of theater can coexist. The well-established Shakespeare festivals of Stratford, Ontario; Ashland, Oregon; and Santa Cruz, California, have added well-equipped indoor theaters to their outdoor acting spaces, and an indoor auditorium is projected as an addition to Shakespeare's Globe in London. A reconstruction of the Blackfriars Playhouse opened in Staunton, Virginia, in 2001.

Although it has been impossible to discuss the theatrical fortunes of every Shakespeare play, it may be interesting to end by reflecting how greatly these have fluctuated. If some plays, like *Hamlet* and *Macbeth*, have always been popular, the history of others is more checkered. Some of the comedies most popular today, such as *As You Like It* and *Twelfth Night*, were regarded as insipid in the eighteenth century, redeemed only by their scenes of low comedy and occasional sententious speeches. *The Merry Wives of Windsor* was the most popular comedy during the Restoration; *King John* and *Henry VIII* were more popular in the nineteenth century than *Richard II* or *2 Henry IV*. *Othello* was acted without the "willow scene" (4.3) for most of the eighteenth and nineteenth centuries, and *Troilus and Cressida* and *Titus Andronicus* were performed, if at all, only in heavily adapted versions. It is arguable that the attitude to Shakespeare that Bernard Shaw ridiculed as "Bardolatry" reached its height, not in the Victorian age, but at the end of the twentieth century, a time when any Shakespeare play, however minor, was likely to find a director and an audience. One reason might be that the subsidized theaters had been giving fewer controversial productions since 1980, emphasizing instead what the plays have in common with musical comedies and films. An important American contribution to Shakespeare in performance has taken the form of musicals like *The Boys from Syracuse* (1938), *Kiss Me, Kate* (1948), and *West Side Story* (1957), based respectively on *The Comedy of Errors*, *The Taming of the Shrew*, and *Romeo and Juliet*; now, many productions of the comedies followed the Restoration practice of filling them with popular music. What was new was not the practice of adaptation but the attitude toward it. In the mid century, the plays were taken to be fixed quantities: the job of the theater director, as of the critic, was to uncover the "real" work, whether through more authentic staging, a more accurate text, or a better understanding of its meaning. By the end of the millennium, when some theorists were insisting that the text itself was unknowable, it is not surprising to find a much greater tolerance for re-creations and explorations of the plays in other forms.

David Garrick in the role of King Lear in the storm, as painted by Benjamin Wilson.

V&A IMAGES, LONDON / ART RESOURCE, NY

Appendix 4

Films and Videos as a Guide to the Study of Shakespeare

by David Bevington

The general introduction to this volume makes the point that seeing a Shakespeare play in production is often a very good way to start with the study of that play. Aspects of Shakespeare that might seem daunting at first—the occasionally unfamiliar vocabulary and idiom, unusual Elizabethan grammatical constructions, and other difficulties of meaning—can disappear as a problem when good actors interpret for us. Watching a production can be fun and exciting. It erases much of the distance of time between Shakespeare's day and our own. And, since film and video versions are far more readily available than live stage performances, productions on screen are likely to be our best choice.

The choices are surprisingly numerous. One can find a worthwhile screen interpretation of virtually every play Shakespeare wrote. For the better known plays, multiple versions are available, so that comparisons can be made of varying styles and interpretations. What follows here is a brief history of Shakespeare on film and video, stressing the highlights, as a way of indicating what is available and what are perhaps the best choices today. This brief history is followed by a selective filmography—that is, a bibliography of film and video, listing the best and most available versions, play by play.

Silent film versions of Shakespeare's plays are numerous in the early twentieth century. They are, of course, of interest to the specialist, but are omitted here since this account is aimed at providing a practical listing of screen productions best suited to the reader wishing to gain a lively acquaintance with a play or plays. The story begins early in the days of talking movies.

Mary Pickford and Douglas Fairbanks Sr. starred as Kate and Petruchio in the first full-length talking film of any Shakespeare play, Sam Taylor's *The Taming of the Shrew*, 1929. *A Midsummer Night's Dream* enjoyed real box-office success in Max Reinhardt's 1935 film, starring a young Mickey Rooney as Puck, James Cagney as Bottom the Weaver, and Olivia de Havilland as Hermia, along with some other notable Hollywood favorites. Franco Zeffirelli scored a great hit with his film version of *The Taming* in 1967, starring Richard Burton and Elizabeth Taylor as Petruchio and Kate.

Laurence Olivier achieved an artistic breakthrough in 1944 with his full-length color film of *Henry V*, produced during World War II to keep up morale on the home front. Olivier's *Hamlet,* 1948, *Richard III,* 1955, and *Othello,* 1965, were similar triumphs. Orson Welles's *Macbeth,* 1948, and *Othello,* 1952, were conscious and serious attempts to show that the United States could challenge Olivier at his own game. Welles's *Chimes at Midnight* (1965), with himself in the role of Falstaff, combined elements of *1* and *2 Henry IV* and bits of *The Merry Wives of Windsor* into a moving account of the ultimate rejection of Falstaff by Prince Hal.

Another wave of film revivals of Shakespeare began in 1989 with Kenneth Branagh's highly successful *Henry V.* Young, brash, superbly self-confident, Branagh deliberately chose *Henry V* as a way of confronting the legendary Olivier on his own turf. Olivier's film had been patriotic and upbeat, albeit with an awareness of the grim aspects of war. Branagh's version, in the aftermath of Vietnam and the Falklands military engagement, was more wary of patriotic fervor. Branagh followed up this triumph in 1993 with *Much Ado About Nothing,* starring himself as Benedick and his then-wife Emma Thompson as Beatrice, along with Denzel Washington as Don Pedro, Keanu Reeves as Don John, and Michael Keaton as Dogberry. The age of star turns in Shakespeare films was by now in full swing. Branagh repeated this surefire box-office stratagem with his four-hour *Hamlet* in 1996, with himself as Hamlet, Julie Christie as Gertrude, Kate Winslet as Ophelia, Derek Jacobi as Claudius, and a host of cameo appearances by Jack Lemmon (Marcellus), Gérard Depardieu (Reynaldo), Robin Williams (Osric), Billy Crystal (the Gravedigger), and Charlton Heston (the Player King).

Not to be outdone in this contest of the stars, Franco Zeffirelli had already cast Mel Gibson as Hamlet, Glenn Close as Gertrude, Helena Bonham Carter as Ophelia, Ian Holm as Polonius, Alan Bates as Claudius, and Paul Scofield as the Ghost in his 1990 *Hamlet*.

Zeffirelli had scored a great success earlier, in 1968, with his visually gorgeous *Romeo and Juliet*, starring Olivia Hussey as Juliet, Leonard Whiting as Romeo, and Michael York as Tybalt. With brief and tactful nudity, and a handsome couple in the title roles, this film could not fail. No less popular with the younger set particularly was Baz Luhrmann's *Romeo + Juliet*, 1996, starring Claire Danes and Leonardo DiCaprio. Filmed in Mexico City in such a way as to suggest a major U.S. sunbelt city like Miami or Los Angeles, this version updates its story with panache: Tybalt and his cohorts are Hispanic gang members, the Capulets are nouveau riche, and Friar Laurence is a New Age priest.

Many other Shakespeare films are eminently worth studying, with well-known stars in key roles. *Julius Caesar*, produced in 1953 by John Houseman with Joseph L. Mankiewicz as director, Marlon Brando as Mark Antony, James Mason as Brutus, John Gielgud as Cassius, Louis Calhern as Julius Caesar, Greer Garson as Calpurnia, and Deborah Kerr as Portia, is a Hollywood extravaganza, bringing together famous actors from the UK and the United States. Trevor Nunn's *Twelfth Night*, 1996, stars Imogen Stubbs as Viola, Helena Bonham Carter as Olivia, Nigel Hawthorne as Malvolio, and Ben Kingsley as Feste, along with some spectacularly handsome Cornish scenery. Ian McKellen and Judi Dench are outstanding in Trevor Nunn's *Macbeth*, 1979. Roman Polanski's film version of the same play in 1971, for Playboy Productions, is quirky but interesting. Al Pacino as Shylock, Jeremy Irons as Antonio, and Joseph Fiennes as Bassanio are admirable in Michael Radford's *The Merchant of Venice*, 2004. No less excellent are Laurence Olivier and Joan Plowright in Jonathan Sichel's 1969 film of this same play. Kenneth Branagh's recent *As You Like It* (2006), with Kevin Kline as Jaques, has some lively moments. Even some lesser plays occasionally get in on the act: Julie Taymor's film version of *Titus Andronicus* (1999) has excellent performances by Anthony Hopkins as Titus, Jessica Lange as Tamora, Harry Lennix as Aaron, and still others. Branagh's *Love's Labour's Lost* (2000) enlivens this little-known play by adapting some hit tunes by Irving Berlin, Jerome Kern, the Gershwins, and Cole Porter.

At least three film *Othello* are eminently worth watching, in addition to that of Laurence Olivier in 1965 mentioned above. Janet Suzman's film version is based on a stage production in Johannesburg, South Africa, in 1988, shortly before the end of Apartheid, with John Kani as Othello, Joanna Weinberg as Desdemona, and Richard Haddon Haines as Iago. Trevor Nunn's 1990 film stars Willard White as Othello, Imogen Stubbs as Desdemona, and Ian McKellen as Iago. Oliver Parker's 1995 *Othello* features notable performances by Laurence Fishburne as Othello, Kenneth Branagh as Iago, and Irène Jacob as Desdemona. The availability of several excellent films on a single play offers the opportunity for comparison and contrast of acting styles, interpretation, and filming techniques.

The same is even more true of *Hamlet*, where we have the versions discussed above by Olivier, Zeffirelli, and Branagh, along with Richard Burton as Hamlet in John Gielgud's 1964 film, a Russian *Hamlet* by Grigori Kozintsev in 1964, Nicol Williamson in the lead role in 1969 as directed by Tony Richardson, Richard Chamberlain in 1970 as directed by Peter Wood, and Kevin Kline in an especially intelligent production of 1990 as directed by Kirk Browning and Kevin Kline. Michael Almereyda's *Hamlet* (2000), set in midtown Manhattan at the turn of the twentieth century, stars Ethan Hawke as Hamlet, Diane Venora as Gertrude, Julia Stiles as Ophelia, Kyle MacLachlan as Claudius, Bill Murray as Polonius, and Sam Shepard as the Ghost.

King Lear also affords several worthy film versions for comparison, notably Kozintsev's 1970 film with music by Dimitri Shostakovich, Peter Brook's starkly pessimistic version of 1971 with Paul Scofield in the title role, and Michael Elliott's version for Granada Television in 1983 starring Laurence Olivier. *Richard III* offers brilliant choices to compare, including the Olivier discussed above and Richard Loncraine's film version, 1995, set in 1930s London with Ian McKellen as Richard. Still other plays are available in multiple interpretations on film; see the selected filmography at the end of this essay.

Film adaptations attest no less eloquently to the popularity of Shakespeare today on film, stressing as they do the appeal of adapting the original to current mores and cultural preoccupations. Akira Kurosawa's black-and-white *Throne of Blood*, 1957, transfers the story of *Macbeth* to late medieval warlord Japan. His *Ran*, 1985, colorfully retells *King Lear* as a saga about an aging King and his three sons (rather than daughters). These are among the finest films Kurosawa ever produced. *West Side Story* triumphantly entered the world of film in 1961, based on the stage musical adaptation of *Romeo and Juliet*, with Leonard Bernstein as the composer and Stephen Sondheim as lyricist. *Kiss Me, Kate*, 1953, has proven to be no less immortal in its reworking of *The Taming of the Shrew*.

The same play was relocated to the world of high-school dating and jealous rivalries in Gil Junger's *10 Things I Hate About You*, 1999, with Julia Stiles as Katharine Stratford. *Othello* also has been resituated in a high-school setting in Tim Blake Nelson's *O*, 2001, with Julia Stiles this time as Desi Brable, the Desdemona equivalent. *Hamlet* has been given a modern twist in Kurosawa's *The Bad Sleep Well* (1960). *Shakespeare in Love* (1998), scripted by Tom Stoppard and Marc Norman, contains some radiant moments from *Romeo and Juliet*, with Gwyneth Paltrow as Juliet and Joseph Fiennes as Romeo.

A Selected Filmography

(Compiled by David Bevington with special thanks to David Scott Kastan)

Here is a listing, play by play, of some interesting and generally successful film or video versions of Shakespeare's plays. Most are available in video and DVD. Comparison of one or more versions can offer invaluable insights into the potential range of various interpretations. Also included here are some adaptations and spin-offs. BBC/Time-Life Television has produced videos of all the plays; those of special note are described here.

ANTONY AND CLEOPATRA

A Royal Shakespeare Company/ITC production, 1974, directed by Trevor Nunn and Jon Scoffield, with Richard Johnson as Antony, Janet Suzman as Cleopatra, Patrick Stewart as Enobarbus, Corin Redgrave as Octavius, Rosemary McHale as Charmian, Raymond Westfall as Lepidus, Ben Kingsley as Thidias, Mary Rutherford as Octavia, and Tim Pigott-Smith as Proculeius. (Charlton Heston directed a film version in 1972, with himself as Antony and Hildegard Neil as Cleopatra, but it is generally accounted a failure.)

A Merchant-Ivory production, 1965, of *Shakespeare Wallah*, directed by James Ivory, with Felicity and Geoffrey Kendal. An adaptation, with scenes from *Antony and Cleopatra*.

AS YOU LIKE IT

A Twentieth Century British Fox production, directed by Paul Czinner, 1936, with Laurence Olivier and Elisabeth Bergner as Orlando and Rosalind, Felix Aylmer as Duke Frederick, Sophie Stewart as Celia, John Laurie as Oliver, MacKenzie Ward as Touchstone, Leon Quartermaine as Jaques, Henry Ainley as Duke Senior, Dorice Fordred as Audrey, and J. Fisher White as Adam. A flawed production, but notable for the casting of a very young Olivier.

A BBC-TV production with the Royal Shakespeare Company, 1963, directed by Ronald Eyre for TV, based on a stage production by Michael Elliott, with Patrick Allen and Vanessa Redgrave as Orlando and Rosalind, Tony Church as Duke Frederick, Paul Hardwick as Duke Senior, Patrick Wymark as Touchstone, Max Adrian as Jaques, Rosalind Knight as Celia, David Buck as Oliver, Russell Hunter as Corin, Peter Gill as Silvius, Jeanne Hepple as Phoebe, Gordon Gostelow as William, Patsy Byrne as Audrey, and Ian Richardson as Le Beau.

A BBC Shakespeare Collection television version of 1978, produced by Cedric Messina and directed by Basil Coleman, shot mostly on location and outdoors in Masterpiece Theatre style with stately aristocratic homes and leafy forests; with Helen Mirren as Rosalind, Angharad Rees as Celia, Brian Stirner as Orlando, Clive Francis as Oliver, Tony Church as Duke Senior, Richard Easton as Duke Frederick, John Quentin as Le Beau, James Bolan as Touchstone, Richard Pasco as Jaques, Maynard Williams as Silvius, Victoria Plucknett as Phoebe, Marilyn Le Conte as Audrey, David Lloyd Meredith as Corin, Arthur Hewlett as Adam, and Tom McDonnell as Amiens.

A Sands Films production, 1992, directed by Christine Edzard, modernized, with Andrew Tiernan and Emma Croft as Orlando and Rosalind, Celia Bannerman as Celia, James Fox as Jaques, Don Henderson as Duke Senior and Duke Frederick, Cyril Cusack as Adam, Valerie Gogan as Phoebe, Miriam Margolyes as Audrey, and Griff Rhys Jones as Touchstone.

An HBO production, 2006, directed by Kenneth Branagh, with Bryce Dallas Howard as Rosalind, David Oyelowo as Orlando, Alfred Molina as Touchstone, Kevin Kline as Jaques, Brian Blessed as Duke Senior and Duke Frederick, Romola Garai as Celia, Adrian Lester as Oliver, Richard Clifford as Le Beau, Richard Briers as Adam, Jimmy Yuill as Corin, Alex Wyndham as Silvius, Jade Jefferies as Phoebe, Paul Chan as William, and Janet McTeer as Audrey.

A film version, 2010, based on Thea Sharrock's London Globe Theatre production of 2009, with Naomi Frederick as Rosalind, Jack Laskey as Orlando, Dominic Rowan as Touchstone, Tim McMullan as Jaques, Philip Bird as Duke Senior, Trevor Martin as old Adam, Laura Rogers as Celia, Jamie Parker as Oliver, Brendon Hughes as Duke Frederick, Michael Benz as Silvius, Sophie Duval as Audrey, Gregory Dudgeon as Le Beau and William, Trevor Martin as Adam, and Jade Williams as Phoebe.

HAMLET

A Two Cities Films production, 1948, directed by Laurence Olivier, with Olivier as Hamlet, Basil Sydney as Claudius, Eileen Herlie as Gertrude, Felix Aylmer as Polonius, Jean Simmons as Ophelia, Norman Wooland as Horatio, Terence Morgan as Laertes, and Stanley Holloway as the First Gravedigger.

A Classic Cinemas filming of a stage performance at the Lunt-Fontaine Theatre, 1964, directed by John Gielgud on stage and Bill Colleran on film, with Richard Burton as Hamlet, Alfred Drake as Claudius, Eileen Herlie as Gertrude, Hume Cronyn as Polonius, Linda Marsh as Ophelia, John Cullum as Laertes, Robert Milli as Horatio, and John Gielgud as the voice of the Ghost.

A Lenfilm production, 1964, in Russian with subtitles, directed by Grigori Kozintsev, with Innokenti Smoktunovsky as Hamlet, Mikhail Nazvanov as Claudius, Elza Radzina-Szolkonis as Gertrude, Yuri Tolubeyev as Polonius, Anastasia Vertinskaya as Ophelia, Stepan Oleksenko as Laertes, Vladimir Erenberg as Horatio, and V. Kolpakor as the Gravedigger.

A Woodfall Productions/Columbia Pictures production, 1969, directed by Tony Richardson, with Nicol Williamson as Hamlet, Anthony Hopkins as Claudius, Judy Parfitt as Gertrude, Mark Dignam as Polonius, Marianne Faithfull as Ophelia, Michael Pennington as Laertes, Gordon Jackson as Horatio, Roger Livesay as the First Player and the Gravedigger, Ben Aris as Rosencrantz, and Clive Graham as Guildenstern.

A Hallmark Hall of Fame production, 1970, directed by Peter Wood, with Richard Chamberlain as Hamlet, Richard Johnson as Claudius, Margaret Leighton as Gertrude, Michael Redgrave as Polonius, Ciaran Madden as Ophelia, Martin Shaw as Horatio, Nicholas Jones as Laertes, John Gielgud as the Ghost, and Alan Bennett as Osric.

A Warner Brothers production, 1990, directed by Franco Zeffirelli, with Mel Gibson as Hamlet, Alan Bates as Claudius, Glenn Close as Gertrude, Ian Holm as Polonius, Helena Bonham Carter as Ophelia, Nathaniel Parker as Laertes, Stephen Dillane as Horatio, Michael Maloney as Rosencrantz, Sean Murray as Guildenstern, Pete Postlethwaite as the Player King, John McEnery as Osric, and Paul Scofield as the Ghost.

A PBS Television Great Performances production, 1990, not shown in movie theaters, directed by Kirk Browning and Kevin Kline, with Kevin Kline as Hamlet, Brian Murray as Claudius, Dana Ivey as Gertrude, Michael Krumpsty as Laertes, Diane Venora as Ophelia, Peter Francis James as Horatio, Philip Goodwin as Rosencrantz, Reg E. Cathey as Guildenstern, Don Reilly as Fortinbras, and Leo Burmester as Osric.

A Columbia production, 1996, four hours in length, essentially uncut, directed by Kenneth Branagh, with Kenneth Branagh as Hamlet, Derek Jacobi as Claudius, Julie Christie as Gertrude, Richard Briers as Polonius, Kate Winslet as Ophelia, Michael Maloney as Laertes, Nicholas Farrell as Horatio, Jack Lemmon as Marcellus, Gérard Depardieu as Reynaldo, Charlton Heston as the Player King, Robin Williams as Osric, Billy Crystal as the First Gravedigger, and Brian Blessed as the Ghost.

A Miramax production, 2000, directed by Michael Almereyda, with Ethan Hawke as Hamlet, Kyle MacLachlan as Claudius, Diane Venora as Gertrude, Bill Murray as Polonius, Julia Stiles as Ophelia, Liev Schreiber as Laertes, Karl Geary as Horatio, and Sam Shepard as the Ghost.

A Hallmark Entertainment production directed for TV by Campbell Scott and Eric Simonson in 2000, starring Campbell Scott as Hamlet, Jamey Sheridan as Claudius, Blair Brown as Gertrude, Roscoe Lee Browne as Polonius, LisaGay Hamilton as Ophelia, Roger Guenveur Smith as Laertes, John Benjamin Hickey as Horatio, Bill Buell as Bernardo, John Campion as Marcellus, David Debesse as Francisco, Marcus Giamatti as Guildenstern, Michael Imperioli as Rosencrantz, Lewis Arlt as Voltemand, Dan Moran as the Gravedigger, Denis O'Hare as Osric, Byron Jennings as the Ghost of Hamlet's father and First Player, and Sam Robards as Fortinbras.

A production by Bethan Jones, David Horn, Denise Wood, John Wyver, and Seb Grant, based on a highly praised stage production by the Royal Shakespeare Company as directed by Gregory Doran, filmed in 2009, with David Tennant as Hamlet, Patrick Stewart as Claudius, Penny Downie as Gertrude, Oliver Ford Davies as Polonius, Mariah Gale as Ophelia, Edward Bennett as Laertes, Peter De Jersey as Horatio, Sam Alexander as Rosencrantz and the Second Gravedigger, Tom Davey as Guildenstern, and Mark Hadfield as the Gravedigger.

A filming of 2010, based on the stage production at the National's Olivier Theatre in London, set in a modern police state, directed by Nicholas Hytner, starring Rory Kinnear as Hamlet, Clare Higgins as an alcoholic Gertrude, Patrick Malahide as a cold-blooded and ruthless Claudius, David Calder as Polonius, Ruth Negga as Ophelia, Alex Lanipekun as Laertes, and James Laurenson as the Ghost and Player King.

The much-acclaimed 2009 London production of *Hamlet* starring Jude Law appears to be included (in portions, at least) in the Video Library of the New York Times. An interview about it is available on British Universities Film.

Kurosawa Productions, 1960, of *The Bad Sleep Well*, directed by Akiria Kurosawa, with Toshiro Mifune as the Hamlet-like hero and Takeshi Kato as the Claudius-like villain. An adaptation.

A production of *Rosencrantz and Guildenstern Are Dead*, 1990, based on the stage play by Tom Stoppard, with Gary Oldman as Rosencrantz, Tim Roth as Guildenstern, Richard Dreyfuss as the Player, Iain Glen as Hamlet, Joanna Miles as Gertrude, Donald Sumpter as Claudius, Joanna Roth as Ophelia, and Ian Richardson as Polonius. A witty excursion into the world of

Hamlet from the point of view of Hamlet's two youthful companions.

HENRY IV PART I

An Internacional Films/Alpine Films production, *Chimes at Midnight*, 1966, directed by Orson Welles, with Welles as Falstaff, John Gielgud as King Henry IV, Keith Baxter as Prince Hal, Tony Beckley as Poins, Norman Rodway as Hotspur, Fernando Rey as Mortimer, Michael Aldridge as Pistol, Alan Webb as Justice Shallow, and Margaret Rutherford as Mistress Quickly. A synthesis of *1* and *2 Henry IV*, with parts of *The Merry Wives of Windsor*.

A BBC/Time-Life Television production, 1979–80, directed by David Giles, with David Gwillim as Prince Hal, Anthony Quayle as Falstaff, Jon Finch as King Henry IV, Tim Pigott-Smith as Hotspur, David Buck as Westmorland, Clive Percy as Worcester, Robert Brown as Blunt, Bruce Purchase as Northumberland, Robert Morris as the Earl of March, Michele Dotrice as Lady Percy, and Brenda Bruce as Mistress Quickly.

A New Line Cinema production, 1991, of *My Own Private Idaho*, directed by Gus Van Sant, with Keanu Reeves as the Hal-like Scott Favor, William Richert as the Falstaff-like Bob, and River Phoenix as Scott's friend Mike Waters. An adaptation of *1* and *2 Henry IV*.

A film version staged during a production at London's Globe Theatre, 2011 (in tandem with a production of *2 Henry IV*), directed by Dominic Dromgoole, with Roger Allam as Falstaff, Oliver Cotton as King Henry IV, Jamie Parker as Prince Hal, Sam Crane as Hotspur, William Gaunt as Worcester, Daon Broni as Mortimer, Christopher Godwin as Northumberland, Jason Baughan as Westmorland, Sean Kearns as Glendower, Barbara Marten as Mistress Quickly, Danny Lee Wynter as Poins, Paul Rider as Bardolph, Joseph Timms as Francis, Kevork Malikyan as Vernon, Lorna Stuart as Lady Percy, Jade Williams as Lady Mortimer, James Lalley as Mowbray and Gadshill, and Phil Cheadle as the Earl of Douglas.

HENRY V

A Two Cities Films Ltd. production, directed by Laurence Olivier, 1944, with Olivier as King Henry, Renée Asherson as the Princess Katharine, Felix Aylmer as the Archbishop of Canterbury, Robert Helpmann as the Bishop of Ely, Nicholas Hannen as Exeter, Michael Shepley as Captain Gower, John Laurie as Captain Jamy, Niall MacGinnis as Captain MacMorris, Harcourt Williams as the French King, Max Adrian as the Dauphin, Leo Genn as the Constable of France, Francis Lister as the Duke of Orleans, Ralph Truman as Mountjoy, Valentine Dyall as the Duke of Burgundy, Esmond Knight as Fluellen, Robert Newton as Pistol, Roy Emmerton as Bardolph, Freda Jackson as Mistress Quickly, Ivy St. Helier as Alice, and Leslie Banks as the Chorus.

A BBC/Renaissance Films production, 1989, directed by Kenneth Branagh, with Branagh as King Henry, Derek Jacobi as the Chorus, Emma Thompson as the Princess Katharine, Brian Blessed as Exeter, Charles Kay as the Archbishop of Canterbury, Alec McCowen as the Bishop of Ely, Danny Webb as Captain Gower, Jimmy Yuill as Captain Jamy, John Sessions as Captain MacMorris, Paul Scofield as the French King, Michael Maloney as the Dauphin, Richard Easton as the Constable of France, Christopher Ravenscroft as Mountjoy, Ian Holm as Fluellen, Robert Stephens as Pistol, Richard Briers as Bardolph, Judi Dench as Mistress Quickly, and Geraldine McEwan as Alice.

JULIUS CAESAR

An MGM John Houseman production, 1953, directed by Joseph L. Mankiewicz, with Marlon Brando as Mark Antony, James Mason as Brutus, John Gielgud as Cassius, Louis Calhern as Julius Caesar, Greer Garson as Calpurnia, Edmond O'Brien as Casca, Richard Hale as the Sooothsayer, and Deborah Kerr as Portia.

A production by Peter Snell, 1969–70, directed by Stuart Burge, with Charlton Heston as Mark Antony, Jason Robards as Brutus, Richard Johnson as Cassius, John Gielgud as Caesar, Richard Chamberlain as Octavius Caesar, Diana Rigg as Portia, Jill Bennett as Calpurnia, and Robert Vaughn as Casca.

KING LEAR

A Lenfilm production, 1970, directed by Grigori Kozintsev, in Russian (*Karol Lir*), with subtitles, with Yuri Yarvet as Lear, Valentina Shendrikova as Cordelia, Elze Radzina as Goneril, Galina Volchek as Regan, Oleg Dal as the Fool, Vladimir Yemelyanov as Kent, Karl Sebris as Gloucester, Regimantas Adomaitis as Edmund, and Leonard Merzin as Edgar.

A Filmways production, 1971, directed by Peter Brook, with Paul Scofield as Lear, Anne-lise Gabold as Cordelia, Jack MacGowran as the Fool, Cyril Cusack as Albany, Irene Worth as Goneril, Susan Engel as Regan, Patrick Magee as Cornwall, Tom Fleming as Kent, Alan Webb as Gloucester, Ian Hogg as Edmund, and Robert Lloyd as Edgar.

A Granada Television production, 1983, directed by Michael Elliott, with Laurence Olivier as Lear, Anna Calder-Marshall as Cordelia, Dorothy Tutin as Goneril, Diana Rigg as Regan, John Hurt as the Fool, David Threlfall as Edgar, Robert Lindsay as Edmund, Colin Blakely as Kent, Robert Lang as Albany, Jeremy Kemp as Cornwall, and Leo McKern as Gloucester,

A Great Performances version, directed by Trevor Nunn in 2009 and based on a stage production by the Royal Shakespeare Company, with Ian McKellen as King Lear, William Gaunt as Gloucester, Philip

Winchester as Edmund, Ben Meyjes as Edgar, Frances Barber as Goneril, Monica Dolan as Regan, Romola Garai as Cordelia, Sylvester McCoy as the Fool, Jonathan Hyde as Kent, Guy Williams as Cornwall, Julian Harries as Albany, John Heffernan as Oswald, and Peter Hinton as Burgundy.

A film of the play called *The Dresser*, 1983–5, with Albert Finney as Sir and Tom Courtney as the Dresser (Norman). An adaptation, based loosely on the career of the Shakespearan actor-manager Donald Wolfit, with scenes from *King Lear*.

An Orion Classics production, 1985, directed by Akira Kurosawa, in Japanese (*Ran*), with subtitles. With Tatsuya Nakadai as the Lear-like Hidetora Ichimonji; his three sons Akira Terao as the Goneril-like Taro, Jinpachi Nezu as the Regan-like Jiro, and Daisuke Ryu as the Cordelia-like Saburo; Meiko Harada as the daunting Lady Kaede, wife of Taro; Peter as the Fool-like Kyoami; Masayuki Yui as the Kent-like Tango; Yoshiko Miyazaki as Lady Sue, the saintly wife of Jiro; and Takeshi Nomura as the Edgar-and Gloucester-like Tsurmaru, brother of Lady Sue. An adaptation.

MACBETH

A Republic Pictures and Mercury Films production, 1948, directed by Orson Welles, with Welles as Macbeth, Jeanette Nolan as Lady Macbeth, Dan O'Herlihy as Macduff, Edgar Barrier as Banquo, Erskine Sanford as Duncan, and Roddy McDowall as Malcolm.

Playboy Productions and Columbia Pictures, 1971, directed by Roman Polanski, with Jon Finch as Macbeth, Francesca Annis as Lady Macbeth, Terence Bayler as Macduff, Martin Shaw as Banquo, Nicholas Selby as Duncan, Stephan Chase as Malcolm, Sydney Bromley as the Porter, Andrew Laurence as Lennox, Noel Davis as Seyton, and John Stride as Ross.

A Thames Television production, 1979, based on a Royal Shakespeare stage and then TV production of 1976, directed by Trevor Nunn on stage and Philip Casson on TV, with Ian McKellen as Macbeth, Judi Dench as Lady Macbeth, Bob Peck as Macduff, Griffith Jones as Duncan, Roger Rees as Malcolm, Ian McDiarmid as Ross and the Porter, and John Woodvine as Banquo.

A televised version, directed by Gregory Doran, based on a 2001 production by the Royal Shakespeare Company and shot in 2004 at London's Roundhouse, using edgy fly-on-the-wall documentary technique, starring Antony Sher as Macbeth, Harriet Walter as Lady Macbeth, Richard Armitage as Angus, Joseph O'Conor as Duncan, Ken Bones, and Nigel Cooke, with Noma Dumezweni, Polly Kemp, and Diane Beck as the three Weird Sisters.

A production (2011) directed by Rupert Goold, based on a stage production by the Royal Shakespeare Company, starring Patrick Stewart as Macbeth, Kate Fleetwood

as Lady Macbeth, Scott Handy, Martin Turner, and Oliver Burch.

A 2005 adaptation in the "Shakespeare Re-told" series, by screenwriter Peter Moffat, directed by Mark Brozel and set in a three-star London restaurant, with James McAvoy as Joe Macbeth, Keeley Hawes as his wife and scheming hostess Ella, Vincent Regan as Duncan Docherty the chief restauranteur (cf. Duncan), Joseph Millson as Billy (Banquo), Richard Armitage as Peter Macduff, and the avenging headwaiter Toby Kebbell as Malcolm.

A Toho Company Ltd. production of *Throne of Blood*, 1957, directed by Akira Kurosawa, with Toshiro Mifune as the Macbeth-like Washizu, Isuzu Yamada as the Lady Macbeth-like Asaji, Minoru Chiaki as the Banquo-like Miki, Takamaru Sasaki as the Duncan-like Tsuzuki, Takashi Shimura as the Macduff-like Noriyasu, Akira Kubo as the Fleance-like Yoshiteru, Yoichi Tachikawa as the Malcolm-like Kunimaru, and Chieko Naniwa as the Evil Spirit. An adaptation.

MEASURE FOR MEASURE

A BBC/Time-Life Television production, 1979, directed by Desmond Davis, with Tim Pigott-Smith as Angelo, Kate Nelligan as Isabella, Kenneth Colley as Duke Vincentio, Christopher Strauli as Claudio, John McEnery as Lucio, Frank Middlemass as Pompey, Adrienne Corri as Mistress Overdone, Ellis Jones as Elbow, Alun Armstrong as the Provost, and Kevin Stoney as Escalus.

A contemporary adaptation, 1994–5, made for BBC's new TV Performance series, with considerable use of closed-circuit television, directed by David Thacker, with Tom Wilkinson as a dejected Duke watching (in the opening scene) a TV montage of Vienna in moral decline, Corin Redgrave as Angelo, Juliet Aubrey as Isabella, Ben Miles as Claudio, Rob Edwards as Lucio, Ian Bannen as the Provost, Sue Johnston as Mistress Overdone, and Henry Goodman as Pompey.

A 2006 adaptation, Lucky Strike Productions, in a script by Gian Carlo Rossi and others, set in a modern-day British army barracks, directed by Bob Komar; with Daniel Roberts as Angelo, Josephine Rogers as Isabella, Simon Phillips as the Duke, Kristopher Milnes as the Provost, Dawn Murphy as Escalus, Simon Brandon (Simon Nuckley) as Claudio, Emma Agerwal (Emma Ager) as Mariana, Robert Anderson as Froth, Leah Grayson as Pompey, Luke Leeves as Lucio, Piers Pereira as Elbow, Hanne Steen as Mistress Overdone, Kate Sullington as Juliet, and Roberto Argenti as a priest.

THE MERCHANT OF VENICE

A Precision Video production, directed by John Sichel, based on a stage production directed by Jonathan Miller,

1969 (1973–4 in the U.S.), with Laurence Olivier as Shylock, Joan Plowright as Portia, Jeremy Brett as Bassanio, Anthony Nicholls as Antonio, Michael Jayston as Gratiano, Anna Carteret as Nerissa, Louise Purnell as Jessica, and Malcolm Reid as Lorenzo.

A BBC Masterpiece Theatre television production by Chris Hunt, Andy Picheta, and Richard Price, directed by Trevor Nunn, based on the Royal National Theatre's Cottesloe production of 1999, which was then moved to the Olivier Theatre; then filmed by Chris Hunt and Trevor Nunn in 2001, with Henry Goodman as Shylock, Derbhle Crotty as Portia, Alex Kelly as Nerissa, Alexander Hanson as Bassanio, David Bamber as Antonio, Richard Henders as Gratiano, Peter De Jersey as Salerio, Mark Umbers as Solanio, Jack James as Lorenzo, Gabrielle Jourdan as Jessica, Andrew French as Launcelot Gobbo, Oscar James as Old Gobbo, Chu Omambala as the Prince of Morocco, and Raymon Coulthard as the Prince of Aragon.

An Arclight Films/Sony Picture Classics production, directed by Michael Radford, 2004, with Al Pacino as Shylock, Jeremy Irons as Antonio, Joseph Fiennes as Bassanio, Lynn Collins as Portia, Zuleikha Robinson as Jessica, Charlie Cox as Lorenzo, Mackenzie Crook as Launcelot Gobbo, Allan Corduner as Tubal, Kris Marshall as Gratiano, John Sessions as Salerio, and Gregor Fisher as Solanio.

A 2011 video recording of Rupert Goold's stage production for the Royal Shakespeare Company, set in modern-day Las Vegas, with Patrick Stewart as Shylock, Susannah Fielding as Portia in a Dolly Parton hairdo, Emily Plumtree as Nerissa, Scott Handy as Antonio (a homosexual professional gambler), Richard Riddell as Bassanio, Caroline Martin as Jessica, Daniel Percival as Lorenzo, Jamie Beamish (an Elvis Presley impersonator) as Launcelot Gobbo, Chris Jarman as the Prince of Morocco, Jason Morell as the Prince of Aragon, Howard Charles as Gratiano, Aidan Kelly as Solanio, and Steve Toussaint as Salerio.

A Grandfather Films adaptation, directed by Douglas Morse for the ADC Theatre at the University of Cambridge in 2008, somewhat in the style of Monty Python's Flying Circus, with Thomas Yarrow as Shylock, Lizzy Crarer as Portia, Natalie Kasterton as Nerissa, Edward Martineau as Bassanio, Molly Goyer Gorman as Gratiano, Mark Corbin as Lorenzo, Stephanie Bain as Jessica, James Everest as Launcelot Gobbo, and Dan Martin as the Princes of Morocco and Aragon.

A MIDSUMMER NIGHT'S DREAM

A Warner Brothers production, 1935, directed by Max Reinhardt and William Dieterle, with Mickey Rooney as Puck, James Cagney as Bottom, Ian Hunter as Theseus, Verree Teasdale as Hippolyta, Dick Powell as Lysander,

Ross Alexander as Demetrius, Olivia de Havilland as Hermia, Jean Muir as Helena, Victor Jory as Oberon, Anita Louise as Titania, and Joe E. Brown as Flute/Thisbe.

A Royal Shakespeare Enterprise production, 1969, directed by Peter Hall, with Derek Godfrey as Theseus, Barbara Jefford as Titania, Paul Rogers as Bottom, Helen Mirren as Hermia, Diana Rigg as Helena, Michael Jayston as Demetrius, David Warner as Lysander, Judi Dench as Titania, Ian Richardson as Oberon, Ian Holm as Puck, and Sebastian Shaw as Peter Quince.

A Lindsay Kemp/David Haughton counterculture production, 1984, directed by Celestino Coronado, with Lindsay Kemp as Puck, Jack Birkett (a.k.a. The Incredible Orlando) as Hippolyta and Titania in drag, François Testory as the Changeling Indian boy, and Michael Matou as Theseus and Oberon, and with an explicit rape of the Amazons by Theseus's soldiers. Some stunning effects in a mix of high camp and low burlesque.

A Fox Searchlight Pictures production, 1999, directed by Michael Hoffman, with David Strathairn as Theseus, Sophie Marceau as Hippolyta, Christian Bale as Demetrius, Dominic West as Lysander, Anna Friel as Hermia, Calista Flockhart as Helena, Stanley Tucci as Puck, Kevin Kline as Bottom, Michelle Pfeiffer as Titania, and Rupert Everett as Oberon.

A 1996 production directed by Adrian Noble for the Royal Shakespeare Company, with Alex Jennings as Theseus and Oberon, Lindsay Duncan as Hippolyta and Titania, Desmond Barrit as Bottom, Finbar Lynch as Puck and Philostrate, Emily Raymond as Helena, Monica Dolan as Hermia, Daniel Evans as Lysander, Kevin Doyle as Demetrius, Alfred Burke as Egeus, and Osheen Jones as the changeling boy.

An Oliver Stockman production, directed by Christine Edzard, of *The Children's Midsummer Night's Dream*, 2001, with Dominic Haywood-Benge as Oberon, Rajouana Zalal as Titania, Leane Lyson as Puck, Oliver Szczypka as Bottom, Danny Bishop as Lysander, John Heyfron as Demetrius, Jamie Peachey as Hermia, Jessica Fowler as Helena, David Joyce as Flute, Daniel Rouse as Quince, Hassan Lahrech as Snug, Jack Nottage as Snout, and Mathew Zelic as Starveling.

A 2006 updating in the "Shakespeare Re-told" series, scripted by Peter Bowker and directed by Ed Fraiman, with Bill Paterson and Imelda Staunton as Theo and Polly, hosts of a party in Dream Park to celebrate the engagement of their daughter Hermia (played by Zoë Tapper) to James (William Ash), until Xander (Rupert Evans), Hermia's preferred choice, shows up. With Sharon Small as Titania, Lennie James as Oberon, Dean Lennox Kelly as Puck, and Johnny Vegas as Bottom, a security guard at Dream Park.

A delightful filming of Benjamin Britten's operatic adaptation, with dialogue entirely from Shakespeare's play, available in DVD as conducted by Bernard Haitink and directed by Peter Hall for the Glyndebourne Festival, 1981, and filmed under Peter Hall's direction in 2004. With Ileanna Cotrubas, James Bowman, Curt Appelgren, Felicity Lott, and Isobel Buchanan.

MUCH ADO ABOUT NOTHING

A New York Shakespeare Festival production, filming a stage production, 1973, directed by A. J. Antoon, with Sam Waterston and Kathleen Widdoes as Benedick and Beatrice, Barnard Hughes as Dogberry, Glenn Walken as Claudio, April Shawnhan as Hero, and Douglas Watson as Don Pedro.

A Samuel Goldwyn Company production, 1993, directed by Kenneth Branagh, with Branagh and Emma Thompson as Benedick and Beatrice, Denzel Washington as Don Pedro, Keanu Reeves as Don John, Michael Keaton as Dogberry, Richard Briers as Leonato, Robert Sean Leonard as Claudio, Kate Beckinsale as Hero, and Imelda Staunton as Margaret.

A 2005 modern adaptation, in the "Shakespeare Retold" series, directed by Brian Percival, set in a television news studio, with Sarah Parish and Damian Lewis as Beatrice and Benedick, and with Billie Piper as Hero, Tom Ellis as Claude (Claudio), Martin Jarvis as Leonard (Leonardo), and Derek Riddell as Don (Don John). Adapted by screenwriter David Nicholls.

OTHELLO

Film Marceau/Mercury Productions, 1952, directed by Orson Welles, with Welles as Othello, Suzanne Cloutier as Desdemona, Michael MacLiammóir as Iago, Michael Lawrence as Cassio, Fay Compton as Emilia, Robert Coote as Roderigo, Hilton Edwards as Brabantio, Nicholas Bruce as Lodovico, Doris Dowling as Bianca, Joseph Cotten as a Senator, and Joan Fontaine as a Page.

A Mosfilm production, in Russian, with subtitles, 1955, directed by Sergei Yutkevich, with Sergei Bondarchuk as Othello, Irina Skobtseva as Desdemona, Andrei Popov as Iago, Vladimir Soshalsky as Cassio, A. Maximova as Emilia, E. Vesnik as Roderigo, and E. Teterin as Brabantio.

A production by Anthony Havelock-Allan and John Brabourne, 1965, directed by Stuart Burge, based on the National Theatre's successful stage production of 1964 directed by John Dexter, with Laurence Olivier as Othello in blackface, Maggie Smith as Desdemona, Frank Finlay as Iago, Derek Jacobi as Cassio, Joyce Redman as Emilia, Robert Lang as Roderigo, Anthony Nicholls as Brabantio, and Sheila Reid as Bianca.

Othello Productions, Inc., 1988, adapted from a stage production at Market Place Theatre, Johannesburg, 1987, directed by Janet Suzman, with John Kani as Othello, Joanna Weinberg as Desdemona, Richard

Haddon Haines as Iago, Stuart Brown as Brabantio, Dorothy Gould as Emilia, Neil McCarthy as Cassio, Frantz Dobrowsky as Roderigo, and Gaynor Young as Bianca.

A production by Greg Smith, 1990, directed by Trevor Nunn, with Willard White as Othello, Imogen Stubbs as Desdemona, Ian McKellen as Iago, Zoë Wanamaker as Emilia, Sean Baker as Cassio, Michael Grandage as Roderigo, and Clive Swift as Brabantio, and Marsha Hunt as Bianca.

A Castle Rock production, 1995, directed by Oliver Parker, with Laurence Fishburne as Othello, Irène Jacob as Desdemona, Kenneth Branagh as Iago, Nathaniel Parker as Cassio, Anne Patrick as Emilia, Michael Maloney as Roderigo, and Pierre Vaneck as Brabantio.

A Merchant-Ivory production, 1965, of *Shakespeare Wallah*, directed by James Ivory, with Felicity Kendal. An adaptation, with scenes from *Othello*.

A production by Michael J. Levy and William Shively of *O*, 2001, with Mekhi Phifer as the Othello-like Odin James, Julia Stiles as the Desdemona-like Desi Brable, and Josh Hartnett as the Iago-like Hugo Goulding. An adaptation.

A 2001 British television adaptation, scripted by Andrew Davies (not using the language of Shakespeare's text) and directed by Geoffrey Sax, with Eamonn Walker as a black police officer in modern-day London named John Othello, Christopher Eccleston as Ben Jago, jealous of Othello's promotion to commissioner of his precinct, Keeley Hawes as Dessie Brabant (Desdemona), Richard Coyle as Michael Cass (Cassio), Rachael Stirling as Lulu (Emilia), Joss Ackland as James Brabant (Brabantio), and Bill Paterson as the London Metropolitan Police Commissioner Sinclair Carver (cf. the Duke of Venice).

A London Globe Theatre production, recorded for television in 2007 as directed by Wilson Milam, with Eamonn Walker as Othello, Tim McInnerny as Iago, Zoë Tapper as Desdemona, Sam Crane as Roderigo, Nick Barber as Cassio, Lorraine Burroughs as Emilia, Zawe Ashton as Bianca, John Stahl as Brabantio, Jonathan Newth as the Duke of Venice, Michael O'Hagan as Gratiano, Nigel Hastings as Montano, and Dickon Tyrrell as Lodovico.

A Canadian Broadcasting Corporation (CBC) television movie of 2008, directed by Zaib Shaikh, with Carlo Rota as Othello, Christine Horne as Desdemona, Matthew Deslippe as Iago, Graham Abbey as Cassio, Emma Campbell as Emilia, Ryan Hollyman as Roderigo, Peter Donaldson as Brabantio, Jonathan Goad as Montano, Nazneen Contractor as Bianca, and John Gilbert as the Duke of Venice.

A film of Verdi's opera, *Otello*, directed by Franco Zeffirelli, 1986, with Placido Domingo as Otello and Justino Diaz as Iago.

RICHARD II

A BBC/Time-Life Television production, 1978–9, directed by David Giles, with Derek Jacobi as King Richard, Janet Maw as the Queen, Jon Finch as Bolingbroke, John Gielgud as John of Gaunt, Charles Gray as the Duke of York, David Swift as Northumberland, Wendy Hiller as the Duchess of York, and Mary Morris as the Duchess of Gloucester.

A BBC/The Globe Theatre production, 2003, in an all-male cast, directed by Tim Carroll, with Mark Rylance as King Richard, Liam Brennan as Bolingbroke, John McEnery as John of Gaunt, Michael Brown as the Queen, Terence McGinty as Mowbray, Chu Omambala as Aumerle, William Osbourne as the Duchess of Gloucester, and Bill Stewart as the Duke of York.

RICHARD III

A London Films Productions, 1955, directed by Laurence Olivier, with Olivier as Richard, Claire Bloom as the Lady Anne, Cedric Hardwicke as King Edward IV, Ralph Richardson as the Duke of Buckingham, John Gielgud as the Duke of Clarence, Alec Clunes as Lord Hastings, Norman Wooland as Catesby, Esmond Knight as Ratcliffe, Mary Kerridge as Queen Elizabeth, Helen Haye as the Duchess of York, Pamela Brown as Jane Shore, Laurence Naismith as Lord Stanley, and Stanley Baker as the Earl of Richmond.

A Bayly-Paré Productions/United Artists production, 1995–6, directed by Richard Loncraine, with Ian McKellen as Richard, Kristin Scott Thomas as the Lady Anne, Jim Broadbent as the Duke of Buckingham, Nigel Hawthorne as the Duke of Clarence, John Wood as King Edward IV, Jim Carter as Hastings, Tim McInnerny as Catesby, Annette Bening as Queen Elizabeth, Maggie Smith as the Duchess of York, Robert Downey Jr. as Lord Rivers, Adrian Dunbar as Tyrell, Bill Patterson as Ratcliffe, Edward Harwicke as Stanley, Kate Stevenson-Payne as Princess Elizabeth of York, and Dominic West as the Earl of Richmond.

A Twentieth Century Fox production, *Looking for Richard*, 1996, directed by Al Pacino. A documentary about Pacino's stage interpretation of Richard. With Pacino as Richard, Winona Ryder as the Lady Anne, Kevin Spacey as the Duke of Buckingham, Alec Baldwin as Clarence, and Aidan Quinn as the Earl of Richmond.

ROMEO AND JULIET

Verona Productions, 1954, directed by Renato Castallani, with John Gielgud as Chorus, Laurence Harvey and Susan Shentall as Romeo and Juliet, Ubaldo Zollo as Mercutio, Enzo Fiermonte as Tybalt, Flora Robson as the Nurse, Norman Wooland as Paris, Mervyn Johns as Friar Laurence, Bill Travers as Benvolio, Sebastian Cabot as Capulet, and Lydia Sherwood as Capulet's wife.

A Paramount production, 1968, directed by Franco Zeffirelli, with Leonard Whiting and Olivia Hussy as Romeo and Juliet, Michael York as Tybalt, John McEnery as Mercutio, Pat Heywood as the Nurse, Milo O'Shea as Friar Laurence, Bruce Robinson as Benvolio, Paul Hardwick as Capulet, Natasha Parry as Capulet's wife, Roberto Bisacco as Count Paris, and Robert Stephens as Prince Escalus.

A Twentieth Century Fox production, 1996, *Romeo + Juliet*, directed by Baz Luhrmann, with Leonardo DiCaprio and Claire Danes as Romeo and Juliet, Harold Perrineau as Mercutio, Miriam Margolyes as the Nurse, Pete Postlethwaite as Friar Laurence, John Leguizamo as Tybalt, Jesse Bradford as Benvolio, Paul Sorvino as Fulgencio Capulet, Diane Venora as Gloria Capulet, Paul Rudd as Dave Paris, Brian Dennehy as Ted Montague, and Vondie Curtis-Hall as the Prince.

A film version, based on a popular London Globe Theatre production directed by Dominic Dromgoole, 2009, with Adetomiwa Edun as Romeo, Ellie Kendrick as Juliet, Philip Cumbus as Mercutio, Jack Farthing as Benvolio, Ukweli Roach as Tybalt, Rawiri Paratene as Friar Laurence, Tom Stuart as Count Paris, Michael O'Hagan as Montague, Holly Atkins as Montague's wife, Ian Redford as Capulet, Miranda Foster as Capulet's wife, Penny Layden as the Nurse, Graham Vick as Abraham and the Apothecary, and Andrew Vincent as the Prince.

A United Artists production of *West Side Story*, 1961, directed by Jerome Robbins and Robert Wise, with Richard Beymer as Tony, Natalie Wood as Maria, and Rita Moreno as Anita. An adaptation.

A production by David Parfitt, Marc Norman, and others, of *Shakespeare in Love*, 1998, directed by John Madden, with Joseph Fiennes as Shakespeare/Romeo, Gwyneth Paltrow as Viola de Lesseps/Thomas Kent/Juliet, Colin Firth as Lord Wessex, Imelda Staunton as the Nurse, Ben Affleck as Ned Alleyn, Geoffrey Rush as Philip Henslowe, Rupert Everett as Christopher Marlowe, Tom Wilkinson as Fennyman, Martin Clunes as Richard Burbage, and Judi Dench as Queen Elizabeth I. An adaptation by Tom Stoppard containing scenes from *Romeo and Juliet*.

THE TAMING OF THE SHREW

A United Artists/Pickford Corporation production, 1929, directed by Sam Taylor, with Douglas Fairbanks Sr. and Mary Pickford as Petruchio and Kate, Edwin Maxwell as Baptista Minola, Dorothy Jordan as Bianca, Geoffrey Wardell as Hortensio, Joseph Cawthorn as Gremio, and Clyde Cook as Grumio.

A Royal Films International production, 1966–7, directed by Franco Zeffirelli, with Richard Burton and Elizabeth Taylor as Petruchio and Kate, Natasha Pyne as

Bianca, Michael Hordern as Baptista Minola, Michael York as Lucentio, Alfred Lynch as Tranio, Victor Spinetti as Hortensio, Alan Webb as Gremio, Cyril Cusack as Grumio, and Bice Valori as the Widow.

A NET/American Conservatory Theatre production, 1976, in commedia dell'arte style, directed by William Ball and Kirk Browning, with Marc Singer and Fredi Olster as Petruchio and Kate, Stephen St. Paul as Lucentio, Raye Birk as Gremio, Ronald Boussom as Grumio, Rick Hamilton as Tranio, William Paterson as Baptista Minola, and Sandra Shotwell as Bianca.

Bard Productions, 1983, directed by John Allison, with Franklyn Seales and Karen Austin as Petruchio and Kate, Larry Drake as Baptista Minola, Bruce Davison as Tranio, Jeremy Lawrence as Grumio, Kay E. Kuter as Gremio, Charles Berendt as Hortensio, and Kathryn Jonson as Bianca.

A Metro-Goldwyn-Mayer production of *Kiss Me, Kate,* 1953, directed by George Sidney, with Howard Keel as Fred Graham/Petruchio, Kathryn Grayson as Lili Vanessi/Kate, Ann Miller as Lois Lane/Bianca, Tommy Rall as Bill Calhoun/Lucentio, Ron Randell as Cole Porter, Keenan Wynn as Lippy, and James Whitmore as Slug. An adaptation.

A Jaret Entertainment production of *10 Things I Hate About You,* 1999, directed by Gil Junger, with Julia Stiles as Katharina 'Kat' Stratford, Heath Ledger as the Petruchio-like Patrick Verona, Larisa Oleynik as Bianca Stratford, Larry Miller as the girls' father (Dr. Walter Stratford), David Krumholtz as the Tranio-like Michael Eckman, Joseph Gordon-Leavitt as the Lucentio-like Cameron James, and Andrew Keegan as the Hortensio- and Grumio-like Joey Donner. An adaptation.

A 2005 modern adaptation, in the "Shakespeare Retold" series, directed by David Richard, with Shirley Henderson as Katharine Minola, member of Parliament and aspiring prime minister, Jaime Murray as her sister and supermodel Bianca, Rufus Sewell as a spendthrift Petruchio, Stephen Tompkinson as Harry (cf. Hortensio), Twiggy as Kate and Bianca's mother (not in Shakespeare's play), and David Mitchell as Kate's hapless secretary, Tim. Adapted by screenwriter Sally Wainwright.

THE TEMPEST

A BBC/Time-Life Television production, 1981, directed by John Gorrie, with Michael Hordern as Prospero, Pippa Guard as Miranda, David Dixon as Ariel, Christopher Guard as Ferdinand, Derek Godfrey as Antonio, David Waller as Alonso, Warren Clarke as Caliban, Nigel Hawthorne as Stephano, and Andrew Sachs as Trinculo. Reviewers were generally disappointed; it is listed here in the absence of any other reliable "straight" interpretation of the play on film.

A Boyd's Company production, 1979–80, directed by Derek Jarman, with Heathcote Williams as Prospero, Toyah Willcox as Miranda, David Meyer as Ferdinand, Karl Johnson as Ariel, Jack Birkett (a.k.a. the Incredible Orlando) as Caliban, Christopher Biggins as Stephano, Peter Turner as Trinculo, Peter Bull as Alonso, Richard Warwick as Antonio, Neil Cunningham as Sebastian, Ken Campbell as Gonzalo, and Elisabeth Welch as a goddess singing "Stormy Weather." A starkly transgressive and postmodern film that some viewers find offensive, but compelling.

A production by Kees Kasander, 1991, *Prospero's Books,* directed by Peter Greenaway, in which John Gielgud as Prospero speaks most of the lines. With Isabelle Pasco as Miranda, Mark Rylance as Ferdinand, Michael Clark as Caliban, and several figures representing Ariel. Strange but fascinating.

A film adaptation of 2010, shot on the Hawaiian island of Lanai, directed by Julie Taymor, starring Helen Mirren as Prospera, the Duchess of Milan, with Felicity Jones as Miranda, Reeve Carney as Ferdinand, Djimon Hounsou as Caliban, Ben Whishaw as Ariel, Russell Brand as Trinculo, Alfred Molina as Stephano, Chris Cooper as Antonio, Alan Cumming as Sebastian, David Strathairn as Alonso, Tom Conti as Gonzalo, Jude Akuwudike as the Boatswain, and David Scott Klein as Prospera's husband.

A production by Nicholas Nayfack, 1956, of *Forbidden Planet,* an adaptation of *The Tempest* as a journey into space, directed by Fred McLeod Wilcox, with Walter Pidgeon as the Prospero-like Doctor Morbius, Anne Francis as the Miranda-like Altaira, Leslie Nielsen as the Ferdinand-like Commander J. J. Adams, and Robby the Robot as the Ariel-like servant to Doctor Morbius.

A Columbia Pictures production, 1982, an adaptation in a twentieth-century setting, with John Cassavetes as the Prospero-like Philip, Molly Ringwald as Miranda, Raul Julia as Kalianos, and Susan Sarandon as the Ariel-like Aretha.

TWELFTH NIGHT

An Incorporated Television Company production, 1970, directed by John Sichel, with Joan Plowright as Viola, Gary Raymond as Orsino, Adrienne Corri as Olivia, Alec Guinness as Malvolio, Tommy Steele as Feste, John Moffat as Sir Andrew Aguecheek, Ralph Richardson as Sir Toby Belch, and Sheila Reid as Maria.

A 1988 production directed by Kenneth Branagh for the Renaissance Theatre Company, with Richard Briers as Malvolio, Caroline Langrishe as Olivia, Frances Barber as Viola, Anton Lesser as Feste, Christopher Ravenscroft as Orsino, James Saxon as Sir Toby, James Simmons as Sir Andrew, Christopher Hollis as Sebastian and

Curio, Tim Barker as Antonio and the Sea Captain, Abigail McKern as Maria, and Shaun Prendergast as Fabian. With original music by Paul McCartney and Pat Doyle.

A Renaissance Films/Summit Entertainment production, 1996, directed by Trevor Nunn, with Imogen Stubbs as Viola, Helena Bonham Carter as Olivia, Toby Stephens as Orsino, Ben Kingsley as Feste, Nigel Hawthorne as Malvolio, Imelda Staunton as Maria, Stephen Mackintosh as Sebastian, Mel Smith as Sir Toby Belch, Richard E. Grant as Sir Andrew Aguecheek, and Peter Gunn as Fabian.

THE WINTER'S TALE

A BBC/Time-Life Television production, 1980–1, directed by Jane Howell, with Jeremy Kemp as Leontes,

Anna Calder-Marshall as Hermione, Robert Stephens as Polixenes, Debbie Farrington as Perdita, Robin Kermode as Florizel, David Burke as Camillo, Margaret Tyzack as Paulina, Cyril Luckham as Antigonus, Rikki Fulton as Autolycus, and Paul Jesson as the Young Shepherd or Clown.

A version filmed for TV and based on the Royal Shakespeare Company's 1999 production at the Barbican Theatre, London, directed by Robin Lough and Gregory Doran, with Antony Sher as Leontes, Alexandra Gilbreath as Hermione, Emily Bruni as Perdita, Ryan McCluskey as Florizel, Estelle Kohler as Paulina, Jeffrey Wickham as Antigonus, Ken Bones as Polixenes, Geoffrey Freshwater as Camillo, Ian Hughes as Autolycus, James Hayes as the Old Shepherd, and Christopher Brand as the Young Shepherd.

THE ROYAL GENEALOGY OF ENGLAND, 1154–1625

THE PLANTAGENET KINGS

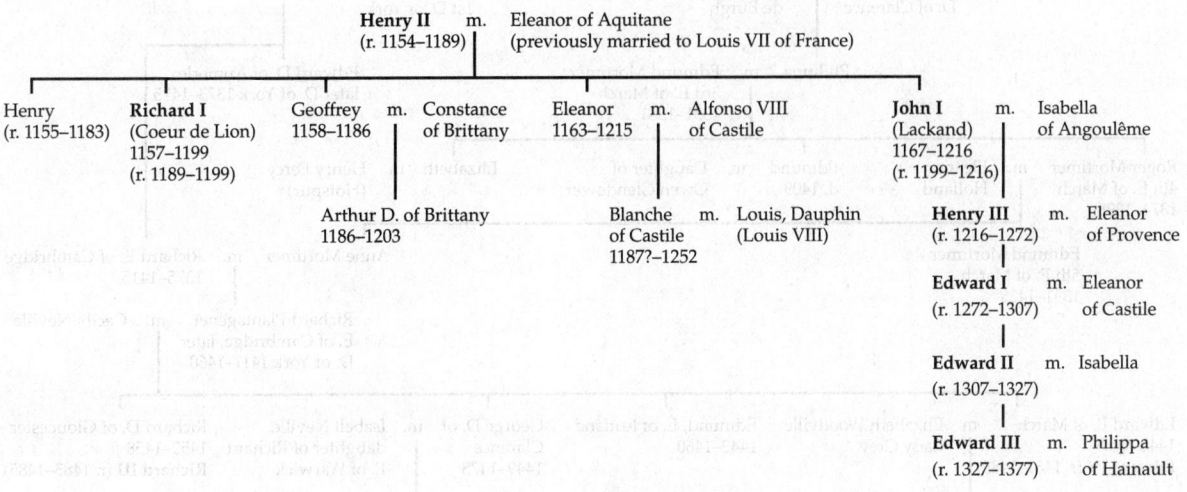

THE LANCASTRIAN KINGS

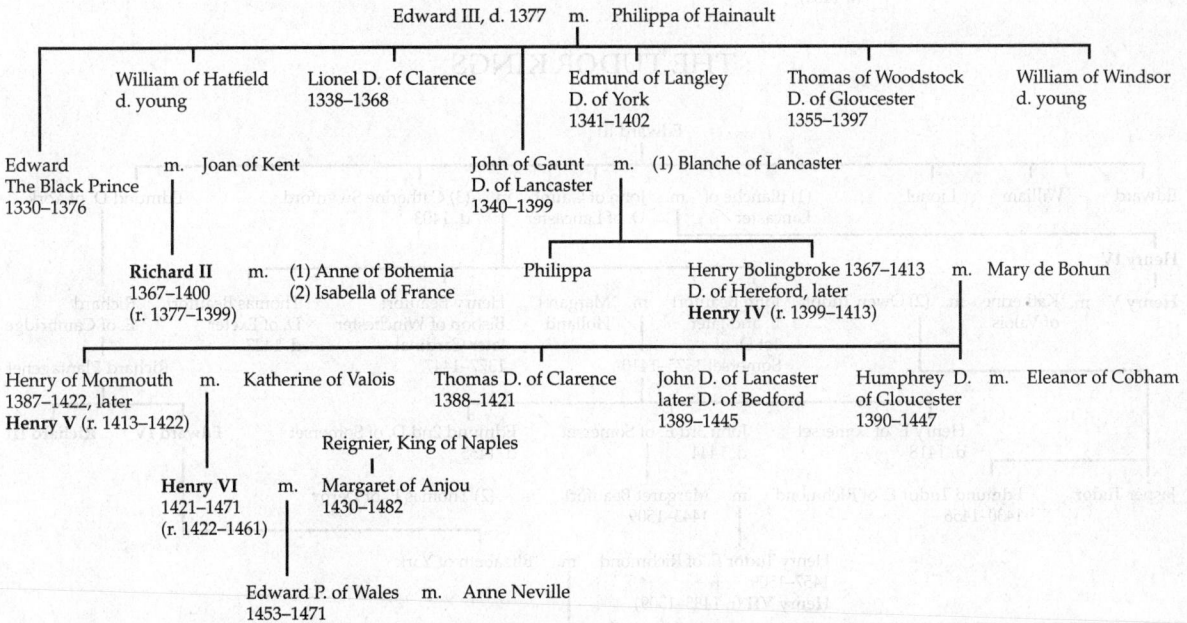

In these diagrams, reigning dates are given in parentheses; other dates indicate life span. Abbreviations: P., Prince, D., Duke, E., Earl; b., born, d., died, m., married, r., reigned. English monarchs are printed in boldface type. The spatial arrangement of names in a family indicates order of birth.

In 1 Henry IV, Shakespeare confuses the Edmund Mortimer who married Glendower's daughter and died in 1409 with his nephew Edmund, fifth Earl of March, who asserted a claim to the English throne (see "The Yorkist Kings"). Shakespeare also refers to Henry Percy's (Hotspur's) wife as "Kate," though historically she was named Elizabeth.

Catherine Swynford, third wife of John of Gaunt (see "The Tudor Kings"), bore him children before their eventual marriage. These Beauforts, although later legitimized, were specifically barred from any claim to the English throne.

THE YORKIST KINGS

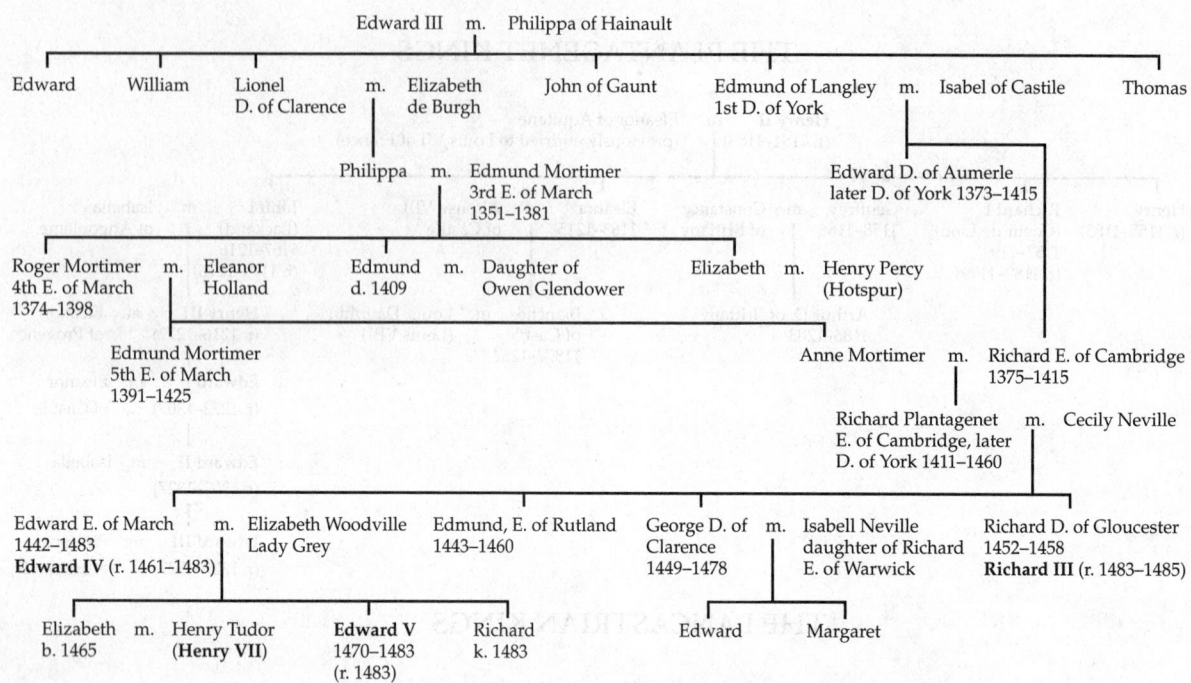

Edward III m. Philippa of Hainault

Edward   William   Lionel   m. Elizabeth   John of Gaunt   Edmund of Langley m. Isabel of Castile   Thomas
D. of Clarence   de Burgh   1st D. of York

Philippa m. Edmund Mortimer   Edward D. of Aumerle
3rd E. of March   later D. of York 1373–1415
1351–1381

Roger Mortimer m. Eleanor   Edmund m. Daughter of   Elizabeth m. Henry Percy
4th E. of March   Holland   d. 1409   Owen Glendower   (Hotspur)
1374–1398

Edmund Mortimer   Anne Mortimer m. Richard E. of Cambridge
5th E. of March   1375–1415
1391–1425

Richard Plantagenet m. Cecily Neville
E. of Cambridge, later
D. of York 1411–1460

Edward E. of March m. Elizabeth Woodville   Edmund, E. of Rutland   George D. of m. Isabell Neville   Richard D. of Gloucester
1442–1483   Lady Grey   1443–1460   Clarence   daughter of Richard   1452–1458
Edward IV (r. 1461–1483)   1449–1478   E. of Warwick   **Richard III** (r. 1483–1485)

Elizabeth m. Henry Tudor   **Edward V**   Richard   Edward   Margaret
b. 1465   (**Henry VII**)   1470–1483   k. 1483
(r. 1483)

THE TUDOR KINGS

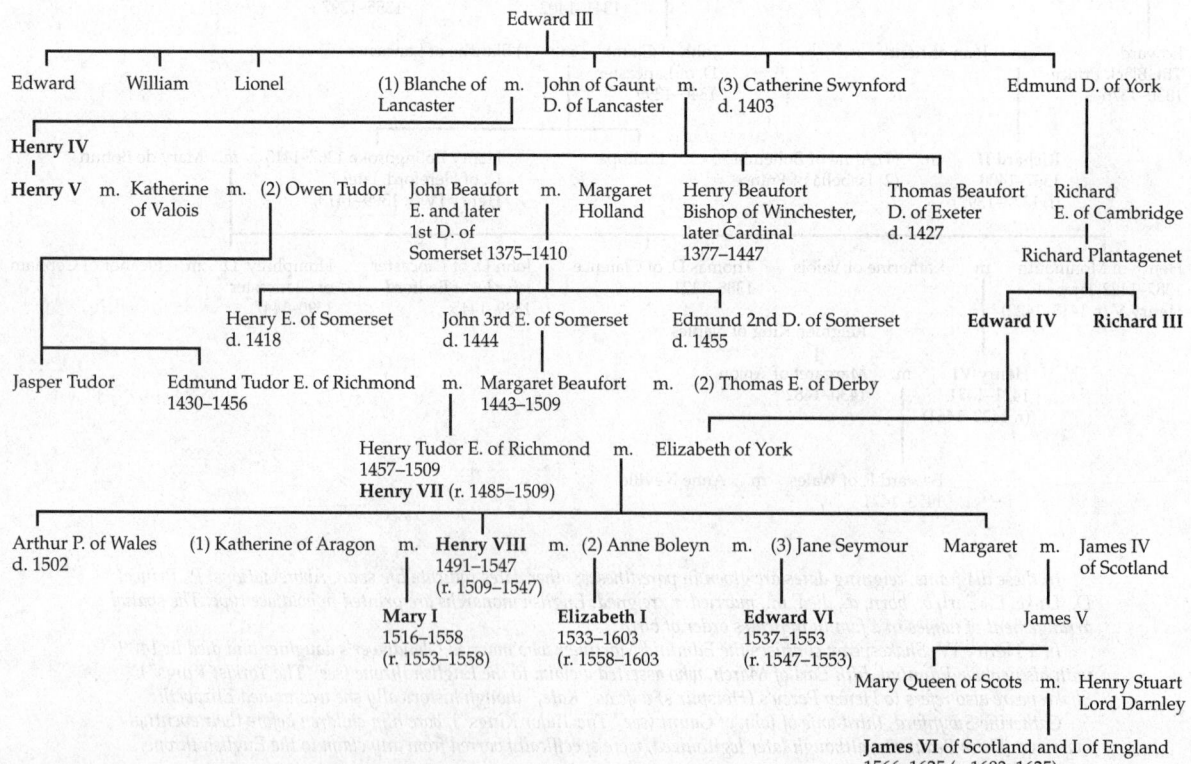

Edward III

Edward   William   Lionel   (1) Blanche of m. John of Gaunt m. (3) Catherine Swynford   Edmund D. of York
Lancaster   D. of Lancaster   d. 1403

Henry IV

Henry V m. Katherine m. (2) Owen Tudor   John Beaufort m. Margaret   Henry Beaufort   Thomas Beaufort   Richard
of Valois   E. and later   Holland   Bishop of Winchester,   D. of Exeter   E. of Cambridge
1st D. of   later Cardinal   d. 1427
Somerset 1375–1410   1377–1447   Richard Plantagenet

Henry E. of Somerset   John 3rd E. of Somerset   Edmund 2nd D. of Somerset   **Edward IV**   **Richard III**
d. 1418   d. 1444   d. 1455

Jasper Tudor   Edmund Tudor E. of Richmond m. Margaret Beaufort m. (2) Thomas E. of Derby
1430–1456   1443–1509

Henry Tudor E. of Richmond m. Elizabeth of York
1457–1509
Henry VII (r. 1485–1509)

Arthur P. of Wales   (1) Katherine of Aragon m. **Henry VIII** m. (2) Anne Boleyn m. (3) Jane Seymour   Margaret m. James IV
d. 1502   1491–1547   of Scotland
(r. 1509–1547)

Mary I   **Elizabeth I**   **Edward VI**   James V
1516–1558   1533–1603   1537–1553
(r. 1553–1558)   (r. 1558–1603)   (r. 1547–1553)

Mary Queen of Scots m. Henry Stuart
Lord Darnley

James VI of Scotland and I of England
1566–1625 (r. 1603–1625)

Maps

A map of London (below) of Shakespeare's time shows the prominent landmarks, as well as the theaters and other places where plays were performed.

A map of England and western France (opposite) gives the locations for the scenes of Shakespeare's history plays.

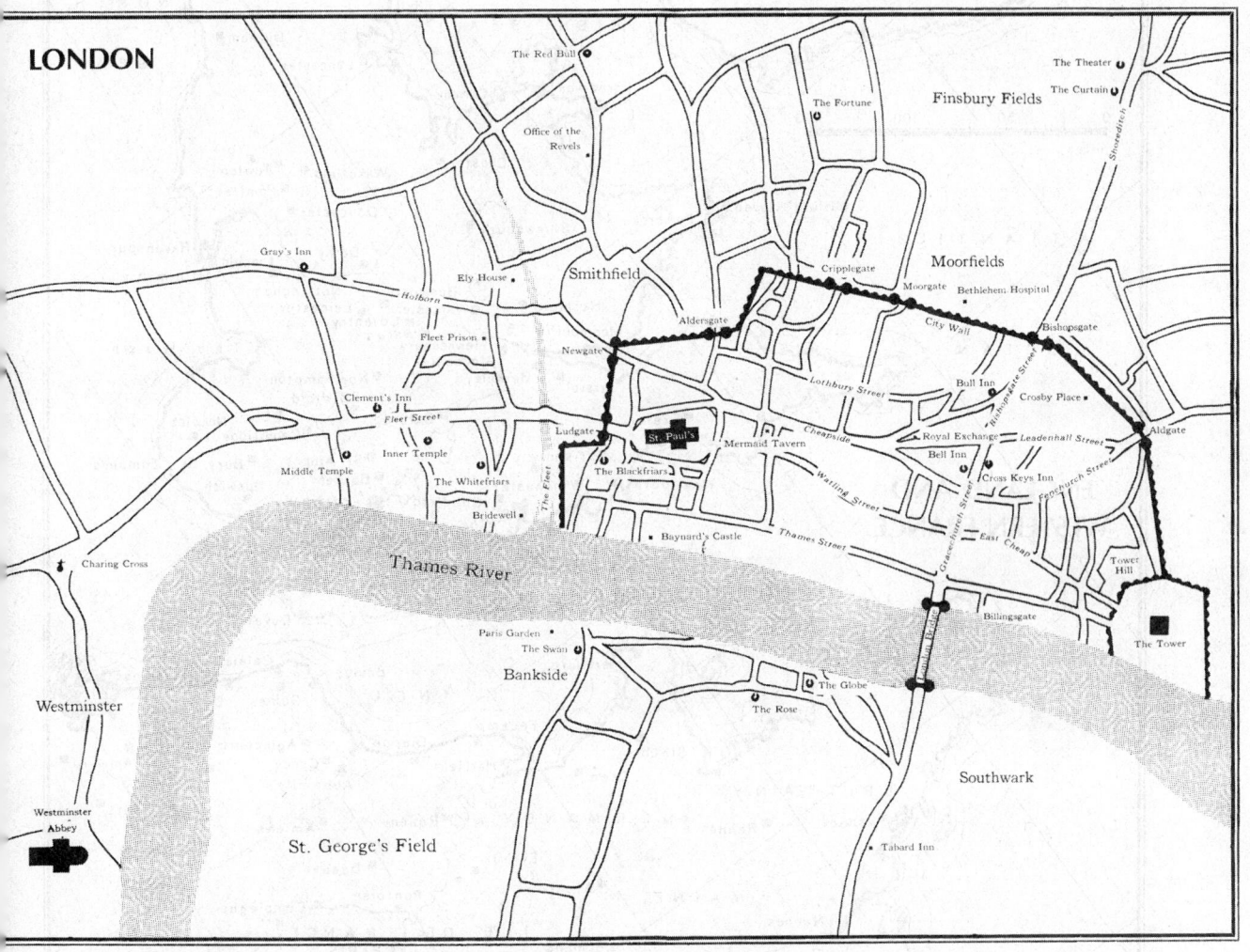

LONDON

The Red Bull
The Theater
The Curtain
The Fortune
Office of the Revels
Finsbury Fields
Shoreditch
Gray's Inn
Cripplegate
Moorfields
Moorgate
Bethlehem Hospital
Ely House
Smithfield
Aldersgate
City Wall
Bishopsgate
Holborn
Fleet Prison
Newgate
Bull Inn
Crosby Place
Clement's Inn
Lothbury Street
Bishopsgate Street
Fleet Street
Ludgate
St. Paul's
Mermaid Tavern
Cheapside
Royal Exchange
Leadenhall Street
Aldgate
Inner Temple
Middle Temple
The Whitefriars
The Blackfriars
Watling Street
Bell Inn
Cross Keys Inn
Fenchurch Street
The Fleet
Bridewell
Baynard's Castle
Thames Street
East Cheap
Tower Hill
Charing Cross
Billingsgate
The Tower
Paris Garden
The Swan
Bankside
The Globe
The Rose
Westminster
Southwark
Westminster Abbey
St. George's Field
Tabard Inn
Thames River
Gracechurch Street
London Bridge

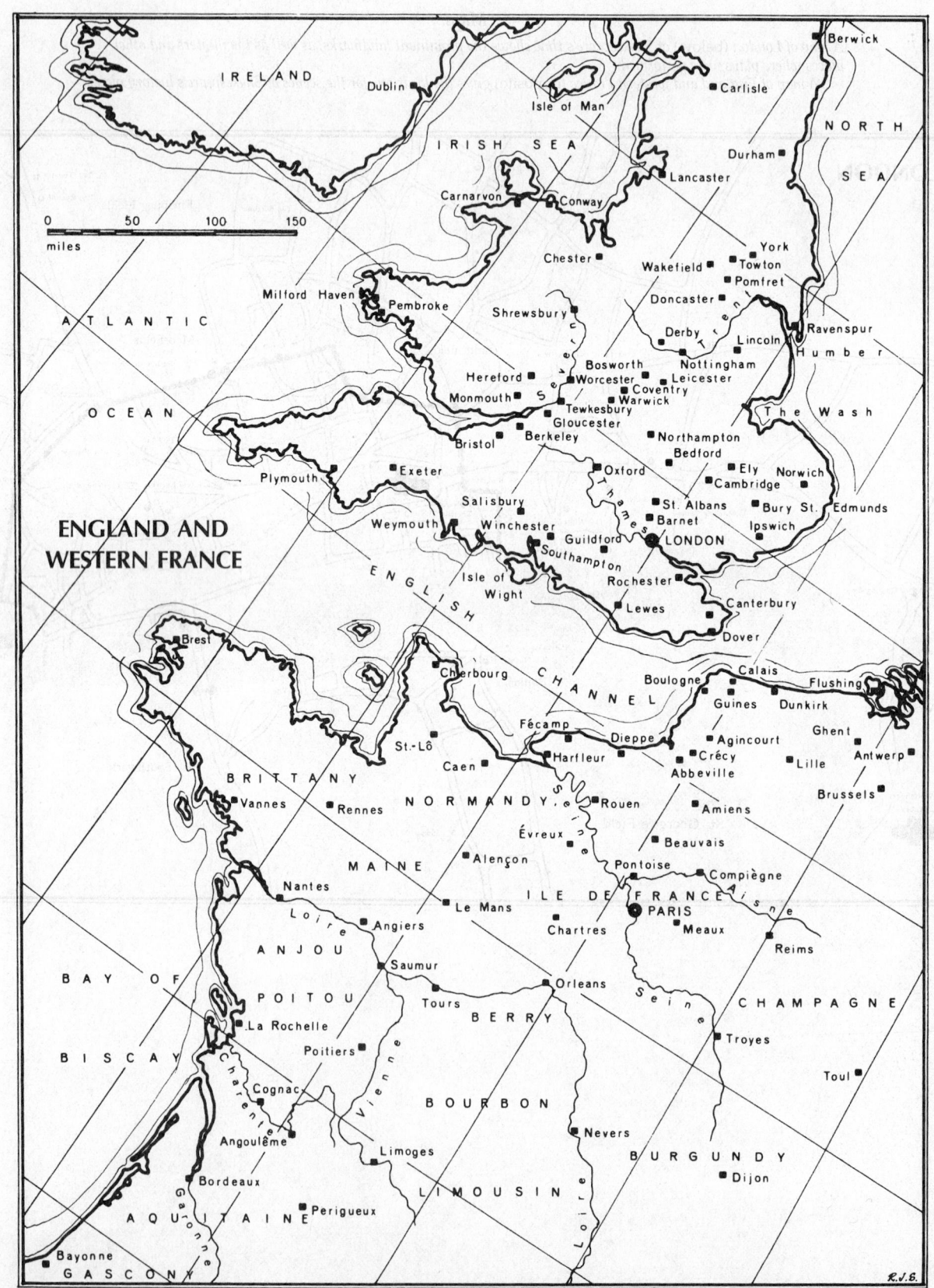

ENGLAND AND WESTERN FRANCE

IRELAND

Dublin

Isle of Man

IRISH SEA

Carlisle
Berwick

NORTH SEA

Durham
Lancaster

Carnarvon
Conway

York
Chester
Wakefield
Towton
Pomfret
Doncaster
Shrewsbury
Derby
Lincoln
Ravenspur
Milford Haven
Pembroke
Humber
Bosworth
Nottingham
Hereford
Worcester
Leicester
Coventry
Monmouth
Warwick
The Wash
Tewkesbury
Gloucester
Northampton
Bristol
Berkeley
Bedford
Ely
Norwich
Exeter
Oxford
Cambridge
Plymouth
Bury St. Edmunds
Salisbury
St. Albans
Weymouth
Winchester
Barnet
Ipswich
Guildford
LONDON
Southampton
Rochester
Canterbury
Isle of Wight
Lewes
Dover

ATLANTIC OCEAN

ENGLISH CHANNEL

Brest
Cherbourg
Boulogne
Calais
Flushing
Guines
Dunkirk
Fécamp
Ghent
Antwerp
St.-Lô
Dieppe
Agincourt
Harfleur
Crécy
Lille
Caen
Abbeville
Brussels
BRITTANY
NORMANDY
Vannes
Rouen
Rennes
Amiens
MAINE
Évreux
Beauvais
Alençon
Pontoise
Compiègne
Nantes
ILE DE FRANCE
PARIS
Le Mans
Aisne
Angiers
Chartres
Meaux
Reims
ANJOU
Saumur
Orleans
POITOU
Tours
BERRY
CHAMPAGNE
La Rochelle
Troyes
Poitiers
Toul
BAY OF BISCAY
Cognac
BOURBON
Angoulême
Nevers
Limoges
BURGUNDY
Bordeaux
Dijon
LIMOUSIN
AQUITAINE
Bayonne
Perigueux
GASCONY

Loire
Charente
Vienne
Garonne
Seine
Thames
Trent
Severn

0   50   100   150
miles

R.J.S.

Bibliography

Abbreviations Used

English Literary History	ELH
Publications of the Modern Language Association of America	PMLA
Shakespeare Quarterly	SQ
Shakespeare Studies	ShakS
Shakespeare Survey	ShS

Works of Reference

Abbott, E. A. *A Shakespearian Grammar*. New ed., London, 1870.

Allen, Michael J. B., and Kenneth Muir, eds. *Shakespeare's Plays in Quarto*. Berkeley, 1981.

Bentley, G. E. *The Jacobean and Caroline Stage*. 7 vols. Oxford, 1941–1968.

Berger, Thomas L., William C. Bradford, and Sidney L. Sondergard, eds. *An Index of Characters in Early Modern English Drama: Printed Plays, 1500–1660*. Cambridge, Eng., 1998.

Bergeron, David M. *Shakespeare: A Study and Research Guide*. New York, 1975; 2nd ed., rev. David Bergeron and Geraldo de Sousa. Lawrence, Kans., 1987.

Bullough, Geoffrey, ed. *Narrative and Dramatic Sources of Shakespeare*. 8 vols. London, 1957–1975.

Chambers, E. K. *The Elizabethan Stage*. 4 vols. Oxford, 1923; rev., 1945.

———. *The Mediaeval Stage*. 2 vols. Oxford, 1903.

———. *William Shakespeare: A Study of Facts and Problems*. 2 vols. Oxford, 1930.

Dent, R. W. *Shakespeare's Proverbial Language: An Index*. Berkeley, 1981.

Edelman, Charles. *Shakespeare's Military Language: A Dictionary*. London and New Brunswick, 2000.

Garland Shakespeare Bibliographies, gen. ed. William Godshalk. Published in separate volumes for various plays, at varying dates. Garland: New York.

Gillespie, Stuart. *Shakespeare's Books: A Dictionary of Shakespeare's Resources*. London, 2001.

Greg, W. W. *A Bibliography of the English Printed Drama to the Restoration*. 4 vols. London, 1939–1959.

———, ed. *Shakespeare Quarto Facsimiles*. London, 1939–. (An incomplete set; Greg's work has been supplemented by Charlton Hinman.)

Harbage, Alfred. *Annals of English Drama, 975–1700*. Rev. S. Schoenbaum. Philadelphia, 1964; 3rd ed., Sylvia Stoler Wagonheim, 1989.

Hinman, Charlton, ed. *The Norton Facsimile: The First Folio of Shakespeare*. New York, 1968.

Hosley, Richard, ed. *Shakespeare's Holinshed*. New York, 1968.

Kökeritz, Helge. *Shakespeare's Names*. New Haven, 1959.

———. *Shakespeare's Pronunciation*. New Haven, 1953.

Long, John. *Shakespeare's Use of Music: Comedies*. Gainesville, Fla., 1955. *Final Comedies*, 1961; *Histories and Tragedies*, 1971.

McDonald, Russ. *The Bedford Companion to Shakespeare: An Introduction with Documents*. Boston, 1996; 2nd ed., 2001.

McManaway, James G., and Jeanne Addison Roberts, compilers. *A Selective Bibliography of Shakespeare*. Charlottesville, Va., 1975.

Muir, Kenneth. *Shakespeare's Sources*. 2 vols. London, 1957.

———, and S. Schoenbaum, eds. *A New Companion to Shakespeare Studies*. London and New York, 1971.

Munro, John, ed. *The Shakespeare Allusion Book*. 2 vols. London and New York, 1909; reissued 1932.

Naylor, Edward W. *Shakespeare and Music*. New ed., London, 1931.

Noble, Richmond. *Shakespeare's Biblical Knowledge and Use of the Book of Common Prayer*. London, 1935.

———. *Shakespeare's Use of Song*. London, 1923.

Onions, C. T. *A Shakespeare Glossary*. Rev. and enlgd. R. D. Eagleson. Oxford, 1986.

Pegasus Shakespeare Bibliographies. Annotated bibliographies of Shakespeare studies in a 12-volume series, gen. ed. Richard L. Nochimson, including *Love's Labor's Lost, A Midsummer Night's Dream*, and *The Merchant of Venice* (Clifford Chalmers Huffman), *Richard II, Henry IV, I and II*, and *Henry V* (Joseph Candido), *Hamlet* (Michael E. Mooney), *The Rape of Lucrece, Titus Andronicus, Julius Caesar, Antony and Cleopatra*, and *Coriolanus* (Clifford Chalmers Huffman and John W. Velz), *King Lear* and *Macbeth* (Rebecca W. Bushnell), and *Shakespeare and the Renaissance Stage to 1616* and *Shakespearean Stage History 1616 to 1998* (Hugh Macrae Richmond). Binghamton, N.Y., 1995, and Asheville, N.C., 1996—.

Publications of the Modern Language Association of America (PMLA). Annual Bibliography.

Rothwell, Kenneth S., and Annabelle Henkin Melzer. *Shakespeare on Screen: An International Filmography and Videography*. New York and London, 1990.

Schmidt, Alexander. *Shakespeare-Lexicon*. 5th ed. Berlin, 1962.

Seager, H. W. *Natural History in Shakespeare's Time*. London, 1896.

Seng, Peter J. *The Vocal Songs in the Plays of Shakespeare*. Cambridge, Mass., 1967.

Shaheen, Naseeb. *Biblical References in Shakespeare's Plays*. Newark, Del., and London, 1999.

Shakespeare Bulletin.

Shakespeare-Jahrbuch.

Shakespeare Newsletter.

Shakespeare Quarterly. Annual Bibliography.

Shakespeare Studies.

Shakespeare Survey.

Spencer, T. J. B., ed. *Shakespeare's Plutarch*. Harmondsworth, Eng., 1964.

Spevack, Marvin. *The Harvard Concordance to Shakespeare*. Cambridge, Mass., 1973.

Thomson, J. A. K. *Shakespeare and the Classics*. London, 1952.

Wells, Stanley, ed. *Shakespeare: Select Bibliographical Guides*. London, 1973.
———, ed. *The Cambridge Companion to Shakespeare Studies*. Cambridge, Eng., 1986.

Life in Shakespeare's England

Allen, Don Cameron. *The Star-Crossed Renaissance*. Durham, N.C., 1941.

Appelbaum, Robert. *Aguecheek's Beef, Belch's Hiccup, and Other Gastronomic Interjections: Literature, Culture, and Food Among the Early Moderns*. Chicago, 2006.

Baker, Herschel. *The Image of Man: A Study of the Idea of Human Dignity in Classical Antiquity, the Middle Ages, and the Renaissance*. Cambridge, Mass., 1961. (First published in 1947 as *The Dignity of Man*.)

———. *The Wars of Truth: Studies in the Decay of Christian Humanism in the Earlier Seventeenth Century*. Cambridge, Mass., 1952.

Bakhtin, Mikhail M. *Rabelais and His World*, trans. H. Iswolsky. Cambridge, Mass., 1968.

Barkan, Leonard. *Nature's Work of Art: The Human Body as Image of the World*. New Haven, 1975.

———. *The Gods Made Flesh: Metamorphosis and the Pursuit of Paganism*. New Haven, 1986.

Barkan, Leonard, Bradin Cormack, and Sean Keilen, eds. *The Forms of Renaissance Thought: New Essays in Literature and Culture*. Basingstoke, Hampshire, 2009.

Barroll, J. Leeds. *Politics, Plague, and Shakespeare's Theater: The Stuart Years*. Ithaca, N.Y., 1991.

Bertram, Benjamin. *The Time Is Out of Joint: Skepticism in Shakespeare's England*. Newark, Del., and Cranbury, N.J., 2004.

Bindoff, S. T., et al., eds. *Elizabethan Government and Society*. Essays presented to Sir John Neale. London, 1961.

Brown, Georgia. *Redefining Elizabethan Literature*. Cambridge, Eng., 2004

Bush, Douglas. *The Renaissance and English Humanism*. Toronto, 1939.

Buxton, John. *Elizabethan Taste*. London, 1963.

Byrne, Muriel St. Clare. *Elizabethan Life in Town and Country*. 8th ed. London, 1970.

Camden, Carroll. *The Elizabethan Woman*. Houston, 1952.

Caspari, Fritz. *Humanism and the Social Order in Tudor England*. Chicago, 1954.

Cassirer, Ernst. *The Platonic Renaissance in England*, trans. J. E. Pettegrove. Austin, Tex., 1953.

Cefalu, Paul. *Moral Identity in Early Modern English Literature*. Cambridge, Eng., 2004.

Clark, Glenn, Judith Owens, and Greg T. Smith. *City Limits: Perspectives on the Historical European City*. Montreal, 2010.

Cormack, Bradin. *A Power to Do Justice: Jurisdiction, English Literature, and the Rise of Common Law, 1509-1625*. Chicago, 2007.

Crockett, Bryan. *The Play of Paradox: Stage and Sermon in Renaissance England*. Philadelphia, 1995.

Curran, Kevin. *Marriage, Performance, and Politics at the Jacobean Court*. Farnham, Surrey, 2009.

De Grazia, Margreta, Maureen Quilligan, and Peter Stallybrass, eds. *Subject and Object in Renaissance Culture*. Cambridge, Eng., 1996.

Dobranski, Stephen B. *Readers and Authorship in Early Modern England*. Cambridge, Eng., 2005.

Dubrow, Heather, and Richard Strier, eds. *The Historical Renaissance: New Essays on Tudor and Stuart Literature and Culture*. Chicago, 1988.

Einstein, Lewis. *Tudor Ideals*. New York, 1921.

Elizabeth I. *Collected Works*, eds. Leah S. Marcus, Janel Mueller, and Mary Beth Rose. Chicago, 2000.

Elton, G. R. *The Tudor Revolution in Government*. Cambridge, Eng., 1959.

Fisher, Will. *Materializing Gender in Early Modern English Literature and Culture*. Cambridge, Eng., 2006.

Fumerton, Patricia, and Simon Hunt, eds. *Renaissance Culture and the Everyday*. Philadelphia, 1999.

Gallagher, Lowell. *Medusa's Gaze: Casuistry and Conscience in the Renaissance*. Stanford, 1991.

Hackel, Heidi Brayman. *Reading Material in Early Modern England: Print, Gender, and Literacy*. Cambridge, Eng., 2005.

Harrison, G. B. *An Elizabethan Journal*. London, 1928; supplements.

———. *A Jacobean Journal . . . 1603–1606*. London, 1941.

———. *A Second Jacobean Journal . . . 1607 to 1610*. Ann Arbor, Mich., 1958.

Haydn, Hiram. *The Counter-Renaissance*. New York, 1950.

Helgerson, Richard. *Forms of Nationhood: The Elizbethan Writing of England*. Chicago, 1992.

———. *Adulterous Alliances: Home, State, and History in Early Modern European Drama and Painting*. Chicago, 2000.

Heninger, S. K., Jr. *A Handbook of Renaissance Meteorology*. Durham, N.C., 1960.

Hirst, Derek. *Authority and Conflict: England, 1603–1658*. Cambridge, Mass., 1986.

Hirst, Derek, and Richard Strier, eds. *Writing and Political Engagement in Seventeenth-Century England*. Cambridge, Eng., 1999.

Huizinga, Johan. *The Waning of the Middle Ages*. London, 1924; Baltimore, 1955.

Hurstfield, Joel, *Elizabeth I and the Unity of England*. London, 1960.

Jones, Ann Rosalind, and Peter Stallybrass. *Renaissance Clothing and the Materials of Memory*. Cambridge, Eng., 2000.

Jordan, Constance. *Renaissance Feminism: Literary Texts and Political Models*. Ithaca, N.Y., 1990.

Judges, A. V., ed. *The Elizabethan Underworld*. London and New York, 1930. Rpt., London, 1965.

Kewes, Paulina, ed. *Plagiarism in Early Modern England*. Basingstoke, Hampshire, Eng., 2003.

Kingsley-Smith, Jane. *Cupid in Early Modern Literature and Culture*. Cambridge, Eng., 2010.

Knapp, Jeffrey. *Shakespeare's Tribe: Church, Nation, and Theater in Renaissance England*. Chicago, 2002.

Knights, L. C. *Drama and Society in the Age of Jonson*. London, 1937.

Kocher, Paul. *Science and Religion in Elizabethan England*. San Marino, Calif., 1953.

Landreth, David. *The Face of Mammon: The Matter of Money in English Renaissance Literature*. Oxford, 2012.

Lee, Morris. *Great Britain's Solomon: James VI and I in His Three Kingdoms*. Urbana, Ill., 1990.

Lemon, Rebecca. *Treason by Words: Literature, Law, and Rebellion in Shakespeare's England*. Ithaca, N.Y., 2006.

Leinwand, Theodore B. *Theatre, Finance and Society in Early Modern England*. Cambridge, Eng., 1999.

Lockey, Brian C. *Law and Empire in English Renaissance Literature*. Cambridge, Eng., 2006.

Loewenstein, David, and John Marshall, eds. *Heresy, Literature, and Politics in Early Modern English Culture*. Cambridge, Eng., 2006.

Longfellow, Erica. *Women and Religious Writing in Early Modern England*. Cambridge, Eng., 2004.

Lovejoy, A. O. *The Great Chain of Being*. Cambridge, Mass., 1936.

MacCaffrey, Wallace T. *The Shaping of the Elizabethan Regime*. Princeton, 1968.

MacFaul, Tom. *Poetry and Paternity in Renaissance England: Sidney, Spenser, Shakespeare, Donne, and Jonson*. Cambridge, Eng., 2010.

Maquerlot, Jean-Pierre, and Michéle Willems. *Travel and Drama in Shakespeare's Time*. Cambridge, Eng., 1996.

Marotti, Arthur F., ed. *Catholicism and Anti-Catholicism in Early Modern English Texts*. Basingstoke, Hampshire, Eng., 1999.

Matar, Nabil. *Turks, Moors, and Englishmen in the Age of Discovery*. New York, 1999.

Mattingly, Garrett. *The Armada*. Boston, 1959.

McEachern, Claire, and Debora Shuger, eds. *Religion and Culture in Renaissance England*. Cambridge, Eng., 1997.

McElwee, W. *The Wisest Fool in Christendom*. [About James VI and I.] New York, 1958.

McPeek, James A. S. *The Black Book of Knaves and Unthrifts in Shakespeare and Other Renaissance Authors*. Storrs, Conn., 1969.

Monta, Susannah Brietz. *Martyrdom and Literature in Early Modern England*. Cambridge, Eng., 2005.

Montrose, Louis. *The Subject of Elizabeth: Authority, Gender, and Representation*. Chicago, 2006.

Neale, John E. *Elizabeth I and Her Parliaments*. 2 vols. London and New York, 1953–1958.

———. *The Elizabethan House of Commons*. London, 1949.

———. *Queen Elizabeth I*. London, 1934; New York, 1957.

Nichols, John, ed. *The Progresses and Public Processions of Queen Elizabeth*. 3 vols. London, 1823.

Orlin, Lena Cowen, ed. *Material London, ca. 1600*. Philadelphia, 2000.

Patterson, Annabel M. *Reading Holinshed's Chronicles*. Chicago, 1994.

Peck, Linda Levy. *Court Patronage and Corruption in Early Stuart England*. Boston, 1990.

Penrose, Boies. *Travel and Discovery in the Renaissance, 1420–1620*. Cambridge, Mass., 1955.

Perry, Curtis. *Literature and Favoritism in Early Modern England*. Cambridge, Eng., 2006.

Porter, Stephen. *Shakespeare's London: Everyday Life in London 1580–1616*. Stroud, Gloucestershire, 2009.

Quinones, Ricardo J. *The Renaissance Discovery of Time*. Cambridge, Mass., 1972.

Rowse, A. L. *The England of Elizabeth: The Structure of Society*. London, 1951.

Schwyzer, Philip. *Literature, Nationalism, and Memory in Early Modern England and Wales*. Cambridge, Eng., 2004.

Spiller, Elizabeth. *Science, Reading, and Renaissance Literature: The Art of Making Knowledge*. Cambridge, Eng., 2005.

Stallybrass, Peter, and Allon White. *The Politics and Poetics of Transgression*. Ithaca, N.Y., and London, 1986.

Stone, Lawrence. *The Crisis of the Aristocracy, 1558–1641*. Oxford, 1965.

———. *The Family, Sex and Marriage in England, 1500–1800*. London, 1977.

Stow, John. *Survey of London*, ed. C. L. Kingsford. Oxford, 1971.

Strier, Richard. *Resistant Structures: Particularity, Radicalism, and Renaissance Texts*. Berkeley, 1995.

———. *The Unrepentant Renaissance: From Petrarch to Shakespeare to Milton*. Chicago, 2011.

Targoff, Ramie. *Common Prayer: The Language of Public Devotion in Early Modern England*. Chicago, 2001.

Tawney, R. H. *Religion and the Rise of Capitalism*. New York, 1926, 1962.

Tillyard, E. M. W. *The Elizabethan World Picture*. London, 1943, 1967.

Trevor, Douglas. *The Poetics of Melancholy in Early Modern England*. Cambridge, Eng., 2004.

Underdown, David. *Revel, Riot, and Rebellion: Popular Politics and Culture in England, 1603–1660*. Oxford, 1985.

Whigham, Frank. *Ambition and Privilege: The Social Tropes of Elizabethan Courtesy Theory*. Berkeley, 1984.

Willson, David Harris. *King James VI & I*. New York, 1956.

Wilson, F. P. *Elizabethan and Jacobean*. Oxford, 1945.

Wilson, J. Dover, ed. *Life in Shakespeare's England*. Cambridge, Eng., 1911; 2nd ed., 1926.

Woodbridge, Linda. *Vagrancy, Homelessness, and English Renaissance Literature*. Urbana, Ill., 2001.

Wright, Louis B. *Middle-Class Culture in Elizabethan England*. Chapel Hill, N.C., 1935.

Wrightson, Keith. *English Society, 1580–1680*. New Brunswick, N.J., 1982.

Wyatt, Michael. *The Italian Encounter with Tudor England: A Cultural Politics of Translation*. Cambridge, Eng., 2005.

Zeeveld, W. Gordon. *Foundations of Tudor Policy*. Cambridge, Mass., 1948.

Shakespeare's Predecessors and Contemporaries

See also, under *Works of Reference*, Bentley, Chambers, Greg, and Harbage; under *London Theaters and Dramatic Companies*, McMillin and MacLean; under *Shakespeare Criticism Since 1980*, Dollimore, Garber (*Cannibals*), Goldberg, Greenblatt, Jardine, Loomba, Mullaney, Newman, and Skura; under *The Histories*, Ribner; and under *The Tragedies*, Bushnell.

Alford, John A. *From Page to Performance: Essays in Early English Drama*. East Lansing, Mich., 1995.

Altman, Joel B. *The Tudor Play of Mind: Rhetorical Inquiry and the Development of Elizabethan Drama*. Berkeley, 1978.

Bamford, Karen. *Sexual Violence on the Jacobean Stage*. New York, 2000.

Barber, C. L. *Creating Elizabethan Tragedy: The Theater of Kyd and Marlowe*. Chicago, 1988.

Bartels, Emily C. *Spectacles of Strangeness: Imperialism, Alienation, and Marlowe*. Philadelphia, 1993.

Bednarz, James P. *Shakespeare and the Poets' War*. New York, 2001.

Belsey, Catherine. *The Subject of Tragedy: Identity and Difference in Renaissance Drama*. London, 1985.

Bentley, G. E. *Shakespeare and Jonson: Their Reputations in the Seventeenth Century Compared*. 2 vols. Chicago, 1945.

Bergeron, David M. *Practicing Renaissance Scholarship Plays and Pageants, Patrons and Politics*. Pittsburgh, 2000.

Berry, Philippa. *Of Chastity and Power: Elizabethan Literature and the Unmarried Queen*. London and New York, 1989.

Bevington, David. *From "Mankind" to Marlowe: Growth of Structure in the Popular Drama of Tudor England*. Cambridge, Mass., 1962.

———. *Tudor Drama and Politics*. Cambridge, Mass., 1968.

———, and Peter Holbrook, eds. *The Politics of the Stuart Court Masque*. Cambridge, Eng., 1991.

———, Lars Engle, Katharine Eisaman Maus, and Eric Rasmussen, eds. *English Renaissance Drama: A Norton Anthology*. New York, 2002.

———, Martin Butler, and Ian Donaldson, gen. eds. *The Cambridge Edition of the Complete Works of Ben Jonson*. 7 vols. Cambridge, Eng., 2012.

Bowers, Fredson T. *Elizabethan Revenge Tragedy, 1587–1642*. Princeton, 1940.

Braden, Gordon. *Renaissance Tragedy and the Senecan Tradition*. New Haven, 1985.

Braunmuller, A. R., and Michael Hattaway, eds. *The Cambridge Companion to English Renaissance Drama*. Cambridge, Eng., 1990; 2nd ed., 2003.

Bristol, Michael D. *Carnival and Theater: Plebeian Culture and the Structure of Authority in Renaissance England*. London, 1985.

Bromley, James M. *Intimacy and Sexuality in the Age of Shakespeare*. Cambridge, Eng., 2012.

Brooke, C. F. Tucker, ed. *The Shakespeare Apocrypha*. Oxford, 1908.

Brooks, Douglas A. *From Playhouse to Printing House: Drama and Authorship in Early Modern England*. Cambridge, Eng., 2000.

Bruster, Douglas. *Drama and the Market in the Age of Shakespeare*. Cambridge, Eng., 1992.

Burt, Richard. *Licensed by Authority: Ben Jonson and the Discourses of Censorship*. Ithaca, N.Y., 1993.

Bushnell, Rebecca W. *Tragedies of Tyrants: Political Thought and Theater in the English Renaissance*. Ithaca, N.Y., 1990.

Butterworth, Philip. *Theatre of Fire: Special Effects in Early English and Scottish Theatre*. London, 1998.

Caputi, Anthony. *John Marston, Satirist*. Ithaca, N.Y., 1961.

Cohen, Walter. *Drama of a Nation: Public Theater in Renaissance England and Spain*. Ithaca, N.Y., 1985.

Comensoli, Viviana, and Anna Russell, eds. *Enacting Gender on the English Renaissance Stage*. Urbana, Ill., 1999.

Cousins, A. D., and Alison V. Scott, eds. *Ben Jonson and the Politics of Genre*. Cambridge, Eng., 2009.

Cox, John D., and David Scott Kastan, eds. *A New History of Early English Drama*. New York, 1997.

Craik, T. W. *The Tudor Interlude*. Leicester, 1958, 1962.

Dawson, Anthony B., and Paul Yachnin. *The Culture of Playgoing in Shakespeare's England: A Collaborative Debate*. Cambridge, Eng., 2001.

Deats, Sara Munson. *Sex, Gender, and Desire in the Plays of Christopher Marlowe*. Newark, Del., 1997.

Dessen, Alan C. *Elizabethan Drama and the Viewer's Eye*. Chapel Hill, N.C., 1977.

Diehl, Huston. *Staging Reform, Reforming the Stage: Protestantism and Popular Theater in Early Modern England*. Ithaca, N.Y., 1997.

Dillon, Janette. *Theatre, Court and City, 1595–1610: Drama and Social Space in London*. Cambridge, Eng., 2000.

———. *The Cambridge Introduction to Early English Theatre*. Cambridge, Eng., 2006.

DiGangi, Mario. *The Homoerotics of Early Modern Drama*. Cambridge, Eng., 1997.

Dolan, Frances E. *Dangerous Familiars: Representations of Domestic Crime in England, 1550–1700*. Ithaca, N.Y., 1994.

Doran, Madeleine. *Endeavors of Art: A Study of Form in Elizabethan Drama*. Madison, Wis., 1954, 1972.

Erickson, Peter, and Clark Hulse, eds. *Early Modern Visual Culture: Representation, Race, and Empire in Renaissance England*. Philadelphia, 2000.

Erne, Lukas. *Beyond "The Spanish Tragedy": A Study of the Works of Thomas Kyd*. Manchester, 2001.

Esche, Edward J. *Shakespeare and His Contemporaries in Performance*. Aldershot, Hants., 2000.

Falco, Raphael. *Charismatic Authority in Early Modern English Tragedy*. Baltimore, 2000.

Farley-Hills, David. *Shakespeare and the Rival Playwrights, 1600–1606*. London, 1990.

Findlay, Alison. *A Feminist Perspective on Renaissance Drama*. Oxford, 1999.

———. *Illegitimate Power: Bastards in Renaissance Drama*. Manchester, Eng., 1994.

———. *Playing Spaces in Early Women's Drama*. Cambridge, Eng., 2006.

Finkelpearl, Philip. *John Marston of the Middle Temple*. Cambridge, Mass., 1969.

Freer, Coburn. *The Poetics of Jacobean Drama*. Baltimore, 1981.

Gardiner, H. C. *Mysteries' End*. New Haven, 1946.

Gibbons, Brian. *Jacobean City Comedy*. London, 1968.

Gossett, Suzanne, ed. *Thomas Middleton in Context*. Cambridge, Eng., 2011.

Hall, Kim F. *Things of Darkness: Economies of Race and Gender in Early Modern England*. Ithaca, N.Y., 1995.

Hardison, O. B., Jr. *Christian Rite and Christian Drama in the Middle Ages*. Baltimore, 1965.

Hart, Jonathan. *Shakespeare and His Contemporaries*. New York, 2010.

Hassel, R. Chris. *Renaissance Drama and the English Church Year*. Lincoln, Neb., 1979.

Hattaway, Michael. *Elizabethan Popular Theatre: Plays in Performance*. London, 1982.

Hawkins, Harriett. *Likenesses of Truth in Elizabethan and Restoration Drama*. Oxford, 1972.

Helgerson, Richard. *Adulterous Alliances: Home, State, and History in Early Modern European Drama and Painting*. Chicago, 2000.

Hendricks, Margo, and Patricia Parker, eds. *Women, "Race," and Writing in the Early Modern Period*. London and New York, 1994.

Hillman, Richard. *Shakespeare, Marlowe, and the Politics of France*. Houndmills, Eng., 2002.

Holbrook, Peter. *Literature and Degree in Renaissance England: Nashe, Bourgeois Tragedy, Shakespeare*. Newark, Del., 1994.

Honigmann, E. A. J., ed. *Shakespeare and His Contemporaries: Essays in Comparison*. Manchester, 1986.

Howard, Jean. *The Stage and Social Struggle in Early Modern England*. London and New York, 1994.

Hunter, G. K. *John Lyly: The Humanist as Courtier*. Cambridge, Mass., 1962.

Jankowski, Theodora A. *Pure Resistance: Queer Virginity in Early Modern English Drama*. Philadelphia, 2000.

Kastan, David Scott, and Peter Stallybrass, eds. *Staging the Renaissance: Reinterpretations of Elizabethan and Jacobean Drama*. New York and London, 1991.

Kernan, Alvin. *The Cankered Muse: Satire of the English Renaissance*. New Haven, 1959.

Kerrigan, John. *Revenge Tragedy: Aeschylus to Armageddon*. Oxford, 1998.

———. *Archipelagic English: Literature, History, and Politics, 1603–1707*. Oxford, 2008, 2010.

Kiefer, Frederick. *Writing on the Renaissance Stage: Written Words, Printed Pages, Metaphoric Books*. Newark, Del., 1996.

Kirsch, Arthur C. *Jacobean Dramatic Perspectives*. Charlottesville, Va., 1972.

Kitch, Aaron. *Political Economy and the States of Literature in Early Modern England*. Farnham, Surrey, 2009.

Knapp, Jeffrey. *Shakespeare's Tribe: Church, Nation, and Theater in Renaissance England*. Chicago, 2002.

Kolve, V. A. *The Play Called Corpus Christi*. Palo Alto and London, 1966.

Kuriyama, Constance Brown. *Christopher Marlowe: A Renaissance Life*. Ithaca, N.Y., 2002.

Leggatt, Alexander. *Citizen Comedy in the Age of Shakespeare*. Toronto, 1973.

———. *Introduction to English Renaissance Comedy*. Manchester, 1999.

———. *Jacobean Public Theatre*. London, 1992.

Leishman, J. B., ed. *The Three Parnassus Plays (1598–1601)*. London, 1949.

Lesser, Zachary. *Renaissance Drama and the Politics of Publication: Readings in the English Book Trade*. Cambridge, Eng., 2004.

Levin, Harry. *The Overreacher: A Study of Christopher Marlowe*. Cambridge, Mass., 1952, 1964.

Levin, Richard. *The Multiple Plot in English Renaissance Drama*. Chicago, 1971.

Liebler, Naomi Conn, ed. *The Female Tragic Hero in English Renaissance Drama*. New York and Basingstoke, Eng., 2002.

Limon, Jerzy, and Jay L. Halio, eds. *Shakespeare and His Contemporaries: Eastern and Central European Studies*. Newark, Del., 1993.

Logan, Robert P., and Denzell S. Smith. *The Predecessors of Shakespeare: A Survey and Bibliography of Recent Studies in English Renaissance Drama*. Lincoln, Neb., 1973.

Low, Jennifer. *Manhood and the Duel: Masculinity in Early Modern Drama and Culture*. New York and Basingstoke, Eng., 2003.

MacFoul, Thomas. *Male Friendship in Shakespeare and His Contemporaries*. Cambridge, Eng., 2007.

Maguire, Nancy Klein. *Renaissance Tragicomedy: Explorations in Genre and Politics*. New York, 1987.

Malay, Jessica L. *Prophecy and Sibylline Imagery in the Renaissance: Shakespeare's Sibyls*. New York, 2010.

Mardock, James D. *Our Scene Is London: Ben Jonson's City and the Space of the Author*. New York and London, 2008.

Margeson, J. M. R. *The Origins of English Tragedy*. Oxford, 1967.

Marrapodi, Michele, ed., with A. J. Hoenselaars. *The Italian World of English Renaissance Drama: Cultural Exchange and Intertextuality*. Newark, Del., 1998.

Maul, Victoria. *Jonson, Horace, and the Classical Tradition*. Cambridge, Eng., 2010.

Maus, Katharine Eisaman. *Inwardness and Theater in the English Renaissance Drama*. Chicago, 1995.

McAlindon, T. *English Renaissance Tragedy*. London, 1986.

McDonald, Russ. *Shakespeare and Jonson, Jonson and Shakespeare*. Lincoln, Neb., 1988.

McLuskie, Kathleen. *Renaissance Dramatists*. (Feminist Readings.) Atlantic Highlands, N.J., 1989.

McMahan, Chris. *Family and the State in Early Modern Revenge Drama*. New York, 2012.

McManus, Clare. *Women on the Renaissance Stage: Anna of Denmark and Female Masquing in the Stuart Court (1590–1619)*. Manchester, 2002.

Mukherji, Subha. *Law and Representation in Early Modern Drama*. Cambridge, Eng., 2006.

Neill, Michael. *Putting History to the Question: Power, Politics, and Society in English Renaissance Drama*. New York, 2000.

Orgel, Stephen. *The Illusion of Power: Political Theater in the English Renaissance*. Berkeley, 1975.

———. *Impersonations: The Performance of Gender in Shakespeare's England*. Cambridge, Eng., 1996.

Orgel, Stephen, and Roy Strong. *Inigo Jones: The Theatre of the Stuart Court*. 2 vols. London and Berkeley, 1973.

Ornstein, Robert. *The Moral Vision of Jacobean Tragedy*. Madison, Wis., 1960.

Panek, Jennifer. *Widows and Suitors in Early Modern English Comedy*. Cambridge, Eng., 2004.

Rabkin, Norman, ed: *Reinterpretations of Elizabethan Drama*. New York, 1969.

Rasmussen, Mark David, ed. *Renaissance Literature and Its Formal Engagements*. Basingstoke, Hampshire, 2002.

Rose, Mary Beth. *The Expense of Spirit: Love and Sexuality in English Renaissance Drama*. Ithaca, N.Y., 1988.

———. *Gender and Heroism in Early Modern English Literature*. Chicago, 2002.

———. ed. *Renaissance Drama as Cultural History*. Evanston, Ill., 1990.

Sanders, Julie. *Ben Jonson in Context*. Cambridge, Eng., 2010.

Sanders, Wilbur. *The Dramatist and the Received Idea: Studies in the Plays of Marlowe and Shakespeare*. Cambridge, Eng., 1968.

Shannon, Laurie. *Sovereign Amity: Figures of Friendship in Shakespearean Contexts*. Chicago, 2002.

Shapiro, James. *Rival Playwrights: Marlowe, Jonson, Shakespeare*. New York, 1991.

Simon, Eckehard, ed. *The Theatre of Medieval Europe: New Research in Early Drama*. Cambridge, Eng., 1991.

Smith, Bruce R. *The Acoustic World of Early Modern England*. Chicago, 1999.

Smith, David L., Richard Strier, and David Bevington, eds. *The Theatrical City: Culture, Theatre and Politics in London, 1567–1649*. Cambridge, Eng., 1995.

Smith, Emma, and Garrett A. Sullivan, Jr. *The Cambridge Companion to English Renaissance Tragedy*. Cambridge, Eng., 2010.

Southern, Richard. *The Medieval Theatre in the Round*. London, 1957.

Spivack, Bernard. *Shakespeare and the Allegory of Evil*. New York, 1958.

Straznicky, Marta. *Privacy, Playreading, and Women's Closet Drama, 1550–1700*. Cambridge, Eng., 2004.

Sullivan, Jr., Garrett A. *Memory and Forgetting in English Renaissance Drama: Shakespeare, Marlowe, Webster*. Cambridge, Eng., 2005.

Traub, Valerie, M. Lindsay Kaplan, and Dympna C. Callaghan, eds. *Feminist Readings of Early Modern Culture: Emerging Subjects*. Cambridge, Eng., 1996.

Vickers, Brian. *"Counterfeiting" Shakespeare: Evidence, Authorship, and John Ford's "Funerall Elegye."* Cambridge, Eng., 2002.

Waith, Eugene M. *The Herculean Hero in Marlowe, Chapman, Shakespeare, and Dryden*. New York, 1962.

Wall, Wendy. *Staging Domesticity: Household Work and English Identity in Early Modern Drama*. Cambridge, Eng., 2002.

Wells, Stanley. *Shakespeare & Co.: Christopher Marlowe, Thomas Dekker, Ben Jonson, Thomas Middleton, John Fletcher, and the Other Players in His Story*. New York, 2007.

Whigham, Frank. *Seizures of the Will in Early Modern English Drama*. Cambridge, Eng., 1996.

White, Paul Whitfield. *Marlowe, History, and Sexuality: New Critical Essays on Christopher Marlowe*. New York, 1998.

———, *Theatre and Reformation: Protestantism, Patronage and Playing in Tudor England*. Cambridge, Eng., 1993.

Whitney, Charles. *Early Responses to Renaissance Drama*. Cambridge, Eng., 2006.

Wickham, Glynne. *Early English Stages, 1300 to 1660*. 3 vols. London, 1959–1972.

Wiggins, Martin. *Shakespeare and the Drama of His Time*. Oxford, 2000.

———, and Catherine Richardson, compilers. *British Drama, 1533–1642: A Catalogue*. Vol. 1. Oxford, 2012.

Wilson, F. P. *Marlowe and the Early Shakespeare*. Oxford, 1953.

Wilson, Luke. *Theaters of Intention: Drama and the Law in Early Modern England*. Stanford, Calif., 2000.

Wong, Katrine K. *Music and Gender in English Renaissance Drama*. New York, 2012.

Woodbridge, Linda. *Women and the English Renaissance: Literature and the Nature of Womankind, 1540–1620*. Urbana, Ill., 1984.

———. *English Revenge Drama: Money, Resistance, Equality*. Cambridge, Eng., 2010.

Woolf, Rosemary. *The English Mystery Plays*. Berkeley and Los Angeles, 1972.

Yachnin, Paul. *Stage-Wrights: Shakespeare, Jonson, Middleton, and the Making of Theatrical Value*. Philadelphia, 1997.

Zimmerman, Susan, ed. *Erotic Politics: Desire on the Renaissance Stage*. London and New York, 1992.

Zucker, Adam. *The Places of Wit in Early Modern English Comedy*. Cambridge, Eng., 2011.

London Theaters and Dramatic Companies

See also, under *Works of Reference*, Bentley, and Chambers (*Elizabethan Stage*).

Astington, John H., ed. *The Development of Shakespeare's Theater*. New York, 1992.

Beckerman, Bernard. *Shakespeare at the Globe, 1599–1609*. New York, 1962, 1967.

Bentley, Gerald Eades. *The Profession of Dramatist in Shakespeare's Time, 1590–1642*. Princeton, 1971.

———. *The Profession of Player in Shakespeare's Time, 1590–1642*. Princeton, 1984.

Berry, Herbert. *Shakespeare's Playhouses*. New York, 1987.

Bradley, David. *From Text to Performance in the Elizabethan Theatre: Preparing the Play for the Stage*. Cambridge, Eng., 1992.

Clare, Janet. *"Art Made Tongue-Tied by Authority": Elizabethan and Jacobean Dramatic Censorship*. Manchester, 1990; 2nd ed., 1999.

Cook, Ann Jennalie. *The Privileged Playgoers of Shakespeare's London, 1576–1642*. Princeton, 1981.

Dillon, Janet. *The Language of Space in Court Performance, 1400–1625*. Cambridge, Eng., 2010.

Dutton, Richard. *Mastering the Revels: The Regulation and Censorship of English Renaissance Drama*. Iowa City, 1991.

———, ed. *The Oxford Handbook of Early Modern Theatre*. Oxford, 2012.

Feuillerat, Albert, ed. *Documents Relating to the Office of the Revels in the Time of Queen Elizabeth*. Louvain (Louven), Belgium, 1908.

Foakes, R. A., ed. *The Henslowe Papers: The Diary, Theatre Papers, and Bear Garden Papers*. In full and in facsimile. 3 vols. in 2. London, 1976.

Foakes, R. A., and R. T. Rickert, eds. *Henslowe's Diary*. London, 1961.

Gair, W. Reavley. *The Children of Paul's*. Cambridge, Eng., 1982.

Greg, W. W., ed. *Dramatic Documents from the Elizabethan Playhouses: Stage Plots; Actors' Parts; Prompt Books*. 2 vols. Oxford, 1931.

Gurr, Andrew. *Playgoing in Shakespeare's London*. Cambridge, Eng., 1987; 2nd ed., 1996.

———. *The Shakespeare Company, 1594–1642*. Cambridge, Eng., 2004.

———. *The Shakespearian Playing Companies*. Oxford, 1996.

———. *The Shakespearean Stage, 1574–1642*. Cambridge, Eng., 1970; 2nd ed., 1980.

———. *Shakespeare's Opposites: The Admiral's Company, 1594–1625*. Cambridge, Eng., 2009.

———, and John Orrell. *Rebuilding Shakespeare's Globe*. London and New York, 1989.

———, and Mariko Ichikawa. *Staging in Shakespeare's Theatres*. Oxford, 2000.

Harbage, Alfred. *Shakespeare's Audience*. New York, 1941.

Hill, Janet. *Stages and Playgoers: From Guild Plays to Shakespeare*. Montreal and Kingston, 2002.

Hodges, C. Walter. *The Globe Restored*. London, 1953; 2nd ed., New York, 1968.

Hosley, Richard. "Was There a Music-room in Shakespeare's Globe?" *ShS 13* (1960), 113–23.

Ingram, William. *The Business of Playing: The Beginnings of the Adult Professional Theater in Elizabethan London*. Ithaca, N.Y., 1992.

Jones, Ann Rosalind, and Peter Stallybrass. *Renaissance Clothing and the Materials of Memory*. Cambridge, Eng., 2000.

Kathman, David. "Grocers, Goldsmiths, and Drapers: Freemen and Apprentices in the Elizabethan Theater," *SQ 55* (2004), 1–49.

King, T. J. *Casting Shakespeare's Plays: London Actors and Their Roles, 1590–1642*. Cambridge, Eng., 1992.

———. *Shakespearean Staging, 1599–1642*. Cambridge, Mass., 1971.

Knutson, Roslyn Lander. *The Repertory of Shakespeare's Company, 1594–1613*. Fayetteville, Ark., 1991.

———. *Playing Companies and Commerce in Shakespeare's Time*. Cambridge, Eng., 2001.

Linthicum, Marie C. *Costume in the Drama of Shakespeare and His Contemporaries*. Oxford, 1936.

Mann, David. *The Elizabethan Player: Contemporary Stage Representation*. London, 1991.

McMillin, Scott. *The Elizabethan Theatre and "The Book of Sir Thomas More."* Ithaca, N.Y., 1987.

McMillin, Scott, and Sally-Beth MacLean. *The Queen's Men and Their Plays*. Cambridge, Eng., 1998.

Munro, Lucy. *Children of the Queen's Revels: A Jacobean Theatre Repertory*. Cambridge, Eng., 2005.

Nelson, Alan H. *Early Cambridge Theatres: College, University, and Town Stages, 1464–1720*. Cambridge, Eng., 1994.

Nungezer, Edwin. *A Dictionary of Actors*. London and New Haven, 1929.

Shapiro, Michael. *Children of the Revels: The Boys' Companies of Shakespeare's Time and Their Plays*. New York, 1977.

Turner, Henry S. *The English Renaissance Stage: Geometry, Poetics, and the Practical Spatial Arts*. Oxford, 2006.

Vaughan, Virginia Mason. *Performing Blackness on English Stages, 1500–1800*. Cambridge, Eng., 2005.

West, Russell. *Spatial Representations and the Jacobean Stage: From Shakespeare to Webster*. Basingstoke, Eng., and New York, 2002.

White, Paul Whitfield, and Suzanne R. Westfall, eds. *Shakespeare and Theatrical Patronage in Early Modern England*. Cambridge, Eng., 2002.

Wickham, Glynne. *Early English Stages, 1300 to 1660*. 3 vols. London, 1959–1972.

Shakespeare's Life and Work

Alexander, Peter. *Shakespeare's Life and Art*. New ed., New York, 1961.

Baldwin, T. W. *William Shakspere's Small Latine and Lesse Greeke*. 2 vols. Urbana, Ill., 1944.

Bate, Jonathan. *Soul of the Age: A Biography of the Mind of William Shakespeare*. New York, 2009.

Bevington, David. *Shakespeare and Biography*. Oxford, 2010.

Chambers, E. K. *William Shakespeare: A Study of Facts and Problems*. 2 vols. Oxford, 1930.

Duncan-Jones, Katherine. *Ungentle Shakespeare: Scenes from His Life*. London, 2001.

Eccles, Mark. *Shakespeare in Warwickshire*. Madison, Wis., 1961.

Greenblatt, Stephen. *Will in the World: How Shakespeare Became Shakespeare*. New York, 2004.

Greer, Germaine. *Shakespeare*. Oxford, 1986.

———. *Shakespeare's Wife*. London and New York, 2007.

Honan, Park. *Shakespeare: A Life*. Oxford, 1998.

Matus, Irvin Leigh, *Shakespeare, In Fact*. New York, 1994.

Nicholl, Charles. *The Lodger Shakespeare: His Life on Silver Street*. New York, 2007.

Pogue, Kate Emery. *Shakespeare's Family*. Westport, Conn., and London, 2008.

Potter, Lois. *The Life of William Shakespeare*. Oxford, 2012.

Schoenbaum, S. *Shakespeare's Lives*. Oxford and New York, 1970.

———. *William Shakespeare: A Documentary Life*. Oxford, 1975. Also published with fewer illustrations and a slightly revised text as *A Compact Documentary Life*. 1977.

———. *William Shakespeare: Records and Images*. Oxford, 1981.

Shapiro, James S. *A Year in the Life of William Shakespeare, 1599*. New York, 2005.

———. *Contested Will: Who Wrote Shakespeare?* New York, 2010.

Wells, Stanley. *Shakespeare: A Life in Drama*. New York and London, 1995.

———. *Shakespeare: For All Time*. Oxford, 2003.

Wheeler, Richard P. "Deaths in the Family: The Loss of a Son and the Rise of Shakespearean Comedy," *SQ* 51 (2000), 127–53.

Shakespeare's Language: His Development as Poet and Dramatist

See also, under *Works of Reference*, Abbott, Onions, and Schmidt; and under *The Comedies*, Elam.

Adamson, Sylvia, Gavin Alexander, and Katrin Ettenhuber, eds. *Renaissance Figures of Speech*. Cambridge, Eng., 2007.

Alexander, Catherine M. S., ed. *Shakespeare and Language*. Cambridge, Eng., 2004.

Barton, Anne. "Shakespeare and the Limits of Language," *ShS* 24 (1971), 19–30.

Byrne, Muriel St. Clare. "The Foundations of Elizabethan Language," *ShS* 17 (1964), 223–39.

Cercignani, Fausto. *Shakespeare's Works and Elizabethan Pronunciation*. Oxford, 1981.

Charney, Maurice. *Shakespeare's Roman Plays: The Function of Imagery in the Drama*. Cambridge, Mass., 1961.

———. *Style in Hamlet*. Princeton, 1969.

Clemen, Wolfgang H. *The Development of Shakespeare's Imagery*. Cambridge, Mass., 1951.

Coleman, E. A. M. *The Dramatic Use of Bawdy in Shakespeare*. London, 1974.

Cruttwell, Patrick. *The Shakespearean Moment and Its Place in the Poetry of the Seventeenth Century*. London, 1954.

Crystal, David. *Pronouncing Shakespeare: The Globe Experiment*. Cambridge, Eng., 2005.

———, and Ben Crystal. *Shakespeare's Words: A Glossary and Language Companion*. London and New York, 2002.

Desmet, Christy. *Reading Shakespeare's Characters: Rhetoric, Ethics, and Identity*. Amherst, Mass., 1992.

Dobson, E. J. *English Pronunciation, 1500–1700*. 2 vols. 2nd ed. Oxford, 1968.

Donawerth, Jane. *Shakespeare and the Sixteenth-Century Study of Language*. Urbana, Ill., 1984.

Doran, Madeleine. *Shakespeare's Dramatic Language*. Madison, Wis., 1976.

Empson, William. *The Structure of Complex Words*. London, 1951; 3rd ed., 1977.

Hazard, Mary E. *Elizabethan Silent Language*. Lincoln, Neb., 2000.

Hirsch, James E. *Shakespeare and the History of Soliloquies*. Madison, N.J., and London, 2003.

Hoenselaars, Ton, ed. *Shakespeare and the Language of Translation*. London, 2004.

———. *Shakespeare's Grammar*. London, 2003.

Hope, Jonathan. *Shakespeare and Language: Reason, Eloquence, and Artifice in the Renaissance*. London, 2010.

Hulme, Hilda M. *Explorations in Shakespeare's Language*. London, 1962.

Kermode, Frank. *Shakespeare's Language*. New York, 2000.

Kökeritz, Helge. *Shakespeare's Names*. New Haven, 1959.

———. *Shakespeare's Pronunciation*. New Haven, 1953.

Lanham, Richard A. *The Motives of Eloquence: Literary Rhetoric in the Renaissance*. New Haven, 1976.

Lyne, Raphael. *Shakespeare, Rhetoric, and Cognition*. Cambridge, Eng., 2011.

Magnussen, Lynne. *Shakespeare and Social Dialogue: Dramatic Language and Elizabethan Letters*. Cambridge, Eng., 1999.

Mahood, M. M. *Shakespeare's Wordplay*. London, 1957.

———. *Shakespeare and the Arts of Language*. Oxford, 2001.

McDonald, Russ. *Shakespeare's Late Style*. Cambridge, Eng., 2006.

Miriam Joseph, Sister. *Shakespeare's Use of the Arts of Language*. New York, 1947. Rpt. in part as *Rhetoric in Shakespeare's Time*. 1962.

Nares, Robert. *A Glossary ... of Shakespeare and His Contemporaries*. New ed. J. O. Halliwell and Thomas Wright. 2 vols. London, 1859, 1905, Rpt. Detroit, 1966.

Partridge, Eric. *Shakespeare's Bawdy*. London, 1947, 1955.

Perng, Ching-Hsi. *Dialogue with Monologue: A Study in Shakespearean Soliloquy*. Taiwan, 2011.

Pogue, Kate Emery. *Shakespeare's Figures of Speech: A Reader's Guide*. New York and Bloomington, Ind., 2009.

Rhodes, Neil. *Shakespeare and the Origins of English*. Oxford, 2004.

Siemon, James R. *Word Against Word: Shakespearian Utterance*. Amherst and Boston, 2002.

Sokol, B. J., and Mary Sokol. *Shakespeare's Legal Language: A Dictionary*. London and New Brunswick, N.J., 2000.

Spurgeon, Caroline. *Shakespeare's Imagery and What it Tells Us*. Cambridge, Eng., 1935.

Thompson, Ann and John O. *Shakespeare: Meaning and Metaphor*. Iowa City, 1987.

Thorne, Alison. *Vision and Rhetoric in Shakespeare: Looking Through Language*. Basingstoke and New York, 2000.

Trousdale, Marion. *Shakespeare and the Rhetoricians*. Chapel Hill, N.C., 1982.

Vickers, Brian. *The Artistry of Shakespeare's Prose*. London, 1968.

Willbern, David. *Poetic Will: Shakespeare and the Play of Language*. Philadelphia, 1997.

Willcock, Gladys D. "Shakespeare and Elizabethan English," *ShS* 7 (1954), 12–24.

———. *Shakespeare and Rhetoric*. Oxford, 1944.

Williams, Gordon. *A Dictionary of Sexual Language and Imagery in Shakespearean and Stuart Literature*. 3 vols. London, 1994.

Wright, George T. *Shakespeare's Metrical Art*. Berkeley, 1988.

Textual Criticism and Bibliography

See also under *Shakespeare's Predecessors and Contemporaries*, Cox and Kastan (essay by Blayney); and, under *King Lear*, Urkowitz.

Alexander, Peter. *Shakespeare's "Henry VI" and "Richard III."* Cambridge, Eng., 1929.

Blayney, Peter W. M. *The First Folio of Shakespeare*. Washington D.C., 1991.

———. *The Texts of "King Lear" and Their Origins*. Vol. 1. Cambridge, Eng., 1982.

Bowers, Fredson. *Bibliography and Textual Criticism*. Oxford, 1964.

———. *On Editing Shakespeare*. Charlottesville, Va., 1966.

———. *Principles of Bibliographical Description*. Princeton, 1949.

———. *Textual and Literary Criticism*. Cambridge, Eng., 1959.

Chambers, E. K. *William Shakespeare: A Study of Facts and Problems*. 2 vols. Oxford, 1930.

De Grazia, Margreta. *Shakespeare Verbatim: The Reproduction of Authenticity and the 1790 Apparatus*. Oxford, 1991.

Doran, Madeleine. *"Henry VI," Parts II and III: Their Relation to "The Contention" and "The True Tragedy."* Iowa City, 1928.

Duthie, G. I. *Elizabethan Shorthand and the First Quarto of "King Lear."* Oxford, 1949.

Erne, Lukas. *Shakespeare as Literary Dramatist*. Cambridge, Eng., 2003.

———. "Shakespeare and the Publication of His Plays," *SQ* 53.1 (2002), 1–20.

———, ed. *Textual Performances: The Modern Reproduction of Shakespeare's Drama*. Cambridge, Eng., 2004.

Gaskell, Philip. *A New Introduction to Bibliography*. New York and Oxford, 1972.

Greg, W. W. *The Editorial Problem in Shakespeare*. 3rd ed. Oxford, 1954.

———. *Principles of Emendation in Shakespeare*. London, 1928.

———. *The Shakespeare First Folio: Its Bibliographical and Textual History*. Oxford, 1955.

Hart, Alfred. *Stolne and Surreptitious Copies: A Comparative Study of Shakespeare's Bad Quartos*. Melbourne and London, 1942.

Hinman, Charlton. *The Printing and Proof-Reading of the First Folio of Shakespeare*. 2 vols. Oxford, 1963.

Honigmann, E. A. J. *The Stability of Shakespeare's Text*. London and Lincoln, Neb., 1965.

Jowett, John. *Shakespeare and Text*. Oxford, 2007.

Long, William B. "'A bed for woodstock': A Warning for the Unwary," *Medieval and Renaissance Drama in England* 2 (1985), 91–118.

Maguire, Laurie E., and Thomas L. Berger, eds. *Textual Formations and Reformations*. Newark, Del., 1998.

Massai, Sonia. *Shakespeare and the Rise of the Editor*. Cambridge, Eng., 2007.

Masten, Jeffrey. *Textual Intercourse: Collaboration, Authorship, and Sexualities in Renaissance Drama*. Cambridge, Eng., 1997.

McKerrow, Ronald B. *An Introduction to Bibliography for Literary Students*. Oxford, 1927.

———. *Prolegomena for the Oxford Shakespeare*. Oxford, 1939.

McLeod, Randall, ed. *Crisis in Editing: Texts of the English Renaissance*. New York, 1994.

McMillin, Scott, ed. *The First Quarto of "Othello."* Cambridge, Eng., 2001.

Mowat, Barbara, and Paul Werstine, eds. *The New Folger Library Shakespeare*. New York, 1992–.

Murphy, Andrew. *Shakespeare in Print: A History and Chronology of Shakespeare Publishing*. Cambridge, Eng., 2003.

Nosworthy, J. M. *Shakespeare's Occasional Plays: Their Origin and Transmission*. London and New York, 1965.

Pechter, Edward, ed. *Textual and Theatrical Shakespeare: Questions of Evidence*. Iowa City, 1996.

Peterson, Lene B. *Shakespeare's Errant Texts: Textual Form and Linguistic Style in Shakespeare's "Bad" Quartos and Co-authored Plays*. Cambridge, Eng., 2010.

Pollard, Alfred W. *Shakespeare Folios and Quartos: A Study in the Bibliography of Shakespeare's Plays, 1594–1685*. London, 1909.

———. *Shakespeare's Fight with the Pirates and the Problems of the Transmission of His Text*. Rev. ed. Cambridge, Eng., 1937.

Proudfoot, Richard. *Shakespeare: Text, Stage, and Canon*. London, 2001.

Sisson, C. J. *New Readings in Shakespeare*. 2 vols. Cambridge, Eng., 1956.

Taylor, Gary. *Shakespeare Reshaped, 1606–1623*. Oxford, 1993.

———, and Michael Warren, eds. *The Division of the Kingdoms: Shakespeare's Two Versions of "King Lear."* Oxford, 1983.

Vickers, Brian. *Appropriating Shakespeare: Contemporary Critical Quarrels*. New Haven, 1993.

———. *Shakespeare, Co-Author: A Historical Study of Five Collaborative Plays*. Oxford, 2002.

Walker, Alice. *Textual Problems of the First Folio*. Cambridge, Eng., 1953.

Wells, Stanley. *Re-editing Shakespeare for the Modern Reader*. Oxford, 1984.

Wells, Stanley, and Gary Taylor. *Modernizing Shakespeare's Spelling*. Oxford, 1979.

Werstine, Paul. "'Foul Papers' and 'Prompt-books': Printer's Copy for Shakespeare's *Comedy of Errors*," *Studies in Bibliography* 41 (1988), 232–46.

West, Anthony James. *The Shakespeare First Folio: The History of the Book*. Oxford, 2001.

Shakespeare Criticism to the 1930s

Badawi, M. M. *Coleridge: Critic of Shakespeare*. Cambridge, Eng., 1973.

Bradby, Anne, ed. *Shakespeare Criticism, 1919–35*. London, 1936.

Coleridge, S. T. *Coleridge on Shakespeare: The Text of the Lectures of 1811–12*, ed. R. A. Foakes. Charlottesville, Va., 1971.

———. *Coleridge's Writings on Shakespeare*, ed. Terence Hawkes. New York, 1959.

Dowden, Edward. *Shakspere: A Critical Study of His Mind and Art*. 3rd ed. London, 1905.

Evans, G. Blakemore, ed. *Shakespeare: Aspects of Influence*. Cambridge, Mass., 1976.

Hazlitt, William. *Characters of Shakespear's Plays*. London, 1817.

Johnson, Samuel. *Johnson on Shakespeare*, ed. Arthur Sherbo. Vol. 7 of *The Yale Edition of the Works of Samuel Johnson*. New Haven, 1968.

Kermode, Frank, ed. *Four Centuries of Shakespearean Criticism*. New York, 1965.

Knight, G. Wilson. *The Shakespearian Tempest*. London, 1932, 1953.

Muir, Kenneth. "Fifty Years of Shakespearian Criticism: 1900–1950," *ShS* 4 (1951), 1–25.

Rabkin, Norman, ed. *Approaches to Shakespeare*. New York, 1964.

Ralli, Augustus. *A History of Shakespearian Criticism*. 2 vols. London, 1932.

Raysor, T. M., ed. *Samuel Taylor Coleridge: Shakespearean Criticism*. 2 vols. 2nd ed. London, 1960.

Schlegel, August Wilhelm. *Lectures on Dramatic Art and Literature*, trans. John Black, 1846. Rpt., New York, 1965.

Schücking, Levin L. *Character Problems in Shakespeare's Plays*. London, 1917; trans., 1922.

Shaw, G. B. *Shaw on Shakespeare*, ed. Edwin Wilson. New York, 1961.

Sherbo, Arthur. *Samuel Johnson, Editor of Shakespeare*. Urbana, Ill., 1956.

Smith, David Nichol, ed. *Shakespeare Criticism: A Selection*. World's Classics, Oxford, 1916.

———, ed. *Eighteenth Century Essays on Shakespeare*. 2nd ed. Oxford, 1963.

Stoll, E. E. *Art and Artifice in Shakespeare*. Cambridge, Eng., 1933, 1962.

Vickers, Brian, ed. *Shakespeare: The Critical Heritage*. Several volumes. London and Boston, 1974–.

Welsford, Enid. *The Fool: His Social and Literary History*. London, 1935; rpt. 1966.

Westfall, A. V. *American Shakespearean Criticism, 1607–1865*. New York, 1939.

Shakespeare Criticism from the 1940s to the 1970s

Armstrong, Edward A. *Shakespeare's Imagination: A Study of the Psychology of Association and Inspiration*. London, 1946.

Barton, Anne. See Righter, Anne.

Bethell, S. L. *Shakespeare and the Popular Dramatic Tradition*. London and Durham, N.C., 1944.

Bevington, David, and Jay L. Halio, eds. *Shakespeare: Pattern of Excelling Nature*. Newark, Del., 1978.

Bloom, Allan, with Harry V. Jaffa. *Shakespeare's Politics*. New York and London, 1964.

Brown, John Russell. *Shakespeare's Plays in Performance*. London, 1966.

Bryant, J. A., Jr. *Hippolyta's View: Some Christian Aspects of Shakespeare's Plays*. Lexington, Ky., 1961.

Burckhardt, Sigurd. *Shakespearean Meanings*. Princeton, 1968.

Burke, Kenneth. *Language as Symbolic Action*. Berkeley, 1966.

Bush, Geoffrey. *Shakespeare and the Natural Condition*. Cambridge, Mass., 1956.

Calderwood, James L. *Shakespearean Metadrama*. Minneapolis, 1971.

Coghill, Neville. *Shakespeare's Professional Skills*. Cambridge, Eng., 1964.

Colie, Rosalie L. *Shakespeare's Living Art*. Princeton, 1974.

Council, Norman. *When Honour's at the Stake: Ideas of Honour in Shakespeare's Plays*. London, 1973.

Danby, John F. *Poets on Fortune's Hill: Studies in Sidney, Shakespeare, and Beaumont and Fletcher*. London, 1952.

Dean, Leonard F., ed. *Shakespeare: Modern Essays in Criticism*. New York, 1967.

Driver, Tom F. *The Sense of History in Greek and Shakespearean Drama*. New York, 1960.

Dusinberre, Juliet. *Shakespeare and the Nature of Women*. New York, 1975; 2nd ed., 1996.

Eagleton, Terence. *Shakespeare and Society*. New York and London, 1967.

Edwards, Philip. *Shakespeare and the Confines of Art*. London and New York, 1968.

Empson, William. *The Structure of Complex Words*. London, 1951.

Falconer, Alexander Frederick. *Shakespeare and the Sea*. London, 1964.

Fiedler, Leslie A. *The Stranger in Shakespeare*. New York, 1972.

Fly, Richard. *Shakespeare's Mediated World*. Amherst, Mass., 1976.

Frye, Roland M. *Shakespeare and Christian Doctrine*. Princeton, 1963.

Garber, Marjorie B. *Dream in Shakespeare: From Metaphor to Metamorphosis*. New Haven and London, 1974.

Goddard, Harold C. *The Meaning of Shakespeare*. Chicago, 1951.

Goldman, Michael. *Shakespeare and the Energies of Drama*. Princeton, 1972.

Granville-Barker, Harley. *Prefaces to Shakespeare*. 2 vols. Princeton, 1946–1947.

Harbage, Alfred. *As They Liked it*. New York, 1947.

———. *Shakespeare and the Rival Traditions*. New York, 1952.

Hawkes, Terence. *Shakespeare's Talking Animals: Language and Drama in Society*. London, 1973.

Hawkins, Harriett. *Poetic Freedom and Poetic Truth: Chaucer, Shakespeare, Marlowe, Milton*. Oxford, 1976.

Holland, Norman. *Psychoanalysis and Shakespeare*. New York, 1966.

———. *The Shakespearean Imagination*. New York, 1964.

Hunter, Robert Grams. *Shakespeare and the Mystery of God's Judgments*. Athens, Ga., 1976.

Jones, Emrys. *The Origins of Shakespeare*. Oxford, 1977.

Jorgensen, Paul A. *Shakespeare's Military World*. Berkeley and Los Angeles, 1956.

Kernan, Alvin B. *The Playwright as Magician: Shakespeare's Image of the Poet in the English Public Theater*. New Haven, 1979.

———, ed. *Modern Shakespearean Criticism*. New York, 1970.

Kettle, Arnold, ed. *Shakespeare in a Changing World*. London and New York, 1964.

Knights, L. C. *Some Shakespearean Themes*. London, 1959.

Kott, Jan. *Shakespeare Our Contemporary*. New York, 1964.

Leavis, F. R. *The Common Pursuit*. London, 1952.

Levin, Harry. *Shakespeare and the Revolution of the Times: Perspectives and Commentaries*. Oxford, 1976.

Levin, Richard. *New Readings vs. Old Plays: Recent Trends in the Reinterpretation of English Renaissance Drama*. Chicago, 1979.

McAlindon, T. *Shakespeare and Decorum*. London and New York, 1973.

Rabkin, Norman. *Shakespeare and the Common Understanding*. New York, 1967.

Righter, Anne. *Shakespeare and the Idea of the Play*. London, 1962.

Rossiter, A. P. *Angel with Horns*. London, 1961.

Sanders, Wilbur. *The Dramatist and the Received Idea: Studies in the Plays of Marlowe and Shakespeare*. Cambridge, Eng., 1968.

Sewell, Arthur. *Character and Society in Shakespeare*. London, 1951.

Soellner, Rolf. *Shakespeare's Patterns of Self-Knowledge*. Columbus, Ohio, 1972.

Spencer, Theodore. *Shakespeare and the Nature of Man*. New York, 1942.

Spivack, Bernard. *Shakespeare and the Allegory of Evil*. New York, 1958.

Stewart, J. I. M. *Character and Motive in Shakespeare*. London, 1949.

Stirling, Brents. *The Populace in Shakespeare*. New York, 1949.

Traversi, Derek. *An Approach to Shakespeare*. 2 vols. Rev. ed. London, 1968.

Turner, Frederick. *Shakespeare and the Nature of Time: Moral and Philosophical Themes in Some Plays and Poems of William Shakespeare*. Oxford, 1971.

Van Laan, Thomas F. *Role-Playing in Shakespeare*. Toronto, 1978.

Vyvyan, John. *Shakespeare and the Rose of Love: A Study of the Early Plays in Relation to the Medieval Philosophy of Love*. London, 1960.

Watson, Curtis Brown. *Shakespeare and the Renaissance Concept of Honor*. Princeton, 1960.

Weimann, Robert. *Shakespeare and the Popular Tradition in the Theater*, ed. Robert Schwartz. Baltimore, 1978.

Whitaker, Virgil K. *Shakespeare's Use of Learning*. San Marino, Calif., 1953.

Zeeveld, W. Gordon. *The Temper of Shakespeare's Thought*. New Haven and London, 1974.

Shakespeare Criticism Since 1980, Including New Historicism, Gender Studies, and Poststructuralism

See also, under *Shakespeare's Predecessors and Contemporaries*, Bednarz, Belsey, Braden, Bristol, Bruster, Cohen, Dolan, Farley-Hills, Findlay (two items), Freer, McLuskie, Orgel, Rasmussen, Rose, Shannon, Sullivan, and Vickers; and under *Shakespeare Criticism from the 1940s to the 1970s*, Weimann.

Adelman, Janet. *Suffocating Mothers: Fantasies of Maternal Origin in Shakespeare's Plays, "Hamlet" to "The Tempest."* Chicago, 1992.

Alexander, Catherine M. S., ed. *Shakespeare and Politics*. Cambridge, Eng., 2004.

———, and Stanley Wells, eds. *Shakespeare and Race*. Cambridge, Eng., 2000.

———, eds. *Shakespeare and Sexuality*. Cambridge, Eng., 2001.

Archer, John Michael. *Citizen Shakespeare: Freemen and Aliens in the Language of the Plays*. New York, 2005.

Aridge, Anthony. *Shakespeare and the Prince of Love: The Feast of Misrule in the Middle Temple*. London, 2000.

Armitage, David, Conal Condren, and Andrew Fitzmaurice, eds. *Shakespeare and Early Modern Political Thought*. Cambridge, 2009.

Armstrong, Philip. *Shakespeare in Psychoanalysis*. London and New York, 2001.

Atkins, G. Douglas, and David Bergeron, eds. *Shakespeare and Deconstruction*. New York, 1988.

Auden, W. H. *Lectures on Shakespeare*, ed. Arthur Kirsch. Princeton, 2000.

Bach, Rebecca Ann. *Shakespeare and Renaissance Literature before Heterosexuality*. New York, 2007.

Bache, William B., and Vernon P. Loggins. *Shakespeare's Deliberate Art*. Lanham, Md., 1996.

Bamber, Linda. *Comic Women, Tragic Men: A Study of Gender and Genre in Shakespeare*. Stanford, 1982.

Barber, C. L. *The Whole Journey: Shakespeare's Power of Development*. Berkeley, 1986.

Bate, Jonathan. *The Genius of Shakespeare*. Oxford, 1997.

———. *Shakespeare and Ovid*. Oxford, 1993.

———. *Shakespeare and the English Romantic Imagination*. Oxford, 1986, 1989.

———. *Shakespearean Constitutions: Politics, Theatre, Criticism, 1730–1830*. Oxford, 1989.

———, ed. *The Romantics on Shakespeare*. New York and London, 1992.

———, Jill L. Levenson, and Dieter Mehl, eds. *Shakespeare and the Twentieth Century: The Selected Proceedings of the International Shakespeare Association World Congress, Los Angeles, 1996*. Newark, Del., 1998.

Bates, Robin E. *Shakespeare and the Cultural Colonization of Ireland*. New York, 2008.

Belsey, Catherine. *Shakespeare and the Loss of Eden: The Construction of Family Values in Early Modern Culture*. New Brunswick, N.J., 1999.

———. *Shakespeare in Theory and Practice*. Edinburgh, 2008.

Berger, Harry, Jr. *Making Trifles of Terrors: Redistributing Complicities in Shakespeare*. ed. Peter Erickson. Stanford, 1997.

Bergeron, David, ed. *Pageantry in the Shakespearean Theater*. Athens, Ga., 1985.

Berry, Edward. *Shakespeare and the Hunt: A Cultural and Social Study*. Cambridge, Eng., 2001.

Berryman, John. *Shakespeare*. New York, 1999.

Bevington, David. *Shakespeare*. Oxford, 2002.

———. *Shakespeare's Ideas: More Things in Heaven and Earth*. Oxford, 2008.

Blank, Paula. *Shakespeare and the Mismeasure of Renaissance Man*. Ithaca, N.Y., 2006.

Bloom, Allan David. *Shakespeare on Love and Friendship*. Chicago, 2000.

Bloom, Harold. *Shakespeare: The Invention of the Human.* New York, 1998.

Boehrer, Bruce Thomas. *Shakespeare among the Animals: Nature and Society in the Drama of Early Modern England.* New York, 2002.

Boose, Lynda E. "The Father and the Bride in Shakespeare," *PMLA* 97 (1982), 325–47.

Bretzius, Stephen. *Shakespeare in Theory: The Postmodern Academy and the Early Modern Theater.* Ann Arbor, Mich., 1997.

Bristol, Michael. *Shakespeare's America, America's Shakespeare.* London and New York, 1990.

Bruster, Douglas. *Shakespeare and the Question of Culture: Early Modern Literature and the Cultural Turn.* New York, 2003.

Bulman, James C., ed. *Shakespeare, Theory, and Performance.* London and New York, 1996.

Burnett, Mark Thorton. *Constructing "Monsters" in Shakespearian Drama and Early Modern Culture.* Houndmills, Basingstoke, UK, and New York, 2002.

———, and Ramona Wray. *Shakespeare and Ireland: History, Politics, Culture.* New York, 1997.

Burt, Richard. *Shakespeare and Mass Media.* New York and Basingstoke, Eng., 2002.

Calderwood, James. *Shakespeare and the Denial of Death.* Amherst, Mass., 1987.

Callaghan, Dympna C. *Shakespeare Without Women: Representing Gender and Race on the Renaissance Stage.* London and New York, 2000.

———, ed. *A Feminist Companion to Shakespeare.* Oxford, 2000.

Callaghan, Dympna, Lorraine Helms, and Jyotsna Singh. *The Weyward Sisters: Shakespeare and Feminist Politics.* Cambridge, Eng., 1994.

Canino, Catherine Grace. *Shakespeare and the Nobility: The Negotiation of Lineage.* Cambridge, Eng., 2007.

Carey, John, ed. *English Renaissance Studies.* Oxford, 1980.

Cartelli, Thomas. *Repositioning Shakespeare: National Formations, Postcolonial Appropriations.* London and New York, 1999.

Cavell, Stanley. *Disowning Knowledge in Six Plays of Shakespeare.* Cambridge, Eng., 1987.

Charnes, Linda. *Notorious Identity: Materializing the Subject in Shakespeare.* Cambridge, Mass., 1993.

Chedgzoy, Kate, ed. *Shakespeare, Feminism, and Gender.* Basingstoke, Hants., New York, 2001.

———, Susanne Greenhaigh, and Robert Shaughnessy, eds. *Shakespeare and Childhood.* Cambridge, 2007.

Cheney, Patrick. *Shakespeare, National Poet-Playwright.* Cambridge, Eng., 2004.

———. *Shakespeare's Literary Authorship.* Cambridge, Eng., 2008.

Chernaik, Warren. *The Myth of Rome in Shakespeare and His Contemporaries.* Cambridge, Eng., 2011.

Clayton, Tom, Susan Brock, and Vincente Forés, eds. *Shakespeare and the Mediterranean: The Selected Proceedings of the International Shakespeare Association World Congress, Valencia, 2001.* Newark, Del., 2004.

Cohen, Adam Max. *Shakespeare and Technology: Dramatizing Early Modern Technological Revolutions.* New York, 2006.

Cook, Ann Jennalie. *Making a Match: Courtship in Shakespeare and His Society.* Princeton, 1991.

Cooper, Helen. *Shakespeare and the Medieval World.* London, 2010.

Corcoran, Neil. *Shakespeare and the Modern Poet.* Cambridge, Eng., 2010.

Cox, John D. *Shakespeare and the Dramaturgy of Power.* Princeton, 1989.

———. *Seeming Knowledge: Shakespeare and Skeptical Faith.* Waco, Tex., 2007.

Crane, Mary Thomas. *Shakespeare's Brain: Reading with Cognitive Theory.* Princeton, 2001.

Daileader, Celia R. *Eroticism on the Renaissance Stage: Transcendence, Desire, and the Limits of the Visible.* Cambridge, Eng., 1998.

Danson, Lawrence. *Shakespeare's Dramatic Genres.* Oxford, 2000.

Dawson, Anthony B. *Indirections: Shakespeare and the Art of Illusion.* Toronto, 1984.

Davis, Philip. *Shakespeare Thinking.* London, 2007.

De Cook, Travis, and Alan Galey, eds. *Shakespeare, the Bible, and the Form of the Book: Contested Scriptures.* New York, 2012.

De Grazia, Margreta, Maureen Quilligan, and Peter Stallybrass, eds. *Subject and Object in Renaissance Culture.* Cambridge, Eng., 1996.

De Grazia, Margreta, and Stanley Wells, eds. *The Cambridge Companion to Shakespeare.* Cambridge, Eng., 2nd ed., 2011.

Delabastita, Dirk, Jozef de Vos, and Paul Franssen, eds. *Shakespeare and European Politics.* Newark, Del., 2008.

Desmet, Christy. *Reading Shakespeare's Characters: Rhetoric, Ethics, and Identity.* Amherst, Mass., 1992.

Desmet, Christy, and Robert Sawyer, eds. *Shakespeare and Appropriation.* London and New York, 1999.

DiPietro, Cary. *Shakespeare and Modernism.* Cambridge, Eng., 2006.

Dobson, Michael. *The Making of the National Poet: Shakespeare, Adaptation, and Authorship, 1660–1769.* Oxford, 1992.

———, and Stanley Wells, eds. *The Oxford Companion to Shakespeare.* Oxford, 2001.

Dolan, Frances E. *Dangerous Familiars: Representations of Domestic Crime in England, 1550–1700.* Ithaca, N.Y., 1994.

Dollimore, Jonathan. *Radical Tragedy: Religion, Ideology and Power in the Drama of Shakespeare and His Contemporaries.* Chicago, 1984; New York, 1989.

Dollimore, Jonathan, and Alan Sinfield, eds. *Political Shakespeare: New Essays in Cultural Materialism.* Manchester, Eng., 1985.

Donaldson, E. Talbot. *The Swan at the Well: Shakespeare Reading Chaucer.* New Haven, 1985.

———, ed. *Alternative Shakespeares.* London, 1985.

Drakakis, John, and Dale Townshend. *Gothic Shakespeares.* New York, 2008.

Driver, Martha A., and Sid Ray, eds. *Shakespeare and the Middle Ages: Essays on the Performance and Adaptation of the Plays with Medieval Sources or Settings.* Jefferson, N.C., 2009.

Dubrow, Heather. *Shakespeare and Domestic Loss: Forms of Deprivation, Mourning, and Recuperation.* Cambridge, Eng., 1999 and 2004.

———, and Richard Strier, eds. *The Historical Renaissance: New Essays on Tudor and Stuart Literature and Culture.* Chicago, 1988.

Eagleton, Terence. *William Shakespeare.* Oxford, 1986.

Edwards, Philip. *Shakespeare: A Writer's Progress.* Oxford, 1986.

———, et al., eds. *Shakespeare's Styles.* Cambridge, Eng., 1980.

Egan, Gabriel. *Shakespeare and Marx.* Oxford, 2004.

Engle, Lars. *Shakespearean Pragmatism: Market of His Time.* Chicago, 1993.

Enterline, Lynn. *The Rhetoric of the Body from Ovid to Shakespeare.* Cambridge, Eng., 2000.

Erickson, Peter. *Patriarchal Structures in Shakespeare's Drama.* Berkeley, 1985.

Erickson, Peter, and Coppélia Kahn, eds. *Shakespeare's Rough Magic: Essays in Honor of C. L. Barber.* Newark, Del., 1985.

Erne, Lukas. *Shakespeare's Modern Collaborators.* London, 2008.

———. *Shakespeare as Literary Dramatist.* Cambridge, Eng., 2003.

Fernie, Ewan. *Spiritual Shakespeare.* London and New York, 2005.

———. *Shame in Shakespeare.* London and New York, 2001.

Foakes, R. A. *Shakespeare and Violence.* Cambridge, Eng., 2003.

Frazer, Elizabeth. *Shakespeare and the Political Way.* London, 2007.

French, Marilyn. *Shakespeare's Division of Experience.* New York, 1981.

Frye, Northrop. *Northrop Frye on Shakespeare,* ed. Robert Sandler. New Haven, 1986.

Fumerton, Patricia, and Simon Hunt, eds. *Renaissance Culture and the Everyday.* Philadelphia, 1999.

Gager, Valerie L. *Shakespeare and Dickens: The Dynamics of Influence.* Cambridge, Eng., 1996.

Garber, Marjorie. *Coming of Age in Shakespeare.* London, 1981.

———. *Shakespeare's Ghost Writers: Literature as Uncanny Causality.* London and New York, 1987.

———. *Shakespeare After All.* New York, 2004.

———, ed. *Cannibals, Witches, and Divorce: Estranging the Renaissance.* Baltimore, 1987.

———. *Profiling Shakespeare.* New York, 2008.

———. *Shakespeare and Modern Culture.* New York, 2008.

Garner, Shirley Nelson, Claire Kehane, and Madelon Sprengnether, eds. *The (M)other Tongue: Essays in Feminist Psychoanalytic Interpretation.* Ithaca, N.Y., 1985.

Ghose, Indira. *Shakespeare and Laughter: A Cultural History.* Manchester, 2008.

Gibbons, Brian. *Shakespeare and Multiplicity.* Cambridge, Eng., 1993.

Gillespie, Stuart, and Neil Rhodes. *Shakespeare and Elizabethan Popular Culture.* London, 2006.

Gillies, John. *Shakespeare and the Geography of Difference.* Cambridge, Eng., 1994.

Goldberg, Jonathan. *James I and the Politics of Literature: Jonson, Shakespeare, Donne, and Their Contemporaries.* Baltimore, 1983.

————. *Sodometries: Renaissance Texts, Modern Sexualities.* Stanford, 1992.

Gonzáles, José Manuel, and Holger Klein, eds. *Shakespeare and Spain.* Lewiston, Maine, 2002.

Grady, Hugh. *Shakespeare, Machiavelli, and Montaigne: Power and Subjectivity from "Richard II" to "Hamlet."* Oxford, 2002.

————, ed. *Shakespeare and Modernity: Early Modern to Millennium.* London and New York, 2000.

————. *Shakespeare's Universal Wolf: Postmodernist Studies in Early Modern Reification.* Oxford, 1996.

————. *Shakespeare and Modernity: Early Modern to Millennium.* London and New York, 2000.

————. *Shakespeare and Impure Aesthetics.* Cambridge, 2009.

Graham, Kenneth J. E., and Philip D. Colington, eds. *Shakespeare and Religious Change.* Basingstoke, Hants., and New York, 2009.

Grav, Peter F. *Shakespeare and the Economic Imperative: What's Aught but as 'Tis Valued?* New York, 2008.

Greenblatt, Stephen. *Learning to Curse: Essays in Early Modern Culture.* London and New York, 1990.

————. *Marvelous Possessions: The Wonder of the New World.* Chicago, 1991.

————. *Renaissance Self-Fashioning: From More to Shakespeare.* Chicago, 1980.

————. *Shakespearean Negotiations: The Circulation of Social Energy in Renaissance England.* Berkeley, 1988.

————. *Shakespeare's Freedom.* Chicago, 2010.

————. *Will in the World: How Shakespeare Became Shakespeare.* New York, 2004.

Guneratne, Anthony R. *Shakespeare and Genre: From Early Inheritances to Postmodern Legacies.* Basingstoke, Hants., and New York, 2011.

Habib, Imtiaz. *Shakespeare and Race: Postcolonial Praxis in the Early Modern Period.* Lanham and Oxford, 2000.

Hackett, Helen. *Shakespeare and Elizabeth: The Meeting of Two Myths.* Princeton, 2009.

Hadfield, Andrew. *Shakespeare and Republicanism.* Cambridge, Eng., 2004.

————. *Shakespeare and Renaissance Politics.* London, 2004.

————. *Shakespeare, Spenser, and the Matter of Britain.* Basingstoke, Hants, and New York, 2004.

————, and Paul Hammond, eds. *Shakespeare and Renaissance Europe.* London, 2004.

Hall, Kim F. *Things of Darkness: Economies of Race and Gender in Early Modern England.* Ithaca, N.Y., 1994.

Hallett, Charles A. and Elaine S. *Analyzing Shakespeare's Action: Scene versus Sequence.* Cambridge, Eng., 1991.

Halpern, Richard. *Shakespeare Among the Moderns.* Ithaca, N.Y., 1997.

Hamilton, Donna B. *Shakespeare and the Politics of Protestant England.* Lexington, Ky., 1992.

Hamlin, William M. *The Image of America in Montaigne, Spenser, and Shakespeare: Renaissance Ethnography and Literary Tradition.* New York, 1995.

Hapgood, Robert. *Shakespeare the Theatre-Poet.* Oxford, 1991.

Hardy, Barbara. *Shakespeare's Storytellers: Dramatic Narration.* London and Chester Springs, 1997.

Harris, Jonathan Gil. *Shakespeare and Literary Theory.* Oxford, 2010.

Hart, Jonathan. *Columbus, Shakespeare, and the Interpretation of the New World.* New York, 2003.

Haverkamp, Anselm. *Shakespearean Genealogies of Power: A Whispering of Nothing in Hamlet, Richard II, Julius Caesar, Macbeth, The Merchant of Venice, and The Winter's Tale.* New York, 2011.

Hawkes, Terence. *Meaning by Shakespeare.* London and New York, 1992.

————, ed. *Alternative Shakespeares.* Vol. 2. London and New York, 1996.

Hawkins, Harriet. *The Devil's Party: Critical Counter-interpretations of Shakespearian Drama.* Oxford, 1985.

Hillman, Richard. *Shakespeare, Marlowe, and the Politics of France.* Basingstoke, Hants., and New York, 2002.

Hofele, Andreas. *Stage, Stake, and Scaffold: Humans and Animals in Shakespeare's Theatre.* Oxford, 2011.

Holbrook, Peter. *Shakespeare's Individualism.* Cambridge, Eng., 2010.

Holderness, Graham. *Shakespeare and Venice.* Farnham, Surrey, Burlington, Vermont, 2010.

Holland, Norman, et al., eds. *Shakespeare's Personality.* Berkeley, 1989.

Holland, Peter. *Shakespeare and Narrative.* Cambridge, Eng., 2000.

Hopkins, Lisa. *Shakespeare on the Edge: Border-Crossing in the Tragedies and the Henriad.* Aldershot and Burlington, Vt., 2005.

Howard, Jean E. *Shakespeare's Art of Orchestration: Stage Technique and Audience Response.* Urbana, Ill., 1984.

————. *The Stage and Social Struggle in Early Modern England.* London, 1994.

————, and Marion F. O'Connor, eds. *Shakespeare Reproduced: The Text in History and Ideology.* London and New York, 1987.

————, and Scott Cutler Shershow, eds. *Marxist Shakespeares.* London and New York, 2001.

Huang, Alexander C.Y. *Chinese Shakespeares: Two Centuries of Cultural Exchange.* New York, 2009.

Hughes, Ted. *Shakespeare and the Goddess of Complete Being.* London, 1992.

Hulbert, Jennifer. *Shakespeare and Youth Culture.* New York, 2006.

Jacobus, Lee A. *Shakespeare and the Dialectic of Certainty.* New York, 1992.

James, Heather. *Shakespeare's Troy: Drama, Politics, and the Translation of Empire.* Cambridge, Eng., 1997.

Jardine, Lisa. *Reading Shakespeare Historically.* London and New York, 1996.

————. *Still Harping on Daughters: Women and Drama in the Age of Shakespeare.* Sussex and Totowa, N.J., 1983; New York, 1989.

Johnson, David, ed. *Shakespeare and South Africa.* Oxford, 1996.

Jones, John. *Shakespeare at Work.* Oxford, 1995, 2000.

Joughlin, John J. *Shakespeare and National Culture.* Manchester, 1997.

Kahn, Coppélia. *Man's Estate: Masculine Identity in Shakespeare.* Berkeley, 1981.

————. *Roman Shakespeare: Warriors, Wounds, and Women.* London and New York, 1997.

Kamps, Ivo, ed. *Materialist Shakespeare: A History.* London, 1995.

————, ed. *Shakespeare Left and Right.* New York and London, 1991.

Kastan, David Scott. *Shakespeare After Theory.* London, 1999.

————. *Shakespeare and the Book.* Cambridge, Eng., 2001.

————. *Shakespeare and the Shapes of Time.* Hanover, N.H., 1982.

————, ed. *A Companion to Shakespeare.* Oxford, 1999.

Keevak, Michael. *Sexual Shakespeare: Forgery, Authorship, Portraiture.* Detroit, 2001.

Kehler, Dorothea. *Shakespeare's Widows.* New York, 2009.

Kendall, Gillian Murray, ed. *Shakespearean Power and Punishment: A Volume of Essays.* Madison, N.J., London, 1998.

Kermode, Frank. *On Shakespeare's Learning.* Manchester, 1965.

Kernan, Alvin. *Shakespeare, the King's Playwright: Theater in the Stuart Court, 1603–1613.* New Haven, 1995.

Kerrigan, William. *Shakespeare's Promises.* Baltimore, 1999.

————. *On Shakespeare and Early Modern Literature: Essays.* Oxford, 2001.

Kidnie, Margaret Jane. *Shakespeare and the Problem of Adaptation.* Abingdon, Oxon., New York, 2009.

Kiefer, Frederick. *Shakespeare's Visual Theatre: Staging the Personified Characters.* Cambridge, Eng., 2003.

King, Ros, and Paul J. C. M. Fanssen. *Shakespeare and War.* Basingstoke, Hants., and New York, 2008.

Kinney, Arthur F. *Shakespeare and Cognition: Aristotle's Legacy and Shakespearean Drama.* New York, 2006.

————. *Shakespeare's Webs: Networks of Meaning in Renaissance Drama.* New York, 2004.

————, ed. *The Oxford Handbook of Shakespeare.* Oxford, 2012.

Kirsch, Arthur. *Shakespeare and the Experience of Love.* Cambridge, Eng., 1981.

Kishi, Tetsuo, and Graham Bradshaw. *Shakespeare in Japan*. London and New York, 2005.

Klein, Holger, and Jean-Marie Maguin. *Shakespeare and France*. Lewiston, N.Y., 1995.

———, and James L. Harner, eds. *Shakespeare and the Visual Arts*. Lewiston, Maine, 2000.

———. *Shakespeare Only*. Chicago, 2009.

Knapp, Robert S. *Shakespeare—The Theater and the Book*. Princeton, 1989.

Knowles, Richard, ed. *Shakespeare and Carnival: After Bakhtin*. London and New York, 1998.

Korda, Natasha. *Shakespeare's Domestic Economies: Gender and Property in Early Modern England*. Philadelphia, 2002.

Kosthová, Marcela. *Shakespeare in Transition: Political Appropriations in the Postcommunist Czech Republic*. Basingstoke, Hants., New York, 2010.

Krier, Theresa M. *Birth Passages: Maternity and Nostalgia, Antiquity to Shakespeare*. Ithaca, N.Y., 2001.

Lanier, Douglas. *Shakespeare and Modern Popular Culture*. Oxford, 2002.

Lenz, Carolyn, et al., eds. *The Woman's Part: Feminist Criticism of Shakespeare*. Urbana, Ill., 1980.

Levin, Carole, and John Watkins. *Shakespeare's Foreign Words: National and Transnational Identities in the Elizabethan Age*. Ithaca, N.Y., 2009.

Levin, Richard A. *Shakespeare's Secret Schemers: The Study of an Early Modern Dramatic Device*. Newark, Del., 2002.

Lindley, David. *Shakespeare and Music*. London, 2006.

Little, Arthur L., Jr. *Shakespeare Jungle Fever: National-Imperial Re-Visions of Race, Rape, and Sacrifice*. Stanford, 2000.

Loomba, Ania. *Gender, Race, Renaissance Drama*. Manchester, Eng., 1989.

———. *Shakespeare, Race, and Colonialism*. Oxford, 2002.

Loomba, Ania, and Martin Orkin, eds. *Post-colonial Shakespeares*. London and New York, 1998.

Loxley, James, and Mark Robson. *Shakespeare, Jonson, and the Claims of the Performative*. New York, 2012.

Lupton, Julia Reinhard. *Citizen-Saints: Shakespeare and Political Theology*. Chicago, 2005.

Maguire, Laurie E. *Shakespeare's Names*. Oxford, 2007.

Mahon, John W., and Thomas A. Pendleton, eds. *"Fanned and Winnowed Opinion": Shakespearean Essays Presented to Harold Jenkins*. London, 1987.

Makaryk, Irena R., and Joseph G. Price, eds. *Shakespeare and the Worlds of Communism and Socialism*. Toronto, 2006.

Maley, Willy, and Andrew Murphy, eds. *Shakespeare and Scotland*. Manchester, 2004.

———, and Philip Schwyer. *Shakespeare and Wales: From the Marches to the Assembly*. Farnham, Eng., and Burlington, Vermont, 2010.

Mallin, Eric. *Inscribing the Time: Shakespeare and the End of Elizabethan England*. Berkeley, 1995.

Marcus, Leah. *Puzzling Shakespeare: Local Reading and its Discontents*. Berkeley, 1988.

Marrapodi, Michele, ed. *Shakespeare and Renaissance Literary Theories: Anglo-Italian Translations*. Aldershot, Eng., and Burlington, Vermont, 2010.

———, ed. *Shakespeare, Italy, and Intertextuality*. Manchester, 2004.

Marshall, Gail. *Shakespeare in the Nineteenth Century*. Cambridge, Eng., 2012.

———. *Shakespeare and Victorian Women*. Cambridge, Eng., 2009.

Martindale, Charles, and A. B. Taylor, eds. *Shakespeare and the Classics*. Cambridge, Eng., 2004.

Martindale, Charles and Michelle. *Shakespeare and the Uses of Antiquity*. London and New York, 1990.

Marx, Steven. *Shakespeare and the Bible*. Oxford, 2000.

Mazzio, Carla, and Douglas Trevor, eds. *Historicism, Psychoanalysis, and Early Modern Culture*. London and New York, 2000.

McAlindon, T. *Shakespeare Minus "Theory."* Aldershot, Hants., and Burlington, Vermont, 2004.

McDonald, Russ, ed. *Shakespeare Reread: The Texts in New Contexts*. Ithaca, N.Y., 1994.

McMullan, Gordon, and Jonathan Hope, eds. *The Politics of Tragicomedy: Shakespeare and After*. London and New York, 1992.

McNeill, Fiona. *Poor Women in Shakespeare*. Cambridge, Eng., 2007.

McPherson, David C. *Shakespeare, Jonson, and the Myth of Venice*. Newark, Del., 1990.

Melchiori, Giorgio. *Shakespeare's Garter Plays: "Edward III" to "Merry Wives of Windsor."* Newark, Del., 1994.

Meron, Theodor. *Bloody Constraint: War, and Chivalry in Shakespeare*. Oxford, 1998.

———. *Henry's Wars and Shakespeare's Laws: Perspectives on the Law of War in the Later Middle Ages*. Oxford, 1994.

Milwes, Geoffrey. *Shakespeare and the Constant Romans*. Oxford, 1996.

Miola, Robert S. *Shakespeare's Reading*. Oxford and New York, 2000.

———. *Shakespeare's Rome*. Cambridge, Eng., 1983.

Montrose, Louis. *The Purpose of Playing: Shakespeare and Cultural Politics of the Elizabethan Theatre*. Chicago, 1996.

Mullaney, Steven. *The Place of the Stage: License, Play, and Power in Renaissance England*. Chicago, 1988.

Murphy, Andrew. *Shakespeare for the People: Working-Class Readers, 1800–1900*. Cambridge, Eng., 2008.

Nagarajan, S., and S. Viswanathan, eds. *Shakespeare in India*. Oxford, 1987.

Neely, Carol Thomas. *Broken Nuptials in Shakespeare's Plays*. New Haven, 1985.

Newman, Karen. *Fashioning Femininity and the English Renaissance Drama*. Chicago, 1991.

Nordlund, Marcus. *Shakespeare and the Nature of Love: Literature, Culture, Evolution*. Evanston, Ill., 2007.

Novy, Marianne. *Love's Argument: Gender Relations in Shakespeare*. Chapel Hill, N.C., 1984.

———, ed. *Women's Re-Visions of Shakespeare*. Urbana, Ill., 1990.

———, ed. *Transforming Shakespeare: Contemporary Women's Re-Visions in Literature and Performance*. New York, 1999.

Nuttall, A. D. *A New Mimesis: Shakespeare and the Representation of Reality*. London, 1983.

———. *Shakespeare the Thinker*. New Haven, 2007.

Orgel, Stephen. *The Authentic Shakespeare and Other Problems of the Early Modern Stage*. London and New York, 2002.

———. *Imagining Shakespeare: A History of Texts and Visions*. Basingstoke, Eng., and New York, 2003.

Orgel, Stephen, and Sean Keilen, eds. *Shakespeare and History; Post-modern Shakespeare; Shakespeare and the Interpretive Tradition; Shakespeare and the Literary Tradition; Shakespeare and Gender; Political Shakespeare; Shakespeare and the Arts, Shakespeare and the Editorial Tradition*. In separate volumes, New York, 1999.

O'Rourke, James. *Retheorizing Shakespeare Through Presentist Readings*. New York, 2012.

Palfrey, Simon. *Shakespeare in Parts*. Oxford, 2007.

Parker, Patricia. *Shakespeare from the Margins: Language, Culture, Context*. Chicago, 1996.

———, and Geoffrey Hartman, eds. *Shakespeare and the Question of Theory*. London, 1985, 1990.

Paster, Gail Kern. *The Body Embarrassed: Drama and the Disciplines of Shame in Early Modern England*. Ithaca, N.Y., 1993.

———. *Humoring the Body: Emotions and the Renaissance Stage*. Chicago, 2004.

Patterson, Annabel. *Shakespeare and the Popular Voice*. Oxford, 1989.

Pechter, Edward. *Shakespeare Studies Today: Romanticism Lost*. Basingstoke, Hants., 2011.

Perry, Curtis, and John Watkins. *Shakespeare and the Middle Ages*. Oxford, 2009.

Pettigrew, Todd Howard James. *Shakespeare and the Practice of Physics: Medical Narratives on the Early Modern English Stage*. Newark, Del., 2007.

Platt, Peter G. *Shakespeare and the Culture of Paradox*. Farnham, Eng., and Burlington, Vermont, 2009.

Polka, Brayton. *Shakespeare and Interpretation, or What You Will*. Newark, Del., 2011.

Poole, Kristen. *Radical Religion from Shakespeare to Milton*. Cambridge, Eng., 2000.

Pugliatti, Paola. *Shakespeare and the Just War Tradition*. Farnham, Eng., and Burlington, Vermont, 2010.

Pye, Christopher. *The Vanishing: Shakespeare, the Subject, and Early Modern Culture*. Durham, N.C., 2000.

Rabkin, Norman. *Shakespeare and the Problem of Meaning.* Chicago, 1981.

Rackin, Phyllis. *Shakespeare and Women.* Oxford, 2005.

Raffield, Paul, and Gary Watt, eds. *Shakespeare and the Law.* Oxford, 2008.

Rasmussen, Eric, and Aaron Santesso, eds. *Comparative Excellence: New Essays on Shakespeare and Johnson.* New York, 2007.

Richardson, Catherine. *Shakespeare and Material Culture.* Oxford, 2011.

Ritchie, Fiona, and Peter Sabor, eds. *Shakespeare in the Eighteenth Century.* Cambridge, Eng., 2012.

Roberts, Jeanne Addison. *Literary Criticism as Dream Analysis: Essays on Renaissance and Modern Writers.* Baltimore, 2009.

Roe, John. *Shakespeare and Machiavelli.* Cambridge, Eng., 2002.

Rozmovits, Linda. *Shakespeare and the Politics of Culture in Late Victorian England.* Baltimore, 1998.

Sabor, Peter, and Paul Yachnin. *Shakespeare and the Eighteenth Century.* Aldershot, Eng., and Burlington, Vermont, 2008.

Salingar, Leo. *Dramatic Form in Shakespeare and the Jacobeans.* Cambridge, Eng., 1986.

Sanders, Julie. *Shakespeare and Music: Afterlives and Borrowings.* Cambridge, Eng., and Malden, Mass., 2007.

Schalkwyk, David. *Shakespeare, Love, and Service.* Cambridge, Eng., 2008.

Schmidgall, Gary. *Shakespeare and Opera.* Oxford, 1990.

Schoch, Richard W. *Not Shakespeare: Bardolatry and Burlesque in the Nineteenth Century.* Cambridge, Eng., 2002.

Schwartz, Murray, and Coppélia Kahn, eds. *Representing Shakespeare: New Psychoanalytic Essays.* Baltimore, 1980.

Scott, Charlotte. *Shakespeare and the Idea of the Book.* Oxford, 2007.

Scott, Michael. *Shakespeare and the Modern Dramatist.* New York, 1989.

Shannon, Laurie. *Sovereign Amity: Figures of Friendship in Shakespeare's Contexts.* Chicago, 2002.

Shapiro, James S. *Shakespeare and the Jews.* New York, 1996.

———. *A Year in the Life of William Shakespeare, 1599.* New York, 2005.

Shaughnessy, Robert, ed. *The Cambridge Companion to Shakespeare and Popular Culture.* Cambridge, Eng., 2007.

Shell, Alison. *Shakespeare and Religion.* London, 2005.

Shurbanov, Aleksandŭr. *Shakespeare's Lyricized Drama.* Newark, Del., 2010.

Siemon, James R. *Shakespearean Iconoclasm.* Berkeley, 1985.

Sillars, Suart. *Painting Shakespeare: The Artist as Critic, 1720–1820.* Cambridge, Eng., 2006.

Sinfield, Alan. *Faultlines: Cultural Materialism and the Politics of Dissident Reading.* Berkeley, 1992.

Skura, Meredith Anne. *The Literary Use of the Psychoanalytic Process.* New Haven, 1981.

———. *Shakespeare the Actor and the Purposes of Playing.* Chicago, 1993.

Smith, Bruce R. *Homosexual Desire in Shakespeare's England.* Chicago, 1991.

———. *Shakespeare and Masculinity.* Oxford, 2000.

Smith, Emma. *The Cambridge Shakespeare Guide.* Cambridge, 2012.

Snyder, Susan. *Shakespeare: A Wayward Journey.* Newark, Del., 2002.

Sokol, B. J. *Shakespeare and Tolerance.* Cambridge, Eng., 2008.

———, and Mary Sokol. *Shakespeare, Law, and Marriage.* Cambridge, Eng., 2003.

Stapleton, M. L. *Fated Sky: The "Femina Furens" in Shakespeare.* Newark, Del., and London, 2000.

Stewart, Alan. *Shakespeare's Letters.* Oxford, 2008.

Stewart, Stanley. *Shakespeare and Philosophy.* New York, 2010.

Stockholder, Kay. *Dream Works: Lovers and Families in Shakespeare's Plays.* Toronto, 1987.

Stříbrný, Zdeněk. *Shakespeare and Eastern Europe.* Oxford, 2000.

Sturgess, Kim C. *Shakespeare and the American Nation.* Cambridge, Eng., 2004.

Tanner, Tony. *Prefaces to Shakespeare.* Cambridge, Mass., 2010.

Taylor, A. B. *Shakespeare's Ovid: The Metamorphoses in the Plays and Poems.* Cambridge, Eng., 2000.

Taylor, Dennis, and David Beauregard, eds. *Shakespeare and the Culture of Christianity in Early Modern England.* New York, 2003.

Taylor, Gary. *Reinventing Shakespeare: A Cultural History from the Restoration to the Present.* New York, 1989.

Taylor, Mark. *Shakespeare's Imitations.* Newark, Del., 2002.

Taylor, Michael. *Shakespeare Criticism in the Twentieth Century.* Oxford, 2001.

Tetsuo, Kiski, and Graham Bradshaw. *Shakespeare in Japan.* London, 2005.

Traub, Valerie. *Desire and Anxiety: Circulations of Sexuality in Shakespearean Drama.* London, 1992.

Trawick, Buckner B. *Shakespeare and Alcohol.* Amsterdam, 1976.

Trudeau-Clayton, Margaret. *Jonson, Shakespeare, and Early Modern Virgil.* Cambridge, Eng., 1998.

Tucker, Kenneth. *Shakespeare and Jungian Typology: A Reading of the Plays.* Jefferson, N.C., 2003.

Turner, Henry. *Shakespeare's Double Helix.* London, 2007.

Usher, Peter D. *Shakespeare and the Dawn of Modern Science.* Amherst, N.Y., 2010.

Wagner, Matthew D. *Shakespeare, Theatre, and Time.* New York, 2012.

Ward, Ian. *Shakespeare and the Legal Imagination.* London, 1999.

Watson, Robert N. *The Rest is Silence: Death as Annihilation in the English Renaissance.* Berkeley, 1994.

———. *Shakespeare and the Hazards of Ambition.* Cambridge, Mass., 1984.

Wayne, Valerie, ed. *The Matter of Difference: Materialist Feminist Criticism of Shakespeare.* Ithaca, N.Y., 1991.

Weil, Judith. *Service and Dependency in Shakespeare's Plays.* Cambridge, Eng., 2005.

Weimann, Robert. *Author's Pen and Actor's Voice: Playing and Writing in Shakespeare's Theatre.* Cambridge, Eng., 2000.

Wells, Robin Headlam. *Shakespeare on Masculinity.* Cambridge, Eng., 2000.

———. *Shakespeare, Politics, and the State.* London, 1986.

———. *Shakespeare's Humanism.* Cambridge, Eng., 2005.

Wells, Stanley. *Shakespeare: For All Time.* Oxford, 2003.

———. *Shakespeare, Sex, and Love.* Oxford, 2010.

Wells, Stanley, and Lena Cowen Orlin, eds. *Shakespeare: An Oxford Guide.* Oxford, 2003.

Wheeler, Richard P. *Shakespeare's Development and the Problem Comedies: Turn and Counter-Turn.* Berkeley, 1981.

White, Paul Whitfield, and Suzanne R. Westfall, eds. *Shakespeare and Theatrical Patronage in Early Modern England.* Cambridge, Eng., 2002.

Wiggins, Martin. *Shakespeare and the Drama of His Time.* Oxford, 2000.

Williams, Gordon. *Shakespeare, Sex, and the Print Revolution.* London and Atlantic Highlands, N.J., 1996.

Witmore, Michael. *Shakespeare's Metaphysics.* London, 2007.

Woodbridge, Linda. *The Scythe of Saturn: Shakespeare and Magical Thinking.* Urbana, Ill., 1994.

Woodbridge, Linda, and Edward Berry, eds. *True Rites and Maimed Rites: Ritual and Anti-Ritual in Shakespeare and His Age.* Urbana, Ill., 1992.

Yachnin, Paul, and Jessica Sights, eds. *Shakespeare and Character: Theory, History, Performance, and Theatrical Persons.* New York, 2009.

———, and Patricia Badir, eds. *Shakespeare and the Culture of Performance.* Aldershot, Eng., and Burlington, Vermont, 2008.

Young, Alan R. *Hamlet and the Visual Arts, 1709–1900.* Newark, Del., and London, 2003.

Ziegler, Georgianna, ed. *Shakespeare's Unruly Women.* Washington, D.C., 1997.

Zurcher, Andrew. *Shakespeare and Law.* London, 2010.

Shakespeare in Performance; Dramaturgy; Shakespeare in Film and Video

See also, under *Shakespeare Criticism from the 1940s to the 1970s,* Goldman and Granville-Barker; and under *Shakespeare Criticism Since 1980,* Weimann.

Aebischer, Pascale. *Shakespeare's Violated Bodies: Stage and Screen Performance*. Cambridge, Eng., 2004.

Astington, John. *Actors and Acting in Shakespeare's Time: The Art of Stage Playing*. Cambridge, Eng., 2010.

Bartholomeusz, Dennis. *Macbeth and the Players*. Cambridge, Eng., 1969.

Barton, John. *Playing Shakespeare*. London, 1984.

Bate, Jonathan, and Russell Jackson, eds. *Shakespeare: An Illustrated Stage History*. Oxford, 1996.

Beckerman, Bernard. *Shakespeare at the Globe, 1599–1609*. New York, 1962.

Berger, Harry. *Imaginary Audition: Shakespeare on Stage and Page*. Berkeley, 1989.

Bevington, David. *Action is Eloquence: Shakespeare's Language of Gesture*. Cambridge, Mass., 1984.

——. *This Wide and Universal Theater: Shakespeare in Performance Then and Now*. Chicago, 2007.

Bristol, Michael, and Kathleen McLuskie, eds., with Christopher Holmes. *Shakespeare and Modern Theatre: The Performance of Modernity*. London and New York, 2001.

Brockbank, Philip, ed. *Players of Shakespeare*. Cambridge, Eng., 1985.

Brode, Douglas. *Shakespeare in the Movies: From the Silent Era to "Shakespeare in Love."* Oxford, 2000.

Brooks, Douglas A., and Lingui Yang, eds. *Shakespeare and Asia*. Lewiston, Maine, 2010.

Brown, Ivor. *Shakespeare and the Actors*. London, 1970.

Brown, John Russell. *Shakespeare's Plays in Performance*. London, 1966.

——. *Shakespeare's Dramatic Style*. London, 1970.

——. *Shakespeare and the Theatrical Event*. Basingstoke, Eng., and New York, 2002.

——. *Shakespeare Dancing: A Theatrical Study of the Plays*. Basingstoke, Hants., New York, 2005.

——. ed. *The Routledge Companion to Directors' Shakespeare*. New York, 2008.

——, and Kevin Ewart, eds. *The Routledge Companion to Actors' Shakespeare*. New York and Abingdon, Eng., 2012.

Brydon, Diana, and Irena R. Makaryk, eds. *Shakespeare in Canada: A World Elsewhere*. Toronto, 2002.

Buchanan, Judith. *Shakespeare on Silent Film: An Excellent Dumb Discourse*. Cambridge, Eng., 2009.

Buhler, Stephen M. *Shakespeare in the Cinema: Ocular Proof*. Albany, N.Y., 2002.

Bulman, James C., ed. *Shakespeare Re-dressed: Cross-Gender Casting in Contemporary Performance*. Madison, N.J., 2008.

Bulman, J. C., and H. R. Coursen, eds. *Shakespeare on Television*. Hanover, N.H., 1988.

Burt, Richard, and Lynda E. Boose, eds. *Shakespeare, the Movie, I and II: Popularizing the Plays on Film, TV, Video, and DVD*. London and New York, 1997 and 2003.

Carlisle, Carol Jones. *Shakespeare from the Greenroom: Actors' Criticisms of Four Major Tragedies*. Chapel Hill, N.C., 1969.

Coghill, Nevill. *Shakespeare's Professional Skills*. Cambridge, Eng., 1964.

Cohn, Ruby. *Modern Shakespeare Offshoots*. Princeton, 1976.

Cook, Judith. *Shakespeare's Players*. London, 1983.

Crowl, Samuel. *Shakespeare and Film: A Norton Guide*. New York, 2008.

Coursen, Herbert R. *Shakespeare in Space: Recent Productions on Screen*. New York, 2002.

D'Amico, Jack. *Shakespeare and Italy: The City and the Stage*. Gainesville, Fla., 2001.

Davies, Anthony, and Stanley Wells, eds. *Shakespeare and the Moving Image: The Plays on Film and Television*. Cambridge, Eng., 1994.

Dessen, Alan C. *Recovering Shakespeare's Theatrical Vocabulary*. Cambridge, Eng., 1995.

——. *Rescripting Shakespeare: The Text, the Director, and Modern Productions*. Cambridge, Eng., 2002.

——, and Leslie Thomson. *A Dictionary of Stage Directions in English Drama, 1580–1642*. Cambridge, Eng., 1999.

Dobson, Michael. *Performing Shakespeare's Tragedies Today: The Actor's Perspective*. Cambridge, Eng., 2006.

——. *Shakespeare and Amateur Performance: A Cultural History*. Cambridge, Eng., 2011.

Donohue, Joseph W., Jr. *Dramatic Character in the English Romantic Age*. Princeton, 1970.

Downer, Alan S. *The Eminent Tragedian, William Charles Macready*. Cambridge, Mass., 1966.

Dymkowski, Christine, and Christie Carson, eds. *Shakespeare in Stages: New Theatre Histories*. Cambridge, Eng., 2010.

Edelman, Charles. *Brawl Ridiculous: Swordfighting in Shakespeare's Plays*. Manchester, Eng., 1992.

Escolme, Bridget. *Talking to the Audience: Shakespeare, Performance, Self*. Abingdon, Eng., 2005.

Fitter, Chris. *Radical Shakespeare: Politics and Stagecraft in the Early Career*. New York, 2012.

Flachmann, Michael. *Shakespeare in Performance: Inside the Creative Process*. Salt Lake City, Utah, 2011.

Fontane, Theodor. *Shakespeare in the London Theatre 1855–58*, trans. Russell Jackson. London, 1999.

Foulkes, Richard. *Performing Shakespeare in the Age of Empire*. Cambridge, Eng., 2002.

——, ed. *Shakespeare and the Victorian Age*. Cambridge, Eng., 1986.

Gregor, Keith. *Shakespeare in the Spanish Theatre: 1772 to the Present*. London, 2010.

Guneratne, Anthony R. *Shakespeare, Film Studies, and the Visual Cultures of Modernity*. New York, 2008.

Harris, Jonathan Gil, and Natasha Korda. *Staged Properties in Early Modern English Drama*. Cambridge, Eng., 2002.

Hatchuel, Sarah. *Shakespeare: From Stage to Screen*. Cambridge, Eng., 2004.

——, and Nathalie Vienne-Guerrin, eds. *Shakespeare on Screen: Television Shakespeare: Essays in Honour of Michele Willems*. Mont-Saint-Aignan, 2008.

Hattaway, Michael, Boika Sokolova, and Derek Roper, eds. *Shakespeare in the New Europe*. Sheffield, Eng., 1994.

Hill, Errol. *Shakespeare in Sable: A History of Black Shakespearean Actors*. Amherst, Mass., 1984.

Hodgdon, Barbara. *The Shakespeare Trade: Performances and Appropriations*. Philadelphia, 1998.

Hogan, Charles B. *Shakespeare in the Theatre, 1701–1800*. 2 vols. Oxford, 1952–1957.

Holland, Peter. *Shakespeare, Memory, and Performance*. Cambridge, Eng., 2006.

Huang, Alexander C.Y., and Charles S. Ross, eds. *Shakespeare in Hollywood, Asia, and Cyberspace*. West Lafayette, Ind., 2009.

Hunter, Lynette, and Peter Lichtenfels, eds. *Shakespeare, Language, and the Stage: The Fifth Wall, Approaches to Shakespeare from Criticism, Performance, and Theatre Studies*. London, 2005.

Jackson, Russell, ed. *The Cambridge Companion to Shakespeare on Film*. Cambridge, Eng., 2000.

——, *Shakespeare Films in the Making: Vision, Production, and Reception*. Cambridge, Eng., 2007.

——, and Robert Smallwood, eds. *Players of Shakespeare 2*. Cambridge, Eng., 1988. Followed by vols. 3 (1993); and 4, ed. Smallwood (1998).

Jones, Emrys. *Scenic Form in Shakespeare*. Oxford, 1971.

Jorgens, Jack L. *Shakespeare on Film*. Bloomington, Ind., 1977.

Kanelos, Peter, and Matt Kozusko, eds. *Thunder at a Playhouse: Essaying Shakespeare and the Early Modern Stage*. Selinsgrove, Penn., 2010.

Kennedy, Dennis, and Li Lan Yong, eds. *Shakespeare in Asia: Contemporary Performance*. Cambridge, Eng., 2010.

Kiefer, Frederick. *Shakespeare's Visual Theatre: Staging the Personified Characters*. Cambridge, Eng., 2003.

Lehmann, Courtney. *Shakespeare Remains: Theater to Film, Early Modern to Postmodern*. Ithaca, N.Y., 2002.

Levith, Murray J. *Shakespeare in China*. London, 2004.

Lopez, Jeremy. *Theatrical Convention and Audience Response in Early Modern England*. Cambridge, Eng., 2003.

MacKay, Ellen. *Persecution, Plague, and Fire: Fugitive Histories of the Stage in Early Modern England*. Chicago, 2011.

Magnus, Laury, and Walter W. Cannon, eds. *Who Hears in Shakespeare? Auditory Worlds on Stage and Screen*. Madison, N.J., 2012.

Mann, David. *Shakespeare's Women: Performance and Conception*. Cambridge, Eng., 2008.

Manvell, Roger. *Shakespeare and the Film.* London and New York, 1971.

McGuire, Philip C. *Speechless Dialect: Shakespeare's Open Silences.* Berkeley, 1985.

McGuire, Philip C., and David A. Samuelson. *Shakespeare: The Theatrical Dimension.* New York, 1979.

McLuskie, Kathleen, and Michael Bristol, with Christopher Holmes. *Shakespeare and Modern Theatre: The Performance of Modernity.* London and New York, 2001.

Murray, Barbara A., ed. *Shakespeare Adaptations from the Restoration: Five Plays.* Madison, N.J., 2005.

Occhiogrosso, Frank, ed. *Shakespeare in Performance: A Collection of Essays.* Newark, Del., 2003.

Odell, George C. D. *Shakespeare from Betterton to Irving.* 2 vols. New York, 1920, 1966.

Poel, William. *Shakespeare in the Theatre.* London, 1913, 1968.

Price, Joseph G., ed. *The Triple Bond: Plays, Mainly Shakespearean, in Performance.* University Park, Pa., 1975.

Quince, Rohan. *Shakespeare in South Africa: Stage Productions During the Apartheid Era.* New York, 2000.

Rokison, Abigail. *Shakespearean Verse Speaking: Text and Theatre Practice.* Cambridge, Eng., 2009.

Rothwell, Kenneth S. *A History of Shakespeare on Screen: A Century of Film and Television.* Cambridge, Eng., 1999; 2nd ed., 2005.

———, and Annabella Hankin Melzer. *Shakespeare on Screen: An International Filmography and Videography.* New York, 1990.

Rutter, Carol Chillington. *Enter the Body: Women and Representation on Shakespeare's Stage.* London and New York, 2001.

———. *Shakespeare and Child's Play: Performing Lost Boys on Stage and Screen.* London and New York, 2007.

———, ed. *Documents of the Rose Playhouse.* Manchester, Eng., 1999.

———, et al. *Clamorous Voices: Shakespeare's Women Today.* New York, 1989.

Sammons, Eddie. *Shakespeare: A Hundred Years on Film.* Lanham, Md., 2004.

Samuelson, David A., ed. *Shakespeare: The Theatrical Dimension.* New York, 1959.

Sasayama, Takashi, J. R. Mulryne, and Margaret Shewring, eds. *Shakespeare and the Japanese Stage.* Cambridge, Eng., 1998.

Schalkwyk, David. *Speech and Performance in Shakespeare's Sonnets and Plays.* Cambridge, Eng., 2002.

Schoch, Richard W. *Shakespeare's Victorian Stage: Performing History in the Theatre of Charles Kean.* Cambridge, Eng., 1998.

Shapiro, Michael. *Gender in Play on the Shakespearean Stage: Boy Heroines and Female Pages.* Ann Arbor, Mich., 1994.

Shattuck, Charles H. *The Shakespeare Promptbooks: A Descriptive Catalogue.* Urbana, Ill., 1965.

———. *Shakespeare on the American Stage from the Hallams to Edwin Booth.* Washington, D.C., 1976; *from Booth and Barrett to Sothern and Marlowe,* Washington, D.C., 1987.

Shaughnessy, Robert. *Shakespeare in Performance.* New York, 2000.

Sheen, Erica. *Shakespeare and the Institution of Theatre: The Best in This Kind.* Basingstoke, Hants., and New York, 2009.

Slater, Ann Pasternak. *Shakespeare the Director.* Brighton, Sussex, and Totowa, N.J., 1982.

Speaight, Robert. *William Poel and the Elizabethan Revival.* London, 1954.

Spencer, Hazelton. *Shakespeare Improved: The Restoration Versions in Quarto and on the Stage.* Cambridge, Mass., 1927.

Sprague, Arthur Colby. *Shakespeare and the Actors.* Cambridge, Mass., 1944.

———. *Shakespearian Players and Performances.* Cambridge, Mass., 1953.

Styan, J. L. *Shakespeare's Stagecraft.* Cambridge, Eng., 1967.

Teague, Frances. *Shakespeare and the American Popular Stage.* Cambridge, Eng., 2006.

Thompson, Marvin and Ruth, eds. *Shakespeare and the Sense of Performance: Essays in the Tradition of Performance Criticism in Honor of Bernard Beckerman.* Newark, Del., 1989.

Van Laan, Thomas F. *Role-Playing in Shakespeare.* Toronto, 1958.

Weimann, Robert. *Shakespeare and the Power of Performance: Stage and Page in Elizabethan Theatre.* Cambridge, Eng., 2008.

Wells, Stanley. *Royal Shakespeare: Four Major Productions at Stratford-upon-Avon.* Manchester, Eng., 1977.

———, and Sarah Stanton, eds. *The Cambridge Companion to Shakespeare on Stage.* Cambridge, Eng., 2002.

Werner, Sarah. *Shakespeare and Feminist Performance: Ideology on Stage.* London and New York, 2001.

Wilder, Lina Perkins. *Shakespeare's Memory Theatre: Recollection, Properties, and Character.* Cambridge, Eng., 2010.

Wilson, Robert Frank. *Shakespeare in Hollywood.* Madison, N.J., and London, 2000.

Worthen, W. B. *Shakespeare and the Force of Modern Performance.* Cambridge, Eng., 2003.

The Comedies

See also, under *Shakespeare Criticism Since 1980,* Drakakis (essay by Belsey), Erickson and Kahn (essay by Adelman), and Paster (Chapter 7).

Anderson, Linda. *A Kind of Wild Justice: Revenge in Shakespeare's Comedies.* Newark, Del., 1987.

Barber, C. L. *Shakespeare's Festive Comedy.* Princeton, 1959.

Barton, Anne. *The Names of Comedy.* Toronto, 1990.

Berry, Edward. *Shakespeare's Comic Rites.* Cambridge, Eng., 1984.

Berry, Ralph. *Shakespeare's Comedies: Explorations in Form.* Princeton, 1972.

———. *The Shakespearean Metaphor: Studies in Language and Form.* Totowa, N.J., 1978.

Bloom, Harold, ed., *William Shakespeare: Comedies and Romances.* New York, 1986.

Bradbury, Malcolm, and David Palmer, eds. *Shakespearian Comedy.* London, 1972.

Brown, John Russell. *Shakespeare and His Comedies.* London, 1957, 1968.

Brown, John Russell, and Bernard Harris, eds. *Early Shakespeare.* Stratford-upon-Avon Studies 3. London, 1961. (Including an essay by Frank Kermode on "The Mature Comedies.")

Bryant, J. A., Jr. *Shakespeare and the Uses of Comedy.* Lexington, Ky., 1986.

Burke, William Kenneth. *A New Approach to Shakespeare's Early Comedies: Theoretical Foundations.* New York, 1998.

Carroll, William C. *The Metamorphoses of Shakespearean Comedy.* Princeton, 1985.

Champion, Larry S. *The Evolution of Shakespeare's Comedy.* Cambridge, Mass., 1970.

Charlton, H. B. *Shakespearian Comedy.* London, 1938.

Charney, Maurice, ed. *Shakespearean Comedy.* New York, 1980.

Cody, Richard. *The Landscape of the Mind: Pastoralism and Platonic Theory in Tasso's "Aminta" and Shakespeare's Early Comedies.* Oxford, 1969.

Collins, Michael J., ed. *Shakespeare's Sweet Thunder: Essays on the Early Comedies.* Newark, Del., 1997.

Cook, Ann Jennalie. *Making a Match: Courtship in Shakespeare and His Society.* Princeton, 1991.

Cordner, Michael, Peter Holland, and John Kerrigan, eds. *English Comedy.* Cambridge, Eng., 1994.

Draper, Ronald P. *Shakespeare: The Comedies.* New York, 2000.

Elam, Keir. *Shakespeare's Universe of Discourse: Language-Games in the Comedies.* Cambridge, Eng., 1984.

Evans, Bertrand. *Shakespeare's Comedies.* Oxford, 1960.

Freedman, Barbara. *Staging the Gaze: Postmodernism, Psychoanalysis, and Shakespearean Comedy.* Ithaca, N.Y., 1991.

Friedman, Michael D. *"The World Must Be Peopled": Shakespeare's Comedies of Forgiveness.* Madison, N. J., and London, 2002.

Frye, Northrop. "The Argument of Comedy," *English Institute Essays 1948.* New York, 1949.

———. *A Natural Perspective: The Development of Shakespearean Comedy and Romance.* New York, 1965.

Hale, John K. *The Shakespeare of the Comedies: A Multiple Approach.* Bern, N.Y., 1996.

Hall, Jonathan. *Anxious Pleasures: Shakespearean Comedy and the Nation-State.* Madison, N. J., 1995.

Hamilton, A. C. *The Early Shakespeare.* San Marino, Calif., 1967.

Hassel, R. Chris. *Faith and Folly in Shakespeare's Romantic Comedies.* Athens, Ga., 1980.

Hawkins, Sherman H. "The Two Worlds of Shakespearean Comedy," *ShakS* 3 (1967), 62–80.

Hunter, Robert G. *Shakespeare and the Comedy of Forgiveness*. New York, 1965.

Huston, J. Dennis. *Shakespeare's Comedies of Play*. New York, 1981.

Jensen, Ejner J. *Shakespeare and the Ends of Comedy*. Bloomington, Ind., 1991.

Leggatt, Alexander. *English Stage Comedy, 1490–1990: Five Centuries of a Genre*. London and New York, 1998.

——. *Shakespeare's Comedy of Love*. London and New York, 1974.

——, ed. *The Cambridge Companion to Shakespearean Comedy*. Cambridge, Eng., 2002.

Lerner, Laurence, ed. *Shakespeare's Comedies: An Anthology of Modern Criticism*. Baltimore, 1967.

Levin, Richard A. *Love and Society in Shakespearean Comedy: A Study of Dramatic Form and Content*. Newark, Del., 1985.

Maslen, R. W. *Shakespeare and Comedy*. London, 2005.

Miola, Robert S. *Shakespeare and Classical Comedy: The Influence of Plautus and Terence*. Oxford, 1994.

Nevo, Ruth. *Comic Transformations in Shakespeare*. London, 1980.

Newman, Karen. *Shakespeare's Rhetoric of Comic Character*. New York and London, 1985.

Palmer, David J., and Malcolm Bradbury, eds. *Shakespearian Comedy*. Statford-upon-Avon Studies 1. London, 1972.

Palmer, John. *Comic Characters of Shakespeare*. London, 1946.

Pettet, E. C. *Shakespeare and the Romance Tradition*. London, 1949.

Phialas, Peter G. *Shakespeare's Romantic Comedies*. Chapel Hill, N.C., 1966.

Richmond, Hugh M. *Shakespeare's Sexual Comedy*. Indianapolis, 1971.

Salingar, Leo. *Shakespeare and the Traditions of Comedy*. Cambridge, Eng., 1974.

Shaheen, Naseeb. *Biblical References in Shakespeare's Comedies*. Newark, Del., 1993.

Smidt, Kristian. *Unconformities in Shakespeare's Early Comedies*. London, 1986.

Smith, Emma, ed. *Shakespeare's Comedies*. Malden, Mass., and Oxford, 2004.

Stevenson, David L. *The Love-Game Comedy*. New York, 1946.

Traversi, Derek. *Shakespeare: The Early Comedies*. London, 1960.

Turner, Robert Y. *Shakespeare's Apprenticeship*. Chicago, 1974.

Westlund, Joseph. *Shakespeare's Reparative Comedies: A Psychoanalytic View of the Middle Plays*. Chicago, 1984.

Wheeler, Richard P. "Deaths in the Family: The Loss of a Son and the Rise of Shakespearean Comedy," *SQ* 51 (2000), 127–53.

Williamson, Marilyn. *The Patriarchy of Shakespeare's Comedies*. Detroit, 1986.

The Problem Plays

Bentley, Greg W. *Shakespeare and the New Disease: The Dramatic Function of Syphilis in "Troilus and Cressida," "Measure for Measure," and "Timon of Athens."* New York and Bern, 1989.

Campbell, Oscar James. *Shakespeare's Satire*. London and New York, 1943, 1963.

Foakes, R. A. *Shakespeare, The Dark Comedies to the Last Plays: From Satire to Celebration*. Charlottesville, Va., 1971.

Frye, Northrop. *The Myth of Deliverance: Reflections on Shakespeare's Problem Comedies*. Toronto, 1983.

Hawkes, Terry. *Shakespeare and the Reason: A Study of the Tragedies and the Problem Plays*. London and New York, 1964.

Jamieson, Michael. "The Problem Plays, 1920–1970: A Retrospect," *ShS* 25 (1972), 1–10.

Lawrence, W. W. *Shakespeare's Problem Comedies*. New York, 1931, 1960.

Maquerlot, Jean-Pierre. *Shakespeare and the Mannerist Tradition: A Reading of Five Problem Plays*. Cambridge, Eng., 1995. (Includes consideration of *Julius Caesar* and *Hamlet*.)

McCandless, David. *Gender and Performance in Shakespeare's Problem Comedies*. Bloomington, Ind., 1997.

Muir, Kenneth, and Stanley Wells, eds. *Aspects of Shakespeare's "Problem Plays": Articles Reprinted from "Shakespeare Survey."* Cambridge, Eng., 1982.

Schanzer, Ernest. *The Problem Plays of Shakespeare*. New York, 1963.

Thomas, Vivian. *The Moral Universe of Shakespeare's Problem Plays*. New York, 1987.

Tillyard, E. M. W. *Shakespeare's Problem Plays*. Toronto, 1949.

Wheeler, Richard P. *Shakespeare's Development and the Problem Comedies: Turn and Counter-Turn*. Berkeley, 1981.

Ure, Peter. *William Shakespeare: The Problem Plays*. London, 1961.

The Taming of the Shrew

See also, under *Shakespeare's Predecessors and Contemporaries*, Marrapodi (essay by Bevington); under *Shakespeare Criticism from the 1940s to the 1970s*, Garber; under *Shakespeare Criticism Since 1980*, Auden, Fumerton and Hunt (essay by Dolan), Kahn, Lenz et al. (essay by Bean), McDonald (essay by Boose), Novy (*Love's Argument*), and Parker and Hartman (essay by Fineman); under *Shakespeare in Performance*, Rutter; and under *The Comedies*, R. Berry, Charlton, Collins (essays by Dessen and Rutter), Evans, Hawkins, Huston, Leggatt, Nevo, and Stevenson.

Boose, Lynda E. "'Scolding Brides and Bridling Scolds': Taming the Woman's Unruly Member," *SQ* 42 (1991), 179–213.

Brunvand, Jan Harold. "The Folktale Origin of *The Taming of the Shrew*," *SQ* 17 (1966), 345–59.

Crocker, Holly A. "Performing Passivity and Playing A-Part in *The Taming of the Shrew*," *SQ* 54 (2003), 142–59.

Dolan, Frances E., ed. *"The Taming of the Shrew": Text and Contexts*. New York, 1996.

Haring-Smith, Tori. *From Farce to Metadrama; A Stage History of "The Taming of the Shrew," 1594–1983*. Westport, Conn., 1985.

Hosley, Richard. "Was There a 'Dramatic Epilogue' to *The Taming of the Shrew?*" *Studies in English Literature* 1:2 (1961), 17–34.

Hutson, Lorna. *The Usurer's Daughter: Male Friendship and Fictions of Women in Sixteenth-Century England*. London and New York, 1994.

Jayne, Sears. "The Dreaming of *The Shrew*," *SQ* 17 (1966), 41–56.

Korda, Natasha. "Household Kates: Domesticating Commodities in *The Taming of the Shrew*," *SQ* 47 (1996), 109–31.

Maguire, Laurie E. "Cultural Control in *The Taming of the Shrew*," *Renaissance Drama* n.s. 26 (1995), 83–104.

Marcus, Leah. "The Shakespearean Editor as Shrew-Tamer," *English Literary Rennaisance* 22 (1922), 177–200.

Newman, Karen. "Renaissance Family Politics and Shakespeare's *The Taming of the Shrew*," *English Literary Renaissance* 16 (1986), 86–100.

Saccio, Peter. "Shrewd and Kindly Farce," *ShS* 37 (1984), 33–40.

Thompson, Ann, ed., *The Taming of the Shrew*. Cambridge, Eng., 1984.

Thorne, W. B. "Folk Elements in *The Taming of the Shrew*," *Queen's Quarterly* 75 (1968), 482–96.

A Midsummer Night's Dream

See also, under *Life in Shakespeare's England*, De Grazia, Quilligan, and Stallybrass (essay by Parker); under *Shakespeare Criticism from the 1940s to the 1970s*, Calderwood, Coghill, Garber, Granville-Barker, and Kott; under *Shakespeare Criticism Since 1980*, Callaghan (*A Feminist Companion*, essay by Loomba), Mazzio and Trevor (essay by Maus), Montrose, Parker, Paster, and Patterson (Chapter 3); and under *The Comedies*, Barber, Bloom (essay by Girard), Brown and Harris (essays by Kermode and Merchant), Carroll, Collins (essay by Halio), Evans, Huston, Leggatt, Lerner, Palmer and Bradbury (essay by Wells), and Smidt.

Bevington, David. "'But We Are Spirits of Another Sort': The Dark Side of Love and Magic in *A Midsummer Night's Dream*," *Medieval and Renaissance Studies*, ed. Siegfried Wenzel. Chapel Hill, N.C., 1978.

Donaldson, E. Talbot. *The Swan at the Well: Shakespeare Reads Chaucer*. New Haven, 1985.

Garner, Shirley Nelson. "*A Midsummer Night's Dream:* 'Jack Shall Have Jill; Nought Shall Go Ill,'" *Women's Studies* 9 (1981), 47–63.

Girard, René. "Myth and Ritual in Shakespeare's *A Midsummer Night's Dream*," *Textual Strategies: Perspectives in Post-Structuralist Criticism*, ed. Josué V. Harari. Ithaca, N.Y., 1979.

Howard, Skiles. "Hands, Feet, and Bottoms: Decentering the Cosmic Dance in *A Midsummer Night's Dream*," *SQ* 44 (1993), 325–42.

Lamb, Mary Ellen. "*A Midsummer Night's Dream*: The Myth of Theseus and the Minotaur," *Texas Studies in Literature and Language* 21 (1979), 478–91.

———. "'Taken by the Fairies': Fairy Practices and the Production of Popular Culture in *A Midsummer Night's Dream*," *SQ* 51 (2000), 277–312.

Montrose, Louis Adrian. "'Shaping Fantasies': Figurations of Gender and Power in Elizabethan Culture," *Representations* 2 (1.2, Spring 1983), 61–94.

Nuttall, A. D. "*A Midsummer Night's Dream*: Comedy as *Apotrope* of Myth," *ShS* 53 (2000), 49–59.

Olson, Paul A. "*A Midsummer Night's Dream* and the Meaning of Court Marriage," *ELH* 24 (1957), 95–119.

Ormerod, David. "*A Midsummer Night's Dream*: The Monster in the Labyrinth," *ShakS* 11 (1978), 39–52.

Paster, Gail Kern, and Howard Skiles, eds. *A Midsummer Night's Dream: Texts and Contexts*. Boston and New York, 1999.

Pearson, D'Orsay W. "'Unkinde' Theseus: A Study in Renaissance Mythography," *English Literary Renaissance* 4 (1974), 276–98.

Wall, Wendy. "Why Does Puck Sweep?: Fairylore, Merry Wives, and Social Struggle," *SQ* 52 (2001), 67–106.

Warren, Roger. *"A Midsummer Night's Dream": Text and Performance*. Text and Performance. London, 1983.

Williams, Gary Jay. *Our Moonlight Revels: "A Midsummer Night's Dream" in the Theatre*. Ames, Iowa, 1997.

Young, David P. *Something of Great Constancy: The Art of "A Midsummer Night's Dream."* New Haven, 1966.

The Merchant of Venice

See also, under *Shakespeare's Predecessors and Contemporaries*, Rose (ed. *Renaissance Drama*, essay by Whigham); under *Shakespeare's Language*, Donawerth; under *Shakespeare Criticism from the 1940s to the 1970s*, Burkhardt, Fiedler, and Granville-Barker; under *Shakespeare Criticism Since 1980*, Auden, Callaghan (*A Feminist Companion*, essay by Singh), Dawson, Erickson and Kahn (essays by Kahn and Wheeler), Garber (*Cannibals*, essay by Mullaney), Grady (essays by Drakakis, Freinkel, and Mallin), Howard and O'Connor (essay by Moisan), Mazzio and Trevor (essay by Siemon), Novy (*Love's Argument*, Chapter 4), Rabkin, and Wayne (essay by Leventen); and under *The Comedies*, Barber, Bradbury and Palmer (essay by Palmer), Brown and Harris (essays by J. R. Brown and Kermode), Evans, Leggatt, Levin, Nevo, and Smidt.

Adelman, Janet. *Blood Relations: Christian and Jew in "The Merchant of Venice."* Chicago, 2008.

Auden, W. H. "Brothers and Others," *"The Dyer's Hand" and Other Essays*. New York, 1948.

Berger, Harry, Jr. "Marriage and Mercifixion in *The Merchant of Venice*: The Casket Scene Revisited," *SQ* 32 (1981), 155–62.

———. *A Fury in the Words: Love and Embarrassment in Shakespeare's Venice*. New York, 2012.

Boose, Lynda E. "The Comic Contract and Portia's Golden Ring," *ShakS* 20 (1988), 241–54.

Bulman, James C. *The Merchant of Venice*. Shakespeare in Performance. Manchester, Eng., 1991.

Cohen, Walter. "*The Merchant of Venice* and the Possibilities of Historical Criticism," *ELH* 49 (1982), 765–89.

Danson, Lawrence. *The Harmonies of "The Merchant of Venice."* New Haven and London, 1978.

Dessen, Alan C. "The Elizabethan Stage Jew and Christian Example: Gerontus, Barabas, and Shylock," *Modern Language Quarterly* 35 (1974), 231–45.

Edelman, Charles. "Which is the Jew that Shakespeare Knew? Shylock on the Elizabethan Stage," *ShS* 52 (1999), 99–106.

Engle, Lars. "'Thrift is Blessing': Exchange and Explanation in *The Merchant of Venice*," *SQ* 37 (1986), 20–37.

Freud, Sigmund. "The Theme of the Three Caskets," *Complete Psychological Works of Sigmund Freud*, trans. James Strachey et al. London, 1973–4.

Girard, René. "'To Entrap the Wisest': A Reading of *The Merchant of Venice*," *Literature and Society*. Selected Papers from the English Institute, 1978, ed. Edward W. Said. Baltimore, 1980.

Gross, Kenneth. *Shylock Is Shakespeare*. Chicago, 2006.

Hutson, Lorna. *The Usurer's Daughter: Male Friendship and Fictions of Women in Sixteenth-Century England*. London and New York, 1994.

Jardine, Lisa. "Cultural Confusion and Shakespeare's Learned Heroines: 'These Are Old Paradoxes,'" *SQ* 38 (1987), 1–18.

Kaplan, Lindsay M. "Jessica's Mother: Medieval Constructions of Jewish Race and Gender in *The Merchant of Venice*," *SQ* 58 (2007), 1–30.

Lever, J. W. "Shylock, Portia, and the Values of Shakespearian Comedy," *SQ* 3 (1952), 383–6.

Lewalski, Barbara K. "Biblical Allusion and Allegory in *The Merchant of Venice*," *SQ* 13 (1962), 327–43.

MacKay, Maxine. "*The Merchant of Venice*: A Reflection of the Early Conflict Between Courts of Law and Courts of Equity," *SQ* 15:4 (1964), 371–5.

Mahon, John W., and Ellen MacLeod Mahon, eds. *"The Merchant of Venice": New Critical Essays*. London, 2002.

Moody, A. D. *Shakespeare: "The Merchant of Venice."* London, 1964.

Newman, Karen. "Portia's Ring: Unruly Women and Structures of Exchange in *The Merchant of Venice*," *SQ* 38 (1987), 19–33.

Normand, Lawrence. "Reading the Body in *The Merchant of Venice*," *Textual Practice* 5 (1991), 55–73.

Overton, Bill. *"The Merchant of Venice": Text and Performance*. Atlantic Highlands, N.J., 1987.

Parten, Anne. "Re-establishing Sexual Order: The Ring Episode in *The Merchant of Venice*," *Women's Studies* 9 (1982), 145–55.

Pettet, E. C. "*The Merchant of Venice* and the Problem of Usury," *English Association Essays and Studies* 31 (1945), 19–33.

Shapiro, James. *Shakespeare and the Jews*. New York, 1996.

Turner, Henry S. "The Problem of the More-Than-One: Friendship, Calculation, and Political Association in *The Merchant of Venice*," *SQ* 57 (2006), 413–42.

Whigham, Frank. "Ideology and Class Conduct in *The Merchant of Venice*," *Renaissance Drama* 10 (1979), 93–115.

Yaffe, Martin D. *Shylock and the Jewish Question*. Baltimore, 1997.

Much Ado About Nothing

See also, under *Shakespeare's Predecessors and Contemporaries*, Marrapodi (essay by Salingar); under *The Comedies*, R. Berry, Brown, Cordner et al. (essay by Everett), Evans, Hunter, Huston, Leggatt, Levin, Nevo, Newman, Salingar, and Stevenson; under *Shakespeare Criticism from the 1940s to the 1970s*, Rossiter; and under *Shakespeare Criticism Since 1980*, Howard and O'Connor (essay by Howard), Kirsch, Lenz et al. (essay by Hays), and Neely.

Barish, Jonas A. "Pattern and Purpose in the Prose of *Much Ado About Nothing*," *Rice U. Studies* 60:2 (1974), 19–30.

Berger, Harry, Jr. "Against the Sink-a-Pace: Sexual and Family Politics in *Much Ado About Nothing*," *SQ* 33 (1982), 302–13.

Cook, Carol. "'The Sign and Semblance of Her Honor': Reading Gender Difference in *Much Ado about Nothing*," *PMLA* 101 (1986), 186–202.

Dawson, Anthony B. "Much Ado about Signifying," *Studies in English Literature* 22 (1982), 211–21.

Dusinberre, Juliet. "Much Ado about Lying," *Shakespeare Readers, Audiences, Players*, eds. R. S. White, Charles Edelman, and Christopher Wortham. Nedlands, Australia, 1998.

Everett, Barbara. "*Much Ado About Nothing*," *Critical Quarterly* 3 (1961), 319–35.

Friedman, Michael D. "Male Bonds and Marriage in *All's Well* and *Much Ado*," *Studies in English Literature* 35 (1995), 231–49.

Jorgensen, Paul A. "*Much Ado About Nothing*," *SQ* 5 (1954), 287–95. Rpt. in *Redeeming Shakespeare's Words*. Berkeley, 1962.

Lane, Robert. "'Foremost in report': Social Identity and Masculinity in *Much Ado About Nothing*," *Upstart Crow* 16 (1996), 31–47.

Lewalski, Barbara K. "Love, Appearance, and Reality: Much Ado About Something," *Studies in English Literature* 8 (1968), 235–51.

Mason, Pamela. *"Much Ado About Nothing"*: *Text and Performance*. Basingstoke, 1992.

Ormerod, David. "Faith and Fashion in *Much Ado About Nothing*," *ShS* 25 (1972), 93–105.

Taylor, Michael. "*Much Ado About Nothing*: The Individual in Society," *Essays in Criticism* 23 (1973), 146–53.

As You Like It

See also, under *The Comedies*, Barber, R. Berry, Bradbury and Palmer (essay by Anne Barton), Brown, Hunter, Leggatt, Nevo, and Salingar; and under *Shakespeare Criticism Since 1980*, Belsey, Callaghan (*A Feminist Companion*, essay by Neely), Erickson, Lenz et al. (essay by Park), Mahon and Pendleton (essay by Gibbons), and McDonald (essay by Wofford).

Alpers, Paul. *What Is Pastoral?* Chicago, 1996.

Barnet, Sylvan. "Strange Events: Improbability in *As You Like It*," *ShakS* 4 (1968), 119–31.

Bono, Barbara J. "Mixed Gender, Mixed Genre in Shakespeare's *As You Like It*," *Renaissance Genres: Essays on Theory, History, and Interpretation*, ed. Barbara Kiefer Lewalski. Cambridge, Mass., 1986.

Debax, Jean-Paul, and Yves Peyré, eds. "*As You Like It*": *Essais critiques*. Toulouse, 1998.

Doran, Madeleine. "'Yet Am I Inland Bred,'" *SQ* 15:2 (1964), 99–114.

Fortin, René E. "'Tongues in Trees': Symbolic Patterns in *As You Like it*," *Texas Studies in Literature and Language* 14 (1973), 569–82.

Gardner, Helen. "*As You Like It*," *More Talking of Shakespeare*, ed. John Garrett. London and New York, 1959.

Halio, Jay L. "'No Clock in the Forest': Time in *As You Like It*," *Studies in English Literature* 2 (1962), 197–207.

Hayles, Nancy K. "Sexual Disguise in *As You Like It* and *Twelfth Night*," *ShS* 32 (1979), 63–72.

Howard, Jean E. "Crossdressing, The Theatre, and Gender Struggle in Early Modern England," *SQ* 39 (1988), 418–40.

Kernan, Alvin B. *The Cankered Muse*. New Haven, 1959.

Knowles, Richard. "Myth and Type in *As You Like It*," *ELH* 33 (1966), 1–22.

Marshall, Cynthia. "The Doubled Jaques and Constructions of Negation in *As You Like It*," *SQ* 49 (1998), 375–92.

———, ed. *Shakespeare in Production: "As You Like It."* Cambridge, Eng., 2004.

Montrose, Louis Adrian. "'The Place of a Brother' in *As You Like It*: Social Process and Comic Form," *SQ* 32 (1981), 28–54.

Ronk, Martha. "Locating the Visual in *As You Like It*," *SQ* 52 (2001), 255–76.

Schleiner, Louise. "Voice, Ideology, and Gendered Subjects: The Case of *As You Like It* and *Two Gentlemen*," *SQ* 50 (1999), 285–309.

Young, David. *The Heart's Forest*. New Haven, 1972.

Twelfth Night

See also, under *The Comedies*, Barber, E. Berry, Bradbury and Palmer (essay by Anne Barton), Brown, Brown and Harris (essay by Kermode), Hunter, Leggatt, Levin, Nevo, and Salingar; and under *Shakespeare Criticism Since 1980*, Callaghan (*A Feminist Companion*, essay by Neely), Erickson and Kahn (essay by Booth), Greenblatt (*Shakespearean Negotiations*, Chapter 3), Hamilton (Chapter 4), Hawkes (essay by Elam), Howard, and Parker and Hartman (essay by Hartman).

Arlidge, Anthony. *Shakespeare and the Prince of Love: The Feast of Misrule in the Middle Temple*. London, 2000.

Auden, W. H. "Music in Shakespeare," "*The Dyer's Hand" and Other Essays*. New York, 1948.

Bloom, Harold, ed. *Modern Critical Interpretations of "Twelfth Night."* New York, 1987.

Booth, Stephen. *Precious Nonsense: The Gettysburg Address, Ben Jonson's Epitaphs on His Children, and "Twelfth Night."* Berkeley, 1998.

Brown, John Russell. "Directions for *Twelfth Night*, or What You Will," *Tulane Drama Review* 5:4 (1961), 77–88.

Downer, Alan S. "Feste's Night," *College English* 13 (1952), 258–65.

Eagleton, Terence. "Language and Reality in *Twelfth Night*," *Critical Quarterly* 9 (1967), 217–28.

Elam, Keir. "The Fertile Eunuch: *Twelfth Night*, Early Modern Intercourse, and the Fruits of Castration," *SQ* 47 (1996), 1–36.

Hollander, John. "*Twelfth Night* and the Morality of Indulgence," *Sewanee Review* 67 (1959), 220–38.

Hutson, Lorna. "On Not Being Deceived: Rhetoric and the Body in *Twelfth Night*," *Texas Studies in Literature and Language* 38 (1996), 140–74.

Kerrigan, John. "Secrecy and Gossip in *Twelfth Night*," *ShS* 50 (1997), 65–80.

Leech, Clifford. "*Twelfth Night*" and *Shakespearian Comedy*. Toronto, 1965.

Lewalski, Barbara K. "Thematic Patterns in *Twelfth Night*," *ShakS* 1 (1965), 168–81.

Potter, Lois. "*Twelfth Night*": *Text and Performance*. London, 1985.

Salingar, L. D. "The Design of *Twelfth Night*," *SQ* 9 (1958), 117–39.

Schalkwyk, David. "Love and Service in *Twelfth Night* and the Sonnets," *SQ* 56 (2005), 76–100.

Schiffer, James, ed. "*Twelfth Night*": *New Critical Essays*. London and New York, 2011.

Shannon, Laurie J. "Nature's Bias: Renaissance Homonormativity and Elizabethan Likeness," *Modern Philology* 98 (2000), 183–210.

Wells, Stanley. *Royal Shakespeare*. Manchester, Eng., 1977. (Includes an account of John Barton's production of *Twelfth Night*.)

Welsford, Enid. *The Fool: His Social and Literary History*. London, 1935.

Williams, Porter, Jr. "Mistakes in *Twelfth Night* and Their Resolution," *PMLA* 76 (1961), 193–9.

Measure for Measure

See also, under *The Comedies*, Hunter and Newman; under *The Problem Plays*, Frye, Schanzer, and Wheeler; under *Shakespeare Criticism from the 1940s to the 1970s*, Empson, Fly, Holland, Levin (pp. 171–93), and Sewell; and under *Shakespeare Criticism Since 1980*, Cox, Dollimore, Dollimore and Sinfield (essays by Dollimore and McLuskie), Drakakis (essay by Rose), Goldberg (Chapter 5), Grady (*Shakespeare and Modernity*, essay by Engle), Hamilton (Chapter 5), Holland et al. (essay by Adelman), Kirsch, Marcus, Mullaney (Chapter 4), and Skura (pp. 243–70).

Bennett, Josephine Waters. "*Measure for Measure*" *as Royal Entertainment*. New York, 1966.

Bennett, Robert B. *Romance and Reformation: The Erasmian Spirit of Shakespeare's "Measure for Measure."* Newark, Del., 2000.

Brown, Carolyn E. "The Wooing of Duke Vincentio and Isabella of *Measure for Measure*: The Image of It Gives [Them] Content,'" *ShakS* 22 (1994), 189–219.

Cacicedo, Alberto. "'She is fast my wife': Sex, Marriage, and Ducal Authority in *Measure for Measure*," *ShakS* 23 (1995), 187–209.

Chamberlain, Stephanie. "Defrocking Ecclesiastical Authority: *Measure for Measure* and the Struggle for Matrimonial Reform in Early Modern England," *Ben Jonson Journal* 7 (2000), 115–28.

Chambers, R. W. "The Jacobean Shakespeare and *Measure for Measure*," *Proceedings of the British Academy* 23 (1937), 135–92.

Coghill, Nevill. "Comic Form in *Measure for Measure*," *ShS* 8 (1955), 14–27.

Desens, Marliss C. *The Bed-Trick in English Renaissance Drama: Explorations in Gender, Sexuality, and Power*. Newark, Del., 1994.

Fergusson, Francis. *The Human Image in Dramatic Literature*. Garden City, N.Y., 1957.

Gless, Darryl. "*Measure for Measure*," *the Law, and the Convent*. Princeton, 1979.

Lascelles, Mary. *Shakespeare's "Measure for Measure."* London, 1953.

Leavis, F. R. "The Greatness of *Measure for Measure*," *Scrutiny* 10 (1942), 234–47.

Leggatt, Alexander. "Substitution in *Measure for Measure*," *SQ* 39 (1988), 342–59.

Nagarajan, S. "*Measure for Measure* and Elizabethan Betrothals," *SQ* 14 (1963), 115–19.

Shell, Marc. *The End of Kinship: "Measure for Measure," Incest, and the Ideal of Universal Siblinghood*. Stanford, 1988.

Shuger, Debora Kuller. *Political Theologies in Shakespeare's England: The Sacred and the State in "Measure for Measure."* Basingstoke, Eng., and New York, 2001.

Stevenson, David L. *The Achievement of "Measure for Measure."* Ithaca, N.Y., 1966.

Wilson, Harold S. "Action and Symbol in *Measure for Measure* and *The Tempest*." *SQ* 4 (1953), 375–84.

Wood, Nigel. "*Measure for Measure*." Theory in Practice Series. Buckingham and Philadelphia, 1996.

The Histories

See also, under *Shakespeare's Predecessors and Contemporaries*, Hillman.

Alexander, Peter. *Shakespeare's, "Henry VI" and "Richard III."* Cambridge, Eng., 1929.

Baldo, Jonathan. *Memory in Shakespeare's Histories: Stages of Forgetting in Early Modern England.* New York, 2012.

Berry, Edward I. *Patterns of Decay: Shakespeare's Early Histories.* Charlottesville, Va., 1975.

Blanpied, John W. *Time and the Artist in Shakespeare's English Histories.* Newark, Del., 1983.

Calderwood, James L. *Metadrama in Shakespeare's Henriad: "Richard II" to "Henry V."* Berkeley, 1979.

Campbell, Lily B. *Shakespeare's "Histories": Mirrors of Elizabethan Policy.* San Marino, Calif., 1947.

Cavanagh, Dermot, Stuart Hampton-Ross, and Stephen Longstaffe, eds. *Shakespeare's Histories and Counter-Histories.* Manchester, 2006.

Champion, Larry S. *"The Noise of Threatening Drum": Dramatic Strategy and Political Ideology in Shakespeare and the English Chronicle Plays.* Newark, Del., 1990.

———. *Perspective in Shakespeare's English Histories.* Athens, Ga., 1980.

Dillon, Janette. *Shakespeare and the Staging of English History.* Oxford, 2012.

Dorius, R. J. "A Little More Than a Little," *SQ* 11 (1960), 13–26.

Edwards, Philip. "The Hidden King: Shakespeare's History Plays," *Threshold of a Nation: A Study in English and Irish Drama.* Cambridge, Eng., 1979.

Forker, Charles R. "Shakespeare's Chronicle Plays as Historical-Pastoral," *ShakS* 1 (1965), 85–104.

Goy-Blanquet, Dominique. *Shakespeare's Early History Plays.* Oxford, 2003.

Grene, Nicholas. *Shakespeare's Serial History Plays.* Cambridge, Eng., 2002.

Hattaway, Michael, ed. *The Cambridge Companion to Shakespeare's History Plays.* Cambridge, Eng., 2002.

Heller, Agnes. *The Time Is Out of Joint: Shakespeare as Philosopher of History.* Lanham, Md., 2002.

Hodgdon, Barbara. *The End Crowns All: Closure and Contradiction in Shakespeare's History.* Princeton, 1991.

Hoenselaars, Ton, ed. *Shakespeare's History Plays: Performance, Translation, and Adaptation in Britain and Abroad.* Cambridge, Eng., 2004.

Holderness, Graham. *Shakespeare's History.* New York, 1985. Largely reprinted in *Shakespeare Recycled: The Making of Historical Drama.* Hempstead, Eng., New York, 1992.

———. *Shakespeare—The Histories.* New York, 2000.

———, ed. *Shakespeare's History Plays: "Richard II" to "Henry V."* London, 1992.

Howard, Jean E., and Phyllis Rackin. *Engendering a Nation: A Feminist Account of Shakespeare's English Histories.* London and New York, 1997.

Jenkins, Harold. "Shakespeare's History Plays: 1900–1951," *ShS* 6 (1953), 1–15.

Jorgensen, Paul A. *Shakespeare's Military World.* Berkeley and Los Angeles, 1956.

Kantorowicz, Ernst. *The King's Two Bodies: A Study in Mediaeval Political Theology.* Princeton, 1957.

Kastan, David Scott. *Shakespeare and the Shapes of Time.* Hanover, N. H., 1982.

Kelly, Henry A. *Divine Providence in the England of Shakespeare's Histories.* Cambridge, Mass., 1970.

Knights, L. C. "Shakespeare's Politics: With Some Reflections on the Nature of Tradition," *Proceedings of the British Academy* 43 (1957), 115–32.

Knowles, Roland. *Shakespeare's Arguments with History.* Basingstoke, Eng., and New York, 2002.

Leggatt, Alexander. *Shakespeare's Political Drama: The History Plays and the Roman Plays.* London, 1988.

Levine, Nina S. *Women's Matters: Politics, Gender, and Nation in Shakespeare's Early History Plays.* Newark, Del., 1998.

Manheim, Michael. *The Weak King Dilemma in the Shakespearean History Play.* Syracuse, N.Y., 1973.

Mayer, Jean-Christophe. *Shakespeare's Hybrid Faith: Religion and the Stage.* Basingstoke, Hants., and New York, 2006.

McAlindon, Tom. *Shakespeare's Tudor History: A Study of Henry IV, Parts 1 and 2.* Aldershot, Eng., and Burlington, Vt., 2001.

Norwich, John Julius. *Shakespeare's Kings: The Great Plays and the History of England in the Middle Ages: 1337–1485.* London, 1999; New York, 2000.

Orgel, Stephen, and Sean Kellen, eds. *Shakespeare and History.* New York, 1999.

Ornstein, Robert. *A Kingdom for a Stage.* Cambridge, Mass., 1972.

Palmer, John. *Political Characters of Shakespeare.* London, 1945.

Paris, Bernard J. *Character as a Subversive Force in Shakespeare: The History and Roman Plays.* Rutherford, N.J., and London, 1991.

Patterson, Annabel. *Reading Holinshed's Chronicles.* Chicago, 1994.

Pierce, Robert B. *Shakespeare's History Plays: The Family and the State.* Columbus, Ohio, 1971.

Pilkington, Ace G. *Screening Shakespeare from "Richard II" to "Henry V."* Newark, Del., 1991.

Porter, Joseph. *The Drama of Speech Acts: Shakespeare's Lancastrian Tetralogy.* Berkeley, 1979.

Prior, Moody E. *The Drama of Power: Studies in Shakespeare's History Plays.* Evanston, Ill., 1973.

Pugliatti, Paola. *Shakespeare the Historian.* New York, 1996.

Pye, Christopher. *The Regal Phantasm: Shakespeare and the Politics of Spectacle.* London, 1990.

Rackin, Phyllis. "Anti-Historians: Women's Roles in Shakespeare's Histories," *Theatre Journal* 37 (1985), 329–44.

———. *Stages of History: Shakespeare's English Chronicles.* Ithaca, N.Y., 1990.

Raffield, Paul. *Shakespeare's Imaginary Constitution: Late Elizabethan Politics and the Theatre of Law.* Oxford, 2010.

Reese, M. M. *The Cease of Majesty.* London and New York, 1961.

Ribner, Irving. *The English History Play in the Age of Shakespeare*, Rev. ed., London, 1965.

Rossiter, A. P. "Ambivalence: The Dialectic of the Histories," *Talking of Shakespeare,* ed. John Garrett. London, 1954.

Saccio, Peter. *Shakespeare's English Kings: History, Chronicle, and Drama.* New York, 1977.

Shafer, Ronald G. *Shakespeare and English History: Interdisciplinary Perspectives.* Bloomington, Ind., 1976.

Shaheen, Naseeb. *Biblical References in Shakespeare's History Plays.* Newark, Del., 1989.

Smith, Emma, ed. *Shakespeare's Histories.* Malden, Mass., 2004.

Sprague, Arthur Colby. *Shakespeare's Histories: Plays for the Stage.* London, 1964.

Sterling, Eric. *The Movement Towards Subversion: The English History Play from Skelton to Shakespeare.* Lanham, Md., 1996.

Tillyard, E. M. W. *Shakespeare's History Plays.* London, 1944, 1961.

Traversi, Derek. *Shakespeare from "Richard II" to "Henry V."* London, 1957.

Velz, John W., ed. *Shakespeare's English Histories: A Quest for Form and Genre.* Binghamton, N.Y., 1996.

Walsh, Brian. *Shakespeare, the Queen's Men, and the Elizabethan Performance of History.* Cambridge, Eng., 2009.

Winny, James. *The Player King: A Theme of Shakespeare's Histories.* London, 1968.

Yeats, William Butler. "At Stratford-upon-Avon," *Ideas of Good and Evil.* London, 1903.

Richard III

See also, under *The Histories*, Alexander, Berry, Campbell, Kelly, Ornstein, Prior, Ribner, and Saccio; under *Shakespeare's Predecessors and Contemporaries,* Sanders; under *Shakespeare Criticism from the 1940s to the 1970s,* Jones, Rossiter, and Spivack; under *Shakespeare Criticism since 1980,* Dubrow and Strier (essay by Garber), and Lenz et al. (essay by Miner); under *The Tragedies,* Garner and Sprengnether (essay by Rackin), and Hunter; and under *The Henry VI Plays,* Watson.

Anderson, Judith H. "Shakespeare's *Richard III:* The Metamorphosis of Biographical Truth to Fiction," *Biographical Truth: The Representation of Historical Persons in Tudor-Stuart Writing.* New Haven, 1984.

Bevington, David. " 'Why Should Calamity Be Full of Words?' The Efficacy of Cursing in *Richard III," Iowa State Journal of Research* 56:1 (1981), 9–21.

Colley, Scott. *"Richard's Himself Again": A Stage History of "Richard III."* New York, 1992.

French, A. L. "The World of *Richard III*," *ShakS 4* (1968), 25–39.

Hankey, Julie, ed. *Plays in Performance: "Richard III."* Bristol, 1981; 2nd ed., 1988.

Hassel, R. Chris, Jr. *Songs of Death: Performance, Interpretation, and the Text of "Richard III."* Lincoln, Neb., 1987.

Hunter, Robert G. *Shakespeare and the Mystery of God's Judgments.* Athens, Ga., 1976.

Kendall, Paul Murray. *Richard the Third.* New York and London, 1956.

Krieger, Murray. "The Dark Generations of *Richard III*," *Criticism* 1 (1959), 32–48.

Neill, Michael. "Shakespeare's Halle of Mirrors: Play, Politics, and Psychology in *Richard III*," *ShakS 8* (1975), 99–129.

Sher, Antony. *Year of the King: An Actor's Diary and Sketchbook.* London, 1985.

Torrey, Michael. "'The plain devil and dissembling looks': Ambivalent Physiognomy and Shakespeare's *Richard III*," *English Literary Renaissance* 30 (2000), 123–53.

Wheeler, Richard P. "History, Character, and Conscience in *Richard III*," *Comparative Drama* 5 (1971–1972), 301–21.

Richard II

See also, under *The Histories*, Calderwood, Campbell, Dorius, Forker, Ornstein, Palmer, Porter, Reese, Ribner, Saccio and Tillyard; under *Shakespeare's Predecessors and Contemporaries*, Sanders; under *Shakespeare's Language*, Mahood; under *Shakespeare Criticism to the 1930s*, Coleridge (*Coleridge's Writings*); under *Shakespeare Criticism from the 1940s to the 1970s*, Bryant, Calderwood, Hawkes, Kernan (essay on the "Major History Plays"), and Rabkin (pp. 81–98); under *Shakespeare Criticism Since 1980*, Bergeron (essay by Black), Parker and Hartman (essay by Berger), and Woodbridge and Berry (essay by Liebler); under *Shakespeare in Performance*, McGuire and Samuelson (essay by McGuire); and under *The Tragedies*, Nevo.

Barkan, Leonard. "The Theatrical Consistency of *Richard II*," *SQ* 29 (1978), 5–19.

Berger, Harry, Jr. "Textual Dramaturgy: Representing the Limits of Theatre in *Richard II*," *Theatre Journal* 39 (1987), 135–55.

Bergeron, David M. "*Richard II*: Internal and External Evidence," *Practicing Renaissance Scholarship: Plays and Pageants, Patrons and Politics.* Pittsburgh, Pa., 2000.

Dorius, R. J. "A Little More Than a Little," *SQ* 11 (1960), 13–26.

Elliott, John R., Jr. "History and Tragedy in *Richard II*," *Studies in English Literature* 8 (1968), 253–71.

Forker, Charles. *Shakespeare: The Critical Tradition: Richard II.* London, 1998.

Gaudet, Paul. "The 'Parasitical' Counselors in Shakespeare's *Richard II*: A Problem in Dramatic Interpretation," *SQ* 33 (1982), 142–54.

Halvorson, John. "The Lamentable Comedy of *Richard II*," *English Literary Renaissance* 24 (1994), 343–69.

Harris, Kathryn Montgomery. "Sun and Water Imagery in *Richard II*: Its Dramatic Function," *SQ* 21 (1970), 157–65.

Heninger, S. K., Jr. "The Sun-King Analogy in *Richard II*," *SQ* 11 (1960), 319–27.

Humphreys, A. R. *Shakespeare: "Richard II."* London, 1967.

Kantorowicz, Ernst H. *The King's Two Bodies: A Study in Medieval Political Theology.* Princeton, 1957.

Lisak, Catherine. "In Search of *Richard II*: Shakespeare's Use of Eyewitness Accounts of the Revolution (1399–1400); Conflicting Tales and the Dramatic Structure of the Play," *Shakespeare et le Moyen-Âge*. Actes du colloque international de la Société française Shakespeare, gen. ed. Jean-Marie Maguin. Montpellier, France, 2002.

Lopez, Jeremy, ed. "*Richard II*": New Critical Essays. London and New York, 2012.

MacKenzie, Clayton G. "Paradise and Paradise Lost in *Richard II*," *SQ* 37 (1986), 318–39.

McMillin, Scott. "Shakespeare's *Richard II*: Eyes of Sorrow, Eyes of Desire," *SQ* 35 (1984), 40–52.

Page, Malcolm. *Text and Performance: "Richard II."* Atlantic Highlands, N.J., 1987.

Potter, Lois. "The Antic Disposition of Richard II," *ShS* 27 (1974), 33–41.

Schoenbaum, S. "*Richard II* and the Realities of Power," *ShS* 28 (1975), 1–13.

Shewring, Margaret. *Shakespeare in Performance: "King Richard II."* Manchester, 1996.

Stirling, Brents. "Bolingbroke's 'Decision,'" *SQ* 2 (1951), 27–34.

Syme, Holger Schott. *Theatre and Testimony in Shakespeare's England: A Culture of Mediation.* New York, 2012.

Yeats, W. B. "At Stratford-upon-Avon," *Ideas of Good and Evil*, collected in *Essays and Introductions.* New York, 1961.

Zitner, Sheldon P. "Aumerle's Conspiracy," *Studies in English Literature* 14 (1974), 239–57.

The Henry IV Plays

See also, under *The Histories*, Blanpied, Calderwood, Campbell, Dorius, Kelly, Manheim, Ornstein, Palmer, Porter, Prior, Reese, Saccio, Sprague, Tillyard, and Velz (essay by Rumrich); under *Shakespeare Criticism to the 1930s*, Johnson and Smith (*Eighteenth Century*, essay by Morgann); under *Shakespeare Criticism from the 1940s to the 1970s*, Bevington and Halio (essay by R. G. Hunter), Bryant, Burckhardt, Council, Goldman, Kernan (essay on the "Major History Plays"), Spivack, and Stewart; and under *Shakespeare Criticism Since 1980*, Auden, Dollimore and Sinfield (essay by Greenblatt, originally published by *Glyph 8* and in *Shakespearean Negotiations*), Hopkins, Nuttall, and Watson; and under *The Comedies*, Barber.

Abrams, Richard. "Rumor's Reign in *2 Henry IV*: The Scope of a Personification," *English Literary Renaissance* 16 (1986), 467–95.

Auden, W. H. "The Prince's Dog," *"The Dyer's Hand" and Other Essays*. New York, 1948.

Barber, C. L. "Rule and Misrule in *Henry IV*," *Shakespeare's Festive Comedy*. Princeton, 1959.

Barish, Jonas A. "The Turning Away of Prince Hal," *ShakS 1* (1965), 9–17.

Barker, Roberta. "Tragical-Comical-Historical Hotspur," *SQ* 54 (2003), 288–307.

Berger, Harry, Jr. "Sneak's Noise, or Rumor and Detextualization in *2 Henry IV*," *Kenyon Review* n.s. 6:4 (1984), 58–78.

Berry, Edward I. "The Rejection Scene in *2 Henry IV*," *Studies in English Literature* 17 (1977), 201–18.

Bradley, A. C. "The Rejection of Falstaff," *Oxford Lectures on Poetry*. London, 1909, 1961.

Bryant, J. A., Jr., "Prince Hal and the Ephesians," *Sewanee Review* 67 (1959), 204–19.

Cohen, Derek. "The Rite of Violence in *1 Henry IV*," *ShS 38* (1985), 77–84.

Dessen, Alan. "Dual Protagonists in *1 Henry IV*," *Shakespeare and the Late Moral Plays*. Lincoln, Neb., 1986.

Doran, Madeleine. "Imagery in *Richard II* and in *Henry IV*," *Modern Language Review* 37 (1942), 113–22.

Dorius, R. J., ed. *Twentieth Century Interpretations of "Henry IV Part I."* Englewood Cliffs, N.J., 1970.

Empson, William. "Falstaff and Mr. Dover Wilson," *Kenyon Review* 15 (1953), 213–62.

Everett, Barbara. "The Fatness of Falstaff: Shakespeare and Character," *Proceedings of the British Academy* 76 (1990), 109–28.

Gottschalk, Paul A. "Hal and the 'Play Extempore' in *1 Henry IV*," *Texas Studies in Literature and Language* 15 (1974), 605–14.

Hawkins, Sherman H. "Virtue and Kingship in Shakespeare's *Henry IV*," *English Literary Renaissance* 5 (1975), 313–43.

Hodgdon, Barbara. *Shakespeare in Performance: "Henry IV, Part Two."* Manchester, 1993.

Hunter, G. K. "*Henry IV* and the Elizabethan Two-Part Play," *Review of English Studies* n.s. 5 (1954), 236–48.

———. "Shakespeare's Politics and the Rejection of Falstaff," *Critical Quarterly* 1 (1959), 229–36.

Jenkins, Harold. *The Structural Problem in Shakespeare's "Henry the Fourth."* London, 1956.

Jorgensen, Paul A. "The 'Dastardly Treachery' of Prince John of Lancaster," *PMLA* 76 (1961), 488–92.

Knowles, Richard. "Unquiet and the Double Plot of *2 Henry IV*," *ShakS 2* (1966), 133–40.

Kris, Ernst. "Prince Hal's Conflict," *Psychoanalytic Explorations in Art*. New York, 1964.

Levine, Nina. "Extending Credit in the *Henry IV Plays,*" *SQ* 51 (2000), 403–31.

Manley, Frank. "The Unity of Betrayal in *2 Henry IV,*" *Studies in the Literary Imagination* 5:1 (1972), 91–110.

McAlindon, Tom. *Shakespeare's Tudor History: A Study of "Henry IV, Parts 1 and 2."* Aldershot, Eng., 2001.

McLuhan, Herbert Marshall. "*Henry IV,* A Mirror for Magistrates," *University of Toronto Quarterly* 17 (1947–1948), 152–60.

McMillin, Scott. *Shakespeare in Performance: "Henry IV, Part One."* Manchester, Eng., 1991.

Palmer, D. J. "Casting Off the Old Man: History and St. Paul in *Henry IV,*" *Critical Quarterly* 12 (1970), 267–83.

Poole, Kristen. "Saints Alive! Falstaff, Martin Marprelate, and the Staging of Puritanism," *SQ* 46 (1995), 47–75.

Somerset, J. A. B. "Falstaff, the Prince, and the Pattern of *2 Henry IV,*" *ShS* 30 (1977), 35–45.

Toliver, Harold E. "Falstaff, the Prince, and the History Play," *SQ* 16 (1965), 63–80.

Wharton, T. F. *"Henry the Fourth, Parts 1 and 2": Text and Performance.* London, 1983.

Wilson, J. Dover. *The Fortunes of Falstaff.* Cambridge, Eng., 1943.

Womersley, David. "Why Is Falstaff Fat?" *Review of English Studies* n.s. 47 (1996), 1–22.

Henry V

See also, under *The Histories,* Calderwood, Campbell, Jorgensen, Kastan, Ornstein, Porter, Prior, Reese, Ribner, Saccio, and Traversi; under *Shakespeare Criticism to the 1930s,* Hazlitt and Schlegel; under *Shakespeare Criticism from the 1940s to the 1970s,* Burckhardt, Goddard, Goldman, and Kernan (essay on the "Major History Plays"); under *Shakespeare Criticism Since 1980,* Dollimore and Sinfield (essays by Greenblatt and Tennenhouse), Drakakis (essay by Dollimore and Sinfield), Erickson, Mahon and Pendleton (essay by Hammond), Patterson (Chapter 4), and Rabkin (Chapter 2); and under *Shakespeare in Performance,* Price (essay by Barton).

Altman, Joel B. "'Vile Participation': The Amplification of Violence in the Theater of *Henry V,*" *SQ* 42 (1991), 1–32.

Beauman, Sally, ed. *"King Henry V": The Royal Shakespeare Company's Production of "Henry V" for the Centenary Season at the Royal Shakespeare Theatre.* Oxford, 1976. (Includes information on Terry Hands's *Henry V.*)

Cubeta, Paul M. "Falstaff and the Art of Dying," *Studies in English Literature* 27 (1987), 197–211.

Eggert, Katherine. "Nostalgia and the Not Yet Late Queen: Refusing Female Rule in *Henry V,*" *ELH* 61 (1994), 523–50.

Granville-Barker, Harley. "From *Henry V* to *Hamlet,*" *Proceedings of the British Academy* 11 (1925), 283–309.

Gurr, Andrew. "*Henry V* and the Bees' Commonwealth," *ShS* 30 (1977): 61–72.

Levin, Richard. "Hazlitt on *Henry V,* and the Appropriation of Shakespeare," *SQ* 35 (1984), 134–41.

McEachern, Claire. *The Poetics of English Nationhood, 1590–1612.* Cambridge, Eng., 1996.

The Tragedies

See also, under *Shakespeare's Predecessors and Contemporaries,* Belsey, Falco, and Liebler; and under *Shakespeare Criticism Since 1980,* Dollimore and Hopkins.

Alfar, Cristina León. *Fantasies of Female Evil: The Dynamics of Gender and Power in Shakespearean Tragedy.* Newark, Del., and London, 2003.

Armstrong, Philip. *Shakespeare's Visual Regime: Tragedy, Psychoanalysis, and the Gaze.* Basingstoke and New York, 2000.

Baldo, Jonathan. *The Unmasking of Drama: Contested Representation in Shakespeare's Tragedies.* Detroit, 1996.

Barker, Francis, ed. *The Culture of Violence: Essays on Tragedy and History.* Chicago, 1993.

Barroll, J. Leeds. *Artificial Persons: The Formation of Character in the Tragedies of Shakespeare.* Columbia, S. C., 1974.

Bayley, John. *Shakespeare and Tragedy.* London, 1981.

Bell, Millicent. *Shakespeare's Tragic Skepticism.* New Haven, 2002.

Berry, Philippa. *Shakespeare's Feminine Endings: Disfiguring Death in the Tragedies.* London and New York, 1999.

Berry, Ralph. *Tragic Instance: The Sequence of Shakespeare's Tragedies.* Newark, Del., 1999.

Bradley, A. C. *Shakespearean Tragedy.* London, 1904. (*Hamlet, Othello, King Lear, Macbeth.*)

Brooke, Nicholas. *Shakespeare's Early Tragedies.* London and New York, 1968.

Brown, John Russell, and Bernard Harris, eds. *Early Shakespeare.* London, 1961.

Bulman, James C. *The Heroic Idiom of Shakespearean Tragedy.* Newark, Del., 1985.

Bushnell, Rebecca. *Tragedies of Tyrants: Political Thought and Theater in the English Renaissance.* Ithaca, N.Y., 1990.

Campbell, Lily B. *Shakespeare's Tragic Heroes: Slaves of Passion.* Cambridge, Eng., 1930.

Champion, Larry S. *Shakespeare's Tragic Perspective.* Athens, Ga., 1976.

Charlton, H. B. *Shakespearian Tragedy.* Cambridge, Eng., 1948.

Cunningham, I.V. *Woe or Wonder: The Emotional Effect of Shakespearean Tragedy.* Denver, 1951. Rpt. in *Tradition and Poetic Structure.* Denver, 1960.

Danson, Lawrence. *Tragic Alphabet: Shakespeare's Drama of Language.* New Haven and London, 1974.

Dickey, Franklin M. *Not Wisely But Too Well: Shakespeare's Love Tragedies.* San Marino, Calif., 1957.

Dobson, Michael. *Performing Shakespeare's Tragedies Today: The Actor's Perspective.* Cambridge, Eng., 2006.

Eliot, T. S. "Shakespeare and the Stoicism of Seneca," *Selected Essays, 1917–1932.* London, 1932.

Everett, Barbara. *Young Hamlet: Essays on Shakespeare's Tragedies.* Oxford, 1989.

Falco, Raphael. *Charismatic Authority in Early Modern English Tragedy.* Baltimore, 2000.

Farnham, Willard. *Shakespeare's Tragic Frontier.* Berkeley, 1950.

Frye, Northrop. *Fools of Time: Studies in Shakespearean Tragedy.* Toronto, 1967.

Gajowski, Evelyn. *The Art of Loving: Female Subjectivity and Male Discursive Traditions in Shakespeare's Tragedies.* Newark, Del., 1992.

Garner, Shirley Nelson, and Madelon Sprengnether, eds. *Shakespearean Tragedy and Gender.* Bloomington, Ind., 1996.

Goldman, Michael. *Acting and Action in Shakespearean Tragedy.* Princeton, 1985.

Grene, Nicholas. *Shakespeare's Tragic Imagination.* New York, 1992.

Hawkes, Terence. *Shakespeare and the Reason: A Study of the Tragedies and the Problem Plays.* London, 1964.

Hays, Michael L. *Shakespearean Tragedy as Chivalric Romance: Rethinking Macbeth, Hamlet, Othello, and King Lear.* Cambridge, Eng., 2003.

Held, George F. *The Good That Lives After Them: A Pattern in Shakespeare's Tragedies.* Heidelberg, 1995.

Holloway, John. *The Story of the Night: Studies in Shakespeare's Major Tragedies.* London and Lincoln, Neb., 1961.

Honigmann, E. A. J. *Myriad-Minded Shakespeare: Essays, Chiefly on the Tragedies and Problem Comedies.* New York, 1989.

———. *Shakespeare: Seven Tragedies Revisited: The Dramatist's Manipulation of Response.* London and New York, 1976; 2nd ed., 2002.

Hopkins, Lisa. *The Female Hero in English Renaissance Tragedy.* Basingstoke, Eng., and New York, 2002.

Hunter, Robert Grams. *Shakespeare and the Mystery of God's Judgments.* Athens, Ga., 1976.

Ide, Richard S. *Possessed with Greatness: The Heroic Tragedies of Chapman and Shakespeare.* Chapel Hill, N.C., 1980.

Kiefer, Frederick. *Fortune and Elizabethan Tragedy.* San Marino, Calif., 1983.

Kirsch, Arthur. *The Passions of Shakespeare's Tragic Heroes.* Charlottesville, Va., 1990.

Knight, G. Wilson. *The Wheel of Fire.* London, 1930, 1965.

Lawlor, John. *The Tragic Sense in Shakespeare.* London, 1960.

Leech, Clifford. *Shakespeare's Tragedies and Other Studies in Seventeenth-Century Drama.* London, 1950.

———, ed. *Shakespeare: The Tragedies.* Chicago, 1965.

Leggatt, Alexander. *Shakespeare's Tragedies: Violation and Identity.* Cambridge, Eng., 2005.

Liebler, Naomi Conn. *Shakespeare's Festive Tragedy: The Ritual Foundations of Genre.* London and New York, 1995.

Mack, Maynard. *Everybody's Shakespeare: Reflections Chiefly on the Tragedies.* Lincoln, Neb., 1993.

———. "The Jacobean Shakespeare: Some Observations on the Construction of the Tragedies," *Jacobean Theatre,* eds. John Russell Brown and Bernard Harris. Stratford-upon-Avon Studies 1. London, 1960.

Mack, Maynard, Jr. *Killing the King: Three Studies in Shakespeare's Tragic Structure.* New Haven and London, 1973.

Margolies, David. *Monsters of the Deep: Social Dissolution in Shakespeare's Tragedies.* Manchester, Eng., 1992.

McAlindon, T. *Shakespeare's Tragic Cosmos.* Cambridge, 1991.

McEachern, Claire, ed. *The Cambridge Companion to Shakespearean Tragedy.* Cambridge, Eng., 2002.

Miola, Robert S. *Shakespeare and Classical Tragedy: The Influence of Seneca.* Oxford, 1992.

Neill, Michael. *Issues of Death: Mortality and Identity in English Renaissance Tragedy.* Oxford, 1997.

Nevo, Ruth. *Tragic Form in Shakespeare.* Princeton, 1972.

Proser, Matthew N. *The Heroic Image in Five Shakespearean Tragedies.* Princeton, 1965.

Rackin, Phyllis. *Shakespeare's Tragedies.* New York, 1978.

Reid, Robert Lanier. *Shakespeare's Tragic Form: Spirit in the Wheel.* Newark, Del., 2000.

Ribner, Irving, *Patterns in Shakespearean Tragedy.* New York, 1960.

Rosen, William. *Shakespeare and the Craft of Tragedy.* Cambridge, Mass., 1960.

Sanders, Wilbur, and Howard Jacobson. *Shakespeare's Magnanimity: Four Tragic Heroes, Their Friends and Families.* Oxford, 1978.

Shaheen, Naseeb. *Biblical References in Shakespeare's Tragedies.* Newark, Del., 1987.

Smith, Emma. *Shakespeare's Tragedies.* Malden, Mass., 2004.

Smith, Molly. *The Darker World Within: Evil in the Tragedies of Shakespeare and His Successors.* Newark, Del., 1991.

Snyder, Susan. *The Comic Matrix of Shakespeare's Tragedies.* Princeton, 1979.

Spivack, Bernard. *Shakespeare and the Allegory of Evil.* New York, 1958.

Sternfeld, Frederick W. *Music in Shakespearean Tragedy.* London, 1963, 1967.

Whitaker, Virgil. *The Mirror up to Nature.* San Marino, Calif., 1965.

Wilson, Harold S. *On the Design of Shakespearian Tragedy.* Toronto, 1957.

Young, David. *The Action to the Word: Structure and Style in Shakespearean Tragedy.* New Haven, 1990.

The Greek and Roman Tragedies

See also, under *Shakespeare Criticism Since 1980,* Paster (Chapter 3).

Brower, Reuben A. *Hero and Saint: Shakespeare and the Graeco-Roman Heroic Tradition.* New York and Oxford, 1971.

Cantor, Paul A. *Shakespeare's Rome: Republic and Empire.* Ithaca, N.Y., 1976.

Charney, Maurice, ed. *Discussions of Shakespeare's Roman Plays.* Boston, 1964.

———. *Shakespeare's Roman Plays: The Function of Imagery in the Drama.* Cambridge, Mass., 1961.

Knight, G. Wilson. *The Imperial Theme: Further Interpretations of Shakespeare's Tragedies Including the Roman Plays.* London, 1931, 1953.

Leggatt, Alexander. *Shakespeare's Political Drama: The History Plays and the Roman Plays.* London and New York, 1988.

MacCallum, M. W. *Shakespeare's Roman Plays and Their Background.* London, 1910.

Maxwell, J. C. "Shakespeare's Roman Plays: 1900–1956," *ShS* 10 (1957), 1–11.

Miles, Geoffrey. *Shakespeare and the Constant Romans.* Oxford, 1996.

Miola, Robert S. *Shakespeare's Rome.* Cambridge, Eng., 1983.

Nicoll, Allardyce, ed. *Shakespeare Survey 10* (1957).

Paris, Bernard J. *Character as a Subversive Force in Shakespeare: The History and Roman Plays.* Rutherford, N.J., and London, 1991.

Phillips, James E., Jr. *The State in Shakespeare's Greek and Roman Plays.* New York, 1940.

Simmons, J. L. *Shakespeare's Pagan World: The Roman Tragedies.* Charlottesville, Va., 1973.

Thomas, Vivian. *Shakespeare's Roman Worlds.* London, 1989.

Thomson, J. A. K. *Shakespeare and the Classics.* London, 1952.

Traversi, Derek. *Shakespeare: The Roman Plays.* Palo Alto, Calif., 1963.

Velz, John W. "The Ancient World in Shakespeare: Authenticity or Anachronism? A Retrospect," *ShS* 31 (1978), 1–12.

———. *Shakespeare and the Classical Tradition: A Critical Guide to Commentary, 1660–1960.* Minneapolis, 1968.

Romeo and Juliet

See also, under *The Tragedies,* Brooke, Brown and Harris (essay by Lawlor), Charlton, Dickey, Nevo, Ribner, and Snyder; under *Shakespeare's Language,* Mahood; under *Shakespeare Criticism to the 1930s,* Hazlitt; under *Shakespeare Criticism from the 1940s to the 1970s,* Calderwood, Granville-Barker, and Rabkin (pp. 162–84); under *Shakespeare Criticism Since 1980,* Callaghan (*A Feminist Companion,* essay by Berry), Daileader, Edwards et al. (essay by Wells), Erickson and Kahn (essay by Snow), Lenz et al. (essay by Kahn), and Novy (*Love's Argument*); and under *Shakespeare in Performance,* Brockbank (essay by Brenda Bruce).

Appelbaum, Robert. "'Standing to the wall': The Pressures of Masculinity in *Romeo and Juliet,*" *SQ* 48 (1997), 251–72.

Auden, W. H. "Commentary on the Poetry and Tragedy of *Romeo and Juliet.*" The Laurel Shakespeare, gen. ed. Francis Fergusson. New York, 1958.

Evans, Bertrand. "The Brevity of Friar Lawrence," *PMLA* 65 (1950), 841–65.

Evans, Robert O. *The Osier Cage: Rhetorical Devices in "Romeo and Juliet."* Lexington, Ky., 1966.

Everett, Barbara. "*Romeo and Juliet:* The Nurse's Story," *Critical Quarterly* 14 (1972), 129–39.

Halio, Jay, ed. *"Romeo and Juliet": Texts, Contexts, and Interpretation.* Newark, Del., 1995.

Hosley, Richard. "The Use of the Upper Stage in *Romeo and Juliet,*" *SQ* 5 (1954), 371–9.

Levenson, Jill L. *Shakespeare in Performance: "Romeo and Juliet."* Manchester, Eng., 1987.

Melchiori, Giorgio. "Peter, Balthasar, and Shakespeare's Art of Doubling," *Modern Language Review* 78 (1983), 777–92.

Williams, George W., ed. *The Most Excellent and Lamentable Tragedie of Romeo and Juliet.* Durham, N.C., 1964.

Julius Caesar

See also, under *The Greek and Roman Tragedies,* Brower, Charney (both titles), Knight, Miola, and Traversi; under *Shakespeare's Language,* Doran; under *Shakespeare Criticism to the 1930s,* Shaw; under *Shakespeare Criticism from the 1940s to the 1970s,* Burckhardt, Council, Goldman (Chapter 4), Granville-Barker, Kernan (essay by Mack), Rabkin (pp. 105–19), and Stirling; under *Shakespeare Criticism Since 1980,* Kahn; under *The Problem Plays,* Schanzer; and under *The Histories,* Palmer.

Blits, Jan H. *The End of the Ancient Republic: Essays on "Julius Caesar."* Durham, N.C., 1982.

Burke, Kenneth. "Antony in Behalf of the Play," *Southern Review* 1 (1935), 308–19. Rpt. in *The Philosophy of Literary Form.* Baton Rouge, La., 1941.

Knights, L. C. "Shakespeare and Political Wisdom: A Note on the Personalism of *Julius Caesar* and *Coriolanus,*" *Sewanee Review* 61 (1953), 43–55.

Liebler, Naomi Conn. "'Thou Bleeding Piece of Earth': The Ritual Ground of *Julius Caesar,*" *ShakS* 14 (1981), 175–96.

Miola, Robert S. "*Julius Caesar* and the Tyrannicide Debate," *Renaissance Quarterly* 38 (1985), 271–89.

Ornstein, Robert. "Seneca and the Political Drama of *Julius Caesar,*" *Journal of English and Germanic Philology* 57 (1958), 51–6.

Parker, Barbara L. "'A Thing Unfirm': Plato's *Republic* and Shakespeare's *Julius Caesar,*" *SQ* 44 (1993), 30–43.

Paster, Gail Kern." 'In the spirit of men there is no blood': Blood as Trope of Gender in *Julius Caesar,*" *SQ* 40 (1989), 284–98.

Ribner, Irving."Political Issues in *Julius Caesar,*" *Journal of English and Germanic Philology* 56 (1957), 10–22.

Ripley, John. *"Julius Caesar" on Stage in England and America, 1599–1973.* Cambridge, Eng., 1980.

Rose, Mark."Conjuring Caesar: Ceremony, History, and Authority in 1599," *English Literary Renaissance* 19 (1989), 291–304.

Velz, John W."Clemency, Will, and Just Cause in *Julius Caesar,*" *ShS* 22 (1969), 109–18.

———." 'If I Were Brutus Now . . . ': Role-Playing in *Julius Caesar,*" *ShakS* 4 (1968), 149–59.

———."Undular Structure in *Julius Caesar,*" *Modern Language Review* 66 (1971), 21–30.

Hamlet

See also, under *Shakespeare's Language,* Donawerth; under *The Tragedies,* Barker, Bradley, Brooke, Goldman, Holloway, Kirsch, Mack, Mack Jr., Rosen, and Whitaker; under *The Greek and Roman Tragedies,* Brower; under *Shakespeare's Predecessors and Contemporaries,* Bowers, and Rabkin (essay by Booth); under *Shakespeare Criticism to the 1930s,* Coleridge (*Coleridge's Writings*); under *Shakespeare Criticism from the 1940s to the 1970s,* Granville-Barker, Hawkes, and Righter; under *Shakespeare Criticism Since 1980,* Cavell (Chapter 5), Drakakis (essay by Rose), Erickson, Garber (*Shakespeare's Ghost Writers,* Chapter 6), Loomba and Orkin (essay by Bertoldi), Mazzio and Trevor (essays by De Grazia and Guillory), McDonald (essay by Parker), Parker and Hartman (essays by Weimann, Ferguson, and Hawkes), Patterson (Chapters 1 and 5), and Schwartz and Kahn (essays by Fineman and Leverenz); under *Shakespeare in Performance,* Bevington; and under *The Problem Plays,* Tillyard.

Bertram, Paul, and Bernice W. Kliman, eds. *The Three-Text "Hamlet": Parallel Texts of the First and Second Quartos and First Folio.* New York, 1991.

Bevington, David. *Murder Most Foul: Hamlet Through the Ages.* Oxford, 2012.

Bowers, Fredson T."Hamlet as Minister and Scourge," *PMLA* 70 (1955), 740–9.

Bruster, Douglas. *To Be or Not To Be.* London, 2007.

Calderwood, James L. *To Be and Not to Be: Negation and Metadrama in "Hamlet."* New York, 1983.

Charney, Maurice. *Style in "Hamlet."* Princeton, 1969.

Clayton, Thomas, ed. *The "Hamlet" First Published (Q1, 1603): Origin, Form, Intertextualities.* Newark, Del., 1992.

Dawson, Anthony B. *Hamlet.* Shakespeare in Performance. Manchester, Eng., 1995.

De Grazia, Margreta."*Hamlet" without Hamlet.* Cambridge, Eng., 2007.

Eliot, T. S."Hamlet and His Problems," *Selected Essays, 1917–1932.* London and New York, 1932.

Erlich, Avi. *Hamlet's Absent Father.* Princeton, 1977.

Ewbank, Inga-Stina."Hamlet and the Power of Words," *ShS* 30 (1977), 85–102.

Fergusson, Francis. *The Idea of a Theater.* Princeton, 1949.

Foakes, R. A. *"Hamlet" versus "Lear": Cultural Politics and Shakespeare's Art.* Cambridge, Eng., 1993.

Frye, Roland Mushat. *The Renaissance "Hamlet": Issues and Responses in 1600.* Princeton, 1984.

Gallagher, Catherine, and Stephen Greenblatt, "The Mousetrap," in *Practicing New Historicism.* Chicago, 2000.

Greenblatt, Stephen. *Hamlet in Purgatory.* Princeton, 2001.

Heilbrun, Carolyn G. *Hamlet's Mother and Other Women.* New York, 1990.

Hirschfeld, Heather Anne."Hamlet's 'first corse': Repetition, Trauma, and the Displacement of Redemptive Typology," *SQ* 54 (2003), 424–48.

Howard, Tony. *Woman as Hamlet: Performance and Interpretation in Theatre, Film and Fiction.* Cambridge, Eng., 2007.

James, D. G. *The Dream of Learning.* Oxford, 1951.

Jones, Ernest. *Hamlet and Oedipus.* Rev. ed. New York, 1949, 1954.

Joseph, Bertram. *Conscience and the King.* London, 1953.

Kerrigan, William. *Hamlet's Perfection.* Baltimore, 1994.

Kinney, Arthur E., ed. *Hamlet: New Critical Essays.* New York and London, 2002.

Kitto, H. D. F. *Form and Meaning in Drama.* London, 1956.

Knights, L. C. *An Approach to Hamlet.* London, 1960.

Lacan, Jacques."Desire and the Interpretation of Desire in *Hamlet,*" *Yale French Studies* 55/56 (1977), 11–52.

Landau, Aaron. " 'Let Me Not Burst in Ignorance': Skepticism and Anxiety in *Hamlet,*" *English Studies,* 82 (2001), 218–29.

Lee, John. *Shakespeare's "Hamlet" and the Controversies of Self.* Oxford, 2000.

Levin, Harry. *The Question of Hamlet.* New York and London, 1959.

Lewis, C. S."Hamlet: The Prince or the Poem?" *Proceedings of the British Academy* 28 (1942), 139–54.

Litvin, Margaret. *Hamlet's Arab Journey: Shakespeare's Prince and Nasser's Ghost.* Princeton, 2011.

Mack, Maynard."The World of Hamlet," *Yale Review* 41 (1952), 502–23.

McCoy, Richard C."A Wedding and Four Funerals: Conjunction and Commemoration in *Hamlet,*" *ShS* 54 (2001), 122–39.

McGee, Arthur. *The Elizabethan Hamlet.* New Haven, 1987.

Muir, Kenneth, and Stanley Wells, eds., *Aspects of "Hamlet": Articles Reprinted from "Shakespeare Survey."* Cambridge, Eng., 1979. (Especially essay by Inga-Stina Ewbank.)

Murray, Gilbert. *Hamlet and Orestes.* Annual Shakespeare Lecture for the British Academy, 1914. London, 1919.

Nicoll, Allardyce, ed. *Shakespeare Survey 9* (1956).

Nietzsche, Friedrich."The Birth of Tragedy or: Hellenism and Pessimism" (1872), *The Birth of Tragedy and The Case of Wagner,* trans. Walter Kaufmann. New York, 1967.

Rose, Mark."Hamlet and the Shape of Revenge," *English Literary Renaissance* 1 (1971), 132–43.

Rosenberg, Marvin. *The Masks of "Hamlet."* Newark, Del., 1992.

Russell, John. *Hamlet and Narcissus.* Cranbury, N.J., 1995.

Skulsky, Harold." 'I Know My Course': Hamlet's Confidence," *PMLA* 89 (1974), 477–86.

Stallybrass, Peter."Hamlet's Tables and the Technologies of Writing in Renaissance England," *SQ* 55 (2004), 379–419.

States, Bert O. *"Hamlet" and the Concept of Character.* Baltimore, 1992.

Tronch-Pérez, Jesús. *A Synoptic "Hamlet": A Critical-Synoptic Edition of the Second Quarto and First Folio Texts of "Hamlet."* Valencia, Spain, 2002.

Welsh, Alexander. *Hamlet in His Modern Guises.* Princeton, 2001.

Wilson, J. Dover. *What Happens in "Hamlet."* London and New York, 1935, 1951.

Wright, George T."Hendiadys and *Hamlet,*" *PMLA* 96 (1981), 168–93.

Young, David."Hamlet, Son of Hamlet," *Perspectives on "Hamlet,"* eds. William G. Holzberger and Peter B. Waldock. Lewisburg, Pa., and London, 1975.

Othello

See also, under *The Tragedies,* Philippa Berry, Bradley, Dickey, Garner and Sprengnether (essays by Orlin, Hendricks, and Rose), Goldman, Hawkes, Holloway, Knight, Snyder, and Spivack; under *Shakespeare's Language,* Doran; under *Shakespeare's Predecessors and Contemporaries,* Hendricks and Parker (essays by Boose and Parker); under *Shakespeare Criticism to the 1930s,* Coleridge (*Coleridge's Writings*) and Johnson; under *Shakespeare Criticism from the 1940s to the 1970s,* Empson, Fiedler, Granville-Barker, and Sewell; and under *Shakespeare Criticism Since 1980,* Cavell (Chapter 3), Daileder, Erickson, Erickson and Kahn (essay by Wheeler), Greenblatt (*Renaissance Self-Fashioning,* Chapter 6), Howard and O'Connor (essay by Newman), Kirsch, Lenz et al. (essay by Neely), Loomba and Orkin (essay by Burton), McDonald (essay by Parker), Novy (*Love's Argument,* Chapter 7), and Parker and Hartman (essays by Parker and Showalter).

Adamson, Jane. *"Othello" as Tragedy: Some Problems of Judgment and Feeling*. Cambridge, Eng., 1980.

Altman, Joel B. " 'Preposterous Conclusions': Eros, *Enargeia*, and the Composition of *Othello*," *Representations* 18 (1987), 129–57.

———. *The Improbability of "Othello": Rhetorical Anthropology and Shakespearean Selfhood*. Chicago, 2010.

Bartels, Emily C. "Making More of the Moor: Aaron, Othello, and Renaissance Refashionings of Race," *SQ* 41 (1990), 433–54.

Bates, Catherine. "Weaving and Writing in *Othello*," *SQ* 46 (1995), 51–60.

Bayley, John. *The Characters of Love*. London, 1960.

Boose, Lynda E. "Othello's Handkerchief: 'The Recognizance and Pledge of Love,'" *English Literary Renaissance* 5 (1975), 360–74.

Calderwood, James L. *The Properties of "Othello."* Amherst, Mass., 1989.

Daileader, Celia R. *Racism, Misogyny, and the "Othello" Myth: Interracial Couples from Shakespeare to Spike Lee*. Cambridge, Eng., 2005.

Dean, Leonard F., ed. *A Casebook on "Othello."* New York, 1961.

Evans, Robert C. "Friendship in Shakespeare's *Othello*," *Ben Jonson Journal* 6 (1999), 109–46.

Everett, Barbara. "Inside *Othello*." *ShS* 53 (2000), 184–95.

———. "Reflections on the Sentimentalist's *Othello*," *Critical Quarterly* 3 (1961), 127–39. (A comment on the Leavis article below.)

Garner, S. N. "Shakespeare's Desdemona," *ShakS* 9 (1976), 233–52.

Hankey, Julie, ed. *Plays in Performance: "Othello."* Bristol, 1987.

Heilman, Robert B. *Magic in the Web: Action and Language in "Othello."* Lexington, Ky., 1956.

Honigmann, E. A. J. *The Texts of "Othello" and Shakespearian Revision*. London, 1996.

Hyman, Stanley Edgar. *Iago: Some Approaches to the Illusion of His Motivation*. New York, 1970.

Jones, Eldred. *Othello's Countrymen: The African in English Renaissance Drama*. London, 1965.

Kolin, Philip C. *Othello: New Critical Essays*. New York and London, 2002.

Korda, Natasha. *Shakespeare's Domestic Economies: Gender and Property in Early Modern England*. Philadelphia, 2002 (Chapter 4).

Leavis, F. R. "Diabolic Intellect and the Noble Hero: Or The Sentimentalist's Othello," *The Common Pursuit*. London, 1952.

Muir, Kenneth, ed. *Shakespeare Survey 21* (1968).

Nowottny, Winifred M. T. "Justice and Love in *Othello*," *University of Toronto Quarterly* 21 (1952), 330–44.

Orkin, Martin. "Othello and the 'plain face' of Racism," *SQ* 38 (1987), 166–88.

Orlin, Lena Cowen. *Private Matters and Public Culture in Post-Reformation England*. Ithaca, N.Y., 1994.

Pechter, Edward. *"Othello" and Interpretive Traditions*. Iowa City, 1999.

Potter, Lois. *Shakespeare in Performance: "Othello."* Manchester, 2002.

Rosenberg, Marvin. *The Masks of "Othello."* Berkeley, 1961.

Saunders, Ben. "Iago's Clyster: Purgation, Anality, and the Civilizing Process," *SQ* 55 (2004), 148–76.

Seltzer, Daniel. "Elizabethan Acting in *Othello*," *SQ* 10 (1959), 201–10.

Snyder, Susan, ed. *"Othello": Critical Essays*. New York, 1988.

Stoll, E. E. *"Othello": An Historical and Comparative Study*. Minneapolis, 1915. Rpt. New York, 1964.

Vaughan, Virginia Mason. *Performing Blackness on English Stages, 1500–1800*. Cambridge, Eng., 2005.

Wine, Martin L. *"Othello": Text and Performance*. London, 1984.

King Lear

See also, under *Life in Shakespeare's England*, De Grazia, Quilligan, and Stallybrass (essay by De Grazia); under *The Tragedies*, Bradley, Cunningham, Frye, Goldman, Holloway, Hunter, Kirsch, Knight, and Rosen; under *The Greek and Roman Tragedies*, Brower; under *Textual Criticism and Bibliography*, Blayney, and Taylor and Warren; under *Shakespeare's Language*, Doran; under *Shakespeare Criticism to the 1930s*, Hazlitt, Johnson, and Stoll; under *Shakespeare Criticism from the 1940s to the 1970s*, Bloom (essay by Jaffa), Burckhardt, Empson, Fly, Granville-Barker, Knights, Kott, and Sewell; under *Shakespeare Criticism Since 1980*, Auden, Boose, Cavell (Chapter 2, identical with the Cavell entry below), Dollimore, Dollimore and Sinfield (essay by McLuskie), Dubrow and Strier (essay by Strier), Erickson, Erickson and Kahn (essay by Berger), Garber (*Shakespeare's Ghost Writers*, Chapter 5), Greenblatt (*Shakespearean Negotiations*, Chapter 4), Loomba and Orkin (essay by Visser), Novy (*Love's Argument*), Patterson (Chapter 5), and Wayne (essay by Thompson); and under *The Romances*, Felperin and Young.

Alpers, Paul J. "*King Lear* and the Theory of the 'Sight Pattern,'" *In Defense of Reading*, ed. Reuben A. Brower and Richard Poirier. New York, 1962.

Berger, Harry, Jr. *"King Lear"*: The Lear Family Romance," *Centennial Review* 23 (1979), 348–76.

Booth, Stephen. *"King Lear,"* "Macbeth," Indefinition, and Tragedy, New Haven, 1983.

Brownlow, F. W. *Shakespeare, Harsnett, and the Devils of Denham*. Newark, Del., 1993.

Cavell, Stanley. "The Avoidance of Love: A Reading of *King Lear*," *Must We Mean What We Say?* New York, 1969. Rpt. in *Disowning Knowledge in Six Plays of Shakespeare*. Cambridge, Eng., 1987.

Colie, Rosalie L., and F. T. Flahiff, eds. *Some Facets of "King Lear."* Toronto, 1974.

Craig, Leon Harold. *Of Philosophers and Kings: Political Philosophy in Shakespeare's "Macbeth" and "King Lear."* Toronto, 2001.

Danby, John F. *Shakespeare's Doctrine of Nature: A Study of King Lear*. London, 1949.

Delany, Paul. *"King Lear"* and the Decline of Feudalism," *PMLA* 92 (1977), 429–40.

Elton, William R. *King Lear and the Gods*. San Marino, Calif., 1966. Rpt. Lexington, Ky., 1988.

Everett, Barbara. "The New *King Lear*," *Critical Quarterly* 2 (1960), 325–39.

Foakes, R. A. *"Hamlet" Versus "Lear": Cultural Politics and Shakespeare's Art*. Cambridge, Eng., 1993.

Freud, Sigmund. "The Theme of the Three Caskets," *Complete Psychological Works of Sigmund Freud* 12 (1911–1913), pp. 291–301. London, 1958.

Goldberg, S. L. *An Essay on "King Lear."* Cambridge, Eng., 1974.

Graham, Kenneth J. E. " 'Without the form of justice': Plainness and the Performance of Love in *King Lear*," *SQ* 42 (1991), 438–61.

Halio, Jay L. *King Lear: A Guide to the Play*. Greenwood, Conn., 2001.

Hardison, O. B., Jr. "Myth and History in *King Lear*," *SQ* 26 (1975), 227–42.

Heilman, Robert B. *This Great Stage: Image and Structure in "King Lear."* Baton Rouge, La., 1948. Rpt. Seattle, 1963.

Heinemann, Margot. " 'Demystifying the Mystery of State': *King Lear* and the World Upside Down," *ShS* 44 (1992), 75–83.

James, D. G. *The Dream of Learning*. Oxford, 1951.

Jorgensen, Paul A. *Lear's Self-Discovery*, Berkeley, 1967.

Kahn, Coppélia. "The Absent Mother in *King Lear*," *Rewriting the Renaissance: The Discourses of Sexual Difference in Early Modern Europe*, eds. Margaret W. Ferguson et al. Chicago, 1986.

Kahn, Paul W. *Law and Love: The Trials of King Lear*. New Haven, 2000.

Kernan, Alvin. "Formalism and Realism in Elizabethan Drama: The Miracles in *King Lear*," *Renaissance Drama* 9 (1966), 59–66.

Kirsch, Arthur. "The Emotional Landscape of *King Lear*," *SQ* 39 (1988), 154–70.

Kronenfeld, Judy. *King Lear and the Naked Truth: Rethinking the Language of Religion and Resistance*. Durham, N.C., 1998.

Leggatt, Alexander. *King Lear*. Shakespeare in Performance. Manchester, Eng., 1991.

Lothian, J. M. *"King Lear": A Tragic Reading of Life*. Toronto, 1949.

Lusardi, James P., and June Schlueter. *Reading Shakespeare in Performance: "King Lear."* Rutherford, N.J., 1991.

Mack, Maynard. *King Lear in Our Time*. Berkeley, 1965.

Maclean, Norman. "Episode, Scene, Speech, and Word: The Madness of Lear," *Critics and Criticism*, ed. R. S. Crane. Chicago, 1952.

Matchett, William H. "Some Dramatic Techniques in *King Lear*," in *Shakespeare: The*

Theatrical Dimension, eds. Philip G. McGuire and David A. Samuelson. New York, 1959.

Michie, Donald M., ed. *A Critical Edition of "The True Chronicle History of King Leir and His Three Daughters, Gonorill, Ragan and Cordella."* New York, 1991.

Murphy, John L. *Darkness and Devils: Exorcism and "King Lear."* Athens, Ohio, 1984.

Reibetanz, John. *The "Lear" World: A Study of "King Lear" in Its Dramatic Context.* Toronto, 1977.

Rosenberg, Marvin. *The Masks of "King Lear."* Berkeley, 1972.

Scott, William O. "Contracts of Love and Affection: Lear, Old Age, and Kingship," *ShS* 55 (2002), 36–42.

Sewall, Richard B. *The Vision of Tragedy.* New Haven, 1959.

Snyder, Susan. "*King Lear* and the Psychology of Dying," *SQ* 33 (1982), 449–60.

Soellner, Rolf. "*King Lear* and the Magic of the Wheel," *SQ* 35 (1984), 274–89.

Tate, Nahum. *The History of King Lear* (1681), ed. James Black. Lincoln, Neb. 1975.

Taylor, Gary, and Michael Warren, eds. *The Division of the Kingdoms: Shakespeare's Two Versions of "King Lear."* Oxford, 1983.

Urkowitz, Steven. *Shakespeare's Revision of "King Lear."* Princeton, 1980.

Warren, Michael, preparer. *The Parallel "King Lear," 1608–1623: Parallel Texts of the First Quarto (1608) and the First Folio (1623).* Berkeley, 1989.

Wittreich, Joseph. *"Image of that Horror": History, Prophecy, and Apocalypse in "King Lear."* San Marino, Calif., 1984.

Macbeth

See also, under *The Tragedies*, Berry, Bradley, Garner and Sprengnether (essay by Adelman), Goldman, Holloway, Hunter, Kirsch, Mack, Mack Jr., and Rosen; under *Shakespeare Criticism to the 1930s*, Smith (essay by De Quincey); under *Shakespeare Criticism from the 1940s to the 1970s*, Sanders and Sewell; under *Shakespeare Criticism Since 1980*, Garber (*Cannibals*, essay by Adelman), Howard and O'Connor (essay by Goldberg), Mullaney (Chapter 5), Schwartz and Kahn (essay by Gohlke), Watson, and Woodbridge and Berry (essay by Willis); and under *The Histories*, Pye.

Aitchison, Nick. *Macbeth: Man and Myth.* Stroud, Eng., 1999.

Bartholomeusz, Dennis. *"Macbeth" and the Players.* Cambridge, Eng., 1969.

Booth, Stephen. *"King Lear," "Macbeth," Indefinition, and Tragedy.* New Haven, 1983.

Brooks, Cleanth. "The Naked Babe and the Cloak of Manliness," *The Well Wrought Urn.* New York, 1947.

Calderwood, James L. *If It Were Done: "Macbeth" and Tragic Action.* Amherst, 1986.

Carroll, William C. *Macbeth: Texts and Contexts.* Boston and New York, 1999.

Craig, Leon Harold. *Of Philosophers and Kings: Political Philosophy in Shakespeare's "Macbeth" and "King Lear."* Toronto, 2001.

Driver, Tom. *The Sense of History in Greek and Shakespearean Drama.* New York, 1960.

Elliott, G. R. *Dramatic Providence in "Macbeth."* Princeton, 1958.

Fergusson, Francis. "*Macbeth* as the Imitation of an Action," *English Institute Essays 1951* (1952), 31–43.

Freud, Sigmund. "Some Character-Types Met with in Psycho-Analytic Work," trans. E. Cobern Mayne, *Collected Papers.* Vol. 4, pp. 326–32. London, 1925.

Gardner, Helen. "Milton's 'Satan' and the Theme of Damnation in Elizabethan Tragedy," *English Association Essays and Studies* n.s. 1 (1948), 46–66.

Jorgensen, Paul A. *Our Naked Frailties: Sensational Art and Meaning in "Macbeth."* Berkeley, 1971.

Kinney, Arthur F. *Lies Like Truth: Shakespeare, Macbeth, and the Cultural Moment.* Detroit, 2001.

Kliman, Bernice W. *Macbeth.* Shakespeare in Performance. Manchester, Eng., 1992.

Knights, L. C. "How Many Children Had Lady Macbeth? An Essay in the Theory and Practice of Shakespeare Criticism," *Explorations.* London, 1946. Rpt. Westport, Conn., 1975.

Norbrook, David. "*Macbeth* and the Politics of Historiography," *Politics of Discourse: The Literature and History of Seventeenth-Century England*, eds. Kevin Sharpe and Steven Zwicker, pp. 78–116. Berkeley, 1987.

Orgel, Stephen. "*Macbeth* and the Antic Round," *ShS* 52 (1999), 143–53. Rpt. in Orgel, under *Shakespeare Criticism Since 1980*.

Paul, Henry N. *The Royal Play of Macbeth.* New York, 1950.

Purkiss, Diane. *The Witch in History: Early Modern and Twentieth-Century Representations.* London and New York, 1996.

Rosenberg, Marvin. *The Masks of "Macbeth."* Berkeley, 1978.

Sinfield, Alan. "*Macbeth*: History, Ideology and Intellectuals," *Critical Quarterly* 28 (1986), 63–77.

Spender, Stephen. "Time, Violence, and *Macbeth*," *Penguin New Writing*, 3. London, 1940–1941.

Wilders, John, ed. *Shakespeare in Production: "Macbeth."* Cambridge, Eng., 2004.

Williams, Raymond. "Monologue in *Macbeth*," *Teaching the Text*, eds. Susanne Kappeler and Norman Bryson. London, 1983.

Wills, Garry. *Witches and Jesuits: Shakespeare's "Macbeth."* Oxford, 1995.

Antony and Cleopatra

See also, under *The Tragedies*, Frye, Garner and Sprengnether (essays by Cook and Charnes), Goldman, Holloway, Mack, and Rosen; under *The Greek and Roman Tragedies*, Brower, Cantor, Charney, Miola, and Traversi; under *Shakespeare's Predecessors and Contemporaries*, Comensoli and Russell (essay by Adelman), and Waith; under *Shakespeare's Language*, Doran; under *Shakespeare Criticism to the 1930s*, Coleridge (*Coleridge's Writings*); under *Shakespeare Criticism from the 1940s to the 1970s*, Bethell, Burke, Colie, Granville-Barker, Kettle (essay by Nandy), McAlindon, and Van Laan; under *Shakespeare Criticism Since 1980*, Auden, Bamber, Cavell (pp. 18–37), Charnes, Dollimore (*Radical Tragedy*), Edwards et al. (essay by Hibbard), Erickson (Chapter 4), Holland et al. (essay by Sprengnether), and Neely; under *The Problem Plays*, Schanzer; under *The Histories*, Palmer; and under *The Romances*, Brown and Harris (essay by Ornstein), Danby, and Felperin.

Adelman, Janet. *The Common Liar: An Essay on "Antony and Cleopatra."* New Haven, 1973.

Barroll, J. Leeds. *Shakespearean Tragedy: Genre, Tradition, and Change in "Antony and Cleopatra,"* Washington, D.C., 1984.

Bono, Barbara J. "The Shakespearean Synthesis: *Antony and Cleopatra," Literary Transvaluation: From Vergilian Epic to Shakespearean Tragicomedy.* Berkeley, 1984.

Bradley, A. C. *Oxford Lectures on Poetry.* London, 1909, 1961.

Drakakis, John, ed. "*Antony and Cleopatra.*" Basingstoke, 1994.

Fitz, L. T. [Linda Woodbridge], "Egyptian Queens and Male Reviewers: Sexist Attitudes in *Antony and Cleopatra* Criticism," *SQ* 28 (1977), 297–316.

Hatchuel, Sarah. *Shakespeare and the Cleopatra/Caesar Intertext: Sequel, Conflation, Remake.* Madison, N.J., and Lanham, Md., 2011.

Kaula, David. "The Time Sense of *Antony and Cleopatra," SQ* 15:3 (1964), 211–23.

Knights, L. C. *Some Shakespearean Themes.* London, 1959.

Lamb, Margaret. *"Antony and Cleopatra" on the English Stage.* Rutherford, N.J., and London, 1980.

Leavis, F. R. "*Antony and Cleopatra* and *All for Love*: A Critical Exercise," *Scrutiny* 5 (1936–1937), 158–69.

Levine, Laura. *Men in Women's Clothing: Anti-Theatricality and Effeminization, 1579–1642.* Cambridge, Eng., 1994.

Lloyd, Michael. "Cleopatra as Isis," *ShS* 12 (1959), 88–94.

Mack, Maynard. "*Antony and Cleopatra*: The Stillness and the Dance," *Shakespeare's Art: Seven Essays*, ed. Milton Crane. Chicago, 1973.

Madelaine, Richard, ed. *Antony and Cleopatra.* Shakespeare in Production. Cambridge, Eng., 1998.

Markels, Julian. *The Pillar of the World: "Antony and Cleopatra" in Shakespeare's Development.* Columbus, Ohio, 1968.

Mayer, Jean-Christophe, ed. *Lectures de Shakespeare: "Antony and Cleopatra."* Rennes, France, 2000.

Rackin, Phyllis. "Shakespeare's Boy Cleopatra, the Decorum of Nature, and the Golden World of Poetry," *PMLA* 87 (1972), 201–12.

Reimer, A. P. *A Reading of Shakespeare's "Antony and Cleopatra."* Sydney, 1968.

Scott, Michael. *Antony and Cleopatra.* Text and Peformance. London, 1983.

Steppat, Michael. *The Critical Reception of Shakespeare's "Antony and Cleopatra" from 1607 to 1905.* Amsterdam, 1980.

Williamson, Marilyn L. *Infinite Variety: "Antony and Cleopatra" in Renaissance Drama and Earlier Tradition.* Mystic, Conn., 1974.

Wood, Nigel, ed. *"Antony and Cleopatra."* Theory in Practice. Buckingham and Philadelphia, 1996.

Yachnin, Paul. "Shakespeare's Politics of Loyalty: Sovereignty and Subjectivity in *Antony and Cleopatra," Studies in English Literature* 33 (1993), 343–63.

The Romances

See also, under *Shakespeare Criticism Since 1980,* McMullan and Hope.

Beckwith, Sarah. *Shakespeare and the Grammar of Forgiveness.* Ithaca, N.Y., 2011.

Bergeron, David M. *Shakespeare's Romances and the Royal Family.* Lawrence, Kans., 1985.

Bishop, T. G. *Shakespeare and the Theatre of Wonder.* Cambridge, Eng., 1996.

Brown, John Russell, and Bernard Harris, eds. *Later Shakespeare.* Stratford-upon-Avon Studies 8. London, 1966.

Danby, John F. *Poets on Fortune's Hill.* London, 1952. Reprinted as *Elizabethan and Jacobean Poets.* London, 1964.

Edwards, Philip. "Shakespeare's Romances: 1900–1957," *ShS* 11 (1958), 1–18. See also other articles in this issue.

Fawkner, H. W. *Shakespeare's Miracle Plays: "Pericles," "Cymbeline," and "The Winter's Tale."* Rutherford, N.J., 1992.

Felperin, Howard. *Shakespearean Romance.* Princeton, 1972.

Foakes, R. A. *Shakespeare: From the Dark Comedies to the Last Plays.* London and Charlottesville, Va., 1971.

Frye, Northrop. *Anatomy of Criticism.* Princeton, 1957.

———. *A Natural Perspective: The Development of Shakespearean Comedy and Romance.* New York, 1965.

———. *The Secular Scripture: A Study of the Structure of Romance.* Cambridge, Mass., 1976.

Gesner, Carol. *Shakespeare and the Greek Romance: A Study of Origins.* Lexington, Ky., 1970.

Hartwig, Joan. *Shakespeare's Tragicomic Vision.* Baton Rouge, La., 1972.

Hunter, Robert Grams. *Shakespeare and the Comedy of Forgiveness.* New York, 1965.

James, D. G. "The Failure of the Ballad-Makers," *Scepticism and Poetry.* London, 1937.

Jordan, Constance. *Shakespeare's Monarchies: Ruler and Subject in the Romances.* Ithaca, N.Y., 1997.

Kermode, Frank. *William Shakespeare: The Final Plays.* London, 1963.

Knight, G. Wilson. *The Crown of Life.* London, 1947, 1966.

———. *The Shakespearian Tempest.* London, 1932, 1953.

Leavis, F. R. "A Criticism of Shakespeare's Last Plays," *Scrutiny* 10 (1942), 339–45. Rpt. in *The Common Pursuit.* London, 1952.

Lyne, Raphael. *Shakespeare's Late Work.* Oxford, 2007.

Marsh, D. R. C. *The Recurring Miracle: A Study of "Cymbeline" and the Last Plays.* Pietermaritzburg, Natal, 1962, 1964.

Marshall, Cynthia. *Last Things and Last Plays: Shakespearean Eschatology.* Carbondale, Ill., 1991.

McMullan, Gordon. *Shakespeare and the Idea of Late Writing: Authorship in the Proximity of Death.* Cambridge, Eng., 2007.

Mincoff, Marco. *Things Supernatural and Causeless: Shakespearean Romance.* Newark, Del., 1992.

Mowat, Barbara A. *The Dramaturgy of Shakespeare's Romances.* Athens, Ga., 1976.

Nevo, Ruth. *Shakespeare's Other Language.* New York and London, 1987.

Palfrey, Simon. *Late Shakespeare: A New World of Words.* Oxford, 1997.

Peterson, Douglas L. *Time, Tide, and Tempest: A Study of Shakespeare's Romances.* San Marino, Calif., 1973.

Pettet, E. C. *Shakespeare and the Romance Tradition.* London, 1949.

Platt, Peter G. *Reason Diminished: Shakespeare and the Marvelous.* Lincoln, Neb., 1997.

Richards, Jennifer, and James Knowles, eds. *Shakespeare's Late Plays: New Readings.* Edinburgh, 1999.

Ryan, Kiernan, ed. *Shakespeare: The Late Plays.* New York, 1999.

Smith, Hallett. *Shakespeare's Romances.* San Marino, Calif., 1972.

Smith, Stephen W. *Shakespeare's Last Plays: Essays in Literature and Politics.* Lanham, Md., and Oxford, 2002.

Strachey, Lytton. "Shakespeare's Final Period," *Books and Characters.* London, 1922.

Traversi, Derek. *Shakespeare: The Last Phase.* New York, 1954.

Yates, Frances A. *Shakespeare's Last Plays: A New Approach.* London, 1975.

Young, David. *The Heart's Forest: A Study of Shakespeare's Pastoral Plays.* New Haven and London, 1972.

The Winter's Tale

See also, under *The Romances,* Felperin, Foakes, Hartwig, Hunter, Knight (*Crown of Life*), Mowat, and Young; and under *Shakespeare Criticism Since 1980,* Cavell (Chapter 6), Erickson, Neely, and Parker and Hartman (essay by Felperin).

Alpers, Paul. *What Is Pastoral?* Chicago, 1996.

Barber, C. L. "'Thou That Beget'st Him That Did Thee Beget': Transformation in *Pericles* and *The Winter's Tale," ShS* 22 (1969), 59–67.

Bartholomeusz, Dennis. *"The Winter's Tale" in Performance in England and America, 1611–1976.* Cambridge, Eng., 1982.

Bethell, S. L. *The Winter's Tale: A Study.* London, 1947.

Bishop, T. G. *Shakespeare and the Theatre of Wonder.* Cambridge, Eng., 1996.

Coghill, Nevill. "Six Points of Stage-Craft in *The Winter's Tale," ShS* 11 (1958), 31–41.

Draper, R. P. *"The Winter's Tale": Text and Performance.* London, 1985.

Ewbank, Inga-Stina. "The Triumph of Time in *The Winter's Tale," Review of English Literature* 5:2 (1964), 83–100.

Frey, Charles. *Shakespeare's Vast Romance: A Study of "The Winter's Tale."* Columbia, Mo., 1980.

Frye, Northrop. "Recognition in *The Winter's Tale," Essays on Shakespeare and Elizabethan Drama in Honor of Hardin Craig,* ed. R. Hosley, pp. 235–46. Columbia, Mo., 1962.

Jensen, Phebe. "Singing Psalms to Hornpipes: Festivity, Iconoclasm, and Catholicism in *The Winter's Tale," SQ* 55 (2004), 279–306.

Kaplan, Lindsay M., and Katherine Eggert. "'Good queen, my lord, good queen': Sexual Slanders and the Trials of Female Authority in *The Winter's Tale," Renaissance Drama* n.s. 25 (1994), 89–118.

Knapp, James A. "Visual and Ethical Truth in *The Winter's Tale," SQ* 55 (2004), 253–78.

Lindenbaum, Peter. "Time, Sexual Love, and the Uses of Pastoral in *The Winter's Tale," Modern Language Quarterly* 33 (1972), 3–22.

Matchett, William H. "Some Dramatic Techniques in *The Winter's Tale," ShS* 22 (1969), 93–107.

Siemon, James Edward. " 'But It Appears She Lives': Iteration in *The Winter's Tale," PMLA* 89 (1974), 10–16.

Snyder, Susan. "Mamillius and Gender Polarization in *The Winter's Tale," SQ* 50 (1999), 1–8.

Sokol, B. J. *Art and Illusion in "The Winter's Tale."* Manchester, Eng., 1994.

Syme, Holger Schott. *Theatre and Testimony in Shakespeare's England: A Culture of Mediation.* Cambridge, Eng., 2012.

Tayler, Edward W. *Nature and Art in Renaissance Literature.* New York, 1964.

Wickham, Glynne. "Romance and Emblem: A Study in the Dramatic Structure of *The Winter's Tale," The Elizabethan Theatre III,* ed. David Galloway. Hamden, Conn., 1973.

Williams, John Anthony. *The Natural Work of Art: The Experience of Romance in Shakespeare's "Winter's Tale."* Cambridge, Mass., 1967.

The Tempest

See also, under *The Romances*, Brown and Harris (essay by Brockbank), Felperin, Frye (*Natural Perspective*), Hartwig, Kermode, Mowat, Peterson, and Young; under *Shakespeare's Predecessors and Contemporaries*, Bevington and Holbrook (essay by Bevington); under *Shakespeare Criticism to the 1930s*, Coleridge (*Coleridge's Writings*); under *Shakespeare Criticism from the 1940s to the 1970s*, Fiedler, Kernan (*Playwright as Magician*, Chapter 6), and Kott; under *Shakespeare Criticism Since 1980*, Dollimore and Sinfield (essay by Brown), Drakakis (essay by Barker and Hulme), Garber (*Cannibals*, essay by Orgel), Greenblatt (*Shakespearean Negotiations*, Chapter 5), Hamlin, Howard and O'Connor (essay by Cartelli), Lenz et al. (essay by Leininger), Loomba and Orkin (essay by Brotton), McMullan and Hope (essay by Norbrook), and Schwartz and Kahn (essay by Sundelson); and under *The Comedies*, Palmer and Bradbury (essay by Wells).

Auden, W. H. "The Sea and the Mirror: A Commentary on Shakespeare's *The Tempest*," *The Collected Poetry*. New York, 1945.

Berger, Harry, Jr. "Miraculous Harp: A Reading of Shakespeare's *Tempest*," *ShakS* 5 (1969), 253–83.

Demaray, John G. *Shakespeare and the Spectacles of Strangeness: "The Tempest" and the Transformation of Renaissance Theatrical Forms*. Pittsburgh, Pa., 1998.

Frey, Charles. "*The Tempest* and the New World," *SQ* 30 (1979), 29–41.

Hamilton, Donna. *Virgil and "The Tempest": The Politics of Imitation*. Columbus, Ohio, 1990.

Hulme, Peter, and William H. Sherman, eds. *"The Tempest" and Its Travels*. Philadelphia, 2000.

James, D. G. *The Dream of Prospero*. Oxford, 1967.

James, Henry. "Introduction to *The Tempest*." Rpt. in *Henry James: Selected Literary Criticism*, ed. Morris Shapiro. London, 1963.

Mebane, John S. *Renaissance Magic and the Return of the Golden Age: The Occult Tradition and Marlowe, Jonson, and Shakespeare*. Lincoln, Neb., 1989.

Mowat, Barbara A. "Prospero's Book," *SQ* 52 (2001), 1–33.

Orgel, Stephen. "New Uses of Adversity: Tragic Experience in *The Tempest*," *In Defense of Reading*, eds. Reuben A. Brower and Richard Poirier. New York, 1962.

———. "Prospero's Wife," *Representations* 8 (1984), 1–13. Rpt. in Orgel, under *Shakespeare Criticism Since 1980*.

Skura, Meredith Anne. "Discourse and the Individual: The Case of Colonialism in *The Tempest*," *SQ* 40 (1989), 42–69.

Strier, Richard. "'I am Power': Normal and Magical Politics in *The Tempest*," in *Writing and Political Engagement in Seventeenth-Century England*, eds. Derek Hirst and Richard Strier. Cambridge, Eng., 1999.

Thompson, Ann. "'Miranda, where's your sister?': Reading Shakespeare's *The Tempest*," *Feminist Criticism: Theory and Practice*, ed. Susan Sellers. New York, 1991.

Vaughan, Alden T. "Shakespeare's Indian: The Americanization of Caliban," *SQ* 39 (1988), 137–53.

Vaughan, Alden T., and Virginia Mason Vaughan. *Shakespeare's Caliban: A Cultural History*. Cambridge, Eng., 1991.

Vaughan, Virginia Mason, and Alden T. Vaughan, eds. *Critical Essays on Shakespeare's "The Tempest."* New York and London, 1998.

William, David. "*The Tempest* on the Stage," *Jacobean Theatre*, eds. John Russell Brown and Bernard Harris, pp. 133–57. Stratford-upon-Avon Studies 1. London, 1960.

Potter, Lois. "Topicality or Politics? *The Two Noble Kinsmen*, 1613–34," *The Politics of Tragicomedy: Shakespeare and After*, eds. Gordon McMullan and Jonathan Hope. London, 1992.

Shannon, Laurie J. "Emilia's Argument: Friendship and 'Human Title' in *The Two Noble Kinsmen*," *ELH* 64 (1997), 657–82.

Waith, Eugene. "Shakespeare and Fletcher on Love and Friendship," *ShakS* 18 (1986), 235–49.

The Poems

Cheney, Patrick, ed. *The Cambridge Companion to Shakespeare's Poetry*. Cambridge, Eng., 2007.

Dubrow, Heather. *Captive Victors: Shakespeare's Narrative Poems and Sonnets*. Ithaca, N.Y., 1987.

Hulse, Clarke. *Metamorphic Verse: The Elizabethan Minor Epic*. Princeton, 1981.

Schoenfeldt, Michael Carl. *The Cambridge Introduction to Shakespeare's Poetry*. Cambridge, Eng., 2010.

Shakespeare Survey 15 (1962). Devoted chiefly to the poems and music, including the sonnets.

Vickers, Brian. *Counterfeiting Shakespeare: Evidence, Authorship, and John Ford's "Funerall Elegye."* Cambridge, Eng., 2002.

Sonnets

See also, under *The Poems*, Dubrow; under *Shakespeare's Predecessors and Contemporaries*, Rasmussen (essay by Alpers); under *Shakespeare Criticism from the 1940s to the 1970s*, Colie, and Kernan (*Playwright as Magician*, Chapter 2); under *Shakespeare Criticism Since 1980*, Loomba and Orkin (essay by Hall), McDonald (essay by Vendler), Parker and Hartman (essay by Greene), and Wheeler (pp. 179–90); and, under *Twelfth Night*, Schalkwyk.

Allen, Michael J. B. "Shakespeare's Man Descending a Staircase: Sonnets 126 to 154," *ShS* 31 (1978), 127–38.

Booth, Stephen. *An Essay on Shakespeare's Sonnets*. New Haven, 1969.

———, ed. *Shakespeare's Sonnets, Edited with Analytic Commentary*. New Haven, 1977.

Bradley, A. C. *Oxford Lectures on Poetry*. London, 1909, 1961.

Brown, Richard Danson, and David Johnson, eds. *Cymbeline and The Sonnets*. New York, 2000.

Callaghan, Dympna. *Shakespeare's Sonnets*. Malden, Mass., 2007.

Cheney, Patrick. "'O, let my books be . . . dumb presagers': Poetry and Theater in Shakespeare's Sonnets," *SQ* 52 (2001), 222–54.

Clark, S. H. *Sordid Images: The Poetry of Masculine Desire*. London and New York, 1994.

Cousins, A. D. *Shakespeare's Sonnets and Narrative Poems*. Harlow, Eng., 2000.

De Grazia, Margreta. "The Scandal of Shakespeare's Sonnets," *ShS* 46 (1994), 35–49.

Dubrow, Heather. *Echoes of Desire: English Petrarchism and Its Counterdiscourses*. Ithaca, N.Y., 1995.

Edmundson, Paul, and Stanley Wells. *Shakespeare's Sonnets*. Oxford, 2004.

Fineman, Joel. *Shakespeare's Perjured Eye: The Invention of Poetic Subjectivity in the Sonnets*. Berkeley, 1986.

Giroux, Robert. *The Book Known as Q: A Consideration of Shakespeare's Sonnets*. New York, 1982.

Halpern, Richard. *Shakespeare's Perfume: Sodomy and Sublimity in the Sonnets, Wilde, Freud, and Lacan*. Philadelphia, 2002.

Healy, Margaret. *Shakespeare's Alchemy and the Creative Imagination: The Sonnets and "A Lover's Complaint."* Cambridge, Eng., 2011.

Hopkins, Lisa. *Shakespeare's "The Tempest": The Relationship between Text and Film*. London, 2008.

Hubler, Edward, Northrop Frye, Leslie A. Fiedler, Stephen Spender, and R. P. Blackmur. *The Riddle of Shakespeare's Sonnets*. New York, 1962.

Ingram, W. G., and Theodore Redpath, eds. *Shakespeare's Sonnets*. London, 1964.

Innes, Paul. *Shakespeare and the English Renaissance Sonnet: Verses of Feigning Love*. Basingstoke and New York, 1997.

Knight, G. Wilson. *The Mutual Flame: On Shakespeare's Sonnets and "The Phoenix and the Turtle."* London, 1955.

Krieger, Murray. *A Window to Criticism: Shakespeare's Sonnets and Modern Poetics*. Princeton, 1964.

Landry, Hilton. *Interpretations in Shakespeare's Sonnets*. Berkeley, 1963.

———, ed. *New Essays on Shakespeare's Sonnets*. New York, 1976.

Leishman, J. B. *Themes and Variations in Shakespeare's Sonnets*. London, 1961.

Lever, J. W. *The Elizabethan Love Sonnet*. London, 1956.

Melchiori, Giorgio. *Shakespeare's Dramatic Meditations: An Experiment in Criticism*. Oxford, 1976.

Muir, Kenneth. *Shakespeare's Sonnets*. London, 1979.

Paterson, Don. *Reading Shakespeare's Sonnets: A New Commentary*. London, 2010.

Pequigney, Joseph. *Such is My Love: A Study of Shakespeare's Sonnets*. Chicago, 1985.

Ramsay, Paul. *The Fickle Glass: A Study of Shakespeare's Sonnets*. New York, 1979.

Ransom, John Crowe. *The World's Body*. New York and London, 1938, 1968.

Schalkwyk, David. *Speech and Performance in Shakespeare's Sonnets and Plays*. Cambridge, Eng., 2002.

Schiffer, James, ed. *Shakespeare's Sonnets: Critical Essays*. New York, 1999.

Vendler, Helen. *The Art of Shakespeare's Sonnets*. Cambridge, Mass., 1997.

Warley, Christopher. *Sonnet Sequences and Social Distinction in Renaissance England*. Cambridge, Eng., 2005.

Textual Notes

These textual notes do not offer an historical collation, either of the early quartos and folios or of more recent editions; they are simply a record of departures in this edition from the copy text. For most plays the notes give the adopted reading of this edition in bold face, followed by the rejected reading in the relevant copy text. Where two substantive early texts are involved, or where a reading from some other earlier edition has been adopted, the notes provide information on the source of the reading in square brackets. In a few texts, adopted readings of editions more recent than the First Folio are indicated by [eds.]. Alterations in lineation are not indicated, nor are some minor and obvious typographical errors; changes in punctuation are indicated when the resulting change in meaning is substantive.

Abbreviations used:

F The First Folio
Q quarto
O octavo
s.d. stage direction
s.p. speech prefix

The Taming of the Shrew

Copy Text: The First Folio. The act and scene divisions are missing in the Folio except for Act 1 (before the first Induction), Act 3, Act 4 (at 4.3), and Act 5 (at 5.2).

Ind.1. 0.1 *Christopher Sly* [printed at the end of the s.d. in F as "Christophero Sly"] **1 [and elsewhere]** SLY *Begger* **10–11 thirdborough** Headborough **16 Breathe** Brach **21 [and elsewhere]** FIRST HUNTSMAN *Hunts.* **81 FIRST PLAYER** *2. Player* **87 SECOND PLAYER** *Sincklo* **99 FIRST PLAYER** *Plai.* **134 peasant.** peasant,
Ind. 2. 2 Lordship Lord **18 Sly's** Sies **26 [and elsewhere]** THIRD SERVINGMAN *3. Man* **27 [and elsewhere]** SECOND SERVINGMAN *2 Man* **47 [and elsewhere]** FIRST SERVINGMAN *1 Man* **53 wi'th'** with **93 Greet** Greece **98 lose** loose **99 [and elsewhere]** PAGE *Lady* **125 SERVINGMAN** *Mes.* **133 it. Is** it is
1.1. 3 fore for **13 Vincentio** *Vincentio's* **14 brought** brough **24 satiety** sacietie **25** *Mi perdonate* Me *Pardonato* **33 Ovid be** *Ouid;* be **146 s.d.** *Manent* Manet **163** *captum* captam **208 colored** Conlord **227 time.** time **244 your** you **248.2** *speak* speakes
1.2. 17.1 *wrings* rings **18 masters** mistris **24** *Con . . . trovato* Contutti *le core bene trobatto* **25** *ben* bene **26** *Molto* multo *onorato* honorata

33 pip peepe **45 this's** this **51 grows. But** growes but **few**, few. **72 me, were she** me. Were she is **119 me and other more,** me. Other more **170 help me** helpe one **188 Antonio's** *Butonios* **189 his** my **211 ours** yours **264 feat** seeke **279** *ben* Been
2.1. 8 thee tell tel **75–6 wooing.—Neighbors,** wooing neighbors: **79 unto you** vnto **104 Pisa. By report** *Pisa* by report, **153 struck** stroke **157 rascal fiddler** Rascall, Fidler **168 s.d.** *Exeunt* Exit **186 bonny** bony **244 askance** a sconce **322 s.d.** *Exeunt* Exit **328 in me** 352 *Valance* Vallens **355 pail** pale **373 Marseilles** Marcellus
3.1. 28 *Sigeia* sigeria [also at lines 33 and 42] **43** *steterat* staterat **47 [Aside]** *Luc.* **50 BIANCA** [not in F] **51 LUCENTIO** *Bian.* **53 BIANCA** *Hort.* **74** *B mi* Beeme **76 clef** Cliffe **80 change** charge **odd** old **81 SERVANT** *Nicke*
3.2. 13 behavior. behaviour, **14 man,** man; **29 of thy** of **30 old news** newes **33 hear** heard **54 swayed** Waid **56 cheeked** chekt **60 velour** velure **128 to love** Loue **130 As I** As **150 e'er** ere **182 s.d.** *Music plays* [after line 183 in F] **199 GREMIO** *Gra.*
4.1. 23 CURTIS *Gru.* **59 Imprimis** Inprimis **81 sleekly** slickely **106 GRUMIO** *Gre.* **168.1** *Curtis* Curtis *a Seruant* [after line 169 in F]
4.2. 4 HORTENSIO *Luc.* **6 LUCENTIO** *Hor.* [and at line 8] **7 you? First resolve** you first, resolue **8 read that I profess,** *The* reade, that I professe the **13 none** me **31 her** them **72 Take . . . alone** [assigned to "*Par.*" in F] **in** me
4.[3] [F has "*Actus Quartus. Scena Prima*" here] **48 to** too **62.1** *Enter Haberdasher* [after 61 in F] **63 HABERDASHER** *Fel.* **81 is a** is **88 like a** like **146 where,** where **148 mete-yard** meat-yard **177 account'st** accountedst
4.4. 0.2 [*booted*] [appears at line 18.2 in F] **1 Sir** Sirs **18.2 bareheaded** *booted and bare headed* **68.1** *Exit* [after line 67 in F; F also adds a s.d., "*Enter Peter,*" after line 68] **78 he's** has **91 except** expect **93** *solum* solem
4.5. 14 An And **18 is** in **35 make a** make the **37 Whither** Whether **where** whether **77 she be** she
5.1. 4 [F has "*Exit*" here] **6 master's** mistris **42 brought** brough **50 master's** Mistris **62 copintank** copataine **104.1** *Exeunt* Exit **139 No** Mo **143 than never** then vever
5.[2] [F has "*Actus Quintus*" here] **2 done** come **37 thee, lad** the lad **39 butt** But **40 butt! An** but an **45 bitter** better **two** too **52 TRANIO** *Tri.* **57 Oho** Oh, oh **62 two** too **65 for sir** **93.1** *Enter Biondello* [after "Do what you can" in 93 in F] **132 a** fiue **136 you're** your **152 maintenance commits** maintenance. Commits

A Midsummer Night's Dream

Copy text: the first quarto of 1600. The act and scene divisions are absent from the quarto; the Folio provides act divisions only.

1.1. 4 wanes waues   **10 New** Now   **19.1 Lysander** Lysander *and* Helena   **24 Stand forth, Demetrius** [printed as s.d. in Q]   **26 Stand forth, Lysander** [printed as s.d. in Q]   **74 their** there   **114 [and elsewhere] lose** loose   **132 Ay** Eigh   **133 hear** here   **136 low** loue   **187 Yours would** Your words   **191 I'd** ile   **216 sweet** sweld   **219 stranger companies** strange companions   **224 s.d. Exit Hermia** [after line 223 in Q]

2.1. 1 [and elsewhere] PUCK *Robin*   **61 [and elsewhere] TITANIA** *Qu.*   **61 Fairies** Fairy   **79 Aegles** Eagles   **109 thin** chinne   **158 the west** west   **183 off** of   **190 slay** stay   **slayeth** stayeth   **194 thee** the   **201 not nor** not, not   **206 lose** loose   **246.1** [after line 247 in Q]

2.2. 4 leathern lethren   **9 FIRST FAIRY** [not in Q]   **13 CHORUS** [not in Q; also at line 24]   **44 comfort** comfor   **45 Be** Bet   **49 good** god   **53 is it** 63 human humane   **155 ate** eate

3.1. 52 BOTTOM *Cet.*   **72 PUCK** *Ro.*   **77 BOTTOM** *Pyra.* [also at lines 79 and 98]   **78 Odors, odors** Odours, odorous   **83 PUCK** *Quin.*   **84 FLUTE** *Thys.* [also at lines 88 and 97]   **120 ousel** Woosell   **144 own** owe   **156 [and elsewhere] Mote** *Moth*   **157–8 Ready ... go** [assigned to FAIRIES in Q]   **170 PEASEBLOSSOM** *1. Fai.*   **171 COBWEB** [not in Q]   **172 MOTE** *2. Fair.*   **173 MUSTARDSEED** *3. Fai.*   **190 you of** you   **196.1 Exeunt** Exit

3.2. 0.1 [Q: *Enter King of Fairies, and* Robin goodfellow]   **3.1** [See previous note.]   **6–7 love. / Near ... bower,** loue, / Neere ... bower.   **15–16 brake. / When ... take,** brake, / When ... take: **19 mimic** Minnick   **38 [and elsewhere] PUCK** *Rob.*   **80 I so** I   **85 sleep** slippe   **213 like** life   **215 rend** rent   **220 passionate words** words   **250 prayers** praise   **260 off** of   **299 gentlemen** gentleman   **313 too to** 326 but hut   **344 s.d. Exit** Exeunt   **406 Speak! In some bush?** Speake in some bush.   **426 shalt** shat   **451 To your** your

4.1. 5 [and elsewhere] BOTTOM *Clown*   **20 courtesy** curtsie   **24 marvelous** maruailes   **54 flowerets'** flouriets   **64 off** of   **71 or** o'er or   **81 five** fine   **82 ho** howe   **116 Seemed** Seeme   **127 this is** this   **132 rite** right   **137.2 Wind ...** *up they all start vp.* Winde hornes   **171 saw** see   **177 hear** here   **190 found** fonnd   **198 let us** lets   **205 to expound** expound   **208 a patched** patcht a   **213 ballad** Ballet

4.2. 0.1 [*Snout, and Starveling*] Thisby *and the rabble*   **3 STARVELING** *Flut.*   **5 FLUTE** *Thys.* [and at lines 9, 13, 19]   **29 no** not   **34 ribbons** ribands

5.1. 34 our Or   **107 [and elsewhere] THESEUS** *Duk.*   **122 his** this   **150.1 Exeunt** Exit [after line 153 in Q]   **155 Snout** Flute   **190 up in thee** now againe   **193 love! Thou art my** loue thou art, my   **205 mural down** Moon vsed   **209 [and elsewhere] HIPPOLYTA** *Dutch.*   **216 beasts in, a** beasts, in a   **265.1 Enter Pyramus** [after 267 in Q]   **270 gleams** beames   **309 before** before?   **315 mote** moth   **317 warrant** warnd   **325 tomb** tumbe   **347 BOTTOM** *Lyon*   **363 gait** gate (also at 411)   **366 lion** Lyons   **367 behowls** beholds   **414–15 And ... rest** [these lines are transposed in Q]

The Merchant of Venice

Copy text: the first quarto of 1600 [Q]. The act and scene divisions are absent from the quarto; the Folio provides act divisions only.

1.1. 0.1 Salerio Salaryno [and also elsewhere *Salarino*, and abbreviated *Salar.*, *Sala.*, and *Sal.*]   **Solanio** Salanio [and abbreviated elsewhere *Sola.* and *Sol.*]   **19 Peering** Piring   **27 docked** docks   **84 alabaster** Alablaster   **85 jaundice** *Iaundies*   **112 tongue** togue   **113 Is** It is   **128 off** of   **151 back** bake

1.2. 44 Palatine Palentine [and at line 57]   **53 Bone** *Boune*   **58 throstle** Trassell   **119.1 Enter a Servingman** [after line 120 in Q]

1.3. 28 [and elsewhere] SHYLOCK *Iew*   **76 compromised** compremyzd   **82 peeled** pyld   **110 spit** spet [also at lines 124 and 129]   **125 day, another time** day another time,

2.1. 0.2 Morocco Morochus   **25 Sophy ... prince,** Sophy, and a Persian Prince   **31 thee** the   **35 page** rage

2.2. 1 [and elsewhere] LAUNCELOT *Clowne*   **3 [and elsewhere in this scene] Gobbo** *Iobbe*   **42 By** Be   **76 murder** muder   **91 fill horse** philhorse   **94 last** lost   **165.1 Exit Leonardo** [after line 164 in Q]   **168 a suit** sute   **180 [and elsewhere] lose** loose

2.3. 11 did doe

2.4. 8 o'clock of clocke   **9 s.d.** [after line 9 in Q]   **14 Love news,** Loue, newes   **20.1 Exit clown** [after line 23 in Q]   **39 s.d. Exeunt** Exit

2.5. 44 Jewess' Iewes

2.6. 26 Ho! Who's Howe whose   **35 night, you** night you   **59 gentlemen** gentleman   **61 Who's** Whose

2.7. 18 threatens. Men threatens men   **45 Spits** Spets   **69 tombs** *timber*

2.8. 8 gondola Gondylo   **39 Slubber** slumber

2.9. 6 rites rights   **48 chaff** chaft   **49 varnished** varnist   **64 judgment** *iudement*   **73** [Q provides a s.p.: *Arrag.*]

3.1. 19 [and elsewhere] lest least   **21.1 Enter Shylock** [after line 22 in Q]   **46 courtesy** cursie   **70 MAN** [not in Q]   **74.1** [Q repeats the s.d. "*Enter Tuball*"]   **100 Heard** heere   **114 turquoise** Turkies

3.2. 23 eke ech   **61 live. With** liue with   **67 eyes** *eye*   **81 vice** voyce   **84 stairs** stayers   **99 Veiling** vailing   **101 Therefore** Therefore then   **110 shuddering** shyddring   **117 whether** whither   **199 loved; for intermission,** lou'd for intermission,   **204 roof** rough   **217.1–2** [after line 219 in Q]   **315 BASSANIO** [not in Q]   **336 e'er** ere

3.3. 0.1 Solanio Salerio   **24 SOLANIO** *Sal.*

3.4. 13 equal egall   **23 Hear other things:** heere other things   **49 Padua** Mantua   **50 cousin's** cosin   **53 traject** Tranect   **80 near** nere   **81 my** my my

3.5. 20 enough enow   **e'en** in   **26 comes** come   **74 merit it,** meane it, it   **81 a wife** wife   **85 howsome'er** how so mere   **87 s.d. Exeunt** Exit

4.1. 30 his state this states   **31 flint** flints   **35 [and elsewhere in this scene] SHYLOCK** *Iewe*   **50 urine; for affection,** vrine for affection.   **51 Mistress** Maisters   **73 You may as well** well   **74 Why he hath made the** the   **bleat** bleake   **75 pines** of Pines   **81 more** moe   **100 is** as   **123 sole ... soul** soule ... soule   **136 whilst** whilest   **228 No, not** Not not   **233 tenor** tenure   **270 off** of   **322 off** of   **396 GRATIANO** *Shy.*   **405.1 Exeunt** Exit

5.1. 26 STEPHANO *Messen.* [also *Mess.* at lines 28 and 33]   **41 Lorenzo** Lorenzo, &   **49 Sweet soul** [assigned in Q to Lancelot]   **51 Stephano** Stephen   **62 choiring** quiring   **87 Erebus** Terebus   **106 wren** Renne   **109 ho!** how   **152 give it** giue   **233 my** mine

Much Ado About Nothing

Copy text: the quarto of 1600. The act and scene divisions are missing from the quarto; the Folio provides act divisions only.

1.1. 0.1 Messina Messina, Innogen, his wife   **2 Pedro** Peter [also in line 9]   **40 bird-bolt** Burbolt   **84 Benedick** Benedict   **141 all, Leonato.** Signor all: Leonato, signior   **194.1 Pedro** Pedro, Iohn the bastard   **239 [and elsewhere] lose** loose

1.2. 3 [and elsewhere] ANTONIO *Old*   **6 event** euents   **24 skill** shill

1.3. 46 brother's bothers   **70 s.d. Exeunt** exit

2.1. 0.1 Hero his wife, Hero   **0.3 Ursula** [Q adds"*and a kinsman*"]   **2 [and elsewhere] ANTONIO** brother   **37 bearward** Berrord   **44 Peter, for the heavens;** Peter: for the heauens,   **50, 53 curtsy** cursie   **67 hear** here   **79.3. and Don** or dumb   **80 a bout** about   **94 BALTHASAR** *Bene.* [also at lines 97 and 99]   **187 drover** Drouier   **201.2 Leonato** Leonato, Iohn and Borachio, and Conrade   **311 [and elsewhere] DON PEDRO** Prince   **369 s.d. Exeunt** exit

2.3. 7 s.d. [at line 5 in Q]   **25 an** and   **35.1 Claudio** Claudio, Musicke   **61 BALTHASAR** [not in Q]   **73–6 but ...** nonny &c.   **84 lief** liue   **91 s.d.** [after line 90 in Q]   **139 us of** of vs   **171 doffed** daft

3.1. 0.2. Ursula Ursley   **23 s.d.** [after line 25 in Q]   **63 antic** antique   **111 on; I** on I

3.2. 27 can cannot   **51 DON PEDRO** *Bene.*   **74 [and elsewhere] DON JOHN** Bastard   **75 e'en** den   **91–2 manifest. For my brother, I ... heart hath** manifest, for my brother (I ... heart) hath   **108 her then, tomorrow** her, then to morrow   **118 her, tomorrow** her to morrow

3.3. 17 SEACOAL *Watch* 2 [also at line 27]   **87** SEACOAL *Watch* [also at lines 95, 105, 125]   **134 reechy** rechie   **161** SEACOAL *Watch* 1 [also at line 165]   **162** FIRST WATCH *Watch* 2 [also at line 168]   **171** SEACOAL [missing in Q]

3.4. 17 in it

3.5. 2 [and elsewhere] DOGBERRY *Const. Dog.*   **7** [and elsewhere] VERGES *Headb.*   **9 off** of   **32 talking. As** talking as   **50** [Q provides an "*exit*" at this point]

4.1. 4 FRIAR *Fran.*   **28** DON PEDRO *Princn*   **167 tenor** tenure   **202 princes** princesse

4.2. 0.1–3 [Q reads "*Enter the Constables, Borachio, and the Towne clearke in gownes.*"]   **1** DOGBERRY *Keeper*   **2** [and elsewhere in this scene] VERGES *Cowley*   **4** DOGBERRY *Andrew*   **9** [and elsewhere in this scene] DOGBERRY *Kemp*   **18** CONRADE, BORACHIO *Both*   **39** SEACOAL *Watch* 1 [also at line 53]   **47** FIRST WATCH *Watch* 2   **51** VERGES *Const.*   **67** [and elsewhere] DOGBERRY *Constable*   **69** CONRADE [missing in Q]   **Off** of   **73** CONRADE *Couley*   **86.1** *Exeunt exit*

5.1. 16 Bid And   **97 anticly** antiquely, and   **98 off** of   **116 like** likt   **167 there's** theirs   **179 on** one   **189 Lackbeard there, he** Lacke-beard, there hee   **201.1.2** [after line 197 in Q]   **252** VERGES *Con.* 2

5.2. 41.1 [after line 42 in Q]   **81 myself. So** my self so   **97 s.d.** *Exeunt exit*

5.3. 2 A LORD *Lord*   **3** CLAUDIO [missing in Q]   **10 dumb** dead   **11** [Q provides a s.p. "*Claudio*" here]   **12** BALTHASAR [missing in Q]   **23** CLAUDIO *Lo.*   **24 rite** right   **32 speed's** speeds

5.4. 54 ANTONIO *Leo.*   **97** BENEDICK *Leon.*

As You Like It

Copy text: the First Folio. Act and scene divisions follow the Folio text throughout.

1.1. 105 she hee   **154** OLIVER [not in F]   **154 s.d.** *Exit* [at line 153 in F]

1.2. 3 I were were   **51 goddesses and** goddesses   **53** [and elsewhere] **whither** whether   **55** [and elsewhere] TOUCHSTONE *Clow.*   **56 father** farher   **80** CELIA *Ros.*   **88 Le** the   **233 love** loue;   **251.1** [at line 249 in F]   **280** [and occasionally elsewhere] **Rosalind** *Rosaline*

1.3. 55 likelihood likelihoods   **76 her** per   **87.1** *with Lords &c*   **124 be** by   **129 travel** trauaile   **131** [and elsewhere] **woo** woe   **135 we in** in we

2.1. 31 antique anticke   **49 much** must   **50 friends** friend   **59 of the** of

2.3. 10 some seeme   **16** ORLANDO [not in F]   **29** ORLANDO *Ad.*   **71 seventeen** seauentie

2.4. 1 weary merry   **42 thy wound** they would   **65 you,** your

2.5. 1 AMIENS [not in F; also at line 35]   **38.1** *All together here* [before line 35 in F]   **41–2 No . . . weather** *&c*   **46** JAQUES *Amy.*

2.7. 0.1 *Lords Lord*   **38 brain** braiue   **55 Not to seem** Seeme   **87 comes** come   **161 treble, pipes** trebble pipes,   **174** AMIENS [not in F]   **182 Then** *The*   **190–3 heigh-ho . . . jolly** *&c.*   **201 master** masters

3.2. 26 good pood   **115 graft** graffe [twice]   **123 a desert** *Desert*   **143 her** his   **190 whooping** hooping   **234 such fruit** fruite   **241 thy** the   **254** [and elsewhere] **b'wi'you** buy you   **340 lectures** Lectors   **354 deifying** defying   **362 are** art

3.3. 52–3 so. Poor men alone? No so poore men alone: No   **88** TOUCHSTONE *Ol.*   **99 s.d.** *Exit Exeunt*

3.4. 29 a lover Louer   **41 puny** puisny

3.5. 11 pretty, sure pretty sure   **65 hear** here   **105 erewhile** yere-while   **128 I have** Haue

4.1. 1 me be me   **18 my** by   **27 travel** trauaile   **36 gondola** Gundello   **44 thousandth** thousand   **72 warrant** warne   **148 hyena** Hyen   **202 it** in

4.2. 2 FIRST LORD *Lord*   **7** SECOND LORD *Lord*   **10** SECOND LORD [not in F]

4.3. 5.1 [after line 3 in F]   **8 bid** did bid   **12 tenor** tenure   **79–80 bottom; bottom** 104–5 **itself:** it selfe   **143 In** I   **156 his** this

5.1. 14 gi' ye   **37 sir** sit   **56 policy** police

5.2. 7 nor her nor   **31 overcame** ouercome

5.3. 15 BOTH PAGES [not in F]   **18 In** *In the*   **ring** rang   **24–6 In . . . spring** *In spring time, &c* [also at lines 30–2 and 36–8]   **33–8** [this stanza comes after line 20 in F]

5.4. 25.1. *Exeunt Exit*   **34.1** [after line 33 in F]   **80 so to** the so ro   **113 her** *his*   **150** JAQUES DE BOYS 2 *Bro.* [also at line 182]   **163 them** him   **170 were** vvete   **196 rites** rights   **197 trust they'll end, in** trust, they'l end in   **197.1** *Exeunt Exit*

Twelfth Night

Copy text: the First Folio. Act and scene divisions follow the Folio text throughout.

1.1. 1 [and throughout] ORSINO *Duke*   **10 capacity** capacitie,   **11 sea, naught** sea. Nought   **22 s.d.** [after 22 in F]

1.2. 15 Arion Orion

1.3. 51 SIR ANDREW *Ma.*   **54 Mary Accost** *Mary,* accost   **96 curl by** coole my   **98 me** we   **132 dun** dam'd   **set** sit   **136 That's** That

1.5. 5 [and throughout] FESTE *Clo.*   **85 gagged** gag'd [also at 5.1. 376]   **144 He's** Ha's   **163.1** *Viola Uiolenta*   **296 County's** Countes   **306 s.d.** [F adds "*Finis, Actus primus*"]

2.2. 20 That sure That   **31 our** O   **32 made of, such** made, if such

2.3. 2 diluculo Deliculo   **25 leman** Lemon   **39** FESTE (sings) *Clowne sings.*   **119 stoop** stope   **133 a nayword** an ayword

2.4. 51 FESTE [not in F]   **53 Fly . . . fly** Fye . . . fie   **55 yew** Ew   **88 I** It

2.5. 14 metal Mettle   **112 staniel** stallion   **118 portend?** portend,   **142 born** become   **achieve** atcheeues   **156–7 Unhappy." Daylight** vnhappy daylight   **173 dear** deero   **203 s.d.** [F adds "*Finis Actus secundus*"]

3.1. 8 king Kings   **68 wise men** wisemens   **91 all ready** already   **124 grece** grize

3.2. 7 thee the the   **64 nine** mine

3.4. 15.1–2 s.d. [at line 14 in F, after "hither"]   **25** OLIVIA *Mal.*   **65.1** *Exeunt exit*   **72 tang** langer   **106 lose** loose   **175 You** Yon   **222 thee** the   **228 sir. I am sure no** sir I am sure, no   **249 competent** computent   **397.1** *Exeunt Exit*

4.1. 34 struck stroke

4.2. 6 in in in   **38 clerestories** cleere stores   **71 sport to** sport   **101 b'wi'** buy

4.3. 1 SEBASTIAN [not in F]   **35 s.d.** [F adds "*Finis Actus Quartus*"]

5.1. 5 freight fraught   **141 Whither** Whether   **173 He's** H'as   **190.1** [after line 187 in F]   **195 He's** has   **200 pavane** panyn   **205 help? An** helpe an   **207 to** too   **285 He's** has   **389 tiny** tine   **406 With hey** *hey*

Measure for Measure

Copy text: the First Folio. Act and scene divisions are from the Folio except as indicated below.

The Names of All the Actors [at the end of the play in F]

1.1. 76 s.d. [at line 75 in F]

1.2. 58 [and elsewhere] MISTRESS OVERDONE *Bawd*   **83.1** [after line 84 in F]   **85** [and elsewhere] POMPEY *Clo.*   **115** [F begins "*Scena Tertia*" here]   **134 morality** mortality

1.3. [F labels as "*Scena Quarta*"]   **20 steeds** weedes   **27 Becomes more** More   **48** [and elsewhere] **More** Moe   **54.1** *Exeunt Exit*

1.4. [F labels as "*Scena Quinta*"]   **0.1** [and elsewhere] ISABELLA *Isabell*   **2** [and throughout] FRANCISCA *Nun*   **5 sisterhood** Sisterstood   **17 stead** steed [also at 3.2. 252]   **54 givings-out** giuing-out   **61–2 mind, study, and fast. / He** minde: Studie, and fast / He   **72 He's** Has   **78** [and elsewhere] **lose** loose

2.1. 12 your our   **39 breaks** brakes   **90** [and elsewhere] **prunes** prewyns   **139.1** [at line 138 in F]

2.2. 63 back again againe   **104 ere** here

2.3. 31 [and elsewhere] **lest** least

2.4. 9 sere feard   **17 s.d.** *Enter Servant* [after line 17 in F]   **30 s.d.**
Enter Isabella [after line 30 in F]   **48 metal** mettle   **53 or** and
75 craftily crafty   **76 me be** be   **94 all-binding** all-building
3.1. 29 thee sire, thee, fire   **31 serpigo** Sapego   **52 me to hear them**
them to heare me   **68 Though** Through   **91 enew** emmew
96 damned'st damnest   **131 penury** periury   **200 advisings. To . . .**
good a aduisings, to . . . good; a   **216 by oath** oath
3.2. 0 [not marked as a new scene in F]   **8 law a** Law; a   **9 on** and
26 eat, array eate away   **48 it clutched** clutch'd   **74–5 bondage.**
If . . . patiently, why bondage if . . . patiently: Why   **109 ungenera-**
tive generatiue   **147 dearer** deare   **214 See** Sea
4.1. 1 BOY [not in F]   **49.1** [after line 48 in F]   **61 quests** Quest
64 s.d. *Enter . . . Isabella* [after line 64 in F]
4.2. 43–7 If . . . thief [assigned in F to *Clo.*]   **58 yare** y'are   **60.1** [at line
59 in F]   **72 s.d.** *Enter Duke* [after line 72 in F]   **100 This . . . man**
[assigned in F to *Duke*]   **Lordship's** Lords   **101 DUKE** *Pro.*
120 PROVOST [not in F]
4.3. 92.1 [at line 91 in F]   **93 Varrius** *Angelo*   **100 well** weale
4.4. 6 redeliver reliuer   **15–16 proclaimed. Betimes** proclaim'd
betimes   **19 s.d.** [at line 18 in F]
4.5. 6 Flavius' *Flauia's*
5.1. 14 me we   **34 hear!** heere.   **173 s.d.** *Enter Mariana* [after line 173
in F]   **174 her face** your face   **226 promised** promis'd   **268 s.d.** [at
line 267 in F]   **288.1** [after line 286 in F]   **407 s.d.** *Mariana* Maria
431 confiscation confutation   **488.2** *Juliet* Iulietta   **550 that's** that

Richard III

Copy text: the First Folio, except for two passages, 3.1.1–158 and 5.3.48
to end of play, for which Q1 is copy text. Unless otherwise indicated, the
adopted readings are from the first quarto of 1597 [Q1]. Act and scene
divisions are marked in the copy text except as indicated below.
1.1. 1 RICHARD [not in F]   **41.1** *Enter . . . Brackenbury* [eds.] *Enter*
Clarence, and Brackenbury, guarded   **45 the** th'   **52 for** but   **65 tem-**
pers him to this tempts him to this harsh   **75 to her for his** for her
88 An 't and   **103 I** I do   **124 the** this   **133 prey** play
1.2. 27 life [eds.] death   **38 HALBERDIER** [eds.] *Gen.*   **39 stand** Stand'st
78 of a of   **80 t'accuse** [eds.] to curse   **94 hand** hands   **141 thee** the
171 words word   **204 RICHARD** [not in F]   **205** [not in F]
227.1 Exeunt [eds.] *Exit* [also at line 229]   **228 RICHARD** Sirs . . .
corpse [not in F]   **229.1** *Exeunt* Exit
1.3. 17 come comes   **lords** Lord   **19** [and elsewhere] **STANLEY** *Der.*
54 whom who   **69** [not in F]   **109.1** [after line 110 in F]   **114** [not in
F]   **155 Ah, little** A little   **160 of** off   **309 QUEEN ELIZABETH** *Mar.*
342 FIRST MURDERER *Vil.* [also at lines 350 and 355]   **351 doers. Be**
assured dooers, be assur'd:
1.4. 13 Thence There   **22 waters** water   **22, 23 my** mine   **25 Ten** A
39 seek find   **41 Which** Who   **64 my lord** Lord   **99 s.d.** *Exit* [at
line 97 in F]   **100 I** we   **122 Faith** [not in F]   **126 Zounds** Come
147 Zounds [not in F]   **152 Tut** [not in F]   **192 to have redemption**
for any goodnesse   **193** [not in F]   **240** [not in F]   **242 of** on
269 [in F, printed after line 263]   **272 s.d.** *Stabs him* [after line 272 in F]
2.1. 0.3 Buckingham [eds.] *Buckingham, Wooduill*   **5 in** to   **7 Rivers**
and Hastings *Dorset* and *Riuers*   **39 God** heauen   **57 unwittingly**
vnwillingly   **59 By** To   **68** [F follows with a line: "Of you Lord
Wooduill, and Lord *Scales* of you"]   **93 but** and   **108 at** and
2.2. 1 BOY *Edw.*   **3** [and throughout scene] **GIRL** [eds.] *Daugh.*   **3 do**
you do   **26 his** a   **47 have I** haue   **83 weep** weepes   **84–5 Clarence**
. . . they *Clarence* weep, so do they   **87 Pour** Power   **142 Ludlow**
London [also at line 154]   **145** [not in F]   **145.1 Manent** [eds.] *Manet*
2.3. 44 Ensuing Pursuing [but the catchword on page 184 in F is "Ensuing"]
2.4. 1 hear heard   **9 young** good   **21 ARCHBISHOP** *Car.* [Q1] *Yor.* [F]
65 death earth
3.1. 1–158 [based on Q1 as copy text]   **2** [and elsewhere] **RICHARD** *Glo.*
60.1 [bracketed s.d. from F]   **111 With all** withall [Q1]   **150.1** [*A sen-*
net] [from F]   **150.2 Hastings** Hast. Dors.   **Manent** [F2] manet

3.2. 20 councils Councell   **78 as you do** as
3.3. 1 [not in F]
3.4. 9 methinks we thinke   **58** [not in F]   **79.1 Exeunt** [at line 78 in F]
Manent Manet   **82 raze** rowse
3.5. 4 wert were   **20 innocence** Innocencie   **34 Look . . . Mayor** [not
in F; after line 26 in Q1]   **56 we I**   **hear** heard   **66 cause** case
74 meet'st advantage meetest vantage   **104 Penker** [eds.] *Peuker*
105.1. Exeunt [eds.] *Exit*   **109 s.d. Exit** Exeunt
3.7. 7 insatiate vnsatiate   **20 mine** my   **33 spake** spoke   **40 wisdoms**
wisdome   **43** [not in F]   **44 RICHARD** [not in F]   **54 we'll** we
83 My lord [not in F]   **125 her** his [also in lines 126 and 127]
214 whe'er where [also in line 229]   **219 Zounds! I'll** we will
220 [not in F]   **224 stone** Stones   **240 Richard** *King Richard*
241 MAYOR AND CITIZENS *All*   **247 cousin** Cousins
4.1. 0.1–5 [F: *Enter the Queene, Anne Duchesse of Gloucester, the Duchesse of*
Yorke, and Marquesse Dorset]   **15 BRACKENBURY** *Lieu.* [and at lines 18
and 26]
4.2. 36 My Lord [not in F]   **72 there** then   **87 to** vnto   **90 Hereford**
Hertford   **98–118 perhaps . . . today** [not in F]
4.3. 0 [scene division not in F]   **4 whom** who   **5 ruthless** ruthfull
13 Which And   **15 once** one   **20 gone; with . . . remorse** gone with
. . . Remorse,   **31 at** and   **33 thee** the   **40 Breton** Britaine   **53 leads**
leds
4.4. 0 [*Scena Tertia* in F]   **10 unblown** vnblowed   **39** [not in F]   **o'er**
over [Q1]   **41 Harry** [eds.] Husband   **45 holp'st** hop'st   **52–3** [lines
reversed in F]   **64 Thy** The   **112 weary** wearied   **118 nights . . .**
days night . . . day   **128 intestate** intestine   **141 Where** Where't
225 lanced [eds.] lanch'd   **239 or** and   **268 would I** I would
284 This is this   **324 Of ten** [eds.] Often   **364–5** [lines reversed in F,
and the s.p. *Queen Elizabeth* is missing]   **366 KING RICHARD** [not in F]
377 God Heauen   **God's** Heavens   **392 in** with   **396 o'erpast**
repast   **417 fond** found   **430.1 Exit Queen** [at line 429 in F]
431.1 Enter Ratcliffe [below line 432 in F]   **444 Ratcliffe** [eds.]
Catesby   **498 FIRST MESSENGER** *Mess.*   **503 SECOND MESSENGER**
Mess.   **506 THIRD MESSENGER** *Mess.* [also at lines 509 and 517]
518 FOURTH MESSENGER *Mess.*   **534 tidings** Newes, but
4.5. 0 [*Scena Quarta in F*]
5.1. 11 is, my lord is
5.2. 11 center Centry   **12 Near** Ne're   **17 swords** men
5.3. 0 [scene not marked in F]   **20 track** Tract   **28 you** [eds.] your
48 ff. [to the end of the play] [copy text is Q1]   **54 sentinels** [F]
centinell [Q1]   **59 CATESBY** [eds.] *Rat.*   **79 sit** [F] set [Q1; also at line
131]   **85 that. The** that the [Q1]   **100 sundered** sundried [Q1]
107.1 [*Richmond remains*] [substantially from F]   **119 stabbed'st**
stabst   **139 GHOST OF RIVERS** *King* [Q1]   **141 GHOST OF GREY** *Gray*
142 GHOST OF VAUGHAN *Vaugh.*   **145 Will** Wel [Q1]   **145.2–150**
[after line 158 in Q1]   **151 GHOSTS** [F] *Ghost* [Q1]   **159 GHOST** [not
in Q1]   **167 GHOST** [not in Q1]   **176 fall** [F] fals [Q1]   **183 am** and
[Q1]   **209 My** Ratcliffe, my   **223 LORDS** *Lo.* [Q1]   **226, 235 A LORD**
Lo. [Q1]   **243 Richard except,** Richard, except   **270.1** *Ratcliffe Rat.*
& c.   **299 main** [F] matne [Q1]   **301 boot** bootes [Q1]   **304 KING**
RICHARD [at line 306 ("King") in Q1]   **324 Brittany** Brittaine
351 them! Victory them victorie [Q1]
5.5. 13 STANLEY [not in Q1]   **13 Ferrers** *Ferri* [Q1]   **15 becomes**
become [Q1]   **41 s.d.** *Exeunt* [F; not in Q1]

Richard II

Copy text: the first quarto of 1597 as press-corrected in all four extant
copies [Q1]; and, for the deposition scene, 4.1. 155–321, the First Folio.
Act and scene divisions, absent in Q1, are from F except that F provides
no scene marking at 5.4 and labels 5.5 and 5.6 as "*Scoena Quarta*" and
"*Scoena Quinta*," respectively.
1.1. 15 presence. Face presence face   **19.1** [and throughout]
Bolingbroke Bullingbrooke   **118 by my** [F] by   **139 But** Ah but
152 gentlemen [F] gentleman   **162–3 Harry, when? / Obedience**
bids Harry? when obedience bids. / Obedience bids   **176 gage. My**

gage, my   **178 reputation; that** Reputation that   **192 parle** parlee
205.1 *Exeunt Exit*
1.2. 25 him. Thou him, thou   **42 alas** [not in Q]   **47 sit** [F] set
48 butcher [Qb, F] butchers [Qa]   **58 it** [Q2–5, F] is   **59 empty** [Qb,
F] emptines, [Qa]   **60 begun** begone   **70 hear** [F] cheere
1.3. 15 thee the   **33 comest** [Q5] comes   **58 thee** the   **104 FIRST HER-
ALD** *Herald*   **108 his God** [F] God   **128 civil** [Qb, F] cruel [Qa]
133 Draws [Qb] Draw [Qa]   **136 wrathful iron** [Qb, F] harsh
resounding [Qa]   **172 then but** [F] but   **180 you owe** [F] y'owe
193 far fare   **222 night** [Q4–5, F] nightes   **239 had it** had't
241 sought ought   **269 world** world:
1.4. 0.1 *Bagot* [F] *Bushie*   **20 our cousin,** [F] our Coosens   **23 Bagot
here, and Green** [Q6; not in Q1]   **27 What** [Qb, F] With [Qa]
47 hand. If hand if   **52.1** *Enter Bushy* [F] *Enter Bushie with newes*
53 Bushy, what news [F; not in Q1]   **65 ALL** [not in Q1]
2.1. 15 life's liues   **18 fond** found   **30** [and elsewhere] **lose** loose
48 as a [Q4–5, F] as   **68.1–2** [after line 70 in Q1]   **70 reined** ragde
102 encagèd [F] inraged   **113 not** not, not   **124 brother** brothers
156 kerns [Qb, F] kerne   **161 coin** [Qb, F] coines [Qa]   **168 my** [Qb,
F] mine   **177 the** [F] a   **209 seize** cease   **239 more** mo   **257 King's**
[Q3–5, F] King   **277 Port le Blanc** le Port Blan   **278 Brittany**
Brittaine [also in 285]   **284 Coint** Coines
2.2. 19 Show [Q6, F] Shows [Qa]   **31 though** [Q2–5, F] thought
53 Harry H.
2.3. 9 Cotswold Cotshall   **30 Lordship** Lo: **36 Hereford** [Q3–5, F]
Herefords   **75 raze** race   **99 the lord** [F] Lord   **164** [and elsewhere]
Bristol Bristow
2.4. 1 WELSH CAPTAIN *Welsh* [also at line 7]
3.2. 32 succor succors   **40 boldly** bouldy   **72 O'erthrows** [F]
Ouerthrowes   **86 name! A** name a   **170 through** [Q2–5, F] thorough
3.3. 13 brief with you [F] briefe   **31 lord** [F] Lords   **59 rain** raigne.
60 waters—on water's on   **100 pastures'** pastors   **119 a prince and
princesse**   **127 ourself** our selues
3.4. 11 joy griefe   **26 pins** [F] pines   **27 state, for** state for   **28 change;
woe** change woe   **29 apricots** Aphricokes   **34 too** [F] two   **48 hath**
htah   **55 seized** ceasde   **57 We at** at   **80 Cam'st** [Q2–5, F] Canst
4.1. 23 him [Q3–5, F] them   **44 Fitzwater** [F] Fitzwaters   **55 As** As it
56 sun to sun sinne to sinne   **63 true. You** true you   **77 my bond**
[Q3–5, F] bond   **110 thee** [Q2–5, F] the   **146 you** yon   **155–321**
[This deposition scene is based on the First Folio text; Q1 has only:
"Let it be so, and loe on wednesday next, / We solemnly proclaime our
Coronation, / Lords be ready all." Unless otherwise indicated all the
departures in F from lines 155–321 are taken from Q4.]   **184 and on**
on   **252 and** a   **256 Nor** No, nor   **297 manners** manner
321.2 *Carlisle Caleil*
5.1. 11 model modle   **41 thee** [Q2–5, F] the   **84 NORTHUMBERLAND** [F]
King
5.2. 2 off [F] of   **11 thee** [F] the [also at lines 17 and 94]   **78 my troth**
by my troth   **94 thee the** [F] And An
5.3. 0.1 *King the King*   **10 While** Which   **31 the** my   **36 I may** [Q2–5,
F] May   **68 And** An   **75 shrill-voiced** shril voice   **111 KING HENRY**
yorke   **135–6 With . . . him** I pardon him with al my heart
5.4. 0.1 *Enter* [F] *Manet*   *Exton* Exton, *etc.*
5.5. 20 through [F] thorow   **22 cannot, die** cannot die   **27 sit** [Q3–5,
F] set   **33 treason makes** treasons make   **55 sounds that tell**
sound that telles   **56 that** which   **58 hours, and times** times,
and houres
5.6. 8 Salisbury, Spencer [F] Oxford, Salisbury   **12.1** *Fitzwater
Fitzwaters*   **43 through the** [F] through

1 Henry IV

Copy text: the first complete quarto of 1598 [Q1]; and, for 1.3.201
through 2.2.110, the fragment of an earlier Quarto [Q0]. The act and
scene divisions, missing in Q0 and Q1, are based on F except that F
provides no break at 5.3.

1.1. 22 levy leauy   **39 Herdfordshire** Herdforshire   **62 a dear** deere
69 blood, did bloud. Did   **70 plains. Of** plaines, of   **76 In faith, it is**
[assigned in Q1 to King]
1.2. 16 king a king   **33 proof, now:** proofe. Now   **78 similes** smiles
154 thou the   **158 Peto, Bardolph** Haruey, Rossill
1.3. 12 too to,   **137** [and throughout] **Bolingbroke** Bullingbrooke
194 good night god-night   **201 HOTSPUR** [missing in Q0–Q4]
222 holler hollow   **238 whipped** [Q1] whip [Q0]
2.1. 34 FIRST CARRIER *Car.*   **48.1** [below line 47 in Q0]   **56 Weald** wild
70 Trojans Troyans
2.2. 0.1 Poins, Peto, and *Poines, and Peto &c*   **12 square** squire
16 two-and-twenty xxii: **20 Bardolph** Bardol [and thus, or
"Bardoll," throughout the play]   **34 mine** [Q1] my [Q0]   **42 Go hang**
[F] Hang [Q0]   **51 BARDOLPH What news** [all assigned as continuation of Poins's speech in line 50]   **52 GADSHILL** *Bar.*   **78 FIRST
TRAVELER** *Trauel.*   **82 TRAVELERS** *Trauel.*   **86 TRAVELERS** *Tra.*
2.3. 1 HOTSPUR [not in Q1]   **4 In** the   **48 thee** the   **69 A roan**
Roane
2.4. 33 precedent present   **36 POINS** *Prin.*   **121 sun's** soanes
171 PRINCE *Gad*   **172 GADSHILL** *Ross.* [also at lines 174 and 178]
226 keech catch   **242 eel-skin** elsskin   **322.1** [after line 321 in Q1]
337 Owen O   **390 tristful** trustfull   **398 yet** so   **468 lean** lane
518 Good God [also at line 519]   **526 s.d. pockets** pocket   **530 PETO**
[not in Q1]   **535 PRINCE** [not in Q1]
3.1. 55 coz coose [also at line 75]   **97 cantle** scantle   **126 meter** miter
129 on an   **183 Loseth** Looseth   **261 hot Lord** Hot. Lord
3.2. 32 Council counsell   **59 won** wan   **84 gorged** gordge   **96 then**
than   **145 northern** Northren   **161.1** [after line 162 in Q1]
3.3. 35 that's that   **57 tithe** tight   **119 no thing** nothing   **135 owed**
ought   **173 guests** ghesse   **201 o'clock** of clocke
4.1. 1 [and elsewhere] **HOTSPUR** *Per.*   **20 lord** mind   **55 is** tis
96 doffed daft   **105 cuisses** cushes   **108 dropped** drop   **116 altar**
altars   **123 ne'er** neare   **126 cannot** can   **127 yet** it   **134 merrily**
merely
4.2. 3 Coldfield cop-hill   **15 yeomen's** Yeomans   **31 feazed** fazd
33–4 tattered tottered   **80 s.d.** *Exit Exeunt*
4.3. 23 horse horses   **74 heirs . . . followed** heires, as Pages followed
84 country's Countrey
4.4. 0.1 [and throughout] *Michael Mighell*   **18 o'erruled** ouerrulde
36 not, ere not ere   **37 power he** power, he
5.1. 0.2 *Lancaster Lancaster, Earle of Westmerland*   **2 bosky** bulky
3 southern Southren   **88 off** of   **138 will it** wil
5.2. 3 undone vnder on   **8 Suspicion** Supposition   **12 merrily**
merely   **25.1** *Hotspur Percy*   **79 FIRST MESSENGER** *Mes.*   **89 SECOND
MESSENGER** *Mes.*   **94–5 withal / . . . day.** withall. / . . . day,
5.3. 1 in the in   **22 A** Ah   **35–6 ragamuffins** rag of Muffins
5.4. 4 [and elsewhere] **LANCASTER** *P. John*   **68 Nor** Now   **76.1** *who he*
92 enough. This inough, this   **thee** the
5.5. 36 bend you bend, you

Henry V

Copy text: the First Folio. Act and scene divisions are for the most part
editorially supplied; F marks "*Actus Secundus*" at Act 3, "*Actus Tertius*" at
Act 4, "*Actus Quartus*" at 4.7, and "*Actus Quintus*" at Act 5.
Prologue. 1 CHORUS [not in F, but is in prologues to other acts]
1.2. 38 succedant succedaul   **45 Elbe** Elue [also at line 52]   **76** [and
elsewhere] **Lewis** *Lewes*   **82 Ermengard** Ermengare   **90–1 day, /
Howbeit** day. / Howbeit,   **115 ELY** *Bish.*   **131 blood** Bloods.
163 her their   **166 A LORD** *Bish. Ely*   **197 majesty** Maiesties
212 End [Q] And   **221** [and elsewhere] **Dauphin** Dolphin
237 FIRST AMBASSADOR *Amb.* [also at line 245]   **310.1** *Flourish* [at
the beginning of 2.0 in F]
2.1. 23 mare [Q] name   **28 NYM** [Q; not in F]   **42, 43 Iceland** Island
73 thee defy [Q] defie thee   **80 enough** enough to   **83 you** your
105–6 [Q; not in F]   **betting** [Q] beating   **116 that's** that

2.2. 29 GREY *Kni.*   **86 furnish him** [Q] furnish   **106 a** an   **107 whoop** hoope   **113 All** And   **138 mark the** make thee   **139 suspicion . . . thee;** suspition, . . . thee.   **146 Henry** [Q] *Thomas*   **147 Masham** [Q] *Marsham*   **158 Which I** Which   **175 have sought** [Q] sought   **180.1 Exeunt** *Exit*

2.3. 16–17 'a babbled a Table   **24 upward** vp-peer'd   **32 HOSTESS** *Woman*   **48 word** world

2.4. 0.2 Brittany *Britaine*   **1 [and elsewhere] FRENCH KING** *King*   **132 Louvre** Louer   **146.1 Flourish** [at the beginning of 3.0 in F]

3.0. 6 fanning fayning   **17 [and elsewhere] Harfleur** Harflew   **35 eke** eech

3.1. 7 conjure commune   **17 noblest** Noblish   **24 men** me   **32 Straining** Straying

3.2. 25 runs wins   **67 [and elsewhere in scene] FLUELLEN** *Welch*   **82 [and elsewhere in scene] JAMY** *Scot*   **87 [and elsewhere in scene] MACMORRIS** *Irish*   **102 quite** quit   **112 Chrish** Christ

3.3. 32 heady headly   **35 Defile** Desire   **43** [here F has s.d. "*Enter Gouernour*"]   **54 all. For** all for

3.4. 2 parles *parlas* [throughout the play, the French has been somewhat modernized, besides the emendations listed here]   **7 Elle** *il*   **8 Et les doigts** [assigned to Alice in F]   **9 ALICE** *Kat.*   **les doigts** *e doyt*   **10 souviendrai** *souemeray*   **12 KATHARINE** *Alice*   **13 j'ai** *Kath. I'ay*   **14 les** *le*   **16 Nous** [not in F]   **40 pas déjà** *y desia*   **42 Non** *Nome*   **46 Sauf** *Sans*   **51 les** *le* [also in line 52]

3.5. 11 de du   **26 "Poor" may** Poore   **43 Vaudemont** *Vandemont*   **45 Foix . . . Boucicault** *Loys, Lestrale, Bouciquall*   **46 knights** Kings

3.6. 31 her [Q] his   **37 is make** [Q] makes   **110–11 lenity** Leuitie

3.7. 12 pasterns postures   **14 qui a** *ches*   **59 lief** liue   **65 et est** *truie leuye*

4.0. 16 name nam'd   **20 cripple** creeple   **27 Presenteth** Presented

4.1. 3 Good God   **95 Thomas** *Iohn*   **158 deaths** [Q] death   **propose** purpose   **227 s.d. Exeunt** *Exit* [at line 222 in F]   **243 What is** What? is   **adoration** Odoration   **251 Think'st** Thinks   **273 Hyperion** *Hiperio*   **289 reck'ning, ere . . . numbers** reckning of . . . numbers: **307 friends** friend

4.2. 4 eaux ewes   **6 Cieux** *Cein*   **11 dout** doubt   **47 drooping** dropping   **49 gimmaled** Iymold   **52 all impatient** all, impatient

4.3. 12 [placed after line 14 in F]   **48** [Q; not in F]   **124 'em** vm

4.4. 15 Or for   **36 à cette heure** asture   **37 couper** couppes   **54 l'avez** layt a   **57 remerciments** remercious   **58 j'ai tombé** le intombe   **59 très-distinguè** tres distinie   **68 Suivez-vous** *Saaue vous*

4.5. 2 perdu . . . perdu perdia . . . perdie   **3 Mort de** *Mor Dieu*   **16 by a** [Q] a base   **24.1 Exeunt** *Exit*

4.6. 34 mistful mixtfull   **38 s.d. Exeunt** *Exit*

4.7. 22 e'en in   **69 [and elsewhere in this scene] MONTJOY** *Her.*   **77 the** with   **109 countryman** Countrymen   **114 God** Good   **123 'a live** aliue   **126 'a lived** aliue   **161 [and elsewhere] an't** and

4.8. 77 Boucicault *Bouchiquald*   **99 Foix** Foyes   **100 Vaudemont** *Vandemont*   **Lestrelles** *Lestrale*   **104 Keighley** *Ketly*   **110–11 loss / On . . . other?** losse? / On . . . other,   **113 we** me   **121 in my** [Q] my   **122 rites** Rights

5.0. 29 but but by

5.1. 39 By Jesu [Q] I say   **69 begun** began   **88 swear** swore   **5.2. 1 [and elsewhere] KING HENRY** *King*   **12 [and throughout scene] QUEEN ISABEL** *Quee.*   **12 England** Ireland   **21 [also elsewhere] KING HENRY** *Eng.*   **45 fumitory** Femetary   **50 all** withall   **61 diffused** defus'd   **72 tenors** Tenures   **77 cursitory** curselarie   **93 Haply** Happily   **98 s.d. Manent** Manet   **114 [and elsewhere] ALICE** *Lady*   **190 meilleur** melieus   **255 grandeur** grandeus   **261 noces** nopcese   **264 les** le   **265 baiser** buisse   **267 entend** entendre   **323 hath never** hath   **332 then** in in   **364 paction** Pation

Epilogue CHORUS [not in F]

Romeo and Juliet

Copy text: the second quarto of 1599, except for 1.2.53–1.3.34, for which Q1 (the first quarto) is the prior authority. Act and scene divisions are absent from the second quarto and the Folio.

1.1. 27 it in [Q1] it   **38 side** sides   **73 CITIZENS** *Offi.*   **76 CAPULET'S WIFE** *Wife*   **92 Verona's** *Neronas*   **120 drave** driue   **147 his** is   **153 sun** same   **177 create** [Q1] created   **179 well-seeming** [Q1] welseeing   **189 grief to** [Q1] grief, too   **192 lovers'** louing   **202 Bid a** [Q1] A   **make** [Q1] makes   **206 markman** mark man   **211 unharmed** [Q1] vncharmd   **218 makes** make

1.2. 14 The earth Earth   **32 on** one   **38–9 written here** written. Here   **46 One** [Q1] on   **56 Good e'en** Goddess   **57 God gi' good e'en** Godgigoden   **70 and Livia** [Q1] Liuia [Q2]   **79 thee** [Q1] you [Q2]   **91 fires** fier [Q1]

1.3. 12 an [Q2] a [Q1]   **18 shall** [Q1] stal [Q2]   **33 wi' th'** [Q1: *with*] with the [Q2]   **50 [and elsewhere] WIFE** *Old La.*   **66 disposition** [F] dispositions   **67, 68 honor** [Q1] houre   **100 it fly** [Q1] flie   **105 [and elsewhere] WIFE** *Mo.*

1.4. 7–8 [Q1; not in Q2]   **23 MERCUTIO** *Horatio*   **31 quote** cote   **39 done** [Q1] dum   **42 Of** Or   **45 like lamps** [Q1] lights lights   **47 five** fine   **57 atomi** [Q1] ottamie   **59–61** [these lines follow line 69 in Q2]   **66 film** Philome   **69 maid** [Q1] man   **72 O'er** [Q1] On   **74 on** one   **76 breaths** [Q1] breath   **80 parson's** Persons   **81 dreams he** [Q1] he dreams   **90 elflocks** Elklocks   **111 forfeit** [Q1] fofreit

1.5. 0.1 [Q2 adds: "*Enter Romeo*"]   **1 FIRST SERVINGMAN** *Ser.* [also at lines 6 and 12]   **3 SECOND SERVINGMAN** 1   **7 court cupboard** Courtcubbert   **11 THIRD SERVINGMAN** 2   **14 FOURTH SERVINGMAN** 3   **15 longest** longer   **17 CAPULET** 1. *Capu.* [also at lines 35 and 40]   **18 a bout** about   **57 antic** anticque   **96 ready** [Q1] did readie

2.0. Chorus 1 CHORUS [not in Q2]   **4 matched** match

2.1. 7 Nay . . . too [assigned in Q2 to Benvolio]   **10 one** [Q1] on   **11 Pronounce** [Q1] prouaunt   **dove** [Q1] day   **13 heir** [Q1] her   **14 trim** [Q1] true   **39 open-arse, and** open, or   **pop'ring** Poprin

2.2. 16 do [Q1] to   **20 eyes** [Q1] eye   **41–2 nor any . . . name** ô be some other name / Belonging to a man   **45 were** [Q1] wene   **82 pilot** Pylat   **83 washed** [Q1] washeth   **92–3 false . . . They** false at louers periuries. / They   **99 havior** behauiour   **101 more cunning** coying   **110 circled** [Q1] circle   **146 [and elsewhere] rite** right   **151 NURSE** [not in Q2]   **150, 151 JULIET** [not in Q2]   **163 than mine** then   **168 nyas** Neece   **180 gyves** giues   **187 Sleep . . . breast** [Q1; assigned in Q2 to Juliet]   **189–90** [preceded in Q2 by an earlier version of lines 1–4 of the next scene, in which "fleckled darkness" reads "darknesse fleckted" and "and Titan's fiery wheels" reads "made by *Tytans* wheels"]

2.3. 2 Check'ring [Q1] Checking   **22 sometime's** sometime   **50 me** me: **51 wounded. Both our** wounded both, our   **85 not. She whom** [Q1] me not, her

2.4. 18 BENVOLIO [Q1] *Ro.*   **28 antic** antique   **28–9 phantasimes** phantacies   **33 pardon-me's** pardons mees   **40 but a a**   **68 Switch . . . switch** Swits . . . swits   **113–14 for himself** [Q1] himself   **205 dog's** dog   **212 s.d. Exeunt** *Exit*

2.5. 11 three there   **15 And** *M.* And   **26 I had** [Q1] I

2.6. 18 gossamer gossamours   **27 music's** musicke

3.1. 2 Capels are *Capels*   **67 injured** iniuried   **73 stoccada** stucatho   **90 your houses** houses   **107 soundly too. Your** soundly, to your   **121 Alive** He gan   **123 fire-eyed** [Q1] fier end   **136 FIRST CITIZEN** *Citti.*   **138 FIRST CITIZEN** *Citi.*   **141 all** all: **165 agile** [Q1] aged   **183 MONTAGUE** *Capu.*   **187 hate's** heart's   **191 I** [Q1] it   **196.1 Exeunt** *Exit*

3.2. 1 JULIET [not in Q2]   **9 By** And by   **12 [and elsewhere] lose** loose   **15 grown** grow   **47 darting** arting   **49 shut** shot   **51 Brief sounds** Briefe, sounds,   **of my** my   **54 [and elsewhere] corpse** coarse   **60 one** on   **72 It . . . day** it did [assigned in Q2 to Juliet]   **73 O . . . face** [assigned in Q2 to Nurse]   **76 Dove-feathered** Rauenous doue-featherd   **79 damnèd** dimme   **143.1 Exeunt** *Exit*

3.3. 0.1 [Q2 has "*Enter Friar and Romeo*"]   **39** [Q2 follows with a line: "This may flyes do, when I from this must flie"]   **43** [printed in Q2 before line 40]   **52 Thou** [Q1] Then   **61 madmen** [Q1] mad man   **70.1** *Knock* Enter Nurse, and knocke   **73 s.d.** *Knock* They knocke   **74 Who's** whose   **75.1** *Knock* Slud knock   **80.1** *Enter Nurse* [below line 78 in Q2]   **110 denote** [Q1] deuote   **117 lives** [Q1] lies   **144 pout'st upon** puts vp   **168 disguised** disguise
3.4. 10 [and elsewhere] WIFE *La.*   13 be [Q1] me   23 We'll keep Well, keepe
3.5. 13 exhaled exhale   19 the the the   31 changed change   36.1 *Enter Nurse Enter Madame and Nurse*   54 JULIET *Ro.*   67.1 [bracketed s.d. from Q1]   82 pardon him padon   130–1 body . . . a bark body? / Thou counterfeits. A Barke   133–4 is, . . . flood; is: . . . floud,   139 gives giue   142 How? Will How will   151–2 proud . . . Thank proud mistresse minion you? / Thanke   160 [and elsewhere] CAPULET *Fa.*   172 CAPULET Oh, God-i'-good-e'en Father, Godigeden   173 NURSE [not in Q2]   181 liened liand
4.1. 7 talked [Q1] talke   45 cure [Q1] care   46 Ah [Q1] O   72 slay [Q1] stay   78 off [Q1] of   83 chopless [Q1] chapels   85 his tomb his   98 breath [Q1] breast   100 To wanny Too many   110 In Is [Q2 follows with a line: "Be borne to buriall in thy kindreds graue"]   111 shalt shall   115 and he an he   116 waking walking   126 s.d. *Exeunt Exit*
4.2. 3, 6 SERVINGMAN *Ser.*   14 willed wield   26 becomèd becomd   38 [and elsewhere] WIFE *Mo.*   47.1 *Exeunt Exit*
4.3. 20 vial Violl   49 wake walke
4.4. 1 [and elsewhere] WIFE *La.*   12.1 *Exeunt Exit*   13.1–2 [after line 14 in Q2]   15 FIRST SERVINGMAN *Fel.*   18 SECOND SERVIN GMAN *Fel.*   21 Thou Twou   faith father   23 s.d. [after line 21 in Q2]
4.5. 40 all; life all life   41 long [Q1] loue   51 behold bedold   65 cure care   65–6 not . . . Heaven not, / In these confusions heauen   82 fond some   96 FIRST MUSICIAN *Musi.*   98 s.d. *Exit Exit omnes* [below line 99]   99, 103 FIRST MUSICIAN *Fid.*   99 by [Q1] my   99.1 *Enter Peter Enter Will Kemp*   107 FIRST MUSICIAN *Minstrels* [and subsequently in this scene indicated by *Minst.* or *Minstrel*]   123 Then . . . wit [assigned in Q2 to 2 *M*]   127 And . . . oppress [Q1; not in Q2]   133, 136 Pretty [Q1] Prates   145 s.d. *Exeunt Exit*
5.1. 15 fares my [Q1] doth my Lady   17, 27, 32 BALTHASAR *Man*   24 e'en in   defy [Q1] denie   33.1 [at line 32, after "good lord," in Q2]   76 pay [Q1] pray   86 s.d. *Exit Exeunt*
5.3. 3 yew [Q1] young   21.2 [*Balthasar*] [Q1] Peter   25 light. Upon light vpon   40, 43 BALTHASAR *Pet.*   68 conjuration commiration   71 PAGE *Boy* [Q1; s.p. missing in Q2 and line treated as a s.d.]   102 fair faire? I will beleeue   107 palace pallat   108 [Q2 has four undeleted lines here: "Depart againe, come lye thou in my arme, / Heer's to thy health, where ere thou tumblest in. / O true Appothecarie! / Thy drugs are quicke. Thus with a kisse I die."]   123 [and elsewhere] BALTHASAR *Man*   137 yew yong   168 FIRST WATCH *Watch* [also at lines 172, 195, 199]   171 PAGE *Watch boy*   182 SECOND WATCH *Watch*   183, 187 FIRST WATCH *Chief. watch*   187 too too too   190 shrieked shrike   194 our your   199 slaughtered Slaughter   201 [Q2 has a s.d. here: "Enter Capulet and his wife"]   209 more early [Q1] now earling   232 that thats   274–5 place . . . This place. To this same monument / This   281 PAGE *Boy*   299 raise raie

Julius Caesar

Copy text: the First Folio. Act divisions are marked in the Folio; scene divisions are editorially supplied.
1.1. 0.1 [and elsewhere] *Marullus Murellus*   37 Pompey? . . . oft *Pompey* many a time and oft?   61 [and elsewhere] whe'er where
1.2. 0.1 [and elsewhere] *Calpurnia Calphurnia*   24.1 *Manent Manet*   124 [and elsewhere] lose loose   254 like. He like he   301 digest disgest
1.3. 129 In favor's like Is Fauors, like

2.1. 28 [and elsewhere] lest least   40 ides first   67 of of a   83 put path   122 women, then, women. Then   136 oath, when Oath. When   214 eighth eight   268 his hit   281 the tho   310.1 *Enter Lucius and Ligarius* [after "with haste" in line 310 in F]   314 [and through line 322] LIGARIUS *Cai.*
2.2. 23 did neigh do neigh   46 are heare   81 Of And   120 to blame too blame
2.3. 1 ARTEMIDORUS [not in F]
3.1. 40 law lane   114 states State   116 lies lye   201 [and elsewhere] corpse Coarse [also Course and Corpes]   256 ANTONY [not in F]   277.1 *Octavius' Octauio's* [also at 5.2.4]   285 for from
3.2. 106 art are   205 ALL [not in F]   222 wit writ   260 s.d. *Exeunt Exit*   262 s.d. *Enter Servant* [after "fellow" in F]
3.3. 6 Whither Whether
4.2. 34–6 FIRST, SECOND, THIRD SOLDIER [not in F]   50 Lucius *Lucillius*   52 Lucilius *Lucius*   52.1 *Manent Manet*
4.3. 209–10 off / If off. / If   230 s.d. *Enter Lucius* [before line 230 in F]   244, 246 [and throughout] Claudius *Claudio*   246 [and throughout] Varro *Varrus*   252 will will it   303, 307 VARRO, CLAUDIUS *Both*
5.1. 42 teeth teethes   67.1 *Exeunt Exit*   70 [F has s.d.: "*Lucillius and Messala stand forth*"]   71 LUCILIUS (stands forth) *Luc.*   73 MESSALA (stands forth) *Messa.*   99 rest rests
5.3. 99 fare far   104 Thasos *Tharsus*   108 Flavius *Flauio*
5.4. 7 LUCILIUS [not in F]   9 O *Luc.* O   12, 15 FIRST SOLDIER *Sold.*   16.1 *Enter Antony* [before line 16 in F]   17 the news thee newes
5.5. 33 too, Strato to *Strato*   77 With all Withall

Hamlet

Copy text: the second quarto of 1604–1605 [Q2]. The First Folio text also represents an independently authoritative text; although seemingly not the correct choice for copy text, the Folio text is considerably less marred by typographical errors than is Q2. The adopted readings in these notes are from F unless otherwise indicated; [eds.] means that the adopted reading was first proposed by some editor since the time of F. Some readings also are supplied from the first quarto of 1603 [Q1]. Act and scene divisions are missing in Q$_q$ 1–2; the Folio provides such markings only through 1.3 and at Act 2.

1.1. 1 Who's Whose   19 soldier [F, Q1] souldiers   44 off [Q1] of   48 harrows horrowes   67 sledded Polacks [eds.] sleaded pollax   77 why [F, Q1] with   cast cost   91 heraldry [F, Q1] heraldy   92 those [F, Q1] these   95 returned returne   97 cov'nant comart   98 designed [eds.] desseigne   113 e'en so [eds.] enso   116 mote [eds.] moth   119 tenantless tennatlesse   125 feared [eds.] feare   142 you [F, Q1] your   144 at it it   181 conveniently [F, Q1] conuenient
1.2. 0.2 [and elsewhere] *Gertrude Gertrad*   1 KING *Claud.*   67 so so much   77 good coold   82 shapes [Q3] chapes   83 denote deuote   96 a or   105 corpse [eds.] course   112 you. For you for   114 retrograde retrograd   129 sullied [eds.] sallied [Q2] solid [F]   132 self seale   133 weary wary   137 to this thus   140 satyr [F4] satire   143 would [F, Q1] should   149 even she [F; not in Q2]   175 to drink deep [F, Q1] for to drinke   178 to see [F, Q1] to   199 waste [F2] wast [Q2, F]   206 jelly with . . . fear, gelly, with . . . feare   210 Where, as [Q5] Whereas   225 Indeed, indeed [F, Q1] Indeede   241 Very like, very like [F, Q1] Very like   242 hundred hundreth   243 MARCELLUS, BERNARDO [eds.] *Both*   247 tonight to nigh   256 fare farre   257 eleven a leauen   259.1 *Exeunt* [at line 258 in Q2]   262 Foul [F, Q1] fonde
1.3. 3 convoy is conuay, in   12 bulk bulkes   18 [F; not in Q2]   29 weigh way   49 like a a   74 Are Or   75 be boy   76 loan loue   110 Running [eds.] Wrong [Q2] Roaming [F]   116 springes springs   126 tether tider   130 implorators imploratotors   131 bawds [eds.] bonds   132 beguile beguide
1.4. 2 is a is   6.1 go off [eds.] goes of   17 revel [Q3] reueale   19 clepe clip   36 evil [eds.] eale [Q2] ease [Q3]   37 often dout [eds.] of a

doubt **49 inurned** interr'd [Q2, Q1] **61, 79 wafts** waues **80 off** of **82 artery** arture **86.1** *Exeunt Exit* **87 imagination** [F, Q1] imagion

1.5. 1 Whither [eds.] Whether **20 on** [eds.] an **21 fretful porcupine** [F, Q1] fearfull Porpentine **44 wit** [eds.] wits **48 what a** what **56 lust** [F, Q1] but **angel** Angle **57 sate** [F] sort **59 scent** [eds.] sent **68 alleys** [eds.] allies **69 posset** possesse **96 stiffly** swiftly **119 bird** and **128 HORATIO, MARCELLUS** *Booth* [also at line 151] heaven, my lord heauen **138 Look you, I'll** I will **157 s.d.** *cries Ghost cries* **179 some'er** so mere **185 Well** well, well [Q1, Q2]

2.1 0.1 man [eds.] *man or two* **3 marvelous** meruiles **29 Faith, no** Fayth **41 warrant** wit **42 sullies** sallies **43 wi' th'** with **60 o'ertook** or tooke **64 takes** take **76 s.d.** *Exit Reynaldo. Enter Ophelia* [after line 75 in Q2] **107 passion** passions **114 quoted** [eds.] coted

2.2. 0.1 [and elsewhere] *Rosencrantz Rosencraus* **57 o'erhasty** hastie **73 three** [F, Q1] threescore **90 since brevity** breuitie **125 This** [Q2 has a speech prefix: *Pol.* This] **126 above** about **137 winking** working **143 his** her **148 watch** wath **149 to a** to **151 'tis** [F, Q1; not in Q2] **170.1** [at line 169 in Q2] *Exeunt* [eds.] *Exit* **210 sanity** sanctity **212–13 and suddenly . . . him** [F; not in Q2] **213 honorable lord** Lord **214 most humbly take** take **215 cannot, sir** cannot **216 more** not more **224 excellent** extent **228–9 overhappy. / On** euer happy on **229 cap** lap **240–70 Let . . . attended** [F; not in Q2] **267 ROSENCRANTZ, GUILDENSTERN** *Both* [F] **273 even** euer **288 could** can **292 off** of **304 What a** What **306–7 admirable, in action how . . . angel, in** [F, eds.] admirable in action, how . . . Angell in **310 no, nor** nor **314 you** yee **321 of** on **324–5 the clown . . . sear** [F; not in Q2] **tickle** [eds.] tickled [F] **326 blank** black **337–62 How . . . too** [F; not in Q2] **342 berattle** [eds.] be-ratled [F] **349 most like** [eds.] like most [F] **373 lest my** let me **381 too** to **398–9 tragical-historical, tragical-comical-historical-pastoral** [F; not in Q2] **401 light . . . these** [eds.] light for the lawe of writ, and the liberty: these **425 By 'r** by **429 e'en to 't** ento't **French falconers** friendly Fankners **433 [and elsewhere] FIRST PLAYER** *Player* **436–7 caviare** cauiary **443 affectation** affection **446 tale** [F, Q1] talke **456 heraldry** [F, Q1] heraldy **dismal. Head** dismall head **474 Then senseless Ilium** [F; not in Q2] **481 And, like** Like **495 fellies** [F4] follies [Q2] Fallies [F] **504 "Moblèd queen" is good** [F; not in Q2; F reads "Inobled"] **506 bisson** *Bison* **514 husband's** [F, Q1] husband **519 whe'er** where **540 a** [F; not in Q2] **541 or** [F, Q1] lines, or **546 s.d.** *Exeunt players* [see textual note at line 548.1] **547 till** tell **548.1** *Exeunt* [F; Q2 has "*Exeunt Pol. and Players*" after line 547] **554 his** the **556 and** an **559 to Hecuba** [F, Q1] to her **561 the cue** that **582 Oh, vengeance** [F; not in Q2] **584 father** [Q1, Q3, Q4; not in Q2, F] **588 scullion** [F] stallyon [Q2] scalion [Q1] **600 the devil** a deale the devil the deale

3.1. 1 And An **28 too** two **32 lawful espials** [F; not in Q2] **33 Will** Wee'le **46 loneliness** lowlines **to** too **56 Let's withdraw** with-draw **56.2** *Enter Hamlet* [after line 55 in Q2] **65 wished. To** wisht to **73 disprized** despiz'd **84 of us all** [F, Q1; not in Q2] **86 sicklied** sickled **93 well, well, well** well **100 the** these **108 your honesty** you **119 inoculate** euocutat **122 to a** a a **130 knaves all** knaues **144 paintings too** [Q1] paintings **146 jig, you amble** gig & amble **147 lisp** list **148 your ignorance** [F, Q1] ignorance **155 Th'expectancy** Th'expectation **159 music** musickt **160 that** what **161 tune** time **162 feature** stature **164** [Q2 has "*Exit*" at the end of this line] **191 unwatched** vnmatcht

3.2. 10 tatters totters **split** [F, Q1] spleet **27 of the** of **29 praise** praysd **37 sir** [F; not in Q2] **45.1** *Enter . . . Rosencrantz* [after line 47 in Q2] **88 detecting** detected **96 now. My lord,** now, my Lord. **107 [and elsewhere] QUEEN** *Ger.* **108 metal** mettle **112–13** [F; not in Q2] **127 devil** deule [Q2] Diuel [F] **133.1** *sound* [eds.] *sounds* **133.7** *Anon comes* anon come **135 miching** [F, Q1] munching **140 keep counsel** [F, Q1] keepe **153 [and throughout scene] PLAYER KING** *King* **154 orbèd** orb'd the **159 [and throughout scene] PLAYER QUEEN** *Quee.* **162 your** our **164** [Q2 follows here with an extraneous unrhymed line: "For women feare too much, euen as they

loue"] **165 For** And **166 In** Eyther none, in **167 love** Lord **179 Wormwood, wormwood** That's wormwood **180 PLAYER QUEEN** [not in Q2] **188 like** the **197 joys** joy **217 An** And **221 a widow** [F, Q1] I be a widow **be** [F] be a **226.1** *Exit* [F, Q1] *Exeunt* **240 wince** [Q1] winch [Q2, F] **241.1** [after line 242 in Q2] **254 Confederate** [F, Q1] Considerat **256 infected** [F, Q1, Q4] inuected **258 usurp** vsurps **264** [F; not in Q2] **274 with two** with **288.1** [F; after line 293 in Q2] **308 start** stare **317 of my** of **343.1** [after line 341 in Q2] **357 thumb** the vmber **366 to the top of** to **370 can fret me** [F] fret me not [Q2] can fret me, yet [Q1] **371.1** [after line 372 in Q2] **385 POLONIUS** [F; not in Q2] **386 Leave me, friends** [so F; Q2 places before "I will say so," and assigns both to Hamlet] **388 breathes** breakes **390 bitter . . . day** business as the bitter day **395 daggers** [F, Q1] dagger

3.3. 19 huge hough **22 ruin** raine **23 but with** but **35.1** *Exit* [after "I know" in F] **50 pardoned** pardon **58 Offense's** [eds.] Offences **shove** showe **73 pat . . . a-praying** but now a is a praying **75 revenged** reuendge **79 hire and salary** base and silly **81 With all** Withall

3.4. 5–6 with him . . . Mother, Mother, Mother [F; not in Q2] **7 warrant** wait **8.1** *Enter Hamlet* [at line 5 in Q2] **21 inmost** most **23 Help, ho!** Helpe how **43 off of** 51 tristful heated **53** [assigned in Q2 to Hamlet] **60 heaven-kissing** heaue, a kissing **89 panders** pardons **91 mine . . . soul** my very eyes into my soule **92 grainèd** greeued **93 not leave** leaue there **100 tithe** kyth **146 Ecstasy** [F; not in Q2] **150 I the** the **165 live** leaue **172 Refrain tonight** to refraine night **193 ravel** rouell **205 to breathe** [eds.] to breath **222 a** [F, Q1] a most **224.1** *Exeunt* [eds.] *Exit*

4.1. 32.1 [at 31 in Q2]

4.2. 0.1 [Q2: "Enter Hamlet, Rosencraus, and others."] **2–3** [F; not in Q2; the s.p. in F is "Gentlemen"] **4 HAMLET** [not in Q2] **5.1** [F; not in Q2] **7 Compounded** Compound **18–19 an ape** [not in Q2] **31–2 Hide . . . after** [F; not in Q2]

4.3. 44 With fiery quickness [F; not in Q2] **56 and so** so **72 were** will **begun** begin

4.4. 20–1 name. To name To

4.5. 16 Let . . . in [assigned in Q2 to Horatio] **20.1** [after line 16 in Q2] **38 with all** with **52 clothes** close **57 Indeed, la** Indeede **62 to** too **83 in their** in **98** [F; not in Q2] **100.1** [below line 97 in Q2] **103 impetuous** [Q3, F2] impitious [Q2] impittious [F] **109 They** The **146 swoopstake** [eds.] soopstake [Q1 reads "Swoop-stake-like"] **158 Let her come in** [assigned in Q2 to Laertes and placed before "How now, what noyse is that?"] **s.d.** *Enter Ophelia* [after line 157 in Q2] **162 Till** Tell **165 an old** [F, Q1] a poore **166–8, 170** [F; not in Q2] **186 must** [F, Q1] may **191 affliction** [F, Q1] afflictions **199 All flaxen** Flaxen **203 Christian** [F] Christians **souls, I pray God** [F, Q1] soules **204 you see** you **217 trophy, sword** trophe sword

4.6. 7, 9 FIRST SAILOR *Say.* **9 an't** and **22 good turn** turne **26 bore** bord **30 He** So **31 will give** will

4.7. 6 proceeded proceede **7 crimeful** criminall **15 conjunctive** concliue **22 gyves** Giues **23 loud a wind** loued Arm'd **25 had** haue **37 How . . . Hamlet** [F; not in Q2] **38 This** These **46–7 your pardon** you pardon **48 and more strange** [F; not in Q2] **Hamlet** [F; not in Q2] **56 shall live** [F, Q1] liue **62 checking** the King **78 ribbon** [eds.] ribaud **89 my** me **101 escrimers** [eds.] Scrimures **116 wick** [eds.] weeke **123 spendthrift** [Q5] spend thrifts **135 on** ore **139 pass** pace **141 for that** for **151 shape. If** shape if **157 ha 't** hate **160 prepared** prefard **168 hoar** horry **172 cold** cull-cold **192 douts** [F "doubts"] drownes

5.1. 1 [and throughout] FIRST CLOWN *Clowne* **3 [and throughout] SECOND CLOWN** *Other* **9 se offendendo** so offended **12 and to** to **Argal** or all **34–7 SECOND CLOWN: Why . . . arms?** [F; not in Q2] **43 that frame** that **55.1** [before line 65 in Q2] **60 stoup** soope **70 daintier** dintier **85 meant** [F, Q1, Q3] went **89 mazard** massene **106–7 Is . . . recoveries** [F; not in Q2] **107–8 Will his** will

109 double ones too doubles   **120 Oh** or   **121** [F; not in Q2]
143 Of all Of   **165 nowadays** [F; not in Q2]   **183 Let me see** [F; not in Q]   **192 chamber** [F, Q1] table   **208–9 As thus** [F; not in Q2]
216 winter's waters   **226, 235 PRIEST** Doct.   **231 Shards, flints** Flints   **246 t' have** haue   **247 treble** double   **262 and rash** rash   **288 thus** this   **296.1** [*Exit*] *Horatio and Horatio*   **301 shortly** thereby   **302 Till** Tell

5.2. 5 Methought my thought   **6 bilboes** bilbo   **9 pall** fall   **17 unseal** vnfold   **19 Ah,** [eds.] A   **29 villainies** villaines   **30 Ere** Or   **43 "as"es** as sir   **52 Subscribed** Subscribe   **57, 68–80** [F; not in Q2]   **73 interim is** [eds.] *interim's* [F]   **78 court** [eds.] count [F]   **81** [and throughout] OSRIC *Cour.*   **82 humbly** humble   **93 Put your** your   **98 sultry** sully **for** or   **107 gentleman** [eds.] gentlemen   **109 feelingly** [Q4] fellingly   **114 dozy** [eds.] dazzie   **yaw** [eds.] raw   **141 his** [eds.] this   **142 him by** them, him, by them   **149 hangers** hanger   **156 carriages** carriage   **159 might be** be might   **162 impawned, as** [eds.] all [Q2] impon'd, as [F]   **174 purpose, I** purpose; I   **181–2 Yours, yours. 'A does** Yours doo's   **186 comply** so sir   **190 yeasty** histy   **191 fanned** [eds.] prophane [Q2] fond [F]   **winnowed** trennowed   **210 But thou** thou   **218 be now** be   **220 will come** well come   **238** [F; not in Q2]   **248 To keep** To till all   **252 foils. Come on** foiles.   **255 off** of   **261 bettered** better   **270 union** Vnice ["Onixe" in some copies]   **288 A touch, a touch,** I I   **302 afeard** sure   **316 Hamlet. Hamlet** *Hamlet*   **319 thy** [F, Q1] my   **327 murderous** [F; not in Q2]   **328 off** of   **thy union** [F, Q1] the Onixe   **345 ha 't** [eds.] hate [Q2] have 't [F]   **366 proud** prou'd   **369 FIRST AMBASSADOR** *Embas.*   **381 th' yet** yet   **385 forced** for no   **394 on** no

Passages contained only in F and omitted from Q2 are noted in the textual notes above. Listed below are the more important instances in which Q2 contains words, lines, and passages omitted in F.

1.1. 112–29 BERNARDO I think . . . countrymen
1.2. 58–60 wrung . . . consent
1.3. 9 perfume and
1.4. 17–38 This heavy-headed . . . scandal   **75–8** The very . . . beneath
2.1. 122 Come
2.2. 17 Whether . . . thus   **217** except my life   **363** very   **366** 'Sblood (and some other profanity passim)   **371** then   **444–5** as wholesome . . . fine   **521–2** of this   **589** Hum
3.2. 169–70 Where . . . there   **216–17** To . . . scope
3.4. 72–7 Sense . . . difference   **79–82** Eyes . . . mope   **168–72** That monster . . . put on   **174–7** the next . . . potency   **187** One word . . . lady   **209–17** There's . . . meet
4.1. 4 Bestow . . . while   **41–4** Whose . . . air
4.2. 4 But soft
4.3. 26–9 KING Alas . . . worm
4.4. 9–67 *Enter Hamlet* . . . worth
4.5. 33 Oho
4.7. 68–82 LAERTES My lord . . . graveness   **101–3** Th' escrimers . . . them   **115–24** There . . . ulcer
5.1. 154 There
5.2. 106–42 here is . . . unfellowed (replaced in F by "you are not ignorant of what excellence Laertes is at his weapon")   **154–5** HORATIO [*to Hamlet*] I knew . . . done   **193–207** *Enter a Lord* . . . lose, my lord (replaced in F by "You will lose this wager, my lord")   **222** Let be

Othello

Copy text: the First Folio. The adopted readings are from the quarto of 1622 [Q1], unless otherwise indicated; [eds.] means that the adopted reading was first proposed by some editor subsequent to the First Folio. Act and scene divisions are marked in the Folio with the exception of 2.3.

1.1. 1 Tush, never Neuer   **4 'Sblood, but** But   **16 And, in conclusion** [Q1; not in F]   **26 togaed** Tongued   **30 other** others   **34 God bless** blesse   **68 full** fall   **thick-lips** Thicks-lips   **74 changes** chances   **75** [and elsewhere] **lose** [eds.] loose   **81 Thieves, thieves, thieves** Theeues, Theeues   **83.1** *Brabantio above* [in F, printed as a speech

prefix to line 84]   **88 Zounds, sir** Sir [also at line 111]   **103 bravery** knauerie   **119 are now** are   **158 pains** apines   **161 sign. That** [eds.] signe) that   **186 night** might

1.2. 34 Duke Dukes   **50 carrack** Carract   **64 her!** [eds.] her   **69 darlings** Deareling   **89 I do** do

1.3. 1 There is There's   **these** this   **61 DUKE AND SENATORS** [*All* Q1] *Sen.*   **101 maimed** main'd   **108 upon** vp on   **DUKE** [Q1; not in F]   **109 overt** ouer   **112** [and elsewhere] **FIRST SENATOR** *Sen.*   **124 till** tell   **132 battles** Battaile   **fortunes** Fortune   **141 travels'** Trauellours   **143 rocks, and** Rocks   **heads** head   **145 other** others   **146 Anthropophagi** *Antropophague*   **147 Do grow** Grew   **149 thence** hence   **157 intentively** instinctiuely   **161 sighs** kisses   **203 grece** grise   **204 Into your favor** [Q1; not in F]   **222 piercèd** pierc'd   **ear** eares   **227 sovereign** more soueraigne   **233 couch** [eds.] Coach [F] Cooch [Q1]   **237 These** [eds.] This   **244 Nor I. I would not** Nor would I   **251 did love** loue   **267 me** [eds.] my   **273 instruments** Instrument   **281 DESDEMONA Tonight, my lord?** DUKE This night [Q1; not in F]   **285 With** And   **294 FIRST SENATOR** *Sen.*   **296.1 Exeunt** *Exit*   **302 matters** matter   **303 the the** the th   **329 beam** [eds.] braine [F] ballance [Q1]   **333–4 our unbitted** or vnbitted   **335 scion** [eds.] Seyen [F] syen [Q1]   **353 error** errors   **354 She . . . she must** [Q1; not in F]   **358 a supersubtle** super-subtle   **378–82 RODERIGO What . . . purse** [Q1; not in F]   **386 a snipe** Snpe   **389 He's** [Ha's Q1] She ha's   **396 ear** eares

2.1. 35 prays praye   **36 heaven** Heauens   **42 THIRD GENTLEMAN** *Gent.*   **44 arrivance** Arriuancie   **45 this the** *Gent.* [also at lines 61, 68, and 95]   **58 SECOND GENTLEMAN**   **72 clog** enclogge   **84 And . . . comfort** [Q1; not in F]   **90 tell me** tell   **94 the sea** Sea   **96 their** this   **107 list** leaue   **111 doors** doore   **156** [and elsewhere] **ne'er** neu'r   **158 such wight** *such wightes*   **170 gyve** [eds.] giue   **174 An** and   **175 courtesy** Curtsie   **176 clyster pipes** Cluster-pipes   **214.1 Exeunt** [eds.] *Exit*   **217 hither** thither   **230 again** a game   **240 fortune** Forune   **242–3 compassing** compasse   **244–5 finder out** finder   **245 occasions** occasion   **has** he's   **264 mutualities** mutabilities   **301 for wife** for wift   **308 rank** right   **309 nightcap** Night-Cape

2.2. 6 addiction [eds.] addition   **10 Heaven bless** Blesse

2.3. 27 stoup [eds.] stope   **38 unfortunate** infortunate   **52 lads** else   **57 to put** put to   **61, 71 God** heauen   **76 Englishman** Englishmen   **91 Then . . . auld** [*Then . . . owd* Q1] And take thy awl'd   **93 'Fore God** Why   **97 God's** heau'ns   **106 God forgive** Forgiue   **110 speak I** speake   **123 the** his   **138 s.d. Cry within**: Help! Help! [from Q1: "Helpe, helpe, within"]   **139 Zounds, you** You   **152 God's will** Alas   **153 Montano—sir** *Montano*   **156 God's will, Lieutenant, hold** Fie, fie Lieutenant   **158 Zounds,** I I   **161 sense of place** [eds.] place of sense   **184 wont be** wont to be   **201 Zounds, if I** If I once   **212 leagued** [eds.] league   **218 Thus** This   **227 the** then   **246 well now** well   **250 vile** vil'd   **255 God** Heauen   **260 thought** had thought   **283 Oh, God** Oh   **308 I'll** I   **311 denotement** [eds.] deuotement   **325–6 me here** me   **337 were't** were   **356 s.d. Enter Roderigo** [after line 356 in F]   **369 hast** hath   **372 By the Mass** Introth   **378 on;** [on Q1] on   **379 the while** [eds.] a while

3.1. 1 Musicians [eds.] *Musicians, and Clowne*   **5** [and at lines 7, 9, and 15] **A MUSICIAN** *Mus.*   **21 s.d. Exeunt** [eds.] *Exit*   **22 hear** heare me   **26 General's wife** Generall   **31 CASSIO Do, good my friend** [Q1; not in F]   **42 s.d. Exit** [at line 41 in F]   **52 To . . . front** [Q1; not in F]

3.3. 16 circumstance Circumstances   **41 you** your   **55 Yes, faith** I sooth   **66 or** on   **80 By'r Lady** Trust me   **103 you** he   **118 By heaven** Alas   **124 In** Of   **148 that all** that: All   **free to** free   **152 But some** Wherein   **160 oft** of   **161 wisdom then** wisdome   **175 By heaven, I'll** Ile   **183 fondly** [eds.] soundly [F] strongly [Q1]   **188 God** Heauen   **194 Is once** is   **196 blown** blow'd   **199 dances well** Dances   **216 God** Heauen   **218 keep't** [eds.] keepe [Q1] kept [F]   **225** [and elsewhere] **to** too   **230 I'faith** Trust me   **232 my** your   **249 disproportion** disproportions   **264 to hold** to   **275 qualities** Quantities   **276 human** humane   **289 of** to   **294 oh, then heaven mocks** Heauen mock'd   **301 Faith** Why   **305.1 Exit** [at line 304 in F]   **328 faith** but   **345 s.d. Enter Othello** [after "I did say so" in F]   **354 of her** in her   **385 remorse;** [remorce. Q1] remorse   **407 see, sir** see   **411 supervisor**

super-vision   **439 then laid** laid   **440 Over** ore   **sighed** sigh
kissed kisse   **441 Cried** cry   **455 any that was** [eds.] any, it was
468 mind perhaps minde   **471 Ne'er feels** [eds.] Neu'r keepes
3.4. 23 that the   **37 It yet** It   **56 faith** indeed   **77 I'faith** Indeed
79 God Heauen   **83 Heaven bless** Blesse   **88 can, sir** can
94–5 DESDEMONA I pray . . . Cassio. OTHELLO The handkerchief!
[Q1; not in F]   **99 I'faith** Insooth   **100 Zounds** Away   **142 s.d.** *Exit*
[after line 141 in F]   **164 that** the   **169.1** *Exit* [after line 168 in F]
172 I'faith Indeed   **182 friend.** [eds.] Friend,   **183 absence** [eds.]
absence, [Q1] Absence: [F]   **188 by my faith** in good troth
4.1. 32 Faith Why   **36 Zounds, that's** that's   **45 work** workes   **52 No,**
forbear [Q1; not in F]   **72 couch** [Coach Q1] Cowch;   **79 unsuiting**
[Q1 corrected] vnfitting [Q1 uncorrected] **resulting** [F]   **81 'scuse**
scuses   **97 clothes** Cloath   **103 conster** conserue   **105 you now** you
109 power dowre   **113 a woman** woman   **114 i'faith** indeed
121 Do you triumph, Roman? Do ye triumph, Romaine?
122 marry her marry   **125 win** [eds.] winnes   **126 Faith** Why   **shall**
marry marry   **133 beckons** becomes   **138 by this hand, she** [Q1;
not in F]   **166 Faith, I** I   **168 Faith** Yes   **215.1** [after line 212 in F]
218 God save Saue   **241 By my troth** Trust me   **254 Truly, an** Truely
287 denote deonte [F uncorrected] deuote [F corrected]
4.2. 32 Nay May   **33 knees** knee   **35 But not the words** [Q1; not in F]
51 kinds kind   **56 A** The   **66 Ay, there** [eds.] I heere   **71 ne'er**
neuer   **83 Impudent strumpet** [Q1; not in F]   **96 keep** [eds.] keepes
s.d. *Enter Emilia* [after line 94 in F]   **155 O God** Alas   **162 them in**
[eds.] them: or   **174 And . . . you** [Q1; not in F]   **177 you to** to
190 Faith, I I   **for** and   **201 By this hand** Nay   **232 takes** taketh
236 of [Q1; not in F]
4.3. 10.1 *Exit* [after line 9 in F]   **22 favor in them** fauour   **25 faith**
Father   **26 before thee** before   **35 Barbary** *Braberie*   **43 sighing**
[eds.] *singing* [F corrected] *sining* [F uncorrected]   **73 Good troth**
Introth   **74 By my troth** Introth   **78 Uds pity** why   **107 God** Heauen
5.1. 1 bulk Barke   **22 Be't** But   **hear** heard   **36 Forth** For   **50 Did** Do
91 Oh, heaven Yes, 'tis   **106 out o'** o'   **113 'Las, what's . . . What's**
Alas, what is . . . What is   **116 dead** quite dead   **126 Faugh! Fie** Fie
5.2. 34 heaven Heauens   **37 say so** say   **56 Yes, presently** Presently
61 Then Lord O Heauen   **96 here** high   **104 Should** Did
108 s.d. Enter Emilia [after line 108 in F]   **121 Oh, Lord** Alas
131 heard heare   **148 Nay, had** had   **225 Oh, God! Oh, heavenly**
God Oh Heauen! oh heauenly Powres   **226 Zounds** Come
248 have here haue   **317 not. Here** [not: here Q1] not) heere
357 Indian Iudean

King Lear

Copy text: the First Folio, except for those 300 or so lines found only in
the first quarto of 1608 [Q1]. Unless otherwise indicated, adopted readings are from the corrected state (Qb) of Q1. A few readings are supplied
from the second quarto of 1619 [Q2]. All readings subsequent to 1619
are marked as supplied by"eds."Act and scene divisions are as marked
in F, except that F does not mark 2.3 and 2.4, and omits 4.3 entirely, so
that 4.4 is marked"Scena Tertia"and similarly with 4.5 and 4.6 (though
4.7 is marked"Scena Septima").
1.1. 5 equalities qualities   **20–2 account . . . yet** [eds.] account, though
. . . for: yet   **35 liege** Lord   **55 words** word   **66 issue** issues
68 Speak [Q1; not in F]   **74 possesses** professes   **85 interessed**
[eds.] interest   **104** [Q1; not in F]   **110 mysteries** [eds.] miseries [F]
mistresse [Q1]   **135 turns** turne   **156 as a** as   **157 nor** nere
161 LEAR Kear   **162 KENT** Lent   **165 CORNWALL** [eds.] Cor.   **166 the**
thy   **173 sentence** sentences   **191 GLOUCESTER** Cor.   **217 best**
object obiect   **229 well** will   **252 respects of fortune** respect and
Fortunes   **272 Ye** [eds.] The   **285 shame them** with shame
286.1 Exeunt [eds.] Exit   **293 hath** not hath   **306 hit** sit
1.2. 1 [and elsewhere] EDMUND Bast.   **21 top** [eds.] to'   **56 waked**
wake   **97–9 EDMUND Nor . . . earth** [Q1; not in F]   **134 Fut, I** I
136 Edgar [Q1; not in F]   **137 and pat** [Q1] Pat [F] and out [Q1]
147–55 as . . . come, [Q1; not in F]   **182 s.d.** [at line 181 in F]

1.3. 3 [and elsewhere] OSWALD [eds.] *Ste.*   **17–21** [Q1; not in F]
26–7 I would . . . speak [Q1; not in F]   **28 very** [Q1; not in F]
1.4. 1 well will   **31 canst** canst thou   **43.1** *Enter steward* [eds.; after
line 44 in F]   **50 daughter** Daughters   **76.1** *Enter steward* [eds.;
after line 77 in F]   **96 KENT** Lear   **Fool** my Boy   **135 Dost** Do'st thou
138–53 That . . . snatching [Q1; not in F]   **158 crown** Crownes
175 fools Foole   **195 nor crumb** not crum   **214 it had** it's had
229–32 [Q1; not in F]   **255 Oh . . . come** [Q1; not in F]   **303 Yea . . .**
this [Q1; not in F]   **343 You're** Your are   **attasked** at task
1.5. 0.1 *Kent Kent, Gentleman*   **51 s.d.** *Exit* Exeunt
2.1. 2 you your   **19.1** [after line 18 in F]   **39 stand 's** stand   **69 I should**
should I   **70 ay, though** though   **78 I never got him** [Q1; not in F]
78 s.d. [at line 76 in F, after"seeke it"]   **79 why** wher   **87 strange**
news strangenesse   **100 spoil** wast   **122 poise** prize   **125 least**
thought best though   **132** *Flourish. Exeunt* [eds.] *Exeunt. Flourish*
2.2. 22 clamorous clamours   **45 an** if   **52 What's** What is   **66 you'll**
you will   **78 Bring . . . their** Being . . . the   **79 Renege** Reuenge
80 gale gall   **83 Smile** Smoile   **84 an** if   **101 take't** take it   **109 flick-**
ering flicking   **124 dread** dead   **127 their** there   **132 respect** respects
142.1 [at line 140 in F]   **144–8 His . . . with** [Q1; not in F]   **146 con-**
temned'st [eds.] temnest [Q1]   **148 King** King his Master, needs
153 [Q1; not in F]   **154 Come . . . away** [assigned in F to Cornwall]
good [Q1; not in F]   **154.1** *Exeunt* [eds.] Exit   **155 Duke's** Duke
2.3. 18 sheepcotes Sheeps-Coates
2.4. 2 messenger Messengers   **9 man's** man   **18–19** [Q1; not in F]
30 panting painting   **33 whose** those   **56 Hysterica** [eds.] *Historica*
62 the the the   **74 have** hause   **128 you** your   **130 mother's** Mother
183 s.d. [after line 182 in F]   **185.1** [at line 183 in F, after"Stockes"]
187 fickle fickly   **190 s.d.** [after line 188 in F]   **213 hot-blooded**
hot-bloodied   **285 s.d.** [after"weeping"in line 286 in F]   **297 s.d.** [after
line 296 in F]   **298 Whither** Whether [also in line 299]   **302 bleak** high
3.1. 7–15 tears . . . all [Q1; not in F]   **10 outstorm** [eds.] outscorne [Q1]
30–42 [Q1; not in F]
3.2. 3 drowned drown   **38.1** [after line 36 in F]   **50 pother** pudder
85–6 [these lines follow line 92 in F]
3.3. 17 for 't for it
3.4. 7 skin. So 'tis skinso: 'tis   **10 thy** they   **12 This** the   **27 s.d.** [at
line 26 in F]   **31 looped** lop'd   **38.1** *Enter Fool* [F, after line 36:
"*Enter Edgar, and Foole*"]   **44.1** [after line 36 in F]   **46 blows the cold**
wind blow the windes   **51 through fire** though Fire   **52 ford** Sword
57, 58 Bless Blisse   **90 deeply** deerely   **99 sessa** [eds.] *Sesey*
112.1 [after line 108 in F]   **114 fiend** [Q1; not in F]   **115 till the** at
116 squinnies [eds.] squints [F] squemes [Q1]   **134 stock-punished**
stockt, punish'd   **hath had** hath   **173 in th'** into th'
3.5. 11 he which hee   **26 dearer** deere
3.6. 5.1 *Exit* [at line 3 in F]   **17–55** [Q1; not in F]   **21 justicer** [eds.]
Iustice [Q1]   **22 Now** [Q2] no [Q1]   **24 eyes at trial, madam?** eyes,
at tral madam   **25 burn** [eds.] broome [Q1]   **34 cushions** [eds.]
cushings [Q1]   **36 robèd** robbed   **51 joint** ioyne [Q1]   **53 on**
[eds.] an [Q1]   **67 mongrel grim** Mongrill, Grim   **68 lym** [eds.]
Hym   **69 Bobtail tike or trundle-tail** Or Bobtaile tight, or Troudle
taile   **73 Sessa** sese   **76 makes** make   **85.1** [after line 80 in F]
97–101 KENT Oppressèd . . . behind [Q1; not in F]   **101 GLOUCESTER**
[not in F]   **102–15** [Q1; not in F]
3.7. 10 festinate [eds.] festiuate   **18 lord's dependents** Lords,
dependents   **23 s.d. Exeunt** [eds.] Exit [at line 22 in F]   **61 rash**
sticke   **66 dern** sterne   **75 FIRST SERVANT** Seru. [also Seru. or Ser. at
lines 79, 82, 84]   **83** [F provides a stage direction:"Killes him"]
102–10 [Q1; not in F]   **102 SECOND SERVANT** Seruant [and called"1 Ser"
at line 106 in Q1]   **103 THIRD SERVANT** 2 Seruant [Q1]   **107 Roguish**
[Qa; not in Qb]   **109 THIRD SERVANT** 2 Ser.   **110.1 Exeunt** Exit
4.1. 2 flattered. To be worst flattered to be worst,   **41 Then . . . gone**
Get thee away   **57–62 Five . . . master** [Q1; not in F]   **60 Flibberti-**
gibbet [eds.] Stiberdigebit [Q1]   **60–1 mopping and mowing** [eds.]
Mobing, & Mohing [Q1]
4.2. 0.1 *Bastard* Bastard, and Steward   **2 s.d.** steward [Q1; placed at
scene beginning in F]   **30 whistling** whistle   **32–51 I fear . . . deep**

[Q1; not in F]   **33 its** [eds.] ith [Q1]   **48 these** [eds.] this [Q1]
54–60 that . . . so [Q1; not in F]   **58 to threat** thereat [Q1 corrected]
61 shows seemes   **63–9, 70** [Q1; not in F]   **76 thereat enraged**
threat-enrag'd   **80 justicers** [Q1 corrected] Iustices
4.3. 1–57 [scene omitted in F]   **11 sir** [eds.] say [Q1]   **16 strove** [eds.]
streme [Q1]   **20 seemed** [eds.] seeme [Q1]   **22 dropped. In** dropt in
32 then her, then   **44 benediction, turned her** benediction turnd
her,   **57 s.d. Exeunt** [eds.] Exit [Q1]
4.4 [F reads *"Scena Tertia"*]   **3 fumiter** [eds.] femiter [Q1] Fenitar [F]
6 century Centery   **18 distress** desires   **28 right** Rite
4.5 [F reads *"Scena Quarta"*]   **8 letters** Letter   **23 Something** Some
things   **27 oeillades** [eds.] Eliads   **41 meet him** meet
4.6 [F reads *"Scena Quinta"*]   **17 walk** walk'd   **57 summit** Somnet
66–7 strangeness. / Upon . . . cliff what [eds.] strangenesse, /Vpon
. . . Cliffe. What   **71 enridgèd** enraged   **83 coining** crying
97 white the white   **124 they're** they are   **161 thine** thy
164 Through Thorough   **small** great   **165 Plate sin** [eds.] Place
sinnes   **197 Ay . . . dust** [Q1; not in F]   **205 one** a   **218.1 Exit** [after
"moved on" in line 218 in F]   **235 Durst** Dar'st   **238 'cagion** 'casion
263–4 not. / To not / To   **269 done if . . . conqueror. Then** [eds.] *done.*
If . . . Conqueror then   **274 and . . . venture** [Q1; not in F]   **275 indistinguished** indinguish'd   **288 s.d. Drum afar off** [after line 286 in F]
4.7. 25 doubt not doubt   **25–6 CORDELIA Very . . . there** [Q1; not in
F]   **33 warring** iarring   **34–7 To stand . . . helm** [Q1; not in F]
59 hands hand   **60 No, sir** [Q1; not in F]   **83–4 and . . . lost** [Q1; not
in F]   **91–103** [Q1; not in F]
5.1. 12–14 [Q1; not in F]   **18 me not** not   **19–20** [Q1; not in F]
24–9 Where . . . nobly [Q1; not in F]   **35** [Q1; not in F]
41 s.d. Exeunt . . . armies [after line 39 in F]   **48 love** loues
5.3. 13 and hear poor rogues and heare (poore Rogues)   **39–40** [Q1; not
in F]   **49 and appointed guard** [Q1 corrected; not in F]   **56–61 At . . .
place** [Q1; not in F]   **57 We** [Q1 corrected] mee [Q1 uncorrected]
59 sharpness [Q1 corrected] sharpes [Q1 uncorrected]   **72 GONERIL**
Alb.   **85 attaint** arrest   **86 sister** Sisters   **87 bar** [eds.] bare   **100 he is**
hes   **105 EDMUND A herald, ho, a herald** [Q1; not in F]   **105.1 Enter a**
Herald [after line 104 in F]   **106 ALBANY** [not in F]   **112 CAPTAIN**
Sound, trumpet [Q1; not in F]   **118 EDMUND Sound** [Q1; not in F]
124–5 lost, / By . . . canker-bit. lost / By . . . Treasons tooth: bare-gnawne,
and Canker-bit,   **132 the** my priuiledge, The   **135 Despite** Despise
146 tongue some say of tongue (some say) of   **149 those** these
151 scarcely scarely   **153.1 Fight** [eds.] Fights. ["*Alarums. Fights*" is
opposite "Saue him, saue him," in line 154 in F.]   **155 arms** Warre
158 stopple stop   **163 GONERIL** *Bast.*   **163 s.d. Exit** [at line 162 after
"'t" in F]   **208–25 This . . . slave** [Q1; not in F]   **217 him** [eds.] me
[Q1]   **241.1** [after line 234 in F]   **255 The captain** [Q1; not in F]
262 you your   **280 CAPTAIN** *Gent.*   **282 them** him   **294 You are** [eds.]
Your are [F] You'r [Q1]   **299.1** [after "to him" in line 299 in F]
320 rack wracke

The above textual notes list all instances in which material not in F is
included from Q1. To enable the reader to compare further the F and Q1
texts, a list is provided here of material not in Q1 that is to be found in F.
There are some 100 lines in all.
1.1. 40–5 while . . . now   **49–50** Since . . . state   **64–5** and . . . rivers
83–5 to whose . . . interested   **88–9** LEAR Nothing? CORDELIA Nothing
165 ALBANY, CORNWALL Dear sir, forbear.
1.2. 112–17 This . . . graves   **169–75** I pray . . . brother
1.4. 260 ALBANY Pray . . . patient   **273** Of . . . you   **321–33** This . . .
unfitness
2.4. 6 KENT No, my lord   **21** KENT By Juno . . . ay   **45–54** FOOL Winter's . . .
year   **96–7** GLOUCESTER Well . . . man   **101–2** Are they . . . Fiery? The
139–44 LEAR Say . . . blame   **298–9** CORNWALL Whither . . . horse
3.1. 22–9 Who . . . furnishings
3.2. 79–96 FOOL This . . . time. *Exit*
3.4. 17–18 In . . . endure   **26–7** In . . . sleep   **37–8** Fathom . . . Tom
3.6. 12–14 FOOL No . . . him   **85** FOOL And . . . noon
4.1. 6–9 Welcome . . . blasts

4.2. 26 Oh, the . . . man
4.6. 165–70 Plate . . . lips
5.2. 11 GLOUCESTER And . . . too
5.3. 78 Dispose . . . thine   **91** GONERIL An interlude   **147** What . . . delay
226 ALBANY Speak, man   **316–17** Do you . . . look there

Macbeth

Copy text: the First Folio. Act and scene divisions follow the Folio text,
except that 5.8 is not marked in the Folio.
1.1. 9 SECOND WITCH *All*   **10 THIRD WITCH** [not in F]   **11 ALL** [at line 9
in F]
1.2. 1 [and elsewhere] DUNCAN *King*   **13 gallowglasses** Gallowgrosses
14 quarrel Quarry   **21 ne'er** neu'r   **26 thunders break** Thunders
1.3. 32 Weird weyward [elsewhere in F spelled "weyard"]   **39 Forres**
Soris   **97 death. As** death, as   **98 Came** Can   **111 lose** loose
1.4. 1 Are Or
1.5. 1 [and elsewhere] LADY MACBETH *Lady*   **12 lose** loose   **47 it** hit
1.6. 4 martlet Barlet   **9 most** must
1.7. 6 shoal Schoole   **48 do** no
2.1. 56 strides sides   **57 sure** sowre   **58 way they** they may
2.2. 13.1 [at line 8 in F, after "die"]
2.3. 41.1 [after line 40 in F]   **142 nea'er** neere
3.1. 76 MURDERERS *Murth.*   **116 BOTH MURDERERS** *Murth.* [also at line
141]   **142.1 Exeunt** [at line 144 in F]
3.3. 7 and end
3.4. 79 time times   **122.1 Exeunt** Exit
3.6. 24 son Sonnes   **38 the** their
4.1. 34 cauldron Cawdron   **38.1 to** and   **59 germens** Germaine
93 Dunsinane Dunsmane   **94 s.d. Descends** Descend   **98 Birnam**
Byrnan [also spelled "Byrnam" at line 93 and "Birnan," "Byrnane,"
and "Birnane" in Act 5]   **119 eighth** eight
4.2. 1 [and throughout] LADY MACDUFF *Wife*   **22 none** moue
70–1 ones . . . methinks, ones / To fright you thus. Me thinkes
80 s.d. Enter Murderers [after "What are these faces" in F]
81 [and throughout scene] FIRST MURDERER *Mur.*   **84 shag-haired**
shagge-ear'd
4.3. 4 downfall'n downfall   **15 deserve** discerne   **35 Fare** Far
108 accurst accust   **124 detraction, here** detraction. Heere   **134 thy**
they   **144 essay** assay   **146.1** [after "amend" in F]   **161 not** nor
237 tune time
5.1. 38 fear who feare? who
5.3. 41 Cure her Cure   **54 pristine** pristiue   **57 senna** Cyme
62.1 Exeunt [at line 64 in F]
5.4. 16 SIWARD *Sey.*

Antony and Cleopatra

Copy text: the First Folio. Act and scene divisions, missing in the Folio,
are editorially supplied.
1.1. 41 On One   **52 whose** who
1.2. 4 charge change   **41 fertile** fore-tell   **64 Alexas** [printed in F as
s.p.]   **83 Saw** Saue   **90 Alexas** *Alexias*   **93** [and through line 118]
FIRST MESSENGER *Messen.* (or *Mess.*)   **116 minds** windes   **119 ho**
how   **120 SECOND MESSENGER** 1. *Mes.*   **121 THIRD MESSENGER** 2.
Mes.   **124 FOURTH MESSENGER** 3. *Mes.*   **126 FOURTH MESSENGER**
Mes.   **137.1 Enter Enobarbus** [after "hatch," line 137, in F]   **144 occasion** an occasion   **162 travel** Trauaile   **186 leave** loue   **191 Hath**
Haue   **200 hair** heire   **202 place is** places   **requires** require
1.3. 2 who's Whose   **20 What, says** What sayes   **43 services** Seruicles
63 vials Violles   **80 blood. No more.** blood no more?   **82 by**
my by
1.4. 3 Our One   **8 Vouchsafed** vouchsafe   **9 abstract** abstracts
34 FIRST MESSENGER *Mes.*   **44 deared** fear'd   **46 lackeying** lacking
48 SECOND MESSENGER *Mes.*   **57 wassails** Vassailes   **58 Modena**
Medena   **59 Pansa** *Pausa*   **77 we** me

1.5. 3 **mandragora** *Mandragoru* 5 **time** time: 35.1 *Alexas Alexas from Caesar* 52 **dumbed** dumbe 53, **What, was** What was 64 **man** mans

2.1. 2 **[and throughout scene]** MENAS *Mene.* 22 **joined** ioyne 39 **ne'er** neere 42 **warred** wan'd 44–5 **greater. . . . all,** greater, . . . all:

2.2. 77 **Alexandria; you** Alexandria you 113 **soldier only. Speak** Souldier, onely speak 128 **so** say 129 **reproof** proofe 180.1 *Exeunt Exit omnes Manent Manet* 204 **lovesick . . . The** Loue-sicke. With them the 214 **glow** gloue 216 **gentlewomen** Gentlewoman 233 **heard** hard

2.3. 23 **afeard** a feare 25 **thee; . . . to thee.** thee no more but: when to thee, 31 **away** alway 32 **[and elsewhere]** Ventidius *Ventigius* 41 s.d. *Enter Ventidius* [after "Ventigius," line 41, in F]

2.4. 6 **th' Mount** Mount 9 MAECENAS, AGRIPPA *Both*

2.5. 2 ALL *Omnes* 10 **river. There** Riuer there 11 **off, I** off. I 12 **finned** fine 23 s.d. *Enter a Messenger* [after "Italy," line 23, in F] 28 **him, there** him. / There 44 **is** 'tis 85 s.d. *Enter . . . again* [after "sir" line 85, in F]

2.6. 0.1 *Menas* [listed after *Agrippa* in F] 16 **th'all-honored** all-honor'd 19 **is** his 39 CAESAR, ANTONY, LEPIDUS *Omnes* 42–3 **impatience. Though . . . telling,** impatience: though . . . telling. 58 **composition** composition 67 **meanings** meaning 71 **more of** more 83 CAESAR, ANTONY, LEPIDUS *All* 83.1 *Manent Manet*

2.7. 1 **their** th'their 4 **colored** Conlord 39 s.d. *whispers in 's ear* [at line 41 in F] 93 **is** he is 101 **grows** grow 113 **bear** beate 115 BOY [not in F] 119 ALL [not in F] 122 **off. Our** of our 126 **Splits** Spleet's 130 **father's** Father 132 MENAS [not in F]

3.1. 5 **[and throughout scene]** SILIUS *Romaine* 8 **[and elsewhere] whither** whether

3.2. 10 AGRIPPA *Ant.* 16 **figures** Figure 49 **full** the full 60 **wept** weepe

3.3. 2 s.d. *Enter . . . before* [after "sir," line 2, in F] 19 **looked'st** look'st

3.4. 8 **them,** then 9 **took't** look't 24 **yours** your 30 **Your** You 38 **has** he's

3.5. 13 **world** would **hast** hadst **chops** chaps 15 **grind the one** grind

3.6. 13 **he there** hither **the kings** the King 30 **being, that** being that, 62 **obstruct** abstract 73 **Adallas** *Adullas* 74 **Manchus** *Mauchus* 76 **Comagene** Comageat **Polemon** *Polemen* 77 **Lycaonia** Licoania

3.7. 4 **it is** it it 14 **Photinus, an** *Photinus* an 19 s.d. *Canidius Camidias* [also spelled "*Camidius*" in this scene and elsewhere] 21 **Brundusium** Brandusium 23 **Toryne** Troine 29 **[and elsewhere]** CANIDIUS *Cam.* 36 **muleteers** Militers 52 **Actium** Action 57 **impossible;** impossible 67.1 *Exeunt exit* 70 **leader's** led Leaders leade 73 CANIDIUS *Ven.* 80 **Well I** Well, I 82 **in** with

3.8. 6 s.d. *Exeunt exit*

3.9. 4 s.d. *Exeunt exit*

3.10. 0.5. *Enobarbus Enobarbus and Scarus* 14 **June** Inne 28 **he** his

3.11. 6 ALL *Omnes* 19 **that** them 46 **seize** cease 50 **led** lead 57 **tow** stowe 58 **Thy** The

3.12. 0.1. *Dolabella Dollabello* 13 **lessens** Lessons

3.13. 26 **caparisons** Comparisons 34 **alike. That** alike, that 55 **Caesar** *Caesars* 74 **deputation** disputation 76 **kneel / Till** kneele. / Tell him, 94 s.d. *Enter a Servant* [after "him," in line 94, in F] 104 **This** the 114–15 **eyes, / In . . . filth** eyes / In . . . filth, 133 s.d. *Enter . . . Thidias* [after "whipped," in line 133, in F] 140 **whipped . . . Henceforth** whipt. For following him, henceforth 165 **smite** smile 168 **discandying** discandering 171 **sits** sets 202 **on** in 204 s.d. *Exit Exeunt*

4.2. 1 *Domitius Domitian* 20 ALL *Omnes*

4.3. 8 THIRD 1 25, 31 ALL *Omnes*

4.4. 5 **too** too, *Anthony* 6 ANTONY [not in F, or mistakenly placed in line 5 as part of Cleopatra's speech] 8 CLEOPATRA [not in F] 24 CAPTAIN *Alex.* 32–3 **compliment . . . Now** Complement, Ile leaue thee. / Now

4.5. 1, 3, 6 SOLDIER *Eros* 17 **Dispatch.—Enobarbus** Dispatch *Enobarbus* 17.1 *Exeunt Exit*

4.6. 37–8 **do 't . . . I** doo't. I feele / I

4.7. 3 s.d. *Exeunt Exit* 8 s.d. [after "heads," line 6, in F]

4.8. 2 **gests** guests 18 **My** Mine 23 **favoring** sauouring

4.12. 3 s.d. *Alarum . . . fight* [at 0.1 in F] 4 **augurers** Auguries 21 **spanieled** pannelled

4.13. 10 **death. To** death to'

4.14. 4 **towered** toward 10 **dislimns** dislimes 19 **Caesar** *Caesars* 104 **ho** how 119 DERCETUS *Decre.* 145.1 *Exeunt Exit*

4.15. 26–7 **me. If . . . operation,** me, if . . . operation. 56 **lived the** liued. The 78 **e'en** in 96.1 *off of*

5.1. 0.1 *Maecenas Menas* 3.1 *Dercetus Decretas* 5, 13, 19 DERCETUS *Dec.* 5 **Dercetus** *Decretas* 26 **you sad, friends?** you sad Friends, 28, 31 AGRIPPA *Dol.* 48.1 [after "says," line 51, in F] 54 **intents desires** intents, desires, 59 **live** leaue

5.2. 26 **dependency** dependacie 35 [F repeats s.p. *Pro.*] 55 **varletry** Varlotarie 69.1 [after "to him" in F] 80 **O, the** o'th' 86 **autumn 'twas** *Anthony* it was 102 **success but** successe: But 103 **smites suites** 144 **seal** seele 156 **soulless villain** Soule-lesse, Villain 178 **merits in our name,** merits, in our name 207 s.d. *Exit* [at line 206 in F] 216 **Ballad** Ballads 223 **my** mine 228 **Cydnus** *Cidrus* 318 **awry** away 319.1 *in in, and Dolabella* 342–3 **diadem . . . mistress;** Diadem; . . . Mistris

The Winter's Tale

Copy text: the First Folio. Characters' names are groups at the heads of scenes throughout the play. Act and scene divisions are as marked in the Folio.

The Names of the Actors [printed in F at the end of the play] ARCHIDAMUS [after *Autoclycus* in F]

1.1. 9 **us, we** vs: we

1.2. 104 **And** A 121 **hast** has't 137–8 **be?— / Affection, thy** be / Affection? thy 148 **What . . . brother** [assigned in F to Leontes] 151–3 **its folly, . . . Its tenderness, . . . bosoms!** it's folly? . . . It's tendernesse? . . . bosomes? 158 **do** do's 202–3 **powerful, think it, . . . south. Be** powrefull: thinke it: . . . South, be 208 **you, they** you 253 **forth. In . . . lord,** forth in . . . (my Lord.) 275 **hobbyhorse** Holy-Horse 386 **How? Caught** How caught 461 **off. Hence!** off, hence:

2.1. 2 **[and throughout scene]** FIRST LADY *Lady* 91 **fedarie** Federarie

2.2. 32–3 **me. / If . . . blister** me, / If . . . blister.

2.3. 2 **thus, mere weakness. If** thus: meere weaknesse, if 39 **What Who** 61 **good, so** good so,

3.2. 10 **Silence** [printed in F as a s.d.] 10.1–2 *Hermione, as to her trial . . . Ladies* [at start of scene in F, as generally with the s.d. in this play] 33 **Who** Whom 99 **Starred** Star'd 156 **woo** woe

3.3. 64 **scar'd** scarr'd 116 **made** mad

4.2. 13 **thee. Thou,** thee, thou

4.3. 1 AUTOLYCUS [not in F] 7 **on** *an* 10 **With heigh, with heigh** With heigh 38 **currants** Currence

4.4. 12 **Digest it** Digest 13 **swoon** sworne 60 **a fire** o'fire 83 **bastards. Of** bastards) of 93 **scion** Sien 98 **your** you 160 **out** on't 218 AUTOLYCUS [not in F] 244 **kilnhole** kill-hole 297 AUTOLYCUS [in F, appears at line 298] 299 **Whither** Whether [and similarly throughout song] 310 **gentleman** Gent. 316 **cape** Crpe 339 **square** squire 355 **reply, at least** reply at least, 361 **who** whom 421 **acknowledged** acknowledge 425 **who** whom 430 **see** neuer see 441 **hoop** hope 470 **your** my 473 **sight as yet, I fear.** sight, as yet I feare; 485–6 **fancy. If . . . obedient,** fancie, if . . . obedient: I 503 **our** her 614 **could** would **filed** fill'd **off** of 644 **flayed** fled 708 **know not** know 738 **to** at 833 s.d. *Exeunt* [at 845 in F]

5.1. 6 **Whilst** Whilest [also at line 169] 59 **Where . . . appear** (Where we Offendors now appeare) 61 **just** just such 75 **I have done** [assigned in F to Cleomenes] 84 s.d. *Gentleman Seruant* 85 **[and through line 110]** GENTLEMAN *Ser.* 114 s.d. *Exit* [after "us" in line 115 in F] 160 **his, parting** his parting

5.2. 113 s.d. *Exeunt Exit*

5.3. 18 **Lonely** Louely 67 **fixture** fixure

The Tempest

Copy text: the First Folio. Characters' names are grouped at the heads of scenes throughout. Act and scene divisions are as marked in the Folio.

Names of the Actors [printed in F at the end of the play]

1.1. 8.1 Ferdinand *Ferdinando*   **34 s.d. *Exeunt*** *Exit*   **36 [and elsewhere] wi' the** with   **38.1** [at line 37 in F]

1.2. 99 exact, like exact. Like   **166 steaded much.** steeded much,   **174 princes** Princesse   **201 bowsprit** Bore-spritt   **213 me. The** me the   **230 Bermudas** *Bermoothes*   **284 she** he   **288 service. Thou** service, thou   **330 forth at** for that   **377.5, 399.1 Ariel's** Ariel (or Ariell)   **385 s.d. *Burden, dispersedly*** [before "Hark, hark!" in line 384 in F]   **387** [F provides a speech prefix, *Ar.*]   **400 ARIEL** [not in F]

2.1. 38 ANTONIO *Seb.*   **39 SEBASTIAN** *Ant.*   **183 mettle** mettal   **232 throes** throwes

2.2. 9 mow moe   **116 spirits** sprights

3.1. 2 sets set

3.2. 51–2 isle; / From me he Isle / From me, he   **122 scout** *cout*

3.3. 15 travel trauaile   **17.1–2 Solemn . . . invisible** [after "they are fresh" in F, and followed by the s.d. at line 19, *Enter . . . depart*]   **28 me** me?   **29 islanders?** Islands;   **33 human** humaine   **65 plume** plumbe

4.1. 9 off of   **13 gift** guest   **25 love as 'tis now, the** loue, as 'tis now the   **61 vetches** Fetches   **68 poll-clipped** pole-clipt   **74 Her** here   **110 CERES** [not in F]   **124.1–2** [after line 127 in F]   **163.1 *Exeunt*** *Exit*   **193 s.d. *Enter Ariel . . . etc.*** [after "on this line" in F, and followed by *Enter* Caliban . . . *all wet*]   **193 them on** on them   **232 Let't** let's

5.1. 16 run runs   **60 boiled** boile   **72 Didst** Did   **75 entertained** entertaine   **82 lies** ly   **88 ARIEL** [not in F]   **111 Whe'er** Where   **236 horrible,** horrible.   **238 her** our   **249 business. At** businesse, at   **250 Which . . . single** (Which shall be shortly single)   **260 coraggio** Corasio

The Sonnets

Copy text: the quarto of 1609 [Q].

2.4 tattered totter'd [also at 26.11]   **2.14 cold** could   **6.4 beauty's** beautits   **8.10 Strikes** Strike [in some copies]   **12.4 all** or

13.7 Yourself You selfe   **15.8 wear** were   **17.12 meter** miter   **17.14 twice, in it and** twise in it, and   **18.10 [and elsewhere] lose** loose   **19.3 jaws** yawes   **20.2 Hast** Haste   **22.3 furrows** forrwes   **23.6 rite** right   **23.14 with** wit   wit wiht   **24.1 stelled** steeld   **25.9 fight** worth   **26.12 thy** their [also at 27.10, 35.8 (twice), 37.7, 43.11, 45.12, 46.3, 46.8, 46.13, 46.14, 69.5, 70.6, 85.3, 128.11, 128.14]   **27.2 travel** trauaill   **28.12 gild'st** guil'st   **28.14 strength** length   **31.8 thee** there   **34.2 travel** trauaile   **34.12 cross** losse   **34.13 sheds** sheeds   **38.2 pour'st** poor'st   **38.3 too** to   **39.12 doth** dost   **41.7 woos** woes   **42.10 losing** loosing   **44.12 attend time's** attend, times   **44.13 naught** naughts   **45.9 life's** liues   **46.9 'cide** side   **46.12 the** he [in some copies]   **47.2 other.** other,   **47.4 smother,** smother;   **47.11 no nor** nor   **50.6 dully** duly   **51.10 perfect'st** perfects   **55.1 monuments** monument   **56.3 [and elsewhere] today** too daie   **58.7 patience-tame to suffrance** patience tame, to sufferance   **59.6 hundred** hundreth   **59.11 whe'er** where   **61.14 off** of   too to   **62.10 chapped** chopt   **63.5 traveled** trauaild   **65.12 of** or   **67.6 seeming** seeing   **69.3 due** end   **69.14 soil** solye   **71.13 Lest** Least [also at 72.1, 72.9, and elsewhere]   **73.4 ruined** rn'wd   **choirs** quiers   **76.7 tell** fel   **77.1 wear** were   **77.10 blanks** blacks   **82.8 these** the   **83.7 too** to   **88.8 losing** loosing   **90.11 shall** stall   **91.9 better** bitter   **93.5 there** their   **98.11 were** weare   **99.4 dwells** dwells?   **99.9 One** Our   **99.13 ate** eate   **102.8 her** his   **106.12 skill** still   **111.1 with** wish   **112.14 are** y'are   **113.6 latch** lack   **113.13 more, replete with** more repleat, with   **113.14 mine eye** mine   **116** [numbered 119 in Q]   **117.10 surmise accumulate;** surmise, accumilate   **118.5 ne'er-cloying** nere cloying   **118.10 were not, grew** were, not grew   **119.4 losing** loosing   **121.11 bevel.** beuel   **125.6 rent, rent** rent   **125.7 sweet forgoing** sweet; Forgoing   **126.2 sickle hour;** sickle, hower: **126.8 minutes** mynuit   **127.2 were** weare   **127.10 brows** eyes   **129.9 Mad** Made   **129.10 quest to have,** quest, to haue   **129.11 proved, a** proud and   **132.6 the east** th'East   **132.9 mourning** morning   **138.12 to have** t'haue   **140.5 were** weare   **144.6 side** [adopted from *The Passionate Pilgrim*] sight   **144.9 fiend** [adopted from *The Passionate Pilgrim*] finde   **146.2 Thrall to** My sinfull earth   **147.7 approve** approoue   **153.14 eyes** eye

Glossary

Shakespearean Words and Meanings of Frequent Occurrence

A

'A: he (unaccented form).

Abate: lessen, diminish; blunt, reduce; deprive; bar, leave out of account, except; depreciate; humble.

Abuse (N): insult, error, misdeed, offense, crime; imposture, deception; also the modern sense.

Abuse (V): deceive, misapply, put to a bad use; maltreat; frequently the modern sense.

Addition: something added to one's name to denote rank; mark of distinction; title.

Admiration: wonder; object of wonder.

Admire: wonder at.

Advantage (N): profit, convenience, benefit; opportunity, favorable opportunity; pecuniary profit; often shades toward the modern sense.

Advantage (V): profit, be of benefit to, benefit; augment.

Advice: reflection, consideration, deliberation, consultation.

Affect: aim at, aspire to, incline toward; fond of, be inclined; love; act upon contagiously (as a disease). (PAST PART.) **Affected**: disposed, inclined, in love, loved.

Affection: passion, love; emotion, feeling, mental tendency, disposition; wish, inclination; affectation.

Alarum: signal calling soldiers to arms (in stage directions).

An: if; but; **an if:** if, though, even if.

Anon: at once, soon; presently, by and by.

Answer: return, requite; atone for; render an account of, account for; obey, agree with; also the modern sense.

Apparent: evident, plain; seeming.

Argument: subject, theme, reason, cause; story; excuse.

As: according as; as far as; namely; as if; in the capacity of; that; so that; that is, that they.

Assay: try, attempt; accost, address; challenge.

Atone: reconcile; set at one.

Attach: arrest, seize.

Aweful, awful: commanding reverential fear or respect; profoundly respectful or reverential.

B

Band: bond, fetters, manacle (leash for a dog). **Band** and **bond** are etymologically the same word; **band** was formerly used in both senses.

Basilisk: fabulous reptile said to kill by its look. The basilisk of popular superstition was a creature with legs, wings, a serpentine and winding tail, and a crest or comb somewhat like a cock. It was the offspring of a cock's egg hatched under a toad or serpent.

Bate: blunt, abate, reduce; deduct, except.

Battle: army; division of an army.

Beshrew: curse, blame; used as a mild curse, "Bad or ill luck to."

Bias: tendency, bent, inclination, swaying influence; term in bowling applied to the form of the bowl, the oblique line in which it runs, and the kind of impetus given to cause it to run obliquely.

Blood: nature, vigor; supposed source of emotion; passion; spirit, animation; one of the four humors (see **humor**).

Boot (N): advantage, profit; something given in addition to the bargain; booty, plunder.

Boot (V): profit, avail.

Brave (ADJ.): fine, gallant; splendid, finely arrayed, showy; ostentatiously defiant.

Brave (V): challenge, defy; make splendid.

Brook: tolerate, endure.

C

Can: can do; know; be skilled; sometimes used for *did*.

Capable: comprehensive; sensible, impressible, susceptible; capable of; gifted, intelligent.

Careful: anxious, full of care; provident; attentive.

Carry: manage, execute; be successful, win; conquer; sustain; endure.

Censure (N): judgment, opinion; critical opinion, unfavorable opinion.

Censure (V): judge, estimate; pass sentence or judgment.

Character (N): writing, printing, record; handwriting; cipher; face, features (bespeaking inward qualities).

Character (V): write, engrave, inscribe.

Check (N): reproof; restraint.

Check (V): reprove, restrain, keep from; control.

Circumstance: condition, state of affairs, particulars; adjunct details; detailed narration, argument, or discourse; formality, ceremony.

Clip: embrace; surround.

Close: secret, private; concealed; uncommunicative; enclosed.

Cog: cheat.

Coil: noise, disturbance, turmoil; fuss, to-do, bustle.

Color: appearance; pretext, pretense; excuse.

Companion: fellow (used contemptuously).

Complete: accomplished, fully endowed; perfect, perfect in quality; also frequently the modern sense.

Complexion: external appearance; temperament, disposition; the four complexions—sanguine, choleric, phlegmatic, and melancholy—corresponding to the four humors (see **humor**); also the modern sense.

Composition: compact, agreement, constitution.

Compound: settle, agree.

Conceit: conception, idea, thought; mental faculty, wit; fancy, imagination; opinion, estimate; device, invention, design.

Condition: temperament, disposition; characteristic, property, quality; social or official position, rank or status; covenant, treaty, contract.

Confound: waste, spend, invalidate, destroy; undo, ruin; mingle indistinguishably, mix, blend.

Confusion: destruction, overthrow, ruin; mental agitation.

Continent: that which contains or encloses; earth, globe; sum, summary.

Contrive: plot; plan; spend or pass (time).

Conversation: conduct, deportment; social intercourse, association.

Converse: hold intercourse; associate with, have to do with.

Cope: encounter, meet; have to do with.

Copy: model, pattern; example; minutes or memoranda.

Cousin: any relative not belonging to one's immediate family.

Cry you mercy: beg your pardon.

Cuckold: husband whose wife is unfaithful.

Curious: careful, fastidious; anxious, concerned; made with care, skillfully, intricately, or daintily wrought; particular.

Cursed, curst: shrewish, perverse, spiteful.

D

Dainty: minute; scrupulous, particular; particular about (with **of**); refined, elegant; also the modern sense.

Date: duration, termination, term of existence; limit or end of a term or period; term.

Dear: precious; best; costly; important; affectionate; hearty; grievous, dire; also the modern sense.

Debate: discuss; fight.

Decay (N): downfall, ruin; cause of ruin.

Decay (V): perish, be destroyed; destroy.

Defeat (N): destruction, ruin.

Defeat (V): destroy, disfigure, ruin.

Defy: challenge, challenge to a fight; reject; despise.

Demand (N): inquiry; request.

Demand (V): inquire, question; request.

Deny: refuse (to do something); refuse permission; refuse to accept; refuse admittance; disown.

Depart (N): departure.

Depart (V): part; go away from, leave, quit; take leave (of one another); **depart with, withal:** part with, give up.

Derive: gain, obtain; draw upon, direct (to); descend; pass by descent, be descended or inherited; trace the origin of.

Difference: diversity of opinion, disagreement, dissension, dispute; characteristic or distinguishing feature; alteration or addition to a coat of arms to distinguish a younger or lateral branch of a family.

Digest: arrange, perfect; assimilate, amalgamate; disperse, dissipate; comprehend, understand; put up with (FIG. from the physical sense of digesting food).

Discourse (N): reasoning, reflection; talk, act of conversing, conversation; faculty of conversing; familiar intercourse; relating (as by speech).

Discourse (V): speak, talk, converse; pass (the time) in talk; say, utter, tell, give forth; narrate, relate.

Discover: uncover, expose to view; divulge, reveal, make known; spy out, reconnoiter; betray; distinguish, discern; also the modern sense.

Dispose (N): disposal; temperament, bent of mind, disposition; external manner.

Dispose (V): distribute, manage, make use of; deposit, put or stow away; regulate, order, direct; come to terms. (PAST PART.) **Disposed:** in a good frame of mind; inclined to be merry.

Dispute: discuss, reason; strive against, resist.

Distemper (V): disturb; (N): disorder, ill humor; illness.

Doit: old Dutch coin, one-half an English farthing.

Doubt (N): suspicion, apprehension; fear, danger, risk; also the modern sense.

Doubt (V): suspect, apprehend; fear; also the modern sense.

Doubtful: inclined to suspect, suspicious, apprehensive; not to be relied on; almost certain.

Duty: reverence, respect, expression of respect; submission to authority, obedience; due.

E

Earnest: money paid as an installment to secure a bargain; partial payment; often used with *quibble* in the modern sense.

Ease: comfort, assistance, leisure; idleness, sloth, inactivity; also the modern sense.

Ecstasy: frenzy, madness, state of being beside oneself, excitement, bewilderment; swoon; rapture.

Element: used to refer to the simple substances of which all material bodies were thought to be composed; specifically earth, air, fire, and water, corresponding to the four humors (see **humor**); atmosphere, sky; atmospheric agencies or powers; that one of the four elements which is the natural abode of a creature; hence, natural surroundings, sphere.

Engage: pledge, pawn, mortgage; bind by a promise, swear to; entangle, involve; enlist; embark on an enterprise.

Engine: mechanical contrivance; artifice, device, plot.

Enlarge: give free scope to; set at liberty, release.

Entertain: keep up, maintain, accept; take into one's service; treat; engage (someone's) attention or thought; occupy, while or pass away pleasurably; engage (as an enemy); receive.

Envious: malicious, spiteful, malignant.

Envy: ill-will, malice; hate; also the modern sense.

Even: uniform; direct, straightforward; exact, precise; equable, smooth, comfortable; equal, equally balanced.

Event: outcome; affair, business; also frequently the modern sense.

Exclaim: protest, rail; accuse, blame (with **on**), reproach.

Excursion: stage battle or skirmish (in stage directions).

Excuse: seek to extenuate (a fault); maintain the innocence of; clear oneself, justify or vindicate oneself; decline.

F

Fact: deed, act; crime.

Faction: party, class, group, set (of persons); party strife, dissension; factious quarrel, intrigue.

Fail: die, die out; err, be at fault; omit, leave undone.

Fair (N): fair thing; one of the fair sex; someone beloved; beauty (the abstract concept).

Fair (ADJ.): just; clear, distinct; beautiful; of light complexion or color of hair.

Fair (ADV): fairly.

Fairly: beautifully, handsomely; courteously, civilly; properly, honorably, honestly; becomingly, appropriately; favorably, fortunately; softly, gently, kindly.

Fall: let fall, drop; happen, come to pass; befall; shades frequently toward the modern senses.

Falsely: wrongly; treacherously; improperly.

Fame: report; rumor; reputation.

Familiar (N): intimate friend; familiar or attendant spirit, demon associated with, and obedient to, a person.

Familiar (ADJ.): intimate, friendly; belonging to household or family, domestic; well-known; habitual, ordinary, trivial; plain, easily understood.

Fancy: fantasticalness; imaginative conception, flight of imagination; amorous inclination or passion, love; liking, taste.

Fantasy: fancy, imagination; caprice, whim.

Favor: countenance, face; complexion; aspect, appearance; leave, permission, pardon; attraction, charm, good will; **in favor:** benevolently.

Fear (N): dread, apprehension; dreadfulness; object of dread or fear.

Fear (v): be apprehensive or concerned about, mistrust, doubt; frighten, make afraid.

Fearful: exciting or inspiring fear, terrible, dreadful; timorous, apprehensive, full of fear.

Feature: shape or form of body, figure; shapeliness, comeliness.

Fellow: companion; partaker, sharer (of); equal, match; customary form of address to a servant or an inferior (sometimes used contemptuously or condescendingly).

Fine (N): end, conclusion; **in fine:** finally.

Fine (ADJ.): highly accomplished or skillful; exquisitely fashioned, delicate; refined, subtle; frequently the modern sense.

Flaw: fragment; crack, fissure; tempest, squall, gust of wind; outburst of passion.

Flesh (v): reward a hawk or hound with a piece of flesh of the game killed to excite its eagerness of the chase; hence, to inflame by a foretaste of success; initiate or inure to bloodshed (used for a first time in battle); harden, train.

Flourish: fanfare of trumpets (in stage directions).

Fond: foolish, doting; **fond of:** eager for; also the modern sense.

Fool: term of endearment and pity; frequently the modern sense.

For that, for why: because.

Forfend: forbid, avert.

Free: generous, magnanimous; candid, open; guiltless, innocent.

Front: forehead, face; foremost line of battle; beginning.

Furnish: equip, fit out (furnish forth); endow; dress, decorate, embellish.

G

Gear: apparel, dress; stuff, substance, thing, article; discourse, talk; matter, business, affair.

Get: beget.

Gloss: specious fair appearance; lustrous surface.

Go to: expression of remonstrance, impatience, disapprobation, or derision.

Grace (N): kindness, favor, charm, divine favor; fortune, luck; beneficent virtue; sense of duty or propriety; mercy, pardon; embellish; **do grace:** reflect credit on, do honor to, do a favor for.

Grace (v): gratify, delight; honor, favor.

Groat: coin equal to four pence.

H

Habit: dress, garb, costume; bearing, demeanor, manner; occasionally in the modern sense.

Happily: haply, perchance, perhaps; fortunately.

Hardly: with difficulty.

Have at: I shall come at (you) (i.e., listen to me), I shall attack (a person or thing); let me at.

Have with: I shall go along with; let me go along with; come along.

Having: possession, property, wealth, estate; endowments, accomplishments.

Head: armed force.

Hind: servant, slave; rustic, boor, clown.

His: its. **His** was historically the possessive form of both the masculine and neuter pronouns. **Its,** although not common in Shakespeare's time, occurs in the plays occasionally.

Holp: helped (archaic past tense).

Home: fully, satisfactorily, thoroughly, plainly, effectually; to the quick.

Honest: holding an honorable position, honorable, respectable; decent, kind, seemly, befitting, proper; chaste; genuine; loosely used as an epithet of approbation.

Humor: mood, temper, cast of mind, temperament, disposition; vagary, fancy, whim; moisture (the literal sense); a physiological and, by transference, a psychological term applied to the four chief fluids of the human body—phlegm, blood, bile or choler, and black bile or melancholy. A person's disposition and temporary state of mind were determined according to the relative proportions of these fluids in the body; consequently, a person was said to be phlegmatic, sanguine, choleric, or melancholy.

I

Image: likeness; visible form; representation; embodiment, type; mental picture, creation of the imagination.

Influence: supposed flowing from the stars or heavens of an ethereal fluid, acting upon the characters and destinies of men (used metaphorically).

Inform: take shape, give form to, imbue, inspire; instruct, teach; charge (against).

Instance: evidence, proof, sign, confirmation; motive, cause.

Invention: power of mental creation, the creative faculty; work of the imagination, artistic creation, premeditated design; device, plan, scheme.

J

Jar (N): discord in music; quarrel, discord.

Jar (V): be out of tune; be discordant, quarrel.

Jump: agree, tally, coincide, fit exactly; risk, hazard.

K

Keep: continue, carry on; dwell, lodge, guard, defend, care for, employ, be with; restrain, control; confine in prison.

Kind (N): nature, established order of things; manner, fashion, respect; race, class, kindred, family; **by kind:** naturally.

Kind (ADJ.): natural; favorable; affectionate.

Kindly (ADJ.): natural, appropriate; agreeable; innate; benign.

Kindly (ADV): naturally; gently, courteously.

L

Large: liberal, bounteous, lavish; free, unrestrained; **at large:** at length, in full; in full detail, as a whole, in general.

Late: lately.

Learn: teach; inform (someone of something); also the modern sense.

Let: hinder.

Level: aim; also shades toward the modern sense.

Liberal: possessed of the characteristics and qualities of wellborn persons; genteel, becoming, refined; free in speech; unrestrained by prudence or decorum; licentious.

Lie: be in bed; be still; be confined, be kept in prison; dwell, sojourn, reside, lodge.

Like: please, feel affection; liken, compare.

List (N): strip of cloth, selvedge; limit, boundary; desire.

List (V): choose, desire, please; listen to.

Liver: the seat of love and of violent passions generally (see also **spleen**).

'Long of: owing to, on account of.

Look: power to see; take care, see to it; expect; seek, search for.

M

Make: do; have to do (with); consider; go; be effective, make up, complete; also the modern sense.

Manage: management, conduct, administration; action and paces to which a horse is trained; short gallop at full speed.

Marry: mild interjection equivalent to "Indeed!" Originally, an oath by the Virgin Mary.

May: can; also frequently the modern sense to denote probability; **might** has corresponding meanings and uses.

Mean, means (N): instrument, agency, method; effort; opportunity (for doing something); something interposed or intervening; money, wealth (frequently in the plural form); middle position, medium; tenor or alto part in singing (usually in the singular form).

Mean (ADJ.): average, moderate, middle; of low degree, station, or position; undignified, base.

Measure (N): grave or stately dance, graceful motion; tune, melody, musical accompaniment; treatment meted out; moderation, proportion; limit; distance, reach.

Measure (V): judge, estimate; traverse.

Mere: absolute, sheer; pure, unmixed; downright, sincere.

Mew (up): coop up (as used of a hawk), shut up, imprison, confine.

Mind (N): thoughts, judgment, opinion, message; purpose, intention, desire; disposition; also the modern sense of the mental faculty.

Mind (V): remind; perceive, notice, attend; intend.

Minion: saucy woman, hussy; follower; favorite, favored person, darling (often used contemptuously).

Misdoubt (N): suspicion.

Misdoubt (V): mistrust, suspect.

Model: pattern, replica, likeness.

Modern: ordinary, commonplace, everyday.

Modest: moderate, marked by moderation, becoming; characterized by decency and propriety; chaste.

Moiety: half; share; small part, lesser share; portion, part of.

Mortal: fatal; deadly, of or for death; belonging to mankind; human, pertaining to human affairs.

Motion: power of movement; suggestion, proposal; movement of the soul; impulse, prompting; also the modern sense.

Move: make angry; urge, incite, instigate, arouse, prompt; propose, make a pro-

posal to, apply to, appeal to, suggest; also the modern sense.

Muse: wonder, marvel; grumble, complain.

N

Napkin: handkerchief.

Natural: related by blood; having natural or kindly feeling; also the modern sense.

Naught: useless, worthless; wicked, naughty.

Naughty: wicked; good for nothing, worthless.

Nerves: sinews.

Nice: delicate; fastidious, dainty, particular, scrupulous; minute, subtle; shy, coy; reluctant, unwilling; unimportant, insignificant, trivial; accurate, precise; wanton, lascivious.

Nothing (ADJ.): not at all.

O

Of: from, away from; during; on; by; as regards; instead of; **out of:** compelled by; made from.

Offer: make an attack; menace; venture, dare, presume.

Opinion: censure; reputation or credit; favorable estimate of oneself; self-conceit, arrogance; self-confidence; public opinion, reputation; also the modern sense.

Or: before; also used conjunctively where no alternative is implied; **or . . . or:** either . . . or; whether . . . or.

Out (ADV): without, outside; abroad; fully, quite; at an end, finished; at variance, aligned the wrong way.

Out (INTERJ.): an expression of reproach, impatience, indignation, or anger.

Owe: own; also the modern sense.

P

Pack (V): load; depart, begone; conspire.

Pageant: show, spectacle, spectacular entertainment; device on a moving carriage.

Pain: punishment, penalty; labor, trouble, effort; also frequently the modern sense.

Painted: specious, unreal, counterfeit.

Parle (N): parley, conference, talk; bugle call for parley.

Part (V): depart, part from; divide.

Particular (N): detail; personal interest or concern; details of a private nature; single person.

Party: faction, side, part, cause; partner, ally.

Pass (V): pass through, traverse; exceed; surpass; pledge.

Passing (ADJ. and ADV.): surpassing, surpassingly, exceedingly.

Passion (N): powerful or violent feeling, violent sorrow or grief; painful affection or disorder of the body; sorrow; feelings or desires of love; passionate speech or outburst.

Passion (V): sorrow, grieve.

Peevish: silly, senseless, childish; perverse, obstinate, stubborn; sullen.

Perforce: by violence or compulsion; forcibly; necessarily.

Phoenix: mythical Arabian bird believed to be the only one of its kind; it lived five or six hundred years, after which it burned itself to ashes and reemerged to live through another cycle.

Physic: medical faculty; healing art, medical treatment; remedy, medicine, healing property.

Pitch: height; specifically, the height to which a falcon soars before swooping on its prey (often used figuratively); tarlike substance.

Policy: conduct of affairs (especially public affairs); prudent management; stratagem, trick; contrivance; craft, cunning.

Port: bearing, demeanor; state, style of living, social station; gate.

Possess: have or give possession or command (of something); inform, acquaint; also the modern sense.

Post (N): courier, messenger; post-horse; haste.

Post (V): convey swiftly; hasten, ignore through haste (with **over** or **off**).

Practice (N): execution; exercise (especially for instruction); stratagem, intrigue; conspiracy, plot, treachery.

Practice (V): perform, take part in; use stratagem, craft, or artifice; scheme, plot; play a joke on.

Pregnant: resourceful; disposed, inclined; clear, obvious.

Present (ADJ.): ready, immediate, prompt, instant.

Present (V): represent.

Presently: immediately, at once.

Prevent: forestall, anticipate, foresee; also the modern sense.

Process: drift, tenor, gist; narrative, story; formal command, mandate.

Proof: test, trial, experiment; experience; issue, result; proved or tested strength of armor or arms; also the modern sense.

Proper: (one's or its) own; peculiar, exclusive; excellent; honest, respectable; handsome, elegant, fine, good-looking.

Proportion: symmetry; size; form, carriage, appearance, shape; portion, allotment; rhythm.

Prove: make trial of; put to test; show or find out by experience.

Purchase (N): acquisition; spoil, booty.

Purchase (V): acquire, gain, obtain; strive, exert oneself; redeem, exempt.

Q

Quaint: skilled, clever; pretty, fine, dainty; handsome, elegant; carefully or ingeniously wrought or elaborated.

Quality: that which constitutes (something); essential being; good natural gifts; accomplishment, attainment, property; art, skill; rank, position; profession, occupation, business; party, side; manner, style; cause, occasion.

Quick: living (used substantively to mean "living flesh"); alive; lively, sharp, piercing; hasty, impatient; with child.

Quillets: verbal niceties, subtle distinctions.

Quit: requite, reward; set at liberty; acquit, remit; pay for, clear off.

R

Rack (V): stretch or strain beyond normal extent or capacity to endure; strain oneself; distort.

Rage (N): madness, insanity; vehement pain; angry disposition; violent passion or appetite; poetic enthusiasm; warlike ardor or fury.

Rage (V): behave wantonly or riotously; act with fury or violence; enrage; pursue furiously.

Range: extend or lie in the same plane (with); occupy a position; rove, roam; be inconstant; traverse.

Rank (ADJ.): coarsely luxuriant; puffed up, swollen, fat, abundant; full, copious; rancid; lustful; corrupt, foul.

Rate (N): estimate; value or worth; estimation, consideration; standard, style.

Rate (V): allot; calculate, estimate, compute; reckon, consider; be of equal value (with); chide, scold, berate; drive away by chiding or scolding.

Recreant (N): traitor, coward, cowardly wretch (also as ADJ.).

Remorse: pity, compassion; also the modern sense.

Remove: removal, absence; period of absence; change.

Require: ask, inquire of, request.

Resolve: dissolve, melt, dissipate; answer; free from doubt or uncertainty, convince; inform; decide; also the modern sense.

Respect (N): consideration, reflection, act of seeing, view; attention, notice; decency, modest deportment; also the modern sense.

Respect (V): esteem, value, prize; regard, consider; heed, pay attention to; also the modern sense.

Round: spherical; plain, direct, brusque; fair; honest.

Roundly: plainly, unceremoniously.

Rub: obstacle (a term in the game of bowls); unevenness; inequality.

S

Sack: generic term for Spanish and Canary wines; sweet white wine.

Sad: grave, serious; also the modern sense.

Sadness: seriousness; also the modern sense.

Sans: without (French preposition).

Scope: object, aim, limit; freedom, license; free play.

Seal: bring to completion or conclusion; conclude, confirm, ratify, stamp; also the modern sense.

Sennet: a series of notes sounded on a trumpet to herald the approach or departure of a procession (used in stage directions).

Sense: mental faculty, mind; mental perception, import, rational meaning; physical perception; sensual nature; **common sense:** ordinary or untutored perception, observation or knowledge.

Sensible: capable of physical feeling or perception, sensitive; capable of or exhibiting emotion; rational; capable of being perceived.

Serve: be sufficient; be favorable; succeed; satisfy the need for; serve a turn; answer the purpose.

Several: separate, distinct, different; particular, private; various.

Shadow: shade, shelter; reflection; likeness, image; ghost; representation, picture of the imagination, phantom; also the modern sense.

Shift: change; stratagem, strategy, trick, contrivance, device to serve a purpose; **make shift:** manage.

Shrewd: malicious, mischievous, ill-natured; shrewish; bad, of evil import, grievous; severe.

Sirrah: ordinary or customary form of address to inferiors or servants; disrespectful form of address.

Sith: since.

Smock: woman's undergarment; used typically for "a woman."

Something: somewhat.

Sometime: sometimes, from time to time; once, formerly; at times, at one time.

Speed (N): fortune, success; protecting and assisting power; also the modern sense.

Speed (V): fare (well or ill); succeed; be successful; assist, guard, favor.

Spleen: the seat of emotions and passions; violent passion; fiery temper; malice; anger, rage; impulse, fit of passion; caprice; impetuosity (see also **liver**).

Spoil: destruction, ruin; plunder; slaughter, massacre.

Starve: die of cold or hunger; be benumbed with cold; paralyze, disable; allow or cause to die.

State: degree, rank; social position, station; pomp, splendor, outward display, clothes; court, household of a great person; shades into the modern sense.

Stay: wait, wait for; sustain; stand; withhold, withstand; stop.

Stead: assist; be of use to, benefit, help.

Still: always, ever, continuously or continually, constant or constantly; silent, mute; also modern senses.

Stomach: appetite, inclination, disposition; resentment; angry temper, resentful feeling; proud spirit, courage.

Straight: immediately.

Strange: belonging to another country or person, foreign, unfriendly; new, fresh; ignorant; estranged.

Success: issue, outcome (good or bad); sequel, succession, descent (as from father to son).

Suggest: tempt; prompt; seduce.

Suggestion: temptation.

T

Table: memorandum, tablet; surface on which something is written or drawn.

Take: strike; bewitch; charm; infect; destroy; repair to for refuge; modern senses.

Tall: goodly, fine; strong in fight, valiant.

Target: shield.

Tax: censure, blame, accuse.

Tell: count; relate.

Thorough: through.

Throughly: thoroughly.

Toward: in preparation; forthcoming, about to take place; modern senses.

Toy: trifle, idle fancy; folly.

Train: lure, entice, allure, attract.

Trencher: wooden dish or plate.

Trow: think, suppose, believe; know.

U

Undergo: undertake, perform; modern sense.

Undo: ruin.

Unfold: disclose, tell, make known, reveal; communicate.

Unhappy: evil, mischievous; fatal, ill-fated; miserable.

Unjust: untrue, dishonest; unjustified, groundless; faithless, false.

Unkind: unnatural, cruel, faulty; compare **kind.**

Use (N): custom, habit; interest paid.

Use (V): make practice of; be accustomed; put out at interest.

V

Vail: lower, let fall.

Vantage: advantage; opportunity; benefit, profit; superiority.

Virtue: general excellence; valor, bravery; merit, goodness, honor; good accomplishment, excellence in culture; power; essence, essential part.

W

Want: lack; be in need of; be without.

Watch: be awake, lie awake, sit up at night, lose sleep; keep from sleep (TRANS.).

Weed: garment, clothes.

Welkin: sky, heavens.

Wink: close the eyes; close the eyes in sleep; have the eyes closed; seem not to see.

Withal: with; with it, this, or these; together with this; at the same time.

Wot: know.

Index

Page ranges in **bold** indicate the page range for the entire play. Page references followed by *n* indicate a footnote.

Porter, Joseph, critic, xcvlli

Portia, rich heiress (*Mer. Ven.*), xxix, xcv, xcvii, 4, 74, 75, 76, 77, 78, 82*n*, 85*n*, 91*n*, 93*n*, 95*n*, 97*n*, 100*n*, 101*n*, 107*n*, 108*n*, 110*n*, 153, 154, 192, 506, A-3

Portia, wife of Brutus (*J.C.*), 81*n*, 506, 507, 509, 510, 521*n*, 537*n*, A-26

Porto, Luigi da (1486–1529), *Historia novellamente ritrovata di due Nobili Amanti*, 460, A-25

Posthumus Leonatus, husband of Imogen (*Cymb.*), 846

Postlethwaite, Pete, actor, A-51, A-56

Potpan, servant of Capulets (*R. and J.*), 464

Potter, Lois, scholar, c

Powell, Dick, actor, A-54

Prendergast, Shaun, actor, A-58Prester John, legendary Eastern king, 125*n*

Preston, Thomas (1537–1598?), *Cambyses*, xxxvii, 389*n*, A-16

Price, Richard, producer, A-54

Princess's Theatre, A-41

Pritchard, Hannah (1711–1768), actress, 116, A-40

Procne, 55*n*. *See also* Philomela

Procris. *See* Cephalus and Procris

Proculeius, follower of Octavius (*Ant. and Cleo.*), 752, A-33

Prodigal Son, biblical, xxxix, 77, 90*n*, 156*n*

Prometheus, xlii, 650*n*

Proserpina (Persephone), 73*n*, 170*n*, 804, 828*n*, 847, 848, 871*n*, A-15

Prospero (*Temp.*), xxxiii, xlix, lxix, 804, 845, 846, 847, 848, 849, 850*n*, 851*n*, 854*n*, 855*n*, 863*n*, 864*n*, 869*n*, 872*n*, 873*n*, 875*n*, 876*n*, 878*n*, A-35

Prospero's Books, 1991 film, 849, A-57

Proteus, ancient one of the sea, 270

Provost (*Meas. Meas.*), 231

Prynne, William (1600–1669), *Histrio-Mastix: The Player's Scourge or Actor's Tragedy*, xlviii

Ptolemy of Alexandria (*fl.* 127–151 A.D.), astronomer, xxviii, xxix

Ptolemy XIII, brother and husband to Cleopatra, 749, 758*n*, 761*n*

Publius, senator (*J.C.*), 510, 526*n*, 533*n*

Puck, fairy (*Mids. Dr.*), 2, 43, 44, 45, 46, 51*n*, 64*n*, 73*n*, A-15, A-16, A-35, A-44

Purchase, Bruce, actor, A-52

Puritan, The, anonymous comedy, A-12

Purnell, Louise, actress, A-54

Putti, young male angel, 722*n*

Pygmalion, legendary sculptor, 250*n*, A-34

Pym, John (1584–1643), statesman, xxviii

Pyne, Natasha, actress, A-56

Pyramus and Thisbe, story of, 42, 43, 45, 57*n*, 67*n*, 78, 108*n*, 480*n*, A-3, A15, A-16, A-25, A-38, A-44

Pyrrha, wife of Deucalion, 513*n*

Pyrrhus, King of Epirus, 571*n*

Pythagoras (*fl.* 580 B.C.), Greek philosopher, lxvii, 104*n*, 172*n*, 220*n*, A-1

Pythias. *See* Damon and Pythias

Quartermaine, Leon, actor, A-50

Quayle, Anthony, actor and director, 116, 371, 507, A-52

Queen (Isabella) (*Rich. II*), 330, 331, 333*n*, 344*n*, 346*n*, A-6, A-22

Queen Mab, Fairy Queen, 472*n*

Queen's Men, lv, lvi, c, A-30

Quickly, Mistress (*1 and 2 Hen. IV, Hen. V*, and *Mer. Wives*), lxviii, 372, 373, 399*n*, 414, 416, 427*n*, 452*n*, A-24, A-25, A-38

Quince, Peter, carpenter (*Mids. Dr.*), 46, 57*n*, 70*n*

Quiney, Thomas (*fl.* 1616), Shakespeare's son-in-law, lxxx

Quinn, Aidan, actor, 273, 551, A-54

Rabelais, François (1490?–1553?), 172*n*, 689*n*

Racine, Jean Baptiste (1639–1699), French tragedian, xlii, lxxxix, 660

Rackin, Phyllis, critic, xcvii, c

Radford, Michael, filmmaker, xii, A-49, A-54, A-56

Radzina, Eliza, actress, A-50, A-52

Ragozine, prisoner (*Meas. Meas.*), 227

Ralegh, Sir Walter (1553?–1618), xxviii, A-35

Raleigh, Sir Walter (1861–1922), xci

Rall, Tommy, actor, A-57

Rambures, Lord (*Hen. V*), 416

Ramus, Petrus (1515?–1572), humanist, xxxi

Ran, Kurosawa's 1985 film, xii, 661, A-46, A-49, A-53

Randell, Ron, actor, A-57

Rannius (*Ant. and Cleo.*), 753*n*

Rape of Lucrece, The, lxii, lxiii, lxvii, lxxvii, 20*n*, 171*n*, 506, 509, 880, 881, 889*n*, A-1, A-2, A-3, A-13

Rastell, John (1475?–1536), humanist and author, xxxix, 124*n*
Of Gentleness and Nobility, xxxix; *The Nature of the Four Elements*, xxxix

Rastell, William, son of John Rastell, printer, xxxix

Ratcliffe, Sir Richard, follower of Richard (*Rich. III*), 274

Ravenscroft, Christopher, actor, A-55, A-57

Raymond, Emily, actress, A-54

Raymond, Gary, actor, A-57

Reagan, Ronald, US president, 551

Redford, Ian, actor, A-56

Redgrave, Corin, actor, A-53

Redgrave, Michael, actor, 330, 751, A-51

Redgrave, Vanessa, actress, 751, A-50

Redman, Joyce, actress, A-55

Rees, Angharad, actress, A-50

Rees, Roger, actor, A-53

Reese, M. M., critic, xcii

Reeves, Keanu, actor, xii, A-48, A-52, A-55

Regan, daughter of King Lear (*K. Lear*), 657, 658, 659, 660, 661, 662, 670*n*, 671*n*, 674*n*, 679*n*, 690*n*, 700*n*, 704*n*, A-11

Regan, Vincent, actor, A-53

Reid, Malcolm, actor, A-54

Reid, Sheila, actress, A-55, A-57

Reilly, Don, actor, A-51

Reinhardt, Max, filmmaker, xi, A-54

Respublica, anonymous play, xxxvii

Return from Parnassus, The, xlviii, lxix, lxxiii

Rey, Fernando, actor, A-52

Reynaldo, servant of Polonius (*Ham.*), 552, A-43

Reynard the Fox, medieval beast epic, 480*n*, 817*n*

Ribner, Irving, scholar and editor, xcii

Rich, Richard, *New from Virginia*, 845

Richard, David, director, A-57

Richard, Duke of Gloucester, after Richard III (*2 and 3 Hen. VI* and *Rich. III*), xxii, xxvii, xxxiii, xxxvii, xlvi, lxxv, 270, 271, 272, 273, 274, 275*n*, 276*n*, 277*n*, 278*n*, 279*n*, 280*n*, 281*n*, 283*n*, 285*n*, 290*n*, 291*n*, 294*n*, 296*n*, 297*n*, 298*n*, 302*n*, 303*n*, 305*n*, 306*n*, 307*n*, 308*n*, 310*n*, 311*n*, 313*n*, 314*n*, 318*n*, 319*n*, 320*n*, 321*n*, 322*n*, 323*n*, 324*n*, 326, 607, A-21, A-22, A-37, A-40, A-41, A-45

Richard, Duke of York, son of Edward IV (*Rich. III*), 274, 311*n*, 312*n*, A-39

Richard, Earl of Cambridge. *See* Cambridge, Richard Langley, Earl of

Richard II, Carroll's 2003 production of, A-56

Richard II, Giles's TV production of, A-56

Richard II, King of England (*Rich. II*), xxvii, xxxiii, lxxv, xcv, 271, 272, 326, 327, 328, 329, 330, 331, 333*n*, 334*n*, 335*n*, 336*n*, 337*n*, 339*n*, 341*n*, 342*n*, 343*n*, 344*n*, 346*n*, 347*n*, 348*n*, 350*n*, 351*n*, 352*n*, 353*n*, 355*n*, 357*n*, 358*n*, 359*n*, 360*n*, 362*n*, 363*n*, 367*n*, 370, 378*n*, 379*n*, 396*n*, 403*n*, 442*n*, 506, A-1, A-6, A-22, A-23, A-44, A-45

Richard II, The Tragedy of King, xxvi, xxvii, xlvi, lxxi, lxxv, xciii, xcv, xcviii, **326–69**, 370, 372, 374*n*, 380*n*, 404*n*, 412, 460, 507, A-1, A-3, A-6, A-8, A-22–A-23, A-24, A-39, A-44, A-45, A-47

Richard III. *See* Richard, Duke of Gloucester

Richard III, Loncraine's 1995 film, 273, A-49, A-56

Richard III, Olivier's 1955 film, xi, 273, A-39, A-48, A-49, A-56

Richard III, The Tragedy of King, xii, xxii, xxvii, xxxiii, xxxvii, xlvi, lv, lxiv, lxix, lxxi, lxxv, xcii, **270–325**, 413, 506, 710, A-1, A-5–A-6, A-21–A-22, A-22, A-39, A-41, A-44, A-45

Richard III, True Tragedy of. See True Tragedy of Richard III

Richardson, Catherine, scholars, c

Richardson, Ian, actor, 330, A-50, A-54

Richardson, Ralph, actor, A-54, A-56, A-57

Richardson, Tony, director, A-49, A-51

Richardson, William (1743–1814), critic, lxxxix

Riche, Barnabe (1540?–1617), *Riche His Farewell to Military Profession*, 190, 191, A-20

Richert, William, actor, A-52

Richmond, Edmund Tudor, Earl of, 281*n*

Richmond, Henry Tudor, Earl of. *See* Henry Tudor

Richmond, Margaret Beaufort, Countess of (1443–1509), 281*n*

Riddell, Derek, actor, A-55

Riddell, Richard, actor, A-54

Scoffield, Jon, director, A-50

Scofield, Paul, actor, viii, ix, 330, 610, 661, A-44, A-49, A-50, A-51, A-52

Scoloker, Anthony, *Diaphantus* (1604), lxxv

Scot, Reginald (1538?–1599), *The Discovery of Witchcraft*, xxix, A-16

Scott, Campbell, TV producer and actor, A-51

Scott, George C., actor, 78

Scroop, Henry, third Baron Scroop of Masham (*Hen. V*), 404*n*, 413, 416, 424*n*, 426*n*

Scroop, Sir Stephen (*Rich. II*), 331, 404*n*

Scylla and Charybdis, 101*n*

Seacoal, Francis, sexton (*Much Ado*), 117, 137*n*

Seacoal, George, watchman (*Much Ado*), 117, 133*n*, 137*n*, 141*n*

Seales, Franklyn, actor, A-57

Sebastian, brother of Alonso (*Temp.*), 846, 847, 849, 858*n*, 859*n*, 860*n*

Sebastian, brother of Viola (*12th Night*), 192, 218*n*, A-20

Sebris, Karl, actor, A-52

Secchi, Nicolò (*fl.* 1547) *Gl'Inganni*, A-19, A-20; *L'Interesse*, A-19, A-20

Selby, Nicholas, actor, A-53

Seleucus, Egyptian (*Ant. and Cleo.*), 752

Semiramis, Queen of Assyria, 8*n*, 57*n*

Seneca, Lucius Annaeus (3? B.C.–65 A.D.), xxxix, xli, xlii, xliv, xlv, lx, lxiv, lxvi, lxvii, lxxvi, lxxxvi, 571*n*, A-1, A-28
Hercules Furens, 50*n*; *Medea*, A-32

Senior, Duke, living in banishment (*A.Y.L.*), 150, 152, 153, 154, 155, 166*n*, 167*n*, 187*n*, 188*n*

Sessions, John, actor, A-52, A-54

Setebos, pagan god (mentioned in *Temp.*), 845, 856*n*

Sewell, Rufus, actor, A-57

Sextus, Tarquinius (*The Rape of Lucrece*). *See* Tarquinius Sextus

Sextus Pompeius (*Ant. and Cleo.*), 748, 749, 750, 752, 756*n*, 757*n*, 760*n*, 768*n*, 769*n*, 775*n*, A-33

Seymour, Jane, queen of Henry VIII, xxiii

Seyton (*Macb.*), 715

Shadwell, Thomas (1642?–1692), poet, A-39

Shaikh, Zaib, director, A-55

Shakespeare, Anne, wife. *See* Hathaway, Anne

Shakespeare, Edmund (d. 1607), brother, lxxiv

Shakespeare, Elizabeth, grandchild, lxxiv

Shakespeare, Gilbert (*fl.* 1602), brother, lxxiv

Shakespeare, Hamnet (1585–1596), son, lxii, lxx

Shakespeare, John (d. 1601), father, lviii, lix, lxii, lxiii, lxx, lxxiv

Shakespeare, Judith (b. 1585), daughter, lxii, lxxx

Shakespeare, Richard (d. ca. 1561), grandfather, lvii

Shakespeare, Susanna (b. 1583), daughter, lxii, lxxiv, lxxx, lxxxi

Shakespeare in Love, 1998 film, xii, A-50, A-54

Shakespeare Wallah, 1965 film, A-50, A-55

Shallow, Robert, country justice (*2 Hen. IV* and *Mer. Wives*), xxxvii, lxii, lxviii, lxxi

Shannon, Laurie, critic, xcvii, c

Shapiro, James S., scholar, cxiii

Shaw, Doctor (mentioned in *Rich. III*), 303*n*

Shaw, Fiona, actress, 330, A-45

Shaw, George Bernard, playwright (1856–1950), 114, 116, 412, A-42, A-43, A-47

Shaw, Glen Byam, director, 507, 714, 751

Shaw, Martin, actor, A-51, A-53

Shaw, Sebastian, actor, A-54

Shawnhan, April, actress, A-55

Shendrikova, Valentina, actress, A-52

Shentall, Susan, actress, A-56

Shepard, Sam, actor, 552, A-49, A-51

Shepley, Michael, actor, A-52

Sher, Antony, actor, xii, 273, A-53, A-58

Sheridan, Alan, translator, xciv

Sheridan, Jamey, actor, A-51

Sherwood, Lydia, actress, A-56

Shimura, Takashi, actor, A-53

Shirley, Sir Anthony, English adventurer, A-4

Shively, William, producer, A-55

Shore, Jane, mistress of Edward IV (1445?–1527), 276*n*, 297*n*, A-22

Short, Peter, printer, A-6

Shostakovich, Dimitri, composer, A-49

Shotwell, Sandra, actress, A-57

Shylock, rich Jew (*Mer. Ven.*), 74, 75, 76, 77, 78, 79, 83*n*, 85*n*, 88*n*, 89*n*, 90*n*, 94*n*, 95*n*, 99*n*, 107*n*, A-3, A-17, A-40, A-41, A-42, A-46, A-49, A-54

Sibyl of Cumae, 13*n*, 83*n*

Sichel, Jonathan, filmmaker, A-49, A-53, A-57

Siddons, Sarah (1755–1831), actress, A-41

Sidney, George, director, A-57

Sidney, Sir Philip (1554–1586), xli, xlii, xliii, lxxv, lxxxiii, 507, 884; *Arcadia*, 151, 190, 656, A-15, A-19, A-20, A-31; *Astrophel and Stella*, 880, 882; *The Defense of Poesy*, xlii

Sigismund, Holy Roman Emperor, 451*n*

Silence, country justice (*2 Hen. IV*), lxviii

Silius, in Ventidius's army (*Ant. and Cleo.*), 752

Silvius, shepherd (*A.Y.L.*), 150, 151, 153, 155, 177*n*, 182*n*, 188*n*, 191, A-19

Simmons, James, actor, A-57

Simmons, Jean, actress, A-50

Simonson, Eric, TV producer, A-51

Sims, Valentine (*fl.* 1599–1605), printer, A-4, A-5, A-6

Sinden, Donald, actor, 116, 661

Sinel, father of Macbeth, 718*n*

Sinfield, Alan, critic, xcvi, c

Singer, Marc, actor, A-57

Singh, Jyotsna, critic, xcvii

Sinon, deceiver of Trojans with wooden horse, 270

Sir Clyomon and Sir Clamydes, anonymous play, 190, A-20

Sir John Oldcastle, play (Drayton, et al.), lxviii, lxxi

Sir Thomas More, play (Munday, et al.), lxxi

Siward, Earl of Northumberland (*Macb.*), 714, 715, A-31

Siward, Young, son of Siward (*Macb.*), 715, 746*n*

Sixtus V, Pope, 882

Skelton, John (1460?–1529), *Magnificence*, xxxvi, xxxvii

Skobtseva, Irina, actress, A-55

Skura, Meredith, critic, xciv, xcvii, c

Slater, Ann Pasternak, critic, xciii

Slaughter of the Innocents, The, cycle play, 576*n*

Slender, Abraham, cousin of Shallow (*Mer. Wives*), lxxi

Sly, Christopher, tinker (*Tam. Shrew*), lxxxiii, 2, 3, 5, 5*n*, 9*n*, A-14, A-45

Sly, Stephen, Stratford citizen, 8*n*

Sly, William (*fl.* 1590–1608), actor, lxxii, lxxiv

Small, Sharon, actress, A-54

Smethwick, John (*fl.* 1607–1623), printer, A-9

Smiley, Jan, *A Thousand Acres*, 661

Smith, Bruce R., scholar, xcvii, c

Smith, Greg, producer, A-55

Smith, Irwin (b. 1892), scholar, xcii

Smith, Maggie, actress, 116, 610, A-55, A-56

Smith, Mel, actor, A-58

Smith, Roger Guenveur, actor, A-51

Smith, Warren D., scholar, A-7

Smith, William (*fl.* 1596), *Chloris*, 880

Smoktunovsky, Innonkenti, actor, A-51

Snell, Peter, producer, A-52

Snout, Tom, tinker (*Mids. Dr.*), 46

Snug, joiner (*Mids. Dr.*), 46

Socrates (470–399 B.C.), lxxxi

Sokol, B.J. and Mary, scholars, c

Solanio, friend of Antonio (*Mer. Ven.*), 77, 79, 94*n*

Solyman, Turkish sultan, 86*n*

Sondheim, Stephen, composer and lyricist, A-49

Sonnets, lxvii, lxxi, xciv, 750, **880–916**, A-1, A-13, A-35

Soothsayer (*Ant. and Cleo.*), 748, 752, 753*n*, 754*n*, A-33

Soothsayer (*J.C.*), 510, A-26

Sophocles (496?–405 B.C.), Greek tragedian, xliv, lxxxvi

Sophy, Shah of Persia, 86*n*, 209*n*, A-4

Sorvino, Paul, actor, A-56

Soshalsky, Vladimir, actor, A-55

Southampton, Countess of. *See* Vernon, Lady Elizabeth

Southampton, Henry Wriothesley, third Earl of (1573–1624), lxxxii, 880, 881, A-3

Southampton, Mary, Countess of, lxviii, 881, A-3

Spacey, Kevin, actor, 273, A-56

Speght, Thomas, publisher of Chaucer, lxviii, A-10

Spencer, T. J. B., editor, xcii